Gene B. Bates

Inu J. Bates

This **Holy Bible**

is presented to

by

on

Church Record

EVENT

MINISTER

CHURCH DATE

EVENT

MINISTER

CHURCH DATE

EVENT

MINISTER

CHURCH DATE

EVENT

MINISTER

CHURCH DATE

EVENT

MINISTER

CHURCH DATE

EVENT

MINISTER

CHURCH DATE

Marriages

HUSBAND

WIFE

PLACE DATE

HUSBAND

WIFE

PLACE DATE

HUSBAND

WIFE

PLACE DATE

HUSBAND

WIFE

PLACE DATE

HUSBAND

WIFE

PLACE DATE

HUSBAND

WIFE

PLACE DATE

Wife's Family Tree

NAME

BIRTHPLACE _____ DATE _____

BROTHERS AND SISTERS _____

PARENTS

FATHER _____ MOTHER

NAME _____ NAME _____

BIRTHPLACE _____ DATE ____ BIRTHPLACE _____ DATE ____

GRANDPARENTS

PATERNAL _____ MATERNAL

GRANDFATHER _____ GRANDFATHER _____

BIRTHPLACE _____ DATE ____ BIRTHPLACE _____ DATE ____

GRANDMOTHER _____ GRANDMOTHER _____

BIRTHPLACE _____ DATE ____ BIRTHPLACE _____ DATE ____

GREAT-GRANDPARENTS

PATERNAL _____ MATERNAL

GRANDFATHER'S FATHER _____ GRANDFATHER'S FATHER _____

BIRTHPLACE _____ DATE ____ BIRTHPLACE _____ DATE ____

GRANDFATHER'S MOTHER _____ GRANDFATHER'S MOTHER _____

BIRTHPLACE _____ DATE ____ BIRTHPLACE _____ DATE ____

GRANDMOTHER'S FATHER _____ GRANDMOTHER'S FATHER _____

BIRTHPLACE _____ DATE ____ BIRTHPLACE _____ DATE ____

GRANDMOTHER'S MOTHER _____ GRANDMOTHER'S MOTHER _____

BIRTHPLACE _____ DATE ____ BIRTHPLACE _____ DATE ____

Husband's Family Tree

NAME _____

BIRTHPLACE _____ DATE _____

BROTHERS AND SISTERS _____

PARENTS

FATHER	MOTHER
NAME _____	NAME _____
BIRTHPLACE _____ DATE ___	BIRTHPLACE _____ DATE ___

GRANDPARENTS

PATERNAL	MATERNAL
GRANDFATHER _____	GRANDFATHER _____
BIRTHPLACE _____ DATE ___	BIRTHPLACE _____ DATE ___
GRANDMOTHER _____	GRANDMOTHER _____
BIRTHPLACE _____ DATE ___	BIRTHPLACE _____ DATE ___

GREAT-GRANDPARENTS

PATERNAL	MATERNAL
GRANDFATHER'S FATHER _____	GRANDFATHER'S FATHER _____
BIRTHPLACE _____ DATE ___	BIRTHPLACE _____ DATE ___
GRANDFATHER'S MOTHER _____	GRANDFATHER'S MOTHER _____
BIRTHPLACE _____ DATE ___	BIRTHPLACE _____ DATE ___
GRANDMOTHER'S FATHER _____	GRANDMOTHER'S FATHER _____
BIRTHPLACE _____ DATE ___	BIRTHPLACE _____ DATE ___
GRANDMOTHER'S MOTHER _____	GRANDMOTHER'S MOTHER _____
BIRTHPLACE _____ DATE ___	BIRTHPLACE _____ DATE ___

Births

NAME _____ DATE _____

BORN TO _____

NAME _____ DATE _____

BORN TO _____

NAME _____ DATE _____

BORN TO _____

NAME _____ DATE _____

BORN TO _____

NAME _____ DATE _____

BORN TO _____

NAME _____ DATE _____

BORN TO _____

NAME _____ DATE _____

BORN TO _____

NAME _____ DATE _____

BORN TO _____

NAME _____ DATE _____

BORN TO _____

Deaths

NAME

DATE

NAME

DATE

NAME

DATE

NAME

DATE

NAME

DATE

NAME

DATE

NAME

DATE

NAME

DATE

NAME

DATE

Special Events

EVENT _____

PLACE _____ DATE _____

EVENT _____

PLACE _____ DATE _____

EVENT _____

PLACE _____ DATE _____

EVENT _____

PLACE _____ DATE _____

EVENT _____

PLACE _____ DATE _____

EVENT _____

PLACE _____ DATE _____

HOLY BIBLE

New Revised Standard Version

HOLY BIBLE

New Revised Standard Version

containing the
OLD AND NEW TESTAMENTS

ZONDERVAN BIBLE PUBLISHERS
GRAND RAPIDS, MICHIGAN

The Names And Order Of The
BOOKS OF THE BIBLE

The Old Testament

The New Testament

Study Helps
Promises and Perspectives
Concordance
Map Index

MAPS AND CHARTS

ABBREVIATIONS

The following abbreviations are used for the books of the Bible:

The Old Testament

Gen	Genesis	2 Chr	2 Chronicles	Dan	Daniel
Ex	Exodus	Ezra	Ezra	Hos	Hosea
Lev	Leviticus	Neh	Nehemiah	Joel	Joel
Num	Numbers	Esth	Esther	Am	Amos
Deut	Deuteronomy	Job	Job	Ob	Obadiah
Josh	Joshua	Ps	Psalms	Jon	Jonah
Judg	Judges	Prov	Proverbs	Mic	Micah
Ruth	Ruth	Eccl	Ecclesiastes	Nah	Nahum
1 Sam	1 Samuel	Song	Song of Solomon	Hab	Habakkuk
2 Sam	2 Samuel	Isa	Isaiah	Zeph	Zephaniah
1 Kings	1 Kings	Jer	Jeremiah	Hag	Haggai
2 Kings	2 Kings	Lam	Lamentations	Zech	Zechariah
1 Chr	1 Chronicles	Ezek	Ezekiel	Mal	Malachi

The New Testament

Mt	Matthew	Eph	Ephesians	Heb	Hebrews
Mk	Mark	Phil	Philippians	Jas	James
Lk	Luke	Col	Colossians	1 Pet	1 Peter
Jn	John	1 Thess	1 Thessalonians	2 Pet	2 Peter
Acts	Acts of the Apostles	2 Thess	2 Thessalonians	1 Jn	1 John
Rom	Romans	1 Tim	1 Timothy	2 Jn	2 John
1 Cor	1 Corinthians	2 Tim	2 Timothy	3 Jn	3 John
2 Cor	2 Corinthians	Titus	Titus	Jude	Jude
Gal	Galatians	Philem	Philemon	Rev	Revelation

In the notes to the books of the Old Testament the following abbreviations are used:

Ant.	Josephus, *Antiquities of the Jews*
Aram	Aramaic
Ch, chs	Chapter, chapters
Cn	Correction; made where the text has suffered in transmission and the versions provide no satisfactory restoration but where the Standard Bible Committee agrees with the judgment of competent scholars as to the most probable reconstruction of the original text.
Gk	Septuagint, Greek version of the Old Testament
Heb	Hebrew of the consonantal Masoretic Text of the Old Testament
Josephus	Flavius Josephus (Jewish historian, about A.D. 37 to about 95)
Macc.	The book(s) of the Maccabees
Ms(s)	Manuscript(s)
MT	The Hebrew of the pointed Masoretic Text of the Old Testament
OL	Old Latin
Q Ms(s)	Manuscript(s) found at Qumran by the Dead Sea
Sam	Samaritan Hebrew text of the Old Testament
Syr	Syriac Version of the Old Testament
Syr H	Syriac Version of Origen's Hexapla
Tg	Targum
Vg	Vulgate, Latin Version of the Old Testament

To The
READER

This preface is addressed to you by the Committee of translators, who wish to explain, as briefly as possible, the origin and character of our work. The publication of our revision is yet another step in the long, continual process of making the Bible available in the form of the English language that is most widely current in our day. To summarize in a single sentence: the New Revised Standard Version of the Bible is an authorized revision of the Revised Standard Version, published in 1952, which was a revision of the American Standard Version, published in 1901, which, in turn, embodied earlier revisions of the King James Version, published in 1611.

In the course of time, the King James Version came to be regarded as "the Authorized Version." With good reason it has been termed "the noblest monument of English prose," and it has entered, as no other book has, into the making of the personal character and the public institutions of the English-speaking peoples. We owe to it an incalculable debt.

Yet the King James Version has serious defects. By the middle of the nineteenth century, the development of biblical studies and the discovery of many biblical manuscripts more ancient than those on which the King James Version was based made it apparent that these defects were so many as to call for revision. The task was begun, by authority of the Church of England, in 1870. The (British) Revised Version of the Bible was published in 1881-1885; and the American Standard Version, its variant embodying the preferences of the American scholars associated with the work, was published, as was mentioned above, in 1901. In 1928 the copyright of the latter was acquired by the International Council of Religious Education and thus passed into the ownership of the churches of the United States and Canada that were associated in this Council through their boards of education and publication.

The Council appointed a committee of scholars to have charge of the text of the American Standard Version and to undertake inquiry concerning the need for further revision. After studying the questions whether or not revision should be undertaken, and if so, what its nature and extent should be, in 1937 the Council authorized a revision. The scholars who served as members of the Committee worked in two sections, one dealing with the Old Testament and one with the New Testament. In 1946 the Revised Standard Version of the New Testament was published. The publication of the Revised Standard Version of the Bible, containing the Old and New Testaments, took place on September 30, 1952. A translation of the Apocryphal/Deuterocanonical Books of the Old Testament followed in 1957. In 1977 this collection was issued in an expanded edition, containing three additional texts received by Eastern Orthodox communions (3 and 4 Maccabees and Psalm 151). Thereafter the Revised Standard Version gained the distinction of being officially authorized for use by all major Christian churches: Protestant, Anglican, Roman Catholic, and Eastern Orthodox.

The Revised Standard Version Bible Committee is a continuing body, comprising about thirty members, both men and women. Ecumenical in representation, it includes scholars affiliated with various Protestant denominations, as well as several Roman Catholic members, an Eastern Orthodox member, and a Jewish member who serves in the Old Testament section. For a period of time the Committee included several members from Canada and from England.

Because no translation of the Bible is perfect or is acceptable to all groups of readers, and because discoveries of older manuscripts and further investigation of linguistic features of the text continue to become available, renderings of the Bible have proliferated. During the years following the publication of the Revised Standard Version, twenty-six other English translations and revisions of the Bible were produced by committees and by individual scholars—not to mention twenty-five other translations and revisions of the New Testament alone. One of the latter was the second edition of the RSV New Testament, issued in 1971, twenty-five years after its initial publication.

Following the publication of the RSV Old Testament in 1952, significant advances were made in the discovery and interpretation of documents in Semitic languages related to Hebrew. In addition to the information that had become available in the late 1940s from the Dead Sea texts of Isaiah and Habakkuk, subsequent acquisitions from the same area brought to light many other early copies of all the books of the Hebrew Scriptures (except Esther), though most of these copies are fragmentary. During the same period early Greek manuscript copies of books of the New Testament also became available.

In order to take these discoveries into account, along with recent studies of documents in Semitic languages related to Hebrew, in 1974 the Policies Committee of the Revised Standard Version, which is a standing committee of the National Council of the Churches of Christ in the U.S.A., authorized the preparation of a revision of the entire RSV Bible.

For the Old Testament the Committee has made use of the *Biblia Hebraica Stuttgartensia* (1977; ed. sec. emendata, 1983). This is an edition of the Hebrew and Aramaic text as current early in the Christian era and fixed by Jewish scholars (the "Masoretes") of the sixth to the ninth centuries. The vowel signs, which were added by the Masoretes, are accepted in the main, but where a more probable and convincing reading can be obtained by assuming different vowels, this has been done. No notes are given in such cases, because the vowel points are less ancient and reliable than the consonants. When an alternative reading given by the Masoretes is translated in a footnote, this is identified by the words "Another reading is."

Departures from the consonantal text of the best manuscripts have been made only where it seems clear that errors in copying had been made before the text was standardized. Most of the corrections adopted are based on the ancient versions (translations into Greek, Aramaic, Syriac, and Latin), which were made prior to the time of the work of the Masoretes and which therefore may reflect earlier forms of the Hebrew text. In such instances a footnote specifies the version or versions from which the correction has been derived and also gives a translation of the Masoretic Text. Where it was deemed appropriate to do so, information is supplied in footnotes from subsidiary Jewish traditions concerning other textual readings (the *Tiqqune Sopherim*, "emendations of the scribes"). These are identified in the footnotes as "Ancient Heb tradition."

Occasionally it is evident that the text has suffered in transmission and that none of the versions provides a satisfactory restoration. Here we can only follow the best judgment of competent scholars as to the most probable reconstruction of the original text. Such reconstructions are indicated in footnotes by the abbreviation Cn ("Correction"), and a translation of the Masoretic Text is added.

For the New Testament the Committee has based its work on the most recent edition of *The Greek New Testament*, prepared by an interconfessional and international committee and published by the United Bible Societies (1966; 3rd ed. corrected, 1983; information concerning changes to be introduced into the critical apparatus of the forthcoming 4th edition was available to the Committee). As in that edition, double brackets are used to enclose a few passages that are generally regarded to be later additions to the text, but which we have

retained because of their evident antiquity and their importance in the textual tradition. Only in very rare instances have we replaced the text or the punctuation of the Bible Societies' edition by an alternative that seemed to us to be superior. Here and there in the footnotes the phrase, "Other ancient authorities read," identifies alternative readings preserved by Greek manuscripts and early versions. In both Testaments, alternative renderings of the text are indicated by the word "Or."

As for the style of English adopted for the present revision, among the mandates given to the Committee in 1980 by the Division of Education and Ministry of the National Council of Churches of Christ (which now holds the copyright of the RSV Bible) was the directive to continue in the tradition of the King James Bible, but to introduce such changes as are warranted on the basis of accuracy, clarity, euphony, and current English usage. Within the constraints set by the original texts and by the mandates of the Division, the Committee has followed the maxim, "As literal as possible, as free as necessary." As a consequence, the New Revised Standard Version (NRSV) remains essentially a literal translation. Paraphrastic renderings have been adopted only sparingly, and then chiefly to compensate for a deficiency in the English language—the lack of a common gender third person singular pronoun.

During the almost half a century since the publication of the RSV, many in the churches have become sensitive to the danger of linguistic sexism arising from the inherent bias of the English language towards the masculine gender, a bias that in the case of the Bible has often restricted or obscured the meaning of the original text. The mandates from the Division specified that, in references to men and women, masculine-oriented language should be eliminated as far as this can be done without altering passages that reflect the historical situation of ancient patriarchal culture. As can be appreciated, more than once the Committee found that the several mandates stood in tension and even in conflict. The various concerns had to be balanced case by case in order to provide a faithful and acceptable rendering without using contrived English. Only very occasionally has the pronoun "he" or "him" been retained in passages where the reference may have been to a woman as well as to a man; for example, in several legal texts in Leviticus and Deuteronomy. In such instances of formal, legal language, the options of either putting the passage in the plural or of introducing additional nouns to avoid masculine pronouns in English seemed to the Committee to obscure the historic structure and literary character of the original. In the vast majority of cases, however, inclusiveness has been attained by simple rephrasing or by introducing plural forms when this does not distort the meaning of the passage. Of course, in narrative and in parable no attempt was made to generalize the sex of individual persons.

Another aspect of style will be detected by readers who compare the more stately English rendering of the Old Testament with the less formal rendering adopted for the New Testament. For example, the traditional distinction between *shall* and *will* in English has been retained in the Old Testament as appropriate in rendering a document that embodies what may be termed the classic form of Hebrew, while in the New Testament the abandonment of such distinctions in the usage of the future tense in English reflects the more colloquial nature of the koine Greek used by most New Testament authors except when they are quoting the Old Testament.

Careful readers will notice that here and there in the Old Testament the word LORD (or in certain cases GOD) is printed in capital letters. This represents the traditional manner in English versions of rendering the Divine Name, the "Tetragrammaton" (see the notes on Exodus 3.14, 15), following the precedent of the ancient Greek and Latin translators and the long established practice in the reading of the Hebrew Scriptures in the synagogue. While it is almost if not quite

certain that the Name was originally pronounced "Yahweh," this pronunciation was not indicated when the Masoretes added vowel sounds to the consonantal Hebrew text. To the four consonants YHWH of the Name, which had come to be regarded as too sacred to be pronounced, they attached vowel signs indicating that in its place should be read the Hebrew word *Adonai* meaning "Lord" (or *Elohim* meaning "God"). Ancient Greek translators employed the word *Kyrios* ("Lord") for the Name. The Vulgate likewise used the Latin word *Dominus* ("Lord"). The form "Jehovah" is of late medieval origin; it is a combination of the consonants of the Divine Name and the vowels attached to it by the Masoretes but belonging to an entirely different word. Although the American Standard Version (1901) had used "Jehovah" to render the Tetragrammaton (the sound of Y being represented by J and the sound of W by V, as in Latin), for two reasons the Committees that produced the RSV and the NRSV returned to the more familiar usage of the King James Version. (1) The word "Jehovah" does not accurately represent any form of the Name ever used in Hebrew. (2) The use of any proper name for the one and only God, as though there were other gods from whom the true God had to be distinguished, began to be discontinued in Judaism before the Christian era and is inappropriate for the universal faith of the Christian Church.

It will be seen that in the Psalms and in other prayers addressed to God the archaic second person singular pronouns (*thee, thou, thine*) and verb forms (*art, hast, hadst*) are no longer used. Although some readers may regret this change, it should be pointed out that in the original languages neither the Old Testament nor the New makes any linguistic distinction between addressing a human being and addressing the Deity. Furthermore, in the tradition of the King James Version one will not expect to find the use of capital letters for pronouns that refer to the Deity — such capitalization is an unnecessary innovation that has only recently been introduced into a few English translations of the Bible. Finally, we have left to the discretion of the licensed publishers such matters as section headings, cross-references, and clues to the pronunciation of proper names.

This new version seeks to preserve all that is best in the English Bible as it has been known and used through the years. It is intended for use in public reading and congregational worship, as well as in private study, instruction, and meditation. We have resisted the temptation to introduce terms and phrases that merely reflect current moods, and have tried to put the message of the Scriptures in simple, enduring words and expressions that are worthy to stand in the great tradition of the King James Bible and its predecessors.

In traditional Judaism and Christianity, the Bible has been more than a historical document to be preserved or a classic of literature to be cherished and admired; it is recognized as the unique record of God's dealings with people over the ages. The Old Testament sets forth the call of a special people to enter into covenant relation with the God of justice and steadfast love and to bring God's law to the nations. The New Testament records the life and work of Jesus Christ, the one in whom "the Word became flesh," as well as describes the rise and spread of the early Christian Church. The Bible carries its full message, not to those who regard it simply as a noble literary heritage of the past or who wish to use it to enhance political purposes and advance otherwise desirable goals, but to all persons and communities who read it so that they may discern and understand what God is saying to them. That message must not be disguised in phrases that are no longer clear, or hidden under words that have changed or lost their meaning; it must be presented in language that is direct and plain and meaningful to people today. It is the hope and prayer of the translators that this version of the Bible may continue to hold a large place in congregational life and to speak to all readers, young and old alike, helping them to understand and believe and respond to its message.

For the Committee,

Bruce M. Metzger

THE HEBREW SCRIPTURES
commonly called

THE OLD TESTAMENT

Genesis

Title and Background

The first phrase in the Hebrew text of Genesis 1.1 means "In the beginning." The book of Genesis is about many beginnings—the beginning of the universe, the beginning of man and woman, the beginning of human sin, and the beginning of God's promises and plans for salvation.

Author and Date of Writing

Traditionally, Jews and Christians alike have held that Moses was the author/compiler of Genesis, the first of the five books of the Old Testament known as the Pentateuch (meaning "five-volumed book"). More recently, scholars have suggested that though Moses may have written parts of the Pentateuch, these five books did not take their final form until later on in Israelite history.

There are two possibilities for the historical period during which Moses lived. The older view puts Moses in the fifteenth century B.C.; this is based primarily on 1 Kings 6.1, which states that "the fourth year of Solomon's reign over Israel" was the same as "the four hundred eightieth year after the Israelites came out of the land of Egypt." The other view, based largely on archaeological evidence for the date of the exodus, places Moses in the thirteenth century B.C.

Theme and Message

The message of Genesis is rich and complex but it is mainly a book of relationships—between God and nature, between God and the human race, and between various people. It stresses the fact that the one true God is sovereign over all that exists, whether good or evil. It introduces us to the way in which God initiates and enters into covenants with his chosen people, pledging his love and faithfulness to them.

Outline

I. Primeval History: Four Great Events (1.1–11.32)
 A. The Creation of the Universe, Adam, and Eve (1.1–2.25)
 B. The Human Race's First Sin and Its Results (3.1–5.32)
 C. The Great Flood (6.1–9.29)
 D. The Scattering of the Nations (10.1–11.32)
II. Patriarchal History: Four Great Characters (12.1–50.26)
 A. The Life of Abraham (12.1–20.18)
 B. The Life of Isaac (21.1–26.35)
 C. The Life of Jacob (27.1–37.1)
 D. The Life of Joseph (37.2–50.26)

Six Days of Creation and the Sabbath

1 In the beginning when God created[a] the heavens and the earth, [2] the earth was a formless void and darkness covered the face of the deep, while a wind from God[b] swept over the face of the waters. [3] Then God said, "Let there be light"; and there was light. [4] And God saw that the light was good; and God separated the light from the darkness. [5] God called the light Day, and the darkness he called

1.1 Jn 1.1,2; Ps 8.3; Isa 44.24; 42.5; 45.18 **1.2** Jer 4.23; Ps 104.30 **1.3** Ps 33.6,9; 2 Cor 4.6

1.4 Isa 45.7 **1.5** Ps 74.16

a Or when God began to create or In the beginning God created b Or while the spirit of God or while a mighty wind

Night. And there was evening and there was morning, the first day.

6 And God said, "Let there be a dome in the midst of the waters, and let it separate the waters from the waters." [7] So God made the dome and separated the waters that were under the dome from the waters that were above the dome. And it was so. [8] God called the dome Sky. And there was evening and there was morning, the second day.

9 And God said, "Let the waters under the sky be gathered together into one place, and let the dry land appear." And it was so. [10] God called the dry land Earth, and the waters that were gathered together he called Seas. And God saw that it was good. [11] Then God said, "Let the earth put forth vegetation: plants yielding seed, and fruit trees of every kind on earth that bear fruit with the seed in it." And it was so. [12] The earth brought forth vegetation: plants yielding seed of every kind, and trees of every kind bearing fruit with the seed in it. And God saw that it was good. [13] And there was evening and there was morning, the third day.

14 And God said, "Let there be lights in the dome of the sky to separate the day from the night; and let them be for signs and for seasons and for days and years, [15] and let them be lights in the dome of the sky to give light upon the earth." And it was so. [16] God made the two great lights—the greater light to rule the day and the lesser light to rule the night—and the stars. [17] God set them in the dome of the sky to give light upon the earth, [18] to rule over the day and over the night, and to separate the light from the darkness. And God saw that it was good. [19] And there was evening and there was morning, the fourth day.

20 And God said, "Let the waters bring forth swarms of living creatures, and let birds fly above the earth across the dome of the sky." [21] So God created the great sea monsters and every living creature that moves, of every kind, with which the waters swarm, and every winged bird of every kind. And God saw that it was good. [22] God blessed them, saying, "Be fruitful and multiply and fill the waters in the seas, and let birds multiply on the earth." [23] And there was evening and there was morning, the fifth day.

24 And God said, "Let the earth bring forth living creatures of every kind: cattle and creeping things and wild animals of the earth of every kind." And it was so. [25] God made the wild animals of the earth of every kind, and the cattle of every kind, and everything that creeps upon the ground of every kind. And God saw that it was good.

26 Then God said, "Let us make humankind[c] in our image, according to our likeness; and let them have dominion over the fish of the sea, and over the birds of the air, and over the cattle, and over all the wild animals of the earth,[d] and over every creeping thing that creeps upon the earth."

27 So God created humankind[c]
 in his image,
 in the image of God he
 created them;[e]
 male and female he
 created them.

28 God blessed them, and God said to them, "Be fruitful and multiply, and fill the earth and subdue it; and have dominion over the fish of the sea and over the birds of the air and over every living thing that moves upon the earth." [29] God said, "See, I have given you every plant yielding seed that is upon the face of all the earth, and every tree with seed in its fruit; you shall have them for food. [30] And to every beast of the earth, and to every bird of the air, and to everything that creeps on the earth, everything that has the breath of life, I have given every green plant for food." And it was so. [31] God saw everything that he

1.6
Jer 10.12
1.7
Prov 8.28;
Ps 148.4
1.9
Job 26.10;
Prov 8.29;
Jer 5.22;
2 Pet 3.5
1.10
Ps 33.7
1.11
Lk 6.44
1.14
Ps 74.16;
104.19
1.16
Ps 136.8,9;
Job 38.7
1.18
Jer 31.35
1.21
Ps 104.25,
26

1.22
Gen 8.17
1.25
Jer 27.5
1.26
Ps 100.3;
Acts 17.26,
28,29;
Col 3.10
1.27
1 Cor 11.7;
Gen 5.2;
Mt 19.4
1.28
Gen 9.1,7;
Lev 26.9
1.29
Ps 104.14,
15; 136.25
1.30
Ps 145.15;
Job 38.41
1.31
Ps 104.24

[c] Heb *adam* [d] Syr: Heb *and over all the earth* [e] Heb *him*

had made, and indeed, it was very good. And there was evening and there was morning, the sixth day.

2 Thus the heavens and the earth were finished, and all their multitude. ²And on the seventh day God finished the work that he had done, and he rested on the seventh day from all the work that he had done. ³So God blessed the seventh day and hallowed it, because on it God rested from all the work that he had done in creation.

4 These are the generations of the heavens and the earth when they were created.

Another Account of the Creation

In the day that the LORD God made the earth and the heavens, ⁵when no plant of the field was yet in the earth and no herb of the field had yet sprung up—for the LORD God had not caused it to rain upon the earth, and there was no one to till the ground; ⁶but a stream would rise from the earth, and water the whole face of the ground— ⁷then the LORD God formed man from the dust of the ground,ᶠ and breathed into his nostrils the breath of life; and the man became a living being. ⁸And the LORD God planted a garden in Eden, in the east; and there he put the man whom he had formed. ⁹Out of the ground the LORD God made to grow every tree that is pleasant to the sight and good for food, the tree of life also in the midst of the garden, and the tree of the knowledge of good and evil.

10 A river flows out of Eden to water the garden, and from there it divides and becomes four branches. ¹¹The name of the first is Pishon; it is the one that flows around the whole land of Havilah, where there is gold; ¹²and the gold of that land is good; bdellium and onyx stone are there. ¹³The name of the second river is Gihon; it is the one that flows around the whole land of Cush. ¹⁴The name of the third river is Tigris, which flows

2.1
Ps 33.6
2.2
Ex 20.11;
Heb 4.4
2.3
Isa 58.13
2.5
Gen 1.12;
Job 38.26-28
2.7
Gen 3.19;
Ps 103.14;
Job 33.4;
Acts 17.25;
1 Cor 15.45
2.8
Isa 51.3;
Gen 3.24;
4.16
2.9
Ezek 31.8;
Gen 3.22;
Rev 2.7;
22.2,14
2.12
Num 11.7
2.14
Dan 10.4

2.17
Deut 30.15,
19,20;
Rom 6.23;
Jas 1.15
2.18
1 Cor 11.9
2.19
Gen 1.20,
24; Ps 8.7
2.21
1 Sam 26.12
2.23
Eph 5.30;
1 Cor 11.8
2.24
Mt 19.5;
Mk 10.7,8;
1 Cor 6.16;
Eph 5.31
2.25
Gen 3.7,10,
11
3.1
2 Cor 11.3;
Rev 12.9;
20.2

east of Assyria. And the fourth river is the Euphrates.

15 The LORD God took the man and put him in the garden of Eden to till it and keep it. ¹⁶And the LORD God commanded the man, "You may freely eat of every tree of the garden; ¹⁷but of the tree of the knowledge of good and evil you shall not eat, for in the day that you eat of it you shall die."

18 Then the LORD God said, "It is not good that the man should be alone; I will make him a helper as his partner." ¹⁹So out of the ground the LORD God formed every animal of the field and every bird of the air, and brought them to the man to see what he would call them; and whatever the man called every living creature, that was its name. ²⁰The man gave names to all cattle, and to the birds of the air, and to every animal of the field; but for the manᵍ there was not found a helper as his partner. ²¹So the LORD God caused a deep sleep to fall upon the man, and he slept; then he took one of his ribs and closed up its place with flesh. ²²And the rib that the LORD God had taken from the man he made into a woman and brought her to the man. ²³Then the man said,

"This at last is bone of my
 bones
 and flesh of my flesh;
 this one shall be called
 Woman,ʰ
 for out of Manⁱ this one
 was taken."

²⁴Therefore a man leaves his father and his mother and clings to his wife, and they become one flesh. ²⁵And the man and his wife were both naked, and were not ashamed.

The First Sin and Its Punishment

3 Now the serpent was more crafty than any other wild animal that the LORD God had made. He said to the woman, "Did God

ᶠ Or formed a man (Heb adam) of dust from the ground (Heb adamah) ᵍ Or for Adam
ʰ Heb ishshah ⁱ Heb ish

say, 'You shall not eat from any tree in the garden'?" ²The woman said to the serpent, "We may eat of the fruit of the trees in the garden; ³but God said, 'You shall not eat of the fruit of the tree that is in the middle of the garden, nor shall you touch it, or you shall die.' " ⁴But the serpent said to the woman, "You will not die; ⁵for God knows that when you eat of it your eyes will be opened, and you will be like God,ⁱ knowing good and evil." ⁶So when the woman saw that the tree was good for food, and that it was a delight to the eyes, and that the tree was to be desired to make one wise, she took of its fruit and ate; and she also gave some to her husband, who was with her, and he ate. ⁷Then the eyes of both were opened, and they knew that they were naked; and they sewed fig leaves together and made loincloths for themselves.

8 They heard the sound of the Lord God walking in the garden at the time of the evening breeze, and the man and his wife hid themselves from the presence of the Lord God among the trees of the garden. ⁹But the Lord God called to the man, and said to him, "Where are you?" ¹⁰He said, "I heard the sound of you in the garden, and I was afraid, because I was naked; and I hid myself." ¹¹He said, "Who told you that you were naked? Have you eaten from the tree of which I commanded you not to eat?" ¹²The man said, "The woman whom you gave to be with me, she gave me fruit from the tree, and I ate." ¹³Then the Lord God said to the woman, "What is this that you have done?" The woman said, "The serpent tricked me, and I ate." ¹⁴The Lord God said to the serpent,

"Because you have done this,
 cursed are you among all
 animals
 and among all wild
 creatures;
upon your belly you shall go,
 and dust you shall eat
 all the days of your life.

3.3
2 Cor 11.3
3.4
Jn 8.44
3.6
1 Tim 2.14
3.8
Job 31.33;
Jer 23.24
3.10
1 Jn 3.20
3.12
Prov 28.13
3.13
2 Cor 11.3;
1 Tim 2.14
3.14
Isa 65.25;
Mic 7.17

3.15
Jn 8.44;
Acts 13.10;
1 Jn 3.8;
Isa 7.14;
Mt 1.23;
Rom 16.20;
Rev 12.7
3.16
Isa 13.8;
Gen 4.7;
1 Cor 11.3;
Eph 5.22
3.17
1 Sam 15.23;
Gen 2.17;
Rom 8.20-22
3.18
Ps 104.14
3.19
Gen 2.7;
Ps 90.3;
104.29;
Eccl 12.7
3.22
Rev 22.2
3.23
Gen 4.2

¹⁵ I will put enmity between
 you and the woman,
 and between your offspring
 and hers;
he will strike your head,
 and you will strike his
 heel."
¹⁶To the woman he said,
"I will greatly increase your
 pangs in childbearing;
in pain you shall bring
 forth children,
yet your desire shall be for
 your husband,
and he shall rule over you."
¹⁷And to the manᵏ he said,
"Because you have listened
 to the voice of your
 wife,
and have eaten of the tree
about which I commanded
 you,
'You shall not eat of it,'
cursed is the ground because
 of you;
in toil you shall eat of it all
 the days of your life;
¹⁸ thorns and thistles it shall
 bring forth for you;
and you shall eat the
 plants of the field.
¹⁹ By the sweat of your face
 you shall eat bread
until you return to the
 ground,
for out of it you were
 taken;
you are dust,
 and to dust you shall
 return."

20 The man named his wife Eve,¹ because she was the mother of all living. ²¹And the Lord God made garments of skins for the manᵐ and for his wife, and clothed them.

22 Then the Lord God said, "See, the man has become like one of us, knowing good and evil; and now, he might reach out his hand and take also from the tree of life, and eat, and live forever"— ²³therefore the Lord God sent him forth from the garden of Eden, to

ⁱ Or *gods* ᵏ Or *to Adam* ¹ In Heb *Eve* resembles the word for *living* ᵐ Or *for Adam*

till the ground from which he was taken. [24] He drove out the man; and at the east of the garden of Eden he placed the cherubim, and a sword flaming and turning to guard the way to the tree of life.

Cain Murders Abel

4 Now the man knew his wife Eve, and she conceived and bore Cain, saying, "I have produced[n] a man with the help of the LORD." [2] Next she bore his brother Abel. Now Abel was a keeper of sheep, and Cain a tiller of the ground. [3] In the course of time Cain brought to the LORD an offering of the fruit of the ground, [4] and Abel for his part brought of the firstlings of his flock, their fat portions. And the LORD had regard for Abel and his offering, [5] but for Cain and his offering he had no regard. So Cain was very angry, and his countenance fell. [6] The LORD said to Cain, "Why are you angry, and why has your countenance fallen? [7] If you do well, will you not be accepted? And if you do not do well, sin is lurking at the door; its desire is for you, but you must master it."

[8] Cain said to his brother Abel, "Let us go out to the field."[o] And when they were in the field, Cain rose up against his brother Abel, and killed him. [9] Then the LORD said to Cain, "Where is your brother Abel?" He said, "I do not know; am I my brother's keeper?" [10] And the LORD said, "What have you done? Listen; your brother's blood is crying out to me from the ground! [11] And now you are cursed from the ground, which has opened its mouth to receive your brother's blood from your hand. [12] When you till the ground, it will no longer yield to you its strength; you will be a fugitive and a wanderer on the earth." [13] Cain said to the LORD, "My punishment is greater than I can bear! [14] Today you have driven me away from the soil, and I shall be hidden from your face; I shall be a fugitive and a wanderer on the earth, and anyone who meets me may kill me." [15] Then the LORD said

to him, "Not so![p] Whoever kills Cain will suffer a sevenfold vengeance." And the LORD put a mark on Cain, so that no one who came upon him would kill him. [16] Then Cain went away from the presence of the LORD, and settled in the land of Nod,[q] east of Eden.

Beginnings of Civilization

[17] Cain knew his wife, and she conceived and bore Enoch; and he built a city, and named it Enoch after his son Enoch. [18] To Enoch was born Irad; and Irad was the father of Mehujael, and Mehujael the father of Methushael, and Methushael the father of Lamech. [19] Lamech took two wives; the name of the one was Adah, and the name of the other Zillah. [20] Adah bore Jabal; he was the ancestor of those who live in tents and have livestock. [21] His brother's name was Jubal; he was the ancestor of all those who play the lyre and pipe. [22] Zillah bore Tubal-cain, who made all kinds of bronze and iron tools. The sister of Tubal-cain was Naamah.

[23] Lamech said to his wives:
"Adah and Zillah, hear my
voice;
you wives of Lamech, listen
to what I say:
I have killed a man for
wounding me,
a young man for striking
me.
[24] If Cain is avenged sevenfold,
truly Lamech
seventy-sevenfold."

[25] Adam knew his wife again, and she bore a son and named him Seth, for she said, "God has appointed[r] for me another child instead of Abel, because Cain killed him." [26] To Seth also a son was born, and he named him Enosh. At that time people began to invoke the name of the LORD.

3.24
Gen 2.8,9
4.2
Lk 11.50,51
4.3
Num 18.12
4.4
Num 18.17;
Lev 3.16;
Heb 11.4
4.5
Isa 3.9;
Jude 11
4.8
Mt 23.35;
1 Jn 3.12
4.10
Heb 12.24;
Rev 6.10
4.12
v. 14
4.14
Ps 51.11;
Gen 9.6;
Num 35.19,
21,27
4.15
Ps 79.12;
Ezek 9.4,6

4.17
Ps 49.11
4.18
Gen 5.25,
28,30
4.23
Ex 20.13;
Lev 19.18;
Deut 32.35;
Lk 3.36;
v. 18
4.24
v. 15
4.25
Gen 5.3;
v. 8
4.26
1 Kings 18.24;
Ps 116.17;
Joel 2.32;
Zeph 3.9;
1 Cor 1.2

[n] The verb in Heb resembles the word for *Cain* [o] Sam Gk Syr Compare Vg: MT lacks *Let us go out to the field* [p] Gk Syr Vg: Heb *Therefore* [q] That is *Wandering* [r] The verb in Heb resembles the word for *Seth*

Adam's Descendants to Noah and His Sons

5 This is the list of the descendants of Adam. When God created humankind,[s] he made them[t] in the likeness of God. [2] Male and female he created them, and he blessed them and named them "Humankind"[s] when they were created.

3 When Adam had lived one hundred thirty years, he became the father of a son in his likeness, according to his image, and named him Seth. [4] The days of Adam after he became the father of Seth were eight hundred years; and he had other sons and daughters. [5] Thus all the days that Adam lived were nine hundred thirty years; and he died.

6 When Seth had lived one hundred five years, he became the father of Enosh. [7] Seth lived after the birth of Enosh eight hundred seven years, and had other sons and daughters. [8] Thus all the days of Seth were nine hundred twelve years; and he died.

9 When Enosh had lived ninety years, he became the father of Kenan. [10] Enosh lived after the birth of Kenan eight hundred fifteen years, and had other sons and daughters. [11] Thus all the days of Enosh were nine hundred five years; and he died.

12 When Kenan had lived seventy years, he became the father of Mahalalel. [13] Kenan lived after the birth of Mahalalel eight hundred and forty years, and had other sons and daughters. [14] Thus all the days of Kenan were nine hundred and ten years; and he died.

15 When Mahalalel had lived sixty-five years, he became the father of Jared. [16] Mahalalel lived after the birth of Jared eight hundred thirty years, and had other sons and daughters. [17] Thus all the days of Mahalalel were eight hundred ninety-five years; and he died.

18 When Jared had lived one hundred sixty-two years he became the father of Enoch. [19] Jared lived after the birth of Enoch eight hundred years, and had other sons and daughters. [20] Thus all the days of Jared were nine hundred sixty-two years; and he died.

21 When Enoch had lived sixty-five years, he became the father of Methuselah. [22] Enoch walked with God after the birth of Methuselah three hundred years, and had other sons and daughters. [23] Thus all the days of Enoch were three hundred sixty-five years. [24] Enoch walked with God; then he was no more, because God took him.

25 When Methuselah had lived one hundred eighty-seven years, he became the father of Lamech. [26] Methuselah lived after the birth of Lamech seven hundred eighty-two years, and had other sons and daughters. [27] Thus all the days of Methuselah were nine hundred sixty-nine years; and he died.

28 When Lamech had lived one hundred eighty-two years, he became the father of a son; [29] he named him Noah, saying, "Out of the ground that the LORD has cursed this one shall bring us relief from our work and from the toil of our hands." [30] Lamech lived after the birth of Noah five hundred ninety-five years, and had other sons and daughters. [31] Thus all the days of Lamech were seven hundred seventy-seven years; and he died.

32 After Noah was five hundred years old, Noah became the father of Shem, Ham, and Japheth.

The Wickedness of Humankind

6 When people began to multiply on the face of the ground, and daughters were born to them, [2] the sons of God saw that they were fair; and they took wives for themselves of all that they chose. [3] Then the LORD said, "My spirit shall not abide[u] in mortals forever, for they are flesh; their days shall be one hundred twenty years." [4] The Nephilim were on the earth in those days—and also afterward—

5.1 Gen 1.26; Eph 4.24; Col 3.10
5.2 Gen 1.27
5.3 Gen 4.25
5.5 Gen 3.19; Heb 9.27
5.6 Gen 4.26
5.7 Lk 3.38
5.11 1 Chr 1.1
5.12 1 Chr 1.2
5.15 1 Chr 1.2
5.18 Jude 14,15

5.21 1 Chr 1.3; Lk 3.37; Jude 14
5.24 2 Kings 2.11; Heb 11.5
5.26 Lk 3.36
5.29 Gen 3.17-19
5.32 Gen 6.10; 10.21
6.1 Gen 1.28
6.2 Deut 7.1-4
6.3 1 Pet 3.19; Ps 78.39

s Heb *adam* t Heb *him* u Meaning of Heb uncertain

when the sons of God went in to the daughters of humans, who bore children to them. These were the heroes that were of old, warriors of renown.

5 The Lord saw that the wickedness of humankind was great in the earth, and that every inclination of the thoughts of their hearts was only evil continually. 6 And the Lord was sorry that he had made humankind on the earth, and it grieved him to his heart. 7 So the Lord said, "I will blot out from the earth the human beings I have created—people together with animals and creeping things and birds of the air, for I am sorry that I have made them." 8 But Noah found favor in the sight of the Lord.

Noah Pleases God

9 These are the descendants of Noah. Noah was a righteous man, blameless in his generation; Noah walked with God. 10 And Noah had three sons, Shem, Ham, and Japheth.

11 Now the earth was corrupt in God's sight, and the earth was filled with violence. 12 And God saw that the earth was corrupt; for all flesh had corrupted its ways upon the earth. 13 And God said to Noah, "I have determined to make an end of all flesh, for the earth is filled with violence because of them; now I am going to destroy them along with the earth. 14 Make yourself an ark of cypress^v wood; make rooms in the ark, and cover it inside and out with pitch. 15 This is how you are to make it: the length of the ark three hundred cubits, its width fifty cubits, and its height thirty cubits. 16 Make a roof^w for the ark, and finish it to a cubit above; and put the door of the ark in its side; make it with lower, second, and third decks. 17 For my part, I am going to bring a flood of waters on the earth, to destroy from under heaven all flesh in which is the breath of life; everything that is on the earth shall die. 18 But I will establish my covenant with you; and you shall come into

the ark, you, your sons, your wife, and your sons' wives with you. 19 And of every living thing, of all flesh, you shall bring two of every kind into the ark, to keep them alive with you; they shall be male and female. 20 Of the birds according to their kinds, and of the animals according to their kinds, of every creeping thing of the ground according to its kind, two of every kind shall come in to you, to keep them alive. 21 Also take with you every kind of food that is eaten, and store it up; and it shall serve as food for you and for them." 22 Noah did this; he did all that God commanded him.

The Great Flood

7 Then the Lord said to Noah, "Go into the ark, you and all your household, for I have seen that you alone are righteous before me in this generation. 2 Take with you seven pairs of all clean animals, the male and its mate; and a pair of the animals that are not clean, the male and its mate; 3 and seven pairs of the birds of the air also, male and female, to keep their kind alive on the face of all the earth. 4 For in seven days I will send rain on the earth for forty days and forty nights; and every living thing that I have made I will blot out from the face of the ground." 5 And Noah did all that the Lord had commanded him.

6 Noah was six hundred years old when the flood of waters came on the earth. 7 And Noah with his sons and his wife and his sons' wives went into the ark to escape the waters of the flood. 8 Of clean animals, and of animals that are not clean, and of birds, and of everything that creeps on the ground, 9 two and two, male and female, went into the ark with Noah, as God had commanded Noah. 10 And after seven days the waters of the flood came on the earth.

11 In the six hundredth year of Noah's life, in the second month, on the seventeenth day of the

Cross-references (center column):

6.5 Gen 8.21
6.6 1 Sam 15.11, 29; 2 Sam 24.16; Mal 3.6; Jas 1.17; Isa 63.10
6.8 Gen 19.19; Ex 33.12; Lk 1.30; Acts 7.46
6.9 Gen 17.1; Ezek 14.14, 20; Heb 11.7; 2 Pet 2.5; Gen 5.22
6.10 Gen 5.32
6.11 Rom 2.13; Ezek 8.17
6.12 Ps 14.1-3
6.13 Ezek 7.2,3; v. 17
6.14 Heb 11.7; 1 Pet 3.20
6.17 Gen 7.4, 21-23
6.18 Gen 7.1,7, 13; 1 Pet 3.20; 2 Pet 2.5
6.19 Gen 7.8,9, 15,16
6.20 Gen 7.9,15
6.22 Heb 11.7; Gen 7.5
7.1 Mt 24.38; Lk 17.26
7.2 Lev ch. 11; 10.10; Ezek 44.23
7.7 Gen 6.22; v. 1
7.11 Gen 8.2; Prov 8.28; Ezek 26.19

^v Meaning of Heb uncertain ^w Or *window*

month, on that day all the fountains of the great deep burst forth, and the windows of the heavens were opened. 12 The rain fell on the earth forty days and forty nights. 13 On the very same day Noah with his sons, Shem and Ham and Japheth, and Noah's wife and the three wives of his sons entered the ark, 14 they and every wild animal of every kind, and all domestic animals of every kind, and every creeping thing that creeps on the earth, and every bird of every kind—every bird, every winged creature. 15 They went into the ark with Noah, two and two of all flesh in which there was the breath of life. 16 And those that entered, male and female of all flesh, went in as God had commanded him; and the LORD shut him in.

17 The flood continued forty days on the earth; and the waters increased, and bore up the ark, and it rose high above the earth. 18 The waters swelled and increased greatly on the earth; and the ark floated on the face of the waters. 19 The waters swelled so mightily on the earth that all the high mountains under the whole heaven were covered; 20 the waters swelled above the mountains, covering them fifteen cubits deep. 21 And all flesh died that moved on the earth, birds, domestic animals, wild animals, all swarming creatures that swarm on the earth, and all human beings; 22 everything on dry land in whose nostrils was the breath of life died. 23 He blotted out every living thing that was on the face of the ground, human beings and animals and creeping things and birds of the air; they were blotted out from the earth. Only Noah was left, and those that were with him in the ark. 24 And the waters swelled on the earth for one hundred fifty days.

The Flood Subsides

8 But God remembered Noah and all the wild animals and all the domestic animals that were with him in the ark. And God made a wind blow over the earth, and the

waters subsided; 2 the fountains of the deep and the windows of the heavens were closed, the rain from the heavens was restrained, 3 and the waters gradually receded from the earth. At the end of one hundred fifty days the waters had abated; 4 and in the seventh month, on the seventeenth day of the month, the ark came to rest on the mountains of Ararat. 5 The waters continued to abate until the tenth month; in the tenth month, on the first day of the month, the tops of the mountains appeared.

6 At the end of forty days Noah opened the window of the ark that he had made 7 and sent out the raven; and it went to and fro until the waters were dried up from the earth. 8 Then he sent out the dove from him, to see if the waters had subsided from the face of the ground; 9 but the dove found no place to set its foot, and it returned to him to the ark, for the waters were still on the face of the whole earth. So he put out his hand and took it and brought it into the ark with him. 10 He waited another seven days, and again he sent out the dove from the ark; 11 and the dove came back to him in the evening, and there in its beak was a freshly plucked olive leaf; so Noah knew that the waters had subsided from the earth. 12 Then he waited another seven days, and sent out the dove; and it did not return to him any more.

13 In the six hundred first year, in the first month, the first day of the month, the waters were dried up from the earth; and Noah removed the covering of the ark, and looked, and saw that the face of the ground was drying. 14 In the second month, on the twenty-seventh day of the month, the earth was dry. 15 Then God said to Noah, 16 "Go out of the ark, you and your wife, and your sons and your sons' wives with you. 17 Bring out with you every living thing that is with you of all flesh—birds and animals and every creeping thing that creeps on the earth—so that they may

7.12
vv. 4,17
7.13
vv. 1,7; 6.18
7.15
Gen 6.20
7.16
vv. 2,3
7.17
vv. 4,12
7.18
Ps 104.26
7.21
Gen 6.13,17
7.22
Gen 2.7
7.23
1 Pet 3.20;
2 Pet 2.5
7.24
Gen 8.3
8.1
Gen 19.29;
Ex 2.24;
1 Sam 1.19;
Ex 14.21;
Job 12.15;
Ps 29.10;
Isa 44.27;
Nah 1.4

8.2
Gen 7.11;
Job 38.37
8.3
Gen 7.24
8.4
Jer 51.27
8.6
2 Pet 2.5
8.7
1 Kings 17.4,
6
8.11
Mt 10.16
8.13
2 Pet 3.5,6
8.16
Gen 7.13
8.17
Gen 1.22

abound on the earth, and be fruitful and multiply on the earth." 18 So Noah went out with his sons and his wife and his sons' wives. 19 And every animal, every creeping thing, and every bird, everything that moves on the earth, went out of the ark by families.

God's Promise to Noah

20 Then Noah built an altar to the LORD, and took of every clean animal and of every clean bird, and offered burnt offerings on the altar. 21 And when the LORD smelled the pleasing odor, the LORD said in his heart, "I will never again curse the ground because of humankind, for the inclination of the human heart is evil from youth; nor will I ever again destroy every living creature as I have done.

22 As long as the earth endures,
　　seedtime and harvest, cold
　　　　and heat,
　　summer and winter, day and
　　　　night,
　　shall not cease."

The Covenant with Noah

9 God blessed Noah and his sons, and said to them, "Be fruitful and multiply, and fill the earth. 2 The fear and dread of you shall rest on every animal of the earth, and on every bird of the air, on everything that creeps on the ground, and on all the fish of the sea; into your hand they are delivered. 3 Every moving thing that lives shall be food for you; and just as I gave you the green plants, I give you everything. 4 Only, you shall not eat flesh with its life, that is, its blood. 5 For your own lifeblood I will surely require a reckoning: from every animal I will require it and from human beings, each one for the blood of another, I will require a reckoning for human life.
6 Whoever sheds the blood of
　　a human,
　　by a human shall that
　　　　person's blood be shed;
　　for in his own image
　　God made humankind.
7 And you, be fruitful and multiply,

abound on the earth and multiply in it."

8 Then God said to Noah and to his sons with him, 9 "As for me, I am establishing my covenant with you and your descendants after you, 10 and with every living creature that is with you, the birds, the domestic animals, and every animal of the earth with you, as many as came out of the ark.ˣ 11 I establish my covenant with you, that never again shall all flesh be cut off by the waters of a flood, and never again shall there be a flood to destroy the earth." 12 God said, "This is the sign of the covenant that I make between me and you and every living creature that is with you, for all future generations: 13 I have set my bow in the clouds, and it shall be a sign of the covenant between me and the earth. 14 When I bring clouds over the earth and the bow is seen in the clouds, 15 I will remember my covenant that is between me and you and every living creature of all flesh; and the waters shall never again become a flood to destroy all flesh. 16 When the bow is in the clouds, I will see it and remember the everlasting covenant between God and every living creature of all flesh that is on the earth." 17 God said to Noah, "This is the sign of the covenant that I have established between me and all flesh that is on the earth."

Noah and His Sons

18 The sons of Noah who went out of the ark were Shem, Ham, and Japheth. Ham was the father of Canaan. 19 These three were the sons of Noah; and from these the whole earth was peopled.

20 Noah, a man of the soil, was the first to plant a vineyard. 21 He drank some of the wine and became drunk, and he lay uncovered in his tent. 22 And Ham, the father of Canaan, saw the nakedness of his father, and told his two brothers outside. 23 Then Shem and Japheth took a garment, laid it on both their shoulders, and walked

ˣ Gk: Heb adds *every animal of the earth*

8.20
Gen 12.7,8;
13.18; 22.9;
7.2; 22.2;
Ex 10.25
8.21
Lev 1.9;
2 Cor 2.15;
Gen 3.17;
6.17; 9.11,15
8.22
Isa 54.9;
Jer 33.20,25
9.1
v. 7;
Gen 1.28
9.3
Deut 12.15;
Gen 1.29
9.4
Lev 17.10-16;
Deut 12.23;
1 Sam 14.33
9.5
Ex 21.28;
Gen 4.9,10
9.6
Ex 21.12,
14;
Lev 24.17;
Mt 26.52;
Gen 1.27
9.7
vv. 1,19

9.9
Gen 6.18;
Isa 54.9
9.10
Ps 149.9
9.11
Isa 54.9
9.12
Gen 17.11
9.13
Ezek 1.28;
Rev 4.3
9.15
Lev 26.42,
45; Deut 7.9
9.16
Gen 17.13,
19
9.18
Gen 10.6
9.19
Gen 5.32
9.23
Ex 20.12

backward and covered the nakedness of their father; their faces were turned away, and they did not see their father's nakedness. 24When Noah awoke from his wine and knew what his youngest son had done to him, 25he said,

"Cursed be Canaan;
　lowest of slaves shall he be
　　to his brothers."
26He also said,
"Blessed by the Lord my God
　be Shem;
and let Canaan be his
　slave.
27 May God make space fory
　Japheth,
and let him live in the
　tents of Shem;
and let Canaan be his
　slave."

28 After the flood Noah lived three hundred fifty years. 29All the days of Noah were nine hundred fifty years; and he died.

Nations Descended from Noah

10 These are the descendants of Noah's sons, Shem, Ham, and Japheth; children were born to them after the flood.

2 The descendants of Japheth: Gomer, Magog, Madai, Javan, Tubal, Meshech, and Tiras. 3The descendants of Gomer: Ashkenaz, Riphath, and Togarmah. 4The descendants of Javan: Elishah, Tarshish, Kittim, and Rodanim.z 5From these the coastland peoples spread. These are the descendants of Japhetha in their lands, with their own language, by their families, in their nations.

6 The descendants of Ham: Cush, Egypt, Put, and Canaan. 7The descendants of Cush: Seba, Havilah, Sabtah, Raamah, and Sabteca. The descendants of Raamah: Sheba and Dedan. 8Cush became the father of Nimrod; he was the first on earth to become a mighty warrior. 9He was a mighty hunter before the Lord; therefore it is said, "Like Nimrod a mighty hunter before the Lord." 10The beginning of his kingdom was Babel, Erech, and Accad, all of them in the land of

Shinar. 11From that land he went into Assyria, and built Nineveh, Rehoboth-ir, Calah, and 12Resen between Nineveh and Calah; that is the great city. 13Egypt became the father of Ludim, Anamim, Lehabim, Naphtuhim, 14Pathrusim, Casluhim, and Caphtorim, from which the Philistines come.b

15 Canaan became the father of Sidon his firstborn, and Heth, 16and the Jebusites, the Amorites, the Girgashites, 17the Hivites, the Arkites, the Sinites, 18the Arvadites, the Zemarites, and the Hamathites. Afterward the families of the Canaanites spread abroad. 19And the territory of the Canaanites extended from Sidon, in the direction of Gerar, as far as Gaza, and in the direction of Sodom, Gomorrah, Admah, and Zeboiim, as far as Lasha. 20These are the descendants of Ham, by their families, their languages, their lands, and their nations.

21 To Shem also, the father of all the children of Eber, the elder brother of Japheth, children were born. 22The descendants of Shem: Elam, Asshur, Arpachshad, Lud, and Aram. 23The descendants of Aram: Uz, Hul, Gether, and Mash. 24Arpachshad became the father of Shelah; and Shelah became the father of Eber. 25To Eber were born two sons: the name of the one was Peleg,c for in his days the earth was divided, and his brother's name was Joktan. 26Joktan became the father of Almodad, Sheleph, Hazarmaveth, Jerah, 27Hadoram, Uzal, Diklah, 28Obal, Abimael, Sheba, 29Ophir, Havilah, and Jobab; all these were the descendants of Joktan. 30The territory in which they lived extended from Mesha in the direction of Sephar, the hill country of the east. 31These are the descendants of Shem, by their families, their lan-

Cross references

9.25 Deut 27.16
9.26 Ps 144.15
9.27 Eph 2.13, 14; 3.6
10.2 1 Chr 1.5-7
10.5 Gen 5.32
10.6 1 Chr 1.8-10
10.9 Mic 5.6
10.10 Mic 5.6
10.13 1 Chr 1.8, 11
10.15 1 Chr 1.13
10.18 1 Chr 1.16; 18.3
10.19 Num 34.2-12
10.22 1 Chr 1.17; Gen 14.1,9; 2 Kings 15.29; Gen 11.10; Isa 66.19
10.23 Job 1.1
10.24 Gen 11.12; Lk 3.35
10.25 1 Chr 1.19
10.26-29 1 Chr 1.20-23

y Heb yapht, a play on Japheth
z Heb Mss Sam Gk See 1 Chr 1.7: MT Dodanim　a Compare verses 20, 31. Heb lacks These are the descendants of Japheth　b Cn: Heb Casluhim, from which the Philistines come, and Caphtorim　c That is Division

guages, their lands, and their nations.

32 These are the families of Noah's sons, according to their genealogies, in their nations; and from these the nations spread abroad on the earth after the flood.

The Tower of Babel

11 Now the whole earth had one language and the same words. ²And as they migrated from the east,d they came upon a plain in the land of Shinar and settled there. ³And they said to one another, "Come, let us make bricks, and burn them thoroughly." And they had brick for stone, and bitumen for mortar. ⁴Then they said, "Come, let us build ourselves a city, and a tower with its top in the heavens, and let us make a name for ourselves; otherwise we shall be scattered abroad upon the face of the whole earth." ⁵The Lord came down to see the city and the tower, which mortals had built. ⁶And the Lord said, "Look, they are one people, and they have all one language; and this is only the beginning of what they will do; nothing that they propose to do will now be impossible for them. ⁷Come, let us go down, and confuse their language there, so that they will not understand one another's speech." ⁸So the Lord scattered them abroad from there over the face of all the earth, and they left off building the city. ⁹Therefore it was called Babel, because there the Lord confusede the language of all the earth; and from there the Lord scattered them abroad over the face of all the earth.

Descendants of Shem

10 These are the descendants of Shem. When Shem was one hundred years old, he became the father of Arpachshad two years after the flood; ¹¹and Shem lived after the birth of Arpachshad five hundred years, and had other sons and daughters.

12 When Arpachshad had lived thirty-five years, he became the fa-

ther of Shelah; ¹³and Arpachshad lived after the birth of Shelah four hundred three years, and had other sons and daughters.

14 When Shelah had lived thirty years, he became the father of Eber; ¹⁵and Shelah lived after the birth of Eber four hundred three years, and had other sons and daughters.

16 When Eber had lived thirty-four years, he became the father of Peleg; ¹⁷and Eber lived after the birth of Peleg four hundred thirty years, and had other sons and daughters.

18 When Peleg had lived thirty years, he became the father of Reu; ¹⁹and Peleg lived after the birth of Reu two hundred nine years, and had other sons and daughters.

20 When Reu had lived thirty-two years, he became the father of Serug; ²¹and Reu lived after the birth of Serug two hundred seven years, and had other sons and daughters.

22 When Serug had lived thirty years, he became the father of Nahor; ²³and Serug lived after the birth of Nahor two hundred years, and had other sons and daughters.

24 When Nahor had lived twenty-nine years, he became the father of Terah; ²⁵and Nahor lived after the birth of Terah one hundred nineteen years, and had other sons and daughters.

26 When Terah had lived seventy years, he became the father of Abram, Nahor, and Haran.

Descendants of Terah

27 Now these are the descendants of Terah. Terah was the father of Abram, Nahor, and Haran; and Haran was the father of Lot. ²⁸Haran died before his father Terah in the land of his birth, in Ur of the Chaldeans. ²⁹Abram and Nahor took wives; the name of Abram's wife was Sarai, and the name of Nahor's wife was Milcah. She was the daughter of Haran the father of

10.32
v. 1
11.2
Ex 1.11,14;
5.7-19
11.4ff
Deut 1.28
11.5
Gen 18.21
11.6
Acts 17.26;
Gen 9.19
11.7
Gen 1.26;
42.23;
Ex 4.11;
1 Cor 14.2,
11
11.8
Lk 1.51;
Gen 10.25,
32
11.9
Gen 10.10
11.10
Gen 10.22;
1 Chr 1.17
11.12
Lk 3.36

11.16
1 Chr 1.19
11.20
Lk 3.35
11.24
Lk 3.34
11.26
Josh 24.2
11.29
Gen 24.10;
17.15; 20.12;
22.20

d Or migrated eastward e Heb balal, meaning to confuse

Milcah and Iscah. 30 Now Sarai was barren; she had no child.

31 Terah took his son Abram and his grandson Lot son of Haran, and his daughter-in-law Sarai, his son Abram's wife, and they went out together from Ur of the Chaldeans to go into the land of Canaan; but when they came to Haran, they settled there. 32 The days of Terah were two hundred five years; and Terah died in Haran.

The Call of Abram

12 Now the LORD said to Abram, "Go from your country and your kindred and your father's house to the land that I will show you. 2 I will make of you a great nation, and I will bless you, and make your name great, so that you will be a blessing. 3 I will bless those who bless you, and the one who curses you I will curse; and in you all the families of the earth shall be blessed."f

4 So Abram went, as the LORD had told him; and Lot went with him. Abram was seventy-five years old when he departed from Haran. 5 Abram took his wife Sarai and his brother's son Lot, and all the possessions that they had gathered, and the persons whom they had acquired in Haran; and they set forth to go to the land of Canaan. When they had come to the land of Canaan, 6 Abram passed through the land to the place at Shechem, to the oakg of Moreh. At that time the Canaanites were in the land. 7 Then the LORD appeared to Abram, and said, "To your offspringh I will give this land." So he built there an altar to the LORD, who had appeared to him. 8 From there he moved on to the hill country on the east of Bethel, and pitched his tent, with Bethel on the west and Ai on the east; and there he built an altar to the LORD and invoked the name of the LORD. 9 And Abram journeyed on by stages toward the Negeb.

Abram and Sarai in Egypt

10 Now there was a famine in the land. So Abram went down to Egypt to reside there as an alien, for the famine was severe in the land. 11 When he was about to enter Egypt, he said to his wife Sarai, "I know well that you are a woman beautiful in appearance; 12 and when the Egyptians see you, they will say, 'This is his wife'; then they will kill me, but they will let you live. 13 Say you are my sister, so that it may go well with me because of you, and that my life may be spared on your account." 14 When Abram entered Egypt the Egyptians saw that the woman was very beautiful. 15 When the officials of Pharaoh saw her, they praised her to Pharaoh. And the woman was taken into Pharaoh's house. 16 And for her sake he dealt well with Abram; and he had sheep, oxen, male donkeys, male and female slaves, female donkeys, and camels.

17 But the LORD afflicted Pharaoh and his house with great plagues because of Sarai, Abram's wife. 18 So Pharaoh called Abram, and said, "What is this you have done to me? Why did you not tell me that she was your wife? 19 Why did you say, 'She is my sister,' so that I took her for my wife? Now then, here is your wife, take her, and be gone." 20 And Pharaoh gave his men orders concerning him; and they set him on the way, with his wife and all that he had.

Abram and Lot Separate

13 So Abram went up from Egypt, he and his wife, and all that he had, and Lot with him, into the Negeb.

2 Now Abram was very rich in livestock, in silver, and in gold. 3 He journeyed on by stages from the Negeb as far as Bethel, to the place where his tent had been at the beginning, between Bethel and Ai, 4 to the place where he had made an altar at the first; and there Abram called on the name of the LORD. 5 Now Lot, who went with

Cross-references

11.30 Gen 16.1
11.31 Gen 15.7; Neh 9.7; Acts 7.4
12.1 Acts 7.3; Heb 11.8
12.2 Gen 15.5; 17.4,5; 18.18; 22.17; 28.14; 32.12; 35.11; 46.3
12.3 Gen 27.29; Ex 23.22; Num 24.9; Gen 18.18; 22.18; 26.4; Acts 3.25; Gal 3.8
12.4 Gen 11.27, 31
12.5 Gen 14.14; 11.31
12.6 Heb 11.9; Deut 11.30; Gen 10.18, 19
12.7 Gen 17.1; 13.15; 17.8; Ps 105.9; Gen 13.4
12.8 Gen 13.4

12.12 Gen 20.11
12.13 Gen 20.5,13
12.15 Gen 20.2
12.16 Gen 20.14
12.17 Gen 20.18; 1 Chr 16.21; Ps 105.14
12.18 Gen 20.9,10
12.20 Prov 21.1
13.1 Gen 12.9
13.3 Gen 12.8,9
13.4 Gen 12.7,8

f Or by you all the families of the earth shall bless themselves g Or terebinth h Heb seed

Abram, also had flocks and herds and tents, ⁶so that the land could not support both of them living together; for their possessions were so great that they could not live together, ⁷and there was strife between the herders of Abram's livestock and the herders of Lot's livestock. At that time the Canaanites and the Perizzites lived in the land.

8 Then Abram said to Lot, "Let there be no strife between you and me, and between your herders and my herders; for we are kindred. ⁹Is not the whole land before you? Separate yourself from me. If you take the left hand, then I will go to the right; or if you take the right hand, then I will go to the left." ¹⁰Lot looked about him, and saw that the plain of the Jordan was well watered everywhere like the garden of the LORD, like the land of Egypt, in the direction of Zoar; this was before the LORD had destroyed Sodom and Gomorrah. ¹¹So Lot chose for himself all the plain of the Jordan, and Lot journeyed eastward; thus they separated from each other. ¹²Abram settled in the land of Canaan, while Lot settled among the cities of the Plain and moved his tent as far as Sodom. ¹³Now the people of Sodom were wicked, great sinners against the LORD.

14 The LORD said to Abram, after Lot had separated from him, "Raise your eyes now, and look from the place where you are, northward and southward and eastward and westward; ¹⁵for all the land that you see I will give to you and to your offspring[i] forever. ¹⁶I will make your offspring like the dust of the earth; so that if one can count the dust of the earth, your offspring also can be counted. ¹⁷Rise up, walk through the length and the breadth of the land, for I will give it to you." ¹⁸So Abram moved his tent, and came and settled by the oaks[j] of Mamre, which are at Hebron; and there he built an altar to the LORD.

13.7
Gen 26.20
13.8
Prov 15.18;
20.3
13.10
Gen 19.17-29;
Deut 34.3;
Gen 2.8;
47.6; 14.8
13.12
Gen 19.29
13.13
Gen 18.20;
2 Pet 2.7,8
13.14
Gen 28.14;
Deut 3.27
13.15
Gen 12.7;
17.8;
Deut 34.3;
Acts 7.5;
2 Chr 20.7
13.16
Gen 16.10;
28.14
13.17
Num 13.17-24
13.18
Gen 14.13;
35.27

14.1
Isa 11.11;
Dan 8.2
14.2
Gen 10.19;
Deut 29.23;
Gen 13.10
14.3
Num 34.12;
Deut 3.17;
Josh 3.16
14.5
Gen 15.20;
Deut 2.20
14.6
Deut 2.12,
22
14.7
2 Chr 20.2
14.11
vv. 16,21
14.12
Gen 12.5;
13.12
14.13
Gen 13.18;
v. 24

Lot's Captivity and Rescue

14 In the days of King Amraphel of Shinar, King Arioch of Ellasar, King Chedorlaomer of Elam, and King Tidal of Goiim, ²these kings made war with King Bera of Sodom, King Birsha of Gomorrah, King Shinab of Admah, King Shemeber of Zeboiim, and the king of Bela (that is, Zoar). ³All these joined forces in the Valley of Siddim (that is, the Dead Sea).[k] ⁴Twelve years they had served Chedorlaomer, but in the thirteenth year they rebelled. ⁵In the fourteenth year Chedorlaomer and the kings who were with him came and subdued the Rephaim in Ashteroth-karnaim, the Zuzim in Ham, the Emim in Shaveh-kiriathaim, ⁶and the Horites in the hill country of Seir as far as El-paran on the edge of the wilderness; ⁷then they turned back and came to En-mishpat (that is, Kadesh), and subdued all the country of the Amalekites, and also the Amorites who lived in Hazazon-tamar. ⁸Then the king of Sodom, the king of Gomorrah, the king of Admah, the king of Zeboiim, and the king of Bela (that is, Zoar) went out, and they joined battle in the Valley of Siddim ⁹with King Chedorlaomer of Elam, King Tidal of Goiim, King Amraphel of Shinar, and King Arioch of Ellasar, four kings against five. ¹⁰Now the Valley of Siddim was full of bitumen pits; and as the kings of Sodom and Gomorrah fled, some fell into them, and the rest fled to the hill country. ¹¹So the enemy took all the goods of Sodom and Gomorrah, and all their provisions, and went their way; ¹²they also took Lot, the son of Abram's brother, who lived in Sodom, and his goods, and departed.

13 Then one who had escaped came and told Abram the Hebrew, who was living by the oaks[j] of Mamre the Amorite, brother of Eshcol and of Aner; these were al-

[i] Heb *seed* [j] Or *terebinths* [k] Heb *Salt Sea*

lies of Abram. [14]When Abram heard that his nephew had been taken captive, he led forth his trained men, born in his house, three hundred eighteen of them, and went in pursuit as far as Dan. [15]He divided his forces against them by night, he and his servants, and routed them and pursued them to Hobah, north of Damascus. [16]Then he brought back all the goods, and also brought back his nephew Lot with his goods, and the women and the people.

Abram Blessed by Melchizedek

[17] After his return from the defeat of Chedorlaomer and the kings who were with him, the king of Sodom went out to meet him at the Valley of Shaveh (that is, the King's Valley). [18]And King Melchizedek of Salem brought out bread and wine; he was priest of God Most High.[1] [19]He blessed him and said,

"Blessed be Abram by God
　Most High,[1]
maker of heaven and earth;
[20] and blessed be God Most
　High,[1]
　who has delivered your
　　enemies into your
　　hand!"

And Abram gave him one tenth of everything. [21] Then the king of Sodom said to Abram, "Give me the persons, but take the goods for yourself." [22] But Abram said to the king of Sodom, "I have sworn to the LORD, God Most High,[1] maker of heaven and earth, [23] that I would not take a thread or a sandal-thong or anything that is yours, so that you might not say, 'I have made Abram rich.' [24] I will take nothing but what the young men have eaten, and the share of the men who went with me—Aner, Eshcol, and Mamre. Let them take their share."

God's Covenant with Abram

15 After these things the word of the LORD came to Abram in a vision, "Do not be afraid, Abram, I am your shield; your reward shall be very great." [2] But Abram said, "O Lord GOD, what

14.14
Gen 13.8;
15.3
14.16
vv. 11,12
14.17
1 Sam 18.6,
18
14.18
Heb 7.1;
Ps 110.4;
Heb 5.6,10
14.19
v. 22;
Mt 11.25
14.20
Gen 24.27;
Heb 7.4
14.22
Dan 12.7;
v. 19
14.23
2 Kings 5.16
15.1
Dan 10.1;
Gen 21.17;
26.24;
Deut 33.29;
Prov 11.8
15.2f
Acts 7.5

15.3
Gen 14.14
15.4
Gal 4.28
15.5
Ps 147.4;
Jer 33.22;
Gen 22.17;
Rom 4.18;
Heb 11.12
15.7
Gen 11.31;
13.15,17
15.8
Lk 1.18
15.10
Jer 34.18;
Lev 1.17
15.12
Gen 2.21
15.13
Acts 7.6;
Ex 12.40
15.14
Ex 12.36
15.15
Gen 25.8
15.16
1 Kings 21.26
15.17
Jer 34.18,19

will you give me, for I continue childless, and the heir of my house is Eliezer of Damascus?"[m] [3]And Abram said, "You have given me no offspring, and so a slave born in my house is to be my heir." [4]But the word of the LORD came to him, "This man shall not be your heir; no one but your very own issue shall be your heir." [5]He brought him outside and said, "Look toward heaven and count the stars, if you are able to count them." Then he said to him, "So shall your descendants be." [6]And he believed the LORD; and the LORD[n] reckoned it to him as righteousness.

[7] Then he said to him, "I am the LORD who brought you from Ur of the Chaldeans, to give you this land to possess." [8]But he said, "O Lord GOD, how am I to know that I shall possess it?" [9]He said to him, "Bring me a heifer three years old, a female goat three years old, a ram three years old, a turtledove, and a young pigeon." [10]He brought him all these and cut them in two, laying each half over against the other; but he did not cut the birds in two. [11]And when birds of prey came down on the carcasses, Abram drove them away.

[12] As the sun was going down, a deep sleep fell upon Abram, and a deep and terrifying darkness descended upon him. [13]Then the LORD[n] said to Abram, "Know this for certain, that your offspring shall be aliens in a land that is not theirs, and shall be slaves there, and they shall be oppressed for four hundred years; [14]but I will bring judgment on the nation that they serve, and afterward they shall come out with great possessions. [15]As for yourself, you shall go to your ancestors in peace; you shall be buried in a good old age. [16]And they shall come back here in the fourth generation; for the iniquity of the Amorites is not yet complete."

[17] When the sun had gone down

[1]Heb El Elyon　　[m]Meaning of Heb
uncertain　　[n]Heb he

and it was dark, a smoking fire pot and a flaming torch passed between these pieces. ¹⁸On that day the LORD made a covenant with Abram, saying, "To your descendants I give this land, from the river of Egypt to the great river, the river Euphrates, ¹⁹the land of the Kenites, the Kenizzites, the Kadmonites, ²⁰the Hittites, the Perizzites, the Rephaim, ²¹the Amorites, the Canaanites, the Girgashites, and the Jebusites."

The Birth of Ishmael

16 Now Sarai, Abram's wife, bore him no children. She had an Egyptian slave-girl whose name was Hagar, ²and Sarai said to Abram, "You see that the LORD has prevented me from bearing children; go in to my slave-girl; it may be that I shall obtain children by her." And Abram listened to the voice of Sarai. ³So, after Abram had lived ten years in the land of Canaan, Sarai, Abram's wife, took Hagar the Egyptian, her slave-girl, and gave her to her husband Abram as a wife. ⁴He went in to Hagar, and she conceived; and when she saw that she had conceived, she looked with contempt on her mistress. ⁵Then Sarai said to Abram, "May the wrong done to me be on you! I gave my slave-girl to your embrace, and when she saw that she had conceived, she looked on me with contempt. May the LORD judge between you and me!" ⁶But Abram said to Sarai, "Your slave-girl is in your power; do to her as you please." Then Sarai dealt harshly with her, and she ran away from her.

7 The angel of the LORD found her by a spring of water in the wilderness, the spring on the way to Shur. ⁸And he said, "Hagar, slave-girl of Sarai, where have you come from and where are you going?" She said, "I am running away from my mistress Sarai." ⁹The angel of the LORD said to her, "Return to your mistress, and submit to her." ¹⁰The angel of the LORD also said to her, "I will so greatly multiply your

offspring that they cannot be counted for multitude." ¹¹And the angel of the LORD said to her,

"Now you have conceived
 and shall bear a son;
 you shall call him
 Ishmael,°
 for the LORD has given heed
 to your affliction.
¹² He shall be a wild ass of a
 man,
 with his hand against
 everyone,
 and everyone's hand
 against him;
 and he shall live at odds
 with all his kin."

¹³So she named the LORD who spoke to her, "You are El-roi;ᵖ for she said, "Have I really seen God and remained alive after seeing him?"�q ¹⁴Therefore the well was called Beer-lahai-roi;ʳ it lies between Kadesh and Bered.

15 Hagar bore Abram a son; and Abram named his son, whom Hagar bore, Ishmael. ¹⁶Abram was eighty-six years old when Hagar bore himˢ Ishmael.

The Sign of the Covenant

17 When Abram was ninety-nine years old, the LORD appeared to Abram, and said to him, "I am God Almighty;ᵗ walk before me, and be blameless. ²And I will make my covenant between me and you, and will make you exceedingly numerous." ³Then Abram fell on his face; and God said to him, ⁴"As for me, this is my covenant with you: You shall be the ancestor of a multitude of nations. ⁵No longer shall your name be Abram,ᵘ but your name shall be Abraham;ᵛ for I have made you the ancestor of a multitude of nations. ⁶I will make you exceedingly fruitful; and I will make nations of you, and kings shall come from you. ⁷I will establish my covenant be-

with

15.18
Gen 24.7;
12.7;
Ex 23.31;
Num 34.3;
Deut 11.24;
Josh 1.4
16.1
Gen 11.30;
21.9;
Gal 4.24
16.2
Gen 30.3,4,
9,10
16.3
Gen 12.5
16.5
Gen 31.53
16.7
Gen 21.17,
18; 22.11,15;
31.11; 20.1
16.10
Gen 17.20

16.11
Ex 3.7,9
16.12
Gen 25.18
16.13
Gen 32.30
16.15
Gal 4.22
17.1
Gen 28.3;
Ex 6.3;
Deut 18.13
17.2
Gen 15.18
17.4
Gen 35.11;
48.19
17.5
Neh 9.7;
Rom 4.17
17.6
Gen 35.11;
Mt 1.6
17.7
Gal 3.17;
Gen 26.24;
28.13;
Rom 9.8

° That is *God hears* ᵖ Perhaps *God of seeing* or *God who sees* q Meaning of Heb uncertain ʳ That is *the Well of the Living One who sees me* ˢ Heb *Abram* ᵗ Traditional rendering of Heb *El Shaddai* ᵘ That is *exalted ancestor* ᵛ Here taken to mean *ancestor of a multitude*

tween me and you, and your offspring after you throughout their generations, for an everlasting covenant, to be God to you and to your offspring[w] after you. [8]And I will give to you, and to your offspring after you, the land where you are now an alien, all the land of Canaan, for a perpetual holding; and I will be their God."

9 God said to Abraham, "As for you, you shall keep my covenant, you and your offspring after you throughout their generations. [10]This is my covenant, which you shall keep, between me and you and your offspring after you: Every male among you shall be circumcised. [11]You shall circumcise the flesh of your foreskins, and it shall be a sign of the covenant between me and you. [12]Throughout your generations every male among you shall be circumcised when he is eight days old, including the slave born in your house and the one bought with your money from any foreigner who is not of your offspring. [13]Both the slave born in your house and the one bought with your money must be circumcised. So shall my covenant be in your flesh an everlasting covenant. [14]Any uncircumcised male who is not circumcised in the flesh of his foreskin shall be cut off from his people; he has broken my covenant."

15 God said to Abraham, "As for Sarah your wife, you shall not call her Sarai, but Sarah shall be her name. [16]I will bless her, and moreover I will give you a son by her. I will bless her, and she shall give rise to nations; kings of peoples shall come from her." [17]Then Abraham fell on his face and laughed, and said to himself, "Can a child be born to a man who is a hundred years old? Can Sarah, who is ninety years old, bear a child?" [18]And Abraham said to God, "O that Ishmael might live in your sight!" [19]God said, "No, but your wife Sarah shall bear you a son, and you shall name him Isaac.[x] I will establish my covenant with him as an ev-

erlasting covenant for his offspring after him. [20]As for Ishmael, I have heard you; I will bless him and make him fruitful and exceedingly numerous; he shall be the father of twelve princes, and I will make him a great nation. [21]But my covenant I will establish with Isaac, whom Sarah shall bear to you at this season next year." [22]And when he had finished talking with him, God went up from Abraham.

23 Then Abraham took his son Ishmael and all the slaves born in his house or bought with his money, every male among the men of Abraham's house, and he circumcised the flesh of their foreskins that very day, as God had said to him. [24]Abraham was ninety-nine years old when he was circumcised in the flesh of his foreskin. [25]And his son Ishmael was thirteen years old when he was circumcised in the flesh of his foreskin. [26]That very day Abraham and his son Ishmael were circumcised; [27]and all the men of his house, slaves born in the house and those bought with money from a foreigner, were circumcised with him.

A Son Promised to Abraham and Sarah

18 The Lord appeared to Abraham[y] by the oaks[z] of Mamre, as he sat at the entrance of his tent in the heat of the day. [2]He looked up and saw three men standing near him. When he saw them, he ran from the tent entrance to meet them, and bowed down to the ground. [3]He said, "My lord, if I find favor with you, do not pass by your servant. [4]Let a little water be brought, and wash your feet, and rest yourselves under the tree. [5]Let me bring a little bread, that you may refresh yourselves, and after that you may pass on— since you have come to your servant." So they said, "Do as you have said." [6]And Abraham hastened into the tent to Sarah, and said, "Make ready quickly three

17.8
Gen 12.7;
Ps 105.9,11;
Gen 23.4;
28.4;
Ex 6.7;
Lev 26.12
17.10
Acts 7.8
17.11
Ex 12.48;
Deut 10.16;
Rom 4.11
17.12
Lev 12.3;
Lk 2.21
17.14
Ex 4.24
17.16
Gen 18.10;
35.11;
Gal 4.31
17.17
Gen 18.12;
21.6
17.19
Gen 18.10;
21.2; 26.2-5

17.20
Gen 16.10;
25.12,16
17.23
Gen 14.14
17.24
Rom 4.11
18.1
Gen 13.18;
14.13
18.2
vv. 16,22;
Gen 32.24;
Josh 5.13;
Judg 13.6-11
18.4
Gen 19.2;
43.24
18.5
Judg 6.18,
19; 13.15,16

w Heb seed x That is he laughs
y Heb him z Or terebinths

measures[a] of choice flour, knead it, and make cakes." 7 Abraham ran to the herd, and took a calf, tender and good, and gave it to the servant, who hastened to prepare it. 8 Then he took curds and milk and the calf that he had prepared, and set it before them; and he stood by them under the tree while they ate.

9 They said to him, "Where is your wife Sarah?" And he said, "There, in the tent." 10 Then one said, "I will surely return to you in due season, and your wife Sarah shall have a son." And Sarah was listening at the tent entrance behind him. 11 Now Abraham and Sarah were old, advanced in age; it had ceased to be with Sarah after the manner of women. 12 So Sarah laughed to herself, saying, "After I have grown old, and my husband is old, shall I have pleasure?" 13 The LORD said to Abraham, "Why did Sarah laugh, and say, 'Shall I indeed bear a child, now that I am old?' 14 Is anything too wonderful for the LORD? At the set time I will return to you, in due season, and Sarah shall have a son." 15 But Sarah denied, saying, "I did not laugh"; for she was afraid. He said, "Oh yes, you did laugh."

Judgment Pronounced on Sodom

16 Then the men set out from there, and they looked toward Sodom; and Abraham went with them to set them on their way. 17 The LORD said, "Shall I hide from Abraham what I am about to do, 18 seeing that Abraham shall become a great and mighty nation, and all the nations of the earth shall be blessed in him?[b] 19 No, for I have chosen[c] him, that he may charge his children and his household after him to keep the way of the LORD by doing righteousness and justice; so that the LORD may bring about for Abraham what he has promised him." 20 Then the LORD said, "How great is the outcry against Sodom and Gomorrah and how very grave their sin! 21 I must go down and see whether they have done altogether

according to the outcry that has come to me; and if not, I will know."

22 So the men turned from there, and went toward Sodom, while Abraham remained standing before the LORD. [d] 23 Then Abraham came near and said, "Will you indeed sweep away the righteous with the wicked? 24 Suppose there are fifty righteous within the city; will you then sweep away the place and not forgive it for the fifty righteous who are in it? 25 Far be it from you to do such a thing, to slay the righteous with the wicked, so that the righteous fare as the wicked! Far be that from you! Shall not the Judge of all the earth do what is just?" 26 And the LORD said, "If I find at Sodom fifty righteous in the city, I will forgive the whole place for their sake." 27 Abraham answered, "Let me take it upon myself to speak to the Lord, I who am but dust and ashes. 28 Suppose five of the fifty righteous are lacking? Will you destroy the whole city for lack of five?" And he said, "I will not destroy it if I find forty-five there." 29 Again he spoke to him, "Suppose forty are found there." He answered, "For the sake of forty I will not do it." 30 Then he said, "Oh do not let the Lord be angry if I speak. Suppose thirty are found there." He answered, "I will not do it, if I find thirty there." 31 He said, "Let me take it upon myself to speak to the Lord. Suppose twenty are found there." He answered, "For the sake of twenty I will not destroy it." 32 Then he said, "Oh do not let the Lord be angry if I speak just once more. Suppose ten are found there." He answered, "For the sake of ten I will not destroy it." 33 And the LORD went his way, when he had finished speaking to Abraham; and Abraham returned to his place.

a Heb seahs　　b Or and all the nations of the earth shall bless themselves by him
c Heb known　　d Another ancient tradition reads while the LORD remained standing before Abraham

18.8
Gen 19.3
18.10
Rom 9.9
18.11
Gen 17.17;
Rom 4.19
18.12ff
1 Pet 3.6
18.14
Jer 32.17,
27;
Zech 8.6;
Mt 3.9;
Lk 1.37
18.18
Gal 3.8
18.19
Deut 4.9,10;
6.7;
Josh 24.15;
Eph 6.4
18.20
Gen 19.13;
Ezek 16.49,
50
18.21
Gen 11.5

18.22
Gen 19.1
18.23
Heb 10.22;
Num 16.22
18.24
Jer 5.1
18.25
Job 8.20;
Isa 3.10,11;
Rom 3.6
18.27
Gen 3.19;
Job 4.19;
30.19; 42.6;
2 Cor 5.1
18.32
Judg 6.39;
Jas 5.16

The Depravity of Sodom

19 The two angels came to Sodom in the evening, and Lot was sitting in the gateway of Sodom. When Lot saw them, he rose to meet them, and bowed down with his face to the ground. ²He said, "Please, my lords, turn aside to your servant's house and spend the night, and wash your feet; then you can rise early and go on your way." They said, "No; we will spend the night in the square." ³But he urged them strongly; so they turned aside to him and entered his house; and he made them a feast, and baked unleavened bread, and they ate. ⁴But before they lay down, the men of the city, the men of Sodom, both young and old, all the people to the last man, surrounded the house; ⁵and they called to Lot, "Where are the men who came to you tonight? Bring them out to us, so that we may know them." ⁶Lot went out of the door to the men, shut the door after him, ⁷and said, "I beg you, my brothers, do not act so wickedly. ⁸Look, I have two daughters who have not known a man; let me bring them out to you, and do to them as you please; only do nothing to these men, for they have come under the shelter of my roof." ⁹But they replied, "Stand back!" And they said, "This fellow came here as an alien, and he would play the judge! Now we will deal worse with you than with them." Then they pressed hard against the man Lot, and came near the door to break it down. ¹⁰But the men inside reached out their hands and brought Lot into the house with them, and shut the door. ¹¹And they struck with blindness the men who were at the door of the house, both small and great, so that they were unable to find the door.

Sodom and Gomorrah Destroyed

12 Then the men said to Lot, "Have you anyone else here? Sons-in-law, sons, daughters, or anyone you have in the city—bring them out of the place. ¹³For we are about to destroy this place, because the outcry against its people has become great before the LORD, and the LORD has sent us to destroy it." ¹⁴So Lot went out and said to his sons-in-law, who were to marry his daughters, "Up, get out of this place; for the LORD is about to destroy the city." But he seemed to his sons-in-law to be jesting.

15 When morning dawned, the angels urged Lot, saying, "Get up, take your wife and your two daughters who are here, or else you will be consumed in the punishment of the city." ¹⁶But he lingered; so the men seized him and his wife and his two daughters by the hand, the LORD being merciful to him, and they brought him out and left him outside the city. ¹⁷When they had brought them outside, they^e said, "Flee for your life; do not look back or stop anywhere in the Plain; flee to the hills, or else you will be consumed." ¹⁸And Lot said to them, "Oh, no, my lords; ¹⁹your servant has found favor with you, and you have shown me great kindness in saving my life; but I cannot flee to the hills, for fear the disaster will overtake me and I die. ²⁰Look, that city is near enough to flee to, and it is a little one. Let me escape there—is it not a little one?—and my life will be saved!" ²¹He said to him, "Very well, I grant you this favor too, and will not overthrow the city of which you have spoken. ²²Hurry, escape there, for I can do nothing until you arrive there." Therefore the city was called Zoar.^f ²³The sun had risen on the earth when Lot came to Zoar.

24 Then the LORD rained on Sodom and Gomorrah sulfur and fire from the LORD out of heaven; ²⁵and he overthrew those cities, and all the Plain, and all the inhabitants of the cities, and what grew on the ground. ²⁶But Lot's wife, behind him, looked back, and she became a pillar of salt.

27 Abraham went early in the morning to the place where he had

Cross references (center column)

19.1 Gen 18.22; 18.1ff
19.2 Heb 13.2; Gen 18.4
19.3 Gen 18.8
19.5 Isa 3.9; Judg 19.22; Rom 1.24
19.6 Judg 19.23
19.8 Judg 19.24
19.9 2 Pet 2.7, 8; Ex 2.14
19.11 2 Kings 6.18; Acts 13.11
19.12 Gen 7.1; 2 Pet 2.7,9
19.13 Gen 18.20; 1 Chr 21.15
19.14 Num 16.21; Ex 9.21; Lk 17.28
19.15 Num 16.24, 26; Rev 18.4
19.16 Lk 18.13; Ps 34.22
19.17 1 Kings 19.3; Jer 48.6; v. 26
19.21 Job 42.8,9; Ps 145.9
19.24 Deut 29.23; Isa 13.19; Lk 17.29; Jude 7
19.25 Ps 107.34
19.26 Lk 17.32
19.27 Gen 18.22

^e Gk Syr Vg: Heb *he* ^f That is *Little*

stood before the LORD; 28 and he looked down toward Sodom and Gomorrah and toward all the land of the Plain and saw the smoke of the land going up like the smoke of a furnace.

29 So it was that, when God destroyed the cities of the Plain, God remembered Abraham, and sent Lot out of the midst of the overthrow, when he overthrew the cities in which Lot had settled.

The Shameful Origin of Moab and Ammon

30 Now Lot went up out of Zoar and settled in the hills with his two daughters, for he was afraid to stay in Zoar; so he lived in a cave with his two daughters. 31 And the firstborn said to the younger, "Our father is old, and there is not a man on earth to come in to us after the manner of all the world. 32 Come, let us make our father drink wine, and we will lie with him, so that we may preserve offspring through our father." 33 So they made their father drink wine that night; and the firstborn went in, and lay with her father; he did not know when she lay down or when she rose. 34 On the next day, the firstborn said to the younger, "Look, I lay last night with my father; let us make him drink wine tonight also; then you go in and lie with him, so that we may preserve offspring through our father." 35 So they made their father drink wine that night also; and the younger rose, and lay with him; and he did not know when she lay down or when she rose. 36 Thus both the daughters of Lot became pregnant by their father. 37 The firstborn bore a son, and named him Moab; he is the ancestor of the Moabites to this day. 38 The younger also bore a son and named him Ben-ammi; he is the ancestor of the Ammonites to this day.

Abraham and Sarah at Gerar

20 From there Abraham journeyed toward the region of the Negeb, and settled between Kadesh and Shur. While residing in Gerar as an alien, 2 Abraham said of his wife Sarah, "She is my sister." And King Abimelech of Gerar sent and took Sarah. 3 But God came to Abimelech in a dream by night, and said to him, "You are about to die because of the woman whom you have taken; for she is a married woman." 4 Now Abimelech had not approached her; so he said, "Lord, will you destroy an innocent people? 5 Did he not himself say to me, 'She is my sister'? And she herself said, 'He is my brother.' I did this in the integrity of my heart and the innocence of my hands." 6 Then God said to him in the dream, "Yes, I know that you did this in the integrity of your heart; furthermore it was I who kept you from sinning against me. Therefore I did not let you touch her. 7 Now then, return the man's wife; for he is a prophet, and he will pray for you and you shall live. But if you do not restore her, know that you shall surely die, you and all that are yours."

8 So Abimelech rose early in the morning, and called all his servants and told them all these things; and the men were very much afraid. 9 Then Abimelech called Abraham, and said to him, "What have you done to us? How have I sinned against you, that you have brought such great guilt on me and my kingdom? You have done things to me that ought not to be done." 10 And Abimelech said to Abraham, "What were you thinking of, that you did this thing?" 11 Abraham said, "I did it because I thought, There is no fear of God at all in this place, and they will kill me because of my wife. 12 Besides, she is indeed my sister, the daughter of my father but not the daughter of my mother; and she became my wife. 13 And when God caused me to wander from my father's house, I said to her, 'This is the kindness you must do me: at every place to which we come, say of me, He is my brother.' " 14 Then Abimelech took sheep and oxen, and male and female slaves, and gave them to Abraham, and restored his wife

19.28
Rev 9.2;
18.9
19.29
2 Pet 2.7
19.31
Gen 38.8,9;
Deut 25.5
19.32
Mk 12.19
19.37
Deut 2.9
19.38
Deut 2.19
20.1
Gen 18.1;
16.7,14; 26.6

20.2
v. 12;
Gen 12.13,
15
20.3
Ps 105.14;
Job 33.15;
Gen 26.11
20.5
1 Kings 9.4;
2 Kings 20.3
20.7
1 Sam 7.5;
Job 42.8
20.9
Gen 26.10;
Ex 32.21;
Josh 7.25;
Gen 34.7
20.11
Ps 36.1;
Gen 12.12;
26.7
20.13
v. 5
20.14
Gen 12.16

Sarah to him. [15] Abimelech said, "My land is before you; settle where it pleases you." [16] To Sarah he said, "Look, I have given your brother a thousand pieces of silver; it is your exoneration before all who are with you; you are completely vindicated." [17] Then Abraham prayed to God; and God healed Abimelech, and also healed his wife and female slaves so that they bore children. [18] For the LORD had closed fast all the wombs of the house of Abimelech because of Sarah, Abraham's wife.

The Birth of Isaac

21 The LORD dealt with Sarah as he had said, and the LORD did for Sarah as he had promised. [2] Sarah conceived and bore Abraham a son in his old age, at the time of which God had spoken to him. [3] Abraham gave the name Isaac to his son whom Sarah bore him. [4] And Abraham circumcised his son Isaac when he was eight days old, as God had commanded him. [5] Abraham was a hundred years old when his son Isaac was born to him. [6] Now Sarah said, "God has brought laughter for me; everyone who hears will laugh with me." [7] And she said, "Who would ever have said to Abraham that Sarah would nurse children? Yet I have borne him a son in his old age."

Hagar and Ishmael Sent Away

8 The child grew, and was weaned; and Abraham made a great feast on the day that Isaac was weaned. [9] But Sarah saw the son of Hagar the Egyptian, whom she had borne to Abraham, playing with her son Isaac.[g] [10] So she said to Abraham, "Cast out this slave woman with her son; for the son of this slave woman shall not inherit along with my son Isaac." [11] The matter was very distressing to Abraham on account of his son. [12] But God said to Abraham, "Do not be distressed because of the boy and because of your slave woman; whatever Sarah says to you, do as she tells you, for it is

through Isaac that offspring shall be named for you. [13] As for the son of the slave woman, I will make a nation of him also, because he is your offspring." [14] So Abraham rose early in the morning, and took bread and a skin of water, and gave it to Hagar, putting it on her shoulder, along with the child, and sent her away. And she departed, and wandered about in the wilderness of Beer-sheba.

15 When the water in the skin was gone, she cast the child under one of the bushes. [16] Then she went and sat down opposite him a good way off, about the distance of a bowshot; for she said, "Do not let me look on the death of the child." And as she sat opposite him, she lifted up her voice and wept. [17] And God heard the voice of the boy; and the angel of God called to Hagar from heaven, and said to her, "What troubles you, Hagar? Do not be afraid; for God has heard the voice of the boy where he is. [18] Come, lift up the boy and hold him fast with your hand, for I will make a great nation of him." [19] Then God opened her eyes and she saw a well of water. She went, and filled the skin with water, and gave the boy a drink.

20 God was with the boy, and he grew up; he lived in the wilderness, and became an expert with the bow. [21] He lived in the wilderness of Paran; and his mother got a wife for him from the land of Egypt.

Abraham and Abimelech Make a Covenant

22 At that time Abimelech, with Phicol the commander of his army, said to Abraham, "God is with you in all that you do; [23] now therefore swear to me here by God that you will not deal falsely with me or with my offspring or with my posterity, but as I have dealt loyally with you, you will deal with me and with the land where you have resided as an alien." [24] And Abraham said, "I swear it."

25 When Abraham complained

20.15	Gen 13.9
20.17	Num 12.13; Job 42.9
20.18	Gen 12.17
21.1	1 Sam 2.21; Gen 17.16, 21; Gal 4.23
21.2	Acts 7.8; Gal 4.22; Heb 11.11; Gen 17.21
21.3	Gen 17.19
21.4	Gen 17.12; Acts 7.8
21.5	Gen 17.17
21.6	Ps 126.2; Isa 54.1
21.7	Gen 18.13
21.9	Gen 16.15; Gal 4.29
21.10	Gal 4.30
21.11	Gen 17.18
21.12	Rom 9.7; Heb 11.18
21.13	v. 18; Gen 16.10; 17.20
21.17	Ex 3.7
21.18	v. 13
21.19	Num 22.31
21.20	Gen 28.15; 39.2,3,21
21.21	Gen 24.4
21.22	Gen 20.2; 26.26,28
21.25	Gen 26.15; 18,20-22

g Gk Vg: Heb lacks *with her son Isaac*

to Abimelech about a well of water that Abimelech's servants had seized, [26] Abimelech said, "I do not know who has done this; you did not tell me, and I have not heard of it until today." [27] So Abraham took sheep and oxen and gave them to Abimelech, and the two men made a covenant. [28] Abraham set apart seven ewe lambs of the flock. [29] And Abimelech said to Abraham, "What is the meaning of these seven ewe lambs that you have set apart?" [30] He said, "These seven ewe lambs you shall accept from my hand, in order that you may be a witness for me that I dug this well." [31] Therefore that place was called Beer-sheba;[h] because there both of them swore an oath. [32] When they had made a covenant at Beer-sheba, Abimelech, with Phicol the commander of his army, left and returned to the land of the Philistines. [33] Abraham[i] planted a tamarisk tree in Beer-sheba, and called there on the name of the Lord, the Everlasting God.[j] [34] And Abraham resided as an alien many days in the land of the Philistines.

The Command to Sacrifice Isaac

22 After these things God tested Abraham. He said to him, "Abraham!" And he said, "Here I am." [2] He said, "Take your son, your only son Isaac, whom you love, and go to the land of Moriah, and offer him there as a burnt offering on one of the mountains that I shall show you." [3] So Abraham rose early in the morning, saddled his donkey, and took two of his young men with him, and his son Isaac; he cut the wood for the burnt offering, and set out and went to the place in the distance that God had shown him. [4] On the third day Abraham looked up and saw the place far away. [5] Then Abraham said to his young men, "Stay here with the donkey; the boy and I will go over there; we will worship, and then we will come back to you." [6] Abraham took the wood of the burnt offering and laid it on his son Isaac, and he himself carried the

fire and the knife. So the two of them walked on together. [7] Isaac said to his father Abraham, "Father!" And he said, "Here I am, my son." He said, "The fire and the wood are here, but where is the lamb for a burnt offering?" [8] Abraham said, "God himself will provide the lamb for a burnt offering, my son." So the two of them walked on together.

9 When they came to the place that God had shown him, Abraham built an altar there and laid the wood in order. He bound his son Isaac, and laid him on the altar, on top of the wood. [10] Then Abraham reached out his hand and took the knife to kill[k] his son. [11] But the angel of the Lord called to him from heaven, and said, "Abraham, Abraham!" And he said, "Here I am." [12] He said, "Do not lay your hand on the boy or do anything to him; for now I know that you fear God, since you have not withheld your son, your only son, from me." [13] And Abraham looked up and saw a ram, caught in a thicket by its horns. Abraham went and took the ram and offered it up as a burnt offering instead of his son. [14] So Abraham called that place "The Lord will provide";[l] as it is said to this day, "On the mount of the Lord it shall be provided."[m]

15 The angel of the Lord called to Abraham a second time from heaven, [16] and said, "By myself I have sworn, says the Lord: Because you have done this, and have not withheld your son, your only son, [17] I will indeed bless you, and I will make your offspring as numerous as the stars of heaven and as the sand that is on the seashore. And your offspring shall possess the gate of their enemies, [18] and by your offspring shall all the nations of the earth gain blessing for themselves, because you have obeyed my voice." [19] So Abraham returned

21.27
Gen 26.31
21.30
Gen 31.48,
52
21.31
Gen 26.33
21.33
Gen 4.26;
Deut 33.27
22.2
Heb 11.17;
2 Chr 3.1
22.6
Jn 19.17

22.7
Jn 1.29,36;
Rev 13.8
22.9
Heb 11.17-19
22.12
Gen 26.5;
1 Sam 15.22
22.16
Heb 6.13,14
22.17
Gen 15.5;
26.4; 32.12;
24.60
22.18
Gal 3.8,16;
Acts 3.25;
Gen 18.19

h That is *Well of seven* or *Well of the oath*
i Heb *He* j Or the Lord, *El Olam*
k Or *to slaughter* l Or *will see*; Heb traditionally transliterated *Jehovah Jireh*
m Or *he shall be seen*

to his young men, and they arose and went together to Beer-sheba; and Abraham lived at Beer-sheba.

The Children of Nahor

20 Now after these things it was told Abraham, "Milcah also has borne children, to your brother Nahor: 21Uz the firstborn, Buz his brother, Kemuel the father of Aram, 22Chesed, Hazo, Pildash, Jidlaph, and Bethuel." 23Bethuel became the father of Rebekah. These eight Milcah bore to Nahor, Abraham's brother. 24Moreover, his concubine, whose name was Reumah, bore Tebah, Gaham, Tahash, and Maacah.

Sarah's Death and Burial

23 Sarah lived one hundred twenty-seven years; this was the length of Sarah's life. 2And Sarah died at Kiriath-arba (that is, Hebron) in the land of Canaan; and Abraham went in to mourn for Sarah and to weep for her. 3Abraham rose up from beside his dead, and said to the Hittites, 4"I am a stranger and an alien residing among you; give me property among you for a burying place, so that I may bury my dead out of my sight." 5The Hittites answered Abraham, 6"Hear us, my lord; you are a mighty prince among us. Bury your dead in the choicest of our burial places; none of us will withhold from you any burial ground for burying your dead." 7Abraham rose and bowed to the Hittites, the people of the land. 8He said to them, "If you are willing that I should bury my dead out of my sight, hear me, and entreat for me Ephron son of Zohar, 9so that he may give me the cave of Machpelah, which he owns; it is at the end of his field. For the full price let him give it to me in your presence as a possession for a burying place." 10Now Ephron was sitting among the Hittites; and Ephron the Hittite answered Abraham in the hearing of the Hittites, of all who went in at the gate of his city, 11"No, my lord, hear me; I give you the field, and I give you the

cave that is in it; in the presence of my people I give it to you; bury your dead." 12Then Abraham bowed down before the people of the land. 13He said to Ephron in the hearing of the people of the land, "If you only will listen to me! I will give the price of the field; accept it from me, so that I may bury my dead there." 14Ephron answered Abraham, 15"My lord, listen to me; a piece of land worth four hundred shekels of silver—what is that between you and me? Bury your dead." 16Abraham agreed with Ephron; and Abraham weighed out for Ephron the silver that he had named in the hearing of the Hittites, four hundred shekels of silver, according to the weights current among the merchants.

17 So the field of Ephron in Machpelah, which was to the east of Mamre, the field with the cave that was in it and all the trees that were in the field, throughout its whole area, passed 18to Abraham as a possession in the presence of the Hittites, in the presence of all who went in at the gate of his city. 19After this, Abraham buried Sarah his wife in the cave of the field of Machpelah facing Mamre (that is, Hebron) in the land of Canaan. 20The field and the cave that is in it passed from the Hittites into Abraham's possession as a burying place.

The Marriage of Isaac and Rebekah

24 Now Abraham was old, well advanced in years; and the LORD had blessed Abraham in all things. 2Abraham said to his servant, the oldest of his house, who had charge of all that he had, "Put your hand under my thigh 3and I will make you swear by the LORD, the God of heaven and earth, that you will not get a wife for my son from the daughters of the Canaanites, among whom I live, 4but will go to my country and to my kindred and get a wife for my son Isaac." 5The servant said to him, "Perhaps the woman may not be

22.23
Gen 24.15
23.2
Josh 14.15;
v. 19;
Gen 13.18
23.4
1 Chr 29.15;
Ps 105.12;
Heb 11.9,13
23.6
Gen 14.14;
24.35
23.8
Gen 25.9
23.10
Gen 24.20,
24; Ruth 4.4
23.11
2 Sam 24.21-24

23.15
Ex 30.13;
Ezek 45.12
23.16
Jer 32.9;
Zech 11.12
23.17
Gen 25.9;
49.30-32;
50.13;
Acts 7.16
24.1
v. 35;
Gen 13.2
24.2
Gen 47.29
24.3
Gen 14.22;
10.18,19;
26.34,35;
28.1,2,8
24.4
Gen 28.2;
12.1

willing to follow me to this land; must I then take your son back to the land from which you came?" [6] Abraham said to him, "See to it that you do not take my son back there. [7] The LORD, the God of heaven, who took me from my father's house and from the land of my birth, and who spoke to me and swore to me, 'To your offspring I will give this land,' he will send his angel before you, and you shall take a wife for my son from there. [8] But if the woman is not willing to follow you, then you will be free from this oath of mine; only you must not take my son back there." [9] So the servant put his hand under the thigh of Abraham his master and swore to him concerning this matter.

10 Then the servant took ten of his master's camels and departed, taking all kinds of choice gifts from his master; and he set out and went to Aram-naharaim, to the city of Nahor. [11] He made the camels kneel down outside the city by the well of water; it was toward evening, the time when women go out to draw water. [12] And he said, "O LORD, God of my master Abraham, please grant me success today and show steadfast love to my master Abraham. [13] I am standing here by the spring of water, and the daughters of the townspeople are coming out to draw water. [14] Let the girl to whom I shall say, 'Please offer your jar that I may drink,' and who shall say, 'Drink, and I will water your camels'—let her be the one whom you have appointed for your servant Isaac. By this I shall know that you have shown steadfast love to my master."

15 Before he had finished speaking, there was Rebekah, who was born to Bethuel son of Milcah, the wife of Nahor, Abraham's brother, coming out with her water jar on her shoulder. [16] The girl was very fair to look upon, a virgin, whom no man had known. She went down to the spring, filled her jar, and came up. [17] Then the servant ran to meet her and said,

"Please let me sip a little water from your jar," she said, [18] "Drink, my lord," she said, and quickly lowered her jar upon her hand and gave him a drink. [19] When she had finished giving him a drink, she said, "I will draw for your camels also, until they have finished drinking." [20] So she quickly emptied her jar into the trough and ran again to the well to draw, and she drew for all his camels. [21] The man gazed at her in silence to learn whether or not the LORD had made his journey successful.

22 When the camels had finished drinking, the man took a gold nose-ring weighing a half shekel, and two bracelets for her arms weighing ten gold shekels, [23] and said, "Tell me whose daughter you are. Is there room in your father's house for us to spend the night?" [24] She said to him, "I am the daughter of Bethuel son of Milcah, whom she bore to Nahor." [25] She added, "We have plenty of straw and fodder and a place to spend the night." [26] The man bowed his head and worshiped the LORD [27] and said, "Blessed be the LORD, the God of my master Abraham, who has not forsaken his steadfast love and his faithfulness toward my master. As for me, the LORD has led me on the way to the house of my master's kin."

28 Then the girl ran and told her mother's household about these things. [29] Rebekah had a brother whose name was Laban; and Laban ran out to the man, to the spring. [30] As soon as he had seen the nose-ring, and the bracelets on his sister's arms, and when he heard the words of his sister Rebekah, "Thus the man spoke to me," he went to the man; and there he was, standing by the camels at the spring. [31] He said, "Come in, O blessed of the LORD. Why do you stand outside when I have prepared the house and a place for the camels?" [32] So the man came into the house; and Laban unloaded the camels, and gave him straw and fodder for the camels, and water to wash his feet

24.7
Gen 12.7;
13.15; 15.18;
Ex 23.20,23
24.9
v. 2
24.10
Gen 11.31,
32; 27.43
24.11
1 Sam 9.11
24.12
v. 27;
Gen 26.24;
Ex 3.6
24.13
v. 43
24.14
Judg 6.17,
37;
1 Sam 6.7
24.15
v. 45;
Gen 22.20,
23
24.16
Gen 26.7

24.18
vv. 14,16
24.19
v. 14
24.21
vv. 12-14;
56
24.22
v. 47
24.24
v. 15
24.26
vv. 48,52
24.27
vv. 42,48,21
24.29
Gen 29.5,13
24.31
Gen 26.29
24.32
Gen 43.24;
Judg 19.21

and the feet of the men who were with him. 33 Then food was set before him to eat; but he said, "I will not eat until I have told my errand." He said, "Speak on."

34 So he said, "I am Abraham's servant. 35 The LORD has greatly blessed my master, and he has become wealthy; he has given him flocks and herds, silver and gold, male and female slaves, camels and donkeys. 36 And Sarah my master's wife bore a son to my master when she was old; and he has given him all that he has. 37 My master made me swear, saying, 'You shall not take a wife for my son from the daughters of the Canaanites, in whose land I live; 38 but you shall go to my father's house, to my kindred, and get a wife for my son.' 39 I said to my master, 'Perhaps the woman will not follow me.' 40 But he said to me, 'The LORD, before whom I walk, will send his angel with you and make your way successful. You shall get a wife for my son from my kindred, from my father's house. 41 Then you will be free from my oath, when you come to my kindred; even if they will not give her to you, you will be free from my oath.'

42 "I came today to the spring, and said, 'O LORD, the God of my master Abraham, if now you will only make successful the way I am going! 43 I am standing here by the spring of water; let the young woman who comes out to draw, to whom I shall say, "Please give me a little water from your jar to drink," 44 and who will say to me, "Drink, and I will draw for your camels also"—let her be the woman whom the LORD has appointed for my master's son.'

45 "Before I had finished speaking in my heart, there was Rebekah coming out with her water jar on her shoulder; and she went down to the spring, and drew. I said to her, 'Please let me drink.' 46 She quickly let down her jar from her shoulder, and said, 'Drink, and I will also water your camels.' So I drank, and she also watered the camels.

47 Then I asked her, 'Whose daughter are you?' She said, 'The daughter of Bethuel, Nahor's son, whom Milcah bore to him.' So I put the ring on her nose, and the bracelets on her arms. 48 Then I bowed my head and worshiped the LORD, and blessed the LORD, the God of my master Abraham, who had led me by the right way to obtain the daughter of my master's kinsman for his son. 49 Now then, if you will deal loyally and truly with my master, tell me; and if not, tell me, so that I may turn either to the right hand or to the left."

50 Then Laban and Bethuel answered, "The thing comes from the LORD; we cannot speak to you anything bad or good. 51 Look, Rebekah is before you, take her and go, and let her be the wife of your master's son, as the LORD has spoken."

52 When Abraham's servant heard their words, he bowed himself to the ground before the LORD. 53 And the servant brought out jewelry of silver and of gold, and garments, and gave them to Rebekah; he also gave to her brother and to her mother costly ornaments. 54 Then he and the men who were with him ate and drank, and they spent the night there. When they rose in the morning, he said, "Send me back to my master." 55 Her brother and her mother said, "Let the girl remain with us a while, at least ten days; after that she may go." 56 But he said to them, "Do not delay me, since the LORD has made my journey successful; let me go that I may go to my master." 57 They said, "We will call the girl, and ask her." 58 And they called Rebekah, and said to her, "Will you go with this man?" She said, "I will." 59 So they sent away their sister Rebekah and her nurse along with Abraham's servant and his men. 60 And they blessed Rebekah and said to her,

"May you, our sister, become
　　thousands of myriads;
may your offspring gain
　　possession
of the gates of their foes."

24.35 v. 1; Gen 13.2
24.36 Gen 21.2, 10; 25.5
24.37 vv. 2-4
24.38 v. 4
24.39 v. 5
24.40 v. 7
24.41 v. 8
24.42 vv. 11,12
24.43 vv. 13,14
24.45 vv. 15,17; 1 Sam 1.13
24.46 v. 18

24.47 vv. 23,24
24.48 vv. 26,27
24.49 Gen 47.29; Josh 2.14
24.50 Ps 118.23; Gen 31.24
24.52 v. 26
24.53 vv. 10,22
24.54 vv. 56,59
24.59 Gen 35.8
24.60 Gen 17.16; 22.17

[61] Then Rebekah and her maids rose up, mounted the camels, and followed the man; thus the servant took Rebekah, and went his way.

62 Now Isaac had come from[n] Beer-lahai-roi, and was settled in the Negeb. [63] Isaac went out in the evening to walk[o] in the field; and looking up, he saw camels coming. [64] And Rebekah looked up, and when she saw Isaac, she slipped quickly from the camel, [65] and said to the servant, "Who is the man over there, walking in the field to meet us?" The servant said, "It is my master." So she took her veil and covered herself. [66] And the servant told Isaac all the things that he had done. [67] Then Isaac brought her into his mother Sarah's tent. He took Rebekah, and she became his wife; and he loved her. So Isaac was comforted after his mother's death.

Abraham Marries Keturah

25 Abraham took another wife, whose name was Keturah. [2] She bore him Zimran, Jokshan, Medan, Midian, Ishbak, and Shuah. [3] Jokshan was the father of Sheba and Dedan. The sons of Dedan were Asshurim, Letushim, and Leummim. [4] The sons of Midian were Ephah, Epher, Hanoch, Abida, and Eldaah. All these were the children of Keturah. [5] Abraham gave all he had to Isaac. [6] But to the sons of his concubines Abraham gave gifts, while he was still living, and he sent them away from his son Isaac, eastward to the east country.

The Death of Abraham

7 This is the length of Abraham's life, one hundred seventy-five years. [8] Abraham breathed his last and died in a good old age, an old man and full of years, and was gathered to his people. [9] His sons Isaac and Ishmael buried him in the cave of Machpelah, in the field of Ephron son of Zohar the Hittite, east of Mamre, [10] the field that Abraham purchased from the Hittites. There Abraham was buried,

with his wife Sarah. [11] After the death of Abraham God blessed his son Isaac. And Isaac settled at Beer-lahai-roi.

Ishmael's Descendants

12 These are the descendants of Ishmael, Abraham's son, whom Hagar the Egyptian, Sarah's slave-girl, bore to Abraham. [13] These are the names of the sons of Ishmael, named in the order of their birth: Nebaioth, the firstborn of Ishmael; and Kedar, Adbeel, Mibsam, [14] Mishma, Dumah, Massa, [15] Hadad, Tema, Jetur, Naphish, and Kedemah. [16] These are the sons of Ishmael and these are their names, by their villages and by their encampments, twelve princes according to their tribes. [17] (This is the length of the life of Ishmael, one hundred thirty-seven years; he breathed his last and died, and was gathered to his people.) [18] They settled from Havilah to Shur, which is opposite Egypt in the direction of Assyria; he settled down[p] alongside of[q] all his people.

The Birth and Youth of Esau and Jacob

19 These are the descendants of Isaac, Abraham's son: Abraham was the father of Isaac, [20] and Isaac was forty years old when he married Rebekah, daughter of Bethuel the Aramean of Paddan-aram, sister of Laban the Aramean. [21] Isaac prayed to the LORD for his wife, because she was barren; and the LORD granted his prayer, and his wife Rebekah conceived. [22] The children struggled together within her; and she said, "If it is to be this way, why do I live?"[r] So she went to inquire of the LORD. [23] And the LORD said to her,

"Two nations are in your
 womb,
and two peoples born of
 you shall be divided;
the one shall be stronger
 than the other,

24.62
Gen 16.14;
25.11; 20.1
24.63
Ps 1.2;
77.12;
119.15;
143.5; 145.5
24.67
Gen 29.18;
23.1,2; 25.20
25.2
1 Chr 1.32,
33
25.5
Gen 24.35,
36
25.8
Gen 15.15;
35.29; 49.29,
33
25.10
Gen 23.16

25.11
Gen 24.62
25.12
Gen 16.15
25.13
1 Chr 1.29-31
25.16
Gen 17.20
25.17
v. 8
25.18
Gen 16.12
25.20
Gen 24.15,
29
25.21
1 Sam 1.17;
Ps 127.3
25.23
Gen 17.16;
Num 20.14;
Gen 27.29;
Mal 1.3;
Rom 9.12

[n] Syr Tg: Heb *from coming to* [o] Meaning of Heb word is uncertain [p] Heb *he fell* [q] Or *down in opposition to* [r] Syr: Meaning of Heb uncertain

the elder shall serve the younger."

24 When her time to give birth was at hand, there were twins in her womb. 25 The first came out red, all his body like a hairy mantle; so they named him Esau. 26 Afterward his brother came out, with his hand gripping Esau's heel; so he was named Jacob.s Isaac was sixty years old when she bore them.

27 When the boys grew up, Esau was a skillful hunter, a man of the field, while Jacob was a quiet man, living in tents. 28 Isaac loved Esau, because he was fond of game; but Rebekah loved Jacob.

Esau Sells His Birthright

29 Once when Jacob was cooking a stew, Esau came in from the field, and he was famished. 30 Esau said to Jacob, "Let me eat some of that red stuff, for I am famished!" (Therefore he was called Edom.t) 31 Jacob said, "First sell me your birthright." 32 Esau said, "I am about to die; of what use is a birthright to me?" 33 Jacob said, "Swear to me first."u So he swore to him, and sold his birthright to Jacob. 34 Then Jacob gave Esau bread and lentil stew, and he ate and drank, and rose and went his way. Thus Esau despised his birthright.

Isaac and Abimelech

26 Now there was a famine in the land, besides the former famine that had occurred in the days of Abraham. And Isaac went to Gerar, to King Abimelech of the Philistines. 2 The LORD appeared to Isaacv and said, "Do not go down to Egypt; settle in the land that I shall show you. 3 Reside in this land as an alien, and I will be with you, and I will bless you; for to you and to your descendants I will give all these lands, and I will fulfill the oath that I swore to your father Abraham. 4 I will make your offspring as numerous as the stars of heaven, and will give to your offspring all these lands; and all the nations of the earth shall gain blessing for themselves through

your offspring, 5 because Abraham obeyed my voice and kept my charge, my commandments, my statutes, and my laws."

6 So Isaac settled in Gerar. 7 When the men of the place asked him about his wife, he said, "She is my sister"; for he was afraid to say, "My wife," thinking, "or else the men of the place might kill me for the sake of Rebekah, because she is attractive in appearance." 8 When Isaac had been there a long time, King Abimelech of the Philistines looked out of a window and saw him fondling his wife Rebekah. 9 So Abimelech called for Isaac, and said, "So she is your wife! Why then did you say, 'She is my sister'?" Isaac said to him, "Because I thought I might die because of her." 10 Abimelech said, "What is this you have done to us? One of the people might easily have lain with your wife, and you would have brought guilt upon us." 11 So Abimelech warned all the people, saying, "Whoever touches this man or his wife shall be put to death."

12 Isaac sowed seed in that land, and in the same year reaped a hundredfold. The LORD blessed him, 13 and the man became rich; he prospered more and more until he became very wealthy. 14 He had possessions of flocks and herds, and a great household, so that the Philistines envied him. 15 (Now the Philistines had stopped up and filled with earth all the wells that his father's servants had dug in the days of his father Abraham.) 16 And Abimelech said to Isaac, "Go away from us; you have become too powerful for us."

17 So Isaac departed from there and camped in the valley of Gerar and settled there. 18 Isaac dug again the wells of water that had been dug in the days of his father Abraham; for the Philistines had stopped them up after the death of Abraham; and he gave them the names that his father had given

Cross references

25.25 Gen 27.11
25.26 Hos 12.3; Gen 27.36
25.27 Gen 27.3,5
25.33 Heb 12.16
26.1 Gen 12.10; 20.1,2
26.2 Gen 12.7; 17.1; 18.1; 19.1
26.3 Gen 20.1; 12.2,7; 13.15; 15.18; 22.16-18
26.4 Gen 15.5; 22.17; Ex 32.15; Gen 12.3; 22.18; Gal 3.8
26.7 Gen 12.13; 20.2,12,13
26.10 Gen 20.9
26.12 v. 3
26.14 Gen 24.35; 37.11
26.15 Gen 21.25, 30
26.18 Gen 21.31

s That is *He takes by the heel* or *He supplants* t That is *Red* u Heb *today* v Heb *him*

them. 19 But when Isaac's servants dug in the valley and found there a well of spring water, 20 the herders of Gerar quarreled with Isaac's herders, saying, "The water is ours." So he called the well Esek,ʷ because they contended with him. 21 Then they dug another well, and they quarreled over that one also; so he called it Sitnah.ˣ 22 He moved from there and dug another well, and they did not quarrel over it; so he called it Rehoboth,ʸ saying, "Now the LORD has made room for us, and we shall be fruitful in the land."

23 From there he went up to Beer-sheba. 24 And that very night the LORD appeared to him and said, "I am the God of your father Abraham; do not be afraid, for I am with you and will bless you and make your offspring numerous for my servant Abraham's sake." 25 So he built an altar there, called on the name of the LORD, and pitched his tent there. And there Isaac's servants dug a well.

26 Then Abimelech went to him from Gerar, with Ahuzzath his adviser and Phicol the commander of his army. 27 Isaac said to them, "Why have you come to me, seeing that you hate me and have sent me away from you?" 28 They said, "We see plainly that the LORD has been with you; so we say, let there be an oath between you and us, and let us make a covenant with you 29 so that you will do us no harm, just as we have not touched you and have done to you nothing but good and have sent you away in peace. You are now the blessed of the LORD." 30 So he made them a feast, and they ate and drank. 31 In the morning they rose early and exchanged oaths; and Isaac set them on their way, and they departed from him in peace. 32 That same day Isaac's servants came and told him about the well that they had dug, and said to him, "We have found water!" 33 He called it Shibah;ᶻ therefore the name of the city is Beer-shebaᵃ to this day.

26.22 Gen 17.6
26.24 Gen 17.7; 24.12; Ex 3.6
26.25 Gen 12.7,8; 13.4,18; Ps 116.17
26.26 Gen 21.22
26.27 v. 16
26.28 Gen 21.22, 23
26.31 Gen 21.31
26.33 Gen 21.31
26.34 Gen 28.8; 36.2
26.35 Gen 27.46
27.1 Gen 48.10; 1 Sam 3.2
27.2 Gen 47.29
27.3 Gen 25.27, 28
27.4 v. 27; Gen 48.9, 15; 49.28
27.8 v. 13
27.11 Gen 25.25
27.12 vv. 21,22
27.13 v. 8; Mt 27.25

Esau's Hittite Wives

34 When Esau was forty years old, he married Judith daughter of Beeri the Hittite, and Basemath daughter of Elon the Hittite; 35 and they made life bitter for Isaac and Rebekah.

Isaac Blesses Jacob

27 When Isaac was old and his eyes were dim so that he could not see, he called his elder son Esau and said to him, "My son"; and he answered, "Here I am." 2 He said, "See, I am old; I do not know the day of my death. 3 Now then, take your weapons, your quiver and your bow, and go out to the field, and hunt game for me. 4 Then prepare for me savory food, such as I like, and bring it to me to eat, so that I may bless you before I die."

5 Now Rebekah was listening when Isaac spoke to his son Esau. So when Esau went to the field to hunt for game and bring it, 6 Rebekah said to her son Jacob, "I heard your father say to your brother Esau, 7 'Bring me game, and prepare for me savory food to eat, that I may bless you before the LORD before I die.' 8 Now therefore, my son, obey my word as I command you. 9 Go to the flock, and get me two choice kids, so that I may prepare from them savory food for your father, such as he likes; 10 and you shall take it to your father to eat, so that he may bless you before he dies." 11 But Jacob said to his mother Rebekah, "Look, my brother Esau is a hairy man, and I am a man of smooth skin. 12 Perhaps my father will feel me, and I shall seem to be mocking him, and bring a curse on myself and not a blessing." 13 His mother said to him, "Let your curse be on me, my son; only obey my word, and go, get them for me." 14 So he went and got them and brought them to his mother; and his mother prepared

ʷ That is *Contention* ˣ That is *Enmity*
ʸ That is *Broad places* or *Room* ᶻ A word resembling the word for *oath* ᵃ That is *Well of the oath* or *Well of seven*

savory food, such as his father loved. ¹⁵Then Rebekah took the best garments of her elder son Esau, which were with her in the house, and put them on her younger son Jacob; ¹⁶and she put the skins of the kids on his hands and on the smooth part of his neck. ¹⁷Then she handed the savory food, and the bread that she had prepared, to her son Jacob.

18 So he went in to his father, and said, "My father"; and he said, "Here I am; who are you, my son?" ¹⁹Jacob said to his father, "I am Esau your firstborn. I have done as you told me; now sit up and eat of my game, so that you may bless me." ²⁰But Isaac said to his son, "How is it that you have found it so quickly, my son?" He answered, "Because the LORD your God granted me success." ²¹Then Isaac said to Jacob, "Come near, that I may feel you, my son, to know whether you are really my son Esau or not." ²²So Jacob went up to his father Isaac, who felt him and said, "The voice is Jacob's voice, but the hands are the hands of Esau." ²³He did not recognize him, because his hands were hairy like his brother Esau's hands; so he blessed him. ²⁴He said, "Are you really my son Esau?" He answered, "I am." ²⁵Then he said, "Bring it to me, that I may eat of my son's game and bless you." So he brought it to him, and he ate; and he brought him wine, and he drank. ²⁶Then his father Isaac said to him, "Come near and kiss me, my son." ²⁷So he came near and kissed him; and he smelled the smell of his garments, and blessed him, and said,

"Ah, the smell of my son
 is like the smell of a field
 that the LORD has
 blessed.
²⁸ May God give you of the dew
 of heaven,
 and of the fatness of the
 earth,
 and plenty of grain and
 wine.
²⁹ Let peoples serve you,

and nations bow down to
 you.
Be lord over your brothers,
 and may your mother's
 sons bow down to you.
Cursed be everyone who
 curses you,
 and blessed be everyone
 who blesses you!"

Esau's Lost Blessing

30 As soon as Isaac had finished blessing Jacob, when Jacob had scarcely gone out from the presence of his father Isaac, his brother Esau came in from his hunting. ³¹He also prepared savory food, and brought it to his father. And he said to his father, "Let my father sit up and eat of his son's game, so that you may bless me." ³²His father Isaac said to him, "Who are you?" He answered, "I am your firstborn son, Esau." ³³Then Isaac trembled violently, and said, "Who was it then that hunted game and brought it to me, and I ate it all[b] before you came, and I have blessed him?—yes, and blessed he shall be!" ³⁴When Esau heard his father's words, he cried out with an exceedingly great and bitter cry, and said to his father, "Bless me, me also, father!" ³⁵But he said, "Your brother came deceitfully, and he has taken away your blessing." ³⁶Esau said, "Is he not rightly named Jacob?[c] For he has supplanted me these two times. He took away my birthright; and look, now he has taken away my blessing." Then he said, "Have you not reserved a blessing for me?" ³⁷Isaac answered Esau, "I have already made him your lord, and I have given him all his brothers as servants, and with grain and wine I have sustained him. What then can I do for you, my son?" ³⁸Esau said to his father, "Have you only one blessing, father? Bless me, me also, father!" And Esau lifted up his voice and wept.

39 Then his father Isaac answered him:

27.15
v. 27
27.19
v. 4
27.21
v. 12
27.23
v. 16
27.25
vv. 4,10,19,
31
27.27
Heb 11.20;
Song 4.11
27.28
Deut 33.13,
28;
Gen 45.18
27.29
Gen 9.25;
25.23; 49.8;
12.3;
Num 24.9;
Zeph 2.8

27.31
v. 4
27.32
v. 18
27.33
Gen 28.3,4;
Rom 11.29
27.34
Heb 12.17
27.37
vv. 28,29
27.38
Heb 12.17
27.39
v. 28

b Cn: Heb of all c That is He supplants or
He takes by the heel

"See, away from[d] the fatness
 of the earth shall your
 home be,
and away from[e] the dew of
 heaven on high.
40 By your sword you shall live,
 and you shall serve your
 brother;
but when you break loose,[f]
 you shall break his yoke
 from your neck."

Jacob Escapes Esau's Fury

41 Now Esau hated Jacob because of the blessing with which his father had blessed him, and Esau said to himself, "The days of mourning for my father are approaching; then I will kill my brother Jacob." 42 But the words of her elder son Esau were told to Rebekah; so she sent and called her younger son Jacob and said to him, "Your brother Esau is consoling himself by planning to kill you. 43 Now therefore, my son, obey my voice; flee at once to my brother Laban in Haran, 44 and stay with him a while, until your brother's fury turns away— 45 until your brother's anger against you turns away, and he forgets what you have done to him; then I will send, and bring you back from there. Why should I lose both of you in one day?"

46 Then Rebekah said to Isaac, "I am weary of my life because of the Hittite women. If Jacob marries one of the Hittite women such as these, one of the women of the land, what good will my life be to me?"

28 Then Isaac called Jacob and blessed him, and charged him, "You shall not marry one of the Canaanite women. 2 Go at once to Paddan-aram to the house of Bethuel, your mother's father; and take as wife from there one of the daughters of Laban, your mother's brother. 3 May God Almighty[g] bless you and make you fruitful and numerous, that you may become a company of peoples. 4 May he give to you the blessing of Abraham, to you and to your off-

spring with you, so that you may take possession of the land where you now live as an alien—land that God gave to Abraham." 5 Thus Isaac sent Jacob away; and he went to Paddan-aram, to Laban son of Bethuel the Aramean, the brother of Rebekah, Jacob's and Esau's mother.

Esau Marries Ishmael's Daughter

6 Now Esau saw that Isaac had blessed Jacob and sent him away to Paddan-aram to take a wife from there, and that as he blessed him he charged him, "You shall not marry one of the Canaanite women," 7 and that Jacob had obeyed his father and his mother and gone to Paddan-aram. 8 So when Esau saw that the Canaanite women did not please his father Isaac, 9 Esau went to Ishmael and took Mahalath daughter of Abraham's son Ishmael, and sister of Nebaioth, to be his wife in addition to the wives he had.

Jacob's Dream at Bethel

10 Jacob left Beer-sheba and went toward Haran. 11 He came to a certain place and stayed there for the night, because the sun had set. Taking one of the stones of the place, he put it under his head and lay down in that place. 12 And he dreamed that there was a ladder[h] set up on the earth, the top of it reaching to heaven; and the angels of God were ascending and descending on it. 13 And the LORD stood beside him[i] and said, "I am the LORD, the God of Abraham your father and the God of Isaac; the land on which you lie I will give to you and to your offspring; 14 and your offspring shall be like the dust of the earth, and you shall spread abroad to the west and to the east and to the north and to the south; and all the families of the earth shall be blessed[j] in you and in

Cross references (center column):

27.40 Gen 25.23; 2 Kings 8.20-22
27.41 Gen 32.3-11
27.43 vv. 8,13; Gen 24.29
27.46 Gen 26.34, 35
28.1 Gen 24.3,4
28.2 Gen 25.20
28.3 Gen 17.1,6
28.4 Gen 12.2; 17.8

28.6 v. 1
28.8 Gen 24.3; 26.35
28.9 Gen 36.3
28.12 Jn 1.51
28.13 Gen 35.1; 48.3; 26.24; 13.15; 35.12
28.14 Gen 13.14-16; 22.17; 12.3; 18.18; 22.18; 26.4

Footnotes:

d Or *See, of* e Or *and of* f Meaning of Heb uncertain g Traditional rendering of Heb *El Shaddai* h Or *stairway* or *ramp* i Or *stood above it* j Or *shall bless themselves*

your offspring. 15 Know that I am with you and will keep you wherever you go, and will bring you back to this land; for I will not leave you until I have done what I have promised you." 16 Then Jacob woke from his sleep and said, "Surely the LORD is in this place—and I did not know it!" 17 And he was afraid, and said, "How awesome is this place! This is none other than the house of God, and this is the gate of heaven."

18 So Jacob rose early in the morning, and he took the stone that he had put under his head and set it up for a pillar and poured oil on the top of it. 19 He called that place Bethel;k but the name of the city was Luz at the first. 20 Then Jacob made a vow, saying, "If God will be with me, and will keep me in this way that I go, and will give me bread to eat and clothing to wear, 21 so that I come again to my father's house in peace, then the LORD shall be my God, 22 and this stone, which I have set up for a pillar, shall be God's house; and of all that you give me I will surely give one tenth to you."

Jacob Meets Rachel

29 Then Jacob went on his journey, and came to the land of the people of the east. 2 As he looked, he saw a well in the field and three flocks of sheep lying there beside it; for out of that well the flocks were watered. The stone on the well's mouth was large, 3 and when all the flocks were gathered there, the shepherds would roll the stone from the mouth of the well, and water the sheep, and put the stone back in its place on the mouth of the well.

4 Jacob said to them, "My brothers, where do you come from?" They said, "We are from Haran." 5 He said to them, "Do you know Laban son of Nahor?" They said, "We do." 6 He said to them, "Is it well with him?" "Yes," they replied, "and here is his daughter Rachel, coming with the sheep." 7 He said, "Look, it is still broad

28.15
Gen 26.3;
Num 6.24;
Ps 121.7,8;
Gen 48.21;
Deut 31.6,8
28.16
Ex 3.5;
Josh 5.15
28.18
Gen 35.14;
Lev 8.10-12
28.19
Judg 1.23,
26;
Hos 4.15
28.20ff
Gen 31.13;
v. 15;
1 Tim 6.8
28.21
Judg 11.31;
2 Sam 19.24,
30;
Deut 26.17;
2 Sam 15.8
28.22
Gen 35.7,
14;
Lev 27.30
29.1
Judg 6.3,33
29.4
Gen 28.10
29.5
Gen 24.24,
29
29.6
Gen 43.27

29.9
Ex 2.16
29.10
Ex 2.17
29.12
Gen 13.8;
14.14,16;
24.28
29.13
Gen 24.29,
31; 33.4
29.14
Judg 9.2
29.18
Hos 12.12

daylight; it is not time for the animals to be gathered together. Water the sheep, and go, pasture them." 8 But they said, "We cannot until all the flocks are gathered together, and the stone is rolled from the mouth of the well; then we water the sheep."

9 While he was still speaking with them, Rachel came with her father's sheep; for she kept them. 10 Now when Jacob saw Rachel, the daughter of his mother's brother Laban, and the sheep of his mother's brother Laban, Jacob went up and rolled the stone from the well's mouth, and watered the flock of his mother's brother Laban. 11 Then Jacob kissed Rachel, and wept aloud. 12 And Jacob told Rachel that he was her father's kinsman, and that he was Rebekah's son; and she ran and told her father.

13 When Laban heard the news about his sister's son Jacob, he ran to meet him; he embraced him and kissed him, and brought him to his house. Jacobl told Laban all these things, 14 and Laban said to him, "Surely you are my bone and my flesh!" And he stayed with him a month.

Jacob Marries Laban's Daughters

15 Then Laban said to Jacob, "Because you are my kinsman, should you therefore serve me for nothing? Tell me, what shall your wages be?" 16 Now Laban had two daughters; the name of the elder was Leah, and the name of the younger was Rachel. 17 Leah's eyes were lovely,m and Rachel was graceful and beautiful. 18 Jacob loved Rachel; so he said, "I will serve you seven years for your younger daughter Rachel." 19 Laban said, "It is better that I give her to you than that I should give her to any other man; stay with me." 20 So Jacob served seven years for Rachel, and they seemed to him but a few days because of the love he had for her.

k That is House of God l Heb He
m Meaning of Heb uncertain

21 Then Jacob said to Laban, "Give me my wife that I may go in to her, for my time is completed." 22 So Laban gathered together all the people of the place, and made a feast. 23 But in the evening he took his daughter Leah and brought her to Jacob; and he went in to her. 24 (Laban gave his maid Zilpah to his daughter Leah to be her maid.) 25 When morning came, it was Leah! And Jacob said to Laban, "What is this you have done to me? Did I not serve with you for Rachel? Why then have you deceived me?" 26 Laban said, "This is not done in our country—giving the younger before the firstborn. 27 Complete the week of this one, and we will give you the other also in return for serving me another seven years." 28 Jacob did so, and completed her week; then Laban gave him his daughter Rachel as a wife. 29 (Laban gave his maid Bilhah to his daughter Rachel to be her maid.) 30 So Jacob went in to Rachel also, and he loved Rachel more than Leah. He served Laban^n for another seven years.

31 When the Lord saw that Leah was unloved, he opened her womb; but Rachel was barren. 32 Leah conceived and bore a son, and she named him Reuben;^o for she said, "Because the Lord has looked on my affliction; surely now my husband will love me." 33 She conceived again and bore a son, and said, "Because the Lord has heard^p that I am hated, he has given me this son also"; and she named him Simeon. 34 Again she conceived and bore a son, and said, "Now this time my husband will be joined^q to me, because I have borne him three sons"; therefore he was named Levi. 35 She conceived again and bore a son, and said, "This time I will praise^r the Lord"; therefore she named him Judah; then she ceased bearing.

30 When Rachel saw that she bore Jacob no children, she envied her sister; and she said to Jacob, "Give me children, or I shall die!" 2 Jacob became very angry

29.21
Judg 15.1
29.22
Judg 14.10;
Jn 2.1,2
29.27
Judg 14.12
29.30
vv. 17,18
29.31
Ps 127.3;
Gen 30.1
29.32
Gen 16.11;
31.42
29.34
Gen 49.5
29.35
Gen 49.8;
Mt 1.2
30.1
1 Sam 1.5,
6
30.2
Gen 20.18;
29.31

30.3
Gen 16.2
30.4
Gen 16.3,4
30.6
Lam 3.59
30.8
Mt 4.13
30.9
v. 4
30.13
Prov 31.28
30.14
Gen 25.30
30.15
Num 16.9,
13

with Rachel and said, "Am I in the place of God, who has withheld from you the fruit of the womb?" 3 Then she said, "Here is my maid Bilhah; go in to her, that she may bear upon my knees and that I too may have children through her." 4 So she gave him her maid Bilhah as a wife; and Jacob went in to her. 5 And Bilhah conceived and bore Jacob a son. 6 Then Rachel said, "God has judged me, and has also heard my voice and given me a son"; therefore she named him Dan.^s 7 Rachel's maid Bilhah conceived again and bore Jacob a second son. 8 Then Rachel said, "With mighty wrestlings I have wrestled^t with my sister, and have prevailed"; so she named him Naphtali.

9 When Leah saw that she had ceased bearing children, she took her maid Zilpah and gave her to Jacob as a wife. 10 Then Leah's maid Zilpah bore Jacob a son. 11 And Leah said, "Good fortune!" so she named him Gad.^u 12 Leah's maid Zilpah bore Jacob a second son. 13 And Leah said, "Happy am I! For the women will call me happy"; so she named him Asher.^v

14 In the days of wheat harvest Reuben went and found mandrakes in the field, and brought them to his mother Leah. Then Rachel said to Leah, "Please give me some of your son's mandrakes." 15 But she said to her, "Is it a small matter that you have taken away my husband? Would you take away my son's mandrakes also?" Rachel said, "Then he may lie with you tonight for your son's mandrakes." 16 When Jacob came from the field in the evening, Leah went out to meet him, and said, "You must come in to me; for I have hired you with my son's mandrakes." So he lay with her that night. 17 And God heeded Leah, and she conceived and bore Jacob a fifth son. 18 Leah

^n Heb *him* ^o That is *See, a son*
^p Heb *shama* ^q Heb *lawah*
^r Heb *hodah* ^s That is *He judged*
^t Heb *niphtal* ^u That is *Fortune* ^v That is *Happy*

said, "God has given me my hire[w] because I gave my maid to my husband"; so she named him Issachar. [19]And Leah conceived again, and she bore Jacob a sixth son. [20]Then Leah said, "God has endowed me with a good dowry; now my husband will honor[x] me, because I have borne him six sons"; so she named him Zebulun. [21]Afterwards she bore a daughter, and named her Dinah.

22 Then God remembered Rachel, and God heeded her and opened her womb. [23]She conceived and bore a son, and said, "God has taken away my reproach"; [24]and she named him Joseph,[y] saying, "May the LORD add to me another son!"

Jacob Prospers at Laban's Expense

25 When Rachel had borne Joseph, Jacob said to Laban, "Send me away, that I may go to my own home and country. [26]Give me my wives and my children for whom I have served you, and let me go; for you know very well the service I have given you." [27]But Laban said to him, "If you will allow me to say so, I have learned by divination that the LORD has blessed me because of you; [28]name your wages, and I will give it." [29]Jacob said to him, "You yourself know how I have served you, and how your cattle have fared with me. [30]For you had little before I came, and it has increased abundantly; and the LORD has blessed you wherever I turned. But now when shall I provide for my own household also?" [31]He said, "What shall I give you?" Jacob said, "You shall not give me anything; if you will do this for me, I will again feed your flock and keep it: [32]let me pass through all your flock today, removing from it every speckled and spotted sheep and every black lamb, and the spotted and speckled among the goats; and such shall be my wages. [33]So my honesty will answer for me later, when you come to look into my wages with you. Every one that is

not speckled and spotted among the goats and black among the lambs, if found with me, shall be counted stolen." [34]Laban said, "Good! Let it be as you have said." [35]But that day Laban removed the male goats that were striped and spotted, and all the female goats that were speckled and spotted, every one that had white on it, and every lamb that was black, and put them in charge of his sons; [36]and he set a distance of three days' journey between himself and Jacob, while Jacob was pasturing the rest of Laban's flock.

37 Then Jacob took fresh rods of poplar and almond and plane, and peeled white streaks in them, exposing the white of the rods. [38]He set the rods that he had peeled in front of the flocks in the troughs, that is, the watering places, where the flocks came to drink. And since they bred when they came to drink, [39]the flocks bred in front of the rods, and so the flocks produced young that were striped, speckled, and spotted. [40]Jacob separated the lambs, and set the faces of the flocks toward the striped and the completely black animals in the flock of Laban; and he put his own droves apart, and did not put them with Laban's flock. [41]Whenever the stronger of the flock were breeding, Jacob laid the rods in the troughs before the eyes of the flock, that they might breed among the rods, [42]but for the feebler of the flock he did not lay them there; so the feebler were Laban's, and the stronger Jacob's. [43]Thus the man grew exceedingly rich, and had large flocks, and male and female slaves, and camels and donkeys.

Jacob Flees with Family and Flocks

31 Now Jacob heard that the sons of Laban were saying, "Jacob has taken all that was our father's; he has gained all this wealth from what belonged to our

30.20
Mt 4.13
30.22
1 Sam 1.19, 20;
Gen 29.31
30.23
Isa 4.1;
Lk 1.25
30.24
Gen 35.17
30.25
Gen 24.54, 56
30.26
Gen 29.20, 30;
Hos 12.12
30.27
Gen 39.3,5
30.28
Gen 29.15
30.29
Gen 31.38-40
30.30
1 Tim 5.8
30.32
Gen 31.8
30.33
Ps 37.6

30.37
Gen 31.9-12
30.43
Gen 12.16;
13.2; 24.35;
26.13,14

[w]Heb *sakar*　　[x]Heb *zabal*　　[y]That is *He adds*

father." ²And Jacob saw that Laban did not regard him as favorably as he did before. ³Then the LORD said to Jacob, "Return to the land of your ancestors and to your kindred, and I will be with you." ⁴So Jacob sent and called Rachel and Leah into the field where his flock was, ⁵and said to them, "I see that your father does not regard me as favorably as he did before. But the God of my father has been with me. ⁶You know that I have served your father with all my strength; ⁷yet your father has cheated me and changed my wages ten times, but God did not permit him to harm me. ⁸If he said, 'The speckled shall be your wages,' then all the flock bore speckled; and if he said, 'The striped shall be your wages,' then all the flock bore striped. ⁹Thus God has taken away the livestock of your father, and given them to me.

10 During the mating of the flock I once had a dream in which I looked up and saw that the male goats that leaped upon the flock were striped, speckled, and mottled. ¹¹Then the angel of God said to me in the dream, 'Jacob,' and I said, 'Here I am!' ¹²And he said, 'Look up and see that all the goats that leap on the flock are striped, speckled, and mottled; for I have seen all that Laban is doing to you. ¹³I am the God of Bethel,ᶻ where you anointed a pillar and made a vow to me. Now leave this land at once and return to the land of your birth.' " ¹⁴Then Rachel and Leah answered him, "Is there any portion or inheritance left to us in our father's house? ¹⁵Are we not regarded by him as foreigners? For he has sold us, and he has been using up the money given for us. ¹⁶All the property that God has taken away from our father belongs to us and to our children; now then, do whatever God has said to you."

17 So Jacob arose, and set his children and his wives on camels; ¹⁸and he drove away all his livestock, all the property that he had gained, the livestock in his posses-

sion that he had acquired in Paddan-aram, to go to his father Isaac in the land of Canaan.

19 Now Laban had gone to shear his sheep, and Rachel stole her father's household gods. ²⁰And Jacob deceived Laban the Aramean, in that he did not tell him that he intended to flee. ²¹So he fled with all that he had; starting out he crossed the Euphrates,ᵃ and set his face toward the hill country of Gilead.

Laban Overtakes Jacob

22 On the third day Laban was told that Jacob had fled. ²³So he took his kinsfolk with him and pursued him for seven days until he caught up with him in the hill country of Gilead. ²⁴But God came to Laban the Aramean in a dream by night, and said to him, "Take heed that you say not a word to Jacob, either good or bad."

25 Laban overtook Jacob. Now Jacob had pitched his tent in the hill country, and Laban with his kinsfolk camped in the hill country of Gilead. ²⁶Laban said to Jacob, "What have you done? You have deceived me, and carried away my daughters like captives of the sword. ²⁷Why did you flee secretly and deceive me and not tell me? I would have sent you away with mirth and songs, with tambourine and lyre. ²⁸And why did you not permit me to kiss my sons and my daughters farewell? What you have done is foolish. ²⁹It is in my power to do you harm; but the God of your father spoke to me last night, saying, 'Take heed that you speak to Jacob neither good nor bad.' ³⁰Even though you had to go because you longed greatly for your father's house, why did you steal my gods?" ³¹Jacob answered Laban, "Because I was afraid, for I thought that you would take your daughters from me by force. ³²But anyone with whom you find your gods shall not live. In the presence of our kinsfolk, point out what I

31.3
Gen 28.15, 20,21; 32.9
31.5
vv. 3,42; Gen 48.15
31.7
v. 41; Job 19.3; Ps 37.28; 105.14
31.8
Gen 30.32
31.11
Gen 48.16
31.13
Gen 28.13, 18,20
31.14
Gen 29.15, 27

31.19
vv. 30,34; Judg 17.5; 1 Sam 19.13; Hos 3.4
31.21
Gen 37.25
31.23
Gen 13.8
31.24
Gen 20.3; Job 33.15; Gen 24.50
31.26
1 Sam 30.2
31.27
v. 55; Ruth 1.9,14; Acts 20.37
31.29
vv. 53,24
31.30
v. 19
31.32
Gen 44.9

ᶻ Cn: Meaning of Heb uncertain
ᵃ Heb *the river*

have that is yours, and take it."
Now Jacob did not know that Rachel had stolen the gods.[b]

33 So Laban went into Jacob's tent, and into Leah's tent, and into the tent of the two maids, but he did not find them. And he went out of Leah's tent, and entered Rachel's. [34] Now Rachel had taken the household gods and put them in the camel's saddle, and sat on them. Laban felt all about in the tent, but did not find them. [35] And she said to her father, "Let not my lord be angry that I cannot rise before you, for the way of women is upon me." So he searched, but did not find the household gods.

36 Then Jacob became angry, and upbraided Laban. Jacob said to Laban, "What is my offense? What is my sin, that you have hotly pursued me? [37] Although you have felt about through all my goods, what have you found of all your household goods? Set it here before my kinsfolk and your kinsfolk, so that they may decide between us two. [38] These twenty years I have been with you; your ewes and your female goats have not miscarried, and I have not eaten the rams of your flocks. [39] That which was torn by wild beasts I did not bring to you; I bore the loss of it myself; of my hand you required it, whether stolen by day or stolen by night. [40] It was like this with me: by day the heat consumed me, and the cold by night, and my sleep fled from my eyes. [41] These twenty years I have been in your house; I served you fourteen years for your two daughters, and six years for your flock, and you have changed my wages ten times. [42] If the God of my father, the God of Abraham and the Fear[c] of Isaac, had not been on my side, surely now you would have sent me away empty-handed. God saw my affliction and the labor of my hands, and rebuked you last night."

Laban and Jacob Make a Covenant

43 Then Laban answered and

said to Jacob, "The daughters are my daughters, the children are my children, the flocks are my flocks, and all that you see is mine. But what can I do today about these daughters of mine, or about their children whom they have borne? [44] Come now, let us make a covenant, you and I; and let it be a witness between you and me." [45] So Jacob took a stone, and set it up as a pillar. [46] And Jacob said to his kinsfolk, "Gather stones," and they took stones, and made a heap; and they ate there by the heap. [47] Laban called it Jegar-sahadutha:[d] but Jacob called it Galeed.[e] [48] Laban said, "This heap is a witness between you and me today." Therefore he called it Galeed, [49] and the pillar[f] Mizpah,[g] for he said, "The LORD watch between you and me, when we are absent one from the other. [50] If you ill-treat my daughters, or if you take wives in addition to my daughters, though no one else is with us, remember that God is witness between you and me."

51 Then Laban said to Jacob, "See this heap and see the pillar, which I have set between you and me. [52] This heap is a witness, and the pillar is a witness, that I will not pass beyond this heap to you, and you will not pass beyond this heap and this pillar to me, for harm. [53] May the God of Abraham and the God of Nahor"—the God of their father—"judge between us." So Jacob swore by the Fear[c] of his father Isaac, [54] and Jacob offered a sacrifice on the height and called his kinsfolk to eat bread; and they ate bread and tarried all night in the hill country.

55 [h]Early in the morning Laban rose up, and kissed his grandchildren and his daughters and blessed them; then he departed and returned home.

32 Jacob went on his way and the angels of God met him;

Cross references

31.35 Ex 20.12; Lev 19.32
31.39 Ex 22.10-13
31.41 Gen 29.27, 30; v. 7
31.42 Ps 124.1,2; v. 53; Isa 8.13; Gen 29.32; 1 Chr 12.17
31.44 Gen 21.27, 32; 26.28; Josh 24.27
31.45 Gen 28.18
31.48 Josh 24.27
31.49 Judg 11.29; 1 Sam 7.5
31.53 Gen 16.5; 21.23; 28.13; v. 42
31.55 Gen 18.33; 30.25
32.1 Ps 34.7; 91.11; Heb 1.14

Footnotes

[b] Heb *them* [c] Meaning of Heb uncertain
[d] In Aramaic *The heap of witness*
[e] In Hebrew *The heap of witness*
[f] Compare Sam: MT lacks *the pillar* [g] That is *Watchpost* [h] Ch 32.1 in Heb

JACOB'S JOURNEYS

Carchemish

Til Barsip

Aleppo

Haran

Balikh R.

Alalakh

Euphrates R.

Orontes R.

Ugarit

PADDAN ARAM

Jacob's journey took him from
Beersheba in Canaan to the home of
his uncle Laban near Haran and back
to Canaan. His route back (after twenty
years in Haran) likely took him toward
Aleppo, then to Damascus and Edrei
before reaching Peniel on the Jabbok
River. From Peniel he camped at Suc-
coth, finally reentering Canaan and
settling at Shechem, where he built
an altar to the Lord.

Damascus

Ramoth
Gilead

Edrei

Peniel

CANAAN

Bethel

SEIR

Miles 0 20 40 60 80 100
Kms 0 40 80 120

Ramoth
Gilead

Mizpah?

Peniel

Shechem

Mahanaim

Succoth

Jabbok R.

CANAAN

GILEAD

Jordan River

Bethel

Ephrath

Salt
Sea

Mamre

Kiriath
Arba

Miles 0 10 20
Kms 0 10 20 30

Beersheba

2 and when Jacob saw them he said, "This is God's camp!" So he called that place Mahanaim.[i]

Jacob Sends Presents to Appease Esau

3 Jacob sent messengers before him to his brother Esau in the land of Seir, the country of Edom, 4 instructing them, "Thus you shall say to my lord Esau: Thus says your servant Jacob, 'I have lived with Laban as an alien, and stayed until now; 5 and I have oxen, donkeys, flocks, male and female slaves; and I have sent to tell my lord, in order that I may find favor in your sight.' "

6 The messengers returned to Jacob, saying, "We came to your brother Esau, and he is coming to meet you, and four hundred men are with him." 7 Then Jacob was greatly afraid and distressed; and he divided the people that were with him, and the flocks and herds and camels, into two companies, 8 thinking, "If Esau comes to the one company and destroys it, then the company that is left will escape."

9 And Jacob said, "O God of my father Abraham and God of my father Isaac, O LORD who said to me, 'Return to your country and to your kindred, and I will do you good,' 10 I am not worthy of the least of all the steadfast love and all the faithfulness that you have shown to your servant, for with only my staff I crossed this Jordan; and now I have become two companies. 11 Deliver me, please, from the hand of my brother, from the hand of Esau, for I am afraid of him; he may come and kill us all, the mothers with the children. 12 Yet you have said, 'I will surely do you good, and make your offspring as the sand of the sea, which cannot be counted because of their number.' "

13 So he spent that night there, and from what he had with him he took a present for his brother Esau, 14 two hundred female goats and twenty male goats, two hundred ewes and twenty rams, 15 thirty

milch camels and their colts, forty cows and ten bulls, twenty female donkeys and ten male donkeys. 16 These he delivered into the hand of his servants, every drove by itself, and said to his servants, "Pass on ahead of me, and put a space between drove and drove." 17 He instructed the foremost, "When Esau my brother meets you, and asks you, 'To whom do you belong? Where are you going? And whose are these ahead of you?' 18 then you shall say, 'They belong to your servant Jacob; they are a present sent to my lord Esau; and moreover he is behind us.' " 19 He likewise instructed the second and the third and all who followed the droves, "You shall say the same thing to Esau when you meet him, 20 and you shall say, 'Moreover your servant Jacob is behind us.' " For he thought, "I may appease him with the present that goes ahead of me, and afterwards I shall see his face; perhaps he will accept me." 21 So the present passed on ahead of him; and he himself spent that night in the camp.

Jacob Wrestles at Peniel

22 The same night he got up and took his two wives, his two maids, and his eleven children, and crossed the ford of the Jabbok. 23 He took them and sent them across the stream, and likewise everything that he had. 24 Jacob was left alone; and a man wrestled with him until daybreak. 25 When the man saw that he did not prevail against Jacob, he struck him on the hip socket; and Jacob's hip was put out of joint as he wrestled with him. 26 Then he said, "Let me go, for the day is breaking." But Jacob said, "I will not let you go, unless you bless me." 27 So he said to him, "What is your name?" And he said, "Jacob." 28 Then the man[j] said, "You shall no longer be called Jacob, but Israel,[k] for you have striven with God and with humans,[l]

i Here taken to mean *Two camps* j Heb *he*
k That is *The one who strives with God* or *God strives* l Or *with divine and human beings*

and have prevailed." ²⁹Then Jacob asked him, "Please tell me your name." But he said, "Why is it that you ask my name?" And there he blessed him. ³⁰So Jacob called the place Peniel,^m saying, "For I have seen God face to face, and yet my life is preserved." ³¹The sun rose upon him as he passed Penuel, limping because of his hip. ³²Therefore to this day the Israelites do not eat the thigh muscle that is on the hip socket, because he struck Jacob on the hip socket at the thigh muscle.

Jacob and Esau Meet

33 Now Jacob looked up and saw Esau coming, and four hundred men with him. So he divided the children among Leah and Rachel and the two maids. ²He put the maids with their children in front, then Leah with her children, and Rachel and Joseph last of all. ³He himself went on ahead of them, bowing himself to the ground seven times, until he came near his brother.

⁴But Esau ran to meet him, and embraced him, and fell on his neck and kissed him, and they wept. ⁵When Esau looked up and saw the women and children, he said, "Who are these with you?" Jacob said, "The children whom God has graciously given your servant." ⁶Then the maids drew near, they and their children, and bowed down; ⁷Leah likewise and her children drew near and bowed down; and finally Joseph and Rachel drew near, and they bowed down. ⁸Esau said, "What do you mean by all this company that I met?" Jacob answered, "To find favor with my lord." ⁹But Esau said, "I have enough, my brother; keep what you have for yourself." ¹⁰Jacob said, "No, please; if I find favor with you, then accept my present from my hand; for truly to see your face is like seeing the face of God—since you have received me with such favor. ¹¹Please accept my gift that is brought to you, because God has dealt graciously with me, and be-

cause I have everything I want." So he urged him, and he took it.

12 Then Esau said, "Let us journey on our way, and I will go alongside you." ¹³But Jacob said to him, "My lord knows that the children are frail and that the flocks and herds, which are nursing, are a care to me; and if they are overdriven for one day, all the flocks will die. ¹⁴Let my lord pass on ahead of his servant, and I will lead on slowly, according to the pace of the cattle that are before me and according to the pace of the children, until I come to my lord in Seir."

15 So Esau said, "Let me leave with you some of the people who are with me." But he said, "Why should my lord be so kind to me?" ¹⁶So Esau returned that day on his way to Seir. ¹⁷But Jacob journeyed to Succoth,ⁿ and built himself a house, and made booths for his cattle; therefore the place is called Succoth.

Jacob Reaches Shechem

18 Jacob came safely to the city of Shechem, which is in the land of Canaan, on his way from Paddanaram; and he camped before the city. ¹⁹And from the sons of Hamor, Shechem's father, he bought for one hundred pieces of money^o the plot of land on which he had pitched his tent. ²⁰There he erected an altar and called it El-Elohe-Israel.^p

The Rape of Dinah

34 Now Dinah the daughter of Leah, whom she had borne to Jacob, went out to visit the women of the region. ²When Shechem son of Hamor the Hivite, prince of the region, saw her, he seized her and lay with her by force. ³And his soul was drawn to Dinah daughter of Jacob; he loved the girl, and spoke tenderly to her. ⁴So Shechem spoke to his father Hamor, saying, "Get me this girl to be my wife."

Cross references

32.29 Judg 13.17, 18
32.30 Gen 16.13; Ex 24.11; Num 12.8; Judg 6.22; 13.22
33.1 Gen 32.6
33.3 Gen 18.2; 42.6
33.4 Gen 45.14, 15
33.5 Gen 48.9; Ps 127.3; Isa 8.18
33.8 Gen 32.14-16
33.10 Gen 43.3; 2 Sam 3.13
33.11 1 Sam 25.27

33.14 Gen 32.3
33.15 Gen 34.11; 47.25; Ruth 2.13
33.17 Judg 8.5,14
33.18 Josh 24.1; Judg 9.1; Gen 25.20; 28.2
33.19 Josh 24.32; Jn 4.5
34.1 Gen 30.21
34.4 Judg 14.2

^mThat is *The face of God* ⁿThat is *Booths*
^oHeb *one hundred qesitah* ^pThat is *God, the God of Israel*

5 Now Jacob heard that Shechem[q] had defiled his daughter Dinah; but his sons were with his cattle in the field, so Jacob held his peace until they came. 6 And Hamor the father of Shechem went out to Jacob to speak with him, 7 just as the sons of Jacob came in from the field. When they heard of it, the men were indignant and very angry, because he had committed an outrage in Israel by lying with Jacob's daughter, for such a thing ought not to be done.

8 But Hamor spoke with them, saying, "The heart of my son Shechem longs for your daughter; please give her to him in marriage; 9 Make marriages with us; give your daughters to us, and take our daughters for yourselves. 10 You shall live with us; and the land shall be open to you; live and trade in it, and get property in it." 11 Shechem also said to her father and to her brothers, "Let me find favor with you, and whatever you say to me I will give. 12 Put the marriage present and gift as high as you like, and I will give whatever you ask me; only give me the girl to be my wife."

13 The sons of Jacob answered Shechem and his father Hamor deceitfully, because he had defiled their sister Dinah. 14 They said to them, "We cannot do this thing, to give our sister to one who is uncircumcised, for that would be a disgrace to us. 15 Only on this condition will we consent to you: that you will become as we are and every male among you be circumcised. 16 Then we will give our daughters to you, and we will take your daughters for ourselves, and we will live among you and become one people. 17 But if you will not listen to us and be circumcised, then we will take our daughter and be gone."

18 Their words pleased Hamor and Hamor's son Shechem. 19 And the young man did not delay to do the thing, because he was delighted with Jacob's daughter. Now he was the most honored of all his

family. 20 So Hamor and his son Shechem came to the gate of their city and spoke to the men of their city, saying, 21 "These people are friendly with us; let them live in the land and trade in it, for the land is large enough for them; let us take their daughters in marriage, and let us give them our daughters. 22 Only on this condition will they agree to live among us, to become one people: that every male among us be circumcised as they are circumcised. 23 Will not their livestock, their property, and all their animals be ours? Only let us agree with them, and they will live among us." 24 And all who went out of the city gate heeded Hamor and his son Shechem; and every male was circumcised, all who went out of the gate of his city.

Dinah's Brothers Avenge Their Sister

25 On the third day, when they were still in pain, two of the sons of Jacob, Simeon and Levi, Dinah's brothers, took their swords and came against the city unawares, and killed all the males. 26 They killed Hamor and his son Shechem with the sword, and took Dinah out of Shechem's house, and went away. 27 And the other sons of Jacob came upon the slain, and plundered the city, because their sister had been defiled. 28 They took their flocks and their herds, their donkeys, and whatever was in the city and in the field. 29 All their wealth, all their little ones and their wives, all that was in the houses, they captured and made their prey. 30 Then Jacob said to Simeon and Levi, "You have brought trouble on me by making me odious to the inhabitants of the land, the Canaanites and the Perizzites; my numbers are few, and if they gather themselves against me and attack me, I shall be destroyed, both I and my household." 31 But they said, "Should our sister be treated like a whore?"

34.7
Deut 22.21;
Josh 7.15;
Judg 20.6;
2 Sam 13.12
34.10
Gen 13.9;
20.15
34.12
Ex 22.16;
Deut 22.29;
1 Sam 18.25
34.14
Gen 17.14
34.19
1 Chr 4.9

34.24
Gen 23.10
34.25
Gen 49.5-7
34.30
Gen 49.6;
Ex 5.21;
Gen 36.26,
27

q Heb *he*

Jacob Returns to Bethel

35 God said to Jacob, "Arise, go up to Bethel, and settle there. Make an altar there to the God who appeared to you when you fled from your brother Esau." ²So Jacob said to his household and to all who were with him, "Put away the foreign gods that are among you, and purify yourselves, and change your clothes; ³then come, let us go up to Bethel, that I may make an altar there to the God who answered me in the day of my distress and has been with me wherever I have gone." ⁴So they gave to Jacob all the foreign gods that they had, and the rings that were in their ears; and Jacob hid them under the oak that was near Shechem.

5 As they journeyed, a terror from God fell upon the cities all around them, so that no one pursued them. ⁶Jacob came to Luz (that is, Bethel), which is in the land of Canaan, he and all the people who were with him, ⁷and there he built an altar and called the place El-bethel,ʳ because it was there that God had revealed himself to him when he fled from his brother. ⁸And Deborah, Rebekah's nurse, died, and she was buried under an oak below Bethel. So it was called Allon-bacuth.ˢ

9 God appeared to Jacob again when he came from Paddan-aram, and he blessed him. ¹⁰God said to him, "Your name is Jacob; no longer shall you be called Jacob, but Israel shall be your name." So he was called Israel. ¹¹God said to him, "I am God Almighty:ᵗ be fruitful and multiply; a nation and a company of nations shall come from you, and kings shall spring from you. ¹²The land that I gave to Abraham and Isaac I will give to you, and I will give the land to your offspring after you." ¹³Then God went up from him at the place where he had spoken with him. ¹⁴Jacob set up a pillar in the place where he had spoken with him, a pillar of stone; and he poured out a

drink offering on it, and poured oil on it. ¹⁵So Jacob called the place where God had spoken with him Bethel.

The Birth of Benjamin and the Death of Rachel

16 Then they journeyed from Bethel; and when they were still some distance from Ephrath, Rachel was in childbirth, and she had hard labor. ¹⁷When she was in her hard labor, the midwife said to her, "Do not be afraid; for now you will have another son." ¹⁸As her soul was departing (for she died), she named him Ben-oni;ᵘ but his father called him Benjamin.ᵛ ¹⁹So Rachel died, and she was buried on the way to Ephrath (that is, Bethlehem), ²⁰and Jacob set up a pillar at her grave; it is the pillar of Rachel's tomb, which is there to this day. ²¹Israel journeyed on, and pitched his tent beyond the tower of Eder.

22 While Israel lived in that land, Reuben went and lay with Bilhah his father's concubine; and Israel heard of it.

Now the sons of Jacob were twelve. ²³The sons of Leah: Reuben (Jacob's firstborn), Simeon, Levi, Judah, Issachar, and Zebulun. ²⁴The sons of Rachel: Joseph and Benjamin. ²⁵The sons of Bilhah, Rachel's maid: Dan and Naphtali. ²⁶The sons of Zilpah, Leah's maid: Gad and Asher. These were the sons of Jacob who were born to him in Paddan-aram.

The Death of Isaac

27 Jacob came to his father Isaac at Mamre, or Kiriath-arba (that is, Hebron), where Abraham and Isaac had resided as aliens. ²⁸Now the days of Isaac were one hundred eighty years. ²⁹And Isaac breathed his last; he died and was gathered to his people, old and full of days; and his sons Esau and Jacob buried him.

ʳThat is *God of Bethel* ˢThat is *Oak of weeping* ᵗTraditional rendering of Heb *El Shaddai* ᵘThat is *Son of my sorrow*
ᵛThat is *Son of the right hand* or *Son of the South*

35.1
Gen 28.19, 13; 27.43
35.2
Gen 31.19, 30,34;
Ex 19.10,14
35.3
Gen 32.7, 24; 28.20-22; 28.15
35.4
Hos 2.13; Josh 24.26
35.6
Gen 28.19; 48.3
35.7
Gen 28.13
35.8
Gen 24.59
35.9
Hos 12.4; Gen 32.29
35.10
Gen 32.28
35.11
Gen 17.1; 28.3; 48.4; 17.6,16; 36.31
35.12
Gen 13.15; 26.3; 28.13
35.13
Gen 17.22
35.14
Gen 28.18

35.15
Gen 28.19
35.17
Gen 30.24
35.19
Gen 48.7; Ruth 1.2; Mic 5.2; Mt 2.6
35.20
1 Sam 10.2; 35.5; Ex 15.16; Deut 2.25; 11.25
35.22
Gen 49.2; 1 Chr 5.1; 1 Cor 5.1
35.27
Gen 18.1; 23.9
35.29
Gen 25.8; 15.15

Esau's Descendants

36 These are the descendants of Esau (that is, Edom). [2] Esau took his wives from the Canaanites: Adah daughter of Elon the Hittite, Oholibamah daughter of Anah son[w] of Zibeon the Hivite, [3] and Basemath, Ishmael's daughter, sister of Nebaioth. [4] Adah bore Eliphaz to Esau; Basemath bore Reuel; [5] and Oholibamah bore Jeush, Jalam, and Korah. These are the sons of Esau who were born to him in the land of Canaan.

6 Then Esau took his wives, his sons, his daughters, and all the members of his household, his cattle, all his livestock, and all the property he had acquired in the land of Canaan; and he moved to a land some distance from his brother Jacob. [7] For their possessions were too great for them to live together; the land where they were staying could not support them because of their livestock. [8] So Esau settled in the hill country of Seir; Esau is Edom.

9 These are the descendants of Esau, ancestor of the Edomites, in the hill country of Seir. [10] These are the names of Esau's sons: Eliphaz son of Adah the wife of Esau; Reuel, the son of Esau's wife Basemath. [11] The sons of Eliphaz were Teman, Omar, Zepho, Gatam, and Kenaz. [12] (Timna was a concubine of Eliphaz, Esau's son; she bore Amalek to Eliphaz.) These were the sons of Adah, Esau's wife. [13] These were the sons of Reuel: Nahath, Zerah, Shammah, and Mizzah. These were the sons of Esau's wife, Basemath. [14] These were the sons of Esau's wife Oholibamah, daughter of Anah son[x] of Zibeon: she bore to Esau Jeush, Jalam, and Korah.

Clans and Kings of Edom

15 These are the clans[y] of the sons of Esau. The sons of Eliphaz the firstborn of Esau: the clans[y] Teman, Omar, Zepho, Kenaz, [16] Korah, Gatam, and Amalek; these are the clans[y] of Eliphaz in the land of Edom; they are the sons

of Adah. [17] These are the sons of Esau's son Reuel: the clans[y] Nahath, Zerah, Shammah, and Mizzah; these are the clans[y] of Reuel in the land of Edom; they are the sons of Esau's wife Basemath. [18] These are the sons of Esau's wife Oholibamah: the clans[y] Jeush, Jalam, and Korah; these are the clans[y] born of Esau's wife Oholibamah, the daughter of Anah. [19] These are the sons of Esau (that is, Edom), and these are their clans.[y]

20 These are the sons of Seir the Horite, the inhabitants of the land: Lotan, Shobal, Zibeon, Anah, [21] Dishon, Ezer, and Dishan; these are the clans[y] of the Horites, the sons of Seir in the land of Edom. [22] The sons of Lotan were Hori and Heman; and Lotan's sister was Timna. [23] These are the sons of Shobal: Alvan, Manahath, Ebal, Shepho, and Onam. [24] These are the sons of Zibeon: Aiah and Anah; he is the Anah who found the springs[z] in the wilderness, as he pastured the donkeys of his father Zibeon. [25] These are the children of Anah: Dishon and Oholibamah daughter of Anah. [26] These are the sons of Dishon: Hemdan, Eshban, Ithran, and Cheran. [27] These are the sons of Ezer: Bilhan, Zaavan, and Akan. [28] These are the sons of Dishan: Uz and Aran. [29] These are the clans[y] of the Horites: the clans[y] Lotan, Shobal, Zibeon, Anah, [30] Dishon, Ezer, and Dishan; these are the clans[y] of the Horites, clan by clan[a] in the land of Seir.

31 These are the kings who reigned in the land of Edom, before any king reigned over the Israelites. [32] Bela son of Beor reigned in Edom, the name of his city being Dinhabah. [33] Bela died, and Jobab son of Zerah of Bozrah succeeded him as king. [34] Jobab died, and Husham of the land of the Temanites succeeded him as king. [35] Husham died, and Hadad son of Bedad, who defeated Midian in the country of

36.1 Gen 25.30
36.2 Gen 26.34; 28.9
36.6 Gen 12.5
36.7 Gen 13.6, 11; 17.8; 28.4
36.8 Gen 32.3
36.10 1 Chr 1.35
36.12 Ex 17.8,14
36.15 1 Chr 1.34

36.17 1 Chr 1.35, 37
36.18 v. 25; 1 Chr 1.52
36.20 Gen 14.6; Deut 2.12, 22;
1 Chr 1.38
36.25 v. 18;
1 Chr 1.52
36.27 1 Chr 1.42
36.31 1 Chr 1.43

w Sam Gk Syr: Heb *daughter* x Gk Syr:
Heb *daughter* y Or *chiefs* z Meaning of
Heb uncertain a Or *chief by chief*

Moab, succeeded him as king, the name of his city being Avith. ³⁶Hadad died, and Samlah of Masrekah succeeded him as king. ³⁷Samlah died, and Shaul of Rehoboth on the Euphrates succeeded him as king. ³⁸Shaul died, and Baal-hanan son of Achbor succeeded him as king. ³⁹Baal-hanan son of Achbor died, and Hadar succeeded him as king, the name of his city being Pau; his wife's name was Mehetabel, the daughter of Matred, daughter of Me-zahab.

40 These are the names of the clansᵇ of Esau, according to their families and their localities by their names: the clansᵇ Timna, Alvah, Jetheth, ⁴¹Oholibamah, Elah, Pinon, ⁴²Kenaz, Teman, Mibzar, ⁴³Magdiel, and Iram; these are the clansᵇ of Edom (that is, Esau, the father of Edom), according to their settlements in the land that they held.

Joseph Dreams of Greatness

37 Jacob settled in the land where his father had lived as an alien, the land of Canaan. ²This is the story of the family of Jacob.

Joseph, being seventeen years old, was shepherding the flock with his brothers; he was a helper to the sons of Bilhah and Zilpah, his father's wives; and Joseph brought a bad report of them to their father. ³Now Israel loved Joseph more than any other of his children, because he was the son of his old age; and he had made him a long robe with sleeves.ᶜ ⁴But when his brothers saw that their father loved him more than all his brothers, they hated him, and could not speak peaceably to him.

5 Once Joseph had a dream, and when he told it to his brothers, they hated him even more. ⁶He said to them, "Listen to this dream that I dreamed. ⁷There we were, binding sheaves in the field. Suddenly my sheaf rose and stood upright; then your sheaves gathered around it, and bowed down to my sheaf." ⁸His brothers said to him, "Are you

indeed to reign over us? Are you indeed to have dominion over us?" So they hated him even more because of his dreams and his words.

9 He had another dream, and told it to his brothers, saying, "Look, I have had another dream: the sun, the moon, and eleven stars were bowing down to me." ¹⁰But when he told it to his father and to his brothers, his father rebuked him, and said to him, "What kind of dream is this that you have had? Shall we indeed come, I and your mother and your brothers, and bow to the ground before you?" ¹¹So his brothers were jealous of him, but his father kept the matter in mind.

Joseph Is Sold by His Brothers

12 Now his brothers went to pasture their father's flock near Shechem. ¹³And Israel said to Joseph, "Are not your brothers pasturing the flock at Shechem? Come, I will send you to them." He answered, "Here I am." ¹⁴So he said to him, "Go now, see if it is well with your brothers and with the flock; and bring word back to me." So he sent him from the valley of Hebron.

He came to Shechem, ¹⁵and a man found him wandering in the fields; the man asked him, "What are you seeking?" ¹⁶"I am seeking my brothers," he said; "tell me, please, where they are pasturing the flock." ¹⁷The man said, "They have gone away, for I heard them say, 'Let us go to Dothan.' " So Joseph went after his brothers, and found them at Dothan. ¹⁸They saw him from a distance, and before he came near to them, they conspired to kill him. ¹⁹They said to one another, "Here comes this dreamer. ²⁰Come now, let us kill him and throw him into one of the pits; then we shall say that a wild animal has devoured him, and we shall see what will become of his dreams." ²¹But when Reuben heard it, he delivered him out of their hands, say-

ᵇ Or chiefs ᶜ Traditional rendering (compare Gk): a coat of many colors; Meaning of Heb uncertain

ing, "Let us not take his life."
²²Reuben said to them, "Shed no
blood; throw him into this pit here
in the wilderness, but lay no hand
on him"—that he might rescue
him out of their hand and restore
him to his father. ²³So when Jo-
seph came to his brothers, they
stripped him of his robe, the long
robe with sleeves^d that he wore;
²⁴and they took him and threw him
into a pit. The pit was empty; there
was no water in it.

25 Then they sat down to eat;
and looking up they saw a caravan
of Ishmaelites coming from Gilead,
with their camels carrying gum,
balm, and resin, on their way to
carry it down to Egypt. ²⁶Then Ju-
dah said to his brothers, "What
profit is it if we kill our brother and
conceal his blood? ²⁷Come, let us
sell him to the Ishmaelites, and not
lay our hands on him, for he is our
brother, our own flesh." And his
brothers agreed. ²⁸When some
Midianite traders passed by, they
drew Joseph up, lifting him out of
the pit, and sold him to the Ishma-
elites for twenty pieces of silver.
And they took Joseph to Egypt.

29 When Reuben returned to
the pit and saw that Joseph was not
in the pit, he tore his clothes. ³⁰He
returned to his brothers, and said,
"The boy is gone; and I, where can
I turn?" ³¹Then they took Joseph's
robe, slaughtered a goat, and
dipped the robe in the blood.
³²They had the long robe with
sleeves^d taken to their father, and
they said, "This we have found; see
now whether it is your son's robe or
not." ³³He recognized it, and said,
"It is my son's robe! A wild animal
has devoured him; Joseph is with-
out doubt torn to pieces." ³⁴Then
Jacob tore his garments, and put
sackcloth on his loins, and
mourned for his son many days.
³⁵All his sons and all his daughters
sought to comfort him; but he re-
fused to be comforted, and said,
"No, I shall go down to Sheol to my
son, mourning." Thus his father
bewailed him. ³⁶Meanwhile the
Midianites had sold him in Egypt

37.25
vv. 28,36;
Gen 43.11;
Jer 8.22
37.26
v. 20;
Gen 4.10;
Job 16.18
37.27
Gen 42.21
37.28
Judg 6.3;
Gen 45.4,5;
Acts 7.9;
Gen 39.1
37.29
Gen 44.13
37.30
Gen 42.13,
36
37.31
vv. 3,23
37.33
v. 20;
Gen 44.28
37.34
v. 29;
2 Sam 3.31
37.35
2 Sam 12.17;
Gen 42.38;
44.29,31
37.36
Gen 39.1

38.3
Gen 46.12;
Num 26.19
38.7
1 Chr 2.3
38.8
Deut 25.5;
Mt 22.24
38.9
Deut 25.6
38.11
Ruth 1.12,
13
38.12
Josh 15.10,
57

to Potiphar, one of Pharaoh's offi-
cials, the captain of the guard.

Judah and Tamar

38 It happened at that time
that Judah went down from
his brothers and settled near a cer-
tain Adullamite whose name was
Hirah. ²There Judah saw the
daughter of a certain Canaanite
whose name was Shua; he married
her and went in to her. ³She con-
ceived and bore a son; and he
named him Er. ⁴Again she con-
ceived and bore a son whom she
named Onan. ⁵Yet again she bore a
son, and she named him Shelah.
She^e was in Chezib when she bore
him. ⁶Judah took a wife for Er his
firstborn; her name was Tamar.
⁷But Er, Judah's firstborn, was
wicked in the sight of the LORD, and
the LORD put him to death. ⁸Then
Judah said to Onan, "Go in to your
brother's wife and perform the duty
of a brother-in-law to her; raise up
offspring for your brother." ⁹But
since Onan knew that the offspring
would not be his, he spilled his se-
men on the ground whenever he
went in to his brother's wife, so
that he would not give offspring to
his brother. ¹⁰What he did was dis-
pleasing in the sight of the LORD,
and he put him to death also.
¹¹Then Judah said to his daughter-
in-law Tamar, "Remain a widow in
your father's house until my son
Shelah grows up"—for he feared
that he too would die, like his
brothers. So Tamar went to live in
her father's house.

12 In course of time the wife of
Judah, Shua's daughter, died;
when Judah's time of mourning
was over,^f he went up to Timnah
to his sheepshearers, he and his
friend Hirah the Adullamite.
¹³When Tamar was told, "Your
father-in-law is going up to Timnah
to shear his sheep," ¹⁴she put off
her widow's garments, put on a
veil, wrapped herself up, and sat
down at the entrance to Enaim,
which is on the road to Timnah.

^d See note on 37.3 ^e Gk: Heb *He*
^f Heb *when Judah was comforted*

She saw that Shelah was grown up, yet she had not been given to him in marriage. 15When Judah saw her, he thought her to be a prostitute, for she had covered her face. 16He went over to her at the road side, and said, "Come, let me come in to you," for he did not know that she was his daughter-in-law. She said, "What will you give me, that you may come in to me?" 17He answered, "I will send you a kid from the flock." And she said, "Only if you give me a pledge, until you send it." 18He said, "What pledge shall I give you?" She replied, "Your signet and your cord, and the staff that is in your hand." So he gave them to her, and went in to her, and she conceived by him. 19Then she got up and went away, and taking off her veil she put on the garments of her widowhood.

20 When Judah sent the kid by his friend the Adullamite, to recover the pledge from the woman, he could not find her. 21He asked the townspeople, "Where is the temple prostitute who was at Enaim by the wayside?" But they said, "No prostitute has been here." 22So he returned to Judah, and said, "I have not found her; moreover the townspeople said, 'No prostitute has been here.'" 23Judah replied, "Let her keep the things as her own, otherwise we will be laughed at; you see, I sent this kid, and you could not find her."

24 About three months later Judah was told, "Your daughter-in-law Tamar has played the whore; moreover she is pregnant as a result of whoredom." And Judah said, "Bring her out, and let her be burned." 25As she was being brought out, she sent word to her father-in-law, "It was the owner of these who made me pregnant." And she said, "Take note, please, whose these are, the signet and the cord and the staff." 26Then Judah acknowledged them and said, "She is more in the right than I, since I did not give her to my son Shelah." And he did not lie with her again. 27 When the time of her deliv-

38.17
Ezek 16.33;
v. 20
38.18
v. 25
38.19
v. 14
38.24
Lev 21.9;
Deut 22.21
38.25
v. 18
38.26
1 Sam 24.17;
v. 14

38.29
Gen 46.12;
Num 26.20;
Mt 1.3
39.1
Gen 37.28,
36;
Ps 105.17
39.2
vv. 3,21,23
39.3
Gen 21.22;
26.28;
Acts 7.9
39.4
vv. 8,22
39.5
Gen 30.27
39.7
2 Sam 13.11;
Prov 7.15-20
39.9
Gen 20.6;
42.18;
2 Sam 12.13

ery came, there were twins in her womb. 28While she was in labor, one put out a hand; and the midwife took and bound on his hand a crimson thread, saying, "This one came out first." 29But just then he drew back his hand, and out came his brother; and she said, "What a breach you have made for yourself!" Therefore he was named Perez. g 30Afterward his brother came out with the crimson thread on his hand; and he was named Zerah. h

Joseph and Potiphar's Wife

39 Now Joseph was taken down to Egypt, and Potiphar, an officer of Pharaoh, the captain of the guard, an Egyptian, bought him from the Ishmaelites who had brought him down there. 2The LORD was with Joseph, and he became a successful man; he was in the house of his Egyptian master. 3His master saw that the LORD was with him, and that the LORD caused all that he did to prosper in his hands. 4So Joseph found favor in his sight and attended him; he made him overseer of his house and put him in charge of all that he had. 5From the time that he made him overseer in his house and over all that he had, the LORD blessed the Egyptian's house for Joseph's sake; the blessing of the LORD was on all that he had, in house and field. 6So he left all that he had in Joseph's charge; and, with him there, he had no concern for anything but the food that he ate.

Now Joseph was handsome and good-looking. 7And after a time his master's wife cast her eyes on Joseph and said, "Lie with me." 8But he refused and said to his master's wife, "Look, with me here, my master has no concern about anything in the house, and he has put everything that he has in my hand. 9He is not greater in this house than I am, nor has he kept back anything from me except yourself, because you are his wife. How then could I do this great wickedness, and sin

g That is *A breach* h That is *Brightness;* perhaps alluding to the crimson thread

against God?" 10 And although she spoke to Joseph day after day, he would not consent to lie beside her or to be with her. 11 One day, however, when he went into the house to do his work, and while no one else was in the house, 12 she caught hold of his garment, saying, "Lie with me!" But he left his garment in her hand, and fled and ran outside. 13 When she saw that he had left his garment in her hand and had fled outside, 14 she called out to the members of her household and said to them, "See, my husband[i] has brought among us a Hebrew to insult us! He came in to me to lie with me, and I cried out with a loud voice; 15 and when he heard me raise my voice and cry out, he left his garment beside me, and fled outside." 16 Then she kept his garment by her until his master came home, 17 and she told him the same story, saying, "The Hebrew servant, whom you have brought among us, came in to me to insult me; 18 but as soon as I raised my voice and cried out, he left his garment beside me, and fled outside."

19 When his master heard the words that his wife spoke to him, saying, "This is the way your servant treated me," he became enraged. 20 And Joseph's master took him and put him into the prison, the place where the king's prisoners were confined; he remained there in prison. 21 But the LORD was with Joseph and showed him steadfast love; he gave him favor in the sight of the chief jailer. 22 The chief jailer committed to Joseph's care all the prisoners who were in the prison, and whatever was done there, he was the one who did it. 23 The chief jailer paid no heed to anything that was in Joseph's care, because the LORD was with him; and whatever he did, the LORD made it prosper.

The Dreams of Two Prisoners

40 Some time after this, the cupbearer of the king of Egypt and his baker offended their lord the king of Egypt. 2 Pharaoh was angry with his two officers, the chief cupbearer and the chief baker, 3 and he put them in custody in the house of the captain of the guard, in the prison where Joseph was confined. 4 The captain of the guard charged Joseph with them, and he waited on them; and they continued for some time in custody. 5 One night they both dreamed—the cupbearer and the baker of the king of Egypt, who were confined in the prison—each his own dream, and each dream with its own meaning. 6 When Joseph came to them in the morning, he saw that they were troubled. 7 So he asked Pharaoh's officers, who were with him in custody in his master's house, "Why are your faces downcast today?" 8 They said to him, "We have had dreams, and there is no one to interpret them." And Joseph said to them, "Do not interpretations belong to God? Please tell them to me."

9 So the chief cupbearer told his dream to Joseph, and said to him, "In my dream there was a vine before me, 10 and on the vine there were three branches. As soon as it budded, its blossoms came out and the clusters ripened into grapes. 11 Pharaoh's cup was in my hand; and I took the grapes and pressed them into Pharaoh's cup, and placed the cup in Pharaoh's hand." 12 Then Joseph said to him, "This is its interpretation: the three branches are three days; 13 within three days Pharaoh will lift up your head and restore you to your office; and you shall place Pharaoh's cup in his hand, just as you used to do when you were his cupbearer. 14 But remember me when it is well with you; please do me the kindness to make mention of me to Pharaoh, and so get me out of this place. 15 For in fact I was stolen out of the land of the Hebrews; and here also I have done nothing that they should have put me into the dungeon."

16 When the chief baker saw

Cross references:
39.12 Prov 7.13-25
39.17 Ex 23.1; Ps 120.3
39.19 Prov 6.34,35
39.20 Ps 105.18
39.21 v.21; Ps 105.19; Ex 3.21; Dan 1.9
39.22 v. 4
39.23 vv. 2,3,8
40.1 vv. 11,13
40.3 Gen 39.20, 23
40.8 Gen 41.16; Dan 2.27,28
40.12 Gen 41.12, 25; Dan 2.36; 4.19
40.14 Lk 23.42; Josh 2.12
40.15 Gen 37.26-28

i Heb *he*

that the interpretation was favorable, he said to Joseph, "I also had a dream: there were three cake baskets on my head, [17] and in the uppermost basket there were all sorts of baked food for Pharaoh, but the birds were eating it out of the basket on my head." [18] And Joseph answered, "This is its interpretation: the three baskets are three days; [19] within three days Pharaoh will lift up your head—from you!—and hang you on a pole; and the birds will eat the flesh from you."

20 On the third day, which was Pharaoh's birthday, he made a feast for all his servants, and lifted up the head of the chief cupbearer and the head of the chief baker among his servants. [21] He restored the chief cupbearer to his cupbearing, and he placed the cup in Pharaoh's hand; [22] but the chief baker he hanged, just as Joseph had interpreted to them. [23] Yet the chief cupbearer did not remember Joseph, but forgot him.

Joseph Interprets Pharaoh's Dream

41 After two whole years, Pharaoh dreamed that he was standing by the Nile, [2] and there came up out of the Nile seven sleek and fat cows, and they grazed in the reed grass. [3] Then came other cows, ugly and thin, came up out of the Nile after them, and stood by the other cows on the bank of the Nile. [4] The ugly and thin cows ate up the seven sleek and fat cows. And Pharaoh awoke. [5] Then he fell asleep and dreamed a second time; seven ears of grain, plump and good, were growing on one stalk. [6] Then seven ears, thin and blighted by the east wind, sprouted after them. [7] The thin ears swallowed up the seven plump and full ears. Pharaoh awoke, and it was a dream. [8] In the morning his spirit was troubled; so he sent and called for all the magicians of Egypt and all its wise men. Pharaoh told them his dreams, but there was no one who could interpret them to Pharaoh.

40.18
v. 12
40.19
v. 13
40.20
vv. 13,19
40.21
v. 13
40.22
v. 19
41.8
Dan 2.1,3;
4.5,19;
Ex 7.11,22;
Dan 2.27;
4.7

41.10
Gen 40.2,3
41.11
Gen 40.5
41.12
Gen 40.12ff
41.13
Gen 40.21,
22
41.14
Ps 105.20;
Dan 2.25;
Ps 113.7,8
41.15
v. 12
41.16
Dan 2.30;
Acts 3.12;
2 Cor 3.5;
Gen 40.8
41.24
v. 8

9 Then the chief cupbearer said to Pharaoh, "I remember my faults today. [10] Once Pharaoh was angry with his servants, and put me and the chief baker in custody in the house of the captain of the guard. [11] We dreamed on the same night, he and I, each having a dream with its own meaning. [12] A young Hebrew was there with us, a servant of the captain of the guard. When we told him, he interpreted our dreams to us, giving an interpretation to each according to his dream. [13] As he interpreted to us, so it turned out; I was restored to my office, and the baker was hanged."

14 Then Pharaoh sent for Joseph, and he was hurriedly brought out of the dungeon. When he had shaved himself and changed his clothes, he came in before Pharaoh. [15] And Pharaoh said to Joseph, "I have had a dream, and there is no one who can interpret it. I have heard it said of you that when you hear a dream you can interpret it." [16] Joseph answered Pharaoh, "It is not I; God will give Pharaoh a favorable answer." [17] Then Pharaoh said to Joseph, "In my dream I was standing on the banks of the Nile; [18] and seven cows, fat and sleek, came up out of the Nile and fed in the reed grass. [19] Then seven other cows came up after them, poor, very ugly, and thin. Never had I seen such ugly ones in all the land of Egypt. [20] The thin and ugly cows ate up the first seven fat cows, [21] but when they had eaten them no one would have known that they had done so, for they were still as ugly as before. Then I awoke. [22] I fell asleep a second time[j] and I saw in my dream seven ears of grain, full and good, growing on one stalk, [23] and seven ears, withered, thin, and blighted by the east wind, sprouting after them; [24] and the thin ears swallowed up the seven good ears. But when I told it to

[j] Gk Syr Vg: Heb lacks *I fell asleep a second time*

the magicians, there was no one who could explain it to me."

25 Then Joseph said to Pharaoh, "Pharaoh's dreams are one and the same; God has revealed to Pharaoh what he is about to do. [26] The seven good cows are seven years, and the seven good ears are seven years; the dreams are one. [27] The seven lean and ugly cows that came up after them are seven years, as are the seven empty ears blighted by the east wind. They are seven years of famine. [28] It is as I told Pharaoh; God has shown to Pharaoh what he is about to do. [29] There will come seven years of great plenty throughout all the land of Egypt. [30] After them there will arise seven years of famine, and all the plenty will be forgotten in the land of Egypt; the famine will consume the land. [31] The plenty will no longer be known in the land because of the famine that will follow, for it will be very grievous. [32] And the doubling of Pharaoh's dream means that the thing is fixed by God, and God will shortly bring it about. [33] Now therefore let Pharaoh select a man who is discerning and wise, and set him over the land of Egypt. [34] Let Pharaoh proceed to appoint overseers over the land, and take one-fifth of the produce of the land of Egypt during the seven plenteous years. [35] Let them gather all the food of these good years that are coming, and lay up grain under the authority of Pharaoh for food in the cities, and let them keep it. [36] That food shall be a reserve for the land against the seven years of famine that are to befall the land of Egypt, so that the land may not perish through the famine."

Joseph's Rise to Power

37 The proposal pleased Pharaoh and all his servants. [38] Pharaoh said to his servants, "Can we find anyone else like this—one in whom is the spirit of God?" [39] So Pharaoh said to Joseph, "Since God has shown you all this, there is no one so discerning and wise as

you. [40] You shall be over my house, and all my people shall order themselves as you command; only with regard to the throne will I be greater than you." [41] And Pharaoh said to Joseph, "See, I have set you over all the land of Egypt." [42] Removing his signet ring from his hand, Pharaoh put it on Joseph's hand; he arrayed him in garments of fine linen, and put a gold chain around his neck. [43] He had him ride in the chariot of his second-in-command; and they cried out in front of him, "Bow the knee!"[k] Thus he set him over all the land of Egypt. [44] Moreover Pharaoh said to Joseph, "I am Pharaoh, and without your consent no one shall lift up hand or foot in all the land of Egypt." [45] Pharaoh gave Joseph the name Zaphenath-paneah; and he gave him Asenath daughter of Potiphera, priest of On, as his wife. Thus Joseph gained authority over the land of Egypt.

46 Joseph was thirty years old when he entered the service of Pharaoh king of Egypt. And Joseph went out from the presence of Pharaoh, and went through all the land of Egypt. [47] During the seven plenteous years the earth produced abundantly. [48] He gathered up all the food of the seven years when there was plenty[l] in the land of Egypt, and stored up food in the cities; he stored up in every city the food from the fields around it. [49] So Joseph stored up grain in such abundance—like the sand of the sea—that he stopped measuring it; it was beyond measure.

50 Before the years of famine came, Joseph had two sons, whom Asenath daughter of Potiphera, priest of On, bore to him. [51] Joseph named the firstborn Manasseh,[m] "For," he said, "God has made me forget all my hardship and all my father's house." [52] The second he named Ephraim,[n] "For God has

41.25
vv. 28,32
41.27
2 Kings 8.1
41.28
vv. 25,32
41.29
v. 47
41.30
vv. 54,56;
Gen 47.13
41.32
Num 23.19;
Isa 46.10,11
41.35
v. 48
41.38
Num 27.18;
Dan 4.8,18

41.40
Ps 105.21,
22;
Acts 7.10
41.41
Gen 42.6
41.42
Esther 3.10;
Dan 5.7,16,
29
41.43
Esther 6.9
41.44
Ps 105.22
41.46
Gen 37.2
41.50
Gen 46.20
41.52
Gen 17.6;
28.3; 49.22

k *Abrek*, apparently an Egyptian word similar in sound to the Hebrew word meaning *to kneel* l Sam Gk: MT *the seven years that were* m That is *Making to forget* n From a Hebrew word meaning *to be fruitful*

made me fruitful in the land of my misfortunes."

53 The seven years of plenty that prevailed in the land of Egypt came to an end; 54 and the seven years of famine began to come, just as Joseph had said. There was famine in every country, but throughout the land of Egypt there was bread. 55 When all the land of Egypt was famished, the people cried to Pharaoh for bread. Pharaoh said to all the Egyptians, "Go to Joseph; what he says to you, do." 56 And since the famine had spread over all the land, Joseph opened all the storehouses,º and sold to the Egyptians, for the famine was severe in the land of Egypt. 57 Moreover, all the world came to Joseph in Egypt to buy grain, because the famine became severe throughout the world.

Joseph's Brothers Go to Egypt

42 When Jacob learned that there was grain in Egypt, he said to his sons, "Why do you keep looking at one another? 2 I have heard," he said, "that there is grain in Egypt; go down and buy grain for us there, that we may live and not die." 3 So ten of Joseph's brothers went down to buy grain in Egypt. 4 But Jacob did not send Joseph's brother Benjamin with his brothers, for he feared that harm might come to him. 5 Thus the sons of Israel were among the other people who came to buy grain, for the famine had reached the land of Canaan.

6 Now Joseph was governor over the land; it was he who sold to all the people of the land. And Joseph's brothers came and bowed themselves before him with their faces to the ground. 7 When Joseph saw his brothers, he recognized them, but he treated them like strangers and spoke harshly to them. "Where do you come from?" he said. They said, "From the land of Canaan, to buy food." 8 Although Joseph had recognized his brothers, they did not recognize him. 9 Joseph also remembered the

dreams that he had dreamed about them. He said to them, "You are spies; you have come to see the nakedness of the land!" 10 They said to him, "No, my lord; your servants have come to buy food. 11 We are all sons of one man; we are honest men; your servants have never been spies." 12 But he said to them, "No, you have come to see the nakedness of the land!" 13 They said, "We, your servants, are twelve brothers, the sons of a certain man in the land of Canaan; the youngest, however, is now with our father, and one is no more." 14 But Joseph said to them, "It is just as I have said to you; you are spies! 15 Here is how you shall be tested: as Pharaoh lives, you shall not leave this place unless your youngest brother comes here! 16 Let one of you go and bring your brother, while the rest of you remain in prison, in order that your words may be tested, whether there is truth in you; or else, as Pharaoh lives, surely you are spies." 17 And he put them all together in prison for three days.

18 On the third day Joseph said to them, "Do this and you will live, for I fear God: 19 if you are honest men, let one of your brothers stay here where you are imprisoned. The rest of you shall go and carry grain for the famine of your households, 20 and bring your youngest brother to me. Thus your words will be verified, and you shall not die." And they agreed to do so. 21 They said to one another, "Alas, we are paying the penalty for what we did to our brother; we saw his anguish when he pleaded with us, but we would not listen. That is why this anguish has come upon us." 22 Then Reuben answered them, "Did I not tell you not to wrong the boy? But you would not listen. So now there comes a reckoning for his blood." 23 They did not know that Joseph understood them, since he spoke with them through an interpreter. 24 He turned away

41.54
v. 30;
Ps 105.16;
Acts 7.11
41.56
Gen 42.6
42.1
Acts 7.12
42.2
Gen 43.8
42.4
Gen 35.24
42.5
Gen 41.57;
Acts 7.11
42.6
Gen 41.41,
55; 37.7
42.7
v. 30
42.9
Gen 37.6-9

42.13
Gen 43.7;
37.30
42.18
Lev 25.43
42.20
v. 34
42.21
Hos 5.15;
Prov 21.13
42.22
Gen 37.22;
9.5,6
42.24
Gen 43.30;
45.14,15;
43.14,23

º Gk Vg Compare Syr: Heb *opened all that was in* (or, *among*) *them*

from them and wept; then he returned and spoke to them. And he picked out Simeon and had him bound before their eyes. 25 Joseph then gave orders to fill their bags with grain, to return every man's money to his sack, and to give them provisions for their journey. This was done for them.

Joseph's Brothers Return to Canaan

26 They loaded their donkeys with their grain, and departed. 27 When one of them opened his sack to give his donkey fodder at the lodging place, he saw his money at the top of the sack. 28 He said to his brothers, "My money has been put back; here it is in my sack!" At this they lost heart and turned trembling to one another, saying, "What is this that God has done to us?"

29 When they came to their father Jacob in the land of Canaan, they told him all that had happened to them, saying, 30 "The man, the lord of the land, spoke harshly to us, and charged us with spying on the land. 31 But we said to him, 'We are honest men, we are not spies. 32 We are twelve brothers, sons of our father; one is no more, and the youngest is now with our father in the land of Canaan.' 33 Then the man, the lord of the land, said to us, 'By this I shall know that you are honest men: leave one of your brothers with me, take grain for the famine of your households, and go your way. 34 Bring your youngest brother to me, and I shall know that you are not spies but honest men. Then I will release your brother to you, and you may trade in the land.' "

35 As they were emptying their sacks, there in each one's sack was his bag of money. When they and their father saw their bundles of money, they were dismayed. 36 And their father Jacob said to them, "I am the one you have bereaved of children: Joseph is no more, and Simeon is no more, and now you would take Benjamin. All this has

42.25
Gen 44.1;
Rom 12.17,
20,21
42.26
Gen 37.31-35
42.30
v. 7
42.31
v. 11
42.33
Gen 15.19,
20
42.35
Gen 43.12,
15
42.36
Gen 43.14

42.38
Gen 37.33,
35; 44.31
43.1
Gen 41.56,
57
43.3
Gen 42.20;
44.23
43.7
v. 27;
Gen 42.13
43.9
Gen 42.37;
44.32;
Philem 18,
19
43.11
Gen 32.20;
Prov 18.16;
Gen 37.25;
Jer 8.22

happened to me!" 37 Then Reuben said to his father, "You may kill my two sons if I do not bring him back to you. Put him in my hands, and I will bring him back to you." 38 But he said, "My son shall not go down with you, for his brother is dead, and he alone is left. If harm should come to him on the journey that you are to make, you would bring down my gray hairs with sorrow to Sheol."

The Brothers Come Again, Bringing Benjamin

43 Now the famine was severe in the land. 2 And when they had eaten up the grain that they had brought from Egypt, their father said to them, "Go again, buy us a little more food." 3 But Judah said to him, "The man solemnly warned us, saying, 'You shall not see my face unless your brother is with you.' 4 If you will send our brother with us, we will go down and buy you food; 5 but if you will not send him, we will not go down, for the man said to us, 'You shall not see my face, unless your brother is with you.' " 6 Israel said, "Why did you treat me so badly as to tell the man that you had another brother?" 7 They replied, "The man questioned us carefully about ourselves and our kindred, saying, 'Is your father still alive? Have you another brother?' What we told him was in answer to these questions. Could we in any way know that he would say, 'Bring your brother down'?" 8 Then Judah said to his father Israel, "Send the boy with me, and let us be on our way, so that we may live and not die — you and we and also our little ones. 9 I myself will be surety for him; you can hold me accountable for him. If I do not bring him back to you and set him before you, then let me bear the blame forever. 10 If we had not delayed, we would now have returned twice."

11 Then their father Israel said to them, "If it must be so, then do this: take some of the choice fruits of the land in your bags, and carry

them down as a present to the man—a little balm and a little honey, gum, resin, pistachio nuts, and almonds. ¹²Take double the money with you. Carry back with you the money that was returned in the top of your sacks; perhaps it was an oversight. ¹³Take your brother also, and be on your way again to the man; ¹⁴may God Almightyᵖ grant you mercy before the man, so that he may send back your other brother and Benjamin. As for me, if I am bereaved of my children, I am bereaved." ¹⁵So the men took the present, and they took double the money with them, as well as Benjamin. Then they went on their way down to Egypt, and stood before Joseph.

16 When Joseph saw Benjamin with them, he said to the steward of his house, "Bring the men into the house, and slaughter an animal and make ready, for the men are to dine with me at noon." ¹⁷The man did as Joseph said, and brought the men to Joseph's house. ¹⁸Now the men were afraid because they were brought to Joseph's house, and they said, "It is because of the money, replaced in our sacks the first time, that we have been brought in, so that he may have an opportunity to fall upon us, to make slaves of us and take our donkeys." ¹⁹So they went up to the steward of Joseph's house and spoke with him at the entrance to the house. ²⁰They said, "Oh, my lord, we came down the first time to buy food; ²¹and when we came to the lodging place we opened our sacks, and there was each one's money in the top of his sack, our money in full weight. So we have brought it back with us. ²²Moreover we have brought down with us additional money to buy food. We do not know who put our money in our sacks." ²³He replied, "Rest assured, do not be afraid; your God and the God of your father must have put treasure in your sacks for you; I received your money." Then he brought Simeon out to them. ²⁴When the steward�q had brought

the men into Joseph's house, and given them water, and they had washed their feet, and when he had given their donkeys fodder, ²⁵they made the present ready for Joseph's coming at noon, for they had heard that they would dine there.

26 When Joseph came home, they brought him the present that they had carried into the house, and bowed to the ground before him. ²⁷He inquired about their welfare, and said, "Is your father well, the old man of whom you spoke? Is he still alive?" ²⁸They said, "Your servant our father is well; he is still alive." And they bowed their heads and did obeisance. ²⁹Then he looked up and saw his brother Benjamin, his mother's son, and said, "Is this your youngest brother, of whom you spoke to me? God be gracious to you, my son!" ³⁰With that, Joseph hurried out, because he was overcome with affection for his brother, and he was about to weep. So he went into a private room and wept there. ³¹Then he washed his face and came out; and controlling himself he said, "Serve the meal." ³²They served him by himself, and them by themselves, and the Egyptians who ate with him by themselves, because the Egyptians could not eat with the Hebrews, for that is an abomination to the Egyptians. ³³When they were seated before him, the firstborn according to his birthright and the youngest according to his youth, the men looked at one another in amazement. ³⁴Portions were taken to them from Joseph's table, but Benjamin's portion was five times as much as any of theirs. So they drank and were merry with him.

Joseph Detains Benjamin

44 Then he commanded the steward of his house, "Fill the men's sacks with food, as much as they can carry, and put each man's money in the top of his sack.

43.12
Gen 42.35;
vv. 21,22
43.14
Gen 17.1;
28.3; 35.11;
Ps 106.46;
Gen 42.24
43.16
Gen 44.1
43.20
Gen 42.3,10
43.21
Gen 42.35;
vv. 12,15
43.23
Gen 42.24
43.24
Gen 18.4;
19.2; 24.32

43.26
Gen 37.7,10
43.27
v. 7;
Gen 45.3
43.28
Gen 37.7,10
43.29
Gen 35.17,
18; 42.13;
Num 6.25;
Ps 67.1
43.30
Gen 42.24;
45.2,14,15;
46.29
43.31
Gen 45.1
43.32
Gen 46.34
43.34
Gen 45.22
44.1
Gen 42.25

p Traditional rendering of Heb El Shaddai
q Heb the man

² Put my cup, the silver cup, in the top of the sack of the youngest, with his money for the grain." And he did as Joseph told him. ³ As soon as the morning was light, the men were sent away with their donkeys. ⁴ When they had gone only a short distance from the city, Joseph said to his steward, "Go, follow after the men; and when you overtake them, say to them, 'Why have you returned evil for good? Why have you stolen my silver cup?'ʳ ⁵ Is it not from this that my lord drinks? Does he not indeed use it for divination? You have done wrong in doing this.' "

6 When he overtook them, he repeated these words to them. ⁷ They said to him, "Why does my lord speak such words as these? Far be it from your servants that they should do such a thing! ⁸ Look, the money that we found at the top of our sacks, we brought back to you from the land of Canaan; why then would we steal silver or gold from your lord's house? ⁹ Should it be found with any one of your servants, let him die; moreover the rest of us will become my lord's slaves." ¹⁰ He said, "Even so; in accordance with your words, let it be: he with whom it is found shall become my slave, but the rest of you shall go free." ¹¹ Then each one quickly lowered his sack to the ground, and each opened his sack. ¹² He searched, beginning with the eldest and ending with the youngest; and the cup was found in Benjamin's sack. ¹³ At this they tore their clothes. Then each one loaded his donkey, and they returned to the city.

14 Judah and his brothers came to Joseph's house while he was still there; and they fell to the ground before him. ¹⁵ Joseph said to them, "What deed is this that you have done? Do you not know that one such as I can practice divination?" ¹⁶ And Judah said, "What can we say to my lord? What can we speak? How can we clear ourselves? God has found out the guilt of your servants; here we are then, my lord's

44.5
v. 15;
Lev 19.26;
Deut 18.10-14
44.8
Gen 43.21
44.9
Gen 31.32
44.13
Gen 37.29,
34;
Num 14.6
44.14
Gen 37.7,10
44.15
v. 5
44.16
v. 9

44.18
Gen 37.7,8;
41.40-44
44.20
v. 30;
Gen 43.8;
37.33; 42.13,
38
44.23
Gen 43.3
44.28
Gen 37.31-35
44.29
Gen 42.36,
38

slaves, both we and also the one in whose possession the cup has been found." ¹⁷ But he said, "Far be it from me that I should do so! Only the one in whose possession the cup was found shall be my slave; but as for you, go up in peace to your father."

Judah Pleads for Benjamin's Release

18 Then Judah stepped up to him and said, "O my lord, let your servant please speak a word in my lord's ears, and do not be angry with your servant; for you are like Pharaoh himself. ¹⁹ My lord asked his servants, saying, 'Have you a father or a brother?' ²⁰ And we said to my lord, 'We have a father, an old man, and a young brother, the child of his old age. His brother is dead; he alone is left of his mother's children, and his father loves him.' ²¹ Then you said to your servants, 'Bring him down to me, so that I may set my eyes on him.' ²² We said to my lord, 'The boy cannot leave his father, for if he should leave his father, his father would die.' ²³ Then you said to your servants, 'Unless your youngest brother comes down with you, you shall see my face no more.' ²⁴ When we went back to your servant my father we told him the words of my lord. ²⁵ And when our father said, 'Go again, buy us a little food,' ²⁶ we said, 'We cannot go down. Only if our youngest brother goes with us, will we go down; for we cannot see the man's face unless our youngest brother is with us.' ²⁷ Then your servant my father said to us, 'You know that my wife bore me two sons; ²⁸ one left me, and I said, Surely he has been torn to pieces; and I have never seen him since. ²⁹ If you take this one also from me, and harm comes to him, you will bring down my gray hairs in sorrow to Sheol.' ³⁰ Now therefore, when I come to your servant my father and the boy is not with us, then, as his life is bound up in

ʳ Gk Compare Vg: Heb lacks *Why have you stolen my silver cup?*

the boy's life, [31] when he sees that the boy is not with us, he will die; and your servants will bring down the gray hairs of your servant our father with sorrow to Sheol. [32] For your servant became surety for the boy to my father, saying, 'If I do not bring him back to you, then I will bear the blame in the sight of my father all my life.' [33] Now therefore, please let your servant remain as a slave to my lord in place of the boy; and let the boy go back with his brothers. [34] For how can I go back to my father if the boy is not with me? I fear to see the suffering that would come upon my father."

Joseph Reveals Himself to His Brothers

45 Then Joseph could no longer control himself before all those who stood by him, and he cried out, "Send everyone away from me." So no one stayed with him when Joseph made himself known to his brothers. [2] And he wept so loudly that the Egyptians heard it, and the household of Pharaoh heard it. [3] Joseph said to his brothers, "I am Joseph. Is my father still alive?" But his brothers could not answer him, so dismayed were they at his presence.

4 Then Joseph said to his brothers, "Come closer to me." And they came closer. He said, "I am your brother, Joseph, whom you sold into Egypt. [5] And now do not be distressed, or angry with yourselves, because you sold me here; for God sent me before you to preserve life. [6] For the famine has been in the land these two years; and there are five more years in which there will be neither plowing nor harvest. [7] God sent me before you to preserve for you a remnant on earth, and to keep alive for you many survivors. [8] So it was not you who sent me here, but God; he has made me a father to Pharaoh, and lord of all his house and ruler over all the land of Egypt. [9] Hurry and go up to my father and say to him, 'Thus says your son Joseph, God has made me lord of all Egypt; come

down to me, do not delay. [10] You shall settle in the land of Goshen, and you shall be near me, you and your children and your children's children, as well as your flocks, your herds, and all that you have. [11] I will provide for you there— since there are five more years of famine to come—so that you and your household, and all that you have, will not come to poverty.' [12] And now your eyes and the eyes of my brother Benjamin see that it is my own mouth that speaks to you. [13] You must tell my father how greatly I am honored in Egypt, and all that you have seen. Hurry and bring my father down here." [14] Then he fell upon his brother Benjamin's neck and wept, while Benjamin wept upon his neck. [15] And he kissed all his brothers and wept upon them; and after that his brothers talked with him.

16 When the report was heard in Pharaoh's house, "Joseph's brothers have come," Pharaoh and his servants were pleased. [17] Pharaoh said to Joseph, "Say to your brothers, 'Do this: load your animals and go back to the land of Canaan. [18] Take your father and your households and come to me, so that I may give you the best of the land of Egypt, and you may enjoy the fat of the land.' [19] You are further charged to say, 'Do this: take wagons from the land of Egypt for your little ones and for your wives, and bring your father, and come. [20] Give no thought to your possessions, for the best of all the land of Egypt is yours.'"

21 The sons of Israel did so. Joseph gave them wagons according to the instruction of Pharaoh, and he gave them provisions for the journey. [22] To each one of them he gave a set of garments; but to Benjamin he gave three hundred pieces of silver and five sets of garments. [23] To his father he sent the following: ten donkeys loaded with the good things of Egypt, and ten female donkeys loaded with grain, bread, and provision for his father on the journey. [24] Then he sent his

Center reference column

44.32
Gen 43.9
45.1
Acts 7.13
45.2
vv. 14,15;
Gen 46.29
45.3
Gen 43.27
45.4
Gen 37.28
45.5
Isa 40.2;
Gen 37.28;
44.20; 50.20
45.8
Gen 41.43

45.10
Gen 46.28,
34; 47.1
45.13
Acts 7.14
45.18
Gen 27.28;
Num 18.12,
29
45.22
Gen 43.34

brothers on their way, and as they were leaving he said to them, "Do not quarrel[s] along the way."

25 So they went up out of Egypt and came to their father Jacob in the land of Canaan. [26] And they told him, "Joseph is still alive! He is even ruler over all the land of Egypt." He was stunned; he could not believe them. [27] But when they told him all the words of Joseph that he had said to them, and when he saw the wagons that Joseph had sent to carry him, the spirit of their father Jacob revived. [28] Israel said, "Enough! My son Joseph is still alive. I must go and see him before I die."

Jacob Brings His Whole Family to Egypt

46 When Israel set out on his journey with all that he had and came to Beer-sheba, he offered sacrifices to the God of his father Isaac. [2] God spoke to Israel in visions of the night, and said, "Jacob, Jacob." And he said, "Here I am." [3] Then he said, "I am God,[t] the God of your father; do not be afraid to go down to Egypt, for I will make of you a great nation there. [4] I myself will go down with you to Egypt, and I will also bring you up again; and Joseph's own hand shall close your eyes."

5 Then Jacob set out from Beer-sheba; and the sons of Israel carried their father Jacob, their little ones, and their wives, in the wagons that Pharaoh had sent to carry him. [6] They also took their livestock and the goods that they had acquired in the land of Canaan, and they came into Egypt, Jacob and all his offspring with him, [7] his sons, and his sons' sons with him, his daughters, and his sons' daughters; all his offspring he brought with him into Egypt.

8 Now these are the names of the Israelites, Jacob and his offspring, who came to Egypt. Reuben, Jacob's firstborn, [9] and the children of Reuben: Hanoch, Pallu, Hezron, and Carmi. [10] The children of Simeon: Jemuel, Jamin, Ohad,

Jachin, Zohar, and Shaul,[u] the son of a Canaanite woman. [11] The children of Levi: Gershon, Kohath, and Merari. [12] The children of Judah: Er, Onan, Shelah, Perez, and Zerah (but Er and Onan died in the land of Canaan); and the children of Perez were Hezron and Hamul. [13] The children of Issachar: Tola, Puvah, Jashub,[v] and Shimron. [14] The children of Zebulun: Sered, Elon, and Jahleel [15] (these are the sons of Leah, whom she bore to Jacob in Paddan-aram, together with his daughter Dinah; in all his sons and his daughters numbered thirty-three). [16] The children of Gad: Ziphion, Haggi, Shuni, Ezbon, Eri, Arodi, and Areli. [17] The children of Asher: Imnah, Ishvah, Ishvi, Beriah, and their sister Serah. The children of Beriah: Heber and Malchiel [18] (these are the children of Zilpah, whom Laban gave to his daughter Leah; and these she bore to Jacob—sixteen persons). [19] The children of Jacob's wife Rachel: Joseph and Benjamin. [20] To Joseph in the land of Egypt were born Manasseh and Ephraim, whom Asenath daughter of Potiphera, priest of On, bore to him. [21] The children of Benjamin: Bela, Becher, Ashbel, Gera, Naaman, Ehi, Rosh, Muppim, Huppim, and Ard [22] (these are the children of Rachel, who were born to Jacob—fourteen persons in all). [23] The children of Dan: Hashum.[w] [24] The children of Naphtali: Jahzeel, Guni, Jezer, and Shillem [25] (these are the children of Bilhah, whom Laban gave to his daughter Rachel, and these she bore to Jacob—seven persons in all). [26] All the persons belonging to Jacob who came into Egypt, who were his own offspring, not including the wives of his sons, were sixty-six persons in all. [27] The children of Joseph, who were born to him in Egypt, were two; all the persons of the house of Jacob who came into Egypt were seventy.

46.1 Gen 28.10; 26.24; 28.13
46.2 Job 33.14, 15; Gen 22.11; 31.11
46.3 Gen 28.13; 12.2
46.4 Gen 28.15; 50.13,24,25; Ex 3.8; Gen 50.1
46.5 Gen 45.19, 21
46.6 Acts 7.15; Deut 26.5; Josh 24.4; Ps 105.23; Isa 52.4
46.8 Ex 1.1
46.10 Ex 6.15
46.11 1 Chr 6.1, 16
46.12 1 Chr 2.3; 4.21; 38.3,7, 10,29
46.17 1 Chr 7.30
46.18 Gen 30.10; 29.24
46.19 Gen 44.27
46.20 Gen 41.50
46.21 1 Chr 7.6; 8.1
46.23 1 Chr 7.12
46.24 1 Chr 7.13
46.25 Gen 30.5,7; 29.29
46.26 Ex 1.5
46.27 Deut 10.22; Acts 7.14

s Or be agitated t Heb the God
u Or Saul v Compare Sam Gk Num 26.24
1 Chr 7.1: MT Iob w Gk: Heb Hushim

Jacob Settles in Goshen

28 Israel[x] sent Judah ahead to Joseph to lead the way before him into Goshen. When they came to the land of Goshen, [29] Joseph made ready his chariot and went up to meet his father Israel in Goshen. He presented himself to him, fell on his neck, and wept on his neck a good while. [30] Israel said to Joseph, "I can die now, having seen for myself that you are still alive." [31] Joseph said to his brothers and to his father's household, "I will go up and tell Pharaoh, and will say to him, 'My brothers and my father's household, who were in the land of Canaan, have come to me. [32] The men are shepherds, for they have been keepers of livestock; and they have brought their flocks, and their herds, and all that they have.' [33] When Pharaoh calls you, and says, 'What is your occupation?' [34] you shall say, 'Your servants have been keepers of livestock from our youth even until now, both we and our ancestors'—in order that you may settle in the land of Goshen, because all shepherds are abhorrent to the Egyptians."

47 So Joseph went and told Pharaoh, "My father and my brothers, with their flocks and herds and all that they possess, have come from the land of Canaan; they are now in the land of Goshen." [2] From among his brothers he took five men and presented them to Pharaoh. [3] Pharaoh said to his brothers, "What is your occupation?" And they said to Pharaoh, "Your servants are shepherds, as our ancestors were." [4] They said to Pharaoh, "We have come to reside as aliens in the land; for there is no pasture for your servants' flocks because the famine is severe in the land of Canaan. Now, we ask you, let your servants settle in the land of Goshen." [5] Then Pharaoh said to Joseph, "Your father and your brothers have come to you. [6] The land of Egypt is before you; settle your father and your brothers in the best part of the land; let them live

in the land of Goshen; and if you know that there are capable men among them, put them in charge of my livestock."

7 Then Joseph brought in his father Jacob, and presented him before Pharaoh, and Jacob blessed Pharaoh. [8] Pharaoh said to Jacob, "How many are the years of your life?" [9] Jacob said to Pharaoh, "The years of my earthly sojourn are one hundred thirty; few and hard have been the years of my life. They do not compare with the years of the life of my ancestors during their long sojourn." [10] Then Jacob blessed Pharaoh, and went out from the presence of Pharaoh. [11] Joseph settled his father and his brothers, and granted them a holding in the land of Egypt, in the best part of the land, in the land of Rameses, as Pharaoh had instructed. [12] And Joseph provided his father, his brothers, and all his father's household with food, according to the number of their dependents.

The Famine in Egypt

13 Now there was no food in all the land, for the famine was very severe. The land of Egypt and the land of Canaan languished because of the famine. [14] Joseph collected all the money to be found in the land of Egypt and in the land of Canaan, in exchange for the grain that they bought; and Joseph brought the money into Pharaoh's house. [15] When the money from the land of Egypt and from the land of Canaan was spent, all the Egyptians came to Joseph, and said, "Give us food! Why should we die before your eyes? For our money is gone." [16] And Joseph answered, "Give me your livestock, and I will give you food in exchange for your livestock, if your money is gone." [17] So they brought their livestock to Joseph; and Joseph gave them food in exchange for the horses, the flocks, the herds, and the donkeys. That year he supplied them with food in exchange for all their livestock. [18] When that year was ended, they

46.28
Gen 47.1
46.29
Gen 45.14, 15
46.31
Gen 47.1
46.33
Gen 47.2,3
46.34
Gen 13.7,8; 26.20; 37.2; 45.10,18; Ex 8.26
47.1
Gen 46.31
47.3
Gen 46.33, 34
47.4
Gen 15.13; Deut 26.5; Gen 43.1; 46.34
47.6
v. 11; Gen 45.10, 18

47.8
Ps 39.12; Heb 11.9, 13; Job 14.1; Gen 25.7; 35.28
47.10
v. 7
47.11
Ex 1.11; 12.37; 6.27
47.13
Gen 41.30; Acts 7.11
47.14
Gen 41.56
47.15
v. 19

x Heb *He*

came to him the following year, and said to him, "We can not hide from my lord that our money is all spent; and the herds of cattle are my lord's. There is nothing left in the sight of my lord but our bodies and our lands. [19] Shall we die before your eyes, both we and our land? Buy us and our land in exchange for food. We with our land will become slaves to Pharaoh; just give us seed, so that we may live and not die, and that the land may not become desolate."

20 So Joseph bought all the land of Egypt for Pharaoh. All the Egyptians sold their fields, because the famine was severe upon them; and the land became Pharaoh's. [21] As for the people, he made slaves of them[y] from one end of Egypt to the other. [22] Only the land of the priests he did not buy; for the priests had a fixed allowance from Pharaoh, and lived on the allowance that Pharaoh gave them; therefore they did not sell their land. [23] Then Joseph said to the people, "Now that I have this day bought you and your land for Pharaoh, here is seed for you; sow the land. [24] And at the harvests you shall give one-fifth to Pharaoh, and four-fifths shall be your own, as seed for the field and as food for yourselves and your households, and as food for your little ones." [25] They said, "You have saved our lives; may it please my lord, we will be slaves to Pharaoh." [26] So Joseph made it a statute concerning the land of Egypt, and it stands to this day, that Pharaoh should have the fifth. The land of the priests alone did not become Pharaoh's.

The Last Days of Jacob

27 Thus Israel settled in the land of Egypt, in the region of Goshen; and they gained possessions in it, and were fruitful and multiplied exceedingly. [28] Jacob lived in the land of Egypt seventeen years; so the days of Jacob, the years of his life, were one hundred forty-seven years.

29 When the time of Israel's

death drew near, he called his son Joseph and said to him, "If I have found favor with you, put your hand under my thigh and promise to deal loyally and truly with me. Do not bury me in Egypt. [30] When I lie down with my ancestors, carry me out of Egypt and bury me in their burial place." He answered, "I will do as you have said." [31] And he said, "Swear to me"; and he swore to him. Then Israel bowed himself on the head of his bed.

Jacob Blesses Joseph's Sons

48 After this Joseph was told, "Your father is ill." So he took with him his two sons, Manasseh and Ephraim. [2] When Jacob was told, "Your son Joseph has come to you," he[z] summoned his strength and sat up in bed. [3] And Jacob said to Joseph, "God Almighty[a] appeared to me at Luz in the land of Canaan, and he blessed me, [4] and said to me, 'I am going to make you fruitful and increase your numbers; I will make of you a company of peoples, and will give this land to your offspring after you for a perpetual holding.' [5] Therefore your two sons, who were born to you in the land of Egypt before I came to you in Egypt, are now mine; Ephraim and Manasseh shall be mine, just as Reuben and Simeon are. [6] As for the offspring born to you after them, they shall be yours. They shall be recorded under the names of their brothers with regard to their inheritance. [7] For when I came from Paddan, Rachel, alas, died in the land of Canaan on the way, while there was still some distance to go to Ephrath; and I buried her there on the way to Ephrath" (that is, Bethlehem).

8 When Israel saw Joseph's sons, he said, "Who are these?" [9] Joseph said to his father, "They are my sons, whom God has given me here." And he said, "Bring them to me, please, that I may bless them." [10] Now the eyes of Israel

Cross references (center column)

47.22 Ezra 7.24
47.24 Gen 41.34
47.25 Gen 33.15
47.26 v. 22
47.27 v. 11; Gen 46.3; Ex 1.7
47.29 Deut 31.14; Gen 24.2,49
47.30 Gen 49.29; 50.5,13
47.31 Gen 21.23, 24; 24.3; 31.53; 50.25
48.3 Gen 35.9-12; 28.19; 35.6
48.4 Gen 18.8
48.5 Gen 46.20; Josh 13.7; 14.4
48.7 Gen 33.18; 35.19,20
48.9 Gen 33.5
48.10 Gen 27.1,27

y Sam Gk Compare Vg: MT *He removed them to the cities* z Heb *Israel* a Traditional rendering of Heb *El Shaddai*

were dim with age, and he could not see well. So Joseph brought them near him; and he kissed them and embraced them. [11] Israel said to Joseph, "I did not expect to see your face; and here God has let me see your children also." [12] Then Joseph removed them from his father's knees,[b] and he bowed himself with his face to the earth. [13] Joseph took them both, Ephraim in his right hand toward Israel's left, and Manasseh in his left hand toward Israel's right, and brought them near him. [14] But Israel stretched out his right hand and laid it on the head of Ephraim, who was the younger, and his left hand on the head of Manasseh, crossing his hands, for Manasseh was the firstborn. [15] He blessed Joseph, and said,

> "The God before whom my
> ancestors Abraham and
> Isaac walked,
> the God who has been my
> shepherd all my life to
> this day,
> [16] the angel who has redeemed
> me from all harm, bless
> the boys;
> and in them let my name be
> perpetuated, and the
> name of my ancestors
> Abraham and Isaac;
> and let them grow into a
> multitude on the
> earth."

17 When Joseph saw that his father laid his right hand on the head of Ephraim, it displeased him; so he took his father's hand, to remove it from Ephraim's head to Manasseh's head. [18] Joseph said to his father, "Not so, my father! Since this one is the firstborn, put your right hand on his head." [19] But his father refused, and said, "I know, my son, I know; he also shall become a people, and he also shall be great. Nevertheless his younger brother shall be greater than he, and his offspring shall become a multitude of nations." [20] So he blessed them that day, saying,

> "By you[c] Israel will invoke
> blessings, saying,

> 'God make you[c] like
> Ephraim and like
> Manasseh.' "

So he put Ephraim ahead of Manasseh. [21] Then Israel said to Joseph, "I am about to die, but God will be with you and will bring you again to the land of your ancestors. [22] I now give to you one portion[d] more than to your brothers, the portion[d] that I took from the hand of the Amorites with my sword and with my bow."

Jacob's Last Words to His Sons

49 Then Jacob called his sons, and said: "Gather around, that I may tell you what will happen to you in days to come.
> [2] Assemble and hear, O sons
> of Jacob;
> listen to Israel your father.

> [3] Reuben, you are my
> firstborn,
> my might and the first
> fruits of my vigor,
> excelling in rank and
> excelling in power.
> [4] Unstable as water, you shall
> no longer excell
> because you went up onto
> your father's bed;
> then you defiled it—you[e]
> went up onto my
> couch!

> [5] Simeon and Levi are
> brothers;
> weapons of violence are
> their swords.
> [6] May I never come into their
> council;
> may I not be joined to their
> company—
> for in their anger they killed
> men,
> and at their whim they
> hamstrung oxen.
> [7] Cursed be their anger, for it
> is fierce,
> and their wrath, for it is
> cruel!

48.11
Gen 45.26
48.14
v. 19
48.15
Gen 17.1;
Heb 11.21
48.16
Gen 28.15;
31.11,13,24;
28.14; 46.3
48.17
v. 14
48.19
v. 14;
Num 1.33,
35

48.21
Gen 26.3;
28.15; 46.4;
50.24
48.22
Josh 24.32;
Jn 4.5
49.1
Num 24.14
49.3
Gen 29.32;
Deut 21.17
49.4
Gen 35.22;
Deut 27.20
49.5
Gen 34.25-30
49.6
Prov 1.15;
Eph 5.11;
Gen 34.26
49.7
Josh 19.1,9;
21.1-42

b Heb *from his knees* c *you* here is singular in Heb d Or *mountain slope* (Heb *shekem*, a play on the name of the town and district of Shechem) e Gk Syr Tg: Heb *he*

I will divide them in Jacob,
and scatter them in Israel.

8 Judah, your brothers shall
praise you;
your hand shall be on the
neck of your enemies;
your father's sons shall
bow down before you.
9 Judah is a lion's whelp;
from the prey, my son, you
have gone up.
He crouches down, he
stretches out like a
lion,
like a lioness—who dares
rouse him up?
10 The scepter shall not depart
from Judah,
nor the ruler's staff from
between his feet,
until tribute comes to him;[f]
and the obedience of the
peoples is his.
11 Binding his foal to the vine
and his donkey's colt to
the choice vine,
he washes his garments in
wine
and his robe in the blood
of grapes;
12 his eyes are darker than
wine,
and his teeth whiter than
milk.

13 Zebulun shall settle at the
shore of the sea;
he shall be a haven for
ships,
and his border shall be at
Sidon.

14 Issachar is a strong donkey,
lying down between the
sheepfolds;
15 he saw that a resting place
was good,
and that the land was
pleasant;
so he bowed his shoulder to
the burden,
and became a slave at
forced labor.

16 Dan shall judge his people

as one of the tribes of
Israel.
17 Dan shall be a snake by the
roadside,
a viper along the path,
that bites the horse's heels
so that its rider falls
backward.

18 I wait for your salvation,
O Lord.

19 Gad shall be raided by
raiders,
but he shall raid at their
heels.

20 Asher's[g] food shall be rich,
and he shall provide royal
delicacies.

21 Naphtali is a doe let loose
that bears lovely fawns.[h]

22 Joseph is a fruitful bough,
a fruitful bough by a
spring;
his branches run over the
wall.[i]
23 The archers fiercely attacked
him;
they shot at him and
pressed him hard.
24 Yet his bow remained taut,
and his arms[j] were made
agile
by the hands of the Mighty
One of Jacob,
by the name of the
Shepherd, the Rock of
Israel,
25 by the God of your father,
who will help you,
by the Almighty[k] who will
bless you
with blessings of heaven
above,
blessings of the deep that
lies beneath,
blessings of the breasts and
of the womb.

[f] Or until Shiloh comes or until he comes to
Shiloh or (with Syr) until he comes to whom it
belongs [g] Gk Vg Syr: Heb From Asher
[h] Or that gives beautiful words [i] Meaning
of Heb uncertain [j] Heb the arms of his
hands [k] Traditional rendering of Heb
Shaddai

49.8
Deut 33.7;
1 Chr 5.2
49.9
Ezek 19.5-7;
Mic 5.8
49.10
Num 24.17;
Ps 60.7;
Lk 1.32;
Isa 2.2; 11.1
49.13
Deut 33.18,
19;
Josh 19.10,
11
49.16
Deut 33.22;
Judg 18.1,2

49.17
Judg 18.26,
27
49.18
Ex 15.2;
Ps 25.5;
119.166,174;
Isa 25.9;
Mic 7.7
49.19
Deut 33.20;
1 Chr 5.18
49.20
Deut 33.24,
25;
Josh 19.24
49.21
Deut 33.23
49.22
Deut 33.13-17
49.23
Gen 37.4,
24,28
49.24
Ps 18.34;
Isa 41.10;
Ps 132.2,5;
Isa 1.24;
Ps 23.1;
Isa 28.16;
1 Pet 2.6-8
49.25
Gen 28.3,
13; 32.9;
48.3; 27.28

26 The blessings of your father
　　are stronger than the
　　　blessings of the eternal
　　　　mountains,
　　the bounties[1] of the
　　　everlasting hills;
　may they be on the head of
　　Joseph,
　　on the brow of him who
　　　was set apart from his
　　　brothers.

27 Benjamin is a ravenous wolf,
　　in the morning devouring
　　　the prey,
　　and at evening dividing the
　　　spoil."

28 All these are the twelve
tribes of Israel, and this is what
their father said to them when he
blessed them, blessing each one of
them with a suitable blessing.

Jacob's Death and Burial

29 Then he charged them, say-
ing to them, "I am about to be gath-

49.26
Deut 33.15, 16
49.28
Gen 23.16-20
49.29
Gen 25.8; 47.30

49.30
Gen 23.16
49.31
Gen 23.19; 25.9; 35.29
49.33
Gen 25.8; Acts 7.15; v. 29
50.1
Gen 46.4
50.2
v. 26
50.3
v. 10; Num 20.29; Deut 34.8

ered to my people. Bury me with
my ancestors—in the cave in the
field of Ephron the Hittite, 30 in the
cave in the field at Machpelah,
near Mamre, in the land of Canaan,
in the field that Abraham bought
from Ephron the Hittite as a burial
site. 31 There Abraham and his wife
Sarah were buried; there Isaac and
his wife Rebekah were buried; and
there I buried Leah— 32 the field
and the cave that is in it were pur-
chased from the Hittites." 33 When
Jacob ended his charge to his sons,
he drew up his feet into the bed,
breathed his last, and was gathered
to his people.

50 Then Joseph threw himself
on his father's face and
wept over him and kissed him. 2 Jo-
seph commanded the physicians in
his service to embalm his father. So
the physicians embalmed Israel;
3 they spent forty days in doing this,

[1] Cn Compare Gk: Heb of my progenitors to the boundaries

THE TRIBES OF ISRAEL

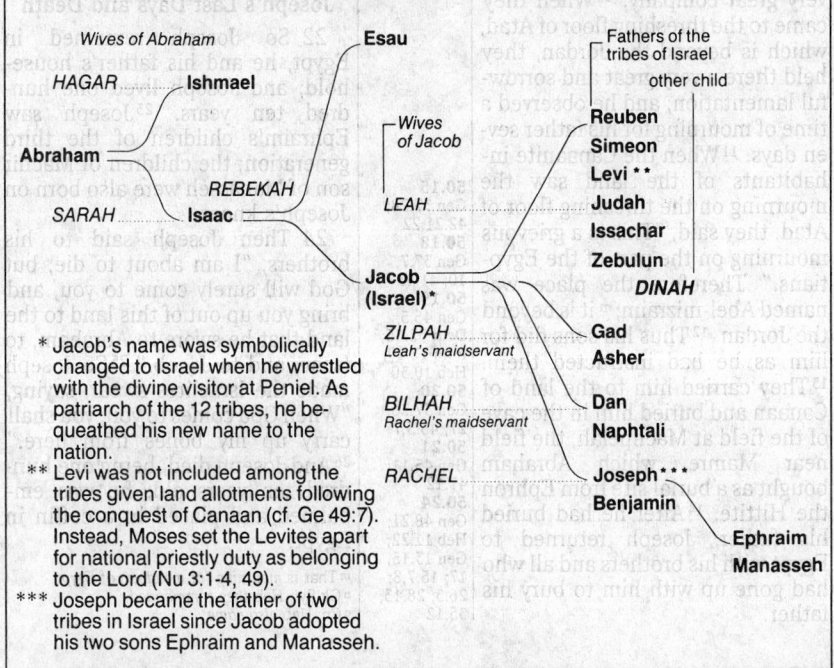

Wives of Abraham

HAGAR **Ishmael**

Abraham

　　　　REBEKAH

SARAH **Isaac**

Esau

　Wives
　of Jacob

LEAH

**Jacob
(Israel)***

ZILPAH
Leah's maidservant

BILHAH
Rachel's maidservant

RACHEL

Fathers of the
tribes of Israel
other child

Reuben
Simeon
Levi *
Judah
Issachar
Zebulun
DINAH
Gad
Asher
Dan
Naphtali
Joseph***
Benjamin
　　Ephraim
　　Manasseh

* Jacob's name was symbolically
changed to Israel when he wrestled
with the divine visitor at Peniel. As
patriarch of the 12 tribes, he be-
queathed his new name to the
nation.
** Levi was not included among the
tribes given land allotments following
the conquest of Canaan (cf. Ge 49:7).
Instead, Moses set the Levites apart
for national priestly duty as belonging
to the Lord (Nu 3:1-4, 49).
*** Joseph became the father of two
tribes in Israel since Jacob adopted
his two sons Ephraim and Manasseh.

for that is the time required for embalming. And the Egyptians wept for him seventy days.

4 When the days of weeping for him were past, Joseph addressed the household of Pharaoh, "If now I have found favor with you, please speak to Pharaoh as follows: [5]My father made me swear an oath; he said, 'I am about to die. In the tomb that I hewed out for myself in the land of Canaan, there you shall bury me.' Now therefore let me go up, so that I may bury my father; then I will return." [6]Pharaoh answered, "Go up, and bury your father, as he made you swear to do."

7 So Joseph went up to bury his father. With him went up all the servants of Pharaoh, the elders of his household, and all the elders of the land of Egypt, [8]as well as all the household of Joseph, his brothers, and his father's household. Only their children, their flocks, and their herds were left in the land of Goshen. [9]Both chariots and charioteers went up with him. It was a very great company. [10]When they came to the threshing floor of Atad, which is beyond the Jordan, they held there a very great and sorrowful lamentation; and he observed a time of mourning for his father seven days. [11]When the Canaanite inhabitants of the land saw the mourning on the threshing floor of Atad, they said, "This is a grievous mourning on the part of the Egyptians." Therefore the place was named Abel-mizraim;[m] it is beyond the Jordan. [12]Thus his sons did for him as he had instructed them. [13]They carried him to the land of Canaan and buried him in the cave of the field at Machpelah, the field near Mamre, which Abraham bought as a burial site from Ephron the Hittite. [14]After he had buried his father, Joseph returned to Egypt with his brothers and all who had gone up with him to bury his father.

50.5
Gen 47.29-31
50.8
Ex 8.22
50.10
2 Sam 1.17;
1 Sam 31.13;
Job 2.13
50.13
Gen 49.29,
30; 23.16

50.15
Gen 37.28;
42.21,22
50.18
Gen 37.7,
10; 41.43
50.19
Gen 45.5;
Deut 32.35;
Rom 12.19;
Heb 10.30
50.20
Gen 37.26,
27; 45.5,7
50.21
Gen 45.11;
47.12
50.24
Gen 48.21;
Heb 11.22;
Gen 13.15,
17; 15.7,8;
26.3; 28.13;
35.12

Joseph Forgives His Brothers

15 Realizing that their father was dead, Joseph's brothers said, "What if Joseph still bears a grudge against us and pays us back in full for all the wrong that we did to him?" [16]So they approached[n] Joseph, saying, "Your father gave this instruction before he died, [17]'Say to Joseph: I beg you, forgive the crime of your brothers and the wrong they did in harming you.' Now therefore please forgive the crime of the servants of the God of your father." Joseph wept when they spoke to him. [18]Then his brothers also wept,[o] fell down before him, and said, "We are here as your slaves." [19]But Joseph said to them, "Do not be afraid! Am I in the place of God? [20]Even though you intended to do harm to me, God intended it for good, in order to preserve a numerous people, as he is doing today. [21]So have no fear; I myself will provide for you and your little ones." In this way he reassured them, speaking kindly to them.

Joseph's Last Days and Death

22 So Joseph remained in Egypt, he and his father's household; and Joseph lived one hundred ten years. [23]Joseph saw Ephraim's children of the third generation; the children of Machir son of Manasseh were also born on Joseph's knees.

24 Then Joseph said to his brothers, "I am about to die; but God will surely come to you, and bring you up out of this land to the land that he swore to Abraham, to Isaac, and to Jacob." [25]So Joseph made the Israelites swear, saying, "When God comes to you, you shall carry up my bones from here." [26]And Joseph died, being one hundred ten years old; he was embalmed and placed in a coffin in Egypt.

[m] That is *mourning* (or *meadow*) *of Egypt*
[n] Gk Syr: Heb *they commanded*
[o] Cn: Heb *also came*

Exodus

Title and Background

Exodus is a Latin word (derived from the Greek) that means "exit," "departure." This book describes the greatest miracle in the Old Testament record of Israel's history–their "going out" from Egypt and slavery. While the story of the Israelites began with Abraham in Genesis, Exodus is the history of their early years as God's chosen nation, committed to him according to the terms of the Mosaic covenant given at Mount Sinai. The book of Exodus was not intended to exist separately, but was thought of as a continuation of a narrative that began in Genesis and moves on through Leviticus, Numbers, and Deuteronomy.

Author and Date of Writing

Several verses in Exodus state that Moses wrote certain sections of the book (see 17.14; 24.4; 34.27). The New Testament also mentions Mosaic authorship for various passages in Exodus (see, e.g., Mk 7.10; 12.26; Lk 2.22-23). It seems likely, however, that the final form of Exodus took place at a later time in Israel's history.

Using 1 Kings 6.1 as a basis for dating places the exodus at approximately 1446 B.C. This date is by no means certain, however, for a significant amount of archaeological evidence tends to date Moses and the exodus in the thirteenth century B.C.

Theme and Message

Exodus lays the foundation for a theology of God's revelation of his name, his attributes, his redemption, his law, and his worship. It also reports the appointment and work of the first covenant mediator (Moses), describes the beginning of the priesthood, defines the role of the prophet, and relates how the ancient covenant relationship between God and his people came under a new administration (the Sinai covenant).

Outline

I. Preparation for Israel's Deliverance from Slavery (1.1–4.31)
II. Israel's Deliverance from Egyptian Slavery (5.1–18.27)
 A. Pharaoh's Resistance and the Lord's Reassurance (5.1–6.27)
 B. The Ten Plagues on Egypt (6.28–12.36)
 C. The Exodus: From Egypt to Mount Sinai (12.37–18.27)
III. The Covenant at Sinai (19.1–24.18)
IV. The Tabernacle for Worship (25.1–40.38)

1 These are the names of the sons of Israel who came to Egypt with Jacob, each with his household: ²Reuben, Simeon, Levi, and Judah, ³Issachar, Zebulun, and Benjamin, ⁴Dan and Naphtali, Gad and Asher. ⁵The total number of people born to Jacob was seventy. Joseph was already in Egypt. ⁶Then Joseph died, and all his brothers, and that whole generation. ⁷But the Israelites were fruitful and prolific; they multiplied and grew exceedingly strong, so that the land was filled with them.

The Israelites Are Oppressed

8 Now a new king arose over Egypt, who did not know Joseph. ⁹He said to his people, "Look, the Israelite people are more numerous and more powerful than we. ¹⁰Come, let us deal shrewdly with

1.1
Gen 46.8-27
1.5
Gen 46.27
1.6
Gen 50.26
1.7
Gen 46.3;
47.27;
Acts 7.17
1.8
Acts 7.18,19
1.9
Ps 105.24,
25

them, or they will increase and, in the event of war, join our enemies and fight against us and escape from the land." ¹¹ Therefore they set taskmasters over them to oppress them with forced labor. They built supply cities, Pithom and Rameses, for Pharaoh. ¹² But the more they were oppressed, the more they multiplied and spread, so that the Egyptians came to dread the Israelites. ¹³ The Egyptians became ruthless in imposing tasks on the Israelites, ¹⁴ and made their lives bitter with hard service in mortar and brick and in every kind of field labor. They were ruthless in all the tasks that they imposed on them.

15 The king of Egypt said to the Hebrew midwives, one of whom was named Shiphrah and the other Puah, ¹⁶ "When you act as midwives to the Hebrew women, and see them on the birthstool, if it is a boy, kill him; but if it is a girl, she shall live." ¹⁷ But the midwives feared God; they did not do as the king of Egypt commanded them, but they let the boys live. ¹⁸ So the king of Egypt summoned the midwives and said to them, "Why have you done this, and allowed the boys to live?" ¹⁹ The midwives said to Pharaoh, "Because the Hebrew women are not like the Egyptian women; for they are vigorous and give birth before the midwife comes to them." ²⁰ So God dealt well with the midwives; and the people multiplied and became very strong. ²¹ And because the midwives feared God, he gave them families. ²² Then Pharaoh commanded all his people, "Every boy that is born to the Hebrews[a] you shall throw into the Nile, but you shall let every girl live."

Birth and Youth of Moses

2 Now a man from the house of Levi went and married a Levite woman. ² The woman conceived and bore a son; and when she saw that he was a fine baby, she hid him three months. ³ When she could hide him no longer she got a papy-

1.11
Ex 3.7; 5.6
1.14
Ps 81.6
1.16
Acts 7.19
1.17
v. 21
1.20
v. 12;
Isa 3.10
1.21
1 Sam 2.35
1.22
Acts 7.19
2.1
Ex 6.19,20
2.2
Acts 7.20;
Heb 11.23

2.4
Ex 15.20;
Num 26.59
2.10
Acts 7.21
2.11
Acts 7.23;
Heb 11.24-26
2.12
Acts 7.24
2.13
Acts 7.26-28
2.14
Gen 19.9;
Acts 7.27
2.15
Acts 7.29;
Gen 24.11;
29.2

rus basket for him, and plastered it with bitumen and pitch; she put the child in it and placed it among the reeds on the bank of the river. ⁴ His sister stood at a distance, to see what would happen to him.

5 The daughter of Pharaoh came down to bathe at the river, while her attendants walked beside the river. She saw the basket among the reeds and sent her maid to bring it. ⁶ When she opened it, she saw the child. He was crying, and she took pity on him, "This must be one of the Hebrews' children," she said. ⁷ Then his sister said to Pharaoh's daughter, "Shall I go and get you a nurse from the Hebrew women to nurse the child for you?" ⁸ Pharaoh's daughter said to her, "Yes." So the girl went and called the child's mother. ⁹ Pharaoh's daughter said to her, "Take this child and nurse it for me, and I will give you your wages." So the woman took the child and nursed it. ¹⁰ When the child grew up, she brought him to Pharaoh's daughter, and she took him as her son. She named him Moses,[b] "because," she said, "I drew him out[c] of the water."

Moses Flees to Midian

11 One day, after Moses had grown up, he went out to his people and saw their forced labor. He saw an Egyptian beating a Hebrew, one of his kinsfolk. ¹² He looked this way and that, and seeing no one he killed the Egyptian and hid him in the sand. ¹³ When he went out the next day, he saw two Hebrews fighting; and he said to the one who was in the wrong, "Why do you strike your fellow Hebrew?" ¹⁴ He answered, "Who made you a ruler and judge over us? Do you mean to kill me as you killed the Egyptian?" Then Moses was afraid and thought, "Surely the thing is known." ¹⁵ When Pharaoh heard of it, he sought to kill Moses.

But Moses fled from Pharaoh. He settled in the land of Midian,

a Sam Gk Tg: Heb lacks *to the Hebrews*
b Heb *Mosheh*　　c Heb *mashah*

and sat down by a well. [16]The priest of Midian had seven daughters. They came to draw water, and filled the troughs to water their father's flock. [17]But some shepherds came and drove them away. Moses got up and came to their defense and watered their flock. [18]When they returned to their father Reuel, he said, "How is it that you have come back so soon today?" [19]They said, "An Egyptian helped us against the shepherds; he even drew water for us and watered the flock." [20]He said to his daughters, "Where is he? Why did you leave the man? Invite him to break bread." [21]Moses agreed to stay with the man, and he gave Moses his daughter Zipporah in marriage. [22]She bore a son, and he named him Gershom; for he said, "I have been an alien[d] residing in a foreign land."

23 After a long time the king of Egypt died. The Israelites groaned under their slavery, and cried out. Out of the slavery their cry for help rose up to God. [24]God heard their groaning, and God remembered his covenant with Abraham, Isaac, and Jacob. [25]God looked upon the Israelites, and God took notice of them.

Moses at the Burning Bush

3 Moses was keeping the flock of his father-in-law Jethro, the priest of Midian; he led his flock beyond the wilderness, and came to Horeb, the mountain of God. [2]There the angel of the Lord appeared to him in a flame of fire out of a bush; he looked, and the bush was blazing, yet it was not consumed. [3]Then Moses said, "I must turn aside and look at this great sight, and see why the bush is not burned up." [4]When the Lord saw that he had turned aside to see, God called to him out of the bush, "Moses, Moses!" And he said, "Here I am." [5]Then he said, "Come no closer! Remove the sandals from your feet, for the place on which you are standing is holy ground." [6]He said further, "I am the God of

2.16
Ex 3.1;
18.12;
Gen 24.13,
19
2.17
Gen 29.3,10
2.18
Ex 3.1;
Num 10.29
2.20
Gen 31.54
2.21
Acts 7.29;
Gen 4.25;
18.2
2.22
Ex 18.3;
Heb 11.13,
14
2.23
Acts 7.30;
Deut 26.7;
Ex 3.9;
Jas 5.4
2.24
Ex 6.5;
Ps 105.8,42;
Gen 22.16-18
2.25
Ex 4.31;
3.7; 4.27;
18.5
3.1
Ex 2.18
3.2
Deut 33.16;
Mk 12.26
3.3
Acts 7.31
3.5
Josh 5.15;
Acts 7.33
3.6
Mt 22.31,
32;
Mk 12.26;
Lk 20.37;
Acts 7.32

3.7
Ex 2.25;
Neh 9.9;
Acts 7.34
3.8
Gen 50.24,
25; v. 17;
Josh 24.11
3.9
Ex 2.23;
1.13,14
3.10
Mic 6.4
3.12
Gen 31.3;
Josh 1.5
3.14
Ex 6.3;
Jn 8.58;
Heb 13.8
3.15
Ps 135.13;
Hos 12.5

your father, the God of Abraham, the God of Isaac, and the God of Jacob." And Moses hid his face, for he was afraid to look at God.

7 Then the Lord said, "I have observed the misery of my people who are in Egypt; I have heard their cry on account of their taskmasters. Indeed, I know their sufferings, [8]and I have come down to deliver them from the Egyptians, and to bring them up out of that land to a good and broad land, a land flowing with milk and honey, to the country of the Canaanites, the Hittites, the Amorites, the Perizzites, the Hivites, and the Jebusites. [9]The cry of the Israelites has now come to me; I have also seen how the Egyptians oppress them. [10]So come, I will send you to Pharaoh to bring my people, the Israelites, out of Egypt." [11]But Moses said to God, "Who am I that I should go to Pharaoh, and bring the Israelites out of Egypt?" [12]He said, "I will be with you; and this shall be the sign for you that it is I who sent you: when you have brought the people out of Egypt, you shall worship God on this mountain."

The Divine Name Revealed

13 But Moses said to God, "If I come to the Israelites and say to them, 'The God of your ancestors has sent me to you,' and they ask me, 'What is his name?' what shall I say to them?" [14]God said to Moses, "I am who I am."[e] He said further, "Thus you shall say to the Israelites, 'I am has sent me to you.' " [15]God also said to Moses, "Thus you shall say to the Israelites, 'The Lord,[f] the God of your ancestors, the God of Abraham, the God of Isaac, and the God of Jacob, has sent me to you':

This is my name forever,
and this my title for all
generations.

[16]Go and assemble the elders of Israel, and say to them, 'The Lord,

[d] Heb ger [e] Or *I am what I am* or *I will be what I will be* [f] The word "Lord" when spelled with capital letters stands for the divine name, *YHWH*, which is here connected with the verb *hayah*, "to be"

the God of your ancestors, the God of Abraham, of Isaac, and of Jacob, has appeared to me, saying: I have given heed to you and to what has been done to you in Egypt. 17 I declare that I will bring you up out of the misery of Egypt, to the land of the Canaanites, the Hittites, the Amorites, the Perizzites, the Hivites, and the Jebusites, a land flowing with milk and honey.' 18 They will listen to your voice; and you and the elders of Israel shall go to the king of Egypt and say to him, 'The LORD, the God of the Hebrews, has met with us; let us now go a three days' journey into the wilderness, so that we may sacrifice to the LORD our God.' 19 I know, however, that the king of Egypt will not let you go unless compelled by a mighty hand. g 20 So I will stretch out my hand and strike Egypt with all my wonders that I will perform in it; after that he will let you go. 21 I will bring this people into such favor with the Egyptians that, when you go, you will not go empty-handed; 22 each woman shall ask her neighbor and any woman living in the neighbor's house for jewelry of silver and of gold, and clothing, and you shall put them on your sons and on your daughters; and so you shall plunder the Egyptians."

Moses' Miraculous Power

4 Then Moses answered, "But suppose they do not believe me or listen to me, but say, 'The LORD did not appear to you.' " 2 The LORD said to him, "What is that in your hand?" He said, "A staff." 3 And he said, "Throw it on the ground." So he threw the staff on the ground, and it became a snake; and Moses drew back from it. 4 Then the LORD said to Moses, "Reach out your hand, and seize it by the tail" — so he reached out his hand and grasped it, and it became a staff in his hand — 5 "so that they may believe that the LORD, the God of their ancestors, the God of Abraham, the God of Isaac, and the God of Jacob, has appeared to you."

6 Again, the LORD said to him,

"Put your hand inside your cloak." He put his hand into his cloak; and when he took it out, his hand was leprous, h as white as snow. 7 Then God said, "Put your hand back into your cloak" — so he put his hand back into his cloak, and when he took it out, it was restored like the rest of his body — 8 "If they will not believe you or heed the first sign, they may believe the second sign. 9 If they will not believe even these two signs or heed you, you shall take some water from the Nile and pour it on the dry ground; and the water that you shall take from the Nile will become blood on the dry ground."

10 But Moses said to the LORD, "O my Lord, I have never been eloquent, neither in the past nor even now that you have spoken to your servant; but I am slow of speech and slow of tongue." 11 Then the LORD said to him, "Who gives speech to mortals? Who makes them mute or deaf, seeing or blind? Is it not I, the LORD? 12 Now go, and I will be with your mouth and teach you what you are to speak." 13 But he said, "O my Lord, please send someone else." 14 Then the anger of the LORD was kindled against Moses and he said, "What of your brother Aaron, the Levite? I know that he can speak fluently; even now he is coming out to meet you, and when he sees you his heart will be glad. 15 You shall speak to him and put the words in his mouth; and I will be with your mouth and with his mouth, and will teach you what you shall do. 16 He indeed shall speak for you to the people; he shall serve as a mouth for you, and you shall serve as God for him. 17 Take in your hand this staff, with which you shall perform the signs."

Moses Returns to Egypt

18 Moses went back to his father-in-law Jethro and said to him, "Please let me go back to my kindred in Egypt and see whether

3.17
Gen 15.14, 16;
Josh 24.11
3.18
Ex 4.31;
5.1,3
3.19
Ex 5.2; 6.1
3.20
Ex 6.6;
9.15;
Deut 6.22;
Neh 9.10;
Ex 12.31
3.21
Ex 11.3;
12.36
3.22
Ex 11.2,3;
12.35,36
4.1
Ex 3.18;
6.30
4.2
vv. 17,20
4.6
Num 12.10;
2 Kings 5.27

4.7
Num 12.13, 14;
Deut 32.39;
2 Kings 5.14;
Mt 8.3
4.9
Ex 7.19
4.10
Ex 6.12;
Jer 1.6
4.11
Ps 94.9;
Mt 11.5
4.12
Isa 50.4;
Jer 1.9;
Mt 10.19;
Mk 13.11;
Lk 12.11,12;
21.14,15
4.14
v. 27
4.15
Ex 7.1,2;
Num 25.5,
12,16;
Deut 5.31
4.17
v. 2;
Ex 7.9-20

g Gk Vg: Heb no, not by a mighty hand h A term for several skin diseases; precise meaning uncertain

they are still living." And Jethro said to Moses, "Go in peace." [19]The LORD said to Moses in Midian, "Go back to Egypt; for all those who were seeking your life are dead." [20]So Moses took his wife and his sons, put them on a donkey and went back to the land of Egypt; and Moses carried the staff of God in his hand.

21 And the LORD said to Moses, "When you go back to Egypt, see that you perform before Pharaoh all the wonders that I have put in your power; but I will harden his heart, so that he will not let the people go. [22]Then you shall say to Pharaoh, 'Thus says the LORD: Israel is my firstborn son. [23]I said to you, "Let my son go that he may worship me." But you refused to let him go; now I will kill your firstborn son.' "

24 On the way, at a place where they spent the night, the LORD met him and tried to kill him. [25]But Zipporah took a flint and cut off her son's foreskin, and touched Moses'[i] feet with it, and said, "Truly you are a bridegroom of blood to me!" [26]So he let him alone. It was then she said, "A bridegroom of blood by circumcision."

27 The LORD said to Aaron, "Go into the wilderness to meet Moses." So he went; and he met him at the mountain of God and kissed him. [28]Moses told Aaron all the words of the LORD with which he had sent him, and all the signs with which he had charged him. [29]Then Moses and Aaron went and assembled all the elders of the Israelites. [30]Aaron spoke all the words that the LORD had spoken to Moses, and performed the signs in the sight of the people. [31]The people believed; and when they heard that the LORD had given heed to the Israelites and that he had seen their misery, they bowed down and worshiped.

Bricks without Straw

5 Afterward Moses and Aaron went to Pharaoh and said, "Thus says the LORD, the God of Israel, 'Let my people go, so that they

may celebrate a festival to me in the wilderness.' " [2]But Pharaoh said, "Who is the LORD, that I should heed him and let Israel go? I do not know the LORD, and I will not let Israel go." [3]Then they said, "The God of the Hebrews has revealed himself to us; let us go a three days' journey into the wilderness to sacrifice to the LORD our God, or he will fall upon us with pestilence or sword." [4]But the king of Egypt said to them, "Moses and Aaron, why are you taking the people away from their work? Get to your labors!" [5]Pharaoh continued, "Now they are more numerous than the people of the land[j] and yet you want them to stop working!" [6]That same day Pharaoh commanded the taskmasters of the people, as well as their supervisors, [7]"You shall no longer give the people straw to make bricks, as before; let them go and gather straw for themselves. [8]But you shall require of them the same quantity of bricks as they have made previously; do not diminish it, for they are lazy; that is why they cry, 'Let us go and offer sacrifice to our God.' [9]Let heavier work be laid on them; then they will labor at it and pay no attention to deceptive words."

10 So the taskmasters and the supervisors of the people went out and said to the people, "Thus says Pharaoh, 'I will not give you straw. [11]Go and get straw yourselves, wherever you can find it; but your work will not be lessened in the least.' " [12]So the people scattered throughout the land of Egypt, to gather stubble for straw. [13]The taskmasters were urgent, saying, "Complete your work, the same daily assignment as when you were given straw." [14]And the supervisors of the Israelites, whom Pharaoh's taskmasters had set over them, were beaten, and were asked, "Why did you not finish the required quantity of bricks yesterday and today, as you did before?"

4.19
Ex 2.15,23
4.20
Ex 17.9;
Num 20.8
4.21
Ex 7.3,13;
9.12,35; 10.1;
14.8;
Deut 2.30;
Jn 12.40;
Rom 19.18
4.22
Isa 63.16;
64.8;
Hos 11.1;
Rom 9.4;
Jer 31.9
4.23
Ex 5.1;
6.11; 7.16;
12.29
4.24ff
Num 22.22;
Gen 17.14
4.25
Josh 5.2,3
4.27
v. 14;
Ex 3.1
4.28
vv. 15,16;
8.9
4.29
Ex 3.16
4.30
v. 16
4.31
v. 8,9;
Ex 3.18;
2.25; 3.7;
12.27
5.1
Ex 3.18;
4.23; 10.9

5.2
Job 21.15;
Ex 3.19
5.3
Ex 3.18
5.4
Ex 1.11;
2.11; 6.6,7
5.5
Ex 1.7,9
5.6
Ex 1.11; 3.7
5.8
v. 17
5.10
v. 6
5.14
v. 6;
Isa 10.24

[i] Heb *his* [j] Sam: Heb *The people of the land are now many*

15 Then the Israelite supervisors came to Pharaoh and cried, "Why do you treat your servants like this? 16 No straw is given to your servants, yet they say to us, 'Make bricks!' Look how your servants are beaten! You are unjust to your own people."k 17 He said, "You are lazy, lazy; that is why you say, 'Let us go and sacrifice to the LORD.' 18 Go now, and work; for no straw shall be given you, but you shall still deliver the same number of bricks." 19 The Israelite supervisors saw that they were in trouble when they were told, "You shall not lessen your daily number of bricks." 20 As they left Pharaoh, they came upon Moses and Aaron who were waiting to meet them. 21 They said to them, "The LORD look upon you and judge! You have brought us into bad odor with Pharaoh and his officials, and have put a sword in their hand to kill us."

22 Then Moses turned again to the LORD and said, "O LORD, why have you mistreated this people? Why did you ever send me? 23 Since I first came to Pharaoh to speak in your name, he has mistreated this people, and you have done nothing at all to deliver your people."

Israel's Deliverance Assured

6 Then the LORD said to Moses, "Now you shall see what I will do to Pharaoh: Indeed, by a mighty hand he will let them go; by a mighty hand he will drive them out of his land."

2 God also spoke to Moses and said to him: "I am the LORD. 3 I appeared to Abraham, Isaac, and Jacob as God Almighty,l but by my name 'The LORD'm I did not make myself known to them. 4 I also established my covenant with them, to give them the land of Canaan, the land in which they resided as aliens. 5 I have also heard the groaning of the Israelites whom the Egyptians are holding as slaves, and I have remembered my covenant. 6 Say therefore to the Israelites, 'I am the LORD, and I will free

you from the burdens of the Egyptians and deliver you from slavery to them. I will redeem you with an outstretched arm and with mighty acts of judgment. 7 I will take you as my people, and I will be your God. You shall know that I am the LORD your God, who has freed you from the burdens of the Egyptians. 8 I will bring you into the land that I swore to give to Abraham, Isaac, and Jacob; I will give it to you for a possession. I am the LORD.' " 9 Moses told this to the Israelites; but they would not listen to Moses, because of their broken spirit and their cruel slavery.

10 Then the LORD spoke to Moses, 11 "Go and tell Pharaoh king of Egypt to let the Israelites go out of his land." 12 But Moses spoke to the LORD, "The Israelites have not listened to me; how then shall Pharaoh listen to me, poor speaker that I am?"n 13 Thus the LORD spoke to Moses and Aaron, and gave them orders regarding the Israelites and Pharaoh king of Egypt, charging them to free the Israelites from the land of Egypt.

The Genealogy of Moses and Aaron

14 The following are the heads of their ancestral houses: the sons of Reuben, the firstborn of Israel: Hanoch, Pallu, Hezron, and Carmi; these are the families of Reuben. 15 The sons of Simeon: Jemuel, Jamin, Ohad, Jachin, Zohar, and Shaul,o the son of a Canaanite woman; these are the families of Simeon. 16 The following are the names of the sons of Levi according to their genealogies: Gershon,p Kohath, and Merari, and the length of Levi's life was one hundred thirty-seven years. 17 The sons of Gershon:p Libni and Shimei, by their families. 18 The sons of Kohath: Amram, Izhar, Hebron, and Uzziel, and the length of Kohath's life was one hundred thirty-three years. 19 The

5.17
v. 8
5.21
Ex 14.11;
15.24;
Gen 16.5;
34.30
5.22
Num 11.11;
Jer 4.10
5.23
Ex 3.8
6.1
Ex 3.19,20;
7.4,5; 12.31,
33,39
6.3
Ps 68.4;
83.18;
Isa 52.6;
Jer 16.21;
Ezek 37.6,
13
6.4
Gen 15.18;
28.4
6.5
Ex 2.24
6.6
Deut 26.8

6.7
Deut 4.20;
26.8;
Ps 81.6;
Isa 41.20
6.8
Gen 15.18
6.14
Gen 46.9;
Num 26.5-11
6.15
Gen 46.10;
1 Chr 4.24
6.16
Gen 46.11;
Num 3.17
6.17
1 Chr 6.17
6.18
1 Chr 6.2,
18
6.19
1 Chr 6.19

k Gk Compare Syr Vg: Heb beaten, and the sin of your people l Traditional rendering of Heb El Shaddai m Heb YHWH; see note at 3.15 n Heb me? I am uncircumcised of lips o Or Saul p Also spelled Gershom; see 2.22

sons of Merari: Mahli and Mushi. These are the families of the Levites according to their genealogies. 20 Amram married Jochebed his father's sister and she bore him Aaron and Moses, and the length of Amram's life was one hundred thirty-seven years. 21 The sons of Izhar: Korah, Nepheg, and Zichri. 22 The sons of Uzziel: Mishael, Elzaphan, and Sithri. 23 Aaron married Elisheba, daughter of Amminadab and sister of Nahshon, and she bore him Nadab, Abihu, Eleazar, and Ithamar. 24 The sons of Korah: Assir, Elkanah, and Abiasaph; these are the families of the Korahites. 25 Aaron's son Eleazar married one of the daughters of Putiel, and she bore him Phinehas. These are the heads of the ancestral houses of the Levites by their families.

26 It was this same Aaron and Moses to whom the LORD said, "Bring the Israelites out of the land of Egypt, company by company." 27 It was they who spoke to Pharaoh king of Egypt to bring the Israelites out of Egypt, the same Moses and Aaron.

Moses and Aaron Obey God's Commands

28 On the day when the LORD spoke to Moses in the land of Egypt, 29 he said to him, "I am the LORD; tell Pharaoh king of Egypt all that I am speaking to you." 30 But Moses said in the LORD's presence, "Since I am a poor speaker, q why would Pharaoh listen to me?"

7 The LORD said to Moses, "See, I have made you like God to Pharaoh, and your brother Aaron shall be your prophet. 2 You shall speak all that I command you, and your brother Aaron shall tell Pharaoh to let the Israelites go out of his land. 3 But I will harden Pharaoh's heart, and I will multiply my signs and wonders in the land of Egypt. 4 When Pharaoh does not listen to you, I will lay my hand upon Egypt and bring my people the Israelites, company by company, out of the land of Egypt by great acts of judgment. 5 The Egyptians

shall know that I am the LORD, when I stretch out my hand against Egypt and bring the Israelites out from among them." 6 Moses and Aaron did so; they did just as the LORD commanded them. 7 Moses was eighty years old and Aaron eighty-three when they spoke to Pharaoh.

Aaron's Miraculous Rod

8 The LORD said to Moses and Aaron, 9 "When Pharaoh says to you, 'Perform a wonder,' then you shall say to Aaron, 'Take your staff and throw it down before Pharaoh, and it will become a snake.' " 10 So Moses and Aaron went to Pharaoh and did as the LORD had commanded; Aaron threw down his staff before Pharaoh and his officials, and it became a snake. 11 Then Pharaoh summoned the wise men and the sorcerers; and they also, the magicians of Egypt, did the same by their secret arts. 12 Each one threw down his staff, and they became snakes; but Aaron's staff swallowed up theirs. 13 Still Pharaoh's heart was hardened, and he would not listen to them, as the LORD had said.

The First Plague: Water Turned to Blood

14 Then the LORD said to Moses, "Pharaoh's heart is hardened; he refuses to let the people go. 15 Go to Pharaoh in the morning, as he is going out to the water; stand by at the river bank to meet him, and take in your hand the staff that was turned into a snake. 16 Say to him, 'The LORD, the God of the Hebrews, sent me to you to say, "Let my people go, so that they may worship me in the wilderness." But until now you have not listened.' 17 Thus says the LORD, "By this you shall know that I am the LORD." See, with the staff that is in my hand I will strike the water that is in the Nile, and it shall be turned to blood. 18 The fish in the river shall die, the river itself shall stink, and the Egyptians shall be unable to drink

6.20
Ex 2.1,2;
Num 26.59
6.21
Num 16.1;
1 Chr 6.37,
38
6.22
Lev 10.4;
Num 3.30
6.24
Num 26.11
6.25
Josh 24.33;
Num 25.7-11;
Ps 106.30
6.29
v. 11;
Ex 7.2
6.30
v. 12;
Ex 4.10
7.1
Ex 4.16
7.2
Ex 4.15
7.3
Ex 4.21;
11.9
7.4
Ex 3.19,20;
10.1; 11.9;
12.51; 13.3,9;
6.6
7.5
v. 17;
Ex 8.19;
3.20
7.6
v. 2
7.7
Deut 34.7;
Acts 7.23,30
7.9
Isa 7.11;
Jn 2.18;
Ex 4.2,17
7.10
v. 9;
Ex 4.3
7.11
Gen 41.8;
v. 22;
Ex 8.7,18
7.13
v. 4;
Ex 4.21
7.14
Ex 8.15;
10.1,20,27
7.15
v. 10;
Ex 4.2,3
7.16
Ex 3.12,18;
5.1,3
7.17
v. 5;
Ex 5.2; 4.9;
Rev 11.6;
16.4,6
7.18
vv. 21,24

q Heb *am uncircumcised of lips*; see 6.12

water from the Nile.' " ¹⁹ The LORD said to Moses, "Say to Aaron, 'Take your staff and stretch out your hand over the waters of Egypt— over its rivers, its canals, and its ponds, and all its pools of water— so that they may become blood; and there shall be blood throughout the whole land of Egypt, even in vessels of wood and in vessels of stone.' "

20 Moses and Aaron did just as the LORD commanded. In the sight of Pharaoh and of his officials he lifted up the staff and struck the water in the river, and all the water in the river was turned into blood, ²¹ and the fish in the river died. The river stank so that the Egyptians could not drink its water, and there was blood throughout the whole land of Egypt. ²² But the magicians of Egypt did the same by their secret arts; so Pharaoh's heart remained hardened, and he would not listen to them; as the LORD had said. ²³ Pharaoh turned and went into his house, and he did not take even this to heart. ²⁴ And all the Egyptians had to dig along the Nile for water to drink, for they could not drink the water of the river.

25 Seven days passed after the LORD had struck the Nile.

The Second Plague: Frogs

8 ʳ Then the LORD said to Moses, "Go to Pharaoh and say to him, 'Thus says the LORD: Let my people go, so that they may worship me. ² If you refuse to let them go, I will plague your whole country with frogs. ³ The river shall swarm with frogs; they shall come up into your palace, into your bedchamber and your bed, and into the houses of your officials and of your people,ˢ and into your ovens and your kneading bowls. ⁴ The frogs shall come up on you and on your people and on all your officials.' " ⁵ᵗ And the LORD said to Moses, "Say to Aaron, 'Stretch out your hand with your staff over the rivers, the canals, and the pools, and make frogs come up on the land of Egypt.' " ⁶ So Aaron stretched out his hand

7.19
Ex 8.5,6,16;
9.22; 10.12,
21; 14.21,26
7.20
Ps 78.44;
105.29
7.21
v. 18
7.22
v. 11;
Ex 8.7
8.1
Ex 3.12,18
8.3
Ps 105.30
8.5
Ex 7.19
8.6
Ps 78.45;
105.30

8.7
Ex 7.11
8.8
vv. 25,28;
Ex 9.27,28;
10.17
8.10
Ex 9.14;
Deut 33.26;
Ps 86.8;
Isa 46.9;
Jer 10.6,7
8.12
v. 30;
Ex 9.33;
10.18
8.15
Ex 7.4
8.17
Ps 105.31
8.18
Ex 7.11

over the waters of Egypt; and the frogs came up and covered the land of Egypt. ⁷ But the magicians did the same by their secret arts, and brought frogs up on the land of Egypt.

8 Then Pharaoh called Moses and Aaron, and said, "Pray to the LORD to take away the frogs from me and my people, and I will let the people go to sacrifice to the LORD." ⁹ Moses said to Pharaoh, "Kindly tell me when I am to pray for you and for your officials and for your people, that the frogs may be removed from you and your houses and be left only in the Nile." ¹⁰ And he said, "Tomorrow." Moses said, "As you say! So that you may know that there is no one like the LORD our God, ¹¹ the frogs shall leave you and your houses and your officials and your people; they shall be left only in the Nile." ¹² Then Moses and Aaron went out from Pharaoh; and Moses cried out to the LORD concerning the frogs that he had brought upon Pharaoh.ᵘ ¹³ And the LORD did as Moses requested: the frogs died in the houses, the courtyards, and the fields. ¹⁴ And they gathered them together in heaps, and the land stank. ¹⁵ But when Pharaoh saw that there was a respite, he hardened his heart, and would not listen to them, just as the LORD had said.

The Third Plague: Gnats

16 Then the LORD said to Moses, "Say to Aaron, 'Stretch out your staff and strike the dust of the earth, so that it may become gnats throughout the whole land of Egypt.' " ¹⁷ And they did so; Aaron stretched out his hand with his staff and struck the dust of the earth, and gnats came on humans and animals alike; all the dust of the earth turned into gnats throughout the whole land of Egypt. ¹⁸ The magicians tried to produce gnats by their secret arts, but they could not. There were

ʳ Ch 7.26 in Heb ˢ Gk: Heb *upon your people* ᵗ Ch 8.1 in Heb ᵘ Or *frogs, as he had agreed with Pharaoh*

gnats on both humans and animals. [19] And the magicians said to Pharaoh, "This is the finger of God!" But Pharaoh's heart was hardened, and he would not listen to them, just as the LORD had said.

The Fourth Plague: Flies

20 Then the LORD said to Moses, "Rise early in the morning and present yourself before Pharaoh, as he goes out to the water, and say to him, 'Thus says the LORD: Let my people go, so that they may worship me. [21] For if you will not let my people go, I will send swarms of flies on you, your officials, and your people, and into your houses; and the houses of the Egyptians shall be filled with swarms of flies; so also the land where they live. [22] But on that day I will set apart the land of Goshen, where my people live, so that no swarms of flies shall be there, that you may know that I the LORD am in this land. [23] Thus I will make a distinction[v] between my people and your people. This sign shall appear tomorrow.' " [24] The LORD did so, and great swarms of flies came into the house of Pharaoh and into his officials' houses; in all of Egypt the land was ruined because of the flies.

25 Then Pharaoh summoned Moses and Aaron, and said, "Go, sacrifice to your God within the land." [26] But Moses said, "It would not be right to do so; for the sacrifices that we offer to the LORD our God are offensive to the Egyptians. If we offer in the sight of the Egyptians sacrifices that are offensive to them, will they not stone us? [27] We must go a three days' journey into the wilderness and sacrifice to the LORD our God as he commands us." [28] So Pharaoh said, "I will let you go to sacrifice to the LORD your God in the wilderness, provided you do not go very far away. Pray for me." [29] Then Moses said, "As soon as I leave you, I will pray to the LORD that the swarms of flies may depart tomorrow from Pharaoh, from his officials, and from his people; only do not let Pharaoh again deal false-

ly by not letting the people go to sacrifice to the LORD."

30 So Moses went out from Pharaoh and prayed to the LORD. [31] And the LORD did as Moses asked: he removed the swarms of flies from Pharaoh, from his officials, and from his people; not one remained. [32] But Pharaoh hardened his heart this time also, and would not let the people go.

The Fifth Plague: Livestock Diseased

9 Then the LORD said to Moses, "Go to Pharaoh, and say to him, 'Thus says the LORD, the God of the Hebrews: Let my people go, so that they may worship me. [2] For if you refuse to let them go and still hold them, [3] the hand of the LORD will strike with a deadly pestilence your livestock in the field: the horses, the donkeys, the camels, the herds, and the flocks. [4] But the LORD will make a distinction between the livestock of Israel and the livestock of Egypt, so that nothing shall die of all that belongs to the Israelites.' " [5] The LORD set a time, saying, "Tomorrow the LORD will do this thing in the land." [6] And on the next day the LORD did so; all the livestock of the Egyptians died, but of the livestock of the Israelites not one died. [7] Pharaoh inquired and found that not one of the livestock of the Israelites was dead. But the heart of Pharaoh was hardened, and he would not let the people go.

The Sixth Plague: Boils

8 Then the LORD said to Moses and Aaron, "Take handfuls of soot from the kiln, and let Moses throw it in the air in the sight of Pharaoh. [9] It shall become fine dust all over the land of Egypt, and shall cause festering boils on humans and animals throughout the whole land of Egypt." [10] So they took soot from the kiln, and stood before Pharaoh, and Moses threw it in the air, and it caused festering boils on humans and animals. [11] The magicians

8.19
Ex 7.5; 10.7
8.20
Ex 9.13;
7.15; v. 1
8.22
Ex 9.4,6,26;
10.23; 11.6,7
8.24
Ps 78.45;
105.31
8.27
Ex 3.18; 5.3
8.28
vv. 8,15,29,
32
8.29
vv. 8,15

8.32
vv. 8,15;
Ex 4.21
9.1
Ex 8.1
9.2
Ex 8.2
9.4
Ex 8.22
9.6
Ex 11.5;
v. 4
9.7
Ex 7.14;
8.32
9.9
Rev 16.2

v Gk Vg: Heb *will set redemption*

could not stand before Moses because of the boils, for the boils afflicted the magicians as well as all the Egyptians. 12 But the Lord hardened the heart of Pharaoh, and he would not listen to them, just as the Lord had spoken to Moses.

The Seventh Plague: Thunder and Hail

13 Then the Lord said to Moses, "Rise early in the morning and present yourself before Pharaoh, and say to him, 'Thus says the Lord, the God of the Hebrews: Let my people go, so that they may worship me. 14 For this time I will send all my plagues upon you yourself, and upon your officials, and upon your people, so that you may know that there is no one like me in all the earth. 15 For by now I could have stretched out my hand and struck you and your people with pestilence, and you would have been cut off from the earth. 16 But this is why I have let you live: to show you my power, and to make my name resound through all the earth. 17 You are still exalting yourself against my people, and will not let them go. 18 Tomorrow at this time I will cause the heaviest hail to fall that has ever fallen in Egypt from the day it was founded until now. 19 Send, therefore, and have your livestock and everything that you have in the open field brought to a secure place; every human or animal that is in the open field and is not brought under shelter will die when the hail comes down upon them.' " 20 Those officials of Pharaoh who feared the word of the Lord hurried their slaves and livestock off to a secure place. 21 Those who did not regard the word of the Lord left their slaves and livestock in the open field.

22 The Lord said to Moses, "Stretch out your hand toward heaven so that hail may fall on the whole land of Egypt, on humans and animals and all the plants of the field in the land of Egypt." 23 Then Moses stretched out his staff toward heaven, and the Lord

sent thunder and hail, and fire came down on the earth. And the Lord rained hail on the land of Egypt; 24 there was hail with fire flashing continually in the midst of it, such heavy hail as had never fallen in all the land of Egypt since it became a nation. 25 The hail struck down everything that was in the open field throughout all the land of Egypt, both human and animal; the hail also struck down all the plants of the field, and shattered every tree in the field. 26 Only in the land of Goshen, where the Israelites were, there was no hail.

27 Then Pharaoh summoned Moses and Aaron, and said to them, "This time I have sinned; the Lord is in the right, and I and my people are in the wrong. 28 Pray to the Lord! Enough of God's thunder and hail! I will let you go; you need stay no longer." 29 Moses said to him, "As soon as I have gone out of the city, I will stretch out my hands to the Lord; the thunder will cease, and there will be no more hail, so that you may know that the earth is the Lord's. 30 But as for you and your officials, I know that you do not yet fear the Lord God." 31 (Now the flax and the barley were ruined, for the barley was in the ear and the flax was in bud. 32 But the wheat and the spelt were not ruined, for they are late in coming up.) 33 So Moses left Pharaoh, went out of the city, and stretched out his hands to the Lord; then the thunder and the hail ceased, and the rain no longer poured down on the earth. 34 But when Pharaoh saw that the rain and the hail and the thunder had ceased, he sinned once more and hardened his heart, he and his officials. 35 So the heart of Pharaoh was hardened, and he would not let the Israelites go, just as the Lord had spoken through Moses.

The Eighth Plague: Locusts

10 Then the Lord said to Moses, "Go to Pharaoh; for I have hardened his heart and the heart of his officials, in order that I may show these signs of mine

9.12
Ex 4.21
9.13
Ex 8.20
9.14
Ex 8.10
9.15
Ex 3.20
9.16
Rom 9.17
9.18
vv. 23,24
9.20
Prov 13.13
9.22
Rev 16.21
9.23
Gen 19.24;
Josh 10.11;
Ps 78.47;
Isa 30.30;
Ezek 38.22;
Rev 8.7

9.25
v. 19;
Ps 78.47;
105.32,33
9.26
Ex 8.22;
9.4,6; 10.23;
11.7; 12.13
9.27
Ex 8.8;
10.16,17;
2 Chr 12.6;
Ps 129.4
9.28
Ex 8.8;
10.17
9.29
1 Kings 8.22;
Ps 143.6;
Ex 8.22;
19.5; 20.11;
Ps 24.1
9.35
Ex 4.21
10.1
Ex 4.21;
7.14

among them, ²and that you may tell your children and grandchildren how I have made fools of the Egyptians and what signs I have done among them—so that you may know that I am the LORD."

3 So Moses and Aaron went to Pharaoh, and said to him, "Thus says the LORD, the God of the Hebrews, 'How long will you refuse to humble yourself before me? Let my people go, so that they may worship me. ⁴For if you refuse to let my people go, tomorrow I will bring locusts into your country. ⁵They shall cover the surface of the land, so that no one will be able to see the land. They shall devour the last remnant left you after the hail, and they shall devour every tree of yours that grows in the field. ⁶They shall fill your houses, and the houses of all your officials and of all the Egyptians—something that neither your parents nor your grandparents have seen, from the day they came on earth to this day.' " Then he turned and went out from Pharaoh.

7 Pharaoh's officials said to him, "How long shall this fellow be a snare to us? Let the people go, so that they may worship the LORD their God; do you not yet understand that Egypt is ruined?" ⁸So Moses and Aaron were brought back to Pharaoh, and he said to them, "Go, worship the LORD your God! But which ones are to go?" ⁹Moses said, "We will go with our young and our old; we will go with our sons and daughters and with our flocks and herds, because we have the LORD's festival to celebrate." ¹⁰He said to them, "The LORD indeed will be with you, if ever I let your little ones go with you! Plainly, you have some evil purpose in mind. ¹¹No, never! Your men may go and worship the LORD, for that is what you are asking." And they were driven out from Pharaoh's presence.

12 Then the LORD said to Moses, "Stretch out your hand over the land of Egypt, so that the locusts may come upon it and eat every

plant in the land, all that the hail has left." ¹³So Moses stretched out his staff over the land of Egypt, and the LORD brought an east wind upon the land all that day and all that night; when morning came, the east wind had brought the locusts. ¹⁴The locusts came upon all the land of Egypt and settled on the whole country of Egypt, such a dense swarm of locusts as had never been before, nor ever shall be again. ¹⁵They covered the surface of the whole land, so that the land was black; and they ate all the plants in the land and all the fruit of the trees that the hail had left; nothing green was left, no tree, no plant in the field, in all the land of Egypt. ¹⁶Pharaoh hurriedly summoned Moses and Aaron and said, "I have sinned against the LORD your God, and against you. ¹⁷Do forgive my sin just this once, and pray to the LORD your God that at the least he remove this deadly thing from me." ¹⁸So he went out from Pharaoh and prayed to the LORD. ¹⁹The LORD changed the wind into a very strong west wind, which lifted the locusts and drove them into the Red Sea;ʷ not a single locust was left in all the country of Egypt. ²⁰But the LORD hardened Pharaoh's heart, and he would not let the Israelites go.

The Ninth Plague: Darkness

21 Then the LORD said to Moses, "Stretch out your hand toward heaven so that there may be darkness over the land of Egypt, a darkness that can be felt." ²²So Moses stretched out his hand toward heaven, and there was dense darkness in all the land of Egypt for three days. ²³People could not see one another, and for three days they could not move from where they were; but all the Israelites had light where they lived. ²⁴Then Pharaoh summoned Moses, and said, "Go, worship the LORD. Only your flocks and your herds shall remain behind. Even your children may go with you." ²⁵But Moses

10.2
Ex 12.26,
27; 13.8,14,
15;
Deut 4.9;
Ps 44.1;
Ex 7.5,15
10.3
Jas 4.10;
1 Pet 5.6;
Ex 4.23
10.4
Rev 9.3
10.5
Ex 9.32;
Joel 1.4;
2.25
10.6
Ex 8.3,21
10.7
Ex 7.5;
8.19; 12.33
10.8
Ex 8.8,25
10.9
Ex 12.37,
38; v. 26;
Ex 5.1
10.11
v. 28
10.12
Ex 7.19;
vv. 4,5

10.14
Ps 78.46;
105.34;
Joel 2.1-11
10.15
v. 5;
Ps 105.35
10.16
Ex 9.27
10.17
Ex 8.8,29
10.20
Ex 4.21;
11.10
10.21
Deut 28.29
10.22
Ps 105.28
10.24
vv. 8,10

ʷ Or *Sea of Reeds*

said, "You must also let us have sacrifices and burnt offerings to sacrifice to the LORD our God. ²⁶Our livestock also must go with us; not a hoof shall be left behind, for we must choose some of them for the worship of the LORD our God, and we will not know what to use to worship the LORD until we arrive there." ²⁷But the LORD hardened Pharaoh's heart, and he was unwilling to let them go. ²⁸Then Pharaoh said to him, "Get away from me! Take care that you do not see my face again, for on the day you see my face you shall die." ²⁹Moses said, "Just as you say! I will never see your face again."

Warning of the Final Plague

11 The LORD said to Moses, "I will bring one more plague upon Pharaoh and upon Egypt; afterwards he will let you go from here; indeed, when he lets you go, he will drive you away. ²Tell the people that every man is to ask his neighbor and every woman is to ask her neighbor for objects of silver and gold." ³The LORD gave the people favor in the sight of the Egyptians. Moreover, Moses himself was a man of great importance in the land of Egypt, in the sight of Pharaoh's officials and in the sight of the people.

4 Moses said, "Thus says the LORD: About midnight I will go out through Egypt. ⁵Every firstborn in the land of Egypt shall die, from the firstborn of Pharaoh who sits on his throne to the firstborn of the female slave who is behind the handmill, and all the firstborn of the livestock. ⁶Then there will be a loud cry throughout the whole land of Egypt, such as has never been or will ever be again. ⁷But not a dog shall growl at any of the Israelites—not at people, not at animals—so that you may know that the LORD makes a distinction between Egypt and Israel. ⁸Then all these officials of yours shall come down to me, and bow low to me, saying, 'Leave us, you and all the people who follow you.' After

10.26
v. 9
10.27
v. 20
10.28
v. 11
10.29
Heb 11.27
11.1
Ex 12.31,
33,39
11.2
Ex 3.22;
12.35,36
11.3
Ex 3.21;
12.36;
Deut 34.10-12
11.4
Ex 12.29
11.5
Ex 12.12,
29;
Ps 78.51;
105.36;
135.8; 136.10
11.6
Ex 12.30
11.7
Ex 8.22
11.8
Ex 12.31-33

11.9
Ex 7.3,4
11.10
Ex 4.21;
10.20,27
12.2
Ex 13.4;
Deut 16.1
12.5
Lev 22.18-20
12.6
Lev 23.5;
Num 9.3;
Deut 16.1,6
12.8
Ex 34.25;
Num 9.11,
12;
Deut 16.7
12.10
Ex 23.18;
34.25
12.11
v. 27
12.12
Ex 11.4,5;
Num 33.4

that I will leave." And in hot anger he left Pharaoh.

9 The LORD said to Moses, "Pharaoh will not listen to you, in order that my wonders may be multiplied in the land of Egypt." ¹⁰Moses and Aaron performed all these wonders before Pharaoh; but the LORD hardened Pharaoh's heart, and he did not let the people of Israel go out of his land.

The First Passover Instituted

12 The LORD said to Moses and Aaron in the land of Egypt: ²This month shall mark for you the beginning of months; it shall be the first month of the year for you. ³Tell the whole congregation of Israel that on the tenth of this month they are to take a lamb for each family, a lamb for each household. ⁴If a household is too small for a whole lamb, it shall join its closest neighbor in obtaining one; the lamb shall be divided in proportion to the number of people who eat of it. ⁵Your lamb shall be without blemish, a year-old male; you may take it from the sheep or from the goats. ⁶You shall keep it until the fourteenth day of this month; then the whole assembled congregation of Israel shall slaughter it at twilight. ⁷They shall take some of the blood and put it on the two doorposts and the lintel of the houses in which they eat it. ⁸They shall eat the lamb that same night; they shall eat it roasted over the fire with unleavened bread and bitter herbs. ⁹Do not eat any of it raw or boiled in water, but roasted over the fire, with its head, legs, and inner organs. ¹⁰You shall let none of it remain until the morning; anything that remains until the morning you shall burn. ¹¹This is how you shall eat it: your loins girded, your sandals on your feet, and your staff in your hand; and you shall eat it hurriedly. It is the passover of the LORD. ¹²For I will pass through the land of Egypt that night, and I will strike down every firstborn in the land of Egypt, both human beings and animals; on all the gods of

HEBREW CALENDAR AND SELECTED EVENTS

Sacred Sequence Begins	Hebrew Name	Modern Equivalent	Biblical References	Agriculture	Feasts
1	Abib; Nisan	March-April	Ex 12:2; 13:4; 23:15; 34:18; Dt 16:1; Ne 2:1; Est 3:7	Spring (later) rains; barley and flax harvest begins	Passover; Unleavened Bread; Firstfruits
2	Ziv (Iyyar)*	April-May	1 Ki 6:1,37	Barley harvest; dry season begins	
3	Sivan	May-June	Est 8:9	Wheat harvest	Pentecost (Weeks)
4	(Tammuz)*	June-July		Tending vines	
5	(Ab)*	July-August		Ripening of grapes, figs and olives	
6	Elul	August-September	Ne 6:15	Processing grapes, figs and olives	
7	Ethanim (Tishri)*	September-October	1 Ki 8:2	Autumn (early) rains begin; plowing	Trumpets; Atonement; Tabernacles (Booths)
8	Bul (Marcheshvan)*	October-November	1 Ki 6:38	Sowing of wheat and barley	
9	Kislev	November-December	Ne 1:1, Zec 7:1	Winter rains begin (snow in some areas)	Hanukkah ("Dedication")
10	Tebeth	December-January	Est 2:16		
11	Shebat	January-February	Zec 1:7		
12	Adar	February-March	Ezr 6:15; Est 3:7,13; 8:12; 9:1,15,17,19,21	Almond trees bloom; citrus fruit harvest	Purim
	(Adar Sheni)* Second Adar				

This intercalary month was added about every three years so the lunar calendar would correspond to the solar year.

* Names in parentheses are not in the Bible

Egypt I will execute judgments: I am the Lord. 13 The blood shall be a sign for you on the houses where you live: when I see the blood, I will pass over you, and no plague shall destroy you when I strike the land of Egypt.

14 This day shall be a day of remembrance for you. You shall celebrate it as a festival to the Lord; throughout your generations you shall observe it as a perpetual ordinance. 15 Seven days you shall eat unleavened bread; on the first day you shall remove leaven from your houses, for whoever eats leavened bread from the first day until the seventh day shall be cut off from Israel. 16 On the first day you shall hold a solemn assembly, and on the seventh day a solemn assembly; no work shall be done on those days; only what everyone must eat, that alone may be prepared by you. 17 You shall observe the festival of unleavened bread, for on this very day I brought your companies out of the land of Egypt: you shall observe this day throughout your generations as a perpetual ordinance. 18 In the first month, from the evening of the fourteenth day until the evening of the twenty-first day, you shall eat unleavened bread. 19 For seven days no leaven shall be found in your houses; for whoever eats what is leavened shall be cut off from the congregation of Israel, whether an alien or a native of the land. 20 You shall eat nothing leavened; in all your settlements you shall eat unleavened bread.

21 Then Moses called all the elders of Israel and said to them, "Go, select lambs for your families, and slaughter the passover lamb. 22 Take a bunch of hyssop, dip it in the blood that is in the basin, and touch the lintel and the two doorposts with the blood in the basin. None of you shall go outside the door of your house until morning. 23 For the Lord will pass through to strike down the Egyptians; when he sees the blood on the lintel and on the two doorposts, the Lord will pass over that door and will not al-

low the destroyer to enter your houses to strike you down. 24 You shall observe this rite as a perpetual ordinance for you and your children. 25 When you come to the land that the Lord will give you, as he has promised, you shall keep this observance. 26 And when your children ask you, 'What do you mean by this observance?' 27 you shall say, 'It is the passover sacrifice to the Lord, for he passed over the houses of the Israelites in Egypt, when he struck down the Egyptians but spared our houses.' " And the people bowed down and worshiped.

28 The Israelites went and did just as the Lord had commanded Moses and Aaron.

The Tenth Plague: Death of the Firstborn

29 At midnight the Lord struck down all the firstborn in the land of Egypt, from the firstborn of Pharaoh who sat on his throne to the firstborn of the prisoner who was in the dungeon, and all the firstborn of the livestock. 30 Pharaoh arose in the night, he and all his officials and all the Egyptians; and there was a loud cry in Egypt, for there was not a house without someone dead. 31 Then he summoned Moses and Aaron in the night, and said, "Rise up, go away from my people, both you and the Israelites! Go, worship the Lord, as you said. 32 Take your flocks and your herds, as you said, and be gone. And bring a blessing on me too!"

The Exodus: From Rameses to Succoth

33 The Egyptians urged the people to hasten their departure from the land, for they said, "We shall all be dead." 34 So the people took their dough before it was leavened, with their kneading bowls wrapped up in their cloaks on their shoulders. 35 The Israelites had done as Moses told them; they had asked the Egyptians for jewelry of silver and gold, and for clothing, 36 and the Lord had given the people favor

12.14
v. 6;
Ex 13.9;
v. 17;
Ex 13.10
12.15
Ex 23.15;
34.18;
Lev 23.5,6;
Deut 16.3;
v. 19;
Num 9.13
12.16
Lev 23.7,8
12.17
v. 41;
Ex 13.3
12.18
v. 2;
Lev 23.5-8;
Num 28.16-25
12.19
v. 15
12.21
Heb 11.28;
v. 11;
Num 9.4
12.22
v. 7
12.23
vv. 12,13

12.24
Ex 13.5,10
12.26
Ex 13.14,
15; Josh 4.6
12.27
v. 11;
Ex 4.31
12.29
Ex 11.4;
4.23; 9.6;
Ps 78.51;
105.36
12.30
Ex 11.6
12.31
Ex 8.8,25
12.32
Ex 10.9,26
12.33
v. 39;
Ex 10.7;
11.1;
Ps 105.38
12.35
Ex 3.21,22;
11.2,3
12.36
Ex 3.22

in the sight of the Egyptians, so that they let them have what they asked. And so they plundered the Egyptians.

37 The Israelites journeyed from Rameses to Succoth, about six hundred thousand men on foot, besides children. 38 A mixed crowd also went up with them, and livestock in great numbers, both flocks and herds. 39 They baked unleavened cakes of the dough that they had brought out of Egypt; it was not leavened, because they were driven out of Egypt and could not wait, nor had they prepared any provisions for themselves.

40 The time that the Israelites had lived in Egypt was four hundred thirty years. 41 At the end of four hundred thirty years, on that very day, all the companies of the LORD went out from the land of Egypt. 42 That was for the LORD a night of vigil, to bring them out of the land of Egypt. That same night is a vigil to be kept for the LORD by all the Israelites throughout their generations.

Directions for the Passover

43 The LORD said to Moses and Aaron: This is the ordinance for the passover: no foreigner shall eat of it, 44 but any slave who has been purchased may eat of it after he has been circumcised; 45 no bound or hired servant may eat of it. 46 It shall be eaten in one house; you shall not take any of the animal outside the house, and you shall not break any of its bones. 47 The whole congregation of Israel shall celebrate it. 48 If an alien who resides with you wants to celebrate the passover to the LORD, all his males shall be circumcised; then he may draw near to celebrate it; he shall be regarded as a native of the land. But no uncircumcised person shall eat of it; 49 there shall be one law for the native and for the alien who resides among you.

50 All the Israelites did just as the LORD had commanded Moses and Aaron. 51 That very day the LORD brought the Israelites out of

the land of Egypt, company by company.

13

The LORD said to Moses: 2 Consecrate to me all the firstborn; whatever is the first to open the womb among the Israelites, of human beings and animals, is mine.

The Festival of Unleavened Bread

3 Moses said to the people, "Remember this day on which you came out of Egypt, out of the house of slavery, because the LORD brought you out from there by strength of hand; no leavened bread shall be eaten. 4 Today, in the month of Abib, you are going out. 5 When the LORD brings you into the land of the Canaanites, the Hittites, the Amorites, the Hivites, and the Jebusites, which he swore to your ancestors to give you, a land flowing with milk and honey, you shall keep this observance in this month. 6 Seven days you shall eat unleavened bread, and on the seventh day there shall be a festival to the LORD. 7 Unleavened bread shall be eaten for seven days; no leavened bread shall be seen in your possession, and no leaven shall be seen among you in all your territory. 8 You shall tell your child on that day, 'It is because of what the LORD did for me when I came out of Egypt.' 9 It shall serve for you as a sign on your hand and as a reminder on your forehead, so that the teaching of the LORD may be on your lips; for with a strong hand the LORD brought you out of Egypt. 10 You shall keep this ordinance at its proper time from year to year.

The Consecration of the Firstborn

11 "When the LORD has brought you into the land of the Canaanites, as he swore to you and your ancestors, and has given it to you, 12 you shall set apart to the LORD all that first opens the womb. All the firstborn of your livestock that are males shall be the LORD's. 13 But every firstborn donkey you shall re-

12.37
Num 33.3,4;
Ex 38.26;
Num 1.46;
11.21
12.38
Num 11.4;
Ex 17.3
12.39
vv. 31-33;
Ex 11.1
12.40
Gen 15.13;
Acts 7.6;
Gal 3.17
12.41
v. 17;
Ex 3.8,10;
6.6
12.42
Ex 13.10;
Deut 16.1
12.43
vv. 11,48
12.44
Gen 17.12,
13;
Lev 22.11
12.46
Num 9.12;
Jn 19.33,36
12.47
Num 9.13,
14
12.49
Num 15.15,
16; Gal 3.28
12.51
v. 41

13.2
vv. 12,13,
15;
Ex 22.29;
Lk 2.23
13.3
Ex 3.20;
6.1; 12.19
13.5
Ex 3.8;
12.25,26
13.6
Ex 12.15-20
13.8
v. 14;
Ex 10.2
13.9
v. 16;
Ex 12.14;
Deut 6.8;
11.18
13.10
Ex 12.24,25
13.12
v. 2;
Ex 22.29;
34.19
13.13
Ex 34.20;
Num 18.15,
16

deem with a sheep; if you do not redeem it, you must break its neck. Every firstborn male among your children you shall redeem. ¹⁴When in the future your child asks you, 'What does this mean?' you shall answer, 'By strength of hand the LORD brought us out of Egypt, from the house of slavery. ¹⁵When Pharaoh stubbornly refused to let us go, the LORD killed all the firstborn in the land of Egypt, from human firstborn to the firstborn of animals. Therefore I sacrifice to the LORD every male that first opens the womb, but every firstborn of my sons I redeem.' ¹⁶It shall serve as a sign on your hand and as an emblemˣ on your forehead that by strength of hand the LORD brought us out of Egypt."

The Pillars of Cloud and Fire

17 When Pharaoh let the people go, God did not lead them by way of the land of the Philistines, although that was nearer; for God thought, "If the people face war, they may change their minds and return to Egypt." ¹⁸So God led the people by the roundabout way of the wilderness toward the Red Sea.ʸ The Israelites went up out of the land of Egypt prepared for battle. ¹⁹And Moses took with him the bones of Joseph who had required a solemn oath of the Israelites, saying, "God will surely take notice of you, and then you must carry my bones with you from here." ²⁰They set out from Succoth, and camped at Etham, on the edge of the wilderness. ²¹The LORD went in front of them in a pillar of cloud by day, to lead them along the way, and in a pillar of fire by night, to give them light, so that they might travel by day and by night. ²²Neither the pillar of cloud by day nor the pillar of fire by night left its place in front of the people.

Crossing the Red Sea

14 Then the LORD said to Moses: ²Tell the Israelites to turn back and camp in front of Pi-hahiroth, between Migdol and the

sea, in front of Baal-zephon; you shall camp opposite it, by the sea. ³Pharaoh will say of the Israelites, 'They are wandering aimlessly in the land; the wilderness has closed in on them.' ⁴I will harden Pharaoh's heart, and he will pursue them, so that I will gain glory for myself over Pharaoh and all his army; and the Egyptians shall know that I am the LORD. And they did so.

5 When the king of Egypt was told that the people had fled, the minds of Pharaoh and his officials were changed toward the people, and they said, "What have we done, letting Israel leave our service?" ⁶So he had his chariot made ready, and took his army with him; ⁷he took six hundred picked chariots and all the other chariots of Egypt with officers over all of them. ⁸The LORD hardened the heart of Pharaoh king of Egypt and he pursued the Israelites, who were going out boldly. ⁹The Egyptians pursued them, all Pharaoh's horses and chariots, his chariot drivers and his army; they overtook them camped by the sea, by Pi-hahiroth, in front of Baal-zephon.

10 As Pharaoh drew near, the Israelites looked back, and there were the Egyptians advancing on them. In great fear the Israelites cried out to the LORD. ¹¹They said to Moses, "Was it because there were no graves in Egypt that you have taken us away to die in the wilderness? What have you done to us, bringing us out of Egypt? ¹²Is this not the very thing we told you in Egypt, 'Let us alone and let us serve the Egyptians'? For it would have been better for us to serve the Egyptians than to die in the wilderness." ¹³But Moses said to the people, "Do not be afraid, stand firm, and see the deliverance that the LORD will accomplish for you today; for the Egyptians whom you see today you shall never see again.

13.14
Ex 12.26, 27;
Deut 6.20;
vv. 3,9
13.15
Ex 12.29
13.16
v. 9
13.17
Ex 14.11, 12;
Num 14.1-4;
Deut 17.16
13.19
Gen 50.25, 26;
Josh 24.32;
Acts 7.16
13.20
Num 33.6-8
13.21f
Ex 14.19, 24; 33.9,10;
Ps 78.14;
105.39;
1 Cor 10.1
14.2
Num 33.7,8

14.4
v. 17;
Ex 4.21; 7.5
14.8
v. 4;
Num 33.3;
Acts 13.17
14.9
Ex 15.9
14.10
Neh 9.9
14.11
Ps 106.7,8
14.13
Gen 15.1;
v. 30;
Ex 15.2

ˣOr *as a frontlet*; Meaning of Heb uncertain
ʸOr *Sea of Reeds*

14 The LORD will fight for you, and you have only to keep still."

15 Then the LORD said to Moses, "Why do you cry out to me? Tell the Israelites to go forward. 16 But you lift up your staff, and stretch out your hand over the sea and divide it, that the Israelites may go into the sea on dry ground. 17 Then I will harden the hearts of the Egyptians so that they will go in after them; and so I will gain glory for myself over Pharaoh and all his army, his chariots, and his chariot drivers. 18 And the Egyptians shall know that I am the LORD, when I have gained glory for myself over Pharaoh, his chariots, and his chariot drivers."

19 The angel of God who was going before the Israelite army moved and went behind them; and the pillar of cloud moved from in front of them and took its place behind them. 20 It came between the army of Egypt and the army of Israel. And so the cloud was there with the darkness, and it lit up the night; one did not come near the other all night.

21 Then Moses stretched out his hand over the sea. The LORD drove the sea back by a strong east wind all night, and turned the sea into dry land; and the waters were divided. 22 The Israelites went into the sea on dry ground, the waters forming a wall for them on their right and on their left. 23 The Egyptians pursued, and went into the sea after them, all of Pharaoh's horses, chariots, and chariot drivers. 24 At the morning watch the LORD in the pillar of fire and cloud looked down upon the Egyptian army, and threw the Egyptian army into panic. 25 He clogged[z] their chariot wheels so that they turned with difficulty. The Egyptians said, "Let us flee from the Israelites, for the LORD is fighting for them against Egypt."

The Pursuers Drowned

26 Then the LORD said to Moses, "Stretch out your hand over the sea, so that the water may come

back upon the Egyptians, upon their chariots and chariot drivers." 27 So Moses stretched out his hand over the sea, and at dawn the sea returned to its normal depth. As the Egyptians fled before it, the LORD tossed the Egyptians into the sea. 28 The waters returned and covered the chariots and the chariot drivers, the entire army of Pharaoh that had followed them into the sea; not one of them remained. 29 But the Israelites walked on dry ground through the sea, the waters forming a wall for them on their right and on their left.

30 Thus the LORD saved Israel that day from the Egyptians; and Israel saw the Egyptians dead on the seashore. 31 Israel saw the great work that the LORD did against the Egyptians. So the people feared the LORD and believed in the LORD and in his servant Moses.

The Song of Moses

15 Then Moses and the Israelites sang this song to the LORD:

> "I will sing to the LORD, for
> he has triumphed
> gloriously;
> horse and rider he has
> thrown into the sea.
> 2 The LORD is my strength and
> my might,[a]
> and he has become my
> salvation;
> this is my God, and I will
> praise him,
> my father's God, and I will
> exalt him.
> 3 The LORD is a warrior;
> the LORD is his name.
>
> 4 "Pharaoh's chariots and his
> army he cast into the
> sea;
> his picked officers were
> sunk in the Red Sea.[b]
> 5 The floods covered them;
> they went down into the
> depths like a stone.
> 6 Your right hand, O LORD,
> glorious in power—

14.14
Ex 15.3;
Deut 1.30;
3.22;
Isa 30.15
14.16
Ex 4.17;
Num 20.8,9,
11;
Isa 10.26
14.17
v. 4
14.18
v. 25
14.19
Ex 13.21,22
14.21
v. 16;
Ps 106.9;
114.3,5;
Isa 63.12,13
14.22
Ex 15.19;
Neh 9.11;
Heb 11.29
14.24
Ex 13.21
14.25
vv. 4,18

14.27
Ex 15.1,7
14.28
Ps 78.53;
106.11
14.29
Ex 15.19;
Neh 9.11;
Heb 11.29
14.30
Ps 106.8
14.31
Ps 106.12
15.1
Ps 106.12;
Rev 15.3
15.2
Ps 59.17;
Ex 3.15,16
15.3
Ps 24.8;
83.18
15.4
Ex 14.6,7,
17,28
15.5
v. 10;
Neh 9.11
15.6
Ps 118.15

z Sam Gk Syr: MT removed a Or song
b Or Sea of Reeds

your right hand, O LORD,
 shattered the enemy.
7 In the greatness of your
 majesty you overthrew
 your adversaries;
you sent out your fury, it
 consumed them like
 stubble.
8 At the blast of your nostrils
 the waters piled up,
the floods stood up in a
 heap;
the deeps congealed in the
 heart of the sea.
9 The enemy said, 'I will
 pursue, I will overtake,
I will divide the spoil, my
 desire shall have its fill
 of them.
I will draw my sword, my
 hand shall destroy
 them.'
10 You blew with your wind, the
 sea covered them;
they sank like lead in the
 mighty waters.

11 "Who is like you, O LORD,
 among the gods?
Who is like you, majestic
 in holiness,
awesome in splendor,
 doing wonders?
12 You stretched out your right
 hand,
the earth swallowed them.

13 "In your steadfast love you
 led the people whom
 you redeemed;
you guided them by your
 strength to your holy
 abode.
14 The peoples heard, they
 trembled;
pangs seized the
 inhabitants of Philistia.
15 Then the chiefs of Edom
 were dismayed;
trembling seized the
 leaders of Moab;
all the inhabitants of
 Canaan melted away.
16 Terror and dread fell upon
 them;
by the might of your arm,

15.7
Ex 14.27;
Ps 78.49,50
15.8
Ex 14.22,
29; Ps 78.13
15.9
Ex 14.5
15.10
Ex 14.28
15.11
Ex 8.10;
Deut 3.24;
Isa 6.3;
Rev 4.8;
Ps 22.23;
72.18
15.13
Neh 9.12;
Ps 77.15;
78.54
15.14
Deut 2.25;
Hab 3.7
15.15
Gen 36.15;
Num 22.3;
Josh 5.1
15.16
Ex 23.27;
1 Sam 25.37;
Ps 74.2

15.17
Ps 44.2;
78.54
15.18
Ps 10.16
15.19
Ex 14.23,28
15.20
Judg 4.4;
Num 26.59;
1 Sam 18.6;
Ps 30.11;
150.4
15.21
v. 1
15.22
Ps 77.20;
Num 33.8
15.23
Num 33.8
15.24
Ex 14.11;
Ps 106.13
15.25
Ex 14.10;
Ps 50.15

they became still as a
 stone
until your people, O LORD,
 passed by,
until the people whom you
 acquired passed by.
17 You brought them in and
 planted them on the
 mountain of your own
 possession,
the place, O LORD, that you
 made your abode,
the sanctuary, O LORD, that
 your hands have
 established.
18 The LORD will reign forever
 and ever."

19 When the horses of Pharaoh
with his chariots and his chariot
drivers went into the sea, the LORD
brought back the waters of the sea
upon them; but the Israelites
walked through the sea on dry
ground.

The Song of Miriam

20 Then the prophet Miriam,
Aaron's sister, took a tambourine
in her hand; and all the women
went out after her with tambou-
rines and with dancing. 21 And Mir-
iam sang to them:

"Sing to the LORD, for he has
 triumphed gloriously;
horse and rider he has
 thrown into the sea."

Bitter Water Made Sweet

22 Then Moses ordered Israel to
set out from the Red Sea,[c] and
they went into the wilderness of
Shur. They went three days in the
wilderness and found no water.
23 When they came to Marah, they
could not drink the water of Marah
because it was bitter. That is why it
was called Marah.[d] 24 And the peo-
ple complained against Moses, say-
ing, "What shall we drink?" 25 He
cried out to the LORD; and the LORD
showed him a piece of wood;[e] he
threw it into the water, and the wa-
ter became sweet.

There the LORD[f] made for them
a statute and an ordinance and

c Or *Sea of Reeds* d That is *Bitterness*
e Or *a tree* f Heb *he*

there he put them to the test. 26 He said, "If you will listen carefully to the voice of the LORD your God, and do what is right in his sight, and give heed to his commandments and keep all his statutes, I will not bring upon you any of the diseases that I brought upon the Egyptians; for I am the LORD who heals you."

27 Then they came to Elim, where there were twelve springs of water and seventy palm trees; and they camped there by the water.

Bread from Heaven

16 The whole congregation of the Israelites set out from Elim; and Israel came to the wilderness of Sin, which is between Elim and Sinai, on the fifteenth day of the second month after they had departed from the land of Egypt. 2 The whole congregation of the Israelites complained against Moses and Aaron in the wilderness. 3 The Israelites said to them, "If only we had died by the hand of the LORD in the land of Egypt, when we sat by the fleshpots and ate our fill of bread; for you have brought us out into this wilderness to kill this whole assembly with hunger."

4 Then the LORD said to Moses, "I am going to rain bread from heaven for you, and each day the people shall go out and gather enough for that day. In that way I will test them, whether they will follow my instruction or not. 5 On the sixth day, when they prepare what they bring in, it will be twice as much as they gather on other days." 6 So Moses and Aaron said to all the Israelites, "In the evening you shall know that it was the LORD who brought you out of the land of Egypt, 7 and in the morning you shall see the glory of the LORD, because he has heard your complaining against the LORD. For what are we, that you complain against us?" 8 And Moses said, "When the LORD gives you meat to eat in the evening and your fill of bread in the morning, because the LORD has heard the complaining that you utter against

him—what are we? Your complaining is not against us but against the LORD."

9 Then Moses said to Aaron, "Say to the whole congregation of the Israelites, 'Draw near to the LORD, for he has heard your complaining.' " 10 And as Aaron spoke to the whole congregation of the Israelites, they looked toward the wilderness, and the glory of the LORD appeared in the cloud. 11 The LORD spoke to Moses and said, 12 "I have heard the complaining of the Israelites; say to them, 'At twilight you shall eat meat, and in the morning you shall have your fill of bread; then you shall know that I am the LORD your God.' "

13 In the evening quails came up and covered the camp; and in the morning there was a layer of dew around the camp. 14 When the layer of dew lifted, there on the surface of the wilderness was a fine flaky substance, as fine as frost on the ground. 15 When the Israelites saw it, they said to one another, "What is it?"g For they did not know what it was. Moses said to them, "It is the bread that the LORD has given you to eat. 16 This is what the LORD has commanded: 'Gather as much of it as each of you needs, an omer to a person according to the number of persons, all providing for those in their own tents.' " 17 The Israelites did so, some gathering more, some less. 18 But when they measured it with an omer, those who gathered much had nothing over, and those who gathered little had no shortage; they gathered as much as each of them needed. 19 And Moses said to them, "Let no one leave any of it over until morning." 20 But they did not listen to Moses; some left part of it until morning, and it bred worms and became foul. And Moses was angry with them. 21 Morning by morning they gathered it, as much as each needed; but when the sun grew hot, it melted.

15.26
Deut 7.12;
28.27
15.27
Num 33.9,
10
16.1
Num 33.11,
12
16.2
Ex 14.11;
1 Cor 10.10
16.3
Ex 17.3;
Num 11.4,5
16.4
Jn 6.31;
1 Cor 10.3;
Deut 8.2,16
16.5
v. 22
16.7
v. 12;
Num 14.27;
16.11

16.9
Num 16.16
16.10
v. 7;
Num 16.19
16.13
Num 11.31;
Ps 78.27,28;
105.40
16.14
Num 11.7-9;
v. 31
16.15
v. 4
16.18
2 Cor 8.15
16.19
v. 23;
Ex 12.10;
23.18

g Or "It is manna" (Heb man hu, see verse 31)

22 On the sixth day they gathered twice as much food, two omers apiece. When all the leaders of the congregation came and told Moses, 23 he said to them, "This is what the LORD has commanded: 'Tomorrow is a day of solemn rest, a holy sabbath to the LORD; bake what you want to bake and boil what you want to boil, and all that is left over put aside to be kept until morning.' " 24 So they put it aside until morning, as Moses commanded them; and it did not become foul, and there were no worms in it. 25 Moses said, "Eat it today, for today is a sabbath to the LORD; today you will not find it in the field. 26 Six days you shall gather it; but on the seventh day, which is a sabbath, there will be none."

27 On the seventh day some of the people went out to gather, and they found none. 28 The LORD said to Moses, "How long will you refuse to keep my commandments and instructions? 29 See! The LORD has given you the sabbath, therefore on the sixth day he gives you food for two days; each of you stay where you are; do not leave your place on the seventh day." 30 So the people rested on the seventh day.

31 The house of Israel called it manna; it was like coriander seed, white, and the taste of it was like wafers made with honey. 32 Moses said, "This is what the LORD has commanded: 'Let an omer of it be kept throughout your generations, in order that they may see the food with which I fed you in the wilderness, when I brought you out of the land of Egypt.' " 33 And Moses said to Aaron, "Take a jar, and put an omer of manna in it, and place it before the LORD, to be kept throughout your generations." 34 As the LORD commanded Moses, so Aaron placed it before the covenant,h for safekeeping. 35 The Israelites ate manna forty years, until they came to a habitable land; they ate manna, until they came to the border of the land of Canaan. 36 An omer is a tenth of an ephah.

16.22
v. 5;
Ex 34.31
16.23ff
Ex 20.8;
23.12
16.24
v. 20
16.28
Ps 78.10
16.31
Num 11.6-9
16.33
Heb 9.4
16.34
Ex 25.16,21
16.35
Josh 5.12;
Neh 9.20,21

17.1
Ex 16.1
17.2
Num 20.3;
Deut 6.16;
1 Cor 10.9
17.3
Ex 16.2,3
17.4
Ex 14.15;
Num 14.10;
1 Sam 30.6
17.5
Ex 3.16,18;
7.20
17.6
Num 20.10;
Ps 114.8;
1 Cor 10.4
17.7
Ps 81.7
17.8
Num 24.20;
Deut 25.17-19
17.9
Ex 4.20

Water from the Rock

17 From the wilderness of Sin the whole congregation of the Israelites journeyed by stages, as the LORD commanded. They camped at Rephidim, but there was no water for the people to drink. 2 The people quarreled with Moses, and said, "Give us water to drink." Moses said to them, "Why do you quarrel with me? Why do you test the LORD?" 3 But the people thirsted there for water; and the people complained against Moses and said, "Why did you bring us out of Egypt, to kill us and our children and livestock with thirst?" 4 So Moses cried out to the LORD, "What shall I do with this people? They are almost ready to stone me." 5 The LORD said to Moses, "Go on ahead of the people, and take some of the elders of Israel with you; take in your hand the staff with which you struck the Nile, and go. 6 I will be standing there in front of you on the rock at Horeb. Strike the rock, and water will come out of it, so that the people may drink." Moses did so, in the sight of the elders of Israel. 7 He called the place Massahi and Meribah,j because the Israelites quarreled and tested the LORD, saying, "Is the LORD among us or not?"

Amalek Attacks Israel and Is Defeated

8 Then Amalek came and fought with Israel at Rephidim. 9 Moses said to Joshua, "Choose some men for us and go out, fight with Amalek. Tomorrow I will stand on the top of the hill with the staff of God in my hand." 10 So Joshua did as Moses told him, and fought with Amalek, while Moses, Aaron, and Hur went up to the top of the hill. 11 Whenever Moses held up his hand, Israel prevailed; and whenever he lowered his hand, Amalek prevailed. 12 But Moses' hands grew weary; so they took a stone and put it under him, and he

h Or treaty or testimony; Heb eduth i That is Test j That is Quarrel

sat on it. Aaron and Hur held up his hands, one on one side, and the other on the other side; so his hands were steady until the sun set. [13] And Joshua defeated Amalek and his people with the sword.

14 Then the LORD said to Moses, "Write this as a reminder in a book and recite it in the hearing of Joshua: I will utterly blot out the remembrance of Amalek from under heaven." [15] And Moses built an altar and called it, The LORD is my banner. [16] He said, "A hand upon the banner of the LORD![k] The LORD will have war with Amalek from generation to generation."

Jethro's Advice

18 Jethro, the priest of Midian, Moses' father-in-law, heard of all that God had done for Moses and for his people Israel, how the LORD had brought Israel out of Egypt. [2] After Moses had sent away his wife Zipporah, his father-in-law Jethro took her back, [3] along with her two sons. The name of the one was Gershom (for he said, "I have been an alien[l] in a foreign land"), [4] and the name of the other, Eliezer[m] (for he said, "The God of my father was my help, and delivered me from the sword of Pharaoh"). [5] Jethro, Moses' father-in-law, came into the wilderness where Moses was encamped at the mountain of God, bringing Moses' sons and wife to him. [6] He sent word to Moses, "I, your father-in-law Jethro, am coming to you, with your wife and her two sons." [7] Moses went out to meet his father-in-law; he bowed down and kissed him; each asked after the other's welfare, and they went into the tent. [8] Then Moses told his father-in-law all that the LORD had done to Pharaoh and to the Egyptians for Israel's sake, all the hardship that had beset them on the way, and how the LORD had delivered them. [9] Jethro rejoiced for all the good that the LORD had done to Israel, in delivering them from the Egyptians.

10 Jethro said, "Blessed be the LORD, who has delivered you from the Egyptians and from Pharaoh. [11] Now I know that the LORD is greater than all gods, because he delivered the people from the Egyptians,[n] when they dealt arrogantly with them." [12] And Jethro, Moses' father-in-law, brought a burnt offering and sacrifices to God; and Aaron came with all the elders of Israel to eat bread with Moses' father-in-law in the presence of God.

13 The next day Moses sat as judge for the people, while the people stood around him from morning until evening. [14] When Moses' father-in-law saw all that he was doing for the people, he said, "What is this that you are doing for the people? Why do you sit alone, while all the people stand around you from morning until evening?" [15] Moses said to his father-in-law, "Because the people come to me to inquire of God. [16] When they have a dispute, they come to me and I decide between one person and another, and I make known to them the statutes and instructions of God." [17] Moses' father-in-law said to him, "What you are doing is not good. [18] You will surely wear yourself out, both you and these people with you. For the task is too heavy for you; you cannot do it alone. [19] Now listen to me. I will give you counsel, and God be with you! You should represent the people before God, and you should bring their cases before God; [20] teach them the statutes and instructions and make known to them the way they are to go and the things they are to do. [21] You should also look for able men among all the people, men who fear God, are trustworthy, and hate dishonest gain; set such men over them as officers over thousands, hundreds, fifties and tens. [22] Let them sit as judges for the people at all times; let them bring every important case to you, but

Cross references (center column):

17.14
Ex 34.27;
Num 24.20;
Deut 29.19
18.1
Ex 2.16; 3.1
18.2
Ex 4.25
18.3
Acts 7.29;
Ex 2.22
18.5
Ex 3.1,12
18.7
Gen 43.26-28;
Ex 4.27
18.8
Ps 81.7
18.10
Ps 68.19,20

18.11
Ex 12.12;
15.11;
1 Sam 2.3
18.15
Num 9.8;
Deut 17.8-13
18.18
Num 11.14,
17
18.19
Ex 3.12;
Num 27.5
18.20
Deut 1.18
18.21ff
v. 25;
Deut 1.13,
15
18.22
Deut 1.17,
18;
Num 11.17

[k] Cn: Meaning of Heb uncertain
[l] Heb *ger* [m] Heb *Eli*, my God; *ezer*, help
[n] The clause *because . . . Egyptians* has been transposed from verse 10

decide every minor case themselves. So it will be easier for you, and they will bear the burden with you. [23] If you do this, and God so commands you, then you will be able to endure, and all these people will go to their home in peace."

24 So Moses listened to his father-in-law and did all that he had said. [25] Moses chose able men from all Israel and appointed them as heads over the people, as officers over thousands, hundreds, fifties, and tens. [26] And they judged the people at all times; hard cases they brought to Moses, but any minor case they decided themselves. [27] Then Moses let his father-in-law depart, and he went off to his own country.

The Israelites Reach Mount Sinai

19 On the third new moon after the Israelites had gone out of the land of Egypt, on that very day, they came into the wilderness of Sinai. [2] They had journeyed from Rephidim, entered the wilderness of Sinai, and camped in the wilderness; Israel camped there in front of the mountain. [3] Then Moses went up to God; the LORD called to him from the mountain, saying, "Thus you shall say to the house of Jacob, and tell the Israelites: [4] You have seen what I did to the Egyptians, and how I bore you on eagles' wings and brought you to myself. [5] Now therefore, if you obey my voice and keep my covenant, you shall be my treasured possession out of all the peoples. Indeed, the whole earth is mine, [6] but you shall be for me a priestly kingdom and a holy nation. These are the words that you shall speak to the Israelites."

7 So Moses came, summoned the elders of the people, and set before them all these words that the LORD had commanded him. [8] The people all answered as one: "Everything that the LORD has spoken we will do." Moses reported the words of the people to the LORD. [9] Then the LORD said to Moses, "I am going to come to you in a dense cloud, in order that the people may hear when I speak with you and so trust you ever after."

The People Consecrated

When Moses had told the words of the people to the LORD, [10] the LORD said to Moses: "Go to the people and consecrate them today and tomorrow. Have them wash their clothes [11] and prepare for the third day, because on the third day the LORD will come down upon Mount Sinai in the sight of all the people. [12] You shall set limits for the people all around, saying, 'Be careful not to go up the mountain or to touch the edge of it. Any who touch the mountain shall be put to death. [13] No hand shall touch them, but they shall be stoned or shot with arrows; [o] whether animal or human being, they shall not live.' When the trumpet sounds a long blast, they may go up on the mountain." [14] So Moses went down from the mountain to the people. He consecrated the people, and they washed their clothes. [15] And he said to the people, "Prepare for the third day; do not go near a woman."

16 On the morning of the third day there was thunder and lightning, as well as a thick cloud on the mountain, and a blast of a trumpet so loud that all the people who were in the camp trembled. [17] Moses brought the people out of the camp to meet God. They took their stand at the foot of the mountain. [18] Now Mount Sinai was wrapped in smoke, because the LORD had descended upon it in fire; the smoke went up like the smoke of a kiln, while the whole mountain shook violently. [19] As the blast of the trumpet grew louder and louder, Moses would speak and God would answer him in thunder. [20] When the LORD descended upon Mount Sinai, to the top of the mountain, the LORD summoned Moses to the top of the mountain, and Moses went up. [21] Then the LORD said to Moses, "Go down and warn the people not

[o] Heb lacks *with arrows*

18.25
Deut 1.15
18.26
v. 22
18.27
Num 10.29, 30
19.2
Ex 17.1; 18.5
19.3
Ex 20;21; Acts 7.38
19.4
Deut 29.2; Isa 63.9
19.5ff
Deut 5.2; 7.6; 10.14
19.6
1 Pet 2.5; Rev 1.6; 5.10; Deut 14.21; 26.19
19.8
Ex 24.3,7
19.9
v. 16; Ex 24.15

19.10
Lev 11.44, 45; Heb 10.22; Gen 35.2; Num 8.7; 19.19
19.11
v. 16
19.12
Heb 12.20
19.13
v. 17
19.16
Heb 12.18, 19; Ex 40.34
19.18
Ps 104.32; Heb 12.18; Gen 19.28; Ps 68.7,8
19.19
Heb 12.21; Ps 81.7
19.21
Ex 3.5

to break through to the LORD to look; otherwise many of them will perish. 22 Even the priests who approach the LORD must consecrate themselves or the LORD will break out against them." 23 Moses said to the LORD, "The people are not permitted to come up to Mount Sinai; for you yourself warned us, saying, 'Set limits around the mountain and keep it holy.' " 24 The LORD said to him, "Go down, and come up bringing Aaron with you; but do not let either the priests or the people break through to come up to the LORD; otherwise he will break out against them." 25 So Moses went down to the people and told them.

The Ten Commandments

20 Then God spoke all these words:

2 I am the LORD your God, who brought you out of the land of Egypt, out of the house of slavery; 3 you shall have no other gods beforeᴾ me.

4 You shall not make for yourself an idol, whether in the form of anything that is in heaven above, or that is on the earth beneath, or that is in the water under the earth. 5 You shall not bow down to them or worship them; for I the LORD your God am a jealous God, punishing children for the iniquity of parents, to the third and the fourth generation of those who reject me, 6 but showing steadfast love to the thousandth generation�q of those who love me and keep my commandments.

7 You shall not make wrongful use of the name of the LORD your God, for the LORD will not acquit anyone who misuses his name.

8 Remember the sabbath day, and keep it holy. 9 Six days you shall labor and do all your work. 10 But the seventh day is a sabbath to the LORD your God; you shall not do any work—you, your son or your daughter, your male or female slave, your livestock, or the alien resident in your towns. 11 For in six days the LORD made heaven and earth, the sea, and all that is in

them, but rested the seventh day; therefore the LORD blessed the sabbath day and consecrated it.

12 Honor your father and your mother, so that your days may be long in the land that the LORD your God is giving you.

13 You shall not murder.ʳ

14 You shall not commit adultery.

15 You shall not steal.

16 You shall not bear false witness against your neighbor.

17 You shall not covet your neighbor's house; you shall not covet your neighbor's wife, or male or female slave, or ox, or donkey, or anything that belongs to your neighbor.

18 When all the people witnessed the thunder and lightning, the sound of the trumpet, and the mountain smoking, they were afraidˢ and trembled and stood at a distance, 19 and said to Moses, "You speak to us, and we will listen; but do not let God speak to us, or we will die." 20 Moses said to the people, "Do not be afraid; for God has come only to test you and to put the fear of him upon you so that you do not sin." 21 Then the people stood at a distance, while Moses drew near to the thick darkness where God was.

The Law concerning the Altar

22 The LORD said to Moses: Thus you shall say to the Israelites: "You have seen for yourselves that I spoke with you from heaven. 23 You shall not make gods of silver alongside me, nor shall you make for yourselves gods of gold. 24 You need make for me only an altar of earth and sacrifice on it your burnt offerings and your offerings of well-being, your sheep and your oxen; in every place where I cause my name to be remembered I will come to you and bless you. 25 But if you make for me an altar of stone, do not build it of hewn stones; for if you use a chisel upon it you profane it. 26 You shall not go up by

Cross references (center column)

19.22 Lev 10.3; 2 Sam 6.7
19.23 v. 12
20.1 Deut 5.22
20.2 Deut 5.6; 7.8
20.3 Jer 35.15
20.4 Lev 26.1; Deut 4.15-19; Ps 97.7
20.5 Isa 44.15, 19; Deut 4.24; Jer 32.18
20.6 Deut 7.9
20.7 Lev 19.12; Mt 5.33
20.8 Ex 23.12; 31.15
20.9 Ex 34.21; Lk 13.14
20.11 Gen 2.2,3

20.12 Lev 19.3; Mt 15.4; Mk 7.10; Eph 6.2
20.13 Rom 13.9
20.14 Mt 19.18
20.15 Mt 19.18
20.16 Ex 23.1; Mt 19.18
20.17 Rom 7.7; 13.9
20.18 Heb 12.18; Ex 19.18
20.19 Deut 5.23-27
20.20 Ex 14.13; 15.25; Deut 4.10
20.21 Deut 5.22
20.22 Neh 9.13
20.23 v. 3; Ex 32.1,2,4
20.24 Lev 1.2; Deut 12.5; Gen 12.2
20.25 Deut 27.5,6

ᴾ Or besides q Or to thousands
ʳ Or kill ˢ Sam Gk Syr Vg: MT they saw

steps to my altar, so that your nakedness may not be exposed on it."

The Law concerning Slaves

21 These are the ordinances that you shall set before them:

2 When you buy a male Hebrew slave, he shall serve six years, but in the seventh he shall go out a free person, without debt. ³ If he comes in single, he shall go out single; if he comes in married, then his wife shall go out with him. ⁴ If his master gives him a wife and she bears him sons or daughters, the wife and her children shall be her master's and he shall go out alone. ⁵ But if the slave declares, "I love my master, my wife, and my children; I will not go out a free person," ⁶ then his master shall bring him before God.ᵗ He shall be brought to the door or the doorpost; and his master shall pierce his ear with an awl; and he shall serve him for life.

7 When a man sells his daughter as a slave, she shall not go out as the male slaves do. ⁸ If she does not please her master, who designated her for himself, then he shall let her be redeemed; he shall have no right to sell her to a foreign people, since he has dealt unfairly with her. ⁹ If he designates her for his son, he shall deal with her as with a daughter. ¹⁰ If he takes another wife to himself, he shall not diminish the food, clothing, or marital rights of the first wife.ᵘ ¹¹ And if he does not do these three things for her, she shall go out without debt, without payment of money.

The Law concerning Violence

12 Whoever strikes a person mortally shall be put to death. ¹³ If it was not premeditated, but came about by an act of God, then I will appoint for you a place to which the killer may flee. ¹⁴ But if someone willfully attacks and kills another by treachery, you shall take the killer from my altar for execution.

15 Whoever strikes father or mother shall be put to death.

16 Whoever kidnaps a person, whether that person has been sold or is still held in possession, shall be put to death.

17 Whoever curses father or mother shall be put to death.

18 When individuals quarrel and one strikes the other with a stone or fist so that the injured party, though not dead, is confined to bed, ¹⁹ but recovers and walks around outside with the help of a staff, then the assailant shall be free of liability, except to pay for the loss of time, and to arrange for full recovery.

20 When a slaveowner strikes a male or female slave with a rod and the slave dies immediately, the owner shall be punished. ²¹ But if the slave survives a day or two, there is no punishment; for the slave is the owner's property.

22 When people who are fighting injure a pregnant woman so that there is a miscarriage, and yet no further harm follows, the one responsible shall be fined what the woman's husband demands, paying as much as the judges determine. ²³ If any harm follows, then you shall give life for life, ²⁴ eye for eye, tooth for tooth, hand for hand, foot for foot, ²⁵ burn for burn, wound for wound, stripe for stripe.

26 When a slaveowner strikes the eye of a male or female slave, destroying it, the owner shall let the slave go, a free person, to compensate for the eye. ²⁷ If the owner knocks out a tooth of a male or female slave, the slave shall be let go, a free person, to compensate for the tooth.

Laws concerning Property

28 When an ox gores a man or a woman to death, the ox shall be stoned, and its flesh shall not be eaten; but the owner of the ox shall not be liable. ²⁹ If the ox has been accustomed to gore in the past, and its owner has been warned but has not restrained it, and it kills a man or a woman, the ox shall be stoned, and its owner also shall be

21.1
Deut 4.14
21.2
Lev 25.39-41;
Deut 15.12-18
21.6
Ex 22.8,9,
28
21.7
Neh 5.5;
vv. 2,3
21.10
1 Cor 7.3,
5
21.12
Gen 9.6;
Lev 24.17
21.13
Num 35.22;
Deut 19.4,5
21.14
Deut 19.11,
12;
Heb 10.26;
1 Kings 2.28-
34

21.16
Deut 24.7
21.17
Lev 20.9;
Mt 15.4;
Mk 7.10
21.21
Lev 25.45,
46
21.23ff
Lev 24.19
21.24
Mt 5.38
21.28
Gen 9.5

ᵗ Or to the judges ᵘ Heb of her

put to death. ³⁰If a ransom is imposed on the owner, then the owner shall pay whatever is imposed for the redemption of the victim's life. ³¹If it gores a boy or a girl, the owner shall be dealt with according to this same rule. ³²If the ox gores a male or female slave, the owner shall pay to the slaveowner thirty shekels of silver, and the ox shall be stoned.

33 If someone leaves a pit open, or digs a pit and does not cover it, and an ox or a donkey falls into it, ³⁴the owner of the pit shall make restitution, giving money to its owner, but keeping the dead animal.

35 If someone's ox hurts the ox of another, so that it dies, then they shall sell the live ox and divide the price of it; and the dead animal they shall also divide. ³⁶But if it was known that the ox was accustomed to gore in the past, and its owner has not restrained it, the owner shall restore ox for ox, but keep the dead animal.

Laws of Restitution

22 ᵛ When someone steals an ox or a sheep, and slaughters it or sells it, the thief shall pay five oxen for an ox, and four sheep for a sheep.ʷ The thief shall make restitution, but if unable to do so, shall be sold for the theft. ⁴When the animal, whether ox or donkey or sheep, is found alive in the thief's possession, the thief shall pay double.

2 ˣIf a thief is found breaking in, and is beaten to death, no bloodguilt is incurred; ³but if it happens after sunrise, bloodguilt is incurred.

5 When someone causes a field or vineyard to be grazed over, or lets livestock loose to graze in someone else's field, restitution shall be made from the best in the owner's field or vineyard.

6 When fire breaks out and catches in thorns so that the stacked grain or the standing grain or the field is consumed, the one who started the fire shall make full restitution.

7 When someone delivers to a neighbor money or goods for safekeeping, and they are stolen from the neighbor's house, then the thief, if caught, shall pay double. ⁸If the thief is not caught, the owner of the house shall be brought before God,ʸ to determine whether or not the owner had laid hands on the neighbor's goods.

9 In any case of disputed ownership involving ox, donkey, sheep, clothing, or any other loss, of which one party says, "This is mine," the case of both parties shall come before God;ʸ the one whom God condemnsᶻ shall pay double to the other.

10 When someone delivers to another a donkey, ox, sheep, or any other animal for safekeeping, and it dies or is injured or is carried off, without anyone seeing it, ¹¹an oath before the LORD shall decide between the two of them that the one has not laid hands on the property of the other; the owner shall accept the oath, and no restitution shall be made. ¹²But if it was stolen, restitution shall be made to its owner. ¹³If it was mangled by beasts, let it be brought as evidence; restitution shall not be made for the mangled remains.

14 When someone borrows an animal from another and it is injured or dies, the owner not being present, full restitution shall be made. ¹⁵If the owner was present, there shall be no restitution; if it was hired, only the hiring fee is due.

Social and Religious Laws

16 When a man seduces a virgin who is not engaged to be married, and lies with her, he shall give the bride-price for her and make her his wife. ¹⁷But if her father refuses to give her to him, he shall pay an

21.30 v. 22
21.32 Zech 11.12, 13;
Mt 26.15
21.33 Lk 14.5
22.1 2 Sam 12.6
22.2 Mt 24.43;
Num 35.27
22.3 Ex 21.2

22.7 v. 4
22.8 v. 28;
Ex 21.6;
Deut 17.8,9;
19.17
22.9 vv. 8,28
22.11 Heb 6.16
22.12 Gen 31.39
22.16 Deut 22.28, 29
22.17 Deut 22.29

amount equal to the bride-price for virgins.

18 You shall not permit a female sorcerer to live.

19 Whoever lies with an animal shall be put to death.

20 Whoever sacrifices to any god, other than the LORD alone, shall be devoted to destruction.

21 You shall not wrong or oppress a resident alien, for you were aliens in the land of Egypt. 22 You shall not abuse any widow or orphan. 23 If you do abuse them, when they cry out to me, I will surely heed their cry; 24 my wrath will burn, and I will kill you with the sword, and your wives shall become widows and your children orphans.

25 If you lend money to my people, to the poor among you, you shall not deal with them as a creditor; you shall not exact interest from them. 26 If you take your neighbor's cloak in pawn, you shall restore it before the sun goes down; 27 for it may be your neighbor's only clothing to use as cover; in what else shall that person sleep? And if your neighbor cries out to me, I will listen, for I am compassionate.

28 You shall not revile God, or curse a leader of your people.

29 You shall not delay to make offerings from the fullness of your harvest and from the outflow of your presses. a

The firstborn of your sons you shall give to me. 30 You shall do the same with your oxen and with your sheep: seven days it shall remain with its mother; on the eighth day you shall give it to me.

31 You shall be people consecrated to me; therefore you shall not eat any meat that is mangled by beasts in the field; you shall throw it to the dogs.

Justice for All

23 You shall not spread a false report. You shall not join hands with the wicked to act as a malicious witness. 2 You shall not follow a majority in wrongdoing; when you bear witness in a lawsuit,

you shall not side with the majority so as to pervert justice; 3 nor shall you be partial to the poor in a lawsuit.

4 When you come upon your enemy's ox or donkey going astray, you shall bring it back.

5 When you see the donkey of one who hates you lying under its burden and you would hold back from setting it free, you must help to set it free. a

6 You shall not pervert the justice due to your poor in their lawsuits. 7 Keep far from a false charge, and do not kill the innocent and those in the right, for I will not acquit the guilty. 8 You shall take no bribe, for a bribe blinds the officials, and subverts the cause of those who are in the right.

9 You shall not oppress a resident alien; you know the heart of an alien, for you were aliens in the land of Egypt.

Sabbatical Year and Sabbath

10 For six years you shall sow your land and gather in its yield; 11 but the seventh year you shall let it rest and lie fallow, so that the poor of your people may eat; and what they leave the wild animals may eat. You shall do the same with your vineyard, and with your olive orchard.

12 Six days you shall do your work, but on the seventh day you shall rest, so that your ox and your donkey may have relief, and your homeborn slave and the resident alien may be refreshed. 13 Be attentive to all that I have said to you. Do not invoke the names of other gods; do not let them be heard on your lips.

The Annual Festivals

14 Three times in the year you shall hold a festival for me. 15 You shall observe the festival of unleavened bread; as I commanded you, you shall eat unleavened bread for seven days at the appointed time in the month of Abib, for in it you came out of Egypt.

a Meaning of Heb uncertain

Cross references (center column)

22.18
Lev 20.27;
Deut 18.10
22.19
Lev 18.23;
Deut 27.21
22.20
Deut 17.2,3,5
22.21
Lev 19.33;
Deut 10.19
22.22
Deut 24.17,18
22.23
Deut 15.9;
Lk 18.7;
Ps 18.6
22.24
Ps 69.24;
109.9
22.25
Lev 25.35-37;
Deut 23.19,20
22.28
Lev 24.15,16;
Acts 23.5
22.29
Ex 23.16;
13.2,12
22.30
Deut 15.19;
Lev 22.27
22.31
Lev 19.6;
22.8
23.1
Ex 20.16;
Ps 35.11
23.2
Deut 16.19

23.4
Deut 22.1
23.5
Deut 22.4
23.6
vv. 2,3
23.7
Rom 1.18
23.8
Deut 10.17;
16.19
23.9
Ex 22.21
23.10
Lev 25.3
23.12
Ex 20.8-11
23.13
Ps 39.1;
Eph 5.15
23.14
Ex 34.23
23.15
Ex 12.15;
34.20

No one shall appear before me empty-handed.

16 You shall observe the festival of harvest, of the first fruits of your labor, of what you sow in the field. You shall observe the festival of in-gathering at the end of the year, when you gather in from the field the fruit of your labor. 17 Three times in the year all your males shall appear before the Lord GOD.

18 You shall not offer the blood of my sacrifice with anything leavened, or let the fat of my festival remain until the morning.

19 The choicest of the first fruits of your ground you shall bring into the house of the LORD your God.

You shall not boil a kid in its mother's milk.

The Conquest of Canaan Promised

20 I am going to send an angel in front of you, to guard you on the way and to bring you to the place that I have prepared. 21 Be attentive to him and listen to his voice; do not rebel against him, for he will not pardon your transgression; for my name is in him.

22 But if you listen attentively to his voice and do all that I say, then I will be an enemy to your enemies and a foe to your foes.

23 When my angel goes in front of you, and brings you to the Amorites, the Hittites, the Perizzites, the Canaanites, the Hivites, and the Jebusites, and I blot them out, 24 you shall not bow down to their gods, or worship them, or follow their practices, but you shall utterly demolish them and break their pillars in pieces. 25 You shall worship the LORD your God, and I b will bless your bread and your water; and I will take sickness away from among you. 26 No one shall miscarry or be barren in your land; I will fulfill the number of your days. 27 I will send my terror in front of you, and will throw into confusion all the people against whom you shall come, and I will make all your enemies turn their backs to you. 28 And

I will send the pestilence c in front of you, which shall drive out the Hivites, the Canaanites, and the Hittites from before you. 29 I will not drive them out from before you in one year, or the land would become desolate and the wild animals would multiply against you. 30 Little by little I will drive them out from before you, until you have increased and possess the land. 31 I will set your borders from the Red Sea d to the sea of the Philistines, and from the wilderness to the Euphrates; for I will hand over to you the inhabitants of the land, and you shall drive them out before you. 32 You shall make no covenant with them and their gods. 33 They shall not live in your land, or they will make you sin against me; for if you worship their gods, it will surely be a snare to you.

The Blood of the Covenant

24 Then he said to Moses, "Come up to the LORD, you and Aaron, Nadab, and Abihu, and seventy of the elders of Israel, and worship at a distance. 2 Moses alone shall come near the LORD; but the others shall not come near, and the people shall not come up with him."

3 Moses came and told the people all the words of the LORD and all the ordinances; and all the people answered with one voice, and said, "All the words that the LORD has spoken we will do." 4 And Moses wrote down all the words of the LORD. He rose early in the morning, and built an altar at the foot of the mountain, and set up twelve pillars, corresponding to the twelve tribes of Israel. 5 He sent young men of the people of Israel, who offered burnt offerings and sacrificed oxen as offerings of well-being to the LORD. 6 Moses took half of the blood and put it in basins, and half of the blood he dashed against the altar. 7 Then he took the book of the covenant, and read it in the hearing of the people; and they

23.16
Ex 34.22;
Deut 16.13
23.17
Deut 16.16
23.18
Ex 34.25
23.19
Ex 22.29;
Deut 14.21
23.20
Ex 32.34;
15.16,17
23.21
Num 14.11;
Ps 78.40,56;
Num 14.35
23.22
Gen 12.2
23.23
Josh 24.8,
11
23.24
Ex 20.5;
Lev 18.3;
Ex 34.13
23.25
Deut 6.13;
Mt 4.10;
Deut 28.5;
Ex 15.26
23.26
Deut 7.14;
Mal 3.11;
Job 5.26
23.27
Ex 15.14,
16;
Deut 7.23
23.28
Deut 7.20;
Josh 24.12

23.29
Deut 7.22
23.31
Gen 15.18;
Josh 21.44;
24.12,18
23.32
Deut 7.2;
v. 13,24
23.33
Deut 7.1-5,
16
24.1
Lev 10.1,2;
Num 11.16
24.3
v. 7;
Ex 19.8
24.4
Deut 31.9;
Gen 28.18
24.6
Heb 9.18
24.7
Heb 9.19;
v. 3

b Gk Vg: Heb *he* c Or *hornets*: Meaning of Heb uncertain d Or *Sea of Reeds*

said, "All that the LORD has spoken we will do, and we will be obedient." ⁸Moses took the blood and dashed it on the people, and said, "See the blood of the covenant that the LORD has made with you in accordance with all these words."

On the Mountain with God

9 Then Moses and Aaron, Nadab, and Abihu, and seventy of the elders of Israel went up, ¹⁰and they saw the God of Israel. Under his feet there was something like a pavement of sapphire stone, like the very heaven for clearness. ¹¹Gode did not lay his hand on the chief men of the people of Israel; also they beheld God, and they ate and drank.

12 The LORD said to Moses, "Come up to me on the mountain, and wait there; and I will give you the tablets of stone, with the law and the commandment, which I have written for their instruction." ¹³So Moses set out with his assistant Joshua, and Moses went up into the mountain of God. ¹⁴To the elders he had said, "Wait here for us, until we come to you again; for Aaron and Hur are with you; whoever has a dispute may go to them."

15 Then Moses went up on the mountain, and the cloud covered the mountain. ¹⁶The glory of the LORD settled on Mount Sinai, and the cloud covered it for six days; on the seventh day he called to Moses out of the cloud. ¹⁷Now the appearance of the glory of the LORD was like a devouring fire on the top of the mountain in the sight of the people of Israel. ¹⁸Moses entered the cloud, and went up on the mountain. Moses was on the mountain for forty days and forty nights.

Offerings for the Tabernacle

25 The LORD said to Moses: ²Tell the Israelites to take for me an offering; from all whose hearts prompt them to give you shall receive the offering for me. ³This is the offering that you shall receive from them: gold, silver, and

bronze, ⁴blue, purple, and crimson yarns and fine linen, goats' hair, ⁵tanned rams' skins, fine leather,f acacia wood, ⁶oil for the lamps, spices for the anointing oil and for the fragrant incense, ⁷onyx stones and gems to be set in the ephod and for the breastpiece. ⁸And have them make me a sanctuary, so that I may dwell among them. ⁹In accordance with all that I show you concerning the pattern of the tabernacle and of all its furniture, so you shall make it.

The Ark of the Covenant

10 They shall make an ark of acacia wood; it shall be two and a half cubits long, a cubit and a half wide, and a cubit and a half high. ¹¹You shall overlay it with pure gold, inside and outside you shall overlay it, and you shall make a molding of gold upon it all around. ¹²You shall cast four rings of gold for it and put them on its four feet, two rings on the one side of it, and two rings on the other side. ¹³You shall make poles of acacia wood, and overlay them with gold. ¹⁴And you shall put the poles into the rings on the sides of the ark, by which to carry the ark. ¹⁵The poles shall remain in the rings of the ark; they shall not be taken from it. ¹⁶You shall put into the ark the covenantg that I shall give you.

17 Then you shall make a mercy seath of pure gold; two cubits and a half shall be its length, and a cubit and a half its width. ¹⁸You shall make two cherubim of gold; you shall make them of hammered work, at the two ends of the mercy seat.i ¹⁹Make one cherub at the one end, and one cherub at the other; of one piece with the mercy seati you shall make the cherubim at its two ends. ²⁰The cherubim shall spread out their wings above, overshadowing the mercy seati with their wings. They shall face one to another; the faces of the cherubim shall be turned toward

24.8 Heb 9.20; 1 Pet 1.2
24.9 v. 1
24.10 Ezek 1.26; Rev 4.3; Mt 17.2
24.11 Ex 19.21; Gen 32.30; 31.54
24.12 vv. 2,15; Ex 32.15,16
24.13 Ex 17.9-14; 3.1
24.15 Ex 19.9
24.16 Ex 16.10
24.17 Ex 3.2; Deut 4.36; Heb 12.18, 29
24.18 Ex 34.28; Deut 9.9
25.2 Ex 35.5,21; 2 Cor 8.12; 9.7
25.6 Ex 27.20; 30.23,34
25.7 Ex 28.4,6, 15
25.8 Ex 36.1,3,4; Heb 9.1,2; Ex 29.45; Rev 21.3
25.9 v. 40; Acts 7.44; Heb 8.2,5
25.10 Ex 37.1-9
25.16 Deut 31.26; Heb 9.4
25.17 Ex 37.6; Rom 3.25; Heb 9.5
25.20 1 Kings 8.7; Heb 9.5

e Heb He f Meaning of Heb uncertain g Or treaty, or testimony; Heb eduth h Or a cover i Or the cover

the mercy seat.^j ^21 You shall put the mercy seat^j on the top of the ark; and in the ark you shall put the covenant^k that I shall give you. ^22 There I will meet with you, and from above the mercy seat,^j from between the two cherubim that are on the ark of the covenant,^k I will deliver to you all my commands for the Israelites.

The Table for the Bread of the Presence

23 You shall make a table of acacia wood, two cubits long, one cubit wide, and a cubit and a half high. ^24 You shall overlay it with pure gold, and make a molding of gold around it. ^25 You shall make around it a rim a handbreadth wide, and a molding of gold around the rim. ^26 You shall make for it four rings of gold, and fasten the rings to the four corners at its four legs. ^27 The rings that hold the poles used for carrying the table shall be close to the rim. ^28 You shall make the poles of acacia wood, and overlay them with gold, and the table shall be carried with these. ^29 You shall make its plates and dishes for incense, and its flagons and bowls with which to pour drink offerings; you shall make them of pure gold. ^30 And you shall set the bread of the Presence on the table before me always.

The Lampstand

31 You shall make a lampstand of pure gold. The base and the shaft of the lampstand shall be made of hammered work; its cups, its calyxes, and its petals shall be of one piece with it; ^32 and there shall be six branches going out of its sides, three branches of the lampstand out of one side of it and three branches of the lampstand out of the other side of it; ^33 three cups shaped like almond blossoms, each with calyx and petals, on one branch, and three cups shaped like almond blossoms, each with calyx and petals, on the other branch—so for the six branches going out of the lamp-

stand. ^34 On the lampstand itself there shall be four cups shaped like almond blossoms, each with its calyxes and petals. ^35 There shall be a calyx of one piece with it under the first pair of branches, a calyx of one piece with it under the next pair of branches, and a calyx of one piece with it under the last pair of branches—so for the six branches that go out of the lampstand. ^36 Their calyxes and their branches shall be of one piece with it, the whole of it one hammered piece of pure gold. ^37 You shall make the seven lamps for it; and the lamps shall be set up so as to give light on the space in front of it. ^38 Its snuffers and trays shall be of pure gold. ^39 It, and all these utensils, shall be made from a talent of pure gold. ^40 And see that you make them according to the pattern for them, which is being shown you on the mountain.

The Tabernacle

26 Moreover you shall make the tabernacle with ten curtains of fine twisted linen, and blue, purple, and crimson yarns; you shall make them with cherubim skillfully worked into them. ^2 The length of each curtain shall be twenty-eight cubits, and the width of each curtain four cubits; all the curtains shall be of the same size. ^3 Five curtains shall be joined to one another; and the other five curtains shall be joined to one another. ^4 You shall make loops of blue on the edge of the outermost curtain in the first set; and likewise you shall make loops on the edge of the outermost curtain in the second set. ^5 You shall make fifty loops on the one curtain, and you shall make fifty loops on the edge of the curtain that is in the second set; the loops shall be opposite one another. ^6 You shall make fifty clasps of gold, and join the curtains to one another with the clasps, so that the tabernacle may be one whole.

7 You shall also make curtains

25.21
Ex 26.34;
v. 16
25.22
Ex 29.42,
43; 30.6,36;
Num 7.89;
Ps 80.1
25.23
Ex 37.10-16;
Heb 9.2
25.29
Ex 37.16;
Num 4.7
25.30
Lev 24.5-9
25.31
Ex 37.17;
Heb 9.2;
Rev 1.12
25.32
Ex 38.18

25.34
Ex 37.20
25.37
Ex 27.21;
Lev 24.3,4
25.40
Ex 26.30;
Acts 7.44;
Heb 8.5
26.1
Ex 36.8
26.3
Ex 36.10
26.5
Ex 36.12
26.7
Ex 36.14

^i Or *the cover* ^k Or *treaty*, or *testimony*; Heb *eduth*

of goats' hair for a tent over the tabernacle; you shall make eleven curtains. ⁸The length of each curtain shall be thirty cubits, and the width of each curtain four cubits; the eleven curtains shall be of the same size. ⁹You shall join five curtains by themselves, and six curtains by themselves, and the sixth curtain you shall double over at the front of the tent. ¹⁰You shall make fifty loops on the edge of the curtain that is outermost in one set, and fifty loops on the edge of the curtain that is outermost in the second set.

11 You shall make fifty clasps of bronze, and put the clasps into the loops, and join the tent together, so that it may be one whole. ¹²The part that remains of the curtains of the tent, the half curtain that remains, shall hang over the back of the tabernacle. ¹³The cubit on the one side, and the cubit on the other side, of what remains in the length of the curtains of the tent, shall hang over the sides of the tabernacle, on this side and that side, to cover it. ¹⁴You shall make for the tent a covering of tanned rams' skins and an outer covering of fine leather.[1]

The Framework

15 You shall make upright frames of acacia wood for the tabernacle. ¹⁶Ten cubits shall be the length of a frame, and a cubit and a half the width of each frame. ¹⁷There shall be two pegs in each frame to fit the frames together; you shall make these for all the frames of the tabernacle. ¹⁸You shall make the frames for the tabernacle: twenty frames for the south side; ¹⁹and you shall make forty bases of silver under the twenty frames, two bases under the first frame for its two pegs, and two bases under the next frame for its two pegs; ²⁰and for the second side of the tabernacle, on the north side twenty frames, ²¹and their forty bases of silver, two bases under the first frame, and two bases under the next frame; ²²and for the rear of

the tabernacle westward you shall make six frames. ²³You shall make two frames for corners of the tabernacle in the rear; ²⁴they shall be separate beneath, but joined at the top, at the first ring; it shall be the same with both of them; they shall form the two corners. ²⁵And so there shall be eight frames, with their bases of silver, sixteen bases; two bases under the first frame, and two bases under the next frame.

26 You shall make bars of acacia wood, five for the frames of the one side of the tabernacle, ²⁷and five bars for the frames of the other side of the tabernacle, and five bars for the frames of the side of the tabernacle at the rear westward. ²⁸The middle bar, halfway up the frames, shall pass through from end to end. ²⁹You shall overlay the frames with gold, and shall make their rings of gold to hold the bars; and you shall overlay the bars with gold. ³⁰Then you shall erect the tabernacle according to the plan for it that you were shown on the mountain.

The Curtain

31 You shall make a curtain of blue, purple, and crimson yarns, and of fine twisted linen; it shall be made with cherubim skillfully worked into it. ³²You shall hang it on four pillars of acacia overlaid with gold, which have hooks of gold and rest on four bases of silver. ³³You shall hang the curtain under the clasps, and bring the ark of the covenant[m] in there, within the curtain; and the curtain shall separate for you the holy place from the most holy. ³⁴You shall put the mercy seat[n] on the ark of the covenant[m] in the most holy place. ³⁵You shall set the table outside the curtain, and the lampstand on the south side of the tabernacle opposite the table; and you shall put the table on the north side.

36 You shall make a screen for the entrance of the tent, of blue, purple, and crimson yarns, and of

26.11
Ex 36.18
26.14
Ex 36.19
26.15
Ex 36.20
26.20
Ex 36.23

26.25
Ex 36.30
26.30
Ex 25.9,40;
27.8;
Acts 7.44;
Heb 8.5
26.31
Ex 36.35;
Mt 27.51;
Heb 9.3
26.33
Ex 25.16;
40.21;
Lev 16.2;
Heb 9.2,3
26.34
Ex 25.21;
40.20;
Heb 9.5
26.35
Ex 40.22,
24; Heb 9.2
26.36
Ex 36.37

[1] Meaning of Heb uncertain [m] Or *treaty*, or *testimony*; Heb *eduth* [n] Or *the cover*

fine twisted linen, embroidered with needlework. [37] You shall make for the screen five pillars of acacia, and overlay them with gold; their hooks shall be of gold, and you shall cast five bases of bronze for them.

The Altar of Burnt Offering

27 You shall make the altar of acacia wood, five cubits long and five cubits wide; the altar shall be square, and it shall be three cubits high. [2] You shall make horns for it on its four corners; its horns shall be of one piece with it, and you shall overlay it with bronze. [3] You shall make pots for it to receive its ashes, and shovels and basins and forks and firepans; you shall make all its utensils of bronze. [4] You shall also make for it a grating, a network of bronze; and on the net you shall make four bronze rings at its four corners. [5] You shall set it under the ledge of the altar so that the net shall extend halfway down the altar. [6] You shall make poles for the altar, poles of acacia wood, and overlay them with bronze; [7] the poles shall be put through the rings, so that the poles shall be on the two sides of the altar when it is carried. [8] You shall make it hollow, with boards. They shall be made just as you were shown on the mountain.

The Court and Its Hangings

[9] You shall make the court of the tabernacle. On the south side the court shall have hangings of fine twisted linen one hundred cubits long for that side; [10] its twenty pillars and their twenty bases shall be of bronze, but the hooks of the pillars and their bands shall be of silver. [11] Likewise for its length on the north side there shall be hangings one hundred cubits long, their pillars twenty and their bases twenty, of bronze, but the hooks of the pillars and their bands shall be of silver. [12] For the width of the court on the west side there shall be fifty cubits of hangings, with ten pillars and ten bases. [13] The width

of the court on the front to the east shall be fifty cubits. [14] There shall be fifteen cubits of hangings on the one side, with three pillars and three bases. [15] There shall be fifteen cubits of hangings on the other side, with three pillars and three bases. [16] For the gate of the court there shall be a screen twenty cubits long, of blue, purple, and crimson yarns, and of fine twisted linen, embroidered with needlework; it shall have four pillars and with them four bases. [17] All the pillars around the court shall be banded with silver; their hooks shall be of silver, and their bases of bronze. [18] The length of the court shall be one hundred cubits, the width fifty, and the height five cubits, with hangings of fine twisted linen and bases of bronze. [19] All the utensils of the tabernacle for every use, and all its pegs and all the pegs of the court, shall be of bronze.

The Oil for the Lamp

[20] You shall further command the Israelites to bring you pure oil of beaten olives for the light, so that a lamp may be set up to burn regularly. [21] In the tent of meeting, outside the curtain that is before the covenant,º Aaron and his sons shall tend it from evening to morning before the LORD. It shall be a perpetual ordinance to be observed throughout their generations by the Israelites.

Vestments for the Priesthood

28 Then bring near to you your brother Aaron, and his sons with him, from among the Israelites, to serve me as priests—Aaron and Aaron's sons, Nadab and Abihu, Eleazar and Ithamar. [2] You shall make sacred vestments for the glorious adornment of your brother Aaron. [3] And you shall speak to all who have ability, whom I have endowed with skill, that they make Aaron's vestments to consecrate him for my priesthood. [4] These are the vestments that they shall make: a breastpiece, an

º Or *treaty,* or *testimony;* Heb *eduth*

26.37
Ex 36.38
27.1
Ex 38.1;
Ezek 43.13
27.3
Num 4.14
27.8
Ex 25.40;
26.30
27.9
Ex 38.9
27.10
Ex 38.17

27.14
Ex 38.15
27.16
Ex 36.37
27.20
Lev 24.2
27.21
Ex 26.31,
33; 30.8;
28.43;
Lev 3.17;
16.34
28.1
Num 18.7;
Heb 5.1,4
28.2
Ex 29.5,29;
31.10
28.3
Ex 31.3,6
28.4
see vv. 6,15,
31,39

ephod, a robe, a checkered tunic, a turban, and a sash. When they make these sacred vestments for your brother Aaron and his sons to serve me as priests, ⁵they shall use gold, blue, purple, and crimson yarns, and fine linen.

The Ephod

6 They shall make the ephod of gold, of blue, purple, and crimson yarns, and of fine twisted linen, skillfully worked. ⁷It shall have two shoulder-pieces attached to its two edges, so that it may be joined together. ⁸The decorated band on it shall be of the same workmanship and materials, of gold, of blue, purple, and crimson yarns, and of fine twisted linen. ⁹You shall take two onyx stones, and engrave on them the names of the sons of Israel, ¹⁰six of their names on the one stone, and the names of the remaining six on the other stone, in the order of their birth. ¹¹As a gem-cutter engraves signets, so you shall engrave the two stones with the names of the sons of Israel; you shall mount them in settings of gold filigree. ¹²You shall set the two stones on the shoulder-pieces of the ephod, as stones of remembrance for the sons of Israel; and Aaron shall bear their names before the LORD on his two shoulders for remembrance. ¹³You shall make settings of gold filigree, ¹⁴and two chains of pure gold, twisted like cords; and you shall attach the corded chains to the settings.

The Breastplate

15 You shall make a breastpiece of judgment, in skilled work; you shall make it in the style of the ephod; of gold, of blue and purple and crimson yarns, and of fine twisted linen you shall make it. ¹⁶It shall be square and doubled, a span in length and a span in width. ¹⁷You shall set in it four rows of stones. A row of carnelian,ᵖ chrysolite, and emerald shall be the first row; ¹⁸and the second row a turquoise, a sapphire�۹ and a moonstone; ¹⁹and the third row a jacinth, an agate, and an amethyst; ²⁰and the fourth row a beryl, an onyx, and a jasper; they shall be set in gold filigree. ²¹There shall be twelve stones with names corresponding to the names of the sons of Israel; they shall be like signets, each engraved with its name, for the twelve tribes. ²²You shall make for the breastpiece chains of pure gold, twisted like cords; ²³and you shall make for the breastpiece two rings of gold, and put the two rings on the two edges of the breastpiece. ²⁴You shall put the two cords of gold in the two rings at the edges of the breastpiece; ²⁵the two ends of the two cords you shall attach to the two settings, and so attach it in front to the shoulder-pieces of the ephod. ²⁶You shall make two rings of gold, and put them at the two ends of the breastpiece, on its inside edge next to the ephod. ²⁷You shall make two rings of gold, and attach them in front to the lower part of the two shoulder-pieces of the ephod, at its joining above the decorated band of the ephod. ²⁸The breastpiece shall be bound by its rings to the rings of the ephod with a blue cord, so that it may lie on the decorated band of the ephod, and so that the breastpiece shall not come loose from the ephod. ²⁹So Aaron shall bear the names of the sons of Israel in the breastpiece of judgment on his heart when he goes into the holy place, for a continual remembrance before the LORD. ³⁰In the breastpiece of judgment you shall put the Urim and the Thummim, and they shall be on Aaron's heart when he goes in before the LORD; thus Aaron shall bear the judgment of the Israelites on his heart before the LORD continually.

Other Priestly Vestments

31 You shall make the robe of the ephod all of blue. ³²It shall

28.6
Ex 39.2
28.9
1 Cor 9.22
28.12
v. 29;
Ex 39.7
28.15
Ex 39.8
28.17
Ex 39.10ff

28.21
Ex 39.14
28.24
Ex 39.17
28.26
Ex 39.17
28.29
v. 12
28.30
Lev 8.8;
Num 27.21
28.31
Ex 39.22

ᵖ The identity of several of these stones is uncertain ۹Or *lapis lazuli*

have an opening for the head in the middle of it, with a woven binding around the opening, like the opening in a coat of mail,ʳ so that it may not be torn. ³³On its lower hem you shall make pomegranates of blue, purple, and crimson yarns, all around the lower hem, with bells of gold between them all around—³⁴a golden bell and a pomegranate alternating all around the lower hem of the robe. ³⁵Aaron shall wear it when he ministers, and its sound shall be heard when he goes into the holy place before the LORD, and when he comes out, so that he may not die.

36 You shall make a rosette of pure gold, and engrave on it, like the engraving of a signet, "Holy to the LORD." ³⁷You shall fasten it on the turban with a blue cord; it shall be on the front of the turban. ³⁸It shall be on Aaron's forehead, and Aaron shall take on himself any guilt incurred in the holy offering that the Israelites consecrate as their sacred donations; it shall always be on his forehead, in order that they may find favor before the LORD.

39 You shall make the checkered tunic of fine linen, and you shall make a turban of fine linen, and you shall make a sash embroidered with needlework.

40 For Aaron's sons you shall make tunics and sashes and headdresses; you shall make them for their glorious adornment. ⁴¹You shall put them on your brother Aaron, and on his sons with him, and shall anoint them and ordain them and consecrate them, so that they may serve me as priests. ⁴²You shall make for them linen undergarments to cover their naked flesh; they shall reach from the hips to the thighs; ⁴³Aaron and his sons shall wear them when they go into the tent of meeting, or when they come near the altar to minister in the holy place; or they will bring guilt on themselves and die. This shall be a perpetual ordinance for him and for his descendants after him.

28.36
Ex 39.30,31
28.38
v. 43;
Lev 10.17;
Num 18.1;
Heb 9.28;
1 Pet 2.24
28.40
v. 4;
Ex 39.27-29
28.41
Ex 29.7-9;
30.30;
Lev ch. 8;
Heb 7.28
28.42
Ex 39.28
28.43
Ex 20.26;
Lev 20.19,
20;
Ex 27.21;
Lev 17.7

29.1
Lev 8.2
29.2
Lev 6.19-23
29.4
Ex 40.12;
Heb 10.22
29.5
Ex 28.2,8
29.6
Lev 8.9
29.7
Lev 8.12
29.8
Lev 8.13
29.9
Num 18.7;
Ex 28.41
29.10
Lev 1.4;
8.14
29.12
Lev 8.15;
Ex 27.2
29.13
Lev 3.3
29.14
Lev 4.11,12,
21

The Ordination of the Priests

29 Now this is what you shall do to them to consecrate them, so that they may serve me as priests. Take one young bull and two rams without blemish, ²and unleavened bread, unleavened cakes mixed with oil, and unleavened wafers spread with oil. You shall make them of choice wheat flour. ³You shall put them in one basket and bring them in the basket, and bring the bull and the two rams. ⁴You shall bring Aaron and his sons to the entrance of the tent of meeting, and wash them with water. ⁵Then you shall take the vestments, and put on Aaron the tunic and the robe of the ephod, and the ephod, and the breastpiece, and gird him with the decorated band of the ephod; ⁶and you shall set the turban on his head, and put the holy diadem on the turban. ⁷You shall take the anointing oil, and pour it on his head and anoint him. ⁸Then you shall bring his sons, and put tunics on them, ⁹and you shall gird them with sashesˢ and tie headdresses on them; and the priesthood shall be theirs by a perpetual ordinance. You shall then ordain Aaron and his sons.

10 You shall bring the bull in front of the tent of meeting. Aaron and his sons shall lay their hands on the head of the bull, ¹¹and you shall slaughter the bull before the LORD, at the entrance of the tent of meeting, ¹²and shall take some of the blood of the bull and put it on the horns of the altar with your finger, and all the rest of the blood you shall pour out at the base of the altar. ¹³You shall take all the fat that covers the entrails, and the appendage of the liver, and the two kidneys with the fat that is on them, and turn them into smoke on the altar. ¹⁴But the flesh of the bull, and its skin, and its dung, you shall burn with fire outside the camp; it is a sin offering.

ʳ Meaning of Heb uncertain ˢ Gk: Heb sashes, Aaron and his sons

15 Then you shall take one of the rams, and Aaron and his sons shall lay their hands on the head of the ram, [16] and you shall slaughter the ram, and shall take its blood and dash it against all sides of the altar. [17] Then you shall cut the ram into its parts, and wash its entrails and its legs, and put them with its parts and its head, [18] and turn the whole ram into smoke on the altar; it is a burnt offering to the LORD; it is a pleasing odor, an offering by fire to the LORD.

19 You shall take the other ram; and Aaron and his sons shall lay their hands on the head of the ram, [20] and you shall slaughter the ram, and take some of its blood and put it on the lobe of Aaron's right ear and on the lobes of the right ears of his sons, and on the thumbs of their right hands, and on the big toes of their right feet, and dash the rest of the blood against all sides of the altar. [21] Then you shall take some of the blood that is on the altar, and some of the anointing oil, and sprinkle it on Aaron and his vestments and on his sons and his sons' vestments with him; then he and his vestments shall be holy, as well as his sons and his sons' vestments.

22 You shall also take the fat of the ram, the fat tail, the fat that covers the entrails, the appendage of the liver, the two kidneys with the fat that is on them, and the right thigh (for it is a ram of ordination), [23] and one loaf of bread, one cake of bread made with oil, and one wafer, out of the basket of unleavened bread that is before the LORD; [24] and you shall place all these on the palms of Aaron and on the palms of his sons, and raise them as an elevation offering before the LORD. [25] Then you shall take them from their hands, and turn them into smoke on the altar on top of the burnt offering of pleasing odor before the LORD; it is an offering by fire to the LORD.

26 You shall take the breast of the ram of Aaron's ordination and raise it as an elevation offering be-

fore the LORD; and it shall be your portion. [27] You shall consecrate the breast that was raised as an elevation offering and the thigh that was raised as an elevation offering from the ram of ordination, from that which belonged to Aaron and his sons. [28] These things shall be a perpetual ordinance for Aaron and his sons from the Israelites, for this is an offering; and it shall be an offering by the Israelites from their sacrifice of offerings of well-being, their offering to the LORD.

29 The sacred vestments of Aaron shall be passed on to his sons after him; they shall be anointed in them and ordained in them. [30] The son who is priest in his place shall wear them seven days, when he comes into the tent of meeting to minister in the holy place.

31 You shall take the ram of ordination, and boil its flesh in a holy place; [32] and Aaron and his sons shall eat the flesh of the ram and the bread that is in the basket, at the entrance of the tent of meeting. [33] They themselves shall eat the food by which atonement is made, to ordain and consecrate them, but no one else shall eat of them, because they are holy. [34] If any of the flesh for the ordination, or of the bread, remains until the morning, then you shall burn the remainder with fire; it shall not be eaten, because it is holy.

35 Thus you shall do to Aaron and to his sons, just as I have commanded you; through seven days you shall ordain them. [36] Also every day you shall offer a bull as a sin offering for atonement. Also you shall offer a sin offering for the altar, when you make atonement for it, and shall anoint it, to consecrate it. [37] Seven days you shall make atonement for the altar, and consecrate it, and the altar shall be most holy; whatever touches the altar shall become holy.

The Daily Offerings

38 Now this is what you shall offer on the altar: two lambs a year old regularly each day. [39] One lamb

29.18
Gen 8.21
29.21
Ex 30.25,
31; v. 1;
Heb 9.22
29.23
Lev 8.26
29.24
Lev 7.30
29.25
Lev 8.28
29.26
Lev 8.29

29.27
Lev 7.31,34;
Deut 18.3
29.28
Lev 10.15
29.29
Num 20.26,
28; 18.8
29.30
Num 20.28;
Lev 8.35;
9.1,8
29.31
Lev 8.31
29.32
Mt 12.4
29.33
Lev 10.14,
15,17; 22.10
29.34
Lev 8.32
29.35
Lev 8.33
29.36
Heb 10.11;
Ex 40.10
29.37
Ex 40.10;
Mt 23.19
29.38
Num 28.3

you shall offer in the morning, and the other lamb you shall offer in the evening; 40 and with the first lamb one-tenth of a measure of choice flour mixed with one-fourth of a hin of beaten oil, and one-fourth of a hin of wine for a drink offering. 41 And the other lamb you shall offer in the evening, and shall offer with it a grain offering and its drink offering, as in the morning, for a pleasing odor, an offering by fire to the Lord. 42 It shall be a regular burnt offering throughout your generations at the entrance of the tent of meeting before the Lord, where I will meet with you, to speak to you there. 43 I will meet with the Israelites there, and it shall be sanctified by my glory; 44 I will consecrate the tent of meeting and the altar; Aaron also and his sons I will consecrate, to serve me as priests. 45 I will dwell among the Israelites, and I will be their God. 46 And they shall know that I am the Lord their God, who brought them out of the land of Egypt that I might dwell among them; I am the Lord their God.

The Altar of Incense

30 You shall make an altar on which to offer incense; you shall make it of acacia wood. 2 It shall be one cubit long, and one cubit wide; it shall be square, and shall be two cubits high; its horns shall be of one piece with it. 3 You shall overlay it with pure gold, its top, and its sides all around and its horns; and you shall make for it a molding of gold all around. 4 And you shall make two golden rings for it; under its molding on two opposite sides of it you shall make them, and they shall hold the poles with which to carry it. 5 You shall make the poles of acacia wood, and overlay them with gold. 6 You shall place it in front of the curtain that is above the ark of the covenant,[t] in front of the mercy seat[u] that is over the covenant,[t] where I will meet with you. 7 Aaron shall offer fragrant incense on it; every morning when he dresses the lamps he

shall offer it, 8 and when Aaron sets up the lamps in the evening, he shall offer it, a regular incense offering before the Lord throughout your generations. 9 You shall not offer unholy incense on it, or a burnt offering, or a grain offering; and you shall not pour a drink offering on it. 10 Once a year Aaron shall perform the rite of atonement on its horns. Throughout your generations he shall perform the atonement for it once a year with the blood of the atoning sin offering. It is most holy to the Lord.

The Half Shekel for the Sanctuary

11 The Lord spoke to Moses: 12 When you take a census of the Israelites to register them, at registration all of them shall give a ransom for their lives to the Lord, so that no plague may come upon them for being registered. 13 This is what each one who is registered shall give: half a shekel according to the shekel of the sanctuary (the shekel is twenty gerahs), half a shekel as an offering to the Lord. 14 Each one who is registered, from twenty years old and upward, shall give the Lord's offering. 15 The rich shall not give more, and the poor shall not give less, than the half shekel, when you bring this offering to the Lord to make atonement for your lives. 16 You shall take the atonement money from the Israelites and shall designate it for the service of the tent of meeting; before the Lord it will be a reminder to the Israelites of the ransom given for your lives.

The Bronze Basin

17 The Lord spoke to Moses: 18 You shall make a bronze basin with a bronze stand for washing. You shall put it between the tent of meeting and the altar, and you shall put water in it; 19 with the water[v] Aaron and his sons shall wash their hands and their feet. 20 When they go into the tent of meeting, or

29.42
Ex 30.8
29.43
1 Kings 8.11
29.44
Lev 21.15
29.45
Ex 25.8;
Lev 26.12;
Rev 21.3
29.46
Ex 20.2
30.1
Ex 37.25
30.6
Ex 25.21,22
30.7
vv. 34,35;
Ex 27.21

30.9
Lev 10.1
30.10
Lev 16.18
30.12
Num 1.2,5;
31.50;
Mt 20.28;
2 Sam 24.15
30.13
Mt 17.24
30.15
Prov 22.2
30.16
Ex 38.25;
Num 16.40
30.18
Ex 38.8;
40.7,30
30.19
Ex 40.31,32

t Or treaty, or testimony; Heb eduth
u Or the cover　v Heb it

when they come near the altar to minister, to make an offering by fire to the LORD, they shall wash with water, so that they may not die. 21 They shall wash their hands and their feet, so that they may not die: it shall be a perpetual ordinance for them, for him and for his descendants throughout their generations.

The Anointing Oil and Incense

22 The LORD spoke to Moses: 23 Take the finest spices: of liquid myrrh five hundred shekels, and of sweet-smelling cinnamon half as much, that is, two hundred fifty, and two hundred fifty of aromatic cane, 24 and five hundred of cassia—measured by the sanctuary shekel—and a hin of olive oil; 25 and you shall make of these a sacred anointing oil blended as by the perfumer; it shall be a holy anointing oil. 26 With it you shall anoint the tent of meeting and the ark of the covenant,w 27 and the table and all its utensils, and the lampstand and its utensils, and the altar of incense, 28 and the altar of burnt offering with all its utensils, and the basin with its stand; 29 you shall consecrate them, so that they may be most holy; whatever touches them will become holy. 30 You shall anoint Aaron and his sons, and consecrate them, in order that they may serve me as priests. 31 You shall say to the Israelites, "This shall be my holy anointing oil throughout your generations. 32 It shall not be used in any ordinary anointing of the body, and you shall make no other like it in composition; it is holy, and it shall be holy to you. 33 Whoever compounds any like it or whoever puts any of it on an unqualified person shall be cut off from the people."

34 The LORD said to Moses: Take sweet spices, stacte, and onycha, and galbanum, sweet spices with pure frankincense (an equal part of each), 35 and make an incense blended as by the perfumer, seasoned with salt, pure and holy;

36 and you shall beat some of it into powder, and put part of it before the covenantw in the tent of meeting where I shall meet with you; it shall be for you most holy. 37 When you make incense according to this composition, you shall not make it for yourselves; it shall be regarded by you as holy to the LORD. 38 Whoever makes any like it to use as perfume shall be cut off from the people.

Bezalel and Oholiab

31 The LORD spoke to Moses: 2 See, I have called by name Bezalel son of Uri son of Hur, of the tribe of Judah: 3 and I have filled him with divine spirit,x with ability, intelligence, and knowledge in every kind of craft, 4 to devise artistic designs, to work in gold, silver, and bronze, 5 in cutting stones for setting, and in carving wood, in every kind of craft. 6 Moreover, I have appointed with him Oholiab son of Ahisamach, of the tribe of Dan; and I have given skill to all the skillful, so that they may make all that I have commanded you: 7 the tent of meeting, and the ark of the covenant,w and the mercy seaty that is on it, and all the furnishings of the tent, 8 the table and its utensils, and the pure lampstand with all its utensils, and the altar of incense, 9 and the altar of burnt offering with all its utensils, and the basin with its stand, 10 and the finely worked vestments, the holy vestments for the priest Aaron and the vestments of his sons, for their service as priests, 11 and the anointing oil and the fragrant incense for the holy place. They shall do just as I have commanded you.

The Sabbath Law

12 The LORD said to Moses: 13 You yourself are to speak to the Israelites: "You shall keep my sabbaths, for this is a sign between me and you throughout your generations, given in order that you may know that I, the LORD, sanctify you.

30.21
Ex 28.43
30.25
Ex 37.29;
40.9
30.26
Lev 8.10
30.29
Ex 29.37
30.30
Lev 8.12,30
30.32
vv. 25,37
30.33
v. 38;
Ex 12.15
30.35
v. 25

30.36
Ex 29.42;
Lev 16.2;
v. 32;
Ex 29.37;
Lev 2.3
31.2
Ex 35.30-36.1
31.6
Ex 35.34
31.7
Ex 36.8;
37.1,6
31.8
Ex 37.10,17
31.11
Ex 30.25,
31; 37.29;
30.34
31.13
Lev 19.3,30;
Ezek 20.12,
20

w Or treaty, or testimony; Heb eduth
x Or with the spirit of God y Or the cover

¹⁴You shall keep the sabbath, because it is holy for you; everyone who profanes it shall be put to death; whoever does any work on it shall be cut off from among the people. ¹⁵Six days shall work be done, but the seventh day is a sabbath of solemn rest, holy to the LORD; whoever does any work on the sabbath day shall be put to death. ¹⁶Therefore the Israelites shall keep the sabbath, observing the sabbath throughout their generations, as a perpetual covenant. ¹⁷It is a sign forever between me and the people of Israel that in six days the LORD made heaven and earth, and on the seventh day he rested, and was refreshed."

The Two Tablets of the Covenant

18 When God[z] finished speaking with Moses on Mount Sinai, he gave him the two tablets of the covenant,[a] tablets of stone, written with the finger of God.

The Golden Calf

32 When the people saw that Moses delayed to come down from the mountain, the people gathered around Aaron, and said to him, "Come, make gods for us, who shall go before us; as for this Moses, the man who brought us up out of the land of Egypt, we do not know what has become of him." ²Aaron said to them, "Take off the gold rings that are on the ears of your wives, your sons, and your daughters, and bring them to me." ³So all the people took off the gold rings from their ears, and brought them to Aaron. ⁴He took the gold from them, formed it in a mold,[b] and cast an image of a calf; and they said, "These are your gods, O Israel, who brought you up out of the land of Egypt!" ⁵When Aaron saw this, he built an altar before it; and Aaron made proclamation and said, "Tomorrow shall be a festival to the LORD." ⁶They rose early the next day, and offered burnt offerings and brought sacrifices of well-being; and the people

sat down to eat and drink, and rose up to revel.

7 The LORD said to Moses, "Go down at once! Your people, whom you brought up out of the land of Egypt, have acted perversely; ⁸they have been quick to turn aside from the way that I commanded them; they have cast for themselves an image of a calf, and have worshiped it and sacrificed to it, and said, 'These are your gods, O Israel, who brought you up out of the land of Egypt!' " ⁹The LORD said to Moses, "I have seen this people, how stiff-necked they are. ¹⁰Now let me alone, so that my wrath may burn hot against them and I may consume them; and of you I will make a great nation."

11 But Moses implored the LORD his God, and said, "O LORD, why does your wrath burn hot against your people, whom you brought out of the land of Egypt with great power and with a mighty hand? ¹²Why should the Egyptians say, 'It was with evil intent that he brought them out to kill them in the mountains, and to consume them from the face of the earth'? Turn from your fierce wrath; change your mind and do not bring disaster on your people. ¹³Remember Abraham, Isaac, and Israel, your servants, how you swore to them by your own self, saying to them, 'I will multiply your descendants like the stars of heaven, and all this land that I have promised I will give to your descendants, and they shall inherit it forever.' " ¹⁴And the LORD changed his mind about the disaster that he planned to bring on his people.

15 Then Moses turned and went down from the mountain, carrying the two tablets of the covenant[a] in his hands, tablets that were written on both sides, written on the front and on the back. ¹⁶The tablets were the work of God, and the writing was the writing of God, engraved upon the tablets. ¹⁷When

31.14
Ex 35.2;
Num 15.32,
35
31.15
Ex 16.23;
20.9,10
31.17
v. 13;
Gen 2.2,3
31.18
Ex 24.12;
32.15,16;
34.1,28
32.1
Ex 24.18;
Deut 9.9;
Acts 7.40;
Ex 13.21
32.2
Ex 35.22
32.4
Deut 9.16;
Acts 7.41
32.6
1 Cor 10.7

32.7
Deut 9.12;
Dan 9.24;
Gen 6.11,12
32.8
Ex 20.3,4,
23;
1 Kings 12.28
32.9
Num 14.11-20;
Ex 33.3,5;
34.9;
Acts 7.31
32.10
Deut 9.14;
Num 14.12
32.11
Deut 9.18
32.12
Num 14.13;
Deut 9.28;
v. 14
32.13
Gen 22.16;
Heb 6.13;
Gen 12.7;
13.15;
Ex 13.5
32.14
Ps 106.45
32.15
Deut 9.15
32.16
Ex 31.18

[z] Heb *he* [a] Or *treaty*, or *testimony*; Heb *eduth* [b] Or *fashioned it with a graving tool*; Meaning of Heb uncertain

Joshua heard the noise of the people as they shouted, he said to Moses, "There is a noise of war in the camp." [18] But he said,

"It is not the sound made by
 victors,
or the sound made by losers;
it is the sound of revelers
 that I hear."

[19] As soon as he came near the camp and saw the calf and the dancing, Moses' anger burned hot, and he threw the tablets from his hands and broke them at the foot of the mountain. [20] He took the calf that they had made, burned it with fire, ground it to powder, scattered it on the water, and made the Israelites drink it.

21 Moses said to Aaron, "What did this people do to you that you have brought so great a sin upon them?" [22] And Aaron said, "Do not let the anger of my lord burn hot; you know the people, that they are bent on evil. [23] They said to me, 'Make us gods, who shall go before us; as for this Moses, the man who brought us up out of the land of Egypt, we do not know what has become of him.' [24] So I said to them, 'Whoever has gold, take it off'; so they gave it to me, and I threw it into the fire, and out came this calf!"

25 When Moses saw that the people were running wild (for Aaron had let them run wild, to the derision of their enemies), [26] then Moses stood in the gate of the camp, and said, "Who is on the LORD's side? Come to me!" And all the sons of Levi gathered around him. [27] He said to them, "Thus says the LORD, the God of Israel, 'Put your sword on your side, each of you! Go back and forth from gate to gate throughout the camp, and each of you kill your brother, your friend, and your neighbor.' " [28] The sons of Levi did as Moses commanded, and about three thousand of the people fell on that day. [29] Moses said, "Today you have ordained yourselves[c] for the service of the LORD, each one at the cost of a son or a brother, and so have

brought a blessing on yourselves this day."

30 On the next day Moses said to the people, "You have sinned a great sin. But now I will go up to the LORD; perhaps I can make atonement for your sin." [31] So Moses returned to the LORD and said, "Alas, this people has sinned a great sin; they have made for themselves gods of gold. [32] But now, if you will only forgive their sin—but if not, blot me out of the book that you have written." [33] But the LORD said to Moses, "Whoever has sinned against me I will blot out of my book. [34] But now go, lead the people to the place about which I have spoken to you; see, my angel shall go in front of you. Nevertheless, when the day comes for punishment, I will punish them for their sin."

35 Then the LORD sent a plague on the people, because they made the calf—the one that Aaron made.

The Command to Leave Sinai

33 The LORD said to Moses, "Go, leave this place, you and the people whom you have brought up out of the land of Egypt, and go to the land of which I swore to Abraham, Isaac, and Jacob, saying, 'To your descendants I will give it.' [2] I will send an angel before you, and I will drive out the Canaanites, the Amorites, the Hittites, the Perizzites, the Hivites, and the Jebusites. [3] Go up to a land flowing with milk and honey; but I will not go up among you, or I would consume you on the way, for you are a stiff-necked people."

4 When the people heard these harsh words, they mourned, and no one put on ornaments. [5] For the LORD had said to Moses, "Say to the Israelites, 'You are a stiff-necked people; if for a single moment I should go up among you, I would consume you. So now take off your ornaments, and I will decide what to do to you.' " [6] Therefore the Isra-

32.19 Deut 9.16, 17
32.20 Deut 9.21
32.21 Gen 26.10
32.22 Deut 9.24
32.23 v. 1
32.24 v. 4
32.27 Num 25.7-13; Deut 33.9

32.30 1 Sam 12.20, 23; 2 Sam 16.12; Num 25.13
32.31 Deut 9.18; Ex 20.23
32.32 Ps 69.28; Rom 9.3; Dan 12.1; Rev 3.5; 13.8; 17.8; 21.27
32.33 Deut 29.20; Ps 9.5
32.34 Ex 3.17; 23.20; Ps 99.8
32.35 vv. 4,24,28
33.1 Ex 32.7,13; Gen 12.7
33.2 Ex 32.34; 23.27-31
33.3 Ex 3.8,17; 32.9,10
33.4 Num 14.1, 39
33.5 v. 3

c Gk Vg Compare Tg: Heb *Today ordain yourselves*

elites stripped themselves of their ornaments, from Mount Horeb onward.

The Tent outside the Camp

7 Now Moses used to take the tent and pitch it outside the camp, far off from the camp; he called it the tent of meeting. And everyone who sought the LORD would go out to the tent of meeting, which was outside the camp. ⁸Whenever Moses went out to the tent, all the people would rise and stand, each of them, at the entrance of their tents and watch Moses until he had gone into the tent. ⁹When Moses entered the tent, the pillar of cloud would descend and stand at the entrance of the tent, and the LORD would speak with Moses. ¹⁰When all the people saw the pillar of cloud standing at the entrance of the tent, all the people would rise and bow down, all of them, at the entrance of their tent. ¹¹Thus the LORD used to speak to Moses face to face, as one speaks to a friend. Then he would return to the camp; but his young assistant, Joshua son of Nun, would not leave the tent.

Moses' Intercession

12 Moses said to the LORD, "See, you have said to me, 'Bring up this people'; but you have not let me know whom you will send with me. Yet you have said, 'I know you by name, and you have also found favor in my sight.' ¹³Now if I have found favor in your sight, show me your ways, so that I may know you and find favor in your sight. Consider too that this nation is your people." ¹⁴He said, "My presence will go with you, and I will give you rest." ¹⁵And he said to him, "If your presence will not go, do not carry us up from here. ¹⁶For how shall it be known that I have found favor in your sight, I and your people, unless you go with us? In this way, we shall be distinct, I and your people, from every people on the face of the earth."

17 The LORD said to Moses, "I will do the very thing that you have

asked; for you have found favor in my sight, and I know you by name." ¹⁸Moses said, "Show me your glory, I pray." ¹⁹And he said, "I will make all my goodness pass before you, and will proclaim before you the name, 'The LORD';ᵈ and I will be gracious to whom I will be gracious, and will show mercy on whom I will show mercy. ²⁰But," he said, "you cannot see my face; for no one shall see me and live." ²¹And the LORD continued, "See, there is a place by me where you shall stand on the rock; ²²and while my glory passes by I will put you in a cleft of the rock, and I will cover you with my hand until I have passed by; ²³then I will take away my hand, and you shall see my back; but my face shall not be seen."

Moses Makes New Tablets

34 The LORD said to Moses, "Cut two tablets of stone like the former ones, and I will write on the tablets the words that were on the former tablets, which you broke. ²Be ready in the morning, and come up in the morning to Mount Sinai and present yourself there to me, on the top of the mountain. ³No one shall come up with you, and do not let anyone be seen throughout all the mountain; and do not let flocks or herds graze in front of that mountain." ⁴So Moses cut two tablets of stone like the former ones; and he rose early in the morning and went up on Mount Sinai, as the LORD had commanded him, and took in his hand the two tablets of stone. ⁵The LORD descended in the cloud and stood with him there, and proclaimed the name, "The LORD."ᵈ ⁶The LORD passed before him, and proclaimed,

"The LORD, the LORD,
a God merciful and gracious,
 slow to anger,
and abounding in steadfast
 love and faithfulness,

ᵈ Heb *YHWH*; see note at 3.15

33.7
Ex 29.42, 43;
Deut 4.29
33.8
Num 16.27
33.9
Ex 25.22;
31.18;
Ps 99.7
33.11
Num 12.8;
Deut 34.10;
Ex 24.13
33.12
Ex 32.34;
v. 17;
Jer 1.5;
Jn 10.14,15;
2 Tim 2.19
33.13
Ex 34.9;
Ps 25.4;
Deut 9.26, 29
33.14
Isa 63.9;
Josh 22.4
33.16
Num 14.14;
Ex 34.10
33.17
v. 12

33.18
vv. 20,23
33.19
Rom 9.15, 16,18
33.20
Gen 32.20;
Isa 6.5
33.23
Jn 1.18
34.1
Ex 32.16, 19; v. 28
34.2
Ex 19.20
34.3
Ex 19.12, 13,21
34.5
Ex 33.19
34.6
Num 14.18;
Neh 9.17;
Ps 86.15;
103.8

7 keeping steadfast love for the
 thousandth
 generation,[e]
forgiving iniquity and
 transgression and sin,
yet by no means clearing the
 guilty,
but visiting the iniquity of
 the parents
upon the children
and the children's children,
to the third and the fourth
 generation."

8 And Moses quickly bowed his head toward the earth, and worshiped. 9 He said, "If now I have found favor in your sight, O Lord, I pray, let the Lord go with us. Although this is a stiff-necked people, pardon our iniquity and our sin, and take us for your inheritance."

The Covenant Renewed

10 He said: I hereby make a covenant. Before all your people I will perform marvels, such as have not been performed in all the earth or in any nation; and all the people among whom you live shall see the work of the LORD; for it is an awesome thing that I will do with you. 11 Observe what I command you today. See, I will drive out before you the Amorites, the Canaanites, the Hittites, the Perizzites, the Hivites, and the Jebusites. 12 Take care not to make a covenant with the inhabitants of the land to which you are going, or it will become a snare among you. 13 You shall tear down their altars, break their pillars, and cut down their sacred poles[f] 14 (for you shall worship no other god, because the LORD, whose name is Jealous, is a jealous God). 15 You shall not make a covenant with the inhabitants of the land, for when they prostitute themselves to their gods and sacrifice to their gods, someone among them will invite you, and you will eat of the sacrifice. 16 And you will take wives from among their daughters for your sons, and their daughters who prostitute themselves to their gods will make your

34.7
Ex 20.6,7;
Ps 103.3;
Dan 9.9;
Eph 4.32
34.8
Ex 4.31
34.9
Ex 33.3,15,
16
34.10
Deut 5.2;
4.32
34.11
Deut 6.3;
Ex 33.2
34.12
Ex 23.32,33
34.13
Ex 23.24;
2 Kings 18.4
34.14
Ex 20.3,5;
Deut 4.24
34.15
Judg 2.17;
Num 25.2;
1 Cor 8.4,
7,10
34.16
Deut 7.3;
Num 25.1

34.17
Ex 32.8
34.18
Ex 12.2,
15-17; 13.4
34.19
Ex 13.2;
22.29
34.20
Ex 13.13;
23.15
34.21
Ex 20.9;
Lk 13.14
34.22
Ex 23.16
34.23
Ex 23.14-17
34.25
Ex 23.18;
12.10
34.26
Ex 23.19
34.27
Ex 17.14;
24.4
34.28
Ex 24.18;
31.18; 34.1;
Deut 4.13;
10.4

sons also prostitute themselves to their gods.

17 You shall not make cast idols.

18 You shall keep the festival of unleavened bread. Seven days you shall eat unleavened bread, as I commanded you, at the time appointed in the month of Abib; for in the month of Abib you came out from Egypt.

19 All that first opens the womb is mine, all your male[g] livestock, the firstborn of cow and sheep. 20 The firstborn of a donkey you shall redeem with a lamb, or if you will not redeem it you shall break its neck. All the firstborn of your sons you shall redeem.

No one shall appear before me empty-handed.

21 Six days you shall work, but on the seventh day you shall rest; even in plowing time and in harvest time you shall rest. 22 You shall observe the festival of weeks, the first fruits of wheat harvest, and the festival of ingathering at the turn of the year. 23 Three times in the year all your males shall appear before the LORD God, the God of Israel. 24 For I will cast out nations before you, and enlarge your borders; no one shall covet your land when you go up to appear before the LORD your God three times in the year.

25 You shall not offer the blood of my sacrifice with leaven, and the sacrifice of the festival of the passover shall not be left until the morning.

26 The best of the first fruits of your ground you shall bring to the house of the LORD your God.

You shall not boil a kid in its mother's milk.

27 The LORD said to Moses: Write these words; in accordance with these words I have made a covenant with you and with Israel. 28 He was there with the LORD forty days and forty nights; he neither ate bread nor drank water. And he wrote on the tablets the words of

[e] Or *for thousands* [f] Heb *Asherim*
[g] Gk Theodotion Vg Tg: Meaning of Heb uncertain

the covenant, the ten commandments. [h]

The Shining Face of Moses

29 Moses came down from Mount Sinai. As he came down from the mountain with the two tablets of the covenant[i] in his hand, Moses did not know that the skin of his face shone because he had been talking with God. 30 When Aaron and all the Israelites saw Moses, the skin of his face was shining, and they were afraid to come near him. 31 But Moses called to them; and Aaron and all the leaders of the congregation returned to him, and Moses spoke with them. 32 Afterward all the Israelites came near, and he gave them in commandment all that the LORD had spoken with him on Mount Sinai. 33 When Moses had finished speaking with them, he put a veil on his face; 34 but whenever Moses went in before the LORD to speak with him, he would take the veil off, until he came out; and when he came out, and told the Israelites what he had been commanded, 35 the Israelites would see the face of Moses, that the skin of his face was shining; and Moses would put the veil on his face again, until he went in to speak with him.

Sabbath Regulations

35 Moses assembled all the congregation of the Israelites and said to them: These are the things that the LORD has commanded you to do:
2 Six days shall work be done, but on the seventh day you shall have a holy sabbath of solemn rest to the LORD; whoever does any work on it shall be put to death. 3 You shall kindle no fire in all your dwellings on the sabbath day.

Preparations for Making the Tabernacle

4 Moses said to all the congregation of the Israelites: This is the thing that the LORD has commanded: 5 Take from among you an offering to the LORD; let whoever is of a generous heart bring the LORD's of-

fering: gold, silver, and bronze; 6 blue, purple, and crimson yarns, and fine linen; goats' hair, 7 tanned rams' skins, and fine leather;[i] acacia wood, 8 oil for the light, spices for the anointing oil and for the fragrant incense, 9 and onyx stones and gems to be set in the ephod and the breastpiece.

10 All who are skillful among you shall come and make all that the LORD has commanded: the tabernacle, 11 its tent and its covering, its clasps and its frames, its bars, its pillars, and its bases; 12 the ark with its poles, the mercy seat,[k] and the curtain for the screen; 13 the table with its poles and all its utensils, and the bread of the Presence; 14 the lampstand also for the light, with its utensils and its lamps, and the oil for the light; 15 and the altar of incense, with its poles, and the anointing oil and the fragrant incense, and the screen for the entrance, the entrance of the tabernacle; 16 the altar of burnt offering, with its grating of bronze, its poles, and all its utensils, the basin with its stand; 17 the hangings of the court, its pillars and its bases, and the screen for the gate of the court; 18 the pegs of the tabernacle and the pegs of the court, and their cords; 19 the finely worked vestments for ministering in the holy place, the holy vestments for the priest Aaron, and the vestments of his sons, for their service as priests.

Offerings for the Tabernacle

20 Then all the congregation of the Israelites withdrew from the presence of Moses. 21 And they came, everyone whose heart was stirred, and everyone whose spirit was willing, and brought the LORD's offering to be used for the tent of meeting, and for all its service, and for the sacred vestments. 22 So they came, both men and women; all who were of a willing heart brought brooches and earrings and signet rings and pendants, all sorts of gold

34.29
Ex 32.15;
Mt 17.2;
2 Cor 3.7,
13
34.32
Ex 24.3
34.33
2 Cor 3.13
34.34
2 Cor 3.16
35.1
Ex 34.32
35.2
Ex 31.15
35.3
Ex 16.23
35.4
Ex 25.1-9

35.10
Ex 31.6
35.11
Ex 26.1ff
35.13
Ex 25.23,
30;
Lev 24.5,6
35.15
Ex 30.1
35.19
Ex 31.10
35.21
Ex 25.2

h Heb *words* i Or *treaty,* or *testimony;*
Heb *eduth* j Meaning of Heb uncertain
k Or *the cover*

objects, everyone bringing an offering of gold to the LORD. ²³And everyone who possessed blue or purple or crimson yarn or fine linen or goats' hair or tanned rams' skins or fine leather,¹ brought them. ²⁴Everyone who could make an offering of silver or bronze brought it as the LORD's offering; and everyone who possessed acacia wood of any use in the work, brought it. ²⁵All the skillful women spun with their hands, and brought what they had spun in blue and purple and crimson yarns and fine linen; ²⁶all the women whose hearts moved them to use their skill spun the goats' hair. ²⁷And the leaders brought onyx stones and gems to be set in the ephod and the breastpiece, ²⁸and spices and oil for the light, and for the anointing oil, and for the fragrant incense. ²⁹All the Israelite men and women whose hearts made them willing to bring anything for the work that the LORD had commanded by Moses to be done, brought it as a freewill offering to the LORD.

Bezalel and Oholiab

30 Then Moses said to the Israelites: See, the LORD has called by name Bezalel son of Uri son of Hur, of the tribe of Judah; ³¹he has filled him with divine spirit,ᵐ with skill, intelligence, and knowledge in every kind of craft, ³²to devise artistic designs, to work in gold, silver, and bronze, ³³in cutting stones for setting, and in carving wood, in every kind of craft. ³⁴And he has inspired him to teach, both him and Oholiab son of Ahisamach, of the tribe of Dan. ³⁵He has filled them with skill to do every kind of work done by an artisan or by a designer or by an embroiderer in blue, purple, and crimson yarns, and in fine linen, or by a weaver—by any sort of artisan or skilled designer.

36 Bezalel and Oholiab and every skillful one to whom the LORD has given skill and understanding to know how to do any work in the construction of the sanctuary shall work in accordance

with all that the LORD has commanded.

2 Moses then called Bezalel and Oholiab and every skillful one to whom the the LORD had given skill, everyone whose heart was stirred to come to do the work; ³and they received from Moses all the freewill offerings that the Israelites had brought for doing the work on the sanctuary. They still kept bringing him freewill offerings every morning, ⁴so that all the artisans who were doing every sort of task on the sanctuary came, each from the task being performed, ⁵and said to Moses, "The people are bringing much more than enough for doing the work that the LORD has commanded us to do." ⁶So Moses gave command, and word was proclaimed throughout the camp: "No man or woman is to make anything else as an offering for the sanctuary." So the people were restrained from bringing; ⁷for what they had already brought was more than enough to do all the work.

Construction of the Tabernacle

8 All those with skill among the workers made the tabernacle with ten curtains; they were made of fine twisted linen, and blue, purple, and crimson yarns, with cherubim skillfully worked into them. ⁹The length of each curtain was twenty-eight cubits, and the width of each curtain four cubits; all the curtains were of the same size.

10 He joined five curtains to one another, and the other five curtains he joined to one another. ¹¹He made loops of blue on the edge of the outermost curtain of the first set; likewise he made them on the edge of the outermost curtain of the second set; ¹²he made fifty loops on the one curtain, and he made fifty loops on the edge of the curtain that was in the second set; the loops were opposite one another. ¹³And he made fifty clasps of gold, and joined the curtains one to

35.23
1 Chr 29.8
35.25
Ex 28.3
35.27
1 Chr 29.6;
Ezra 2.68
35.28
Ex 30.23
35.29
v. 21
35.30
Ex 31.1-6
35.35
v. 31
36.1
Ex 25.8

36.2
Ex 35.21, 26;
1 Chr 29.5
36.3
Ex 35.27
36.5
2 Chr 24.14;
31.6-10;
2 Cor 8.23
36.8
Ex 26.1-14
36.12
Ex 26.5

¹Meaning of Heb uncertain ᵐOr *the spirit of God*

the other with clasps; so the tabernacle was one whole.

14 He also made curtains of goats' hair for a tent over the tabernacle; he made eleven curtains. ¹⁵The length of each curtain was thirty cubits, and the width of each curtain four cubits; the eleven curtains were of the same size. ¹⁶He joined five curtains by themselves, and six curtains by themselves. ¹⁷He made fifty loops on the edge of the outermost curtain of the one set, and fifty loops on the edge of the other connecting curtain. ¹⁸He made fifty clasps of bronze to join the tent together so that it might be one whole. ¹⁹And he made for the tent a covering of tanned rams' skins and an outer covering of fine leather.[n]

20 Then he made the upright frames for the tabernacle of acacia wood. ²¹Ten cubits was the length of a frame, and a cubit and a half the width of each frame. ²²Each frame had two pegs for fitting together; he did this for all the frames of the tabernacle. ²³The frames for the tabernacle he made in this way: twenty frames for the south side; ²⁴and he made forty bases of silver under the twenty frames, two bases under the first frame for its two pegs, and two bases under the next frame for its two pegs. ²⁵For the second side of the tabernacle, on the north side, he made twenty frames ²⁶and their forty bases of silver, two bases under the first frame and two bases under the next frame. ²⁷For the rear of the tabernacle westward he made six frames. ²⁸He made two frames for corners of the tabernacle in the rear. ²⁹They were separate beneath, but joined at the top, at the first ring; he made two of them in this way, for the two corners. ³⁰There were eight frames with their bases of silver: sixteen bases, under every frame two bases.

31 He made bars of acacia wood, five for the frames of the one side of the tabernacle, ³²and five bars for the frames of the other side of the tabernacle, and five bars for

36.14
Ex 26.7
36.19
Ex 26.14
36.20
Ex 26.15-29
36.24
Ex 26.21
36.27
Ex 26.22
36.31
Ex 26.26

the frames of the tabernacle at the rear westward. ³³He made the middle bar to pass through from end to end halfway up the frames. ³⁴And he overlaid the frames with gold, and made rings of gold for them to hold the bars, and overlaid the bars with gold.

35 He made the curtain of blue, purple, and crimson yarns, and fine twisted linen, with cherubim skillfully worked into it. ³⁶For it he made four pillars of acacia, and overlaid them with gold; their hooks were of gold, and he cast for them four bases of silver. ³⁷He also made a screen for the entrance to the tent, of blue, purple, and crimson yarns, and fine twisted linen, embroidered with needlework; ³⁸and its five pillars with their hooks. He overlaid their capitals and their bases with gold, but their five bases were of bronze.

Making the Ark of the Covenant

37 Bezalel made the ark of acacia wood; it was two and a half cubits long, a cubit and a half wide, and a cubit and a half high. ²He overlaid it with pure gold inside and outside, and made a molding of gold around it. ³He cast for it four rings of gold for its four feet, two rings on its one side and two rings on its other side. ⁴He made poles of acacia wood, and overlaid them with gold, ⁵and put the poles into the rings on the sides of the ark, to carry the ark. ⁶He made a mercy seat[o] of pure gold; two cubits and a half was its length, and a cubit and a half its width. ⁷He made two cherubim of hammered gold; at the two ends of the mercy seat[p] he made them, ⁸one cherub at the one end, and one cherub at the other end; of one piece with the mercy seat[p] he made the cherubim at its two ends. ⁹The cherubim spread out their wings above, overshadowing the mercy seat[p] with their wings. They faced one another; the faces of the

36.35
Ex 26.31-37
37.1
Ex 25.10-20
37.3
Ex 25.12
37.6
Ex 25.17

[n] Meaning of Heb uncertain [o] Or *a cover* [p] Or *the cover*

cherubim were turned toward the mercy seat.�ۅ

Making the Table for the Bread of the Presence

10 He also made the table of acacia wood, two cubits long, one cubit wide, and a cubit and a half high. ¹¹He overlaid it with pure gold, and made a molding of gold around it. ¹²He made around it a rim a handbreadth wide, and made a molding of gold around the rim. ¹³He cast for it four rings of gold, and fastened the rings to the four corners at its four legs. ¹⁴The rings that held the poles used for carrying the table were close to the rim. ¹⁵He made the poles of acacia wood to carry the table, and overlaid them with gold. ¹⁶And he made the vessels of pure gold that were to be on the table, its plates and dishes for incense, and its bowls and flagons with which to pour drink offerings.

Making the Lampstand

17 He also made the lampstand of pure gold. The base and the shaft of the lampstand were made of hammered work; its cups, its calyxes, and its petals were of one piece with it. ¹⁸There were six branches going out of its sides, three branches of the lampstand out of one side of it and three branches of the lampstand out of the other side of it; ¹⁹three cups shaped like almond blossoms, each with calyx and petals, on one branch, and three cups shaped like almond blossoms, each with calyx and petals, on the other branch— so for the six branches going out of the lampstand. ²⁰On the lampstand itself there were four cups shaped like almond blossoms, each with its calyxes and petals. ²¹There was a calyx of one piece with it under the first pair of branches, a calyx of one piece with it under the next pair of branches, and a calyx of one piece with it under the last pair of branches. ²²Their calyxes and their branches were of one piece with it, the whole

37.16
Ex 25.29
37.17
Ex 25.31-39
37.19
Ex 25.33
37.21
Ex 25.35

37.25
Ex 30.1-5
37.29
Ex 30.23,34
38.1
Ex 27.1-8
38.8
Ex 30.18

of it one hammered piece of pure gold. ²³He made its seven lamps and its snuffers and its trays of pure gold. ²⁴He made it and all its utensils of a talent of pure gold.

Making the Altar of Incense

25 He made the altar of incense of acacia wood, one cubit long, and one cubit wide; it was square, and was two cubits high; its horns were of one piece with it. ²⁶He overlaid it with pure gold, its top, and its sides all around, and its horns; and he made for it a molding of gold all around, ²⁷and made two golden rings for it under its molding, on two opposite sides of it, to hold the poles with which to carry it. ²⁸And he made the poles of acacia wood, and overlaid them with gold.

Making the Anointing Oil and the Incense

29 He made the holy anointing oil also, and the pure fragrant incense, blended as by the perfumer.

Making the Altar of Burnt Offering

38 He made the altar of burnt offering also of acacia wood; it was five cubits long, and five cubits wide; it was square, and three cubits high. ²He made horns for it on its four corners; its horns were of one piece with it, and he overlaid it with bronze. ³He made all the utensils of the altar, the pots, the shovels, the basins, the forks, and the firepans: all its utensils he made of bronze. ⁴He made for the altar a grating, a network of bronze, under its ledge, extending halfway down. ⁵He cast four rings on the four corners of the bronze grating to hold the poles; ⁶he made the poles of acacia wood, and overlaid them with bronze. ⁷And he put the poles through the rings on the sides of the altar, to carry it with them; he made it hollow, with boards.

8 He made the basin of bronze with its stand of bronze, from the mirrors of the women who served

�ۅOr *the cover*

at the entrance to the tent of meeting.

Making the Court of the Tabernacle

9 He made the court; for the south side the hangings of the court were of fine twisted linen, one hundred cubits long; ¹⁰its twenty pillars and their twenty bases were of bronze, but the hooks of the pillars and their bands were of silver. ¹¹For the north side there were hangings one hundred cubits long; its twenty pillars and their twenty bases were of bronze, but the hooks of the pillars and their bands were of silver. ¹²For the west side there were hangings fifty cubits long, with ten pillars and ten bases; the hooks of the pillars and their bands were of silver. ¹³And for the front to the east, fifty cubits. ¹⁴The hangings for one side of the gate were fifteen cubits, with three pillars and three bases. ¹⁵And so for the other side; on each side of the gate of the court were hangings of fifteen cubits, with three pillars and three bases. ¹⁶All the hangings around the court were of fine twisted linen. ¹⁷The bases for the pillars were of bronze, but the hooks of the pillars and their bands were of silver; the overlaying of their capitals was also of silver, and all the pillars of the court were banded with silver. ¹⁸The screen for the entrance to the court was embroidered with needlework in blue, purple, and crimson yarns and fine twisted linen. It was twenty cubits long and, along the width of it, five cubits high, corresponding to the hangings of the court. ¹⁹There were four pillars; their four bases were of bronze, their hooks of silver, and the overlaying of their capitals and their bands of silver. ²⁰All the pegs for the tabernacle and for the court all around were of bronze.

Materials of the Tabernacle

21 These are the records of the tabernacle, the tabernacle of the covenant,ʳ which were drawn up at the commandment of Moses,

the work of the Levites being under the direction of Ithamar son of the priest Aaron. ²²Bezalel son of Uri son of Hur, of the tribe of Judah, made all that the LORD commanded Moses; ²³and with him was Oholiab son of Ahisamach, of the tribe of Dan, engraver, designer, and embroiderer in blue, purple, and crimson yarns, and in fine linen.

24 All the gold that was used for the work, in all the construction of the sanctuary, the gold from the offering, was twenty-nine talents and seven hundred thirty shekels, measured by the sanctuary shekel. ²⁵The silver from those of the congregation who were counted was one hundred talents and one thousand seven hundred seventy-five shekels, measured by the sanctuary shekel; ²⁶a beka a head (that is, half a shekel, measured by the sanctuary shekel), for everyone who was counted in the census, from twenty years old and upward, for six hundred three thousand, five hundred fifty men. ²⁷The hundred talents of silver were for casting the bases of the sanctuary, and the bases of the curtain; one hundred bases for the hundred talents, a talent for a base. ²⁸Of the thousand seven hundred seventy-five shekels he made hooks for the pillars, and overlaid their capitals and made bands for them. ²⁹The bronze that was contributed was seventy talents, and two thousand four hundred shekels; ³⁰with it he made the bases for the entrance of the tent of meeting, the bronze altar and the bronze grating for it and all the utensils of the altar, ³¹the bases all around the court, and the bases of the gate of the court, all the pegs of the tabernacle, and all the pegs around the court.

Making the Vestments for the Priesthood

39 Of the blue, purple, and crimson yarns they made finely worked vestments, for ministering in the holy place; they made the sacred vestments for Aaron; as

38.9
Ex 27.9-19
38.11
Ex 27.11
38.14
Ex 27.14
38.18
Ex 27.16
38.21
Num 4.28, 33

38.22
Ex 31.2,6
38.24
Ex 30.13
38.25
Ex 30.11-16
38.26
Ex 30.13, 15;
Num 1.46
38.27
Ex 26.19, 21,25,32
39.1
Ex 35.23; 28.4

ʳ Or treaty, or testimony; Heb eduth

the LORD had commanded Moses.

2 He made the ephod of gold, of blue, purple, and crimson yarns, and of fine twisted linen. ³ Gold leaf was hammered out and cut into threads to work into the blue, purple, and crimson yarns and into the fine twisted linen, in skilled design. ⁴ They made for the ephod shoulder-pieces, joined to it at its two edges. ⁵ The decorated band on it was of the same materials and workmanship, of gold, of blue, purple, and crimson yarns, and of fine twisted linen; as the LORD had commanded Moses.

6 The onyx stones were prepared, enclosed in settings of gold filigree and engraved like the engravings of a signet, according to the names of the sons of Israel. ⁷ He set them on the shoulder-pieces of the ephod, to be stones of remembrance for the sons of Israel; as the LORD had commanded Moses.

8 He made the breastpiece, in skilled work, like the work of the ephod, of gold, of blue, purple, and crimson yarns, and of fine twisted linen. ⁹ It was square; the breastpiece was made double, a span in length and a span in width when doubled. ¹⁰ They set in it four rows of stones. A row of carnelian,ˢ chrysolite, and emerald was the first row; ¹¹ and the second row, a turquoise, a sapphire,ᵗ and a moonstone; ¹² and the third row, a jacinth, an agate, and an amethyst; ¹³ and the fourth row, a beryl, an onyx, and a jasper; they were enclosed in settings of gold filigree. ¹⁴ There were twelve stones with names corresponding to the names of the sons of Israel; they were like signets, each engraved with its name, for the twelve tribes. ¹⁵ They made on the breastpiece chains of pure gold, twisted like cords; ¹⁶ and they made two settings of gold filigree and two gold rings, and put the two rings on the two edges of the breastpiece; ¹⁷ and they put the two cords of gold in the two rings at the edges of the breastpiece. ¹⁸ Two ends of the two cords they had attached to the two settings of fili-

gree; in this way they attached it in front to the shoulder-pieces of the ephod. ¹⁹ Then they made two rings of gold, and put them at the two ends of the breastpiece, on its inside edge next to the ephod. ²⁰ They made two rings of gold, and attached them in front to the lower part of the two shoulder-pieces of the ephod, at its joining above the decorated band of the ephod. ²¹ They bound the breastpiece by its rings to the rings of the ephod with a blue cord, so that it should lie on the decorated band of the ephod, and that the breastpiece should not come loose from the ephod; as the LORD had commanded Moses.

22 He also made the robe of the ephod woven all of blue yarn; ²³ and the opening of the robe in the middle of it was like the opening in a coat of mail,ᵘ with a binding around the opening, so that it might not be torn. ²⁴ On the lower hem of the robe they made pomegranates of blue, purple, and crimson yarns, and of fine twisted linen. ²⁵ They also made bells of pure gold, and put the bells between the pomegranates on the lower hem of the robe all around, between the pomegranates; ²⁶ a bell and a pomegranate, a bell and a pomegranate all around on the lower hem of the robe for ministering; as the LORD had commanded Moses.

27 They also made the tunics, woven of fine linen, for Aaron and his sons, ²⁸ and the turban of fine linen, and the head-dresses of fine linen, and the linen undergarments of fine twisted linen, ²⁹ and the sash of fine twisted linen, and of blue, purple, and crimson yarns, embroidered with needlework; as the LORD had commanded Moses.

30 They made the rosette of the holy diadem of pure gold, and wrote on it an inscription, like the engraving of a signet, "Holy to the LORD." ³¹ They tied to it a blue cord, to fasten it on the turban above; as

39.2
Ex 28.6-12
39.6
Ex 28.9
39.7
Ex 28.12
39.8
Ex 28.15-28
39.11
Ex 28.18
39.14
Ex 28.21
39.16
Ex 28.24

39.19
Ex 28.26
39.22
Ex 28.31-34
39.27
Ex 28.39,
40,42
39.30
Ex 28.36,37

ˢ The identification of several of these stones is uncertain ᵗ Or *lapis lazuli* ᵘ Meaning of Heb uncertain

the LORD had commanded Moses.

The Work Completed

32 In this way all the work of the tabernacle of the tent of meeting was finished; the Israelites had done everything just as the LORD had commanded Moses. 33 Then they brought the tabernacle to Moses, the tent and all its utensils, its hooks, its frames, its bars, its pillars, and its bases; 34 the covering of tanned rams' skins and the covering of fine leather,v and the curtain for the screen; 35 the ark of the covenantw with its poles and the mercy seat;x 36 the table with all its utensils, and the bread of the Presence; 37 the pure lampstand with its lamps set on it and all its utensils, and the oil for the light; 38 the golden altar, the anointing oil and the fragrant incense, and the screen for the entrance of the tent; 39 the bronze altar, and its grating of bronze, its poles, and all its utensils; the basin with its stand; 40 the hangings of the court, its pillars, and its bases, and the screen for the gate of the court, its cords, and its pegs; and all the utensils for the service of the tabernacle, for the tent of meeting; 41 the finely worked vestments for ministering in the holy place, the sacred vestments for the priest Aaron, and the vestments of his sons to serve as priests. 42 The Israelites had done all of the work just as the LORD had commanded Moses. 43 When Moses saw that they had done all the work just as the LORD had commanded, he blessed them.

The Tabernacle Erected and Its Equipment Installed

40 The LORD spoke to Moses: 2 On the first day of the first month you shall set up the tabernacle of the tent of meeting. 3 You shall put in it the ark of the covenant,w and you shall screen the ark with the curtain. 4 You shall bring in the table, and arrange its setting; and you shall bring in the lampstand, and set up its lamps. 5 You shall put the golden altar for in-

39.32
vv. 42,43;
Ex 25.40
39.35
Ex 25.16;
30.6
39.41
Ex 26.33
39.43
Lev 9.22,23
40.2
Ex 12.2;
13.4; v. 17
40.3
vv. 21-30

40.9
Ex 30.26
40.10
Ex 29.36,37
40.12
Lev 8.1-13
40.13
Ex 28.41
40.15
Num 25.13
40.20
Ex 25.16
40.21
Ex 26.33;
35.12

cense before the ark of the covenant,w and set up the screen for the entrance of the tabernacle. 6 You shall set the altar of burnt offering before the entrance of the tabernacle of the tent of meeting, 7 and place the basin between the tent of meeting and the altar, and put water in it. 8 You shall set up the court all around, and hang up the screen for the gate of the court. 9 Then you shall take the anointing oil, and anoint the tabernacle and all that is in it, and consecrate it and all its furniture, so that it shall become holy. 10 You shall also anoint the altar of burnt offering and all its utensils, and consecrate the altar, so that the altar shall be most holy. 11 You shall also anoint the basin with its stand, and consecrate it. 12 Then you shall bring Aaron and his sons to the entrance of the tent of meeting, and shall wash them with water, 13 and put on Aaron the sacred vestments, and you shall anoint him and consecrate him, so that he may serve me as priest. 14 You shall bring his sons also and put tunics on them, 15 and anoint them, as you anointed their father, that they may serve me as priests: and their anointing shall admit them to a perpetual priesthood throughout all generations to come.

16 Moses did everything just as the LORD had commanded him. 17 In the first month in the second year, on the first day of the month, the tabernacle was set up. 18 Moses set up the tabernacle; he laid its bases, and set up its frames, and put in its poles, and raised up its pillars; 19 and he spread the tent over the tabernacle, and put the covering of the tent over it; as the LORD had commanded Moses. 20 He took the covenantw and put it into the ark, and put the poles on the ark, and set the mercy seatx above the ark; 21 and he brought the ark into the tabernacle, and set up the curtain for screening, and screened

v Meaning of Heb uncertain w Or treaty, or testimony; Heb eduth x Or the cover

the ark of the covenant;y as the Lord had commanded Moses. 22 He put the table in the tent of meeting, on the north side of the tabernacle, outside the curtain, 23 and set the bread in order on it before the Lord; as the Lord had commanded Moses. 24 He put the lampstand in the tent of meeting, opposite the table on the south side of the tabernacle, 25 and set up the lamps before the Lord; as the Lord had commanded Moses. 26 He put the golden altar in the tent of meeting before the curtain, 27 and offered fragrant incense on it; as the Lord had commanded Moses. 28 He also put in place the screen for the entrance of the tabernacle. 29 He set the altar of burnt offering at the entrance of the tabernacle of the tent of meeting, and offered on it the burnt offering and the grain offering as the Lord had commanded Moses. 30 He set the basin between the tent of meeting and the altar, and put water in it for washing, 31 with which Moses and Aaron and his sons washed their hands and their feet. 32 When they went into the tent of meeting, and when they approached the altar, they washed; as the Lord had commanded Moses. 33 He set up the court around the tabernacle and the altar, and put up the screen at the gate of the court. So Moses finished the work.

The Cloud and the Glory

34 Then the cloud covered the tent of meeting, and the glory of the Lord filled the tabernacle. 35 Moses was not able to enter the tent of meeting because the cloud settled upon it, and the glory of the Lord filled the tabernacle. 36 Whenever the cloud was taken up from the tabernacle, the Israelites would set out on each stage of their journey; 37 but if the cloud was not taken up, then they did not set out until the day that it was taken up. 38 For the cloud of the Lord was on the tabernacle by day, and fire was in the cloudz by night, before the eyes of all the house of Israel at each stage of their journey.

y Or *treaty*, or *testimony*; Heb *eduth*
z Heb *it*

40.22
Ex 26.35
40.23
v. 4
40.25
Ex 25.37
40.26
v. 5
40.28
Ex 26.36
40.30
v. 7
40.32
Ex 30.19,20

40.34
Num 9.15-23
40.36
Num 9.17;
10.11;
Neh 9.19
40.38
Ex 13.21;
Num 9.15

Leviticus

Title and Background

Leviticus receives its name from the Septuagint (the Greek translation of the Old Testament) and means "relating to the Levites." Although Leviticus does not deal only with the special duties of the Levites, it is so named because it is concerned mainly with the service of worship at the tabernacle. Exodus had given the directions for building the tabernacle. Leviticus gives the laws and regulations for worship at the tabernacle, along with instructions on ceremonial cleanness, moral laws, holy days, the sabbath year, the year of jubilee, etc.

Author and Date of Writing

Leviticus 1.1 states that the contents of Leviticus were given to Moses by God. In more than fifty places in the book it is said that the Lord spoke to Moses. For the date of Moses and the exodus, see the Introductions to Genesis and Exodus.

Theme and Message

The key thought of Leviticus is holiness—the holiness of God and his people. The command to be holy is stated in 11.45—"you shall be holy, for I am holy." The instructions or laws in the book were given to help the Israelites worship and live as God's holy people.

Some of the instructions deal with such things as offering sacrifices, handling everyday problems concerning cleanliness, and observing special holidays. The Levitical priests are given special instructions for making sacrifices and carrying out God's commands.

Outline

The Burnt Offering

1 The Lord summoned Moses and spoke to him from the tent of meeting, saying: ²Speak to the people of Israel and say to them: When any of you bring an offering of livestock to the Lord, you shall bring your offering from the herd or from the flock.

3 If the offering is a burnt offering from the herd, you shall offer a male without blemish; you shall bring it to the entrance of the tent of meeting, for acceptance in your behalf before the Lord. ⁴You shall lay your hand on the head of the burnt offering, and it shall be acceptable in your behalf as atonement for you. ⁵The bull shall be slaughtered before the Lord; and Aaron's sons the priests shall offer the blood, dashing the blood against all sides of the altar that is at the entrance of the tent of meeting. ⁶The burnt offering shall be flayed and cut up into its parts. ⁷The sons of the priest Aaron shall put fire on the altar and arrange wood on the fire. ⁸Aaron's sons the priests shall arrange the parts, with the head and the suet, on the wood

1.1
Num 7.89
1.2f
Lev 22.18, 19
1.3
Deut 15.21;
Heb 9.14;
1 Pet 1.19
1.4f
Ex 29.10;
Lev 9.7;
Num 15.25

1.5
Ex 29.11;
Heb 10.11;
12.24;
1 Pet 1.2
1.7
Lev 6.8-13

that is on the fire on the altar; ⁹but its entrails and its legs shall be washed with water. Then the priest shall turn the whole into smoke on the altar as a burnt offering, an offering by fire of pleasing odor to the LORD.

10 If your gift for a burnt offering is from the flock, from the sheep or goats, your offering shall be a male without blemish. ¹¹It shall be slaughtered on the north side of the altar before the LORD, and Aaron's sons the priests shall dash its blood against all sides of the altar. ¹²It shall be cut up into its parts, with its head and its suet, and the priest shall arrange them on the wood that is on the fire on the altar; ¹³but the entrails and the legs shall be washed with water. Then the priest shall offer the whole and turn it into smoke on the altar; it is a burnt offering, an offering by fire of pleasing odor to the LORD.

14 If your offering to the LORD is a burnt offering of birds, you shall choose your offering from turtledoves or pigeons. ¹⁵The priest shall bring it to the altar and wring off its head, and turn it into smoke on the altar; and its blood shall be drained out against the side of the altar. ¹⁶He shall remove its crop with its contentsᵃ and throw it at the east side of the altar, in the place for ashes. ¹⁷He shall tear it open by its wings without severing it. Then the priest shall turn it into smoke on the altar, on the wood that is on the fire; it is a burnt offering, an offering by fire of pleasing odor to the LORD.

Grain Offerings

2 When anyone presents a grain offering to the LORD, the offering shall be of choice flour; the worshiper shall pour oil on it, and put frankincense on it, ²and bring it to Aaron's sons the priests. After taking from it a handful of the choice flour and oil, with all its frankincense, the priest shall turn this token portion into smoke on the altar, an offering by fire of

pleasing odor to the LORD. ³And what is left of the grain offering shall be for Aaron and his sons, a most holy part of the offerings by fire to the LORD.

4 When you present a grain offering baked in the oven, it shall be of choice flour: unleavened cakes mixed with oil, or unleavened wafers spread with oil. ⁵If your offering is grain prepared on a griddle, it shall be of choice flour mixed with oil, unleavened; ⁶break it in pieces, and pour oil on it; it is a grain offering. ⁷If your offering is grain prepared in a pan, it shall be made of choice flour in oil. ⁸You shall bring to the LORD the grain offering that is prepared in any of these ways; and when it is presented to the priest, he shall take it to the altar. ⁹The priest shall remove from the grain offering its token portion and turn this into smoke on the altar, an offering by fire of pleasing odor to the LORD. ¹⁰And what is left of the grain offering shall be for Aaron and his sons; it is a most holy part of the offerings by fire to the LORD.

11 No grain offering that you bring to the LORD shall be made with leaven, for you must not turn any leaven or honey into smoke as an offering by fire to the LORD. ¹²You may bring them to the LORD as an offering of choice products, but they shall not be offered on the altar for a pleasing odor. ¹³You shall not omit from your grain offerings the salt of the covenant with your God; with all your offerings you shall offer salt.

14 If you bring a grain offering of first fruits to the LORD, you shall bring as the grain offering of your first fruits coarse new grain from fresh ears, parched with fire. ¹⁵You shall add oil to it and lay frankincense on it; it is a grain offering. ¹⁶And the priest shall turn a token portion of it into smoke—some of the coarse grain and oil with all its frankincense; it is an offering by fire to the LORD.

ᵃ Meaning of Heb uncertain

1.9
Num 15.8-10;
Eph 5.2
1.11
v. 5
1.14
Lev 5.7
1.15
Lev 5.9
1.16
Lev 6.10
1.17
Lev 5.8;
Gen 15.10
2.1
Lev 6.14
2.2
vv. 9,16;
Lev 5.12;
6.15;
Acts 10.4

2.3
Lev 6.16;
10.12,13
2.9
v. 2;
Ex 29.18
2.10
v. 3
2.11
Lev 6.16,17;
Ex 23.18;
34.25
2.12
Lev 7.13;
23.10,11
2.13
Mk 9.49;
Num 18.19
2.14
Lev 23.10,
14
2.16
v. 2

Offerings of Well-Being

3 If the offering is a sacrifice of well-being, if you offer an animal of the herd, whether male or female, you shall offer one without blemish before the LORD. ²You shall lay your hand on the head of the offering and slaughter it at the entrance of the tent of meeting; and Aaron's sons the priests shall dash the blood against all sides of the altar. ³You shall offer from the sacrifice of well-being, as an offering by fire to the LORD, the fat that covers the entrails and all the fat that is around the entrails; ⁴the two kidneys with the fat that is on them at the loins, and the appendage of the liver, which he shall remove with the kidneys. ⁵Then Aaron's sons shall turn these into smoke on the altar, with the burnt offering that is on the wood on the fire, as an offering by fire of pleasing odor to the LORD.

6 If your offering for a sacrifice of well-being to the LORD is from the flock, male or female, you shall offer one without blemish. ⁷If you present a sheep as your offering, you shall bring it before the LORD ⁸and lay your hand on the head of the offering. It shall be slaughtered before the tent of meeting, and Aaron's sons shall dash its blood against all sides of the altar. ⁹You shall present its fat from the sacrifice of well-being, as an offering by fire to the LORD: the whole broad tail, which shall be removed close to the backbone, the fat that covers the entrails, and all the fat that is around the entrails; ¹⁰the two kidneys with the fat that is on them at the loins, and the appendage of the liver, which you shall remove with the kidneys. ¹¹Then the priest shall turn these into smoke on the altar as a food offering by fire to the LORD.

12 If your offering is a goat, you shall bring it before the LORD ¹³and lay your hand on its head; it shall be slaughtered before the tent of meeting; and the sons of Aaron shall dash its blood against all

sides of the altar. ¹⁴You shall present as your offering from it, as an offering by fire to the LORD, the fat that covers the entrails, and all the fat that is around the entrails; ¹⁵the two kidneys with the fat that is on them at the loins, and the appendage of the liver, which you shall remove with the kidneys. ¹⁶Then the priest shall turn these into smoke on the altar as a food offering by fire for a pleasing odor.

All fat is the LORD's. ¹⁷It shall be a perpetual statute throughout your generations, in all your settlements: you must not eat any fat or any blood.

Sin Offerings

4 The LORD spoke to Moses, saying, ²Speak to the people of Israel, saying: When anyone sins unintentionally in any of the LORD's commandments about things not to be done, and does any one of them:

3 If it is the anointed priest who sins, thus bringing guilt on the people, he shall offer for the sin that he has committed a bull of the herd without blemish as a sin offering to the LORD. ⁴He shall bring the bull to the entrance of the tent of meeting before the LORD and lay his hand on the head of the bull; the bull shall be slaughtered before the LORD. ⁵The anointed priest shall take some of the blood of the bull and bring it into the tent of meeting. ⁶The priest shall dip his finger in the blood and sprinkle some of the blood seven times before the LORD in front of the curtain of the sanctuary. ⁷The priest shall put some of the blood on the horns of the altar of fragrant incense that is in the tent of meeting before the LORD; and the rest of the blood of the bull he shall pour out at the base of the altar of burnt offering, which is at the entrance of the tent of meeting. ⁸He shall remove all the fat from the bull of sin offering: the fat that covers the entrails and all the fat that is around the entrails; ⁹the two kidneys with the fat that is on them at the loins; and the

Cross references

3.1 Lev 7.11,19; 22.21
3.2 Lev 1.4; Ex 29.11, 16,20
3.3 Ex 29.13,22
3.5 Lev 7.28-34; Ex 29.13
3.6 v. 1
3.7 Lev 17.8,9
3.8 Lev 1.4,5; v. 2
3.10 v. 4
3.11 vv. 5,16; Lev 21.6,8, 17

3.16 Lev 7.23-25
3.17 Gen 9.4; Lev 17.10, 14; Deut 12.16
4.2 Lev 5.15-18; Ps 19.12
4.3ff vv. 14,23,28
4.4 Lev 1.4
4.5 Lev 16.14
4.7 Lev 8.15; 9.9; Lev 5.9
4.8 Lev 3.3-5

OLD TESTAMENT SACRIFICES

Sacrifice	OT References	Elements	Purpose
BURNT OFFERING	Lev 1; 6:8-13; 8:18-21; 16:24	Bull, ram or male bird (dove or young pigeon for poor); wholly consumed; no defect	Voluntary act of worship; atonement for unintentional sin in general; expression of devotion, commitment and complete surrender to God
GRAIN OFFERING	Lev 2; 6:14-23	Grain, fine flour, olive oil, incense, baked bread (cakes or wafers), salt; no yeast or honey; accompanied burnt offering and fellowship offering (along with drink offering)	Voluntary act of worship; recognition of God's goodness and provisions; devotion to God
FELLOWSHIP OFFERING	Lev 3; 7:11-34	Any animal without defect from herd or flock; variety of breads	Voluntary act of worship; thanksgiving and fellowship (it included a communal meal)
SIN OFFERING	Lev 4:1-5:13; 6:24-30; 8:14-17; 16:3-22	1. Young bull: for high priest and congregation 2. Male goat: for leader 3. Female goat or lamb: for common person 4. Dove or pigeon: for the poor 5. Tenth of an ephah of fine flour: for the very poor	Mandatory atonement for specific unintentional sin; confession of sin; forgiveness of sin; cleansing from defilement
GUILT OFFERING	Lev 5:14-6:7; 7:1-6	Ram or lamb	Mandatory atonement for unintentional sin requiring restitution; cleansing from defilement; make restitution; pay 20% fine

When more than one kind of offering was presented (as in Nu 7:16, 17), the procedure was usually as follows: (1) sin offering or guilt offering, (2) burnt offering, (3) fellowship offering and grain offering (along with a drink offering). This sequence furnishes part of the spiritual significance of the sacrificial system. First, sin had to be dealt with (sin offering or guilt offering). Second, the worshiper committed himself completely to God (burnt offering and grain offering). Third, fellowship or communion between the Lord, the priest and the worshiper (fellowship offering) was established.

appendage of the liver, which he shall remove with the kidneys, [10]just as these are removed from the ox of the sacrifice of well-being. The priest shall turn them into smoke upon the altar of burnt offering. [11]But the skin of the bull and all its flesh, as well as its head, its legs, its entrails, and its dung— [12]all the rest of the bull—he shall carry out to a clean place outside the camp, to the ash heap, and shall burn it on a wood fire; at the ash heap it shall be burned.

[13] If the whole congregation of Israel errs unintentionally and the matter escapes the notice of the assembly, and they do any one of the things that by the LORD's commandments ought not to be done and incur guilt; [14]when the sin that they have committed becomes known, the assembly shall offer a bull of the herd for a sin offering and bring it before the tent of meeting. [15]The elders of the congregation shall lay their hands on the head of the bull before the LORD, and the bull shall be slaughtered before the LORD. [16]The anointed priest shall bring some of the blood of the bull into the tent of meeting, [17]and the priest shall dip his finger in the blood and sprinkle it seven times before the LORD, in front of the curtain. [18]He shall put some of the blood on the horns of the altar that is before the LORD in the tent of meeting; and the rest of the blood he shall pour out at the base of the altar of burnt offering that is at the entrance of the tent of meeting. [19]He shall remove all its fat and turn it into smoke on the altar. [20]He shall do with the bull just as is done with the bull of sin offering; he shall do the same with this. The priest shall make atonement for them, and they shall be forgiven. [21]He shall carry the bull outside the camp, and burn it as he burned the first bull; it is the sin offering for the assembly.

[22] When a ruler sins, doing unintentionally any one of all the things that by commandments of the LORD his God ought not to be

done and incurs guilt, [23]once the sin that he has committed is made known to him, he shall bring as his offering a male goat without blemish. [24]He shall lay his hand on the head of the goat; it shall be slaughtered at the spot where the burnt offering is slaughtered before the LORD; it is a sin offering. [25]The priest shall take some of the blood of the sin offering with his finger and put it on the horns of the altar of burnt offering, and pour out the rest of its blood at the base of the altar of burnt offering. [26]All its fat he shall turn into smoke on the altar, like the fat of the sacrifice of well-being. Thus the priest shall make atonement on his behalf for his sin, and he shall be forgiven.

[27] If anyone of the ordinary people among you sins unintentionally in doing any one of the things that by the LORD's commandments ought not to be done and incurs guilt, [28]when the sin that you have committed is made known to you, you shall bring a female goat without blemish as your offering, for the sin that you have committed. [29]You shall lay your hand on the head of the sin offering; and the sin offering shall be slaughtered at the place of the burnt offering. [30]The priest shall take some of its blood with his finger and put it on the horns of the altar of burnt offering, and he shall pour out the rest of its blood at the base of the altar. [31]He shall remove all its fat, as the fat is removed from the offering of well-being, and the priest shall turn it into smoke on the altar for a pleasing odor to the LORD. Thus the priest shall make atonement on your behalf, and you shall be forgiven.

[32] If the offering you bring as a sin offering is a sheep, you shall bring a female without blemish. [33]You shall lay your hand on the head of the sin offering; and it shall be slaughtered as a sin offering at the spot where the burnt offering is slaughtered. [34]The priest shall take some of the blood of the sin offering with his finger and put it on the

4.12
Lev 6.11;
Heb 13.11
4.13
Num 15.24-26;
Lev 5.2-4,17
4.14
vv. 3,23,28
4.15
Lev 1.4
4.17
v. 6
4.20
Rom 5.11;
Heb 2.17;
10.10-12
4.22
vv. 2,13

4.23
v. 14
4.25
vv. 7,18,30,
34
4.26
vv. 19,20
4.27
v. 2
4.28
v. 23
4.29
Lev 1.4,5
4.32
v. 28

horns of the altar of burnt offering, and pour out the rest of its blood at the base of the altar. 35 You shall remove all its fat, as the fat of the sheep is removed from the sacrifice of well-being, and the priest shall turn it into smoke on the altar, with the offerings by fire to the LORD. Thus the priest shall make atonement on your behalf for the sin that you have committed, and you shall be forgiven.

5 When any of you sin in that you have heard a public adjuration to testify and—though able to testify as one who has seen or learned of the matter—does not speak up, you are subject to punishment. 2 Or when any of you touch any unclean thing—whether the carcass of an unclean beast or the carcass of unclean livestock or the carcass of an unclean swarming thing—and are unaware of it, you have become unclean, and are guilty. 3 Or when you touch human uncleanness—any uncleanness by which one can become unclean—and are unaware of it, when you come to know it, you shall be guilty. 4 Or when any of you utter aloud a rash oath for a bad or a good purpose, whatever people utter in an oath, and are unaware of it, when you come to know it, you shall in any of these be guilty. 5 When you realize your guilt in any of these, you shall confess the sin that you have committed. 6 And you shall bring to the LORD, as your penalty for the sin that you have committed, a female from the flock, a sheep or a goat, as a sin offering; and the priest shall make atonement on your behalf for your sin.

7 But if you cannot afford a sheep, you shall bring to the LORD, as your penalty for the sin that you have committed, two turtledoves or two pigeons, one for a sin offering and the other for a burnt offering. 8 You shall bring them to the priest, who shall offer first the one for the sin offering, wringing its head at the nape without severing it. 9 He shall sprinkle some of the

4.35
Lev 3.5;
vv. 26,31
5.1
Prov 29.24;
v. 17
5.2
Lev 11.24-39;
Num 19.11-16
5.5
Lev 16.21;
26.40;
Num 5.7;
Prov 28.13
5.7
Lev 12.8;
14.21
5.8
Lev 1.15,17
5.9
Lev 4.7,18,
30,34

5.10
Lev 1.14-17
5.11
Lev 2.1,2
5.13
Lev 4.26;
2.3
5.14
Lev 22.14;
7.1-10;
Ex 30.13
5.16
Lev 6.5;
22.14;
Num 5.7,8;
Lev 4.26
5.17
v. 15; 4.2,
13,22,27
5.18
vv. 15-17

blood of the sin offering on the side of the altar, while the rest of the blood shall be drained out at the base of the altar; it is a sin offering. 10 And the second he shall offer for a burnt offering according to the regulation. Thus the priest shall make atonement on your behalf for the sin that you have committed, and you shall be forgiven.

11 But if you cannot afford two turtledoves or two pigeons, you shall bring as your offering for the sin that you have committed one-tenth of an ephah of choice flour for a sin offering; you shall not put oil on it or lay frankincense on it, for it is a sin offering. 12 You shall bring it to the priest, and the priest shall scoop up a handful of it as its memorial portion, and turn this into smoke on the altar, with the offerings by fire to the LORD; it is a sin offering. 13 Thus the priest shall make atonement on your behalf for whichever of these sins you have committed, and you shall be forgiven. Like the grain offering, the rest shall be for the priest.

Offerings with Restitution

14 The LORD spoke to Moses, saying: 15 When any of you commit a trespass and sins unintentionally in any of the holy things of the LORD, you shall bring, as your guilt offering to the LORD, a ram without blemish from the flock, convertible into silver by the sanctuary shekel; it is a guilt offering. 16 And you shall make restitution for the holy thing in which you were remiss, and shall add one-fifth to it and give it to the priest. The priest shall make atonement on your behalf with the ram of the guilt offering, and you shall be forgiven.

17 If any of you sin without knowing it, doing any of the things that by the LORD's commandments ought not to be done, you have incurred guilt, and are subject to punishment. 18 You shall bring to the priest a ram without blemish from the flock, or the equivalent, as a guilt offering; and the priest shall make atonement on your behalf for

the error that you committed unintentionally, and you shall be forgiven. [19] It is a guilt offering; you have incurred guilt before the LORD.

6 [b] The LORD spoke to Moses, saying: [2] When any of you sin and commit a trespass against the LORD by deceiving a neighbor in a matter of a deposit or a pledge, or by robbery, or if you have defrauded a neighbor, [3] or have found something lost and lied about it—if you swear falsely regarding any of the various things that one may do and sin thereby— [4] when you have sinned and realize your guilt, and would restore what you took by robbery or by fraud or the deposit that was committed to you, or the lost thing that you found, [5] or anything else about which you have sworn falsely, you shall repay the principal amount and shall add one-fifth to it. You shall pay it to its owner when you realize your guilt. [6] And you shall bring to the priest, as your guilt offering to the LORD, a ram without blemish from the flock, or its equivalent, for a guilt offering. [7] The priest shall make atonement on your behalf before the LORD, and you shall be forgiven for any of the things that one may do and incur guilt thereby.

Instructions concerning Sacrifices

8 [c] The LORD spoke to Moses, saying: [9] Command Aaron and his sons, saying: This is the ritual of the burnt offering. The burnt offering itself shall remain on the hearth upon the altar all night until the morning, while the fire on the altar shall be kept burning. [10] The priest shall put on his linen vestments after putting on his linen undergarments next to his body; and he shall take up the ashes to which the fire has reduced the burnt offering on the altar, and place them beside the altar. [11] Then he shall take off his vestments and put on other garments, and carry the ashes out to a clean place outside the camp. [12] The fire on the altar shall be kept burning; it shall not

go out. Every morning the priest shall add wood to it, lay out the burnt offering on it, and turn into smoke the fat pieces of the offerings of well-being. [13] A perpetual fire shall be kept burning on the altar; it shall not go out.

14 This is the ritual of the grain offering: The sons of Aaron shall offer it before the LORD, in front of the altar. [15] They shall take from it a handful of the choice flour and oil of the grain offering, with all the frankincense that is on the offering, and they shall turn its memorial portion into smoke on the altar as a pleasing odor to the LORD. [16] Aaron and his sons shall eat what is left of it; it shall be eaten as unleavened cakes in a holy place; in the court of the tent of meeting they shall eat it. [17] It shall not be baked with leaven. I have given it as their portion of my offerings by fire; it is most holy, like the sin offering and the guilt offering. [18] Every male among the descendants of Aaron shall eat of it, as their perpetual due throughout your generations, from the LORD's offerings by fire; anything that touches them shall become holy.

19 The LORD spoke to Moses, saying: [20] This is the offering that Aaron and his sons shall offer to the LORD on the day when he is anointed: one-tenth of an ephah of choice flour as a regular offering, half of it in the morning and half in the evening. [21] It shall be made with oil on a griddle; you shall bring it well soaked, as a grain offering of baked[d] pieces, and you shall present it as a pleasing odor to the LORD. [22] And so the priest, anointed from among Aaron's descendants as a successor, shall prepare it; it is the LORD's—a perpetual due—to be turned entirely into smoke. [23] Every grain offering of a priest shall be wholly burned; it shall not be eaten.

24 The LORD spoke to Moses, saying: [25] Speak to Aaron and his

6.2
Num 5.6;
Acts 5.4;
Col 3.9;
Ex 22.7,10;
Prov 24.28
6.3
Deut 22.1-3
6.5
Lev 5.16;
Num 5.7,8
6.6
Lev 5.16
6.7
Lev 4.26
6.10
Ex 28.39-41,
43; 39.27,28

6.14
Lev 2.1,2
6.16
Lev 2.3
6.17
Lev 2.11;
vv. 26,29,30
6.18
v. 29;
Num 18.10;
v. 27
6.20
Ex 29.1,2
6.21
Lev 2.5
6.25
Lev 4.2,24,
29,33; 1.3,5,
11

[b] Ch 5.20 in Heb [c] Ch 6.1 in Heb
[d] Meaning of Heb uncertain

sons, saying: This is the ritual of the sin offering. The sin offering shall be slaughtered before the Lord at the spot where the burnt offering is slaughtered; it is most holy. 26 The priest who offers it as a sin offering shall eat of it; it shall be eaten in a holy place, in the court of the tent of meeting. 27 Whatever touches its flesh shall become holy; and when any of its blood is spattered on a garment, you shall wash the bespattered part in a holy place. 28 An earthen vessel in which it was boiled shall be broken; but if it is boiled in a bronze vessel, that shall be scoured and rinsed in water. 29 Every male among the priests shall eat of it; it is most holy. 30 But no sin offering shall be eaten from which any blood is brought into the tent of meeting for atonement in the holy place; it shall be burned with fire.

7 This is the ritual of the guilt offering. It is most holy; 2 at the spot where the burnt offering is slaughtered, they shall slaughter the guilt offering, and its blood shall be dashed against all sides of the altar. 3 All its fat shall be offered: the broad tail, the fat that covers the entrails, 4 the two kidneys with the fat that is on them at the loins, and the appendage of the liver, which shall be removed with the kidneys. 5 The priest shall turn them into smoke on the altar as an offering by fire to the Lord; it is a guilt offering. 6 Every male among the priests shall eat of it; it shall be eaten in a holy place; it is most holy.

7 The guilt offering is like the sin offering, there is the same ritual for them; the priest who makes atonement with it shall have it. 8 So, too, the priest who offers anyone's burnt offering shall keep the skin of the burnt offering that he has offered. 9 And every grain offering baked in the oven, and all that is prepared in a pan or on a griddle, shall belong to the priest who offers it. 10 But every other grain offering, mixed with oil or dry, shall

belong to all the sons of Aaron equally.

Further Instructions

11 This is the ritual of the sacrifice of the offering of well-being that one may offer to the Lord. 12 If you offer it for thanksgiving, you shall offer with the thank offering unleavened cakes mixed with oil, unleavened wafers spread with oil, and cakes of choice flour well soaked in oil. 13 With your thanksgiving sacrifice of well-being you shall bring your offering with cakes of leavened bread. 14 From this you shall offer one cake from each offering, as a gift to the Lord; it shall belong to the priest who dashes the blood of the offering of well-being. 15 And the flesh of your thanksgiving sacrifice of well-being shall be eaten on the day it is offered; you shall not leave any of it until morning. 16 But if the sacrifice you offer is a votive offering or a freewill offering, it shall be eaten on the day that you offer your sacrifice, and what is left of it shall be eaten the next day; 17 but what is left of the flesh of the sacrifice shall be burned up on the third day. 18 If any of the flesh of your sacrifice of well-being is eaten on the third day, it shall not be acceptable, nor shall it be credited to the one who offers it; it shall be an abomination, and the one who eats of it shall incur guilt.

19 Flesh that touches any unclean thing shall not be eaten; it shall be burned up. As for other flesh, all who are clean may eat such flesh. 20 But those who eat flesh from the Lord's sacrifice of well-being while in a state of uncleanness shall be cut off from their kin. 21 When any one of you touches any unclean thing— human uncleanness or an unclean animal or any unclean creature— and then eats flesh from the Lord's sacrifice of well-being, you shall be cut off from your kin.

22 The Lord spoke to Moses, saying: 23 Speak to the people of Israel, saying: You shall eat no fat of ox or sheep or goat. 24 The fat of an

6.26
Lev 10.17, 18; v. 16
6.27
Ex 29.37
6.28
Ex 11.33; 15.12
6.29
vv. 18,25
6.30
Lev 4.1,7, 11,12,18,21
7.1
Lev 5.14-6.7
7.2
Lev 1.11
7.4
Lev 3.4
7.6
Lev 6.16-18; 2.3
7.7
Lev 6.25,26
7.9
Lev 2.3,10

7.14
Num 18.8, 11,19
7.15
Lev 22.30
7.16
Lev 19.6-8
7.18
Lev 19.7; Num 18.27
7.20
Lev 22.3
7.21
Lev 11.24, 28
7.23
Lev 3.17

animal that died or was torn by wild animals may be put to any use, but you must not eat it. ²⁵ If any one of you eats the fat from an animal of which an offering by fire may be made to the LORD, you who eat it shall be cut off from your kin. ²⁶ You must not eat any blood whatever, either of bird or of animal, in any of your settlements. ²⁷ Any one of you who eats any blood shall be cut off from your kin.

28 The LORD spoke to Moses, saying: ²⁹ Speak to the people of Israel, saying: Any one of you who would offer to the LORD your sacrifice of well-being must yourself bring to the LORD your offering from your sacrifice of well-being. ³⁰ Your own hands shall bring the LORD's offering by fire; you shall bring the fat with the breast, so that the breast may be raised as an elevation offering before the LORD. ³¹ The priest shall turn the fat into smoke on the altar, but the breast shall belong to Aaron and his sons. ³² And the right thigh from your sacrifices of well-being you shall give to the priest as an offering; ³³ the one among the sons of Aaron who offers the blood and fat of the offering of well-being shall have the right thigh for a portion. ³⁴ For I have taken the breast of the elevation offering, and the thigh that is offered, from the people of Israel, from their sacrifices of well-being, and have given them to Aaron the priest and to his sons, as a perpetual due from the people of Israel. ³⁵ This is the portion allotted to Aaron and to his sons from the offerings made by fire to the LORD, once they have been brought forward to serve the LORD as priests; ³⁶ these the LORD commanded to be given them, when he anointed them, as a perpetual due from the people of Israel throughout their generations.

37 This is the ritual of the burnt offering, the grain offering, the sin offering, the guilt offering, the offering of ordination, and the sacrifice of well-being, ³⁸ which the LORD commanded Moses on Mount Si-

nai, when he commanded the people of Israel to bring their offerings to the LORD, in the wilderness of Sinai.

The Rites of Ordination

8 The LORD spoke to Moses, saying: ² Take Aaron and his sons with him, the vestments, the anointing oil, the bull of sin offering, the two rams, and the basket of unleavened bread; ³ and assemble the whole congregation at the entrance of the tent of meeting. ⁴ And Moses did as the LORD commanded him. When the congregation was assembled at the entrance of the tent of meeting, ⁵ Moses said to the congregation, "This is what the LORD has commanded to be done."

6 Then Moses brought Aaron and his sons forward, and washed them with water. ⁷ He put the tunic on him, fastened the sash around him, clothed him with the robe, and put the ephod on him. He then put the decorated band of the ephod around him, tying the ephod to him with it. ⁸ He placed the breastpiece on him, and in the breastpiece he put the Urim and the Thummim. ⁹ And he set the turban on his head, and on the turban, in front, he set the golden ornament, the holy crown, as the LORD commanded Moses.

10 Then Moses took the anointing oil and anointed the tabernacle and all that was in it, and consecrated them. ¹¹ He sprinkled some of it on the altar seven times, and anointed the altar and all its utensils, and the basin and its base, to consecrate them. ¹² He poured some of the anointing oil on Aaron's head and anointed him, to consecrate him. ¹³ And Moses brought forward Aaron's sons, and clothed them with tunics, and fastened sashes around them, and tied headdresses on them, as the LORD commanded Moses.

14 He led forward the bull of sin offering; and Aaron and his sons laid their hands upon the head of the bull of sin offering, ¹⁵ and it was slaughtered. Moses took the blood

7.26
Lev 17.10-14
7.29
Lev 3.1
7.31
v. 34
7.34
Num 18.18, 19
7.37
Lev 6.9,14, 20,25; vv. 1, 11
7.38
Lev 1.1,2

8.2
Ex 29.1-3; 28.2,4; 30.24, 25
8.6
Ex 29.4-6
8.8
Ex 28.30
8.9
Ex 28.36,37
8.10
v. 2
8.12
Ex 30.30; Ps 133.2
8.13
Ex 29.8,9
8.14
Ex 29.10; Lev 4.4
8.15
Lev 4.7; Heb 9.22

and with his finger put some on each of the horns of the altar, purifying the altar; then he poured out the blood at the base of the altar. Thus he consecrated it, to make atonement for it. [16] Moses took all the fat that was around the entrails, and the appendage of the liver, and the two kidneys with their fat, and turned them into smoke on the altar. [17] But the bull itself, its skin and flesh and its dung, he burned with fire outside the camp, as the LORD commanded Moses.

18 Then he brought forward the ram of burnt offering. Aaron and his sons laid their hands on the head of the ram, [19] and it was slaughtered. Moses dashed the blood against all sides of the altar. [20] The ram was cut into its parts, and Moses turned into smoke the head and the parts and the suet. [21] And after the entrails and the legs were washed with water, Moses turned into smoke the whole ram on the altar; it was a burnt offering for a pleasing odor, an offering by fire to the LORD, as the LORD commanded Moses.

22 Then he brought forward the second ram, the ram of ordination. Aaron and his sons laid their hands on the head of the ram, [23] and it was slaughtered. Moses took some of its blood and put it on the lobe of Aaron's right ear and on the thumb of his right hand and on the big toe of his right foot. [24] After Aaron's sons were brought forward, Moses put some of the blood on the lobes of their right ears and on the thumbs of their right hands and on the big toes of their right feet; and Moses dashed the rest of the blood against all sides of the altar. [25] He took the fat—the broad tail, all the fat that was around the entrails, the appendage of the liver, and the two kidneys with their fat—and the right thigh. [26] From the basket of unleavened bread that was before the LORD, he took one cake of unleavened bread, one cake of bread with oil, and one wafer, and placed them on the fat and on the right thigh. [27] He placed all

these on the palms of Aaron and on the palms of his sons, and raised them as an elevation offering before the LORD. [28] Then Moses took them from their hands and turned them into smoke on the altar with the burnt offering. This was an ordination offering for a pleasing odor, an offering by fire to the LORD. [29] Moses took the breast and raised it as an elevation offering before the LORD; it was Moses' portion of the ram of ordination, as the LORD commanded Moses.

30 Then Moses took some of the anointing oil and some of the blood that was on the altar and sprinkled them on Aaron and his vestments, and also on his sons and their vestments. Thus he consecrated Aaron and his vestments, and also his sons and their vestments.

31 And Moses said to Aaron and his sons, "Boil the flesh at the entrance of the tent of meeting, and eat it there with the bread that is in the basket of ordination offerings, as I was commanded, 'Aaron and his sons shall eat it'; [32] and what remains of the flesh and the bread you shall burn with fire. [33] You shall not go outside the entrance of the tent of meeting for seven days, until the day when your period of ordination is completed. For it will take seven days to ordain you; [34] as has been done today, the LORD has commanded to be done to make atonement for you. [35] You shall remain at the entrance of the tent of meeting day and night for seven days, keeping the LORD's charge so that you do not die; for so I am commanded." [36] Aaron and his sons did all the things that the LORD commanded through Moses.

Aaron's Priesthood Inaugurated

9 On the eighth day Moses summoned Aaron and his sons and the elders of Israel. [2] He said to Aaron, "Take a bull calf for a sin offering and a ram for a burnt offering, without blemish, and offer them before the LORD. [3] And say to the people of Israel, 'Take a male goat for a sin offering; a calf and a lamb,

8.16
Lev 4.8
8.17
Lev 4.11,12
8.18
Ex 29.15
8.21
Ex 29.18
8.22
Ex 29.19,31
8.25
Ex 29.22
8.26
Ex 29.23

8.28
Ex 29.25
8.29
Ex 29.26
8.30
Ex 30.30;
Num 3.3
8.31
Ex 29.31,32
8.32
Ex 29.34
8.33
Ex 29.30,35
8.34
Heb 7.16
9.2
Lev 8.18;
Ex 29.1
9.3
Lev 4.23

yearlings without blemish, for a burnt offering; [4] and an ox and a ram for an offering of well-being to sacrifice before the LORD; and a grain offering mixed with oil. For today the LORD will appear to you.' " [5] They brought what Moses commanded to the front of the tent of meeting; and the whole congregation drew near and stood before the LORD. [6] And Moses said, "This is the thing that the LORD commanded you to do, so that the glory of the LORD may appear to you." [7] Then Moses said to Aaron, "Draw near to the altar and sacrifice your sin offering and your burnt offering, and make atonement for yourself and for the people; and sacrifice the offering of the people, and make atonement for them; as the LORD has commanded."

8 Aaron drew near to the altar, and slaughtered the calf of the sin offering, which was for himself. [9] The sons of Aaron presented the blood to him, and he dipped his finger in the blood and put it on the horns of the altar; and the rest of the blood he poured out at the base of the altar. [10] But the fat, the kidneys, and the appendage of the liver from the sin offering he turned into smoke on the altar, as the LORD commanded Moses; [11] and the flesh and the skin he burned with fire outside the camp.

12 Then he slaughtered the burnt offering. Aaron's sons brought him the blood, and he dashed it against all sides of the altar. [13] And they brought him the burnt offering piece by piece, and the head, which he turned into smoke on the altar. [14] He washed the entrails and the legs and, with the burnt offering, turned them into smoke on the altar.

15 Next he presented the people's offering. He took the goat of the sin offering that was for the people, and slaughtered it, and presented it as a sin offering like the first one. [16] He presented the burnt offering, and sacrificed it according to regulation. [17] He presented the grain offering, and, taking a handful of it, he turned it into smoke on the altar, in addition to the burnt offering of the morning.

18 He slaughtered the ox and the ram as a sacrifice of well-being for the people. Aaron's sons brought him the blood, which he dashed against all sides of the altar, [19] and the fat of the ox and of the ram—the broad tail, the fat that covers the entrails, the two kidneys and the fat on them, [e] and the appendage of the liver. [20] They first laid the fat on the breasts, and the fat was turned into smoke on the altar; [21] and the breasts and the right thigh Aaron raised as an elevation offering before the LORD, as Moses had commanded.

22 Aaron lifted his hands toward the people and blessed them; and he came down after sacrificing the sin offering, the burnt offering, and the offering of well-being. [23] Moses and Aaron entered the tent of meeting, and then came out and blessed the people; and the glory of the LORD appeared to all the people. [24] Fire came out from the LORD and consumed the burnt offering and the fat on the altar; and when all the people saw it, they shouted and fell on their faces.

Nadab and Abihu

10 Now Aaron's sons, Nadab and Abihu, each took his censer, put fire in it, and laid incense on it; and they offered unholy fire before the LORD, such as he had not commanded them. [2] And fire came out from the presence of the LORD and consumed them, and they died before the LORD. [3] Then Moses said to Aaron, "This is what the LORD meant when he said,

'Through those who are near
 me
 I will show myself holy,
 and before all the people
 I will be glorified.' "
And Aaron was silent.

4 Moses summoned Mishael and Elzaphan, sons of Uzziel the

Cross references (center column):

9.6
v. 23
9.7
Heb 5.1,3
9.8
Lev 4.1-12
9.9
vv. 12,18
9.11
Lev 4.11;
8.17
9.15
Lev 4.27-31
9.16
Lev 1.3,10
9.17
Lev 2.1,2;
3.5

9.18
Lev 3.1-11
9.21
Lev 7.30-34
9.23
v. 6;
Num 14.10
9.24
1 Kings 18.38,
39
10.1
Num 3.3,4;
Lev 16.12;
Ex 30.9
10.2
Num 3.4;
26.61
10.3
Ex 19.22;
30.30;
Lev 21.6
10.4
Ex 6.18,22;
Acts 5.6,9,
10

[e] Gk: Heb *the broad tail, and that which covers, and the kidneys*

uncle of Aaron, and said to them, "Come forward, and carry your kinsmen away from the front of the sanctuary to a place outside the camp." 5They came forward and carried them by their tunics out of the camp, as Moses had ordered. 6And Moses said to Aaron and to his sons Eleazar and Ithamar, "Do not dishevel your hair, and do not tear your vestments, or you will die and wrath will strike all the congregation; but your kindred, the whole house of Israel, may mourn the burning that the Lord has sent. 7You shall not go outside the entrance of the tent of meeting, or you will die; for the anointing oil of the Lord is on you." And they did as Moses had ordered.

8 And the Lord spoke to Aaron: 9Drink no wine or strong drink, neither you nor your sons, when you enter the tent of meeting, that you may not die; it is a statute forever throughout your generations. 10You are to distinguish between the holy and the common, and between the unclean and the clean; 11and you are to teach the people of Israel all the statutes that the Lord has spoken to them through Moses.

12 Moses spoke to Aaron and to his remaining sons, Eleazar and Ithamar: Take the grain offering that is left from the Lord's offerings by fire, and eat it unleavened beside the altar, for it is most holy; 13you shall eat it in a holy place, because it is your due and your sons' due, from the offerings by fire to the Lord; for so I am commanded. 14But the breast that is elevated and the thigh that is raised, you and your sons and daughters as well may eat in any clean place; for they have been assigned to you and your children from the sacrifices of the offerings of well-being of the people of Israel. 15The thigh that is raised and the breast that is elevated they shall bring, together with the offerings by fire of the fat, to raise for an elevation offering before the Lord; they are to be your due and that of your children for-

ever, as the Lord has commanded.

16 Then Moses made inquiry about the goat of the sin offering, and—it had already been burned! He was angry with Eleazar and Ithamar, Aaron's remaining sons, and said, 17"Why did you not eat the sin offering in the sacred area? For it is most holy, and God[f] has given it to you that you may remove the guilt of the congregation, to make atonement on their behalf before the Lord. 18Its blood was not brought into the inner part of the sanctuary. You should certainly have eaten it in the sanctuary, as I commanded." 19And Aaron spoke to Moses, "See, today they offered their sin offering and their burnt offering before the Lord; and yet such things as these have befallen me! If I had eaten the sin offering today, would it have been agreeable to the Lord?" 20And when Moses heard that, he agreed.

Clean and Unclean Foods

11 The Lord spoke to Moses and Aaron, saying to them: 2Speak to the people of Israel, saying:

From among all the land animals, these are the creatures that you may eat. 3Any animal that has divided hoofs and is cleft-footed and chews the cud—such you may eat. 4But among those that chew the cud or have divided hoofs, you shall not eat the following: the camel, for even though it chews the cud, it does not have divided hoofs; it is unclean for you. 5The rock badger, for even though it chews the cud, it does not have divided hoofs; it is unclean for you. 6The hare, for even though it chews the cud, it does not have divided hoofs; it is unclean for you. 7The pig, for even though it has divided hoofs and is cleft-footed, it does not chew the cud; it is unclean for you. 8Of their flesh you shall not eat, and their carcasses you shall not touch; they are unclean for you.

9 These you may eat, of all that

f Heb he

are in the waters. Everything in the waters that has fins and scales, whether in the seas or in the streams—such you may eat. [10] But anything in the seas or the streams that does not have fins and scales, of the swarming creatures in the waters and among all the other living creatures that are in the waters—they are detestable to you [11] and detestable they shall remain. Of their flesh you shall not eat, and their carcasses you shall regard as detestable. [12] Everything in the waters that does not have fins and scales is detestable to you.

13 These you shall regard as detestable among the birds. They shall not be eaten; they are an abomination: the eagle, the vulture, the osprey, [14] the buzzard, the kite of any kind; [15] every raven of any kind; [16] the ostrich, the nighthawk, the sea gull, the hawk of any kind; [17] the little owl, the cormorant, the great owl, [18] the water hen, the desert owl,g the carrion vulture, [19] the stork, the heron of any kind, the hoopoe, and the bat. h

20 All winged insects that walk upon all fours are detestable to you. [21] But among the winged insects that walk on all fours you may eat those that have jointed legs above their feet, with which to leap on the ground. [22] Of them you may eat: the locust according to its kind, the bald locust according to its kind, the cricket according to its kind, and the grasshopper according to its kind. [23] But all other winged insects that have four feet are detestable to you.

Unclean Animals

24 By these you shall become unclean; whoever touches the carcass of any of them shall be unclean until the evening, [25] and whoever carries any part of the carcass of any of them shall wash his clothes and be unclean until the evening. [26] Every animal that has divided hoofs but is not cleft-footed or does not chew the cud is unclean for you; everyone who

touches one of them shall be unclean. [27] All that walk on their paws, among the animals that walk on all fours, are unclean for you; whoever touches the carcass of any of them shall be unclean until the evening, [28] and the one who carries the carcass shall wash his clothes and be unclean until the evening; they are unclean for you.

29 These are unclean for you among the creatures that swarm upon the earth: the weasel, the mouse, the great lizard according to its kind, [30] the gecko, the land crocodile, the lizard, the sand lizard, and the chameleon. [31] These are unclean for you among all that swarm; whoever touches one of them when they are dead shall be unclean until the evening. [32] And anything upon which any of them falls when they are dead shall be unclean, whether an article of wood or cloth or skin or sacking, any article that is used for any purpose; it shall be dipped into water, and it shall be unclean until the evening, and then it shall be clean. [33] And if any of them falls into any earthen vessel, all that is in it shall be unclean, and you shall break the vessel. [34] Any food that could be eaten shall be unclean if water from any such vessel comes upon it; and any liquid that could be drunk shall be unclean if it was in any such vessel. [35] Everything on which any part of the carcass falls shall be unclean; whether an oven or stove, it shall be broken in pieces; they are unclean, and shall remain unclean for you. [36] But a spring or a cistern holding water shall be clean, while whatever touches the carcass in it shall be unclean. [37] If any part of their carcass falls upon any seed set aside for sowing, it is clean; [38] but if water is put on the seed and any part of their carcass falls on it, it is unclean for you.

39 If an animal of which you may eat dies, anyone who touches

11.10
Lev 7.18;
Deut 14.3
11.13
Deut 14.12
11.22
Mt 3.4;
Mk 1.6
11.25
v. 40

11.29
Isa 66.17
11.32
Lev 15.12
11.33
Lev 6.28;
15.12

g Or pelican h Identification of several of the birds in verses 13-19 is uncertain

its carcass shall be unclean until the evening. 40 Those who eat of its carcass shall wash their clothes and be unclean until the evening; and those who carry the carcass shall wash their clothes and be unclean until the evening.

41 All creatures that swarm upon the earth are detestable; they shall not be eaten. 42 Whatever moves on its belly, and whatever moves on all fours, or whatever has many feet, all the creatures that swarm upon the earth, you shall not eat; for they are detestable. 43 You shall not make yourselves detestable with any creature that swarms; you shall not defile yourselves with them, and so become unclean. 44 For I am the LORD your God; sanctify yourselves therefore, and be holy, for I am holy. You shall not defile yourselves with any swarming creature that moves on the earth. 45 For I am the LORD who brought you up from the land of Egypt, to be your God; you shall be holy, for I am holy.

46 This is the law pertaining to land animal and bird and every living creature that moves through the waters and every creature that swarms upon the earth, 47 to make a distinction between the unclean and the clean, and between the living creature that may be eaten and the living creature that may not be eaten.

Purification of Women after Childbirth

12 The LORD spoke to Moses, saying: 2 Speak to the people of Israel, saying:

If a woman conceives and bears a male child, she shall be ceremonially unclean seven days; as at the time of her menstruation, she shall be unclean. 3 On the eighth day the flesh of his foreskin shall be circumcised. 4 Her time of blood purification shall be thirty-three days; she shall not touch any holy thing, or come into the sanctuary, until the days of her purification are completed. 5 If she bears a female child, she shall be unclean

two weeks, as in her menstruation; her time of blood purification shall be sixty-six days.

6 When the days of her purification are completed, whether for a son or for a daughter, she shall bring to the priest at the entrance of the tent of meeting a lamb in its first year for a burnt offering, and a pigeon or a turtledove for a sin offering. 7 He shall offer it before the LORD, and make atonement on her behalf; then she shall be clean from her flow of blood. This is the law for her who bears a child, male or female. 8 If she cannot afford a sheep, she shall take two turtledoves or two pigeons, one for a burnt offering and the other for a sin offering; and the priest shall make atonement on her behalf, and she shall be clean.

Leprosy, Varieties and Symptoms

13 The LORD spoke to Moses and Aaron, saying:

2 When a person has on the skin of his body a swelling or an eruption or a spot, and it turns into a leprous[i] disease on the skin of his body, he shall be brought to Aaron the priest or to one of his sons the priests. 3 The priest shall examine the disease on the skin of his body, and if the hair in the diseased area has turned white and the disease appears to be deeper than the skin of his body, it is a leprous[i] disease; after the priest has examined him he shall pronounce him ceremonially unclean. 4 But if the spot is white in the skin of his body, and appears no deeper than the skin, and the hair in it has not turned white, the priest shall confine the diseased person for seven days. 5 The priest shall examine him on the seventh day, and if he sees that the disease is checked and the disease has not spread in the skin, then the priest shall confine him seven days more. 6 The priest shall examine him again on the seventh day, and if the disease has abated

[i] A term for several skin diseases; precise meaning uncertain

11.40
Lev 17.15;
22.8
11.41
v. 29
11.43
Lev 20.25
11.44
Ex 6.7;
19.6;
Lev 19.2;
1 Pet 1.15,
16
11.45
Ex 6.7
11.47
Lev 10.10
12.2
Lev 15.19;
18.19
12.3
Gen 17.12

12.6
Lk 2.22
12.8
Lk 2.22-24;
Lev 5.7;
4.26
13.2
Deut 24.8
13.4
v. 21
13.6
Lev 11.25;
14.8

and the disease has not spread in the skin, the priest shall pronounce him clean; it is only an eruption; and he shall wash his clothes, and be clean. ⁷But if the eruption spreads in the skin after he has shown himself to the priest for his cleansing, he shall appear again before the priest. ⁸The priest shall make an examination, and if the eruption has spread in the skin, the priest shall pronounce him unclean; it is a leprousʲ disease.

9 When a person contracts a leprousʲ disease, he shall be brought to the priest. ¹⁰The priest shall make an examination, and if there is a white swelling in the skin that has turned the hair white, and there is quick raw flesh in the swelling, ¹¹it is a chronic leprousʲ disease in the skin of his body. The priest shall pronounce him unclean; he shall not confine him, for he is unclean. ¹²But if the disease breaks out in the skin, so that it covers all the skin of the diseased person from head to foot, so far as the priest can see, ¹³then the priest shall make an examination, and if the disease has covered all his body, he shall pronounce him clean of the disease; since it has all turned white, he is clean. ¹⁴But if raw flesh ever appears on him, he shall be unclean; ¹⁵the priest shall examine the raw flesh and pronounce him unclean. Raw flesh is unclean, for it is a leprousʲ disease. ¹⁶But if the raw flesh again turns white, he shall come to the priest; ¹⁷the priest shall examine him, and if the disease has turned white, the priest shall pronounce the diseased person clean. He is clean.

18 When there is on the skin of one's body a boil that has healed, ¹⁹and in the place of the boil there appears a white swelling or a reddish-white spot, it shall be shown to the priest. ²⁰The priest shall make an examination, and if it appears deeper than the skin and its hair has turned white, the priest shall pronounce him unclean; this is a leprousʲ disease, broken out in

the boil. ²¹But if the priest examines it and the hair on it is not white, nor is it deeper than the skin but has abated, the priest shall confine him seven days. ²²If it spreads in the skin, the priest shall pronounce him unclean; it is diseased. ²³But if the spot remains in one place and does not spread, it is the scar of the boil; the priest shall pronounce him clean.

24 Or, when the body has a burn on the skin and the raw flesh of the burn becomes a spot, reddish-white or white, ²⁵the priest shall examine it. If the hair in the spot has turned white and it appears deeper than the skin, it is a leprousʲ disease; it has broken out in the burn, and the priest shall pronounce him unclean. This is a leprousʲ disease. ²⁶But if the priest examines it and the hair in the spot is not white, and it is no deeper than the skin but has abated, the priest shall confine him seven days. ²⁷The priest shall examine him the seventh day; if it is spreading in the skin, the priest shall pronounce him unclean. This is a leprousʲ disease. ²⁸But if the spot remains in one place and does not spread in the skin but has abated, it is a swelling from the burn, and the priest shall pronounce him clean; for it is the scar of the burn.

29 When a man or woman has a disease on the head or in the beard, ³⁰the priest shall examine the disease. If it appears deeper than the skin and the hair in it is yellow and thin, the priest shall pronounce him unclean; it is an itch, a leprousʲ disease of the head or the beard. ³¹If the priest examines the itching disease, and it appears no deeper than the skin and there is no black hair in it, the priest shall confine the person with the itching disease for seven days. ³²On the seventh day the priest shall examine the itch; if the itch has not spread, and there is no yellow hair in it, and the itch appears to be no

13.7
Lk 5.14
13.10
Num 12.10;
2 Kings 5.27;
2 Chr 26.20
13.12
Lk 5.12
13.15
Mt 8.3
13.18
Ex 9.9
13.19
v. 43

13.21
Num 12.14,
15
13.25
v. 15
13.27
v. 5
13.29
v. 44
13.32
v. 5

ʲA term for several skin diseases; precise meaning uncertain

deeper than the skin, ³³he shall shave, but the itch he shall not shave. The priest shall confine the person with the itch for seven days more. ³⁴On the seventh day the priest shall examine the itch; if the itch has not spread in the skin and it appears to be no deeper than the skin, the priest shall pronounce him clean. He shall wash his clothes and be clean. ³⁵But if the itch spreads in the skin after he was pronounced clean, ³⁶the priest shall examine him. If the itch has spread in the skin, the priest need not seek for the yellow hair; he is unclean. ³⁷But if in his eyes the itch is checked, and black hair has grown in it, the itch is healed, he is clean; and the priest shall pronounce him clean.

38 When a man or a woman has spots on the skin of the body, white spots, ³⁹the priest shall make an examination, and if the spots on the skin of the body are of a dull white, it is a rash that has broken out on the skin; he is clean.

40 If anyone loses the hair from his head, he is bald but he is clean. ⁴¹If he loses the hair from his forehead and temples, he has baldness of the forehead but he is clean. ⁴²But if there is on the bald head or the bald forehead a reddish-white diseased spot, it is a leprous^k disease breaking out on his bald head or his bald forehead. ⁴³The priest shall examine him; if the diseased swelling is reddish-white on his bald head or on his bald forehead, which resembles a leprous^k disease in the skin of the body, ⁴⁴he is leprous,^k he is unclean. The priest shall pronounce him unclean; the disease is on his head.

45 The person who has the leprous^k disease shall wear torn clothes and let the hair of his head be disheveled; and he shall cover his upper lip and cry out, "Unclean, unclean." ⁴⁶He shall remain unclean as long as he has the disease; he is unclean. He shall live alone; his dwelling shall be outside the camp.

47 Concerning clothing: when a

leprous^k disease appears in it, in woolen or linen cloth, ⁴⁸in warp or woof of linen or wool, or in a skin or in anything made of skin, ⁴⁹if the disease shows greenish or reddish in the garment, whether in warp or woof or in skin or in anything made of skin, it is a leprous^k disease and shall be shown to the priest. ⁵⁰The priest shall examine the disease, and put the diseased article aside for seven days. ⁵¹He shall examine the disease on the seventh day. If the disease has spread in the cloth, in warp or woof, or in the skin, whatever be the use of the skin, this is a spreading leprous^k disease; it is unclean. ⁵²He shall burn the clothing, whether diseased in warp or woof, woolen or linen, or anything of skin, for it is a spreading leprous^k disease; it shall be burned in fire.

53 If the priest makes an examination, and the disease has not spread in the clothing, in warp or woof or in anything of skin, ⁵⁴the priest shall command them to wash the article in which the disease appears, and he shall put it aside seven days more. ⁵⁵The priest shall examine the diseased article after it has been washed. If the diseased spot has not changed color, though the disease has not spread, it is unclean; you shall burn it in fire, whether the leprous^k spot is on the inside or on the outside.

56 If the priest makes an examination, and the disease has abated after it is washed, he shall tear the spot out of the cloth, in warp or woof, or out of skin. ⁵⁷If it appears again in the garment, in warp or woof, or in anything of skin, it is spreading; you shall burn with fire that in which the disease appears. ⁵⁸But the cloth, warp or woof, or anything of skin from which the disease disappears when you have washed it, shall then be washed a second time, and it shall be clean.

59 This is the ritual for a leprous^k disease in a cloth of wool or

13.34
Lev 14.8
13.36
v. 30
13.40
Ezek 29.18
13.44
v. 29
13.45
Ezek 24.17, 22; Mic 3.7; Lam 4.15
13.46
Num 5.2; 12.14; 2 Kings 7.3; 15.5; Lk 17.12

13.51
Lev 14.44
13.52
Lev 14.44
13.54
v. 4
13.56
Lev 14.8

^kA term for several skin diseases; precise meaning uncertain

linen, either in warp or woof, or in anything of skin, to decide whether it is clean or unclean.

Purification of Lepers and Leprous Houses

14 The LORD spoke to Moses, saying: ²This shall be the ritual for the leprous[1] person at the time of his cleansing:

He shall be brought to the priest; ³the priest shall go out of the camp, and the priest shall make an examination. If the disease is healed in the leprous[1] person, ⁴the priest shall command that two living clean birds and cedarwood and crimson yarn and hyssop be brought for the one who is to be cleansed. ⁵The priest shall command that one of the birds be slaughtered over fresh water in an earthen vessel. ⁶He shall take the living bird with the cedarwood and the crimson yarn and the hyssop, and dip them and the living bird in the blood of the bird that was slaughtered over the fresh water. ⁷He shall sprinkle it seven times upon the one who is to be cleansed of the leprous[1] disease; then he shall pronounce him clean, and he shall let the living bird go into the open field. ⁸The one who is to be cleansed shall wash his clothes, and shave off all his hair, and bathe himself in water, and he shall be clean. After that he shall come into the camp, but shall live outside his tent seven days. ⁹On the seventh day he shall shave all his hair: of head, beard, eyebrows; he shall shave all his hair. Then he shall wash his clothes, and bathe his body in water, and he shall be clean.

10 On the eighth day he shall take two male lambs without blemish, and one ewe lamb in its first year without blemish, and a grain offering of three-tenths of an ephah of choice flour mixed with oil, and one log[m] of oil. ¹¹The priest who cleanses shall set the person to be cleansed, along with these things, before the LORD, at the entrance of the tent of meeting.

¹²The priest shall take one of the lambs, and offer it as a guilt offering, along with the log[m] of oil, and raise them as an elevation offering before the LORD. ¹³He shall slaughter the lamb in the place where the sin offering and the burnt offering are slaughtered in the holy place; for the guilt offering, like the sin offering, belongs to the priest: it is most holy. ¹⁴The priest shall take some of the blood of the guilt offering and put it on the lobe of the right ear of the one to be cleansed, and on the thumb of the right hand, and on the big toe of the right foot. ¹⁵The priest shall take some of the log[m] of oil and pour it into the palm of his own left hand, ¹⁶and dip his right finger in the oil that is in his left hand and sprinkle some oil with his finger seven times before the LORD. ¹⁷Some of the oil that remains in his hand the priest shall put on the lobe of the right ear of the one to be cleansed, and on the thumb of the right hand, and on the big toe of the right foot, on top of the blood of the guilt offering. ¹⁸The rest of the oil that is in the priest's hand he shall put on the head of the one to be cleansed. Then the priest shall make atonement on his behalf before the LORD: ¹⁹the priest shall offer the sin offering, to make atonement for the one to be cleansed from his uncleanness. Afterward he shall slaughter the burnt offering; ²⁰and the priest shall offer the burnt offering and the grain offering on the altar. Thus the priest shall make atonement on his behalf and he shall be clean.

21 But if he is poor and cannot afford so much, he shall take one male lamb for a guilt offering to be elevated, to make atonement on his behalf, and one-tenth of an ephah of choice flour mixed with oil for a grain offering and a log[m] of oil; ²²also two turtledoves or two pigeons, such as he can afford, one for a sin offering and the other for

14.2 Mt 8.2,4; Mk 1.40,44; Lk 5.12,14; 17.14
14.4 vv. 6,49,51, 52; Num 19.6
14.7 2 Kings 5.10, 14
14.8 Lev 13.6; Num 8.7
14.10 Mt 8.4; Mk 1.44; Lk 5.14
14.12 Lev 5.2,8; 6.6,7; Ex 29.24
14.13 Lev 1.5,11; 6.24-30; 2.3; 7.6
14.14 Lev 8.23
14.18 Lev 4.26
14.19 v. 12
14.21 Lev 5.7,11; 12.8; v. 22
14.22 Lev 12.8; 15.14,15

[1]A term for several skin diseases; precise meaning uncertain [m]A liquid measure

a burnt offering. 23 On the eighth day he shall bring them for his cleansing to the priest, to the entrance of the tent of meeting, before the LORD; 24 and the priest shall take the lamb of the guilt offering and the log[n] of oil, and the priest shall raise them as an elevation offering before the LORD. 25 The priest shall slaughter the lamb of the guilt offering and shall take some of the blood of the guilt offering, and put it on the lobe of the right ear of the one to be cleansed, and on the thumb of the right hand, and on the big toe of the right foot. 26 The priest shall pour some of the oil into the palm of his own left hand, 27 and shall sprinkle with his right finger some of the oil that is in his left hand seven times before the LORD. 28 The priest shall put some of the oil that is in his hand on the lobe of the right ear of the one to be cleansed, and on the thumb of the right hand, and the big toe of the right foot, where the blood of the guilt offering was placed. 29 The rest of the oil that is in the priest's hand he shall put on the head of the one to be cleansed, to make atonement on his behalf before the LORD. 30 And he shall offer, of the turtledoves or pigeons such as he can afford, 31 one[o] for a sin offering and the other for a burnt offering, along with a grain offering; and the priest shall make atonement before the LORD on behalf of the one being cleansed. 32 This is the ritual for the one who has a leprous[p] disease, who cannot afford the offerings for his cleansing.

33 The LORD spoke to Moses and Aaron, saying:

34 When you come into the land of Canaan, which I give you for a possession, and I put a leprous[p] disease in a house in the land of your possession, 35 the owner of the house shall come and tell the priest, saying, "There seems to me to be some sort of disease in my house." 36 The priest shall command that they empty the house before the priest goes to examine the disease, or all that is in the

house will become unclean; and afterward the priest shall go in to inspect the house. 37 He shall examine the disease; if the disease is in the walls of the house with greenish or reddish spots, and if it appears to be deeper than the surface, 38 the priest shall go outside to the door of the house and shut up the house seven days. 39 The priest shall come again on the seventh day and make an inspection; if the disease has spread in the walls of the house, 40 the priest shall command that the stones in which the disease appears be taken out and thrown into an unclean place outside the city. 41 He shall have the inside of the house scraped thoroughly, and the plaster that is scraped off shall be dumped in an unclean place outside the city. 42 They shall take other stones and put them in the place of those stones, and take other plaster and plaster the house.

43 If the disease breaks out again in the house, after he has taken out the stones and scraped the house and plastered it, 44 the priest shall go and make inspection; if the disease has spread in the house, it is a spreading leprous[p] disease in the house; it is unclean. 45 He shall have the house torn down, its stones and timber and all the plaster of the house, and taken outside the city to an unclean place. 46 All who enter the house while it is shut up shall be unclean until the evening; 47 and all who sleep in the house shall wash their clothes; and all who eat in the house shall wash their clothes.

48 If the priest comes and makes an inspection, and the disease has not spread in the house after the house was plastered, the priest shall pronounce the house clean; the disease is healed. 49 For the cleansing of the house he shall take two birds, with cedarwood and crimson yarn and hyssop, 50 and

Center reference column:

14.23
vv. 10,11
14.24
v. 12
14.25
v. 14
14.28
Lev 5.6
14.30
v. 22;
Lev 15.15
14.31
Lev 5.7
14.34
Gen 17.8;
Num 32.22;
Deut 7.1
14.35
Ps 91.10;
Prov 3.33

14.38
Num 12.15
14.40
v. 45
14.44
Lev 13.51
14.49
v. 4

n A liquid measure o Gk Syr: Heb *afford,* 31*such as he can afford, one* p A term for several skin diseases; precise meaning uncertain

shall slaughter one of the birds over fresh water in an earthen vessel, [51] and shall take the cedarwood and the hyssop and the crimson yarn, along with the living bird, and dip them in the blood of the slaughtered bird and the fresh water, and sprinkle the house seven times. [52] Thus he shall cleanse the house with the blood of the bird, and with the fresh water, and with the living bird, and with the cedarwood and hyssop and crimson yarn; [53] and he shall let the living bird go out of the city into the open field; so he shall make atonement for the house, and it shall be clean.

54 This is the ritual for any leprousq disease: for an itch, [55] for leprousq diseases in clothing and houses, [56] and for a swelling or an eruption or a spot, [57] to determine when it is unclean and when it is clean. This is the ritual for leprousq diseases.

Concerning Bodily Discharges

15 The LORD spoke to Moses and Aaron, saying: [2] Speak to the people of Israel and say to them:

When any man has a discharge from his member,r his discharge makes him ceremonially unclean. [3] The uncleanness of his discharge is this: whether his memberr flows with his discharge, or his memberr is stopped from discharging, it is uncleanness for him. [4] Every bed on which the one with the discharge lies shall be unclean; and everything on which he sits shall be unclean. [5] Anyone who touches his bed shall wash his clothes, and bathe in water, and be unclean until the evening. [6] All who sit on anything on which the one with the discharge has sat shall wash their clothes, and bathe in water, and be unclean until the evening. [7] All who touch the body of the one with the discharge shall wash their clothes, and bathe in water, and be unclean until the evening. [8] If the one with the discharge spits on persons who are clean, then they shall wash their clothes, and bathe in water,

and be unclean until the evening. [9] Any saddle on which the one with the discharge rides shall be unclean. [10] All who touch anything that was under him shall be unclean until the evening, and all who carry such a thing shall wash their clothes, and bathe in water, and be unclean until the evening. [11] All those whom the one with the discharge touches without his having rinsed his hands in water shall wash their clothes, and bathe in water, and be unclean until the evening. [12] Any earthen vessel that the one with the discharge touches shall be broken; and every vessel of wood shall be rinsed in water.

13 When the one with a discharge is cleansed of his discharge, he shall count seven days for his cleansing; he shall wash his clothes and bathe his body in fresh water, and he shall be clean. [14] On the eighth day he shall take two turtledoves or two pigeons and come before the LORD to the entrance of the tent of meeting and give them to the priest. [15] The priest shall offer them, one for a sin offering and the other for a burnt offering; and the priest shall make atonement on his behalf before the LORD for his discharge.

16 If a man has an emission of semen, he shall bathe his whole body in water, and be unclean until the evening. [17] Everything made of cloth or of skin on which the semen falls shall be washed with water, and be unclean until the evening. [18] If a man lies with a woman and has an emission of semen, both of them shall bathe in water, and be unclean until the evening.

19 When a woman has a discharge of blood that is her regular discharge from her body, she shall be in her impurity for seven days, and whoever touches her shall be unclean until the evening. [20] Everything upon which she lies during her impurity shall be unclean; everything also upon which she sits

14.51
Ps 51.7
14.53
v. 20
14.54
Lev 13.30
14.56
Lev 13.2
15.2
Lev 22.4;
Num 5.2;
2 Sam 3.29;
Mt 9.20
15.7
Num 19.19

15.10
Num 19.10
15.12
Lev 6.28;
11.32,33
15.13
v. 28
15.14
Lev 14.22,
23
15.15
Lev 14.30,
31
15.16
Lev 22.4;
Deut 23.10
15.18
1 Sam 21.4
15.19
Lev 12.2

qA term for several skin diseases; precise meaning uncertain rHeb *flesh*

shall be unclean. [21]Whoever touches her bed shall wash his clothes, and bathe in water, and be unclean until the evening. [22]Whoever touches anything upon which she sits shall wash his clothes, and bathe in water, and be unclean until the evening; [23]whether it is the bed or anything upon which she sits, when he touches it he shall be unclean until the evening. [24]If any man lies with her, and her impurity falls on him, he shall be unclean seven days; and every bed on which he lies shall be unclean.

25 If a woman has a discharge of blood for many days, not at the time of her impurity, or if she has a discharge beyond the time of her impurity, all the days of the discharge she shall continue in uncleanness; as in the days of her impurity, she shall be unclean. [26]Every bed on which she lies during all the days of her discharge shall be treated as the bed of her impurity; and everything on which she sits shall be unclean, as in the uncleanness of her impurity. [27]Whoever touches these things shall be unclean, and shall wash his clothes, and bathe in water, and be unclean until the evening. [28]If she is cleansed of her discharge, she shall count seven days, and after that she shall be clean. [29]On the eighth day she shall take two turtledoves or two pigeons and bring them to the priest to the entrance of the tent of meeting. [30]The priest shall offer one for a sin offering and the other for a burnt offering; and the priest shall make atonement on her behalf before the LORD for her unclean discharge.

31 Thus you shall keep the people of Israel separate from their uncleanness, so that they do not die in their uncleanness by defiling my tabernacle that is in their midst.

32 This is the ritual for those who have a discharge: for him who has an emission of semen, becoming unclean thereby, [33]for her who is in the infirmity of her period, for anyone, male or female, who has a

discharge, and for the man who lies with a woman who is unclean.

The Day of Atonement

16 The LORD spoke to Moses after the death of the two sons of Aaron, when they drew near before the LORD and died. [2]The LORD said to Moses:

Tell your brother Aaron not to come just at any time into the sanctuary inside the curtain before the mercy seat[s] that is upon the ark, or he will die; for I appear in the cloud upon the mercy seat.[s] [3]Thus shall Aaron come into the holy place: with a young bull for a sin offering and a ram for a burnt offering. [4]He shall put on the holy linen tunic, and shall have the linen undergarments next to his body, fasten the linen sash, and wear the linen turban; these are the holy vestments. He shall bathe his body in water, and then put them on. [5]He shall take from the congregation of the people of Israel two male goats for a sin offering, and one ram for a burnt offering.

6 Aaron shall offer the bull as a sin offering for himself, and shall make atonement for himself and for his house. [7]He shall take the two goats and set them before the LORD at the entrance of the tent of meeting; [8]and Aaron shall cast lots on the two goats, one lot for the LORD and the other lot for Azazel.[t] [9]Aaron shall present the goat on which the lot fell for the LORD, and offer it as a sin offering; [10]but the goat on which the lot fell for Azazel[t] shall be presented alive before the LORD to make atonement over it, that it may be sent away into the wilderness to Azazel.[t]

11 Aaron shall present the bull as a sin offering for himself, and shall make atonement for himself and for his house; he shall slaughter the bull as a sin offering for himself. [12]He shall take a censer full of coals of fire from the altar before the LORD, and two handfuls of crushed sweet incense, and he

Center reference column:

15.21
v. 27
15.24
Lev 20.18
15.25
Mt 9.20;
Mk 5.25;
Lk 8.43
15.27
v. 21
15.29
Gen 15.9
15.31
Ezek 44.23;
Num 5.3;
19.13,20;
Ezek 5.11;
23.38
15.32
vv. 2,16
15.33
vv. 19,24,25

16.1
Lev 10.1,2
16.2
Ex 30.10;
Heb 9.7;
10.19;
Ex 25.21,22
16.3
Heb 9.7,12,
24,25;
Lev 4.3
16.4
Ex 28.39,
42,43; v. 24
16.5
Lev 4.13-21
16.6
Lev 9.7;
Heb 5.2;
7.27,28; 9.7
16.11
Heb 7.27;
9.7
16.12
Lev 10.1;
Ex 30.34

[s]Or *the cover* [t]Traditionally rendered *a scapegoat*

shall bring it inside the curtain ¹³and put the incense on the fire before the Lord, that the cloud of the incense may cover the mercy seat ᵘ that is upon the covenant,ᵛ or he will die. ¹⁴He shall take some of the blood of the bull, and sprinkle it with his finger on the front of the mercy seat, ᵘ and before the mercy seat ᵘ he shall sprinkle the blood with his finger seven times.

15 He shall slaughter the goat of the sin offering that is for the people and bring its blood inside the curtain, and do with its blood as he did with the blood of the bull, sprinkling it upon the mercy seat ᵘ and before the mercy seat. ᵘ ¹⁶Thus he shall make atonement for the sanctuary, because of the uncleannesses of the people of Israel, and because of their transgressions, all their sins; and so he shall do for the tent of meeting, which remains with them in the midst of their uncleannesses. ¹⁷No one shall be in the tent of meeting from the time he enters to make atonement in the sanctuary until he comes out and has made atonement for himself and for his house and for all the assembly of Israel. ¹⁸Then he shall go out to the altar that is before the Lord and make atonement on its behalf, and shall take some of the blood of the bull and of the blood of the goat, and put it on each of the horns of the altar. ¹⁹He shall sprinkle some of the blood on it with his finger seven times, and cleanse it and hallow it from the uncleannesses of the people of Israel.

20 When he has finished atoning for the holy place and the tent of meeting and the altar, he shall present the live goat. ²¹Then Aaron shall lay both his hands on the head of the live goat, and confess over it all the iniquities of the people of Israel, and all their transgressions, all their sins, putting them on the head of the goat, and sending it away into the wilderness by means of someone designated for the task. ʷ ²²The goat shall bear on itself all their iniquities to a barren

region; and the goat shall be set free in the wilderness.

23 Then Aaron shall enter the tent of meeting, and shall take off the linen vestments that he put on when he went into the holy place, and shall leave them there. ²⁴He shall bathe his body in water in a holy place, and put on his vestments; then he shall come out and offer his burnt offering and the burnt offering of the people, making atonement for himself and for the people. ²⁵The fat of the sin offering he shall turn into smoke on the altar. ²⁶The one who sets the goat free for Azazelˣ shall wash his clothes and bathe his body in water, and afterward may come into the camp. ²⁷The bull of the sin offering and the goat of the sin offering, whose blood was brought in to make atonement in the holy place, shall be taken outside the camp; their skin and their flesh and their dung shall be consumed in fire. ²⁸The one who burns them shall wash his clothes and bathe his body in water, and afterward may come into the camp.

29 This shall be a statute to you forever: In the seventh month, on the tenth day of the month, you shall deny yourselves,ʸ and shall do no work, neither the citizen nor the alien who resides among you. ³⁰For on this day atonement shall be made for you, to cleanse you; from all your sins you shall be clean before the Lord. ³¹It is a sabbath of complete rest to you, and you shall deny yourselves;ʸ it is a statute forever. ³²The priest who is anointed and consecrated as priest in his father's place shall make atonement, wearing the linen vestments, the holy vestments. ³³He shall make atonement for the sanctuary, and he shall make atonement for the tent of meeting and for the altar, and he shall make atonement for the priests and for all the people of the assembly.

16.13
Lev 22.9
16.14
Heb 9.13, 25; Lev 4.6, 17
16.15
Heb 9.3,7, 12
16.16
Ex 29.36; Heb 2.17
16.18
Lev 4.25; Ezek 43.20, 22
16.19
v. 14
16.21
Isa 53.6
16.22
Isa 53.11,12

16.23
v. 4; Ezek 42.14; 44.19
16.24
vv. 3-5
16.27
Lev 4.12,21; 6.30; Heb 13.11
16.29
Lev 23.27; Num 29.7
16.31
Lev 23.32; Isa 58.3,5
16.32
v. 4; Num 20.26, 28
16.33
vv. 6,16-18, 24

ᵘ Or *the cover* ᵛ Or *treaty,* or *testament;* Heb *eduth* ʷ Meaning of Heb uncertain ˣ Traditionally rendered *a scapegoat* ʸ Or *shall fast*

34 This shall be an everlasting statute for you, to make atonement for the people of Israel once in the year for all their sins. And Moses did as the LORD had commanded him.

The Slaughtering of Animals

17 The LORD spoke to Moses: 2 Speak to Aaron and his sons and to all the people of Israel and say to them: This is what the LORD has commanded. 3 If anyone of the house of Israel slaughters an ox or a lamb or a goat in the camp, or slaughters it outside the camp, 4 and does not bring it to the entrance of the tent of meeting, to present it as an offering to the LORD before the tabernacle of the LORD, he shall be held guilty of bloodshed; he has shed blood, and he shall be cut off from the people. 5 This is in order that the people of Israel may bring their sacrifices that they offer in the open field, that they may bring them to the LORD, to the priest at the entrance of the tent of meeting, and offer them as sacrifices of well-being to the LORD. 6 The priest shall dash the blood against the altar of the LORD at the entrance of the tent of meeting, and turn the fat into smoke as a pleasing odor to the LORD, 7 so that they may no longer offer their sacrifices for goat-demons, to whom they prostitute themselves. This shall be a statute forever to them throughout their generations.

8 And say to them further: Anyone of the house of Israel or of the aliens who reside among them who offers a burnt offering or sacrifice, 9 and does not bring it to the entrance of the tent of meeting, to sacrifice it to the LORD, shall be cut off from the people.

Eating Blood Prohibited

10 If anyone of the house of Israel or of the aliens who reside among them eats any blood, I will set my face against that person who eats blood, and will cut that person off from the people. 11 For the life of the flesh is in the blood;

and I have given it to you for making atonement for your lives on the altar; for, as life, it is the blood that makes atonement. 12 Therefore I have said to the people of Israel: No person among you shall eat blood, nor shall any alien who resides among you eat blood. 13 And anyone of the people of Israel, or of the aliens who reside among them, who hunts down an animal or bird that may be eaten shall pour out its blood and cover it with earth.

14 For the life of every creature—its blood is its life; therefore I have said to the people of Israel: You shall not eat the blood of any creature, for the life of every creature is its blood; whoever eats it shall be cut off. 15 All persons, citizens or aliens, who eat what dies of itself or what has been torn by wild animals, shall wash their clothes, and bathe themselves in water, and be unclean until the evening; then they shall be clean. 16 But if they do not wash themselves or bathe their body, they shall bear their guilt.

Sexual Relations

18 The LORD spoke to Moses, saying: 2 Speak to the people of Israel and say to them: I am the LORD your God. 3 You shall not do as they do in the land of Egypt, where you lived, and you shall not do as they do in the land of Canaan, to which I am bringing you. You shall not follow their statutes. 4 My ordinances you shall observe and my statutes you shall keep, following them: I am the LORD your God. 5 You shall keep my statutes and my ordinances; by doing so one shall live: I am the LORD.

6 None of you shall approach anyone near of kin to uncover nakedness: I am the LORD. 7 You shall not uncover the nakedness of your father, which is the nakedness of your mother; she is your mother, you shall not uncover her nakedness. 8 You shall not uncover the nakedness of your father's wife; it is the nakedness of your father.

16.34
Heb 9.7,25
17.4
Deut 12.5-21;
Rom 5.13
17.6
Lev 3.2;
Num 18.17
17.7
Ex 22.20;
32.8; 34.15;
Deut 32.17;
2 Chr 11.15
17.9
v. 4
17.10
Lev 3.17;
Deut 12.16,
23
17.11
v. 14;
Gen 9.4;
Heb 9.22

17.13
Lev 7.26;
Deut 12.16
17.14
v. 11
17.15
Ex 22.31;
Deut 14.21
18.2
Ex 6.7;
Lev 11.44
18.3
Ezek 20.7,8;
Ex 23.24;
Lev 20.23
18.5
Ezek 20.11;
Lk 10.28;
Rom 10.5;
Gal 3.12
18.7
Lev 20.11

9 You shall not uncover the nakedness of your sister, your father's daughter or your mother's daughter, whether born at home or born abroad. 10 You shall not uncover the nakedness of your son's daughter or of your daughter's daughter, for their nakedness is your own nakedness. 11 You shall not uncover the nakedness of your father's wife's daughter, begotten by your father, since she is your sister. 12 You shall not uncover the nakedness of your father's sister; she is your father's flesh. 13 You shall not uncover the nakedness of your mother's sister, for she is your mother's flesh. 14 You shall not uncover the nakedness of your father's brother, that is, you shall not approach his wife; she is your aunt. 15 You shall not uncover the nakedness of your daughter-in-law: she is your son's wife; you shall not uncover her nakedness. 16 You shall not uncover the nakedness of your brother's wife; it is your brother's nakedness. 17 You shall not uncover the nakedness of a woman and her daughter, and you shall not take[z] her son's daughter or her daughter's daughter to uncover her nakedness; they are your[a] flesh; it is depravity. 18 And you shall not take[z] a woman as a rival to her sister, uncovering her nakedness while her sister is still alive.

19 You shall not approach a woman to uncover her nakedness while she is in her menstrual uncleanness. 20 You shall not have sexual relations with your kinsman's wife, and defile yourself with her. 21 You shall not give any of your offspring to sacrifice them[b] to Molech, and so profane the name of your God: I am the LORD. 22 You shall not lie with a male as with a woman; it is an abomination. 23 You shall not have sexual relations with any animal and defile yourself with it, nor shall any woman give herself to an animal to have sexual relations with it: it is perversion.

24 Do not defile yourselves in any of these ways, for by all these practices the nations I am casting out before you have defiled themselves; 25 Thus the land became defiled; and I punished it for its iniquity, and the land vomited out its inhabitants. 26 But you shall keep my statutes and my ordinances and commit none of these abominations, either the citizen or the alien who resides among you 27 (for the inhabitants of the land, who were before you, committed all of these abominations, and the land became defiled); 28 otherwise the land will vomit you out for defiling it, as it vomited out the nation that was before you. 29 For whoever commits any of these abominations shall be cut off from their people. 30 So keep my charge not to commit any of these abominations that were done before you, and not to defile yourselves by them: I am the LORD your God.

Ritual and Moral Holiness

19 The LORD spoke to Moses, saying:

2 Speak to all the congregation of the people of Israel and say to them: You shall be holy, for I the LORD your God am holy. 3 You shall each revere your mother and father, and you shall keep my sabbaths: I am the LORD your God. 4 Do not turn to idols or make cast images for yourselves: I am the LORD your God.

5 When you offer a sacrifice of well-being to the LORD, offer it in such a way that it is acceptable on your behalf. 6 It shall be eaten on the same day you offer it, or on the next day; and anything left over until the third day shall be consumed in fire. 7 If it is eaten at all on the third day, it is an abomination; it will not be acceptable. 8 All who eat it shall be subject to punishment, because they have profaned what is holy to the LORD; and any such person shall be cut off from the people.

9 When you reap the harvest of your land, you shall not reap to the

18.9
Lev 20.17
18.12
Lev 20.19
18.14
Lev 20.20
18.15
Lev 20.12
18.16
Lev 20.21
18.17
Lev 20.14
18.19
Lev 15.24;
20.18
18.20
Lev 20.10;
Ex 20.14;
Prov 6.32;
Mt 5.27
18.21
Lev 20.2-5;
19.12; 21.6
18.22
Lev 20.13;
Rom 1.27
18.23
Ex 22.19;
Lev 20.15;
Deut 27.21
18.24
v. 3;
Lev 20.23

18.25
Lev 20.23;
Deut 9.5;
18.12; v. 28
18.30
Lev 22.9;
Deut 11.1;
v. 2
19.2
1 Pet 1.16
19.3
Ex 20.8,12;
Lev 11.44
19.4
Lev 26.1;
Ps 96.5;
Ex 20.23;
34.17
19.9
Lev 23.22;
Deut 24.20-22

z Or marry a Gk: Heb lacks your
b Heb to pass them over

very edges of your field, or gather the gleanings of your harvest. [10]You shall not strip your vineyard bare, or gather the fallen grapes of your vineyard; you shall leave them for the poor and the alien: I am the LORD your God.

11 You shall not steal; you shall not deal falsely; and you shall not lie to one another. [12]And you shall not swear falsely by my name, profaning the name of your God: I am the LORD.

13 You shall not defraud your neighbor; you shall not steal; and you shall not keep for yourself the wages of a laborer until morning. [14]You shall not revile the deaf or put a stumbling block before the blind; you shall fear your God: I am the LORD.

15 You shall not render an unjust judgment; you shall not be partial to the poor or defer to the great: with justice you shall judge your neighbor. [16]You shall not go around as a slanderer[c] among your people, and you shall not profit by the blood[d] of your neighbor: I am the LORD.

17 You shall not hate in your heart anyone of your kin; you shall reprove your neighbor, or you will incur guilt yourself. [18]You shall not take vengeance or bear a grudge against any of your people, but you shall love your neighbor as yourself: I am the LORD.

19 You shall keep my statutes. You shall not let your animals breed with a different kind; you shall not sow your field with two kinds of seed; nor shall you put on a garment made of two different materials.

20 If a man has sexual relations with a woman who is a slave, designated for another man but not ransomed or given her freedom, an inquiry shall be held. They shall not be put to death, since she has not been freed; [21]but he shall bring a guilt offering for himself to the LORD, at the entrance of the tent of meeting, a ram as guilt offering. [22]And the priest shall make atonement for him with the ram of guilt offering before the LORD for his sin that he committed; and the sin he committed shall be forgiven him.

23 When you come into the land and plant all kinds of trees for food, then you shall regard their fruit as forbidden;[e] three years it shall be forbidden[f] to you, it must not be eaten. [24]In the fourth year all their fruit shall be set apart for rejoicing in the LORD. [25]But in the fifth year you may eat of their fruit, that their yield may be increased for you: I am the LORD your God.

26 You shall not eat anything with its blood. You shall not practice augury or witchcraft. [27]You shall not round off the hair on your temples or mar the edges of your beard. [28]You shall not make any gashes in your flesh for the dead or tattoo any marks upon you: I am the LORD.

29 Do not profane your daughter by making her a prostitute, that the land not become prostituted and full of depravity. [30]You shall keep my sabbaths and reverence my sanctuary: I am the LORD.

31 Do not turn to mediums or wizards; do not seek them out, to be defiled by them: I am the LORD your God.

32 You shall rise before the aged, and defer to the old; and you shall fear your God: I am the LORD.

33 When an alien resides with you in your land, you shall not oppress the alien. [34]The alien who resides with you shall be to you as the citizen among you; you shall love the alien as yourself, for you were aliens in the land of Egypt: I am the LORD your God.

35 You shall not cheat in measuring length, weight, or quantity. [36]You shall have honest balances, honest weights, an honest ephah, and an honest hin: I am the LORD your God, who brought you out of the land of Egypt. [37]You shall keep all my statutes and all my ordinances, and observe them: I am the LORD.

19.11
Ex 20.15;
Lev 6.2;
Eph 4.25;
Col 3.9
19.12
Ex 20.7;
Lev 18.21
19.13
Ex 22.7-15;
21-27;
Deut 24.15;
Jas 5.4
19.14
Deut 27.18
19.15
Ex 23.6;
Deut 1.17
19.16
Ps 15.3;
Ezek 22.9;
Ex 23.7
19.17
1 Jn 2.9,
11; 3.15;
Lk 17.3;
Gal 6.1
19.18
Rom 12.19;
Ps 103.9;
Mt 19.19;
Mk 12.31;
Rom 13.9
19.19
Deut 22.9,
11
19.21
Lev 5.15

19.24
Deut 12.17,
18; Prov 3.9
19.26
Lev 17.10;
Deut 18.10
19.27
Lev 21.5
19.28
Lev 21.5
19.29
Deut 23.17
19.30
v. 3;
Lev 26.2
19.31
Lev 20.6,27;
Deut 18.10,
11
19.33
Ex 22.21
19.34
Ex 12.48,
49;
Deut 10.19

c Meaning of Heb uncertain d Heb *stand against the blood* e Heb *as their uncircumcision* f Heb *uncircumcision*

Penalties for Violations of Holiness

20 The Lord spoke to Moses, saying: ²Say further to the people of Israel:

Any of the people of Israel, or of the aliens who reside in Israel, who give any of their offspring to Molech shall be put to death; the people of the land shall stone them to death. ³I myself will set my face against them, and will cut them off from the people, because they have given of their offspring to Molech, defiling my sanctuary and profaning my holy name. ⁴And if the people of the land should ever close their eyes to them, when they give of their offspring to Molech, and do not put them to death, ⁵I myself will set my face against them and against their family, and will cut them off from among their people, them and all who follow them in prostituting themselves to Molech.

6 If any turn to mediums and wizards, prostituting themselves to them, I will set my face against them, and will cut them off from the people. ⁷Consecrate yourselves therefore, and be holy; for I am the Lord your God. ⁸Keep my statutes, and observe them; I am the Lord; I sanctify you. ⁹All who curse father or mother shall be put to death; having cursed father or mother, their blood is upon them.

10 If a man commits adultery with the wife of[g] his neighbor, both the adulterer and the adulteress shall be put to death. ¹¹The man who lies with his father's wife has uncovered his father's nakedness; both of them shall be put to death; their blood is upon them. ¹²If a man lies with his daughter-in-law, both of them shall be put to death; they have committed perversion, their blood is upon them. ¹³If a man lies with a male as with a woman, both of them have committed an abomination; they shall be put to death; their blood is upon them. ¹⁴If a man takes a wife and her mother also, it is depravity; they shall be burned to death, both

he and they, that there may be no depravity among you. ¹⁵If a man has sexual relations with an animal, he shall be put to death; and you shall kill the animal. ¹⁶If a woman approaches any animal and has sexual relations with it, you shall kill the woman and the animal; they shall be put to death, their blood is upon them.

17 If a man takes his sister, a daughter of his father or a daughter of his mother, and sees her nakedness, and she sees his nakedness, it is a disgrace, and they shall be cut off in the sight of their people; he has uncovered his sister's nakedness, he shall be subject to punishment. ¹⁸If a man lies with a woman having her sickness and uncovers her nakedness, he has laid bare her flow and she has laid bare her flow of blood; both of them shall be cut off from their people. ¹⁹You shall not uncover the nakedness of your mother's sister or of your father's sister, for that is to lay bare one's own flesh; they shall be subject to punishment. ²⁰If a man lies with his uncle's wife, he has uncovered his uncle's nakedness; they shall be subject to punishment; they shall die childless. ²¹If a man takes his brother's wife, it is impurity; he has uncovered his brother's nakedness; they shall be childless.

22 You shall keep all my statutes and all my ordinances, and observe them, so that the land to which I bring you to settle in may not vomit you out. ²³You shall not follow the practices of the nation that I am driving out before you. Because they did all these things, I abhorred them. ²⁴But I have said to you: You shall inherit their land, and I will give it to you to possess, a land flowing with milk and honey. I am the Lord your God; I have separated you from the peoples. ²⁵You shall therefore make a distinction between the clean animal and the unclean, and between the unclean bird and the clean; you

20.2
Lev 18.21
20.3
Lev 15.31; 18.21
20.4
Deut 17.2,3, 5
20.6
Lev 19.31
20.7
1 Pet 1.16
20.8
Lev 19.37; Ex 31.13
20.9
Ex 21.17; Deut 27.16
20.10
Lev 18.20; Deut 22.22
20.11
Lev 18.7,8
20.12
Lev 18.15
20.13
Lev 18.22
20.14
Deut 27.23

20.15
Lev 18.23
20.17
Lev 18.9
20.18
Lev 18.19
20.19
Lev 18.12, 13
20.20
Lev 18.14
20.21
Lev 18.16
20.22
Lev 18.25, 26,28
20.23
Lev 18.3,24, 27,30
20.24
Ex 13.5; 33.3,16; v. 26
20.25
Lev 11.1-47; Deut 14.3-21

g Heb repeats *if a man commits adultery with the wife of*

shall not bring abomination on yourselves by animal or by bird or by anything with which the ground teems, which I have set apart for you to hold unclean. 26You shall be holy to me; for I the LORD am holy, and I have separated you from the other peoples to be mine.

27 A man or a woman who is a medium or a wizard shall be put to death; they shall be stoned to death, their blood is upon them.

The Holiness of Priests

21 The LORD said to Moses: Speak to the priests, the sons of Aaron, and say to them:

No one shall defile himself for a dead person among his relatives, 2except for his nearest kin: his mother, his father, his son, his daughter, his brother; 3likewise, for a virgin sister, close to him because she has had no husband, he may defile himself for her. 4But he shall not defile himself as a husband among his people and so profane himself. 5They shall not make bald spots upon their heads, or shave off the edges of their beards, or make any gashes in their flesh. 6They shall be holy to their God, and not profane the name of their God; for they offer the LORD's offerings by fire, the food of their God; therefore they shall be holy. 7They shall not marry a prostitute or a woman who has been defiled; neither shall they marry a woman divorced from her husband. For they are holy to their God, 8and you shall treat them as holy, since they offer the food of your God; they shall be holy to you, for I the LORD, I who sanctify you, am holy. 9When the daughter of a priest profanes herself through prostitution, she profanes her father; she shall be burned to death.

10 The priest who is exalted above his fellows, on whose head the anointing oil has been poured and who has been consecrated to wear the vestments, shall not dishevel his hair, nor tear his vestments. 11He shall not go where there is a dead body; he shall not

defile himself even for his father or mother. 12He shall not go outside the sanctuary and thus profane the sanctuary of his God; for the consecration of the anointing oil of his God is upon him: I am the LORD. 13He shall marry only a woman who is a virgin. 14A widow, or a divorced woman, or a woman who has been defiled, a prostitute, these he shall not marry. He shall marry a virgin of his own kin, 15that he may not profane his offspring among his kin; for I am the LORD; I sanctify him.

16 The LORD spoke to Moses, saying: 17Speak to Aaron and say: No one of your offspring throughout their generations who has a blemish may approach to offer the food of his God. 18For no one who has a blemish shall draw near, one who is blind or lame, or one who has a mutilated face or a limb too long, 19or one who has a broken foot or a broken hand, 20or a hunchback, or a dwarf, or a man with a blemish in his eyes or an itching disease or scabs or crushed testicles. 21No descendant of Aaron the priest who has a blemish shall come near to offer the LORD's offerings by fire; since he has a blemish, he shall not come near to offer the food of his God. 22He may eat the food of his God, of the most holy as well as of the holy. 23But he shall not come near the curtain or approach the altar, because he has a blemish, that he may not profane my sanctuaries; for I am the LORD; I sanctify them. 24Thus Moses spoke to Aaron and to his sons and to all the people of Israel.

The Use of Holy Offerings

22 The LORD spoke to Moses, saying: 2Direct Aaron and his sons to deal carefully with the sacred donations of the people of Israel, which they dedicate to me, so that they may not profane my holy name; I am the LORD. 3Say to them: If anyone among all your offspring throughout your generations comes near the sacred donations, which the people of Israel

20.26
v. 24
20.27
Lev 19.31
21.1
Lev 19.28;
Ezek 44.25
21.5
Deut 14.1;
Ezek 44.20;
Lev 19.27
21.6
Lev 18.21;
3.11
21.7
vv. 13,14
21.10
Lev 16.32;
10.6,7
21.11
Lev 19.28

21.12
Lev 10.7;
Ex 29.6,7
21.13
v. 7;
Ezek 44.22
21.17ff
v. 6
21.18
Lev 22.23
21.20
Deut 23.1
21.21
v. 6
21.23
v. 12
22.3
Lev 7.20

dedicate to the Lord, while he is in a state of uncleanness, that person shall be cut off from my presence: I am the Lord. [4] No one of Aaron's offspring who has a leprous[h] disease or suffers a discharge may eat of the sacred donations until he is clean. Whoever touches anything made unclean by a corpse or a man who has had an emission of semen, [5] and whoever touches any swarming thing by which he may be made unclean or any human being by whom he may be made unclean — whatever his uncleanness may be — [6] the person who touches any such shall be unclean until evening and shall not eat of the sacred donations unless he has washed his body in water. [7] When the sun sets he shall be clean; and afterward he may eat of the sacred donations, for they are his food. [8] That which died or was torn by wild animals he shall not eat, becoming unclean by it: I am the Lord. [9] They shall keep my charge, so that they may not incur guilt and die in the sanctuary[i] for having profaned it: I am the Lord; I sanctify them.

10 No lay person shall eat of the sacred donations. No bound or hired servant of the priest shall eat of the sacred donations; [11] but if a priest acquires anyone by purchase, the person may eat of them; and those that are born in his house may eat of his food. [12] If a priest's daughter marries a layman, she shall not eat of the offering of the sacred donations; [13] but if a priest's daughter is widowed or divorced, without offspring, and returns to her father's house, as in her youth, she may eat of her father's food. No lay person shall eat of it. [14] If a man eats of the sacred donation unintentionally, he shall add one-fifth of its value to it, and give the sacred donation to the priest. [15] No one shall profane the sacred donations of the people of Israel, which they offer to the Lord, [16] causing them to bear guilt requiring a guilt offering, by eating their sacred donations: for I am the Lord; I sanctify them.

Acceptable Offerings

17 The Lord spoke to Moses, saying: [18] Speak to Aaron and his sons and all the people of Israel and say to them: When anyone of the house of Israel or of the aliens residing in Israel presents an offering, whether in payment of a vow or as a freewill offering that is offered to the Lord as a burnt offering, [19] to be acceptable in your behalf it shall be a male without blemish, of the cattle or the sheep or the goats. [20] You shall not offer anything that has a blemish, for it will not be acceptable in your behalf.

21 When anyone offers a sacrifice of well-being to the Lord, in fulfillment of a vow or as a freewill offering, from the herd or from the flock, to be acceptable it must be perfect; there shall be no blemish in it. [22] Anything blind, or injured, or maimed, or having a discharge or an itch or scabs — these you shall not offer to the Lord or put any of them on the altar as offerings by fire to the Lord. [23] An ox or a lamb that has a limb too long or too short you may present for a freewill offering; but it will not be accepted for a vow. [24] Any animal that has its testicles bruised or crushed or torn or cut, you shall not offer to the Lord; such you shall not do within your land, [25] nor shall you accept any such animals from a foreigner to offer as food to your God; since they are mutilated, with a blemish in them, they shall not be accepted in your behalf.

26 The Lord spoke to Moses, saying: [27] When an ox or a sheep or a goat is born, it shall remain seven days with its mother, and from the eighth day on it shall be acceptable as the Lord's offering by fire. [28] But you shall not slaughter, from the herd or the flock, an animal with its young on the same day. [29] When you sacrifice a thanksgiving offering to the Lord, you shall sacrifice it so that it may be acceptable in

22.4
Lev 14.1-32;
Num 19.11,
12; 15.16,17
22.5
Lev 11.24,
43,44; 15.7,
19
22.8
Ex 22.31;
Lev 17.15
22.9
Lev 18.30;
v. 16
22.10
v. 13
22.13
v. 10
22.14
Lev 5.15,16
22.16
v. 9

22.19
Lev 1.3
22.20
Deut 15.21;
17.1;
Heb 9.14;
1 Pet 1.19
22.21
Lev 3.1,6
22.25
Lev 21.6,17
22.27
Ex 22.30
22.28
Deut 22.6,7
22.29
Lev 7.12

[h] A term for several skin diseases; precise meaning uncertain [i] Vg: Heb incur guilt for it and die in it

your behalf. ³⁰It shall be eaten on the same day; you shall not leave any of it until morning: I am the LORD.

31 Thus you shall keep my commandments and observe them: I am the LORD. ³²You shall not profane my holy name, that I may be sanctified among the people of Israel: I am the LORD; I sanctify you, ³³I who brought you out of the land of Egypt to be your God: I am the LORD.

Appointed Festivals

23 The LORD spoke to Moses, saying: ²Speak to the people of Israel and say to them: These are the appointed festivals of the LORD that you shall proclaim as holy convocations, my appointed festivals.

The Sabbath, Passover, and Unleavened Bread

3 Six days shall work be done; but the seventh day is a sabbath of complete rest, a holy convocation; you shall do no work: it is a sabbath to the LORD throughout your settlements.

4 These are the appointed festivals of the LORD, the holy convocations, which you shall celebrate at the time appointed for them. ⁵In the first month, on the fourteenth day of the month, at twilight,ⁱ there shall be a passover offering to the LORD, ⁶and on the fifteenth day of the same month is the festival of unleavened bread to the LORD; seven days you shall eat unleavened bread. ⁷On the first day you shall have a holy convocation; you shall not work at your occupations. ⁸For seven days you shall present the LORD's offerings by fire; on the seventh day there shall be a holy convocation: you shall not work at your occupations.

The Offering of First Fruits

9 The LORD spoke to Moses: ¹⁰Speak to the people of Israel and say to them: When you enter the land that I am giving you and you reap its harvest, you shall bring the sheaf of the first fruits of your har-

22.30
Lev 7.15
22.31
Lev 19.37
22.32
Lev 18.21;
10.3
22.33
Ex 6.7;
Lev 11.45
23.2
vv. 4,37,44;
Num 29.39
23.3
Lev 19.3;
Ex 31.13-17;
Deut 5.13
23.4
v. 2
23.5
Ex 12.18,
19;
Num 28.16,
17
23.8
vv. 8,21,25,
35,36
23.10
Ex 23.16,
19; 34.22,26

23.13
Lev 2.14-16
23.15
Deut 16.9
23.16
Num 28.26
23.17
Lev 2.12;
7.13
23.19
Num 28.30;
Lev 3.1
23.21
v. 7

vest to the priest. ¹¹He shall raise the sheaf before the LORD, that you may find acceptance; on the day after the sabbath the priest shall raise it. ¹²On the day when you raise the sheaf, you shall offer a lamb a year old, without blemish, as a burnt offering to the LORD. ¹³And the grain offering with it shall be two-tenths of an ephah of choice flour mixed with oil, an offering by fire of pleasing odor to the LORD; and the drink offering with it shall be of wine, one-fourth of a hin. ¹⁴You shall eat no bread or parched grain or fresh ears until that very day, until you have brought the offering of your God: it is a statute forever throughout your generations in all your settlements.

The Festival of Weeks

15 And from the day after the sabbath, from the day on which you bring the sheaf of the elevation offering, you shall count off seven weeks; they shall be complete. ¹⁶You shall count until the day after the seventh sabbath, fifty days; then you shall present an offering of new grain to the LORD. ¹⁷You shall bring from your settlements two loaves of bread as an elevation offering, each made of two-tenths of an ephah; they shall be of choice flour, baked with leaven, as first fruits to the LORD. ¹⁸You shall present with the bread seven lambs a year old without blemish, one young bull, and two rams; they shall be a burnt offering to the LORD, along with their grain offering and their drink offerings, an offering by fire of pleasing odor to the LORD. ¹⁹You shall also offer one male goat for a sin offering, and two male lambs a year old as a sacrifice of well-being. ²⁰The priest shall raise them with the bread of the first fruits as an elevation offering before the LORD, together with the two lambs; they shall be holy to the LORD for the priest. ²¹On that same day you shall make proclamation; you shall hold a holy convocation; you shall not work at your

ⁱ Heb *between the two evenings*

occupations. This is a statute forever in all your settlements throughout your generations.

22 When you reap the harvest of your land, you shall not reap to the very edges of your field, or gather the gleanings of your harvest; you shall leave them for the poor and for the alien: I am the LORD your God.

The Festival of Trumpets

23 The LORD spoke to Moses, saying: 24 Speak to the people of Israel, saying: In the seventh month, on the first day of the month, you shall observe a day of complete rest, a holy convocation commemorated with trumpet blasts. 25 You shall not work at your occupations; and you shall present the LORD's offering by fire.

The Day of Atonement

26 The LORD spoke to Moses, saying: 27 Now, the tenth day of this seventh month is the day of atonement; it shall be a holy convocation for you: you shall deny yourselves[k] and present the LORD's offering by fire; 28 and you shall do no work during that entire day; for it is a day of atonement, to make atonement on your behalf before the LORD your God. 29 For anyone who does not practice self-denial[l] during that entire day shall be cut off from the people. 30 And anyone who does any work during that entire day, such a one I will destroy from the midst of the people. 31 You shall do no work: it is a statute forever throughout your generations in all your settlements. 32 It shall be to you a sabbath of complete rest, and you shall deny yourselves;[k] on the ninth day of the month at evening, from evening to evening you shall keep your sabbath.

The Festival of Booths

33 The LORD spoke to Moses, saying: 34 Speak to the people of Israel, saying: On the fifteenth day of this seventh month, and lasting seven days, there shall be the festival of booths[m] to the LORD. 35 The first day shall be a holy convoca-

tion; you shall not work at your occupations. 36 Seven days you shall present the LORD's offerings by fire; on the eighth day you shall observe a holy convocation and present the LORD's offerings by fire; it is a solemn assembly; you shall not work at your occupations.

37 These are the appointed festivals of the LORD, which you shall celebrate as times of holy convocation, for presenting to the LORD offerings by fire—burnt offerings and grain offerings, sacrifices and drink offerings, each on its proper day— 38 apart from the sabbaths of the LORD, and apart from your gifts, and apart from all your votive offerings, and apart from all your freewill offerings, which you give to the LORD.

39 Now, the fifteenth day of the seventh month, when you have gathered in the produce of the land, you shall keep the festival of the LORD, lasting seven days; a complete rest on the first day, and a complete rest on the eighth day. 40 On the first day you shall take the fruit of majestic[n] trees, branches of palm trees, boughs of leafy trees, and willows of the brook; and you shall rejoice before the LORD your God for seven days. 41 You shall keep it as a festival to the LORD seven days in the year; you shall keep it in the seventh month as a statute forever throughout your generations. 42 You shall live in booths for seven days; all that are citizens in Israel shall live in booths, 43 so that your generations may know that I made the people of Israel live in booths when I brought them out of the land of Egypt: I am the LORD your God.

44 Thus Moses declared to the people of Israel the appointed festivals of the LORD.

The Lamp

24 The LORD spoke to Moses, saying: 2 Command the people of Israel to bring you pure oil of beaten olives for the lamp,

23.22
Lev 19.9
23.24
Num 29.1;
Lev 25.9
23.27
Lev 16.29,
30
23.29
Gen 17.14
23.30
Lev 20.3,5,6
23.34
Ex 23.16;
Num 29.12;
vv. 42,43

23.36
Num 29.12-38
23.37
v. 2,4
23.39
Ex 23.16;
Deut 16.13
23.40
Neh 8.15;
Deut 16.14,
15
23.42
Neh 8.14-16
23.44
vv. 2,37
24.2
Ex 27.20,21

k Or *shall fast* l Or *does not fast* m Or *tabernacles*: Heb *succoth* n Meaning of Heb uncertain

that a light may be kept burning regularly. ³Aaron shall set it up in the tent of meeting, outside the curtain of the covenant,° to burn from evening to morning before the LORD regularly; it shall be a statute forever throughout your generations. ⁴He shall set up the lamps on the lampstand of pure goldᴾ before the LORD regularly.

The Bread for the Tabernacle

5 You shall take choice flour, and bake twelve loaves of it; two-tenths of an ephah shall be in each loaf. ⁶You shall place them in two rows, six in a row, on the table of pure gold.�q ⁷You shall put pure frankincense with each row, to be a token offering for the bread, as an offering by fire to the LORD. ⁸Every sabbath day Aaron shall set them in order before the LORD regularly as a commitment of the people of Israel, as a covenant forever. ⁹They shall be for Aaron and his descendants, who shall eat them in a holy place, for they are most holy portions for him from the offerings by fire to the LORD, a perpetual due.

Blasphemy and Its Punishment

10 A man whose mother was an Israelite and whose father was an Egyptian came out among the people of Israel; and the Israelite woman's son and a certain Israelite began fighting in the camp. ¹¹The Israelite woman's son blasphemed the Name in a curse. And they brought him to Moses—now his mother's name was Shelomith, daughter of Dibri, of the tribe of Dan— ¹²and they put him in custody, until the decision of the LORD should be made clear to them.

13 The LORD said to Moses, saying: ¹⁴Take the blasphemer outside the camp; and let all who were within hearing lay their hands on his head, and let the whole congregation stone him. ¹⁵And speak to the people of Israel, saying: Anyone who curses God shall bear the sin. ¹⁶One who blasphemes the name of the LORD shall be put to death; the whole congregation shall stone

the blasphemer. Aliens as well as citizens, when they blaspheme the Name, shall be put to death. ¹⁷Anyone who kills a human being shall be put to death. ¹⁸Anyone who kills an animal shall make restitution for it, life for life. ¹⁹Anyone who maims another shall suffer the same injury in return: ²⁰fracture for fracture, eye for eye, tooth for tooth; the injury inflicted is the injury to be suffered. ²¹One who kills an animal shall make restitution for it; but one who kills a human being shall be put to death. ²²You shall have one law for the alien and for the citizen: for I am the LORD your God. ²³Moses spoke thus to the people of Israel; and they took the blasphemer outside the camp, and stoned him to death. The people of Israel did as the LORD had commanded Moses.

The Sabbatical Year

25 The LORD spoke to Moses on Mount Sinai, saying: ²Speak to the people of Israel and say to them: When you enter the land that I am giving you, the land shall observe a sabbath for the LORD. ³Six years you shall sow your field, and six years you shall prune your vineyard, and gather in their yield; ⁴but in the seventh year there shall be a sabbath of complete rest for the land, a sabbath for the LORD: you shall not sow your field or prune your vineyard. ⁵You shall not reap the aftergrowth of your harvest or gather the grapes of your unpruned vine: it shall be a year of complete rest for the land. ⁶You may eat what the land yields during its sabbath—you, your male and female slaves, your hired and your bound laborers who live with you; ⁷for your livestock also, and for the wild animals in your land all its yield shall be for food.

The Year of Jubilee

8 You shall count off seven weeksʳ of years, seven times seven

Cross references

24.4 Ex 31.8; 39.37
24.5 Ex 25.30
24.6 Ex 25.24; 1 Kings 7.48
24.8 Num 4.7; 1 Chr 9.32; 2 Chr 2.4
24.9 Mt 12.4; Mk 2.26; Lk 6.4; Lev 8.31
24.11 v. 16
24.12 Num 15.34; Ex 18.15,16
24.14 Deut 13.9; 17.7; Lev 20.2,27; Deut 21.21
24.16 1 Kings 21.10, 13; Mt 12.31; Mk 3.28

24.17 Ex 21.12; Num 35.30, 31; Deut 19.11, 12
24.18 v. 21
24.20 Ex 21.23, 24; Deut 19.21; Mt 5.38
24.21 vv. 17,18
24.22 Ex 12.49; Num 15.16
25.2 Ex 23.10,11
25.6 vv. 20,21

° Or treaty, or testament; Heb eduth ᴾ Heb pure lampstand q Heb pure table ʳ Or sabbaths

years, so that the period of seven weeks of years gives forty-nine years. ⁹Then you shall have the trumpet sounded loud; on the tenth day of the seventh month — on the day of atonement — you shall have the trumpet sounded throughout all your land. ¹⁰And you shall hallow the fiftieth year and you shall proclaim liberty throughout the land to all its inhabitants. It shall be a jubilee for you: you shall return, every one of you, to your property and every one of you to your family. ¹¹That fiftieth year shall be a jubilee for you: you shall not sow, or reap the aftergrowth, or harvest the unpruned vines. ¹²For it is a jubilee; it shall be holy to you: you shall eat only what the field itself produces.

13 In this year of jubilee you shall return, every one of you, to your property. ¹⁴When you make a sale to your neighbor or buy from your neighbor, you shall not cheat one another. ¹⁵When you buy from your neighbor, you shall pay only for the number of years since the jubilee; the seller shall charge you only for the remaining crop years. ¹⁶If the years are more, you shall increase the price, and if the years are fewer, you shall diminish the price; for it is a certain number of harvests that are being sold to you. ¹⁷You shall not cheat one another, but you shall fear your God; for I am the LORD your God.

18 You shall observe my statutes and faithfully keep my ordinances, so that you may live on the land securely. ¹⁹The land will yield its fruit, and you will eat your fill and live on it securely. ²⁰Should you ask, What shall we eat in the seventh year, if we may not sow or gather in our crop? ²¹I will order my blessing for you in the sixth year, so that it will yield a crop for three years. ²²When you sow in the eighth year, you will be eating from the old crop; until the ninth year, when its produce comes in, you shall eat the old. ²³The land shall not be sold in perpetuity, for the land is mine; with me you are but

aliens and tenants. ²⁴Throughout the land that you hold, you shall provide for the redemption of the land.

25 If anyone of your kin falls into difficulty and sells a piece of property, then the next of kin shall come and redeem what the relative has sold. ²⁶If the person has no one to redeem it, but then prospers and finds sufficient means to do so, ²⁷the years since its sale shall be computed and the difference shall be refunded to the person to whom it was sold, and the property shall be returned. ²⁸But if there is not sufficient means to recover it, what was sold shall remain with the purchaser until the year of jubilee; in the jubilee it shall be released, and the property shall be returned.

29 If anyone sells a dwelling house in a walled city, it may be redeemed until a year has elapsed since its sale; the right of redemption shall be one year. ³⁰If it is not redeemed before a full year has elapsed, a house that is in a walled city shall pass in perpetuity to the purchaser, throughout the generations; it shall not be released in the jubilee. ³¹But houses in villages that have no walls around them shall be classed as open country; they may be redeemed, and they shall be released in the jubilee. ³²As for the cities of the Levites, the Levites shall forever have the right of redemption of the houses in the cities belonging to them. ³³Such property as may be redeemed from the Levites — houses sold in a city belonging to them — shall be released in the jubilee; because the houses in the cities of the Levites are their possession among the people of Israel. ³⁴But the open land around their cities may not be sold; for that is their possession for all time.

35 If any of your kin fall into difficulty and become dependent on you,ˢ you shall support them; they shall live with you as though resident aliens. ³⁶Do not take interest

25.9
Lev 23.24, 27
25.10
vv. 13,28,54
25.13
v. 10
25.14
Lev 19.13; 1 Sam 12.3, 4;
1 Cor 6.8
25.15
Lev 27.18, 23
25.17
v. 14;
Lev 19.14, 32
25.18
Lev 19.37; 26.4,5
25.20
vv. 4,5
25.22
Lev 26.10
25.23
Ex 19.5;
Gen 23.4;
1 Chr 29.15;
Ps 39.12

25.25
Ruth 2.20; 4.4,6
25.27
vv. 50-52
25.28
v. 13
25.32
Num 35.1-8
25.35
Deut 15.7-11;
Ps 37.26;
Lk 6.35
25.36
Ex 22.25;
Deut 23.19, 20

ˢ Meaning of Heb uncertain

in advance or otherwise make a profit from them, but fear your God; let them live with you. ³⁷You shall not lend them your money at interest taken in advance, or provide them food at a profit. ³⁸I am the LORD your God, who brought you out of the land of Egypt, to give you the land of Canaan, to be your God.

39 If any who are dependent on you become so impoverished that they sell themselves to you, you shall not make them serve as slaves. ⁴⁰They shall remain with you as hired or bound laborers. They shall serve with you until the year of the jubilee. ⁴¹Then they and their children with them shall be free from your authority; they shall go back to their own family and return to their ancestral property. ⁴²For they are my servants, whom I brought out of the land of Egypt; they shall not be sold as slaves are sold. ⁴³You shall not rule over them with harshness, but shall fear your God. ⁴⁴As for the male and female slaves whom you may have, it is from the nations around you that you may acquire male and female slaves. ⁴⁵You may also acquire them from among the aliens residing with you, and from their families that are with you, who have been born in your land; and they may be your property. ⁴⁶You may keep them as a possession for your children after you, for them to inherit as property. These you may treat as slaves, but as for your fellow Israelites, no one shall rule over the other with harshness.

47 If resident aliens among you prosper, and if any of your kin fall into difficulty with one of them and sell themselves to an alien, or to a branch of the alien's family, ⁴⁸after they have sold themselves they shall have the right of redemption; one of their brothers may redeem them, ⁴⁹or their uncle or their uncle's son may redeem them, or anyone of their family who is of their own flesh may redeem them; or if they prosper they may redeem themselves. ⁵⁰They shall compute

with the purchaser the total from the year when they sold themselves to the alien until the jubilee year; the price of the sale shall be applied to the number of years: the time they were with the owner shall be rated as the time of a hired laborer. ⁵¹If many years remain, they shall pay for their redemption in proportion to the purchase price; ⁵²and if few years remain until the jubilee year, they shall compute thus: according to the years involved they shall make payment for their redemption. ⁵³As a laborer hired by the year they shall be under the alien's authority, who shall not, however, rule with harshness over them in your sight. ⁵⁴And if they have not been redeemed in any of these ways, they and their children with them shall go free in the jubilee year. ⁵⁵For to me the people of Israel are servants; they are my servants whom I brought out from the land of Egypt: I am the LORD your God.

Rewards for Obedience

26 You shall make for yourselves no idols and erect no carved images or pillars, and you shall not place figured stones in your land, to worship at them; for I am the LORD your God. ²You shall keep my sabbaths and reverence my sanctuary: I am the LORD.

3 If you follow my statutes and keep my commandments and observe them faithfully, ⁴I will give you your rains in their season, and the land shall yield its produce, and the trees of the field shall yield their fruit. ⁵Your threshing shall overtake the vintage, and the vintage shall overtake the sowing; you shall eat your bread to the full, and live securely in your land. ⁶And I will grant peace in the land, and you shall lie down, and no one shall make you afraid; I will remove dangerous animals from the land, and no sword shall go through your land. ⁷You shall give chase to your enemies, and they shall fall before you by the sword. ⁸Five of you shall give chase to a hundred, and a hun-

Cross references (center column)

25.38 Lev 11.45
25.39 Ex 21.2; Deut 15.12; 1 Kings 9.22
25.41 Ex 21.3; v. 28
25.43 vv. 46,53; Ex 1.13,14
25.45 Isa 56.3,6
25.46 v. 43
25.48 Neh 5.5
25.49 v. 26
25.50 Job 7.1; Isa 16.14; 21.16

25.51 Jer 32.7
25.54 vv. 10,13,28
26.1 Ex 20.4,5; Lev 19.4; Deut 5.8
26.2 Lev 19.30
26.3 Deut 28.1
26.5 Am 9.13; Lev 25.18, 19
26.6 Ps 29.11; 147.14; Zeph 3.13; vv. 22,25
26.8 Deut 32.30; Josh 23.10

dred of you shall give chase to ten thousand; your enemies shall fall before you by the sword. ⁹I will look with favor upon you and make you fruitful and multiply you; and I will maintain my covenant with you. ¹⁰You shall eat old grain long stored, and you shall have to clear out the old to make way for the new. ¹¹I will place my dwelling in your midst, and I shall not abhor you. ¹²And I will walk among you, and will be your God, and you shall be my people. ¹³I am the LORD your God who brought you out of the land of Egypt, to be their slaves no more; I have broken the bars of your yoke and made you walk erect.

Penalties for Disobedience

14 But if you will not obey me, and do not observe all these commandments, ¹⁵if you spurn my statutes, and abhor my ordinances, so that you will not observe all my commandments, and you break my covenant, ¹⁶I in turn will do this to you: I will bring terror on you; consumption and fever that waste the eyes and cause life to pine away. You shall sow your seed in vain, for your enemies shall eat it. ¹⁷I will set my face against you, and you shall be struck down by your enemies; your foes shall rule over you, and you shall flee though no one pursues you. ¹⁸And if in spite of this you will not obey me, I will continue to punish you sevenfold for your sins. ¹⁹I will break your proud glory, and I will make your sky like iron and your earth like copper. ²⁰Your strength shall be spent to no purpose: your land shall not yield its produce, and the trees of the land shall not yield their fruit.

21 If you continue hostile to me, and will not obey me, I will continue to plague you sevenfold for your sins. ²²I will let loose wild animals against you, and they shall bereave you of your children and destroy your livestock; they shall make you few in number, and your roads shall be deserted.

26.9
Gen 17.6,7;
22.17;
Neh 9.23
26.10
Lev 25.22
26.11
Ex 25.8;
Ps 76.2
26.12
2 Cor 6.16
26.14
Deut 28.15;
Mal 2.2
26.16
Deut 28.22;
1 Sam 2.33;
Deut 28.35,
51
26.17
Lev 17.10;
Deut 28.25;
Ps 106.41;
53.5; vv. 36,
37
26.18
vv. 21,24,28
26.19
Isa 25.11;
Deut 28.23
26.20
Isa 17.10,
11;
Deut 11.17
26.21
vv. 18,24,
27,40
26.22
Deut 32.24

26.23
Jer 2.30; 5.3
26.24
vv. 21,28,41
26.25
Ezek 5.17;
Num 14.12
26.26
Ps 105.16;
Isa 3.1;
Mic 6.14
26.28
vv. 24,41
26.29
Deut 28.53
26.30
2 Chr 34.3;
Ezek 6.3-6,
13
26.31
Ps 74.7;
Isa 63.18
26.32
Jer 9.11;
19.18
26.33
Deut 4.27;
Ezek 12.15
26.34
v. 43;
2 Chr 36.21
26.36
Ezek 21.7
26.37
Josh 7.12,
13

23 If in spite of these punishments you have not turned back to me, but continue hostile to me, ²⁴then I too will continue hostile to you: I myself will strike you sevenfold for your sins. ²⁵I will bring the sword against you, executing vengeance for the covenant; and if you withdraw within your cities, I will send pestilence among you, and you shall be delivered into enemy hands. ²⁶When I break your staff of bread, ten women shall bake your bread in a single oven, and they shall dole out your bread by weight; and though you eat, you shall not be satisfied.

27 But if, despite this, you disobey me, and continue hostile to me, ²⁸I will continue hostile to you in fury; I in turn will punish you myself sevenfold for your sins. ²⁹You shall eat the flesh of your sons, and you shall eat the flesh of your daughters. ³⁰I will destroy your high places and cut down your incense altars; I will heap your carcasses on the carcasses of your idols. I will abhor you. ³¹I will lay your cities waste, will make your sanctuaries desolate, and I will not smell your pleasing odors. ³²I will devastate the land, so that your enemies who come to settle in it shall be appalled at it. ³³And you I will scatter among the nations, and I will unsheathe the sword against you; your land shall be a desolation, and your cities a waste.

34 Then the land shall enjoy[t] its sabbath years as long as it lies desolate, while you are in the land of your enemies; then the land shall rest, and enjoy[t] its sabbath years. ³⁵As long as it lies desolate, it shall have the rest it did not have on your sabbaths when you were living on it. ³⁶And as for those of you who survive, I will send faintness into their hearts in the lands of their enemies; the sound of a driven leaf shall put them to flight, and they shall flee as one flees from the sword, and they shall fall though no one pursues. ³⁷They

[t] Or *make up for*

shall stumble over one another, as if to escape a sword, though no one pursues; and you shall have no power to stand against your enemies. [38]You shall perish among the nations, and the land of your enemies shall devour you. [39]And those of you who survive shall languish in the land of your enemies because of their iniquities; also they shall languish because of the iniquities of their ancestors.

40 But if they confess their iniquity and the iniquity of their ancestors, in that they committed treachery against me and, moreover, that they continued hostile to me— [41]so that I, in turn, continued hostile to them and brought them into the land of their enemies; if then their uncircumcised heart is humbled and they make amends for their iniquity, [42]then will I remember my covenant with Jacob; I will remember also my covenant with Isaac and also my covenant with Abraham, and I will remember the land. [43]For the land shall be deserted by them, and enjoy[u] its sabbath years by lying desolate without them, while they shall make amends for their iniquity, because they dared to spurn my ordinances, and they abhorred my statutes. [44]Yet for all that, when they are in the land of their enemies, I will not spurn them, or abhor them so as to destroy them utterly and break my covenant with them; for I am the LORD their God; [45]but I will remember in their favor the covenant with their ancestors whom I brought out of the land of Egypt in the sight of the nations, to be their God: I am the LORD.

46 These are the statutes and ordinances and laws that the LORD established between himself and the people of Israel on Mount Sinai through Moses.

Votive Offerings

27 The LORD spoke to Moses, saying: [2]Speak to the people of Israel and say to them: When a person makes an explicit vow to the LORD concerning the equivalent

for a human being, [3]the equivalent for a male shall be: from twenty to sixty years of age the equivalent shall be fifty shekels of silver by the sanctuary shekel. [4]If the person is a female, the equivalent is thirty shekels. [5]If the age is from five to twenty years of age, the equivalent is twenty shekels for a male and ten shekels for a female. [6]If the age is from one month to five years, the equivalent for a male is five shekels of silver, and for a female the equivalent is three shekels of silver. [7]And if the person is sixty years old or over, then the equivalent for a male is fifteen shekels, and for a female ten shekels. [8]If any cannot afford the equivalent, they shall be brought before the priest and the priest shall assess them; the priest shall assess them according to what each one making a vow can afford.

9 If it concerns an animal that may be brought as an offering to the LORD, any such that may be given to the LORD shall be holy. [10]Another shall not be exchanged or substituted for it, either good for bad or bad for good; and if one animal is substituted for another, both that one and its substitute shall be holy. [11]If it concerns any unclean animal that may not be brought as an offering to the LORD, the animal shall be presented before the priest. [12]The priest shall assess it: whether good or bad, according to the assessment of the priest, so it shall be. [13]But if it is one-fifth must be added to the assessment.

14 If a person consecrates a house to the LORD, the priest shall assess it: whether good or bad, as the priest assesses it, so it shall stand. [15]And if the one who consecrates the house wishes to redeem it, one-fifth shall be added to its assessed value, and it shall revert to the original owner.

16 If a person consecrates to the LORD any inherited landholding, its assessment shall be in accordance with its seed requirements: fifty

26.38
Deut 4.26
26.39
Deut 4.27;
Ezek 4.17
26.40ff
Jer 3.12-15;
Lk 15.18;
1 Jn 1.9
26.41
Ezek 44.9;
2 Chr 12.6,
7
26.42
Gen 28.13-15;
26.2-5;
22.15-18
26.43
vv. 34,35,15
26.44
Deut 4.31;
Rom 11.2
26.45
Ex 6.6-8;
Lev 25.38;
Gen 17.7
26.46
Lev 7.38;
27.34; 25.1

27.3
Ex 30.13
27.6
Num 18.16
27.8
v. 12
27.12
v. 8
27.13
vv. 15,19
27.15
v. 20

[u] Or make up for

shekels of silver to a homer of barley seed. [17] If the person consecrates the field as of the year of jubilee, that assessment shall stand; [18] but if the field is consecrated after the jubilee, the priest shall compute the price for it according to the years that remain until the year of jubilee, and the assessment shall be reduced. [19] And if the one who consecrates the field wishes to redeem it, then one-fifth shall be added to its assessed value, and it shall revert to the original owner; [20] but if the field is not redeemed, or if it has been sold to someone else, it shall no longer be redeemable. [21] But when the field is released in the jubilee, it shall be holy to the LORD as a devoted field; it becomes the priest's holding. [22] If someone consecrates to the LORD a field that has been purchased, which is not a part of the inherited landholding, [23] the priest shall compute for it the proportionate assessment up to the year of jubilee, and the assessment shall be paid as of that day, a sacred donation to the LORD. [24] In the year of jubilee the field shall return to the one from whom it was bought, whose holding the land is. [25] All assessments shall be by the sanctuary shekel: twenty gerahs shall make a shekel.

26 A firstling of animals, however, which as a firstling belongs to the LORD, cannot be consecrated by anyone; whether ox or sheep, it is the LORD's. [27] If it is an unclean animal, it shall be ransomed at its assessment, with one-fifth added; if it is not redeemed, it shall be sold at its assessment.

28 Nothing that a person owns that has been devoted to destruction for the LORD, be it human or animal, or inherited landholding, may be sold or redeemed; every devoted thing is most holy to the LORD. [29] No human beings who have been devoted to destruction can be ransomed; they shall be put to death.

30 All tithes from the land, whether the seed from the ground or the fruit from the tree, are the LORD's; they are holy to the LORD. [31] If persons wish to redeem any of their tithes, they must add one-fifth to them. [32] All tithes of herd and flock, every tenth one that passes under the shepherd's staff, shall be holy to the LORD. [33] Let no one inquire whether it is good or bad, or make substitution for it; if one makes substitution for it, then both it and the substitute shall be holy and cannot be redeemed.

34 These are the commandments that the LORD gave to Moses for the people of Israel on Mount Sinai.

27.18
Lev 25.15, 16
27.21
Lev 25.10, 28,31;
Num 18.14
27.23
v. 18
27.24
Lev 25.28
27.25
Ex 30.13
27.26
Ex 13.2,12

27.27
vv. 11,12
27.28
Josh 6.17-19
27.30
Gen 28.22;
Mal 3.8,10
27.31
v. 13
27.33
v. 10
27.34
Lev 26.46;
Deut 4.5

Numbers

Title and Background

The book of Numbers gets its name from the two numberings or countings of the people of Israel during their forty years of wandering in the desert. These countings are found in chapters 1 and 26. Numbers presents an account of that wandering in the desert following the establishment of the covenant at Sinai.

Author and Date of Writing

Numbers has been traditionally ascribed to Moses, though like the other books of the Pentateuch, the final form of the first five books of the Bible may not have taken place until later on in Israel's history. The New Testament consistently ascribes quotations from the Pentateuch to Moses (e.g., Mt 19.8; Jn 5.46-47; Rom 10.5).

Theme and Message

Numbers relates the story of Israel's journey from Mount Sinai to the plains of Moab on the border of Canaan. It tells of the murmuring and rebellion of God's people and of their subsequent judgment. They were condemned to live out their lives in the desert; only their children would enjoy the fulfillment of the promise that had originally been theirs.

Throughout the years in the desert, one thing became clear to Israel—God's constant care for them. Not only did he meet their needs but he also loved and forgave his people continually.

Outline

 I. Israel at Sinai, Preparing to Go to Canaan (1.1–10.10)
 II. From Sinai to Kadesh (10.11–12.16)
 III. Israel at Kadesh, the Delay Resulting from Rebellion (13.1–20.13)
 IV. From Kadesh to the Plains of Moab (20.14–22.1)
 V. Israel on the Plains of Moab (22.2–32.42)
 VI. Supplements Dealing with Various Matters (33.1–36.13)

The First Census of Israel

1 The LORD spoke to Moses in the wilderness of Sinai, in the tent of meeting, on the first day of the second month, in the second year after they had come out of the land of Egypt, saying: ² Take a census of the whole congregation of Israelites, in their clans, by ancestral houses, according to the number of names, every male individually; ³ from twenty years old and upward, everyone in Israel able to go to war. You and Aaron shall enroll them, company by company. ⁴ A man from each tribe shall be with you, each man the head of his ancestral house. ⁵ These are the names of the men who shall assist you:

From Reuben, Elizur son of Shedeur.
⁶ From Simeon, Shelumiel son of Zurishaddai.
⁷ From Judah, Nahshon son of Amminadab.
⁸ From Issachar, Nethanel son of Zuar.
⁹ From Zebulun, Eliab son of Helon.
¹⁰ From the sons of Joseph:
from Ephraim, Elishama son of Ammihud;
from Manasseh, Gamaliel son of Pedahzur.

1.1 Ex 19.1; 40.2,17
1.2 Ex 38.26; Num 26.2
1.4 v. 16

11 From Benjamin, Abidan son of Gideoni.

12 From Dan, Ahiezer son of Ammishaddai.

13 From Asher, Pagiel son of Ochran.

14 From Gad, Eliasaph son of Deuel.

15 From Naphtali, Ahira son of Enan.

16 These were the ones chosen from the congregation, the leaders of their ancestral tribes, the heads of the divisions of Israel.

17 Moses and Aaron took these men who had been designated by name, 18 and on the first day of the second month they assembled the whole congregation together. They registered themselves in their clans, by their ancestral houses, according to the number of names from twenty years old and upward, individually, 19 as the LORD commanded Moses. So he enrolled them in the wilderness of Sinai.

20 The descendants of Reuben, Israel's firstborn, their lineage, in their clans, by their ancestral houses, according to the number of names, individually, every male from twenty years old and upward, everyone able to go to war: 21 those enrolled of the tribe of Reuben were forty-six thousand five hundred.

22 The descendants of Simeon, their lineage, in their clans, by their ancestral houses, those of them that were numbered, according to the number of names, individually, every male from twenty years old and upward, everyone able to go to war: 23 those enrolled of the tribe of Simeon were fifty-nine thousand three hundred.

24 The descendants of Gad, their lineage, in their clans, by their ancestral houses, according to the number of the names, from twenty years old and upward, everyone able to go to war: 25 those enrolled of the tribe of Gad were forty-five thousand six hundred fifty.

26 The descendants of Judah, their lineage, in their clans, by

their ancestral houses, according to the number of names, from twenty years old and upward, everyone able to go to war: 27 those enrolled of the tribe of Judah were seventy-four thousand six hundred.

28 The descendants of Issachar, their lineage, in their clans, by their ancestral houses, according to the number of names, from twenty years old and upward, everyone able to go to war: 29 those enrolled of the tribe of Issachar were fifty-four thousand four hundred.

30 The descendants of Zebulun, their lineage, in their clans, by their ancestral houses, according to the number of names, from twenty years old and upward, everyone able to go to war: 31 those enrolled of the tribe of Zebulun were fifty-seven thousand four hundred.

32 The descendants of Joseph, namely, the descendants of Ephraim, their lineage, in their clans, by their ancestral houses, according to the number of names, from twenty years old and upward, everyone able to go to war: 33 those enrolled of the tribe of Ephraim were forty thousand five hundred.

34 The descendants of Manasseh, their lineage, in their clans, by their ancestral houses, according to the number of names, from twenty years old and upward, everyone able to go to war: 35 those enrolled of the tribe of Manasseh were thirty-two thousand two hundred.

36 The descendants of Benjamin, their lineage, in their clans, by their ancestral houses, according to the number of names, from twenty years old and upward, everyone able to go to war: 37 those enrolled of the tribe of Benjamin were thirty-five thousand four hundred.

38 The descendants of Dan, their lineage, in their clans, by their ancestral houses, according to the number of names, from twenty years old and upward, ev-

1.14
Num 2.14
1.16
Num 16.2;
26.9
1.20
Num 26.5-11
1.22
Num 26.12-14
1.24
Num 26.15-18
1.26
Num 26.19-22

1.28
Num 26.23-25
1.30
Num 26.26,
27
1.32
Num 26.35-37
1.34
Num 26.28-34
1.36
Num 26.38-41
1.38
Num 26.42,
43

eryone able to go to war: 39 those enrolled of the tribe of Dan were sixty-two thousand seven hundred.

40 The descendants of Asher, their lineage, in their clans, by their ancestral houses, according to the number of names, from twenty years old and upward, everyone able to go to war: 41 those enrolled of the tribe of Asher were forty-one thousand five hundred.

42 The descendants of Naphtali, their lineage, in their clans, by their ancestral houses, according to the number of names, from twenty years old and upward, everyone able to go to war: 43 those enrolled of the tribe of Naphtali were fifty-three thousand four hundred.

44 These are those who were enrolled, whom Moses and Aaron enrolled with the help of the leaders of Israel, twelve men, each representing his ancestral house. 45 So the whole number of the Israelites, by their ancestral houses, from twenty years old and upward, everyone able to go to war in Israel— 46 their whole number was six hundred three thousand five hundred fifty. 47 The Levites, however, were not numbered by their ancestral tribe along with them.

48 The LORD had said to Moses: 49 Only the tribe of Levi you shall not enroll, and you shall not take a census of them with the other Israelites. 50 Rather you shall appoint the Levites over the tabernacle of the covenant,a and over all its equipment, and over all that belongs to it; they are to carry the tabernacle and all its equipment, and they shall tend it, and shall camp around the tabernacle. 51 When the tabernacle is to set out, the Levites shall take it down; and when the tabernacle is to be pitched, the Levites shall set it up. And any outsider who comes near shall be put to death. 52 The other Israelites shall camp in their respective regimental camps, by companies; 53 but the Levites shall camp around the tabernacle of the covenant,a that there may be no wrath on the con-

1.40
Num 26.44-47
1.42
Num 26.48-50
1.44
Num 26.64
1.46
Num 2.32;
26.51;
Ex 12.37;
38.26
1.47
Num 2.33;
chs. 3,4;
26.57
1.50
Num 3.25-37
1.51
Num 4.1-33
1.52
Num 2.2
1.53
v. 50

2.2
Num 1.52
2.3
Num 10;14
2.5
Num 1.8
2.9
Num 10.14
2.10
Num 1.5
2.12
Num 1.6
2.14
Num 1.14,

gregation of the Israelites; and the Levites shall perform the guard duty of the tabernacle of the covenant.a 54 The Israelites did so; they did just as the LORD commanded Moses.

The Order of Encampment and Marching

2 The LORD spoke to Moses and Aaron, saying: 2 The Israelites shall camp each in their respective regiments, under ensigns by their ancestral houses; they shall camp facing the tent of meeting on every side. 3 Those to camp on the east side toward the sunrise shall be of the regimental encampment of Judah by companies. The leader of the people of Judah shall be Nahshon son of Amminadab, 4 with a company as enrolled of seventy-four thousand six hundred. 5 Those to camp next to him shall be the tribe of Issachar. The leader of the Issacharites shall be Nethanel son of Zuar, 6 with a company as enrolled of fifty-four thousand four hundred. 7 Then the tribe of Zebulun: The leader of the Zebulunites shall be Eliab son of Helon, 8 with a company as enrolled of fifty-seven thousand four hundred. 9 The total enrollment of the camp of Judah, by companies, is one hundred eighty-six thousand four hundred. They shall set out first on the march.

10 On the south side shall be the regimental encampment of Reuben by companies. The leader of the Reubenites shall be Elizur son of Shedeur, 11 with a company as enrolled of forty-six thousand five hundred. 12 And those to camp next to him shall be the tribe of Simeon. The leader of the Simeonites shall be Shelumiel son of Zurishaddai, 13 with a company as enrolled of fifty-nine thousand three hundred. 14 Then the tribe of Gad: The leader of the Gadites shall be Eliasaph son of Reuel, 15 with a company as enrolled of forty-five thousand six hundred fifty. 16 The total enrollment of the camp of

a Or *treaty*, or *testimony*; Heb *eduth*

Reuben, by companies, is one hundred fifty-one thousand four hundred fifty. They shall set out second.

17 The tent of meeting, with the camp of the Levites, shall set out in the center of the camps; they shall set out just as they camp, each in position, by their regiments.

18 On the west side shall be the regimental encampment of Ephraim by companies. The leader of the people of Ephraim shall be Elishama son of Ammihud, 19 with a company as enrolled of forty thousand five hundred. 20 Next to him shall be the tribe of Manasseh. The leader of the people of Manasseh shall be Gamaliel son of Pedahzur, 21 with a company as enrolled of thirty-two thousand two hundred. 22 Then the tribe of Benjamin: The leader of the Benjaminites shall be Abidan son of Gideoni, 23 with a company as enrolled of thirty-five thousand four hundred. 24 The total enrollment of the camp of Ephraim, by companies, is one hundred eight thousand one hundred. They shall set out third on the march.

25 On the north side shall be the regimental encampment of Dan by companies. The leader of the Danites shall be Ahiezer son of Ammishaddai, 26 with a company as enrolled of sixty-two thousand seven hundred. 27 Those to camp next to him shall be the tribe of Asher. The leader of the Asherites shall be Pagiel son of Ochran, 28 with a company as enrolled of forty-one thousand five hundred. 29 Then the tribe of Naphtali: The leader of the Naphtalites shall be Ahira son of Enan, 30 with a company as enrolled of fifty-three thousand four hundred. 31 The total enrollment of the camp of Dan is one hundred fifty-seven thousand six hundred. They shall set out last, by companies. b

32 This was the enrollment of the Israelites by their ancestral houses; the total enrollment in the camps by their companies was six hundred three thousand five hundred fifty. 33 Just as the LORD had

commanded Moses, the Levites were not enrolled among the other Israelites.

34 The Israelites did just as the LORD had commanded Moses: They camped by regiments, and they set out the same way, everyone by clans, according to ancestral houses.

The Sons of Aaron

3 This is the lineage of Aaron and Moses at the time when the LORD spoke with Moses on Mount Sinai. 2 These are the names of the sons of Aaron: Nadab the firstborn, and Abihu, Eleazar, and Ithamar; 3 these are the names of the sons of Aaron, the anointed priests, whom he ordained to minister as priests. 4 Nadab and Abihu died before the LORD when they offered illicit fire before the LORD in the wilderness of Sinai, and they had no children. Eleazar and Ithamar served as priests in the lifetime of their father Aaron.

The Duties of the Levites

5 Then the LORD spoke to Moses, saying: 6 Bring the tribe of Levi near, and set them before Aaron the priest, so that they may assist him. 7 They shall perform duties for him and for the whole congregation in front of the tent of meeting, doing service at the tabernacle; 8 they shall be in charge of all the furnishings of the tent of meeting, and attend to the duties for the Israelites as they do service at the tabernacle. 9 You shall give the Levites to Aaron and his descendants; they are unreservedly given to him from among the Israelites. 10 But you shall make a register of Aaron and his descendants; it is they who shall attend to the priesthood, and any outsider who comes near shall be put to death.

11 Then the LORD spoke to Moses, saying: 12 I hereby accept the Levites from among the Israelites as substitutes for all the firstborn that open the womb among the Is-

2.17
Num 1.53
2.20
Num 1.10
2.24
Num 10.22
2.25
Num 1.12
2.27
Num 1.13
2.31
Num 10.25
2.32
Num 1.46;
Ex 38.26
2.33
Num 1.47

3.2
Num 26.60
3.4
Num 26.61
3.6
Num 8.6-22;
18.1-7
3.9
Num 18.6
3.10
Ex 29.9;
Num 1.51
3.12
v. 41;
Num 8.16;
18.6

b Compare verses 9, 16, 24: Heb *by their regiments*

raelites. The Levites shall be mine, [13] for all the firstborn are mine; when I killed all the firstborn in the land of Egypt, I consecrated for my own all the firstborn in Israel, both human and animal; they shall be mine. I am the LORD.

A Census of the Levites

14 Then the LORD spoke to Moses in the wilderness of Sinai, saying: [15] Enroll the Levites by ancestral houses and by clans. You shall enroll every male from a month old and upward. [16] So Moses enrolled them according to the word of the LORD, as he was commanded. [17] The following were the sons of Levi, by their names: Gershon, Kohath, and Merari. [18] These are the names of the sons of Gershon by their clans: Libni and Shimei. [19] The sons of Kohath by their clans: Amram, Izhar, Hebron, and Uzziel. [20] The sons of Merari by their clans: Mahli and Mushi. These are the clans of the Levites, by their ancestral houses.

21 To Gershon belonged the clan of the Libnites and the clan of the Shimeites; these were the clans of the Gershonites. [22] Their enrollment, counting all the males from a month old and upward, was seven thousand five hundred. [23] The clans of the Gershonites were to camp behind the tabernacle on the west, [24] with Eliasaph son of Lael as head of the ancestral house of the Gershonites. [25] The responsibility of the sons of Gershon in the tent of meeting was to be the tabernacle, the tent with its covering, the screen for the entrance of the tent of meeting, [26] the hangings of the court, the screen for the entrance of the court that is around the tabernacle and the altar, and its cords—all the service pertaining to these.

27 To Kohath belonged the clan of the Amramites, the clan of the Izharites, the clan of the Hebronites, and the clan of the Uzzielites; these are the clans of the Kohathites. [28] Counting all the males, from a month old and upward, there

3.13
Ex 13.2,12, 15;
Num 8.17
3.15
v. 39
3.17
Ex 6.16-22
3.20
Gen 46.11
3.21
Ex 6.17
3.25
Num 4.24-26;
Ex 25.9
3.27
1 Chr 26.23

3.29
Ex 6.18
3.33
Ex 6.19
3.36
Num 4.29-32
3.38
Num 18.5;
vv. 7,8,10
3.39
Num 26.62
3.41
vv. 12,45

were eight thousand six hundred, attending to the duties of the sanctuary. [29] The clans of the Kohathites were to camp on the south side of the tabernacle, [30] with Elizaphan son of Uzziel as head of the ancestral house of the clans of the Kohathites. [31] Their responsibility was to be the ark, the table, the lampstand, the altars, the vessels of the sanctuary with which the priests minister, and the screen—all the service pertaining to these. [32] Eleazar son of Aaron the priest was to be chief over the leaders of the Levites, and to have oversight of those who had charge of the sanctuary.

33 To Merari belonged the clan of the Mahlites and the clan of the Mushites: these are the clans of Merari. [34] Their enrollment, counting all the males from a month old and upward, was six thousand two hundred. [35] The head of the ancestral house of the clans of Merari was Zuriel son of Abihail; they were to camp on the north side of the tabernacle. [36] The responsibility assigned to the sons of Merari was to be the frames of the tabernacle, the bars, the pillars, the bases, and all their accessories—all the service pertaining to these; [37] also the pillars of the court all around, with their bases and pegs and cords.

38 Those who were to camp in front of the tabernacle on the east—in front of the tent of meeting toward the east—were Moses and Aaron and Aaron's sons, having charge of the rites within the sanctuary, whatever had to be done for the Israelites; and any outsider who came near was to be put to death. [39] The total enrollment of the Levites whom Moses and Aaron enrolled at the commandment of the LORD, by their clans, all the males from a month old and upward, was twenty-two thousand.

The Redemption of the Firstborn

40 Then the LORD said to Moses: Enroll all the firstborn males of the Israelites, from a month old and upward, and count their names. [41] But you shall accept the Levites

for me—I am the LORD—as substitutes for all the firstborn among the Israelites, and the livestock of the Levites as substitutes for all the firstborn among the livestock of the Israelites. ⁴²So Moses enrolled all the firstborn among the Israelites, as the LORD commanded him. ⁴³The total enrollment, all the firstborn males from a month old and upward, counting the number of names, was twenty-two thousand two hundred seventy-three.

44 Then the LORD spoke to Moses, saying: ⁴⁵Accept the Levites as substitutes for all the firstborn among the Israelites, and the livestock of the Levites as substitutes for their livestock; and the Levites shall be mine. I am the LORD. ⁴⁶As the price of redemption of the two hundred seventy-three of the firstborn of the Israelites, over and above the number of the Levites, ⁴⁷you shall accept five shekels apiece, reckoning by the shekel of the sanctuary, a shekel of twenty gerahs. ⁴⁸Give to Aaron and his sons the money by which the excess number of them is redeemed. ⁴⁹So Moses took the redemption money from those who were over and above those redeemed by the Levites; ⁵⁰from the firstborn of the Israelites he took the money, one thousand three hundred sixty-five shekels, reckoned by the shekel of the sanctuary; ⁵¹and Moses gave the redemption money to Aaron and his sons, according to the word of the LORD, as the LORD had commanded Moses.

The Kohathites

4 The LORD spoke to Moses and Aaron, saying: ²Take a census of the Kohathites separate from the other Levites, by their clans and their ancestral houses, ³from thirty years old up to fifty years old, all who qualify to do work relating to the tent of meeting. ⁴The service of the Kohathites relating to the tent of meeting concerns the most holy things.

5 When the camp is to set out, Aaron and his sons shall go in and

take down the screening curtain, and cover the ark of the covenant[c] with it; ⁶then they shall put on it a covering of fine leather,[d] and spread over that a cloth all of blue, and shall put its poles in place. ⁷Over the table of the bread of the Presence they shall spread a blue cloth, and put on it the plates, the dishes for incense, the bowls, and the flagons for the drink offering; the regular bread also shall be on it; ⁸then they shall spread over them a crimson cloth, and cover it with a covering of fine leather,[d] and shall put its poles in place. ⁹They shall take a blue cloth, and cover the lampstand for the light, with its lamps, its snuffers, its trays, and all the vessels for oil with which it is supplied; ¹⁰and they shall put it with all its utensils in a covering of fine leather,[d] and put it on the carrying frame. ¹¹Over the golden altar they shall spread a blue cloth, and cover it with a covering of fine leather,[d] and shall put its poles in place; ¹²and they shall take all the utensils of the service that are used in the sanctuary, and put them in a blue cloth, and cover them with a covering of fine leather,[d] and put them on the carrying frame. ¹³They shall take away the ashes from the altar, and spread a purple cloth over it; ¹⁴and they shall put on it all the utensils of the altar, which are used for the service there, the firepans, the forks, the shovels, and the basins, all the utensils of the altar; and they shall spread on it a covering of fine leather,[d] and shall put its poles in place. ¹⁵When Aaron and his sons have finished covering the sanctuary and all the furnishings of the sanctuary, as the camp sets out, after that the Kohathites shall come to carry these, but they must not touch the holy things, or they will die. These are the things of the tent of meeting that the Kohathites are to carry.

16 Eleazar son of Aaron the

3.43
v. 39
3.45
vv. 12,41
3.46
Ex 13.13;
Num 18.15
3.47
Ex 30.13
3.50
vv. 46-48
4.3
Num 8.24;
vv. 23,30,35

4.6
v. 25
4.7
Ex 25.23,
29,30;
Lev 24.5-9
4.9
Ex 25.31,
37,38
4.11
Ex 30.1,3
4.15
Num 7.9;
2 Sam 6.6,
7
4.16
Lev 24.1-3;
Ex 30.34;
29.40; 30.23

[c] Or *treaty*, or *testimony*; Heb *eduth*
[d] Meaning of Heb uncertain

priest shall have charge of the oil for the light, the fragrant incense, the regular grain offering, and the anointing oil, the oversight of all the tabernacle and all that is in it, in the sanctuary and in its utensils.

17 Then the LORD spoke to Moses and Aaron, saying: 18 You must not let the tribe of the clans of the Kohathites be destroyed from among the Levites. 19 This is how you must deal with them in order that they may live and not die when they come near to the most holy things: Aaron and his sons shall go in and assign each to a particular task or burden. 20 But the Kohathites[e] must not go in to look on the holy things even for a moment; otherwise they will die.

The Gershonites and Merarites

21 Then the LORD spoke to Moses, saying: 22 Take a census of the Gershonites also, by their ancestral houses and by their clans; 23 from thirty years old up to fifty years old you shall enroll them, all who qualify to do work in the tent of meeting. 24 This is the service of the clans of the Gershonites, in serving and bearing burdens: 25 They shall carry the curtains of the tabernacle, and the tent of meeting with its covering, and the outer covering of fine leather[f] that is on top of it, and the screen for the entrance of the tent of meeting, 26 and the hangings of the court, and the screen for the entrance of the gate of the court that is around the tabernacle and the altar, and their cords, and all the equipment for their service; and they shall do all that needs to be done with regard to them. 27 All the service of the Gershonites shall be at the command of Aaron and his sons, in all that they are to carry, and in all that they have to do; and you shall assign to their charge all that they are to carry. 28 This is the service of the clans of the Gershonites relating to the tent of meeting, and their responsibilities are to be under the oversight of Ithamar son of Aaron the priest.

29 As for the Merarites, you shall enroll them by their clans and their ancestral houses; 30 from thirty years old up to fifty years old you shall enroll them, everyone who qualifies to do the work of the tent of meeting. 31 This is what they are charged to carry, as the whole of their service in the tent of meeting: the frames of the tabernacle, with its bars, pillars, and bases, 32 and the pillars of the court all around with their bases, pegs, and cords, with all their equipment and all their related service; and you shall assign by name the objects that they are required to carry. 33 This is the service of the clans of the Merarites, the whole of their service relating to the tent of meeting, under the hand of Ithamar son of Aaron the priest.

Census of the Levites

34 So Moses and Aaron and the leaders of the congregation enrolled the Kohathites, by their clans and their ancestral houses, 35 from thirty years old up to fifty years old, everyone who qualified for work relating to the tent of meeting; 36 and their enrollment by clans was two thousand seven hundred fifty. 37 This was the enrollment of the clans of the Kohathites, all who served at the tent of meeting, whom Moses and Aaron enrolled according to the commandment of the LORD by Moses.

38 The enrollment of the Gershonites, by their clans and their ancestral houses, 39 from thirty years old up to fifty years old, everyone who qualified for work relating to the tent of meeting— 40 their enrollment by their clans and their ancestral houses was two thousand six hundred thirty. 41 This was the enrollment of the clans of the Gershonites, all who served at the tent of meeting, whom Moses and Aaron enrolled according to the commandment of the LORD.

42 The enrollment of the clans of the Merarites, by their clans and

4.19
vv. 4,15
4.23
v. 3
4.25
Num 3.25, 26
4.27
Num 3.21

4.30
v. 3
4.31
Num 3.36, 37
4.33
v. 28
4.34
v. 2
4.37
Num 3.27
4.38
Gen 46.11
4.41
v. 22

[e] Heb *they* [f] Meaning of Heb uncertain

their ancestral houses, ⁴³from thirty years old up to fifty years old, everyone who qualified for work relating to the tent of meeting—⁴⁴their enrollment by their clans was three thousand two hundred. ⁴⁵This is the enrollment of the clans of the Merarites, whom Moses and Aaron enrolled according to the commandment of the LORD by Moses.

46 All those who were enrolled of the Levites, whom Moses and Aaron and the leaders of Israel enrolled, by their clans and their ancestral houses, ⁴⁷from thirty years old up to fifty years old, everyone who qualified to do the work of service and the work of bearing burdens relating to the tent of meeting, ⁴⁸their enrollment was eight thousand five hundred eighty. ⁴⁹According to the commandment of the LORD through Moses they were appointed to their several tasks of serving or carrying; thus they were enrolled by him, as the LORD commanded Moses.

Unclean Persons

5 The LORD spoke to Moses, saying: ²Command the Israelites to put out of the camp everyone who is leprous,ᵍ or has a discharge, and everyone who is unclean through contact with a corpse; ³you shall put out both male and female, putting them outside the camp; they must not defile their camp, where I dwell among them. ⁴The Israelites did so, putting them outside the camp; as the LORD had spoken to Moses, so the Israelites did.

Confession and Restitution

5 The LORD spoke to Moses, saying: ⁶Speak to the Israelites: When a man or a woman wrongs another, breaking faith with the LORD, that person incurs guilt ⁷and shall confess the sin that has been committed. The person shall make full restitution for the wrong, adding one fifth to it, and giving it to the one who was wronged. ⁸If the injured party has no next of kin to whom

restitution may be made for the wrong, the restitution for wrong shall go to the LORD for the priest, in addition to the ram of atonement with which atonement is made for the guilty party. ⁹Among all the sacred donations of the Israelites, every gift that they bring to the priest shall be his. ¹⁰The sacred donations of all are their own; whatever anyone gives to the priest shall be his.

Concerning an Unfaithful Wife

11 The LORD spoke to Moses, saying: ¹²Speak to the Israelites and say to them: If any man's wife goes astray and is unfaithful to him, ¹³if a man has had intercourse with her but it is hidden from her husband, so that she is undetected though she has defiled herself, and there is no witness against her since she was not caught in the act; ¹⁴if a spirit of jealousy comes on him, and he is jealous of his wife who has defiled herself; or if a spirit of jealousy comes on him, and he is jealous of his wife, though she has not defiled herself; ¹⁵then the man shall bring his wife to the priest. And he shall bring the offering required for her, one-tenth of an ephah of barley flour. He shall pour no oil on it and put no frankincense on it, for it is a grain offering of jealousy, a grain offering of remembrance, bringing iniquity to remembrance.

16 Then the priest shall bring her near, and set her before the LORD; ¹⁷the priest shall take holy water in an earthen vessel, and take some of the dust that is on the floor of the tabernacle and put it into the water. ¹⁸The priest shall set the woman before the LORD, dishevel the woman's hair, and place in her hands the grain offering of remembrance, which is the grain offering of jealousy. In his own hand the priest shall have the water of bitterness that brings the curse. ¹⁹Then the priest shall make her take an oath, saying, "If no man

Cross references (center column):
4.45
v. 29
4.47
w. 3,23,30
5.2ff
Lev 13.3,46;
15.2; 19.11
5.3
Lev 26.11,
12;
2 Cor 6.16
5.6
Lev 6.2,3
5.7
Lev 5.5;
26.40; 6.5
5.8
Lev 6.6,7;
7.7

5.9
Lev 6.17,18,
26; 7.6-14
5.10
Lev 10.13
5.12
Ex 20.14
5.13
Lev 18.20
5.15
Ezek 29.16
5.18
1 Cor 11.6

ᵍA term for several skin diseases; precise meaning uncertain

has lain with you, if you have not turned aside to uncleanness while under your husband's authority, be immune to this water of bitterness that brings the curse. ²⁰ But if you have gone astray while under your husband's authority, if you have defiled yourself and some man other than your husband has had intercourse with you," ²¹ —let the priest make the woman take the oath of the curse and say to the woman— "the LORD make you an execration and an oath among your people, when the LORD makes your uterus drop, your womb discharge; ²² now may this water that brings the curse enter your bowels and make your womb discharge, your uterus drop!" And the woman shall say, "Amen. Amen."

23 Then the priest shall put these curses in writing, and wash them off into the water of bitterness. ²⁴ He shall make the woman drink the water of bitterness that brings the curse, and the water that brings the curse shall enter her and cause bitter pain. ²⁵ The priest shall take the grain offering of jealousy out of the woman's hand, and shall elevate the grain offering before the LORD and bring it to the altar; ²⁶ and the priest shall take a handful of the grain offering, as its memorial portion, and turn it into smoke on the altar, and afterward shall make the woman drink the water. ²⁷ When he has made her drink the water, then, if she has defiled herself and has been unfaithful to her husband, the water that brings the curse shall enter into her and cause bitter pain, and her womb shall discharge, her uterus drop, and the woman shall become an execration among her people. ²⁸ But if the woman has not defiled herself and is clean, then she shall be immune and be able to conceive children.

29 This is the law in cases of jealousy, when a wife, while under her husband's authority, goes astray and defiles herself, ³⁰ or when a spirit of jealousy comes on a man and he is jealous of his wife;

5.21
Josh 6.26;
1 Sam 14.24;
Neh 10.29
5.22
Deut 27.15;
Ps 109.18
5.25
Lev 8.27
5.27
Jer 29.18;
42.18;
Zech 8.13
5.29
vv. 12,19

then he shall set the woman before the LORD, and the priest shall apply this entire law to her. ³¹ The man shall be free from iniquity, but the woman shall bear her iniquity.

The Nazirites

6 The LORD spoke to Moses, saying: ²Speak to the Israelites and say to them: When either men or women make a special vow, the vow of a nazirite,ʰ to separate themselves to the LORD, ³ they shall separate themselves from wine and strong drink; they shall drink no wine vinegar or other vinegar, and shall not drink any grape juice or eat grapes, fresh or dried. ⁴ All their days as naziritesⁱ they shall eat nothing that is produced by the grapevine, not even the seeds or the skins.

5 All the days of their nazirite vow no razor shall come upon the head; until the time is completed for which they separate themselves to the LORD, they shall be holy; they shall let the locks of the head grow long.

6 All the days that they separate themselves to the LORD they shall not go near a corpse. ⁷ Even if their father or mother, brother or sister, should die, they may not defile themselves; because their consecration to God is upon the head. ⁸ All their days as naziritesⁱ they are holy to the LORD.

9 If someone dies very suddenly nearby, defiling the consecrated head, then they shall shave the head on the day of their cleansing; on the seventh day they shall shave it. ¹⁰ On the eighth day they shall bring two turtledoves or two young pigeons to the priest at the entrance of the tent of meeting, ¹¹ and the priest shall offer one as a sin offering and the other as a burnt offering, and make atonement for them, because they incurred guilt by reason of the corpse. They shall sanctify the head that same day, ¹² and separate themselves to the LORD for their days as nazirites,ⁱ

6.2
Judg 13.5;
16.17;
Am 2.11,12
6.5
1 Sam 1.11
6.6
Lev 19.11-22;
21.1-3
6.10
Lev 5.7
6.12
Lev 5.6

ʰ That is *one separated* or *one consecrated*
ⁱ That is *those separated* or *those consecrated*

and bring a male lamb a year old as a guilt offering. The former time shall be void, because the consecrated head was defiled.

13 This is the law for the nazirites[j] when the time of their consecration has been completed: they shall be brought to the entrance of the tent of meeting, 14 and they shall offer their gift to the LORD, one male lamb a year old without blemish as a burnt offering, one ewe lamb a year old without blemish as a sin offering, one ram without blemish as an offering of well-being, 15 and a basket of unleavened bread, cakes of choice flour mixed with oil and unleavened wafers spread with oil, with their grain offering and their drink offerings. 16 The priest shall present them before the LORD and offer their sin offering and burnt offering, 17 and shall offer the ram as a sacrifice of well-being to the LORD, with the basket of unleavened bread; the priest also shall make the accompanying grain offering and drink offering. 18 Then the nazirites[j] shall shave the consecrated head at the entrance of the tent of meeting, and shall take the hair from the consecrated head and put it on the fire under the sacrifice of well-being. 19 The priest shall take the shoulder of the ram, when it is boiled, and one unleavened cake out of the basket, and one unleavened wafer, and shall put them in the palms of the nazirites,[j] after they have shaved the consecrated head. 20 Then the priest shall elevate them as an elevation offering before the LORD; they are a holy portion for the priest, together with the breast that is elevated and the thigh that is offered. After that the nazirites[j] may drink wine.

21 This is the law for the nazirites[j] who take a vow. Their offering to the LORD must be in accordance with the nazirite[k] vow, apart from what else they can afford. In accordance with whatever vow they take, so they shall do, following the law for their consecration.

6.13
Acts 21.26
6.14
Num 15.27;
Lev 14.10
6.15
Num 15.1-7
6.18
v. 9;
Acts 21.24

6.23
1 Chr 23.13
6.24
Deut 28.3-6
6.25
Ps 80.3,7,
19; 119.135;
Gen 43.29
6.26
Ps 4.6; 44.3;
Jn 14.27
6.27
Deut 28.10;
2 Chr 7.14
7.1
Ex 40.18
7.2
Num 1.5-16
7.7
Num 4.25
7.8
Num 4.28,
31,33
7.9
Num 4.5-15
7.10
2 Chr 7.9

The Priestly Benediction

22 The LORD spoke to Moses, saying: 23 Speak to Aaron and his sons, saying, Thus you shall bless the Israelites: You shall say to them,

24 The LORD bless you and keep
 you;
25 the LORD make his face to
 shine upon you, and be
 gracious to you;
26 the LORD lift up his
 countenance upon you,
 and give you peace.

27 So they shall put my name on the Israelites, and I will bless them.

Offerings of the Leaders

7 On the day when Moses had finished setting up the tabernacle, and had anointed and consecrated it with all its furnishings, and had anointed and consecrated the altar with all its utensils, 2 the leaders of Israel, heads of their ancestral houses, the leaders of the tribes, who were over those who were enrolled, made offerings. 3 They brought their offerings before the LORD, six covered wagons and twelve oxen, a wagon for every two of the leaders, and for each one an ox; they presented them before the tabernacle. 4 Then the LORD said to Moses: 5 Accept these from them, that they may be used in doing the service of the tent of meeting, and give them to the Levites, to each according to his service. 6 So Moses took the wagons and the oxen, and gave them to the Levites. 7 Two wagons and four oxen he gave to the Gershonites, according to their service; 8 and four wagons and eight oxen he gave to the Merarites, according to their service, under the direction of Ithamar son of Aaron the priest. 9 But to the Kohathites he gave none, because they were charged with the care of the holy things that had to be carried on the shoulders.

10 The leaders also presented offerings for the dedication of the

j That is *those separated* or *those consecrated*
k That is *one separated* or *one consecrated*

altar at the time when it was anointed; the leaders presented their offering before the altar. [11] The LORD said to Moses: They shall present their offerings, one leader each day, for the dedication of the altar.

12 The one who presented his offering the first day was Nahshon son of Amminadab, of the tribe of Judah; [13] his offering was one silver plate weighing one hundred thirty shekels, one silver basin weighing seventy shekels, according to the shekel of the sanctuary, both of them full of choice flour mixed with oil for a grain offering; [14] one golden dish weighing ten shekels, full of incense; [15] one young bull, one ram, one male lamb a year old, for a burnt offering; [16] one male goat for a sin offering; [17] and for the sacrifice of well-being, two oxen, five rams, five male goats, and five male lambs a year old. This was the offering of Nahshon son of Amminadab.

18 On the second day Nethanel son of Zuar, the leader of Issachar, presented an offering; [19] he presented for his offering one silver plate weighing one hundred thirty shekels, one silver basin weighing seventy shekels, according to the shekel of the sanctuary, both of them full of choice flour mixed with oil for a grain offering; [20] one golden dish weighing ten shekels, full of incense; [21] one young bull, one ram, one male lamb a year old, as a burnt offering; [22] one male goat as a sin offering; [23] and for the sacrifice of well-being, two oxen, five rams, five male goats, and five male lambs a year old. This was the offering of Nethanel son of Zuar.

24 On the third day Eliab son of Helon, the leader of the Zebulunites: [25] his offering was one silver plate weighing one hundred thirty shekels, one silver basin weighing seventy shekels, according to the shekel of the sanctuary, both of them full of choice flour mixed with oil for a grain offering; [26] one golden dish weighing ten shekels, full of incense; [27] one young bull,

one ram, one male lamb a year old, for a burnt offering; [28] one male goat for a sin offering; [29] and for the sacrifice of well-being, two oxen, five rams, five male goats, and five male lambs a year old. This was the offering of Eliab son of Helon.

30 On the fourth day Elizur son of Shedeur, the leader of the Reubenites: [31] his offering was one silver plate weighing one hundred thirty shekels, one silver basin weighing seventy shekels, according to the shekel of the sanctuary, both of them full of choice flour mixed with oil for a grain offering; [32] one golden dish weighing ten shekels, full of incense; [33] one young bull, one ram, one male lamb a year old, for a burnt offering; [34] one male goat for a sin offering; [35] and for the sacrifice of well-being, two oxen, five rams, five male goats, and five male lambs a year old. This was the offering of Elizur son of Shedeur.

36 On the fifth day Shelumiel son of Zurishaddai, the leader of the Simeonites: [37] his offering was one silver plate weighing one hundred thirty shekels, one silver basin weighing seventy shekels, according to the shekel of the sanctuary, both of them full of choice flour mixed with oil for a grain offering; [38] one golden dish weighing ten shekels, full of incense; [39] one young bull, one ram, one male lamb a year old, for a burnt offering; [40] one male goat for a sin offering; [41] and for the sacrifice of well-being, two oxen, five rams, five male goats, and five male lambs a year old. This was the offering of Shelumiel son of Zurishaddai.

42 On the sixth day Eliasaph son of Deuel, the leader of the Gadites: [43] his offering was one silver plate weighing one hundred thirty shekels, one silver basin weighing seventy shekels, according to the shekel of the sanctuary, both of them full of choice flour mixed with oil for a grain offering; [44] one golden dish weighing ten shekels, full of incense; [45] one young bull, one ram, one male lamb a year old,

7.13 Num 3.47
7.14 Ex 30.34
7.17 Lev 3.1
7.18 Num 1.8
7.23 v. 18
7.24 Num 1.9

7.29 Lev 7.32
7.30 Num 1.5
7.34 Heb 10.4
7.36 Num 1.6
7.40 v. 34
7.42 Num 1.14

for a burnt offering; 46 one male goat for a sin offering; 47 and for the sacrifice of well-being, two oxen, five rams, five male goats, and five male lambs a year old. This was the offering of Eliasaph son of Deuel.

48 On the seventh day Elishama son of Ammihud, the leader of the Ephraimites: 49 his offering was one silver plate weighing one hundred thirty shekels, one silver basin weighing seventy shekels, according to the shekel of the sanctuary, both of them full of choice flour mixed with oil for a grain offering; 50 one golden dish weighing ten shekels, full of incense; 51 one young bull, one ram, one male lamb a year old, for a burnt offering; 52 one male goat for a sin offering; 53 and for the sacrifice of well-being, two oxen, five rams, five male goats, and five male lambs a year old. This was the offering of Elishama son of Ammihud.

54 On the eighth day Gamaliel son of Pedahzur, the leader of the Manassites: 55 his offering was one silver plate weighing one hundred thirty shekels, one silver basin weighing seventy shekels, according to the shekel of the sanctuary, both of them full of choice flour mixed with oil for a grain offering; 56 one golden dish weighing ten shekels, full of incense; 57 one young bull, one ram, one male lamb a year old, for a burnt offering; 58 one male goat for a sin offering; 59 and for the sacrifice of well-being, two oxen, five rams, five male goats, and five male lambs a year old. This was the offering of Gamaliel son of Pedahzur.

60 On the ninth day Abidan son of Gideoni, the leader of the Benjaminites: 61 his offering was one silver plate weighing one hundred thirty shekels, one silver basin weighing seventy shekels, according to the shekel of the sanctuary, both of them full of choice flour mixed with oil for a grain offering; 62 one golden dish weighing ten shekels, full of incense; 63 one young bull, one ram, one male lamb a year old, for a burnt offer-

ing; 64 one male goat for a sin offering; 65 and for the sacrifice of well-being, two oxen, five rams, five male goats, and five male lambs a year old. This was the offering of Abidan son of Gideoni.

66 On the tenth day Ahiezer son of Ammishaddai, the leader of the Danites: 67 his offering was one silver plate weighing one hundred thirty shekels, one silver basin weighing seventy shekels, according to the shekel of the sanctuary, both of them full of choice flour mixed with oil for a grain offering; 68 one golden dish weighing ten shekels, full of incense; 69 one young bull, one ram, one male lamb a year old, for a burnt offering; 70 one male goat for a sin offering; 71 and for the sacrifice of well-being, two oxen, five rams, five male goats, and five male lambs a year old. This was the offering of Ahiezer son of Ammishaddai.

72 On the eleventh day Pagiel son of Ochran, the leader of the Asherites: 73 his offering was one silver plate weighing one hundred thirty shekels, one silver basin weighing seventy shekels, according to the shekel of the sanctuary, both of them full of choice flour mixed with oil for a grain offering; 74 one golden dish weighing ten shekels, full of incense; 75 one young bull, one ram, one male lamb a year old, for a burnt offering; 76 one male goat for a sin offering; 77 and for the sacrifice of well-being, two oxen, five rams, five male goats, and five male lambs a year old. This was the offering of Pagiel son of Ochran.

78 On the twelfth day Ahira son of Enan, the leader of the Naphtalites: 79 his offering was one silver plate weighing one hundred thirty shekels, one silver basin weighing seventy shekels, according to the shekel of the sanctuary, both of them full of choice flour mixed with oil for a grain offering; 80 one golden dish weighing ten shekels, full of incense; 81 one young bull, one ram, one male lamb a year old, for a burnt offering; 82 one male

7.46
v. 34
7.48
Num 1.10
7.52
Heb 10.4
7.54
Num 1.10
7.58
v. 52
7.60
Num 1.11

7.64
v. 52
7.66
Num 1.12
7.70
Heb 10.4
7.72
Num 1.13
7.76
v. 70
7.78
Num 1.15
7.82
v. 70

goat for a sin offering; [83] and for the sacrifice of well-being, two oxen, five rams, five male goats, and five male lambs a year old. This was the offering of Ahira son of Enan.

84 This was the dedication offering for the altar, at the time when it was anointed, from the leaders of Israel: twelve silver plates, twelve silver basins, twelve golden dishes, [85] each silver plate weighing one hundred thirty shekels and each basin seventy, all the silver of the vessels two thousand four hundred shekels according to the shekel of the sanctuary, [86] the twelve golden dishes, full of incense, weighing ten shekels apiece according to the shekel of the sanctuary, all the gold of the dishes being one hundred twenty shekels; [87] all the livestock for the burnt offering twelve bulls, twelve rams, twelve male lambs a year old, with their grain offering; and twelve male goats for a sin offering; [88] and all the livestock for the sacrifice of well-being twenty-four bulls, the rams sixty, the male goats sixty, the male lambs a year old sixty. This was the dedication offering for the altar, after it was anointed.

89 When Moses went into the tent of meeting to speak with the LORD,[1] he would hear the voice speaking to him from above the mercy seat[m] that was on the ark of the covenant[n] from between the two cherubim; thus it spoke to him.

The Seven Lamps

8 The LORD spoke to Moses, saying: [2] Speak to Aaron and say to him: When you set up the lamps, the seven lamps shall give light in front of the lampstand. [3] Aaron did so; he set up its lamps to give light in front of the lampstand, as the LORD had commanded Moses. [4] Now this was how the lampstand was made, out of hammered work of gold. From its base to its flowers, it was hammered work; according to the pattern that the LORD had shown Moses, so he made the lampstand.

7.84
vv. 1,10
7.87
Gen 8.20
7.89
Ex 33.9,11;
25.21,22
8.2
Ex 25.37;
Lev 24.2,4
8.4
Ex 25.31-40;
25.18

8.7
Num 19.9,
17,18;
Lev 14.8,9;
v. 21
8.8
Lev 2.1
8.9
Lev 8.3
8.12
Ex 29.10
8.14
Num 3.12,
45
8.15
vv. 11,13
8.16
Num 3.12,
45

Consecration and Service of the Levites

5 The LORD spoke to Moses, saying: [6] Take the Levites from among the Israelites and cleanse them. [7] Thus you shall do to them, to cleanse them: sprinkle the water of purification on them, have them shave their whole body with a razor and wash their clothes, and so cleanse themselves. [8] Then let them take a young bull and its grain offering of choice flour mixed with oil, and you shall take another young bull for a sin offering. [9] You shall bring the Levites before the tent of meeting, and assemble the whole congregation of the Israelites. [10] When you bring the Levites before the LORD, the Israelites shall lay their hands on the Levites, [11] and Aaron shall present the Levites before the LORD as an elevation offering from the Israelites, that they may do the service of the LORD. [12] The Levites shall lay their hands on the heads of the bulls, and he shall offer the one for a sin offering and the other for a burnt offering to the LORD, to make atonement for the Levites. [13] Then you shall have the Levites stand before Aaron and his sons, and you shall present them as an elevation offering to the LORD.

14 Thus you shall separate the Levites from among the other Israelites, and the Levites shall be mine. [15] Thereafter the Levites may go in to do service at the tent of meeting, once you have cleansed them and presented them as an elevation offering. [16] For they are unreservedly given to me from among the Israelites; I have taken them for myself, in place of all that open the womb, the firstborn of all the Israelites. [17] For all the firstborn among the Israelites are mine, both human and animal. On the day that I struck down all the firstborn in the land of Egypt I consecrated them for myself, [18] but I have taken the Levites in place of all the firstborn

[1]Heb him [m]Or the cover [n]Or treaty, or testimony; Heb eduth

among the Israelites. ¹⁹Moreover, I have given the Levites as a gift to Aaron and his sons from among the Israelites, to do the service for the Israelites at the tent of meeting, and to make atonement for the Israelites, in order that there may be no plague among the Israelites for coming too close to the sanctuary.

20 Moses and Aaron and the whole congregation of the Israelites did with the Levites accordingly; the Israelites did with the Levites just as the LORD had commanded Moses concerning them. ²¹The Levites purified themselves from sin and washed their clothes; then Aaron presented them as an elevation offering before the LORD, and Aaron made atonement for them to cleanse them. ²²Thereafter the Levites went in to do their service in the tent of meeting in attendance on Aaron and his sons. As the LORD had commanded Moses concerning the Levites, so they did with them.

23 The LORD spoke to Moses, saying: ²⁴This applies to the Levites: from twenty-five years old and upward they shall begin to do duty in the service of the tent of meeting; ²⁵and from the age of fifty years they shall retire from the duty of the service and serve no more. ²⁶They may assist their brothers in the tent of meeting in carrying out their duties, but they shall perform no service. Thus you shall do with the Levites in assigning their duties.

The Passover at Sinai

9 The LORD spoke to Moses in the wilderness of Sinai, in the first month of the second year after they had come out of the land of Egypt, saying: ²Let the Israelites keep the passover at its appointed time. ³On the fourteenth day of this month, at twilight,° you shall keep it at its appointed time; according to all its statutes and all its regulations you shall keep it. ⁴So Moses told the Israelites that they should keep the passover. ⁵They

kept the passover in the first month, on the fourteenth day of the month, at twilight,° in the wilderness of Sinai. Just as the LORD had commanded Moses, so the Israelites did. ⁶Now there were certain people who were unclean through touching a corpse, so that they could not keep the passover on that day. They came before Moses and Aaron on that day, ⁷and said to him, "Although we are unclean through touching a corpse, why must we be kept from presenting the LORD's offering at its appointed time among the Israelites?" ⁸Moses spoke to them, "Wait, so that I may hear what the LORD will command concerning you."

9 The LORD spoke to Moses, saying: ¹⁰Speak to the Israelites, saying: Anyone of you or your descendants who is unclean through touching a corpse, or is away on a journey, shall still keep the passover to the LORD. ¹¹In the second month on the fourteenth day, at twilight,° they shall keep it; they shall eat it with unleavened bread and bitter herbs. ¹²They shall leave none of it until morning, nor break a bone of it; according to all the statute for the passover they shall keep it. ¹³But anyone who is clean and is not on a journey, and yet refrains from keeping the passover, shall be cut off from the people for not presenting the LORD's offering at its appointed time; such a one shall bear the consequences for the sin. ¹⁴Any alien residing among you who wishes to keep the passover to the LORD shall do so according to the statute of the passover and according to its regulation; you shall have one statute for both the resident alien and the native.

The Cloud and the Fire

15 On the day the tabernacle was set up, the cloud covered the tabernacle, the tent of the covenant;ᴾ and from evening until morning it was over the tabernacle,

8.19
Num 1.53
8.21
vv. 7,11,12
8.24
Num 4.3
9.1
Num 1.1
9.2
Ex 12.6
9.5
Josh 5.10

9.6
Num 19.11-22
9.8
Ex 18.15;
Num 27.5
9.11
Ex 12.8
9.12
Ex 12.10,
43,46;
Jn 19.36
9.13
v. 7;
Ex 12.15
9.14
Ex 12.48,49
9.15
Ex 40.34;
Neh 9.12,
19; Ps 78.4;
Ex 13.21;
40.38

° Heb *between the two evenings*
ᴾ Or *treaty,* or *testimony;* Heb *eduth*

having the appearance of fire. ¹⁶It was always so: the cloud covered it by day⁹ and the appearance of fire by night. ¹⁷Whenever the cloud lifted from over the tent, then the Israelites would set out; and in the place where the cloud settled down, there the Israelites would camp. ¹⁸At the command of the LORD the Israelites would set out, and at the command of the LORD they would camp. As long as the cloud rested over the tabernacle, they would remain in camp. ¹⁹Even when the cloud continued over the tabernacle many days, the Israelites would keep the charge of the LORD, and would not set out. ²⁰Sometimes the cloud would remain a few days over the tabernacle, and according to the command of the LORD they would remain in camp; then according to the command of the LORD they would set out. ²¹Sometimes the cloud would remain from evening until morning; and when the cloud lifted in the morning, they would set out, or if it continued for a day and a night, when the cloud lifted they would set out. ²²Whether it was two days, or a month, or a longer time, that the cloud continued over the tabernacle, resting upon it, the Israelites would remain in camp and would not set out; but when it lifted they would set out. ²³At the command of the LORD they would camp, and at the command of the LORD they would set out. They kept the charge of the LORD, at the command of the LORD by Moses.

The Silver Trumpets

10 The LORD spoke to Moses, saying: ²Make two silver trumpets; you shall make them of hammered work; and you shall use them for summoning the congregation, and for breaking camp. ³When both are blown, the whole congregation shall assemble before you at the entrance of the tent of meeting. ⁴But if only one is blown, then the leaders, the heads of the tribes of Israel, shall assemble before you. ⁵When you blow an

alarm, the camps on the east side shall set out; ⁶when you blow a second alarm, the camps on the south side shall set out. An alarm is to be blown whenever they are to set out. ⁷But when the assembly is to be gathered, you shall blow, but you shall not sound an alarm. ⁸The sons of Aaron, the priests, shall blow the trumpets; this shall be a perpetual institution for you throughout your generations. ⁹When you go to war in your land against the adversary who oppresses you, you shall sound an alarm with the trumpets, so that you may be remembered before the LORD your God and be saved from your enemies. ¹⁰Also on your days of rejoicing, at your appointed festivals, and at the beginnings of your months, you shall blow the trumpets over your burnt offerings and over your sacrifices of well-being; they shall serve as a reminder on your behalf before the LORD your God: I am the LORD your God.

Departure from Sinai

11 In the second year, in the second month, on the twentieth day of the month, the cloud lifted from over the tabernacle of the covenant.ʳ ¹²Then the Israelites set out by stages from the wilderness of Sinai, and the cloud settled down in the wilderness of Paran. ¹³They set out for the first time at the command of the LORD by Moses. ¹⁴The standard of the camp of Judah set out first, company by company, and over the whole company was Nahshon son of Amminadab. ¹⁵Over the company of the tribe of Issachar was Nethanel son of Zuar; ¹⁶and over the company of the tribe of Zebulun was Eliab son of Helon.

17 Then the tabernacle was taken down, and the Gershonites and the Merarites, who carried the tabernacle, set out. ¹⁸Next the standard of the camp of Reuben set out, company by company; and over the whole company was Elizur son of

9.17
Num 10.11, 12;
Ex 40.36-38
9.18
1 Cor 10.1
9.19
Num 1.53; 3.8
9.22
Ex 40.36,37
10.3
Jer 4.5
10.5
v. 14

10.6
v. 18
10.8
Num 31.6
10.9
Num 31.6;
Judg 2.18;
Ps 106.4
10.10
Num 29.1;
Lev 23.24;
Ps 81.3-5
10.11
Num 9.17
10.13
Deut 1.6
10.14
Num 2.3-9
10.17
Num 4.21-32
10.18
Num 2.10-16

⁹Gk Syr Vg: Heb lacks *by day* ʳOr *treaty*, or *testimony*; Heb *eduth*

Shedeur. ¹⁹Over the company of the tribe of Simeon was Shelumiel son of Zurishaddai, ²⁰and over the company of the tribe of Gad was Eliasaph son of Deuel.

21 Then the Kohathites, who carried the holy things, set out; and the tabernacle was set up before their arrival. ²²Next the standard of the Ephraimite camp set out, company by company, and over the whole company was Elishama son of Ammihud. ²³Over the company of the tribe of Manasseh was Gamaliel son of Pedahzur, ²⁴and over the company of the tribe of Benjamin was Abidan son of Gideoni.

25 Then the standard of the camp of Dan, acting as the rear guard of all the camps, set out, company by company, and over the whole company was Ahiezer son of Ammishaddai. ²⁶Over the company of the tribe of Asher was Pagiel son of Ochran, ²⁷and over the company of the tribe of Naphtali was Ahira son of Enan. ²⁸This was the order of march of the Israelites, company by company, when they set out.

29 Moses said to Hobab son of Reuel the Midianite, Moses' father-in-law, "We are setting out for the place of which the LORD said, 'I will give it to you'; come with us, and we will treat you well; for the LORD has promised good to Israel." ³⁰But he said to him, "I will not go, but I will go back to my own land and to my kindred." ³¹He said, "Do not leave us, for you know where we should camp in the wilderness, and you will serve as eyes for us. ³²Moreover, if you go with us, whatever good the LORD does for us, the same we will do for you."

33 So they set out from the mount of the LORD three days' journey with the ark of the covenant of the LORD going before them three days' journey, to seek out a resting place for them, ³⁴the cloud of the LORD being over them by day when they set out from the camp.

35 Whenever the ark set out, Moses would say,

"Arise, O LORD, let your
 enemies be scattered,
 and your foes flee before
 you."

³⁶And whenever it came to rest, he would say,

"Return, O LORD of the ten
 thousand thousands of
 Israel."ˢ

Complaining in the Desert

11 Now when the people complained in the hearing of the LORD about their misfortunes, the LORD heard it and his anger was kindled. Then the fire of the LORD burned against them, and consumed some outlying parts of the camp. ²But the people cried out to Moses; and Moses prayed to the LORD, and the fire abated. ³So that place was called Taberah,ᵗ because the fire of the LORD burned against them.

4 The rabble among them had a strong craving; and the Israelites also wept again, and said, "If only we had meat to eat! ⁵We remember the fish we used to eat in Egypt for nothing, the cucumbers, the melons, the leeks, the onions, and the garlic; ⁶but now our strength is dried up, and there is nothing at all but this manna to look at."

7 Now the manna was like coriander seed, and its color was like the color of gum resin. ⁸The people went around and gathered it, ground it in mills or beat it in mortars, then boiled it in pots and made cakes of it; and the taste of it was like the taste of cakes baked with oil. ⁹When the dew fell on the camp in the night, the manna would fall with it.

10 Moses heard the people weeping throughout their families, all at the entrances of their tents. Then the LORD became very angry, and Moses was displeased. ¹¹So Moses said to the LORD, "Why have you treated your servant so badly? Why have I not found favor in your sight, that you lay the burden of all this people on me? ¹²Did I con-

10.21
Num 4.4-20
10.22
Num 2.18-24
10.25
Num 2.25-31;
Josh 6.9,13
10.29
Judg 4.11;
Ex 2.18;
Gen 12.7;
32.12;
Ex 3.8
10.32
Ps 22.27-31;
Lev 19.34
10.33
v. 11;
Deut 1.33;
Isa 11.10
10.34
Num 9.15-23
10.35
Ps 68.1,2;
Deut 7.10;
32.41

11.1
Num 14.2;
16.11; 17.5;
16.35;
Lev 10.2
11.2
Num 21.7
11.4
Ex 12.38;
Ps 78.18;
1 Cor 10.6
11.5
Ex 16.3
11.6
Lev 21.5
11.7
Ex 16.14,31
11.9
Ex 16.13,14
11.10
Ps 78.21
11.12
Isa 40.11;
49.23;
Gen 26.3;
Ex 13.5

ˢMeaning of Heb uncertain ᵗThat is *Burning*

ceive all this people? Did I give birth to them, that you should say to me, 'Carry them in your bosom, as a nurse carries a sucking child,' to the land that you promised on oath to their ancestors? [13] Where am I to get meat to give to all this people? For they come weeping to me and say, 'Give us meat to eat!' [14] I am not able to carry all this people alone, for they are too heavy for me. [15] If this is the way you are going to treat me, put me to death at once — if I have found favor in your sight — and do not let me see my misery."

The Seventy Elders

16 So the LORD said to Moses, "Gather for me seventy of the elders of Israel, whom you know to be the elders of the people and officers over them; bring them to the tent of meeting, and have them take their place there with you. [17] I will come down and talk with you there; and I will take some of the spirit that is on you and put it on them; and they shall bear the burden of the people along with you so that you will not bear it all by yourself. [18] And say to the people: Consecrate yourselves for tomorrow, and you shall eat meat; for you have wailed in the hearing of the LORD, saying, 'If only we had meat to eat! Surely it was better for us in Egypt.' Therefore the LORD will give you meat, and you shall eat. [19] You shall eat not only one day, or two days, or five days, or ten days, or twenty days, [20] but for a whole month — until it comes out of your nostrils and becomes loathsome to you — because you have rejected the LORD who is among you, and have wailed before him, saying, 'Why did we ever leave Egypt?' " [21] But Moses said, "The people I am with number six hundred thousand on foot; and you say, 'I will give them meat, that they may eat for a whole month'! [22] Are there enough flocks and herds to slaughter for them? Are there enough fish in the sea to catch for them?" [23] The LORD said to Moses, "Is the LORD's power

limited?[u] Now you shall see whether my word will come true for you or not."

24 So Moses went out and told the people the words of the LORD; and he gathered seventy elders of the people, and placed them all around the tent. [25] Then the LORD came down in the cloud and spoke to him, and took some of the spirit that was on him and put it on the seventy elders; and when the spirit rested upon them, they prophesied. But they did not do so again.

26 Two men remained in the camp, one named Eldad, and the other named Medad, and the spirit rested on them; they were among those registered, but they had not gone out to the tent, and so they prophesied in the camp. [27] And a young man ran and told Moses, "Eldad and Medad are prophesying in the camp." [28] And Joshua son of Nun, the assistant of Moses, one of his chosen men,[v] said, "My lord Moses, stop them!" [29] But Moses said to him, "Are you jealous for my sake? Would that all the LORD's people were prophets, and that the LORD would put his spirit on them!" [30] And Moses and the elders of Israel returned to the camp.

The Quails

31 Then a wind went out from the LORD, and it brought quails from the sea and let them fall beside the camp, about a day's journey on this side and a day's journey on the other side, all around the camp, about two cubits deep on the ground. [32] So the people worked all that day and night and all the next day, gathering the quails; the least anyone gathered was ten homers; and they spread them out for themselves all around the camp. [33] But while the meat was still between their teeth, before it was consumed, the anger of the LORD was kindled against the people, and the LORD struck the people with a very great plague. [34] So that place was called Kibroth-

11.13
vv. 21,22;
Jn 6.5-9
11.14
Ex 18.18
11.15
1 Kings 19.4;
Jon 4.3
11.16
Ex 24.1,9;
Deut 16.18
11.17
v. 25;
Ex 19.20;
1 Sam 10.6;
2 Kings 2.15
11.18
Ex 19.10;
16.7; v. 5;
Acts 7.39
11.19
Ps 78.29;
106.15;
Num 21.5
11.22
Mt 15.33
11.23
Isa 50.2;
59.1;
Num 23.19

11.24
v. 16
11.25
v. 17;
Num 12.5;
1 Sam 10.5,
6,10;
Acts 2.17,18
11.26
1 Sam 10.6;
20.26
11.28
Mk 9.38-40
11.29
1 Cor 14.5
11.31
Ex 16.13;
Ps 78.26-28;
105.40
11.33
Ps 78.30,31;
106.15
11.34
Deut 9.22

u Heb LORD's hand too short? v Or of
Moses from his youth

hattaavah,ʷ because there they buried the people who had the craving. ³⁵From Kibroth-hattaavah the people journeyed to Hazeroth.

Aaron and Miriam Jealous of Moses

12 While they were at Hazeroth, Miriam and Aaron spoke against Moses because of the Cushite woman whom he had married (for he had indeed married a Cushite woman); ²and they said, "Has the LORD spoken only through Moses? Has he not spoken through us also?" And the LORD heard it. ³Now the man Moses was very humble,ˣ more so than anyone else on the face of the earth. ⁴Suddenly the LORD said to Moses, Aaron, and Miriam, "Come out, you three, to the tent of meeting." So the three of them came out. ⁵Then the LORD came down in a pillar of cloud, and stood at the entrance of the tent, and called Aaron and Miriam; and they both came forward. ⁶And he said, "Hear my words:

When there are prophets
 among you,
I the LORD make myself
 known to them in
 visions;
I speak to them in dreams.
⁷ Not so with my servant
 Moses;
 he is entrusted with all my
 house.
⁸ With him I speak face to
 face—
 clearly, not in riddles;
 and he beholds the form of
 the LORD.
Why then were you not afraid to speak against my servant Moses?" ⁹And the anger of the LORD was kindled against them, and he departed.

10 When the cloud went away from over the tent, Miriam had become leprous,ʸ as white as snow. And Aaron turned towards Miriam and saw that she was leprous. ¹¹Then Aaron said to Moses, "Oh, my lord, do not punish usᶻ for a sin that we have so foolishly committed. ¹²Do not let her be like one

stillborn, whose flesh is half consumed when it comes out of its mother's womb." ¹³And Moses cried to the LORD, "O God, please heal her." ¹⁴But the LORD said to Moses, "If her father had but spit in her face, would she not bear her shame for seven days? Let her be shut out of the camp for seven days, and after that she may be brought in again." ¹⁵So Miriam was shut out of the camp for seven days; and the people did not set out on the march until Miriam had been brought in again. ¹⁶After that the people set out from Hazeroth, and camped in the wilderness of Paran.

Spies Sent into Canaan

13 The LORD said to Moses, ²"Send men to spy out the land of Canaan, which I am giving to the Israelites; from each of their ancestral tribes you shall send a man, every one a leader among them." ³So Moses sent them from the wilderness of Paran, according to the command of the LORD, all of them leading men among the Israelites. ⁴These were their names: From the tribe of Reuben, Shammua son of Zaccur; ⁵from the tribe of Simeon, Shaphat son of Hori; ⁶from the tribe of Judah, Caleb son of Jephunneh; ⁷from the tribe of Issachar, Igal son of Joseph; ⁸from the tribe of Ephraim, Hoshea son of Nun; ⁹from the tribe of Benjamin, Palti son of Raphu; ¹⁰from the tribe of Zebulun, Gaddiel son of Sodi; ¹¹from the tribe of Joseph (that is, from the tribe of Manasseh), Gaddi son of Susi; ¹²from the tribe of Dan, Ammiel son of Gemalli; ¹³from the tribe of Asher, Sethur son of Michael; ¹⁴from the tribe of Naphtali, Nahbi son of Vophsi; ¹⁵from the tribe of Gad, Geuel son of Machi. ¹⁶These were the names of the men whom Moses sent to spy out the land. And Moses changed

11.35
Num 33.17
12.1
Ex 2.21
12.2
Num 16.3
12.3
Mt 11.29
12.5
Num 11.25;
16.19
12.6
Gen 46.2;
31.10,11;
1 Kings 3.5
12.7
Ps 105.26;
Heb 3.2,5
12.8
Ex 33.11;
Deut 34.10;
Ex 33.19
12.10
Deut 24.9;
2 Kings 5.27;
15.5
12.11
2 Sam 19.19;
24.10

12.14
Lev 13.46;
Num 5.2,3
13.2
Deut 1.22
13.8
v. 16
13.16
v. 8

ʷ That is *Graves of craving* ˣ Or *devout*
ʸ A term for several skin diseases; precise meaning uncertain ᶻ Heb *do not lay sin upon us*

the name of Hoshea son of Nun to Joshua.

17 Moses sent them to spy out the land of Canaan, and said to them, "Go up there into the Negeb, and go up into the hill country, [18] and see what the land is like, and whether the people who live in it are strong or weak, whether they are few or many, [19] and whether the land they live in is good or bad, and whether the towns that they live in are unwalled or fortified, [20] and whether the land is rich or poor, and whether there are trees in it or not. Be bold, and bring some of the fruit of the land." Now it was the season of the first ripe grapes.

21 So they went up and spied out the land from the wilderness of Zin to Rehob, near Lebo-hamath. [22] They went up into the Negeb, and came to Hebron; and Ahiman, Sheshai, and Talmai, the Anakites, were there. (Hebron was built seven years before Zoan in Egypt.) [23] And they came to the Wadi Eshcol, and cut down from there a branch with a single cluster of grapes, and they carried it on a pole between two of them. They also brought some pomegranates and figs. [24] That place was called the Wadi Eshcol,[a] because of the cluster that the Israelites cut down from there.

The Report of the Spies

25 At the end of forty days they returned from spying out the land. [26] And they came to Moses and Aaron and to all the congregation of the Israelites in the wilderness of Paran, at Kadesh; they brought back word to them and to all the congregation, and showed them the fruit of the land. [27] And they told him, "We came to the land to which you sent us; it flows with milk and honey, and this is its fruit. [28] Yet the people who live in the land are strong, and the towns are fortified and very large; and besides, we saw the descendants of Anak there. [29] The Amalekites live in the land of the Negeb; the Hittites, the Jebusites, and the Amo-

13.17
v. 21
13.20
Deut 1.24, 25; 31.6,23
13.22
Josh 15.13, 14; vv. 28, 33; Ps 78.12
13.26
v. 3;
Num 20.1, 16; 32.8
13.27
Ex 3.8;
Deut 1.25
13.28
Deut 1.28
13.29
Num 14.43

13.30
Num 14.6, 24
13.31
Deut 1.28
13.32
Num 14.36;
Ps 106.24;
Am 2.9
13.33
Deut 1.28;
9.2
14.2
Num 11.1,5
14.5
Num 16.4, 22
14.7
Num 13.27;
Deut 1.25
14.8
Deut 10.15;
Num 13.27
14.9
Deut 9.7,23, 24; 7.18;
20.1,3,4

rites live in the hill country; and the Canaanites live by the sea, and along the Jordan."

30 But Caleb quieted the people before Moses, and said, "Let us go up at once and occupy it, for we are well able to overcome it." [31] Then the men who had gone up with him said, "We are not able to go up against this people, for they are stronger than we." [32] So they brought to the Israelites an unfavorable report of the land that they had spied out, saying, "The land that we have gone through as spies is a land that devours its inhabitants; and all the people that we saw in it are of great size. [33] There we saw the Nephilim (the Anakites come from the Nephilim); and to ourselves we seemed like grasshoppers, and so we seemed to them."

The People Rebel

14 Then all the congregation raised a loud cry, and the people wept that night. [2] And all the Israelites complained against Moses and Aaron; the whole congregation said to them, "Would that we had died in the land of Egypt! Or would that we had died in this wilderness! [3] Why is the LORD bringing us into this land to fall by the sword? Our wives and our little ones will become booty; would it not be better for us to go back to Egypt?" [4] So they said to one another, "Let us choose a captain, and go back to Egypt."

5 Then Moses and Aaron fell on their faces before all the assembly of the congregation of the Israelites. [6] And Joshua son of Nun and Caleb son of Jephunneh, who were among those who had spied out the land, tore their clothes [7] and said to all the congregation of the Israelites, "The land that we went through as spies is an exceedingly good land. [8] If the LORD is pleased with us, he will bring us into this land and give it to us, a land that flows with milk and honey. [9] Only, do not rebel against the LORD; and do not fear the people of the land,

[a] That is Cluster

for they are no more than bread for us; their protection is removed from them, and the LORD is with us; do not fear them." 10 But the whole congregation threatened to stone them.

Then the glory of the LORD appeared at the tent of meeting to all the Israelites. 11 And the LORD said to Moses, "How long will this people despise me? And how long will they refuse to believe in me, in spite of all the signs that I have done among them? 12 I will strike them with pestilence and disinherit them, and I will make of you a nation greater and mightier than they."

Moses Intercedes for the People

13 But Moses said to the LORD, "Then the Egyptians will hear of it, for in your might you brought up this people from among them, 14 and they will tell the inhabitants of this land. They have heard that you, O LORD, are in the midst of this people; for you, O LORD, are seen face to face, and your cloud stands over them and you go in front of them, in a pillar of cloud by day and in a pillar of fire by night. 15 Now if you kill this people all at one time, then the nations who have heard about you will say, 16 'It is because the LORD was not able to bring this people into the land he swore to give them that he has slaughtered them in the wilderness.' 17 And now, therefore, let the power of the LORD be great in the way that you promised when you spoke, saying,
18 'The LORD is slow to anger,
 and abounding in steadfast
 love,
 forgiving iniquity and
 transgression,
 but by no means clearing the
 guilty,
 visiting the iniquity of the
 parents
 upon the children
 to the third and the fourth
 generation.'
19 Forgive the iniquity of this people according to the greatness of

your steadfast love, just as you have pardoned this people, from Egypt even until now."

20 Then the LORD said, "I do forgive, just as you have asked; 21 nevertheless — as I live, and as all the earth shall be filled with the glory of the LORD — 22 none of the people who have seen my glory and the signs that I did in Egypt and in the wilderness, and yet have tested me these ten times and have not obeyed my voice, 23 shall see the land that I swore to give to their ancestors; none of those who despised me shall see it. 24 But my servant Caleb, because he has a different spirit and has followed me wholeheartedly, I will bring into the land into which he went, and his descendants shall possess it. 25 Now, since the Amalekites and the Canaanites live in the valleys, turn tomorrow and set out for the wilderness by the way to the Red Sea."[b]

An Attempted Invasion is Repulsed

26 And the LORD spoke to Moses and to Aaron, saying: 27 How long shall this wicked congregation complain against me? I have heard the complaints of the Israelites, which they complain against me. 28 Say to them, "As I live," says the LORD, "I will do to you the very things I heard you say: 29 your dead bodies shall fall in this very wilderness; and of all your number, included in the census, from twenty years old and upward, who have complained against me, 30 not one of you shall come into the land in which I swore to settle you, except Caleb son of Jephunneh and Joshua son of Nun. 31 But your little ones, who you said would become booty, I will bring in, and they shall know the land that you have despised. 32 But as for you, your dead bodies shall fall in this wilderness. 33 And your children shall be shepherds in the wilderness for forty years, and shall suffer for your faithlessness, until the last of your

b Or Sea of Reeds

14.10
Ex 17.4;
16.10;
Lev 9.23
14.11
Deut 9.7,8;
Ps 78.22;
106.24
14.12
Ex 32.10
14.13
Ps 106.23
14.14
Ex 15.14;
Josh 2.9,10;
Ex 13.21
14.16
Deut 9.28
14.18
Ex 34.6,7;
Ps 103.8;
Ex 20.5
14.19
Ex 34.9;
Ps 106.45;
78.38

14.20
Ps 106.23
14.21
Ps 72.19
14.24
vv. 7-9;
Num 32.12;
Josh 14.6-15
14.25
Deut 1.40
14.27
Num 11.1;
Ex 16.12
14.28
v. 21;
Deut 1.35;
see v. 2
14.29
Num 1.45;
26.64
14.30
v. 24;
Deut 1.36
14.31
Deut 1.39;
Ps 106.24
14.32
1 Cor 10.5
14.33
Num 32.13;
Ps 107.40

dead bodies lies in the wilderness. ³⁴According to the number of the days in which you spied out the land, forty days, for every day a year, you shall bear your iniquity, forty years, and you shall know my displeasure." ³⁵I the LORD have spoken; surely I will do thus to all this wicked congregation gathered together against me: in this wilderness they shall come to a full end, and there they shall die.

36 And the men whom Moses sent to spy out the land, who returned and made all the congregation complain against him by bringing a bad report about the land— ³⁷the men who brought an unfavorable report about the land died by a plague before the LORD. ³⁸But Joshua son of Nun and Caleb son of Jephunneh alone remained alive, of those men who went to spy out the land.

39 When Moses told these words to all the Israelites, the people mourned greatly. ⁴⁰They rose early in the morning and went up to the heights of the hill country, saying, "Here we are. We will go up to the place that the LORD has promised, for we have sinned." ⁴¹But Moses said, "Why do you continue to transgress the command of the LORD? That will not succeed. ⁴²Do not go up, for the LORD is not with you; do not let yourselves be struck down before your enemies. ⁴³For the Amalekites and the Canaanites will confront you there, and you shall fall by the sword; because you have turned back from following the LORD, the LORD will not be with you." ⁴⁴But they presumed to go up to the heights of the hill country, even though the ark of the covenant of the LORD, and Moses, had not left the camp. ⁴⁵Then the Amalekites and the Canaanites who lived in that hill country came down and defeated them, pursuing them as far as Hormah.

Various Offerings

15 The LORD spoke to Moses, saying: ²Speak to the Israelites and say to them: When you come into the land you are to inhabit, which I am giving you, ³and you make an offering by fire to the LORD from the herd or from the flock—whether a burnt offering or a sacrifice, to fulfill a vow or as a freewill offering or at your appointed festivals—to make a pleasing odor for the LORD, ⁴then whoever presents such an offering to the LORD shall present also a grain offering, one-tenth of an ephah of choice flour, mixed with one-fourth of a hin of oil. ⁵Moreover, you shall offer one-fourth of a hin of wine as a drink offering with the burnt offering or the sacrifice, for each lamb. ⁶For a ram, you shall offer a grain offering, two-tenths of an ephah of choice flour mixed with one-third of a hin of oil; ⁷and as a drink offering you shall offer one-third of a hin of wine, a pleasing odor to the LORD. ⁸When you offer a bull as a burnt offering or a sacrifice, to fulfill a vow or as an offering of well-being to the LORD, ⁹then you shall present with the bull a grain offering, three-tenths of an ephah of choice flour, mixed with half a hin of oil, ¹⁰and you shall present as a drink offering half a hin of wine, as an offering by fire, a pleasing odor to the LORD.

11 Thus it shall be done for each ox or ram, or for each of the male lambs or the kids. ¹²According to the number that you offer, so you shall do with each and every one. ¹³Every native Israelite shall do these things in this way, in presenting an offering by fire, a pleasing odor to the LORD. ¹⁴An alien who lives with you, or who takes up permanent residence among you, and wishes to offer an offering by fire, a pleasing odor to the LORD, shall do as you do. ¹⁵As for the assembly, there shall be for both you and the resident alien a single statute, a perpetual statute throughout your generations; you and the alien shall be alike before the LORD. ¹⁶You and the alien who resides with you shall have the same law and the same ordinance.

17 The LORD spoke to Moses,

Center reference column:

14.34
Num 13.25;
Ps 95.10
14.35
Num 23.19;
26.65
14.36
Num 13.4-16,
32
14.38
Josh 14.6
14.39
Ex 33.4
14.40
Deut 1.41
14.42
Deut 1.42
14.44
Deut 1.43
14.45
Deut 1.44;
Num 21.3
15.2
v. 18

15.3
Lev 23.1-44
15.4
Lev 2.1;
6.14;
Ex 29.40;
Lev 23.13;
14.10;
Num 28.5
15.5
Num 28.7,
14
15.6
Num 28.12,
14
15.8
Lev 7.11
15.9
Num 28.12,
14
15.15
v. 29;
Num 9.14

saying: [18]Speak to the Israelites and say to them: After you come into the land to which I am bringing you, [19]whenever you eat of the bread of the land, you shall present a donation to the LORD. [20]From your first batch of dough you shall present a loaf as a donation; you shall present it just as you present a donation from the threshing floor. [21]Throughout your generations you shall give to the LORD a donation from the first of your batch of dough.

22 But if you unintentionally fail to observe all these commandments that the LORD has spoken to Moses— [23]everything that the LORD has commanded you by Moses, from the day the LORD gave commandment and thereafter, throughout your generations— [24]then if it was done unintentionally without the knowledge of the congregation, the whole congregation shall offer one young bull for a burnt offering, a pleasing odor to the LORD, together with its grain offering and its drink offering, according to the ordinance, and one male goat for a sin offering. [25]The priest shall make atonement for all the congregation of the Israelites, and they shall be forgiven; it was unintentional, and they have brought their offering, an offering by fire to the LORD, and their sin offering before the LORD, for their error. [26]All the congregation of the Israelites shall be forgiven, as well as the aliens residing among them, because the whole people was involved in the error.

27 An individual who sins unintentionally shall present a female goat a year old for a sin offering. [28]And the priest shall make atonement before the LORD for the one who commits an error, when it is unintentional, to make atonement for the person, who then shall be forgiven. [29]For both the native among the Israelites and the alien residing among them—you shall have the same law for anyone who acts in error. [30]But whoever acts high-handedly, whether a native or

an alien, affronts the LORD, and shall be cut off from among the people. [31]Because of having despised the word of the LORD and broken his commandment, such a person shall be utterly cut off and bear the guilt.

Penalty for Violating the Sabbath

32 When the Israelites were in the wilderness, they found a man gathering sticks on the sabbath day. [33]Those who found him gathering sticks brought him to Moses, Aaron, and to the whole congregation. [34]They put him in custody, because it was not clear what should be done to him. [35]Then the LORD said to Moses, "The man shall be put to death; all the congregation shall stone him outside the camp." [36]The whole congregation brought him outside the camp and stoned him to death, just as the LORD had commanded Moses.

Fringes on Garments

37 The LORD said to Moses: [38]Speak to the Israelites, and tell them to make fringes on the corners of their garments throughout their generations and to put a blue cord on the fringe at each corner. [39]You have the fringe so that, when you see it, you will remember all the commandments of the LORD and do them, and not follow the lust of your own heart and your own eyes. [40]So you shall remember and do all my commandments, and you shall be holy to your God. [41]I am the LORD your God, who brought you out of the land of Egypt, to be your God: I am the LORD your God.

Revolt of Korah, Dathan, and Abiram

16 Now Korah son of Izhar son of Kohath son of Levi, along with Dathan and Abiram sons of Eliab, and On son of Peleth—descendants of Reuben— took [2]two hundred fifty Israelite men, leaders of the congregation, chosen from the assembly, well-

15.18
v. 2
15.19
Josh 5.11, 12
15.20
Deut 26.2, 10; Lev 2.14
15.22
Lev 4.2
15.24
Lev 4.13; vv. 8-10
15.25
Lev 4.20
15.27
Lev 4.27,28
15.28
Lev 4.35
15.29
v. 15

15.31
2 Sam 12.9; Lev 5.1; Ezek 18.20
15.32
Ex 31.14, 15; 35.2,3
15.34
Lev 24.12
15.35
Ex 31.14, 15;
Lev 24.14; Acts 7.58
15.38
Deut 22.12; Mt 23.5
15.39
Deut 4.23; Ps 73.27
15.40
Lev 11.44; Rom 12.1; Col 1.22; 1 Pet 1.15, 16
16.1
Ex 6.21; Jude 11
16.2
Num 26.9

known men,c and they confronted Moses. ³They assembled against Moses and against Aaron, and said to them, "You have gone too far! All the congregation are holy, every-one of them, and the LORD is among them. So why then do you exalt yourselves above the assembly of the LORD?" ⁴When Moses heard it, he fell on his face. ⁵Then he said to Korah and all his company, "In the morning the LORD will make known who is his, and who is holy, and who will be allowed to approach him; the one whom he will choose he will allow to approach him. ⁶Do this: take censers, Korah and all yourd company, ⁷and tomorrow put fire in them, and lay incense on them before the LORD; and the man whom the LORD chooses shall be the holy one. You Levites have gone too far!" ⁸Then Moses said to Korah, "Hear now, you Levites! ⁹Is it too little for you that the God of Israel has separated you from the congregation of Israel, to allow you to approach him in order to per-form the duties of the LORD's taber-nacle, and to stand before the con-gregation and serve them? ¹⁰He has allowed you to approach him, and all your brother Levites with you; yet you seek the priesthood as well! ¹¹Therefore you and all your company have gathered together against the LORD. What is Aaron that you rail against him?"

12 Moses sent for Dathan and Abiram sons of Eliab; but they said, "We will not come! ¹³Is it too little that you have brought us up out of a land flowing with milk and honey to kill us in the wilderness, that you must also lord it over us? ¹⁴It is clear you have not brought us into a land flowing with milk and hon-ey, or given us an inheritance of fields and vineyards. Would you put out the eyes of these men? We will not come!"

15 Moses was very angry and said to the LORD, "Pay no attention to their offering. I have not taken one donkey from them, and I have not harmed any one of them." ¹⁶And Moses said to Korah, "As for

you and all your company, be present tomorrow before the LORD, you and they and Aaron; ¹⁷and let each one of you take his censer, and put incense on it, and each one of you present his censer before the LORD, two hundred fifty censers; you also, and Aaron, each his cen-ser." ¹⁸So each man took his cen-ser, and they put fire in the censers and laid incense on them, and they stood at the entrance of the tent of meeting with Moses and Aaron. ¹⁹Then Korah assembled the whole congregation against them at the entrance of the tent of meet-ing. And the glory of the LORD ap-peared to the whole congregation.

20 Then the LORD spoke to Mo-ses and to Aaron, saying: ²¹Sepa-rate yourselves from this congrega-tion, so that I may consume them in a moment. ²²They fell on their faces, and said, "O God, the God of the spirits of all flesh, shall one person sin and you become angry with the whole congregation?"

23 And the LORD spoke to Mo-ses, saying: ²⁴Say to the congrega-tion: Get away from the dwellings of Korah, Dathan, and Abiram. ²⁵So Moses got up and went to Da-than and Abiram; the elders of Isra-el followed him. ²⁶He said to the congregation, "Turn away from the tents of these wicked men, and touch nothing of theirs, or you will be swept away for all their sins." ²⁷So they got away from the dwell-ings of Korah, Dathan, and Abiram; and Dathan and Abiram came out and stood at the entrance of their tents, together with their wives, their children, and their little ones. ²⁸And Moses said, "This is how you shall know that the LORD has sent me to do all these works; it has not been of my own accord: ²⁹If these people die a natural death, or if a natural fate comes on them, then the LORD has not sent me. ³⁰But if the LORD creates something new, and the ground opens its mouth and swallows them up, with all that

16.3
Ps 106.16;
Ex 19.6;
Num 14.14
16.4
Num 14.5
16.5
Lev 10.3;
Ps 65.4;
Num 17.5,8
16.9
Num 3.6,9;
8.14;
Deut 10.8
16.11
Ex 16.7,8;
1 Cor 10.10
16.13
Num 11.4-6;
Ex 2.14;
Acts 7.27,35
16.14
Lev 20.24
16.15
Gen 4.4,5;
1 Sam 12.3
16.16
vv. 6,7

16.19
v. 42;
Num 14.10;
Ex 16.7,10;
Lev 9.6,23
16.21
v. 45;
Ex 32.10,12
16.22
v. 45;
Num 14.5
16.26
Gen 19.12,
14
16.28
Ex 3.12;
Jn 5.36;
Num 24.13;
Jn 6.38
16.30
v. 33;
Ps 55.15

c Cn: Heb and they confronted Moses, and two hundred fifty men . . . well-known men
d Heb his

belongs to them, and they go down alive into Sheol, then you shall know that these men have despised the LORD."

31 As soon as he finished speaking all these words, the ground under them was split apart. ³²The earth opened its mouth and swallowed them up, along with their households—everyone who belonged to Korah and all their goods. ³³So they with all that belonged to them went down alive into Sheol; the earth closed over them, and they perished from the midst of the assembly. ³⁴All Israel around them fled at their outcry, for they said, "The earth will swallow us too!" ³⁵And fire came out from the LORD and consumed the two hundred fifty men offering the incense.

36ᵉThen the LORD spoke to Moses, saying: ³⁷Tell Eleazar son of Aaron the priest to take the censers out of the blaze; then scatter the fire far and wide. ³⁸For the censers of these sinners have become holy at the cost of their lives. Make them into hammered plates as a covering for the altar, for they presented them before the LORD and they became holy. Thus they shall be a sign to the Israelites. ³⁹So Eleazar the priest took the bronze censers that had been presented by those who were burned; and they were hammered out as a covering for the altar— ⁴⁰a reminder to the Israelites that no outsider, who is not of the descendants of Aaron, shall approach to offer incense before the LORD, so as not to become like Korah and his company—just as the LORD had said to him through Moses.

41 On the next day, however, the whole congregation of the Israelites rebelled against Moses and against Aaron, saying, "You have killed the people of the LORD." ⁴²And when the congregation had assembled against them, Moses and Aaron turned toward the tent of meeting; the cloud had covered it and the glory of the LORD appeared. ⁴³Then Moses and Aaron

came to the front of the tent of meeting, ⁴⁴and the LORD spoke to Moses, saying, ⁴⁵"Get away from this congregation, so that I may consume them in a moment." And they fell on their faces. ⁴⁶Moses said to Aaron, "Take your censer, put fire on it from the altar and lay incense on it, and carry it quickly to the congregation and make atonement for them. For wrath has gone out from the LORD; the plague has begun." ⁴⁷So Aaron took it as Moses had ordered, and ran into the middle of the assembly, where the plague had already begun among the people. He put on the incense, and made atonement for the people. ⁴⁸He stood between the dead and the living; and the plague was stopped. ⁴⁹Those who died by the plague were fourteen thousand seven hundred, besides those who died in the affair of Korah. ⁵⁰When the plague was stopped, Aaron returned to Moses at the entrance of the tent of meeting.

The Budding of Aaron's Rod

17ᶠ The LORD spoke to Moses, saying: ²Speak to the Israelites, and get twelve staffs from them, one for each ancestral house, from all the leaders of their ancestral houses. Write each man's name on his staff, ³and write Aaron's name on the staff of Levi. For there shall be one staff for the head of each ancestral house. ⁴Place them in the tent of meeting before the covenant,ᵍ where I meet with you. ⁵And the staff of the man whom I choose shall sprout; thus I will put a stop to the complaints of the Israelites that they continually make against you. ⁶Moses spoke to the Israelites; and all their leaders gave him staffs, one for each leader, according to their ancestral houses, twelve staffs; and the staff of Aaron was among theirs. ⁷So Moses placed the staffs before the LORD in the tent of the covenant.ᵍ

8 When Moses went into the

16.31
Num 26.10
16.32
Num 26.11
16.35
Num 11.1-3;
26.10
16.38
Prov 20.2;
Num 26.10
16.40
Num 3.10;
2 Chr 26.18
16.41
v. 3
16.42
Ex 40.34;
v. 19;
Num 20.6

16.45
vv. 21,24
16.46
Num 8.19;
Ps 106.29
16.47
Num 25.7,8,
13
16.48
Ps 106.30
16.49
vv. 32,35
17.4
Ex 25.22;
29.42,43
17.5
Num 16.5,
11
17.7
Num 18.2;
Acts 7.44

ᵉCh 17.1 in Heb　　ᶠCh 17.16 in Heb
ᵍOr treaty, or testimony; Heb eduth

tent of the covenant[h] on the next day, the staff of Aaron for the house of Levi had sprouted. It put forth buds, produced blossoms, and bore ripe almonds. ⁹Then Moses brought out all the staffs from before the LORD to all the Israelites; and they looked, and each man took his staff. ¹⁰And the LORD said to Moses, "Put back the staff of Aaron before the covenant,[h] to be kept as a warning to rebels, so that you may make an end of their complaints against me, or else they will die." ¹¹Moses did so; just as the LORD commanded him, so he did.

12 The Israelites said to Moses, "We are perishing; we are lost, all of us are lost! ¹³Everyone who approaches the tabernacle of the LORD will die. Are we all to perish?"

Responsibility of Priests and Levites

18 The LORD said to Aaron: You and your sons and your ancestral house with you shall bear responsibility for offenses connected with the sanctuary, while you and your sons alone shall bear responsibility for offenses connected with the priesthood. ²So bring with you also your brothers of the tribe of Levi, your ancestral tribe, in order that they may be joined to you, and serve you while you and your sons with you are in front of the tent of the covenant.[h] ³They shall perform duties for you and for the whole tent. But they must not approach either the utensils of the sanctuary or the altar, otherwise both they and you will die. ⁴They are attached to you in order to perform the duties of the tent of meeting, for all the service of the tent; no outsider shall approach you. ⁵You yourselves shall perform the duties of the sanctuary and the duties of the altar, so that wrath may never again come upon the Israelites. ⁶It is I who now take your brother Levites from among the Israelites; they are now yours as a gift, dedicated to the LORD, to perform the service of the tent of meeting. ⁷But you and your sons

with you shall diligently perform your priestly duties in all that concerns the altar and the area behind the curtain. I give your priesthood as a gift;[i] any outsider who approaches shall be put to death.

The Priests' Portion

8 The LORD spoke to Aaron: I have given you charge of the offerings made to me, all the holy gifts of the Israelites; I have given them to you and your sons as a priestly portion due you in perpetuity. ⁹This shall be yours from the most holy things, reserved from the fire: every offering of theirs that they render to me as a most holy thing, whether grain offering, sin offering, or guilt offering, shall belong to you and your sons. ¹⁰As a most holy thing you shall eat it; every male may eat it; it shall be holy to you. ¹¹This also is yours: I have given to you, together with your sons and daughters, as a perpetual due, whatever is set aside from the gifts of all the elevation offerings of the Israelites; everyone who is clean in your house may eat them. ¹²All the best of the oil and all the best of the wine and of the grain, the choice produce that they give to the LORD, I have given to you. ¹³The first fruits of all that is in their land, which they bring to the LORD, shall be yours; everyone who is clean in your house may eat of it. ¹⁴Every devoted thing in Israel shall be yours. ¹⁵The first issue of the womb of all creatures, human and animal, which is offered to the LORD, shall be yours; but the firstborn of human beings you shall redeem, and the firstborn of unclean animals you shall redeem. ¹⁶Their redemption price, reckoned from one month of age, you shall fix at five shekels of silver, according to the shekel of the sanctuary (that is, twenty gerahs). ¹⁷But the firstborn of a cow, or the firstborn of a sheep, or the firstborn of a goat, you shall not redeem; they are holy. You shall dash their blood on the altar,

17.10
Heb 9.4;
v. 5
17.13
Num 1.51,
53
18.1
Ex 28.38
18.2
Num 3.5-10
18.3
Num 3.25,
31,36; 4.15
18.4
Num 3.10
18.5
Num 16.46
18.6
Num 3.9,12,
45
18.7
Num 3.10;
Heb 9.3,6

18.8
Lev 6.16,18;
7.6,32;
Ex 29.29;
40.13,15
18.9
Lev 2.2,3;
10.12,13;
6.25,26; 7.7
18.10
Lev 6.16,26
18.11
Ex 29.27,
28;
Lev 22.1-16
18.12
Ex 23.19;
Deut 18.4;
Neh 10.35;
Ex 22.29
18.13
Ex 22.29;
23.19; 34.26
18.14
Lev 27.28
18.15
Ex 13.2;
Lev 27.26;
Ex 13.13
18.16
Lev 27.6
18.17
Lev 3.2,5

[h] Or treaty, or testimony; Heb eduth
[i] Heb as a service of gift

and shall turn their fat into smoke as an offering by fire for a pleasing odor to the LORD; ¹⁸but their flesh shall be yours, just as the breast that is elevated and as the right thigh are yours. ¹⁹All the holy offerings that the Israelites present to the LORD I have given to you, together with your sons and daughters, as a perpetual due; it is a covenant of salt forever before the LORD for you and your descendants as well. ²⁰Then the LORD said to Aaron: You shall have no allotment in their land, nor shall you have any share among them; I am your share and your possession among the Israelites.

21 To the Levites I have given every tithe in Israel for a possession in return for the service that they perform, the service in the tent of meeting. ²²From now on the Israelites shall no longer approach the tent of meeting, or else they will incur guilt and die. ²³But the Levites shall perform the service of the tent of meeting, and they shall bear responsibility for their own offenses; it shall be a perpetual statute throughout your generations. But among the Israelites they shall have no allotment, ²⁴because I have given to the Levites as their portion the tithe of the Israelites, which they set apart as an offering to the LORD. Therefore I have said of them that they shall have no allotment among the Israelites.

25 Then the LORD spoke to Moses, saying: ²⁶You shall speak to the Levites, saying: When you receive from the Israelites the tithe that I have given you from them for your portion, you shall set apart an offering from it to the LORD, a tithe of the tithe. ²⁷It shall be reckoned to you as your gift, the same as the grain of the threshing floor and the fullness of the wine press. ²⁸Thus you also shall set apart an offering to the LORD from all the tithes that you receive from the Israelites; and from them you shall give the LORD's offering to the priest Aaron. ²⁹Out of all the gifts to you, you shall set apart every offering due to the

LORD; the best of all of them is the part to be consecrated. ³⁰Say also to them: When you have set apart the best of it, then the rest shall be reckoned to the Levites as produce of the threshing floor, and as produce of the wine press. ³¹You may eat it in any place, you and your households; for it is your payment for your service in the tent of meeting. ³²You shall incur no guilt by reason of it, when you have offered the best of it. But you shall not profane the holy gifts of the Israelites, on pain of death.

Ceremony of the Red Heifer

19 The LORD spoke to Moses and Aaron, saying: ²This is a statute of the law that the LORD has commanded: Tell the Israelites to bring you a red heifer without defect, in which there is no blemish and on which no yoke has been laid. ³You shall give it to the priest Eleazar, and it shall be taken outside the camp and slaughtered in his presence. ⁴The priest Eleazar shall take some of its blood with his finger and sprinkle it seven times towards the front of the tent of meeting. ⁵Then the heifer shall be burned in his sight; its skin, its flesh, and its blood, with its dung, shall be burned. ⁶The priest shall take cedarwood, hyssop, and crimson material, and throw them into the fire in which the heifer is burning. ⁷Then the priest shall wash his clothes and bathe his body in water, and afterwards he may come into the camp; but the priest shall remain unclean until evening. ⁸The one who burns the heiferⁱ shall wash his clothes in water and bathe his body in water; he shall remain unclean until evening. ⁹Then someone who is clean shall gather up the ashes of the heifer, and deposit them outside the camp in a clean place; and they shall be kept for the congregation of the Israelites for the water for cleansing. It is a purification offering. ¹⁰The one who gathers the ashes of the

heifer shall wash his clothes and be unclean until evening.

This shall be a perpetual statute for the Israelites and for the alien residing among them. [11] Those who touch the dead body of any human being shall be unclean seven days. [12] They shall purify themselves with the water on the third day and on the seventh day, and so be clean; but if they do not purify themselves on the third day and on the seventh day, they will not become clean. [13] All who touch a corpse, the body of a human being who has died, and do not purify themselves, defile the tabernacle of the LORD; such persons shall be cut off from Israel. Since water for cleansing was not dashed on them, they remain unclean; their uncleanness is still on them.

14 This is the law when someone dies in a tent: everyone who comes into the tent, and everyone who is in the tent, shall be unclean seven days. [15] And every open vessel with no cover fastened on it is unclean. [16] Whoever in the open field touches one who has been killed by a sword, or who has died naturally,[k] or a human bone, or a grave, shall be unclean seven days. [17] For the unclean they shall take some ashes of the burnt purification offering, and running water shall be added in a vessel; [18] then a clean person shall take hyssop, dip it in the water, and sprinkle it on the tent, on all the furnishings, on the persons who were there, and on whoever touched the bone, the slain, the corpse, or the grave. [19] The clean person shall sprinkle the unclean ones on the third day and on the seventh day, thus purifying them on the seventh day. Then they shall wash their clothes and bathe themselves in water, and at evening they shall be clean. [20] Any who are unclean but do not purify themselves, those persons shall be cut off from the assembly, for they have defiled the sanctuary of the LORD. Since the water for cleansing has not been dashed on them, they are unclean.

21 It shall be a perpetual statute for them. The one who sprinkles the water for cleansing shall wash his clothes, and whoever touches the water for cleansing shall be unclean until evening. [22] Whatever the unclean person touches shall be unclean, and anyone who touches it shall be unclean until evening.

The Waters of Meribah

20 The Israelites, the whole congregation, came into the wilderness of Zin in the first month, and the people stayed in Kadesh. Miriam died there, and was buried there.

2 Now there was no water for the congregation; so they gathered together against Moses and against Aaron. [3] The people quarreled with Moses and said, "Would that we had died when our kindred died before the LORD! [4] Why have you brought the assembly of the LORD into this wilderness for us and our livestock to die here? [5] Why have you brought us up out of Egypt, to bring us to this wretched place? It is no place for grain, or figs, or vines, or pomegranates; and there is no water to drink." [6] Then Moses and Aaron went away from the assembly to the entrance of the tent of meeting; they fell on their faces, and the glory of the LORD appeared to them. [7] The LORD spoke to Moses, saying: [8] Take the staff, and assemble the congregation, you and your brother Aaron, and command the rock before their eyes to yield its water. Thus you shall bring water out of the rock for them; thus you shall provide drink for the congregation and their livestock.

9 So Moses took the staff from before the LORD, as he had commanded him. [10] Moses and Aaron gathered the assembly together before the rock, and he said to them, "Listen, you rebels, shall we bring water for you out of this rock?" [11] Then Moses lifted up his hand and struck the rock twice with his staff; water came out abundantly,

Cross references (center column):

19.11
Num 5.2;
Lev 21.1;
Acts 21.26,
27
19.12
v. 19;
Num 31.19
19.13
v. 20;
Lev 15.31;
v. 9;
Num 8.7;
Lev 7.20;
22.3
19.16
v. 11
19.17
v. 9
19.19
Ezek 36.25;
Heb 10.22
19.20
v. 13

19.22
Hag 2.13,14
20.1
Num 33.36
20.2
Ex 17.1
20.3
Ex 17.2;
Num 14.2,3;
16.31-35
20.4
Ex 17.3
20.6
Num 14.5,
10
20.8
Ex 17.5;
Neh 9.15;
Isa 43.20;
48.21
20.10
Ps 106.32,
33
20.11
Ps 78.16;
Isa 48.21;
1 Cor 10.14

k Heb lacks *naturally*

and the congregation and their livestock drank. [12] But the Lord said to Moses and Aaron, "Because you did not trust in me, to show my holiness before the eyes of the Israelites, therefore you shall not bring this assembly into the land that I have given them." [13] These are the waters of Meribah,[1] where the people of Israel quarreled with the Lord, and by which he showed his holiness.

Passage through Edom Refused

[14] Moses sent messengers from Kadesh to the king of Edom, "Thus says your brother Israel: You know all the adversity that has befallen us: [15] how our ancestors went down to Egypt, and we lived in Egypt a long time; and the Egyptians oppressed us and our ancestors; [16] and when we cried to the Lord, he heard our voice, and sent an angel and brought us out of Egypt; and here we are in Kadesh, a town on the edge of your territory. [17] Now let us pass through your land. We will not pass through field or vineyard, or drink water from any well; we will go along the King's Highway, not turning aside to the right hand or to the left until we have passed through your territory." [18] But Edom said to him, "You shall not pass through, or we will come out with the sword against you." [19] The Israelites said to him, "We will stay on the highway; and if we drink of your water, we and our livestock, then we will pay for it. It is only a small matter; just let us pass through on foot." [20] But he said, "You shall not pass through." And Edom came out against them with a large force, heavily armed. [21] Thus Edom refused to give Israel passage through their territory; so Israel turned away from them.

The Death of Aaron

[22] They set out from Kadesh, and the Israelites, the whole congregation, came to Mount Hor. [23] Then the Lord said to Moses and Aaron at Mount Hor, on the border of the land of Edom, [24] "Let Aaron

be gathered to his people. For he shall not enter the land that I have given to the Israelites, because you rebelled against my command at the waters of Meribah. [25] Take Aaron and his son Eleazar, and bring them up Mount Hor; [26] strip Aaron of his vestments, and put them on his son Eleazar. But Aaron shall be gathered to his people,[m] and shall die there." [27] Moses did as the Lord had commanded; they went up Mount Hor in the sight of the whole congregation. [28] Moses stripped Aaron of his vestments, and put them on his son Eleazar; and Aaron died there on the top of the mountain. Moses and Eleazar came down from the mountain. [29] When all the congregation saw that Aaron had died, all the house of Israel mourned for Aaron thirty days.

The Bronze Serpent

21 When the Canaanite, the king of Arad, who lived in the Negeb, heard that Israel was coming by the way of Atharim, he fought against Israel and took some of them captive. [2] Then Israel made a vow to the Lord and said, "If you will indeed give this people into our hands, then we will utterly destroy their towns." [3] The Lord listened to the voice of Israel, and handed over the Canaanites; and they utterly destroyed them and their towns; so the place was called Hormah.[n]

[4] From Mount Hor they set out by the way to the Red Sea,[o] to go around the land of Edom; but the people became impatient on the way. [5] The people spoke against God and against Moses, "Why have you brought us up out of Egypt to die in the wilderness? For there is no food and no water, and we detest this miserable food." [6] Then the Lord sent poisonous[p] serpents among the people, and they bit the people, so that many Israelites died. [7] The people came to Moses

Cross references

20.12 Num 27.14; Deut 1.37; 3.26,27; Lev 10.3
20.13 Deut 33.8; Ps 95.8
20.14 Deut 2.4
20.15 Gen 46.6; Acts 7.15, 19; Ex 12.40; Deut 26.6
20.16 Ex 2.23; 14.19
20.19 Deut 2.6,28
20.21 Judg 11.17; Deut 2.8
20.22 Num 33.37; 21.4
20.24 Gen 25.8; v. 12
20.25 Num 33.38; Deut 32.50
20.28 Num 33.38; Deut 10.6
21.1 Num 33.40; Judg 1.16; Num 13.21
21.4 Num 20.22
21.5 Ps 78.19; Ex 16.3; 17.3; Num 11.6
21.6 Deut 8.15; 1 Cor 10.9
21.7 Ps 78.34

[1] That is *Quarrel* [m] Heb lacks *to his people*
[n] Heb *Destruction* [o] Or *Sea of Reeds*
[p] Or *fiery*; Heb *seraphim*

and said, "We have sinned by speaking against the LORD and against you; pray to the LORD to take away the serpents from us." So Moses prayed for the people. [8] And the LORD said to Moses, "Make a poisonous[q] serpent, and set it on a pole; and everyone who is bitten shall look at it and live." [9] So Moses made a serpent of bronze, and put it upon a pole; and whenever a serpent bit someone, that person would look at the serpent of bronze and live.

The Journey to Moab

[10] The Israelites set out, and camped in Oboth. [11] They set out from Oboth, and camped at Iye-abarim, in the wilderness bordering Moab toward the sunrise. [12] From there they set out, and camped in the Wadi Zered. [13] From there they set out, and camped on the other side of the Arnon, in[r] the wilderness that extends from the boundary of the Amorites; for the Arnon is the boundary of Moab, between Moab and the Amorites. [14] Wherefore it is said in the Book of the Wars of the LORD,

"Waheb in Suphah and the
 wadis.
The Arnon [15] and the slopes of
 the wadis
that extend to the seat of Ar,
and lie along the border of
 Moab."[s]

[16] From there they continued to Beer;[t] that is the well of which the LORD said to Moses, "Gather the people together, and I will give them water." [17] Then Israel sang this song:

"Spring up, O well!—Sing to
 it!—
[18] the well that the leaders
 sank,
that the nobles of the people
 dug,
with the scepter, with the
 staff."

From the wilderness to Mattanah, [19] from Mattanah to Nahaliel, from Nahaliel to Bamoth, [20] and from Bamoth to the valley lying in the

21.9
2 Kings 18.4;
Jn 3.14,15
21.10
Num 33.43
21.11
Num 33.44
21.12
Deut 2.13
21.15
v. 28;
Deut 2.18,
29

21.21
Deut 2.26,
27
21.22
Num 20.16,
17
21.23
Num 20.21;
Deut 2.32
21.24
Deut 2.33;
Josh 12.1,2;
Ps 135.10,
11
21.28
Jer 48.45,
46;
Deut 2.9,18;
Isa 15.1
21.29
Judg 11.24;
1 Kings 11.7,
33;
2 Kings 23.13;
Jer 48.7,13
21.30
Num 32.3,
34;
Jer 48.18,22

region of Moab by the top of Pisgah that overlooks the wasteland. [u]

King Sihon Defeated

[21] Then Israel sent messengers to King Sihon of the Amorites, saying, [22] "Let me pass through your land; we will not turn aside into field or vineyard; we will not drink the water of any well; we will go by the King's Highway until we have passed through your territory." [23] But Sihon would not allow Israel to pass through his territory. Sihon gathered all his people together, and went out against Israel to the wilderness; he came to Jahaz, and fought against Israel. [24] Israel put him to the sword, and took possession of his land from the Arnon to the Jabbok, as far as to the Ammonites; for the boundary of the Ammonites was strong. [25] Israel took all these towns, and Israel settled in all the towns of the Amorites, in Heshbon, and in all its villages. [26] For Heshbon was the city of King Sihon of the Amorites, who had fought against the former king of Moab and captured all his land as far as the Arnon. [27] Therefore the ballad singers say,

"Come to Heshbon, let it be
 built;
let the city of Sihon be
 established.
[28] For fire came out from
 Heshbon,
flame from the city of
 Sihon.
It devoured Ar of Moab,
and swallowed up[v] the
 heights of the Arnon.
[29] Woe to you, O Moab!
You are undone, O people
 of Chemosh!
He has made his sons
 fugitives,
and his daughters captives,
 to an Amorite king, Sihon.
[30] So their posterity perished
 from Heshbon[w] to Dibon,

q Or fiery; Heb seraph r Gk: Heb which is in s Meaning of Heb uncertain t That is Well u Or Jeshimon v Gk: Heb and the lords of w Gk: Heb we have shot at them; Heshbon has perished

and we laid waste until fire spread to Medeba."ˣ

31 Thus Israel settled in the land of the Amorites. ³²Moses sent to spy out Jazer; and they captured its villages, and dispossessed the Amorites who were there.

King Og Defeated

33 Then they turned and went up the road to Bashan; and King Og of Bashan came out against them, he and all his people, to battle at Edrei. ³⁴But the LORD said to Moses, "Do not be afraid of him; for I have given him into your hand, with all his people, and all his land. You shall do to him as you did to King Sihon of the Amorites, who ruled in Heshbon." ³⁵So they killed him, his sons, and all his people, until there was no survivor left; and they took possession of his land.

Balak Summons Balaam to Curse Israel

22 The Israelites set out, and camped in the plains of Moab across the Jordan from Jericho. ²Now Balak son of Zippor saw all that Israel had done to the Amorites. ³Moab was in great dread of the people, because they were so numerous; Moab was overcome with fear of the people of Israel. ⁴And Moab said to the elders of Midian, "This horde will now lick up all that is around us, as an ox licks up the grass of the field." Now Balak son of Zippor was king of Moab at that time. ⁵He sent messengers to Balaam son of Beor at Pethor, which is on the Euphrates, in the land of Amaw,ʸ to summon him, saying, "A people has come out of Egypt; they have spread over the face of the earth, and they have settled next to me. ⁶Come now, curse this people for me, since they are stronger than I; perhaps I shall be able to defeat them and drive them from the land; for I know that whomever you bless is blessed, and whomever you curse is cursed."

7 So the elders of Moab and the elders of Midian departed with the fees for divination in their hand; and they came to Balaam, and gave him Balak's message. ⁸He said to them, "Stay here tonight, and I will bring back word to you, just as the LORD speaks to me"; so the officials of Moab stayed with Balaam. ⁹God came to Balaam and said, "Who are these men with you?" ¹⁰Balaam said to God, "King Balak son of Zippor of Moab, has sent me this message: ¹¹'A people has come out of Egypt and has spread over the face of the earth; now come, curse them for me; perhaps I shall be able to fight against them and drive them out.' " ¹²God said to Balaam, "You shall not go with them; you shall not curse the people, for they are blessed." ¹³So Balaam rose in the morning, and said to the officials of Balak, "Go to your own land, for the LORD has refused to let me go with you." ¹⁴So the officials of Moab rose and went to Balak, and said, "Balaam refuses to come with us."

15 Once again Balak sent officials, more numerous and more distinguished than these. ¹⁶They came to Balaam and said to him, "Thus says Balak son of Zippor: 'Do not let anything hinder you from coming to me; ¹⁷for I will surely do you great honor, and whatever you say to me I will do; come, curse this people for me.' " ¹⁸But Balaam replied to the servants of Balak, "Although Balak were to give me his house full of silver and gold, I could not go beyond the command of the LORD my God, to do less or more. ¹⁹You remain here, as the others did, so that I may learn what more the LORD may say to me." ²⁰That night God came to Balaam and said to him, "If the men have come to summon you, get up and go with them; but do only what I tell you to do." ²¹So Balaam got up in the morning, saddled his donkey, and went with the officials of Moab.

21.32
Num 32.1;
Jer 48.32
21.33
Deut 3.1-7;
Josh 13.12
21.34
Deut 3.2;
v. 24
22.1
Num 33.48
22.3
Ex 15.15
22.4
Num 31.1-3,
8
22.5
Num 23.7;
Josh 24.9;
Deut 23.4
22.6
v. 17;
Num 23.7

22.7
Num 23.23;
24.1
22.8
v. 19
22.12
Num 23.20
22.17
v. 6
22.18
Num 24.13;
1 Kings 22.14;
2 Chr 18.13
22.20
v. 35;
Num 23.12,
26; 24.13
22.21
2 Pet 2.15

ˣ Compare Sam Gk: Meaning of MT uncertain
ʸ Or *land of his kinsfolk*

Balaam, the Donkey, and the Angel

22 God's anger was kindled because he was going, and the angel of the LORD took his stand in the road as his adversary. Now he was riding on the donkey, and his two servants were with him. 23 The donkey saw the angel of the LORD standing in the road, with a drawn sword in his hand; so the donkey turned off the road, and went into the field; and Balaam struck the donkey, to turn it back onto the road. 24 Then the angel of the LORD stood in a narrow path between the vineyards, with a wall on either side. 25 When the donkey saw the angel of the LORD, it scraped against the wall, and scraped Balaam's foot against the wall; so he struck it again. 26 Then the angel of the LORD went ahead, and stood in a narrow place, where there was no way to turn either to the right or to the left. 27 When the donkey saw the angel of the LORD, it lay down under Balaam; and Balaam's anger was kindled, and he struck the donkey with his staff. 28 Then the LORD opened the mouth of the donkey, and it said to Balaam, "What have I done to you, that you have struck me these three times?" 29 Balaam said to the donkey, "Because you have made a fool of me! I wish I had a sword in my hand! I would kill you right now!" 30 But the donkey said to Balaam, "Am I not your donkey, which you have ridden all your life to this day? Have I been in the habit of treating you this way?" And he said, "No."

31 Then the LORD opened the eyes of Balaam, and he saw the angel of the LORD standing in the road, with his drawn sword in his hand; and he bowed down, falling on his face. 32 The angel of the LORD said to him, "Why have you struck your donkey these three times? I have come out as an adversary, because your way is perverse[z] before me. 33 The donkey saw me, and turned away from me these three times. If it had not turned away

from me, surely just now I would have killed you and let it live." 34 Then Balaam said to the angel of the LORD, "I have sinned, for I did not know that you were standing in the road to oppose me. Now therefore, if it is displeasing to you, I will return home." 35 The angel of the LORD said to Balaam, "Go with the men; but speak only what I tell you to speak." So Balaam went on with the officials of Balak.

36 When Balak heard that Balaam had come, he went out to meet him at Ir-moab, on the boundary formed by the Arnon, at the farthest point of the boundary. 37 Balak said to Balaam, "Did I not send to summon you? Why did you not come to me? Am I not able to honor you?" 38 Balaam said to Balak, "I have come to you now, but do I have power to say just anything? The word God puts in my mouth, that is what I must say." 39 Then Balaam went with Balak, and they came to Kiriath-huzoth. 40 Balak sacrificed oxen and sheep, and sent them to Balaam and to the officials who were with him.

Balaam's First Oracle

41 On the next day Balak took Balaam and brought him up to Bamoth-baal; and from there he could see part of the people of Israel.[a] 1 Then Balaam said to Balak, "Build me seven altars here, and prepare seven bulls and seven rams for me." 2 Balak did as Balaam had said; and Balak and Balaam offered a bull and a ram on each altar. 3 Then Balaam said to Balak, "Stay here beside your burnt offerings while I go aside. Perhaps the LORD will come to meet me. Whatever he shows me I will tell you." And he went to a bare height. 4 Then God met Balaam; and Balaam said to him, "I have arranged the seven altars, and have offered a bull and a ram on each altar." 5 The LORD put a word in Balaam's mouth, and said, "Return to Balak, and this is what you must

22.23 2 Pet 2.16
22.24 Judg 6.12
22.28 2 Pet 2.16
22.29 Prov 12.10
22.30 2 Pet 2.16
22.31 Josh 5.13-15

22.34 Num 14.40; 1 Sam 15.24, 30; 2 Sam 12.13
22.35 v. 20
22.37 v. 17;
Num 24.11
22.38 v. 18;
Num 23.26; 24.13
22.41 Deut 12.2
23.1 v. 29
23.2 vv. 14,30
23.3 v. 15
23.4 v. 16
23.5 v. 16;
Num 22.35;
Deut 18.18;
Jer 1.9

z Meaning of Heb uncertain a Heb lacks *of Israel*

say." ⁶So he returned to Balak,ᵇ who was standing beside his burnt offerings with all the officials of Moab. ⁷Then Balaamᶜ uttered his oracle, saying:

"Balak has brought me from
 Aram,
 the king of Moab from the
 eastern mountains:
'Come, curse Jacob for me;
 Come, denounce Israel!'
⁸ How can I curse whom God
 has not cursed?
 How can I denounce those
 whom the LORD has not
 denounced?
⁹ For from the top of the crags
 I see him,
 from the hills I behold
 him;
 Here is a people living alone,
 and not reckoning itself
 among the nations!
¹⁰ Who can count the dust of
 Jacob,
 or number the dust-cloudᵈ
 of Israel?
 Let me die the death of the
 upright,
 and let my end be like
 his!"

¹¹ Then Balak said to Balaam, "What have you done to me? I brought you to curse my enemies, but now you have done nothing but bless them." ¹²He answered, "Must I not take care to say what the LORD puts into my mouth?"

Balaam's Second Oracle

13 So Balak said to him, "Come with me to another place from which you may see them; you shall see only part of them, and shall not see them all; then curse them for me from there." ¹⁴So he took him to the field of Zophim, to the top of Pisgah. He built seven altars, and offered a bull and a ram on each altar. ¹⁵Balaam said to Balak, "Stand here beside your burnt offerings, while I meet the LORD over there. ¹⁶The LORD met Balaam, put a word into his mouth, and said, "Return to Balak, and this is what you shall say." ¹⁷When he came to him, he was standing beside his

burnt offerings with the officials of Moab. Balak said to him, "What has the LORD said?" ¹⁸Then Balaam uttered his oracle, saying:

"Rise, Balak, and hear;
 listen to me, O son of
 Zippor:
¹⁹ God is not a human being,
 that he should lie,
 or a mortal, that he should
 change his mind.
 Has he promised, and will he
 not do it?
 Has he spoken, and will he
 not fulfill it?
²⁰ See, I received a command
 to bless;
 he has blessed, and I
 cannot revoke it.
²¹ He has not beheld
 misfortune in Jacob;
 nor has he seen trouble in
 Israel.
 The LORD their God is with
 them,
 acclaimed as a king among
 them.
²² God, who brings them out of
 Egypt,
 is like the horns of a wild
 ox for them.
²³ Surely there is no
 enchantment against
 Jacob,
 no divination against Israel;
 now it shall be said of Jacob
 and Israel,
 'See what God has done!'
²⁴ Look, a people rising up like
 a lioness,
 and rousing itself like a
 lion!
 It does not lie down until it
 has eaten the prey
 and drunk the blood of the
 slain."

25 Then Balak said to Balaam, "Do not curse them at all, and do not bless them at all." ²⁶But Balaam answered Balak, "Did I not tell you, 'Whatever the LORD says, that is what I must do'?"

27 So Balak said to Balaam, "Come now, I will take you to another place; perhaps it will please

23.7
v. 18;
Num 24.3,
15,23;
Job 27.1;
29.1;
Ps 78.2;
Num 22.6
23.8
Num 22.12
23.9
Ex 33.16;
Deut 32.8;
33.28
23.10
Gen 13.16;
Ps 116.15
23.11
Num 24.10
23.12
Num 22.20,
38
23.14
vv. 1,2
23.16
Num 22.20

23.19
1 Sam 15.29;
Mal 3.6;
Rom 11.29;
Titus 1.2;
Jas 1.17
23.20
Isa 43.13
23.21
Ps 32.2,5;
Rom 4.7,8;
Isa 40.2;
Ex 29.45,
46; Ps 89.15
23.22
Num 24.8
23.24
Gen 49.9,27
23.26
v. 12;
Num 22.38
23.27
v. 13

ᵇ Heb *him* ᶜ Heb *he* ᵈ Or *fourth part*

God that you may curse them for me from there." [28]So Balak took Balaam to the top of Peor, which overlooks the wasteland.[e] [29]Balaam said to Balak, "Build me seven altars here, and prepare seven bulls and seven rams for me." [30]So Balak did as Balaam had said, and offered a bull and a ram on each altar.

Balaam's Third Oracle

24 Now Balaam saw that it pleased the LORD to bless Israel, so he did not go, as at other times, to look for omens, but set his face toward the wilderness. [2]Balaam looked up and saw Israel camping tribe by tribe. Then the spirit of God came upon him, [3]and he uttered his oracle, saying:

"The oracle of Balaam son of Beor,
 the oracle of the man
 whose eye is clear,[f]
[4] the oracle of one who hears
 the words of God,
 who sees the vision of the Almighty,[g]
 who falls down, but with
 eyes uncovered:
[5] how fair are your tents,
 O Jacob,
 your encampments,
 O Israel!
[6] Like palm-groves that stretch
 far away,
 like gardens beside a river,
 like aloes that the LORD has
 planted,
 like cedar trees beside the
 waters.
[7] Water shall flow from his
 buckets,
 and his seed shall have
 abundant water,
 his king shall be higher than
 Agag,
 and his kingdom shall be
 exalted.
[8] God who brings him out of
 Egypt,
 is like the horns of a wild
 ox for him;
 he shall devour the nations
 that are his foes
 and break their bones.

He shall strike with his
 arrows.[h]
[9] He crouched, he lay down
 like a lion,
 and like a lioness; who will
 rouse him up?
 Blessed is everyone who
 blesses you,
 and cursed is everyone who
 curses you."

10 Then Balak's anger was kindled against Balaam, and he struck his hands together. Balak said to Balaam, "I summoned you to curse my enemies, but instead you have blessed them these three times. [11]Now be off with you! Go home! I said, 'I will reward you richly,' but the LORD has denied you any reward." [12]And Balaam said to Balak, "Did I not tell your messengers whom you sent to me, [13]'If Balak should give me his house full of silver and gold, I would not be able to go beyond the word of the LORD, to do either good or bad of my own will; what the LORD says, that is what I will say'? [14]So now, I am going to my people; let me advise you what this people will do to your people in days to come."

Balaam's Fourth Oracle

15 So he uttered his oracle, saying:

"The oracle of Balaam son of
 Beor,
 the oracle of the man
 whose eye is clear,[f]
[16] the oracle of one who hears
 the words of God,
 and knows the knowledge
 of the Most High,[i]
 who sees the vision of the
 Almighty,[g]
 who falls down, but with
 his eyes uncovered:
[17] I see him, but not now;
 I behold him, but not
 near—
 a star shall come out of
 Jacob,

Cross references

23.29
v. 1
24.1
Num 23.3, 15
24.2
Num 11.25, 26; 1 Sam 10.10; 2 Chr 15.1
24.3
Num 23.7, 18
24.4
Num 22.20; 12.6
24.6
Ps 1.3; 104.16
24.7
v. 20; 1 Sam 15.8, 9; 2 Sam 5.12; 1 Chr 14.2
24.8
Num 23.22, 24; Ps 2.9; 45.5; Jer 50.9,17
24.9
Gen 49.9; 12.3; 27.29
24.11
Num 22.17, 37
24.13
Num 22.18, 20
24.14
Gen 49.1; Dan 2.28; Mic 6.5
24.17
Rev 1.7; Mt 2.2; Gen 49.10

[e] Or *overlooks Jeshimon* [f] Or *closed* or *open* [g] Traditional rendering of Heb *Shaddai* [h] Meaning of Heb uncertain [i] Or *of Elyon*

and a scepter shall rise out
 of Israel;
it shall crush the
 borderlands[j] of Moab,
and the territory[k] of all the
 Shethites.
18 Edom will become a
 possession,
Seir a possession of its
 enemies,[l]
while Israel does valiantly.
19 One out of Jacob shall rule,
 and destroy the survivors of
 Ir."

20 Then he looked on Amalek,
and uttered his oracle, saying:
"First among the nations was
 Amalek,
but its end is to perish
 forever."
21 Then he looked on the Ke-
nite, and uttered his oracle, saying:
"Enduring is your dwelling
 place,
and your nest is set in the
 rock;
22 yet Kain is destined for
 burning.
How long shall Asshur take
 you away captive?"
23 Again he uttered his oracle,
saying:
"Alas, who shall live when
 God does this?
24 But ships shall come from
 Kittim
and shall afflict Asshur and
 Eber;
and he also shall perish
 forever."
25 Then Balaam got up and
went back to his place, and Balak
also went his way.

Worship of Baal of Peor

25 While Israel was staying at
 Shittim, the people began
to have sexual relations with the
women of Moab. 2 These invited
the people to the sacrifices of their
gods, and the people ate and
bowed down to their gods. 3 Thus
Israel yoked itself to the Baal of
Peor, and the LORD's anger was kin-
dled against Israel. 4 The LORD said
to Moses, "Take all the chiefs of
the people, and impale them in the

sun before the LORD, in order that
the fierce anger of the LORD may
turn away from Israel." 5 And Mo-
ses said to the judges of Israel,
"Each of you shall kill any of your
people who have yoked themselves
to the Baal of Peor."

6 Just then one of the Israelites
came and brought a Midianite
woman into his family, in the sight
of Moses and in the sight of the
whole congregation of the Israel-
ites, while they were weeping at
the entrance of the tent of meeting.
7 When Phinehas son of Eleazar,
son of Aaron the priest, saw it, he
got up and left the congregation.
Taking a spear in his hand, 8 he
went after the Israelite man into
the tent, and pierced the two of
them, the Israelite and the woman,
through the belly. So the plague
was stopped among the people of
Israel. 9 Nevertheless those that
died by the plague were twenty-
four thousand.

10 The LORD spoke to Moses,
saying: 11 "Phinehas son of Eleazar,
son of Aaron the priest, has turned
back my wrath from the Israelites
by manifesting such zeal among
them on my behalf that in my jeal-
ousy I did not consume the Israel-
ites. 12 Therefore say, 'I hereby
grant him my covenant of peace.
13 It shall be for him and for his de-
scendants after him a covenant of
perpetual priesthood, because he
was zealous for his God, and made
atonement for the Israelites.' "

14 The name of the slain Israel-
ite man, who was killed with the
Midianite woman, was Zimri son of
Salu, head of an ancestral house
belonging to the Simeonites. 15 The
name of the Midianite woman who
was killed was Cozbi daughter of
Zur, who was the head of a clan, an
ancestral house in Midian.

16 The LORD said to Moses,
17 "Harass the Midianites, and de-
feat them; 18 for they have harassed
you by the trickery with which they
deceived you in the affair of Peor,

24.18
2 Sam 8.14
24.19
Gen 49.10;
Mic 5.2
24.20
Ex 17.8,14,
16
24.24
Gen 10.4,
21; v. 20
24.25
Num 31.8
25.1
Mic 6.5;
Num 31.16;
1 Cor 10.8;
Rev 2.14
25.2
Ex 34.15;
20.5;
1 Cor 10.20
25.3
Ps 106.28,
29;
Hos 9.10
25.4
Deut 4.3

25.7
Ps 106.30
25.9
Deut 4.3;
1 Cor 10.8
25.11
Ps 106.30;
Ex 20.5;
Deut 32.16,
21
25.12
Isa 54.10;
Mal 2.4,5
25.13
Ex 40.15;
Num 16.46;
Heb 2.17
25.15
Num 31.8
25.17
Num 31.2
25.18
Num 31.16

i Or *forehead* k Some Mss read *skull*
l Heb *Seir, its enemies, a possession*

and in the affair of Cozbi, the daughter of a leader of Midian, their sister; she was killed on the day of the plague that resulted from Peor."

A Census of the New Generation

26 After the plague the LORD said to Moses and to Eleazar son of Aaron the priest, 2 "Take a census of the whole congregation of the Israelites, from twenty years old and upward, by their ancestral houses, everyone in Israel able to go to war." 3 Moses and Eleazar the priest spoke with them in the plains of Moab by the Jordan opposite Jericho, saying, 4 "Take a census of the people,m from twenty years old and upward," as the LORD commanded Moses.

The Israelites, who came out of the land of Egypt, were:

5 Reuben, the firstborn of Israel. The descendants of Reuben: of Hanoch, the clan of the Hanochites; of Pallu, the clan of the Palluites; 6 of Hezron, the clan of the Hezronites; of Carmi, the clan of the Carmites. 7 These are the clans of the Reubenites; the number of those enrolled was forty-three thousand seven hundred thirty. 8 And the descendants of Pallu: Eliab. 9 The descendants of Eliab: Nemuel, Dathan, and Abiram. These are the same Dathan and Abiram, chosen from the congregation, who rebelled against Moses and Aaron in the company of Korah, when they rebelled against the LORD, 10 and the earth opened its mouth and swallowed them up along with Korah, when that company died, when the fire devoured two hundred fifty men; and they became a warning. 11 Notwithstanding, the sons of Korah did not die.

12 The descendants of Simeon by their clans: of Nemuel, the clan of the Nemuelites; of Jamin, the clan of the Jaminites; of Jachin, the clan of the Jachinites; 13 of Zerah, the clan of the Zerahites; of Shaul, the clan of the Shaulites.n 14 These are the clans of the Sime-

onites, twenty-two thousand two hundred.

15 The children of Gad by their clans: of Zephon, the clan of the Zephonites; of Haggi, the clan of the Haggites; of Shuni, the clan of the Shunites; 16 of Ozni, the clan of the Oznites; of Eri, the clan of the Erites; 17 of Arod, the clan of the Arodites; of Areli, the clan of the Arelites. 18 These are the clans of the Gadites: the number of those enrolled was forty thousand five hundred.

19 The sons of Judah: Er and Onan; Er and Onan died in the land of Canaan. 20 The descendants of Judah by their clans were: of Shelah, the clan of the Shelanites; of Perez, the clan of the Perezites; of Zerah, the clan of the Zerahites. 21 The descendants of Perez were: of Hezron, the clan of the Hezronites; of Hamul, the clan of the Hamulites. 22 These are the clans of Judah: the number of those enrolled was seventy-six thousand five hundred.

23 The descendants of Issachar by their clans: of Tola, the clan of the Tolaites; of Puvah, the clan of the Punites; 24 of Jashub, the clan of the Jashubites; of Shimron, the clan of the Shimronites. 25 These are the clans of Issachar: sixty-four thousand three hundred enrolled.

26 The descendants of Zebulun by their clans: of Sered, the clan of the Seredites; of Elon, the clan of the Elonites; of Jahleel, the clan of the Jahleelites. 27 These are the clans of the Zebulunites; the number of those enrolled was sixty thousand five hundred.

28 The sons of Joseph by their clans: Manasseh and Ephraim. 29 The descendants of Manasseh: of Machir, the clan of the Machirites; and Machir was the father of Gilead; of Gilead, the clan of the Gileadites. 30 These are the descendants of Gilead: of Iezer, the clan of the Iezerites; of Helek, the clan of the Helekites; 31 and of Asriel, the

26.2
Ex 30.12;
38.25,26;
Num 1.2
26.5
Ex 6.14
26.9
Num 16.1,2
26.10
Num 16.32,
35,38
26.11
Deut 24.16
26.12
Ex 6.15;
1 Chr 4.24
26.13
Gen 46.10

26.15
Gen 46.16
26.16
Gen 46.16
26.17
Gen 46.16
26.18
Num 1.25
26.22
Num 1.27
26.24
Gen 46.13
26.25
Num 1.29
26.27
Num 1.31
26.30
see
Josh 17.2

m Heb lacks *take a census of the people*: Compare verse 2 n Or *Saul . . . Saulites*

clan of the Asrielites; and of Shechem, the clan of the Shechemites; ³²and of Shemida, the clan of the Shemidaites; and of Hepher, the clan of the Hepherites. ³³Now Zelophehad son of Hepher had no sons, but daughters: and the names of the daughters of Zelophehad were Mahlah, Noah, Hoglah, Milcah, and Tirzah. ³⁴These are the clans of Manasseh; the number of those enrolled was fifty-two thousand seven hundred.

35 These are the descendants of Ephraim according to their clans: of Shuthelah, the clan of the Shuthelahites; of Becher, the clan of the Becherites; of Tahan, the clan of the Tahanites. ³⁶And these are the descendants of Shuthelah: of Eran, the clan of the Eranites. ³⁷These are the clans of the Ephraimites: the number of those enrolled was thirty-two thousand five hundred. These are the descendants of Joseph by their clans.

38 The descendants of Benjamin by their clans: of Bela, the clan of the Belaites; of Ashbel, the clan of the Ashbelites; of Ahiram, the clan of the Ahiramites; ³⁹of Shephupham, the clan of the Shuphamites; of Hupham, the clan of the Huphamites. ⁴⁰And the sons of Bela were Ard and Naaman: of Ard, the clan of the Ardites; of Naaman, the clan of the Naamites. ⁴¹These are the descendants of Benjamin by their clans; the number of those enrolled was forty-five thousand six hundred.

42 These are the descendants of Dan by their clans: of Shuham, the clan of the Shuhamites. These are the clans of Dan by their clans. ⁴³All the clans of the Shuhamites: sixty-four thousand four hundred enrolled.

44 The descendants of Asher by their families: of Imnah, the clan of the Imnites; of Ishvi, the clan of the Ishvites; of Beriah, the clan of the Beriites. ⁴⁵Of the descendants of Beriah: of Heber, the clan of the Heberites; of Malchiel, the clan of the Malchielites. ⁴⁶And the name of the daughter of Asher was Serah.

⁴⁷These are the clans of the Asherites: the number of those enrolled was fifty-three thousand four hundred.

48 The descendants of Naphtali by their clans: of Jahzeel, the clan of the Jahzeelites; of Guni, the clan of the Gunites; ⁴⁹of Jezer, the clan of the Jezerites; of Shillem, the clan of the Shillemites. ⁵⁰These the Naphtalites^o by their clans: the number of those enrolled was forty-five thousand four hundred.

51 This was the number of the Israelites enrolled: six hundred and one thousand seven hundred thirty.

52 The Lord spoke to Moses, saying: ⁵³To these the land shall be apportioned for inheritance according to the number of names. ⁵⁴To a large tribe you shall give a large inheritance, and to a small tribe you shall give a small inheritance; every tribe shall be given its inheritance according to its enrollment. ⁵⁵But the land shall be apportioned by lot; according to the names of their ancestral tribes they shall inherit. ⁵⁶Their inheritance shall be apportioned according to lot between the larger and the smaller.

57 This is the enrollment of the Levites by their clans: of Gershon, the clan of the Gershonites; of Kohath, the clan of the Kohathites; of Merari, the clan of the Merarites. ⁵⁸These are the clans of Levi: the clan of the Libnites, the clan of the Hebronites, the clan of the Mahlites, the clan of the Mushites, the clan of the Korahites. Now Kohath was the father of Amram. ⁵⁹The name of Amram's wife was Jochebed daughter of Levi, who was born to Levi in Egypt; and she bore to Amram: Aaron, Moses, and their sister Miriam. ⁶⁰To Aaron were born Nadab, Abihu, Eleazar, and Ithamar. ⁶¹But Nadab and Abihu died when they offered illicit fire before the Lord. ⁶²The number of those enrolled was twenty-three thousand, every male one month

o Heb *clans of Naphtali*

26.35
1 Chr 7.20
26.37
Num 1.33
26.38
Gen 46.21
26.39
Gen 46.21
26.40
1 Chr 8.3
26.41
Num 1.37
26.42
Gen 46.23
26.43
Num 1.39

26.47
Num 1.41
26.50
Num 1.43
26.53
Josh 11.23;
14.1
26.54
Num 33.54
26.55
Num 33.54;
34.13
26.59
Ex 6.20
26.60
Num 3.2
26.61
Lev 10.1,2;
Num 3.4
26.62
Num 1.47;
18.20,23,24

old and up; for they were not enrolled among the Israelites because there was no allotment given to them among the Israelites.

63 These were those enrolled by Moses and Eleazar the priest, who enrolled the Israelites in the plains of Moab by the Jordan opposite Jericho. 64 Among these there was not one of those enrolled by Moses and Aaron the priest, who had enrolled the Israelites in the wilderness of Sinai. 65 For the LORD had said of them, "They shall die in the wilderness." Not one of them was left, except Caleb son of Jephunneh and Joshua son of Nun.

The Daughters of Zelophehad

27 Then the daughters of Zelophehad came forward. Zelophehad was son of Hepher son of Gilead son of Machir son of Manasseh son of Joseph, a member of the Manassite clans. The names of his daughters were: Mahlah, Noah, Hoglah, Milcah, and Tirzah. 2 They stood before Moses, Eleazar the priest, the leaders, and all the congregation, at the entrance of the tent of meeting, and they said, 3 "Our father died in the wilderness; he was not among the company of those who gathered themselves together against the LORD in the company of Korah, but died for his own sin; and he had no sons. 4 Why should the name of our father be taken away from his clan because he had no son? Give to us a possession among our father's brothers."

5 Moses brought their case before the LORD. 6 And the LORD spoke to Moses, saying: 7 The daughters of Zelophehad are right in what they are saying; you shall indeed let them possess an inheritance among their father's brothers and pass the inheritance of their father on to them. 8 You shall also say to the Israelites, "If a man dies, and has no son, then you shall pass his inheritance on to his daughter. 9 If he has no daughter, then you shall give his inheritance to his brothers. 10 If he has no brothers, then you

shall give his inheritance to his father's brothers. 11 And if his father has no brothers, then you shall give his inheritance to the nearest kinsman of his clan, and he shall possess it. It shall be for the Israelites a statute and ordinance, as the LORD commanded Moses."

Joshua Appointed Moses' Successor

12 The LORD said to Moses, "Go up this mountain of the Abarim range, and see the land that I have given to the Israelites. 13 When you have seen it, you also shall be gathered to your people, as your brother Aaron was, 14 because you rebelled against my word in the wilderness of Zin when the congregation quarreled with me.p You did not show my holiness before their eyes at the waters." (These are the waters of Meribah of Kadesh in the wilderness of Zin.) 15 Moses spoke to the LORD, saying, 16 "Let the LORD, the God of the spirits of all flesh, appoint someone over the congregation 17 who shall go out before them and come in before them, who shall lead them out and bring them in, so that the congregation of the LORD may not be like sheep without a shepherd." 18 So the LORD said to Moses, "Take Joshua son of Nun, a man in whom is the spirit, and lay your hand upon him; 19 have him stand before Eleazar the priest and all the congregation, and commission him in their sight. 20 You shall give him some of your authority, so that all the congregation of the Israelites may obey. 21 But he shall stand before Eleazar the priest, who shall inquire for him by the decision of the Urim before the LORD; at his word they shall go out, and at his word they shall come in, both he and all the Israelites with him, the whole congregation." 22 So Moses did as the LORD commanded him. He took Joshua and had him stand before Eleazar the priest and the whole congregation; 23 he laid his hands on him and commis-

Cross references (center column):

26.64 Deut 2.14, 15
26.65 Num 14.28, 29; 1 Cor 10.5, 6; Num 14.30
27.1ff Num 26.33; 36.1
27.3 Num 26.64, 65; 26.33; 16.1,2
27.4 Josh 17.4
27.5 Num 9.8
27.6 Num 36.2

27.12 Num 33.47; Deut 32.49
27.13 Num 31.2
27.14 Num 20.12; Ex 17.7
27.16 Num 16.22
27.17 Deut 31.2; Mt 9.36; Mk 6.34
27.18 Num 11.25-29; Deut 34.9
27.19 Deut 31.3,7, 8,23
27.20 Josh 1.16, 17
27.21 Ex 28.30

p Heb lacks *with me*

sioned him—as the LORD had directed through Moses.

Daily Offerings

28 The LORD spoke to Moses, saying: ²Command the Israelites, and say to them: My offering, the food for my offerings by fire, my pleasing odor, you shall take care to offer to me at its appointed time. ³And you shall say to them, This is the offering by fire that you shall offer to the LORD: two male lambs a year old without blemish, daily, as a regular offering. ⁴One lamb you shall offer in the morning, and the other lamb you shall offer at twilight⁹ ⁵also one-tenth of an ephah of choice flour for a grain offering, mixed with one-fourth of a hin of beaten oil. ⁶It is a regular burnt offering, ordained at Mount Sinai for a pleasing odor, an offering by fire to the LORD. ⁷Its drink offering shall be one-fourth of a hin for each lamb; in the sanctuary you shall pour out a drink offering of strong drink to the LORD. ⁸The other lamb you shall offer at twilight⁹ with a grain offering and a drink offering like the one in the morning; you shall offer it as an offering by fire, a pleasing odor to the LORD.

Sabbath Offerings

9 On the sabbath day: two male lambs a year old without blemish, and two-tenths of an ephah of choice flour for a grain offering, mixed with oil, and its drink offering— ¹⁰this is the burnt offering for every sabbath, in addition to the regular burnt offering and its drink offering.

Monthly Offerings

11 At the beginnings of your months you shall offer a burnt offering to the LORD: two young bulls, one ram, seven male lambs a year old without blemish; ¹²also three-tenths of an ephah of choice flour for a grain offering, mixed with oil, for each bull; and two-tenths of choice flour for a grain offering, mixed with oil, for the one ram; ¹³and one-tenth of choice flour

mixed with oil as a grain offering for every lamb—a burnt offering of pleasing odor, an offering by fire to the LORD. ¹⁴Their drink offerings shall be half a hin of wine for a bull, one-third of a hin for a ram, and one-fourth of a hin for a lamb. This is the burnt offering of every month throughout the months of the year. ¹⁵And there shall be one male goat for a sin offering to the LORD; it shall be offered in addition to the regular burnt offering and its drink offering.

Offerings at Passover

16 On the fourteenth day of the first month there shall be a passover offering to the LORD. ¹⁷And on the fifteenth day of this month is a festival; seven days shall unleavened bread be eaten. ¹⁸On the first day there shall be a holy convocation. You shall not work at your occupations. ¹⁹You shall offer an offering by fire, a burnt offering to the LORD: two young bulls, one ram, and seven male lambs a year old; see that they are without blemish. ²⁰Their grain offering shall be of choice flour mixed with oil: three-tenths of an ephah shall you offer for a bull, and two-tenths for a ram; ²¹one-tenth shall you offer for each of the seven lambs; ²²also one male goat for a sin offering, to make atonement for you. ²³You shall offer these in addition to the burnt offering of the morning, which belongs to the regular burnt offering. ²⁴In the same way you shall offer daily, for seven days, the food of an offering by fire, a pleasing odor to the LORD; it shall be offered in addition to the regular burnt offering and its drink offering. ²⁵And on the seventh day you shall have a holy convocation; you shall not work at your occupations.

Offerings at the Festival of Weeks

26 On the day of the first fruits, when you offer a grain offering of new grain to the LORD at your festival of weeks, you shall have a holy

28.2
Lev 3.11
28.3
Ex 29.38
28.7
Ex 29.42
28.10
v. 3
28.11
Num 10.10;
Ezek 45.17;
46.6
28.12
Num 15.4-12

28.15
v. 3
28.16
Ex 12.6,18;
Lev 23.5;
Deut 16.1
28.17
Lev 23.6
28.18
Ex 12.16;
Lev 23.7
28.23
v. 3
28.25
Ex 12.16
28.26
Ex 23.16;
34.22;
Lev 23.10,
15;
Deut 16.10

⁹ Heb *between the two evenings*

convocation; you shall not work at your occupations. 27 You shall offer a burnt offering, a pleasing odor to the LORD: two young bulls, one ram, seven male lambs a year old. 28 Their grain offering shall be of choice flour mixed with oil, three-tenths of an ephah for each bull, two-tenths for one ram, 29 one-tenth for each of the seven lambs; 30 with one male goat, to make atonement for you. 31 In addition to the regular burnt offering with its grain offering, you shall offer them and their drink offering. They shall be without blemish.

Offerings at the Festival of Trumpets

29 On the first day of the seventh month you shall have a holy convocation; you shall not work at your occupations. It is a day for you to blow the trumpets, 2 and you shall offer a burnt offering, a pleasing odor to the LORD: one young bull, one ram, seven male lambs a year old without blemish. 3 Their grain offering shall be of choice flour mixed with oil, three-tenths of one ephah for the bull, two-tenths for the ram, 4 and one-tenth for each of the seven lambs; 5 with one male goat for a sin offering, to make atonement for you. 6 These are in addition to the burnt offering of the new moon and its grain offering, and the regular burnt offering and its grain offering, and their drink offerings, according to the ordinance for them, a pleasing odor, an offering by fire to the LORD.

Offerings on the Day of Atonement

7 On the tenth day of this seventh month you shall have a holy convocation, and deny yourselves;ʳ you shall do no work. 8 You shall offer a burnt offering to the LORD, a pleasing odor: one young bull, one ram, seven male lambs a year old. They shall be without blemish. 9 Their grain offering shall be of choice flour mixed with oil, three-tenths of an ephah for the

28.31
vv. 3,19
29.1
Ex 23.16;
34.22;
Lev 23.24
29.6
Num 28.3,
11
29.7
Lev 16.29-34;
23.26-32

29.11
Lev 16.3,5;
Num 28.3
29.12
Lev 23.33-35
29.16
v. 11
29.18
vv. 3,4,9,10;
Num 15.12;
28.7,14
29.22
Num 28.15

bull, two-tenths for the one ram, 10 one-tenth for each of the seven lambs; 11 with one male goat for a sin offering, in addition to the sin offering of atonement, and the regular burnt offering and its grain offering, and their drink offerings.

Offerings at the Festival of Booths

12 On the fifteenth day of the seventh month you shall have a holy convocation; you shall not work at your occupations. You shall celebrate a festival to the LORD seven days. 13 You shall offer a burnt offering, an offering by fire, a pleasing odor to the LORD: thirteen young bulls, two rams, fourteen male lambs a year old. They shall be without blemish. 14 Their grain offering shall be of choice flour mixed with oil, three-tenths of an ephah for each of the thirteen bulls, two-tenths for each of the two rams, 15 and one-tenth for each of the fourteen lambs; 16 also one male goat for a sin offering, in addition to the regular burnt offering, its grain offering and its drink offering.

17 On the second day: twelve young bulls, two rams, fourteen male lambs a year old without blemish, 18 with the grain offering and the drink offerings for the bulls, for the rams, and for the lambs, as prescribed in accordance with their number; 19 also one male goat for a sin offering, in addition to the regular burnt offering and its grain offering, and their drink offerings.

20 On the third day: eleven bulls, two rams, fourteen male lambs a year old without blemish, 21 with the grain offering and the drink offerings for the bulls, for the rams, and for the lambs, as prescribed in accordance with their number; 22 also one male goat for a sin offering, in addition to the regular burnt offering and its grain offering and its drink offering.

23 On the fourth day: ten bulls, two rams, fourteen male lambs a

ʳ Or and fast

year old without blemish, 24 with the grain offering and the drink offerings for the bulls, for the rams, and for the lambs, as prescribed in accordance with their number; 25 also one male goat for a sin offering, in addition to the regular burnt offering, its grain offering and its drink offering.

26 On the fifth day: nine bulls, two rams, fourteen male lambs a year old without blemish, 27 with the grain offering and the drink offerings for the bulls, for the rams, and for the lambs, as prescribed in accordance with their number; 28 also one male goat for a sin offering, in addition to the regular burnt offering and its grain offering and its drink offering.

29 On the sixth day: eight bulls, two rams, fourteen male lambs a year old without blemish, 30 with the grain offering and the drink offerings for the bulls, for the rams, and for the lambs, as prescribed in accordance with their number; 31 also one male goat for a sin offering, in addition to the regular burnt offering, its grain offering, and its drink offerings.

32 On the seventh day: seven bulls, two rams, fourteen male lambs a year old without blemish, 33 with the grain offering and the drink offerings for the bulls, for the rams, and for the lambs, as prescribed in accordance with their number; 34 also one male goat for a sin offering, besides the regular burnt offering, its grain offering, and its drink offering.

35 On the eighth day you shall have a solemn assembly; you shall not work at your occupations. 36 You shall offer a burnt offering, an offering by fire, a pleasing odor to the LORD: one bull, one ram, seven male lambs a year old without blemish, 37 and the grain offering and the drink offerings for the bull, for the ram, and for the lambs, as prescribed in accordance with their number; 38 also one male goat for a sin offering, in addition to the regular burnt offering and its grain offering and its drink offering.

39 These you shall offer to the LORD at your appointed festivals, in addition to your votive offerings and your freewill offerings, as your burnt offerings, your grain offerings, your drink offerings, and your offerings of well-being.

40 s So Moses told the Israelites everything just as the LORD had commanded Moses.

Vows Made by Women

30 Then Moses said to the heads of the tribes of the Israelites: This is what the LORD has commanded. 2 When a man makes a vow to the LORD, or swears an oath to bind himself by a pledge, he shall not break his word; he shall do according to all that proceeds out of his mouth.

3 When a woman makes a vow to the LORD, or binds herself by a pledge, while within her father's house, in her youth, 4 and her father hears of her vow or her pledge by which she has bound herself, and says nothing to her; then all her vows shall stand, and any pledge by which she has bound herself shall stand. 5 But if her father expresses disapproval to her at the time that he hears of it, no vow of hers, and no pledge by which she has bound herself, shall stand; and the LORD will forgive her, because her father had expressed to her his disapproval.

6 If she marries, while obligated by her vows or any thoughtless utterance of her lips by which she bound herself, 7 and her husband hears of it and says nothing to her at the time that he hears, then her vows shall stand, and her pledges by which she has bound herself shall stand. 8 But if, at the time that her husband hears of it, he expresses disapproval to her, then he shall nullify the vow by which she was obligated, or the thoughtless utterance of her lips, by which she bound herself; and the LORD will forgive her. 9 (But every vow of a widow or of a divorced woman, by which she has bound herself, shall

Cross references (center column):

29.28
Num 15.24
29.31
v. 22;
Gen 8.20
29.35
Lev 23.36

29.39
Lev 23.2;
1 Chr 23.31;
2 Chr 31.3;
Lev 7.11,16
30.2
Deut 23.21;
Mt 5.23
30.5
Eccl 5.4
30.6
Ps 56.12
30.8
Gen 3.16

s Ch 30.1 in Heb

be binding upon her.) ¹⁰And if she made a vow in her husband's house, or bound herself by a pledge with an oath, ¹¹and her husband heard it and said nothing to her, and did not express disapproval to her, then all her vows shall stand, and any pledge by which she bound herself shall stand. ¹²But if her husband nullifies them at the time that he hears them, then whatever proceeds out of her lips concerning her vows, or concerning her pledge of herself, shall not stand. Her husband has nullified them, and the LORD will forgive her. ¹³Any vow or any binding oath to deny herself,ᵗ her husband may allow to stand, or her husband may nullify. ¹⁴But if her husband says nothing to her from day to day,ᵘ then he validates all her vows, or all her pledges, by which she is obligated; he has validated them, because he said nothing to her at the time that he heard of them. ¹⁵But if he nullifies them some time after he has heard of them, then he shall bear her guilt.

16 These are the statutes that the LORD commanded Moses concerning a husband and his wife, and a father and his daughter while she is still young and in her father's house.

War against Midian

31 The LORD spoke to Moses, saying, ²"Avenge the Israelites on the Midianites; afterward you shall be gathered to your people." ³So Moses said to the people, "Arm some of your number for the war, so that they may go against Midian, to execute the LORD's vengeance on Midian. ⁴You shall send a thousand from each of the tribes of Israel to the war." ⁵So out of the thousands of Israel, a thousand from each tribe were conscripted, twelve thousand armed for battle. ⁶Moses sent them to the war, a thousand from each tribe, along with Phinehas son of Eleazar the priest,ᵛ with the vessels of the sanctuary and the trumpets for sounding the alarm in his hand. ⁷They did battle against Midian, as

30.12
Eph 5.22
30.15
Col 3.18
30.16
Ex 15.26
31.2
Num 25.1, 16,17; 27.13
31.6
Num 10.9

31.8
Josh 13.21, 22; v. 16
31.11
Deut 20.14
31.16
Num 25.1-9; 24.14;
2 Pet 2.15;
Rev 2.14
31.17
Judg 21.11
31.19
Num 19.11-22

the LORD had commanded Moses, and killed every male. ⁸They killed the kings of Midian: Evi, Rekem, Zur, Hur, and Reba, the five kings of Midian, in addition to others who were slain by them; and they also killed Balaam son of Beor with the sword. ⁹The Israelites took the women of Midian and their little ones captive; and they took all their cattle, their flocks, and all their goods as booty. ¹⁰All their towns where they had settled, and all their encampments, they burned, ¹¹but they took all the spoil and all the booty, both people and animals. ¹²Then they brought the captives and the booty and the spoil to Moses, to Eleazar the priest, and to the congregation of the Israelites, at the camp on the plains of Moab by the Jordan at Jericho.

Return from the War

13 Moses, Eleazar the priest, and all the leaders of the congregation went to meet them outside the camp. ¹⁴Moses became angry with the officers of the army, the commanders of thousands and the commanders of hundreds, who had come from service in the war. ¹⁵Moses said to them, "Have you allowed all the women to live? ¹⁶These women here, on Balaam's advice, made the Israelites act treacherously against the LORD in the affair of Peor, so that the plague came among the congregation of the LORD. ¹⁷Now therefore, kill every male among the little ones, and kill every woman who has known a man by sleeping with him. ¹⁸But all the young girls who have not known a man by sleeping with him, keep alive for yourselves. ¹⁹Camp outside the camp seven days; whoever of you has killed any person or touched a corpse, purify yourselves and your captives on the third and on the seventh day. ²⁰You shall purify every garment, every article of skin, everything made of

ᵗOr to fast ᵘOr from that day to the next
ᵛGk: Heb adds to the war

goats' hair, and every article of wood."

21 Eleazar the priest said to the troops who had gone to battle: "This is the statute of the law that the LORD has commanded Moses: ²²gold, silver, bronze, iron, tin, and lead— ²³everything that can withstand fire, shall be passed through fire, and it shall be clean. Nevertheless it shall also be purified with the water for purification; and whatever cannot withstand fire, shall be passed through the water. ²⁴You must wash your clothes on the seventh day, and you shall be clean; afterward you may come into the camp."

Disposition of Captives and Booty

25 The LORD spoke to Moses, saying, ²⁶"You and Eleazar the priest and the heads of the ancestral houses of the congregation make an inventory of the booty captured, both human and animal. ²⁷Divide the booty into two parts, between the warriors who went out to battle and all the congregation. ²⁸From the share of the warriors who went out to battle, set aside as tribute for the LORD, one item out of every five hundred, whether persons, oxen, donkeys, sheep, or goats. ²⁹Take it from their half and give it to Eleazar the priest as an offering to the LORD. ³⁰But from the Israelites' half you shall take one out of every fifty, whether persons, oxen, donkeys, sheep, or goats— all the animals—and give them to the Levites who had charge of the tabernacle of the LORD."

31 Then Moses and Eleazar the priest did as the LORD had commanded Moses:

32 The booty remaining from the spoil that the troops had taken totaled six hundred seventy-five thousand sheep, ³³seventy-two thousand oxen, ³⁴sixty-one thousand donkeys, ³⁵and thirty-two thousand persons in all, women who had not known a man by sleeping with him.

36 The half-share, the portion

of those who had gone out to war, was in number three hundred thirty-seven thousand five hundred sheep and goats, ³⁷and the LORD's tribute of sheep and goats was six hundred seventy-five. ³⁸The oxen were thirty-six thousand, of which the LORD's tribute was seventy-two. ³⁹The donkeys were thirty thousand five hundred, of which the LORD's tribute was sixty-one. ⁴⁰The persons were sixteen thousand, of which the LORD's tribute was thirty-two persons. ⁴¹Moses gave the tribute, the offering for the LORD, to Eleazar the priest, as the LORD had commanded Moses.

42 As for the Israelites' half, which Moses separated from that of the troops, ⁴³the congregation's half was three hundred thirty-seven thousand five hundred sheep and goats, ⁴⁴thirty-six thousand oxen, ⁴⁵thirty thousand five hundred donkeys, ⁴⁶and sixteen thousand persons. ⁴⁷From the Israelites' half Moses took one of every fifty, both of persons and of animals, and gave them to the Levites who had charge of the tabernacle of the LORD; as the LORD had commanded Moses.

48 Then the officers who were over the thousands of the army, the commanders of thousands and the commanders of hundreds, approached Moses, ⁴⁹and said to Moses, "Your servants have counted the warriors who are under our command, and not one of us is missing. ⁵⁰And we have brought the LORD's offering, what each of us found, articles of gold, armlets and bracelets, signet rings, earrings, and pendants, to make atonement for ourselves before the LORD." ⁵¹Moses and Eleazar the priest received the gold from them, all in the form of crafted articles. ⁵²And all the gold of the offering that they offered to the LORD, from the commanders of thousands and the commanders of hundreds, was sixteen thousand seven hundred fifty shekels. ⁵³(The troops had all taken plunder for themselves.) ⁵⁴So Moses and Eleazar the priest re-

31.23
Num 19.9, 17
31.24
Lev 11.25
31.28
Num 18.21-30
31.30
Num 3.7,8, 25; 18.3,4
31.32
Gen 49.27; Ex 15.9
31.37
vv. 38,41
31.41
Num 18.8,9
31.47
v. 30
31.50
Ex 30.12,16
31.53
v. 52; Deut 20.14
31.54
Ex 30.16

ceived the gold from the commanders of thousands and of hundreds, and brought it into the tent of meeting as a memorial for the Israelites before the LORD.

Conquest and Division of Transjordan

32 Now the Reubenites and the Gadites owned a very great number of cattle. When they saw that the land of Jazer and the land of Gilead was a good place for cattle, ²the Gadites and the Reubenites came and spoke to Moses, to Eleazar the priest, and to the leaders of the congregation, saying, ³"Ataroth, Dibon, Jazer, Nimrah, Heshbon, Elealeh, Sebam, Nebo, and Beon— ⁴the land that the LORD subdued before the congregation of Israel—is a land for cattle; and your servants have cattle." ⁵They continued, "If we have found favor in your sight, let this land be given to your servants for a possession; do not make us cross the Jordan."

6 But Moses said to the Gadites and to the Reubenites, "Shall your brothers go to war while you sit here? ⁷Why will you discourage the hearts of the Israelites from going over into the land that the LORD has given them? ⁸Your fathers did this, when I sent them from Kadesh-barnea to see the land. ⁹When they went up to the Wadi Eshcol and saw the land, they discouraged the hearts of the Israelites from going into the land that the LORD had given them. ¹⁰The LORD's anger was kindled on that day and he swore, saying, ¹¹'Surely none of the people who came up out of Egypt, from twenty years old and upward, shall see the land that I swore to give to Abraham, to Isaac, and to Jacob, because they have not unreservedly followed me— ¹²none except Caleb son of Jephunneh the Kenizzite and Joshua son of Nun, for they have unreservedly followed the LORD.' ¹³And the LORD's anger was kindled against Israel, and he made them wander in the wilderness for forty years, until all the generation that had done evil in

the sight of the LORD had disappeared. ¹⁴And now you, a brood of sinners, have risen in place of your fathers, to increase the LORD's fierce anger against Israel! ¹⁵If you turn away from following him, he will again abandon them in the wilderness; and you will destroy all this people."

16 Then they came up to him and said, "We will build sheepfolds here for our flocks, and towns for our little ones, ¹⁷but we will take up arms as a vanguardᵂ before the Israelites, until we have brought them to their place. Meanwhile our little ones will stay in the fortified towns because of the inhabitants of the land. ¹⁸We will not return to our homes until all the Israelites have obtained their inheritance. ¹⁹We will not inherit with them on the other side of the Jordan and beyond, because our inheritance has come to us on this side of the Jordan to the east."

20 So Moses said to them, "If you do this—if you take up arms to go before the LORD for the war, ²¹and all those of you who bear arms cross the Jordan before the LORD, until he has driven out his enemies from before him ²²and the land is subdued before the LORD— then after that you may return and be free of obligation to the LORD and to Israel, and this land shall be your possession before the LORD. ²³But if you do not do this, you have sinned against the LORD; and be sure your sin will find you out. ²⁴Build towns for your little ones, and folds for your flocks; but do what you have promised."

25 Then the Gadites and the Reubenites said to Moses, "Your servants will do as my lord commands. ²⁶Our little ones, our wives, our flocks, and all our livestock shall remain there in the towns of Gilead; ²⁷but your servants will cross over, everyone armed for war, to do battle for the LORD, just as my lord orders."

28 So Moses gave command

Cross-references

32.1
Ex 12.38;
Num 21.32
32.7
Num 13.27-
14.4
32.8
Num 13.3,
26
32.10
Num 14.11,
21;
Deut 1.34
32.11
Num 14.28-30;
Deut 1.35
32.12
Num 14.24;
Deut 1.36
32.13
Num 14.33-35;
26.64,65

32.15
Deut 30.17,
18
32.17
Josh 4.12,
13
32.18
Josh 22.1-4
32.19
v. 33
32.20
Deut 3.18
32.22
Deut 3.12-20
32.24
vv. 16,34
32.26
Josh 1.14
32.27
Josh 4.12
32.28
Josh 1.13

ᵂ Cn: Heb *hurrying*

concerning them to Eleazar the priest, to Joshua son of Nun, and to the heads of the ancestral houses of the Israelite tribes. ²⁹ And Moses said to them, "If the Gadites and the Reubenites, everyone armed for battle before the LORD, will cross over the Jordan with you and the land shall be subdued before you, then you shall give them the land of Gilead for a possession; ³⁰ but if they will not cross over with you armed, they shall have possessions among you in the land of Canaan." ³¹ The Gadites and the Reubenites answered, "As the LORD has spoken to your servants, so we will do. ³² We will cross over armed before the LORD into the land of Canaan, but the possession of our inheritance shall remain with us on this side of^x the Jordan."

³³ Moses gave to them—to the Gadites and to the Reubenites and to the half-tribe of Manasseh son of Joseph—the kingdom of King Sihon of the Amorites and the kingdom of King Og of Bashan, the land and its towns, with the territories of the surrounding towns. ³⁴ And the Gadites rebuilt Dibon, Ataroth, Aroer, ³⁵ Atroth-shophan, Jazer, Jogbehah, ³⁶ Beth-nimrah, and Beth-haran, fortified cities, and folds for sheep. ³⁷ And the Reubenites rebuilt Heshbon, Elealeh, Kiriathaim, ³⁸ Nebo, and Baal-meon (some names being changed), and Sibmah; and they gave names to the towns that they rebuilt. ³⁹ The descendants of Machir son of Manasseh went to Gilead, captured it, and dispossessed the Amorites who were there; ⁴⁰ so Moses gave Gilead to Machir son of Manasseh, and he settled there. ⁴¹ Jair son of Manasseh went and captured their villages, and renamed them Havvoth-jair.^y ⁴² And Nobah went and captured Kenath and its villages, and renamed it Nobah after himself.

The Stages of Israel's Journey from Egypt

33 These are the stages by which the Israelites went

out of the land of Egypt in military formation under the leadership of Moses and Aaron. ² Moses wrote down their starting points, stage by stage, by command of the LORD; and these are their stages according to their starting places. ³ They set out from Rameses in the first month, on the fifteenth day of the first month; on the day after the passover the Israelites went out boldly in the sight of all the Egyptians, ⁴ while the Egyptians were burying all their firstborn, whom the LORD had struck down among them. The LORD executed judgments even against their gods.

5 So the Israelites set out from Rameses, and camped at Succoth. ⁶ They set out from Succoth, and camped at Etham, which is on the edge of the wilderness. ⁷ They set out from Etham, and turned back to Pi-hahiroth, which faces Baal-zephon; and they camped before Migdol. ⁸ They set out from Pi-hahiroth, passed through the sea into the wilderness, went a three days' journey in the wilderness of Etham, and camped at Marah. ⁹ They set out from Marah and came to Elim; at Elim there were twelve springs of water and seventy palm trees, and they camped there. ¹⁰ They set out from Elim and camped by the Red Sea.^z ¹¹ They set out from the Red Sea^z and camped in the wilderness of Sin. ¹² They set out from the wilderness of Sin and camped at Dophkah. ¹³ They set out from Dophkah and camped at Alush. ¹⁴ They set out from Alush and camped at Rephidim, where there was no water for the people to drink. ¹⁵ They set out from Rephidim and camped in the wilderness of Sinai. ¹⁶ They set out from the wilderness of Sinai and camped at Kibroth-hattaavah. ¹⁷ They set out from Kibroth-hattaavah and camped at Hazeroth. ¹⁸ They set out from Hazeroth and camped at Rithmah. ¹⁹ They set out from Rithmah and camped

32.29
v. 1
32.33
Deut 3.12-17;
Josh 12.1-6;
Num 21.24,
33,35
32.41
Judg 10.4
33.1
Ps 77.20;
Mic 6.4

33.3
Ex 12.37;
14.8
33.4
Ex 12.12
33.6
Ex 13.20
33.7
Ex 14.2,9
33.8
Ex 14.22
33.9
Ex 15.27
33.11
Ex 16.1
33.14
Ex 17.1
33.15
Ex 19.1
33.16
Num 11.34
33.17
Num 11.35

^x Heb *beyond* ^y That is *the villages of Jair*
^z Or *Sea of Reeds*

at Rimmon-perez. 20 They set out from Rimmon-perez and camped at Libnah. 21 They set out from Libnah and camped at Rissah. 22 They set out from Rissah and camped at Kehelathah. 23 They set out from Kehelathah and camped at Mount Shepher. 24 They set out from Mount Shepher and camped at Haradah. 25 They set out from Haradah and camped at Makheloth. 26 They set out from Makheloth and camped at Tahath. 27 They set out from Tahath and camped at Terah. 28 They set out from Terah and camped at Mithkah. 29 They set out from Mithkah and camped at Hashmonah. 30 They set out from Hashmonah and camped at Moseroth. 31 They set out from Moseroth and camped at Bene-jaakan. 32 They set out from Bene-jaakan and camped at Hor-haggidgad. 33 They set out from Hor-haggidgad and camped at Jotbathah. 34 They set out from Jotbathah and camped at Abronah. 35 They set out from Abronah and camped at Ezion-geber. 36 They set out from Ezion-geber and camped in the wilderness of Zin (that is, Kadesh). 37 They set out from Kadesh and camped at Mount Hor, on the edge of the land of Edom.

38 Aaron the priest went up Mount Hor at the command of the LORD and died there in the fortieth year after the Israelites had come out of the land of Egypt, on the first day of the fifth month. 39 Aaron was one hundred twenty-three years old when he died on Mount Hor.

40 The Canaanite, the king of Arad, who lived in the Negeb in the land of Canaan, heard of the coming of the Israelites.

41 They set out from Mount Hor and camped at Zalmonah. 42 They set out from Zalmonah and camped at Punon. 43 They set out from Punon and camped at Oboth. 44 They set out from Oboth and camped at Iye-abarim, in the territory of Moab. 45 They set out from Iyim and camped at Dibon-gad. 46 They set out from Dibon-gad and camped at Almon-diblathaim.

47 They set out from Almon-diblathaim and camped in the mountains of Abarim, before Nebo. 48 They set out from the mountains of Abarim and camped in the plains of Moab by the Jordan at Jericho; 49 they camped by the Jordan from Beth-jeshimoth as far as Abel-shittim in the plains of Moab.

Directions for the Conquest of Canaan

50 In the plains of Moab by the Jordan at Jericho, the LORD spoke to Moses, saying: 51 Speak to the Israelites, and say to them: When you cross over the Jordan into the land of Canaan, 52 you shall drive out all the inhabitants of the land from before you, destroy all their figured stones, destroy all their cast images, and demolish all their high places. 53 You shall take possession of the land and settle in it, for I have given you the land to possess. 54 You shall apportion the land by lot according to your clans; to a large one you shall give a large inheritance, and to a small one you shall give a small inheritance; the inheritance shall belong to the person on whom the lot falls; according to your ancestral tribes you shall inherit. 55 But if you do not drive out the inhabitants of the land from before you, then those whom you let remain shall be as barbs in your eyes and thorns in your sides; they shall trouble you in the land where you are settling. 56 And I will do to you as I thought to do to them.

The Boundaries of the Land

34 The LORD spoke to Moses, saying: 2 Command the Israelites, and say to them: When you enter the land of Canaan (this is the land that shall fall to you for an inheritance, the land of Canaan, defined by its boundaries), 3 your south sector shall extend from the wilderness of Zin along the side of Edom. Your southern boundary shall begin from the end of the Dead Sea[a] on the east; 4 your

a Heb Salt Sea

33.20
see
Josh 10.29
33.30
Deut 10.6
33.33
Deut 10.7
33.35
Deut 2.8
33.36
Num 20.1
33.37
Num 20.16, 22; 21.4
33.38
Num 20.25, 28;
Deut 10.6
33.40
Num 21.1
33.43
Num 21.10
33.44
Num 21.11

33.47
Num 27.12
33.48
Num 22.1
33.49
Num 25.1
33.52
Ex 23.24, 33; 34.13;
Deut 7.2,5;
12.3;
Josh 11.12
33.54
Num 26.53-55
33.55
Josh 23.13;
Ps 106.34, 36
34.2
Gen 17.8;
Deut 1.7;
Ps 78.55;
Ezek 47.15
34.3
Josh 15.1-3

boundary shall turn south of the ascent of Akrabbim, and cross to Zin, and its outer limit shall be south of Kadesh-barnea; then it shall go on to Hazar-addar, and cross to Azmon; ⁵the boundary shall turn from Azmon to the Wadi of Egypt, and its termination shall be at the Sea.

6 For the western boundary, you shall have the Great Sea and its[b] coast; this shall be your western boundary.

7 This shall be your northern boundary: from the Great Sea you shall mark out your line to Mount Hor; ⁸from Mount Hor you shall mark it out to Lebo-hamath, and the outer limit of the boundary shall be at Zedad; ⁹then the boundary shall extend to Ziphron, and its end shall be at Hazar-enan; this shall be your northern boundary.

10 You shall mark out your eastern boundary from Hazar-enan to Shepham; ¹¹and the boundary shall continue down from Shepham to Riblah on the east side of Ain; and the boundary shall go down, and reach the eastern slope of the sea of Chinnereth; ¹²and the boundary shall go down to the Jordan, and its end shall be at the Dead Sea.[c] This shall be your land with its boundaries all around.

13 Moses commanded the Israelites, saying: This is the land that you shall inherit by lot, which the Lord has commanded to give to the nine tribes and to the half-tribe; ¹⁴for the tribe of the Reubenites by their ancestral houses and the tribe of the Gadites by their ancestral houses have taken their inheritance, and also the half-tribe of Manasseh; ¹⁵the two tribes and the half-tribe have taken their inheritance beyond the Jordan at Jericho eastward, toward the sunrise.

Tribal Leaders

16 The Lord spoke to Moses, saying: ¹⁷These are the names of the men who shall apportion the land to you for inheritance: the priest Eleazar and Joshua son of Nun. ¹⁸You shall take one leader of

every tribe to apportion the land for inheritance. ¹⁹These are the names of the men: Of the tribe of Judah, Caleb son of Jephunneh. ²⁰Of the tribe of the Simeonites, Shemuel son of Ammihud. ²¹Of the tribe of Benjamin, Elidad son of Chislon. ²²Of the tribe of the Danites a leader, Bukki son of Jogli. ²³Of the Josephites: of the tribe of the Manassites a leader, Hanniel son of Ephod, ²⁴and of the tribe of the Ephraimites a leader, Kemuel son of Shiphtan. ²⁵Of the tribe of the Zebulunites a leader, Eli-zaphan son of Parnach. ²⁶Of the tribe of the Issacharites a leader, Paltiel son of Azzan. ²⁷And of the tribe of the Asherites a leader, Ahihud son of Shelomi. ²⁸Of the tribe of the Naphtalites a leader, Pedahel son of Ammihud. ²⁹These were the ones whom the Lord commanded to apportion the inheritance for the Israelites in the land of Canaan.

Cities for the Levites

35 In the plains of Moab by the Jordan at Jericho, the Lord spoke to Moses, saying: ²Command the Israelites to give, from the inheritance that they possess, towns for the Levites to live in; you shall also give to the Levites pasture lands surrounding the towns. ³The towns shall be theirs to live in, and their pasture lands shall be for their cattle, for their livestock, and for all their animals. ⁴The pasture lands of the towns, which you shall give to the Levites, shall reach from the wall of the town outward a thousand cubits all around. ⁵You shall measure, outside the town, for the east side two thousand cubits, for the south side two thousand cubits, for the west side two thousand cubits, and for the north side two thousand cubits, with the town in the middle; this shall belong to them as pasture land for their towns.

6 The towns that you give to the Levites shall include the six cities of refuge, where you shall permit a slayer to flee, and in addition to

34.5
Gen 15.18;
Josh 15.4,
47
34.7
Ezek 47.15-17
34.8
Num 13.21
34.11
2 Kings 23.33;
Deut 3.17;
Josh 11.2
34.13
Josh 14.1,2
34.14
Num 32.33;
Josh 14.2,3
34.17
Josh 14.1
34.18
Num 1.4,16

35.2
Lev 25.32-34;
Josh 14.3,4
35.6
Josh 20.7-9;
21.3,13,21,
27,32,36,38

b Syr: Heb lacks *its* c Heb *Salt Sea*

them you shall give forty-two towns. 7 The towns that you give to the Levites shall total forty-eight, with their pasture lands. 8 And as for the towns that you shall give from the possession of the Israelites, from the larger tribes you shall take many, and from the smaller tribes you shall take few; each, in proportion to the inheritance that it obtains, shall give of its towns to the Levites.

Cities of Refuge

9 The LORD spoke to Moses, saying: 10 Speak to the Israelites, and say to them: When you cross the Jordan into the land of Canaan, 11 then you shall select cities to be cities of refuge for you, so that a slayer who kills a person without intent may flee there. 12 The cities shall be for you a refuge from the avenger, so that the slayer may not die until there is a trial before the congregation.

13 The cities that you designate shall be six cities of refuge for you: 14 you shall designate three cities beyond the Jordan, and three cities in the land of Canaan, to be cities of refuge. 15 These six cities shall serve as refuge for the Israelites, for the resident or transient alien among them, so that anyone who kills a person without intent may flee there.

Concerning Murder and Blood Revenge

16 But anyone who strikes another with an iron object, and death ensues, is a murderer; the murderer shall be put to death. 17 Or anyone who strikes another with a stone in hand that could cause death, and death ensues, is a murderer; the murderer shall be put to death. 18 Or anyone who strikes another with a weapon of wood in hand that could cause death, and death ensues, is a murderer; the murderer shall be put to death. 19 The avenger of blood is the one who shall put the murderer to death; when they meet, the avenger of blood shall execute the

sentence. 20 Likewise, if someone pushes another from hatred, or hurls something at another, lying in wait, and death ensues, 21 or in enmity strikes another with the hand, and death ensues, then the one who struck the blow shall be put to death; that person is a murderer; the avenger of blood shall put the murderer to death, when they meet.

22 But if someone pushes another suddenly without enmity, or hurls any object without lying in wait, 23 or, while handling any stone that could cause death, unintentionally[d] drops it on another and death ensues, though they were not enemies, and no harm was intended, 24 then the congregation shall judge between the slayer and the avenger of blood, in accordance with these ordinances; 25 and the congregation shall rescue the slayer from the avenger of blood. Then the congregation shall send the slayer back to the original city of refuge. The slayer shall live in it until the death of the high priest who was anointed with the holy oil. 26 But if the slayer shall at any time go outside the bounds of the original city of refuge, 27 and is found by the avenger of blood outside the bounds of the city of refuge, and is killed by the avenger, no bloodguilt shall be incurred. 28 For the slayer must remain in the city of refuge until the death of the high priest; but after the death of the high priest the slayer may return home.

29 These things shall be a statute and ordinance for you throughout your generations wherever you live.

30 If anyone kills another, the murderer shall be put to death on the evidence of witnesses; but no one shall be put to death on the testimony of a single witness. 31 Moreover you shall accept no ransom for the life of a murderer who is subject to the death penalty; a murderer must be put to death.

35.8 Num 26.54; Lev 25.32-34; Josh 21.1-42
35.11 Deut 19.1-13; Ex 21.13
35.12 Josh 20.2-6
35.15 v. 11
35.16 Ex 21.12, 14; Lev 24.17
35.19 vv. 21,24,27

35.22 v. 11; Ex 21.13
35.24 v. 12
35.30 v. 16; Deut 17.6; 19.15; Mt 18.16; 2 Cor 13.1; Heb 10.28

d Heb without seeing

³²Nor shall you accept ransom for one who has fled to a city of refuge, enabling the fugitive to return to live in the land before the death of the high priest. ³³You shall not pollute the land in which you live; for blood pollutes the land, and no expiation can be made for the land, for the blood that is shed in it, except by the blood of the one who shed it. ³⁴You shall not defile the land in which you live, in which I also dwell; for I the LORD dwell among the Israelites.

Marriage of Female Heirs

36 The heads of the ancestral houses of the clans of the descendants of Gilead son of Machir son of Manasseh, of the Josephite clans, came forward and spoke in the presence of Moses and the leaders, the heads of the ancestral houses of the Israelites; ²they said, "The LORD commanded my lord to give the land for inheritance by lot to the Israelites; and my lord

was commanded by the LORD to give the inheritance of our brother Zelophehad to his daughters. ³But if they are married into another Israelite tribe, then their inheritance will be taken from the inheritance of our ancestors and added to the inheritance of the tribe into which they marry; so it will be taken away from the alloted portion of our inheritance. ⁴And when the jubilee of the Israelites comes, then their inheritance will be added to the inheritance of the tribe into which they have married; and their inheritance will be taken from the inheritance of our ancestral tribe."

5 Then Moses commanded the Israelites according to the word of the LORD, saying, "The descendants of the tribe of Joseph are right in what they are saying. ⁶This is what the LORD commands concerning the daughters of Zelophehad, 'Let them marry whom they think best; only it must be into a clan of their father's tribe that they are married,

Cross-references (center column):
35.33
Ps 106.38;
Gen 9.6
35.34
Lev 18.25;
Ex 29.45,46
36.1
Num 26.29;
27.1
36.2
Num 26.55;
33.54; 27.1,7

36.4
Lev 25.10
36.6
v. 12

CITIES OF REFUGE

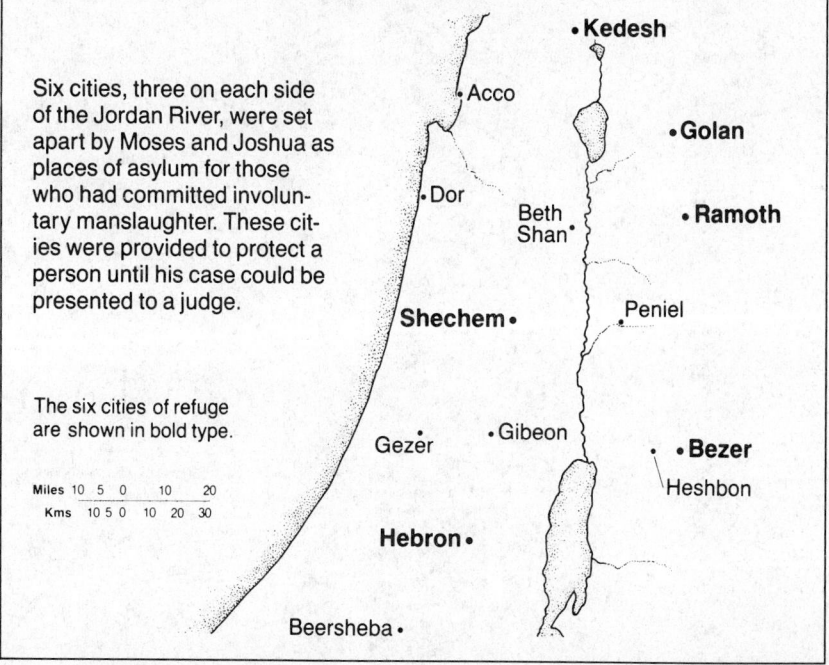

Six cities, three on each side of the Jordan River, were set apart by Moses and Joshua as places of asylum for those who had committed involuntary manslaughter. These cities were provided to protect a person until his case could be presented to a judge.

The six cities of refuge are shown in bold type.

Miles 10 5 0 10 20
Kms 10 5 0 10 20 30

• **Kedesh**

• Acco

• **Golan**

• Dor

Beth Shan•

• **Ramoth**

Shechem •

Peniel

Gezer •

• Gibeon

• **Bezer**

Heshbon

Hebron •

Beersheba •

⁷so that no inheritance of the Israelites shall be transferred from one tribe to another; for all Israelites shall retain the inheritance of their ancestral tribes. ⁸Every daughter who possesses an inheritance in any tribe of the Israelites shall marry one from the clan of her father's tribe, so that all Israelites may continue to possess their ancestral inheritance. ⁹No inheritance shall be transferred from one tribe to another; for each of the tribes of the Israelites shall retain its own inheritance.' "

10 The daughters of Zelophe-

had did as the Lord had commanded Moses. ¹¹Mahlah, Tirzah, Hoglah, Milcah, and Noah, the daughters of Zelophehad, married sons of their father's brothers. ¹²They were married into the clans of the descendants of Manasseh son of Joseph, and their inheritance remained in the tribe of their father's clan.

13 These are the commandments and the ordinances that the Lord commanded through Moses to the Israelites in the plains of Moab by the Jordan at Jericho.

36.8
1 Chr 23.22

36.11
Num 27.1
36.13
Num 22.1;
Lev 26.46;
27.34

Deuteronomy

Title and Background

Deuteronomy means "repetition of the law." After forty years the Israelites were about to enter Canaan. But before they did, Moses wanted to remind them of their history, all that God had done for them, and the laws they had to continue to obey as God's chosen people.

Author and Date of Writing

This book is cast as a speech that Moses gave to the nation of Israel as they gathered on the other side of the Jordan, waiting for their entry into Canaan (1.5; 4.44; 5.1; 27.1). The time of this speech would be shortly before his death, recorded in the last chapter. See the Introductions to Genesis and Exodus for the two possible dates for Moses.

Theme and Message

Moses reminded the people of God's goodness to them through their journey and his giving them the land of Canaan. He also summarized God's laws, including the Ten Commandments. One subject that pervades the whole book is the love relationship of the Lord to his people and that of the people to the Lord as their sovereign God.

Outline

I. Preamble (1.1-5)
II. Historical Prologue (1.6–4.43)
III. Stipulations of the Covenant (4.44–26.19)
 A. Primary Demands (4.44–11.32)
 B. Additional Requirements (12.1–26.19)
IV. Curses and Blessings, and Renewal of the Covenant (27.1–30.20)
V. Succession under the Covenant (31.1-29)
VI. Moses' Song, Final Blessing, and Death (31.30–34.12)

Events at Horeb Recalled

1 These are the words that Moses spoke to all Israel beyond the Jordan—in the wilderness, on the plain opposite Suph, between Paran and Tophel, Laban, Hazeroth, and Di-zahab. ² (By the way of Mount Seir it takes eleven days to reach Kadesh-barnea from Horeb.) ³ In the fortieth year, on the first day of the eleventh month, Moses spoke to the Israelites just as the LORD had commanded him to speak to them. ⁴ This was after he had defeated King Sihon of the Amorites, who reigned in Heshbon, and King Og of Bashan, who reigned in Ashtaroth andᵃ in Edrei. ⁵ Beyond the Jordan in the land of Moab, Moses undertook to expound this law as follows:

6 The LORD our God spoke to us at Horeb, saying, "You have stayed long enough at this mountain. ⁷ Resume your journey, and go into the hill country of the Amorites as well as into the neighboring regions—the Arabah, the hill country, the Shephelah, the Negeb, and the seacoast—the land of the Canaanites and the Lebanon, as far as the great river, the river

1.3 Num 33.38
1.4 Num 21.24, 33
1.6 Ex 3.1; Num 10.11-13

ᵃ Gk Syr Vg Compare Josh 12.4: Heb lacks *and*

Euphrates. 8 See, I have set the land before you; go in and take possession of the land that I[b] swore to your ancestors, to Abraham, to Isaac, and to Jacob, to give to them and to their descendants after them."

Appointment of Tribal Leaders

9 At that time I said to you, "I am unable by myself to bear you. 10 The LORD your God has multiplied you, so that today you are as numerous as the stars of heaven. 11 May the LORD, the God of your ancestors, increase you a thousand times more and bless you, as he has promised you! 12 But how can I bear the heavy burden of your disputes all by myself? 13 Choose for each of your tribes individuals who are wise, discerning, and reputable to be your leaders." 14 You answered me, "The plan you have proposed is a good one." 15 So I took the leaders of your tribes, wise and reputable individuals, and installed them as leaders over you, commanders of thousands, commanders of hundreds, commanders of fifties, commanders of tens, and officials, throughout your tribes. 16 I charged your judges at that time: "Give the members of your community a fair hearing, and judge rightly between one person and another, whether citizen or resident alien. 17 You must not be partial in judging: hear out the small and the great alike; you shall not be intimidated by anyone, for the judgment is God's. Any case that is too hard for you, bring to me, and I will hear it." 18 So I charged you at that time with all the things that you should do.

Israel's Refusal to Enter the Land

19 Then, just as the LORD our God had ordered us, we set out from Horeb and went through all that great and terrible wilderness that you saw, on the way to the hill country of the Amorites, until we reached Kadesh-barnea. 20 I said to you, "You have reached the hill country of the Amorites, which the LORD our God is giving us. 21 See, the LORD your God has given the land to you; go up, take possession, as the LORD, the God of your ancestors, has promised you; do not fear or be dismayed."

22 All of you came to me and said, "Let us send men ahead of us to explore the land for us and bring back a report to us regarding the route by which we should go up and the cities we will come to." 23 The plan seemed good to me, and I selected twelve of you, one from each tribe. 24 They set out and went up into the hill country, and when they reached the Valley of Eshcol they spied it out 25 and gathered some of the land's produce, which they brought down to us. They brought back a report to us, and said, "It is a good land that the LORD our God is giving us."

26 But you were unwilling to go up. You rebelled against the command of the LORD your God; 27 you grumbled in your tents and said, "It is because the LORD hates us that he has brought us out of the land of Egypt, to hand us over to the Amorites to destroy us. 28 Where are we headed? Our kindred have made our hearts melt by reporting, 'The people are stronger and taller than we; the cities are large and fortified up to heaven! We actually saw there the offspring of the Anakim!'" 29 I said to you, "Have no dread or fear of them. 30 The LORD your God, who goes before you, is the one who will fight for you, just as he did for you in Egypt before your very eyes, 31 and in the wilderness, where you saw how the LORD your God carried you, just as one carries a child, all the way that you traveled until you reached this place. 32 But in spite of this, you have no trust in the LORD your God, 33 who goes before you on the way to seek out a place for you to camp, in fire by night, and in the cloud by day, to show you the route you should take."

1.8 Gen 12.7; 15.18; 17.7,8; 26.4; 28.13
1.9 Ex 18.18
1.10 Gen 15.5; Deut 10.22
1.11 Gen 22.17; Ex 32.13
1.13 Ex 18.21
1.15 Ex 18.25
1.16 Deut 16.18; Lev 24.22
1.17 Lev 19.15; Jas 2.1; Ex 18.19-26
1.19 v. 2; Deut 8.15; Num 13.26
1.21 Josh 1.9
1.23 Num 13.1-3
1.24 Num 13.22-24
1.25 Num 13.27
1.26 Num 14.1-4
1.27 Deut 9.28; Ps 106.25
1.28 Num 13.28, 31-33; Deut 9.1,2
1.30 Ex 14.14; Deut 3.22
1.31 Deut 32.11, 12; Acts 13.18
1.32 Ps 106.24
1.33 Ex 13.21; Num 10.33

b Sam Gk: MT the LORD

The Penalty for Israel's Rebellion

34 When the Lord heard your words, he was wrathful and swore: ³⁵ "Not one of these—not one of this evil generation—shall see the good land that I swore to give to your ancestors, ³⁶ except Caleb son of Jephunneh. He shall see it, and to him and to his descendants I will give the land on which he set foot, because of his complete fidelity to the Lord." ³⁷ Even with me the Lord was angry on your account, saying, "You also shall not enter there. ³⁸ Joshua son of Nun, your assistant, shall enter there; encourage him, for he is the one who will secure Israel's possession of it. ³⁹ And as for your little ones, who you thought would become booty, your children, who today do not yet know right from wrong, they shall enter there; to them I will give it, and they shall take possession of it. ⁴⁰ But as for you, journey back into the wilderness, in the direction of the Red Sea."ᶜ

41 You answered me, "We have sinned against the Lord! We are ready to go up and fight, just as the Lord our God commanded us." So all of you strapped on your battle gear, and thought it easy to go up into the hill country. ⁴² The Lord said to me, "Say to them, 'Do not go up and do not fight, for I am not in the midst of you; otherwise you will be defeated by your enemies.' " ⁴³ Although I told you, you would not listen. You rebelled against the command of the Lord and presumptuously went up into the hill country. ⁴⁴ The Amorites who lived in that hill country then came out against you and chased you as bees do. They beat you down in Seir as far as Hormah. ⁴⁵ When you returned and wept before the Lord, the Lord would neither heed your voice nor pay you any attention.

The Desert Years

46 After you had stayed at Kadesh as many days as you did,

2 ¹ we journeyed back into the wilderness, in the direction of the Red Sea,ᶜ as the Lord had told me and skirted Mount Seir for many days. ² Then the Lord said to me: ³ "You have been skirting this hill country long enough. Head north, ⁴ and charge the people as follows: You are about to pass through the territory of your kindred, the descendants of Esau, who live in Seir. They will be afraid of you, so, be very careful ⁵ not to engage in battle with them, for I will not give you even so much as a foot's length of their land, since I have given Mount Seir to Esau as a possession. ⁶ You shall purchase food from them for money, so that you may eat; and you shall also buy water from them for money, so that you may drink. ⁷ Surely the Lord your God has blessed you in all your undertakings; he knows your going through this great wilderness. These forty years the Lord your God has been with you; you have lacked nothing." ⁸ So we passed by our kin, the descendants of Esau who live in Seir, leaving behind the route of the Arabah, and leaving behind Elath and Eziongeber.

When we had headed out along the route of the wilderness of Moab, ⁹ the Lord said to me: "Do not harass Moab or engage them in battle, for I will not give you any of its land as a possession, since I have given Ar as a possession to the descendants of Lot." ¹⁰ (The Emim—a large and numerous people, as tall as the Anakim—had formerly inhabited it. ¹¹ Like the Anakim, they are usually reckoned as Rephaim, though the Moabites call them Emim. ¹² Moreover, the Horim had formerly inhabited Seir, but the descendants of Esau dispossessed them, destroying them and settling in their place, as Israel has done in the land that the Lord gave them as a possession.) ¹³ "Now then, proceed to cross over the Wadi Zered."

ᶜ Or *Sea of Reeds*

1.34
Num 14.22-30
1.37
Num 20.12;
Deut 3.26;
Ps 106.32
1.38
Num 14.30;
Deut 3.28;
31.7
1.39
Num 14.3,
31
1.40
Num 14.25
1.41
Num 14.40
1.42
Num 14.42
1.43
Num 14.44,
45
1.44
Ps 118.12

2.1
Num 21.4
2.4
Num 20.14
2.5
Josh 24.4
2.7
Deut 8.2-4
2.8
Judg 11.18
2.9
v. 18;
Num 21.28;
Gen 19.36,
37
2.10ff
Gen 14.5;
Num 13.22,
33
2.12
v. 22

So we crossed over the Wadi Zered. ¹⁴And the length of time we had traveled from Kadesh-barnea until we crossed the Wadi Zered was thirty-eight years, until the entire generation of warriors had perished from the camp, as the LORD had sworn concerning them. ¹⁵Indeed, the LORD's own hand was against them, to root them out from the camp, until all had perished.

16 Just as soon as all the warriors had died off from among the people, ¹⁷the LORD spoke to me, saying, ¹⁸"Today you are going to cross the boundary of Moab at Ar. ¹⁹When you approach the frontier of the Ammonites, do not harass them or engage them in battle, for I will not give the land of the Ammonites to you as a possession, because I have given it to the descendants of Lot." ²⁰(It also is usually reckoned as a land of Rephaim. Rephaim formerly inhabited it, though the Ammonites call them Zamzummim, ²¹a strong and numerous people, as tall as the Anakim. But the LORD destroyed them from before the Ammonites so that they could dispossess them and settle in their place. ²²He did the same for the descendants of Esau, who live in Seir, by destroying the Horim before them so that they could dispossess them and settle in their place even to this day. ²³As for the Avvim, who had lived in settlements in the vicinity of Gaza, the Caphtorim, who came from Caphtor, destroyed them and settled in their place.) ²⁴"Proceed on your journey and cross the Wadi Arnon. See, I have handed over to you King Sihon the Amorite of Heshbon, and his land. Begin to take possession by engaging him in battle. ²⁵This day I will begin to put the dread and fear of you upon the peoples everywhere under heaven; when they hear report of you, they will tremble and be in anguish because of you."

Defeat of King Sihon

26 So I sent messengers from the wilderness of Kedemoth to King Sihon of Heshbon with the following terms of peace: ²⁷"If you let me pass through your land, I will travel only along the road; I will turn aside neither to the right nor to the left. ²⁸You shall sell me food for money, so that I may eat, and supply me water for money, so that I may drink. Only allow me to pass through on foot— ²⁹just as the descendants of Esau who live in Seir have done for me and likewise the Moabites who live in Ar— until I cross the Jordan into the land that the LORD our God is giving us." ³⁰But King Sihon of Heshbon was not willing to let us pass through, for the LORD your God had hardened his spirit and made his heart defiant in order to hand him over to you, as he has now done.

31 The LORD said to me, "See, I have begun to give Sihon and his land over to you. Begin now to take possession of his land." ³²So when Sihon came out against us, he and all his people for battle at Jahaz, ³³the LORD our God gave him over to us; and we struck him down, along with his offspring and all his people. ³⁴At that time we captured all his towns, and in each town we utterly destroyed men, women, and children. We left not a single survivor. ³⁵Only the livestock we kept as spoil for ourselves, as well as the plunder of the towns that we had captured. ³⁶From Aroer on the edge of the Wadi Arnon (including the town that is in the wadi itself) as far as Gilead, there was no citadel too high for us. The LORD our God gave everything to us. ³⁷You did not encroach, however, on the land of the Ammonites, avoiding the whole upper region of the Wadi Jabbok as well as the towns of the hill country, just as ᵈ the LORD our God had charged.

Defeat of King Og

3 When we headed up the road to Bashan, King Og of Bashan came out against us, he and all his people, for battle at Edrei. ²The

ᵈ Gk Tg: Heb and all

2.14
Num 13.26;
14.29-35;
26.64;
Deut 1.34,
35
2.15
Ps 106.26
2.19
v. 9
2.21
v. 10
2.22
Gen 36.8;
v. 12
2.23
Josh 13.3;
Gen 10.14;
Am 9.7
2.24
Judg 11.18
2.25
Ex 15.14,
15;
Deut 11.25;
Josh 2.9,10
2.26
Deut 20.10

2.27
Num 21.21,
22
2.28
Num 20.19
2.30
Num 21.23
2.31
Deut 1.8
2.32
Num 21.23,
24;
Deut 7.2;
20.16
2.34
Deut 3.6
2.36
Deut 3.12;
4.48;
Ps 44.3
2.37
Num 21.24
3.1
Num 21.33-35
3.2
Num 21.34

LORD said to me, "Do not fear him, for I have handed him over to you, along with his people and his land. Do to him as you did to King Sihon of the Amorites, who reigned in Heshbon." ³So the LORD our God also handed over to us King Og of Bashan and all his people. We struck him down until not a single survivor was left. ⁴At that time we captured all his towns; there was no citadel that we did not take from them—sixty towns, the whole region of Argob, the kingdom of Og in Bashan. ⁵All these were fortress towns with high walls, double gates, and bars, besides a great many villages. ⁶And we utterly destroyed them, as we had done to King Sihon of Heshbon, in each city utterly destroying men, women, and children. ⁷But all the livestock and the plunder of the towns we kept as spoil for ourselves.

8 So at that time we took from the two kings of the Amorites the land beyond the Jordan, from the Wadi Arnon to Mount Hermon ⁹(the Sidonians call Hermon Sirion, while the Amorites call it Senir), ¹⁰all the towns of the tableland, the whole of Gilead, and all of Bashan, as far as Salecah and Edrei, towns of Og's kingdom in Bashan. ¹¹(Now only King Og of Bashan was left of the remnant of the Rephaim. In fact his bed, an iron bed, can still be seen in Rabbah of the Ammonites. By the common cubit it is nine cubits long and four cubits wide.) ¹²As for the land that we took possession of at that time, I gave to the Reubenites and Gadites the territory north of Aroer,ᵉ that is on the edge of the Wadi Arnon, as well as half the hill country of Gilead with its towns, ¹³and I gave to the half-tribe of Manasseh the rest of Gilead and all of Bashan, Og's kingdom. (The whole region of Argob: all that portion of Bashan used to be called a land of Rephaim; ¹⁴Jair the Manassite acquired the whole region of Argob as far as the border of the Geshurites and the Maacathites, and he named them—that is, Bashan—after him-

self, Havvoth-jair,ᶠ as it is to this day.) ¹⁵To Machir I gave Gilead. ¹⁶And to the Reubenites and the Gadites I gave the territory from Gilead as far as the Wadi Arnon, with the middle of the wadi as a boundary, and up to the Jabbok, the wadi being boundary of the Ammonites; ¹⁷the Arabah also, with the Jordan and its banks, from Chinnereth down to the sea of the Arabah, the Dead Sea,ᵍ with the lower slopes of Pisgah on the east.

18 At that time, I charged you as follows: "Although the LORD your God has given you this land to occupy, all your troops shall cross over armed as the vanguard of your Israelite kin. ¹⁹Only your wives, your children, and your livestock—I know that you have much livestock—shall stay behind in the towns that I have given to you. ²⁰When the LORD gives rest to your kindred, as to you, and they too have occupied the land that the LORD your God is giving them beyond the Jordan, then each of you may return to the property that I have given to you." ²¹And I charged Joshua as well at that time, saying: "Your own eyes have seen everything that the LORD your God has done to these two kings; so the LORD will do to all the kingdoms into which you are about to cross. ²²Do not fear them, for it is the LORD your God who fights for you."

Moses Views Canaan from Pisgah

23 At that time, too, I entreated the LORD, saying: ²⁴"O Lord GOD, you have only begun to show your servant your greatness and your might; what god in heaven or on earth can perform deeds and mighty acts like yours! ²⁵Let me cross over to see the good land beyond the Jordan, that good hill country and the Lebanon." ²⁶But the LORD was angry with me on your account and would not heed me. The LORD said to me, "Enough from you! Never speak to me of this mat-

3.3 Num 21.35
3.4 1 Kings 4.13
3.6 Deut 2.24, 34
3.9 Ps 29.6
3.11 Am 2.9; Gen 14.5; 2 Sam 12.26; Jer 49.2
3.12 Deut 2.36; Num 32.32-38; Josh 13.8-13
3.14 Num 32.41; 1 Chr 2.22

3.15 Num 32.39, 40
3.17 Num 34.11; Josh 13.27
3.18 Num 32.20
3.20 Josh 22.4
3.22 Deut 1.30
3.24 Ex 15.11; Ps 86.8
3.26 Deut 1.37; 31.2

ᵉ Heb *territory from Aroer* ᶠ That is *Settlement of Jair* ᵍ Heb *Salt Sea*

ter again! 27 Go up to the top of Pisgah and look around you to the west, to the north, to the south, and to the east. Look well, for you shall not cross over this Jordan. 28 But charge Joshua, and encourage and strengthen him, because it is he who shall cross over at the head of this people and who shall secure their possession of the land that you will see." 29 So we remained in the valley opposite Beth-peor.

Moses Commands Obedience

4 So now, Israel, give heed to the statutes and ordinances that I am teaching you to observe, so that you may live to enter and occupy the land that the LORD, the God of your ancestors, is giving you. 2 You must neither add anything to what I command you nor take away anything from it, but keep the commandments of the LORD your God with which I am charging you. 3 You have seen for yourselves what the LORD did with regard to the Baal of Peor—how the LORD your God destroyed from among you everyone who followed the Baal of Peor, 4 while those of you who held fast to the LORD your God are all alive today.

5 See, just as the LORD my God has charged me, I now teach you statutes and ordinances for you to observe in the land that you are about to enter and occupy. 6 You must observe them diligently, for this will show your wisdom and discernment to the peoples, who, when they hear all these statutes, will say, "Surely this great nation is a wise and discerning people!" 7 For what other great nation has a god so near to it as the LORD our God is whenever we call to him? 8 And what other great nation has statutes and ordinances as just as this entire law that I am setting before you today?

9 But take care and watch yourselves closely, so as neither to forget the things that your eyes have seen nor to let them slip from your mind all the days of your life; make

them known to your children and your children's children— 10 how you once stood before the LORD your God at Horeb, when the LORD said to me, "Assemble the people for me, and I will let them hear my words, so that they may learn to fear me as long as they live on the earth, and may teach their children so"; 11 you approached and stood at the foot of the mountain while the mountain was blazing up to the very heavens, shrouded in dark clouds. 12 Then the LORD spoke to you out of the fire. You heard the sound of words but saw no form; there was only a voice. 13 He declared to you his covenant, which he charged you to observe, that is, the ten commandments;h and he wrote them on two stone tablets. 14 And the LORD charged me at that time to teach you statutes and ordinances for you to observe in the land that you are about to cross into and occupy.

15 Since you saw no form when the LORD spoke to you at Horeb out of the fire, take care and watch yourselves closely, 16 so that you do not act corruptly by making an idol for yourselves, in the form of any figure—the likeness of male or female, 17 the likeness of any animal that is on the earth, the likeness of any winged bird that flies in the air, 18 the likeness of anything that creeps on the ground, the likeness of any fish that is in the water under the earth. 19 And when you look up to the heavens and see the sun, the moon, and the stars, all the host of heaven, do not be led astray and bow down to them and serve them, things that the LORD your God has allotted to all the peoples everywhere under heaven. 20 But the LORD has taken you and brought you out of the iron-smelter, out of Egypt, to become a people of his very own possession, as you are now.

21 The LORD was angry with me because of you, and he vowed that I should not cross the Jordan and

h Heb the ten words

Cross-references

3.27 Num 27.12
3.28 Num 27.18, 23; Deut 31.3,7
3.29 Deut 4.46; 34.6
4.1 Deut 5.33; 8.1; 16.20; 30.16,19
4.2 Deut 12.32; Josh 1.7; Rev 22.18, 19
4.3 Num 25.4; Ps 106.28, 29
4.6 Deut 30.19, 20; 32.46,47
4.7 2 Sam 7.23; Ps 46.1; Isa 55.6
4.9 Prov 4.23; Gen 18.19; Deut 6.7; 11.19; Ps 78.5,6; Eph 6.4

4.10 Ex 19.9,16
4.11 Ex 19.18; Heb 12.18, 19
4.12 Deut 5.4,22; Ex 20.22
4.13 Deut 9.9,11; Ex 34.28; 24.12; 31.18
4.16 Ex 32.7; 20.4,5; Deut 5.8
4.19 Deut 17.3; 2 Kings 17.16; Rom 1.25
4.20 1 Kings 8.51; Jer 11.4; Deut 9.29
4.21 Deut 1.37

that I should not enter the good land that the LORD your God is giving for your possession. ²²For I am going to die in this land without crossing over the Jordan, but you are going to cross over to take possession of that good land. ²³So be careful not to forget the covenant that the LORD your God made with you, and not to make for yourselves an idol in the form of anything that the LORD your God has forbidden you. ²⁴For the LORD your God is a devouring fire, a jealous God.

25 When you have had children and children's children, and become complacent in the land, if you act corruptly by making an idol in the form of anything, thus doing what is evil in the sight of the LORD your God, and provoking him to anger, ²⁶I call heaven and earth to witness against you today that you will soon utterly perish from the land that you are crossing the Jordan to occupy; you will not live long on it, but will be utterly destroyed. ²⁷The LORD will scatter you among the peoples; only a few of you will be left among the nations where the LORD will lead you. ²⁸There you will serve other gods made by human hands, objects of wood and stone that neither see, nor hear, nor eat, nor smell. ²⁹From there you will seek the LORD your God, and you will find him if you search after him with all your heart and soul. ³⁰In your distress, when all these things have happened to you in time to come, you will return to the LORD your God and heed him. ³¹Because the LORD your God is a merciful God, he will neither abandon you nor destroy you; he will not forget the covenant with your ancestors that he swore to them.

32 For ask now about former ages, long before your own, ever since the day that God created human beings on the earth; ask from one end of heaven to the other: has anything so great as this ever happened or has its like ever been heard of? ³³Has any people ever heard the voice of a god speaking

out of a fire, as you have heard, and lived? ³⁴Or has any god ever attempted to go and take a nation for himself from the midst of another nation, by trials, by signs and wonders, by war, by a mighty hand and an outstretched arm, and by terrifying displays of power, as the LORD your God did for you in Egypt before your very eyes? ³⁵To you it was shown so that you would acknowledge that the LORD is God; there is no other besides him. ³⁶From heaven he made you hear his voice to discipline you. On earth he showed you his great fire, while you heard his words coming out of the fire. ³⁷And because he loved your ancestors, he chose their descendants after them. He brought you out of Egypt with his own presence, by his great power, ³⁸driving out before you nations greater and mightier than yourselves, to bring you in, giving you their land for a possession, as it is still today. ³⁹So acknowledge today and take to heart that the LORD is God in heaven above and on the earth beneath; there is no other. ⁴⁰Keep his statutes and his commandments, which I am commanding you today for your own well-being and that of your descendants after you, so that you may long remain in the land that the LORD your God is giving you for all time.

Cities of Refuge East of the Jordan

41 Then Moses set apart on the east side of the Jordan three cities ⁴²to which a homicide could flee, someone who unintentionally kills another person, the two not having been at enmity before; the homicide could flee to one of these cities and live: ⁴³Bezer in the wilderness on the tableland belonging to the Reubenites, Ramoth in Gilead belonging to the Gadites, and Golan in Bashan belonging to the Manassites.

Transition to the Second Address

44 This is the law that Moses set

4.22
Deut 3.25, 27
4.23
vv. 9,16;
Ex 20.4,5
4.24
Ex 24.17;
Deut 9.3;
Heb 12.29;
Deut 6.15
4.25
vv. 16,23;
2 Kings 17.17
4.26
Deut 30.18, 19
4.27
Deut 28.62, 64
4.28
Deut 28.64;
1 Sam 26.19;
Ps 115.4,5
4.29
Deut 30.1-3;
2 Chr 15.4;
Isa 55.6,7;
Jer 29.12-14
4.31
2 Chr 30.9;
Ps 116.5
4.32
Deut 32.7;
Gen 1.27;
Deut 28.64
4.33
Ex 20.22;
Deut 5.24, 26
4.34
Deut 7.19;
Ex 7.3;
13.3; 6.6;
Deut 26.8;
34.12
4.35
Deut 32.39;
1 Sam 2.2;
Isa 45.5,18;
Mk 12.29
4.36
Ex 19.9,19;
Heb 12.18
4.37
Deut 10.15;
Ex 13.3,9, 14
4.38
Deut 7.1;
9.1,4,5
4.39
v. 35;
Josh 2.11
4.40
Lev 22.31;
Deut 5.16, 29,33;
Eph 6.2,3
4.41
Num 35.6

before the Israelites. 45 These are the decrees and the statutes and ordinances that Moses spoke to the Israelites when they had come out of Egypt, 46 beyond the Jordan in the valley opposite Beth-peor, in the land of King Sihon of the Amorites, who reigned at Heshbon, whom Moses and the Israelites defeated when they came out of Egypt. 47 They occupied his land and the land of King Og of Bashan, the two kings of the Amorites on the eastern side of the Jordan: 48 from Aroer, which is on the edge of the Wadi Arnon, as far as Mount Sirion[i] (that is, Hermon), 49 together with all the Arabah on the east side of the Jordan as far as the Sea of the Arabah, under the slopes of Pisgah.

The Ten Commandments

5 Moses convened all Israel, and said to them:

Hear, O Israel, the statutes and ordinances that I am addressing to you today; you shall learn them and observe them diligently. 2 The Lord our God made a covenant with us at Horeb. 3 Not with our ancestors did the Lord make this covenant, but with us, who are all of us here alive today. 4 The Lord spoke with you face to face at the mountain, out of the fire. 5 (At that time I was standing between the Lord and you to declare to you the words[i] of the Lord; for you were afraid because of the fire and did not go up the mountain.) And he said:

6 I am the Lord your God, who brought you out of the land of Egypt, out of the house of slavery; 7 you shall have no other gods before[k] me.

8 You shall not make for yourself an idol, whether in the form of anything that is in heaven above, or that is on the earth beneath, or that is in the water under the earth. 9 You shall not bow down to them or worship them; for I the Lord your God am a jealous God, punishing children for the iniquity of parents, to the third and fourth generation of those who reject me, 10 but showing steadfast love to the thousandth generation[l] of those who love me and keep my commandments.

11 You shall not make wrongful use of the name of the Lord your God, for the Lord will not acquit anyone who misuses his name.

12 Observe the sabbath day and keep it holy, as the Lord your God commanded you. 13 Six days you shall labor and do all your work. 14 But the seventh day is a sabbath to the Lord your God; you shall not do any work—you, or your son or your daughter, or your male or female slave, or your ox or your donkey, or any of your livestock, or the resident alien in your towns, so that your male and female slave may rest as well as you. 15 Remember that you were a slave in the land of Egypt, and the Lord your God brought you out from there with a mighty hand and an outstretched arm; therefore the Lord your God commanded you to keep the sabbath day.

16 Honor your father and your mother, as the Lord your God commanded you, so that your days may be long and that it may go well with you in the land that the Lord your God is giving you.

17 You shall not murder.[m]

18 Neither shall you commit adultery.

19 Neither shall you steal.

20 Neither shall you bear false witness against your neighbor.

21 Neither shall you covet your neighbor's wife.

Neither shall you desire your neighbor's house, or field, or male or female slave, or ox, or donkey, or anything that belongs to your neighbor.

Moses the Mediator of God's Will

22 These words the Lord spoke

Cross references

4.46 Deut 3.29; Num 21.21-25
4.48 Deut 2.36; 3.12
5.2 Ex 19.5
5.4 Ex 19.9,19; Deut 4.33, 36
5.5 Ex 20.18,21
5.6 Ex 20.2-17
5.9 Ex 34.7
5.10 Jer 32.18
5.14 Gen 2.2; Ex 16.29,30
5.15 Deut 15.16; 4.34,37
5.21 Rom 7.7; 13.9
5.22 Ex 31.18; Deut 4.13

with a loud voice to your whole assembly at the mountain, out of the fire, the cloud, and the thick darkness, and he added no more. He wrote them on two stone tablets, and gave them to me. 23 When you heard the voice out of the darkness, while the mountain was burning with fire, you approached me, all the heads of your tribes and your elders; 24 and you said, "Look, the LORD our God has shown us his glory and greatness, and we have heard his voice out of the fire. Today we have seen that God may speak to someone and the person may still live. 25 So now why should we die? For this great fire will consume us; if we hear the voice of the LORD our God any longer, we shall die. 26 For who is there of all flesh that has heard the voice of the living God speaking out of fire, as we have, and remained alive? 27 Go near, you yourself, and hear all that the LORD our God will say. Then tell us everything that the LORD our God tells you, and we will listen and do it."

28 The LORD heard your words when you spoke to me, and the LORD said to me: "I have heard the words of this people, which they have spoken to you; they are right in all that they have spoken. 29 If only they had such a mind as this, to fear me and to keep all my commandments always, so that it might go well with them and with their children forever! 30 Go say to them, 'Return to your tents.' 31 But you, stand here by me, and I will tell you all the commandments, the statutes and the ordinances, that you shall teach them, so that they may do them in the land that I am giving them to possess." 32 You must therefore be careful to do as the LORD your God has commanded you; you shall not turn to the right or to the left. 33 You must follow exactly the path that the LORD your God has commanded you, so that you may live, and that it may go well with you, and that you may live long in the land that you are to possess.

5.24
Ex 19.19
5.25
Deut 18.16
5.26
Deut 4.33
5.28
Deut 18.17
5.29
Ps 81.13;
Isa 48.18;
Deut 4.40
5.31
Ex 24.12
5.32
Deut 17.20;
28.14;
Josh 1.7;
23.6
5.33
Deut 4.40

6.2
Ex 20.20;
Deut 10.12,
13
6.3
Deut 5.33;
Gen 15.5;
Ex 3.8
6.4ff
Mk 12.29,
32; Jn 17.3;
1 Cor 8.4,
6
6.5
Deut 10.12;
Mt 22.37;
Lk 10.27
6.7
Deut 4.9;
Eph 6.4
6.8
Ex 13.9,16;
Deut 11.18
6.9
Deut 11.20
6.10
Deut 9.1;
Josh 24.13
6.11
Deut 8.10
6.13
Deut 10.20

The Great Commandment

6 Now this is the commandment—the statutes and the ordinances—that the LORD your God charged me to teach you to observe in the land that you are about to cross into and occupy, 2 so that you and your children and your children's children, may fear the LORD your God all the days of your life, and keep all his decrees and his commandments that I am commanding you, so that your days may be long. 3 Hear therefore, O Israel, and observe them diligently, so that it may go well with you, and so that you may multiply greatly in a land flowing with milk and honey, as the LORD, the God of your ancestors, has promised you.

4 Hear, O Israel: The LORD is our God, the LORD alone.[n] 5 You shall love the LORD your God with all your heart, and with all your soul, and with all your might. 6 Keep these words that I am commanding you today in your heart. 7 Recite them to your children and talk about them when you are at home and when you are away, when you lie down and when you rise. 8 Bind them as a sign on your hand, fix them as an emblem[o] on your forehead, 9 and write them on the doorposts of your house and on your gates.

Caution against Disobedience

10 When the LORD your God has brought you into the land that he swore to your ancestors, to Abraham, to Isaac, and to Jacob, to give you—a land with fine, large cities that you did not build, 11 houses filled with all sorts of goods that you did not fill, hewn cisterns that you did not hew, vineyards and olive groves that you did not plant—and when you have eaten your fill, 12 take care that you do not forget the LORD, who brought you out of the land of Egypt, out of the house of slavery. 13 The LORD your God you shall fear; him you shall serve, and

[n] Or *The LORD our God is one LORD,* or *The LORD our God, the LORD is one,* or *The LORD is our God, the LORD is one* [o] Or *as a frontlet*

by his name alone you shall swear. ¹⁴Do not follow other gods, any of the gods of the peoples who are all around you, ¹⁵because the Lord your God, who is present with you, is a jealous God. The anger of the Lord your God would be kindled against you and he would destroy you from the face of the earth.

16 Do not put the Lord your God to the test, as you tested him at Massah. ¹⁷You must diligently keep the commandments of the Lord your God, and his decrees, and his statutes that he has commanded you. ¹⁸Do what is right and good in the sight of the Lord, so that it may go well with you, and so that you may go in and occupy the good land that the Lord swore to your ancestors to give you, ¹⁹thrusting out all your enemies from before you, as the Lord has promised.

20 When your children ask you in time to come, "What is the meaning of the decrees and the statutes and the ordinances that the Lord our God has commanded you?" ²¹then you shall say to your children, "We were Pharaoh's slaves in Egypt, but the Lord brought us out of Egypt with a mighty hand. ²²The Lord displayed before our eyes great and awesome signs and wonders against Egypt, against Pharaoh and all his household. ²³He brought us out from there in order to bring us in, to give us the land that he promised on oath to our ancestors. ²⁴Then the Lord commanded us to observe all these statutes, to fear the Lord our God, for our lasting good, so as to keep us alive, as is now the case. ²⁵If we diligently observe this entire commandment before the Lord our God, as he has commanded us, we will be in the right."

A Chosen People

7 When the Lord your God brings you into the land that you are about to enter and occupy, and he clears away many nations before you—the Hittites, the Girgashites, the Amorites, the Ca-

naanites, the Perizzites, the Hivites, and the Jebusites, seven nations mightier and more numerous than you— ²and when the Lord your God gives them over to you and you defeat them, then you must utterly destroy them. Make no covenant with them and show them no mercy. ³Do not intermarry with them, giving your daughters to their sons or taking their daughters for your sons, ⁴for that would turn away your children from following me, to serve other gods. Then the anger of the Lord would be kindled against you, and he would destroy you quickly. ⁵But this is how you must deal with them: break down their altars, smash their pillars, hew down their sacred poles,ᴾ and burn their idols with fire. ⁶For you are a people holy to the Lord your God; the Lord your God has chosen you out of all the peoples on earth to be his people, his treasured possession.

7 It was not because you were more numerous than any other people that the Lord set his heart on you and chose you—for you were the fewest of all peoples. ⁸It was because the Lord loved you and kept the oath that he swore to your ancestors, that the Lord has brought you out with a mighty hand, and redeemed you from the house of slavery, from the hand of Pharaoh king of Egypt. ⁹Know therefore that the Lord your God is God, the faithful God who maintains covenant loyalty with those who love him and keep his commandments, to a thousand generations, ¹⁰and who repays in their own person those who reject him. He does not delay but repays in their own person those who reject him. ¹¹Therefore, observe diligently the commandment—the statutes, and the ordinances—that I am commanding you today.

Blessings for Obedience

12 If you heed these ordinances, by diligently observing them, the Lord your God will maintain with

6.15 Deut 4.24
6.16 Mt 4.7;
Ex 17.2,7
6.17 Deut 11.22
6.18 Deut 4.40
6.20 Ex 13.14
6.24 Deut 10.12
6.25 Deut 24.13
7.1 Deut 31.3;
Acts 13.19

7.2 Ex 23.32;
Deut 13.8
7.3 Ex 34.15,16
7.4 Deut 6.15
7.5 Ex 23.24
7.6 Ex 19.5,6;
Deut 14.2
7.7 Deut 10.22
7.8 Deut 10.15;
Ex 32.13;
13.3,14
7.9 Deut 4.35,
39; Neh 1.5
7.12 Lev 26.3;
Deut 28.1;
Ps 105.8,9

ᴾ Heb Asherim

you the covenant loyalty that he swore to your ancestors; [13]he will love you, bless you, and multiply you; he will bless the fruit of your womb and the fruit of your ground, your grain and your wine and your oil, the increase of your cattle and the issue of your flock, in the land that he swore to your ancestors to give you. [14]You shall be the most blessed of peoples, with neither sterility nor barrenness among you or your livestock. [15]The LORD will turn away from you every illness; all the dread diseases of Egypt that you experienced, he will not inflict on you, but he will lay them on all who hate you. [16]You shall devour all the peoples that the LORD your God is giving over to you, showing them no pity; you shall not serve their gods, for that would be a snare to you.

17 If you say to yourself, "These nations are more numerous than I; how can I dispossess them?" [18]do not be afraid of them. Just remember what the LORD your God did to Pharaoh and to all Egypt, [19]the great trials that your eyes saw, the signs and wonders, the mighty hand and the outstretched arm by which the LORD your God brought you out. The LORD your God will do the same to all the peoples of whom you are afraid. [20]Moreover, the LORD your God will send the pestilence[q] against them, until even the survivors and the fugitives are destroyed. [21]Have no dread of them, for the LORD your God, who is present with you, is a great and awesome God. [22]The LORD your God will clear away these nations before you little by little; you will not be able to make a quick end of them, otherwise the wild animals would become too numerous for you. [23]But the LORD your God will give them over to you, and throw them into great panic, until they are destroyed. [24]He will hand their kings over to you and you shall blot out their name from under heaven; no one will be able to stand against you, until you have destroyed them. [25]The images of their gods

you shall burn with fire. Do not covet the silver or the gold that is on them and take it for yourself, because you could be ensnared by it; for it is abhorrent to the LORD your God. [26]Do not bring an abhorrent thing into your house, or you will be set apart for destruction like it. You must utterly detest and abhor it, for it is set apart for destruction.

A Warning Not to Forget God in Prosperity

8 This entire commandment that I command you today you must diligently observe, so that you may live and increase, and go in and occupy the land that the LORD promised on oath to your ancestors. [2]Remember the long way that the LORD your God has led you these forty years in the wilderness, in order to humble you, testing you to know what was in your heart, whether or not you would keep his commandments. [3]He humbled you by letting you hunger, then by feeding you with manna, with which neither you nor your ancestors were acquainted, in order to make you understand that one does not live by bread alone, but by every word that comes from the mouth of the LORD.[r] [4]The clothes on your back did not wear out and your feet did not swell these forty years. [5]Know then in your heart that as a parent disciplines a child so the LORD your God disciplines you. [6]Therefore keep the commandments of the LORD your God, by walking in his ways and by fearing him. [7]For the LORD your God is bringing you into a good land, a land with flowing streams, with springs and underground waters welling up in valleys and hills, [8]a land of wheat and barley, of vines and fig trees and pomegranates, a land of olive trees and honey, [9]a land where you may eat bread without scarcity, where you will lack nothing, a land whose stones are iron and from whose hills you may

7.13
Deut 28.4
7.14
Ex 23.26
7.15
Ex 15.26
7.16
v. 2;
Ex 23.33
7.18
Deut 31.6
7.19
Deut 4.34
7.20
Ex 23.28;
Josh 24.12
7.21
Deut 10.17
7.22
Ex 23.29,30
7.24
v. 16
7.25
1 Chr 14.12;
Josh 7.1,21;
Judg 8.27

8.1
Deut 4.1
8.2
Deut 29.5;
13.3
8.3
Ex 16.2,3,
12,14,35;
Mt 4.4;
Lk 4.7
8.4
Deut 29.5
8.5
Prov 3.12;
Heb 12.5,6
8.6
Deut 5.33
8.7
Deut 11.10-12

[q]Or *hornets*: Meaning of Heb uncertain
[r]Or *by anything that the LORD decrees*

mine copper. 10You shall eat your fill and bless the Lord your God for the good land that he has given you.

11 Take care that you do not forget the Lord your God, by failing to keep his commandments, his ordinances, and his statutes, which I am commanding you today. 12When you have eaten your fill and have built fine houses and live in them, 13and when your herds and flocks have multiplied, and your silver and gold is multiplied, and all that you have is multiplied, 14then do not exalt yourself, forgetting the Lord your God, who brought you out of the land of Egypt, out of the house of slavery, 15who led you through the great and terrible wilderness, an arid wasteland with poisonouss snakes and scorpions. He made water flow for you from flint rock, 16and fed you in the wilderness with manna that your ancestors did not know, to humble you and to test you, and in the end to do you good. 17Do not say to yourself, "My power and the might of my own hand have gotten me this wealth." 18But remember the Lord your God, for it is he who gives you power to get wealth, so that he may confirm his covenant that he swore to your ancestors, as he is doing today. 19If you do forget the Lord your God and follow other gods to serve and worship them, I solemnly warn you today that you shall surely perish. 20Like the nations that the Lord is destroying before you, so shall you perish, because you would not obey the voice of the Lord your God.

The Consequences of Rebelling against God

9 Hear, O Israel! You are about to cross the Jordan today, to go in and dispossess nations larger and mightier than you, great cities, fortified to the heavens, 2a strong and tall people, the offspring of the Anakim, whom you know. You have heard it said of them, "Who can stand up to the Anakim?" 3Know then today that the Lord

your God is the one who crosses over before you as a devouring fire; he will defeat them and subdue them before you, so that you may dispossess and destroy them quickly, as the Lord has promised you.

4 When the Lord your God thrusts them out before you, do not say to yourself, "It is because of my righteousness that the Lord has brought me in to occupy this land"; it is rather because of the wickedness of these nations that the Lord is dispossessing them before you. 5It is not because of your righteousness or the uprightness of your heart that you are going in to occupy their land; but because of the wickedness of these nations the Lord your God is dispossessing them before you, in order to fulfill the promise that the Lord made on oath to your ancestors, to Abraham, to Isaac, and to Jacob.

6 Know, then, that the Lord your God is not giving you this good land to occupy because of your righteousness; for you are a stubborn people. 7Remember and do not forget how you provoked the Lord your God to wrath in the wilderness; you have been rebellious against the Lord from the day you came out of the land of Egypt until you came to this place.

8 Even at Horeb you provoked the Lord to wrath, and the Lord was so angry with you that he was ready to destroy you. 9When I went up the mountain to receive the stone tablets, the tablets of the covenant that the Lord made with you, I remained on the mountain forty days and forty nights; I neither ate bread nor drank water. 10And the Lord gave me the two stone tablets written with the finger of God; on them were all the words that the Lord had spoken to you at the mountain out of the fire on the day of the assembly. 11At the end of forty days and forty nights the Lord gave me the two stone tablets, the tablets of the covenant. 12Then the Lord said

8.10
Deut 6.11, 12
8.14
Ps 106.21
8.15
Num 21.6; 20.11;
Ps 78.15; 114.8
8.16
vv. 2,3;
Ex 16.15
8.18
Prov 10.22;
Hos 2.8
8.19
Deut 4.26; 30.18
9.1
Deut 11.31
9.2
Num 13.22, 28,32,33
9.3
Deut 31.3; 4.24; 7.23,24

9.4
Deut 8.17; 18.12;
Lev 18.24, 25
9.5
Gen 12.7
9.6
v. 13;
Ex 32.9;
Deut 31.27
9.8
Ex 32.7-10
9.9
Ex 24.12, 15,18
9.10
Ex 31.18;
Deut 4.13
9.12
Ex 32.7,8;
Deut 31.29

s Or *fiery*; Heb *seraph*

to me, "Get up, go down quickly from here, for your people whom you have brought from Egypt have acted corruptly. They have been quick to turn from the way that I commanded them; they have cast an image for themselves." [13] Furthermore the LORD said to me, "I have seen that this people is indeed a stubborn people. [14] Let me alone that I may destroy them and blot out their name from under heaven; and I will make of you a nation mightier and more numerous than they."

15 So I turned and went down from the mountain, while the mountain was ablaze; the two tablets of the covenant were in my two hands. [16] Then I saw that you had indeed sinned against the LORD your God, by casting for yourselves an image of a calf; you had been quick to turn from the way that the LORD had commanded you. [17] So I took hold of the two tablets and flung them from my two hands, smashing them before your eyes. [18] Then I lay prostrate before the LORD as before, forty days and forty nights; I neither ate bread nor drank water, because of all the sin you had committed, provoking the LORD by doing what was evil in his sight. [19] For I was afraid that the anger that the LORD bore against you was so fierce that he would destroy you. But the LORD listened to me that time also. [20] The LORD was so angry with Aaron that he was ready to destroy him, but I interceded also on behalf of Aaron at that same time. [21] Then I took the sinful thing you had made, the calf, and burned it with fire and crushed it, grinding it thoroughly, until it was reduced to dust; and I threw the dust of it into the stream that runs down the mountain.

22 At Taberah also, and at Massah, and at Kibroth-hattaavah, you provoked the LORD to wrath. [23] And when the LORD sent you from Kadesh-barnea, saying, "Go up and occupy the land that I have given you," you rebelled against the command of the LORD your God, neither

trusting him nor obeying him. [24] You have been rebellious against the LORD as long as he has[t] known you.

25 Throughout the forty days and forty nights that I lay prostrate before the LORD when the LORD intended to destroy you, [26] I prayed to the LORD and said, "Lord GOD, do not destroy the people who are your very own possession, whom you redeemed in your greatness, whom you brought out of Egypt with a mighty hand. [27] Remember your servants, Abraham, Isaac, and Jacob; pay no attention to the stubbornness of this people, their wickedness and their sin, [28] otherwise the land from which you have brought us might say, 'Because the LORD was not able to bring them into the land that he promised them, and because he hated them, he has brought them out to let them die in the wilderness.' [29] For they are the people of your very own possession, whom you brought out by your great power and by your outstretched arm."

The Second Pair of Tablets

10 At that time the LORD said to me, "Carve out two tablets of stone like the former ones, and come up to me on the mountain, and make an ark of wood. [2] I will write on the tablets the words that were on the former tablets, which you smashed, and you shall put them in the ark." [3] So I made an ark of acacia wood, cut two tablets of stone like the former ones, and went up the mountain with the two tablets in my hand. [4] Then he wrote on the tablets the same words as before, the ten commandments[u] that the LORD had spoken to you on the mountain out of the fire on the day of the assembly; and the LORD gave them to me. [5] So I turned and came down from the mountain, and put the tablets in the ark that I had made; and there they are, as the LORD commanded me.

6 (The Israelites journeyed from

9.13
Ex 32.9;
v. 6
9.14
Ex 32.10;
Deut 29.20;
Num 14.12
9.15
Ex 32.15-19;
19.18
9.16
Ex 32.19
9.18
Ex 34.28
9.19
Ex 32.10-14
9.21
Ex 32.20
9.22
Num 11.3,
34; Ex 17.7

9.24
v. 7;
Deut 31.27
9.25
v. 18
9.26
Ex 32.11-13
9.29
Deut 4.20,
34
10.1
Ex 34.1,2;
25.10
10.2
Deut 4.13;
Ex 25.16,21
10.3
Ex 37.1;
34.4
10.4
Ex 20.1
10.5
Ex 40.20
10.6
Num 33.30,
31,38

[t] Sam Gk: MT *I have*　　[u] Heb *the ten words*

Beeroth Bene-jaakan[v] to Moserah. There Aaron died, and there he was buried; his son Eleazar succeeded him as priest. [7]From there they journeyed to Gudgodah, and from Gudgodah to Jotbathah, a land with flowing streams. [8]At that time the Lord set apart the tribe of Levi to carry the ark of the covenant of the Lord, to stand before the Lord to minister to him, and to bless in his name, to this day. [9]Therefore Levi has no allotment or inheritance with his kindred; the Lord is his inheritance, as the Lord your God promised him.)

10 I stayed on the mountain forty days and forty nights, as I had done the first time. And once again the Lord listened to me. The Lord was unwilling to destroy you. [11]The Lord said to me, "Get up, go on your journey at the head of the people, that they may go in and occupy the land that I swore to their ancestors to give them."

The Essence of the Law

12 So now, O Israel, what does the Lord your God require of you? Only to fear the Lord your God, to walk in all his ways, to love him, to serve the Lord your God with all your heart and with all your soul, [13]and to keep the commandments of the Lord your God[w] and his decrees that I am commanding you today, for your own well-being. [14]Although heaven and the heaven of heavens belong to the Lord your God, the earth with all that is in it, [15]yet the Lord set his heart in love on your ancestors alone and chose you, their descendants after them, out of all the peoples, as it is today. [16]Circumcise, then, the foreskin of your heart, and do not be stubborn any longer. [17]For the Lord your God is God of gods and Lord of lords, the great God, mighty and awesome, who is not partial and takes no bribe, [18]who executes justice for the orphan and the widow, and who loves the strangers, providing them food and clothing. [19]You shall also love the stranger, for you were strangers in the land

of Egypt. [20]You shall fear the Lord your God; him alone you shall worship; to him you shall hold fast, and by his name you shall swear. [21]He is your praise; he is your God, who has done for you these great and awesome things that your own eyes have seen. [22]Your ancestors went down to Egypt seventy persons; and now the Lord your God has made you as numerous as the stars in heaven.

Rewards for Obedience

11 You shall love the Lord your God, therefore, and keep his charge, his decrees, his ordinances, and his commandments always. [2]Remember today that it was not your children (who have not known or seen the discipline of the Lord your God), but it is you who must acknowledge his greatness, his mighty hand and his outstretched arm, [3]his signs and his deeds that he did in Egypt to Pharaoh, the king of Egypt, and to all his land; [4]what he did to the Egyptian army, to their horses and chariots, how he made the water of the Red Sea[x] flow over them as they pursued you, so that the Lord has destroyed them to this day; [5]what he did to you in the wilderness, until you came to this place; [6]and what he did to Dathan and Abiram, sons of Eliab son of Reuben, how in the midst of all Israel the earth opened its mouth and swallowed them up, along with their households, their tents, and every living being in their company; [7]for it is your own eyes that have seen every great deed that the Lord did.

8 Keep, then, this entire commandment that I am commanding you today, so that you may have strength to go in and occupy the land that you are crossing over to occupy, [9]and so that you may live long in the land that the Lord swore to your ancestors to give them and to their descendants, a land flowing with milk and honey.

10.7
Num 33.32-34
10.8
Num 3.6;
4.15;
Deut 18.5;
21.5
10.9
Num 18.20,
24
10.10
Deut 9.18,
25;
Ex 33.17
10.12
Mic 6.8;
Deut 6.13;
5.33; 6.5
10.14
1 Kings 8.27;
Ex 19.5
10.15
Deut 4.37
10.16
Jer 4.4;
Deut 9.6
10.17
Josh 22.22;
Rev 19.16;
Acts 10.34
10.18
Ps 68.5
10.19
Lev 19.34

10.20
Mt 4.10;
Deut 11.22;
Ps 63.11
10.21
Ex 15.2;
Ps 106.21,
22
10.22
Gen 46.27;
Deut 1.10
11.1
Deut 10.12;
Zech 3.7
11.2
Deut 8.5;
5.24
11.4
Ex 14.27,28
11.6
Num 16.31-33
11.8
Josh 1.6,7
11.9
Deut 4.40;
9.5; Ex 3.8

[v]Or the wells of the Bene-jaakan [w]Q Ms Gk Syr: MT lacks your God [x]Or Sea of Reeds

10 For the land that you are about to enter to occupy is not like the land of Egypt, from which you have come, where you sow your seed and irrigate by foot like a vegetable garden. 11 But the land that you are crossing over to occupy is a land of hills and valleys, watered by rain from the sky, 12 a land that the LORD your God looks after. The eyes of the LORD your God are always on it, from the beginning of the year to the end of the year.

13 If you will only heed his every commandment[y] that I am commanding you today—loving the LORD your God, and serving him with all your heart and with all your soul— 14 then he[z] will give the rain for your land in its season, the early rain and the later rain, and you will gather in your grain, your wine, and your oil; 15 and he[z] will give grass in your fields for your livestock, and you will eat your fill. 16 Take care, or you will be seduced into turning away, serving other gods and worshiping them, 17 for then the anger of the LORD will be kindled against you and he will shut up the heavens, so that there will be no rain and the land will yield no fruit; then you will perish quickly off the good land that the LORD is giving you.

18 You shall put these words of mine in your heart and soul, and you shall bind them as a sign on your hand, and fix them as an emblem[a] on your forehead. 19 Teach them to your children, talking about them when you are at home and when you are away, when you lie down and when you rise. 20 Write them on the doorposts of your house and on your gates, 21 so that your days and the days of your children may be multiplied in the land that the LORD swore to your ancestors to give them, as long as the heavens are above the earth.

22 If you will diligently observe this entire commandment that I am commanding you, loving the LORD your God, walking in all his ways, and holding fast to him, 23 then the LORD will drive out all these nations before you, and you will dispossess nations larger and mightier than yourselves. 24 Every place on which you set foot shall be yours; your territory shall extend from the wilderness to the Lebanon and from the River, the river Euphrates, to the Western Sea. 25 No one will be able to stand against you; the LORD your God will put the fear and dread of you on all the land on which you set foot, as he promised you.

26 See, I am setting before you today a blessing and a curse: 27 the blessing, if you obey the commandments of the LORD your God that I am commanding you today; 28 and the curse, if you do not obey the commandments of the LORD your God, but turn from the way that I am commanding you today, to follow other gods that you have not known.

29 When the LORD your God has brought you into the land that you are entering to occupy, you shall set the blessing on Mount Gerizim and the curse on Mount Ebal. 30 As you know, they are beyond the Jordan, some distance to the west, in the land of the Canaanites who live in the Arabah, opposite Gilgal, beside the oak[b] of Moreh.

31 When you cross the Jordan to go in to occupy the land that the LORD your God is giving you, and when you occupy it and live in it, 32 you must diligently observe all the statutes and ordinances that I am setting before you today.

Pagan Shrines to Be Destroyed

12 These are the statutes and ordinances that you must diligently observe in the land that the LORD, the God of your ancestors, has given you to occupy all the days that you live on the earth.

2 You must demolish completely all the places where the nations whom you are about to dispossess served their gods, on the mountain

11.11
Deut 8.7
11.13
v. 22;
Deut 6.17;
10.12
11.14
Deut 28.12;
Joel 2.23
11.15
Deut 6.11
11.16
Deut 29.18;
8.19
11.17
Deut 6.15;
1 Kings 8.35;
Deut 4.26
11.18
Deut 6.6,8
11.19
Deut 4.9,10;
6.7
11.20
Deut 6.9
11.22
Deut 6.17;
10.20
11.23
Deut 9.1,5

11.24
Josh 1.3;
Gen 15.18;
Ex 23.31
11.25
Deut 7.24;
Ex 23.27
11.26
Deut 30.1,
19
11.27
Deut 28.2
11.28
Deut 28.15
11.29
Deut 27.12;
Josh 8.33
11.30
Josh 4.19;
Gen 12.6
11.31
Deut 9.1;
Josh 1.11
12.1
Deut 4.9,10

y Compare Gk: Heb *my commandments*
z Sam Gk Vg: MT *I* a Or *as a frontlet*
b Gk Syr: Compare Gen 12.6; Heb *oaks* or *terebinths*

heights, on the hills, and under every leafy tree. ³ Break down their altars, smash their pillars, burn their sacred poles^c with fire, and hew down the idols of their gods, and thus blot out their name from their places. ⁴ You shall not worship the Lord your God in such ways. ⁵ But you shall seek the place that the Lord your God will choose out of all your tribes as his habitation to put his name there. You shall go there, ⁶ bringing there your burnt offerings and your sacrifices, your tithes and your donations, your votive gifts, your freewill offerings, and the firstlings of your herds and flocks. ⁷ And you shall eat there in the presence of the Lord your God, you and your households together, rejoicing in all the undertakings in which the Lord your God has blessed you.

8 You shall not act as we are acting here today, all of us according to our own desires, ⁹ for you have not yet come into the rest and the possession that the Lord your God is giving you. ¹⁰ When you cross over the Jordan and live in the land that the Lord your God is allotting to you, and when he gives you rest from your enemies all around so that you live in safety, ¹¹ then you shall bring everything that I command you to the place that the Lord your God will choose as a dwelling for his name: your burnt offerings and your sacrifices, your tithes and your donations, and all your choice votive gifts that you vow to the Lord. ¹² And you shall rejoice before the Lord your God, you together with your sons and your daughters, your male and female slaves, and the Levites who reside in your towns (since they have no allotment or inheritance with you).

A Prescribed Place of Worship

13 Take care that you do not offer your burnt offerings at any place you happen to see. ¹⁴ But only at the place that the Lord will choose in one of your tribes—there you shall offer your burnt offerings and

there you shall do everything I command you.

15 Yet whenever you desire you may slaughter and eat meat within any of your towns, according to the blessing that the Lord your God has given you; the unclean and the clean may eat of it, as they would of gazelle or deer. ¹⁶ The blood, however, you must not eat; you shall pour it out on the ground like water. ¹⁷ Nor may you eat within your towns the tithe of your grain, your wine, and your oil, the firstlings of your herds and your flocks, any of your votive gifts that you vow, your freewill offerings, or your donations; ¹⁸ these you shall eat in the presence of the Lord your God at the place that the Lord your God will choose, you together with your son and your daughter, your male and female slaves, and the Levites resident in your towns, rejoicing in the presence of the Lord your God in all your undertakings. ¹⁹ Take care that you do not neglect the Levite as long as you live in your land.

20 When the Lord your God enlarges your territory, as he has promised you, and you say, "I am going to eat some meat," because you wish to eat meat, you may eat meat whenever you have the desire. ²¹ If the place where the Lord your God will choose to put his name is too far from you, and you slaughter as I have commanded you any of your herd or flock that the Lord has given you, then you may eat within your towns whenever you desire. ²² Indeed, just as gazelle or deer is eaten, so you may eat it; the unclean and the clean alike may eat it. ²³ Only be sure that you do not eat the blood; for the blood is the life, and you shall not eat the life with the meat. ²⁴ Do not eat it; you shall pour it out on the ground like water. ²⁵ Do not eat it, so that all may go well with you and your children after you, because you do what is right in the sight of the Lord. ²⁶ But the sacred donations that are due from you, and

Cross references (center column)

12.3 Deut 7.5
12.5 v. 11
12.7 Deut 14.26; vv. 12,18
12.10 Deut 11.31
12.11 v. 5
12.12 v. 7; Deut 10.9
12.14 v. 11

12.15 vv. 20-23; Deut 14.5
12.16 Lev 17.10-12
12.18 vv. 5,7,12
12.19 Deut 14.27
12.20 Gen 15.18
12.22 v. 15
12.23 v. 16; Lev 17.11, 14
12.25 Deut 4.40; 13.18
12.26 v. 17

^c Heb *Asherim*

your votive gifts, you shall bring to the place that the LORD will choose. [27] You shall present your burnt offerings, both the meat and the blood, on the altar of the LORD your God; the blood of your other sacrifices shall be poured out beside[d] the altar of the LORD your God, but the meat you may eat.

28 Be careful to obey all these words that I command you today,[e] so that it may go well with you and with your children after you forever, because you will be doing what is good and right in the sight of the LORD your God.

Warning against Idolatry

29 When the LORD your God has cut off before you the nations whom you are about to enter to dispossess them, when you have dispossessed them and live in their land, [30] take care that you are not snared into imitating them, after they have been destroyed before you: do not inquire concerning their gods, saying, "How did these nations worship their gods? I also want to do the same." [31] You must not do the same for the LORD your God, because every abhorrent thing that the LORD hates they have done for their gods. They would even burn their sons and their daughters in the fire to their gods. [32][f] You must diligently observe everything that I command you; do not add to it or take anything from it.

13 [g] If prophets or those who divine by dreams appear among you and promise you omens or portents, [2] and the omens or the portents declared by them take place, and they say, "Let us follow other gods" (whom you have not known) "and let us serve them," [3] you must not heed the words of those prophets or those who divine by dreams; for the LORD your God is testing you, to know whether you indeed love the LORD your God with all your heart and soul. [4] The LORD your God you shall follow, him alone you shall fear, his command-

ments you shall keep, his voice you shall obey, him you shall serve, and to him you shall hold fast. [5] But those prophets or those who divine by dreams shall be put to death for having spoken treason against the LORD your God—who brought you out of the land of Egypt and redeemed you from the house of slavery—to turn you from the way in which the LORD your God commanded you to walk. So you shall purge the evil from your midst.

6 If anyone secretly entices you—even if it is your brother, your father's son or[h] your mother's son, or your own son or daughter, or the wife you embrace, or your most intimate friend—saying, "Let us go worship other gods," whom neither you nor your ancestors have known, [7] any of the gods of the peoples that are around you, whether near you or far away from you, from one end of the earth to the other, [8] you must not yield to or heed any such persons. Show them no pity or compassion and do not shield them. [9] But you shall surely kill them; your own hand shall be first against them to execute them, and afterwards the hand of all the people. [10] Stone them to death for trying to turn you away from the LORD your God, who brought you out of the land of Egypt, out of the house of slavery. [11] Then all Israel shall hear and be afraid, and never again do any such wickedness.

12 If you hear it said about one of the towns that the LORD your God is giving you to live in, [13] that scoundrels from among you have gone out and led the inhabitants of the town astray, saying, "Let us go and worship other gods," whom you have not known, [14] then you shall inquire and make a thorough investigation. If the charge is established that such an abhorrent thing has been done among you, [15] you shall put the inhabitants of that town to the sword, utterly de-

12.28
v. 25;
Deut 4.40
12.31
Deut 9.5;
18.10
12.32
Deut 4.2
13.1
Mt 24.24;
Mk 13.22
13.2
vv. 6,13
13.3
Deut 8.2,16
13.4
2 Kings 23.3;
Deut 10.20

13.5
Deut 18.20;
17.7
13.6
Deut 17.2-7;
29.18
13.9
Deut 17.5,7
13.11
Deut 19.20
13.13
vv. 2,6; see
1 Jn 2.19
13.15
Ex 22.20

d Or on e Gk Sam Syr: MT lacks *today*
f Ch 13.1 in Heb g Ch 13.2 in Heb
h Sam Gk Compare Tg: MT lacks *your father's son or*

stroying it and everything in it—even putting its livestock to the sword. 16All of its spoil you shall gather into its public square; then burn the town and all its spoil with fire, as a whole burnt offering to the LORD your God. It shall remain a perpetual ruin, never to be rebuilt. 17Do not let anything devoted to destruction stick to your hand, so that the LORD may turn from his fierce anger and show you compassion, and in his compassion multiply you, as he swore to your ancestors, 18if you obey the voice of the LORD your God by keeping all his commandments that I am commanding you today, doing what is right in the sight of the LORD your God.

Pagan Practices Forbidden

14 You are children of the LORD your God. You must not lacerate yourselves or shave your forelocks for the dead. 2For you are a people holy to the LORD your God; it is you the LORD has chosen out of all the peoples on earth to be his people, his treasured possession.

Clean and Unclean Foods

3 You shall not eat any abhorrent thing. 4These are the animals you may eat: the ox, the sheep, the goat, 5the deer, the gazelle, the roebuck, the wild goat, the ibex, the antelope, and the mountain-sheep. 6Any animal that divides the hoof and has the hoof cleft in two, and chews the cud, among the animals, you may eat. 7Yet of those that chew the cud or have the hoof cleft you shall not eat these: the camel, the hare, and the rock badger, because they chew the cud but do not divide the hoof; they are unclean for you. 8And the pig, because it divides the hoof but does not chew the cud, is unclean for you. You shall not eat their meat, and you shall not touch their carcasses.

9 Of all that live in water you may eat these: whatever has fins and scales you may eat. 10And whatever does not have fins and

scales you shall not eat; it is unclean for you.

11 You may eat any clean birds. 12But these are the ones that you shall not eat: the eagle, the vulture, the osprey, 13the buzzard, the kite, of any kind; 14every raven of any kind; 15the ostrich, the nighthawk, the sea gull, the hawk, of any kind; 16the little owl and the great owl, the water hen 17and the desert owl,i the carrion vulture and the cormorant, 18the stork, the heron, of any kind; the hoopoe and the bat.j 19And all winged insects are unclean for you; they shall not be eaten. 20You may eat any clean winged creature.

21 You shall not eat anything that dies of itself; you may give it to aliens residing in your towns for them to eat, or you may sell it to a foreigner. For you are a people holy to the LORD your God.

You shall not boil a kid in its mother's milk.

Regulations concerning Tithes

22 Set apart a tithe of all the yield of your seed that is brought in yearly from the field. 23In the presence of the LORD your God, in the place that he will choose as a dwelling for his name, you shall eat the tithe of your grain, your wine, and your oil, as well as the firstlings of your herd and flock, so that you may learn to fear the LORD your God always. 24But if, when the LORD your God has blessed you, the distance is so great that you are unable to transport it, because the place where the LORD your God will choose to set his name is too far away from you, 25then you may turn it into money. With the money secure in hand, go to the place that the LORD your God will choose; 26spend the money for whatever you wish—oxen, sheep, wine, strong drink, or whatever you desire. And you shall eat there in the presence of the LORD your God, you and your household rejoicing together. 27As for the Levites resi-

Cross references

13.16 Josh 6.24; 8.28
13.17 Num 25.4; Deut 30.3; 7.13
13.18 Deut 12.28
14.1 Rom 8;16; Lev 21.5
14.2 Deut 7.6
14.4 Lev 11.2-45; Acts 10.14
14.8 Lev 11.26, 27
14.9 Lev 11.9

14.12 Lev 11.3
14.19 Lev 11.20
14.21 Lev 17.15; v. 2; Ex 29.19; 34.26
14.22ff Lev 27.30
14.23 Deut 12.5-7; 4.10
14.24 Deut 12.5, 21
14.26 Deut 12.7, 18
14.27 Deut 12.12; Num 18.20

i Or pellican j Identification of several of the birds in verses 12-18 is uncertain

dent in your towns, do not neglect them, because they have no allotment or inheritance with you.

28 Every third year you shall bring out the full tithe of your produce for that year, and store it within your towns; 29 the Levites, because they have no allotment or inheritance with you, as well as the resident aliens, the orphans, and the widows in your towns, may come and eat their fill so that the LORD your God may bless you in all the work that you undertake.

Laws concerning the Sabbatical Year

15 Every seventh year you shall grant a remission of debts. 2 And this is the manner of the remission: every creditor shall remit the claim that is held against a neighbor, not exacting it of a neighbor who is a member of the community, because the LORD's remission has been proclaimed. 3 Of a foreigner you may exact it, but you must remit your claim on whatever any member of your community owes you. 4 There will, however, be no one in need among you, because the LORD is sure to bless you in the land that the LORD your God is giving you as a possession to occupy, 5 if only you will obey the LORD your God by diligently observing this entire commandment that I command you today. 6 When the LORD your God has blessed you, as he promised you, you will lend to many nations, but you will not borrow; you will rule over many nations, but they will not rule over you.

7 If there is among you anyone in need, a member of your community in any of your towns within the land that the LORD your God is giving you, do not be hard-hearted or tight-fisted toward your needy neighbor. 8 You should rather open your hand, willingly lending enough to meet the need, whatever it may be. 9 Be careful that you do not entertain a mean thought, thinking, "The seventh year, the year of remission, is near," and

therefore view your needy neighbor with hostility and give nothing; your neighbor might cry to the LORD against you, and you would incur guilt. 10 Give liberally and be ungrudging when you do so, for on this account the LORD your God will bless you in all your work and in all that you undertake. 11 Since there will never cease to be some in need on the earth, I therefore command you, "Open your hand to the poor and needy neighbor in your land."

12 If a member of your community, whether a Hebrew man or a Hebrew woman, is sold[k] to you and works for you six years, in the seventh year you shall set that person free. 13 And when you send a male slave[l] out from you a free person, you shall not send him out empty-handed. 14 Provide liberally out of your flock, your threshing floor, and your wine press, thus giving to him some of the bounty with which the LORD your God has blessed you. 15 Remember that you were a slave in the land of Egypt, and the LORD your God redeemed you; for this reason I lay this command upon you today. 16 But if he says to you, "I will not go out from you," because he loves you and your household, since he is well off with you, 17 then you shall take an awl and thrust it through his earlobe into the door, and he shall be your slave[m] forever.

You shall do the same with regard to your female slave.[n]

18 Do not consider it a hardship when you send them out from you free persons, because for six years they have given you services worth the wages of hired laborers; and the LORD your God will bless you in all that you do.

The Firstborn of Livestock

19 Every firstling male born of your herd and flock you shall consecrate to the LORD your God; you shall not do work with your firstling ox nor shear the firstling of your flock. 20 You shall eat it, you to-

Center reference column

14.28
Deut 26.12
14.29
Deut 26.12;
v. 27;
Deut 15.10
15.1
Deut 31.10
15.5
Deut 28.1
15.6
Deut 28.12, 13
15.7
1 Jn 3.17
15.8
Lev 25.35
15.9
v. 1;
Deut 24.15

15.10
2 Cor 9.5, 7;
Deut 24.19
15.11
Mt 26.11;
Mk 14.7;
Jn 12.8
15.12
Ex 21.2;
Lev 25.39
15.15
Deut 5.15;
16.12
15.16
Ex 21.5,6
15.19
Ex 13.2
15.20
Deut 12.5-7, 17

k Or *sells himself or herself*　l Heb *him*　m Or *bondman*　n Or *bondwoman*

gether with your household, in the presence of the LORD your God year by year at the place that the LORD will choose. 21 But if it has any defect—any serious defect, such as lameness or blindness—you shall not sacrifice it to the LORD your God; 22 within your towns you may eat it, the unclean and the clean alike, as you would a gazelle or deer. 23 Its blood, however, you must not eat; you shall pour it out on the ground like water.

The Passover Reviewed

16 Observe the month° of Abib by keeping the passover for the LORD your God, for in the month of Abib the LORD your God brought you out of Egypt by night. 2 You shall offer the passover sacrifice for the LORD your God, from the flock and the herd, at the place that the LORD will choose as a dwelling for his name. 3 You must not eat with it anything leavened. For seven days you shall eat unleavened bread with it—the bread of affliction—because you came out of the land of Egypt in great haste, so that all the days of your life you may remember the day of your departure from the land of Egypt. 4 No leaven shall be seen with you in all your territory for seven days; and none of the meat of what you slaughter on the evening of the first day shall remain until morning. 5 You are not permitted to offer the passover sacrifice within any of your towns that the LORD your God is giving you. 6 But at the place that the LORD your God will choose as a dwelling for his name, only there shall you offer the passover sacrifice, in the evening at sunset, the time of day when you departed from Egypt. 7 You shall cook it and eat it at the place that the LORD your God will choose; the next morning you may go back to your tents. 8 For six days you shall continue to eat unleavened bread, and on the seventh day there shall be a solemn assembly for the LORD your God, when you shall do no work.

The Festival of Weeks Reviewed

9 You shall count seven weeks; begin to count the seven weeks from the time the sickle is first put to the standing grain. 10 Then you shall keep the festival of weeks for the LORD your God, contributing a freewill offering in proportion to the blessing that you have received from the LORD your God. 11 Rejoice before the LORD your God—you and your sons and your daughters, your male and female slaves, the Levites resident in your towns, as well as the strangers, the orphans, and the widows who are among you—at the place that the LORD your God will choose as a dwelling for his name. 12 Remember that you were a slave in Egypt, and diligently observe these statutes.

The Festival of Booths Reviewed

13 You shall keep the festival of booths p for seven days, when you have gathered in the produce from your threshing floor and your wine press. 14 Rejoice during your festival, you and your sons and your daughters, your male and female slaves, as well as the Levites, the strangers, the orphans, and the widows resident in your towns. 15 Seven days you shall keep the festival for the LORD your God at the place that the LORD will choose; for the LORD your God will bless you in all your produce and in all your undertakings, and you shall surely celebrate.

16 Three times a year all your males shall appear before the LORD your God at the place that he will choose: at the festival of unleavened bread, at the festival of weeks, and at the festival of booths. p They shall not appear before the LORD empty-handed; 17 all shall give as they are able, according to the blessing of the LORD your God that he has given you.

Municipal Judges and Officers

18 You shall appoint judges and officials throughout your tribes, in

Cross references (center column)

15.21
Lev 22.19-25
15.22
Deut 12.15, 22
15.23
Deut 12.16, 23
16.1
Ex 12.2,29, 42; 13.4
16.2
Deut 12.5, 26
16.3
Ex 12.8,15
16.4
Ex 13.7; 12.10
16.6
Deut 12.5; Ex 12.6
16.7
Ex 12.8,9
16.8
Ex 12.16
16.9
Ex 23.16; 34.22; Lev 23.15; Num 28.26
16.11
Deut 12.7, 12
16.12
Deut 15.15
16.13
Ex 23.16; Lev 23.34
16.14
v. 11
16.15
Lev 23.39
16.16
Ex 23.14-17; 34.20,23
16.18
Deut 1.16

° Or new moon p Or tabernacles; Heb succoth

all your towns that the LORD your God is giving you, and they shall render just decisions for the people. [19] You must not distort justice; you must not show partiality; and you must not accept bribes, for a bribe blinds the eyes of the wise and subverts the cause of those who are in the right. [20] Justice, and only justice, you shall pursue, so that you may live and occupy the land that the LORD your God is giving you.

Forbidden Forms of Worship

21 You shall not plant any tree as a sacred pole[q] beside the altar that you make for the LORD your God; [22] nor shall you set up a stone pillar—things that the LORD your God hates.

17 You must not sacrifice to the LORD your God an ox or a sheep that has a defect, anything seriously wrong; for that is abhorrent to the LORD your God.

2 If there is found among you, in one of your towns that the LORD your God is giving you, a man or woman who does what is evil in the sight of the LORD your God, and transgresses his covenant [3] by going to serve other gods and worshiping them—whether the sun or the moon or any of the host of heaven, which I have forbidden— [4] and if it is reported to you or you hear of it, and you make a thorough inquiry, and the charge is proved true that such an abhorrent thing has occurred in Israel, [5] then you shall bring out to your gates that man or that woman who has committed this crime and you shall stone the man or woman to death. [6] On the evidence of two or three witnesses the death sentence shall be executed; a person must not be put to death on the evidence of only one witness. [7] The hands of the witnesses shall be the first raised against the person to execute the death penalty, and afterward the hands of all the people. So you shall purge the evil from your midst.

Legal Decisions by Priests and Judges

8 If a judicial decision is too difficult for you to make between one kind of bloodshed and another, one kind of legal right and another, or one kind of assault and another—any such matters of dispute in your towns—then you shall immediately go up to the place that the LORD your God will choose, [9] where you shall consult with the levitical priests and the judge who is in office in those days; they shall announce to you the decision in the case. [10] Carry out exactly the decision that they announce to you from the place that the LORD will choose, diligently observing everything they instruct you. [11] You must carry out fully the law that they interpret for you or the ruling that they announce to you; do not turn aside from the decision that they announce to you, either to the right or to the left. [12] As for anyone who presumes to disobey the priest appointed to minister there to the LORD your God, or the judge, that person shall die. So you shall purge the evil from Israel. [13] All the people will hear and be afraid, and will not act presumptuously again.

Limitations of Royal Authority

14 When you have come into the land that the LORD your God is giving you, and have taken possession of it and settled in it, and you say, "I will set a king over me, like all the nations that are around me," [15] you may indeed set over you a king whom the LORD your God will choose. One of your own community you may set as king over you; you are not permitted to put a foreigner over you, who is not of your own community. [16] Even so, he must not acquire many horses for himself, or return the people to Egypt in order to acquire more horses, since the LORD has said to you, "You must never return that way again." [17] And he must not ac-

16.19
Deut 1.17;
Ex 23.8
16.21
Ex 34.13;
Deut 7.5
17.1
Deut 15.21;
Mal 1.8,13
17.2
Deut 13.6
17.4
Deut 13.12,
14
17.6
Num 35.30;
Deut 19.15;
Mt 18.16
17.7
Deut 13.5,9

17.8
Deut 12.5
17.9
Deut 19.17;
Ezek 44.24
17.11
Deut 25.1
17.13
Deut 13.11;
19.20
17.14
Deut 11.31;
1 Sam 8.5,
19,20
17.15
Jer 30.21
17.16ff
1 Kings 4.26;
10.26,28;
Isa 31.1;
Ezek 17.15
17.17
cf.
1 Kings 11.3,
4

q Heb *Asherah*

quire many wives for himself, or else his heart will turn away; also silver and gold he must not acquire in great quantity for himself. [18] When he has taken the throne of his kingdom, he shall have a copy of this law written for him in the presence of the levitical priests. [19] It shall remain with him and he shall read in it all the days of his life, so that he may learn to fear the LORD his God, diligently observing all the words of this law and these statutes, [20] neither exalting himself above other members of the community nor turning aside from the commandment, either to the right or to the left, so that he and his descendants may reign long over his kingdom in Israel.

Privileges of Priests and Levites

18 The levitical priests, the whole tribe of Levi, shall have no allotment or inheritance within Israel. They may eat the sacrifices that are the LORD's portion[r] [2] but they shall have no inheritance among the other members of the community; the LORD is their inheritance, as he promised them.

[3] This shall be the priests' due from the people, from those offering a sacrifice, whether an ox or a sheep: they shall give to the priest the shoulder, the two jowls, and the stomach. [4] The first fruits of your grain, your wine, and your oil, as well as the first of the fleece of your sheep, you shall give him. [5] For the LORD your God has chosen Levi[s] out of all your tribes, to stand and minister in the name of the LORD, him and his sons for all time.

[6] If a Levite leaves any of your towns, from wherever he has been residing in Israel, and comes to the place that the LORD will choose (and he may come whenever he wishes), [7] then he may minister in the name of the LORD his God, like all his fellow-Levites who stand to minister there before the LORD. [8] They shall have equal portions to eat, even though they have income

Cross references (center column)

17.18 Deut 31.24-26
17.19 Josh 1.8
17.20 Deut 5.32
18.1 Deut 10.9; 1 Cor 9.13
18.3 Lev 7.30-34
18.4 Ex 22.29; Num 18.12
18.5 Ex 28.1; Deut 10.8
18.8 Neh 12.44, 47
18.9 Deut 12.29-31
18.10 Deut 12.31; Lev 19.26, 31
18.12 Deut 9.4
18.15ff Jn 1.21; Acts 3.22; 7.37
18.16 Deut 5.23-27; Ex 20.19
18.17 Deut 5.28
18.18 v. 15; Isa 51.16; Jn 4.25,26
18.19 Acts 3.23
18.20 Deut 13.1,2, 5

from the sale of family possessions.[r]

Child-Sacrifice, Divination, and Magic Prohibited

[9] When you come into the land that the LORD your God is giving you, you must not learn to imitate the abhorrent practices of those nations. [10] No one shall be found among you who makes a son or daughter pass through fire, or who practices divination, or is a soothsayer, or an augur, or a sorcerer, [11] or one who casts spells, or who consults ghosts or spirits, or who seeks oracles from the dead. [12] For whoever does these things is abhorrent to the LORD; it is because of such abhorrent practices that the LORD your God is driving them out before you. [13] You must remain completely loyal to the LORD your God. [14] Although these nations that you are about to dispossess do give heed to soothsayers and diviners, as for you, the LORD your God does not permit you to do so.

A New Prophet Like Moses

[15] The LORD your God will raise up for you a prophet[t] like me from among your own people; you shall heed such a prophet.[u] [16] This is what you requested of the LORD your God at Horeb on the day of the assembly when you said: "If I hear the voice of the LORD my God any more, or ever again see this great fire, I will die." [17] Then the LORD replied to me: "They are right in what they have said. [18] I will raise up for them a prophet[t] like you from among their own people; I will put my words in the mouth of the prophet,[v] who shall speak to them everything that I command. [19] Anyone who does not heed the words that the prophet[w] shall speak in my name, I myself will hold accountable. [20] But any prophet who speaks in the name of other gods, or who presumes to speak in my name a word that I have not com-

r Meaning of Heb uncertain s Heb him
t Or prophets u Or such prophets
v Or mouths of the prophets w Heb he

manded the prophet to speak—that prophet shall die." [21] You may say to yourself, "How can we recognize a word that the LORD has not spoken?" [22] If a prophet speaks in the name of the LORD but the thing does not take place or prove true, it is a word that the LORD has not spoken. The prophet has spoken it presumptuously; do not be frightened by it.

Laws concerning the Cities of Refuge

19 When the LORD your God has cut off the nations whose land the LORD your God is giving you, and you have dispossessed them and settled in their towns and in their houses, [2] you shall set apart three cities in the land that the LORD your God is giving you to possess. [3] You shall calculate the distances[x] and divide into three regions the land that the LORD your God gives you as a possession, so that any homicide can flee to one of them.

[4] Now this is the case of a homicide who might flee there and live, that is, someone who has killed another person unintentionally when the two had not been at enmity before: [5] Suppose someone goes into the forest with another to cut wood, and when one of them swings the ax to cut down a tree, the head slips from the handle and strikes the other person who then dies; the killer may flee to one of these cities and live. [6] But if the distance is too great, the avenger of blood in hot anger might pursue and overtake and put the killer to death, although a death sentence was not deserved, since the two had not been at enmity before. [7] Therefore I command you: You shall set apart three cities.

[8] If the LORD your God enlarges your territory, as he swore to your ancestors—and he will give you all the land that he promised your ancestors to give you, [9] provided you diligently observe this entire commandment that I command you today, by loving the LORD your God

and walking always in his ways—then you shall add three more cities to these three, [10] so that the blood of an innocent person may not be shed in the land that the LORD your God is giving you as an inheritance, thereby bringing bloodguilt upon you.

[11] But if someone at enmity with another lies in wait and attacks and takes the life of that person, and flees into one of these cities, [12] then the elders of the killer's city shall send to have the culprit taken from there and handed over to the avenger of blood to be put to death. [13] Show no pity; you shall purge the guilt of innocent blood from Israel, so that it may go well with you.

Property Boundaries

[14] You must not move your neighbor's boundary marker, set up by former generations, on the property that will be allotted to you in the land that the LORD your God is giving you to possess.

Law concerning Witnesses

[15] A single witness shall not suffice to convict a person of any crime or wrongdoing in connection with any offense that may be committed. Only on the evidence of two or three witnesses shall a charge be sustained. [16] If a malicious witness comes forward to accuse someone of wrongdoing, [17] then both parties to the dispute shall appear before the LORD, before the priests and the judges who are in office in those days, [18] and the judges shall make a thorough inquiry. If the witness is a false witness, having testified falsely against another, [19] then you shall do to the false witness just as the false witness had meant to do to the other. So you shall purge the evil from your midst. [20] The rest shall hear and be afraid, and a crime such as this shall never again be committed among you. [21] Show no pity: life for life, eye for eye,

18.22
Jer 28.9;
v. 20
19.1
Deut 12.29
19.2
Num 35.10, 14
19.4
Num 35.15
19.6
Num 35.12
19.9
Josh 20.7,8

19.10
Deut 21.1-9;
Num 35.33
19.13
Deut 7.2
19.14
Deut 27.17
19.15
Num 35.30;
Deut 17.6;
Mt 18.16;
2 Cor 13.1
19.16
Ex 23.1;
Ps 27.12
19.17
Deut 17.9
19.19
Prov 19.5,9
19.21
v. 13;
Ex 21.23;
Lev 24.20;
Mt 5.38

[x] Or *prepare roads to them*

tooth for tooth, hand for hand, foot for foot.

Rules of Warfare

20 When you go out to war against your enemies, and see horses and chariots, an army larger than your own, you shall not be afraid of them; for the LORD your God is with you, who brought you up from the land of Egypt. ²Before you engage in battle, the priest shall come forward and speak to the troops, ³and shall say to them: "Hear, O Israel! Today you are drawing near to do battle against your enemies. Do not lose heart, or be afraid, or panic, or be in dread of them; ⁴for it is the LORD your God who goes with you, to fight for you against your enemies, to give you victory." ⁵Then the officials shall address the troops, saying, "Has anyone built a new house but not dedicated it? He should go back to his house, or he might die in the battle and another dedicate it. ⁶Has anyone planted a vineyard but not yet enjoyed its fruit? He should go back to his house, or he might die in the battle and another be first to enjoy its fruit. ⁷Has anyone become engaged to a woman but not yet married her? He should go back to his house, or he might die in the battle and another marry her." ⁸The officials shall continue to address the troops, saying, "Is anyone afraid or disheartened? He should go back to his house, or he might cause the heart of his comrades to melt like his own." ⁹When the officials have finished addressing the troops, then the commanders shall take charge of them.

10 When you draw near to a town to fight against it, offer it terms of peace. ¹¹If it accepts your terms of peace and surrenders to you, then all the people in it shall serve you at forced labor. ¹²If it does not submit to you peacefully, but makes war against you, then you shall besiege it; ¹³and when the LORD your God gives it into your hand, you shall put all its males to the sword. ¹⁴You may, however,

take as your booty the women, the children, livestock, and everything else in the town, all its spoil. You may enjoy the spoil of your enemies, which the LORD your God has given you. ¹⁵Thus you shall treat all the towns that are very far from you, which are not towns of the nations here. ¹⁶But as for the towns of these peoples that the LORD your God is giving you as an inheritance, you must not let anything that breathes remain alive. ¹⁷You shall annihilate them—the Hittites and the Amorites, the Canaanites and the Perizzites, the Hivites and the Jebusites—just as the LORD your God has commanded, ¹⁸so that they may not teach you to do all the abhorrent things that they do for their gods, and you thus sin against the LORD your God.

19 If you besiege a town for a long time, making war against it in order to take it, you must not destroy its trees by wielding an ax against them. Although you may take food from them, you must not cut them down. Are trees in the field human beings that they should come under siege from you? ²⁰You may destroy only the trees that you know do not produce food; you may cut them down for use in building siegeworks against the town that makes war with you, until it falls.

Law concerning Murder by Persons Unknown

21 If, in the land that the LORD your God is giving you to possess, a body is found lying in open country, and it is not known who struck the person down, ²then your elders and your judges shall come out to measure the distances to the towns that are near the body. ³The elders of the town nearest the body shall take a heifer that has never been worked, one that has not pulled in the yoke; ⁴the elders of that town shall bring the heifer down to a wadi with running water, which is neither plowed nor sown, and shall break the heifer's neck there in the wadi. ⁵Then the

20.1
Deut 31.6,8
20.3
v. 1;
Josh 23.10
20.4
Deut 1.30
20.6
1 Cor 9.7
20.7
Deut 24.5
20.8
Judg 7.3
20.10ff
Lk 14.31
20.14
Josh 8.2;
22.8

20.16
Deut 7.1,2;
Josh 11.14
20.18
Ex 23.33
21.1
Josh 1.6
21.5
Deut 17.8-11

priests, the sons of Levi, shall come forward, for the LORD your God has chosen them to minister to him and to pronounce blessings in the name of the LORD, and by their decision all cases of dispute and assault shall be settled. 6 All the elders of that town nearest the body shall wash their hands over the heifer whose neck was broken in the wadi, 7 and they shall declare: "Our hands did not shed this blood, nor were we witnesses to it. 8 Absolve, O LORD, your people Israel, whom you redeemed; do not let the guilt of innocent blood remain in the midst of your people Israel." Then they will be absolved of bloodguilt. 9 So you shall purge the guilt of innocent blood from your midst, because you must do what is right in the sight of the LORD.

Female Captives

10 When you go out to war against your enemies, and the LORD your God hands them over to you and you take them captive, 11 suppose you see among the captives a beautiful woman whom you desire and want to marry, 12 and so you bring her home to your house: she shall shave her head, pare her nails, 13 discard her captive's garb, and shall remain in your house a full month, mourning for her father and mother; after that you may go in to her and be her husband, and she shall be your wife. 14 But if you are not satisfied with her, you shall let her go free and not sell her for money. You must not treat her as a slave, since you have dishonored her.

The Right of the Firstborn

15 If a man has two wives, one of them loved and the other disliked, and if both the loved and the disliked have borne him sons, the firstborn being the son of the one who is disliked, 16 then on the day when he wills his possessions to his sons, he is not permitted to treat the son of the loved as the firstborn in preference to the son of the disliked, who is the firstborn.

17 He must acknowledge as firstborn the son of the one who is disliked, giving him a double portion[y] of all that he has; since he is the first issue of his virility, the right of the firstborn is his.

Rebellious Children

18 If someone has a stubborn and rebellious son who will not obey his father and mother, who does not heed them when they discipline him, 19 then his father and his mother shall take hold of him and bring him out to the elders of his town at the gate of that place. 20 They shall say to the elders of his town, "This son of ours is stubborn and rebellious. He will not obey us. He is a glutton and a drunkard." 21 Then all the men of the town shall stone him to death. So you shall purge the evil from your midst; and all Israel will hear, and be afraid.

Miscellaneous Laws

22 When someone is convicted of a crime punishable by death and is executed, and you hang him on a tree, 23 his corpse must not remain all night upon the tree; you shall bury him that same day, for anyone hung on a tree is under God's curse. You must not defile the land that the LORD your God is giving you for possession.

22 You shall not watch your neighbor's ox or sheep straying away and ignore them; you shall take them back to their owner. 2 If the owner does not reside near you or you do not know who the owner is, you shall bring it to your own house, and it shall remain with you until the owner claims it; then you shall return it. 3 You shall do the same with a neighbor's donkey; you shall do the same with a neighbor's garment; and you shall do the same with anything else that your neighbor loses and you find. You may not withhold your help.

4 You shall not see your neighbor's donkey or ox fallen on the

21.8
Jon 1.8
21.9
Deut 19.13
21.12
Lev 14.8,9;
Num 6.9
21.16
1 Chr 26.10

21.17
Gen 49.3
21.18
Isa 30.1
21.21
Deut 13.5,
11
21.23
Josh 8.29;
10.26,27;
Jn 19.31;
Gal 3.13
22.1
Ex 23.4
22.4
Ex 23.5

y Heb *two-thirds*

road and ignore it; you shall help to lift it up.

5 A woman shall not wear a man's apparel, nor shall a man put on a woman's garment; for whoever does such things is abhorrent to the LORD your God.

6 If you come on a bird's nest, in any tree or on the ground, with fledglings or eggs, with the mother sitting on the fledglings or on the eggs, you shall not take the mother with the young. 7 Let the mother go, taking only the young for yourself, in order that it may go well with you and you may live long.

8 When you build a new house, you shall make a parapet for your roof; otherwise you might have bloodguilt on your house, if anyone should fall from it.

9 You shall not sow your vineyard with a second kind of seed, or the whole yield will have to be forfeited, both the crop that you have sown and the yield of the vineyard itself.

10 You shall not plow with an ox and a donkey yoked together.

11 You shall not wear clothes made of wool and linen woven together.

12 You shall make tassels on the four corners of the cloak with which you cover yourself.

Laws concerning Sexual Relations

13 Suppose a man marries a woman, but after going in to her, he dislikes her 14 and makes up charges against her, slandering her by saying, "I married this woman; but when I lay with her, I did not find evidence of her virginity." 15 The father of the young woman and her mother shall then submit the evidence of the young woman's virginity to the elders of the city at the gate. 16 The father of the young woman shall say to the elders: "I gave my daughter in marriage to this man but he dislikes her; 17 now he has made up charges against her, saying, 'I did not find evidence of your daughter's virginity.' But here is the evidence of my daugh-

ter's virginity." Then they shall spread out the cloth before the elders of the town. 18 The elders of that town shall take the man and punish him; 19 they shall fine him one hundred shekels of silver (which they shall give to the young woman's father) because he has slandered a virgin of Israel. She shall remain his wife; he shall not be permitted to divorce her as long as he lives.

20 If, however, this charge is true, that evidence of the young woman's virginity was not found, 21 then they shall bring the young woman out to the entrance of her father's house and the men of her town shall stone her to death, because she committed a disgraceful act in Israel by prostituting herself in her father's house. So you shall purge the evil from your midst.

22 If a man is caught lying with the wife of another man, both of them shall die, the man who lay with the woman as well as the woman. So you shall purge the evil from Israel.

23 If there is a young woman, a virgin already engaged to be married, and a man meets her in the town and lies with her, 24 you shall bring both of them to the gate of that town and stone them to death, the young woman because she did not cry for help in the town and the man because he violated his neighbor's wife. So you shall purge the evil from your midst.

25 But if the man meets the engaged woman in the open country, and the man seizes her and lies with her, then only the man who lay with her shall die. 26 You shall do nothing to the young woman; the young woman has not committed an offense punishable by death, because this case is like that of someone who attacks and murders a neighbor. 27 Since he found her in the open country, the engaged woman may have cried for help, but there was no one to rescue her.

28 If a man meets a virgin who is not engaged, and seizes her and

Cross references (center column):

22.6 Lev 22.28
22.7
Deut 4.40
22.9 Lev 19.19
22.11 Lev 19.19
22.12 Num 15.37-41; Mt 23.5
22.13 Deut 24.1
22.15 v. 23ff

22.21 Deut 23.17, 18; 13.5
22.22 Lev 20.10; Jn 8.5
22.24 vv. 21,22
22.25 Jn 8.1-11
22.28 Ex 22.16,17

lies with her, and they are caught in the act, [29] the man who lay with her shall give fifty shekels of silver to the young woman's father, and she shall become his wife. Because he violated her he shall not be permitted to divorce her as long as he lives.

30 [z] A man shall not marry his father's wife, thereby violating his father's rights. [a]

Those Excluded from the Assembly

23 No one whose testicles are crushed or whose penis is cut off shall be admitted to the assembly of the LORD.

2 Those born of an illicit union shall not be admitted to the assembly of the LORD. Even to the tenth generation, none of their descendants shall be admitted to the assembly of the LORD.

3 No Ammonite or Moabite shall be admitted to the assembly of the LORD. Even to the tenth generation, none of their descendants shall be admitted to the assembly of the LORD, [4] because they did not meet you with food and water on your journey out of Egypt, and because they hired against you Balaam son of Beor, from Pethor of Mesopotamia, to curse you. [5] (Yet the LORD your God refused to heed Balaam; the LORD your God turned the curse into a blessing for you, because the LORD your God loved you.) [6] You shall never promote their welfare or their prosperity as long as you live.

7 You shall not abhor any of the Edomites, for they are your kin. You shall not abhor any of the Egyptians, because you were an alien residing in their land. [8] The children of the third generation that are born to them may be admitted to the assembly of the LORD.

Sanitary, Ritual, and Humanitarian Precepts

9 When you are encamped against your enemies you shall guard against any impropriety.

10 If one of you becomes un-

clean because of a nocturnal emission, then he shall go outside the camp; he must not come within the camp. [11] When evening comes, he shall wash himself with water, and when the sun has set, he may come back into the camp.

12 You shall have a designated area outside the camp to which you shall go. [13] With your utensils you shall have a trowel; when you relieve yourself outside, you shall dig a hole with it and then cover up your excrement. [14] Because the LORD your God travels along with your camp, to save you and to hand over your enemies to you, therefore your camp must be holy, so that he may not see anything indecent among you and turn away from you.

15 Slaves who have escaped to you from their owners shall not be given back to them. [16] They shall reside with you, in your midst, in any place they choose in any one of your towns, wherever they please; you shall not oppress them.

17 None of the daughters of Israel shall be a temple prostitute; none of the sons of Israel shall be a temple prostitute. [18] You shall not bring the fee of a prostitute or the wages of a male prostitute [b] into the house of the LORD your God in payment for any vow, for both of these are abhorrent to the LORD your God.

19 You shall not charge interest on loans to another Israelite, interest on money, interest on provisions, interest on anything that is lent. [20] On loans to a foreigner you may charge interest, but on loans to another Israelite you may not charge interest, so that the LORD your God may bless you in all your undertakings in the land that you are about to enter and possess.

21 If you make a vow to the LORD your God, do not postpone fulfilling it; for the LORD your God will surely require it of you, and you would incur guilt. [22] But if you re-

22.30
Deut 27.20
23.3
Neh 13.1,2
23.4
Num 22.5,6
23.7
Gen 25.24-26
23.10
Lev 15.16

23.14
Lev 26.12
23.17
Deut 22.21
23.19
Ex 22.25;
Lev 25.36,
37
23.20
Deut 28.12
23.21
Num 30.2;
Mt 5.33

[z] Ch 23.1 in Heb [a] Heb *uncovering his father's skirt* [b] Heb *a dog*

MAJOR SOCIAL CONCERNS IN THE COVENANT

1. PERSONHOOD
Everyone's person is to be secure (Ex 20:13; Dt 5:17; Ex 21:16-21, 26-31; Lev 19:14; Dt 24:7; 27:18).

2. FALSE ACCUSATION
Everyone is to be secure against slander and false accusation (Ex 20:16; Dt 5:20; Ex 23:1-3; Lev 19:16; Dt 19:15-21).

3. WOMAN
No woman is to be taken advantage of within her subordinate status in society (Ex 21:7-11, 20, 26-32; 22:16-17; Dt. 21:10-14; 22:13-30; 24:1-5).

4. PUNISHMENT
Punishment for wrongdoing shall not be excessive so that the culprit is dehumanized (Dt 25:1-5).

5. DIGNITY
Every Israelite's dignity and right to be God's freedman and servant are to be honored and safeguarded (Ex 21:2, 5-6; Lev 25; Dt 15:12-18).

6. INHERITANCE
Every Israelite's inheritance in the promised land is to be secure (Lev 25; Nu 27:5-7; 36:1-9; Dt 25:5-10).

7. PROPERTY
Everyone's property is to be secure (Ex 20:15; Dt 5:19; Ex 21:33-36; 22:1-15; 23:4-5; Lev 19:35-36; Dt 22:1-4; 25:13-15).

8. FRUIT OF LABOR
Everyone is to receive the fruit of his labors (Lev 19:13; Dt 24:14; 25:4).

9. FRUIT OF THE GROUND
Everyone is to share the fruit of the ground (Ex 23:10-11; Lev 19:9-10; 23:22; 25:3-55; Dt. 14:28-29; 24:19-21).

10. REST ON SABBATH
Everyone, down to the humblest servant and the resident alien, is to share in the weekly rest of God's Sabbath (Ex 20:8-11; Dt 5:12-15; Ex 23:12).

11. MARRIAGE
The marriage relationship is to be kept inviolate (Ex 20:14; Dt 5:18; see also Lev 18:6-23; 20:10-21; Dt 22:13-30).

12. EXPLOITATION
No one, however disabled, impoverished or powerless, is to be oppressed or exploited (Ex 22:21-27; Lev 19:14, 33-34; 25:35-36; Dt 23:19; 24:6, 12-15, 17; 27:18).

13. FAIR TRIAL
Everyone is to have free access to the courts and is to be afforded a fair trial (Ex 23:6,8; Lev 19:15; Dt 1:17; 10:17-18; 16:18-20; 17:8-13; 19:15-21).

14. SOCIAL ORDER
Every person's God-given place in the social order is to be honored (Ex 20:12; Dt 5:16; Ex 21:15, 17; 22:28; Lev 19:3, 32; 20:9; Dt 17:8-13; 21:15-21; 27:16).

15. LAW
No one shall be above the law, not even the king (Dt 17:18-20).

16. ANIMALS
Concern for the welfare of other creatures is to be extended to the animal world (Ex 23:5, 11; Lev 25:7, Dt 22:4, 6-7; 25:4).

frain from vowing, you will not incur guilt. [23]Whatever your lips utter you must diligently perform, just as you have freely vowed to the LORD your God with your own mouth.

24 If you go into your neighbor's vineyard, you may eat your fill of grapes, as many as you wish, but you shall not put any in a container.

25 If you go into your neighbor's standing grain, you may pluck the ears with your hand, but you shall not put a sickle to your neighbor's standing grain.

Laws concerning Marriage and Divorce

24 Suppose a man enters into marriage with a woman, but she does not please him because he finds something objectionable about her, and so he writes her a certificate of divorce, puts it in her hand, and sends her out of his house; she then leaves his house [2]and goes off to become another man's wife. [3]Then suppose the second man dislikes her, writes her a bill of divorce, puts it in her hand, and sends her out of his house (or the second man who married her dies); [4]her first husband, who sent her away, is not permitted to take her again to be his wife after she has been defiled; for that would be abhorrent to the LORD, and you shall not bring guilt on the land that the LORD your God is giving you as a possession.

Miscellaneous Laws

5 When a man is newly married, he shall not go out with the army or be charged with any related duty. He shall be free at home one year, to be happy with the wife whom he has married.

6 No one shall take a mill or an upper millstone in pledge, for that would be taking a life in pledge.

7 If someone is caught kidnaping another Israelite, enslaving or selling the Israelite, then that kidnaper shall die. So you shall purge the evil from your midst.

23.25
Mt 12.1;
Mk 2.23;
Lk 6.1
24.1
Deut 22.13-21;
Mt 5.31;
19.7;
Mk 10.4
24.4
Jer 3.1
24.5
Deut 20.7
24.7
Ex 21.16

24.8
Lev 13.2;
14.2
24.9
Num 12.10
24.13
Ex 22.26;
Deut 6.25
24.14
Lev 25.35-43;
Deut 15.7-18
24.15
Lev 19.13;
Jas 5.4;
Deut 15.9
24.16
2 Kings 14.6;
2 Chr 25.4;
Jer 31.29,
30;
Ezek 18.20
24.17
Deut 1.17;
10.17; 16.19
24.18
Deut 16.12
24.19
Lev 19.9,10;
23.22
24.20
Lev 19.10

8 Guard against an outbreak of a leprous[c] skin disease by being very careful; you shall carefully observe whatever the levitical priests instruct you, just as I have commanded them. [9]Remember what the LORD your God did to Miriam on your journey out of Egypt.

10 When you make your neighbor a loan of any kind, you shall not go into the house to take the pledge. [11]You shall wait outside, while the person to whom you are making the loan brings the pledge out to you. [12]If the person is poor, you shall not sleep in the garment given you as[d] the pledge. [13]You shall give the pledge back by sunset, so that your neighbor may sleep in the cloak and bless you; and it will be to your credit before the LORD your God.

14 You shall not withhold the wages of poor and needy laborers, whether other Israelites or aliens who reside in your land in one of your towns. [15]You shall pay them their wages daily before sunset, because they are poor and their livelihood depends on them; otherwise they might cry to the LORD against you, and you would incur guilt.

16 Parents shall not be put to death for their children, nor shall children be put to death for their parents; only for their own crimes may persons be put to death.

17 You shall not deprive a resident alien or an orphan of justice; you shall not take a widow's garment in pledge. [18]Remember that you were a slave in Egypt and the LORD your God redeemed you from there; therefore I command you to do this.

19 When you reap your harvest in your field and forget a sheaf in the field, you shall not go back to get it; it shall be left for the alien, the orphan, and the widow, so that the LORD your God may bless you in all your undertakings. [20]When you beat your olive trees, do not strip

[c] A term for several skin diseases; precise meaning uncertain [d] Heb lacks *the garment given you as*

what is left; it shall be for the alien, the orphan, and the widow.

21 When you gather the grapes of your vineyard, do not glean what is left; it shall be for the alien, the orphan, and the widow. 22 Remember that you were a slave in the land of Egypt; therefore I am commanding you to do this.

25 Suppose two persons have a dispute and enter into litigation, and the judges decide between them, declaring one to be in the right and the other to be in the wrong. 2 If the one in the wrong deserves to be flogged, the judge shall make that person lie down and be beaten in his presence with the number of lashes proportionate to the offense. 3 Forty lashes may be given but not more; if more lashes than these are given, your neighbor will be degraded in your sight.

4 You shall not muzzle an ox while it is treading out the grain.

Levirate Marriage

5 When brothers reside together, and one of them dies and has no son, the wife of the deceased shall not be married outside the family to a stranger. Her husband's brother shall go in to her, taking her in marriage, and performing the duty of a husband's brother to her, 6 and the firstborn whom she bears shall succeed to the name of the deceased brother, so that his name may not be blotted out of Israel. 7 But if the man has no desire to marry his brother's widow, then his brother's widow shall go up to the elders at the gate and say, "My husband's brother refuses to perpetuate his brother's name in Israel; he will not perform the duty of a husband's brother to me." 8 Then the elders of his town shall summon him and speak to him. If he persists, saying, "I have no desire to marry her," 9 then his brother's wife shall go up to him in the presence of the elders, pull his sandal off his foot, spit in his face, and declare, "This is what is done to the man who does not build up his brother's house." 10 Throughout Israel his

24.22
v. 18
25.1
Deut 19.17;
1.16,17
25.3
2 Cor 11.24
25.4
1 Cor 9.9;
1 Tim 5.18
25.5ff
Mt 22.24;
Mk 12.19;
Lk 20.28
25.6
Gen 38.9;
Ruth 4.10
25.7
Ruth 4.1,2
25.8
Ruth 4.6
25.9f
Ruth 4.7,11

25.13
Lev 19.35-37
25.16
Prov 11.1
25.17
Ex 17.8
25.19
1 Sam 15.2,
3
26.2
Ex 22.29;
23.16,19;
Num 18.13

family shall be known as "the house of him whose sandal was pulled off."

Various Commands

11 If men get into a fight with one another, and the wife of one intervenes to rescue her husband from the grip of his opponent by reaching out and seizing his genitals, 12 you shall cut off her hand; show no pity.

13 You shall not have in your bag two kinds of weights, large and small. 14 You shall not have in your house two kinds of measures, large and small. 15 You shall have only a full and honest weight; you shall have only a full and honest measure, so that your days may be long in the land that the LORD your God is giving you. 16 For all who do such things, all who act dishonestly, are abhorrent to the LORD your God.

17 Remember what Amalek did to you on your journey out of Egypt, 18 how he attacked you on the way, when you were faint and weary, and struck down all who lagged behind you; he did not fear God. 19 Therefore when the LORD your God has given you rest from all your enemies on every hand, in the land that the LORD your God is giving you as an inheritance to possess, you shall blot out the remembrance of Amalek from under heaven; do not forget.

First Fruits and Tithes

26 When you have come into the land that the LORD your God is giving you as an inheritance to possess, and you possess it, and settle in it, 2 you shall take some of the first of all the fruit of the ground, which you harvest from the land that the LORD your God is giving you, and you shall put it in a basket and go to the place that the LORD your God will choose as a dwelling for his name. 3 You shall go to the priest who is in office at that time, and say to him, "Today I declare to the LORD your God that I have come into the land that the LORD swore to our ancestors to give

us." [4]When the priest takes the basket from your hand and sets it down before the altar of the LORD your God, [5]you shall make this response before the LORD your God: "A wandering Aramean was my ancestor; he went down into Egypt and lived there as an alien, few in number, and there he became a great nation, mighty and populous. [6]When the Egyptians treated us harshly and afflicted us, by imposing hard labor on us, [7]we cried to the LORD, the God of our ancestors; the LORD heard our voice and saw our affliction, our toil, and our oppression. [8]The LORD brought us out of Egypt with a mighty hand and an outstretched arm, with a terrifying display of power, and with signs and wonders; [9]and he brought us into this place and gave us this land, a land flowing with milk and honey. [10]So now I bring the first of the fruit of the ground that you, O LORD, have given me." You shall set it down before the LORD your God and bow down before the LORD your God. [11]Then you, together with the Levites and the aliens who reside among you, shall celebrate with all the bounty that the LORD your God has given to you and to your house.

[12] When you have finished paying all the tithe of your produce in the third year (which is the year of the tithe), giving it to the Levites, the aliens, the orphans, and the widows, so that they may eat their fill within your towns, [13]then you shall say before the LORD your God: "I have removed the sacred portion from the house, and I have given it to the Levites, the resident aliens, the orphans, and the widows, in accordance with your entire commandment that you commanded me; I have neither transgressed nor forgotten any of your commandments: [14]I have not eaten of it while in mourning; I have not removed any of it while I was unclean; and I have not offered any of it to the dead. I have obeyed the LORD my God, doing just as you commanded me. [15]Look down

from your holy habitation, from heaven, and bless your people Israel and the ground that you have given us, as you swore to our ancestors—a land flowing with milk and honey."

Concluding Exhortation

[16] This very day the LORD your God is commanding you to observe these statutes and ordinances; so observe them diligently with all your heart and with all your soul. [17]Today you have obtained the LORD's agreement: to be your God; and for you to walk in his ways, to keep his statutes, his commandments, and his ordinances, and to obey him. [18]Today the LORD has obtained your agreement: to be his treasured people, as he promised you, and to keep his commandments; [19]for him to set you high above all nations that he has made, in praise and in fame and in honor; and for you to be a people holy to the LORD your God, as he promised.

The Inscribed Stones and Altar on Mount Ebal

27 Then Moses and the elders of Israel charged all the people as follows: Keep the entire commandment that I am commanding you today. [2]On the day that you cross over the Jordan into the land that the LORD your God is giving you, you shall set up large stones and cover them with plaster. [3]You shall write on them all the words of this law when you have crossed over, to enter the land that the LORD your God is giving you, a land flowing with milk and honey, as the LORD, the God of your ancestors, promised you. [4]So when you have crossed over the Jordan, you shall set up these stones, about which I am commanding you today, on Mount Ebal, and you shall cover them with plaster. [5]And you shall build an altar there to the LORD your God, an altar of stones on which you have not used an iron tool. [6]You must build the altar of the LORD your God of unhewn[e]

26.5
Hos 12.12;
Gen 43.1,2;
45.7,11;
46.27;
Deut 10.22
26.6
Ex 1.11,14
26.7
Ex 2.23-25
26.8
Deut 4.34
26.9
Ex 3.8
26.11
Deut 12.7
26.12
Deut 14.28,
29; Heb 7.5,
9,10
26.13
Ps 119.141,
153,176
26.14
Lev 7.20;
Hos 9.4

26.16
Deut 4.29
26.18
Deut 7.6
26.19
Deut 28.1;
Ps 148.14;
Deut 7.6
27.2
Josh 8.30-32
27.3
Deut 26.9
27.5
Ex 20.25;
Josh 8.31

[e] Heb *whole*

stones. Then offer up burnt offerings on it to the LORD your God, [7] make sacrifices of well-being, and eat them there, rejoicing before the LORD your God. [8] You shall write on the stones all the words of this law very clearly. .

9 Then Moses and the levitical priests spoke to all Israel, saying: Keep silence and hear, O Israel! This very day you have become the people of the LORD your God. [10] Therefore obey the LORD your God, observing his commandments and his statutes that I am commanding you today.

Twelve Curses

11 The same day Moses charged the people as follows: [12] When you have crossed over the Jordan, these shall stand on Mount Gerizim for the blessing of the people: Simeon, Levi, Judah, Issachar, Joseph, and Benjamin. [13] And these shall stand on Mount Ebal for the curse: Reuben, Gad, Asher, Zebulun, Dan, and Naphtali. [14] Then the Levites shall declare in a loud voice to all the Israelites:

15 "Cursed be anyone who makes an idol or casts an image, anything abhorrent to the LORD, the work of an artisan, and sets it up in secret." All the people shall respond, saying, "Amen!"

16 "Cursed be anyone who dishonors father or mother." All the people shall say, "Amen!"

17 "Cursed be anyone who moves a neighbor's boundary marker." All the people shall say, "Amen!"

18 "Cursed be anyone who misleads a blind person on the road." All the people shall say, "Amen!"

19 "Cursed be anyone who deprives the alien, the orphan, and the widow of justice." All the people shall say, "Amen!"

20 "Cursed be anyone who lies with his father's wife, because he has violated his father's rights." [f] All the people shall say, "Amen!"

21 "Cursed be anyone who lies with any animal." All the people shall say, "Amen!"

22 "Cursed be anyone who lies with his sister, whether the daughter of his father or the daughter of his mother." All the people shall say, "Amen!"

23 "Cursed be anyone who lies with his mother-in-law." All the people shall say, "Amen!"

24 "Cursed be anyone who strikes down a neighbor in secret." All the people shall say, "Amen!"

25 "Cursed be anyone who takes a bribe to shed innocent blood." All the people shall say, "Amen!"

26 "Cursed be anyone who does not uphold the words of this law by observing them." All the people shall say, "Amen!"

Blessings for Obedience

28 If you will only obey the LORD your God, by diligently observing all his commandments that I am commanding you today, the LORD your God will set you high above all the nations of the earth; [2] all these blessings shall come upon you and overtake you, if you obey the LORD your God:

3 Blessed shall you be in the city, and blessed shall you be in the field.

4 Blessed shall be the fruit of your womb, the fruit of your ground, and the fruit of your livestock, both the increase of your cattle and the issue of your flock.

5 Blessed shall be your basket and your kneading bowl.

6 Blessed shall you be when you come in, and blessed shall you be when you go out.

7 The LORD will cause your enemies who rise against you to be defeated before you; they shall come out against you one way, and flee before you seven ways. [8] The LORD will command the blessing upon you in your barns, and in all that you undertake; he will bless you in the land that the LORD your God is giving you. [9] The LORD will establish you as his holy people, as he has sworn to you, if you keep the commandments of the LORD your God

27.9
Deut 26.18
27.12
Josh 8.33-35
27.15
Ex 20.4,23;
34.17
27.16
Ex 21.17;
Lev 20.9
27.17
Lev 19.14
27.18
Lev 19.14
27.19
Deut 10.18;
24.17
27.20
Lev 18.8;
Deut 22.30
27.21
Lev 18.23

27.22
Lev 18.9;
20.17
27.23
Lev 20.14
27.24
Lev 24.17;
Num 35.31
27.25
Ex 23.7,8
27.26
Deut 28.15;
Gal 3.10
28.1
Deut 7.12-26;
26.19
28.3
Gen 39.5;
Ps 128.14
28.4
Gen 49.25;
Ps 107.38;
Prov 10.22
28.7
Lev 26.7,8
28.9
Deut 7.6

[f] Heb *uncovered his father's skirt*

and walk in his ways. 10 All the peoples of the earth shall see that you are called by the name of the LORD, and they shall be afraid of you. 11 The LORD will make you abound in prosperity, in the fruit of your womb, in the fruit of your livestock, and in the fruit of your ground in the land that the LORD swore to your ancestors to give you. 12 The LORD will open for you his rich storehouse, the heavens, to give the rain of your land in its season and to bless all your undertakings. You will lend to many nations, but you will not borrow. 13 The LORD will make you the head, and not the tail; you shall be only at the top, and not at the bottom—if you obey the commandments of the LORD your God, which I am commanding you today, by diligently observing them, 14 and if you do not turn aside from any of the words that I am commanding you today, either to the right or to the left, following other gods to serve them.

Warnings against Disobedience

15 But if you will not obey the LORD your God by diligently observing all his commandments and decrees, which I am commanding you today, then all these curses shall come upon you and overtake you:

16 Cursed shall you be in the city, and cursed shall you be in the field.

17 Cursed shall be your basket and your kneading bowl.

18 Cursed shall be the fruit of your womb, the fruit of your ground, the increase of your cattle and the issue of your flock.

19 Cursed shall you be when you come in, and cursed shall you be when you go out.

20 The LORD will send upon you disaster, panic, and frustration in everything you attempt to do, until you are destroyed and perish quickly, on account of the evil of your deeds, because you have forsaken me. 21 The LORD will make the pestilence cling to you until it has consumed you off the land that you are entering to possess. 22 The

LORD will afflict you with consumption, fever, inflammation, with fiery heat and drought, and with blight and mildew; they shall pursue you until you perish. 23 The sky over your head shall be bronze, and the earth under you iron. 24 The LORD will change the rain of your land into powder, and only dust shall come down upon you from the sky until you are destroyed.

25 The LORD will cause you to be defeated before your enemies; you shall go out against them one way and flee before them seven ways. You shall become an object of horror to all the kingdoms of the earth. 26 Your corpses shall be food for every bird of the air and animal of the earth, and there shall be no one to frighten them away. 27 The LORD will afflict you with the boils of Egypt, with ulcers, scurvy, and itch, of which you cannot be healed. 28 The LORD will afflict you with madness, blindness, and confusion of mind; 29 you shall grope about at noon as blind people grope in darkness, but you shall be unable to find your way; and you shall be continually abused and robbed, without anyone to help. 30 You shall become engaged to a woman, but another man shall lie with her. You shall build a house, but not live in it. You shall plant a vineyard, but not enjoy its fruit. 31 Your ox shall be butchered before your eyes, but you shall not eat of it. Your donkey shall be stolen in front of you, and shall not be restored to you. Your sheep shall be given to your enemies, without anyone to help you. 32 Your sons and daughters shall be given to another people, while you look on; you will strain your eyes looking for them all day but be powerless to do anything. 33 A people whom you do not know shall eat up the fruit of your ground and of all your labors; you shall be continually abused and crushed, 34 and driven mad by the sight that your eyes shall see. 35 The LORD will strike you on the knees and on the legs with grievous boils of which you cannot be

Cross references (center column)

28.10
2 Chr 7.14
28.11
Deut 30.9
28.12
Lev 26.4;
Deut 15.6
28.14
Deut 5.32
28.15
Lev 26.14;
Josh 23.15;
Mal 2.2
28.20
Deut 4.26
28.21
Lev 26.25;
Jer 24.10
28.22
Lev 26.16;
Am 4.9

28.23
Lev 26.19
28.25
Lev 26.17,
37; Jer 15.4
28.26
Jer 7.33;
16.4; 34.20
28.27
vv. 60,61
28.29
Job 5.14;
Isa 59.10
28.30
Jer 8.10;
12.13;
Am 5.11
28.32
v. 41
28.33
Jer 5.17
28.35
v. 27

healed, from the sole of your foot to the crown of your head. ³⁶ The LORD will bring you, and the king whom you set over you, to a nation that neither you nor your ancestors have known, where you shall serve other gods, of wood and stone. ³⁷ You shall become an object of horror, a proverb, and a byword among all the peoples where the LORD will lead you.

38 You shall carry much seed into the field but shall gather little in, for the locust shall consume it. ³⁹ You shall plant vineyards and dress them, but you shall neither drink the wine nor gather the grapes, for the worm shall eat them. ⁴⁰ You shall have olive trees throughout all your territory, but you shall not anoint yourself with the oil, for your olives shall drop off. ⁴¹ You shall have sons and daughters, but they shall not remain yours, for they shall go into captivity. ⁴² All your trees and the fruit of your ground the cicada shall take over. ⁴³ Aliens residing among you shall ascend above you higher and higher, while you shall descend lower and lower. ⁴⁴ They shall lend to you but you shall not lend to them; they shall be the head and you shall be the tail.

45 All these curses shall come upon you, pursuing and overtaking you until you are destroyed, because you did not obey the LORD your God, by observing the commandments and the decrees that he commanded you. ⁴⁶ They shall be among you and your descendants as a sign and a portent forever.

47 Because you did not serve the LORD your God joyfully and with gladness of heart for the abundance of everything, ⁴⁸ therefore you shall serve your enemies whom the LORD will send against you, in hunger and thirst, in nakedness and lack of everything. He will put an iron yoke on your neck until he has destroyed you. ⁴⁹ The LORD will bring a nation from far away, from the end of the earth, to swoop down on you like an eagle, a nation

28.36
2 Kings 17.4, 6; 24.12,14; 25.7,11; Deut 4.28
28.37
Jer 24.9; Ps 44.14
28.38
Mic 6.15
28.41
v. 32
28.42
v. 38
28.43
v. 13
28.44
vv. 12,13
28.45
v. 15
28.47
Deut 32.15
28.48
Jer 28.13,14
28.49
Jer 5.15

28.51
v. 33
28.52
Jer 10.17, 18; Zeph 1.15, 16; Josh 1.4
28.53
Lev 26.29; Jer 19.9; Lam 2.20
28.56
v. 54
28.58
Ex 6.3
28.60
v. 27

whose language you do not understand, ⁵⁰ a grim-faced nation showing no respect to the old or favor to the young. ⁵¹ It shall consume the fruit of your livestock and the fruit of your ground until you are destroyed, leaving you neither grain, wine, and oil, nor the increase of your cattle and the issue of your flock, until it has made you perish. ⁵² It shall besiege you in all your towns until your high and fortified walls, in which you trusted, come down throughout your land; it shall besiege you in all your towns throughout the land that the LORD your God has given you. ⁵³ In the desperate straits to which the enemy siege reduces you, you will eat the fruit of your womb, the flesh of your own sons and daughters whom the LORD your God has given you. ⁵⁴ Even the most refined and gentle of men among you will begrudge food to his own brother, to the wife whom he embraces, and to the last of his remaining children, ⁵⁵ giving to none of them any of the flesh of his children whom he is eating, because nothing else remains to him, in the desperate straits to which the enemy siege will reduce you in all your towns. ⁵⁶ She who is the most refined and gentle among you, so gentle and refined that she does not venture to set the sole of her foot on the ground, will begrudge food to the husband whom she embraces, to her own son, and to her own daughter, ⁵⁷ begrudging even the afterbirth that comes out from between her thighs, and the children that she bears, because she is eating them in secret for lack of anything else, in the desperate straits to which the enemy siege will reduce you in your towns.

58 If you do not diligently observe all the words of this law that are written in this book, fearing this glorious and awesome name, the LORD your God, ⁵⁹ then the LORD will overwhelm both you and your offspring with severe and lasting afflictions and grievous and lasting maladies. ⁶⁰ He will bring back

upon you all the diseases of Egypt, of which you were in dread, and they shall cling to you. 61 Every other malady and affliction, even though not recorded in the book of this law, the LORD will inflict on you until you are destroyed. 62 Although once you were as numerous as the stars in heaven, you shall be left few in number, because you did not obey the LORD your God. 63 And just as the LORD took delight in making you prosperous and numerous, so the LORD will take delight in bringing you to ruin and destruction; you shall be plucked off the land that you are entering to possess. 64 The LORD will scatter you among all peoples, from one end of the earth to the other; and there you shall serve other gods, of wood and stone, which neither you nor your ancestors have known. 65 Among those nations you shall find no ease, no resting place for the sole of your foot. There the LORD will give you a trembling heart, failing eyes, and a languishing spirit. 66 Your life shall hang in doubt before you; night and day you shall be in dread, with no assurance of your life. 67 In the morning you shall say, "If only it were evening!" and at evening you shall say, "If only it were morning!"— because of the dread that your heart shall feel and the sights that your eyes shall see. 68 The LORD will bring you back in ships to Egypt, by a route that I promised you would never see again; and there you shall offer yourselves for sale to your enemies as male and female slaves, but there will be no buyer.

29 g These are the words of the covenant that the LORD commanded Moses to make with the Israelites in the land of Moab, in addition to the covenant that he had made with them at Horeb.

The Covenant Renewed in Moab

2 h Moses summoned all Israel and said to them: You have seen all that the LORD did before your eyes in the land of Egypt, to Pharaoh and to all his servants and to all his

land, 3 the great trials that your eyes saw, the signs, and those great wonders. 4 But to this day the LORD has not given you a mind to understand, or eyes to see, or ears to hear. 5 I have led you forty years in the wilderness. The clothes on your back have not worn out, and the sandals on your feet have not worn out; 6 you have not eaten bread, and you have not drunk wine or strong drink— so that you may know that I am the LORD your God. 7 When you came to this place, King Sihon of Heshbon and King Og of Bashan came out against us for battle, but we defeated them. 8 We took their land and gave it as an inheritance to the Reubenites, the Gadites, and the half-tribe of Manasseh. 9 Therefore diligently observe the words of this covenant, in order that you may succeed i in everything that you do.

10 You stand assembled today, all of you, before the LORD your God—the leaders of your tribes, j your elders, and your officials, all the men of Israel, 11 your children, your women, and the aliens who are in your camp, both those who cut your wood and those who draw your water— 12 to enter into the covenant of the LORD your God, sworn by an oath, which the LORD your God is making with you today; 13 in order that he may establish you today as his people, and that he may be your God, as he promised you and as he swore to your ancestors, to Abraham, to Isaac, and to Jacob. 14 I am making this covenant, sworn by an oath, not only with you who stand here with us today before the LORD our God, 15 but also with those who are not here with us today. 16 You know how we lived in the land of Egypt, and how we came through the midst of the nations through which you passed. 17 You have seen their detestable things, the filthy idols of wood and stone, of silver and gold, that were among them. 18 It may be

28.61
Deut 4.25, 26
28.62
Deut 4.27; 10.22
28.63
Jer 12.14; 45.4
28.64
Deut 4.27, 28
28.65
Lev 26.16, 36
28.67
v. 34
29.1
Deut 5.2,3
29.2
Ex 19.4

29.4
Isa 6.9,10; Acts 28.26, 27; Eph 4.18
29.5
Deut 8.4
29.6
Deut 8.3
29.7
Num 21.21-24, 33-35; Deut 2.32; 3.1
29.8
Num 32.33; Deut 3.12, 13
29.9
Deut 4.6; Josh 1.7
29.11
Josh 9.21, 23,27
29.13
Deut 28.9; Ex 6.7; Gen 17.7
29.17
Deut 28.26
29.18
Deut 11.16; Heb 12.15

g Ch 28.69 in Heb h Ch 29.1 in Heb
i Or deal wisely j Gk Syr: Heb your leaders, your tribes

that there is among you a man or woman, or a family or tribe, whose heart is already turning away from the LORD our God to serve the gods of those nations. It may be that there is among you a root sprouting poisonous and bitter growth. [19] All who hear the words of this oath and bless themselves, thinking in their hearts, "We are safe even though we go our own stubborn ways" (thus bringing disaster on moist and dry alike)[k]— [20] the LORD will be unwilling to pardon them, for the LORD's anger and passion will smoke against them. All the curses written in this book will descend on them, and the LORD will blot out their names from under heaven. [21] The LORD will single them out from all the tribes of Israel for calamity, in accordance with all the curses of the covenant written in this book of the law. [22] The next generation, your children who rise up after you, as well as the foreigner who comes from a distant country, will see the devastation of that land and the afflictions with which the LORD has afflicted it— [23] all its soil burned out by sulfur and salt, nothing planted, nothing sprouting, unable to support any vegetation, like the destruction of Sodom and Gomorrah, Admah and Zeboiim, which the LORD destroyed in his fierce anger— [24] they and indeed all the nations will wonder, "Why has the LORD done thus to this land? What caused this great display of anger?" [25] They will conclude, "It is because they abandoned the covenant of the LORD, the God of their ancestors, which he made with them when he brought them out of the land of Egypt. [26] They turned and served other gods, worshiping them, gods whom they had not known and whom he had not allotted to them; [27] so the anger of the LORD was kindled against that land, bringing on it every curse written in this book. [28] The LORD uprooted them from their land in anger, fury, and great wrath, and cast them into another land, as is now the case." [29] The se-

cret things belong to the LORD God, but the revealed things long to us and to our children ever, to observe all the word this law.

God's Fidelity Assured

30 When all these things happened to you, the bl ings and the curses that I have before you, if you call them to m among all the nations where LORD your God has driven you, [2] return to the LORD your God, you and your children obey with all your heart and with all y soul, just as I am commanding today, [3] then the LORD your God restore your fortunes and h compassion on you, gathering again from all the peoples am whom the LORD your God has s tered you. [4] Even if you are exile the ends of the world,[1] from th the LORD your God will gather y and from there he will bring back. [5] The LORD your God bring you into the land that y ancestors possessed, and you possess it; he will make you n prosperous and numerous t your ancestors.

[6] Moreover, the LORD your C will circumcise your heart and heart of your descendants, so you will love the LORD your C with all your heart and with all y soul, in order that you may [7] The LORD your God will put these curses on your enemies on the adversaries who took ad tage of you. [8] Then you shall a obey the LORD, observing all commandments that I am c manding you today, [9] and the L your God will make you abund ly prosperous in all your under ings, in the fruit of your body the fruit of your livestock, an the fruit of your soil. For the L will again take delight in pros ing you, just as he delighted prospering your ancestors, [10] w you obey the LORD your God by serving his commandments

29.20 Ps 74.1; 79.5; Deut 9.14; Ex 32.33
29.21 Mt 24.51
29.22 Jer 19.8
29.23 Gen 19.24; Isa 34.9; Jer 20.16
29.24 Jer 22.8,9
29.28 1 Kings 14.15; 2 Chr 7.20

30.1 vv. 15,19; Deut 11.26; 28.64; 29.28
30.2 Deut 4.29, 30
30.3 Jer 29.14; 32.37
30.4 Neh 1.9; Isa 43.6
30.6 Jer 32.39
30.9 Deut 28.11; Jer 32.41

[k] Meaning of Heb uncertain　[1] Heb *of heaven*

decrees that are written in this book of the law, because you turn to the Lord your God with all your heart and with all your soul.

Exhortation to Choose Life

11 Surely, this commandment that I am commanding you today is not too hard for you, nor is it too far away. [12] It is not in heaven, that you should say, "Who will go up to heaven for us, and get it for us so that we may hear it and observe it?" [13] Neither is it beyond the sea, that you should say, "Who will cross to the other side of the sea for us, and get it for us so that we may hear it and observe it?" [14] No, the word is very near to you; it is in your mouth and in your heart for you to observe.

15 See, I have set before you today life and prosperity, death and adversity. [16] If you obey the commandments of the Lord your God[m] that I am commanding you today, by loving the Lord your God, walking in his ways, and observing his commandments, decrees, and ordinances, then you shall live and become numerous, and the Lord your God will bless you in the land that you are entering to possess. [17] But if your heart turns away and you do not hear, but are led astray to bow down to other gods and serve them, [18] I declare to you today that you shall perish; you shall not live long in the land that you are crossing the Jordan to enter and possess. [19] I call heaven and earth to witness against you today that I have set before you life and death, blessings and curses. Choose life so that you and your descendants may live, [20] loving the Lord your God, obeying him, and holding fast to him; for that means life to you and length of days, so that you may live in the land that the Lord swore to give to your ancestors, to Abraham, to Isaac, and to Jacob.

Joshua Becomes Moses' Successor

31 When Moses had finished speaking all[n] these words

to all Israel, [2] he said to them: "I am now one hundred twenty years old. I am no longer able to get about, and the Lord has told me, 'You shall not cross over this Jordan.' [3] The Lord your God himself will cross over before you. He will destroy these nations before you, and you shall dispossess them. Joshua also will cross over before you, as the Lord promised. [4] The Lord will do to them as he did to Sihon and Og, the kings of the Amorites, and to their land, when he destroyed them. [5] The Lord will give them over to you and you shall deal with them in full accord with the command that I have given to you. [6] Be strong and bold; have no fear or dread of them, because it is the Lord your God who goes with you; he will not fail you or forsake you."

7 Then Moses summoned Joshua and said to him in the sight of all Israel: "Be strong and bold, for you are the one who will go with this people into the land that the Lord has sworn to their ancestors to give them; and you will put them in possession of it. [8] It is the Lord who goes before you. He will be with you; he will not fail you or forsake you. Do not fear or be dismayed."

The Law to Be Read Every Seventh Year

9 Then Moses wrote down this law, and gave it to the priests, the sons of Levi, who carried the ark of the covenant of the Lord, and to all the elders of Israel. [10] Moses commanded them: "Every seventh year, in the scheduled year of remission, during the festival of booths,[o] [11] when all Israel comes to appear before the Lord your God at the place that he will choose, you shall read this law before all Israel in their hearing. [12] Assemble the people—men, women, and children, as well as the aliens residing in your towns—so that they may hear and learn to fear the Lord

30.11
Isa 45.19
30.12
Rom 10.6-8
30.15
vv. 1,19
30.18
Deut 4.26
30.19
Deut 4.26;
v. 1
30.20
Deut 6.5;
10.20;
Ps 27.1;
Jn 11.25

31.2
Deut 34.7;
3.27
31.3
Deut 9.3;
3.28
31.5
Deut 7.2
31.6
Josh 10.25;
Deut 1.29;
20.4;
Heb 13.5
31.7
Deut 1.38;
3.28
31.8
v. 6
31.9
v. 25;
Num 4.15
31.10
Deut 15.1;
Lev 23.34
31.11
Deut 16.16;
Josh 8.34,
35
31.12
Deut 4.10

m Gk: Heb lacks *If you obey the commandments of the Lord your God*
n Q Ms Gk: MT *Moses went and spoke*
o Or *tabernacles*; Heb *succoth*

your God and to observe diligently all the words of this law, 13 and so that their children, who have not known it, may hear and learn to fear the LORD your God, as long as you live in the land that you are crossing over the Jordan to possess."

Moses and Joshua Receive God's Charge

14 The LORD said to Moses, "Your time to die is near; call Joshua and present yourselves in the tent of meeting, so that I may commission him." So Moses and Joshua went and presented themselves in the tent of meeting, 15 and the LORD appeared at the tent in a pillar of cloud; the pillar of cloud stood at the entrance to the tent.

16 The LORD said to Moses, "Soon you will lie down with your ancestors. Then this people will begin to prostitute themselves to the foreign gods in their midst, the gods of the land into which they are going; they will forsake me, breaking my covenant that I have made with them. 17 My anger will be kindled against them in that day. I will forsake them and hide my face from them; they will become easy prey, and many terrible troubles will come upon them. In that day they will say, 'Have not these troubles come upon us because our God is not in our midst?' 18 On that day I will surely hide my face on account of all the evil they have done by turning to other gods. 19 Now therefore write this song, and teach it to the Israelites; put it in their mouths, in order that this song may be a witness for me against the Israelites. 20 For when I have brought them into the land flowing with milk and honey, which I promised on oath to their ancestors, and they have eaten their fill and grown fat, they will turn to other gods and serve them, despising me and breaking my covenant. 21 And when many terrible troubles come upon them, this song will confront them as a witness, because it will not be lost

31.13
Deut 11.2;
Ps 78.6,7
31.14
Deut 32.49,
50; v. 23
31.15
Ex 33.9
31.16
Judg 2.11,
12; 10.6,13
31.17
Judg 2.14;
6.13;
Deut 32.20;
Num 14.42
31.20
Deut 6.10-12;
32.15-17;
v. 16
31.21
v. 17;
Hos 5.3

31.22
v. 19
31.23
v. 7;
Josh 1.6
31.25
v. 9
31.26
v. 19
31.27
Deut 9.6,24
31.28
Deut 4.26
31.29
Deut 32.5;
28.15
32.1
Isa 1.2
32.2
Isa 55.10,11

from the mouths of their descendants. For I know what they are inclined to do even now, before I have brought them into the land that I promised them on oath." 22 That very day Moses wrote this song and taught it to the Israelites.

23 Then the LORD commissioned Joshua son of Nun and said, "Be strong and bold, for you shall bring the Israelites into the land that I promised them; I will be with you."

24 When Moses had finished writing down in a book the words of this law to the very end, 25 Moses commanded the Levites who carried the ark of the covenant of the LORD, saying, 26 "Take this book of the law and put it beside the ark of the covenant of the LORD your God; let it remain there as a witness against you. 27 For I know well how rebellious and stubborn you are. If you already have been so rebellious toward the LORD while I am still alive among you, how much more after my death! 28 Assemble to me all the elders of your tribes and your officials, so that I may recite these words in their hearing and call heaven and earth to witness against them. 29 For I know that after my death you will surely act corruptly, turning aside from the way that I have commanded you. In time to come trouble will befall you, because you will do what is evil in the sight of the LORD, provoking him to anger through the work of your hands."

The Song of Moses

30 Then Moses recited the words of this song, to the very end, in the hearing of the whole assembly of Israel:

32 Give ear, O heavens, and I will speak;
 let the earth hear the words of my mouth.
2 May my teaching drop like the rain,
 my speech condense like the dew;
 like gentle rain on grass,

like showers on new growth.

3 For I will proclaim the name of the LORD;
ascribe greatness to our God!

4 The Rock, his work is perfect,
and all his ways are just.
A faithful God, without deceit,
just and upright is he;

5 yet his degenerate children have dealt falsely with him,p
a perverse and crooked generation.

6 Do you thus repay the LORD, O foolish and senseless people?
Is not he your father, who created you,
who made you and established you?

7 Remember the days of old, consider the years long past;
ask your father, and he will inform you;
your elders, and they will tell you.

8 When the Most Highq apportioned the nations,
when he divided humankind,
he fixed the boundaries of the peoples
according to the number of the gods;r

9 the LORD's own portion was his people,
Jacob his allotted share.

10 He sustaineds him in a desert land,
in a howling wilderness waste;
he shielded him, cared for him,
guarded him as the apple of his eye.

11 As an eagle stirs up its nest, and hovers over its young;
as it spreads its wings, takes them up,

and bears them aloft on its pinions;

12 the LORD alone guided him;
no foreign god was with him.

13 He set him atop the heights of the land,
and fed him witht produce of the field;
he nursed him with honey from the crags,
with oil from flinty rock;

14 curds from the herd, and milk from the flock,
with fat of lambs and rams;
Bashan bulls and goats,
together with the choicest wheat—
you drank fine wine from the blood of grapes.

15 Jacob ate his fill;u
Jeshurun grew fat, and kicked.
You grew fat, bloated, and gorged!
He abandoned God who made him,
and scoffed at the Rock of his salvation.

16 They made him jealous with strange gods,
with abhorrent things they provoked him.

17 They sacrificed to demons, not God,
to deities they had never known,
to new ones recently arrived,
whom your ancestors had not feared.

18 You were unmindful of the Rock that bore you;v
you forgot the God who gave you birth.

19 The LORD saw it, and was jealousw
he spurnedx his sons and daughters.

32.3
Ex 33.19; Deut 3.24
32.4
vv. 15,18, 30; Deut 7.9; Ps 92.15
32.5
Deut 31.29; Lk 9.41
32.6
Deut 1.31
32.7
Ex 13.14
32.8
Gen 11.8; Acts 17.26
32.9
1 Kings 8.51, 53; Jer 10.16
32.10
Jer 2.6; Zech 2.8
32.11
Ex 19.4; Isa 31.5
32.12
v. 39
32.13
Isa 58.14; Job 29.6
32.14
Ps 147.14
32.15
Deut 33.5, 26; Isa 1.4; vv. 6,4
32.16
Ps 78.58; 1 Cor 10.22
32.17
Ps 106.37; Deut 28.64; Judg 5.8
32.18
Isa 17.10; Ps 106.21
32.19
Ps 106.40; Jer 44.21-23

p Meaning of Heb uncertain q Traditional rendering of Heb *Elyon* r Q Ms Compare Gk Tg: MT *the Israelites* s Sam Gk Compare Tg: MT *found* t Sam Gk Syr Tg: MT *he ate* u Q Mss Sam Gk: MT lacks *Jacob ate his fill* v Or *that begot you* w Q Mss Gk: MT lacks *was jealous* x Cn: Heb *he spurned because of provocation*

20 He said: I will hide my face
 from them,
 I will see what their end
 will be;
 for they are a perverse
 generation,
 children in whom there is
 no faithfulness.
21 They made me jealous with
 what is no god,
 provoked me with their
 idols.
 So I will make them jealous
 with what is no people,
 provoke them with a
 foolish nation.
22 For a fire is kindled by my
 anger,
 and burns to the depths of
 Sheol;
 it devours the earth and its
 increase,
 and sets on fire the
 foundations of the
 mountains.
23 I will heap disasters upon
 them,
 spend my arrows against
 them:
24 wasting hunger,
 burning consumption,
 bitter pestilence.
 The teeth of beasts I will
 send against them,
 with venom of things
 crawling in the dust.
25 In the street the sword shall
 bereave,
 and in the chambers terror,
 for young man and woman
 alike,
 nursing child and old gray
 head.
26 I thought to scatter them[y]
 and blot out the memory of
 them from humankind;
27 but I feared provocation by
 the enemy,
 for their adversaries might
 misunderstand
 and say, "Our hand is
 triumphant;
 it was not the LORD who
 did all this."

28 They are a nation void of
 sense;

there is no understanding
 in them.
29 If they were wise, they would
 understand this;
 they would discern what
 the end would be.
30 How could one have routed a
 thousand,
 and two put a myriad to
 flight,
 unless their Rock had sold
 them,
 the LORD had given them
 up?
31 Indeed their rock is not like
 our Rock;
 our enemies are fools.[y]
32 Their vine comes from the
 vinestock of Sodom,
 from the vineyards of
 Gomorrah;
 their grapes are grapes of
 poison,
 their clusters are bitter;
33 their wine is the poison of
 serpents,
 the cruel venom of asps.

34 Is not this laid up in store
 with me,
 sealed up in my treasuries?
35 Vengeance is mine, and
 recompense,
 for the time when their
 foot shall slip;
 because the day of their
 calamity is at hand,
 their doom comes swiftly.

36 Indeed the LORD will
 vindicate his people,
 have compassion on his
 servants,
 when he sees that their
 power is gone,
 neither bond nor free
 remaining.
37 Then he will say: Where are
 their gods,
 the rock in which they took
 refuge,
38 who ate the fat of their
 sacrifices,
 and drank the wine of the
 libations?

32.20
Deut 31.17,
29; v. 5
32.21
v. 16;
Rom 10.19
32.22
Jer 15.14
32.23
Deut 29.21;
Ezek 5.16
32.24
Deut 28.22;
Lev 26.22;
v. 33
32.25
Ezek 7.15;
2 Chr 36.17
32.26
Deut 4.27;
Ps 34.16
32.27
Deut 9.26-28;
Isa 10.13

32.29
Ps 81.13
32.30
Lev 26.7,8;
v. 4
32.31
1 Sam 2.2;
4.8
32.33
Ps 58.4
32.34
Hos 13.12
32.35
Rom 12.19;
Heb 10.30
32.36
Ps 135.14;
106.45;
Judg 2.18;
Joel 2.14
32.37
Jer 2.28

y Gk: Meaning of Heb uncertain

Let them rise up and help
you,
let them be your
protection!

39 See now that I, even I, am
he;
there is no god beside me.
I kill and I make alive;
I wound and I heal;
and no one can deliver
from my hand.
40 For I lift up my hand to
heaven,
and swear: As I live forever,
41 when I whet my flashing
sword,
and my hand takes hold on
judgment;
I will take vengeance on my
adversaries,
and will repay those who
hate me.
42 I will make my arrows drunk
with blood,
and my sword shall devour
flesh—
with the blood of the slain
and the captives,
from the long-haired
enemy.

43 Praise, O heavens,z his
people,
worship him, all you
gods!a
For he will avenge the blood
of his children,b
and take vengeance on his
adversaries;
he will repay those who hate
him,a
and cleanse the land for
his people.c

44 Moses came and recited all
the words of this song in the hear-
ing of the people, he and Joshuad
son of Nun. 45When Moses had fin-
ished reciting all these words to all
Israel, 46he said to them: "Take to
heart all the words that I am giving
in witness against you today; give
them as a command to your chil-
dren, so that they may diligently
observe all the words of this law.
47This is no trifling matter for you,
but rather your very life; through it

32.39
Isa 41.4;
Ps 50.22
32.41
Ezek 21.9,
10
32.42
Jer 46.10
32.43
Rom 15.10;
Rev 19.2;
Ps 85.1
32.46
Deut 6.6;
Ezek 40.4
32.47
Deut 30.20

32.49
Num 27.12-14
32.51
Num 20.11-13;
27.14
32.52
Deut 34.1-3;
1.37
33.1
Josh 14.6
33.2
Hab 3.3;
Dan 7.10;
Acts 7.53;
Gal 3.19;
Rev 5.11
33.3
Hos 11.1;
Deut 14.2
33.4
Jn 1.17;
Ps 119.111

you may live long in the land that
you are crossing over the Jordan to
possess."

Moses' Death Foretold

48 On that very day the LORD ad-
dressed Moses as follows: 49"As-
cend this mountain of the Abarim,
Mount Nebo, which is in the land
of Moab, across from Jericho, and
view the land of Canaan, which I
am giving to the Israelites for a pos-
session; 50you shall die there on
the mountain that you ascend and
shall be gathered to your kin, as
your brother Aaron died on Mount
Hor and was gathered to his kin;
51because both of you broke faith
with me among the Israelites at the
waters of Meribath-kadesh in the
wilderness of Zin, by failing to
maintain my holiness among the
Israelites. 52Although you may
view the land from a distance, you
shall not enter it—the land that I
am giving to the Israelites."

Moses' Final Blessing on Israel

33 This is the blessing with
which Moses, the man of
God, blessed the Israelites before
his death. 2 He said:
The LORD came from Sinai,
and dawned from Seir upon
us;e
he shone forth from Mount
Paran.
With him were myriads of
holy ones;f
at his right, a host of his
own.g
3 Indeed, O favorite amongh
peoples,
all his holy ones were in
your charge;
they marched at your heels,
accepted direction from
you.
4 Moses charged us with the
law,

z Q Ms Gk: MT nations a Q Ms Gk: MT
lacks this line b Q Ms Gk: MT his servants
c Q Ms Sam Gk Vg: MT his land his people
d Sam Gk Syr Vg: MT Hoshea e Gk Syr
Vg Compare Tg: Heb upon them
f Cn Compare Gk Sam Syr Vg: MT He came
from Ribeboth-kadesh, g Cn Compare Gk:
meaning of Heb uncertain h Or O lover
of the

as a possession for the
assembly of Jacob.

5 There arose a king in
Jeshurun,
when the leaders of the
people assembled—
the united tribes of Israel.

6 May Reuben live, and not die
out,
even though his numbers
are few.

7 And this he said of Judah:
O Lord, give heed to Judah,
and bring him to his
people;
strengthen his hands for
him,[i]
and be a help against his
adversaries.

8 And of Levi he said:
Give to Levi[j] your
Thummim,
and your Urim to your loyal
one,
whom you tested at Massah,
with whom you contended
at the waters of
Meribah;
9 who said of his father and
mother,
"I regard them not";
he ignored his kin,
and did not acknowledge
his children.
For they observed your word,
and kept your covenant.
10 They teach Jacob your
ordinances,
and Israel your law;
they place incense before
you,
and whole burnt offerings
on your altar.
11 Bless, O Lord, his substance,
and accept the work of his
hands;
crush the loins of his
adversaries,
of those that hate him, so
that they do not rise
again.

12 Of Benjamin he said:

The beloved of the Lord rests
in safety—
the High God[k] surrounds
him all day long—
the beloved[l] rests between
his shoulders.

13 And of Joseph he said:
Blessed by the Lord be his
land,
with the choice gifts of
heaven above,
and of the deep that lies
beneath;
14 with the choice fruits of the
sun,
and the rich yield of the
months;
15 with the finest produce of
the ancient mountains,
and the abundance of the
everlasting hills;
16 with the choice gifts of the
earth and its fullness,
and the favor of the one
who dwells on Sinai.[m]
Let these come on the head
of Joseph,
on the brow of the prince
among his brothers.
17 A firstborn[n] bull—majesty is
his!
His horns are the horns of
a wild ox;
with them he gores the
peoples,
driving them to[o] the ends
of the earth;
such are the myriads of
Ephraim,
such the thousands of
Manasseh.

18 And of Zebulun he said:
Rejoice, Zebulun, in your
going out;
and Issachar, in your tents.
19 They call peoples to the
mountain;
there they offer the right
sacrifices;

Cross references

33.7
Gen 49.8-12
33.8
Ex 28.30;
17.7
33.9
Ex 32.26-29
33.10
Deut 31.9-13;
Ex 30.7,8;
Ps 51.19
33.11
2 Sam 24.23;
Ps 20.3

33.13
Gen 49.25;
27.28
33.15
Gen 49.26
33.16
Ex 3.2,4;
Acts 7.30,35
33.17
Num 23.22;
Ps 44.5
33.18
Gen 49.13-15
33.19
Isa 2.3;
Ps 4.5

[i] Cn: Heb *with his hands he contended*
[j] Q Ms Gk: MT lacks *Give to Levi*
[k] Heb *above him* [l] Heb *he* [m] Cn: Heb
in the bush [n] Q Ms Gk Syr Vg: MT *His
firstborn* [o] Cn: Heb *the peoples, together*

for they suck the affluence of
the seas
and the hidden treasures of
the sand.

20 And of Gad he said:
Blessed be the enlargement
of Gad!
Gad lives like a lion;
he tears at arm and scalp.
21 He chose the best for
himself,
for there a commander's
allotment was reserved;
he came at the head of the
people,
he executed the justice of
the LORD,
and his ordinances for
Israel.

22 And of Dan he said:
Dan is a lion's whelp
that leaps forth from
Bashan.

23 And of Naphtali he said:
O Naphtali, sated with favor,
full of the blessing of the
LORD,
possess the west and the
south.

24 And of Asher he said:
Most blessed of sons be
Asher;
may he be the favorite of
his brothers,
and may he dip his foot in
oil.
25 Your bars are iron and
bronze;
and as your days, so is your
strength.

26 There is none like God,
O Jeshurun,
who rides through the
heavens to your help,
majestic through the skies.
27 He subdues the ancient
gods, p
shatters q the forces of
old; r
he drove out the enemy
before you,
and said, "Destroy!"

33.20
Gen 49.19
33.21
Num 32.1-5,
31,32;
Josh 4.12;
22.1-3
33.22
Gen 49.16
33.23
Gen 49.21
33.24
Gen 49.20;
Job 29;6
33.25
Deut 4.40;
32.49
33.26
Ex 15.11;
Ps 68.33,34
33.27
Ps 90.1,2;
Josh 24.18

33.28
Num 23.9;
Gen 27.28
33.29
Ps 144.15;
2 Sam 7.23;
Ps 18.14;
Deut 32.13
34.1
Deut 32.49,
52
34.4
Gen 12.7;
28.13
34.5
Deut 32.50;
Josh 1.1,2
34.7
Deut 31.2
34.9
Isa 11.2;
Num 27.18,
23

28 So Israel lives in safety,
untroubled is Jacob's
abode s
in a land of grain and wine,
where the heavens drop
down dew.
29 Happy are you, O Israel! Who
is like you,
a people saved by the LORD,
the shield of your help,
and the sword of your
triumph!
Your enemies shall come
fawning to you,
and you shall tread on
their backs.

Moses Dies and Is Buried in the Land of Moab

34 Then Moses went up from
the plains of Moab to
Mount Nebo, to the top of Pisgah,
which is opposite Jericho, and the
LORD showed him the whole land:
Gilead as far as Dan, 2 all Naphtali,
the land of Ephraim and Manas-
seh, all the land of Judah as far as
the Western Sea, 3 the Negeb, and
the Plain—that is, the valley of Jer-
icho, the city of palm trees—as far
as Zoar. 4 The LORD said to him,
"This is the land of which I swore to
Abraham, to Isaac, and to Jacob,
saying, 'I will give it to your descen-
dants'; I have let you see it with
your eyes, but you shall not cross
over there." 5 Then Moses, the ser-
vant of the LORD, died there in the
land of Moab, at the LORD's com-
mand. 6 He was buried in a valley in
the land of Moab, opposite Beth-
peor, but no one knows his burial
place to this day. 7 Moses was one
hundred twenty years old when he
died; his sight was unimpaired and
his vigor had not abated. 8 The Isra-
elites wept for Moses in the plains
of Moab thirty days; then the peri-
od of mourning for Moses was end-
ed.

9 Joshua son of Nun was full of
the spirit of wisdom, because Mo-
ses had laid his hands on him; and

p Or *The eternal God is a dwelling place*
q Cn: Heb *from underneath* r Or *the
everlasting arms* s Or *fountain*

the Israelites obeyed him, doing as the LORD had commanded Moses.

10 Never since has there arisen a prophet in Israel like Moses, whom the LORD knew face to face. [11] He was unequaled for all the signs and wonders that the LORD

34.10
Num 12.6,8
34.11
Deut 4.34

sent him to perform in the land of Egypt, against Pharaoh and all his servants and his entire land, [12] and for all the mighty deeds and all the terrifying displays of power that Moses performed in the sight of all Israel.

Joshua

Title and Background

This book is named after its leading character, Joshua, whom God named as the leader of Israel before Moses' death. Where Deuteronomy ends the book of Joshua begins, with the tribes still camped on the east side of the Jordan River, ready to enter Canaan.

Author and Date of Writing

The earliest Jewish traditions (Talmud) claim that Joshua wrote his own book, except the final section about his funeral, which is assigned to Eleazar son of Aaron. Others think that Samuel may have shaped or compiled the materials of the book. However, we have no sure knowledge of who the author was. The book of Joshua was probably written, at least in its early form, sometime before 1000 B.C.

Theme and Message

The theme of this book is the establishment of the nation of Israel in the promised land. With God's help the people crossed the Jordan River and took possession of all the main areas of Canaan. Toward the end of the book Joshua reminded the people of God's covenant promises to them and instructed them to keep on loving and obeying God.

Outline

I. Preparation for Possession of Canaan (1.1–5.12)
II. The Conquest of Canaan (5.13–12.24)
III. The Distribution of Land to Tribes (13.1–21.45)
IV. Farewell and Death of Joshua (22.1–24.33)

God's Commission to Joshua

1 After the death of Moses the servant of the Lord, the Lord spoke to Joshua son of Nun, Moses' assistant, saying, [2] "My servant Moses is dead. Now proceed to cross the Jordan, you and all this people, into the land that I am giving to them, to the Israelites. [3] Every place that the sole of your foot will tread upon I have given to you, as I promised to Moses. [4] From the wilderness and the Lebanon as far as the great river, the river Euphrates, all the land of the Hittites, to the Great Sea in the west shall be your territory. [5] No one shall be able to stand against you all the days of your life. As I was with Moses, so I will be with you; I will not fail you or forsake you. [6] Be strong and courageous; for you shall put this people in possession of the land that I swore to their ancestors to give them. [7] Only be strong and very courageous, being careful to act in accordance with all the law that my servant Moses commanded you; do not turn from it to the right hand or to the left, so that you may be successful wherever you go. [8] This book of the law shall not depart out of your mouth; you shall meditate on it day and night, so that you may be careful to act in accordance with all that is written in it. For then you shall make your way prosperous, and then you shall be successful. [9] I hereby command you: Be strong and courageous; do not be frightened or dismayed, for the Lord your God is with you wherever you go."

Preparations for the Invasion

10 Then Joshua commanded the officers of the people, [11] "Pass

1.2 Num 12.7; Deut 34.5; v. 11
1.3 Deut 11.24
1.4 Gen 15.18
1.5 Deut 7.24; 31.6-8
1.7 Deut 5.32; 28.14
1.8 Deut 17.8,9; Ps 1.1-3
1.9 Deut 31.7,8, 23; Jer 1.8
1.11 Joel 3.2

through the camp, and command the people: 'Prepare your provisions; for in three days you are to cross over the Jordan, to go in to take possession of the land that the LORD your God gives you to possess.'"

12 To the Reubenites, the Gadites, and the half-tribe of Manasseh Joshua said, 13 "Remember the word that Moses the servant of the LORD commanded you, saying, 'The LORD your God is providing you a place of rest, and will give you this land.' 14 Your wives, your little ones, and your livestock shall remain in the land that Moses gave you beyond the Jordan. But all the warriors among you shall cross over armed before your kindred and shall help them, 15 until the LORD gives rest to your kindred as well as to you, and they too take possession of the land that the LORD your God is giving them. Then you shall return to your own land and take possession of it, the land that Moses the servant of the LORD gave you beyond the Jordan to the east."

16 They answered Joshua: "All that you have commanded us we will do, and wherever you send us we will go. 17 Just as we obeyed Moses in all things, so we will obey you. Only may the LORD your God be with you, as he was with Moses! 18 Whoever rebels against your orders and disobeys your words, whatever you command, shall be put to death. Only be strong and courageous."

Spies Sent to Jericho

2 Then Joshua son of Nun sent two men secretly from Shittim as spies, saying, "Go, view the land, especially Jericho." So they went, and entered the house of a prostitute whose name was Rahab, and spent the night there. 2 The king of Jericho was told, "Some Israelites have come here tonight to search out the land." 3 Then the king of Jericho sent orders to Rahab, "Bring out the men who have come to you, who entered your house, for they have come only to search out

the whole land." 4 But the woman took the two men and hid them. Then she said, "True, the men came to me, but I did not know where they came from. 5 And when it was time to close the gate at dark, the men went out. Where the men went I do not know. Pursue them quickly, for you can overtake them." 6 She had, however, brought them up to the roof and hidden them with the stalks of flax that she had laid out on the roof. 7 So the men pursued them on the way to the Jordan as far as the fords. As soon as the pursuers had gone out, the gate was shut.

8 Before they went to sleep, she came up to them on the roof 9 and said to the men: "I know that the LORD has given you the land, and that dread of you has fallen on us, and that all the inhabitants of the land melt in fear before you. 10 For we have heard how the LORD dried up the water of the Red Sea[a] before you when you came out of Egypt, and what you did to the two kings of the Amorites that were beyond the Jordan, to Sihon and Og, whom you utterly destroyed. 11 As soon as we heard it, our hearts melted, and there was no courage left in any of us because of you. The LORD your God is indeed God in heaven above and on earth below. 12 Now then, since I have dealt kindly with you, swear to me by the LORD that you in turn will deal kindly with my family. Give me a sign of good faith 13 that you will spare my father and mother, my brothers and sisters, and all who belong to them, and deliver our lives from death." 14 The men said to her, "Our life for yours! If you do not tell this business of ours, then we will deal kindly and faithfully with you when the LORD gives us the land."

15 Then she let them down by a rope through the window, for her house was on the outer side of the city wall and she resided within the wall itself. 16 She said to them, "Go toward the hill country, so that the

Cross references (center column):

1.12 Num 32.20-22
1.13 Deut 3.18-20
1.15 Josh 22.1-4
1.17 vv. 5,9
2.1 Num 25.1; Heb 11.31; Jas 2.25

2.6 Jas 2.25
2.9 Ex 23.27; Deut 2.25
2.10 Ex 14.21; Num 21.24, 34,35
2.11 Ex 15.14, 15; Josh 5.1; Deut 4.39
2.12 v. 18
2.14 Judg 1.24
2.16 Jas 2.25

[a] Or *Sea of Reeds*

pursuers may not come upon you. Hide yourselves there three days, until the pursuers have returned; then afterward you may go your way." ¹⁷The men said to her, "We will be released from this oath that you have made us swear to you ¹⁸if we invade the land and you do not tie this crimson cord in the window through which you let us down, and you do not gather into your house your father and mother, your brothers, and all your family. ¹⁹If any of you go out of the doors of your house into the street, they shall be responsible for their own death, and we shall be innocent; but if a hand is laid upon any who are with you in the house, we shall bear the responsibility for their death. ²⁰But if you tell this business of ours, then we shall be released from this oath that you made us swear to you." ²¹She said, "According to your words, so be it." She sent them away and they departed. Then she tied the crimson cord in the window.

22 They departed and went into the hill country and stayed there three days, until the pursuers returned. The pursuers had searched all along the way and found nothing. ²³Then the two men came down again from the hill country. They crossed over, came to Joshua son of Nun, and told him all that had happened to them. ²⁴They said to Joshua, "Truly the LORD has given all the land into our hands; moreover all the inhabitants of the land melt in fear before us."

Israel Crosses the Jordan

3 Early in the morning Joshua rose and set out from Shittim with all the Israelites, and they came to the Jordan. They camped there before crossing over. ²At the end of three days the officers went through the camp ³and commanded the people, "When you see the ark of the covenant of the LORD your God being carried by the levitical priests, then you shall set out from your place. Follow it, ⁴so that you may know the way you should

go, for you have not passed this way before. Yet there shall be a space between you and it, a distance of about two thousand cubits; do not come any nearer to it." ⁵Then Joshua said to the people, "Sanctify yourselves; for tomorrow the LORD will do wonders among you." ⁶To the priests Joshua said, "Take up the ark of the covenant, and pass on in front of the people." So they took up the ark of the covenant and went in front of the people.

7 The LORD said to Joshua, "This day I will begin to exalt you in the sight of all Israel, so that they may know that I will be with you as I was with Moses. ⁸You are the one who shall command the priests who bear the ark of the covenant, 'When you come to the edge of the waters of the Jordan, you shall stand still in the Jordan.' " ⁹Joshua then said to the Israelites, "Draw near and hear the words of the LORD your God." ¹⁰Joshua said, "By this you shall know that among you is the living God who without fail will drive out from before you the Canaanites, Hittites, Hivites, Perizzites, Girgashites, Amorites, and Jebusites: ¹¹the ark of the covenant of the Lord of all the earth is going to pass before you into the Jordan. ¹²So now select twelve men from the tribes of Israel, one from each tribe. ¹³When the soles of the feet of the priests who bear the ark of the LORD, the Lord of all the earth, rest in the waters of the Jordan, the waters of the Jordan flowing from above shall be cut off; they shall stand in a single heap."

14 When the people set out from their tents to cross over the Jordan, the priests bearing the ark of the covenant were in front of the people. ¹⁵Now the Jordan overflows all its banks throughout the time of harvest. So when those who bore the ark had come to the Jordan, and the feet of the priests bearing the ark were dipped in the edge of the water, ¹⁶the waters flowing from above stood still, rising up in a single heap far off at Adam, the city that is beside Zare-

Cross references

2.17 Gen 24.8
2.18 Josh 6.23
2.19 Ezek 33.4
2.24 v. 9; Josh 6.2
3.1 Josh 2.1
3.2 Josh 1.11
3.3 Deut 31.9
3.5 Ex 19.10, 14; Josh 7.13
3.7 Josh 4.7; 1.5
3.8 vv. 3,17
3.10 Deut 7.1
3.12 Josh 4.2
3.13 Ex 15.8; Ps 78.13
3.15 Josh 4.18
3.16 Ps 66.6; 74.15; v. 13

than, while those flowing toward the sea of the Arabah, the Dead Sea,ᵇ were wholly cut off. Then the people crossed over opposite Jericho. ¹⁷While all Israel were crossing over on dry ground, the priests who bore the ark of the covenant of the Lord stood on dry ground in the middle of the Jordan, until the entire nation finished crossing over the Jordan.

Twelve Stones Set Up at Gilgal

4 When the entire nation had finished crossing over the Jordan, the Lord said to Joshua: ²"Select twelve men from the people, one from each tribe, ³and command them, 'Take twelve stones from here out of the middle of the Jordan, from the place where the priests' feet stood, carry them over with you, and lay them down in the place where you camp tonight.'" ⁴Then Joshua summoned the twelve men from the Israelites, whom he had appointed, one from each tribe. ⁵Joshua said to them, "Pass on before the ark of the Lord your God into the middle of the Jordan, and each of you take up a stone on his shoulder, one for each of the tribes of the Israelites, ⁶so that this may be a sign among you. When your children ask in time to come, 'What do those stones mean to you?' ⁷then you shall tell them that the waters of the Jordan were cut off in front of the ark of the covenant of the Lord. When it crossed over the Jordan, the waters of the Jordan were cut off. So these stones shall be to the Israelites a memorial forever."

8 The Israelites did as Joshua commanded. They took up twelve stones out of the middle of the Jordan, according to the number of the tribes of the Israelites, as the Lord told Joshua, carried them over with them to the place where they camped, and laid them down there. ⁹(Joshua set up twelve stones in the middle of the Jordan, in the place where the feet of the priests bearing the ark of the cove-

nant had stood; and they are there to this day.)

10 The priests who bore the ark remained standing in the middle of the Jordan, until everything was finished that the Lord commanded Joshua to tell the people, according to all that Moses had commanded Joshua. The people crossed over in haste. ¹¹As soon as all the people had finished crossing over, the ark of the Lord, and the priests, crossed over in front of the people. ¹²The Reubenites, the Gadites, and the half-tribe of Manasseh crossed over armed before the Israelites, as Moses had ordered them. ¹³About forty thousand armed for war crossed over before the Lord to the plains of Jericho for battle.

14 On that day the Lord exalted Joshua in the sight of all Israel; and they stood in awe of him, as they had stood in awe of Moses, all the days of his life.

15 The Lord said to Joshua, ¹⁶"Command the priests who bear the ark of the covenant,ᶜ to come up out of the Jordan." ¹⁷Joshua therefore commanded the priests, "Come up out of the Jordan." ¹⁸When the priests bearing the ark of the covenant of the Lord came up from the middle of the Jordan, and the soles of the priests' feet touched dry ground, the waters of the Jordan returned to their place and overflowed all its banks, as before.

19 The people came up out of the Jordan on the tenth day of the first month, and they camped in Gilgal on the east border of Jericho. ²⁰Those twelve stones, which they had taken out of the Jordan, Joshua set up in Gilgal, ²¹saying to the Israelites, "When your children ask their parents in time to come, 'What do these stones mean?' ²²then you shall let your children know, 'Israel crossed over the Jordan here on dry ground.' ²³For the Lord your God dried up the waters

3.17
Ex 14.29
4.2
Josh 3.12
4.3
vv. 19,20
4.6
v. 21;
Ex 12.26;
13.14
4.7
Josh 3.13
4.8
vv. 19,20
4.9
Ex 28.21

4.12
Num 32.17
4.14
Josh 3.7
4.18
Josh 3.15
4.19
Josh 5.9
4.20
vv. 3,8
4.21
v. 6
4.22
Josh 3.17
4.23
Ex 14.21

ᵇ Heb Salt Sea ᶜ Or treaty, or testimony; Heb eduth

of the Jordan for you until you crossed over, as the LORD your God did to the Red Sea,[d] which he dried up for us until we crossed over, 24 so that all the peoples of the earth may know that the hand of the LORD is mighty, and so that you may fear the LORD your God forever."

The New Generation Circumcised

5 When all the kings of the Amorites beyond the Jordan to the west, and all the kings of the Canaanites by the sea, heard that the LORD had dried up the waters of the Jordan for the Israelites until they had crossed over, their hearts melted, and there was no longer any spirit in them, because of the Israelites.

2 At that time the LORD said to Joshua, "Make flint knives and circumcise the Israelites a second time." 3 So Joshua made flint knives, and circumcised the Israelites at Gibeath-haaraloth.[e] 4 This is the reason why Joshua circumcised them: all the males of the people who came out of Egypt, all the warriors, had died during the journey through the wilderness after they had come out of Egypt. 5 Although all the people who came out had been circumcised, yet all the people born on the journey through the wilderness after they had come out of Egypt had not been circumcised. 6 For the Israelites traveled forty years in the wilderness, until all the nation, the warriors who came out of Egypt, perished, not having listened to the voice of the LORD. To them the LORD swore that he would not let them see the land that he had sworn to their ancestors to give us, a land flowing with milk and honey. 7 So it was their children, whom he raised up in their place, that Joshua circumcised; for they were uncircumcised, because they had not been circumcised on the way.

8 When the circumcising of all the nation was done, they remained in their places in the camp

until they were healed. 9 The LORD said to Joshua, "Today I have rolled away from you the disgrace of Egypt." And so that place is called Gilgal[f] to this day.

The Passover at Gilgal

10 While the Israelites were camped in Gilgal they kept the passover in the evening on the fourteenth day of the month in the plains of Jericho. 11 On the day after the passover, on that very day, they ate the produce of the land, unleavened cakes and parched grain. 12 The manna ceased on the day they ate the produce of the land, and the Israelites no longer had manna; they ate the crops of the land of Canaan that year.

Joshua's Vision

13 Once when Joshua was by Jericho, he looked up and saw a man standing before him with a drawn sword in his hand. Joshua went to him and said to him, "Are you one of us, or one of our adversaries?" 14 He replied, "Neither; but as commander of the army of the LORD I have now come." And Joshua fell on his face to the earth and worshiped, and he said to him, "What do you command your servant, my lord?" 15 The commander of the army of the LORD said to Joshua, "Remove the sandals from your feet, for the place where you stand is holy." And Joshua did so.

Jericho Taken and Destroyed

6 Now Jericho was shut up inside and out because of the Israelites; no one came out and no one went in. 2 The LORD said to Joshua, "See, I have handed Jericho over to you, along with its king and soldiers. 3 You shall march around the city, all the warriors circling the city once. Thus you shall do for six days, 4 with seven priests bearing seven trumpets of rams' horns before the ark. On the seventh day you shall march around the city seven times, the priests blowing the trumpets. 5 When they

Cross references (center column)

4.24
1 Kings 8.42, 43;
Ps 89.13;
Ex 14.31
5.1
Num 13.29;
Josh 2.9-11
5.2
Ex 4.25
5.4
Deut 2.16
5.6
Deut 2.7,14;
Num 14.23

5.10
Ex 12.6,8
5.12
Ex 16.35
5.13
Gen 18.2;
32.24;
Num 22.31
5.14
Gen 17.3
5.15
Ex 3.5
6.2
Josh 2.9,24;
Deut 7.24
6.4
Num 10.8
6.5
Lev 25.9

d Or *Sea of Reeds* e That is *the Hill of the Foreskins* f Related to Heb *galal* to roll

make a long blast with the ram's horn, as soon as you hear the sound of the trumpet, then all the people shall shout with a great shout; and the wall of the city will fall down flat, and all the people shall charge straight ahead." [6] So Joshua son of Nun summoned the priests and said to them, "Take up the ark of the covenant, and have seven priests carry seven trumpets of rams' horns in front of the ark of the Lord." [7] To the people he said, "Go forward and march around the city; have the armed men pass on before the ark of the Lord."

8 As Joshua had commanded the people, the seven priests carrying the seven trumpets of rams' horns before the Lord went forward, blowing the trumpets, with the ark of the covenant of the Lord following them. [9] And the armed men went before the priests who blew the trumpets; the rear guard came after the ark, while the trumpets blew continually. [10] To the people Joshua gave this command: "You shall not shout or let your voice be heard, nor shall you utter a word, until the day I tell you to shout. Then you shall shout." [11] So the ark of the Lord went around the city, circling it once; and they came into the camp, and spent the night in the camp.

12 Then Joshua rose early in the morning, and the priests took up the ark of the Lord. [13] The seven priests carrying the seven trumpets of rams' horns before the ark of the Lord passed on, blowing the trumpets continually. The armed men went before them, and the rear guard came after the ark of the Lord, while the trumpets blew continually. [14] On the second day they marched around the city once and then returned to the camp. They did this for six days.

15 On the seventh day they rose early, at dawn, and marched around the city in the same manner seven times. It was only on that day that they marched around the city seven times. [16] And at the seventh time, when the priests had blown

the trumpets, Joshua said to the people, "Shout! For the Lord has given you the city. [17] The city and all that is in it shall be devoted to the Lord for destruction. Only Rahab the prostitute and all who are with her in her house shall live because she hid the messengers we sent. [18] As for you, keep away from the things devoted to destruction, so as not to covet[g] and take any of the devoted things and make the camp of Israel an object for destruction, bringing trouble upon it. [19] But all silver and gold, and vessels of bronze and iron, are sacred to the Lord; they shall go into the treasury of the Lord." [20] So the people shouted, and the trumpets were blown. As soon as the people heard the sound of the trumpets, they raised a great shout, and the wall fell down flat; so the people charged straight ahead into the city and captured it. [21] Then they devoted to destruction by the edge of the sword all in the city, both men and women, young and old, oxen, sheep, and donkeys.

22 Joshua said to the two men who had spied out the land, "Go into the prostitute's house, and bring the woman out of it and all who belong to her, as you swore to her." [23] So the young men who had been spies went in and brought Rahab out, along with her father, her mother, her brothers, and all who belonged to her—they brought all her kindred out—and set them outside the camp of Israel. [24] They burned down the city, and everything in it; only the silver and gold, and the vessels of bronze and iron, they put into the treasury of the house of the Lord. [25] But Rahab the prostitute, with her family and all who belonged to her, Joshua spared. Her family[h] has lived in Israel ever since. For she hid the messengers whom Joshua sent to spy out Jericho.

26 Joshua then pronounced this oath, saying,

6.7
Ex 14.15
6.9
v. 13;
Isa 52.12
6.13
vv. 4,9

6.17
Lev 27.28;
Josh 2.4
6.18
Josh 7.1,25
6.20
v. 5;
Heb 11.30
6.21
Deut 7.2;
20.16
6.22
Josh 2.14;
Heb 11.31
6.23
Josh 2.13
6.24
v. 19
6.25
Heb 11.31
6.26
1 Kings 16.34

g Gk: Heb *devote to destruction* Compare 7.21
h Heb *She*

"Cursed before the Lord be
 anyone who tries
to build this city—this
 Jericho!
At the cost of his firstborn
 he shall lay its
 foundation,
and at the cost of his
 youngest he shall set up
 its gates!"

27 So the Lord was with Joshua;
and his fame was in all the land.

The Sin of Achan and Its Punishment

7 But the Israelites broke faith
in regard to the devoted
things: Achan son of Carmi son of
Zabdi son of Zerah, of the tribe of
Judah, took some of the devoted
things; and the anger of the Lord
burned against the Israelites.

2 Joshua sent men from Jericho
to Ai, which is near Beth-aven, east
of Bethel, and said to them, "Go up
and spy out the land." And the men
went up and spied out Ai. ³Then
they returned to Joshua and said to
him, "Not all the people need go
up; about two or three thousand
men should go up and attack Ai.
Since they are so few, do not make
the whole people toil up there."
⁴So about three thousand of the
people went up there; and they fled
before the men of Ai. ⁵The men of
Ai killed about thirty-six of them,
chasing them from outside the gate
as far as Shebarim and killing them
on the slope. The hearts of the peo-
ple melted and turned to water.

6 Then Joshua tore his clothes,
and fell to the ground on his face
before the ark of the Lord until the
evening, he and the elders of Israel;
and they put dust on their heads.
⁷Joshua said, "Ah, Lord God! Why
have you brought this people
across the Jordan at all, to hand us
over to the Amorites so as to de-
stroy us? Would that we had been
content to settle beyond the Jor-
dan! ⁸O Lord, what can I say, now
that Israel has turned their backs
to their enemies! ⁹The Canaanites
and all the inhabitants of the land
will hear of it, and surround us, and

cut off our name from the earth.
Then what will you do for your
great name?"

10 The Lord said to Joshua,
"Stand up! Why have you fallen
upon your face? ¹¹Israel has
sinned; they have transgressed my
covenant that I imposed on them.
They have taken some of the devot-
ed things; they have stolen, they
have acted deceitfully, and they
have put them among their own be-
longings. ¹²Therefore the Israelites
are unable to stand before their en-
emies; they turn their backs to
their enemies, because they have
become a thing devoted for de-
struction themselves. I will be with
you no more, unless you destroy
the devoted things from among
you. ¹³Proceed to sanctify the peo-
ple, and say, 'Sanctify yourselves
for tomorrow; for thus says the
Lord, the God of Israel, "There are
devoted things among you,
O Israel; you will be unable to
stand before your enemies until
you take away the devoted things
from among you." ¹⁴In the morning
therefore you shall come forward
tribe by tribe. The tribe that the
Lord takes shall come near by
clans, the clan that the Lord takes
shall come near by households,
and the household that the Lord
takes shall come near one by one.
¹⁵And the one who is taken as hav-
ing the devoted things shall be
burned with fire, together with all
that he has, for having transgressed
the covenant of the Lord, and for
having done an outrageous thing in
Israel.' "

16 So Joshua rose early in the
morning, and brought Israel near
tribe by tribe, and the tribe of Ju-
dah was taken. ¹⁷He brought near
the clans of Judah, and the clan of
the Zerahites was taken; and he
brought near the clan of the Zera-
hites, family by family,[i] and Zabdi
was taken. ¹⁸And he brought near
his household one by one, and
Achan son of Carmi son of Zabdi
son of Zerah, of the tribe of Judah,

6.27
Josh 1.5;
9.1,3
7.1
Josh 6.17-19
7.4
Lev 26.17;
28.25
7.6
Job 2.12;
Rev 18.19
7.7
Ex 5.22
7.9
Ex 32.12;
Deut 9.28

7.11
v. 1;
Josh 6.18,
19; Acts 5.1,2
7.13
Josh 3.5;
6.18
7.15
v. 11
7.17
Num 26.20

[i] Mss Syr: MT *man by man*

was taken. ¹⁹ Then Joshua said to Achan, "My son, give glory to the LORD God of Israel and make confession to him. Tell me now what you have done; do not hide it from me." ²⁰ And Achan answered Joshua, "It is true; I am the one who sinned against the LORD God of Israel. This is what I did: ²¹ when I saw among the spoil a beautiful mantle from Shinar, and two hundred shekels of silver, and a bar of gold weighing fifty shekels, then I coveted them and took them. They now lie hidden in the ground inside my tent, with the silver underneath."

22 So Joshua sent messengers, and they ran to the tent; and there it was, hidden in his tent with the silver underneath. ²³ They took them out of the tent and brought them to Joshua and all the Israelites; and they spread them out before the LORD. ²⁴ Then Joshua and all Israel with him took Achan son of Zerah, with the silver, the mantle, and the bar of gold, with his sons and daughters, with his oxen, donkeys, and sheep, and his tent and all that he had; and they brought them up to the Valley of Achor. ²⁵ Joshua said, "Why did you bring trouble on us? The LORD is bringing trouble on you today." And all Israel stoned him to death; they burned them with fire, cast stones on them, ²⁶ and raised over him a great heap of stones that remains to this day. Then the LORD turned from his burning anger. Therefore that place to this day is called the Valley of Achor.ⁱ

Ai Captured by a Stratagem and Destroyed

8 Then the LORD said to Joshua, "Do not fear or be dismayed; take all the fighting men with you, and go up now to Ai. See, I have handed over to you the king of Ai with his people, his city, and his land. ² You shall do to Ai and its king as you did to Jericho and its king; only its spoil and its livestock you may take as booty for your-

7.19
Jer 13.16;
Jn 9.24;
Num 5.6,7;
1 Sam 14.43
7.20
Josh 22.20;
1 Chr 2.7
7.24
Josh 15.7
7.25
Josh 6.18;
Deut 17.5
7.26
Deut 13.17;
Isa 65.10;
Hos 2.15
8.1
Deut 1.21;
7.18;
Josh 1.9;
6.2
8.2
v. 27;
Deut 20.14

8.4
Judg 20.29-32
8.8
v. 2
8.10
v. 33
8.14
Josh 3.16;
Judg 20.34

selves. Set an ambush against the city, behind it."

3 So Joshua and all the fighting men set out to go up against Ai. Joshua chose thirty thousand warriors and sent them out by night ⁴ with the command, "You shall lie in ambush against the city, behind it; do not go very far from the city, but all of you stay alert. ⁵ I and all the people who are with me will approach the city. When they come out against us, as before, we shall flee from them. ⁶ They will come out after us until we have drawn them away from the city; for they will say, 'They are fleeing from us, as before.' While we flee from them, ⁷ you shall rise up from the ambush and seize the city; for the LORD your God will give it into your hand. ⁸ And when you have taken the city, you shall set the city on fire, doing as the LORD has ordered; see, I have commanded you." ⁹ So Joshua sent them out; and they went to the place of ambush, and lay between Bethel and Ai, to the west of Ai; but Joshua spent that night in the camp.ᵏ

10 In the morning Joshua rose early and mustered the people, and went up, with the elders of Israel, before the people to Ai. ¹¹ All the fighting men who were with him went up, and drew near before the city, and camped on the north side of Ai, with a ravine between them and Ai. ¹² Taking about five thousand men, he set them in ambush between Bethel and Ai, to the west of the city. ¹³ So they stationed the forces, the main encampment that was north of the city and its rear guard west of the city. But Joshua spent that night in the valley. ¹⁴ When the king of Ai saw this, he and all his people, the inhabitants of the city, hurried out early in the morning to the meeting place facing the Arabah to meet Israel in battle; but he did not know that there was an ambush against him behind the city. ¹⁵ And Joshua and all Israel made a pretense of being

ⁱ That is *Trouble* ᵏ Heb *among the people*

beaten before them, and fled in the direction of the wilderness. [16] So all the people who were in the city were called together to pursue them, and as they pursued Joshua they were drawn away from the city. [17] There was not a man left in Ai or Bethel who did not go out after Israel; they left the city open, and pursued Israel.

18 Then the LORD said to Joshua, "Stretch out the sword that is in your hand toward Ai; for I will give it into your hand." And Joshua stretched out the sword that was in his hand toward the city. [19] As soon as he stretched out his hand, the troops in ambush rose quickly out of their place and rushed forward. They entered the city, took it, and at once set the city on fire. [20] So when the men of Ai looked back, the smoke of the city was rising to the sky. They had no power to flee this way or that, for the people who fled to the wilderness turned back against the pursuers. [21] When Joshua and all Israel saw that the ambush had taken the city and that the smoke of the city was rising, then they turned back and struck down the men of Ai. [22] And the others came out from the city against them; so they were surrounded by Israelites, some on one side, and some on the other; and Israel struck them down until no one was left who survived or escaped. [23] But the king of Ai was taken alive and brought to Joshua.

24 When Israel had finished slaughtering all the inhabitants of Ai in the open wilderness where they pursued them, and when all of them to the very last had fallen by the edge of the sword, all Israel returned to Ai, and attacked it with the edge of the sword. [25] The total of those who fell that day, both men and women, was twelve thousand—all the people of Ai. [26] For Joshua did not draw back his hand, with which he stretched out the sword, until he had utterly destroyed all the inhabitants of Ai. [27] Only the livestock and the spoil of that city Israel took as their boo-

ty, according to the word of the LORD that he had issued to Joshua. [28] So Joshua burned Ai, and made it forever a heap of ruins, as it is to this day. [29] And he hanged the king of Ai on a tree until evening; and at sunset Joshua commanded, and they took his body down from the tree, threw it down at the entrance of the gate of the city, and raised over it a great heap of stones, which stands there to this day.

Joshua Renews the Covenant

30 Then Joshua built on Mount Ebal an altar to the LORD, the God of Israel, [31] just as Moses the servant of the LORD had commanded the Israelites, as it is written in the book of the law of Moses, "an altar of unhewn[1] stones, on which no iron tool has been used"; and they offered on it burnt offerings to the LORD, and sacrificed offerings of well-being. [32] And there, in the presence of the Israelites, Joshua[m] wrote on the stones a copy of the law of Moses, which he had written. [33] All Israel, alien as well as citizen, with their elders and officers and their judges, stood on opposite sides of the ark in front of the levitical priests who carried the ark of the covenant of the LORD, half of them in front of Mount Gerizim and half of them in front of Mount Ebal, as Moses the servant of the LORD had commanded at the first, that they should bless the people of Israel. [34] And afterward he read all the words of the law, blessings and curses, according to all that is written in the book of the law. [35] There was not a word of all that Moses commanded that Joshua did not read before all the assembly of Israel, and the women, and the little ones, and the aliens who resided among them.

The Gibeonites Save Themselves by Trickery

9 Now when all the kings who were beyond the Jordan in the hill country and in the lowland all along the coast of the Great Sea to-

8.18
v. 26;
Ex 14.16;
17.9-13
8.19
v. 8
8.22
Deut 7.2
8.25
Deut 20.16-18
8.26
Ex 17.11,12
8.27
v. 2;
Num 31.22

8.28
Deut 13.16
8.29
Deut 21.22,
23
8.30
Deut 27.2-8
8.31
Ex 20.24,
25;
Deut 27.5,6
8.32
Deut 27.2,8
8.33
Deut 31.9,
12; 27.11-14
8.34f
Deut 31.11;
Josh 1.8
8.35
Deut 31.12
9.1
Josh 3.10

[1] Heb *whole* [m] Heb *he*

ward Lebanon—the Hittites, the Amorites, the Canaanites, the Perizzites, the Hivites, and the Jebusites—heard of this, ²they gathered together with one accord to fight Joshua and Israel.

3 But when the inhabitants of Gibeon heard what Joshua had done to Jericho and to Ai, ⁴they on their part acted with cunning: they went and prepared provisions,ⁿ and took worn-out sacks for their donkeys, and wineskins, worn-out and torn and mended, ⁵with worn-out, patched sandals on their feet, and worn-out clothes; and all their provisions were dry and moldy. ⁶They went to Joshua in the camp at Gilgal, and said to him and to the Israelites, "We have come from a far country; so now make a treaty with us." ⁷But the Israelites said to the Hivites, "Perhaps you live among us; then how can we make a treaty with you?" ⁸They said to Joshua, "We are your servants." And Joshua said to them, "Who are you? And where do you come from?" ⁹They said to him, "Your servants have come from a very far country, because of the name of the Lord your God; for we have heard a report of him, of all that he did in Egypt, ¹⁰and of all that he did to the two kings of the Amorites who were beyond the Jordan, King Sihon of Heshbon, and King Og of Bashan who lived in Ashtaroth. ¹¹So our elders and all the inhabitants of our country said to us, 'Take provisions in your hand for the journey; go to meet them, and say to them, "We are your servants; come now, make a treaty with us." ' ¹²Here is our bread; it was still warm when we took it from our houses as our food for the journey, on the day we set out to come to you, but now, see, it is dry and moldy; ¹³these wineskins were new when we filled them, and see, they are burst; and these garments and sandals of ours are worn out from the very long journey." ¹⁴So the leadersᵒ partook of their provisions, and did not ask direction from the Lord. ¹⁵And Joshua made

peace with them, guaranteeing their lives by a treaty; and the leaders of the congregation swore an oath to them.

16 But when three days had passed after they had made a treaty with them, they heard that they were their neighbors and were living among them. ¹⁷So the Israelites set out and reached their cities on the third day. Now their cities were Gibeon, Chephirah, Beeroth, and Kiriath-jearim. ¹⁸But the Israelites did not attack them, because the leaders of the congregation had sworn to them by the Lord, the God of Israel. Then all the congregation murmured against the leaders. ¹⁹But all the leaders said to all the congregation, "We have sworn to them by the Lord, the God of Israel, and now we must not touch them. ²⁰This is what we will do to them: We will let them live, so that wrath may not come upon us, because of the oath that we swore to them." ²¹The leaders said to them, "Let them live." So they became hewers of wood and drawers of water for all the congregation, as the leaders had decided concerning them.

22 Joshua summoned them, and said to them, "Why did you deceive us, saying, 'We are very far from you,' while in fact you are living among us? ²³Now therefore you are cursed, and some of you shall always be slaves, hewers of wood and drawers of water for the house of my God." ²⁴They answered Joshua, "Because it was told to your servants for a certainty that the Lord your God had commanded his servant Moses to give you all the land, and to destroy all the inhabitants of the land before you; so we were in great fear for our lives because of you, and did this thing. ²⁵And now we are in your hand: do as it seems good and right in your sight to do to us." ²⁶This is what he did for them: he saved them from the Israelites; and they did not kill them. ²⁷But on that day Joshua

9.3
Josh 10.2;
6.27
9.6
Josh 5.10
9.7
v. 2;
Josh 11.19;
Ex 23.32
9.8
Deut 20.11
9.9
Deut 20.15;
vv. 16,17,
24;
Josh 2.9,10
9.10
Num 21.24,
33
9.14
Num 27.21
9.15
Ex 23.32

9.17
Josh 18.25-28;
Ezra 2.25
9.18
Ps 15.4;
Eccl 5.2
9.21
v. 15
9.22
vv. 6,9,16,
17
9.23
Gen 9.25;
vv. 21,27
9.24
Deut 7.1,2
9.25
Gen 16.6
9.27
vv. 21,23;
Deut 12.5

ⁿCn: Meaning of Heb uncertain
ᵒGk: Heb men

made them hewers of wood and drawers of water for the congregation and for the altar of the LORD, to continue to this day, in the place that he should choose.

The Sun Stands Still

10 When King Adoni-zedek of Jerusalem heard how Joshua had taken Ai, and had utterly destroyed it, doing to Ai and its king as he had done to Jericho and its king, and how the inhabitants of Gibeon had made peace with Israel and were among them, ²he p became greatly frightened, because Gibeon was a large city, like one of the royal cities, and was larger than Ai, and all its men were warriors. ³So King Adoni-zedek of Jerusalem sent a message to King Hoham of Hebron, to King Piram of Jarmuth, to King Japhia of Lachish, and to King Debir of Eglon, saying, ⁴"Come up and help me, and let us attack Gibeon; for it has made peace with Joshua and with the Israelites." ⁵Then the five kings of the Amorites—the king of Jerusalem, the king of Hebron, the king of Jarmuth, the king of Lachish, and the king of Eglon—gathered their forces, and went up with all their armies and camped against Gibeon, and made war against it.

6 And the Gibeonites sent to Joshua at the camp in Gilgal, saying, "Do not abandon your servants; come up to us quickly, and save us, and help us; for all the kings of the Amorites who live in the hill country are gathered against us." ⁷So Joshua went up from Gilgal, he and all the fighting force with him, all the mighty warriors. ⁸The LORD said to Joshua, "Do not fear them, for I have handed them over to you; not one of them shall stand before you." ⁹So Joshua came upon them suddenly, having marched up all night from Gilgal. ¹⁰And the LORD threw them into a panic before Israel, who inflicted a great slaughter on them at Gibeon, chased them by the way of the ascent of Beth-horon, and struck them down as far as Azekah

and Makkedah. ¹¹As they fled before Israel, while they were going down the slope of Beth-horon, the LORD threw down huge stones from heaven on them as far as Azekah, and they died; there were more who died because of the hailstones than the Israelites killed with the sword.

12 On the day when the LORD gave the Amorites over to the Israelites, Joshua spoke to the LORD; and he said in the sight of Israel,
"Sun, stand still at Gibeon,
 and Moon, in the valley of
 Aijalon."
¹³ And the sun stood still, and
 the moon stopped,
 until the nation took
 vengeance on their
 enemies.
Is this not written in the Book of Jashar? The sun stopped in mid-heaven, and did not hurry to set for about a whole day. ¹⁴There has been no day like it before or since, when the LORD heeded a human voice; for the LORD fought for Israel.

15 Then Joshua returned, and all Israel with him, to the camp at Gilgal.

Five Kings Defeated

16 Meanwhile, these five kings fled and hid themselves in the cave at Makkedah. ¹⁷And it was told Joshua, "The five kings have been found, hidden in the cave at Makkedah." ¹⁸Joshua said, "Roll large stones against the mouth of the cave, and set men by it to guard them; ¹⁹but do not stay there yourselves; pursue your enemies, and attack them from the rear. Do not let them enter their towns, for the LORD your God has given them into your hand." ²⁰When Joshua and the Israelites had finished inflicting a very great slaughter on them, until they were wiped out, and when the survivors had entered into the fortified towns, ²¹all the people returned safe to Joshua in the camp at Makkedah; no one dared to speak q against any of the Israelites.

10.1 Josh 6.21; 8.22,26,28; 9.15
10.4 v. 1
10.5 Josh 9.2
10.8 Josh 1.5,9; 11.6
10.10 Deut 7.23

10.11 Ps 18.13,14; Isa 30.30
10.12 Hab 3.11
10.13 2 Sam 1.18; Isa 38.8
10.14 v. 42
10.15 v. 43
10.16 v. 5
10.20 Deut 20.16
10.21 Ex 11.7

p Heb *they* q Heb *moved his tongue*

22 Then Joshua said, "Open the mouth of the cave, and bring those five kings out to me from the cave." ²³They did so, and brought the five kings out to him from the cave, the king of Jerusalem, the king of Hebron, the king of Jarmuth, the king of Lachish, and the king of Eglon. ²⁴When they brought the kings out to Joshua, Joshua summoned all the Israelites, and said to the chiefs of the warriors who had gone with him, "Come near, put your feet on the necks of these kings." Then they came near and put their feet on their necks. ²⁵And Joshua said to them, "Do not be afraid or dismayed; be strong and courageous; for thus the LORD will do to all the enemies against whom you fight." ²⁶Afterward Joshua struck them down and put them to death, and he hung them on five trees. And they hung on the trees until evening. ²⁷At sunset Joshua commanded, and they took them down from the trees and threw them into the cave where they had hidden themselves; they set large stones against the mouth of the cave, which remain to this very day.

28 Joshua took Makkedah on that day, and struck it and its king with the edge of the sword; he utterly destroyed every person in it; he left no one remaining. And he did to the king of Makkedah as he had done to the king of Jericho.

29 Then Joshua passed on from Makkedah, and all Israel with him, to Libnah, and fought against Libnah. ³⁰The LORD gave it also and its king into the hand of Israel; and he struck it with the edge of the sword, and every person in it; he left no one remaining in it; and he did to its king as he had done to the king of Jericho.

31 Next Joshua passed on from Libnah, and all Israel with him, to Lachish, and laid siege to it, and assaulted it. ³²The LORD gave Lachish into the hand of Israel, and he took it on the second day, and struck it with the edge of the sword, and every person in it, as he had done to Libnah.

33 Then King Horam of Gezer came up to help Lachish; and Joshua struck him and his people, leaving him no survivors.

34 From Lachish Joshua passed on with all Israel to Eglon; and they laid siege to it, and assaulted it; ³⁵and they took it that day, and struck it with the edge of the sword; and every person in it he utterly destroyed that day, as he had done to Lachish.

36 Then Joshua went up with all Israel from Eglon to Hebron; they assaulted it, ³⁷and took it, and struck it with the edge of the sword, and its king and its towns, and every person in it; he left no one remaining, just as he had done to Eglon, and utterly destroyed it with every person in it.

38 Then Joshua, with all Israel, turned back to Debir and assaulted it, ³⁹and he took it with its king and all its towns; they struck them with the edge of the sword, and utterly destroyed every person in it; he left no one remaining; just as he had done to Hebron, and, as he had done to Libnah and its king, so he did to Debir and its king.

40 So Joshua defeated the whole land, the hill country and the Negeb and the lowland and the slopes, and all their kings; he left no one remaining, but utterly destroyed all that breathed, as the LORD God of Israel commanded. ⁴¹And Joshua defeated them from Kadesh-barnea to Gaza, and all the country of Goshen, as far as Gibeon. ⁴²Joshua took all these kings and their land at one time, because the LORD God of Israel fought for Israel. ⁴³Then Joshua returned, and all Israel with him, to the camp at Gilgal.

The United Kings of Northern Canaan Defeated

11 When King Jabin of Hazor heard of this, he sent to King Jobab of Madon, to the king of Shimron, to the king of Achshaph, ²and to the kings who were in the northern hill country, and in the Arabah south of Chinneroth,

10.22 Deut 7.24
10.24 Ps 110.5; Isa 26.5,6; Mal 4.3
10.25 v. 8
10.26 Josh 8.29
10.27 Deut 21.23; Josh 8.9
10.28 Deut 20.16; Josh 6.21
10.29 1 Chr 6.57
10.31 2 Kings 14.19

10.36 Josh 14.13; 15.13; Judg 1.10
10.38 Josh 15.15; Judg 1.11
10.40 Deut 1.7; 7.24; 20.16, 17
10.41 Josh 11.16; 15.51
10.42 v. 14
11.1 v. 10
11.2 Josh 12.3ff

and in the lowland, and in Naphoth-dor on the west, ³to the Canaanites in the east and the west, the Amorites, the Hittites, the Perizzites, and the Jebusites in the hill country, and the Hivites under Hermon in the land of Mizpah. ⁴They came out, with all their troops, a great army, in number like the sand on the seashore, with very many horses and chariots. ⁵All these kings joined their forces, and came and camped together at the waters of Merom, to fight with Israel.

6 And the LORD said to Joshua, "Do not be afraid of them, for to-morrow at this time I will hand over all of them, slain, to Israel; you shall hamstring their horses, and burn their chariots with fire." ⁷So Joshua came suddenly upon them with all his fighting force, by the waters of Merom, and fell upon them. ⁸And the LORD handed them over to Israel, who attacked them and chased them as far as Great Sidon and Misrephoth-maim, and eastward as far as the valley of Mizpeh. They struck them down, until they had left no one remaining. ⁹And Joshua did to them as the LORD commanded him; he hamstrung their horses, and burned their chariots with fire.

10 Joshua turned back at that time, and took Hazor, and struck its king down with the sword. Before that time Hazor was the head of all those kingdoms. ¹¹And they put to the sword all who were in it, utterly destroying them; there was no one left who breathed, and he burned Hazor with fire. ¹²And all the towns of those kings, and all their kings, Joshua took, and struck them with the edge of the sword, utterly destroying them, as Moses the servant of the LORD had commanded. ¹³But Israel burned none of the towns that stood on mounds except Hazor, which Joshua did burn. ¹⁴All the spoil of these towns, and the livestock, the Israelites took for their booty; but all the people they struck down with the edge of the sword, until they

11.4
Judg 7.12
11.6
Josh 10.8;
2 Sam 8.4
11.8
Josh 13.6
11.9
v. 6
11.11
Deut 20.16,
17
11.14
Num 31.11,
12

11.15
Ex 34.11,
12;
Deut 7.2;
Josh 1.7
11.16
Josh 10.40,
41; v. 2
11.17
Josh 12.7;
Deut 7.24
11.19
Josh 9.3,7
11.20
Deut 2.30;
Rom 9.18;
Deut 20.16,
17
11.21
Num 13.33;
Deut 9.2
11.23
Num 34.2ff
12.1
Deut 3.8,9

had destroyed them, and they did not leave any who breathed. ¹⁵As the LORD had commanded his servant Moses, so Moses commanded Joshua, and so Joshua did; he left nothing undone of all that the LORD had commanded Moses.

Summary of Joshua's Conquests

16 So Joshua took all that land: the hill country and all the Negeb and all the land of Goshen and the lowland and the Arabah and the hill country of Israel and its lowland, ¹⁷from Mount Halak, which rises toward Seir, as far as Baal-gad in the valley of Lebanon below Mount Hermon. He took all their kings, struck them down, and put them to death. ¹⁸Joshua made war a long time with all those kings. ¹⁹There was not a town that made peace with the Israelites, except the Hivites, the inhabitants of Gibeon; all were taken in battle. ²⁰For it was the LORD's doing to harden their hearts so that they would come against Israel in battle, in order that they might be utterly destroyed, and might receive no mercy, but be exterminated, just as the LORD had commanded Moses.

21 At that time Joshua came and wiped out the Anakim from the hill country, from Hebron, from Debir, from Anab, and from all the hill country of Judah, and from all the hill country of Israel; Joshua utterly destroyed them with their towns. ²²None of the Anakim was left in the land of the Israelites; some remained only in Gaza, in Gath, and in Ashdod. ²³So Joshua took the whole land, according to all that the LORD had spoken to Moses; and Joshua gave it for an inheritance to Israel according to their tribal allotments. And the land had rest from war.

The Kings Conquered by Moses

12 Now these are the kings of the land, whom the Israelites defeated, whose land they occupied beyond the Jordan toward the east, from the Wadi Arnon to Mount Hermon, with all the Ara-

bah eastward: ² King Sihon of the
Amorites who lived at Heshbon,
and ruled from Aroer, which is on
the edge of the Wadi Arnon, and
from the middle of the valley as far
as the river Jabbok, the boundary
of the Ammonites, that is, half of
Gilead, ³ and the Arabah to the Sea
of Chinneroth eastward, and in the
direction of Beth-jeshimoth, to the
sea of the Arabah, the Dead Sea,ʳ
southward to the foot of the slopes
of Pisgah; ⁴ and King Ogˢ of Ba-
shan, one of the last of the Repha-
im, who lived at Ashtaroth and at
Edrei ⁵ and ruled over Mount Her-
mon and Salecah and all Bashan to
the boundary of the Geshurites and
the Maacathites, and over half of
Gilead to the boundary of King Si-
hon of Heshbon. ⁶ Moses, the ser-
vant of the LORD, and the Israelites
defeated them; and Moses the ser-
vant of the LORD gave their land for
a possession to the Reubenites and
the Gadites and the half-tribe of
Manasseh.

The Kings Conquered by Joshua

7 The following are the kings of
the land whom Joshua and the Is-
raelites defeated on the west side
of the Jordan, from Baal-gad in the
valley of Lebanon to Mount Halak,
that rises toward Seir (and Joshua
gave their land to the tribes of Isra-
el as a possession according to
their allotments, ⁸ in the hill coun-
try, in the lowland, in the Arabah,
in the slopes, in the wilderness,
and in the Negeb, the land of the
Hittites, Amorites, Canaanites,
Perizzites, Hivites, and Jebusites):

⁹ the king of Jericho	one
the king of Ai, which is	
next to Bethel	one
¹⁰ the king of Jerusalem	one
the king of Hebron	one
¹¹ the king of Jarmuth	one
the king of Lachish	one
¹² the king of Eglon	one
the king of Gezer	one
¹³ the king of Debir	one
the king of Geder	one
¹⁴ the king of Hormah	one
the king of Arad	one
¹⁵ the king of Libnah	one

the king of Adullam	one
¹⁶ the king of Makkedah	one
the king of Bethel	one
¹⁷ the king of Tappuah	one
the king of Hepher	one
¹⁸ the king of Aphek	one
the king of Lasharon	one
¹⁹ the king of Madon	one
the king of Hazor	one
²⁰ the king of Shimron-	
meron	one
the king of Achshaph	one
²¹ the king of Taanach	one
the king of Megiddo	one
²² the king of Kedesh	one
the king of Jokneam in	
Carmel	one
²³ the king of Dor in	
Naphath-dor	one
the king of Goiim in	
Galilee,ᵗ	one
²⁴ the king of Tirzah	one
thirty-one kings in all.	

The Parts of Canaan Still Unconquered

13 Now Joshua was old and
advanced in years; and the
LORD said to him, "You are old and
advanced in years, and very much
of the land still remains to be pos-
sessed. ² This is the land that still
remains: all the regions of the Phil-
istines, and all those of the Geshu-
rites ³ (from the Shihor, which is
east of Egypt, northward to the
boundary of Ekron, it is reckoned
as Canaanite; there are five rulers
of the Philistines, those of Gaza,
Ashdod, Ashkelon, Gath, and Ek-
ron), and those of the Avvim, ⁴ in
the south, all the land of the Ca-
naanites, and Mearah that belongs
to the Sidonians, to Aphek, to the
boundary of the Amorites, ⁵ and the
land of the Gebalites, and all Leba-
non, toward the east, from Baal-
gad below Mount Hermon to Lebo-
hamath, ⁶ all the inhabitants of the
hill country from Lebanon to
Misrephoth-maim, even all the Si-
donians. I will myself drive them
out from before the Israelites; only
allot the land to Israel for an inheri-
tance, as I have commanded you.

12.2
Deut 2.33,
36
12.3
Josh 11.2;
13.20
12.4
Deut 3.11
12.5
Deut 3.8ff
12.6
Num 21.24,
33; 32.29,33
12.7
Josh 11.17,
23
12.8
Josh 11.16
12.9ff
Josh 6.2;
8.29
12.12
Josh 10.33
12.13
Josh 10.38

12.24
Deut 7.24
13.1
Josh 14.10
13.3
Judg 3.3;
Deut 2.23
13.6
Josh 11.8

ʳ Heb Salt Sea ˢ Gk: Heb the boundary of
King Og ᵗ Gk: Heb Gilgal

7 Now therefore divide this land for an inheritance to the nine tribes and the half-tribe of Manasseh."

The Territory East of the Jordan

8 With the other half-tribe of Manasseh[u] the Reubenites and the Gadites received their inheritance, which Moses gave them, beyond the Jordan eastward, as Moses the servant of the LORD gave them: 9 from Aroer, which is on the edge of the Wadi Arnon, and the town that is in the middle of the valley, and all the tableland from[v] Medeba as far as Dibon; 10 and all the cities of King Sihon of the Amorites, who reigned in Heshbon, as far as the boundary of the Ammonites; 11 and Gilead, and the region of the Geshurites and Maacathites, and all Mount Hermon, and all Bashan to Salecah; 12 all the kingdom of Og in Bashan, who reigned in Ashtaroth and in Edrei (he alone was left of the survivors of the Rephaim); these Moses had defeated and driven out. 13 Yet the Israelites did not drive out the Geshurites or the Maacathites; but Geshur and Maacath live within Israel to this day.

14 To the tribe of Levi alone Moses gave no inheritance; the offerings by fire to the LORD God of Israel are their inheritance, as he said to them.

The Territory of Reuben

15 Moses gave an inheritance to the tribe of the Reubenites according to their clans. 16 Their territory was from Aroer, which is on the edge of the Wadi Arnon, and the town that is in the middle of the valley, and all the tableland by Medeba; 17 with Heshbon, and all its towns that are in the tableland; Dibon, and Bamoth-baal, and Beth-baal-meon, 18 and Jahaz, and Kedemoth, and Mephaath, 19 and Kiriathaim, and Sibmah, and Zereth-shahar on the hill of the valley, 20 and Beth-peor, and the slopes of Pisgah, and Beth-jeshimoth, 21 that is, all the towns of the tableland, and all the king-

dom of King Sihon of the Amorites, who reigned in Heshbon, whom Moses defeated with the leaders of Midian, Evi and Rekem and Zur and Hur and Reba, as princes of Sihon, who lived in the land. 22 Along with the rest of those they put to death, the Israelites also put to the sword Balaam son of Beor, who practiced divination. 23 And the border of the Reubenites was the Jordan and its banks. This was the inheritance of the Reubenites, according to their families with their towns and villages.

The Territory of Gad

24 Moses gave an inheritance also to the tribe of the Gadites, according to their families. 25 Their territory was Jazer, and all the towns of Gilead, and half the land of the Ammonites, to Aroer, which is east of Rabbah, 26 and from Heshbon to Ramath-mizpeh and Betonim, and from Mahanaim to the territory of Debir,[w] 27 and in the valley Beth-haram, Beth-nimrah, Succoth, and Zaphon, the rest of the kingdom of King Sihon of Heshbon, the Jordan and its banks, as far as the lower end of the Sea of Chinnereth, eastward beyond the Jordan. 28 This is the inheritance of the Gadites according to their clans, with their towns and villages.

The Territory of the Half-Tribe of Manasseh (East)

29 Moses gave an inheritance to the half-tribe of Manasseh; it was allotted to the half-tribe of the Manassites according to their families. 30 Their territory extended from Mahanaim, through all Bashan, the whole kingdom of King Og of Bashan, and all the settlements of Jair, which are in Bashan, sixty towns, 31 and half of Gilead, and Ashtaroth, and Edrei, the towns of the kingdom of Og in Bashan; these were allotted to the people of Machir son of Manasseh

13.8 Josh 12.1-6
13.9 v. 16
13.10 Num 21.24, 25
13.12 Deut 3.11; Num 21.24, 35
13.14 Deut 18.1,2
13.16 Josh 12.2
13.21 Num 31.8

13.22 Num 31.8
13.25 Num 21.32
13.27 Num 34.11
13.30 Num 32.41

u Cn: Heb *With it* v Compare Gk: Heb lacks *from* w Gk Syr Vg: Heb *Lidebir*

according to their clans—for half the Machirites.

32 These are the inheritances that Moses distributed in the plains of Moab, beyond the Jordan east of Jericho. 33 But to the tribe of Levi Moses gave no inheritance; the LORD God of Israel is their inheritance, as he said to them.

The Distribution of Territory West of the Jordan

14 These are the inheritances that the Israelites received in the land of Canaan, which the priest Eleazar, and Joshua son of Nun, and the heads of the families of the tribes of the Israelites distributed to them. 2 Their inheritance was by lot, as the LORD had commanded Moses for the nine and one-half tribes. 3 For Moses had given an inheritance to the two and one-half tribes beyond the Jordan; but to the Levites he gave no inheritance among them. 4 For the people of Joseph were two tribes, Manasseh and Ephraim; and no portion was given to the Levites in the land, but only towns to live in, with their pasture lands for their flocks and herds. 5 The Israelites did as the LORD commanded Moses; they allotted the land.

Hebron Allotted to Caleb

6 Then the people of Judah came to Joshua at Gilgal; and Caleb son of Jephunneh the Kenizzite said to him, "You know what the LORD said to Moses the man of God in Kadesh-barnea concerning you and me. 7 I was forty years old when Moses the servant of the LORD sent me from Kadesh-barnea to spy out the land; and I brought him an honest report. 8 But my companions who went up with me made the heart of the people melt; yet I wholeheartedly followed the LORD my God. 9 And Moses swore on that day, saying, 'Surely the land on which your foot has trodden shall be an inheritance for you and your children forever, because you have wholeheartedly followed the LORD my God.' 10 And now, as you see,

the LORD has kept me alive, as he said, these forty-five years since the time that the LORD spoke this word to Moses, while Israel was journeying through the wilderness; and here I am today, eighty-five years old. 11 I am still as strong today as I was on the day that Moses sent me; my strength now is as my strength was then, for war, and for going and coming. 12 So now give me this hill country of which the LORD spoke on that day; for you heard on that day how the Anakim were there, with great fortified cities; it may be that the LORD will be with me, and I shall drive them out, as the LORD said."

13 Then Joshua blessed him, and gave Hebron to Caleb son of Jephunneh for an inheritance. 14 So Hebron became the inheritance of Caleb son of Jephunneh the Kenizzite to this day, because he wholeheartedly followed the LORD, the God of Israel. 15 Now the name of Hebron formerly was Kiriath-arba;[x] this Arba was[y] the greatest man among the Anakim. And the land had rest from war.

The Territory of Judah

15 The lot for the tribe of the people of Judah according to their families reached southward to the boundary of Edom, to the wilderness of Zin at the farthest south. 2 And their south boundary ran from the end of the Dead Sea,[z] from the bay that faces southward; 3 it goes out southward of the ascent of Akrabbim, passes along to Zin, and goes up south of Kadesh-barnea, along by Hezron, up to Addar, makes a turn to Karka, 4 passes along to Azmon, goes out by the Wadi of Egypt, and comes to its end at the sea. This shall be your south boundary. 5 And the east boundary is the Dead Sea,[z] to the mouth of the Jordan. And the boundary on the north side runs from the bay of the sea at the mouth of the Jordan; 6 and the boundary goes up to Beth-hoglah,

Cross references (center column)

13.33
v. 14;
Num 18.20;
Deut 10.9;
18.1,2
14.1
Num 34.17,
18
14.2
Num 26.55
14.3
Num 32.33;
Josh 13.14
14.4
Gen 48.5
14.6
Num 13.6,
26,30; 14.6,
24,30
14.7
Num 13.6;
14.6
14.8
Num 13.31,
32; 14.24
14.9
Deut 1.36
14.10
Num 14.30

14.12
Num 13.33
14.14
Josh 22.6;
vv. 8,9
14.15
Josh 11.23
15.1
Num 34.3,4;
33.36
15.3
Num 34.4
15.4
Num 34.5
15.6
Josh 18.17,
19

x That is *the city of Arba* y Heb lacks *this Arba was* z Heb *Salt Sea*

and passes along north of Beth-arabah; and the boundary goes up to the Stone of Bohan, Reuben's son; [7] and the boundary goes up to Debir from the Valley of Achor, and so northward, turning toward Gilgal, which is opposite the ascent of Adummim, which is on the south side of the valley; and the boundary passes along to the waters of En-shemesh, and ends at En-rogel; [8] then the boundary goes up by the valley of the son of Hinnom at the southern slope of the Jebusites (that is, Jerusalem); and the boundary goes up to the top of the mountain that lies over against the valley of Hinnom, on the west, at the northern end of the valley of Rephaim; [9] then the boundary extends from the top of the mountain to the spring of the Waters of Nephtoah, and from there to the towns of Mount Ephron; then the boundary bends around to Baalah (that is, Kiriath-jearim); [10] and the boundary circles west of Baalah to Mount Seir, passes along to the northern slope of Mount Jearim (that is, Chesalon), and goes down to Beth-shemesh, and passes along by Timnah; [11] the boundary goes out to the slope of the hill north of Ekron, then the boundary bends around to Shikkeron, and passes along to Mount Baalah, and goes out to Jabneel; then the boundary comes to an end at the sea. [12] And the west boundary was the Mediterranean with its coast. This is the boundary surrounding the people of Judah according to their families.

Caleb Occupies His Portion

[13] According to the commandment of the LORD to Joshua, he gave to Caleb son of Jephunneh a portion among the people of Judah, Kiriath-arba,[a] that is, Hebron (Arba was the father of Anak). [14] And Caleb drove out from there the three sons of Anak: Sheshai, Ahiman, and Talmai, the descendants of Anak. [15] From there he went up against the inhabitants of Debir; now the name of Debir for-

merly was Kiriath-sepher. [16] And Caleb said, "Whoever attacks Kiriath-sepher and takes it, to him I will give my daughter Achsah as wife." [17] Othniel son of Kenaz, the brother of Caleb, took it; and he gave him his daughter Achsah as wife. [18] When she came to him, she urged him to ask her father for a field. As she dismounted from her donkey, Caleb said to her, "What do you wish?" [19] She said to him, "Give me a present; since you have set me in the land of the Negeb, give me springs of water as well." So Caleb gave her the upper springs and the lower springs.

The Towns of Judah

[20] This is the inheritance of the tribe of the people of Judah according to their families. [21] The towns belonging to the tribe of the people of Judah in the extreme South, toward the boundary of Edom, were Kabzeel, Eder, Jagur, [22] Kinah, Dimonah, Adadah, [23] Kedesh, Hazor, Ithnan, [24] Ziph, Telem, Bealoth, [25] Hazor-hadattah, Kerioth-hezron (that is, Hazor), [26] Amam, Shema, Moladah, [27] Hazar-gaddah, Heshmon, Beth-pelet, [28] Hazar-shual, Beer-sheba, Biziothiah, [29] Baalah, Iim, Ezem, [30] Eltolad, Chesil, Hormah, [31] Ziklag, Madmannah, Sansannah, [32] Lebaoth, Shilhim, Ain, and Rimmon: in all, twenty-nine towns, with their villages.

[33] And in the Lowland, Eshtaol, Zorah, Ashnah, [34] Zanoah, Engannim, Tappuah, Enam, [35] Jarmuth, Adullam, Socoh, Azekah, [36] Shaaraim, Adithaim, Gederah, Gederothaim: fourteen towns with their villages.

[37] Zenan, Hadashah, Migdalgad, [38] Dilan, Mizpeh, Jokthe-el, [39] Lachish, Bozkath, Eglon, [40] Cabbon, Lahmam, Chitlish, [41] Gederoth, Beth-dagon, Naamah, and Makkedah: sixteen towns with their villages.

[42] Libnah, Ether, Ashan, [43] Iphtah, Ashnah, Nezib, [44] Keilah, Achzib, and Mareshah: nine towns with their villages.

15.7 Josh 7.24
15.8 v. 63
15.9 Josh 18.15
15.10 Judg 14.1
15.12 v. 47
15.13 Jn 14.13-15
15.14 Josh 11.21, 22;
Num 13.22
15.15 Josh 10.38
15.16 Judg 1.12, 13; 3.9
15.18 Judg 1.14
15.28 Gen 21.31
15.31 1 Sam 27.6
15.33 Judg 13.25; 16.31
15.35 1 Sam 22.1
15.38 2 Kings 14.7
15.39 Josh 10.3; 2 Kings 14.19

a That is the city of Arba

45 Ekron, with its dependencies and its villages; 46 from Ekron to the sea, all that were near Ashdod, with their villages.

47 Ashdod, its towns and its villages; Gaza, its towns and its villages; to the Wadi of Egypt, and the Great Sea with its coast.

48 And in the hill country, Shamir, Jattir, Socoh, 49 Dannah, Kiriath-sannah (that is, Debir), 50 Anab, Eshtemoh, Anim, 51 Goshen, Holon, and Giloh: eleven towns with their villages.

52 Arab, Dumah, Eshan, 53 Janim, Beth-tappuah, Aphekah, 54 Humtah, Kiriath-arba (that is, Hebron), and Zior: nine towns with their villages.

55 Maon, Carmel, Ziph, Juttah, 56 Jezreel, Jokdeam, Zanoah, 57 Kain, Gibeah, and Timnah: ten towns with their villages.

58 Halhul, Beth-zur, Gedor, 59 Maarath, Beth-anoth, and Eltekon: six towns with their villages.

60 Kiriath-baal (that is, Kiriath-jearim), and Rabbah: two towns with their villages.

61 In the wilderness, Beth-arabah, Middin, Secacah, 62 Nibshan, the City of Salt, and En-gedi: six towns with their villages.

63 But the people of Judah could not drive out the Jebusites, the inhabitants of Jerusalem; so the Jebusites live with the people of Judah in Jerusalem to this day.

The Territory of Ephraim

16 The allotment of the Josephites went from the Jordan by Jericho, east of the waters of Jericho, into the wilderness, going up from Jericho into the hill country to Bethel; 2 then going from Bethel to Luz, it passes along to Ataroth, the territory of the Archites; 3 then it goes down westward to the territory of the Japhletites, as far as the territory of Lower Beth-horon, then to Gezer, and it ends at the sea.

4 The Josephites—Manasseh and Ephraim—received their inheritance.

5 The territory of the Ephraim-

ites by their families was as follows: the boundary of their inheritance on the east was Ataroth-addar as far as Upper Beth-horon, 6 and the boundary goes from there to the sea; on the north is Michmethath; then on the east the boundary makes a turn toward Taanath-shiloh, and passes along beyond it on the east to Janoah, 7 then it goes down from Janoah to Ataroth and to Naarah, and touches Jericho, ending at the Jordan. 8 From Tappuah the boundary goes westward to the Wadi Kanah, and ends at the sea. Such is the inheritance of the tribe of the Ephraimites by their families, 9 together with the towns that were set apart for the Ephraimites within the inheritance of the Manassites, all those towns with their villages. 10 They did not, however, drive out the Canaanites who lived in Gezer: so the Canaanites have lived within Ephraim to this day but have been made to do forced labor.

The Other Half-Tribe of Manasseh (West)

17 Then allotment was made to the tribe of Manasseh, for he was the firstborn of Joseph. To Machir the firstborn of Manasseh, the father of Gilead, were allotted Gilead and Bashan, because he was a warrior. 2 And allotments were made to the rest of the tribe of Manasseh, by their families, Abiezer, Helek, Asriel, Shechem, Hepher, and Shemida; these were the male descendants of Manasseh son of Joseph, by their families.

3 Now Zelophehad son of Hepher son of Gilead son of Machir son of Manasseh had no sons, but only daughters; and these are the names of his daughters: Mahlah, Noah, Hoglah, Milcah, and Tirzah. 4 They came before the priest Eleazar and Joshua son of Nun and the leaders, and said, "The LORD commanded Moses to give us an inheritance along with our male kin." So according to the commandment of the LORD he gave them an inheritance among the kinsmen of their

15.47
v. 4;
Num 34.6
15.51
Josh 10.41;
11.16
15.60
Josh 18.14
15.63
Judg 1.21;
2 Sam 5.6
16.1
Josh 18.12
16.2
Josh 18.13
16.3
Josh 18.13;
2 Chr 8.5
16.5
Josh 18.13

16.6
Josh 17.7
16.7
1 Chr 7.28
16.8
Josh 17.8,9
16.10
Judg 1.29;
1 Kings 9.16;
Josh 17.12,
13
17.1
Gen 41.41;
50.23;
Deut 3.15
17.2
Num 26.29-32
17.3
Num 26.33;
27.1-7
17.4
Num 27.5-7

father. ⁵Thus there fell to Manasseh ten portions, besides the land of Gilead and Bashan, which is on the other side of the Jordan, ⁶because the daughters of Manasseh received an inheritance along with his sons. The land of Gilead was allotted to the rest of the Manassites.

7 The territory of Manasseh reached from Asher to Michmethath, which is east of Shechem; then the boundary goes along southward to the inhabitants of En-tappuah. ⁸The land of Tappuah belonged to Manasseh, but the town of Tappuah on the boundary of Manasseh belonged to the Ephraimites. ⁹Then the boundary went down to the Wadi Kanah. The towns here, to the south of the wadi, among the towns of Manasseh, belong to Ephraim. Then the boundary of Manasseh goes along the north side of the wadi and ends at the sea. ¹⁰The land to the south is Ephraim's and that to the north is Manasseh's, with the sea forming its boundary; on the north Asher is reached, and on the east Issachar. ¹¹Within Issachar and Asher, Manasseh had Beth-shean and its villages, Ibleam and its villages, the inhabitants of Dor and its villages, the inhabitants of En-dor and its villages, the inhabitants of Taanach and its villages, and the inhabitants of Megiddo and its villages (the third is Naphath).ᵇ ¹²Yet the Manassites could not take possession of those towns; but the Canaanites continued to live in that land. ¹³But when the Israelites grew strong, they put the Canaanites to forced labor, but did not utterly drive them out.

The Tribe of Joseph Protests

14 The tribe of Joseph spoke to Joshua, saying, "Why have you given me but one lot and one portion as an inheritance, since we are a numerous people, whom all along the LORD has blessed?" ¹⁵And Joshua said to them, "If you are a numerous people, go up to the forest, and clear ground there for yourselves in the land of the Perizzites

17.6
Josh 13.30, 31
17.7
Josh 16.6
17.8
Josh 16.8
17.9
Josh 16.8,9
17.11
1 Chr 7.29
17.12
Judg 1.27, 28
17.13
Josh 16.10
17.14
Num 26.34, 37

17.16
Judg 1.19; 4.3
18.1
Josh 19.51; Jer 7.12; Judg 18.31
18.3
Judg 18.9
18.5
Josh 15.1; 16.1,4
18.7
Josh 13.33; 13.8

and the Rephaim, since the hill country of Ephraim is too narrow for you." ¹⁶The tribe of Joseph said, "The hill country is not enough for us; yet all the Canaanites who live in the plain have chariots of iron, both those in Beth-shean and its villages and those in the Valley of Jezreel." ¹⁷Then Joshua said to the house of Joseph, to Ephraim and Manasseh, "You are indeed a numerous people, and have great power; you shall not have one lot only, ¹⁸but the hill country shall be yours, for though it is a forest, you shall clear it and possess it to its farthest borders; for you shall drive out the Canaanites, though they have chariots of iron, and though they are strong."

The Territories of the Remaining Tribes

18 Then the whole congregation of the Israelites assembled at Shiloh, and set up the tent of meeting there. The land lay subdued before them.

2 There remained among the Israelites seven tribes whose inheritance had not yet been apportioned. ³So Joshua said to the Israelites, "How long will you be slack about going in and taking possession of the land that the LORD, the God of your ancestors, has given you? ⁴Provide three men from each tribe, and I will send them out that they may begin to go throughout the land, writing a description of it with a view to their inheritances. Then come back to me. ⁵They shall divide it into seven portions, Judah continuing in its territory on the south, and the house of Joseph in their territory on the north. ⁶You shall describe the land in seven divisions and bring the description here to me; and I will cast lots for you here before the LORD our God. ⁷The Levites have no portion among you, for the priesthood of the LORD is their heritage; and Gad and Reuben and the half-tribe of Manasseh have received their inheritance beyond

ᵇ Meaning of Heb uncertain

the Jordan eastward, which Moses the servant of the LORD gave them."

8 So the men started on their way; and Joshua charged those who went to write the description of the land, saying, "Go throughout the land and write a description of it, and come back to me; and I will cast lots for you here before the LORD in Shiloh." 9 So the men went and traversed the land and set down in a book a description of it by towns in seven divisions; then they came back to Joshua in the camp at Shiloh, 10 and Joshua cast lots for them in Shiloh before the LORD; and there Joshua apportioned the land to the Israelites, to each a portion.

The Territory of Benjamin

11 The lot of the tribe of Benjamin according to its families came up, and the territory allotted to it fell between the tribe of Judah and the tribe of Joseph. 12 On the north side their boundary began at the Jordan; then the boundary goes up to the slope of Jericho on the north, then up through the hill country westward; and it ends at the wilderness of Beth-aven. 13 From there the boundary passes along southward in the direction of Luz, to the slope of Luz (that is, Bethel), then the boundary goes down to Ataroth-addar, on the mountain that lies south of Lower Beth-horon. 14 Then the boundary goes in another direction, turning on the western side southward from the mountain that lies to the south, opposite Beth-horon, and it ends at Kiriath-baal (that is, Kiriath-jearim), a town belonging to the tribe of Judah. This forms the western side. 15 The southern side begins at the outskirts of Kiriath-jearim; and the boundary goes from there to Ephron, c to the spring of the Waters of Nephtoah; 16 then the boundary goes down to the border of the mountain that overlooks the valley of the son of Hinnom, which is at the north end of the valley of Rephaim; and it then goes down the valley of Hin-

nom, south of the slope of the Jebusites, and downward to En-rogel; 17 then it bends in a northerly direction going on to En-shemesh, and from there goes to Geliloth, which is opposite the ascent of Adummim; then it goes down to the Stone of Bohan, Reuben's son; 18 and passing on to the north of the slope of Beth-arabah d it goes down to the Arabah; 19 then the boundary passes on to the north of the slope of Beth-hoglah; and the boundary ends at the northern bay of the Dead Sea, e at the south end of the Jordan: this is the southern border. 20 The Jordan forms its boundary on the eastern side. This is the inheritance of the tribe of Benjamin, according to its families, boundary by boundary all around.

21 Now the towns of the tribe of Benjamin according to their families were Jericho, Beth-hoglah, Emek-keziz, 22 Beth-arabah, Zemaraim, Bethel, 23 Avvim, Parah, Ophrah, 24 Chephar-ammoni, Ophni, and Geba — twelve towns with their villages: 25 Gibeon, Ramah, Beeroth, 26 Mizpeh, Chephirah, Mozah, 27 Rekem, Irpeel, Taralah, 28 Zela, Haeleph, Jebus f (that is, Jerusalem), Gibeah g and Kiriath-jearim h — fourteen towns with their villages. This is the inheritance of the tribe of Benjamin according to its families.

The Territory of Simeon

19 The second lot came out for Simeon, for the tribe of Simeon, according to its families; its inheritance lay within the inheritance of the tribe of Judah. 2 It had for its inheritance Beer-sheba, Sheba, Moladah, 3 Hazar-shual, Balah, Ezem, 4 Eltolad, Bethul, Hormah, 5 Ziklag, Beth-marcaboth, Hazar-susah, 6 Beth-lebaoth, and Sharuhen — thirteen towns with their villages; 7 Ain, Rimmon, Ether, and Ashan — four towns with their villages; 8 together with all the

18.8
v. 1;
Judg 18.31
18.10
Josh 19.51
18.13
Gen 28.19;
Josh 16.3
18.14
Josh 15.9
18.15
Josh 15.5-9
18.16
2 Kings 23.10

18.20
Josh 21.4,
17
18.28
Josh 15.8
19.1
v. 9
19.5
1 Sam 30.1

c Cn See 15.9. Heb *westward* d Gk: Heb *to the slope over against the Arabah* e Heb *Salt Sea* f Gk Syr Vg: Heb *the Jebusite* g Heb *Gibeath* h Gk: Heb *Kiriath*

villages all around these towns as far as Baalath-beer, Ramah of the Negeb. This was the inheritance of the tribe of Simeon according to its families. ⁹The inheritance of the tribe of Simeon formed part of the territory of Judah; because the portion of the tribe of Judah was too large for them, the tribe of Simeon obtained an inheritance within their inheritance.

The Territory of Zebulun

10 The third lot came up for the tribe of Zebulun, according to its families. The boundary of its inheritance reached as far as Sarid; ¹¹then its boundary goes up westward, and on to Maralah, and touches Dabbesheth, then the wadi that is east of Jokneam; ¹²from Sarid it goes in the other direction eastward toward the sunrise to the boundary of Chisloth-tabor; from there it goes to Daberath, then up to Japhia; ¹³from there it passes along on the east toward the sunrise to Gath-hepher, to Eth-kazin, and going on to Rimmon it bends toward Neah; ¹⁴then on the north the boundary makes a turn to Hannathon, and it ends at the valley of Iphtah-el; ¹⁵and Kattath, Nahalal, Shimron, Idalah, and Bethlehem—twelve towns with their villages. ¹⁶This is the inheritance of the tribe of Zebulun, according to its families— these towns with their villages.

The Territory of Issachar

17 The fourth lot came out for Issachar, for the tribe of Issachar, according to its families. ¹⁸Its territory included Jezreel, Chesulloth, Shunem, ¹⁹Hapharaim, Shion, Anaharath, ²⁰Rabbith, Kishion, Ebez, ²¹Remeth, En-gannim, En-haddah, Beth-pazzez; ²²the boundary also touches Tabor, Shahazu-mah, and Beth-shemesh, and its boundary ends at the Jordan— sixteen towns with their villages. ²³This is the inheritance of the tribe of Issachar, according to its families—the towns with their villages.

19.9
v. 1
19.11
Josh 21.34
19.15
Mic 5.2
19.17
2 Sam 2.9

19.28
Josh 11.8
19.30
Josh 21.31
19.34
Deut 33.23

The Territory of Asher

24 The fifth lot came out for the tribe of Asher according to its families. ²⁵Its boundary included Helkath, Hali, Beten, Achshaph, ²⁶Allammelech, Amad, and Mishal; on the west it touches Carmel and Shihor-libnath, ²⁷then it turns eastward, goes to Beth-dagon, and touches Zebulun and the valley of Iphtah-el northward to Beth-emek and Neiel; then it continues in the north to Cabul, ²⁸Ebron, Rehob, Hammon, Kanah, as far as Sidon the Great; ²⁹then the boundary turns to Ramah, reaching to the fortified city of Tyre; then the boundary turns to Hosah, and it ends at the sea; Mahalab,ⁱ Achzib, ³⁰Ummah, Aphek, and Rehob— twenty-two towns with their villages. ³¹This is the inheritance of the tribe of Asher according to its families—these towns with their villages.

The Territory of Naphtali

32 The sixth lot came out for the tribe of Naphtali, for the tribe of Naphtali, according to its families. ³³And its boundary ran from Heleph, from the oak in Zaanannim, and Adami-nekeb, and Jabneel, as far as Lakkum; and it ended at the Jordan; ³⁴then the boundary turns westward to Aznoth-tabor, and goes from there to Hukkok, touching Zebulun at the south, and Asher on the west, and Judah on the east at the Jordan. ³⁵The fortified towns are Ziddim, Zer, Hammath, Rakkath, Chinnereth, ³⁶Adamah, Ramah, Hazor, ³⁷Kedesh, Edrei, En-hazor, ³⁸Iron, Migdal-el Horem, Beth-anath, and Beth-shemesh—nineteen towns with their villages. ³⁹This is the inheritance of the tribe of Naphtali according to its families—the towns with their villages.

The Territory of Dan

40 The seventh lot came out for the tribe of Dan, according to its families. ⁴¹The territory of its inheritance included Zorah, Eshtaol,

ⁱ Cn Compare Gk: Heb Mehebel

Ir-shemesh, ⁴²Shaalabbin, Aijalon, Ithlah, ⁴³Elon, Timnah, Ekron, ⁴⁴Eltekeh, Gibbethon, Baalath, ⁴⁵Jehud, Bene-berak, Gath-rimmon, ⁴⁶Me-jarkon, and Rakkon at the border opposite Joppa. ⁴⁷When the territory of the Danites was lost to them, the Danites went up and fought against Leshem, and after capturing it and putting it to the sword, they took possession of it and settled in it, calling Leshem, Dan, after their ancestor Dan. ⁴⁸This is the inheritance of the tribe of Dan, according to their families—these towns with their villages.

Joshua's Inheritance

49 When they had finished distributing the several territories of the land as inheritances, the Israelites gave an inheritance among them to Joshua son of Nun. ⁵⁰By command of the LORD they gave him the town that he asked for, Timnath-serah in the hill country of Ephraim; he rebuilt the town, and settled in it.

51 These are the inheritances that the priest Eleazar and Joshua son of Nun and the heads of the families of the tribes of the Israelites distributed by lot at Shiloh before the LORD, at the entrance of the tent of meeting. So they finished dividing the land.

The Cities of Refuge

20 Then the LORD spoke to Joshua, saying, ²"Say to the Israelites, 'Appoint the cities of refuge, of which I spoke to you through Moses, ³so that anyone who kills a person without intent or by mistake may flee there; they shall be for you a refuge from the avenger of blood. ⁴The slayer shall flee to one of these cities and shall stand at the entrance of the gate of the city, and explain the case to the elders of that city; then the fugitive shall be taken into the city, and given a place, and shall remain with them. ⁵And if the avenger of blood is in pursuit, they shall not give up the slayer, because the neighbor

was killed by mistake, there having been no enmity between them before. ⁶The slayer shall remain in that city until there is a trial before the congregation, until the death of the one who is high priest at the time: then the slayer may return home, to the town in which the deed was done.' "

7 So they set apart Kedesh in Galilee in the hill country of Naphtali, and Shechem in the hill country of Ephraim, and Kiriath-arba (that is, Hebron) in the hill country of Judah. ⁸And beyond the Jordan east of Jericho, they appointed Bezer in the wilderness on the table-land, from the tribe of Reuben, and Ramoth in Gilead, from the tribe of Gad, and Golan in Bashan, from the tribe of Manasseh. ⁹These were the cities designated for all the Israelites, and for the aliens residing among them, that anyone who killed a person without intent could flee there, so as not to die by the hand of the avenger of blood, until there was a trial before the congregation.

Cities Allotted to the Levites

21 Then the heads of the families of the Levites came to the priest Eleazar and to Joshua son of Nun and to the heads of the families of the tribes of the Israelites; ²they said to them at Shiloh in the land of Canaan, "The LORD commanded through Moses that we be given towns to live in, along with their pasture lands for our livestock." ³So by command of the LORD the Israelites gave to the Levites the following towns and pasture lands out of their inheritance.

4 The lot came out for the families of the Kohathites. So those Levites who were descendants of Aaron the priest received by lot thirteen towns from the tribes of Judah, Simeon, and Benjamin.

5 The rest of the Kohathites received by lot ten towns from the families of the tribe of Ephraim, from the tribe of Dan, and the half-tribe of Manasseh.

6 The Gershonites received by

19.42
Judg 1.35
19.47
Judg 18.27-31
19.50
Josh 24.30
19.51
Josh 14.1;
18.1,10
20.2
Num 35.6-34;
Deut 4.41;
19.2
20.4
Ruth 4.1,2
20.5
Num 35.12

20.6
Num 35.25
20.7
Josh 21.32;
1 Chr 6.76;
Josh 21.11;
Lk 1.39
20.8
Josh 21.27,
36,38
20.9
Num 35.15;
v. 6
21.1
Num 35.1-8
21.2
Num 35.2
21.4
vv. 8,19
21.5
v. 20ff
21.6
v. 27ff

lot thirteen towns from the families of the tribe of Issachar, from the tribe of Asher, from the tribe of Naphtali, and from the half-tribe of Manasseh in Bashan.

7 The Merarites according to their families received twelve towns from the tribe of Reuben, the tribe of Gad, and the tribe of Zebulun.

8 These towns and their pasture lands the Israelites gave by lot to the Levites, as the LORD had commanded through Moses.

9 Out of the tribe of Judah and the tribe of Simeon they gave the following towns mentioned by name, 10 which went to the descendants of Aaron, one of the families of the Kohathites who belonged to the Levites, since the lot fell to them first. 11 They gave them Kiriath-arba (Arba being the father of Anak), that is Hebron, in the hill country of Judah, along with the pasture lands around it. 12 But the fields of the town and its villages had been given to Caleb son of Jephunneh as his holding.

13 To the descendants of Aaron the priest they gave Hebron, the city of refuge for the slayer, with its pasture lands, Libnah with its pasture lands, 14 Jattir with its pasture lands, Eshtemoa with its pasture lands, 15 Holon with its pasture lands, Debir with its pasture lands, 16 Ain with its pasture lands, Juttah with its pasture lands, and Bethshemesh with its pasture lands — nine towns out of these two tribes. 17 Out of the tribe of Benjamin: Gibeon with its pasture lands, Geba with its pasture lands, 18 Anathoth with its pasture lands, and Almon with its pasture lands — four towns. 19 The towns of the descendants of Aaron — the priests — were thirteen in all, with their pasture lands.

20 As to the rest of the Kohathites belonging to the Kohathite families of the Levites, the towns allotted to them were out of the tribe of Ephraim. 21 To them were given Shechem, the city of refuge for the slayer, with its pasture

21.7
v. 34ff
21.8
v. 3
21.11
Josh 15.13,
14;
1 Chr 6.55
21.13
Josh 15.42,
54; 20.7;
1 Chr 6.57
21.15
Josh 15.49,
51;
1 Chr 6.58
21.16
Josh 15.10,
15;
1 Chr 6.59
21.18
1 Chr 6.60
21.21
Josh 20.7

21.27
v. 6
21.32
Josh 20.7
21.34
v. 7
21.36
Josh 20.8

lands in the hill country of Ephraim, Gezer with its pasture lands, 22 Kibzaim with its pasture lands, and Beth-horon with its pasture lands — four towns. 23 Out of the tribe of Dan: Elteke with its pasture lands, Gibbethon with its pasture lands, 24 Aijalon with its pasture lands, Gath-rimmon with its pasture lands — four towns. 25 Out of the half-tribe of Manasseh: Taanach with its pasture lands, and Gath-rimmon with its pasture lands — two towns. 26 The towns of the families of the rest of the Kohathites were ten in all, with their pasture lands.

27 To the Gershonites, one of the families of the Levites, were given out of the half-tribe of Manasseh, Golan in Bashan with its pasture lands, the city of refuge for the slayer, and Beeshterah with its pasture lands — two towns. 28 Out of the tribe of Issachar: Kishion with its pasture lands, Daberath with its pasture lands, 29 Jarmuth with its pasture lands, En-gannim with its pasture lands — four towns; 30 Out of the tribe of Asher: Mishal with its pasture lands, Abdon with its pasture lands, 31 Helkath with its pasture lands, and Rehob with its pasture lands — four towns. 32 Out of the tribe of Naphtali: Kedesh in Galilee with its pasture lands, the city of refuge for the slayer, Hammoth-dor with its pasture lands, and Kartan with its pasture lands — three towns. 33 The towns of the several families of the Gershonites were in all thirteen, with their pasture lands.

34 To the rest of the Levites — the Merarite families — were given out of the tribe of Zebulun: Jokneam with its pasture lands, Kartah with its pasture lands, 35 Dimnah with its pasture lands, Nahalal with its pasture lands — four towns. 36 Out of the tribe of Reuben: Bezer with its pasture lands, Jahzah with its pasture lands, 37 Kedemoth with its pasture lands, and Mephaath with its pasture lands — four towns. 38 Out of the tribe of Gad: Ramoth in Gilead with its pasture lands,

the city of refuge for the slayer, Mahanaim with its pasture lands, ³⁹Heshbon with its pasture lands, Jazer with its pasture lands—four towns in all. ⁴⁰As for the towns of the several Merarite families, that is, the remainder of the families of the Levites, those allotted to them were twelve in all.

41 The towns of the Levites within the holdings of the Israelites were in all forty-eight towns with their pasture lands. ⁴²Each of these towns had its pasture lands around it; so it was with all these towns.

43 Thus the LORD gave to Israel all the land that he swore to their ancestors that he would give them; and having taken possession of it, they settled there. ⁴⁴And the LORD gave them rest on every side just as he had sworn to their ancestors; not one of all their enemies had withstood them, for the LORD had given all their enemies into their hands. ⁴⁵Not one of all the good promises that the LORD had made to the house of Israel had failed; all came to pass.

The Eastern Tribes Return to Their Territory

22 Then Joshua summoned the Reubenites, the Gadites, and the half-tribe of Manasseh, ²and said to them, "You have observed all that Moses the servant of the LORD commanded you, and have obeyed me in all that I have commanded you; ³you have not forsaken your kindred these many days, down to this day, but have been careful to keep the charge of the LORD your God. ⁴And now the LORD your God has given rest to your kindred, as he promised them; therefore turn and go to your tents in the land where your possession lies, which Moses the servant of the LORD gave you on the other side of the Jordan. ⁵Take good care to observe the commandment and instruction that Moses the servant of the LORD commanded you, to love the LORD your God, to walk in all his ways, to keep his commandments, and to hold fast to him, and to

serve him with all your heart and with all your soul." ⁶So Joshua blessed them and sent them away, and they went to their tents.

7 Now to the one half of the tribe of Manasseh Moses had given a possession in Bashan; but to the other half Joshua had given a possession beside their fellow Israelites in the land west of the Jordan. And when Joshua sent them away to their tents and blessed them, ⁸he said to them, "Go back to your tents with much wealth, and with very much livestock, with silver, gold, bronze, and iron, and with a great quantity of clothing; divide the spoil of your enemies with your kindred." ⁹So the Reubenites and the Gadites and the half-tribe of Manasseh returned home, parting from the Israelites at Shiloh, which is in the land of Canaan, to go to the land of Gilead, their own land of which they had taken possession by command of the LORD through Moses.

A Memorial Altar East of the Jordan

10 When they came to the region[j] near the Jordan that lies in the land of Canaan, the Reubenites and the Gadites and the half-tribe of Manasseh built there an altar by the Jordan, an altar of great size. ¹¹The Israelites heard that the Reubenites and the Gadites and the half-tribe of Manasseh had built an altar at the frontier of the land of Canaan, in the region[k] near the Jordan, on the side that belongs to the Israelites. ¹²And when the people of Israel heard of it, the whole assembly of the Israelites gathered at Shiloh, to make war against them.

13 Then the Israelites sent the priest Phinehas son of Eleazar to the Reubenites and the Gadites and the half-tribe of Manasseh, in the land of Gilead, ¹⁴and with him ten chiefs, one from each of the tribal families of Israel, every one of them the head of a family among the clans of Israel. ¹⁵They came to

21.41 Num 35.7
21.43ff Gen 13.15; Deut 11.31
21.44 Josh 1.13; 11.23; Deut 7.24
21.45 Josh 23.14
22.2 Num 32.20
22.4 Num 32.18; Deut 3.20
22.5 Deut 6.6,17; 10.12

22.7 Num 32.33; Josh 17.5
22.9 Num 32.1, 26,29
22.11 v. 19
22.12 Josh 18.1
22.13 Deut 13.14; Num 25.7

j Or to Geliloth k Or at Geliloth

the Reubenites, the Gadites, and the half-tribe of Manasseh, in the land of Gilead, and they said to them, [16] "Thus says the whole congregation of the LORD, 'What is this treachery that you have committed against the God of Israel in turning away today from following the LORD, by building yourselves an altar today in rebellion against the LORD? [17] Have we not had enough of the sin at Peor from which even yet we have not cleansed ourselves, and for which a plague came upon the congregation of the LORD, [18] that you must turn away today from following the LORD! If you rebel against the LORD today, he will be angry with the whole congregation of Israel tomorrow. [19] But now, if your land is unclean, cross over into the LORD's land where the LORD's tabernacle now stands, and take for yourselves a possession among us; only do not rebel against the LORD, or rebel against us[1] by building yourselves an altar other than the altar of the LORD our God. [20] Did not Achan son of Zerah break faith in the matter of the devoted things, and wrath fell upon all the congregation of Israel? And he did not perish alone for his iniquity!' "

[21] Then the Reubenites, the Gadites, and the half-tribe of Manasseh said in answer to the heads of the families of Israel, [22] "The LORD, God of gods! The LORD, God of gods! He knows; and let Israel itself know! If it was in rebellion or in breach of faith toward the LORD, do not spare us today [23] for building an altar to turn away from following the LORD; or if we did so to offer burnt offerings or grain offerings or offerings of well-being on it, may the LORD himself take vengeance. [24] No! We did it from fear that in time to come your children might say to our children, 'What have you to do with the LORD, the God of Israel? [25] For the LORD has made the Jordan a boundary between us and you, you Reubenites and Gadites; you have no portion in the LORD.' So your children might make our children cease to worship the LORD.

22.16
v. 11;
Deut 12.13, 14
22.17
Num 25.1-9
22.19
v. 11
22.20
Josh 7.1-26
22.22
Deut 10.17;
1 Kings 8.39
22.23
Deut 18.19;
1 Sam 20.16

22.27
Josh 24.27
22.29
Deut 12.13, 14
22.31
Lev 26.11, 12;
2 Chr 15.2
22.33
1 Chr 29.20
22.34
Josh 24.27

[26] Therefore we said, 'Let us now build an altar, not for burnt offering, nor for sacrifice, [27] but to be a witness between us and you, and between the generations after us, that we do perform the service of the LORD in his presence with our burnt offerings and sacrifices and offerings of well-being; so that your children may never say to our children in time to come, "You have no portion in the LORD." ' [28] And we thought, If this should be said to us or to our descendants in time to come, we could say, 'Look at this copy of the altar of the LORD, which our ancestors made, not for burnt offerings, nor for sacrifice, but to be a witness between us and you.' [29] Far be it from us that we should rebel against the LORD, and turn away this day from following the LORD by building an altar for burnt offering, grain offering, or sacrifice, other than the altar of the LORD our God that stands before his tabernacle!"

[30] When the priest Phinehas and the chiefs of the congregation, the heads of the families of Israel who were with him, heard the words that the Reubenites and the Gadites and the Manassites spoke, they were satisfied. [31] The priest Phinehas son of Eleazar said to the Reubenites and the Gadites and the Manassites, "Today we know that the LORD is among us, because you have not committed this treachery against the LORD; now you have saved the Israelites from the hand of the LORD."

[32] Then the priest Phinehas son of Eleazar and the chiefs returned from the Reubenites and the Gadites in the land of Gilead to the land of Canaan, to the Israelites, and brought back word to them. [33] The report pleased the Israelites; and the Israelites blessed God and spoke no more of making war against them, to destroy the land where the Reubenites and the Gadites were settled. [34] The Reubenites and the Gadites called the altar

[1] Or *make rebels of us*

Witness;[m] "For," said they, "it is a witness between us that the LORD is God."

Joshua Exhorts the People

23 A long time afterward, when the LORD had given rest to Israel from all their enemies all around, and Joshua was old and well advanced in years, [2] Joshua summoned all Israel, their elders and heads, their judges and officers, and said to them, "I am now old and well advanced in years; [3] and you have seen all that the LORD your God has done to all these nations for your sake, for it is the LORD your God who has fought for you. [4] I have allotted to you as an inheritance for your tribes those nations that remain, along with all the nations that I have already cut off, from the Jordan to the Great Sea in the west. [5] The LORD your God will push them back before you, and drive them out of your sight; and you shall possess their land, as the LORD your God promised you. [6] Therefore be very steadfast to observe and do all that is written in the book of the law of Moses, turning aside from it neither to the right nor to the left, [7] so that you may not be mixed with these nations left here among you, or make mention of the names of their gods, or swear by them, or serve them, or bow yourselves down to them, [8] but hold fast to the LORD your God, as you have done to this day. [9] For the LORD has driven out before you great and strong nations; and as for you, no one has been able to withstand you to this day. [10] One of you puts to flight a thousand, since it is the LORD your God who fights for you, as he promised you. [11] Be very careful, therefore, to love the LORD your God. [12] For if you turn back, and join the survivors of these nations left here among you, and intermarry with them, so that you marry their women and they yours, [13] know assuredly that the LORD your God will not continue to drive out these nations before you; but they shall be a

snare and a trap for you, a scourge on your sides, and thorns in your eyes, until you perish from this good land that the LORD your God has given you.

14 "And now I am about to go the way of all the earth, and you know in your hearts and souls, all of you, that not one thing has failed of all the good things that the LORD your God promised concerning you; all have come to pass for you, not one of them has failed. [15] But just as all the good things that the LORD your God promised concerning you have been fulfilled for you, so the LORD will bring upon you all the bad things, until he has destroyed you from this good land that the LORD your God has given you. [16] If you transgress the covenant of the LORD your God, which he enjoined on you, and go and serve other gods and bow down to them, then the anger of the LORD will be kindled against you, and you shall perish quickly from the good land that he has given to you."

The Tribes Renew the Covenant

24 Then Joshua gathered all the tribes of Israel to Shechem, and summoned the elders, the heads, the judges, and the officers of Israel; and they presented themselves before God. [2] And Joshua said to all the people, "Thus says the LORD, the God of Israel: Long ago your ancestors—Terah and his sons Abraham and Nahor—lived beyond the Euphrates and served other gods. [3] Then I took your father Abraham from beyond the River and led him through all the land of Canaan and made his offspring many. I gave him Isaac; [4] and to Isaac I gave Jacob and Esau. I gave Esau the hill country of Seir to possess, but Jacob and his children went down to Egypt. [5] Then I sent Moses and Aaron, and I plagued Egypt with what I did in its midst; and afterwards I brought you out. [6] When I brought your ancestors out of Egypt, you came to

23.1 Josh 21.44; 13.1
23.2 Josh 24.1
23.3 Josh 10.14, 42
23.5 Num 33.53
23.6 Deut 5.32; Josh 1.7
23.7 Ex 23.33; Deut 7.2,3; Ex 23.13; Ps 16.4
23.8 Deut 10.20
23.9 Deut 11.23; Josh 1.5
23.10 Lev 26.8; v. 3; Deut 3.22
23.12 Ex 34.15, 16; Deut 7.3
23.13 Judg 2.3; Ex 23.33; Num 33.55

23.14 1 Kings 2.2; Josh 21.45
23.15 Lev 26.16; Deut 28.15
24.1 Josh 23.2
24.2 Gen 11.27-32
24.3 Gen 12.1; 15.5; 21.3
24.4 Gen 25.25, 26; Deut 2.5; Gen 46.6,7
24.5 Ex 3.10
24.6 Ex 12.51; 14.2-31

[m] Cn Compare Syr: Heb lacks *Witness*

the sea; and the Egyptians pursued your ancestors with chariots and horsemen to the Red Sea. ⁿ ⁷When they cried out to the LORD, he put darkness between you and the Egyptians, and made the sea come upon them and cover them; and your eyes saw what I did to Egypt. Afterwards you lived in the wilderness a long time. ⁸Then I brought you to the land of the Amorites, who lived on the other side of the Jordan; they fought with you, and I handed them over to you, and you took possession of their land, and I destroyed them before you. ⁹Then King Balak son of Zippor of Moab, set out to fight against Israel. He sent and invited Balaam son of Beor to curse you, ¹⁰but I would not listen to Balaam; therefore he blessed you; so I rescued you out of his hand. ¹¹When you went over the Jordan and came to Jericho, the citizens of Jericho fought against you, and also the Amorites, the Perizzites, the Canaanites, the Hittites, the Girgashites, the Hivites, and the Jebusites; and I handed them over to you. ¹²I sent the hornetᵒ ahead of you, which drove out before you the two kings of the Amorites; it was not by your sword or by your bow. ¹³I gave you a land on which you had not labored, and towns that you had not built, and you live in them; you eat the fruit of vineyards and olive-yards that you did not plant.

14 "Now therefore revere the LORD, and serve him in sincerity and in faithfulness; put away the gods that your ancestors served beyond the River and in Egypt, and serve the LORD. ¹⁵Now if you are unwilling to serve the LORD, choose this day whom you will serve, whether the gods your ancestors served in the region beyond the River or the gods of the Amorites in whose land you are living; but as for me and my household, we will serve the LORD."

16 Then the people answered, "Far be it from us that we should forsake the LORD to serve other gods; ¹⁷for it is the LORD our God

24.8
Num 21.21-35
24.9
Num 22.2,5
24.11
Josh 3.16,
17; 6.1
24.12
Ex 23.28;
Deut 7.20;
Ps 44.3,6
24.13
Deut 6.10,
11
24.14
Deut 10.12;
18.13;
2 Cor 1.12
24.15
Ruth 1.15;
1 Kings 18.21;
Ezek 20.39

24.19
Lev 19.2;
Ex 20.5;
23.21
24.20
1 Chr 28.9;
Josh 23.15
24.23
Judg 10.16
24.24
Ex 19.8;
24.3,7;
Deut 5.27
24.25
Ex 24.8
24.27
Josh 22.27
24.29
Judg 2.8
24.30
Josh 19.50

who brought us and our ancestors up from the land of Egypt, out of the house of slavery, and who did those great signs in our sight. He protected us along all the way that we went, and among all the peoples through whom we passed; ¹⁸and the LORD drove out before us all the peoples, the Amorites who lived in the land. Therefore we also will serve the LORD, for he is our God."

19 But Joshua said to the people, "You cannot serve the LORD, for he is a holy God. He is a jealous God; he will not forgive your transgressions or your sins. ²⁰If you forsake the LORD and serve foreign gods, then he will turn and do you harm, and consume you, after having done you good." ²¹And the people said to Joshua, "No, we will serve the LORD!" ²²Then Joshua said to the people, "You are witnesses against yourselves that you have chosen the LORD, to serve him." And they said, "We are witnesses." ²³He said, "Then put away the foreign gods that are among you, and incline your hearts to the LORD, the God of Israel." ²⁴The people said to Joshua, "The LORD our God we will serve, and him we will obey." ²⁵So Joshua made a covenant with the people that day, and made statutes and ordinances for them at Shechem. ²⁶Joshua wrote these words in the book of the law of God; and he took a large stone, and set it up there under the oak in the sanctuary of the LORD. ²⁷Joshua said to all the people, "See, this stone shall be a witness against us; for it has heard all the words of the LORD that he spoke to us; therefore it shall be a witness against you, if you deal falsely with your God." ²⁸So Joshua sent the people away to their inheritances.

Death of Joshua and Eleazar

29 After these things Joshua son of Nun, the servant of the LORD, died, being one hundred ten years old. ³⁰They buried him in his own

ⁿ Or *Sea of Reeds* ᵒ Meaning of Heb uncertain

inheritance at Timnath-serah, which is in the hill country of Ephraim, north of Mount Gaash.

31 Israel served the LORD all the days of Joshua, and all the days of the elders who outlived Joshua and had known all the work that the LORD did for Israel.

32 The bones of Joseph, which the Israelites had brought up from Egypt, were buried at Shechem, in the portion of ground that Jacob

had bought from the children of Hamor, the father of Shechem, for one hundred pieces of money;P it became an inheritance of the descendants of Joseph.

33 Eleazar son of Aaron died; and they buried him at Gibeah, the town of his son Phinehas, which had been given him in the hill country of Ephraim.

P Heb one hundred qesitah

24.31
Judg 2.7
24.32
Gen 50.24, 25;
Ex 13.19;
Gen 33.19

24.33
Josh 22.13

Judges

Title and Background

The title describes the type of leaders Israel had from the time of the elders who outlived Joshua until the time of the monarchy. Their principal purpose for having these leaders is best expressed in 2.16. "Then the LORD raised up judges, who delivered them out of the power of those who plundered them." The book tells of Israel's history for the period between the death of Joshua and the ministry of Samuel.

Author and Date of Writing

According to tradition, Samuel wrote the book, but actual authorship is uncertain. It is possible that Samuel assembled some of the accounts from the period of the judges and that some of the prophets had a hand in shaping and editing the material (see 1Ch 29.29). The date of composition was undoubtedly sometime after 1000 B.C.

Theme and Message

On the one hand, the book of Judges tells how the Israelites frequently departed from the Lord to serve idols, provoking God's chastening. On the other hand, it is an account of urgent appeals to God in times of crisis, moving the Lord to raise up leaders (judges) through whom he threw off foreign oppressors and restored the land to peace. It contains several accounts of this recurring cycle (turning to idols, oppression, crying to the Lord, and deliverance). Judges reveals an age when "there was no king in Israel; all the people did what was right in their own eyes" (21.25).

Outline

I. Introduction: Incomplete Conquest and Apostasy (1.1–3.6)
 A. First Episode (1.1–2.5)
 B. Second Episode (2.6–3.6)
II. Oppression by Nations and Deliverance by Judges (3.7–16.31)
III. Epilogue: Religious and Moral Disorder (17.1–21.25)
 A. First Episode (17.1–18.31)
 B. Second Episode (19.1–21.25)

Israel's Failure to Complete the Conquest of Canaan

1 After the death of Joshua, the Israelites inquired of the LORD, "Who shall go up first for us against the Canaanites, to fight against them?" ²The LORD said, "Judah shall go up. I hereby give the land into his hand." ³Judah said to his brother Simeon, "Come up with me into the territory allotted to me, that we may fight against the Canaanites; then I too will go with you into the territory allotted to you." So Simeon went with him.

1.1
Num 27.21
1.3
v. 17

1.4
Gen 13.7

⁴Then Judah went up and the LORD gave the Canaanites and the Perizzites into their hand; and they defeated ten thousand of them at Bezek. ⁵They came upon Adoni-bezek at Bezek, and fought against him, and defeated the Canaanites and the Perizzites. ⁶Adoni-bezek fled; but they pursued him, and caught him, and cut off his thumbs and big toes. ⁷Adoni-bezek said, "Seventy kings with their thumbs and big toes cut off used to pick up scraps under my table; as I have done, so God has paid me back." They

brought him to Jerusalem, and he died there.

8 Then the people of Judah fought against Jerusalem and took it. They put it to the sword and set the city on fire. 9 Afterward the people of Judah went down to fight against the Canaanites who lived in the hill country, in the Negeb, and in the lowland. 10 Judah went against the Canaanites who lived in Hebron (the name of Hebron was formerly Kiriath-arba); and they defeated Sheshai and Ahiman and Talmai.

11 From there they went against the inhabitants of Debir (the name of Debir was formerly Kiriath-sepher). 12 Then Caleb said, "Whoever attacks Kiriath-sepher and takes it, I will give him my daughter Achsah as wife." 13 And Othniel son of Kenaz, Caleb's younger brother, took it; and he gave him his daughter Achsah as wife. 14 When she came to him, she urged him to ask her father for a field. As she dismounted from her donkey, Caleb said to her, "What do you wish?" 15 She said to him, "Give me a present; since you have set me in the land of the Negeb, give me also Gulloth-mayim." a So Caleb gave her Upper Gulloth and Lower Gulloth.

16 The descendants of Hobab b the Kenite, Moses' father-in-law, went up with the people of Judah from the city of palms into the wilderness of Judah, which lies in the Negeb near Arad. Then they went and settled with the Amalekites. c 17 Judah went with his brother Simeon, and they defeated the Canaanites who inhabited Zephath, and devoted it to destruction. So the city was called Hormah. 18 Judah took Gaza with its territory, Ashkelon with its territory, and Ekron with its territory. 19 The LORD was with Judah, and he took possession of the hill country, but could not drive out the inhabitants of the plain, because they had chariots of iron. 20 Hebron was given to Caleb, as Moses had said; and he drove out from it the three sons

of Anak. 21 But the Benjaminit did not drive out the Jebusites w lived in Jerusalem; so the Jebusit have lived in Jerusalem among t Benjaminites to this day.

22 The house of Joseph al went up against Bethel; and t LORD was with them. 23 The hou of Joseph sent out spies to Beth (the name of the city was former Luz). 24 When the spies saw a m coming out of the city, they said him, "Show us the way into t city, and we will deal kindly wi you." 25 So he showed them the w into the city; and they put the ci to the sword, but they let the m and all his family go. 26 So the m went to the land of the Hittites a built a city, and named it Luz; th is its name to this day.

27 Manasseh did not drive (the inhabitants of Beth-shean a its villages, or Taanach and its ▾ lages, or the inhabitants of Dor a its villages, or the inhabitants of leam and its villages, or the inha tants of Megiddo and its villag but the Canaanites continued live in that land. 28 When Isr grew strong, they put the Cana ites to forced labor, but did no fact drive them out.

29 And Ephraim did not dr out the Canaanites who lived Gezer; but the Canaanites li among them in Gezer.

30 Zebulun did not drive out inhabitants of Kitron, or the inh itants of Nahalol; but the Cana ites lived among them, and beca subject to forced labor.

31 Asher did not drive out inhabitants of Acco, or the inha tants of Sidon, or of Ahlab, or Achzib, or of Helbah, or of Ap or of Rehob; 32 but the Asher lived among the Canaanites, inhabitants of the land; for they not drive them out.

33 Naphtali did not drive the inhabitants of Beth-sheme or the inhabitants of Beth-an but lived among the Canaani

1.8
v. 21;
Josh 15.63
1.10
Josh 15.13-19
1.13
Judg 3.9
1.14
Josh 15.18, 19
1.16
Judg 4.11, 17;
Deut 34.3;
Judg 3.13
1.17
v. 3;
Num 21.3
1.19
v. 2;
Josh 17.16, 18
1.20
Josh 14.9;
15.13,14;
v. 10

1.21
Josh 15.63
1.23
Gen 28.19
1.25
Josh 6.25
1.27
Josh 17.11-13
1.29
Josh 16.10
1.31
Judg 10.6

a That is Basins of Water b Gk: Heb lacl Hobab c See 1 Sam 15.6: Heb people

the inhabitants of the land; nevertheless the inhabitants of Bethshemesh and of Beth-anath became subject to forced labor for them.

34 The Amorites pressed the Danites back into the hill country; they did not allow them to come down to the plain. 35 The Amorites continued to live in Har-heres, in Aijalon, and in Shaalbim, but the hand of the house of Joseph rested heavily on them, and they became subject to forced labor. 36 The border of the Amorites ran from the ascent of Akrabbim, from Sela and upward.

Israel's Disobedience

2 Now the angel of the LORD went up from Gilgal to Bochim, and said, "I brought you up from Egypt, and brought you into the land that I had promised to your ancestors. I said, 'I will never break my covenant with you. 2 For your part, do not make a covenant with the inhabitants of this land; tear down their altars.' But you have not obeyed my command. See what you have done! 3 So now I say, I will not drive them out before you; but they shall become adversaries d to you, and their gods shall be a snare to you." 4 When the angel of the LORD spoke these words to all the Israelites, the people lifted up their voices and wept. 5 So they named that place Bochim, e and there they sacrificed to the LORD.

Death of Joshua

6 When Joshua dismissed the people, the Israelites all went to their own inheritances to take possession of the land. 7 The people worshiped the LORD all the days of Joshua, and all the days of the elders who outlived Joshua, who had seen all the great work that the LORD had done for Israel. 8 Joshua son of Nun, the servant of the LORD, died at the age of one hundred ten years. 9 So they buried him within the bounds of his inheritance in Timnath-heres, in the hill country

of Ephraim, north of Mount Gaash. 10 Moreover, that whole generation was gathered to their ancestors, and another generation grew up after them, who did not know the LORD or the work that he had done for Israel.

Israel's Unfaithfulness

11 Then the Israelites did what was evil in the sight of the LORD and worshiped the Baals; 12 and they abandoned the LORD, the God of their ancestors, who had brought them out of the land of Egypt; they followed other gods, from among the gods of the peoples who were all around them, and bowed down to them; and they provoked the LORD to anger. 13 They abandoned the LORD, and worshiped Baal and the Astartes. 14 So the anger of the LORD was kindled against Israel, and he gave them over to plunderers who plundered them, and he sold them into the power of their enemies all around, so that they could no longer withstand their enemies. 15 Whenever they marched out, the hand of the LORD was against them to bring misfortune, as the LORD had warned them and sworn to them; and they were in great distress.

16 Then the LORD raised up judges, who delivered them out of the power of those who plundered them. 17 Yet they did not listen even to their judges; for they lusted after other gods and bowed down to them. They soon turned aside from the way in which their ancestors had walked, who had obeyed the commandments of the LORD; they did not follow their example. 18 Whenever the LORD raised up judges for them, the LORD was with the judge, and he delivered them from the hand of their enemies all the days of the judge; for the LORD would be moved to pity by their groaning because of those who persecuted and oppressed them. 19 But whenever the judge died, they would relapse and behave worse

Cross-references

1.34
Ex 3.17
1.36
Josh 15.3
2.1
v. 5;
Judg 6.11;
Ex 20.2;
Gen 17.7;
Deut 7.9
2.2
Ex 23.32;
34.12,13
2.3
Josh 23.13;
Judg 3.6;
Deut 7.16;
Ps 106.36
2.6
Josh 24.28-31

2.10
1 Sam 2.12;
1 Chr 28.9;
Gal 4.8
2.11
Judg 3.7,12;
4.1; 6.1,25;
8.33; 10.6
2.12
Deut 31.16
2.13
Judg 10.6
2.14
Judg 3.8;
Ps 106.40-42;
Deut 28.25
2.16
Ps 106.43-45;
Acts 13.20
2.17
v. 7
2.19
Judg 3.12;
4.1; 8.33

d OL Vg Compare Gk: Heb sides e That is Weepers

than their ancestors, following other gods, worshiping them and bowing down to them. They would not drop any of their practices or their stubborn ways. 20 So the anger of the LORD was kindled against Israel; and he said, "Because this people have transgressed my covenant that I commanded their ancestors, and have not obeyed my voice, 21 I will no longer drive out before them any of the nations that Joshua left when he died." 22 In order to test Israel, whether or not they would take care to walk in the way of the LORD as their ancestors did, 23 the LORD had left those nations, not driving them out at once, and had not handed them over to Joshua.

Nations Remaining in the Land

3 Now these are the nations that the LORD left to test all those in Israel who had no experience of any war in Canaan 2 (it was only that successive generations of Israelites might know war, to teach those who had no experience of it before): 3 the five lords of the Philistines, and all the Canaanites, and the Sidonians, and the Hivites who lived on Mount Lebanon, from Mount Baal-hermon as far as Lebo-hamath. 4 They were for the testing of Israel, to know whether Israel would obey the commandments of the LORD, which he commanded their ancestors by Moses. 5 So the Israelites lived among the Canaanites, the Hittites, the Amorites, the Perizzites, the Hivites, and the Jebusites; 6 and they took their daughters as wives for themselves, and their own daughters they gave to their sons; and they worshiped their gods.

Othniel

7 The Israelites did what was evil in the sight of the LORD, forgetting the LORD their God, and worshiping the Baals and the Asherahs. 8 Therefore the anger of the LORD was kindled against Israel, and he sold them into the hand of

2.20
v. 14;
Josh 23.16
2.21
Josh 23.13
2.22
Judg 3.1,4
3.1
Judg 2.21,
22
3.3
Josh 13.3
3.4
Deut 8.2;
Judg 2.22
3.6
Ex 34.16;
Deut 7.3,4
3.7
Judg 2.11,
13; Deut 4.9

3.9
v. 15;
Judg 1.13
3.10
Num 11.25,
29; 24.2;
Judg 6.34
3.12
Judg 2.11,
14
3.13
Judg 1.16
3.15
Ps 107.13
3.17
v. 12

King Cushan-rishathaim of Aram Naharaim; and the Israelites served Cushan-rishathaim eight years. 9 But when the Israelites cried out to the LORD, the LORD raised up a deliverer for the Israelites, who delivered them, Othniel son of Kenaz, Caleb's younger brother. 10 The spirit of the LORD came upon him, and he judged Israel; he went out to war, and the LORD gave King Cushan-rishathaim of Aram into his hand; and his hand prevailed over Cushan-rishathaim. 11 So the land had rest forty years. Then Othniel son of Kenaz died.

Ehud

12 The Israelites again did what was evil in the sight of the LORD; and the LORD strengthened King Eglon of Moab against Israel, because they had done what was evil in the sight of the LORD. 13 In alliance with the Ammonites and the Amalekites, he went and defeated Israel; and they took possession of the city of palms. 14 So the Israelites served King Eglon of Moab eighteen years.

15 But when the Israelites cried out to the LORD, the LORD raised up for them a deliverer, Ehud son of Gera, the Benjaminite, a left-handed man. The Israelites sent tribute by him to King Eglon of Moab. 16 Ehud made for himself a sword with two edges, a cubit in length; and he fastened it on his right thigh under his clothes. 17 Then he presented the tribute to King Eglon of Moab. Now Eglon was a very fat man. 18 When Ehud had finished presenting the tribute, he sent the people who carried the tribute on their way. 19 But he himself turned back at the sculptured stones near Gilgal, and said, "I have a secret message for you, O king." So the king said,[f] "Silence!" and all his attendants went out from his presence. 20 Ehud came to him, while he was sitting alone in his cool roof chamber, and

f Heb _he said_

said, "I have a message from God for you." So he rose from his seat. ²¹ Then Ehud reached with his left hand, took the sword from his right thigh, and thrust it into Eglon's[g] belly; ²² the hilt also went in after the blade, and the fat closed over the blade, for he did not draw the sword out of his belly; and the dirt came out.[h] ²³ Then Ehud went out into the vestibule,[i] and closed the doors of the roof chamber on him, and locked them.

24 After he had gone, the servants came. When they saw that the doors of the roof chamber were locked, they thought, "He must be relieving himself[j] in the cool chamber." ²⁵ So they waited until they were embarrassed. When he still did not open the doors of the roof chamber, they took the key and opened them. There was their lord lying dead on the floor.

26 Ehud escaped while they delayed, and passed beyond the sculptured stones, and escaped to Seirah. ²⁷ When he arrived, he sounded the trumpet in the hill country of Ephraim; and the Israelites went down with him from the hill country, having him at their head. ²⁸ He said to them, "Follow after me; for the Lord has given your enemies the Moabites into your hand." So they went down after him, and seized the fords of the Jordan against the Moabites, and allowed no one to cross over. ²⁹ At that time they killed about ten thousand of the Moabites, all strong, able-bodied men; no one escaped. ³⁰ So Moab was subdued that day under the hand of Israel. And the land had rest eighty years.

Shamgar

31 After him came Shamgar son of Anath, who killed six hundred of the Philistines with an oxgoad. He too delivered Israel.

Deborah and Barak

4 The Israelites again did what was evil in the sight of the Lord, after Ehud died. ² So the Lord sold them into the hand of King Jabin of Canaan, who reigned in Hazor; the commander of his army was Sisera, who lived in Harosheth-ha-goiim. ³ Then the Israelites cried out to the Lord for help; for he had nine hundred chariots of iron, and had oppressed the Israelites cruelly twenty years.

4 At that time Deborah, a prophetess, wife of Lappidoth, was judging Israel. ⁵ She used to sit under the palm of Deborah between Ramah and Bethel in the hill country of Ephraim; and the Israelites came up to her for judgment. ⁶ She sent and summoned Barak son of Abinoam from Kedesh in Naphtali, and said to him, "The Lord, the God of Israel, commands you, 'Go, take position at Mount Tabor, bringing ten thousand from the tribe of Naphtali and the tribe of Zebulun. ⁷ I will draw out Sisera, the general of Jabin's army, to meet you by the Wadi Kishon with his chariots and his troops; and I will give him into your hand.' " ⁸ Barak said to her, "If you will go with me, I will go; but if you will not go with me, I will not go." ⁹ And she said, "I will surely go with you; nevertheless, the road on which you are going will not lead to your glory, for the Lord will sell Sisera into the hand of a woman." Then Deborah got up and went with Barak to Kedesh. ¹⁰ Barak summoned Zebulun and Naphtali to Kedesh; and ten thousand warriors went up behind him; and Deborah went up with him.

11 Now Heber the Kenite had separated from the other Kenites,[k] that is, the descendants of Hobab the father-in-law of Moses, and had encamped as far away as Elon-bezaanannim, which is near Kedesh.

12 When Sisera was told that Barak son of Abinoam had gone up to Mount Tabor, ¹³ Sisera called out all his chariots, nine hundred char-

3.24 1 Sam 24.3
3.25 2 Kings 2.17; 8.11
3.28 Judg 7.9,15, 24; 12.5
3.30 v. 11
3.31 Judg 5.6
4.1 Judg 2.19
4.2 Josh 11.1, 10; vv. 13, 16; Ps 83.9
4.3 Judg 1.19
4.6 Heb 11.32
4.7 Ps 83.9
4.9 v. 21
4.10 Judg 5.18; v. 14;
Judg 5.15
4.11 Judg 1.16; v. 6
4.13 v. 3

g Heb his h With Tg Vg: Meaning of Heb uncertain i Meaning of Heb uncertain j Heb covering his feet k Heb from the Kain

iots of iron, and all the troops who were with him, from Harosheth-hagoiim to the Wadi Kishon. [14]Then Deborah said to Barak, "Up! For this is the day on which the LORD has given Sisera into your hand. The LORD is indeed going out before you." So Barak went down from Mount Tabor with ten thousand warriors following him. [15]And the LORD threw Sisera and all his chariots and all his army into a panic[1] before Barak; Sisera got down from his chariot and fled away on foot, [16]while Barak pursued the chariots and the army to Harosheth-hagoiim. All the army of Sisera fell by the sword; no one was left.

17 Now Sisera had fled away on foot to the tent of Jael wife of Heber the Kenite; for there was peace between King Jabin of Hazor and the clan of Heber the Kenite. [18]Jael came out to meet Sisera, and said to him, "Turn aside, my lord, turn aside to me; have no fear." So he turned aside to her into the tent, and she covered him with a rug. [19]Then he said to her, "Please give me a little water to drink; for I am thirsty." So she opened a skin of milk and gave him a drink and covered him. [20]He said to her, "Stand at the entrance of the tent, and if anybody comes and asks you, 'Is anyone here?' say, 'No.' " [21]But Jael wife of Heber took a tent peg, and took a hammer in her hand, and went softly to him and drove the peg into his temple, until it went down into the ground—he was lying fast asleep from weariness—and he died. [22]Then, as Barak came in pursuit of Sisera, Jael went out to meet him, and said to him, "Come, and I will show you the man whom you are seeking." So he went into her tent; and there was Sisera lying dead, with the tent peg in his temple.

23 So on that day God subdued King Jabin of Canaan before the Israelites. [24]Then the hand of the Israelites bore harder and harder on King Jabin of Canaan, until they destroyed King Jabin of Canaan.

4.14
Deut 9.3
4.15
Josh 10.10
4.16
Ps 83.9
4.19
Judg 5.25
4.21
Judg 5.26

5.1
Ex 15.1
5.2
Deut 32.41
5.3
Ps 27.6
5.4
Deut 33.2;
Ps 68.7-9
5.5
Ps 97.5;
Isa 64.1,3;
Ps 68.8
5.6
Judg 3.31;
4.17
5.8
Deut 32.17

The Song of Deborah

5 Then Deborah and Barak son of Abinoam sang on that day, saying:

[2] "When locks are long in
 Israel,
 when the people offer
 themselves willingly—
 bless [m] the LORD!

[3] "Hear, O kings; give ear,
 O princes;
 to the LORD I will sing,
 I will make melody to the
 LORD, the God of Israel.

[4] "LORD, when you went out
 from Seir,
 when you marched from
 the region of Edom,
 the earth trembled,
 and the heavens poured,
 the clouds indeed poured
 water.

[5] The mountains quaked
 before the LORD, the
 One of Sinai,
 before the LORD, the God of
 Israel.

[6] "In the days of Shamgar son
 of Anath,
 in the days of Jael,
 caravans ceased
 and travelers kept to the
 byways.

[7] The peasantry prospered in
 Israel,
 they grew fat on plunder,
 because you arose, Deborah,
 arose as a mother in Israel.

[8] When new gods were chosen,
 then war was in the gates.
 Was shield or spear to be
 seen
 among forty thousand in
 Israel?

[9] My heart goes out to the
 commanders of Israel
 who offered themselves
 willingly among the
 people.
 Bless the LORD.

[1]Heb adds *to the sword*; compare verse 16
[m] Or *You who offer yourselves willingly among the people, bless*

10 "Tell of it, you who ride on
 white donkeys,
 you who sit on rich
 carpets[n]
 and you who walk by the
 way.
11 To the sound of musicians[n]
 at the watering places,
 there they repeat the
 triumphs of the LORD,
 the triumphs of his
 peasantry in Israel.

"Then down to the gates
 marched the people of
 the LORD.

12 "Awake, awake, Deborah!
 Awake, awake, utter a
 song!
 Arise, Barak, lead away your
 captives,
 O son of Abinoam.
13 Then down marched the
 remnant of the noble;
 the people of the LORD
 marched down for him[o]
 against the mighty.
14 From Ephraim they set out[p]
 into the valley,[q]
 following you, Benjamin,
 with your kin;
 from Machir marched down
 the commanders,
 and from Zebulun those
 who bear the marshal's
 staff;
15 the chiefs of Issachar came
 with Deborah,
 and Issachar faithful to
 Barak;
 into the valley they rushed
 out at his heels.
 Among the clans of Reuben
 there were great searchings
 of heart.
16 Why did you tarry among the
 sheepfolds,
 to hear the piping for the
 flocks?
 Among the clans of Reuben
 there were great searchings
 of heart.
17 Gilead stayed beyond the
 Jordan;
 and Dan, why did he abide
 with the ships?

Asher sat still at the coast of
 the sea,
 settling down by his
 landings.
18 Zebulun is a people that
 scorned death;
 Naphtali too, on the
 heights of the field.

19 "The kings came, they
 fought;
 then fought the kings of
 Canaan,
 at Taanach, by the waters of
 Megiddo;
 they got no spoils of silver.
20 The stars fought from
 heaven,
 from their courses they
 fought against Sisera.
21 The torrent Kishon swept
 them away,
 the onrushing torrent, the
 torrent Kishon.
 March on, my soul, with
 might!

22 "Then loud beat the horses'
 hoofs
 with the galloping,
 galloping of his steeds.

23 "Curse Meroz, says the angel
 of the LORD,
 curse bitterly its
 inhabitants,
 because they did not come
 to the help of the LORD,
 to the help of the LORD
 against the mighty.

24 "Most blessed of women be
 Jael,
 the wife of Heber the
 Kenite,
 of tent-dwelling women
 most blessed.
25 He asked water and she gave
 him milk,
 she brought him curds in a
 lordly bowl.
26 She put her hand to the tent
 peg

5.11
1 Sam 12.7;
Mic 6.5
5.12
Ps 57.8;
68.18
5.14
Judg 3.13,
27;
Num 32.39
5.15
Judg 4.10
5.16
Num 32.1
5.17
Josh 13.24-
28; 19.29,46

5.18
Judg 4.6,10
5.19ff
Josh 11.1,2;
Judg 1.27
5.20
Josh 10.11-14
5.21
Judg 4.7
5.24
Judg 4.17,
19-21
5.25
Judg 4.19
5.26
Judg 4.21

[n] Meaning of Heb uncertain [o] Gk: Heb me
[p] Cn: Heb From Ephraim their root
[q] Gk: Heb in Amalek

and her right hand to the
 workmen's mallet;
she struck Sisera a blow,
 she crushed his head,
 she shattered and pierced
 his temple.
27 He sank, he fell,
 he lay still at her feet;
 at her feet he sank, he fell;
 where he sank, there he
 fell dead.

28 "Out of the window she
 peered,
 the mother of Sisera
 gazed[r] through the
 lattice:
'Why is his chariot so long in
 coming?
 Why tarry the hoofbeats of
 his chariots?'
29 Her wisest ladies make
 answer,
 indeed, she answers the
 question herself:
30 'Are they not finding and
 dividing the spoil?—
 A girl or two for every man;
spoil of dyed stuffs for
 Sisera,
 spoil of dyed stuffs
 embroidered,
 two pieces of dyed work
 embroidered for my
 neck as spoil?'

31 "So perish all your enemies,
 O LORD!
 But may your friends be
 like the sun as it rises
 in its might."

And the land had rest forty years.

The Midianite Oppression

6 The Israelites did what was
 evil in the sight of the LORD,
and the LORD gave them into the
hand of Midian seven years. 2 The
hand of Midian prevailed over Isra-
el; and because of Midian the Isra-
elites provided for themselves hid-
ing places in the mountains, caves
and strongholds. 3 For whenever
the Israelites put in seed, the Midi-
anites and the Amalekites and the
people of the East would come up

5.28
Prov 7.6
5.30
Ex 15.9
5.31
Ps 68.2;
92.9; 19.4,5;
Judg 3.11
6.1
Judg 2.11,
19;
Num 25.15-18;
31.1-3
6.3
Judg 3.13

6.4
Lev 26.16;
Deut 28.30,
33,51
6.5
Judg 7.12
6.6
Judg 3.15
6.8
Judg 2.1,2
6.9
Ps 44.2,3
6.11
Josh 17.2
6.12
Josh 1.5
6.13
Ps 44.1;
2 Chr 15.2
6.14
Heb 11.32,
34; Judg 4.6

against them. 4 They would en-
camp against them and destroy the
produce of the land, as far as the
neighborhood of Gaza, and leave
no sustenance in Israel, and no
sheep or ox or donkey. 5 For they
and their livestock would come up,
and they would even bring their
tents, as thick as locusts; neither
they nor their camels could be
counted; so they wasted the land as
they came in. 6 Thus Israel was
greatly impoverished because of
Midian; and the Israelites cried out
to the LORD for help.

7 When the Israelites cried to
the LORD on account of the Midian-
ites, 8 the LORD sent a prophet to
the Israelites; and he said to them,
"Thus says the LORD, the God of Is-
rael: I led you up from Egypt, and
brought you out of the house of
slavery; 9 and I delivered you from
the hand of the Egyptians, and
from the hand of all who oppressed
you, and drove them out before
you, and gave you their land; 10 and
I said to you, 'I am the LORD your
God; you shall not pay reverence to
the gods of the Amorites, in whose
land you live.' But you have not giv-
en heed to my voice."

The Call of Gideon

11 Now the angel of the LORD
came and sat under the oak at
Ophrah, which belonged to Joash
the Abiezrite, as his son Gideon
was beating out wheat in the wine
press, to hide it from the Midian-
ites. 12 The angel of the LORD ap-
peared to him and said to him,
"The LORD is with you, you mighty
warrior." 13 Gideon answered him,
"But sir, if the LORD is with us, why
then has all this happened to us?
And where are all his wonderful
deeds that our ancestors recounted
to us, saying, 'Did not the LORD
bring us up from Egypt?' But now
the LORD has cast us off, and given
us into the hand of Midian."
14 Then the LORD turned to him and
said, "Go in this might of yours and
deliver Israel from the hand of Mid-
ian; I hereby commission you."

r Gk Compare Tg: Heb *exclaimed*

¹⁵He responded, "But sir, how can I deliver Israel? My clan is the weakest in Manasseh, and I am the least in my family." ¹⁶The LORD said to him, "But I will be with you, and you shall strike down the Midianites, every one of them." ¹⁷Then he said to him, "If now I have found favor with you, then show me a sign that it is you who speak with me. ¹⁸Do not depart from here until I come to you, and bring out my present, and set it before you." And he said, "I will stay until you return."

19 So Gideon went into his house and prepared a kid, and unleavened cakes from an ephah of flour; the meat he put in a basket, and the broth he put in a pot, and brought them to him under the oak and presented them. ²⁰The angel of God said to him, "Take the meat and the unleavened cakes, and put them on this rock, and pour out the broth." And he did so. ²¹Then the angel of the LORD reached out the tip of the staff that was in his hand, and touched the meat and the unleavened cakes; and fire sprang up from the rock and consumed the meat and the unleavened cakes; and the angel of the LORD vanished from his sight. ²²Then Gideon perceived that it was the angel of the LORD; and Gideon said, "Help me, Lord GOD! For I have seen the angel of the LORD face to face." ²³But the LORD said to him, "Peace be to you; do not fear, you shall not die." ²⁴Then Gideon built an altar there to the LORD, and called it, The LORD is peace. To this day it still stands at Ophrah, which belongs to the Abiezrites.

25 That night the LORD said to him, "Take your father's bull, the second bull seven years old, and pull down the altar of Baal that belongs to your father, and cut down the sacred poleˢ that is beside it; ²⁶and build an altar to the LORD your God on the top of the stronghold here, in proper order; then take the second bull, and offer it as a burnt offering with the wood of the sacred poleˢ that you shall cut

down." ²⁷So Gideon took ten of his servants, and did as the LORD had told him; but because he was too afraid of his family and the townspeople to do it by day, he did it by night.

Gideon Destroys the Altar of Baal

28 When the townspeople rose early in the morning, the altar of Baal was broken down, and the sacred poleˢ beside it was cut down, and the second bull was offered on the altar that had been built. ²⁹So they said to one another, "Who has done this?" After searching and inquiring, they were told, "Gideon son of Joash did it." ³⁰Then the townspeople said to Joash, "Bring out your son, so that he may die, for he has pulled down the altar of Baal and cut down the sacred poleˢ beside it." ³¹But Joash said to all who were arrayed against him, "Will you contend for Baal? Or will you defend his cause? Whoever contends for him shall be put to death by morning. If he is a god, let him contend for himself, because his altar has been pulled down." ³²Therefore on that day Gideonᵗ was called Jerubbaal, that is to say, "Let Baal contend against him," because he pulled down his altar.

33 Then all the Midianites and the Amalekites and the people of the East came together, and crossing the Jordan they encamped in the Valley of Jezreel. ³⁴But the spirit of the LORD took possession of Gideon; and he sounded the trumpet, and the Abiezrites were called out to follow him. ³⁵He sent messengers throughout all Manasseh, and they too were called out to follow him. He also sent messengers to Asher, Zebulun, and Naphtali, and they went up to meet them.

The Sign of the Fleece

36 Then Gideon said to God, "In order to see whether you will deliver Israel by my hand, as you have

6.15
Ex 3.11;
1 Sam 9.21
6.16
Ex 3.12;
Josh 1.5
6.17
vv. 36,37;
Isa 38.7,8
6.19
Gen 18.6-8
6.20
Judg 13.19
6.21
Lev 9.24
6.22
Judg 13.21
6.25
Ex 34.13;
Deut 7.5

6.28
1 Kings 16.32
6.32
Judg 7.1;
1 Sam 12.11
6.33
v. 3;
Josh 17.16
6.34
Judg 3.10,
27;
1 Chr 12.18;
2 Chr 24.20

ˢHeb *Asherah* ᵗHeb *he*

said, [37] I am going to lay a fleece of wool on the threshing floor; if there is dew on the fleece alone, and it is dry on all the ground, then I shall know that you will deliver Israel by my hand, as you have said." [38] And it was so. When he rose early next morning and squeezed the fleece, he wrung enough dew from the fleece to fill a bowl with water. [39] Then Gideon said to God, "Do not let your anger burn against me, let me speak one more time; let me, please, make trial with the fleece just once more; let it be dry only on the fleece, and on all the ground let there be dew." [40] And God did so that night. It was dry on the fleece only, and on all the ground there was dew.

Gideon Surprises and Routs the Midianites

7 Then Jerubbaal (that is, Gideon) and all the troops that were with him rose early and encamped beside the spring of Harod; and the camp of Midian was north of them, below[u] the hill of Moreh, in the valley.

2 The Lord said to Gideon, "The troops with you are too many for me to give the Midianites into their hand. Israel would only take the credit away from me, saying, 'My own hand has delivered me.' [3] Now therefore proclaim this in the hearing of the troops, 'Whoever is fearful and trembling, let him return home.'" Thus Gideon sifted them out;[v] twenty-two thousand returned, and ten thousand remained.

4 Then the Lord said to Gideon, "The troops are still too many; take them down to the water and I will sift them out for you there. When I say, 'This one shall go with you,' he shall go with you; and when I say, 'This one shall not go with you,' he shall not go." [5] So he brought the troops down to the water; and the Lord said to Gideon, "All those who lap the water with their tongues, as a dog laps, you shall put to one side; all those who kneel down to drink, putting their hands

to their mouths,[w] you shall put to the other side." [6] The number of those that lapped was three hundred; but all the rest of the troops knelt down to drink water. [7] Then the Lord said to Gideon, "With the three hundred that lapped I will deliver you, and give the Midianites into your hand. Let all the others go to their homes." [8] So he took the jars of the troops from their hands,[x] and their trumpets; and he sent all the rest of Israel back to their own tents, but retained the three hundred. The camp of Midian was below him in the valley.

9 That same night the Lord said to him, "Get up, attack the camp; for I have given it into your hand. [10] But if you fear to attack, go down to the camp with your servant Purah; [11] and you shall hear what they say, and afterward your hands shall be strengthened to attack the camp." Then he went down with his servant Purah to the outposts of the armed men that were in the camp. [12] The Midianites and the Amalekites and all the people of the East lay along the valley as thick as locusts; and their camels were without number, countless as the sand on the seashore. [13] When Gideon arrived, there was a man telling a dream to his comrade; and he said, "I had a dream, and in it a cake of barley bread tumbled into the camp of Midian, and came to the tent, and struck it so that it fell; it turned upside down, and the tent collapsed." [14] And his comrade answered, "This is no other than the sword of Gideon son of Joash, a man of Israel; into his hand God has given Midian and all the army."

15 When Gideon heard the telling of the dream and its interpretation, he worshiped; and he returned to the camp of Israel, and said, "Get up; for the Lord has given the army of Midian into your hand." [16] After he divided the three

Cross references
6.37 Ex 4.3-7
6.39 Gen 18.32
7.1 Judg 6.32
7.2 Deut 8.17; Isa 10.13; 2 Cor 4.7
7.3 Deut 20.8
7.4 1 Sam 14.6
7.7 1 Sam 14.6
7.9 Josh 2.24; 10.8; 11.6
7.11 vv. 13-15
7.12 Judg 6.5; 8.10; Josh 11.4
7.14 v. 20
7.15 1 Sam 15.31

u Heb from v Cn: Heb home, and depart from Mount Gilead' " w Heb places the words putting their hands to their mouths after the word lapped in verse 6 x Cn: Heb So the people took provisions in their hands

hundred men into three companies, and put trumpets into the hands of all of them, and empty jars, with torches inside the jars, ¹⁷he said to them, "Look at me, and do the same; when I come to the outskirts of the camp, do as I do. ¹⁸When I blow the trumpet, I and all who are with me, then you also blow the trumpets around the whole camp, and shout, 'For the LORD and for Gideon!' "

19 So Gideon and the hundred who were with him came to the outskirts of the camp at the beginning of the middle watch, when they had just set the watch; and they blew the trumpets and smashed the jars that were in their hands. ²⁰So the three companies blew the trumpets and broke the jars, holding in their left hands the torches, and in their right hands the trumpets to blow; and they cried, "A sword for the LORD and for Gideon!" ²¹Every man stood in his place all around the camp, and all the men in camp ran; they cried out and fled. ²²When they blew the three hundred trumpets, the LORD set every man's sword against his fellow and against all the army; and the army fled as far as Beth-shittah toward Zererah,^y as far as the border of Abel-meholah, by Tabbath. ²³And the men of Israel were called out from Naphtali and from Asher and from all Manasseh, and they pursued after the Midianites.

24 Then Gideon sent messengers throughout all the hill country of Ephraim, saying, "Come down against the Midianites and seize the waters against them, as far as Beth-barah, and also the Jordan." So all the men of Ephraim were called out, and they seized the waters as far as Beth-barah, and also the Jordan. ²⁵They captured the two captains of Midian, Oreb and Zeeb; they killed Oreb at the rock of Oreb, and Zeeb they killed at the wine press of Zeeb, as they pursued the Midianites. They brought the heads of Oreb and Zeeb to Gideon beyond the Jordan.

7.18 vv. 14,20
7.20 v. 14
7.21 2 Kings 7.7
7.22 Josh 6.4; 16.20; 1 Sam 14.20
7.23 Judg 6.35
7.24 Judg 3.27, 28
7.25 Judg 8.3,4; Ps 83.11; Isa 10.26
8.1 Judg 12.1
8.3 Judg 7.24, 25
8.5 Gen 33.17
8.6 v. 15
8.7 Judg 7.15
8.8 Gen 32.30, 31
8.9 v. 18
8.12 Ps 83.11

Gideon's Triumph and Vengeance

8 Then the Ephraimites said to him, "What have you done to us, not to call us when you went to fight against the Midianites?" And they upbraided him violently. ²So he said to them, "What have I done now in comparison with you? Is not the gleaning of the grapes of Ephraim better than the vintage of Abiezer? ³God has given into your hands the captains of Midian, Oreb and Zeeb; what have I been able to do in comparison with you?" When he said this, their anger against him subsided.

4 Then Gideon came to the Jordan and crossed over, he and the three hundred who were with him, exhausted and famished.^z ⁵So he said to the people of Succoth, "Please give some loaves of bread to my followers, for they are exhausted, and I am pursuing Zebah and Zalmunna, the kings of Midian." ⁶But the officials of Succoth said, "Do you already have in your possession the hands of Zebah and Zalmunna, that we should give bread to your army?" ⁷Gideon replied, "Well then, when the LORD has given Zebah and Zalmunna into my hand, I will trample your flesh on the thorns of the wilderness and on briers." ⁸From there he went up to Penuel, and made the same request of them; and the people of Penuel answered him as the people of Succoth had answered. ⁹So he said to the people of Penuel, "When I come back victorious, I will break down this tower."

10 Now Zebah and Zalmunna were in Karkor with their army, about fifteen thousand men, all who were left of all the army of the people of the East; for one hundred twenty thousand men bearing arms had fallen. ¹¹So Gideon went up by the caravan route east of Nobah and Jogbehah, and attacked the army; for the army was off its guard. ¹²Zebah and Zalmunna fled; and

^yAnother reading is *Zeredah* ^zGk: Heb *pursuing*

he pursued them and took the two kings of Midian, Zebah and Zalmunna, and threw all the army into a panic.

13 When Gideon son of Joash returned from the battle by the ascent of Heres, [14] he caught a young man, one of the people of Succoth, and questioned him; and he listed for him the officials and elders of Succoth, seventy-seven people. [15] Then he came to the people of Succoth, and said, "Here are Zebah and Zalmunna, about whom you taunted me, saying, 'Do you already have in your possession the hands of Zebah and Zalmunna, that we should give bread to your troops who are exhausted?' " [16] So he took the elders of the city and he took thorns of the wilderness and briers and with them he trampled[a] the people of Succoth. [17] He also broke down the tower of Penuel, and killed the men of the city.

18 Then he said to Zebah and Zalmunna, "What about the men whom you killed at Tabor?" They answered, "As you are, so were they, every one of them; they resembled the sons of a king." [19] And he replied, "They were my brothers, the sons of my mother; as the LORD lives, if you had saved them alive, I would not kill you." [20] So he said to Jether his firstborn, "Go kill them!" But the boy did not draw his sword, for he was afraid, because he was still a boy. [21] Then Zebah and Zalmunna said, "You come and kill us; for as the man is, so is his strength." So Gideon proceeded to kill Zebah and Zalmunna; and he took the crescents that were on the necks of their camels.

Gideon's Idolatry

22 Then the Israelites said to Gideon, "Rule over us, you and your son and your grandson also; for you have delivered us out of the hand of Midian." [23] Gideon said to them, "I will not rule over you, and my son will not rule over you; the LORD will rule over you." [24] Then Gideon said to them, "Let me make a request of you; each of you

give me an earring he has taken as booty." (For the enemy[b] had golden earrings, because they were Ishmaelites.) [25] "We will willingly give them," they answered. So they spread a garment, and each threw into it an earring he had taken as booty. [26] The weight of the golden earrings that he requested was one thousand seven hundred shekels of gold (apart from the crescents and the pendants and the purple garments worn by the kings of Midian, and the collars that were on the necks of their camels). [27] Gideon made an ephod of it and put it in his town, in Ophrah; and all Israel prostituted themselves to it there, and it became a snare to Gideon and to his family. [28] So Midian was subdued before the Israelites, and they lifted up their heads no more. So the land had rest forty years in the days of Gideon.

Death of Gideon

29 Jerubbaal son of Joash went to live in his own house. [30] Now Gideon had seventy sons, his own offspring, for he had many wives. [31] His concubine who was in Shechem also bore him a son, and he named him Abimelech. [32] Then Gideon son of Joash died at a good old age, and was buried in the tomb of his father Joash at Ophrah of the Abiezrites.

33 As soon as Gideon died, the Israelites relapsed and prostituted themselves with the Baals, making Baal-berith their god. [34] The Israelites did not remember the LORD their God, who had rescued them from the hand of all their enemies on every side; [35] and they did not exhibit loyalty to the house of Jerubbaal (that is, Gideon) in return for all the good that he had done to Israel.

Abimelech Attempts to Establish a Monarchy

9 Now Abimelech son of Jerubbaal went to Shechem to his mother's kinsfolk and said to them

Cross references

8.15 v. 6
8.16 v. 7
8.17 v. 9
8.18 Judg 4.6
8.21 Ps 83.11; v. 26
8.23 1 Sam 8.7; 10.19; 12.12
8.27 Judg 17.5; Ps 106.39; Deut 7.16
8.28 Judg 5.31
8.29 Judg 7.1
8.30 Judg 9.2,5
8.31 Judg 9.1
8.33 Judg 2.17, 19; 9.4,46
8.34 Judg 3.7; Deut 4.9
9.1 Judg 8.31

a With verse 7, Compare Gk: Heb *he taught*
b Heb *they*

and to the whole clan of his mother's family, [2] "Say in the hearing of all the lords of Shechem, 'Which is better for you, that all seventy of the sons of Jerubbaal rule over you, or that one rule over you?' Remember also that I am your bone and your flesh." [3] So his mother's kinsfolk spoke all these words on his behalf in the hearing of all the lords of Shechem; and their hearts inclined to follow Abimelech, for they said, "He is our brother." [4] They gave him seventy pieces of silver out of the temple of Baal-berith with which Abimelech hired worthless and reckless fellows, who followed him. [5] He went to his father's house at Ophrah, and killed his brothers the sons of Jerubbaal, seventy men, on one stone; but Jotham, the youngest son of Jerubbaal, survived, for he hid himself. [6] Then all the lords of Shechem and all Beth-millo came together, and they went and made Abimelech king, by the oak of the pillar[c] at Shechem.

The Parable of the Trees

[7] When it was told to Jotham, he went and stood on the top of Mount Gerizim, and cried aloud and said to them, "Listen to me, you lords of Shechem, so that God may listen to you.

[8] The trees once went out
 to anoint a king over
 themselves.
So they said to the olive tree,
 'Reign over us.'
[9] The olive tree answered
 them,
 'Shall I stop producing my
 rich oil
 by which gods and
 mortals are honored,
 and go to sway over the
 trees?'
[10] Then the trees said to the fig
 tree,
 'You come and reign over
 us.'
[11] But the fig tree answered
 them,
 'Shall I stop producing my
 sweetness

and my delicious fruit,
 and go to sway over the
 trees?'
[12] Then the trees said to the
 vine,
 'You come and reign over
 us.'
[13] But the vine said to them,
 'Shall I stop producing my
 wine
 that cheers gods and
 mortals,
 and go to sway over the
 trees?'
[14] So all the trees said to the
 bramble,
 'You come and reign over
 us.'
[15] And the bramble said to the
 trees,
 'If in good faith you are
 anointing me king over
 you,
 then come and take
 refuge in my shade;
 but if not, let fire come out
 of the bramble
 and devour the cedars of
 Lebanon.'
[16] "Now therefore, if you acted in good faith and honor when you made Abimelech king, and if you have dealt well with Jerubbaal and his house, and have done to him as his actions deserved— [17] for my father fought for you, and risked his life, and rescued you from the hand of Midian; [18] but you have risen up against my father's house this day, and have killed his sons, seventy men on one stone, and have made Abimelech, the son of his slave woman, king over the lords of Shechem, because he is your kinsman— [19] if, I say, you have acted in good faith and honor with Jerubbaal and with his house this day, then rejoice in Abimelech, and let him also rejoice in you; [20] but if not, let fire come out from Abimelech, and devour the lords of Shechem, and Beth-millo; and let fire come out from the lords of Shechem, and from Beth-millo, and devour Abimelech." [21] Then Jotham ran away

9.2
Judg 8.30;
Gen 29.14
9.4
Judg 8.33
9.5
v. 2
9.7
Deut 11.29;
27.12;
Jn 4.20

9.15
Isa 30.2;
v. 20
9.16
Judg 8.35
9.18
vv. 5,6;
Judg 8.31
9.19
Judg 8.35

c Cn: Meaning of Heb uncertain

and fled, going to Beer, where he remained for fear of his brother Abimelech.

The Downfall of Abimelech

22 Abimelech ruled over Israel three years. 23 But God sent an evil spirit between Abimelech and the lords of Shechem; and the lords of Shechem dealt treacherously with Abimelech. 24 This happened so that the violence done to the seventy sons of Jerubbaal might be avenged[d] and their blood be laid on their brother Abimelech, who killed them, and on the lords of Shechem, who strengthened his hands to kill his brothers. 25 So, out of hostility to him, the lords of Shechem set ambushes on the mountain tops. They robbed all who passed by them along that way; and it was reported to Abimelech.

26 When Gaal son of Ebed moved into Shechem with his kinsfolk, the lords of Shechem put confidence in him. 27 They went out into the field and gathered the grapes from their vineyards, trod them, and celebrated. Then they went into the temple of their god, ate and drank, and ridiculed Abimelech. 28 Gaal son of Ebed said, "Who is Abimelech, and who are we of Shechem, that we should serve him? Did not the son of Jerubbaal and Zebul his officer serve the men of Hamor father of Shechem? Why then should we serve him? 29 If only this people were under my command! Then I would remove Abimelech; I would say[e] to him, 'Increase your army, and come out.'"

30 When Zebul the ruler of the city heard the words of Gaal son of Ebed, his anger was kindled. 31 He sent messengers to Abimelech at Arumah,[f] saying, "Look, Gaal son of Ebed and his kinsfolk have come to Shechem, and they are stirring up[g] the city against you. 32 Now therefore, go by night, you and the troops that are with you, and lie in wait in the fields. 33 Then early in the morning, as soon as the sun rises, get up and rush on the city;

and when he and the troops that are with him come out against you, you may deal with them as best you can."

34 So Abimelech and all the troops with him got up by night and lay in wait against Shechem in four companies. 35 When Gaal son of Ebed went out and stood in the entrance of the gate of the city, Abimelech and the troops with him rose from the ambush. 36 And when Gaal saw them, he said to Zebul, "Look, people are coming down from the mountain tops!" And Zebul said to him, "The shadows on the mountains look like people to you." 37 Gaal spoke again and said, "Look, people are coming down from Tabbur-erez, and one company is coming from the direction of Elon-meonenim."[h] 38 Then Zebul said to him, "Where is your boast[i] now, you who said, 'Who is Abimelech, that we should serve him?' Are not these the troops you made light of? Go out now and fight with them." 39 So Gaal went out at the head of the lords of Shechem, and fought with Abimelech. 40 Abimelech chased him, and he fled before him. Many fell wounded, up to the entrance of the gate. 41 So Abimelech resided at Arumah; and Zebul drove out Gaal and his kinsfolk, so that they could not live on at Shechem.

42 On the following day the people went out into the fields. When Abimelech was told, 43 he took his troops and divided them into three companies, and lay in wait in the fields. When he looked and saw the people coming out of the city, he rose against them and killed them. 44 Abimelech and the company that was[j] with him rushed forward and stood at the entrance of the gate of the city, while the two companies rushed on all who were in the fields and killed them. 45 Abimelech fought against

Cross references

9.23 1 Sam 16.14; 18.9,10
9.24 vv. 56,57; Deut 27.25; Num 35.33
9.27 Judg 8.33
9.28 Gen 34.2,6
9.29 2 Sam 15.4
9.33 1 Sam 10.7
9.37 Ezek 38.12
9.38 vv. 28,29
9.39 Gen 35.4
9.45 v. 20; Deut 29.23

d Heb might come e Gk: Heb and he said f Cn See 9.41. Heb Tormah g Cn: Heb are besieging h That is Diviners' Oak i Heb mouth j Vg and some Gk Mss: Heb companies that were

the city all that day; he took the city, and killed the people that were in it; and he razed the city and sowed it with salt.

46 When all the lords of the Tower of Shechem heard of it, they entered the stronghold of the temple of El-berith. 47 Abimelech was told that all the lords of the Tower of Shechem were gathered together. 48 So Abimelech went up to Mount Zalmon, he and all the troops that were with him. Abimelech took an ax in his hand, cut down a bundle of brushwood, and took it up and laid it on his shoulder. Then he said to the troops with him, "What you have seen me do, do quickly, as I have done." 49 So every one of the troops cut down a bundle and following Abimelech put it against the stronghold, and they set the stronghold on fire over them, so that all the people of the Tower of Shechem also died, about a thousand men and women.

50 Then Abimelech went to Thebez, and encamped against Thebez, and took it. 51 But there was a strong tower within the city, and all the men and women and all the lords of the city fled to it and shut themselves in; and they went to the roof of the tower. 52 Abimelech came to the tower, and fought against it, and came near to the entrance of the tower to burn it with fire. 53 But a certain woman threw an upper millstone on Abimelech's head, and crushed his skull. 54 Immediately he called to the young man who carried his armor and said to him, "Draw your sword and kill me, so people will not say about me, 'A woman killed him.'" So the young man thrust him through, and he died. 55 When the Israelites saw that Abimelech was dead, they all went home. 56 Thus God repaid Abimelech for the crime he committed against his father in killing his seventy brothers; 57 and God also made all the wickedness of the people of Shechem fall back on their heads, and on them came the curse of Jotham son of Jerubbaal.

9.46
Judg 8.33
9.48
Ps 68.14
9.50
2 Sam 11.21
9.53
v. 50
9.56
v. 24;
Ps 94.23
9.57
v. 20

10.1
Judg 2.16
10.4
Num 32.41
10.6
Judg 2.11-13;
Deut 31.16,
17; 32.15
10.7
Judg 2.14
10.10
1 Sam 12.10
10.11
Ex 14.30;
Num 21.21;
24.25;
Judg 3.12,
13,31
10.12
Judg 5.19;
Ps 106.42,
43

Tolah and Jair

10 After Abimelech, Tola son of Puah son of Dodo, a man of Issachar, who lived at Shamir in the hill country of Ephraim, rose to deliver Israel. 2 He judged Israel twenty-three years. Then he died, and was buried at Shamir.

3 After him came Jair the Gileadite, who judged Israel twenty-two years. 4 He had thirty sons who rode on thirty donkeys; and they had thirty towns, which are in the land of Gilead, and are called Havvoth-jair to this day. 5 Jair died, and was buried in Kamon.

Oppression by the Ammonites

6 The Israelites again did what was evil in the sight of the LORD, worshiping the Baals and the Astartes, the gods of Aram, the gods of Sidon, the gods of Moab, the gods of the Ammonites, and the gods of the Philistines. Thus they abandoned the LORD, and did not worship him. 7 So the anger of the LORD was kindled against Israel, and he sold them into the hand of the Philistines and into the hand of the Ammonites, 8 and they crushed and oppressed the Israelites that year. For eighteen years they oppressed all the Israelites that were beyond the Jordan in the land of the Amorites, which is in Gilead. 9 The Ammonites also crossed the Jordan to fight against Judah and against Benjamin and against the house of Ephraim; so that Israel was greatly distressed.

10 So the Israelites cried to the LORD, saying, "We have sinned against you, because we have abandoned our God and have worshiped the Baals." 11 And the LORD said to the Israelites, "Did I not deliver you[k] from the Egyptians and from the Amorites, from the Ammonites and from the Philistines? 12 The Sidonians also, and the Amalekites, and the Maonites, oppressed you; and you cried to me, and I delivered you out of their hand. 13 Yet you have abandoned me and wor-

[k] Heb lacks *Did I not deliver you*

shiped other gods; therefore I will deliver you no more. ¹⁴Go and cry to the gods whom you have chosen; let them deliver you in the time of your distress." ¹⁵And the Israelites said to the LORD, "We have sinned; do to us whatever seems good to you; but deliver us this day!" ¹⁶So they put away the foreign gods from among them and worshiped the LORD; and he could no longer bear to see Israel suffer.

17 Then the Ammonites were called to arms, and they encamped in Gilead; and the Israelites came together, and they encamped at Mizpah. ¹⁸The commanders of the people of Gilead said to one another, "Who will begin the fight against the Ammonites? He shall be head over all the inhabitants of Gilead."

Jephthah

11 Now Jephthah the Gileadite, the son of a prostitute, was a mighty warrior. Gilead was the father of Jephthah. ²Gilead's wife also bore him sons; and when his wife's sons grew up, they drove Jephthah away, saying to him, "You shall not inherit anything in our father's house; for you are the son of another woman." ³Then Jephthah fled from his brothers and lived in the land of Tob. Outlaws collected around Jephthah and went raiding with him.

4 After a time the Ammonites made war against Israel. ⁵And when the Ammonites made war against Israel, the elders of Gilead went to bring Jephthah from the land of Tob. ⁶They said to Jephthah, "Come and be our commander, so that we may fight with the Ammonites." ⁷But Jephthah said to the elders of Gilead, "Are you not the very ones who rejected me and drove me out of my father's house? So why do you come to me now when you are in trouble?" ⁸The elders of Gilead said to Jephthah, "Nevertheless, we have now turned back to you, so that you may go with us and fight with the Ammonites, and become head over us,

over all the inhabitants of Gilead." ⁹Jephthah said to the elders of Gilead, "If you bring me home again to fight with the Ammonites, and the LORD gives them over to me, I will be your head." ¹⁰And the elders of Gilead said to Jephthah, "The LORD will be witness between us; we will surely do as you say." ¹¹So Jephthah went with the elders of Gilead, and the people made him head and commander over them; and Jephthah spoke all his words before the LORD at Mizpah.

12 Then Jephthah sent messengers to the king of the Ammonites and said, "What is there between you and me, that you have come to me to fight against my land?" ¹³The king of the Ammonites answered the messengers of Jephthah, "Because Israel, on coming from Egypt, took away my land from the Arnon to the Jabbok and to the Jordan; now therefore restore it peaceably." ¹⁴Once again Jephthah sent messengers to the king of the Ammonites ¹⁵and said to him: "Thus says Jephthah: Israel did not take away the land of Moab or the land of the Ammonites, ¹⁶but when they came up from Egypt, Israel went through the wilderness to the Red Sea¹ and came to Kadesh. ¹⁷Israel then sent messengers to the king of Edom, saying, 'Let us pass through your land'; but the king of Edom would not listen. They also sent to the king of Moab, but he would not consent. So Israel remained at Kadesh. ¹⁸Then they journeyed through the wilderness, went around the land of Edom and the land of Moab, arrived on the east side of the land of Moab, and camped on the other side of the Arnon. They did not enter the territory of Moab, for the Arnon was the boundary of Moab. ¹⁹Israel then sent messengers to King Sihon of the Amorites, king of Heshbon; and Israel said to him, 'Let us pass through your land to our country.' ²⁰But Sihon did not trust Israel to

10.14
Deut 32.37
10.15
1 Sam 3.18
10.16
Josh 24.23;
Jer 18.7,8;
Deut 32.36;
Ps 106.44,
45
10.17
Judg 11.29
10.18
Judg 11.8,
11
11.1
Heb 11.32
11.3
2 Sam 10.6,
8
11.4
Judg 10.9,
17
11.8
Judg 10.18

11.10
Jer 42.5
11.11
v. 8;
Judg 10.17
11.13
Num 21.24-26
11.15
Deut 2.9,19
11.16
Num 14.25;
20.1,14-21
11.18
Num 21.4;
Deut 2.1-9,
18,19
11.19
Num 21.21,
22;
Deut 2.26,
27
11.20
Num 21.23;
Deut 2.32

¹Or *Sea of Reeds*

pass through his territory; so Sihon gathered all his people together, and encamped at Jahaz, and fought with Israel. 21 Then the LORD, the God of Israel, gave Sihon and all his people into the hand of Israel, and they defeated them; so Israel occupied all the land of the Amorites, who inhabited that country. 22 They occupied all the territory of the Amorites from the Arnon to the Jabbok and from the wilderness to the Jordan. 23 So now the LORD, the God of Israel, has conquered the Amorites for the benefit of his people Israel. Do you intend to take their place? 24 Should you not possess what your god Chemosh gives you to possess? And should we not be the ones to possess everything that the LORD our God has conquered for our benefit? 25 Now are you any better than King Balak son of Zippor of Moab? Did he ever enter into conflict with Israel, or did he ever go to war with them? 26 While Israel lived in Heshbon and its villages, and in Aroer and its villages, and in all the towns that are along the Arnon, three hundred years, why did you not recover them within that time? 27 It is not I who have sinned against you, but you are the one who does me wrong by making war on me. Let the LORD, who is judge, decide today for the Israelites or for the Ammonites." 28 But the king of the Ammonites did not heed the message that Jephthah sent him.

Jephthah's Vow

29 Then the spirit of the LORD came upon Jephthah, and he passed through Gilead and Manasseh. He passed on to Mizpah of Gilead, and from Mizpah of Gilead he passed on to the Ammonites. 30 And Jephthah made a vow to the LORD, and said, "If you will give the Ammonites into my hand, 31 then whoever comes out of the doors of my house to meet me, when I return victorious from the Ammonites, shall be the LORD's, to be offered up by me as a burnt offering." 32 So Jephthah crossed over to the

Ammonites to fight against them; and the LORD gave them into his hand. 33 He inflicted a massive defeat on them from Aroer to the neighborhood of Minnith, twenty towns, and as far as Abel-keramim. So the Ammonites were subdued before the people of Israel.

Jephthah's Daughter

34 Then Jephthah came to his home at Mizpah; and there was his daughter coming out to meet him with timbrels and with dancing. She was his only child; he had no son or daughter except her. 35 When he saw her, he tore his clothes, and said, "Alas, my daughter! You have brought me very low; you have become the cause of great trouble to me. For I have opened my mouth to the LORD, and I cannot take back my vow." 36 She said to him, "My father, if you have opened your mouth to the LORD, do to me according to what has gone out of your mouth, now that the LORD has given you vengeance against your enemies, the Ammonites." 37 And she said to her father, "Let this thing be done for me: Grant me two months, so that I may go and wander^m on the mountains, and bewail my virginity, my companions and I." 38 "Go," he said and sent her away for two months. So she departed, she and her companions, and bewailed her virginity on the mountains. 39 At the end of two months, she returned to her father, who did with her according to the vow he had made. She had never slept with a man. So there arose an Israelite custom that 40 for four days every year the daughters of Israel would go out to lament the daughter of Jephthah the Gileadite.

Intertribal Dissension

12 The men of Ephraim were called to arms, and they crossed to Zaphon and said to Jephthah, "Why did you cross over to fight against the Ammonites, and did not call us to go with you?

11.21
Num 21.24, 25;
Deut 2.33, 34
11.22
Deut 2.36
11.24
Num 21.29;
1 Kings 11.7;
Josh 3.10
11.25
Num 22.2;
Josh 24.9
11.26
Num 21.25;
Deut 2.36
11.27
Gen 16.5;
18.25; 31.53;
1 Sam 24.12, 15
11.29
Judg 3.10

11.33
Ezek 27.17
11.34
Judg 10.17;
Ex 15.20;
1 Sam 18.6;
Jer 31.4
11.35
Num 30.2;
Eccl 5.2,4,5
11.36
Num 30.2;
2 Sam 18.19, 31; Lk 1.38
12.1
Judg 8.1

m Cn: Heb go down

We will burn your house down over you!" [2] Jephthah said to them, "My people and I were engaged in conflict with the Ammonites who oppressed us[n] severely. But when I called you, you did not deliver me from their hand. [3] When I saw that you would not deliver me, I took my life in my hand, and crossed over against the Ammonites, and the LORD gave them into my hand. Why then have you come up to me this day, to fight against me?" [4] Then Jephthah gathered all the men of Gilead and fought with Ephraim; and the men of Gilead defeated Ephraim, because they said, "You are fugitives from Ephraim, you Gileadites—in the heart of Ephraim and Manasseh."[o] [5] Then the Gileadites took the fords of the Jordan against the Ephraimites. Whenever one of the fugitives of Ephraim said, "Let me go over," the men of Gilead would say to him, "Are you an Ephraimite?" When he said, "No," [6] they said to him, "Then say Shibboleth," and he said, "Sibboleth," for he could not pronounce it right. Then they seized him and killed him at the fords of the Jordan. Forty-two thousand of the Ephraimites fell at that time.

[7] Jephthah judged Israel six years. Then Jephthah the Gileadite died, and was buried in his town in Gilead.[p]

Ibzan, Elon, and Abdon

[8] After him Ibzan of Bethlehem judged Israel. [9] He had thirty sons. He gave his thirty daughters in marriage outside his clan and brought in thirty young women from outside for his sons. He judged Israel seven years. [10] Then Ibzan died, and was buried at Bethlehem.

[11] After him Elon the Zebulunite judged Israel; and he judged Israel ten years. [12] Then Elon the Zebulunite died, and was buried at Aijalon in the land of Zebulun.

[13] After him Abdon son of Hillel the Pirathonite judged Israel. [14] He had forty sons and thirty grand-

sons, who rode on seventy donkeys; he judged Israel eight years. [15] Then Abdon son of Hillel the Pirathonite died, and was buried at Pirathon in the land of Ephraim, in the hill country of the Amalekites.

The Birth of Samson

13 The Israelites again did what was evil in the sight of the LORD, and the LORD gave them into the hand of the Philistines forty years.

2 There was a certain man of Zorah, of the tribe of the Danites, whose name was Manoah. His wife was barren, having borne no children. [3] And the angel of the LORD appeared to the woman and said to her, "Although you are barren, having borne no children, you shall conceive and bear a son. [4] Now be careful not to drink wine or strong drink, or to eat anything unclean, [5] for you shall conceive and bear a son. No razor is to come on his head, for the boy shall be a nazirite[q] to God from birth. It is he who shall begin to deliver Israel from the hand of the Philistines." [6] Then the woman came and told her husband, "A man of God came to me, and his appearance was like that of an angel[r] of God, most awe-inspiring; I did not ask him where he came from, and he did not tell me his name; [7] but he said to me, 'You shall conceive and bear a son. So then drink no wine or strong drink, and eat nothing unclean, for the boy shall be a nazirite[q] to God from birth to the day of his death.' "

8 Then Manoah entreated the LORD, and said, "O, LORD, I pray, let the man of God whom you sent come to us again and teach us what we are to do concerning the boy who will be born." [9] God listened to Manoah, and the angel of God came again to the woman as she sat in the field; but her husband Manoah was not with her. [10] So the

Cross references

12.3: 1 Sam 19.5; 28.21; Job 13.14
12.4: Judg 3.28; 7.24
12.5: Judg 3.28; 7.24; Josh 22.11
12.7: Heb 11.32
12.14: Judg 5.10; 10.4
13.1: Judg 2.11; 1 Sam 12.9
13.2: Josh 19.41
13.3: vv. 6,8,10; Judg 6.12
13.4: v. 14; Num 6.2,3
13.5: Lk 1.15; Num 6.2,5
13.6: 1 Sam 2.27; Mt 28.3; vv. 17,18
13.8: vv. 3,7

Footnotes

n Gk OL, Syr H: Heb lacks *who oppressed us*
o Meaning of Heb uncertain: Gk omits *because . . . Manasseh* p Gk: Heb *in the towns of Gilead* q That is *one separated* or *one consecrated* r Or *the angel*

woman ran quickly and told her husband, "The man who came to me the other day has appeared to me." ¹¹Manoah got up and followed his wife, and came to the man and said to him, "Are you the man who spoke to this woman?" And he said, "I am." ¹²Then Manoah said, "Now when your words come true, what is to be the boy's rule of life; what is he to do?" ¹³The angel of the Lord said to Manoah, "Let the woman give heed to all that I said to her. ¹⁴She may not eat of anything that comes from the vine. She is not to drink wine or strong drink, or eat any unclean thing. She is to observe everything that I commanded her."

15 Manoah said to the angel of the Lord, "Allow us to detain you, and prepare a kid for you." ¹⁶The angel of the Lord said to Manoah, "If you detain me, I will not eat your food; but if you want to prepare a burnt offering, then offer it to the Lord." (For Manoah did not know that he was the angel of the Lord.) ¹⁷Then Manoah said to the angel of the Lord, "What is your name, so that we may honor you when your words come true?" ¹⁸But the angel of the Lord said to him, "Why do you ask my name? It is too wonderful."

19 So Manoah took the kid with the grain offering, and offered it on the rock to the Lord, to him who works^s wonders.^t ²⁰When the flame went up toward heaven from the altar, the angel of the Lord ascended in the flame of the altar while Manoah and his wife looked on; and they fell on their faces to the ground. ²¹The angel of the Lord did not appear again to Manoah and his wife. Then Manoah realized that it was the angel of the Lord. ²²And Manoah said to his wife, "We shall surely die, for we have seen God." ²³But his wife said to him, "If the Lord had meant to kill us, he would not have accepted a burnt offering and a grain offering at our hands, or shown us all these things, or now announced to us such things as these."

24 The woman bore a son, and named him Samson. The boy grew, and the Lord blessed him. ²⁵The spirit of the Lord began to stir him in Mahaneh-dan, between Zorah and Eshtaol.

Samson's Marriage

14 Once Samson went down to Timnah, and at Timnah he saw a Philistine woman. ²Then he came up, and told his father and mother, "I saw a Philistine woman at Timnah; now get her for me as my wife." ³But his father and mother said to him, "Is there not a woman among your kin, or among all our^u people, that you must go to take a wife from the uncircumcised Philistines?" But Samson said to his father, "Get her for me, because she pleases me." ⁴His father and mother did not know that this was from the Lord; for he was seeking a pretext to act against the Philistines. At that time the Philistines had dominion over Israel.

5 Then Samson went down with his father and mother to Timnah. When he came to the vineyards of Timnah, suddenly a young lion roared at him. ⁶The spirit of the Lord rushed on him, and he tore the lion apart barehanded as one might tear apart a kid. But he did not tell his father or his mother what he had done. ⁷Then he went down and talked with the woman, and she pleased Samson. ⁸After a while he returned to marry her, and he turned aside to see the carcass of the lion, and there was a swarm of bees in the body of the lion, and honey. ⁹He scraped it out into his hands, and went on, eating as he went. When he came to his father and mother, he gave some to them, and they ate it. But he did not tell them that he had taken the honey from the carcass of the lion.

10 His father went down to the woman, and Samson made a feast there as the young men were accustomed to do. ¹¹When the people

13.13
vv. 4,11
13.14
Num 6.4
13.15
v. 3
13.16
Judg 6.20
13.17
Gen 32.29
13.18
Isa 9.6
13.19
Judg 6.20, 21
13.20
Lev 9.24
13.21
v. 16
13.22
Judg 6.22; Deut 5.26

13.24
Heb 11.32; 1 Sam 3.19
13.25
Judg 3.10; 18.11
14.2
Gen 21.21; 34.4
14.4
Josh 11.20; Judg 13.1
14.6
Judg 3.10; 13.25
14.7
v. 3

^s Gk Vg: Heb *and working* ^t Heb *wonders, while Manoah and his wife looked on*
^u Cn: Heb *my*

saw him, they brought thirty companions to be with him. 12 Samson said to them, "Let me now put a riddle to you. If you can explain it to me within the seven days of the feast, and find it out, then I will give you thirty linen garments and thirty festal garments. 13 But if you cannot explain it to me, then you shall give me thirty linen garments and thirty festal garments." So they said to him, "Ask your riddle; let us hear it." 14 He said to them,

"Out of the eater came
 something to eat.
Out of the strong came
 something sweet."

But for three days they could not explain the riddle.

15 On the fourthᵛ day they said to Samson's wife, "Coax your husband to explain the riddle to us, or we will burn you and your father's house with fire. Have you invited us here to impoverish us?" 16 So Samson's wife wept before him, saying, "You hate me; you do not really love me. You have asked a riddle of my people, but you have not explained it to me." He said to her, "Look, I have not told my father or my mother. Why should I tell you?" 17 She wept before him the seven days that their feast lasted; and because she nagged him, on the seventh day he told her. Then she explained the riddle to her people. 18 The men of the town said to him on the seventh day before the sun went down,

"What is sweeter than
 honey?
What is stronger than a
 lion?"

And he said to them,

"If you had not plowed with
 my heifer,
you would not have found
 out my riddle."

19 Then the spirit of the LORD rushed on him, and he went down to Ashkelon. He killed thirty men of the town, took their spoil, and gave the festal garments to those who had explained the riddle. In hot anger he went back to his father's house. 20 And Samson's wife

14.12
1 Kings 10.2;
Ezek 17.2;
Gen 29.27
14.15
Judg 16.5;
15.6
14.18
v. 14
14.19
Judg 3.10
14.20
Judg 15.2;
Jn 3.29

15.2
Judg 14.20
15.6
Judg 14.15
15.9
v. 19
15.11
Judg 13.1;
14.4

was given to his companion, who had been his best man.

Samson Defeats the Philistines

15 After a while, at the time of the wheat harvest, Samson went to visit his wife, bringing along a kid. He said, "I want to go into my wife's room." But her father would not allow him to go in. 2 Her father said, "I was sure that you had rejected her; so I gave her to your companion. Is not her younger sister prettier than she? Why not take her instead?" 3 Samson said to them, "This time, when I do mischief to the Philistines, I will be without blame." 4 So Samson went and caught three hundred foxes, and took some torches; and he turned the foxesʷ tail to tail, and put a torch between each pair of tails. 5 When he had set fire to the torches, he let the foxes go into the standing grain of the Philistines, and burned up the shocks and the standing grain, as well as the vineyards andˣ olive groves. 6 Then the Philistines asked, "Who has done this?" And they said, "Samson, the son-in-law of the Timnite, because he has taken Samson's wife and given her to his companion." So the Philistines came up, and burned her and her father. 7 Samson said to them, "If this is what you do, I swear I will not stop until I have taken revenge on you." 8 He struck them down hip and thigh with great slaughter; and he went down and stayed in the cleft of the rock of Etam.

9 Then the Philistines came up and encamped in Judah, and made a raid on Lehi. 10 The men of Judah said, "Why have you come up against us?" They said, "We have come up to bind Samson, to do to him as he did to us." 11 Then three thousand men of Judah went down to the cleft of the rock of Etam, and they said to Samson, "Do you not know that the Philistines are rulers over us? What then have you done to us?" He replied, "As they did to

ᵛ Gk Syr: Heb *seventh* ʷ Heb *them*
ˣ Gk Tg Vg: Heb lacks *and*

me, so I have done to them." ¹²They said to him, "We have come down to bind you, so that we may give you into the hands of the Philistines." Samson answered them, "Swear to me that you yourselves will not attack me." ¹³They said to him, "No, we will only bind you and give you into their hands; we will not kill you." So they bound him with two new ropes, and brought him up from the rock.

14 When he came to Lehi, the Philistines came shouting to meet him; and the spirit of the LORD rushed on him, and the ropes that were on his arms became like flax that has caught fire, and his bonds melted off his hands. ¹⁵Then he found a fresh jawbone of a donkey, reached down and took it, and with it he killed a thousand men. ¹⁶And Samson said,

"With the jawbone of a
 donkey,
 heaps upon heaps,
 with the jawbone of a
 donkey
 I have slain a thousand
 men."

¹⁷When he had finished speaking, he threw away the jawbone; and that place was called Ramath-lehi.^y

18 By then he was very thirsty, and he called on the LORD, saying, "You have granted this great victory by the hand of your servant. Am I now to die of thirst, and fall into the hands of the uncircumcised?" ¹⁹So God split open the hollow place that is at Lehi, and water came from it. When he drank, his spirit returned, and he revived. Therefore it was named En-hakkore,^z which is at Lehi to this day. ²⁰And he judged Israel in the days of the Philistines twenty years.

Samson and Delilah

16 Once Samson went to Gaza, where he saw a prostitute and went in to her. ²The Gazites were told,^a "Samson has come here." So they circled around and lay in wait for him all night at

15.14
Judg 14.19;
1 Sam 11.6
15.15
Lev 26.8;
Josh 23.10;
Judg 3.31
15.18
Judg 16.28
15.19
Gen 45.27;
Isa 40.29
15.20
Heb 11.32;
Judg 13.1;
16.31
16.2
Ps 118.10-12

16.5
Judg 14.15
16.10
vv. 13,15

the city gate. They kept quiet all night, thinking, "Let us wait until the light of the morning; then we will kill him." ³But Samson lay only until midnight. Then at midnight he rose up, took hold of the doors of the city gate and the two posts, pulled them up, bar and all, put them on his shoulders, and carried them to the top of the hill that is in front of Hebron.

4 After this he fell in love with a woman in the valley of Sorek, whose name was Delilah. ⁵The lords of the Philistines came to her and said to her, "Coax him, and find out what makes his strength so great, and how we may overpower him, so that we may bind him in order to subdue him; and we will each give you eleven hundred pieces of silver." ⁶So Delilah said to Samson, "Please tell me what makes your strength so great, and how you could be bound, so that one could subdue you." ⁷Samson said to her, "If they bind me with seven fresh bowstrings that are not dried out, then I shall become weak, and be like anyone else." ⁸Then the lords of the Philistines brought her seven fresh bowstrings that had not dried out, and she bound him with them. ⁹While men were lying in wait in an inner chamber, she said to him, "The Philistines are upon you, Samson!" But he snapped the bowstrings, as a strand of fiber snaps when it touches the fire. So the secret of his strength was not known.

10 Then Delilah said to Samson, "You have mocked me and told me lies; please tell me how you could be bound." ¹¹He said to her, "If they bind me with new ropes that have not been used, then I shall become weak, and be like anyone else." ¹²So Delilah took new ropes and bound him with them, and said to him, "The Philistines are upon you, Samson!" (The men lying in wait were in an inner

^yThat is *The Hill of the Jawbone* ^zThat is *The Spring of the One who Called* ^aGk: Heb lacks *were told*

chamber.) But he snapped the ropes off his arms like a thread.

13 Then Delilah said to Samson, "Until now you have mocked me and told me lies; tell me how you could be bound." He said to her, "If you weave the seven locks of my head with the web and make it tight with the pin, then I shall become weak, and be like anyone else." [14] So while he slept, Delilah took the seven locks of his head and wove them into the web, [b] and made them tight with the pin. Then she said to him, "The Philistines are upon you, Samson!" But he awoke from his sleep, and pulled away the pin, the loom, and the web.

15 Then she said to him, "How can you say, 'I love you,' when your heart is not with me? You have mocked me three times now and have not told me what makes your strength so great." [16] Finally, after she had nagged him with her words day after day, and pestered him, he was tired to death. [17] So he told her his whole secret, and said to her, "A razor has never come upon my head; for I have been a nazirite[c] to God from my mother's womb. If my head were shaved, then my strength would leave me; I would become weak, and be like anyone else."

18 When Delilah realized that he had told her his whole secret, she sent and called the lords of the Philistines, saying, "This time come up, for he has told his whole secret to me." Then the lords of the Philistines came up to her, and brought the money in their hands. [19] She let him fall asleep on her lap; and she called a man, and had him shave off the seven locks of his head. He began to weaken,[d] and his strength left him. [20] Then she said, "The Philistines are upon you, Samson!" When he awoke from his sleep, he thought, "I will go out as at other times, and shake myself free." But he did not know that the LORD had left him. [21] So the Philistines seized him and gouged out his eyes. They brought him

down to Gaza and bound him with bronze shackles; and he ground at the mill in the prison. [22] But the hair of his head began to grow again after it had been shaved.

Samson's Death

23 Now the lords of the Philistines gathered to offer a great sacrifice to their god Dagon, and to rejoice; for they said, "Our god has given Samson our enemy into our hand." [24] When the people saw him, they praised their god; for they said, "Our god has given our enemy into our hand, the ravager of our country, who has killed many of us." [25] And when their hearts were merry, they said, "Call Samson, and let him entertain us." So they called Samson out of the prison, and he performed for them. They made him stand between the pillars; [26] and Samson said to the attendant who held him by the hand, "Let me feel the pillars on which the house rests, so that I may lean against them." [27] Now the house was full of men and women; all the lords of the Philistines were there, and on the roof there were about three thousand men and women, who looked on while Samson performed.

28 Then Samson called to the LORD and said, "Lord GOD, remember me and strengthen me only this once, O God, so that with this one act of revenge I may pay back the Philistines for my two eyes."[e] [29] And Samson grasped the two middle pillars on which the house rested, and he leaned his weight against them, his right hand on the one and his left hand on the other. [30] Then Samson said, "Let me die with the Philistines." He strained with all his might; and the house fell on the lords and all the people who were in it. So those he killed at his death were more than those he had killed during his life. [31] Then

Cross references (center column)

16.13
vv. 10,15
16.15
Judg 14.16
16.17
Mic 7.5;
Num 6.5;
Judg 13.5
16.19
Prov 7.26,27
16.20
Josh 7.12;
1 Sam 16.14;
18.12

16.23
1 Sam 5.2
16.24
Dan 5.4
16.25
Judg 9.27
16.27
Deut 22.8
16.28
Judg 15.18;
Jer 15.15
16.31
Judg 15.20

Footnotes

b Compare Gk: in verses 13-14, Heb lacks and make it tight . . . into the web c That is one separated or one consecrated
d Gk: Heb She began to torment him
e Or so that I may be avenged upon the Philistines for one of my two eyes

his brothers and all his family came down and took him and brought him up and buried him between Zorah and Eshtaol in the tomb of his father Manoah. He had judged Israel twenty years.

The Sanctuary and Idolatry of Dan

17 There was a man in the hill country of Ephraim whose name was Micah. [2] He said to his mother, "The eleven hundred pieces of silver that were taken from you, about which you uttered a curse, and even spoke it in my hearing,—that silver is in my possession; I took it; but now I will return it to you."[f] And his mother said, "May my son be blessed by the Lord!" [3] Then he returned the eleven hundred pieces of silver to his mother; and his mother said, "I consecrate the silver to the Lord from my hand for my son, to make an idol of cast metal." [4] So when he returned the money to his mother, his mother took two hundred pieces of silver, and gave it to the silversmith, who made it into an idol of cast metal; and it was in the house of Micah. [5] This man Micah had a shrine, and he made an ephod and teraphim, and installed one of his sons, who became his priest. [6] In those days there was no king in Israel; all the people did what was right in their own eyes.

[7] Now there was a young man of Bethlehem in Judah, of the clan of Judah. He was a Levite residing there. [8] This man left the town of Bethlehem in Judah, to live wherever he could find a place. He came to the house of Micah in the hill country of Ephraim to carry on his work.[g] [9] Micah said to him, "From where do you come?" He replied, "I am a Levite of Bethlehem in Judah, and I am going to live wherever I can find a place." [10] Then Micah said to him, "Stay with me, and be to me a father and a priest, and I will give you ten pieces of silver a year, a set of clothes, and your living."[h] [11] The Levite agreed to stay with the man; and the young man

became to him like one of his sons. [12] So Micah installed the Levite, and the young man became his priest, and was in the house of Micah. [13] Then Micah said, "Now I know that the Lord will prosper me, because the Levite has become my priest."

The Migration of Dan

18 In those days there was no king in Israel. And in those days the tribe of the Danites was seeking for itself a territory to live in; for until then no territory among the tribes of Israel had been allotted to them. [2] So the Danites sent five valiant men from the whole number of their clan, from Zorah and from Eshtaol, to spy out the land and to explore it; and they said to them, "Go, explore the land." When they came to the hill country of Ephraim, to the house of Micah, they stayed there. [3] While they were at Micah's house, they recognized the voice of the young Levite; so they went over and asked him, "Who brought you here? What are you doing in this place? What is your business here?" [4] He said to them, "Micah did such and such for me, and he hired me, and I have become his priest." [5] Then they said to him, "Inquire of God that we may know whether the mission we are undertaking will succeed." [6] The priest replied, "Go in peace. The mission you are on is under the eye of the Lord."

[7] The five men went on, and when they came to Laish, they observed the people who were there living securely, after the manner of the Sidonians, quiet and unsuspecting, lacking[i] nothing on earth, and possessing wealth.[j] Furthermore, they were far from the Sidonians and had no dealings with Aram.[k] [8] When they came to their kinsfolk at Zorah and Eshtaol,

Cross references

17.3 Ex 20.4,23; 34.17; Lev 19.4
17.5 Judg 18.24; 8.27; 18.14; Gen 31.19
17.6 Judg 18.1; 19.1; Deut 12.8
17.7 Judg 19.1; Ruth 1.1,2; Mic 5.2; Mt 2.1
17.10 Judg 18.19
17.12 v. 5; Judg 13.25
18.1 Judg 17.6; 19.1; Josh 19.47
18.2 Judg 13.25; Josh 2.1; Judg 17.1
18.4 Judg 17.10, 12
18.5 1 Kings 22.5
18.6 1 Kings 22.6
18.7 vv. 27,28; Josh 19.47
18.8 v. 2

f The words *but now I will return it to you* are transposed from the end of verse 3 in Heb
g Or *Ephraim, continuing his journey*
h Heb *living, and the Levite went*
i Cn Compare 18.10: Meaning of Heb uncertain
j Meaning of Heb uncertain
k Symmachus: Heb *with anyone*

they said to them, "What do you report?" [9] They said, "Come, let us go up against them; for we have seen the land, and it is very good. Will you do nothing? Do not be slow to go, but enter in and possess the land. [10] When you go, you will come to an unsuspecting people. The land is broad—God has indeed given it into your hands—a place where there is no lack of anything on earth."

11 Six hundred men of the Danite clan, armed with weapons of war, set out from Zorah and Eshtaol, [12] and went up and encamped at Kiriath-jearim in Judah. On this account that place is called Mahaneh-dan[l] to this day; it is west of Kiriath-jearim. [13] From there they passed on to the hill country of Ephraim, and came to the house of Micah.

14 Then the five men who had gone to spy out the land (that is, Laish) said to their comrades, "Do you know that in these buildings there are an ephod, teraphim, and an idol of cast metal? Now therefore consider what you will do." [15] So they turned in that direction and came to the house of the young Levite, at the home of Micah, and greeted him. [16] While the six hundred men of the Danites, armed with their weapons of war, stood by the entrance of the gate, [17] the five men who had gone to spy out the land proceeded to enter and take the idol of cast metal, the ephod, and the teraphim. [m] The priest was standing by the entrance of the gate with the six hundred men armed with weapons of war. [18] When the men went into Micah's house and took the idol of cast metal, the ephod, and the teraphim, the priest said to them, "What are you doing?" [19] They said to him, "Keep quiet! Put your hand over your mouth, and come with us, and be to us a father and a priest. Is it better for you to be priest to the house of one person, or to be priest to a tribe and clan in Israel?" [20] Then the priest accepted the offer. He took the ephod, the

teraphim, and the idol, and went along with the people.

21 So they resumed their journey, putting the little ones, the livestock, and the goods in front of them. [22] When they were some distance from the home of Micah, the men who were in the houses near Micah's house were called out, and they overtook the Danites. [23] They shouted to the Danites, who turned around and said to Micah, "What is the matter that you come with such a company?" [24] He replied, "You take my gods that I made, and the priest, and go away, and what have I left? How then can you ask me, 'What is the matter?' " [25] And the Danites said to him, "You had better not let your voice be heard among us or else hot-tempered fellows will attack you, and you will lose your life and the lives of your household." [26] Then the Danites went their way. When Micah saw that they were too strong for him, he turned and went back to his home.

The Danites Settle in Laish

27 The Danites, having taken what Micah had made, and the priest who belonged to him, came to Laish, to a people quiet and unsuspecting, put them to the sword, and burned down the city. [28] There was no deliverer, because it was far from Sidon and they had no dealings with Aram. [n] It was in the valley that belongs to Beth-rehob. They rebuilt the city, and lived in it. [29] They named the city Dan, after their ancestor Dan, who was born to Israel; but the name of the city was formerly Laish. [30] Then the Danites set up the idol for themselves. Jonathan son of Gershom, son of Moses, [o] and his sons were priests to the tribe of the Danites until the time the land went into captivity. [31] So they maintained as

18.9
Num 13.30;
1 Kings 22.3
18.10
vv. 7,27;
Deut 8.9
18.12
Judg 13.25
18.13
v. 2
18.14
Judg 17.5
18.16
v. 11
18.17
vv. 2,14
18.19
Job 21.5;
Judg 17.10

18.24
Judg 17.5
18.27
vv. 7,10;
Josh 19.47
18.28
v. 7;
2 Sam 10.6
18.29
Josh 19.47
18.30
Judg 17.3,5;
Ex 2.22
18.31
Josh 18.1

l That is *Camp of Dan* m Compare 17.4, 5;
18.14: Heb *teraphim and the cast metal*
n Cn Compare verse 7: Heb *with anyone*
o Another reading is *son of Manasseh*

their own Micah's idol that he had
made, as long as the house of God
was at Shiloh.

The Levite's Concubine

19 In those days, when there
was no king in Israel, a cer-
tain Levite, residing in the remote
parts of the hill country of Ephra-
im, took to himself a concubine
from Bethlehem in Judah. ² But his
concubine became angry withᴾ
him, and she went away from him
to her father's house at Bethlehem
in Judah, and was there some four
months. ³ Then her husband set
out after her, to speak tenderly to
her and bring her back. He had
with him his servant and a couple
of donkeys. When he reached�q her
father's house, the girl's father saw
him and came with joy to meet
him. ⁴ His father-in-law, the girl's
father, made him stay, and he re-
mained with him three days; so
they ate and drank, and heʳ stayed
there. ⁵ On the fourth day they got
up early in the morning, and he
prepared to go; but the girl's father
said to his son-in-law, "Fortify
yourself with a bit of food, and after
that you may go." ⁶ So the two men
sat and ate and drank together; and
the girl's father said to the man,
"Why not spend the night and en-
joy yourself?" ⁷ When the man got
up to go, his father-in-law kept
urging him until he spent the night
there again. ⁸ On the fifth day he
got up early in the morning to
leave; and the girl's father said,
"Fortify yourself." So they lin-
geredˢ until the day declined, and
the two of them ate and drank.ᵗ
⁹ When the man with his concubine
and his servant got up to leave, his
father-in-law, the girl's father, said
to him, "Look, the day has worn on
until it is almost evening. Spend
the night. See, the day has drawn to
a close. Spend the night here and
enjoy yourself. Tomorrow you can
get up early in the morning for your
journey, and go home."

10 But the man would not
spend the night; he got up and de-
parted, and arrived opposite Jebus

(that is, Jerusalem). He had with
him a couple of saddled donkeys,
and his concubine was with him.
¹¹ When they were near Jebus, the
day was far spent, and the servant
said to his master, "Come now, let
us turn aside to this city of the Jeb-
usites, and spend the night in it."
¹² But his master said to him, "We
will not turn aside into a city of for-
eigners, who do not belong to the
people of Israel; but we will contin-
ue on to Gibeah." ¹³ Then he said to
his servant, "Come, let us try to
reach one of these places, and
spend the night at Gibeah or at Ra-
mah." ¹⁴ So they passed on and
went their way; and the sun went
down on them near Gibeah, which
belongs to Benjamin. ¹⁵ They
turned aside there, to go in and
spend the night at Gibeah. He went
in and sat down in the open square
of the city, but no one took them in
to spend the night.

16 Then at evening there was an
old man coming from his work in
the field. The man was from the hill
country of Ephraim, and he was re-
siding in Gibeah. (The people of
the place were Benjaminites.)
¹⁷ When the old man looked up and
saw the wayfarer in the open
square of the city, he said, "Where
are you going and where do you
come from?" ¹⁸ He answered him,
"We are passing from Bethlehem in
Judah to the remote parts of the
hill country of Ephraim, from
which I come. I went to Bethlehem
in Judah; and I am going to my
home.ᵘ Nobody has offered to take
me in. ¹⁹ We your servants have
straw and fodder for our donkeys,
with bread and wine for me and the
woman and the young man along
with us. We need nothing more."
²⁰ The old man said, "Peace be to
you. I will care for all your wants;
only do not spend the night in the
square." ²¹ So he brought him into

Cross references

19.1 Judg 18.1
19.3 Gen 34.3; 50.21
19.5 v. 8; Gen 18.5
19.6 vv. 9,22
19.10 1 Chr 11.4, 5
19.11 Judg 1.21
19.12 Heb 11.13
19.15 Heb 13.2
19.16 Ps 104.23; v. 14
19.18 Judg 18.31; 20.18
19.21 Gen 24.32, 33

ᴾ Gk OL: Heb *prostituted herself against*
q Gk: Heb *she brought him* ʳ Compare
verse 7 and Gk: Heb *they* ˢ Cn: Heb *Linger*
ᵗ Gk: Heb lacks *and drank* ᵘ Gk Compare
19.29. Heb *to the house of the* Lᴏʀᴅ

his house, and fed the donkeys; they washed their feet, and ate and drank.

Gibeah's Crime

22 While they were enjoying themselves, the men of the city, a perverse lot, surrounded the house, and started pounding on the door. They said to the old man, the master of the house, "Bring out the man who came into your house, so that we may have intercourse with him." 23 And the man, the master of the house, went out to them and said to them, "No, my brothers, do not act so wickedly. Since this man is my guest, do not do this vile thing. 24 Here are my virgin daughter and his concubine; let me bring them out now. Ravish them and do whatever you want to them; but against this man do not do such a vile thing." 25 But the men would not listen to him. So the man seized his concubine, and put her out to them. They wantonly raped her, and abused her all through the night until the morning. And as the dawn began to break, they let her go. 26 As morning appeared, the woman came and fell down at the door of the man's house where her master was, until it was light.

27 In the morning her master got up, opened the doors of the house, and when he went out to go on his way, there was his concubine lying at the door of the house, with her hands on the threshold. 28 "Get up," he said to her, "we are going." But there was no answer. Then he put her on the donkey; and the man set out for his home. 29 When he had entered his house, he took a knife, and grasping his concubine he cut her into twelve pieces, limb by limb, and sent her throughout all the territory of Israel. 30 Then he commanded the men whom he sent, saying, "Thus shall you say to all the Israelites, 'Has such a thing ever happened v since the day that the Israelites came up from the land of Egypt until this day? Consider it, take counsel, and speak out.'"

19.22 Gen 19.4; Deut 13.13; Rom 1.26, 27
19.23 Gen 34.7; Deut 22.21; 2 Sam 13.12
19.24 Gen 19.8; Deut 21.14
19.28 Judg 20.5
19.29 1 Sam 11.7
19.30 Judg 20.7

20.1 Judg 21.5; 1 Sam 7.5
20.4 Judg 19.15
20.5 Judg 19.22, 25,26
20.6 Judg 19.29; Josh 7.15
20.7 Judg 19.30
20.12 Deut 13.14, 15

The Other Tribes Attack Benjamin

20 Then all the Israelites came out, from Dan to Beer-sheba, including the land of Gilead, and the congregation assembled in one body before the LORD at Mizpah. 2 The chiefs of all the people, of all the tribes of Israel, presented themselves in the assembly of the people of God, four hundred thousand foot-soldiers bearing arms. 3 (Now the Benjaminites heard that the people of Israel had gone up to Mizpah.) And the Israelites said, "Tell us, how did this criminal act come about?" 4 The Levite, the husband of the woman who was murdered, answered, "I came to Gibeah that belongs to Benjamin, I and my concubine, to spend the night. 5 The lords of Gibeah rose up against me, and surrounded the house at night. They intended to kill me, and they raped my concubine until she died. 6 Then I took my concubine and cut her into pieces, and sent her throughout the whole extent of Israel's territory; for they have committed a vile outrage in Israel. 7 So now, you Israelites, all of you, give your advice and counsel here.

8 All the people got up as one, saying, "We will not any of us go to our tents, nor will any of us return to our houses. 9 But now this is what we will do to Gibeah: we will go up w against it by lot. 10 We will take ten men of a hundred throughout all the tribes of Israel, and a hundred of a thousand, and a thousand of ten thousand, to bring provisions for the troops, who are going to repay x Gibeah of Benjamin for all the disgrace that they have done in Israel." 11 So all the men of Israel gathered against the city, united as one.

12 The tribes of Israel sent men through all the tribe of Benjamin, saying, "What crime is this that has been committed among you?

v Compare Gk: Heb 30And all who saw it said, "Such a thing has not happened or been seen w Gk: Heb lacks we will go up x Compare Gk: Meaning of Heb uncertain

13 Now then, hand over those scoundrels in Gibeah, so that we may put them to death, and purge the evil from Israel." But the Benjaminites would not listen to their kinsfolk, the Israelites. 14 The Benjaminites came together out of the towns to Gibeah, to go out to battle against the Israelites. 15 On that day the Benjaminites mustered twenty-six thousand armed men from their towns, besides the inhabitants of Gibeah. 16 Of all this force, there were seven hundred picked men who were left-handed; every one could sling a stone at a hair, and not miss. 17 And the Israelites, apart from Benjamin, mustered four hundred thousand armed men, all of them warriors.

18 The Israelites proceeded to go up to Bethel, where they inquired of God, "Which of us shall go up first to battle against the Benjaminites?" And the LORD answered, "Judah shall go up first."

19 Then the Israelites got up in the morning, and encamped against Gibeah. 20 The Israelites went out to battle against Benjamin; and the Israelites drew up the battle line against them at Gibeah. 21 The Benjaminites came out of Gibeah, and struck down on that day twenty-two thousand of the Israelites. 23 y The Israelites went up and wept before the LORD until the evening; and they inquired of the LORD, "Shall we again draw near to battle against our kinsfolk the Benjaminites?" And the LORD said, "Go up against them." 22 The Israelites took courage, and again formed the battle line in the same place where they had formed it on the first day. 24 So the Israelites advanced against the Benjaminites the second day. 25 Benjamin moved out against them from Gibeah the second day, and struck down eighteen thousand of the Israelites, all of them armed men. 26 Then all the Israelites, the whole army, went back to Bethel and wept, sitting there before the LORD; they fasted that day until evening. Then they offered burnt offerings and sacrifices

of well-being before the LORD. 27 And the Israelites inquired of the LORD (for the ark of the covenant of God was there in those days, 28 and Phinehas son of Eleazar, son of Aaron, ministered before it in those days), saying, "Shall we go out once more to battle against our kinsfolk the Benjaminites, or shall we desist?" The LORD answered, "Go up, for tomorrow I will give them into your hand."

29 So Israel stationed men in ambush around Gibeah. 30 Then the Israelites went up against the Benjaminites on the third day, and set themselves in array against Gibeah, as before. 31 When the Benjaminites went out against the army, they were drawn away from the city. As before they began to inflict casualties on the troops, along the main roads, one of which goes up to Bethel and the other to Gibeah, as well as in the open country, killing about thirty men of Israel. 32 The Benjaminites thought, "They are being routed before us, as previously." But the Israelites said, "Let us retreat and draw them away from the city toward the roads." 33 The main body of the Israelites drew back its battle line to Baal-tamar, while those Israelites who were in ambush rushed out of their place west z of Geba. 34 There came against Gibeah ten thousand picked men out of all Israel, and the battle was fierce. But the Benjaminites did not realize that disaster was close upon them.

35 The LORD defeated Benjamin before Israel; and the Israelites destroyed twenty-five thousand one hundred men of Benjamin that day, all of them armed.

36 Then the Benjaminites saw that they were defeated. a

The Israelites gave ground to Benjamin, because they trusted to the troops in ambush that they had stationed against Gibeah. 37 The troops in ambush rushed quickly upon Gibeah. Then they put the

20.13
Judg 19.22
20.16
Judg 3.15;
1 Chr 12.2
20.18
vv. 23,26,
27;
Num 27.21
20.21
v. 25
20.23
v. 18
20.25
v. 21
20.26
v. 23;
Judg 21.2

20.27
Josh 18.1
20.28
Josh 24.33;
Deut 18.5;
Judg 7.9
20.29
Josh 8.4
20.31
Josh 8.16
20.33
Josh 8.19
20.34
Josh 8.14
20.36
Josh 8.15
20.37
Josh 8.19

y Verses 22 and 23 are transposed　　z Gk Vg: Heb *in the plain*　　a This sentence is continued by verse 45.

whole city to the sword. 38 Now the agreement between the main body of Israel and the men in ambush was that when they sent up a cloud of smoke out of the city 39 the main body of Israel should turn in battle. But Benjamin had begun to inflict casualties on the Israelites, killing about thirty of them; so they thought, "Surely they are defeated before us, as in the first battle." 40 But when the cloud, a column of smoke, began to rise out of the city, the Benjaminites looked behind them—and there was the whole city going up in smoke toward the sky! 41 Then the main body of Israel turned, and the Benjaminites were dismayed, for they saw that disaster was close upon them. 42 Therefore they turned away from the Israelites in the direction of the wilderness; but the battle overtook them, and those who came out of the city[b] were slaughtering them in between.[c] 43 Cutting down[d] the Benjaminites, they pursued them from Nohah[e] and trod them down as far as a place east of Gibeah. 44 Eighteen thousand Benjaminites fell, all of them courageous fighters. 45 When they turned and fled toward the wilderness to the rock of Rimmon, five thousand of them were cut down on the main roads, and they were pursued as far as Gidom, and two thousand of them were slain. 46 So all who fell that day of Benjamin were twenty-five thousand arms-bearing men, all of them courageous fighters. 47 But six hundred turned and fled toward the wilderness to the rock of Rimmon, and remained at the rock of Rimmon for four months. 48 Meanwhile, the Israelites turned back against the Benjaminites, and put them to the sword—the city, the people, the animals, and all that remained. Also the remaining towns they set on fire.

The Benjaminites Saved from Extinction

21 Now the Israelites had sworn at Mizpah, "No one of us shall give his daughter in marriage to Benjamin." 2 And the people came to Bethel, and sat there until evening before God, and they lifted up their voices and wept bitterly. 3 They said, "O LORD, the God of Israel, why has it come to pass that today there should be one tribe lacking in Israel?" 4 On the next day, the people got up early, and built an altar there, and offered burnt offerings and sacrifices of well-being. 5 Then the Israelites said, "Which of all the tribes of Israel did not come up in the assembly to the LORD?" For a solemn oath had been taken concerning whoever did not come up to the LORD to Mizpah, saying, "That one shall be put to death." 6 But the Israelites had compassion for Benjamin their kin, and said, "One tribe is cut off from Israel this day. 7 What shall we do for wives for those who are left, since we have sworn by the LORD that we will not give them any of our daughters as wives?"

8 Then they said, "Is there anyone from the tribes of Israel who did not come up to the LORD to Mizpah?" It turned out that no one from Jabesh-gilead had come to the camp, to the assembly. 9 For when the roll was called among the people, not one of the inhabitants of Jabesh-gilead was there. 10 So the congregation sent twelve thousand soldiers there and commanded them, "Go, put the inhabitants of Jabesh-gilead to the sword, including the women and the little ones. 11 This is what you shall do; every male and every woman that has lain with a male you shall devote to destruction." 12 And they found among the inhabitants of Jabesh-gilead four hundred young virgins who had never slept with a man and brought them to the camp at Shiloh, which is in the land of Canaan.

13 Then the whole congregation sent word to the Benjaminites who were at the rock of Rimmon, and

Cross-reference column

20.38
Josh 8.20
20.39
v. 32
20.40
Josh 8.20
20.45
Judg 21.13
20.47
Judg 21.13
21.1
vv. 7,18

21.2
Judg 20.18, 26
21.4
2 Sam 24.25
21.7
v. 1
21.11
Num 31.17
21.13
Judg 20.47; Deut 20.10

Footnotes

b Compare Vg and some Gk Mss: Heb *cities*
c Compare Syr: Meaning of Heb uncertain
d Gk: Heb *Surrounding* e Gk: Heb *pursued them at their resting place*

proclaimed peace to them. ¹⁴Benjamin returned at that time; and they gave them the women whom they had saved alive of the women of Jabesh-gilead; but they did not suffice for them.

15 The people had compassion on Benjamin because the Lᴏʀᴅ had made a breach in the tribes of Israel. ¹⁶So the elders of the congregation said, "What shall we do for wives for those who are left, since there are no women left in Benjamin?" ¹⁷And they said, "There must be heirs for the survivors of Benjamin, in order that a tribe may not be blotted out from Israel. ¹⁸Yet we cannot give any of our daughters to them as wives." For the Israelites had sworn, "Cursed be anyone who gives a wife to Benjamin." ¹⁹So they said, "Look, the yearly festival of the Lᴏʀᴅ is taking place at Shiloh, which is north of Bethel, on the east of the highway that goes up from Bethel to Shechem, and south of Lebonah." ²⁰And they instructed the Benja-

minites, saying, "Go and lie in wait in the vineyards, ²¹and watch; when the young women of Shiloh come out to dance in the dances, then come out of the vineyards and each of you carry off a wife for himself from the young women of Shiloh, and go to the land of Benjamin. ²²Then if their fathers or their brothers come to complain to us, we will say to them, 'Be generous and allow us to have them; because we did not capture in battle a wife for each man. But neither did you incur guilt by giving your daughters to them.' " ²³The Benjaminites did so; they took wives for each of them from the dancers whom they abducted. Then they went and returned to their territory, and rebuilt the towns, and lived in them. ²⁴So the Israelites departed from there at that time by tribes and families, and they went out from there to their own territories.

25 In those days there was no king in Israel; all the people did what was right in their own eyes.

Ruth

Title and Background

This book is named after the leading character whose story is told here. Ruth was the great-grandmother of David and was included in the genealogy of Jesus (Mt 1.1,5). The story is set in the time of the judges and reflects a temporary time of peace between Israel and Moab. It gives a series of intimate glances into the private lives of the members of an Israelite family and presents a delightful account of a remnant of true faith and piety during this period.

Author and Date of Writing

The author is unknown, although Jewish tradition points to Samuel. This is unlikely because the mention of David (4.17,22) implies a later date. The literary style of the Hebrew text suggests it was written during the monarchy, probably sometime after 1000 B.C.

Theme and Message

Redemption is a key concept throughout the book; the Hebrew word in its various forms occurs twenty-three times. The word shows how God is working out his plan of salvation. The book of Ruth also illustrates love and devotion—self-giving love that fulfills God's law, and God's love in blessing the lives of his children.

Outline

 I. Introduction: Naomi Emptied (1.1-5)
 II. Naomi Returns from Moab (1.6-22)
 III. Ruth and Boaz Meet in the Harvest Fields (2.1-23)
 IV. Ruth Goes to Boaz at the Threshing Floor (3.1-18)
 V. Boaz Arranges to Marry Ruth (4.1-12)
 VI. Conclusion: Naomi Filled (4.13-17)
VII. Epilogue: Genealogy of David (4.18-22)

Elimelech's Family Goes to Moab

1 In the days when the judges ruled, there was a famine in the land, and a certain man of Bethlehem in Judah went to live in the country of Moab, he and his wife and two sons. ² The name of the man was Elimelech and the name of his wife Naomi, and the names of his two sons were Mahlon and Chilion; they were Ephrathites from Bethlehem in Judah. They went into the country of Moab and remained there. ³ But Elimelech, the husband of Naomi, died, and she was left with her two sons. ⁴ These took Moabite wives; the name of the one was Orpah and the name of the other Ruth. When they had lived there about ten years, ⁵ both Mahlon and Chilion also died, so that the woman was left without her two sons and her husband.

Naomi and Her Moabite Daughters-in-Law

6 Then she started to return with her daughters-in-law from the country of Moab, for she had heard in the country of Moab that the Lord had considered his people and given them food. ⁷ So she set out from the place where she had been living, she and her two daughters-in-law, and they went on their way to go back to the land of Judah. ⁸ But Naomi said to her two

1.1
Judg 2.16
1.2
Gen 35.19;
Judg 3.30

1.6
Ex 4.31
1.8
v. 5;
Ruth 2.20

daughters-in-law, "Go back each of you to your mother's house. May the LORD deal kindly with you, as you have dealt with the dead and with me. [9]The LORD grant that you may find security, each of you in the house of your husband." Then she kissed them, and they wept aloud. [10]They said to her, "No, we will return with you to your people." [11]But Naomi said, "Turn back, my daughters, why will you go with me? Do I still have sons in my womb that they may become your husbands? [12]Turn back, my daughters, go your way, for I am too old to have a husband. Even if I thought there was hope for me, even if I should have a husband tonight and bear sons, [13]would you then wait until they were grown? Would you then refrain from marrying? No, my daughters, it has been far more bitter for me than for you, because the hand of the LORD has turned against me." [14]Then they wept aloud again. Orpah kissed her mother-in-law, but Ruth clung to her.

15 So she said, "See, your sister-in-law has gone back to her people and to her gods; return after your sister-in-law." [16]But Ruth said,

"Do not press me to leave you
or to turn back from
 following you!
Where you go, I will go;
Where you lodge, I will
 lodge;
your people shall be my
 people,
and your God my God.
[17] Where you die, I will die—
 there will I be buried.
May the LORD do thus and so
 to me,
 and more as well,
if even death parts me from
 you!"

[18]When Naomi saw that she was determined to go with her, she said no more to her.

19 So the two of them went on until they came to Bethlehem. When they came to Bethlehem, the whole town was stirred because of

1.9
Ruth 3.1
1.11
Deut 25.5
1.13
Judg 2.15;
Ps 32.4
1.16
2 Kings 2.2,
4,6;
Ruth 2.11,
12
1.18
Acts 21.14

1.20
Ex 6.3;
Job 6.4
1.21
Job 1.21
1.22
Ex 9.31,32;
Ruth 2.23
2.1
Ruth 1.2;
3.2,12
2.2
v. 7;
Lev 19.9;
Deut 24.19
2.4
Ps 129.7,8;
Lk 1.28
2.6
Ruth 1.22

them; and the women said, "Is this Naomi?" [20]She said to them,
"Call me no longer Naomi,[a]
 call me Mara,[b]
 for the Almighty[c] has dealt
 bitterly with me.
[21] I went away full,
 but the LORD has brought
 me back empty;
 why call me Naomi
 when the LORD has dealt
 harshly with[d] me,
 and the Almighty[c] has
 brought calamity upon
 me?"

22 So Naomi returned together with Ruth the Moabite, her daughter-in-law, who came back with her from the country of Moab. They came to Bethlehem at the beginning of the barley harvest.

Ruth Meets Boaz

2 Now Naomi had a kinsman on her husband's side, a prominent rich man, of the family of Elimelech, whose name was Boaz. [2]And Ruth the Moabite said to Naomi, "Let me go to the field and glean among the ears of grain, behind someone in whose sight I may find favor." She said to her, "Go, my daughter." [3]So she went. She came and gleaned in the field behind the reapers. As it happened, she came to the part of the field belonging to Boaz, who was of the family of Elimelech. [4]Just then Boaz came from Bethlehem. He said to the reapers, "The LORD be with you." They answered, "The LORD bless you." [5]Then Boaz said to his servant who was in charge of the reapers, "To whom does this young woman belong?" [6]The servant who was in charge of the reapers answered, "She is the Moabite who came back with Naomi from the country of Moab. [7]She said, 'Please, let me glean and gather among the sheaves behind the reapers.' So she came, and she has been on her feet from early this

[a] That is *Pleasant* [b] That is *Bitter*
[c] Traditional rendering of Heb *Shaddai*
[d] Or *has testified against*

morning until now, without resting even for a moment."e

8 Then Boaz said to Ruth, "Now listen, my daughter, do not go to glean in another field or leave this one, but keep close to my young women. 9 Keep your eyes on the field that is being reaped, and follow behind them. I have ordered the young men not to bother you. If you get thirsty, go to the vessels and drink from what the young men have drawn." 10 Then she fell prostrate, with her face to the ground, and said to him, "Why have I found favor in your sight, that you should take notice of me, when I am a foreigner?" 11 But Boaz answered her, "All that you have done for your mother-in-law since the death of your husband has been fully told me, and how you left your father and mother and your native land and came to a people that you did not know before. 12 May the LORD reward you for your deeds, and may you have a full reward from the LORD, the God of Israel, under whose wings you have come for refuge!" 13 Then she said, "May I continue to find favor in your sight, my lord, for you have comforted me and spoken kindly to your servant, even though I am not one of your servants."

14 At mealtime Boaz said to her, "Come here, and eat some of this bread, and dip your morsel in the sour wine." So she sat beside the reapers, and he heaped up for her some parched grain. She ate until she was satisfied, and she had some left over. 15 When she got up to glean, Boaz instructed his young men, "Let her glean even among the standing sheaves, and do not reproach her. 16 You must also pull out some handfuls for her from the bundles, and leave them for her to glean, and do not rebuke her."

17 So she gleaned in the field until evening. Then she beat out what she had gleaned, and it was about an ephah of barley. 18 She picked it up and came into the town, and her mother-in-law saw how much she had gleaned. Then

she took out and gave her what was left over after she herself had been satisfied. 19 Her mother-in-law said to her, "Where did you glean today? And where have you worked? Blessed be the man who took notice of you." So she told her mother-in-law with whom she had worked, and said, "The name of the man with whom I worked today is Boaz." 20 Then Naomi said to her daughter-in-law, "Blessed be he by the LORD, whose kindness has not forsaken the living or the dead!" Naomi also said to her, "The man is a relative of ours, one of our nearest kin."f 21 Then Ruth the Moabite said, "He even said to me, 'Stay close by my servants, until they have finished all my harvest.'" 22 Naomi said to Ruth, her daughter-in-law, "It is better, my daughter, that you go out with his young women, otherwise you might be bothered in another field." 23 So she stayed close to the young women of Boaz, gleaning until the end of the barley and wheat harvests; and she lived with her mother-in-law.

Ruth and Boaz at the Threshing Floor

3 Naomi her mother-in-law said to her, "My daughter, I need to seek some security for you, so that it may be well with you. 2 Now here is our kinsman Boaz, with whose young women you have been working. See, he is winnowing barley tonight at the threshing floor. 3 Now wash and anoint yourself, and put on your best clothes and go down to the threshing floor; but do not make yourself known to the man until he has finished eating and drinking. 4 When he lies down, observe the place where he lies; then, go and uncover his feet and lie down; and he will tell you what to do." 5 She said to her, "All that you tell me I will do."

6 So she went down to the

2.10
1 Sam 25.23
2.11
Ruth 1.14,
16,17
2.12
1 Sam 24.19;
Ps 17.8;
Ruth 1.16
2.14
v. 18
2.18
v. 14

2.19
v. 10
2.20
Ruth 3.10;
Prov 17.17;
Ruth 3.9;
4.6
2.23
Deut 16.9
3.1
Ruth 1.9
3.2
Deut 25.5-10;
Ruth 2.8
3.3
2 Sam 14.2

e Compare Gk Vg: Meaning of Heb uncertain
f Or one with the right to redeem

threshing floor and did just as her mother-in-law had instructed her. ⁷When Boaz had eaten and drunk, and he was in a contented mood, he went to lie down at the end of the heap of grain. Then she came stealthily and uncovered his feet, and lay down. ⁸At midnight the man was startled, and turned over, and there, lying at his feet, was a woman! ⁹He said, "Who are you?" And she answered, "I am Ruth, your servant; spread your cloak over your servant, for you are next-of-kin."ᵍ ¹⁰He said, "May you be blessed by the Lᴏʀᴅ, my daughter; this last instance of your loyalty is better than the first; you have not gone after young men, whether poor or rich. ¹¹And now, my daughter, do not be afraid, I will do for you all that you ask, for all the assembly of my people know that you are a worthy woman. ¹²But now, though it is true that I am a near kinsman, there is another kinsman more closely related than I. ¹³Remain this night, and in the morning, if he will act as next-of-kinᵍ for you, good; let him do it. If he is not willing to act as next-of-kinᵍ for you, then, as the Lᴏʀᴅ lives, I will act as next-of-kinᵍ for you. Lie down until the morning."

14 So she lay at his feet until morning, but got up before one person could recognize another; for he said, "It must not be known that the woman came to the threshing floor." ¹⁵Then he said, "Bring the cloak you are wearing and hold it out." So she held it, and he measured out six measures of barley, and put it on her back; then he went into the city. ¹⁶She came to her mother-in-law, who said, "How did things go with you,ʰ my daughter?" Then she told her all that the man had done for her, ¹⁷saying, "He gave me these six measures of barley, for he said, 'Do not go back to your mother-in-law empty-handed.' " ¹⁸She replied, "Wait, my daughter, until you learn how the matter turns out, for the man will not rest, but will settle the matter today."

3.7
Judg 19.6,9, 22;
2 Sam 13.28
3.9
v. 12;
Ruth 2.20
3.11
Prov 12.4
3.12
v. 9;
Ruth 4.1
3.13
Ruth 4.5
3.18
Ps 37.3-5

4.1
Ruth 3.12
4.3
Lev 25.25
4.4
Jer 32.7,8;
Lev 25.25
4.5ff
Deut 25.5,6
4.6
Ruth 3.12, 13
4.7
Deut 25.7,9
4.10
Deut 25.6

The Marriage of Boaz and Ruth

4 No sooner had Boaz gone up to the gate and sat down there than the next-of-kin,ᵍ of whom Boaz had spoken, came passing by. So Boaz said, "Come over, friend; sit down here." And he went over and sat down. ²Then Boaz took ten men of the elders of the city, and said, "Sit down here"; so they sat down. ³He then said to the next-of-kin,ᵍ "Naomi, who has come back from the country of Moab, is selling the parcel of land that belonged to our kinsman Elimelech. ⁴So I thought I would tell you of it, and say: Buy it in the presence of those sitting here, and in the presence of the elders of my people. If you will redeem it, redeem it; but if you will not, tell me, so that I may know; for there is no one prior to you to redeem it, and I come after you." So he said, "I will redeem it." ⁵Then Boaz said, "The day you acquire the field from the hand of Naomi, you are also acquiring Ruthⁱ the Moabite, the widow of the dead man, to maintain the dead man's name on his inheritance." ⁶At this, the next-of-kinᵍ said, "I cannot redeem it for myself without damaging my own inheritance. Take my right of redemption yourself, for I cannot redeem it."

7 Now this was the custom in former times in Israel concerning redeeming and exchanging: to confirm a transaction, the one took off a sandal and gave it to the other; this was the manner of attesting in Israel. ⁸So when the next-of-kinᵍ said to Boaz, "Acquire it for yourself," he took off his sandal. ⁹Then Boaz said to the elders and all the people, "Today you are witnesses that I have acquired from the hand of Naomi all that belonged to Elimelech and all that belonged to Chilion and Mahlon. ¹⁰I have also acquired Ruth the Moabite, the wife of Mahlon, to be my wife, to maintain the dead man's name on his

ᵍ Or *one with the right to redeem*
ʰ Or *"Who are you,* ⁱ OL Vg: Heb *from the hand of Naomi and from Ruth*

inheritance, in order that the name of the dead may not be cut off from his kindred and from the gate of his native place; today you are witnesses." [11] Then all the people who were at the gate, along with the elders, said, "We are witnesses. May the LORD make the woman who is coming into your house like Rachel and Leah, who together built up the house of Israel. May you produce children in Ephrathah and bestow a name in Bethlehem; [12] and, through the children that the LORD will give you by this young woman, may your house be like the house of Perez, whom Tamar bore to Judah."

The Genealogy of David

13 So Boaz took Ruth and she became his wife. When they came together, the LORD made her conceive, and she bore a son. [14] Then the women said to Naomi, "Blessed be the LORD, who has not left you this day without next-of-kin;[i] and may his name be renowned in Israel! [15] He shall be to you a restorer of life and a nourisher of your old age; for your daughter-in-law who loves you, who is more to you than seven sons, has borne him." [16] Then Naomi took the child and laid him in her bosom, and became his nurse. [17] The women of the neighborhood gave him a name, saying, "A son has been born to Naomi." They named him Obed; he became the father of Jesse, the father of David.

18 Now these are the descendants of Perez: Perez became the father of Hezron, [19] Hezron of Ram, Ram of Amminadab, [20] Amminadab of Nahshon, Nahshon of Salmon, [21] Salmon of Boaz, Boaz of Obed, [22] Obed of Jesse, and Jesse of David.

i Or *one with the right to redeem*

4.11 Ps 127.3
4.12 v. 18; Gen 38.29
4.13 Ruth 3.11; Gen 29.31; 33.5
4.14 Lk 1.58
4.15 Ruth 1.16, 17; 2.11,12
4.18 Mt 1.3-6

1 Samuel

Title and Background

1 and 2 Samuel are named after the individual whom God used to establish kingship in Israel. These two books were originally one book, but it was divided into two parts by the translators of the Septuagint (Greek version of the Old Testament). The book of 1 Samuel records the lives of Samuel and Saul, and most of the life of David before he became king.

Author and Date of Writing

Who the author was is uncertain because the book itself does not identify anyone. The author probably wrote some time after the division of the kingdom that followed upon the death of Solomon in 930 B.C. Some scholars place its composition as late as the exile (seventh century B.C.).

Theme and Message

1 Samuel portrays the establishment of kingship in Israel. When the people demanded a king, Samuel was led by God to anoint Saul as the first king of Israel. But Saul was disobedient to God, and God rejected him as king. Then Samuel secretly anointed David to take Saul's place. The struggles between Saul and David make up the rest of the book. The weaknesses and sins of these leaders of Israel are shown, but so are Samuel's and David's goodness and obedience to God.

Outline

I. Background for the Establishment of Kingship in Israel (1.1–7.17)
II. Establishment of Kingship in Israel (8.1–12.25)
III. Failure of Saul's Kingship (13.1–15.35)
IV. David and Saul (16.1–30.31)
V. Death of Saul (31.1-13)

Samuel's Birth and Dedication

1 There was a certain man of Ramathaim, a Zuphite[a] from the hill country of Ephraim, whose name was Elkanah son of Jeroham son of Elihu son of Tohu son of Zuph, an Ephraimite. 2 He had two wives; the name of the one was Hannah, and the name of the other Peninnah. Peninnah had children, but Hannah had no children.

3 Now this man used to go up year by year from his town to worship and to sacrifice to the LORD of hosts at Shiloh, where the two sons of Eli, Hophni and Phinehas, were priests of the LORD. 4 On the day when Elkanah sacrificed, he would give portions to his wife Peninnah and to all her sons and daughters;

5 but to Hannah he gave a double portion,[b] because he loved her, though the LORD had closed her womb. 6 Her rival used to provoke her severely, to irritate her, because the LORD had closed her womb. 7 So it went on year by year; as often as she went up to the house of the LORD, she used to provoke her. Therefore Hannah wept and would not eat. 8 Her husband Elkanah said to her, "Hannah, why do you weep? Why do you not eat? Why is your heart sad? Am I not more to you than ten sons?"

9 After they had eaten and drunk at Shiloh, Hannah rose and presented herself before the

1.1 Josh 17.17, 18; 1 Chr 6.27
1.2 Deut 21.15-17; Lk 2.36
1.3 Ex 34.23; Deut 12.5; Josh 18.1
1.4 Deut 12.17
1.5 Gen 16.1; 30.2
1.6 Job 24.21
1.8 Ruth 4.15
1.9 1 Sam 3.3

a Compare Gk and 1 Chr 6.35-36: Heb *Ramathaim-zophim* b Syr: Meaning of Heb uncertain

LORD.[c] Now Eli the priest was sitting on the seat beside the doorpost of the temple of the LORD. [10] She was deeply distressed and prayed to the LORD, and wept bitterly. [11] She made this vow: "O LORD of hosts, if only you will look on the misery of your servant, and remember me, and not forget your servant, but will give to your servant a male child, then I will set him before you as a nazirite[d] until the day of his death. He shall drink neither wine nor intoxicants,[e] and no razor shall touch his head."

12 As she continued praying before the LORD, Eli observed her mouth. [13] Hannah was praying silently; only her lips moved, but her voice was not heard; therefore Eli thought she was drunk. [14] So Eli said to her, "How long will you make a drunken spectacle of yourself? Put away your wine." [15] But Hannah answered, "No, my lord; I am a woman deeply troubled; I have drunk neither wine nor strong drink, but I have been pouring out my soul before the LORD. [16] Do not regard your servant as a worthless woman, for I have been speaking out of my great anxiety and vexation all this time." [17] Then Eli answered, "Go in peace; the God of Israel grant the petition you have made to him." [18] And she said, "Let your servant find favor in your sight." Then the woman went to her quarters,[f] ate and drank with her husband,[g] and her countenance was sad no longer.[h]

19 They rose early in the morning and worshiped before the LORD; then they went back to their house at Ramah. Elkanah knew his wife Hannah, and the LORD remembered her. [20] In due time Hannah conceived and bore a son. She named him Samuel, for she said, "I have asked him of the LORD."

21 The man Elkanah and all his household went up to offer to the LORD the yearly sacrifice, and to pay his vow. [22] But Hannah did not go up, for she said to her husband, "As soon as the child is weaned, I will bring him, that he may appear in the presence of the LORD, and remain there forever; I will offer him as a nazirite[d] for all time."[i] [23] Her husband Elkanah said to her, "Do what seems best to you, wait until you have weaned him; only—may the LORD establish his word."[j] So the woman remained and nursed her son, until she weaned him. [24] When she had weaned him, she took him up with her, along with a three-year-old bull,[k] an ephah of flour, and a skin of wine. She brought him to the house of the LORD at Shiloh; and the child was young. [25] Then they slaughtered the bull, and they brought the child to Eli. [26] And she said, "Oh, my lord! As you live, my lord, I am the woman who was standing here in your presence, praying to the LORD. [27] For this child I prayed; and the LORD has granted me the petition that I made to him. [28] Therefore I have lent him to the LORD; as long as he lives, he is given to the LORD."

She left him there for[l] the LORD.

Hannah's Prayer

2 Hannah prayed and said,
"My heart exults in the
 LORD;
my strength is exalted in
 my God.[m]
My mouth derides my
 enemies,
because I rejoice in my[n]
 victory.

2 "There is no Holy One like
 the LORD,
no one besides you;
there is no Rock like our
 God.

1.11 Gen 28.20; 29.32; Num 6.5; Judg 13.5
1.13 Gen 24.42-45
1.14 Acts 2.4,13
1.15 Ps 62.8
1.17 Judg 18.6; 1 Sam 25.35; Mk 5.34
1.18 Ruth 2.13; Eccl 9.7
1.19 Gen 4.1; 30.22
1.20 Gen 41.51, 52; Ex 2.10, 22
1.21 v. 3
1.22 Lk 2.22; 1 Sam 2.11, 18
1.23 Num 30.7; v. 17
1.24 Deut 12.5; Josh 18.1
1.25 Lev 1.5;
1.26 Lk 2.22
1.26 2 Kings 2.2
1.27 vv. 11-13
1.28 vv. 11,22
2.1 Lk 1.46-55; Ps 89.17; Isa 12.2,3
2.2 Lev 19.2; 2 Sam 22.32; Deut 32.30, 31

[c] Gk: Heb lacks *and presented herself before the LORD* [d] That is *one separated* or *one consecrated* [e] Cn Compare Gk Q Ms 1.22: MT *then I will give him to the LORD all the days of his life* [f] Gk: Heb *went her way* [g] Gk: Heb lacks *and drank with her husband* [h] Gk: Meaning of Heb uncertain [i] Cn Compare Q Ms: MT lacks *I will offer him as a nazirite for all time* [j] MT: Q Ms Gk Compare Syr *that which goes out of your mouth* [k] Q Ms Gk Syr: MT *three bulls* [l] Gk (Compare Q Ms) and Gk at 2.11: MT *And he* (that is, Elkanah) *worshiped there before* [m] Gk: Heb *the LORD* [n] Q Ms: MT *your*

3 Talk no more so very
proudly,
let not arrogance come
from your mouth;
for the LORD is a God of
knowledge,
and by him actions are
weighed.
4 The bows of the mighty are
broken,
but the feeble gird on
strength.
5 Those who were full have
hired themselves out for
bread,
but those who were hungry
are fat with spoil.
The barren has borne seven,
but she who has many
children is forlorn.
6 The LORD kills and brings to
life;
he brings down to Sheol
and raises up.
7 The LORD makes poor and
makes rich;
he brings low, he also
exalts.
8 He raises up the poor from
the dust;
he lifts the needy from the
ash heap,
to make them sit with
princes
and inherit a seat of
honor.°
For the pillars of the earth
are the LORD's,
and on them he has set the
world.

9 "He will guard the feet of his
faithful ones,
but the wicked shall be cut
off in darkness;
for not by might does one
prevail.
10 The LORD! His adversaries
shall be shattered;
the Most High* will
thunder in heaven.
The LORD will judge the ends
of the earth;
he will give strength to his
king,
and exalt the power of his
anointed."

2.3
Prov 8.13;
1 Sam 16.7;
1 Kings 8.39;
Prov 16.2;
24.12
2.4
Ps 76.3
2.5
Ps 113.9;
Jer 15.9
2.6
Deut 32.39;
Isa 26.19
2.7
Deut 8.17,
18;
Job 5.11;
Ps 75.6,7
2.8
Ps 113.7,8;
Job 36.7;
38.4,5
2.9
Ps 91.11,12;
Mt 8.12;
Ps 33.16,17
2.10
Ps 2.9;
18.13; 96.13;
21.1,7; 89.24

2.11
1 Sam 3.1
2.12
Jer 2.8; 9.3,
6
2.13
Lev 7.29-34
2.15
Lev 3.3,4
2.17
Mal 2.7-9
2.18
vv. 11,28;
1 Sam 3.1
2.19
1 Sam 1.3
2.20
Lk 2.34;
1 Sam 1.11,
27,28
2.21
Gen 21.1;
v. 26;
1 Sam 3.19;
Lk 2.40

Eli's Wicked Sons

11 Then Elkanah went home to
Ramah, while the boy remained to
minister to the LORD, in the pres-
ence of the priest Eli.

12 Now the sons of Eli were
scoundrels; they had no regard for
the LORD 13 or for the duties of the
priests to the people. When anyone
offered sacrifice, the priest's ser-
vant would come, while the meat
was boiling, with a three-pronged
fork in his hand, 14 and he would
thrust it into the pan, or kettle, or
caldron, or pot; all that the fork
brought up the priest would take
for himself.q This is what they did
at Shiloh to all the Israelites who
came there. 15 Moreover, before the
fat was burned, the priest's servant
would come and say to the one who
was sacrificing, "Give meat for the
priest to roast; for he will not ac-
cept boiled meat from you, but
only raw." 16 And if the man said to
him, "Let them burn the fat first,
and then take whatever you wish,"
he would say, "No, you must give it
now; if not, I will take it by force."
17 Thus the sin of the young men
was very great in the sight of the
LORD; for they treated the offerings
of the LORD with contempt.

The Child Samuel at Shiloh

18 Samuel was ministering be-
fore the LORD, a boy wearing a linen
ephod. 19 His mother used to make
for him a little robe and take it to
him each year, when she went up
with her husband to offer the yearly
sacrifice. 20 Then Eli would bless
Elkanah and his wife, and say,
"May the LORD repayr you with
children by this woman for the gift
that she made to s the LORD"; and
then they would return to their
home.

21 Andt the LORD took note of
Hannah; she conceived and bore
three sons and two daughters. And

° Gk (Compare Q Ms) adds *He grants the
vow of the one who vows, and blesses the years
of the just*　º Cn Heb *against him he*
q Gk Syr Vg: Heb *with it*　r Q Ms Gk: MT
give　s Q Ms Gk: MT *for the petition that
she asked of*　t Q Ms Gk: MT *When*

the boy Samuel grew up in the presence of the LORD.

Prophecy against Eli's Household

22 Now Eli was very old. He heard all that his sons were doing to all Israel, and how they lay with the women who served at the entrance to the tent of meeting. 23 He said to them, "Why do you do such things? For I hear of your evil dealings from all these people. 24 No, my sons; it is not a good report that I hear the people of the LORD spreading abroad. 25 If one person sins against another, someone can intercede for the sinner with the LORD;ᵘ but if someone sins against the LORD, who can make intercession?" But they would not listen to the voice of their father; for it was the will of the LORD to kill them.

26 Now the boy Samuel continued to grow both in stature and in favor with the LORD and with the people.

27 A man of God came to Eli and said to him, "Thus the LORD has said, 'I revealedᵛ myself to the family of your ancestor in Egypt when they were slavesʷ to the house of Pharaoh. 28 I chose him out of all the tribes of Israel to be my priest, to go up to my altar, to offer incense, to wear an ephod before me; and I gave to the family of your ancestor all my offerings by fire from the people of Israel. 29 Why then look with greedy eyeˣ at my sacrifices and my offerings that I commanded, and honor your sons more than me by fattening yourselves on the choicest parts of every offering of my people Israel?' 30 Therefore the LORD the God of Israel declares: 'I promised that your family and the family of your ancestor should go in and out before me forever'; but now the LORD declares: 'Far be it from me; for those who honor me I will honor, and those who despise me shall be treated with contempt. 31 See, a time is coming when I will cut off your strength and the strength of your ancestor's family, so that no

one in your family will live t[o] age. 32 Then in distress you look with greedy eyeʸ on al[l] prosperity that shall be beste[d] upon Israel; and no one in family shall ever live to old 33 The only one of you whom I not cut off from my altar sha[ll] spared to weep out hisᶻ eyes grieve hisᵃ heart; all the men of your household shall die b[y] sword.ᵇ 34 The fate of your sons, Hophni and Phinehas, be the sign to you—both of [them] shall die on the same day. 35 I raise up for myself a faithful p[riest] who shall do according to wh[at] in my heart and in my mind. [I will] build him a sure house, an[d he] shall go in and out before anointed one forever. 36 Ever[y one] who is left in your family come to implore him for a pie[ce of] silver or a loaf of bread, and say, Please put me in one o[f the] priest's places, that I may e[at a] morsel of bread.' "

Samuel's Calling and Proph[etic] Activity

3 Now the boy Samuel was [min]istering to the LORD unde[r Eli]. The word of the LORD was ra[re in] those days; visions were not v[ide]spread.

2 At that time Eli, whose sight had begun to grow dim s[o that] he could not see, was lying dow[n in] his room; 3 the lamp of God ha[d] yet gone out, and Samuel was [lying] down in the temple of the [LORD,] where the ark of God was. 4 T[hen] the LORD called, "Samuel! [Sam]uel!"ᶜ and he said, "Here I [am!"] 5 and ran to Eli, and said, "H[ere I] am, for you called me." But he [said,] "I did not call; lie down again[." So] he went and lay down. 6 The [LORD] called again, "Samuel!" Samue[l rose] up and went to Eli, and said, "[Here I]

ᵘ Gk Compare Q Ms: MT *another, God w[ill] mediate for him* ᵛ Gk Tg Syr: Heb *Did reveal* ʷ Q Ms Gk: MT lacks *slaves* ˣ Q Ms Gk: MT *then kick* ʸ Q Ms Gk: MT *will kick* ᶻ Q Ms Gk: MT *your* ᵃ Q [Ms] Gk: Heb *your* ᵇ Q Ms See Gk: MT *die mortals* ᶜ Q Ms Gk See 3.10: MT *the L[ORD] called Samuel*

Cross references (center column):

2.22 Ex 38.8
2.24 1 Kings 15.26
2.25 Deut 1.17; Num 15.30; Josh 11.20
2.26 v. 21; Lk 2.52
2.27 1 Kings 13.1; Ex 4.14-16
2.28 Ex 28.1-4; Lev 8.7,8
2.29 vv. 13-17; Deut 12.5; Mt 10.37
2.30 Ex 29.9; Ps 91.14; Mal 2.9
2.31 1 Sam 4.11-18; 22.17-20
2.32 1 Kings 2.26, 27; Zech 8.4
2.34 1 Kings 13.3; 1 Sam 4.11
2.35 1 Kings 2.35; 2 Sam 7.11, 27; 1 Kings 11.38; 1 Sam 12.3; 16.13
2.36 1 Kings 2.27
3.1 1 Sam 2.11, 18; Ps 74.9; Am 8.11
3.2 1 Sam 4.15
3.3 Lev 24.2-4
3.4 Isa 6.8

I am, for you called me." But he said, "I did not call, my son; lie down again." [7] Now Samuel did not yet know the LORD, and the word of the LORD had not yet been revealed to him. [8] The LORD called Samuel again, a third time. And he got up and went to Eli, and said, "Here I am, for you called me." Then Eli perceived that the LORD was calling the boy. [9] Therefore Eli said to Samuel, "Go, lie down; and if he calls you, you shall say, 'Speak, LORD, for your servant is listening.'" So Samuel went and lay down in his place.

10 Now the LORD came and stood there, calling as before, "Samuel! Samuel!" And Samuel said, "Speak, for your servant is listening." [11] Then the LORD said to Samuel, "See, I am about to do something in Israel that will make both ears of anyone who hears of it tingle. [12] On that day I will fulfill against Eli all that I have spoken concerning his house, from beginning to end. [13] For I have told him that I am about to punish his house forever, for the iniquity that he knew, because his sons were blaspheming God,[d] and he did not restrain them. [14] Therefore I swear to the house of Eli that the iniquity of Eli's house shall not be expiated by sacrifice or offering forever."

15 Samuel lay there until morning; then he opened the doors of the house of the LORD. Samuel was afraid to tell the vision to Eli. [16] But Eli called Samuel and said, "Samuel, my son." He said, "Here I am." [17] Eli said, "What was it that he told you? Do not hide it from me. May God do so to you and more also, if you hide anything from me of all that he told you." [18] So Samuel told him everything and hid nothing from him. Then he said, "It is the LORD; let him do what seems good to him."

19 As Samuel grew up, the LORD was with him and let none of his words fall to the ground. [20] And all Israel from Dan to Beer-sheba knew that Samuel was a trustworthy prophet of the LORD. [21] The LORD

continued to appear at Shiloh, for the LORD revealed himself to Samuel at Shiloh by the word of the LORD. [1] And the word of Samuel came to all Israel.

The Ark of God Captured

4 In those days the Philistines mustered for war against Israel,[e] and Israel went out to battle against them;[f] they encamped at Ebenezer, and the Philistines encamped at Aphek. [2] The Philistines drew up in line against Israel, and when the battle was joined,[g] Israel was defeated by the Philistines, who killed about four thousand men on the field of battle. [3] When the troops came to the camp, the elders of Israel said, "Why has the LORD put us to rout today before the Philistines? Let us bring the ark of the covenant of the LORD here from Shiloh, so that he may come among us and save us from the power of our enemies." [4] So the people sent to Shiloh, and brought from there the ark of the covenant of the LORD of hosts, who is enthroned on the cherubim. The two sons of Eli, Hophni and Phinehas, were there with the ark of the covenant of God.

5 When the ark of the covenant of the LORD came into the camp, all Israel gave a mighty shout, so that the earth resounded. [6] When the Philistines heard the noise of the shouting, they said, "What does this great shouting in the camp of the Hebrews mean?" When they learned that the ark of the LORD had come to the camp, [7] the Philistines were afraid; for they said, "Gods have[h] come into the camp." They also said, "Woe to us! For nothing like this has happened before. [8] Woe to us! Who can deliver us from the power of these mighty gods? These are the gods who struck the Egyptians with every sort of plague in the wilderness. [9] Take courage, and be men,

3.7
Acts 19.2
3.11
2 Kings 21.12;
Jer 19.3
3.12
1 Sam 2.30-36
3.13
1 Sam 2.12,
17,22,29-31
3.14
Lev 15.30,
31;
Isa 22.14
3.17
Ruth 1.17;
2 Sam 3.35
3.18
Job 2.10;
Isa 39.8
3.19
1 Sam 2.21;
Gen 21.22;
39.2;
1 Sam 9.6
3.20
Judg 20.1
3.21
v. 10

4.1
1 Sam 7.12
4.3
Josh 7.7,8;
Num 10.35
4.4
2 Sam 6.2;
Ex 25.18,22
4.5
Josh 6.5,20
4.6
Ex 15.14
4.9
1 Cor 16.13;
Judg 13.1

d Another reading is for themselves
e Gk: Heb lacks In those days the Philistines mustered for war against Israel f Gk: Heb against the Philistines g Meaning of Heb uncertain h Or A god has

O Philistines, in order not to become slaves to the Hebrews as they have been to you; be men and fight."

10 So the Philistines fought; Israel was defeated, and they fled, everyone to his home. There was a very great slaughter, for there fell of Israel thirty thousand foot soldiers. [11] The ark of God was captured; and the two sons of Eli, Hophni and Phinehas, died.

Death of Eli

12 A man of Benjamin ran from the battle line, and came to Shiloh the same day, with his clothes torn and with earth upon his head. [13] When he arrived, Eli was sitting upon his seat by the road watching, for his heart trembled for the ark of God. When the man came into the city and told the news, all the city cried out. [14] When Eli heard the sound of the outcry, he said, "What is this uproar?" Then the man came quickly and told Eli. [15] Now Eli was ninety-eight years old and his eyes were set, so that he could not see. [16] The man said to Eli, "I have just come from the battle; I fled from the battle today." He said, "How did it go, my son?" [17] The messenger replied, "Israel has fled before the Philistines, and there has also been a great slaughter among the troops; your two sons also, Hophni and Phinehas, are dead, and the ark of God has been captured." [18] When he mentioned the ark of God, Eli[i] fell over backward from his seat by the side of the gate; and his neck was broken and he died, for he was an old man, and heavy. He had judged Israel forty years.

19 Now his daughter-in-law, the wife of Phinehas, was pregnant, about to give birth. When she heard the news that the ark of God was captured, and that her father-in-law and her husband were dead, she bowed and gave birth; for her labor pains overwhelmed her. [20] As she was about to die, the women attending her said to her, "Do not be afraid, for you have borne a

son." But she did not answer or give heed. [21] She named the child Ichabod, meaning, "The glory has departed from Israel," because the ark of God had been captured and because of her father-in-law and her husband. [22] She said, "The glory has departed from Israel, for the ark of God has been captured."

The Philistines and the Ark

5 When the Philistines captured the ark of God, they brought it from Ebenezer to Ashdod; [2] then the Philistines took the ark of God and brought it into the house of Dagon and placed it beside Dagon. [3] When the people of Ashdod rose early the next day, there was Dagon, fallen on his face to the ground before the ark of the LORD. So they took Dagon and put him back in his place. [4] But when they rose early on the next morning, Dagon had fallen on his face to the ground before the ark of the LORD, and the head of Dagon and both his hands were lying cut off upon the threshold; only the trunk of[j] Dagon was left to him. [5] This is why the priests of Dagon and all who enter the house of Dagon do not step on the threshold of Dagon in Ashdod to this day.

6 The hand of the LORD was heavy upon the people of Ashdod, and he terrified and struck them with tumors, both in Ashdod and in its territory. [7] And when the inhabitants of Ashdod saw how things were, they said, "The ark of the God of Israel must not remain with us; for his hand is heavy on us and on our god Dagon." [8] So they sent and gathered together all the lords of the Philistines, and said, "What shall we do with the ark of the God of Israel?" The inhabitants of Gath replied, "Let the ark of God be moved on to us."[k] So they moved the ark of the God of Israel to Gath.[l] [9] But after they had brought it to Gath,[m] the hand of the LORD

4.10
v. 2;
Deut 28.25;
2 Sam 18.17;
2 Kings 14.12
4.11
1 Sam 2.34;
Ps 78.56-64
4.12
Josh 7.6;
2 Sam 1.2;
Neh 9.1
4.13
v. 18;
1 Sam 1.9
4.15
1 Sam 3.2
4.16
2 Sam 1.4
4.18
v. 13
4.20
Gen 35.16-19

4.22
Jer 2.11;
v. 11
5.1
1 Sam 4.1;
7.12
5.2
Judg 16.23
5.3
Isa 19.1;
46.1,2,7
5.4
Ezek 6.4,6
5.6
vv. 7,11;
Ex 9.3;
1 Sam 6.5;
Deut 28.27;
Ps 78.66
5.8
v. 11
5.9
vv. 6,11;
1 Sam 7.13;
Ps 78.66

i Heb he j Heb lacks *the trunk of*
k Gk Compare Q Ms: MT *They answered,
"Let the ark of the God of Israel be brought
around to Gath."* l Gk: Heb lacks *to Gath*
m Q Ms: MT lacks *to Gath*

was against the city, causing a very great panic; he struck the inhabitants of the city, both young and old, so that tumors broke out on them. [10] So they sent the ark of the God of Israel[n] to Ekron. But when the ark of God came to Ekron, the people of Ekron cried out, "Why[o] have they brought around to us[p] the ark of the God of Israel to kill us[p] and our[q] people?" [11] They sent therefore and gathered together all the lords of the Philistines, and said, "Send away the ark of the God of Israel, and let it return to its own place, that it may not kill us and our people." For there was a deathly panic[r] throughout the whole city. The hand of God was very heavy there; [12] those who did not die were stricken with tumors, and the cry of the city went up to heaven.

The Ark Returned to Israel

6 The ark of the LORD was in the country of the Philistines seven months. [2] Then the Philistines called for the priests and the diviners and said, "What shall we do with the ark of the LORD? Tell us what we should send with it to its place." [3] They said, "If you send away the ark of the God of Israel, do not send it empty, but by all means return him a guilt offering. Then you will be healed and will be ransomed;[s] will not his hand then turn from you?" [4] And they said, "What is the guilt offering that we shall return to him?" They answered, "Five gold tumors and five gold mice, according to the number of the lords of the Philistines; for the same plague was upon all of you and upon your lords. [5] So you must make images of your tumors and images of your mice that ravage the land, and give glory to the God of Israel; perhaps he will lighten his hand on you and your gods and your land. [6] Why should you harden your hearts as the Egyptians and Pharaoh hardened their hearts? After he had made fools of them, did they not let the people go, and they departed? [7] Now then,

get ready a new cart and two milch cows that have never borne a yoke, and yoke the cows to the cart, but take their calves home, away from them. [8] Take the ark of the LORD and place it on the cart, and put in a box at its side the figures of gold, which you are returning to him as a guilt offering. Then send it off, and let it go its way. [9] And watch; if it goes up on the way to its own land, to Beth-shemesh, then it is he who has done us this great harm; but if not, then we shall know that it is not his hand that struck us; it happened to us by chance."

10 The men did so; they took two milch cows and yoked them to the cart, and shut up their calves at home. [11] They put the ark of the LORD on the cart, and the box with the gold mice and the images of their tumors. [12] The cows went straight in the direction of Beth-shemesh along one highway, lowing as they went; they turned neither to the right nor to the left, and the lords of the Philistines went after them as far as the border of Beth-shemesh.

13 Now the people of Beth-shemesh were reaping their wheat harvest in the valley. When they looked up and saw the ark, they went with rejoicing to meet it.[t] [14] The cart came into the field of Joshua of Beth-shemesh, and stopped there. A large stone was there; so they split up the wood of the cart and offered the cows as a burnt offering to the LORD. [15] The Levites took down the ark of the LORD and the box that was beside it, in which were the gold objects, and set them upon the large stone. Then the people of Beth-shemesh offered burnt offerings and presented sacrifices on that day to the LORD. [16] When the five lords of the Philistines saw it, they returned that day to Ekron.

17 These are the gold tumors,

Cross-references (center column)

5.11 vv. 6,8,9
6.2 Gen 41.8; Ex 7.11; Isa 2.6
6.3 Ex 23.15; Deut 16.16; Lev 5.15,16
6.4 vv. 17,18; Josh 13.3; Judg 3.3
6.5 1 Sam 5.3-11; Josh 7.19; Isa 42.12
6.6 Ex 8.15; 9.34; 12.31
6.7 2 Sam 6.3; Num 19.2
6.8 vv. 3-5
6.9 Josh 15.10; v. 3
6.12 v. 9; Num 20.19
6.14 2 Sam 24.22; 1 Kings 19.21
6.16 Josh 13.3
6.17 v. 4

Footnotes

[n] Q Ms Gk: MT lacks *of Israel* [o] Q Ms Gk: MT lacks *Why* [p] Heb *me* [q] Heb *my* [r] Q Ms reads *a panic from the* LORD [s] Q Ms Gk: MT *and it will be known to you* [t] Gk: Heb *rejoiced to see it*

which the Philistines returned as a guilt offering to the LORD: one for Ashdod, one for Gaza, one for Ashkelon, one for Gath, one for Ekron; 18 also the gold mice, according to the number of all the cities of the Philistines belonging to the five lords, both fortified cities and unwalled villages. The great stone, beside which they set down the ark of the LORD, is a witness to this day in the field of Joshua of Beth-shemesh.

The Ark at Kiriath-jearim

19 The descendants of Jeconiah did not rejoice with the people of Beth-shemesh when they greeted^u the ark of the LORD; and he killed seventy men of them.^v The people mourned because the LORD had made a great slaughter among the people. 20 Then the people of Beth-shemesh said, "Who is able to stand before the LORD, this holy God? To whom shall he go so that we may be rid of him?" 21 So they sent messengers to the inhabitants of Kiriath-jearim, saying, "The Philistines have returned the ark of the LORD. Come down and take it up to you." 1 And the people of Kiriath-jearim came and took up the ark of the LORD, and brought it to the house of Abinadab on the hill. They consecrated his son, Eleazar, to have charge of the ark of the LORD.

2 From the day that the ark was lodged at Kiriath-jearim, a long time passed, some twenty years, and all the house of Israel lamented^w after the LORD.

Samuel as Judge

3 Then Samuel said to all the house of Israel, "If you are returning to the LORD with all your heart, then put away the foreign gods and the Astartes from among you. Direct your heart to the LORD, and serve him only, and he will deliver you out of the hand of the Philistines." 4 So Israel put away the Baals and the Astartes, and they served the LORD only.

5 Then Samuel said, "Gather all

Israel at Mizpah, and I will pra the LORD for you." 6 So they g ered at Mizpah, and drew w and poured it out before the L They fasted that day, and said, have sinned against the LORD." Samuel judged the people of Is at Mizpah.

7 When the Philistines h that the people of Israel had g ered at Mizpah, the lords of Philistines went up against Is And when the people of I heard of it they were afraid of Philistines. 8 The people of Is said to Samuel, "Do not ceas cry out to the LORD our God fo and pray that he may save us f the hand of the Philistines." Samuel took a sucking lamb offered it as a whole burnt off to the LORD; Samuel cried o the LORD for Israel, and the LOR swered him. 10 As Samuel was c ing up the burnt offering, the istines drew near to attack Is but the LORD thundered wi mighty voice that day against Philistines and threw them confusion; and they were ro before Israel. 11 And the men rael went out of Mizpah and sued the Philistines, and st them down as far as beyond F car.

12 Then Samuel took a s and set it up between Mizpah Jeshanah,^x and named it Eb ezer;^y for he said, "Thus far the has helped us." 13 So the Philis were subdued and did not enter the territory of Israel hand of the LORD was agains Philistines all the days of Sar 14 The towns that the Philis had taken from Israel were res to Israel, from Ekron to Gath Israel recovered their territory the hand of the Philistines. T was peace also between Israel the Amorites.

15 Samuel judged Israel a

6.18
vv. 14,15
6.19
Num 4.5,15,20;
2 Sam 6.7
6.20
Lev 11.44,45;
2 Sam 6.9
6.21
Josh 9.17;
15.9,60
7.1
2 Sam 6.3,4
7.3
Joel 2.2;
Josh 24.14;
Judg 2.13;
Deut 6.13;
Mt 4.10

7.6
Ps 62.8;
Neh 9.1;
Judg 10.10
7.7
1 Sam 17.11
7.8
Isa 37.4
7.9
Ps 99.6;
Jer 15.1
7.10
Josh 10.10;
1 Sam 2.10;
2 Sam 22.14,15
7.12
Gen 35.14;
Josh 4.9
7.13
Judg 13.1;
1 Sam 13.5
7.15
v. 6;
1 Sam 12.11

u Gk: Heb And he killed some of the peopl
Beth-shemesh, because they looked into
v Heb killed seventy men, fifty thousand m
w Meaning of Heb uncertain x Gk Syr
Shen y That is Stone of Help

days of his life. [16] He went on a circuit year by year to Bethel, Gilgal, and Mizpah; and he judged Israel in all these places. [17] Then he would come back to Ramah, for his home was there; he administered justice there to Israel, and built there an altar to the LORD.

Israel Demands a King

8 When Samuel became old, he made his sons judges over Israel. [2] The name of his firstborn son was Joel, and the name of his second, Abijah; they were judges in Beer-sheba. [3] Yet his sons did not follow in his ways, but turned aside after gain; they took bribes and perverted justice.

[4] Then all the elders of Israel gathered together and came to Samuel at Ramah, [5] and said to him, "You are old and your sons do not follow in your ways; appoint for us, then, a king to govern us, like other nations." [6] But the thing displeased Samuel when they said, "Give us a king to govern us." Samuel prayed to the LORD, [7] and the LORD said to Samuel, "Listen to the voice of the people in all that they say to you; for they have not rejected you, but they have rejected me from being king over them. [8] Just as they have done to me,[z] from the day I brought them up out of Egypt to this day, forsaking me and serving other gods, so also they are doing to you. [9] Now then, listen to their voice; only—you shall solemnly warn them, and show them the ways of the king who shall reign over them."

[10] So Samuel reported all the words of the LORD to the people who were asking him for a king. [11] He said, "These will be the ways of the king who will reign over you: he will take your sons and appoint them to his chariots and to be his horsemen, and to run before his chariots; [12] and he will appoint for himself commanders of thousands and commanders of fifties, and some to plow his ground and to reap his harvest, and to make his implements of war and the equip-

ment of his chariots. [13] He will take your daughters to be perfumers and cooks and bakers. [14] He will take the best of your fields and vineyards and olive orchards and give them to his courtiers. [15] He will take one-tenth of your grain and of your vineyards and give it to his officers and his courtiers. [16] He will take your male and female slaves, and the best of your cattle[a] and donkeys, and put them to his work. [17] He will take one-tenth of your flocks, and you shall be his slaves. [18] And in that day you will cry out because of your king, whom you have chosen for yourselves; but the LORD will not answer you in that day."

Israel's Request for a King Granted

[19] But the people refused to listen to the voice of Samuel; they said, "No! but we are determined to have a king over us, [20] so that we also may be like other nations, and that our king may govern us and go out before us and fight our battles." [21] When Samuel had heard all the words of the people, he repeated them in the ears of the LORD. [22] The LORD said to Samuel, "Listen to their voice and set a king over them." Samuel then said to the people of Israel, "Each of you return home."

Saul Chosen to be King

9 There was a man of Benjamin whose name was Kish son of Abiel son of Zeror son of Becorath son of Aphiah, a Benjaminite, a man of wealth. [2] He had a son whose name was Saul, a handsome young man. There was not a man among the people of Israel more handsome than he; he stood head and shoulders above everyone else.

[3] Now the donkeys of Kish, Saul's father, had strayed. So Kish said to his son Saul, "Take one of the boys with you; go and look for the donkeys." [4] He passed through the hill country of Ephraim and

7.17
1 Sam 1.19;
7.5;
Judg 20.1;
1 Sam 8.6
8.1
Deut 16.18,
19
8.3
Ex 23.6,8;
Deut 16.19;
Ps 15.5
8.4
1 Sam 7.17
8.5ff
Deut 17.14,
15
8.6
1 Sam 15.11
8.7
1 Sam 10.19;
Ex 16.8
8.9
v. 11
8.11
1 Sam 14.52;
2 Sam 15.1
8.12
1 Sam 22.7

8.14
1 Kings 21.7;
Ezek 46.18
8.18
Prov 1.25-28;
Mic 3.4
8.20
v. 5
8.22
v. 7
9.1
1 Sam 14.51;
1 Chr 9.36-39
9.2
1 Sam 10.23,
24
9.4
Josh 24.33;
2 Kings 4.42;
Josh 19.42

[z] Gk: Heb lacks to me
men

[a] Gk: Heb young

passed through the land of Shalishah, but they did not find them. And they passed through the land of Shaalim, but they were not there. Then he passed through the land of Benjamin, but they did not find them.

5 When they came to the land of Zuph, Saul said to the boy who was with him, "Let us turn back, or my father will stop worrying about the donkeys and worry about us." ⁶But he said to him, "There is a man of God in this town; he is a man held in honor. Whatever he says always comes true. Let us go there now; perhaps he will tell us about the journey on which we have set out." ⁷Then Saul replied to the boy, "But if we go, what can we bring the man? For the bread in our sacks is gone, and there is no present to bring to the man of God. What have we?" ⁸The boy answered Saul again, "Here, I have with me a quarter shekel of silver; I will give it to the man of God, to tell us our way." ⁹(Formerly in Israel, anyone who went to inquire of God would say, "Come, let us go to the seer"; for the one who is now called a prophet was formerly called a seer.) ¹⁰Saul said to the boy, "Good; come, let us go." So they went to the town where the man of God was.

11 As they went up the hill to the town, they met some girls coming out to draw water, and said to them, "Is the seer here?" ¹²They answered, "Yes, there he is just ahead of you. Hurry; he has come just now to the town, because the people have a sacrifice today at the shrine. ¹³As soon as you enter the town, you will find him, before he goes up to the shrine to eat. For the people will not eat until he comes, since he must bless the sacrifice; afterward those eat who are invited. Now go up, for you will meet him immediately." ¹⁴So they went up to the town. As they were entering the town, they saw Samuel coming out toward them on his way up to the shrine.

15 Now the day before Saul

came, the LORD had revealed to Samuel: ¹⁶"Tomorrow about this time I will send to you a man from the land of Benjamin, and you shall anoint him to be ruler over my people Israel. He shall save my people from the hand of the Philistines; for I have seen the suffering of ᵇ my people, because their outcry has come to me." ¹⁷When Samuel saw Saul, the LORD told him, "Here is the man of whom I spoke to you. He it is who shall rule over my people." ¹⁸Then Saul approached Samuel inside the gate, and said, "Tell me, please, where is the house of the seer?" ¹⁹Samuel answered Saul, "I am the seer; go up before me to the shrine, for today you shall eat with me, and in the morning I will let you go and will tell you all that is on your mind. ²⁰As for your donkeys that were lost three days ago, give no further thought to them, for they have been found. And on whom is all Israel's desire fixed, if not on you and on all your ancestral house?" ²¹Saul answered, "I am only a Benjaminite, from the least of the tribes of Israel, and my family is the humblest of all the families of the tribe of Benjamin. Why then have you spoken to me in this way?"

22 Then Samuel took Saul and his servant-boy and brought them into the hall, and gave them a place at the head of those who had been invited, of whom there were about thirty. ²³And Samuel said to the cook, "Bring the portion I gave you, the one I asked you to put aside." ²⁴The cook took up the thigh and what went with it ᶜ and set them before Saul. Samuel said, "See, what was kept is set before you. Eat; for it is set ᵈ before you at the appointed time, so that you might eat with the guests." ᵉ

So Saul ate with Samuel that day. ²⁵When they came down from the shrine into the town, a bed was

9.5
1 Sam 10.2
9.6
Deut 33.1;
1 Sam 3.19
9.7
1 Kings 14.3;
2 Kings 8.8
9.9
2 Sam 24.11;
1 Chr 26.28;
Isa 30.10
9.11
Gen 24.15
9.12
Num 28.11-15;
1 Sam 7.17;
10.5

9.16
1 Sam 10.1;
Ex 3.7,9
9.17
1 Sam 16.12
9.20
v. 3;
1 Sam 8.5;
12.13
9.21
1 Sam 15.17;
Judg 20.46,
48
9.24
Lev 7.32,33;
Num 18.18
9.25
Deut 22.8;
Acts 10.9

ᵇGk: Heb lacks *the suffering of* ᶜMeaning of Heb uncertain ᵈQ Ms Gk: MT *it was kept* ᵉCn: Heb *it was kept for you, saying, I have invited the people*

spread for Saul[f] on the roof, and he lay down to sleep.[g] 26 Then at the break of dawn[h] Samuel called to Saul upon the roof, "Get up, so that I may send you on your way." Saul got up, and both he and Samuel went out into the street.

Samuel Anoints Saul

27 As they were going down to the outskirts of the town, Samuel said to Saul, "Tell the boy to go on before us, and when he has passed on, stop here yourself for a while, that I may make known to you the word of God." 1 Samuel took a vial of oil and poured it on his head, and kissed him; he said, "The LORD has anointed you ruler over his people Israel. You shall reign over the people of the LORD and you will save them from the hand of their enemies all around. Now this shall be the sign to you that the LORD has anointed you ruler[i] over his heritage: 2 When you depart from me today you will meet two men by Rachel's tomb in the territory of Benjamin at Zelzah; they will say to you, 'The donkeys that you went to seek are found, and now your father has stopped worrying about them and is worrying about you, saying: What shall I do about my son?' 3 Then you shall go on from there further and come to the oak of Tabor; three men going up to God at Bethel will meet you there, one carrying three kids, another carrying three loaves of bread, and another carrying a skin of wine. 4 They will greet you and give you two loaves of bread, which you shall accept from them. 5 After that you shall come to Gibeath-elohim,[j] at the place where the Philistine garrison is; there, as you come to the town, you will meet a band of prophets coming down from the shrine with harp, tambourine, flute, and lyre playing in front of them; they will be in a prophetic frenzy. 6 Then the spirit of the LORD will possess you, and you will be in a prophetic frenzy along with them and be turned into a different person. 7 Now when

these signs meet you, do whatever you see fit to do, for God is with you. 8 And you shall go down to Gilgal ahead of me; then I will come down to you to present burnt offerings and offer sacrifices of well-being. Seven days you shall wait, until I come to you and show you what you shall do."

Saul Prophesies

9 As he turned away to leave Samuel, God gave him another heart; and all these signs were fulfilled that day. 10 When they were going from there[k] to Gibeah,[l] a band of prophets met him; and the spirit of God possessed him, and he fell into a prophetic frenzy along with them. 11 When all who knew him before saw how he prophesied with the prophets, the people said to one another, "What has come over the son of Kish? Is Saul also among the prophets?" 12 A man of the place answered, "And who is their father?" Therefore it became a proverb, "Is Saul also among the prophets?" 13 When his prophetic frenzy had ended, he went home.[m]

14 Saul's uncle said to him and to the boy, "Where did you go?" And he replied, "To seek the donkeys; and when we saw they were not to be found, we went to Samuel." 15 Saul's uncle said, "Tell me what Samuel said to you." 16 Saul said to his uncle, "He told us that the donkeys had been found." But about the matter of the kingship, of which Samuel had spoken, he did not tell him anything.

Saul Proclaimed King

17 Samuel summoned the people to the LORD at Mizpah 18 and said to them,[n] "Thus says the LORD, the God of Israel, 'I brought up Israel out of Egypt, and I rescued you from the hand of the Egyptians and from the hand of all

10.1
1 Sam 16.13;
2 Kings 9.3,
6; Ps 2.11;
Deut 32.9;
Ps 78.71
10.2
Gen 35.19,
20;
1 Sam 9.3-5
10.3
Gen 28.22;
35.1,3,7,8
10.5
1 Sam 13.3;
9.12; 19.20;
2 Kings 3.15
10.6
Num 11.25,
29; v. 10;
1 Sam 19.23,
24
10.7
Josh 1.5;
Judg 6.12

10.8
1 Sam 11.15;
13.8
10.9
v. 6
10.10
w. 5,6;
1 Sam 19.20
10.11
1 Sam 19.24;
Mt 13.54,
55; Jn 7.15
10.16
1 Sam 9.20
10.17
1 Sam 7.5,
6
10.18
Judg 6.8,9

[f] Gk: Heb *and he spoke with Saul*
[g] Gk: Heb lacks *and he lay down to sleep*
[h] Gk: Heb *and they arose early and at break of dawn* [i] Gk: Heb *over his people Israel. You shall . . . anointed you ruler*
[j] Or *the Hill of God* [k] Gk: Heb *they came there* [l] Or *the hill* [m] Cn: Heb *he came to the shrine* [n] Heb *to the people of Israel*

the kingdoms that were oppressing you.' [19] But today you have rejected your God, who saves you from all your calamities and your distresses; and you have said, 'No! but set a king over us.' Now therefore present yourselves before the LORD by your tribes and by your clans."

20 Then Samuel brought all the tribes of Israel near, and the tribe of Benjamin was taken by lot. [21] He brought the tribe of Benjamin near by its families, and the family of the Matrites was taken by lot. Finally he brought the family of the Matrites near man by man,[o] and Saul the son of Kish was taken by lot. But when they sought him, he could not be found. [22] So they inquired again of the LORD, "Did the man come here?"[p] and the LORD said, "See, he has hidden himself among the baggage." [23] Then they ran and brought him from there. When he took his stand among the people, he was head and shoulders taller than any of them. [24] Samuel said to all the people, "Do you see the one whom the LORD has chosen? There is no one like him among all the people." And all the people shouted, "Long live the king!"

25 Samuel told the people the rights and duties of the kingship; and he wrote them in a book and laid it up before the LORD. Then Samuel sent all the people back to their homes. [26] Saul also went to his home at Gibeah, and with him went warriors whose hearts God had touched. [27] But some worthless fellows said, "How can this man save us?" They despised him and brought him no present. But he held his peace.

Now Nahash, king of the Ammonites, had been grievously oppressing the Gadites and the Reubenites. He would gouge out the right eye of each of them and would not grant Israel a deliverer. No one was left of the Israelites across the Jordan whose right eye Nahash, king of the Ammonites, had not gouged out. But there were seven thousand men who had escaped from the Ammonites and had entered Jabesh-gilead.[q]

Saul Defeats the Ammonites

11 About a month later,[r] Nahash the Ammonite went up and besieged Jabesh-gilead; and all the men of Jabesh said to Nahash, "Make a treaty with us, and we will serve you." [2] But Nahash the Ammonite said to them, "On this condition I will make a treaty with you, namely that I gouge out everyone's right eye, and thus put disgrace upon all Israel." [3] The elders of Jabesh said to him, "Give us seven days' respite that we may send messengers through all the territory of Israel. Then, if there is no one to save us, we will give ourselves up to you." [4] When the messengers came to Gibeah of Saul, they reported the matter in the hearing of the people; and all the people wept aloud.

5 Now Saul was coming from the field behind the oxen; and Saul said, "What is the matter with the people, that they are weeping?" So they told him the message from the inhabitants of Jabesh. [6] And the spirit of God came upon Saul in power when he heard these words, and his anger was greatly kindled. [7] He took a yoke of oxen, and cut them in pieces and sent them throughout all the territory of Israel by messengers, saying, "Whoever does not come out after Saul and Samuel, so shall it be done to his oxen!" Then the dread of the LORD fell upon the people, and they came out as one. [8] When he mustered them at Bezek, those from Israel were three hundred thousand, and those from Judah seventy[s] thousand. [9] They said to the messengers who had come, "Thus shall you say to the inhabitants of Jabesh-gilead: 'Tomorrow, by the time the sun is hot, you shall have deliverance.' " When the messen-

10.19 1 Sam 8.6, 7; Josh 24.1
10.20 Josh 7.14, 16,17
10.22 1 Sam 23.2, 4,9-11
10.23 1 Sam 9.2
10.24 2 Sam 21.6; 1 Kings 1.25, 39
10.25 1 Sam 8.11-18; Deut 17.14-20
10.26 1 Sam 11.4
10.27 1 Kings 10.25; 2 Chr 17.5

11.1 1 Sam 12.12; Judg 21.8; 1 Kings 20.34; Ezek 17.13
11.2 Num 16.14; 1 Sam 17.26
11.4 1 Sam 10.26; 15.34; 30.4; Judg 2.4
11.6 Judg 3.10; 6.34; 13.25; 14.6; 1 Sam 10.10; 16.13
11.7 Judg 19.29; 21.5,8,10
11.8 Judg 1.5; 20.2

o Gk: Heb lacks *Finally . . . man by man*
p Gk: Heb *Is there yet a man to come here?*
q Q Ms Compare Josephus, *Antiquities* VI.v.1 (68-71): MT lacks *Now Nahash . . . entered Jabesh-gilead.* r Q Ms Gk: MT lacks *About a month later* s Q Ms Gk: MT *thirty*

gers came and told the inhabitants of Jabesh, they rejoiced. 10 So the inhabitants of Jabesh said, "To-morrow we will give ourselves up to you, and you may do to us whatever seems good to you." 11 The next day Saul put the people in three com-panies. At the morning watch they came into the camp and cut down the Ammonites until the heat of the day; and those who survived were scattered, so that no two of them were left together.

12 The people said to Samuel, "Who is it that said, 'Shall Saul reign over us?' Give them to us so that we may put them to death." 13 But Saul said, "No one shall be put to death this day, for today the Lord has brought deliverance to Is-rael."

14 Samuel said to the people, "Come, let us go to Gilgal and there renew the kingship." 15 So all the people went to Gilgal, and there they made Saul king before the Lord in Gilgal. There they sacri-ficed offerings of well-being before the Lord, and there Saul and all the Israelites rejoiced greatly.

Samuel's Farewell Address

12 Samuel said to all Israel, "I have listened to you in all that you have said to me, and have set a king over you. 2 See, it is the king who leads you now; I am old and gray, but my sons are with you. I have led you from my youth until this day. 3 Here I am; testify against me before the Lord and before his anointed. Whose ox have I taken? Or whose donkey have I taken? Or whom have I defrauded? Whom have I oppressed? Or from whose hand have I taken a bribe to blind my eyes with it? Testify against me[t] and I will restore it to you." 4 They said, "You have not defraud-ed us or oppressed us or taken any-thing from the hand of anyone." 5 He said to them, "The Lord is wit-ness against you, and his anointed is witness this day, that you have not found anything in my hand." And they said, "He is witness."

6 Samuel said to the people,

"The Lord is witness, who[u] ap-pointed Moses and Aaron and brought your ancestors up out of the land of Egypt. 7 Now therefore take your stand, so that I may enter into judgment with you before the Lord, and I will declare to you[v] all the saving deeds of the Lord that he performed for you and for your an-cestors. 8 When Jacob went into Egypt and the Egyptians oppressed them,[w] then your ancestors cried to the Lord and the Lord sent Mo-ses and Aaron, who brought forth your ancestors out of Egypt, and settled them in this place. 9 But they forgot the Lord their God; and he sold them into the hand of Sis-era, commander of the army of King Jabin of[x] Hazor, and into the hand of the Philistines, and into the hand of the king of Moab; and they fought against them. 10 Then they cried to the Lord, and said, 'We have sinned, because we have forsaken the Lord, and have served the Baals and the Astartes; but now rescue us out of the hand of our en-emies, and we will serve you.' 11 And the Lord sent Jerubbaal and Barak,[y] and Jephthah, and Sam-son,[z] and rescued you out of the hand of your enemies on every side; and you lived in safety. 12 But when you saw that King Nahash of the Ammonites came against you, you said to me, 'No, but a king shall reign over us,' though the Lord your God was your king. 13 See, here is the king whom you have chosen, for whom you have asked; see, the Lord has set a king over you. 14 If you will fear the Lord and serve him and heed his voice and not rebel against the com-mandment of the Lord, and if both you and the king who reigns over you will follow the Lord your God, it will be well; 15 but if you will not heed the voice of the Lord, but re-bel against the commandment of

11.10
v. 3
11.11
Judg 7.16
11.12
1 Sam 10.27;
Lk 19.27
11.13
2 Sam 19.22;
Ex 14.13;
1 Sam 19.5
11.14
1 Sam 10.8,
25
11.15
1 Sam 10.8,
17
12.1
1 Sam 8.7,
9,22; 10.24;
11.14,15
12.2
1 Sam 8.1,
5,20
12.3
1 Sam 10.1;
24.6;
2 Sam 1.14;
Num 16.15;
Acts 20.33;
Deut 16.19
12.5
Acts 23.9;
24.20;
Ex 22.4
12.6
Ex 6.26

12.7
Isa 1.18;
Mic 6.1-5
12.8
Ex 2.23;
3.10; 4.16
12.9
Judg 3.7;
4.2; 10.7;
13.1; 3.12
12.10
Judg 10.10;
2.13; 10.15
12.11
Judg 6.14,
32; 4.6; 11.1
12.12
1 Sam 11.1;
8.6,19;
Judg 8.23
12.13
1 Sam 10.24;
8.5;
Hos 13.11
12.14
Josh 24.14
12.15
Josh 24.20

t Gk: Heb lacks *Testify against me*
u Gk: Heb lacks *is witness, who*
v Gk: Heb lacks *and I will declare to you*
w Gk: Heb lacks *and the Egyptians oppressed them* x Gk: Heb lacks *Jabin king of*
y Gk Syr: Heb *Bedan* z Gk: Heb *Samuel*

the LORD, then the hand of the LORD will be against you and your king.[a] [16]Now therefore take your stand and see this great thing that the LORD will do before your eyes. [17]Is it not the wheat harvest today? I will call upon the LORD, that he may send thunder and rain; and you shall know and see that the wickedness that you have done in the sight of the LORD is great in demanding a king for yourselves." [18]So Samuel called upon the LORD, and the LORD sent thunder and rain that day; and all the people greatly feared the LORD and Samuel.

19 All the people said to Samuel, "Pray to the LORD your God for your servants, so that we may not die; for we have added to all our sins the evil of demanding a king for ourselves." [20]And Samuel said to the people, "Do not be afraid; you have done all this evil, yet do not turn aside from following the LORD, but serve the LORD with all your heart; [21]and do not turn aside after useless things that cannot profit or save, for they are useless. [22]For the LORD will not cast away his people, for his great name's sake, because it has pleased the LORD to make you a people for himself. [23]Moreover as for me, far be it from me that I should sin against the LORD by ceasing to pray for you; and I will instruct you in the good and the right way. [24]Only fear the LORD, and serve him faithfully with all your heart; for consider what great things he has done for you. [25]But if you still do wickedly, you shall be swept away, both you and your king."

Saul's Unlawful Sacrifice

13 Saul was ...[b] years old when he began to reign; and he reigned ... and two[c] years over Israel.

2 Saul chose three thousand out of Israel; two thousand were with Saul in Michmash and the hill country of Bethel, and a thousand were with Jonathan in Gibeah of Benjamin; the rest of the people he

sent home to their tents. [3]Jonathan defeated the garrison of the Philistines that was at Geba; and the Philistines heard of it. And Saul blew the trumpet throughout all the land, saying, "Let the Hebrews hear!" [4]When all Israel heard that Saul had defeated the garrison of the Philistines, and also that Israel had become odious to the Philistines, the people were called out to join Saul at Gilgal.

5 The Philistines mustered to fight with Israel, thirty thousand chariots, and six thousand horsemen, and troops like the sand on the seashore in multitude; they came up and encamped at Michmash, to the east of Beth-aven. [6]When the Israelites saw that they were in distress (for the troops were hard pressed), the people hid themselves in caves and in holes and in rocks and in tombs and in cisterns. [7]Some Hebrews crossed the Jordan to the land of Gad and Gilead. Saul was still at Gilgal, and all the people followed him trembling.

8 He waited seven days, the time appointed by Samuel; but Samuel did not come to Gilgal, and the people began to slip away from Saul.[d] [9]So Saul said, "Bring the burnt offering here to me, and the offerings of well-being." And he offered the burnt offering. [10]As soon as he had finished offering the burnt offering, Samuel arrived; and Saul went out to meet him and salute him. [11]Samuel said, "What have you done?" Saul replied, "When I saw that the people were slipping away from me, and that you did not come within the days appointed, and that the Philistines were mustering at Michmash, [12]I said, 'Now the Philistines will come down upon me at Gilgal, and I have not entreated the favor of the LORD'; so I forced myself, and offered the burnt offering." [13]Samuel

Cross references

12.16 Ex 14.13,31
12.17 Prov 26.1; 1 Sam 7.9, 10; 8.7
12.18 Ex 14.31
12.19 v. 23; Ex 9.28; Jas 5.15
12.21 Deut 11.16; Jer 16.19; Hab 2.18
12.22 1 Kings 6.13; Josh 7.9; Deut 7.7,8
12.23 Rom 1.9; Col 1.9; 2 Tim 1.3; 1 Kings 8.36
12.24 Eccl 12.13; Deut 10.21
12.25 Josh 24.20; 1 Sam 31.1-5
13.2 1 Sam 10.26
13.3 1 Sam 10.5
13.5 Josh 11.4
13.6 Judg 6.2
13.8 1 Sam 10.8
13.9 2 Sam 24.25
13.10 1 Sam 15.13
13.11 vv. 2,5,16, 23
13.13 2 Chr 16.9; 1 Sam 15.11, 22

[a] Gk: Heb *and your ancestors* [b] The number is lacking in the Heb text (the verse is lacking in the Septuagint). [c] *Two* is not the entire number; something has dropped out. [d] Heb *him*

said to Saul, "You have done foolishly; you have not kept the commandment of the LORD your God, which he commanded you. The LORD would have established your kingdom over Israel forever, [14] but now your kingdom will not continue; the LORD has sought out a man after his own heart; and the LORD has appointed him to be ruler over his people, because you have not kept what the LORD commanded you." [15] And Samuel left and went on his way from Gilgal. [e] The rest of the people followed Saul to join the army; they went up from Gilgal toward Gibeah of Benjamin. [f]

Preparations for Battle

Saul counted the people who were present with him, about six hundred men. [16] Saul, his son Jonathan, and the people who were present with them stayed in Geba of Benjamin; but the Philistines encamped at Michmash. [17] And raiders came out of the camp of the Philistines in three companies; one company turned toward Ophrah, to the land of Shual, [18] another company turned toward Beth-horon, and another company turned toward the mountain[g] that looks down upon the valley of Zeboim toward the wilderness.

[19] Now there was no smith to be found throughout all the land of Israel; for the Philistines said, "The Hebrews must not make swords or spears for themselves"; [20] so all the Israelites went down to the Philistines to sharpen their plowshare, mattocks, axes, or sickles; [h] [21] The charge was two-thirds of a shekel [i] for the plowshares and for the mattocks, and one-third of a shekel for sharpening the axes and for setting the goads. [j] [22] So on the day of the battle neither sword nor spear was to be found in the possession of any of the people with Saul and Jonathan; but Saul and his son Jonathan had them.

Jonathan Surprises and Routs the Philistines

[23] Now a garrison of the Philis-

13.14
1 Sam 15.28;
Acts 13.22
13.15
1 Sam 14.2
13.17
1 Sam 14.15
13.18
Josh 18.13,
14;
Neh 11.34
13.19
2 Kings 24.14
13.22
Judg 5.8

14.2
1 Sam 13.15
14.3
1 Sam 22.9-12,
20; 4.21; 2.28
14.4
1 Sam 13.23
14.6
Judg 7.4,7;
1 Sam 17.46,
47
14.10
Gen 24.14;
Judg 6.36,
37
14.11
1 Sam 13.6

tines had gone out to the pass of Michmash. [1] One day Jonathan son of Saul said to the young man who carried his armor, "Come, let us go over to the Philistine garrison on the other side." But he did not tell his father. [2] Saul was staying in the outskirts of Gibeah under the pomegranate tree that is at Migron; the troops that were with him were about six hundred men, [3] along with Ahijah son of Ahitub, Ichabod's brother, son of Phinehas son of Eli, the priest of the LORD in Shiloh, carrying an ephod. Now the people did not know that Jonathan had gone. [4] In the pass, [k] by which Jonathan tried to go over to the Philistine garrison, there was a rocky crag on one side and a rocky crag on the other; the name of the one was Bozez, and the name of the other Seneh. [5] One crag rose on the north in front of Michmash, and the other on the south in front of Geba.

[6] Jonathan said to the young man who carried his armor, "Come, let us go over to the garrison of these uncircumcised; it may be that the LORD will act for us; for nothing can hinder the LORD from saving by many or by few." [7] His armor-bearer said to him, "Do all that your mind inclines to. [l] I am with you; as your mind is, so is mine." [m] [8] Then Jonathan said, "Now we will cross over to those men and will show ourselves to them. [9] If they say to us, 'Wait until we come to you,' then we will stand still in our place, and we will not go up to them. [10] But if they say, 'Come up to us,' then we will go up; for the LORD has given them into our hand. That will be the sign for us." [11] So both of them showed themselves to the garrison of the Philistines; and the Philistines

[e] Gk: Heb *went up from Gilgal to Gibeah of Benjamin* [f] Gk: Heb lacks *The rest . . . of Benjamin* [g] Cn Compare Gk: Heb *toward the border* [h] Gk: Heb *plowshare* [i] Heb *was a pim* [j] Cn: Meaning of Heb uncertain [k] Heb *Between the passes* [l] Gk: Heb *Do all that is in your mind. Turn* [m] Gk: Heb lacks *so is mine*

said, "Look, Hebrews are coming out of the holes where they have hidden themselves." [12] The men of the garrison hailed Jonathan and his armor-bearer, saying, "Come up to us, and we will show you something." Jonathan said to his armor-bearer, "Come up after me; for the LORD has given them into the hand of Israel." [13] Then Jonathan climbed up on his hands and feet, with his armor-bearer following after him. The Philistines[n] fell before Jonathan, and his armor-bearer, coming after him, killed them. [14] In that first slaughter Jonathan and his armor-bearer killed about twenty men within an area about half a furrow long in an acre[o] of land. [15] There was a panic in the camp, in the field, and among all the people; the garrison and even the raiders trembled; the earth quaked; and it became a very great panic.

[16] Saul's lookouts in Gibeah of Benjamin were watching as the multitude was surging back and forth.[p] [17] Then Saul said to the troops that were with him, "Call the roll and see who has gone from us." When they had called the roll, Jonathan and his armor-bearer were not there. [18] Saul said to Ahijah, "Bring the ark[q] of God here." For at that time the ark[q] of God went with the Israelites. [19] While Saul was talking to the priest, the tumult in the camp of the Philistines increased more and more; and Saul said to the priest, "Withdraw your hand." [20] Then Saul and all the people who were with him rallied and went into the battle; and every sword was against the other, so that there was very great confusion. [21] Now the Hebrews who previously had been with the Philistines and had gone up with them into the camp turned and joined the Israelites who were with Saul and Jonathan. [22] Likewise, when all the Israelites who had gone into hiding in the hill country of Ephraim heard that the Philistines were fleeing, they too followed closely after them in the bat-

tle. [23] So the LORD gave Israel the victory that day.

The battle passed beyond Bethaven, and the troops with Saul numbered altogether about ten thousand men. The battle spread out over the hill country of Ephraim.

Saul's Rash Oath

24 Now Saul committed a very rash act on that day.[r] He had laid an oath on the troops, saying, "Cursed be anyone who eats food before it is evening and I have been avenged on my enemies." So none of the troops tasted food. [25] All the troops[s] came upon a honeycomb; and there was honey on the ground. [26] When the troops came upon the honeycomb, the honey was dripping out; but they did not put their hands to their mouths, for they feared the oath. [27] But Jonathan had not heard his father charge the troops with the oath; so he extended the staff that was in his hand, and dipped the tip of it in the honeycomb, and put his hand to his mouth; and his eyes brightened. [28] Then one of the soldiers said, "Your father strictly charged the troops with an oath, saying, 'Cursed be anyone who eats food this day.' And so the troops are faint." [29] Then Jonathan said, "My father has troubled the land; see how my eyes have brightened because I tasted a little of this honey. [30] How much better if today the troops had eaten freely of the spoil taken from their enemies; for now the slaughter among the Philistines has not been great."

31 After they had struck down the Philistines that day from Michmash to Aijalon, the troops were very faint; [32] so the troops flew upon the spoil, and took sheep and oxen and calves, and slaughtered them on the ground; and the troops ate them with the blood. [33] Then it was reported to Saul, "Look, the

14.12
1 Sam 17.43, 44;
2 Sam 5.24
14.15
2 Kings 7.6, 7;
1 Sam 13.17
14.16
2 Sam 18.24
14.19
Num 27.21
14.20
Judg 7.22;
2 Chr 20.23
14.22
1 Sam 13.6

14.23
Ex 14.30;
Ps 44.6,7;
1 Sam 13.5
14.24
Josh 6.26
14.27
1 Sam 30.12
14.29
1 Kings 18.18
14.32
1 Sam 15.19;
Lev 17.10-14

n Heb They　o Heb yoke　p Gk: Heb
they went and there　q Gk the ephod
r Gk: Heb The Israelites were distressed that
day　s Heb land

troops are sinning against the LORD by eating with the blood." And he said, "You have dealt treacherously; roll a large stone before me here."ᵗ ³⁴Saul said, "Disperse yourselves among the troops, and say to them, 'Let all bring their oxen or their sheep, and slaughter them here, and eat; and do not sin against the LORD by eating with the blood.'" So all of the troops brought their oxen with them that night, and slaughtered them there. ³⁵And Saul built an altar to the LORD; it was the first altar that he built to the LORD.

Jonathan in Danger of Death

36 Then Saul said, "Let us go down after the Philistines by night and despoil them until the morning light; let us not leave one of them." They said, "Do whatever seems good to you." But the priest said, "Let us draw near to God here." ³⁷So Saul inquired of God, "Shall I go down after the Philistines? Will you give them into the hand of Israel?" But he did not answer him that day. ³⁸Saul said, "Come here, all you leaders of the people; and let us find out how this sin has arisen today. ³⁹For as the LORD lives who saves Israel, even if it is in my son Jonathan, he shall surely die!" But there was no one among all the people who answered him. ⁴⁰He said to all Israel, "You shall be on one side, and I and my son Jonathan will be on the other side." The people said to Saul, "Do what seems good to you." ⁴¹Then Saul said, "O LORD God of Israel, why have you not answered your servant today? If this guilt is in me or in my son Jonathan, O LORD God of Israel, give Urim; but if this guilt is in your people Israel,ᵘ give Thummim." And Jonathan and Saul were indicated by the lot, but the people were cleared. ⁴²Then Saul said, "Cast the lot between me and my son Jonathan." And Jonathan was taken.

43 Then Saul said to Jonathan, "Tell me what you have done."

Jonathan told him, "I tasted a little honey with the tip of the staff that was in my hand; here I am, I will die." ⁴⁴Saul said, "God do so to me and more also; you shall surely die, Jonathan!" ⁴⁵Then the people said to Saul, "Shall Jonathan die, who has accomplished this great victory in Israel? Far from it! As the LORD lives, not one hair of his head shall fall to the ground; for he has worked with God today." So the people ransomed Jonathan, and he did not die. ⁴⁶Then Saul withdrew from pursuing the Philistines; and the Philistines went to their own place.

Saul's Continuing Wars

47 When Saul had taken the kingship over Israel, he fought against all his enemies on every side—against Moab, against the Ammonites, against Edom, against the kings of Zobah, and against the Philistines; wherever he turned he routed them. ⁴⁸He did valiantly, and struck down the Amalekites, and rescued Israel out of the hands of those who plundered them.

49 Now the sons of Saul were Jonathan, Ishvi, and Malchishua; and the names of his two daughters were these: the name of the firstborn was Merab, and the name of the younger, Michal. ⁵⁰The name of Saul's wife was Ahinoam daughter of Ahimaaz. And the name of the commander of his army was Abner son of Ner, Saul's uncle; ⁵¹Kish was the father of Saul, and Ner the father of Abner was the son of Abiel.

52 There was hard fighting against the Philistines all the days of Saul; and when Saul saw any strong or valiant warrior, he took him into his service.

Saul Defeats the Amalekites but Spares Their King

15 Samuel said to Saul, "The LORD sent me to anoint you king over his people Israel; now therefore listen to the words of the

14.35
1 Sam 7.17
14.37
1 Sam 10.22;
28.6
14.38
Josh 7.14;
1 Sam 10.19
14.39
2 Sam 12.5
14.41
Prov 16.33;
Acts 1.24
14.43
Josh 7.19;
v. 23

14.44
Ruth 1.17;
v. 39
14.45
2 Sam 14.11;
1 Kings 1.52;
Acts 27.34
14.47
1 Sam 11.1-13;
2 Sam 10.6;
v. 52
14.48
1 Sam 15.3,
7
14.49
1 Sam 31.2;
1 Chr 8.33;
1 Sam 18.17-
20
14.50
2 Sam 2.8
14.51
1 Sam 9.1
14.52
1 Sam 8.11
15.1
1 Sam 9.16

ᵗ Gk: Heb *me this day* ᵘ Vg Compare Gk: Heb ⁴¹*Saul said to the LORD, the God of Israel*

LORD. ²Thus says the LORD of hosts, 'I will punish the Amalekites for what they did in opposing the Israelites when they came up out of Egypt. ³Now go and attack Amalek, and utterly destroy all that they have; do not spare them, but kill both man and woman, child and infant, ox and sheep, camel and donkey.' "

4 So Saul summoned the people, and numbered them in Telaim, two hundred thousand foot soldiers, and ten thousand soldiers of Judah. ⁵Saul came to the city of the Amalekites and lay in wait in the valley. ⁶Saul said to the Kenites, "Go! Leave! Withdraw from among the Amalekites, or I will destroy you with them; for you showed kindness to all the people of Israel when they came up out of Egypt." So the Kenites withdrew from the Amalekites. ⁷Saul defeated the Amalekites, from Havilah as far as Shur, which is east of Egypt. ⁸He took King Agag of the Amalekites alive, but utterly destroyed all the people with the edge of the sword. ⁹Saul and the people spared Agag, and the best of the sheep and of the cattle and of the fatlings, and the lambs, and all that was valuable, and would not utterly destroy them; all that was despised and worthless they utterly destroyed.

Saul Rejected as King

10 The word of the LORD came to Samuel: ¹¹"I regret that I made Saul king, for he has turned back from following me, and has not carried out my commands." Samuel was angry; and he cried out to the LORD all night. ¹²Samuel rose early in the morning to meet Saul, and Samuel was told, "Saul went to Carmel, where he set up a monument for himself, and on returning he passed on down to Gilgal." ¹³When Samuel came to Saul, Saul said to him, "May you be blessed by the LORD; I have carried out the command of the LORD." ¹⁴But Samuel said, "What then is this bleating of sheep in my ears, and the lowing of cattle that I hear?" ¹⁵Saul

said, "They have brought them from the Amalekites; for the people spared the best of the sheep and the cattle, to sacrifice to the LORD your God; but the rest we have utterly destroyed." ¹⁶Then Samuel said to Saul, "Stop! I will tell you what the LORD said to me last night." He replied, "Speak."

17 Samuel said, "Though you are little in your own eyes, are you not the head of the tribes of Israel? The LORD anointed you king over Israel. ¹⁸And the LORD sent you on a mission, and said, 'Go, utterly destroy the sinners, the Amalekites, and fight against them until they are consumed.' ¹⁹Why then did you not obey the voice of the LORD? Why did you swoop down on the spoil, and do what was evil in the sight of the LORD?" ²⁰Saul said to Samuel, "I have obeyed the voice of the LORD, I have gone on the mission on which the LORD sent me, I have brought Agag the king of Amalek, and I have utterly destroyed the Amalekites. ²¹But from the spoil the people took sheep and cattle, the best of the things devoted to destruction, to sacrifice to the LORD your God in Gilgal." ²²And Samuel said,

"Has the LORD as great
 delight in burnt
 offerings and sacrifices,
 as in obeying the voice of
 the LORD?
Surely, to obey is better than
 sacrifice,
 and to heed than the fat of
 rams.
²³ For rebellion is no less a sin
 than divination,
 and stubbornness is like
 iniquity and idolatry.
Because you have rejected
 the word of the LORD,
 he has also rejected you
 from being king."

24 Saul said to Samuel, "I have sinned; for I have transgressed the commandment of the LORD and your words, because I feared the people and obeyed their voice. ²⁵Now therefore, I pray, pardon my sin, and return with me, so that I

Cross references

15.2 Ex 17.8-14; Num 24.20; Deut 25.17-19
15.3 Num 24.20; Deut 20.16-18; 1 Sam 22.19
15.6 Judg 1.16; 4.11; Ex 18.10, 19; Num 10.29-32
15.7 1 Sam 14.48; Gen 16.7; 25.17,18; Ex 15.22
15.8 1 Kings 20.34ff; 1 Sam 30.1
15.9 vv. 3,15
15.11 Gen 6.6,7; 2 Sam 24.16; 1 Kings 9.6, 7; 1 Sam 16.1
15.12 Josh 15.55
15.13 Gen 14.19; Judg 17.2
15.15 vv. 9,21; Gen 3.12
15.17 1 Sam 9.21
15.18 v. 3
15.19 1 Sam 14.32
15.20 v. 13
15.21 v. 15
15.22 Isa 1.11-13; Mic 6.6-8; Heb 10.6-9; Hos 6.6; Mk 12.33
15.23 1 Sam 13.14
15.24 2 Sam 12.13; Prov 29.25; Isa 51.12,13

may worship the LORD." [26] Samuel said to Saul, "I will not return with you; for you have rejected the word of the LORD, and the LORD has rejected you from being king over Israel." [27] As Samuel turned to go away, Saul caught hold of the hem of his robe, and it tore. [28] And Samuel said to him, "The LORD has torn the kingdom of Israel from you this very day, and has given it to a neighbor of yours, who is better than you. [29] Moreover the Glory of Israel will not recant[v] or change his mind; for he is not a mortal, that he should change his mind." [30] Then Saul[w] said, "I have sinned; yet honor me now before the elders of my people and before Israel, and return with me, so that I may worship the LORD your God." [31] So Samuel turned back after Saul; and Saul worshiped the LORD.

32 Then Samuel said, "Bring Agag king of the Amalekites here to me." And Agag came to him haltingly.[x] Agag said, "Surely this is the bitterness of death."[y] [33] But Samuel said,

"As your sword has made
　　women childless,
so your mother shall be
　　childless among
　　women."

And Samuel hewed Agag in pieces before the LORD in Gilgal.

34 Then Samuel went to Ramah; and Saul went up to his house in Gibeah of Saul. [35] Samuel did not see Saul again until the day of his death, but Samuel grieved over Saul. And the LORD was sorry that he had made Saul king over Israel.

David Anointed as King

16 The LORD said to Samuel, "How long will you grieve over Saul? I have rejected him from being king over Israel. Fill your horn with oil and set out; I will send you to Jesse the Bethlehemite, for I have provided for myself a king among his sons." [2] Samuel said, "How can I go? If Saul hears of it, he will kill me." And the LORD said, "Take a heifer with you, and say, 'I have come to sacrifice to the

LORD.' [3] Invite Jesse to the sacrifice, and I will show you what you shall do; and you shall anoint for me the one whom I name to you." [4] Samuel did what the LORD commanded, and came to Bethlehem. The elders of the city came to meet him trembling, and said, "Do you come peaceably?" [5] He said, "Peaceably; I have come to sacrifice to the LORD; sanctify yourselves and come with me to the sacrifice." And he sanctified Jesse and his sons and invited them to the sacrifice.

6 When they came, he looked on Eliab and thought, "Surely the LORD's anointed is now before the LORD."[z] [7] But the LORD said to Samuel, "Do not look on his appearance or on the height of his stature, because I have rejected him; for the LORD does not see as mortals see; they look on the outward appearance, but the LORD looks on the heart." [8] Then Jesse called Abinadab, and made him pass before Samuel. He said, "Neither has the LORD chosen this one." [9] Then Jesse made Shammah pass by. And he said, "Neither has the LORD chosen this one." [10] Jesse made seven of his sons pass before Samuel, and Samuel said to Jesse, "The LORD has not chosen any of these." [11] Samuel said to Jesse, "Are all your sons here?" And he said, "There remains yet the youngest, but he is keeping the sheep." And Samuel said to Jesse, "Send and bring him; for we will not sit down until he comes here." [12] He sent and brought him in. Now he was ruddy, and had beautiful eyes, and was handsome. The LORD said, "Rise and anoint him; for this is the one." [13] Then Samuel took the horn of oil, and anointed him in the presence of his brothers; and the spirit of the LORD came mightily upon David from that day forward. Samuel then set out and went to Ramah.

15.26
1 Sam 13.14
15.27
1 Kings 11.30, 31
15.28
1 Sam 28.17
15.29
1 Chr 29.11; Num 23.19; Ezek 24.14
15.30
Jn 12.43; Isa 29.13
15.33
Gen 9.6; Judg 1.7
15.34
1 Sam 7.17; 11.4
15.35
1 Sam 19.24; 16.1
16.1
1 Sam 15.23, 35; 9.16; 2 Kings 9.1; Ps 78.70; Acts 13.22
16.2
1 Sam 20.29

16.3
Ex 4.15; 1 Sam 9.16
16.4
Lk 2.4; 1 Kings 2.13; 2 Kings 9.22
16.5
Ex 19.10
16.6
1 Sam 17.13
16.7
Isa 55.8; 1 Kings 8.39; 1 Chr 28.9
16.8
1 Sam 17.13
16.9
1 Sam 17.13
16.11
1 Sam 17.12
16.12
1 Sam 17.42; 9.17
16.13
1 Sam 10.1, 6,9,10; Judg 11.29

[v] Q Ms Gk: MT *deceive*　　[w] Heb *he*
[x] Cn Compare Gk: Meaning of Heb uncertain
[y] Q Ms Gk: MT *Surely the bitterness of death is past*　　[z] Heb *him*

David Plays the Lyre for Saul

14 Now the spirit of the LORD departed from Saul, and an evil spirit from the LORD tormented him. [15] And Saul's servants said to him, "See now, an evil spirit from God is tormenting you. [16] Let our lord now command the servants who attend you to look for someone who is skillful in playing the lyre; and when the evil spirit from God is upon you, he will play it, and you will feel better." [17] So Saul said to his servants, "Provide for me someone who can play well, and bring him to me." [18] One of the young men answered, "I have seen a son of Jesse the Bethlehemite who is skillful in playing, a man of valor, a warrior, prudent in speech, and a man of good presence; and the LORD is with him." [19] So Saul sent messengers to Jesse, and said, "Send me your son David who is with the sheep." [20] Jesse took a donkey loaded with bread, a skin of wine, and a kid, and sent them by his son David to Saul. [21] And David came to Saul, and entered his service. Saul loved him greatly, and he became his armor-bearer. [22] Saul sent to Jesse, saying, "Let David remain in my service, for he has found favor in my sight." [23] And whenever the evil spirit from God came upon Saul, David took the lyre and played it with his hand, and Saul would be relieved and feel better, and the evil spirit would depart from him.

David and Goliath

17 Now the Philistines gathered their armies for battle; they were gathered at Socoh, which belongs to Judah, and encamped between Socoh and Azekah, in Ephes-dammim. [2] Saul and the Israelites gathered and encamped in the valley of Elah, and formed ranks against the Philistines. [3] The Philistines stood on the mountain on the one side, and Israel stood on the mountain on the other side, with a valley between them. [4] And there came out from the camp of the Philistines a champion named Goliath, of Gath, whose height was six[a] cubits and a span. [5] He had a helmet of bronze on his head, and he was armed with a coat of mail; the weight of the coat was five thousand shekels of bronze. [6] He had greaves of bronze on his legs and a javelin of bronze slung between his shoulders. [7] The shaft of his spear was like a weaver's beam, and his spear's head weighed six hundred shekels of iron; and his shield-bearer went before him. [8] He stood and shouted to the ranks of Israel, "Why have you come out to draw up for battle? Am I not a Philistine, and are you not servants of Saul? Choose a man for yourselves, and let him come down to me. [9] If he is able to fight with me and kill me, then we will be your servants; but if I prevail against him and kill him, then you shall be our servants and serve us." [10] And the Philistine said, "Today I defy the ranks of Israel! Give me a man, that we may fight together." [11] When Saul and all Israel heard these words of the Philistine, they were dismayed and greatly afraid.

12 Now David was the son of an Ephrathite of Bethlehem in Judah, named Jesse, who had eight sons. In the days of Saul the man was already old and advanced in years.[b] [13] The three eldest sons of Jesse had followed Saul to the battle; the names of his three sons who went to the battle were Eliab the firstborn, and next to him Abinadab, and the third Shammah. [14] David was the youngest; the three eldest followed Saul, [15] but David went back and forth from Saul to feed his father's sheep at Bethlehem. [16] For forty days the Philistine came forward and took his stand, morning and evening.

17 Jesse said to his son David, "Take for your brothers an ephah of this parched grain and these ten loaves, and carry them quickly to the camp to your brothers; [18] also take these ten cheeses to the com-

Cross references (center column)

16.14
Judg 16.20;
1 Sam 18.10
16.16
v. 23;
1 Sam 18.10;
19.9;
2 Kings 3.15
16.18
1 Sam 17.32-
36; 3.19
16.20
1 Sam 10.27;
Prov 18.16
16.21f
Gen 41.46;
Prov 22.29
16.23
vv. 14-16
17.1
1 Sam 13.5;
2 Chr 28.18
17.2
1 Sam 21.9
17.4
2 Sam 21.19;
Josh 11.21,
22

17.6
v. 45
17.7
2 Sam 21.19;
v. 41
17.8
1 Sam 8.17
17.10
vv. 26,36,45
17.12
Ruth 4.22;
1 Sam 16.18;
Gen 35.19;
1 Sam 16.10,
11;
1 Chr 2.13-15
17.13
1 Sam 16.6,
8,9
17.15
1 Sam 16.19
17.18
Gen 37.14

[a] MT: Q Ms Gk *four* [b] Gk Syr: Heb *among men*

DAVID'S FAMILY TREE

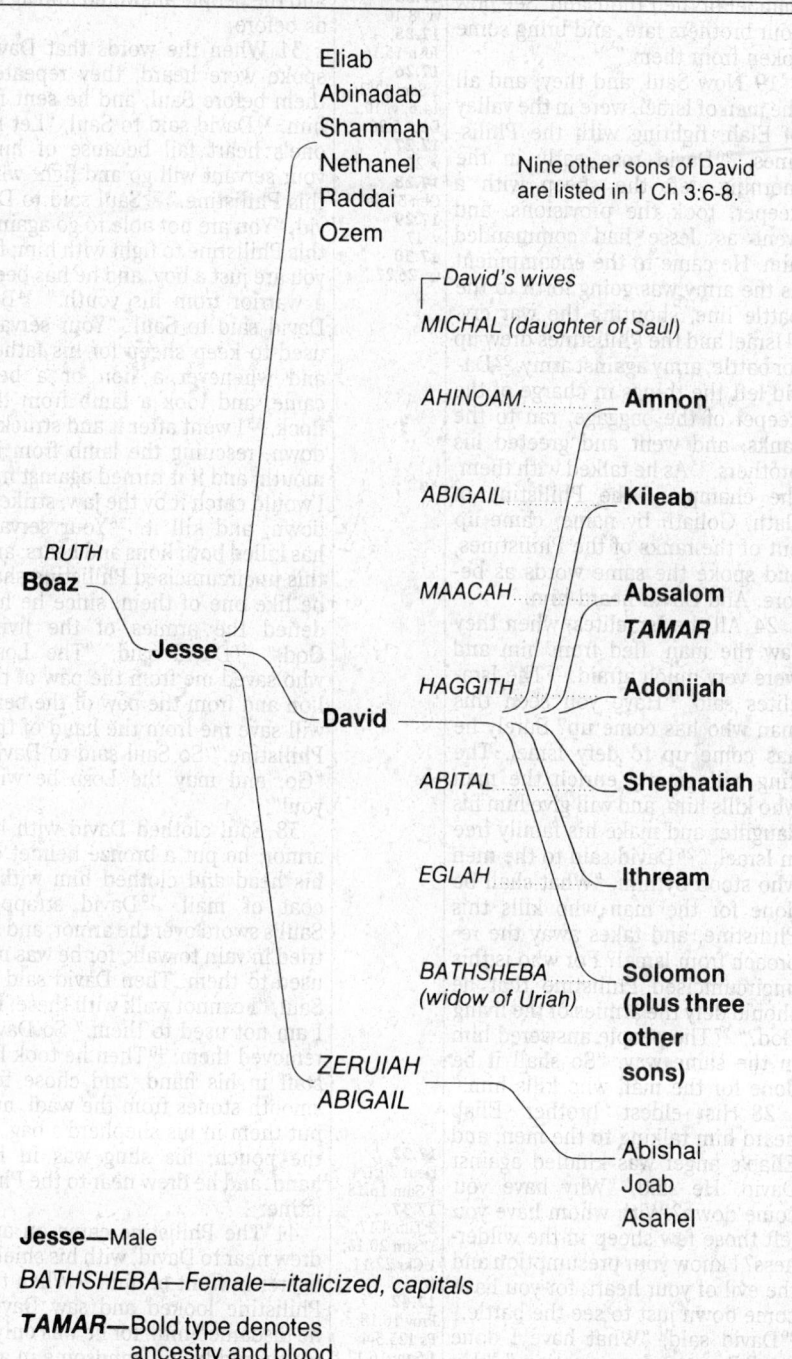

Eliab
Abinadab
Shammah
Nethanel
Raddai
Ozem

Nine other sons of David
are listed in 1 Ch 3:6-8.

RUTH
Boaz

Jesse

David's wives

MICHAL (daughter of Saul)

AHINOAM **Amnon**

ABIGAIL **Kileab**

MAACAH **Absalom**
TAMAR

HAGGITH **Adonijah**

David

ABITAL **Shephatiah**

EGLAH **Ithream**

BATHSHEBA
(widow of Uriah) **Solomon
(plus three
other
sons)**

ZERUIAH
ABIGAIL

Abishai
Joab
Asahel

Jesse—Male

BATHSHEBA—Female—italicized, capitals

TAMAR—Bold type denotes
ancestry and blood
line of David

mander of their thousand. See how your brothers fare, and bring some token from them."

19 Now Saul, and they, and all the men of Israel, were in the valley of Elah, fighting with the Philistines. ²⁰David rose early in the morning, left the sheep with a keeper, took the provisions, and went as Jesse had commanded him. He came to the encampment as the army was going forth to the battle line, shouting the war cry. ²¹Israel and the Philistines drew up for battle, army against army. ²²David left the things in charge of the keeper of the baggage, ran to the ranks, and went and greeted his brothers. ²³As he talked with them, the champion, the Philistine of Gath, Goliath by name, came up out of the ranks of the Philistines, and spoke the same words as before. And David heard him.

24 All the Israelites, when they saw the man, fled from him and were very much afraid. ²⁵The Israelites said, "Have you seen this man who has come up? Surely he has come up to defy Israel. The king will greatly enrich the man who kills him, and will give him his daughter and make his family free in Israel." ²⁶David said to the men who stood by him, "What shall be done for the man who kills this Philistine, and takes away the reproach from Israel? For who is this uncircumcised Philistine that he should defy the armies of the living God?" ²⁷The people answered him in the same way, "So shall it be done for the man who kills him."

28 His eldest brother Eliab heard him talking to the men; and Eliab's anger was kindled against David. He said, "Why have you come down? With whom have you left those few sheep in the wilderness? I know your presumption and the evil of your heart; for you have come down just to see the battle." ²⁹David said, "What have I done now? It was only a question." ³⁰He turned away from him toward another and spoke in the same way;

17.23
vv. 8-10
17.25
Josh 15.16
17.26
1 Sam 11.2;
14.6; v. 10;
Deut 5.26
17.27
v. 25
17.28
Gen 37.4ff
17.29
v. 17
17.30
vv. 26,27

17.32
Deut 20.1-4;
1 Sam 16.18
17.37
2 Tim 4.17;
1 Sam 20.13;
1 Chr 22.11,
16
17.42
Prov 16.18;
Ps 123.3,4;
1 Sam 16.12
17.43
1 Sam 24.14;
2 Sam 3.8

and the people answered him again as before.

31 When the words that David spoke were heard, they repeated them before Saul; and he sent for him. ³²David said to Saul, "Let no one's heart fail because of him; your servant will go and fight with this Philistine." ³³Saul said to David, "You are not able to go against this Philistine to fight with him; for you are just a boy, and he has been a warrior from his youth." ³⁴But David said to Saul, "Your servant used to keep sheep for his father; and whenever a lion or a bear came, and took a lamb from the flock, ³⁵I went after it and struck it down, rescuing the lamb from its mouth; and if it turned against me, I would catch it by the jaw, strike it down, and kill it. ³⁶Your servant has killed both lions and bears; and this uncircumcised Philistine shall be like one of them, since he has defied the armies of the living God." ³⁷David said, "The LORD, who saved me from the paw of the lion and from the paw of the bear, will save me from the hand of this Philistine." So Saul said to David, "Go, and may the LORD be with you!"

38 Saul clothed David with his armor; he put a bronze helmet on his head and clothed him with a coat of mail. ³⁹David strapped Saul's sword over the armor, and he tried in vain to walk, for he was not used to them. Then David said to Saul, "I cannot walk with these; for I am not used to them." So David removed them. ⁴⁰Then he took his staff in his hand, and chose five smooth stones from the wadi, and put them in his shepherd's bag, in the pouch; his sling was in his hand, and he drew near to the Philistine.

41 The Philistine came on and drew near to David, with his shield-bearer in front of him. ⁴²When the Philistine looked and saw David, he disdained him, for he was only a youth, ruddy and handsome in appearance. ⁴³The Philistine said to David, "Am I a dog, that you come

to me with sticks?" And the Philistine cursed David by his gods. [44] The Philistine said to David, "Come to me, and I will give your flesh to the birds of the air and to the wild animals of the field." [45] But David said to the Philistine, "You come to me with sword and spear and javelin; but I come to you in the name of the LORD of hosts, the God of the armies of Israel, whom you have defied. [46] This very day the LORD will deliver you into my hand, and I will strike you down and cut off your head; and I will give the dead bodies of the Philistine army this very day to the birds of the air and to the wild animals of the earth, so that all the earth may know that there is a God in Israel, [47] and that all this assembly may know that the LORD does not save by sword and spear; for the battle is the LORD's and he will give you into our hand."

48 When the Philistine drew nearer to meet David, David ran quickly toward the battle line to meet the Philistine. [49] David put his hand in his bag, took out a stone, slung it, and struck the Philistine on his forehead; the stone sank into his forehead, and he fell face down on the ground.

50 So David prevailed over the Philistine with a sling and a stone, striking down the Philistine and killing him; there was no sword in David's hand. [51] Then David ran and stood over the Philistine; he grasped his sword, drew it out of its sheath, and killed him; then he cut off his head with it.

When the Philistines saw that their champion was dead, they fled. [52] The troops of Israel and Judah rose up with a shout and pursued the Philistines as far as Gath[c] and the gates of Ekron, so that the wounded Philistines fell on the way from Shaaraim as far as Gath and Ekron. [53] The Israelites came back from chasing the Philistines, and they plundered their camp. [54] David took the head of the Philistine and brought it to Jerusalem; but he put his armor in his tent.

55 When Saul saw David go out against the Philistine, he said to Abner, the commander of the army, "Abner, whose son is this young man?" Abner said, "As your soul lives, O king, I do not know." [56] The king said, "Inquire whose son the stripling is." [57] On David's return from killing the Philistine, Abner took him and brought him before Saul, with the head of the Philistine in his hand. [58] Saul said to him, "Whose son are you, young man?" And David answered, "I am the son of your servant Jesse the Bethlehemite."

Jonathan's Covenant with David

18 When David[d] had finished speaking to Saul, the soul of Jonathan was bound to the soul of David, and Jonathan loved him as his own soul. [2] Saul took him that day and would not let him return to his father's house. [3] Then Jonathan made a covenant with David, because he loved him as his own soul. [4] Jonathan stripped himself of the robe that he was wearing, and gave it to David, and his armor, and even his sword and his bow and his belt. [5] David went out and was successful wherever Saul sent him; as a result, Saul set him over the army. And all the people, even the servants of Saul, approved.

6 As they were coming home, when David returned from killing the Philistine, the women came out of all the towns of Israel, singing and dancing, to meet King Saul, with tambourines, with songs of joy, and with musical instruments.[e] [7] And the women sang to one another as they made merry,

> "Saul has killed his
> thousands,
> and David his ten
> thousands."

8 Saul was very angry, for this saying displeased him. He said, "They have ascribed to David ten thousands, and to me they have ascribed thousands; what more can

17.44
1 Kings 20.10
17.45
2 Chr 32.8;
Ps 124.8;
Heb 11.34
17.46
1 Kings 18.36;
2 Kings 19.19;
Isa 52.10
17.47
1 Sam 14.6;
2 Chr 14.11;
Ps 44.6,7
17.51
1 Sam 21.9;
Heb 11.34
17.52
Josh 15.36

17.55
1 Sam 16.21,
22
17.57
v. 54
17.58
v. 12
18.1
Gen 44.30;
Deut 13.6;
1 Sam 20.17;
2 Sam 1.26
18.2
1 Sam 17.15
18.6
Ex 15.20;
Judg 11.34;
Ps 68.25
18.7
Ex 15.21;
1 Sam 21.11
18.8
1 Sam 15.8

c Gk Syr: Heb Gai　d Heb he
e Or triangles, or three-stringed instruments

he have but the kingdom?" ⁹ So Saul eyed David from that day on.

Saul Tries to Kill David

10 The next day an evil spirit from God rushed upon Saul, and he raved within his house, while David was playing the lyre, as he did day by day. Saul had his spear in his hand; ¹¹ and Saul threw the spear, for he thought, "I will pin David to the wall." But David eluded him twice.

12 Saul was afraid of David, because the LORD was with him but had departed from Saul. ¹³ So Saul removed him from his presence, and made him a commander of a thousand; and David marched out and came in, leading the army. ¹⁴ David had success in all his undertakings; for the LORD was with him. ¹⁵ When Saul saw that he had great success, he stood in awe of him. ¹⁶ But all Israel and Judah loved David; for it was he who marched out and came in leading them.

David Marries Michal

17 Then Saul said to David, "Here is my elder daughter Merab; I will give her to you as a wife; only be valiant for me and fight the LORD's battles." For Saul thought, "I will not raise a hand against him; let the Philistines deal with him." ¹⁸ David said to Saul, "Who am I and who are my kinsfolk, my father's family in Israel, that I should be son-in-law to the king?" ¹⁹ But at the time when Saul's daughter Merab should have been given to David, she was given to Adriel the Meholathite as a wife.

20 Now Saul's daughter Michal loved David. Saul was told, and the thing pleased him. ²¹ Saul thought, "Let me give her to him that she may be a snare for him and that the hand of the Philistines may be against him." Therefore Saul said to David a second time,ᶠ "You shall now be my son-in-law." ²² Saul commanded his servants, "Speak to David in private and say, 'See, the king is delighted with you,

and all his servants love you; now then, become the king's son-in-law.' " ²³ So Saul's servants reported these words to David in private. And David said, "Does it seem to you a little thing to become the king's son-in-law, seeing that I am a poor man and of no repute?" ²⁴ The servants of Saul told him, "This is what David said." ²⁵ Then Saul said, "Thus shall you say to David, 'The king desires no marriage present except a hundred foreskins of the Philistines, that he may be avenged on the king's enemies.' " Now Saul planned to make David fall by the hand of the Philistines. ²⁶ When his servants told David these words, David was well pleased to be the king's son-in-law. Before the time had expired, ²⁷ David rose and went, along with his men, and killed one hundredᵍ of the Philistines; and David brought their foreskins, which were given in full number to the king, that he might become the king's son-in-law. Saul gave him his daughter Michal as a wife. ²⁸ But when Saul realized that the LORD was with David, and that Saul's daughter Michal loved him, ²⁹ Saul was still more afraid of David. So Saul was David's enemy from that time forward.

30 Then the commanders of the Philistines came out to battle; and as often as they came out, David had more success than all the servants of Saul, so that his fame became very great.

Jonathan Intercedes for David

19 Saul spoke with his son Jonathan and with all his servants about killing David. But Saul's son Jonathan took great delight in David. ² Jonathan told David, "My father Saul is trying to kill you; therefore be on guard tomorrow morning; stay in a secret place and hide yourself. ³ I will go out and stand beside my father in the field where you are, and I will speak to my father about you; if I learn any-

18.10
1 Sam 16.14, 23; 19.9,23, 24
18.11
1 Sam 19.10; 20.33
18.12
vv. 15,29; 1 Sam 16.13, 14,18
18.13
v. 16; 2 Sam 5.2
18.14
1 Sam 16.18; Gen 39.2,3, 23
18.16
v. 5
18.17
1 Sam 17.25; 25.28; vv. 21,25
18.18
v. 23; 1 Sam 9.21; 2 Sam 7.18
18.19
2 Sam 21.8; Judg 7.22
18.20
v. 28
18.21
vv. 17,26

18.25
Ex 22.17; 1 Sam 14.24; v. 17
18.26
v. 21
18.27
v. 13; 2 Sam 3.14
18.30
v. 5
19.1
1 Sam 18.1-3, 8,9
19.3
1 Sam 20.9, 13

ᶠ Heb by two ᵍ Gk Compare 2 Sam 3.14: Heb two hundred

thing I will tell you." ⁴Jonathan spoke well of David to his father Saul, saying to him, "The king should not sin against his servant David, because he has not sinned against you, and because his deeds have been of good service to you; ⁵for he took his life in his hand when he attacked the Philistine, and the LORD brought about a great victory for all Israel. You saw it, and rejoiced; why then will you sin against an innocent person by killing David without cause?" ⁶Saul heeded the voice of Jonathan; Saul swore, "As the LORD lives, he shall not be put to death." ⁷So Jonathan called David and related all these things to him. Jonathan then brought David to Saul, and he was in his presence as before.

Michal Helps David Escape from Saul

8 Again there was war, and David went out to fight the Philistines. He launched a heavy attack on them, so that they fled before him. ⁹Then an evil spirit from the LORD came upon Saul, as he sat in his house with his spear in his hand, while David was playing music. ¹⁰Saul sought to pin David to the wall with the spear; but he eluded Saul, so that he struck the spear into the wall. David fled and escaped that night.

11 Saul sent messengers to David's house to keep watch over him, planning to kill him in the morning. David's wife Michal told him, "If you do not save your life tonight, tomorrow you will be killed." ¹²So Michal let David down through the window; he fled away and escaped. ¹³Michal took an idolʰ and laid it on the bed; she put a netⁱ of goats' hair on its head, and covered it with the clothes. ¹⁴When Saul sent messengers to take David, she said, "He is sick." ¹⁵Then Saul sent the messengers to see David for themselves. He said, "Bring him up to me in the bed, that I may kill him." ¹⁶When the messengers came in, the idolⁱ was in the bed, with the

covering‍ⁱ of goats' hair on its head. ¹⁷Saul said to Michal, "Why have you deceived me like this, and let my enemy go, so that he has escaped?" Michal answered Saul, "He said to me, 'Let me go; why should I kill you?'"

David Joins Samuel in Ramah

18 Now David fled and escaped; he came to Samuel at Ramah, and told him all that Saul had done to him. He and Samuel went and settled at Naioth. ¹⁹Saul was told, "David is at Naioth in Ramah." ²⁰Then Saul sent messengers to take David. When they saw the company of the prophets in a frenzy, with Samuel standing in charge ofⁱ them, the spirit of God came upon the messengers of Saul, and they also fell into a prophetic frenzy. ²¹When Saul was told, he sent other messengers, and they also fell into a frenzy. Saul sent messengers again the third time, and they also fell into a frenzy. ²²Then he himself went to Ramah. He came to the great well that is in Secu;ᵏ he asked, "Where are Samuel and David?" And someone said, "They are at Naioth in Ramah." ²³He went there, toward Naioth in Ramah; and the spirit of God came upon him. As he was going, he fell into a prophetic frenzy, until he came to Naioth in Ramah. ²⁴He too stripped off his clothes, and he too fell into a frenzy before Samuel. He lay naked all that day and all that night. Therefore it is said, "Is Saul also among the prophets?"

The Friendship of David and Jonathan

20 David fled from Naioth in Ramah. He came before Jonathan and said, "What have I done? What is my guilt? And what is my sin against your father that he is trying to take my life?" ²He said to him, "Far from it! You shall not die. My father does nothing either great or small without disclosing it

Cross references (center column):

19.4
1 Sam 20.32;
Gen 42.22
19.5
1 Sam 17.49,
50; 11.13;
20.32
19.7
1 Sam 16.21;
18.2,13
19.9
1 Sam 16.14;
18.10,11
19.10
1 Sam 18.11
19.12
Josh 2.15;
Acts 9.24,25
19.14
Josh 2.5

19.18
1 Sam 7.17
19.20
vv. 11,14;
1 Sam 10.5,
6;
Num 11.25
19.23
Isa 20.2;
1 Sam 10.10-
12
20.1
1 Sam 24.9

ʰ Heb *took the teraphim* ⁱ Meaning of Heb uncertain ʲ Heb *the teraphim* ᵏ Gk reads *to the well of the threshing floor on the bare height*

to me; and why should my father hide this from me? Never!" ³But David also swore, "Your father knows well that you like me; and he thinks, 'Do not let Jonathan know this, or he will be grieved.' But truly, as the LORD lives and as you yourself live, there is but a step between me and death." ⁴Then Jonathan said to David, "Whatever you say, I will do for you." ⁵David said to Jonathan, "Tomorrow is the new moon, and I should not fail to sit with the king at the meal; but let me go, so that I may hide in the field until the third evening. ⁶If your father misses me at all, then say, 'David earnestly asked leave of me to run to Bethlehem his city; for there is a yearly sacrifice there for all the family.' ⁷If he says, 'Good!' it will be well with your servant; but if he is angry, then know that evil has been determined by him. ⁸Therefore deal kindly with your servant, for you have brought your servant into a sacred covenant¹ with you. But if there is guilt in me, kill me yourself; why should you bring me to your father?" ⁹Jonathan said, "Far be it from you! If I knew that it was decided by my father that evil should come upon you, would I not tell you?" ¹⁰Then David said to Jonathan, "Who will tell me if your father answers you harshly?" ¹¹Jonathan replied to David, "Come, let us go out into the field." So they both went out into the field.

12 Jonathan said to David, "By the LORD, the God of Israel! When I have sounded out my father, about this time tomorrow, or on the third day, if he is well disposed toward David, shall I not then send and disclose it to you? ¹³But if my father intends to do you harm, the LORD do so to Jonathan, and more also, if I do not disclose it to you, and send you away, so that you may go in safety. May the LORD be with you, as he has been with my father. ¹⁴If I am still alive, show me the faithful love of the LORD; but if I die,ᵐ ¹⁵never cut off your faithful love from my house, even if the

LORD were to cut off every one of the enemies of David from the face of the earth." ¹⁶Thus Jonathan made a covenant with the house of David, saying, "May the LORD seek out the enemies of David." ¹⁷Jonathan made David swear again by his love for him; for he loved him as he loved his own life.

18 Jonathan said to him, "Tomorrow is the new moon; you will be missed, because your place will be empty. ¹⁹On the day after tomorrow, you shall go a long way down; go to the place where you hid yourself earlier, and remain beside the stone there.ᵐ ²⁰I will shoot three arrows to the side of it, as though I shot at a mark. ²¹Then I will send the boy, saying, 'Go, find the arrows.' If I say to the boy, 'Look, the arrows are on this side of you, collect them,' then you are to come, for, as the LORD lives, it is safe for you and there is no danger. ²²But if I say to the young man, 'Look, the arrows are beyond you,' then go; for the LORD has sent you away. ²³As for the matter about which you and I have spoken, the LORD is witnessⁿ between you and me forever."

24 So David hid himself in the field. When the new moon came, the king sat at the feast to eat. ²⁵The king sat upon his seat, as at other times, upon the seat by the wall. Jonathan stood, while Abner sat by Saul's side; but David's place was empty. 26 Saul did not say anything that day; for he thought, "Something has befallen him; he is not clean, surely he is not clean." ²⁷But on the second day, the day after the new moon, David's place was empty. And Saul said to his son Jonathan, "Why has the son of Jesse not come to the feast, either yesterday or today?" ²⁸Jonathan answered Saul, "David earnestly asked leave of me to go to Bethlehem; ²⁹he said, 'Let me go; for our family is holding a sacrifice in the city, and

20.5
Num 10.10;
28.11;
1 Sam 19.2
20.6
1 Sam 17.58;
Deut 12.5
20.8
1 Sam 18.3;
23.18;
2 Sam 14.32
20.13
1 Sam 3.17;
Ruth 1.17;
1 Sam 17.37
20.15
2 Sam 9.1

20.17
1 Sam 18.1
20.18
vv. 5,25
20.19
1 Sam 19.2
20.22
v. 37
20.23
vv. 14,15;
Gen 31.49,
53
20.25
v. 18
20.26
1 Sam 16.5;
Lev 7.20,21
20.28
v. 6

¹Heb *a covenant of the LORD* ᵐMeaning of Heb uncertain ⁿGk: Heb lacks *witness*

my brother has commanded me to be there. So now, if I have found favor in your sight, let me get away, and see my brothers.' For this reason he has not come to the king's table."

30 Then Saul's anger was kindled against Jonathan. He said to him, "You son of a perverse, rebellious woman! Do I not know that you have chosen the son of Jesse to your own shame, and to the shame of your mother's nakedness? 31 For as long as the son of Jesse lives upon the earth, neither you nor your kingdom shall be established. Now send and bring him to me, for he shall surely die." 32 Then Jonathan answered his father Saul, "Why should he be put to death? What has he done?" 33 But Saul threw his spear at him to strike him; so Jonathan knew that it was the decision of his father to put David to death. 34 Jonathan rose from the table in fierce anger and ate no food on the second day of the month, for he was grieved for David, and because his father had disgraced him.

35 In the morning Jonathan went out into the field to the appointment with David, and with him was a little boy. 36 He said to the boy, "Run and find the arrows that I shoot." As the boy ran, he shot an arrow beyond him. 37 When the boy came to the place where Jonathan's arrow had fallen, Jonathan called after the boy and said, "Is the arrow not beyond you?" 38 Jonathan called after the boy, "Hurry, be quick, do not linger." So Jonathan's boy gathered up the arrows and came to his master. 39 But the boy knew nothing; only Jonathan and David knew the arrangement. 40 Jonathan gave his weapons to the boy and said to him, "Go and carry them to the city." 41 As soon as the boy had gone, David rose from beside the stone heap o and prostrated himself with his face to the ground. He bowed three times, and they kissed each other, and wept with each other; David wept the more. p 42 Then Jonathan

said to David, "Go in peace, since both of us have sworn in the name of the LORD, saying, 'The LORD shall be between me and you, and between my descendants and your descendants, forever.' " He got up and left; and Jonathan went into the city. q

David and the Holy Bread

21 r David came to Nob to the priest Ahimelech. Ahimelech came trembling to meet David, and said to him, "Why are you alone, and no one with you?" 2 David said to the priest Ahimelech, "The king has charged me with a matter, and said to me, 'No one must know anything of the matter about which I send you, and with which I have charged you.' I have made an appointment s with the young men for such and such a place. 3 Now then, what have you at hand? Give me five loaves of bread, or whatever is here." 4 The priest answered David, "I have no ordinary bread at hand, only holy bread—provided that the young men have kept themselves from women." 5 David answered the priest, "Indeed women have been kept from us as always when I go on an expedition; the vessels of the young men are holy even when it is a common journey; how much more today will their vessels be holy?" 6 So the priest gave him the holy bread; for there was no bread there except the bread of the Presence, which is removed from before the LORD, to be replaced by hot bread on the day it is taken away.

7 Now a certain man of the servants of Saul was there that day, detained before the LORD; his name was Doeg the Edomite, the chief of Saul's shepherds.

8 David said to Ahimelech, "Is there no spear or sword here with you? I did not bring my sword or my weapons with me, because the king's business required haste."

20.30
Deut 21.20
20.32
1 Sam 19.5;
Mt 27.23;
Lk 23.22
20.33
v. 7
20.36
vv. 20,21
20.37
v. 22
20.42
1 Sam 1.17;
v. 22

21.1
1 Sam 22.19;
14.3; 16.4
21.4
Lev 24.5-9;
Mt 12.4
21.5
Ex 19.14,15
21.6
Mt 12.3,4;
Mk 2.25,26;
Lev 24.8,9
21.7
1 Sam 22.9

o Gk: Heb *from beside the south* p Vg: Meaning of Heb uncertain q This sentence is 21.1 in Heb r Ch 21.2 in Heb s Q Ms Vg Compare Gk: Meaning of MT uncertain

9 The priest said, "The sword of Goliath the Philistine, whom you killed in the valley of Elah, is here wrapped in a cloth behind the ephod; if you will take that, take it, for there is none here except that one." David said, "There is none like it; give it to me."

David Flees to Gath

10 David rose and fled that day from Saul; he went to King Achish of Gath. 11 The servants of Achish said to him, "Is this not David the king of the land? Did they not sing to one another of him in dances,

'Saul has killed his
 thousands,
 and David his ten
 thousands'?"

12 David took these words to heart and was very much afraid of King Achish of Gath. 13 So he changed his behavior before them; he pretended to be mad when in their presence.[t] He scratched marks on the doors of the gate, and let his spittle run down his beard. 14 Achish said to his servants, "Look, you see the man is mad; why then have you brought him to me? 15 Do I lack madmen, that you have brought this fellow to play the madman in my presence? Shall this fellow come into my house?"

David and His Followers at Adullam

22 David left there and escaped to the cave of Adullam; when his brothers and all his father's house heard of it, they went down there to him. 2 Everyone who was in distress, and everyone who was in debt, and everyone who was discontented gathered to him; and he became captain over them. Those who were with him numbered about four hundred.

3 David went from there to Mizpeh of Moab. He said to the king of Moab, "Please let my father and mother come[u] to you, until I know what God will do for me." 4 He left them with the king of Moab, and they stayed with him all the time that David was in the stronghold.

21.9
1 Sam 17.2, 51
21.11
1 Sam 18.7; 29.5
21.12
1 Sam 2.19
22.1
2 Sam 23.13
22.2
1 Sam 23.13; 25.13

22.5
2 Sam 24.11; 1 Chr 29.29; 2 Chr 29.25
22.7
1 Sam 8.14
22.8
1 Sam 18.3; 20.16
22.9
1 Sam 21.1; 14.3
22.10
1 Sam 10.22; 21.6,9
22.14
1 Sam 19.4, 5

5 Then the prophet Gad said to David, "Do not remain in the stronghold; leave, and go into the land of Judah." So David left, and went into the forest of Hereth.

Saul Slaughters the Priests at Nob

6 Saul heard that David and those who were with him had been located. Saul was sitting at Gibeah, under the tamarisk tree on the height, with his spear in his hand, and all his servants were standing around him. 7 Saul said to his servants who stood around him, "Hear now, you Benjaminites; will the son of Jesse give every one of you fields and vineyards, will he make you all commanders of thousands and commanders of hundreds? 8 Is that why all of you have conspired against me? No one discloses to me when my son makes a league with the son of Jesse, none of you is sorry for me or discloses to me that my son has stirred up my servant against me, to lie in wait, as he is doing today." 9 Doeg the Edomite, who was in charge of Saul's servants, answered, "I saw the son of Jesse coming to Nob, to Ahimelech son of Ahitub; 10 he inquired of the LORD for him, gave him provisions, and gave him the sword of Goliath the Philistine."

11 The king sent for the priest Ahimelech son of Ahitub and for all his father's house, the priests who were at Nob; and all of them came to the king. 12 Saul said, "Listen now, son of Ahitub." He answered, "Here I am, my lord." 13 Saul said to him, "Why have you conspired against me, you and the son of Jesse, by giving him bread and a sword, and by inquiring of God for him, so that he has risen against me, to lie in wait, as he is doing today?"

14 Then Ahimelech answered the king, "Who among all your servants is so faithful as David? He is the king's son-in-law, and is quick[v] to do your bidding, and is

[t] Heb in their hands [u] Syr Vg: Heb come out [v] Heb and turns aside

honored in your house. [15] Is today the first time that I have inquired of God for him? By no means! Do not let the king impute anything to his servant or to any member of my father's house; for your servant has known nothing of all this, much or little." [16] The king said, "You shall surely die, Ahimelech, you and all your father's house." [17] The king said to the guard who stood around him, "Turn and kill the priests of the LORD, because their hand also is with David; they knew that he fled, and did not disclose it to me." But the servants of the king would not raise their hand to attack the priests of the LORD. [18] Then the king said to Doeg, "You, Doeg, turn and attack the priests." Doeg the Edomite turned and attacked the priests; on that day he killed eighty-five who wore the linen ephod. [19] Nob, the city of the priests, he put to the sword; men and women, children and infants, oxen, donkeys, and sheep, he put to the sword.

[20] But one of the sons of Ahimelech son of Ahitub, named Abiathar, escaped and fled after David. [21] Abiathar told David that Saul had killed the priests of the LORD. [22] David said to Abiathar, "I knew on that day, when Doeg the Edomite was there, that he would surely tell Saul. I am responsible[w] for the lives of all your father's house. [23] Stay with me, and do not be afraid; for the one who seeks my life seeks your life; you will be safe with me."

David Saves the City of Keilah

23 Now they told David, "The Philistines are fighting against Keilah, and are robbing the threshing floors." [2] David inquired of the LORD, "Shall I go and attack these Philistines?" The LORD said to David, "Go and attack the Philistines and save Keilah." [3] But David's men said to him, "Look, we are afraid here in Judah; how much more then if we go to Keilah against the armies of the Philistines?" [4] Then David inquired of the LORD again. The LORD answered him, "Yes, go down to Keilah; for I will give the Philistines into your hand." [5] So David and his men went to Keilah, fought with the Philistines, brought away their livestock, and dealt them a heavy defeat. Thus David rescued the inhabitants of Keilah.

6 When Abiathar son of Ahimelech fled to David at Keilah, he came down with an ephod in his hand. [7] Now it was told Saul that David had come to Keilah. And Saul said, "God has given[x] him into my hand; for he has shut himself in by entering a town that has gates and bars." [8] Saul summoned all the people to war, to go down to Keilah, to besiege David and his men. [9] When David learned that Saul was plotting evil against him, he said to the priest Abiathar, "Bring the ephod here." [10] David said, "O LORD, the God of Israel, your servant has heard that Saul seeks to come to Keilah, to destroy the city on my account. [11] And now, will[y] Saul come down as your servant has heard? O LORD, the God of Israel, I beseech you, tell your servant." The LORD said, "He will come down." [12] Then David said, "Will the men of Keilah surrender me and my men into the hand of Saul?" The LORD said, "They will surrender you." [13] Then David and his men, who were about six hundred, set out and left Keilah; they wandered wherever they could go. When Saul was told that David had escaped from Keilah, he gave up the expedition. [14] David remained in the strongholds in the wilderness, in the hill country of the Wilderness of Ziph. Saul sought him every day, but the LORD[z] did not give him into his hand.

David Eludes Saul in the Wilderness

15 David was in the Wilderness of Ziph at Horesh when he learned

Cross references (center column):

22.17
Ex 1.17
22.18
1 Sam 2.18,
31
22.20
1 Sam 23.6,
9; 2.33
22.22
1 Sam 21.7
22.23
1 Kings 2.26
23.1
Josh 15.44
23.2
vv. 4,6,9;
2 Sam 5.19,
23
23.4
Josh 8.7;
Judg 7.7

23.6
1 Sam 22.20
23.9
v. 6;
1 Sam 30.7
23.12
v. 20
23.13
1 Sam 22.2;
25.13
23.14
Josh 15.15;
Ps 54.3,4

w Gk Vg: Meaning of Heb uncertain
x Gk Tg: Heb made a stranger of y Q Ms
Compare Gk: MT Will the men of Keilah
surrender me into his hand? Will z Q Ms
Gk: MT God

that[a] Saul had come out to seek his life. [16] Saul's son Jonathan set out and came to David at Horesh; there he strengthened his hand through the LORD.[b] [17] He said to him, "Do not be afraid; for the hand of my father Saul shall not find you; you shall be king over Israel, and I shall be second to you; my father Saul also knows that this is so." [18] Then the two of them made a covenant before the LORD; David remained at Horesh, and Jonathan went home.

19 Then some Ziphites went up to Saul at Gibeah and said, "David is hiding among us in the strongholds of Horesh, on the hill of Hachilah, which is south of Jeshimon. [20] Now, O king, whenever you wish to come down, do so; and our part will be to surrender him into the king's hand." [21] Saul said, "May you be blessed by the LORD for showing me compassion! [22] Go and make sure once more; find out exactly where he is, and who has seen him there; for I am told that he is very cunning. [23] Look around and learn all the hiding places where he lurks, and come back to me with sure information. Then I will go with you; and if he is in the land, I will search him out among all the thousands of Judah." [24] So they set out and went to Ziph ahead of Saul.

David and his men were in the wilderness of Maon, in the Arabah to the south of Jeshimon. [25] Saul and his men went to search for him. When David was told, he went down to the rock and stayed in the wilderness of Maon. When Saul heard that, he pursued David into the wilderness of Maon. [26] Saul went on one side of the mountain, and David and his men on the other side of the mountain. David was hurrying to get away from Saul, while Saul and his men were closing in on David and his men to capture them. [27] Then a messenger came to Saul, saying, "Hurry and come; for the Philistines have made a raid on the land." [28] So Saul stopped pursuing David, and went against the Philistines; therefore

23.16
1 Sam 30.6
23.17
1 Sam 20.31;
24.20
23.18
1 Sam 18.3;
20.16,42;
2 Sam 9.1;
21.7
23.19
1 Sam 26.1
23.20
v. 12
23.21
1 Sam 22.8
23.24
Josh 15.55;
1 Sam 25.2
23.26
Ps 17.9

23.29
2 Chr 20.2
24.1
1 Sam 23.28,
29
24.2
1 Sam 26.2
24.3
Judg 3.24
24.4
1 Sam 23.17;
25.28-30
24.5
2 Sam 24.10
24.6
1 Sam 26.11
24.8
1 Sam 25.23,
24

that place was called the Rock of Escape.[c] [29][d] David then went up from there, and lived in the strongholds of En-gedi.

David Spares Saul's Life

24 When Saul returned from following the Philistines, he was told, "David is in the wilderness of En-gedi." [2] Then Saul took three thousand chosen men out of all Israel, and went to look for David and his men in the direction of the Rocks of the Wild Goats. [3] He came to the sheepfolds beside the road, where there was a cave; and Saul went in to relieve himself.[e] Now David and his men were sitting in the innermost parts of the cave. [4] The men of David said to him, "Here is the day of which the LORD said to you, 'I will give your enemy into your hand, and you shall do to him as it seems good to you.' " Then David went and stealthily cut off a corner of Saul's cloak. [5] Afterward David was stricken to the heart because he had cut off a corner of Saul's cloak. [6] He said to his men, "The LORD forbid that I should do this thing to my lord, the LORD's anointed, to raise my hand against him; for he is the LORD's anointed." [7] So David scolded his men severely and did not permit them to attack Saul. Then Saul got up and left the cave, and went on his way.

8 Afterwards David also rose up and went out of the cave and called after Saul, "My lord the king!" When Saul looked behind him, David bowed with his face to the ground, and did obeisance. [9] David said to Saul, "Why do you listen to the words of those who say, 'David seeks to do you harm'? [10] This very day your eyes have seen how the LORD gave you into my hand in the cave; and some urged me to kill you, but I spared[f] you. I said, 'I will not raise my hand against my lord; for he is the LORD's anointed.'

a Or saw that b Compare Q Ms Gk: MT
God c Or Rock of Division; Meaning of
Heb uncertain d Ch 24.1 in Heb
e Heb to cover his feet f Gk Syr Tg Vg:
Heb it (my eye) spared

[11] See, my father, see the corner of your cloak in my hand; for by the fact that I cut off the corner of your cloak, and did not kill you, you may know for certain that there is no wrong or treason in my hands. I have not sinned against you, though you are hunting me to take my life. [12] May the LORD judge between me and you! May the LORD avenge me on you; but my hand shall not be against you. [13] As the ancient proverb says, 'Out of the wicked comes forth wickedness'; but my hand shall not be against you. [14] Against whom has the king of Israel come out? Whom do you pursue? A dead dog? A single flea? [15] May the LORD therefore be judge, and give sentence between me and you. May he see to it, and plead my cause, and vindicate me against you."

16 When David had finished speaking these words to Saul, Saul said, "Is this your voice, my son David?" Saul lifted up his voice and wept. [17] He said to David, "You are more righteous than I; for you have repaid me good, whereas I have repaid you evil. [18] Today you have explained how you have dealt well with me, in that you did not kill me when the LORD put me into your hands. [19] For who has ever found an enemy, and sent the enemy safely away? So may the LORD reward you with good for what you have done to me this day. [20] Now I know that you shall surely be king, and that the kingdom of Israel shall be established in your hand. [21] Swear to me therefore by the LORD that you will not cut off my descendants after me, and that you will not wipe out my name from my father's house." [22] So David swore this to Saul. Then Saul went home; but David and his men went up to the stronghold.

Death of Samuel

25 Now Samuel died; and all Israel assembled and mourned for him. They buried him at his home in Ramah.

Then David got up and went down to the wilderness of Paran.

David and the Wife of Nabal

2 There was a man in Maon, whose property was in Carmel. The man was very rich; he had three thousand sheep and a thousand goats. He was shearing his sheep in Carmel. [3] Now the name of the man was Nabal, and the name of his wife Abigail. The woman was clever and beautiful, but the man was surly and mean; he was a Calebite. [4] David heard in the wilderness that Nabal was shearing his sheep. [5] So David sent ten young men; and David said to the young men, "Go up to Carmel, and go to Nabal, and greet him in my name. [6] Thus you shall salute him: 'Peace be to you, and peace be to your house, and peace be to all that you have. [7] I hear that you have shearers; now your shepherds have been with us, and we did them no harm, and they missed nothing, all the time they were in Carmel. [8] Ask your young men, and they will tell you. Therefore let my young men find favor in your sight; for we have come on a feast day. Please give whatever you have at hand to your servants and to your son David.' "

9 When David's young men came, they said all this to Nabal in the name of David; and then they waited. [10] But Nabal answered David's servants, "Who is David? Who is the son of Jesse? There are many servants today who are breaking away from their masters. [11] Shall I take my bread and my water and the meat that I have butchered for my shearers, and give it to men who come from I do not know where?" [12] So David's young men turned away, and came back and told him all this. [13] David said to his men, "Every man strap on his sword!" And every one of them strapped on his sword; David also strapped on his sword; and about four hundred men went up after David, while two hundred remained with the baggage. 14 But one of the young men

Cross references (center column):

24.11 Ps 7.3; 35.7; 1 Sam 23.14, 23; 26.20
24.12 Gen 31.53; Judg 11.27; 1 Sam 26.10; Job 5.8
24.13 Mt 7.16-20
24.14 1 Sam 17.43; 26.20
24.15 v. 12; Ps 35.1; Mic 7.9
24.16 1 Sam 26.17
24.17 1 Sam 26.21; Mt 5.44
24.18 1 Sam 26.23
24.20 1 Sam 23.17
24.21 Gen 21.23; 2 Sam 21.6-8
24.22 1 Sam 23.29
25.1 1 Sam 28.3; Deut 34.8; 2 Chr 33.20; Gen 21.21

25.2 1 Sam 23.24; Josh 15.55
25.6 1 Chr 12.18
25.7 2 Sam 13.23, 24; vv. 15, 21
25.8 Neh 8.10-12
25.10 Judg 9.28
25.13 1 Sam 23.13; 30.24

told Abigail, Nabal's wife, "David sent messengers out of the wilderness to salute our master; and he shouted insults at them. [15]Yet the men were very good to us, and we suffered no harm, and we never missed anything when we were in the fields, as long as we were with them; [16]they were a wall to us both by night and by day, all the while we were with them keeping the sheep. [17]Now therefore know this and consider what you should do; for evil has been decided against our master and against all his house; he is so ill-natured that no one can speak to him."

18 Then Abigail hurried and took two hundred loaves, two skins of wine, five sheep ready dressed, five measures of parched grain, one hundred clusters of raisins, and two hundred cakes of figs. She loaded them on donkeys [19]and said to her young men, "Go on ahead of me; I am coming after you." But she did not tell her husband Nabal. [20]As she rode on the donkey and came down under cover of the mountain, David and his men came down toward her; and she met them. [21]Now David had said, "Surely it was in vain that I protected all that this fellow has in the wilderness, so that nothing was missed of all that belonged to him; but he has returned me evil for good. [22]God do so to David[g] and more also, if by morning I leave so much as one male of all who belong to him."

23 When Abigail saw David, she hurried and alighted from the donkey, fell before David on her face, bowing to the ground. [24]She fell at his feet and said, "Upon me alone, my lord, be the guilt; please let your servant speak in your ears, and hear the words of your servant. [25]My lord, do not take seriously this ill-natured fellow, Nabal; for as his name is, so is he; Nabal[h] is his name, and folly is with him; but I, your servant, did not see the young men of my lord, whom you sent. 26 Now then, my lord, as the LORD lives, and as you yourself live,

since the LORD has restrained you from bloodguilt and from taking vengeance with your own hand, now let your enemies and those who seek to do evil to my lord be like Nabal. [27]And now let this present that your servant has brought to my lord be given to the young men who follow my lord. [28]Please forgive the trespass of your servant; for the LORD will certainly make my lord a sure house, because my lord is fighting the battles of the LORD; and evil shall not be found in you so long as you live. [29]If anyone should rise up to pursue you and to seek your life, the life of my lord shall be bound in the bundle of the living under the care of the LORD your God; but the lives of your enemies he shall sling out as from the hollow of a sling. [30]When the LORD has done to my lord according to all the good that he has spoken concerning you, and has appointed you prince over Israel, [31]my lord shall have no cause of grief, or pangs of conscience, for having shed blood without cause or for having saved himself. And when the LORD has dealt well with my lord, then remember your servant."

32 David said to Abigail, "Blessed be the LORD, the God of Israel, who sent you to meet me today! [33]Blessed be your good sense, and blessed be you, who have kept me today from bloodguilt and from avenging myself by my own hand! [34]For as surely as the LORD the God of Israel lives, who has restrained me from hurting you, unless you had hurried and come to meet me, truly by morning there would not have been left to Nabal so much as one male." [35]Then David received from her hand what she had brought him; he said to her, "Go up to your house in peace; see, I have heeded your voice, and I have granted your petition."

36 Abigail came to Nabal; he was holding a feast in his house, like the feast of a king. Nabal's

25.15
v. 7
25.16
Ex 14.22
25.18
2 Sam 16.1;
1 Chr 12.40
25.19
Gen 32.16,
20
25.21
Ps 109.5
25.22
1 Sam 3.17;
20.13;
1 Kings 14.10
25.23
1 Sam 20.41
25.26
Heb 10.30;
2 Sam 18.32

25.27
Gen 33.11;
1 Sam 30.26
25.28
2 Sam 7.11,
27; 18.17;
24.11
25.29
Jer 10.18
25.30
1 Sam 13.14
25.32
Ex 18.10
25.33
v. 26
25.34
v. 26
25.35
1 Sam 20.42;
2 Kings 5.19;
Gen 19.21
25.36
2 Sam 13.23

g Gk Compare Syr: Heb *the enemies of David*
h That is *Fool*

heart was merry within him, for he was very drunk; so she told him nothing at all until the morning light. [37] In the morning, when the wine had gone out of Nabal, his wife told him these things, and his heart died within him; he became like a stone. [38] About ten days later the LORD struck Nabal, and he died.

39 When David heard that Nabal was dead, he said, "Blessed be the LORD who has judged the case of Nabal's insult to me, and has kept back his servant from evil; the LORD has returned the evil-doing of Nabal upon his own head." Then David sent and wooed Abigail, to make her his wife. [40] When David's servants came to Abigail at Carmel, they said to her, "David has sent us to you to take you to him as his wife." [41] She rose and bowed down, with her face to the ground, and said, "Your servant is a slave to wash the feet of the servants of my lord." [42] Abigail got up hurriedly and rode away on a donkey; her five maids attended her. She went after the messengers of David and became his wife.

43 David also married Ahinoam of Jezreel; both of them became his wives. [44] Saul had given his daughter Michal, David's wife, to Palti son of Laish, who was from Gallim.

David Spares Saul's Life a Second Time

26 Then the Ziphites came to Saul at Gibeah, saying, "David is in hiding on the hill of Hachilah, which is opposite Jeshimon."[i] [2] So Saul rose and went down to the Wilderness of Ziph, with three thousand chosen men of Israel, to seek David in the Wilderness of Ziph. [3] Saul encamped on the hill of Hachilah, which is opposite Jeshimon[i] beside the road. But David remained in the wilderness. When he learned that Saul came after him into the wilderness, [4] David sent out spies, and learned that Saul had indeed arrived. [5] Then David set out and came to the place where Saul had encamped; and David saw the place

25.39
1 Sam 24.15;
vv. 26,34;
1 Kings 2.44
25.41
Ruth 2.10,
13; Mk 1.7
25.42
Gen 24.61-67
25.43
Josh 15.56;
1 Sam 27.3
25.44
2 Sam 3.14;
Isa 10.30
26.1
1 Sam 23.19
26.2
1 Sam 13.2;
24.2
26.5
1 Sam 14.50;
17.55

26.6
1 Chr 2.16;
Judg 7.10,
11
26.9
1 Sam 24.6,
7;
2 Sam 1.16
26.10
1 Sam 25.38;
Deut 31.14;
1 Sam 31.6
26.11
1 Sam 24.6,
12
26.12
Gen 2.21;
16.12

where Saul lay, with Abner son of Ner, the commander of his army. Saul was lying within the encampment, while the army was encamped around him.

6 Then David said to Ahimelech the Hittite, and to Joab's brother Abishai son of Zeruiah, "Who will go down with me into the camp to Saul?" Abishai said, "I will go down with you." [7] So David and Abishai went to the army by night; there Saul lay sleeping within the encampment, with his spear stuck in the ground at his head; and Abner and the army lay around him. [8] Abishai said to David, "God has given your enemy into your hand today; now therefore let me pin him to the ground with one stroke of the spear; I will not strike him twice." [9] But David said to Abishai, "Do not destroy him; for who can raise his hand against the LORD's anointed, and be guiltless?" [10] David said, "As the LORD lives, the LORD will strike him down; or his day will come to die; or he will go down into battle and perish. [11] The LORD forbid that I should raise my hand against the LORD's anointed; but now take the spear that is at his head, and the water jar, and let us go." [12] So David took the spear that was at Saul's head and the water jar, and they went away. No one saw it, or knew it, nor did anyone awake; for they were all asleep, because a deep sleep from the LORD had fallen upon them.

13 Then David went over to the other side, and stood on top of a hill far away, with a great distance between them. [14] David called to the army and to Abner son of Ner, saying, "Abner! Will you not answer?" Then Abner replied, "Who are you that calls to the king?" [15] David said to Abner, "Are you not a man? Who is like you in Israel? Why then have you not kept watch over your lord the king? For one of the people came in to destroy your lord the king. [16] This thing that you have done is not good. As the LORD

i Or *opposite the wasteland*

lives, you deserve to die, because you have not kept watch over your lord, the Lord's anointed. See now, where is the king's spear, or the water jar that was at his head?"

17 Saul recognized David's voice, and said, "Is this your voice, my son David?" David said, "It is my voice, my lord, O king." 18 And he added, "Why does my lord pursue his servant? For what have I done? What guilt is on my hands? 19 Now therefore let my lord the king hear the words of his servant. If it is the Lord who has stirred you up against me, may he accept an offering; but if it is mortals, may they be cursed before the Lord, for they have driven me out today from my share in the heritage of the Lord, saying, 'Go, serve other gods.' 20 Now therefore, do not let my blood fall to the ground, away from the presence of the Lord; for the king of Israel has come out to seek a single flea, like one who hunts a partridge in the mountains."

21 Then Saul said, "I have done wrong; come back, my son David, for I will never harm you again, because my life was precious in your sight today; I have been a fool, and have made a great mistake." 22 David replied, "Here is the spear, O king! Let one of the young men come over and get it. 23 The Lord rewards everyone for his righteousness and his faithfulness; for the Lord gave you into my hand today, but I would not raise my hand against the Lord's anointed. 24 As your life was precious today in my sight, so may my life be precious in the sight of the Lord, and may he rescue me from all tribulation." 25 Then Saul said to David, "Blessed be you, my son David! You will do many things and will succeed in them." So David went his way, and Saul returned to his place.

David Serves King Achish of Gath

27 David said in his heart, "I shall now perish one day by

26.17
1 Sam 24.16
26.18
1 Sam 24.9, 11-14
26.19
2 Sam 16.11
26.20
1 Sam 24.14
26.21
1 Sam 15.24; 24.17
26.22
1 Sam 24.12, 19
26.24
Ps 54.7

27.2
1 Sam 25.13; 21.10
27.3
1 Sam 30.3; 25.42,43
27.6
Josh 15.31; 19.5
27.7
1 Sam 29.3
27.8
Josh 13.2, 13; Ex 17.8; 1 Sam 15.7, 8; Ex 15.22
27.9
1 Sam 15.3
27.10
1 Chr 2.9, 25; Judg 1.16

the hand of Saul; there is nothing better for me than to escape to the land of the Philistines; then Saul will despair of seeking me any longer within the borders of Israel, and I shall escape out of his hand." 2 So David set out and went over, he and the six hundred men who were with him, to King Achish son of Maoch of Gath. 3 David stayed with Achish at Gath, he and his troops, every man with his household, and David with his two wives, Ahinoam of Jezreel, and Abigail of Carmel, Nabal's widow. 4 When Saul was told that David had fled to Gath, he no longer sought for him.

5 Then David said to Achish, "If I have found favor in your sight, let a place be given me in one of the country towns, so that I may live there; for why should your servant live in the royal city with you?" 6 So that day Achish gave him Ziklag; therefore Ziklag has belonged to the kings of Judah to this day. 7 The length of time that David lived in the country of the Philistines was one year and four months.

8 Now David and his men went up and made raids on the Geshurites, the Girzites, and the Amalekites; for these were the landed settlements from Telam[i] on the way to Shur and on to the land of Egypt. 9 David struck the land, leaving neither man nor woman alive, but took away the sheep, the oxen, the donkeys, the camels, and the clothing, and came back to Achish. 10 When Achish asked, "Against whom[k] have you made a raid today?" David would say, "Against the Negeb of Judah," or "Against the Negeb of the Jerahmeelites," or, "Against the Negeb of the Kenites." 11 David left neither man nor woman alive to be brought back to Gath, thinking, "They might tell about us, and say, 'David has done so and so.' " Such was his practice all the time he lived in the country of the Philistines. 12 Achish trusted David, thinking, "He has

i Compare Gk 15.4: Heb *from of old*
k Q Ms Gk Vg: MT lacks *whom*

made himself utterly abhorrent to his people Israel; therefore he shall always be my servant."

28 In those days the Philistines gathered their forces for war, to fight against Israel. Achish said to David, "You know, of course, that you and your men are to go out with me in the army." ²David said to Achish, "Very well, then you shall know what your servant can do." Achish said to David, "Very well, I will make you my bodyguard for life."

Saul Consults a Medium

3 Now Samuel had died, and all Israel had mourned for him and buried him in Ramah, his own city. Saul had expelled the mediums and the wizards from the land. ⁴The Philistines assembled, and came and encamped at Shunem. Saul gathered all Israel, and they encamped at Gilboa. ⁵When Saul saw the army of the Philistines, he was afraid, and his heart trembled greatly. ⁶When Saul inquired of the LORD, the LORD did not answer him, not by dreams, or by Urim, or by prophets. ⁷Then Saul said to his servants, "Seek out for me a woman who is a medium, so that I may go to her and inquire of her." His servants said to him, "There is a medium at Endor."

8 So Saul disguised himself and put on other clothes and went there, he and two men with him. They came to the woman by night. And he said, "Consult a spirit for me, and bring up for me the one whom I name to you." ⁹The woman said to him, "Surely you know what Saul has done, how he has cut off the mediums and the wizards from the land. Why then are you laying a snare for my life to bring about my death?" ¹⁰But Saul swore to her by the LORD, "As the LORD lives, no punishment shall come upon you for this thing." ¹¹Then the woman said, "Whom shall I bring up for you?" He answered, "Bring up Samuel for me." ¹²When the woman saw Samuel, she cried out with a loud voice; and the woman said

to Saul, "Why have you deceived me? You are Saul!" ¹³The king said to her, "Have no fear; what do you see?" The woman said to Saul, "I see a divine being¹ coming up out of the ground." ¹⁴He said to her, "What is his appearance?" She said, "An old man is coming up; he is wrapped in a robe." So Saul knew that it was Samuel, and he bowed with his face to the ground, and did obeisance.

15 Then Samuel said to Saul, "Why have you disturbed me by bringing me up?" Saul answered, "I am in great distress, for the Philistines are warring against me, and God has turned away from me and answers me no more, either by prophets or by dreams; so I have summoned you to tell me what I should do." ¹⁶Samuel said, "Why then do you ask me, since the LORD has turned from you and become your enemy? ¹⁷The LORD has done to you just as he spoke by me; for the LORD has torn the kingdom out of your hand, and given it to your neighbor, David. ¹⁸Because you did not obey the voice of the LORD, and did not carry out his fierce wrath against Amalek, therefore the LORD has done this thing to you today. ¹⁹Moreover the LORD will give Israel along with you into the hands of the Philistines; and tomorrow you and your sons shall be with me; the LORD will also give the army of Israel into the hands of the Philistines."

20 Immediately Saul fell full length on the ground, filled with fear because of the words of Samuel; and there was no strength in him, for he had eaten nothing all day and all night. ²¹The woman came to Saul, and when she saw that he was terrified, she said to him, "Your servant has listened to you; I have taken my life in my hand, and have listened to what you have said to me. ²²Now therefore, you also listen to your servant; let me set a morsel of bread before you. Eat, that you may have

28.1f
1 Sam 29.1
28.3
1 Sam 25.1;
7.17; 15.23;
Lev 19.31;
Deut 18.10,
11
28.4
2 Kings 4.8;
1 Sam 31.1
28.6
1 Chr 10.13,
14;
Prov 1.28;
Ex 28.30
28.7
Acts 16.16;
Josh 17.11
28.8
Isa 8.19;
Deut 18.10,
11
28.9
v. 3

28.14
1 Sam 15.27;
24.8
28.15
1 Sam 18.12;
v. 6
28.17
1 Sam 15.28
28.18
1 Sam 15.9,
20,26
28.19
1 Sam 31.2
28.21
1 Sam 19.5;
Judg 12.3

¹Or *a god*; or *gods*

strength when you go on your way." [23] He refused, and said, "I will not eat." But his servants, together with the woman, urged him; and he listened to their words. So he got up from the ground and sat on the bed. [24] Now the woman had a fatted calf in the house. She quickly slaughtered it, and she took flour, kneaded it, and baked unleavened cakes. [25] She put them before Saul and his servants, and they ate. Then they rose and went away that night.

The Philistines Reject David

29 Now the Philistines gathered all their forces at Aphek, while the Israelites were encamped by the fountain that is in Jezreel. [2] As the lords of the Philistines were passing on by hundreds and by thousands, and David and his men were passing on in the rear with Achish, [3] the commanders of the Philistines said, "What are these Hebrews doing here?" Achish said to the commanders of the Philistines, "Is this not David, the servant of King Saul of Israel, who has been with me now for days and years? Since he deserted to me I have found no fault in him to this day." [4] But the commanders of the Philistines were angry with him; and the commanders of the Philistines said to him, "Send the man back, so that he may return to the place that you have assigned to him; he shall not go down with us to battle, or else he may become an adversary to us in the battle. For how could this fellow reconcile himself to his lord? Would it not be with the heads of the men here? [5] Is this not David, of whom they sing to one another in dances,

'Saul has killed his thousands,
 and David his ten thousands'?"

6 Then Achish called David and said to him, "As the LORD lives, you have been honest, and to me it seems right that you should march out and in with me in the campaign; for I have found nothing

wrong in you from the day of your coming to me until today. Nevertheless the lords do not approve of you. [7] So go back now; and go peaceably; do nothing to displease the lords of the Philistines." [8] David said to Achish, "But what have I done? What have you found in your servant from the day I entered your service until now, that I should not go and fight against the enemies of my lord the king?" [9] Achish replied to David, "I know that you are as blameless in my sight as an angel of God; nevertheless, the commanders of the Philistines have said, 'He shall not go up with us to the battle.' [10] Now then rise early in the morning, you and the servants of your lord who came with you, and go to the place that I appointed for you. As for the evil report, do not take it to heart, for you have done well before me.[m] Start early in the morning, and leave as soon as you have light." [11] So David set out with his men early in the morning, to return to the land of the Philistines. But the Philistines went up to Jezreel.

David Avenges the Destruction of Ziklag

30 Now when David and his men came to Ziklag on the third day, the Amalekites had made a raid on the Negeb and on Ziklag. They had attacked Ziklag, burned it down, [2] and taken captive the women and all[n] who were in it, both small and great; they killed none of them, but carried them off, and went their way. [3] When David and his men came to the city, they found it burned down, and their wives and sons and daughters taken captive. [4] Then David and the people who were with him raised their voices and wept, until they had no more strength to weep. [5] David's two wives also had been taken captive, Ahinoam of Jezreel, and Abigail the widow of Nabal of

28.23
2 Kings 5.13
29.1
1 Sam 28.1;
4.1;
Josh 12.18
29.2
1 Sam 28.1,
2
29.3
1 Sam 27.7;
Dan 6.5
29.4
1 Chr 12.19;
1 Sam 14.21
29.5
1 Sam 18.7;
21.11
29.6
v. 3

29.9
2 Sam 14.17,
20; 19.27;
v. 4
29.10
1 Chr 12.19,
22
30.1
1 Sam 29.4,
11; 15.7; 27.8
30.5
1 Sam 25.42,
43

m Gk: Heb lacks *and go to the place* . . . *done well before me* n Gk: Heb lacks *and all*

Carmel. 6 David was in great danger; for the people spoke of stoning him, because all the people were bitter in spirit for their sons and daughters. But David strengthened himself in the LORD his God.

7 David said to the priest Abiathar son of Ahimelech, "Bring me the ephod." So Abiathar brought the ephod to David. 8 David inquired of the LORD, "Shall I pursue this band? Shall I overtake them?" He answered him, "Pursue; for you shall surely overtake and shall surely rescue." 9 So David set out, he and the six hundred men who were with him. They came to the Wadi Besor, where those stayed who were left behind. 10 But David went on with the pursuit, he and four hundred men; two hundred stayed behind, too exhausted to cross the Wadi Besor.

11 In the open country they found an Egyptian, and brought him to David. They gave him bread and he ate, they gave him water to drink; 12 they also gave him a piece of fig cake and two clusters of raisins. When he had eaten, his spirit revived; for he had not eaten bread or drunk water for three days and three nights. 13 Then David said to him, "To whom do you belong? Where are you from?" He said, "I am a young man of Egypt, servant to an Amalekite. My master left me behind because I fell sick three days ago. 14 We had made a raid on the Negeb of the Cherethites and on that which belongs to Judah and on the Negeb of Caleb; and we burned Ziklag down." 15 David said to him, "Will you take me down to this raiding party?" He said, "Swear to me by God that you will not kill me, or hand me over to my master, and I will take you down to them."

16 When he had taken him down, they were spread out all over the ground, eating and drinking and dancing, because of the great amount of spoil they had taken from the land of the Philistines and from the land of Judah. 17 David attacked them from twilight until the evening of the next day. Not one of

them escaped, except four hundred young men, who mounted camels and fled. 18 David recovered all that the Amalekites had taken; and David rescued his two wives. 19 Nothing was missing, whether small or great, sons or daughters, spoil or anything that had been taken; David brought back everything. 20 David also captured all the flocks and herds, which were driven ahead of the other cattle; people said, "This is David's spoil."

21 Then David came to the two hundred men who had been too exhausted to follow David, and who had been left at the brook Besor. They went out to meet David and to meet the people who were with him. When David drew near to the people he saluted them. 22 Then all the corrupt and worthless fellows among the men who had gone with David said, "Because they did not go with us, we will not give them any of the spoil that we have recovered, except that each man may take his wife and children, and leave." 23 But David said, "You shall not do so, my brothers, with what the LORD has given us; he has preserved us and handed over to us the raiding party that attacked us. 24 Who would listen to you in this matter? For the share of the one who goes down into the battle shall be the same as the share of the one who stays by the baggage; they shall share alike." 25 From that day forward he made it a statute and an ordinance for Israel; it continues to the present day.

26 When David came to Ziklag, he sent part of the spoil to his friends, the elders of Judah, saying, "Here is a present for you from the spoil of the enemies of the LORD"; 27 it was for those in Bethel, in Ramoth of the Negeb, in Jattir, 28 in Aroer, in Siphmoth, in Eshtemoa, 29 in Racal, in the towns of the Jerahmeelites, in the towns of the Kenites, 30 in Hormah, in Borashan, in Athach, 31 in Hebron, all the places where David and his men had roamed.

30.6
Ex 17.4;
Ps 27.14;
56.3,4,11
30.7
1 Sam 23.9
30.8
1 Sam 23.2,
4; v. 18
30.9
1 Sam 27.2
30.10
vv. 9,21
30.12
Judg 15.19
30.14
vv. 1,16;
2 Sam 8.18;
Ezek 25.16;
Josh 14.13
30.16
v. 14
30.17
1 Sam 15.3

30.19
v. 8
30.20
vv. 26-31
30.21
v. 10
30.24
Num 31.27;
Josh 22.8
30.27
Josh 15.30;
19.8; 15.48
30.28
Josh 13.16;
15.50
30.29
1 Sam 27.10;
15.16
30.30
Judg 1.17
30.31
Josh 14.13

The Death of Saul and His Sons

31 Now the Philistines fought against Israel; and the men of Israel fled before the Philistines, and many fell° on Mount Gilboa. ²The Philistines overtook Saul and his sons; and the Philistines killed Jonathan and Abinadab and Malchishua, the sons of Saul. ³The battle pressed hard upon Saul; the archers found him, and he was badly wounded by them. ⁴Then Saul said to his armor-bearer, "Draw your sword and thrust me through with it, so that these uncircumcised may not come and thrust me through, and make sport of me." But his armor-bearer was unwilling; for he was terrified. So Saul took his own sword and fell upon it. ⁵When his armor-bearer saw that Saul was dead, he also fell upon his sword and died with him. ⁶So Saul and his three sons and his armor-bearer and all his men died together on the same day. ⁷When the men of Israel who were on the other side of the valley and those beyond the Jordan saw that the men of Israel had fled and that Saul and his sons

were dead, they forsook their towns and fled; and the Philistines came and occupied them.

8 The next day, when the Philistines came to strip the dead, they found Saul and his three sons fallen on Mount Gilboa. ⁹They cut off his head, stripped off his armor, and sent messengers throughout the land of the Philistines to carry the good news to the houses of their idols and to the people. ¹⁰They put his armor in the temple of Astarte;ᴾ and they fastened his body to the wall of Beth-shan. ¹¹But when the inhabitants of Jabesh-gilead heard what the Philistines had done to Saul, ¹²all the valiant men set out, traveled all night long, and took the body of Saul and the bodies of his sons from the wall of Beth-shan. They came to Jabesh and burned them there. ¹³Then they took their bones and buried them under the tamarisk tree in Jabesh, and fasted seven days.

31.1
1 Chr 10.1-12;
1 Sam 28.4
31.3
2 Sam 1.6
31.4
Judg 9.54;
2 Sam 1.6,
10

31.9
2 Sam 1.20
31.10
1 Sam 7.3;
Judg 2.13;
2 Sam 21.12;
Josh 17.11
31.11
1 Sam 11.3,
9,11
31.12
2 Sam 2.4-7;
2 Chr 16.14
31.13
2 Sam 21.12-
14;
1 Sam 22.6;
2 Sam 1.12

°Heb *and they fell slain* ᴾHeb plural

2 Samuel

Title and Background

1 and 2 Samuel were originally one book (see Introduction to 1 Samuel).

Author and Date of Writing

See Introduction to 1 Samuel.

Theme and Message

2 Samuel depicts David as a true (though imperfect) representative of the ideal theocratic king. Under David's rule the Lord caused the nation to prosper, and he helped the Israelites defeat their enemies. In chapter 7 God established his covenant with David and promised that David's dynasty would endure forever.

Outline

David Mourns for Saul and Jonathan

1 After the death of Saul, when David had returned from defeating the Amalekites, David remained two days in Ziklag. ²On the third day, a man came from Saul's camp, with his clothes torn and dirt on his head. When he came to David, he fell to the ground and did obeisance. ³David said to him, "Where have you come from?" He said to him, "I have escaped from the camp of Israel." ⁴David said to him, "How did things go? Tell me!" He answered, "The army fled from the battle, but also many of the army fell and died; and Saul and his son Jonathan also died." ⁵Then David asked the young man who was reporting to him, "How do you know that Saul and his son Jonathan died?" ⁶The young man reporting to him said, "I happened to be on Mount Gilboa; and there was Saul leaning on his spear, while the chariots and the horsemen drew close to him. ⁷When he looked behind him, he saw me, and called to me. I answered, 'Here sir.' ⁸And he said to me, 'Who are you?' I answered him, 'I am an Amalekite.' ⁹He said to me, 'Come, stand over me and kill me; for convulsions have seized me, and yet my life still lingers.' ¹⁰So I stood over him, and killed him, for I knew that he could not live after he had fallen. I took the crown that was on his head and the armlet that was on his arm, and I have brought them here to my lord."

11 Then David took hold of his clothes and tore them; and all the men who were with him did the same. ¹²They mourned and wept, and fasted until evening for Saul and for his son Jonathan, and for the army of the LORD and for the house of Israel, because they had fallen by the sword. ¹³David said to the young man who had reported to him, "Where do you come from?" He answered, "I am the son of a resident alien, an Amalekite." ¹⁴David said to him, "Were you not afraid to lift your hand to destroy the LORD's anointed?" ¹⁵Then David called one of the young men

1.1 1 Sam 31.6; 30.17,26
1.2 1 Sam 4.10, 12
1.6 1 Sam 31.2-4
1.8 1 Sam 15.3
1.10 Judg 9.54
1.11 2 Sam 3.31; 13.31
1.12 2 Sam 3.35
1.13 v. 8
1.14 1 Sam 24.6; 26.9
1.15 2 Sam 4.10, 12

and said, "Come here and strike him down." So he struck him down and he died. ¹⁶David said to him, "Your blood be on your head; for your own mouth has testified against you, saying, 'I have killed the LORD's anointed.' "

17 David intoned this lamentation over Saul and his son Jonathan. ¹⁸(He ordered that The Song of the Bow^a be taught to the people of Judah; it is written in the Book of Jashar.) He said:

¹⁹ Your glory, O Israel, lies
 slain upon your high
 places!
 How the mighty have
 fallen!
²⁰ Tell it not in Gath,
 proclaim it not in the
 streets of Ashkelon;
 or the daughters of the
 Philistines will rejoice,
 the daughters of the
 uncircumcised will
 exult.

²¹ You mountains of Gilboa,
 let there be no dew or rain
 upon you,
 nor bounteous fields!^b
 For there the shield of the
 mighty was defiled,
 the shield of Saul, anointed
 with oil no more.

²² From the blood of the
 slain,
 from the fat of the mighty,
 the bow of Jonathan did not
 turn back,
 nor the sword of Saul
 return empty.

²³ Saul and Jonathan, beloved
 and lovely!
 In life and in death they
 were not divided;
 they were swifter than
 eagles,
 they were stronger than
 lions.

²⁴ O daughters of Israel, weep
 over Saul,
 who clothed you with
 crimson, in luxury,

1.16
2 Sam 3.28, 29; v. 10
1.17
2 Chr 35.25
1.18
1 Sam 31.3; Josh 10.13
1.19
v. 27
1.20
1 Sam 31.9; Mic 1.10; Ex 15.20; 1 Sam 18.6; 31.4
1.21
1 Sam 31.1; Job 3.3,4; Isa 21.5
1.22
Isa 34.6; 1 Sam 18.4
1.23
Jer 4.13; Judg 14.18

1.25
vv. 19,27
1.26
1 Sam 18.1-4
1.27
vv. 19,25; 1 Sam 2.4
2.1
1 Sam 23.2, 4,9-12; 30.31
2.2
1 Sam 30.5
2.3
1 Sam 30.9; 1 Chr 12.1
2.4
2 Sam 5.3, 5; 1 Sam 31.11-13
2.5
1 Sam 23.21

 who put ornaments of gold
 on your apparel.

²⁵ How the mighty have fallen
 in the midst of the battle!

 Jonathan lies slain upon
 your high places.
²⁶ I am distressed for you, my
 brother Jonathan;
 greatly beloved were you to
 me;
 your love to me was
 wonderful,
 passing the love of women.

²⁷ How the mighty have fallen,
 and the weapons of war
 perished!

David Anointed King of Judah

2 After this David inquired of the LORD, "Shall I go up into any of the cities of Judah?" The LORD said to him, "Go up." David said, "To which shall I go up?" He said, "To Hebron." ²So David went up there, along with his two wives, Ahinoam of Jezreel, and Abigail the widow of Nabal of Carmel. ³David brought up the men who were with him, every one with his household; and they settled in the towns of Hebron. ⁴Then the people of Judah came, and there they anointed David king over the house of Judah.

When they told David, "It was the people of Jabesh-gilead who buried Saul," ⁵David sent messengers to the people of Jabesh-gilead, and said to them, "May you be blessed by the LORD, because you showed this loyalty to Saul your lord, and buried him! ⁶Now may the LORD show steadfast love and faithfulness to you! And I too will reward you because you have done this thing. ⁷Therefore let your hands be strong, and be valiant; for Saul your lord is dead, and the house of Judah has anointed me king over them."

^aHeb *that The Bow* ^bMeaning of Heb uncertain

Ish-bosheth King of Israel

8 But Abner son of Ner, commander of Saul's army, had taken Ishbaal[c] son of Saul, and brought him over to Mahanaim. [9] He made him king over Gilead, the Ashurites, Jezreel, Ephraim, Benjamin, and over all Israel. [10] Ishbaal,[c] Saul's son, was forty years old when he began to reign over Israel, and he reigned two years. But the house of Judah followed David. [11] The time that David was king in Hebron over the house of Judah was seven years and six months.

The Battle of Gibeon

12 Abner son of Ner, and the servants of Ishbaal[c] son of Saul, went out from Mahanaim to Gibeon. [13] Joab son of Zeruiah, and the servants of David, went out and met them at the pool of Gibeon. One group sat on one side of the pool, while the other sat on the other side of the pool. [14] Abner said to Joab, "Let the young men come forward and have a contest before us." Joab said, "Let them come forward." [15] So they came forward and were counted as they passed by, twelve for Benjamin and Ishbaal[c] son of Saul, and twelve of the servants of David. [16] Each grasped his opponent by the head, and thrust his sword in his opponent's side; so they fell down together. Therefore that place was called Helkath-hazzurim,[d] which is at Gibeon. [17] The battle was very fierce that day; and Abner and the men of Israel were beaten by the servants of David.

18 The three sons of Zeruiah were there, Joab, Abishai, and Asahel. Now Asahel was as swift of foot as a wild gazelle. [19] Asahel pursued Abner, turning neither to the right nor to the left as he followed him. [20] Then Abner looked back and said, "Is it you, Asahel?" He answered, "Yes, it is." [21] Abner said to him, "Turn to your right or to your left, and seize one of the young men, and take his spoil." But Asahel would not turn away from following him. [22] Abner said again to Asahel, "Turn away from following me; why should I strike you to the ground? How then could I show my face to your brother Joab?" [23] But he refused to turn away. So Abner struck him in the stomach with the butt of his spear, so that the spear came out at his back. He fell there, and died where he lay. And all those who came to the place where Asahel had fallen and died, stood still.

24 But Joab and Abishai pursued Abner. As the sun was going down they came to the hill of Ammah, which lies before Giah on the way to the wilderness of Gibeon. [25] The Benjaminites rallied around Abner and formed a single band; they took their stand on the top of a hill. [26] Then Abner called to Joab, "Is the sword to keep devouring forever? Do you not know that the end will be bitter? How long will it be before you order your people to turn from the pursuit of their kinsmen?" [27] Joab said, "As God lives, if you had not spoken, the people would have continued to pursue their kinsmen, not stopping until morning." [28] Joab sounded the trumpet and all the people stopped; they no longer pursued Israel or engaged in battle any further.

29 Abner and his men traveled all that night through the Arabah; they crossed the Jordan, and, marching the whole forenoon,[e] they came to Mahanaim. [30] Joab returned from the pursuit of Abner; and when he had gathered all the people together, there were missing of David's servants nineteen men besides Asahel. [31] But the servants of David had killed of Benjamin three hundred sixty of Abner's men. [32] They took up Asahel and buried him in the tomb of his father, which was at Bethlehem. Joab and his men marched all night, and the day broke upon them at Hebron.

Cross references (center column)

2.8
2 Sam 14.50
2.9
Judg 1.32;
1 Sam 29.1
2.11
2 Sam 5.5
2.12
Josh 18.25
2.13
1 Chr 2.16
2.17
2 Sam 3.1
2.18
1 Chr 2.16;
12.8
2.22
2 Sam 3.27

2.23
2 Sam 3.27;
4.6; 20.10
2.24
Josh 10.41
2.27
v. 14
2.29
v. 8

c Gk Compare 1 Chr 8.33; 9.39: Heb *Ish-bosheth*, "man of shame" d That is *Field of Sword-edges* e Meaning of Heb uncertain

Abner Defects to David

3 There was a long war between the house of Saul and the house of David; David grew stronger and stronger, while the house of Saul became weaker and weaker.

2 Sons were born to David at Hebron: his firstborn was Amnon, of Ahinoam of Jezreel; [3] his second, Chileab, of Abigail the widow of Nabal of Carmel; the third, Absalom son of Maacah, daughter of King Talmai of Geshur; [4] the fourth, Adonijah son of Haggith; the fifth, Shephatiah son of Abital; [5] and the sixth, Ithream, of David's wife Eglah. These were born to David in Hebron.

6 While there was war between the house of Saul and the house of David, Abner was making himself strong in the house of Saul. [7] Now Saul had a concubine whose name was Rizpah daughter of Aiah. And Ishbaal[f] said to Abner, "Why have you gone in to my father's concubine?" [8] The words of Ishbaal[g] made Abner very angry; he said, "Am I a dog's head for Judah? Today I keep showing loyalty to the house of your father Saul, to his brothers, and to his friends, and have not given you into the hand of David; and yet you charge me now with a crime concerning this woman. [9] So may God do to Abner and so may he add to it! For just what the LORD has sworn to David, that will I accomplish for him, [10] to transfer the kingdom from the house of Saul, and set up the throne of David over Israel and over Judah, from Dan to Beer-sheba." [11] And Ishbaal[f] could not answer Abner another word, because he feared him.

12 Abner sent messengers to David at Hebron,[h] saying, "To whom does the land belong? Make your covenant with me, and I will give you my support to bring all Israel over to you." [13] He said, "Good; I will make a covenant with you. But one thing I require of you: you shall never appear in my presence unless you bring Saul's daughter Michal when you come to see me." [14] Then David sent messengers to Saul's son Ishbaal,[i] saying, "Give me my wife Michal, to whom I became engaged at the price of one hundred foreskins of the Philistines." [15] Ishbaal[i] sent and took her from her husband Paltiel the son of Laish. [16] But her husband went with her, weeping as he walked behind her all the way to Bahurim. Then Abner said to him, "Go back home!" So he went back.

17 Abner sent word to the elders of Israel, saying, "For some time past you have been seeking David as king over you. [18] Now then bring it about; for the LORD has promised David: Through my servant David I will save my people Israel from the hand of the Philistines, and from all their enemies." [19] Abner also spoke directly to the Benjaminites; then Abner went to tell David at Hebron all that Israel and the whole house of Benjamin were ready to do.

20 When Abner came with twenty men to David at Hebron, David made a feast for Abner and the men who were with him. [21] Abner said to David, "Let me go and rally all Israel to my lord the king, in order that they may make a covenant with you, and that you may reign over all that your heart desires." So David dismissed Abner, and he went away in peace.

Abner Is Killed by Joab

22 Just then the servants of David arrived with Joab from a raid, bringing much spoil with them. But Abner was not with David at Hebron, for David[j] had dismissed him, and he had gone away in peace. [23] When Joab and all the army that was with him came, it was told Joab, "Abner son of Ner came to the king, and he has dismissed him, and he has gone away in peace." [24] Then Joab went to the

3.2 1 Chr 3.1-3; 1 Sam 25.42, 43
3.3 1 Sam 27.8; 2 Sam 13.37
3.4 1 Kings 1.5
3.7 2 Sam 21.8-11; 16.21
3.8 1 Sam 24.14; 2 Sam 9.8
3.9 1 Kings 19.2; 1 Sam 15.8
3.10 Judg 20.1; 1 Sam 3.20
3.13 Gen 43.3; 1 Sam 18.20
3.14 1 Sam 18.25, 27
3.15 1 Sam 25.44
3.16 2 Sam 16.5
3.18 1 Sam 9.16; 15.28
3.19 1 Sam 10.20, 21
3.21 vv. 10,12; 1 Kings 11.37
3.22 1 Sam 27.8

f Heb And he g Gk Compare 1 Chr 8.33; 9.39: Heb Ish-bosheth, "man of shame"
h Gk: Heb where he was
i Heb Ish-bosheth j Heb he

king and said, "What have you done? Abner came to you; why did you dismiss him, so that he got away? [25]You know that Abner son of Ner came to deceive you, and to learn your comings and goings and to learn all that you are doing."

26 When Joab came out from David's presence, he sent messengers after Abner, and they brought him back from the cistern of Sirah; but David did not know about it. [27]When Abner returned to Hebron, Joab took him aside in the gateway to speak with him privately, and there he stabbed him in the stomach. So he died for shedding[k] the blood of Asahel, Joab's[l] brother. [28]Afterward, when David heard of it, he said, "I and my kingdom are forever guiltless before the LORD for the blood of Abner son of Ner. [29]May the guilt[m] fall on the head of Joab, and on all his father's house; and may the house of Joab never be without one who has a discharge, or who is leprous,[n] or who holds a spindle, or who falls by the sword, or who lacks food!" [30]So Joab and his brother Abishai murdered Abner because he had killed their brother Asahel in the battle at Gibeon.

31 Then David said to Joab and to all the people who were with him, "Tear your clothes, and put on sackcloth, and mourn over Abner." And King David followed the bier. [32]They buried Abner at Hebron. The king lifted up his voice and wept at the grave of Abner, and all the people wept. [33]The king lamented for Abner, saying,

"Should Abner die as a fool dies?
[34] Your hands were not bound,
 your feet were not fettered;
as one falls before the
 wicked
you have fallen."

And all the people wept over him again. [35]Then all the people came to persuade David to eat something while it was still day; but David swore, saying, "So may God do to me, and more, if I taste bread or anything else before the sun goes

down!" [36]All the people took notice of it, and it pleased them; just as everything the king did pleased all the people. [37]So all the people and all Israel understood that day that the king had no part in the killing of Abner son of Ner. [38]And the king said to his servants, "Do you not know that a prince and a great man has fallen this day in Israel? [39]Today I am powerless, even though anointed king; these men, the sons of Zeruiah, are too violent for me. The LORD pay back the one who does wickedly in accordance with his wickedness!"

Ish-bosheth Assassinated

4 When Saul's son Ishbaal[o] heard that Abner had died at Hebron, his courage failed, and all Israel was dismayed. [2]Saul's son had two captains of raiding bands; the name of the one was Baanah, and the name of the other Rechab. They were sons of Rimmon a Benjaminite from Beeroth — for Beeroth is considered to belong to Benjamin. [3](Now the people of Beeroth had fled to Gittaim and are there as resident aliens to this day).

4 Saul's son Jonathan had a son who was crippled in his feet. He was five years old when the news about Saul and Jonathan came from Jezreel. His nurse picked him up and fled; and, in her haste to flee, it happened that he fell and became lame. His name was Mephibosheth.[p]

5 Now the sons of Rimmon the Beerothite, Rechab and Baanah, set out, and about the heat of the day they came to the house of Ishbaal,[q] while he was taking his noonday rest. [6]They came inside the house as though to take wheat, and they struck him in the stomach; then Rechab and his brother Baanah escaped.[r] [7]Now they had come into the house while he was lying on his couch in his bedcham-

Cross-references (center column):

3.25
1 Sam 29.6;
Isa 37.28
3.27
2 Sam 2.23;
4.6; 20.9,10;
1 Kings 2.5
3.29
1 Kings 2.32,
33; Lev 15.2
3.30
2 Sam 2.23
3.31
Gen 37.34;
2 Sam 1.2,
11
3.33
2 Sam 1.17
3.35
2 Sam 12.17;
1 Sam 3.17;
2 Sam 1.12

3.39
2 Sam 19.5-7;
1 Kings 2.5,
6,33,34
4.1
2 Sam 3.27;
Ezra 4.4
4.2
Josh 18.25
4.3
Neh 11.33
4.4
2 Sam 9.3,
6;
1 Sam 31.1-4
4.5
2 Sam 2.8
4.6
2 Sam 2.23

k Heb lacks *shedding* l Heb *his*
m Heb *May it* n A term for several skin diseases; precise meaning uncertain
o Heb lacks *Ishbaal* p In 1 Chr 8.34 and 9.40, *Merib-baal* q Heb *Ish-bosheth*
r Meaning of Heb of verse 6 uncertain

ber; they attacked him, killed him, and beheaded him. Then they took his head and traveled by way of the Arabah all night long. ⁸ They brought the head of Ishbaalˢ to David at Hebron and said to the king, "Here is the head of Ishbaal,ˢ son of Saul, your enemy, who sought your life; the LORD has avenged my lord the king this day on Saul and on his offspring."

9 David answered Rechab and his brother Baanah, the sons of Rimmon the Beerothite, "As the LORD lives, who has redeemed my life out of every adversity, ¹⁰ when the one who told me, 'See, Saul is dead,' thought he was bringing good news, I seized him and killed him at Ziklag—this was the reward I gave him for his news. ¹¹ How much more then, when wicked men have killed a righteous man on his bed in his own house! And now shall I not require his blood at your hand, and destroy you from the earth?" ¹² So David commanded the young men, and they killed them; they cut off their hands and feet, and hung their bodies beside the pool at Hebron. But the head of Ishbaalˢ they took and buried in the tomb of Abner at Hebron.

David Anointed King of All Israel

5 Then all the tribes of Israel came to David at Hebron, and said, "Look, we are your bone and flesh. ² For some time, while Saul was king over us, it was you who led out Israel and brought it in. The LORD said to you: It is you who shall be shepherd of my people Israel, you who shall be ruler over Israel." ³ So all the elders of Israel came to the king at Hebron; and King David made a covenant with them at Hebron before the LORD, and they anointed David king over Israel. ⁴ David was thirty years old when he began to reign, and he reigned forty years. ⁵ At Hebron he reigned over Judah seven years and six months; and at Jerusalem he reigned over all Israel and Judah thirty-three years.

4.8
1 Sam 23.15;
25.29
4.9
1 Kings 1.29
4.10
2 Sam 1.2,
4,15
4.11
Gen 9.5,6
4.12
2 Sam 1.15;
3.32
5.1
1 Chr 11.1;
2 Sam 19.13
5.2
1 Sam 18.13;
16.1,12;
25.30
5.3
1 Chr 11.3;
2 Sam 3.21;
2.4
5.4
Num 4.3;
Lk 3.23;
1 Chr 26.31
5.5
2 Sam 2.11

5.6
Josh 15.63;
Judg 1.8,21
5.8
v. 9;
2 Sam 6.12,
16;
1 Kings 2.10
5.9
v. 7
5.10
2 Sam 3.1
5.11
1 Chr 14.1
5.13
Deut 17.17;
1 Chr 3.9
5.14
1 Chr 3.5-8
5.17
2 Sam 23.14
5.18
Josh 15.18;
17.15; 18.16
5.19
1 Sam 23.2;
2 Sam 2.1

Jerusalem Made Capital of the United Kingdom

6 The king and his men marched to Jerusalem against the Jebusites, the inhabitants of the land, who said to David, "You will not come in here, even the blind and the lame will turn you back"— thinking, "David cannot come in here." ⁷ Nevertheless David took the stronghold of Zion, which is now the city of David. ⁸ David had said on that day, "Whoever would strike down the Jebusites, let him get up the water shaft to attack the lame and the blind, those whom David hates."ᵗ Therefore it is said, "The blind and the lame shall not come into the house." ⁹ David occupied the stronghold, and named it the city of David. David built the city all around from the Millo inward. ¹⁰ And David became greater and greater, for the LORD, the God of hosts, was with him.

11 King Hiram of Tyre sent messengers to David, along with cedar trees, and carpenters and masons who built David a house. ¹² David then perceived that the LORD had established him king over Israel, and that he had exalted his kingdom for the sake of his people Israel.

13 In Jerusalem, after he came from Hebron, David took more concubines and wives; and more sons and daughters were born to David. ¹⁴ These are the names of those who were born to him in Jerusalem: Shammua, Shobab, Nathan, Solomon, ¹⁵ Ibhar, Elishua, Nepheg, Japhia, ¹⁶ Elishama, Eliada, and Eliphelet.

Philistine Attack Repulsed

17 When the Philistines heard that David had been anointed king over Israel, all the Philistines went up in search of David; but David heard about it and went down to the stronghold. ¹⁸ Now the Philistines had come and spread out in the valley of Rephaim. ¹⁹ David in-

ˢ Heb *Ish-bosheth* ᵗ Another reading is *those who hate David*

quired of the LORD, "Shall I go up against the Philistines? Will you give them into my hand?" The LORD said to David, "Go up; for I will certainly give the Philistines into your hand." [20] So David came to Baal-perazim, and David defeated them there. He said, "The LORD has burst forth against[u] my enemies before me, like a bursting flood." Therefore that place is called Baal-perazim. [v] [21] The Philistines abandoned their idols there, and David and his men carried them away.

22 Once again the Philistines came up, and were spread out in the valley of Rephaim. [23] When David inquired of the LORD, he said, "You shall not go up; go around to their rear, and come upon them opposite the balsam trees. [24] When you hear the sound of marching in the tops of the balsam trees, then be on the alert; for then the LORD has gone out before you to strike down the army of the Philistines." [25] David did just as the LORD had commanded him; and he struck down the Philistines from Geba all the way to Gezer.

David Brings the Ark to Jerusalem

6 David again gathered all the chosen men of Israel, thirty thousand. [2] David and all the people with him set out and went from Baale-judah, to bring up from there the ark of God, which is called by the name of the LORD of hosts who is enthroned on the cherubim. [3] They carried the ark of God on a new cart, and brought it out of the house of Abinadab, which was on the hill. Uzzah and Ahio,[w] the sons of Abinadab, were driving the new cart [4] with the ark of God;[x] and Ahio[w] went in front of the ark. [5] David and all the house of Israel were dancing before the LORD with all their might, with songs[y] and lyres and harps and tambourines and castanets and cymbals.

6 When they came to the threshing floor of Nacon, Uzzah reached out his hand to the ark of God and took hold of it, for the oxen shook

5.20
Isa 28.21
5.21
1 Chr 14.12
5.22
v. 18
5.23
v. 19
5.24
2 Kings 7.6;
Judg 4.14
5.25
Josh 12.12;
1 Chr 14.16
6.2
1 Chr 13.5,
6;
Lev 24.16;
1 Sam 4.4
6.3
1 Sam 6.7
6.4
1 Sam 7.1
6.5
1 Sam 18.6,
7;
1 Chr 13.8
6.6
1 Chr 13.9;
Num 4.15,
19,20

6.7
1 Sam 6.19
6.10
1 Chr 13.13
6.11
1 Chr 13.14
6.12
1 Chr 15.25;
1 Kings 8.1
6.14
Ex 15.20;
1 Sam 2.18
6.15
1 Chr 15.28
6.16
1 Chr 15.29
6.17
1 Chr 15.1;
16.1;
1 Kings 8.62-65
6.18
1 Kings 8.14,
15

it. [7] The anger of the LORD was kindled against Uzzah; and God struck him there because he reached out his hand to the ark;[z] and he died there beside the ark of God. [8] David was angry because the LORD had burst forth with an outburst upon Uzzah; so that place is called Perez-uzzah,[a] to this day. [9] David was afraid of the LORD that day; he said, "How can the ark of the LORD come into my care?" [10] So David was unwilling to take the ark of the LORD into his care in the city of David; instead David took it to the house of Obed-edom the Gittite. [11] The ark of the LORD remained in the house of Obed-edom the Gittite three months; and the LORD blessed Obed-edom and all his household.

12 It was told King David, "The LORD has blessed the household of Obed-edom and all that belongs to him, because of the ark of God." So David went and brought up the ark of God from the house of Obed-edom to the city of David with rejoicing; [13] and when those who bore the ark of the LORD had gone six paces, he sacrificed an ox and a fatling. [14] David danced before the LORD with all his might; David was girded with a linen ephod. [15] So David and all the house of Israel brought up the ark of the LORD with shouting, and with the sound of the trumpet.

16 As the ark of the LORD came into the city of David, Michal daughter of Saul looked out of the window, and saw King David leaping and dancing before the LORD; and she despised him in her heart.

17 They brought in the ark of the LORD, and set it in its place, inside the tent that David had pitched for it; and David offered burnt offerings and offerings of well-being before the LORD. [18] When David had finished offering the

[u] Heb *paraz* [v] That is *Lord of Bursting Forth* [w] Or *and his brother* [x] Compare Gk: Heb *and brought it out of the house of Abinadab, which was on the hill with the ark of God* [y] Q Ms Gk 1 Chr 13.8: Heb *fir-trees* [z] 1 Chr 13.10 Compare Q Ms: Meaning of Heb uncertain [a] That is *Bursting Out Against Uzzah*

burnt offerings and the offerings of well-being, he blessed the people in the name of the LORD of hosts, [19]and distributed food among all the people, the whole multitude of Israel, both men and women, to each a cake of bread, a portion of meat,[b] and a cake of raisins. Then all the people went back to their homes.

20 David returned to bless his household. But Michal the daughter of Saul came out to meet David, and said, "How the king of Israel honored himself today, uncovering himself today before the eyes of his servants' maids, as any vulgar fellow might shamelessly uncover himself!" [21]David said to Michal, "It was before the LORD, who chose me in place of your father and all his household, to appoint me as prince over Israel, the people of the LORD, that I have danced before the LORD. [22]I will make myself yet more contemptible than this, and I will be abased in my own eyes; but by the maids of whom you have spoken, by them I shall be held in honor." [23]And Michal the daughter of Saul had no child to the day of her death.

God's Covenant with David

7 Now when the king was settled in his house, and the LORD had given him rest from all his enemies around him, [2]the king said to the prophet Nathan, "See now, I am living in a house of cedar, but the ark of God stays in a tent." [3]Nathan said to the king, "Go, do all that you have in mind; for the LORD is with you."

4 But that same night the word of the LORD came to Nathan: [5]Go and tell my servant David: Thus says the LORD: Are you the one to build me a house to live in? [6]I have not lived in a house since the day I brought up the people of Israel from Egypt to this day, but I have been moving about in a tent and a tabernacle. [7]Wherever I have moved about among all the people of Israel, did I ever speak a word with any of the tribal leaders[c] of

Israel, whom I commanded to shepherd my people Israel, saying, "Why have you not built me a house of cedar?" [8]Now therefore thus you shall say to my servant David: Thus says the LORD of hosts: I took you from the pasture, from following the sheep to be prince over my people Israel; [9]and I have been with you wherever you went, and have cut off all your enemies from before you; and I will make for you a great name, like the name of the great ones of the earth. [10]And I will appoint a place for my people Israel and will plant them, so that they may live in their own place, and be disturbed no more; and evildoers shall afflict them no more, as formerly, [11]from the time that I appointed judges over my people Israel; and I will give you rest from all your enemies. Moreover the LORD declares to you that the LORD will make you a house. [12]When your days are fulfilled and you lie down with your ancestors, I will raise up your offspring after you, who shall come forth from your body, and I will establish his kingdom. [13]He shall build a house for my name, and I will establish the throne of his kingdom forever. [14]I will be a father to him, and he shall be a son to me. When he commits iniquity, I will punish him with a rod such as mortals use, with blows inflicted by human beings. [15]But I will not take[d] my steadfast love from him, as I took it from Saul, whom I put away from before you. [16]Your house and your kingdom shall be made sure forever before me;[e] your throne shall be established forever. [17]In accordance with all these words and with all this vision, Nathan spoke to David.

David's Prayer

18 Then King David went in and sat before the LORD, and said, "Who am I, O Lord GOD, and what is my house, that you have brought me

Cross references

6.20 vv. 14,16; 1 Sam 19.24
6.21 1 Sam 13.14; 15.28
7.1 1 Chr 17.1ff
7.2 2 Sam 5.11; Acts 7.46; Ex 26.1
7.3 1 Kings 8.17, 18
7.5 1 Kings 5.3, 4; 8.19
7.6 1 Kings 8.16; Ex 40.18,34
7.7 Lev 26.11, 12; Deut 23.14; 2 Sam 5.2
7.8 1 Sam 16.11, 12; Ps 78.70; 2 Sam 6.21
7.9 1 Sam 18.14; 2 Sam 5.10; Ps 18.37-42
7.10 Ex 15.17; Isa 5.2,7; Ps 89.22; Isa 60.18
7.11 Judg 2.16; 1 Sam 12.9-11; vv. 1,27; 1 Sam 25.28
7.12 1 Kings 2.1
7.13 1 Kings 5.5; Ps 89.4,29; 36.37; Isa 9.7
7.14 Ps 89.26,27; Heb 1.5; Ps 89.30-33
7.15 1 Sam 15.23, 28
7.16 Ps 89.36,37
7.18 Ex 3.11; 1 Sam 18.18

b Vg: Meaning of Heb uncertain c Or *any of the tribes* d Gk Syr Vg 1 Chr 17.13: Heb *shall not depart* e Gk Heb Mss: MT *before you*; Compare 2 Sam 7.26, 29

thus far? [19]And yet this was a small thing in your eyes, O Lord God; you have spoken also of your servant's house for a great while to come. May this be instruction for the people,[f] O Lord God! [20]And what more can David say to you? For you know your servant, O Lord God! [21]Because of your promise, and according to your own heart, you have wrought all this greatness, so that your servant may know it. [22]Therefore you are great, O Lord God; for there is no one like you, and there is no God besides you, according to all that we have heard with our ears. [23]Who is like your people, like Israel? Is there another[g] nation on earth whose God went to redeem it as a people, and to make a name for himself, doing great and awesome things for them,[h] by driving out[i] before his people nations and their gods?[j] [24]And you established your people Israel for yourself to be your people forever; and you, O Lord, became their God. [25]And now, O Lord God, as for the word that you have spoken concerning your servant and concerning his house, confirm it forever; do as you have promised. [26]Thus your name will be magnified forever in the saying, 'The Lord of hosts is God over Israel'; and the house of your servant David will be established before you. [27]For you, O Lord of hosts, the God of Israel, have made this revelation to your servant, saying, 'I will build you a house'; therefore your servant has found courage to pray this prayer to you. [28]And now, O Lord God, you are God, and your words are true, and you have promised this good thing to your servant; [29]now therefore may it please you to bless the house of your servant, so that it may continue forever before you; for you, O Lord God, have spoken, and with your blessing shall the house of your servant be blessed forever."

David's Wars

8 Some time afterward, David attacked the Philistines and

subdued them; David took Methegammah out of the hand of the Philistines.

2 He also defeated the Moabites and, making them lie down on the ground, measured them off with a cord; he measured two lengths of cord for those who were to be put to death, and one length[k] for those who were to be spared. And the Moabites became servants to David and brought tribute.

3 David also struck down King Hadadezer son of Rehob of Zobah, as he went to restore his monument[l] at the river Euphrates. [4]David took from him one thousand seven hundred horsemen, and twenty thousand foot soldiers. David hamstrung all the chariot horses, but left enough for a hundred chariots. [5]When the Arameans of Damascus came to help King Hadadezer of Zobah, David killed twenty-two thousand men of the Arameans. [6]Then David put garrisons among the Arameans of Damascus; and the Arameans became servants to David and brought tribute. The Lord gave victory to David wherever he went. [7]David took the gold shields that were carried by the servants of Hadadezer, and brought them to Jerusalem. [8]From Betah and from Berothai, towns of Hadadezer, King David took a great amount of bronze.

9 When King Toi of Hamath heard that David had defeated the whole army of Hadadezer, [10]Toi sent his son Joram to King David, to greet him and to congratulate him because he had fought against Hadadezer and defeated him. Now Hadadezer had often been at war with Toi. Joram brought with him articles of silver, gold, and bronze; [11]these also King David dedicated to the Lord, together with the silver and gold that he dedicated from all the nations he subdued, [12]from

7.19
Isa 55.8
7.20
1 Sam 16.7;
Jn 21.17
7.22
Ps 48.1;
86.10;
Ex 15.11;
Deut 3.24;
Ps 44.1
7.23
Deut 4.7,
32-38; 10.21;
15.15; 9.26
7.24
Deut 26.18;
Ps 48.14
7.26
Ps 72.18,19
7.27
v. 13
7.28
Jn 17.17
7.29
Num 6.24-26

8.2
Num 24.17
8.3
2 Sam 10.15-19
8.4
Josh 11.6,9
8.5
1 Kings 11.23-25
8.6
v. 14;
2 Sam 7.9
8.7
1 Kings 10.16
8.10
1 Chr 18.10
8.11
1 Kings 7.51;
1 Chr 18.11;
26.25

f Meaning of Heb uncertain g Gk: Heb one h Heb you i Gk 1 Chr 17.21: Heb for your land j Cn: Heb before your people, whom you redeemed for yourself from Egypt, nations and its gods k Heb one full length l Compare 1 Sam 15.12 and 2 Sam 18.18

Edom, Moab, the Ammonites, the Philistines, Amalek, and from the spoil of King Hadadezer son of Rehob of Zobah.

13 David won a name for himself. When he returned, he killed eighteen thousand Edomites[m] in the Valley of Salt. [14] He put garrisons in Edom; throughout all Edom he put garrisons, and all the Edomites became David's servants. And the LORD gave victory to David wherever he went.

David's Officers

15 So David reigned over all Israel; and David administered justice and equity to all his people. [16] Joab son of Zeruiah was over the army; Jehoshaphat son of Ahilud was recorder; [17] Zadok son of Ahitub and Ahimelech son of Abiathar were priests; Seraiah was secretary; [18] Benaiah son of Jehoiada was over[n] the Cherethites and the Pelethites; and David's sons were priests.

David's Kindness to Mephibosheth

9 David asked, "Is there still anyone left of the house of Saul to whom I may show kindness for Jonathan's sake?" [2] Now there was a servant of the house of Saul whose name was Ziba, and he was summoned to David. The king said to him, "Are you Ziba?" And he said, "At your service!" [3] The king said, "Is there anyone remaining of the house of Saul to whom I may show the kindness of God?" Ziba said to the king, "There remains a son of Jonathan; he is crippled in his feet." [4] The king said to him, "Where is he?" Ziba said to the king, "He is in the house of Machir son of Ammiel, at Lo-debar." [5] Then King David sent and brought him from the house of Machir son of Ammiel, at Lo-debar. [6] Mephibosheth[o] son of Jonathan son of Saul came to David, and fell on his face and did obeisance. David said, "Mephibosheth!"[o] He answered, "I am your servant." [7] David said to him, "Do not be afraid, for I will

show you kindness for the sake of your father Jonathan; I will restore to you all the land of your grandfather Saul, and you yourself shall eat at my table always." [8] He did obeisance and said, "What is your servant, that you should look upon a dead dog such as I?"

9 Then the king summoned Saul's servant Ziba, and said to him, "All that belonged to Saul and to all his house I have given to your master's grandson. [10] You and your sons and your servants shall till the land for him, and shall bring in the produce, so that your master's grandson may have food to eat; but your master's grandson Mephibosheth[o] shall always eat at my table." Now Ziba had fifteen sons and twenty servants. [11] Then Ziba said to the king, "According to all that my lord the king commands his servant, so your servant will do." Mephibosheth[o] ate at David's[p] table, like one of the king's sons. [12] Mephibosheth[o] had a young son whose name was Mica. And all who lived in Ziba's house became Mephibosheth's[q] servants. [13] Mephibosheth[o] lived in Jerusalem, for he always ate at the king's table. Now he was lame in both his feet.

The Ammonites and Arameans Are Defeated

10 Some time afterward, the king of the Ammonites died, and his son Hanun succeeded him. [2] David said, "I will deal loyally with Hanun son of Nahash, just as his father dealt loyally with me." So David sent envoys to console him concerning his father. When David's envoys came into the land of the Ammonites, [3] the princes of the Ammonites said to their lord Hanun, "Do you really think that David is honoring your father just because he has sent messengers with condolences to you? Has not David sent his envoys to you to

8.13
2 Ki 14.7
8.14
Gen 27.29,
37,40;
Num 24.17,
18; v. 6
8.16
2 Sam 19.13;
1 Kings 4.3;
2 Kings 18.18,
37
8.17
1 Chr 24.3
8.18
1 Sam 30.14
9.1
1 Sam 20.14-
17, 42
9.2
2 Sam 16.1-4;
19.17,29
9.3
1 Sam 20.14;
2 Sam 4.4
9.4
2 Sam 17.27
9.6
2 Sam 16.4;
19.24-30
9.7
vv. 1,3;
2 Sam 12.8;
19.28

9.8
2 Sam 16.9
9.9
2 Sam 16.4;
19.29
9.10
vv. 7,11,13;
2 Sam 19.28
9.12
1 Chr 8.34
9.13
vv. 3,7,10
10.1
1 Chr 19.1ff

m Gk: Heb *returned from striking down eighteen thousand Arameans* n Syr Tg Vg 20.23; 1 Chr 18.17: Heb lacks *was over* o Or *Merib-baal:* See 4.4 note p Gk: Heb *my* q Or *Merib-baal's:* See 4.4 note

search the city, to spy it out, and to overthrow it?" ⁴So Hanun seized David's envoys, shaved off half the beard of each, cut off their garments in the middle at their hips, and sent them away. ⁵When David was told, he sent to meet them, for the men were greatly ashamed. The king said, "Remain at Jericho until your beards have grown, and then return."

6 When the Ammonites saw that they had become odious to David, the Ammonites sent and hired the Arameans of Beth-rehob and the Arameans of Zobah, twenty thousand foot soldiers, as well as the king of Maacah, one thousand men, and the men of Tob, twelve thousand men. ⁷When David heard of it, he sent Joab and all the army with the warriors. ⁸The Ammonites came out and drew up in battle array at the entrance of the gate; but the Arameans of Zobah and of Rehob, and the men of Tob and Maacah, were by themselves in the open country.

9 When Joab saw that the battle was set against him both in front and in the rear, he chose some of the picked men of Israel, and arrayed them against the Arameans; ¹⁰the rest of his men he put in the charge of his brother Abishai, and he arrayed them against the Ammonites. ¹¹He said, "If the Arameans are too strong for me, then you shall help me; but if the Ammonites are too strong for you, then I will come and help you. ¹²Be strong, and let us be courageous for the sake of our people, and for the cities of our God; and may the Lord do what seems good to him." ¹³So Joab and the people who were with him moved forward into battle against the Arameans; and they fled before him. ¹⁴When the Ammonites saw that the Arameans fled, they likewise fled before Abishai, and entered the city. Then Joab returned from fighting against the Ammonites, and came to Jerusalem.

15 But when the Arameans saw that they had been defeated by Is-

rael, they gathered themselves together. ¹⁶Hadadezer sent and brought out the Arameans who were beyond the Euphrates; and they came to Helam, with Shobach the commander of the army of Hadadezer at their head. ¹⁷When it was told David, he gathered all Israel together, and crossed the Jordan, and came to Helam. The Arameans arrayed themselves against David and fought with him. ¹⁸The Arameans fled before Israel; and David killed of the Arameans seven hundred chariot teams, and forty thousand horsemen,ʳ and wounded Shobach the commander of their army, so that he died there. ¹⁹When all the kings who were servants of Hadadezer saw that they had been defeated by Israel, they made peace with Israel, and became subject to them. So the Arameans were afraid to help the Ammonites any more.

David Commits Adultery with Bathsheba

11 In the spring of the year, the time when kings go out to battle, David sent Joab with his officers and all Israel with him; they ravaged the Ammonites, and besieged Rabbah. But David remained at Jerusalem.

2 It happened, late one afternoon, when David rose from his couch and was walking about on the roof of the king's house, that he saw from the roof a woman bathing; the woman was very beautiful. ³David sent someone to inquire about the woman. It was reported, "This is Bathsheba daughter of Eliam, the wife of Uriah the Hittite." ⁴So David sent messengers to get her, and she came to him, and he lay with her. (Now she was purifying herself after her period.) Then she returned to her house. ⁵The woman conceived; and she sent and told David, "I am pregnant."

6 So David sent word to Joab, "Send me Uriah the Hittite." And Joab sent Uriah to David. ⁷When

Cross references (center column):

10.4 Isa 15.2; 20.4
10.6 Gen 34.30; 2 Sam 8.3, 5;
Judg 18.28
10.8 1 Chr 19.9; Judg 11.3,5
10.12 Deut 31.6; 1 Cor 16.13; 1 Sam 3.18
10.13 1 Kings 20.13-21

10.16 2 Sam 8.3; 1 Chr 19.16
10.18 1 Chr 19.18; 2 Sam 8.6
11.1 1 Chr 20.1; 1 Kings 20.22, 26; 2 Sam 12.26-28
11.2 Deut 22.8; Mt 5.28
11.3 2 Sam 23.39
11.4 Lev 15.19, 28; 18.19
11.5 Lev 20.10

ʳ 1 Chr 19.18 and some Gk Mss read *foot soldiers*

Uriah came to him, David asked how Joab and the people fared, and how the war was going. [8] Then David said to Uriah, "Go down to your house, and wash your feet." Uriah went out of the king's house, and there followed him a present from the king. [9] But Uriah slept at the entrance of the king's house with all the servants of his lord, and did not go down to his house. [10] When they told David, "Uriah did not go down to his house," David said to Uriah, "You have just come from a journey. Why did you not go down to your house?" [11] Uriah said to David, "The ark and Israel and Judah remain in booths; [s] and my lord Joab and the servants of my lord are camping in the open field; shall I then go to my house, to eat and to drink, and to lie with my wife? As you live, and as your soul lives, I will not do such a thing." [12] Then David said to Uriah, "Remain here today also, and tomorrow I will send you back." So Uriah remained in Jerusalem that day. On the next day, [13] David invited him to eat and drink in his presence and made him drunk; and in the evening he went out to lie on his couch with the servants of his lord, but he did not go down to his house.

David Has Uriah Killed

[14] In the morning David wrote a letter to Joab, and sent it by the hand of Uriah. [15] In the letter he wrote, "Set Uriah in the forefront of the hardest fighting, and then draw back from him, so that he may be struck down and die." [16] As Joab was besieging the city, he assigned Uriah to the place where he knew there were valiant warriors. [17] The men of the city came out and fought with Joab; and some of the servants of David among the people fell. Uriah the Hittite was killed as well. [18] Then Joab sent and told David all the news about the fighting; [19] and he instructed the messenger, "When you have finished telling the king all the news about the fighting, [20] then, if the king's anger rises, and if he says to you,

'Why did you go so near the city to fight? Did you not know that they would shoot from the wall? [21] Who killed Abimelech son of Jerubbaal? [t] Did not a woman throw an upper millstone on him from the wall, so that he died at Thebez? Why did you go so near the wall?' then you shall say, 'Your servant Uriah the Hittite is dead too.' "

22 So the messenger went, and came and told David all that Joab had sent him to tell. [23] The messenger said to David, "The men gained an advantage over us, and came out against us in the field; but we drove them back to the entrance of the gate. [24] Then the archers shot at your servants from the wall; some of the king's servants are dead; and your servant Uriah the Hittite is dead also." [25] David said to the messenger, "Thus you shall say to Joab, 'Do not let this matter trouble you, for the sword devours now one and now another; press your attack on the city, and overthrow it.' And encourage him."

26 When the wife of Uriah heard that her husband was dead, she made lamentation for him. [27] When the mourning was over, David sent and brought her to his house, and she became his wife, and bore him a son.

Nathan Condemns David

12 But the thing that David had done displeased the LORD, [1] and the LORD sent Nathan to David. He came to him, and said to him, "There were two men in a certain city, the one rich and the other poor. [2] The rich man had very many flocks and herds; [3] but the poor man had nothing but one little ewe lamb, which he had bought. He brought it up, and it grew up with him and with his children; it used to eat of his meager fare, and drink from his cup, and lie in his bosom, and it was like a daughter to him. [4] Now there came a traveler to the rich man, and he was loath to take one of his own flock or herd

11.8
Gen 43.24;
Lk 7.44
11.10
2 Sam 7.2,
6; 20.6
11.13
v. 9
11.14
1 Kings 21.8-
10
11.15
2 Sam 12.9
11.17
v. 21

11.21
Judg 9.50-54
11.26
Deut 34.8;
1 Sam 31.13
11.27
2 Sam 12.9;
Ps 51.4,5
12.1
2 Sam 14.4-7;
1 Kings 20.35-
40

s Or at *Succoth* t Gk Syr Judg 7.1: Heb *Jerubbesheth*

to prepare for the wayfarer who had come to him, but he took the poor man's lamb, and prepared that for the guest who had come to him." [5] Then David's anger was greatly kindled against the man. He said to Nathan, "As the LORD lives, the man who has done this deserves to die; [6] he shall restore the lamb fourfold, because he did this thing, and because he had no pity."

[7] Nathan said to David, "You are the man! Thus says the LORD, the God of Israel: I anointed you king over Israel, and I rescued you from the hand of Saul; [8] I gave you your master's house, and your master's wives into your bosom, and gave you the house of Israel and of Judah; and if that had been too little, I would have added as much more. [9] Why have you despised the word of the LORD, to do what is evil in his sight? You have struck down Uriah the Hittite with the sword, and have taken his wife to be your wife, and have killed him with the sword of the Ammonites. [10] Now therefore the sword shall never depart from your house, for you have despised me, and have taken the wife of Uriah the Hittite to be your wife. [11] Thus says the LORD: I will raise up trouble against you from within your own house; and I will take your wives before your eyes, and give them to your neighbor, and he shall lie with your wives in the sight of this very sun. [12] For you did it secretly; but I will do this thing before all Israel, and before the sun." [13] David said to Nathan, "I have sinned against the LORD." Nathan said to David, "Now the LORD has put away your sin; you shall not die. [14] Nevertheless, because by this deed you have utterly scorned the LORD,[u] the child that is born to you shall die." [15] Then Nathan went to his house.

Bathsheba's Child Dies

The LORD struck the child that Uriah's wife bore to David, and it became very ill. [16] David therefore pleaded with God for the child; David fasted, and went in and lay all night on the ground. [17] The elders of his house stood beside him, urging him to rise from the ground; but he would not, nor did he eat food with them. [18] On the seventh day the child died. And the servants of David were afraid to tell him that the child was dead; for they said, "While the child was still alive, we spoke to him, and he did not listen to us; how then can we tell him the child is dead? He may do himself some harm." [19] But when David saw that his servants were whispering together, he perceived that the child was dead; and David said to his servants, "Is the child dead?" They said, "He is dead."

[20] Then David rose from the ground, washed, anointed himself, and changed his clothes. He went into the house of the LORD, and worshiped; he then went to his own house; and when he asked, they set food before him and he ate. [21] Then his servants said to him, "What is this thing that you have done? You fasted and wept for the child while it was alive; but when the child died, you rose and ate food." [22] He said, "While the child was still alive, I fasted and wept; for I said, 'Who knows? The LORD may be gracious to me, and the child may live.' [23] But now he is dead; why should I fast? Can I bring him back again? I shall go to him, but he will not return to me."

Solomon Is Born

[24] Then David consoled his wife Bathsheba, and went to her, and lay with her; and she bore a son, and he named him Solomon. The LORD loved him, [25] and sent a message by the prophet Nathan; so he named him Jedidiah,[v] because of the LORD.

The Ammonites Crushed

[26] Now Joab fought against Rabbah of the Ammonites, and took the royal city. [27] Joab sent

Cross references (center column)

12.5 1 Kings 20.39, 41
12.6 Ex 22.1; Lk 19.8
12.7 1 Kings 20.42; 1 Sam 16.13
12.9 1 Sam 15.19; 2 Sam 11.15-17, 27
12.10 2 Sam 13.28; 18.14; 1 Kings 2.25
12.11 Deut 28.30; 2 Sam 16.22
12.12 2 Sam 11.4-15; 16.22
12.13 1 Sam 15.24; 2 Sam 24.10; Prov 28.13; Mic 7.18
12.14 Isa 52.5; Rom 2.24
12.15 1 Sam 25.38
12.16 2 Sam 13.31
12.20 Job 1.20
12.22 Isa 38.1,5; Jon 3.9
12.23 Gen 37.35; Job 7.8-10
12.24 Mt 1.6; 1 Chr 22.9
12.26 1 Chr 20.1-3

[u] Ancient scribal tradition: Compare 1 Sam 25.22 note: Heb *scorned the enemies of the LORD*　[v] That is *Beloved of the LORD*

messengers to David, and said, "I have fought against Rabbah; moreover, I have taken the water city. 28 Now, then, gather the rest of the people together, and encamp against the city, and take it; or I myself will take the city, and it will be called by my name." 29 So David gathered all the people together and went to Rabbah, and fought against it and took it. 30 He took the crown of Milcomᵂ from his head; the weight of it was a talent of gold, and in it was a precious stone; and it was placed on David's head. He also brought forth the spoil of the city, a very great amount. 31 He brought out the people who were in it, and set them to work with saws and iron picks and iron axes, or sent them to the brickworks. Thus he did to all the cities of the Ammonites. Then David and all the people returned to Jerusalem.

Amnon and Tamar

13 Some time passed. David's son Absalom had a beautiful sister whose name was Tamar; and David's son Amnon fell in love with her. 2 Amnon was so tormented that he made himself ill because of his sister Tamar, for she was a virgin and it seemed impossible to Amnon to do anything to her. 3 But Amnon had a friend whose name was Jonadab, the son of David's brother Shimeah; and Jonadab was a very crafty man. 4 He said to him, "O son of the king, why are you so haggard morning after morning? Will you not tell me?" Amnon said to him, "I love Tamar, my brother Absalom's sister." 5 Jonadab said to him, "Lie down on your bed, and pretend to be ill; and when your father comes to see you, say to him, 'Let my sister Tamar come and give me something to eat, and prepare the food in my sight, so that I may see it and eat it from her hand.'" 6 So Amnon lay down, and pretended to be ill; and when the king came to see him, Amnon said to the king, "Please let my sister Tamar come and make a couple of

12.30
1 Chr 20.2
13.1
2 Sam 3.2, 3;
1 Chr 3.9
13.3
1 Sam 16.9
13.6
Gen 18.6

13.9
Gen 45.1
13.11
Gen 39.12
13.12
Lev 20.17;
Judg 19.23;
20.6
13.13
Gen 20.12;
Lev 18.9,11
13.14
Deut 22.25
13.18
Gen 37.3;
Judg 5.30

cakes in my sight, so that I may eat from her hand."

7 Then David sent home to Tamar, saying, "Go to your brother Amnon's house, and prepare food for him." 8 So Tamar went to her brother Amnon's house, where he was lying down. She took dough, kneaded it, made cakes in his sight, and baked the cakes. 9 Then she took the pan and set themˣ out before him, but he refused to eat. Amnon said, "Send out everyone from me." So everyone went out from him. 10 Then Amnon said to Tamar, "Bring the food into the chamber, so that I may eat from your hand." So Tamar took the cakes she had made, and brought them into the chamber to Amnon her brother. 11 But when she brought them near him to eat, he took hold of her, and said to her, "Come, lie with me, my sister." 12 She answered him, "No, my brother, do not force me; for such a thing is not done in Israel; do not do anything so vile! 13 As for me, where could I carry my shame? And as for you, you would be as one of the scoundrels in Israel. Now therefore, I beg you, speak to the king; for he will not withhold me from you." 14 But he would not listen to her; and being stronger than she, he forced her and lay with her.

15 Then Amnon was seized with a very great loathing for her; indeed, his loathing was even greater than the lust he had felt for her. Amnon said to her, "Get out!" 16 But she said to him, "No, my brother;ʸ for this wrong in sending me away is greater than the other that you did to me." But he would not listen to her. 17 He called the young man who served him and said, "Put this woman out of my presence, and bolt the door after her." 18 (Now she was wearing a long robe with sleeves; for this is how the virgin daughters of the king were clothed in earlier

ᵂ Gk See 1 Kings 11.5, 33: Heb *their kings*
ˣ Heb *and poured* ʸ Cn Compare Gk Vg: Meaning of Heb uncertain

times. z) So his servant put her out, and bolted the door after her. 19 But Tamar put ashes on her head, and tore the long robe that she was wearing; she put her hand on her head, and went away, crying aloud as she went.

20 Her brother Absalom said to her, "Has Amnon your brother been with you? Be quiet for now, my sister; he is your brother; do not take this to heart." So Tamar remained, a desolate woman, in her brother Absalom's house. 21 When King David heard of all these things, he became very angry, but he would not punish his son Amnon, because he loved him, for he was his firstborn. a 22 But Absalom spoke to Amnon neither good nor bad; for Absalom hated Amnon, because he had raped his sister Tamar.

Absalom Avenges the Violation of His Sister

23 After two full years Absalom had sheepshearers at Baal-hazor, which is near Ephraim, and Absalom invited all the king's sons. 24 Absalom came to the king, and said, "Your servant has sheepshearers; will the king and his servants please go with your servant?" 25 But the king said to Absalom, "No, my son, let us not all go, or else we will be burdensome to you." He pressed him, but he would not go but gave him his blessing. 26 Then Absalom said, "If not, please let my brother Amnon go with us." The king said to him, "Why should he go with you?" 27 But Absalom pressed him until he let Amnon and all the king's sons go with him. Absalom made a feast like a king's feast. b 28 Then Absalom commanded his servants, "Watch when Amnon's heart is merry with wine, and when I say to you, 'Strike Amnon,' then kill him. Do not be afraid; have I not myself commanded you? Be courageous and valiant." 29 So the servants of Absalom did to Amnon as Absalom had commanded. Then all the

king's sons rose, and each mounted his mule and fled.

30 While they were on the way, the report came to David that Absalom had killed all the king's sons, and not one of them was left. 31 The king rose, tore his garments, and lay on the ground; and all his servants who were standing by tore their garments. 32 But Jonadab, the son of David's brother Shimeah, said, "Let not my lord suppose that they have killed all the young men the king's sons; Amnon alone is dead. This has been determined by Absalom from the day Amnon c raped his sister Tamar. 33 Now therefore, do not let my lord the king take it to heart, as if all the king's sons were dead; for Amnon alone is dead."

34 But Absalom fled. When the young man who kept watch looked up, he saw many people coming from the Horonaim road d by the side of the mountain. 35 Jonadab said to the king, "See, the king's sons have come; as your servant said, so it has come about." 36 As soon as he had finished speaking, the king's sons arrived, and raised their voices and wept; and the king and all his servants also wept very bitterly.

37 But Absalom fled, and went to Talmai son of Ammihud, king of Geshur. David mourned for his son day after day. 38 Absalom, having fled to Geshur, stayed there three years. 39 And the heart of e the king went out, yearning for Absalom; for he was now consoled over the death of Amnon.

Absalom Returns to Jerusalem

14 Now Joab son of Zeruiah perceived that the king's mind was on Absalom. 2 Joab sent to Tekoa and brought from there a wise woman. He said to her, "Pretend to be a mourner; put on mourning garments, do not anoint

Cross-references

13.19
1 Sam 4.12;
2 Sam 1.2;
Jer 2.37
13.20
2 Sam 14.24
13.22
Gen 31.24;
Lev 19.17, 18
13.28
Judg 19.6,9, 22;
1 Sam 25.36
13.29
2 Sam 18.9;
1 Kings 1.33, 38

13.31
2 Sam 1.11;
12.16
13.32
v. 3
13.33
2 Sam 19.19
13.34
vv. 37,38;
2 Sam 18.24
13.37
v. 34;
2 Sam 3.3;
14.23,32
13.39
2 Sam 12.19-23
14.1
2 Sam 13.39
14.2
2 Chr 11.6;
1 Kings 20.35-43;
2 Sam 12.20

z Cn: Heb *were clothed in robes* a Q Ms Gk: MT lacks *but he would not punish . . . firstborn* b Gk Compare Q Ms: MT lacks *Absalom made a feast like a king's feast* c Heb *he* d Cn Compare Gk: Heb *the road behind him* e Q Ms Gk: MT *And David*

yourself with oil, but behave like a woman who has been mourning many days for the dead. ³Go to the king and speak to him as follows." And Joab put the words into her mouth.

4 When the woman of Tekoa came to the king, she fell on her face to the ground and did obeisance, and said, "Help, O king!" ⁵The king asked her, "What is your trouble?" She answered, "Alas, I am a widow; my husband is dead. ⁶Your servant had two sons, and they fought with one another in the field; there was no one to part them, and one struck the other and killed him. ⁷Now the whole family has risen against your servant. They say, 'Give up the man who struck his brother, so that we may kill him for the life of his brother whom he murdered, even if we destroy the heir as well.' Thus they would quench my one remaining ember, and leave to my husband neither name nor remnant on the face of the earth."

8 Then the king said to the woman, "Go to your house, and I will give orders concerning you." ⁹The woman of Tekoa said to the king, "On me be the guilt, my lord the king, and on my father's house; let the king and his throne be guiltless." ¹⁰The king said, "If anyone says anything to you, bring him to me, and he shall never touch you again." ¹¹Then she said, "Please, may the king keep the LORD your God in mind, so that the avenger of blood may kill no more, and my son not be destroyed." He said, "As the LORD lives, not one hair of your son shall fall to the ground."

12 Then the woman said, "Please let your servant speak a word to my lord the king." He said, "Speak." ¹³The woman said, "Why then have you planned such a thing against the people of God? For in giving this decision the king convicts himself, inasmuch as the king does not bring his banished one home again. ¹⁴We must all die; we are like water spilled on the ground, which cannot be gathered

14.3
v. 19
14.4
2 Sam 1.2;
2 Kings 6.26-28
14.5
2 Sam 12.1-7
14.7
Num 35.19;
Deut 19.12;
Mt 21.38
14.9
1 Sam 25.24;
Mt 27.25;
1 Kings 2.33
14.11
Num 35.19;
1 Sam 14.45
14.13
2 Sam 12.7;
1 Kings 20.40-42;
2 Sam 13.37, 38
14.14
Job 34.15;
Heb 9.27;
Num 35.15, 25,28

up. But God will not take away a life; he will devise plans so as not to keep an outcast banished forever from his presence.ᶠ ¹⁵Now I have come to say this to my lord the king because the people have made me afraid; your servant thought, 'I will speak to the king; it may be that the king will perform the request of his servant. ¹⁶For the king will hear, and deliver his servant from the hand of the man who would cut both me and my son off from the heritage of God.' ¹⁷Your servant thought, 'The word of my lord the king will set me at rest'; for my lord the king is like the angel of God, discerning good and evil. The LORD your God be with you!"

18 Then the king answered the woman, "Do not withhold from me anything I ask you." The woman said, "Let my lord the king speak." ¹⁹The king said, "Is the hand of Joab with you in all this?" The woman answered and said, "As surely as you live, my lord the king, one cannot turn right or left from anything that my lord the king has said. For it was your servant Joab who commanded me; it was he who put all these words into the mouth of your servant. ²⁰In order to change the course of affairs your servant Joab did this. But my lord has wisdom like the wisdom of the angel of God to know all things that are on the earth."

21 Then the king said to Joab, "Very well, I grant this; go, bring back the young man Absalom." ²²Joab prostrated himself with his face to the ground and did obeisance, and blessed the king; and Joab said, "Today your servant knows that I have found favor in your sight, my lord the king, in that the king has granted the request of his servant." ²³So Joab set off, went to Geshur, and brought Absalom to Jerusalem. ²⁴The king said, "Let him go to his own house; he is not to come into my presence." So Absalom went to his own house, and

14.17
v. 20;
2 Sam 19.27
14.19
v. 3
14.20
v. 17;
2 Sam 19.27
14.23
2 Sam 13.37, 38
14.24
2 Sam 3.13

ᶠMeaning of Heb uncertain

did not come into the king's presence.

David Forgives Absalom

25 Now in all Israel there was no one to be praised so much for his beauty as Absalom; from the sole of his foot to the crown of his head there was no blemish in him. 26When he cut the hair of his head (for at the end of every year he used to cut it; when it was heavy on him, he cut it), he weighed the hair of his head, two hundred shekels by the king's weight. 27There were born to Absalom three sons, and one daughter whose name was Tamar; she was a beautiful woman.

28 So Absalom lived two full years in Jerusalem, without coming into the king's presence. 29Then Absalom sent for Joab to send him to the king; but Joab would not come to him. He sent a second time, but Joab would not come. 30Then he said to his servants, "Look, Joab's field is next to mine, and he has barley there; go and set it on fire." So Absalom's servants set the field on fire. 31Then Joab rose and went to Absalom at his house, and said to him, "Why have your servants set my field on fire?" 32Absalom answered Joab, "Look, I sent word to you: Come here, that I may send you to the king with the question, 'Why have I come from Geshur? It would be better for me to be there still.' Now let me go into the king's presence; if there is guilt in me, let him kill me!" 33Then Joab went to the king and told him; and he summoned Absalom. So he came to the king and prostrated himself with his face to the ground before the king; and the king kissed Absalom.

Absalom Usurps the Throne

15 After this Absalom got himself a chariot and horses, and fifty men to run ahead of him. 2Absalom used to rise early and stand beside the road into the gate; and when anyone brought a suit before the king for judgment, Absalom would call out and say,

"From what city are you?" When the person said, "Your servant is of such and such a tribe in Israel," 3Absalom would say, "See, your claims are good and right; but there is no one deputed by the king to hear you." 4Absalom said moreover, "If only I were judge in the land! Then all who had a suit or cause might come to me, and I would give them justice." 5Whenever people came near to do obeisance to him, he would put out his hand and take hold of them, and kiss them. 6Thus Absalom did to every Israelite who came to the king for judgment; so Absalom stole the hearts of the people of Israel.

7 At the end of fourᵍ years Absalom said to the king, "Please let me go to Hebron and pay the vow that I have made to the LORD. 8For your servant made a vow while I lived at Geshur in Aram: If the LORD will indeed bring me back to Jerusalem, then I will worship the LORD in Hebron."ʰ 9The king said to him, "Go in peace." So he got up, and went to Hebron. 10But Absalom sent secret messengers throughout all the tribes of Israel, saying, "As soon as you hear the sound of the trumpet, then shout: Absalom has become king at Hebron!" 11Two hundred men from Jerusalem went with Absalom; they were invited guests, and they went in their innocence, knowing nothing of the matter. 12While Absalom was offering the sacrifices, he sent forⁱ Ahithophel the Gilonite, David's counselor, from his city Giloh. The conspiracy grew in strength, and the people with Absalom kept increasing.

David Flees from Jerusalem

13 A messenger came to David, saying, "The hearts of the Israelites have gone after Absalom." 14Then David said to all his officials who were with him at Jerusalem, "Get up! Let us flee, or there will be no escape for us from Absalom. Hurry,

Cross references (center column)

14.25
Isa 1.6
14.26
Ezek 44.20
14.27
2 Sam 18.18
14.28
v. 24
14.32
1 Sam 20.8
14.33
Gen 33.4;
Lk 15.20
15.1
2 Sam 12.11;
1 Kings 1.5
15.2
2 Sam 19.8

15.4
Judg 9.29
15.6
Rom 16.18
15.7ff
2 Sam 3.2,
3
15.8
2 Sam 13.37,
38;
Gen 28.20,
21
15.11
1 Sam 9.13;
22.15
15.12
v. 31;
Josh 15.51;
Ps 3.1
15.13
v. 6;
Judg 9.3
15.14
2 Sam 12.11;
19.9

ᵍ Gk Syr: Heb forty ʰ Gk Mss: Heb lacks in Hebron ⁱ Or he sent

or he will soon overtake us, and bring disaster down upon us, and attack the city with the edge of the sword." ¹⁵The king's officials said to the king, "Your servants are ready to do whatever our lord the king decides." ¹⁶So the king left, followed by all his household, except ten concubines whom he left behind to look after the house. ¹⁷The king left, followed by all the people; and they stopped at the last house. ¹⁸All his officials passed by him; and all the Cherethites, and all the Pelethites, and all the six hundred Gittites who had followed him from Gath, passed on before the king.

19 Then the king said to Ittai the Gittite, "Why are you also coming with us? Go back, and stay with the king; for you are a foreigner, and also an exile from your home. ²⁰You came only yesterday, and shall I today make you wander about with us, while I go wherever I can? Go back, and take your kinsfolk with you; and may the LORD show[j] steadfast love and faithfulness to you." ²¹But Ittai answered the king, "As the LORD lives, and as my lord the king lives, wherever my lord the king may be, whether for death or for life, there also your servant will be." ²²David said to Ittai, "Go then, march on." So Ittai the Gittite marched on, with all his men and all the little ones who were with him. ²³The whole country wept aloud as all the people passed by; the king crossed the Wadi Kidron, and all the people moved on toward the wilderness.

24 Abiathar came up, and Zadok also, with all the Levites, carrying the ark of the covenant of God. They set down the ark of God, until the people had all passed out of the city. ²⁵Then the king said to Zadok, "Carry the ark of God back into the city. If I find favor in the eyes of the LORD, he will bring me back and let me see both it and the place where it stays. ²⁶But if he says, 'I take no pleasure in you,' here I am, let him do to me what seems good to him." ²⁷The king also said to the priest

Zadok, "Look,[k] go back to the city in peace, you and Abiathar,[l] with your two sons, Ahimaaz your son, and Jonathan son of Abiathar. ²⁸See, I will wait at the fords of the wilderness until word comes from you to inform me." ²⁹So Zadok and Abiathar carried the ark of God back to Jerusalem, and they remained there.

30 But David went up the ascent of the Mount of Olives, weeping as he went, with his head covered and walking barefoot; and all the people who were with him covered their heads and went up, weeping as they went. ³¹David was told that Ahithophel was among the conspirators with Absalom. And David said, "O LORD, I pray you, turn the counsel of Ahithophel into foolishness."

Hushai Becomes David's Spy

32 When David came to the summit, where God was worshiped, Hushai the Archite came to meet him with his coat torn and earth on his head. ³³David said to him, "If you go on with me, you will be a burden to me. ³⁴But if you return to the city and say to Absalom, 'I will be your servant, O king; as I have been your father's servant in time past, so now I will be your servant,' then you will defeat for me the counsel of Ahithophel. ³⁵The priests Zadok and Abiathar will be with you there. So whatever you hear from the king's house, tell it to the priests Zadok and Abiathar. ³⁶Their two sons are with them there, Zadok's son Ahimaaz and Abiathar's son Jonathan; and by them you shall report to me everything you hear." ³⁷So Hushai, David's friend, came into the city, just as Absalom was entering Jerusalem.

David's Adversaries

16 When David had passed a little beyond the summit, Ziba the servant of Mephibosheth[m]

Cross references (center column):

15.16
2 Sam 16.21, 22
15.18
2 Sam 8.18
15.19
2 Sam 18.2
15.20
1 Sam 23.13
15.21
Ruth 1.16, 17
15.24
2 Sam 8.17; Num 4.15; 1 Sam 22.20
15.25
Ps 43.3;
Jer 25.30
15.26
2 Sam 22.20; 1 Kings 10.9; 1 Sam 3.18
15.27
1 Sam 9.6-9; 2 Sam 17.17
15.28
2 Sam 17.16
15.30
Esther 6.12; 2 Sam 19.4; Isa 20.2-4; Ps 126.6
15.31
v. 12;
2 Sam 16.23; 17.14,23
15.32
Josh 16.2; 2 Sam 1.2
15.33
2 Sam 19.35
15.34
2 Sam 16.19
15.35
2 Sam 17.15, 16
15.36
v. 27;
2 Sam 17.17
15.37
2 Sam 16.16, 17;
1 Chr 27.33
16.1
2 Sam 15.32; 9.2-13

i Gk Compare 2.6: Heb lacks *may the LORD show* k Gk: Heb *Are you a seer* or *Do you see?* l Cn: Heb lacks *and Abiathar*
m Or *Merib-baal*: See 4.4 note

met him, with a couple of donkeys saddled, carrying two hundred loaves of bread, one hundred bunches of raisins, one hundred of summer fruits, and one skin of wine. [2] The king said to Ziba, "Why have you brought these?" Ziba answered, "The donkeys are for the king's household to ride, the bread and summer fruit for the young men to eat, and the wine is for those to drink who faint in the wilderness." [3] The king said, "And where is your master's son?" Ziba said to the king, "He remains in Jerusalem; for he said, 'Today the house of Israel will give me back my grandfather's kingdom.'" [4] Then the king said to Ziba, "All that belonged to Mephibosheth[n] is now yours." Ziba said, "I do obeisance; let me find favor in your sight, my lord the king."

Shimei Curses David

5 When King David came to Bahurim, a man of the family of the house of Saul came out whose name was Shimei son of Gera; he came out cursing. [6] He threw stones at David and at all the servants of King David; now all the people and all the warriors were on his right and on his left. [7] Shimei shouted while he cursed, "Out! Out! Murderer! Scoundrel! [8] The LORD has avenged on all of you the blood of the house of Saul, in whose place you have reigned; and the LORD has given the kingdom into the hand of your son Absalom. See, disaster has overtaken you; for you are a man of blood."

9 Then Abishai son of Zeruiah said to the king, "Why should this dead dog curse my lord the king? Let me go over and take off his head." [10] But the king said, "What have I to do with you, you sons of Zeruiah? If he is cursing because the LORD has said to him, 'Curse David,' who then shall say, 'Why have you done so?'" [11] David said to Abishai and to all his servants, "My own son seeks my life; how much more now may this Benjaminite! Let him alone, and let him

16.2
2 Sam 17.29
16.3
2 Sam 9.9,
10; 19.26,27
16.5
2 Sam 3.16-18;
19.16-23;
1 Kings 2.8
16.7
2 Sam 12.9
16.8
2 Sam 21.1-9
2 Sam 19.21;
9.8;
Ex 22.28
16.10
2 Sam 19.22;
1 Pet 2.23;
2 Kings 18.25;
Rom 9.20
16.11
2 Sam 12.11;
Gen 45.5

16.12
Rom 8.28
16.15
2 Sam 15.37
16.16
2 Sam 15.37
16.17
2 Sam 19.25
16.19
2 Sam 15.34
16.21
2 Sam 15.16;
1 Sam 13.4;
2 Sam 2.7
16.22
2 Sam 12.11,
12
16.23
2 Sam 15.12

curse; for the LORD has bidden him. [12] It may be that the LORD will look on my distress,[o] and the LORD will repay me with good for this cursing of me today." [13] So David and his men went on the road, while Shimei went along on the hillside opposite him and cursed as he went, throwing stones and flinging dust at him. [14] The king and all the people who were with him arrived weary at the Jordan;[p] and there he refreshed himself.

The Counsel of Ahithophel

15 Now Absalom and all the Israelites[q] came to Jerusalem; Ahithophel was with him. [16] When Hushai the Archite, David's friend, came to Absalom, Hushai said to Absalom, "Long live the king! Long live the king!" [17] Absalom said to Hushai, "Is this your loyalty to your friend? Why did you not go with your friend?" [18] Hushai said to Absalom, "No; but the one whom the LORD and this people and all the Israelites have chosen, his I will be, and with him I will remain. [19] Moreover, whom should I serve? Should it not be his son? Just as I have served your father, so I will serve you."

20 Then Absalom said to Ahithophel, "Give us your counsel; what shall we do?" [21] Ahithophel said to Absalom, "Go in to your father's concubines, the ones he has left to look after the house; and all Israel will hear that you have made yourself odious to your father, and the hands of all who are with you will be strengthened." [22] So they pitched a tent for Absalom upon the roof; and Absalom went in to his father's concubines in the sight of all Israel. [23] Now in those days the counsel that Ahithophel gave was as if one consulted the oracle[r] of God; so all the counsel of Ahithophel was esteemed, both by David and by Absalom.

[n] Or *Merib-baal*: See 4.4 note　[o] Gk Vg:
Heb *iniquity*　[p] Gk: Heb lacks *at the Jordan*
[q] Gk: Heb *all the people, the men of Israel*
[r] Heb *word*

17 Moreover Ahithophel said to Absalom, "Let me choose twelve thousand men, and I will set out and pursue David tonight. [2] I will come upon him while he is weary and discouraged, and throw him into a panic; and all the people who are with him will flee. I will strike down only the king, [3] and I will bring all the people back to you as a bride comes home to her husband. You seek the life of only one man, [s] and all the people will be at peace." [4] The advice pleased Absalom and all the elders of Israel.

The Counsel of Hushai

[5] Then Absalom said, "Call Hushai the Archite also, and let us hear too what he has to say." [6] When Hushai came to Absalom, Absalom said to him, "This is what Ahithophel has said; shall we do as he advises? If not, you tell us." [7] Then Hushai said to Absalom, "This time the counsel that Ahithophel has given is not good." [8] Hushai continued, "You know that your father and his men are warriors, and that they are enraged, like a bear robbed of her cubs in the field. Besides, your father is expert in war; he will not spend the night with the troops. [9] Even now he has hidden himself in one of the pits, or in some other place. And when some of our troops[t] fall at the first attack, whoever hears it will say, 'There has been a slaughter among the troops who follow Absalom.' [10] Then even the valiant warrior, whose heart is like the heart of a lion, will utterly melt with fear; for all Israel knows that your father is a warrior, and that those who are with him are valiant warriors. [11] But my counsel is that all Israel be gathered to you, from Dan to Beer-sheba, like the sand by the sea for multitude, and that you go to battle in person. [12] So we shall come upon him in whatever place he may be found, and we shall light on him as the dew falls on the ground; and he will not survive, nor will any of those with him. [13] If he withdraws into a city, then all Israel will bring ropes to that city, and we shall drag it into the valley, until not even a pebble is to be found there." [14] Absalom and all the men of Israel said, "The counsel of Hushai the Archite is better than the counsel of Ahithophel." For the Lord had ordained to defeat the good counsel of Ahithophel, so that the Lord might bring ruin on Absalom.

Hushai Warns David to Escape

[15] Then Hushai said to the priests Zadok and Abiathar, "Thus and so did Ahithophel counsel Absalom and the elders of Israel; and thus and so I have counseled. [16] Therefore send quickly and tell David, 'Do not lodge tonight at the fords of the wilderness, but by all means cross over; otherwise the king and all the people who are with him will be swallowed up.' " [17] Jonathan and Ahimaaz were waiting at En-rogel; a servant girl used to go and tell them, and they would go and tell King David; for they could not risk being seen entering the city. [18] But a boy saw them, and told Absalom; so both of them went away quickly, and came to the house of a man at Bahurim, who had a well in his courtyard; and they went down into it. [19] The man's wife took a covering, stretched it over the well's mouth, and spread out grain on it; and nothing was known of it. [20] When Absalom's servants came to the woman at the house, they said, "Where are Ahimaaz and Jonathan?" The woman said to them, "They have crossed over the brook[u] of water." And when they had searched and could not find them, they returned to Jerusalem.

[21] After they had gone, the men came up out of the well, and went and told King David. They said to David, "Go and cross the water quickly; for thus and so has Ahithophel counseled against you." [22] So

17.2
2 Sam 16.14;
1 Kings 22.31
17.5
2 Sam 15.32-34
17.8
Hos 13.8;
1 Sam 16.18
17.10
Josh 2.11

17.14
2 Sam 15.31, 34
17.15
2 Sam 15.35
17.16
2 Sam 15.28
17.17
2 Sam 15.27, 36;
Josh 15.7;
18.16
17.18
2 Sam 16.5
17.19
Josh 2.4-6
17.20
Josh 2.3-5;
1 Sam 19.12-17
17.21
vv. 15,16

s Gk: Heb *like the return of the whole (is) the man whom you seek* t Gk Mss: Heb *some of them* u Meaning of Heb uncertain

David and all the people who were with him set out and crossed the Jordan; by daybreak not one was left who had not crossed the Jordan.

23 When Ahithophel saw that his counsel was not followed, he saddled his donkey and went off home to his own city. He set his house in order, and hanged himself; he died and was buried in the tomb of his father.

24 Then David came to Mahanaim, while Absalom crossed the Jordan with all the men of Israel. 25 Now Absalom had set Amasa over the army in the place of Joab. Amasa was the son of a man named Ithra the Ishmaelite,ᵛ who had married Abigal daughter of Nahash, sister of Zeruiah, Joab's mother. 26 The Israelites and Absalom encamped in the land of Gilead.

27 When David came to Mahanaim, Shobi son of Nahash from Rabbah of the Ammonites, and Machir son of Ammiel from Lodebar, and Barzillai the Gileadite from Rogelim, 28 brought beds, basins, and earthen vessels, wheat, barley, meal, parched grain, beans and lentils,ʷ 29 honey and curds, sheep, and cheese from the herd, for David and the people with him to eat; for they said, "The troops are hungry and weary and thirsty in the wilderness."

The Defeat and Death of Absalom

18 Then David mustered the men who were with him, and set over them commanders of thousands and commanders of hundreds. 2 And David divided the army into three groups:ˣ one third under the command of Joab, one third under the command of Abishai son of Zeruiah, Joab's brother, and one third under the command of Ittai the Gittite. The king said to the men, "I myself will also go out with you." 3 But the men said, "You shall not go out. For if we flee, they will not care about us. If half of us die, they will not care about us. But

you are worth ten thousand of us;ʸ therefore it is better that you send us help from the city." 4 The king said to them, "Whatever seems best to you I will do." So the king stood at the side of the gate, while all the army marched out by hundreds and by thousands. 5 The king ordered Joab and Abishai and Ittai, saying, "Deal gently for my sake with the young man Absalom." And all the people heard when the king gave orders to all the commanders concerning Absalom.

6 So the army went out into the field against Israel; and the battle was fought in the forest of Ephraim. 7 The men of Israel were defeated there by the servants of David, and the slaughter there was great on that day, twenty thousand men. 8 The battle spread over the face of all the country; and the forest claimed more victims that day than the sword.

9 Absalom happened to meet the servants of David. Absalom was riding on his mule, and the mule went under the thick branches of a great oak. His head caught fast in the oak, and he was left hangingᶻ between heaven and earth, while the mule that was under him went on. 10 A man saw it, and told Joab, "I saw Absalom hanging in an oak." 11 Joab said to the man who told him, "What, you saw him! Why then did you not strike him there to the ground? I would have been glad to give you ten pieces of silver and a belt." 12 But the man said to Joab, "Even if I felt in my hand the weight of a thousand pieces of silver, I would not raise my hand against the king's son; for in our hearing the king commanded you and Abishai and Ittai, saying: For my sake protect the young man Absalom! 13 On the other hand, if I had dealt treacherously against his lifeᵃ (and there is nothing hidden

Cross-references (center column)

17.23
2 Sam 15.12;
2 Kings 20.1;
Mt 27.5
17.24
Gen 32.2;
2 Sam 2.8
17.25
2 Sam 19.13;
20.9-12
17.27
2 Sam 10.1,
2; 12.26,29;
19.31,32;
1 Kings 2.7
17.29
2 Sam 16.2
18.1
Ex 18.25;
1 Sam 22.7
18.2
1 Sam 11.11;
2 Sam 15.19
18.3
2 Sam 21.17

18.4
v. 24
18.5
v. 12
18.6
Josh 17.15,
18
18.9
2 Sam 14.26
18.12
v. 5

ᵛ1 Chr 2.17: Heb *Israelite* ʷHeb *and lentils and parched grain* ˣGk: Heb *sent forth the army* ʸGk Vg Symmachus: Heb *for now there are ten thousand such as we* ᶻGk Syr Tg: Heb *was put* ᵃAnother reading is *at the risk of my life*

from the king), then you yourself would have stood aloof." ¹⁴Joab said, "I will not waste time like this with you." He took three spears in his hand, and thrust them into the heart of Absalom, while he was still alive in the oak. ¹⁵And ten young men, Joab's armor-bearers, surrounded Absalom and struck him, and killed him.

16 Then Joab sounded the trumpet, and the troops came back from pursuing Israel, for Joab restrained the troops. ¹⁷They took Absalom, threw him into a great pit in the forest, and raised over him a very great heap of stones. Meanwhile all the Israelites fled to their homes. ¹⁸Now Absalom in his lifetime had taken and set up for himself a pillar that is in the King's Valley, for he said, "I have no son to keep my name in remembrance"; he called the pillar by his own name. It is called Absalom's Monument to this day.

David Hears of Absalom's Death

19 Then Ahimaaz son of Zadok said, "Let me run, and carry tidings to the king that the LORD has delivered him from the power of his enemies." ²⁰Joab said to him, "You are not to carry tidings today; you may carry tidings another day, but today you shall not do so, because the king's son is dead." ²¹Then Joab said to a Cushite, "Go, tell the king what you have seen." The Cushite bowed before Joab, and ran. ²²Then Ahimaaz son of Zadok said again to Joab, "Come what may, let me also run after the Cushite." And Joab said, "Why will you run, my son, seeing that you have no reward ᵇ for the tidings?" ²³"Come what may," he said, "I will run." So he said to him, "Run." Then Ahimaaz ran by the way of the Plain, and outran the Cushite.

24 Now David was sitting between the two gates. The sentinel went up to the roof of the gate by the wall, and when he looked up, he saw a man running alone. ²⁵The sentinel shouted and told the king. The king said, "If he is alone, there are tidings in his mouth." He kept coming, and drew near. ²⁶Then the sentinel saw another man running; and the sentinel called to the gatekeeper and said, "See, another man running alone!" The king said, "He also is bringing tidings." ²⁷The sentinel said, "I think the running of the first one is like the running of Ahimaaz son of Zadok." The king said, "He is a good man, and comes with good tidings."

28 Then Ahimaaz cried out to the king, "All is well!" He prostrated himself before the king with his face to the ground, and said, "Blessed be the LORD your God, who has delivered up the men who raised their hand against my lord the king." ²⁹The king said, "Is it well with the young man Absalom?" Ahimaaz answered, "When Joab sent your servant,ᶜ I saw a great tumult, but I do not know what it was." ³⁰The king said, "Turn aside, and stand here." So he turned aside, and stood still.

31 Then the Cushite came; and the Cushite said, "Good tidings for my lord the king! For the LORD has vindicated you this day, delivering you from the power of all who rose up against you." ³²The king said to the Cushite, "Is it well with the young man Absalom?" The Cushite answered, "May the enemies of my lord the king, and all who rise up to do you harm, be like that young man."

David Mourns for Absalom

33ᵈThe king was deeply moved, and went up to the chamber over the gate, and wept; and as he went, he said, "O my son Absalom, my son, my son Absalom! Would I had died instead of you, O Absalom, my son, my son!"

19 It was told Joab, "The king is weeping and mourning for Absalom." ²So the victory that day was turned into mourning for all the troops; for the troops heard that day, "The king is grieving for

18.14
2 Sam 14.30
18.16
2 Sam 2.28;
20.22
18.17
Josh 7.26;
8.29;
2 Sam 19.8
18.18
1 Sam 15.12;
Gen 14.17;
2 Sam 14.27
18.19
2 Sam 15.36;
v. 31
18.24
2 Sam 19.8;
13.34;
2 Kings 9.17

18.28
2 Sam 14.4;
1 Sam 25.23;
17.46
18.29
v. 22
18.31
v. 19;
Judg 5.31
18.32
1 Sam 25.26
18.33
2 Sam 19.4;
Ex 32.32;
Rom 9.3
19.1
2 Sam 18.33

ᵇ Meaning of Heb uncertain ᶜ Heb the king's servant, your servant ᵈ Ch 19.1 in Heb

his son." ³The troops stole into the city that day as soldiers steal in who are ashamed when they flee in battle. ⁴The king covered his face, and the king cried with a loud voice, "O my son Absalom, O Absalom, my son, my son!" ⁵Then Joab came into the house to the king, and said, "Today you have covered with shame the faces of all your officers who have saved your life today, and the lives of your sons and your daughters, and the lives of your wives and your concubines, ⁶for love of those who hate you and for hatred of those who love you. You have made it clear today that commanders and officers are nothing to you; for I perceive that if Absalom were alive and all of us were dead today, then you would be pleased. ⁷So go out at once and speak kindly to your servants; for I swear by the Lord, if you do not go, not a man will stay with you this night; and this will be worse for you than any disaster that has come upon you from your youth until now." ⁸Then the king got up and took his seat in the gate. The troops were all told, "See, the king is sitting in the gate"; and all the troops came before the king.

David Recalled to Jerusalem

Meanwhile, all the Israelites had fled to their homes. ⁹All the people were disputing throughout all the tribes of Israel, saying, "The king delivered us from the hand of our enemies, and saved us from the hand of the Philistines; and now he has fled out of the land because of Absalom. ¹⁰But Absalom, whom we anointed over us, is dead in battle. Now therefore why do you say nothing about bringing the king back?"

11 King David sent this message to the priests Zadok and Abiathar, "Say to the elders of Judah, 'Why should you be the last to bring the king back to his house? The talk of all Israel has come to the king.ᵉ ¹²You are my kin, you are my bone and my flesh; why then should you be the last to bring back the king?'

¹³And say to Amasa, 'Are you not my bone and my flesh? So may God do to me, and more, if you are not the commander of my army from now on, in place of Joab.' " ¹⁴Amasaᶠ swayed the hearts of all the people of Judah as one, and they sent word to the king, "Return, both you and all your servants." ¹⁵So the king came back to the Jordan; and Judah came to Gilgal to meet the king and to bring him over the Jordan.

16 Shimei son of Gera, the Benjaminite, from Bahurim, hurried to come down with the people of Judah to meet King David; ¹⁷with him were a thousand people from Benjamin. And Ziba, the servant of the house of Saul, with his fifteen sons and his twenty servants, rushed down to the Jordan ahead of the king, ¹⁸while the crossing was taking place,ᵍ to bring over the king's household, and to do his pleasure.

David's Mercy to Shimei

Shimei son of Gera fell down before the king, as he was about to cross the Jordan, ¹⁹and said to the king, "May my lord not hold me guilty or remember how your servant did wrong on the day my lord the king left Jerusalem; may the king not bear it in mind. ²⁰For your servant knows that I have sinned; therefore, see, I have come this day, the first of all the house of Joseph to come down to meet my lord the king." ²¹Abishai son of Zeruiah answered, "Shall not Shimei be put to death for this, because he cursed the Lord's anointed?" ²²But David said, "What have I to do with you, you sons of Zeruiah, that you should today become an adversary to me? Shall anyone be put to death in Israel this day? For do I not know that I am this day king over Israel?" ²³The king said to Shimei, "You shall not die." And the king gave him his oath.

19.4
2 Sam 15.30;
18.33
19.6
Mt 5.46
19.8
2 Sam 15.2;
18.4
19.9
2 Sam 8.1-14;
5.20; 15.14
19.12
2 Sam 5.1

19.13
2 Sam 17.25;
1 Kings 19.2;
8.16; vv. 5-7
19.14
Judg 20.1
19.15
Josh 5.9
19.16
2 Sam 16.5;
1 Kings 2.8
19.17
2 Sam 16.1,
2
19.19
1 Sam 22.15;
2 Sam 16.6-8;
13.33
19.20
2 Sam 16.5
19.21
2 Sam 16.7,
8; Ex 22.28
19.22
2 Sam 16.10;
1 Sam 11.13
19.23
1 Kings 2.8

ᵉ Gk: Heb *to the king, to his house*
ᶠ Heb *He* ᵍ Cn: Heb *the ford crossed*

David and Mephibosheth Meet

24 Mephibosheth[h] grandson of Saul came down to meet the king; he had not taken care of his feet, or trimmed his beard, or washed his clothes, from the day the king left until the day he came back in safety. [25] When he came from Jerusalem to meet the king, the king said to him, "Why did you not go with me, Mephibosheth?"[h] [26] He answered, "My lord, O king, my servant deceived me; for your servant said to him, 'Saddle a donkey for me,[i] so that I may ride on it and go with the king.' For your servant is lame. [27] He has slandered your servant to my lord the king. But my lord the king is like the angel of God; do therefore what seems good to you. [28] For all my father's house were doomed to death before my lord the king; but you set your servant among those who eat at your table. What further right have I, then, to appeal to the king?" [29] The king said to him, "Why speak any more of your affairs? I have decided: you and Ziba shall divide the land." [30] Mephibosheth[h] said to the king, "Let him take it all, since my lord the king has arrived home safely."

David's Kindness to Barzillai

31 Now Barzillai the Gileadite had come down from Rogelim; he went on with the king to the Jordan, to escort him over the Jordan. [32] Barzillai was a very aged man, eighty years old. He had provided the king with food while he stayed at Mahanaim, for he was a very wealthy man. [33] The king said to Barzillai, "Come over with me, and I will provide for you in Jerusalem at my side." [34] But Barzillai said to the king, "How many years have I still to live, that I should go up with the king to Jerusalem? [35] Today I am eighty years old; can I discern what is pleasant and what is not? Can your servant taste what he eats or what he drinks? Can I still listen to the voice of singing men and singing women? Why then should your servant be an added burden to my lord the king? [36] Your servant will go a little way over the Jordan with the king. Why should the king recompense me with such a reward? [37] Please let your servant return, so that I may die in my own town, near the graves of my father and my mother. But here is your servant Chimham; let him go over with my lord the king; and do for him whatever seems good to you." [38] The king answered, "Chimham shall go over with me, and I will do for him whatever seems good to you; and all that you desire of me I will do for you." [39] Then all the people crossed over the Jordan, and the king crossed over; the king kissed Barzillai and blessed him, and he returned to his own home. [40] The king went on to Gilgal, and Chimham went on with him; all the people of Judah, and also half the people of Israel, brought the king on his way.

41 Then all the people of Israel came to the king, and said to him, "Why have our kindred the people of Judah stolen you away, and brought the king and his household over the Jordan, and all David's men with him?" [42] All the people of Judah answered the people of Israel, "Because the king is near of kin to us. Why then are you angry over this matter? Have we eaten at all at the king's expense? Or has he given us any gift?" [43] But the people of Israel answered the people of Judah, "We have ten shares in the king, and in David also we have more than you. Why then did you despise us? Were we not the first to speak of bringing back our king?" But the words of the people of Judah were fiercer than the words of the people of Israel.

The Rebellion of Sheba

20 Now a scoundrel named Sheba son of Bichri, a Benjaminite, happened to be there. He sounded the trumpet and cried out,

Cross references (center column)

19.24 2 Sam 9.6-10
19.25 2 Sam 16.17
19.26 2 Sam 9.3
19.27 2 Sam 16.3; 14.17,20
19.28 2 Sam 21.6-9; 9.7,10,13
19.31 1 Kings 2.7
19.32 1 Sam 17.27
19.35 Ps 90.10; Isa 5.11,12

19.37 v. 40; 1 Kings 2.7; Jer 41.17
19.39 Gen 31.55
19.41 v. 15
19.42 v. 12
19.43 1 Kings 11.30, 31
20.1 2 Sam 19.43; 1 Kings 12.16; 2 Chr 10.16

h Or *Merib-baal*: See 4.4 note i Gk Syr Vg: Heb *said, I will saddle a donkey for myself*

"We have no portion in
 David,
no share in the son of Jesse!
Everyone to your tents,
 O Israel!"

2 So all the people of Israel withdrew from David and followed Sheba son of Bichri; but the people of Judah followed their king steadfastly from the Jordan to Jerusalem.

3 David came to his house at Jerusalem; and the king took the ten concubines whom he had left to look after the house, and put them in a house under guard, and provided for them, but did not go in to them. So they were shut up until the day of their death, living as if in widowhood.

4 Then the king said to Amasa, "Call the men of Judah together to me within three days, and be here yourself." 5 So Amasa went to summon Judah; but he delayed beyond the set time that had been appointed him. 6 David said to Abishai, "Now Sheba son of Bichri will do us more harm than Absalom; take your lord's servants and pursue him, or he will find fortified cities for himself, and escape from us." 7 Joab's men went out after him, along with the Cherethites, the Pelethites, and all the warriors; they went out from Jerusalem to pursue Sheba son of Bichri. 8 When they were at the large stone that is in Gibeon, Amasa came to meet them. Now Joab was wearing a soldier's garment and over it was a belt with a sword in its sheath fastened at his waist; as he went forward it fell out. 9 Joab said to Amasa, "Is it well with you, my brother?" And Joab took Amasa by the beard with his right hand to kiss him. 10 But Amasa did not notice the sword in Joab's hand; Joab struck him in the belly so that his entrails poured out on the ground, and he died. He did not strike a second blow.

Then Joab and his brother Abishai pursued Sheba son of Bichri. 11 And one of Joab's men took his stand by Amasa, and said,

"Whoever favors Joab, and whoever is for David, let him follow Joab." 12 Amasa lay wallowing in his blood on the highway, and the man saw that all the people were stopping. Since he saw that all who came by him were stopping, he carried Amasa from the highway into a field, and threw a garment over him. 13 Once he was removed from the highway, all the people went on after Joab to pursue Sheba son of Bichri.

14 Sheba[j] passed through all the tribes of Israel to Abel of Beth-maacah;[k] and all the Bichrites[l] assembled, and followed him inside. 15 Joab's forces[m] came and besieged him in Abel of Beth-maacah; they threw up a siege-ramp against the city, and it stood against the rampart. Joab's forces were battering the wall to break it down. 16 Then a wise woman called from the city, "Listen! Listen! Tell Joab, 'Come here, I want to speak to you.' " 17 He came near her; and the woman said, "Are you Joab?" He answered, "I am." Then she said to him, "Listen to the words of your servant." He answered, "I am listening." 18 Then she said, "They used to say in the old days, 'Let them inquire at Abel'; and so they would settle a matter. 19 I am one of those who are peaceable and faithful in Israel; you seek to destroy a city that is a mother in Israel; why will you swallow up the heritage of the LORD?" 20 Joab answered, "Far be it from me, far be it, that I should swallow up or destroy! 21 That is not the case! But a man of the hill country of Ephraim, called Sheba son of Bichri, has lifted up his hand against King David; give him up alone, and I will withdraw from the city." The woman said to Joab, "His head shall be thrown over the wall to you." 22 Then the woman went to all the people with her wise plan. And they cut off the head of Sheba son of Bichri, and threw it out to Joab. So he blew the

20.3
2 Sam 15.16;
16.21,22
20.4
2 Sam 19.13
20.6
2 Sam 11.11;
1 Kings 1.33
20.7
2 Sam 8.18;
1 Kings 1.38;
2 Sam 15.18
20.9
Mt 26.49
20.10
2 Sam 2.23;
3.27;
1 Kings 2.5

20.15
1 Kings 15.20;
2 Kings 19.32
20.16
2 Sam 14.2
20.19
1 Sam 26.19;
2 Sam 21.3
20.21
v. 2
20.22
Eccl 9.13-16;
v. 1

j Heb He k Compare 20.15: Heb and
Beth-maacah; l Compare Gk Vg: Heb Berites
m Heb They

trumpet, and they dispersed from the city, and all went to their homes, while Joab returned to Jerusalem to the king.

23 Now Joab was in command of all the army of Israel;[n] Benaiah son of Jehoiada was in command of the Cherethites and the Pelethites; 24 Adoram was in charge of the forced labor; Jehoshaphat son of Ahilud was the recorder; 25 Sheva was secretary; Zadok and Abiathar were priests; 26 and Ira the Jairite was also David's priest.

David Avenges the Gibeonites

21 Now there was a famine in the days of David for three years, year after year; and David inquired of the LORD. The LORD said, "There is bloodguilt on Saul and on his house, because he put the Gibeonites to death." 2 So the king called the Gibeonites and spoke to them. (Now the Gibeonites were not of the people of Israel, but of the remnant of the Amorites; although the people of Israel had sworn to spare them, Saul had tried to wipe them out in his zeal for the people of Israel and Judah.) 3 David said to the Gibeonites, "What shall I do for you? How shall I make expiation, that you may bless the heritage of the LORD?" 4 The Gibeonites said to him, "It is not a matter of silver or gold between us and Saul or his house; neither is it for us to put anyone to death in Israel." He said, "What do you say that I should do for you?" 5 They said to the king, "The man who consumed us and planned to destroy us, so that we should have no place in all the territory of Israel — 6 let seven of his sons be handed over to us, and we will impale them before the LORD at Gibeon on the mountain of the LORD."[o] The king said, "I will hand them over."

7 But the king spared Mephibosheth,[p] the son of Saul's son Jonathan, because of the oath of the LORD that was between them, between David and Jonathan son of Saul. 8 The king took the two sons of Rizpah daughter of Aiah, whom she bore to Saul, Armoni and Mephibosheth;[p] and the five sons of Merab[q] daughter of Saul, whom she bore to Adriel son of Barzillai the Meholathite; 9 he gave them into the hands of the Gibeonites, and they impaled them on the mountain before the LORD. The seven of them perished together. They were put to death in the first days of harvest, at the beginning of barley harvest.

10 Then Rizpah the daughter of Aiah took sackcloth, and spread it on a rock for herself, from the beginning of harvest until rain fell on them from the heavens; she did not allow the birds of the air to come on the bodies[r] by day, or the wild animals by night. 11 When David was told what Rizpah daughter of Aiah, the concubine of Saul, had done, 12 David went and took the bones of Saul and the bones of his son Jonathan from the people of Jabesh-gilead, who had stolen them from the public square of Beth-shan, where the Philistines had hung them up, on the day the Philistines killed Saul on Gilboa. 13 He brought up from there the bones of Saul and the bones of his son Jonathan; and they gathered the bones of those who had been impaled. 14 They buried the bones of Saul and of his son Jonathan in the land of Benjamin in Zela, in the tomb of his father Kish; they did all that the king commanded. After that, God heeded supplications for the land.

Exploits of David's Men

15 The Philistines went to war again with Israel, and David went down together with his servants. They fought against the Philistines, and David grew weary. 16 Ishbi-benob, one of the descendants of the giants, whose spear weighed three hundred shekels of bronze, and who was fitted out

Cross references

20.23　2 Sam 8.16-18
20.25　2 Sam 8.17
20.26　2 Sam 23.38
21.2　Josh 9.3, 15-17
21.3　2 Sam 20.19
21.4　Num 35.31, 32
21.5　1 Sam 10.24, 26
21.7　2 Sam 4.4; 9.10; 1 Sam 18.3; 20.8,15; 23.18
21.8　2 Sam 3.7

21.10　v. 8; Deut 21.23; 1 Sam 17.44, 46
21.12　1 Sam 31.10-13
21.14　Josh 18.28; 7.26; 2 Sam 24.25

Footnotes

n Cn: Heb *Joab to all the army, Israel*
o Cn Compare Gk and 21.9: Heb *at Gibeah of Saul, the chosen of the* LORD
p Or *Merib-baal*: See 4.4 note　q Two Heb Mss Syr Compare Gk: MT *Michal*
r Heb *them*

with new weapons,ˢ said he would kill David. 17But Abishai son of Zeruiah came to his aid, and attacked the Philistine and killed him. Then David's men swore to him, "You shall not go out with us to battle any longer, so that you do not quench the lamp of Israel."

18 After this a battle took place with the Philistines, at Gob; then Sibbecai the Hushathite killed Saph, who was one of the descendants of the giants. 19Then there was another battle with the Philistines at Gob; and Elhanan son of Jaare-oregim, the Bethlehemite, killed Goliath the Gittite, the shaft of whose spear was like a weaver's beam. 20There was again war at Gath, where there was a man of great size, who had six fingers on each hand, and six toes on each foot, twenty-four in number; he too was descended from the giants. 21When he taunted Israel, Jonathan son of David's brother Shimei, killed him. 22These four were descended from the giants in Gath; they fell by the hands of David and his servants.

David's Song of Thanksgiving

22 David spoke to the LORD the words of this song on the day when the LORD delivered him from the hand of all his enemies, and from the hand of Saul. 2He said:

The LORD is my rock, my
 fortress, and my
 deliverer,
3 my God, my rock, in whom
 I take refuge,
 my shield and the horn of
 my salvation,
 my stronghold and my
 refuge,
 my savior; you save me
 from violence.
4 I call upon the LORD, who is
 worthy to be praised,
 and I am saved from my
 enemies.

5 For the waves of death
 encompassed me,

 the torrents of perdition
 assailed me;
6 the cords of Sheol entangled
 me,
 the snares of death
 confronted me.

7 In my distress I called upon
 the LORD;
 to my God I called.
 From his temple he heard
 my voice,
 and my cry came to his
 ears.

8 Then the earth reeled and
 rocked;
 the foundations of the
 heavens trembled
 and quaked, because he
 was angry.
9 Smoke went up from his
 nostrils,
 and devouring fire from his
 mouth;
 glowing coals flamed forth
 from him.
10 He bowed the heavens, and
 came down;
 thick darkness was under
 his feet.
11 He rode on a cherub, and
 flew;
 he was seen upon the
 wings of the wind.
12 He made darkness around
 him a canopy,
 thick clouds, a gathering of
 water.
13 Out of the brightness before
 him
 coals of fire flamed forth.
14 The LORD thundered from
 heaven;
 the Most High uttered his
 voice.
15 He sent out arrows, and
 scattered them
 —lightning, and routed
 them.
16 Then the channels of the sea
 were seen,
 the foundations of the
 world were laid bare
 at the rebuke of the LORD,

21.17
2 Sam 18.3;
6.17
21.18
1 Chr 20.4;
11.29
21.19
1 Chr 20.5
21.20
1 Chr 20.6
21.21
see
1 Sam 16.9
21.22
1 Chr 20.8
22.1
Ex 15.1;
Judg 5.1;
Ps 18.2-50
22.2
Deut 32.4;
Ps 31.3;
71.3; 91.2;
144.2
22.3
Heb 2.13;
Gen 15.1;
Lk 1.69;
Ps 9.9; 14.6;
Jer 16.19
22.4
Ps 48.1
22.5
Ps 93.4;
Jon 2.3;
Ps 69.14,15
22.6
Ps 116.3
22.7
Ps 116.4;
120.1; 34.6,
15
22.8
Judg 5.4;
Ps 77.18;
Job 26.11
22.9
Ps 97.3;
Heb 12.29
22.10
Ex 19.16;
1 Kings 8.12;
Ps 97.2
22.11
Ps 104.3
22.12
Ps 97.2
22.13
v. 9
22.14
1 Sam 2.10
22.16
Hab 3.11

ˢ Heb *was belted anew*

at the blast of the breath
of his nostrils.

17 He reached from on high, he
took me,
he drew me out of mighty
waters.

18 He delivered me from my
strong enemy,
from those who hated me;
for they were too mighty
for me.

19 They came upon me in the
day of my calamity,
but the LORD was my stay.

20 He brought me out into a
broad place;
he delivered me, because
he delighted in me.

21 The LORD rewarded me
according to my
righteousness;
according to the cleanness
of my hands he
recompensed me.

22 For I have kept the ways of
the LORD,
and have not wickedly
departed from my God.

23 For all his ordinances were
before me,
and from his statutes I did
not turn aside.

24 I was blameless before him,
and I kept myself from
guilt.

25 Therefore the LORD has
recompensed me
according to my
righteousness,
according to my cleanness
in his sight.

26 With the loyal you show
yourself loyal;
with the blameless you
show yourself
blameless;

27 with the pure you show
yourself pure,
and with the crooked you
show yourself perverse.

28 You deliver a humble people,
but your eyes are upon the
haughty to bring them
down.

29 Indeed, you are my lamp,
O LORD,
the LORD lightens my
darkness.

30 By you I can crush a troop,
and by my God I can leap
over a wall.

31 This God—his way is
perfect;
the promise of the LORD
proves true;
he is a shield for all who
take refuge in him.

32 For who is God, but the
LORD?
And who is a rock, except
our God?

33 The God who has girded me
with strength[t]
has opened wide my path.[u]

34 He made my[v] feet like the
feet of deer,
and set me secure on the
heights.

35 He trains my hands for war,
so that my arms can bend
a bow of bronze.

36 You have given me the shield
of your salvation,
and your help[w] has made
me great.

37 You have made me stride
freely,
and my feet do not slip;

38 I pursued my enemies and
destroyed them,
and did not turn back until
they were consumed.

39 I consumed them; I struck
them down, so that
they did not rise;
they fell under my feet.

40 For you girded me with
strength for the battle;
you made my assailants
sink under me.

41 You made my enemies turn
their backs to me,
those who hated me, and I
destroyed them.

42 They looked, but there was
no one to save them;

22.17
Ps 144.7;
32.6
22.19
Ps 23.4
22.20
Ps 31.8;
22.8
22.21
1 Kings 8.32;
Ps 24.4
22.22
Gen 18.19;
Ps 128.1
22.23
Deut 6.6-9
22.24
Gen 7.1;
17.1;
Eph 1.4
22.25
v. 21
22.26
Mt 5.7
22.27
Lev 26.23
22.28
Ps 72.12;
Isa 2.11,12,
17

22.29
Ps 27.1
22.31
Deut 32.4;
Mt 5.48;
Ps 12.6;
v. 3
22.32
1 Sam 2.2;
v. 2
22.33
Ps 27.1;
Ps 101.2,6
22.34
Hab 3.19;
Deut 32.13
22.35
Ps 144.1
22.37
Prov 4.12
22.39
Mal 4.3
22.40
Ps 44.5
22.41
Ex 23.27;
Josh 10.24
22.42
Ps 50.22;
1 Sam 28.6

[t] Q Ms Gk Syr Vg Compare Ps 18.32: MT *God
is my strong refuge* [u] Meaning of Heb
uncertain [v] Another reading is *his*
[w] Q Ms: MT *your answering*

they cried to the LORD, but
he did not answer
them.
43 I beat them fine like the
dust of the earth,
I crushed them and
stamped them down
like the mire of the
streets.

44 You delivered me from strife
with the peoples;ˣ
you kept me as the head of
the nations;
people whom I had not
known served me.
45 Foreigners came cringing to
me;
as soon as they heard of
me, they obeyed me.
46 Foreigners lost heart,
and came trembling out of
their strongholds.

47 The LORD lives! Blessed be
my rock,
and exalted be my God,
the rock of my
salvation,
48 the God who gave me
vengeance
and brought down peoples
under me,
49 who brought me out from my
enemies;
you exalted me above my
adversaries,
you delivered me from the
violent.

50 For this I will extol you,
O LORD, among the
nations,
and sing praises to your
name.
51 He is a tower of salvation for
his king,
and shows steadfast love to
his anointed,
to David and his
descendants forever.

The Last Words of David

23 Now these are the last
words of David:

22.43
Ps 18.42;
Isa 10;6
22.44
2 Sam 3.1;
Deut 28.13;
Isa 55.5
22.45
Ps 66.3
22.46
Mic 7.17
22.47
Ps 89.26
22.48
Ps 94.1;
144.2
22.49
Ps 44.5;
140.1
22.50
Rom 15.9
22.51
Ps 144.10;
89.20,29;
2 Sam 7.12-16
23.1
2 Sam 7.8,
9; Ps 78.70;
89.27;
1 Sam 16.12,
13; Ps 89.20

23.2
2 Pet 1.21
23.3
Deut 32.4;
2 Sam 22.2,
32;
Ex 18.21;
2 Chr 19.7,
9
23.4
Judg 5.31;
Ps 89.36
23.5
Ps 89.29;
Isa 55.3
23.6
Mt 13.42

The oracle of David, son of
Jesse,
the oracle of the man
whom God exalted,ʸ
the anointed of the God of
Jacob,
the favorite of the Strong
One of Israel:

2 The spirit of the LORD speaks
through me,
his word is upon my
tongue.
3 The God of Israel has
spoken,
the Rock of Israel has said
to me:
One who rules over people
justly,
ruling in the fear of God,
4 is like the light of morning,
like the sun rising on a
cloudless morning,
gleaming from the rain on
the grassy land.

5 Is not my house like this
with God?
For he has made with me
an everlasting covenant,
ordered in all things and
secure.
Will he not cause to prosper
all my help and my desire?
6 But the godless areᶻ all like
thorns that are thrown
away;
for they cannot be picked
up with the hand;
7 to touch them one uses an
iron bar
or the shaft of a spear.
And they are entirely
consumed in fire on the
spot.ᵃ

David's Mighty Men

8 These are the names of the
warriors whom David had: Josheb-
basshebeth a Tahchemonite; he
was chief of the Three;ᵇ he wield-

ˣ Gk: Heb *from strife with my people*
ʸ Q Ms: MT *who was raised on high*
ᶻ Heb *But worthlessness* ᵃ Heb *in sitting*
ᵇ Gk Vg Compare 1 Chr 11.11: Meaning of
Heb uncertain

ed his spear[c] against eight hundred whom he killed at one time.

9 Next to him among the three warriors was Eleazar son of Dodo son of Ahohi. He was with David when they defied the Philistines who were gathered there for battle. The Israelites withdrew, [10]but he stood his ground. He struck down the Philistines until his arm grew weary, though his hand clung to the sword. The LORD brought about a great victory that day. Then the people came back to him—but only to strip the dead.

11 Next to him was Shammah son of Agee, the Hararite. The Philistines gathered together at Lehi, where there was a plot of ground full of lentils; and the army fled from the Philistines. [12]But he took his stand in the middle of the plot, defended it, and killed the Philistines; and the LORD brought about a great victory.

13 Towards the beginning of harvest three of the thirty[d] chiefs went down to join David at the cave of Adullam, while a band of Philistines was encamped in the valley of Rephaim. [14]David was then in the stronghold; and the garrison of the Philistines was then at Bethlehem. [15]David said longingly, "O that someone would give me water to drink from the well of Bethlehem that is by the gate!" [16]Then the three warriors broke through the camp of the Philistines, drew water from the well of Bethlehem that was by the gate, and brought it to David. But he would not drink of it; he poured it out to the LORD, [17]for he said, "The LORD forbid that I should do this. Can I drink the blood of the men who went at the risk of their lives?" Therefore he would not drink it. The three warriors did these things.

18 Now Abishai son of Zeruiah, the brother of Joab, was chief of the Thirty.[e] With his spear he fought against three hundred men and killed them, and won a name beside the Three. [19]He was the most renowned of the Thirty,[f] and

became their commander; but he did not attain to the Three.

20 Benaiah son of Jehoiada was a valiant warrior[g] from Kabzeel, a doer of great deeds; he struck down two sons of Ariel[h] of Moab. He also went down and killed a lion in a pit on a day when snow had fallen. [21]And he killed an Egyptian, a handsome man. The Egyptian had a spear in his hand; but Benaiah went against him with a staff, snatched the spear out of the Egyptian's hand, and killed him with his own spear. [22]Such were the things Benaiah son of Jehoiada did, and won a name beside the three warriors. [23]He was renowned among the Thirty, but he did not attain to the Three. And David put him in charge of his bodyguard.

24 Among the Thirty were Asahel brother of Joab; Elhanan son of Dodo of Bethlehem; [25]Shammah of Harod; Elika of Harod; [26]Helez the Paltite; Ira son of Ikkesh of Tekoa; [27]Abiezer of Anathoth; Mebunnai the Hushathite; [28]Zalmon the Ahohite; Maharai of Netophah; [29]Heleb son of Baanah of Netophah; Ittai son of Ribai of Gibeah of the Benjaminites; [30]Benaiah of Pirathon; Hiddai of the torrents of Gaash; [31]Abi-albon the Arbathite; Azmaveth of Bahurim; [32]Eliahba of Shaalbon; the sons of Jashen: Jonathan [33]son of[i] Shammah the Hararite; Ahiam son of Sharar the Hararite; [34]Eliphelet son of Ahasbai of Maacah; Eliam son of Ahithophel the Gilonite; [35]Hezro[j] of Carmel; Paarai the Arbite; [36]Igal son of Nathan of Zobah; Bani the Gadite; [37]Zelek the Ammonite; Naharai of Beeroth, the armor-bearer of Joab son of Zeruiah; [38]Ira the Ithrite; Gareb the Ithrite; [39]Uriah the Hittite—thirty-seven in all.

23.9
1 Chr 27.4
23.10
1 Chr 11.12-14
23.11
1 Chr 11.27
23.13
1 Sam 22.1;
2 Sam 5.18
23.14
1 Sam 22.4,5
23.17
Lev 17.10
23.18
2 Sam 10.10,14;
1 Chr 11.20

23.20
2 Sam 8.18;
20.33;
Josh 15.21
23.23
2 Sam 8.18;
20.23
23.24
2 Sam 2.18
23.25
1 Chr 11.27
23.38
2 Sam 20.26
23.39
2 Sam 11.3,6

c 1 Chr 11.11: Meaning of Heb uncertain
d Heb adds *head* e Two Heb Mss Syr: MT *Three* f Syr Compare 1 Chr 11.25: Heb *Was he the most renowned of the Three?*
g Another reading is *the son of Ish-hai*
h Gk: Heb lacks *sons of* i Gk: Heb lacks *son of* j Another reading is *Hezrai*

David's Census of Israel and Judah

24 Again the anger of the Lord was kindled against Israel, and he incited David against them, saying, "Go, count the people of Israel and Judah." ² So the king said to Joab and the commanders of the army,ᵏ who were with him, "Go through all the tribes of Israel, from Dan to Beer-sheba, and take a census of the people, so that I may know how many there are." ³ But Joab said to the king, "May the Lord your God increase the number of the people a hundredfold, while the eyes of my lord the king can still see it! But why does my lord the king want to do this?" ⁴ But the king's word prevailed against Joab and the commanders of the army. So Joab and the commanders of the army went out from the presence of the king to take a census of the people of Israel. ⁵ They crossed the Jordan, and began fromˡ Aroer and from the city that is in the middle of the valley, toward Gad and on to Jazer. ⁶ Then they came to Gilead, and to Kadesh in the land of the Hittites;ᵐ and they came to Dan, and from Danⁿ they went around to Sidon, ⁷ and came to the fortress of Tyre and to all the cities of the Hivites and Canaanites; and they went out to the Negeb of Judah at Beer-sheba. ⁸ So when they had gone through all the land, they came back to Jerusalem at the end of nine months and twenty days. ⁹ Joab reported to the king the number of those who had been recorded: in Israel there were eight hundred thousand soldiers able to draw the sword, and those of Judah were five hundred thousand.

Judgment on David's Sin

10 But afterward, David was stricken to the heart because he had numbered the people. David said to the Lord, "I have sinned greatly in what I have done. But now, O Lord, I pray you, take away the guilt of your servant; for I have done very foolishly." ¹¹ When David

24.1
2 Sam 20.1, 2;
1 Chr 27.23, 24
24.2
2 Sam 3.10; Judg 20.1
24.5
Deut 2.36; Josh 13.9, 16;
Num 32.1,3
24.6
Josh 19.28
24.7
Josh 11.3; Gen 21.22-33
24.9
1 Chr 21.5
24.10
1 Sam 24.5; 2 Sam 12.13; 1 Sam 13.13
24.11
1 Sam 22.5; 9.9;
1 Chr 29.29

24.12
1 Chr 21.12
24.14
Ps 103.8,13, 14
24.15
1 Chr 21.14; 27.24
24.16
Ex 12.23; Gen 6.6;
1 Sam 15.11
24.17
v. 10;
1 Chr 21.17
24.18
1 Chr 21.18ff

rose in the morning, the word of the Lord came to the prophet Gad, David's seer, saying, ¹² "Go and say to David: Thus says the Lord: Three things I offerᵒ you; choose one of them, and I will do it to you." ¹³ So Gad came to David and told him; he asked him, "Shall threeᵖ years of famine come to you on your land? Or will you flee three months before your foes while they pursue you? Or shall there be three days' pestilence in your land? Now consider, and decide what answer I shall return to the one who sent me." ¹⁴ Then David said to Gad, "I am in great distress; let us fall into the hand of the Lord, for his mercy is great; but let me not fall into human hands."

15 So the Lord sent a pestilence on Israel from that morning until the appointed time; and seventy thousand of the people died, from Dan to Beer-sheba. ¹⁶ But when the angel stretched out his hand toward Jerusalem to destroy it, the Lord relented concerning the evil, and said to the angel who was bringing destruction among the people, "It is enough; now stay your hand." The angel of the Lord was then by the threshing floor of Araunah the Jebusite. ¹⁷ When David saw the angel who was destroying the people, he said to the Lord, "I alone have sinned, and I alone have done wickedly; but these sheep, what have they done? Let your hand, I pray, be against me and against my father's house."

David's Altar on the Threshing Floor

18 That day Gad came to David and said to him, "Go up and erect an altar to the Lord on the threshing floor of Araunah the Jebusite." ¹⁹ Following Gad's instructions, David went up, as the Lord had commanded. ²⁰ When Araunah looked down, he saw the king and

ᵏ 1 Chr 21.2 Gk: Heb *to Joab the commander of the army* ˡ Gk Mss: Heb *encamped in Aroer south of* ᵐ Gk: Heb *to the land of Tahtim-hodshi* ⁿ Cn Compare Gk: Heb *they came to Dan-jaan and* ᵒ Or *hold over* ᵖ 1 Chr 21.12 Gk: Heb *seven*

his servants coming toward him; and Araunah went out and prostrated himself before the king with his face to the ground. ²¹Araunah said, "Why has my lord the king come to his servant?" David said, "To buy the threshing floor from you in order to build an altar to the LORD, so that the plague may be averted from the people." ²²Then Araunah said to David, "Let my lord the king take and offer up what seems good to him; here are the oxen for the burnt offering, and the threshing sledges and the yokes of the oxen for the wood. ²³All this, O king, Araunah gives to the king."

24.21
Num 16.48, 50
24.22
1 Kings 19.21
24.23
Ezek 20.40, 41

24.24
1 Chr 21.24, 25
24.25
2 Sam 21.14; v. 21

And Araunah said to the king, "May the LORD your God respond favorably to you."

24 But the king said to Araunah, "No, but I will buy them from you for a price; I will not offer burnt offerings to the LORD my God that cost me nothing." So David bought the threshing floor and the oxen for fifty shekels of silver. ²⁵David built there an altar to the LORD, and offered burnt offerings and offerings of well-being. So the LORD answered his supplication for the land, and the plague was averted from Israel.

1 Kings

Title and Background

1 and 2 Kings (like 1,2 Samuel) are actually one literary work, called in Hebrew tradition simply "Kings." The division into two books was first done in the Septuagint (Greek translation of the Old Testament). Together Samuel and Kings relate the whole history of the monarchy, from its rise under the ministry of Samuel to its destruction at the hands of the Babylonians. Beginning with Solomon's reign, 1 Kings records the history of Israel through the divided kingdom to the death of Ahab.

Author and Date of Writing

There is little conclusive evidence as to the author of 1 and 2 Kings. Whoever the author may have been, this person was clearly familiar with the book of Deuteronomy—as were many of Israel's prophets. The book was probably written subsequent to Jehoiachin's release from prison (562 B.C.) and prior to the end of the Babylonian exile in 539.

Theme and Message

1 and 2 Kings contain no explicit statement of purpose or theme. In general, these two books describe the history of the kings of Israel and Judah in the light of God's covenants. The author was primarily concerned with Israel's faithfulness to the covenants, and consequently recorded the activities of each ruler as to his/her obedience to the covenant. Obedience to God brought peace and prosperity; disobedience and idol worship resulted in war and disaster. 2 Kings also carries stories of several prophets, notably Elijah.

Outline

The Struggle for the Succession

1.3 Josh 19.18

1 King David was old and advanced in years; and although they covered him with clothes, he could not get warm. ²So his servants said to him, "Let a young virgin be sought for my lord the king, and let her wait on the king, and be his attendant; let her lie in your bosom, so that my lord the king may be warm." ³So they searched for a beautiful girl throughout all the territory of Israel, and found Abishag the Shunammite, and brought her to the king. ⁴The girl was very beautiful. She became the king's attendant and served him, but the king did not know her sexually.

5 Now Adonijah son of Haggith exalted himself, saying, "I will be king"; he prepared for himself chariots and horsemen, and fifty men to run before him. ⁶His father had never at any time displeased him by asking, "Why have you done thus and so?" He was also a very handsome man, and he was born next after Absalom. ⁷He conferred with Joab son of Zeruiah and with the priest Abiathar, and they supported Adonijah. ⁸But the priest Zadok, and Benaiah son of Jehoiada, and the prophet Nathan, and

1.5 2 Sam 3.4; 15.1
1.6 2 Sam 3.3, 4
1.7 1 Chr 11.6; 2 Sam 20.25; 1 Kings 2.22, 28
1.8 2 Sam 20.25; 8.18; 12.1; 23.8

Shimei, and Rei, and David's own warriors did not side with Adonijah.

9 Adonijah sacrificed sheep, oxen, and fatted cattle by the stone Zoheleth, which is beside En-rogel, and he invited all his brothers, the king's sons, and all the royal officials of Judah, 10 but he did not invite the prophet Nathan or Benaiah or the warriors or his brother Solomon.

11 Then Nathan said to Bathsheba, Solomon's mother, "Have you not heard that Adonijah son of Haggith has become king and our lord David does not know it? 12 Now therefore come, let me give you advice, so that you may save your own life and the life of your son Solomon. 13 Go in at once to King David, and say to him, 'Did you not, my lord the king, swear to your servant, saying: Your son Solomon shall succeed me as king, and he shall sit on my throne? Why then is Adonijah king?' 14 Then while you are still there speaking with the king, I will come in after you and confirm your words."

15 So Bathsheba went to the king in his room. The king was very old; Abishag the Shunammite was attending the king. 16 Bathsheba bowed and did obeisance to the king, and the king said, "What do you wish?" 17 She said to him, "My lord, you swore to your servant by the LORD your God, saying: Your son Solomon shall succeed me as king, and he shall sit on my throne. 18 But now suddenly Adonijah has become king, though you, my lord the king, do not know it. 19 He has sacrificed oxen, fatted cattle, and sheep in abundance, and has invited all the children of the king, the priest Abiathar, and Joab the commander of the army; but your servant Solomon he has not invited. 20 But you, my lord the king—the eyes of all Israel are on you to tell them who shall sit on the throne of my lord the king after him. 21 Otherwise it will come to pass, when my lord the king sleeps with his ancestors, that my son Solomon

1.9
2 Sam 17.17
1.10
2 Sam 12.24
1.11
2 Sam 3.4
1.13
v. 30;
1 Chr 22.9-13
1.15
v. 1
1.17
vv. 13,30
1.19
v. 9
1.21
Deut 31.16;
1 Kings 2.10

1.25
v. 9;
1 Sam 10.24
1.26
vv. 8,10
1.29
2 Sam 4.9
1.30
vv. 13,17
1.31
Neh 2.3;
Dan 2.4
1.33
2 Sam 20.6,
7
1.34
1 Sam 10.1;
16.3,12;
2 Sam 15.10;
v. 25

and I will be counted offenders."

22 While she was still speaking with the king, the prophet Nathan came in. 23 The king was told, "Here is the prophet Nathan." When he came in before the king, he did obeisance to the king, with his face to the ground. 24 Nathan said, "My lord the king, have you said, 'Adonijah shall succeed me as king, and he shall sit on my throne'? 25 For today he has gone down and has sacrificed oxen, fatted cattle, and sheep in abundance, and has invited all the king's children, Joab the commander[a] of the army, and the priest Abiathar, who are now eating and drinking before him, and saying, 'Long live King Adonijah!' 26 But he did not invite me, your servant, and the priest Zadok, and Benaiah son of Jehoiada, and your servant Solomon. 27 Has this thing been brought about by my lord the king and you have not let your servants know who should sit on the throne of my lord the king after him?"

The Accession of Solomon

28 King David answered, "Summon Bathsheba to me." So she came into the king's presence, and stood before the king. 29 The king swore, saying, "As the LORD lives, who has saved my life from every adversity, 30 as I swore to you by the LORD, the God of Israel, 'Your son Solomon shall succeed me as king, and he shall sit on my throne in my place,' so will I do this day." 31 Then Bathsheba bowed with her face to the ground, and did obeisance to the king, and said, "May my lord King David live forever!"

32 King David said, "Summon to me the priest Zadok, the prophet Nathan, and Benaiah son of Jehoiada." When they came before the king, 33 the king said to them, "Take with you the servants of your lord, and have my son Solomon ride on my own mule, and bring him down to Gihon. 34 There let the

a Gk: Heb *the commanders*

priest Zadok and the prophet Nathan anoint him king over Israel; then blow the trumpet, and say, 'Long live King Solomon!' 35 You shall go up following him. Let him enter and sit on my throne; he shall be king in my place; for I have appointed him to be ruler over Israel and over Judah." 36 Benaiah son of Jehoiada answered the king, "Amen! May the LORD, the God of my lord the king, so ordain. 37 As the LORD has been with my lord the king, so may he be with Solomon, and make his throne greater than the throne of my lord King David."

38 So the priest Zadok, the prophet Nathan, and Benaiah son of Jehoiada, and the Cherethites and the Pelethites, went down and had Solomon ride on King David's mule, and led him to Gihon. 39 There the priest Zadok took the horn of oil from the tent and anointed Solomon. Then they blew the trumpet, and all the people said, "Long live King Solomon!" 40 And all the people went up following him, playing on pipes and rejoicing with great joy, so that the earth quaked at their noise.

41 Adonijah and all the guests who were with him heard it as they finished feasting. When Joab heard the sound of the trumpet, he said, "Why is the city in an uproar?" 42 While he was still speaking, Jonathan son of the priest Abiathar arrived. Adonijah said, "Come in, for you are a worthy man and surely you bring good news." 43 Jonathan answered Adonijah, "No, for our lord King David has made Solomon king; 44 the king has sent with him the priest Zadok, the prophet Nathan, and Benaiah son of Jehoiada, and the Cherethites and the Pelethites; and they had him ride on the king's mule; 45 the priest Zadok and the prophet Nathan have anointed him king at Gihon; and they have gone up from there rejoicing, so that the city is in an uproar. This is the noise that you heard. 46 Solomon now sits on the royal throne. 47 Moreover the king's servants came to congratulate our lord King David, saying, 'May God make the name of Solomon more famous than yours, and make his throne greater than your throne.' The king bowed in worship on the bed 48 and went on to pray thus, 'Blessed be the LORD, the God of Israel, who today has granted one of my offspring[b] to sit on my throne and permitted me to witness it.' "

49 Then all the guests of Adonijah got up trembling and went their own ways. 50 Adonijah, fearing Solomon, got up and went to grasp the horns of the altar. 51 Solomon was informed, "Adonijah is afraid of King Solomon; see, he has laid hold of the horns of the altar, saying, 'Let King Solomon swear to me first that he will not kill his servant with the sword.' " 52 So Solomon responded, "If he proves to be a worthy man, not one of his hairs shall fall to the ground; but if wickedness is found in him, he shall die." 53 Then King Solomon sent to have him brought down from the altar. He came to do obeisance to King Solomon; and Solomon said to him, "Go home."

David's Instruction to Solomon

2 When David's time to die drew near, he charged his son Solomon, saying: 2 "I am about to go the way of all the earth. Be strong, be courageous, 3 and keep the charge of the LORD your God, walking in his ways and keeping his statutes, his commandments, his ordinances, and his testimonies, as it is written in the law of Moses, so that you may prosper in all that you do and wherever you turn. 4 Then the LORD will establish his word that he spoke concerning me: 'If your heirs take heed to their way, to walk before me in faithfulness with all their heart and with all their soul, there shall not fail you a successor on the throne of Israel.'

5 "Moreover you know also what Joab son of Zeruiah did to me, how he dealt with the two commanders of the armies of Israel, Abner son of Ner, and Amasa son of

b Gk: Heb one

Cross references

1.37 Josh 1.5,17; 1 Sam 20.13; v. 47
1.38 vv. 8,33; 2 Sam 8.18
1.39 Ex 30.23-32; Ps 89.20; 1 Chr 29.22; v. 34
1.42 2 Sam 15.27, 36; 18.27
1.45 v. 40
1.46 1 Chr 29.23
1.47 v. 37; Gen 47.31
1.48 1 Kings 3.6; 2 Sam 7.12
1.50 1 Kings 2.28
1.52 1 Sam 14.45; 2 Sam 14.11
2.1 Gen 47.29; Deut 31.14
2.2 Josh 23.14; Deut 31.7, 23; Josh 1.6,7
2.3 Josh 1.7; 1 Chr 22.12, 13
2.4 2 Sam 7.25; Ps 132.12; 2 Kings 20.3; 2 Sam 7.12, 13
2.5 2 Sam 18.5, 12,14; 3.27; 20.10

Jether, whom he murdered, retaliating in time of peace for blood that had been shed in war, and putting the blood of war on the belt around his waist, and on the sandals on his feet. ⁶Act therefore according to your wisdom, but do not let his gray head go down to Sheol in peace. ⁷Deal loyally, however, with the sons of Barzillai the Gileadite, and let them be among those who eat at your table; for with such loyalty they met me when I fled from your brother Absalom. ⁸There is also with you Shimei son of Gera, the Benjaminite from Bahurim, who cursed me with a terrible curse on the day when I went to Mahanaim; but when he came down to meet me at the Jordan, I swore to him by the Lord, 'I will not put you to death with the sword.' ⁹Therefore do not hold him guiltless, for you are a wise man; you will know what you ought to do to him, and you must bring his gray head down with blood to Sheol."

Death of David

10 Then David slept with his ancestors, and was buried in the city of David. ¹¹The time that David reigned over Israel was forty years; he reigned seven years in Hebron, and thirty-three years in Jerusalem. ¹²So Solomon sat on the throne of his father David; and his kingdom was firmly established.

Solomon Consolidates His Reign

13 Then Adonijah son of Haggith came to Bathsheba, Solomon's mother. She asked, "Do you come peaceably?" He said, "Peaceably." ¹⁴Then he said, "May I have a word with you?" She said, "Go on." ¹⁵He said, "You know that the kingdom was mine, and that all Israel expected me to reign; however, the kingdom has turned about and become my brother's, for it was his from the Lord. ¹⁶And now I have one request to make of you; do not refuse me." She said to him, "Go on." ¹⁷He said, "Please ask King Solomon—he will not refuse you—to give me Abishag the Shunam-

mite as my wife." ¹⁸Bathsheba said, "Very well; I will speak to the king on your behalf."

19 So Bathsheba went to King Solomon, to speak to him on behalf of Adonijah. The king rose to meet her, and bowed down to her; then he sat on his throne, and had a throne brought for the king's mother, and she sat on his right. ²⁰Then she said, "I have one small request to make of you; do not refuse me." And the king said to her, "Make your request, my mother; for I will not refuse you." ²¹She said, "Let Abishag the Shunammite be given to your brother Adonijah as his wife." ²²King Solomon answered his mother, "And why do you ask Abishag the Shunammite for Adonijah? Ask for him the kingdom as well! For he is my elder brother; ask not only for him but also for the priest Abiathar and for Joab son of Zeruiah!" ²³Then King Solomon swore by the Lord, "So may God do to me, and more also, for Adonijah has devised this scheme at the risk of his life! ²⁴Now therefore as the Lord lives, who has established me and placed me on the throne of my father David, and who has made me a house as he promised, today Adonijah shall be put to death." ²⁵So King Solomon sent Benaiah son of Jehoiada; he struck him down, and he died.

26 The king said to the priest Abiathar, "Go to Anathoth, to your estate; for you deserve death. But I will not at this time put you to death, because you carried the ark of the Lord God before my father David, and because you shared in all the hardships my father endured." ²⁷So Solomon banished Abiathar from being priest to the Lord, thus fulfilling the word of the Lord that he had spoken concerning the house of Eli in Shiloh.

28 When the news came to Joab—for Joab had supported Adonijah though he had not supported Absalom—Joab fled to the tent of the Lord and grasped the horns of the altar. ²⁹When it was told

2.6
v. 6
2.7
2 Sam 19.31,
38; 9.7,10;
17.27
2.8
2 Sam 16.5-8;
19.18-23
2.9
v. 6
2.10
Acts 2.29;
2 Sam 5.7
2.11
2 Sam 5.4;
1 Chr 29.26,
27
2.12
1 Chr 29.23;
2 Chr 1.1
2.13
1 Sam 16.4
2.15
1 Kings 1.5;
1 Chr 22.9,
10; 28.5-7
2.17
1 Kings 1.3,
4

2.19
Ps 45.9
2.20
v. 16
2.21
1 Kings 1.3,
4
2.22
2 Sam 12.8;
1 Kings 1.6,
7
2.23
Ruth 1.17
2.24
2 Sam 7.11,
13;
1 Chr 22.10
2.26
Josh 21.18;
1 Sam 23.6;
2 Sam 15.24-
29;
1 Sam 22.20-
23
2.27
1 Sam 2.31-35
2.28
1 Kings 1.7,
50
2.29
v. 25

King Solomon, "Joab has fled to the tent of the LORD and now is beside the altar," Solomon sent Benaiah son of Jehoiada, saying, "Go, strike him down." 30 So Benaiah came to the tent of the LORD and said to him, "The king commands, 'Come out.' " But he said, "No, I will die here." Then Benaiah brought the king word again, saying, "Thus said Joab, and thus he answered me." 31 The king replied to him, "Do as he has said, strike him down and bury him; and thus take away from me and from my father's house the guilt for the blood that Joab shed without cause. 32 The LORD will bring back his bloody deeds on his own head, because, without the knowledge of my father David, he attacked and killed with the sword two men more righteous and better than himself, Abner son of Ner, commander of the army of Israel, and Amasa son of Jether, commander of the army of Judah. 33 So shall their blood come back on the head of Joab and on the head of his descendants forever; but to David, and to his descendants, and to his house, and to his throne, there shall be peace from the LORD forevermore." 34 Then Benaiah son of Jehoiada went up and struck him down and killed him; and he was buried at his own house near the wilderness. 35 The king put Benaiah son of Jehoiada over the army in his place, and the king put the priest Zadok in the place of Abiathar.

36 Then the king sent and summoned Shimei, and said to him, "Build yourself a house in Jerusalem, and live there, and do not go out from there to any place whatever. 37 For on the day you go out, and cross the Wadi Kidron, know for certain that you shall die; your blood shall be on your own head." 38 And Shimei said to the king, "The sentence is fair; as my lord the king has said, so will your servant do." So Shimei lived in Jerusalem many days.

39 But it happened at the end of three years that two of Shimei's slaves ran away to King Achish son of Maacah of Gath. When it was told Shimei, "Your slaves are in Gath," 40 Shimei arose and saddled a donkey, and went to Achish in Gath, to search for his slaves; Shimei went and brought his slaves from Gath. 41 When Solomon was told that Shimei had gone from Jerusalem to Gath and returned, 42 the king sent and summoned Shimei, and said to him, "Did I not make you swear by the LORD, and solemnly adjure you, saying, 'Know for certain that on the day you go out and go to any place whatever, you shall die'? And you said to me, 'The sentence is fair; I accept.' 43 Why then have you not kept your oath to the LORD and the commandment with which I charged you?" 44 The king also said to Shimei, "You know in your own heart all the evil that you did to my father David; so the LORD will bring back your evil on your own head. 45 But King Solomon shall be blessed, and the throne of David shall be established before the LORD forever." 46 Then the king commanded Benaiah son of Jehoiada; and he went out and struck him down, and he died.

So the kingdom was established in the hand of Solomon.

Solomon's Prayer for Wisdom

3 Solomon made a marriage alliance with Pharaoh king of Egypt; he took Pharaoh's daughter and brought her into the city of David, until he had finished building his own house and the house of the LORD and the wall around Jerusalem. 2 The people were sacrificing at the high places, however, because no house had yet been built for the name of the LORD.

3 Solomon loved the LORD, walking in the statutes of his father David; only, he sacrificed and offered incense at the high places. 4 The king went to Gibeon to sacrifice there, for that was the principal

2.31
Ex 21.14;
Num 35.33;
Deut 19.13
2.32
Judg 9.24,
57; Ps 7.16;
2 Chr 21.13;
2 Sam 3.27;
20.10
2.33
2 Sam 3.29;
Prov 25.5
2.35
1 Kings 4.4;
1 Chr 29.22;
v. 27
2.36
v. 8
2.37
2 Sam 15.23;
Lev 20.9;
2 Sam 1.16

2.39
1 Sam 27.2
2.40
2 Sam 19.16-
23
2.44
2 Sam 16.5-13;
1 Sam 25.39;
Ezek 17.19
2.45
2 Sam 7.13
2.46
vv. 12,25,
34;
2 Chr 1.1
3.1
1 Kings 7.8;
9.24;
2 Sam 5.7;
1 Kings 7.1;
ch. 6; 9.15,19
3.2
Lev 17.3-5;
Deut 12.2,4,
5
3.3f
Deut 6.5;
Ps 31.23;
1 Kings 2.3;
9.4; 11.4,6,38
3.4
2 Chr 1.3;
1 Chr 16.39

high place; Solomon used to offer a thousand burnt offerings on that altar. ⁵At Gibeon the Lord appeared to Solomon in a dream by night; and God said, "Ask what I should give you." ⁶And Solomon said, "You have shown great and steadfast love to your servant my father David, because he walked before you in faithfulness, in righteousness, and in uprightness of heart toward you; and you have kept for him this great and steadfast love, and have given him a son to sit on his throne today. ⁷And now, O Lord my God, you have made your servant king in place of my father David, although I am only a little child; I do not know how to go out or come in. ⁸And your servant is in the midst of the people whom you have chosen, a great people, so numerous they cannot be numbered or counted. ⁹Give your servant therefore an understanding mind to govern your people, able to discern between good and evil; for who can govern this your great people?"

10 It pleased the Lord that Solomon had asked this. ¹¹God said to him, "Because you have asked this, and have not asked for yourself long life or riches, or for the life of your enemies, but have asked for yourself understanding to discern what is right, ¹²I now do according to your word. Indeed I give you a wise and discerning mind; no one like you has been before you and no one like you shall arise after you. ¹³I give you also what you have not asked, both riches and honor all your life; no other king shall compare with you. ¹⁴If you will walk in my ways, keeping my statutes and my commandments, as your father David walked, then I will lengthen your life."

15 Then Solomon awoke; it had been a dream. He came to Jerusalem where he stood before the ark of the covenant of the Lord. He offered up burnt offerings and offerings of well-being, and provided a feast for all his servants.

3.5
1 Kings 9.2;
2 Chr 1.7;
Num 12.6;
Mt 1.20
3.6
2 Chr 1.8ff;
1 Kings 2.4;
9.4; 1.48
3.7
1 Chr 2.9-13;
29.1;
Num 27.17
3.8
Deut 7.6;
Gen 13.16;
15.5
3.9
2 Chr 1.10;
Prov 2.3-9;
Jas 1.5;
Ps 72.1,2
3.11
Jas 4.3
3.12
1 Jn 5.14,
15;
1 Kings 4.29-31
3.13
Mt 6.33;
1 Kings 4.21-24
3.14
v. 6
3.15
Gen 41.7;
1 Kings 8.65;
Esther 1.3;
Dan 5.1;
Mk 6.21

3.17
Num 27.2
3.20
Ruth 4.16
3.26
Gen 43.30;
Isa 49.15;
Jer 31.20
3.28
vv. 9,11,12

Solomon's Wisdom in Judgment

16 Later, two women who were prostitutes came to the king and stood before him. ¹⁷The one woman said, "Please, my lord, this woman and I live in the same house; and I gave birth while she was in the house. ¹⁸Then on the third day after I gave birth, this woman also gave birth. We were together; there was no one else with us in the house, only the two of us were in the house. ¹⁹Then this woman's son died in the night, because she lay on him. ²⁰She got up in the middle of the night and took my son from beside me while your servant slept. She laid him at her breast, and laid her dead son at my breast. ²¹When I rose in the morning to nurse my son, I saw that he was dead; but when I looked at him closely in the morning, clearly it was not the son I had borne." ²²But the other woman said, "No, the living son is mine, and the dead son is yours." The first said, "No, the dead son is yours, and the living son is mine." So they argued before the king.

23 Then the king said, "The one says, 'This is my son that is alive, and your son is dead'; while the other says, 'Not so! Your son is dead, and my son is the living one.' " ²⁴So the king said, "Bring me a sword," and they brought a sword before the king. ²⁵The king said, "Divide the living boy in two; then give half to the one, and half to the other." ²⁶But the woman whose son was alive said to the king—because compassion for her son burned within her— "Please, my lord, give her the living boy; certainly do not kill him!" The other said, "It shall be neither mine nor yours; divide it." ²⁷Then the king responded: "Give the first woman the living boy; do not kill him. She is his mother." ²⁸All Israel heard of the judgment that the king had rendered; and they stood in awe of the king, because they perceived that the wisdom of God was in him, to execute justice.

Solomon's Administrative Officers

4 King Solomon was king over all Israel, ²and these were his high officials: Azariah son of Zadok was the priest; ³Elihoreph and Ahijah sons of Shisha were secretaries; Jehoshaphat son of Ahilud was recorder; ⁴Benaiah son of Jehoiada was in command of the army; Zadok and Abiathar were priests; ⁵Azariah son of Nathan was over the officials; Zabud son of Nathan was priest and king's friend; ⁶Ahishar was in charge of the palace; and Adoniram son of Abda was in charge of the forced labor.

7 Solomon had twelve officials over all Israel, who provided food for the king and his household; each one had to make provision for one month in the year. ⁸These were their names: Ben-hur, in the hill country of Ephraim; ⁹Ben-deker, in Makaz, Shaalbim, Beth-shemesh, and Elon-beth-hanan; ¹⁰Benhesed, in Arubboth (to him belonged Socoh and all the land of Hepher); ¹¹Ben-abinadab, in all Naphath-dor (he had Taphath, Solomon's daughter, as his wife); ¹²Baana son of Ahilud, in Taanach, Megiddo, and all Beth-shean, which is beside Zarethan below Jezreel, and from Beth-shean to Abel-meholah, as far as the other side of Jokmeam; ¹³Ben-geber, in Ramoth-gilead (he had the villages of Jair son of Manasseh, which are in Gilead, and he had the region of Argob, which is in Bashan, sixty great cities with walls and bronze bars); ¹⁴Ahinadab son of Iddo, in Mahanaim; ¹⁵Ahimaaz, in Naphtali (he had taken Basemath, Solomon's daughter, as his wife); ¹⁶Baana son of Hushai, in Asher and Bealoth; ¹⁷Jehoshaphat son of Paruah, in Issachar; ¹⁸Shimei son of Ela, in Benjamin; ¹⁹Geber son of Uri, in the land of Gilead, the country of King Sihon of the Amorites and of King Og of Bashan. And there was one official in the land of Judah.

Center references

4.5
v. 7
4.8
Josh 24.33
4.9
Josh 1.35;
21.16
4.10
Josh 15.35;
12.17
4.11
Josh 11.1,2
4.12
Josh 5.19;
17.11; 3.16;
1 Kings 19.16;
1 Chr 6.68
4.13
Num 32.41;
Deut 3.4
4.14
Josh 13.26
4.15
2 Sam 15.27
4.16
2 Sam 15.32
4.18
1 Kings 1.8
4.19
Deut 3.8-10

4.20
Gen 32.12;
1 Kings 3.8
4.21
2 Chr 9.26;
Gen 15.18;
Ps 68.29;
72.10,11
4.24
Ps 72.11;
1 Chr 22.9
4.25
Jer 23.6;
Mic 4.4;
Zech 3.10;
Judg 20.1
4.26
1 Kings 10.26;
2 Chr 1.14
4.27
v. 7
4.29
1 Kings 3.12
4.30
Gen 25.6;
Acts 7.22
4.31
1 Kings 3.12;
1 Chr 15.19;
2.6; 6.33
4.32
Prov 1.1;
Eccl 12.9;
Song 1.1

Magnificence of Solomon's Rule

20 Judah and Israel were as numerous as the sand by the sea; they ate and drank and were happy. ²¹ᶜSolomon was sovereign over all the kingdoms from the Euphrates to the land of the Philistines, even to the border of Egypt; they brought tribute and served Solomon all the days of his life.

22 Solomon's provision for one day was thirty cors of choice flour, and sixty cors of meal, ²³ten fat oxen, and twenty pasture-fed cattle, one hundred sheep, besides deer, gazelles, roebucks, and fatted fowl. ²⁴For he had dominion over all the region west of the Euphrates from Tiphsah to Gaza, over all the kings west of the Euphrates; and he had peace on all sides. ²⁵During Solomon's lifetime Judah and Israel lived in safety, from Dan even to Beer-sheba, all of them under their vines and fig trees. ²⁶Solomon also had forty thousand stalls of horses for his chariots, and twelve thousand horsemen. ²⁷Those officials supplied provisions for King Solomon and for all who came to King Solomon's table, each one in his month; they let nothing be lacking. ²⁸They also brought to the required place barley and straw for the horses and swift steeds, each according to his charge.

Fame of Solomon's Wisdom

29 God gave Solomon very great wisdom, discernment, and breadth of understanding as vast as the sand on the seashore, ³⁰so that Solomon's wisdom surpassed the wisdom of all the people of the east, and all the wisdom of Egypt. ³¹He was wiser than anyone else, wiser than Ethan the Ezrahite, and Heman, Calcol, and Darda, children of Mahol; his fame spread throughout all the surrounding nations. ³²He composed three thousand proverbs, and his songs numbered a thousand and five. ³³He would speak of trees, from the cedar that is in the Lebanon to the hyssop

ᶜCh 5.1 in Heb

that grows in the wall; he would speak of animals, and birds, and reptiles, and fish. [34] People came from all the nations to hear the wisdom of Solomon; they came from all the kings of the earth who had heard of his wisdom.

Preparations and Materials for the Temple

5 [d] Now King Hiram of Tyre sent his servants to Solomon, when he heard that they had anointed him king in place of his father; for Hiram had always been a friend to David. [2] Solomon sent word to Hiram, saying, [3] "You know that my father David could not build a house for the name of the LORD his God because of the warfare with which his enemies surrounded him, until the LORD put them under the soles of his feet. [e] [4] But now the LORD my God has given me rest on every side; there is neither adversary nor misfortune. [5] So I intend to build a house for the name of the LORD my God, as the LORD said to my father David, 'Your son, whom I will set on your throne in your place, shall build the house for my name.' [6] Therefore command that cedars from the Lebanon be cut for me. My servants will join your servants, and I will give you whatever wages you set for your servants; for you know that there is no one among us who knows how to cut timber like the Sidonians."

[7] When Hiram heard the words of Solomon, he rejoiced greatly, and said, "Blessed be the LORD today, who has given to David a wise son to be over this great people." [8] Hiram sent word to Solomon, "I have heard the message that you have sent to me; I will fulfill all your needs in the matter of cedar and cypress timber. [9] My servants shall bring it down to the sea from the Lebanon; I will make it into rafts to go by sea to the place you indicate. I will have them broken up there for you to take away. And you shall meet my needs by providing food for my household." [10] So Hiram supplied Solomon's every

need for timber of cedar and cypress. [11] Solomon in turn gave Hiram twenty thousand cors of wheat as food for his household, and twenty cors of fine oil. Solomon gave this to Hiram year by year. [12] So the LORD gave Solomon wisdom, as he promised him. There was peace between Hiram and Solomon; and the two of them made a treaty.

[13] King Solomon conscripted forced labor out of all Israel; the levy numbered thirty thousand men. [14] He sent them to the Lebanon, ten thousand a month in shifts; they would be a month in the Lebanon and two months at home; Adoniram was in charge of the forced labor. [15] Solomon also had seventy thousand laborers and eighty thousand stonecutters in the hill country, [16] besides Solomon's three thousand three hundred supervisors who were over the work, having charge of the people who did the work. [17] At the king's command, they quarried out great, costly stones in order to lay the foundation of the house with dressed stones. [18] So Solomon's builders and Hiram's builders and the Giblites did the stonecutting and prepared the timber and the stone to build the house.

Solomon Builds the Temple

6 In the four hundred eightieth year after the Israelites came out of the land of Egypt, in the fourth year of Solomon's reign over Israel, in the month of Ziv, which is the second month, he began to build the house of the LORD. [2] The house that King Solomon built for the LORD was sixty cubits long, twenty cubits wide, and thirty cubits high. [3] The vestibule in front of the nave of the house was twenty cubits wide, across the width of the house. Its depth was ten cubits in front of the house. [4] For the house he made windows with recessed frames. [f] [5] He also built a structure against the wall of the house, run-

4.34
1 Kings 10.1;
2 Chr 9.23
5.1
vv. 10,18;
2 Chr 2.3;
2 Sam 5.11;
1 Chr 14.1
5.3
1 Chr 22.8;
28.3
5.4
1 Kings 4.24;
1 Chr 22.9
5.5
2 Sam 7.12,
13;
1 Chr 17.12;
22.10
5.9
2 Chr 2.16;
Ezra 3.7;
Ezek 27.17;
Acts 12.20

5.11
cf.
2 Chr 2.10
5.12
1 Kings 3.12
5.14
1 Kings 4.6
5.15
1 Kings 9.20-
22;
2 Chr 2.17,
18
5.17
1 Chr 22.2
6.1
2 Chr 3.1,
2; Acts 7.47
6.2
cf.
Ezek 41.1ff
6.4
Ezek 40.16;
41.16
6.5
Ezek 41.6;
vv. 16,
19-21,31

d Ch 5.15 in Heb e Gk Tg Vg: Heb *my feet* or *his feet* f Gk: Meaning of Heb uncertain

ning around the walls of the house, both the nave and the inner sanctuary; and he made side chambers all around. 6 The lowest story[g] was five cubits wide, the middle one was six cubits wide, and the third was seven cubits wide; for around the outside of the house he made offsets on the wall in order that the supporting beams should not be inserted into the walls of the house.

7 The house was built with stone finished at the quarry, so that neither hammer nor ax nor any tool of iron was heard in the temple while it was being built.

8 The entrance for the middle story was on the south side of the house: one went up by winding stairs to the middle story, and from the middle story to the third. 9 So he built the house, and finished it; he roofed the house with beams and planks of cedar. 10 He built the structure against the whole house, each story[h] five cubits high, and it was joined to the house with timbers of cedar.

11 Now the word of the LORD came to Solomon, 12 "Concerning this house that you are building, if you will walk in my statutes, obey my ordinances, and keep all my commandments by walking in them, then I will establish my promise with you, which I made to your father David. 13 I will dwell among the children of Israel, and will not forsake my people Israel."

14 So Solomon built the house, and finished it. 15 He lined the walls of the house on the inside with boards of cedar; from the floor of the house to the rafters of the ceiling, he covered them on the inside with wood; and he covered the floor of the house with boards of cypress. 16 He built twenty cubits of the rear of the house with boards of cedar from the floor to the rafters, and he built this within as an inner sanctuary, as the most holy place. 17 The house, that is, the nave in front of the inner sanctuary, was forty cubits long. 18 The cedar within the house had carvings of gourds and open flowers; all was cedar, no

6.7
Deut 27.5,6
6.9
vv. 14,38
6.12
1 Kings 2.4;
9.4
6.13
Ex 25.8;
Deut 31.6
6.14
vv. 9,38
6.16
Ex 26.33;
Lev 16.2;
1 Kings 8.6;
2 Chr 3.8
6.18
1 Kings 7.24

6.22
Ex 30.1,3,6
6.23
2 Chr 3.10-12
6.27
Ex 25.20;
37.9;
1 Kings 8.7;
2 Chr 5.8

stone was seen. 19 The inner sanctuary he prepared in the innermost part of the house, to set there the ark of the covenant of the LORD. 20 The interior of the inner sanctuary was twenty cubits long, twenty cubits wide, and twenty cubits high; he overlaid it with pure gold. He also overlaid the altar with cedar.[i] 21 Solomon overlaid the inside of the house with pure gold, then he drew chains of gold across, in front of the inner sanctuary, and overlaid it with gold. 22 Next he overlaid the whole house with gold, in order that the whole house might be perfect; even the whole altar that belonged to the inner sanctuary he overlaid with gold.

The Furnishings of the Temple

23 In the inner sanctuary he made two cherubim of olivewood, each ten cubits high. 24 Five cubits was the length of one wing of the cherub, and five cubits the length of the other wing of the cherub; it was ten cubits from the tip of one wing to the tip of the other. 25 The other cherub also measured ten cubits; both cherubim had the same measure and the same form. 26 The height of one cherub was ten cubits, and so was that of the other cherub. 27 He put the cherubim in the innermost part of the house; the wings of the cherubim were spread out so that a wing of one was touching the one wall, and a wing of the other cherub was touching the other wall; their other wings toward the center of the house were touching wing to wing. 28 He also overlaid the cherubim with gold.

29 He carved the walls of the house all around about with carved engravings of cherubim, palm trees, and open flowers, in the inner and outer rooms. 30 The floor of the house he overlaid with gold, in the inner and outer rooms.

31 For the entrance to the inner sanctuary he made doors of olivewood; the lintel and the doorposts

g Gk: Heb *structure* h Heb lacks *each story* i Meaning of Heb uncertain

were five-sided.ⁱ ³²He covered the two doors of olivewood with carvings of cherubim, palm trees, and open flowers; he overlaid them with gold, and spread gold on the cherubim and on the palm trees.

33 So also he made for the entrance to the nave doorposts of olivewood, four-sided each, ³⁴and two doors of cypress wood; the two leaves of the one door were folding, and the two leaves of the other door were folding. ³⁵He carved cherubim, palm trees, and open flowers, overlaying them with gold evenly applied upon the carved work. ³⁶He built the inner court with three courses of dressed stone to one course of cedar beams.

37 In the fourth year the foundation of the house of the LORD was laid, in the month of Ziv. ³⁸In the eleventh year, in the month of Bul, which is the eighth month, the house was finished in all its parts, and according to all its specifications. He was seven years in building it.

Solomon's Palace and Other Buildings

7 Solomon was building his own house thirteen years, and he finished his entire house.

2 He built the House of the Forest of the Lebanon one hundred cubits long, fifty cubits wide, and thirty cubits high, built on four rows of cedar pillars, with cedar beams on the pillars. ³It was roofed with cedar on the forty-five rafters, fifteen in each row, which were on the pillars. ⁴There were window frames in the three rows, facing each other in the three rows. ⁵All the doorways and doorposts had four-sided frames, opposite, facing each other in the three rows.

6 He made the Hall of Pillars fifty cubits long and thirty cubits wide. There was a porch in front with pillars, and a canopy in front of them.

7 He made the Hall of the Throne where he was to pronounce judgment, the Hall of Justice, covered with cedar from floor to floor.

8 His own house where he would reside, in the other court back of the hall, was of the same construction. Solomon also made a house like this hall for Pharaoh's daughter, whom he had taken in marriage.

9 All these were made of costly stones, cut according to measure, sawed with saws, back and front, from the foundation to the coping, and from outside to the great court. ¹⁰The foundation was of costly stones, huge stones, stones of eight and ten cubits. ¹¹There were costly stones above, cut to measure, and cedarwood. ¹²The great court had three courses of dressed stone to one layer of cedar beams all around; so had the inner court of the house of the LORD, and the vestibule of the house.

Products of Hiram the Bronzeworker

13 Now King Solomon invited and received Hiram from Tyre. ¹⁴He was the son of a widow of the tribe of Naphtali, whose father, a man of Tyre, had been an artisan in bronze; he was full of skill, intelligence, and knowledge in working bronze. He came to King Solomon, and did all his work.

15 He cast two pillars of bronze. Eighteen cubits was the height of the one, and a cord of twelve cubits would encircle it; the second pillar was the same.ᵏ ¹⁶He also made two capitals of molten bronze, to set on the tops of the pillars; the height of the one capital was five cubits, and the height of the other capital was five cubits. ¹⁷There were nets of checker work with wreaths of chain work for the capitals on the tops of the pillars; sevenˡ for the one capital, and sevenˡ for the other capital. ¹⁸He made the columns with two rows around each latticework to cover the capitals that were above the pomegranates; he did the same with the other capital. ¹⁹Now the capitals that

Cross references (center column)

6.34
Ezek 41.23-25
6.36
1 Kings 7.12
6.37
v. 1
7.1
1 Kings 9.10;
2 Chr 8.1
7.2
1 Kings 10.17,
21
7.7
1 Kings 6.15,
16

7.8
1 Kings 3.1;
2 Chr 8.11
7.12
1 Kings 6.36;
v. 6
7.13
2 Chr 4.11
7.14
2 Chr 2.14;
4.16;
Ex 31.3-5;
35.31
7.15
2 Kings 25.17;
2 Chr 3.15

ⁱ Meaning of Heb uncertain ᵏ Cn: Heb and a cord of twelve cubits encircled the second pillar; Compare Jer 52.21 ˡ Heb: Gk a net

were on the tops of the pillars in the vestibule were of lily-work, four cubits high. ²⁰ The capitals were on the two pillars and also above the rounded projection that was beside the latticework; there were two hundred pomegranates in rows all around; and so with the other capital. ²¹ He set up the pillars at the vestibule of the temple; he set up the pillar on the south and called it Jachin; and he set up the pillar on the north and called it Boaz. ²² On the tops of the pillars was lily-work. Thus the work of the pillars was finished.

23 Then he made the molten sea; it was round, ten cubits from brim to brim, and five cubits high. A line of thirty cubits would encircle it completely. ²⁴ Under its brim were panels all around it, each of ten cubits, surrounding the sea; there were two rows of panels, cast when it was cast. ²⁵ It stood on twelve oxen, three facing north, three facing west, three facing south, and three facing east; the sea was set on them. The hindquarters of each were toward the inside. ²⁶ Its thickness was a handbreadth; its brim was made like the brim of a cup, like the flower of a lily; it held two thousand baths.ᵐ

27 He also made the ten stands of bronze; each stand was four cubits long, four cubits wide, and three cubits high. ²⁸ This was the construction of the stands: they had borders; the borders were within the frames; ²⁹ on the borders that were set in the frames were lions, oxen, and cherubim. On the frames, both above and below the lions and oxen, there were wreaths of beveled work. ³⁰ Each stand had four bronze wheels and axles of bronze; at the four corners were supports for a basin. The supports were cast with wreaths at the side of each. ³¹ Its opening was within the crown whose height was one cubit; its opening was round, as a pedestal is made; it was a cubit and a half wide. At its opening there were carvings; its borders were four-sided, not round. ³² The four

wheels were underneath the borders; the axles of the wheels were in the stands; and the height of a wheel was a cubit and a half. ³³ The wheels were made like a chariot wheel; their axles, their rims, their spokes, and their hubs were all cast. ³⁴ There were four supports at the four corners of each stand; the supports were of one piece with the stands. ³⁵ On the top of the stand there was a round band half a cubit high; on the top of the stand, its stays and its borders were of one piece with it. ³⁶ On the surfaces of its stays and on its borders he carved cherubim, lions, and palm trees, where each had space, with wreaths all around. ³⁷ In this way he made the ten stands; all of them were cast alike, with the same size and the same form.

38 He made ten basins of bronze; each basin held forty baths,ᵐ each basin measured four cubits; there was a basin for each of the ten stands. ³⁹ He set five of the stands on the south side of the house, and five on the north side of the house; he set the sea on the southeast corner of the house.

40 Hiram also made the pots, the shovels, and the basins. So Hiram finished all the work that he did for King Solomon on the house of the Lord: ⁴¹ the two pillars, the two bowls of the capitals that were on the tops of the pillars, the two latticeworks to cover the two bowls of the capitals that were on the tops of the pillars; ⁴² the four hundred pomegranates for the two latticeworks, two rows of pomegranates for each latticework, to cover the two bowls of the capitals that were on the pillars; ⁴³ the ten stands, the ten basins on the stands; ⁴⁴ the one sea, and the twelve oxen underneath the sea.

45 The pots, the shovels, and the basins, all these vessels that Hiram made for King Solomon for the house of the Lord were of burnished bronze. ⁴⁶ In the plain of the Jordan the king cast them, in the

7.20
2 Chr 3.16;
4.13;
Jer 52.23
7.21
2 Chr 3.17;
1 Kings 6.3
7.23
2 Kings 25.13;
2 Chr 4.2;
Jer 52.17
7.24
1 Kings 6.18;
2 Chr 4.3
7.25
2 Chr 4.4,
5; Jer 52.20
7.27
v. 38;
2 Chr 4.14
7.30
2 Kings 16.17;
25.13,16

7.37
2 Chr 4.14
7.38
2 Chr 4.6
7.41
vv. 17,18
7.42
v. 20
7.44
vv. 23,25
7.45
2 Chr 4.16
7.46
2 Chr 4.17;
Josh 13.27;
3.16

ᵐ A Heb measure of volume

clay ground between Succoth and Zarethan. 47 Solomon left all the vessels unweighed, because there were so many of them; the weight of the bronze was not determined.

48 So Solomon made all the vessels that were in the house of the LORD: the golden altar, the golden table for the bread of the Presence, 49 the lampstands of pure gold, five on the south side and five on the north, in front of the inner sanctuary; the flowers, the lamps, and the tongs, of gold; 50 the cups, snuffers, basins, dishes for incense, and firepans, of pure gold; the sockets for the doors of the innermost part of the house, the most holy place, and for the doors of the nave of the temple, of gold.

51 Thus all the work that King Solomon did on the house of the LORD was finished. Solomon brought in the things that his father David had dedicated, the silver, the gold, and the vessels, and stored them in the treasuries of the house of the LORD.

Dedication of the Temple

8 Then Solomon assembled the elders of Israel and all the heads of the tribes, the leaders of the ancestral houses of the Israelites, before King Solomon in Jerusalem, to bring up the ark of the covenant of the LORD out of the city of David, which is Zion. 2 All the people of Israel assembled to King Solomon at the festival in the month Ethanim, which is the seventh month. 3 And all the elders of Israel came, and the priests carried the ark. 4 So they brought up the ark of the LORD, the tent of meeting, and all the holy vessels that were in the tent; the priests and the Levites brought them up. 5 King Solomon and all the congregation of Israel, who had assembled before him, were with him before the ark, sacrificing so many sheep and oxen that they could not be counted or numbered. 6 Then the priests brought the ark of the covenant of the LORD to its place, in the inner sanctuary of the house, in the most

holy place, underneath the wings of the cherubim. 7 For the cherubim spread out their wings over the place of the ark, so that the cherubim made a covering above the ark and its poles. 8 The poles were so long that the ends of the poles were seen from the holy place in front of the inner sanctuary; but they could not be seen from outside; they are there to this day. 9 There was nothing in the ark except the two tablets of stone that Moses had placed there at Horeb, where the LORD made a covenant with the Israelites, when they came out of the land of Egypt. 10 And when the priests came out of the holy place, a cloud filled the house of the LORD, 11 so that the priests could not stand to minister because of the cloud; for the glory of the LORD filled the house of the LORD.

12 Then Solomon said,

"The LORD has said that he
 would dwell in thick
 darkness.
13 I have built you an exalted
 house,
 a place for you to dwell in
 forever."

Solomon's Speech

14 Then the king turned around and blessed all the assembly of Israel, while all the assembly of Israel stood. 15 He said, "Blessed be the LORD, the God of Israel, who with his hand has fulfilled what he promised with his mouth to my father David, saying, 16 'Since the day that I brought my people Israel out of Egypt, I have not chosen a city from any of the tribes of Israel in which to build a house, that my name might be there; but I chose David to be over my people Israel.' 17 My father David had it in mind to build a house for the name of the LORD, the God of Israel. 18 But the LORD said to my father David, 'You did well to consider building a house for my name; 19 nevertheless you shall not build the house, but your son who shall be born to you shall build the house for my name.' 20 Now the LORD has upheld the

7.48
Ex 37.10ff
7.49
Ex 31-38
7.51
2 Sam 8.11;
2 Chr 5.1
8.1
2 Chr 5.2;
2 Sam 6.17;
5.7,9
8.2
Lev 23.34;
2 Chr 7.8
8.3
Num 7.9
8.4
1 Kings 3.4;
2 Chr 1.3
8.5
2 Sam 6.13
8.6
2 Sam 6.17;
1 Kings 6.19,
27
8.8
Ex 25.14
8.9
Ex 25.21;
Deut 10.2-5;
Heb 9.4;
Ex 24.7,8
8.10
Ex 40.34,
35;
2 Chr 7.1,
2
8.12
2 Chr 6.1;
Ps 97.2
8.13
2 Sam 7.13;
Ps 132.14
8.14
2 Sam 6.18
8.15
1 Chr 29.10,
20; Neh 9.5;
2 Sam 7.12,
13
8.16
2 Sam 7.4-6;
Deut 12.11;
1 Sam 16.1;
2 Sam 7.8
8.17
2 Sam 7.2;
1 Chr 17.1
8.19
2 Sam 7.5;
12.13;
1 Kings 5.3,
5
8.20
1 Chr 28.5,
6

promise that he made; for I have risen in the place of my father David; I sit on the throne of Israel, as the LORD promised, and have built the house for the name of the LORD, the God of Israel. [21] There I have provided a place for the ark, in which is the covenant of the LORD that he made with our ancestors when he brought them out of the land of Egypt."

Solomon's Prayer of Dedication

22 Then Solomon stood before the altar of the LORD in the presence of all the assembly of Israel, and spread out his hands to heaven. [23] He said, "O LORD, God of Israel, there is no God like you in heaven above or on earth beneath, keeping covenant and steadfast love for your servants who walk before you with all their heart, [24] the covenant that you kept for your servant my father David as you declared to him; you promised with your mouth and have this day fulfilled with your hand. [25] Therefore, O LORD, God of Israel, keep for your servant my father David that which you promised him, saying, 'There shall never fail you a successor before me to sit on the throne of Israel, if only your children look to their way, to walk before me as you have walked before me.' [26] Therefore, O God of Israel, let your word be confirmed, which you promised to your servant my father David.

27 "But will God indeed dwell on the earth? Even heaven and the highest heaven cannot contain you, much less this house that I have built! [28] Regard your servant's prayer and his plea, O LORD my God, heeding the cry and the prayer that your servant prays to you today; [29] that your eyes may be open night and day toward this house, the place of which you said, 'My name shall be there,' that you may heed the prayer that your servant prays toward this place. [30] Hear the plea of your servant and of your people Israel when they pray toward this place; O hear in heaven your dwelling place; heed and forgive.

31 "If someone sins against a neighbor and is given an oath to swear, and comes and swears before your altar in this house, [32] then hear in heaven, and act, and judge your servants, condemning the guilty by bringing their conduct on their own head, and vindicating the righteous by rewarding them according to their righteousness.

33 "When your people Israel, having sinned against you, are defeated before an enemy but turn again to you, confess your name, pray and plead with you in this house, [34] then hear in heaven, forgive the sin of your people Israel, and bring them again to the land that you gave to their ancestors.

35 "When heaven is shut up and there is no rain because they have sinned against you, and then they pray toward this place, confess your name, and turn from their sin, because you punish[n] them, [36] then hear in heaven, and forgive the sin of your servants, your people Israel, when you teach them the good way in which they should walk; and grant rain on your land, which you have given to your people as an inheritance.

37 "If there is famine in the land, if there is plague, blight, mildew, locust, or caterpillar; if their enemy besieges them in any[o] of their cities; whatever plague, whatever sickness there is; [38] whatever prayer, whatever plea there is from any individual or from all your people Israel, all knowing the afflictions of their own hearts so that they stretch out their hands toward this house; [39] then hear in heaven your dwelling place, forgive, act, and render to all whose hearts you know—according to all their ways, for only you know what is in every human heart— [40] so that they may fear you all the days that they live in the land that you gave to our ancestors.

Cross references

8.21 v. 9
8.22 2 Chr 6.12ff; Ex 9.33; Ezra 9.5
8.23 1 Sam 2.2; 2 Sam 7.22; Deut 7.9; Neh 1.5,9, 32
8.25 2 Sam 7.12, 16; 1 Kings 2.4
8.26 2 Sam 7.25
8.27 2 Chr 2.6; Isa 66.1; Jer 23.24; Acts 7.49
8.29 Deut 12.11; Dan 6.10
8.30 Neh 1.6
8.31 Ex 22.11
8.32 Deut 25.1
8.33 Lev 26.17; Deut 28.25; Lev 26.39
8.35 Lev 26.19; Deut 28.23
8.36 1 Sam 12.23; Ps 27.11; 94.12
8.37 Lev 26.16, 25,26; Deut 28.21-23, 38-42
8.39 1 Sam 16.7; 1 Chr 28.9; Ps 11.4; Jer 17.10
8.40 Ps 130.4

[n] Or *when you answer*　[o] Gk Syr: Heb *in the land*

41 "Likewise when a foreigner, who is not of your people Israel, comes from a distant land because of your name [42] —for they shall hear of your great name, your mighty hand, and your outstretched arm—when a foreigner comes and prays toward this house, [43] then hear in heaven your dwelling place, and do according to all that the foreigner calls to you, so that all the peoples of the earth may know your name and fear you, as do your people Israel, and so that they may know that your name has been invoked on this house that I have built.

44 "If your people go out to battle against their enemy, by whatever way you shall send them, and they pray to the Lord toward the city that you have chosen and the house that I have built for your name, [45] then hear in heaven their prayer and their plea, and maintain their cause.

46 "If they sin against you—for there is no one who does not sin—and you are angry with them and give them to an enemy, so that they are carried away captive to the land of the enemy, far off or near; [47] yet if they come to their senses in the land to which they have been taken captive, and repent, and plead with you in the land of their captors, saying, 'We have sinned, and have done wrong; we have acted wickedly'; [48] if they repent with all their heart and soul in the land of their enemies, who took them captive, and pray to you toward their land, which you gave to their ancestors, the city that you have chosen, and the house that I have built for your name; [49] then hear in heaven your dwelling place their prayer and their plea, maintain their cause [50] and forgive your people who have sinned against you, and all their transgressions that they have committed against you; and grant them compassion in the sight of their captors, so that they may have compassion on them [51] (for they are your people and heritage, which you brought out of Egypt, from the

midst of the iron-smelter). [52] Let your eyes be open to the plea of your servant, and to the plea of your people Israel, listening to them whenever they call to you. [53] For you have separated them from among all the peoples of the earth, to be your heritage, just as you promised through Moses, your servant, when you brought our ancestors out of Egypt, O Lord God."

Solomon Blesses the Assembly

54 Now when Solomon finished offering all this prayer and this plea to the Lord, he arose from facing the altar of the Lord, where he had knelt with hands outstretched toward heaven; [55] he stood and blessed all the assembly of Israel with a loud voice:

56 "Blessed be the Lord, who has given rest to his people Israel according to all that he promised; not one word has failed of all his good promise, which he spoke through his servant Moses. [57] The Lord our God be with us, as he was with our ancestors; may he not leave us or abandon us, [58] but incline our hearts to him, to walk in all his ways, and to keep his commandments, his statutes, and his ordinances, which he commanded our ancestors. [59] Let these words of mine, with which I pleaded before the Lord, be near to the Lord our God day and night, and may he maintain the cause of his servant and the cause of his people Israel, as each day requires; [60] so that all the peoples of the earth may know that the Lord is God; there is no other. [61] Therefore devote yourselves completely to the Lord our God, walking in his statutes and keeping his commandments, as at this day."

Solomon Offers Sacrifices

62 Then the king, and all Israel with him, offered sacrifice before the Lord. [63] Solomon offered as sacrifices of well-being to the Lord twenty-two thousand oxen and one hundred twenty thousand sheep. So the king and all the people of

Cross references
8.42 Deut 3.24
8.43 1 Sam 17.46; 2 Kings 19.19; Ps 102.15
8.46 2 Chr 6.36; Prov 20.9; 1 Jn 1.8-10; Lev 26.34-39; Deut 28.36, 64
8.47 Lev 26.40; Neh 1.6; Ps 106.6; Dan 9.5
8.48 Jer 29.12-14; Dan 6.10
8.50 2 Chr 30.9; Ps 106.46
8.51 Deut 9.29; Neh 1.10; Deut 4.20; Jer 11.4
8.53 Ex 19.5; Deut 9.26-29
8.55 v. 14
8.56 Josh 21.45; 23.14
8.57 Josh 1.5; Rom 8.28; Heb 13.5
8.58 Ps 119.36
8.60 1 Kings 18.39; Jer 10.10-12
8.61 1 Kings 11.4; 15.3,14; 2 Kings 20.3
8.62 2 Chr 7.4ff

Israel dedicated the house of the LORD. 64 The same day the king consecrated the middle of the court that was in front of the house of the LORD; for there he offered the burnt offerings and the grain offerings and the fat pieces of the sacrifices of well-being, because the bronze altar that was before the LORD was too small to receive the burnt offerings and the grain offerings and the fat pieces of the sacrifices of well-being.

65 So Solomon held the festival at that time, and all Israel with him—a great assembly, people from Lebo-hamath to the Wadi of Egypt—before the LORD our God, seven days. p 66 On the eighth day he sent the people away; and they blessed the king, and went to their tents, joyful and in good spirits because of all the goodness that the LORD had shown to his servant David and to his people Israel.

God Appears Again to Solomon

9 When Solomon had finished building the house of the LORD and the king's house and all that Solomon desired to build, 2 the LORD appeared to Solomon a second time, as he had appeared to him at Gibeon. 3 The LORD said to him, "I have heard your prayer and your plea, which you made before me; I have consecrated this house that you have built, and put my name there forever; my eyes and my heart will be there for all time. 4 As for you, if you will walk before me, as David your father walked, with integrity of heart and uprightness, doing according to all that I have commanded you, and keeping my statutes and my ordinances, 5 then I will establish your royal throne over Israel forever, as I promised your father David, saying, 'There shall not fail you a successor on the throne of Israel.'

6 "If you turn aside from following me, you or your children, and do not keep my commandments and my statutes that I have set before you, but go and serve other gods and worship them, 7 then I will

cut Israel off from the land that I have given them; and the house that I have consecrated for my name I will cast out of my sight; and Israel will become a proverb and a taunt among all peoples. 8 This house will become a heap of ruins; q everyone passing by it will be astonished, and will hiss; and they will say, 'Why has the LORD done such a thing to this land and to this house?' 9 Then they will say, 'Because they have forsaken the LORD their God, who brought their ancestors out of the land of Egypt, and embraced other gods, worshiping them and serving them; therefore the LORD has brought this disaster upon them.' "

10 At the end of twenty years, in which Solomon had built the two houses, the house of the LORD and the king's house, 11 King Hiram of Tyre having supplied Solomon with cedar and cypress timber and gold, as much as he desired, King Solomon gave to Hiram twenty cities in the land of Galilee. 12 But when Hiram came from Tyre to see the cities that Solomon had given him, they did not please him. 13 Therefore he said, "What kind of cities are these that you have given me, my brother?" So they are called the land of Cabul r to this day. 14 But Hiram had sent to the king one hundred twenty talents of gold.

Other Acts of Solomon

15 This is the account of the forced labor that King Solomon conscripted to build the house of the LORD and his own house, the Millo and the wall of Jerusalem, Hazor, Megiddo, Gezer 16 (Pharaoh king of Egypt had gone up and captured Gezer and burned it down, had killed the Canaanites who lived in the city, and had given it as dowry to his daughter, Solomon's wife; 17 so Solomon rebuilt Gezer), Lower Beth-horon, 18 Baalath, Tamar in the wilderness, within the

Cross-references

8.64
2 Chr 7.7;
4.1
8.65
v. 2;
Lev 23.34;
Num 34.8;
Josh 13.5;
Gen 15.18;
2 Chr 7.8
9.1
2 Chr 7.11ff;
1 Kings 7.1;
2 Chr 8.6
9.2
1 Kings 3.5
9.3
2 Kings 20.5;
1 Kings 8.29;
Deut 11.12
9.4
Gen 17.1;
1 Kings 15.5
9.5
2 Sam 7.12, 16;
1 Kings 2.4;
1 Chr 22.10
9.6
2 Sam 7.14;
2 Chr 7.19, 20
9.7
2 Kings 17.23;
25.21;
Jer 7.14;
Deut 28.37;
Ps 44.14

9.8
2 Chr 7.21;
Deut 29.24-26;
Jer 22.8,9
9.10
1 Kings 6.37, 38; 7.1;
2 Chr 8.1
9.11
2 Chr 8.2
9.13
Josh 19.27
9.15
1 Kings 5.13;
v. 24;
2 Sam 5.9;
Josh 19.36;
17.11; 16.10
9.16
Josh 16.10
9.17
Josh 16.3;
2 Chr 8.5

p Compare Gk: Heb seven days and seven days, fourteen days q Syr Old Latin: Heb will become high r Perhaps meaning a land good for nothing

land, [19] as well as all of Solomon's storage cities, the cities for his chariots, the cities for his cavalry, and whatever Solomon desired to build, in Jerusalem, in Lebanon, and in all the land of his dominion. [20] All the people who were left of the Amorites, the Hittites, the Perizzites, the Hivites, and the Jebusites, who were not of the people of Israel— [21] their descendants who were still left in the land, whom the Israelites were unable to destroy completely—these Solomon conscripted for slave labor, and so they are to this day. [22] But of the Israelites Solomon made no slaves; they were the soldiers, they were his officials, his commanders, his captains, and the commanders of his chariotry and cavalry.

23 These were the chief officers who were over Solomon's work: five hundred fifty, who had charge of the people who carried on the work.

24 But Pharaoh's daughter went up from the city of David to her own house that Solomon had built for her; then he built the Millo.

25 Three times a year Solomon used to offer up burnt offerings and sacrifices of well-being on the altar that he built for the Lord, offering incense[s] before the Lord. So he completed the house.

Solomon's Commercial Activity

26 King Solomon built a fleet of ships at Ezion-geber, which is near Eloth on the shore of the Red Sea,[t] in the land of Edom. [27] Hiram sent his servants with the fleet, sailors who were familiar with the sea, together with the servants of Solomon. [28] They went to Ophir, and imported from there four hundred twenty talents of gold, which they delivered to King Solomon.

Visit of the Queen of Sheba

10 When the queen of Sheba heard of the fame of Solomon, (fame due to[u] the name of the Lord), she came to test him with hard questions. [2] She came to Jerusalem with a very great reti-

nue, with camels bearing spices, and very much gold, and precious stones; and when she came to Solomon, she told him all that was on her mind. [3] Solomon answered all her questions; there was nothing hidden from the king that he could not explain to her. [4] When the queen of Sheba had observed all the wisdom of Solomon, the house that he had built, [5] the food of his table, the seating of his officials, and the attendance of his servants, their clothing, his valets, and his burnt offerings that he offered at the house of the Lord, there was no more spirit in her.

6 So she said to the king, "The report was true that I heard in my own land of your accomplishments and of your wisdom, [7] but I did not believe the reports until I came and my own eyes had seen it. Not even half had been told me; your wisdom and prosperity far surpass the report that I had heard. [8] Happy are your wives![v] Happy are these your servants, who continually attend you and hear your wisdom! [9] Blessed be the Lord your God, who has delighted in you and set you on the throne of Israel! Because the Lord loved Israel forever, he has made you king to execute justice and righteousness." [10] Then she gave the king one hundred twenty talents of gold, a great quantity of spices, and precious stones; never again did spices come in such quantity as that which the queen of Sheba gave to King Solomon.

11 Moreover, the fleet of Hiram, which carried gold from Ophir, brought from Ophir a great quantity of almug wood and precious stones. [12] From the almug wood the king made supports for the house of the Lord, and for the king's house, lyres also and harps for the singers; no such almug wood has come or been seen to this day.

13 Meanwhile King Solomon gave to the queen of Sheba every

9.19 1 Kings 4.26; v. 1
9.20 2 Chr 8.7
9.21 Judg 1.21, 27,29; Josh 15.63; 17.12; Judg 1.21; Gen 9.25, 26; Ezra 2.55,58
9.22 Lev 25.39
9.23 2 Chr 8.10
9.24 1 Kings 3.1; 7.8; 11.27; 2 Chr 32.5
9.25 2 Chr 8.12, 13,16
9.26 2 Chr 8.17, 18; Num 33.35; Deut 2.8; 1 Kings 22.48
9.27 1 Kings 10.11
9.28 1 Chr 29.4
10.1 2 Chr 9.1ff; Mt 12.42; Judg 14.12
10.5 1 Chr 26.16
10.9 1 Kings 5.7; 2 Sam 8.15
10.10 v. 2
10.11 1 Kings 9.27, 28
10.12 2 Chr 9.10, 11

s Gk: Heb *offering incense with it that was* t Or *Sea of Reeds* u Meaning of Heb uncertain v Gk Syr: Heb *men*

desire that she expressed, as well as what he gave her out of Solomon's royal bounty. Then she returned to her own land, with her servants.

14 The weight of gold that came to Solomon in one year was six hundred sixty-six talents of gold, 15 besides that which came from the traders and from the business of the merchants, and from all the kings of Arabia and the governors of the land. 16 King Solomon made two hundred large shields of beaten gold; six hundred shekels of gold went into each large shield. 17 He made three hundred shields of beaten gold; three minas of gold went into each shield; and the king put them in the House of the Forest of Lebanon. 18 The king also made a great ivory throne, and overlaid it with the finest gold. 19 The throne had six steps. The top of the throne was rounded in the back, and on each side of the seat were arm rests and two lions standing beside the arm rests, 20 while twelve lions were standing, one on each end of a step on the six steps. Nothing like it was ever made in any kingdom. 21 All King Solomon's drinking vessels were of gold, and all the vessels of the House of the Forest of Lebanon were of pure gold; none were of silver—it was not considered as anything in the days of Solomon. 22 For the king had a fleet of ships of Tarshish at sea with the fleet of Hiram. Once every three years the fleet of ships of Tarshish used to come bringing gold, silver, ivory, apes, and peacocks. w

23 Thus King Solomon excelled all the kings of the earth in riches and in wisdom. 24 The whole earth sought the presence of Solomon to hear his wisdom, which God had put into his mind. 25 Every one of them brought a present, objects of silver and gold, garments, weaponry, spices, horses, and mules, so much year by year.

26 Solomon gathered together chariots and horses; he had fourteen hundred chariots and twelve

thousand horses, which he stationed in the chariot cities and with the king in Jerusalem. 27 The king made silver as common in Jerusalem as stones, and he made cedars as numerous as the sycamores of the Shephelah. 28 Solomon's import of horses was from Egypt and Kue, and the king's traders received them from Kue at a price. 29 A chariot could be imported from Egypt for six hundred shekels of silver, and a horse for one hundred fifty; so through the king's traders they were exported to all the kings of the Hittites and the kings of Aram.

Solomon's Errors

11 King Solomon loved many foreign women along with the daughter of Pharaoh: Moabite, Ammonite, Edomite, Sidonian, and Hittite women, 2 from the nations concerning which the LORD had said to the Israelites, "You shall not enter into marriage with them, neither shall they with you; for they will surely incline your heart to follow their gods"; Solomon clung to these in love. 3 Among his wives were seven hundred princesses and three hundred concubines; and his wives turned away his heart. 4 For when Solomon was old, his wives turned away his heart after other gods; and his heart was not true to the LORD his God, as was the heart of his father David. 5 For Solomon followed Astarte the goddess of the Sidonians, and Milcom the abomination of the Ammonites. 6 So Solomon did what was evil in the sight of the LORD, and did not completely follow the LORD, as his father David had done. 7 Then Solomon built a high place for Chemosh the abomination of Moab, and for Molech the abomination of the Ammonites, on the mountain east of Jerusalem. 8 He did the same for all his foreign wives, who offered incense and sacrificed to their gods.

9 Then the LORD was angry with Solomon, because his heart had

Cross references (center column):

10.14
2 Chr 9.13-28
10.16
1 Kings 14.26-28
10.17
1 Kings 7.2
10.18
2 Chr 9.17ff
10.22
1 Kings 9.26-28; 22.48;
2 Chr 20.36
10.23
1 Kings 3.12, 13; 4.30
10.24
1 Kings 3.9, 12,28
10.26
1 Kings 4.26;
2 Chr 1.14;
9.25;
1 Kings 9.19

10.28
2 Chr 1.16;
9.28
10.29
2 Kings 7.6, 7
11.1
Neh 13.26;
Deut 17.17
11.2
Ex 34.16;
Deut 7.3,4
11.4
1 Kings 8.61;
9.4
11.5
v. 33;
Judg 2.13;
2 Kings 23.13
11.7
Num 21.29;
Judg 11.24;
2 Kings 23.13
11.9
vv. 2,3;
1 Kings 3.5;
9.2

w Or baboons

turned away from the LORD, the God of Israel, who had appeared to him twice, [10] and had commanded him concerning this matter, that he should not follow other gods; but he did not observe what the LORD commanded. [11] Therefore the LORD said to Solomon, "Since this has been your mind and you have not kept my covenant and my statutes that I have commanded you, I will surely tear the kingdom from you and give it to your servant. [12] Yet for the sake of your father David I will not do it in your lifetime; I will tear it out of the hand of your son. [13] I will not, however, tear away the entire kingdom; I will give one tribe to your son, for the sake of my servant David and for the sake of Jerusalem, which I have chosen."

Adversaries of Solomon

14 Then the LORD raised up an adversary against Solomon, Hadad the Edomite; he was of the royal house in Edom. [15] For when David was in Edom, and Joab the commander of the army went up to bury the dead, he killed every male in Edom [16] (for Joab and all Israel remained there six months, until he had eliminated every male in Edom); [17] but Hadad fled to Egypt with some Edomites who were servants of his father. He was a young boy at that time. [18] They set out from Midian and came to Paran; they took people with them from Paran and came to Egypt, to Pharaoh king of Egypt, who gave him a house, assigned him an allowance of food, and gave him land. [19] Hadad found great favor in the sight of Pharaoh, so that he gave him his sister-in-law for a wife, the sister of Queen Tahpenes. [20] The sister of Tahpenes gave birth by him to his son Genubath, whom Tahpenes weaned in Pharaoh's house; Genubath was in Pharaoh's house among the children of Pharaoh. [21] When Hadad heard in Egypt that David slept with his ancestors and that Joab the commander of the army was dead, Hadad said to

Pharaoh, "Let me depart, that I may go to my own country." [22] But Pharaoh said to him, "What do you lack with me that you now seek to go to your own country?" And he said, "No, do let me go."

23 God raised up another adversary against Solomon,[x] Rezon son of Eliada, who had fled from his master, King Hadadezer of Zobah. [24] He gathered followers around him and became leader of a marauding band, after the slaughter by David; they went to Damascus, settled there, and made him king in Damascus. [25] He was an adversary of Israel all the days of Solomon, making trouble as Hadad did; he despised Israel and reigned over Aram.

Jeroboam's Rebellion

26 Jeroboam son of Nebat, an Ephraimite of Zeredah, a servant of Solomon, whose mother's name was Zeruah, a widow, rebelled against the king. [27] The following was the reason he rebelled against the king. Solomon built the Millo, and closed up the gap in the wall[y] of the city of his father David. [28] The man Jeroboam was very able, and when Solomon saw that the young man was industrious he gave him charge over all the forced labor of the house of Joseph. [29] About that time, when Jeroboam was leaving Jerusalem, the prophet Ahijah the Shilonite found him on the road. Ahijah had clothed himself with a new garment. The two of them were alone in the open country [30] when Ahijah laid hold of the new garment he was wearing and tore it into twelve pieces. [31] He then said to Jeroboam: Take for yourself ten pieces; for thus says the LORD, the God of Israel, "See, I am about to tear the kingdom from the hand of Solomon, and will give you ten tribes. [32] One tribe will remain his, for the sake of my servant David and for the sake of Jerusalem, the city that I have chosen out of all the tribes of Israel. [33] This is

11.10
1 Kings 6.12; 9.6,7
11.11
v. 31;
1 Kings 12.15, 16
11.13
2 Sam 7.15;
1 Kings 12.20;
Deut 12.11
11.15
2 Sam 8.14;
1 Chr 18.12, 13
11.21
1 Kings 2.10

11.23
v. 14;
2 Sam 8.3
11.24
2 Sam 8.3;
10.8,18
11.26
1 Kings 12.2;
2 Chr 13.6;
2 Sam 20.21
11.27
1 Kings 9.24
11.29
1 Kings 14.2
11.30
1 Sam 15.27, 28
11.31
vv. 11-13
11.33
vv. 5-7

x Heb him y Heb lacks *in the wall*

because he has[z] forsaken me, worshiped Astarte the goddess of the Sidonians, Chemosh the god of Moab, and Milcom the god of the Ammonites, and has[z] not walked in my ways, doing what is right in my sight and keeping my statutes and my ordinances, as his father David did. [34]Nevertheless I will not take the whole kingdom away from him but will make him ruler all the days of his life, for the sake of my servant David whom I chose and who did keep my commandments and my statutes; [35]but I will take the kingdom away from his son and give it to you—that is, the ten tribes. [36]Yet to his son I will give one tribe, so that my servant David may always have a lamp before me in Jerusalem, the city where I have chosen to put my name. [37]I will take you, and you shall reign over all that your soul desires; you shall be king over Israel. [38]If you will listen to all that I command you, walk in my ways, and do what is right in my sight by keeping my statutes and my commandments, as David my servant did, I will be with you, and will build you an enduring house, as I built for David, and I will give Israel to you. [39]For this reason I will punish the descendants of David, but not forever." [40]Solomon sought therefore to kill Jeroboam; but Jeroboam promptly fled to Egypt, to King Shishak of Egypt, and remained in Egypt until the death of Solomon.

Death of Solomon

41 Now the rest of the acts of Solomon, all that he did as well as his wisdom, are they not written in the Book of the Acts of Solomon? [42]The time that Solomon reigned in Jerusalem over all Israel was forty years. [43]Solomon slept with his ancestors and was buried in the city of his father David; and his son Rehoboam succeeded him.

The Northern Tribes Secede

12 Rehoboam went to Shechem, for all Israel had come to Shechem to make him king. [2]When Jeroboam son of Nebat heard of it (for he was still in Egypt, where he had fled from King Solomon), then Jeroboam returned from[a] Egypt. [3]And they sent and called him; and Jeroboam and all the assembly of Israel came and said to Rehoboam, [4]"Your father made our yoke heavy. Now therefore lighten the hard service of your father and his heavy yoke that he placed on us, and we will serve you." [5]He said to them, "Go away for three days, then come again to me." So the people went away.

6 Then King Rehoboam took counsel with the older men who had attended his father Solomon while he was still alive, saying, "How do you advise me to answer this people?" [7]They answered him, "If you will be a servant to this people today and serve them, and speak good words to them when you answer them, then they will be your servants forever." [8]But he disregarded the advice that the older men gave him, and consulted with the young men who had grown up with him and now attended him. [9]He said to them, "What do you advise that we answer this people who have said to me, 'Lighten the yoke that your father put on us'?" [10]The young men who had grown up with him said to him, "Thus you should say to this people who spoke to you, 'Your father made our yoke heavy, but you must lighten it for us'; thus you should say to them, 'My little finger is thicker than my father's loins. [11]Now, whereas my father laid on you a heavy yoke, I will add to your yoke. My father disciplined you with whips, but I will discipline you with scorpions.' "

12 So Jeroboam and all the people came to Rehoboam the third day, as the king had said, "Come to me again the third day." [13]The king answered the people harshly. He disregarded the advice that the older men had given him [14]and spoke

Cross references (center column):

11.35
1 Kings 12.16, 17
11.36
v. 13;
1 Kings 15.4;
2 Kings 8.19
11.38
Josh 1.5;
2 Sam 7.11, 27
11.41
2 Chr 9.29
11.42
2 Chr 9.30
11.43
2 Chr 9.31;
1 Kings 14.21
12.1
2 Chr 10.1ff

12.2
1 Kings 11.26, 40
12.4
1 Sam 8.11-18;
1 Kings 4.7
12.5
v. 12
12.7
2 Chr 10.7
12.8
Lev 19.32
12.12
v. 5
12.14
Ex 1.13,14;
5.5-9,16-18

[z] Gk Syr Vg: Heb they have [a] Gk Vg Compare 2 Chr 10.2: Heb lived in

to them according to the advice of the young men, "My father made your yoke heavy, but I will add to your yoke; my father disciplined you with whips, but I will discipline you with scorpions." 15 So the king did not listen to the people, because it was a turn of affairs brought about by the LORD that he might fulfill his word, which the LORD had spoken by Ahijah the Shilonite to Jeroboam son of Nebat.

16 When all Israel saw that the king would not listen to them, the people answered the king,

"What share do we have in
 David?
We have no inheritance in
 the son of Jesse.
To your tents, O Israel!
Look now to your own
 house, O David."

So Israel went away to their tents. 17 But Rehoboam reigned over the Israelites who were living in the towns of Judah. 18 When King Rehoboam sent Adoram, who was taskmaster over the forced labor, all Israel stoned him to death. King Rehoboam then hurriedly mounted his chariot to flee to Jerusalem. 19 So Israel has been in rebellion against the house of David to this day.

First Dynasty: Jeroboam Reigns over Israel

20 When all Israel heard that Jeroboam had returned, they sent and called him to the assembly and made him king over all Israel. There was no one who followed the house of David, except the tribe of Judah alone.

21 When Rehoboam came to Jerusalem, he assembled all the house of Judah and the tribe of Benjamin, one hundred eighty thousand chosen troops to fight against the house of Israel, to restore the kingdom to Rehoboam son of Solomon. 22 But the word of God came to Shemaiah the man of God: 23 Say to King Rehoboam of Judah, son of Solomon, and to all the house of Judah and Benjamin, and to the rest of the people,

24 "Thus says the LORD, You shall not go up or fight against your kindred the people of Israel. Let everyone go home, for this thing is from me." So they heeded the word of the LORD and went home again, according to the word of the LORD.

Jeroboam's Golden Calves

25 Then Jeroboam built Shechem in the hill country of Ephraim, and resided there; he went out from there and built Penuel. 26 Then Jeroboam said to himself, "Now the kingdom may well revert to the house of David. 27 If this people continues to go up to offer sacrifices in the house of the LORD at Jerusalem, the heart of this people will turn again to their master, King Rehoboam of Judah; they will kill me and return to King Rehoboam of Judah." 28 So the king took counsel, and made two calves of gold. He said to the people,[b] "You have gone up to Jerusalem long enough. Here are your gods, O Israel, who brought you up out of the land of Egypt." 29 He set one in Bethel, and the other he put in Dan. 30 And this thing became a sin, for the people went to worship before the one at Bethel and before the other as far as Dan.[c] 31 He also made houses[d] on high places, and appointed priests from among all the people, who were not Levites. 32 Jeroboam appointed a festival on the fifteenth day of the eighth month like the festival that was in Judah, and he offered sacrifices on the altar; so he did in Bethel, sacrificing to the calves that he had made. And he placed in Bethel the priests of the high places that he had made. 33 He went up to the altar that he had made in Bethel on the fifteenth day in the eighth month, in the month that he alone had devised; he appointed a festival for the people of Israel, and he went up to the altar to offer incense.

12.15
v. 24;
Judg 14.4;
2 Chr 10.15;
22.7; 25.20;
1 Kings 11.11,
31
12.16
2 Sam 20.1
12.17
1 Kings 11.13,
36
12.18
1 Kings 4.6;
5.14
12.19
2 Kings 17.21
12.20
1 Kings 11.13,
32
12.21
2 Chr 11.1ff

12.24
v. 15
12.25
Judg 9.45;
8.17
12.27
Deut 12.5,6
12.28
2 Kings 10.29;
17.16;
Ex 32.4,8
12.29
Gen 28.19;
Judg 18.29
12.30
1 Kings 13.34;
2 Kings 17.21
12.31
1 Kings 13.32,
33;
Num 3.10;
2 Kings 17.32
12.32
Lev 23.33,
34;
Num 29.12;
Am 7.13
12.33
1 Kings 13.1

b Gk: Heb to them c Compare Gk: Heb went up to the one as far as Dan d Gk Vg Compare 13.32: Heb a house

A Man of God from Judah

13 While Jeroboam was standing by the altar to offer incense, a man of God came out of Judah by the word of the Lord to Bethel ²and proclaimed against the altar by the word of the Lord, and said, "O altar, altar, thus says the Lord: 'A son shall be born to the house of David, Josiah by name; and he shall sacrifice on you the priests of the high places who offer incense on you, and human bones shall be burned on you.'" ³He gave a sign the same day, saying, "This is the sign that the Lord has spoken: 'The altar shall be torn down, and the ashes that are on it shall be poured out.'" ⁴When the king heard what the man of God cried out against the altar at Bethel, Jeroboam stretched out his hand from the altar, saying, "Seize him!" But the hand that he stretched out against him withered so that he could not draw it back to himself. ⁵The altar also was torn down, and the ashes poured out from the altar, according to the sign that the man of God had given by the word of the Lord. ⁶The king said to the man of God, "Entreat now the favor of the Lord your God, and pray for me, so that my hand may be restored to me." So the man of God entreated the Lord; and the king's hand was restored to him, and became as it was before. ⁷Then the king said to the man of God, "Come home with me and dine, and I will give you a gift." ⁸But the man of God said to the king, "If you give me half your kingdom, I will not go in with you; nor will I eat food or drink water in this place. ⁹For thus I was commanded by the word of the Lord: You shall not eat food, or drink water, or return by the way that you came." ¹⁰So he went another way, and did not return by the way that he had come to Bethel.

11 Now there lived an old prophet in Bethel. One of his sons came and told him all that the man of God had done that day in Bethel;

the words also that he had spoken to the king, they told to their father. ¹²Their father said to them, "Which way did he go?" And his sons showed him the way that the man of God who came from Judah had gone. ¹³Then he said to his sons, "Saddle a donkey for me." So they saddled a donkey for him, and he mounted it. ¹⁴He went after the man of God, and found him sitting under an oak tree. He said to him, "Are you the man of God who came from Judah?" He answered, "I am." ¹⁵Then he said to him, "Come home with me and eat some food." ¹⁶But he said, "I cannot return with you, or go in with you; nor will I eat food or drink water with you in this place; ¹⁷for it was said to me by the word of the Lord: You shall not eat food or drink water there, or return by the way that you came." ¹⁸Then the other ᵉ said to him, "I also am a prophet as you are, and an angel spoke to me by the word of the Lord: Bring him back with you into your house so that he may eat food and drink water." But he was deceiving him. ¹⁹Then the man of God ᵉ went back with him, and ate food and drank water in his house.

20 As they were sitting at the table, the word of the Lord came to the prophet who had brought him back; ²¹and he proclaimed to the man of God who came from Judah, "Thus says the Lord: Because you have disobeyed the word of the Lord, and have not kept the commandment that the Lord your God commanded you, ²²but have come back and have eaten food and drunk water in the place of which he said to you, 'Eat no food, and drink no water,' your body shall not come to your ancestral tomb." ²³After the man of God ᵉ had eaten food and had drunk, they saddled for him a donkey belonging to the prophet who had brought him back. ²⁴Then as he went away, a lion met him on the road and killed him. His body was thrown in the road, and the donkey stood beside

Cross-references (center column):

13.1 — 2 Kings 23.17; 1 Kings 12.32, 33
13.2 — 2 Kings 23.15, 16
13.3 — Isa 7.14; Judg 6.17
13.6 — Ex 8.8; 9.28; Acts 8.24; Lk 6.27,28
13.7 — 1 Sam 9.7, 8; 2 Kings 5.15
13.8 — vv. 16,17; Num 22.18; 24.13
13.11 — v. 25
13.16 — vv. 8,9
13.17 — 1 Kings 20.35
13.21 — 1 Sam 15.26
13.24 — 1 Kings 20.36

ᵉ Heb *he*

it; the lion also stood beside the body. ²⁵People passed by and saw the body thrown in the road, with the lion standing by the body. And they came and told it in the town where the old prophet lived.

26 When the prophet who had brought him back from the way heard of it, he said, "It is the man of God who disobeyed the word of the LORD; therefore the LORD has given him to the lion, which has torn him and killed him according to the word that the LORD spoke to him." ²⁷Then he said to his sons, "Saddle a donkey for me." So they saddled one, ²⁸and he went and found the body thrown in the road, with the donkey and the lion standing beside the body. The lion had not eaten the body or attacked the donkey. ²⁹The prophet took up the body of the man of God, laid it on the donkey, and brought it back to the city,^f to mourn and to bury him. ³⁰He laid the body in his own grave; and they mourned over him, saying, "Alas, my brother!" ³¹After he had buried him, he said to his sons, "When I die, bury me in the grave in which the man of God is buried; lay my bones beside his bones. ³²For the saying that he proclaimed by the word of the LORD against the altar in Bethel, and against all the houses of the high places that are in the cities of Samaria, shall surely come to pass."

33 Even after this event Jeroboam did not turn from his evil way, but made priests for the high places again from among all the people; any who wanted to be priests he consecrated for the high places. ³⁴This matter became sin to the house of Jeroboam, so as to cut it off and to destroy it from the face of the earth.

Judgment on the House of Jeroboam

14 At that time Abijah son of Jeroboam fell sick. ²Jeroboam said to his wife, "Go, disguise yourself, so that it will not be known that you are the wife of Jeroboam, and go to Shiloh; for the

prophet Ahijah is there, who said of me that I should be king over this people. ³Take with you ten loaves, some cakes, and a jar of honey, and go to him; he will tell you what shall happen to the child."

4 Jeroboam's wife did so; she set out and went to Shiloh, and came to the house of Ahijah. Now Ahijah could not see, for his eyes were dim because of his age. ⁵But the LORD said to Ahijah, "The wife of Jeroboam is coming to inquire of you concerning her son; for he is sick. Thus and thus you shall say to her."

When she came, she pretended to be another woman. ⁶But when Ahijah heard the sound of her feet, as she came in at the door, he said, "Come in, wife of Jeroboam; why do you pretend to be another? For I am charged with heavy tidings for you. ⁷Go, tell Jeroboam, 'Thus says the LORD, the God of Israel: Because I exalted you from among the people, made you leader over my people Israel, ⁸and tore the kingdom away from the house of David to give it to you; yet you have not been like my servant David, who kept my commandments and followed me with all his heart, doing only that which was right in my sight, ⁹but you have done evil above all those who were before you and have gone and made for yourself other gods, and cast images, provoking me to anger, and have thrust me behind your back; ¹⁰therefore, I will bring evil upon the house of Jeroboam. I will cut off from Jeroboam every male, both bond and free in Israel, and will consume the house of Jeroboam, just as one burns up dung until it is all gone. ¹¹Anyone belonging to Jeroboam who dies in the city, the dogs shall eat; and anyone who dies in the open country, the birds of the air shall eat; for the LORD has spoken.' ¹²Therefore set out, go to your house. When your feet enter the city, the child shall die. ¹³All

13.25 v. 11
13.26 v. 21
13.30 Jer 22.18
13.31 2 Kings 23.17, 18
13.32 v. 2; 2 Kings 23.16, 17,19; see 1 Kings 16.24
13.33 1 Kings 12.31, 32; 2 Chr 11.15; 13.9
13.34 1 Kings 12.30; 14.10
14.2 1 Sam 28.8; 2 Sam 14.2; 1 Kings 11.29-31

14.3 1 Sam 9.7, 8
14.4 1 Kings 11.29; 1 Sam 3.2; 4.15
14.5 2 Sam 14.2
14.7 1 Kings 11.28-31;16.2
14.8 1 Kings 11.31ff
14.9 1 Kings 12.28; 2 Chr 11.15; Ps 50.17; Ex 34.17; Ezek 23.35
14.10 1 Kings 15.29; 21.21; 2 Kings 9.8; Deut 32.36; 2 Kings 14.26
14.11 1 Kings 16.4; 21.24
14.12 v. 17
14.13 2 Chr 12.12

^fGk: Heb *he came to the town of the old prophet*

Israel shall mourn for him and bury him; for he alone of Jeroboam's family shall come to the grave, because in him there is found something pleasing to the LORD, the God of Israel, in the house of Jeroboam. [14]Moreover the LORD will raise up for himself a king over Israel, who shall cut off the house of Jeroboam today, even right now![g]

15 "The LORD will strike Israel, as a reed is shaken in the water; he will root up Israel out of this good land that he gave to their ancestors, and scatter them beyond the Euphrates, because they have made their sacred poles,[h] provoking the LORD to anger. [16]He will give Israel up because of the sins of Jeroboam, which he sinned and which he caused Israel to commit."

17 Then Jeroboam's wife got up and went away, and she came to Tirzah. As she came to the threshold of the house, the child died. [18]All Israel buried him and mourned for him, according to the word of the LORD, which he spoke by his servant the prophet Ahijah.

Death of Jeroboam

19 Now the rest of the acts of Jeroboam, how he warred and how he reigned, are written in the Book of the Annals of the Kings of Israel. [20]The time that Jeroboam reigned was twenty-two years; then he slept with his ancestors, and his son Nadab succeeded him.

Rehoboam Reigns over Judah

21 Now Rehoboam son of Solomon reigned in Judah. Rehoboam was forty-one years old when he began to reign, and he reigned seventeen years in Jerusalem, the city that the LORD had chosen out of all the tribes of Israel, to put his name there. His mother's name was Naamah the Ammonite. [22]Judah did what was evil in the sight of the LORD; they provoked him to jealousy with their sins that they committed, more than all that their ancestors had done. [23]For they also built for themselves high places, pillars, and sacred poles[h] on every high

hill and under every green tree; [24]there were also male temple prostitutes in the land. They committed all the abominations of the nations that the LORD drove out before the people of Israel.

25 In the fifth year of King Rehoboam, King Shishak of Egypt came up against Jerusalem; [26]he took away the treasures of the house of the LORD and the treasures of the king's house; he took everything. He also took away all the shields of gold that Solomon had made; [27]so King Rehoboam made shields of bronze instead, and committed them to the hands of the officers of the guard, who kept the door of the king's house. [28]As often as the king went into the house of the LORD, the guard carried them and brought them back to the guardroom.

29 Now the rest of the acts of Rehoboam, and all that he did, are they not written in the Book of the Annals of the Kings of Judah? [30]There was war between Rehoboam and Jeroboam continually. [31]Rehoboam slept with his ancestors and was buried with his ancestors in the city of David. His mother's name was Naamah the Ammonite. His son Abijam succeeded him.

Abijam Reigns over Judah: Idolatry and War

15 Now in the eighteenth year of King Jeroboam son of Nebat, Abijam began to reign over Judah. [2]He reigned for three years in Jerusalem. His mother's name was Maacah daughter of Abishalom. [3]He committed all the sins that his father did before him; his heart was not true to the LORD his God, like the heart of his father David. [4]Nevertheless for David's sake the LORD his God gave him a lamp in Jerusalem, setting up his son after him, and establishing Jerusalem; [5]because David did what was right in the sight of the LORD, and did not turn aside from anything that he commanded him all the

14.14
1 Kings 15.27-29
14.15
2 Kings 17.6; Josh 23.15, 16;
2 Kings 15.29; Ex 34.13; Deut 12.3,4
14.16
1 Kings 12.30; 13.34; 15.30, 34
14.17
1 Kings 16.6-9
14.18
v. 13
14.19
2 Chr 13.2-20
14.21
2 Chr 12.13; 1 Kings 11.32, 36; v. 31
14.22
2 Chr 12.1; Deut 32.21
14.23
Deut 12.2; Ezek 16.24, 25;
2 Kings 17.9, 10; Isa 57.5

14.24
Deut 23.17; 1 Kings 15.12; 2 Kings 23.7
14.25
1 Kings 11.40; 2 Chr 12.2, 9-11
14.26
1 Kings 15.18; 10.17
14.29
2 Chr 12.15
14.30
1 Kings 12.21-24; 15.6
14.31
2 Chr 12.16; v. 21
15.1
2 Chr 13.1, 2
15.3
1 Kings 11.4
15.4
1 Kings 11.36; 2 Chr 21.7
15.5
1 Kings 14.8; 2 Sam 11.4, 15-17; 12.9

[g]Meaning of Heb uncertain [h]Heb *Asherim*

days of his life, except in the matter of Uriah the Hittite. [6] The war begun between Rehoboam and Jeroboam continued all the days of his life. [7] The rest of the acts of Abijam, and all that he did, are they not written in the Book of the Annals of the Kings of Judah? There was war between Abijam and Jeroboam. [8] Abijam slept with his ancestors, and they buried him in the city of David. Then his son Asa succeeded him.

Asa Reigns over Judah

9 In the twentieth year of King Jeroboam of Israel, Asa began to reign over Judah; [10] he reigned forty-one years in Jerusalem. His mother's name was Maacah daughter of Abishalom. [11] Asa did what was right in the sight of the LORD, as his father David had done. [12] He put away the male temple prostitutes out of the land, and removed all the idols that his ancestors had made. [13] He also removed his mother Maacah from being queen mother, because she had made an abominable image for Asherah; Asa cut down her image and burned it at the Wadi Kidron. [14] But the high places were not taken away. Nevertheless the heart of Asa was true to the LORD all his days. [15] He brought into the house of the LORD the votive gifts of his father and his own votive gifts—silver, gold, and utensils.

Alliance with Aram against Israel

16 There was war between Asa and King Baasha of Israel all their days. [17] King Baasha of Israel went up against Judah, and built Ramah, to prevent anyone from going out or coming in to King Asa of Judah. [18] Then Asa took all the silver and the gold that were left in the treasures of the house of the LORD and the treasures of the king's house, and gave them into the hands of his servants. King Asa sent them to King Ben-hadad son of Tabrimmon son of Hezion of Aram, who resided in Damascus,

saying, [19] "Let there be an alliance between me and you, like that between my father and your father: I am sending you a present of silver and gold; go, break your alliance with King Baasha of Israel, so that he may withdraw from me." [20] Benhadad listened to King Asa, and sent the commanders of his armies against the cities of Israel. He conquered Ijon, Dan, Abel-bethmaacah, and all Chinneroth, with all the land of Naphtali. [21] When Baasha heard of it, he stopped building Ramah and lived in Tirzah. [22] Then King Asa made a proclamation to all Judah, none was exempt: they carried away the stones of Ramah and its timber, with which Baasha had been building; with them King Asa built Geba of Benjamin and Mizpah. [23] Now the rest of all the acts of Asa, all his power, all that he did, and the cities that he built, are they not written in the Book of the Annals of the Kings of Judah? But in his old age he was diseased in his feet. [24] Then Asa slept with his ancestors, and was buried with his ancestors in the city of his father David; his son Jehoshaphat succeeded him.

Nadab Reigns over Israel

25 Nadab son of Jeroboam began to reign over Israel in the second year of King Asa of Judah; he reigned over Israel two years. [26] He did what was evil in the sight of the LORD, walking in the way of his ancestor and in the sin that he caused Israel to commit.

27 Baasha son of Ahijah, of the house of Issachar, conspired against him; and Baasha struck him down at Gibbethon, which belonged to the Philistines; for Nadab and all Israel were laying siege to Gibbethon. [28] So Baasha killed Nadab[i] in the third year of King Asa of Judah, and succeeded him. [29] As soon as he was king, he killed all the house of Jeroboam; he left to the house of Jeroboam not one that breathed, until he had destroyed it, according to the word of

15.6
1 Kings 14.30
15.7
2 Chr 13.2, 3,22
15.8
2 Chr 14.1
15.10
v. 2
15.11
2 Chr 14.2
15.12
1 Kings 14.24; 22.46
15.13
2 Chr 15.16-18; Ex 32.20
15.14
1 Kings 22.43; 2 Chr 15.17, 18; v. 3
15.15
1 Kings 7.51
15.16
v. 32
15.17
2 Chr 16.1ff; Josh 18.25; 1 Kings 12.27
15.18
v. 15; 2 Chr 16.2; 1 Kings 11.23, 24

15.20
2 Kings 15.29; Judg 18.29; 2 Sam 20.14
15.22
2 Chr 16.6; Josh 21.17
15.23
2 Chr 16.11-14
15.24
2 Chr 17.1
15.25
1 Kings 14.20
15.26
1 Kings 12.30; 14.16
15.27
1 Kings 14.14; Josh 19.44; 21.23
15.29
1 Kings 14.10, 14

i Heb him

the LORD that he spoke by his servant Ahijah the Shilonite— ³⁰because of the sins of Jeroboam that he committed and that he caused Israel to commit, and because of the anger to which he provoked the LORD, the God of Israel.

31 Now the rest of the acts of Nadab, and all that he did, are they not written in the Book of the Annals of the Kings of Israel? ³²There was war between Asa and King Baasha of Israel all their days.

Second Dynasty: Baasha Reigns over Israel

33 In the third year of King Asa of Judah, Baasha son of Ahijah began to reign over all Israel at Tirzah; he reigned twenty-four years. ³⁴He did what was evil in the sight of the LORD, walking in the way of Jeroboam and in the sin that he caused Israel to commit.

16 The word of the LORD came to Jehu son of Hanani against Baasha, saying, ² "Since I exalted you out of the dust and made you leader over my people Israel, and you have walked in the way of Jeroboam, and have caused my people Israel to sin, provoking me to anger with their sins, ³ therefore, I will consume Baasha and his house, and I will make your house like the house of Jeroboam son of Nebat. ⁴Anyone belonging to Baasha who dies in the city the dogs shall eat; and anyone of his who dies in the field the birds of the air shall eat."

5 Now the rest of the acts of Baasha, what he did, and his power, are they not written in the Book of the Annals of the Kings of Israel? ⁶Baasha slept with his ancestors, and was buried at Tirzah; and his son Elah succeeded him. ⁷Moreover the word of the LORD came by the prophet Jehu son of Hanani against Baasha and his house, both because of all the evil that he did in the sight of the LORD, provoking him to anger with the work of his hands, in being like the house of Jeroboam, and also because he destroyed it.

15.30
1 Kings 14.9,
16
15.31
v. 16
15.34
1 Kings 12.28,
29; 13.33;
14.16
16.1
v. 7;
2 Chr 19.2;
20.34
16.2
1 Kings 14.7;
15.34
16.3
v. 11;
1 Kings 14.10;
15.29
16.4
1 Kings 14.11
16.5
1 Kings 14.19;
15.31
16.6
1 Kings 14.17;
15.21
16.7
v. 1;
1 Kings 15.27,
29

16.9
2 Kings 9.30-
33
16.12
v. 3;
2 Chr 19.2;
20.34
16.13
Deut 32.21;
1 Sam 12.21;
Isa 41.29
16.14
v. 5
16.15
1 Kings 15.27
16.18
1 Sam 31.4,
5;
2 Sam 17.23
16.19
1 Kings 12.28;
15.26,34

Elah Reigns over Israel

8 In the twenty-sixth year of King Asa of Judah, Elah son of Baasha began to reign over Israel in Tirzah; he reigned two years. ⁹But his servant Zimri, commander of half his chariots, conspired against him. When he was at Tirzah, drinking himself drunk in the house of Arza, who was in charge of the palace at Tirzah, ¹⁰Zimri came in and struck him down and killed him, in the twenty-seventh year of King Asa of Judah, and succeeded him.

11 When he began to reign, as soon as he had seated himself on his throne, he killed all the house of Baasha; he did not leave him a single male of his kindred or his friends. ¹²Thus Zimri destroyed all the house of Baasha, according to the word of the LORD, which he spoke against Baasha by the prophet Jehu— ¹³because of all the sins of Baasha and the sins of his son Elah that they committed, and that they caused Israel to commit, provoking the LORD God of Israel to anger with their idols. ¹⁴Now the rest of the acts of Elah, and all that he did, are they not written in the Book of the Annals of the Kings of Israel?

Third Dynasty: Zimri Reigns over Israel

15 In the twenty-seventh year of King Asa of Judah, Zimri reigned seven days in Tirzah. Now the troops were encamped against Gibbethon, which belonged to the Philistines, ¹⁶and the troops who were encamped heard it said, "Zimri has conspired, and he has killed the king"; therefore all Israel made Omri, the commander of the army, king over Israel that day in the camp. ¹⁷So Omri went up from Gibbethon, and all Israel with him, and they besieged Tirzah. ¹⁸When Zimri saw that the city was taken, he went into the citadel of the king's house; he burned down the king's house over himself with fire, and died— ¹⁹because of the sins that he committed, doing evil in the sight of the LORD, walking in the

way of Jeroboam, and for the sin that he committed, causing Israel to sin. 20 Now the rest of the acts of Zimri, and the conspiracy that he made, are they not written in the Book of the Annals of the Kings of Israel?

Fourth Dynasty: Omri Reigns over Israel

21 Then the people of Israel were divided into two parts; half of the people followed Tibni son of Ginath, to make him king, and half followed Omri. 22 But the people who followed Omri overcame the people who followed Tibni son of Ginath; so Tibni died, and Omri became king. 23 In the thirty-first year of King Asa of Judah, Omri began to reign over Israel; he reigned for twelve years, six of them in Tirzah.

Samaria the New Capital

24 He bought the hill of Samaria from Shemer for two talents of silver; he fortified the hill, and called the city that he built, Samaria, after the name of Shemer, the owner of the hill.
25 Omri did what was evil in the sight of the Lord; he did more evil than all who were before him. 26 For he walked in all the way of Jeroboam son of Nebat, and in the sins that he caused Israel to commit, provoking the Lord, the God of Israel, to anger by their idols. 27 Now the rest of the acts of Omri that he did, and the power that he showed, are they not written in the Book of the Annals of the Kings of Israel? 28 Omri slept with his ancestors, and was buried in Samaria; his son Ahab succeeded him.

Ahab Reigns over Israel

29 In the thirty-eighth year of King Asa of Judah, Ahab son of Omri began to reign over Israel; Ahab son of Omri reigned over Israel in Samaria twenty-two years. 30 Ahab son of Omri did evil in the sight of the Lord more than all who were before him.

16.20
vv. 5,14,27
16.23
1 Kings 15.21
16.24
1 Kings 13.32;
Jn 4.4
16.26
Mic 6.16;
v. 19
16.30
v. 25;
1 Kings 14.9

16.31
Deut 7.3;
2 Kings 10.18;
17.16
16.32
2 Kings 10.21,
26,27
16.33
2 Kings 13.6;
vv. 29,30
16.34
Josh 6.26
17.1
2 Kings 3.14;
Deut 10.8;
1 Kings 18.1;
Jas 5.17;
Lk 4.25
17.9
Ob 20;
Lk 4.26

Ahab Marries Jezebel and Worships Baal

31 And as if it had been a light thing for him to walk in the sins of Jeroboam son of Nebat, he took as his wife Jezebel daughter of King Ethbaal of the Sidonians, and went and served Baal, and worshiped him. 32 He erected an altar for Baal in the house of Baal, which he built in Samaria. 33 Ahab also made a sacred pole.i Ahab did more to provoke the anger of the Lord, the God of Israel, than had all the kings of Israel who were before him. 34 In his days Hiel of Bethel built Jericho; he laid its foundation at the cost of Abiram his firstborn, and set up its gates at the cost of his youngest son Segub, according to the word of the Lord, which he spoke by Joshua son of Nun.

Elijah Predicts a Drought

17 Now Elijah the Tishbite, of Tishbe k in Gilead, said to Ahab, "As the Lord the God of Israel lives, before whom I stand, there shall be neither dew nor rain these years, except by my word." 2 The word of the Lord came to him, saying, 3 "Go from here and turn eastward, and hide yourself by the Wadi Cherith, which is east of the Jordan. 4 You shall drink from the wadi, and I have commanded the ravens to feed you there." 5 So he went and did according to the word of the Lord; he went and lived by the Wadi Cherith, which is east of the Jordan. 6 The ravens brought him bread and meat in the morning, and bread and meat in the evening; and he drank from the wadi. 7 But after a while the wadi dried up, because there was no rain in the land.

The Widow of Zarephath

8 Then the word of the Lord came to him, saying, 9 "Go now to Zarephath, which belongs to Sidon, and live there; for I have commanded a widow there to feed you." 10 So he set out and went to Zarephath. When he came to the

i Heb Asherah k Gk: Heb of the settlers

gate of the town, a widow was there gathering sticks; he called to her and said, "Bring me a little water in a vessel, so that I may drink." ¹¹As she was going to bring it, he called to her and said, "Bring me a morsel of bread in your hand." ¹²But she said, "As the LORD your God lives, I have nothing baked, only a handful of meal in a jar, and a little oil in a jug; I am now gathering a couple of sticks, so that I may go home and prepare it for myself and my son, that we may eat it, and die." ¹³Elijah said to her, "Do not be afraid; go and do as you have said; but first make me a little cake of it and bring it to me, and afterwards make something for yourself and your son. ¹⁴For thus says the LORD the God of Israel: The jar of meal will not be emptied and the jug of oil will not fail until the day that the LORD sends rain on the earth." ¹⁵She went and did as Elijah said, so that she as well as he and her household ate for many days. ¹⁶The jar of meal was not emptied, neither did the jug of oil fail, according to the word of the LORD that he spoke by Elijah.

Elijah Revives the Widow's Son

17 After this the son of the woman, the mistress of the house, became ill; his illness was so severe that there was no breath left in him. ¹⁸She then said to Elijah, "What have you against me, O man of God? You have come to me to bring my sin to remembrance, and to cause the death of my son!" ¹⁹But he said to her, "Give me your son." He took him from her bosom, carried him up into the upper chamber where he was lodging, and laid him on his own bed. ²⁰He cried out to the LORD, "O LORD my God, have you brought calamity even upon the widow with whom I am staying, by killing her son?" ²¹Then he stretched himself upon the child three times, and cried out to the LORD, "O LORD my God, let this child's life come into him again." ²²The LORD listened to the voice of Elijah; the life of the child

came into him again, and he revived. ²³Elijah took the child, brought him down from the upper chamber into the house, and gave him to his mother; then Elijah said, "See, your son is alive." ²⁴So the woman said to Elijah, "Now I know that you are a man of God, and that the word of the LORD in your mouth is truth."

Elijah's Message to Ahab

18 After many days the word of the LORD came to Elijah, in the third year of the drought,¹ saying, "Go, present yourself to Ahab; I will send rain on the earth." ²So Elijah went to present himself to Ahab. The famine was severe in Samaria. ³Ahab summoned Obadiah, who was in charge of the palace. (Now Obadiah revered the LORD greatly; ⁴when Jezebel was killing off the prophets of the LORD, Obadiah took a hundred prophets, hid them fifty to a cave, and provided them with bread and water.) ⁵Then Ahab said to Obadiah, "Go through the land to all the springs of water and to all the wadis; perhaps we may find grass to keep the horses and mules alive, and not lose some of the animals." ⁶So they divided the land between them to pass through it; Ahab went in one direction by himself, and Obadiah went in another direction by himself.

7 As Obadiah was on the way, Elijah met him; Obadiah recognized him, fell on his face, and said, "Is it you, my lord Elijah?" ⁸He answered him, "It is I. Go, tell your lord that Elijah is here." ⁹And he said, "How have I sinned, that you would hand your servant over to Ahab, to kill me? ¹⁰As the LORD your God lives, there is no nation or kingdom to which my lord has not sent to seek you; and when they would say, 'He is not here,' he would require an oath of the kingdom or nation, that they had not found you. ¹¹But now you say, 'Go, tell your lord that Elijah is here.' ¹²As soon as I have gone from you,

17.12
v. 1;
2 Kings 4.2-7
17.14
Lk 4.25,26
17.18
2 Kings 3.13
17.21
2 Kings 4.34,
35; Acts 20.10
17.22
Heb 11.25

17.24
Jn 3.2;
16.30
18.1
1 Kings 17.1;
Lk 4.25;
Jas 5.17
18.4
v. 13
18.7
2 Kings 1.6-8
18.10
1 Kings 17.1
18.12
2 Kings 2.16;
Ezek 3.12,
14;
Acts 8.39

¹Heb lacks *of the drought*

the spirit of the Lord will carry you I know not where; so, when I come and tell Ahab and he cannot find you, he will kill me, although I your servant have revered the Lord from my youth. 13 Has it not been told my lord what I did when Jezebel killed the prophets of the Lord, how I hid a hundred of the Lord's prophets fifty to a cave, and provided them with bread and water? 14 Yet now you say, 'Go, tell your lord that Elijah is here'; he will surely kill me." 15 Elijah said, "As the Lord of hosts lives, before whom I stand, I will surely show myself to him today." 16 So Obadiah went to meet Ahab, and told him; and Ahab went to meet Elijah.

17 When Ahab saw Elijah, Ahab said to him, "Is it you, you troubler of Israel?" 18 He answered, "I have not troubled Israel; but you have, and your father's house, because you have forsaken the commandments of the Lord and followed the Baals. 19 Now therefore have all Israel assemble for me at Mount Carmel, with the four hundred fifty prophets of Baal and the four hundred prophets of Asherah, who eat at Jezebel's table."

Elijah's Triumph over the Priests of Baal

20 So Ahab sent to all the Israelites, and assembled the prophets at Mount Carmel. 21 Elijah then came near to all the people, and said, "How long will you go limping with two different opinions? If the Lord is God, follow him; but if Baal, then follow him." The people did not answer him a word. 22 Then Elijah said to the people, "I, even I only, am left a prophet of the Lord; but Baal's prophets number four hundred fifty. 23 Let two bulls be given to us; let them choose one bull for themselves, cut it in pieces, and lay it on the wood, but put no fire to it; I will prepare the other bull and lay it on the wood, but put no fire to it. 24 Then you call on the name of your god and I will call on the name of the Lord; the god who answers by fire is indeed God." All the

people answered, "Well spoken!" 25 Then Elijah said to the prophets of Baal, "Choose for yourselves one bull and prepare it first, for you are many; then call on the name of your god, but put no fire to it." 26 So they took the bull that was given them, prepared it, and called on the name of Baal from morning until noon, crying, "O Baal, answer us!" But there was no voice, and no answer. They limped about the altar that they had made. 27 At noon Elijah mocked them, saying, "Cry aloud! Surely he is a god; either he is meditating, or he has wandered away, or he is on a journey, or perhaps he is asleep and must be awakened." 28 Then they cried aloud and, as was their custom, they cut themselves with swords and lances until the blood gushed out over them. 29 As midday passed, they raved on until the time of the offering of the oblation, but there was no voice, no answer, and no response.

30 Then Elijah said to all the people, "Come closer to me"; and all the people came closer to him. First he repaired the altar of the Lord that had been thrown down; 31 Elijah took twelve stones, according to the number of the tribes of the sons of Jacob, to whom the word of the Lord came, saying, "Israel shall be your name"; 32 with the stones he built an altar in the name of the Lord. Then he made a trench around the altar, large enough to contain two measures of seed. 33 Next he put the wood in order, cut the bull in pieces, and laid it on the wood. He said, "Fill four jars with water and pour it on the burnt offering and on the wood." 34 Then he said, "Do it a second time"; and they did it a second time. Again he said, "Do it a third time"; and they did it a third time, 35 so that the water ran all around the altar, and filled the trench also with water.

36 At the time of the offering of the oblation, the prophet Elijah came near and said, "O Lord, God of Abraham, Isaac, and Israel, let it

18.13
v. 4
18.15
1 Kings 17.1
18.17
1 Kings 21.20;
Josh 7.25;
Acts 16.20
18.18
2 Chr 15.2;
1 Kings 16.31;
21.25,26
18.19
Josh 19.26;
1 Kings 16.33
18.21
2 Kings 17.41;
Mt 6.24;
Josh 24.15
18.22
1 Kings 19.10,
14; v. 19
18.24
v. 38;
1 Chr 21.26;
Acts 20.10

18.26
Ps 115.5;
Jer 10.5;
1 Cor 8.4;
12.2
18.28
Lev 19.28;
Deut 14.1
18.29
v. 26
18.30
1 Kings 19.10,
14
18.31
Gen 32.28;
35.10;
2 Kings 17.34
18.32
Col 3.17
18.33
Gen 22.9;
Lev 1.6-8
18.36
Ex 3.6;
1 Kings 8.43;
2 Kings 19.19;
Num 16.28

be known this day that you are God in Israel, that I am your servant, and that I have done all these things at your bidding. 37 Answer me, O LORD, answer me, so that this people may know that you, O LORD, are God, and that you have turned their hearts back." 38 Then the fire of the LORD fell and consumed the burnt offering, the wood, the stones, and the dust, and even licked up the water that was in the trench. 39 When all the people saw it, they fell on their faces and said, "The LORD indeed is God; the LORD indeed is God." 40 Elijah said to them, "Seize the prophets of Baal; do not let one of them escape." Then they seized them; and Elijah brought them down to the Wadi Kishon, and killed them there.

The Drought Ends

41 Elijah said to Ahab, "Go up, eat and drink; for there is a sound of rushing rain." 42 So Ahab went up to eat and to drink. Elijah went up to the top of Carmel; there he bowed himself down upon the earth and put his face between his knees. 43 He said to his servant, "Go up now, look toward the sea." He went up and looked, and said, "There is nothing." Then he said, "Go again seven times." 44 At the seventh time he said, "Look, a little cloud no bigger than a person's hand is rising out of the sea." Then he said, "Go say to Ahab, 'Harness your chariot and go down before the rain stops you.'" 45 In a little while the heavens grew black with clouds and wind; there was a heavy rain. Ahab rode off and went to Jezreel. 46 But the hand of the LORD was on Elijah; he girded up his loins and ran in front of Ahab to the entrance of Jezreel.

Elijah Flees from Jezebel

19 Ahab told Jezebel all that Elijah had done, and how he had killed all the prophets with the sword. 2 Then Jezebel sent a messenger to Elijah, saying, "So may the gods do to me, and more

also, if I do not make your life like the life of one of them by this time tomorrow." 3 Then he was afraid; he got up and fled for his life, and came to Beer-sheba, which belongs to Judah; he left his servant there.

4 But he himself went a day's journey into the wilderness, and came and sat down under a solitary broom tree. He asked that he might die: "It is enough; now, O LORD, take away my life, for I am no better than my ancestors." 5 Then he lay down under the broom tree and fell asleep. Suddenly an angel touched him and said to him, "Get up and eat." 6 He looked, and there at his head was a cake baked on hot stones, and a jar of water. He ate and drank, and lay down again. 7 The angel of the LORD came a second time, touched him, and said, "Get up and eat, otherwise the journey will be too much for you." 8 He got up, and ate and drank; then he went in the strength of that food forty days and forty nights to Horeb the mount of God. 9 At that place he came to a cave, and spent the night there.

Then the word of the LORD came to him, saying, "What are you doing here, Elijah?" 10 He answered, "I have been very zealous for the LORD, the God of hosts; for the Israelites have forsaken your covenant, thrown down your altars, and killed your prophets with the sword. I alone am left, and they are seeking my life, to take it away."

Elijah Meets God at Horeb

11 He said, "Go out and stand on the mountain before the LORD, for the LORD is about to pass by." Now there was a great wind, so strong that it was splitting mountains and breaking rocks in pieces before the LORD, but the LORD was not in the wind; and after the wind an earthquake, but the LORD was not in the earthquake; 12 and after the earthquake a fire, but the LORD was not in the fire; and after the fire a sound of sheer silence. 13 When Elijah heard it, he wrapped his face in his mantle and went out and

18.38
Lev 9.24;
1 Chr 21.26;
2 Chr 7.1
18.39
vv. 21,24
18.40
Deut 13.5;
18.20;
2 Kings 10.24,
25
18.42
vv. 19,20;
Jas 5.17,18
18.46
2 Kings 3.15;
4.29
19.1
1 Kings 18.40
19.2
1 Kings 20.10;
2 Kings 6.31

19.4
Num 11.15;
Jon 4.3,8
19.8
Ex 34.28;
Deut 9.9-11,
18; Mt 4.2;
Ex 3.1
19.10
Rom 11.3;
1 Kings 18.4,
22
19.11
Ex 24.12;
Ezek 1.4;
37.7
19.13
Ex 3.6;
v. 9

stood at the entrance of the cave. Then there came a voice to him that said, "What are you doing here, Elijah?" ¹⁴He answered, "I have been very zealous for the LORD, the God of hosts; for the Israelites have forsaken your covenant, thrown down your altars, and killed your prophets with the sword. I alone am left, and they are seeking my life, to take it away." ¹⁵Then the LORD said to him, "Go, return on your way to the wilderness of Damascus; when you arrive, you shall anoint Hazael as king over Aram. ¹⁶Also you shall anoint Jehu son of Nimshi as king over Israel; and you shall anoint Elisha son of Shaphat of Abel-meholah as prophet in your place. ¹⁷Whoever escapes from the sword of Hazael, Jehu shall kill; and whoever escapes from the sword of Jehu, Elisha shall kill. ¹⁸Yet I will leave seven thousand in Israel, all the knees that have not bowed to Baal, and every mouth that has not kissed him."

Elisha Becomes Elijah's Disciple

19 So he set out from there, and found Elisha son of Shaphat, who was plowing. There were twelve yoke of oxen ahead of him, and he was with the twelfth. Elijah passed by him and threw his mantle over him. ²⁰He left the oxen, ran after Elijah, and said, "Let me kiss my father and my mother, and then I will follow you." Then Elijah^m said to him, "Go back again; for what have I done to you?" ²¹He returned from following him, took the yoke of oxen, and slaughtered them; using the equipment from the oxen, he boiled their flesh, and gave it to the people, and they ate. Then he set out and followed Elijah, and became his servant.

Ahab's Wars with the Arameans

20 King Ben-hadad of Aram gathered all his army together; thirty-two kings were with him, along with horses and chariots. He marched against Samaria, laid siege to it, and attacked it.

19.14
v. 10
19.15
2 Kings 8.12, 13
19.16
2 Kings 9.1-3; vv. 19-21;
2 Kings 2.9, 15
19.17
2 Kings 8.12; 9.14ff; 13.3, 22
19.18
Rom 11.4; Hos 13.2
19.19
2 Kings 2.8, 13
19.20
Mt 8.21,22; Lk 9.61,62
19.21
2 Sam 24.22
20.1
1 Kings 15.18, 20;
2 Kings 6.24;
1 Kings 22.31;
2 Kings 6.24-29

20.7
2 Kings 5.7
20.10
1 Kings 19.2
20.11
Prov 27.1
20.12
v. 16
20.13
v. 28

²Then he sent messengers into the city to King Ahab of Israel, and said to him: "Thus says Ben-hadad: ³Your silver and gold are mine; your fairest wives and children also are mine." ⁴The king of Israel answered, "As you say, my lord, O king, I am yours, and all that I have." ⁵The messengers came again and said: "Thus says Ben-hadad: I sent to you, saying, 'Deliver to me your silver and gold, your wives and children'; ⁶nevertheless I will send my servants to you tomorrow about this time, and they shall search your house and the houses of your servants, and lay hands on whatever pleases them,^n and take it away."

7 Then the king of Israel called all the elders of the land, and said, "Look now! See how this man is seeking trouble; for he sent to me for my wives, my children, my silver, and my gold; and I did not refuse him." ⁸Then all the elders and all the people said to him, "Do not listen or consent." ⁹So he said to the messengers of Ben-hadad, "Tell my lord the king: All that you first demanded of your servant I will do; but this thing I cannot do." The messengers left and brought him word again. ¹⁰Ben-hadad sent to him and said, "The gods do so to me, and more also, if the dust of Samaria will provide a handful for each of the people who follow me." ¹¹The king of Israel answered, "Tell him: One who puts on armor should not brag like one who takes it off." ¹²When Ben-hadad heard this message—now he had been drinking with the kings in the booths—he said to his men, "Take your positions!" And they took their positions against the city.

Prophetic Opposition to Ahab

13 Then a certain prophet came up to King Ahab of Israel and said, "Thus says the LORD, Have you seen all this great multitude? Look, I will give it into your hand today; and you shall know that I am the LORD." ¹⁴Ahab said, "By whom?"

^m Heb he ^n Gk Syr Vg: Heb you

He said, "Thus says the Lord, By the young men who serve the district governors." Then he said, "Who shall begin the battle?" He answered, "You." 15 Then he mustered the young men who serve the district governors, two hundred thirty-two; after them he mustered all the people of Israel, seven thousand.

16 They went out at noon, while Ben-hadad was drinking himself drunk in the booths, he and the thirty-two kings allied with him. 17 The young men who serve the district governors went out first. Ben-hadad had sent out scouts,°and they reported to him, "Men have come out from Samaria." 18 He said, "If they have come out for peace, take them alive; if they have come out for war, take them alive."

19 But these had already come out of the city: the young men who serve the district governors, and the army that followed them. 20 Each killed his man; the Arameans fled and Israel pursued them, but King Ben-hadad of Aram escaped on a horse with the cavalry. 21 The king of Israel went out, attacked the horses and chariots, and defeated the Arameans with a great slaughter. 22 Then the prophet approached the king of Israel and said to him, "Come, strengthen yourself, and consider well what you have to do; for in the spring the king of Aram will come up against you."

The Arameans Are Defeated

23 The servants of the king of Aram said to him, "Their gods are gods of the hills, and so they were stronger than we; but let us fight against them in the plain, and surely we shall be stronger than they. 24 Also do this: remove the kings, each from his post, and put commanders in place of them; 25 and muster an army like the army that you have lost, horse for horse, and chariot for chariot; then we will fight against them in the plain, and

surely we shall be stronger than they." He heeded their voice, and did so.

26 In the spring Ben-hadad mustered the Arameans and went up to Aphek to fight against Israel. 27 After the Israelites had been mustered and provisioned, they went out to engage them; the people of Israel encamped opposite them like two little flocks of goats, while the Arameans filled the country. 28 A man of God approached and said to the king of Israel, "Thus says the Lord: Because the Arameans have said, 'The Lord is a god of the hills but he is not a god of the valleys,' therefore I will give all this great multitude into your hand, and you shall know that I am the Lord." 29 They encamped opposite one another seven days. Then on the seventh day the battle began; the Israelites killed one hundred thousand Aramean foot soldiers in one day. 30 The rest fled into the city of Aphek; and the wall fell on twenty-seven thousand men that were left.

Ben-hadad also fled, and entered the city to hide. 31 His servants said to him, "Look, we have heard that the kings of the house of Israel are merciful kings; let us put sackcloth around our waists and ropes on our heads, and go out to the king of Israel; perhaps he will spare your life." 32 So they tied sackcloth around their waists, put ropes on their heads, went to the king of Israel, and said, "Your servant Ben-hadad says, 'Please let me live.' " And he said, "Is he still alive? He is my brother." 33 Now the men were watching for an omen; they quickly took it up from him and said, "Yes, Ben-hadad is your brother." Then he said, "Go and bring him." So Ben-hadad came out to him; and he had him come up into the chariot. 34 Ben-hadadᴾ said to him, "I will restore the towns that my father took from your father; and you may establish bazaars for yourself in Damascus, as my father did in

Cross references (center column)

20.16
v. 12
20.18
2 Kings 14.8-12
20.22
vv. 13,26;
2 Sam 11.1
20.23
1 Kings 14.23

20.26
v. 22;
2 Kings 13.7
20.28
v. 13
20.30
v. 26;
1 Kings 22.25;
2 Chr 18.24
20.31
Gen 37.34
20.32
vv. 3-6
20.34
1 Kings 15.20

° Heb lacks *scouts* ᴾ Heb *He*

Samaria." The king of Israel responded,q "I will let you go on those terms." So he made a treaty with him and let him go.

A Prophet Condemns Ahab

35 At the command of the LORD a certain member of a company of prophetsr said to another, "Strike me!" But the man refused to strike him. 36 Then he said to him, "Because you have not obeyed the voice of the LORD, as soon as you have left me, a lion will kill you." And when he had left him, a lion met him and killed him. 37 Then he found another man and said, "Strike me!" So the man hit him, striking and wounding him. 38 Then the prophet departed, and waited for the king along the road, disguising himself with a bandage over his eyes. 39 As the king passed by, he cried to the king and said, "Your servant went out into the thick of the battle; then a soldier turned and brought a man to me, and said, 'Guard this man; if he is missing, your life shall be given for his life, or else you shall pay a talent of silver.' 40 While your servant was busy here and there, he was gone." The king of Israel said to him, "So shall your judgment be; you yourself have decided it." 41 Then he quickly took the bandage away from his eyes. The king of Israel recognized him as one of the prophets. 42 Then he said to him, "Thus says the LORD, 'Because you have let the man go whom I had devoted to destruction, therefore your life shall be for his life, and your people for his people.' " 43 The king of Israel set out toward home, resentful and sullen, and came to Samaria.

Naboth's Vineyard

21 Later the following events took place: Naboth the Jezreelite had a vineyard in Jezreel, beside the palace of King Ahab of Samaria. 2 And Ahab said to Naboth, "Give me your vineyard, so that I may have it for a vegetable garden, because it is near my house; I will give you a better vine-

yard for it; or, if it seems good to you, I will give you its value in money." 3 But Naboth said to Ahab, "The LORD forbid that I should give you my ancestral inheritance." 4 Ahab went home resentful and sullen because of what Naboth the Jezreelite had said to him; for he had said, "I will not give you my ancestral inheritance." He lay down on his bed, turned away his face, and would not eat.

5 His wife Jezebel came to him and said, "Why are you so depressed that you will not eat?" 6 He said to her, "Because I spoke to Naboth the Jezreelite and said to him, 'Give me your vineyard for money; or else, if you prefer, I will give you another vineyard for it'; but he answered, 'I will not give you my vineyard.' " 7 His wife Jezebel said to him, "Do you now govern Israel? Get up, eat some food, and be cheerful; I will give you the vineyard of Naboth the Jezreelite."

8 So she wrote letters in Ahab's name and sealed them with his seal; she sent the letters to the elders and the nobles who lived with Naboth in his city. 9 She wrote in the letters, "Proclaim a fast, and seat Naboth at the head of the assembly; 10 seat two scoundrels opposite him, and have them bring a charge against him, saying, 'You have cursed God and the king.' Then take him out, and stone him to death." 11 The men of his city, the elders and the nobles who lived in his city, did as Jezebel had sent word to them. Just as it was written in the letters that she had sent to them, 12 they proclaimed a fast and seated Naboth at the head of the assembly. 13 The two scoundrels came in and sat opposite him; and the scoundrels brought a charge against Naboth, in the presence of the people, saying, "Naboth cursed God and the king." So they took him outside the city, and stoned him to death. 14 Then they sent to

20.35
2 Kings 2.3-7;
1 Kings 13.17,
18
20.36
1 Kings 13.24
20.39
2 Kings 10.24
20.42
v. 39;
1 Kings 22.31-
37
20.43
1 Kings 21.4
21.1
1 Kings 18.45,
46
21.2
1 Sam 8.14

21.3
Lev 25.23;
Num 36.7;
Ezek 46.18
21.4
1 Kings 20.43
21.7
1 Sam 8.14
21.8
Esther 3.12;
8.8,10
21.10
Ex 22.28;
Lev 24.15,
16;
Acts 6.11
21.13
2 Kings 9.26

q Heb lacks The king of Israel responded
r Heb of the sons of the prophets

Jezebel, saying, "Naboth has been stoned; he is dead."

15 As soon as Jezebel heard that Naboth had been stoned and was dead, Jezebel said to Ahab, "Go, take possession of the vineyard of Naboth the Jezreelite, which he refused to give you for money; for Naboth is not alive, but dead." 16 As soon as Ahab heard that Naboth was dead, Ahab set out to go down to the vineyard of Naboth the Jezreelite, to take possession of it.

Elijah Pronounces God's Sentence

17 Then the word of the Lord came to Elijah the Tishbite, saying: 18 Go down to meet King Ahab of Israel, who rules s in Samaria; he is now in the vineyard of Naboth, where he has gone to take possession. 19 You shall say to him, "Thus says the Lord: Have you killed, and also taken possession?" You shall say to him, "Thus says the Lord: In the place where dogs licked up the blood of Naboth, dogs will also lick up your blood."

20 Ahab said to Elijah, "Have you found me, O my enemy?" He answered, "I have found you. Because you have sold yourself to do what is evil in the sight of the Lord, 21 I will bring disaster on you; I will consume you, and will cut off from Ahab every male, bond or free, in Israel; 22 and I will make your house like the house of Jeroboam son of Nebat, and like the house of Baasha son of Ahijah, because you have provoked me to anger and have caused Israel to sin. 23 Also concerning Jezebel the Lord said, 'The dogs shall eat Jezebel within the bounds of Jezreel.' 24 Anyone belonging to Ahab who dies in the city the dogs shall eat; and anyone of his who dies in the open country the birds of the air shall eat."

25 (Indeed, there was no one like Ahab, who sold himself to do what was evil in the sight of the Lord, urged on by his wife Jezebel. 26 He acted most abominably in going after idols, as the Amorites had

21.17
Ps 9.12
21.18
1 Kings 16.29
21.19
1 Kings 22.38;
2 Kings 9.8
21.20
1 Kings 18.17;
v. 25
21.21
1 Kings 14.10;
2 Kings 9.8
21.22
1 Kings 15.29
21.23
2 Kings 9.10,
30-37
21.24
1 Kings 14.11;
16.4
21.25
v. 20;
1 Kings 16.30-
33
21.26
Gen 15.16;
Lev 18.25-30

21.27
2 Sam 3.31;
2 Kings 6.30
21.29
2 Kings 9.25
22.2
2 Chr 18.2ff;
1 Kings 15.24
22.3
Deut 4.43;
Josh 21.38
22.4
2 Kings 3.7
22.6
1 Kings 18.19
22.7
2 Kings 3.11
22.10
v. 6

done, whom the Lord drove out before the Israelites.)

27 When Ahab heard those words, he tore his clothes and put sackcloth over his bare flesh; he fasted, lay in the sackcloth, and went about dejectedly. 28 Then the word of the Lord came to Elijah the Tishbite: 29 "Have you seen how Ahab has humbled himself before me? Because he has humbled himself before me, I will not bring the disaster in his days; but in his son's days I will bring the disaster on his house."

Joint Campaign with Judah against Aram

22 For three years Aram and Israel continued without war. 2 But in the third year King Jehoshaphat of Judah came down to the king of Israel. 3 The king of Israel said to his servants, "Do you know that Ramoth-gilead belongs to us, yet we are doing nothing to take it out of the hand of the king of Aram?" 4 He said to Jehoshaphat, "Will you go with me to battle at Ramoth-gilead?" Jehoshaphat replied to the king of Israel, "I am as you are; my people are your people, my horses are your horses."

5 But Jehoshaphat also said to the king of Israel, "Inquire first for the word of the Lord." 6 Then the king of Israel gathered the prophets together, about four hundred of them, and said to them, "Shall I go to battle against Ramoth-gilead, or shall I refrain?" They said, "Go up; for the Lord will give it into the hand of the king." 7 But Jehoshaphat said, "Is there no other prophet of the Lord here of whom we may inquire?" 8 The king of Israel said to Jehoshaphat, "There is still one other by whom we may inquire of the Lord, Micaiah son of Imlah; but I hate him, for he never prophesies anything favorable about me, but only disaster." Jehoshaphat said, "Let the king not say such a thing." 9 Then the king of Israel summoned an officer and said, "Bring quickly Micaiah son of Imlah." 10 Now the

s Heb *who is*

king of Israel and King Jehoshaphat of Judah were sitting on their thrones, arrayed in their robes, at the threshing floor at the entrance of the gate of Samaria; and all the prophets were prophesying before them. ¹¹Zedekiah son of Chenaanah made for himself horns of iron, and he said, "Thus says the LORD: With these you shall gore the Arameans until they are destroyed." ¹²All the prophets were prophesying the same and saying, "Go up to Ramoth-gilead and triumph; the LORD will give it into the hand of the king."

Micaiah Predicts Failure

13 The messenger who had gone to summon Micaiah said to him, "Look, the words of the prophets with one accord are favorable to the king; let your word be like the word of one of them, and speak favorably." ¹⁴But Micaiah said, "As the LORD lives, whatever the LORD says to me, that I will speak."

15 When he had come to the king, the king said to him, "Micaiah, shall we go to Ramoth-gilead to battle, or shall we refrain?" He answered him, "Go up and triumph; the LORD will give it into the hand of the king." ¹⁶But the king said to him, "How many times must I make you swear to tell me nothing but the truth in the name of the LORD?" ¹⁷Then Micaiah[t] said, "I saw all Israel scattered on the mountains, like sheep that have no shepherd; and the LORD said, 'These have no master; let each one go home in peace.'" ¹⁸The king of Israel said to Jehoshaphat, "Did I not tell you that he would not prophesy anything favorable about me, but only disaster?"

19 Then Micaiah[t] said, "Therefore hear the word of the LORD: I saw the LORD sitting on his throne, with all the host of heaven standing beside him to the right and to the left of him. ²⁰And the LORD said, 'Who will entice Ahab, so that he may go up and fall at Ramoth-gilead?' Then one said one thing,

22.11
Zech 1.18-21;
Deut 33.17
22.14
1 Kings 18.10, 15;
Num 22.18;
24.13
22.15
v. 12
22.17
vv. 34-36
22.18
v. 8
22.19
Isa 6.1;
Dan 7.9,10

22.22
Judg 9.23;
1 Sam 16.14;
18.10; 19.9;
2 Thes 2.11
22.23
Ezek 14.9
22.24
2 Chr 18.23
22.25
1 Kings 20.30
22.27
2 Chr 18.25-27
22.28
Deut 18.22
22.29
vv. 3,4
22.30
2 Chr 25.32
22.31
2 Chr 18.30
22.32
2 Chr 18.31

and another said another, ²¹until a spirit came forward and stood before the LORD, saying, 'I will entice him.' ²²'How?' the LORD asked him. He replied, 'I will go out and be a lying spirit in the mouth of all his prophets.' Then the LORD[t] said, 'You are to entice him, and you shall succeed; go out and do it.' ²³So you see, the LORD has put a lying spirit in the mouth of all these your prophets; the LORD has decreed disaster for you."

24 Then Zedekiah son of Chenaanah came up to Micaiah, slapped him on the cheek, and said, "Which way did the spirit of the LORD pass from me to speak to you?" ²⁵Micaiah replied, "You will find out on that day when you go in to hide in an inner chamber." ²⁶The king of Israel then ordered, "Take Micaiah, and return him to Amon the governor of the city and to Joash the king's son, ²⁷and say, 'Thus says the king: Put this fellow in prison, and feed him on reduced rations of bread and water until I come in peace.'" ²⁸Micaiah said, "If you return in peace, the LORD has not spoken by me." And he said, "Hear, you peoples, all of you!"

Defeat and Death of Ahab

29 So the king of Israel and King Jehoshaphat of Judah went up to Ramoth-gilead. ³⁰The king of Israel said to Jehoshaphat, "I will disguise myself and go into battle, but you wear your robes." So the king of Israel disguised himself and went into battle. ³¹Now the king of Aram had commanded the thirty-two captains of his chariots, "Fight with no one small or great, but only with the king of Israel." ³²When the captains of the chariots saw Jehoshaphat, they said, "It is surely the king of Israel." So they turned to fight against him; and Jehoshaphat cried out. ³³When the captains of the chariots saw that it was not the king of Israel, they turned back from pursuing him. ³⁴But a certain man drew his bow and un-

[t]Heb *he*

knowingly struck the king of Israel between the scale armor and the breastplate; so he said to the driver of his chariot, "Turn around, and carry me out of the battle, for I am wounded." 35 The battle grew hot that day, and the king was propped up in his chariot facing the Arameans, until at evening he died; the blood from the wound had flowed into the bottom of the chariot. 36 Then about sunset a shout went through the army, "Every man to his city, and every man to his country!"

37 So the king died, and was brought to Samaria; they buried the king in Samaria. 38 They washed the chariot by the pool of Samaria; the dogs licked up his blood, and the prostitutes washed themselves in it,ᵘ according to the word of the LORD that he had spoken. 39 Now the rest of the acts of Ahab, and all that he did, and the ivory house that he built, and all the cities that he built, are they not written in the Book of the Annals of the Kings of Israel? 40 So Ahab slept with his ancestors; and his son Ahaziah succeeded him.

Jehoshaphat Reigns over Judah

41 Jehoshaphat son of Asa began to reign over Judah in the fourth year of King Ahab of Israel. 42 Jehoshaphat was thirty-five years old when he began to reign, and he reigned twenty-five years in Jerusalem. His mother's name was Azubah daughter of Shilhi. 43 He walked in all the way of his father Asa; he did not turn aside from it, doing what was right in the sight of the LORD; yet the high places were

not taken away, and the people still sacrificed and offered incense on the high places. 44 Jehoshaphat also made peace with the king of Israel.

45 Now the rest of the acts of Jehoshaphat, and his power that he showed, and how he waged war, are they not written in the Book of the Annals of the Kings of Judah? 46 The remnant of the male temple prostitutes who were still in the land in the days of his father Asa, he exterminated.

47 There was no king in Edom; a deputy was king. 48 Jehoshaphat made ships of the Tarshish type to go to Ophir for gold; but they did not go, for the ships were wrecked at Ezion-geber. 49 Then Ahaziah son of Ahab said to Jehoshaphat, "Let my servants go with your servants in the ships," but Jehoshaphat was not willing. 50 Jehoshaphat slept with his ancestors and was buried with his ancestors in the city of his father David; his son Jehoram succeeded him.

Ahaziah Reigns over Israel

51 Ahaziah son of Ahab began to reign over Israel in Samaria in the seventeenth year of King Jehoshaphat of Judah; he reigned two years over Israel. 52 He did what was evil in the sight of the LORD, and walked in the way of his father and mother, and in the way of Jeroboam son of Nebat, who caused Israel to sin. 53 He served Baal and worshiped him; he provoked the LORD, the God of Israel, to anger, just as his father had done.

ᵘ Heb lacks *in it*

22.38
1 Kings 21.19
22.39
Am 3.15
22.41
2 Chr 20.31
22.43
2 Chr 17.3;
1 Kings 15.14;
2 Kings 12.3

22.44
2 Chr 19.2
22.45
2 Chr 20.34
22.46
1 Kings 14.24;
15.12
22.47
2 Sam 8.14;
2 Kings 3.9
22.48
2 Chr 20.35ff;
1 Kings 10.22
22.50
2 Chr 21.1
22.51
v. 40
22.52
1 Kings 15.26;
21.25
22.53
1 Kings 16.30-
32

2 Kings

Title and Background

See Introduction to 1 Kings.

Author and Date of Writing

See Introduction to 1 Kings.

Theme and Message

2 Kings continues the stories of the great prophets Elijah and Elisha. It also tells the history of the northern and southern kingdoms until they were both finally conquered. In both kingdoms God's prophets kept warning the people that God would punish them if they did not repent of their sins.

Outline

 I. Elijah and Elisha (1.1–8.15)
 II. Israel and Judah from Joram/Jehoram to Israel's Exile (8.16–17.41)
 III. Judah from Hezekiah to the Babylonian Exile (18.1–25.30)

Elijah Denounces Ahaziah

1 After the death of Ahab, Moab rebelled against Israel.

2 Ahaziah had fallen through the lattice in his upper chamber in Samaria, and lay injured; so he sent messengers, telling them, "Go, inquire of Baal-zebub, the god of Ekron, whether I shall recover from this injury." ³But the angel of the LORD said to Elijah the Tishbite, "Get up, go to meet the messengers of the king of Samaria, and say to them, 'Is it because there is no God in Israel that you are going to inquire of Baal-zebub, the god of Ekron?' ⁴Now therefore thus says the LORD, 'You shall not leave the bed to which you have gone, but you shall surely die.' " So Elijah went.

5 The messengers returned to the king, who said to them, "Why have you returned?" ⁶They answered him, "There came a man to meet us, who said to us, 'Go back to the king who sent you, and say to him: Thus says the LORD: Is it because there is no God in Israel that you are sending to inquire of Baal-zebub, the god of Ekron? Therefore you shall not leave the bed to

which you have gone, but shall surely die.' " ⁷He said to them, "What sort of man was he who came to meet you and told you these things?" ⁸They answered him, "A hairy man, with a leather belt around his waist." He said, "It is Elijah the Tishbite."

9 Then the king sent to him a captain of fifty with his fifty men. He went up to Elijah, who was sitting on the top of a hill, and said to him, "O man of God, the king says, 'Come down.' " ¹⁰But Elijah answered the captain of fifty, "If I am a man of God, let fire come down from heaven and consume you and your fifty." Then fire came down from heaven, and consumed him and his fifty.

11 Again the king sent to him another captain of fifty with his fifty. He went up[a] and said to him, "O man of God, this is the king's order: Come down quickly!" ¹²But Elijah answered them, "If I am a man of God, let fire come down from heaven and consume you and your fifty." Then the fire of God

1.1
2 Sam 8.2;
2 Kings 3.5
1.2
vv. 3,6;
Mt 10.25;
2 Kings 8.7-10
1.4
vv. 6,16

1.8
Zech 13.4;
Mt 3.4
1.10
1 Kings 18.36-
38;
Lk 9.54

a Gk Compare verses 9, 13: Heb *He answered*

came down from heaven and consumed him and his fifty.

13 Again the king sent the captain of a third fifty with his fifty. So the third captain of fifty went up, and came and fell on his knees before Elijah, and entreated him, "O man of God, please let my life, and the life of these fifty servants of yours, be precious in your sight. [14] Look, fire came down from heaven and consumed the two former captains of fifty men with their fifties; but now let my life be precious in your sight." [15] Then the angel of the LORD said to Elijah, "Go down with him; do not be afraid of him." So he set out and went down with him to the king, [16] and said to him, "Thus says the LORD: Because you have sent messengers to inquire of Baal-zebub, the god of Ekron, —is it because there is no God in Israel to inquire of his word?—therefore you shall not leave the bed to which you have gone, but you shall surely die."

Death of Ahaziah

17 So he died according to the word of the LORD that Elijah had spoken. His brother,[b] Jehoram succeeded him as king in the second year of King Jehoram son of Jehoshaphat of Judah, because Ahaziah had no son. [18] Now the rest of the acts of Ahaziah that he did, are they not written in the Book of the Annals of the Kings of Israel?

Elijah Ascends to Heaven

2 Now when the LORD was about to take Elijah up to heaven by a whirlwind, Elijah and Elisha were on their way from Gilgal. [2] Elijah said to Elisha, "Stay here; for the LORD has sent me as far as Bethel." But Elisha said, "As the LORD lives, and as you yourself live, I will not leave you." So they went down to Bethel. [3] The company of prophets[c] who were in Bethel came out to Elisha, and said to him, "Do you know that today the LORD will take your master away from you?" And he said, "Yes, I know; keep silent."

4 Elijah said to him, "Elisha,

stay here; for the LORD has sent me to Jericho." But he said, "As the LORD lives, and as you yourself live, I will not leave you." So they came to Jericho. [5] The company of prophets[c] who were at Jericho drew near to Elisha, and said to him, "Do you know that today the LORD will take your master away from you?" And he answered, "Yes, I know; be silent."

6 Then Elijah said to him, "Stay here; for the LORD has sent me to the Jordan." But he said, "As the LORD lives, and as you yourself live, I will not leave you." So the two of them went on. [7] Fifty men of the company of prophets[c] also went, and stood at some distance from them, as they both were standing by the Jordan. [8] Then Elijah took his mantle and rolled it up, and struck the water; the water was parted to the one side and to the other, until the two of them crossed on dry ground.

9 When they had crossed, Elijah said to Elisha, "Tell me what I may do for you, before I am taken from you." Elisha said, "Please let me inherit a double share of your spirit." [10] He responded, "You have asked a hard thing; yet, if you see me as I am being taken from you, it will be granted you; if not, it will not." [11] As they continued walking and talking, a chariot of fire and horses of fire separated the two of them, and Elijah ascended in a whirlwind into heaven. [12] Elisha kept watching and crying out, "Father, father! The chariots of Israel and its horsemen!" But when he could no longer see him, he grasped his own clothes and tore them in two pieces.

Elisha Succeeds Elijah

13 He picked up the mantle of Elijah that had fallen from him, and went back and stood on the bank of the Jordan. [14] He took the mantle of Elijah that had fallen from him, and struck the water, saying, "Where is the LORD, the God

1.13
1 Sam 26.21;
Ps 72.14
1.15
v. 3
1.16
v. 3
1.17
2 Kings 3.1;
8.16
2.1
Gen 5.24;
Heb 11.5;
1 Kings 19.21
2.2
Ruth 1.15,
16; vv. 4,6;
1 Sam 1.26;
2 Kings 4.30
2.3
vv. 5,7,15;
2 Kings 4.1,
38
2.4
v. 2;
Josh 6.26

2.5
v. 3
2.6
v. 3;
Josh 3.8,
15-17
2.7
vv. 15,16
2.8
1 Kings 19.13,
19; v. 14;
Ex 14.21,22
2.11
2 Kings 6.17;
Ps 104.4
2.12
2 Kings 13.14
2.14
v. 8

b Gk Syr: Heb lacks *His brother*
c Heb *sons of the prophets*

of Elijah?" When he had struck the water, the water was parted to the one side and to the other, and Elisha went over.

15 When the company of prophets[d] who were at Jericho saw him at a distance, they declared, "The spirit of Elijah rests on Elisha." They came to meet him and bowed to the ground before him. 16 They said to him, "See now, we have fifty strong men among your servants; please let them go and seek your master; it may be that the spirit of the LORD has caught him up and thrown him down on some mountain or into some valley." He responded, "No, do not send them." 17 But when they urged him until he was ashamed, he said, "Send them." So they sent fifty men who searched for three days but did not find him. 18 When they came back to him (he had remained at Jericho), he said to them, "Did I not say to you, Do not go?"

Elisha Performs Miracles

19 Now the people of the city said to Elisha, "The location of this city is good, as my lord sees; but the water is bad, and the land is unfruitful." 20 He said, "Bring me a new bowl, and put salt in it." So they brought it to him. 21 Then he went to the spring of water and threw the salt into it, and said, "Thus says the LORD, I have made this water wholesome; from now on neither death nor miscarriage shall come from it." 22 So the water has been wholesome to this day, according to the word that Elisha spoke.

23 He went up from there to Bethel; and while he was going up on the way, some small boys came out of the city and jeered at him, saying, "Go away, baldhead! Go away, baldhead!" 24 When he turned around and saw them, he cursed them in the name of the LORD. Then two she-bears came out of the woods and mauled forty-two of the boys. 25 From there he went on to Mount Carmel, and then returned to Samaria.

Jehoram Reigns over Israel

3 In the eighteenth year of King Jehoshaphat of Judah, Jehoram son of Ahab became king over Israel in Samaria; he reigned twelve years. 2 He did what was evil in the sight of the LORD, though not like his father and mother, for he removed the pillar of Baal that his father had made. 3 Nevertheless he clung to the sin of Jeroboam son of Nebat, which he caused Israel to commit; he did not depart from it.

War with Moab

4 Now King Mesha of Moab was a sheep breeder, who used to deliver to the king of Israel one hundred thousand lambs, and the wool of one hundred thousand rams. 5 But when Ahab died, the king of Moab rebelled against the king of Israel. 6 So King Jehoram marched out of Samaria at that time and mustered all Israel. 7 As he went he sent word to King Jehoshaphat of Judah, "The king of Moab has rebelled against me; will you go with me to battle against Moab?" He answered, "I will; I am with you, my people are your people, my horses are your horses." 8 Then he asked, "By which way shall we march?" Jehoram answered, "By the way of the wilderness of Edom."

9 So the king of Israel, the king of Judah, and the king of Edom set out; and when they had made a roundabout march of seven days, there was no water for the army or for the animals that were with them. 10 Then the king of Israel said, "Alas! The LORD has summoned us, three kings, only to be handed over to Moab." 11 But Jehoshaphat said, "Is there no prophet of the LORD here, through whom we may inquire of the LORD?" Then one of the servants of the king of Israel answered, "Elisha son of Shaphat, who used to pour water on the hands of Elijah, is here." 12 Jehoshaphat said, "The word of the LORD is with him." So the king of Israel and Jehoshaphat and the

2.15
v. 7
2.16
1 Kings 18.12;
Acts 8.39
2.17
2 Kings 8.11
2.21
Ex 15.25;
2 Kings 4.41;
6.6
2.24
Neh 13.25-27
2.25
2 Kings 4.25;
1 Kings 18.19,
20

3.1
2 Kings 1.17
3.2
2 Kings 10.18,
26-28;
1 Kings 16.31,
32
3.3
1 Kings 12.28-
32; 14.9,16
3.4
2 Sam 8.2;
Isa 16.1
3.5
2 Kings 1.1
3.7
1 Kings 22.4
3.9
vv. 1,7;
1 Kings 22.47
3.11
1 Kings 22.7;
19.21

d Heb sons of the prophets

king of Edom went down to him.
13 Elisha said to the king of Is-
rael, "What have I to do with you?
Go to your father's prophets or to
your mother's." But the king of Is-
rael said to him, "No; it is the LORD
who has summoned us, three
kings, only to be handed over to
Moab." 14 Elisha said, "As the LORD
of hosts lives, whom I serve, were it
not that I have regard for King Je-
hoshaphat of Judah, I would give
you neither a look nor a glance.
15 But get me a musician." And
then, while the musician was play-
ing, the power of the LORD came on
him. 16 And he said, "Thus says the
LORD, 'I will make this wadi full of
pools.' 17 For thus says the LORD,
'You shall see neither wind nor
rain, but the wadi shall be filled
with water, so that you shall drink,
you, your cattle, and your animals.'
18 This is only a trifle in the sight of
the LORD, for he will also hand
Moab over to you. 19 You shall con-
quer every fortified city and every
choice city; every good tree you
shall fell, all springs of water you
shall stop up, and every good piece
of land you shall ruin with stones."
20 The next day, about the time of
the morning offering, suddenly wa-
ter began to flow from the direction
of Edom, until the country was
filled with water.

21 When all the Moabites heard
that the kings had come up to fight
against them, all who were able to
put on armor, from the youngest to
the oldest, were called out and
were drawn up at the frontier.
22 When they rose early in the
morning, and the sun shone upon
the water, the Moabites saw the
water opposite them as red as
blood. 23 They said, "This is blood;
the kings must have fought togeth-
er, and killed one another. Now
then, Moab, to the spoil!" 24 But
when they came to the camp of Is-
rael, the Israelites rose up and at-
tacked the Moabites, who fled be-
fore them; as they entered Moab
they continued the attack.e 25 The
cities they overturned, and on ev-
ery good piece of land everyone

threw a stone, until it was covered;
every spring of water they stopped
up, and every good tree they felled.
Only at Kir-hareseth did the stone
walls remain, until the slingers sur-
rounded and attacked it. 26 When
the king of Moab saw that the bat-
tle was going against him, he took
with him seven hundred swords-
men to break through, opposite the
king of Edom; but they could not.
27 Then he took his firstborn son
who was to succeed him, and of-
fered him as a burnt offering on the
wall. And great wrath came upon
Israel, so they withdrew from him
and returned to their own land.

Elisha and the Widow's Oil

4 Now the wife of a member of
the company of prophetsf
cried to Elisha, "Your servant my
husband is dead; and you know
that your servant feared the LORD,
but a creditor has come to take my
two children as slaves." 2 Elisha
said to her, "What shall I do for
you? Tell me, what do you have in
the house?" She answered, "Your
servant has nothing in the house,
except a jar of oil." 3 He said, "Go
outside, borrow vessels from all
your neighbors, empty vessels and
not just a few. 4 Then go in, and
shut the door behind you and your
children, and start pouring into all
these vessels; when each is full, set
it aside." 5 So she left him and shut
the door behind her and her chil-
dren; they kept bringing vessels to
her, and she kept pouring. 6 When
the vessels were full, she said to her
son, "Bring me another vessel."
But he said to her, "There are no
more." Then the oil stopped flow-
ing. 7 She came and told the man of
God, and he said, "Go sell the oil
and pay your debts, and you and
your children can live on the rest."

Elisha Raises the Shunammite's Son

8 One day Elisha was passing
through Shunem, where a wealthy
woman lived, who urged him to

e Compare Gk Syr: Meaning of Heb uncertain
f Heb the sons of the prophets

3.13 Ezek 14.3-5; 1 Kings 18.19
3.14 1 Kings 17.1; 2 Kings 5.16
3.15 1 Sam 16.23; Ezek 1.3
3.19 v. 25
3.20 Ex 29.39,40
3.21 Gen 19.37
3.25 v. 19; Isa 16.7,11; Jer 48.31,36
3.27 Am 2.1; Mic 6.7
4.1 2 Kings 2.3; Lev 25.39; Mt 18.25
4.7 1 Kings 12.22
4.8 Josh 19.18

have a meal. So whenever he passed that way, he would stop there for a meal. ⁹She said to her husband, "Look, I am sure that this man who regularly passes our way is a holy man of God. ¹⁰Let us make a small roof chamber with walls, and put there for him a bed, a table, a chair, and a lamp, so that he can stay there whenever he comes to us."

11 One day when he came there, he went up to the chamber and lay down there. ¹²He said to his servant Gehazi, "Call the Shunammite woman." When he had called her, she stood before him. ¹³He said to him, "Say to her, Since you have taken all this trouble for us, what may be done for you? Would you have a word spoken on your behalf to the king or to the commander of the army?" She answered, "I live among my own people." ¹⁴He said, "What then may be done for her?" Gehazi answered, "Well, she has no son, and her husband is old." ¹⁵He said, "Call her." When he had called her, she stood at the door. ¹⁶He said, "At this season, in due time, you shall embrace a son." She replied, "No, my lord, O man of God; do not deceive your servant."

17 The woman conceived and bore a son at that season, in due time, as Elisha had declared to her.

18 When the child was older, he went out one day to his father among the reapers. ¹⁹He complained to his father, "Oh, my head, my head!" The father said to his servant, "Carry him to his mother." ²⁰He carried him and brought him to his mother; the child sat on her lap until noon, and he died. ²¹She went up and laid him on the bed of the man of God, closed the door on him, and left. ²²Then she called to her husband, and said, "Send me one of the servants and one of the donkeys, so that I may quickly go to the man of God and come back again." ²³He said, "Why go to him today? It is neither new moon nor sabbath." She said, "It will be all right."

4.9
v. 7
4.12
vv. 29-31;
2 Kings 5.20-
27; 8.4,5
4.16
Gen 18.10,
14; v. 28
4.21
vv. 7,32
4.23
Num 10.10;
28.11;
1 Chr 23.31

4.25
2 Kings 2.25
4.28
v. 16
4.29
1 Kings 18.46;
2 Kings 9.1;
Lk 10.4;
Ex 7.19;
14.16;
2 Kings 2.8,
14
4.30
2 Kings 2.2
4.33
v. 4;
Mt 6.6;
1 Kings 17.20
4.34
1 Kings 17.21;
Acts 20.10
4.35
1 Kings 17.21;
2 Kings 8.1,
5

²⁴Then she saddled the donkey and said to her servant, "Urge the animal on; do not hold back for me unless I tell you." ²⁵So she set out, and came to the man of God at Mount Carmel.

When the man of God saw her coming, he said to Gehazi his servant, "Look, there is the Shunammite woman; ²⁶run at once to meet her, and say to her, Are you all right? Is your husband all right? Is the child all right?" She answered, "It is all right." ²⁷When she came to the man of God at the mountain, she caught hold of his feet. Gehazi approached to push her away. But the man of God said, "Let her alone, for she is in bitter distress; the LORD has hidden it from me and has not told me." ²⁸Then she said, "Did I ask my lord for a son? Did I not say, Do not mislead me?" ²⁹He said to Gehazi, "Gird up your loins, and take my staff in your hand, and go. If you meet anyone, give no greeting, and if anyone greets you, do not answer; and lay my staff on the face of the child." ³⁰Then the mother of the child said, "As the LORD lives, and as you yourself live, I will not leave without you." So he rose up and followed her. ³¹Gehazi went on ahead and laid the staff on the face of the child, but there was no sound or sign of life. He came back to meet him and told him, "The child has not awakened."

32 When Elisha came into the house, he saw the child lying dead on his bed. ³³So he went in and closed the door on the two of them, and prayed to the LORD. ³⁴Then he got up on the bed^g and lay upon the child, putting his mouth upon his mouth, his eyes upon his eyes, and his hands upon his hands; and while he lay bent over him, the flesh of the child became warm. ³⁵He got down, walked once to and fro in the room, then got up again and bent over him; the child sneezed seven times, and the child opened his eyes. ³⁶Elisha^h summoned Gehazi and said, "Call the

^g Heb lacks *on the bed* ^h Heb *he*

Shunammite woman." So he called her. When she came to him, he said, "Take your son." [37] She came and fell at his feet, bowing to the ground; then she took her son and left.

Elisha Purifies the Pot of Stew

38 When Elisha returned to Gilgal, there was a famine in the land. As the company of prophets was[i] sitting before him, he said to his servant, "Put the large pot on, and make some stew for the company of prophets."[i] [39] One of them went out into the field to gather herbs; he found a wild vine and gathered from it a lapful of wild gourds, and came and cut them up into the pot of stew, not knowing what they were. [40] They served some for the men to eat. But while they were eating the stew, they cried out, "O man of God, there is death in the pot!" They could not eat it. [41] He said, "Then bring some flour." He threw it into the pot, and said, "Serve the people and let them eat." And there was nothing harmful in the pot.

Elisha Feeds One Hundred Men

42 A man came from Baalshalishah, bringing food from the first fruits to the man of God: twenty loaves of barley and fresh ears of grain in his sack. Elisha said, "Give it to the people and let them eat." [43] But his servant said, "How can I set this before a hundred people?" So he repeated, "Give it to the people and let them eat, for thus says the Lord, 'They shall eat and have some left.' " [44] He set it before them, they ate, and had some left, according to the word of the Lord.

The Healing of Naaman

5 Naaman, commander of the army of the king of Aram, was a great man and in high favor with his master, because by him the Lord had given victory to Aram. The man, though a mighty warrior, suffered from leprosy.[k] [2] Now the Arameans on one of their raids had taken a young girl captive from the land of Israel, and she served Naa-

man's wife. [3] She said to her mistress, "If only my lord were with the prophet who is in Samaria! He would cure him of his leprosy."[k] [4] So Naaman[l] went in and told his lord just what the girl from the land of Israel had said. [5] And the king of Aram said, "Go then, and I will send along a letter to the king of Israel."

He went, taking with him ten talents of silver, six thousand shekels of gold, and ten sets of garments. [6] He brought the letter to the king of Israel, which read, "When this letter reaches you, know that I have sent to you my servant Naaman, that you may cure him of his leprosy."[k] [7] When the king of Israel read the letter, he tore his clothes and said, "Am I God, to give death or life, that this man sends word to me to cure a man of his leprosy?[k] Just look and see how he is trying to pick a quarrel with me."

8 But when Elisha the man of God heard that the king of Israel had torn his clothes, he sent a message to the king, "Why have you torn your clothes? Let him come to me, that he may learn that there is a prophet in Israel." [9] So Naaman came with his horses and chariots, and halted at the entrance of Elisha's house. [10] Elisha sent a messenger to him, saying, "Go, wash in the Jordan seven times, and your flesh shall be restored and you shall be clean." [11] But Naaman became angry and went away, saying, "I thought that for me he would surely come out, and stand and call on the name of the Lord his God, and would wave his hand over the spot, and cure the leprosy![k] [12] Are not Abana[m] and Pharpar, the rivers of Damascus, better than all the waters of Israel? Could I not wash in them, and be clean?" He turned and went away in a rage. [13] But his servants approached and said to him, "Father, if the prophet had

Cross references

4.37
1 Kings 17.23;
Heb 11.35
4.38
2 Kings 2.1,
3; 8.1;
Lk 10.39;
Acts 22.3
4.41
Ex 15.25;
2 Kings 2.21
4.42
1 Sam 9.4,
7
4.44
Mt 14.16-21;
15.32-38
5.1
Lk 4.27

5.5
1 Sam 9.8;
2 Kings 8.8,
9
5.7
Gen 37.29;
30.2;
Deut 32.39;
1 Sam 2.6;
1 Kings 20.7
5.8
1 Kings 12.22
5.10
Jn 9.7
5.13
2 Kings 6.21;
8.9;
1 Sam 28.23

Footnotes

i Heb sons of the prophets were
i Heb sons of the prophets k A term for several skin diseases; precise meaning uncertain l Heb he m Another reading is Amana

commanded you to do something difficult, would you not have done it? How much more, when all he said to you was, 'Wash, and be clean'?" [14] So he went down and immersed himself seven times in the Jordan, according to the word of the man of God; his flesh was restored like the flesh of a young boy, and he was clean.

15 Then he returned to the man of God, he and all his company; he came and stood before him and said, "Now I know that there is no God in all the earth except in Israel; please accept a present from your servant." [16] But he said, "As the LORD lives, whom I serve, I will accept nothing!" He urged him to accept, but he refused. [17] Then Naaman said, "If not, please let two mule-loads of earth be given to your servant; for your servant will no longer offer burnt offering or sacrifice to any god except the LORD. [18] But may the LORD pardon your servant on one count: when my master goes into the house of Rimmon to worship there, leaning on my arm, and I bow down in the house of Rimmon, when I do bow down in the house of Rimmon, may the LORD pardon your servant on this one count." [19] He said to him, "Go in peace."

Gehazi's Greed

But when Naaman had gone from him a short distance, [20] Gehazi, the servant of Elisha the man of God, thought, "My master has let that Aramean Naaman off too lightly by not accepting from him what he offered. As the LORD lives, I will run after him and get something out of him." [21] So Gehazi went after Naaman. When Naaman saw someone running after him, he jumped down from the chariot to meet him and said, "Is everything all right?" [22] He replied, "Yes, but my master has sent me to say, 'Two members of a company of prophets[n] have just come to me from the hill country of Ephraim; please give them a talent of silver and two changes of clothing.' " [23] Naaman

said, "Please accept two talents." He urged him, and tied up two talents of silver in two bags, with two changes of clothing, and gave them to two of his servants, who carried them in front of Gehazi.[o] [24] When he came to the citadel, he took the bags[p] from them, and stored them inside; he dismissed the men, and they left.

25 He went in and stood before his master; and Elisha said to him, "Where have you been, Gehazi?" He answered, "Your servant has not gone anywhere at all." [26] But he said to him, "Did I not go with you in spirit when someone left his chariot to meet you? Is this a time to accept money and to accept clothing, olive orchards and vineyards, sheep and oxen, and male and female slaves? [27] Therefore the leprosy[q] of Naaman shall cling to you, and to your descendants forever." So he left his presence leprous,[q] as white as snow.

The Miracle of the Ax Head

6 Now the company of prophets[n] said to Elisha, "As you see, the place where we live under your charge is too small for us. [2] Let us go to the Jordan, and let us collect logs there, one for each of us, and build a place there for us to live." He answered, "Do so." [3] Then one of them said, "Please come with your servants." And he answered, "I will." [4] So he went with them. When they came to the Jordan, they cut down trees. [5] But as one was felling a log, his ax head fell into the water; he cried out, "Alas, master! It was borrowed." [6] Then the man of God said, "Where did it fall?" When he showed him the place, he cut off a stick, and threw it in there, and made the iron float. [7] He said, "Pick it up." So he reached out his hand and took it.

The Aramean Attack Is Thwarted

8 Once when the king of Aram

Cross-references (center column)

5.14
v. 10;
Job 33.25;
Lk 4.27
5.15
1 Sam 15.46,
47;
Dan 2.47;
3.29;
1 Sam 25.27
5.16
2 Kings 3.14;
vv. 20,26;
Gen 14.22,
23
5.18
2 Kings 7.2,
17
5.20
2 Kings 4.12,
31,36
5.22
2 Kings 4.26;
Josh 24.33

5.25
v. 22
5.26
v. 16
5.27
Ex 4.6;
Num 12.10;
2 Kings 15.5
6.1
2 Kings 4.38
6.6
2 Kings 2.21

[n] Heb sons of the prophets　　[o] Heb him
[p] Heb lacks the bags　　[q] A term for several skin diseases; precise meaning uncertain

was at war with Israel, he took counsel with his officers. He said, "At such and such a place shall be my camp." 9 But the man of God sent word to the king of Israel, "Take care not to pass this place, because the Arameans are going down there." 10 The king of Israel sent word to the place of which the man of God spoke. More than once or twice he warned such a place[r] so that it was on the alert.

11 The mind of the king of Aram was greatly perturbed because of this; he called his officers and said to them, "Now tell me who among us sides with the king of Israel?" 12 Then one of his officers said, "No one, my lord king. It is Elisha, the prophet in Israel, who tells the king of Israel the words that you speak in your bedchamber." 13 He said, "Go and find where he is; I will send and seize him." He was told, "He is in Dothan." 14 So he sent horses and chariots there and a great army; they came by night, and surrounded the city.

15 When an attendant of the man of God rose early in the morning and went out, an army with horses and chariots was all around the city. His servant said, "Alas, master! What shall we do?" 16 He replied, "Do not be afraid, for there are more with us than there are with them." 17 Then Elisha prayed: "O LORD, please open his eyes that he may see." So the LORD opened the eyes of the servant, and he saw; the mountain was full of horses and chariots of fire all around Elisha. 18 When the Arameans[s] came down against him, Elisha prayed to the LORD, and said, "Strike this people, please, with blindness." So he struck them with blindness as Elisha had asked. 19 Elisha said to them, "This is not the way, and this is not the city; follow me, and I will bring you to the man whom you seek." And he led them to Samaria.

20 As soon as they entered Samaria, Elisha said, "O LORD, open the eyes of these men so that they may see." The LORD opened their eyes, and they saw that they were

inside Samaria. 21 When the king of Israel saw them he said to Elisha, "Father, shall I kill them? Shall I kill them?" 22 He answered, "No! Did you capture with your sword and your bow those whom you want to kill? Set food and water before them so that they may eat and drink; and let them go to their master." 23 So he prepared for them a great feast; after they ate and drank, he sent them on their way, and they went to their master. And the Arameans no longer came raiding into the land of Israel.

Ben-hadad's Siege of Samaria

24 Some time later King Benhadad of Aram mustered his entire army; he marched against Samaria and laid siege to it. 25 As the siege continued, famine in Samaria became so great that a donkey's head was sold for eighty shekels of silver, and one-fourth of a kab of dove's dung for five shekels of silver. 26 Now as the king of Israel was walking on the city wall, a woman cried out to him, "Help, my lord king!" 27 He said, "No! Let the LORD help you. How can I help you? From the threshing floor or from the wine press?" 28 But then the king asked her, "What is your complaint?" She answered, "This woman said to me, 'Give up your son; we will eat him today, and we will eat my son tomorrow.' 29 So we cooked my son and ate him. The next day I said to her, 'Give up your son and we will eat him.' But she has hidden her son." 30 When the king heard the words of the woman he tore his clothes—now since he was walking on the city wall, the people could see that he had sackcloth on his body underneath— 31 and he said, "So may God do to me, and more, if the head of Elisha son of Shaphat stays on his shoulders today." 32 So he dispatched a man from his presence.

Now Elisha was sitting in his house, and the elders were sitting with him. Before the messenger arrived, Elisha said to the elders,

6.9
v. 12
6.13
Gen 37.17
6.16
2 Chr 32.7,
8; Ps 55.18;
Rom 8.31
6.17
2 Kings 2.11;
Ps 68.17;
Zech 6.1-7
6.18
Gen 19.11
6.20
v. 17

6.21
2 Kings 2.12;
5.13; 8.9
6.22
Deut 20.11-16;
Rom 12.20
6.23
vv. 8,9;
2 Kings 5.2
6.24
1 Kings 20.1
6.29
Lev 26.27-29;
Deut 28.52,
53,57
6.30
1 Kings 21.27
6.31
Ruth 1.17;
1 Kings 19.2
6.32
Ezek 8.1;
20.1;
1 Kings 18.4,
13,14

[r] Heb *warned it* [s] Heb *they*

"Are you aware that this murderer has sent someone to take off my head? When the messenger comes, see that you shut the door and hold it closed against him. Is not the sound of his master's feet behind him?" [33] While he was still speaking with them, the king[t] came down to him and said, "This trouble is from the LORD! Why should I hope in the LORD any longer?"

7 [1] But Elisha said, "Hear the word of the LORD: thus says the LORD, Tomorrow about this time a measure of choice meal shall be sold for a shekel, and two measures of barley for a shekel, at the gate of Samaria." [2] Then the captain on whose hand the king leaned said to the man of God, "Even if the LORD were to make windows in the sky, could such a thing happen?" But he said, "You shall see it with your own eyes, but you shall not eat from it."

The Arameans Flee

3 Now there were four leprous[u] men outside the city gate, who said to one another, "Why should we sit here until we die? [4] If we say, 'Let us enter the city,' the famine is in the city, and we shall die there; but if we sit here, we shall also die. Therefore, let us desert to the Aramean camp; if they spare our lives, we shall live; and if they kill us, we shall but die." [5] So they arose at twilight to go to the Aramean camp; but when they came to the edge of the Aramean camp, there was no one there at all. [6] For the Lord had caused the Aramean army to hear the sound of chariots, and of horses, the sound of a great army, so that they said to one another, "The king of Israel has hired the kings of the Hittites and the kings of Egypt to fight against us." [7] So they fled away in the twilight and abandoned their tents, their horses, and their donkeys leaving the camp just as it was, and fled for their lives. [8] When these leprous[u] men had come to the edge of the camp, they went into a tent, ate and drank, carried off silver, gold,

and clothing, and went and hid them. Then they came back, entered another tent, carried off things from it, and went and hid them.

9 Then they said to one another, "What we are doing is wrong. This is a day of good news; if we are silent and wait until the morning light, we will be found guilty; therefore let us go and tell the king's household." [10] So they came and called to the gatekeepers of the city, and told them, "We went to the Aramean camp, but there was no one to be seen or heard there, nothing but the horses tied, the donkeys tied, and the tents as they were." [11] Then the gatekeepers called out and proclaimed it to the king's household. [12] The king got up in the night, and said to his servants, "I will tell you what the Arameans have prepared against us. They know that we are starving; so they have left the camp to hide themselves in the open country, thinking, 'When they come out of the city, we shall take them alive and get into the city.'" [13] One of his servants said, "Let some men take five of the remaining horses, since those left here will suffer the fate of the whole multitude of Israel that have perished already;[v] let us send and find out." [14] So they took two mounted men, and the king sent them after the Aramean army, saying, "Go and find out." [15] So they went after them as far as the Jordan; the whole way was littered with garments and equipment that the Arameans had thrown away in their haste. So the messengers returned, and told the king.

16 Then the people went out, and plundered the camp of the Arameans. So a measure of choice meal was sold for a shekel, and two measures of barley for a shekel, according to the word of the LORD. [17] Now the king had appointed the captain on whose hand he leaned

Cross references (center column):

6.33
Job 2.9
7.1
v. 18
7.2
vv. 17,19, 20;
Mal 3.10
7.3
Lev 13.46
7.4
2 Kings 6.24
7.6
2 Sam 5.24;
19.7;
1 Kings 10.29
7.7
Ps 48.4-6

7.9
2 Sam 18.27
7.12
2 Kings 6.25-29
7.16
v. 1
7.17
v. 2;
2 Kings 6.32

tSee 7.2: Heb *messenger* uA term for several skin diseases; precise meaning uncertain vCompare Gk Syr Vg: Meaning of Heb uncertain

to have charge of the gate; the people trampled him to death in the gate, just as the man of God had said when the king came down to him. [18] For when the man of God had said to the king, "Two measures of barley shall be sold for a shekel, and a measure of choice meal for a shekel, about this time tomorrow in the gate of Samaria," [19] the captain had answered the man of God, "Even if the LORD were to make windows in the sky, could such a thing happen?" And he had answered, "You shall see it with your own eyes, but you shall not eat from it." [20] It did indeed happen to him; the people trampled him to death in the gate.

The Shunammite Woman's Land Restored

8 Now Elisha had said to the woman whose son he had restored to life, "Get up and go with your household, and settle wherever you can; for the LORD has called for a famine, and it will come on the land for seven years." [2] So the woman got up and did according to the word of the man of God; she went with her household and settled in the land of the Philistines seven years. [3] At the end of the seven years, when the woman returned from the land of the Philistines, she set out to appeal to the king for her house and her land. [4] Now the king was talking with Gehazi the servant of the man of God, saying, "Tell me all the great things that Elisha has done." [5] While he was telling the king how Elisha had restored a dead person to life, the woman whose son he had restored to life appealed to the king for her house and her land. Gehazi said, "My lord king, here is the woman, and here is her son whom Elisha restored to life." [6] When the king questioned the woman, she told him. So the king appointed an official for her, saying, "Restore all that was hers, together with all the revenue of the fields from the day that she left the land until now."

Cross references

7.18
v. 1
7.19
v. 2
8.1
2 Kings 4.35;
Ps 105.16;
Hag 1.11
8.4
2 Kings 4.12;
5.20-27
8.5
2 Kings 4.35

8.7
1 Kings 11.24;
2 Kings 6.24
8.8
1 Kings 19.15;
14.3;
2 Kings 1.2
8.10
vv. 14,15
8.12
2 Kings 10.32;
12.17; 13.3,7;
15.16;
Hos 13.16;
Am 1.13
8.13
1 Sam 17.43;
1 Kings 19.15
8.15
v. 10
8.16
2 Kings 1.17;
3.1;
2 Chr 21.3,
4
8.17
2 Chr 21.5-10

Death of Ben-hadad

7 Elisha went to Damascus while King Ben-hadad of Aram was ill. When it was told him, "The man of God has come here," [8] the king said to Hazael, "Take a present with you and go to meet the man of God. Inquire of the LORD through him, whether I shall recover from this illness." [9] So Hazael went to meet him, taking a present with him, all kinds of goods of Damascus, forty camel loads. When he entered and stood before him, he said, "Your son King Ben-hadad of Aram has sent me to you, saying, 'Shall I recover from this illness?'" [10] Elisha said to him, "Go, say to him, 'You shall certainly recover'; but the LORD has shown me that he shall certainly die." [11] He fixed his gaze and stared at him, until he was ashamed. Then the man of God wept. [12] Hazael asked, "Why does my lord weep?" He answered, "Because I know the evil that you will do to the people of Israel; you will set their fortresses on fire, you will kill their young men with the sword, dash in pieces their little ones, and rip up their pregnant women." [13] Hazael said, "What is your servant, who is a mere dog, that he should do this great thing?" Elisha answered, "The LORD has shown me that you are to be king over Aram." [14] Then he left Elisha, and went to his master Ben-hadad,[w] who said to him, "What did Elisha say to you?" And he answered, "He told me that you would certainly recover." [15] But the next day he took the bed-cover and dipped it in water and spread it over the king's face, until he died. And Hazael succeeded him.

Jehoram Reigns over Judah

16 In the fifth year of King Joram son of Ahab of Israel,[x] Jehoram son of King Jehoshaphat of Judah began to reign. [17] He was thirty-two years old when he became king, and he reigned eight

[w] Heb lacks *Ben-hadad* [x] Gk Syr: Heb adds *Jehoshaphat being king of Judah,*

years in Jerusalem. ¹⁸ He walked in the way of the kings of Israel, as the house of Ahab had done, for the daughter of Ahab was his wife. He did what was evil in the sight of the LORD. ¹⁹ Yet the LORD would not destroy Judah, for the sake of his servant David, since he had promised to give a lamp to him and to his descendants forever.

20 In his days Edom revolted against the rule of Judah, and set up a king of their own. ²¹ Then Joram crossed over to Zair with all his chariots. He set out by night and attacked the Edomites and their chariot commanders who had surrounded him;ʸ but his army fled home. ²² So Edom has been in revolt against the rule of Judah to this day. Libnah also revolted at the same time. ²³ Now the rest of the acts of Joram, and all that he did, are they not written in the Book of the Annals of the Kings of Judah? ²⁴ So Joram slept with his ancestors, and was buried with them in the city of David; his son Ahaziah succeeded him.

Ahaziah Reigns over Judah

25 In the twelfth year of King Joram son of Ahab of Israel, Ahaziah son of King Jehoram of Judah began to reign. ²⁶ Ahaziah was twenty-two years old when he began to reign; he reigned one year in Jerusalem. His mother's name was Athaliah, a granddaughter of King Omri of Israel. ²⁷ He also walked in the way of the house of Ahab, doing what was evil in the sight of the LORD, as the house of Ahab had done, for he was son-in-law to the house of Ahab.

28 He went with Joram son of Ahab to wage war against King Hazael of Aram at Ramoth-gilead, where the Arameans wounded Joram. ²⁹ King Joram returned to be healed in Jezreel of the wounds that the Arameans had inflicted on him at Ramah, when he fought against King Hazael of Aram. King Ahaziah son of Jehoram of Judah went down to see Joram son of

8.18
v. 27
8.19
2 Sam 7.13;
1 Kings 11.36;
2 Chr 21.7
8.20
1 Kings 22.4;
2 Kings 3.27;
2 Chr 21.8-10
8.21
2 Sam 18.17;
19.8
8.22
2 Chr 21.10
8.24
2 Chr 21.20;
22.1
8.25
2 Chr 22.1-6
8.28
v. 15;
1 Kings 22.3,
29
8.29
2 Kings 9.15;
2 Chr 22.6,
7

9.1
2 Kings 2.3;
4.29; 8.28,29
9.2
vv. 5,11
9.3
2 Chr 22.7
9.6
v. 3;
1 Kings 19.16;
2 Chr 22.7
9.7
Deut 32.35;
1 Kings 18.4;
21.15;
vv. 32,37
9.8
2 Kings 10.17;
1 Kings 21.21;
1 Sam 25.22;
Deut 32.36;
2 Kings 14.26
9.9
1 Kings 14.10;
15.29; 16.3-5,
11,12
9.10
vv. 35,36;
1 Kings 21.23
9.11
Jer 29.26;
Jn 10.20;
Acts 26.24

Ahab in Jezreel, because he was wounded.

Anointing of Jehu

9 Then the prophet Elisha called a member of the company of prophetsᶻ and said to him, "Gird up your loins; take this flask of oil in your hand, and go to Ramoth-gilead. ²When you arrive, look there for Jehu son of Jehoshaphat, son of Nimshi; go in and get him to leave his companions, and take him into an inner chamber. ³Then take the flask of oil, pour it on his head, and say, 'Thus says the LORD: I anoint you king over Israel.' Then open the door and flee; do not linger."

4 So the young man, the young prophet, went to Ramoth-gilead. ⁵He arrived while the commanders of the army were in council, and he announced, "I have a message for you, commander." "For which one of us?" asked Jehu. "For you, commander." ⁶So Jehuᵃ got up and went inside; the young man poured the oil on his head, saying to him, "Thus says the LORD the God of Israel: I anoint you king over the people of the LORD, over Israel. ⁷You shall strike down the house of your master Ahab, so that I may avenge on Jezebel the blood of my servants the prophets, and the blood of all the servants of the LORD. ⁸For the whole house of Ahab shall perish; I will cut off from Ahab every male, bond or free, in Israel. ⁹I will make the house of Ahab like the house of Jeroboam son of Nebat, and like the house of Baasha son of Ahijah. ¹⁰The dogs shall eat Jezebel in the territory of Jezreel, and no one shall bury her." Then he opened the door and fled.

11 When Jehu came back to his master's officers, they said to him, "Is everything all right? Why did that madman come to you?" He answered them, "You know the sort and how they babble." ¹²They said, "Liar! Come on, tell us!" So he said, "This is just what he said to me:

ʸ Meaning of Heb uncertain ᶻ Heb sons of the prophets ᵃ Heb he

'Thus says the LORD, I anoint you king over Israel.' " [13] Then hurriedly they all took their cloaks and spread them for him on the bare[b] steps; and they blew the trumpet, and proclaimed, "Jehu is king."

Joram of Israel Killed

14 Thus Jehu son of Jehoshaphat son of Nimshi conspired against Joram. Joram with all Israel had been on guard at Ramoth-gilead against King Hazael of Aram; [15] but King Joram had returned to be healed in Jezreel of the wounds that the Arameans had inflicted on him, when he fought against King Hazael of Aram. So Jehu said, "If this is your wish, then let no one slip out of the city to go and tell the news in Jezreel." [16] Then Jehu mounted his chariot and went to Jezreel, where Joram was lying ill. King Ahaziah of Judah had come down to visit Joram.

17 In Jezreel, the sentinel standing on the tower spied the company of Jehu arriving, and said, "I see a company." Joram said, "Take a horseman; send him to meet them, and let him say, 'Is it peace?' " [18] So the horseman went to meet him; he said, "Thus says the king, 'Is it peace?' " Jehu responded, "What have you to do with peace? Fall in behind me." The sentinel reported, saying, "The messenger reached them, but he is not coming back." [19] Then he sent out a second horseman, who came to them and said, "Thus says the king, 'Is it peace?' " Jehu answered, "What have you to do with peace? Fall in behind me." [20] Again the sentinel reported, "He reached them, but he is not coming back. It looks like the driving of Jehu son of Nimshi; for he drives like a maniac."

21 Joram said, "Get ready." And they got his chariot ready. Then King Joram of Israel and King Ahaziah of Judah set out, each in his chariot, and went to meet Jehu; they met him at the property of Naboth the Jezreelite. [22] When Joram saw Jehu, he said, "Is it peace,

Jehu?" He answered, "What peace can there be, so long as the many whoredoms and sorceries of your mother Jezebel continue?" [23] Then Joram reined about and fled, saying to Ahaziah, "Treason, Ahaziah!" [24] Jehu drew his bow with all his strength, and shot Joram between the shoulders, so that the arrow pierced his heart; and he sank in his chariot. [25] Jehu said to his aide Bidkar, "Lift him out, and throw him on the plot of ground belonging to Naboth the Jezreelite; for remember, when you and I rode side by side behind his father Ahab how the LORD uttered this oracle against him: [26] 'For the blood of Naboth and for the blood of his children that I saw yesterday, says the LORD, I swear I will repay you on this very plot of ground.' Now therefore lift him out and throw him on the plot of ground, in accordance with the word of the LORD."

Ahaziah of Judah Killed

27 When King Ahaziah of Judah saw this, he fled in the direction of Beth-haggan. Jehu pursued him, saying, "Shoot him also!" And they shot him[c] in the chariot at the ascent to Gur, which is by Ibleam. Then he fled to Megiddo, and died there. [28] His officers carried him in a chariot to Jerusalem, and buried him in his tomb with his ancestors in the city of David.

29 In the eleventh year of Joram son of Ahab, Ahaziah began to reign over Judah.

Jezebel's Violent Death

30 When Jehu came to Jezreel, Jezebel heard of it; she painted her eyes, and adorned her head, and looked out of the window. [31] As Jehu entered the gate, she said, "Is it peace, Zimri, murderer of your master?" [32] He looked up to the window and said, "Who is on my side? Who?" Two or three eunuchs looked out at him. [33] He said, "Throw her down." So they threw her down; some of her blood spat-

9.13
Mt 21.7;
2 Sam 15.10;
1 Kings 1.34, 39
9.14
2 Kings 8.28
9.15
2 Kings 8.29
9.16
2 Kings 8.29
9.18
vv. 19,22
9.20
2 Sam 18.27;
1 Kings 19.17
9.21
2 Chr 22.7;
v. 26;
1 Kings 21.1-7, 15-19
9.22
1 Kings 16.30-33; 18.19;
2 Chr 21.13

9.23
2 Kings 11.24
9.24
1 Kings 22.34
9.25
1 Kings 21.1, 19,24-29
9.26
1 Kings 21.19
9.27
2 Chr 22.9
9.28
2 Kings 23.30
9.30
Jer 4.30;
Ezek 23.40
9.31
1 Kings 16.9-20

b Meaning of Heb uncertain　c Syr Vg
Compare Gk: Heb lacks *and they shot him*

tered on the wall and on the horses, which trampled on her. 34 Then he went in and ate and drank; he said, "See to that cursed woman and bury her; for she is a king's daughter." 35 But when they went to bury her, they found no more of her than the skull and the feet and the palms of her hands. 36 When they came back and told him, he said, "This is the word of the LORD, which he spoke by his servant Elijah the Tishbite, 'In the territory of Jezreel the dogs shall eat the flesh of Jezebel; 37 the corpse of Jezebel shall be like dung on the field in the territory of Jezreel, so that no one can say, This is Jezebel.' "

Massacre of Ahab's Descendants

10 Now Ahab had seventy sons in Samaria. So Jehu wrote letters and sent them to Samaria, to the rulers of Jezreel,d to the elders, and to the guardians of the sons ofe Ahab, saying, 2 "Since your master's sons are with you and you have at your disposal chariots and horses, a fortified city, and weapons, 3 select the son of your master who is the best qualified, set him on his father's throne, and fight for your master's house." 4 But they were utterly terrified and said, "Look, two kings could not withstand him; how then can we stand?" 5 So the steward of the palace, and the governor of the city, along with the elders and the guardians, sent word to Jehu: "We are your servants; we will do anything you say. We will not make anyone king; do whatever you think right." 6 Then he wrote them a second letter, saying, "If you are on my side, and if you are ready to obey me, take the heads of your master's sons and come to me at Jezreel tomorrow at this time." Now the king's sons, seventy persons, were with the leaders of the city, who were charged with their upbringing. 7 When the letter reached them, they took the king's sons and killed them, seventy persons; they put their heads in baskets and sent them to him at Jezre-

el. 8 When the messenger came and told him, "They have brought the heads of the king's sons," he said, "Lay them in two heaps at the entrance of the gate until the morning." 9 Then in the morning when he went out, he stood and said to all the people, "You are innocent. It was I who conspired against my master and killed him; but who struck down all these? 10 Know then that there shall fall to the earth nothing of the word of the LORD, which the LORD spoke concerning the house of Ahab; for the LORD has done what he said through his servant Elijah." 11 So Jehu killed all who were left of the house of Ahab in Jezreel, all his leaders, close friends, and priests, until he left him no survivor.

12 Then he set out and went to Samaria. On the way, when he was at Beth-eked of the Shepherds, 13 Jehu met relatives of King Ahaziah of Judah and said, "Who are you?" They answered, "We are kin of Ahaziah; we have come down to visit the royal princes and the sons of the queen mother." 14 He said, "Take them alive." They took them alive, and slaughtered them at the pit of Beth-eked, forty-two in all; he spared none of them.

15 When he left there, he met Jehonadab son of Rechab coming to meet him; he greeted him, and said to him, "Is your heart as true to mine as mine is to yours?"f Jehonadab answered, "It is." Jehu said,g "If it is, give me your hand." So he gave him his hand. Jehu took him up with him into the chariot. 16 He said, "Come with me, and see my zeal for the LORD." So heh had him ride in his chariot. 17 When he came to Samaria, he killed all who were left to Ahab in Samaria, until he had wiped them out, according to the word of the LORD that he spoke to Elijah.

9.34
1 Kings 21.25; 16.31
9.36
1 Kings 21.23
9.37
Jer 8.1-3
10.1
1 Kings 16.24-29
10.5
1 Kings 20.4, 32
10.7
1 Kings 21.21

10.9
2 Kings 9.14-24; v. 6
10.10
2 Kings 9.7-10; 1 Kings 21.19-29
10.13
2 Kings 8.24, 29; 2 Chr 22.8
10.15
Jer 35.6ff; 1 Chr 2.55; Ezra 10.19
10.16
1 Kings 19.10
10.17
2 Kings 9.8; 2 Chr 22.8; v. 10

d Or of the city; Vg Compare Gk
e Gk: Heb lacks of the sons of f Gk: Heb Is it right with your heart, as my heart is with your heart? g Gk: Heb lacks Jehu said
h Gk Syr Tg: Heb they

Slaughter of Worshipers of Baal

18 Then Jehu assembled all the people and said to them, "Ahab offered Baal small service; but Jehu will offer much more. [19] Now therefore summon to me all the prophets of Baal, all his worshipers, and all his priests; let none be missing, for I have a great sacrifice to offer to Baal; whoever is missing shall not live." But Jehu was acting with cunning in order to destroy the worshipers of Baal. [20] Jehu decreed, "Sanctify a solemn assembly for Baal." So they proclaimed it. [21] Jehu sent word throughout all Israel; all the worshipers of Baal came, so that there was no one left who did not come. They entered the temple of Baal, until the temple of Baal was filled from wall to wall. [22] He said to the keeper of the wardrobe, "Bring out the vestments for all the worshipers of Baal." So he brought out the vestments for them. [23] Then Jehu entered the temple of Baal with Jehonadab son of Rechab; he said to the worshipers of Baal, "Search and see that there is no worshiper of the LORD here among you, but only worshipers of Baal." [24] Then they proceeded to offer sacrifices and burnt offerings.

Now Jehu had stationed eighty men outside, saying, "Whoever allows any of those to escape whom I deliver into your hands shall forfeit his life." [25] As soon as he had finished presenting the burnt offering, Jehu said to the guards and to the officers, "Come in and kill them; let no one escape." So they put them to the sword. The guards and the officers threw them out, and then went into the citadel of the temple of Baal. [26] They brought out the pillar[i] that was in the temple of Baal, and burned it. [27] Then they demolished the pillar of Baal, and destroyed the temple of Baal, and made it a latrine to this day.

28 Thus Jehu wiped out Baal from Israel. [29] But Jehu did not turn aside from the sins of Jeroboam son of Nebat, which he caused Isra-

el to commit—the golden calves that were in Bethel and in Dan. [30] The LORD said to Jehu, "Because you have done well in carrying out what I consider right, and in accordance with all that was in my heart have dealt with the house of Ahab, your sons of the fourth generation shall sit on the throne of Israel." [31] But Jehu was not careful to follow the law of the LORD the God of Israel with all his heart; he did not turn from the sins of Jeroboam, which he caused Israel to commit.

Death of Jehu

32 In those days the LORD began to trim off parts of Israel. Hazael defeated them throughout the territory of Israel: [33] from the Jordan eastward, all the land of Gilead, the Gadites, the Reubenites, and the Manassites, from Aroer, which is by the Wadi Arnon, that is, Gilead and Bashan. [34] Now the rest of the acts of Jehu, all that he did, and all his power, are they not written in the Book of the Annals of the Kings of Israel? [35] So Jehu slept with his ancestors, and they buried him in Samaria. His son Jehoahaz succeeded him. [36] The time that Jehu reigned over Israel in Samaria was twenty-eight years.

Athaliah Reigns over Judah

11 Now when Athaliah, Ahaziah's mother, saw that her son was dead, she set about to destroy all the royal family. [2] But Jehosheba, King Joram's daughter, Ahaziah's sister, took Joash son of Ahaziah, and stole him away from among the king's children who were about to be killed; she put[i] him and his nurse in a bedroom. Thus she[k] hid him from Athaliah, so that he was not killed; [3] he remained with her six years, hidden in the house of the LORD, while Athaliah reigned over the land.

Jehoiada Anoints the Child Joash

4 But in the seventh year Jehoi-

Cross references

10.18
1 Kings 16.31,
32
10.19
1 Kings 22.6
10.20
Joel 1.14;
Ex 32.4-6
10.21
1 Kings 16.32;
2 Kings 11.18
10.24
1 Kings 20.39
10.25
1 Kings 18.40
10.26
1 Kings 14.23
10.27
Ezra 6.11;
Dan 2.5;
3.29
10.29
1 Kings 12.28,
29

10.30
v. 35;
2 Kings 15.8,
12
10.31
v. 29
10.32
2 Kings 8.12
10.34
Am 1.3-5
11.1
2 Chr 22.10-12
11.4
2 Chr 23.1ff;
v. 19

i Gk Vg Syr Tg: Heb *pillars* i With 2 Chr 22.11: Heb lacks *she put* k Gk Syr Vg Compare 2 Chr 22.11: Heb *they*

ada summoned the captains of the Carites and of the guards and had them come to him in the house of the LORD. He made a covenant with them and put them under oath in the house of the LORD; then he showed them the king's son. ⁵He commanded them, "This is what you are to do: one-third of you, those who go off duty on the sabbath and guard the king's house ⁶(another third being at the gate Sur and a third at the gate behind the guards), shall guard the palace; ⁷and your two divisions that come on duty in force on the sabbath and guard the house of the LORD[1] ⁸shall surround the king, each with weapons in hand; and whoever approaches the ranks is to be killed. Be with the king in his comings and goings."

9 The captains did according to all that the priest Jehoiada commanded; each brought his men who were to go off duty on the sabbath, with those who were to come on duty on the sabbath, and came to the priest Jehoiada. ¹⁰The priest delivered to the captains the spears and shields that had been King David's, which were in the house of the LORD; ¹¹the guards stood, every man with his weapons in his hand, from the south side of the house to the north side of the house, around the altar and the house, to guard the king on every side. ¹²Then he brought out the king's son, put the crown on him, and gave him the covenant;[m] they proclaimed him king, and anointed him; they clapped their hands and shouted, "Long live the king!"

Death of Athaliah

13 When Athaliah heard the noise of the guard and of the people, she went into the house of the LORD to the people; ¹⁴when she looked, there was the king standing by the pillar, according to custom, with the captains and the trumpeters beside the king, and all the people of the land rejoicing and blowing trumpets. Athaliah tore her clothes and cried, "Treason! Trea-

son!" ¹⁵Then the priest Jehoiada commanded the captains who were set over the army, "Bring her out between the ranks, and kill with the sword anyone who follows her." For the priest said, "Let her not be killed in the house of the LORD." ¹⁶So they laid hands on her; she went through the horses' entrance to the king's house, and there she was put to death.

17 Jehoiada made a covenant between the LORD and the king and people, that they should be the LORD's people; also between the king and the people. ¹⁸Then all the people of the land went to the house of Baal, and tore it down; his altars and his images they broke in pieces, and they killed Mattan, the priest of Baal, before the altars. The priest posted guards over the house of the LORD. ¹⁹He took the captains, the Carites, the guards, and all the people of the land; then they brought the king down from the house of the LORD, marching through the gate of the guards to the king's house. He took his seat on the throne of the kings. ²⁰So all the people of the land rejoiced; and the city was quiet after Athaliah had been killed with the sword at the king's house.

21 ⁿJehoashº was seven years old when he began to reign.

The Temple Repaired

12 In the seventh year of Jehu, Jehoash began to reign; he reigned forty years in Jerusalem. His mother's name was Zibiah of Beer-sheba. ²Jehoash did what was right in the sight of the LORD all his days, because the priest Jehoiada instructed him. ³Nevertheless the high places were not taken away; the people continued to sacrifice and make offerings on the high places.

4 Jehoash said to the priests, "All the money offered as sacred donations that is brought into the house of the LORD, the money for

11.5
1 Chr 9.25
11.9
2 Chr 23.8
11.10
2 Sam 8.7;
1 Chr 18.7
11.12
1 Sam 10.24
11.13
2 Chr 23.12ff
11.14
2 Kings 23.3;
2 Chr 34.31;
1 Kings 1.39,
40;
2 Kings 9.23

11.17
2 Chr 23.16;
15.12-14;
2 Sam 5.3
11.18
2 Kings 10.26;
Deut 12.3;
2 Chr 23.17ff
11.19
vv. 4,6
11.21
2 Chr 24.1
12.3
2 Kings 14.4;
15.35
12.4
2 Kings 22.4;
Ex 35.5;
1 Chr 29.3-9

[1]Heb the LORD to the king m Or treaty or testimony; Heb eduth n Ch 12.1 in Heb º Another spelling is Joash; see verse 19

which each person is assessed — the money from the assessment of persons — and the money from the voluntary offerings brought into the house of the LORD, ⁵let the priests receive from each of the donors; and let them repair the house wherever any need of repairs is discovered." ⁶But by the twenty-third year of King Jehoash the priests had made no repairs on the house. ⁷Therefore King Jehoash summoned the priest Jehoiada with the other priests and said to them, "Why are you not repairing the house? Now therefore do not accept any more money from your donors but hand it over for the repair of the house." ⁸So the priests agreed that they would neither accept more money from the people nor repair the house.

9 Then the priest Jehoiada took a chest, made a hole in its lid, and set it beside the altar on the right side as one entered the house of the LORD; the priests who guarded the threshold put in it all the money that was brought into the house of the LORD. ¹⁰Whenever they saw that there was a great deal of money in the chest, the king's secretary and the high priest went up, counted the money that was found in the house of the LORD, and tied it up in bags. ¹¹They would give the money that was weighed out into the hands of the workers who had the oversight of the house of the LORD; then they paid it out to the carpenters and the builders who worked on the house of the LORD, ¹²to the masons and the stonecutters, as well as to buy timber and quarried stone for making repairs on the house of the LORD, as well as for any outlay for repairs of the house. ¹³But for the house of the LORD no basins of silver, snuffers, bowls, trumpets, or any vessels of gold, or of silver, were made from the money that was brought into the house of the LORD, ¹⁴for that was given to the workers who were repairing the house of the LORD with it. ¹⁵They did not ask an accounting from those into whose hand they deliv-

12.6
2 Chr 24.5
12.7
2 Chr 24.6
12.9
2 Chr 24.8;
Mk 12.41;
Lk 21.1
12.10
2 Kings 19.2
12.12
2 Kings 22.5,
6
12.13
2 Chr 24.14;
1 Kings 7.48,
50
12.15
2 Kings 22.7

12.16
Lev 5.15-18;
4.24,29;
Num 18.9,
19
12.17
2 Kings 8.12;
2 Chr 24.23
12.18
1 Kings 15.18;
2 Kings 18.15,
16
12.20
2 Kings 14.5;
2 Chr 24.25;
1 Kings 11.27
12.21
2 Chr 24.26,
27;
2 Kings 14.1
13.2
1 Kings 12.26-
33
13.3
Judg 2.14;
2 Kings 8.12;
12.17
13.4
Num 21.7-9;
Ps 78.34;
Ex 3.7;
2 Kings 14.26

ered the money to pay out to the workers, for they dealt honestly. ¹⁶The money from the guilt offerings and the money from the sin offerings was not brought into the house of the LORD; it belonged to the priests.

Hazael Threatens Jerusalem

17 At that time King Hazael of Aram went up, fought against Gath, and took it. But when Hazael set his face to go up against Jerusalem, ¹⁸King Jehoash of Judah took all the votive gifts that Jehoshaphat, Jehoram, and Ahaziah, his ancestors, the kings of Judah, had dedicated, as well as his own votive gifts, all the gold that was found in the treasuries of the house of the LORD and of the king's house, and sent these to King Hazael of Aram. Then Hazael withdrew from Jerusalem.

Death of Joash

19 Now the rest of the acts of Joash, and all that he did, are they not written in the Book of the Annals of the Kings of Judah? ²⁰His servants arose, devised a conspiracy, and killed Joash in the house of Millo, on the way that goes down to Silla. ²¹It was Jozacar son of Shimeath and Jehozabad son of Shomer, his servants, who struck him down, so that he died. He was buried with his ancestors in the city of David; then his son Amaziah succeeded him.

Jehoahaz Reigns over Israel

13 In the twenty-third year of King Joash son of Ahaziah of Judah, Jehoahaz son of Jehu began to reign over Israel in Samaria; he reigned seventeen years. ²He did what was evil in the sight of the LORD, and followed the sins of Jeroboam son of Nebat, which he caused Israel to sin; he did not depart from them. ³The anger of the LORD was kindled against Israel, so that he gave them repeatedly into the hand of King Hazael of Aram, then into the hand of Ben-hadad son of Hazael. ⁴But Jehoahaz entreated the LORD, and the LORD

heeded him; for he saw the oppression of Israel, how the king of Aram oppressed them. [5] Therefore the LORD gave Israel a savior, so that they escaped from the hand of the Arameans; and the people of Israel lived in their homes as formerly. [6] Nevertheless they did not depart from the sins of the house of Jeroboam, which he caused Israel to sin, but walked[p] in them; the sacred pole[q] also remained in Samaria. [7] So Jehoahaz was left with an army of not more than fifty horsemen, ten chariots and ten thousand footmen; for the king of Aram had destroyed them and made them like the dust at threshing. [8] Now the rest of the acts of Jehoahaz and all that he did, including his might, are they not written in the Book of the Annals of the Kings of Israel? [9] So Jehoahaz slept with his ancestors, and they buried him in Samaria; then his son Joash succeeded him.

Jehoash Reigns over Israel

10 In the thirty-seventh year of King Joash of Judah, Jehoash son of Jehoahaz began to reign over Israel in Samaria; he reigned sixteen years. [11] He also did what was evil in the sight of the LORD; he did not depart from all the sins of Jeroboam son of Nebat, which he caused Israel to sin, but he walked in them. [12] Now the rest of the acts of Joash, and all that he did, as well as the might with which he fought against King Amaziah of Judah, are they not written in the Book of the Annals of the Kings of Israel? [13] So Joash slept with his ancestors, and Jeroboam sat upon his throne; Joash was buried in Samaria with the kings of Israel.

Death of Elisha

14 Now when Elisha had fallen sick with the illness of which he was to die, King Joash of Israel went down to him, and wept before him, crying, "My father, my father! The chariots of Israel and its horsemen!" [15] Elisha said to him, "Take a bow and arrows"; so he took a

bow and arrows. [16] Then he said to the king of Israel, "Draw the bow"; and he drew it. Elisha laid his hands on the king's hands. [17] Then he said, "Open the window eastward"; and he opened it. Elisha said, "Shoot"; and he shot. Then he said, "The LORD's arrow of victory, the arrow of victory over Aram! For you shall fight the Arameans in Aphek until you have made an end of them." [18] He continued, "Take the arrows"; and he took them. He said to the king of Israel, "Strike the ground with them"; he struck three times, and stopped. [19] Then the man of God was angry with him, and said, "You should have struck five or six times; then you would have struck down Aram until you had made an end of it, but now you will strike down Aram only three times."

20 So Elisha died, and they buried him. Now bands of Moabites used to invade the land in the spring of the year. [21] As a man was being buried, a marauding band was seen and the man was thrown into the grave of Elisha; as soon as the man touched the bones of Elisha, he came to life and stood on his feet.

Israel Recaptures Cities from Aram

22 Now King Hazael of Aram oppressed Israel all the days of Jehoahaz. [23] But the LORD was gracious to them and had compassion on them; he turned toward them, because of his covenant with Abraham, Isaac, and Jacob, and would not destroy them; nor has he banished them from his presence until now.

24 When King Hazael of Aram died, his son Ben-hadad succeeded him. [25] Then Jehoash son of Jehoahaz took again from Ben-hadad son of Hazael the towns that he had taken from his father Jehoahaz in war. Three times Joash defeated him and recovered the towns of Israel.

Cross references (center column)

13.5
v. 25;
2 Kings 14.25,
27
13.6
v. 2;
1 Kings 16.33
13.7
Am 1.3
13.9
2 Kings 10.35
13.12
vv. 14-19;
2 Kings 14.8-
15;
2 Chr 25.17ff
13.14
2 Kings 2.12

13.17
1 Kings 20.26
13.19
v. 25
13.20
2 Kings 3.7;
24.2
13.22
2 Kings 8.12
13.23
2 Kings 14.27;
Ex 2.24,25;
Gen 13.16,
17
13.25
2 Kings 10.32,
33; 14.25;
vv. 18,19

p Gk Syr Tg Vg: Heb *he walked*
q Heb *Asherah*

Amaziah Reigns over Judah

14 In the second year of King Joash son of Joahaz of Israel, King Amaziah son of Joash of Judah, began to reign. ² He was twenty-five years old when he began to reign, and he reigned twenty-nine years in Jerusalem. His mother's name was Jehoaddin of Jerusalem. ³ He did what was right in the sight of the LORD, yet not like his ancestor David; in all things he did as his father Joash had done. ⁴ But the high places were not removed; the people still sacrificed and made offerings on the high places. ⁵ As soon as the royal power was firmly in his hand he killed his servants who had murdered his father the king. ⁶ But he did not put to death the children of the murderers; according to what is written in the book of the law of Moses, where the LORD commanded, "The parents shall not be put to death for the children, or the children be put to death for the parents; but all shall be put to death for their own sins."

7 He killed ten thousand Edomites in the Valley of Salt and took Sela by storm; he called it Joktheel, which is its name to this day.

8 Then Amaziah sent messengers to King Jehoash son of Jehoahaz, son of Jehu, of Israel, saying, "Come, let us look one another in the face." ⁹ King Jehoash of Israel sent word to King Amaziah of Judah, "A thorn bush on Lebanon sent to a cedar on Lebanon, saying, 'Give your daughter to my son for a wife'; but a wild animal of Lebanon passed by and trampled down the thorn bush. ¹⁰ You have indeed defeated Edom, and your heart has lifted you up. Be content with your glory, and stay at home; for why should you provoke trouble so that you fall, you and Judah with you?"

11 But Amaziah would not listen. So King Jehoash of Israel went up; he and King Amaziah of Judah faced one another in battle at Beth-shemesh, which belongs to Judah. ¹² Judah was defeated by Israel; everyone fled home. ¹³ King Jehoash of Israel captured King Amaziah of Judah son of Jehoash, son of Ahaziah, at Beth-shemesh; he came to Jerusalem, and broke down the wall of Jerusalem from the Ephraim Gate to the Corner Gate, a distance of four hundred cubits. ¹⁴ He seized all the gold and silver, and all the vessels that were found in the house of the LORD and in the treasuries of the king's house, as well as hostages; then he returned to Samaria.

15 Now the rest of the acts that Jehoash did, his might, and how he fought with King Amaziah of Judah, are they not written in the Book of the Annals of the Kings of Israel? ¹⁶ Jehoash slept with his ancestors, and was buried in Samaria with the kings of Israel; then his son Jeroboam succeeded him.

17 King Amaziah son of Joash of Judah lived fifteen years after the death of King Jehoash son of Jehoahaz of Israel. ¹⁸ Now the rest of the deeds of Amaziah, are they not written in the Book of the Annals of the Kings of Judah? ¹⁹ They made a conspiracy against him in Jerusalem, and he fled to Lachish. But they sent after him to Lachish, and killed him there. ²⁰ They brought him on horses; he was buried in Jerusalem with his ancestors in the city of David. ²¹ All the people of Judah took Azariah, who was sixteen years old, and made him king to succeed his father Amaziah. ²² He rebuilt Elath and restored it to Judah, after King Amaziah[r] slept with his ancestors.

Jeroboam II Reigns over Israel

23 In the fifteenth year of King Amaziah son of Joash of Judah, King Jeroboam son of Joash of Israel began to reign in Samaria; he reigned forty-one years. ²⁴ He did what was evil in the sight of the LORD; he did not depart from all the sins of Jeroboam son of Nebat, which he caused Israel to sin. ²⁵ He restored the border of Israel from Lebo-hamath as far as the Sea of

14.1
2 Kings 13.10;
2 Chr 25.1
14.4
2 Kings 12.3;
16.4
14.5
2 Kings 12.20
14.6
Deut 24.16;
Ezek 18.4,
20
14.7
2 Chr 25.11;
2 Sam 8.13;
Josh 15.38
14.8
2 Chr 25.17-24
14.9
Judg 9.8-15
14.10
v. 7;
Deut 8.14;
2 Chr 26.16;
32.25
14.11
Josh 19.38
14.12
2 Sam 18.17

14.13
Neh 8.16;
12.39;
2 Chr 25.23
14.14
2 Kings 12.18
14.15
2 Kings 13.12
14.17
2 Chr 25.25-28
14.19
Josh 10.31;
2 Kings 18.14,
17
14.22
2 Kings 16.6;
2 Chr 26.2
14.25
2 Kings 10.32;
1 Kings 8.65;
Deut 3.17;
Jon 1.1;
Mt 12.39,
40;
Josh 19.13

r Heb *the king*

the Arabah, according to the word of the LORD, the God of Israel, which he spoke by his servant Jonah son of Amittai, the prophet, who was from Gath-hepher. ²⁶For the LORD saw that the distress of Israel was very bitter; there was no one left, bond or free, and no one to help Israel. ²⁷But the LORD had not said that he would blot out the name of Israel from under heaven, so he saved them by the hand of Jeroboam son of Joash.

28 Now the rest of the acts of Jeroboam, and all that he did, and his might, how he fought, and how he recovered for Israel Damascus and Hamath, which had belonged to Judah, are they not written in the Book of the Annals of the Kings of Israel? ²⁹Jeroboam slept with his ancestors, the kings of Israel; his son Zechariah succeeded him.

Azariah Reigns over Judah

15 In the twenty-seventh year of King Jeroboam of Israel King Azariah son of Amaziah of Judah began to reign. ²He was sixteen years old when he began to reign, and he reigned fifty-two years in Jerusalem. His mother's name was Jecoliah of Jerusalem. ³He did what was right in the sight of the LORD, just as his father Amaziah had done. ⁴Nevertheless the high places were not taken away; the people still sacrificed and made offerings on the high places. ⁵The LORD struck the king, so that he was leprous ˢ to the day of his death, and lived in a separate house. Jotham the king's son was in charge of the palace, governing the people of the land. ⁶Now the rest of the acts of Azariah, and all that he did, are they not written in the Book of the Annals of the Kings of Judah? ⁷Azariah slept with his ancestors; they buried him with his ancestors in the city of David; his son Jotham succeeded him.

Zechariah Reigns over Israel

8 In the thirty-eighth year of King Azariah of Judah, Zechariah son of Jeroboam reigned over Israel

in Samaria six months. ⁹He did what was evil in the sight of the LORD, as his ancestors had done. He did not depart from the sins of Jeroboam son of Nebat, which he caused Israel to sin. ¹⁰Shallum son of Jabesh conspired against him, and struck him down in public and killed him, and reigned in place of him. ¹¹Now the rest of the deeds of Zechariah are written in the Book of the Annals of the Kings of Israel. ¹²This was the promise of the LORD that he gave to Jehu, "Your sons shall sit on the throne of Israel to the fourth generation." And so it happened.

Shallum Reigns over Israel

13 Shallum son of Jabesh began to reign in the thirty-ninth year of King Uzziah of Judah; he reigned one month in Samaria. ¹⁴Then Menahem son of Gadi came up from Tirzah and came to Samaria; he struck down Shallum son of Jabesh in Samaria and killed him; he reigned in place of him. ¹⁵Now the rest of the deeds of Shallum, including the conspiracy that he made, are written in the Book of the Annals of the Kings of Israel. ¹⁶At that time Menahem sacked Tiphsah, all who were in it and its territory from Tirzah on; because they did not open it to him, he sacked it. He ripped open all the pregnant women in it.

Menahem Reigns over Israel

17 In the thirty-ninth year of King Azariah of Judah, Menahem son of Gadi began to reign over Israel; he reigned ten years in Samaria. ¹⁸He did what was evil in the sight of the LORD; he did not depart all his days from any of the sins of Jeroboam son of Nebat, which he caused Israel to sin. ¹⁹King Pul of Assyria came against the land; Menahem gave Pul a thousand talents of silver, so that he might help him confirm his hold on the royal power. ²⁰Menahem exacted the money from Israel, that is, from all

14.26
2 Kings 13.4;
Deut 32.36
14.27
2 Kings 13.5,
23
14.28
2 Sam 8.6;
1 Kings 11.24;
2 Chr 8.3
14.29
2 Kings 15.8
15.1
2 Kings 14.21;
2 Chr 26.1,
3,4
15.2
2 Chr 26.3,
4
15.4
2 Kings 12.3;
14.4
15.5
2 Chr 26.19-21
15.7
2 Chr 26.23

15.10
Am 7.9
15.12
2 Kings 10.30
15.13
vv. 1,8
15.14
1 Kings 14.17
15.16
1 Kings 4.24;
2 Kings 8.12
15.17
vv. 1,8,13
15.19
1 Chr 5.26

ˢA term for several skin diseases; precise meaning uncertain

the wealthy, fifty shekels of silver from each one, to give to the king of Assyria. So the king of Assyria turned back, and did not stay there in the land. 21 Now the rest of the deeds of Menahem, and all that he did, are they not written in the Book of the Annals of the Kings of Israel? 22 Menahem slept with his ancestors, and his son Pekahiah succeeded him.

Pekahiah Reigns over Israel

23 In the fiftieth year of King Azariah of Judah, Pekahiah son of Menahem began to reign over Israel in Samaria; he reigned two years. 24 He did what was evil in the sight of the LORD; he did not turn away from the sins of Jeroboam son of Nebat, which he caused Israel to sin. 25 Pekah son of Remaliah, his captain, conspired against him with fifty of the Gileadites, and attacked him in Samaria, in the citadel of the palace along with Argob and Arieh; he killed him, and reigned in place of him. 26 Now the rest of the deeds of Pekahiah, and all that he did, are written in the Book of the Annals of the Kings of Israel.

Pekah Reigns over Israel

27 In the fifty-second year of King Azariah of Judah, Pekah son of Remaliah began to reign over Israel in Samaria; he reigned twenty years. 28 He did what was evil in the sight of the LORD; he did not depart from the sins of Jeroboam son of Nebat, which he caused Israel to sin. 29 In the days of King Pekah of Israel, King Tiglath-pileser of Assyria came and captured Ijon, Abel-beth-maacah, Janoah, Kedesh, Hazor, Gilead, and Galilee, all the land of Naphtali; and he carried the people captive to Assyria. 30 Then Hoshea son of Elah made a conspiracy against Pekah son of Remaliah, attacked him, and killed him; he reigned in place of him, in the twentieth year of Jotham son of Uzziah. 31 Now the rest of the acts of Pekah, and all that he did, are

written in the Book of the Annals of the Kings of Israel.

Jotham Reigns over Judah

32 In the second year of King Pekah son of Remaliah of Israel, King Jotham son of Uzziah of Judah began to reign. 33 He was twenty-five years old when he began to reign and reigned sixteen years in Jerusalem. His mother's name was Jerusha daughter of Zadok. 34 He did what was right in the sight of the LORD, just as his father Uzziah had done. 35 Nevertheless the high places were not removed; the people still sacrificed and made offerings on the high places. He built the upper gate of the house of the LORD. 36 Now the rest of the acts of Jotham, and all that he did, are they not written in the Book of the Annals of the Kings of Judah? 37 In those days the LORD began to send King Rezin of Aram and Pekah son of Remaliah against Judah. 38 Jotham slept with his ancestors, and was buried with his ancestors in the city of David, his ancestor; his son Ahaz succeeded him.

Ahaz Reigns over Judah

16 In the seventeenth year of Pekah son of Remaliah, King Ahaz son of Jotham of Judah began to reign. 2 Ahaz was twenty years old when he began to reign; he reigned sixteen years in Jerusalem. He did not do what was right in the sight of the LORD his God, as his ancestor David had done, 3 but he walked in the way of the kings of Israel. He even made his son pass through fire, according to the abominable practices of the nations whom the LORD drove out before the people of Israel. 4 He sacrificed and made offerings on the high places, on the hills, and under every green tree.

5 Then King Rezin of Aram and King Pekah son of Remaliah of Israel came up to wage war on Jerusalem; they besieged Ahaz but could not conquer him. 6 At that

Cross references

15.23
vv. 1,8,13, 17
15.25
1 Kings 16.18
15.27
v. 23;
Isa 7.1
15.29
v. 19;
2 Kings 17.6;
1 Chr 5.26

15.32
2 Chr 27.1ff
15.34
v. 3;
2 Chr 26.4, 5
15.35
v. 4;
2 Chr 27.3
15.37
2 Kings 16.5;
Isa 7.1;
v. 27
16.1
2 Chr 28.1ff
16.3
Lev 18.21;
2 Kings 17.17;
21.6;
Deut 12.31;
2 Kings 21.2, 11
16.4
Deut 12.2;
2 Kings 14.4
16.5
2 Kings 15.37;
Isa 7.1;
2 Chr 28.5, 6
16.6
2 Kings 14.22;
2 Chr 26.2

time the king of Edom[t] recovered Elath for Edom,[u] and drove the Judeans from Elath; and the Edomites came to Elath, where they live to this day. [7] Ahaz sent messengers to King Tiglath-pileser of Assyria, saying, "I am your servant and your son. Come up, and rescue me from the hand of the king of Aram and from the hand of the king of Israel, who are attacking me." [8] Ahaz also took the silver and gold found in the house of the LORD and in the treasures of the king's house, and sent a present to the king of Assyria. [9] The king of Assyria listened to him; the king of Assyria marched up against Damascus, and took it, carrying its people captive to Kir; then he killed Rezin.

10 When King Ahaz went to Damascus to meet King Tiglath-pileser of Assyria, he saw the altar that was at Damascus. King Ahaz sent to the priest Uriah a model of the altar, and its pattern, exact in all its details. [11] The priest Uriah built the altar; in accordance with all that King Ahaz had sent from Damascus, just so did the priest Uriah build it, before King Ahaz arrived from Damascus. [12] When the king came from Damascus, the king viewed the altar. Then the king drew near to the altar, went up on it, [13] and offered his burnt offering and his grain offering, poured his drink offering, and dashed the blood of his offerings of well-being against the altar. [14] The bronze altar that was before the LORD he removed from the front of the house, from the place between his altar and the house of the LORD, and put it on the north side of his altar. [15] King Ahaz commanded the priest Uriah, saying, "Upon the great altar offer the morning burnt offering, and the evening grain offering, and the king's burnt offering, and his grain offering, with the burnt offering of all the people of the land, their grain offering, and their drink offering; then dash against it all the blood of the burnt offering, and all the blood of the sacrifice; but the bronze altar shall be for me to in-

quire by." [16] The priest Uriah did everything that King Ahaz commanded.

17 Then King Ahaz cut off the frames of the stands, and removed the laver from them; he removed the sea from the bronze oxen that were under it, and put it on a pediment of stone. [18] The covered portal for use on the sabbath that had been built inside the palace, and the outer entrance for the king he removed from[v] the house of the LORD. He did this because of the king of Assyria. [19] Now the rest of the acts of Ahaz that he did, are they not written in the Book of the Annals of the Kings of Judah? [20] Ahaz slept with his ancestors, and was buried with his ancestors in the city of David; his son Hezekiah succeeded him.

Hoshea Reigns over Israel

17 In the twelfth year of King Ahaz of Judah, Hoshea son of Elah began to reign in Samaria over Israel; he reigned nine years. [2] He did what was evil in the sight of the LORD, yet not like the kings of Israel who were before him. [3] King Shalmaneser of Assyria came up against him; Hoshea became his vassal, and paid him tribute. [4] But the king of Assyria found treachery in Hoshea; for he had sent messengers to King So of Egypt, and offered no tribute to the king of Assyria, as he had done year by year; therefore the king of Assyria confined him and imprisoned him.

Israel Carried Captive to Assyria

5 Then the king of Assyria invaded all the land and came to Samaria; for three years he besieged it. [6] In the ninth year of Hoshea the king of Assyria captured Samaria; he carried the Israelites away to Assyria. He placed them in Halah, on the Habor, the river of Gozan, and in the cities of the Medes.

7 This occurred because the people of Israel had sinned against the LORD their God, who had

16.7
2 Chr 28.16ff;
2 Kings 15.29
16.8
2 Kings 12.17,
18
16.9
2 Chr 28.21;
Am 1.3-5
16.10
2 Kings 15.29;
Isa 8.2
16.14
2 Chr 4.1
16.15
Ex 29.39-41

16.17
1 Kings 7.23-
28
16.20
2 Chr 28.27
17.1
2 Kings 15.30
17.3
2 Kings 18.9-
12
17.5
Hos 13.16
17.6
Hos 13.16;
Deut 28.64;
29.27,28;
1 Chr 5.26;
2 Kings 18.10,
11
17.7
Josh 23.16;
Ex 14.15-30;
Judg 6.10

t Cn: Heb *King Rezin of Aram* u Cn: Heb *Aram* v Cn: Heb lacks *from*

brought them up out of the land of Egypt from under the hand of Pharaoh king of Egypt. They had worshiped other gods [8] and walked in the customs of the nations whom the LORD drove out before the people of Israel, and in the customs that the kings of Israel had introduced.[w] [9] The people of Israel secretly did things that were not right against the LORD their God. They built for themselves high places at all their towns, from watchtower to fortified city; [10] they set up for themselves pillars and sacred poles[x] on every high hill and under every green tree; [11] there they made offerings on all the high places, as the nations did whom the LORD carried away before them. They did wicked things, provoking the LORD to anger; [12] they served idols, of which the LORD had said to them, "You shall not do this." [13] Yet the LORD warned Israel and Judah by every prophet and every seer, saying, "Turn from your evil ways and keep my commandments and my statutes, in accordance with all the law that I commanded your ancestors and that I sent to you by my servants the prophets." [14] They would not listen but were stubborn, as their ancestors had been, who did not believe in the LORD their God. [15] They despised his statutes, and his covenant that he made with their ancestors, and the warnings that he gave them. They went after false idols and became false; they followed the nations that were around them, concerning whom the LORD had commanded them that they should not do as they did. [16] They rejected all the commandments of the LORD their God and made for themselves cast images of two calves; they made a sacred pole,[y] worshiped all the host of heaven, and served Baal. [17] They made their sons and their daughters pass through fire; they used divination and augury; and they sold themselves to do evil in the sight of the LORD, provoking him to anger. [18] Therefore the LORD was very angry with Israel and re-

moved them out of his sight; none was left but the tribe of Judah alone.

[19] Judah also did not keep the commandments of the LORD their God but walked in the customs that Israel had introduced. [20] The LORD rejected all the descendants of Israel; he punished them and gave them into the hand of plunderers, until he had banished them from his presence.

[21] When he had torn Israel from the house of David, they made Jeroboam son of Nebat king. Jeroboam drove Israel from following the LORD and made them commit great sin. [22] The people of Israel continued in all the sins that Jeroboam committed; they did not depart from them [23] until the LORD removed Israel out of his sight, as he had foretold through all his servants the prophets. So Israel was exiled from their own land to Assyria until this day.

Assyria Resettles Samaria

[24] The king of Assyria brought people from Babylon, Cuthah, Avva, Hamath, and Sepharvaim, and placed them in the cities of Samaria in place of the people of Israel; they took possession of Samaria, and settled in its cities. [25] When they first settled there, they did not worship the LORD; therefore the LORD sent lions among them, which killed some of them. [26] So the king of Assyria was told, "The nations that you have carried away and placed in the cities of Samaria do not know the law of the god of the land; therefore he has sent lions among them; they are killing them, because they do not know the law of the god of the land." [27] Then the king of Assyria commanded, "Send there one of the priests whom you carried away from there; let him[z] go and live there, and teach them the law of the god of the land." [28] So one of the priests whom they had carried away from Samaria came

17.8
Lev 18.3;
Deut 18.9;
2 Kings 16.3
17.9
2 Kings 18.8
17.10
Ex 34.12-14;
1 Kings 14.23;
Mic 5.14
17.12
Ex 20.3,4
17.13
1 Sam 9.9;
Jer 18.11;
25.5; 35.15
17.14
Ex 32.9;
Deut 31.27;
Acts 7.51
17.15
Jer 8.9;
Deut 29.25;
32.21;
Deut 12.30,
31
17.16
1 Kings 12.28;
14.15,23;
2 Kings 21.3;
1 Kings 16.31
17.17
Lev 19.26;
2 Kings 16.3;
Deut 18.10-12;
1 Kings 21.20
17.18
v. 6;
1 Kings 11.13,
32,36

17.19
1 Kings 14.22,
23;
2 Kings 16.3
17.20
2 Kings 15.29
17.21
1 Kings 11.11,
31; 12.20,
28-33
17.23
vv. 6,13
17.24
Ezra 4.2,10;
2 Kings 18.34
17.27
Mic 3.11

[w] Meaning of Heb uncertain [x] Heb *Asherim* [y] Heb *Asherah* [z] Syr Vg: Heb *them*

and lived in Bethel; he taught them how they should worship the Lord.

29 But every nation still made gods of its own and put them in the shrines of the high places that the people of Samaria had made, every nation in the cities in which they lived; 30 the people of Babylon made Succoth-benoth, the people of Cuth made Nergal, the people of Hamath made Ashima; 31 the Avvites made Nibhaz and Tartak; the Sepharvites burned their children in the fire to Adrammelech and Anammelech, the gods of Sepharvaim. 32 They also worshiped the Lord and appointed from among themselves all sorts of people as priests of the high places, who sacrificed for them in the shrines of the high places. 33 So they worshiped the Lord but also served their own gods, after the manner of the nations from among whom they had been carried away. 34 To this day they continue to practice their former customs.

They do not worship the Lord and they do not follow the statutes or the ordinances or the law or the commandment that the Lord commanded the children of Jacob, whom he named Israel. 35 The Lord had made a covenant with them and commanded them, "You shall not worship other gods or bow yourselves to them or serve them or sacrifice to them, 36 but you shall worship the Lord, who brought you out of the land of Egypt with great power and with an outstretched arm; you shall bow yourselves to him, and to him you shall sacrifice. 37 The statutes and the ordinances and the law and the commandment that he wrote for you, you shall always be careful to observe. You shall not worship other gods; 38 you shall not forget the covenant that I have made with you. You shall not worship other gods, 39 but you shall worship the Lord your God; he will deliver you out of the hand of all your enemies." 40 They would not listen, however, but they continued to practice their former custom.

41 So these nations worshiped the Lord, but also served their carved images; to this day their children and their children's children continue to do as their ancestors did.

Hezekiah's Reign over Judah

18 In the third year of King Hoshea son of Elah of Israel, Hezekiah son of King Ahaz of Judah began to reign. 2 He was twenty-five years old when he began to reign; he reigned twenty-nine years in Jerusalem. His mother's name was Abi daughter of Zechariah. 3 He did what was right in the sight of the Lord just as his ancestor David had done. 4 He removed the high places, broke down the pillars, and cut down the sacred pole.[a] He broke in pieces the bronze serpent that Moses had made, for until those days the people of Israel had made offerings to it; it was called Nehushtan. 5 He trusted in the Lord the God of Israel; so that there was no one like him among all the kings of Judah after him, or among those who were before him. 6 For he held fast to the Lord; he did not depart from following him but kept the commandments that the Lord commanded Moses. 7 The Lord was with him; wherever he went, he prospered. He rebelled against the king of Assyria and would not serve him. 8 He attacked the Philistines as far as Gaza and its territory, from watchtower to fortified city.

9 In the fourth year of King Hezekiah, which was the seventh year of King Hoshea son of Elah of Israel, King Shalmaneser of Assyria came up against Samaria, besieged it, 10 and at the end of three years, took it. In the sixth year of Hezekiah, which was the ninth year of King Hoshea of Israel, Samaria was taken. 11 The king of Assyria carried the Israelites away to Assyria, settled them in Halah, on the Habor, the river of Gozan, and in the cities of the Medes, 12 because they did not obey the voice of the Lord

17.30
v. 24
17.31
vv. 17,24
17.32
1 Kings 12.31
17.33
Zeph 1.5
17.34
Gen 32.28; 35.10
17.35
Judg 6.10; Ex 20.5
17.36
Ex 6.6; Deut 10.20
17.37
Deut 5.32
17.38
Deut 4.23

17.41
vv. 32,33
18.1
2 Kings 17.1; 2 Chr 28.27
18.2
2 Chr 29.1, 2
18.4
2 Chr 31.1; Num 21.8,9
18.5
2 Kings 19.10; 23.25
18.6
Deut 10.20
18.7
Gen 39.2,3; 1 Sam 18.14; 2 Kings 16.7
18.8
1 Chr 4.41; Isa 14.29; 2 Kings 17.9
18.9
2 Kings 17.3
18.10
2 Kings 17.6
18.11
2 Kings 17.6

a Heb *Asherah*

their God but transgressed his covenant—all that Moses the servant of the LORD had commanded; they neither listened nor obeyed.

Sennacherib Invades Judah

13 In the fourteenth year of King Hezekiah, King Sennacherib of Assyria came up against all the fortified cities of Judah and captured them. ¹⁴ King Hezekiah of Judah sent to the king of Assyria at Lachish, saying, "I have done wrong; withdraw from me; whatever you impose on me I will bear." The king of Assyria demanded of King Hezekiah of Judah three hundred talents of silver and thirty talents of gold. ¹⁵ Hezekiah gave him all the silver that was found in the house of the LORD and in the treasuries of the king's house. ¹⁶ At that time Hezekiah stripped the gold from the doors of the temple of the LORD, and from the doorposts that King Hezekiah of Judah had overlaid and gave it to the king of Assyria. ¹⁷ The king of Assyria sent the Tartan, the Rab-saris, and the Rabshakeh with a great army from Lachish to King Hezekiah at Jerusalem. They went up and came to Jerusalem. When they arrived, they came and stood by the conduit of the upper pool, which is on the highway to the Fuller's Field. ¹⁸ When they called for the king, there came out to them Eliakim son of Hilkiah, who was in charge of the palace, and Shebnah the secretary, and Joah son of Asaph, the recorder.

19 The Rabshakeh said to them, "Say to Hezekiah: Thus says the great king, the king of Assyria: On what do you base this confidence of yours? ²⁰ Do you think that mere words are strategy and power for war? On whom do you now rely, that you have rebelled against me? ²¹ See, you are relying now on Egypt, that broken reed of a staff, which will pierce the hand of anyone who leans on it. Such is Pharaoh king of Egypt to all who rely on him. ²² But if you say to me, 'We rely on the LORD our God,' is it not

he whose high places and altars Hezekiah has removed, saying to Judah and to Jerusalem, 'You shall worship before this altar in Jerusalem'? ²³ Come now, make a wager with my master the king of Assyria: I will give you two thousand horses, if you are able on your part to set riders on them. ²⁴ How then can you repulse a single captain among the least of my master's servants, when you rely on Egypt for chariots and for horsemen? ²⁵ Moreover, is it without the LORD that I have come up against this place to destroy it? The LORD said to me, Go up against this land, and destroy it."

26 Then Eliakim son of Hilkiah, and Shebnah, and Joah said to the Rabshakeh, "Please speak to your servants in the Aramaic language, for we understand it; do not speak to us in the language of Judah within the hearing of the people who are on the wall." ²⁷ But the Rabshakeh said to them, "Has my master sent me to speak these words to your master and to you, and not to the people sitting on the wall, who are doomed with you to eat their own dung and to drink their own urine?"

28 Then the Rabshakeh stood and called out in a loud voice in the language of Judah, "Hear the word of the great king, the king of Assyria! ²⁹ Thus says the king: 'Do not let Hezekiah deceive you, for he will not be able to deliver you out of my hand. ³⁰ Do not let Hezekiah make you rely on the LORD by saying, The LORD will surely deliver us, and this city will not be given into the hand of the king of Assyria.' ³¹ Do not listen to Hezekiah; for thus says the king of Assyria: 'Make your peace with me and come out to me; then every one of you will eat from your own vine and your own fig tree, and drink water from your own cistern, ³² until I come and take you away to a land like your own land, a land of grain and wine, a land of bread and vineyards, a land of olive oil and honey, that you may live and not die. Do not listen to Hezekiah when he misleads you by saying,

Cross references (center column)

18.13
2 Chr 32.1ff;
Isa 36.1ff
18.15
2 Kings 16.8
18.17
Isa 20.1; 7.3
18.18
2 Kings 19.2;
Isa 22.15,20
18.19
2 Chr 32.10ff
18.21
Ezek 29.6,7
18.22
v. 4;
2 Chr 31.1;
32.12

18.24
Isa 31.1
18.26
Ezra 4.7
18.29
2 Chr 32.15
18.31
1 Kings 4.20,
25
18.32
Deut 8.7-9

The LORD will deliver us. 33 Has any of the gods of the nations ever delivered its land out of the hand of the king of Assyria? 34 Where are the gods of Hamath and Arpad? Where are the gods of Sepharvaim, Hena, and Ivvah? Have they delivered Samaria out of my hand? 35 Who among all the gods of the countries have delivered their countries out of my hand, that the LORD should deliver Jerusalem out of my hand?' "

36 But the people were silent and answered him not a word, for the king's command was, "Do not answer him." 37 Then Eliakim son of Hilkiah, who was in charge of the palace, and Shebna the secretary, and Joah son of Asaph, the recorder, came to Hezekiah with their clothes torn and told him the words of the Rabshakeh.

Hezekiah Consults Isaiah

19 When King Hezekiah heard it, he tore his clothes, covered himself with sackcloth, and went into the house of the LORD. 2 And he sent Eliakim, who was in charge of the palace, and Shebna the secretary, and the senior priests, covered with sackcloth, to the prophet Isaiah son of Amoz. 3 They said to him, "Thus says Hezekiah, This day is a day of distress, of rebuke, and of disgrace; children have come to the birth, and there is no strength to bring them forth. 4 It may be that the LORD your God heard all the words of the Rabshakeh, whom his master the king of Assyria has sent to mock the living God, and will rebuke the words that the LORD your God has heard; therefore lift up your prayer for the remnant that is left." 5 When the servants of King Hezekiah came to Isaiah, 6 Isaiah said to them, "Say to your master, 'Thus says the LORD: Do not be afraid because of the words that you have heard, with which the servants of the king of Assyria have reviled me. 7 I myself will put a spirit in him, so that he shall hear a rumor and return to his own land; I will cause him to

fall by the sword in his own land.' "

Sennacherib's Threat

8 The Rabshakeh returned, and found the king of Assyria fighting against Libnah; for he had heard that the king had left Lachish. 9 When the king[b] heard concerning King Tirhakah of Ethiopia,[c] "See, he has set out to fight against you," he sent messengers again to Hezekiah, saying, 10 "Thus shall you speak to King Hezekiah of Judah: Do not let your God on whom you rely deceive you by promising that Jerusalem will not be given into the hand of the king of Assyria. 11 See, you have heard what the kings of Assyria have done to all lands, destroying them utterly. Shall you be delivered? 12 Have the gods of the nations delivered them, the nations that my predecessors destroyed, Gozan, Haran, Rezeph, and the people of Eden who were in Telassar? 13 Where is the king of Hamath, the king of Arpad, the king of the city of Sepharvaim, the king of Hena, or the king of Ivvah?"

Hezekiah's Prayer

14 Hezekiah received the letter from the hand of the messengers and read it; then Hezekiah went up to the house of the LORD and spread it before the LORD. 15 And Hezekiah prayed before the LORD, and said: "O LORD the God of Israel, who are enthroned above the cherubim, you are God, you alone, of all the kingdoms of the earth; you have made heaven and earth. 16 Incline your ear, O LORD, and hear; open your eyes, O LORD, and see; hear the words of Sennacherib, which he has sent to mock the living God. 17 Truly, O LORD, the kings of Assyria have laid waste the nations and their lands, 18 and have hurled their gods into the fire, though they were no gods but the work of human hands—wood and stone—and so they were destroyed. 19 So now, O LORD our God, save us, I pray you, from his hand, so that all the kingdoms of the earth may know

b Heb he c Or Nubia; Heb Cush

Cross references

18.33
2 Kings 19.12;
2 Chr 32.14;
Isa 10.10,11
18.34
2 Kings 19.13;
17.24
18.37
vv. 18,26;
2 Kings 6.30
19.1
2 Chr 32.20-22;
Isa 37.1-38;
2 Kings 18.37;
1 Kings 21.27
19.2
Isa 1.1; 2.1
19.4
2 Sam 16.12;
2 Kings 18.35;
1.9
19.6
Isa 37.6ff;
2 Kings 18.17ff
19.7
vv. 35-37

19.8
Josh 10.29;
2 Kings 18.14
19.10
2 Kings 18.5,30
19.12
2 Kings 18.33
19.13
2 Kings 18.34
19.14
Isa 37.14
19.15
1 Sam 4.4;
1 Kings 18.39
19.16
Ps 31.2;
2 Chr 6.40;
v. 4
19.18
Ps 115.4;
Jer 10.3
19.19
Ps 83.18;
v. 15

that you, O Lord, are God alone."

20 Then Isaiah son of Amoz sent to Hezekiah, saying, "Thus says the Lord, the God of Israel: I have heard your prayer to me about King Sennacherib of Assyria. 21 This is the word that the Lord has spoken concerning him:

She despises you, she scorns
 you—
 virgin daughter Zion;
she tosses her head—behind
 your back,
 daughter Jerusalem.

22 Whom have you mocked and
 reviled?
 Against whom have you
 raised your voice
and haughtily lifted your
 eyes?
 Against the Holy One of
 Israel!
23 By your messengers you have
 mocked the Lord,
 and you have said, 'With
 my many chariots
I have gone up the heights of
 the mountains,
 to the far recesses of
 Lebanon;
I felled its tallest cedars,
 its choicest cypresses;
I entered its farthest retreat,
 its densest forest.
24 I dug wells
 and drank foreign waters,
I dried up with the sole of
 my foot
 all the streams of Egypt.'
25 Have you not heard
 that I determined it long
 ago?
I planned from days of old
 what now I bring to pass,
that you should make
 fortified cities
 crash into heaps of ruins,
26 while their inhabitants,
 shorn of strength,
 are dismayed and
 confounded;
they have become like plants
 of the field
 and like tender grass,
like grass on the housetops,

blighted before it is grown.

27 "But I know your rising[d] and
 your sitting,
 your going out and coming
 in,
 and your raging against me.
28 Because you have raged
 against me
 and your arrogance has
 come to my ears,
I will put my hook in your
 nose
 and my bit in your mouth;
I will turn you back on the
 way
 by which you came.

29 "And this shall be the sign for you: This year you shall eat what grows of itself, and in the second year what springs from that; then in the third year sow, reap, plant vineyards, and eat their fruit. 30 The surviving remnant of the house of Judah shall again take root downward, and bear fruit upward; 31 for from Jerusalem a remnant shall go out, and from Mount Zion a band of survivors. The zeal of the Lord of hosts will do this.

32 "Therefore thus says the Lord concerning the king of Assyria: He shall not come into this city, shoot an arrow there, come before it with a shield, or cast up a siege-ramp against it. 33 By the way that he came, by the same he shall return; he shall not come into this city, says the Lord. 34 For I will defend this city to save it, for my own sake and for the sake of my servant David."

Sennacherib's Defeat and Death

35 That very night the angel of the Lord set out and struck down one hundred eighty-five thousand in the camp of the Assyrians; when morning dawned, they were all dead bodies. 36 Then King Sennacherib of Assyria left, went home, and lived at Nineveh. 37 As he was worshiping in the house of his god Nisroch, his sons Adram-

19.20 2 Kings 20.5; Isa 37.21
19.21 Lam 2.13; Job 16.4; Ps 22.7,8
19.22 vv. 4,6; Ps 71.22; Isa 5.24
19.23 2 Kings 18.17; Ps 20.7; Isa 10.18
19.24 Isa 19.6
19.25 Isa 45.7; 10.5
19.26 Ps 129.6

19.28 Job 41.2; Ezek 29.4; vv. 33,36
19.29 1 Sam 2.34; 2 Kings 20.8, 9; Lk 2.12
19.30 2 Chr 32.22, 23
19.31 Isa 9.7
19.33 v. 28
19.34 2 Kings 20.6; 1 Kings 11.12, 13
19.35 2 Chr 32.21; Isa 37.36
19.36 vv. 7,28,33; Jon 1.2
19.37 2 Chr 32.21; v. 7; Ezra 4.2

[d] Gk Compare Isa 37.27 Q Ms: MT lacks *rising*

melech and Sharezer killed him with the sword, and they escaped into the land of Ararat. His son Esar-haddon succeeded him.

Hezekiah's Illness

20 In those days Hezekiah became sick and was at the point of death. The prophet Isaiah son of Amoz came to him, and said to him, "Thus says the LORD: Set your house in order, for you shall die; you shall not recover." 2 Then Hezekiah turned his face to the wall and prayed to the LORD: 3 "Remember now, O LORD, I implore you, how I have walked before you in faithfulness with a whole heart, and have done what is good in your sight." Hezekiah wept bitterly. 4 Before Isaiah had gone out of the middle court, the word of the LORD came to him: 5 "Turn back, and say to Hezekiah prince of my people, Thus says the LORD, the God of your ancestor David: I have heard your prayer, I have seen your tears; indeed, I will heal you; on the third day you shall go up to the house of the LORD. 6 I will add fifteen years to your life. I will deliver you and this city out of the hand of the king of Assyria; I will defend this city for my own sake and for my servant David's sake." 7 Then Isaiah said, "Bring a lump of figs. Let them take it and apply it to the boil, so that he may recover."

8 Hezekiah said to Isaiah, "What shall be the sign that the LORD will heal me, and that I shall go up to the house of the LORD on the third day?" 9 Isaiah said, "This is the sign to you from the LORD, that the LORD will do the thing that he has promised: the shadow has now advanced ten intervals; shall it retreat ten intervals?" 10 Hezekiah answered, "It is normal for the shadow to lengthen ten intervals; rather let the shadow retreat ten intervals." 11 The prophet Isaiah cried to the LORD; and he brought the shadow back the ten intervals, by which the sun[e] had declined on the dial of Ahaz.

Envoys from Babylon

12 At that time King Merodach-baladan son of Baladan of Babylon sent envoys with letters and a present to Hezekiah, for he had heard that Hezekiah had been sick. 13 Hezekiah welcomed them;[f] showed them all his treasure house, the silver, the gold, the spices, the precious oil, his armory, all that was found in his storehouses; there was nothing in his house or in all his realm that Hezekiah did not show them. 14 Then the prophet Isaiah came to King Hezekiah, and said to him, "What did these men say? From where did they come to you?" Hezekiah answered, "They have come from a far country, from Babylon." 15 He said, "What have they seen in your house?" Hezekiah answered, "They have seen all that is in my house; there is nothing in my storehouses that I did not show them."

16 Then Isaiah said to Hezekiah, "Hear the word of the LORD: 17 Days are coming when all that is in your house, and that which your ancestors have stored up until this day, shall be carried to Babylon; nothing shall be left, says the LORD. 18 Some of your own sons who are born to you shall be taken away; they shall be eunuchs in the palace of the king of Babylon." 19 Then Hezekiah said to Isaiah, "The word of the LORD that you have spoken is good." For he thought, "Why not, if there will be peace and security in my days?"

Death of Hezekiah

20 The rest of the deeds of Hezekiah, all his power, how he made the pool and the conduit and brought water into the city, are they not written in the Book of the Annals of the Kings of Judah? 21 Hezekiah slept with his ancestors; and his son Manasseh succeeded him.

20.1 2 Chr 32.24; Isa 38.1; 2 Sam 17.23
20.3 Neh 13.22; 2 Kings 18.3-6
20.5 1 Sam 9.16; 10.1; 2 Kings 19.20; Ps 39.12
20.6 2 Kings 19.34
20.7 Isa 38.21
20.11 Josh 10.12-14

20.12 Isa 39.1ff
20.13 2 Chr 32.27
20.15 v. 13
20.17 2 Kings 24.13; 25.13; Jer 52.17
20.18 2 Kings 24.12; 2 Chr 33.1; Dan 1.3-7
20.19 1 Sam 3.18
20.20 2 Chr 32.32; Neh 3.16
20.21 2 Chr 32.33

e Syr See Isa 38.8 and Tg: Heb *it* f Gk Vg Syr: Heb *When Hezekiah heard about them*

Manasseh Reigns over Judah

21 Manasseh was twelve years old when he began to reign; he reigned fifty-five years in Jerusalem. His mother's name was Hephzibah. ² He did what was evil in the sight of the LORD, following the abominable practices of the nations that the LORD drove out before the people of Israel. ³ For he rebuilt the high places that his father Hezekiah had destroyed; he erected altars for Baal, made a sacred pole,ᵍ as King Ahab of Israel had done, worshiped all the host of heaven, and served them. ⁴ He built altars in the house of the LORD, of which the LORD had said, "In Jerusalem I will put my name." ⁵ He built altars for all the host of heaven in the two courts of the house of the LORD. ⁶ He made his son pass through fire; he practiced soothsaying and augury, and dealt with mediums and with wizards. He did much evil in the sight of the LORD, provoking him to anger. ⁷ The carved image of Asherah that he had made he set in the house of which the LORD said to David and to his son Solomon, "In this house, and in Jerusalem, which I have chosen out of all the tribes of Israel, I will put my name forever; ⁸ I will not cause the feet of Israel to wander any more out of the land that I gave to their ancestors, if only they will be careful to do according to all that I have commanded them, and according to all the law that my servant Moses commanded them." ⁹ But they did not listen; Manasseh misled them to do more evil than the nations had done that the LORD destroyed before the people of Israel.

10 The LORD said by his servants the prophets, ¹¹ "Because King Manasseh of Judah has committed these abominations, has done things more wicked than all that the Amorites did, who were before him, and has caused Judah also to sin with his idols; ¹² therefore thus says the LORD, the God of Israel, I am bringing upon Jerusalem and Judah such evil that the ears of everyone who hears of it will tingle. ¹³ I will stretch over Jerusalem the measuring line for Samaria, and the plummet for the house of Ahab; I will wipe Jerusalem as one wipes a dish, wiping it and turning it upside down. ¹⁴ I will cast off the remnant of my heritage, and give them into the hand of their enemies; they shall become a prey and a spoil to all their enemies, ¹⁵ because they have done what is evil in my sight and have provoked me to anger, since the day their ancestors came out of Egypt, even to this day."

16 Moreover Manasseh shed very much innocent blood, until he had filled Jerusalem from one end to another, besides the sin that he caused Judah to sin so that they did what was evil in the sight of the LORD.

17 Now the rest of the acts of Manasseh, all that he did, and the sin that he committed, are they not written in the Book of the Annals of the Kings of Judah? ¹⁸ Manasseh slept with his ancestors, and was buried in the garden of his house, in the garden of Uzza. His son Amon succeeded him.

Amon Reigns over Judah

19 Amon was twenty-two years old when he began to reign; he reigned two years in Jerusalem. His mother's name was Meshullemeth daughter of Haruz of Jotbah. ²⁰ He did what was evil in the sight of the LORD, as his father Manasseh had done. ²¹ He walked in all the way in which his father walked, served the idols that his father served, and worshiped them; ²² he abandoned the LORD, the God of his ancestors, and did not walk in the way of the LORD. ²³ The servants of Amon conspired against him, and killed the king in his house. ²⁴ But the people of the land killed all those who had conspired against King Amon, and the people of the land made his son Josiah king in place of him. ²⁵ Now the rest of the acts of Amon that he did, are they not written in the

Cross-references (center column):

21.1
2 Chr 33.1ff
21.2
2 Kings 16.3
21.3
2 Kings 18.4;
1 Kings 16.32,
33;
2 Kings 17.16;
Deut 17.3
21.4
Jer 32.34;
2 Sam 7.13;
1 Kings 8.29
21.6
Lev 18.21;
2 Kings 16.3;
17.17;
Lev 19.26,
31;
Deut 18.20,
11
21.7
1 Kings 8.29;
9.3;
2 Kings 23.27;
Jer 32.34
21.8
2 Sam 7.10
21.9
Prov 29.12
21.11
2 Kings 24.3,
4;
1 Kings 21.26;
v. 16
21.12
1 Sam 3.11;
Jer 19.3

21.13
Isa 34.11;
Am 7.7,8
21.16
2 Kings 24.4
21.17
2 Chr 33.11-19
21.18
2 Chr 33.20
21.19
2 Chr 33.21-23
21.20
vv. 2-6,11,
16
21.22
1 Kings 11.33
21.23
2 Chr 33.24,
25

ᵍ Heb *Asherah*

Book of the Annals of the Kings of Judah? 26He was buried in his tomb in the garden of Uzza; then his son Josiah succeeded him.

Josiah Reigns over Judah

22 Josiah was eight years old when he began to reign; he reigned thirty-one years in Jerusalem. His mother's name was Jedidah daughter of Adaiah of Bozkath. 2He did what was right in the sight of the LORD, and walked in all the way of his father David; he did not turn aside to the right or to the left.

Hilkiah Finds the Book of the Law

3 In the eighteenth year of King Josiah, the king sent Shaphan son of Azaliah, son of Meshullam, the secretary, to the house of the LORD, saying, 4"Go up to the high priest Hilkiah, and have him count the entire sum of the money that has been brought into the house of the LORD, which the keepers of the threshold have collected from the people; 5let it be given into the hand of the workers who have the oversight of the house of the LORD; let them give it to the workers who are at the house of the LORD, repairing the house, 6that is, to the carpenters, to the builders, to the masons; and let them use it to buy timber and quarried stone to repair the house. 7But no accounting shall be asked from them for the money that is delivered into their hand, for they deal honestly."

8 The high priest Hilkiah said to Shaphan the secretary, "I have found the book of the law in the house of the LORD." When Hilkiah gave the book to Shaphan, he read it. 9Then Shaphan the secretary came to the king, and reported to the king, "Your servants have emptied out the money that was found in the house, and have delivered it into the hand of the workers who have oversight of the house of the LORD." 10Shaphan the secretary informed the king, "The priest Hilkiah has given me a book." Shaphan then read it aloud to the king.

21.26
v. 18
22.1
2 Chr 34.1;
Josh 15.39
22.2
Deut 5.32
22.3
2 Chr 34.8ff
22.4
2 Kings 12.4,
9,10
22.5
2 Kings 12.11-
14
22.7
2 Kings 12.15
22.8
Deut 31.24-26;
2 Chr 34.14,
15

22.12
2 Kings 25.22;
2 Chr 34.20
22.13
Deut 29.27
22.14
2 Chr 34.22
22.17
Deut 29.25-27
22.19
Ps 51.17;
Isa 57.15;
1 Kings 21.29;
Lev 26.31;
Jer 26.6

11 When the king heard the words of the book of the law, he tore his clothes. 12Then the king commanded the priest Hilkiah, Ahikam son of Shaphan, Achbor son of Micaiah, Shaphan the secretary, and the king's servant Asaiah, saying, 13"Go, inquire of the LORD for me, for the people, and for all Judah, concerning the words of this book that has been found; for great is the wrath of the LORD that is kindled against us, because our ancestors did not obey the words of this book, to do according to all that is written concerning us."

14 So the priest Hilkiah, Ahikam, Achbor, Shaphan, and Asaiah went to the prophetess Huldah the wife of Shallum son of Tikvah, son of Harhas, keeper of the wardrobe; she resided in Jerusalem in the Second Quarter, where they consulted her. 15She declared to them, "Thus says the LORD, the God of Israel: Tell the man who sent you to me, 16Thus says the LORD, I will indeed bring disaster on this place and on its inhabitants—all the words of the book that the king of Judah has read. 17Because they have abandoned me and have made offerings to other gods, so that they have provoked me to anger with all the work of their hands, therefore my wrath will be kindled against this place, and it will not be quenched. 18But as to the king of Judah, who sent you to inquire of the LORD, thus shall you say to him, Thus says the LORD, the God of Israel: Regarding the words that you have heard, 19because your heart was penitent, and you humbled yourself before the LORD, when you heard how I spoke against this place, and against its inhabitants, that they should become a desolation and a curse, and because you have torn your clothes and wept before me, I also have heard you, says the LORD. 20Therefore, I will gather you to your ancestors, and you shall be gathered to your grave in peace; your eyes shall not see all the disaster that I will bring on this

place." They took the message back to the king.

Josiah's Reformation

23 Then the king directed that all the elders of Judah and Jerusalem should be gathered to him. ² The king went up to the house of the LORD, and with him went all the people of Judah, all the inhabitants of Jerusalem, the priests, the prophets, and all the people, both small and great; he read in their hearing all the words of the book of the covenant that had been found in the house of the LORD. ³ The king stood by the pillar and made a covenant before the LORD, to follow the LORD, keeping his commandments, his decrees, and his statutes, with all his heart and all his soul, to perform the words of this covenant that were written in this book. All the people joined in the covenant.

4 The king commanded the high priest Hilkiah, the priests of the second order, and the guardians of the threshold, to bring out of the temple of the LORD all the vessels made for Baal, for Asherah, and for all the host of heaven; he burned them outside Jerusalem in the fields of the Kidron, and carried their ashes to Bethel. ⁵ He deposed the idolatrous priests whom the kings of Judah had ordained to make offerings in the high places at the cities of Judah and around Jerusalem; those also who made offerings to Baal, to the sun, the moon, the constellations, and all the host of the heavens. ⁶ He brought out the image of[h] Asherah from the house of the LORD, outside Jerusalem, to the Wadi Kidron, burned it at the Wadi Kidron, beat it to dust and threw the dust of it upon the graves of the common people. ⁷ He broke down the houses of the male temple prostitutes that were in the house of the LORD, where the women did weaving for Asherah. ⁸ He brought all the priests out of the towns of Judah, and defiled the high places where the priests had made offer-

ings, from Geba to Beer-sheba; he broke down the high places of the gates that were at the entrance of the gate of Joshua the governor of the city, which were on the left at the gate of the city. ⁹ The priests of the high places, however, did not come up to the altar of the LORD in Jerusalem, but ate unleavened bread among their kindred. ¹⁰ He defiled Topheth, which is in the valley of Ben-hinnom, so that no one would make a son or a daughter pass through fire as an offering to Molech. ¹¹ He removed the horses that the kings of Judah had dedicated to the sun, at the entrance to the house of the LORD, by the chamber of the eunuch Nathan-melech, which was in the precincts;[i] then he burned the chariots of the sun with fire. ¹² The altars on the roof of the upper chamber of Ahaz, which the kings of Judah had made, and the altars that Manasseh had made in the two courts of the house of the LORD, he pulled down from there and broke in pieces, and threw the rubble into the Wadi Kidron. ¹³ The king defiled the high places that were east of Jerusalem, to the south of the Mount of Destruction, which King Solomon of Israel had built for Astarte the abomination of the Sidonians, for Chemosh the abomination of Moab, and for Milcom the abomination of the Ammonites. ¹⁴ He broke the pillars in pieces, cut down the sacred poles,[i] and covered the sites with human bones.

15 Moreover, the altar at Bethel, the high place erected by Jeroboam son of Nebat, who caused Israel to sin— he pulled down that altar along with the high place. He burned the high place, crushing it to dust; he also burned the sacred pole.[k] ¹⁶ As Josiah turned, he saw the tombs there on the mount; and he sent and took the bones out of the tombs, and burned them on the altar, and defiled it, according to

23.1
2 Chr 34.29-32
23.2
Deut 31.10-13;
2 Kings 22.8
23.3
2 Kings 11.14,
17;
Deut 13.4
23.4ff
2 Kings 21.3,
7
23.7
1 Kings 14.24;
15.12;
Ezek 16.16
23.8
1 Kings 15.22

23.9
Ezek 44.10-14
23.10
Isa 30.33;
Jer 7.31;
Lev 18.21;
Deut 18.10
23.12
Jer 19.13;
Zeph 1.5;
2 Kings 21.5;
vv. 4,6
23.13
1 Kings 11.7
23.14
Ex 23.24;
Deut 7.5,25
23.15
1 Kings 12.28-
33
23.16
1 Kings 13.2

h Heb lacks *image of* i Meaning of Heb uncertain i Heb *Asherim*
k Heb *Asherah*

the word of the Lord that the man of God proclaimed,[1] when Jeroboam stood by the altar at the festival; he turned and looked up at the tomb of the man of God who had predicted these things. 17 Then he said, "What is that monument that I see?" The people of the city told him, "It is the tomb of the man of God who came from Judah and predicted these things that you have done against the altar at Bethel." 18 He said, "Let him rest; let no one move his bones." So they let his bones alone, with the bones of the prophet who came out of Samaria. 19 Moreover, Josiah removed all the shrines of the high places that were in the towns of Samaria, which kings of Israel had made, provoking the Lord to anger; he did to them just as he had done at Bethel. 20 He slaughtered on the altars all the priests who were there, and burned human bones on them. Then he returned to Jerusalem.

The Passover Celebrated

21 The king commanded all the people, "Keep the passover to the Lord your God as prescribed in this book of the covenant." 22 No such passover had been kept since the days of the judges who judged Israel, or during all the days of the kings of Israel or of the kings of Judah; 23 but in the eighteenth year of King Josiah this passover was kept to the Lord in Jerusalem.

24 Moreover Josiah put away the mediums, wizards, teraphim,[m] idols, and all the abominations that were seen in the land of Judah and in Jerusalem, so that he established the words of the law that were written in the book that the priest Hilkiah had found in the house of the Lord. 25 Before him there was no king like him, who turned to the Lord with all his heart, with all his soul, and with all his might, according to all the law of Moses; nor did any like him arise after him.

26 Still the Lord did not turn from the fierceness of his great wrath, by which his anger was kindled against Judah, because of all the provocations with which Manasseh had provoked him. 27 The Lord said, "I will remove Judah also out of my sight, as I have removed Israel; and I will reject this city that I have chosen, Jerusalem, and the house of which I said, My name shall be there."

Josiah Dies in Battle

28 Now the rest of the acts of Josiah, and all that he did, are they not written in the Book of the Annals of the Kings of Judah? 29 In his days Pharaoh Neco king of Egypt went up to the king of Assyria to the river Euphrates. King Josiah went to meet him; but when Pharaoh Neco met him at Megiddo, he killed him. 30 His servants carried him dead in a chariot from Megiddo, brought him to Jerusalem, and buried him in his own tomb. The people of the land took Jehoahaz son of Josiah, anointed him, and made him king in place of his father.

Reign and Captivity of Jehoahaz

31 Jehoahaz was twenty-three years old when he began to reign; he reigned three months in Jerusalem. His mother's name was Hamutal daughter of Jeremiah of Libnah. 32 He did what was evil in the sight of the Lord, just as his ancestors had done. 33 Pharaoh Neco confined him at Riblah in the land of Hamath, so that he might not reign in Jerusalem, and imposed tribute on the land of one hundred talents of silver and a talent of gold. 34 Pharaoh Neco made Eliakim son of Josiah king in place of his father Josiah, and changed his name to Jehoiakim. But he took Jehoahaz away; he came to Egypt, and died there. 35 Jehoiakim gave the silver and the gold to Pharaoh, but he taxed the land in order to meet Pharaoh's demand for money. He exacted the silver and the gold from the people of the land,

23.17
1 Kings 13.1, 30
23.18
1 Kings 13.31
23.19
2 Chr 34.6, 7
23.20
2 Kings 10.25; 11.18;
2 Chr 34.5
23.21
2 Chr 35.1;
Ex 12.3;
Num 9.2;
Deut 16.2
23.22
2 Chr 35.18, 19
23.24
2 Kings 21.6, 11,21;
Deut 18.10-12
23.25
2 Kings 18.5
23.26
2 Kings 21.11, 12; Jer 15.4

23.27
2 Kings 18.11; 21.13,14
23.29
2 Chr 35.20; Zech 12.11
23.30
2 Chr 35.24; 36.1
23.31
1 Chr 3.15; Jer 22.11; 2 Kings 24.18
23.33
2 Kings 25.6; Jer 52.27; 2 Chr 36.3
23.34
2 Chr 36.4; 2 Kings 24.17; Ezek 19.3,4
23.35
v. 33

[1] Gk: Heb *proclaimed, who had predicted these things* m Or *household gods*

from all according to their assessment, to give it to Pharaoh Neco.

Jehoiakim Reigns over Judah

36 Jehoiakim was twenty-five years old when he began to reign; he reigned eleven years in Jerusalem. His mother's name was Zebidah daughter of Pedaiah of Rumah. [37] He did what was evil in the sight of the Lord, just as all his ancestors had done.

Judah Overrun by Enemies

24 In his days King Nebuchadnezzar of Babylon came up; Jehoiakim became his servant for three years; then he turned and rebelled against him. [2] The Lord sent against him bands of the Chaldeans, bands of the Arameans, bands of the Moabites, and bands of the Ammonites; he sent them against Judah to destroy it, according to the word of the Lord that he spoke by his servants the prophets. [3] Surely this came upon Judah at the command of the Lord, to remove them out of his sight, for the sins of Manasseh, for all that he had committed, [4] and also for the innocent blood that he had shed; for he filled Jerusalem with innocent blood, and the Lord was not willing to pardon. [5] Now the rest of the deeds of Jehoiakim, and all that he did, are they not written in the Book of the Annals of the Kings of Judah? [6] So Jehoiakim slept with his ancestors; then his son Jehoiachin succeeded him. [7] The king of Egypt did not come again out of his land, for the king of Babylon had taken over all that belonged to the king of Egypt from the Wadi of Egypt to the River Euphrates.

Reign and Captivity of Jehoiachin

8 Jehoiachin was eighteen years old when he began to reign; he reigned three months in Jerusalem. His mother's name was Nehushta daughter of Elnathan of Jerusalem. [9] He did what was evil in the sight of the Lord, just as his father had done.

10 At that time the servants of

King Nebuchadnezzar of Babylon came up to Jerusalem, and the city was besieged. [11] King Nebuchadnezzar of Babylon came to the city, while his servants were besieging it; [12] King Jehoiachin of Judah gave himself up to the king of Babylon, himself, his mother, his servants, his officers, and his palace officials. The king of Babylon took him prisoner in the eighth year of his reign.

Capture of Jerusalem

13 He carried off all the treasures of the house of the Lord, and the treasures of the king's house; he cut in pieces all the vessels of gold in the temple of the Lord, which King Solomon of Israel had made, all this as the Lord had foretold. [14] He carried away all Jerusalem, all the officials, all the warriors, ten thousand captives, all the artisans and the smiths; no one remained, except the poorest people of the land. [15] He carried away Jehoiachin to Babylon; the king's mother, the king's wives, his officials, and the elite of the land, he took into captivity from Jerusalem to Babylon. [16] The king of Babylon brought captive to Babylon all the men of valor, seven thousand, the artisans and the smiths, one thousand, all of them strong and fit for war. [17] The king of Babylon made Mattaniah, Jehoiachin's uncle, king in his place, and changed his name to Zedekiah.

Zedekiah Reigns over Judah

18 Zedekiah was twenty-one years old when he began to reign; he reigned eleven years in Jerusalem. His mother's name was Hamutal daughter of Jeremiah of Libnah. [19] He did what was evil in the sight of the Lord, just as Jehoiakim had done. [20] Indeed, Jerusalem and Judah so angered the Lord that he expelled them from his presence.

The Fall and Captivity of Judah

Zedekiah rebelled against the **25** king of Babylon. [1] And in the ninth year of his reign, in the tenth month, on the tenth

23.36
2 Chr 36.5
24.1
2 Chr 36.6;
Jer 25.1
24.2
Jer 25.9;
35.11;
2 Kings 23.27
24.3
2 Kings 18.25;
23.26
24.4
2 Kings 21.16
24.6
Jer 22.18,19
24.7
Jer 37.5-7;
46.2
24.8
1 Chr 3.16;
2 Chr 36.9
24.10
Dan 1.1

24.12
Jer 24.1;
29.1,2; 25.1;
2 Kings 25.27;
Jer 52.28
24.13
2 Kings 20.17;
Isa 39.6;
2 Kings 25.13-
15; Jer 20.5
24.14
Jer 24.1;
52.28;
2 Kings 25.12;
Jer 40.7
24.15
2 Chr 36.10;
Jer 22.24-28
24.16
Jer 52.28
24.17
Jer 37.1;
1 Chr 3.15;
2 Chr 36.4,
10
24.18
2 Chr 36.11;
Jer 52.1ff;
2 Kings 23.31
24.19
2 Chr 36.12
24.20
2 Chr 36.13
25.1
2 Chr 36.13,
17-20;
Jer 39.1-7;
Ezek 24.1,2

day of the month, King Nebuchadnezzar of Babylon came with all his army against Jerusalem, and laid siege to it; they built siegeworks against it all around. [2] So the city was besieged until the eleventh year of King Zedekiah. [3] On the ninth day of the fourth month the famine became so severe in the city that there was no food for the people of the land. [4] Then a breach was made in the city wall;[n] the king with all the soldiers fled[o] by night by the way of the gate between the two walls, by the king's garden, though the Chaldeans were all around the city. They went in the direction of the Arabah. [5] But the army of the Chaldeans pursued the king, and overtook him in the plains of Jericho; all his army was scattered, deserting him. [6] Then they captured the king and brought him up to the king of Babylon at Riblah, who passed sentence on him. [7] They slaughtered the sons of Zedekiah before his eyes, then put out the eyes of Zedekiah; they bound him in fetters and took him to Babylon.

8 In the fifth month, on the seventh day of the month—which was the nineteenth year of King Nebuchadnezzar, king of Babylon—Nebuzaradan, the captain of the bodyguard, a servant of the king of Babylon, came to Jerusalem. [9] He burned the house of the LORD, the king's house, and all the houses of Jerusalem; every great house he burned down. [10] All the army of the Chaldeans who were with the captain of the guard broke down the walls around Jerusalem. [11] Nebuzaradan the captain of the guard carried into exile the rest of the people who were left in the city and the deserters who had defected to the king of Babylon—all the rest of the population. [12] But the captain of the guard left some of the poorest people of the land to be vinedressers and tillers of the soil.

13 The bronze pillars that were in the house of the LORD, as well as the stands and the bronze sea that were in the house of the LORD, the

Chaldeans broke in pieces, and carried the bronze to Babylon. [14] They took away the pots, the shovels, the snuffers, the dishes for incense, and all the bronze vessels used in the temple service, [15] as well as the firepans and the basins. What was made of gold the captain of the guard took away for the gold, and what was made of silver, for the silver. [16] As for the two pillars, the one sea, and the stands, which Solomon had made for the house of the LORD, the bronze of all these vessels was beyond weighing. [17] The height of the one pillar was eighteen cubits, and on it was a bronze capital; the height of the capital was three cubits; latticework and pomegranates, all of bronze, were on the capital all around. The second pillar had the same, with the latticework.

18 The captain of the guard took the chief priest Seraiah, the second priest Zephaniah, and the three guardians of the threshold; [19] from the city he took an officer who had been in command of the soldiers, and five men of the king's council who were found in the city; the secretary who was the commander of the army who mustered the people of the land; and sixty men of the people of the land who were found in the city. [20] Nebuzaradan the captain of the guard took them, and brought them to the king of Babylon at Riblah. [21] The king of Babylon struck them down and put them to death at Riblah in the land of Hamath. So Judah went into exile out of its land.

Gedaliah Made Governor of Judah

22 He appointed Gedaliah son of Ahikam son of Shaphan as governor over the people who remained in the land of Judah, whom King Nebuchadnezzar of Babylon had left. [23] Now when all the captains of the forces and their men heard that the king of Babylon had appointed Gedaliah as governor,

25.3 Jer 39.1,2
25.4 Jer 39.4-7
25.6 Jer 34.21, 22;
2 Kings 23.33
25.7 Jer 39.6,7;
Ezek 12.13
25.8 Jer 52.12-14;
39.9
25.9 2 Chr 36.19;
Ps 74.3-7;
Am 2.5
25.10 Neh 1.3;
Jer 52.14
25.11 2 Chr 36.20;
Jer 39.9;
52.15
25.12 2 Kings 24.14;
Jer 40.7
25.13 2 Chr 36.18

25.14 1 Kings 7.47-50
25.16 1 Kings 7.47
25.17 1 Kings 7.15-22
25.18 1 Chr 6.14;
Ezra 7.1;
Jer 21.1;
29.25
25.21 Deut 28.64;
2 Kings 23.27
25.22 Jer 40.5
25.23 Jer 40.7-9

[n] Heb lacks *wall* [o] Gk Compare Jer 39.4;
52.7: Heb lacks *the king* and lacks *fled*

they came with their men to Gedaliah at Mizpah, namely, Ishmael son of Nethaniah, Johanan son of Kareah, Seraiah son of Tanhumeth the Netophathite, and Jaazaniah son of the Maacathite. ²⁴ Gedaliah swore to them and their men, saying, "Do not be afraid because of the Chaldean officials; live in the land, serve the king of Babylon, and it shall be well with you." ²⁵ But in the seventh month, Ishmael son of Nethaniah son of Elishama, of the royal family, came with ten men; they struck down Gedaliah so that he died, along with the Judeans and Chaldeans who were with him at Mizpah. ²⁶ Then all the people, high and low[p] and the captains of the forces set out and went to Egypt; for they were afraid of the Chaldeans.

25.25
Jer 41.1,2
25.26
Jer 43.4-7

25.27
Jer 52.31-34;
Gen 40.13,
20
25.29
2 Sam 9.7

Jehoiachin Released from Prison

27 In the thirty-seventh year of the exile of King Jehoiachin of Judah, in the twelfth month, on the twenty-seventh day of the month, King Evil-merodach of Babylon, in the year that he began to reign, released King Jehoiachin of Judah from prison; ²⁸ he spoke kindly to him, and gave him a seat above the other seats of the kings who were with him in Babylon. ²⁹ So Jehoiachin put aside his prison clothes. Every day of his life he dined regularly in the king's presence. ³⁰ For his allowance, a regular allowance was given him by the king, a portion every day, as long as he lived.

p Or *young and old*

1 Chronicles

Title and Background

The Hebrew title can be translated "the events (or annals) of the days (or years)." The Septuagint translators dubbed the book "the things omitted," indicating that they regarded it as a supplement to Samuel and Kings.

Author and Date of Writing

According to ancient Jewish tradition, Ezra wrote Chronicles, but this cannot be established with certainty. A growing consensus dates Chronicles in the latter half of the fifth century B.C., thus possibly within Ezra's lifetime. It must be acknowledged that the author, if not Ezra, at least shared many basic concerns with that reforming priest.

Theme and Message

Chronicles was written for the exiles who had returned to Israel after the Babylonian captivity, to remind them that they were still God's chosen people. The burning issue was the question of continuity with the past: Is God still interested in us? Are his covenants still in force? Now that we have no Davidic king and are subject to Persia, do God's promises to David still have meaning for us?

Outline

I. Genealogies: From Creation to Restoration (1.1–9.44)
II. The Death of Saul (10.1-14)
III. The Reign of David (11.1–29.30)

From Adam to Abraham

1 Adam, Seth, Enosh; [2]Kenan, Mahalalel, Jared; [3]Enoch, Methuselah, Lamech; [4]Noah, Shem, Ham, and Japheth.

5 The descendants of Japheth: Gomer, Magog, Madai, Javan, Tubal, Meshech, and Tiras. [6]The descendants of Gomer: Ashkenaz, Diphath,[a] and Togarmah. [7]The descendants of Javan: Elishah, Tarshish, Kittim, and Rodanim.[b]

8 The descendants of Ham: Cush, Egypt, Put, and Canaan. [9]The descendants of Cush: Seba, Havilah, Sabta, Raama, and Sabteca. The descendants of Raamah: Sheba and Dedan. [10]Cush became the father of Nimrod; he was the first to be a mighty one on the earth.

11 Egypt became the father of Ludim, Anamim, Lehabim, Naphtuhim, [12]Pathrusim, Casluhim, and Caphtorim, from whom the Philistines come.[c]

13 Canaan became the father of Sidon his firstborn, and Heth, [14]and the Jebusites, the Amorites, the Girgashites, [15]the Hivites, the Arkites, the Sinites, [16]the Arvadites, the Zemarites, and the Hamathites.

17 The descendants of Shem: Elam, Asshur, Arpachshad, Lud, Aram, Uz, Hul, Gether, and Meshech.[d] [18]Arpachshad became the father of Shelah; and Shelah became the father of Eber. [19]To Eber were born two sons: the name of the one was Peleg (for in his days the earth was divided), and the name of his brother Joktan. [20]Joktan became the father of Almodad, Sheleph, Hazarmaveth, Jerah,

1.1 Gen 4.25; 5.32
1.5 Gen 10.2-4
1.8 Gen 10.6ff
1.10 Gen 10.8, 13ff
1.17 Gen 10.22ff

a Gen 10.3 *Ripath;* See Gk Vg b Gen 10.4 *Dodanim;* See Syr Vg c Heb *Casluhim, from which the Philistines come, Caphtorim;* See Am 9.7, Jer 47.4 d *Mash* in Gen 10.23

²¹ Hadoram, Uzal, Diklah, ²² Ebal, Abimael, Sheba, ²³ Ophir, Havilah, and Jobab; all these were the descendants of Joktan.

24 Shem, Arpachshad, Shelah; ²⁵ Eber, Peleg, Reu; ²⁶ Serug, Nahor, Terah; ²⁷ Abram, that is, Abraham.

From Abraham to Jacob

28 The sons of Abraham: Isaac and Ishmael. ²⁹ These are their genealogies: the firstborn of Ishmael, Nebaioth; and Kedar, Adbeel, Mibsam, ³⁰ Mishma, Dumah, Massa, Hadad, Tema, ³¹ Jetur, Naphish, and Kedemah. These are the sons of Ishmael. ³² The sons of Keturah, Abraham's concubine: she bore Zimran, Jokshan, Medan, Midian, Ishbak, and Shuah. The sons of Jokshan: Sheba and Dedan. ³³ The sons of Midian: Ephah, Epher, Hanoch, Abida, and Eldaah. All these were the descendants of Keturah.

34 Abraham became the father of Isaac. The sons of Isaac: Esau and Israel. ³⁵ The sons of Esau: Eliphaz, Reuel, Jeush, Jalam, and Korah. ³⁶ The sons of Eliphaz: Teman, Omar, Zephi, Gatam, Kenaz, Timna, and Amalek. ³⁷ The sons of Reuel: Nahath, Zerah, Shammah, and Mizzah.

38 The sons of Seir: Lotan, Shobal, Zibeon, Anah, Dishon, Ezer, and Dishan. ³⁹ The sons of Lotan: Hori and Homam; and Lotan's sister was Timna. ⁴⁰ The sons of Shobal: Alian, Manahath, Ebal, Shephi, and Onam. The sons of Zibeon: Aiah and Anah. ⁴¹ The sons of Anah: Dishon. The sons of Dishon: Hamran, Eshban, Ithran, and Cheran. ⁴² The sons of Ezer: Bilhan, Zaavan, and Jaakan.^e The sons of Dishan:^f Uz and Aran.

43 These are the kings who reigned in the land of Edom before any king reigned over the Israelites: Bela son of Beor, whose city was called Dinhabah. ⁴⁴ When Bela died, Jobab son of Zerah of Bozrah succeeded him. ⁴⁵ When Jobab died, Husham of the land of the Temanites succeeded him. ⁴⁶ When Husham died, Hadad son of Bedad, who defeated Midian in the country of Moab, succeeded him; and the name of his city was Avith. ⁴⁷ When Hadad died, Samlah of Masrekah succeeded him. ⁴⁸ When Samlah died, Shaul^g of Rehoboth on the Euphrates succeeded him. ⁴⁹ When Shaul^g died, Baal-hanan son of Achbor succeeded him. ⁵⁰ When Baal-hanan died, Hadad succeeded him; the name of his city was Pai, and his wife's name Mehetabel daughter of Matred, daughter of Me-zahab. ⁵¹ And Hadad died.

The clans^h of Edom were: clans^h Timna, Aliah,ⁱ Jetheth, ⁵² Oholibamah, Elah, Pinon, ⁵³ Kenaz, Teman, Mibzar, ⁵⁴ Magdiel, and Iram; these are the clans^h of Edom.

The Sons of Israel and the Descendants of Judah

2 These are the sons of Israel: Reuben, Simeon, Levi, Judah, Issachar, Zebulun, ² Dan, Joseph, Benjamin, Naphtali, Gad, and Asher. ³ The sons of Judah: Er, Onan, and Shelah; these three the Canaanite woman Bath-shua bore to him. Now Er, Judah's firstborn, was wicked in the sight of the LORD, and he put him to death. ⁴ His daughter-in-law Tamar also bore him Perez and Zerah. Judah had five sons in all.

5 The sons of Perez: Hezron and Hamul. ⁶ The sons of Zerah: Zimri, Ethan, Heman, Calcol, and Dara,ⁱ five in all. ⁷ The sons of Carmi: Achar, the troubler of Israel, who transgressed in the matter of the devoted thing; ⁸ and Ethan's son was Azariah.

9 The sons of Hezron, who were born to him: Jerahmeel, Ram, and Chelubai. ¹⁰ Ram became the father of Amminadab, and Amminadab became the father of Nahshon, prince of the sons of Judah. ¹¹ Nahshon became the father of Salma, Salma of Boaz, ¹² Boaz of Obed,

1.24
Gen 11.10ff
1.29
Gen 25.13-16
1.32
Gen 25.1-4
1.34
Gen 21.2,3;
25.25,26
1.35
Gen 36.9,10
1.38
Gen 36.20-28
1.43
Gen 36.31-43

2.1
Gen 35.23-26;
46.8-25
2.2
Gen 38.2-10
2.4
Gen 38.29,
30
2.5
Gen 46.12
2.6
Josh 7.1;
1 Kings 4.31
2.7
Josh 6.18;
7.1
2.10
Ruth 4.19,
20; Mt 1.4

e Or and Akan; See Gen 36.27 f See 1.38: Heb Dishon g Or Saul h Or chiefs i Or Alvah; See Gen 36.40 j Or Darda; Compare Syr Tg some Gk Mss; See 1 Kings 4.31

RULERS OF ISRAEL AND JUDAH

Biblical References	Kings	Years of Reign	Dates of Reign	Notes
1. 1 Ki 12:1-24 14:21-31	Rehoboam (J)	17 years	930-913	
2. 1 Ki 12:25–14:20	Jeroboam I (I)	22 years	930-909	
3. 1 Ki 15:1-8	Abijah (J)	3 years	913-910	
4. 1 Ki 15:9-24	Asa (J)	41 years	910-869	
5. 1 Ki 15:25-31	Nadab (I)	2 years	909-908	
6. 1 Ki 15:32–16:7	Baasha (I)	24 years	908-886	
7. 1 Ki 16:8-14	Elah (I)	2 years	886-885	
8. 1 Ki 16:15-20	Zimri (I)	7 days	885	
9. 1 Ki 16:21-22	Tibni (I)		885-880	Overlap with Omri
10. 1 Ki 16:23-28	Omri (I)		885	Made king by the people
			885-880	Overlap with Tibni
		12 years	885-874	Official reign = 11 actual years
11. 1 Ki 16:29–22:40	Ahab (I)	22 years	874-853	Official reign = 21 actual years
12. 1 Ki 22:41-50	Jehoshaphat (J)		872-869	Co-regency with Asa
		25 years	872-848	Official reign
			869	Beginning of sole reign
			853-848	Has Jehoram as regent
13. 1 Ki 22:51–2 Ki 1:18	Ahaziah (I)	2 years	853-852	Official reign = 1 yr. actual reign
14. 2 Ki 1:17 2 Ki 3:1–8:15	Joram (I)		852	
		12 years	852-841	Official reign = 11 actual years
15. 2 Ki 8:16-24	Jehoram (J)		848	Beginning of sole reign
		8 years	848-841	Official reign = 7 actual years
16. 2 Ki 8:25-29	Ahaziah (J)	1 year	841	Nonaccession-year reckoning
2 Ki 9:29			841	Accession-year reckoning
17. 2 Ki 9:30–10:36	Jehu (I)	28 years	841-814	
18. 2 Ki 11	Athaliah (J)	7 years	841-835	
19. 2 Ki 12	Josah (J)	40 years	835-796	
20. 2 Ki 13:1-9	Jehoahaz (I)	17 years	814-798	
21. 2 Ki 13:10-25	Jehoash (I)	16 years	798-782	

Biblical References	Kings	Years of Reign	Dates of Reign	Notes
22. 2 Ki 14:1-22	**Amaziah** (J)	29 years	**796-767**	
			792-767	Overlap with Azariah
23. 2 Ki 14:23-29	Jeroboam II (I)		**793-782**	Co-regency with Jehoash
		41 years	**793-753**	Total reign
24. 2 Ki 15:1-7	**Azariah** (J)		792-767	Overlap with Amaziah
		52 years	**792-740**	Total reign
			767	Beginning of sole reign
25. 2 Ki 15:8-12	Zechariah (I)	6 months	**753**	
26. 2 Ki 15:13-15	Shallum (I)	1 month	**752**	
27. 2 Ki 15:16-22	Menahem (I)	10 years	**752-742**	Ruled in Samaria
28. 2 Ki 15:23-26	Pekahiah (I)	2 years	**742-740**	
29. 2 Ki 15:27-31	Pekah (I)		752-740	In Gilead; overlapping years
		20 years	**752-732**	Total reign
			740	Beginning of sole reign
30. 2 Ki 15:32-38 2 Ki 15:30	**Jotham** (J)		750-740	Co-regency with Azariah
		16 years	**750-735**	Official reign
			750-732	Reign to his 20th year
			750	Beginning of co-regency
31. 2 Ki 16	**Ahaz** (J)		735-715	Total reign
		16 years	**732-715**	From 20th of Jotham
32. 2 Ki 15:30 2 Ki 17	Hoshea (I)		732	20th of Jotham
		9 years	**732-722**	
33. 2 Ki 18:1–20:21	**Hezekiah** (J)	29 years	**715-686**	
34. 2 Ki 21:1-18	**Manasseh** (J)		697-686	Co-regency with Hezekiah
		55 years	697-642	Total reign
35. 2 Ki 21:19-26	**Amon** (J)	2 years	**642-640**	
36. 2 Ki 22:1–23:30	**Josiah** (J)	31 years	**640-609**	
37. 2 Ki 23:31-33	**Jehoahaz** (J)	3 months	**609**	
38. 2 Ki 23:34–24:7	**Jehoiakim** (J)	11 years	**609-598**	
39. 2 Ki 24:8-17	**Jehoiachin** (J)	3 months	**598-597**	
40. 2 Ki 24:18–25:26	**Zedekiah** (J)	11 years	**597-586**	

Data and dates in order of sequence
(J) Italics denote kings of **Judah**. (I) non-italic type denotes kings of **Israel**.
Adapted from: *A Chronology of the Hebrew Kings* by Edwin R. Thiele.
© 1977 by The Zondervan Corporation. Used by permission.

Obed of Jesse. ¹³Jesse became the father of Eliab his firstborn, Abinadab the second, Shimea the third, ¹⁴Nethanel the fourth, Raddai the fifth, ¹⁵Ozem the sixth, David the seventh; ¹⁶and their sisters were Zeruiah and Abigail. The sons of Zeruiah: Abishai, Joab, and Asahel, three. ¹⁷Abigail bore Amasa, and the father of Amasa was Jether the Ishmaelite.

18 Caleb son of Hezron had children by his wife Azubah, and by Jerioth; these were her sons: Jesher, Shobab, and Ardon. ¹⁹When Azubah died, Caleb married Ephrath, who bore him Hur. ²⁰Hur became the father of Uri, and Uri became the father of Bezalel.

21 Afterward Hezron went in to the daughter of Machir father of Gilead, whom he married when he was sixty years old; and she bore him Segub; ²²and Segub became the father of Jair, who had twenty-three towns in the land of Gilead. ²³But Geshur and Aram took from them Havvoth-jair, Kenath and its villages, sixty towns. All these were descendants of Machir, father of Gilead. ²⁴After the death of Hezron, in Caleb-ephrathah, Abijah wife of Hezron bore him Ashhur, father of Tekoa.

25 The sons of Jerahmeel, the firstborn of Hezron: Ram his firstborn, Bunah, Oren, Ozem, and Ahijah. ²⁶Jerahmeel also had another wife, whose name was Atarah; she was the mother of Onam. ²⁷The sons of Ram, the firstborn of Jerahmeel: Maaz, Jamin, and Eker. ²⁸The sons of Onam: Shammai and Jada. The sons of Shammai: Nadab and Abishur. ²⁹The name of Abishur's wife was Abihail, and she bore him Ahban and Molid. ³⁰The sons of Nadab: Seled and Appaim; and Seled died childless. ³¹The sonᵏ of Appaim: Ishi. The sonᵏ of Ishi: Sheshan. The sonᵏ of Sheshan: Ahlai. ³²The sons of Jada, Shammai's brother: Jether and Jonathan; and Jether died childless. ³³The sons of Jonathan: Peleth and Zaza. These were the descendants of Jerahmeel. ³⁴Now

Sheshan had no sons, only daughters; but Sheshan had an Egyptian slave, whose name was Jarha. ³⁵So Sheshan gave his daughter in marriage to his slave Jarha; and she bore him Attai. ³⁶Attai became the father of Nathan, and Nathan of Zabad. ³⁷Zabad became the father of Ephlal, and Ephlal of Obed. ³⁸Obed became the father of Jehu, and Jehu of Azariah. ³⁹Azariah became the father of Helez, and Helez of Eleasah. ⁴⁰Eleasah became the father of Sismai, and Sismai of Shallum. ⁴¹Shallum became the father of Jekamiah, and Jekamiah of Elishama.

42 The sons of Caleb brother of Jerahmeel: Meshaˡ his firstborn, who was father of Ziph. The sons of Mareshah father of Hebron. ⁴³The sons of Hebron: Korah, Tappuah, Rekem, and Shema. ⁴⁴Shema became father of Raham, father of Jorkeam; and Rekem became the father of Shammai. ⁴⁵The son of Shammai: Maon; and Maon was the father of Beth-zur. ⁴⁶Ephah also, Caleb's concubine, bore Haran, Moza, and Gazez; and Haran became the father of Gazez. ⁴⁷The sons of Jahdai: Regem, Jotham, Geshan, Pelet, Ephah, and Shaaph. ⁴⁸Maacah, Caleb's concubine, bore Sheber and Tirhanah. ⁴⁹She also bore Shaaph father of Madmannah, Sheva father of Machbenah and father of Gibea; and the daughter of Caleb was Achsah. ⁵⁰These were the descendants of Caleb.

The sonsᵐ of Hur the firstborn of Ephrathah: Shobal father of Kiriath-jearim, ⁵¹Salma father of Bethlehem, and Hareph father of Beth-gader. ⁵²Shobal father of Kiriath-jearim had other sons: Haroeh, half of the Menuhoth. ⁵³And the families of Kiriath-jearim: the Ithrites, the Puthites, the Shumathites, and the Mishraites; from these came the Zorathites and the Eshtaolites. ⁵⁴The sons of Salma: Bethlehem, the Netophathites, Atroth-beth-joab, and half of the

2.13
1 Sam 16.6, 9
2.16
2 Sam 2.18
2.17
2 Sam 17.25
2.19
v. 50
2.20
Ex 31.2
2.21
Num 27.1
2.23
Num 32.41;
Deut 3.14;
Josh 13.30
2.24
1 Chr 4.5
2.31
vv. 34,35

2.36
1 Chr 11.41
2.42
1 Chr 2.18, 19
2.50
1 Chr 4.4

ᵏHeb sons ˡGk reads Mareshah
ᵐGk Vg: Heb son

Manahathites, the Zorites. [55] The families also of the scribes that lived at Jabez: the Tirathites, the Shimeathites, and the Sucathites. These are the Kenites who came from Hammath, father of the house of Rechab.

Descendants of David and Solomon

3 These are the sons of David who were born to him in Hebron: the firstborn Amnon, by Ahinoam the Jezreelite; the second Daniel, by Abigail the Carmelite; [2] the third Absalom, son of Maacah, daughter of King Talmai of Geshur; the fourth Adonijah, son of Haggith; [3] the fifth Shephatiah, by Abital; the sixth Ithream, by his wife Eglah; [4] six were born to him in Hebron, where he reigned for seven years and six months. And he reigned thirty-three years in Jerusalem. [5] These were born to him in Jerusalem: Shimea, Shobab, Nathan, and Solomon, four by Bathshua, daughter of Ammiel; [6] then Ibhar, Elishama, Eliphelet, [7] Nogah, Nepheg, Japhia, [8] Elishama, Eliada, and Eliphelet, nine. [9] All these were David's sons, besides the sons of the concubines; and Tamar was their sister.

10 The descendants of Solomon: Rehoboam, Abijah his son, Asa his son, Jehoshaphat his son, [11] Joram his son, Ahaziah his son, Joash his son, [12] Amaziah his son, Azariah his son, Jotham his son, [13] Ahaz his son, Hezekiah his son, Manasseh his son, [14] Amon his son, Josiah his son. [15] The sons of Josiah: Johanan the firstborn, the second Jehoiakim, the third Zedekiah, the fourth Shallum. [16] The descendants of Jehoiakim: Jeconiah his son, Zedekiah his son; [17] and the sons of Jeconiah, the captive: Shealtiel his son, [18] Malchiram, Pedaiah, Shenazzar, Jekamiah, Hoshama, and Nedabiah; [19] The sons of Pedaiah: Zerubbabel and Shimei; and the sons of Zerubbabel: Meshullam and Hananiah, and Shelomith was their sister; [20] and Hashubah, Ohel, Berechiah, Hasadiah,

and Jushab-hesed, five. [21] The sons of Hananiah: Pelatiah and Jeshaiah, his son[n] Rephaiah, his son[n] Arnan, his son[n] Obadiah, his son[n] Shecaniah. [22] The son[o] of Shecaniah: Shemaiah. And the sons of Shemaiah: Hattush, Igal, Bariah, Neariah, and Shaphat, six. [23] The sons of Neariah: Elioenai, Hizkiah, and Azrikam, three. [24] The sons of Elioenai: Hodaviah, Eliashib, Pelaiah, Akkub, Johanan, Delaiah, and Anani, seven.

Descendants of Judah

4 The sons of Judah: Perez, Hezron, Carmi, Hur, and Shobal. [2] Reaiah son of Shobal became the father of Jahath, and Jahath became the father of Ahumai and Lahad. These were the families of the Zorathites. [3] These were the sons[p] of Etam: Jezreel, Ishma, and Idbash; and the name of their sister was Hazzelelponi, [4] and Penuel was the father of Gedor, and Ezer the father of Hushah. These were the sons of Hur, the firstborn of Ephrathah, the father of Bethlehem. [5] Ashhur father of Tekoa had two wives, Helah and Naarah; [6] Naarah bore him Ahuzzam, Hepher, Temeni, and Haahashtari.[q] These were the sons of Naarah. [7] The sons of Helah: Zereth, Izhar,[r] and Ethnan. [8] Koz became the father of Anub, Zobebah, and the families of Aharhel son of Harum. [9] Jabez was honored more than his brothers; and his mother named him Jabez, saying, "Because I bore him in pain." [10] Jabez called on the God of Israel, saying, "Oh that you would bless me and enlarge my border, and that your hand might be with me, and that you would keep me from hurt and harm!" And God granted what he asked. [11] Chelub the brother of Shuhah became the father of Mehir, who was the father of Eshton. [12] Eshton became the father of Beth-rapha, Paseah, and Tehinnah the father of Irnahash. These are

2.55
Judg 1.16;
Jer 35.2
3.1
2 Sam 3.2,
3;
Josh 15.56
3.3
2 Sam 3.5
3.4
2 Sam 2.11;
5.5
3.5
2 Sam 5.14-16;
2 Sam 12.24;
11.3
3.9
2 Sam 13.1
3.10
1 Kings 11.43
3.16
Mt 1.11

3.22
Ezek 8.2
4.1
Gen 46.12
4.4
1 Chr 2.50
4.5
1 Chr 2.24
4.9
Gen 34.19

n Gk Compare Syr Vg: Heb *sons of*
o Heb *sons* p Gk Compare Vg: Heb *the father* q Or *Ahashtari* r Another reading is *Zohar*

the men of Recah. 13 The sons of Kenaz: Othniel and Seraiah; and the sons of Othniel: Hathath and Meonothai.s 14 Meonothai became the father of Ophrah; and Seraiah became the father of Joab father of Ge-harashim,t so-called because they were artisans. 15 The sons of Caleb son of Jephunneh: Iru, Elah, and Naam; and the sonu of Elah: Kenaz. 16 The sons of Jehallelel: Ziph, Ziphah, Tiria, and Asarel. 17 The sons of Ezrah: Jether, Mered, Epher, and Jalon. These are the sons of Bithiah, daughter of Pharaoh, whom Mered married;v and she conceived and borew Miriam, Shammai, and Ishbah father of Eshtemoa. 18 And his Judean wife bore Jered father of Gedor, Heber father of Soco, and Jekuthiel father of Zanoah. 19 The sons of the wife of Hodiah, the sister of Naham, were the fathers of Keilah the Garmite and Eshtemoa the Maacathite. 20 The sons of Shimon: Amnon, Rinnah, Ben-hanan, and Tilon. The sons of Ishi: Zoheth and Ben-zoheth. 21 The sons of Shelah son of Judah: Er father of Lecah, Laadah father of Mareshah, and the families of the guild of linen workers at Beth-ashbea; 22 and Jokim, and the men of Cozeba, and Joash, and Saraph, who married into Moab but returned to Lehemx (now the recordsy are ancient). 23 These were the potters and inhabitants of Netaim and Gederah; they lived there with the king in his service.

Descendants of Simeon

24 The sons of Simeon: Nemuel, Jamin, Jarib, Zerah, Shaul;z 25 Shallum was his son, Mibsam his son, Mishma his son. 26 The sons of Mishma: Hammuel his son, Zaccur his son, Shimei his son. 27 Shimei had sixteen sons and six daughters; but his brothers did not have many children, nor did all their family multiply like the Judeans. 28 They lived in Beer-sheba, Moladah, Hazar-shual, 29 Bilhah, Ezem, Tolad, 30 Bethuel, Hormah, Ziklag, 31 Beth-marcaboth, Hazar-susim, Beth-biri, and Shaaraim. These

4.13
Josh 15.17
4.14
Neh 11.35
4.21
Gen 38.1,5
4.24
Gen 29.33
4.28
Josh 19.2
4.30
1 Chr 12.1

4.40
Judg 18.7-10
4.41
2 Kings 18.8
4.43
1 Sam 15.8;
30.17;
2 Sam 8.12
5.1f
Gen 29.32;
35.22; 49.4;
48.15,22
5.2
Gen 49.8,
10; Mic 5.2;
Mt 2.6

were their towns until David became king. 32 And their villages were Etam, Ain, Rimmon, Tochen, and Ashan, five towns, 33 along with all their villages that were around these towns as far as Baal. These were their settlements. And they kept a genealogical record.

34 Meshobab, Jamlech, Joshah son of Amaziah, 35 Joel, Jehu son of Joshibiah son of Seraiah son of Asiel, 36 Elioenai, Jaakobah, Jeshohaiah, Asaiah, Adiel, Jesimiel, Benaiah, 37 Ziza son of Shiphi son of Allon son of Jedaiah son of Shimri son of Shemaiah— 38 these mentioned by name were leaders in their families, and their clans increased greatly. 39 They journeyed to the entrance of Gedor, to the east side of the valley, to seek pasture for their flocks, 40 where they found rich, good pasture, and the land was very broad, quiet, and peaceful; for the former inhabitants there belonged to Ham. 41 These, registered by name, came in the days of King Hezekiah of Judah, and attacked their tents and the Meunim who were found there, and exterminated them to this day, and settled in their place, because there was pasture there for their flocks. 42 And some of them, five hundred men of the Simeonites, went to Mount Seir, having as their leaders Pelatiah, Neariah, Rephaiah, and Uzziel, sons of Ishi; 43 they destroyed the remnant of the Amalekites that had escaped, and they have lived there to this day.

Descendants of Reuben

5 The sons of Reuben the firstborn of Israel. (He was the firstborn, but because he defiled his father's bed his birthright was given to the sons of Joseph son of Israel, so that he is not enrolled in the genealogy according to the birthright; 2 though Judah became prominent among his brothers and

s Gk Vg: Heb lacks and Meonothai t That is Valley of artisans u Heb sons v The clause: These are . . . married is transposed from verse 18 w Heb lacks and bore x Vg Compare Gk: Heb and Jashubi-lahem y Or matters z Or Saul

a ruler came from him, yet the birthright belonged to Joseph.) ³The sons of Reuben, the firstborn of Israel: Hanoch, Pallu, Hezron, and Carmi. ⁴The sons of Joel: Shemaiah his son, Gog his son, Shimei his son, ⁵Micah his son, Reaiah his son, Baal his son, ⁶Beerah his son, whom King Tilgath-pilneser of Assyria carried away into exile; he was a chieftain of the Reubenites. ⁷And his kindred by their families, when the genealogy of their generations was reckoned: the chief, Jeiel, and Zechariah, ⁸and Bela son of Azaz, son of Shema, son of Joel, who lived in Aroer, as far as Nebo and Baal-meon. ⁹He also lived to the east as far as the beginning of the desert this side of the Euphrates, because their cattle had multiplied in the land of Gilead. ¹⁰And in the days of Saul they made war on the Hagrites, who fell by their hand; and they lived in their tents throughout all the region east of Gilead.

Descendants of Gad

11 The sons of Gad lived beside them in the land of Bashan as far as Salecah: ¹²Joel the chief, Shapham the second, Janai, and Shaphat in Bashan. ¹³And their kindred according to their clans: Michael, Meshullam, Sheba, Jorai, Jacan, Zia, and Eber, seven. ¹⁴These were the sons of Abihail son of Huri, son of Jaroah, son of Gilead, son of Michael, son of Jeshishai, son of Jahdo, son of Buz; ¹⁵Ahi son of Abdiel, son of Guni, was chief in their clan; ¹⁶and they lived in Gilead, in Bashan and in its towns, and in all the pasture lands of Sharon to their limits. ¹⁷All of these were enrolled by genealogies in the days of King Jotham of Judah, and in the days of King Jeroboam of Israel.

18 The Reubenites, the Gadites, and the half-tribe of Manasseh had valiant warriors, who carried shield and sword, and drew the bow, expert in war, forty-four thousand seven hundred sixty, ready for service. ¹⁹They made war on the Hagrites, Jetur, Naphish, and Nodab;

²⁰and when they received help against them, the Hagrites and all who were with them were given into their hands, for they cried to God in the battle, and he granted their entreaty because they trusted in him. ²¹They captured their livestock: fifty thousand of their camels, two hundred fifty thousand sheep, two thousand donkeys, and one hundred thousand captives. ²²Many fell slain, because the war was of God. And they lived in their territory until the exile.

The Half-Tribe of Manasseh

23 The members of the half-tribe of Manasseh lived in the land; they were very numerous from Bashan to Baal-hermon, Senir, and Mount Hermon. ²⁴These were the heads of their clans: Epher,ᵃ Ishi, Eliel, Azriel, Jeremiah, Hodaviah, and Jahdiel, mighty warriors, famous men, heads of their clans. ²⁵But they transgressed against the God of their ancestors, and prostituted themselves to the gods of the peoples of the land, whom God had destroyed before them. ²⁶So the God of Israel stirred up the spirit of King Pul of Assyria, the spirit of King Tilgath-pilneser of Assyria, and he carried them away, namely, the Reubenites, the Gadites, and the half-tribe of Manasseh, and brought them to Halah, Habor, Hara, and the river Gozan, to this day.

Descendants of Levi

6ᵇ The sons of Levi: Gershom,ᶜ Kohath, and Merari. ²The sons of Kohath: Amram, Izhar, Hebron, and Uzziel. ³The children of Amram: Aaron, Moses, and Miriam. The sons of Aaron: Nadab, Abihu, Eleazar, and Ithamar. ⁴Eleazar became the father of Phinehas, Phinehas of Abishua, ⁵Abishua of Bukki, Bukki of Uzzi, ⁶Uzzi of Zerahiah, Zerahiah of Meraioth, ⁷Meraioth of Amariah, Amariah of Ahitub, ⁸Ahitub of Zadok, Zadok of Ahimaaz, ⁹Ahimaaz of Azariah, Az-

Cross-references (center column)

5.3 Gen 46.9; Num 26.5
5.7 v. 17
5.8 Josh 13.15, 16
5.9 Josh 22.9
5.10 vv. 18-21
5.11 Josh 13.11, 24
5.16 1 Chr 27.29
5.17 2 Kings 15.5, 32; 14.16,28
5.19 v. 10; 1 Chr 1.31
5.20 2 Chr 4.11-13; Ps 22.4,5
5.22 2 Kings 15.29; 17.6
5.25 2 Kings 17.7
5.26 2 Kings 15.19, 29; 17.6; 18.11
6.1 Ex 6.16; Num 26.57; 1 Chr 23.6
6.3 Lev 10.1
6.8 2 Sam 8.17; 15.27

ᵃ Gk Vg: Heb *and Epher*　ᵇ Ch 5.27 in Heb
ᶜ Heb *Gershon*, variant of *Gershom*; See 6.16

ariah of Johanan, [10] and Johanan of Azariah (it was he who served as priest in the house that Solomon built in Jerusalem). [11] Azariah became the father of Amariah, Amariah of Ahitub, [12] Ahitub of Zadok, Zadok of Shallum, [13] Shallum of Hilkiah, Hilkiah of Azariah, [14] Azariah of Seraiah, Seraiah of Jehozadak; [15] and Jehozadak went into exile when the LORD sent Judah and Jerusalem into exile by the hand of Nebuchadnezzar.

[16] [d] The sons of Levi: Gershom, Kohath, and Merari. [17] These are the names of the sons of Gershom: Libni and Shimei. [18] The sons of Kohath: Amram, Izhar, Hebron, and Uzziel. [19] The sons of Merari: Mahli and Mushi. These are the clans of the Levites according to their ancestry. [20] Of Gershom: Libni his son, Jahath his son, Zimmah his son, [21] Joah his son, Iddo his son, Zerah his son, Jeatherai his son. [22] The sons of Kohath: Amminadab his son, Korah his son, Assir his son, [23] Elkanah his son, Ebiasaph his son, Assir his son, [24] Tahath his son, Uriel his son, Uzziah his son, and Shaul his son. [25] The sons of Elkanah: Amasai and Ahimoth, [26] Elkanah his son, Zophai his son, Nahath his son, [27] Eliab his son, Jeroham his son, Elkanah his son. [28] The sons of Samuel: Joel[e] his firstborn, the second Abijah.[f] [29] The sons of Merari: Mahli, Libni his son, Shimei his son, Uzzah his son, [30] Shimea his son, Haggiah his son, and Asaiah his son.

Musicians Appointed by David

[31] These are the men whom David put in charge of the service of song in the house of the LORD, after the ark came to rest there. [32] They ministered with song before the tabernacle of the tent of meeting, until Solomon had built the house of the LORD in Jerusalem; and they performed their service in due order. [33] These are the men who served; and their sons were: Of the Kohathites: Heman, the singer, son of Joel, son of Samuel, [34] son of Elkanah, son of Jeroham, son of

Eliel, son of Toah, [35] son of Zuph, son of Elkanah, son of Mahath, son of Amasai, [36] son of Elkanah, son of Joel, son of Azariah, son of Zephaniah, [37] son of Tahath, son of Assir, son of Ebiasaph, son of Korah, [38] son of Izhar, son of Kohath, son of Levi, son of Israel; [39] and his brother Asaph, who stood on his right, namely, Asaph son of Berechiah, son of Shimea, [40] son of Michael, son of Baaseiah, son of Malchijah, [41] son of Ethni, son of Zerah, son of Adaiah, [42] son of Ethan, son of Zimmah, son of Shimei, [43] son of Jahath, son of Gershom, son of Levi. [44] On the left were their kindred the sons of Merari: Ethan son of Kishi, son of Abdi, son of Malluch, [45] son of Hashabiah, son of Amaziah, son of Hilkiah, [46] son of Amzi, son of Bani, son of Shemer, [47] son of Mahli, son of Mushi, son of Merari, son of Levi; [48] and their kindred the Levites were appointed for all the service of the tabernacle of the house of God.

49 But Aaron and his sons made offerings on the altar of burnt offering and on the altar of incense, doing all the work of the most holy place, to make atonement for Israel, according to all that Moses the servant of God had commanded. [50] These are the sons of Aaron: Eleazar his son, Phinehas his son, Abishua his son, [51] Bukki his son, Uzzi his son, Zerahiah his son, [52] Meraioth his son, Amariah his son, Ahitub his son, [53] Zadok his son, Ahimaaz his son.

Settlements of the Levites

54 These are their dwelling places according to their settlements within their borders: to the sons of Aaron of the families of Kohathites—for the lot fell to them first— [55] to them they gave Hebron in the land of Judah and its surrounding pasture lands, [56] but the fields of the city and its villages

6.14
Neh 11.11
6.15
2 Kings 25.18
6.16
Ex 6.16
6.20
v. 42
6.25
vv. 35,36
6.26
v. 34
6.31
1 Chr 15.16-
16.6

6.37
Ex 6.24
6.41
v. 21
6.49
Ex 27.1-8;
30.1-7,10
6.50
vv. 4-8
6.54
Josh 21.4,
10
6.55
Josh 21.11,
12
6.56
Josh 14.13;
15.13

d Ch 6.1 in Heb e Gk Syr Compare verse 33 and 1 Sam 8.2: Heb lacks *Joel*
f Heb reads *Vashni, and Abijah* for *the second Abijah*, taking *the second* as a proper name

they gave to Caleb son of Jephunneh. 57To the sons of Aaron they gave the cities of refuge: Hebron, Libnah with its pasture lands, Jattir, Eshtemoa with its pasture lands, 58Hilenᵍ with its pasture lands, Debir with its pasture lands, 59Ashan with its pasture lands, and Beth-shemesh with its pasture lands. 60From the tribe of Benjamin, Geba with its pasture lands, Alemeth with its pasture lands, and Anathoth with its pasture lands. All their towns throughout their families were thirteen.

61 To the rest of the Kohathites were given by lot out of the family of the tribe, out of the half-tribe, the half of Manasseh, ten towns. 62To the Gershomites according to their families were allotted thirteen towns out of the tribes of Issachar, Asher, Naphtali, and Manasseh in Bashan. 63To the Merarites according to their families were allotted twelve towns out of the tribes of Reuben, Gad, and Zebulun. 64So the people of Israel gave the Levites the towns with their pasture lands. 65They also gave them by lot out of the tribes of Judah, Simeon, and Benjamin these towns that are mentioned by name.

66 And some of the families of the sons of Kohath had towns of their territory out of the tribe of Ephraim. 67They were given the cities of refuge: Shechem with its pasture lands in the hill country of Ephraim, Gezer with its pasture lands, 68Jokmeam with its pasture lands, Beth-horon with its pasture lands, 69Aijalon with its pasture lands, Gath-rimmon with its pasture lands; 70and out of the half-tribe of Manasseh, Aner with its pasture lands, and Bileam with its pasture lands, for the rest of the families of the Kohathites.

71 To the Gershomites: out of the half-tribe of Manasseh: Golan in Bashan with its pasture lands and Ashtaroth with its pasture lands; 72and out of the tribe of Issachar: Kedesh with its pasture lands, Daberathʰ with its pasture lands, 73Ramoth with its pasture

lands, and Anem with its pasture lands; 74out of the tribe of Asher: Mashal with its pasture lands, Abdon with its pasture lands, 75Hukok with its pasture lands, and Rehob with its pasture lands; 76and out of the tribe of Naphtali: Kedesh in Galilee with its pasture lands, Hammon with its pasture lands, and Kiriathaim with its pasture lands. 77To the rest of the Merarites out of the tribe of Zebulun: Rimmono with its pasture lands, Tabor with its pasture lands, 78and across the Jordan from Jericho, on the east side of the Jordan, out of the tribe of Reuben: Bezer in the steppe with its pasture lands, Jahzah with its pasture lands, 79Kedemoth with its pasture lands, and Mephaath with its pasture lands; 80and out of the tribe of Gad: Ramoth in Gilead with its pasture lands, Mahanaim with its pasture lands, 81Heshbon with its pasture lands, and Jazer with its pasture lands.

Descendants of Issachar

7 The sonsⁱ of Issachar: Tola, Puah, Jashub, and Shimron, four. 2The sons of Tola: Uzzi, Rephaiah, Jeriel, Jahmai, Ibsam, and Shemuel, heads of their ancestral houses, namely of Tola, mighty warriors of their generations, their number in the days of David being twenty-two thousand six hundred. 3The sonʲ of Uzzi: Izrahiah. And the sons of Izrahiah: Michael, Obadiah, Joel, and Isshiah, five, all of them chiefs; 4and along with them, by their generations, according to their ancestral houses, were units of the fighting force, thirty-six thousand, for they had many wives and sons. 5Their kindred belonging to all the families of Issachar were in all eighty-seven thousand mighty warriors, enrolled by genealogy.

Descendants of Benjamin

6 The sons of Benjamin: Bela,

6.57 Josh 21.13
6.61 vv. 66-70;
Josh 21.5
6.63 Josh 21.7, 34
6.64 Josh 21.3, 41,42
6.65 vv. 57-60
6.66 v. 61
6.67 Josh 21.21
6.68 see Josh 21.22-35 where some names are differently given
6.73 Josh 21.29; 19.21

6.76 v. 62
6.77 v. 63
7.1 Gen 46.13; Num 26.23
7.2 2 Sam 24.1, 2
7.5 1 Chr 6.62, 72
7.6 Gen 46.21; Num 26.38; 1 Chr 8.1-40

ᵍOther readings Hilez, Holon; See Josh 21.15 ᵸOr Dobrath ⁱSyr Compare Vg: Heb And to the sons ʲHeb sons

Becher, and Jediael, three. [7] The sons of Bela: Ezbon, Uzzi, Uzziel, Jerimoth, and Iri, five, heads of ancestral houses, mighty warriors; and their enrollment by genealogies was twenty-two thousand thirty-four. [8] The sons of Becher: Zemirah, Joash, Eliezer, Elioenai, Omri, Jeremoth, Abijah, Anathoth, and Alemeth. All these were the sons of Becher; [9] and their enrollment by genealogies, according to their generations, as heads of their ancestral houses, mighty warriors, was twenty thousand two hundred. [10] The sons of Jediael: Bilhan. And the sons of Bilhan: Jeush, Benjamin, Ehud, Chenaanah, Zethan, Tarshish, and Ahishahar. [11] All these were the sons of Jediael according to the heads of their ancestral houses, mighty warriors, seventeen thousand two hundred, ready for service in war. [12] And Shuppim and Huppim were the sons of Ir, Hushim the son[k] of Aher.

Descendants of Naphtali

13 The descendants of Naphtali: Jahziel, Guni, Jezer, and Shallum, the descendants of Bilhah.

Descendants of Manasseh

14 The sons of Manasseh: Asriel, whom his Aramean concubine bore; she bore Machir the father of Gilead. [15] And Machir took a wife for Huppim and for Shuppim. The name of his sister was Maacah. And the name of the second was Zelophehad; and Zelophehad had daughters. [16] Maacah the wife of Machir bore a son, and she named him Peresh; the name of his brother was Sheresh; and his sons were Ulam and Rekem. [17] The son[k] of Ulam: Bedan. These were the sons of Gilead son of Machir, son of Manasseh. [18] And his sister Hammolecheth bore Ishhod, Abiezer, and Mahlah. [19] The sons of Shemida were Ahian, Shechem, Likhi, and Aniam.

Descendants of Ephraim

20 The sons of Ephraim: Shuthelah, and Bered his son, Tahath his son, Eleadah his son, Tahath

his son, [21] Zabad his son, Shuthelah his son, and Ezer and Elead. Now the people of Gath, who were born in the land, killed them, because they came down to raid their cattle. [22] And their father Ephraim mourned many days, and his brothers came to comfort him. [23] Ephraim[l] went in to his wife, and she conceived and bore a son; and he named him Beriah, because disaster[m] had befallen his house. [24] His daughter was Sheerah, who built both Lower and Upper Beth-horon, and Uzzen-sheerah. [25] Rephah was his son, Resheph his son, Telah his son, Tahan his son, [26] Ladan his son, Ammihud his son, Elishama his son, [27] Nun[n] his son, Joshua his son. [28] Their possessions and settlements were Bethel and its towns, and eastward Naaran, and westward Gezer and its towns, Shechem and its towns, as far as Ayyah and its towns; [29] also along the borders of the Manassites, Beth-shean and its towns, Taanach and its towns, Megiddo and its towns, Dor and its towns. In these lived the sons of Joseph son of Israel.

Descendants of Asher

30 The sons of Asher: Imnah, Ishvah, Ishvi, Beriah, and their sister Serah. [31] The sons of Beriah: Heber and Malchiel, who was the father of Birzaith. [32] Heber became the father of Japhlet, Shomer, Hotham, and their sister Shua. [33] The sons of Japhlet: Pasach, Bimhal, and Ashvath. These are the sons of Japhlet. [34] The sons of Shemer: Ahi, Rohgah, Hubbah, and Aram. [35] The sons of Helem[o] his brother: Zophah, Imna, Shelesh, and Amal. [36] The sons of Zophah: Suah, Harnepher, Shual, Beri, Imrah, [37] Bezer, Hod, Shamma, Shilshah, Ithran, and Beera. [38] The sons of Jether: Jephunneh, Pispa, and Ara. [39] The sons of Ulla: Arah, Hanniel, and Rizia. [40] All of these were men of Asher, heads of ancestral houses, select mighty warriors,

7.12 Num 26.39
7.13 Gen 46.24
7.17 1 Sam 12.11
7.20 Num 26.35

7.24 Josh 16.3,5
7.27 Ex 17.9-14; 24.13
7.28 Josh 16.7
7.30 Gen 46.17; Num 26.44
7.40 v. 30

k Heb sons l Heb He m Heb beraah
n Here spelled Non; see Exod 33.33
o Or Hotham; see 7.32

chief of the princes. Their number enrolled by genealogies, for service in war, was twenty-six thousand men.

Descendants of Benjamin

8 Benjamin became the father of Bela his firstborn, Ashbel the second, Aharah the third, [2]Nohah the fourth, and Rapha the fifth. [3]And Bela had sons: Addar, Gera, Abihud,[p] [4]Abishua, Naaman, Ahoah, [5]Gera, Shephuphan, and Huram. [6]These are the sons of Ehud (they were heads of ancestral houses of the inhabitants of Geba, and they were carried into exile to Manahath): [7]Naaman,[q] Ahijah, and Gera, that is, Heglam,[r] who became the father of Uzza and Ahihud. [8]And Shaharaim had sons in the country of Moab after he had sent away his wives Hushim and Baara. [9]He had sons by his wife Hodesh: Jobab, Zibia, Mesha, Malcam, [10]Jeuz, Sachia, and Mirmah. These were his sons, heads of ancestral houses. [11]He also had sons by Hushim: Abitub and Elpaal. [12]The sons of Elpaal: Eber, Misham, and Shemed, who built Ono and Lod with its towns, [13]and Beriah and Shema (they were heads of ancestral houses of the inhabitants of Aijalon, who put to flight the inhabitants of Gath); [14]and Ahio, Shashak, and Jeremoth. [15]Zebadiah, Arad, Eder, [16]Michael, Ishpah, and Joha were sons of Beriah. [17]Zebadiah, Meshullam, Hizki, Heber, [18]Ishmerai, Izliah, and Jobab were the sons of Elpaal. [19]Jakim, Zichri, Zabdi, [20]Elienai, Zillethai, Eliel, [21]Adaiah, Beraiah, and Shimrath were the sons of Shimei. [22]Ishpan, Eber, Eliel, [23]Abdon, Zichri, Hanan, [24]Hananiah, Elam, Anthothijah, [25]Iphdeiah, and Penuel were the sons of Shashak. [26]Shamsherai, Shehariah, Athaliah, [27]Jaareshiah, Elijah, and Zichri were the sons of Jeroham. [28]These were the heads of ancestral houses, according to their generations, chiefs. These lived in Jerusalem.

[29]Jeiel[s] the father of Gibeon lived in Gibeon, and the name of his wife was Maacah. [30]His firstborn son: Abdon, then Zur, Kish, Baal,[t] Nadab, [31]Gedor, Ahio, Zecher, [32]and Mikloth, who became the father of Shimeah. Now these also lived opposite their kindred in Jerusalem, with their kindred. [33]Ner became the father of Kish, Kish of Saul,[u] Saul[u] of Jonathan, Malchishua, Abinadab, and Eshbaal; [34]and the son of Jonathan was Merib-baal; and Merib-baal became the father of Micah. [35]The sons of Micah: Pithon, Melech, Tarea, and Ahaz. [36]Ahaz became the father of Jehoaddah; and Jehoaddah became the father of Alemeth, Azmaveth, and Zimri; Zimri became the father of Moza. [37]Moza became the father of Binea; Raphah was his son, Eleasah his son, Azel his son. [38]Azel had six sons, and these are their names: Azrikam, Bocheru, Ishmael, Sheariah, Obadiah, and Hanan; all these were the sons of Azel. [39]The sons of his brother Eshek: Ulam his firstborn, Jeush the second, and Eliphelet the third. [40]The sons of Ulam were mighty warriors, archers, having many children and grandchildren, one hundred fifty. All these were Benjaminites.

9 So all Israel was enrolled by genealogies; and these are written in the Book of the Kings of Israel. And Judah was taken into exile in Babylon because of their unfaithfulness. [2]Now the first to live again in their possessions in their towns were Israelites, priests, Levites, and temple servants.

Inhabitants of Jerusalem after the Exile

3 And some of the people of Judah, Benjamin, Ephraim, and Manasseh lived in Jerusalem: [4]Uthai son of Ammihud, son of Omri, son of Imri, son of Bani, from the sons of Perez son of Judah. [5]And of the Shilonites: Asaiah the firstborn, and his sons. [6]Of the sons of Zerah:

8.1 Gen 46.21; 1 Chr 7.6
8.6 1 Chr 2.52
8.13 v. 21
8.21 v. 13
8.29 1 Chr 9.35

8.33 1 Chr 9.35-38
8.34 2 Sam 9.12
9.1 1 Chr 5.25, 26
9.2 Neh 11.3-22; Ezra 2.43;
8.20
9.3 Neh 11.1

[p]Or *father of Ehud*; see 8.6 [q]Heb *and Naaman* [r]Or *he carried them into exile* [s]Compare 9.35: Heb lacks *Jeiel* [t]Gk Ms adds *Ner*; Compare 8.33 and 9.36 [u]Or *Shaul*

Jeuel and their kin, six hundred ninety. [7] Of the Benjaminites: Sallu son of Meshullam, son of Hodaviah, son of Hassenuah, [8] Ibneiah son of Jeroham, Elah son of Uzzi, son of Michri, and Meshullam son of Shephatiah, son of Reuel, son of Ibnijah; [9] and their kindred according to their generations, nine hundred fifty-six. All these were heads of families according to their ancestral houses.

Priestly Families

[10] Of the priests: Jedaiah, Jehoiarib, Jachin, [11] and Azariah son of Hilkiah, son of Meshullam, son of Zadok, son of Meraioth, son of Ahitub, the chief officer of the house of God; [12] and Adaiah son of Jeroham, son of Pashhur, son of Malchijah, and Maasai son of Adiel, son of Jahzerah, son of Meshullam, son of Meshillemith, son of Immer; [13] besides their kindred, heads of their ancestral houses, one thousand seven hundred sixty, qualified for the work of the service of the house of God.

Levitical Families

[14] Of the Levites: Shemaiah son of Hasshub, son of Azrikam, son of Hashabiah, of the sons of Merari; [15] and Bakbakkar, Heresh, Galal, and Mattaniah son of Mica, son of Zichri, son of Asaph; [16] and Obadiah son of Shemaiah, son of Galal, son of Jeduthun, and Berechiah son of Asa, son of Elkanah, who lived in the villages of the Netophathites.

[17] The gatekeepers were: Shallum, Akkub, Talmon, Ahiman; and their kindred Shallum was the chief, [18] stationed previously in the king's gate on the east side. These were the gatekeepers of the camp of the Levites. [19] Shallum son of Kore, son of Ebiasaph, son of Korah, and his kindred of his ancestral house, the Korahites, were in charge of the work of the service, guardians of the thresholds of the tent, as their ancestors had been in charge of the camp of the LORD, guardians of the entrance. [20] And

9.10 Neh 11.10-14
9.14 Neh 11.15-19
9.18 Ezek 46.1,2
9.20 Num 25.7-13
9.21 1 Chr 26.2, 14
9.22 1 Chr 26.1, 2;
2 Chr 31.15, 18
9.25 v. 16;
2 Kings 11.5, 7;
2 Chr 23.8
9.27 1 Chr 23.30-32
9.29 1 Chr 23.29
9.30 Ex 30.23-25
9.32 Lev 24.8
9.33 1 Chr 6.31; 25.1;
Ps 134.1

Phinehas son of Eleazar was chief over them in former times; the LORD was with him. [21] Zechariah son of Meshelemiah was gatekeeper at the entrance of the tent of meeting. [22] All these, who were chosen as gatekeepers at the thresholds, were two hundred twelve. They were enrolled by genealogies in their villages. David and the seer Samuel established them in their office of trust. [23] So they and their descendants were in charge of the gates of the house of the LORD, that is, the house of the tent, as guards. [24] The gatekeepers were on the four sides, east, west, north, and south; [25] and their kindred who were in their villages were obliged to come in every seven days, in turn, to be with them; [26] for the four chief gatekeepers, who were Levites, were in charge of the chambers and the treasures of the house of God. [27] And they would spend the night near the house of God; for on them lay the duty of watching, and they had charge of opening it every morning.

[28] Some of them had charge of the utensils of service, for they were required to count them when they were brought in and taken out. [29] Others of them were appointed over the furniture, and over all the holy utensils, also over the choice flour, the wine, the oil, the incense, and the spices. [30] Others, of the sons of the priests, prepared the mixing of the spices, [31] and Mattithiah, one of the Levites, the firstborn of Shallum the Korahite, was in charge of making the flat cakes. [32] Also some of their kindred of the Kohathites had charge of the rows of bread, to prepare them for each sabbath.

[33] Now these are the singers, the heads of ancestral houses of the Levites, living in the chambers of the temple free from other service, for they were on duty day and night. [34] These were heads of ancestral houses of the Levites, according to their generations; these leaders lived in Jerusalem.

The Family of King Saul

35 In Gibeon lived the father of Gibeon, Jeiel, and the name of his wife was Maacah. 36His firstborn son was Abdon, then Zur, Kish, Baal, Ner, Nadab, 37Gedor, Ahio, Zechariah, and Mikloth; 38and Mikloth became the father of Shimeam; and these also lived opposite their kindred in Jerusalem, with their kindred. 39Ner became the father of Kish, Kish of Saul, Saul of Jonathan, Malchishua, Abinadab, and Esh-baal; 40and the son of Jonathan was Merib-baal; and Merib-baal became the father of Micah. 41The sons of Micah: Pithon, Melech, Tahrea, and Ahaz;v 42and Ahaz became the father of Jarah, and Jarah of Alemeth, Azmaveth, and Zimri; and Zimri became the father of Moza. 43Moza became the father of Binea; and Rephaiah was his son, Eleasah his son, Azel his son. 44Azel had six sons, and these are their names: Azrikam, Bocheru, Ishmael, Sheariah, Obadiah, and Hanan; these were the sons of Azel.

Death of Saul and His Sons

10 Now the Philistines fought against Israel; and the men of Israel fled before the Philistines, and fell slain on Mount Gilboa. 2The Philistines overtook Saul and his sons; and the Philistines killed Jonathan and Abinadab and Malchishua, sons of Saul. 3The battle pressed hard on Saul; and the archers found him, and he was wounded by the archers. 4Then Saul said to his armor-bearer, "Draw your sword, and thrust me through with it, so that these uncircumcised may not come and make sport of me." But his armor-bearer was unwilling, for he was terrified. So Saul took his own sword and fell on it. 5When his armor-bearer saw that Saul was dead, he also fell on his sword and died. 6Thus Saul died; he and his three sons and all his house died together. 7When all the men of Israel who were in the valley saw that the armyw had fled and that Saul and his sons were dead,

they abandoned their towns and fled; and the Philistines came and occupied them.

8 The next day when the Philistines came to strip the dead, they found Saul and his sons fallen on Mount Gilboa. 9They stripped him and took his head and his armor, and sent messengers throughout the land of the Philistines to carry the good news to their idols and to the people. 10They put his armor in the temple of their gods, and fastened his head in the temple of Dagon. 11But when all Jabesh-gilead heard everything that the Philistines had done to Saul, 12all the valiant warriors got up and took away the body of Saul and the bodies of his sons, and brought them to Jabesh. Then they buried their bones under the oak in Jabesh, and fasted seven days.

13 So Saul died for his unfaithfulness; he was unfaithful to the LORD in that he did not keep the command of the LORD; moreover, he had consulted a medium, seeking guidance, 14and did not seek guidance from the LORD. Therefore the LORDx put him to death and turned the kingdom over to David son of Jesse.

David Anointed King of All Israel

11 Then all Israel gathered together to David at Hebron and said, "See, we are your bone and flesh. 2For some time now, even while Saul was king, it was you who commanded the army of Israel. The LORD your God said to you: It is you who shall be shepherd of my people Israel, you who shall be ruler over my people Israel." 3So all the elders of Israel came to the king at Hebron, and David made a covenant with them at Hebron before the LORD. And they anointed David king over Israel, according to the word of the LORD by Samuel.

Jerusalem Captured

4 David and all Israel marched

Cross-references (margin)

9.35 · 1 Chr 8.29
9.39 · 1 Chr 8.33
9.41 · 1 Chr 8.35
10.1 · 1 Sam 31.1, 2
10.4 · cf. 1 Sam 31.4-7
10.10 · 1 Sam 31.10
10.13 · 1 Sam 13.13; 15.23; 28.7
10.14 · 1 Sam 15.28; 1 Chr 12.23
11.1 · 2 Sam 5.1
11.2 · 2 Sam 5.2; Ps 78.71
11.3 · 2 Sam 5.3; 1 Sam 16.1, 12,13
11.4 · Judg 1.21; 19.10

v Compare 8.35: Heb lacks *and Ahaz* w Heb *they* x Heb *he*

to Jerusalem, that is Jebus, where the Jebusites were, the inhabitants of the land. 5 The inhabitants of Jebus said to David, "You will not come in here." Nevertheless David took the stronghold of Zion, now the city of David. 6 David had said, "Whoever attacks the Jebusites first shall be chief and commander." And Joab son of Zeruiah went up first, so he became chief. 7 David resided in the stronghold; therefore it was called the city of David. 8 He built the city all around, from the Millo in complete circuit; and Joab repaired the rest of the city. 9 And David became greater and greater, for the LORD of hosts was with him.

David's Mighty Men and Their Exploits

10 Now these are the chiefs of David's warriors, who gave him strong support in his kingdom, together with all Israel, to make him king, according to the word of the LORD concerning Israel. 11 This is an account of David's mighty warriors: Jashobeam, son of Hachmoni, y was chief of the Three; z he wielded his spear against three hundred whom he killed at one time.

12 And next to him among the three warriors was Eleazar son of Dodo, the Ahohite. 13 He was with David at Pas-dammim when the Philistines were gathered there for battle. There was a plot of ground full of barley. Now the people had fled from the Philistines, 14 but he and David took their stand in the middle of the plot, defended it, and killed the Philistines; and the LORD saved them by a great victory.

15 Three of the thirty chiefs went down to the rock to David at the cave of Adullam, while the army of Philistines was encamped in the valley of Rephaim. 16 David was then in the stronghold; and the garrison of the Philistines was then at Bethlehem. 17 David said longingly, "O that someone would give me water to drink from the well of Bethlehem that is by the gate!" 18 Then the Three broke through

the camp of the Philistines, and drew water from the well of Bethlehem that was by the gate, and they brought it to David. But David would not drink of it; he poured it out to the LORD, 19 and said, "My God forbid that I should do this. Can I drink the blood of these men? For at the risk of their lives they brought it." Therefore he would not drink it. The three warriors did these things.

20 Now Abishai,a the brother of Joab, was chief of the Thirty.b With his spear he fought against three hundred and killed them, and won a name beside the Three. 21 He was the most renownedc of the Thirty,b and became their commander; but he did not attain to the Three.

22 Benaiah son of Jehoiada was a valiant mand of Kabzeel, a doer of great deeds; he struck down two sons ofe Ariel of Moab. He also went down and killed a lion in a pit on a day when snow had fallen. 23 And he killed an Egyptian, a man of great stature, five cubits tall. The Egyptian had in his hand a spear like a weaver's beam; but Benaiah went against him with a staff, snatched the spear out of the Egyptian's hand, and killed him with his own spear. 24 Such were the things Benaiah son of Jehoiada did, and he won a name beside the three warriors. 25 He was renowned among the Thirty, but he did not attain to the Three. And David put him in charge of his bodyguard.

26 The warriors of the armies were Asahel brother of Joab, Elhanan son of Dodo of Bethlehem, 27 Shammoth of Harod,f Helez the Pelonite, 28 Ira son of Ikkesh of Tekoa, Abiezer of Anathoth, 29 Sibbecai the Hushathite, Ilai the Ahohite, 30 Maharai of Netophah, Heled son of Baanah of Netophah,

Cross references (center column)

11.6 2 Sam 8.16
11.9 2 Sam 3.1
11.10 2 Sam 23.8-39; v. 3
11.11 2 Sam 23.8
11.13 2 Sam 23.11, 12
11.15 2 Sam 23.13; 1 Chr 14.9

11.20 2 Sam 23.18
11.21 2 Sam 23.19
11.22 2 Sam 23.20
11.23 1 Sam 17.7
11.26 2 Sam 23.24

y Or a Hachmonite z Compare 2 Sam 23.8: Heb Thirty or captains a Gk Vg Tg Compare 2 Sam 23.18: Heb Abishai b Syr: Heb Three c Compare 2 Sam 23.19: Heb more renowned among the two d Syr: Heb the son of a valiant man e See 2 Sam 23.20: Heb lacks sons of f Compare 2 Sam 23.25: Heb the Harorite

³¹Ithai son of Ribai of Gibeah of the Benjaminites, Benaiah of Pirathon, ³²Hurai of the wadis of Gaash, Abiel the Arbathite, ³³Azmaveth of Baharum, Eliahba of Shaalbon, ³⁴Hashem[g] the Gizonite, Jonathan son of Shagee the Hararite, ³⁵Ahiam son of Sachar the Hararite, Eliphal son of Ur, ³⁶Hepher the Mecherathite, Ahijah the Pelonite, ³⁷Hezro of Carmel, Naarai son of Ezbai, ³⁸Joel the brother of Nathan, Mibhar son of Hagri, ³⁹Zelek the Ammonite, Naharai of Beeroth, the armor-bearer of Joab son of Zeruiah, ⁴⁰Ira the Ithrite, Gareb the Ithrite, ⁴¹Uriah the Hittite, Zabad son of Ahlai, ⁴²Adina son of Shiza the Reubenite, a leader of the Reubenites, and thirty with him, ⁴³Hanan son of Maacah, and Joshaphat the Mithnite, ⁴⁴Uzzia the Ashterathite, Shama and Jeiel sons of Hotham the Aroerite, ⁴⁵Jediael son of Shimri, and his brother Joha the Tizite, ⁴⁶Eliel the Mahavite, and Jeribai and Joshaviah sons of Elnaam, and Ithmah the Moabite, ⁴⁷Eliel, and Obed, and Jaasiel the Mezobaite.

David's Followers in the Desert

12 The following are those who came to David at Ziklag, while he could not move about freely because of Saul son of Kish; they were among the mighty warriors who helped him in war. ²They were archers, and could shoot arrows and sling stones with either the right hand or the left; they were Benjaminites, Saul's kindred. ³The chief was Ahiezer, then Joash, both sons of Shemaah of Gibeah; also Jeziel and Pelet sons of Azmaveth; Beracah, Jehu of Anathoth, ⁴Ishmaiah of Gibeon, a warrior among the Thirty and a leader over the Thirty; Jeremiah,[h] Jahaziel, Johanan, Jozabad of Gederah, ⁵Eluzai,[i] Jerimoth, Bealiah, Shemariah, Shephatiah the Haruphite; ⁶Elkanah, Isshiah, Azarel, Joezer, and Jashobeam, the Korahites; ⁷and Joelah and Zebadiah, sons of Jeroham of Gedor.

8 From the Gadites there went over to David at the stronghold in the wilderness mighty and experienced warriors, expert with shield and spear, whose faces were like the faces of lions, and who were swift as gazelles on the mountains: ⁹Ezer the chief, Obadiah second, Eliab third, ¹⁰Mishmannah fourth, Jeremiah fifth, ¹¹Attai sixth, Eliel seventh, ¹²Johanan eighth, Elzabad ninth, ¹³Jeremiah tenth, Machbannai eleventh. ¹⁴These Gadites were officers of the army, the least equal to a hundred and the greatest to a thousand. ¹⁵These are the men who crossed the Jordan in the first month, when it was overflowing all its banks, and put to flight all those in the valleys, to the east and to the west.

16 Some Benjaminites and Judahites came to the stronghold to David. ¹⁷David went out to meet them and said to them, "If you have come to me in friendship, to help me, then my heart will be knit to you; but if you have come to betray me to my adversaries, though my hands have done no wrong, then may the God of our ancestors see and give judgment." ¹⁸Then the spirit came upon Amasai, chief of the Thirty, and he said,

> "We are yours, O David;
> and with you, O son of
> Jesse!
> Peace, peace to you,
> and peace to the one who
> helps you!
> For your God is the one
> who helps you."

Then David received them, and made them officers of his troops.

19 Some of the Manassites deserted to David when he came with the Philistines for the battle against Saul. (Yet he did not help them, for the rulers of the Philistines took counsel and sent him away, saying, "He will desert to his master Saul at the cost of our heads.") ²⁰As he went to Ziklag

Cross references (center column):

11.39
1 Chr 18.15
12.1
1 Sam 27.2-6
12.2
Judg 20.16
12.8
2 Sam 2.18

12.15
Josh 3.15
12.18
Judg 6.34;
2 Sam 17.25
12.19
1 Sam 29.2, 4

g Compare Gk and 2 Sam 23.32: Heb *the sons of Hashem* h Heb verse 5 i Heb verse 6

these Manassites deserted to him: Adnah, Jozabad, Jediael, Michael, Jozabad, Elihu, and Zillethai, chiefs of the thousands in Manasseh. ²¹They helped David against the band of raiders,ⁱ for they were all warriors and commanders in the army. ²²Indeed from day to day people kept coming to David to help him, until there was a great army, like an army of God.

David's Army at Hebron

23 These are the numbers of the divisions of the armed troops who came to David in Hebron to turn the kingdom of Saul over to him, according to the word of the LORD. ²⁴The people of Judah bearing shield and spear numbered six thousand eight hundred armed troops. ²⁵Of the Simeonites, mighty warriors, seven thousand one hundred. ²⁶Of the Levites four thousand six hundred. ²⁷Jehoiada, leader of the house of Aaron, and with him three thousand seven hundred. ²⁸Zadok, a young warrior, and twenty-two commanders from his own ancestral house. ²⁹Of the Benjaminites, the kindred of Saul, three thousand, of whom the majority had continued to keep their allegiance to the house of Saul. ³⁰Of the Ephraimites, twenty thousand eight hundred, mighty warriors, notables in their ancestral houses. ³¹Of the half-tribe of Manasseh, eighteen thousand, who were expressly named to come and make David king. ³²Of Issachar, those who had understanding of the times, to know what Israel ought to do, two hundred chiefs, and all their kindred under their command. ³³Of Zebulun, fifty thousand seasoned troops, equipped for battle with all the weapons of war, to help Davidᵏ with singleness of purpose. ³⁴Of Naphtali, a thousand commanders, with whom there were thirty-seven thousand armed with shield and spear. ³⁵Of the Danites, twenty-eight thousand six hundred equipped for battle. ³⁶Of Asher, forty thousand seasoned troops

ready for battle. ³⁷Of the Reubenites and Gadites and the half-tribe of Manasseh from beyond the Jordan, one hundred twenty thousand armed with all the weapons of war.

38 All these, warriors arrayed in battle order, came to Hebron with full intent to make David king over all Israel; likewise all the rest of Israel were of a single mind to make David king. ³⁹They were there with David for three days, eating and drinking, for their kindred had provided for them. ⁴⁰And also their neighbors, from as far away as Issachar and Zebulun and Naphtali, came bringing food on donkeys, camels, mules, and oxen— abundant provisions of meal, cakes of figs, clusters of raisins, wine, oil, oxen, and sheep, for there was joy in Israel.

The Ark Brought from Kiriath-jearim

13 David consulted with the commanders of the thousands and of the hundreds, with every leader. ²David said to the whole assembly of Israel, "If it seems good to you, and if it is the will of the LORD our God, let us send abroad to our kindred who remain in all the land of Israel, including the priests and Levites in the cities that have pasture lands, that they may come together to us. ³Then let us bring again the ark of our God to us; for we did not turn to it in the days of Saul." ⁴The whole assembly agreed to do so, for the thing pleased all the people.

5 So David assembled all Israel from the Shihor of Egypt to Lebohamath, to bring the ark of God from Kiriath-jearim. ⁶And David and all Israel went up to Baalah, that is, to Kiriath-jearim, which belongs to Judah, to bring up from there the ark of God, the LORD, who is enthroned on the cherubim, which is called by hisˡ name. ⁷They carried the ark of God on a new cart, from the house of Abina-

Reference column:

12.21 1 Sam 30.1, 9,10
12.23 2 Sam 2.3, 4; 1 Chr 11.1; 10.14; 1 Sam 16.1, 3
12.28 2 Sam 8.17
12.29 2 Sam 2.8, 9
12.32 Esther 1.13
12.33 Ps 12.2
12.38 2 Sam 5.1-3
12.40 1 Sam 25.18
13.2 1 Sam 31.1; Isa 37.4
13.3 1 Sam 7.1, 2
13.5 2 Sam 6.1; 1 Chr 15.3; 1 Sam 6.21; 7.1
13.6 Josh 15.9; 2 Kings 19.15
13.7 1 Sam 7.1

ⁱ Or as officers of his troops ᵏ Gk: Heb lacks David ˡ Heb lacks his

dab, and Uzzah and Ahio[m] were driving the cart. [8]David and all Israel were dancing before God with all their might, with song and lyres and harps and tambourines and cymbals and trumpets.

9 When they came to the threshing floor of Chidon, Uzzah put out his hand to hold the ark, for the oxen shook it. [10]The anger of the LORD was kindled against Uzzah; he struck him down because he put out his hand to the ark; and he died there before God. [11]David was angry because the LORD had burst out against Uzzah; so that place is called Perez-uzzah[n] to this day. [12]David was afraid of God that day; he said, "How can I bring the ark of God into my care?" [13]So David did not take the ark into his care into the city of David; he took it instead to the house of Obed-edom the Gittite. [14]The ark of God remained with the household of Obed-edom in his house three months, and the LORD blessed the household of Obed-edom and all that he had.

David Established at Jerusalem

14 King Hiram of Tyre sent messengers to David, along with cedar logs, and masons and carpenters to build a house for him. [2]David then perceived that the LORD had established him as king over Israel, and that his kingdom was highly exalted for the sake of his people Israel.

3 David took more wives in Jerusalem, and David became the father of more sons and daughters. [4]These are the names of the children whom he had in Jerusalem: Shammua, Shobab, and Nathan; Solomon, [5]Ibhar, Elishua, and Elpelet; [6]Nogah, Nepheg, and Japhia; [7]Elishama, Beeliada, and Eliphelet.

Defeat of the Philistines

8 When the Philistines heard that David had been anointed king over all Israel, all the Philistines went up in search of David; and David heard of it and went out against them. [9]Now the Philistines had

come and made a raid in the valley of Rephaim. [10]David inquired of God, "Shall I go up against the Philistines? Will you give them into my hand?" The LORD said to him, "Go up, and I will give them into your hand." [11]So he went up to Baal-perazim, and David defeated them there. David said, "God has burst out[o] against my enemies by my hand, like a bursting flood." Therefore that place is called Baal-perazim.[p] [12]They abandoned their gods there, and at David's command they were burned.

13 Once again the Philistines made a raid in the valley. [14]When David again inquired of God, God said to him, "You shall not go up after them; go around and come on them opposite the balsam trees. [15]When you hear the sound of marching in the tops of the balsam trees, then go out to battle; for God has gone out before you to strike down the army of the Philistines." [16]David did as God had commanded him, and they struck down the Philistine army from Gibeon to Gezer. [17]The fame of David went out into all lands, and the LORD brought the fear of him on all nations.

The Ark Brought to Jerusalem

15 David[q] built houses for himself in the city of David, and he prepared a place for the ark of God and pitched a tent for it. [2]Then David commanded that no one but the Levites were to carry the ark of God, for the LORD had chosen them to carry the ark of the LORD and to minister to him forever. [3]David assembled all Israel in Jerusalem to bring up the ark of the LORD to its place, which he had prepared for it. [4]Then David gathered together the descendants of Aaron and the Levites: [5]of the sons of Kohath, Uriel the chief, with one hundred twenty of his kindred; [6]of the sons of Merari, Asaiah the chief, with two hundred twenty of his kindred; [7]of the sons of Gershom, Joel

13.8
2 Sam 6.5
13.9
2 Sam 6.6
13.10
1 Chr 15.13, 15
13.14
1 Chr 26.4, 5
14.1
2 Sam 5.11
14.4
1 Chr 3.5
14.8
2 Sam 5.17
14.9
1 Chr 11.15

14.13
v. 9;
2 Sam 5.22
14.14
2 Sam 5.23
14.16
2 Sam 5.25
14.17
2 Chr 26.8;
Deut 2.25
15.1
1 Chr 16.1
15.2
Num 4.15;
Deut 10.8;
31.9
15.3
Josh 6.27;
1 Kings 8.1;
1 Chr 13.5

[m] Or *and his brother* [n] That is *Bursting Out Against Uzzah* [o] Heb *paraz* [p] That is *Lord of Bursting Out* [q] Heb *He*

the chief, with one hundred thirty of his kindred; [8] of the sons of Elizaphan, Shemaiah the chief, two hundred of his kindred; [9] of the sons of Hebron, Eliel the chief, with eighty of his kindred; [10] of the sons of Uzziel, Amminadab the chief, with one hundred twelve of his kindred.

11 David summoned the priests Zadok and Abiathar, and the Levites Uriel, Asaiah, Joel, Shemaiah, Eliel, and Amminadab. [12] He said to them, "You are the heads of families of the Levites; sanctify yourselves, you and your kindred, so that you may bring up the ark of the LORD, the God of Israel, to the place that I have prepared for it. [13] Because you did not carry it the first time,[r] the LORD our God burst out against us, because we did not give it proper care." [14] So the priests and the Levites sanctified themselves to bring up the ark of the LORD, the God of Israel. [15] And the Levites carried the ark of God on their shoulders with the poles, as Moses had commanded according to the word of the LORD.

16 David also commanded the chiefs of the Levites to appoint their kindred as the singers to play on musical instruments, on harps and lyres and cymbals, to raise loud sounds of joy. [17] So the Levites appointed Heman son of Joel; and of his kindred Asaph son of Berechiah; and of the sons of Merari, their kindred, Ethan son of Kushaiah; [18] and with them their kindred of the second order, Zechariah, Jaaziel, Shemiramoth, Jehiel, Unni, Eliab, Benaiah, Maaseiah, Mattithiah, Eliphelehu, and Mikneiah, and the gatekeepers Obed-edom and Jeiel. [19] The singers Heman, Asaph, and Ethan were to sound bronze cymbals; [20] Zechariah, Aziel, Shemiramoth, Jehiel, Unni, Eliab, Maaseiah, and Benaiah were to play harps according to Alamoth; [21] but Mattithiah, Eliphelehu, Mikneiah, Obed-edom, Jeiel, and Azaziah were to lead with lyres according to the Sheminith. [22] Chenaniah, leader of the Levites in music, was

to direct the music, for he understood it. [23] Berechiah and Elkanah were to be gatekeepers for the ark. [24] Shebaniah, Joshaphat, Nethanel, Amasai, Zechariah, Benaiah, and Eliezer, the priests, were to blow the trumpets before the ark of God. Obed-edom and Jehiah also were to be gatekeepers for the ark.

25 So David and the elders of Israel, and the commanders of the thousands, went to bring up the ark of the covenant of the LORD from the house of Obed-edom with rejoicing. [26] And because God helped the Levites who were carrying the ark of the covenant of the LORD, they sacrificed seven bulls and seven rams. [27] David was clothed with a robe of fine linen, as also were all the Levites who were carrying the ark, and the singers, and Chenaniah the leader of the music of the singers; and David wore a linen ephod. [28] So all Israel brought up the ark of the covenant of the LORD with shouting, to the sound of the horn, trumpets, and cymbals, and made loud music on harps and lyres.

29 As the ark of the covenant of the LORD came to the city of David, Michal daughter of Saul looked out of the window, and saw King David leaping and dancing; and she despised him in her heart.

The Ark Placed in the Tent

16 They brought in the ark of God, and set it inside the tent that David had pitched for it; and they offered burnt offerings and offerings of well-being before God. [2] When David had finished offering the burnt offerings and the offerings of well-being, he blessed the people in the name of the LORD; [3] and he distributed to every person in Israel—man and woman alike—to each a loaf of bread, a portion of meat,[s] and a cake of raisins.

4 He appointed certain of the Levites as ministers before the ark of the LORD, to invoke, to thank, and to praise the LORD, the God of

15.8
Ex 6.22
15.9
Ex 6.18
15.11
1 Chr 12.28;
1 Sam 22.20-
23
15.12
Ex 19.14,
15;
2 Chr 35.6
15.13
2 Sam 6.3;
1 Chr 13.7,
10,11
15.14
v. 12
15.15
Ex 25.14;
Num 4.5
15.16
1 Chr 25.1
15.17
1 Chr 6.33,
39,44

15.24
v. 28;
1 Chr 16.6
15.25
2 Sam 6.12,
15;
1 Chr 13.13
15.28
1 Chr 13.8
15.29
2 Sam 6.16
16.1
2 Sam 6.17-19

r Meaning of Heb uncertain s Compare Gk Syr Vg: Meaning of Heb uncertain

Israel. ⁵Asaph was the chief, and second to him Zechariah, Jeiel, Shemiramoth, Jehiel, Mattithiah, Eliab, Benaiah, Obed-edom, and Jeiel, with harps and lyres; Asaph was to sound the cymbals, ⁶and the priests Benaiah and Jahaziel were to blow trumpets regularly, before the ark of the covenant of God.

David's Psalm of Thanksgiving

7 Then on that day David first appointed the singing of praises to the Lord by Asaph and his kindred.

⁸ O give thanks to the Lord,
 call on his name,
make known his deeds
 among the peoples.
⁹ Sing to him, sing praises to
 him,
tell of all his wonderful
 works.
¹⁰ Glory in his holy name;
 let the hearts of those who
 seek the Lord rejoice.
¹¹ Seek the Lord and his
 strength,
seek his presence
 continually.
¹² Remember the wonderful
 works he has done,
his miracles, and the
 judgments he uttered,
¹³ O offspring of his servant
 Israel,^t
children of Jacob, his
 chosen ones.

¹⁴ He is the Lord our God;
 his judgments are in all the
 earth.
¹⁵ Remember his covenant
 forever,
the word that he
 commanded, for a
 thousand generations,
¹⁶ the covenant that he made
 with Abraham,
his sworn promise to Isaac,
¹⁷ which he confirmed to Jacob
 as a statute,
to Israel as an everlasting
 covenant,
¹⁸ saying, "To you I will give
 the land of Canaan

as your portion for an
 inheritance."

¹⁹ When they were few in
 number,
of little account, and
 strangers in the land,^u
²⁰ wandering from nation to
 nation,
from one kingdom to
 another people,
²¹ he allowed no one to oppress
 them;
he rebuked kings on their
 account,
²² saying, "Do not touch my
 anointed ones;
do my prophets no harm."

²³ Sing to the Lord, all the
 earth.
Tell of his salvation from
 day to day.
²⁴ Declare his glory among the
 nations,
his marvelous works among
 all the peoples.
²⁵ For great is the Lord, and
 greatly to be praised;
he is to be revered above
 all gods.
²⁶ For all the gods of the
 peoples are idols,
but the Lord made the
 heavens.
²⁷ Honor and majesty are
 before him;
strength and joy are in his
 place.

²⁸ Ascribe to the Lord,
 O families of the
 peoples,
ascribe to the Lord glory
 and strength.
²⁹ Ascribe to the Lord the glory
 due his name;
bring an offering, and come
 before him.
Worship the Lord in holy
 splendor;
³⁰ tremble before him, all the
 earth.

Cross-references:

16.5 Ps ch. 50; 73
16.7 2 Sam 23.1
16.8 Ps 105.1-15
16.11 Ps 24.6
16.12 Ps 77.11; 78.43-68
16.14 Isa 26.9
16.16 Gen 17.2; 26.3; 28.13; 35.11
16.17 Gen 35.11, 12
16.19 Gen 34.30
16.21 Gen 12.17; 20.3; Ex 7.15-18
16.23 Ps 96.1-13
16.25 Ps 48.1; 89.7
16.26 Ps 96.5
16.28 Ps 29.1,2

^tAnother reading is *Abraham* (compare Ps 105.6) ^uHeb *in it*

The world is firmly
　established; it shall
　never be moved.
31 Let the heavens be glad, and
　let the earth rejoice,
　and let them say among
　　the nations, "The LORD
　　is king!"
32 Let the sea roar, and all that
　fills it;
　let the field exult, and
　everything in it.
33 Then shall the trees of the
　forest sing for joy
　before the LORD, for he
　comes to judge the
　earth.
34 O give thanks to the LORD,
　for he is good;
　for his steadfast love
　endures forever.

35 Say also:
"Save us, O God of our
　salvation,
　and gather and rescue us
　　from among the nations,
　that we may give thanks to
　　your holy name,
　and glory in your praise.
36 Blessed be the LORD, the God
　of Israel,
　from everlasting to
　everlasting."
Then all the people said "Amen!"
and praised the LORD.

Regular Worship Maintained

37 David left Asaph and his
kinsfolk there before the ark of the
covenant of the LORD to minister
regularly before the ark as each day
required, 38 and also Obed-edom
and his[v] sixty-eight kinsfolk; while
Obed-edom son of Jeduthun and
Hosah were to be gatekeepers.
39 And he left the priest Zadok and
his kindred the priests before the
tabernacle of the LORD in the high
place that was at Gibeon, 40 to offer
burnt offerings to the LORD on the
altar of burnt offering regularly,
morning and evening, according to
all that is written in the law of the
LORD that he commanded Israel.
41 With them were Heman and Je-
duthun, and the rest of those cho-

sen and expressly named to render
thanks to the LORD, for his steadfast
love endures forever. 42 Heman and
Jeduthun had with them trumpets
and cymbals for the music, and in-
struments for sacred song. The
sons of Jeduthun were appointed
to the gate.

43 Then all the people departed
to their homes, and David went
home to bless his household.

God's Covenant with David

17 Now when David settled in
his house, David said to the
prophet Nathan, "I am living in a
house of cedar, but the ark of the
covenant of the LORD is under a
tent." 2 Nathan said to David, "Do
all that you have in mind, for God
is with you."

3 But that same night the word
of the LORD came to Nathan, say-
ing: 4 Go and tell my servant David:
Thus says the LORD: You shall not
build me a house to live in. 5 For I
have not lived in a house since the
day I brought out Israel to this very
day, but I have lived in a tent and
a tabernacle.[w] 6 Wherever I have
moved about among all Israel, did
I ever speak a word with any of the
judges of Israel, whom I command-
ed to shepherd my people, saying,
Why have you not built me a house
of cedar? 7 Now therefore thus you
shall say to my servant David: Thus
says the LORD of hosts: I took you
from the pasture, from following
the sheep, to be ruler over my peo-
ple Israel; 8 and I have been with
you wherever you went, and have
cut off all your enemies before you;
and I will make for you a name, like
the name of the great ones of the
earth. 9 I will appoint a place for my
people Israel, and will plant them,
so that they may live in their own
place, and be disturbed no more;
and evildoers shall wear them
down no more, as they did former-
ly, 10 from the time that I appointed
judges over my people Israel; and I
will subdue all your enemies.

16.31
Isa 49.13;
Ps 93.1
16.32
Ps 98.7
16.34
Ps 106.1
16.35
Ps 106.47,
48
16.36
1 Kings 8.15;
Deut 27.15
16.37
vv. 4,5;
2 Chr 8.14
16.38
1 Chr 13.14;
26.10
16.39
1 Chr 15.11;
1 Kings 3.4
16.40
Ex 29.38;
Num 28.3
16.41
1 Chr 6.33;
25.1-6;
2 Chr 5.13

17.1
2 Sam 7.1-29
17.4
1 Chr 28.2,
3
17.5
2 Sam 7.6
17.6
2 Sam 7.7
17.10
Judg 2.16

v Gk Syr Vg: Heb *their*　　w Gk 2 Sam 7.6:
Heb *but I have been from tent to tent and from
tabernacle*

Moreover I declare to you that the LORD will build you a house. ¹¹When your days are fulfilled to go to be with your ancestors, I will raise up your offspring after you, one of your own sons, and I will establish his kingdom. ¹²He shall build a house for me, and I will establish his throne forever. ¹³I will be a father to him, and he shall be a son to me. I will not take my steadfast love from him, as I took it from him who was before you, ¹⁴but I will confirm him in my house and in my kingdom forever, and his throne shall be established forever. ¹⁵In accordance with all these words and all this vision, Nathan spoke to David.

David's Prayer

16 Then King David went in and sat before the LORD, and said, "Who am I, O LORD God, and what is my house, that you have brought me thus far? ¹⁷And even this was a small thing in your sight, O God; you have also spoken of your servant's house for a great while to come. You regard me as someone of high rank,ˣ O LORD God! ¹⁸And what more can David say to you for honoring your servant? You know your servant. ¹⁹For your servant's sake, O LORD, and according to your own heart, you have done all these great deeds, making known all these great things. ²⁰There is no one like you, O LORD, and there is no God besides you, according to all that we have heard with our ears. ²¹Who is like your people Israel, one nation on the earth whom God went to redeem to be his people, making for yourself a name for great and terrible things, in driving out nations before your people whom you redeemed from Egypt? ²²And you made your people Israel to be your people forever; and you, O LORD, became their God.

23 And now, O LORD, as for the word that you have spoken concerning your servant and concerning his house, let it be established forever, and do as you have promised. ²⁴Thus your name will be es-

tablished and magnified forever in the saying, 'The LORD of hosts, the God of Israel, is Israel's God'; and the house of your servant David will be established in your presence. ²⁵For you, my God, have revealed to your servant that you will build a house for him; therefore your servant has found it possible to pray before you. ²⁶And now, O LORD, you are God, and you have promised this good thing to your servant; ²⁷therefore may it please you to bless the house of your servant, that it may continue forever before you. For you, O LORD, have blessed and are blessedʸ forever."

David's Kingdom Established and Extended

18 Some time afterward, David attacked the Philistines and subdued them; he took Gath and its villages from the Philistines.

2 He defeated Moab, and the Moabites became subject to David and brought tribute.

3 David also struck down King Hadadezer of Zobah, toward Hamath,ˣ as he went to set up a monument at the river Euphrates. ⁴David took from him one thousand chariots, seven thousand cavalry, and twenty thousand foot soldiers. David hamstrung all the chariot horses, but left one hundred of them. ⁵When the Arameans of Damascus came to help King Hadadezer of Zobah, David killed twenty-two thousand Arameans. ⁶Then David put garrisonsᶻ in Aram of Damascus; and the Arameans became subject to David, and brought tribute. The LORD gave victory to David wherever he went. ⁷David took the gold shields that were carried by the servants of Hadadezer, and brought them to Jerusalem. ⁸From Tibhath and from Cun, cities of Hadadezer, David took a vast quantity of bronze; with it Solomon made the bronze

Cross-references (center column):

17.13
2 Sam 7.14,
15; Heb 1.5
17.14
Lk 1.33
17.16
2 Sam 7.18
17.19
Isa 37.35
17.22
Ex 19.5,6
17.24
Ps 46.7,11

18.1
2 Sam 8.1-18
18.5
1 Chr 19.6
18.8
1 Kings 7.15,
23;
2 Chr 4.12,
15,16

ˣMeaning of Heb uncertain ʸOr and it is blessed ᶻGk Vg 2 Sam 8.6 Compare Syr: Heb lacks garrisons

sea and the pillars and the vessels of bronze.

9 When King Tou of Hamath heard that David had defeated the whole army of King Hadadezer of Zobah, [10] he sent his son Hadoram to King David, to greet him and to congratulate him, because he had fought against Hadadezer and defeated him. Now Hadadezer had often been at war with Tou. He sent all sorts of articles of gold, of silver, and of bronze; [11] these also King David dedicated to the LORD, together with the silver and gold that he had carried off from all the nations, from Edom, Moab, the Ammonites, the Philistines, and Amalek.

12 Abishai son of Zeruiah killed eighteen thousand Edomites in the Valley of Salt. [13] He put garrisons in Edom; and all the Edomites became subject to David. And the LORD gave victory to David wherever he went.

David's Administration

14 So David reigned over all Israel; and he administered justice and equity to all his people. [15] Joab son of Zeruiah was over the army; Jehoshaphat son of Ahilud was recorder; [16] Zadok son of Ahitub and Ahimelech son of Abiathar were priests; Shavsha was secretary; [17] Benaiah son of Jehoiada was over the Cherethites and the Pelethites; and David's sons were the chief officials in the service of the king.

Defeat of the Ammonites and Arameans

19 Some time afterward, King Nahash of the Ammonites died, and his son succeeded him. [2] David said, "I will deal loyally with Hanun son of Nahash, for his father dealt loyally with me." So David sent messengers to console him concerning his father. When David's servants came to Hanun in the land of the Ammonites, to console him, [3] the officials of the Ammonites said to Hanun, "Do you think, because David has sent consolers to you, that he is honoring

18.10 2 Sam 10.16 **18.12** **18.13** 2 Sam 8.13 **18.15** 1 Chr 11.6 **18.17** 2 Sam 8.18 **19.1** 2 Sam 10.1 **19.3** 2 Sam 10.3
19.4 2 Sam 10.4 **19.6** 1 Chr 18.5, 9 **19.7** Num 21.30; Josh 13.9, 16 **19.8** 2 Sam 10.7 **19.11** 2 Sam 10.10 **19.12** 2 Sam 10.11 **19.14** 2 Sam 10.13

your father? Have not his servants come to you to search and to overthrow and to spy out the land?" [4] So Hanun seized David's servants, shaved them, cut off their garments in the middle at their hips, and sent them away; [5] and they departed. When David was told about the men, he sent messengers to them, for they felt greatly humiliated. The king said, "Remain at Jericho until your beards have grown, and then return."

6 When the Ammonites saw that they had made themselves odious to David, Hanun and the Ammonites sent a thousand talents of silver to hire chariots and cavalry from Mesopotamia, from Aram-maacah and from Zobah. [7] They hired thirty-two thousand chariots and the king of Maacah with his army, who came and camped before Medeba. And the Ammonites were mustered from their cities and came to battle. [8] When David heard of it, he sent Joab and all the army of the warriors. [9] The Ammonites came out and drew up in battle array at the entrance of the city, and the kings who had come were by themselves in the open country.

10 When Joab saw that the line of battle was set against him both in front and in the rear, he chose some of the picked men of Israel and arrayed them against the Arameans; [11] the rest of his troops he put in the charge of his brother Abishai, and they were arrayed against the Ammonites. [12] He said, "If the Arameans are too strong for me, then you shall help me; but if the Ammonites are too strong for you, then I will help you. [13] Be strong, and let us be courageous for our people and for the cities of our God; and may the LORD do what seems good to him." [14] So Joab and the troops who were with him advanced toward the Arameans for battle; and they fled before him. [15] When the Ammonites saw that the Arameans fled, they likewise fled before Abishai, Joab's brother,

and entered the city. Then Joab came to Jerusalem.

16 But when the Arameans saw that they had been defeated by Israel, they sent messengers and brought out the Arameans who were beyond the Euphrates, with Shophach the commander of the army of Hadadezer at their head. [17]When David was informed, he gathered all Israel together, crossed the Jordan, came to them, and drew up his forces against them. When David set the battle in array against the Arameans, they fought with him. [18]The Arameans fled before Israel; and David killed seven thousand Aramean charioteers and forty thousand foot soldiers, and also killed Shophach the commander of their army. [19]When the servants of Hadadezer saw that they had been defeated by Israel, they made peace with David, and became subject to him. So the Arameans were not willing to help the Ammonites any more.

Siege and Capture of Rabbah

20 In the spring of the year, the time when kings go out to battle, Joab led out the army, ravaged the country of the Ammonites, and came and besieged Rabbah. But David remained at Jerusalem. Joab attacked Rabbah, and overthrew it. [2]David took the crown of Milcom[a] from his head; he found that it weighed a talent of gold, and in it was a precious stone; and it was placed on David's head. He also brought out the booty of the city, a very great amount. [3]He brought out the people who were in it, and set them to work[b] with saws and iron picks and axes. [c] Thus David did to all the cities of the Ammonites. Then David and all the people returned to Jerusalem.

Exploits against the Philistines

4 After this, war broke out with the Philistines at Gezer; then Sibbecai the Hushathite killed Sippai, who was one of the descendants of the giants; and the Philistines were subdued. [5]Again there was war

with the Philistines; and Elhanan son of Jair killed Lahmi the brother of Goliath the Gittite, the shaft of whose spear was like a weaver's beam. [6]Again there was war at Gath, where there was a man of great size, who had six fingers on each hand, and six toes on each foot, twenty-four in number; he also was descended from the giants. [7]When he taunted Israel, Jonathan son of Shimea, David's brother, killed him. [8]These were descended from the giants in Gath; they fell by the hand of David and his servants.

The Census and Plague

21 Satan stood up against Israel, and incited David to count the people of Israel. [2]So David said to Joab and the commanders of the army, "Go, number Israel, from Beer-sheba to Dan, and bring me a report, so that I may know their number." [3]But Joab said, "May the LORD increase the number of his people a hundredfold! Are they not, my lord the king, all of them my lord's servants? Why then should my lord require this? Why should he bring guilt on Israel?" [4]But the king's word prevailed against Joab. So Joab departed and went throughout all Israel, and came back to Jerusalem. [5]Joab gave the total count of the people to David. In all Israel there were one million one hundred thousand men who drew the sword, and in Judah four hundred seventy thousand who drew the sword. [6]But he did not include Levi and Benjamin in the numbering, for the king's command was abhorrent to Joab.

7 But God was displeased with this thing, and he struck Israel. [8]David said to God, "I have sinned greatly in that I have done this thing. But now, I pray you, take away the guilt of your servant; for I have done very foolishly." [9]The LORD spoke to Gad, David's seer, saying, [10]"Go and say to David,

19.16
2 Sam 10.15
19.17
2 Sam 10.17
19.18
2 Sam 10.18
19.19
2 Sam 10.19
20.1ff
2 Sam 11.1;
12.26
20.2
2 Sam 12.30,
31
20.3
2 Sam 12.31
20.4
2 Sam 21.18
20.5
2 Sam 21.19;
1 Sam 17.7

20.6
2 Sam 21.20
21.1
2 Sam 24.1-25
21.2
1 Chr 27.23
21.3
Deut 1.11
21.5
cf.
2 Sam 24.9
21.6
1 Chr 27.24
21.8
2 Sam 24.10;
12.13
21.10
1 Chr 29.29;
1 Sam 9.9

a Gk Vg See 1 Kings 11.5, 33: MT *of their king* b Compare 2 Sam 12.31: Heb *and he sawed* c Compare 2 Sam 12.31: Heb *saws*

'Thus says the LORD: Three things I offer you; choose one of them, so that I may do it to you.' " ¹¹ So Gad came to David and said to him, "Thus says the LORD, 'Take your choice: ¹² either three years of famine; or three months of devastation by your foes, while the sword of your enemies overtakes you; or three days of the sword of the LORD, pestilence on the land, and the angel of the LORD destroying throughout all the territory of Israel.' Now decide what answer I shall return to the one who sent me." ¹³ Then David said to Gad, "I am in great distress; let me fall into the hand of the LORD, for his mercy is very great; but let me not fall into human hands."

14 So the LORD sent a pestilence on Israel; and seventy thousand persons fell in Israel. ¹⁵ And God sent an angel to Jerusalem to destroy it; but when he was about to destroy it, the LORD took note and relented concerning the calamity; he said to the destroying angel, "Enough! Stay your hand." The angel of the LORD was then standing by the threshing floor of Ornan the Jebusite. ¹⁶ David looked up and saw the angel of the LORD standing between earth and heaven, and in his hand a drawn sword stretched out over Jerusalem. Then David and the elders, clothed in sackcloth, fell on their faces. ¹⁷ And David said to God, "Was it not I who gave the command to count the people? It is I who have sinned and done very wickedly. But these sheep, what have they done? Let your hand, I pray, O LORD my God, be against me and against my father's house; but do not let your people be plagued!"

David's Altar and Sacrifice

18 Then the angel of the LORD commanded Gad to tell David that he should go up and erect an altar to the LORD on the threshing floor of Ornan the Jebusite. ¹⁹ So David went up following Gad's instructions, which he had spoken in the

21.12
2 Sam 24.13
21.13
Ps 51.1;
130.4,7
21.14
1 Chr 27.24
21.15
2 Sam 24.16
21.16
2 Chr 3.1
21.17
2 Sam 7.8;
Ps 74.1
21.18
2 Chr 3.1

21.21
2 Chr 3.1
21.25
2 Sam 24.24
21.26
Lev 9.24;
Judg 6.21
21.29
1 Chr 16.39;
1 Kings 3.4
22.1
1 Chr 21.18-
29;
2 Chr 3.1

name of the LORD. ²⁰ Ornan turned and saw the angel; and while his four sons who were with him hid themselves, Ornan continued to thresh wheat. ²¹ As David came to Ornan, Ornan looked and saw David; he went out from the threshing floor, and did obeisance to David with his face to the ground. ²² David said to Ornan, "Give me the site of the threshing floor that I may build on it an altar to the LORD — give it to me at its full price — so that the plague may be averted from the people." ²³ Then Ornan said to David, "Take it; and let my lord the king do what seems good to him; see, I present the oxen for burnt offerings, and the threshing sledges for the wood, and the wheat for a grain offering. I give it all." ²⁴ But King David said to Ornan, "No; I will buy them for the full price. I will not take for the LORD what is yours, nor offer burnt offerings that cost me nothing." ²⁵ So David paid Ornan six hundred shekels of gold by weight for the site. ²⁶ David built there an altar to the LORD and presented burnt offerings and offerings of well-being. He called upon the LORD, and he answered him with fire from heaven on the altar of burnt offering. ²⁷ Then the LORD commanded the angel, and he put his sword back into its sheath.

The Place Chosen for the Temple

28 At that time, when David saw that the LORD had answered him at the threshing floor of Ornah the Jebusite, he made his sacrifices there. ²⁹ For the tabernacle of the LORD, which Moses had made in the wilderness, and the altar of burnt offering were at that time in the high place at Gibeon; ³⁰ but David could not go before it to inquire of God, for he was afraid of the sword of the angel of the LORD.

22 ¹ Then David said, "Here shall be the house of the LORD God and here the altar of burnt offering for Israel."

David Prepares to Build the Temple

2 David gave orders to gather together the aliens who were residing in the land of Israel, and he set stonecutters to prepare dressed stones for building the house of God. [3] David also provided great stores of iron for nails for the doors of the gates and for clamps, as well as bronze in quantities beyond weighing, [4] and cedar logs without number—for the Sidonians and Tyrians brought great quantities of cedar to David. [5] For David said, "My son Solomon is young and inexperienced, and the house that is to be built for the LORD must be exceedingly magnificent, famous and glorified throughout all lands; I will therefore make preparation for it." So David provided materials in great quantity before his death.

David's Charge to Solomon and the Leaders

6 Then he called for his son Solomon and charged him to build a house for the LORD, the God of Israel. [7] David said to Solomon, "My son, I had planned to build a house to the name of the LORD my God. [8] But the word of the LORD came to me, saying, 'You have shed much blood and have waged great wars; you shall not build a house to my name, because you have shed so much blood in my sight on the earth. [9] See, a son shall be born to you; he shall be a man of peace. I will give him peace from all his enemies on every side; for his name shall be Solomon,[d] and I will give peace[e] and quiet to Israel in his days. [10] He shall build a house for my name. He shall be a son to me, and I will be a father to him, and I will establish his royal throne in Israel forever.' [11] Now, my son, the LORD be with you, so that you may succeed in building the house of the LORD your God, as he has spoken concerning you. [12] Only, may the LORD grant you discretion and understanding, so that when he gives you charge over Israel you may keep the law of the LORD your

God. [13] Then you will prosper if you are careful to observe the statutes and the ordinances that the LORD commanded Moses for Israel. Be strong and of good courage. Do not be afraid or dismayed. [14] With great pains I have provided for the house of the LORD one hundred thousand talents of gold, one million talents of silver, and bronze and iron beyond weighing, for there is so much of it; timber and stone too I have provided. To these you must add more. [15] You have an abundance of workers: stonecutters, masons, carpenters, and all kinds of artisans without number, skilled in working [16] gold, silver, bronze, and iron. Now begin the work, and the LORD be with you."

17 David also commanded all the leaders of Israel to help his son Solomon, saying, [18] "Is not the LORD your God with you? Has he not given you peace on every side? For he has delivered the inhabitants of the land into my hand; and the land is subdued before the LORD and his people. [19] Now set your mind and heart to seek the LORD your God. Go and build the sanctuary of the LORD God so that the ark of the covenant of the LORD and the holy vessels of God may be brought into a house built for the name of the LORD."

Families of the Levites and Their Functions

23 When David was old and full of days, he made his son Solomon king over Israel.

2 David assembled all the leaders of Israel and the priests and the Levites. [3] The Levites, thirty years old and upward, were counted, and the total was thirty-eight thousand. [4] "Twenty-four thousand of these," David said, "shall have charge of the work in the house of the LORD, six thousand shall be officers and judges, [5] four thousand gatekeepers, and four thousand shall offer praises to the LORD with the instruments that I have made for praise." [6] And David organized them in divi-

22.2
1 Kings 9.21;
5.17,18
22.3
1 Chr 29.2,
7; v. 14
22.4
1 Kings 5.6
22.5
1 Chr 29.1
22.7
2 Sam 7.2;
1 Chr 17.1;
Deut 12.5,
11
22.8
1 Kings 5.3;
1 Chr 28.3
22.9
1 Kings 4.20,
25;
2 Sam 12.24,
25
22.10
2 Sam 7.13;
1 Chr 17.12,
13
22.11
v. 16
22.12
1 Kings 3.9-12;
2 Chr 1.10

22.13
1 Chr 28.7;
Josh 1.6-9;
1 Chr 28.20
22.14
v. 3
22.16
v. 11
22.17
1 Chr 28.1-6
22.18
2 Sam 7.1;
1 Chr 23.25
22.19
1 Chr 28.9;
1 Kings 8.6;
2 Chr 5.7;
v. 7
23.1
1 Kings 1.33-
39;
1 Chr 29.28;
28.5
23.3
Num 4.3-49;
v. 24
23.4
2 Chr 19.8
23.5
1 Chr 15.16
23.6
2 Chr 8.14;
29.25

d Heb Shelomoh e Heb shalom

sions corresponding to the sons of Levi: Gershon,[f] Kohath, and Merari.

7 The sons of Gershon[g] were Ladan and Shimei. 8 The sons of Ladan: Jehiel the chief, Zetham, and Joel, three. 9 The sons of Shimei: Shelomoth, Haziel, and Haran, three. These were the heads of families of Ladan. 10 And the sons of Shimei: Jahath, Zina, Jeush, and Beriah. These four were the sons of Shimei. 11 Jahath was the chief, and Zizah the second; but Jeush and Beriah did not have many sons, so they were enrolled as a single family.

12 The sons of Kohath: Amram, Izhar, Hebron, and Uzziel, four. 13 The sons of Amram: Aaron and Moses. Aaron was set apart to consecrate the most holy things, so that he and his sons forever should make offerings before the LORD, and minister to him and pronounce blessings in his name forever; 14 but as for Moses the man of God, his sons were to be reckoned among the tribe of Levi. 15 The sons of Moses: Gershom and Eliezer. 16 The sons of Gershom: Shebuel the chief. 17 The sons of Eliezer: Rehabiah the chief; Eliezer had no other sons, but the sons of Rehabiah were very numerous. 18 The sons of Izhar: Shelomith the chief. 19 The sons of Hebron: Jeriah the chief, Amariah the second, Jahaziel the third, and Jekameam the fourth. 20 The sons of Uzziel: Micah the chief and Isshiah the second.

21 The sons of Merari: Mahli and Mushi. The sons of Mahli: Eleazar and Kish. 22 Eleazar died having no sons, but only daughters; their kindred, the sons of Kish, married them. 23 The sons of Mushi: Mahli, Eder, and Jeremoth, three.

24 These were the sons of Levi by their ancestral houses, the heads of families as they were enrolled according to the number of the names of the individuals from twenty years old and upward who were to do the work for the service of the house of the LORD. 25 For Da-

vid said, "The LORD, the God of Israel, has given rest to his people; and he resides in Jerusalem forever. 26 And so the Levites no longer need to carry the tabernacle or any of the things for its service"— 27 for according to the last words of David these were the number of the Levites from twenty years old and upward— 28 "but their duty shall be to assist the descendants of Aaron for the service of the house of the LORD, having the care of the courts and the chambers, the cleansing of all that is holy, and any work for the service of the house of God; 29 to assist also with the rows of bread, the choice flour for the grain offering, the wafers of unleavened bread, the baked offering, the offering mixed with oil, and all measures of quantity or size. 30 And they shall stand every morning, thanking and praising the LORD, and likewise at evening, 31 and whenever burnt offerings are offered to the LORD on sabbaths, new moons, and appointed festivals, according to the number required of them, regularly before the LORD. 32 Thus they shall keep charge of the tent of meeting and the sanctuary, and shall attend the descendants of Aaron, their kindred, for the service of the house of the LORD."

Divisions of the Priests

24 The divisions of the descendants of Aaron were these. The sons of Aaron: Nadab, Abihu, Eleazar, and Ithamar. 2 But Nadab and Abihu died before their father, and had no sons; so Eleazar and Ithamar became the priests. 3 Along with Zadok of the sons of Eleazar, and Ahimelech of the sons of Ithamar, David organized them according to the appointed duties in their service. 4 Since more chief men were found among the sons of Eleazar than among the sons of Ithamar, they organized them under sixteen heads of ancestral houses

23.12
Ex 6.18
23.13
Ex 6.20;
28.1; 30.6-10;
Deut 21.5
23.16
1 Chr 26.24ff
23.21
1 Chr 24.26ff
23.24
Num 10.17,
21; v. 3
23.25
1 Chr 22.18

23.26
Num 4.5
23.29
Lev 23.5-9;
Ex 25.30;
Lev 6.20;
2.4-7; 19.35
23.31
Isa 1.13,14;
Lev 23.24
23.32
Num 1.53;
1 Chr 9.27;
Num 3.6
24.1
Ex 6.23
24.2
Lev 10.2;
Num 3.4

f Or Gershom; See 1 Chr 6.1, note, and 23.15 g Vg Compare Gk Syr: Heb to the Gershonite

of the sons of Eleazar, and eight of the sons of Ithamar. ⁵They organized them by lot, all alike, for there were officers of the sanctuary and officers of God among both the sons of Eleazar and the sons of Ithamar. ⁶The scribe Shemaiah son of Nethanel, a Levite, recorded them in the presence of the king, and the officers, and Zadok the priest, and Ahimelech son of Abiathar, and the heads of ancestral houses of the priests and of the Levites; one ancestral house being chosen for Eleazar and one chosen for Ithamar.

7 The first lot fell to Jehoiarib, the second to Jedaiah, ⁸the third to Harim, the fourth to Seorim, ⁹the fifth to Malchijah, the sixth to Mijamin, ¹⁰the seventh to Hakkoz, the eighth to Abijah, ¹¹the ninth to Jeshua, the tenth to Shecaniah, ¹²the eleventh to Eliashib, the twelfth to Jakim, ¹³the thirteenth to Huppah, the fourteenth to Jeshebeab, ¹⁴the fifteenth to Bilgah, the sixteenth to Immer, ¹⁵the seventeenth to Hezir, the eighteenth to Happizzez, ¹⁶the nineteenth to Pethahiah, the twentieth to Jehezkel, ¹⁷the twenty-first to Jachin, the twenty-second to Gamul, ¹⁸the twenty-third to Delaiah, the twenty-fourth to Maaziah. ¹⁹These had as their appointed duty in their service to enter the house of the LORD according to the procedure established for them by their ancestor Aaron, as the LORD God of Israel had commanded him.

Other Levites

20 And of the rest of the sons of Levi: of the sons of Amram, Shubael; of the sons of Shubael, Jehdeiah. ²¹Of Rehabiah: of the sons of Rehabiah, Isshiah the chief. ²²Of the Izharites, Shelomoth; of the sons of Shelomoth, Jahath. ²³The sons of Hebron:ʰ Jeriah the chief,ⁱ Amariah the second, Jahaziel the third, Jekameam the fourth. ²⁴The sons of Uzziel, Micah; of the sons of Micah, Shamir. ²⁵The brother of Micah, Isshiah; of the sons of Isshiah, Zechariah. ²⁶The sons of Merari: Mahli and

Mushi. The sons of Jaaziah: Beno.ⁱ ²⁷The sons of Merari: of Jaaziah, Beno,ⁱ Shoham, Zaccur, and Ibri. ²⁸Of Mahli: Eleazar, who had no sons. ²⁹Of Kish, the sons of Kish: Jerahmeel. ³⁰The sons of Mushi: Mahli, Eder, and Jerimoth. These were the sons of the Levites according to their ancestral houses. ³¹These also cast lots corresponding to their kindred, the descendants of Aaron, in the presence of King David, Zadok, Ahimelech, and the heads of ancestral houses of the priests and of the Levites, the chief as well as the youngest brother.

The Temple Musicians

25 David and the officers of the army also set apart for the service the sons of Asaph, and of Heman, and of Jeduthun, who should prophesy with lyres, harps, and cymbals. The list of those who did the work and of their duties was: ²Of the sons of Asaph: Zaccur, Joseph, Nethaniah, and Asarelah, sons of Asaph, under the direction of Asaph, who prophesied under the direction of the king. ³Of Jeduthun, the sons of Jeduthun: Gedaliah, Zeri, Jeshaiah, Shimei,ᵏ Hashabiah, and Mattithiah, six, under the direction of their father Jeduthun, who prophesied with the lyre in thanksgiving and praise to the LORD. ⁴Of Heman, the sons of Heman: Bukkiah, Mattaniah, Uzziel, Shebuel, and Jerimoth, Hananiah, Hanani, Eliathah, Giddalti, and Romamti-ezer, Joshbekashah, Mallothi, Hothir, Mahazioth. ⁵All these were the sons of Heman the king's seer, according to the promise of God to exalt him; for God had given Heman fourteen sons and three daughters. ⁶They were all under the direction of their father for the music in the house of the LORD with cymbals, harps, and lyres for the service of the house of God. Asaph, Jeduthun, and Heman

24.5
v. 31
24.10
Neh 12.4, 17; Lk 1.5
24.19
1 Chr 9.25
24.21
1 Chr 23.17
24.23
1 Chr 23.19
24.26
1 Chr 23.21

24.31
vv. 5,6
25.1
1 Chr 6.33, 39; 15.16
25.3
1 Chr 16.41, 42
25.4
1 Chr 6.33;
v. 25
25.6
1 Chr 15.16, 19

ʰ See 23.19: Heb lacks *Hebron* ⁱ See 23.19: Heb lacks *the chief* ⁱ Or *his son*: Meaning of Heb uncertain ᵏ One Ms: Gk: MT lacks *Shimei*

were under the order of the king. ⁷They and their kindred, who were trained in singing to the LORD, all of whom were skillful, numbered two hundred eighty-eight. ⁸And they cast lots for their duties, small and great, teacher and pupil alike.

9 The first lot fell for Asaph to Joseph; the second to Gedaliah, to him and his brothers and his sons, twelve; ¹⁰the third to Zaccur, his sons and his brothers, twelve; ¹¹the fourth to Izri, his sons and his brothers, twelve; ¹²the fifth to Nethaniah, his sons and his brothers, twelve; ¹³the sixth to Bukkiah, his sons and his brothers, twelve; ¹⁴the seventh to Jesarelah,¹ his sons and his brothers, twelve; ¹⁵the eighth to Jeshaiah, his sons and his brothers, twelve; ¹⁶the ninth to Mattaniah, his sons and his brothers, twelve; ¹⁷the tenth to Shimei, his sons and his brothers, twelve; ¹⁸the eleventh to Azarel, his sons and his brothers, twelve; ¹⁹the twelfth to Hashabiah, his sons and his brothers, twelve; ²⁰to the thirteenth, Shubael, his sons and his brothers, twelve; ²¹to the fourteenth, Mattithiah, his sons and his brothers, twelve; ²²to the fifteenth, to Jeremoth, his sons and his brothers, twelve; ²³to the sixteenth, to Hananiah, his sons and his brothers, twelve; ²⁴to the seventeenth, to Joshbekashah, his sons and his brothers, twelve; ²⁵to the eighteenth, to Hanani, his sons and his brothers, twelve; ²⁶to the nineteenth, to Mallothi, his sons and his brothers, twelve; ²⁷to the twentieth, to Eliathah, his sons and his brothers, twelve; ²⁸to the twenty-first, to Hothir, his sons and his brothers, twelve; ²⁹to the twenty-second, to Giddalti, his sons and his brothers, twelve; ³⁰to the twenty-third, to Mahazioth, his sons and his brothers, twelve; ³¹to the twenty-fourth, to Romamti-ezer, his sons and his brothers, twelve.

The Gatekeepers

26 As for the divisions of the gatekeepers: of the Korah-ites, Meshelemiah son of Kore, of the sons of Asaph. ²Meshelemiah had sons: Zechariah the firstborn, Jediael the second, Zebadiah the third, Jathniel the fourth, ³Elam the fifth, Jehohanan the sixth, Eliehoenai the seventh. ⁴Obed-edom had sons: Shemaiah the firstborn, Jehozabad the second, Joah the third, Sachar the fourth, Nethanel the fifth, ⁵Ammiel the sixth, Issachar the seventh, Peullethai the eighth; for God blessed him. ⁶Also to his son Shemaiah sons were born who exercised authority in their ancestral houses, for they were men of great ability. ⁷The sons of Shemaiah: Othni, Rephael, Obed, and Elzabad, whose brothers were able men, Elihu and Semachiah. ⁸All these, sons of Obed-edom with their sons and brothers, were able men qualified for the service; sixty-two of Obed-edom. ⁹Meshelemiah had sons and brothers, able men, eighteen. ¹⁰Hosah, of the sons of Merari, had sons: Shimri the chief (for though he was not the firstborn, his father made him chief), ¹¹Hilkiah the second, Tebaliah the third, Zechariah the fourth: all the sons and brothers of Hosah totaled thirteen.

12 These divisions of the gatekeepers, corresponding to their leaders, had duties, just as their kindred did, ministering in the house of the LORD; ¹³and they cast lots by ancestral houses, small and great alike, for their gates. ¹⁴The lot for the east fell to Shelemiah. They cast lots also for his son Zechariah, a prudent counselor, and his lot came out for the north. ¹⁵Obed-edom's came out for the south, and to his sons was allotted the storehouse. ¹⁶For Shuppim and Hosah it came out for the west, at the gate of Shallecheth on the ascending road. Guard corresponded to guard. ¹⁷On the east there were six Levites each day,ᵐ on the north four each day, on the south four each day, as well as two and two at

Cross references (center column)

25.8
1 Chr 26.13
25.9
1 Chr 6.39
25.16
v. 4
25.23
v. 4
25.25
v. 4
26.1
v. 19

26.4
1 Chr 15.18
26.10
1 Chr 16.38
26.12
v. 1
26.13
1 Chr 24.5, 31; 25.8

¹Or *Asarelah*; see 25.2 ᵐGk: Heb lacks *each day*

the storehouse; [18] and for the colonnade[n] on the west there were four at the road and two at the colonnade.[n] [19] These were the divisions of the gatekeepers among the Korahites and the sons of Merari.

The Treasurers, Officers, and Judges

20 And of the Levites, Ahijah had charge of the treasuries of the house of God and the treasuries of the dedicated gifts. [21] The sons of Ladan, the sons of the Gershonites belonging to Ladan, the heads of families belonging to Ladan the Gershonite: Jehieli.[o] 22 The sons of Jehieli, Zetham and his brother Joel, were in charge of the treasuries of the house of the LORD. [23] Of the Amramites, the Izharites, the Hebronites, and the Uzzielites: [24] Shebuel son of Gershom, son of Moses, was chief officer in charge of the treasuries. [25] His brothers: from Eliezer were his son Rehabiah, his son Jeshaiah, his son Joram, his son Zichri, and his son Shelomoth. [26] This Shelomoth and his brothers were in charge of all the treasuries of the dedicated gifts that King David, and the heads of families, and the officers of the thousands and the hundreds, and the commanders of the army, had dedicated. [27] From booty won in battles they dedicated gifts for the maintenance of the house of the LORD. [28] Also all that Samuel the seer, and Saul son of Kish, and Abner son of Ner, and Joab son of Zeruiah had dedicated — all dedicated gifts were in the care of Shelomoth[p] and his brothers.

29 Of the Izharites, Chenaniah and his sons were appointed to outside duties for Israel, as officers and judges. [30] Of the Hebronites, Hashabiah and his brothers, one thousand seven hundred men of ability, had the oversight of Israel west of the Jordan for all the work of the LORD and for the service of the king. [31] Of the Hebronites, Jerijah was chief of the Hebronites. (In the fortieth year of David's reign

search was made, of whatever genealogy or family, and men of great ability among them were found at Jazer in Gilead.) [32] King David appointed him and his brothers, two thousand seven hundred men of ability, heads of families, to have the oversight of the Reubenites, the Gadites, and the half-tribe of the Manassites for everything pertaining to God and for the affairs of the king.

The Military Divisions

27 This is the list of the people of Israel, the heads of families, the commanders of the thousands and the hundreds, and their officers who served the king in all matters concerning the divisions that came and went, month after month throughout the year, each division numbering twenty-four thousand:

2 Jashobeam son of Zabdiel was in charge of the first division in the first month; in his division were twenty-four thousand. [3] He was a descendant of Perez, and was chief of all the commanders of the army for the first month. [4] Dodai the Ahohite was in charge of the division of the second month; Mikloth was the chief officer of his division. In his division were twenty-four thousand. [5] The third commander, for the third month, was Benaiah son of the priest Jehoiada, as chief; in his division were twenty-four thousand. [6] This is the Benaiah who was a mighty man of the Thirty and in command of the Thirty; his son Ammizabad was in charge of his division.[q] [7] Asahel brother of Joab was fourth, for the fourth month, and his son Zebadiah after him; in his division were twenty-four thousand. [8] The fifth commander, for the fifth month, was Shamhuth, the Izrahite; in his division were twenty-four thousand. [9] Sixth, for the sixth month, was Ira son of Ikkesh the Tekoite; in his di-

26.20
1 Chr 28.12
26.24
1 Chr 23.16
26.25
1 Chr 23.18
26.26
2 Sam 8.11
26.28
1 Sam 9.9
26.29
Neh 11.16;
1 Chr 23.4
26.30
1 Chr 27.17
26.31
1 Chr 23.19

26.32
2 Chr 19.11
27.2
2 Sam 23.8-50;
1 Chr 11.11-31
27.6
1 Chr 11.22ff
27.7
1 Chr 11.26
27.9
1 Chr 11.28

[n] Heb *parbar*: meaning uncertain
[o] The Hebrew text of verse 21 is confused
[p] Gk Compare 26.28: Heb *Shelomith*
[q] Gk Vg: Heb *Ammizabad was his division*

vision were twenty-four thousand. [10] Seventh, for the seventh month, was Helez the Pelonite, of the Ephraimites; in his division were twenty-four thousand. [11] Eighth, for the eighth month, was Sibbecai the Hushathite, of the Zerahites; in his division were twenty-four thousand. [12] Ninth, for the ninth month, was Abiezer of Anathoth, a Benjaminite; in his division were twenty-four thousand. [13] Tenth, for the tenth month, was Maharai of Netophah, of the Zerahites; in his division were twenty-four thousand. [14] Eleventh, for the eleventh month, was Benaiah of Pirathon, of the Ephraimites; in his division were twenty-four thousand. [15] Twelfth, for the twelfth month, was Heldai the Netophathite, of Othniel; in his division were twenty-four thousand.

Leaders of Tribes

16 Over the tribes of Israel, for the Reubenites, Eliezer son of Zichri was chief officer; for the Simeonites, Shephatiah son of Maacah; [17] for Levi, Hashabiah son of Kemuel; for Aaron, Zadok; [18] for Judah, Elihu, one of David's brothers; for Issachar, Omri son of Michael; [19] for Zebulun, Ishmaiah son of Obadiah; for Naphtali, Jerimoth son of Azriel; [20] for the Ephraimites, Hoshea son of Azaziah; for the half-tribe of Manasseh, Joel son of Pedaiah; [21] for the half-tribe of Manasseh in Gilead, Iddo son of Zechariah; for Benjamin, Jaasiel son of Abner; [22] for Dan, Azarel son of Jeroham. These were the leaders of the tribes of Israel. [23] David did not count those below twenty years of age, for the LORD had promised to make Israel as numerous as the stars of heaven. [24] Joab son of Zeruiah began to count them, but did not finish; yet wrath came upon Israel for this, and the number was not entered into the account of the Annals of King David.

Other Civic Officials

25 Over the king's treasuries was Azmaveth son of Adiel. Over

27.10
1 Chr 11.27
27.11
1 Chr 11.29
27.12
1 Chr 11.28
27.13
1 Chr 11.30
27.14
1 Chr 11.31
27.22
1 Chr 28.1
27.23
Gen 15.5
27.24
2 Sam 24.15;
1 Chr 21.7

27.28
1 Kings 10.27;
2 Chr 1.15
27.33
2 Sam 15.12,
32,37
27.34
1 Kings 1.7;
1 Chr 11.6
28.1
1 Chr 27.1-31;
11.10-47
28.2
2 Sam 7.2;
1 Chr 17.1,
2; Ps 132.7
28.3
2 Sam 7.5,
13;
1 Chr 22.8
28.4
1 Sam 16.6-13;
1 Chr 17.23,
27; 5.2;
Gen 49.8-10

the treasuries in the country, in the cities, in the villages and in the towers, was Jonathan son of Uzziah. [26] Over those who did the work of the field, tilling the soil, was Ezri son of Chelub. [27] Over the vineyards was Shimei the Ramathite. Over the produce of the vineyards for the wine cellars was Zabdi the Shiphmite. [28] Over the olive and sycamore trees in the Shephelah was Baal-hanan the Gederite. Over the stores of oil was Joash. [29] Over the herds that pastured in Sharon was Shitrai the Sharonite. Over the herds in the valleys was Shaphat son of Adlai. [30] Over the camels was Obil the Ishmaelite. Over the donkeys was Jehdeiah the Meronothite. Over the flocks was Jaziz the Hagrite. [31] All these were stewards of King David's property.

32 Jonathan, David's uncle, was a counselor, being a man of understanding and a scribe; Jehiel son of Hachmoni attended the king's sons. [33] Ahithophel was the king's counselor, and Hushai the Archite was the king's friend. [34] After Ahithophel came Jehoiada son of Benaiah, and Abiathar. Joab was commander of the king's army.

Solomon Instructed to Build the Temple

28 David assembled at Jerusalem all the officials of Israel, the officials of the tribes, the officers of the divisions that served the king, the commanders of the thousands, the commanders of the hundreds, the stewards of all the property and cattle of the king and his sons, together with the palace officials, the mighty warriors, and all the warriors. [2] Then King David rose to his feet and said: "Hear me, my brothers and my people. I had planned to build a house of rest for the ark of the covenant of the LORD, for the footstool of our God; and I made preparations for building. [3] But God said to me, 'You shall not build a house for my name, for you are a warrior and have shed blood.' [4] Yet the LORD God of Israel chose me from all my ancestral house to

be king over Israel forever; for he chose Judah as leader, and in the house of Judah my father's house, and among my father's sons he took delight in making me king over all Israel. ⁵And of all my sons, for the LORD has given me many, he has chosen my son Solomon to sit upon the throne of the kingdom of the LORD over Israel. ⁶He said to me, 'It is your son Solomon who shall build my house and my courts, for I have chosen him to be a son to me, and I will be a father to him. ⁷I will establish his kingdom forever if he continues resolute in keeping my commandments and my ordinances, as he is today.' ⁸Now therefore in the sight of all Israel, the assembly of the LORD, and in the hearing of our God, observe and search out all the commandments of the LORD your God; that you may possess this good land, and leave it for an inheritance to your children after you forever.

9 "And you, my son Solomon, know the God of your father, and serve him with single mind and willing heart; for the LORD searches every mind, and understands every plan and thought. If you seek him, he will be found by you; but if you forsake him, he will abandon you forever. ¹⁰Take heed now, for the LORD has chosen you to build a house as the sanctuary; be strong, and act."

11 Then David gave his son Solomon the plan of the vestibule of the temple, and of its houses, its treasuries, its upper rooms, and its inner chambers, and of the room for the mercy seat;ʳ ¹²and the plan of all that he had in mind: for the courts of the house of the LORD, all the surrounding chambers, the treasuries of the house of God, and the treasuries for dedicated gifts; ¹³for the divisions of the priests and of the Levites, and all the work of the service in the house of the LORD; for all the vessels for the service in the house of the LORD, ¹⁴the weight of gold for all golden vessels for each service, the weight of silver vessels for each service, ¹⁵the

weight of the golden lampstands and their lamps, the weight of gold for each lampstand and its lamps, the weight of silver for a lampstand and its lamps, according to the use of each in the service, ¹⁶the weight of gold for each table for the rows of bread, the silver for the silver tables, ¹⁷and pure gold for the forks, the basins, and the cups; for the golden bowls and the weight of each; for the silver bowls and the weight of each; ¹⁸for the altar of incense made of refined gold, and its weight; also his plan for the golden chariot of the cherubim that spread their wings and covered the ark of the covenant of the LORD.

19 "All this, in writing at the LORD's direction, he made clear to me—the plan of all the works."

20 David said further to his son Solomon, "Be strong and of good courage, and act. Do not be afraid or dismayed; for the LORD God, my God, is with you. He will not fail you or forsake you, until all the work for the service of the house of the LORD is finished. ²¹Here are the divisions of the priests and the Levites for all the service of the house of God; and with you in all the work will be every volunteer who has skill for any kind of service; also the officers and all the people will be wholly at your command."

Offerings for Building the Temple

29 King David said to the whole assembly, "My son Solomon, whom alone God has chosen, is young and inexperienced, and the work is great; for the templeˢ will not be for mortals but for the LORD God. ²So I have provided for the house of my God, so far as I was able, the gold for the things of gold, the silver for the things of silver, and the bronze for the things of bronze, the iron for the things of iron, and wood for the things of wood, besides great quantities of onyx and stones for setting, antimony, colored stones, all sorts of precious stones, and mar-

28.5
1 Chr 3.1-9;
22.9,10
28.6
2 Sam 7.13,
14;
1 Chr 22.9,
10
28.7
1 Chr 22.13
28.9
Jer 9.24;
1 Chr 29.17-
19;
1 Sam 16.7;
2 Chr 15.2;
Jer 29.13
28.10
1 Chr 22.13
28.11
vv. 12,19;
Ex 25.40
28.12
1 Chr 26.20
28.13
1 Chr 24.1;
23.6
28.15
Ex 25.31-39

28.18
Ex 30.1-10;
25.18-22
28.19
vv. 11,12
28.20
Josh 1.6,7,
9;
1 Chr 22.13;
Josh 1.5
28.21
v. 13;
Ex 35.25-35;
36.1,2
29.1
1 Chr 22.5;
v. 19
29.2
1 Chr 22.3-5

ʳ Or *the cover* ˢ Heb *fortress*

ble in abundance. ³Moreover, in addition to all that I have provided for the holy house, I have a treasure of my own of gold and silver, and because of my devotion to the house of my God I give it to the house of my God: ⁴three thousand talents of gold, of the gold of Ophir, and seven thousand talents of refined silver, for overlaying the walls of the house, ⁵and for all the work to be done by artisans, gold for the things of gold and silver for the things of silver. Who then will offer willingly, consecrating themselves today to the LORD?"

6 Then the leaders of ancestral houses made their freewill offerings, as did also the leaders of the tribes, the commanders of the thousands and of the hundreds, and the officers over the king's work. ⁷They gave for the service of the house of God five thousand talents and ten thousand darics of gold, ten thousand talents of silver, eighteen thousand talents of bronze, and one hundred thousand talents of iron. ⁸Whoever had precious stones gave them to the treasury of the house of the LORD, into the care of Jehiel the Gershonite. ⁹Then the people rejoiced because these had given willingly, for with single mind they had offered freely to the LORD; King David also rejoiced greatly.

David's Praise to God

10 Then David blessed the LORD in the presence of all the assembly; David said: "Blessed are you, O LORD, the God of our ancestor Israel, forever and ever. ¹¹Yours, O LORD, are the greatness, the power, the glory, the victory, and the majesty; for all that is in the heavens and on the earth is yours; yours is the kingdom, O LORD, and you are exalted as head above all. ¹²Riches and honor come from you, and you rule over all. In your hand are power and might; and it is in your hand to make great and to give strength to all. ¹³And now, our God, we give thanks to you and praise your glorious name.

14 "But who am I, and what is my people, that we should be able to make this freewill offering? For all things come from you, and of your own have we given you. ¹⁵For we are aliens and transients before you, as were all our ancestors; our days on the earth are like a shadow, and there is no hope. ¹⁶O LORD our God, all this abundance that we have provided for building you a house for your holy name comes from your hand and is all your own. ¹⁷I know, my God, that you search the heart, and take pleasure in uprightness; in the uprightness of my heart I have freely offered all these things, and now I have seen your people, who are present here, offering freely and joyously to you. ¹⁸O LORD, the God of Abraham, Isaac, and Israel, our ancestors, keep forever such purposes and thoughts in the hearts of your people, and direct their hearts toward you. ¹⁹Grant to my son Solomon that with single mind he may keep your commandments, your decrees, and your statutes, performing all of them, and that he may build the temple[t] for which I have made provision."

20 Then David said to the whole assembly, "Bless the LORD your God." And all the assembly blessed the LORD, the God of their ancestors, and bowed their heads and prostrated themselves before the LORD and the king. ²¹On the next day they offered sacrifices and burnt offerings to the LORD, a thousand bulls, a thousand rams, and a thousand lambs, with their libations, and sacrifices in abundance for all Israel; ²²and they ate and drank before the LORD on that day with great joy.

Solomon Anointed King

They made David's son Solomon king a second time; they anointed him as the LORD's prince, and Zadok as priest. ²³Then Solomon sat on the throne of the LORD, succeeding his father David as king; he prospered, and all Israel obeyed

29.4 1 Chr 22.14; 1 Kings 9.28
29.6 1 Chr 27.1; 28.1; 27.25ff
29.7 Ezra 2.69; Neh 7.70
29.8 1 Chr 26.21
29.9 1 Kings 8.61; 2 Cor 9.7
29.11 Mt 6.13; 1 Tim 1.17; Rev 5.13
29.12 2 Chr 1.12; Rom 11.36
29.15 Lev 25.23; Ps 39.12; Heb 11.13; 1 Pet 2.11; Job 14.2
29.17 1 Chr 28.9; Prov 11.20
29.19 1 Chr 28.9; Ps 72.1; v. 2; 1 Chr 22.14
29.21 1 Kings 8.62, 63
29.22 1 Chr 23.1; 1 Kings 1.33-39

[t] Heb *fortress*

him. ²⁴All the leaders and the mighty warriors, and also all the sons of King David, pledged their allegiance to King Solomon. ²⁵The LORD highly exalted Solomon in the sight of all Israel, and bestowed upon him such royal majesty as had not been on any king before him in Israel.

Summary of David's Reign

26 Thus David son of Jesse reigned over all Israel. ²⁷The period that he reigned over Israel was forty years; he reigned seven years in Hebron, and thirty-three years in Jerusalem. ²⁸He died in a good old age, full of days, riches, and honor; and his son Solomon succeeded him. ²⁹Now the acts of King David, from first to last, are written in the records of the seer Samuel, and in the records of the prophet Nathan, and in the records of the seer Gad, ³⁰with accounts of all his rule and his might and of the events that befell him and Israel and all the kingdoms of the earth.

29.25
2 Chr 1.1, 12;
1 Kings 3.13
29.26
1 Chr 18.14
29.27
2 Sam 5.4, 5;
1 Kings 2.11

29.28
Gen 15.15; 25.8;
1 Chr 23.1
29.30
Dan 2.21; 4.23,25

2 Chronicles

Title and Background

See Introduction to 1 Chronicles.

Author and Date of Writing

See Introduction to 1 Chronicles.

Theme and Message

2 Chronicles continues the history of David's royal line. This book, like 1 Chronicles, shows that one's relationship to God was most important, for the author measured the kings of Judah on the basis of their faithfulness to God and his law. The reigns of evil kings receive only a brief account, while the reigns of good kings are described in more detail.

Outline

 I. The Reign of Solomon (1.1–9.31)
 II. The Kings of Judah (10.1–36.14)
 III. The Destruction of Jerusalem (36.15-23)

Solomon Requests Wisdom

1 Solomon son of David established himself in his kingdom; the LORD his God was with him and made him exceedingly great.

2 Solomon summoned all Israel, the commanders of the thousands and of the hundreds, the judges, and all the leaders of all Israel, the heads of families. ³ Then Solomon, and the whole assembly with him, went to the high place that was at Gibeon; for God's tent of meeting, which Moses the servant of the LORD had made in the wilderness, was there. ⁴ (But David had brought the ark of God up from Kiriath-jearim to the place that David had prepared for it; for he had pitched a tent for it in Jerusalem.) ⁵ Moreover the bronze altar that Bezalel son of Uri, son of Hur, had made, was there in front of the tabernacle of the LORD. And Solomon and the assembly inquired at it. ⁶ Solomon went up there to the bronze altar before the LORD, which was at the tent of meeting, and offered a thousand burnt offerings on it.

7 That night God appeared to Solomon, and said to him, "Ask what I should give you." ⁸ Solomon said to God, "You have shown great and steadfast love to my father David, and have made me succeed him as king. ⁹ O LORD God, let your promise to my father David now be fulfilled, for you have made me king over a people as numerous as the dust of the earth. ¹⁰ Give me now wisdom and knowledge to go out and come in before this people, for who can rule this great people of yours?" ¹¹ God answered Solomon, "Because this was in your heart, and you have not asked for possessions, wealth, honor, or the life of those who hate you, and have not even asked for long life, but have asked for wisdom and knowledge for yourself that you may rule my people over whom I have made you king, ¹² wisdom and knowledge are granted to you. I will also give you riches, possessions, and honor, such as none of the kings had who were before you, and none after you shall have the like." ¹³ So Solomon came from[a]

Ref	Cross-reference
1.1	1 Kings 2.12, 46; Gen 39.2; 1 Chr 29.25
1.2	1 Chr 28.1
1.3ff	1 Kings 3.4; Ex 36.8
1.4	2 Sam 6.2, 17; 1 Chr 15.1
1.5	Ex 38.1,2
1.6	1 Kings 3.4
1.7	1 Kings 3.5, 6
1.8	1 Chr 28.5
1.9	1 Kings 3.7, 8
1.10	1 Kings 3.9
1.11	1 Kings 3.11-13
1.12	1 Chr 29.25; 2 Chr 9.22

[a] Gk Vg: Heb to

the high place at Gibeon, from the tent of meeting, to Jerusalem. And he reigned over Israel.

Solomon's Military and Commercial Activity

14 Solomon gathered together chariots and horses; he had fourteen hundred chariots and twelve thousand horses, which he stationed in the chariot cities and with the king in Jerusalem. 15 The king made silver and gold as common in Jerusalem as stone, and he made cedar as plentiful as the sycamore of the Shephelah. 16 Solomon's horses were imported from Egypt and Kue; the king's traders received them from Kue at the prevailing price. 17 They imported from Egypt, and then exported, a chariot for six hundred shekels of silver, and a horse for one hundred fifty; so through them these were exported to all the kings of the Hittites and the kings of Aram.

Preparations for Building the Temple

2 b Solomon decided to build a temple for the name of the LORD, and a royal palace for himself. 2 c Solomon conscripted seventy thousand laborers and eighty thousand stonecutters in the hill country, with three thousand six hundred to oversee them.

Alliance with Huram of Tyre

3 Solomon sent word to King Huram of Tyre: "Once you dealt with my father David and sent him cedar to build himself a house to live in. 4 I am now about to build a house for the name of the LORD my God and dedicate it to him for offering fragrant incense before him, and for the regular offering of the rows of bread, and for burnt offerings morning and evening, on the sabbaths and the new moons and the appointed festivals of the LORD our God, as ordained forever for Israel. 5 The house that I am about to build will be great, for our God is greater than other gods. 6 But who is able to build him a house, since heaven, even highest heaven, can-

not contain him? Who am I to build a house for him, except as a place to make offerings before him? 7 So now send me an artisan skilled to work in gold, silver, bronze, and iron, and in purple, crimson, and blue fabrics, trained also in engraving, to join the skilled workers who are with me in Judah and Jerusalem, whom my father David provided. 8 Send me also cedar, cypress, and algum timber from Lebanon, for I know that your servants are skilled in cutting Lebanon timber. My servants will work with your servants 9 to prepare timber for me in abundance, for the house I am about to build will be great and wonderful. 10 I will provide for your servants, those who cut the timber, twenty thousand cors of crushed wheat, twenty thousand cors of barley, twenty thousand baths d of wine, and twenty thousand baths of oil."

11 Then King Huram of Tyre answered in a letter that he sent to Solomon, "Because the LORD loves his people he has made you king over them." 12 Huram also said, "Blessed be the LORD God of Israel, who made heaven and earth, who has given King David a wise son, endowed with discretion and understanding, who will build a temple for the LORD, and a royal palace for himself.

13 "I have dispatched Huram-abi, a skilled artisan, endowed with understanding, 14 the son of one of the Danite women, his father a Tyrian. He is trained to work in gold, silver, bronze, iron, stone, and wood, and in purple, blue, and crimson fabrics and fine linen, and to do all sorts of engraving and execute any design that may be assigned him, with your artisans, the artisans of my lord, your father David. 15 Now, as for the wheat, barley, oil, and wine, of which my lord has spoken, let him send them to his servants. 16 We will cut whatever timber you need from Lebanon,

Cross references (center column):

1.14ff 1 Kings 4.26; 10.26-29; 2 Chr 9.25
1.15 1 Kings 10.27; 2 Chr 9.27
1.16 1 Kings 10.28, 29; 2 Chr 9.28
2.1 1 Kings 5.5
2.2 v. 18; 1 Kings 5.15, 16
2.3 1 Kings 5.2-11; 1 Chr 14.1
2.4 v. 1; Ex 30.7; 25.30; Num 28.9, 10
2.5 1 Chr 16.25; Ps 135.5
2.6 1 Kings 8.27; 2 Chr 6.18
2.7 vv. 13,14; 1 Chr 22.15
2.8 2 Chr 9.10, 11
2.10 1 Kings 5.11
2.11 1 Kings 10.9; 2 Chr 9.8
2.12 1 Kings 5.7; Ps 33.6; 102.25
2.14 1 Kings 7.13, 14
2.15 v. 10
2.16 1 Kings 5.8, 9

b Ch 1.18 in Heb c Ch 2.1 in Heb d A Hebrew measure of volume

and bring it to you as rafts by sea to Joppa; you will take it up to Jerusalem."

17 Then Solomon took a census of all the aliens who were residing in the land of Israel, after the census that his father David had taken; and there were found to be one hundred fifty-three thousand six hundred. 18 Seventy thousand of them he assigned as laborers, eighty thousand as stonecutters in the hill country, and three thousand six hundred as overseers to make the people work.

Solomon Builds the Temple

3 Solomon began to build the house of the LORD in Jerusalem on Mount Moriah, where the LORD had appeared to his father David, at the place that David had designated, on the threshing floor of Ornan the Jebusite. 2 He began to build on the second day of the second month of the fourth year of his reign. 3 These are Solomon's measurements[e] for building the house of God: the length, in cubits of the old standard, was sixty cubits, and the width twenty cubits. 4 The vestibule in front of the nave of the house was twenty cubits long, across the width of the house;[f] and its height was one hundred twenty cubits. He overlaid it on the inside with pure gold. 5 The nave he lined with cypress, covered it with fine gold, and made palms and chains on it. 6 He adorned the house with settings of precious stones. The gold was gold from Parvaim. 7 So he lined the house with gold—its beams, its thresholds, its walls, and its doors; and he carved cherubim on the walls.

8 He made the most holy place; its length, corresponding to the width of the house, was twenty cubits, and its width twenty cubits; he overlaid it with six hundred talents of fine gold. 9 The weight of the nails was fifty shekels of gold. He overlaid the upper chambers with gold.

10 In the most holy place he

made two carved cherubim and overlaid[g] them with gold. 11 The wings of the cherubim together extended twenty cubits: one wing of the one, five cubits long, touched the wall of the house, and its other wing, five cubits long, touched the wing of the other cherub; 12 and of this cherub, one wing, five cubits long, touched the wall of the house, and the other wing, also five cubits long, was joined to the wing of the first cherub. 13 The wings of these cherubim extended twenty cubits; the cherubim[h] stood on their feet, facing the nave. 14 And Solomon[i] made the curtain of blue and purple and crimson fabrics and fine linen, and worked cherubim into it.

15 In front of the house he made two pillars thirty-five cubits high, with a capital of five cubits on the top of each. 16 He made encircling[j] chains and put them on the tops of the pillars; and he made one hundred pomegranates, and put them on the chains. 17 He set up the pillars in front of the temple, one on the right, the other on the left; the one on the right he called Jachin, and the one on the left, Boaz.

Furnishings of the Temple

4 He made an altar of bronze, twenty cubits long, twenty cubits wide, and ten cubits high. 2 Then he made the molten sea; it was round, ten cubits from rim to rim, and five cubits high. A line of thirty cubits would encircle it completely. 3 Under it were panels all around, each of ten cubits, surrounding the sea; there were two rows of panels, cast when it was cast. 4 It stood on twelve oxen, three facing north, three facing west, three facing south, and three facing east; the sea was set on them. The hindquarters of each were toward the inside. 5 Its thickness was a handbreadth; its rim was made like the rim of a cup, like

2.17
1 Chr 22.2
2.18
v. 2
3.1
1 Kings 6.1ff;
1 Chr 21.18
3.5
1 Kings 6.17
3.7
1 Kings 6.20-
22,29-35
3.8
1 Kings 6.16
3.10
1 Kings 6.23-
28

3.14
Ex 26.31;
Heb 9.3
3.15
1 Kings 7.15-
20
3.17
1 Kings 7.21
4.1
Ex 27.1,2;
2 Kings 16.14
4.2
1 Kings 7.23
4.3
1 Kings 7.24-
26
4.5
1 Kings 7.26

e Syr: Heb *foundations* f Compare 1 Kings 6.3: Meaning of Heb uncertain g Heb *they overlaid* h Heb *they* i Heb *he* j Cn: Heb *in the inner sanctuary*

the flower of a lily; it held three thousand baths. k 6 He also made ten basins in which to wash, and set five on the right side, and five on the left. In these they were to rinse what was used for the burnt offering. The sea was for the priests to wash in.

7 He made ten golden lampstands as prescribed, and set them in the temple, five on the south side and five on the north. 8 He also made ten tables and placed them in the temple, five on the right side and five on the left. And he made one hundred basins of gold. 9 He made the court of the priests, and the great court, and doors for the court; he overlaid their doors with bronze. 10 He set the sea at the southeast corner of the house.

11 And Huram made the pots, the shovels, and the basins. Thus Huram finished the work that he did for King Solomon on the house of God: 12 the two pillars, the bowls, and the two capitals on the top of the pillars; and the two latticeworks to cover the two bowls of the capitals that were on the top of the pillars; 13 the four hundred pomegranates for the two latticeworks, two rows of pomegranates for each latticework, to cover the two bowls of the capitals that were on the pillars. 14 He made the stands, the basins on the stands, 15 the one sea, and the twelve oxen underneath it. 16 The pots, the shovels, the forks, and all the equipment for these Huram-abi made of burnished bronze for King Solomon for the house of the Lord. 17 In the plain of the Jordan the king cast them, in the clay ground between Succoth and Zeredah. 18 Solomon made all these things in great quantities, so that the weight of the bronze was not determined.

19 So Solomon made all the things that were in the house of God: the golden altar, the tables for the bread of the Presence, 20 the lampstands and their lamps of pure gold to burn before the inner sanctuary, as prescribed; 21 the flowers, the lamps, and the tongs, of purest

gold; 22 the snuffers, basins, ladles, and firepans, of pure gold. As for the entrance to the temple: the inner doors to the most holy place and the doors of the nave of the temple were of gold.

5 Thus all the work that Solomon did for the house of the Lord was finished. Solomon brought in the things that his father David had dedicated, and stored the silver, the gold, and all the vessels in the treasuries of the house of God.

The Ark Brought into the Temple

2 Then Solomon assembled the elders of Israel and all the heads of the tribes, the leaders of the ancestral houses of the people of Israel, in Jerusalem, to bring up the ark of the covenant of the Lord out of the city of David, which is Zion. 3 And all the Israelites assembled before the king at the festival that is in the seventh month. 4 And all the elders of Israel came, and the Levites carried the ark. 5 So they brought up the ark, the tent of meeting, and all the holy vessels that were in the tent; the priests and the Levites brought them up. 6 King Solomon and all the congregation of Israel, who had assembled before him, were before the ark, sacrificing so many sheep and oxen that they could not be numbered or counted. 7 Then the priests brought the ark of the covenant of the Lord to its place, in the inner sanctuary of the house, in the most holy place, underneath the wings of the cherubim. 8 For the cherubim spread out their wings over the place of the ark, so that the cherubim made a covering above the ark and its poles. 9 The poles were so long that the ends of the poles were seen from the holy place in front of the inner sanctuary; but they could not be seen from outside; they are there to this day. 10 There was nothing in the ark except the two tablets that Moses put there at Horeb,

4.6 1 Kings 7.38
4.7 1 Kings 7.49; Ex 25.31,40
4.8 1 Kings 7.48
4.9 1 Kings 6.36; 2 Kings 21.5
4.10 1 Kings 7.39
4.11 1 Kings 7.40
4.12 1 Kings 7.41
4.13 1 Kings 7.20
4.14 1 Kings 7.27
4.16 1 Kings 7.14
4.17 1 Kings 7.46
4.18 1 Kings 7.47
4.19 1 Kings 7.48-50; Ex 25.30
4.20 Ex 25.31-37
5.1 1 Kings 7.51
5.2 1 Kings 8.1-9; 2 Sam 6.12
5.4 v. 7
5.9 1 Kings 8.8, 9
5.10 Deut 10.2-5; Heb 9.4

where the LORD made a covenant[1] with the people of Israel after they came out of Egypt.

11 Now when the priests came out of the holy place (for all the priests who were present had sanctified themselves, without regard to their divisions, 12 and all the levitical singers, Asaph, Heman, and Jeduthun, their sons and kindred, arrayed in fine linen, with cymbals, harps, and lyres, stood east of the altar with one hundred twenty priests who were trumpeters). 13 It was the duty of the trumpeters and singers to make themselves heard in unison in praise and thanksgiving to the LORD, and when the song was raised, with trumpets and cymbals and other musical instruments, in praise to the LORD,

"For he is good,
 for his steadfast love
 endures forever,"

the house, the house of the LORD, was filled with a cloud, 14 so that the priests could not stand to minister because of the cloud; for the glory of the LORD filled the house of God.

Dedication of the Temple

6 Then Solomon said, "The LORD has said that he would reside in thick darkness. 2 I have built you an exalted house, a place for you to reside in forever."

3 Then the king turned around and blessed all the assembly of Israel, while all the assembly of Israel stood. 4 And he said, "Blessed be the LORD, the God of Israel, who with his hand has fulfilled what he promised with his mouth to my father David, saying, 5 'Since the day that I brought my people out of the land of Egypt, I have not chosen a city from any of the tribes of Israel in which to build a house, so that my name might be there, and I chose no one as ruler over my people Israel; 6 but I have chosen Jerusalem in order that my name may be there, and I have chosen David to be over my people Israel.' 7 My father David had it in mind to build a house for the name of the LORD,

the God of Israel. 8 But the LORD said to my father David, 'You did well to consider building a house for my name; 9 nevertheless you shall not build the house, but your son who shall be born to you shall build the house for my name.' 10 Now the LORD has fulfilled his promise that he made; for I have succeeded my father David, and sit on the throne of Israel, as the LORD promised, and have built the house for the name of the LORD, the God of Israel. 11 There I have set the ark, in which is the covenant of the LORD that he made with the people of Israel."

Solomon's Prayer of Dedication

12 Then Solomon[m] stood before the altar of the LORD in the presence of the whole assembly of Israel, and spread out his hands. 13 Solomon had made a bronze platform five cubits long, five cubits wide, and three cubits high, and had set it in the court; and he stood on it. Then he knelt on his knees in the presence of the whole assembly of Israel, and spread out his hands toward heaven. 14 He said, "O LORD, God of Israel, there is no God like you, in heaven or on earth, keeping covenant in steadfast love with your servants who walk before you with all their heart— 15 you who have kept for your servant, my father David, what you promised to him. Indeed, you promised with your mouth and this day have fulfilled with your hand. 16 Therefore, O LORD, God of Israel, keep for your servant, my father David, that which you promised him, saying, 'There shall never fail you a successor before me to sit on the throne of Israel, if only your children keep to their way, to walk in my law as you have walked before me.' 17 Therefore, O LORD, God of Israel, let your word be confirmed, which you promised to your servant David.

18 "But will God indeed reside with mortals on earth? Even heaven and the highest heaven cannot

Cross-references (center column):

5.11 1 Chr 24.1-5
5.12 1 Chr 25.1-4; 15.24
5.13 2 Chr 7.3; 1 Chr 16.34, 42
5.14 1 Kings 8.11; 2 Chr 7.2
6.1 1 Kings 8.12-50
6.6 2 Chr 12.13; 1 Chr 28.4
6.7 1 Chr 28.2

6.11 2 Chr 5.10
6.12 1 Kings 8.22
6.13 1 Kings 8.54
6.14 Ex 15.11; Deut 7.9
6.15 1 Chr 22.9, 10
6.16 2 Sam 7.12, 16; 1 Kings 2.4; 2 Chr 7.18
6.18 2 Chr 2.6

[1] Heb lacks *a covenant* [m] Heb *he*

contain you, how much less this house that I have built! [19] Regard your servant's prayer and his plea, O LORD my God, heeding the cry and the prayer that your servant prays to you. [20] May your eyes be open day and night toward this house, the place where you promised to set your name, and may you heed the prayer that your servant prays toward this place. [21] And hear the plea of your servant and of your people Israel, when they pray toward this place; may you hear from heaven your dwelling place; hear and forgive.

[22] "If someone sins against another and is required to take an oath and comes and swears before your altar in this house, [23] may you hear from heaven, and act, and judge your servants, repaying the guilty by bringing their conduct on their own head, and vindicating those who are in the right by rewarding them in accordance with their righteousness.

[24] "When your people Israel, having sinned against you, are defeated before an enemy but turn again to you, confess your name, pray and plead with you in this house, [25] may you hear from heaven, and forgive the sin of your people Israel, and bring them again to the land that you gave to them and to their ancestors.

[26] "When heaven is shut up and there is no rain because they have sinned against you, and then they pray toward this place, confess your name, and turn from their sin, because you punish them, [27] may you hear in heaven, forgive the sin of your servants, your people Israel, when you teach them the good way in which they should walk; and send down rain upon your land, which you have given to your people as an inheritance.

[28] "If there is famine in the land, if there is plague, blight, mildew, locust, or caterpillar; if their enemies besiege them in any of the settlements of the lands; whatever suffering, whatever sickness there is; [29] whatever prayer, whatever

plea from any individual or from all your people Israel, all knowing their own suffering and their own sorrows so that they stretch out their hands toward this house; [30] may you hear from heaven, your dwelling place, forgive, and render to all whose heart you know, according to all their ways, for only you know the human heart. [31] Thus may they fear you and walk in your ways all the days that they live in the land that you gave to our ancestors.

[32] "Likewise when foreigners, who are not of your people Israel, come from a distant land because of your great name, and your mighty hand, and your outstretched arm, when they come and pray toward this house, [33] may you hear from heaven your dwelling place, and do whatever the foreigners ask of you, in order that all the peoples of the earth may know your name and fear you, as do your people Israel, and that they may know that your name has been invoked on this house that I have built.

[34] "If your people go out to battle against their enemies, by whatever way you shall send them, and they pray to you toward this city that you have chosen and the house that I have built for your name, [35] then hear from heaven their prayer and their plea, and maintain their cause.

[36] "If they sin against you—for there is no one who does not sin—and you are angry with them and give them to an enemy, so that they are carried away captive to a land far or near; [37] then if they come to their senses in the land to which they have been taken captive, and repent, and plead with you in the land of their captivity, saying, 'We have sinned, and have done wrong; we have acted wickedly'; [38] if they repent with all their heart and soul in the land of their captivity, to which they were taken captive, and pray toward their land, which you gave to their ancestors, the city that you have chosen, and the

6.21
Mic 7.18
6.22
Mt 5.33
6.24
2 Chr 7.14
6.26
1 Kings 17.1
6.28
2 Chr 20.9

6.30
1 Sam 16.7;
1 Chr 28.9
6.32
Josh 12.20;
Acts 8.27
6.33
2 Chr 7.14
6.36
Job 15.14-16;
Jas 3.2;
1 Jn 1.8-10
6.37
2 Chr 7.14

house that I have built for your name, ³⁹then hear from heaven your dwelling place their prayer and their pleas, maintain their cause and forgive your people who have sinned against you. ⁴⁰Now, O my God, let your eyes be open and your ears attentive to prayer from this place.

⁴¹ "Now rise up, O LORD God,
 and go to your resting
 place,
 you and the ark of your
 might.
 Let your priests, O LORD God,
 be clothed with
 salvation,
 and let your faithful rejoice
 in your goodness.
⁴² O LORD God, do not reject
 your anointed one.
 Remember your steadfast
 love for your servant
 David."

Solomon Dedicates the Temple

7 When Solomon had ended his prayer, fire came down from heaven and consumed the burnt offering and the sacrifices; and the glory of the LORD filled the temple. ²The priests could not enter the house of the LORD, because the glory of the LORD filled the LORD's house. ³When all the people of Israel saw the fire come down and the glory of the LORD on the temple, they bowed down on the pavement with their faces to the ground, and worshiped and gave thanks to the LORD, saying,

"For he is good,
 for his steadfast love
 endures forever."

⁴ Then the king and all the people offered sacrifice before the LORD. ⁵King Solomon offered as a sacrifice twenty-two thousand oxen and one hundred twenty thousand sheep. So the king and all the people dedicated the house of God. ⁶The priests stood at their posts; the Levites also, with the instruments for music to the LORD that King David had made for giving thanks to the LORD—for his steadfast love endures forever—

6.40
2 Chr 7.15;
Ps 17.1
6.41
Ps 132.8-10;
1 Chr 28.2
7.1
1 Kings 8.54;
18.24,38;
2 Chr 5.13,
14
7.2
Deut 12.5,
11
7.3
2 Chr 5.13;
Ps 136.1;
1 Chr 16.41
7.4
1 Kings 8.62,
63
7.6
1 Chr 15.16-
21; 2 Chr 5.12

7.7
1 Kings 8.64-
66
7.8
1 Kings 8.65
7.9
Lev 23.36
7.10
1 Kings 8.66
7.11
1 Kings 9.1-9
7.13
2 Chr 6.26-28
7.14
2 Chr 6.27,
30,37-39
7.15
2 Chr 6.40
7.16
1 Kings 9.3;
2 Chr 6.6;
v. 12

whenever David offered praises by their ministry. Opposite them the priests sounded trumpets; and all Israel stood.

7 Solomon consecrated the middle of the court that was in front of the house of the LORD; for there he offered the burnt offerings and the fat of the offerings of well-being because the bronze altar Solomon had made could not hold the burnt offering and the grain offering and the fat parts.

8 At that time Solomon held the festival for seven days, and all Israel with him, a very great congregation, from Lebo-hamath to the Wadi of Egypt. ⁹On the eighth day they held a solemn assembly; for they had observed the dedication of the altar seven days and the festival seven days. ¹⁰On the twenty-third day of the seventh month he sent the people away to their homes, joyful and in good spirits because of the goodness that the LORD had shown to David and to Solomon and to his people Israel.

11 Thus Solomon finished the house of the LORD and the king's house; all that Solomon had planned to do in the house of the LORD and in his own house he successfully accomplished.

God's Second Appearance to Solomon

12 Then the LORD appeared to Solomon in the night and said to him: "I have heard your prayer, and have chosen this place for myself as a house of sacrifice. ¹³When I shut up the heavens so that there is no rain, or command the locust to devour the land, or send pestilence among my people, ¹⁴if my people who are called by my name humble themselves, pray, seek my face, and turn from their wicked ways, then I will hear from heaven, and will forgive their sin and heal their land. ¹⁵Now my eyes will be open and my ears attentive to the prayer that is made in this place. ¹⁶For now I have chosen and consecrated this house so that my name may be there forever; my eyes and my heart

will be there for all time. [17]As for you, if you walk before me, as your father David walked, doing according to all that I have commanded you and keeping my statutes and my ordinances, [18]then I will establish your royal throne, as I made covenant with your father David saying, 'You shall never lack a successor to rule over Israel.'

19 "But if you[n] turn aside and forsake my statutes and my commandments that I have set before you, and go and serve other gods and worship them, [20]then I will pluck you[o] up from the land that I have given you;[o] and this house, which I have consecrated for my name, I will cast out of my sight, and will make it a proverb and a byword among all peoples. [21]And regarding this house, now exalted, everyone passing by will be astonished, and say, 'Why has the LORD done such a thing to this land and to this house?' [22]Then they will say, 'Because they abandoned the LORD the God of their ancestors who brought them out of the land of Egypt, and they adopted other gods, and worshiped them and served them; therefore he has brought all this calamity upon them.' "

Various Activities of Solomon

8 At the end of twenty years, during which Solomon had built the house of the LORD and his own house, [2]Solomon rebuilt the cities that Huram had given to him, and settled the people of Israel in them.

3 Solomon went to Hamath-zobah, and captured it. [4]He built Tadmor in the wilderness and all the storage towns that he built in Hamath. [5]He also built Upper Beth-horon and Lower Beth-horon, fortified cities, with walls, gates, and bars, [6]and Baalath, as well as all Solomon's storage towns, and all the towns for his chariots, the towns for his cavalry, and whatever Solomon desired to build, in Jerusalem, in Lebanon, and in all the land of his dominion. [7]All the peo-

ple who were left of the Hittites, the Amorites, the Perizzites, the Hivites, and the Jebusites, who were not of Israel, [8]from their descendants who were still left in the land, whom the people of Israel had not destroyed—these Solomon conscripted for forced labor, as is still the case today. [9]But of the people of Israel Solomon made no slaves for his work; they were soldiers, and his officers, the commanders of his chariotry and cavalry. [10]These were the chief officers of King Solomon, two hundred fifty of them, who exercised authority over the people.

11 Solomon brought Pharaoh's daughter from the city of David to the house that he had built for her, for he said, "My wife shall not live in the house of King David of Israel, for the places to which the ark of the LORD has come are holy."

12 Then Solomon offered up burnt offerings to the LORD on the altar of the LORD that he had built in front of the vestibule, [13]as the duty of each day required, offering according to the commandment of Moses for the sabbaths, the new moons, and the three annual festivals—the festival of unleavened bread, the festival of weeks, and the festival of booths. [14]According to the ordinance of his father David, he appointed the divisions of the priests for their service, and the Levites for their offices of praise and ministry alongside the priests as the duty of each day required, and the gatekeepers in their divisions for the several gates; for so David the man of God had commanded. [15]They did not turn away from what the king had commanded the priests and Levites regarding anything at all, or regarding the treasuries.

16 Thus all the work of Solomon was accomplished from[p] the day the foundation of the house of the LORD was laid until the house of the LORD was finished completely.

7.17
1 Kings 9.4ff
7.18
2 Chr 6.16
7.19
Lev 26.14, 33;
Deut 28.15
7.20
Deut 29.28
7.21
Deut 29.24
8.1
1 Kings 9.1-28
8.5
1 Chr 7.24;
2 Chr 14.7

8.8
1 Kings 4.6;
9.21
8.11
1 Kings 3.1;
7.8
8.12
2 Chr 4.1
8.13
Ex 29.38;
Num 28.3;
Ex 23.14-17
8.14
1 Chr 24.1;
25.1; 26.1;
Neh 12.24, 36

n The word *you* in this verse is plural
o Heb *them* p Gk Syr Vg: Heb *to*

17 Then Solomon went to Ezion-geber and Eloth on the shore of the sea, in the land of Edom. [18] Huram sent him, in the care of his servants, ships and servants familiar with the sea. They went to Ophir, together with the servants of Solomon, and imported from there four hundred fifty talents of gold and brought it to King Solomon.

Visit of the Queen of Sheba

9 When the queen of Sheba heard of the fame of Solomon, she came to Jerusalem to test him with hard questions, having a very great retinue and camels bearing spices and very much gold and precious stones. When she came to Solomon, she discussed with him all that was on her mind. [2] Solomon answered all her questions; there was nothing hidden from Solomon that he could not explain to her. [3] When the queen of Sheba had observed the wisdom of Solomon, the house that he had built, [4] the food of his table, the seating of his officials, and the attendance of his servants, and their clothing, his valets, and their clothing, and his burnt offerings[q] that he offered at the house of the LORD, there was no more spirit left in her.

5 So she said to the king, "The report was true that I heard in my own land of your accomplishments and of your wisdom, [6] but I did not believe the[r] reports until I came and my own eyes saw it. Not even half of the greatness of your wisdom had been told to me; you far surpass the report that I had heard. [7] Happy are your people! Happy are these your servants, who continually attend you and hear your wisdom! [8] Blessed be the LORD your God, who has delighted in you and set you on his throne as king for the LORD your God. Because your God loved Israel and would establish them forever, he has made you king over them, that you may execute justice and righteousness." [9] Then she gave the king one hundred twenty talents of gold, a very great

quantity of spices, and precious stones: there were no spices such as those that the queen of Sheba gave to King Solomon.

10 Moreover the servants of Huram and the servants of Solomon who brought gold from Ophir brought algum wood and precious stones. [11] From the algum wood, the king made steps[s] for the house of the LORD and for the king's house, lyres also and harps for the singers; there never was seen the like of them before in the land of Judah.

12 Meanwhile King Solomon granted the queen of Sheba every desire that she expressed, well beyond what she had brought to the king. Then she returned to her own land, with her servants.

Solomon's Great Wealth

13 The weight of gold that came to Solomon in one year was six hundred sixty-six talents of gold, [14] besides that which the traders and merchants brought; and all the kings of Arabia and the governors of the land brought gold and silver to Solomon. [15] King Solomon made two hundred large shields of beaten gold; six hundred shekels of beaten gold went into each large shield. [16] He made three hundred shields of beaten gold; three hundred shekels of gold went into each shield; and the king put them in the House of the Forest of Lebanon. [17] The king also made a great ivory throne, and overlaid it with pure gold. [18] The throne had six steps and a footstool of gold, which were attached to the throne, and on each side of the seat were arm rests and two lions standing beside the arm rests, [19] while twelve lions were standing, one on each end of a step on the six steps. The like of it was never made in any kingdom. [20] All King Solomon's drinking vessels were of gold, and all the vessels of the House of the Forest of Lebanon were of pure gold; silver

8.17
1 Kings 9.26
8.18
1 Kings 9.27;
2 Chr 9.10,
13
9.1
1 Kings 10.1-
13;
Mt 12.42;
Lk 11.31
9.3
1 Kings 5.12
9.5
1 Kings 10.6
9.8
1 Chr 28.5;
29.23;
2 Chr 2.11
9.9
1 Kings 10.10

9.10
2 Chr 8.18
9.13
1 Kings 10.14-
28
9.18
1 Kings 10.18
9.19
1 Kings 10.20

q Gk Syr Vg 1 Kings 10.5: Heb *ascent*
r Heb *their* s Gk Vg: Meaning of Heb uncertain

was not considered as anything in the days of Solomon. ²¹For the king's ships went to Tarshish with the servants of Huram; once every three years the ships of Tarshish used to come bringing gold, silver, ivory, apes, and peacocks.ᵗ

22 Thus King Solomon excelled all the kings of the earth in riches and in wisdom. ²³All the kings of the earth sought the presence of Solomon to hear his wisdom, which God had put into his mind. ²⁴Every one of them brought a present, objects of silver and gold, garments, weaponry, spices, horses, and mules, so much year by year. ²⁵Solomon had four thousand stalls for horses and chariots, and twelve thousand horses, which he stationed in the chariot cities and with the king in Jerusalem. ²⁶He ruled over all the kings from the Euphrates to the land of the Philistines, and to the border of Egypt. ²⁷The king made silver as common in Jerusalem as stone, and cedar as plentiful as the sycamore of the Shephelah. ²⁸Horses were imported for Solomon from Egypt and from all lands.

Death of Solomon

29 Now the rest of the acts of Solomon, from first to last, are they not written in the history of the prophet Nathan, and in the prophecy of Ahijah the Shilonite, and in the visions of the seer Iddo concerning Jeroboam son of Nebat? ³⁰Solomon reigned in Jerusalem over all Israel forty years. ³¹Solomon slept with his ancestors and was buried in the city of his father David; and his son Rehoboam succeeded him.

The Revolt against Rehoboam

10 Rehoboam went to Shechem, for all Israel had come to Shechem to make him king. ²When Jeroboam son of Nebat heard of it (for he was in Egypt, where he had fled from King Solomon), then Jeroboam returned from Egypt. ³They sent and called him; and Jeroboam and all Israel

came and said to Rehoboam, ⁴"Your father made our yoke heavy. Now therefore lighten the hard service of your father and his heavy yoke that he placed on us, and we will serve you." ⁵He said to them, "Come to me again in three days." So the people went away.

6 Then King Rehoboam took counsel with the older men who had attended his father Solomon while he was still alive, saying, "How do you advise me to answer this people?" ⁷They answered him, "If you will be kind to this people and please them, and speak good words to them, then they will be your servants forever." ⁸But he rejected the advice that the older men gave him, and consulted the young men who had grown up with him and now attended him. ⁹He said to them, "What do you advise that we answer this people who have said to me, 'Lighten the yoke that your father put on us'?" ¹⁰The young men who had grown up with him said to him, "Thus should you speak to the people who said to you, 'Your father made our yoke heavy, but you must lighten it for us'; tell them, 'My little finger is thicker than my father's loins. ¹¹Now, whereas my father laid on you a heavy yoke, I will add to your yoke. My father disciplined you with whips, but I will discipline you with scorpions.' "

12 So Jeroboam and all the people came to Rehoboam the third day, as the king had said, "Come to me again the third day." ¹³The king answered them harshly. King Rehoboam rejected the advice of the older men; ¹⁴he spoke to them in accordance with the advice of the young men, "My father made your yoke heavy, but I will add to it; my father disciplined you with whips, but I will discipline you with scorpions." ¹⁵So the king did not listen to the people, because it was a turn of affairs brought about by God so that the LORD might fulfill his word, which he had spoken by Ahijah the

Cross-references:

9.21 2 Chr 20.36, 37
9.22 2 Chr 1.12; 1 Kings 3.13
9.25 1 Kings 4.26; 10.26; 2 Chr 1.14
9.26 1 Kings 4.21; Ps 72.8
9.27 1 Kings 10.27; 2 Chr 1.15
9.28 1 Kings 10.28; 2 Chr 1.16
9.29 1 Kings 11.41; 1 Chr 29.29
9.30 1 Kings 11.42, 43
9.31 1 Kings 2.10
10.1 1 Kings 12.1-20
10.2 1 Kings 11.40

10.6 1 Kings 12.6
10.9 1 Kings 12.9
10.12 v. 5
10.15 1 Kings 12.15, 24; 2 Chr 25.16-20; 1 Kings 11.29

ᵗ Or *baboons*

Shilonite to Jeroboam son of Nebat.

16 When all Israel saw that the king would not listen to them, the people answered the king,

"What share do we have in
 David?
 We have no inheritance in
 the son of Jesse.
 Each of you to your tents,
 O Israel!
 Look now to your own
 house, O David."

So all Israel departed to their tents. 17 But Rehoboam reigned over the people of Israel who were living in the cities of Judah. 18 When King Rehoboam sent Hadoram, who was taskmaster over the forced labor, the people of Israel stoned him to death. King Rehoboam hurriedly mounted his chariot to flee to Jerusalem. 19 So Israel has been in rebellion against the house of David to this day.

Judah and Benjamin Fortified

11 When Rehoboam came to Jerusalem, he assembled one hundred eighty thousand chosen troops of the house of Judah and Benjamin to fight against Israel, to restore the kingdom to Rehoboam. 2 But the word of the LORD came to Shemaiah the man of God: 3 Say to King Rehoboam of Judah, son of Solomon, and to all Israel in Judah and Benjamin, 4 "Thus says the LORD: You shall not go up or fight against your kindred. Let everyone return home, for this thing is from me." So they heeded the word of the LORD and turned back from the expedition against Jeroboam.

5 Rehoboam resided in Jerusalem, and he built cities for defense in Judah. 6 He built up Bethlehem, Etam, Tekoa, 7 Beth-zur, Soco, Adullam, 8 Gath, Mareshah, Ziph, 9 Adoraim, Lachish, Azekah, 10 Zorah, Aijalon, and Hebron, fortified cities that are in Judah and in Benjamin. 11 He made the fortresses strong, and put commanders in them, and stores of food, oil, and wine. 12 He also put large shields

10;16
2 Sam 20.1;
v. 19
10.19
1 Kings 12.19
11.1
1 Kings 12.21-
24
11.2
2 Chr 12.15
11.4
2 Chr 10.15

11.14
Num 35.2-5;
2 Chr 13.9
11.15
1 Kings 12.28-
33; 13.33;
2 Chr 13.9
11.16
2 Chr 15.9
11.17
2 Chr 12.1
11.18
1 Sam 16.6
11.21
Deut 17.17
11.22
Deut 21.15-17

and spears in all the cities, and made them very strong. So he held Judah and Benjamin.

Priests and Levites Support Rehoboam

13 The priests and the Levites who were in all Israel presented themselves to him from all their territories. 14 The Levites had left their common lands and their holdings and had come to Judah and Jerusalem, because Jeroboam and his sons had prevented them from serving as priests of the LORD, 15 and had appointed his own priests for the high places, and for the goat-demons, and for the calves that he had made. 16 Those who had set their hearts to seek the LORD God of Israel came after them from all the tribes of Israel to Jerusalem to sacrifice to the LORD, the God of their ancestors. 17 They strengthened the kingdom of Judah, and for three years they made Rehoboam son of Solomon secure, for they walked for three years in the way of David and Solomon.

Rehoboam's Marriages

18 Rehoboam took as his wife Mahalath daughter of Jerimoth son of David, and of Abihail daughter of Eliab son of Jesse. 19 She bore him sons: Jeush, Shemariah, and Zaham. 20 After her he took Maacah daughter of Absalom, who bore him Abijah, Attai, Ziza, and Shelomith. 21 Rehoboam loved Maacah daughter of Absalom more than all his other wives and concubines (he took eighteen wives and sixty concubines, and became the father of twenty-eight sons and sixty daughters). 22 Rehoboam appointed Abijah son of Maacah as chief prince among his brothers, for he intended to make him king. 23 He dealt wisely, and distributed some of his sons through all the districts of Judah and Benjamin, in all the fortified cities; he gave them abundant provisions, and found many wives for them.

Egypt Attacks Judah

12 When the rule of Rehoboam was established and he grew strong, he abandoned the law of the Lord, he and all Israel with him. [2] In the fifth year of King Rehoboam, because they had been unfaithful to the Lord, King Shishak of Egypt came up against Jerusalem [3] with twelve hundred chariots and sixty thousand cavalry. A countless army came with him from Egypt—Libyans, Sukkiim, and Ethiopians. u [4] He took the fortified cities of Judah and came as far as Jerusalem. [5] Then the prophet Shemaiah came to Rehoboam and to the officers of Judah, who had gathered at Jerusalem because of Shishak, and said to them, "Thus says the Lord: You abandoned me, so I have abandoned you to the hand of Shishak." [6] Then the officers of Israel and the king humbled themselves and said, "The Lord is in the right." [7] When the Lord saw that they humbled themselves, the word of the Lord came to Shemaiah, saying: "They have humbled themselves; I will not destroy them, but I will grant them some deliverance, and my wrath shall not be poured out on Jerusalem by the hand of Shishak. [8] Nevertheless they shall be his servants, so that they may know the difference between serving me and serving the kingdoms of other lands."

[9] So King Shishak of Egypt came up against Jerusalem; he took away the treasures of the house of the Lord and the treasures of the king's house; he took everything. He also took away the shields of gold that Solomon had made; [10] but King Rehoboam made in place of them shields of bronze, and committed them to the hands of the officers of the guard, who kept the door of the king's house. [11] Whenever the king went into the house of the Lord, the guard would come along bearing them, and would then bring them back to the guardroom. [12] Because he humbled himself the wrath of the Lord turned from him, so as not to destroy them completely; moreover, conditions were good in Judah.

Death of Rehoboam

13 So King Rehoboam established himself in Jerusalem and reigned. Rehoboam was forty-one years old when he began to reign; he reigned seventeen years in Jerusalem, the city that the Lord had chosen out of all the tribes of Israel to put his name there. His mother's name was Naamah the Ammonite. [14] He did evil, for he did not set his heart to seek the Lord.

[15] Now the acts of Rehoboam, from first to last, are they not written in the records of the prophet Shemaiah and of the seer Iddo, recorded by genealogy? There were continual wars between Rehoboam and Jeroboam. [16] Rehoboam slept with his ancestors and was buried in the city of David; and his son Abijah succeeded him.

Abijah Reigns over Judah

13 In the eighteenth year of King Jeroboam, Abijah began to reign over Judah. [2] He reigned for three years in Jerusalem. His mother's name was Micaiah daughter of Uriel of Gibeah.

Now there was war between Abijah and Jeroboam. [3] Abijah engaged in battle, having an army of valiant warriors, four hundred thousand picked men; and Jeroboam drew up his line of battle against him with eight hundred thousand picked mighty warriors. [4] Then Abijah stood on the slope of Mount Zemaraim that is in the hill country of Ephraim, and said, "Listen to me, Jeroboam and all Israel! [5] Do you not know that the Lord God of Israel gave the kingship over Israel forever to David and his sons by a covenant of salt? [6] Yet Jeroboam son of Nebat, a servant of Solomon son of David, rose up and rebelled against his lord; [7] and certain worthless scoundrels gathered around him and defied Reho-

12.1
2 Chr 11.17;
1 Kings 14.22-24
12.2
1 Kings 14.24, 25; 11.40
12.3
2 Chr 16.8
12.5
2 Chr 11.2; 15.2;
Deut 28.15
12.6
Ex 9.27;
Dan 9.14
12.7
1 Kings 21.29
12.8
Deut 28.47, 48
12.9
1 Kings 14.25, 26;
2 Chr 9.15, 16
12.12
2 Chr 19.3

12.13
1 Kings 14.21;
2 Chr 6.6
12.14
2 Chr 19.3
12.15
1 Kings 14.29, 30;
2 Chr 9.29
12.16
1 Kings 14.31;
2 Chr 11.20
13.1
1 Kings 15.1, 2
13.2
2 Chr 11.20;
1 Kings 15.7
13.4
Josh 18.22
13.5
2 Sam 7.12, 13,16;
Num 18.19
13.6
1 Kings 11.26

u Or *Nubians*; Heb *Cushites*

boam son of Solomon, when Rehoboam was young and irresolute and could not withstand them.

8 "And now you think that you can withstand the kingdom of the LORD in the hand of the sons of David, because you are a great multitude and have with you the golden calves that Jeroboam made as gods for you. ⁹ Have you not driven out the priests of the LORD, the descendants of Aaron, and the Levites, and made priests for yourselves like the peoples of other lands? Whoever comes to be consecrated with a young bull or seven rams becomes a priest of what are no gods. ¹⁰ But as for us, the LORD is our God, and we have not abandoned him. We have priests ministering to the LORD who are descendants of Aaron, and Levites for their service. ¹¹ They offer to the LORD every morning and every evening burnt offerings and fragrant incense, set out the rows of bread on the table of pure gold, and care for the golden lampstand so that its lamps may burn every evening; for we keep the charge of the LORD our God, but you have abandoned him. ¹² See, God is with us at our head, and his priests have their battle trumpets to sound the call to battle against you. O Israelites, do not fight against the LORD, the God of your ancestors; for you cannot succeed."

13 Jeroboam had sent an ambush around to come on them from behind; thus his troops^v were in front of Judah, and the ambush was behind them. ¹⁴ When Judah turned, the battle was in front of them and behind them. They cried out to the LORD, and the priests blew the trumpets. ¹⁵ Then the people of Judah raised the battle shout. And when the people of Judah shouted, God defeated Jeroboam and all Israel before Abijah and Judah. ¹⁶ The Israelites fled before Judah, and God gave them into their hands. ¹⁷ Abijah and his army defeated them with great slaughter; five hundred thousand picked men of Israel fell slain. ¹⁸ Thus the Israelites were subdued at that

13.8
1 Kings 12.28;
2 Chr 11.15
13.9
2 Chr 11.14;
Ex 29.35;
Jer 2.11; 5.7
13.11
2 Chr 2.4;
Lev 24.5-9
13.12
Num 10.8,9;
Acts 5.39
13.14
2 Chr 14.11
13.15
2 Chr 14.12
13.16
2 Chr 16.8
13.18
1 Chr 5.20;
2 Chr 14.11;
Ps 22.5

13.20
1 Sam 25.38;
1 Kings 14.20
13.22
2 Chr 12.15
14.1
1 Kings 15.8
14.3
Deut 7.5;
1 Kings 15.12-14;
Ex 34.13
14.5
2 Chr 34.4,7
14.6
2 Chr 15.15

time, and the people of Judah prevailed, because they relied on the LORD, the God of their ancestors. ¹⁹ Abijah pursued Jeroboam, and took cities from him: Bethel with its villages and Jeshanah with its villages and Ephron^w with its villages. ²⁰ Jeroboam did not recover his power in the days of Abijah; the LORD struck him down, and he died. ²¹ But Abijah grew strong. He took fourteen wives, and became the father of twenty-two sons and sixteen daughters. ²² The rest of the acts of Abijah, his behavior and his deeds, are written in the story of the prophet Iddo.

Asa Reigns

14 ^x So Abijah slept with his ancestors, and they buried him in the city of David. His son Asa succeeded him. In his days the land had rest for ten years. ² ^y Asa did what was good and right in the sight of the LORD his God. ³ He took away the foreign altars and the high places, broke down the pillars, hewed down the sacred poles,^z ⁴ and commanded Judah to seek the LORD, the God of their ancestors, and to keep the law and the commandment. ⁵ He also removed from all the cities of Judah the high places and the incense altars. And the kingdom had rest under him. ⁶ He built fortified cities in Judah while the land had rest. He had no war in those years, for the LORD gave him peace. ⁷ He said to Judah, "Let us build these cities, and surround them with walls and towers, gates and bars; the land is still ours because we have sought the LORD our God; we have sought him, and he has given us peace on every side." So they built and prospered. ⁸ Asa had an army of three hundred thousand from Judah, armed with large shields and spears, and two hundred eighty thousand troops from Benjamin who carried shields and drew bows; all these were mighty warriors.

^v Heb *they* ^w Another reading is *Ephrain*
^x Ch 13.23 in Heb ^y Ch 14.1 in Heb
^z Heb *Asherim*

Ethiopian Invasion Repulsed

9 Zerah the Ethiopian[a] came out against them with an army of a million men and three hundred chariots, and came as far as Mareshah. 10 Asa went out to meet him, and they drew up their lines of battle in the valley of Zephathah at Mareshah. 11 Asa cried to the LORD his God, "O LORD, there is no difference for you between helping the mighty and the weak. Help us, O LORD our God, for we rely on you, and in your name we have come against this multitude. O LORD, you are our God; let no mortal prevail against you." 12 So the LORD defeated the Ethiopians[b] before Asa and before Judah, and the Ethiopians[b] fled. 13 Asa and the army with him pursued them as far as Gerar, and the Ethiopians[b] fell until no one remained alive; for they were broken before the LORD and his army. The people of Judah[c] carried away a great quantity of booty. 14 They defeated all the cities around Gerar, for the fear of the LORD was on them. They plundered all the cities; for there was much plunder in them. 15 They also attacked the tents of those who had livestock,[d] and carried away sheep and goats in abundance, and camels. Then they returned to Jerusalem.

15 The spirit of God came upon Azariah son of Oded. 2 He went out to meet Asa and said to him, "Hear me, Asa, and all Judah and Benjamin: The LORD is with you, while you are with him. If you seek him, he will be found by you, but if you abandon him, he will abandon you. 3 For a long time Israel was without the true God, and without a teaching priest, and without law; 4 but when in their distress they turned to the LORD, the God of Israel, and sought him, he was found by them. 5 In those times it was not safe for anyone to go or come, for great disturbances afflicted all the inhabitants of the lands. 6 They were broken in pieces, nation against nation and city against city, for God troubled

them with every sort of distress. 7 But you, take courage! Do not let your hands be weak, for your work shall be rewarded."

8 When Asa heard these words, the prophecy of Azariah son of Oded,[e] he took courage, and put away the abominable idols from all the land of Judah and Benjamin and from the towns that he had taken in the hill country of Ephraim. He repaired the altar of the LORD that was in front of the vestibule of the house of the LORD.[f] 9 He gathered all Judah and Benjamin, and those from Ephraim, Manasseh, and Simeon who were residing as aliens with them, for great numbers had deserted to him from Israel when they saw that the LORD his God was with him. 10 They were gathered at Jerusalem in the third month of the fifteenth year of the reign of Asa. 11 They sacrificed to the LORD on that day, from the booty that they had brought, seven hundred oxen and seven thousand sheep. 12 They entered into a covenant to seek the LORD, the God of their ancestors, with all their heart and with all their soul. 13 Whoever would not seek the LORD, the God of Israel, should be put to death, whether young or old, man or woman. 14 They took an oath to the LORD with a loud voice, and with shouting, and with trumpets, and with horns. 15 All Judah rejoiced over the oath; for they had sworn with all their heart, and had sought him with their whole desire, and he was found by them, and the LORD gave them rest all around.

16 King Asa even removed his mother Maacah from being queen mother because she had made an abominable image for Asherah. Asa cut down her image, crushed it, and burned it at the Wadi Kidron. 17 But the high places were not taken out of Israel. Nevertheless the heart of Asa was true all his

14.9 2 Chr 16.8; 11.8
14.11 2 Chr 13.14, 18; 1 Sam 14.6; 17.45
14.12 2 Chr 13.15
14.13 Gen 10.19
14.14 Gen 35.5; 2 Chr 17.10
15.1 Num 24.2; 2 Chr 20.14; 24.20
15.2 Jas 4.8; vv. 4,15; 2 Chr 24.20
15.3 Hos 3.4; Lev 10.11; 2 Chr 17.9
15.4 Deut 4.29
15.5 Judg 5.6
15.6 Mt 24.7
15.7 Josh 1.7,9
15.8 2 Chr 13.19
15.9 2 Chr 11.16
15.11 2 Chr 14.13-15
15.12 2 Chr 23.16; 34.31
15.13 Ex 22.20; Deut 13.5,9, 15
15.15 v. 2; 2 Chr 14.7
15.16 1 Kings 15.13-15; Ex 34.13; 2 Chr 14.2-5

a Or Nubian; Heb Cushite b Or Nubians; Heb Cushites c Heb They d Meaning of Heb uncertain e Compare Syr Vg: Heb the prophecy, the prophet Obed f Heb the vestibule of the LORD

days. 18 He brought into the house of God the votive gifts of his father and his own votive gifts—silver, gold, and utensils. 19 And there was no more war until the thirty-fifth year of the reign of Asa.

Alliance with Aram Condemned

16 In the thirty-sixth year of the reign of Asa, King Baasha of Israel went up against Judah, and built Ramah, to prevent anyone from going out or coming into the territory ofᵍ King Asa of Judah. 2 Then Asa took silver and gold from the treasures of the house of the LORD and the king's house, and sent them to King Ben-hadad of Aram, who resided in Damascus, saying, 3 "Let there be an alliance between me and you, like that between my father and your father; I am sending to you silver and gold; go, break your alliance with King Baasha of Israel, so that he may withdraw from me." 4 Ben-hadad listened to King Asa, and sent the commanders of his armies against the cities of Israel. They conquered Ijon, Dan, Abel-maim, and all the store-cities of Naphtali. 5 When Baasha heard of it, he stopped building Ramah, and let his work cease. 6 Then King Asa brought all Judah, and they carried away the stones of Ramah and its timber, with which Baasha had been building, and with them he built up Geba and Mizpah.

7 At that time the seer Hanani came to King Asa of Judah, and said to him, "Because you relied on the king of Aram, and did not rely on the LORD your God, the army of the king of Aram has escaped you. 8 Were not the Ethiopiansʰ and the Libyans a huge army with exceedingly many chariots and cavalry? Yet because you relied on the LORD, he gave them into your hand. 9 For the eyes of the LORD range throughout the entire earth, to strengthen those whose heart is true to him. You have done foolishly in this; for from now on you will have wars." 10 Then Asa was angry with the seer, and put him in the stocks, in

prison, for he was in a rage with him because of this. And Asa inflicted cruelties on some of the people at the same time.

Asa's Disease and Death

11 The acts of Asa, from first to last, are written in the Book of the Kings of Judah and Israel. 12 In the thirty-ninth year of his reign Asa was diseased in his feet, and his disease became severe; yet even in his disease he did not seek the LORD, but sought help from physicians. 13 Then Asa slept with his ancestors, dying in the forty-first year of his reign. 14 They buried him in the tomb that he had hewn out for himself in the city of David. They laid him on a bier that had been filled with various kinds of spices prepared by the perfumer's art; and they made a very great fire in his honor.

Jehoshaphat's Reign

17 His son Jehoshaphat succeeded him, and strengthened himself against Israel. 2 He placed forces in all the fortified cities of Judah, and set garrisons in the land of Judah, and in the cities of Ephraim that his father Asa had taken. 3 The LORD was with Jehoshaphat, because he walked in the earlier ways of his father;ⁱ he did not seek the Baals, 4 but sought the God of his father and walked in his commandments, and not according to the ways of Israel. 5 Therefore the LORD established the kingdom in his hand. All Judah brought tribute to Jehoshaphat, and he had great riches and honor. 6 His heart was courageous in the ways of the LORD; and furthermore he removed the high places and the sacred polesʲ from Judah.

7 In the third year of his reign he sent his officials, Ben-hail, Obadiah, Zechariah, Nethanel, and Micaiah, to teach in the cities of Judah. 8 With them were the Levites, Shemaiah, Nethaniah, Zebadiah,

Cross references (center column)

16.1
1 Kings 15.17-22
16.4
1 Kings 15.18, 20
16.7
2 Chr 19.2; 14.11; 32.7,8
16.8
2 Chr 14.9; 12.3
16.9
Prov 15.3; Zech 4.10; 1 Sam 13.13

16.11
1 Kings 15.23
16.12
Jer 17.5
16.13
1 Kings 15.24
16.14
Gen 50.2; Jn 19.39,40; 2 Chr 21.19; Jer 34.5
17.1
1 Kings 15.24
17.2
2 Chr 15.8
17.4
1 Kings 12.28
17.5
2 Chr 18.1
17.6
2 Chr 15.17
17.7
2 Chr 15.3
17.8
2 Chr 19.8

ᵍ Heb lacks the territory of ʰ Or Nubians; Heb Cushites ⁱ Another reading is his father David ʲ Heb Asherim

Asahel, Shemiramoth, Jehonathan, Adonijah, Tobijah, and Tobadonijah; and with these Levites, the priests Elishama and Jehoram. 9 They taught in Judah, having the book of the law of the LORD with them; they went around through all the cities of Judah and taught among the people.

10 The fear of the LORD fell on all the kingdoms of the lands around Judah, and they did not make war against Jehoshaphat. 11 Some of the Philistines brought Jehoshaphat presents, and silver for tribute; and the Arabs also brought him seven thousand seven hundred rams and seven thousand seven hundred male goats. 12 Jehoshaphat grew steadily greater. He built fortresses and storage cities in Judah. 13 He carried out great works in the cities of Judah. He had soldiers, mighty warriors, in Jerusalem. 14 This was the muster of them by ancestral houses: Of Judah, the commanders of the thousands: Adnah the commander, with three hundred thousand mighty warriors, 15 and next to him Jehohanan the commander, with two hundred eighty thousand, 16 and next to him Amasiah son of Zichri, a volunteer for the service of the LORD, with two hundred thousand mighty warriors. 17 Of Benjamin: Eliada, a mighty warrior, with two hundred thousand armed with bow and shield, 18 and next to him Jehozabad with one hundred eighty thousand armed for war. 19 These were in the service of the king, besides those whom the king had placed in the fortified cities throughout all Judah.

Micaiah Predicts Failure

18 Now Jehoshaphat had great riches and honor; and he made a marriage alliance with Ahab. 2 After some years he went down to Ahab in Samaria. Ahab slaughtered an abundance of sheep and oxen for him and for the people who were with him, and induced him to go up against Ramoth-gilead. 3 King Ahab of Isra-

Cross references (center column)

17.9 Deut 6.4-9
17.10 2 Chr 14.14
17.11 2 Chr 9.14; 26.8
17.16 Judg 5.2,9; 1 Chr 29.9
18.1 2 Chr 17.5 1 Kings 22.2-35

18.4 1 Sam 23.2, 4,9; 2 Sam 2.1
18.7 1 Kings 22.8
18.9 Ruth 4.1
18.11 2 Chr 22.5
18.13 Num 22.18-20, 35

el said to King Jehoshaphat of Judah, "Will you go with me to Ramoth-gilead?" He answered him, "I am with you, my people are your people. We will be with you in the war."

4 But Jehoshaphat also said to the king of Israel, "Inquire first for the word of the LORD." 5 Then the king of Israel gathered the prophets together, four hundred of them, and said to them, "Shall we go to battle against Ramoth-gilead, or shall I refrain?" They said, "Go up; for God will give it into the hand of the king." 6 But Jehoshaphat said, "Is there no other prophet of the LORD here of whom we may inquire?" 7 The king of Israel said to Jehoshaphat, "There is still one other by whom we may inquire of the LORD, Micaiah son of Imlah; but I hate him, for he never prophesies anything favorable about me, but only disaster." Jehoshaphat said, "Let the king not say such a thing." 8 Then the king of Israel summoned an officer and said, "Bring quickly Micaiah son of Imlah." 9 Now the king of Israel and King Jehoshaphat of Judah were sitting on their thrones, arrayed in their robes; and they were sitting at the threshing floor at the entrance of the gate of Samaria; and all the prophets were prophesying before them. 10 Zedekiah son of Chenaanah made for himself horns of iron, and he said, "Thus says the LORD: With these you shall gore the Arameans until they are destroyed." 11 All the prophets were prophesying the same and saying, "Go up to Ramoth-gilead and triumph; the LORD will give it into the hand of the king."

12 The messenger who had gone to summon Micaiah said to him, "Look, the words of the prophets with one accord are favorable to the king; let your word be like the word of one of them, and speak favorably." 13 But Micaiah said, "As the LORD lives, whatever my God says, that I will speak."

14 When he had come to the king, the king said to him, "Mica-

iah, shall we go to Ramoth-gilead to battle, or shall I refrain?" He answered, "Go up and triumph; they will be given into your hand." 15 But the king said to him, "How many times must I make you swear to tell me nothing but the truth in the name of the LORD?" 16 Then Micaiahᵏ said, "I saw all Israel scattered on the mountains, like sheep without a shepherd; and the LORD said, 'These have no master; let each one go home in peace.' " 17 The king of Israel said to Jehoshaphat, "Did I not tell you that he would not prophesy anything favorable about me, but only disaster?"

18 Then Micaiahᵏ said, "Therefore hear the word of the LORD: I saw the LORD sitting on his throne, with all the host of heaven standing to the right and to the left of him. 19 And the LORD said, 'Who will entice King Ahab of Israel, so that he may go up and fall at Ramoth-gilead?' Then one said one thing, and another said another, 20 until a spirit came forward and stood before the LORD, saying, 'I will entice him.' The LORD asked him, 'How?' 21 He replied, 'I will go out and be a lying spirit in the mouth of all his prophets.' Then the LORDᵏ said, 'You are to entice him, and you shall succeed; go out and do it.' 22 So you see, the LORD has put a lying spirit in the mouth of these your prophets; the LORD has decreed disaster for you."

23 Then Zedekiah son of Chenaanah came up to Micaiah, slapped him on the cheek, and said, "Which way did the spirit of the LORD pass from me to speak to you?" 24 Micaiah replied, "You will find out on that day when you go in to hide in an inner chamber." 25 The king of Israel then ordered, "Take Micaiah, and return him to Amon the governor of the city and to Joash the king's son; 26 and say, 'Thus says the king: Put this fellow in prison, and feed him on reduced rations of bread and water until I return in peace.' " 27 Micaiah said, "If you return in peace, the LORD has not spoken by me." And he

said, "Hear, you peoples, all of you!"

Defeat and Death of Ahab

28 So the king of Israel and King Jehoshaphat of Judah went up to Ramoth-gilead. 29 The king of Israel said to Jehoshaphat, "I will disguise myself and go into battle, but you wear your robes." So the king of Israel disguised himself, and they went into battle. 30 Now the king of Aram had commanded the captains of his chariots, "Fight with no one small or great, but only with the king of Israel." 31 When the captains of the chariots saw Jehoshaphat, they said, "It is the king of Israel." So they turned to fight against him; and Jehoshaphat cried out, and the LORD helped him. God drew them away from him, 32 for when the captains of the chariots saw that it was not the king of Israel, they turned back from pursuing him. 33 But a certain man drew his bow and unknowingly struck the king of Israel between the scale armor and the breastplate; so he said to the driver of his chariot, "Turn around, and carry me out of the battle, for I am wounded." 34 The battle grew hot that day, and the king of Israel propped himself up in his chariot facing the Arameans until evening; then at sunset he died.

19 King Jehoshaphat of Judah returned in safety to his house in Jerusalem. 2 Jehu son of Hanani the seer went out to meet him and said to King Jehoshaphat, "Should you help the wicked and love those who hate the LORD? Because of this, wrath has gone out against you from the LORD. 3 Nevertheless, some good is found in you, for you destroyed the sacred polesˡ out of the land, and have set your heart to seek God."

The Reforms of Jehoshaphat

4 Jehoshaphat resided at Jerusalem; then he went out again among the people, from Beersheba to the hill country of Ephra-

18.16
Num 27.17;
Ezek 34.5-8
18.20
Job 1.6
18.22
Job 12.16;
Ezek 14.9
18.23
Jer 20.2;
Mk 14.65;
Acts 23.2
18.25
v. 8
18.26
2 Chr 16.10
18.27
Mic 1.9

18.31
2 Chr 13.14,
15
18.33
1 Kings 22.34
19.2
1 Kings 16.1;
Ps 139.21;
2 Chr 32.25
19.3
2 Chr 12.12,
14; 17.6;
Ezra 7.10
19.4
2 Chr 15.8-13

ᵏHeb *he* ˡHeb *Asheroth*

im, and brought them back to the LORD, the God of their ancestors. ⁵He appointed judges in the land in all the fortified cities of Judah, city by city, ⁶and said to the judges, "Consider what you are doing, for you judge not on behalf of human beings but on the LORD's behalf; he is with you in giving judgment. ⁷Now, let the fear of the LORD be upon you; take care what you do, for there is no perversion of justice with the LORD our God, or partiality, or taking of bribes."

8 Moreover in Jerusalem Jehoshaphat appointed certain Levites and priests and heads of families of Israel, to give judgment for the LORD and to decide disputed cases. They had their seat at Jerusalem. ⁹He charged them: "This is how you shall act: in the fear of the LORD, in faithfulness, and with your whole heart; ¹⁰whenever a case comes to you from your kindred who live in their cities, concerning bloodshed, law or commandment, statutes or ordinances, then you shall instruct them, so that they may not incur guilt before the LORD and wrath may not come on you and your kindred. Do so, and you will not incur guilt. ¹¹See, Amariah the chief priest is over you in all matters of the LORD; and Zebadiah son of Ishmael, the governor of the house of Judah, in all the king's matters; and the Levites will serve you as officers. Deal courageously, and may the LORD be with the good!"

Invasion from the East

20 After this the Moabites and Ammonites, and with them some of the Meunites,ᵐ came against Jehoshaphat for battle. ²Messengersⁿ came and told Jehoshaphat, "A great multitude is coming against you from Edom,ᵒ from beyond the sea; already they are at Hazazon-tamar (that is, Engedi). ³Jehoshaphat was afraid; he set himself to seek the LORD, and proclaimed a fast throughout all Judah. ⁴Judah assembled to seek help from the LORD; from all the

towns of Judah they came to seek the LORD.

Jehoshaphat's Prayer and Victory

5 Jehoshaphat stood in the assembly of Judah and Jerusalem, in the house of the LORD, before the new court, ⁶and said, "O LORD, God of our ancestors, are you not God in heaven? Do you not rule over all the kingdoms of the nations? In your hand are power and might, so that no one is able to withstand you. ⁷Did you not, O our God, drive out the inhabitants of this land before your people Israel, and give it forever to the descendants of your friend Abraham? ⁸They have lived in it, and in it have built you a sanctuary for your name, saying, ⁹'If disaster comes upon us, the sword, judgment,ᵖ or pestilence, or famine, we will stand before this house, and before you, for your name is in this house, and cry to you in our distress, and you will hear and save.' ¹⁰See now, the people of Ammon, Moab, and Mount Seir, whom you would not let Israel invade when they came from the land of Egypt, and whom they avoided and did not destroy— ¹¹they reward us by coming to drive us out of your possession that you have given us to inherit. ¹²O our God, will you not execute judgment upon them? For we are powerless against this great multitude that is coming against us. We do not know what to do, but our eyes are on you."

13 Meanwhile all Judah stood before the LORD, with their little ones, their wives, and their children. ¹⁴Then the spirit of the LORD came upon Jahaziel son of Zechariah, son of Benaiah, son of Jeiel, son of Mattaniah, a Levite of the sons of Asaph, in the middle of the assembly. ¹⁵He said, "Listen, all Judah and inhabitants of Jerusalem, and King Jehoshaphat: Thus says the LORD to you: 'Do not fear or

19.6
Deut 1.17
19.7
Gen 18.25;
Deut 32.4;
10.17,18;
Rom 2.11;
Col 3.25
19.8
2 Chr 17.8,
9
19.9
2 Sam 23.3
19.10
Deut 17.8;
v. 2
19.11
v. 8;
1 Chr 28.20
20.2
Gen 14.7
20.3
2 Chr 19.3

20.6
Deut 4.39;
Mt 6.9;
1 Chr 29.11,
12; Mt 6.13
20.7
Isa 41.8
20.9
1 Kings 8.33,
37;
2 Chr 6.20,
28-30
20.10
vv. 1,22;
Deut 2.4,9,
19;
Num 20.21
20.11
Ps 83.12
20.12
Judg 11.27;
Ps 25.15;
121.1,2
20.14
2 Chr 15.1;
24.20
20.15
Ex 14.13,
14;
2 Chr 32.7,
8;
1 Sam 17.47

ᵐ Compare 26.7: Heb *Ammonites*
ⁿ Heb *They* ᵒ One Ms: MT *Aram*
ᵖ Or *the sword of judgment*

be dismayed at this great multitude; for the battle is not yours but God's. ¹⁶Tomorrow go down against them; they will come up by the ascent of Ziz; you will find them at the end of the valley, before the wilderness of Jeruel. ¹⁷This battle is not for you to fight; take your position, stand still, and see the victory of the LORD on your behalf, O Judah and Jerusalem.' Do not fear or be dismayed; tomorrow go out against them, and the LORD will be with you."

18 Then Jehoshaphat bowed down with his face to the ground, and all Judah and the inhabitants of Jerusalem fell down before the LORD, worshiping the LORD. ¹⁹And the Levites, of the Kohathites and the Korahites, stood up to praise the LORD, the God of Israel, with a very loud voice.

20 They rose early in the morning and went out into the wilderness of Tekoa; and as they went out, Jehoshaphat stood and said, "Listen to me, O Judah and inhabitants of Jerusalem! Believe in the LORD your God and you will be established; believe his prophets." ²¹When he had taken counsel with the people, he appointed those who were to sing to the LORD and praise him in holy splendor, as they went before the army, saying,

"Give thanks to the LORD,
 for his steadfast love
 endures forever."

²²As they began to sing and praise, the LORD set an ambush against the Ammonites, Moab, and Mount Seir, who had come against Judah, so that they were routed. ²³For the Ammonites and Moab attacked the inhabitants of Mount Seir, destroying them utterly; and when they had made an end of the inhabitants of Seir, they all helped to destroy one another.

24 When Judah came to the watchtower of the wilderness, they looked toward the multitude; they were corpses lying on the ground; no one had escaped. ²⁵When Jehoshaphat and his people came to take the booty from them, they

found livestock�q in great numbers, goods, clothing, and precious things, which they took for themselves until they could carry no more. They spent three days taking the booty, because of its abundance. ²⁶On the fourth day they assembled in the Valley of Beracah, for there they blessed the LORD; therefore that place has been called the Valley of Beracahʳ to this day. ²⁷Then all the people of Judah and Jerusalem, with Jehoshaphat at their head, returned to Jerusalem with joy, for the LORD had enabled them to rejoice over their enemies. ²⁸They came to Jerusalem, with harps and lyres and trumpets, to the house of the LORD. ²⁹The fear of God came on all the kingdoms of the countries when they heard that the LORD had fought against the enemies of Israel. ³⁰And the realm of Jehoshaphat was quiet, for his God gave him rest all around.

The End of Jehoshaphat's Reign

31 So Jehoshaphat reigned over Judah. He was thirty-five years old when he began to reign; he reigned twenty-five years in Jerusalem. His mother's name was Azubah daughter of Shilhi. ³²He walked in the way of his father Asa and did not turn aside from it, doing what was right in the sight of the LORD. ³³Yet the high places were not removed; the people had not yet set their hearts upon the God of their ancestors.

34 Now the rest of the acts of Jehoshaphat, from first to last, are written in the Annals of Jehu son of Hanani, which are recorded in the Book of the Kings of Israel.

35 After this King Jehoshaphat of Judah joined with King Ahaziah of Israel, who did wickedly. ³⁶He joined him in building ships to go to Tarshish; they built the ships in Ezion-geber. ³⁷Then Eliezer son of Dodavahu of Mareshah prophesied against Jehoshaphat, saying, "Because you have joined with Ahaziah, the LORD will destroy what you

20.17
Ex 14.13,
14;
2 Chr 15.2
20.18
Ex 4.31;
2 Chr 7.3
20.20
Isa 7.9
20.21
1 Chr 16.29,
34,41;
Ps 29.2
20.22
Judg 7.22;
2 Chr 13.13
20.23
1 Sam 14.20

20.27
Neh 12.43
20.29
2 Chr 14.14;
17.10
20.30
2 Chr 14.6,
7; 15.15
20.31
1 Kings 22.41-
43
20.33
2 Chr 17.6;
19.3
20.34
1 Kings 16.1,
7
20.35
1 Kings 22.48,
49
20.37
2 Chr 9.21

q Gk: Heb *among them* r That is *Blessing*

have made." And the ships were wrecked and were not able to go to Tarshish.

Jehoram's Reign

21 Jehoshaphat slept with his ancestors and was buried with his ancestors in the city of David; his son Jehoram succeeded him. ² He had brothers, the sons of Jehoshaphat: Azariah, Jehiel, Zechariah, Azariah, Michael, and Shephatiah; all these were the sons of King Jehoshaphat of Judah.ˢ ³ Their father gave them many gifts, of silver, gold, and valuable possessions, together with fortified cities in Judah; but he gave the kingdom to Jehoram, because he was the firstborn. ⁴ When Jehoram had ascended the throne of his father and was established, he put all his brothers to the sword, and also some of the officials of Israel. ⁵ Jehoram was thirty-two years old when he began to reign; he reigned eight years in Jerusalem. ⁶ He walked in the way of the kings of Israel, as the house of Ahab had done; for the daughter of Ahab was his wife. He did what was evil in the sight of the LORD. ⁷ Yet the LORD would not destroy the house of David because of the covenant that he had made with David, and since he had promised to give a lamp to him and to his descendants forever.

Revolt of Edom

8 In his days Edom revolted against the rule of Judah and set up a king of their own. ⁹ Then Jehoram crossed over with his commanders and all his chariots. He set out by night and attacked the Edomites, who had surrounded him and his chariot commanders. ¹⁰ So Edom has been in revolt against the rule of Judah to this day. At that time Libnah also revolted against his rule, because he had forsaken the LORD, the God of his ancestors.

Elijah's Letter

11 Moreover he made high places in the hill country of Judah, and led the inhabitants of Jerusalem into unfaithfulness, and made

Judah go astray. ¹² A letter came to him from the prophet Elijah, saying: "Thus says the LORD, the God of your father David: Because you have not walked in the ways of your father Jehoshaphat or in the ways of King Asa of Judah, ¹³ but have walked in the way of the kings of Israel, and have led Judah and the inhabitants of Jerusalem into unfaithfulness, as the house of Ahab led Israel into unfaithfulness, and because you also have killed your brothers, members of your father's house, who were better than yourself, ¹⁴ see, the LORD will bring a great plague on your people, your children, your wives, and all your possessions, ¹⁵ and you yourself will have a severe sickness with a disease of your bowels, until your bowels come out, day after day, because of the disease."

16 The LORD aroused against Jehoram the anger of the Philistines and of the Arabs who are near the Ethiopians.ᵗ ¹⁷ They came up against Judah, invaded it, and carried away all the possessions they found that belonged to the king's house, along with his sons and his wives, so that no son was left to him except Jehoahaz, his youngest son.

Disease and Death of Jehoram

18 After all this the LORD struck him in his bowels with an incurable disease. ¹⁹ In course of time, at the end of two years, his bowels came out because of the disease, and he died in great agony. His people made no fire in his honor, like the fires made for his ancestors. ²⁰ He was thirty-two years old when he began to reign; he reigned eight years in Jerusalem. He departed with no one's regret. They buried him in the city of David, but not in the tombs of the kings.

Ahaziah's Reign

22 The inhabitants of Jerusalem made his youngest son Ahaziah king as his successor; for

ˢ Gk Syr: Heb *Israel* ᵗ Or *Nubians*; Heb *Cushites*

21.1
1 Kings 22.50
21.3
2 Chr 11.5
21.5
2 Kings 8.17-22
21.7
2 Sam 7.12, 13;
1 Kings 11.36
21.8
2 Kings 8.20-24
21.11
Lev 20.5

21.12
2 Chr 17.3, 4; 14.2-5
21.13
vv. 6,11;
1 Kings 16.31-33;
v. 4
21.15
vv. 18,19
21.16
2 Chr 33.11
21.17
2 Chr 25.23
21.18
v. 15
21.19
2 Chr 16.14
21.20
Jer 22.18, 28;
2 Chr 24.25; 28.27
22.1
2 Kings 8.24-29;
2 Chr 21.16, 17

the troops who came with the Arabs to the camp had killed all the older sons. So Ahaziah son of Jehoram reigned as king of Judah. ²Ahaziah was forty-two years old when he began to reign; he reigned one year in Jerusalem. His mother's name was Athaliah, a granddaughter of Omri. ³He also walked in the ways of the house of Ahab, for his mother was his counselor in doing wickedly. ⁴He did what was evil in the sight of the LORD, as the house of Ahab had done; for after the death of his father they were his counselors, to his ruin. ⁵He even followed their advice, and went with Jehoram son of King Ahab of Israel to make war against King Hazael of Aram at Ramothgilead. The Arameans wounded Joram, ⁶and he returned to be healed in Jezreel of the wounds that he had received at Ramah, when he fought King Hazael of Aram. And Ahaziah son of King Jehoram of Judah went down to see Joram son of Ahab in Jezreel, because he was sick.

7 But it was ordained by God that the downfall of Ahaziah should come about through his going to visit Joram. For when he came there he went out with Jehoram to meet Jehu son of Nimshi, whom the LORD had anointed to destroy the house of Ahab. ⁸When Jehu was executing judgment on the house of Ahab, he met the officials of Judah and the sons of Ahaziah's brothers, who attended Ahaziah, and he killed them. ⁹He searched for Ahaziah, who was captured while hiding in Samaria and was brought to Jehu, and put to death. They buried him, for they said, "He is the grandson of Jehoshaphat, who sought the LORD with all his heart." And the house of Ahaziah had no one able to rule the kingdom.

Athaliah Seizes the Throne

10 Now when Athaliah, Ahaziah's mother, saw that her son was dead, she set about to destroy all the royal family of the house of Ju-

dah. ¹¹But Jehoshabeath, the king's daughter, took Joash son of Ahaziah, and stole him away from among the king's children who were about to be killed; she put him and his nurse in a bedroom. Thus Jehoshabeath, daughter of King Jehoram and wife of the priest Jehoiada—because she was a sister of Ahaziah—hid him from Athaliah, so that she did not kill him; ¹²he remained with them six years, hidden in the house of God, while Athaliah reigned over the land.

23 But in the seventh year Jehoiada took courage, and entered into a compact with the commanders of the hundreds, Azariah son of Jeroham, Ishmael son of Jehohanan, Azariah son of Obed, Maaseiah son of Adaiah, and Elishaphat son of Zichri. ²They went around through Judah and gathered the Levites from all the towns of Judah, and the heads of families of Israel, and they came to Jerusalem. ³Then the whole assembly made a covenant with the king in the house of God. Jehoiadaᵘ said to them, "Here is the king's son! Let him reign, as the LORD promised concerning the sons of David. ⁴This is what you are to do: one third of you, priests and Levites, who come on duty on the sabbath, shall be gatekeepers, ⁵one third shall be at the king's house, and one third at the Gate of the Foundation; and all the people shall be in the courts of the house of the LORD. ⁶Do not let anyone enter the house of the LORD except the priests and ministering Levites; they may enter, for they are holy, but all the otherᵛ people shall observe the instructions of the LORD. ⁷The Levites shall surround the king, each with his weapons in his hand; and whoever enters the house shall be killed. Stay with the king in his comings and goings."

Joash Crowned King

8 The Levites and all Judah did according to all that the priest Jehoiada commanded; each brought

ᵘHeb *He* ᵛHeb lacks *other*

22.2
2 Chr 21.6
22.5
2 Kings 8.28ff
22.6
2 Kings 9.15
22.7
2 Chr 10.15;
2 Kings 9.6, 7,21
22.8
2 Kings 10.10-14
22.9
2 Kings 9.27, 28;
2 Chr 17.4
22.10
2 Kings 11.1-3

23.1
2 Kings 11.4-20
23.3
2 Sam 7.12;
1 Kings 2.4;
2 Chr 6.16;
7.18; 21.7
23.4
1 Chr 9.25
23.7
1 Chr 23.28-32
23.8
1 Chr 24.1

his men, who were to come on duty on the sabbath, with those who were to go off duty on the sabbath; for the priest Jehoiada did not dismiss the divisions. ⁹ The priest Jehoiada delivered to the captains the spears and the large and small shields that had been King David's, which were in the house of God; ¹⁰ and he set all the people as a guard for the king, everyone with weapon in hand, from the south side of the house to the north side of the house, around the altar and the house. ¹¹ Then he brought out the king's son, put the crown on him, and gave him the covenant; ʷ they proclaimed him king, and Jehoiada and his sons anointed him; and they shouted, "Long live the king!"

Athaliah Murdered

12 When Athaliah heard the noise of the people running and praising the king, she went into the house of the Lord to the people; ¹³ and when she looked, there was the king standing by his pillar at the entrance, and the captains and the trumpeters beside the king, and all the people of the land rejoicing and blowing trumpets, and the singers with their musical instruments leading in the celebration. Athaliah tore her clothes, and cried, "Treason! Treason!" ¹⁴ Then the priest Jehoiada brought out the captains who were set over the army, saying to them, "Bring her out between the ranks; anyone who follows her is to be put to the sword." For the priest said, "Do not put her to death in the house of the Lord." ¹⁵ So they laid hands on her; she went into the entrance of the Horse Gate of the king's house, and there they put her to death.

16 Jehoiada made a covenant between himself and all the people and the king that they should be the Lord's people. ¹⁷ Then all the people went to the house of Baal, and tore it down; his altars and his images they broke in pieces, and they killed Mattan, the priest of Baal, in front of the altars. ¹⁸ Jehoi-

ada assigned the care of the house of the Lord to the levitical priests whom David had organized to be in charge of the house of the Lord, to offer burnt offerings to the Lord, as it is written in the law of Moses, with rejoicing and with singing, according to the order of David. ¹⁹ He stationed the gatekeepers at the gates of the house of the Lord so that no one should enter who was in any way unclean. ²⁰ And he took the captains, the nobles, the governors of the people, and all the people of the land, and they brought the king down from the house of the Lord, marching through the upper gate to the king's house. They set the king on the royal throne. ²¹ So all the people of the land rejoiced, and the city was quiet after Athaliah had been killed with the sword.

Joash Repairs the Temple

24 Joash was seven years old when he began to reign; he reigned forty years in Jerusalem; his mother's name was Zibiah of Beer-sheba. ² Joash did what was right in the sight of the Lord all the days of the priest Jehoiada. ³ Jehoiada got two wives for him, and he became the father of sons and daughters.

4 Some time afterward Joash decided to restore the house of the Lord. ⁵ He assembled the priests and the Levites and said to them, "Go out to the cities of Judah and gather money from all Israel to repair the house of your God, year by year; and see that you act quickly." But the Levites did not act quickly. ⁶ So the king summoned Jehoiada the chief, and said to him, "Why have you not required the Levites to bring in from Judah and Jerusalem the tax levied by Moses, the servant of the Lord, on ˣ the congregation of Israel for the tent of the covenant?" ʷ ⁷ For the children of Athaliah, that wicked woman, had broken into the house of God, and had even used all the dedicat-

23.9
v. 1
23.11
Ex 25.16;
1 Sam 10.24
23.12
2 Kings 11.13
23.15
Neh 3.28;
Jer 31.40
23.17
Deut 13.9
23.18
2 Chr 5.5;
1 Chr 23.6,
30,31; 25.1,2,
6

23.19
1 Chr 9.22
23.20
2 Kings 11.19
24.1
2 Kings 11.21;
12.1-15
24.2
2 Chr 26.5
24.4
v. 7
24.6
Ex 30.12-16
24.7
2 Chr 21.17

ʷ Or treaty, or testimony; Heb eduth
ˣ Compare Vg: Heb and

ed things of the house of the LORD for the Baals.

8 So the king gave command, and they made a chest, and set it outside the gate of the house of the LORD. 9 A proclamation was made throughout Judah and Jerusalem to bring in for the LORD the tax that Moses the servant of God laid on Israel in the wilderness. 10 All the leaders and all the people rejoiced and brought their tax and dropped it into the chest until it was full. 11 Whenever the chest was brought to the king's officers by the Levites, when they saw that there was a large amount of money in it, the king's secretary and the officer of the chief priest would come and empty the chest and take it and return it to its place. So they did day after day, and collected money in abundance. 12 The king and Jehoiada gave it to those who had charge of the work of the house of the LORD, and they hired masons and carpenters to restore the house of the LORD, and also workers in iron and bronze to repair the house of the LORD. 13 So those who were engaged in the work labored, and the repairing went forward at their hands, and they restored the house of God to its proper condition and strengthened it. 14 When they had finished, they brought the rest of the money to the king and Jehoiada, and with it were made utensils for the house of the LORD, utensils for the service and for the burnt offerings, and ladles, and vessels of gold and silver. They offered burnt offerings in the house of the LORD regularly all the days of Jehoiada.

Apostasy of Joash

15 But Jehoiada grew old and full of days, and died; he was one hundred thirty years old at his death. 16 And they buried him in the city of David among the kings, because he had done good in Israel, and for God and his house.

17 Now after the death of Jehoiada the officials of Judah came and did obeisance to the king; then the king listened to them. 18 They

abandoned the house of the LORD, the God of their ancestors, and served the sacred poles[y] and the idols. And wrath came upon Judah and Jerusalem for this guilt of theirs. 19 Yet he sent prophets among them to bring them back to the LORD; they testified against them, but they would not listen.

20 Then the spirit of God took possession of[z] Zechariah son of the priest Jehoiada; he stood above the people and said to them, "Thus says God: Why do you transgress the commandments of the LORD, so that you cannot prosper? Because you have forsaken the LORD, he has also forsaken you." 21 But they conspired against him, and by command of the king they stoned him to death in the court of the house of the LORD. 22 King Joash did not remember the kindness that Jehoiada, Zechariah's father, had shown him, but killed his son. As he was dying, he said, "May the LORD see and avenge!"

Death of Joash

23 At the end of the year the army of Aram came up against Joash. They came to Judah and Jerusalem, and destroyed all the officials of the people from among them, and sent all the booty they took to the king of Damascus. 24 Although the army of Aram had come with few men, the LORD delivered into their hand a very great army, because they had abandoned the LORD, the God of their ancestors. Thus they executed judgment on Joash.

25 When they had withdrawn, leaving him severely wounded, his servants conspired against him because of the blood of the son[a] of the priest Jehoiada, and they killed him on his bed. So he died; and they buried him in the city of David, but they did not bury him in the tombs of the kings. 26 Those who conspired against him were Zabad son of Shimeath the Ammonite, and Jehozabad son of

24.9
v. 6
24.11
2 Kings 12.10
24.13
Neh 10.39
24.16
2 Chr 21.2, 20
24.18
v. 4;
Ex 34.12-14;
1 Kings 14.23;
Josh 22.20;
2 Chr 19.2

24.19
Jer 7.25
24.20
2 Chr 20.14;
Num 14.41;
2 Chr 15.2
24.21
Neh 9.26;
Mt 23.35;
Acts 7.58,59
24.22
Gen 9.5
24.23
2 Kings 12.17
24.24
Lev 26.25;
Deut 28.25;
2 Chr 22.8;
Isa 10.5
24.25
2 Kings 12.20;
v. 21

y Heb *Asherim* z Heb *clothed itself with*
a Gk Vg: Heb *sons*

Shimrith the Moabite. ²⁷ Accounts of his sons, and of the many oracles against him, and of the rebuildingᵇ of the house of God are written in the Commentary on the Book of the Kings. And his son Amaziah succeeded him.

Reign of Amaziah

25 Amaziah was twenty-five years old when he began to reign, and he reigned twenty-nine years in Jerusalem. His mother's name was Jehoaddan of Jerusalem. ² He did what was right in the sight of the LORD, yet not with a true heart. ³ As soon as the royal power was firmly in his hand he killed his servants who had murdered his father the king. ⁴ But he did not put their children to death, according to what is written in the law, in the book of Moses, where the LORD commanded, "The parents shall not be put to death for the children, or the children be put to death for the parents; but all shall be put to death for their own sins."

Slaughter of the Edomites

5 Amaziah assembled the people of Judah, and set them by ancestral houses under commanders of the thousands and of the hundreds for all Judah and Benjamin. He mustered those twenty years old and upward, and found that they were three hundred thousand picked troops fit for war, able to handle spear and shield. ⁶ He also hired one hundred thousand mighty warriors from Israel for one hundred talents of silver. ⁷ But a man of God came to him and said, "O king, do not let the army of Israel go with you, for the LORD is not with Israel—all these Ephraimites. ⁸ Rather, go by yourself and act; be strong in battle, or God will fling you down before the enemy; for God has power to help or to overthrow." ⁹ Amaziah said to the man of God, "But what shall we do about the hundred talents that I have given to the army of Israel?" The man of God answered, "The LORD is able to give you much more

than this." ¹⁰ Then Amaziah discharged the army that had come to him from Ephraim, letting them go home again. But they became very angry with Judah, and returned home in fierce anger.

11 Amaziah took courage, and led out his people; he went to the Valley of Salt, and struck down ten thousand men of Seir. ¹² The people of Judah captured another ten thousand alive, took them to the top of Sela, and threw them down from the top of Sela, so that all of them were dashed to pieces. ¹³ But the men of the army whom Amaziah sent back, not letting them go with him to battle, fell on the cities of Judah from Samaria to Bethhoron; they killed three thousand people in them, and took much booty.

14 Now after Amaziah came from the slaughter of the Edomites, he brought the gods of the people of Seir, set them up as his gods, and worshiped them, making offerings to them. ¹⁵ The LORD was angry with Amaziah and sent to him a prophet, who said to him, "Why have you resorted to a people's gods who could not deliver their own people from your hand?" ¹⁶ But as he was speaking the kingᶜ said to him, "Have we made you a royal counselor? Stop! Why should you be put to death?" So the prophet stopped, but said, "I know that God has determined to destroy you, because you have done this and have not listened to my advice."

Israel Defeats Judah

17 Then King Amaziah of Judah took counsel and sent to King Joash son of Jehoahaz son of Jehu of Israel, saying, "Come, let us look one another in the face." ¹⁸ King Joash of Israel sent word to King Amaziah of Judah, "A thorn bush on Lebanon sent to a cedar on Lebanon, saying, 'Give your daughter to my son for a wife'; but a wild animal of Lebanon passed by and trampled down the thorn bush.

24.27
2 Kings 12.18, 21
25.1
2 Kings 14.1-6
25.2
v. 14
25.4
Deut 24.16;
2 Kings 14.6
25.5
Num 1.3
25.8
2 Chr 14.11;
20.6

25.11
2 Kings 14.7
25.14
2 Chr 28.23;
Ex 20.3,5
25.15
Ps 96.5;
vv. 11,12
25.17
2 Kings 14.8-14
25.18
Judg 9.8-15

ᵇ Heb *founding*　ᶜ Heb *he*

¹⁹You say, 'See, I have defeated Edom,' and your heart has lifted you up in boastfulness. Now stay at home; why should you provoke trouble so that you fall, you and Judah with you?"

20 But Amaziah would not listen—it was God's doing, in order to hand them over, because they had sought the gods of Edom. ²¹So King Joash of Israel went up; he and King Amaziah of Judah faced one another in battle at Beth-shemesh, which belongs to Judah. ²²Judah was defeated by Israel; everyone fled home. ²³King Joash of Israel captured King Amaziah of Judah, son of Joash, son of Ahaziah, at Beth-shemesh; he brought him to Jerusalem, and broke down the wall of Jerusalem from the Ephraim Gate to the Corner Gate, a distance of four hundred cubits. ²⁴He seized all the gold and silver, and all the vessels that were found in the house of God, and Obed-edom with them; he seized also the treasuries of the king's house, also hostages; then he returned to Samaria.

Death of Amaziah

25 King Amaziah son of Joash of Judah, lived fifteen years after the death of King Joash son of Jehoahaz of Israel. ²⁶Now the rest of the deeds of Amaziah, from first to last, are they not written in the Book of the Kings of Judah and Israel? ²⁷From the time that Amaziah turned away from the LORD they made a conspiracy against him in Jerusalem, and he fled to Lachish. But they sent after him to Lachish, and killed him there. ²⁸They brought him back on horses; he was buried with his ancestors in the city of David.

Reign of Uzziah

26 Then all the people of Judah took Uzziah, who was sixteen years old, and made him king to succeed his father Amaziah. ²He rebuilt Eloth and restored it to Judah, after the king slept with his ancestors. ³Uzziah was

sixteen years old when he began to reign, and he reigned fifty-two years in Jerusalem. His mother's name was Jecoliah of Jerusalem. ⁴He did what was right in the sight of the LORD, just as his father Amaziah had done. ⁵He set himself to seek God in the days of Zechariah, who instructed him in the fear of God; and as long as he sought the LORD, God made him prosper.

6 He went out and made war against the Philistines, and broke down the wall of Gath and the wall of Jabneh and the wall of Ashdod; he built cities in the territory of Ashdod and elsewhere among the Philistines. ⁷God helped him against the Philistines, against the Arabs who lived in Gur-baal, and against the Meunites. ⁸The Ammonites paid tribute to Uzziah, and his fame spread even to the border of Egypt, for he became very strong. ⁹Moreover Uzziah built towers in Jerusalem at the Corner Gate, at the Valley Gate, and at the Angle, and fortified them. ¹⁰He built towers in the wilderness and hewed out many cisterns, for he had large herds, both in the Shephelah and in the plain, and he had farmers and vinedressers in the hills and in the fertile lands, for he loved the soil. ¹¹Moreover Uzziah had an army of soldiers, fit for war, in divisions according to the numbers in the muster made by the secretary Jeiel and the officer Maaseiah, under the direction of Hananiah, one of the king's commanders. ¹²The whole number of the heads of ancestral houses of mighty warriors was two thousand six hundred. ¹³Under their command was an army of three hundred seven thousand five hundred, who could make war with mighty power, to help the king against the enemy. ¹⁴Uzziah provided for all the army the shields, spears, helmets, coats of mail, bows, and stones for slinging. ¹⁵In Jerusalem he set up machines, invented by skilled workers, on the towers and the corners for shooting arrows and large stones. And his fame spread

Cross references (center column):

25.19
2 Chr 26.16;
32.25
25.20
1 Kings 12.15;
2 Chr 22.7
25.23
2 Chr 21.17;
22.1
25.25
2 Kings 14.17-22
26.1
2 Kings 14.21,
22; 15.2,3

26.5
2 Chr 24.2;
Dan 1.17;
2.19;
2 Chr 15.2
26.6
Isa 14.29
26.7
2 Chr 21.16
26.8
2 Chr 17.11
26.9
2 Chr 25.23;
Neh 3.13
26.13
2 Chr 25.5

far, for he was marvelously helped until he became strong.

Pride and Apostasy

16 But when he had become strong he grew proud, to his destruction. For he was false to the Lord his God, and entered the temple of the Lord to make offering on the altar of incense. ¹⁷But the priest Azariah went in after him, with eighty priests of the Lord who were men of valor; ¹⁸they withstood King Uzziah, and said to him, "It is not for you, Uzziah, to make offering to the Lord, but for the priests the descendants of Aaron, who are consecrated to make offering. Go out of the sanctuary; for you have done wrong, and it will bring you no honor from the Lord God." ¹⁹Then Uzziah was angry. Now he had a censer in his hand to make offering, and when he became angry with the priests a leprous ᵈ disease broke out on his forehead, in the presence of the priests in the house of the Lord, by the altar of incense. ²⁰When the chief priest Azariah, and all the priests, looked at him, he was leprous ᵈ in his forehead. They hurried him out, and he himself hurried to get out, because the Lord had struck him. ²¹King Uzziah was leprous ᵈ to the day of his death, and being leprous ᵈ lived in a separate house, for he was excluded from the house of the Lord. His son Jotham was in charge of the palace of the king, governing the people of the land.

22 Now the rest of the acts of Uzziah, from first to last, the prophet Isaiah son of Amoz wrote. ²³Uzziah slept with his ancestors; they buried him near his ancestors in the burial field that belonged to the kings, for they said, "He is leprous." ᵈ His son Jotham succeeded him.

Reign of Jotham

27 Jotham was twenty-five years old when he began to reign; he reigned sixteen years in Jerusalem. His mother's name was Jerushah daughter of Zadok. ²He did what was right in the sight of the Lord just as his father Uzziah had done—only he did not invade the temple of the Lord. But the people still followed corrupt practices. ³He built the upper gate of the house of the Lord, and did extensive building on the wall of Ophel. ⁴Moreover he built cities in the hill country of Judah, and forts and towers on the wooded hills. ⁵He fought with the king of the Ammonites and prevailed against them. The Ammonites gave him that year one hundred talents of silver, ten thousand cors of wheat and ten thousand of barley. The Ammonites paid him the same amount in the second and the third years. ⁶So Jotham became strong because he ordered his ways before the Lord his God. ⁷Now the rest of the acts of Jotham, and all his wars and his ways, are written in the Book of the Kings of Israel and Judah. ⁸He was twenty-five years old when he began to reign; he reigned sixteen years in Jerusalem. ⁹Jotham slept with his ancestors, and they buried him in the city of David; and his son Ahaz succeeded him.

Reign of Ahaz

28 Ahaz was twenty years old when he began to reign; he reigned sixteen years in Jerusalem. He did not do what was right in the sight of the Lord, as his ancestor David had done, ²but he walked in the ways of the kings of Israel. He even made cast images for the Baals; ³and he made offerings in the valley of the son of Hinnom, and made his sons pass through fire, according to the abominable practices of the nations whom the Lord drove out before the people of Israel. ⁴He sacrificed and made offerings on the high places, on the hills, and under every green tree.

Aram and Israel Defeat Judah

5 Therefore the Lord his God

26.16
Deut 32.15;
2 Chr 25.19;
2 Kings 16.12, 13
26.17
1 Chr 6.10
26.18
Num 16.39, 40; Ex 30.7, 8
26.19
2 Kings 5.25-27
26.21
2 Kings 15.5-7;
Lev 13.46;
Num 5.2
26.22
Isa 1.1
26.23
2 Kings 15.7;
Isa 6.1
27.1
2 Kings 15.33-35

27.2
2 Chr 26.16
27.3
2 Chr 33.14;
Neh 3.26
27.6
2 Chr 26.5
27.7
2 Kings 15.36
27.8
v. 1
28.1
2 Kings 16.2-4
28.2
2 Chr 22.3;
Ex 34.17
28.3
2 Kings 23.10;
Lev 18.21;
2 Kings 16.3;
2 Chr 33.6
28.4
v. 25
28.5
Isa 7.1;
2 Kings 16.5, 6

ᵈ A term for several skin diseases; precise meaning uncertain

gave him into the hand of the king of Aram, who defeated him and took captive a great number of his people and brought them to Damascus. He was also given into the hand of the king of Israel, who defeated him with great slaughter. [6] Pekah son of Remaliah killed one hundred twenty thousand in Judah in one day, all of them valiant warriors, because they had abandoned the LORD, the God of their ancestors. [7] And Zichri, a mighty warrior of Ephraim, killed the king's son Maaseiah, Azrikam the commander of the palace, and Elkanah the next in authority to the king.

Intervention of Oded

8 The people of Israel took captive two hundred thousand of their kin, women, sons, and daughters; they also took much booty from them and brought the booty to Samaria. [9] But a prophet of the LORD was there, whose name was Oded; he went out to meet the army that came to Samaria, and said to them, "Because the LORD, the God of your ancestors, was angry with Judah, he gave them into your hand, but you have killed them in a rage that has reached up to heaven. [10] Now you intend to subjugate the people of Judah and Jerusalem, male and female, as your slaves. But what have you except sins against the LORD your God? [11] Now hear me, and send back the captives whom you have taken from your kindred, for the fierce wrath of the LORD is upon you." [12] Moreover, certain chiefs of the Ephraimites, Azariah son of Johanan, Berechiah son of Meshillemoth, Jehizkiah son of Shallum, and Amasa son of Hadlai, stood up against those who were coming from the war, [13] and said to them, "You shall not bring the captives in here, for you propose to bring on us guilt against the LORD in addition to our present sins and guilt. For our guilt is already great, and there is fierce wrath against Israel." [14] So the warriors left the captives and the booty before the officials and all the assembly. [15] Then

those who were mentioned by name got up and took the captives, and with the booty they clothed all that were naked among them; they clothed them, gave them sandals, provided them with food and drink, and anointed them; and carrying all the feeble among them on donkeys, they brought them to their kindred at Jericho, the city of palm trees. Then they returned to Samaria.

Assyria Refuses to Help Judah

16 At that time King Ahaz sent to the king[e] of Assyria for help. [17] For the Edomites had again invaded and defeated Judah, and carried away captives. [18] And the Philistines had made raids on the cities in the Shephelah and the Negeb of Judah, and had taken Bethshemesh, Aijalon, Gederoth, Soco with its villages, Timnah with its villages, and Gimzo with its villages; and they settled there. [19] For the LORD brought Judah low because of King Ahaz of Israel, for he had behaved without restraint in Judah and had been faithless to the LORD. [20] So King Tilgathpilneser of Assyria came against him, and oppressed him instead of strengthening him. [21] For Ahaz plundered the house of the LORD and the houses of the king and of the officials, and gave tribute to the king of Assyria; but it did not help him.

Apostasy and Death of Ahaz

22 In the time of his distress he became yet more faithless to the LORD—this same King Ahaz. [23] For he sacrificed to the gods of Damascus, which had defeated him, and said, "Because the gods of the kings of Aram helped them, I will sacrifice to them so that they may help me." But they were the ruin of him, and of all Israel. [24] Ahaz gathered together the utensils of the house of God, and cut in pieces the utensils of the house of God. He shut up the doors of the house of the LORD and made himself altars

28.6
2 Kings 15.27
28.8
2 Chr 11.4
28.9
2 Chr 25.15;
Isa 10.5;
47.6;
Ezra 9.6;
Rev 18.5
28.10
Lev 25.39,
42,43,46
28.11
v. 8
28.15
v. 12;
2 Kings 6.22;
Prov 25.21,
22;
Deut 34.3;
Judg 1.16

28.16
2 Kings 16.7
28.18
Ezek 16.57
28.19
2 Chr 21.2
28.20
1 Chr 5.26;
2 Kings 16.8,
9
28.23
2 Chr 25.14;
Jer 44.17,18
28.24
2 Kings 16.17;
2 Chr 29.7;
30.14; 33.3-5

[e] Gk Syr Vg Compare 2 Kings 16.7: Heb *kings*

in every corner of Jerusalem. ²⁵In every city of Judah he made high places to make offerings to other gods, provoking to anger the Lord, the God of his ancestors. ²⁶Now the rest of his acts and all his ways, from first to last, are written in the Book of the Kings of Judah and Israel. ²⁷Ahaz slept with his ancestors, and they buried him in the city, in Jerusalem; but they did not bring him into the tombs of the kings of Israel. His son Hezekiah succeeded him.

Reign of Hezekiah

29 Hezekiah began to reign when he was twenty-five years old; he reigned twenty-nine years in Jerusalem. His mother's name was Abijah daughter of Zechariah. ²He did what was right in the sight of the Lord, just as his ancestor David had done.

The Temple Cleansed

3 In the first year of his reign, in the first month, he opened the doors of the house of the Lord and repaired them. ⁴He brought in the priests and the Levites and assembled them in the square on the east. ⁵He said to them, "Listen to me, Levites! Sanctify yourselves, and sanctify the house of the Lord, the God of your ancestors, and carry out the filth from the holy place. ⁶For our ancestors have been unfaithful and have done what was evil in the sight of the Lord our God; they have forsaken him, and have turned away their faces from the dwelling of the Lord, and turned their backs. ⁷They also shut the doors of the vestibule and put out the lamps, and have not offered incense or made burnt offerings in the holy place to the God of Israel. ⁸Therefore the wrath of the Lord came upon Judah and Jerusalem, and he has made them an object of horror, of astonishment, and of hissing, as you see with your own eyes. ⁹Our fathers have fallen by the sword and our sons and our daughters and our wives are in captivity for this. ¹⁰Now it is in my

heart to make a covenant with the Lord, the God of Israel, so that his fierce anger may turn away from us. ¹¹My sons, do not now be negligent, for the Lord has chosen you to stand in his presence to minister to him, and to be his ministers and make offerings to him."

12 Then the Levites arose, Mahath son of Amasai, and Joel son of Azariah, of the sons of the Kohathites; and of the sons of Merari, Kish son of Abdi, and Azariah son of Jehallelel; and of the Gershonites, Joah son of Zimmah, and Eden son of Joah; ¹³and of the sons of Elizaphan, Shimri and Jeuel; and of the sons of Asaph, Zechariah and Mattaniah; ¹⁴and of the sons of Heman, Jehuel and Shimei; and of the sons of Jeduthun, Shemaiah and Uzziel. ¹⁵They gathered their brothers, sanctified themselves, and went in as the king had commanded, by the words of the Lord, to cleanse the house of the Lord. ¹⁶The priests went into the inner part of the house of the Lord to cleanse it, and they brought out all the unclean things that they found in the temple of the Lord into the court of the house of the Lord; and the Levites took them and carried them out to the Wadi Kidron. ¹⁷They began to sanctify on the first day of the first month, and on the eighth day of the month they came to the vestibule of the Lord; then for eight days they sanctified the house of the Lord, and on the sixteenth day of the first month they finished. ¹⁸Then they went inside to King Hezekiah and said, "We have cleansed all the house of the Lord, the altar of burnt offering and all its utensils, and the table for the rows of bread and all its utensils. ¹⁹All the utensils that King Ahaz repudiated during his reign when he was faithless, we have made ready and sanctified; see, they are in front of the altar of the Lord."

Temple Worship Restored

20 Then King Hezekiah rose early, assembled the officials of the

28.26
2 Kings 16.19, 20
28.27
2 Chr 24.25
29.1
2 Kings 18.1-3
29.2
2 Chr 28.1
29.3
v. 7;
2 Chr 28.24
29.5
vv. 15,34;
2 Chr 35.6
29.6
Jer 2.27;
Ezek 8.16
29.8
2 Chr 24.18;
28.5;
Deut 28.25;
Jer 25.9,18
29.9
2 Chr 28.5-8, 17
29.10
2 Chr 15.12;
23.16

29.11
Num 3.6;
8.14
29.15
v. 5;
2 Chr 30.12;
1 Chr 23.28
29.17
v. 3
29.19
2 Chr 28.24

city, and went up to the house of the LORD. [21] They brought seven bulls, seven rams, seven lambs, and seven male goats for a sin offering for the kingdom and for the sanctuary and for Judah. He commanded the priests the descendants of Aaron to offer them on the altar of the LORD. [22] So they slaughtered the bulls, and the priests received the blood and dashed it against the altar; they slaughtered the rams and their blood was dashed against the altar; they also slaughtered the lambs and their blood was dashed against the altar. [23] Then the male goats for the sin offering were brought to the king and the assembly; they laid their hands on them, [24] and the priests slaughtered them and made a sin offering with their blood at the altar, to make atonement for all Israel. For the king commanded that the burnt offering and the sin offering should be made for all Israel.

25 He stationed the Levites in the house of the LORD with cymbals, harps, and lyres, according to the commandment of David and of Gad the king's seer and of the prophet Nathan, for the commandment was from the LORD through his prophets. [26] The Levites stood with the instruments of David, and the priests with the trumpets. [27] Then Hezekiah commanded that the burnt offering be offered on the altar. When the burnt offering began, the song to the LORD began also, and the trumpets, accompanied by the instruments of King David of Israel. [28] The whole assembly worshiped, the singers sang, and the trumpeters sounded; all this continued until the burnt offering was finished. [29] When the offering was finished, the king and all who were present with him bowed down and worshiped. [30] King Hezekiah and the officials commanded the Levites to sing praises to the LORD with the words of David and of the seer Asaph. They sang praises with gladness, and they bowed down and worshiped.

31 Then Hezekiah said, "You have now consecrated yourselves to the LORD; come near, bring sacrifices and thank offerings to the house of the LORD." The assembly brought sacrifices and thank offerings; and all who were of a willing heart brought burnt offerings. [32] The number of the burnt offerings that the assembly brought was seventy bulls, one hundred rams, and two hundred lambs; all these were for a burnt offering to the LORD. [33] The consecrated offerings were six hundred bulls and three thousand sheep. [34] But the priests were too few and could not skin all the burnt offerings, so, until other priests had sanctified themselves, their kindred, the Levites, helped them until the work was finished—for the Levites were more conscientious[f] than the priests in sanctifying themselves. [35] Besides the great number of burnt offerings there was the fat of the offerings of well-being, and there were the drink offerings for the burnt offerings. Thus the service of the house of the LORD was restored. [36] And Hezekiah and all the people rejoiced because of what God had done for the people; for the thing had come about suddenly.

The Great Passover

30 Hezekiah sent word to all Israel and Judah, and wrote letters also to Ephraim and Manasseh, that they should come to the house of the LORD at Jerusalem, to keep the passover to the LORD the God of Israel. [2] For the king and his officials and all the assembly in Jerusalem had taken counsel to keep the passover in the second month [3] (for they could not keep it at its proper time because the priests had not sanctified themselves in sufficient number, nor had the people assembled in Jerusalem). [4] The plan seemed right to the king and all the assembly. [5] So they decreed to make a proclamation throughout all Israel, from Beer-sheba to Dan, that the

Cross references (center column):

29.21
Lev 4.3-14
29.22
Lev 4.18;
8.14
29.23
Lev 4.15
29.24
Lev 4.26
29.25
1 Chr 25.6;
2 Chr 8.14;
2 Sam 24.11;
7.2
29.26
1 Chr 23.5;
2 Chr 5.12
29.27
2 Chr 23.18
29.29
2 Chr 20.18

29.31
2 Chr 13.9;
Ex 35.5,22
29.34
2 Chr 35.11;
30.3
29.35
v. 32;
Lev 3.16;
Num 15.5-10
30.2
vv. 13,15;
Num 9.10,
11
30.3
Ex 12.6,18;
2 Chr 29.34
30.5
Judg 20.1

f Heb *upright in heart*

people should come and keep the passover to the LORD the God of Israel, at Jerusalem; for they had not kept it in great numbers as prescribed. ⁶So couriers went throughout all Israel and Judah with letters from the king and his officials, as the king had commanded, saying, "O people of Israel, return to the LORD, the God of Abraham, Isaac, and Israel, so that he may turn again to the remnant of you who have escaped from the hand of the kings of Assyria. ⁷Do not be like your ancestors and your kindred, who were faithless to the LORD God of their ancestors, so that he made them a desolation, as you see. ⁸Do not now be stiff-necked as your ancestors were, but yield yourselves to the LORD and come to his sanctuary, which he has sanctified forever, and serve the LORD your God, so that his fierce anger may turn away from you. ⁹For as you return to the LORD, your kindred and your children will find compassion with their captors, and return to this land. For the LORD your God is gracious and merciful, and will not turn away his face from you, if you return to him."

10 So the couriers went from city to city through the country of Ephraim and Manasseh, and as far as Zebulun; but they laughed them to scorn, and mocked them. ¹¹Only a few from Asher, Manasseh, and Zebulun humbled themselves and came to Jerusalem. ¹²The hand of God was also on Judah to give them one heart to do what the king and the officials commanded by the word of the LORD.

13 Many people came together in Jerusalem to keep the festival of unleavened bread in the second month, a very large assembly. ¹⁴They set to work and removed the altars that were in Jerusalem, and all the altars for offering incense they took away and threw into the Wadi Kidron. ¹⁵They slaughtered the passover lamb on the fourteenth day of the second month. The priests and the Levites were ashamed, and they sanctified

30.6
Esther 8.14;
Job 9.25;
Jer 51.31;
2 Chr 20.8
30.7
Ezek 20.18;
2 Chr 29.8
30.8
Ex 32.9;
2 Chr 29.10
30.9
Deut 30.2;
Ex 34.6,7;
Mic 7.18;
Isa 55.7
30.10
2 Chr 36.16
30.11
vv. 18,21,25
30.13
v. 2
30.14
2 Chr 28.24
30.15
vv. 2,3;
2 Chr 29.34

30.16
2 Chr 35.10,
15
30.17
2 Chr 29.34
30.18
vv. 11,25;
Ex 12.43-49
30.19
2 Chr 19.3
30.21
Ex 12.15;
13.6
30.22
2 Chr 32.6;
Ezra 10.11
30.23
1 Kings 8.65
30.24
2 Chr 35.7,
8; 29.34

themselves and brought burnt offerings into the house of the LORD. ¹⁶They took their accustomed posts according to the law of Moses the man of God; the priests dashed the blood that they received ᵍ from the hands of the Levites. ¹⁷For there were many in the assembly who had not sanctified themselves; therefore the Levites had to slaughter the passover lamb for everyone who was not clean, to make it holy to the LORD. ¹⁸For a multitude of the people, many of them from Ephraim, Manasseh, Issachar, and Zebulun, had not cleansed themselves, yet they ate the passover otherwise than as prescribed. But Hezekiah prayed for them, saying, "The good LORD pardon all ¹⁹who set their hearts to seek God, the LORD the God of their ancestors, even though not in accordance with the sanctuary's rules of cleanness." ²⁰The LORD heard Hezekiah, and healed the people. ²¹The people of Israel who were present at Jerusalem kept the festival of unleavened bread seven days with great gladness; and the Levites and the priests praised the LORD day by day, accompanied by loud instruments for the LORD. ²²Hezekiah spoke encouragingly to all the Levites who showed good skill in the service of the LORD. So the people ate the food of the festival for seven days, sacrificing offerings of well-being and giving thanks to the LORD the God of their ancestors.

23 Then the whole assembly agreed together to keep the festival for another seven days; so they kept it for another seven days with gladness. ²⁴For King Hezekiah of Judah gave the assembly a thousand bulls and seven thousand sheep for offerings, and the officials gave the assembly a thousand bulls and ten thousand sheep. The priests sanctified themselves in great numbers. ²⁵The whole assembly of Judah, the priests and the Levites, and the whole assembly that came out of Israel, and the

ᵍ Heb lacks *that they received*

resident aliens who came out of the land of Israel, and the resident aliens who lived in Judah, rejoiced. [26] There was great joy in Jerusalem, for since the time of Solomon son of King David of Israel there had been nothing like this in Jerusalem. [27] Then the priests and the Levites stood up and blessed the people, and their voice was heard; their prayer came to his holy dwelling in heaven.

Pagan Shrines Destroyed

31 Now when all this was finished, all Israel who were present went out to the cities of Judah and broke down the pillars, hewed down the sacred poles,[h] and pulled down the high places and the altars throughout all Judah and Benjamin, and in Ephraim and Manasseh, until they had destroyed them all. Then all the people of Israel returned to their cities, all to their individual properties.

2 Hezekiah appointed the divisions of the priests and of the Levites, division by division, everyone according to his service, the priests and the Levites, for burnt offerings and offerings of well-being, to minister in the gates of the camp of the LORD and to give thanks and praise. [3] The contribution of the king from his own possessions was for the burnt offerings: the burnt offerings of morning and evening, and the burnt offerings for the sabbaths, the new moons, and the appointed festivals, as it is written in the law of the LORD. [4] He commanded the people who lived in Jerusalem to give the portion due to the priests and the Levites, so that they might devote themselves to the law of the LORD. [5] As soon as the word spread, the people of Israel gave in abundance the first fruits of grain, wine, oil, honey, and of all the produce of the field; and they brought in abundantly the tithe of everything. [6] The people of Israel and Judah who lived in the cities of Judah also brought in the tithe of cattle and sheep, and the tithe of the dedicated things that had been consecrat-

ed to the LORD their God, and laid them in heaps. [7] In the third month they began to pile up the heaps, and finished them in the seventh month. [8] When Hezekiah and the officials came and saw the heaps, they blessed the LORD and his people Israel. [9] Hezekiah questioned the priests and the Levites about the heaps. [10] The chief priest Azariah, who was of the house of Zadok, answered him, "Since they began to bring the contributions into the house of the LORD, we have had enough to eat and have plenty to spare; for the LORD has blessed his people, so that we have this great supply left over."

Reorganization of Priests and Levites

11 Then Hezekiah commanded them to prepare store-chambers in the house of the LORD; and they prepared them. [12] Faithfully they brought in the contributions, the tithes and the dedicated things. The chief officer in charge of them was Conaniah the Levite, with his brother Shimei as second; [13] while Jehiel, Azaziah, Nahath, Asahel, Jerimoth, Jozabad, Eliel, Ismachiah, Mahath, and Benaiah were overseers assisting Conaniah and his brother Shimei, by the appointment of King Hezekiah and of Azariah the chief officer of the house of God. [14] Kore son of Imnah the Levite, keeper of the east gate, was in charge of the freewill offerings to God, to apportion the contribution reserved for the LORD and the most holy offerings. [15] Eden, Miniamin, Jeshua, Shemaiah, Amariah, and Shecaniah were faithfully assisting him in the cities of the priests, to distribute the portions to their kindred, old and young alike, by divisions, [16] except those enrolled by genealogy, males from three years old and upwards, all who entered the house of the LORD as the duty of each day required, for their service according to their offices, by their divisions. [17] The enrollment of the priests was according to their an-

30.27
2 Chr 23.18;
Num 6.23;
Deut 26.15;
Ps 68.5
31.1
2 Kings 18.4
31.2
1 Chr 24.1;
23.28-31
31.3
Num 28.29
31.4
Num 18.8;
Neh 13.10
31.5
Neh 13.12
31.6
Lev 27.30;
Deut 14.28

31.10
Mal 3.10
31.13
2 Chr 35.9
31.15
2 Chr 29.12;
Josh 21.9-19
31.16
Ezra 3.4
31.17
1 Chr 23.24

h Heb *Asherim*

cestral houses; that of the Levites from twenty years old and upwards was according to their offices, by their divisions. ¹⁸ The priests were enrolled with all their little children, their wives, their sons, and their daughters, the whole multitude; for they were faithful in keeping themselves holy. ¹⁹ And for the descendants of Aaron, the priests, who were in the fields of common land belonging to their towns, town by town, the people designated by name were to distribute portions to every male among the priests and to everyone among the Levites who was enrolled.

20 Hezekiah did this throughout all Judah; he did what was good and right and faithful before the LORD his God. ²¹ And every work that he undertook in the service of the house of God, and in accordance with the law and the commandments, to seek his God, he did with all his heart; and he prospered.

Sennacherib's Invasion

32 After these things and these acts of faithfulness, King Sennacherib of Assyria came and invaded Judah and encamped against the fortified cities, thinking to win them for himself. ² When Hezekiah saw that Sennacherib had come and intended to fight against Jerusalem, ³ he planned with his officers and his warriors to stop the flow of the springs that were outside the city; and they helped him. ⁴ A great many people were gathered, and they stopped all the springs and the wadi that flowed through the land, saying, "Why should the Assyrian kings come and find water in abundance?" ⁵ Hezekiah^i set to work resolutely and built up the entire wall that was broken down, and raised towers on it,^j and outside it he built another wall; he also strengthened the Millo in the city of David, and made weapons and shields in abundance. ⁶ He appointed combat commanders over the people, and gathered them to-

gether to him in the square at the gate of the city and spoke encouragingly to them, saying, ⁷ "Be strong and of good courage. Do not be afraid or dismayed before the king of Assyria and all the horde that is with him; for there is one greater with us than with him. ⁸ With him is an arm of flesh; but with us is the LORD our God, to help us and to fight our battles." The people were encouraged by the words of King Hezekiah of Judah.

9 After this, while King Sennacherib of Assyria was at Lachish with all his forces, he sent his servants to Jerusalem to King Hezekiah of Judah and to all the people of Judah that were in Jerusalem, saying, ¹⁰ "Thus says King Sennacherib of Assyria: On what are you relying, that you undergo the siege of Jerusalem? ¹¹ Is not Hezekiah misleading you, handing you over to die by famine and by thirst, when he tells you, 'The LORD our God will save us from the hand of the king of Assyria'? ¹² Was it not this same Hezekiah who took away his high places and his altars and commanded Judah and Jerusalem, saying, 'Before one altar you shall worship, and upon it you shall make your offerings'? ¹³ Do you not know what I and my ancestors have done to all the peoples of other lands? Were the gods of the nations of those lands at all able to save their lands out of my hand? ¹⁴ Who among all the gods of those nations that my ancestors utterly destroyed was able to save his people from my hand, that your God should be able to save you from my hand? ¹⁵ Now therefore do not let Hezekiah deceive you or mislead you in this fashion, and do not believe him, for no god of any nation or kingdom has been able to save his people from my hand or from the hand of my ancestors. How much less will your God save you out of my hand!"

16 His servants said still more against the Lord GOD and against

Cross references (center column)

31.19
Lev 25.34;
Num 35.2;
vv. 12-15
31.20
2 Kings 20.3;
22.2
32.1
2 Kings 18.13-
19;
Isa 36.1ff
32.4
2 Kings 20.20;
v. 30
32.5
2 Chr 25.23;
1 Kings 9.24
32.6
2 Chr 30.22

32.7
1 Chr 22.13;
2 Kings 6.16
32.8
Jer 17.5;
2 Chr 13.12;
20.17
32.11
2 Kings 18.30
32.12
2 Kings 18.22;
2 Chr 31.1
32.13
2 Kings 18.33-
35
32.14
Isa 10.9-11
32.15
2 Kings 18.29

^i Heb *He* ^j Vg: Heb *and raised on the towers*

his servant Hezekiah. ¹⁷He also wrote letters to throw contempt on the LORD the God of Israel and to speak against him, saying, "Just as the gods of the nations in other lands did not rescue their people from my hands, so the God of Hezekiah will not rescue his people from my hand." ¹⁸They shouted it with a loud voice in the language of Judah to the people of Jerusalem who were on the wall, to frighten and terrify them, in order that they might take the city. ¹⁹They spoke of the God of Jerusalem as if he were like the gods of the peoples of the earth, which are the work of human hands.

Sennacherib's Defeat and Death

20 Then King Hezekiah and the prophet Isaiah son of Amoz prayed because of this and cried to heaven. ²¹And the LORD sent an angel who cut off all the mighty warriors and commanders and officers in the camp of the king of Assyria. So he returned in disgrace to his own land. When he came into the house of his god, some of his own sons struck him down there with the sword. ²²So the LORD saved Hezekiah and the inhabitants of Jerusalem from the hand of King Sennacherib of Assyria and from the hand of all his enemies; he gave them restk on every side. ²³Many brought gifts to the LORD in Jerusalem and precious things to King Hezekiah of Judah, so that he was exalted in the sight of all nations from that time onward.

Hezekiah's Sickness

24 In those days Hezekiah became sick and was at the point of death. He prayed to the LORD, and he answered him and gave him a sign. ²⁵But Hezekiah did not respond according to the benefit done to him, for his heart was proud. Therefore wrath came upon him and upon Judah and Jerusalem. ²⁶Then Hezekiah humbled himself for the pride of his heart, both he and the inhabitants of Jerusalem, so that the wrath of the

LORD did not come upon them in the days of Hezekiah.

Hezekiah's Prosperity and Achievements

27 Hezekiah had very great riches and honor; and he made for himself treasuries for silver, for gold, for precious stones, for spices, for shields, and for all kinds of costly objects; ²⁸storehouses also for the yield of grain, wine, and oil; and stalls for all kinds of cattle, and sheepfolds.l ²⁹He likewise provided cities for himself, and flocks and herds in abundance; for God had given him very great possessions. ³⁰This same Hezekiah closed the upper outlet of the waters of Gihon and directed them down to the west side of the city of David. Hezekiah prospered in all his works. ³¹So also in the matter of the envoys of the officials of Babylon, who had been sent to him to inquire about the sign that had been done in the land, God left him to himself, in order to test him and to know all that was in his heart.

32 Now the rest of the acts of Hezekiah, and his good deeds, are written in the vision of the prophet Isaiah son of Amoz in the Book of the Kings of Judah and Israel. ³³Hezekiah slept with his ancestors, and they buried him on the ascent to the tombs of the descendants of David; and all Judah and the inhabitants of Jerusalem did him honor at his death. His son Manasseh succeeded him.

Reign of Manasseh

33 Manasseh was twelve years old when he began to reign; he reigned fifty-five years in Jerusalem. ²He did what was evil in the sight of the LORD, according to the abominable practices of the nations whom the LORD drove out before the people of Israel. ³For he rebuilt the high places that his father Hezekiah had pulled down, and erected altars to the Baals, made sacred poles,m worshiped all

Cross references (center column):

32.17 2 Kings 19.9, 12
32.18 2 Kings 18.26-28
32.19 2 Kings 19.18
32.20 2 Kings 19.2, 4,15
32.21 2 Kings 19.35ff
32.23 2 Chr 17.5
32.24 2 Kings 20.1-11; Isa 38.1-8
32.25 Ps 116.12; 2 Chr 26.16; 24.18
32.26 Jer 26.18,19
32.29 1 Chr 29.12
32.30 2 Kings 20.20; 1 Kings 1.33
32.31 2 Kings 20.12; Isa 39.1; Deut 8.2,16
32.33 2 Kings 20.21; Prov 10.7
33.1 2 Kings 21.1-9
33.2 Deut 18.9; 2 Chr 28.3
33.3 2 Chr 31.1; Deut 16.21; 2 Kings 23.5, 6; Deut 17.3

k Gk Vg: Heb *guided them* l Gk Vg: Heb *flocks for folds* m Heb *Asheroth*

the host of heaven, and served them. [4] He built altars in the house of the LORD, of which the LORD had said, "In Jerusalem shall my name be forever." [5] He built altars for all the host of heaven in the two courts of the house of the LORD. [6] He made his son pass through fire in the valley of the son of Hinnom, practiced soothsaying and augury and sorcery, and dealt with mediums and with wizards. He did much evil in the sight of the LORD, provoking him to anger. [7] The carved image of the idol that he had made he set in the house of God, of which God said to David and to his son Solomon, "In this house, and in Jerusalem, which I have chosen out of all the tribes of Israel, I will put my name forever; [8] I will never again remove the feet of Israel from the land that I appointed for your ancestors, if only they will be careful to do all that I have commanded them, all the law, the statutes, and the ordinances given through Moses." [9] Manasseh misled Judah and the inhabitants of Jerusalem, so that they did more evil than the nations whom the LORD had destroyed before the people of Israel.

Manasseh Restored after Repentance

10 The LORD spoke to Manasseh and to his people, but they gave no heed. [11] Therefore the LORD brought against them the commanders of the army of the king of Assyria, who took Manasseh captive in manacles, bound him with fetters, and brought him to Babylon. [12] While he was in distress he entreated the favor of the LORD his God and humbled himself greatly before the God of his ancestors. [13] He prayed to him, and God received his entreaty, heard his plea, and restored him again to Jerusalem and to his kingdom. Then Manasseh knew that the LORD indeed was God.

14 Afterward he built an outer wall for the city of David west of Gihon, in the valley, reaching the entrance at the Fish Gate; he car-

ried it around Ophel, and raised it to a very great height. He also put commanders of the army in all the fortified cities in Judah. [15] He took away the foreign gods and the idol from the house of the LORD, and all the altars that he had built on the mountain of the house of the LORD and in Jerusalem, and he threw them out of the city. [16] He also restored the altar of the LORD and offered on it sacrifices of well-being and of thanksgiving; and he commanded Judah to serve the LORD the God of Israel. [17] The people, however, still sacrificed at the high places, but only to the LORD their God.

Death of Manasseh

18 Now the rest of the acts of Manasseh, his prayer to his God, and the words of the seers who spoke to him in the name of the LORD God of Israel, these are in the Annals of the Kings of Israel. [19] His prayer, and how God received his entreaty, all his sin and his faithlessness, the sites on which he built high places and set up the sacred poles [n] and the images, before he humbled himself, these are written in the records of the seers. [o] [20] So Manasseh slept with his ancestors, and they buried him in his house. His son Amon succeeded him.

Amon's Reign and Death

21 Amon was twenty-two years old when he began to reign; he reigned two years in Jerusalem. [22] He did what was evil in the sight of the LORD, as his father Manasseh had done. Amon sacrificed to all the images that his father Manasseh had made, and served them. [23] He did not humble himself before the LORD, as his father Manasseh had humbled himself, but this Amon incurred more and more guilt. [24] His servants conspired against him and killed him in his house. [25] But the people of the land killed all those who had conspired against King Amon; and the people

Cross-references (center column)

33.4 2 Chr 28.24; 7.16
33.5 2 Chr 4.9
33.6 Lev 18.21; 2 Chr 28.3; Deut 18.10, 11; 2 Kings 21.6
33.7 2 Kings 21.7; vv. 4,15
33.8 2 Sam 7.10
33.11 Deut 28.36; Ps 107.10, 11
33.12 2 Chr 32.26; 1 Pet 5.6
33.13 1 Chr 5.20; Ezra 8.23; Dan 4.25,32
33.14 1 Kings 1.33; Neh 3.3; 2 Chr 27.3
33.15 vv. 3-7
33.17 2 Chr 32.12
33.18 vv. 10,12,18
33.19 vv. 3,13
33.20 2 Kings 21.18
33.21 2 Kings 21.19-24
33.22 vv. 2-7
33.23 v. 12
33.24 2 Chr 25.27

[n] Heb Asherim [o] One Ms Gk: MT of Hozai

of the land made his son Josiah king to succeed him.

Reign of Josiah

34 Josiah was eight years old when he began to reign; he reigned thirty-one years in Jerusalem. 2 He did what was right in the sight of the Lord, and walked in the ways of his ancestor David; he did not turn aside to the right or to the left. 3 For in the eighth year of his reign, while he was still a boy, he began to seek the God of his ancestor David, and in the twelfth year he began to purge Judah and Jerusalem of the high places, the sacred poles,p and the carved and the cast images. 4 In his presence they pulled down the altars of the Baals; he demolished the incense altars that stood above them. He broke down the sacred polesp and the carved and the cast images; he made dust of them and scattered it over the graves of those who had sacrificed to them. 5 He also burned the bones of the priests on their altars, and purged Judah and Jerusalem. 6 In the towns of Manasseh, Ephraim, and Simeon, and as far as Naphtali, in their ruinsq all around, 7 he broke down the altars, beat the sacred polesp and the images into powder, and demolished all the incense altars throughout all the land of Israel. Then he returned to Jerusalem.

Discovery of the Book of the Law

8 In the eighteenth year of his reign, when he had purged the land and the house, he sent Shaphan son of Azaliah, Maaseiah the governor of the city, and Joah son of Joahaz, the recorder, to repair the house of the Lord his God. 9 They came to the high priest Hilkiah and delivered the money that had been brought into the house of God, which the Levites, the keepers of the threshold, had collected from Manasseh and Ephraim and from all the remnant of Israel and from all Judah and Benjamin and from the inhabitants of Jerusalem.

10 They delivered it to the workers who had the oversight of the house of the Lord, and the workers who were working in the house of the Lord gave it for repairing and restoring the house. 11 They gave it to the carpenters and the builders to buy quarried stone, and timber for binders, and beams for the buildings that the kings of Judah had let go to ruin. 12 The people did the work faithfully. Over them were appointed the Levites Jahath and Obadiah, of the sons of Merari, along with Zechariah and Meshullam, of the sons of the Kohathites, to have oversight. Other Levites, all skillful with instruments of music, 13 were over the burden bearers and directed all who did work in every kind of service; and some of the Levites were scribes, and officials, and gatekeepers.

14 While they were bringing out the money that had been brought into the house of the Lord, the priest Hilkiah found the book of the law of the Lord given through Moses. 15 Hilkiah said to the secretary Shaphan, "I have found the book of the law in the house of the Lord"; and Hilkiah gave the book to Shaphan. 16 Shaphan brought the book to the king, and further reported to the king, "All that was committed to your servants they are doing. 17 They have emptied out the money that was found in the house of the Lord and have delivered it into the hand of the overseers and the workers." 18 The secretary Shaphan informed the king, "The priest Hilkiah has given me a book." Shaphan then read it aloud to the king.

19 When the king heard the words of the law he tore his clothes. 20 Then the king commanded Hilkiah, Ahikam son of Shaphan, Abdon son of Micah, the secretary Shaphan, and the king's servant Asaiah: 21 "Go, inquire of the Lord for me and for those who are left in Israel and in Judah, con-

34.1 2 Kings 22.1, 2
34.3 2 Chr 15.2; 1 Kings 13.2; 2 Chr 33.17, 22
34.4 Lev 26.30; 2 Kings 23.4; Ex 32.20
34.5 1 Kings 13.2; 2 Kings 23.20
34.6 2 Kings 23.15, 19
34.7 2 Chr 31.1
34.8 2 Kings 22.3-20
34.9 2 Chr 35.8

34.11 2 Chr 33.4-7
34.12 1 Chr 25.1
34.13 1 Chr 23.4, 5
34.14 v. 9
34.16 v. 8
34.19 Josh 7.6
34.21 2 Chr 29.8

p Heb Asherim q Meaning of Heb uncertain

cerning the words of the book that has been found; for the wrath of the LORD that is poured out on us is great, because our ancestors did not keep the word of the LORD, to act in accordance with all that is written in this book."

The Prophet Huldah Consulted

22 So Hilkiah and those whom the king had sent went to the prophet Huldah, the wife of Shallum son of Tokhath son of Hasrah, keeper of the wardrobe (who lived in Jerusalem in the Second Quarter) and spoke to her to that effect. 23 She declared to them, "Thus says the LORD, the God of Israel: Tell the man who sent you to me, 24 Thus says the LORD: I will indeed bring disaster upon this place and upon its inhabitants, all the curses that are written in the book that was read before the king of Judah. 25 Because they have forsaken me and have made offerings to other gods, so that they have provoked me to anger with all the works of their hands, my wrath will be poured out on this place and will not be quenched. 26 But as to the king of Judah, who sent you to inquire of the LORD, thus shall you say to him: Thus says the LORD, the God of Israel: Regarding the words that you have heard, 27 because your heart was penitent and you humbled yourself before God when you heard his words against this place and its inhabitants, and you have humbled yourself before me, and have torn your clothes and wept before me, I also have heard you, says the LORD. 28 I will gather you to your ancestors and you shall be gathered to your grave in peace; your eyes shall not see all the disaster that I will bring on this place and its inhabitants." They took the message back to the king.

The Covenant Renewed

29 Then the king sent word and gathered together all the elders of Judah and Jerusalem. 30 The king went up to the house of the LORD, with all the people of Judah, the inhabitants of Jerusalem, the priests and the Levites, all the people both great and small; he read in their hearing all the words of the book of the covenant that had been found in the house of the LORD. 31 The king stood in his place and made a covenant before the LORD, to follow the LORD, keeping his commandments, his decrees, and his statutes, with all his heart and all his soul, to perform the words of the covenant that were written in this book. 32 Then he made all who were present in Jerusalem and in Benjamin pledge themselves to it. And the inhabitants of Jerusalem acted according to the covenant of God, the God of their ancestors. 33 Josiah took away all the abominations from all the territory that belonged to the people of Israel, and made all who were in Israel worship the LORD their God. All his days they did not turn away from following the LORD the God of their ancestors.

Celebration of the Passover

35 Josiah kept a passover to the LORD in Jerusalem; they slaughtered the passover lamb on the fourteenth day of the first month. 2 He appointed the priests to their offices and encouraged them in the service of the house of the LORD. 3 He said to the Levites who taught all Israel and who were holy to the LORD, "Put the holy ark in the house that Solomon son of David, king of Israel, built; you need no longer carry it on your shoulders. Now serve the LORD your God and his people Israel. 4 Make preparations by your ancestral houses by your divisions, following the written directions of King David of Israel and the written directions of his son Solomon. 5 Take position in the holy place according to the groupings of the ancestral houses of your kindred the people, and let there be Levites for each division of an ancestral house.r 6 Slaughter the passover lamb, sanctify yourselves, and on

Cross references (center column)

34.22
2 Kings 22.14
34.24
2 Chr 36.14-20;
Deut 28.15-68
34.25
2 Chr 33.3
34.27
2 Chr 12.7;
32.26
34.29
2 Kings 23.1-3
34.30
Neh 8.1-3

34.31
2 Kings 11.14;
23.3;
2 Chr 23.3,
16; 29.10
34.33
vv. 3-7;
2 Chr 33.2-7
35.1
2 Kings 23.21,
22; Ex 12.6;
Num 9.3
35.2
2 Chr 23.18;
29.11
35.3
Deut 33.10;
2 Chr 5.7;
1 Chr 23.26
35.4
1 Chr 9.10-13;
2 Chr 8.14
35.5
Ps 134.1
35.6
v. 1;
2 Chr 29.5,
15;
Ezra 6.20

r Meaning of Heb uncertain

behalf of your kindred make preparations, acting according to the word of the Lord by Moses."

7 Then Josiah contributed to the people, as passover offerings for all that were present, lambs and kids from the flock to the number of thirty thousand, and three thousand bulls; these were from the king's possessions. 8 His officials contributed willingly to the people, to the priests, and to the Levites. Hilkiah, Zechariah, and Jehiel, the chief officers of the house of God, gave to the priests for the passover offerings two thousand six hundred lambs and kids and three hundred bulls. 9 Conaniah also, and his brothers Shemaiah and Nethanel, and Hashabiah and Jeiel and Jozabad, the chiefs of the Levites, gave to the Levites for the passover offerings five thousand lambs and kids and five hundred bulls.

10 When the service had been prepared for, the priests stood in their place, and the Levites in their divisions according to the king's command. 11 They slaughtered the passover lamb, and the priests dashed the blood that they received[s] from them, while the Levites did the skinning. 12 They set aside the burnt offerings so that they might distribute them according to the groupings of the ancestral houses of the people, to offer to the Lord, as it is written in the book of Moses. And they did the same with the bulls. 13 They roasted the passover lamb with fire according to the ordinance; and they boiled the holy offerings in pots, in caldrons, and in pans, and carried them quickly to all the people. 14 Afterward they made preparations for themselves and for the priests, because the priests the descendants of Aaron were occupied in offering the burnt offerings and the fat parts until night; so the Levites made preparations for themselves and for the priests, the descendants of Aaron. 15 The singers, the descendants of Asaph, were in their place according to the command of David, and Asaph, and He-

man, and the king's seer Jeduthun. The gatekeepers were at each gate; they did not need to interrupt their service, for their kindred the Levites made preparations for them.

16 So all the service of the Lord was prepared that day, to keep the passover and to offer burnt offerings on the altar of the Lord, according to the command of King Josiah. 17 The people of Israel who were present kept the passover at that time, and the festival of unleavened bread seven days. 18 No passover like it had been kept in Israel since the days of the prophet Samuel; none of the kings of Israel had kept such a passover as was kept by Josiah, by the priests and the Levites, by all Judah and Israel who were present, and by the inhabitants of Jerusalem. 19 In the eighteenth year of the reign of Josiah this passover was kept.

Defeat by Pharaoh Neco and Death of Josiah

20 After all this, when Josiah had set the temple in order, King Neco of Egypt went up to fight at Carchemish on the Euphrates, and Josiah went out against him. 21 But Neco[t] sent envoys to him, saying, "What have I to do with you, king of Judah? I am not coming against you today, but against the house with which I am at war; and God has commanded me to hurry. Cease opposing God, who is with me, so that he will not destroy you." 22 But Josiah would not turn away from him, but disguised himself in order to fight with him. He did not listen to the words of Neco from the mouth of God, but joined battle in the plain of Megiddo. 23 The archers shot King Josiah; and the king said to his servants, "Take me away, for I am badly wounded." 24 So his servants took him out of the chariot and carried him in his second chariot[u] and brought him to Jerusalem. There he died, and was buried in the tombs of his ancestors. All Judah

35.7	2 Chr 30.24
35.9	2 Chr 31.12
35.10	v. 5; Ezra 6.18
35.11	vv. 1,6; 2 Chr 29.22, 34
35.13	Ex 12.8,9; Lev 6.25; 1 Sam 2.13-15
35.15	1 Chr 25.1; 26.12-19
35.17	Ex 12.15; 2 Chr 30.21
35.18	2 Kings 23.21-23
35.20	2 Kings 23.29, 30; Isa 10.9; Jer 46.2
35.22	2 Chr 18.29; Judg 5.19
35.24	2 Kings 23.30; Zech 12.11

s Heb lacks *that they received* t Heb *he*
u Or *the chariot of his deputy*

and Jerusalem mourned for Josiah.
25 Jeremiah also uttered a lament for Josiah, and all the singing men and singing women have spoken of Josiah in their laments to this day. They made these a custom in Israel; they are recorded in the Laments. 26 Now the rest of the acts of Josiah and his faithful deeds in accordance with what is written in the law of the LORD, 27 and his acts, first and last, are written in the Book of the Kings of Israel and Judah.

Reign of Jehoahaz

36 The people of the land took Jehoahaz son of Josiah and made him king to succeed his father in Jerusalem. 2 Jehoahaz was twenty-three years old when he began to reign; he reigned three months in Jerusalem. 3 Then the king of Egypt deposed him in Jerusalem and laid on the land a tribute of one hundred talents of silver and one talent of gold. 4 The king of Egypt made his brother Eliakim king over Judah and Jerusalem, and changed his name to Jehoiakim; but Neco took his brother Jehoahaz and carried him to Egypt.

Reign and Captivity of Jehoiakim

5 Jehoiakim was twenty-five years old when he began to reign; he reigned eleven years in Jerusalem. He did what was evil in the sight of the LORD his God. 6 Against him King Nebuchadnezzar of Babylon came up, and bound him with fetters to take him to Babylon. 7 Nebuchadnezzar also carried some of the vessels of the house of the LORD to Babylon and put them in his palace in Babylon. 8 Now the rest of the acts of Jehoiakim, and the abominations that he did, and what was found against him, are written in the Book of the Kings of Israel and Judah; and his son Jehoiachin succeeded him.

Reign and Captivity of Jehoiachin

9 Jehoiachin was eight years old

35.25
Lam 4.20;
Jer 22.20
36.1
2 Kings 23.30-34;
Jer 22.11
36.5
2 Kings 23.36, 37
36.6
2 Kings 24.1;
2 Chr 33.11
36.7
2 Kings 24.13
36.8
2 Kings 24.5;
1 Chr 3.16
36.9
2 Kings 24.8-17
36.10
2 Sam 11.1;
Jer 37.1
36.11
2 Kings 24.18-20;
Jer 52.1
36.12
2 Chr 33.23;
Jer 21.3-7
36.13
Jer 52.3;
Ezek 17.15;
2 Kings 17.14;
2 Chr 30.8
36.15
Jer 25.3,4;
35.15; 44.4
36.16
2 Chr 30.10;
Jer 5.12,13;
Prov 1.25;
Ezra 5.12
36.17
2 Kings 25.1-7
36.18
2 Kings 25.13ff

when he began to reign; he reigned three months and ten days in Jerusalem. He did what was evil in the sight of the LORD. 10 In the spring of the year King Nebuchadnezzar sent and brought him to Babylon, along with the precious vessels of the house of the LORD, and made his brother Zedekiah king over Judah and Jerusalem.

Reign of Zedekiah

11 Zedekiah was twenty-one years old when he began to reign; he reigned eleven years in Jerusalem. 12 He did what was evil in the sight of the LORD his God. He did not humble himself before the prophet Jeremiah who spoke from the mouth of the LORD. 13 He also rebelled against King Nebuchadnezzar, who had made him swear by God; he stiffened his neck and hardened his heart against turning to the LORD, the God of Israel. 14 All the leading priests and the people also were exceedingly unfaithful, following all the abominations of the nations; and they polluted the house of the LORD that he had consecrated in Jerusalem.

The Fall of Jerusalem

15 The LORD, the God of their ancestors, sent persistently to them by his messengers, because he had compassion on his people and on his dwelling place; 16 but they kept mocking the messengers of God, despising his words, and scoffing at his prophets, until the wrath of the LORD against his people became so great that there was no remedy.

17 Therefore he brought up against them the king of the Chaldeans, who killed their youths with the sword in the house of their sanctuary, and had no compassion on young man or young woman, the aged or the feeble; he gave them all into his hand. 18 All the vessels of the house of God, large and small, and the treasures of the

house of the LORD, and the treasures of the king and of his officials, all these he brought to Babylon. ¹⁹They burned the house of God, broke down the wall of Jerusalem, burned all its palaces with fire, and destroyed all its precious vessels. ²⁰He took into exile in Babylon those who had escaped from the sword, and they became servants to him and to his sons until the establishment of the kingdom of Persia, ²¹to fulfill the word of the LORD by the mouth of Jeremiah, until the land had made up for its sabbaths. All the days that it lay desolate it kept sabbath, to fulfill seventy years.

36.19
2 Kings 25.9;
Jer 52.13
36.20
2 Kings 25.11;
Jer 27.7
36.21
Jer 29.10;
Lev 26.34;
25.4

36.22
Ezra 1.1;
Jer 25.12;
Isa 44.28
36.23
Ezra 1.2,3

Cyrus Proclaims Liberty for the Exiles

22 In the first year of King Cyrus of Persia, in fulfillment of the word of the LORD spoken by Jeremiah, the LORD stirred up the spirit of King Cyrus of Persia so that he sent a herald throughout all his kingdom and also declared in a written edict: ²³"Thus says King Cyrus of Persia: The LORD, the God of heaven, has given me all the kingdoms of the earth, and he has charged me to build him a house at Jerusalem, which is in Judah. Whoever is among you of all his people, may the LORD his God be with him! Let him go up."

Ezra

Title and Background

The books of Ezra and Nehemiah were one in the earliest Hebrew manuscripts. The separation into two books first began among the church fathers in the third century A.D. Although they were regarded as one book, the caption to Nehemiah 1.1 indicates they were two separate compositions.

Author and Date of Writing

Many scholars have assumed that the author/compiler of Ezra-Nehemiah was also the author of 1,2 Chronicles. This viewpoint is based on certain characteristics common to both. The verses at the end of Chronicles and at the beginning of Ezra are virtually identical, and both of these books exhibit a fondness for lists. But there are also striking differences, so the name of the author cannot be known for certain. The book of Ezra can be dated about 440 B.C.

Theme and Message

Ezra tells about the return of the Jews from exile in Babylon and the rebuilding of the temple. The people completed and dedicated the temple in 516 B.C., after a delay of eighteen years instigated by their enemies from the north. Ezra led a second group of Jews back to the promised land, where he taught the people God's law and reformed their religious life so that the other nations around them could see they were God's chosen nation.

Outline

 I. The First Exiles Return to the Land of Judah (1.1–2.70)
 II. The Temple Is Rebuilt (3.1–6.22)
 III. Ezra's Return and Ministry (7.1–10.44)

End of the Babylonian Captivity

1 In the first year of King Cyrus of Persia, in order that the word of the LORD by the mouth of Jeremiah might be accomplished, the LORD stirred up the spirit of King Cyrus of Persia so that he sent a herald throughout all his kingdom, and also in a written edict declared:

2 "Thus says King Cyrus of Persia: The LORD, the God of heaven, has given me all the kingdoms of the earth, and he has charged me to build him a house at Jerusalem in Judah. 3 Any of those among you who are of his people—may their God be with them!—are now permitted to go up to Jerusalem in Judah, and rebuild the house of the LORD, the God of Israel—he is the God who is in Jerusalem; 4 and let all survivors, in whatever place they reside, be assisted by the people of their place with silver and gold, with goods and with animals, besides freewill offerings for the house of God in Jerusalem."

5 The heads of the families of Judah and Benjamin, and the priests and the Levites—everyone whose spirit God had stirred—got ready to go up and rebuild the house of the LORD in Jerusalem. 6 All their neighbors aided them with silver vessels, with gold, with goods, with animals, and with valuable gifts, besides all that was freely offered. 7 King Cyrus himself brought out the vessels of the house of the LORD that Nebuchadnezzar had carried away from Jerusalem and placed in the house of

Margin references:
1.1ff 2 Chr 36.22, 23; Jer 25.12; 29.10; Ezra 5.13,14
1.2 Isa 44.28; 45.1,12,13
1.3 Dan 6.26
1.5 Phil 2.13
1.7 Ezra 5.14; 6.5; 2 Kings 24.13; 2 Chr 36.7

his gods. ⁸ King Cyrus of Persia had them released into the charge of Mithredath the treasurer, who counted them out to Sheshbazzar the prince of Judah. ⁹ And this was the inventory: gold basins, thirty; silver basins, one thousand; knives,ᵃ twenty-nine; ¹⁰ gold bowls, thirty; other silver bowls, four hundred ten; other vessels, one thousand; ¹¹ the total of the gold and silver vessels was five thousand four hundred. All these Sheshbazzar brought up, when the exiles were brought up from Babylonia to Jerusalem.

List of the Returned Exiles

2 Now these were the people of the province who came from those captive exiles whom King Nebuchadnezzar of Babylon had carried captive to Babylonia; they returned to Jerusalem and Judah, all to their own towns. ² They came with Zerubbabel, Jeshua, Nehemiah, Seraiah, Reelaiah, Mordecai, Bilshan, Mispar, Bigvai, Rehum, and Baanah.

The number of the Israelite people: ³ the descendants of Parosh, two thousand one hundred seventy-two. ⁴ Of Shephatiah, three hundred seventy-two. ⁵ Of Arah, seven hundred seventy-five. ⁶ Of Pahath-moab, namely the descendants of Jeshua and Joab, two thousand eight hundred twelve. ⁷ Of Elam, one thousand two hundred fifty-four. ⁸ Of Zattu, nine hundred forty-five. ⁹ Of Zaccai, seven hundred sixty. ¹⁰ Of Bani, six hundred forty-two. ¹¹ Of Bebai, six hundred twenty-three. ¹² Of Azgad, one thousand two hundred twenty-two. ¹³ Of Adonikam, six hundred sixty-six. ¹⁴ Of Bigvai, two thousand fifty-six. ¹⁵ Of Adin, four hundred fifty-four. ¹⁶ Of Ater, namely of Hezekiah, ninety-eight. ¹⁷ Of Bezai, three hundred twenty-three. ¹⁸ Of Jorah, one hundred twelve. ¹⁹ Of Hashum, two hundred twenty-three. ²⁰ Of Gibbar, ninety-five. ²¹ Of Bethlehem, one hundred

twenty-three. ²² The people of Netophah, fifty-six. ²³ Of Anathoth, one hundred twenty-eight. ²⁴ The descendants of Azmaveth, forty-two. ²⁵ Of Kiriatharim, Chephirah, and Beeroth, seven hundred forty-three. ²⁶ Of Ramah and Geba, six hundred twenty-one. ²⁷ The people of Michmas, one hundred twenty-two. ²⁸ Of Bethel and Ai, two hundred twenty-three. ²⁹ The descendants of Nebo, fifty-two. ³⁰ Of Magbish, one hundred fifty-six. ³¹ Of the other Elam, one thousand two hundred fifty-four. ³² Of Harim, three hundred twenty. ³³ Of Lod, Hadid, and Ono, seven hundred twenty-five. ³⁴ Of Jericho, three hundred forty-five. ³⁵ Of Senaah, three thousand six hundred thirty.

³⁶ The priests: the descendants of Jedaiah, of the house of Jeshua, nine hundred seventy-three. ³⁷ Of Immer, one thousand fifty-two. ³⁸ Of Pashhur, one thousand two hundred forty-seven. ³⁹ Of Harim, one thousand seventeen.

⁴⁰ The Levites: the descendants of Jeshua and Kadmiel, of the descendants of Hodaviah, seventy-four. ⁴¹ The singers: the descendants of Asaph, one hundred twenty-eight. ⁴² The descendants of the gatekeepers: of Shallum, of Ater, of Talmon, of Akkub, of Hatita, and of Shobai, in all one hundred thirty-nine.

⁴³ The temple servants: the descendants of Ziha, Hasupha, Tabbaoth, ⁴⁴ Keros, Siaha, Padon, ⁴⁵ Lebanah, Hagabah, Akkub, ⁴⁶ Hagab, Shamlai, Hanan, ⁴⁷ Giddel, Gahar, Reaiah, ⁴⁸ Rezin, Nekoda, Gazzam, ⁴⁹ Uzza, Paseah, Besai, ⁵⁰ Asnah, Meunim, Nephisim, ⁵¹ Bakbuk, Hakupha, Harhur, ⁵² Bazluth, Mehida, Harsha, ⁵³ Barkos, Sisera, Temah, ⁵⁴ Neziah, and Hatipha.

⁵⁵ The descendants of Solomon's servants: Sotai, Hassophereth, Peruda, ⁵⁶ Jaalah, Darkon, Giddel, ⁵⁷ Shephatiah, Hattil, Pochereth-hazzebaim, and Ami.

ᵃ Vg: Meaning of Heb uncertain

1.8
Ezra 5.14
2.1
Neh 7.6-73;
2 Kings 24.14-16; 25.11;
2 Chr 36.20
2.5
cf. Neh 7.10
2.6
cf. Neh 7.11
2.16
Neh 7.21
2.21
Neh 7.26

2.31
v. 7
2.36
1 Chr 24.7-18
2.38
1 Chr 9.12
2.39
1 Chr 24.8
2.43
1 Chr 9.2
2.48
Neh 7.50
2.55
Neh 7.57;
60; 11.3

RETURN FROM EXILE

Miles 0 100 200 300
Kms 0 100 200 300 400

PERSIAN EMPIRE

3. EZRA won the approval of Artaxerxes I (465-424 B.C.) to return with additional exiles; Nehemiah, to rebuild the walls of Jerusalem.

4. CLAY TABLETS from the Murashu archives at Nippur reveal the presence of Jews remaining a half century after Ezra.

• Ecbatana

• Susa

• Babylon

• Nippur

**Tel Melah
Tel Harsha
Kerub
Addon
Immer**

*Exact
location of
exiles' villages
unknown.*

Euphrates R.

Tigris R.

Euphrates R.

• Haran

• Tiphsah

• Tadmor

TRANS-EUPHRATES

1. RESTORATION of the exiles began under Cyrus (559-530 B.C.), who allowed them to return to Judah with the captured temple treasures.

• Byblos

• Damascus

• Rabbah of the Ammonites

• Tyre

• Jerusalem

2. THE TEMPLE was consecrated by official permission of Darius I (522-486 B.C.).

• Samaria

• Ashdod

• Dumah

58 All the temple servants and the descendants of Solomon's servants were three hundred ninety-two.

59 The following were those who came up from Tel-melah, Tel-harsha, Cherub, Addan, and Immer, though they could not prove their families or their descent, whether they belonged to Israel: 60 the descendants of Delaiah, Tobiah, and Nekoda, six hundred fifty-two. 61 Also, of the descendants of the priests: the descendants of Habaiah, Hakkoz, and Barzillai (who had married one of the daughters of Barzillai the Gileadite, and was called by their name). 62 These looked for their entries in the genealogical records, but they were not found there, and so they were excluded from the priesthood as unclean; 63 the governor told them that they were not to partake of the most holy food, until there should be a priest to consult Urim and Thummim.

64 The whole assembly together was forty-two thousand three hundred sixty, 65 besides their male and female servants, of whom there were seven thousand three hundred thirty-seven; and they had two hundred male and female singers. 66 They had seven hundred thirty-six horses, two hundred forty-five mules, 67 four hundred thirty-five camels, and six thousand seven hundred twenty donkeys.

68 As soon as they came to the house of the LORD in Jerusalem, some of the heads of families made freewill offerings for the house of God, to erect it on its site. 69 According to their resources they gave to the building fund sixty-one thousand darics of gold, five thousand minas of silver, and one hundred priestly robes.

70 The priests, the Levites, and some of the people lived in Jerusalem and its vicinity;b and the singers, the gatekeepers, and the temple servants lived in their towns, and all Israel in their towns.

Worship Restored at Jerusalem

3 When the seventh month came, and the Israelites were in the towns, the people gathered together in Jerusalem. 2 Then Jeshua son of Jozadak, with his fellow priests, and Zerubbabel son of Shealtiel with his kin set out to build the altar of the God of Israel, to offer burnt offerings on it, as prescribed in the law of Moses the man of God. 3 They set up the altar on its foundation, because they were in dread of the neighboring peoples, and they offered burnt offerings upon it to the LORD, morning and evening. 4 And they kept the festival of booths,c as prescribed, and offered the daily burnt offerings by number according to the ordinance, as required for each day, 5 and after that the regular burnt offerings, the offerings at the new moon and at all the sacred festivals of the LORD, and the offerings of everyone who made a freewill offering to the LORD. 6 From the first day of the seventh month they began to offer burnt offerings to the LORD. But the foundation of the temple of the LORD was not yet laid. 7 So they gave money to the masons and the carpenters, and food, drink, and oil to the Sidonians and the Tyrians to bring cedar trees from Lebanon to the sea, to Joppa, according to the grant that they had from King Cyrus of Persia.

Foundation Laid for the Temple

8 In the second year after their arrival at the house of God at Jerusalem, in the second month, Zerubbabel son of Shealtiel and Jeshua son of Jozadak made a beginning, together with the rest of their people, the priests and the Levites and all who had come to Jerusalem from the captivity. They appointed the Levites, from twenty years old and upward, to have the oversight of the work on the house of the LORD. 9 And Jeshua with his sons and his kin, and Kadmiel and

2.58
v. 55
2.61
2 Sam 17.27
2.62
Num 3.10;
16.39,40
2.63
Lev 2.3,10;
Ex 28.30
2.64
Neh 7.66ff
2.69
Ezra 8.25-34

3.1
Neh 7.73;
8.1
3.2
Neh 12.1,8;
Ezra 2.2;
1 Chr 3.17;
Deut 12.5,6
3.3
Ezra 4.4;
Num 28.2-4
3.4
Neh 8.14;
Ex 23.16;
Num 29.12
3.5
Num 28.3,
11,19,26;
29.39
3.7
2 Chr 2.10,
16;
Ezra 1.2;
6.3
3.8
v. 2;
Ezra 4.3;
1 Chr 23.24,
27
3.9
Ezra 2.40

b 1 Esdras 5.46: Heb lacks lived in Jerusalem and its vicinity c Or tabernacles; Heb succoth

his sons, Binnui and Hodaviah[d] along with the sons of Henadad, the Levites, their sons and kin, together took charge of the workers in the house of God.

10 When the builders laid the foundation of the temple of the LORD, the priests in their vestments were stationed to praise the LORD with trumpets, and the Levites, the sons of Asaph, with cymbals, according to the directions of King David of Israel; [11]and they sang responsively, praising and giving thanks to the LORD,

"For he is good,
for his steadfast love endures forever toward Israel."

And all the people responded with a great shout when they praised the LORD, because the foundation of the house of the LORD was laid. [12]But many of the priests and Levites and heads of families, old people who had seen the first house on its foundations, wept with a loud voice when they saw this house, though many shouted aloud for joy, [13]so that the people could not distinguish the sound of the joyful shout from the sound of the people's weeping, for the people shouted so loudly that the sound was heard far away.

Resistance to Rebuilding the Temple

4 When the adversaries of Judah and Benjamin heard that the returned exiles were building a temple to the LORD, the God of Israel, [2]they approached Zerubbabel and the heads of families and said to them, "Let us build with you, for we worship your God as you do, and we have been sacrificing to him ever since the days of King Esar-haddon of Assyria who brought us here." [3]But Zerubbabel, Jeshua, and the rest of the heads of families in Israel said to them, "You shall have no part with us in building a house to our God; but we alone will build to the LORD, the God of Israel, as King Cyrus of Persia has commanded us."

4 Then the people of the land

3.10
1 Chr 16.5, 6,42; 6.31; 25.1
3.11
Ex 15.21; 2 Chr 7.3; Neh 12.24; 1 Chr 16.34, 41
4.1
vv. 7-10
4.2
2 Kings 17.24, 32,33; 19.37
4.3
Neh 2.20; Ezra 1.1-3
4.4
Ezra 3.3

4.6ff
Esther 1.1; Dan 9.1
4.7
2 Kings 18.26;
Dan 2.4
4.10
v. 1
4.12
Ezra 5.3,9
4.13
v. 20;
Ezra 7.24

discouraged the people of Judah, and made them afraid to build, [5]and they bribed officials to frustrate their plan throughout the reign of King Cyrus of Persia and until the reign of King Darius of Persia.

Rebuilding of Jerusalem Opposed

6 In the reign of Ahasuerus, in his accession year, they wrote an accusation against the inhabitants of Judah and Jerusalem.

7 And in the days of Artaxerxes, Bishlam and Mithredath and Tabeel and the rest of their associates wrote to King Artaxerxes of Persia; the letter was written in Aramaic and translated.[e] [8]Rehum the royal deputy and Shimshai the scribe wrote a letter against Jerusalem to King Artaxerxes as follows [9](then Rehum the royal deputy, Shimshai the scribe, and the rest of their associates, the judges, the envoys, the officials, the Persians, the people of Erech, the Babylonians, the people of Susa, that is, the Elamites, [10]and the rest of the nations whom the great and noble Osnappar deported and settled in the cities of Samaria and in the rest of the province Beyond the River wrote— and now [11]this is a copy of the letter that they sent):

"To King Artaxerxes: Your servants, the people of the province Beyond the River, send greeting. And now [12]may it be known to the king that the Jews who came up from you to us have gone to Jerusalem. They are rebuilding that rebellious and wicked city; they are finishing the walls and repairing the foundations. [13]Now may it be known to the king that, if this city is rebuilt and the walls finished, they will not pay tribute, custom, or toll, and the royal revenue will be reduced. [14]Now because we share the salt of the palace and it is

[d] Compare 2.40; Neh 7.43; 1 Esdras 5.58: Heb *sons of Judah* [e] Heb adds *in Aramaic,* indicating that 4.8-6.18 is in Aramaic. Another interpretation is *The letter was written in the Aramaic script and set forth in the Aramaic language*

not fitting for us to witness the king's dishonor, therefore we send and inform the king, ¹⁵so that a search may be made in the annals of your ancestors. You will discover in the annals that this is a rebellious city, hurtful to kings and provinces, and that sedition was stirred up in it from long ago. On that account this city was laid waste. ¹⁶We make known to the king that, if this city is rebuilt and its walls finished, you will then have no possession in the province Beyond the River."

17 The king sent an answer: "To Rehum the royal deputy and Shimshai the scribe and the rest of their associates who live in Samaria and in the rest of the province Beyond the River, greeting. And now ¹⁸the letter that you sent to us has been read in translation before me. ¹⁹So I made a decree, and someone searched and discovered that this city has risen against kings from long ago, and that rebellion and sedition have been made in it. ²⁰Jerusalem has had mighty kings who ruled over the whole province Beyond the River, to whom tribute, custom, and toll were paid. ²¹Therefore issue an order that these people be made to cease, and that this city not be rebuilt, until I make a decree. ²²Moreover, take care not to be slack in this matter; why should damage grow to the hurt of the king?"

23 Then when the copy of King Artaxerxes' letter was read before Rehum and the scribe Shimshai and their associates, they hurried to the Jews in Jerusalem and by force and power made them cease. ²⁴At that time the work on the house of God in Jerusalem stopped and was discontinued until the second year of the reign of King Darius of Persia.

Restoration of the Temple Resumed

5 Now the prophets, Haggai[f] and Zechariah son of Iddo, prophesied to the Jews who were in Judah and Jerusalem, in the name

of the God of Israel who was over them. ²Then Zerubbabel son of Shealtiel and Jeshua son of Jozadak set out to rebuild the house of God in Jerusalem; and with them were the prophets of God, helping them.

3 At the same time Tattenai the governor of the province Beyond the River and Shethar-bozenai and their associates came to them and spoke to them thus, "Who gave you a decree to build this house and to finish this structure?" ⁴They[g] also asked them this, "What are the names of the men who are building this building?" ⁵But the eye of their God was upon the elders of the Jews, and they did not stop them until a report reached Darius and then answer was returned by letter in reply to it.

6 The copy of the letter that Tattenai the governor of the province Beyond the River and Shetharbozenai and his associates the envoys who were in the province Beyond the River sent to King Darius; ⁷they sent him a report, in which was written as follows: "To Darius the king, all peace! ⁸May it be known to the king that we went to the province of Judah, to the house of the great God. It is being built of hewn stone, and timber is laid in the walls; this work is being done diligently and prospers in their hands. ⁹Then we spoke to those elders and asked them, 'Who gave you a decree to build this house and to finish this structure?' ¹⁰We also asked them their names, for your information, so that we might write down the names of the men at their head. ¹¹This was their reply to us: 'We are the servants of the God of heaven and earth, and we are rebuilding the house that was built many years ago, which a great king of Israel built and finished. ¹²But because our ancestors had angered the God of heaven, he gave them into the hand of King Nebuchadnezzar of Babylon, the Chal-

4.18
Neh 8.8
4.20
1 Kings 4.21;
Ps 72.8
5.1
Hag 1.1;
Zech 1.1

5.2
Ezra 3.2
5.3
Ezra 6.6;
v. 9;
Ezra 1.3
5.4
v. 10
5.5
Ezra 7.6,28;
Ps 33.18
5.6
Ezra 4.9
5.9
vv. 3,4
5.11
1 Kings 6.1
5.12
2 Chr 36.16,
17;
2 Kings 24.2;
25.8,9,11

f Aram adds *the prophet* g Gk Syr: Aram *We*

dean, who destroyed this house and carried away the people to Babylonia. ¹³However, King Cyrus of Babylon, in the first year of his reign, made a decree that this house of God should be rebuilt. ¹⁴Moreover, the gold and silver vessels of the house of God, which Nebuchadnezzar had taken out of the temple in Jerusalem and had brought into the temple of Babylon, these King Cyrus took out of the temple of Babylon, and they were delivered to a man named Sheshbazzar, whom he had made governor. ¹⁵He said to him, "Take these vessels; go and put them in the temple in Jerusalem, and let the house of God be rebuilt on its site." ¹⁶Then this Sheshbazzar came and laid the foundations of the house of God in Jerusalem; and from that time until now it has been under construction, and it is not yet finished.' ¹⁷And now, if it seems good to the king, have a search made in the royal archives there in Babylon, to see whether a decree was issued by King Cyrus for the rebuilding of this house of God in Jerusalem. Let the king send us his pleasure in this matter."

The Decree of Darius

6 Then King Darius made a decree, and they searched the archives where the documents were stored in Babylon. ²But it was in Ecbatana, the capital in the province of Media, that a scroll was found on which this was written: "A record. ³In the first year of his reign, King Cyrus issued a decree: Concerning the house of God at Jerusalem, let the house be rebuilt, the place where sacrifices are offered and burnt offerings are brought;ʰ its height shall be sixty cubits and its width sixty cubits, ⁴with three courses of hewn stones and one course of timber; let the cost be paid from the royal treasury. ⁵Moreover, let the gold and silver vessels of the house of God, which Nebuchadnezzar took out of the temple in Jerusalem and brought to Babylon, be restored

and brought back to the temple in Jerusalem, each to its place; you shall put them in the house of God."

6 "Now you, Tattenai, governor of the province Beyond the River, Shethar-bozenai, and you, their associates, the envoys in the province Beyond the River, keep away; ⁷let the work on this house of God alone; let the governor of the Jews and the elders of the Jews rebuild this house of God on its site. ⁸Moreover I make a decree regarding what you shall do for these elders of the Jews for the rebuilding of this house of God: the cost is to be paid to these people, in full and without delay, from the royal revenue, the tribute of the province Beyond the River. ⁹Whatever is needed—young bulls, rams, or sheep for burnt offerings to the God of heaven, wheat, salt, wine, or oil, as the priests in Jerusalem require—let that be given to them day by day without fail, ¹⁰so that they may offer pleasing sacrifices to the God of heaven, and pray for the life of the king and his children. ¹¹Furthermore I decree that if anyone alters this edict, a beam shall be pulled out of the house of the perpetrator, who then shall be impaled on it. The house shall be made a dunghill. ¹²May the God who has established his name there overthrow any king or people that shall put forth a hand to alter this, or to destroy this house of God in Jerusalem. I, Darius, make a decree; let it be done with all diligence."

Completion and Dedication of the Temple

13 Then, according to the word sent by King Darius, Tattenai, the governor of the province Beyond the River, Shethar-bozenai, and their associates did with all diligence what King Darius had ordered. ¹⁴So the elders of the Jews built and prospered, through the prophesying of the prophet Haggai and Zechariah son of Iddo. They

ʰ Meaning of Aram uncertain

5.13
Ezra 1.1
5.14
Ezra 1.7;
6.5;
Dan 5.2;
v. 16;
Ezra 1.8
5.16
Ezra 3.8,10;
6.15
5.17
Ezra 6.1,2
6.1
Ezra 5.17
6.3
Ezra 1.1
6.4
1 Kings 6.36
6.5
Ezra 1.7,8;
5.14

6.6
v. 13;
Ezra 5.3
6.10
Ezra 7.23
6.11
Ezra 7.26;
3.29
6.12
Deut 12.5;
11
6.13
v. 6
6.14
Ezra 5.1,2;
1.1; v. 12;
Ezra 7.1

finished their building by command of the God of Israel and by decree of Cyrus, Darius, and King Artaxerxes of Persia; [15] and this house was finished on the third day of the month of Adar, in the sixth year of the reign of King Darius.

16 The people of Israel, the priests and the Levites, and the rest of the returned exiles, celebrated the dedication of this house of God with joy. [17] They offered at the dedication of this house of God one hundred bulls, two hundred rams, four hundred lambs, and as a sin offering for all Israel, twelve male goats, according to the number of the tribes of Israel. [18] Then they set the priests in their divisions and the Levites in their courses for the service of God at Jerusalem, as it is written in the book of Moses.

The Passover Celebrated

19 On the fourteenth day of the first month the returned exiles kept the passover. [20] For both the priests and the Levites had purified themselves; all of them were clean. So they killed the passover lamb for all the returned exiles, for their fellow priests, and for themselves. [21] It was eaten by the people of Israel who had returned from exile, and also by all who had joined them and separated themselves from the pollutions of the nations of the land to worship the LORD, the God of Israel. [22] With joy they celebrated the festival of unleavened bread seven days; for the LORD had made them joyful, and had turned the heart of the king of Assyria to them, so that he aided them in the work on the house of God, the God of Israel.

The Coming and Work of Ezra

7 After this, in the reign of King Artaxerxes of Persia, Ezra son of Seraiah, son of Azariah, son of Hilkiah, [2] son of Shallum, son of Zadok, son of Ahitub, [3] son of Amariah, son of Azariah, son of Meraioth, [4] son of Zerahiah, son of Uzzi, son of Bukki, [5] son of Abishua, son of Phinehas, son of Eleazar, son of the chief priest Aaron— [6] this Ezra went up from Babylonia. He was a scribe skilled in the law of Moses that the LORD the God of Israel had given; and the king granted him all that he asked, for the hand of the LORD his God was upon him.

7 Some of the people of Israel, and some of the priests and Levites, the singers and gatekeepers, and the temple servants also went up to Jerusalem, in the seventh year of King Artaxerxes. [8] They came to Jerusalem in the fifth month, which was in the seventh year of the king. [9] On the first day of the first month the journey up from Babylon was begun, and on the first day of the fifth month he came to Jerusalem, for the gracious hand of his God was upon him. [10] For Ezra had set his heart to study the law of the LORD, and to do it, and to teach the statutes and ordinances in Israel.

The Letter of Artaxerxes to Ezra

11 This is a copy of the letter that King Artaxerxes gave to the priest Ezra, the scribe, a scholar of the text of the commandments of the LORD and his statutes for Israel: [12] "Artaxerxes, king of kings, to the priest Ezra, the scribe of the law of the God of heaven: Peace.[i] And now [13] I decree that any of the people of Israel or their priests or Levites in my kingdom who freely offers to go to Jerusalem may go with you. [14] For you are sent by the king and his seven counselors to make inquiries about Judah and Jerusalem according to the law of your God, which is in your hand, [15] and also to convey the silver and gold that the king and his counselors have freely offered to the God of Israel, whose dwelling is in Jerusalem, [16] with all the silver and gold that you shall find in the whole province of Babylonia, and with the freewill offerings of the people and the priests, given willingly for the house of their God in Jerusalem. [17] With this money, then, you shall with all diligence buy bulls, rams,

6.16 1 Kings 8.63; 2 Chr 7.5
6.17 Ezra 8.35
6.18 2 Chr 35.5; 1 Chr 23.6; Num 3.6; 8.9
6.19 Ezra 1.11; Ex 12.6
6.20 2 Chr 29.34; 30.15; 35.11
6.21 Neh 9.2; 10.28; Ezra 9.11
6.22 Ex 12.15; Ezra 7.27; 1.1; 6.2
7.1 1 Chr 6.4-14; vv. 12,21; Neh 2.1
7.6 vv. 9,11,12, 21,28
7.7 Ezra 8.1-20
7.9 v. 6
7.10 Ps 119.45; v. 25; Neh 8.1-8
7.12 Ezek 26.7; Dan 2.37
7.14 Esther 1.14
7.15 2 Chr 6.2; Ezra 6.12
7.16 Ezra 8.25; 1 Chr 29.6, 9; Ezra 1.4, 6
7.17 Num 15.4-13; Deut 12.5-11

[i] Syr Vg 1 Esdras 8.9: Aram *Perfect*

and lambs, and their grain offerings and their drink offerings, and you shall offer them on the altar of the house of your God in Jerusalem. [18]Whatever seems good to you and your colleagues to do with the rest of the silver and gold, you may do, according to the will of your God. [19]The vessels that have been given you for the service of the house of your God, you shall deliver before the God of Jerusalem. [20]And whatever else is required for the house of your God, which you are responsible for providing, you may provide out of the king's treasury.

[21] "I, King Artaxerxes, decree to all the treasurers in the province Beyond the River: Whatever the priest Ezra, the scribe of the law of the God of heaven, requires of you, let it be done with all diligence, [22]up to one hundred talents of silver, one hundred cors of wheat, one hundred baths[j] of wine, one hundred baths[j] of oil, and unlimited salt. [23]Whatever is commanded by the God of heaven, let it be done with zeal for the house of the God of heaven, or wrath will come upon the realm of the king and his heirs. [24]We also notify you that it shall not be lawful to impose tribute, custom, or toll on any of the priests, the Levites, the singers, the doorkeepers, the temple servants, or other servants of this house of God.

[25] "And you, Ezra, according to the God-given wisdom you possess, appoint magistrates and judges who may judge all the people in the province Beyond the River who know the laws of your God; and you shall teach those who do not know them. [26]All who will not obey the law of your God and the law of the king, let judgment be strictly executed on them, whether for death or for banishment or for confiscation of their goods or for imprisonment."

[27] Blessed be the LORD, the God of our ancestors, who put such a thing as this into the heart of the king to glorify the house of the LORD in Jerusalem, [28]and who extended to me steadfast love before the king and his counselors, and before all the king's mighty officers. I took courage, for the hand of the LORD my God was upon me, and I gathered leaders from Israel to go up with me.

Heads of Families Who Returned with Ezra

8 These are their family heads, and this is the genealogy of those who went up with me from Babylonia, in the reign of King Artaxerxes: [2]Of the descendants of Phinehas, Gershom. Of Ithamar, Daniel. Of David, Hattush, [3]of the descendants of Shecaniah. Of Parosh, Zechariah, with whom were registered one hundred fifty males. [4]Of the descendants of Pahath-moab, Eliehoenai son of Zerahiah, and with him two hundred males. [5]Of the descendants of Zattu,[k] Shecaniah son of Jahaziel, and with him three hundred males. [6]Of the descendants of Adin, Ebed son of Jonathan, and with him fifty males. [7]Of the descendants of Elam, Jeshaiah son of Athaliah, and with him seventy males. [8]Of the descendants of Shephatiah, Zebadiah son of Michael, and with him eighty males. [9]Of the descendants of Joab, Obadiah son of Jehiel, and with him two hundred eighteen males. [10]Of the descendants of Bani,[l] Shelomith son of Josiphiah, and with him one hundred sixty males. [11]Of the descendants of Bebai, Zechariah son of Bebai, and with him twenty-eight males. [12]Of the descendants of Azgad, Johanan son of Hakkatan, and with him one hundred ten males. [13]Of the descendants of Adonikam, those who came later, their names being Eliphelet, Jeuel, and Shemaiah, and with them sixty males. [14]Of the descendants of Bigvai, Uthai and Zaccur, and with them seventy males.

7.20
Ezra 6.4
7.21
v. 6
7.23
Ezra 6.10
7.25
Ex 18.21;
Deut 16.18;
v. 10
7.27
1 Chr 29.10;
Ezra 6.22

7.28
Ezra 9.9;
vv. 6,9
8.2
1 Chr 3.22
8.3
Ezra 2.3

j A Heb measure of volume k Gk 1 Esdras
8.32: Heb lacks *of Zattu* l Gk 1 Esdras
8.36: Heb lacks *Bani*

Servants for the Temple

15 I gathered them by the river that runs to Ahava, and there we camped three days. As I reviewed the people and the priests, I found there none of the descendants of Levi. 16 Then I sent for Eliezer, Ariel, Shemaiah, Elnathan, Jarib, Elnathan, Nathan, Zechariah, and Meshullam, who were leaders, and for Joiarib and Elnathan, who were wise, 17 and sent them to Iddo, the leader at the place called Casiphia, telling them what to say to Iddo and his colleagues the temple servants at Casiphia, namely, to send us ministers for the house of our God. 18 Since the gracious hand of our God was upon us, they brought us a man of discretion, of the descendants of Mahli son of Levi son of Israel, namely Sherebiah, with his sons and kin, eighteen; 19 also Hashabiah and with him Jeshaiah of the descendants of Merari, with his kin and their sons, twenty; 20 besides two hundred twenty of the temple servants, whom David and his officials had set apart to attend the Levites. These were all mentioned by name.

Fasting and Prayer for Protection

21 Then I proclaimed a fast there, at the river Ahava, that we might deny ourselves[m] before our God, to seek from him a safe journey for ourselves, our children, and all our possessions. 22 For I was ashamed to ask the king for a band of soldiers and cavalry to protect us against the enemy on our way, since we had told the king that the hand of our God is gracious to all who seek him, but his power and his wrath are against all who forsake him. 23 So we fasted and petitioned our God for this, and he listened to our entreaty.

Gifts for the Temple

24 Then I set apart twelve of the leading priests: Sherebiah, Hashabiah, and ten of their kin with them. 25 And I weighed out to them the silver and the gold and the ves-

sels, the offering for the house of our God that the king, his counselors, his lords, and all Israel there present had offered; 26 I weighed out into their hand six hundred fifty talents of silver, and one hundred silver vessels worth . . . talents,[n] and one hundred talents of gold, 27 twenty gold bowls worth a thousand darics, and two vessels of fine polished bronze as precious as gold. 28 And I said to them, "You are holy to the LORD, and the vessels are holy; and the silver and the gold are a freewill offering to the LORD, the God of your ancestors. 29 Guard them and keep them until you weigh them before the chief priests and the Levites and the heads of families in Israel at Jerusalem, within the chambers of the house of the LORD." 30 So the priests and the Levites took over the silver, the gold, and the vessels as they were weighed out, to bring them to Jerusalem, to the house of our God.

The Return to Jerusalem

31 Then we left the river Ahava on the twelfth day of the first month, to go to Jerusalem; the hand of our God was upon us, and he delivered us from the hand of the enemy and from ambushes along the way. 32 We came to Jerusalem and remained there three days. 33 On the fourth day, within the house of our God, the silver, the gold, and the vessels were weighed into the hands of the priest Meremoth son of Uriah, and with him was Eleazar son of Phinehas, and with them were the Levites, Jozabad son of Jeshua and Noadiah son of Binnui. 34 The total was counted and weighed, and the weight of everything was recorded.

35 At that time those who had come from captivity, the returned exiles, offered burnt offerings to the God of Israel, twelve bulls for all Israel, ninety-six rams, seventy-seven lambs, and as a sin offering twelve male goats; all this was a burnt offering to the LORD. 36 They

Cross-references (center column):

8.15
vv. 21,31;
Ezra 7.7
8.17
Ezra 2.43
8.18
Ezra 7.6
8.20
Ezra 2.43
8.21
2 Chr 20.3;
Isa 58.3,5
8.22
Ezra 7.6,9,
28;
Ps 33.18,19;
34.16;
2 Chr 15.2
8.23
2 Chr 33.13
8.25
Ezra 7.15,16

8.26
Ezra 1.9-11
8.28
Lev 21.6-8;
22.2,3
8.29
vv. 33,34
8.31
Ezra 7.6,9,
28
8.32
Neh 2.11
8.33
vv. 26,30
8.35
Ezra 2.1;
6.17
8.36
Ezra 7.21

m Or might fast n The number of talents is lacking

also delivered the king's commissions to the king's satraps and to the governors of the province Beyond the River; and they supported the people and the house of God.

Denunciation of Mixed Marriages

9 After these things had been done, the officials approached me and said, "The people of Israel, the priests, and the Levites have not separated themselves from the peoples of the lands with their abominations, from the Canaanites, the Hittites, the Perizzites, the Jebusites, the Ammonites, the Moabites, the Egyptians, and the Amorites. ²For they have taken some of their daughters as wives for themselves and for their sons. Thus the holy seed has mixed itself with the peoples of the lands, and in this faithlessness the officials and leaders have led the way." ³When I heard this, I tore my garment and my mantle, and pulled hair from my head and beard, and sat appalled. ⁴Then all who trembled at the words of the God of Israel, because of the faithlessness of the returned exiles, gathered around me while I sat appalled until the evening sacrifice.

Ezra's Prayer

5 At the evening sacrifice I got up from my fasting, with my garments and my mantle torn, and fell on my knees, spread out my hands to the LORD my God, ⁶and said,

"O my God, I am too ashamed and embarrassed to lift my face to you, my God, for our iniquities have risen higher than our heads, and our guilt has mounted up to the heavens. ⁷From the days of our ancestors to this day we have been deep in guilt, and for our iniquities we, our kings, and our priests have been handed over to the kings of the lands, to the sword, to captivity, to plundering, and to utter shame, as is now the case. ⁸But now for a brief moment favor has been shown by the LORD our God, who has left us a remnant, and giv-

en us a stake in his holy place, in order that heº may brighten our eyes and grant us a little sustenance in our slavery. ⁹For we are slaves; yet our God has not forsaken us in our slavery, but has extended to us his steadfast love before the kings of Persia, to give us new life to set up the house of our God, to repair its ruins, and to give us a wall in Judea and Jerusalem.

10 "And now, our God, what shall we say after this? For we have forsaken your commandments, ¹¹which you commanded by your servants the prophets, saying, 'The land that you are entering to possess is a land unclean with the pollutions of the peoples of the lands, with their abominations. They have filled it from end to end with their uncleanness. ¹²Therefore do not give your daughters to their sons, neither take their daughters for your sons, and never seek their peace or prosperity, so that you may be strong and eat the good of the land and leave it for an inheritance to your children forever.' ¹³After all that has come upon us for our evil deeds and for our great guilt, seeing that you, our God, have punished us less than our iniquities deserved and have given us such a remnant as this, ¹⁴shall we break your commandments again and intermarry with the peoples who practice these abominations? Would you not be angry with us until you destroy us without remnant or survivor? ¹⁵O LORD, God of Israel, you are just, but we have escaped as a remnant, as is now the case. Here we are before you in our guilt, though no one can face you because of this."

The People's Response

10 While Ezra prayed and made confession, weeping and throwing himself down before the house of God, a very great assembly of men, women, and children gathered to him out of Israel; the people also wept bitterly. ²Shecaniah son of Jehiel, of the de-

ºHeb our God

9.1
Ezra 6.21;
Neh 9.2;
Lev 18.24-30
9.2
Ezra 10.2,
18;
Ex 22.31;
Neh 13.3
9.3
Job 1.20;
Neh 1.4
9.4
Ezra 10.3;
Ex 29.39
9.5
Ex 9.29,33
9.6
Dan 9.7,8;
2 Chr 28.9;
Rev 18.5
9.7
Dan 9.5,6;
Deut 28.36,
64; Dan 9.7,
8
9.8
Isa 22.23;
Ps 13.3;
34.5

9.9
Neh 9.36;
Ezra 7.28
9.11
Ezra 6.21
9.12
Deut 7.3;
23.6;
Prov 13.22
9.13
vv. 6-8
9.14
v. 2;
Neh 13.23,
27;
Deut 9.8,14
9.15
Neh 9.33;
Dan 9.14;
v. 6;
Ps 130.3
10.1
Dan 9.4,20;
2 Chr 20.9
10.2
Ezra 9.2;
Neh 13.27

scendants of Elam, addressed Ezra, saying, "We have broken faith with our God and have married foreign women from the peoples of the land, but even now there is hope for Israel in spite of this. ³So now let us make a covenant with our God to send away all these wives and their children, according to the counsel of my lord and of those who tremble at the commandment of our God; and let it be done according to the law. ⁴Take action, for it is your duty, and we are with you; be strong, and do it." ⁵Then Ezra stood up and made the leading priests, the Levites, and all Israel swear that they would do as had been said. So they swore.

Foreign Wives and Their Children Rejected

6 Then Ezra withdrew from before the house of God, and went to the chamber of Jehohanan son of Eliashib, where he spent the night.ᵖ He did not eat bread or drink water, for he was mourning over the faithlessness of the exiles. ⁷They made a proclamation throughout Judah and Jerusalem to all the returned exiles that they should assemble at Jerusalem, ⁸and that if any did not come within three days, by order of the officials and the elders all their property should be forfeited, and they themselves banned from the congregation of the exiles.

9 Then all the people of Judah and Benjamin assembled at Jerusalem within the three days; it was the ninth month, on the twentieth day of the month. All the people sat in the open square before the house of God, trembling because of this matter and because of the heavy rain. ¹⁰Then Ezra the priest stood up and said to them, "You have trespassed and married foreign women, and so increased the guilt of Israel. ¹¹Now make confession to the LORD the God of your ancestors, and do his will; separate yourselves from the peoples of the land and from the foreign wives." ¹²Then all the assembly answered

with a loud voice, "It is so; we must do as you have said. ¹³But the people are many, and it is a time of heavy rain; we cannot stand in the open. Nor is this a task for one day or for two, for many of us have transgressed in this matter. ¹⁴Let our officials represent the whole assembly, and let all in our towns who have taken foreign wives come at appointed times, and with them the elders and judges of every town, until the fierce wrath of our God on this account is averted from us." ¹⁵Only Jonathan son of Asahel and Jahzeiah son of Tikvah opposed this, and Meshullam and Shabbethai the Levites supported them.

16 Then the returned exiles did so. Ezra the priest selected men,�q heads of families, according to their families, each of them designated by name. On the first day of the tenth month they sat down to examine the matter. ¹⁷By the first day of the first month they had come to the end of all the men who had married foreign women.

18 There were found of the descendants of the priests who had married foreign women, of the descendants of Jeshua son of Jozadak and his brothers: Maaseiah, Eliezer, Jarib, and Gedaliah. ¹⁹They pledged themselves to send away their wives, and their guilt offering was a ram of the flock for their guilt. ²⁰Of the descendants of Immer: Hanani and Zebadiah. ²¹Of the descendants of Harim: Maaseiah, Elijah, Shemaiah, Jehiel, and Uzziah. ²²Of the descendants of Pashhur: Elioenai, Maaseiah, Ishmael, Nethanel, Jozabad, and Elasah.

23 Of the Levites: Jozabad, Shimei, Kelaiah (that is, Kelita), Pethahiah, Judah, and Eliezer. ²⁴Of the singers: Eliashib. Of the gatekeepers: Shallum, Telem, and Uri.

25 And of Israel: of the descendants of Parosh: Ramiah, Izziah,

10.3 2 Chr 34.31; v. 44; Ezra 9.4; Deut 7.2,3
10.4 1 Chr 28.10
10.5 Neh 5.12
10.6 Deut 9.18
10.9 v. 3; Ezra 9.4
10.11 Lev 26.40; v. 3
10.14 2 Chr 29.10; 30.8
10.16 Ezra 4.1
10.19 2 Kings 10.15; 2 Chr 30.8; Lev 5.15; 6.6
10.23 Ex 6.25
10.25 v. 1

ᵖ 1 Esdras 9.2: Heb *where he went*
q 1 Esdras 9.16: Syr: Heb *And there were selected Ezra,*

Malchijah, Mijamin, Eleazar, Hashabiah,[r] and Benaiah. 26 Of the descendants of Elam: Mattaniah, Zechariah, Jehiel, Abdi, Jeremoth, and Elijah. 27 Of the descendants of Zattu: Elioenai, Eliashib, Mattaniah, Jeremoth, Zabad, and Aziza. 28 Of the descendants of Bebai: Jehohanan, Hananiah, Zabbai, and Athlai. 29 Of the descendants of Bani: Meshullam, Malluch, Adaiah, Jashub, Sheal, and Jeremoth. 30 Of the descendants of Pahathmoab: Adna, Chelal, Benaiah, Maaseiah, Mattaniah, Bezalel, Binnui, and Manasseh. 31 Of the descendants of Harim: Eliezer, Isshijah, Malchijah, Shemaiah, Shimeon, 32 Benjamin, Malluch, and Shemariah. 33 Of the descendants of Hashum: Mattenai, Mattattah, Zabad,

Eliphelet, Jeremai, Manasseh, and Shimei. 34 Of the descendants of Bani: Maadai, Amram, Uel, 35 Benaiah, Bedeiah, Cheluhi, 36 Vaniah, Meremoth, Eliashib, 37 Mattaniah, Mattenai, and Jaasu. 38 Of the descendants of Binnui:[s] Shimei, 39 Shelemiah, Nathan, Adaiah, 40 Machnadebai, Shashai, Sharai, 41 Azarel, Shelemiah, Shemariah, 42 Shallum, Amariah, and Joseph. 43 Of the descendants of Nebo: Jeiel, Mattithiah, Zabad, Zebina, Jaddai, Joel, and Benaiah. 44 All these had married foreign women, and they sent them away with their children.[t]

[r] 1 Esdras 9.26 Gk: Heb *Malchijah*
[s] Gk: Heb *Bani, Binnui* [t] 1 Esdras 9.36; Meaning of Heb uncertain

Nehemiah

Title and Background

See Introduction to Ezra.

Author and Date of Writing

See Introduction to Ezra. The book of Nehemiah can be dated about 430 B.C.

Theme and Message

Nehemiah continues the history of the Jews after their return from exile in Babylon where Ezra leaves off. Nehemiah went to Jerusalem in 445 B.C. and inspired the people to repair the city walls. With Ezra he provided religious leadership for the people too. A recurring theme of this book is the importance of prayer to Nehemiah.

Outline

I. Nehemiah Rebuilds the Walls (1.1–7.3)
II. Changes Under Ezra (7.4–10.39)
III. Nehemiah's Plans (11.1–13.31)

Nehemiah Prays for His People

1 The words of Nehemiah son of Hacaliah. In the month of Chislev, in the twentieth year, while I was in Susa the capital, ²one of my brothers, Hanani, came with certain men from Judah; and I asked them about the Jews that survived, those who had escaped the captivity, and about Jerusalem. ³They replied, "The survivors there in the province who escaped captivity are in great trouble and shame; the wall of Jerusalem is broken down, and its gates have been destroyed by fire."

4 When I heard these words I sat down and wept, and mourned for days, fasting and praying before the God of heaven. ⁵I said, "O LORD God of heaven, the great and awesome God who keeps covenant and steadfast love with those who love him and keep his commandments; ⁶let your ear be attentive and your eyes open to hear the prayer of your servant that I now pray before you day and night for your servants, the people of Israel, confessing the sins of the people of Israel, which we have sinned against you. Both I and my family have sinned. ⁷We have offended you deeply, failing to keep the commandments, the statutes, and the ordinances that you commanded your servant Moses. ⁸Remember the word that you commanded your servant Moses, 'If you are unfaithful, I will scatter you among the peoples; ⁹but if you return to me and keep my commandments and do them, though your outcasts are under the farthest skies, I will gather them from there and bring them to the place at which I have chosen to establish my name.' ¹⁰They are your servants and your people, whom you redeemed by your great power and your strong hand. ¹¹O Lord, let your ear be attentive to the prayer of your servant, and to the prayer of your servants who delight in revering your name. Give success to your servant today, and grant him mercy in the sight of this man!"

At the time, I was cupbearer to the king.

1.1 Neh 10.1; 2.1; Esther 1.2; Dan 8.2
1.3 Neh 7.6; 2.17; 2.3
1.4 Ezra 9.3; 10.1; Neh 2.4
1.5 Neh 4.14; 9.32; Ex 20.6
1.6 Dan 9.17; Ezra 10.1; Dan 9.20; 2 Chr 29.6
1.7 Dan 9.5; Deut 28.14, 15
1.8 Lev 26.33
1.9 Deut 30.2-4; 12.5
1.10 Deut 9.29; Dan 9.15
1.11 v. 6

Nehemiah Sent to Judah

2 In the month of Nisan, in the twentieth year of King Artaxerxes, when wine was served him, I carried the wine and gave it to the king. Now, I had never been sad in his presence before. ²So the king said to me, "Why is your face sad, since you are not sick? This can only be sadness of the heart." Then I was very much afraid. ³I said to the king, "May the king live forever! Why should my face not be sad, when the city, the place of my ancestors' graves, lies waste, and its gates have been destroyed by fire?" ⁴Then the king said to me, "What do you request?" So I prayed to the God of heaven. ⁵Then I said to the king, "If it pleases the king, and if your servant has found favor with you, I ask that you send me to Judah, to the city of my ancestors' graves, so that I may rebuild it." ⁶The king said to me (the queen also was sitting beside him), "How long will you be gone, and when will you return?" So it pleased the king to send me, and I set him a date. ⁷Then I said to the king, "If it pleases the king, let letters be given me to the governors of the province Beyond the River, that they may grant me passage until I arrive in Judah; ⁸and a letter to Asaph, the keeper of the king's forest, directing him to give me timber to make beams for the gates of the temple fortress, and for the wall of the city, and for the house that I shall occupy." And the king granted me what I asked, for the gracious hand of my God was upon me.

9 Then I came to the governors of the province Beyond the River, and gave them the king's letters. Now the king had sent officers of the army and cavalry with me. ¹⁰When Sanballat the Horonite and Tobiah the Ammonite official heard this, it displeased them greatly that someone had come to seek the welfare of the people of Israel.

Cross references

2.1
Neh 1.1;
Ezra 7.1;
Neh 1.11
2.2
Prov 15.13
2.3
Dan 2.4;
Neh 1.3
2.4
Neh 1.4
2.6
Neh 5.14;
13.6
2.7
Ezra 7.21;
8.36
2.8
Neh 7.2;
v. 18;
Ezra 7.6
2.9
v. 7;
Ezra 8.22
2.10
v. 19;
Neh 4.1

2.13
Neh 3.13;
vv. 3,17;
Neh 1.3
2.14
Neh 3.15;
2 Kings 20.20
2.17
Neh 1.3
2.18
v. 8;
2 Sam 2.7
2.19
Ps 44.13;
Neh 6.6
2.20
v. 4

Nehemiah's Inspection of the Walls

11 So I came to Jerusalem and was there for three days. ¹²Then I got up during the night, I and a few men with me; I told no one what my God had put into my heart to do for Jerusalem. The only animal I took was the animal I rode. ¹³I went out by night by the Valley Gate past the Dragon's Spring and to the Dung Gate, and I inspected the walls of Jerusalem that had been broken down and its gates that had been destroyed by fire. ¹⁴Then I went on to the Fountain Gate and to the King's Pool; but there was no place for the animal I was riding to continue. ¹⁵So I went up by way of the valley by night and inspected the wall. Then I turned back and entered by the Valley Gate, and so returned. ¹⁶The officials did not know where I had gone or what I was doing; I had not yet told the Jews, the priests, the nobles, the officials, and the rest that were to do the work.

Decision to Restore the Walls

17 Then I said to them, "You see the trouble we are in, how Jerusalem lies in ruins with its gates burned. Come, let us rebuild the wall of Jerusalem, so that we may no longer suffer disgrace." ¹⁸I told them that the hand of my God had been gracious upon me, and also the words that the king had spoken to me. Then they said, "Let us start building!" So they committed themselves to the common good. ¹⁹But when Sanballat the Horonite and Tobiah the Ammonite official, and Geshem the Arab heard of it, they mocked and ridiculed us, saying, "What is this that you are doing? Are you rebelling against the king?" ²⁰Then I replied to them, "The God of heaven is the one who will give us success, and we his servants are going to start building; but you have no share or claim or historic right in Jerusalem."

Organization of the Work

3 Then the high priest Eliashib set to work with his fellow priests and rebuilt the Sheep Gate. They consecrated it and set up its doors; they consecrated it as far as the Tower of the Hundred and as far as the Tower of Hananel. [2] And the men of Jericho built next to him. And next to them[a] Zaccur son of Imri built.

3 The sons of Hassenaah built the Fish Gate; they laid its beams and set up its doors, its bolts, and its bars. [4] Next to them Meremoth son of Uriah son of Hakkoz made repairs. Next to them Meshullam son of Berechiah son of Meshezabel made repairs. Next to them Zadok son of Baana made repairs. [5] Next to them the Tekoites made repairs; but their nobles would not put their shoulders to the work of their Lord.[b]

6 Joiada son of Paseah and Meshullam son of Besodeiah repaired the Old Gate; they laid its beams and set up its doors, its bolts, and its bars. [7] Next to them repairs were made by Melatiah the Gibeonite and Jadon the Meronothite — the men of Gibeon and of Mizpah — who were under the jurisdiction of[c] the governor of the province Beyond the River. [8] Next to them Uzziel son of Harhaiah, one of the goldsmiths, made repairs. Next to him Hananiah, one of the perfumers, made repairs; and they restored Jerusalem as far as the Broad Wall. [9] Next to them Rephaiah son of Hur, ruler of half the district of[d] Jerusalem, made repairs. [10] Next to them Jedaiah son of Harumaph made repairs opposite his house; and next to him Hattush son of Hashabneiah made repairs. [11] Malchijah son of Harim and Hasshub son of Pahath-moab repaired another section and the Tower of the Ovens. [12] Next to him Shallum son of Hallohesh, ruler of half the district of[d] Jerusalem, made repairs, he and his daughters.

13 Hanun and the inhabitants of Zanoah repaired the Valley Gate; they rebuilt it and set up its doors, its bolts, and its bars, and repaired a thousand cubits of the wall, as far as the Dung Gate.

14 Malchijah son of Rechab, ruler of the district of[e] Beth-haccherem, repaired the Dung Gate; he rebuilt it and set up its doors, its bolts, and its bars.

15 And Shallum son of Colhozeh, ruler of the district of[e] Mizpah, repaired the Fountain Gate; he rebuilt it and covered it and set up its doors, its bolts, and its bars; and he built the wall of the Pool of Shelah of the king's garden, as far as the stairs that go down from the City of David. [16] After him Nehemiah son of Azbuk, ruler of half the district of[d] Beth-zur, repaired from a point opposite the graves of David, as far as the artificial pool and the house of the warriors. [17] After him the Levites made repairs: Rehum son of Bani; next to him Hashabiah, ruler of half the district of[d] Keilah, made repairs for his district. [18] After him their kin made repairs: Binnui,[f] son of Henadad, ruler of half the district of[d] Keilah; [19] next to him Ezer son of Jeshua, ruler[g] of Mizpah, repaired another section opposite the ascent to the armory at the Angle. [20] After him Baruch son of Zabbai repaired another section from the Angle to the door of the house of the high priest Eliashib. [21] After him Meremoth son of Uriah son of Hakkoz repaired another section from the door of the house of Eliashib to the end of the house of Eliashib. [22] After him the priests, the men of the surrounding area, made repairs. [23] After them Benjamin and Hasshub made repairs opposite their house. After them Azariah son of Maaseiah son of Ananiah made repairs beside his own house. [24] After him Binnui son of Henadad repaired another section, from the house of Azariah to the Angle and

3.1
vv. 20,32;
Neh 6.1;
7.1; 12.39;
Jer 31.38
3.2
Neh 7.36
3.3
Neh 12.39
3.6
Neh 12.39
3.7
Neh 2.7
3.8
vv. 31,32;
Neh 12.38
3.9
vv. 12,17
3.11
Neh 12.38
3.12
v. 9
3.13
Neh 2.13

3.15
Neh 2.14;
2 Kings 25.4;
Neh 12.37
3.16
vv. 9,12,17;
2 Kings 20.20
3.19
v. 15;
2 Chr 26.9
3.20
v. 1;
Neh 13.7
3.22
Neh 12.28
3.24
v. 19

a Heb *him* b Or *lords* c Meaning of Heb uncertain d Or *supervisor of half the portion assigned to* e Or *supervisor of the portion assigned to* f Gk Syr Compare verse 24, 10.9: Heb *Bavvai* g Or *supervisor*

to the corner. 25Palal son of Uzai repaired opposite the Angle and the tower projecting from the upper house of the king at the court of the guard. After him Pedaiah son of Parosh 26and the temple servants livingh on Ophel made repairs up to a point opposite the Water Gate on the east and the projecting tower. 27After him the Tekoites repaired another section opposite the great projecting tower as far as the wall of Ophel.

28 Above the Horse Gate the priests made repairs, each one opposite his own house. 29After them Zadok son of Immer made repairs opposite his own house. After him Shemaiah son of Shecaniah, the keeper of the East Gate, made repairs. 30After him Hananiah son of Shelemiah and Hanun sixth son of Zalaph repaired another section. After him Meshullam son of Berechiah made repairs opposite his living quarters. 31After him Malchijah, one of the goldsmiths, made repairs as far as the house of the temple servants and of the merchants, opposite the Muster Gate,i and to the upper room of the corner. 32And between the upper room of the corner and the Sheep Gate the goldsmiths and the merchants made repairs.

Hostile Plots Thwarted

4j Now when Sanballat heard that we were building the wall, he was angry and greatly enraged, and he mocked the Jews. 2He said in the presence of his associates and of the army of Samaria, "What are these feeble Jews doing? Will they restore things? Will they sacrifice? Will they finish it in a day? Will they revive the stones out of the heaps of rubbish—and burned ones at that?" 3Tobiah the Ammonite was beside him, and he said, "That stone wall they are building—any fox going up on it would break it down!" 4Hear, O our God, for we are despised; turn their taunt back on their own heads, and give them over as plunder in a land of captivity. 5Do not

cover their guilt, and do not let their sin be blotted out from your sight; for they have hurled insults in the face of the builders.

6 So we rebuilt the wall, and all the wall was joined together to half its height; for the people had a mind to work.

7kBut when Sanballat and Tobiah and the Arabs and the Ammonites and the Ashdodites heard that the repairing of the walls of Jerusalem was going forward and the gaps were beginning to be closed, they were very angry, 8and all plotted together to come and fight against Jerusalem and to cause confusion in it. 9So we prayed to our God, and set a guard as a protection against them day and night.

10 But Judah said, "The strength of the burden bearers is failing, and there is too much rubbish so that we are unable to work on the wall." 11And our enemies said, "They will not know or see anything before we come upon them and kill them and stop the work." 12When the Jews who lived near them came, they said to us ten times, "From all the places where they livel they will come up against us."m 13So in the lowest parts of the space behind the wall, in open places, I stationed the people according to their families,n with their swords, their spears, and their bows. 14After I looked these things over, I stood up and said to the nobles and the officials and the rest of the people, "Do not be afraid of them. Remember the LORD, who is great and awesome, and fight for your kin, your sons, your daughters, your wives, and your homes."

15 When our enemies heard that their plot was known to us, and that God had frustrated it, we all returned to the wall, each to his work. 16From that day on, half of my servants worked on construc-

Cross-references (center column)

3.25 Jer 32.2
3.26 Neh 7.46; 11.21; 8.1
3.28 2 Kings 11.16; 2 Chr 23.15; Jer 31.40
3.31 vv. 8,32
3.32 v. 1
4.1 Neh 2.10,19
4.2 v. 10
4.3 Neh 2.10,19
4.4 Ps 123.3,4; 79.12
4.5 Ps 69.27,28; Jer 18.23

4.7 v. 1
4.9 Ps 50.15
4.13 vv. 17,18
4.14 Num 14.9; Deut 1.29; 2 Sam 10.12
4.15 2 Sam 17.14; Job 5.12

Footnotes

h Cn: Heb were living i Or Hammiphkad Gate jCh 3.33 in Heb kCh 4.1 in Heb lCn: Heb you return mCompare Gk Syr: Meaning of Heb uncertain nMeaning of Heb uncertain

tion, and half held the spears, shields, bows, and body-armor; and the leaders posted themselves behind the whole house of Judah, 17who were building the wall. The burden bearers carried their loads in such a way that each labored on the work with one hand and with the other held a weapon. 18And each of the builders had his sword strapped at his side while he built. The man who sounded the trumpet was beside me. 19And I said to the nobles, the officials, and the rest of the people, "The work is great and widely spread out, and we are separated far from one another on the wall. 20Rally to us wherever you hear the sound of the trumpet. Our God will fight for us."

21 So we labored at the work, and half of them held the spears from break of dawn until the stars came out. 22I also said to the people at that time, "Let every man and his servant pass the night inside Jerusalem, so that they may be a guard for us by night and may labor by day." 23So neither I nor my brothers nor my servants nor the men of the guard who followed me ever took off our clothes; each kept his weapon in his right hand.ᵒ

Nehemiah Deals with Oppression

5 Now there was a great outcry of the people and of their wives against their Jewish kin. 2For there were those who said, "With our sons and our daughters, we are many; we must get grain, so that we may eat and stay alive." 3There were also those who said, "We are having to pledge our fields, our vineyards, and our houses in order to get grain during the famine." 4And there were those who said, "We are having to borrow money on our fields and vineyards to pay the king's tax. 5Now our flesh is the same as that of our kindred; our children are the same as their children; and yet we are forcing our sons and daughters to be slaves, and some of our daughters have been ravished; we are powerless,

and our fields and vineyards now belong to others."

6 I was very angry when I heard their outcry and these complaints. 7After thinking it over, I brought charges against the nobles and the officials; I said to them, "You are all taking interest from your own people." And I called a great assembly to deal with them, 8and said to them, "As far as we were able, we have bought back our Jewish kindred who had been sold to other nations; but now you are selling your own kin, who must then be bought back by us!" They were silent, and could not find a word to say. 9So I said, "The thing that you are doing is not good. Should you not walk in the fear of our God, to prevent the taunts of the nations our enemies? 10Moreover I and my brothers and my servants are lending them money and grain. Let us stop this taking of interest. 11Restore to them, this very day, their fields, their vineyards, their olive orchards, and their houses, and the interest on money, grain, wine, and oil that you have been exacting from them." 12Then they said, "We will restore everything and demand nothing more from them. We will do as you say." And I called the priests, and made them take an oath to do as they had promised. 13I also shook out the fold of my garment and said, "So may God shake out everyone from house and from property who does not perform this promise. Thus may they be shaken out and emptied." And all the assembly said, "Amen," and praised the LORD. And the people did as they had promised.

The Generosity of Nehemiah

14 Moreover from the time that I was appointed to be their governor in the land of Judah, from the twentieth year to the thirty-second year of King Artaxerxes, twelve years, neither I nor my brothers ate the food allowance of the governor. 15The former governors who were before me laid heavy burdens on

ᵒCn: Heb *each his weapon the water*

4.20
Ex 14.14;
Deut 1.30;
Josh 23.10
5.1
Lev 25.35;
Deut 15.7
5.4
Ezra 4.13;
7.24
5.5
Gen 37.27;
Lev 25.39

5.7
Ex 22.25;
Lev 25.36
5.8
Lev 25.48
5.9
2 Sam 12.14;
Neh 4.4;
Rom 2.24
5.12
Ezra 10.5
5.13
Acts 18.6;
Neh 8.6
5.14
Neh 13.6;
Ezra 4.13,14
5.15
v. 9

the people, and took food and wine from them, besides forty shekels of silver. Even their servants lorded it over the people. But I did not do so, because of the fear of God. 16 Indeed, I devoted myself to the work on this wall, and acquired no land; and all my servants were gathered there for the work. 17 Moreover there were at my table one hundred fifty people, Jews and officials, beside those who came to us from the nations around us. 18 Now that which was prepared for one day was one ox and six choice sheep; also fowls were prepared for me, and every ten days skins of wine in abundance; yet with all this I did not demand the food allowance of the governor, because of the heavy burden of labor on the people. 19 Remember for my good, O my God, all that I have done for this people.

Intrigues of Enemies Foiled

6 Now when it was reported to Sanballat and Tobiah and to Geshem the Arab and to the rest of our enemies that I had built the wall and that there was no gap left in it (though up to that time I had not set up the doors in the gates), 2 Sanballat and Geshem sent to me, saying, "Come and let us meet together in one of the villages in the plain of Ono." But they intended to do me harm. 3 So I sent messengers to them, saying, "I am doing a great work and I cannot come down. Why should the work stop while I leave it to come down to you?" 4 They sent to me four times in this way, and I answered them in the same manner. 5 In the same way Sanballat for the fifth time sent his servant to me with an open letter in his hand. 6 In it was written, "It is reported among the nations—and Geshemᴾ also says it—that you and the Jews intend to rebel; that is why you are building the wall; and according to this report you wish to become their king. 7 You have also set up prophets to proclaim in Jerusalem concerning you, 'There is a king in Judah!' And

now it will be reported to the king according to these words. So come, therefore, and let us confer together." 8 Then I sent to him, saying, "No such things as you say have been done; you are inventing them out of your own mind" 9 —for they all wanted to frighten us, thinking, "Their hands will drop from the work, and it will not be done." But now, O God, strengthen my hands.

10 One day when I went into the house of Shemaiah son of Delaiah son of Mehetabel, who was confined to his house, he said, "Let us meet together in the house of God, within the temple, and let us close the doors of the temple, for they are coming to kill you; indeed, tonight they are coming to kill you." 11 But I said, "Should a man like me run away? Would a man like me go into the temple to save his life? I will not go in!" 12 Then I perceived and saw that God had not sent him at all, but he had pronounced the prophecy against me because Tobiah and Sanballat had hired him. 13 He was hired for this purpose, to intimidate me and make me sin by acting in this way, and so they could give me a bad name, in order to taunt me. 14 Remember Tobiah and Sanballat, O my God, according to these things that they did, and also the prophetess Noadiah and the rest of the prophets who wanted to make me afraid.

The Wall Completed

15 So the wall was finished on the twenty-fifth day of the month Elul, in fifty-two days. 16 And when all our enemies heard of it, all the nations around us were afraid�q and fell greatly in their own esteem; for they perceived that this work had been accomplished with the help of our God. 17 Moreover in those days the nobles of Judah sent many letters to Tobiah, and Tobiah's letters came to them. 18 For many in Judah were bound by oath to him, because he was the son-in-law of Shecaniah son of Arah: and his son Jehohanan had married the

5.17
1 Kings 18.19
5.18
1 Kings 4.22, 23;
2 Thes 3.8
5.19
Neh 13.14, 22,31
6.1
Neh 2.10, 19; 4.1,7; 3.1, 3
6.2
1 Chr 8.12
6.6
Neh 2.19

6.10
Jer 36.5
6.12
Ezek 13.22
6.13
v. 6
6.14
Neh 13.29;
Ezek 13.17
6.16
Neh 2.10;
4.1,7;
Ex 14.25;
Ps 126.2

ᴾ Heb *Gashmu* q Another reading is *saw*

daughter of Meshullam son of Berechiah. ¹⁹Also they spoke of his good deeds in my presence, and reported my words to him. And Tobiah sent letters to intimidate me.

7 Now when the wall had been built and I had set up the doors, and the gatekeepers, the singers, and the Levites had been appointed, ²I gave my brother Hanani charge over Jerusalem, along with Hananiah the commander of the citadel—for he was a faithful man and feared God more than many. ³And I said to them, "The gates of Jerusalem are not to be opened until the sun is hot; while the gatekeepersr are still standing guard, let them shut and bar the doors. Appoint guards from among the inhabitants of Jerusalem, some at their watch posts, and others before their own houses." ⁴The city was wide and large, but the people within it were few and no houses had been built.

Lists of the Returned Exiles

5 Then my God put it into my mind to assemble the nobles and the officials and the people to be enrolled by genealogy. And I found the book of the genealogy of those who were the first to come back, and I found the following written in it:

6 These are the people of the province who came up out of the captivity of those exiles whom King Nebuchadnezzar of Babylon had carried into exile; they returned to Jerusalem and Judah, each to his town. ⁷They came with Zerubbabel, Jeshua, Nehemiah, Azariah, Raamiah, Nahamani, Mordecai, Bilshan, Mispereth, Bigvai, Nehum, Baanah.

The number of the Israelite people: ⁸the descendants of Parosh, two thousand one hundred seventy-two. ⁹Of Shephatiah, three hundred seventy-two. ¹⁰Of Arah, six hundred fifty-two. ¹¹Of Pahath-moab, namely the descendants of Jeshua and Joab, two thousand eight hundred eighteen. ¹²Of Elam, one thousand two hundred

fifty-four. ¹³Of Zattu, eight hundred forty-five. ¹⁴Of Zaccai, seven hundred sixty. ¹⁵Of Binnui, six hundred forty-eight. ¹⁶Of Bebai, six hundred twenty-eight. ¹⁷Of Azgad, two thousand three hundred twenty-two. ¹⁸Of Adonikam, six hundred sixty-seven. ¹⁹Of Bigvai, two thousand sixty-seven. ²⁰Of Adin, six hundred fifty-five. ²¹Of Ater, namely of Hezekiah, ninety-eight. ²²Of Hashum, three hundred twenty-eight. ²³Of Bezai, three hundred twenty-four. ²⁴Of Hariph, one hundred twelve. ²⁵Of Gibeon, ninety-five. ²⁶The people of Bethlehem and Netophah, one hundred eighty-eight. ²⁷Of Anathoth, one hundred twenty-eight. ²⁸Of Beth-azmaveth, forty-two. ²⁹Of Kiriath-jearim, Chephirah, and Beeroth, seven hundred forty-three. ³⁰Of Ramah and Geba, six hundred twenty-one. ³¹Of Michmas, one hundred twenty-two. ³²Of Bethel and Ai, one hundred twenty-three. ³³Of the other Nebo, fifty-two. ³⁴The descendants of the other Elam, one thousand two hundred fifty-four. ³⁵Of Harim, three hundred twenty. ³⁶Of Jericho, three hundred forty-five. ³⁷Of Lod, Hadid, and Ono, seven hundred twenty-one. ³⁸Of Senaah, three thousand nine hundred thirty.

39 The priests: the descendants of Jedaiah, namely the house of Jeshua, nine hundred seventy-three. ⁴⁰Of Immer, one thousand fifty-two. ⁴¹Of Pashhur, one thousand two hundred forty-seven. ⁴²Of Harim, one thousand seventeen.

43 The Levites: the descendants of Jeshua, namely of Kadmiel of the descendants of Hodevah, seventy-four. ⁴⁴The singers: the descendants of Asaph, one hundred forty-eight. ⁴⁵The gatekeepers: the descendants of Shallum, of Ater, of Talmon, of Akkub, of Hatita, of Shobai, one hundred thirty-eight.

46 The temple servants: the descendants of Ziha, of Hasupha, of Tabbaoth, ⁴⁷of Keros, of Sia, of Padon, ⁴⁸of Lebana, of Hagaba, of

7.1	Neh 6.1,15
7.2	Neh 2.8
7.6	Ezra 2.1-70
7.7	Ezra 2.2
7.12	Ezra 2.7
7.17	Ezra 2.12
7.23	Ezra 2.17
7.27	Ezra 2.23
7.34	Ezra 2.31
7.39	Ezra 2.36
7.43	Ezra 2.40
7.46	Ezra 2.43

r Heb *while they*

Shalmai, [49] of Hanan, of Giddel, of Gahar, [50] of Reaiah, of Rezin, of Nekoda, [51] of Gazzam, of Uzza, of Paseah, [52] of Besai, of Meunim, of Nephushesim, [53] of Bakbuk, of Hakupha, of Harhur, [54] of Bazlith, of Mehida, of Harsha, [55] of Barkos, of Sisera, of Temah, [56] of Neziah, of Hatipha.

57 The descendants of Solomon's servants: of Sotai, of Sophereth, of Perida, [58] of Jaala, of Darkon, of Giddel, [59] of Shephatiah, of Hattil, of Pochereth-hazzebaim, of Amon.

60 All the temple servants and the descendants of Solomon's servants were three hundred ninety-two.

61 The following were those who came up from Tel-melah, Tel-harsha, Cherub, Addon, and Immer, but they could not prove their ancestral houses or their descent, whether they belonged to Israel: [62] the descendants of Delaiah, of Tobiah, of Nekoda, six hundred forty-two. [63] Also, of the priests: the descendants of Hobaiah, of Hakkoz, of Barzillai (who had married one of the daughters of Barzillai the Gileadite and was called by their name). [64] These sought their registration among those enrolled in the genealogies, but it was not found there, so they were excluded from the priesthood as unclean; [65] the governor told them that they were not to partake of the most holy food, until a priest with Urim and Thummim should come.

66 The whole assembly together was forty-two thousand three hundred sixty, [67] besides their male and female slaves, of whom there were seven thousand three hundred thirty-seven; and they had two hundred forty-five singers, male and female. [68] They had seven hundred thirty-six horses, two hundred forty-five mules, [s] [69] four hundred thirty-five camels, and six thousand seven hundred twenty donkeys.

70 Now some of the heads of ancestral houses contributed to the work. The governor gave to the

7.57
Ezra 2.55
7.60
v. 46
7.63
Ezra 2.61
7.65
Neh 8.9;
10.1
7.70
Neh 8.9

7.71
Ezra 2.69
7.73
Ezra 3.1
8.1
Ezra 3.1;
Neh 3.26;
Ezra 7.6
8.2
Deut 31.11,
12;
Lev 23.24
8.6
Neh 5.13;
Gen 14.22;
Ex 4.31

treasury one thousand darics of gold, fifty basins, and five hundred thirty priestly robes. [71] And some of the heads of ancestral houses gave into the building fund twenty thousand darics of gold and two thousand two hundred minas of silver. [72] And what the rest of the people gave was twenty thousand darics of gold, two thousand minas of silver, and sixty-seven priestly robes.

73 So the priests, the Levites, the gatekeepers, the singers, some of the people, the temple servants, and all Israel settled in their towns.

Ezra Summons the People to Obey the Law

When the seventh month came—the people of Israel being settled in their towns— [1] all **8** the people gathered together into the square before the Water Gate. They told the scribe Ezra to bring the book of the law of Moses, which the LORD had given to Israel. [2] Accordingly, the priest Ezra brought the law before the assembly, both men and women and all who could hear with understanding. This was on the first day of the seventh month. [3] He read from it facing the square before the Water Gate from early morning until midday, in the presence of the men and the women and those who could understand; and the ears of all the people were attentive to the book of the law. [4] The scribe Ezra stood on a wooden platform that had been made for the purpose; and beside him stood Mattithiah, Shema, Anaiah, Uriah, Hilkiah, and Maaseiah on his right hand; and Pedaiah, Mishael, Malchijah, Hashum, Hash-baddanah, Zechariah, and Meshullam on his left hand. [5] And Ezra opened the book in the sight of all the people, for he was standing above all the people; and when he opened it, all the people stood up. [6] Then Ezra blessed the LORD, the great God, and all the people answered, "Amen, Amen," lifting up their hands. Then they bowed

[s] Ezra 2.66 and the margins of some Hebrew Mss: MT lacks *They had . . . forty-five mules*

their heads and worshiped the LORD with their faces to the ground. [7]Also Jeshua, Bani, Sherebiah, Jamin, Akkub, Shabbethai, Hodiah, Maaseiah, Kelita, Azariah, Jozabad, Hanan, Pelaiah, the Levites,[t] helped the people to understand the law, while the people remained in their places. [8]So they read from the book, from the law of God, with interpretation. They gave the sense, so that the people understood the reading.

9 And Nehemiah, who was the governor, and Ezra the priest and scribe, and the Levites who taught the people said to all the people, "This day is holy to the LORD your God; do not mourn or weep." For all the people wept when they heard the words of the law. [10]Then he said to them, "Go your way, eat the fat and drink sweet wine and send portions of them to those for whom nothing is prepared, for this day is holy to our LORD; and do not be grieved, for the joy of the LORD is your strength." [11]So the Levites stilled all the people, saying, "Be quiet, for this day is holy; do not be grieved." [12]And all the people went their way to eat and drink and to send portions and to make great rejoicing, because they had understood the words that were declared to them.

The Festival of Booths Celebrated

13 On the second day the heads of ancestral houses of all the people, with the priests and the Levites, came together to the scribe Ezra in order to study the words of the law. [14]And they found it written in the law, which the LORD had commanded by Moses, that the people of Israel should live in booths[u] during the festival of the seventh month, [15]and that they should publish and proclaim in all their towns and in Jerusalem as follows, "Go out to the hills and bring branches of olive, wild olive, myrtle, palm, and other leafy trees to make booths,[u] as it is written." [16]So the people went out and

brought them, and made booths[u] for themselves, each on the roofs of their houses, and in their courts and in the courts of the house of God, and in the square at the Water Gate and in the square at the Gate of Ephraim. [17]And all the assembly of those who had returned from the captivity made booths[u] and lived in them; for from the days of Jeshua son of Nun to that day the people of Israel had not done so. And there was very great rejoicing. [18]And day by day, from the first day to the last day, he read from the book of the law of God. They kept the festival seven days; and on the eighth day there was a solemn assembly, according to the ordinance.

National Confession

9 Now on the twenty-fourth day of this month the people of Israel were assembled with fasting and in sackcloth, and with earth on their heads.[v] [2]Then those of Israelite descent separated themselves from all foreigners, and stood and confessed their sins and the iniquities of their ancestors. [3]They stood up in their place and read from the book of the law of the LORD their God for a fourth part of the day, and for another fourth they made confession and worshiped the LORD their God. [4]Then Jeshua, Bani, Kadmiel, Shebaniah, Bunni, Sherebiah, Bani, and Chenani stood on the stairs of the Levites and cried out with a loud voice to the LORD their God. [5]Then the Levites, Jeshua, Kadmiel, Bani, Hashabneiah, Sherebiah, Hodiah, Shebaniah, and Pethahiah, said, "Stand up and bless the LORD your God from everlasting to everlasting. Blessed be your glorious name, which is exalted above all blessing and praise."

6 And Ezra said:[w] "You are the LORD, you alone; you have made heaven, the heaven of heavens, with all their host, the earth and all that is on it, the seas and all that is

Cross references (center column)

8.7
2 Chr 17.7-9
8.9
Neh 7.65,
70; 12.26;
Num 29.1;
Deut 16.14,
15
8.10
Deut 26.11,
13
8.12
vv. 10,7,8
8.13
Lev 23.34,
42
8.15
Lev 23.4;
Deut 16.16;
Lev 23.40
8.16
Jer 32.29;
Neh 12.39;
2 Kings 14.13

8.17
2 Chr 30.21
8.18
Deut 31.11;
Lev 23.36;
Num 29.35
9.1
Neh 8.2;
Ezra 8.23;
1 Sam 4.12
9.2
Ezra 10.11;
Neh 13.3,30
9.3
Neh 8.4
9.4
Neh 8.7
9.5
1 Chr 29.13
9.6
2 Kings 19.15;
Gen 1.1;
Ps 36.6;
Col 1.17

[t] 1 Esdras 9.48 Vg: Heb *and the Levites*
[u] Or *tabernacles*; Heb *succoth* [v] Heb *on them* [w] Gk: Heb lacks *And Ezra said*

in them. To all of them you give life, and the host of heaven worships you. 7You are the LORD, the God who chose Abram and brought him out of Ur of the Chaldeans and gave him the name Abraham; 8and you found his heart faithful before you, and made with him a covenant to give to his descendants the land of the Canaanite, the Hittite, the Amorite, the Perizzite, the Jebusite, and the Girgashite; and you have fulfilled your promise, for you are righteous.

9 "And you saw the distress of our ancestors in Egypt and heard their cry at the Red Sea.ˣ 10You performed signs and wonders against Pharaoh and all his servants and all the people of his land, for you knew that they acted insolently against our ancestors. You made a name for yourself, which remains to this day. 11And you divided the sea before them, so that they passed through the sea on dry land, but you threw their pursuers into the depths, like a stone into mighty waters. 12Moreover, you led them by day with a pillar of cloud, and by night with a pillar of fire, to give them light on the way in which they should go. 13You came down also upon Mount Sinai, and spoke with them from heaven, and gave them right ordinances and true laws, good statutes and commandments, 14and you made known your holy sabbath to them and gave them commandments and statutes and a law through your servant Moses. 15For their hunger you gave them bread from heaven, and for their thirst you brought water for them out of the rock, and you told them to go in to possess the land that you swore to give them.

16 "But they and our ancestors acted presumptuously and stiffened their necks and did not obey your commandments; 17they refused to obey, and were not mindful of the wonders that you performed among them; but they stiffened their necks and determined to return to their slavery in Egypt. But you are a God ready to

9.7
Gen 11.31;
12.1; 17.5
9.8
Gen 15.6,
18-21;
Josh 21.43-45
9.9
Ex 3.7;
14.10-12
9.10
Ex 5.2; 9.16
9.11
Ex 14.21;
15.5,10
9.12
Ex 13.21,22
9.13
Ex 19.20;
20.1;
Ps 19.7-9
9.14
Gen 2.3;
Ex 20.8,11
9.15
Ex 16.14;
17.6;
Num 20.7-13;
Deut 1.8
9.16
Ps 106.6;
Deut 31.27
9.17
Ps 78.11;
Num 14.4;
Ex 34.6,7

9.18
Ex 32.4
9.19
vv. 27,31,12
9.20
Num 11.17;
Isa 63.11-14;
Ex 16.15;
17.6
9.21
Deut 2.7;
8.4; 29.5
9.22
Num 21.21-35
9.23
Gen 15.5
9.24
Josh 21.43;
18.1
9.25
Deut 3.9;
Num 13.27;
Deut 6.11;
32.15;
1 Kings 8.66
9.26
Judg 2.11;
1 Kings 14.9;
2 Chr 36.16;
v. 30

forgive, gracious and merciful, slow to anger and abounding in steadfast love, and you did not forsake them. 18Even when they had cast an image of a calf for themselves and said, 'This is your God who brought you up out of Egypt,' and had committed great blasphemies, 19you in your great mercies did not forsake them in the wilderness; the pillar of cloud that led them in the way did not leave them by day, nor the pillar of fire by night that gave them light on the way by which they should go. 20You gave your good spirit to instruct them, and did not withhold your manna from their mouths, and gave them water for their thirst. 21Forty years you sustained them in the wilderness so that they lacked nothing; their clothes did not wear out and their feet did not swell. 22And you gave them kingdoms and peoples, and allotted to them every corner,ʸ so they took possession of the land of King Sihon of Heshbon and the land of King Og of Bashan. 23You multiplied their descendants like the stars of heaven, and brought them into the land that you had told their ancestors to enter and possess. 24So the descendants went in and possessed the land, and you subdued before them the inhabitants of the land, the Canaanites, and gave them into their hands, with their kings and the peoples of the land, to do with them as they pleased. 25And they captured fortress cities and a rich land, and took possession of houses filled with all sorts of goods, hewn cisterns, vineyards, olive orchards, and fruit trees in abundance; so they ate, and were filled and became fat, and delighted themselves in your great goodness.

26 "Nevertheless they were disobedient and rebelled against you and cast your law behind their backs and killed your prophets, who had warned them in order to

ˣ Or *Sea of Reeds* ʸ Meaning of Heb uncertain

turn them back to you, and they committed great blasphemies. ²⁷ Therefore you gave them into the hands of their enemies, who made them suffer. Then in the time of their suffering they cried out to you and you heard them from heaven, and according to your great mercies you gave them saviors who saved them from the hands of their enemies. ²⁸ But after they had rest, they again did evil before you, and you abandoned them to the hands of their enemies, so that they had dominion over them; yet when they turned and cried to you, you heard from heaven, and many times you rescued them according to your mercies. ²⁹ And you warned them in order to turn them back to your law. Yet they acted presumptuously and did not obey your commandments, but sinned against your ordinances, by the observance of which a person shall live. They turned a stubborn shoulder and stiffened their neck and would not obey. ³⁰ Many years you were patient with them, and warned them by your spirit through your prophets; yet they would not listen. Therefore you handed them over to the peoples of the lands. ³¹ Nevertheless, in your great mercies you did not make an end of them or forsake them, for you are a gracious and merciful God.

32 "Now therefore, our God— the great and mighty and awesome God, keeping covenant and steadfast love—do not treat lightly all the hardship that has come upon us, upon our kings, our officials, our priests, our prophets, our ancestors, and all your people, since the time of the kings of Assyria until today. ³³ You have been just in all that has come upon us, for you have dealt faithfully and we have acted wickedly; ³⁴ our kings, our officials, our priests, and our ancestors have not kept your law or heeded the commandments and the warnings that you gave them. ³⁵ Even in their own kingdom, and in the great goodness you bestowed on them, and in the large and rich

land that you set before them, they did not serve you and did not turn from their wicked works. ³⁶ Here we are, slaves to this day—slaves in the land that you gave to our ancestors to enjoy its fruit and its good gifts. ³⁷ Its rich yield goes to the kings whom you have set over us because of our sins; they have power also over our bodies and over our livestock at their pleasure, and we are in great distress."

Those Who Signed the Covenant

38 ᶻBecause of all this we make a firm agreement in writing, and on that sealed document are inscribed the names of our officials, our Levites, and our priests.

10 ᵃ Upon the sealed document are the names of Nehemiah the governor, son of Hacaliah, and Zedekiah; ²Seraiah, Azariah, Jeremiah, ³Pashhur, Amariah, Malchijah, ⁴Hattush, Shebaniah, Malluch, ⁵Harim, Meremoth, Obadiah, ⁶Daniel, Ginnethon, Baruch, ⁷Meshullam, Abijah, Mijamin, ⁸Maaziah, Bilgai, Shemaiah; these are the priests. ⁹And the Levites: Jeshua son of Azaniah, Binnui of the sons of Henadad, Kadmiel; ¹⁰and their associates, Shebaniah, Hodiah, Kelita, Pelaiah, Hanan, ¹¹Mica, Rehob, Hashabiah, ¹²Zaccur, Sherebiah, Shebaniah, ¹³Hodiah, Bani, Beninu. ¹⁴The leaders of the people: Parosh, Pahathmoab, Elam, Zattu, Bani, ¹⁵Bunni, Azgad, Bebai, ¹⁶Adonijah, Bigvai, Adin, ¹⁷Ater, Hezekiah, Azzur, ¹⁸Hodiah, Hashum, Bezai, ¹⁹Hariph, Anathoth, Nebai, ²⁰Magpiash, Meshullam, Hezir, ²¹Meshezabel, Zadok, Jaddua, ²²Pelatiah, Hanan, Anaiah, ²³Hoshea, Hananiah, Hasshub, ²⁴Hallohesh, Pilha, Shobek, ²⁵Rehum, Hashabnah, Maaseiah, ²⁶Ahiah, Hanan, Anan, ²⁷Malluch, Harim, and Baanah.

Summary of the Covenant

28 The rest of the people, the priests, the Levites, the gatekeepers, the singers, the temple servants, and all who have separated

9.27
Judg 2.14;
Deut 4.29;
Judg 2.16,
18
9.28
Judg 3.11;
Ps 106.43
9.29
vv. 26,30,
16;
Lev 18.5;
Zech 7.11
9.30
2 Kings 17.13;
Acts 7.51,52
9.31
Jer 4.27
9.32
Neh 1.5;
2 Kings 15.19;
17.3
9.33
Jer 12.1;
Dan 9.5,6,8
9.35
Deut 28.47

9.36
Deut 28.48
9.37
Deut 28.33
9.38
2 Chr 29.10;
34.31
10.1
Neh 9.38
10.28
Ezra 2.36-58;
Neh 9.2

ᶻCh 10.1 in Heb ᵃCh 10.2 in Heb

themselves from the peoples of the lands to adhere to the law of God, their wives, their sons, their daughters, all who have knowledge and understanding, 29 join with their kin, their nobles, and enter into a curse and an oath to walk in God's law, which was given by Moses the servant of God, and to observe and do all the commandments of the LORD our Lord and his ordinances and his statutes. 30 We will not give our daughters to the peoples of the land or take their daughters for our sons; 31 and if the peoples of the land bring in merchandise or any grain on the sabbath day to sell, we will not buy it from them on the sabbath or on a holy day; and we will forego the crops of the seventh year and the exaction of every debt.

32 We also lay on ourselves the obligation to charge ourselves yearly one-third of a shekel for the service of the house of our God: 33 for the rows of bread, the regular grain offering, the regular burnt offering, the sabbaths, the new moons, the appointed festivals, the sacred donations, and the sin offerings to make atonement for Israel, and for all the work of the house of our God. 34 We have also cast lots among the priests, the Levites, and the people, for the wood offering, to bring it into the house of our God, by ancestral houses, at appointed times, year by year, to burn on the altar of the LORD our God, as it is written in the law. 35 We obligate ourselves to bring the first fruits of our soil and the first fruits of all fruit of every tree, year by year, to the house of the LORD; 36 also to bring to the house of our God, to the priests who minister in the house of our God, the firstborn of our sons and of our livestock, as it is written in the law, and the firstlings of our herds and of our flocks; 37 and to bring the first of our dough, and our contributions, the fruit of every tree, the wine and the oil, to the priests, to the chambers of the house of our God; and to bring to the Levites the tithes from our soil, for it is the Levites who

collect the tithes in all our rural towns. 38 And the priest, the descendant of Aaron, shall be with the Levites when the Levites receive the tithes; and the Levites shall bring up a tithe of the tithes to the house of our God, to the chambers of the storehouse. 39 For the people of Israel and the sons of Levi shall bring the contribution of grain, wine, and oil to the storerooms where the vessels of the sanctuary are, and where the priests that minister, and the gatekeepers and the singers are. We will not neglect the house of our God.

Population of the City Increased

11 Now the leaders of the people lived in Jerusalem; and the rest of the people cast lots to bring one out of ten to live in the holy city Jerusalem, while ninetenths remained in the other towns. 2 And the people blessed all those who willingly offered to live in Jerusalem.

3 These are the leaders of the province who lived in Jerusalem; but in the towns of Judah all lived on their property in their towns: Israel, the priests, the Levites, the temple servants, and the descendants of Solomon's servants. 4 And in Jerusalem lived some of the Judahites and of the Benjaminites. Of the Judahites: Athaiah son of Uzziah son of Zechariah son of Amariah son of Shephatiah son of Mahalalel, of the descendants of Perez; 5 and Maaseiah son of Baruch son of Col-hozeh son of Hazaiah son of Adaiah son of Joiarib son of Zechariah son of the Shilonite. 6 All the descendants of Perez who lived in Jerusalem were four hundred sixty-eight valiant warriors.

7 And these are the Benjaminites: Sallu son of Meshullam son of Joed son of Pedaiah son of Kolaiah son of Maaseiah son of Ithiel son of Jeshaiah. 8 And his brothers[b] Gabbai, Sallai: nine hundred twenty-eight. 9 Joel son of Zichri was their overseer; and Judah son of Hasse-

Cross-references (center column):

10.29
Neh 5.12;
2 Chr 34.31
10.30
Ex 34.16;
Deut 7.3
10.31
Neh 13.15-22;
Ex 23.10,
11;
Deut 15.1,2
10.32
Ex 30.11-16
10.34
Neh 11.1;
13.31
10.35
Ex 23.19;
Deut 26.2
10.36
Ex 13.2;
Num 18.15,
16
10.37
Lev 23.17;
Neh 13.5,9;
Lev 27.30

10.38
Num 18.26;
Neh 13.12,
13
10.39
Deut 12.6;
Neh 13.10,
11
11.1
Neh 10.34;
v. 18;
Isa 48.2
11.3
1 Chr 9.2,
3; v. 20;
Ezra 2.43;
Neh 7.57
11.4
1 Chr 9.3ff
11.7
v. 4

b Gk Mss: Heb And after him

nuah was second in charge of the city.

10 Of the priests: Jedaiah son of Joiarib, Jachin, [11]Seraiah son of Hilkiah son of Meshullam son of Zadok son of Meraioth son of Ahitub, officer of the house of God, [12]and their associates who did the work of the house, eight hundred twenty-two; and Adaiah son of Jeroham son of Pelaliah son of Amzi son of Zechariah son of Pashhur son of Malchijah, [13]and his associates, heads of ancestral houses, two hundred forty-two; and Amashsai son of Azarel son of Ahzai son of Meshillemoth son of Immer, [14]and their associates, valiant warriors, one hundred twenty-eight; their overseer was Zabdiel son of Haggedolim.

15 And of the Levites: Shemaiah son of Hasshub son of Azrikam son of Hashabiah son of Bunni; [16]and Shabbethai and Jozabad, of the leaders of the Levites, who were over the outside work of the house of God; [17]and Mattaniah son of Mica son of Zabdi son of Asaph, who was the leader to begin the thanksgiving in prayer, and Bakbukiah, the second among his associates; and Abda son of Shammua son of Galal son of Jeduthun. [18]All the Levites in the holy city were two hundred eighty-four.

19 The gatekeepers, Akkub, Talmon and their associates, who kept watch at the gates, were one hundred seventy-two. [20]And the rest of Israel, and of the priests and the Levites, were in all the towns of Judah, all of them in their inheritance. [21]But the temple servants lived on Ophel; and Ziha and Gishpa were over the temple servants.

22 The overseer of the Levites in Jerusalem was Uzzi son of Bani son of Hashabiah son of Mattaniah son of Mica, of the descendants of Asaph, the singers, in charge of the work of the house of God. [23]For there was a command from the king concerning them, and a settled provision for the singers, as was required every day. [24]And Pethahiah son of Meshezabel, of

11.10
1 Chr 9.10
11.16
1 Chr 26.29
11.18
v. 1
11.21
Neh 3.26
11.22
vv. 9,14
11.23
Ezra 6.8;
7.20;
Neh 12.47

11.25
Josh 14.15;
13.9,17
12.1
Ezra 2.1,2;
see
Neh 10.2-8
12.7
Ezra 3.2
12.8
Neh 11.17

the descendants of Zerah son of Judah, was at the king's hand in all matters concerning the people.

Villages outside Jerusalem

25 And as for the villages, with their fields, some of the people of Judah lived in Kiriath-arba and its villages, and in Dibon and its villages, and in Jekabzeel and its villages, [26]and in Jeshua and in Moladah and Beth-pelet, [27]in Hazar-shual, in Beer-sheba and its villages, [28]in Ziklag, in Meconah and its villages, [29]in En-rimmon, in Zorah, in Jarmuth, [30]Zanoah, Adullam, and their villages, Lachish and its fields, and Azekah and its villages. So they camped from Beersheba to the valley of Hinnom. [31]The people of Benjamin also lived from Geba onward, at Michmash, Aija, Bethel and its villages, [32]Anathoth, Nob, Ananiah, [33]Hazor, Ramah, Gittaim, [34]Hadid, Zeboim, Neballat, [35]Lod, and Ono, the valley of artisans. [36]And certain divisions of the Levites in Judah were joined to Benjamin.

A List of Priests and Levites

12 These are the priests and the Levites who came up with Zerubbabel son of Shealtiel, and Jeshua: Seraiah, Jeremiah, Ezra, [2]Amariah, Malluch, Hattush, [3]Shecaniah, Rehum, Meremoth, [4]Iddo, Ginnethoi, Abijah, [5]Mijamin, Maadiah, Bilgah, [6]Shemaiah, Joiarib, Jedaiah, [7]Sallu, Amok, Hilkiah, Jedaiah. These were the leaders of the priests and of their associates in the days of Jeshua.

8 And the Levites: Jeshua, Binnui, Kadmiel, Sherebiah, Judah, and Mattaniah, who with his associates was in charge of the songs of thanksgiving. [9]And Bakbukiah and Unno their associates stood opposite them in the service. [10]Jeshua was the father of Joiakim, Joiakim the father of Eliashib, Eliashib the father of Joiada, [11]Joiada the father of Jonathan, and Jonathan the father of Jaddua.

12 In the days of Joiakim the priests, heads of ancestral houses,

were: of Seraiah, Meraiah; of Jeremiah, Hananiah; 13 of Ezra, Meshullam; of Amariah, Jehohanan; 14 of Malluchi, Jonathan; of Shebaniah, Joseph; 15 of Harim, Adna; of Meraioth, Helkai; 16 of Iddo, Zechariah; of Ginnethon, Meshullam; 17 of Abijah, Zichri; of Miniamin, of Moadiah, Piltai; 18 of Bilgah, Shammua; of Shemaiah, Jehonathan; 19 of Joiarib, Mattenai; of Jedaiah, Uzzi; 20 of Sallai, Kallai; of Amok, Eber; 21 of Hilkiah, Hashabiah; of Jedaiah, Nethanel.

22 As for the Levites, in the days of Eliashib, Joiada, Johanan, and Jaddua, there were recorded the heads of ancestral houses; also the priests until the reign of Darius the Persian. 23 The Levites, heads of ancestral houses, were recorded in the Book of the Annals until the days of Johanan son of Eliashib. 24 And the leaders of the Levites: Hashabiah, Sherebiah, and Jeshua son of Kadmiel, with their associates over against them, to praise and to give thanks, according to the commandment of David the man of God, section opposite to section. 25 Mattaniah, Bakbukiah, Obadiah, Meshullam, Talmon, and Akkub were gatekeepers standing guard at the storehouses of the gates. 26 These were in the days of Joiakim son of Jeshua son of Jozadak, and in the days of the governor Nehemiah and of the priest Ezra, the scribe.

Dedication of the City Wall

27 Now at the dedication of the wall of Jerusalem they sought out the Levites in all their places, to bring them to Jerusalem to celebrate the dedication with rejoicing, with thanksgivings and with singing, with cymbals, harps, and lyres. 28 The companies of the singers gathered together from the circuit around Jerusalem and from the villages of the Netophathites; 29 also from Beth-gilgal and from the region of Geba and Azmaveth; for the singers had built for themselves villages around Jerusalem. 30 And the priests and the Levites purified

themselves; and they purified the people and the gates and the wall.

31 Then I brought the leaders of Judah up onto the wall, and appointed two great companies that gave thanks and went in procession. One went to the right on the wall to the Dung Gate; 32 and after them went Hoshaiah and half the officials of Judah, 33 and Azariah, Ezra, Meshullam, 34 Judah, Benjamin, Shemaiah, and Jeremiah, 35 and some of the young priests with trumpets: Zechariah son of Jonathan son of Shemaiah son of Mattaniah son of Micaiah son of Zaccur son of Asaph; 36 and his kindred, Shemaiah, Azarel, Milalai, Gilalai, Maai, Nethanel, Judah, and Hanani, with the musical instruments of David the man of God; and the scribe Ezra went in front of them. 37 At the Fountain Gate, in front of them, they went straight up by the stairs of the city of David, at the ascent of the wall, above the house of David, to the Water Gate on the east.

38 The other company of those who gave thanks went to the left,c and I followed them with half of the people on the wall, above the Tower of the Ovens, to the Broad Wall, 39 and above the Gate of Ephraim, and by the Old Gate, and by the Fish Gate and the Tower of Hananel and the Tower of the Hundred, to the Sheep Gate; and they came to a halt at the Gate of the Guard. 40 So both companies of those who gave thanks stood in the house of God, and I and half of the officials with me; 41 and the priests Eliakim, Maaseiah, Miniamin, Micaiah, Elioenai, Zechariah, and Hananiah, with trumpets; 42 and Maaseiah, Shemaiah, Eleazar, Uzzi, Jehohanan, Malchijah, Elam, and Ezer. And the singers sang with Jezrahiah as their leader. 43 They offered great sacrifices that day and rejoiced, for God had made them rejoice with great joy; the women and children also rejoiced.

c Cn: Heb opposite

12.23
1 Chr 9.14ff
12.24
Neh 11.17
12.25
1 Chr 26.15
12.26
Neh 8.9;
Ezra 7.6,11
12.27
1 Chr 25.6
12.28
1 Chr 9.16
12.30
Neh 13.22, 30

12.31
v. 38;
Neh 2.13;
3.13
12.35
Num 10.2,8
12.36
1 Chr 23.5
12.37
Neh 2.14;
3.15; 3.26
12.38
v. 31;
Neh 3.11;
3.8
12.39
Neh 8.16;
3.6; 3.3; 3.1;
3.25

The joy of Jerusalem was heard far away.

Temple Responsibilities

44 On that day men were appointed over the chambers for the stores, the contributions, the first fruits, and the tithes, to gather into them the portions required by the law for the priests and for the Levites from the fields belonging to the towns; for Judah rejoiced over the priests and the Levites who ministered. 45 They performed the service of their God and the service of purification, as did the singers and the gatekeepers, according to the command of David and his son Solomon. 46 For in the days of David and Asaph long ago there was a leader of the singers, and there were songs of praise and thanksgiving to God. 47 In the days of Zerubbabel and in the days of Nehemiah all Israel gave the daily portions for the singers and the gatekeepers. They set apart that which was for the Levites; and the Levites set apart that which was for the descendants of Aaron.

Foreigners Separated from Israel

13 On that day they read from the book of Moses in the hearing of the people; and in it was found written that no Ammonite or Moabite should ever enter the assembly of God, 2 because they did not meet the Israelites with bread and water, but hired Balaam against them to curse them—yet our God turned the curse into a blessing. 3 When the people heard the law, they separated from Israel all those of foreign descent.

The Reforms of Nehemiah

4 Now before this, the priest Eliashib, who was appointed over the chambers of the house of our God, and who was related to Tobiah, 5 prepared for Tobiah a large room where they had previously put the grain offering, the frankincense, the vessels, and the tithes of grain, wine, and oil, which were given by commandment to the Levites, singers, and gatekeepers, and the contributions for the priests. 6 While this was taking place I was not in Jerusalem, for in the thirty-second year of King Artaxerxes of Babylon I went to the king. After some time I asked leave of the king 7 and returned to Jerusalem. I then discovered the wrong that Eliashib had done on behalf of Tobiah, preparing a room for him in the courts of the house of God. 8 And I was very angry, and I threw all the household furniture of Tobiah out of the room. 9 Then I gave orders and they cleansed the chambers, and I brought back the vessels of the house of God, with the grain offering and the frankincense.

10 I also found out that the portions of the Levites had not been given to them; so that the Levites and the singers, who had conducted the service, had gone back to their fields. 11 So I remonstrated with the officials and said, "Why is the house of God forsaken?" And I gathered them together and set them in their stations. 12 Then all Judah brought the tithe of the grain, wine, and oil into the storehouses. 13 And I appointed as treasurers over the storehouses the priest Shelemiah, the scribe Zadok, and Pedaiah of the Levites, and as their assistant Hanan son of Zaccur son of Mattaniah, for they were considered faithful; and their duty was to distribute to their associates. 14 Remember me, O my God, concerning this, and do not wipe out my good deeds that I have done for the house of my God and for his service.

Sabbath Reforms Begun

15 In those days I saw in Judah people treading wine presses on the sabbath, and bringing in heaps of grain and loading them on donkeys; and also wine, grapes, figs, and all kinds of burdens, which they brought into Jerusalem on the sabbath day; and I warned them at that time against selling food. 16 Tyrians also, who lived in the city, brought in fish and all kinds of merchandise and sold them on the

sabbath to the people of Judah, and in Jerusalem. [17] Then I remonstrated with the nobles of Judah and said to them, "What is this evil thing that you are doing, profaning the sabbath day? [18] Did not your ancestors act in this way, and did not our God bring all this disaster on us and on this city? Yet you bring more wrath on Israel by profaning the sabbath."

[19] When it began to be dark at the gates of Jerusalem before the sabbath, I commanded that the doors should be shut and gave orders that they should not be opened until after the sabbath. And I set some of my servants over the gates, to prevent any burden from being brought in on the sabbath day. [20] Then the merchants and sellers of all kinds of merchandise spent the night outside Jerusalem once or twice. [21] But I warned them and said to them, "Why do you spend the night in front of the wall? If you do so again, I will lay hands on you." From that time on they did not come on the sabbath. [22] And I commanded the Levites that they should purify themselves and come and guard the gates, to keep the sabbath day holy. Remember this also in my favor, O my God, and spare me according to the greatness of your steadfast love.

Mixed Marriages Condemned

[23] In those days also I saw Jews who had married women of Ash-

dod, Ammon, and Moab; [24] and half of their children spoke the language of Ashdod, and they could not speak the language of Judah, but spoke the language of various peoples. [25] And I contended with them and cursed them and beat some of them and pulled out their hair; and I made them take an oath in the name of God, saying, "You shall not give your daughters to their sons, or take their daughters for your sons or for yourselves. [26] Did not King Solomon of Israel sin on account of such women? Among the many nations there was no king like him, and he was beloved by his God, and God made him king over all Israel; nevertheless, foreign women made even him to sin. [27] Shall we then listen to you and do all this great evil and act treacherously against our God by marrying foreign women?"

[28] And one of the sons of Jehoiada, son of the high priest Eliashib, was the son-in-law of Sanballat the Horonite; I chased him away from me. [29] Remember them, O my God, because they have defiled the priesthood, the covenant of the priests and the Levites.

[30] Thus I cleansed them from everything foreign, and I established the duties of the priests and Levites, each in his work; [31] and I provided for the wood offering, at appointed times, and for the first fruits. Remember me, O my God, for good.

13.17
vv. 11,25
13.18
Jer 17.21-23
13.19
Lev 23.32;
Jer 17.21
13.21
v. 15
13.22
Neh 12.30;
vv. 14,31
13.23
Ezra 9.2

13.25
vv. 11,17;
Deut 25.2;
Ezra 10.29,
30
13.26
1 Kings 11.1;
3.13;
2 Chr 1.12;
1 Kings 11.4ff
13.27
v. 23;
Ezra 10.2
13.28
Neh 12.10;
2.10,19
13.29
Neh 6.14;
Num 25.13
13.30
Neh 10.30
13.31
Neh 10.34;
vv. 14,22

Esther

Title and Background

This book has the name of its leading character, a beautiful Jewish girl whom King Ahasuerus of Persia chose to be his queen. The setting is in Susa, the Persian capital at this time (486-465 B.C.).

Author and Date of Writing

We do not know who wrote the book, but it is clear that the author was a Jew, both from the purpose of the book in accounting for the origin of a Jewish festival and from the Jewish nationalism that permeates the story. Many things point to the fact that he was a resident of a Persian city. The earliest date for the book would be shortly after the events narrated, i.e., c. 450 B.C.; the latest date would be before the Persian empire fell to Greece in 331.

Theme and Message

The central purpose of the author was to record the institution of the annual feast of Purim and to keep alive for later generations the memory of the great deliverance of the Jewish people during the reign of Ahasuerus. Although the name of God does not appear in the book, his care for his chosen people is clearly shown. Feasting is a prominent theme in Esther (see Outline).

Outline

I. The Banquet of Ahasuerus (1.1–2.18)
II. The Banquets of Esther (2.19–7.10)
III. The Feast of Purim (8.1–10.3)

King Ahasuerus Deposes Queen Vashti

1 This happened in the days of Ahasuerus, the same Ahasuerus who ruled over one hundred twenty-seven provinces from India to Ethiopia.[a] 2 In those days when King Ahasuerus sat on his royal throne in the citadel of Susa, 3 in the third year of his reign, he gave a banquet for all his officials and ministers. The army of Persia and Media and the nobles and governors of the provinces were present, 4 while he displayed the great wealth of his kingdom and the splendor and pomp of his majesty for many days, one hundred eighty days in all.

5 When these days were completed, the king gave for all the people present in the citadel of Susa, both great and small, a banquet lasting for seven days, in the court of the garden of the king's palace. 6 There were white cotton curtains and blue hangings tied with cords of fine linen and purple to silver rings[b] and marble pillars. There were couches of gold and silver on a mosaic pavement of porphyry, marble, mother-of-pearl, and colored stones. 7 Drinks were served in golden goblets, goblets of different kinds, and the royal wine was lavished according to the bounty of the king. 8 Drinking was by flagons, without restraint; for the king had given orders to all the officials of his palace to do as each one desired. 9 Furthermore, Queen Vashti gave a banquet for the women in the palace of King Ahasuerus.

10 On the seventh day, when the king was merry with wine, he

1.1	Ezra 4.6; Dan 9.1; Esther 8.9; 9.30
1.2	Neh 1.1
1.3	Esther 2.18
1.5	Esther 7.7,8
1.6	Ezek 23.41; Am 6.4
1.7	Esther 2.18
1.10	Judg 16.25; Esther 7.9

a Or Nubia; Heb Cush b Or rods

commanded Mehuman, Biztha, Harbona, Bigtha and Abagtha, Zethar and Carkas, the seven eunuchs who attended him, [11] to bring Queen Vashti before the king, wearing the royal crown, in order to show the peoples and the officials her beauty; for she was fair to behold. [12] But Queen Vashti refused to come at the king's command conveyed by the eunuchs. At this the king was enraged, and his anger burned within him.

13 Then the king consulted the sages who knew the laws[c] (for this was the king's procedure toward all who were versed in law and custom, [14] and those next to him were Carshena, Shethar, Admatha, Tarshish, Meres, Marsena, and Memucan, the seven officials of Persia and Media, who had access to the king, and sat first in the kingdom): [15] "According to the law, what is to be done to Queen Vashti because she has not performed the command of King Ahasuerus conveyed by the eunuchs?" [16] Then Memucan said in the presence of the king and the officials, "Not only has Queen Vashti done wrong to the king, but also to all the officials and all the peoples who are in all the provinces of King Ahasuerus. [17] For this deed of the queen will be made known to all women, causing them to look with contempt on their husbands, since they will say, 'King Ahasuerus commanded Queen Vashti to be brought before him, and she did not come.' [18] This very day the noble ladies of Persia and Media who have heard of the queen's behavior will rebel against[d] the king's officials, and there will be no end of contempt and wrath! [19] If it pleases the king, let a royal order go out from him, and let it be written among the laws of the Persians and the Medes so that it may not be altered, that Vashti is never again to come before King Ahasuerus; and let the king give her royal position to another who is better than she. [20] So when the decree made by the king is proclaimed throughout all his

kingdom, vast as it is, all women will give honor to their husbands, high and low alike."

21 This advice pleased the king and the officials, and the king did as Memucan proposed; [22] he sent letters to all the royal provinces, to every province in its own script and to every people in its own language, declaring that every man should be master in his own house.[e]

Esther Becomes Queen

2 After these things, when the anger of King Ahasuerus had abated, he remembered Vashti and what she had done and what had been decreed against her. [2] Then the king's servants who attended him said, "Let beautiful young virgins be sought out for the king. [3] And let the king appoint commissioners in all the provinces of his kingdom to gather all the beautiful young virgins to the harem in the citadel of Susa under custody of Hegai, the king's eunuch, who is in charge of the women; let their cosmetic treatments be given them. [4] And let the girl who pleases the king be queen instead of Vashti." This pleased the king, and he did so.

5 Now there was a Jew in the citadel of Susa whose name was Mordecai son of Jair son of Shimei son of Kish, a Benjaminite. [6] Kish[f] had been carried away from Jerusalem among the captives carried away with King Jeconiah of Judah, whom King Nebuchadnezzar of Babylon had carried away. [7] Mordecai[g] had brought up Hadassah, that is Esther, his cousin, for she had neither father nor mother; the girl was fair and beautiful, and when her father and her mother died, Mordecai adopted her as his own daughter. [8] So when the king's order and his edict were proclaimed, and when many young women were gathered in the citadel of Susa in custody of Hegai, Es-

1.13
Jer 10.7;
Dan 2.12;
1 Chr 12.32
1.14
2 Kings 25.19
1.17
Eph 5.33
1.19
Esther 8.8;
Dan 6.8
1.20
Eph 5.22;
Col 3.18

1.22
Esther 8.9;
Eph 5.22-24;
1 Tim 2.12
2.1
Esther 7.10;
1.19,20
2.3
vv. 8,15
2.5
Esther 3.2
2.6
2 Kings 24.14,
15; 24.6
2.7
v. 15
2.8
vv. 3,15

[c] Cn: Heb *times* [d] Cn: Heb *will tell*
[e] Heb adds *and speak according to the language of his people* [f] Heb *a Benjamite*
[g] *who* [g] Heb *He*

ther also was taken into the king's palace and put in custody of Hegai, who had charge of the women. [9] The girl pleased him and won his favor, and he quickly provided her with her cosmetic treatments and her portion of food, and with seven chosen maids from the king's palace, and advanced her and her maids to the best place in the harem. [10] Esther did not reveal her people or kindred, for Mordecai had charged her not to tell. [11] Every day Mordecai would walk around in front of the court of the harem, to learn how Esther was and how she fared.

12 The turn came for each girl to go in to King Ahasuerus, after being twelve months under the regulations for the women, since this was the regular period of their cosmetic treatment, six months with oil of myrrh and six months with perfumes and cosmetics for women. [13] When the girl went in to the king she was given whatever she asked for to take with her from the harem to the king's palace. [14] In the evening she went in; then in the morning she came back to the second harem in custody of Shaashgaz, the king's eunuch, who was in charge of the concubines; she did not go in to the king again, unless the king delighted in her and she was summoned by name.

15 When the turn came for Esther daughter of Abihail the uncle of Mordecai, who had adopted her as his own daughter, to go in to the king, she asked for nothing except what Hegai the king's eunuch, who had charge of the women, advised. Now Esther was admired by all who saw her. [16] When Esther was taken to King Ahasuerus in his royal palace in the tenth month, which is the month of Tebeth, in the seventh year of his reign, [17] the king loved Esther more than all the other women; of all the virgins she won his favor and devotion, so that he set the royal crown on her head and made her queen instead of Vashti. [18] Then the king gave a great banquet to all his officials and

2.9
vv. 3,12
2.10
v. 20
2.15
v. 6;
Esther 9.29
2.17
Esther 1.11
2.18
Esther 1.3;
1.7

2.20
v. 10
2.21
Esther 6.2
2.22
Esther 6.1,2
2.23
Esther 10.2
3.1
Esther 5.11;
v. 10
3.2
Esther 2.19;
v. 5
3.3
v. 2
3.5
v. 2;
Esther 5.9
3.6
Ps 83.4

ministers — "Esther's banquet." He also granted a holiday[h] to the provinces, and gave gifts with royal liberality.

Mordecai Discovers a Plot

19 When the virgins were being gathered together,[i] Mordecai was sitting at the king's gate. [20] Now Esther had not revealed her kindred or her people, as Mordecai had charged her; for Esther obeyed Mordecai just as when she was brought up by him. [21] In those days, while Mordecai was sitting at the king's gate, Bigthan and Teresh, two of the king's eunuchs, who guarded the threshold, became angry and conspired to assassinate[j] King Ahasuerus. [22] But the matter came to the knowledge of Mordecai, and he told it to Queen Esther, and Esther told the king in the name of Mordecai. [23] When the affair was investigated and found to be so, both the men were hanged on the gallows. It was recorded in the book of the annals in the presence of the king.

Haman Undertakes to Destroy the Jews

3 After these things King Ahasuerus promoted Haman son of Hammedatha the Agagite, and advanced him and set his seat above all the officials who were with him. [2] And all the king's servants who were at the king's gate bowed down and did obeisance to Haman; for the king had so commanded concerning him. But Mordecai did not bow down or do obeisance. [3] Then the king's servants who were at the king's gate said to Mordecai, "Why do you disobey the king's command?" [4] When they spoke to him day after day and he would not listen to them, they told Haman, in order to see whether Mordecai's words would avail; for he had told them that he was a Jew. [5] When Haman saw that Mordecai did not bow down or do obeisance to him, Haman was infuriated. [6] But he

h Or an amnesty i Heb adds a second time j Heb to lay hands on

thought it beneath him to lay hands on Mordecai alone. So, having been told who Mordecai's people were, Haman plotted to destroy all the Jews, the people of Mordecai, throughout the whole kingdom of Ahasuerus.

7 In the first month, which is the month of Nisan, in the twelfth year of King Ahasuerus, they cast Pur—which means "the lot"—before Haman for the day and for the month, and the lot fell on the thirteenth day[k] of the twelfth month, which is the month of Adar. 8 Then Haman said to King Ahasuerus, "There is a certain people scattered and separated among the peoples in all the provinces of your kingdom; their laws are different from those of every other people, and they do not keep the king's laws, so that it is not appropriate for the king to tolerate them. 9 If it pleases the king, let a decree be issued for their destruction, and I will pay ten thousand talents of silver into the hands of those who have charge of the king's business, so that they may put it into the king's treasuries." 10 So the king took his signet ring from his hand and gave it to Haman son of Hammedatha the Agagite, the enemy of the Jews. 11 The king said to Haman, "The money is given to you, and the people as well, to do with them as it seems good to you."

12 Then the king's secretaries were summoned on the thirteenth day of the first month, and an edict, according to all that Haman commanded, was written to the king's satraps and to the governors over all the provinces and to the officials of all the peoples, to every province in its own script and every people in its own language; it was written in the name of King Ahasuerus and sealed with the king's ring. 13 Letters were sent by couriers to all the king's provinces, giving orders to destroy, to kill, and to annihilate all Jews, young and old, women and children, in one day, the thirteenth day of the twelfth month, which is the month of Adar,

and to plunder their goods. 14 A copy of the document was to be issued as a decree in every province by proclamation, calling on all the peoples to be ready for that day. 15 The couriers went quickly by order of the king, and the decree was issued in the citadel of Susa. The king and Haman sat down to drink; but the city of Susa was thrown into confusion.

Esther Agrees to Help the Jews

4 When Mordecai learned all that had been done, Mordecai tore his clothes and put on sackcloth and ashes, and went through the city, wailing with a loud and bitter cry; 2 he went up to the entrance of the king's gate, for no one might enter the king's gate clothed with sackcloth. 3 In every province, wherever the king's command and his decree came, there was great mourning among the Jews, with fasting and weeping and lamenting, and most of them lay in sackcloth and ashes.

4 When Esther's maids and her eunuchs came and told her, the queen was deeply distressed; she sent garments to clothe Mordecai, so that he might take off his sackcloth; but he would not accept them. 5 Then Esther called for Hathach, one of the king's eunuchs, who had been appointed to attend her, and ordered him to go to Mordecai to learn what was happening and why. 6 Hathach went out to Mordecai in the open square of the city in front of the king's gate, 7 and Mordecai told him all that had happened to him, and the exact sum of money that Haman had promised to pay into the king's treasuries for the destruction of the Jews. 8 Mordecai also gave him a copy of the written decree issued in Susa for their destruction, that he might show it to Esther, explain it to her, and charge her to go to the king to make supplication to him and entreat him for her people.

9 Hathach went and told Esther

3.7
Esther 9.24;
Ezra 6.15
3.8
Ezra 4.12-15;
Acts 16.20
3.10
Esther 8.2;
Gen 41.42;
Esther 7.6
3.12
Esther 8.8-10;
1 Kings 21.8
3.13
Esther 8.10-14

3.14
Esther 8.13,
14
3.15
Esther 8.15
4.1ff
Esther 3.8-10;
Jon 3.5,6;
Ezek 27.30
4.3
Isa 58.5
4.7
Esther 3.9
4.8
Esther 3.14,
15

[k] Cn Compare Gk and verse 13 below: Heb *the twelfth month*

what Mordecai had said. [10]Then Esther spoke to Hathach and gave him a message for Mordecai, saying, [11]"All the king's servants and the people of the king's provinces know that if any man or woman goes to the king inside the inner court without being called, there is but one law—all alike are to be put to death. Only if the king holds out the golden scepter to someone, may that person live. I myself have not been called to come in to the king for thirty days." [12]When they told Mordecai what Esther had said, [13]Mordecai told them to reply to Esther, "Do not think that in the king's palace you will escape any more than all the other Jews. [14]For if you keep silence at such a time as this, relief and deliverance will rise for the Jews from another quarter, but you and your father's family will perish. Who knows? Perhaps you have come to royal dignity for just such a time as this." [15]Then Esther said in reply to Mordecai, [16]"Go, gather all the Jews to be found in Susa, and hold a fast on my behalf, and neither eat nor drink for three days, night or day. I and my maids will also fast as you do. After that I will go to the king, though it is against the law; and if I perish, I perish." [17]Mordecai then went away and did everything as Esther had ordered him.

Esther's Banquet

5 On the third day Esther put on her royal robes and stood in the inner court of the king's palace, opposite the king's hall. The king was sitting on his royal throne inside the palace opposite the entrance to the palace. [2]As soon as the king saw Queen Esther standing in the court, she won his favor and he held out to her the golden scepter that was in his hand. Then Esther approached and touched the top of the scepter. [3]The king said to her, "What is it, Queen Esther? What is your request? It shall be given you, even to the half of my kingdom." [4]Then Esther said, "If it pleases the king, let the king and

Haman come today to a banquet that I have prepared for the king." [5]Then the king said, "Bring Haman quickly, so that we may do as Esther desires." So the king and Haman came to the banquet that Esther had prepared. [6]While they were drinking wine, the king said to Esther, "What is your petition? It shall be granted you. And what is your request? Even to the half of my kingdom, it shall be fulfilled." [7]Then Esther said, "This is my petition and request: [8]If I have won the king's favor, and if it pleases the king to grant my petition and fulfill my request, let the king and Haman come tomorrow to the banquet that I will prepare for them, and then I will do as the king has said."

Haman Plans to Have Mordecai Hanged

[9]Haman went out that day happy and in good spirits. But when Haman saw Mordecai in the king's gate, and observed that he neither rose nor trembled before him, he was infuriated with Mordecai; [10]nevertheless Haman restrained himself and went home. Then he sent and called for his friends and his wife Zeresh, [11]and Haman recounted to them the splendor of his riches, the number of his sons, all the promotions with which the king had honored him, and how he had advanced him above the officials and the ministers of the king. [12]Haman added, "Even Queen Esther let no one but myself come with the king to the banquet that she prepared. Tomorrow also I am invited by her, together with the king. [13]Yet all this does me no good so long as I see the Jew Mordecai sitting at the king's gate." [14]Then his wife Zeresh and all his friends said to him, "Let a gallows fifty cubits high be made, and in the morning tell the king to have Mordecai hanged on it; then go with the king to the banquet in good spirits." This advice pleased Haman, and he had the gallows made.

4.11
Esther 5.1;
6.4;
Dan 2.9;
Esther 5.2;
8.4
4.15
Esther 5.1
5.1
Esther 4.16;
4.11; 6.4
5.2
Prov 21.1;
Esther 4.11;
8.4
5.3
Esther 7.2;
Mk 6.23

5.5
Esther 6.14
5.6
Esther 7.2;
v. 3
5.8
Esther 7.3;
8.5; 6.14
5.9
Esther 2.19;
3.5
5.10
Esther 6.13
5.11
Esther 9.7-10;
3.1
5.12
v. 8
5.13
v. 9
5.14
Esther 6.4;
7.9,10

The King Honors Mordecai

6 On that night the king could not sleep, and he gave orders to bring the book of records, the annals, and they were read to the king. [2] It was found written how Mordecai had told about Bigthana and Teresh, two of the king's eunuchs, who guarded the threshold, and who had conspired to assassinate[1] King Ahasuerus. [3] Then the king said, "What honor or distinction has been bestowed on Mordecai for this?" The king's servants who attended him said, "Nothing has been done for him." [4] The king said, "Who is in the court?" Now Haman had just entered the outer court of the king's palace to speak to the king about having Mordecai hanged on the gallows that he had prepared for him. [5] So the king's servants told him, "Haman is there, standing in the court." The king said, "Let him come in." [6] So Haman came in, and the king said to him, "What shall be done for the man whom the king wishes to honor?" Haman said to himself, "Whom would the king wish to honor more than me?" [7] So Haman said to the king, "For the man whom the king wishes to honor, [8] let royal robes be brought, which the king has worn, and a horse that the king has ridden, with a royal crown on its head. [9] Let the robes and the horse be handed over to one of the king's most noble officials; let him[m] robe the man whom the king wishes to honor, and let him[m] conduct the man on horseback through the open square of the city, proclaiming before him: 'Thus shall it be done for the man whom the king wishes to honor.' " [10] Then the king said to Haman, "Quickly, take the robes and the horse, as you have said, and do so to the Jew Mordecai who sits at the king's gate. Leave out nothing that you have mentioned." [11] So Haman took the robes and the horse and robed Mordecai and led him riding through the open square of the city, proclaiming, "Thus shall it be

done for the man whom the king wishes to honor."

[12] Then Mordecai returned to the king's gate, but Haman hurried to his house, mourning and with his head covered. [13] When Haman told his wife Zeresh and all his friends everything that had happened to him, his advisers and his wife Zeresh said to him, "If Mordecai, before whom your downfall has begun, is of the Jewish people, you will not prevail against him, but will surely fall before him."

Haman's Downfall and Mordecai's Advancement

[14] While they were still talking with him, the king's eunuchs arrived and hurried Haman off to the banquet that Esther had prepared.

7 [1] So the king and Haman went in to feast with Queen Esther. [2] On the second day, as they were drinking wine, the king again said to Esther, "What is your petition, Queen Esther? It shall be granted you. And what is your request? Even to the half of my kingdom, it shall be fulfilled." [3] Then Queen Esther answered, "If I have won your favor, O king, and if it pleases the king, let my life be given me— that is my petition—and the lives of my people—that is my request. [4] For we have been sold, I and my people, to be destroyed, to be killed, and to be annihilated. If we had been sold merely as slaves, men and women, I would have held my peace; but no enemy can compensate for this damage to the king."[n] [5] Then King Ahasuerus said to Queen Esther, "Who is he, and where is he, who has presumed to do this?" [6] Esther said, "A foe and enemy, this wicked Haman!" Then Haman was terrified before the king and the queen. [7] The king rose from the feast in wrath and went into the palace garden, but Haman stayed to beg his life from Queen Esther, for he saw that the king had determined to destroy him. [8] When the king returned from

Cross references

6.1
Dan 6.18;
Esther 2.23;
10.2
6.2
Esther 2.21,
22
6.4
Esther 4.11;
5.1; 5.14
6.6
vv. 7,9,11
6.8
1 Kings 1.33
6.9
Gen 41.43

6.12
2 Sam 15.30
6.13
Esther 5.10
6.14
Esther 5.8
7.2
Esther 5.6;
5.3
7.3
Esther 5.8;
8.5
7.4
Esther 3.9,
13
7.6
Esther 3.10
7.8
Esther 1.6

[1] Heb *to lay hands on* [m] Heb *them*
[n] Meaning of Heb uncertain

the palace garden to the banquet hall, Haman had thrown himself on the couch where Esther was reclining; and the king said, "Will he even assault the queen in my presence, in my own house?" As the words left the mouth of the king, they covered Haman's face. 9 Then Harbona, one of the eunuchs in attendance on the king, said, "Look, the very gallows that Haman has prepared for Mordecai, whose word saved the king, stands at Haman's house, fifty cubits high." And the king said, "Hang him on that." 10 So they hanged Haman on the gallows that he had prepared for Mordecai. Then the anger of the king abated.

Esther Saves the Jews

8 On that day King Ahasuerus gave to Queen Esther the house of Haman, the enemy of the Jews; and Mordecai came before the king, for Esther had told what he was to her. 2 Then the king took off his signet ring, which he had taken from Haman, and gave it to Mordecai. So Esther set Mordecai over the house of Haman.

3 Then Esther spoke again to the king; she fell at his feet, weeping and pleading with him to avert the evil design of Haman the Agagite and the plot that he had devised against the Jews. 4 The king held out the golden scepter to Esther, 5 and Esther rose and stood before the king. She said, "If it pleases the king, and if I have won his favor, and if the thing seems right before the king, and I have his approval, let an order be written to revoke the letters devised by Haman son of Hammedatha the Agagite, which he wrote giving orders to destroy the Jews who are in all the provinces of the king. 6 For how can I bear to see the calamity that is coming on my people? Or how can I bear to see the destruction of my kindred?" 7 Then King Ahasuerus said to Queen Esther and to the Jew Mordecai, "See, I have given Esther the house of Haman, and they have hanged him on the gallows, because he plotted to lay hands on the Jews. 8 You may write as you please with regard to the Jews, in the name of the king, and seal it with the king's ring; for an edict written in the name of the king and sealed with the king's ring cannot be revoked."

9 The king's secretaries were summoned at that time, in the third month, which is the month of Sivan, on the twenty-third day; and an edict was written, according to all that Mordecai commanded, to the Jews and to the satraps and the governors and the officials of the provinces from India to Ethiopia,º one hundred twenty-seven provinces, to every province in its own script and to every people in its own language, and also to the Jews in their script and their language. 10 He wrote letters in the name of King Ahasuerus, sealed them with the king's ring, and sent them by mounted couriers riding on fast steeds bred from the royal herd.ᵖ 11 By these letters the king allowed the Jews who were in every city to assemble and defend their lives, to destroy, to kill, and to annihilate any armed force of any people or province that might attack them, with their children and women, and to plunder their goods 12 on a single day throughout all the provinces of King Ahasuerus, on the thirteenth day of the twelfth month, which is the month of Adar. 13 A copy of the writ was to be issued as a decree in every province and published to all peoples, and the Jews were to be ready on that day to take revenge on their enemies. 14 So the couriers, mounted on their swift royal steeds, hurried out, urged by the king's command. The decree was issued in the citadel of Susa.

15 Then Mordecai went out from the presence of the king, wearing royal robes of blue and white, with a great golden crown and a mantle of fine linen and purple, while the city of Susa shouted

7.9
Esther 1.10;
5.14;
Ps 7.16;
Prov 11.5,6
8.1
Esther 7.6;
2.7
8.2
Esther 3.10
8.4
Esther 4.11;
5.2
8.5
Esther 5.8;
7.3; 3.13
8.6
Esther 7.4;
9.1
8.7
v. 1

8.8
v. 10;
Esther 3.12;
1.19
8.9
Esther 3.12;
1.1; 1.22
8.10
1 Kings 21.8;
Esther 3.12,
13
8.11
Esther 9.2,
10,15,16;
3.13
8.13
Esther 3.14
8.15
Esther 3.15

º Or Nubia; Heb Cush ᵖ Meaning of Heb uncertain

and rejoiced. [16] For the Jews there was light and gladness, joy and honor. [17] In every province and in every city, wherever the king's command and his edict came, there was gladness and joy among the Jews, a festival and a holiday. Furthermore, many of the peoples of the country professed to be Jews, because the fear of the Jews had fallen upon them.

Destruction of the Enemies of the Jews

9 Now in the twelfth month, which is the month of Adar, on the thirteenth day, when the king's command and edict were about to be executed, on the very day when the enemies of the Jews hoped to gain power over them, but which had been changed to a day when the Jews would gain power over their foes, [2] the Jews gathered in their cities throughout all the provinces of King Ahasuerus to lay hands on those who had sought their ruin; and no one could withstand them, because the fear of them had fallen upon all peoples. [3] All the officials of the provinces, the satraps and the governors, and the royal officials were supporting the Jews, because the fear of Mordecai had fallen upon them. [4] For Mordecai was powerful in the king's house, and his fame spread throughout all the provinces as the man Mordecai grew more and more powerful. [5] So the Jews struck down all their enemies with the sword, slaughtering, and destroying them, and did as they pleased to those who hated them. [6] In the citadel of Susa the Jews killed and destroyed five hundred people. [7] They killed Parshandatha, Dalphon, Aspatha, [8] Poratha, Adalia, Aridatha, [9] Parmashta, Arisai, Aridai, Vaizatha, [10] the ten sons of Haman son of Hammedatha, the enemy of the Jews; but they did not touch the plunder.

[11] That very day the number of those killed in the citadel of Susa was reported to the king. [12] The king said to Queen Esther, "In the citadel of Susa the Jews have killed five hundred people and also the ten sons of Haman. What have they done in the rest of the king's provinces? Now what is your petition? It shall be granted you. And what further is your request? It shall be fulfilled." [13] Esther said, "If it pleases the king, let the Jews who are in Susa be allowed tomorrow also to do according to this day's edict, and let the ten sons of Haman be hanged on the gallows." [14] So the king commanded this to be done; a decree was issued in Susa, and the ten sons of Haman were hanged. [15] The Jews who were in Susa gathered also on the fourteenth day of the month of Adar and they killed three hundred persons in Susa; but they did not touch the plunder.

[16] Now the other Jews who were in the king's provinces also gathered to defend their lives, and gained relief from their enemies, and killed seventy-five thousand of those who hated them; but they laid no hands on the plunder. [17] This was on the thirteenth day of the month of Adar, and on the fourteenth day they rested and made that a day of feasting and gladness.

The Feast of Purim Inaugurated

[18] But the Jews who were in Susa gathered on the thirteenth day and on the fourteenth, and rested on the fifteenth day, making that a day of feasting and gladness. [19] Therefore the Jews of the villages, who live in the open towns, hold the fourteenth day of the month of Adar as a day for gladness and feasting, a holiday on which they send gifts of food to one another.

[20] Mordecai recorded these things, and sent letters to all the Jews who were in all the provinces of King Ahasuerus, both near and far, [21] enjoining them that they should keep the fourteenth day of the month Adar and also the fifteenth day of the same month, year by year, [22] as the days on which the Jews gained relief from their ene-

Cross references

8.17
Esther 9.2,
19,27
9.1
Esther 8.12;
v. 17;
Esther 3.13
9.2
vv. 15-18;
Esther 8.11;
Ps 71.13,24;
Esther 8.17
9.3
Ezra 8.36
9.5
2 Sam 3.1;
Prov 4.18
9.10
Esther 5.11;
8.11
9.12
Esther 7.2

9.13
Esther 8.11
9.15
v. 10
9.16
vv. 2,10,15
9.17
vv. 1,21
9.18
vv. 2,21
9.19
Deut 16.11,
14; v. 22;
Neh 8.10
9.22
v. 19

mies, and as the month that had been turned for them from sorrow into gladness and from mourning into a holiday; that they should make them days of feasting and gladness, days for sending gifts of food to one another and presents to the poor. 23 So the Jews adopted as a custom what they had begun to do, as Mordecai had written to them.

24 Haman son of Hammedatha the Agagite, the enemy of all the Jews, had plotted against the Jews to destroy them, and had cast Pur—that is "the lot"—to crush and destroy them; 25 but when Esther came before the king, he gave orders in writing that the wicked plot that he had devised against the Jews should come upon his own head, and that he and his sons should be hanged on the gallows. 26 Therefore these days are called Purim, from the word Pur. Thus because of all that was written in this letter, and of what they had faced in this matter, and of what had happened to them, 27 the Jews established and accepted as a custom for themselves and their descendants and all who joined them, that without fail they would continue to observe these two days every year, as it was written and at the time appointed. 28 These days should be remembered and kept throughout every generation, in every family, province, and city; and these days of Purim should never

fall into disuse among the Jews, nor should the commemoration of these days cease among their descendants.

29 Queen Esther daughter of Abihail, along with the Jew Mordecai, gave full written authority, confirming this second letter about Purim. 30 Letters were sent wishing peace and security to all the Jews, to the one hundred twenty-seven provinces of the kingdom of Ahasuerus, 31 and giving orders that these days of Purim should be observed at their appointed seasons, as the Jew Mordecai and Queen Esther enjoined on the Jews, just as they had laid down for themselves and for their descendants regulations concerning their fasts and their lamentations. 32 The command of Queen Esther fixed these practices of Purim, and it was recorded in writing.

10 King Ahasuerus laid tribute on the land and on the islands of the sea. 2 All the acts of his power and might, and the full account of the high honor of Mordecai, to which the king advanced him, are they not written in the annals of the kings of Media and Persia? 3 For Mordecai the Jew was next in rank to King Ahasuerus, and he was powerful among the Jews and popular with his many kindred, for he sought the good of his people and interceded for the welfare of all his descendants.

Cross references (center column):

9.24 Esther 3.6,7
9.25 Esther 7.4-10; 3.6-15; Ps 7.16
9.26 v. 20
9.27 Esther 8.17; v. 20,21
9.29 Esther 2.15; vv. 20,21
9.30 Esther 1.1
9.31 Esther 4.3
9.32 v. 26
10.1 Isa 24.15
10.2 Esther 8.15; 9.4; 2.23
10.3 Gen 41.40; Neh 2.10

Job

Title and Background

The book of Job is named for its main character, an upright man who was very rich. Even after losing everything he owned and suffering from a terrible sickness, Job still confessed his trust in God.

Author and Date of Writing

Although most of the book consists of the words of Job and his friends, Job himself was not the author. Undoubtedly the author was an Israelite who probably had access to oral and/or written sources from which he composed the book.

Two dates are involved: (1) the date of the man Job and his historical setting, and (2) the date of the inspired writer of the book. The latter could be dated anytime from the reign of Solomon to the exile. The date of the actual events described in this book was most likely between 2000 and 1000 B.C., and probably late in that millennium.

Theme and Message

This book provides a profound statement on the justice of God in light of human suffering. How can the justice of an almighty God be defended in the face of evil, especially human suffering, and even more particularly, the suffering of the innocent? The final answer of this book is that God is in control and that the suffering of the righteous must be seen in the light of the cosmic struggle between God and Satan.

Outline

 I. Prologue (1.1–2.13)
 II. Dialogue-Dispute: Job and His Friends (3.1–27.23)
 III. Interlude on Wisdom (28.1-28)
 IV. Monologues: Job, Elihu, and God (29.1–42.6)
 V. Epilogue (42.7-17)

Job and His Family

1 There was once a man in the land of Uz whose name was Job. That man was blameless and upright, one who feared God and turned away from evil. ² There were born to him seven sons and three daughters. ³ He had seven thousand sheep, three thousand camels, five hundred yoke of oxen, five hundred donkeys, and very many servants; so that this man was the greatest of all the people of the east. ⁴ His sons used to go and hold feasts in one another's houses in turn; and they would send and invite their three sisters to eat and drink with them. ⁵ And when the

feast days had run their course, Job would send and sanctify them, and he would rise early in the morning and offer burnt offerings according to the number of them all; for Job said, "It may be that my children have sinned, and cursed God in their hearts." This is what Job always did.

Attack on Job's Character

6 One day the heavenly beings[a] came to present themselves before the LORD, and Satan[b] also came among them. ⁷ The LORD said to Satan,[b] "Where have you come from?" Satan[b] answered the LORD,

1.1
Jer 25.20;
Ezek 14.14;
Jas 5.11;
Gen 6.9;
17.1;
Ex 18.21
1.2
Job 42.13
1.3
Job 42.12
1.5
Ex 19.10;
Gen 8.20;
1 Kings 21.10,
13
1.6
Job 38.7;
1 Chr 21.1
1.7
1 Pet 5.8

[a] Heb *sons of God* [b] Or *the Accuser;* Heb *ha-satan*

"From going to and fro on the earth, and from walking up and down on it." [8] The Lord said to Satan,[c] "Have you considered my servant Job? There is no one like him on the earth, a blameless and upright man who fears God and turns away from evil." [9] Then Satan[c] answered the Lord, "Does Job fear God for nothing? [10] Have you not put a fence around him and his house and all that he has, on every side? You have blessed the work of his hands, and his possessions have increased in the land. [11] But stretch out your hand now, and touch all that he has, and he will curse you to your face." [12] The Lord said to Satan,[c] "Very well, all that he has is in your power; only do not stretch out your hand against him!" So Satan[c] went out from the presence of the Lord.

Job Loses Property and Children

[13] One day when his sons and daughters were eating and drinking wine in the eldest brother's house, [14] a messenger came to Job and said, "The oxen were plowing and the donkeys were feeding beside them, [15] and the Sabeans fell on them and carried them off, and killed the servants with the edge of the sword; I alone have escaped to tell you." [16] While he was still speaking, another came and said, "The fire of God fell from heaven and burned up the sheep and the servants, and consumed them; I alone have escaped to tell you." [17] While he was still speaking, another came and said, "The Chaldeans formed three columns, made a raid on the camels and carried them off, and killed the servants with the edge of the sword; I alone have escaped to tell you." [18] While he was still speaking, another came and said, "Your sons and daughters were eating and drinking wine in their eldest brother's house, [19] and suddenly a great wind came across the desert, struck the four corners of the house, and it fell on the young people, and they are

dead; I alone have escaped to tell you."

[20] Then Job arose, tore his robe, shaved his head, and fell on the ground and worshiped. [21] He said, "Naked I came from my mother's womb, and naked shall I return there; the Lord gave, and the Lord has taken away; blessed be the name of the Lord."

22 In all this Job did not sin or charge God with wrong-doing.

Attack on Job's Health

2 One day the heavenly beings[d] came to present themselves before the Lord, and Satan[c] also came among them to present himself before the Lord. [2] The Lord said to Satan,[c] "Where have you come from?" Satan[e] answered the Lord, "From going to and fro on the earth, and from walking up and down on it." [3] The Lord said to Satan,[c] "Have you considered my servant Job? There is no one like him on the earth, a blameless and upright man who fears God and turns away from evil. He still persists in his integrity, although you incited me against him, to destroy him for no reason." [4] Then Satan[c] answered the Lord, "Skin for skin! All that people have they will give to save their lives.[f] [5] But stretch out your hand now and touch his bone and his flesh, and he will curse you to your face." [6] The Lord said to Satan,[c] "Very well, he is in your power; only spare his life."

7 So Satan[c] went out from the presence of the Lord, and inflicted loathsome sores on Job from the sole of his foot to the crown of his head. [8] Job[g] took a potsherd with which to scrape himself, and sat among the ashes.

9 Then his wife said to him, "Do you still persist in your integrity? Curse[h] God, and die." [10] But he said to her, "You speak as any foolish woman would speak. Shall we receive the good at the hand of

1.8
Job 42.7,8;
v. 1
1.9
1 Tim 6.5
1.10
Job 29.2-6;
Ps 128.1,2;
Job 31.25
1.11
Job 2.5;
19.21
1.15
Job 6.19
1.16
Gen 19.24;
Lev 10.2;
Num 11.1-3;
2 Kings 1.10
1.17
Gen 11.28,
31
1.18
vv. 4,13
1.19
Jer 4.11;
13.24

1.20
Gen 37.29;
1 Pet 5.6
1.21
Eccl 5.15;
1 Tim 6.7;
Job 2.10;
Eph 5.20;
1 Thes 5.18
1.22
Job 2.10
2.1
Job 1.6
2.2
Job 1.7
2.3
Job 1.1,8;
27.5,6; 9.17
2.5
Job 1.11
2.6
Job 1.12
2.7
Job 7.5
2.8
Job 42.6;
Ezek 27.30;
Mt 11.21
2.10
Job 1.21,22;
Ps 39.1

c Or the Accuser; Heb ha-satan
d Heb sons of God e Or The Accuser; Heb ha-satan f Or All that the man has he will give for his life g Heb He h Heb Bless

God, and not receive the bad?" In all this Job did not sin with his lips.

Job's Three Friends

11 Now when Job's three friends heard of all these troubles that had come upon him, each of them set out from his home— Eliphaz the Temanite, Bildad the Shuhite, and Zophar the Naama-thite. They met together to go and console and comfort him. ¹²When they saw him from a distance, they did not recognize him, and they raised their voices and wept aloud; they tore their robes and threw dust in the air upon their heads. ¹³They sat with him on the ground seven days and seven nights, and no one spoke a word to him, for they saw that his suffering was very great.

Job Curses the Day He Was Born

3 After this Job opened his mouth and cursed the day of his birth. ²Job said:

³ "Let the day perish in which
 I was born,
 and the night that said,
 'A man-child is conceived.'
⁴ Let that day be darkness!
 May God above not seek it,
 or light shine on it.
⁵ Let gloom and deep darkness
 claim it.
 Let clouds settle upon it;
 let the blackness of the day
 terrify it.
⁶ That night—let thick
 darkness seize it!
 let it not rejoice among the
 days of the year;
 let it not come into the
 number of the months.
⁷ Yes, let that night be barren;
 let no joyful cry be heard[i]
 in it.
⁸ Let those curse it who curse
 the Sea,[j]
 those who are skilled to
 rouse up Leviathan.
⁹ Let the stars of its dawn be
 dark;
 let it hope for light, but
 have none;

may it not see the eyelids
 of the morning—
¹⁰ because it did not shut the
 doors of my mother's
 womb,
 and hide trouble from my
 eyes.

¹¹ "Why did I not die at birth,
 come forth from the womb
 and expire?
¹² Why were there knees to
 receive me,
 or breasts for me to suck?
¹³ Now I would be lying down
 and quiet;
 I would be asleep; then I
 would be at rest
¹⁴ with kings and counselors of
 the earth
 who rebuild ruins for
 themselves,
¹⁵ or with princes who have
 gold,
 who fill their houses with
 silver.
¹⁶ Or why was I not buried like
 a stillborn child,
 like an infant that never
 sees the light?
¹⁷ There the wicked cease from
 troubling,
 and there the weary are at
 rest.
¹⁸ There the prisoners are at
 ease together;
 they do not hear the voice
 of the taskmaster.
¹⁹ The small and the great are
 there,
 and the slaves are free
 from their masters.

²⁰ "Why is light given to one in
 misery,
 and life to the bitter in
 soul,
²¹ who long for death, but it
 does not come,
 and dig for it more than for
 hidden treasures;
²² who rejoice exceedingly,
 and are glad when they
 find the grave?

2.11
1 Chr 1.45;
Gen 25.2;
Job 42.11
2.12
Josh 7.6;
Lam 2.10;
Ezek 27.30
2.13
Gen 50.10;
Ezek 3.15
3.3
Job 10.18;
Jer 20.14
3.5
Job 10.21;
Ps 23.4;
Jer 2.6
3.6
Job 23.17
3.8
Job 41.10
3.9
Job 41.18

3.11
Job 10.18
3.12
Gen 30.3;
Isa 66.12
3.14
Job 12.17,
18; 15.28
3.16
Eccl 6.3
3.17
Job 17.16
3.20
1 Sam 1.10;
Prov 31.6;
Isa 38.15;
Ezek 27.31
3.21
Rev 9.6

i Heb *come* j Cn: Heb *day*

23 Why is light given to one
who cannot see the
way,
whom God has fenced in?
24 For my sighing comes like[k]
my bread,
and my groanings are
poured out like water.
25 Truly the thing that I fear
comes upon me,
and what I dread befalls
me.
26 I am not at ease, nor am I
quiet;
I have no rest; but trouble
comes."

Eliphaz Speaks: Job Has Sinned

4 Then Eliphaz the Temanite
answered:
2 "If one ventures a word with
you, will you be
offended?
But who can keep from
speaking?
3 See, you have instructed
many;
you have strengthened the
weak hands.
4 Your words have supported
those who were
stumbling,
and you have made firm
the feeble knees.
5 But now it has come to you,
and you are impatient;
it touches you, and you are
dismayed.
6 Is not your fear of God your
confidence,
and the integrity of your
ways your hope?

7 "Think now, who that was
innocent ever perished?
Or where were the upright
cut off?
8 As I have seen, those who
plow iniquity
and sow trouble reap the
same.
9 By the breath of God they
perish,
and by the blast of his
anger they are
consumed.

10 The roar of the lion, the
voice of the fierce lion,
and the teeth of the young
lions are broken.
11 The strong lion perishes for
lack of prey,
and the whelps of the
lioness are scattered.

12 "Now a word came stealing
to me,
my ear received the
whisper of it.
13 Amid thoughts from visions
of the night,
when deep sleep falls on
mortals,
14 dread came upon me, and
trembling,
which made all my bones
shake.
15 A spirit glided past my face;
the hair of my flesh
bristled.
16 It stood still,
but I could not discern its
appearance.
A form was before my eyes;
there was silence, then I
heard a voice:
17 'Can mortals be righteous
before[l] God?
Can human beings be pure
before[l] their Maker?
18 Even in his servants he puts
no trust,
and his angels he charges
with error;
19 how much more those who
live in houses of clay,
whose foundation is in the
dust,
who are crushed like a
moth.
20 Between morning and
evening they are
destroyed;
they perish forever without
any regarding it.
21 Their tent-cord is plucked up
within them,
and they die devoid of
wisdom.'

3.23
Job 19.6,8,
12; Lam 3.7
3.24
Ps 42.3,4
4.2
Job 32.18-20
4.3
Isa 35.3;
Heb 12.12
4.4
Isa 35.3;
Heb 12.12
4.5
Job 6.14;
19.21
4.6
Job 1.1
4.7
Ps 37.25
4.8
Prov 22.8;
Hos 10.13;
Gal 6.7,8
4.9
Job 15.30;
Isa 30.33;
Ps 59.13

4.10
Ps 58.6
4.11
Ps 34.10
4.12
Job 26.14
4.14
Jer 23.9
4.17
Job 9.2;
35.10
4.18
Job 15.15
4.19
Job 10.9;
22.16
4.20
Ps 90.5,6;
Job 20.7
4.21
Job 36.12

k Heb before l Or more than

Job Is Corrected by God

5 "Call now; is there anyone
who will answer you?
To which of the holy ones
will you turn?

2 Surely vexation kills the fool,
and jealousy slays the
simple.

3 I have seen fools taking root,
but suddenly I cursed their
dwelling.

4 Their children are far from
safety,
they are crushed in the
gate,
and there is no one to
deliver them.

5 The hungry eat their harvest,
and they take it even out
of the thorns;[m]
and the thirsty[n] pant after
their wealth.

6 For misery does not come
from the earth,
nor does trouble sprout
from the ground;

7 but human beings are born
to trouble
just as sparks[o] fly upward.

8 "As for me, I would seek
God,
and to God I would commit
my cause.

9 He does great things and
unsearchable,
marvelous things without
number.

10 He gives rain on the earth
and sends waters on the
fields;

11 he sets on high those who
are lowly,
and those who mourn are
lifted to safety.

12 He frustrates the devices of
the crafty,
so that their hands achieve
no success.

13 He takes the wise in their
own craftiness;
and the schemes of the
wily are brought to a
quick end.

14 They meet with darkness in
the daytime,
and grope at noonday as in
the night.

15 But he saves the needy from
the sword of their
mouth,
from the hand of the
mighty.

16 So the poor have hope,
and injustice shuts its
mouth.

17 "How happy is the one
whom God reproves;
therefore do not despise
the discipline of the
Almighty.[p]

18 For he wounds, but he binds
up;
he strikes, but his hands
heal.

19 He will deliver you from six
troubles;
in seven no harm shall
touch you.

20 In famine he will redeem you
from death,
and in war from the power
of the sword.

21 You shall be hidden from the
scourge of the tongue,
and shall not fear
destruction when it
comes.

22 At destruction and famine
you shall laugh,
and shall not fear the wild
animals of the earth.

23 For you shall be in league
with the stones of the
field,
and the wild animals shall
be at peace with you.

24 You shall know that your
tent is safe,
you shall inspect your fold
and miss nothing.

25 You shall know that your
descendants will be
many,
and your offspring like the
grass of the earth.

26 You shall come to your grave
in ripe old age,

5.1
Job 15.15
5.2
Prov 12.16
5.3
Ps 37.35
5.4
Am 5.12
5.5
Job 18.8-10
5.7
Job 14.1
5.8
Ps 35.23
5.9
Ps 40.5;
72.18
5.10
Ps 65.9
5.11
1 Sam 2.7;
Ps 113.7
5.12
Neh 4.15;
Ps 33.10;
Isa 8.10
5.14
Job 12.25;
Deut 28.29

5.15
Ps 35.10
5.16
Ps 107.42
5.17
Ps 94.12;
Jas 1.12;
Heb 12.5-11
5.18
Isa 30.26
5.19
Ps 34.19;
91.10
5.20
Ps 33.19;
144.10
5.21
Ps 31.20;
91.5,6
5.22
Ps 91.13;
Ezek 34.25
5.23
Ps 91.12;
Isa 11.6-9
5.24
Job 8.6;
21.9
5.25
Ps 72.16;
112.2
5.26
Gen 15.15;
Prov 9.11

m Meaning of Heb uncertain n Aquila
Symmachus Syr Vg: Heb *snare* o Or *birds*;
Heb *sons of Resheph* p Traditional rendering
of Heb *Shaddai*

as a shock of grain comes
up to the threshing
floor in its season.
27 See, we have searched this
out; it is true.
Hear, and know it for
yourself."

Job Replies: My Complaint Is Just

6 Then Job answered:
2 "O that my vexation were
weighed,
and all my calamity laid in
the balances!
3 For then it would be heavier
than the sand of the
sea;
therefore my words have
been rash.
4 For the arrows of the
Almighty^q are in me;
my spirit drinks their
poison;
the terrors of God are
arrayed against me.
5 Does the wild ass bray over
its grass,
or the ox low over its
fodder?
6 Can that which is tasteless
be eaten without salt,
or is there any flavor in the
juice of mallows?^r
7 My appetite refuses to touch
them;
they are like food that is
loathsome to me.^r

8 "O that I might have my
request,
and that God would grant
my desire;
9 that it would please God to
crush me,
that he would let loose his
hand and cut me off!
10 This would be my
consolation;
I would even exult^r in
unrelenting pain;
for I have not denied the
words of the Holy One.
11 What is my strength, that I
should wait?

6.2
Job 31.6
6.3
Prov 27.3
6.4
Ps 38.2;
Job 21.20;
Ps 88.15
6.8
Job 14.13
6.9
1 Kings 19.4
6.10
Job 23.11,
12;
Lev 19.2;
Isa 57.15;
Hos 11.9
6.11
Job 21.4

6.13
Job 26.2,3
6.15
Ps 38.11;
Jer 15.18
6.17
Job 24.19
6.19
Gen 25.15;
Isa 21.14;
1 Kings 10.1
6.20
Jer 14.3

And what is my end, that I
should be patient?
12 Is my strength the strength
of stones,
or is my flesh bronze?
13 In truth I have no help in
me,
and any resource is driven
from me.

14 "Those who withhold^s
kindness from a friend
forsake the fear of the
Almighty.^q
15 My companions are
treacherous like a
torrent-bed,
like freshets that pass
away,
16 that run dark with ice,
turbid with melting snow.
17 In time of heat they
disappear;
when it is hot, they vanish
from their place.
18 The caravans turn aside from
their course;
they go up into the waste,
and perish.
19 The caravans of Tema look,
the travelers of Sheba
hope.
20 They are disappointed
because they were
confident;
they come there and are
confounded.
21 Such you have now become
to me;^t
you see my calamity, and
are afraid.
22 Have I said, 'Make me a
gift'?
Or, 'From your wealth offer
a bribe for me'?
23 Or, 'Save me from an
opponent's hand'?
Or, 'Ransom me from the
hand of oppressors'?

24 "Teach me, and I will be
silent;

^qTraditional rendering of Heb *Shaddai*
^rMeaning of Heb uncertain ^sSyr Vg
Compare Tg: Meaning of Heb uncertain
^tCn Compare Gk Syr: Meaning of Heb
uncertain

make me understand how I
have gone wrong.
25 How forceful are honest
words!
But your reproof, what
does it reprove?
26 Do you think that you can
reprove words,
as if the speech of the
desperate were wind?
27 You would even cast lots
over the orphan,
and bargain over your
friend.

28 "But now, be pleased to look
at me;
for I will not lie to your
face.
29 Turn, I pray, let no wrong be
done.
Turn now, my vindication
is at stake.
30 Is there any wrong on my
tongue?
Cannot my taste discern
calamity?

Job: My Suffering Is without End

7 "Do not human beings have
a hard service on earth,
and are not their days like
the days of a laborer?
2 Like a slave who longs for
the shadow,
and like laborers who look
for their wages,
3 so I am allotted months of
emptiness,
and nights of misery are
apportioned to me.
4 When I lie down I say, 'When
shall I rise?'
But the night is long,
and I am full of tossing
until dawn.
5 My flesh is clothed with
worms and dirt;
my skin hardens, then
breaks out again.
6 My days are swifter than a
weaver's shuttle,
and come to their end
without hope. u

6.25
Eccl 12.10,
11
6.26
Job 8.2
6.27
Joel 3.3;
2 Pet 3.3
6.28
Job 27.4
6.30
Job 27.4;
12.11
7.1
Job 10.17;
14.14;
Isa 40.2;
Job 14.6
7.2
Lev 19.13
7.3
Lam 1.7;
Ps 6.6
7.4
Deut 28.67
7.6
Job 9.25;
13.15; 17.15,
16

7.7
Ps 78.39;
Job 9.25
7.8
Job 20.9;
v. 21
7.9
Job 30.15;
11.8;
2 Sam 12.23
7.10
Job 10.21;
Ps 103.16
7.11
Ps 40.9;
1 Sam 1.10
7.12
Ezek 32.2,3
7.13
Job 9.27
7.14
Job 9.34
7.15
1 Kings 19.4
7.16
Job 10.1;
Eccl 7.15
7.17
Ps 8.4;
144.3;
Heb 2.6
7.20
Job 35.3,6;
v. 12;
Job 16.12

7 "Remember that my life is a
breath;
my eye will never again see
good.
8 The eye that beholds me will
see me no more;
while your eyes are upon
me, I shall be gone.
9 As the cloud fades and
vanishes,
so those who go down to
Sheol do not come up;
10 they return no more to their
houses,
nor do their places know
them any more.

11 "Therefore I will not restrain
my mouth;
I will speak in the anguish
of my spirit;
I will complain in the
bitterness of my soul.
12 Am I the Sea, or the Dragon,
that you set a guard over
me?
13 When I say, 'My bed will
comfort me,
my couch will ease my
complaint,'
14 then you scare me with
dreams
and terrify me with visions,
15 so that I would choose
strangling
and death rather than this
body.
16 I loathe my life; I would not
live forever.
Let me alone, for my days
are a breath.
17 What are human beings, that
you make so much of
them,
that you set your mind on
them,
18 visit them every morning,
test them every moment?
19 Will you not look away from
me for a while,
let me alone until I
swallow my spittle?
20 If I sin, what do I do to you,
you watcher of
humanity?

u Or as the thread runs out

Why have you made me
 your target?
Why have I become a
 burden to you?
21 Why do you not pardon my
 transgression
 and take away my iniquity?
For now I shall lie in the
 earth;
 you will seek me, but I
 shall not be."

Bildad Speaks: Job Should Repent

8 Then Bildad the Shuhite
answered:
2 "How long will you say these
 things,
 and the words of your
 mouth be a great wind?
3 Does God pervert justice?
 Or does the Almighty[v]
 pervert the right?
4 If your children sinned
 against him,
 he delivered them into the
 power of their
 transgression.
5 If you will seek God
 and make supplication to
 the Almighty,[v]
6 if you are pure and upright,
 surely then he will rouse
 himself for you
 and restore to you your
 rightful place.
7 Though your beginning was
 small,
 your latter days will be very
 great.

8 "For inquire now of bygone
 generations,
 and consider what their
 ancestors have found;
9 for we are but of yesterday,
 and we know nothing,
 for our days on earth are
 but a shadow.
10 Will they not teach you and
 tell you
 and utter words out of
 their understanding?

11 "Can papyrus grow where
 there is no marsh?

7.21
Job 10.14;
Ps 104.29;
v. 8
8.3
Gen 18.25;
Deut 32.4;
2 Chr 19.7;
Dan 9.14;
Rom 3.5
8.4
Job 1.5,18,
19
8.5
Job 5.8;
11.13; 9.15
8.6
Ps 7.6
8.7
Job 42.12
8.8
Deut 4.32;
32.7;
Job 15.18
8.9
Gen 47.9;
1 Chr 29.15;
Job 7.5

8.12
Ps 129.6;
Jer 17.6
8.13
Ps 9.17;
Job 11.20;
Prov 10.28
8.14
Isa 59.5,6
8.15
Job 27.18
8.16
Ps 37.35;
80.11
8.18
Job 7.10;
Ps 37.36
8.19
Job 20.5;
Eccl 1.4
8.20
Job 4.7;
21.30
8.21
Ps 126.2;
132.16
8.22
Ps 35.26;
109.29;
v. 15
9.2
Ps 143.2;
Rom 3.20

Can reeds flourish where
 there is no water?
12 While yet in flower and not
 cut down,
 they wither before any
 other plant.
13 Such are the paths of all who
 forget God;
 the hope of the godless
 shall perish.
14 Their confidence is
 gossamer,
 a spider's house their trust.
15 If one leans against its
 house, it will not stand;
 if one lays hold of it, it will
 not endure.
16 The wicked thrive[w] before
 the sun,
 and their shoots spread
 over the garden.
17 Their roots twine around the
 stoneheap;
 they live among the
 rocks.[x]
18 If they are destroyed from
 their place,
 then it will deny them,
 saying, 'I have never
 seen you.'
19 See, these are their happy
 ways,[y]
 and out of the earth still
 others will spring.

20 "See, God will not reject a
 blameless person,
 nor take the hand of
 evildoers.
21 He will yet fill your mouth
 with laughter,
 and your lips with shouts
 of joy.
22 Those who hate you will be
 clothed with shame,
 and the tent of the wicked
 will be no more."

Job Replies: There Is No Mediator

9 Then Job answered:
2 "Indeed I know that this
 is so;

[v] Traditional rendering of Heb *Shaddai*
[w] Heb *He thrives* [x] Gk Vg: Meaning of
Heb uncertain [y] Meaning of Heb uncertain

but how can a mortal be
just before God?
3 If one wished to contend
with him,
one could not answer him
once in a thousand.
4 He is wise in heart, and
mighty in strength
—who has resisted him, and
succeeded?—
5 he who removes mountains,
and they do not know
it,
when he overturns them in
his anger;
6 who shakes the earth out of
its place,
and its pillars tremble;
7 who commands the sun, and
it does not rise;
who seals up the stars;
8 who alone stretched out the
heavens
and trampled the waves of
the Sea;z
9 who made the Bear and
Orion,
the Pleiades and the
chambers of the south;
10 who does great things
beyond understanding,
and marvelous things
without number.
11 Look, he passes by me, and I
do not see him;
he moves on, but I do not
perceive him.
12 He snatches away; who can
stop him?
Who will say to him, 'What
are you doing?'

13 "God will not turn back his
anger;
the helpers of Rahab
bowed beneath him.
14 How then can I answer him,
choosing my words with
him?
15 Though I am innocent, I
cannot answer him;
I must appeal for mercy to
my accuser.a
16 If I summoned him and he
answered me,

I do not believe that he
would listen to my
voice.
17 For he crushes me with a
tempest,
and multiplies my wounds
without cause;
18 he will not let me get my
breath,
but fills me with bitterness.
19 If it is a contest of strength,
he is the strong one!
If it is a matter of justice,
who can summon him?b
20 Though I am innocent, my
own mouth would
condemn me;
though I am blameless, he
would prove me
perverse.
21 I am blameless; I do not
know myself;
I loathe my life.
22 It is all one; therefore I say,
he destroys both the
blameless and the
wicked.
23 When disaster brings sudden
death,
he mocks at the calamityc
of the innocent.
24 The earth is given into the
hand of the wicked;
he covers the eyes of its
judges—
if it is not he, who then is
it?

25 "My days are swifter than a
runner;
they flee away, they see no
good.
26 They go by like skiffs of
reed,
like an eagle swooping on
the prey.
27 If I say, 'I will forget my
complaint;
I will put off my sad
countenance and be of
good cheer,'
28 I become afraid of all my
suffering,

9.4
Job 36.5;
2 Chr 13.12
9.5
Mic 1.4
9.6
Isa 2.19,21;
Hag 2.6;
Heb 12.26;
Job 26.11
9.8
Gen 1.6;
Ps 104.2,3
9.9
Gen 1.16;
Job 38.31;
Am 5.8
9.10
Ps 71.15
9.11
Job 23.8,9;
35.14
9.12
Isa 45.9;
Rom 9.20;
Job 11.10
9.13
Job 26.12;
Isa 30.7
9.14
vv. 3,32
9.15
Job 10.15;
8.5

9.17
Job 16.12,
14; 2.3
9.18
Job 27.2
9.20
vv. 15,29
9.21
Job 1.1;
7.16
9.22
Eccl 9.2,3;
Ezek 21.3
9.23
Ps 64.4;
Heb 11.36;
1 Pet 1.7
9.24
Job 10.3;
12.6; 12.17
9.25
Job 7.6,7
9.26
Hab 1.8
9.27
Job 7.13
9.28
Ps 119.120;
Job 7.21

z Or trampled the back of the sea dragon
a Or for my right b Compare Gk: Heb me
c Meaning of Heb uncertain

for I know you will not
hold me innocent.
29 I shall be condemned;
why then do I labor in
vain?
30 If I wash myself with soap
and cleanse my hands with
lye,
31 yet you will plunge me into
filth,
and my own clothes will
abhor me.
32 For he is not a mortal, as I
am, that I might answer
him,
that we should come to
trial together.
33 There is no umpire d
between us,
who might lay his hand on
us both.
34 If he would take his rod
away from me,
and not let dread of him
terrify me,
35 then I would speak without
fear of him,
for I know I am not what I
am thought to be. e

Job: I Loathe My Life

10 "I loathe my life;
I will give free utterance
to my complaint;
I will speak in the
bitterness of my soul.
2 I will say to God, Do not
condemn me;
let me know why you
contend against me.
3 Does it seem good to you to
oppress,
to despise the work of your
hands
and favor the schemes of
the wicked?
4 Do you have eyes of flesh?
Do you see as humans
see?
5 Are your days like the days
of mortals,
or your years like human
years,
6 that you seek out my
iniquity
and search for my sin,

7 although you know that I am
not guilty,
and there is no one to
deliver out of your
hand?
8 Your hands fashioned and
made me;
and now you turn and
destroy me. f
9 Remember that you
fashioned me like clay;
and will you turn me to
dust again?
10 Did you not pour me out like
milk
and curdle me like
cheese?
11 You clothed me with skin
and flesh,
and knit me together with
bones and sinews.
12 You have granted me life and
steadfast love,
and your care has
preserved my spirit.
13 Yet these things you hid in
your heart;
I know that this was your
purpose.
14 If I sin, you watch me,
and do not acquit me of
my iniquity.
15 If I am wicked, woe to me!
If I am righteous, I cannot
lift up my head,
for I am filled with disgrace
and look upon my
affliction.
16 Bold as a lion you hunt me;
you repeat your exploits
against me.
17 You renew your witnesses
against me,
and increase your vexation
toward me;
you bring fresh troops
against me. g

18 "Why did you bring me forth
from the womb?

9.29
v. 20
9.30
Jer 2.22
9.32
Eccl 6.10;
Rom 9.20;
v. 3;
Ps 143.2
9.33
1 Sam 2.25
9.34
Job 13.21;
Ps 39.10
9.35
Job 13.22
10.1
1 Kings 19.4;
Job 7.16;
7.11
10.2
Job 9.29;
Hos 4.1
10.3
v. 8;
Job 21.16;
22.18
10.4
1 Sam 16.7
10.5
Ps 90.4;
2 Pet 3.8

10.7
Job 9.21;
9.12
10.8
Ps 119.73
10.9
Gen 2.7;
3.19;
Isa 64.8
10.10
Ps 139.14-16
10.12
Job 33.4
10.14
Job 13.27;
9.28
10.15
Isa 3.11;
Job 9.12,15;
Ps 25.8
10.16
Isa 38.13;
Lam 3.10;
Job 5.9
10.17
Job 16.8;
7.1
10.18
Job 3.11

d Another reading is *Would that there were an
umpire* e Cn: Heb *for I am not so in myself*
f Cn Compare Gk Syr: Heb *made me together
all around, and you destroy me*
g Cn Compare Gk: Heb *toward me; changes
and a troop are with me*

Would that I had died
 before any eye had seen
 me,
[19] and were as though I had not
 been,
 carried from the womb to
 the grave.
[20] Are not the days of my life
 few?[h]
Let me alone, that I may
 find a little comfort[i]
[21] before I go, never to return,
 to the land of gloom and
 deep darkness,
[22] the land of gloom[j] and
 chaos,
 where light is like
 darkness."

Zophar Speaks: Job's Guilt Deserves Punishment

11 Then Zophar the Naama-
 thite answered:
[2] "Should a multitude of
 words go unanswered,
 and should one full of talk
 be vindicated?
[3] Should your babble put
 others to silence,
 and when you mock, shall
 no one shame you?
[4] For you say, 'My conduct[k] is
 pure,
 and I am clean in God's[l]
 sight.'
[5] But oh, that God would
 speak,
 and open his lips to you,
[6] and that he would tell you
 the secrets of wisdom!
For wisdom is
 many-sided.[m]
Know then that God exacts
 of you less than your
 guilt deserves.

[7] "Can you find out the deep
 things of God?
 Can you find out the limit
 of the Almighty?[n]
[8] It is higher than
 heaven[o]—what can you
 do?
 Deeper than Sheol—what
 can you know?
[9] Its measure is longer than
 the earth,

10.20
Job 14.1;
7.16,19; 9.27
10.21
Ps 88.12;
23.4
11.2
Job 8.2
11.3
Jas 3.5;
Job 17.2;
21.3
11.4
Job 6.10;
10.7
11.6
Job 28.21;
Ezra 9.13
11.7
Eccl 3.11;
Rom 11.33
11.8
Job 22.12;
17.16

11.10
Job 9.12;
Rev 3.7
11.11
Job 34.21-25;
Ps 10.14
11.13
Ps 78.8;
88.9
11.14
Job 22.23;
Ps 101.3
11.15
1 Jn 3.21;
Ps 27.3
11.16
Isa 65.16;
Job 22.11
11.17
Ps 37.6;
112.4;
Isa 58.8,10
11.18
Ps 3.5;
Prov 3.24
11.19
v. 18
11.20
Deut 28.65;
Jer 15.9

and broader than the sea.
[10] If he passes through, and
 imprisons,
 and assembles for
 judgment, who can
 hinder him?
[11] For he knows those who are
 worthless;
 when he sees iniquity, will
 he not consider it?
[12] But a stupid person will get
 understanding,
 when a wild ass is born
 human.[m]

[13] "If you direct your heart
 rightly,
 you will stretch out your
 hands toward him.
[14] If iniquity is in your hand,
 put it far away,
 and do not let wickedness
 reside in your tents.
[15] Surely then you will lift up
 your face without
 blemish;
 you will be secure, and will
 not fear.
[16] You will forget your misery;
 you will remember it as
 waters that have passed
 away.
[17] And your life will be brighter
 than the noonday;
 its darkness will be like the
 morning.
[18] And you will have
 confidence, because
 there is hope;
 you will be protected[p] and
 take your rest in safety.
[19] You will lie down, and no
 one will make you
 afraid;
 many will entreat your
 favor.
[20] But the eyes of the wicked
 will fail;
 all way of escape will be
 lost to them,

[h] Cn Compare Gk Syr: Heb *Are not my days
few? Let him cease!* [i] Heb *that I may
brighten up a little* [j] Heb *gloom as
darkness, deep darkness* [k] Gk: Heb
teaching [l] Heb *your* [m] Meaning of Heb
uncertain [n] Traditional rendering of Heb
Shaddai [o] Heb *The heights of heaven*
[p] Or *you will look around*

and their hope is to
 breathe their last."

Job Replies: I Am a Laughingstock

12 Then Job answered:
² "No doubt you are the
 people,
and wisdom will die with
 you.
³ But I have understanding as
 well as you;
I am not inferior to
 you.
Who does not know such
 things as these?
⁴ I am a laughingstock to my
 friends;
I, who called upon God
 and he answered me,
a just and blameless man, I
 am a laughingstock.
⁵ Those at ease have contempt
 for misfortune,q
but it is ready for those
 whose feet are unstable.
⁶ The tents of robbers are at
 peace,
and those who provoke
 God are secure,
who bring their god in their
 hands.r

⁷ "But ask the animals, and
 they will teach you;
the birds of the air, and
 they will tell you;
⁸ ask the plants of the earth,s
 and they will teach you;
and the fish of the sea will
 declare to you.
⁹ Who among all these does
 not know
that the hand of the LORD
 has done this?
¹⁰ In his hand is the life of
 every living thing
and the breath of every
 human being.
¹¹ Does not the ear test words
 as the palate tastes food?
¹² Is wisdom with the aged,
 and understanding in
 length of days?
¹³ "With Godt are wisdom and
 strength;

he has counsel and
 understanding.
¹⁴ If he tears down, no one can
 rebuild;
if he shuts someone in, no
 one can open up.
¹⁵ If he withholds the waters,
 they dry up;
if he sends them out, they
 overwhelm the land.
¹⁶ With him are strength and
 wisdom;
the deceived and the
 deceiver are his.
¹⁷ He leads counselors away
 stripped,
and makes fools of judges.
¹⁸ He looses the sash of kings,
and binds a waistcloth on
 their loins.
¹⁹ He leads priests away
 stripped,
and overthrows the mighty.
²⁰ He deprives of speech those
 who are trusted,
and takes away the
 discernment of the
 elders.
²¹ He pours contempt on
 princes,
and looses the belt of the
 strong.
²² He uncovers the deeps out of
 darkness,
and brings deep darkness
 to light.
²³ He makes nations great, then
 destroys them;
he enlarges nations, then
 leads them away.
²⁴ He strips understanding from
 the leadersu of the
 earth,
and makes them wander in
 a pathless waste.
²⁵ They grope in the dark
 without light;
he makes them stagger like
 a drunkard.

13 "Look, my eye has seen
 all this,

12.3
Job 13.2
12.4
Job 6.10,20;
21.3;
Ps 91.15;
Job 6.29
12.5
Ps 123.4
12.6
Job 9.24;
21.9; 22.18
12.9
Isa 41.20
12.10
Acts 17.28;
Job 27.3;
33.4
12.11
Job 34.3
12.12
Job 32.7
12.13
Job 9.4;
11.6

12.14
Job 19.10;
37.7
12.15
1 Kings 8.35;
Gen 7.11
12.16
v. 13;
Job 13.7,9
12.17
Job 3.14;
19.9; 9.24
12.18
Ps 116.16
12.20
Job 32.9
12.21
Ps 107.40;
v. 18
12.22
Dan 2.22;
1 Cor 4.5;
Job 3.5
12.23
Ps 107.38;
Isa 9.3;
Jer 25.9;
Deut 12.20;
Ps 78.61
12.24
v. 20;
Ps 107.40
12.25
Job 5.14;
Ps 107.27
13.1
Job 12.9

q Meaning of Heb uncertain r Or whom
God brought forth by his hand; Meaning of Heb
uncertain s Or speak to the earth
t Heb him u Heb adds of the people

my ear has heard and
understood it.

2 What you know, I also know;
I am not inferior to you.

3 But I would speak to the
Almighty, ᵛ

and I desire to argue my
case with God.

4 As for you, you whitewash
with lies;

all of you are worthless
physicians.

5 If you would only keep
silent,

that would be your
wisdom!

6 Hear now my reasoning,
and listen to the pleadings
of my lips.

7 Will you speak falsely for
God,

and speak deceitfully for
him?

8 Will you show partiality
toward him,

will you plead the case for
God?

9 Will it be well with you when
he searches you out?

Or can you deceive him, as
one person deceives
another?

10 He will surely rebuke you
if in secret you show
partiality.

11 Will not his majesty terrify
you,

and the dread of him fall
upon you?

12 Your maxims are proverbs of
ashes,

your defenses are defenses
of clay.

13 "Let me have silence, and I
will speak,

and let come on me what
may.

14 I will take my flesh in my
teeth,

and put my life in my
hand.ʷ

15 See, he will kill me; I have
no hope;ˣ

but I will defend my ways
to his face.

16 This will be my salvation,

that the godless shall not
come before him.

17 Listen carefully to my words,
and let my declaration be
in your ears.

18 I have indeed prepared my
case;

I know that I shall be
vindicated.

19 Who is there that will
contend with me?

For then I would be silent
and die.

Job's Despondent Prayer

20 Only grant two things to me,
then I will not hide myself
from your face:

21 withdraw your hand far from
me,

and do not let dread of you
terrify me.

22 Then call, and I will answer;
or let me speak, and you
reply to me.

23 How many are my iniquities
and my sins?

Make me know my
transgression and my
sin.

24 Why do you hide your face,
and count me as your
enemy?

25 Will you frighten a
windblown leaf

and pursue dry chaff?

26 For you write bitter things
against me,

and make me reapʸ the
iniquities of my youth.

27 You put my feet in the
stocks,

and watch all my paths;
you set a bound to the
soles of my feet.

28 One wastes away like a
rotten thing,

like a garment that is
moth-eaten.

14 "A mortal, born of
woman, few of days and
full of trouble,

13.2
Job 12.3
13.3
Job 23.3,4;
v. 15
13.4
Ps 119.69;
Jer 23.32
13.5
Prov 17.28
13.7
Job 36.4
13.9
Ps 44.21;
Gal 6.7
13.10
v. 8
13.11
Job 31.23
13.12
Job 15.3
13.13
v. 5
13.14
1 Sam 19.5
13.15
Ps 23.4;
Prov 14.32;
Job 27.5
13.16
Ps 5.5

13.17
Job 21.2
13.18
Job 23.4;
9.2
13.19
Isa 50.8;
Job 40.4
13.20
Job 9.34
13.21
Ps 39.10
13.22
Job 14.15
13.23
1 Sam 26.18
13.24
Deut 32.20;
Ps 13.1;
Job 19.11
13.25
Isa 42.3
13.26
Ps 25.7
13.27
Job 33.11
13.28
Isa 50.9;
Jas 5.2
14.1
Job 5.7;
Eccl 2.23

ᵛ Traditional rendering of Heb *Shaddai*
ʷ Gk: Heb *Why should I take . . . in my
hand?* ˣ Or *Though he kill me, yet I will
trust in him* ʸ Heb *inherit*

2 comes up like a flower and
 withers,
 flees like a shadow and
 does not last.
3 Do you fix your eyes on such
 a one?
 Do you bring me into
 judgment with you?
4 Who can bring a clean thing
 out of an unclean?
 No one can.
5 Since their days are
 determined,
 and the number of their
 months is known to
 you,
 and you have appointed
 the bounds that they
 cannot pass,
6 look away from them, and
 desist,[z]
 that they may enjoy, like
 laborers, their days.

7 "For there is hope for a tree,
 if it is cut down, that it
 will sprout again,
 and that its shoots will not
 cease.
8 Though its root grows old in
 the earth,
 and its stump dies in the
 ground,
9 yet at the scent of water it
 will bud
 and put forth branches like
 a young plant.
10 But mortals die, and are laid
 low;
 humans expire, and where
 are they?
11 As waters fail from a lake,
 and a river wastes away
 and dries up,
12 so mortals lie down and do
 not rise again;
 until the heavens are no
 more, they will not
 awake
 or be roused out of their
 sleep.
13 Oh that you would hide me
 in Sheol,
 that you would conceal me
 until your wrath is past,
 that you would appoint me

a set time, and
 remember me!
14 If mortals die, will they live
 again?
 All the days of my service I
 would wait
 until my release should
 come.
15 You would call, and I would
 answer you;
 you would long for the
 work of your hands.
16 For then you would not[a]
 number my steps,
 you would not keep watch
 over my sin;
17 my transgression would be
 sealed up in a bag,
 and you would cover over
 my iniquity.

18 "But the mountain falls and
 crumbles away,
 and the rock is removed
 from its place;
19 the waters wear away the
 stones;
 the torrents wash away the
 soil of the earth;
 so you destroy the hope of
 mortals.
20 You prevail forever against
 them, and they pass
 away;
 you change their
 countenance, and send
 them away.
21 Their children come to
 honor, and they do not
 know it;
 they are brought low, and
 it goes unnoticed.
22 They feel only the pain of
 their own bodies,
 and mourn only for
 themselves."

Eliphaz Speaks: Job Undermines Religion

15 Then Eliphaz the Temanite answered:
2 "Should the wise answer
 with windy knowledge,

14.2
Ps 90.5,6;
Jas 1.10;
1 Pet 1.24
14.3
Ps 144.3;
143.2
14.4
Ps 51.2,10;
Jn 3.6;
Rom 5.12;
Eph 2.3
14.5
Ps 139.16;
Job 21.21;
Acts 17.26
14.6
Job 7.19;
7.1
14.9
Isa 55.10
14.10
Job 13.19
14.11
Isa 19.5
14.12
Ps 102.26;
Acts 3.21;
Rev 20.11;
21.1
14.13
Isa 26.20

14.14
Job 7.1
14.15
Job 13.22
14.16
Job 10.6;
31.4; 34.21;
Prov 5.21;
Jer 32.19
14.17
Deut 32.34;
Hos 13.12
14.18
Job 18.4
14.19
Job 7.6
14.20
Job 34.20;
Jas 1.10
14.21
Eccl 9.5;
Isa 63.16
15.2
Job 6.26

z Cn: Heb *that they may desist* a Syr: Heb
lacks *not*

and fill themselves with
the east wind?

3 Should they argue in
unprofitable talk,
or in words with which
they can do no good?

4 But you are doing away with
the fear of God,
and hindering meditation
before God.

5 For your iniquity teaches
your mouth,
and you choose the tongue
of the crafty.

6 Your own mouth condemns
you, and not I;
your own lips testify
against you.

7 "Are you the firstborn of the
human race?
Were you brought forth
before the hills?

8 Have you listened in the
council of God?
And do you limit wisdom
to yourself?

9 What do you know that we
do not know?
What do you understand
that is not clear to us?

10 The gray-haired and the aged
are on our side,
those older than your
father.

11 Are the consolations of God
too small for you,
or the word that deals
gently with you?

12 Why does your heart carry
you away,
and why do your eyes
flash,[b]

13 so that you turn your spirit
against God,
and let such words go out
of your mouth?

14 What are mortals, that they
can be clean?
Or those born of woman,
that they can be
righteous?

15 God puts no trust even in his
holy ones,
and the heavens are not
clean in his sight;

16 how much less one who is
abominable and
corrupt,
one who drinks iniquity
like water!

17 "I will show you; listen to
me;
what I have seen I will
declare—

18 what sages have told,
and their ancestors have
not hidden,

19 to whom alone the land was
given,
and no stranger passed
among them.

20 The wicked writhe in pain all
their days,
through all the years that
are laid up for the
ruthless.

21 Terrifying sounds are in their
ears;
in prosperity the destroyer
will come upon them.

22 They despair of returning
from darkness,
and they are destined for
the sword.

23 They wander abroad for
bread, saying, 'Where is
it?'
They know that a day of
darkness is ready at
hand;

24 distress and anguish terrify
them;
they prevail against them,
like a king prepared for
battle.

25 Because they stretched out
their hands against
God,
and bid defiance to the
Almighty,[c]

26 running stubbornly against
him
with a thick-bossed shield;

27 because they have covered
their faces with their
fat,
and gathered fat upon their
loins,

15.5
Ps 36.3;
Prov 16.23;
Job 5.12,13
15.6
Job 9.20;
Lk 19.22
15.7
Job 38.4,21;
Ps 90.2;
Prov 8.25
15.8
Rom 11.34;
Job 12.2
15.9
Job 13.2
15.10
Job 32.6,7
15.11
Job 36.15,
16;
2 Cor 1.3,
4; Zech 1.13
15.13
Job 33.13
15.14
Job 14.4;
Prov 20.9;
Eccl 7.20;
Job 25.4;
Ps 51.5
15.15
Job 4.18;
25.5

15.16
Ps 14.1,3;
Job 34.7
15.18
Job 8.8
15.20
Job 27.13
15.21
Job 18.11;
20.25;
1 Thes 5.3
15.22
v. 30;
Job 27.14
15.23
Ps 59.15;
109.10;
Job 18.12
15.25
Job 36.9
15.27
Ps 17.10

b Meaning of Heb uncertain c Traditional
rendering of Heb *Shaddai*

28 they will live in desolate
cities,
in houses that no one
should inhabit,
houses destined to become
heaps of ruins;
29 they will not be rich, and
their wealth will not
endure,
nor will they strike root in
the earth; d
30 they will not escape from
darkness;
the flame will dry up their
shoots,
and their blossom e will be
swept away f by the
wind.
31 Let them not trust in
emptiness, deceiving
themselves;
for emptiness will be their
recompense.
32 It will be paid in full before
their time,
and their branch will not
be green.
33 They will shake off their
unripe grape, like the
vine,
and cast off their blossoms,
like the olive tree.
34 For the company of the
godless is barren,
and fire consumes the
tents of bribery.
35 They conceive mischief and
bring forth evil
and their heart prepares
deceit."

Job Reaffirms His Innocence

16 Then Job answered:
2 "I have heard many
such things;
miserable comforters are
you all.
3 Have windy words no limit?
Or what provokes you that
you keep on talking?
4 I also could talk as you do,
if you were in my place;
I could join words together
against you,
and shake my head at you.

5 I could encourage you with
my mouth,
and the solace of my lips
would assuage your
pain.
6 "If I speak, my pain is not
assuaged,
and if I forbear, how much
of it leaves me?
7 Surely now God has worn me
out;
he has g made desolate all
my company.
8 And he has g shriveled me
up,
which is a witness against
me;
my leanness has risen up
against me,
and it testifies to my face.
9 He has torn me in his wrath,
and hated me;
he has gnashed his teeth at
me;
my adversary sharpens his
eyes against me.
10 They have gaped at me with
their mouths;
they have struck me
insolently on the cheek;
they mass themselves
together against me.
11 God gives me up to the
ungodly,
and casts me into the
hands of the wicked.
12 I was at ease, and he broke
me in two;
he seized me by the neck
and dashed me to
pieces;
he set me up as his target;
13 his archers surround me.
He slashes open my kidneys,
and shows no mercy;
he pours out my gall on
the ground.
14 He bursts upon me again
and again;
he rushes at me like a
warrior.
15 I have sewed sackcloth upon
my skin,

15.29
Job 27.16,
17
15.30
Job 5.14;
22.20; 4.9
15.31
Isa 59.4
15.32
Job 22.16;
Ps 55.23;
Job 18.16
15.33
Hab 3.17
15.34
Job 16.7;
8.22
15.35
Ps 7.14;
Isa 59.4;
Hos 10.13
16.2
Job 13.4
16.3
Job 6.26
16.4
Ps 22.7;
109.25;
Lam 2.15;
Mt 27.39

16.7
Job 7.3;
v. 20
16.8
Job 10.17;
19.20
16.9
Ps 35.16;
Job 13.24
16.10
Ps 22.13;
Lam 3.30;
Mic 5.1;
Ps 35.15
16.11
Job 1.15,17
16.12
Job 9.17
16.13
Job 19.12;
27.22; 20.25
16.14
Job 9.17;
Joel 2.7
16.15
Gen 37.34;
Job 30.19

d Vg: Meaning of Heb uncertain e Gk: Heb
mouth f Cn: Heb will depart g Heb you
have

and have laid my strength
in the dust.
16 My face is red with weeping,
and deep darkness is on
my eyelids,
17 though there is no violence
in my hands,
and my prayer is pure.

18 "O earth, do not cover my
blood;
let my outcry find no
resting place.
19 Even now, in fact, my
witness is in heaven,
and he that vouches for me
is on high.
20 My friends scorn me;
my eye pours out tears to
God,
21 that he would maintain the
right of a mortal with
God,
as[h] one does for a
neighbor.
22 For when a few years have
come,
I shall go the way from
which I shall not
return.

Job Prays for Relief

17 My spirit is broken, my
days are extinct,
the grave is ready for me.
2 Surely there are mockers
around me,
and my eye dwells on their
provocation.

3 "Lay down a pledge for me
with yourself;
who is there that will give
surety for me?
4 Since you have closed their
minds to
understanding,
therefore you will not let
them triumph.
5 Those who denounce friends
for reward—
the eyes of their children
will fail.

6 "He has made me a byword
of the peoples,

and I am one before whom
people spit.
7 My eye has grown dim from
grief,
and all my members are
like a shadow.
8 The upright are appalled at
this,
and the innocent stir
themselves up against
the godless.
9 Yet the righteous hold to
their way,
and they that have clean
hands grow stronger
and stronger.
10 But you, come back now, all
of you,
and I shall not find a
sensible person among
you.
11 My days are past, my plans
are broken off,
the desires of my heart.
12 They make night into day;
'The light,' they say, 'is
near to the darkness.'[i]
13 If I look for Sheol as my
house,
if I spread my couch in
darkness,
14 if I say to the Pit, 'You are
my father,'
and to the worm, 'My
mother,' or 'My sister,'
15 where then is my hope?
Who will see my hope?
16 Will it go down to the bars of
Sheol?
Shall we descend together
into the dust?"

Bildad Speaks: God Punishes the Wicked

18 Then Bildad the Shuhite
answered:
2 "How long will you hunt for
words?
Consider, and then we
shall speak.
3 Why are we counted as
cattle?
Why are we stupid in your
sight?

16.16
v. 20
16.17
Job 27.4
16.18
Isa 26.21;
Ps 66.18,19
16.19
Rom 1.9
16.20
v. 7;
Lam 2.19
16.21
1 Kings 8.45;
Ps 9.4
16.22
Eccl 12.5
17.1
Ps 88.3,4
17.2
v. 6;
1 Sam 1.6,7
17.3
Ps 119.122;
Prov 6.1
17.4
Job 12.20
17.5
Lev 19.16;
Job 11.20
17.6
Job 30.9,10

17.7
Job 16.16;
16.8
17.8
Job 22.19
17.9
Prov 4.18;
Job 22.30
17.10
Job 12.2
17.11
Job 7.6
17.13
Job 3.13
17.14
Ps 16.10;
Job 21.26;
24.20
17.15
Job 7.6
17.16
Jon 2.6;
Job 3.17-19
18.3
Ps 73.22;
Job 36.14

h Syr Vg Tg: Heb *and* i Meaning of Heb
uncertain

4 You who tear yourself in your
 anger—
 shall the earth be forsaken
 because of you,
 or the rock be removed out
 of its place?

5 "Surely the light of the
 wicked is put out,
 and the flame of their fire
 does not shine.
6 The light is dark in their
 tent,
 and the lamp above them
 is put out.
7 Their strong steps are
 shortened,
 and their own schemes
 throw them down.
8 For they are thrust into a net
 by their own feet,
 and they walk into a pitfall.
9 A trap seizes them by the
 heel;
 a snare lays hold of them.
10 A rope is hid for them in the
 ground,
 a trap for them in the path.
11 Terrors frighten them on
 every side,
 and chase them at their
 heels.
12 Their strength is consumed
 by hunger,ʲ
 and calamity is ready for
 their stumbling.
13 By disease their skin is
 consumed,ᵏ
 the firstborn of Death
 consumes their limbs.
14 They are torn from the tent
 in which they trusted,
 and are brought to the king
 of terrors.
15 In their tents nothing
 remains;
 sulfur is scattered upon
 their habitations.
16 Their roots dry up beneath,
 and their branches wither
 above.
17 Their memory perishes from
 the earth,
 and they have no name in
 the street.
18 They are thrust from light
 into darkness,

and driven out of the
 world.
19 They have no offspring or
 descendant among their
 people,
 and no survivor where they
 used to live.
20 They of the west are
 appalled at their fate,
 and horror seizes those of
 the east.
21 Surely such are the dwellings
 of the ungodly,
 such is the place of those
 who do not know God."

Job Replies: I Know That My Redeemer Lives

19 Then Job answered:
2 "How long will you
 torment me,
 and break me in pieces
 with words?
3 These ten times you have
 cast reproach upon me;
 are you not ashamed to
 wrong me?
4 And even if it is true that I
 have erred,
 my error remains with me.
5 If indeed you magnify
 yourselves against me,
 and make my humiliation
 an argument against
 me,
6 know then that God has put
 me in the wrong,
 and closed his net around
 me.
7 Even when I cry out,
 'Violence!' I am not
 answered;
 I call aloud, but there is no
 justice.
8 He has walled up my way so
 that I cannot pass,
 and he has set darkness
 upon my paths.
9 He has stripped my glory
 from me,
 and taken the crown from
 my head.
10 He breaks me down on every
 side, and I am gone,

18.4
Job 13.14;
14.18
18.5
Prov 13.9;
20.20; 24.20
18.7
Prov 4.12;
Job 5.13
18.8
Job 22.10;
Ps 9.15;
35.8
18.9
Ps 140.5;
Job 5.5
18.10
Ps 69.22
18.11
Job 15.21;
Jer 6.25;
20.3
18.12
Isa 8.21
18.14
Job 8.22;
15.21
18.15
Ps 11.6
18.16
Isa 5.24;
Hos 9.1-16;
Am 2.9;
Mal 4.1;
Job 15.30,
32
18.17
Ps 34.16;
Prov 2.22;
10.7
18.18
Job 5.14;
27.21-23

18.19
Isa 14.22;
Jer 22.30
18.21
Jer 9.3;
1 Thes 4.5
19.4
Job 6.24
19.5
Ps 35.26;
38.16
19.6
Job 27.2;
18.8-10
19.7
Job 30.20
19.8
Job 3.23;
30.26
19.9
Ps 89.44;
89.39
19.10
Job 12.14;
7.6; 24.20

ʲ Or *Disaster is hungry for them* ᵏ Cn: Heb
It consumes the limbs of his skin

he has uprooted my hope
 like a tree.
11 He has kindled his wrath
 against me,
 and counts me as his
 adversary.
12 His troops come on together;
 they have thrown up
 siegeworks¹ against
 me,
 and encamp around my
 tent.
13 "He has put my family far
 from me,
 and my acquaintances are
 wholly estranged from
 me.
14 My relatives and my close
 friends have failed me;
15 the guests in my house
 have forgotten me;
 my serving girls count me as
 a stranger;
 I have become an alien in
 their eyes.
16 I call to my servant, but he
 gives me no answer;
 I must myself plead with
 him.
17 My breath is repulsive to my
 wife;
 I am loathsome to my own
 family.
18 Even young children despise
 me;
 when I rise, they talk
 against me.
19 All my intimate friends
 abhor me,
 and those whom I loved
 have turned against me.
20 My bones cling to my skin
 and to my flesh,
 and I have escaped by the
 skin of my teeth.
21 Have pity on me, have pity
 on me, O you my
 friends,
 for the hand of God has
 touched me!
22 Why do you, like God,
 pursue me,
 never satisfied with my
 flesh?
23 "O that my words were
 written down!

19.11
Job 16:9;
13.24
19.12
Job 30.12
19.14
v. 19
19.15
Gen 14.14;
Eccl 2.7
19.18
2 Kings 2.23
19.19
Ps 38.11;
55.13
19.20
Job 33.21;
Ps 102.5
19.21
Job 6.14;
Ps 38.2
19.22
Job 16.11
19.23
Isa 30.8

19.24
Jer 17.1
19.25
Job 16.19;
Ps 78.35;
Isa 43.14;
Jer 50.34
19.26
Mt 5.8;
1 Cor 13.12;
1 Jn 3.2
19.27
Ps 73.26
19.28
Ps 69.26
19.29
Job 22.4
20.3
Job 19.3
20.4
Deut 4.32
20.5
Ps 37.35;
73.19

O that they were inscribed
 in a book!
24 O that with an iron pen and
 with lead
 they were engraved on a
 rock forever!
25 For I know that my
 Redeemerᵐ lives,
 and that at the last heⁿ
 will stand upon the
 earth;ᵒ
26 and after my skin has been
 thus destroyed,
 then inᵖ my flesh I shall
 see God,�q
27 whom I shall see on my
 side,ʳ
 and my eyes shall behold,
 and not another.
 My heart faints within
 me!
28 If you say, 'How we will
 persecute him!'
 and, 'The root of the
 matter is found in him';
29 be afraid of the sword,
 for wrath brings the
 punishment of the
 sword,
 so that you may know
 there is a judgment."

Zophar Speaks: Wickedness Receives Just Retribution

20 Then Zophar the Naama-
 thite answered:
2 "Pay attention! My thoughts
 urge me to answer,
 because of the agitation
 within me.
3 I hear censure that insults
 me,
 and a spirit beyond my
 understanding answers
 me.
4 Do you not know this from
 of old,
 ever since mortals were
 placed on earth,
5 that the exulting of the
 wicked is short,

¹Cn: Heb *their way* ᵐ Or *Vindicator*
ⁿ Or *that he the Last* ᵒ Heb *dust*
ᵖ Or *without* qMeaning of Heb of this
verse uncertain ʳ Or *for myself*

and the joy of the godless
is but for a moment?

6 Even though they mount up
high as the heavens,
and their head reaches to
the clouds,

7 they will perish forever like
their own dung;
those who have seen them
will say, 'Where are
they?'

8 They will fly away like a
dream, and not be
found;
they will be chased away
like a vision of the
night.

9 The eye that saw them will
see them no more,
nor will their place behold
them any longer.

10 Their children will seek the
favor of the poor,
and their hands will give
back their wealth.

11 Their bodies, once full of
youth,
will lie down in the dust
with them.

12 "Though wickedness is sweet
in their mouth,
though they hide it under
their tongues,

13 though they are loath to let
it go,
and hold it in their
mouths,

14 yet their food is turned in
their stomachs;
it is the venom of asps
within them.

15 They swallow down riches
and vomit them up
again;
God casts them out of their
bellies.

16 They will suck the poison of
asps;
the tongue of a viper will
kill them.

17 They will not look on the
rivers,
the streams flowing with
honey and curds.

18 They will give back the fruit
of their toil,

20.6
Isa 14.13,
14; Ob 3,4
20.7
Job 4.20;
7.10; 8.18
20.8
Ps 73.20;
90.5;
Job 18.18;
27.21-23
20.9
Job 7.8,10
20.10
Job 5.4;
27.16,17
20.11
Job 13.26;
21.26
20.12
Prov 20.17;
Ps 10.7
20.16
Deut 32.24,
33
20.17
Job 29.6;
Deut 32.13,
14
20.18
vv. 10,15

20.19
Job 24.2-4;
35.9
20.20
Eccl 5.13,14
20.21
Job 15.29
20.23
Ps 78.30,31
20.24
Isa 24.18;
Jer 48.43;
Am 5.19
20.25
Job 16.13;
18.11
20.26
Job 18.18;
Ps 21.9
20.27
Deut 31.28
20.28
Deut 28.31;
Job 21.30
20.29
Job 27.13

and will not swallow it
down;
from the profit of their
trading
they will get no enjoyment.

19 For they have crushed and
abandoned the poor,
they have seized a house
that they did not build.

20 "They knew no quiet in their
bellies;
in their greed they let
nothing escape.

21 There was nothing left after
they had eaten;
therefore their prosperity
will not endure.

22 In full sufficiency they will
be in distress;
all the force of misery will
come upon them.

23 To fill their belly to the full
God[s] will send his fierce
anger into them,
and rain it upon them as
their food.[t]

24 They will flee from an iron
weapon;
a bronze arrow will strike
them through.

25 It is drawn forth and comes
out of their body,
and the glittering point
comes out of their gall;
terrors come upon them.

26 Utter darkness is laid up for
their treasures;
a fire fanned by no one will
devour them;
what is left in their tent
will be consumed.

27 The heavens will reveal their
iniquity,
and the earth will rise up
against them.

28 The possessions of their
house will be carried
away,
dragged off in the day of
God's[u] wrath.

29 This is the portion of the
wicked from God,

[s] Heb he [t] Cn: Meaning of Heb uncertain
[u] Heb his

the heritage decreed for
them by God."

Job Replies: The Wicked Often Go Unpunished

21 Then Job answered:
² "Listen carefully to
my words,
and let this be your
consolation.

³ Bear with me, and I will
speak;
then after I have spoken,
mock on.

⁴ As for me, is my complaint
addressed to mortals?
Why should I not be
impatient?

⁵ Look at me, and be appalled,
and lay your hand upon
your mouth.

⁶ When I think of it I am
dismayed,
and shuddering seizes my
flesh.

⁷ Why do the wicked live on,
reach old age, and grow
mighty in power?

⁸ Their children are
established in their
presence,
and their offspring before
their eyes.

⁹ Their houses are safe from
fear,
and no rod of God is upon
them.

¹⁰ Their bull breeds without
fail;
their cow calves and never
miscarries.

¹¹ They send out their little
ones like a flock,
and their children dance
around.

¹² They sing to the tambourine
and the lyre,
and rejoice to the sound of
the pipe.

¹³ They spend their days in
prosperity,
and in peace they go down
to Sheol.

¹⁴ They say to God, 'Leave us
alone!

We do not desire to know
your ways.

¹⁵ What is the Almighty,ᵛ that
we should serve him?
And what profit do we get
if we pray to him?'

¹⁶ Is not their prosperity indeed
their own
achievement?ʷ
The plans of the wicked
are repugnant to me.

¹⁷ "How often is the lamp of
the wicked put out?
How often does calamity
come upon them?
How often does Godˣ
distribute pains in his
anger?

¹⁸ How often are they like
straw before the wind,
and like chaff that the
storm carries away?

¹⁹ You say, 'God stores up their
iniquity for their
children.'
Let it be paid back to
them, so that they may
know it.

²⁰ Let their own eyes see their
destruction,
and let them drink of the
wrath of the Almighty.ᵛ

²¹ For what do they care for
their household after
them,
when the number of their
months is cut off?

²² Will any teach God
knowledge,
seeing that he judges those
that are on high?

²³ One dies in full prosperity,
being wholly at ease and
secure,

²⁴ his loins full of milk
and the marrow of his
bones moist.

²⁵ Another dies in bitterness of
soul,
never having tasted of
good.

²⁶ They lie down alike in the
dust,

21.3
Job 16.10
21.4
Job 6.11
21.5
Judg 18.19;
Job 29.9;
40.4
21.7
Job 12.6;
Ps 73.3,12;
Jer 12.1
21.8
Ps 17.14
21.9
Ps 73.5
21.10
Ex 23.26
21.12
Ps 81.2;
Job 30.31
21.13
Job 36.11
21.14
Job 22.17;
Prov 1.29

21.15
Ex 5.2;
Job 34.9;
Mal 3.14
21.16
Job 22.18
21.17
Job 18.5,6,
12
21.18
Ps 1.4
21.19
Ex 20.5
21.20
Ps 75.8;
Isa 51.17;
Jer 25.15;
Rev 14.10
21.21
Job 14.5
21.22
Isa 40.13,
14;
Rom 11.34
21.26
Eccl 9.2;
Job 24.20

ᵛ Traditional rendering of Heb *Shaddai*
ʷ Heb *in their hand* ˣ Heb *he*

and the worms cover them.

27 "Oh, I know your thoughts,
　　and your schemes to wrong
　　me.

28 For you say, 'Where is the
　　house of the prince?
　　Where is the tent in which
　　the wicked lived?'

29 Have you not asked those
　　who travel the roads,
　　and do you not accept their
　　testimony,

30 that the wicked are spared in
　　the day of calamity,
　　and are rescued in the day
　　of wrath?

31 Who declares their way to
　　their face,
　　and who repays them for
　　what they have done?

32 When they are carried to the
　　grave,
　　a watch is kept over their
　　tomb.

33 The clods of the valley are
　　sweet to them;
　　everyone will follow after,
　　and those who went before
　　are innumerable.

34 How then will you comfort
　　me with empty
　　nothings?
　　There is nothing left of
　　your answers but
　　falsehood."

Eliphaz Speaks: Job's Wickedness Is Great

22 Then Eliphaz the Teman-
ite answered:

2 "Can a mortal be of use to
　　God?
　　Can even the wisest be of
　　service to him?

3 Is it any pleasure to the
　　Almighty[y] if you are
　　righteous,
　　or is it gain to him if you
　　make your ways
　　blameless?

4 Is it for your piety that he
　　reproves you,
　　and enters into judgment
　　with you?

5 Is not your wickedness great?

21.28
Job 12.21;
8.22
21.30
Prov 16.4;
2 Pet 2.9;
Job 20.28;
Rom 2.5
21.33
Job 3.22;
17.16; 3.19;
24.24
21.34
Job 16.2
22.2
Lk 17.10
22.4
Job 14.3;
Ps 143.2
22.5
Job 11.6;
15.5

22.6
Ex 22.26;
Deut 24.6,
17;
Ezek 18.12,
16
22.7
Mt 10.42;
Job 31.31
22.9
Job 24.3;
Isa 10.2
22.11
Job 5.14;
Ps 69.2
22.12
Job 11.7-9
22.13
Ps 10.11
22.14
Job 26.9
22.16
Job 15.32;
14.19;
Mt 7.26,27
22.18
Job 12.6;
21.16

　　There is no end to your
　　iniquities.

6 For you have exacted pledges
　　from your family for no
　　reason,
　　and stripped the naked of
　　their clothing.

7 You have given no water to
　　the weary to drink,
　　and you have withheld
　　bread from the hungry.

8 The powerful possess the
　　land,
　　and the favored live in it.

9 You have sent widows away
　　empty-handed,
　　and the arms of the
　　orphans you have
　　crushed.[z]

10 Therefore snares are around
　　you,
　　and sudden terror
　　overwhelms you,

11 or darkness so that you
　　cannot see;
　　a flood of water covers you.

12 "Is not God high in the
　　heavens?
　　See the highest stars, how
　　lofty they are!

13 Therefore you say, 'What
　　does God know?
　　Can he judge through the
　　deep darkness?

14 Thick clouds enwrap him, so
　　that he does not see,
　　and he walks on the dome
　　of heaven.'

15 Will you keep to the old way
　　that the wicked have trod?

16 They were snatched away
　　before their time;
　　their foundation was
　　washed away by a flood.

17 They said to God, 'Leave us
　　alone,'
　　and 'What can the
　　Almighty[y] do to us?'[a]

18 Yet he filled their houses
　　with good things—
　　but the plans of the wicked
　　are repugnant to me.

y Traditional rendering of Heb Shaddai
z Gk Syr Tg Vg: Heb were crushed
a Gk Syr: Heb them

19 The righteous see it and are
 glad;
 the innocent laugh them to
 scorn,
20 saying, 'Surely our
 adversaries are cut off,
 and what they left, the fire
 has consumed.'
21 "Agree with God,[b] and be at
 peace;
 in this way good will come
 to you.
22 Receive instruction from his
 mouth,
 and lay up his words in
 your heart.
23 If you return to the
 Almighty,[c] you will be
 restored,
 if you remove
 unrighteousness from
 your tents,
24 if you treat gold like dust,
 and gold of Ophir like the
 stones of the
 torrent-bed,
25 and if the Almighty[c] is your
 gold
 and your precious silver,
26 then you will delight yourself
 in the Almighty,[c]
 and lift up your face to
 God.
27 You will pray to him, and he
 will hear you,
 and you will pay your vows.
28 You will decide on a matter,
 and it will be
 established for you,
 and light will shine on your
 ways.
29 When others are humiliated,
 you say it is pride;
 for he saves the humble.
30 He will deliver even those
 who are guilty;
 they will escape because of
 the cleanness of your
 hands."[d]

Job Replies: My Complaint Is Bitter

23 Then Job answered:
 2 "Today also my
 complaint is bitter;[e]

his[f] hand is heavy despite
 my groaning.
3 Oh, that I knew where I
 might find him,
 that I might come even to
 his dwelling!
4 I would lay my case before
 him,
 and fill my mouth with
 arguments.
5 I would learn what he would
 answer me,
 and understand what he
 would say to me.
6 Would he contend with me
 in the greatness of his
 power?
 No; but he would give heed
 to me.
7 There an upright person
 could reason with him,
 and I should be acquitted
 forever by my judge.

8 "If I go forward, he is not
 there;
 or backward, I cannot
 perceive him;
9 on the left he hides, and I
 cannot behold him;
 I turn[g] to the right, but I
 cannot see him.
10 But he knows the way that I
 take;
 when he has tested me, I
 shall come out like
 gold.
11 My foot has held fast to his
 steps;
 I have kept his way and
 have not turned aside.
12 I have not departed from the
 commandment of his
 lips;
 I have treasured in[h] my
 bosom the words of his
 mouth.
13 But he stands alone and who
 can dissuade him?
 What he desires, that he
 does.

22.19
Ps 58.10;
107.42
22.20
Ps 18.39;
Job 15.30
22.21
Jer 9.24;
Gal 4.9
22.22
Ps 138.4
22.23
Job 8.5;
Isa 19.22;
Acts 20.32;
Job 11.14
22.24
Ps 19.10
22.25
Isa 33.6;
Mt 6.20
22.26
Job 27.10;
Isa 58.14
22.27
Job 33.26;
Isa 58.9;
Job 34.28;
Ps 22.25
22.28
Ps 145.19
22.29
Prov 29.23;
Mt 23.12;
1 Pet 5.5
22.30
Job 42.7,8;
2 Sam 22.21
23.2
Job 7.11;
6.2,3

23.3
Deut 4.29;
Ps 9.4
23.4
Job 13.18
23.6
Job 9.4
23.7
Job 13.3,16
23.8
Job 9.11
23.10
Ps 139.1-3
23.11
Ps 44.18
23.12
Jn 4.32,34
23.13
Job 9.12;
12.14;
Ps 115.3

b Heb *him* c Traditional rendering of Heb
Shaddai d Meaning of Heb uncertain
e Syr Vg Tg: Heb *rebellious* f Gk Syr: Heb
my g Syr Vg: Heb *he turns* h Gk Vg: Heb
from

14 For he will complete what he
 appoints for me;
 and many such things are
 in his mind.
15 Therefore I am terrified at
 his presence;
 when I consider, I am in
 dread of him.
16 God has made my heart
 faint;
 the Almighty[i] has terrified
 me;
17 If only I could vanish in
 darkness,
 and thick darkness would
 cover my face![j]

Job Complains of Violence on the Earth

24 "Why are times not kept
 by the Almighty,[i]
 and why do those who
 know him never see his
 days?
2 The wicked[k] remove
 landmarks;
 they seize flocks and
 pasture them.
3 They drive away the donkey
 of the orphan;
 they take the widow's ox
 for a pledge.
4 They thrust the needy off the
 road;
 the poor of the earth all
 hide themselves.
5 Like wild asses in the desert
 they go out to their toil,
 scavenging in the wasteland
 food for their young.
6 They reap in a field not their
 own
 and they glean in the
 vineyard of the wicked.
7 They lie all night naked,
 without clothing,
 and have no covering in
 the cold.
8 They are wet with the rain of
 the mountains,
 and cling to the rock for
 want of shelter.

9 There are those who snatch
 the orphan child from
 the breast,

23.14
1 Thes 3.3
23.16
Ps 22.14;
Jer 51.46
23.17
Job 10.18,
19; 19.8
24.1
Ps 31.15;
Jer 46.10
24.2
Deut 19.14;
27.17; 28.31
24.3
Ex 22.26;
Deut 24.6,
10,12,17;
Job 22.6
24.4
Deut 24.14;
Prov 28.28
24.5
Job 39.5-8;
Ps 104.23
24.7
Ex 22.26;
Job 22.6
24.8
Lam 4.5
24.9
Deut 24.17

24.12
Jer 51.52;
Ezek 26.15;
Job 9.23,24
24.13
Isa 5.20;
Jn 3.19
24.14
Mic 2.1;
Ps 10.8
24.15
Prov 7.9;
Ps 10.11
24.16
Ex 22.2
24.17
Ps 91.5
24.18
Job 9.26;
Ps 90.5
24.19
Job 6.16,17;
21.13

and take as a pledge the
 infant of the poor.
10 They go about naked,
 without clothing;
 though hungry, they carry
 the sheaves;
11 between their terraces[l] they
 press out oil;
 they tread the wine
 presses, but suffer
 thirst.
12 From the city the dying
 groan,
 and the throat of the
 wounded cries for help;
 yet God pays no attention
 to their prayer.

13 "There are those who rebel
 against the light,
 who are not acquainted
 with its ways,
 and do not stay in its
 paths.
14 The murderer rises at dusk
 to kill the poor and needy,
 and in the night is like a
 thief.
15 The eye of the adulterer also
 waits for the twilight,
 saying, 'No eye will see
 me';
 and he disguises his face.
16 In the dark they dig through
 houses;
 by day they shut
 themselves up;
 they do not know the light.
17 For deep darkness is
 morning to all of them;
 for they are friends with
 the terrors of deep
 darkness.

18 "Swift are they on the face of
 the waters;
 their portion in the land is
 cursed;
 no treader turns toward
 their vineyards.
19 Drought and heat snatch
 away the snow waters;

[i] Traditional rendering of Heb *Shaddai*
[j] Or *But I am not destroyed by the darkness;
he has concealed the thick darkness from me*
[k] Gk: Heb *they* [l] Meaning of Heb uncertain

so does Sheol those who
have sinned.

20 The womb forgets them;
the worm finds them
sweet;
they are no longer
remembered;
so wickedness is broken
like a tree.

21 "They harm^m the childless
woman,
and do no good to the
widow.

22 Yet God^n prolongs the life of
the mighty by his
power;
they rise up when they
despair of life.

23 He gives them security, and
they are supported;
his eyes are upon their
ways.

24 They are exalted a little
while, and then are
gone;
they wither and fade like
the mallow;^o
they are cut off like the
heads of grain.

25 If it is not so, who will prove
me a liar,
and show that there is
nothing in what I say?"

Bildad Speaks: How Can a Mortal Be Righteous Before God?

25 Then Bildad the Shuhite
answered:

2 "Dominion and fear are with
God;^p
he makes peace in his high
heaven.

3 Is there any number to his
armies?
Upon whom does his light
not arise?

4 How then can a mortal be
righteous before God?
How can one born of
woman be pure?

5 If even the moon is not
bright
and the stars are not pure
in his sight,

6 how much less a mortal, who
is a maggot,
and a human being, who is
a worm!"

Job Replies: God's Majesty Is Unsearchable

26 Then Job answered:

2 "How you have helped
one who has no power!
How you have assisted the
arm that has no
strength!

3 How you have counseled one
who has no wisdom,
and given much good
advice!

4 With whose help have you
uttered words,
and whose spirit has come
forth from you?

5 The shades below tremble,
the waters and their
inhabitants.

6 Sheol is naked before God,
and Abaddon has no
covering.

7 He stretches out Zaphon^q
over the void,
and hangs the earth upon
nothing.

8 He binds up the waters in
his thick clouds,
and the cloud is not torn
open by them.

9 He covers the face of the full
moon,
and spreads over it his
cloud.

10 He has described a circle on
the face of the waters,
at the boundary between
light and darkness.

11 The pillars of heaven
tremble,
and are astounded at his
rebuke.

12 By his power he stilled the
Sea;
by his understanding he
struck down Rahab.

13 By his wind the heavens
were made fair;

24.20
Ps 31.12;
Prov 10.7
24.21
Job 22.9
24.22
Deut 28.66
24.23
Job 12.6;
11.11
24.24
Ps 37.10;
Job 14.21;
Isa 17.5
24.25
Job 6.28;
27.4
25.2
Job 9.4;
Rev 1.6;
Job 22.12
25.3
Jas 1.17
25.4
Job 4.17;
Ps 143.2;
Job 14.4
25.5
Job 31.26;
15.15

25.6
Job 7.17;
Ps 22.6
26.2
Ps 71.9
26.6
Ps 139.8,11;
Heb 4.13
26.7
Job 9.8
26.8
Prov 30.4
26.9
Ps 97.2
26.10
Job 38.8-11;
Prov 8.29;
Job 38.19,
20,24
26.12
Ex 14.21;
Isa 51.15;
Jer 31.35
26.13
Job 9.8;
Isa 27.1

^m Gk Tg: Heb *feed on* or *associate with*　^n Heb *he*　^o Gk: Heb *like all others*
^p Heb *him*　^q Or *the North*

his hand pierced the
fleeing serpent.
14 These are indeed but the
outskirts of his ways;
and how small a whisper
do we hear of him!
But the thunder of his
power who can
understand?"

Job Maintains His Integrity

27 Job again took up his
discourse and said:
2 "As God lives, who has taken
away my right,
and the Almighty,ʳ who
has made my soul
bitter,
3 as long as my breath is in
me
and the spirit of God is in
my nostrils,
4 my lips will not speak
falsehood,
and my tongue will not
utter deceit.
5 Far be it from me to say that
you are right;
until I die I will not put
away my integrity from
me.
6 I hold fast my righteousness,
and will not let it go;
my heart does not reproach
me for any of my days.

7 "May my enemy be like the
wicked,
and may my opponent be
like the unrighteous.
8 For what is the hope of the
godless when God cuts
them off,
when God takes away their
lives?
9 Will God hear their cry
when trouble comes upon
them?
10 Will they take delight in the
Almighty?ʳ
Will they call upon God at
all times?
11 I will teach you concerning
the hand of God;

26.14
Job 36.29
27.1
Job 13.12;
29.1
27.2
Job 34.5;
9.18
27.3
Job 32.8;
33.4
27.4
Job 6.28
27.5
Job 2.9;
13.15
27.6
Job 2.3;
13.18;
Acts 23.1
27.8
Job 8.13;
11.20
27.9
Job 35.12;
Prov 1.28;
Isa 1.15;
Jer 14.12;
Mic 3.4
27.10
Job 22.26,
27

27.13
Job 20.29;
15.20
27.14
Deut 28.41;
Hos 9.13;
Job 20.10
27.15
Ps 78.64
27.16
Zech 9.3
27.17
Prov 28.8;
Eccl 2.26
27.19
Ezek 29.5;
Job 7.8,21
27.20
Job 15.21;
20.8
27.21
Job 21.18;
7.10
27.22
Jer 13.14;
Ezek 5.11;
Job 11.20
27.23
Lam 2.15;
Job 18.18

that which is with the
Almightyʳ I will not
conceal.
12 All of you have seen it
yourselves;
why then have you become
altogether vain?
13 "This is the portion of the
wicked with God,
and the heritage that
oppressors receive from
the Almighty:ʳ
14 If their children are
multiplied, it is for the
sword;
and their offspring have not
enough to eat.
15 Those who survive them the
pestilence buries,
and their widows make no
lamentation.
16 Though they heap up silver
like dust,
and pile up clothing like
clay—
17 they may pile it up, but the
just will wear it,
and the innocent will
divide the silver.
18 They build their houses like
nests,
like booths made by
sentinels of the
vineyard.
19 They go to bed with wealth,
but will do so no more;
they open their eyes, and it
is gone.
20 Terrors overtake them like a
flood;
in the night a whirlwind
carries them off.
21 The east wind lifts them up
and they are gone;
it sweeps them out of their
place.
22 Itˢ hurls at them without
pity;
they flee from itsᵗ power
in headlong flight.
23 Itˢ claps itsᵗ hands at them,
and hisses at them from
itsᵗ place.

ʳTraditional rendering of Heb *Shaddai*
ˢOr *He* (that is God)　ᵗOr *his*

Interlude: Where Wisdom Is Found

28 "Surely there is a mine for silver,
and a place for gold to be refined.
2 Iron is taken out of the earth,
and copper is smelted from ore.
3 Miners put[u] an end to darkness,
and search out to the farthest bound
the ore in gloom and deep darkness.
4 They open shafts in a valley away from human habitation;
they are forgotten by travelers,
they sway suspended, remote from people.
5 As for the earth, out of it comes bread;
but underneath it is turned up as by fire.
6 Its stones are the place of sapphires,[v]
and its dust contains gold.

7 "That path no bird of prey knows,
and the falcon's eye has not seen it.
8 The proud wild animals have not trodden it;
the lion has not passed over it.
9 "They put their hand to the flinty rock,
and overturn mountains by the roots.
10 They cut out channels in the rocks,
and their eyes see every precious thing.
11 The sources of the rivers they probe;[w]
hidden things they bring to light.

12 "But where shall wisdom be found?

And where is the place of understanding?
13 Mortals do not know the way to it,[x]
and it is not found in the land of the living.
14 The deep says, 'It is not in me,'
and the sea says, 'It is not with me.'
15 It cannot be gotten for gold,
and silver cannot be weighed out as its price.
16 It cannot be valued in the gold of Ophir,
in precious onyx or sapphire.[v]
17 Gold and glass cannot equal it,
nor can it be exchanged for jewels of fine gold.
18 No mention shall be made of coral or of crystal;
the price of wisdom is above pearls.
19 The chrysolite of Ethiopia[y] cannot compare with it,
nor can it be valued in pure gold.

20 "Where then does wisdom come from?
And where is the place of understanding?
21 It is hidden from the eyes of all living,
and concealed from the birds of the air.
22 Abaddon and Death say,
'We have heard a rumor of it with our ears.'

23 "God understands the way to it,
and he knows its place.
24 For he looks to the ends of the earth,
and sees everything under the heavens.
25 When he gave to the wind its weight,
and apportioned out the waters by measure;

28.2
Deut 8.9
28.5
Ps 104.14
28.9
Deut 8.15;
32.13
28.12
vv. 23,28

28.13
Prov 3.15
28.17
Prov 8.10;
16.16
28.18
Prov 3.15;
8.11
28.19
Prov 8.19
28.20
vv. 23,28
28.22
Job 26.6
28.23
vv. 23-28
28.24
Ps 33.13;
Prov 15.3
28.25
Ps 135.7;
Job 12.15

u Heb *He puts* v Or *lapis lazuli*
w Gk Vg: Heb *bind* x Gk: Heb *its price*
y Or *Nubia*; Heb *Cush*

26 when he made a decree for
 the rain,
 and a way for the
 thunderbolt;
27 then he saw it and declared
 it;
 he established it, and
 searched it out.
28 And he said to humankind,
 'Truly, the fear of the Lord,
 that is wisdom;
 and to depart from evil is
 understanding.' "

Job Finishes His Defense

29 Job again took up his
 discourse and said:
2 "Oh, that I were as in the
 months of old,
 as in the days when God
 watched over me;
3 when his lamp shone over
 my head,
 and by his light I walked
 through darkness;
4 when I was in my prime,
 when the friendship of God
 was upon my tent;
5 when the Almighty[z] was still
 with me,
 when my children were
 around me;
6 when my steps were washed
 with milk,
 and the rock poured out for
 me streams of oil!
7 When I went out to the gate
 of the city,
 when I took my seat in the
 square,
8 the young men saw me and
 withdrew,
 and the aged rose up and
 stood;
9 the nobles refrained from
 talking,
 and laid their hands on
 their mouths;
10 the voices of princes were
 hushed,
 and their tongues stuck to
 the roof of their
 mouths.
11 When the ear heard, it
 commended me,

and when the eye saw, it
 approved;
12 because I delivered the poor
 who cried,
 and the orphan who had no
 helper.
13 The blessing of the wretched
 came upon me,
 and I caused the widow's
 heart to sing for joy.
14 I put on righteousness, and
 it clothed me;
 my justice was like a robe
 and a turban.
15 I was eyes to the blind,
 and feet to the lame.
16 I was a father to the needy,
 and I championed the
 cause of the stranger.
17 I broke the fangs of the
 unrighteous,
 and made them drop their
 prey from their teeth.
18 Then I thought, 'I shall die
 in my nest,
 and I shall multiply my
 days like the phoenix;[a]
19 my roots spread out to the
 waters,
 with the dew all night on
 my branches;
20 my glory was fresh with me,
 and my bow ever new in
 my hand.'
21 "They listened to me, and
 waited,
 and kept silence for my
 counsel.
22 After I spoke they did not
 speak again,
 and my word dropped upon
 them like dew.[b]
23 They waited for me as for
 the rain;
 they opened their mouths
 as for the spring rain.
24 I smiled on them when they
 had no confidence;
 and the light of my
 countenance they did
 not extinguish.[c]
25 I chose their way, and sat as
 chief,

28.26
Job 37.6,11,
12; 37.3;
38.25
28.28
Deut 4.6;
Ps 111.10;
Prov 1.7;
9.10
29.1
Job 13.12;
27.1
29.2
Jer 31.28
29.3
Job 11.17
29.4
Ps 25.14
29.6
Job 20.17;
Deut 32.13,
14
29.9
v. 21;
Job 21.5
29.10
v. 22

29.12
Job 31.16,
17,21
29.13
Job 31.19,
20
29.14
Ps 132.9;
Isa 59.17;
61.10;
Eph 6.14
29.16
Prov 29.7
29.17
Ps 3.7
29.18
Ps 30.6
29.19
Job 18.16;
Jer 17.8
29.20
Gen 49.24;
Ps 18.34
29.21
v. 9
29.22
v. 10;
Job 32.2
29.25
Job 1.3;
31.37; 4.4

z Traditional rendering of Heb *Shaddai*
a Or *like sand* b Heb lacks *like dew*
c Meaning of Heb uncertain

and I lived like a king
 among his troops,
like one who comforts
 mourners.

30

"But now they make
 sport of me,
those who are younger than
 I,
whose fathers I would have
 disdained
to set with the dogs of my
 flock.
2 What could I gain from the
 strength of their hands?
 All their vigor is gone.
3 Through want and hard
 hunger
 they gnaw the dry and
 desolate ground,
4 they pick mallow and the
 leaves of bushes,
 and to warm themselves
 the roots of broom.
5 They are driven out from
 society;
 people shout after them as
 after a thief.
6 In the gullies of wadis they
 must live,
 in holes in the ground, and
 in the rocks.
7 Among the bushes they bray;
 under the nettles they
 huddle together.
8 A senseless, disreputable
 brood,
 they have been whipped
 out of the land.

9 "And now they mock me in
 song;
 I am a byword to them.
10 They abhor me, they keep
 aloof from me;
 they do not hesitate to spit
 at the sight of me.
11 Because God has loosed my
 bowstring and humbled
 me,
 they have cast off restraint
 in my presence.
12 On my right hand the rabble
 rise up;
 they send me sprawling,
 and build roads for my
 ruin.

30.1
Job 12.4
30.9
Job 12.4;
17.6
30.10
Num 12.14;
Deut 25.9;
Isa 50.6;
Mt 26.67
30.11
Ruth 1.21;
Ps 88.7
30.12
Ps 140.4,5;
Job 19.12

30.15
Job 3.25;
31.23;
Hos 13.3
30.16
Ps 22.14;
42.4
30.17
v. 30
30.19
Ps 69.2,14
30.20
Ps 19.7
30.21
Job 10.3;
16.9,14; 19.6,
22
30.22
Job 9.17;
27.21
30.23
Job 9.22;
10.8; 3.19;
17.13
30.24
Job 19.7
30.25
Ps 35.13,14;
Rom 12.15

13 They break up my path,
 they promote my calamity;
 no one restrains[d] them.
14 As through a wide breach
 they come;
 amid the crash they roll
 on.
15 Terrors are turned upon me;
 my honor is pursued as by
 the wind,
 and my prosperity has
 passed away like a
 cloud.

16 "And now my soul is poured
 out within me;
 days of affliction have
 taken hold of me.
17 The night racks my bones,
 and the pain that gnaws
 me takes no rest.
18 With violence he seizes my
 garment;[e]
 he grasps me by[f] the
 collar of my tunic.
19 He has cast me into the
 mire,
 and I have become like
 dust and ashes.
20 I cry to you and you do not
 answer me;
 I stand, and you merely
 look at me.
21 You have turned cruel to me;
 with the might of your
 hand you persecute me.
22 You lift me up on the wind,
 you make me ride on it,
 and you toss me about in
 the roar of the storm.
23 I know that you will bring
 me to death,
 and to the house appointed
 for all living.

24 "Surely one does not turn
 against the needy,[g]
 when in disaster they cry
 for help.[h]
25 Did I not weep for those
 whose day was hard?
 Was not my soul grieved
 for the poor?

d Cn: Heb *helps* e Gk: Heb *my garment is
disfigured* f Heb *like* g Heb *ruin*
h Cn: Meaning of Heb uncertain

26 But when I looked for good,
 evil came;
 and when I waited for light,
 darkness came.
27 My inward parts are in
 turmoil, and are never
 still;
 days of affliction come to
 meet me.
28 I go about in sunless gloom;
 I stand up in the assembly
 and cry for help.
29 I am a brother of jackals,
 and a companion of
 ostriches.
30 My skin turns black and falls
 from me,
 and my bones burn with
 heat.
31 My lyre is turned to
 mourning,
 and my pipe to the voice of
 those who weep.

31 "I have made a covenant
 with my eyes;
 how then could I look
 upon a virgin?
2 What would be my portion
 from God above,
 and my heritage from the
 Almighty[i] on high?
3 Does not calamity befall the
 unrighteous,
 and disaster the workers of
 iniquity?
4 Does he not see my ways,
 and number all my steps?

5 "If I have walked with
 falsehood,
 and my foot has hurried to
 deceit—
6 let me be weighed in a just
 balance,
 and let God know my
 integrity!—
7 if my step has turned aside
 from the way,
 and my heart has followed
 my eyes,
 and if any spot has clung
 to my hands;
8 then let me sow, and another
 eat,
 and let what grows for me
 be rooted out.

9 "If my heart has been
 enticed by a woman,
 and I have lain in wait at
 my neighbor's door;
10 then let my wife grind for
 another,
 and let other men kneel
 over her.
11 For that would be a heinous
 crime;
 that would be a criminal
 offense;
12 for that would be a fire
 consuming down to
 Abaddon,
 and it would burn to the
 root all my harvest.

13 "If I have rejected the cause
 of my male or female
 slaves,
 when they brought a
 complaint against me;
14 what then shall I do when
 God rises up?
 When he makes inquiry,
 what shall I answer
 him?
15 Did not he who made me in
 the womb make them?
 And did not one fashion us
 in the womb?

16 "If I have withheld anything
 that the poor desired,
 or have caused the eyes of
 the widow to fail,
17 or have eaten my morsel
 alone,
 and the orphan has not
 eaten from it—
18 for from my youth I reared
 the orphan[j] like a
 father,
 and from my mother's
 womb I guided the
 widow[k]—
19 if I have seen anyone perish
 for lack of clothing,
 or a poor person without
 covering,
20 whose loins have not blessed
 me,

[i] Traditional rendering of Heb Shaddai
[j] Heb him [k] Heb her

30.26 Job 3.25,26; Jer 8.15; Job 19.8 30.28 Ps 38.6; 42.9; 43.2; Job 19.7 30.29 Mic 1.8 30.30 Ps 119.83; Lam 4.8; Ps 102.3 30.31 Ps 107.1,2 31.1 Mt 5.28 31.2 Job 20.29 31.3 Job 21.30; 34.22 31.4 2 Chr 16.9; Prov 5.21 31.5 Mic 2.11 31.6 Job 6.2,3; 27.5,6 31.7 Job 23.11; 9.30 31.8 Lev 26.16; Job 20.18 31.9 Job 24.15 31.10 Jer 8.10 31.11 Gen 38.24; Deut 22.22-24 31.12 Job 15.30; 26.6; 20.28 31.13 Deut 24.14,15 31.15 Mal 2.10 31.16 Job 20.19; 22.7,9 31.17 Job 22.7; 29.12 31.19 Job 22.6; 29.13 31.20 Deut 31.20

and who was not warmed
with the fleece of my
sheep;

21 if I have raised my hand
against the orphan,
because I saw I had
supporters at the gate;

22 then let my shoulder blade
fall from my shoulder,
and let my arm be broken
from its socket.

23 For I was in terror of
calamity from God,
and I could not have faced
his majesty.

24 "If I have made gold my
trust,
or called fine gold my
confidence;

25 if I have rejoiced because my
wealth was great,
or because my hand had
gotten much;

26 if I have looked at the sun¹
when it shone,
or the moon moving in
splendor,

27 and my heart has been
secretly enticed,
and my mouth has kissed
my hand;

28 this also would be an
iniquity to be punished
by the judges,
for I should have been false
to God above.

29 "If I have rejoiced at the ruin
of those who hated me,
or exulted when evil
overtook them—

30 I have not let my mouth sin
by asking for their lives
with a curse—

31 if those of my tent ever said,
'O that we might be sated
with his flesh!'ᵐ—

32 the stranger has not lodged
in the street;
I have opened my doors to
the traveler—

33 if I have concealed my
transgressions as others
do,ⁿ
by hiding my iniquity in my
bosom,

34 because I stood in great fear
of the multitude,
and the contempt of
families terrified me,
so that I kept silence, and
did not go out of
doors—

35 Oh, that I had one to hear
me!
(Here is my signature! let
the Almightyᵒ answer
me!)
Oh, that I had the
indictment written by
my adversary!

36 Surely I would carry it on my
shoulder;
I would bind it on me like
a crown;

37 I would give him an account
of all my steps;
like a prince I would
approach him.

38 "If my land has cried out
against me,
and its furrows have wept
together;

39 if I have eaten its yield
without payment,
and caused the death of its
owners;

40 let thorns grow instead of
wheat,
and foul weeds instead of
barley."

The words of Job are ended.

Elihu Rebukes Job's Friends

32 So these three men ceased
to answer Job, because he
was righteous in his own eyes.
² Then Elihu son of Barachel the
Buzite, of the family of Ram, be-
came angry. He was angry at Job
because he justified himself rather
than God; ³ he was angry also at
Job's three friends because they
had found no answer, though they
had declared Job to be in the
wrong.ᵖ ⁴ Now Elihu had waited to

Cross references (center column):

31.21 Job 22.9
31.22 Job 38.15
31.23 v. 3; Job 13.11
31.24 Mk 10.24
31.25 Ps 62.10
31.26 Deut 4.19; Ezek 8.16
31.28 v. 11
31.29 Prov 17.5
31.30 Mt 5.44
31.31 Job 22.7
31.32 Gen 19.2,3; Rom 12.13
31.33 Gen 3.8; Prov 28.13
31.34 Ex 23.2
31.35 Job 19.7; 30.20,24,28; 35.14
31.37 v. 4; Job 1.3; 29.25
31.38 Gen 4.10,11
31.39 Lev 19.13; 1 Kings 21.19; Jas 5.4
31.40 Gen 3.18
32.1 Job 33.9
32.2 Gen 22.21; Jer 25.23
32.3 Job 11.6; 15.16; 22.5

¹ Heb *the light* ᵐ Meaning of Heb
uncertain ⁿ Or *as Adam did*
ᵒ Traditional rendering of Heb *Shaddai*
ᵖ Another ancient tradition reads *answer, and
had put God in the wrong*

speak to Job, because they were older than he. 5 But when Elihu saw that there was no answer in the mouths of these three men, he became angry.

6 Elihu son of Barachel the Buzite answered:

"I am young in years,
and you are aged;
therefore I was timid and afraid
to declare my opinion to you.
7 I said, 'Let days speak,
and many years teach wisdom.'
8 But truly it is the spirit in a mortal,
the breath of the Almighty,q that makes for understanding.
9 It is not the oldr that are wise,
nor the aged that understand what is right.
10 Therefore I say, 'Listen to me;
let me also declare my opinion.'

11 "See, I waited for your words,
I listened for your wise sayings,
while you searched out what to say.
12 I gave you my attention,
but there was in fact no one that confuted Job,
no one among you that answered his words.
13 Yet do not say, 'We have found wisdom;
God may vanquish him, not a human.'
14 He has not directed his words against me,
and I will not answer him with your speeches.

15 "They are dismayed, they answer no more;
they have not a word to say.
16 And am I to wait, because they do not speak,

because they stand there,
and answer no more?
17 I also will give my answer;
I also will declare my opinion.
18 For I am full of words;
the spirit within me constrains me.
19 My heart is indeed like wine that has no vent;
like new wineskins, it is ready to burst.
20 I must speak, so that I may find relief;
I must open my lips and answer.
21 I will not show partiality to any person
or use flattery toward anyone.
22 For I do not know how to flatter—
or my Maker would soon put an end to me!

Elihu Rebukes Job

33 "But now, hear my speech, O Job,
and listen to all my words.
2 See, I open my mouth;
the tongue in my mouth speaks.
3 My words declare the uprightness of my heart,
and what my lips know they speak sincerely.
4 The spirit of God has made me,
and the breath of the Almightyq gives me life.
5 Answer me, if you can;
set your words in order before me; take your stand.
6 See, before God I am as you are;
I too was formed from a piece of clay.
7 No fear of me need terrify you;
my pressure will not be heavy on you.

q Traditional rendering of Heb *Shaddai*
r Gk Syr Vg: Heb *many*

32.6
Job 15.10
32.8
Job 27.3;
33.4;
1 Kings 3.12;
Prov 2.6
32.9
1 Cor 1.26
32.11
Job 5.27
32.13
Jer 9.23

32.18
Acts 18.5
32.19
Acts 9.17
32.21
Lev 19.15;
Mt 22.16
32.22
1 Thes 2.5
33.3
Job 6.28;
27.4; 36.4
33.4
Gen 2.7;
Job 27.3
33.5
v. 32;
Job 13.18
33.7
Job 9.34;
13.21;
2 Cor 2.5

8 "Surely, you have spoken in
my hearing,
and I have heard the sound
of your words.
9 You say, 'I am clean, without
transgression;
I am pure, and there is no
iniquity in me.
10 Look, he finds occasions
against me,
he counts me as his
enemy;
11 he puts my feet in the
stocks,
and watches all my paths.'

12 "But in this you are not
right. I will answer you:
God is greater than any
mortal.
13 Why do you contend against
him,
saying, 'He will answer
none of my ˢ words'?
14 For God speaks in one way,
and in two, though people
do not perceive it.
15 In a dream, in a vision of the
night,
when deep sleep falls on
mortals,
while they slumber on their
beds,
16 then he opens their ears,
and terrifies them with
warnings,
17 that he may turn them aside
from their deeds,
and keep them from pride,
18 to spare their souls from the
Pit,
their lives from traversing
the River.
19 They are also chastened with
pain upon their beds,
and with continual strife in
their bones,
20 so that their lives loathe
bread,
and their appetites dainty
food.
21 Their flesh is so wasted away
that it cannot be seen;
and their bones, once
invisible, now stick out.
22 Their souls draw near the
Pit,

and their lives to those
who bring death.
23 Then, if there should be for
one of them an angel,
a mediator, one of a
thousand,
one who declares a person
upright,
24 and he is gracious to that
person, and says,
'Deliver him from going
down into the Pit;
I have found a ransom;
25 let his flesh become fresh
with youth;
let him return to the days
of his youthful vigor.'
26 Then he prays to God, and is
accepted by him,
he comes into his presence
with joy,
and God ᵗ repays him for his
righteousness.
27 That person sings to others
and says,
'I sinned, and perverted what
was right,
and it was not paid back to
me.
28 He has redeemed my soul
from going down to the
Pit,
and my life shall see the
light.'

29 "God indeed does all these
things,
twice, three times, with
mortals,
30 to bring back their souls
from the Pit,
so that they may see the
light of life. ᵘ
31 Pay heed, Job, listen to me;
be silent, and I will speak.
32 If you have anything to say,
answer me;
speak, for I desire to justify
you.
33 If not, listen to me;
be silent, and I will teach
you wisdom."

33.9
Job 10.7;
13.23; 16.17
33.10
Job 13.24
33.11
Job 13.27;
14.16
33.13
Job 15.25;
Isa 45.9
33.14
Ps 62.11
33.15
Num 12.6;
Job 4.13
33.16
Job 36.10,
15
33.18
vv. 24,28,30
33.19
Job 30.17
33.20
Ps 107.18
33.21
Job 16.8;
19.20
33.22
Ps 88.3

33.23
Mic 6.8
33.24
Isa 38.17
33.25
2 Kings 5.14
33.26
Job 22.27;
34.28; 22.26;
Ps 51.12
33.27
Lk 15.21;
Rom 6.21
33.28
Ps 103.14;
Job 22.28
33.29
Eph 1.11;
1 Cor 12.6;
Phil 2.13
33.30
Ps 56.13
33.33
Ps 34.11

ˢ Compare Gk: Heb *his* ᵗ Heb *he*
ᵘ Syr: Heb *to be lighted with the light of life*

Elihu Proclaims God's Justice

34 Then Elihu continued and said:

2 "Hear my words, you wise men,
 and give ear to me, you who know;
3 for the ear tests words
 as the palate tastes food.
4 Let us choose what is right;
 let us determine among ourselves what is good.
5 For Job has said, 'I am innocent,
 and God has taken away my right;
6 in spite of being right I am counted a liar;
 my wound is incurable, though I am without transgression.'
7 Who is there like Job,
 who drinks up scoffing like water,
8 who goes in company with evildoers
 and walks with the wicked?
9 For he has said, 'It profits one nothing
 to take delight in God.'

10 "Therefore, hear me, you who have sense,
 far be it from God that he should do wickedness,
 and from the Almighty[v] that he should do wrong.
11 For according to their deeds he will repay them,
 and according to their ways he will make it befall them.
12 Of a truth, God will not do wickedly,
 and the Almighty[v] will not pervert justice.
13 Who gave him charge over the earth
 and who laid on him[w] the whole world?
14 If he should take back his spirit[x] to himself,
 and gather to himself his breath,
15 all flesh would perish together,
 and all mortals return to dust.

16 "If you have understanding, hear this;
 listen to what I say.
17 Shall one who hates justice govern?
 Will you condemn one who is righteous and mighty,
18 who says to a king, 'You scoundrel!'
 and to princes, 'You wicked men!';
19 who shows no partiality to nobles,
 nor regards the rich more than the poor,
 for they are all the work of his hands?
20 In a moment they die;
 at midnight the people are shaken and pass away,
 and the mighty are taken away by no human hand.

21 "For his eyes are upon the ways of mortals,
 and he sees all their steps.
22 There is no gloom of deep darkness
 where evildoers may hide themselves.
23 For he has not appointed a time[y] for anyone
 to go before God in judgment.
24 He shatters the mighty without investigation,
 and sets others in their place.
25 Thus, knowing their works,
 he overturns them in the night, and they are crushed.
26 He strikes them for their wickedness
 while others look on,
27 because they turned aside from following him,

Cross references

34.3 Job 12.11
34.4 1 Thes 5.21
34.5 Job 33.9; 27.2
34.6 Jer 15.18; 30.12
34.7 Job 15.16
34.8 Ps 50.18
34.9 Job 21.15; 35.3
34.10 Job 8.3
34.11 Ps 62.12; Mt 16.27; Rom 2.6; 2 Cor 5.10; Rev 22.12
34.12 Job 8.3
34.13 Job 38.5,6
34.14 Ps 104.29
34.15 Isa 40.6,7; Gen 3.19
34.17 2 Sam 23.3
34.18 Ex 22.28
34.19 Deut 10.17; Gal 2.6; Job 31.15
34.20 Ex 12.29; Job 12.19
34.21 Job 31.4
34.22 Ps 139.12; Am 9.2,3
34.24 Dan 2.21
34.25 vv. 11,20
34.26 Job 26.12
34.27 1 Sam 15.11; Ps 28.5; Isa 5.12

v Traditional rendering of Heb Shaddai w Heb lacks on him x Heb his heart his spirit y Cn: Heb yet

and had no regard for any
of his ways,

28 so that they caused the cry
of the poor to come to
him,
and he heard the cry of the
afflicted—

29 When he is quiet, who can
condemn?
When he hides his face,
who can behold him,
whether it be a nation or
an individual?—

30 so that the godless should
not reign,
or those who ensnare the
people.

31 "For has anyone said to God,
'I have endured
punishment; I will not
offend any more;

32 teach me what I do not see;
if I have done iniquity, I
will do it no more'?

33 Will he then pay back to suit
you,
because you reject it?
For you must choose, and
not I;
therefore declare what you
know.ᶻ

34 Those who have sense will
say to me,
and the wise who hear me
will say,

35 'Job speaks without
knowledge,
his words are without
insight.'

36 Would that Job were tried to
the limit,
because his answers are
those of the wicked.

37 For he adds rebellion to his
sin;
he claps his hands among
us,
and multiplies his words
against God."

Elihu Condemns Self-Righteousness

35 Elihu continued and said:
2 "Do you think this to
be just?

You say, 'I am in the right
before God.'

3 If you ask, 'What advantage
have I?
How am I better off than if
I had sinned?'

4 I will answer you
and your friends with you.

5 Look at the heavens and see;
observe the clouds, which
are higher than you.

6 If you have sinned, what do
you accomplish against
him?
And if your transgressions
are multiplied, what do
you do to him?

7 If you are righteous, what do
you give to him;
or what does he receive
from your hand?

8 Your wickedness affects
others like you,
and your righteousness,
other human beings.

9 "Because of the multitude of
oppressions people cry
out;
they call for help because
of the arm of the
mighty.

10 But no one says, 'Where is
God my Maker,
who gives strength in the
night,

11 who teaches us more than
the animals of the
earth,
and makes us wiser than
the birds of the air?'

12 There they cry out, but he
does not answer,
because of the pride of
evildoers.

13 Surely God does not hear an
empty cry,
nor does the Almightyᵃ
regard it.

14 How much less when you say
that you do not see
him,

34.28
Job 35.9;
Jas 5.4;
Ex 22.23
34.29
1 Chr 22.9
34.30
v. 17
34.32
Job 35.11;
Ps 25.4
34.35
Job 35.16
34.36
Job 23.10;
22.15
35.2
Job 32.2

35.3
Job 34.9;
9.30,31
35.5
Job 22.12
35.6
Prov 8.36;
Jer 7.19
35.7
Job 22.2,3;
Prov 9.12;
Lk 17.10
35.9
Ex 2.23;
Job 12.19
35.10
Job 27.10;
Ps 42.8;
149.5;
Acts 16.25
35.11
Ps 94.12;
Lk 12.24
35.12
Prov 1.28
35.13
Job 27.9;
Prov 15.29;
Isa 1.15;
Jer 11.11
35.14
Ps 37.5,6

ᶻ Meaning of Heb of verses 29-33 uncertain
ᵃ Traditional rendering of Heb *Shaddai*

that the case is before him,
and you are waiting for
him!

15 And now, because his anger
does not punish,
and he does not greatly
heed transgression,[b]

16 Job opens his mouth in
empty talk,
he multiplies words
without knowledge."

Elihu Exalts God's Goodness

36 Elihu continued and said:
2 "Bear with me a little,
and I will show you,
for I have yet something to
say on God's behalf.

3 I will bring my knowledge
from far away,
and ascribe righteousness
to my Maker.

4 For truly my words are not
false;
one who is perfect in
knowledge is with you.

5 "Surely God is mighty and
does not despise any;
he is mighty in strength of
understanding.

6 He does not keep the wicked
alive,
but gives the afflicted their
right.

7 He does not withdraw his
eyes from the righteous,
but with kings on the
throne
he sets them forever, and
they are exalted.

8 And if they are bound in
fetters
and caught in the cords of
affliction,

9 then he declares to them
their work
and their transgressions,
that they are behaving
arrogantly.

10 He opens their ears to
instruction,
and commands that they
return from iniquity.

11 If they listen, and serve him,
they complete their days in
prosperity,

and their years in
pleasantness.

12 But if they do not listen,
they shall perish by the
sword,
and die without knowledge.

13 "The godless in heart cherish
anger;
they do not cry for help
when he binds them.

14 They die in their youth,
and their life ends in
shame.[c]

15 He delivers the afflicted by
their affliction,
and opens their ear by
adversity.

16 He also allured you out of
distress
into a broad place where
there was no constraint,
and what was set on your
table was full of
fatness.

17 "But you are obsessed with
the case of the wicked;
judgment and justice seize
you.

18 Beware that wrath does not
entice you into scoffing,
and do not let the
greatness of the ransom
turn you aside.

19 Will your cry avail to keep
you from distress,
or will all the force of your
strength?

20 Do not long for the night,
when peoples are cut off in
their place.

21 Beware! Do not turn to
iniquity;
because of that you have
been tried by affliction.

22 See, God is exalted in his
power;
who is a teacher like
him?

23 Who has prescribed for him
his way,

35.15
Eccl 8.11
35.16
Job 34.37,
35
36.3
Job 8.3;
37.23
36.4
Job 33.3;
37.16
36.5
Ps 22.24;
Job 12.13
36.6
Job 8.22;
5.15
36.7
Ps 33.18;
113.8
36.8
Ps 107.10;
vv. 15,21
36.9
Job 15.25
36.10
Job 33.16;
2 Kings 17.13
36.11
Isa 1.19,20

36.12
Job 15.22;
4.21
36.13
Rom 2.5
36.14
Job 15.32;
22.16
36.15
Ps 119.67;
v. 10
36.16
Hos 2.14;
Ps 118.5;
23.5
36.18
Job 34.33;
Jon 4.4,9;
Job 33.24
36.20
Job 34.20,
25
36.21
Ps 66.18;
Heb 11.25
36.22
Isa 40.13;
1 Cor 2.16
36.23
Job 34.13;
Job 8.3

b Theodotion Symmachus Compare Vg:
Meaning of Heb uncertain c Heb ends
among the temple prostitutes

or who can say, 'You have done wrong'?

Elihu Proclaims God's Majesty

24 "Remember to extol his work,
　　of which mortals have sung.
25 All people have looked on it;
　　everyone watches it from far away.
26 Surely God is great, and we do not know him;
　　the number of his years is unsearchable.
27 For he draws up the drops of water;
　　he distills[d] his mist in rain,
28 which the skies pour down
　　and drop upon mortals abundantly.
29 Can anyone understand the spreading of the clouds,
　　the thunderings of his pavilion?
30 See, he scatters his lightning around him
　　and covers the roots of the sea.
31 For by these he governs peoples;
　　he gives food in abundance.
32 He covers his hands with the lightning,
　　and commands it to strike the mark.
33 Its crashing[e] tells about him;
　　he is jealous[e] with anger against iniquity.

37 "At this also my heart trembles,
　　and leaps out of its place.
2 Listen, listen to the thunder of his voice
　　and the rumbling that comes from his mouth.
3 Under the whole heaven he lets it loose,
　　and his lightning to the corners of the earth.
4 After it his voice roars;
　　he thunders with his majestic voice

and he does not restrain
　　the lightnings[f] when his voice is heard.
5 God thunders wondrously with his voice;
　　he does great things that we cannot comprehend.
6 For to the snow he says,
　　'Fall on the earth';
　　and the shower of rain, his heavy shower of rain,
7 serves as a sign on everyone's hand,
　　so that all whom he has made may know it.[g]
8 Then the animals go into their lairs
　　and remain in their dens.
9 From its chamber comes the whirlwind,
　　and cold from the scattering winds.
10 By the breath of God ice is given,
　　and the broad waters are frozen fast.
11 He loads the thick cloud with moisture;
　　the clouds scatter his lightning.
12 They turn round and round by his guidance,
　　to accomplish all that he commands them
　　on the face of the habitable world.
13 Whether for correction, or for his land,
　　or for love, he causes it to happen.

14 "Hear this, O Job;
　　stop and consider the wondrous works of God.
15 Do you know how God lays his command upon them,
　　and causes the lightning of his cloud to shine?
16 Do you know the balancings of the clouds,
　　the wondrous works of the one whose knowledge is perfect,

36.24
2 Sam 7.26;
Ps 35.27;
59.16
36.26
Ps 102.24
36.27
Ps 147.8
36.29
Job 37.11,
16; 26.14
36.31
Job 37.13;
Ps 136.25
36.32
Job 37.15
36.33
Job 37.2
37.2
Job 36.33
37.3
v. 12
37.4
Ps 29.3

37.5
Job 5.9;
36.26
37.6
Job 38.22;
36.27
37.7
Job 12.14
37.8
Ps 104.22
37.9
Job 9.9;
Ps 147.17
37.10
Job 38.29;
Ps 147.17
37.11
Job 36.27,
29; v. 15
37.12
Ps 148.8;
Isa 14.21;
27.6;
Prov 8.31
37.13
Ex 9.18;
1 Sam 12.18;
Job 38.26;
1 Kings 18.45
37.14
Ps 111.2
37.16
vv. 5,14,23;
Job 36.4

d Cn: Heb they distill　　e Meaning of Heb uncertain　　f Heb them　　g Meaning of Heb of verse 7 uncertain

17 you whose garments are hot
 when the earth is still
 because of the south
 wind?
18 Can you, like him, spread
 out the skies,
 hard as a molten mirror?
19 Teach us what we shall say
 to him;
 we cannot draw up our
 case because of
 darkness.
20 Should he be told that I
 want to speak?
 Did anyone ever wish to be
 swallowed up?
21 Now, no one can look on the
 light
 when it is bright in the
 skies,
 when the wind has passed
 and cleared them.
22 Out of the north comes
 golden splendor;
 around God is awesome
 majesty.
23 The Almighty[h]—we cannot
 find him;
 he is great in power and
 justice,
 and abundant
 righteousness he will
 not violate.
24 Therefore mortals fear him;
 he does not regard any who
 are wise in their own
 conceit."

The LORD Answers Job

38 Then the LORD answered
 Job out of the whirlwind:
2 "Who is this that darkens
 counsel by words
 without knowledge?
3 Gird up your loins like a
 man,
 I will question you, and
 you shall declare to me.

4 "Where were you when I laid
 the foundation of the
 earth?
 Tell me, if you have
 understanding.

5 Who determined its
 measurements—surely
 you know!
 Or who stretched the line
 upon it?
6 On what were its bases sunk,
 or who laid its cornerstone
7 when the morning stars sang
 together
 and all the heavenly
 beings[i] shouted for joy?

8 "Or who shut in the sea with
 doors
 when it burst out from the
 womb?—
9 when I made the clouds its
 garment,
 and thick darkness its
 swaddling band,
10 and prescribed bounds for it,
 and set bars and doors,
11 and said, 'Thus far shall you
 come, and no farther,
 and here shall your proud
 waves be stopped'?

12 "Have you commanded the
 morning since your days
 began,
 and caused the dawn to
 know its place,
13 so that it might take hold of
 the skirts of the earth,
 and the wicked be shaken
 out of it?
14 It is changed like clay under
 the seal,
 and it is dyed[j] like a
 garment.
15 Light is withheld from the
 wicked,
 and their uplifted arm is
 broken.

16 "Have you entered into the
 springs of the sea,
 or walked in the recesses
 of the deep?
17 Have the gates of death been
 revealed to you,
 or have you seen the gates
 of deep darkness?

37.18
Job 9.8;
Ps 104.2;
Isa 44.24
37.23
1 Tim 6.16;
Job 9.4; 8.3;
Isa 63.9
37.24
Mt 10.28;
11.25;
1 Cor 1.26
38.1
Job 40.6
38.2
Job 42.3;
35.16;
1 Tim 1.7
38.3
Job 40.7
38.4
Ps 104.5;
Prov 8.29
38.6
Job 26.7
38.7
Job 1.6
38.8
Gen 1.9
38.9
Prov 30.4
38.10
Job 26.10
38.11
Ps 89.9
38.12
Ps 74.16
38.13
Ps 104.35
38.15
Job 18.5;
Ps 10.15
38.16
Ps 77.19
38.17
Ps 9.13

h Traditional rendering of Heb *Shaddai*
i Heb *sons of God* j Cn: Heb *and they
stand forth*

18 Have you comprehended the
　　expanse of the earth?
　Declare, if you know all
　　this.

19 "Where is the way to the
　　dwelling of light,
　and where is the place of
　　darkness,
20 that you may take it to its
　　territory
　and that you may discern
　　the paths to its home?
21 Surely you know, for you
　　were born then,
　and the number of your
　　days is great!

22 "Have you entered the
　　storehouses of the
　　snow,
　or have you seen the
　　storehouses of the hail,
23 which I have reserved for the
　　time of trouble,
　for the day of battle and
　　war?
24 What is the way to the place
　　where the light is
　　distributed,
　or where the east wind is
　　scattered upon the
　　earth?

25 "Who has cut a channel for
　　the torrents of rain,
　and a way for the
　　thunderbolt,
26 to bring rain on a land where
　　no one lives,
　on the desert, which is
　　empty of human life,
27 to satisfy the waste and
　　desolate land,
　and to make the ground
　　put forth grass?

28 "Has the rain a father,
　or who has begotten the
　　drops of dew?
29 From whose womb did the
　　ice come forth,
　and who has given birth to
　　the hoarfrost of heaven?
30 The waters become hard like
　　stone,

38.18
Job 28.24
38.20
Job 26.10;
24.13
38.21
Job 15.7
38.22
Job 37.6
38.23
Ex 9.18;
Josh 10.11;
Isa 30.30;
Ezek 13.11,
13;
Rev 16.21
38.24
Job 26.10;
27.21
38.25
Job 28.26
38.26
Job 36.27;
Ps 107.35
38.27
Ps 104.13,
14
38.28
Ps 147.8;
Jer 14.22
38.29
Ps 147.16,
17

38.31
Job 9.9;
Am 5.8
38.33
Job 31.35
38.34
v. 37;
Job 22.11;
36.27,28
38.35
Job 36.32;
37.3
38.36
Job 32.8;
Ps 51.6;
Eccl 2.26;
Job 32.8
38.39
Ps 104.21
38.40
Job 38.8;
Ps 17.12
38.41
Ps 147.9;
Mt 6.26

and the face of the deep is
　　frozen.

31 "Can you bind the chains of
　　the Pleiades,
　or loose the cords of
　　Orion?
32 Can you lead forth the
　　Mazzaroth in their
　　season,
　or can you guide the Bear
　　with its children?
33 Do you know the ordinances
　　of the heavens?
　Can you establish their rule
　　on the earth?

34 "Can you lift up your voice
　　to the clouds,
　so that a flood of waters
　　may cover you?
35 Can you send forth
　　lightnings, so that they
　　may go
　and say to you, 'Here we
　　are'?
36 Who has put wisdom in the
　　inward parts,ᵏ
　or given understanding to
　　the mind?ᵏ
37 Who has the wisdom to
　　number the clouds?
　Or who can tilt the
　　waterskins of the
　　heavens,
38 when the dust runs into a
　　mass
　and the clods cling
　　together?

39 "Can you hunt the prey for
　　the lion,
　or satisfy the appetite of
　　the young lions,
40 when they crouch in their
　　dens,
　or lie in wait in their
　　covert?
41 Who provides for the raven
　　its prey,
　when its young ones cry to
　　God,
　and wander about for lack
　　of food?

ᵏ Meaning of Heb uncertain

39 "Do you know when the mountain goats give birth?
Do you observe the calving of the deer?

2 Can you number the months that they fulfill,
and do you know the time when they give birth,

3 when they crouch to give birth to their offspring,
and are delivered of their young?

4 Their young ones become strong, they grow up in the open;
they go forth, and do not return to them.

5 "Who has let the wild ass go free?
Who has loosed the bonds of the swift ass,

6 to which I have given the steppe for its home,
the salt land for its dwelling place?

7 It scorns the tumult of the city;
it does not hear the shouts of the driver.

8 It ranges the mountains as its pasture,
and it searches after every green thing.

9 "Is the wild ox willing to serve you?
Will it spend the night at your crib?

10 Can you tie it in the furrow with ropes,
or will it harrow the valleys after you?

11 Will you depend on it because its strength is great,
and will you hand over your labor to it?

12 Do you have faith in it that it will return,
and bring your grain to your threshing floor?[l]

13 "The ostrich's wings flap wildly,
though its pinions lack plumage.[m]

14 For it leaves its eggs to the earth,
and lets them be warmed on the ground,

15 forgetting that a foot may crush them,
and that a wild animal may trample them.

16 It deals cruelly with its young, as if they were not its own;
though its labor should be in vain, yet it has no fear;

17 because God has made it forget wisdom,
and given it no share in understanding.

18 When it spreads its plumes aloft,[m]
it laughs at the horse and its rider.

19 "Do you give the horse its might?
Do you clothe its neck with mane?

20 Do you make it leap like the locust?
Its majestic snorting is terrible.

21 It paws[n] violently, exults mightily;
it goes out to meet the weapons.

22 It laughs at fear, and is not dismayed;
it does not turn back from the sword.

23 Upon it rattle the quiver,
the flashing spear, and the javelin.

24 With fierceness and rage it swallows the ground;
it cannot stand still at the sound of the trumpet.

25 When the trumpet sounds, it says 'Aha!'
From a distance it smells the battle,

39.1
Ps 29.9
39.3
1 Sam 4.19
39.5
Job 6.5;
11.12; 24.5
39.6
Job 24.5;
Jer 2.24;
Hos 8.9;
Ps 107.34
39.9
Num 23.22;
Deut 33.17

39.16
Lam 4.3;
v. 22
39.17
Job 35.11
39.19
Ps 147.10
39.20
Joel 2.5;
Jer 8.16
39.21
Jer 8.6
39.24
Jer 4.19;
Ezek 7.14;
Am 3.6
39.25
Josh 6.5;
Am 1.14;
2.2

[l] Heb your grain and your threshing floor
[m] Meaning of Heb uncertain [n] Gk Syr Vg: Heb they dig

the thunder of the
captains, and the
shouting.

26 "Is it by your wisdom that
the hawk soars,
and spreads its wings
toward the south?

27 Is it at your command that
the eagle mounts up
and makes its nest on
high?

28 It lives on the rock and
makes its home
in the fastness of the rocky
crag.

29 From there it spies the prey;
its eyes see it from far
away.

30 Its young ones suck up
blood;
and where the slain are,
there it is."

40

And the LORD said to Job:
2 "Shall a faultfinder
contend with the
Almighty?°
Anyone who argues with
God must respond."

Job's Response to God

3 Then Job answered the LORD:
4 "See, I am of small account;
what shall I answer
you?
I lay my hand on my
mouth.

5 I have spoken once, and I
will not answer;
twice, but will proceed no
further."

God's Challenge to Job

6 Then the LORD answered Job
out of the whirlwind;
7 "Gird up your loins like a
man;
I will question you, and
you declare to me.

8 Will you even put me in the
wrong?
Will you condemn me that
you may be justified?

9 Have you an arm like God,
and can you thunder with a
voice like his?

10 "Deck yourself with majesty
and dignity;
clothe yourself with glory
and splendor.

11 Pour out the overflowings of
your anger,
and look on all who are
proud, and abase them.

12 Look on all who are proud,
and bring them low;
tread down the wicked
where they stand.

13 Hide them all in the dust
together;
bind their faces in the
world below.P

14 Then I will also acknowledge
to you
that your own right hand
can give you victory.

15 "Look at Behemoth,
which I made just as I
made you;
it eats grass like an ox.

16 Its strength is in its loins,
and its power in the
muscles of its belly.

17 It makes its tail stiff like a
cedar;
the sinews of its thighs are
knit together.

18 Its bones are tubes of
bronze,
its limbs like bars of iron.

19 "It is the first of the great
acts of God—
only its Maker can
approach it with the
sword.

20 For the mountains yield food
for it
where all the wild animals
play.

21 Under the lotus plants it lies,
in the covert of the reeds
and in the marsh.

22 The lotus trees cover it for
shade;
the willows of the wadi
surround it.

23 Even if the river is turbulent,
it is not frightened;

39.27
Jer 46.16;
Ob 4
39.30
Mt 24.28;
Lk 17.37
40.1
Job 33.13;
13.3; 23.4;
31.35
40.4
Job 42.6;
29.9
40.5
Job 9.3,15
40.6
Job 38.1
40.7
Job 38.3;
42.4
40.8
Isa 14.27;
Rom 3.4
40.9
2 Chr 32.8;
Jer 17.5;
Job 37.5

40.10
Ps 93.1;
104.1
40.11
Isa 42.25;
2.12;
Dan 4.37
40.12
1 Sam 2.7;
Isa 13.11;
63.3;
Job 36.20
40.14
Ps 20.6;
60.5; 108.6
40.15
v. 19
40.19
Job 41.33;
v. 15
40.20
Ps 104.26
40.22
Isa 44.4

o Traditional rendering of Heb *Shaddai*
P Heb *the hidden place*

it is confident though
Jordan rushes against
its mouth.
24 Can one take it with hooks[q]
or pierce its nose with a
snare?

41 [r] "Can you draw out
Leviathan[s] with a
fishhook,
or press down its tongue
with a cord?
2 Can you put a rope in its
nose,
or pierce its jaw with a
hook?
3 Will it make many
supplications to you?
Will it speak soft words to
you?
4 Will it make a covenant with
you
to be taken as your servant
forever?
5 Will you play with it as with
a bird,
or will you put it on leash
for your girls?
6 Will traders bargain over it?
Will they divide it up
among the merchants?
7 Can you fill its skin with
harpoons,
or its head with fishing
spears?
8 Lay hands on it;
think of the battle; you will
not do it again!
9 [t]Any hope of capturing it[u]
will be disappointed;
were not even the gods[v]
overwhelmed at the
sight of it?
10 No one is so fierce as to dare
to stir it up.
Who can stand before it?[w]
11 Who can confront it[w] and be
safe?[x]
—under the whole heaven,
who?[y]

12 "I will not keep silence
concerning its limbs,
or its mighty strength, or
its splendid frame.
13 Who can strip off its outer
garment?

40.24
Prov 1.17
41.1
Ps 104.26;
Isa 27.1
41.2
Isa 37.29
41.10
Job 3.8
41.11
Rom 11.35;
Ex 19.5;
Deut 10.14;
Ps 24.1;
50.12;
1 Cor 10.26

41.18
Job 3.9

Who can penetrate its
double coat of mail?[z]
14 Who can open the doors of
its face?
There is terror all around
its teeth.
15 Its back[a] is made of shields
in rows,
shut up closely as with a
seal.
16 One is so near to another
that no air can come
between them.
17 They are joined one to
another;
they clasp each other and
cannot be separated.
18 Its sneezes flash forth light,
and its eyes are like the
eyelids of the dawn.
19 From its mouth go flaming
torches;
sparks of fire leap out.
20 Out of its nostrils comes
smoke,
as from a boiling pot and
burning rushes.
21 Its breath kindles coals,
and a flame comes out of
its mouth.
22 In its neck abides strength,
and terror dances before it.
23 The folds of its flesh cling
together;
it is firmly cast and
immovable.
24 Its heart is as hard as stone,
as hard as the lower
millstone.
25 When it raises itself up the
gods are afraid;
at the crashing they are
beside themselves.
26 Though the sword reaches it,
it does not avail,
nor does the spear, the
dart, or the javelin.
27 It counts iron as straw,
and bronze as rotten wood.
28 The arrow cannot make it
flee;

q Cn: Heb in his eyes r Ch 40.25 in Heb
s Or the crocodile t Ch 41.1 in Heb
u Heb of it v Cn Compare Symmachus
Syr: Heb one is w Heb me x Gk: Heb
that I shall repay y Heb to me
z Gk: Heb bridle a Cn Compare Gk Vg:
Heb pride

slingstones, for it, are
turned to chaff.
29 Clubs are counted as chaff;
it laughs at the rattle of
javelins.
30 Its underparts are like sharp
potsherds;
it spreads itself like a
threshing sledge on the
mire.
31 It makes the deep boil like a
pot;
it makes the sea like a pot
of ointment.
32 It leaves a shining wake
behind it;
one would think the deep
to be white-haired.
33 On earth it has no equal,
a creature without fear.
34 It surveys everything that is
lofty;
it is king over all that are
proud."

Job Is Humbled and Satisfied

42 Then Job answered the
Lord:
2 "I know that you can do all
things,
and that no purpose of
yours can be thwarted.
3 'Who is this that hides
counsel without
knowledge?'
Therefore I have uttered
what I did not
understand,
things too wonderful for
me, which I did not
know.
4 'Hear, and I will speak;
I will question you, and
you declare to me.'
5 I had heard of you by the
hearing of the ear,
but now my eye sees you;
6 therefore I despise myself,
and repent in dust and
ashes."

Job's Friends Are Humiliated

7 After the Lord had spoken
these words to Job, the Lord said to

Eliphaz the Temanite: "My wrath is
kindled against you and against
your two friends; for you have not
spoken of me what is right, as my
servant Job has. 8 Now therefore
take seven bulls and seven rams,
and go to my servant Job, and offer
up for yourselves a burnt offering;
and my servant Job shall pray for
you, for I will accept his prayer not
to deal with you according to your
folly; for you have not spoken of me
what is right, as my servant Job has
done." 9 So Eliphaz the Temanite
and Bildad the Shuhite and Zophar
the Naamathite went and did what
the Lord had told them; and the
Lord accepted Job's prayer.

Job's Fortunes Are Restored Twofold

10 And the Lord restored the
fortunes of Job when he had prayed
for his friends; and the Lord gave
Job twice as much as he had be-
fore. 11 Then there came to him all
his brothers and sisters and all who
had known him before, and they
ate bread with him in his house;
they showed him sympathy and
comforted him for all the evil that
the Lord had brought upon him;
and each of them gave him a piece
of money[b] and a gold ring. 12 The
Lord blessed the latter days of Job
more than his beginning; and he
had fourteen thousand sheep, six
thousand camels, a thousand yoke
of oxen, and a thousand donkeys.
13 He also had seven sons and three
daughters. 14 He named the first Je-
mimah, the second Keziah, and the
third Keren-happuch. 15 In all the
land there were no women so beau-
tiful as Job's daughters; and their
father gave them an inheritance
along with their brothers. 16 After
this Job lived one hundred and for-
ty years, and saw his children, and
his children's children, four gener-
ations. 17 And Job died, old and full
of days.

41.33
Job 40.19
42.2
Gen 18.14;
Mt 19.26;
Mk 10.27;
Lk 18.27;
2 Chr 20.6;
Isa 14.27
42.3
Job 38.2;
Ps 40.5;
131.1; 139.6
42.4
Job 38.3;
40.7
42.5
Job 26.14;
Judg 13.22;
Isa 6.5
42.6
Ezra 9.6;
Job 40.4
42.7
Job 32.3;
vv. 1-6;
40.3-5

42.8
Num 23.1;
Job 1.5;
Jas 5.15,16
42.10
Ps 14.7;
126.1
42.11
Job 19.13
42.12
Job 1.10;
8.7; 1.3
42.13
Job 1.2
42.16
Job 5.26;
Prov 3.16
42.17
Gen 25.8

b Heb a qesitah

The Psalms

Title and Background

The names "Psalms" and "Psalter" come from the Septuagint (the Greek translation of the Old Testament). Both originally referred to stringed instruments (e.g., harp, lyre, lute), then to songs sung with their accompaniment. The traditional Hebrew title means "praises," even though many of the psalms are prayers.

Author and Date of Writing

Of the 150 Psalms, 100 of them are thought to be written by the following authors: David–73; Asaph–12; Sons of Korah–10; Solomon–2; Moses–1; Heman the Ezrahite–1; and Ethan the Ezrahite–1. The rest of the Psalms have no recorded author.

The final collection and arrangement of the Psalter was the work of postexilic temple personnel, completed probably in the third century B.C. By the first century A.D. it could be referred to as the "Book of Psalms" (Lk 20.42; Ac 1.20).

Theme and Message

For the most part, the Psalter is a book of prayer and praise, not a book of doctrine. The psalmists pour their hearts out to God in prayer; they go on to praise him and in profess their faith and trust in him. The core teaching of the Psalter is the conviction that the gravitational center not only of life, but of all history and the whole creation, is God. He is the great King over all, and the One to whom all things are subject.

Outline

Book I:	Psalms 1-41
Book II:	Psalms 42-72
Book III:	Psalms 73-89
Book IV:	Psalms 90-106
Book V:	Psalms 107-150

BOOK I

(Psalms 1–41)

Psalm 1

The Two Ways

¹ Happy are those
 who do not follow the
 advice of the wicked,
or take the path that sinners
 tread,
 or sit in the seat of
 scoffers;
² but their delight is in the law
 of the LORD,
 and on his law they
 meditate day and night.

³ They are like trees
 planted by streams of
 water,
 which yield their fruit in its
 season,
 and their leaves do not
 wither.
In all that they do, they
 prosper.

⁴ The wicked are not so,
 but are like chaff that the
 wind drives away.
⁵ Therefore the wicked will not
 stand in the judgment,
 nor sinners in the
 congregation of the
 righteous;

1.1
Prov 4.14;
Job 21.16;
Ps 17.4;
26.5;
Jer 15.17
1.2
Ps 119.35;
Josh 1.8;
Ps 119.1

1.3
Jer 17.8;
Ezek 47.12;
Gen 39.3;
Ps 128.2
1.4
Job 21.18;
Isa 17.13
1.5
Ps 5.5; 9.7;
8.16; 111.1;
149.1

6 for the LORD watches over the
 way of the righteous,
 but the way of the wicked
 will perish.

Psalm 2

God's Promise to His Anointed

1 Why do the nations conspire,
 and the peoples plot in
 vain?
2 The kings of the earth set
 themselves,
 and the rulers take counsel
 together,
 against the LORD and his
 anointed, saying,
3 "Let us burst their bonds
 asunder,
 and cast their cords from
 us."

4 He who sits in the heavens
 laughs;
 the LORD has them in
 derision.
5 Then he will speak to them
 in his wrath,
 and terrify them in his fury,
 saying,
6 "I have set my king on Zion,
 my holy hill."

7 I will tell of the decree of the
 LORD:
 He said to me, "You are my
 son;
 today I have begotten
 you.
8 Ask of me, and I will make
 the nations your
 heritage,
 and the ends of the earth
 your possession.
9 You shall break them with a
 rod of iron,
 and dash them in pieces
 like a potter's vessel."

10 Now therefore, O kings, be
 wise;
 be warned, O rulers of the
 earth.
11 Serve the LORD with fear,

1.6
Ps 37.18;
2 Tim 2.19;
Ps 9.3-6
2.1ff
Acts 4.25;
Ps 21.11
2.2
Ps 48.4-6;
74.18,23;
Jn 1.41
2.3
Jer 5.5
2.4
Ps 59.8;
37.13;
Prov 1.26
2.5
Ps 21.8,9;
78.49,50
2.6
Ps 3.4
2.7
Acts 13.33;
Heb 1.5
2.8
Ps 22.27
2.9
Ps 89.23;
Rev 2.27;
12.5
2.11
Heb 12.28;
Ps 119.119,
120

2.12
Jn 5.23;
Rev 6.16;
Ps 34.8;
Rom 9.33
3.1
2 Sam 15.12
3.2
Ps 71.11
3.3
Ps 28.7;
27.6
3.4
Ps 34.4;
99.9
3.5
Lev 26.6;
Ps 139.18
3.6
Ps 27.3
3.7
Ps 7.6; 6.4;
Job 16.10;
Ps 58.6
3.8
Isa 43.11;
Jer 3.23;
Num 6.23-27

with trembling 12 kiss his
 feet,[a]
 or he will be angry, and you
 will perish in the way;
 for his wrath is quickly
 kindled.

Happy are all who take
 refuge in him.

Psalm 3

Trust in God under Adversity

A Psalm of David, when he fled
 from his son Absalom.

1 O LORD, how many are my
 foes!
 Many are rising against
 me;
2 many are saying to me,
 "There is no help for you[b]
 in God." *Selah*

3 But you, O LORD, are a shield
 around me,
 my glory, and the one who
 lifts up my head.
4 I cry aloud to the LORD,
 and he answers me from
 his holy hill. *Selah*

5 I lie down and sleep;
 I wake again, for the LORD
 sustains me.
6 I am not afraid of ten
 thousands of people
 who have set themselves
 against me all around.

7 Rise up, O LORD!
 Deliver me, O my God!
 For you strike all my
 enemies on the cheek;
 you break the teeth of the
 wicked.

8 Deliverance belongs to the
 LORD;
 may your blessing be on
 your people! *Selah*

[a] Cn: Meaning of Heb of verses 11b and 12a
is uncertain [b] Syr: Heb *him*

Psalm 4

Confident Plea for Deliverance from Enemies

To the leader:
with stringed instruments.
A Psalm of David.

1 Answer me when I call,
O God of my right!
You gave me room when I
was in distress.
Be gracious to me, and
hear my prayer.

2 How long, you people, shall
my honor suffer
shame?
How long will you love vain
words, and seek after
lies? *Selah*
3 But know that the LORD has
set apart the faithful for
himself;
the LORD hears when I call
to him.

4 When you are disturbed,[c] do
not sin;
ponder it on your beds,
and be silent. *Selah*
5 Offer right sacrifices,
and put your trust in the
LORD.

6 There are many who say,
"O that we might see
some good!
Let the light of your face
shine on us, O LORD!"
7 You have put gladness in my
heart
more than when their grain
and wine abound.

8 I will both lie down and
sleep in peace;
for you alone, O LORD,
make me lie down in
safety.

4.1
Ps 27.7;
18.6; 24.5;
18.18; 25.16;
17.6
4.2
Ps 31.6,18
4.3
Ps 31.23;
6.8,9
4.4
Ps 33.8;
Eph 4.26;
Ps 77.6
4.5
Deut 33.19;
Ps 50.14;
37.3
4.6
Num 6.26
4.7
Acts 14.17;
Isa 9.3
4.8
Ps 3.5;
Lev 25.18

5.1
Ps 54.2;
19.14
5.2
Ps 3.4; 84.3
5.3
Ps 88.13;
Hab 2.1
5.4
Ps 11.5;
92.15
5.5
Ps 73.3; 1.5;
11.5
5.6
Rev 21.8;
Ps 55.23
5.7
Ps 69.13;
28.2
5.8
Ps 27.11;
31.1
5.9
Deut 32.20;
Lk 11.44;
Rom 3.13;
Ps 12.2
5.10
Ps 9.16;
Lam 1.5;
Ps 107.10,
11

Psalm 5

Trust in God for Deliverance from Enemies

To the leader: for the flutes. A
Psalm of David.

1 Give ear to my words,
O LORD;
give heed to my sighing.
2 Listen to the sound of my
cry,
my King and my God,
for to you I pray.
3 O LORD, in the morning you
hear my voice;
in the morning I plead my
case to you, and watch.

4 For you are not a God who
delights in wickedness;
evil will not sojourn with
you.
5 The boastful will not stand
before your eyes;
you hate all evildoers.
6 You destroy those who speak
lies;
the LORD abhors the
bloodthirsty and
deceitful.

7 But I, through the
abundance of your
steadfast love,
will enter your house,
I will bow down toward your
holy temple
in awe of you.
8 Lead me, O LORD, in your
righteousness
because of my enemies;
make your way straight
before me.

9 For there is no truth in their
mouths;
their hearts are
destruction;
their throats are open graves;
they flatter with their
tongues.
10 Make them bear their guilt,
O God;

c Or *are angry*

let them fall by their own
counsels;
because of their many
transgressions cast
them out,
for they have rebelled
against you.

11 But let all who take refuge in
you rejoice;
let them ever sing for joy.
Spread your protection over
them,
so that those who love your
name may exult in you.
12 For you bless the righteous,
O Lord;
you cover them with favor
as with a shield.

Psalm 6

Prayer for Recovery from Grave Illness

To the leader: with stringed
instruments; according to The
Sheminith. A Psalm of David.

1 O Lord, do not rebuke me in
your anger,
or discipline me in your
wrath.
2 Be gracious to me, O Lord,
for I am languishing;
O Lord, heal me, for my
bones are shaking with
terror.
3 My soul also is struck with
terror,
while you, O Lord—how
long?

4 Turn, O Lord, save my life;
deliver me for the sake of
your steadfast love.
5 For in death there is no
remembrance of you;
in Sheol who can give you
praise?

6 I am weary with my
moaning;
every night I flood my bed
with tears;
I drench my couch with my
weeping.

5.11
Ps 2.12;
Isa 65.13;
Zech 9.15;
Ps 69.36
5.12
Ps 112.2;
32.7,10
6.1
Ps 38.1; 2.5
6.2
Ps 51.1;
102.4,11;
41.4; 22.14
6.3
Jn 12.27;
Ps 90.13
6.4
Ps 17.13
6.5
Ps 30.9;
Isa 38.18
6.6
Ps 69.3;
22.1; 42.3

6.7
Ps 31.9
6.8
Ps 119.115;
Lk 13.27;
Ps 5.5; 28.6
6.9
Ps 116.1;
66.19,20
6.10
Ps 71.24;
40.14; 73.19
7.1
Ps 11.1;
31.15
7.2
Ps 17.12;
50.22
7.3
2 Sam 16.7;
1 Sam 24.11
7.4
1 Sam 24.7
7.6
Ps 3.7; 94.2;
44.23

7 My eyes waste away because
of grief;
they grow weak because of
all my foes.

8 Depart from me, all you
workers of evil,
for the Lord has heard the
sound of my weeping.
9 The Lord has heard my
supplication;
the Lord accepts my
prayer.
10 All my enemies shall be
ashamed and struck
with terror;
they shall turn back, and in
a moment be put to
shame.

Psalm 7

Plea for Help against Persecutors

A Shiggaion of David, which he
sang to the Lord concerning
Cush, a Benjaminite.

1 O Lord my God, in you I
take refuge;
save me from all my
pursuers, and deliver
me,
2 or like a lion they will tear
me apart;
they will drag me away,
with no one to rescue.

3 O Lord my God, if I have
done this,
if there is wrong in my
hands,
4 if I have repaid my ally with
harm
or plundered my foe
without cause,
5 then let the enemy pursue
and overtake me,
trample my life to the
ground,
and lay my soul in the
dust. Selah

6 Rise up, O Lord, in your
anger;
lift yourself up against the
fury of my enemies;

awake, O my God;[d] you
 have appointed a
 judgment.
7 Let the assembly of the
 peoples be gathered
 around you,
 and over it take your seat[e]
 on high.
8 The Lord judges the peoples;
 judge me, O Lord,
 according to my
 righteousness
 and according to the
 integrity that is in me.

9 O let the evil of the wicked
 come to an end,
 but establish the righteous,
 you who test the minds and
 hearts,
 O righteous God.
10 God is my shield,
 who saves the upright in
 heart.
11 God is a righteous judge,
 and a God who has
 indignation every day.

12 If one does not repent, God[f]
 will whet his sword;
 he has bent and strung his
 bow;
13 he has prepared his deadly
 weapons,
 making his arrows fiery
 shafts.
14 See how they conceive evil,
 and are pregnant with
 mischief,
 and bring forth lies.
15 They make a pit, digging it
 out,
 and fall into the hole that
 they have made.
16 Their mischief returns upon
 their own heads,
 and on their own heads
 their violence descends.

17 I will give to the Lord the
 thanks due to his
 righteousness,
 and sing praise to the
 name of the Lord, the
 Most High.

7.7
Ps 68.18
7.8
Ps 96.13;
18.20; 35.24
7.9
Ps 34.21;
Isa 54.14;
1 Chr 28.9;
Jer 11.20;
Rev 2.23
7.10
Ps 18.2;
125.4
7.11
Ps 50.6;
Isa 34.2
7.12
Ezek 3.19;
33.9;
Deut 32.41;
Ps 21.12
7.13
Ps 64.7
7.14
Isa 59.4;
Jas 1.15
7.15
Job 4.8;
Ps 9.15;
Eccl 10.8
7.16
Ps 140.9;
Esther 9.25
7.17
Ps 71.15,16;
9.2

8.1
Ps 66.2;
148.13; 57.5,
11; 113.4
8.2
Mt 21.16;
Ps 44.16
8.3
Ps 89.11;
102.5; 136.9
8.4
Job 7.17;
Ps 144.3;
Heb 2.6
8.5
Ps 103.4;
21.5;
Heb 2.9
8.6
Gen 1.26;
Heb 2.8
8.9
v. 1

Psalm 8

Divine Majesty and Human Dignity

To the leader: according to The
Gittith. A Psalm of David.

1 O Lord, our Sovereign,
 how majestic is your name
 in all the earth!

You have set your glory
 above the heavens.
2 Out of the mouths of babes
 and infants
you have founded a bulwark
 because of your foes,
 to silence the enemy and
 the avenger.

3 When I look at your heavens,
 the work of your
 fingers,
 the moon and the stars
 that you have
 established;
4 what are human beings that
 you are mindful of
 them,
 mortals[g] that you care for
 them?

5 Yet you have made them a
 little lower than God,[h]
 and crowned them with
 glory and honor.
6 You have given them
 dominion over the
 works of your hands;
 you have put all things
 under their feet,
7 all sheep and oxen,
 and also the beasts of the
 field,
8 the birds of the air, and the
 fish of the sea,
 whatever passes along the
 paths of the seas.

9 O Lord, our Sovereign,
 how majestic is your name
 in all the earth!

d Or awake for me e Cn: Heb return
f Heb he g Heb ben adam, lit. son of man
h Or than the divine beings or angels: Heb
elohim

Psalm 9

God's Power and Justice

To the leader: according to
Muth-labben. A Psalm of David.

1 I will give thanks to the LORD
 with my whole heart;
 I will tell of all your
 wonderful deeds.
2 I will be glad and exult in
 you;
 I will sing praise to your
 name, O Most High.

3 When my enemies turned
 back,
 they stumbled and
 perished before you.
4 For you have maintained my
 just cause;
 you have sat on the throne
 giving righteous
 judgment.

5 You have rebuked the
 nations, you have
 destroyed the wicked;
 you have blotted out their
 name forever and ever.
6 The enemies have vanished
 in everlasting ruins;
 their cities you have rooted
 out;
 the very memory of them
 has perished.

7 But the LORD sits enthroned
 forever,
 he has established his
 throne for judgment.
8 He judges the world with
 righteousness;
 he judges the peoples with
 equity.

9 The LORD is a stronghold for
 the oppressed,
 a stronghold in times of
 trouble.
10 And those who know your
 name put their trust in
 you,

9.1
Ps 86.12;
26.7
9.2
Ps 5.11;
83.18
9.3
Ps 56.9;
27.2
9.4
Ps 140.12;
47.8; 67.4;
1 Pet 2.23
9.5
Deut 9.14
9.6
Ps 40.15;
34.16
9.7
Ps 29.10;
89.14
9.8
Ps 96.13
9.9
Ps 18.2;
32.7; 37.39
9.10
Ps 91.14;
37.28

9.11
Ps 76.2;
105.1
9.12
Gen 9.5;
v. 18
9.13
Ps 50.10;
25.18; 38.19;
30.3
9.14
Ps 106.2;
87.2; 13.5
9.15
Ps 7.15;
35.8
9.16
Isa 64.2;
v. 4
9.17
Ps 49.14;
50.22;
Job 8.13
9.18
v. 12;
Ps 74.19
9.19
Ps 3.7;
2 Chr 14.11;
Ps 110.6
9.20
Ps 83.15;
Isa 31.3

for you, O LORD, have not
 forsaken those who
 seek you.
11 Sing praises to the LORD, who
 dwells in Zion.
 Declare his deeds among
 the peoples.
12 For he who avenges blood is
 mindful of them;
 he does not forget the cry
 of the afflicted.

13 Be gracious to me, O LORD.
 See what I suffer from
 those who hate me;
 you are the one who lifts
 me up from the gates of
 death,
14 so that I may recount all
 your praises,
 and, in the gates of
 daughter Zion,
 rejoice in your deliverance.

15 The nations have sunk in the
 pit that they made;
 in the net that they hid has
 their own foot been
 caught.
16 The LORD has made himself
 known, he has executed
 judgment;
 the wicked are snared in
 the work of their own
 hands. *Higgaion. Selah*

17 The wicked shall depart to
 Sheol,
 all the nations that forget
 God.

18 For the needy shall not
 always be forgotten,
 nor the hope of the poor
 perish forever.

19 Rise up, O LORD! Do not let
 mortals prevail;
 let the nations be judged
 before you.
20 Put them in fear, O LORD;
 let the nations know that
 they are only human.
 Selah

Psalm 10

Prayer for Deliverance from Enemies

1 Why, O LORD, do you stand
far off?
Why do you hide yourself
in times of trouble?
2 In arrogance the wicked
persecute the poor—
let them be caught in the
schemes they have
devised.

3 For the wicked boast of the
desires of their heart,
those greedy for gain curse
and renounce the LORD.
4 In the pride of their
countenance the wicked
say, "God will not seek
it out";
all their thoughts are,
"There is no God."

5 Their ways prosper at all
times;
your judgments are on
high, out of their sight;
as for their foes, they scoff
at them.
6 They think in their heart,
"We shall not be
moved;
throughout all generations
we shall not meet
adversity."

7 Their mouths are filled with
cursing and deceit and
oppression;
under their tongues are
mischief and iniquity.
8 They sit in ambush in the
villages;
in hiding places they
murder the innocent.

Their eyes stealthily watch
for the helpless;
9 they lurk in secret like a
lion in its covert;
they lurk that they may seize
the poor;

they seize the poor and
drag them off in their
net.

10 They stoop, they crouch,
and the helpless fall by
their might.
11 They think in their heart,
"God has forgotten,
he has hidden his face, he
will never see it."

12 Rise up, O LORD; O God, lift
up your hand;
do not forget the
oppressed.
13 Why do the wicked renounce
God,
and say in their hearts,
"You will not call us to
account"?

14 But you do see! Indeed you
note trouble and grief,
that you may take it into
your hands;
the helpless commit
themselves to you;
you have been the helper
of the orphan.

15 Break the arm of the wicked
and evildoers;
seek out their wickedness
until you find none.
16 The LORD is king forever and
ever;
the nations shall perish
from his land.

17 O LORD, you will hear the
desire of the meek;
you will strengthen their
heart, you will incline
your ear
18 to do justice for the orphan
and the oppressed,
so that those from earth
may strike terror no
more.[i]

10.1
Ps 22.1;
13.1
10.2
Ps 109.16;
7.15; 9.16
10.3
Ps 94.4;
Job 1.5,11;
v. 13
10.4
v. 13;
Ps 14.1
10.6
Ps 30.6;
49.11
10.7
Rom 3.14;
Ps 59.12;
73.8; 140.3
10.8
Prov 1.11;
Ps 94.6
10.9
Ps 17.12;
59.3; v. 2;
140.5
10.11
v. 4;
Job 22.13;
Ps 73.11
10.12
Mic 5.9;
Ps 9.12
10.13
v. 3
10.14
Job 11.11;
Jer 51.56;
Ps 37.5;
68.5;
Hos 14.3
10.15
Ps 37.17;
9.12
10.16
Ps 29.10;
Deut 8.20
10.17
Ps 145.19;
1 Chr 29.18;
Ps 34.15
10.18
Ps 82.3; 9.9;
Isa 29.20

i Meaning of Heb uncertain

Psalm 11

Song of Trust in God

To the leader. Of David.

1 In the LORD I take refuge;
 how can you say to me,
 "Flee like a bird to the
 mountains;[i]
2 for look, the wicked bend
 the bow,
 they have fitted their arrow
 to the string,
 to shoot in the dark at the
 upright in heart.
3 If the foundations are
 destroyed,
 what can the righteous
 do?"

4 The LORD is in his holy
 temple;
 the LORD's throne is in
 heaven.
 His eyes behold, his gaze
 examines humankind.
5 The LORD tests the righteous
 and the wicked,
 and his soul hates the lover
 of violence.
6 On the wicked he will rain
 coals of fire and sulfur;
 a scorching wind shall be
 the portion of their cup.
7 For the LORD is righteous;
 he loves righteous deeds;
 the upright shall behold his
 face.

Psalm 12

Plea for Help in Evil Times

To the leader: according to The
Sheminith. A Psalm of David.

1 Help, O LORD, for there is no
 longer anyone who is
 godly;
 the faithful have
 disappeared from
 humankind.
2 They utter lies to each other;
 with flattering lips and a
 double heart they
 speak.

11.1
Ps 56.11
11.2
Ps 7.12;
64.3,4
11.3
Ps 82.5
11.4
Ps 18.6;
103.19;
33.13; 34.15,
16
11.5
Gen 22.1;
Jas 1.12;
Ps 5.5
11.6
Ezek 38.22;
Jer 4.11,12;
Ps 75.8
11.7
Ps 7.9,11;
33.5; 17.15
12.1
Isa 57.1
12.2
Ps 41.6;
55.21;
1 Chr 12.33

12.3
Ps 73.8,9
12.5
Ps 10.18;
3.7; 34.6
12.6
Ps 18.30;
Prov 30.5
12.7
Ps 37.28
12.8
Ps 55.10,11
13.1
Job 13.24;
Ps 44.24;
88.14
13.2
Ps 42.4,9;
94.3
13.3
Ps 5.1;
Ezra 9.8;
Jer 51.39

3 May the LORD cut off all
 flattering lips,
 the tongue that makes
 great boasts,
4 those who say, "With our
 tongues we will prevail;
 our lips are our own—who
 is our master?"

5 "Because the poor are
 despoiled, because the
 needy groan,
 I will now rise up," says
 the LORD;
 "I will place them in the
 safety for which they
 long."
6 The promises of the LORD are
 promises that are pure,
 silver refined in a furnace
 on the ground,
 purified seven times.

7 You, O LORD, will protect us;
 you will guard us from this
 generation forever.
8 On every side the wicked
 prowl,
 as vileness is exalted
 among humankind.

Psalm 13

Prayer for Deliverance from Enemies

To the leader. A Psalm of David.

1 How long, O LORD? Will you
 forget me forever?
 How long will you hide
 your face from me?
2 How long must I bear pain[k]
 in my soul,
 and have sorrow in my
 heart all day long?
 How long shall my enemy be
 exalted over me?

3 Consider and answer me,
 O LORD my God!
 Give light to my eyes, or I
 will sleep the sleep of
 death,

i Gk Syr Jerome Tg: Heb *flee to your
mountain, O bird* k Syr: Heb *hold
counsels*

4 and my enemy will say, "I
 have prevailed";
my foes will rejoice
 because I am shaken.

5 But I trusted in your
 steadfast love;
my heart shall rejoice in
 your salvation.
6 I will sing to the Lord,
 because he has dealt
 bountifully with me.

Psalm 14
Denunciation of Godlessness

To the leader. Of David.

1 Fools say in their hearts,
 "There is no God."
They are corrupt, they do
 abominable deeds;
there is no one who does
 good.

2 The Lord looks down from
 heaven on humankind
to see if there are any who
 are wise,
who seek after God.

3 They have all gone astray,
 they are all alike
 perverse;
there is no one who does
 good,
no, not one.

4 Have they no knowledge, all
 the evildoers
who eat up my people as
 they eat bread,
and do not call upon the
 Lord?

5 There they shall be in great
 terror,
for God is with the
 company of the
 righteous.
6 You would confound the
 plans of the poor,
but the Lord is their
 refuge.

7 O that deliverance for Israel
 would come from Zion!

When the Lord restores the
 fortunes of his people,
Jacob will rejoice; Israel
 will be glad.

Psalm 15
Who Shall Abide in God's Sanctuary?

A Psalm of David.

1 O Lord, who may abide in
 your tent?
Who may dwell on your
 holy hill?

2 Those who walk blamelessly,
 and do what is right,
and speak the truth from
 their heart;
3 who do not slander with
 their tongue,
and do no evil to their
 friends,
nor take up a reproach
 against their neighbors;
4 in whose eyes the wicked are
 despised,
but who honor those who
 fear the Lord;
who stand by their oath even
 to their hurt;
5 who do not lend money at
 interest,
and do not take a bribe
 against the innocent.

Those who do these things
 shall never be moved.

Psalm 16
Song of Trust and Security in God

A Miktam of David.

1 Protect me, O God, for in
 you I take refuge.
2 I say to the Lord, "You are
 my Lord;
I have no good apart from
 you."[1]

13.4
Jer 20.10;
Ps 25.2
13.5
Ps 52.8;
9.14
13.6
Ps 59.16;
116.7
14.1
Ps 10.4;
53.1-6; 73.8;
Rom 3.10-12
14.2
Ps 33.13;
92.6;
Ezra 6.21
14.3
Ps 58.3;
2 Pet 2.7;
Rev 22.11;
Ps 143.2
14.4
Ps 82.5;
27.2; 79.6;
Isa 64.7
14.5
Ps 73.15
14.6
Ps 9.9;
40.17
14.7
Ps 53.6;
Job 42.10

15.1
Ps 24.3-5;
27.5,6; 2.6
15.2
Ps 24.4;
51.6;
Eph 4.25
15.3
Lev 19.16;
Ex 23.1
15.4
2 Tim 3.8;
Acts 28.10;
Judg 11.35
15.5
Ex 22.25;
23.8;
Deut 16.19;
Ps 112.6
16.1
Ps 17.8; 7.1
16.2
Ps 73.25

[1] Jerome Tg: Meaning of Heb uncertain

3 As for the holy ones in the
 land, they are the noble,
in whom is all my delight.

4 Those who choose another
 god multiply their
 sorrows;m
their drink offerings of
 blood I will not pour
 out
or take their names upon
 my lips.

5 The Lord is my chosen
 portion and my cup;
you hold my lot.
6 The boundary lines have
 fallen for me in
 pleasant places;
I have a goodly heritage.

7 I bless the Lord who gives
 me counsel;
in the night also my heart
 instructs me.
8 I keep the Lord always
 before me;
because he is at my right
 hand, I shall not be
 moved.

9 Therefore my heart is glad,
 and my soul rejoices;
my body also rests secure.
10 For you do not give me up to
 Sheol,
or let your faithful one see
 the Pit.

11 You show me the path of
 life.
In your presence there is
 fullness of joy;
in your right hand are
 pleasures forevermore.

Psalm 17

Prayer for Deliverance from Persecutors

A Prayer of David.

1 Hear a just cause, O Lord;
 attend to my cry;
give ear to my prayer from
 lips free of deceit.

16.3
Deut 33.3;
Ps 101.6
16.4
Ps 32.10;
106.37,38;
Ex 23.13
16.5
Ps 73.26;
23.5; 125.3
16.6
Ps 78.55;
Jer 3.19
16.7
Ps 73.24;
77.6
16.8
Ps 54.3;
73.23; 62.2
16.9
Ps 4.7;
30.12; 4.8
16.10
Acts 2.27;
13.35;
Ps 49.9
16.11
Mt 7.14;
Ps 17.15;
36.7,8
17.1
Ps 9.4; 61.1;
55.1;
Isa 29.13

17.2
1 Chr 29.17
17.3
Ps 26.2;
66.10;
Job 23.10;
Jer 50.20;
Ps 39.1
17.4
Prov 1.15
17.5
Ps 44.18;
18.36
17.6
Ps 86.7;
88.2
17.7
Ps 31.21;
20.6
17.8
Deut 32.10;
Ps 36.7
17.9
Ps 31.20;
38.12; 109.3
17.10
Ps 73.7;
1 Sam 2.3;
Ps 31.18
17.11
Ps 88.17;
37.14
17.12
Ps 7.2; 10.9
17.13
Ps 73.18;
22.20; 7.12

2 From you let my vindication
 come;
let your eyes see the right.

3 If you try my heart, if you
 visit me by night,
if you test me, you will find
 no wickedness in me;
my mouth does not
 transgress.
4 As for what others do, by the
 word of your lips
I have avoided the ways of
 the violent.
5 My steps have held fast to
 your paths;
my feet have not slipped.

6 I call upon you, for you will
 answer me, O God;
incline your ear to me,
 hear my words.
7 Wondrously show your
 steadfast love,
O savior of those who seek
 refuge
from their adversaries at
 your right hand.

8 Guard me as the apple of the
 eye;
hide me in the shadow of
 your wings,
9 from the wicked who despoil
 me,
my deadly enemies who
 surround me.
10 They close their hearts to
 pity;
with their mouths they
 speak arrogantly.
11 They track me down;n now
 they surround me;
they set their eyes to cast
 me to the ground.
12 They are like a lion eager to
 tear,
like a young lion lurking in
 ambush.

13 Rise up, O Lord, confront
 them, overthrow them!
By your sword deliver my
 life from the wicked,

m Cn: Meaning of Heb uncertain n One Ms
Compare Syr: MT *Our steps*

14 from mortals — by your hand,
 O LORD —
 from mortals whose portion
 in life is in this world.
 May their bellies be filled
 with what you have
 stored up for them;
 may their children have
 more than enough;
 may they leave something
 over to their little ones.

15 As for me, I shall behold
 your face in
 righteousness;
 when I awake I shall be
 satisfied, beholding
 your likeness.

Psalm 18

Royal Thanksgiving for Victory

To the leader. A Psalm of David
the servant of the LORD, who
addressed the words of this song
to the LORD on the day when the
LORD delivered him from the
hand of all his enemies, and
from the hand of Saul. He said:

1 I love you, O LORD, my
 strength.
2 The LORD is my rock, my
 fortress, and my
 deliverer,
 my God, my rock in whom
 I take refuge,
 my shield, and the horn of
 my salvation, my
 stronghold.
3 I call upon the LORD, who is
 worthy to be praised,
 so I shall be saved from my
 enemies.

4 The cords of death
 encompassed me;
 the torrents of perdition
 assailed me;
5 the cords of Sheol entangled
 me;
 the snares of death
 confronted me.

6 In my distress I called upon
 the LORD;
 to my God I cried for help.

17.14
Lk 16.8;
Ps 73.3-7;
Isa 2.7;
Job 21.11
17.15
1 Jn 3.2;
Ps 4.6,7;
16.11
18.1
Ps 27.1
18.2
Ps 19.14;
91.2; 40.17;
11.1; 59.11;
75.10; 9.9
18.3
Ps 48.1;
Num 10.9
18.4
Ps 116.3;
124.3,4
18.5
Ps 116.3;
Prov 14.27
18.6
Ps 86.7;
11.4; 34.15

18.7
Ps 68.7,8;
114.4,6
18.8
Deut 29.20;
Hab 3.5
18.9
Ps 144.5;
Ex 20.21
18.10
Ps 80.1;
104.3
18.11
Ps 97.2
18.12
Ps 104.2;
Isa 30.30;
Ps 140.10
18.13
Ps 29.3;
104.7
18.14
Ps 7.13;
144.6;
Ex 14.24;
Judg 4.15
18.15
Ps 106.9;
76.6;
Ex 15.8
18.16
Ps 144.7

 From his temple he heard
 my voice,
 and my cry to him reached
 his ears.

7 Then the earth reeled and
 rocked;
 the foundations also of the
 mountains trembled
 and quaked, because he
 was angry.
8 Smoke went up from his
 nostrils,
 and devouring fire from his
 mouth;
 glowing coals flamed forth
 from him.
9 He bowed the heavens, and
 came down;
 thick darkness was under
 his feet.
10 He rode on a cherub, and
 flew;
 he came swiftly upon the
 wings of the wind.
11 He made darkness his
 covering around him,
 his canopy thick clouds
 dark with water.
12 Out of the brightness before
 him
 there broke through his
 clouds
 hailstones and coals of fire.
13 The LORD also thundered in
 the heavens,
 and the Most High uttered
 his voice.°
14 And he sent out his arrows,
 and scattered them;
 he flashed forth lightnings,
 and routed them.
15 Then the channels of the sea
 were seen,
 and the foundations of the
 world were laid bare
 at your rebuke, O LORD,
 at the blast of the breath of
 your nostrils.

16 He reached down from on
 high, he took me;
 he drew me out of mighty
 waters.

° Gk See 2 Sam 22.14: Heb adds *hailstones
and coals of fire*

17 He delivered me from my
 strong enemy,
 and from those who hated
 me;
 for they were too mighty
 for me.
18 They confronted me in the
 day of my calamity;
 but the Lord was my
 support.
19 He brought me out into a
 broad place;
 he delivered me, because
 he delighted in me.

20 The Lord rewarded me
 according to my
 righteousness;
 according to the cleanness
 of my hands he
 recompensed me.
21 For I have kept the ways of
 the Lord,
 and have not wickedly
 departed from my God.
22 For all his ordinances were
 before me,
 and his statutes I did not
 put away from me.
23 I was blameless before him,
 and I kept myself from
 guilt.
24 Therefore the Lord has
 recompensed me
 according to my
 righteousness,
 according to the cleanness
 of my hands in his
 sight.

25 With the loyal you show
 yourself loyal;
 with the blameless you
 show yourself
 blameless;
26 with the pure you show
 yourself pure;
 and with the crooked you
 show yourself perverse.
27 For you deliver a humble
 people,
 but the haughty eyes you
 bring down.
28 It is you who light my lamp;
 the Lord, my God, lights up
 my darkness.
29 By you I can crush a troop,

and by my God I can leap
 over a wall.
30 This God—his way is
 perfect;
 the promise of the Lord
 proves true;
 he is a shield for all who
 take refuge in him.

31 For who is God except the
 Lord?
 And who is a rock besides
 our God?—
32 the God who girded me with
 strength,
 and made my way safe.
33 He made my feet like the
 feet of a deer,
 and set me secure on the
 heights.
34 He trains my hands for war,
 so that my arms can bend
 a bow of bronze.
35 You have given me the shield
 of your salvation,
 and your right hand has
 supported me;
 your help p has made me
 great.
36 You gave me a wide place for
 my steps under me,
 and my feet did not slip.
37 I pursued my enemies and
 overtook them;
 and did not turn back until
 they were consumed.
38 I struck them down, so that
 they were not able to
 rise;
 they fell under my feet.
39 For you girded me with
 strength for the battle;
 you made my assailants
 sink under me.
40 You made my enemies turn
 their backs to me,
 and those who hated me I
 destroyed.
41 They cried for help, but
 there was no one to
 save them;
 they cried to the Lord, but
 he did not answer
 them.

18.41 Ps 50.22; Prov 1.28

p Or *gentleness*

18.17
v. 48;
Ps 35.10
18.18
Ps 59.16;
Isa 10.20
18.19
Ps 31.8;
118.5; 37.23
18.20
Ps 7.8;
1 Kings 8.32;
Ps 24.4
18.21
Ps 119.33;
2 Chr 34.33;
Ps 119.102
18.22
Ps 119.30,
83
18.24
1 Sam 26.23
18.25
Ps 62.12;
Mt 5.7
18.26
Job 25.5;
Prov 3.34
18.27
Ps 72.12;
Prov 6.17
18.28
Job 18.6;
Ps 27.1;
Job 29.3
18.29
2 Cor 12.9;
Heb 11.34

18.30
Deut 32.4;
Ps 12.6;
17.7
18.31
Deut 32.31,
39;
Ps 86.8-10;
Isa 45.5
18.32
Isa 45.5;
Heb 13.21;
1 Pet 5.10
18.33
Hab 3.19;
Deut 32.13
18.34
Ps 144.1;
Job 20.24
18.35
Deut 33.29;
Ps 119.117;
138.6
18.36
Ps 31.8;
71.5
18.37
Ps 44.5;
37.20
18.38
Ps 110.6;
36.12; 47.3
18.39
vv. 32,47
18.40
Ps 21.21;
94.23

42 I beat them fine, like dust
 before the wind;
 I cast them out like the
 mire of the streets.

43 You delivered me from strife
 with the peoples;q
 you made me head of the
 nations;
 people whom I had not
 known served me.
44 As soon as they heard of me
 they obeyed me;
 foreigners came cringing to
 me.
45 Foreigners lost heart,
 and came trembling out of
 their strongholds.

46 The LORD lives! Blessed be
 my rock,
 and exalted be the God of
 my salvation,
47 the God who gave me
 vengeance
 and subdued peoples under
 me;
48 who delivered me from my
 enemies;
 indeed, you exalted me
 above my adversaries;
 you delivered me from the
 violent.

49 For this I will extol you,
 O LORD, among the
 nations,
 and sing praises to your
 name.
50 Great triumphs he gives to
 his king,
 and shows steadfast love to
 his anointed,
 to David and his
 descendants forever.

Psalm 19

God's Glory in Creation and the Law

To the leader. A Psalm of David.

1 The heavens are telling the
 glory of God;
 and the firmamentr
 proclaims his
 handiwork.

2 Day to day pours forth
 speech,
 and night to night declares
 knowledge.
3 There is no speech, nor are
 there words;
 their voice is not heard;
4 yet their voices goes out
 through all the earth,
 and their words to the end
 of the world.

 In the heavenst he has set a
 tent for the sun,
5 which comes out like a
 bridegroom from his
 wedding canopy,
 and like a strong man runs
 its course with joy.
6 Its rising is from the end of
 the heavens,
 and its circuit to the end of
 them;
 and nothing is hid from its
 heat.

7 The law of the LORD is
 perfect,
 reviving the soul;
 the decrees of the LORD are
 sure,
 making wise the simple;
8 the precepts of the LORD are
 right,
 rejoicing the heart;
 the commandment of the
 LORD is clear,
 enlightening the eyes;
9 the fear of the LORD is pure,
 enduring forever;
 the ordinances of the LORD
 are true
 and righteous altogether.
10 More to be desired are they
 than gold,
 even much fine gold;
 sweeter also than honey,
 and drippings of the
 honeycomb.

11 Moreover by them is your
 servant warned;
 in keeping them there is
 great reward.

18.42
Ps 83.13
18.43
Ps 35.1;
Isa 52.15;
55.5
18.44
Ps 66.3
18.46
Ps 42.2;
51.14
18.47
Ps 94.1;
47.3
18.48
Ps 143.9;
27.6; 140.1,4
18.49
Rom 15.9;
Ps 108.1
18.50
Ps 144.10;
28.8; 89.4,29
19.1
Gen 1.6;
Isa 40.22;
Rom 1.19,
20
19.2
Ps 74.16
19.4
Rom 10.18
19.5
Eccl 1.5
19.6
Ps 113.3;
Deut 30.4
19.7
Ps 119.142;
23.3; 93.5;
111.7;
119.98-100
19.8
Ps 119.128;
12.6; 119.30
19.9
Ps 119.42
19.10
Prov 8.10;
16.24
19.11
Ps 17.4;
Prov 29.18

q Gk Tg: Heb *people* r Or *dome*
s Gk Jerome Compare Syr: Heb *line*
t Heb *In them*

12 But who can detect their
 errors?
 Clear me from hidden
 faults.
13 Keep back your servant also
 from the insolent;[u]
 do not let them have
 dominion over me.
 Then I shall be blameless,
 and innocent of great
 transgression.

14 Let the words of my mouth
 and the meditation of
 my heart
 be acceptable to you,
 O LORD, my rock and my
 redeemer.

Psalm 20

Prayer for Victory

To the leader. A Psalm of David.

1 The LORD answer you in the
 day of trouble!
 The name of the God of
 Jacob protect you!
2 May he send you help from
 the sanctuary,
 and give you support from
 Zion.
3 May he remember all your
 offerings,
 and regard with favor your
 burnt sacrifices. *Selah*

4 May he grant you your
 heart's desire,
 and fulfill all your plans.
5 May we shout for joy over
 your victory,
 and in the name of our
 God set up our banners.
 May the LORD fulfill all your
 petitions.

6 Now I know that the LORD
 will help his anointed;
 he will answer him from
 his holy heaven
 with mighty victories by his
 right hand.
7 Some take pride in chariots,
 and some in horses,

but our pride is in the
 name of the LORD our God.
8 They will collapse and fall,
 but we shall rise and stand
 upright.

9 Give victory to the king,
 O LORD;
 answer us when we call.[v]

Psalm 21

Thanksgiving for Victory

To the leader. A Psalm of David.

1 In your strength the king
 rejoices, O LORD,
 and in your help how
 greatly he exults!
2 You have given him his
 heart's desire,
 and have not withheld the
 request of his lips.
 Selah
3 For you meet him with rich
 blessings;
 you set a crown of fine
 gold on his head.
4 He asked you for life; you
 gave it to him—
 length of days forever and
 ever.
5 His glory is great through
 your help;
 splendor and majesty you
 bestow on him.
6 You bestow on him blessings
 forever;
 you make him glad with
 the joy of your
 presence.
7 For the king trusts in the
 LORD,
 and through the steadfast
 love of the Most High
 he shall not be moved.

8 Your hand will find out all
 your enemies;
 your right hand will find
 out those who hate you.
9 You will make them like a
 fiery furnace
 when you appear.

Cross-references

19.12 Ps 139.6; 51.1,2; 90.8
19.13 Ps 119.33; 32.2; 25.11
19.14 Ps 104.34; 18.2; Isa 41.14; 43.14
20.01 Ps 102.2; 91.14; 36.7, 11; 59.1
20.2 Ps 3.4; 119.28
20.3 Ps 51.19
20.4 Ps 21.2; 145.19
20.5 Ps 9.14; 1 Sam 1.17
20.6 Ps 41.11; Isa 58.9; Ps 28.8
20.7 Isa 36.9; 31.1; 2 Chr 32.8

20.8 Ps 37.24
20.9 Ps 3.7
21.1 Ps 59.16,17; 9.14
21.2 Ps 37.4
21.3 Ps 59.10
21.4 Ps 133.3; 91.16
21.5 Ps 18.50; 45.3,4
21.6 1 Chr 17.27; Ps 16.11
21.7 2 Kings 18.5; Ps 16.8
21.8 Isa 10.10
21.9 Mal 4.1; Lam 2.2

u Or *from proud thoughts* v Gk: Heb *give victory, O LORD; let the King answer us when we call*

The LORD will swallow them
up in his wrath,
and fire will consume
them.
10 You will destroy their
offspring from the
earth,
and their children from
among humankind.
11 If they plan evil against you,
if they devise mischief,
they will not succeed.
12 For you will put them to
flight;
you will aim at their faces
with your bows.

13 Be exalted, O LORD, in your
strength!
We will sing and praise
your power.

Psalm 22

Plea for Deliverance from Suffering and Hostility

To the leader: according to The
Deer of the Dawn. A Psalm of
David.

1 My God, my God, why have
you forsaken me?
Why are you so far from
helping me, from the
words of my groaning?
2 O my God, I cry by day, but
you do not answer;
and by night, but find no
rest.

3 Yet you are holy,
enthroned on the praises of
Israel.
4 In you our ancestors trusted;
they trusted, and you
delivered them.
5 To you they cried, and were
saved;
in you they trusted, and
were not put to shame.

6 But I am a worm, and not
human;
scorned by others, and
despised by the people.
7 All who see me mock at me;

they make mouths at me,
they shake their heads;
8 "Commit your cause to the
LORD; let him deliver—
let him rescue the one in
whom he delights!"

9 Yet it was you who took me
from the womb;
you kept me safe on my
mother's breast.
10 On you I was cast from my
birth,
and since my mother bore
me you have been my
God.
11 Do not be far from me,
for trouble is near
and there is no one to
help.

12 Many bulls encircle me,
strong bulls of Bashan
surround me;
13 they open wide their mouths
at me,
like a ravening and roaring
lion.

14 I am poured out like water,
and all my bones are out of
joint;
my heart is like wax;
it is melted within my
breast;
15 my mouth[w] is dried up like a
potsherd,
and my tongue sticks to my
jaws;
you lay me in the dust of
death.

16 For dogs are all around me;
a company of evildoers
encircles me.
My hands and feet have
shriveled;[x]
17 I can count all my bones.
They stare and gloat over
me;
18 they divide my clothes
among themselves,
and for my clothing they
cast lots.

21.10
Deut 28.18;
Ps 37.28
21.11
Ps 2.1-3;
10.2
21.12
Ps 18.40;
7.12,13
21.13
Ps 57.5;
81.1
22.1
Mt 27.46;
Ps 10.1
22.2
Ps 42.3
22.3
Ps 99.9;
35.8
22.5
Ps 107.6;
25.2,3;
Rom 9.33
22.6
Job 25.6;
Isa 41.14;
Ps 31.11;
Isa 49.7
22.7
Mt 27.39;
Mk 15.29

22.8
Mt 27.43;
Mk 1.11
22.9
Ps 71.6
22.10
Isa 46.3
22.11
Ps 72.12
22.12
Ps 68.30;
Deut 32.14
22.13
Ps 35.21;
17.12
22.14
Job 30.16;
Ps 31.10;
107.26
22.15
Ps 58.10;
137.6; 104.29
22.16
Ps 59.6;
Mt 27.35
22.18
Mt 27.35

w Cn: Heb *strength* x Meaning of Heb
uncertain

19 But you, O Lord, do not be
 far away!
 O my help, come quickly
 to my aid!
20 Deliver my soul from the
 sword,
 my life[y] from the power of
 the dog!
21 Save me from the mouth of
 the lion!

From the horns of the wild
 oxen you have rescued[z]
 me.
22 I will tell of your name to my
 brothers and sisters;[a]
 in the midst of the
 congregation I will
 praise you:
23 You who fear the Lord,
 praise him!
 All you offspring of Jacob,
 glorify him;
 stand in awe of him, all
 you offspring of Israel!
24 For he did not despise or
 abhor
 the affliction of the
 afflicted;
 he did not hide his face from
 me,[b]
 but heard when I[c] cried to
 him.

25 From you comes my praise
 in the great
 congregation;
 my vows I will pay before
 those who fear him.
26 The poor[d] shall eat and be
 satisfied;
 those who seek him shall
 praise the Lord.
 May your hearts live
 forever!

27 All the ends of the earth
 shall remember
 and turn to the Lord;
 and all the families of the
 nations
 shall worship before him.[e]
28 For dominion belongs to the
 Lord,
 and he rules over the
 nations.

22.19
v. 11;
Ps 70.5
22.20
Ps 35.17
22.21
v. 13;
Ps 34.4
22.22
Heb 2.12
22.23
Ps 135.19.
86.12; 33.8
22.24
Ps 102.17;
69.17;
Heb 5.7
22.25
Ps 35.18;
66.13
22.26
Ps 107.9;
40.16; 69.32
22.27
Ps 2.8; 86.9
22.28
Ps 47.7,8;
Mt 6.13

22.29
Ps 47.7;
Isa 27.13;
Ps 95.6
22.30
Ps 102.28;
71.18
22.31
Ps 78.6
23.1
Isa 40.11;
Jer 23.4;
Jn 10.11;
1 Pet 2.25;
Phil 4.19
23.2
Ezek 34.14;
Rev 7.17
23.3
Ps 19.7; 5.8;
85.13; 143.11
23.4
Ps 138.7;
Job 3.5;
Ps 27.1;
Isa 43.2
23.5
Ps 78.19;
31.19; 92.10;
16.5
23.6
Ps 25.7,10;
27.4-6

29 To him,[f] indeed, shall all
 who sleep in[g] the earth
 bow down;
 before him shall bow all
 who go down to the
 dust,
 and I shall live for him.[h]
30 Posterity will serve him;
 future generations will be
 told about the Lord,
31 and[i] proclaim his
 deliverance to a people
 yet unborn,
 saying that he has done it.

Psalm 23

The Divine Shepherd

A Psalm of David.

1 The Lord is my shepherd, I
 shall not want.
2 He makes me lie down in
 green pastures;
 he leads me beside still
 waters;[j]
3 he restores my soul.[k]
 He leads me in right paths[l]
 for his name's sake.

4 Even though I walk through
 the darkest valley,[m]
 I fear no evil;
 for you are with me;
 your rod and your staff—
 they comfort me.

5 You prepare a table before
 me
 in the presence of my
 enemies;
 you anoint my head with oil;
 my cup overflows.
6 Surely[n] goodness and
 mercy[o] shall follow me
 all the days of my life,

y Heb *my only one* z Heb *answered*
a Or *kindred* b Heb *him* c Heb *he*
d Or *afflicted* e Gk Syr Jerome: Heb *you*
f Cn: Heb *They have eaten and* g Cn: Heb
all the fat ones h Compare Gk Syr Vg: Heb
and he who cannot keep himself alive
i Compare Gk: Heb *it will be told about the
Lord to the generation, 31they will come and*
j Heb *waters of rest* k Or *life*
l Or *paths of righteousness* m Or *the valley
of the shadow of death* n Or *Only*
o Or *kindness*

and I shall dwell in the
house of the LORD
my whole life long.ᴾ

Psalm 24

Entrance into the Temple

Of David. A Psalm.

1 The earth is the LORD's and
all that is in it,
the world, and those who
live in it;
2 for he has founded it on the
seas,
and established it on the
rivers.

3 Who shall ascend the hill of
the LORD?
And who shall stand in his
holy place?
4 Those who have clean hands
and pure hearts,
who do not lift up their
souls to what is false,
and do not swear
deceitfully.
5 They will receive blessing
from the LORD,
and vindication from the
God of their salvation.
6 Such is the company of
those who seek him,
who seek the face of the
God of Jacob.�q *Selah*

7 Lift up your heads, O gates!
and be lifted up, O ancient
doors!
that the King of glory may
come in.
8 Who is the King of glory?
The LORD, strong and
mighty,
the LORD, mighty in battle.
9 Lift up your heads, O gates!
and be lifted up, O ancient
doors!
that the King of glory may
come in.
10 Who is this King of glory?
The LORD of hosts,
he is the King of glory.
 Selah

24.1
Ex 9.29;
Job 41.11;
1 Cor 10.26;
Ps 89.11
24.3
Ps 15.1; 2.6;
65.4
24.4
Job 17.9;
Mt 5.8;
Ps 15.4
24.5
Deut 11.26,
27;
Isa 46.13;
Ps 25.5
24.6
Ps 27.8
24.7
Isa 26.2;
1 Cor 2.8
24.8
Ps 89.13;
76.3-6
24.9
Zech 9.9;
Mt 21.5

25.1
Ps 86.4
25.2
Ps 31.6;
41.11
25.3
Isa 49.23;
33.1
25.4
Ps 5.8;
86.11
25.5
Jn 16.13;
Ps 24.5;
40.1
25.6
Ps 103.17;
Isa 63.15
25.7
Job 13.26;
Jer 3.25;
Ps 51.1
25.8
Ps 106.1;
92.15; 32.8
25.9
Ps 23.3;
27.11
25.10
Ps 40.11;
103.18

Psalm 25

Prayer for Guidance and for Deliverance

Of David.

1 To you, O LORD, I lift up my
soul.
2 O my God, in you I trust;
do not let me be put to
shame;
do not let my enemies
exult over me.
3 Do not let those who wait for
you be put to shame;
let them be ashamed who
are wantonly
treacherous.

4 Make me to know your ways,
O LORD;
teach me your paths.
5 Lead me in your truth, and
teach me,
for you are the God of my
salvation;
for you I wait all day long.

6 Be mindful of your mercy,
O LORD, and of your
steadfast love,
for they have been from of
old.
7 Do not remember the sins of
my youth or my
transgressions;
according to your steadfast
love remember me,
for your goodness' sake,
O LORD!

8 Good and upright is the
LORD;
therefore he instructs
sinners in the way.
9 He leads the humble in what
is right,
and teaches the humble his
way.
10 All the paths of the LORD are
steadfast love and
faithfulness,

ᴾ Heb *for length of days* q Gk Syr: Heb
your face, O Jacob

for those who keep his
covenant and his
decrees.

11 For your name's sake,
O LORD,
pardon my guilt, for it is
great.
12 Who are they that fear the
LORD?
He will teach them the way
that they should
choose.

13 They will abide in prosperity,
and their children shall
possess the land.
14 The friendship of the LORD is
for those who fear him,
and he makes his covenant
known to them.
15 My eyes are ever toward the
LORD,
for he will pluck my feet
out of the net.

16 Turn to me and be gracious
to me,
for I am lonely and
afflicted.
17 Relieve the troubles of my
heart,
and bring me[r] out of my
distress.
18 Consider my affliction and
my trouble,
and forgive all my sins.

19 Consider how many are my
foes,
and with what violent
hatred they hate me.
20 O guard my life, and deliver
me;
do not let me be put to
shame, for I take refuge
in you.
21 May integrity and
uprightness preserve
me,
for I wait for you.

22 Redeem Israel, O God,
out of all its troubles.

25.11
Ps 31.1;
Rom 5.20
25.13
Prov 19.23;
Ps 37.11
25.14
Prov 3.32;
Jn 7.17
25.15
Ps 141.8
25.16
Ps 69.16
25.17
Ps 88.3;
107.6
25.18
2 Sam 16.12
25.19
Ps 3.1;
27.12
25.20
Ps 86.2
25.21
Ps 41.12;
v. 3
25.22
Ps 130.8

26.1
Ps 7.8;
Prov 20.7;
Ps 25.2;
Heb 10.23
26.2
Ps 7.9;
66.10
26.3
2 Kings 20.3
26.4
Ps 1.1
26.5
Ps 139.21;
1.1
26.6
Ps 73.13
26.7
Ps 35.18;
9.1
26.8
Ps 27.4
26.9
Ps 28.3
26.10
1 Sam 8.3
26.11
v. 1;
Ps 69.18

Psalm 26

Plea for Justice and Declaration of Righteousness

Of David.

1 Vindicate me, O LORD,
for I have walked in my
integrity,
and I have trusted in the
LORD without wavering.
2 Prove me, O LORD, and try
me;
test my heart and mind.
3 For your steadfast love is
before my eyes,
and I walk in faithfulness
to you.[s]

4 I do not sit with the
worthless,
nor do I consort with
hypocrites;
5 I hate the company of
evildoers,
and will not sit with the
wicked.

6 I wash my hands in
innocence,
and go around your altar,
O LORD,
7 singing aloud a song of
thanksgiving,
and telling all your
wondrous deeds.

8 O LORD, I love the house in
which you dwell,
and the place where your
glory abides.
9 Do not sweep me away with
sinners,
nor my life with the
bloodthirsty,
10 those in whose hands are
evil devices,
and whose right hands are
full of bribes.

11 But as for me, I walk in my
integrity;
redeem me, and be
gracious to me.

r Or *The troubles of my heart are enlarged;
bring me* s Or *in your faithfulness*

12 My foot stands on level
ground;
in the great congregation I
will bless the LORD.

Psalm 27

Triumphant Song of Confidence

Of David.

1 The LORD is my light and my
salvation;
whom shall I fear?
The LORD is the stronghold[t]
of my life;
of whom shall I be afraid?

2 When evildoers assail me
to devour my flesh—
my adversaries and foes—
they shall stumble and fall.

3 Though an army encamp
against me,
my heart shall not fear;
though war rise up against
me,
yet I will be confident.

4 One thing I asked of the
LORD,
that will I seek after:
to live in the house of the
LORD
all the days of my life,
to behold the beauty of the
LORD,
and to inquire in his
temple.

5 For he will hide me in his
shelter
in the day of trouble;
he will conceal me under the
cover of his tent;
he will set me high on a
rock.

6 Now my head is lifted up
above my enemies all
around me,
and I will offer in his tent
sacrifices with shouts of
joy;
I will sing and make melody
to the LORD.

26.12
Ps 40.2;
27.11; 22.22
27.1
Isa 60.19;
Ex 15.2;
Ps 62.2
27.2
Ps 14.4
27.3
Ps 3.6
27.4
Ps 26.8;
90.17
27.5
Ps 31.20;
40.2
27.6
Ps 3.3

27.7
Ps 39.12;
13.3
27.8
Ps 24.6
27.9
Ps 69.17
27.10
Isa 49.15;
40.11
27.11
Ps 25.4;
86.11; 5.8
27.12
Ps 41.2;
35.11;
Mt 26.60;
Acts 9.1
27.13
Ps 31.19;
Jer 11.19
27.14
Ps 40.1;
Josh 1.6
28.1
Ps 83.1;
88.4
28.2
Ps 140.6;
5.7; 138.2

7 Hear, O LORD, when I cry
aloud,
be gracious to me and
answer me!
8 "Come," my heart says,
"seek his face!"
Your face, LORD, do I seek.
9 Do not hide your face from
me.

Do not turn your servant
away in anger,
you who have been my
help.
Do not cast me off, do not
forsake me,
O God of my salvation!
10 If my father and mother
forsake me,
the LORD will take me up.

11 Teach me your way, O LORD,
and lead me on a level
path
because of my enemies.
12 Do not give me up to the
will of my adversaries,
for false witnesses have
risen against me,
and they are breathing out
violence.

13 I believe that I shall see the
goodness of the LORD
in the land of the living.
14 Wait for the LORD;
be strong, and let your
heart take courage;
wait for the LORD!

Psalm 28

Prayer for Help and
Thanksgiving for It

Of David.

1 To you, O LORD, I call;
my rock, do not refuse to
hear me,
for if you are silent to me,
I shall be like those who go
down to the Pit.
2 Hear the voice of my
supplication,
as I cry to you for help,

t Or refuge

as I lift up my hands
 toward your most holy
 sanctuary. ᵘ

3 Do not drag me away with
 the wicked,
 with those who are workers
 of evil,
 who speak peace with their
 neighbors,
 while mischief is in their
 hearts.
4 Repay them according to
 their work,
 and according to the evil of
 their deeds;
 repay them according to the
 work of their hands;
 render them their due
 reward.
5 Because they do not regard
 the works of the Lᴏʀᴅ,
 or the work of his
 hands,
 he will break them down and
 build them up no more.

6 Blessed be the Lᴏʀᴅ,
 for he has heard the sound
 of my pleadings.
7 The Lᴏʀᴅ is my strength and
 my shield;
 in him my heart trusts;
 so I am helped, and my heart
 exults,
 and with my song I give
 thanks to him.

8 The Lᴏʀᴅ is the strength of
 his people;
 he is the saving refuge of
 his anointed.
9 O save your people, and
 bless your heritage;
 be their shepherd, and
 carry them forever.

Psalm 29

The Voice of God in a Great
Storm

A Psalm of David.

1 Ascribe to the Lᴏʀᴅ,
 O heavenly beings, ᵛ

28.3
Ps 26.9;
12.2; Jer 9.8
28.4
Rev 18.6
28.5
Isa 5.12
28.6
Ps 116.1
28.7
Ps 18.2;
13.5
28.8
Ps 20.6
28.9
Deut 9.29;
Ezra 1.4
29.1
1 Chr 16.28,
29;
Ps 96.7-9

29.2
2 Chr 20.21
29.3
Job 37.4,5
29.4
Ps 68.33
29.5
Isa 2.13
29.6
Ps 114.4;
Deut 3.9
29.8
Num 13.26
29.9
Ps 26.8
29.10
Ps 10.16
29.11
Ps 28.8;
37.11

 ascribe to the Lᴏʀᴅ glory
 and strength.
2 Ascribe to the Lᴏʀᴅ the glory
 of his name;
 worship the Lᴏʀᴅ in holy
 splendor.

3 The voice of the Lᴏʀᴅ is over
 the waters;
 the God of glory thunders,
 the Lᴏʀᴅ, over mighty
 waters.
4 The voice of the Lᴏʀᴅ is
 powerful;
 the voice of the Lᴏʀᴅ is full
 of majesty.

5 The voice of the Lᴏʀᴅ breaks
 the cedars;
 the Lᴏʀᴅ breaks the cedars
 of Lebanon.
6 He makes Lebanon skip like
 a calf,
 and Sirion like a young
 wild ox.

7 The voice of the Lᴏʀᴅ flashes
 forth flames of fire.
8 The voice of the Lᴏʀᴅ shakes
 the wilderness;
 the Lᴏʀᴅ shakes the
 wilderness of Kadesh.

9 The voice of the Lᴏʀᴅ causes
 the oaks to whirl, ʷ
 and strips the forest
 bare;
 and in his temple all say,
 "Glory!"

10 The Lᴏʀᴅ sits enthroned over
 the flood;
 the Lᴏʀᴅ sits enthroned as
 king forever.
11 May the Lᴏʀᴅ give strength
 to his people!
 May the Lᴏʀᴅ bless his
 people with peace!

ᵘ Heb *your innermost sanctuary*
ᵛ Heb *sons of gods* ʷ Or *causes the deer
to calve*

Psalm 30

Thanksgiving for Recovery from Grave Illness

A Psalm. A Song at the dedication of the temple. Of David.

1 I will extol you, O LORD, for
 you have drawn me up,
and did not let my foes
 rejoice over me.
2 O LORD my God, I cried to
 you for help,
and you have healed me.
3 O LORD, you brought up my
 soul from Sheol,
restored me to life from
 among those gone down
 to the Pit.ˣ

4 Sing praises to the LORD,
 O you his faithful ones,
and give thanks to his holy
 name.
5 For his anger is but for a
 moment;
his favor is for a lifetime.
Weeping may linger for the
 night,
but joy comes with the
 morning.

6 As for me, I said in my
 prosperity,
"I shall never be moved."
7 By your favor, O LORD,
you had established me as
 a strong mountain;
you hid your face;
 I was dismayed.

8 To you, O LORD, I cried,
and to the LORD I made
 supplication:
9 "What profit is there in my
 death,
if I go down to the Pit?
Will the dust praise you?
Will it tell of your
 faithfulness?
10 Hear, O LORD, and be
 gracious to me!
O LORD, be my helper!"

11 You have turned my
 mourning into dancing;
you have taken off my
 sackcloth
and clothed me with joy,
12 so that my soulʸ may praise
 you and not be silent.
O LORD my God, I will give
 thanks to you forever.

Psalm 31

Prayer and Praise for Deliverance from Enemies

To the leader. A Psalm of David.

1 In you, O LORD, I seek refuge;
do not let me ever be put
 to shame;
in your righteousness
 deliver me.
2 Incline your ear to me;
rescue me speedily.
Be a rock of refuge for me,
a strong fortress to save
 me.

3 You are indeed my rock and
 my fortress;
for your name's sake lead
 me and guide me,
4 take me out of the net that
 is hidden for me,
for you are my refuge.
5 Into your hand I commit my
 spirit;
you have redeemed me,
 O LORD, faithful God.

6 You hateᶻ those who pay
 regard to worthless
 idols,
but I trust in the LORD.
7 I will exult and rejoice in
 your steadfast love,
because you have seen my
 affliction;
you have taken heed of my
 adversities,
8 and have not delivered me
 into the hand of the
 enemy;
you have set my feet in a
 broad place.

30.1
Ps 28.9;
25.2
30.2
Ps 88.13;
6.2
30.3
Ps 86.13;
28.1
30.4
Ps 149.1;
50.5; 97.12
30.5
Ps 103.9;
63.3
30.7
Ps 104.29
30.9
Ps 6.5
30.11
Ps 6.8;
Jer 31.4,13;
Ps 4.7

30.12
Ps 16.9;
44.8
31.1
Ps 22.5;
Isa 49.23
31.2
Ps 71.2
31.3
Ps 18.2;
23.3
31.4
Ps 25.15;
28.8
31.5
Lk 23.46;
Acts 7.59
31.6
Jon 2.8
31.7
Ps 90.14;
10.14;
Jn 10.27
31.8
Deut 32.30;
Ps 4.1

ˣ Or *that I should not go down to the Pit*
ʸ Heb *that glory* ᶻ One Heb Ms Gk Syr
Jerome: MT *I hate*

9 Be gracious to me, O LORD,
for I am in distress;
my eye wastes away from
grief,
my soul and body also.
10 For my life is spent with
sorrow,
and my years with sighing;
my strength fails because of
my misery,[a]
and my bones waste away.

11 I am the scorn of all my
adversaries,
a horror[b] to my neighbors,
an object of dread to my
acquaintances;
those who see me in the
street flee from me.
12 I have passed out of mind
like one who is dead;
I have become like a
broken vessel.
13 For I hear the whispering of
many—
terror all around!—
as they scheme together
against me,
as they plot to take my life.

14 But I trust in you, O LORD;
I say, "You are my God."
15 My times are in your hand;
deliver me from the hand
of my enemies and
persecutors.
16 Let your face shine upon
your servant;
save me in your steadfast
love.
17 Do not let me be put to
shame, O LORD,
for I call on you;
let the wicked be put to
shame;
let them go dumbfounded
to Sheol.
18 Let the lying lips be stilled
that speak insolently
against the righteous
with pride and contempt.

19 O how abundant is your
goodness
that you have laid up for
those who fear you,

and accomplished for those
who take refuge in you,
in the sight of everyone!
20 In the shelter of your
presence you hide them
from human plots;
you hold them safe under
your shelter
from contentious tongues.

21 Blessed be the LORD,
for he has wondrously
shown his steadfast love
to me
when I was beset as a city
under siege.
22 I had said in my alarm,
"I am driven far[c] from your
sight."
But you heard my
supplications
when I cried out to you for
help.

23 Love the LORD, all you his
saints.
The LORD preserves the
faithful,
but abundantly repays the
one who acts haughtily.
24 Be strong, and let your heart
take courage,
all you who wait for the
LORD.

Psalm 32

The Joy of Forgiveness

Of David. A Maskil.

1 Happy are those whose
transgression is
forgiven,
whose sin is covered.
2 Happy are those to whom
the LORD imputes no
iniquity,
and in whose spirit there is
no deceit.

3 While I kept silence, my
body wasted away

31.9
Ps 6.7
31.10
Ps 13.2;
39.11; 38.3
31.11
Isa 53.4;
Ps 38.11;
64.8
31.12
Ps 88.4,5
31.13
Jer 20.10;
Lam 2.20;
Mt 27.1
31.14
Ps 140.6
31.15
Job 24.1;
Ps 143.9
31.16
Num 6.25;
Ps 4.6
31.17
Ps 25.2,3
31.18
Ps 120.2;
94.4
31.19
Isa 64.4;
Rom 11.22;
Ps 5.11

31.20
Ps 27.5;
Job 5.21
31.21
Ps 17.7;
1 Sam 23.7
31.22
Ps 116.11;
Lam 3.54
31.23
Ps 34.9;
145.20; 94.2
31.24
Ps 27.14
32.1
Ps 85.2
32.2
2 Cor 5.19;
Jn 1.47
32.3
Ps 39.2,3;
31.10; 38.8

a Gk Syr: Heb *my iniquity* b Cn: Heb
exceedingly c Another reading is *cut off*

through my groaning all
day long.

4 For day and night your hand
was heavy upon me;
my strength was dried up[d]
as by the heat of
summer. *Selah*

5 Then I acknowledged my sin
to you,
and I did not hide my
iniquity;
I said, "I will confess my
transgressions to the
LORD,"
and you forgave the guilt of
my sin. *Selah*

6 Therefore let all who are
faithful
offer prayer to you;
at a time of distress,[e] the
rush of mighty waters
shall not reach them.

7 You are a hiding place for
me;
you preserve me from
trouble;
you surround me with glad
cries of deliverance.
 Selah

8 I will instruct you and teach
you the way you should
go;
I will counsel you with my
eye upon you.

9 Do not be like a horse or a
mule, without
understanding,
whose temper must be
curbed with bit and
bridle,
else it will not stay near
you.

10 Many are the torments of the
wicked,
but steadfast love
surrounds those who
trust in the LORD.

11 Be glad in the LORD and
rejoice, O righteous,
and shout for joy, all you
upright in heart.

32.4
Job 33.7
32.5
Lev 26.40;
Job 31.33;
Prov 28.13;
Ps 103.12
32.6
Ps 69.13;
144.7;
Isa 43.2
32.7
Ps 31.20;
121.7;
Ex 15.1
32.8
Ps 25.8;
33.18
32.9
Jas 3.3
32.10
Rom 2.9;
Prov 16.20
32.11
Ps 64.10

33.1
Ps 32.11;
147.1
33.2
Ps 92.3
33.3
Ps 96.1;
98.4
33.4
Ps 19.8;
119.90
33.5
Ps 11.7;
119.64
33.6
Gen 11.3;
Job 23.13
33.7
Ps 78.13
33.8
Ps 67.7;
96.9
33.9
Gen 1.3;
Ps 148.5
33.10
Isa 8.10;
19.3
33.11
Job 23.13;
Prov 19.21;
Ps 40.5

Psalm 33

The Greatness and Goodness of God

1 Rejoice in the LORD, O you
righteous.
Praise befits the upright.

2 Praise the LORD with the lyre;
make melody to him with
the harp of ten strings.

3 Sing to him a new song;
play skillfully on the
strings, with loud
shouts.

4 For the word of the LORD is
upright,
and all his work is done in
faithfulness.

5 He loves righteousness and
justice;
the earth is full of the
steadfast love of the
LORD.

6 By the word of the LORD the
heavens were made,
and all their host by the
breath of his mouth.

7 He gathered the waters of
the sea as in a bottle;
he put the deeps in
storehouses.

8 Let all the earth fear the
LORD;
let all the inhabitants of
the world stand in awe
of him.

9 For he spoke, and it came to
be;
he commanded, and it
stood firm.

10 The LORD brings the counsel
of the nations to
nothing;
he frustrates the plans of
the peoples.

11 The counsel of the LORD
stands forever,
the thoughts of his heart to
all generations.

[d] Meaning of Heb uncertain [e] Cn: Heb *at
a time of finding only*

¹² Happy is the nation whose
 God is the LORD,
 the people whom he has
 chosen as his heritage.

¹³ The LORD looks down from
 heaven;
 he sees all humankind.
¹⁴ From where he sits
 enthroned he watches
 all the inhabitants of the
 earth—
¹⁵ he who fashions the hearts
 of them all,
 and observes all their
 deeds.
¹⁶ A king is not saved by his
 great army;
 a warrior is not delivered
 by his great strength.
¹⁷ The war horse is a vain hope
 for victory,
 and by its great might it
 cannot save.

¹⁸ Truly the eye of the LORD is
 on those who fear him,
 on those who hope in his
 steadfast love,
¹⁹ to deliver their soul from
 death,
 and to keep them alive in
 famine.

²⁰ Our soul waits for the LORD;
 he is our help and shield.
²¹ Our heart is glad in him,
 because we trust in his
 holy name.
²² Let your steadfast love,
 O LORD, be upon us,
 even as we hope in you.

Psalm 34

Praise for Deliverance from
Trouble

*Of David, when he feigned
madness before Abimelech, so
that he drove him out, and he
went away.*

¹ I will bless the LORD at all
 times;
 his praise shall continually
 be in my mouth.

² My soul makes its boast in
 the LORD;
 let the humble hear and be
 glad.
³ O magnify the LORD with me,
 and let us exalt his name
 together.

⁴ I sought the LORD, and he
 answered me,
 and delivered me from all
 my fears.
⁵ Look to him, and be radiant;
 so your[f] faces shall never
 be ashamed.
⁶ This poor soul cried, and was
 heard by the LORD,
 and was saved from every
 trouble.
⁷ The angel of the LORD
 encamps
 around those who fear him,
 and delivers them.
⁸ O taste and see that the
 LORD is good;
 happy are those who take
 refuge in him.
⁹ O fear the LORD, you his holy
 ones,
 for those who fear him
 have no want.
¹⁰ The young lions suffer want
 and hunger,
 but those who seek the
 LORD lack no good
 thing.

¹¹ Come, O children, listen to
 me;
 I will teach you the fear of
 the LORD.
¹² Which of you desires life,
 and covets many days to
 enjoy good?
¹³ Keep your tongue from evil,
 and your lips from
 speaking deceit.
¹⁴ Depart from evil, and do
 good;
 seek peace, and pursue it.

¹⁵ The eyes of the LORD are on
 the righteous,
 and his ears are open to
 their cry.

33.12
Ps 144.15;
Ex 19.5;
Deut 7.6
33.13
Job 28.24;
Ps 11.4
33.15
Jer 32.19
33.16
Ps 44.6
33.17
Ps 20.7;
Prov 21.31
33.18
Job 36.7;
Ps 34.15;
147.11
33.19
Ps 37.19
33.20
Ps 130.6;
115.9
33.21
Zech 10.7;
Jn 16.22
34.1
Eph 5.20;
Ps 71.6

34.2
Jer 9.24;
Ps 119.74
34.3
Lk 1.46
34.4
Mt 7.7;
vv. 6,17,19
34.5
Ps 36.9;
25.3
34.6
vv. 4,17,19
34.7
Dan 6.22;
2 Kings 6.17
34.8
1 Pet 2.3;
Ps 2.12
34.9
Ps 23.1
34.10
Ps 84.11
34.11
Ps 111.10
34.12
1 Pet 3.10
34.13
1 Pet 2.22
34.14
Ps 37.27;
Heb 12.14
34.15
Job 36.7;
Ps 33.18

[f] Gk Syr Jerome: Heb *their*

16 The face of the LORD is
 against evildoers,
 to cut off the remembrance
 of them from the earth.
17 When the righteous cry for
 help, the LORD hears,
 and rescues them from all
 their troubles.
18 The LORD is near to the
 brokenhearted,
 and saves the crushed in
 spirit.

19 Many are the afflictions of
 the righteous,
 but the LORD rescues them
 from them all.
20 He keeps all their bones;
 not one of them will be
 broken.
21 Evil brings death to the
 wicked,
 and those who hate the
 righteous will be
 condemned.
22 The LORD redeems the life of
 his servants;
 none of those who take
 refuge in him will be
 condemned.

Psalm 35
Prayer for Deliverance from Enemies

Of David.

1 Contend, O LORD, with those
 who contend with me;
 fight against those who
 fight against me!
2 Take hold of shield and
 buckler,
 and rise up to help me!
3 Draw the spear and javelin
 against my pursuers;
 say to my soul,
 "I am your salvation."

4 Let them be put to shame
 and dishonor
 who seek after my life.
 Let them be turned back and
 confounded
 who devise evil against me.
5 Let them be like chaff before
 the wind,

with the angel of the LORD
 driving them on.
6 Let their way be dark and
 slippery,
 with the angel of the LORD
 pursuing them.

7 For without cause they hid
 their net g for me;
 without cause they dug a
 pit h for my life.
8 Let ruin come on them
 unawares.
 And let the net that they hid
 ensnare them;
 let them fall in it — to their
 ruin.

9 Then my soul shall rejoice in
 the LORD,
 exulting in his deliverance.
10 All my bones shall say,
 "O LORD, who is like you?
 You deliver the weak
 from those too strong for
 them,
 the weak and needy from
 those who despoil
 them."

11 Malicious witnesses rise up;
 they ask me about things I
 do not know.
12 They repay me evil for good;
 my soul is forlorn.
13 But as for me, when they
 were sick,
 I wore sackcloth;
 I afflicted myself with
 fasting.
 I prayed with head bowed i
 on my bosom,
14 as though I grieved for a
 friend or a brother;
 I went about as one who
 laments for a mother,
 bowed down and in
 mourning.

15 But at my stumbling they
 gathered in glee,
 they gathered together
 against me;

34.16
Jer 44.11;
Prov 10.7
34.17
Ps 145.19;
v. 19
34.18
Ps 145.18;
Isa 57.15
34.19
Prov 24.16;
vv. 4,6,17
34.20
Jn 19.36
34.21
Ps 94.23
34.22
1 Kings 1.29;
Ps 71.23
35.1
Ps 43.1
35.3
Ps 62.2
35.4
Ps 70.2,3
35.5
Job 21.18;
Ps 1.4;
Isa 29.5

35.6
Ps 73.18;
Jer 23.12
35.7
Ps 9.15
35.8
1 Thes 5.3
35.9
Isa 61.10;
Lk 1.47
35.10
Ex 15.11;
Ps 18.17;
37.14
35.11
Ps 27.12
35.12
Jn 10.32
35.13
Job 30.25;
Ps 69.10
35.15
Job 30.1,8

g Heb *a pit, their net* h The word *pit* is
transposed from the preceding line
i Or *My prayer turned back*

ruffians whom I did not
 know
 tore at me without ceasing;
16 they impiously mocked more
 and more,[i]
 gnashing at me with their
 teeth.

17 How long, O Lord, will you
 look on?
 Rescue me from their
 ravages,
 my life from the lions!
18 Then I will thank you in the
 great congregation;
 in the mighty throng I will
 praise you.

19 Do not let my treacherous
 enemies rejoice over
 me,
 or those who hate me
 without cause wink the
 eye.
20 For they do not speak peace,
 but they conceive deceitful
 words
 against those who are quiet
 in the land.
21 They open wide their mouths
 against me;
 they say, "Aha, Aha,
 our eyes have seen it."

22 You have seen, O Lord; do
 not be silent!
 O Lord, do not be far from
 me!
23 Wake up! Bestir yourself for
 my defense,
 for my cause, my God and
 my Lord!
24 Vindicate me, O Lord, my
 God,
 according to your
 righteousness,
 and do not let them rejoice
 over me.
25 Do not let them say to
 themselves,
 "Aha, we have our heart's
 desire."
 Do not let them say, "We
 have swallowed you[k] up."

26 Let all those who rejoice at
 my calamity

35.16
Lam 2.16
35.17
Hab 1.13;
Ps 22.20
35.18
Ps 22.22,25
35.19
Ps 13.4;
38.19;
Prov 6.13;
Ps 69.4;
Jn 15.25
35.21
Ps 22.13;
40.15
35.22
Ex 3.7;
Ps 28.1;
10.1
35.23
Ps 44.23
35.24
Ps 9.4;
v. 19
35.25
Lam 2.16
35.26
Ps 40.14;
38.16

35.27
Ps 32.11;
9.4; 40.16;
147.11
35.28
Ps 51.14
36.1
Rom 3.18
36.3
Jer 4.22
36.4
Prov 4.16;
Mic 2.1;
Isa 65.2
36.6
Job 11.8;
Ps 77.19;
Rom 11.33

be put to shame and
 confusion;
 let those who exalt
 themselves against me
 be clothed with shame and
 dishonor.

27 Let those who desire my
 vindication
 shout for joy and be glad,
 and say evermore,
 "Great is the Lord,
 who delights in the welfare
 of his servant."
28 Then my tongue shall tell of
 your righteousness
 and of your praise all day
 long.

Psalm 36

Human Wickedness and Divine Goodness

To the leader. Of David, the
 servant of the Lord.

1 Transgression speaks to the
 wicked
 deep in their hearts;
 there is no fear of God
 before their eyes.
2 For they flatter themselves in
 their own eyes
 that their iniquity cannot
 be found out and hated.
3 The words of their mouths
 are mischief and deceit;
 they have ceased to act
 wisely and do good.
4 They plot mischief while on
 their beds;
 they are set on a way that
 is not good;
 they do not reject evil.

5 Your steadfast love, O Lord,
 extends to the heavens,
 your faithfulness to the
 clouds.
6 Your righteousness is like
 the mighty mountains,
 your judgments are like the
 great deep;

i Cn Compare Gk: Heb *like the profanest of
mockers of a cake* k Heb *him*

you save humans and
 animals alike, O Lord.

7 How precious is your
 steadfast love, O God!
 All people may take refuge
 in the shadow of your
 wings.
8 They feast on the abundance
 of your house,
 and you give them drink
 from the river of your
 delights.
9 For with you is the fountain
 of life;
 in your light we see light.

10 O continue your steadfast
 love to those who know
 you,
 and your salvation to the
 upright of heart!
11 Do not let the foot of the
 arrogant tread on me,
 or the hand of the wicked
 drive me away.
12 There the evildoers lie
 prostrate;
 they are thrust down,
 unable to rise.

Psalm 37

Exhortation to Patience and Trust

Of David.

1 Do not fret because of the
 wicked;
 do not be envious of
 wrongdoers,
2 for they will soon fade like
 the grass,
 and wither like the green
 herb.

3 Trust in the Lord, and do
 good;
 so you will live in the land,
 and enjoy security.
4 Take delight in the Lord,
 and he will give you the
 desires of your heart.

5 Commit your way to the
 Lord;

36.7
Ruth 2.12
36.8
Ps 65.4;
Job 20.17;
Rev 22.1
36.9
Jer 2.13;
1 Pet 2.9
36.12
Ps 140.10
37.1
Ps 73.3;
Prov 23.17
37.2
Ps 90.5,6
37.3
Ps 62.8;
Deut 30.20;
Isa 40.11
37.4
Isa 58.14
37.5
Ps 55.22;
Prov 16.3;
1 Pet 5.7

37.6
Job 11.17;
Mic 7.9
37.7
Ps 62.5;
40.1; vv. 1,8
37.8
Ps 73.3;
Eph 4.26
37.9
Isa 60.21
37.10
Job 24.24;
7.10
37.11
Mt 5.5
37.12
Ps 35.16
37.13
Ps 2.4;
1 Sam 26.10
37.14
Ps 11.2;
35.10
37.15
Ps 9.16
37.16
Prov 15.16

 trust in him, and he will
 act.
6 He will make your
 vindication shine like
 the light,
 and the justice of your
 cause like the noonday.

7 Be still before the Lord, and
 wait patiently for him;
 do not fret over those who
 prosper in their way,
 over those who carry out
 evil devices.

8 Refrain from anger, and
 forsake wrath.
 Do not fret — it leads only
 to evil.
9 For the wicked shall be cut
 off,
 but those who wait for the
 Lord shall inherit the
 land.

10 Yet a little while, and the
 wicked will be no more;
 though you look diligently
 for their place, they will
 not be there.
11 But the meek shall inherit
 the land,
 and delight themselves in
 abundant prosperity.

12 The wicked plot against the
 righteous,
 and gnash their teeth at
 them;
13 but the Lord laughs at the
 wicked,
 for he sees that their day is
 coming.

14 The wicked draw the sword
 and bend their bows
 to bring down the poor and
 needy,
 to kill those who walk
 uprightly;
15 their sword shall enter their
 own heart,
 and their bows shall be
 broken.

16 Better is a little that the
 righteous person has

than the abundance of
 many wicked.
17 For the arms of the wicked
 shall be broken,
 but the LORD upholds the
 righteous.

18 The LORD knows the days of
 the blameless,
 and their heritage will
 abide forever;
19 they are not put to shame in
 evil times,
 in the days of famine they
 have abundance.

20 But the wicked perish,
 and the enemies of the
 LORD are like the glory
 of the pastures;
 they vanish — like smoke
 they vanish away.

21 The wicked borrow, and do
 not pay back,
 but the righteous are
 generous and keep
 giving;
22 for those blessed by the LORD
 shall inherit the land,
 but those cursed by him
 shall be cut off.

23 Our steps[l] are made firm by
 the LORD,
 when he delights in our[m]
 way;
24 though we stumble,[n] we[o]
 shall not fall headlong,
 for the LORD holds us[p] by
 the hand.

25 I have been young, and now
 am old,
 yet I have not seen the
 righteous forsaken
 or their children begging
 bread.
26 They are ever giving liberally
 and lending,
 and their children become
 a blessing.

27 Depart from evil, and do
 good;
 so you shall abide forever.
28 For the LORD loves justice;

37.17
Job 38.15;
Ps 10.15
37.18
Ps 1.6
37.19
Job 5.20;
Ps 33.19
37.20
Ps 72.27;
102.3
37.21
Ps 112.5,9
37.22
Prov 3.33;
Job 5.3
37.23
1 Sam 2.9;
Ps 147.11
37.24
Prov 24.16;
Ps 147.6
37.25
Heb 13.5;
Job 15.23
37.26
v. 21;
Ps 147.13
37.27
Ps 34.14;
v. 18
37.28
Ps 11.7;
21.10;
Isa 14.20

37.29
vv. 9,18
37.30
Mt 12.35
37.31
Ps 40.8;
Isa 51.7;
v. 23
37.32
Ps 10.8
37.33
2 Pet 2.9;
Ps 109.31
37.34
Ps 27.14;
52.5,6
37.35
Job 5.3
37.36
Job 20.5
37.37
Isa 57.1,2
37.38
Ps 1.4;
vv. 9,20,28

 he will not forsake his
 faithful ones.

The righteous shall be kept
 safe forever,
 but the children of the
 wicked shall be cut off.
29 The righteous shall inherit
 the land,
 and live in it forever.

30 The mouths of the righteous
 utter wisdom,
 and their tongues speak
 justice.
31 The law of their God is in
 their hearts;
 their steps do not slip.

32 The wicked watch for the
 righteous,
 and seek to kill them.
33 The LORD will not abandon
 them to their power,
 or let them be condemned
 when they are brought
 to trial.

34 Wait for the LORD, and keep
 to his way,
 and he will exalt you to
 inherit the land;
 you will look on the
 destruction of the
 wicked.

35 I have seen the wicked
 oppressing,
 and towering like a cedar
 of Lebanon.[q]
36 Again I[r] passed by, and they
 were no more;
 though I sought them, they
 could not be found.

37 Mark the blameless, and
 behold the upright,
 for there is posterity for the
 peaceable.
38 But transgressors shall be
 altogether destroyed;
 the posterity of the wicked
 shall be cut off.

[l] Heb *a man's steps* [m] Heb *his*
[n] Heb *he stumbles* [o] Heb *he*
[p] Heb *him* [q] Gk: Meaning of Heb
uncertain [r] Gk Syr Jerome: Heb *he*

39 The salvation of the
 righteous is from the
 LORD;
 he is their refuge in the
 time of trouble.
40 The LORD helps them and
 rescues them;
 he rescues them from the
 wicked, and saves
 them,
 because they take refuge in
 him.

Psalm 38

A Penitent Sufferer's Plea for Healing

A Psalm of David, for the
memorial offering.

1 O LORD, do not rebuke me in
 your anger,
 or discipline me in your
 wrath.
2 For your arrows have sunk
 into me,
 and your hand has come
 down on me.

3 There is no soundness in my
 flesh
 because of your
 indignation;
there is no health in my
 bones
 because of my sin.
4 For my iniquities have gone
 over my head;
 they weigh like a burden
 too heavy for me.

5 My wounds grow foul and
 fester
 because of my foolishness;
6 I am utterly bowed down and
 prostrate;
 all day long I go around
 mourning.
7 For my loins are filled with
 burning,
 and there is no soundness
 in my flesh.
8 I am utterly spent and
 crushed;
 I groan because of the
 tumult of my heart.

9 O Lord, all my longing is
 known to you;
 my sighing is not hidden
 from you.
10 My heart throbs, my strength
 fails me;
 as for the light of my
 eyes—it also has gone
 from me.
11 My friends and companions
 stand aloof from my
 affliction,
 and my neighbors stand far
 off.

12 Those who seek my life lay
 their snares;
 those who seek to hurt me
 speak of ruin,
 and meditate treachery all
 day long.

13 But I am like the deaf, I do
 not hear;
 like the mute, who cannot
 speak.
14 Truly, I am like one who
 does not hear,
 and in whose mouth is no
 retort.

15 But it is for you, O LORD,
 that I wait;
 it is you, O LORD my God,
 who will answer.
16 For I pray, "Only do not let
 them rejoice over me,
 those who boast against
 me when my foot
 slips."

17 For I am ready to fall,
 and my pain is ever with
 me.
18 I confess my iniquity;
 I am sorry for my sin.
19 Those who are my foes
 without cause[s] are
 mighty,
 and many are those who
 hate me wrongfully.
20 Those who render me evil for
 good
 are my adversaries because
 I follow after good.

[s] Q Ms: MT *my living foes*

37.39
Ps 3.8; 9.9
37.40
Isa 31.5;
1 Chr 5.20
38.1
Ps 6.1
38.2
Job 6.4;
Ps 32.4
38.3
Isa 1.6;
Ps 6.2
38.4
Ezra 9.6
38.5
Ps 69.5
38.6
Ps 35.14;
42.9
38.7
Ps 102.3;
v. 3
38.8
Job 3.24;
Ps 22.1

38.9
Ps 10.17;
6.6
38.10
Ps 31.10;
6.7
38.11
Ps 31.11;
Lk 23.49
38.12
Ps 54.3;
140.5; 35.4,
20
38.13
Ps 39.2,9
38.15
Ps 39.7;
17.6
38.16
Ps 13.4;
35.26
38.17
Ps 13.2
38.18
Ps 32.5;
2 Cor 7.9
38.19
Ps 18.17;
35.19
38.20
Ps 35.12;
1 Jn 3.12

21 Do not forsake me, O LORD;
 O my God, do not be far
 from me;
22 make haste to help me,
 O Lord, my salvation.

Psalm 39

Prayer for Wisdom and Forgiveness

To the leader: to Jeduthun. A Psalm of David.

1 I said, "I will guard my ways
 that I may not sin with my
 tongue;
 I will keep a muzzle on my
 mouth
 as long as the wicked are
 in my presence."
2 I was silent and still;
 I held my peace to no
 avail;
 my distress grew worse,
3 my heart became hot
 within me.
 While I mused, the fire
 burned;
 then I spoke with my
 tongue:

4 "LORD, let me know my end,
 and what is the measure of
 my days;
 let me know how fleeting
 my life is.
5 You have made my days a
 few handbreadths,
 and my lifetime is as
 nothing in your sight.
 Surely everyone stands as a
 mere breath. *Selah*
6 Surely everyone goes about
 like a shadow.
 Surely for nothing they are in
 turmoil;
 they heap up, and do not
 know who will gather.

7 "And now, O Lord, what do I
 wait for?
 My hope is in you.
8 Deliver me from all my
 transgressions.
 Do not make me the scorn
 of the fool.

9 I am silent; I do not open my
 mouth,
 for it is you who have done
 it.
10 Remove your stroke from me;
 I am worn down by the
 blows[t] of your hand.

11 You chastise mortals
 in punishment for sin,
 consuming like a moth what
 is dear to them;
 surely everyone is a mere
 breath. *Selah*

12 "Hear my prayer, O LORD,
 and give ear to my cry;
 do not hold your peace at
 my tears.
 For I am your passing guest,
 an alien, like all my
 forebears.
13 Turn your gaze away from
 me, that I may smile
 again,
 before I depart and am no
 more."

Psalm 40

Thanksgiving for Deliverance and Prayer for Help

To the leader. Of David. A Psalm.

1 I waited patiently for the
 LORD;
 he inclined to me and
 heard my cry.
2 He drew me up from the
 desolate pit,[u]
 out of the miry bog,
 and set my feet upon a rock,
 making my steps secure.
3 He put a new song in my
 mouth,
 a song of praise to our
 God.
 Many will see and fear,
 and put their trust in the
 LORD.

4 Happy are those who make
 the LORD their trust,
 who do not turn to the
 proud,

38.21
Ps 35.22
38.22
Ps 40.13,17;
27.1
39.1
1 Kings 2.4;
Job 2.10;
Jas 3.2
39.2
Ps 38.13
39.4
Ps 90.12;
103.14
39.5
Ps 89.47;
144.4; 62.9
39.6
1 Pet 1.24;
Ps 127.2;
Job 27.17;
Lk 12.20
39.7
Ps 38.15
39.8
Ps 51.9;
44.13

39.9
v. 2;
Job 2.10
39.10
Job 9.34;
Ps 32.4
39.11
2 Pet 2.16;
Job 13.28;
v. 5
39.12
Ps 102.1;
56.8;
Heb 11.13;
1 Pet 2.11
39.13
Job 10.20;
14.10
40.1
Ps 27.14;
34.15
40.2
Ps 69.2;
27.5
40.3
Ps 33.3
40.4
Ps 84.12

t Heb *hostility* u Cn: Heb *pit of tumult*

to those who go astray
　　after false gods.
5 You have multiplied, O Lᴏʀᴅ
　　my God,
　　your wondrous deeds and
　　　your thoughts toward
　　　us;
　　none can compare with
　　　you.
　　Were I to proclaim and tell
　　　of them,
　　they would be more than
　　　can be counted.

6 Sacrifice and offering you do
　　not desire,
　　but you have given me an
　　　open ear.ᵛ
　　Burnt offering and sin
　　　offering
　　you have not required.
7 Then I said, "Here I am;
　　in the scroll of the book it
　　　is written of me.ʷ
8 I delight to do your will,
　　O my God;
　　your law is within my
　　　heart."

9 I have told the glad news of
　　deliverance
　　in the great congregation;
　　see, I have not restrained my
　　　lips,
　　as you know, O Lᴏʀᴅ.
10 I have not hidden your
　　saving help within my
　　　heart,
　　I have spoken of your
　　　faithfulness and your
　　　salvation;
　　I have not concealed your
　　　steadfast love and your
　　　faithfulness
　　from the great
　　　congregation.

11 Do not, O Lᴏʀᴅ, withhold
　　your mercy from me;
　　let your steadfast love and
　　　your faithfulness
　　keep me safe forever.
12 For evils have encompassed
　　me
　　without number;
　　my iniquities have overtaken
　　　me,

40.5
Ps 136.4;
Isa 55.8;
Ps 139.18
40.6
1 Sam 15.22
40.8
Jn 4.34;
Rom 7.22;
Ps 37.31
40.9
Ps 22.22;
119.13
40.10
Acts 20.20;
Ps 89.1
40.11
Ps 43.3
40.12
Ps 116.3;
38.4; 69.4;
73.26

40.13
Ps 70.1
40.14
Ps 35.4;
63.9
40.15
Ps 70.3
40.16
Ps 70.4;
35.27
40.17
Ps 70.5
41.1
Ps 82.3,4;
Prov 14.21
41.2
Ps 37.22,28;
27.12

　　until I cannot see;
　　they are more than the hairs
　　　of my head,
　　and my heart fails me.

13 Be pleased, O Lᴏʀᴅ, to
　　deliver me;
　　O Lᴏʀᴅ, make haste to help
　　　me.
14 Let all those be put to
　　shame and confusion
　　who seek to snatch away
　　　my life;
　　let those be turned back and
　　　brought to dishonor
　　who desire my hurt.
15 Let those be appalled
　　because of their shame
　　who say to me, "Aha, Aha!"

16 But may all who seek you
　　rejoice and be glad in you;
　　may those who love your
　　　salvation
　　say continually, "Great is
　　　the Lᴏʀᴅ!"
17 As for me, I am poor and
　　needy,
　　but the Lord takes thought
　　　for me.
　　You are my help and my
　　　deliverer;
　　do not delay, O my God.

Psalm 41

Assurance of God's Help and a Plea for Healing

To the leader. A Psalm of David.

1 Happy are those who
　　consider the poor;ˣ
　　the Lᴏʀᴅ delivers them in
　　　the day of trouble.
2 The Lᴏʀᴅ protects them and
　　keeps them alive;
　　they are called happy in
　　　the land.
　　You do not give them up to
　　　the will of their
　　　enemies.

ᵛHeb *ears you have dug for me*　ʷMeaning
of Heb uncertain　ˣOr *weak*

3 The LORD sustains them on
 their sickbed;
 in their illness you heal all
 their infirmities.y

4 As for me, I said, "O LORD,
 be gracious to me;
 heal me, for I have sinned
 against you."
5 My enemies wonder in
 malice
 when I will die, and my
 name perish.
6 And when they come to see
 me, they utter empty
 words,
 while their hearts gather
 mischief;
 when they go out, they tell
 it abroad.
7 All who hate me whisper
 together about me;
 they imagine the worst for
 me.

8 They think that a deadly
 thing has fastened on
 me,
 that I will not rise again
 from where I lie.
9 Even my bosom friend in
 whom I trusted,
 who ate of my bread, has
 lifted the heel against
 me.
10 But you, O LORD, be gracious
 to me,
 and raise me up, that I
 may repay them.

11 By this I know that you are
 pleased with me;
 because my enemy has not
 triumphed over me.
12 But you have upheld me
 because of my integrity,
 and set me in your
 presence forever.

13 Blessed be the LORD, the God
 of Israel,
 from everlasting to
 everlasting.
 Amen and Amen.

41.3
Ps 6.6
41.4
Ps 6.2; 51.4
41.5
Ps 38.12
41.6
Ps 12.2
41.7
Ps 56.5
41.8
Ps 71.10,11
41.9
Job 19.19;
Ps 55.12;
Jn 13.18
41.10
Ps 3.3
41.11
Ps 147.11;
25.2
41.12
Ps 37.17;
Job 36.7
41.13
Ps 106.48

42.1
Ps 119.131
42.2
Ps 63.1;
Jer 10.10;
Ps 43.4
42.3
Ps 80.5;
79.10
42.4
Ps 62.8;
Isa 30.29;
Ps 100.4
42.5
Ps 38.6;
77.3;
Lam 3.24;
Ps 44.3
42.7
Ps 88.7;
Jon 2.3

BOOK II

(Psalms 42–72)

Psalm 42

Longing for God and His Help in Distress

To the leader. A Maskil of the
 Korahites.

1 As a deer longs for flowing
 streams,
 so my soul longs for you,
 O God.
2 My soul thirsts for God,
 for the living God.
 When shall I come and
 behold
 the face of God?
3 My tears have been my food
 day and night,
 while people say to me
 continually,
 "Where is your God?"

4 These things I remember,
 as I pour out my soul:
 how I went with the throng,z
 and led them in procession
 to the house of God,
 with glad shouts and songs
 of thanksgiving,
 a multitude keeping
 festival.
5 Why are you cast down,
 O my soul,
 and why are you disquieted
 within me?
 Hope in God; for I shall
 again praise him,
 my help 6 and my God.

 My soul is cast down within
 me;
 therefore I remember you
 from the land of Jordan and
 of Hermon,
 from Mount Mizar.
7 Deep calls to deep
 at the thunder of your
 cataracts;
 all your waves and your
 billows

y Heb *you change all his bed* z Meaning of
Heb uncertain

have gone over me.
8 By day the LORD commands
 his steadfast love,
 and at night his song is
 with me,
 a prayer to the God of my
 life.

9 I say to God, my rock,
 "Why have you forgotten
 me?
 Why must I walk about
 mournfully
 because the enemy
 oppresses me?"
10 As with a deadly wound in
 my body,
 my adversaries taunt me,
 while they say to me
 continually,
 "Where is your God?"

11 Why are you cast down,
 O my soul,
 and why are you disquieted
 within me?
 Hope in God; for I shall
 again praise him,
 my help and my God.

Psalm 43

Prayer to God in Time of Trouble

1 Vindicate me, O God, and
 defend my cause
 against an ungodly people;
 from those who are deceitful
 and unjust
 deliver me!
2 For you are the God in
 whom I take refuge;
 why have you cast me off?
 Why must I walk about
 mournfully
 because of the oppression
 of the enemy?

3 O send out your light and
 your truth;
 let them lead me;
 let them bring me to your
 holy hill
 and to your dwelling.
4 Then I will go to the altar of
 God,

42.8
Ps 57.3;
Job 35.10;
Ps 63.6;
149.5
42.9
Ps 38.6
42.10
v. 3
42.11
v. 5
43.1
Ps 26.1;
1 Sam 24.15;
Ps 5.6
43.2
Ps 18.1;
44.9; 42.9
43.3
Ps 36.9;
42.4; 84.1
43.4
Ps 26.6;
33.2

43.5
Ps 42.5,11
44.1
Ex 12.26;
Ps 78.3,12
44.2
Ex 15.17;
Ps 78.55;
80.8
44.3
Josh 24.12;
Ps 77.15;
Deut 4.37;
7.7,8
44.4
Ps 74.12;
79.9
44.5
Dan 8.4;
Ps 108.13
44.6
Ps 33.16
44.7
Ps 136.24;
53.5

 to God my exceeding joy;
 and I will praise you with the
 harp,
 O God, my God.

5 Why are you cast down,
 O my soul,
 and why are you disquieted
 within me?
 Hope in God; for I shall
 again praise him,
 my help and my God.

Psalm 44

National Lament and Prayer for Help

To the leader. Of the Korahites.
A Maskil.

1 We have heard with our ears,
 O God,
 our ancestors have told us,
 what deeds you performed in
 their days,
 in the days of old:
2 you with your own hand
 drove out the nations,
 but them you planted;
 you afflicted the peoples,
 but them you set free;
3 for not by their own sword
 did they win the land,
 nor did their own arm give
 them victory;
 but your right hand, and
 your arm,
 and the light of your
 countenance,
 for you delighted in them.

4 You are my King and my
 God;
 you command[a] victories
 for Jacob.
5 Through you we push down
 our foes;
 through your name we
 tread down our
 assailants.
6 For not in my bow do I trust,
 nor can my sword save me.
7 But you have saved us from
 our foes,

a Gk Syr: Heb *You are my King, O God;*
command

and have put to confusion
those who hate us.
8 In God we have boasted
continually,
and we will give thanks to
your name forever.
Selah

9 Yet you have rejected us and
abased us,
and have not gone out with
our armies.
10 You made us turn back from
the foe,
and our enemies have
gotten spoil.
11 You have made us like sheep
for slaughter,
and have scattered us
among the nations.
12 You have sold your people
for a trifle,
demanding no high price
for them.

13 You have made us the taunt
of our neighbors,
the derision and scorn of
those around us.
14 You have made us a byword
among the nations,
a laughingstock[b] among
the peoples.
15 All day long my disgrace is
before me,
and shame has covered my
face
16 at the words of the taunters
and revilers,
at the sight of the enemy
and the avenger.

17 All this has come upon
us,
yet we have not forgotten
you,
or been false to your
covenant.
18 Our heart has not turned
back,
nor have our steps
departed from your way,
19 yet you have broken us in
the haunt of jackals,
and covered us with deep
darkness.

44.8
Ps 34.2;
30.12
44.9
Ps 60.1,10;
74.1
44.10
Lev 26.17;
Josh 7.8;
Ps 89.41
44.11
v. 22;
Deut 4.27;
28.64;
Ps 106.27
44.12
Isa 52.3,4;
Jer 15.13
44.13
Ps 79.4;
80.6
44.14
Jer 24.9;
Ps 109.25
44.16
Ps 74.10;
8.2
44.17
Dan 9.13;
Ps 78.7,57
44.18
Ps 78.57;
Job 23.11
44.19
Ps 51.8;
Job 3.5

44.20
Ps 78.11;
68.31; 81.9
44.21
Ps 139.1,2;
Jer 17.10
44.22
Rom 8.36;
Isa 53.7
44.23
Ps 7.6;
78.65; 77.7
44.24
Job 13.24;
Ps 42.9
44.25
Ps 119.25
44.26
Ps 35.2;
25.22
45.1
Ezra 7.6
45.2
Lk 4.22
45.3
Isa 9.6
45.4
Rev 6.2

20 If we had forgotten the name
of our God,
or spread out our hands to
a strange god,
21 would not God discover this?
For he knows the secrets of
the heart.
22 Because of you we are being
killed all day long,
and accounted as sheep for
the slaughter.

23 Rouse yourself! Why do you
sleep, O Lord?
Awake, do not cast us off
forever!
24 Why do you hide your face?
Why do you forget our
affliction and
oppression?
25 For we sink down to the
dust;
our bodies cling to the
ground.
26 Rise up, come to our help.
Redeem us for the sake of
your steadfast love.

Psalm 45

Ode for a Royal Wedding

To the leader: according to
Lilies. Of the Korahites. A
Maskil. A love song.

1 My heart overflows with a
goodly theme;
I address my verses to the
king;
my tongue is like the pen
of a ready scribe.

2 You are the most handsome
of men;
grace is poured upon your
lips;
therefore God has blessed
you forever.
3 Gird your sword on your
thigh, O mighty one,
in your glory and majesty.

4 In your majesty ride on
victoriously

[b] Heb *a shaking of the head*

for the cause of truth and
to defend^c the right;
let your right hand teach
you dread deeds.
5 Your arrows are sharp
in the heart of the king's
enemies;
the peoples fall under you.

6 Your throne, O God,^d
endures forever and
ever.
Your royal scepter is a
scepter of equity;
7 you love righteousness and
hate wickedness.
Therefore God, your God,
has anointed you
with the oil of gladness
beyond your
companions;
8 your robes are all fragrant
with myrrh and aloes
and cassia.
From ivory palaces stringed
instruments make you
glad;
9 daughters of kings are
among your ladies of
honor;
at your right hand stands
the queen in gold of
Ophir.

10 Hear, O daughter, consider
and incline your ear;
forget your people and your
father's house,
11 and the king will desire
your beauty.
Since he is your lord, bow to
him;
12 the people^e of Tyre will
seek your favor with
gifts,
the richest of the people
13 with all kinds of
wealth.

The princess is decked in her
chamber with
gold-woven robes;^f
14 in many-colored robes she
is led to the king;
behind her the virgins, her
companions, follow.

45.6
Ps 93.2;
Heb 1.8,9;
Ps 98.9
45.7
Ps 33.5;
Isa 61.1;
Ps 79.4;
21.6
45.8
Song 1.3
45.9
Song 6.8;
1 Kings 2.19
45.10
Deut 21.13
45.11
Ps 95.6;
Isa 54.5
45.12
Ps 22.29
45.13
Isa 61.10
45.14
Song 1.4;
v. 9

45.16
1 Pet 2.9;
Rev 1.6;
20.6
45.17
Mal 1.11;
Ps 138.4
46.1
Ps 14.6;
Deut 4.7;
Ps 9.9
46.2
Ps 23.4;
82.5; 18.7
46.3
Ps 93.3,4
46.4
Isa 8.7;
Ps 48.1,8;
Isa 60.14
46.5
Isa 12.6;
Ps 37.40
46.6
Ps 2.1;
68.33;
Mic 1.4

15 With joy and gladness they
are led along
as they enter the palace of
the king.

16 In the place of ancestors
you, O king,^g shall
have sons;
you will make them princes
in all the earth.
17 I will cause your name to be
celebrated in all
generations;
therefore the peoples will
praise you forever and
ever.

Psalm 46

God's Defense of His City and People

*To the leader. Of the Korahites.
According to Alamoth. A Song.*

1 God is our refuge and
strength,
a very present^h help in
trouble.
2 Therefore we will not fear,
though the earth should
change,
though the mountains
shake in the heart of
the sea;
3 though its waters roar and
foam,
though the mountains
tremble with its tumult.
Selah

4 There is a river whose
streams make glad the
city of God,
the holy habitation of the
Most High.
5 God is in the midst of the
city;ⁱ it shall not be
moved;
God will help it when the
morning dawns.
6 The nations are in an uproar,
the kingdoms totter;

^cCn: Heb *and the meekness of* ^dOr *Your
throne is a throne of God, it*
^eHeb *daughter* ^fOr *people.* ¹³*All glorious
is the princess within, gold embroidery is her
clothing* ^gHeb lacks *O king*
^hOr *well proved* ⁱHeb *of it*

he utters his voice, the
earth melts.
7 The LORD of hosts is with us;
the God of Jacob is our
refuge.[i] *Selah*

8 Come, behold the works of
the LORD;
see what desolations he
has brought on the
earth.
9 He makes wars cease to the
end of the earth;
he breaks the bow, and
shatters the spear;
he burns the shields with
fire.
10 "Be still, and know that I am
God!
I am exalted among the
nations,
I am exalted in the earth."
11 The LORD of hosts is with us;
the God of Jacob is our
refuge.[i] *Selah*

Psalm 47

God's Rule over the Nations

To the leader. Of the Korahites.
A Psalm.

1 Clap your hands, all you
peoples;
shout to God with loud
songs of joy.
2 For the LORD, the Most High,
is awesome,
a great king over all the
earth.
3 He subdued peoples under
us,
and nations under our feet.
4 He chose our heritage for us,
the pride of Jacob whom
he loves. *Selah*

5 God has gone up with a
shout,
the LORD with the sound of
a trumpet.
6 Sing praises to God, sing
praises;
sing praises to our King,
sing praises.
7 For God is the king of all the
earth;

46.7
2 Chr 13.12;
Ps 9.9
46.8
Ps 66.5;
Isa 61.4
46.9
Isa 2.4;
Ps 76.3;
Ezek 39.9
46.10
Ps 100.3;
Isa 2.11,17
47.1
Ps 98.8;
Isa 55.12;
Ps 106.47
47.2
Deut 7.21
47.3
Ps 18.47
47.4
1 Pet 1.4
47.5
Ps 68.33;
98.6
47.6
Ps 68.4;
89.18
47.7
1 Cor 14.15

47.8
1 Chr 16.31
47.9
Ps 72.11;
Rom 4.11,
12;
Ps 89.18;
97.9
48.1
Ps 96.4;
Zech 8.3
48.2
Ps 50.2;
Lam 2.15;
Mt 5.35
48.3
Ps 46.7
48.4
2 Sam 10.6-19
48.5
Ex 15.15
48.7
Jer 18.17
48.8
Ps 87.5
48.9
Ps 26.3

sing praises with a psalm.[k]

8 God is king over the nations;
God sits on his holy
throne.
9 The princes of the peoples
gather
as the people of the God of
Abraham.
For the shields of the earth
belong to God;
he is highly exalted.

Psalm 48

The Glory and Strength of Zion

A Song. A Psalm of the
Korahites.

1 Great is the LORD and greatly
to be praised
in the city of our God.
His holy mountain,
2 beautiful in elevation,
is the joy of all the earth,
Mount Zion, in the far north,
the city of the great King.
3 Within its citadels God
has shown himself a sure
defense.

4 Then the kings assembled,
they came on together.
5 As soon as they saw it, they
were astounded;
they were in panic, they
took to flight;
6 trembling took hold of them
there,
pains as of a woman in
labor,
7 as when an east wind
shatters
the ships of Tarshish.
8 As we have heard, so have
we seen
in the city of the LORD of
hosts,
in the city of our God,
which God establishes
forever. *Selah*

9 We ponder your steadfast
love, O God,

i Or *fortress* k Heb *Maskil*

in the midst of your
 temple.
10 Your name, O God, like your
 praise,
reaches to the ends of the
 earth.
Your right hand is filled with
 victory.
11 Let Mount Zion be glad,
let the towns[1] of Judah
 rejoice
because of your judgments.

12 Walk about Zion, go all
 around it,
 count its towers,
13 consider well its ramparts;
 go through its citadels,
that you may tell the next
 generation
14 that this is God,
our God forever and ever.
He will be our guide
 forever.

Psalm 49
The Folly of Trust in Riches

*To the leader. Of the Korahites.
A Psalm.*

1 Hear this, all you peoples;
 give ear, all inhabitants of
 the world,
2 both low and high,
 rich and poor together.
3 My mouth shall speak
 wisdom;
the meditation of my heart
 shall be understanding.
4 I will incline my ear to a
 proverb;
I will solve my riddle to the
 music of the harp.

5 Why should I fear in times of
 trouble,
when the iniquity of my
 persecutors surrounds
 me,
6 those who trust in their
 wealth
and boast of the
 abundance of their
 riches?
7 Truly, no ransom avails for
 one's life,[m]

there is no price one can
 give to God for it.
8 For the ransom of life is
 costly,
 and can never suffice
9 that one should live on
 forever
 and never see the grave.[n]

10 When we look at the wise,
 they die;
fool and dolt perish
 together
and leave their wealth to
 others.
11 Their graves[o] are their
 homes forever,
their dwelling places to all
 generations,
though they named lands
 their own.
12 Mortals cannot abide in their
 pomp;
they are like the animals
 that perish.

13 Such is the fate of the
 foolhardy,
the end of those[p] who are
 pleased with their lot.
 Selah
14 Like sheep they are
 appointed for Sheol;
Death shall be their
 shepherd;
straight to the grave they
 descend,[q]
and their form shall waste
 away;
Sheol shall be their
 home.[r]
15 But God will ransom my soul
 from the power of
 Sheol,
 for he will receive me.
 Selah

16 Do not be afraid when some
 become rich,
when the wealth of their
 houses increases.

48.10
Josh 7.9;
Isa 41.10
48.11
Ps 97.8
48.13
Ps 122.7;
78.5-7
48.14
Ps 23.4
49.1
Ps 78.1;
33.8
49.3
Ps 37.30;
119.130
49.4
Ps 78.2;
Num 12.8
49.5
Ps 23.4
49.6
Job 31.24
49.7
Mt 25.8,9;
Job 36.18

49.8
Mt 16.26
49.9
Ps 22.29;
89.48
49.10
Eccl 2.16,18
49.11
Ps 64.6;
10.6;
Deut 3.14
49.12
v. 20
49.13
Lk 12.20
49.14
Ps 9.17;
Dan 7.18;
Mal 4.3;
1 Cor 6.2;
Rev 2.26;
Job 24.19
49.15
Ps 56.13;
73.24
49.16
Ps 37.7

[1] Heb *daughters* [m] Another reading is *no
one can ransom a brother* [n] Heb *the pit*
[o] Gk Syr Compare Tg: Heb *their inward*
(thought) [p] Tg: Heb *after them*
[q] Cn: Heb *the upright shall have dominion
over them in the morning* [r] Meaning of Heb
uncertain

17 For when they die they will
carry nothing away;
their wealth will not go
down after them.
18 Though in their lifetime they
count themselves happy
—for you are praised when
you do well for
yourself—
19 they[s] will go to the company
of their ancestors,
who will never again see
the light.
20 Mortals cannot abide in their
pomp;
they are like the animals
that perish.

Psalm 50

The Acceptable Sacrifice

A Psalm of Asaph.

1 The mighty one, God the
LORD,
speaks and summons the
earth
from the rising of the sun
to its setting.
2 Out of Zion, the perfection
of beauty,
God shines forth.

3 Our God comes and does not
keep silence,
before him is a devouring
fire,
and a mighty tempest all
around him.
4 He calls to the heavens
above
and to the earth, that he
may judge his people:
5 "Gather to me my faithful
ones,
who made a covenant with
me by sacrifice!"
6 The heavens declare his
righteousness,
for God himself is judge.
 Selah

7 "Hear, O my people, and I
will speak,
O Israel, I will testify
against you.
I am God, your God.

8 Not for your sacrifices do I
rebuke you;
your burnt offerings are
continually before me.
9 I will not accept a bull from
your house,
or goats from your folds.
10 For every wild animal of the
forest is mine,
the cattle on a thousand
hills.
11 I know all the birds of the
air,[t]
and all that moves in the
field is mine.

12 "If I were hungry, I would
not tell you,
for the world and all that is
in it is mine.
13 Do I eat the flesh of bulls,
or drink the blood of goats?
14 Offer to God a sacrifice of
thanksgiving,[u]
and pay your vows to the
Most High.
15 Call on me in the day of
trouble;
I will deliver you, and you
shall glorify me."

16 But to the wicked God says:
"What right have you to
recite my statutes,
or take my covenant on
your lips?
17 For you hate discipline,
and you cast my words
behind you.
18 You make friends with a
thief when you see one,
and you keep company
with adulterers.

19 "You give your mouth free
rein for evil,
and your tongue frames
deceit.
20 You sit and speak against
your kin;
you slander your own
mother's child.
21 These things you have done
and I have been silent;

49.17
Ps 17.14
49.18
Lk 12.19
49.19
Gen 15.15;
Job 33.30
49.20
v. 12
50.1
Josh 22.22;
Ps 113.3
50.2
Ps 48.2;
Deut 33.2
50.3
Ps 96.13;
97.3;
Dan 7.10
50.4
Deut 4.26;
Isa 1.2
50.5
Ps 30.4;
Ex 24.7;
v. 8
50.6
Ps 89.5;
75.7
50.7
Ps 81.8;
Ex 20.2
50.8
Ps 40.6;
Hos 6.6
50.9
Ps 69.31
50.10
Ps 104.24
50.12
Ex 19.5
50.14
Heb 13.15;
Deut 23.21
50.15
Ps 91.15;
81.7; 22.23
50.16
Isa 29.13
50.17
Rom 2.21,
22;
Neh 9.26
50.18
Rom 1.32;
1 Tim 5.22
50.19
Ps 10.7;
52.2
50.20
Mt 10.21
50.21
Eccl 8.11;
Isa 42.14;
Ps 90.8

s Cn: Heb *you* t Gk Syr Tg: Heb
mountains u Or *make thanksgiving your*
sacrifice to God

you thought that I was one
 just like yourself.
But now I rebuke you, and
 lay the charge before
 you.

22 "Mark this, then, you who
 forget God,
 or I will tear you apart, and
 there will be no one to
 deliver.
23 Those who bring
 thanksgiving as their
 sacrifice honor me;
 to those who go the right
 way[v]
 I will show the salvation of
 God."

Psalm 51

Prayer for Cleansing and Pardon

To the leader. A Psalm of David,
when the prophet Nathan came
to him, after he had gone in to
Bathsheba.

1 Have mercy on me, O God,
 according to your steadfast
 love;
 according to your abundant
 mercy
 blot out my transgressions.
2 Wash me thoroughly from
 my iniquity,
 and cleanse me from my
 sin.

3 For I know my
 transgressions,
 and my sin is ever before
 me.
4 Against you, you alone, have
 I sinned,
 and done what is evil in
 your sight,
 so that you are justified in
 your sentence
 and blameless when you
 pass judgment.
5 Indeed, I was born guilty,
 a sinner when my mother
 conceived me.

6 You desire truth in the
 inward being;[w]

therefore teach me wisdom
 in my secret heart.
7 Purge me with hyssop, and I
 shall be clean;
 wash me, and I shall be
 whiter than snow.
8 Let me hear joy and
 gladness;
 let the bones that you have
 crushed rejoice.
9 Hide your face from my sins,
 and blot out all my
 iniquities.

10 Create in me a clean heart,
 O God,
 and put a new and right[x]
 spirit within me.
11 Do not cast me away from
 your presence,
 and do not take your holy
 spirit from me.
12 Restore to me the joy of your
 salvation,
 and sustain in me a
 willing[y] spirit.

13 Then I will teach
 transgressors your ways,
 and sinners will return to
 you.
14 Deliver me from bloodshed,
 O God,
 O God of my salvation,
 and my tongue will sing
 aloud of your
 deliverance.

15 O Lord, open my lips,
 and my mouth will declare
 your praise.
16 For you have no delight in
 sacrifice;
 if I were to give a burnt
 offering, you would not
 be pleased.
17 The sacrifice acceptable to
 God[z] is a broken spirit;
 a broken and contrite
 heart, O God, you will
 not despise.

18 Do good to Zion in your good
 pleasure;

50.22
Job 8.13;
Ps 9.17; 7.2
50.23
v. 14;
Ps 85.13;
91.16
51.1
Ps 4.1;
106.45;
Isa 43.25;
Acts 3.19
51.2
Heb 9.14;
1 Jn 1.7
51.3
Isa 59.12
51.4
Gen 20.6;
Lk 15.21;
Rom 3.4
51.5
Ps 58.3;
Job 14.4
51.6
Ps 15.2;
Prov 2.6

51.7
Lev 14.4;
Heb 9.19;
Isa 1.18
51.8
Ps 35.10
51.9
Jer 16.17
51.10
Acts 15.9;
Eph 2.10;
Ps 78.37
51.11
2 Kings 13.23;
Eph 4.30
51.12
Ps 13.5;
2 Cor 3.17
51.13
Acts 9.21,
22; Ps 22.27
51.14
2 Sam 12.9;
Ps 25.5;
35.28
51.15
Ps 9.14
51.16
1 Sam 15.22;
Ps 40.6
51.17
Ps 34.18
51.18
Isa 51.3;
Ps 102.16

v Heb *who set a way* w Meaning of Heb
uncertain x Or *steadfast* y Or *generous*
z Or *My sacrifice, O God,*

rebuild the walls of
Jerusalem,
19 then you will delight in right
sacrifices,
in burnt offerings and
whole burnt offerings;
then bulls will be offered
on your altar.

Psalm 52

Judgment on the Deceitful

To the leader. A Maskil of David,
when Doeg the Edomite came to
Saul and said to him, "David has
come to the house of
Ahimelech."

1 Why do you boast, O mighty
one,
of mischief done against
the godly?[a]
All day long 2 you are
plotting destruction.
Your tongue is like a sharp
razor,
you worker of treachery.
3 You love evil more than
good,
and lying more than
speaking the truth.
Selah
4 You love all words that
devour,
O deceitful tongue.

5 But God will break you down
forever;
he will snatch and tear you
from your tent;
he will uproot you from the
land of the living. *Selah*
6 The righteous will see, and
fear,
and will laugh at the
evildoer,[b] saying,
7 "See the one who would not
take
refuge in God,
but trusted in abundant
riches,
and sought refuge in
wealth!"[c]

8 But I am like a green olive
tree
in the house of God.

51.19
Ps 4.5;
66.13,15
52.1
1 Sam 22.9;
Ps 94.4
52.2
Ps 50.19;
57.4; 59.7
52.3
Jer 9.4,5
52.4
Ps 120.3
52.5
Prov 2.22;
Ps 27.13
52.6
Job 22.19;
Ps 37.34;
40.3
52.7
Ps 49.6
52.8
Jer 11.16;
Ps 13.5

52.9
Ps 30.12;
54.6
53.1
Ps 14.1-7;
Rom 3.10
53.2
Ps 33.13
53.3
Rom 3.12
53.4
Jer 4.22
53.5
Lev 26.17,
36; Ezek 6.5

I trust in the steadfast love
of God
forever and ever.
9 I will thank you forever,
because of what you have
done.
In the presence of the
faithful
I will proclaim[d] your
name, for it is good.

Psalm 53

Denunciation of Godlessness

To the leader: according to
Mahalath. A Maskil of David.

1 Fools say in their hearts,
"There is no God."
They are corrupt, they
commit abominable
acts;
there is no one who does
good.

2 God looks down from heaven
on humankind
to see if there are any who
are wise,
who seek after God.

3 They have all fallen away,
they are all alike
perverse;
there is no one who does
good,
no, not one.

4 Have they no knowledge,
those evildoers,
who eat up my people as
they eat bread,
and do not call upon God?

5 There they shall be in great
terror,
in terror such as has not
been.
For God will scatter the
bones of the ungodly;[e]

a Cn Compare Syr: Heb *the kindness of God*
b Heb *him* c Syr Tg: Heb *in his destruction*
d Cn: Heb *wait for* e Cn Compare Gk Syr:
Heb *him who encamps against you*

they will be put to
shame,[f] for God has
rejected them.

6 O that deliverance for Israel
would come from Zion!
When God restores the
fortunes of his people,
Jacob will rejoice; Israel
will be glad.

Psalm 54

Prayer for Vindication

To the leader:
with stringed instruments.
A Maskil of David
when the Ziphites went
and told Saul, "David is in
hiding among us."

1 Save me, O God, by your
name,
and vindicate me by your
might.
2 Hear my prayer, O God;
give ear to the words of my
mouth.

3 For the insolent have risen
against me,
the ruthless seek my
life;
they do not set God before
them. *Selah*

4 But surely, God is my
helper;
the Lord is the upholder
of[g] my life.
5 He will repay my enemies for
their evil.
In your faithfulness, put an
end to them.

6 With a freewill offering I will
sacrifice to you;
I will give thanks to your
name, O LORD, for it is
good.
7 For he has delivered me from
every trouble,
and my eye has looked in
triumph on my
enemies.

53.6
Ps 14.7
54.1
Ps 20.1;
2 Chr 20.6
54.2
Ps 55.1; 5.1
54.3
Ps 86.14;
40.14; 36.1
54.4
Ps 118.7;
41.12
54.5
Ps 94.23;
143.12; 89.49
54.6
Ps 50.14;
52.9
54.7
Ps 34.6;
59.10

55.1
Ps 61.1;
27.9
55.2
Ps 66.19;
77.3;
Isa 38.14
55.3
Ps 17.9;
2 Sam 16.7,
8; Ps 71.11
55.4
Ps 116.3
55.5
Ps 119.120;
Job 21.6
55.6
Job 3.13
55.8
Isa 4.6
55.9
Jer 6.7
55.11
Ps 5.9; 10.7

Psalm 55

Complaint about a Friend's Treachery

To the leader: with stringed
instruments. A Maskil of David.

1 Give ear to my prayer,
O God;
do not hide yourself from
my supplication.
2 Attend to me, and answer
me;
I am troubled in my
complaint.
I am distraught 3 by the noise
of the enemy,
because of the clamor of
the wicked.
For they bring[h] trouble upon
me,
and in anger they cherish
enmity against me.

4 My heart is in anguish within
me,
the terrors of death have
fallen upon me.
5 Fear and trembling come
upon me,
and horror overwhelms me.
6 And I say, "O that I had
wings like a dove!
I would fly away and be at
rest;
7 truly, I would flee far away;
I would lodge in the
wilderness; *Selah*
8 I would hurry to find a
shelter for myself
from the raging wind and
tempest."

9 Confuse, O Lord, confound
their speech;
for I see violence and strife
in the city.
10 Day and night they go
around it
on its walls,
and iniquity and trouble are
within it;
11 ruin is in its midst;

[f] Gk: Heb *you will put to shame* [g] Gk Syr
Jerome: Heb *is of those who uphold* or *is with
those who uphold* [h] Cn Compare Gk: Heb
they cause to totter

oppression and fraud
 do not depart from its
 market place.

12 It is not enemies who taunt
 me —
 I could bear that;
 it is not adversaries who deal
 insolently with me —
 I could hide from them.
13 But it is you, my equal,
 my companion, my familiar
 friend,
14 with whom I kept pleasant
 company;
 we walked in the house of
 God with the throng.
15 Let death come upon them;
 let them go down alive to
 Sheol;
 for evil is in their homes
 and in their hearts.

16 But I call upon God,
 and the LORD will save me.
17 Evening and morning and at
 noon
 I utter my complaint and
 moan,
 and he will hear my voice.
18 He will redeem me
 unharmed
 from the battle that I wage,
 for many are arrayed
 against me.
19 God, who is enthroned from
 of old, *Selah*
 will hear, and will humble
 them —
 because they do not change,
 and do not fear God.

20 My companion laid hands on
 a friend
 and violated a covenant
 with me[i]
21 with speech smoother than
 butter,
 but with a heart set on
 war;
 with words that were softer
 than oil,
 but in fact were drawn
 swords.

22 Cast your burden[j] on the
 LORD,

55.12
Ps 41.9
55.13
2 Sam 15.12;
Ps 41.9;
Jer 9.4
55.14
Ps 42.4
55.15
Ps 64.7;
Num 16.30,
33
55.16
Ps 57.2,3
55.17
Ps 141.2;
Dan 6.10;
Acts 3.1;
Ps 5.3
55.18
Ps 103.4;
2 Chr 32.7,8
55.19
Ps 78.59;
Deut 33.27
55.20
Ps 7.4;
89.34
55.21
Ps 28.3;
57.4;
Prov 5.3;
Ps 59.7
55.22
Ps 37.5;
Mt 6.25;
1 Pet 5.7;
Ps 37.24

55.23
Ps 73.18;
5.6;
Job 15.32;
Prov 10.27;
Ps 25.2
56.1
Ps 57.1,3
56.2
Ps 57.3;
35.1
56.3
Ps 55.4,5;
11.1
56.4
Ps 118.6;
Heb 13.6
56.5
Ps 41.7
56.6
Ps 59.3;
140.2; 19.10,
11
56.7
Ps 36.12;
55.23
56.8
Ps 139.3;
39.12;
Mal 3.16

and he will sustain you;
he will never permit
 the righteous to be moved.
23 But you, O God, will cast
 them down
 into the lowest pit;
 the bloodthirsty and
 treacherous
 shall not live out half their
 days.
 But I will trust in you.

Psalm 56

Trust in God under Persecution

To the leader: according to The
Dove on Far-off Terebinths. Of
 David. A Miktam, when the
 Philistines seized him in Gath.

1 Be gracious to me, O God,
 for people trample on
 me;
 all day long foes oppress
 me;
2 my enemies trample on me
 all day long,
 for many fight against me.
 O Most High, 3when I am
 afraid,
 I put my trust in you.
4 In God, whose word I praise,
 in God I trust; I am not
 afraid;
 what can flesh do to me?

5 All day long they seek to
 injure my cause;
 all their thoughts are
 against me for evil.
6 They stir up strife, they lurk,
 they watch my steps.
 As they hoped to have my
 life,
7 so repay[k] them for their
 crime;
 in wrath cast down the
 peoples, O God!

8 You have kept count of my
 tossings;
 put my tears in your bottle.
 Are they not in your
 record?

i Heb lacks *with me* j Or *Cast what he
has given you* k Cn: Heb *rescue*

9 Then my enemies will retreat
 in the day when I call.
 This I know, that[1] God is
 for me.
10 In God, whose word I praise,
 in the LORD, whose word I
 praise,
11 in God I trust; I am not
 afraid.
 What can a mere mortal do
 to me?

12 My vows to you I must
 perform, O God;
 I will render thank
 offerings to you.
13 For you have delivered my
 soul from death,
 and my feet from falling,
so that I may walk before
 God
 in the light of life.

Psalm 57

Praise and Assurance under Persecution

To the leader: Do Not Destroy.
Of David. A Miktam, when he
fled from Saul, in the cave.

1 Be merciful to me, O God,
 be merciful to me,
 for in you my soul takes
 refuge;
in the shadow of your wings
 I will take refuge,
until the destroying storms
 pass by.
2 I cry to God Most High,
 to God who fulfills his
 purpose for me.
3 He will send from heaven
 and save me,
 he will put to shame those
 who trample on me. *Selah*
God will send forth his
 steadfast love and his
 faithfulness.

4 I lie down among lions
 that greedily devour[m]
 human prey;
their teeth are spears and
 arrows,
 their tongues sharp swords.

5 Be exalted, O God, above the
 heavens.
 Let your glory be over all
 the earth.

6 They set a net for my steps;
 my soul was bowed down.
They dug a pit in my path,
 but they have fallen into it
 themselves. *Selah*
7 My heart is steadfast, O God,
 my heart is steadfast.
I will sing and make melody.
8 Awake, my soul!
Awake, O harp and lyre!
 I will awake the dawn.
9 I will give thanks to you,
 O Lord, among the
 peoples;
 I will sing praises to you
 among the nations.
10 For your steadfast love is as
 high as the heavens;
 your faithfulness extends
 to the clouds.

11 Be exalted, O God, above the
 heavens.
 Let your glory be over all
 the earth.

Psalm 58

Prayer for Vengeance

To the leader: Do Not Destroy.
 Of David. A Miktam.

1 Do you indeed decree what
 is right, you gods?[n]
 Do you judge people fairly?
2 No, in your hearts you devise
 wrongs;
 your hands deal out
 violence on earth.

3 The wicked go astray from
 the womb;
 they err from their birth,
 speaking lies.
4 They have venom like the
 venom of a serpent,
 like the deaf adder that
 stops its ear,
5 so that it does not hear the
 voice of charmers

56.9
Ps 9.3;
102.2;
Rom 8.31
56.12
Ps 50.14
56.13
Ps 116.8;
Job 33.30
57.1
Ps 2.12;
17.8;
Isa 26.20
57.2
Ps 138.8
57.3
Ps 18.16;
56.2; 40.11
57.4
Ps 35.17;
Prov 30.14;
Ps 55.21

57.5
Ps 108.5
57.6
Ps 35.7;
145.14; 7.15;
Prov 28.10
57.7
Ps 108.1
57.8
Ps 16.9;
30.12; 150.3
57.9
Ps 108.3
57.10
Ps 36.5
57.11
v. 5
58.1
Ps 82.2
58.2
Mal 3.15;
Ps 94.20
58.3
Ps 51.5;
Isa 48.8;
Ps 53.3
58.4
Ps 140.3;
Eccl 10.11
58.5
Ps 81.11

[1] Or *because* [m] Cn: Heb *are aflame for*
[n] Or *mighty lords*

or of the cunning
enchanter.

6 O God, break the teeth in
their mouths;
tear out the fangs of the
young lions, O Lord!

7 Let them vanish like water
that runs away;
like grass let them be
trodden down° and
wither.

8 Let them be like the snail
that dissolves into
slime;
like the untimely birth that
never sees the sun.

9 Sooner than your pots can
feel the heat of thorns,
whether green or ablaze,
may he sweep them
away!

10 The righteous will rejoice
when they see
vengeance done;
they will bathe their feet in
the blood of the
wicked.

11 People will say, "Surely there
is a reward for the
righteous;
surely there is a God who
judges on earth."

Psalm 59

Prayer for Deliverance from Enemies

To the leader: Do Not Destroy.
Of David. A Miktam, when Saul
ordered his house to be watched
in order to kill him.

1 Deliver me from my enemies,
O my God;
protect me from those who
rise up against me.

2 Deliver me from those who
work evil;
from the bloodthirsty save
me.

3 Even now they lie in wait for
my life;
the mighty stir up strife
against me.

58.6
Job 4.10;
Ps 3.7
58.7
Josh 7.5;
Ps 112.10;
64.3
58.8
Job 3.16
58.9
Ps 118.12;
Prov 10.25
58.10
Ps 64.10;
91.8; 68.23
58.11
Ps 18.20;
9.8
59.1
Ps 143.9
59.2
Ps 28.3;
139.19
59.3
Ps 56.6

59.4
Ps 35.19,23
59.5
Ps 9.5;
Jer 18.23
59.6
v. 14
59.7
Ps 57.4;
10.11
59.8
Ps 37.13;
2.4
59.9
Ps 9.9
59.10
Ps 21.3;
54.7
59.11
Deut 4.9;
Ps 106.27;
84.9
59.12
Prov 12.13;
Zeph 3.11;
Ps 10.7
59.13
Ps 104.35;
83.18

For no transgression or sin of
mine, O Lord,
4 for no fault of mine, they
run and make ready.

Rouse yourself, come to my
help and see!
5 You, Lord God of hosts, are
God of Israel.
Awake to punish all the
nations;
spare none of those who
treacherously plot evil.
Selah

6 Each evening they come
back,
howling like dogs
and prowling about the
city.

7 There they are, bellowing
with their mouths,
with sharp words[p] on their
lips —
for "Who," they think,[q]
"will hear us?"

8 But you laugh at them,
O Lord;
you hold all the nations in
derision.

9 O my strength, I will watch
for you;
for you, O God, are my
fortress.

10 My God in his steadfast love
will meet me;
my God will let me look in
triumph on my
enemies.

11 Do not kill them, or my
people may forget;
make them totter by your
power, and bring them
down,
O Lord, our shield.

12 For the sin of their mouths,
the words of their lips,
let them be trapped in
their pride.
For the cursing and lies that
they utter,
13 consume them in wrath;

° Cn: Meaning of Heb uncertain
p Heb *with swords* q Heb lacks *they think*

consume them until they
are no more.
Then it will be known to the
ends of the earth
that God rules over Jacob.
Selah

14 Each evening they come
back,
howling like dogs
and prowling about the
city.
15 They roam about for food,
and growl if they do not
get their fill.

16 But I will sing of your might;
I will sing aloud of your
steadfast love in the
morning.
For you have been a fortress
for me
and a refuge in the day of
my distress.
17 O my strength, I will sing
praises to you,
for you, O God, are my
fortress,
the God who shows me
steadfast love.

Psalm 60

Prayer for National Victory after Defeat

To the leader: according to the
Lily of the Covenant. A Miktam
of David; for instruction; when he
struggled with Aram-naharaim
and with Aram-zobah, and when
Joab on his return killed twelve
thousand Edomites in the Valley
of Salt.

1 O God, you have rejected us,
broken our defenses;
you have been angry; now
restore us!
2 You have caused the land to
quake; you have torn it
open;
repair the cracks in it, for
it is tottering.
3 You have made your people
suffer hard things;
you have given us wine to
drink that made us reel.

4 You have set up a banner for
those who fear you,
to rally to it out of
bowshot.[r] *Selah*
5 Give victory with your right
hand, and answer us,[s]
so that those whom you
love may be rescued.

6 God has promised in his
sanctuary:[t]
"With exultation I will
divide up Shechem,
and portion out the Vale of
Succoth.
7 Gilead is mine, and
Manasseh is mine;
Ephraim is my helmet;
Judah is my scepter.
8 Moab is my washbasin;
on Edom I hurl my shoe;
over Philistia I shout in
triumph."

9 Who will bring me to the
fortified city?
Who will lead me to Edom?
10 Have you not rejected us,
O God?
You do not go out, O God,
with our armies.
11 O grant us help against the
foe,
for human help is
worthless.
12 With God we shall do
valiantly;
it is he who will tread
down our foes.

Psalm 61

Assurance of God's Protection

To the leader: with stringed
instruments. Of David.

1 Hear my cry, O God;
listen to my prayer.
2 From the end of the earth I
call to you,
when my heart is faint.

Lead me to the rock
that is higher than I;
3 for you are my refuge,

59.14
v. 6
59.16
Ps 21.13;
101.1; 88.13;
v. 9;
Ps 46.1
59.17
vv. 9,10
60.1
Ps 44.9;
2 Sam 5.20;
Ps 79.5;
80.3
60.2
Ps 18.7;
2 Chr 7.14
60.03
Ps 71.20;
Isa 51.17,22

60.4
Ps 20.5
60.5
Ps 108.6;
127.2; 17.7
60.6
Ps 89.35;
Josh 1.6;
Gen 12.6
60.7
Josh 13.31;
Deut 33.17;
Gen 49.10
60.8
2 Sam 8.1
60.10
v. 1;
Ps 44.9
60.11
Ps 146.3
60.12
Num 24.18;
Ps 44.5
61.1
Ps 64.1;
86.6
61.2
Ps 77.3;
18.2
61.3
Ps 62.7;
Prov 18.10

r Gk Syr Jerome: Heb *because of the truth*
s Another reading is *me* t Or *by his holiness*

a strong tower against the
enemy.

4 Let me abide in your tent
forever,
find refuge under the
shelter of your wings.
Selah

5 For you, O God, have heard
my vows;
you have given me the
heritage of those who
fear your name.

6 Prolong the life of the king;
may his years endure to all
generations!

7 May he be enthroned forever
before God;
appoint steadfast love and
faithfulness to watch
over him!

8 So I will always sing praises
to your name,
as I pay my vows day after
day.

Psalm 62
Song of Trust in God Alone

To the leader: according to
Jeduthun. A Psalm of David.

1 For God alone my soul waits
in silence;
from him comes my
salvation.

2 He alone is my rock and my
salvation,
my fortress; I shall never be
shaken.

3 How long will you assail a
person,
will you batter your victim,
all of you,
as you would a leaning
wall, a tottering fence?

4 Their only plan is to bring
down a person of
prominence.
They take pleasure in
falsehood;
they bless with their mouths,
but inwardly they curse.
Selah

61.4
Ps 23.6;
91.4
61.5
Ps 56.12;
86.11
61.6
Ps 21.4
61.7
Ps 41.12;
40.11
61.8
Ps 71.22;
65.1
62.1
Ps 33.20
62.2
Ps 89.26;
v. 6
62.3
Isa 30.13
62.4
Ps 4.2; 28.3

62.6
v. 2
62.7
Ps 85.9;
46.1
62.8
Ps 37.3;
1 Sam 1.15;
Ps 42.4;
Lam 2.19
62.9
Ps 39.5,11;
Isa 40.15,
17; Rom 3.4
62.10
Isa 30.12;
61.8;
Job 31.25;
Ps 52.7;
1 Tim 6.7
62.11
Job 33.14;
1 Chr 29.11
62.12
Job 34.11;
Mt 16.27;
Col 3.25
63.1
Ps 42.2;
84.2
63.2
Ps 27.4

5 For God alone my soul waits
in silence,
for my hope is from him.

6 He alone is my rock and my
salvation,
my fortress; I shall not be
shaken.

7 On God rests my deliverance
and my honor;
my mighty rock, my refuge
is in God.

8 Trust in him at all times,
O people;
pour out your heart before
him;
God is a refuge for us.
Selah

9 Those of low estate are but a
breath,
those of high estate are a
delusion;
in the balances they go up;
they are together lighter
than a breath.

10 Put no confidence in
extortion,
and set no vain hopes on
robbery;
if riches increase, do not
set your heart on them.

11 Once God has spoken;
twice have I heard this:
that power belongs to God,

12 and steadfast love belongs
to you, O Lord.
For you repay to all
according to their work.

Psalm 63
Comfort and Assurance in God's
Presence

A Psalm of David, when he was
in the Wilderness of Judah.

1 O God, you are my God, I
seek you,
my soul thirsts for you;
my flesh faints for you,
as in a dry and weary land
where there is no water.

2 So I have looked upon you in
the sanctuary,

beholding your power and
glory.
3 Because your steadfast love
is better than life,
my lips will praise you.
4 So I will bless you as long as
I live;
I will lift up my hands and
call on your name.

5 My soul is satisfied as with a
rich feast,[u]
and my mouth praises you
with joyful lips
6 when I think of you on my
bed,
and meditate on you in the
watches of the night;
7 for you have been my help,
and in the shadow of your
wings I sing for joy.
8 My soul clings to you;
your right hand upholds
me.

9 But those who seek to
destroy my life
shall go down into the
depths of the earth;
10 they shall be given over to
the power of the sword,
they shall be prey for
jackals.
11 But the king shall rejoice in
God;
all who swear by him shall
exult,
for the mouths of liars will
be stopped.

Psalm 64

Prayer for Protection from Enemies

To the leader. A Psalm of David.

1 Hear my voice, O God, in my
complaint;
preserve my life from the
dread enemy.
2 Hide me from the secret
plots of the wicked,
from the scheming of
evildoers,
3 who whet their tongues like
swords,

63.3
Ps 69.16
63.4
Ps 104.33;
28.2
63.5
Ps 36.8;
71.23
63.6
Ps 42.8
63.7
Ps 27.9
63.8
Ps 18.35
63.9ff
Ps 40.14;
55.15
63.11
Ps 21.1;
Deut 6.13;
Isa 45.23
64.1
Ps 55.2;
140.1
64.2
Ps 56.6;
59.2
64.3
Ps 58.7

64.4
Ps 11.2;
55.19
64.5
Ps 10.11
64.6
Ps 49.11
64.8
Ps 9.3;
Prov 18.7;
Ps 22.7
64.9
Jer 50.28
64.10
Ps 32.11;
25.20
65.1
Ps 116.18
65.2
Isa 66.23

who aim bitter words like
arrows,
4 shooting from ambush at the
blameless;
they shoot suddenly and
without fear.
5 They hold fast to their evil
purpose;
they talk of laying snares
secretly,
thinking, "Who can see us?[v]
6 Who can search out our
crimes?[w]
We have thought out a
cunningly conceived
plot."
For the human heart and
mind are deep.

7 But God will shoot his arrow
at them;
they will be wounded
suddenly.
8 Because of their tongue he
will bring them to
ruin;[x]
all who see them will
shake with horror.
9 Then everyone will fear;
they will tell what God has
brought about,
and ponder what he has
done.

10 Let the righteous rejoice in
the LORD
and take refuge in him.
Let all the upright in heart
glory.

Psalm 65

Thanksgiving for Earth's Bounty

To the leader. A Psalm of David.
A Song.

1 Praise is due to you,
O God, in Zion;
and to you shall vows be
performed,
2 O you who answer prayer!
To you all flesh shall come.

u Heb *with fat and fatness* v Syr: Heb
them w Cn: Heb *They search out crimes*
x Cn: Heb *They will bring him to ruin, their
tongue being against them*

3 When deeds of iniquity
 overwhelm us,
 you forgive our
 transgressions.
4 Happy are those whom you
 choose and bring near
 to live in your courts.
 We shall be satisfied with
 the goodness of your
 house,
 your holy temple.

5 By awesome deeds you
 answer us with
 deliverance,
 O God of our salvation;
 you are the hope of all the
 ends of the earth
 and of the farthest seas.
6 By your[y] strength you
 established the
 mountains;
 you are girded with might.
7 You silence the roaring of
 the seas,
 the roaring of their waves,
 the tumult of the peoples.
8 Those who live at earth's
 farthest bounds are
 awed by your signs;
 you make the gateways of
 the morning and the
 evening shout for joy.

9 You visit the earth and water
 it,
 you greatly enrich it;
 the river of God is full of
 water;
 you provide the people
 with grain,
 for so you have prepared it.
10 You water its furrows
 abundantly,
 settling its ridges,
 softening it with showers,
 and blessing its growth.
11 You crown the year with your
 bounty;
 your wagon tracks overflow
 with richness.
12 The pastures of the
 wilderness overflow,
 the hills gird themselves
 with joy,
13 the meadows clothe
 themselves with flocks,

65.3
Ps 38.4;
Heb 9.14
65.4
Ps 33.12;
4.3; 36.8
65.5
Ps 66.3;
85.4; 22.27;
107.23
65.6
Ps 93.1
65.7
Mt 8.26;
Isa 17.12
65.9
Ps 68.9,10;
46.4; 104.14
65.12
Job 38.26,
27; Ps 98.8
65.13
Ps 144.13;
72.16; 98.8

66.1
Ps 100.1
66.2
Ps 81.1;
79.9
66.3
Ps 65.5;
18.44
66.4
Ps 22.27;
67.3,4
66.5
Ps 46.8;
106.22
66.6
Ex 14.21;
Josh 3.6;
Ps 105.43
66.7
Ps 145.13;
11.4; 140.8
66.8
Ps 98.4
66.9
Ps 121.3
66.10
Ps 17.3;
Isa 48.10;
Zech 13.9;
1 Pet 1.6,7
66.11
Lam 1.13

 the valleys deck themselves
 with grain,
 they shout and sing
 together for joy.

Psalm 66

Praise for God's Goodness to Israel

To the leader. A Song. A Psalm.

1 Make a joyful noise to God,
 all the earth;
2 sing the glory of his name;
 give to him glorious praise.
3 Say to God, "How awesome
 are your deeds!
 Because of your great
 power, your enemies
 cringe before you.
4 All the earth worships you;
 they sing praises to you,
 sing praises to your name."
 Selah

5 Come and see what God has
 done:
 he is awesome in his deeds
 among mortals.
6 He turned the sea into dry
 land;
 they passed through the
 river on foot.
 There we rejoiced in him,
7 who rules by his might
 forever,
 whose eyes keep watch on
 the nations —
 let the rebellious not exalt
 themselves. *Selah*

8 Bless our God, O peoples,
 let the sound of his praise
 be heard,
9 who has kept us among the
 living,
 and has not let our feet
 slip.
10 For you, O God, have tested
 us;
 you have tried us as silver
 is tried.
11 You brought us into the net;
 you laid burdens on our
 backs;

y Gk Jerome: Heb *his*

12 you let people ride over our
 heads;
 we went through fire and
 through water;
 yet you have brought us out
 to a spacious place.z

13 I will come into your house
 with burnt offerings;
 I will pay you my vows,
14 those that my lips uttered
 and my mouth promised
 when I was in trouble.
15 I will offer to you burnt
 offerings of fatlings,
 with the smoke of the
 sacrifice of rams;
 I will make an offering of
 bulls and goats. *Selah*

16 Come and hear, all you who
 fear God,
 and I will tell what he has
 done for me.
17 I cried aloud to him,
 and he was extolled with
 my tongue.
18 If I had cherished iniquity in
 my heart,
 the Lord would not have
 listened.
19 But truly God has listened;
 he has given heed to the
 words of my prayer.

20 Blessed be God,
 because he has not
 rejected my prayer
 or removed his steadfast
 love from me.

Psalm 67

The Nations Called to Praise God

To the leader: with stringed
instruments. A Psalm. A Song.

1 May God be gracious to us
 and bless us
 and make his face to shine
 upon us, *Selah*
2 that your way may be known
 upon earth,
 your saving power among
 all nations.

3 Let the peoples praise you,
 O God;
 let all the peoples praise
 you.

4 Let the nations be glad and
 sing for joy,
 for you judge the peoples
 with equity
 and guide the nations upon
 earth. *Selah*
5 Let the peoples praise you,
 O God;
 let all the peoples praise
 you.

6 The earth has yielded its
 increase;
 God, our God, has blessed
 us.
7 May God continue to bless
 us;
 let all the ends of the earth
 revere him.

Psalm 68

Praise and Thanksgiving

To the leader. Of David. A Psalm.
A Song.

1 Let God rise up, let his
 enemies be scattered;
 let those who hate him flee
 before him.
2 As smoke is driven away, so
 drive them away;
 as wax melts before the
 fire,
 let the wicked perish
 before God.
3 But let the righteous be
 joyful;
 let them exult before God;
 let them be jubilant with
 joy.

4 Sing to God, sing praises to
 his name;
 lift up a song to him who
 rides upon the
 clouds[a] —
 his name is the LORD —
 be exultant before him.

66.12
Isa 51.23;
43.2
66.13
Eccl 5.4
66.14
Ps 18.6
66.15
Ps 51.19;
Num 6.14
66.16
Ps 34.11;
71.15,24
66.18
Job 36.21;
Isa 1.15;
Jas 4.3
66.19
Ps 116.1,2
66.20
Ps 68.35;
22.24
67.1
Num 6.25;
Ps 4.6
67.2
Acts 18.25;
Titus 2.11

67.4
Ps 96.10;
98.9
67.5
v. 3
67.6
Lev 26.4;
Ps 85.12;
Ezek 34.27
67.7
Ps 33.8
68.1
Num 10.35;
Isa 33.3
68.2
Isa 9.18;
Hos 13.3;
Ps 97.5;
Mic 1.4
68.3
Ps 32.11
68.4
Ps 66.2;
Isa 57.14;
40.3;
Ps 83.18

z Cn Compare Gk Syr Jerome Tg: Heb *to a
saturation* a Or *cast up a highway for him
who rides through the deserts*

5 Father of orphans and
　　protector of widows
　is God in his holy
　　habitation.
6 God gives the desolate a
　　home to live in;
　he leads out the prisoners
　　to prosperity,
　but the rebellious live in a
　　parched land.

7 O God, when you went out
　　before your people,
　when you marched through
　　the wilderness,　　*Selah*
8 the earth quaked, the
　　heavens poured down
　　rain
　at the presence of God, the
　　God of Sinai,
　at the presence of God, the
　　God of Israel.
9 Rain in abundance, O God,
　　you showered abroad;
　you restored your heritage
　　when it languished;
10 your flock found a dwelling
　　in it;
　in your goodness, O God,
　　you provided for the
　　needy.

11 The Lord gives the
　　command;
　great is the company of
　　those[b] who bore the
　　tidings:
12 "The kings of the armies,
　　they flee, they flee!"
　The women at home divide
　　the spoil,
13 though they stay among
　　the sheepfolds —
　the wings of a dove covered
　　with silver,
　its pinions with green gold.
14 When the Almighty[c]
　　scattered kings there,
　snow fell on Zalmon.

15 O mighty mountain,
　　mountain of Bashan;
　O many-peaked mountain,
　　mountain of Bashan!
16 Why do you look with envy,
　　O many-peaked
　　mountain,

68.5
Ps 146.9;
Deut 10.18;
26.15
68.6
Ps 113.9;
Acts 21.6;
Ps 107.34
68.7
Ex 13.21;
Judg 4.14
68.8
Ex 19.16,
18; Judg 5.4
68.9
Deut 11.11
68.10
Deut 26.5;
Ps 74.19
68.12
Ps 135.11;
1 Sam 30.24
68.13
Gen 49.14
68.14
Josh 10.10
68.16
Deut 12.5;
Ps 87.1,2

68.17
Deut 33.2;
Dan 7.10
68.18
Acts 1.9;
Eph 4.8;
Judg 5.12;
1 Tim 1.13
68.19
Ps 55.22;
65.5
68.20
Ps 49.15;
56.13
68.21
Ps 110.6;
55.23
68.22
Num 21.33;
Ex 14.22
68.23
Ps 58.10;
1 Kings 21.19
68.24
Ps 77.13;
63.2
68.25
1 Chr 13.8;
Judg 11.34

　　at the mount that God
　　　desired for his abode,
　where the Lord will reside
　　forever?

17 With mighty chariotry, twice
　　ten thousand,
　　thousands upon thousands,
　the Lord came from Sinai
　　into the holy place.[d]
18 You ascended the high
　　mount,
　　leading captives in your
　　　train
　　and receiving gifts from
　　　people,
　even from those who rebel
　　against the Lord God's
　　abiding there.
19 Blessed be the Lord,
　　who daily bears us up;
　God is our salvation.　*Selah*
20 Our God is a God of
　　salvation,
　　and to God, the Lord,
　　belongs escape from
　　death.

21 But God will shatter the
　　heads of his enemies,
　the hairy crown of those
　　who walk in their guilty
　　ways.
22 The Lord said,
　　"I will bring them back
　　　from Bashan,
　I will bring them back from
　　the depths of the sea,
23 so that you may bathe[e] your
　　feet in blood,
　so that the tongues of your
　　dogs may have their
　　share from the foe."

24 Your solemn processions are
　　seen,[f] O God,
　　the processions of my God,
　　my King, into the
　　sanctuary —
25 the singers in front, the
　　musicians last,

[b] Or *company of the women*　[c] Traditional
rendering of Heb *Shaddai*　[d] Cn: Heb *The
Lord among them Sinai in the holy* (place)
[e] Gk Syr Tg: Heb *shatter*　[f] Or *have been
seen*

between them girls playing
tambourines:
26 "Bless God in the great
 congregation,
 the LORD, O you who are of
 Israel's fountain!"
27 There is Benjamin, the least
 of them, in the lead,
 the princes of Judah in a
 body,
 the princes of Zebulun, the
 princes of Naphtali.

28 Summon your might,
 O God;
 show your strength, O God,
 as you have done for us
 before.
29 Because of your temple at
 Jerusalem
 kings bear gifts to you.
30 Rebuke the wild animals
 that live among the
 reeds,
 the herd of bulls with the
 calves of the peoples.
 Trample[g] under foot those
 who lust after tribute;
 scatter the peoples who
 delight in war.[h]
31 Let bronze be brought from
 Egypt;
 let Ethiopia[i] hasten to
 stretch out its hands to
 God.

32 Sing to God, O kingdoms of
 the earth;
 sing praises to the Lord,
 Selah
33 O rider in the heavens, the
 ancient heavens;
 listen, he sends out his
 voice, his mighty voice.
34 Ascribe power to God,
 whose majesty is over
 Israel;
 and whose power is in the
 skies.
35 Awesome is God in his[j]
 sanctuary,
 the God of Israel;
 he gives power and
 strength to his people.

Blessed be God!

68.26
Ps 26.12;
Deut 33.28;
Isa 48.1
68.27
1 Sam 9.21
68.29
Ps 72.10
68.30
Ps 22.12;
89.10
68.31
Isa 19.19;
45.14
68.33
Ps 18.10;
Deut 10.14;
Ps 44.6;
29.4
68.34
Ps 29.1
68.35
Ps 47.2;
29.11; 66.20

69.1
vv. 14,15
69.2
Ps 40.2;
Jon 2.3
69.3
Ps 6.6;
119.82;
Isa 38.14
69.4
Ps 35.19;
Jn 15.25;
Ps 38.19;
35.11
69.5
Ps 58.5;
44.21
69.6
2 Sam 12.14
69.7
Jer 15.15;
Ps 44.15
69.8
Ps 31.11;
Isa 53.3
69.9
Jn 2.17;
Ps 89.50

Psalm 69

Prayer for Deliverance from Persecution

To the leader: according to
Lilies. Of David.

1 Save me, O God,
 for the waters have come
 up to my neck.
2 I sink in deep mire,
 where there is no foothold;
 I have come into deep
 waters,
 and the flood sweeps over
 me.
3 I am weary with my crying;
 my throat is parched.
 My eyes grow dim
 with waiting for my God.

4 More in number than the
 hairs of my head
 are those who hate me
 without cause;
 many are those who would
 destroy me,
 my enemies who accuse
 me falsely.
 What I did not steal
 must I now restore?
5 O God, you know my folly;
 the wrongs I have done are
 not hidden from you.

6 Do not let those who hope in
 you be put to shame
 because of me,
 O Lord GOD of hosts;
 do not let those who seek
 you be dishonored
 because of me,
 O God of Israel.
7 It is for your sake that I have
 borne reproach,
 that shame has covered my
 face.
8 I have become a stranger to
 my kindred,
 an alien to my mother's
 children.

9 It is zeal for your house that
 has consumed me;

g Cn: Heb *Trampling* h Meaning of Heb of
verse 30 is uncertain i Or *Nubia*; Heb
Cush j Gk: Heb *from your*

the insults of those who
insult you have fallen
on me.
10 When I humbled my soul
with fasting, [k]
they insulted me for doing
so.
11 When I made sackcloth my
clothing,
I became a byword to
them.
12 I am the subject of gossip for
those who sit in the
gate,
and the drunkards make
songs about me.

13 But as for me, my prayer is
to you, O LORD.
At an acceptable time,
O God,
in the abundance of your
steadfast love, answer
me.
With your faithful help
14 rescue me
from sinking in the mire;
let me be delivered from my
enemies
and from the deep waters.
15 Do not let the flood sweep
over me,
or the deep swallow me up,
or the Pit close its mouth
over me.

16 Answer me, O LORD, for your
steadfast love is good;
according to your abundant
mercy, turn to me.
17 Do not hide your face from
your servant,
for I am in distress — make
haste to answer me.
18 Draw near to me, redeem
me,
set me free because of my
enemies.

19 You know the insults I
receive,
and my shame and
dishonor;
my foes are all known to
you.
20 Insults have broken my
heart,

so that I am in despair.
I looked for pity, but there
was none;
and for comforters, but I
found none.
21 They gave me poison for
food,
and for my thirst they gave
me vinegar to drink.

22 Let their table be a trap for
them,
a snare for their allies.
23 Let their eyes be darkened
so that they cannot see,
and make their loins
tremble continually.
24 Pour out your indignation
upon them,
and let your burning anger
overtake them.
25 May their camp be a
desolation;
let no one live in their
tents.
26 For they persecute those
whom you have struck
down,
and those whom you have
wounded, they attack
still more.[l]
27 Add guilt to their guilt;
may they have no acquittal
from you.
28 Let them be blotted out of
the book of the living;
let them not be enrolled
among the righteous.
29 But I am lowly and in pain;
let your salvation, O God,
protect me.

30 I will praise the name of God
with a song;
I will magnify him with
thanksgiving.
31 This will please the LORD
more than an ox
or a bull with horns and
hoofs.
32 Let the oppressed see it and
be glad;

69.10
Ps 35.13
69.11
Ps 35.13;
Jer 24.9
69.12
Job 30.9
69.13
Isa 49.8;
2 Cor 6.2;
Ps 51.1
69.14
v. 2;
Ps 144.7
69.15
Ps 124.4,5;
Num 16.33
69.16
Ps 63.3;
51.1; 25.16
69.17
Ps 27.9;
66.14
69.18
Ps 49.15
69.19
Ps 22.6,7;
Isa 53.3
69.20
Jer 23.9;
Isa 63.5;
Job 16.2

69.21
Mt 27.34;
Jn 19.29
69.22
Rom 11.9,10
69.23
Isa 6.9,10;
Dan 5.6
69.24
Ps 79.6
69.25
Mt 23.38;
Acts 1.20
69.26
Isa 53.4
69.28
Ex 32.32;
Phil 4.3;
Lk 10.20
69.29
Ps 70.5;
59.1
69.30
Ps 28.7;
34.3; 50.14
69.31
Ps 50.13,14
69.32
Ps 34.2;
22.26

k Gk Syr: Heb *I wept, with fasting my soul*, or
I made my soul mourn with fasting l Gk Syr: Heb *recount the pain of*

you who seek God, let your
hearts revive.
33 For the LORD hears the
needy,
and does not despise his
own that are in bonds.

34 Let heaven and earth praise
him,
the seas and everything
that moves in them.
35 For God will save Zion
and rebuild the cities of
Judah;
and his servants shall live[m]
there and possess it;
36 the children of his servants
shall inherit it,
and those who love his
name shall live in it.

Psalm 70

Prayer for Deliverance from Enemies

To the leader. Of David, for the memorial offering.

1 Be pleased, O God, to deliver
me.
O LORD, make haste to help
me!
2 Let those be put to shame
and confusion
who seek my life.
Let those be turned back
and brought to dishonor
who desire to hurt me.
3 Let those who say, "Aha,
Aha!"
turn back because of their
shame.

4 Let all who seek you
rejoice and be glad in you.
Let those who love your
salvation
say evermore, "God is
great!"
5 But I am poor and needy;
hasten to me, O God!
You are my help and my
deliverer;
O LORD, do not delay!

69.33
Ps 12.9;
68.6
69.34
Ps 96.11;
148.1;
Isa 44.23;
49.13
69.35
Ps 51.18;
Isa 44.26
69.36
Ps 102.28;
37.29
70.1
Ps 40.13
70.2
Ps 35.4,26
70.3
Ps 40.15
70.5
Ps 40.17;
141.1

71.1
Ps 25.2,3
71.2
Ps 31.1;
17.6
71.3
Ps 31.2,3;
44.4
71.4
Ps 140.1,4
71.5
Jer 17.7
71.6
Ps 22.9,10;
Isa 46.3;
Ps 34.1
71.7
1 Cor 4.9;
Ps 61.3
71.8
Ps 35.28
71.9
v. 18
71.10
Ps 56.6;
Mt 27.1
71.11
Ps 3.2; 7.2

Psalm 71

Prayer for Lifelong Protection and Help

1 In you, O LORD, I take refuge;
let me never be put to
shame.
2 In your righteousness deliver
me and rescue me;
incline your ear to me and
save me.
3 Be to me a rock of refuge,
a strong fortress,[n] to save
me,
for you are my rock and my
fortress.

4 Rescue me, O my God, from
the hand of the wicked,
from the grasp of the
unjust and cruel.
5 For you, O Lord, are my
hope,
my trust, O LORD, from my
youth.
6 Upon you I have leaned from
my birth;
it was you who took me
from my mother's
womb.
My praise is continually of
you.

7 I have been like a portent to
many,
but you are my strong
refuge.
8 My mouth is filled with your
praise,
and with your glory all day
long.
9 Do not cast me off in the
time of old age;
do not forsake me when
my strength is spent.
10 For my enemies speak
concerning me,
and those who watch for
my life consult
together.
11 They say, "Pursue and seize
that person

m Syr: Heb *and they shall live*
n Gk Compare 31.3: Heb *to come continually
you have commanded*

whom God has forsaken,
 for there is no one to
 deliver."

12 O God, do not be far from
 me;
 O my God, make haste to
 help me!
13 Let my accusers be put to
 shame and consumed;
 let those who seek to hurt
 me
 be covered with scorn and
 disgrace.
14 But I will hope continually,
 and will praise you yet
 more and more.
15 My mouth will tell of your
 righteous acts,
 of your deeds of salvation
 all day long,
 though their number is
 past my knowledge.
16 I will come praising the
 mighty deeds of the
 Lord GOD,
 I will praise your
 righteousness, yours
 alone.

17 O God, from my youth you
 have taught me,
 and I still proclaim your
 wondrous deeds.
18 So even to old age and gray
 hairs,
 O God, do not forsake
 me,
 until I proclaim your might
 to all the generations to
 come.º
 Your power 19 and your
 righteousness, O God,
 reach the high heavens.

You who have done great
 things,
 O God, who is like you?
20 You who have made me see
 many troubles and
 calamities
 will revive me again;
 from the depths of the earth
 you will bring me up again.
21 You will increase my honor,
 and comfort me once
 again.

71.12
Ps 35.22;
70.1
71.13
Ps 35.4;
109.29;
v. 24
71.15
Ps 35.28;
40.5
71.16
Ps 106.2;
51.14
71.17
Deut 4.5;
6.7; Ps 26.7
71.18
v. 9
71.19
Ps 57.10;
35.10
71.20
Ps 60.3;
Hos 6.1,2

71.22
Ps 33.2;
78.41
71.23
Ps 5.11;
103.4
71.24
Ps 35.28;
v. 13
72.1
Ps 24.5
72.2
Isa 9.7;
Ps 82.3
72.3
Ps 85.10;
Isa 32.17
72.4
Isa 11.4
72.5
Ps 89.36
72.6
2 Sam 23.4;
Hos 6.3
72.7
Ps 92.12

22 I will also praise you with
 the harp
 for your faithfulness, O my
 God;
 I will sing praises to you with
 the lyre,
 O Holy One of Israel.
23 My lips will shout for joy
 when I sing praises to you;
 my soul also, which you
 have rescued.
24 All day long my tongue will
 talk of your righteous
 help,
 for those who tried to do me
 harm
 have been put to shame,
 and disgraced.

Psalm 72

Prayer for Guidance and Support
for the King

Of Solomon.

1 Give the king your justice,
 O God,
 and your righteousness to a
 king's son.
2 May he judge your people
 with righteousness,
 and your poor with justice.
3 May the mountains yield
 prosperity for the
 people,
 and the hills, in
 righteousness.
4 May he defend the cause of
 the poor of the people,
 give deliverance to the
 needy,
 and crush the oppressor.

5 May he liveP while the sun
 endures,
 and as long as the moon,
 throughout all
 generations.
6 May he be like rain that falls
 on the mown grass,
 like showers that water the
 earth.
7 In his days may
 righteousness flourish

º Gk Compare Syr: Heb *to a generation, to all
that come* P Gk: Heb *may they fear you*

and peace abound, until
the moon is no more.

8 May he have dominion from
sea to sea,
and from the River to the
ends of the earth.
9 May his foes q bow down
before him,
and his enemies lick the
dust.
10 May the kings of Tarshish
and of the isles
render him tribute,
may the kings of Sheba and
Seba
bring gifts.
11 May all kings fall down
before him,
all nations give him
service.

12 For he delivers the needy
when they call,
the poor and those who
have no helper.
13 He has pity on the weak and
the needy,
and saves the lives of the
needy.
14 From oppression and
violence he redeems
their life;
and precious is their blood
in his sight.

15 Long may he live!
May gold of Sheba be given
to him.
May prayer be made for him
continually,
and blessings invoked for
him all day long.
16 May there be abundance of
grain in the land;
may it wave on the tops of
the mountains;
may its fruit be like
Lebanon;
and may people blossom in
the cities
like the grass of the field.
17 May his name endure
forever,
his fame continue as long
as the sun.

72.8
Ex 23.31;
Zech 9.10
72.9
Ps 74.14;
Isa 49.23;
Mic 7.17
72.10
2 Chr 9.21;
Ps 68.29
72.11
Ps 49.23
72.12
Job 29.12
72.14
Ps 116.15
72.15
Isa 60.6
72.16
Ps 104.16;
Job 5.25
72.17
Ps 89.36;
Gen 12.3;
22.18;
Lk 1.48

72.18
Ps 41.13;
106.48; 77.14
72.19
Neh 9.5;
Zech 14.9
73.1
Ps 86.5;
51.10
73.2
Ps 94.18
73.3
Ps 37.1;
Jer 12.1
73.5
Job 21.9
73.6
Ps 109.18
73.7
Job 15.27;
Ps 17.10

May all nations be blessed in
him; r
may they pronounce him
happy.
18 Blessed be the LORD, the God
of Israel,
who alone does wondrous
things.
19 Blessed be his glorious name
forever;
may his glory fill the whole
earth.
Amen and Amen.

20 The prayers of David son of
Jesse are ended.

BOOK III

(Psalms 73–89)

Psalm 73

Plea for Relief from Oppressors

A Psalm of Asaph.

1 Truly God is good to the
upright, s
to those who are pure in
heart.
2 But as for me, my feet had
almost stumbled;
my steps had nearly
slipped.
3 For I was envious of the
arrogant;
I saw the prosperity of the
wicked.

4 For they have no pain;
their bodies are sound and
sleek.
5 They are not in trouble as
others are;
they are not plagued like
other people.
6 Therefore pride is their
necklace;
violence covers them like a
garment.
7 Their eyes swell out with
fatness;

q Cn: Heb *those who live in the wilderness*
r Or *bless themselves by him* s Or *good to
Israel*

their hearts overflow with
 follies.
8 They scoff and speak with
 malice;
 loftily they threaten
 oppression.
9 They set their mouths
 against heaven,
 and their tongues range
 over the earth.

10 Therefore the people turn
 and praise them,[t]
 and find no fault in them.[u]
11 And they say, "How can God
 know?
 Is there knowledge in the
 Most High?"
12 Such are the wicked;
 always at ease, they
 increase in riches.
13 All in vain I have kept my
 heart clean
 and washed my hands in
 innocence.
14 For all day long I have been
 plagued,
 and am punished every
 morning.

15 If I had said, "I will talk on
 in this way,"
 I would have been untrue
 to the circle of your
 children.
16 But when I thought how to
 understand this,
 it seemed to me a
 wearisome task,
17 until I went into the
 sanctuary of God;
 then I perceived their end.
18 Truly you set them in
 slippery places;
 you make them fall to ruin.
19 How they are destroyed in a
 moment,
 swept away utterly by
 terrors!
20 They are[v] like a dream when
 one awakes;
 on awaking you despise
 their phantoms.

21 When my soul was
 embittered,

when I was pricked in
 heart,
22 I was stupid and ignorant;
 I was like a brute beast
 toward you.
23 Nevertheless I am
 continually with you;
 you hold my right hand.
24 You guide me with your
 counsel,
 and afterward you will
 receive me with
 honor.[w]
25 Whom have I in heaven but
 you?
 And there is nothing on
 earth that I desire other
 than you.
26 My flesh and my heart may
 fail,
 but God is the strength[x] of
 my heart and my
 portion forever.

27 Indeed, those who are far
 from you will perish;
 you put an end to those
 who are false to you.
28 But for me it is good to be
 near God;
 I have made the Lord GOD
 my refuge,
 to tell of all your works.

Psalm 74

Plea for Help in Time of National Humiliation

A Maskil of Asaph.

1 O God, why do you cast us
 off forever?
 Why does your anger
 smoke against the
 sheep of your pasture?
2 Remember your
 congregation, which you
 acquired long ago,
 which you redeemed to be
 the tribe of your
 heritage.

73.8
Ps 53.1;
Jude 16
73.11
Job 22.13
73.12
Ps 49.6;
Jer 49.31
73.13
Job 21.15;
34.9; 36.3;
Ps 26.6
73.14
Ps 38.6;
118.18
73.16
Eccl 8.17
73.17
Ps 77.13;
37.38
73.18
Ps 35.6,8
73.19
Num 16.21;
Job 18.11
73.20
Job 20.8;
Ps 78.65;
1 Sam 2.30

73.22
Ps 49.10;
Job 18.3
73.24
Ps 52.8;
48.14
73.25
Phil 3.8
73.26
Ps 84.2;
16.5
73.27
Ps 37.20;
119.155
73.28
Heb 10.22;
Ps 71.7;
40.5
74.1
Ps 44.9,23;
Deut 29.20;
Ps 95.7
74.2
Deut 34.6;
Ps 77.15;
68.16

t Cn: Heb *his people return here*
u Cn: Heb *abundant waters are drained by*
them v Cn: Heb *Lord* w Or *to glory*
x Heb *rock*

Remember Mount Zion,
 where you came to
 dwell.
3 Direct your steps to the
 perpetual ruins;
 the enemy has destroyed
 everything in the
 sanctuary.

4 Your foes have roared within
 your holy place;
 they set up their emblems
 there.
5 At the upper entrance they
 hacked
 the wooden trellis with
 axes.y
6 And then, with hatchets and
 hammers,
 they smashed all its carved
 work.
7 They set your sanctuary on
 fire;
 they desecrated the
 dwelling place of your
 name,
 bringing it to the ground.
8 They said to themselves, "We
 will utterly subdue
 them";
 they burned all the
 meeting places of God
 in the land.

9 We do not see our emblems;
 there is no longer any
 prophet,
 and there is no one among
 us who knows how
 long.
10 How long, O God, is the foe
 to scoff?
 Is the enemy to revile your
 name forever?
11 Why do you hold back your
 hand;
 why do you keep your hand
 inz your bosom?

12 Yet God my King is from of
 old,
 working salvation in the
 earth.
13 You divided the sea by your
 might;

you broke the heads of the
 dragons in the waters.
14 You crushed the heads of
 Leviathan;
 you gave him as fooda for
 the creatures of the
 wilderness.
15 You cut openings for springs
 and torrents;
 you dried up ever-flowing
 streams.
16 Yours is the day, yours also
 the night;
 you established the
 luminariesb and the
 sun.
17 You have fixed all the
 bounds of the earth;
 you made summer and
 winter.

18 Remember this, O LORD, how
 the enemy scoffs,
 and an impious people
 reviles your name.
19 Do not deliver the soul of
 your dove to the wild
 animals;
 do not forget the life of
 your poor forever.

20 Have regard for yourc
 covenant,
 for the dark places of the
 land are full of the
 haunts of violence.
21 Do not let the downtrodden
 be put to shame;
 let the poor and needy
 praise your name.
22 Rise up, O God, plead your
 cause;
 remember how the impious
 scoff at you all day
 long.
23 Do not forget the clamor of
 your foes,
 the uproar of your
 adversaries that goes up
 continually.

74.3
Isa 61.4;
Ps 79.1
74.4
Lam 2.7;
Num 2.2
74.5
Jer 46.22
74.7
2 Kings 25.9
74.8
Ps 83.4
74.9
Ps 78.43;
1 Sam 3.1;
Ps 79.5
74.10
Ps 44.16;
Lev 24.16
74.11
Lam 2.3;
Ps 59.13
74.12
Ps 44.4
74.13
Ex 14.21;
Isa 51.9

74.15
Ex 17.5,6;
Num 20.11;
Josh 3.13
74.16
Ps 104.19
74.17
Gen 8.22
74.18
v. 10;
Ps 39.8
74.19
Song 2.14;
Ps 9.18
74.20
Gen 17.7;
Ps 106.45;
88.6
74.21
Ps 103.6;
35.10
74.22
Ps 43.1;
v. 18
74.23
v. 10;
Ps 65.7

yCn Compare Gk Syr: Meaning of Heb
uncertain zCn: Heb do you consume your
right hand from aHeb food for the people
bOr moon; Heb light cGk Syr: Heb the

Psalm 75

Thanksgiving for God's Wondrous Deeds

To the leader: Do Not Destroy. A Psalm of Asaph. A Song.

1 We give thanks to you,
 O God;
 we give thanks; your name
 is near.
 People tell of your wondrous
 deeds.

2 At the set time that I
 appoint
 I will judge with equity.
3 When the earth totters, with
 all its inhabitants,
 it is I who keep its pillars
 steady. *Selah*
4 I say to the boastful, "Do not
 boast,"
 and to the wicked, "Do not
 lift up your horn;
5 do not lift up your horn on
 high,
 or speak with insolent
 neck."

6 For not from the east or
 from the west
 and not from the
 wilderness comes lifting
 up;
7 but it is God who executes
 judgment,
 putting down one and
 lifting up another.
8 For in the hand of the LORD
 there is a cup
 with foaming wine, well
 mixed;
 he will pour a draught from
 it,
 and all the wicked of the
 earth
 shall drain it down to the
 dregs.
9 But I will rejoice[d] forever;
 I will sing praises to the
 God of Jacob.

10 All the horns of the wicked I
 will cut off,

but the horns of the
 righteous shall be
 exalted.

Psalm 76

Israel's God—Judge of All the Earth

To the leader: with stringed instruments. A Psalm of Asaph. A Song.

1 In Judah God is known,
 his name is great in Israel.
2 His abode has been
 established in Salem,
 his dwelling place in Zion.
3 There he broke the flashing
 arrows,
 the shield, the sword, and
 the weapons of war.
 Selah

4 Glorious are you, more
 majestic
 than the everlasting
 mountains.[e]
5 The stouthearted were
 stripped of their spoil;
 they sank into sleep;
 none of the troops
 was able to lift a hand.
6 At your rebuke, O God of
 Jacob,
 both rider and horse lay
 stunned.

7 But you indeed are awesome!
 Who can stand before
 you
 when once your anger is
 roused?
8 From the heavens you
 uttered judgment;
 the earth feared and was
 still
9 when God rose up to
 establish judgment,
 to save all the oppressed of
 the earth. *Selah*

10 Human wrath serves only to
 praise you,

75.1
Ps 79.13;
145.18; 44.1
75.3
Ps 46.6;
1 Sam 2.8
75.4
Zech 1.21
75.5
Ps 94.4
75.6
Ps 3.3
75.7
Ps 50.6;
1 Sam 2.7;
Dan 2.21
75.8
Job 21.20;
Ps 60.3;
Jer 26.15;
Prov 23.30;
Ps 73.10
75.9
Ps 40.10
75.10
Ps 89.17;
148.14

76.1
Ps 48.3
76.2
Ps 27.5;
9.11
76.3
Ps 46.9
76.5
Isa 46.12;
Ps 13.3
76.6
Ex 15.1,21;
Ps 78.53
76.7
Ps 96.4;
Nah 1.6
76.8
Ezek 38.20;
2 Chr 20.29,
30
76.9
Ps 9.7-9;
72.4
76.10
Ex 9.16;
Rom 9.17

d Gk: Heb *declare* e Gk: Heb *the mountains of prey*

when you bind the last bit
of your[f] wrath around
you.
11 Make vows to the LORD your
God, and perform them;
let all who are around him
bring gifts
to the one who is
awesome,
12 who cuts off the spirit of
princes,
who inspires fear in the
kings of the earth.

Psalm 77

God's Mighty Deeds Recalled

To the leader: according to
Jeduthun. Of Asaph. A Psalm.

1 I cry aloud to God,
aloud to God, that he may
hear me.
2 In the day of my trouble I
seek the Lord;
in the night my hand is
stretched out without
wearying;
my soul refuses to be
comforted.
3 I think of God, and I moan;
I meditate, and my spirit
faints. *Selah*

4 You keep my eyelids from
closing;
I am so troubled that I
cannot speak.
5 I consider the days of old,
and remember the years of
long ago.
6 I commune[g] with my heart
in the night;
I meditate and search my
spirit:[h]
7 "Will the Lord spurn forever,
and never again be
favorable?
8 Has his steadfast love ceased
forever?
Are his promises at an end
for all time?
9 Has God forgotten to be
gracious?
Has he in anger shut up
his compassion?" *Selah*

76.11
Ps 50.14;
68.29
76.12
Ps 68.35
77.1
Ps 3.4
77.2
Ps 50.15;
Isa 26.9,16
77.3
Ps 142.3;
143.4
77.5
Deut 32.7;
Ps 143.5;
Isa 51.9
77.6
Ps 42.8; 4.4
77.7
Ps 74.1;
85.1
77.8
Ps 89.49;
2 Pet 3.9
77.9
Isa 49.15;
Ps 25.6

77.10
Ps 31.22;
44.2,3
77.11
Ps 143.5
77.13
Ps 73.17;
Ex 15.11
77.15
Ex 6.6;
Deut 9.29
77.16
Ex 14.21
77.17
Judg 5.4;
Ps 68.33;
2 Sam 22.15
77.18
2 Sam 22.8
77.19
Hab 3.15;
Ex 14.28
77.20
Ex 13.21;
Isa 63.11-13;
Ex 6.26

10 And I say, "It is my grief
that the right hand of the
Most High has
changed."

11 I will call to mind the deeds
of the LORD;
I will remember your
wonders of old.
12 I will meditate on all your
work,
and muse on your mighty
deeds.
13 Your way, O God, is holy.
What god is so great as our
God?
14 You are the God who works
wonders;
you have displayed your
might among the
peoples.
15 With your strong arm you
redeemed your people,
the descendants of Jacob
and Joseph. *Selah*

16 When the waters saw you,
O God,
when the waters saw you,
they were afraid;
the very deep trembled.
17 The clouds poured out
water;
the skies thundered;
your arrows flashed on
every side.
18 The crash of your thunder
was in the whirlwind;
your lightnings lit up the
world;
the earth trembled and
shook.
19 Your way was through the
sea,
your path, through the
mighty waters;
yet your footprints were
unseen.
20 You led your people like a
flock
by the hand of Moses and
Aaron.

f Heb lacks *your* g Gk Syr: Heb *My music*
h Syr Jerome: Heb *my spirit searches*

Psalm 78

God's Goodness and Israel's Ingratitude

A Maskil of Asaph.

1 Give ear, O my people, to my
 teaching;
 incline your ears to the
 words of my mouth.
2 I will open my mouth in a
 parable;
 I will utter dark sayings
 from of old,
3 things that we have heard
 and known,
 that our ancestors have
 told us.
4 We will not hide them from
 their children;
 we will tell to the coming
 generation
 the glorious deeds of the
 LORD, and his might,
 and the wonders that he
 has done.

5 He established a decree in
 Jacob,
 and appointed a law in
 Israel,
 which he commanded our
 ancestors
 to teach to their children;
6 that the next generation
 might know them,
 the children yet unborn,
 and rise up and tell them to
 their children,
7 so that they should set
 their hope in God,
 and not forget the works of
 God,
 but keep his
 commandments;
8 and that they should not be
 like their ancestors,
 a stubborn and rebellious
 generation,
 a generation whose heart was
 not steadfast,
 whose spirit was not
 faithful to God.

9 The Ephraimites, armed
 with[i] the bow,

turned back on the day of
 battle.
10 They did not keep God's
 covenant,
 but refused to walk
 according to his law.
11 They forgot what he had
 done,
 and the miracles that he
 had shown them.
12 In the sight of their
 ancestors he worked
 marvels
 in the land of Egypt, in the
 fields of Zoan.
13 He divided the sea and let
 them pass through it,
 and made the waters stand
 like a heap.
14 In the daytime he led them
 with a cloud,
 and all night long with a
 fiery light.
15 He split rocks open in the
 wilderness,
 and gave them drink
 abundantly as from the
 deep.
16 He made streams come out
 of the rock,
 and caused waters to flow
 down like rivers.

17 Yet they sinned still more
 against him,
 rebelling against the Most
 High in the desert.
18 They tested God in their
 heart
 by demanding the food
 they craved.
19 They spoke against God,
 saying,
 "Can God spread a table in
 the wilderness?
20 Even though he struck the
 rock so that water
 gushed out
 and torrents overflowed,
 can he also give bread,
 or provide meat for his
 people?"

i Heb *armed with shooting*

78.1 Isa 51.4
78.2 Mt 13.35
78.3 Ps 44.1
78.4 Ex 12.26; Ps 22.30; 71.17
78.5 Ps 147.19; Deut 4.9
78.6 Ps 102.18
78.7 Deut 6.12; 27.1
78.8 Ezek 20.18; Ex 32.9; v. 37
78.9 1 Chr 12.2; Judg 20.39
78.10 2 Kings 18.12; Ps 119.1
78.11 Ps 106.13
78.12 Ex 7-12; Num 13.22; Isa 19.11, 13; Ezek 30.14
78.13 Ex 14.21; 15.8
78.14 Ex 13.21
78.15 Num 20.11; 1 Cor 10.4
78.17 Deut 9.22; Heb 3.16
78.18 Ex 16.2; 1 Cor 10.9
78.19 Num 11.4
78.20 Num 20.11

21 Therefore, when the LORD
 heard, he was full of rage;
 a fire was kindled against
 Jacob,
 his anger mounted against
 Israel,
22 because they had no faith in
 God,
 and did not trust his saving
 power.
23 Yet he commanded the skies
 above,
 and opened the doors of
 heaven;
24 he rained down on them
 manna to eat,
 and gave them the grain of
 heaven.
25 Mortals ate of the bread of
 angels;
 he sent them food in
 abundance.
26 He caused the east wind to
 blow in the heavens,
 and by his power he led
 out the south wind;
27 he rained flesh upon them
 like dust,
 winged birds like the sand
 of the seas;
28 he let them fall within their
 camp,
 all around their dwellings.
29 And they ate and were well
 filled,
 for he gave them what they
 craved.
30 But before they had satisfied
 their craving,
 while the food was still in
 their mouths,
31 the anger of God rose against
 them
 and he killed the strongest
 of them,
 and laid low the flower of
 Israel.

32 In spite of all this they still
 sinned;
 they did not believe in his
 wonders.
33 So he made their days vanish
 like a breath,
 and their years in terror.
34 When he killed them, they
 sought for him;

78.21
Num 11.1
78.22
Heb 3.18
78.23
Mal 3.10
78.24
Jn 6.31
78.26
Num 11.31
78.27
Ps 105.40
78.29
Num 11.20
78.31
Num 11.33
78.32
Num 14.16,
17; v. 22
78.33
Num 14.29,
35
78.34
Hos 5.15

78.35
Deut 32.4;
Isa 41.14
78.36
Ezek 33.31;
Ex 32.7,8
78.38
Num 14.18;
Isa 48.9;
1 Kings 21.29
78.39
Ps 103.14;
Gen 6.3;
Job 7.7,16
78.40
Ps 95.8-10;
Heb 3.16
78.41
Num 14.22;
Ps 89.18
78.44
Ex 7.20
78.45
Ex 8.24;
Ps 105.31;
Ex 8.6
78.47
Ex 9.25

 they repented and sought
 God earnestly.
35 They remembered that God
 was their rock,
 the Most High God their
 redeemer.
36 But they flattered him with
 their mouths;
 they lied to him with their
 tongues.
37 Their heart was not steadfast
 toward him;
 they were not true to his
 covenant.
38 Yet he, being compassionate,
 forgave their iniquity,
 and did not destroy them;
 often he restrained his anger,
 and did not stir up all his
 wrath.
39 He remembered that they
 were but flesh,
 a wind that passes and
 does not come again.
40 How often they rebelled
 against him in the
 wilderness
 and grieved him in the
 desert!
41 They tested God again and
 again,
 and provoked the Holy One
 of Israel.
42 They did not keep in mind
 his power,
 or the day when he
 redeemed them from
 the foe;
43 when he displayed his signs
 in Egypt,
 and his miracles in the
 fields of Zoan.
44 He turned their rivers to
 blood,
 so that they could not
 drink of their streams.
45 He sent among them swarms
 of flies, which devoured
 them,
 and frogs, which destroyed
 them.
46 He gave their crops to the
 caterpillar,
 and the fruit of their labor
 to the locust.
47 He destroyed their vines with
 hail,

and their sycamores with frost.

48 He gave over their cattle to the hail,
and their flocks to thunderbolts.

49 He let loose on them his fierce anger,
wrath, indignation, and distress,
a company of destroying angels.

50 He made a path for his anger;
he did not spare them from death,
but gave their lives over to the plague.

51 He struck all the firstborn in Egypt,
the first issue of their strength in the tents of Ham.

52 Then he led out his people like sheep,
and guided them in the wilderness like a flock.

53 He led them in safety, so that they were not afraid;
but the sea overwhelmed their enemies.

54 And he brought them to his holy hill,
to the mountain that his right hand had won.

55 He drove out nations before them;
he apportioned them for a possession
and settled the tribes of Israel in their tents.

56 Yet they tested the Most High God,
and rebelled against him.
They did not observe his decrees,

57 but turned away and were faithless like their ancestors;
they twisted like a treacherous bow.

58 For they provoked him to anger with their high places;

they moved him to jealousy with their idols.

59 When God heard, he was full of wrath,
and he utterly rejected Israel.

60 He abandoned his dwelling at Shiloh,
the tent where he dwelt among mortals,

61 and delivered his power to captivity,
his glory to the hand of the foe.

62 He gave his people to the sword,
and vented his wrath on his heritage.

63 Fire devoured their young men,
and their girls had no marriage song.

64 Their priests fell by the sword,
and their widows made no lamentation.

65 Then the Lord awoke as from sleep,
like a warrior shouting because of wine.

66 He put his adversaries to rout;
he put them to everlasting disgrace.

67 He rejected the tent of Joseph,
he did not choose the tribe of Ephraim;

68 but he chose the tribe of Judah,
Mount Zion, which he loves.

69 He built his sanctuary like the high heavens,
like the earth, which he has founded forever.

70 He chose his servant David,
and took him from the sheepfolds;

71 from tending the nursing ewes he brought him
to be the shepherd of his people Jacob,
of Israel, his inheritance.

72 With upright heart he tended them,

78.48 Ex 9.23
78.49 Ex 15.7
78.51 Ex 12.29; Ps 106.22
78.52 Ps 77.20
78.53 Ex 14.19,27
78.54 Ex 15.17; Ps 44.3
78.55 Ps 44.2; 105.11
78.56 vv. 18,40
78.57 Ezek 20.27, 28; Hos 7.16
78.58 Deut 32.16, 21; 12.2; 1 Kings 11.7
78.60 1 Sam 4.11
78.61 Judg 18.30
78.62 1 Sam 4.10
78.63 Jer 7.34
78.64 1 Sam 22.18; Job 27.15
78.65 Isa 42.13
78.66 1 Sam 5.6
78.68 Ps 87.2
78.69 1 Sam 6.1-38
78.70 1 Sam 16.11, 12
78.71 2 Sam 7.8; Gen 33.13;
2 Sam 5.2; 1 Chr 11.2
78.72 1 Kings 9.4

and guided them with
skillful hand.

Psalm 79

Plea for Mercy for Jerusalem

A Psalm of Asaph.

1 O God, the nations have
come into your
inheritance;
they have defiled your holy
temple;
they have laid Jerusalem in
ruins.
2 They have given the bodies
of your servants
to the birds of the air for
food,
the flesh of your faithful to
the wild animals of the
earth.
3 They have poured out their
blood like water
all around Jerusalem,
and there was no one to
bury them.
4 We have become a taunt to
our neighbors,
mocked and derided by
those around us.

5 How long, O LORD? Will you
be angry forever?
Will your jealous wrath
burn like fire?
6 Pour out your anger on the
nations
that do not know you,
and on the kingdoms
that do not call on your
name.
7 For they have devoured
Jacob
and laid waste his
habitation.

8 Do not remember against us
the iniquities of our
ancestors;
let your compassion come
speedily to meet us,
for we are brought very
low.
9 Help us, O God of our
salvation,
for the glory of your name;

deliver us, and forgive our
sins,
for your name's sake.
10 Why should the nations say,
"Where is their God?"
Let the avenging of the
outpoured blood of your
servants
be known among the
nations before our eyes.

11 Let the groans of the
prisoners come before
you;
according to your great
power preserve those
doomed to die.
12 Return sevenfold into the
bosom of our neighbors
the taunts with which they
taunted you, O Lord!
13 Then we your people, the
flock of your pasture,
will give thanks to you
forever;
from generation to
generation we will
recount your praise.

Psalm 80

Prayer for Israel's Restoration

*To the leader: on Lilies, a
Covenant. Of Asaph. A Psalm.*

1 Give ear, O Shepherd of
Israel,
you who lead Joseph like a
flock!
You who are enthroned upon
the cherubim, shine
forth
2 before Ephraim and
Benjamin and
Manasseh.
Stir up your might,
and come to save us!

3 Restore us, O God;
let your face shine, that we
may be saved.

4 O LORD God of hosts,
how long will you be angry
with your people's
prayers?

79.1
Ex 15.17;
Ps 74.2;
2 Kings 25.9;
Mic 3.12
79.2
Jer 7.33
79.3
Jer 14.16
79.4
Ps 44.13
79.5
Ps 74.1,9;
Zeph 3.8
79.6
Jer 10.25;
Rev 16.1;
Isa 45.4,5;
2 Thes 1.8
79.8
Isa 64.9
79.9
2 Chr 14.11;
Jer 14.7

79.10
Ps 42.10;
94.1,2
79.11
Ps 102.20
79.12
Isa 65.6,7;
Jer 32.18;
Lk 6.38;
Ps 74.18,22
79.13
Ps 74.1;
95.7;
Isa 43.21
80.1
Ps 23.1;
77.20; 99.1
80.2
Ps 35.23
80.3
Lam 5.21;
Num 6.25
80.4
Ps 85.5

5 You have fed them with the
 bread of tears,
 and given them tears to
 drink in full measure.
6 You make us the scorn[i] of
 our neighbors;
 our enemies laugh among
 themselves.

7 Restore us, O God of
 hosts;
 let your face shine, that we
 may be saved.

8 You brought a vine out of
 Egypt;
 you drove out the nations
 and planted it.
9 You cleared the ground for
 it;
 it took deep root and filled
 the land.
10 The mountains were covered
 with its shade,
 the mighty cedars with its
 branches;
11 it sent out its branches to
 the sea,
 and its shoots to the River.
12 Why then have you broken
 down its walls,
 so that all who pass along
 the way pluck its fruit?
13 The boar from the forest
 ravages it,
 and all that move in the
 field feed on it.

14 Turn again, O God of hosts;
 look down from heaven,
 and see;
 have regard for this vine,
15 the stock that your right
 hand planted.[k]
16 They have burned it with
 fire, they have cut it
 down;[l]
 may they perish at the
 rebuke of your
 countenance.
17 But let your hand be upon
 the one at your right
 hand,
 the one whom you made
 strong for yourself.
18 Then we will never turn back
 from you;

give us life, and we will
 call on your name.

19 Restore us, O LORD God of
 hosts;
 let your face shine, that we
 may be saved.

Psalm 81

God's Appeal to Stubborn Israel

To the leader: according to The
 Gittith. Of Asaph.

1 Sing aloud to God our
 strength;
 shout for joy to the God of
 Jacob.
2 Raise a song, sound the
 tambourine,
 the sweet lyre with the
 harp.
3 Blow the trumpet at the new
 moon,
 at the full moon, on our
 festal day.
4 For it is a statute for Israel,
 an ordinance of the God of
 Jacob.
5 He made it a decree in
 Joseph,
 when he went out over[m]
 the land of Egypt.

I hear a voice I had not
 known:
6 "I relieved your[n] shoulder of
 the burden;
 your[n] hands were freed
 from the basket.
7 In distress you called, and I
 rescued you;
 I answered you in the
 secret place of thunder;
 I tested you at the waters
 of Meribah. Selah
8 Hear, O my people, while I
 admonish you;
 O Israel, if you would but
 listen to me!
9 There shall be no strange
 god among you;

80.5
Ps 42.3;
102.9
80.6
Ps 44.13;
79.4
80.8
Isa 5.1,7;
Jer 2.21;
Ezek 15.6;
Ps 44.2
80.9
Hos 14.5
80.12
Ps 89.40;
Nah 2.2
80.13
Jer 5.6
80.14
Isa 63.15
80.16
Ps 39.11;
76.6
80.17
Ps 89.21
80.18
Isa 50.5;
Ps 71.20

81.1
Ps 59.16;
66.1
81.3
Num 10.10;
Lev 23.24
81.5
Ex 11.4
81.6
Isa 9.4;
10.27
81.7
Ex 2.23;
Ps 50.15;
Ex 19.19;
17.6,7
81.8
Ps 50.7
81.9
Deut 32.12;
Isa 43.12

i Syr: Heb *strife* k Heb adds *from verse
17 and upon the one whom you made strong for
yourself* l Cn: Heb *it is cut down*
m Or *against* n Heb *his*

you shall not bow down to
a foreign god.

10 I am the LORD your God,
who brought you up out of
the land of Egypt.
Open your mouth wide and
I will fill it.

11 "But my people did not
listen to my voice;
Israel would not submit to
me.

12 So I gave them over to their
stubborn hearts,
to follow their own
counsels.

13 O that my people would
listen to me,
that Israel would walk in
my ways!

14 Then I would quickly subdue
their enemies,
and turn my hand against
their foes.

15 Those who hate the LORD
would cringe before
him,
and their doom would last
forever.

16 I would feed you° with the
finest of the wheat,
and with honey from the
rock I would satisfy
you."

Psalm 82

A Plea for Justice

A Psalm of Asaph.

1 God has taken his place in
the divine council;
in the midst of the gods he
holds judgment:

2 "How long will you judge
unjustly
and show partiality to the
wicked? Selah

3 Give justice to the weak and
the orphan;
maintain the right of the
lowly and the destitute.

4 Rescue the weak and the
needy;
deliver them from the hand
of the wicked."

81.10
Ex 20.2;
Ps 103.5
81.11
Ex 32.1
81.12
Acts 7.42;
Rom 1.24
81.13
Deut 5.29;
Isa 48.18;
Ps 128.1
81.14
Ps 47.3;
Am 1.8
81.16
Deut 32.13;
Ps 147.14
82.1
Isa 3.13;
Ex 21.6
82.2
Ps 58.1;
Deut 1.17;
Prov 18.5
82.3
Deut 24.17
82.4
Job 29.12

82.5
Mic 3.1;
Ps 11.3
82.6
Jn 10.34;
Ps 89.26
82.7
Ps 49.12;
Ezek 31.14
82.8
Ps 12.5;
Mic 7.2,7;
Ps 2.8;
Rev 11.15
83.1
Ps 28.1;
109.1
83.2
Ps 2.1;
81.15
83.3
Ps 27.5
83.4
Esther 3.6
83.5
Ps 2.2
83.6
2 Chr 20.1,
10,11

5 They have neither knowledge
nor understanding,
they walk around in
darkness;
all the foundations of the
earth are shaken.

6 I say, "You are gods,
children of the Most High,
all of you;

7 nevertheless, you shall die
like mortals,
and fall like any prince."ᴾ

8 Rise up, O God, judge the
earth;
for all the nations belong
to you!

Psalm 83

Prayer for Judgment on Israel's
Foes

A Song. A Psalm of Asaph.

1 O God, do not keep silence;
do not hold your peace or
be still, O God!

2 Even now your enemies are
in tumult;
those who hate you have
raised their heads.

3 They lay crafty plans against
your people;
they consult together
against those you
protect.

4 They say, "Come, let us wipe
them out as a nation;
let the name of Israel be
remembered no more."

5 They conspire with one
accord;
against you they make a
covenant—

6 the tents of Edom and the
Ishmaelites,
Moab and the Hagrites,

7 Gebal and Ammon and
Amalek,
Philistia with the
inhabitants of Tyre;

8 Assyria also has joined them;

° Cn Compare verse 16b: Heb *he would feed
him* ᴾ Or *fall as one man, O princes*

they are the strong arm of
the children of Lot.
Selah

9 Do to them as you did to
Midian,
as to Sisera and Jabin at
the Wadi Kishon,
10 who were destroyed at
En-dor,
who became dung for the
ground.
11 Make their nobles like Oreb
and Zeeb,
all their princes like Zebah
and Zalmunna,
12 who said, "Let us take the
pastures of God
for our own possession."

13 O my God, make them like
whirling dust,�q
like chaff before the wind.
14 As fire consumes the forest,
as the flame sets the
mountains ablaze,
15 so pursue them with your
tempest
and terrify them with your
hurricane.
16 Fill their faces with shame,
so that they may seek your
name, O LORD.
17 Let them be put to shame
and dismayed forever;
let them perish in disgrace.
18 Let them know that you
alone,
whose name is the LORD,
are the Most High over all
the earth.

Psalm 84

The Joy of Worship in the Temple

To the leader: according to The
Gittith. Of the Korahites.
A Psalm.

1 How lovely is your dwelling
place,
O LORD of hosts!
2 My soul longs, indeed it faints
for the courts of the LORD;
my heart and my flesh sing
for joy

83.9
Judg 4.22,
23
83.11
Judg 8.12,
21
83.12
2 Chr 20.11;
Ps 132.13
83.13
Isa 17.13;
Ps 35.5
83.14
Deut 32.22
83.15
Job 9.17
83.17
Ps 70.2
83.18
Ps 59.13;
Ex 6.3;
Ps 92.8
84.1
Ps 27.4
84.2
Ps 42.1,2

84.3
Ps 43.4; 5.2
84.4
Ps 65.4
84.5
Ps 81.1
84.6
2 Sam 4.23;
Ps 107.35
84.7
Prov 4.18;
2 Cor 3.18;
Deut 16.16;
Ps 42.2
84.9
Gen 15.1;
Ps 2.2
84.10
1 Chr 23.5
84.11
Isa 60.19;
Rev 21.23;
Ps 34.10

to the living God.
3 Even the sparrow finds a
home,
and the swallow a nest for
herself,
where she may lay her
young,
at your altars, O LORD of
hosts,
my King and my God.
4 Happy are those who live in
your house,
ever singing your praise.
Selah

5 Happy are those whose
strength is in you,
in whose heart are the
highways to Zion.ʳ
6 As they go through the valley
of Baca
they make it a place of
springs;
the early rain also covers it
with pools.
7 They go from strength to
strength;
the God of gods will be
seen in Zion.

8 O LORD God of hosts, hear
my prayer;
give ear, O God of Jacob!
Selah
9 Behold our shield, O God;
look on the face of your
anointed.

10 For a day in your courts is
better
than a thousand elsewhere.
I would rather be a
doorkeeper in the
house of my God
than live in the tents of
wickedness.
11 For the LORD God is a sun
and shield;
he bestows favor and
honor.
No good thing does the LORD
withhold
from those who walk
uprightly.

�q Or *a tumbleweed* ʳ Heb lacks *to Zion*

12 O Lord of hosts,
 happy is everyone who
 trusts in you.

Psalm 85

Prayer for the Restoration of God's Favor

To the leader. Of the Korahites.
A Psalm.

1 Lord, you were favorable to
 your land;
 you restored the fortunes
 of Jacob.
2 You forgave the iniquity of
 your people;
 you pardoned all their sin.
 Selah
3 You withdrew all your wrath;
 you turned from your hot
 anger.

4 Restore us again, O God of
 our salvation,
 and put away your
 indignation toward us.
5 Will you be angry with us
 forever?
 Will you prolong your anger
 to all generations?
6 Will you not revive us again,
 so that your people may
 rejoice in you?
7 Show us your steadfast love,
 O Lord,
 and grant us your salvation.

8 Let me hear what God the
 Lord will speak,
 for he will speak peace to
 his people,
 to his faithful, to those
 who turn to him in
 their hearts. [s]
9 Surely his salvation is at
 hand for those who fear
 him,
 that his glory may dwell in
 our land.

10 Steadfast love and
 faithfulness will meet;
 righteousness and peace
 will kiss each other.
11 Faithfulness will spring up
 from the ground,

and righteousness will look
 down from the sky.
12 The Lord will give what is
 good,
 and our land will yield its
 increase.
13 Righteousness will go before
 him,
 and will make a path for
 his steps.

Psalm 86

Supplication for Help against Enemies

A Prayer of David.

1 Incline your ear, O Lord, and
 answer me,
 for I am poor and needy.
2 Preserve my life, for I am
 devoted to you;
 save your servant who
 trusts in you.
 You are my God; 3be
 gracious to me, O Lord,
 for to you do I cry all day
 long.
4 Gladden the soul of your
 servant,
 for to you, O Lord, I lift up
 my soul.
5 For you, O Lord, are good
 and forgiving,
 abounding in steadfast love
 to all who call on you.
6 Give ear, O Lord, to my
 prayer;
 listen to my cry of
 supplication.
7 In the day of my trouble I
 call on you,
 for you will answer me.

8 There is none like you
 among the gods,
 O Lord,
 nor are there any works
 like yours.
9 All the nations you have
 made shall come
 and bow down before you,
 O Lord,
 and shall glorify your
 name.

84.12
Ps 2.12
85.1
Ezra 1.11;
Jer 30.18;
Ezek 39.25
85.2
Ps 103.3;
32.1
85.3
Ps 78.38;
Deut 13.17
85.4
Ps 80.3,7
85.5
Ps 74.1;
79.5; 80.4
85.6
Hab 3.2
85.7
Ps 106.4
85.8
Hab 2.1;
Zech 9.10
85.9
Isa 46.13;
Zech 2.5;
Jn 1.14
85.10
Ps 72.3;
Isa 32.17;
Lk 2.14

85.12
Ps 84.11;
Jas 1.17
85.13
Ps 89.14
86.1
Ps 17.6;
40.17
86.2
Ps 25.20;
4.3; 31.14
86.3
Ps 57.1;
88.9
86.4
Ps 25.1;
143.8
86.5
Ps 130.7;
145.9;
Joel 2.13
86.6
Ps 55.1
86.7
Ps 50.15;
17.6
86.8
Ex 15.11;
Ps 89.6;
Deut 3.24
86.9
Ps 22.31;
Isa 43.7;
Rev 15.4

s Gk: Heb *but let them not turn back to folly*

¹⁰ For you are great and do
wondrous things;
you alone are God.
¹¹ Teach me your way, O LORD,
that I may walk in your
truth;
give me an undivided heart
to revere your name.
¹² I give thanks to you, O Lord
my God, with my whole
heart,
and I will glorify your name
forever.
¹³ For great is your steadfast
love toward me;
you have delivered my soul
from the depths of
Sheol.

¹⁴ O God, the insolent rise up
against me;
a band of ruffians seeks my
life,
and they do not set you
before them.
¹⁵ But you, O Lord, are a God
merciful and gracious,
slow to anger and
abounding in steadfast
love and faithfulness.
¹⁶ Turn to me and be gracious
to me;
give your strength to your
servant;
save the child of your
serving girl.
¹⁷ Show me a sign of your
favor,
so that those who hate me
may see it and be put
to shame,
because you, LORD, have
helped me and
comforted me.

Psalm 87
The Joy of Living in Zion

Of the Korahites. A Psalm.
A Song.

¹ On the holy mount stands
the city he founded;
² the LORD loves the gates of
Zion
more than all the dwellings
of Jacob.

³ Glorious things are spoken of
you,
O city of God. *Selah*

⁴ Among those who know me I
mention Rahab and
Babylon;
Philistia too, and Tyre,
with Ethiopia^t—
"This one was born there,"
they say.

⁵ And of Zion it shall be said,
"This one and that one
were born in it";
for the Most High himself
will establish it.
⁶ The LORD records, as he
registers the peoples,
"This one was born there."
 Selah

⁷ Singers and dancers alike
say,
"All my springs are in you."

Psalm 88
Prayer for Help in Despondency

A Song. A Psalm of the
Korahites. To the leader:
according to Mahalath Leannoth.
A Maskil of Heman the Ezrahite.

¹ O LORD, God of my salvation,
when, at night, I cry out in
your presence,
² let my prayer come before
you;
incline your ear to my cry.

³ For my soul is full of
troubles,
and my life draws near to
Sheol.
⁴ I am counted among those
who go down to the Pit;
I am like those who have
no help,
⁵ like those forsaken among
the dead,
like the slain that lie in the
grave,
like those whom you
remember no more,

^t Or *Nubia*; Heb *Cush*

86.10
Ex 15.11;
Ps 72.18;
Deut 6.4;
Mk 12.29
86.11
Ps 25.4
86.12
Ps 111.1
86.13
Ps 30.3
86.14
Ps 54.3
86.15
Ex 34.6;
Neh 9.17;
Ps 103.8;
Joel 2.13
86.16
Ps 25.16;
68.35; 116.16
86.17
Ps 112.10;
118.13
87.2
Ps 78.67

87.3
Isa 60.1
87.5
Ps 48.8
87.6
Ezek 13.9
87.7
Ps 36.9
88.1
Ps 27.9;
51.14
88.2
Ps 18.6;
86.1
88.3
Ps 107.18,
26
88.4
Ps 28.1
88.5
Isa 53.8

for they are cut off from
your hand.
6 You have put me in the
depths of the Pit,
in the regions dark and
deep.
7 Your wrath lies heavy upon
me,
and you overwhelm me
with all your waves.
Selah

8 You have caused my
companions to shun
me;
you have made me a thing
of horror to them.
I am shut in so that I cannot
escape;
9 my eye grows dim through
sorrow.
Every day I call on you,
O LORD;
I spread out my hands to
you.
10 Do you work wonders for the
dead?
Do the shades rise up to
praise you? *Selah*
11 Is your steadfast love
declared in the grave,
or your faithfulness in
Abaddon?
12 Are your wonders known in
the darkness,
or your saving help in the
land of forgetfulness?

13 But I, O LORD, cry out to you;
in the morning my prayer
comes before you.
14 O LORD, why do you cast me
off?
Why do you hide your face
from me?
15 Wretched and close to death
from my youth up,
I suffer your terrors; I am
desperate.ᵘ
16 Your wrath has swept over
me;
your dread assaults destroy
me.
17 They surround me like a
flood all day long;
from all sides they close in
on me.

88.6
Ps 86.13;
143.3; 69.15
88.7
Ps 42.7
88.8
Job 19.13;
Ps 31.11;
142.4;
Lam 3.7
88.9
Ps 38.10;
86.3;
Job 11.13;
Ps 143.6
88.10
Ps 6.5;
Isa 38.18
88.12
Job 10.21
88.13
Ps 5.3;
119.147
88.14
Job 13.24;
Ps 13.1
88.15
Job 6.4
88.17
Ps 22.16

88.18
Job 19.13;
Ps 31.11;
38.11
89.1
Ps 101.1
89.2
Ps 103.17;
36.5
89.3
1 Kings 8.16;
Ps 132.11
89.4
2 Sam 7.16;
Isa 9.7;
Lk 1.33
89.5
Ps 19.1;
149.1
89.6
Mic 7.18;
Ps 29.1
89.7
Ps 47.2;
96.4
89.8
Ps 71.19
89.9
Ps 65.7

18 You have caused friend and
neighbor to shun me;
my companions are in
darkness.

Psalm 89

God's Covenant with David

A Maskil of Ethan the Ezrahite.

1 I will sing of your steadfast
love, O LORD,ᵛ forever;
with my mouth I will
proclaim your
faithfulness to all
generations.
2 I declare that your steadfast
love is established
forever;
your faithfulness is as firm
as the heavens.

3 You said, "I have made a
covenant with my
chosen one,
I have sworn to my servant
David:
4 'I will establish your
descendants forever,
and build your throne for
all generations.' " *Selah*

5 Let the heavens praise your
wonders, O LORD,
your faithfulness in the
assembly of the holy
ones.
6 For who in the skies can be
compared to the LORD?
Who among the heavenly
beings is like the LORD,
7 a God feared in the council
of the holy ones,
great and awesomeʷ above
all that are around him?
8 O LORD God of hosts,
who is as mighty as you,
O LORD?
Your faithfulness surrounds
you.
9 You rule the raging of the
sea;
when its waves rise, you
still them.

ᵘ Meaning of Heb uncertain ᵛ Gk: Heb *the
steadfast love of the LORD* ʷ Gk Syr: Heb
greatly awesome

10 You crushed Rahab like a
 carcass;
 you scattered your enemies
 with your mighty arm.
11 The heavens are yours, the
 earth also is yours;
 the world and all that is in
 it—you have founded
 them.
12 The north and the
 south[x]—you created
 them;
 Tabor and Hermon joyously
 praise your name.
13 You have a mighty arm;
 strong is your hand, high
 your right hand.
14 Righteousness and justice
 are the foundation of
 your throne;
 steadfast love and
 faithfulness go before
 you.
15 Happy are the people who
 know the festal shout,
 who walk, O LORD, in the
 light of your
 countenance;
16 they exult in your name all
 day long,
 and extol[y] your
 righteousness.
17 For you are the glory of their
 strength;
 by your favor our horn is
 exalted.
18 For our shield belongs to the
 LORD,
 our king to the Holy One
 of Israel.

19 Then you spoke in a vision
 to your faithful one,
 and said:
 "I have set the crown[z] on
 one who is mighty,
 I have exalted one chosen
 from the people.
20 I have found my servant
 David;
 with my holy oil I have
 anointed him;
21 my hand shall always remain
 with him;
 my arm also shall
 strengthen him.

22 The enemy shall not outwit
 him,
 the wicked shall not
 humble him.
23 I will crush his foes before
 him
 and strike down those who
 hate him.
24 My faithfulness and steadfast
 love shall be with him;
 and in my name his horn
 shall be exalted.
25 I will set his hand on the sea
 and his right hand on the
 rivers.
26 He shall cry to me, 'You are
 my Father,
 my God, and the Rock of
 my salvation!'
27 I will make him the
 firstborn,
 the highest of the kings of
 the earth.
28 Forever I will keep my
 steadfast love for him,
 and my covenant with him
 will stand firm.
29 I will establish his line
 forever,
 and his throne as long as
 the heavens endure.
30 If his children forsake my
 law
 and do not walk according
 to my ordinances,
31 if they violate my statutes
 and do not keep my
 commandments,
32 then I will punish their
 transgression with the
 rod
 and their iniquity with
 scourges;
33 but I will not remove from
 him my steadfast love,
 or be false to my
 faithfulness.
34 I will not violate my
 covenant,
 or alter the word that went
 forth from my lips.
35 Once and for all I have
 sworn by my holiness;
 I will not lie to David.

89.10
Ps 87.4;
Isa 51.9;
Ps 68.1
89.11
1 Chr 29.11;
Ps 24.1,2
89.12
Josh 19.22;
12.1
89.13
Ps 98.1
89.14
Ps 97.2;
85.13
89.15
Num 10.10
89.17
Ps 28.8;
75.10
89.18
Ps 47.9;
71.22
89.19
1 Kings 11.34
89.20
Acts 13.22;
1 Sam 16.1,
12

89.22
2 Sam 7.10
89.23
2 Sam 7.9
89.24
2 Sam 7.15
89.26
2 Sam 7.14;
22.47
89.27
Col 1.15;
Num 24.7;
Rev 1.5
89.28
Isa 55.3
89.29
Isa 9.7;
Jer 33.17;
Deut 11.21
89.30
2 Sam 7.14
89.32
2 Sam 7.14
89.33
2 Sam 7.15
89.34
Deut 7.9;
Num 23.19
89.35
Am 4.2

x Or *Zaphon and Yamin* y Cn: Heb *are*
exalted in z Cn: Heb *help*

36 His line shall continue
 forever,
 and his throne endure
 before me like the sun.
37 It shall be established
 forever like the moon,
 an enduring witness in the
 skies." *Selah*

38 But now you have spurned
 and rejected him;
 you are full of wrath
 against your anointed.
39 You have renounced the
 covenant with your
 servant;
 you have defiled his crown
 in the dust.
40 You have broken through all
 his walls;
 you have laid his
 strongholds in ruins.
41 All who pass by plunder
 him;
 he has become the scorn of
 his neighbors.
42 You have exalted the right
 hand of his foes;
 you have made all his
 enemies rejoice.
43 Moreover, you have turned
 back the edge of his
 sword,
 and you have not
 supported him in
 battle.
44 You have removed the
 scepter from his hand,[a]
 and hurled his throne to
 the ground.
45 You have cut short the days
 of his youth;
 you have covered him with
 shame. *Selah*

46 How long, O LORD? Will you
 hide yourself forever?
 How long will your wrath
 burn like fire?
47 Remember how short my
 time is — [b]
 for what vanity you have
 created all mortals!
48 Who can live and never see
 death?
 Who can escape the power
 of Sheol? *Selah*

49 Lord, where is your steadfast
 love of old,
 which by your faithfulness
 you swore to David?
50 Remember, O Lord, how
 your servant is taunted;
 how I bear in my bosom
 the insults of the
 peoples,[c]
51 with which your enemies
 taunt, O LORD,
 with which they taunted
 the footsteps of your
 anointed.

52 Blessed be the LORD forever.
 Amen and Amen.

BOOK IV

(Psalms 90–106)

Psalm 90

God's Eternity and Human Frailty

A Prayer of Moses, the man of God.

1 Lord, you have been our
 dwelling place[d]
 in all generations.
2 Before the mountains were
 brought forth,
 or ever you had formed the
 earth and the world,
 from everlasting to
 everlasting you are God.

3 You turn us[e] back to dust,
 and say, "Turn back, you
 mortals."
4 For a thousand years in your
 sight
 are like yesterday when it
 is past,
 or like a watch in the
 night.

5 You sweep them away; they
 are like a dream,

89.36
Ps 72.5
89.38
1 Chr 28.9;
Deut 32.19
89.39
Lam 5.16
89.40
Ps 80.12;
Lam 2.2,5
89.41
Ps 44.13
89.42
Ps 13.2;
80.6
89.43
Ps 44.10
89.44
Ezek 28.7
89.45
Ps 102.23;
44.15
89.46
Ps 79.5
89.47
Job 7.7;
10.9; 14.1;
Ps 39.5
89.48
Ps 49.9;
Heb 11.5

89.49
2 Sam 7.15;
Ps 54.5
89.50
Ps 69.9,19
89.51
Ps 74.10
89.52
Ps 41.13
90.1
Deut 33.27;
Ezek 11.16
90.2
Prov 8.25;
Ps 102.25;
93.2
90.3
Gen 3.19
90.4
2 Pet 3.8;
Ps 39.5
90.5
Job 27.20;
Ps 73.20;
103.15;
Isa 40.6

a Cn: Heb *removed his cleanness*
b Meaning of Heb uncertain c Cn: Heb
bosom all of many peoples d Another
reading is *our refuge* e Heb *humankind*

like grass that is renewed
in the morning;
6 in the morning it flourishes
and is renewed;
in the evening it fades and
withers.

7 For we are consumed by
your anger;
by your wrath we are
overwhelmed.
8 You have set our iniquities
before you,
our secret sins in the light
of your countenance.

9 For all our days pass away
under your wrath;
our years come to an end[f]
like a sigh.
10 The days of our life are
seventy years,
or perhaps eighty, if we are
strong;
even then their span[g] is only
toil and trouble;
they are soon gone, and we
fly away.

11 Who considers the power of
your anger?
Your wrath is as great as
the fear that is due you.
12 So teach us to count our
days
that we may gain a wise
heart.

13 Turn, O LORD! How long?
Have compassion on your
servants!
14 Satisfy us in the morning
with your steadfast
love,
so that we may rejoice and
be glad all our days.
15 Make us glad as many days
as you have afflicted us,
and as many years as we
have seen evil.
16 Let your work be manifest to
your servants,
and your glorious power to
their children.
17 Let the favor of the Lord our
God be upon us,

90.6
Job 14.2;
Ps 92.7
90.8
Ps 50.21;
Jer 16.17;
Ps 19.12
90.9
Ps 78.33
90.10
Eccl 12.2-7
90.11
Ps 76.7
90.12
Ps 39.4
90.13
Deut 32.26;
Ps 135.14
90.14
Ps 65.4;
85.6
90.16
Hab 3.2;
1 Kings 8.11
90.17
Ps 27.4;
Isa 26.12

91.1
Ps 27.5;
31.20; 17.8
91.2
Ps 142.5
91.3
Ps 124.7
91.4
Isa 51.16;
Ps 57.1;
40.11; 35.2
91.5
Ps 23.4;
Song 3.8;
Ps 64.4
91.6
v. 10;
Job 5.22
91.8
Ps 37.34;
Mal 1.5
91.10
Prov 12.21

and prosper for us the work
of our hands—
O prosper the work of our
hands!

Psalm 91

Assurance of God's Protection

1 You who live in the shelter
of the Most High,
who abide in the shadow of
the Almighty,[h]
2 will say to the LORD, "My
refuge and my fortress;
my God, in whom I trust."
3 For he will deliver you from
the snare of the fowler
and from the deadly
pestilence;
4 he will cover you with his
pinions,
and under his wings you
will find refuge;
his faithfulness is a shield
and buckler.
5 You will not fear the terror of
the night,
or the arrow that flies by
day,
6 or the pestilence that stalks
in darkness,
or the destruction that
wastes at noonday.

7 A thousand may fall at your
side,
ten thousand at your right
hand,
but it will not come near
you.
8 You will only look with your
eyes
and see the punishment of
the wicked.

9 Because you have made the
LORD your refuge,[i]
the Most High your
dwelling place,
10 no evil shall befall you,
no scourge come near your
tent.

f Syr: Heb *we bring our years to an end*
g Cn Compare Gk Syr Jerome Tg: Heb *pride*
h Traditional rendering of Heb *Shaddai*
i Cn: Heb *Because you, LORD, are my refuge;
you have made*

11 For he will command his
　　angels concerning you
　to guard you in all your
　　ways.
12 On their hands they will bear
　　you up,
　so that you will not dash
　　your foot against a
　　stone.
13 You will tread on the lion
　　and the adder,
　the young lion and the
　　serpent you will
　　trample under foot.

14 Those who love me, I will
　　deliver;
　I will protect those who
　　know my name.
15 When they call to me, I will
　　answer them;
　I will be with them in
　　trouble,
　I will rescue them and
　　honor them.
16 With long life I will satisfy
　　them,
　and show them my
　　salvation.

Psalm 92

Thanksgiving for Vindication

A Psalm. A Song for the Sabbath
　　Day.

1 It is good to give thanks to
　　the Lord,
　to sing praises to your
　　name, O Most High;
2 to declare your steadfast love
　　in the morning,
　and your faithfulness by
　　night,
3 to the music of the lute and
　　the harp,
　to the melody of the lyre.
4 For you, O Lord, have made
　　me glad by your work;
　at the works of your hands
　　I sing for joy.

5 How great are your works,
　　O Lord!
　Your thoughts are very
　　deep!
6 The dullard cannot know,

91.11
Ps 34.7;
Mt 4.6;
Lk 4.10;
Heb 1.14
91.13
Lk 10.19
91.14
Ps 145.20;
59.1; 9.10
91.15
Ps 50.15;
1 Sam 2.30;
Jn 12.26
91.16
Ps 21.4;
50.23
92.1
Ps 157.1
92.2
Ps 89.1
92.3
1 Chr 23.5;
Ps 33.2
92.5
Ps 40.5;
Isa 28.29;
Rom 11.33
92.6
Ps 73.22

92.7
Ps 90.5;
94.4; 37.38;
93.4
92.8
Ps 83.18
92.9
Ps 68.1;
89.10
92.10
Ps 89.17;
23.5
92.11
Ps 54.7;
59.10
92.12
Ps 52.8;
Isa 65.22;
Hos 14.5,6;
Ps 104.16
92.13
Ps 80.15;
100.4
92.14
Isa 37.31
92.15
Ps 25.8;
Deut 32.4;
Rom 9.14
93.1
Ps 96.10;
97.1; 99.1;
104.1; 65.6

　the stupid cannot
　　understand this:
7 though the wicked sprout
　　like grass
　and all evildoers flourish,
　they are doomed to
　　destruction forever,
8 but you, O Lord, are on
　　high forever.
9 For your enemies, O Lord,
　for your enemies shall
　　perish;
　all evildoers shall be
　　scattered.

10 But you have exalted my
　　horn like that of the
　　wild ox;
　you have poured over me[j]
　　fresh oil.
11 My eyes have seen the
　　downfall of my
　　enemies;
　my ears have heard the
　　doom of my evil
　　assailants.

12 The righteous flourish like
　　the palm tree,
　and grow like a cedar in
　　Lebanon.
13 They are planted in the
　　house of the Lord;
　they flourish in the courts
　　of our God.
14 In old age they still produce
　　fruit;
　they are always green and
　　full of sap,
15 showing that the Lord is
　　upright;
　he is my rock, and there is
　　no unrighteousness in
　　him.

Psalm 93

The Majesty of God's Rule

1 The Lord is king, he is robed
　　in majesty;
　the Lord is robed, he is
　　girded with strength.
　He has established the
　　world; it shall never be
　　moved;

j Syr: Meaning of Heb uncertain

² your throne is established
from of old;
you are from everlasting.

³ The floods have lifted up,
O Lᴏʀᴅ,
the floods have lifted up
their voice;
the floods lift up their
roaring.
⁴ More majestic than the
thunders of mighty
waters,
more majestic than the
waves[k] of the sea,
majestic on high is the
Lᴏʀᴅ!

⁵ Your decrees are very sure;
holiness befits your house,
O Lᴏʀᴅ, forevermore.

Psalm 94

God the Avenger of the Righteous

¹ O Lᴏʀᴅ, you God of
vengeance,
you God of vengeance,
shine forth!
² Rise up, O judge of the
earth;
give to the proud what they
deserve!
³ O Lᴏʀᴅ, how long shall the
wicked,
how long shall the wicked
exult?

⁴ They pour out their arrogant
words;
all the evildoers boast.
⁵ They crush your people,
O Lᴏʀᴅ,
and afflict your heritage.
⁶ They kill the widow and the
stranger,
they murder the orphan,
⁷ and they say, "The Lᴏʀᴅ does
not see;
the God of Jacob does not
perceive."

⁸ Understand, O dullest of the
people;

fools, when will you be
wise?
⁹ He who planted the ear, does
he not hear?
He who formed the eye, does
he not see?
¹⁰ He who disciplines the
nations,
he who teaches knowledge to
humankind,
does he not chastise?
¹¹ The Lᴏʀᴅ knows our
thoughts,[1]
that they are but an empty
breath.

¹² Happy are those whom you
discipline, O Lᴏʀᴅ,
and whom you teach out of
your law,
¹³ giving them respite from
days of trouble,
until a pit is dug for the
wicked.
¹⁴ For the Lᴏʀᴅ will not forsake
his people;
he will not abandon his
heritage;
¹⁵ for justice will return to the
righteous,
and all the upright in heart
will follow it.

¹⁶ Who rises up for me against
the wicked?
Who stands up for me
against evildoers?
¹⁷ If the Lᴏʀᴅ had not been my
help,
my soul would soon have
lived in the land of
silence.
¹⁸ When I thought, "My foot is
slipping,"
your steadfast love, O Lᴏʀᴅ,
held me up.
¹⁹ When the cares of my heart
are many,
your consolations cheer my
soul.
²⁰ Can wicked rulers be allied
with you,
those who contrive
mischief by statute?

93.2
Ps 45.6;
90.2
93.3
Ps 98.7,8
93.4
Ps 65.7;
89.9
93.5
Ps 19.7;
1 Cor 3.17
94.1
Deut 32.35;
Nah 1.2;
Ps 50.2
94.2
Ps 7.6;
Gen 18.25;
Ps 31.23
94.3
Job 20.5
94.4
Ps 31.18;
10.3
94.6
Isa 10.2
94.7
Ps 10.11
94.8
Ps 92.6

94.9
Ex 4.11;
Prov 20.12
94.10
Ps 44.2;
Job 35.11;
Isa 28.26
94.11
1 Cor 3.20
94.12
Job 5.17;
Heb 12.5
94.13
Ps 49.5;
9.15
94.14
1 Sam 12.22;
Rom 11.1,2
94.16
Isa 28.21;
Ps 59.2
94.17
Ps 124.1
94.18
Ps 38.16
94.19
Isa 66.13
94.20
Am 6.3;
Isa 10.1

k Cn: Heb *majestic are the waves*
1 Heb *the thoughts of humankind*

21 They band together against
　　　the life of the righteous,
　　and condemn the innocent
　　　to death.
22 But the LORD has become my
　　　stronghold,
　　and my God the rock of my
　　　refuge.
23 He will repay them for their
　　　iniquity
　　and wipe them out for their
　　　wickedness;
　　the LORD our God will wipe
　　　them out.

Psalm 95

A Call to Worship and
Obedience

1 O come, let us sing to the
　　　LORD;
　　let us make a joyful noise
　　　to the rock of our
　　　salvation!
2 Let us come into his
　　　presence with
　　　thanksgiving;
　　let us make a joyful noise
　　　to him with songs of
　　　praise!
3 For the LORD is a great God,
　　and a great King above all
　　　gods.
4 In his hand are the depths of
　　　the earth;
　　the heights of the
　　　mountains are his also.
5 The sea is his, for he made
　　　it,
　　and the dry land, which his
　　　hands have formed.

6 O come, let us worship and
　　　bow down,
　　let us kneel before the
　　　LORD, our Maker!
7 For he is our God,
　　and we are the people of
　　　his pasture,
　　and the sheep of his hand.

　O that today you would
　　　listen to his voice!
8 Do not harden your hearts,
　　as at Meribah,

as on the day at Massah in
　　　the wilderness,
9 when your ancestors tested
　　　me,
　　and put me to the proof,
　　　though they had seen
　　　my work.
10 For forty years I loathed that
　　　generation
　　and said, "They are a
　　　people whose hearts go
　　　astray,
　　and they do not regard my
　　　ways."
11 Therefore in my anger I
　　　swore,
　　"They shall not enter my
　　　rest."

Psalm 96

Praise to God Who Comes in
Judgment

1 O sing to the LORD a new
　　　song;
　　sing to the LORD, all the
　　　earth.
2 Sing to the LORD, bless his
　　　name;
　　tell of his salvation from
　　　day to day.
3 Declare his glory among the
　　　nations,
　　his marvelous works among
　　　all the peoples.
4 For great is the LORD, and
　　　greatly to be praised;
　　he is to be revered above
　　　all gods.
5 For all the gods of the
　　　peoples are idols,
　　but the LORD made the
　　　heavens.
6 Honor and majesty are
　　　before him;
　　strength and beauty are in
　　　his sanctuary.

7 Ascribe to the LORD,
　　O families of the
　　　peoples,
　　ascribe to the LORD glory
　　　and strength.
8 Ascribe to the LORD the glory
　　　due his name;

94.21
Ps 56.6;
Mt 27.1;
Prov 17.15
94.22
Ps 59.9;
71.7
94.23
Ps 7.16
95.1
Ps 100.1;
Deut 32.15;
2 Sam 22.47
95.2
Mic 6.6;
Ps 100.4;
81.2
95.3
Ps 96.4;
97.9; 135.5
95.5
Gen 1.9,10
95.6
Ps 99.5,9;
2 Chr 6.13;
Ps 100.3
95.7
Ps 79.13;
100.3;
Heb 3.7-11
95.8
Ex 17.2,7;
Deut 6.16

95.9
Ps 78.18;
1 Cor 10.9
95.10
Heb 3.10,17
95.11
Heb 4.3,5
96.1
1 Chr 16.23-33
96.2
Ps 71.15
96.3
Ps 145.12
96.4
Ps 145.3;
18.3; 95.3
96.5
1 Chr 16.26;
Ps 115.15
96.6
Ps 104.1
96.7
Ps 29.1,2
96.8
Ps 79.9

bring an offering, and come
 into his courts.
9 Worship the LORD in holy
 splendor;
 tremble before him, all the
 earth.

10 Say among the nations, "The
 LORD is king!
 The world is firmly
 established; it shall
 never be moved.
 He will judge the peoples
 with equity."
11 Let the heavens be glad, and
 let the earth rejoice;
 let the sea roar, and all
 that fills it;
12 let the field exult, and
 everything in it.
 Then shall all the trees of
 the forest sing for joy
13 before the LORD; for he is
 coming,
 for he is coming to judge
 the earth.
 He will judge the world with
 righteousness,
 and the peoples with his
 truth.

Psalm 97

The Glory of God's Reign

1 The LORD is king! Let the
 earth rejoice;
 let the many coastlands be
 glad!
2 Clouds and thick darkness
 are all around him;
 righteousness and justice
 are the foundation of
 his throne.
3 Fire goes before him,
 and consumes his
 adversaries on every
 side.
4 His lightnings light up the
 world;
 the earth sees and
 trembles.
5 The mountains melt like wax
 before the LORD,
 before the Lord of all the
 earth.

96.9
Ps 29.2
96.10
Ps 93.1;
67.4
96.11
Ps 97.1;
98.7
96.13
Ps 67.4;
Rev 19.11
97.1
Ps 96.10,11
97.2
1 Kings 8.12;
Ps 18.11;
89.14
97.3
Ps 18.8;
Dan 7.10;
Hab 3.5;
Heb 12.29
97.4
Ps 77.18
97.5
Mic 1.4;
Josh 3.11

97.6
Ps 50.6
97.7
Ex 20.4;
Lev 26.1;
Heb 1.6
97.8
Ps 48.11
97.9
Ps 83.18;
Ex 18.11;
Ps 95.3
97.10
Ps 34.14;
Am 5.15;
Prov 2.8;
Ps 37.39;
Dan 3.28
97.11
Job 22.28;
Ps 112.4
97.12
Ps 32.11;
30.4
98.1
Ps 33.3;
40.5;
Ex 15.6;
Isa 52.10
98.2
Rom 3.25

6 The heavens proclaim his
 righteousness;
 and all the peoples behold
 his glory.
7 All worshipers of images are
 put to shame,
 those who make their boast
 in worthless idols;
 all gods bow down before
 him.
8 Zion hears and is glad,
 and the towns[m] of Judah
 rejoice,
 because of your judgments,
 O God.
9 For you, O LORD, are most
 high over all the earth;
 you are exalted far above
 all gods.

10 The LORD loves those who
 hate[n] evil;
 he guards the lives of his
 faithful;
 he rescues them from the
 hand of the wicked.
11 Light dawns[o] for the
 righteous,
 and joy for the upright in
 heart.
12 Rejoice in the LORD, O you
 righteous,
 and give thanks to his holy
 name!

Psalm 98

Praise the Judge of the World

A Psalm.

1 O sing to the LORD a new
 song,
 for he has done marvelous
 things.
 His right hand and his holy
 arm
 have gotten him victory.
2 The LORD has made known
 his victory;
 he has revealed his
 vindication in the sight
 of the nations.

m Heb *daughters* n Cn: Heb *You who love*
the LORD hate o Gk Syr Jerome: Heb *is*
sown

3 He has remembered his
 steadfast love and
 faithfulness
to the house of Israel.
All the ends of the earth
 have seen
 the victory of our God.

4 Make a joyful noise to the
 LORD, all the earth;
break forth into joyous
 song and sing praises.
5 Sing praises to the LORD with
 the lyre,
with the lyre and the sound
 of melody.
6 With trumpets and the sound
 of the horn
make a joyful noise before
 the King, the LORD.

7 Let the sea roar, and all that
 fills it;
the world and those who
 live in it.
8 Let the floods clap their hands;
let the hills sing together
 for joy
9 at the presence of the LORD,
 for he is coming
 to judge the earth.
He will judge the world with
 righteousness,
and the peoples with
 equity.

Psalm 99

Praise to God for His Holiness

1 The LORD is king; let the
 peoples tremble!
He sits enthroned upon the
 cherubim; let the earth
 quake!
2 The LORD is great in Zion;
he is exalted over all the
 peoples.
3 Let them praise your great
 and awesome name.
Holy is he!
4 Mighty King, p lover of
 justice,
you have established
 equity;
you have executed justice
and righteousness in Jacob.

5 Extol the LORD our God;
worship at his footstool.
Holy is he!

6 Moses and Aaron were
 among his priests,
Samuel also was among
 those who called on his
 name.
They cried to the LORD, and
 he answered them.
7 He spoke to them in the
 pillar of cloud;
they kept his decrees,
and the statutes that he
 gave them.

8 O LORD our God, you
 answered them;
you were a forgiving God to
 them,
but an avenger of their
 wrongdoings.
9 Extol the LORD our God,
and worship at his holy
 mountain;
for the LORD our God is
 holy.

Psalm 100

All Lands Summoned to Praise God

A Psalm of thanksgiving.

1 Make a joyful noise to the
 LORD, all the earth.
2 Worship the LORD with
 gladness;
come into his presence
 with singing.

3 Know that the LORD is God.
It is he that made us, and
 we are his; q
we are his people, and the
 sheep of his pasture.

4 Enter his gates with
 thanksgiving,
and his courts with praise.
Give thanks to him, bless
 his name.

98.3 Lk 1.54; Isa 49.6
98.4 Ps 100.1
98.6 Num 10.10
98.7 Ps 96.11; 24.1
98.8 Ps 93.3; 65.12
98.9 Ps 96.10,13
99.1 Ex 25.22
99.2 Ps 97.9
99.4 Ps 11.7; 17.2; 103.6
99.5 Ps 132.7; Lev 19.2
99.6 Jer 15.1; Ex 14.15; 1 Sam 7.9
99.7 Ex 33.9
99.8 Ps 106.44; Num 14.20; Deut 9.20
99.9 Ps 34.3
100.1 Ps 98.4
100.3 Ps 46.10; 95.6,7
100.4 Ps 95.2; 96.2

p Cn: Heb And a king's strength q Another reading is and not we ourselves

⁵ For the LORD is good;
　　his steadfast love endures
　　　　forever,
　　and his faithfulness to all
　　　　generations.

Psalm 101
A Sovereign's Pledge of Integrity and Justice

Of David. A Psalm.

¹ I will sing of loyalty and of
　　justice;
　　to you, O LORD, I will sing.
² I will study the way that is
　　blameless.
　　When shall I attain it?

　I will walk with integrity of
　　heart
　　within my house;
³ I will not set before my eyes
　　anything that is base.

　I hate the work of those who
　　fall away;
　　it shall not cling to me.
⁴ Perverseness of heart shall
　　be far from me;
　　I will know nothing of evil.

⁵ One who secretly slanders a
　　neighbor
　　I will destroy.
　A haughty look and an
　　arrogant heart
　　I will not tolerate.

⁶ I will look with favor on the
　　faithful in the land,
　　so that they may live with
　　me;
　whoever walks in the way
　　that is blameless
　　shall minister to me.

⁷ No one who practices deceit
　　shall remain in my house;
　no one who utters lies
　　shall continue in my
　　presence.

⁸ Morning by morning I will
　　destroy
　　all the wicked in the land,
　cutting off all evildoers

100.5
Ps 25.8;
119.90
101.1
Ps 89.1
101.2
1 Sam 18.14;
1 Kings 9.4
101.3
Deut 15.9;
Ps 40.4
101.4
Prov 11.20
101.5
Ps 50.20;
Prov 6.17
101.6
Ps 119.1
101.8
Ps 75.10;
118.10-12

102.1
Ex 2.23;
1 Sam 9.16
102.2
Ps 69.17;
71.2
102.3
Jas 4.14;
Job 30.30;
Ps 31.10
102.4
Ps 37.2
102.5
Lam 4.8
102.6
Isa 34.11
102.7
Ps 77.4;
38.11
102.8
Acts 26.11;
23;12
102.9
Ps 42.3
102.10
Ps 38.3;
Job 30.22
102.11
Job 14.2;
v. 4
102.12
Ps 9.7;
Lam 5.19;
Ps 135.13
102.13
Isa 60.10;
Zech 1.12;
Ps 75.2

from the city of the LORD.

Psalm 102
Prayer to the Eternal King for Help

A prayer of one afflicted, when
faint and pleading before the
LORD.

¹ Hear my prayer, O LORD;
　　let my cry come to you.
² Do not hide your face from
　　me
　　in the day of my distress.
　Incline your ear to me;
　　answer me speedily in the
　　day when I call.

³ For my days pass away like
　　smoke,
　　and my bones burn like a
　　furnace.
⁴ My heart is stricken and
　　withered like grass;
　　I am too wasted to eat my
　　bread.
⁵ Because of my loud groaning
　　my bones cling to my skin.
⁶ I am like an owl of the
　　wilderness,
　　like a little owl of the
　　waste places.
⁷ I lie awake;
　　I am like a lonely bird on
　　the housetop.
⁸ All day long my enemies
　　taunt me;
　　those who deride me use
　　my name for a curse.
⁹ For I eat ashes like bread,
　　and mingle tears with my
　　drink,
¹⁰ because of your indignation
　　and anger;
　　for you have lifted me up
　　and thrown me aside.
¹¹ My days are like an evening
　　shadow;
　　I wither away like grass.

¹² But you, O LORD, are
　　enthroned forever;
　　your name endures to all
　　generations.
¹³ You will rise up and have
　　compassion on Zion,

for it is time to favor it;
the appointed time has
come.

14 For your servants hold its
stones dear,
and have pity on its dust.
15 The nations will fear the
name of the LORD,
and all the kings of the
earth your glory.
16 For the LORD will build up
Zion;
he will appear in his
glory.
17 He will regard the prayer of
the destitute,
and will not despise their
prayer.

18 Let this be recorded for a
generation to come,
so that a people yet unborn
may praise the LORD:
19 that he looked down from
his holy height,
from heaven the LORD
looked at the earth,
20 to hear the groans of the
prisoners,
to set free those who were
doomed to die;
21 so that the name of the LORD
may be declared in
Zion,
and his praise in
Jerusalem,
22 when peoples gather
together,
and kingdoms, to worship
the LORD.

23 He has broken my strength
in midcourse;
he has shortened my days.
24 "O my God," I say, "do not
take me away
at the mid-point of my life,
you whose years endure
throughout all
generations."

25 Long ago you laid the
foundation of the earth,
and the heavens are the
work of your hands.
26 They will perish, but you
endure;

they will all wear out like a
garment.
You change them like
clothing, and they pass
away;
27 but you are the same, and
your years have no end.
28 The children of your servants
shall live secure;
their offspring shall be
established in your
presence.

Psalm 103

Thanksgiving for God's Goodness

Of David.

1 Bless the LORD, O my soul,
and all that is within me,
bless his holy name.
2 Bless the LORD, O my soul,
and do not forget all his
benefits—
3 who forgives all your
iniquity,
who heals all your diseases,
4 who redeems your life from
the Pit,
who crowns you with
steadfast love and
mercy,
5 who satisfies you with good
as long as you live[r]
so that your youth is
renewed like the
eagle's.

6 The LORD works vindication
and justice for all who are
oppressed.
7 He made known his ways to
Moses,
his acts to the people of
Israel.
8 The LORD is merciful and
gracious,
slow to anger and
abounding in steadfast
love.
9 He will not always accuse,
nor will he keep his anger
forever.

102.15
1 Kings 8.43;
Ps 138.4
102.16
Isa 60.1,2
102.17
Neh 1.6
102.18
Rom 15.4;
Ps 22.31
102.19
Deut 26.15;
Ps 33.13
102.20
Ps 79.11
102.21
Ps 22.22
102.22
Ps 86.9
102.23
Job 21.21
102.24
Isa 38.10;
Ps 90.2;
Hab 1.12
102.25
Gen 1.1;
Heb 1.10;
Ps 96.5
102.26
Isa 34.4;
Mt 24.35;
2 Pet 3.7,
10;
Rev 20.11

102.27
Mal 3.6;
Heb 13.8;
Jas 1.17
102.28
Ps 69.36;
89.4
103.1
Ps 104.1;
33.21
103.3
Ps 130.8;
Isa 43.25;
Ex 15.26
103.4
Ps 49.15;
5.12
103.5
Isa 40.31
103.8
Ex 34.6;
Neh 9.17;
Ps 145.8
103.9
Ps 30.5;
Isa 57.16;
Jer 3.5

¹⁰ He does not deal with us
according to our sins,
nor repay us according to
our iniquities.
¹¹ For as the heavens are high
above the earth,
so great is his steadfast
love toward those who
fear him;
¹² as far as the east is from the
west,
so far he removes our
transgressions from us.
¹³ As a father has compassion
for his children,
so the LORD has
compassion for those
who fear him.
¹⁴ For he knows how we were
made;
he remembers that we are
dust.

¹⁵ As for mortals, their days are
like grass;
they flourish like a flower
of the field;
¹⁶ for the wind passes over it,
and it is gone,
and its place knows it no
more.
¹⁷ But the steadfast love of the
LORD is from everlasting
to everlasting
on those who fear him,
and his righteousness to
children's children,
¹⁸ to those who keep his
covenant
and remember to do his
commandments.

¹⁹ The LORD has established his
throne in the heavens,
and his kingdom rules over
all.
²⁰ Bless the LORD, O you his
angels,
you mighty ones who do
his bidding,
obedient to his spoken
word.
²¹ Bless the LORD, all his hosts,
his ministers that do his
will.
²² Bless the LORD, all his works,

103.10
Ezra 9.13
103.11
Ps 36.5
103.12
2 Sam 12.13;
Isa 38.17;
Heb 9.26
103.13
Mal 3.17
103.14
Isa 29.16;
Gen 3.19
103.15
1 Pet 1.24;
Job 14.1,2
103.16
Job 7.10
103.18
Deut 7.9
103.19
Ps 11.4;
47.2
103.20
Ps 148.2;
Mt 6.10;
Heb 1.14
103.21
Ps 148.2

104.1
Ps 103.1
104.2
Dan 7.9;
Isa 40.22
104.3
Am 9.6;
Isa 19.1;
Ps 18.10
104.4
Heb 1.7
104.5
Job 26.7;
Ps 24.2
104.6
Gen 7.19
104.8
Ps 33.7
104.9
Job 38.10,
11; Jer 5.22
104.10
Ps 107.35
104.11
Job 39.5

in all places of his
dominion.
Bless the LORD, O my soul.

Psalm 104

God the Creator and Provider

¹ Bless the LORD, O my soul.
O LORD my God, you are
very great.
You are clothed with honor
and majesty,
² wrapped in light as with a
garment.
You stretch out the heavens
like a tent,
³ you set the beams of your^s
chambers on the
waters,
you make the clouds your^s
chariot,
you ride on the wings of
the wind,
⁴ you make the winds your^s
messengers,
fire and flame your^s
ministers.

⁵ You set the earth on its
foundations,
so that it shall never be
shaken.
⁶ You cover it with the deep as
with a garment;
the waters stood above the
mountains.
⁷ At your rebuke they flee;
at the sound of your
thunder they take to
flight.
⁸ They rose up to the
mountains, ran down to
the valleys
to the place that you
appointed for them.
⁹ You set a boundary that they
may not pass,
so that they might not
again cover the earth.

¹⁰ You make springs gush forth
in the valleys;
they flow between the hills,
¹¹ giving drink to every wild
animal;

^s Heb *his*

the wild asses quench their
 thirst.
12 By the streams[t] the birds of
 the air have their
 habitation;
 they sing among the
 branches.
13 From your lofty abode you
 water the mountains;
 the earth is satisfied with
 the fruit of your work.

14 You cause the grass to grow
 for the cattle,
 and plants for people to
 use,[u]
 to bring forth food from the
 earth,
15 and wine to gladden the
 human heart,
 oil to make the face shine,
 and bread to strengthen
 the human heart.
16 The trees of the LORD are
 watered abundantly,
 the cedars of Lebanon that
 he planted.
17 In them the birds build their
 nests;
 the stork has its home in
 the fir trees.
18 The high mountains are for
 the wild goats;
 the rocks are a refuge for
 the coneys.
19 You have made the moon to
 mark the seasons;
 the sun knows its time for
 setting.
20 You make darkness, and it is
 night,
 when all the animals of the
 forest come creeping
 out.
21 The young lions roar for their
 prey,
 seeking their food from
 God.
22 When the sun rises, they
 withdraw
 and lie down in their dens.
23 People go out to their work
 and to their labor until the
 evening.

24 O LORD, how manifold are
 your works!

In wisdom you have made
 them all;
 the earth is full of your
 creatures.
25 Yonder is the sea, great and
 wide,
 creeping things
 innumerable are there,
 living things both small
 and great.
26 There go the ships,
 and Leviathan that you
 formed to sport in it.

27 These all look to you
 to give them their food in
 due season;
28 when you give to them, they
 gather it up;
 when you open your hand,
 they are filled with
 good things.
29 When you hide your face,
 they are dismayed;
 when you take away their
 breath, they die
 and return to their dust.
30 When you send forth your
 spirit,[v] they are
 created;
 and you renew the face of
 the ground.

31 May the glory of the LORD
 endure forever;
 may the LORD rejoice in his
 works—
32 who looks on the earth and
 it trembles,
 who touches the mountains
 and they smoke.
33 I will sing to the LORD as
 long as I live;
 I will sing praise to my God
 while I have being.
34 May my meditation be
 pleasing to him,
 for I rejoice in the LORD.
35 Let sinners be consumed
 from the earth,
 and let the wicked be no
 more.
 Bless the LORD, O my soul.
 Praise the LORD!

104.12
Mt 8.20
104.13
Ps 65.9;
147.8
104.14
Ps 147.8;
Job 38.27;
Gen 1.29;
Job 28.5
104.15
Judg 9.13;
Ps 23.5
104.18
Prov 30.26
104.19
Gen 1.14
104.20
Isa 45.7
104.21
Job 38.39
104.23
Gen 3.19
104.24
Ps 40.5;
Prov 3.19;
Ps 65.9

104.26
Ps 107.23;
Job 41.1
104.27
Ps 136.25;
145.14
104.29
Job 34.14;
Ps 146.4;
Eccl 12.7
104.30
Isa 32.15;
Ezek 37.9
104.31
Gen 1.31
104.32
Ps 97.4,5;
144.5
104.33
Ps 63.4;
146.2
104.35
Ps 59.13;
37.10; v. 1

[t] Heb *By them* [u] Or *to cultivate*
[v] Or *your breath*

Psalm 105

God's Faithfulness to Israel

1 O give thanks to the LORD,
 call on his name,
 make known his deeds
 among the peoples.
2 Sing to him, sing praises to
 him;
 tell of all his wonderful
 works.
3 Glory in his holy name;
 let the hearts of those who
 seek the LORD rejoice.
4 Seek the LORD and his
 strength;
 seek his presence
 continually.
5 Remember the wonderful
 works he has done,
 his miracles, and the
 judgments he uttered,
6 O offspring of his servant
 Abraham,^w
 children of Jacob, his
 chosen ones.

7 He is the LORD our God;
 his judgments are in all the
 earth.
8 He is mindful of his
 covenant forever,
 of the word that he
 commanded, for a
 thousand generations,
9 the covenant that he made
 with Abraham,
 his sworn promise to Isaac,
10 which he confirmed to Jacob
 as a statute,
 to Israel as an everlasting
 covenant,
11 saying, "To you I will give
 the land of Canaan
 as your portion for an
 inheritance."

12 When they were few in
 number,
 of little account, and
 strangers in it,
13 wandering from nation to
 nation,
 from one kingdom to
 another people,

105.1
1 Chr 16.8;
Ps 145.12
105.2
Ps 77.12
105.3
Ps 33.21
105.4
Ps 27.8
105.5
Ps 77.11
105.7
Isa 26.9
105.8
Lk 1.72
105.9
Gen 17.2;
22.16; 26.3
105.10
Gen 28.13-15
105.11
Gen 13.15;
15.18
105.12
Gen 34.30;
Deut 7.7;
Heb 11.9

105.14
Gen 35.5;
12.17
105.16
Gen 41.54;
Lev 26.26;
Isa 3.1;
Ezek 4.16
105.17
Gen 45.5;
37.28,36
105.18
Gen 39.20
105.19
Gen 40.20,
21; Ps 66.10
105.20
Gen 41.14
105.21
Gen 41.40
105.23
Gen 46.6;
Acts 13.17
105.24
Ex 1.7
105.25
Ex 1.8,10
105.26
Ex 3.10;
Num 16.5
105.27
Ex 7-12;
Ps 78.43

14 he allowed no one to oppress
 them;
 he rebuked kings on their
 account,
15 saying, "Do not touch my
 anointed ones;
 do my prophets no harm."

16 When he summoned famine
 against the land,
 and broke every staff of
 bread,
17 he had sent a man ahead of
 them,
 Joseph, who was sold as a
 slave.
18 His feet were hurt with
 fetters,
 his neck was put in a collar
 of iron;
19 until what he had said came
 to pass,
 the word of the LORD kept
 testing him.
20 The king sent and released
 him;
 the ruler of the peoples set
 him free.
21 He made him lord of his
 house,
 and ruler of all his
 possessions,
22 to instruct^x his officials at
 his pleasure,
 and to teach his elders
 wisdom.

23 Then Israel came to Egypt;
 Jacob lived as an alien in
 the land of Ham.
24 And the LORD made his
 people very fruitful,
 and made them stronger
 than their foes,
25 whose hearts he then turned
 to hate his people,
 to deal craftily with his
 servants.

26 He sent his servant Moses,
 and Aaron whom he had
 chosen.
27 They performed his signs
 among them,

^w Another reading is *Israel* (compare 1 Chr
16.13) ^x Gk Syr Jerome: Heb *to bind*

and miracles in the land of
Ham.

28 He sent darkness, and made
the land dark;
they rebelled[y] against his
words.

29 He turned their waters into
blood,
and caused their fish to
die.

30 Their land swarmed with
frogs,
even in the chambers of
their kings.

31 He spoke, and there came
swarms of flies,
and gnats throughout their
country.

32 He gave them hail for rain,
and lightning that flashed
through their land.

33 He struck their vines and fig
trees,
and shattered the trees of
their country.

34 He spoke, and the locusts
came,
and young locusts without
number;

35 they devoured all the
vegetation in their land,
and ate up the fruit of their
ground.

36 He struck down all the
firstborn in their land,
the first issue of all their
strength.

37 Then he brought Israel[z] out
with silver and gold,
and there was no one
among their tribes who
stumbled.

38 Egypt was glad when they
departed,
for dread of them had
fallen upon it.

39 He spread a cloud for a
covering,
and fire to give light by
night.

40 They asked, and he brought
quails,
and gave them food from
heaven in abundance.

41 He opened the rock, and
water gushed out;

105.28
Ex 10.22;
Ps 99.7
105.29
Ex 7.20
105.30
Ex 8.6
105.31
Ex 8.16,21
105.32
Ex 9.23
105.34
Ex 10.4;
Ps 73.46
105.36
Ex 12.29;
Ps 78.51
105.37
Ex 12.35
105.38
Ex 12.33
105.39
Ex 13.21;
Neh 9.12
105.40
Ex 16.12ff;
Ps 78.24ff
105.41
Ex 17.6;
Ps 78.15,16;
1 Cor 10.4

105.42
v. 8
105.44
Deut 6-10;
Josh 13.7
105.45
Deut 6.21-25
106.1
Ps 105.1;
100.5;
1 Chr 16.34
106.2
Ps 145.4,12
106.3
Ps 15.2
106.4
Ps 119.132
106.5
Ps 1.3;
118.15; 105.3
106.6
Dan 9.5

it flowed through the
desert like a river.

42 For he remembered his holy
promise,
and Abraham, his servant.

43 So he brought his people out
with joy,
his chosen ones with
singing.

44 He gave them the lands of
the nations,
and they took possession of
the wealth of the
peoples,

45 that they might keep his
statutes
and observe his laws.
Praise the LORD!

Psalm 106

A Confession of Israel's Sins

1 Praise the LORD!
O give thanks to the LORD,
for he is good;
for his steadfast love
endures forever.

2 Who can utter the mighty
doings of the LORD,
or declare all his praise?

3 Happy are those who observe
justice,
who do righteousness at all
times.

4 Remember me, O LORD, when
you show favor to your
people;
help me when you deliver
them;

5 that I may see the prosperity
of your chosen ones,
that I may rejoice in the
gladness of your nation,
that I may glory in your
heritage.

6 Both we and our ancestors
have sinned;
we have committed
iniquity, have done
wickedly.

y Cn Compare Gk Syr: Heb *they did not rebel*
z Heb *them*

7 Our ancestors, when they
 were in Egypt,
 did not consider your
 wonderful works;
 they did not remember the
 abundance of your
 steadfast love,
 but rebelled against the
 Most High^a at the Red
 Sea.^b
8 Yet he saved them for his
 name's sake,
 so that he might make
 known his mighty
 power.
9 He rebuked the Red Sea,^b
 and it became dry;
 he led them through the
 deep as through a
 desert.
10 So he saved them from the
 hand of the foe,
 and delivered them from
 the hand of the enemy.
11 The waters covered their
 adversaries;
 not one of them was left.
12 Then they believed his
 words;
 they sang his praise.

13 But they soon forgot his
 works;
 they did not wait for his
 counsel.
14 But they had a wanton
 craving in the
 wilderness,
 and put God to the test in
 the desert;
15 he gave them what they
 asked,
 but sent a wasting disease
 among them.

16 They were jealous of Moses
 in the camp,
 and of Aaron, the holy one
 of the LORD.
17 The earth opened and
 swallowed up Dathan,
 and covered the faction of
 Abiram.
18 Fire also broke out in their
 company;
 the flame burned up the
 wicked.

19 They made a calf at Horeb
 and worshiped a cast
 image.
20 They exchanged the glory of
 God^c
 for the image of an ox that
 eats grass.
21 They forgot God, their
 Savior,
 who had done great things
 in Egypt,
22 wondrous works in the land
 of Ham,
 and awesome deeds by the
 Red Sea.^b
23 Therefore he said he would
 destroy them —
 had not Moses, his chosen
 one,
 stood in the breach before
 him,
 to turn away his wrath
 from destroying them.

24 Then they despised the
 pleasant land,
 having no faith in his
 promise.
25 They grumbled in their tents,
 and did not obey the voice
 of the LORD.
26 Therefore he raised his hand
 and swore to them
 that he would make them
 fall in the wilderness,
27 and would disperse^d their
 descendants among the
 nations,
 scattering them over the
 lands.

28 Then they attached
 themselves to the Baal
 of Peor,
 and ate sacrifices offered to
 the dead;
29 they provoked the LORD to
 anger with their deeds,
 and a plague broke out
 among them.
30 Then Phinehas stood up and
 interceded,

106.7
Ps 78.11,42;
Ex 14.11
106.8
Ex 9.16
106.9
Ex 14.21;
Ps 18.15;
78.11,42;
Isa 63.11-14
106.10
Ex 14.30;
Ps 107.2
106.11
Ex 14.28;
15.5
106.12
Ex 14.31;
15.1-21
106.13
Ex 15.24
106.14
1 Cor 10.6,9
106.15
Num 11.31;
Isa 10.16
106.16
Num 16.1-3
106.17
Deut 11.6
106.18
Num 16.35

106.19
Ex 32.14
106.20
Jer 2.11;
Rom 1.23
106.21
Ps 78.11;
Deut 10.21
106.22
Ps 105.27
106.23
Ex 32.10;
32.11-14
106.24
Deut 8.7;
Heb 3.18,19
106.25
Num 14.2
106.26
Num 14.28-35;
Heb 11.3
106.27
Ps 44.11
106.28
Num 25.2,3
106.30
Num 25.7

^a Cn Compare 78.17, 56: Heb *rebelled at the
sea* ^b Or *Sea of Reeds* ^c Compare Gk
Mss: Heb *exchanged their glory*
^d Syr Compare Ezek 20.23: Heb *cause to fall*

and the plague was
 stopped.
31 And that has been reckoned
 to him as righteousness
 from generation to
 generation forever.

32 They angered the LORD[e] at
 the waters of Meribah,
 and it went ill with Moses
 on their account;
33 for they made his spirit
 bitter,
 and he spoke words that
 were rash.

34 They did not destroy the
 peoples,
 as the LORD commanded
 them,
35 but they mingled with the
 nations
 and learned to do as they
 did.
36 They served their idols,
 which became a snare to
 them.
37 They sacrificed their sons
 and their daughters to the
 demons;
38 they poured out innocent
 blood,
 the blood of their sons and
 daughters,
 whom they sacrificed to the
 idols of Canaan;
 and the land was polluted
 with blood.
39 Thus they became unclean
 by their acts,
 and prostituted themselves
 in their doings.

40 Then the anger of the LORD
 was kindled against his
 people,
 and he abhorred his
 heritage;
41 he gave them into the hand
 of the nations,
 so that those who hated
 them ruled over them.
42 Their enemies oppressed
 them,
 and they were brought into
 subjection under their
 power.

43 Many times he delivered
 them,
 but they were rebellious in
 their purposes,
 and were brought low
 through their iniquity.
44 Nevertheless he regarded
 their distress
 when he heard their cry.
45 For their sake he
 remembered his
 covenant,
 and showed compassion
 according to the
 abundance of his
 steadfast love.
46 He caused them to be pitied
 by all who held them
 captive.

47 Save us, O LORD our God,
 and gather us from among
 the nations,
 that we may give thanks to
 your holy name
 and glory in your praise.

48 Blessed be the LORD, the God
 of Israel,
 from everlasting to
 everlasting.
 And let all the people say,
 "Amen."
 Praise the LORD!

BOOK V

(Psalms 107–150)

Psalm 107

Thanksgiving for Deliverance from Many Troubles

1 O give thanks to the LORD,
 for he is good;
 for his steadfast love
 endures forever.
2 Let the redeemed of the
 LORD say so,
 those he redeemed from
 trouble
3 and gathered in from the
 lands,

106.31
Num 25.11-13
106.32
Num 20.3,
13; Ps 81.7
106.33
Num 20.10
106.34
Judg 1.21;
Deut 7.2,16
106.35
Judg 3.5,6
106.36
Judg 2.12
106.37
2 Kings 17.7
106.38
Ps 94.21;
Num 35.33
106.39
Ezek 20.18;
Lev 17.7;
Num 15.39
106.40
Ps 78.59
106.41
Judg 2.14;
Neh 9.27

106.43
Judg 2.16-18
106.44
Judg 3.9;
10.10
106.45
Ps 105.8;
Judg 2.18
106.46
Ezra 9.9;
Jer 42.12
106.47
1 Chr 16.35,
36; Ps 147.2
106.48
Ps 41.13
107.1
Ps 106.1
107.2
Ps 106.10
107.3
Ps 106.47;
Isa 43.5,6

e Heb *him*

from the east and from the
west,
from the north and from
the south.[f]

4 Some wandered in desert
wastes,
finding no way to an
inhabited town;
5 hungry and thirsty,
their soul fainted within
them.
6 Then they cried to the LORD
in their trouble,
and he delivered them from
their distress;
7 he led them by a straight
way,
until they reached an
inhabited town.
8 Let them thank the LORD for
his steadfast love,
for his wonderful works to
humankind.
9 For he satisfies the thirsty,
and the hungry he fills with
good things.

10 Some sat in darkness and in
gloom,
prisoners in misery and in
irons,
11 for they had rebelled against
the words of God,
and spurned the counsel of
the Most High.
12 Their hearts were bowed
down with hard labor;
they fell down, with no one
to help.
13 Then they cried to the LORD
in their trouble,
and he saved them from
their distress;
14 he brought them out of
darkness and gloom,
and broke their bonds
asunder.
15 Let them thank the LORD for
his steadfast love,
for his wonderful works to
humankind.
16 For he shatters the doors of
bronze,
and cuts in two the bars of
iron.

17 Some were sick[g] through
their sinful ways,
and because of their
iniquities endured
affliction;
18 they loathed any kind of
food,
and they drew near to the
gates of death.
19 Then they cried to the LORD
in their trouble,
and he saved them from
their distress;
20 he sent out his word and
healed them,
and delivered them from
destruction.
21 Let them thank the LORD for
his steadfast love,
for his wonderful works to
humankind.
22 And let them offer
thanksgiving sacrifices,
and tell of his deeds with
songs of joy.

23 Some went down to the sea
in ships,
doing business on the
mighty waters;
24 they saw the deeds of the
LORD,
his wondrous works in the
deep.
25 For he commanded and
raised the stormy wind,
which lifted up the waves
of the sea.
26 They mounted up to heaven,
they went down to the
depths;
their courage melted away
in their calamity;
27 they reeled and staggered
like drunkards,
and were at their wits' end.
28 Then they cried to the LORD
in their trouble,
and he brought them out
from their distress;
29 he made the storm be still,
and the waves of the sea
were hushed.
30 Then they were glad because
they had quiet,

107.4 Num 14.33; 32.13
107.6 Ps 50.15
107.7 Ezra 8.21
107.8 vv. 15,21,31
107.9 Ps 22.26; Lk 1.53
107.10 Lk 1.79; Job 36.8
107.11 Ps 106.7; 2 Chr 36.16
107.12 Ps 22.11
107.13 v. 6
107.14 Ps 116.16; Lk 13.16; Acts 12.7
107.15 vv. 8,21,31
107.16 Isa 45.2

107.17 Isa 65.6,7
107.18 Job 33.20, 22; Ps 9.13; 88.3
107.20 Mt 8.8; Ps 30.2; 103.3
107.22 Lev 7.12; Ps 50.14; 9.11; 73.28; 118.17
107.25 Ps 105.31, 34; Jon 1.4; Ps 93.3,4
107.26 Ps 22.14; 119.28
107.27 Job 12.25
107.28 vv. 6,13,19
107.29 Ps 89.9; Mt 8.26

f Cn: Heb *sea* g Cn: Heb *fools*

and he brought them to
their desired haven.
31 Let them thank the Lord for
his steadfast love,
for his wonderful works to
humankind.
32 Let them extol him in the
congregation of the
people,
and praise him in the
assembly of the elders.

33 He turns rivers into a
desert,
springs of water into thirsty
ground,
34 a fruitful land into a salty
waste,
because of the wickedness
of its inhabitants.
35 He turns a desert into pools
of water,
a parched land into springs
of water.
36 And there he lets the hungry
live,
and they establish a town
to live in;
37 they sow fields, and plant
vineyards,
and get a fruitful yield.
38 By his blessing they multiply
greatly,
and he does not let their
cattle decrease.

39 When they are diminished
and brought low
through oppression,
trouble, and sorrow,
40 he pours contempt on
princes
and makes them wander in
trackless wastes;
41 but he raises up the needy
out of distress,
and makes their families
like flocks.
42 The upright see it and are
glad;
and all wickedness stops
its mouth.
43 Let those who are wise give
heed to these things,
and consider the steadfast
love of the Lord.

107.31
vv. 8,15,21
107.32
Ps 22.22,25;
35.18
107.33
Ps 74.15
107.34
Gen 13.10;
14.3; 19.25
107.35
Ps 114.8;
Isa 41.18
107.37
Isa 65.21
107.38
Gen 12.2;
17.16,20;
Ex 1.7
107.39
Ezek 5.11;
Ps 57.6
107.40
Job 12.21,
24
107.41
1 Sam 2.8;
Ps 113.7-9
107.42
Job 22.19;
Ps 52.6;
Job 5.16;
Ps 63.11;
Rom 3.19
107.43
Ps 64.9;
Jer 9.12;
Hos 14.9

108.1
Ps 57.7
108.2
Ps 57.8-11
108.4
Ps 113.4
108.6
Ps 60.5-12
108.8
Ps 60.7
108.11
Ps 44.9

Psalm 108

Praise and Prayer for Victory

A Song. A Psalm of David.

1 My heart is steadfast, O God,
my heart is steadfast;[h]
I will sing and make
melody.
Awake, my soul![i]
2 Awake, O harp and lyre!
I will awake the dawn.
3 I will give thanks to you,
O Lord, among the
peoples,
and I will sing praises to
you among the nations.
4 For your steadfast love is
higher than the
heavens,
and your faithfulness
reaches to the clouds.

5 Be exalted, O God, above the
heavens,
and let your glory be over
all the earth.
6 Give victory with your right
hand, and answer me,
so that those whom you
love may be rescued.

7 God has promised in his
sanctuary:[j]
"With exultation I will
divide up Shechem,
and portion out the Vale of
Succoth.
8 Gilead is mine; Manasseh is
mine;
Ephraim is my helmet;
Judah is my scepter.
9 Moab is my washbasin;
on Edom I hurl my shoe;
over Philistia I shout in
triumph."

10 Who will bring me to the
fortified city?
Who will lead me to Edom?
11 Have you not rejected us,
O God?
You do not go out, O God,
with our armies.

h Heb Mss Gk Syr: MT lacks *my heart is
steadfast* i Compare 57.8: Heb *also my soul*
j Or *by his holiness*

¹² O grant us help against the
　　foe,
　　for human help is
　　　worthless.
¹³ With God we shall do
　　valiantly;
　　it is he who will tread
　　　down our foes.

Psalm 109

Prayer for Vindication and Vengeance

To the leader. Of David. A Psalm.

¹ Do not be silent, O God of
　　my praise.
² For wicked and deceitful
　　mouths are opened
　　against me,
　　speaking against me with
　　　lying tongues.
³ They beset me with words of
　　hate,
　　and attack me without
　　　cause.
⁴ In return for my love they
　　accuse me,
　　even while I make prayer
　　　for them.^k
⁵ So they reward me evil for
　　good,
　　and hatred for my love.

⁶ They say,^l "Appoint a
　　wicked man against
　　him;
　　let an accuser stand on his
　　　right.
⁷ When he is tried, let him be
　　found guilty;
　　let his prayer be counted
　　　as sin.
⁸ May his days be few;
　　may another seize his
　　　position.
⁹ May his children be orphans,
　　and his wife a widow.
¹⁰ May his children wander
　　about and beg;
　　may they be driven out of^m
　　　the ruins they inhabit.
¹¹ May the creditor seize all
　　that he has;
　　may strangers plunder the
　　　fruits of his toil.

109.1
Ps 83.1
109.2
Ps 52.4;
120.2
109.3
Ps 69.4
109.4
Ps 38.20;
69.13
109.5
Ps 35.12;
38.20
109.6
Zech 3.1
109.7
Prov 28.9
109.8
Acts 1.20
109.9
Ex 22.24
109.11
Job 5.5;
18.9

109.12
Isa 9.17
109.13
Ps 37.28;
Prov 10.7
109.14
Ex 20.5;
Neh 4.5;
Jer 18.23
109.15
Ps 34.16
109.16
Ps 37.14,32
109.17
Prov 14.14;
Ezek 35.6
109.18
Ps 73.6;
Num 5.22
109.20
Ps 94.23;
2 Tim 4.14;
Ps 71.10
109.21
Ps 79.9;
69.16
109.22
Ps 40.17;
143.4
109.23
Ps 102.11

¹² May there be no one to do
　　him a kindness,
　　nor anyone to pity his
　　　orphaned children.
¹³ May his posterity be cut off;
　　may his name be blotted
　　　out in the second
　　　generation.
¹⁴ May the iniquity of his
　　fatherⁿ be remembered
　　before the Lord,
　　and do not let the sin of
　　　his mother be blotted
　　　out.
¹⁵ Let them be before the Lord
　　continually,
　　and may his^o memory be
　　　cut off from the earth.
¹⁶ For he did not remember to
　　show kindness,
　　but pursued the poor and
　　　needy
　　and the brokenhearted to
　　　their death.
¹⁷ He loved to curse; let curses
　　come on him.
　　He did not like blessing;
　　may it be far from him.
¹⁸ He clothed himself with
　　cursing as his coat,
　　may it soak into his body
　　　like water,
　　like oil into his bones.
¹⁹ May it be like a garment that
　　he wraps around
　　himself,
　　like a belt that he wears
　　　every day."

²⁰ May that be the reward of
　　my accusers from the
　　Lord,
　　of those who speak evil
　　　against my life.
²¹ But you, O Lord my Lord,
　　act on my behalf for your
　　　name's sake;
　　because your steadfast love
　　　is good, deliver me.
²² For I am poor and needy,
　　and my heart is pierced
　　　within me.
²³ I am gone like a shadow at
　　evening;

^k Syr: Heb *I prayer*　　^l Heb lacks *They say*
^m Gk: Heb *and seek*　　ⁿ Cn: Heb *fathers*
^o Gk: Heb *their*

I am shaken off like a
 locust.
24 My knees are weak through
 fasting;
 my body has become
 gaunt.
25 I am an object of scorn to
 my accusers;
 when they see me, they
 shake their heads.

26 Help me, O LORD my God!
 Save me according to your
 steadfast love.
27 Let them know that this is
 your hand;
 you, O LORD, have done it.
28 Let them curse, but you will
 bless.
 Let my assailants be put to
 shame;p may your
 servant be glad.
29 May my accusers be clothed
 with dishonor;
 may they be wrapped in
 their own shame as in a
 mantle.
30 With my mouth I will give
 great thanks to the
 LORD;
 I will praise him in the
 midst of the throng.
31 For he stands at the right
 hand of the needy,
 to save them from those
 who would condemn
 them to death.

Psalm 110

Assurance of Victory for God's Priest-King

Of David. A Psalm.

1 The LORD says to my lord,
 "Sit at my right hand
 until I make your enemies
 your footstool."

2 The LORD sends out from
 Zion
 your mighty scepter.
 Rule in the midst of your
 foes.
3 Your people will offer
 themselves willingly

109.24
Heb 12.12
109.25
Ps 22.6,7;
Mt 27.39;
Mk 15.29
109.26
Ps 119.86
109.27
Job 37.7
109.28
2 Sam 16.11,
12;
Isa 65.14
109.29
Ps 35.26;
132.18
109.30
Ps 35.18
109.31
Ps 16.8;
121.5
110.1
Mt 22.44;
Mk 12.36;
Lk 20.42;
Acts 2.34;
1 Cor 15.25
110.2
Ps 45.6; 2.9
110.3
Judg 5.2;
Ps 96.9

110.4
Heb 5.6,10;
6.20; 7.11,15,
21
110.5
Ps 16.8; 2.5,
12;
Rom 2.5;
Rev 11.18
110.6
Isa 2.4;
66.24;
Ps 68.21
110.7
Ps 27.6
111.1
Ps 138.1;
149.1
111.2
Ps 92.5
111.3
Ps 145.5
111.4
Ps 86.5;
103.8
111.5
Mt 6.26,33

 on the day you lead your
 forces
 on the holy mountains.q
From the womb of the
 morning,
 like dew, your youthr will
 come to you.
4 The LORD has sworn and will
 not change his mind,
 "You are a priest forever
 according to the order
 of Melchizedek."s

5 The Lord is at your right
 hand;
 he will shatter kings on the
 day of his wrath.
6 He will execute judgment
 among the nations,
 filling them with corpses;
 he will shatter heads
 over the wide earth.
7 He will drink from the
 stream by the path;
 therefore he will lift up his
 head.

Psalm 111

Praise for God's Wonderful Works

1 Praise the LORD!
 I will give thanks to the LORD
 with my whole heart,
 in the company of the
 upright, in the
 congregation.
2 Great are the works of the
 LORD,
 studied by all who delight
 in them.
3 Full of honor and majesty is
 his work,
 and his righteousness
 endures forever.
4 He has gained renown by his
 wonderful deeds;
 the LORD is gracious and
 merciful.
5 He provides food for those
 who fear him;
 he is ever mindful of his
 covenant.

p Gk: Heb *They have risen up and have been
put to shame* q Another reading is *in holy
splendor* r Cn: Heb *the dew of your youth*
s Or *forever, a rightful king by my edict*

⁶ He has shown his people the
 power of his works,
 in giving them the heritage
 of the nations.
⁷ The works of his hands are
 faithful and just;
 all his precepts are
 trustworthy.
⁸ They are established forever
 and ever,
 to be performed with
 faithfulness and
 uprightness.
⁹ He sent redemption to his
 people;
 he has commanded his
 covenant forever.
 Holy and awesome is his
 name.
¹⁰ The fear of the LORD is the
 beginning of wisdom;
 all those who practice it[t]
 have a good
 understanding.
 His praise endures forever.

Psalm 112

Blessings of the Righteous

¹ Praise the LORD!
 Happy are those who fear
 the LORD,
 who greatly delight in his
 commandments.
² Their descendants will be
 mighty in the land;
 the generation of the
 upright will be blessed.
³ Wealth and riches are in
 their houses,
 and their righteousness
 endures forever.
⁴ They rise in the darkness as
 a light for the upright;
 they are gracious, merciful,
 and righteous.
⁵ It is well with those who
 deal generously and
 lend,
 who conduct their affairs
 with justice.
⁶ For the righteous will never
 be moved;
 they will be remembered
 forever.

111.7
Rev 15.3;
Ps 19.7
111.8
Mt 5.18;
Ps 19.9
111.9
Lk 1.68;
Ps 99.3
111.10
Prov 9.10;
3.4;
Ps 145.2
112.1
Ps 128.1;
119.16
112.2
Ps 25.13
112.3
Prov 3.16;
8.18
112.4
Job 11.17;
Ps 97.11
112.5
Ps 37.26
112.6
Prov 10.7

112.7
Prov 1.33;
Ps 57.7
112.8
Ps 59.10;
118.7
112.9
2 Cor 9.9;
Deut 24.13;
Ps 75.10
112.10
Ps 86.17;
37.12; 58.7,8;
Prov 10.28;
11.7
113.1
Ps 135.1
113.2
Dan 2.20
113.3
Ps 50.1
113.4
Ps 97.9;
99.2; 8.1
113.5
Ps 89.6;
103.19
113.6
Ps 11.4;
138.6;
Isa 57.15
113.7
1 Sam 2.8;
Ps 107.41

⁷ They are not afraid of evil
 tidings;
 their hearts are firm,
 secure in the LORD.
⁸ Their hearts are steady, they
 will not be afraid;
 in the end they will look in
 triumph on their foes.
⁹ They have distributed freely,
 they have given to the
 poor;
 their righteousness endures
 forever;
 their horn is exalted in
 honor.
¹⁰ The wicked see it and are
 angry;
 they gnash their teeth and
 melt away;
 the desire of the wicked
 comes to nothing.

Psalm 113

God the Helper of the Needy

¹ Praise the LORD!
 Praise, O servants of the
 LORD;
 praise the name of the
 LORD.

² Blessed be the name of the
 LORD
 from this time on and
 forevermore.
³ From the rising of the sun to
 its setting
 the name of the LORD is to
 be praised.
⁴ The LORD is high above all
 nations,
 and his glory above the
 heavens.

⁵ Who is like the LORD our
 God,
 who is seated on high,
⁶ who looks far down
 on the heavens and the
 earth?
⁷ He raises the poor from the
 dust,
 and lifts the needy from
 the ash heap,

[t] Gk Syr: Heb *them*

8 to make them sit with
 princes,
 with the princes of his
 people.
9 He gives the barren woman a
 home,
 making her the joyous
 mother of children.
Praise the LORD!

Psalm 114

God's Wonders at the Exodus

1 When Israel went out from
 Egypt,
 the house of Jacob from a
 people of strange
 language,
2 Judah became God's[u]
 sanctuary,
 Israel his dominion.

3 The sea looked and fled;
 Jordan turned back.
4 The mountains skipped like
 rams,
 the hills like lambs.

5 Why is it, O sea, that you
 flee?
 O Jordan, that you turn
 back?
6 O mountains, that you skip
 like rams?
 O hills, like lambs?

7 Tremble, O earth, at the
 presence of the LORD,
 at the presence of the God
 of Jacob,
8 who turns the rock into a
 pool of water,
 the flint into a spring of
 water.

Psalm 115

The Impotence of Idols and the Greatness of God

1 Not to us, O LORD, not to us,
 but to your name give
 glory,
 for the sake of your
 steadfast love and your
 faithfulness.
2 Why should the nations say,

"Where is their God?"

3 Our God is in the heavens;
 he does whatever he
 pleases.
4 Their idols are silver and
 gold,
 the work of human hands.
5 They have mouths, but do
 not speak;
 eyes, but do not see.
6 They have ears, but do not
 hear;
 noses, but do not smell.
7 They have hands, but do not
 feel;
 feet, but do not walk;
 they make no sound in
 their throats.
8 Those who make them are
 like them;
 so are all who trust in
 them.

9 O Israel, trust in the LORD!
 He is their help and their
 shield.
10 O house of Aaron, trust in
 the LORD!
 He is their help and their
 shield.
11 You who fear the LORD, trust
 in the LORD!
 He is their help and their
 shield.

12 The LORD has been mindful
 of us; he will bless us;
 he will bless the house of
 Israel;
 he will bless the house of
 Aaron;
13 he will bless those who fear
 the LORD,
 both small and great.

14 May the LORD give you
 increase,
 both you and your
 children.
15 May you be blessed by the
 LORD,
 who made heaven and
 earth.

u Heb his

Cross references

113.8 Job 36.7
113.9 1 Sam 2.5; Ps 68.6; Isa 54.1
114.1 Ex 13.3
114.2 Ex 19.6; 29.45,46
114.3 Ex 14.21; Josh 3.13, 16
114.4 Ps 29.6; Hab 3.6
114.5 Hab 3.6
114.7 Ps 96.9
114.8 Ex 17.6; Num 20.11; Ps 107.35; Deut 8.15
115.1 Isa 48.11; Ezek 36.32; Ps 96.8
115.2 Ps 42.3; 79.10
115.3 Ps 103.19; 135.6; Dan 4.35
115.4 Deut 4.28; Ps 135.15-17; Jer 10.3ff
115.5 Jer 10.5
115.8 Ps 135.18
115.9 Ps 118.2-4; 33.20
115.11 Ps 135.20
115.13 Ps 128.1,4
115.14 Deut 1.11
115.15 Gen 14.19; 1.1; Ps 96.5

16 The heavens are the LORD's
heavens,
 but the earth he has given
 to human beings.
17 The dead do not praise the
LORD,
 nor do any that go down
 into silence.
18 But we will bless the LORD
 from this time on and
 forevermore.
Praise the LORD!

Psalm 116

Thanksgiving for Recovery from Illness

1 I love the LORD, because he
has heard
 my voice and my
 supplications.
2 Because he inclined his ear
to me,
 therefore I will call on him
 as long as I live.
3 The snares of death
 encompassed me;
 the pangs of Sheol laid
 hold on me;
 I suffered distress and
 anguish.
4 Then I called on the name of
the LORD:
 "O LORD, I pray, save my
 life!"

5 Gracious is the LORD, and
righteous;
 our God is merciful.
6 The LORD protects the
simple;
 when I was brought low, he
 saved me.
7 Return, O my soul, to your
rest,
 for the LORD has dealt
 bountifully with you.

8 For you have delivered my
soul from death,
 my eyes from tears,
 my feet from stumbling.
9 I walk before the LORD
 in the land of the living.
10 I kept my faith, even when I
said,

115.16
Ps 89.11;
8.6
115.17
Ps 6.5;
31.17
115.18
Ps 113.2
116.1
Ps 18.1;
66.19
116.2
Ps 40.1
116.3
Ps 18.4-6
116.4
Ps 118.5;
22.20
116.5
Ps 103.8;
Ezra 9.15;
Neh 9.8;
Ps 145.17;
Ex 34.6
116.6
Ps 19.7;
79.8
116.7
Jer 6.16;
Mt 11.29;
Ps 13.6
116.8
Ps 56.13
116.9
Ps 27.13
116.10
2 Cor 4.13

116.11
Ps 31.22;
Rom 3.4
116.13
Ps 16.5;
80.18
116.14
Ps 22.25;
Jon 2.9
116.15
Ps 72.14
116.16
Ps 119.125;
143.12; 86.16
116.17
Ps 50.14;
v. 13
116.18
v. 14
116.19
Ps 96.8;
135.2
117.1
Rom 15.11
117.2
Ps 100.5
118.1
Ps 106.1;
136.1

 "I am greatly afflicted";
11 I said in my consternation,
 "Everyone is a liar."

12 What shall I return to the
LORD
 for all his bounty to me?
13 I will lift up the cup of
salvation
 and call on the name of
 the LORD,
14 I will pay my vows to the
LORD
 in the presence of all his
 people.
15 Precious in the sight of the
LORD
 is the death of his faithful
 ones.
16 O LORD, I am your servant;
 I am your servant, the child
 of your serving girl.
 You have loosed my bonds.
17 I will offer to you a
 thanksgiving sacrifice
 and call on the name of
 the LORD.
18 I will pay my vows to the
LORD
 in the presence of all his
 people,
19 in the courts of the house of
 the LORD,
 in your midst,
 O Jerusalem.
Praise the LORD!

Psalm 117

Universal Call to Worship

1 Praise the LORD, all you
nations!
 Extol him, all you peoples!
2 For great is his steadfast love
toward us,
 and the faithfulness of the
 LORD endures forever.
Praise the LORD!

Psalm 118

A Song of Victory

1 O give thanks to the LORD,
 for he is good;
 his steadfast love endures
 forever!

2 Let Israel say,
 "His steadfast love endures
 forever."
3 Let the house of Aaron say,
 "His steadfast love endures
 forever."
4 Let those who fear the LORD
 say,
 "His steadfast love endures
 forever."

5 Out of my distress I called
 on the LORD;
 the LORD answered me and
 set me in a broad place.
6 With the LORD on my side I
 do not fear.
 What can mortals do to
 me?
7 The LORD is on my side to
 help me;
 I shall look in triumph on
 those who hate me.
8 It is better to take refuge in
 the LORD
 than to put confidence in
 mortals.
9 It is better to take refuge in
 the LORD
 than to put confidence in
 princes.

10 All nations surrounded me;
 in the name of the LORD I
 cut them off!
11 They surrounded me,
 surrounded me on every
 side;
 in the name of the LORD I
 cut them off!
12 They surrounded me like
 bees;
 they blazed[v] like a fire of
 thorns;
 in the name of the LORD I
 cut them off!
13 I was pushed hard,[w] so that
 I was falling,
 but the LORD helped me.
14 The LORD is my strength and
 my might;
 he has become my
 salvation.

15 There are glad songs of
 victory in the tents of
 the righteous:

"The right hand of the LORD
 does valiantly;
16 the right hand of the LORD
 is exalted;
 the right hand of the LORD
 does valiantly."
17 I shall not die, but I shall
 live,
 and recount the deeds of
 the LORD.
18 The LORD has punished me
 severely,
 but he did not give me over
 to death.

19 Open to me the gates of
 righteousness,
 that I may enter through
 them
 and give thanks to the
 LORD.

20 This is the gate of the LORD;
 the righteous shall enter
 through it.

21 I thank you that you have
 answered me
 and have become my
 salvation.
22 The stone that the builders
 rejected
 has become the chief
 cornerstone.
23 This is the LORD's doing;
 it is marvelous in our eyes.
24 This is the day that the LORD
 has made;
 let us rejoice and be glad
 in it.[x]
25 Save us, we beseech you,
 O LORD!
 O LORD, we beseech you,
 give us success!

26 Blessed is the one who
 comes in the name of
 the LORD.[y]
 We bless you from the
 house of the LORD.
27 The LORD is God,
 and he has given us light.

118.2
Ps 115.9
118.5
Ps 120.1;
18.19
118.6
Ps 27.1;
Heb 13.6;
Ps 56.4,11
118.7
Ps 54.4;
59.10
118.8
Ps 40.4;
Jer 17.5
118.9
Ps 146.3
118.10
Ps 3.6;
18.40
118.12
Deut 1.44;
Ps 58.9
118.13
Ps 140.4;
86.17
118.14
Ex 15.2;
Isa 12.2
118.15
Ps 68.3;
89.13

118.16
Ex 15.6
118.17
Hab 1.12;
Ps 73.28
118.18
2 Cor 6.9
118.19
Isa 26.2
118.20
Ps 24.7;
Isa 35.8;
Rev 22.14
118.21
Ps 116.1;
v. 14
118.22
Mt 21.42;
Mk 12.10;
Lk 20.17;
Acts 4.11;
Eph 2.20;
1 Pet 2.4,7
118.26
Mt 21.9;
Mk 11.9;
Lk 13.35;
19.38;
Jn 12.13
118.27
1 Kings 18.39;
Esther 8.16;
1 Pet 2.9

v Gk: Heb were extinguished w Gk Syr
Jerome: Heb You pushed me hard x Or in
him y Or Blessed in the name of the LORD is
the one who comes

Bind the festal procession
with branches,
up to the horns of the
altar. z

28 You are my God, and I will
give thanks to you;
you are my God, I will
extol you.

29 O give thanks to the LORD,
for he is good,
for his steadfast love
endures forever.

Psalm 119

The Glories of God's Law

1 Happy are those whose way
is blameless,
who walk in the law of the
LORD.
2 Happy are those who keep
his decrees,
who seek him with their
whole heart,
3 who also do no wrong,
but walk in his ways.
4 You have commanded your
precepts
to be kept diligently.
5 O that my ways may be
steadfast
in keeping your statutes!
6 Then I shall not be put to
shame,
having my eyes fixed on all
your commandments.
7 I will praise you with an
upright heart,
when I learn your righteous
ordinances.
8 I will observe your statutes;
do not utterly forsake me.

9 How can young people keep
their way pure?
By guarding it according to
your word.
10 With my whole heart I seek
you;
do not let me stray from
your commandments.
11 I treasure your word in my
heart,

118.28
Ex 15.2;
Isa 25.1
118.29
v. 1
119.1
Ps 101.2,6;
128.1
119.2
vv. 22,10;
Deut 6.5
119.3
1 Jn 3.9;
5.18
119.6
v. 80
119.7
v. 62
119.9
2 Chr 6.16
119.10
2 Chr 15.15;
vv. 21,118
119.11
Ps 37.31;
Lk 2.19,51

119.12
vv. 26,64,
68,108,124,
135,171
119.13
Ps 40.9;
v. 72
119.15
vv. 23,48,
78; Ps 1.2
119.16
Ps 1.2
119.17
Ps 13.6
119.19
Gen 47.9;
1 Chr 29.15;
Ps 39.12;
2 Cor 5.6;
Heb 11.13
119.20
Ps 42.1,2
119.21
vv. 10,118
119.22
Ps 39.8
119.23
v. 15
119.24
v. 16
119.25
Ps 44.25;
v. 37
119.26
v. 12

so that I may not sin
against you.
12 Blessed are you, O LORD;
teach me your statutes.
13 With my lips I declare
all the ordinances of your
mouth.
14 I delight in the way of your
decrees
as much as in all riches.
15 I will meditate on your
precepts,
and fix my eyes on your
ways.
16 I will delight in your
statutes;
I will not forget your word.

17 Deal bountifully with your
servant,
so that I may live and
observe your word.
18 Open my eyes, so that I may
behold
wondrous things out of
your law.
19 I live as an alien in the land;
do not hide your
commandments from
me.
20 My soul is consumed with
longing
for your ordinances at all
times.
21 You rebuke the insolent,
accursed ones,
who wander from your
commandments;
22 take away from me their
scorn and contempt,
for I have kept your
decrees.
23 Even though princes sit
plotting against me,
your servant will meditate
on your statutes.
24 Your decrees are my delight,
they are my counselors.

25 My soul clings to the dust;
revive me according to your
word.
26 When I told of my ways, you
answered me;
teach me your statutes.

z Meaning of Heb uncertain

27 Make me understand the
 way of your precepts,
 and I will meditate on your
 wondrous works.
28 My soul melts away for
 sorrow;
 strengthen me according to
 your word.
29 Put false ways far from
 me;
 and graciously teach me
 your law.
30 I have chosen the way of
 faithfulness;
 I set your ordinances
 before me.
31 I cling to your decrees,
 O LORD;
 let me not be put to
 shame.
32 I run the way of your
 commandments,
 for you enlarge my
 understanding.

33 Teach me, O LORD, the way
 of your statutes,
 and I will observe it to the
 end.
34 Give me understanding, that
 I may keep your law
 and observe it with my
 whole heart.
35 Lead me in the path of your
 commandments,
 for I delight in it.
36 Turn my heart to your
 decrees,
 and not to selfish gain.
37 Turn my eyes from looking
 at vanities;
 give me life in your ways.
38 Confirm to your servant your
 promise,
 which is for those who fear
 you.
39 Turn away the disgrace that I
 dread,
 for your ordinances are
 good.
40 See, I have longed for your
 precepts;
 in your righteousness give
 me life.

41 Let your steadfast love come
 to me, O LORD,

119.27
Ps 145.5
119.28
Ps 107.26;
20.2;
1 Pet 5.10
119.31
Deut 11.22
119.32
1 Kings 4.29;
Isa 60.5;
2 Cor 6.11
119.33
vv. 5,12
119.34
v. 73;
Prov 2.6;
Jas 1.5
119.35
v. 16
119.36
1 Kings 8.58;
Lk 12.15
119.37
Isa 33.15;
Ps 71.20
119.38
2 Sam 7.25
119.40
vv. 20,25
119.41
vv. 77,116

119.42
Prov 27.11
119.46
Mt 10.18;
Acts 26.1,2
119.47
v. 16
119.48
v. 15
119.50
Rom 15.4
119.51
Jer 20.7;
v. 157;
Job 23.11;
Ps 44.18
119.52
Ps 103.18
119.53
Ezra 9.3;
Ps 89.30
119.55
Ps 63.6

 your salvation according to
 your promise.
42 Then I shall have an answer
 for those who taunt me,
 for I trust in your word.
43 Do not take the word of
 truth utterly out of my
 mouth,
 for my hope is in your
 ordinances.
44 I will keep your law
 continually,
 forever and ever.
45 I shall walk at liberty,
 for I have sought your
 precepts.
46 I will also speak of your
 decrees before kings,
 and shall not be put to
 shame;
47 I find my delight in your
 commandments,
 because I love them.
48 I revere your
 commandments, which
 I love,
 and I will meditate on your
 statutes.

49 Remember your word to your
 servant,
 in which you have made
 me hope.
50 This is my comfort in my
 distress,
 that your promise gives me
 life.
51 The arrogant utterly deride
 me,
 but I do not turn away
 from your law.
52 When I think of your
 ordinances from of old,
 I take comfort, O LORD.
53 Hot indignation seizes me
 because of the wicked,
 those who forsake your
 law.
54 Your statutes have been my
 songs
 wherever I make my
 home.
55 I remember your name in the
 night, O LORD,
 and keep your law.
56 This blessing has fallen to
 me,

for I have kept your
 precepts.
57 The LORD is my portion;
 I promise to keep your
 words.
58 I implore your favor with all
 my heart;
 be gracious to me
 according to your
 promise.
59 When I think of your ways,
 I turn my feet to your
 decrees;
60 I hurry and do not delay
 to keep your
 commandments.
61 Though the cords of the
 wicked ensnare me,
 I do not forget your law.
62 At midnight I rise to praise
 you,
 because of your righteous
 ordinances.
63 I am a companion of all who
 fear you,
 of those who keep your
 precepts.
64 The earth, O LORD, is full of
 your steadfast love;
 teach me your statutes.

65 You have dealt well with
 your servant,
 O LORD, according to your
 word.
66 Teach me good judgment
 and knowledge,
 for I believe in your
 commandments.
67 Before I was humbled I went
 astray,
 but now I keep your word.
68 You are good and do
 good;
 teach me your statutes.
69 The arrogant smear me with
 lies,
 but with my whole heart I
 keep your precepts.
70 Their hearts are fat and
 gross,
 but I delight in your law.
71 It is good for me that I was
 humbled,
 so that I might learn your
 statutes.

119.57
Ps 16.5;
Deut 33.9
119.58
1 Kings 13.6;
v. 41
119.59
Lk 15.17,18
119.61
Ps 140.5;
v. 83
119.62
Acts 16.25
119.63
Ps 101.6
119.64
Ps 33.5;
v. 12
119.67
v. 71;
Jer 31.18,
19;
Heb 12.11
119.68
Ps 106.1;
Deut 8.16;
v. 12
119.69
Job 13.4;
v. 56
119.70
Ps 17.10;
Isa 6.10;
v. 16

119.72
v. 127;
Ps 19.10;
Prov 8.10,
11,19
119.73
Job 10.8;
Ps 138.8;
v. 34
119.74
Ps 34.2;
v. 43
119.75
Heb 12.10
119.77
vv. 41,47
119.78
Jer 50.32;
vv. 86,15
119.80
vv. 1,46
119.81
Ps 84.2
119.82
Ps 69.3
119.83
Job 30.30
119.84
Ps 39.4;
Rev 6.10

72 The law of your mouth is
 better to me
 than thousands of gold and
 silver pieces.
73 Your hands have made and
 fashioned me;
 give me understanding that
 I may learn your
 commandments.
74 Those who fear you shall see
 me and rejoice,
 because I have hoped in
 your word.
75 I know, O LORD, that your
 judgments are right,
 and that in faithfulness you
 have humbled me.
76 Let your steadfast love
 become my comfort
 according to your promise
 to your servant.
77 Let your mercy come to me,
 that I may live;
 for your law is my delight.
78 Let the arrogant be put to
 shame,
 because they have
 subverted me with
 guile;
 as for me, I will meditate
 on your precepts.
79 Let those who fear you turn
 to me,
 so that they may know
 your decrees.
80 May my heart be blameless
 in your statutes,
 so that I may not be put to
 shame.

81 My soul languishes for your
 salvation;
 I hope in your word.
82 My eyes fail with watching
 for your promise;
 I ask, "When will you
 comfort me?"
83 For I have become like a
 wineskin in the smoke,
 yet I have not forgotten
 your statutes.
84 How long must your servant
 endure?
 When will you judge those
 who persecute me?

85 The arrogant have dug
 pitfalls for me;
 they flout your law.
86 All your commandments are
 enduring;
 I am persecuted without
 cause; help me!
87 They have almost made an
 end of me on earth;
 but I have not forsaken
 your precepts.
88 In your steadfast love spare
 my life,
 so that I may keep the
 decrees of your mouth.

89 The LORD exists forever;
 your word is firmly fixed in
 heaven.
90 Your faithfulness endures to
 all generations;
 you have established the
 earth, and it stands
 fast.
91 By your appointment they
 stand today,
 for all things are your
 servants.
92 If your law had not been my
 delight,
 I would have perished in
 my misery.
93 I will never forget your
 precepts,
 for by them you have given
 me life.
94 I am yours; save me,
 for I have sought your
 precepts.
95 The wicked lie in wait to
 destroy me,
 but I consider your
 decrees.
96 I have seen a limit to all
 perfection,
 but your commandment is
 exceedingly broad.

97 Oh, how I love your law!
 It is my meditation all day
 long.
98 Your commandment makes
 me wiser than my
 enemies,
 for it is always with me.
99 I have more understanding
 than all my teachers,

for your decrees are my
 meditation.
100 I understand more than the
 aged,
 for I keep your precepts.
101 I hold back my feet from
 every evil way,
 in order to keep your word.
102 I do not turn away from
 your ordinances,
 for you have taught me.
103 How sweet are your words
 to my taste,
 sweeter than honey to my
 mouth!
104 Through your precepts I get
 understanding;
 therefore I hate every false
 way.

105 Your word is a lamp to my
 feet
 and a light to my path.
106 I have sworn an oath and
 confirmed it,
 to observe your righteous
 ordinances.
107 I am severely afflicted;
 give me life, O LORD,
 according to your word.
108 Accept my offerings of
 praise, O LORD,
 and teach me your
 ordinances.
109 I hold my life in my hand
 continually,
 but I do not forget your
 law.
110 The wicked have laid a
 snare for me,
 but I do not stray from
 your precepts.
111 Your decrees are my
 heritage forever;
 they are the joy of my
 heart.
112 I incline my heart to
 perform your statutes
 forever, to the end.

113 I hate the double-minded,
 but I love your law.
114 You are my hiding place and
 my shield;
 I hope in your word.
115 Go away from me, you
 evildoers,

119.85
Ps 35.7
119.86
v. 78;
Ps 35.19;
109.26
119.87
Isa 58.2
119.89
Mt 24.34,
35;
1 Pet 1.25
119.90
Ps 36.5;
148.6;
Eccl 1.4
119.91
Jer 33.25
119.92
vv. 16,50
119.93
vv. 16,25
119.94
vv. 146,45
119.97
Ps 1.2
119.98
v. 130;
Deut 4.6
119.99
v. 15

119.100
Job 32.7-9
119.101
Prov 1.15
119.103
Ps 19.10
119.104
vv. 128,130
119.105
Prov 6.23
119.106
Neh 10.29
119.107
v. 25
119.108
Hos 14.2;
Heb 13.15;
v. 12
119.109
Job 13.14;
v. 16
119.110
Ps 140.5;
141.9; v. 10
119.111
Deut 33.4;
vv. 14.162
119.112
v. 33
119.113
Jas 1.8;
v. 47
119.114
Ps 32.7;
91.1; v. 74
119.115
Ps 6.8;
139.19;
Mt 7.23

that I may keep the
commandments of my
God.

116 Uphold me according to
your promise, that I
may live,
and let me not be put to
shame in my hope.

117 Hold me up, that I may be
safe
and have regard for your
statutes continually.

118 You spurn all who go astray
from your statutes;
for their cunning is in
vain.

119 All the wicked of the earth
you count as dross;
therefore I love your
decrees.

120 My flesh trembles for fear of
you,
and I am afraid of your
judgments.

121 I have done what is just and
right;
do not leave me to my
oppressors.

122 Guarantee your servant's
well-being;
do not let the godless
oppress me.

123 My eyes fail from watching
for your salvation,
and for the fulfillment of
your righteous promise.

124 Deal with your servant
according to your
steadfast love,
and teach me your
statutes.

125 I am your servant; give me
understanding,
so that I may know your
decrees.

126 It is time for the LORD to
act,
for your law has been
broken.

127 Truly I love your
commandments
more than gold, more than
fine gold.

128 Truly I direct my steps by
all your precepts;[a]
I hate every false way.

129 Your decrees are wonderful;
therefore my soul keeps
them.

130 The unfolding of your words
gives light;
it imparts understanding to
the simple.

131 With open mouth I pant,
because I long for your
commandments.

132 Turn to me and be gracious
to me,
as is your custom toward
those who love your
name.

133 Keep my steps steady
according to your
promise,
and never let iniquity have
dominion over me.

134 Redeem me from human
oppression,
that I may keep your
precepts.

135 Make your face shine upon
your servant,
and teach me your
statutes.

136 My eyes shed streams of
tears
because your law is not
kept.

137 You are righteous, O LORD,
and your judgments are
right.

138 You have appointed your
decrees in
righteousness
and in all faithfulness.

139 My zeal consumes me
because my foes forget
your words.

140 Your promise is well tried,
and your servant loves it.

141 I am small and despised,
yet I do not forget your
precepts.

142 Your righteousness is an
everlasting
righteousness,
and your law is the truth.

143 Trouble and anguish have
come upon me,

119.116
Ps 54.4;
25.2;
Rom 5.5;
9.33
119.118
v. 21
119.119
Ezek 22.18
119.120
Hab 3.16
119.122
Job 17.3
119.123
vv. 81,82
119.124
v. 12
119.125
Ps 116.16
119.127
Ps 19.10
119.128
v. 104

119.129
vv. 18,22
119.130
Prov 6.23;
Ps 19.7
119.131
Ps 42.1;
v. 20
119.132
Ps 25.16
119.133
Ps 17.15;
19.13
119.134
Ps 142.6
119.135
Ps 4.6;
v. 12
119.136
Jer 9.1;
Ezek 9.4
119.137
Ezra 9.15;
Neh 9.13;
Jer 12.1
119.138
Ps 19.7-9
119.139
Ps 69.9
119.140
Ps 12.6
119.142
Ps 19.9;
vv. 151,160
119.143
vv. 24,77

a Gk Jerome: Meaning of Heb uncertain

but your commandments
are my delight.
144 Your decrees are righteous
forever;
give me understanding that
I may live.

145 With my whole heart I cry;
answer me, O LORD.
I will keep your statutes.
146 I cry to you; save me,
that I may observe your
decrees.
147 I rise before dawn and cry
for help;
I put my hope in your
words.
148 My eyes are awake before
each watch of the
night,
that I may meditate on
your promise.
149 In your steadfast love hear
my voice;
O LORD, in your justice
preserve my life.
150 Those who persecute me
with evil purpose draw
near;
they are far from your
law.
151 Yet you are near, O LORD,
and all your
commandments are
true.
152 Long ago I learned from
your decrees
that you have established
them forever.

153 Look on my misery and
rescue me,
for I do not forget your law.
154 Plead my cause and redeem
me;
give me life according to
your promise.
155 Salvation is far from the
wicked,
for they do not seek your
statutes.
156 Great is your mercy, O LORD;
give me life according to
your justice.
157 Many are my persecutors
and my adversaries,

119.144
Ps 19.9;
vv. 34,73
119.145
vv. 10,22,55
119.148
Ps 5.3
119.149
vv. 40,154
119.151
Ps 145.18;
v. 142
119.152
Lk 21.33
119.153
v. 50;
Prov 3.1
119.154
1 Sam 24.15;
v. 134
119.155
Job 5.4
119.156
2 Sam 24.14
119.157
Ps 7.1;
v. 51

119.158
Ps 139.21
119.159
vv. 47,88
119.160
Ps 139.17;
v. 142
119.161
1 Sam 24.11
119.162
1 Sam 30.16
119.164
vv. 7,160
119.165
Prov 3.2;
Isa 26.3;
32.17
119.166
v. 174;
Gen 49.18
119.168
v. 22;
Prov 5.21
119.169
Ps 18.6;
vv. 27,65
119.170
Ps 28.2;
31.2
119.171
Ps 51.15;
94.12

yet I do not swerve from
your decrees.
158 I look at the faithless with
disgust,
because they do not keep
your commands.
159 Consider how I love your
precepts;
preserve my life according
to your steadfast love.
160 The sum of your word is
truth;
and every one of your
righteous ordinances
endures forever.

161 Princes persecute me
without cause,
but my heart stands in awe
of your words.
162 I rejoice at your word
like one who finds great
spoil.
163 I hate and abhor falsehood,
but I love your law.
164 Seven times a day I praise
you
for your righteous
ordinances.
165 Great peace have those who
love your law;
nothing can make them
stumble.
166 I hope for your salvation,
O LORD,
and I fulfill your
commandments.
167 My soul keeps your
decrees;
I love them exceedingly.
168 I keep your precepts and
decrees,
for all my ways are before
you.

169 Let my cry come before you,
O LORD;
give me understanding
according to your word.
170 Let my supplication come
before you;
deliver me according to
your promise.
171 My lips will pour forth
praise,
because you teach me your
statutes.

172 My tongue will sing of your
 promise,
 for all your commandments
 are right.
173 Let your hand be ready to
 help me,
 for I have chosen your
 precepts.
174 I long for your salvation,
 O LORD,
 and your law is my
 delight.
175 Let me live that I may
 praise you,
 and let your ordinances
 help me.
176 I have gone astray like a
 lost sheep; seek out
 your servant,
 for I do not forget your
 commandments.

Psalm 120

Prayer for Deliverance from Slanderers

A Song of Ascents.

1 In my distress I cry to the
 LORD,
 that he may answer me:
2 "Deliver me, O LORD,
 from lying lips,
 from a deceitful tongue."

3 What shall be given to
 you?
 And what more shall be
 done to you,
 you deceitful tongue?
4 A warrior's sharp arrows,
 with glowing coals of the
 broom tree!

5 Woe is me, that I am an
 alien in Meshech,
 that I must live among the
 tents of Kedar.
6 Too long have I had my
 dwelling
 among those who hate
 peace.
7 I am for peace;
 but when I speak,
 they are for war.

119.173
Ps 37.24
119.174
vv. 166,24
119.175
Isa 55.3
119.176
Isa 53.6;
v. 16
120.1
Ps 102.2;
Jon 2.2
120.2
Prov 12.22;
Ps 52.4
120.4
Ps 45.5;
140.10
120.5
Gen 10.2;
Ezek 27.13;
Gen 25.13;
Jer 49.28
120.7
Ps 55.21

121.2
Ps 124.8;
115.15
121.3
Ps 66.9;
127.1
121.5
Isa 25.4;
Ps 16.8
121.6
Ps 91.5;
Isa 49.10;
Rev 7.16
121.7
Ps 91.10-12
121.8
Deut 28.6
122.1
Isa 2.3;
Zech 8.21
122.3
Ps 48.13

Psalm 121

Assurance of God's Protection

A Song of Ascents.

1 I lift up my eyes to the
 hills—
 from where will my help
 come?
2 My help comes from the
 LORD,
 who made heaven and
 earth.

3 He will not let your foot be
 moved;
 he who keeps you will not
 slumber.
4 He who keeps Israel
 will neither slumber nor
 sleep.

5 The LORD is your keeper;
 the LORD is your shade at
 your right hand.
6 The sun shall not strike you
 by day,
 nor the moon by night.

7 The LORD will keep you from
 all evil;
 he will keep your life.
8 The LORD will keep
 your going out and your
 coming in
 from this time on and
 forevermore.

Psalm 122

Song of Praise and Prayer for Jerusalem

A Song of Ascents. Of David.

1 I was glad when they said to
 me,
 "Let us go to the house of
 the LORD!"
2 Our feet are standing
 within your gates,
 O Jerusalem.

3 Jerusalem—built as a city
 that is bound firmly
 together.

4 To it the tribes go up,
 the tribes of the Lord,
as was decreed for Israel,
 to give thanks to the name
 of the Lord.
5 For there the thrones for
 judgment were set up,
 the thrones of the house of
 David.

6 Pray for the peace of
 Jerusalem:
 "May they prosper who
 love you.
7 Peace be within your walls,
 and security within your
 towers."
8 For the sake of my relatives
 and friends
I will say, "Peace be within
 you."
9 For the sake of the house of
 the Lord our God,
I will seek your good.

Psalm 123

Supplication for Mercy

A Song of Ascents.

1 To you I lift up my eyes,
 O you who are enthroned
 in the heavens!
2 As the eyes of servants
 look to the hand of their
 master,
as the eyes of a maid
 to the hand of her
 mistress,
so our eyes look to the Lord
 our God,
 until he has mercy upon
 us.

3 Have mercy upon us, O Lord,
 have mercy upon us,
for we have had more than
 enough of contempt.
4 Our soul has had more than
 its fill
of the scorn of those who
 are at ease,
of the contempt of the
 proud.

122.4
Deut 16.16;
Ex 16.34
122.5
Deut 17.8;
2 Chr 19.8
122.6
Ps 51.18
122.9
Neh 2.10
123.1
Ps 121.1;
141.8; 2.4;
11.4
123.2
Prov 27.18;
Ps 25.15
123.3
Ps 4.1; 51.1
123.4
Ps 79.4

124.1
Ps 94.17;
129.1
124.3
Ps 56.1;
57.3;
Prov 1.12
124.5
Ps 69.2
124.6
Ps 27.2
124.7
Prov 6.5;
Ps 91.3
124.8
Ps 121.2;
Gen 1.1
125.1
Ps 46.5
125.2
Zech 2.5;
Ps 121.8
125.3
Prov 22.8;
Isa 14.5;
Ps 55.20

Psalm 124

Thanksgiving for Israel's Deliverance

A Song of Ascents. Of David.

1 If it had not been the Lord
 who was on our side
 —let Israel now say—
2 if it had not been the Lord
 who was on our side,
when our enemies attacked
 us,
3 then they would have
 swallowed us up alive,
when their anger was
 kindled against us;
4 then the flood would have
 swept us away,
the torrent would have
 gone over us;
5 then over us would have
 gone
the raging waters.

6 Blessed be the Lord,
 who has not given us
 as prey to their teeth.
7 We have escaped like a bird
 from the snare of the
 fowlers;
the snare is broken,
 and we have escaped.

8 Our help is in the name of
 the Lord,
who made heaven and
 earth.

Psalm 125

The Security of God's People

A Song of Ascents.

1 Those who trust in the Lord
 are like Mount Zion,
which cannot be moved,
 but abides forever.
2 As the mountains surround
 Jerusalem,
so the Lord surrounds his
 people,
from this time on and
 forevermore.
3 For the scepter of
 wickedness shall not
 rest

on the land allotted to the
righteous,
so that the righteous might
not stretch out
their hands to do wrong.
⁴ Do good, O Lord, to those
who are good,
and to those who are
upright in their hearts.
⁵ But those who turn aside to
their own crooked ways
the Lord will lead away
with evildoers.
Peace be upon Israel!

Psalm 126
A Harvest of Joy

A Song of Ascents.

¹ When the Lord restored the
fortunes of Zion,ᵇ
we were like those who
dream.
² Then our mouth was filled
with laughter,
and our tongue with shouts
of joy;
then it was said among the
nations,
"The Lord has done great
things for them."
³ The Lord has done great
things for us,
and we rejoiced.

⁴ Restore our fortunes, O Lord,
like the watercourses in
the Negeb.
⁵ May those who sow in tears
reap with shouts of joy.
⁶ Those who go out weeping,
bearing the seed for
sowing,
shall come home with shouts
of joy,
carrying their sheaves.

Psalm 127
God's Blessings in the Home

A Song of Ascents. Of Solomon.

¹ Unless the Lord builds the
house,
those who build it labor in
vain.

125.4
Ps 119.68;
7.10; 94.15
125.5
Prov 2.15;
Ps 128.6
126.1
Ps 85.1;
Acts 12.9
126.2
Job 8.21;
Ps 51.14;
71.19
126.3
Isa 25.9
126.4
Isa 35.6;
43.19
126.5
Jer 31.16;
Isa 35.10
127.1
Ps 78.69;
121.4

127.2
Gen 3.17;
Job 11.18,
19
127.3
Gen 33.5;
Josh 24.3,4;
Deut 28.4
127.5
Job 5.4;
Prov 27.11
128.1
Ps 112.1;
119.3
128.2
Isa 3.10;
Ezek 23.29;
Eccl 8.12
128.3
Ezek 19.10;
Ps 52.8;
144.12
128.5
Ps 134.3;
20.2; 122.9

Unless the Lord guards the
city,
the guard keeps watch in
vain.
² It is in vain that you rise up
early
and go late to rest,
eating the bread of anxious
toil;
for he gives sleep to his
beloved.ᶜ

³ Sons are indeed a heritage
from the Lord,
the fruit of the womb a
reward.
⁴ Like arrows in the hand of a
warrior
are the sons of one's youth.
⁵ Happy is the man who has
his quiver full of them.
He shall not be put to shame
when he speaks with his
enemies in the gate.

Psalm 128
The Happy Home of the Faithful

A Song of Ascents.

¹ Happy is everyone who fears
the Lord,
who walks in his ways.
² You shall eat the fruit of the
labor of your hands;
you shall be happy, and it
shall go well with you.

³ Your wife will be like a
fruitful vine
within your house;
your children will be like
olive shoots
around your table.
⁴ Thus shall the man be
blessed
who fears the Lord.

⁵ The Lord bless you from
Zion.
May you see the prosperity
of Jerusalem
all the days of your life.

ᵇ Or *brought back those who returned to Zion*
ᶜ Or *for he provides for his beloved during
sleep*

6 May you see your children's
children.
Peace be upon Israel!

Psalm 129
Prayer for the Downfall of Israel's Enemies

A Song of Ascents.

1 "Often have they attacked
me from my youth"
—let Israel now say—
2 "often have they attacked me
from my youth,
yet they have not prevailed
against me.
3 The plowers plowed on my
back;
they made their furrows
long."
4 The LORD is righteous;
he has cut the cords of the
wicked.
5 May all who hate Zion
be put to shame and
turned backward.
6 Let them be like the grass on
the housetops
that withers before it grows
up,
7 with which reapers do not
fill their hands
or binders of sheaves their
arms,
8 while those who pass by do
not say,
"The blessing of the LORD
be upon you!
We bless you in the name
of the LORD!"

Psalm 130
Waiting for Divine Redemption

A Song of Ascents.

1 Out of the depths I cry to
you, O LORD.
2 Lord, hear my voice!
Let your ears be attentive
to the voice of my
supplications!

3 If you, O LORD, should mark
iniquities,
Lord, who could stand?

128.6
Gen 50.23;
Job 42.16;
Ps 125.5
129.1
Ps 88.15;
Hos 2.15;
Ps 124.1
129.2
Mt 16.18
129.4
Ps 119.137
129.5
Mic 4.11;
Ps 71.13
129.6
Ps 37.2
129.8
Ruth 2.4;
Ps 118.26
130.1
Ps 42.7;
69.2
130.2
Ps 64.1;
2 Chr 6.40;
Ps 28.2
130.3
Ps 76.7

130.4
Ex 34.7;
Isa 55.7;
1 Kings 8.40;
Jer 33.8
130.5
Ps 33.20;
Isa 8.17;
Ps 119.81
130.6
Ps 63.6;
119.147
130.7
Ps 131.3;
Isa 55.7
130.8
Lk 1.68
131.1
Ps 101.5;
Isa 5.15;
Rom 12.16
131.2
Ps 62.1;
Mt 18.3;
1 Cor 14.20
131.3
Ps 130.7

4 But there is forgiveness with
you,
so that you may be revered.

5 I wait for the LORD, my soul
waits,
and in his word I hope;
6 my soul waits for the Lord
more than those who
watch for the morning,
more than those who
watch for the morning.

7 O Israel, hope in the LORD!
For with the LORD there is
steadfast love,
and with him is great
power to redeem.
8 It is he who will redeem
Israel
from all its iniquities.

Psalm 131
Song of Quiet Trust

A Song of Ascents. Of David.

1 O LORD, my heart is not
lifted up,
my eyes are not raised too
high;
I do not occupy myself with
things
too great and too
marvelous for me.
2 But I have calmed and
quieted my soul,
like a weaned child with its
mother;
my soul is like the weaned
child that is with me. d

3 O Israel, hope in the LORD
from this time on and
forevermore.

Psalm 132
The Eternal Dwelling of God in Zion

A Song of Ascents.

1 O LORD, remember in David's
favor

d Or my soul within me is like a weaned child

all the hardships he
 endured;

2 how he swore to the LORD
 and vowed to the Mighty
 One of Jacob,

3 "I will not enter my house
 or get into my bed;

4 I will not give sleep to my
 eyes
 or slumber to my eyelids,

5 until I find a place for the
 LORD,
 a dwelling place for the
 Mighty One of Jacob."

6 We heard of it in Ephrathah;
 we found it in the fields of
 Jaar.

7 "Let us go to his dwelling
 place;
 let us worship at his
 footstool."

8 Rise up, O LORD, and go to
 your resting place,
 you and the ark of your
 might.

9 Let your priests be clothed
 with righteousness,
 and let your faithful shout
 for joy.

10 For your servant David's sake
 do not turn away the face
 of your anointed one.

11 The LORD swore to David a
 sure oath
 from which he will not turn
 back:
 "One of the sons of your
 body
 I will set on your throne.

12 If your sons keep my
 covenant
 and my decrees that I shall
 teach them,
 their sons also, forevermore,
 shall sit on your throne."

13 For the LORD has chosen
 Zion;
 he has desired it for his
 habitation:

14 "This is my resting place
 forever;
 here I will reside, for I have
 desired it.

132.2
Gen 49.24
132.4
Prov 6.4
132.5
Acts 7.46
132.6
1 Sam 17.12;
7.1;
1 Chr 13.5
132.7
Ps 4.7; 99.5
132.8
Num 10.35;
2 Chr 6.41;
Ps 78.61
132.9
v. 16;
Job 29.14;
Isa 61.10
132.11
Ps 89.3,4;
2 Sam 7.12;
2 Chr 6.16
132.12
Lk 1.32;
Acts 2.30
132.13
Ps 48.1,2;
68.16
132.14
v. 8

132.15
Ps 147.14;
107.9
132.16
v. 9
132.17
Ezek 29.21;
Lk 1.69;
1 Kings 11.36;
15.4;
2 Chr 21.7
132.18
Ps 35.26;
109.29
133.1
Gen 13.8;
Heb 13.1
133.2
Ex 30.25;
39.24
133.3
Deut 4.48;
Lev 25.21;
Deut 28.8;
Ps 42.8
134.1
Ps 103.21;
135.1,2;
1 Chr 9.33
134.2
Ps 28.2;
1 Tim 2.8
134.3
Ps 124.8;
128.5

15 I will abundantly bless its
 provisions;
 I will satisfy its poor with
 bread.

16 Its priests I will clothe with
 salvation,
 and its faithful will shout
 for joy.

17 There I will cause a horn to
 sprout up for David;
 I have prepared a lamp for
 my anointed one.

18 His enemies I will clothe
 with disgrace,
 but on him, his crown will
 gleam."

Psalm 133

The Blessedness of Unity

A Song of Ascents.

1 How very good and pleasant
 it is
 when kindred live together
 in unity!

2 It is like the precious oil on
 the head,
 running down upon the
 beard,
 on the beard of Aaron,
 running down over the
 collar of his robes.

3 It is like the dew of Hermon,
 which falls on the
 mountains of Zion.
 For there the LORD ordained
 his blessing,
 life forevermore.

Psalm 134

Praise in the Night

A Song of Ascents.

1 Come, bless the LORD, all you
 servants of the LORD,
 who stand by night in the
 house of the LORD!

2 Lift up your hands to the
 holy place,
 and bless the LORD.

3 May the LORD, maker of
 heaven and earth,
 bless you from Zion.

Psalm 135

Praise for God's Goodness and Might

1 Praise the LORD!
 Praise the name of the
 LORD;
 give praise, O servants of
 the LORD,
2 you that stand in the house
 of the LORD,
 in the courts of the house
 of our God.
3 Praise the LORD, for the LORD
 is good;
 sing to his name, for he is
 gracious.
4 For the LORD has chosen
 Jacob for himself,
 Israel as his own
 possession.

5 For I know that the LORD is
 great;
 our Lord is above all gods.
6 Whatever the LORD pleases
 he does,
 in heaven and on earth,
 in the seas and all deeps.
7 He it is who makes the
 clouds rise at the end
 of the earth;
 he makes lightnings for the
 rain
 and brings out the wind
 from his storehouses.

8 He it was who struck down
 the firstborn of Egypt,
 both human beings and
 animals;
9 he sent signs and wonders
 into your midst, O Egypt,
 against Pharaoh and all his
 servants.
10 He struck down many
 nations
 and killed mighty kings —
11 Sihon, king of the Amorites,
 and Og, king of Bashan,
 and all the kingdoms of
 Canaan —
12 and gave their land as a
 heritage,
 a heritage to his people
 Israel.

13 Your name, O LORD, endures
 forever,
 your renown, O LORD,
 throughout all ages.
14 For the LORD will vindicate
 his people,
 and have compassion on
 his servants.

15 The idols of the nations are
 silver and gold,
 the work of human hands.
16 They have mouths, but they
 do not speak;
 they have eyes, but they do
 not see;
17 they have ears, but they do
 not hear,
 and there is no breath in
 their mouths.
18 Those who make them
 and all who trust them
 shall become like them.

19 O house of Israel, bless the
 LORD!
 O house of Aaron, bless
 the LORD!
20 O house of Levi, bless the
 LORD!
 You that fear the LORD,
 bless the LORD!
21 Blessed be the LORD from
 Zion,
 he who resides in
 Jerusalem.
 Praise the LORD!

Psalm 136

God's Work in Creation and in History

1 O give thanks to the LORD,
 for he is good,
 for his steadfast love
 endures forever.
2 O give thanks to the God of
 gods,
 for his steadfast love
 endures forever.
3 O give thanks to the Lord of
 lords,
 for his steadfast love
 endures forever;

135.1
Ps 113.1;
134.1
135.2
Lk 2.37;
Ps 92.13
135.3
Ps 119.68;
147.1
135.4
Deut 7.6,7;
10.15;
Ex 19.5;
1 Pet 2.9
135.5
Ps 48.1;
97.9
135.6
Ps 115.3
135.7
Jer 10.13;
Job 28.25;
Zech 10.1;
Job 38.22
135.8
Ex 12.12;
Ps 78.51
135.9
Ps 78.43;
136.15
135.10
Num 21.24;
Ps 136.17
135.11
Num 21.21-26,
33-35;
Josh 12.7
135.12
Ps 78.55

135.13
Ex 3.15;
Ps 102.12
135.14
Deut 32.36;
Ps 106.45
135.15
Ps 115.4-8
135.19
Ps 115.9
135.20
Ps 118.4
135.21
Ps 134.3;
132.14
136.1
Ps 106.1;
107.1; 118.1;
1 Chr 16.34;
2 Chr 20.21
136.2
Deut 10.17

4 who alone does great
 wonders,
 for his steadfast love
 endures forever;
5 who by understanding made
 the heavens,
 for his steadfast love
 endures forever;
6 who spread out the earth on
 the waters,
 for his steadfast love
 endures forever;
7 who made the great lights,
 for his steadfast love
 endures forever;
8 the sun to rule over the day,
 for his steadfast love
 endures forever;
9 the moon and stars to rule
 over the night,
 for his steadfast love
 endures forever;
10 who struck Egypt through
 their firstborn,
 for his steadfast love
 endures forever;
11 and brought Israel out from
 among them,
 for his steadfast love
 endures forever;
12 with a strong hand and an
 outstretched arm,
 for his steadfast love
 endures forever;
13 who divided the Red Sea[e] in
 two,
 for his steadfast love
 endures forever;
14 and made Israel pass through
 the midst of it,
 for his steadfast love
 endures forever;
15 but overthrew Pharaoh and
 his army in the Red
 Sea,[e]
 for his steadfast love
 endures forever;
16 who led his people through
 the wilderness,
 for his steadfast love
 endures forever;
17 who struck down great kings,
 for his steadfast love
 endures forever;
18 and killed famous kings,

 for his steadfast love
 endures forever;
19 Sihon, king of the Amorites,
 for his steadfast love
 endures forever;
20 and Og, king of Bashan,
 for his steadfast love
 endures forever;
21 and gave their land as a
 heritage,
 for his steadfast love
 endures forever;
22 a heritage to his servant
 Israel,
 for his steadfast love
 endures forever.

23 It is he who remembered us
 in our low estate,
 for his steadfast love
 endures forever;
24 and rescued us from our
 foes,
 for his steadfast love
 endures forever;
25 who gives food to all flesh,
 for his steadfast love
 endures forever.

26 O give thanks to the God of
 heaven,
 for his steadfast love
 endures forever.

Psalm 137

Lament over the Destruction of Jerusalem

1 By the rivers of Babylon—
 there we sat down and
 there we wept
 when we remembered Zion.
2 On the willows[f] there
 we hung up our harps.
3 For there our captors
 asked us for songs,
 and our tormentors asked for
 mirth, saying,
 "Sing us one of the songs
 of Zion!"

4 How could we sing the
 LORD's song
 in a foreign land?
5 If I forget you, O Jerusalem,

e Or *Sea of Reeds* f Or *poplars*

Center column cross-references:

136.4 Ps 72.18
136.5 Gen 1.1; Prov 3.19; Jer 51.15
136.6 Gen 1.9; Ps 24.2; Jer 10.12
136.7 Gen 1.14,16
136.8 Gen 1.16
136.10 Ex 12.29; Ps 135.8
136.11 Ex 12.51
136.12 Ex 6.6; Ps 44.3; Deut 4.34
136.13 Ex 14.21; Ps 78.13
136.14 Ex 14.22
136.15 Ex 14.27; Ps 135.9
136.16 Ex 13.18; 15.22; Deut 8.15
136.17 Ps 135.10-12
136.21 Josh 12.1
136.23 Ps 113.7
136.24 Ps 107.2
136.25 Ps 104.27; 145.15
137.1 Ezek 1.1,3; Neh 1.4
137.3 Ps 80.6

let my right hand wither!
6 Let my tongue cling to the
 roof of my mouth,
 if I do not remember you,
 if I do not set Jerusalem
 above my highest joy.

7 Remember, O LORD, against
 the Edomites
 the day of Jerusalem's fall,
 how they said, "Tear it down!
 Tear it down!
 Down to its foundations!"
8 O daughter Babylon, you
 devastator!g
 Happy shall they be who
 pay you back
 what you have done to us!
9 Happy shall they be who
 take your little ones
 and dash them against the
 rock!

Psalm 138
Thanksgiving and Praise

Of David.

1 I give you thanks, O LORD,
 with my whole heart;
 before the gods I sing your
 praise;
2 I bow down toward your holy
 temple
 and give thanks to your
 name for your steadfast
 love and your
 faithfulness;
 for you have exalted your
 name and your word
 above everything.h
3 On the day I called, you
 answered me,
 you increased my strength
 of soul.i

4 All the kings of the earth
 shall praise you,
 O LORD,
 for they have heard the
 words of your mouth.
5 They shall sing of the ways
 of the LORD,
 for great is the glory of the
 LORD.
6 For though the LORD is high,
 he regards the lowly;

137.6
Ezek 3.26
137.7
Jer 49.7;
Lam 4.22;
Ezek 25.12;
Ob 10-14
137.8
Isa 13.1,6;
Jer 25.12;
50.15;
Rev 18.6
137.9
2 Kings 8.12;
Isa 13.16
138.1
Ps 111.1;
95.3; 96.4
138.2
Ps 28.2;
1 Kings 8.29,
30;
Isa 42.21
138.3
Ps 118.5;
28.7; 46.1
138.4
Ps 102.15
138.6
Ps 113.5,6;
Isa 57.15;
Prov 3.34;
Jas 4.6

138.7
Ps 23.3,4;
71.20;
Jer 41.25;
Ps 20.6
138.8
Ps 57.2;
Phil 1.6;
Ps 136.1;
27.9;
Job 10.3,8;
14.15
139.1
Ps 17.3;
Jer 12.3
139.2
2 Kings 19.27;
Mt 9.4;
Jn 2.24
139.3
Job 31.4
139.4
Heb 4.13
139.5
Ps 34.7;
Job 9.33
139.6
Rom 11.33;
Job 42.3
139.7
Jer 23.24;
Jon 1.3
139.8ff
Am 9.2-4;
Job 26.6;
Prov 15.11

but the haughty he
 perceives from far away.

7 Though I walk in the midst
 of trouble,
 you preserve me against
 the wrath of my
 enemies;
 you stretch out your hand,
 and your right hand
 delivers me.
8 The LORD will fulfill his
 purpose for me;
 your steadfast love, O LORD,
 endures forever.
 Do not forsake the work of
 your hands.

Psalm 139
The Inescapable God

To the leader. Of David. A Psalm.

1 O LORD, you have searched
 me and known me.
2 You know when I sit down
 and when I rise up;
 you discern my thoughts
 from far away.
3 You search out my path and
 my lying down,
 and are acquainted with all
 my ways.
4 Even before a word is on my
 tongue,
 O LORD, you know it
 completely.
5 You hem me in, behind and
 before,
 and lay your hand upon
 me.
6 Such knowledge is too
 wonderful for me;
 it is so high that I cannot
 attain it.

7 Where can I go from your
 spirit?
 Or where can I flee from
 your presence?
8 If I ascend to heaven, you
 are there;

g Or you who are devastated h Cn: Heb
you have exalted your word above all your name
i Syr Compare Gk Tg: Heb you made me
arrogant in my soul with strength

if I make my bed in Sheol,
 you are there.
⁹ If I take the wings of the
 morning
 and settle at the farthest
 limits of the sea,
¹⁰ even there your hand shall
 lead me,
 and your right hand shall
 hold me fast.
¹¹ If I say, "Surely the darkness
 shall cover me,
 and the light around me
 become night,"
¹² even the darkness is not dark
 to you;
 the night is as bright as the
 day,
 for darkness is as light to
 you.

¹³ For it was you who formed
 my inward parts;
 you knit me together in my
 mother's womb.
¹⁴ I praise you, for I am
 fearfully and
 wonderfully made.
 Wonderful are your works;
 that I know very well.
¹⁵ My frame was not hidden
 from you,
 when I was being made in
 secret,
 intricately woven in the
 depths of the earth.
¹⁶ Your eyes beheld my
 unformed substance.
 In your book were written
 all the days that were
 formed for me,
 when none of them as yet
 existed.
¹⁷ How weighty to me are your
 thoughts, O God!
 How vast is the sum of
 them!
¹⁸ I try to count them—they
 are more than the sand;
 I come to the end[j]—I am
 still with you.

¹⁹ O that you would kill the
 wicked, O God,
 and that the bloodthirsty
 would depart from
 me—

²⁰ those who speak of you
 maliciously,
 and lift themselves up
 against you for evil![k]
²¹ Do I not hate those who hate
 you, O Lord?
 And do I not loathe those
 who rise up against
 you?
²² I hate them with perfect
 hatred;
 I count them my enemies.
²³ Search me, O God, and know
 my heart;
 test me and know my
 thoughts.
²⁴ See if there is any wicked[l]
 way in me,
 and lead me in the way
 everlasting.[m]

Psalm 140

Prayer for Deliverance from Enemies

To the leader. A Psalm of David.

¹ Deliver me, O Lord, from
 evildoers;
 protect me from those who
 are violent,
² who plan evil things in their
 minds
 and stir up wars
 continually.
³ They make their tongue
 sharp as a snake's,
 and under their lips is the
 venom of vipers. *Selah*

⁴ Guard me, O Lord, from the
 hands of the wicked;
 protect me from the violent
 who have planned my
 downfall.
⁵ The arrogant have hidden a
 trap for me,
 and with cords they have
 spread a net,[n]

139.10
Ps 23.2,3
139.11
Job 22.13
139.12
Job 34.22;
Dan 2.22;
Heb 4.13
139.13ff
Ps 119.73;
Job 10.11
139.14
Ps 40.5
139.17
Ps 40.5
139.19
Isa 11.4;
Ps 119.115

139.20
Jude 15
139.21
Ps 119.158
139.23
Job 31.6;
Ps 26.2;
Jer 11.20
139.24
Prov 15.9;
Ps 5.8;
143.10
140.1
Ps 17.13;
18.48
140.2
Ps 36.4;
56.6
140.3
Ps 57.4;
68.4;
Jas 3.8
140.4
Ps 71.4
140.5
Ps 35.7;
31.4; 141.9

i Or *I awake* k Cn: Meaning of Heb
uncertain l Heb *hurtful* m Or *the*
ancient way. Compare Jer 6.16 n Or *they*
have spread cords as a net

along the road they have
 set snares for me. *Selah*
6 I say to the LORD, "You are
 my God;
 give ear, O LORD, to the
 voice of my
 supplications."
7 O LORD, my Lord, my strong
 deliverer,
 you have covered my head
 in the day of battle.
8 Do not grant, O LORD, the
 desires of the wicked;
 do not further their evil
 plot.º *Selah*

9 Those who surround me lift
 up their heads;ᴾ
 let the mischief of their
 lips overwhelm them!
10 Let burning coals fall on
 them!
 Let them be flung into pits,
 no more to rise!
11 Do not let the slanderer be
 established in the land;
 let evil speedily hunt down
 the violent!

12 I know that the LORD
 maintains the cause of
 the needy,
 and executes justice for the
 poor.
13 Surely the righteous shall
 give thanks to your
 name;
 the upright shall live in
 your presence.

Psalm 141
Prayer for Preservation
from Evil

A Psalm of David.

1 I call upon you, O LORD;
 come quickly to me;
 give ear to my voice when I
 call to you.
2 Let my prayer be counted as
 incense before you,
 and the lifting up of my
 hands as an evening
 sacrifice.

3 Set a guard over my mouth,
 O LORD;
 keep watch over the door
 of my lips.
4 Do not turn my heart to any
 evil,
 to busy myself with wicked
 deeds
 in company with those who
 work iniquity;
 do not let me eat of their
 delicacies.

5 Let the righteous strike
 me;
 let the faithful correct
 me.
Never let the oil of the
 wicked anoint my
 head,�q
 for my prayer is
 continuallyʳ against
 their wicked deeds.
6 When they are given over to
 those who shall
 condemn them,
 then they shall learn that
 my words were
 pleasant.
7 Like a rock that one breaks
 apart and shatters on
 the land,
 so shall their bones be
 strewn at the mouth of
 Sheol.ˢ

8 But my eyes are turned
 toward you, O GOD, my
 Lord;
 in you I seek refuge; do not
 leave me defenseless.
9 Keep me from the trap that
 they have laid for me,
 and from the snares of
 evildoers.
10 Let the wicked fall into their
 own nets,
 while I alone escape.

140.6
Ps 16.2;
143.1; 116.1
140.7
Ps 28.8;
144.10
140.8
Ps 112.10;
10.2
140.9
Ps 7.16
140.10
Ps 11.6;
21.9; 36.12
140.11
Ps 34.21
140.12
Ps 9.4;
35.10
140.13
Ps 97.12;
11.7
141.1
Ps 22.19;
70.5; 143.1
141.2
Rev 5.8; 8.3;
Ps 134.2;
Ex 29.39

141.4
Ps 119.36;
Prov 23.6
141.5
Prov 9.8;
Ps 23.5;
35.14
141.7
Ps 53.5
141.8
Ps 25.15;
2.12; 27.9
141.9
Ps 38.12;
140.5
141.10
Ps 35.8

º Heb adds *they are exalted*
ᴾ Cn Compare Gk: Heb *those who surround
me are uplifted in head*; Heb divides verses 8
and 9 differently q Gk: Meaning of Heb
uncertain ʳ Cn: Heb *for continually and my
prayer* ˢ Meaning of Heb of verses 5-7 is
uncertain

Psalm 142

Prayer for Deliverance from Persecutors

A Maskil of David. When he was in the cave. A Prayer.

1 With my voice I cry to the
 LORD;
 with my voice I make
 supplication to the
 LORD.
2 I pour out my complaint
 before him;
 I tell my trouble before
 him.
3 When my spirit is faint,
 you know my way.

 In the path where I walk
 they have hidden a trap for
 me.
4 Look on my right hand and
 see —
 there is no one who takes
 notice of me;
 no refuge remains to me;
 no one cares for me.

5 I cry to you, O LORD;
 I say, "You are my refuge,
 my portion in the land of
 the living."
6 Give heed to my cry,
 for I am brought very low.

 Save me from my
 persecutors,
 for they are too strong for
 me.
7 Bring me out of prison,
 so that I may give thanks
 to your name.
 The righteous will surround
 me,
 for you will deal
 bountifully with me.

Psalm 143

Prayer for Deliverance from Enemies

A Psalm of David.

1 Hear my prayer, O LORD;
 give ear to my

142.1
Ps 77.1;
30.8
142.2
Isa 26.16
142.3
Ps 143.4;
140.5
142.4
Ps 31.11;
Job 11.20;
Jer 30.17
142.5
Ps 46.1;
16.5; 27.13
142.6
Ps 17.1;
79.8; 116.6
142.7
Ps 146.7;
13.6
143.1
Ps 140.6;
89.1,2; 71.2

143.2
Job 14.3;
4.17;
Ps 130.3;
Eccl 7.20;
Rom 3.20
143.4
Ps 142.3;
Lam 3.11
143.5
Ps 77.5;
77.12; 105.2
143.6
Ps 88.9;
63.1
143.7
Ps 69.17;
27.9; 28.1
143.8
Ps 90.14;
25.2; 27.11;
25.1
143.9
Ps 31.15
143.10
Ps 25.4,5;
Neh 9.20;
Ps 23.3
143.11
Ps 119.25;
31.1

 supplications in your
 faithfulness;
 answer me in your
 righteousness.
2 Do not enter into judgment
 with your servant,
 for no one living is
 righteous before you.

3 For the enemy has pursued
 me,
 crushing my life to the
 ground,
 making me sit in darkness
 like those long dead.
4 Therefore my spirit faints
 within me;
 my heart within me is
 appalled.

5 I remember the days of old,
 I think about all your
 deeds,
 I meditate on the works of
 your hands.
6 I stretch out my hands to
 you;
 my soul thirsts for you like
 a parched land. *Selah*

7 Answer me quickly, O LORD;
 my spirit fails.
 Do not hide your face from
 me,
 or I shall be like those who
 go down to the Pit.
8 Let me hear of your steadfast
 love in the morning,
 for in you I put my trust.
 Teach me the way I should
 go,
 for to you I lift up my soul.

9 Save me, O LORD, from my
 enemies;
 I have fled to you for
 refuge.[t]
10 Teach me to do your will,
 for you are my God.
 Let your good spirit lead me
 on a level path.

11 For your name's sake,
 O LORD, preserve my
 life.

[t] One Heb Ms Gk: MT *to you I have hidden*

In your righteousness bring
me out of trouble.
12 In your steadfast love cut off
my enemies,
and destroy all my
adversaries,
for I am your servant.

Psalm 144
Prayer for National Deliverance and Security

Of David.

1 Blessed be the LORD, my
rock,
who trains my hands for
war, and my fingers for
battle;
2 my rockᵘ and my fortress,
my stronghold and my
deliverer,
my shield, in whom I take
refuge,
who subdues the peoplesᵛ
under me.

3 O LORD, what are human
beings that you regard
them,
or mortals that you think
of them?
4 They are like a breath;
their days are like a
passing shadow.

5 Bow your heavens, O LORD,
and come down;
touch the mountains so
that they smoke.
6 Make the lightning flash and
scatter them;
send out your arrows and
rout them.
7 Stretch out your hand from
on high;
set me free and rescue me
from the mighty waters,
from the hand of aliens,
8 whose mouths speak lies,
and whose right hands are
false.

9 I will sing a new song to you,
O God;
upon a ten-stringed harp I
will play to you,

143.12
Ps 54.5;
52.5; 116.16
144.1
Ps 18.2,34
144.2
Ps 91.2;
59.9; 84.9;
18.39
144.3
Ps 8.4;
Heb 2.6
144.4
Ps 39.11;
102.11
144.5
Ps 18.9;
Isa 64.1;
Ps 104.32
144.6
Ps 18.13,14;
7.13
144.7
Ps 69.1,14;
18.44
144.8
Ps 12.2;
Isa 44.20
144.9
Ps 33.2,3

144.10
Ps 18.50;
140.7
144.11
Ps 12.2;
Isa 44.20
144.12
Ps 128.3
144.15
Ps 33.12
145.1
Ps 30.1; 5.2;
34.1
145.2
Ps 71.6
145.3
Ps 96.4;
Job 5.9;
Rom 11.33

10 the one who gives victory to
kings,
who rescues his servant
David.
11 Rescue me from the cruel
sword,
and deliver me from the
hand of aliens,
whose mouths speak lies,
and whose right hands are
false.

12 May our sons in their youth
be like plants full grown,
our daughters like corner
pillars,
cut for the building of a
palace.
13 May our barns be filled,
with produce of every kind;
may our sheep increase by
thousands,
by tens of thousands in our
fields,
14 and may our cattle be
heavy with young.
May there be no breach in
the walls,ʷ no exile,
and no cry of distress in
our streets.

15 Happy are the people to
whom such blessings
fall;
happy are the people
whose God is the LORD.

Psalm 145
The Greatness and the Goodness of God

Praise. Of David.

1 I will extol you, my God and
King,
and bless your name
forever and ever.
2 Every day I will bless you,
and praise your name
forever and ever.
3 Great is the LORD, and greatly
to be praised;
his greatness is
unsearchable.

ᵘWith 18.2 and 2 Sam 22.2: Heb *my steadfast
love* ᵛHeb Mss Syr Aquila Jerome: MT *my
people* ʷHeb lacks *in the walls*

⁴ One generation shall laud
 your works to another,
 and shall declare your
 mighty acts.
⁵ On the glorious splendor of
 your majesty,
 and on your wondrous
 works, I will meditate.
⁶ The might of your awesome
 deeds shall be
 proclaimed,
 and I will declare your
 greatness.
⁷ They shall celebrate the
 fame of your abundant
 goodness,
 and shall sing aloud of
 your righteousness.

⁸ The LORD is gracious and
 merciful,
 slow to anger and
 abounding in steadfast
 love.
⁹ The LORD is good to all,
 and his compassion is over
 all that he has made.

¹⁰ All your works shall give
 thanks to you, O LORD,
 and all your faithful shall
 bless you.
¹¹ They shall speak of the glory
 of your kingdom,
 and tell of your power,
¹² to make known to all people
 your^x mighty deeds,
 and the glorious splendor
 of your^y kingdom.
¹³ Your kingdom is an
 everlasting kingdom,
 and your dominion endures
 throughout all
 generations.

 The LORD is faithful in all his
 words,
 and gracious in all his
 deeds.^z
¹⁴ The LORD upholds all who
 are falling,
 and raises up all who are
 bowed down.
¹⁵ The eyes of all look to you,
 and you give them their
 food in due season.
¹⁶ You open your hand,

145.4
Isa 38.19
145.5
v. 12;
Ps 119.27
145.6
Ps 66.3;
Deut 32.3
145.7
Isa 63.7;
Ps 51.14
145.8
Ex 34.6;
Ps 86.5,15
145.9
Ps 100.5;
Nah 1.7
145.10
Ps 19.1;
68.26
145.12
Ps 105.1;
v. 54
145.13
Ps 146.10;
2 Pet 1.11
145.14
Ps 37.24;
146.8
145.15
Ps 104.27
145.16
Ps 124.28

145.18
Deut 4.7;
Jn 4.24
145.19
Ps 37.4;
Prov 15.29
145.20
Ps 31.23;
97.10; 9.5
145.21
Ps 71.8;
65.2; v. 1,2
146.1
Ps 103.1
146.2
Ps 104.33
146.3
Ps 118.8;
Isa 2.22
146.4
Ps 104.29;
Eccl 12.7;
Ps 33.10
146.5
Ps 144.15;
71.5
146.6
Ps 115.15;
Acts 14.15;
Ps 117.2
146.7
Ps 103.6;
107.9; 68.6

satisfying the desire of
 every living thing.
¹⁷ The LORD is just in all his
 ways,
 and kind in all his doings.
¹⁸ The LORD is near to all who
 call on him,
 to all who call on him in
 truth.
¹⁹ He fulfills the desire of all
 who fear him;
 he also hears their cry, and
 saves them.
²⁰ The LORD watches over all
 who love him,
 but all the wicked he will
 destroy.

²¹ My mouth will speak the
 praise of the LORD,
 and all flesh will bless his
 holy name forever and
 ever.

Psalm 146

Praise for God's Help

¹ Praise the LORD!
 Praise the LORD, O my soul!
² I will praise the LORD as long
 as I live;
 I will sing praises to my
 God all my life long.

³ Do not put your trust in
 princes,
 in mortals, in whom there
 is no help.
⁴ When their breath departs,
 they return to the earth;
 on that very day their plans
 perish.

⁵ Happy are those whose help
 is the God of Jacob,
 whose hope is in the LORD
 their God,
⁶ who made heaven and earth,
 the sea, and all that is in
 them;
 who keeps faith forever;
⁷ who executes justice for
 the oppressed;

^x Gk Jerome Syr: Heb *his* ^y Heb *his*
^z These two lines supplied by Q Ms Gk Syr

who gives food to the
hungry.

The Lord sets the prisoners
free;

8 the Lord opens the eyes of
the blind.
The Lord lifts up those who
are bowed down;
the Lord loves the
righteous.

9 The Lord watches over the
strangers;
he upholds the orphan and
the widow,
but the way of the wicked
he brings to ruin.

10 The Lord will reign forever,
your God, O Zion, for all
generations.
Praise the Lord!

Psalm 147

Praise for God's Care for Jerusalem

1 Praise the Lord!
How good it is to sing
praises to our God;
for he is gracious, and a
song of praise is fitting.

2 The Lord builds up
Jerusalem;
he gathers the outcasts of
Israel.

3 He heals the brokenhearted,
and binds up their wounds.

4 He determines the number
of the stars;
he gives to all of them
their names.

5 Great is our Lord, and
abundant in power;
his understanding is
beyond measure.

6 The Lord lifts up the
downtrodden;
he casts the wicked to the
ground.

7 Sing to the Lord with
thanksgiving;
make melody to our God
on the lyre.

146.8
Mt 9.30;
Jn 9.7;
Ps 145.14;
11.7
146.9
Ex 22.21;
Deut 10.18;
Ps 68.5;
147.6
146.10
Ex 15.18;
Ps 10.16;
Rev 11.15
147.1
Ps 135.3;
33.1
147.2
Ps 102.16;
Deut 30.3
147.3
Isa 61.1;
30.26
147.4
Isa 40.26
147.5
Ps 48.1;
Isa 40.28
147.6
Ps 146.8,9
147.7
Ps 33.2

147.8
Job 38.26;
Ps 104.13
147.9
Ps 104.27;
Job 38.41
147.10
Ps 33.16,17;
1 Sam 16.7
147.11
Ps 102.15
147.13
Ps 37.26
147.14
Isa 60.17;
Ps 132.15
147.15
Job 37.12;
Ps 104.4
147.16
Job 37.6;
38.29
147.18
Ps 33.9;
107.25
147.19
Deut 33.2;
Mal 4.4
147.20
Deut 4.32

8 He covers the heavens with
clouds,
prepares rain for the
earth,
makes grass grow on the
hills.

9 He gives to the animals their
food,
and to the young ravens
when they cry.

10 His delight is not in the
strength of the horse,
nor his pleasure in the
speed of a runner;[a]

11 but the Lord takes pleasure
in those who fear him,
in those who hope in his
steadfast love.

12 Praise the Lord,
O Jerusalem!
Praise your God, O Zion!

13 For he strengthens the bars
of your gates;
he blesses your children
within you.

14 He grants peace[b] within
your borders;
he fills you with the finest
of wheat.

15 He sends out his command
to the earth;
his word runs swiftly.

16 He gives snow like wool;
he scatters frost like
ashes.

17 He hurls down hail like
crumbs—
who can stand before his
cold?

18 He sends out his word, and
melts them;
he makes his wind blow,
and the waters flow.

19 He declares his word to
Jacob,
his statutes and ordinances
to Israel.

20 He has not dealt thus with
any other nation;
they do not know his
ordinances.
Praise the Lord!

a Heb legs of a person b Or prosperity

Psalm 148

Praise for God's Universal Glory

1 Praise the LORD!
Praise the LORD from the
heavens;
praise him in the heights!
2 Praise him, all his angels;
praise him, all his host!

3 Praise him, sun and moon;
praise him, all you shining
stars!
4 Praise him, you highest
heavens,
and you waters above the
heavens!

5 Let them praise the name of
the LORD,
for he commanded and
they were created.
6 He established them forever
and ever;
he fixed their bounds,
which cannot be
passed. c

7 Praise the LORD from the
earth,
you sea monsters and all
deeps,
8 fire and hail, snow and frost,
stormy wind fulfilling his
command!

9 Mountains and all hills,
fruit trees and all cedars!
10 Wild animals and all cattle,
creeping things and flying
birds!

11 Kings of the earth and all
peoples,
princes and all rulers of the
earth!
12 Young men and women
alike,
old and young together!

13 Let them praise the name of
the LORD,
for his name alone is
exalted;
his glory is above earth and
heaven.

148.2
Ps 103.20,
21
148.4
1 Kings 8.27;
Gen 1.7
148.5
Gen 1.1;
Ps 33.6,9
148.6
Ps 89.37;
Jer 33.25;
Job 38.33
148.7
Ps 74.13
148.8
Ps 147.15-18
148.9
Isa 44.23;
49.13; 55.12
148.13
Ps 8.1;
Isa 12.4;
Ps 113.4

148.14
Ps 75.10;
Deut 10.21;
Eph 2.17
149.1
Ps 33.3;
35.18
149.2
Ps 95.6;
47.6
149.3
Ps 150.4;
81.2
149.4
Ps 35.27;
132.16
149.5
Ps 132.16;
Job 35.10
149.6
Ps 66.17;
Heb 4.12;
Rev 1.16
149.9
Ezek 28.26;
Ps 148.14
150.1
Ps 102.19;
19.1

14 He has raised up a horn for
his people,
praise for all his faithful,
for the people of Israel who
are close to him.
Praise the LORD!

Psalm 149

Praise for God's Goodness to Israel

1 Praise the LORD!
Sing to the LORD a new song,
his praise in the assembly
of the faithful.
2 Let Israel be glad in its
Maker;
let the children of Zion
rejoice in their King.
3 Let them praise his name
with dancing,
making melody to him with
tambourine and lyre.
4 For the LORD takes pleasure
in his people;
he adorns the humble with
victory.
5 Let the faithful exult in
glory;
let them sing for joy on
their couches.
6 Let the high praises of God
be in their throats
and two-edged swords in
their hands,
7 to execute vengeance on the
nations
and punishment on the
peoples,
8 to bind their kings with
fetters
and their nobles with
chains of iron,
9 to execute on them the
judgment decreed.
This is glory for all his
faithful ones.
Praise the LORD!

Psalm 150

Praise for God's Surpassing Greatness

1 Praise the LORD!
Praise God in his sanctuary;

c Or *he set a law that cannot pass away*

praise him in his mighty
firmament![d]
2 Praise him for his mighty
deeds;
praise him according to
his surpassing
greatness!

3 Praise him with trumpet
sound;
praise him with lute and
harp!

150.2
Ps 145.5,6;
Deut 3.24
150.3
Ps 149.3

150.4
Ex 15.20;
Isa 38.20
150.5
1 Chr 13.8;
15.16
150.6
Ps 145.21

4 Praise him with tambourine
and dance;
praise him with strings and
pipe!
5 Praise him with clanging
cymbals;
praise him with loud
clashing cymbals!
6 Let everything that breathes
praise the LORD!
Praise the LORD!

[d] Or dome

Proverbs

Title and Background

The Hebrew word translated "proverb" is also translated "taunt" (Isa 14.4), "oracle" (Nu 23.7,18) and "allegory" (Eze 17.2), so its meaning is considerably broader than the English term. Most proverbs are short, compact statements that express a truth about human behavior. A common feature of the proverbs is the use of figurative language.

Author and Date of Writing

Although this book begins with a title ascribing the proverbs to Solomon, it is clear from later chapters that he was not the only author of the book (see Outline). Since Solomon had a prominent role in the book, most of Proverbs stem from the tenth century B.C., from the time of Israel's united kingdom. The compliation of these sayings of Solomon began during the reign of Hezekiah (see 25.1), though it may not have been completed until later.

Theme and Message

According to the prologue (1.1-7), Proverbs was written to give "shrewdness to the simple, knowledge and prudence to the young" (1.4), and to make wise men wiser (1.5). Acquiring wisdom and knowing how to avoid the pitfalls of folly lead to health and success. Although Proverbs is a practical book dealing with the art of living, it bases wisdom solidly on the fear of the Lord (1.7).

Outline

1 The proverbs of Solomon son of David, king of Israel:

Prologue

2 For learning about wisdom and instruction,
 for understanding words of insight,
3 for gaining instruction in wise dealing,
 righteousness, justice, and equity;
4 to teach shrewdness to the simple,
 knowledge and prudence to the young—
5 Let the wise also hear and gain in learning,
 and the discerning acquire skill,
6 to understand a proverb and a figure,
 the words of the wise and their riddles.

7 The fear of the Lord is the beginning of knowledge;
 fools despise wisdom and instruction.

1.1
1 Kings 4.32;
Eccl 12.9
1.3
Prov 19.20;
2.9
1.4
Prov 8.5,12;
2.10,11
1.5
Prov 9.9;
14.6
1.6
Ps 78.2
1.7
Job 28.28;
Ps 111.10;
Eccl 12.13

Warnings against Evil Companions

8 Hear, my child, your father's
 instruction,
 and do not reject your
 mother's teaching;
9 for they are a fair garland for
 your head,
 and pendants for your
 neck.
10 My child, if sinners entice
 you,
 do not consent.
11 If they say, "Come with us,
 let us lie in wait for
 blood;
 let us wantonly ambush
 the innocent;
12 like Sheol let us swallow
 them alive
 and whole, like those who
 go down to the Pit.
13 We shall find all kinds of
 costly things;
 we shall fill our houses
 with booty.
14 Throw in your lot among us;
 we will all have one
 purse"—
15 my child, do not walk in
 their way,
 keep your foot from their
 paths;
16 for their feet run to evil,
 and they hurry to shed
 blood.
17 For in vain is the net baited
 while the bird is looking
 on;
18 yet they lie in wait—to kill
 themselves!
 and set an ambush—for
 their own lives!
19 Such is the enda of all who
 are greedy for gain;
 it takes away the life of its
 possessors.

The Call of Wisdom

20 Wisdom cries out in the
 street;
 in the squares she raises
 her voice.
21 At the busiest corner she
 cries out;

1.8
Prov 4.1;
6.20
1.9
Prov 4.9;
Gen 41.42
1.10
Deut 13.8;
Eph 5.11
1.11
Prov 12.6;
v. 18
1.12
Ps 124.3;
28.1
1.15
Ps 1.1;
119.101
1.16
Isa 59.7
1.19
Prov 15.27
1.20
Prov 8.1

1.22
vv. 4,32;
Ps 1.1;
v. 29
1.23
Joel 2.28
1.24
Isa 65.12;
Zech 7.11;
Rom 10.21
1.25
Ps 107.11;
Lk 7.30;
Prov 15.10
1.26
Ps 2.4;
Prov 6.15;
10.24
1.28
Isa 1.15;
Ezek 8.18;
Mic 3.4;
Zech 7.13
1.30
Ps 81.11
1.31
Job 4.8;
Prov 14.14;
Isa 3.11;
Jer 6.19
1.32
Jer 2.19
1.33
Ps 25.12

 at the entrance of the city
 gates she speaks:
22 "How long, O simple ones,
 will you love being
 simple?
 How long will scoffers
 delight in their scoffing
 and fools hate knowledge?
23 Give heed to my reproof;
 I will pour out my thoughts
 to you;
 I will make my words
 known to you.
24 Because I have called and
 you refused,
 have stretched out my
 hand and no one
 heeded,
25 and because you have
 ignored all my counsel
 and would have none of my
 reproof,
26 I also will laugh at your
 calamity;
 I will mock when panic
 strikes you,
27 when panic strikes you like a
 storm,
 and your calamity comes
 like a whirlwind,
 when distress and anguish
 come upon you.
28 Then they will call upon me,
 but I will not answer;
 they will seek me
 diligently, but will not
 find me.
29 Because they hated
 knowledge
 and did not choose the fear
 of the LORD,
30 would have none of my
 counsel,
 and despised all my
 reproof,
31 therefore they shall eat the
 fruit of their way
 and be sated with their
 own devices.
32 For waywardness kills the
 simple,
 and the complacency of
 fools destroys them;
33 but those who listen to me
 will be secure

a Gk: Heb *ways*

and will live at ease,
without dread of
disaster."

The Value of Wisdom

2 My child, if you accept my
words
and treasure up my
commandments within
you,

2 making your ear attentive to
wisdom
and inclining your heart to
understanding;

3 if you indeed cry out for
insight,
and raise your voice for
understanding;

4 if you seek it like silver,
and search for it as for
hidden treasures—

5 then you will understand the
fear of the LORD
and find the knowledge of
God.

6 For the LORD gives wisdom;
from his mouth come
knowledge and
understanding;

7 he stores up sound wisdom
for the upright;
he is a shield to those who
walk blamelessly,

8 guarding the paths of justice
and preserving the way of
his faithful ones.

9 Then you will understand
righteousness and
justice
and equity, every good
path;

10 for wisdom will come into
your heart,
and knowledge will be
pleasant to your soul;

11 prudence will watch over
you;
and understanding will
guard you.

12 It will save you from the way
of evil,
from those who speak
perversely,

13 who forsake the paths of
uprightness

to walk in the ways of
darkness,

14 who rejoice in doing evil
and delight in the
perverseness of evil;

15 those whose paths are
crooked,
and who are devious in
their ways.

16 You will be saved from the
loose[b] woman,
from the adulteress with
her smooth words,

17 who forsakes the partner of
her youth
and forgets her sacred
covenant;

18 for her way[c] leads down to
death,
and her paths to the
shades;

19 those who go to her never
come back,
nor do they regain the
paths of life.

20 Therefore walk in the way of
the good,
and keep to the paths of
the just.

21 For the upright will abide in
the land,
and the innocent will
remain in it;

22 but the wicked will be cut
off from the land,
and the treacherous will be
rooted out of it.

Admonition to Trust and Honor God

3 My child, do not forget my
teaching,
but let your heart keep my
commandments;

2 for length of days and years
of life
and abundant welfare they
will give you.

3 Do not let loyalty and
faithfulness forsake
you;
bind them around your
neck,

2.1
Prov 4.10
2.2
Prov 3.1
2.4
Prov 3.14;
Mt 13.44
2.5
Prov 1.7
2.6
1 Kings 3.9,
12; Jas 1.5
2.7
Ps 84.11
2.8
1 Sam 2.9;
Ps 66.9
2.9
Prov 8.20;
4.18
2.10
Prov 14.33;
22.18
2.11
Prov 6.22
2.13
Jn 3.19

2.14
Prov 10.23;
Jer 11.15
2.15
Ps 125.5
2.16
Prov 6.24;
23.27
2.17
Mal 2.14,15
2.18
Prov 7.27
2.21
Ps 37.29;
28.10
2.22
Ps 37.38;
Deut 28.63
3.1
Prov 4.5;
Ex 20.6;
Deut 30.16
3.2
Prov 4.10;
Ps 119.165
3.3
2 Sam 15.20;
Prov 1.9;
7.3

[b] Heb *strange* [c] Cn: Heb *house*

write them on the tablet of
your heart.
4 So you will find favor and
good repute
in the sight of God and of
people.

5 Trust in the LORD with all
your heart,
and do not rely on your
own insight.
6 In all your ways acknowledge
him,
and he will make straight
your paths.
7 Do not be wise in your own
eyes;
fear the LORD, and turn
away from evil.
8 It will be a healing for your
flesh
and a refreshment for your
body.

9 Honor the LORD with your
substance
and with the first fruits of
all your produce;
10 then your barns will be filled
with plenty,
and your vats will be
bursting with wine.

11 My child, do not despise the
LORD's discipline
or be weary of his reproof,
12 for the LORD reproves the one
he loves,
as a father the son in
whom he delights.

The True Wealth

13 Happy are those who find
wisdom,
and those who get
understanding,
14 for her income is better than
silver,
and her revenue better
than gold.
15 She is more precious than
jewels,
and nothing you desire can
compare with her.
16 Long life is in her right
hand;

3.4
Prov 8.5;
Ps 111.10
3.5
Ps 37.3,5;
Jer 9.23
3.6
1 Chr 28.9;
Isa 45.13
3.7
Rom 12.16;
Prov 16.6
3.8
Job 21.24
3.9
Isa 43.23;
Ex 23.19
3.10
Deut 28.8
3.11
Heb 12.5,6
3.12
Deut 8.5
3.13
Prov 8.32,34
3.14
Job 28.13;
Prov 8.10,19
3.15
Job 28.18;
Prov 8.11
3.16
Prov 8.18

3.17
Prov 16.7
3.18
Prov 11.30;
Gen 2.9
3.19
Ps 104.24
3.20
Gen 7.11;
Job 36.28
3.22
Prov 4.22;
1.9
3.23
Prov 4.12
3.24
Ps 3.5
3.25
Ps 91.5;
Job 5.21
3.27
Rom 13.7;
Gal 6.10
3.28
Lev 19.13

in her left hand are riches
and honor.
17 Her ways are ways of
pleasantness,
and all her paths are
peace.
18 She is a tree of life to those
who lay hold of her;
those who hold her fast are
called happy.

God's Wisdom in Creation

19 The LORD by wisdom founded
the earth;
by understanding he
established the
heavens;
20 by his knowledge the deeps
broke open,
and the clouds drop down
the dew.

The True Security

21 My child, do not let these
escape from your sight:
keep sound wisdom and
prudence,
22 and they will be life for your
soul
and adornment for your
neck.
23 Then you will walk on your
way securely
and your foot will not
stumble.
24 If you sit down,d you will
not be afraid;
when you lie down, your
sleep will be sweet.
25 Do not be afraid of sudden
panic,
or of the storm that strikes
the wicked;
26 for the LORD will be your
confidence
and will keep your foot
from being caught.

27 Do not withhold good from
those to whom it is
due,e
when it is in your power to
do it.
28 Do not say to your neighbor,
"Go, and come again,

d Gk: Heb *lie down* e Heb *from its owners*

tomorrow I will give
it" — when you have it
with you.

29 Do not plan harm against
your neighbor
who lives trustingly beside
you.

30 Do not quarrel with anyone
without cause,
when no harm has been
done to you.

31 Do not envy the violent
and do not choose any of
their ways;

32 for the perverse are an
abomination to the
LORD,
but the upright are in his
confidence.

33 The LORD's curse is on the
house of the wicked,
but he blesses the abode of
the righteous.

34 Toward the scorners he is
scornful,
but to the humble he
shows favor.

35 The wise will inherit honor,
but stubborn fools,
disgrace.

Parental Advice

4 Listen, children, to a
father's instruction,
and be attentive, that you
may gain[f] insight;

2 for I give you good precepts:
do not forsake my
teaching.

3 When I was a son with my
father,
tender, and my mother's
favorite,

4 he taught me, and said to
me,
"Let your heart hold fast my
words;
keep my commandments,
and live.

5 Get wisdom; get insight: do
not forget, nor turn
away
from the words of my
mouth.

6 Do not forsake her, and she
will keep you;

love her, and she will guard
you.

7 The beginning of wisdom is
this: Get wisdom,
and whatever else you get,
get insight.

8 Prize her highly, and she will
exalt you;
she will honor you if you
embrace her.

9 She will place on your head
a fair garland;
she will bestow on you a
beautiful crown."

Admonition to Keep to the Right Path

10 Hear, my child, and accept
my words,
that the years of your life
may be many.

11 I have taught you the way of
wisdom;
I have led you in the paths
of uprightness.

12 When you walk, your step
will not be hampered;
and if you run, you will not
stumble.

13 Keep hold of instruction; do
not let go;
guard her, for she is your
life.

14 Do not enter the path of the
wicked,
and do not walk in the way
of evildoers.

15 Avoid it; do not go on it;
turn away from it and pass
on.

16 For they cannot sleep unless
they have done wrong;
they are robbed of sleep
unless they have made
someone stumble.

17 For they eat the bread of
wickedness
and drink the wine of
violence.

18 But the path of the righteous
is like the light of
dawn,
which shines brighter and
brighter until full day.

3.29 Prov 14.22 **3.30** Rom 12.18 **3.31** Ps 37.1; Prov 24.1 **3.32** Prov 11.20; Ps 25.14 **3.33** Deut 11.28; Mal 2.2; Job 8.6 **3.34** Jas 4.6; 1 Pet 5.5 **4.1** Prov 1.8; 2.2 **4.3** 1 Chr 22.5 **4.4** 1 Chr 28.9; Prov 7.2 **4.5** v. 7; Prov 16.16 **4.6** 2 Thes 2.10 **4.7** Prov 23.23 **4.8** 1 Sam 2.30 **4.9** Prov 1.9 **4.10** Prov 2.1; 3.2 **4.11** 1 Sam 12.23 **4.12** Ps 18.36; Prov 3.23 **4.14** Ps 1.1; Prov 1.15 **4.16** Ps 36.4; Mic 2.1 **4.18** Isa 26.7; 2 Sam 23.4; Dan 12.3

[f] Heb *know*

19 The way of the wicked is like
 deep darkness;
 they do not know what
 they stumble over.
20 My child, be attentive to my
 words;
 incline your ear to my
 sayings.
21 Do not let them escape from
 your sight;
 keep them within your
 heart.
22 For they are life to those
 who find them,
 and healing to all their
 flesh.
23 Keep your heart with all
 vigilance,
 for from it flow the springs
 of life.
24 Put away from you crooked
 speech,
 and put devious talk far
 from you.
25 Let your eyes look directly
 forward,
 and your gaze be straight
 before you.
26 Keep straight the path of
 your feet,
 and all your ways will be
 sure.
27 Do not swerve to the right or
 to the left;
 turn your foot away from
 evil.

Warning against Impurity and Infidelity

5 My child, be attentive to my
 wisdom;
 incline your ear to my
 understanding,
2 so that you may hold on to
 prudence,
 and your lips may guard
 knowledge.
3 For the lips of a loose g
 woman drip honey,
 and her speech is smoother
 than oil;
4 but in the end she is bitter
 as wormwood,
 sharp as a two-edged
 sword.
5 Her feet go down to death;

4.19
Job 18.5;
Isa 59.9,10;
Jer 23.12;
Jn 12.35
4.21
Prov 3.21;
7.1,2
4.22
Prov 3.8;
12.18
4.23
Mt 12.34;
Mk 7.21;
Lk 6.45
4.24
Prov 6.12;
19.1
4.26
Heb 12.13;
Ps 119.5
4.27
Deut 5.32;
28.14;
Prov 1.15
5.1
Prov 4.20;
22.17
5.2
Mal 2.7
5.3
Prov 2.16;
Ps 55.21
5.4
Eccl 7.26;
Ps 57.4
5.5
Prov 7.27

5.7
Prov 7.24;
Ps 119.102
5.8
Prov 7.25;
9.14
5.12
Prov 1.29;
12.1
5.16
Prov 9.17
5.18
Eccl 9.9;
Mal 2.14
5.19
Song 2.9;
4.5; 7.3

 her steps follow the path to
 Sheol.
6 She does not keep straight to
 the path of life;
 her ways wander, and she
 does not know it.
7 And now, my child, h listen
 to me,
 and do not depart from the
 words of my mouth.
8 Keep your way far from her,
 and do not go near the
 door of her house;
9 or you will give your honor
 to others,
 and your years to the
 merciless,
10 and strangers will take their
 fill of your wealth,
 and your labors will go to
 the house of an alien;
11 and at the end of your life
 you will groan,
 when your flesh and body
 are consumed,
12 and you say, "Oh, how I
 hated discipline,
 and my heart despised
 reproof!
13 I did not listen to the voice
 of my teachers
 or incline my ear to my
 instructors.
14 Now I am at the point of
 utter ruin
 in the public assembly."
15 Drink water from your own
 cistern,
 flowing water from your
 own well.
16 Should your springs be
 scattered abroad,
 streams of water in the
 streets?
17 Let them be for yourself
 alone,
 and not for sharing with
 strangers.
18 Let your fountain be blessed,
 and rejoice in the wife of
 your youth,
19 a lovely deer, a graceful
 doe.

g Heb *strange* h Gk Vg: Heb *children*

May her breasts satisfy you
at all times;
may you be intoxicated
always by her love.
20 Why should you be
intoxicated, my son, by
another woman
and embrace the bosom of
an adulteress?
21 For human ways are under
the eyes of the LORD,
and he examines all their
paths.
22 The iniquities of the wicked
ensnare them,
and they are caught in the
toils of their sin.
23 They die for lack of
discipline,
and because of their great
folly they are lost.

Practical Admonitions

6 My child, if you have given
your pledge to your
neighbor,
if you have bound yourself
to another,[i]
2 you are snared by the
utterance of your lips,[i]
caught by the words of
your mouth.
3 So do this, my child, and
save yourself,
for you have come into
your neighbor's power:
go, hurry,[k] and plead with
your neighbor.
4 Give your eyes no sleep
and your eyelids no
slumber;
5 save yourself like a gazelle
from the hunter,[l]
like a bird from the hand
of the fowler.

6 Go to the ant, you lazybones;
consider its ways, and be
wise.
7 Without having any chief
or officer or ruler,
8 it prepares its food in
summer,
and gathers its sustenance
in harvest.
9 How long will you lie there,
O lazybones?

5.20
Prov 2.16;
7.5
5.21
Job 31.4;
34.21;
Prov 15.3;
Jer 16.17;
32.19;
Hos 7.2;
Heb 4.13
5.22
Ps 9.15
5.23
Job 4.21;
36.12
6.1
Prov 11.15;
17.18; 20.16;
22.26; 27.13
6.4
Ps 132.4
6.5
Ps 91.3
6.6
Prov 30.24,
25
6.8
Prov 10.5
6.9
Prov 24.33

6.11
Prov 10.4;
13.4; 20.4
6.12
Prov 16.27;
10.32
6.13
Ps 35.19;
Prov 10.10
6.14
Mic 2.1;
v. 19
6.15
Prov 24.22;
Jer 19.11;
2 Chr 36.16
6.17
Ps 18.27;
120.2;
Isa 1.15
6.18
Gen 6.5;
Prov 1.16
6.19
Ps 27.12;
v. 4
6.20
Prov 7.1;
1.8
6.21
Prov 3.3
6.22
Prov 3.23,24

When will you rise from
your sleep?
10 A little sleep, a little
slumber,
a little folding of the hands
to rest,
11 and poverty will come upon
you like a robber,
and want, like an armed
warrior.

12 A scoundrel and a villain
goes around with crooked
speech,
13 winking the eyes, shuffling
the feet,
pointing the fingers,
14 with perverted mind devising
evil,
continually sowing discord;
15 on such a one calamity will
descend suddenly;
in a moment, damage
beyond repair.

16 There are six things that the
LORD hates,
seven that are an
abomination to him:
17 haughty eyes, a lying tongue,
and hands that shed
innocent blood,
18 a heart that devises wicked
plans,
feet that hurry to run to
evil,
19 a lying witness who testifies
falsely,
and one who sows discord
in a family.

20 My child, keep your father's
commandment,
and do not forsake your
mother's teaching.
21 Bind them upon your heart
always;
tie them around your neck.
22 When you walk, they[m] will
lead you;
when you lie down, they[m]
will watch over you;

i Or a stranger j Cn Compare Gk Syr: Heb
the words of your mouth k Or humble
yourself l Cn: Heb from the hand
m Heb it

and when you awake,
they[n] will talk with
you.

23 For the commandment is a
lamp and the teaching
a light,
and the reproofs of
discipline are the way
of life,

24 to preserve you from the wife
of another,[o]
from the smooth tongue of
the adulteress.

25 Do not desire her beauty in
your heart,
and do not let her capture
you with her eyelashes;

26 for a prostitute's fee is only a
loaf of bread,[p]
but the wife of another
stalks a man's very life.

27 Can fire be carried in the
bosom
without burning one's
clothes?

28 Or can one walk on hot
coals
without scorching the feet?

29 So is he who sleeps with his
neighbor's wife;
no one who touches her
will go unpunished.

30 Thieves are not despised who
steal only
to satisfy their appetite
when they are hungry.

31 Yet if they are caught, they
will pay sevenfold;
they will forfeit all the
goods of their house.

32 But he who commits
adultery has no sense;
he who does it destroys
himself.

33 He will get wounds and
dishonor,
and his disgrace will not be
wiped away.

34 For jealousy arouses a
husband's fury,
and he shows no restraint
when he takes revenge.

35 He will accept no
compensation,
and refuses a bribe no
matter how great.

6.23
Ps 19.8
6.24
Prov 2.16;
5.3
6.25
Mt 5.28
6.26
Prov 29.3;
7.23;
Ezek 13.18
6.29
Ezek 18.6;
33.26
6.31
Ex 22.1-4
6.32
Prov 7.7
6.34
Prov 27.4;
11.4

7.1
Prov 2.1
7.2
Prov 4.4;
Deut 32.10
7.3
Deut 6.8;
Prov 3.3
7.5
Prov 2.16;
5.3; 6.24
7.7
Prov 1.22;
6.32
7.8
vv. 12,27
7.9
Job 24.15
7.11
Prov 9.13;
1 Tim 5.13
7.12
Prov 23.28

The False Attractions of Adultery

7 My child, keep my words
and store up my
commandments with
you;

2 keep my commandments and
live,
keep my teachings as the
apple of your eye;

3 bind them on your fingers,
write them on the tablet of
your heart.

4 Say to wisdom, "You are my
sister,"
and call insight your
intimate friend,

5 that they may keep you from
the loose[q] woman,
from the adulteress with
her smooth words.

6 For at the window of my
house
I looked out through my
lattice,

7 and I saw among the simple
ones,
I observed among the
youths,
a young man without
sense,

8 passing along the street near
her corner,
taking the road to her
house

9 in the twilight, in the
evening,
at the time of night and
darkness.

10 Then a woman comes toward
him,
decked out like a
prostitute, wily of
heart.[r]

11 She is loud and wayward;
her feet do not stay at
home;

12 now in the street, now in the
squares,
and at every corner she lies
in wait.

n Heb it o Gk: MT the evil woman
p Cn Compare Gk Syr Vg Tg: Heb for because
of a harlot to a piece of bread
q Heb strange r Meaning of Heb uncertain

¹³ She seizes him and kisses
him,
and with impudent face
she says to him:
¹⁴ "I had to offer sacrifices,
and today I have paid my
vows;
¹⁵ so now I have come out to
meet you,
to seek you eagerly, and I
have found you!
¹⁶ I have decked my couch with
coverings,
colored spreads of Egyptian
linen;
¹⁷ I have perfumed my bed with
myrrh,
aloes, and cinnamon.
¹⁸ Come, let us take our fill of
love until morning;
let us delight ourselves
with love.
¹⁹ For my husband is not at
home;
he has gone on a long
journey.
²⁰ He took a bag of money with
him;
he will not come home
until full moon."

²¹ With much seductive speech
she persuades him;
with her smooth talk she
compels him.
²² Right away he follows her,
and goes like an ox to the
slaughter,
or bounds like a stag toward
the trap[s]
²³ until an arrow pierces its
entrails.
He is like a bird rushing into
a snare,
not knowing that it will
cost him his life.

²⁴ And now, my children, listen
to me,
and be attentive to the
words of my mouth.
²⁵ Do not let your hearts turn
aside to her ways;
do not stray into her
paths.
²⁶ for many are those she has
laid low,

7.14
Prov 7.11,16
7.16
Prov 31.22;
Isa 19.9
7.21
Prov 5.3
7.23
Eccl 9.12
7.24
Prov 5.7
7.25
Prov 5.8
7.26
Prov 9.18

7.27
Prov 2.18;
5.5; 9.18
8.1
Prov 1.20;
9.3
8.3
Job 29.7
8.5
Prov 1.4,22,
32
8.6
Prov 22.20;
23.16
8.7
Ps 37.30
8.9
Prov 14.6;
3.13
8.10
Prov 3.14,15
8.11
Job 28.18;
Prov 3.15
8.12
v. 5;
Prov 1.4

and numerous are her
victims.
²⁷ Her house is the way to
Sheol,
going down to the
chambers of death.

The Gifts of Wisdom

8 Does not wisdom call,
and does not
understanding raise her
voice?
² On the heights, beside the
way,
at the crossroads she takes
her stand;
³ beside the gates in front of
the town,
at the entrance of the
portals she cries out:
⁴ "To you, O people, I call,
and my cry is to all that
live.
⁵ O simple ones, learn
prudence;
acquire intelligence, you
who lack it.
⁶ Hear, for I will speak noble
things,
and from my lips will come
what is right;
⁷ for my mouth will utter
truth;
wickedness is an
abomination to my lips.
⁸ All the words of my mouth
are righteous;
there is nothing twisted or
crooked in them.
⁹ They are all straight to one
who understands
and right to those who find
knowledge.
¹⁰ Take my instruction instead
of silver,
and knowledge rather than
choice gold;
¹¹ for wisdom is better than
jewels,
and all that you may desire
cannot compare with
her.
¹² I, wisdom, live with
prudence,[t]

[s] Cn Compare Gk: Meaning of Heb uncertain
[t] Meaning of Heb uncertain

and I attain knowledge and
discretion.

13 The fear of the LORD is
hatred of evil.
Pride and arrogance and the
way of evil
and perverted speech I
hate.

14 I have good advice and
sound wisdom;
I have insight, I have
strength.

15 By me kings reign,
and rulers decree what is
just;

16 by me rulers rule,
and nobles, all who govern
rightly.

17 I love those who love me,
and those who seek me
diligently find me.

18 Riches and honor are with
me,
enduring wealth and
prosperity.

19 My fruit is better than gold,
even fine gold,
and my yield than choice
silver.

20 I walk in the way of
righteousness,
along the paths of justice,

21 endowing with wealth those
who love me,
and filling their treasuries.

Wisdom's Part in Creation

22 The LORD created me at the
beginning[u] of his
work,[v]
the first of his acts of long
ago.

23 Ages ago I was set up,
at the first, before the
beginning of the earth.

24 When there were no depths I
was brought forth,
when there were no springs
abounding with water.

25 Before the mountains had
been shaped,
before the hills, I was
brought forth—

26 when he had not yet made
earth and fields,[w]
or the world's first bits of
soil.

27 When he established the
heavens, I was there,
when he drew a circle on
the face of the deep,

28 when he made firm the skies
above,
when he established the
fountains of the deep,

29 when he assigned to the sea
its limit,
so that the waters might
not transgress his
command,
when he marked out the
foundations of the
earth,

30 then I was beside him, like
a master worker;[x]
and I was daily his[y] delight,
rejoicing before him
always,

31 rejoicing in his inhabited
world
and delighting in the
human race.

32 And now, my children, listen
to me:
happy are those who keep
my ways.

33 Hear instruction and be
wise,
and do not neglect it.

34 Happy is the one who listens
to me,
watching daily at my gates,
waiting beside my doors.

35 For whoever finds me finds
life
and obtains favor from the
LORD;

36 but those who miss me
injure themselves;
all who hate me love
death."

Wisdom's Feast

9 Wisdom has built her house,
she has hewn her seven
pillars.

2 She has slaughtered her
animals, she has mixed
her wine,

8.13
Prov 16.6;
16.18; 15.9;
6.12
8.14
Prov 1.25;
2.7;
Eccl 7.19
8.15
Dan 2.21;
Rom 13.1
8.17
1 Sam 2.30;
Ps 91.14;
Jn 14.21;
Jas 1.5
8.18
Prov 3.16;
Mt 6.33
8.19
Prov 3.14;
10.20
8.21
Prov 24.4
8.22
Prov 3.19
8.23
Jn 17.5
8.25
Ps 90.2

8.27
Prov 3.19;
Job 26.10
8.29
Job 38.10;
Ps 104.9;
Job 38.6
8.30
Jn 1.1-3
8.31
Ps 16.3
8.32
Prov 5.7;
Ps 119.1,2;
Lk 11.28
8.33
Prov 4.1
8.34
Prov 3.13,18
8.35
Prov 4.22;
12.2
8.36
Prov 20.2
9.1
Mt 16.18;
Eph 2.20,
22;
1 Pet 2.5
9.2
Mt 22.4;
Lk 14.16,17

u Or *me as the beginning* v Heb *way*
w Meaning of Heb uncertain x Another
reading is *little child* y Gk: Heb lacks *his*

she has also set her table.

3 She has sent out her servant
girls, she calls
from the highest places in
the town,

4 "You that are simple, turn in
here!"
To those without sense she
says,

5 "Come, eat of my bread
and drink of the wine I
have mixed.

6 Lay aside immaturity, z and
live,
and walk in the way of
insight."

General Maxims

7 Whoever corrects a scoffer
wins abuse;
whoever rebukes the
wicked gets hurt.

8 A scoffer who is rebuked will
only hate you;
the wise, when rebuked,
will love you.

9 Give instruction a to the
wise, and they will
become wiser still;
teach the righteous and
they will gain in
learning.

10 The fear of the LORD is the
beginning of wisdom,
and the knowledge of the
Holy One is insight.

11 For by me your days will be
multiplied,
and years will be added to
your life.

12 If you are wise, you are wise
for yourself;
if you scoff, you alone will
bear it.

Folly's Invitation and Promise

13 The foolish woman is loud;
she is ignorant and knows
nothing.

14 She sits at the door of her
house,
on a seat at the high places
of the town,

15 calling to those who pass by,
who are going straight on
their way,

16 "You who are simple, turn in
here!"
And to those without sense
she says,

17 "Stolen water is sweet,
and bread eaten in secret
is pleasant."

18 But they do not know that
the dead b are there,
that her guests are in the
depths of Sheol.

Wise Sayings of Solomon

10 The proverbs of Solomon.

A wise child makes a glad
father,
but a foolish child is a
mother's grief.

2 Treasures gained by
wickedness do not
profit,
but righteousness delivers
from death.

3 The LORD does not let the
righteous go hungry,
but he thwarts the craving
of the wicked.

4 A slack hand causes poverty,
but the hand of the
diligent makes rich.

5 A child who gathers in
summer is prudent,
but a child who sleeps in
harvest brings shame.

6 Blessings are on the head of
the righteous,
but the mouth of the
wicked conceals
violence.

7 The memory of the righteous
is a blessing,
but the name of the wicked
will rot.

8 The wise of heart will heed
commandments,
but a babbling fool will
come to ruin.

9 Whoever walks in integrity
walks securely,
but whoever follows
perverse ways will be
found out.

9.3
Ps 68.11;
Mt 22.3;
Prov 8.1,2
9.4
Prov 8.5;
6.32
9.5
Song 5.1;
Isa 55.1;
Jn 6.27
9.6
Ezek 11.20;
37.24
9.7
Prov 23.9
9.8
Mt 7.6;
Ps 141.5
9.9
Prov 1.5
9.10
Job 28.28;
Prov 1.7
9.11
Prov 3.16;
10.27
9.12
Prov 19.29
9.13
Prov 7.11;
5.6
9.14
v. 3

9.16
v. 4
9.17
Prov 20.17
9.18
Prov 7.27
10.1
Prov 1.1;
15.20; 29.3,
15
10.2
Ps 49.6;
Prov 11.4;
Lk 12.19,20;
Prov 11.4,6
10.3
Ps 34.9,10;
Mt 6.33;
Ps 112.10
10.4
Prov 12.24;
13.4
10.5
Prov 6.8;
17.2
10.6
Esther 7.8
10.7
Ps 9.5,6;
Eccl 8.10
10.8
Prov 13.3
10.9
Ps 23.4;
Prov 28.18;
Isa 33.15;
Prov 26.26

z Or simpleness a Heb lacks instruction
b Heb shades

10 Whoever winks the eye
 causes trouble,
but the one who rebukes
 boldly makes peace.c
11 The mouth of the righteous
 is a fountain of life,
but the mouth of the
 wicked conceals
 violence.
12 Hatred stirs up strife,
 but love covers all offenses.
13 On the lips of one who has
 understanding wisdom
 is found,
but a rod is for the back of
 one who lacks sense.
14 The wise lay up knowledge,
 but the babbling of a fool
 brings ruin near.
15 The wealth of the rich is
 their fortress;
the poverty of the poor is
 their ruin.
16 The wage of the righteous
 leads to life,
the gain of the wicked to
 sin.
17 Whoever heeds instruction is
 on the path to life,
but one who rejects a
 rebuke goes astray.
18 Lying lips conceal hatred,
 and whoever utters slander
 is a fool.
19 When words are many,
 transgression is not
 lacking,
but the prudent are
 restrained in speech.
20 The tongue of the righteous
 is choice silver;
the mind of the wicked is
 of little worth.
21 The lips of the righteous
 feed many,
but fools die for lack of
 sense.
22 The blessing of the LORD
 makes rich,
and he adds no sorrow with
 it.d
23 Doing wrong is like sport to
 a fool,
but wise conduct is
 pleasure to a person of
 understanding.

10.10
Prov 6.13
10.11
Ps 37.30
10.12
1 Pet 4.8
10.13
Prov 26.3
10.14
Prov 9.9;
18.7
10.15
Job 31.24;
Ps 52.7;
Prov 18.11;
19.7
10.17
Prov 6.23
10.18
Prov 26.24;
Ps 15.3
10.19
Prov 18.21;
Eccl 5.3;
Jas 3.2
10.20
Prov 8.19
10.21
v. 11;
Prov 5.23
10.22
Gen 24.35;
Ps 37.22
10.23
Prov 15.21

10.24
Ps 145.19;
Mt 5.6;
1 Jn 5.14,
15
10.25
Prov 12.7;
Ps 15.5;
Mt 7.24;
16.18
10.26
Prov 26.6
10.27
Prov 9.11;
Ps 55.23
10.29
Ps 28.8;
Prov 21.15
10.30
Ps 37.29
10.31
Ps 37.30;
Prov 17.20
11.1
Lev 19.35;
Deut 25.13-16
11.2
Prov 16.18
11.3
Prov 13.6

24 What the wicked dread will
 come upon them,
but the desire of the
 righteous will be
 granted.
25 When the tempest passes,
 the wicked are no more,
but the righteous are
 established forever.
26 Like vinegar to the teeth,
 and smoke to the eyes,
so are the lazy to their
 employers.
27 The fear of the LORD prolongs
 life,
but the years of the wicked
 will be short.
28 The hope of the righteous
 ends in gladness,
but the expectation of the
 wicked comes to
 nothing.
29 The way of the LORD is a
 stronghold for the
 upright,
but destruction for
 evildoers.
30 The righteous will never be
 removed,
but the wicked will not
 remain in the land.
31 The mouth of the righteous
 brings forth wisdom,
but the perverse tongue
 will be cut off.
32 The lips of the righteous
 know what is
 acceptable,
but the mouth of the
 wicked what is
 perverse.

11 A false balance is an
 abomination to the
 LORD,
but an accurate weight is
 his delight.
2 When pride comes, then
 comes disgrace;
but wisdom is with the
 humble.
3 The integrity of the upright
 guides them,

c Gk: Heb but a babbling fool will come to
ruin d Or and toil adds nothing to it

but the crookedness of the
treacherous destroys
them.
4 Riches do not profit in the
day of wrath,
but righteousness delivers
from death.
5 The righteousness of the
blameless keeps their
ways straight,
but the wicked fall by their
own wickedness.
6 The righteousness of the
upright saves them,
but the treacherous are
taken captive by their
schemes.
7 When the wicked die, their
hope perishes,
and the expectation of the
godless comes to
nothing.
8 The righteous are delivered
from trouble,
and the wicked get into it
instead.
9 With their mouths the
godless would destroy
their neighbors,
but by knowledge the
righteous are delivered.
10 When it goes well with the
righteous, the city
rejoices;
and when the wicked
perish, there is
jubilation.
11 By the blessing of the
upright a city is
exalted,
but it is overthrown by the
mouth of the wicked.
12 Whoever belittles another
lacks sense,
but an intelligent person
remains silent.
13 A gossip goes about telling
secrets,
but one who is trustworthy
in spirit keeps a
confidence.
14 Where there is no guidance,
a nation[e] falls,
but in an abundance of
counselors there is
safety.

11.4
Ezek 7.19;
Zeph 1.18;
Gen 7.1
11.6
Eccl 10.8
11.7
Prov 10.28
11.8
Prov 21.18
11.10
Prov 28.12
11.11
Prov 29.8
11.12
Prov 14.21;
10.19
11.13
Lev 19.16;
Prov 20.19;
1 Tim 5.13;
Prov 19.11
11.14
Prov 15.22;
20.18; 24.6

11.16
Prov 31.30
11.17
Mt 5.7;
25.34-36
11.18
Hos 10.12;
Gal 6.8,9
11.20
Prov 12.22;
Ps 119.1
11.21
Prov 16.5;
Ps 112.2
11.23
Rom 2.8,9
11.24
Prov 13.7;
19.17
11.25
2 Cor 9.6-10;
Mt 5.7
11.26
Am 8.5,6;
Job 29.13

15 To guarantee loans for a
stranger brings trouble,
but there is safety in
refusing to do so.
16 A gracious woman gets honor,
but she who hates virtue is
covered with shame.[f]
The timid become
destitute,[g]
but the aggressive gain
riches.
17 Those who are kind reward
themselves,
but the cruel do
themselves harm.
18 The wicked earn no real
gain,
but those who sow
righteousness get a true
reward.
19 Whoever is steadfast in
righteousness will live,
but whoever pursues evil
will die.
20 Crooked minds are an
abomination to the
LORD,
but those of blameless
ways are his delight.
21 Be assured, the wicked will
not go unpunished,
but those who are
righteous will escape.
22 Like a gold ring in a pig's
snout
is a beautiful woman
without good sense.
23 The desire of the righteous
ends only in good;
the expectation of the
wicked in wrath.
24 Some give freely, yet grow all
the richer;
others withhold what is
due, and only suffer
want.
25 A generous person will be
enriched,
and one who gives water
will get water.
26 The people curse those who
hold back grain,
but a blessing is on the
head of those who sell it.

e Or *an army* f Compare Gk Syr: Heb lacks
but she . . . shame g Gk: Heb lacks *The
timid . . . destitute*

27 Whoever diligently seeks
 good seeks favor,
 but evil comes to the one
 who searches for it.
28 Those who trust in their
 riches will wither, h
 but the righteous will
 flourish like green
 leaves.
29 Those who trouble their
 households will inherit
 wind,
 and the fool will be servant
 to the wise.
30 The fruit of the righteous is
 a tree of life,
 but violence i takes lives
 away.
31 If the righteous are repaid on
 earth,
 how much more the wicked
 and the sinner!

12 Whoever loves discipline
 loves knowledge,
 but those who hate to be
 rebuked are stupid.
2 The good obtain favor from
 the LORD,
 but those who devise evil
 he condemns.
3 No one finds security by
 wickedness,
 but the root of the
 righteous will never be
 moved.
4 A good wife is the crown of
 her husband,
 but she who brings shame
 is like rottenness in his
 bones.
5 The thoughts of the
 righteous are just;
 the advice of the wicked is
 treacherous.
6 The words of the wicked are
 a deadly ambush,
 but the speech of the
 upright delivers them.
7 The wicked are overthrown
 and are no more,
 but the house of the
 righteous will stand.
8 One is commended for good
 sense,
 but a perverse mind is
 despised.

9 Better to be despised and
 have a servant,
 than to be self-important
 and lack food.
10 The righteous know the
 needs of their animals,
 but the mercy of the
 wicked is cruel.
11 Those who till their land will
 have plenty of food,
 but those who follow
 worthless pursuits have
 no sense.
12 The wicked covet the
 proceeds of
 wickedness, i
 but the root of the
 righteous bears fruit.
13 The evil are ensnared by the
 transgression of their
 lips,
 but the righteous escape
 from trouble.
14 From the fruit of the mouth
 one is filled with good
 things,
 and manual labor has its
 reward.
15 Fools think their own way is
 right,
 but the wise listen to
 advice.
16 Fools show their anger at
 once,
 but the prudent ignore an
 insult.
17 Whoever speaks the truth
 gives honest evidence,
 but a false witness speaks
 deceitfully.
18 Rash words are like sword
 thrusts,
 but the tongue of the wise
 brings healing.
19 Truthful lips endure forever,
 but a lying tongue lasts
 only a moment.
20 Deceit is in the mind of
 those who plan evil,
 but those who counsel
 peace have joy.
21 No harm happens to the
 righteous,

h Cn: Heb *fall* i Cn Compare Gk Syr: Heb
a wise man i Or *covet the catch of the
wicked*

but the wicked are filled
with trouble.

²² Lying lips are an
abomination to the
Lord,
but those who act faithfully
are his delight.

²³ One who is clever conceals
knowledge,
but the mind of a fool[k]
broadcasts folly.

²⁴ The hand of the diligent will
rule,
while the lazy will be put
to forced labor.

²⁵ Anxiety weighs down the
human heart,
but a good word cheers it
up.

²⁶ The righteous gives good
advice to friends,[l]
but the way of the wicked
leads astray.

²⁷ The lazy do not roast[m] their
game,
but the diligent obtain
precious wealth.[m]

²⁸ In the path of righteousness
there is life,
in walking its path there is
no death.

13 A wise child loves
discipline,[n]
but a scoffer does not
listen to rebuke.

² From the fruit of their words
good persons eat good
things,
but the desire of the
treacherous is for
wrongdoing.

³ Those who guard their
mouths preserve their
lives;
those who open wide their
lips come to ruin.

⁴ The appetite of the lazy
craves, and gets
nothing,
while the appetite of the
diligent is richly
supplied.

⁵ The righteous hate
falsehood,
but the wicked act
shamefully and
disgracefully.

⁶ Righteousness guards one
whose way is upright,
but sin overthrows the
wicked.

⁷ Some pretend to be rich, yet
have nothing;
others pretend to be poor,
yet have great wealth.

⁸ Wealth is a ransom for a
person's life,
but the poor get no threats.

⁹ The light of the righteous
rejoices,
but the lamp of the wicked
goes out.

¹⁰ By insolence the heedless
make strife,
but wisdom is with those
who take advice.

¹¹ Wealth hastily gotten[o] will
dwindle,
but those who gather little
by little will increase it.

¹² Hope deferred makes the
heart sick,
but a desire fulfilled is a
tree of life.

¹³ Those who despise the word
bring destruction on
themselves,
but those who respect the
commandment will be
rewarded.

¹⁴ The teaching of the wise is a
fountain of life,
so that one may avoid the
snares of death.

¹⁵ Good sense wins favor,
but the way of the faithless
is their ruin.[p]

¹⁶ The clever do all things
intelligently,
but the fool displays folly.

¹⁷ A bad messenger brings
trouble,
but a faithful envoy,
healing.

¹⁸ Poverty and disgrace are for
the one who ignores
instruction,
but one who heeds reproof
is honored.

12.22
Prov 6.17;
11.20;
Rev 22.15
12.23
Prov 13.16;
15.2
12.25
Prov 15.13;
Isa 50.4
12.28
Prov 11.19
13.1
Prov 10.1;
15.12
13.2
Prov 12.14
13.3
Ps 39.1;
Jas 3.2
13.4
Prov 10.4

13.6
Prov 11.3,5
13.7
Prov 11.24;
Lk 12.20,21,
33;
2 Cor 6.10
13.9
Job 18.5;
Prov 24.20
13.10
Prov 11.14
13.11
Prov 10.2;
14.23
13.12
v. 19
13.13
2 Chr 36.16
13.14
Prov 10.11;
Ps 18.5
13.15
Prov 3.4;
21.8
13.16
Prov 12.23;
15.2
13.17
Prov 25.13
13.18
Prov 15.5,
31,32

k Heb *the heart of fools*　l Syr: Meaning of
Heb uncertain　m Meaning of Heb uncertain
n Cn: Heb *A wise child the discipline of his
father*　o Gk Vg: Heb *from vanity*
p Cn Compare Gk Syr Vg Tg: Heb *is enduring*

19 A desire realized is sweet to
　　the soul,
　　but to turn away from evil
　　is an abomination to
　　fools.
20 Whoever walks with the wise
　　becomes wise,
　　but the companion of fools
　　suffers harm.
21 Misfortune pursues sinners,
　　but prosperity rewards the
　　righteous.
22 The good leave an
　　inheritance to their
　　children's children,
　　but the sinner's wealth is
　　laid up for the
　　righteous.
23 The field of the poor may
　　yield much food,
　　but it is swept away
　　through injustice.
24 Those who spare the rod
　　hate their children,
　　but those who love them
　　are diligent to
　　discipline them.
25 The righteous have enough
　　to satisfy their appetite,
　　but the belly of the wicked
　　is empty.

14 The wise woman q builds
　　her house,
　　but the foolish tears it
　　down with her own
　　hands.
2 Those who walk uprightly
　　fear the LORD,
　　but one who is devious in
　　conduct despises him.
3 The talk of fools is a rod for
　　their backs,r
　　but the lips of the wise
　　preserve them.
4 Where there are no oxen,
　　there is no grain;
　　abundant crops come by
　　the strength of the ox.
5 A faithful witness does not
　　lie,
　　but a false witness
　　breathes out lies.
6 A scoffer seeks wisdom in
　　vain,
　　but knowledge is easy for
　　one who understands.
7 Leave the presence of a fool,

13.20
Prov 15.31;
28.19
13.21
Ps 32.10
13.22
Job 27.16,
17;
Prov 28.8;
Eccl 2.26
13.23
Prov 12.11
13.24
Prov 19.18;
22.15; 29.15,
17
13.25
Ps 34.10;
37.3
14.1
Prov 24.3
14.2
Prov 19.1;
Rom 2.4
14.3
Prov 12.6
14.5
Ex 20.16;
Prov 6.19;
12.17
14.6
Prov 24.7;
8.9; 17.24

14.8
Prov 15.21;
v. 24
14.11
Prov 3.33;
12.7; 15.25
14.12
Prov 16.25;
Rom 6.21
14.13
Prov 5.4;
Eccl 2.2
14.14
Prov 1.31;
12.14
14.16
Prov 22.3
14.17
v. 29
14.18
Prov 18.15
14.19
Prov 11.29
14.20
Prov 19.7

　　for there you do not find
　　words of knowledge.
8 It is the wisdom of the clever
　　to understand where
　　they go,
　　but the folly of fools
　　misleads.
9 Fools mock at the guilt
　　offering,s
　　but the upright enjoy God's
　　favor.
10 The heart knows its own
　　bitterness,
　　and no stranger shares its
　　joy.
11 The house of the wicked is
　　destroyed,
　　but the tent of the upright
　　flourishes.
12 There is a way that seems
　　right to a person,
　　but its end is the way to
　　death.t
13 Even in laughter the heart is
　　sad,
　　and the end of joy is grief.
14 The perverse get what their
　　ways deserve,
　　and the good, what their
　　deeds deserve.u
15 The simple believe
　　everything,
　　but the clever consider
　　their steps.
16 The wise are cautious and
　　turn away from evil,
　　but the fool throws off
　　restraint and is careless.
17 One who is quick-tempered
　　acts foolishly,
　　and the schemer is hated.
18 The simple are adorned
　　withv folly,
　　but the clever are crowned
　　with knowledge.
19 The evil bow down before
　　the good,
　　the wicked at the gates of
　　the righteous.
20 The poor are disliked even
　　by their neighbors,
　　but the rich have many
　　friends.

q Heb *Wisdom of women*　r Cn: Heb *a rod
of pride*　s Meaning of Heb uncertain
t Heb *ways of death*　u Cn: Heb *from upon
him*　v Or *inherit*

21 Those who despise their
 neighbors are sinners,
 but happy are those who
 are kind to the poor.
22 Do they not err that plan
 evil?
 Those who plan good find
 loyalty and faithfulness.
23 In all toil there is profit,
 but mere talk leads only to
 poverty.
24 The crown of the wise is
 their wisdom,[w]
 but folly is the garland[x] of
 fools.
25 A truthful witness saves
 lives,
 but one who utters lies is a
 betrayer.
26 In the fear of the LORD one
 has strong confidence,
 and one's children will
 have a refuge.
27 The fear of the LORD is a
 fountain of life,
 so that one may avoid the
 snares of death.
28 The glory of a king is a
 multitude of people;
 without people a prince is
 ruined.
29 Whoever is slow to anger has
 great understanding,
 but one who has a hasty
 temper exalts folly.
30 A tranquil mind gives life to
 the flesh,
 but passion makes the
 bones rot.
31 Those who oppress the poor
 insult their Maker,
 but those who are kind to
 the needy honor him.
32 The wicked are overthrown
 by their evil-doing,
 but the righteous find a
 refuge in their
 integrity.[y]
33 Wisdom is at home in the
 mind of one who has
 understanding,
 but it is not[z] known in the
 heart of fools.
34 Righteousness exalts a
 nation,
 but sin is a reproach to any
 people.

14.21
Prov 11.12;
Ps 41.1
14.25
v. 5
14.26
Prov 19.23;
Isa 33.6
14.27
Prov 13.14
14.29
Prov 16.32;
Jas 1.19;
Prov 29.20
14.30
Prov 12.4
14.31
Prov 17.5;
v. 21
14.32
Job 13.15;
Ps 23.4;
2 Cor 1.9;
2 Tim 4.18
14.33
Prov 2.10;
12.16
14.34
Prov 11.11

14.35
Mt 24.45
15.1
Judg 8.1-3;
1 Sam 25.10-
13
15.2
Prov 12.23;
13.16
15.3
Job 34.21;
Heb 4.13
15.5
Prov 13.1,18
15.8
Isa 1.11;
Jer 6.20;
Mic 6.7
15.9
Prov 21.21;
1 Tim 6.11
15.10
Prov 1.29-32;
5.12
15.11
Job 26.6;
Ps 139.8;
2 Chr 6.30
15.12
Prov 13.1;
Am 5.10

35 A servant who deals wisely
 has the king's favor,
 but his wrath falls on one
 who acts shamefully.

15 A soft answer turns away
 wrath,
 but a harsh word stirs up
 anger.
2 The tongue of the wise
 dispenses knowledge,[a]
 but the mouths of fools
 pour out folly.
3 The eyes of the LORD are in
 every place,
 keeping watch on the evil
 and the good.
4 A gentle tongue is a tree of
 life,
 but perverseness in it
 breaks the spirit.
5 A fool despises a parent's
 instruction,
 but the one who heeds
 admonition is prudent.
6 In the house of the righteous
 there is much treasure,
 but trouble befalls the
 income of the wicked.
7 The lips of the wise spread
 knowledge;
 not so the minds of fools.
8 The sacrifice of the wicked is
 an abomination to the
 LORD,
 but the prayer of the
 upright is his delight.
9 The way of the wicked is an
 abomination to the
 LORD,
 but he loves the one who
 pursues righteousness.
10 There is severe discipline for
 one who forsakes the
 way,
 but one who hates a
 rebuke will die.
11 Sheol and Abaddon lie open
 before the LORD,
 how much more human
 hearts!
12 Scoffers do not like to be
 rebuked;

[w] Cn Compare Gk: Heb *riches* [x] Cn: Heb
is the folly [y] Gk Syr: Heb *in their death*
[z] Gk Syr: Heb lacks *not* [a] Cn: Heb *makes*
knowledge good

13 A glad heart makes a
 cheerful countenance,
 but by sorrow of heart the
 spirit is broken.
14 The mind of one who has
 understanding seeks
 knowledge,
 but the mouths of fools
 feed on folly.
15 All the days of the poor are
 hard,
 but a cheerful heart has a
 continual feast.
16 Better is a little with the fear
 of the LORD
 than great treasure and
 trouble with it.
17 Better is a dinner of
 vegetables where love is
 than a fatted ox and hatred
 with it.
18 Those who are hot-tempered
 stir up strife,
 but those who are slow to
 anger calm contention.
19 The way of the lazy is
 overgrown with thorns,
 but the path of the upright
 is a level highway.
20 A wise child makes a glad
 father,
 but the foolish despise
 their mothers.
21 Folly is a joy to one who has
 no sense,
 but a person of
 understanding walks
 straight ahead.
22 Without counsel, plans go
 wrong,
 but with many advisers
 they succeed.
23 To make an apt answer is a
 joy to anyone,
 and a word in season, how
 good it is!
24 For the wise the path of life
 leads upward,
 in order to avoid Sheol
 below.
25 The LORD tears down the
 house of the proud,
 but maintains the widow's
 boundaries.

26 Evil plans are an
 abomination to the
 LORD,
 but gracious words are
 pure.
27 Those who are greedy for
 unjust gain make
 trouble for their
 households,
 but those who hate bribes
 will live.
28 The mind of the righteous
 ponders how to answer,
 but the mouth of the
 wicked pours out evil.
29 The LORD is far from the
 wicked,
 but he hears the prayer of
 the righteous.
30 The light of the eyes rejoices
 the heart,
 and good news refreshes
 the body.
31 The ear that heeds
 wholesome admonition
 will lodge among the wise.
32 Those who ignore instruction
 despise themselves,
 but those who heed
 admonition gain
 understanding.
33 The fear of the LORD is
 instruction in wisdom,
 and humility goes before
 honor.

16 The plans of the mind
 belong to mortals,
 but the answer of the
 tongue is from the
 LORD.
2 All one's ways may be pure
 in one's own eyes,
 but the LORD weighs the
 spirit.
3 Commit your work to the
 LORD,
 and your plans will be
 established.
4 The LORD has made
 everything for its
 purpose,
 even the wicked for the day
 of trouble.
5 All those who are arrogant
 are an abomination to
 the LORD;

15.13
Prov 17.22;
12.25
15.15
v. 13
15.16
Ps 37.16;
Prov 16.8;
1 Tim 6.6
15.17
Prov 17.1
15.18
Prov 26.21;
29.22; 14.29
15.19
Prov 22.5
15.20
Prov 10.1;
30.17
15.21
Prov 10.23;
Eph 5.15
15.22
Prov 11.14;
20.18
15.23
Prov 25.11
15.24
Prov 4.18
15.25
Prov 12.7;
Ps 68.5,6

15.26
Prov 6.16-19;
16.24
15.27
Prov 28.25;
1 Tim 6.10;
Isa 33.15
15.28
1 Pet 3.15
15.29
Ps 34.16;
145.18
15.31
v. 5
15.32
Prov 1.7;
8.36; 15.5
15.33
Prov 1.7;
18.12
16.1
Prov 19.21
16.2
Prov 21.2
16.3
Ps 37.5
16.4
Isa 43.7;
Job 21.30
16.5
Prov 6.17;
11.21

be assured, they will not go
unpunished.

6 By loyalty and faithfulness
iniquity is atoned for,
and by the fear of the LORD
one avoids evil.
7 When the ways of people
please the LORD,
he causes even their
enemies to be at peace
with them.
8 Better is a little with
righteousness
than large income with
injustice.
9 The human mind plans the
way,
but the LORD directs the
steps.
10 Inspired decisions are on the
lips of a king;
his mouth does not sin in
judgment.
11 Honest balances and scales
are the LORD's;
all the weights in the bag
are his work.
12 It is an abomination to kings
to do evil,
for the throne is
established by
righteousness.
13 Righteous lips are the delight
of a king,
and he loves those who
speak what is right.
14 A king's wrath is a
messenger of death,
and whoever is wise will
appease it.
15 In the light of a king's face
there is life,
and his favor is like the
clouds that bring the
spring rain.
16 How much better to get
wisdom than gold!
To get understanding is to
be chosen rather than
silver.
17 The highway of the upright
avoids evil;
those who guard their way
preserve their lives.
18 Pride goes before
destruction,

16.6
Dan 4.27;
Prov 14.16
16.7
2 Chr 17.10
16.9
Ps 37.23;
Prov 20.24;
Jer 10.23
16.11
Prov 11.1
16.12
Prov 25.5
16.13
Prov 14.35
16.14
Prov 19.12
16.15
Job 29.23
16.16
Prov 8.10,19
16.18
Prov 11.2

16.20
Ps 2.12;
34.8;
Jer 17.7
16.22
Prov 13.14;
7.22
16.23
Prov 37.30
16.25
Prov 14.12
16.27
Prov 6.12,
14,18;
Jas 3.6
16.28
Prov 15.18;
17.9
16.29
Prov 1.10
16.31
Prov 20.29
16.32
Prov 19.11

and a haughty spirit before
a fall.
19 It is better to be of a lowly
spirit among the poor
than to divide the spoil
with the proud.
20 Those who are attentive to a
matter will prosper,
and happy are those who
trust in the LORD.
21 The wise of heart is called
perceptive,
and pleasant speech
increases
persuasiveness.
22 Wisdom is a fountain of life
to one who has it,
but folly is the punishment
of fools.
23 The mind of the wise makes
their speech judicious,
and adds persuasiveness to
their lips.
24 Pleasant words are like a
honeycomb,
sweetness to the soul and
health to the body.
25 Sometimes there is a way
that seems to be right,
but in the end it is the way
to death.
26 The appetite of workers
works for them;
their hunger urges them
on.
27 Scoundrels concoct evil,
and their speech is like a
scorching fire.
28 A perverse person spreads
strife,
and a whisperer separates
close friends.
29 The violent entice their
neighbors,
and lead them in a way
that is not good.
30 One who winks the eyes
plans[b] perverse things;
one who compresses the
lips brings evil to pass.
31 Gray hair is a crown of glory;
it is gained in a righteous
life.
32 One who is slow to anger is
better than the mighty,

[b] Gk Syr Vg Tg: Heb *to plan*

and one whose temper is
controlled than one
who captures a city.
33 The lot is cast into the lap,
but the decision is the
Lord's alone.

17

Better is a dry morsel
with quiet
than a house full of
feasting with strife.
2 A slave who deals wisely will
rule over a child who
acts shamefully,
and will share the
inheritance as one of
the family.
3 The crucible is for silver, and
the furnace is for gold,
but the Lord tests the
heart.
4 An evildoer listens to wicked
lips;
and a liar gives heed to a
mischievous tongue.
5 Those who mock the poor
insult their Maker;
those who are glad at
calamity will not go
unpunished.
6 Grandchildren are the crown
of the aged,
and the glory of children is
their parents.
7 Fine speech is not becoming
to a fool;
still less is false speech to
a ruler. c
8 A bribe is like a magic stone
in the eyes of those
who give it;
wherever they turn they
prosper.
9 One who forgives an affront
fosters friendship,
but one who dwells on
disputes will alienate a
friend.
10 A rebuke strikes deeper into
a discerning person
than a hundred blows into
a fool.
11 Evil people seek only
rebellion,
but a cruel messenger will
be sent against them.
12 Better to meet a she-bear
robbed of its cubs

17.1
Prov 15.17
17.2
Prov 10.5
17.3
Prov 27.21;
Ps 26.2
17.5
Prov 14.31;
Job 31.29
17.6
Prov 13.22
17.8
Prov 21.14;
Isa 1.23;
Am 5.12
17.9
Prov 10.12;
Jas 5.20;
1 Pet 4.8;
Prov 16.28
17.12
Hos 13.8

17.13
Ps 109.4,5;
Jer 18.20
17.14
Prov 20.3
17.15
Ex 23.7;
Isa 5.23
17.17
Ruth 1.16;
Prov 18.24
17.18
Prov 6.1
17.19
Prov 29.22;
16.18
17.20
Jas 3.8
17.21
Prov 10.1;
19.13
17.22
Prov 15.13;
Ps 22.15
17.23
Ex 23.8
17.24
Eccl 2.14
17.25
Prov 10.1

than to confront a fool
immersed in folly.
13 Evil will not depart from the
house
of one who returns evil for
good.
14 The beginning of strife is like
letting out water;
so stop before the quarrel
breaks out.
15 One who justifies the wicked
and one who condemns
the righteous
are both alike an
abomination to the
Lord.
16 Why should fools have a
price in hand
to buy wisdom, when they
have no mind to learn?
17 A friend loves at all times,
and kinsfolk are born to
share adversity.
18 It is senseless to give a
pledge,
to become surety for a
neighbor.
19 One who loves transgression
loves strife;
one who builds a high
threshold invites broken
bones.
20 The crooked of mind do not
prosper,
and the perverse of tongue
fall into calamity.
21 The one who begets a fool
gets trouble;
the parent of a fool has no
joy.
22 A cheerful heart is a good
medicine,
but a downcast spirit dries
up the bones.
23 The wicked accept a
concealed bribe
to pervert the ways of
justice.
24 The discerning person looks
to wisdom,
but the eyes of a fool to
the ends of the earth.
25 Foolish children are a grief
to their father

c Or a noble person

and bitterness to her who
bore them.
26 To impose a fine on the
innocent is not right,
or to flog the noble for
their integrity.
27 One who spares words is
knowledgeable;
one who is cool in spirit
has understanding.
28 Even fools who keep silent
are considered wise;
when they close their lips,
they are deemed
intelligent.

18 The one who lives alone
is self-indulgent,
showing contempt for all
who have sound
judgment. d
2 A fool takes no pleasure in
understanding,
but only in expressing
personal opinion.
3 When wickedness comes,
contempt comes also;
and with dishonor comes
disgrace.
4 The words of the mouth are
deep waters;
the fountain of wisdom is a
gushing stream.
5 It is not right to be partial to
the guilty,
or to subvert the innocent
in judgment.
6 A fool's lips bring strife,
and a fool's mouth invites
a flogging.
7 The mouths of fools are their
ruin,
and their lips a snare to
themselves.
8 The words of a whisperer are
like delicious morsels;
they go down into the
inner parts of the body.
9 One who is slack in work
is close kin to a vandal.
10 The name of the LORD is a
strong tower;
the righteous run into it
and are safe.
11 The wealth of the rich is
their strong city;
in their imagination it is
like a high wall.

17.26
Prov 18.5
17.27
Jas 1.19
17.28
Job 13.5
18.2
Prov 12.23
18.4
Prov 20.5;
10.11
18.5
Lev 19.15;
Deut 1.17;
Prov 24.23
18.7
Prov 10.14;
Eccl 10.12
18.8
Prov 26.22
18.9
Prov 28.24
18.10
2 Sam 22.3;
Ps 18.2
18.11
Prov 10.15

18.12
Prov 11.2
18.13
Jn 7.51
18.16
Gen 32.20;
1 Sam 25.27
18.18
Prov 16.33
18.20
Prov 12.14
18.21
Mt 12.37
18.22
Prov 19.14;
8.35
18.23
Jas 2.3
18.24
Prov 17.17
19.1
Prov 28.6

12 Before destruction one's
heart is haughty,
but humility goes before
honor.
13 If one gives answer before
hearing,
it is folly and shame.
14 The human spirit will endure
sickness;
but a broken spirit—who
can bear?
15 An intelligent mind acquires
knowledge,
and the ear of the wise
seeks knowledge.
16 A gift opens doors;
it gives access to the great.
17 The one who first states a
case seems right,
until the other comes and
cross-examines.
18 Casting the lot puts an end
to disputes
and decides between
powerful contenders.
19 An ally offended is stronger
than a city; e
such quarreling is like the
bars of a castle.
20 From the fruit of the mouth
one's stomach is
satisfied;
the yield of the lips brings
satisfaction.
21 Death and life are in the
power of the tongue,
and those who love it will
eat its fruits.
22 He who finds a wife finds a
good thing,
and obtains favor from the
LORD.
23 The poor use entreaties,
but the rich answer
roughly.
24 Some f friends play at
friendship g
but a true friend sticks
closer than one's
nearest kin.

19 Better the poor walking in
integrity

d Meaning of Heb uncertain e Gk Syr Vg
Tg: Meaning of Heb uncertain f Syr Tg: Heb
A man of g Cn Compare Syr Vg Tg:
Meaning of Heb uncertain

than one perverse of
 speech who is a fool.
2 Desire without knowledge is
 not good,
 and one who moves too
 hurriedly misses the
 way.
3 One's own folly leads to
 ruin,
 yet the heart rages against
 the LORD.
4 Wealth brings many friends,
 but the poor are left
 friendless.
5 A false witness will not go
 unpunished,
 and a liar will not escape.
6 Many seek the favor of the
 generous,
 and everyone is a friend to
 a giver of gifts.
7 If the poor are hated even by
 their kin,
 how much more are they
 shunned by their
 friends!
When they call after them,
 they are not there.[h]
8 To get wisdom is to love
 oneself;
 to keep understanding is to
 prosper.
9 A false witness will not go
 unpunished,
 and the liar will perish.
10 It is not fitting for a fool to
 live in luxury,
 much less for a slave to
 rule over princes.
11 Those with good sense are
 slow to anger,
 and it is their glory to
 overlook an offense.
12 A king's anger is like the
 growling of a lion,
 but his favor is like dew on
 the grass.
13 A stupid child is ruin to a
 father,
 and a wife's quarreling is a
 continual dripping of
 rain.
14 House and wealth are
 inherited from parents,
 but a prudent wife is from
 the LORD.

19.3
Prov 11.3;
Ps 37.7
19.4
Prov 14.20
19.5
Ex 23.1;
Prov 6.19
19.6
Prov 29.26;
17.8
19.7
v. 4;
Ps 38.11
19.8
Prov 16.20
19.9
v. 5
19.10
Eccl 10.6,7
19.11
Jas 1.19;
Prov 16.32
19.12
Prov 16.14;
Hos 14.5
19.13
Prov 10.1;
21.9
19.14
2 Cor 12.14;
Prov 18.22

19.15
Prov 6.9;
10.4
19.16
Lk 10.28
19.17
Eccl 11.1;
Mt 10.42;
2 Cor 9.6-8;
Heb 6.10
19.18
Prov 13.24
19.20
Prov 8.33
19.21
Prov 16.1,9;
Ps 33.10,11
19.23
1 Tim 4.8;
Ps 25.13;
Prov 12.21
19.24
Prov 26.15
19.25
Prov 21.11;
9.8
19.26
Prov 28.24;
17.2

15 Laziness brings on deep
 sleep;
 an idle person will suffer
 hunger.
16 Those who keep the
 commandment will live;
 those who are heedless of
 their ways will die.
17 Whoever is kind to the poor
 lends to the LORD,
 and will be repaid in full.
18 Discipline your children
 while there is hope;
 do not set your heart on
 their destruction.
19 A violent tempered person
 will pay the penalty;
 if you effect a rescue, you
 will only have to do it
 again.[h]
20 Listen to advice and accept
 instruction,
 that you may gain wisdom
 for the future.
21 The human mind may devise
 many plans,
 but it is the purpose of the
 LORD that will be
 established.
22 What is desirable in a person
 is loyalty,
 and it is better to be poor
 than a liar.
23 The fear of the LORD is life
 indeed;
 filled with it one rests
 secure
 and suffers no harm.
24 The lazy person buries a
 hand in the dish,
 and will not even bring it
 back to the mouth.
25 Strike a scoffer, and the
 simple will learn
 prudence;
 reprove the intelligent, and
 they will gain
 knowledge.
26 Those who do violence to
 their father and chase
 away their mother
 are children who cause
 shame and bring
 reproach.

[h] Meaning of Heb uncertain

27 Cease straying, my child,
from the words of
knowledge,
in order that you may hear
instruction.
28 A worthless witness mocks at
justice,
and the mouth of the
wicked devours iniquity.
29 Condemnation is ready for
scoffers,
and flogging for the backs
of fools.

20 Wine is a mocker, strong
drink a brawler,
and whoever is led astray
by it is not wise.
2 The dread anger of a king is
like the growling of a
lion;
anyone who provokes him
to anger forfeits life
itself.
3 It is honorable to refrain
from strife,
but every fool is quick to
quarrel.
4 The lazy person does not
plow in season;
harvest comes, and there is
nothing to be found.
5 The purposes in the human
mind are like deep
water,
but the intelligent will
draw them out.
6 Many proclaim themselves
loyal,
but who can find one
worthy of trust?
7 The righteous walk in
integrity—
happy are the children who
follow them!
8 A king who sits on the
throne of judgment
winnows all evil with his
eyes.
9 Who can say, "I have made
my heart clean;
I am pure from my
sin"?
10 Diverse weights and diverse
measures
are both alike an
abomination to the
LORD.

19.28
Job 15.16
19.29
Prov 10.13;
26.3
20.1
Gen 9.21;
Isa 5.22
20.2
Prov 19.12;
8.36;
1 Kings 2.23
20.3
Prov 17.14
20.4
Prov 10.4;
19.15,24
20.5
Prov 18.4
20.6
Prov 25.14;
Mt 6.2;
Lk 18.11;
Ps 12.1;
Lk 18.8
20.7
2 Cor 1.12;
Ps 37.26
20.8
v. 26
20.9
1 Kings 8.46;
1 Jn 1.8
20.10
Deut 25.13;
v. 23

20.11
Mt 7.16
20.12
Ex 4.11
20.13
Prov 6.9,10;
Rom 12.11
20.16
Prov 27.13
20.17
Prov 9.17
20.18
Prov 15.22;
24.6;
Lk 14.31
20.19
Prov 11.13;
Rom 16.18
20.20
Mt 15.4;
Job 18.5
20.21
Prov 28.20
20.22
Rom 12.17;
1 Pet 3.9;
Ps 27.14
20.24
Ps 37.23;
Prov 16.9;
Jer 10.23

11 Even children make
themselves known by
their acts,
by whether what they do is
pure and right.
12 The hearing ear and the
seeing eye—
the LORD has made them
both.
13 Do not love sleep, or else
you will come to
poverty;
open your eyes, and you
will have plenty of
bread.
14 "Bad, bad," says the buyer,
then goes away and boasts.
15 There is gold, and
abundance of costly
stones;
but the lips informed by
knowledge are a
precious jewel.
16 Take the garment of one who
has given surety for a
stranger;
seize the pledge given as
surety for foreigners.
17 Bread gained by deceit is
sweet,
but afterward the mouth
will be full of gravel.
18 Plans are established by
taking advice;
wage war by following wise
guidance.
19 A gossip reveals secrets;
therefore do not associate
with a babbler.
20 If you curse father or
mother,
your lamp will go out in
utter darkness.
21 An estate quickly acquired in
the beginning
will not be blessed in the
end.
22 Do not say, "I will repay
evil";
wait for the LORD, and he
will help you.
23 Differing weights are an
abomination to the LORD,
and false scales are not
good.
24 All our steps are ordered by
the LORD;

how then can we
understand our own
ways?

25 It is a snare for one to say
rashly, "It is holy,"
and begin to reflect only
after making a vow.

26 A wise king winnows the
wicked,
and drives the wheel over
them.

27 The human spirit is the lamp
of the LORD,
searching every innermost
part.

28 Loyalty and faithfulness
preserve the king,
and his throne is upheld by
righteousness.[i]

29 The glory of youths is their
strength,
but the beauty of the aged
is their gray hair.

30 Blows that wound cleanse
away evil;
beatings make clean the
innermost parts.

21

The king's heart is a
stream of water in the
hand of the LORD;
he turns it wherever he
will.

2 All deeds are right in the
sight of the doer,
but the LORD weighs the
heart.

3 To do righteousness and
justice
is more acceptable to the
LORD than sacrifice.

4 Haughty eyes and a proud
heart—
the lamp of the
wicked—are sin.

5 The plans of the diligent
lead surely to
abundance,
but everyone who is hasty
comes only to want.

6 The getting of treasures by a
lying tongue
is a fleeting vapor and a
snare[j] of death.

7 The violence of the wicked
will sweep them away,
because they refuse to do
what is just.

8 The way of the guilty is
crooked,
but the conduct of the
pure is right.

9 It is better to live in a corner
of the housetop
than in a house shared
with a contentious wife.

10 The souls of the wicked
desire evil;
their neighbors find no
mercy in their eyes.

11 When a scoffer is punished,
the simple become
wiser;
when the wise are
instructed, they
increase in knowledge.

12 The Righteous One observes
the house of the
wicked;
he casts the wicked down
to ruin.

13 If you close your ear to the
cry of the poor,
you will cry out and not be
heard.

14 A gift in secret averts anger;
and a concealed bribe in
the bosom, strong
wrath.

15 When justice is done, it is a
joy to the righteous,
but dismay to evildoers.

16 Whoever wanders from the
way of understanding
will rest in the assembly of
the dead.

17 Whoever loves pleasure will
suffer want;
whoever loves wine and oil
will not be rich.

18 The wicked is a ransom for
the righteous,
and the faithless for the
upright.

19 It is better to live in a desert
land
than with a contentious
and fretful wife.

20 Precious treasure remains[k]
in the house of the
wise,
but the fool devours it.

20.25 Eccl 5.4,5
20.26 v. 8
20.27 1 Cor 2.11
20.28 Prov 29.14
20.29 Prov 16.31
21.2 Prov 16.2; 24.12; Lk 16.15
21.3 1 Sam 15.22; Prov 15.8; Isa 1.11-17; Hos 6.6; Mic 6.7,8
21.4 Prov 6.17
21.5 Prov 10.4; 28.22
21.6 2 Pet 2.3
21.7 Prov 10.25
21.9 Prov 25.24
21.10 Prov 2.14; 14.21
21.11 Prov 19.25
21.12 Prov 14.11
21.13 Mt 18.30-34; 1 Jn 3.17; Jas 2.13
21.14 Prov 18.16; 19.6
21.16 Ps 49.14
21.18 Prov 11.8
21.19 v. 9
21.20 Prov 22.4; Job 20.15, 18

i Gk: Heb *loyalty*　　j Gk: Heb *seekers*
k Gk: Heb *and oil*

21 Whoever pursues
　　righteousness and
　　kindness
　will find life[1] and honor.
22 One wise person went up
　　against a city of
　　warriors
　and brought down the
　　stronghold in which
　　they trusted.
23 To watch over mouth and
　　tongue
　is to keep out of trouble.
24 The proud, haughty person,
　　named "Scoffer,"
　acts with arrogant pride.
25 The craving of the lazy
　　person is fatal,
　for lazy hands refuse to
　　labor.
26 All day long the wicked
　　covet,[m]
　but the righteous give and
　　do not hold back.
27 The sacrifice of the wicked is
　　an abomination;
　how much more when
　　brought with evil intent.
28 A false witness will perish,
　but a good listener will
　　testify successfully.
29 The wicked put on a bold
　　face,
　but the upright give
　　thought to[n] their ways.
30 No wisdom, no
　　understanding, no
　　counsel,
　can avail against the LORD.
31 The horse is made ready for
　　the day of battle,
　but the victory belongs to
　　the LORD.

22 A good name is to be
　　chosen rather than
　　great riches,
　and favor is better than
　　silver or gold.
2 The rich and the poor have
　　this in common:
　the LORD is the maker of
　　them all.
3 The clever see danger and
　　hide;
　but the simple go on, and
　　suffer for it.

4 The reward for humility and
　　fear of the LORD
　is riches and honor and
　　life.
5 Thorns and snares are in the
　　way of the perverse;
　the cautious will keep far
　　from them.
6 Train children in the right
　　way,
　and when old, they will not
　　stray.
7 The rich rules over the poor,
　and the borrower is the
　　slave of the lender.
8 Whoever sows injustice will
　　reap calamity,
　and the rod of anger will
　　fail.
9 Those who are generous are
　　blessed,
　for they share their bread
　　with the poor.
10 Drive out a scoffer, and strife
　　goes out;
　quarreling and abuse will
　　cease.
11 Those who love a pure heart
　　and are gracious in
　　speech
　will have the king as a
　　friend.
12 The eyes of the LORD keep
　　watch over knowledge,
　but he overthrows the
　　words of the faithless.
13 The lazy person says, "There
　　is a lion outside!
　I shall be killed in the
　　streets!"
14 The mouth of a loose[o]
　　woman is a deep pit;
　he with whom the LORD is
　　angry falls into it.
15 Folly is bound up in the
　　heart of a boy,
　but the rod of discipline
　　drives it far away.
16 Oppressing the poor in order
　　to enrich oneself,
　and giving to the rich, will
　　lead only to loss.

21.21
Mt 5.6
21.22
Eccl 9.15,16
21.23
Prov 12.13;
Jas 3.2
21.24
Ps 1.1;
Prov 1.22;
Isa 16.6;
Jer 48.29
21.25
Prov 13.4;
20.4
21.26
Ps 37.26;
Mt 5.42;
Eph 4.28
21.27
Isa 66.3;
Jer 6.20;
Am 5.22
21.28
Prov 19.5,9
21.29
Eccl 8.1
21.30
Isa 8.9,10;
Jer 9.23;
Acts 5.39
21.31
Isa 31.1;
Ps 3.8;
1 Cor 15.28
22.1
Eccl 7.1
22.3
Prov 14.16;
27.12

22.5
Prov 15.19
22.6
Eph 6.4
22.7
Prov 18.23;
Jas 2.6
22.8
Prov 24.16;
Ps 125.3
22.9
2 Cor 9.6
22.10
Prov 18.6;
26.20
22.11
Mt 5.8;
Prov 16.13
22.12
Prov 21.12
22.13
Prov 26.13
22.14
Prov 2.16;
5.3; 23.27;
Eccl 7.26
22.15
Prov 13.24;
23.14

[1] Gk: Heb *life and righteousness*
[m] Gk: Heb *all day long one covets covetously*
[n] Another reading is *establish*
[o] Heb *strange*

Sayings of the Wise

17 The words of the wise:

Incline your ear and hear my
words, p
and apply your mind to my
teaching;
18 for it will be pleasant if you
keep them within you,
if all of them are ready on
your lips.
19 So that your trust may be in
the LORD,
I have made them known
to you today—yes, to
you.
20 Have I not written for you
thirty sayings
of admonition and
knowledge,
21 to show you what is right
and true,
so that you may give a true
answer to those who
sent you?

22 Do not rob the poor because
they are poor,
or crush the afflicted at the
gate;
23 for the LORD pleads their
cause
and despoils of life those
who despoil them.
24 Make no friends with those
given to anger,
and do not associate with
hotheads,
25 or you may learn their ways
and entangle yourself in a
snare.
26 Do not be one of those who
give pledges,
who become surety for
debts.
27 If you have nothing with
which to pay,
why should your bed be
taken from under you?
28 Do not remove the ancient
landmark
that your ancestors set
up.
29 Do you see those who are
skillful in their work?
they will serve kings;

22.17
Prov 5.1;
23.12
22.18
Prov 2.10
22.19
Prov 3.5
22.20
Prov 8.6,10
22.21
Lk 1.3,4
22.22
Zech 7.10;
Mal 3.5
22.23
1 Sam 25.39;
Ps 12.5;
35.10;
Prov 23.11
22.26
Prov 11.15
22.28
Prov 23.10
22.29
Rom 12.11;
1 Kings 10.8

23.2
v. 20
23.3
v. 6;
Ps 141.4
23.4
Prov 28.20;
1 Tim 6.9,
10;
Rom 12.16
23.5
Prov 27.24
23.6
Ps 141.4
23.7
Prov 26.24,
25
23.9
Mt 7.6;
Prov 1.7
23.10
Prov 22.28;
Jer 22.3;
Zech 7.10
23.11
Prov 22.23
23.12
Prov 22.17
23.13
Prov 13.24;
19.18; 22.15

they will not serve common
people.

23 When you sit down to eat
with a ruler,
observe carefully what q is
before you,
2 and put a knife to your
throat
if you have a big appetite.
3 Do not desire the ruler's r
delicacies,
for they are deceptive food.
4 Do not wear yourself out to
get rich;
be wise enough to desist.
5 When your eyes light upon
it, it is gone;
for suddenly it takes wings
to itself,
flying like an eagle toward
heaven.
6 Do not eat the bread of the
stingy;
do not desire their
delicacies;
7 for like a hair in the throat,
so are they. s
"Eat and drink!" they say
to you;
but they do not mean it.
8 You will vomit up the little
you have eaten,
and you will waste your
pleasant words.
9 Do not speak in the hearing
of a fool,
who will only despise the
wisdom of your words.
10 Do not remove an ancient
landmark
or encroach on the fields of
orphans,
11 for their redeemer is strong;
he will plead their cause
against you.
12 Apply your mind to
instruction
and your ear to words of
knowledge.
13 Do not withhold discipline
from your children;
if you beat them with a
rod, they will not die.

p Cn Compare Gk: Heb *Incline your ear, and
hear the words of the wise*　q Or *who*
r Heb *his*　s Meaning of Heb uncertain

14 If you beat them with the
 rod,
 you will save their lives
 from Sheol.
15 My child, if your heart is
 wise,
 my heart too will be glad.
16 My soul will rejoice
 when your lips speak what
 is right.
17 Do not let your heart envy
 sinners,
 but always continue in the
 fear of the LORD.
18 Surely there is a future,
 and your hope will not be
 cut off.

19 Hear, my child, and be wise,
 and direct your mind in the
 way.
20 Do not be among
 winebibbers,
 or among gluttonous eaters
 of meat;
21 for the drunkard and the
 glutton will come to
 poverty,
 and drowsiness will clothe
 them with rags.

22 Listen to your father who
 begot you,
 and do not despise your
 mother when she is old.
23 Buy truth, and do not sell it;
 buy wisdom, instruction,
 and understanding.
24 The father of the righteous
 will greatly rejoice;
 he who begets a wise son
 will be glad in him.
25 Let your father and mother
 be glad;
 let her who bore you
 rejoice.

26 My child, give me your heart,
 and let your eyes observe[t]
 my ways.
27 For a prostitute is a deep pit;
 an adulteress[u] is a narrow
 well.
28 She lies in wait like a robber
 and increases the number
 of the faithless.

29 Who has woe? Who has
 sorrow?
 Who has strife? Who has
 complaining?
 Who has wounds without
 cause?
 Who has redness of eyes?
30 Those who linger late over
 wine,
 those who keep trying
 mixed wines.
31 Do not look at wine when it
 is red,
 when it sparkles in the cup
 and goes down smoothly.
32 At the last it bites like a
 serpent,
 and stings like an adder.
33 Your eyes will see strange
 things,
 and your mind utter
 perverse things.
34 You will be like one who lies
 down in the midst of
 the sea,
 like one who lies on the
 top of a mast.[v]
35 "They struck me," you will
 say,[w] "but I was not
 hurt;
 they beat me, but I did not
 feel it.
 When shall I awake?
 I will seek another drink."

24 Do not envy the wicked,
 nor desire to be with
 them;
2 for their minds devise
 violence,
 and their lips talk of
 mischief.

3 By wisdom a house is built,
 and by understanding it is
 established;
4 by knowledge the rooms are
 filled
 with all precious and
 pleasant riches.
5 Wise warriors are mightier
 than strong ones,[x]

23.16
vv. 24,25;
Prov 27.11
23.17
Ps 37.1;
Prov 28.14
23.20
Isa 5.22;
Mt 24.49;
Lk 21.34;
Rom 13.13;
Eph 5.18
23.21
Prov 21.17;
6.10,11
23.22
Prov 1.8;
30.17;
Eph 6.1
23.23
Prov 4.5,7;
Mt 13.44
23.24
Prov 10.1;
15.20
23.26
Prov 3.1;
4.4; Ps 1.2
23.27
Prov 22.14
23.28
Prov 7.12;
Eccl 7.26

23.29
Isa 5.11,22
23.30
Eph 5.18;
Ps 75.8
23.33
Prov 2.12
23.35
Jer 5.3
24.1
Ps 37.1;
73.3;
Prov 3.31
24.2
Jer 22.17;
Job 15.35
24.3
Prov 9.1
24.5
Prov 21.22

[t]Another reading is *delight in* [u]Heb *an
alien woman* [v]Meaning of Heb uncertain
[w]Gk Syr Vg Tg: Heb lacks *you will say*
[x]Gk Compare Syr Tg: Heb *A wise man is
strength*

and those who have
knowledge than those
who have strength;
6 for by wise guidance you can
wage your war,
and in abundance of
counselors there is
victory.
7 Wisdom is too high for
fools;
in the gate they do not
open their mouths.

8 Whoever plans to do evil
will be called a
mischief-maker.
9 The devising of folly is sin,
and the scoffer is an
abomination to all.

10 If you faint in the day of
adversity,
your strength being small;
11 if you hold back from
rescuing those taken
away to death,
those who go staggering to
the slaughter;
12 if you say, "Look, we did not
know this" —
does not he who weighs
the heart perceive it?
Does not he who keeps
watch over your soul
know it?
And will he not repay all
according to their
deeds?

13 My child, eat honey, for it is
good,
and the drippings of the
honeycomb are sweet to
your taste.
14 Know that wisdom is such to
your soul;
if you find it, you will find
a future,
and your hope will not be
cut off.

15 Do not lie in wait like an
outlaw against the
home of the righteous;
do no violence to the place
where the righteous
live;

24.6
Lk 14.31
24.7
Ps 10.5
24.8
Prov 6.14;
Rom 1.30
24.10
Jer 51.46;
Heb 12.3
24.11
Ps 82.4;
Isa 58.6,7
24.12
Prov 21.2;
Eccl 5.8;
Ps 121.3-8;
94.9-11;
Prov 12.14
24.13
Song 5.1
24.14
Prov 2.10
24.15
Ps 10.9,10

24.16
Ps 34.19;
Mic 7.8;
v. 22
24.17
Job 31.29;
Ob 12
24.19
Ps 37.1
24.20
Prov 13.9
24.21
Rom 13.1-7;
1 Pet 2.17
24.23
Prov 1.6;
18.5;
Lev 19.15;
Deut 1.17
24.24
Prov 17.15
24.25
Prov 28.23

16 for though they fall seven
times, they will rise
again;
but the wicked are
overthrown by calamity.

17 Do not rejoice when your
enemies fall,
and do not let your heart
be glad when they
stumble,
18 or else the LORD will see it
and be displeased,
and turn away his anger
from them.

19 Do not fret because of
evildoers.
Do not envy the wicked;
20 for the evil have no future;
the lamp of the wicked will
go out.

21 My child, fear the LORD and
the king,
and do not disobey either
of them;*y*
22 for disaster comes from them
suddenly,
and who knows the ruin
that both can bring?

Further Sayings of the Wise
23 These also are sayings of
the wise:

Partiality in judging is not
good.
24 Whoever says to the wicked,
"You are innocent,"
will be cursed by peoples,
abhorred by nations;
25 but those who rebuke the
wicked will have
delight,
and a good blessing will
come upon them.
26 One who gives an honest
answer
gives a kiss on the lips.

27 Prepare your work outside,
get everything ready for you
in the field;

y Gk: Heb *do not associate with those who
change*

and after that build your
house.

28 Do not be a witness against
your neighbor without
cause,
and do not deceive with
your lips.
29 Do not say, "I will do to
others as they have
done to me;
I will pay them back for
what they have done."

30 I passed by the field of one
who was lazy,
by the vineyard of a stupid
person;
31 and see, it was all overgrown
with thorns;
the ground was covered
with nettles,
and its stone wall was
broken down.
32 Then I saw and considered
it;
I looked and received
instruction.
33 A little sleep, a little
slumber,
a little folding of the hands
to rest,
34 and poverty will come upon
you like a robber,
and want, like an armed
warrior.

Further Wise Sayings of Solomon

25 These are other proverbs of
Solomon that the officials
of King Hezekiah of Judah copied.

2 It is the glory of God to
conceal things,
but the glory of kings is to
search things out.
3 Like the heavens for height,
like the earth for depth,
so the mind of kings is
unsearchable.
4 Take away the dross from
the silver,
and the smith has material
for a vessel;

24.28
Prov 25.18;
Eph 4.25
24.29
Prov 20.22;
Mt 5.39;
Rom 12.17
24.30
Prov 6.6-11
24.33
Prov 6.9;
20.13
25.1
Prov 1.1
25.2
Deut 29.29;
Ezra 6.1
25.4
2 Tim 2.21

25.5
Prov 20.8;
16.12
25.7
Lk 14.7-11
25.8
Mt 5.25
25.9
Mt 18.15;
Prov 11.13
25.11
Prov 15.23
25.12
Prov 15.31;
20.12
25.13
v. 25;
Prov 13.17
25.14
Prov 20.6;
Jude 12
25.15
Gen 32.4;
1 Sam 25.24;
Prov 15.1;
16.14
25.16
v. 27

5 take away the wicked from
the presence of the
king,
and his throne will be
established in
righteousness.
6 Do not put yourself forward
in the king's presence
or stand in the place of the
great;
7 for it is better to be told,
"Come up here,"
than to be put lower in the
presence of a noble.

What your eyes have seen
8 do not hastily bring into
court;
forᶻ what will you do in the
end,
when your neighbor puts
you to shame?
9 Argue your case with your
neighbor directly,
and do not disclose
another's secret;
10 or else someone who hears
you will bring shame
upon you,
and your ill repute will
have no end.

11 A word fitly spoken
is like apples of gold in a
setting of silver.
12 Like a gold ring or an
ornament of gold
is a wise rebuke to a
listening ear.
13 Like the cold of snow in the
time of harvest
are faithful messengers to
those who send them;
they refresh the spirit of
their masters.
14 Like clouds and wind
without rain
is one who boasts of a gift
never given.
15 With patience a ruler may be
persuaded,
and a soft tongue can
break bones.
16 If you have found honey, eat
only enough for you,

ᶻ Cn: Heb *or else*

or else, having too much,
 you will vomit it.
17 Let your foot be seldom in
 your neighbor's house,
 otherwise the neighbor will
 become weary of you
 and hate you.
18 Like a war club, a sword, or
 a sharp arrow
 is one who bears false
 witness against a
 neighbor.
19 Like a bad tooth or a lame
 foot
 is trust in a faithless
 person in time of
 trouble.
20 Like vinegar on a wound[a]
 is one who sings songs to a
 heavy heart.
 Like a moth in clothing or a
 worm in wood,
 sorrow gnaws at the human
 heart.[b]
21 If your enemies are hungry,
 give them bread to eat;
 and if they are thirsty, give
 them water to drink;
22 for you will heap coals of fire
 on their heads,
 and the LORD will reward
 you.
23 The north wind produces
 rain,
 and a backbiting tongue,
 angry looks.
24 It is better to live in a corner
 of the housetop
 than in a house shared
 with a contentious wife.
25 Like cold water to a thirsty
 soul,
 so is good news from a far
 country.
26 Like a muddied spring or a
 polluted fountain
 are the righteous who give
 way before the wicked.
27 It is not good to eat much
 honey,
 or to seek honor on top of
 honor.
28 Like a city breached, without
 walls,
 is one who lacks
 self-control.

25.18
Ps 57.4;
Prov 12.18
25.21
Ex 23.4,5;
Mt 5.44;
Rom 12.20
25.22
2 Sam 16.12
25.23
Ps 101.5
25.24
Prov 21.9
25.25
v. 13;
Prov 15.30
25.26
Ezek 32.2;
34.18,19
25.27
v. 16;
Prov 27.2
25.28
Prov 16.32

26.1
1 Sam 12.17
26.2
Num 23.8;
Deut 23.5
26.3
Ps 32.9
26.4
Prov 23.9;
29.9
26.5
Mt 16.1-4;
21.24-27
26.7
v. 9
26.8
v. 1
26.9
v. 7
26.11
2 Pet 2.22;
Ex 8.15
26.12
v. 5;
Prov 3.7;
29.20
26.13
Prov 22.13

26 Like snow in summer or
 rain in harvest,
 so honor is not fitting for a
 fool.
2 Like a sparrow in its flitting,
 like a swallow in its
 flying,
 an undeserved curse goes
 nowhere.
3 A whip for the horse, a bridle
 for the donkey,
 and a rod for the back of
 fools.
4 Do not answer fools
 according to their folly,
 or you will be a fool
 yourself.
5 Answer fools according to
 their folly,
 or they will be wise in their
 own eyes.
6 It is like cutting off one's
 foot and drinking down
 violence,
 to send a message by a
 fool.
7 The legs of a disabled person
 hang limp;
 so does a proverb in the
 mouth of a fool.
8 It is like binding a stone in a
 sling
 to give honor to a fool.
9 Like a thornbush brandished
 by the hand of a
 drunkard
 is a proverb in the mouth
 of a fool.
10 Like an archer who wounds
 everybody
 is one who hires a passing
 fool or drunkard.[c]
11 Like a dog that returns to its
 vomit
 is a fool who reverts to his
 folly.
12 Do you see persons wise in
 their own eyes?
 There is more hope for
 fools than for them.
13 The lazy person says, "There
 is a lion in the road!

[a] Gk: Heb *Like one who takes off a garment
on a cold day, like vinegar on lye* [b] Gk Syr
Tg: Heb lacks *Like a moth . . . human heart*
[c] Meaning of Heb uncertain

There is a lion in the
streets!"
14 As a door turns on its
hinges,
so does a lazy person in
bed.
15 The lazy person buries a
hand in the dish,
and is too tired to bring it
back to the mouth.
16 The lazy person is wiser in
self-esteem
than seven who can answer
discreetly.
17 Like somebody who takes a
passing dog by the ears
is one who meddles in the
quarrel of another.
18 Like a maniac who shoots
deadly firebrands and
arrows,
19 so is one who deceives a
neighbor
and says, "I am only
joking!"
20 For lack of wood the fire
goes out,
and where there is no
whisperer, quarreling
ceases.
21 As charcoal is to hot embers
and wood to fire,
so is a quarrelsome person
for kindling strife.
22 The words of a whisperer are
like delicious morsels;
they go down into the
inner parts of the body.
23 Like the glaze d covering an
earthen vessel
are smooth e lips with an
evil heart.
24 An enemy dissembles in
speaking
while harboring deceit
within;
25 when an enemy speaks
graciously, do not
believe it,
for there are seven
abominations concealed
within;
26 though hatred is covered
with guile,
the enemy's wickedness
will be exposed in the
assembly.

26.15
Prov 19.24
26.17
Prov 3.30
26.18
Isa 50.11
26.19
Prov 24.28
26.20
Prov 16.28;
22.10
26.21
Prov 15.18
26.22
Prov 18.8
26.24
Prov 10.18;
12.20
26.25
Ps 28.3;
Jer 9.8
26.26
Mt 23.28;
Lk 8.17

26.27
Ps 7.15;
Prov 28.10;
Eccl 10.8
26.28
Prov 29.5
27.1
Lk 12.19,20;
Jas 4.14
27.2
Prov 25.27;
2 Cor 10.12,
18
27.3
Prov 12.16
27.5
Prov 28.23
27.7
Prov 25.16
27.10
2 Chr 10.6-8;
Prov 17.17;
18.24

27 Whoever digs a pit will fall
into it,
and a stone will come back
on the one who starts it
rolling.
28 A lying tongue hates its
victims,
and a flattering mouth
works ruin.

27 Do not boast about
tomorrow,
for you do not know what a
day may bring.
2 Let another praise you, and
not your own mouth—
a stranger, and not your
own lips.
3 A stone is heavy, and sand is
weighty,
but a fool's provocation is
heavier than both.
4 Wrath is cruel, anger is
overwhelming,
but who is able to stand
before jealousy?
5 Better is open rebuke
than hidden love.
6 Well meant are the wounds a
friend inflicts,
but profuse are the kisses
of an enemy.
7 The sated appetite spurns
honey,
but to a ravenous appetite
even the bitter is sweet.
8 Like a bird that strays from
its nest
is one who strays from
home.
9 Perfume and incense make
the heart glad,
but the soul is torn by
trouble. f
10 Do not forsake your friend or
the friend of your
parent;
do not go to the house of
your kindred in the day
of your calamity.
Better is a neighbor who is
nearby
than kindred who are far
away.

d Cn: Heb *silver of dross* e Gk: Heb
burning f Gk: Heb *the sweetness of a friend
is better than one's own counsel*

11 Be wise, my child, and make
　　my heart glad,
　so that I may answer
　　whoever reproaches me.

12 The clever see danger and
　　hide;
　but the simple go on, and
　　suffer for it.

13 Take the garment of one who
　　has given surety for a
　　stranger;
　seize the pledge given as
　　surety for foreigners. g

14 Whoever blesses a neighbor
　　with a loud voice,
　rising early in the morning,
　will be counted as cursing.

15 A continual dripping on a
　　rainy day
　and a contentious wife are
　　alike;

16 to restrain her is to restrain
　　the wind
　or to grasp oil in the right
　　hand. h

17 Iron sharpens iron,
　and one person sharpens
　　the wits i of another.

18 Anyone who tends a fig tree
　　will eat its fruit,
　and anyone who takes care
　　of a master will be
　　honored.

19 Just as water reflects the
　　face,
　so one human heart
　　reflects another.

20 Sheol and Abaddon are never
　　satisfied,
　and human eyes are never
　　satisfied.

21 The crucible is for silver, and
　　the furnace is for gold,
　so a person is tested j by
　　being praised.

22 Crush a fool in a mortar with
　　a pestle
　along with crushed grain,
　but the folly will not be
　　driven out.

23 Know well the condition of
　　your flocks,
　and give attention to your
　　herds;

24 for riches do not last forever,

nor a crown for all
　　generations.

25 When the grass is gone, and
　　new growth appears,
　and the herbage of the
　　mountains is gathered,

26 the lambs will provide your
　　clothing,
　and the goats the price of a
　　field;

27 there will be enough goats'
　　milk for your food,
　for the food of your
　　household
　and nourishment for your
　　servant girls.

28 The wicked flee when no
　　one pursues,
　but the righteous are as
　　bold as a lion.

2 When a land rebels
　it has many rulers;
　but with an intelligent ruler
　　there is lasting order. h

3 A ruler k who oppresses the
　　poor
　is a beating rain that leaves
　　no food.

4 Those who forsake the law
　　praise the wicked,
　but those who keep the law
　　struggle against them.

5 The evil do not understand
　　justice,
　but those who seek the
　　LORD understand it
　　completely.

6 Better to be poor and walk
　　in integrity
　than to be crooked in one's
　　ways even though rich.

7 Those who keep the law are
　　wise children,
　but companions of gluttons
　　shame their parents.

8 One who augments wealth
　　by exorbitant interest
　gathers it for another who
　　is kind to the poor.

9 When one will not listen to
　　the law,
　even one's prayers are an
　　abomination.

27.11
Prov 10.1;
23.15;
Ps 119.42
27.12
Prov 22.3
27.13
Prov 20.16
27.15
Prov 19.13
27.18
1 Cor 9.7;
Lk 12.42-44;
19.17
27.20
Hab 2.5;
Eccl 1.8
27.21
Lk 6.26
27.22
Prov 23.35;
Jer 5.3
27.24
Prov 23.5;
Job 19.9

27.25
Ps 104.14
28.1
Lev 26.17;
Ps 53.5
28.2
Prov 11.11
28.3
Mt 18.28
28.4
Rom 1.32;
1 Kings 18.18
28.5
Ps 92.6;
Jn 7.17;
1 Cor 2.15
28.6
Prov 19.1;
v. 18
28.7
Prov 23.20
28.8
Lev 25.36;
Prov 13.22;
14.31
28.9
Ps 66.18;
Prov 15.8

g Vg and 20.16: Heb *for a foreign woman*
h Meaning of Heb uncertain　i Heb *face*
i Heb lacks *is tested*　k Cn: Heb *A poor
person*

10 Those who mislead the
 upright into evil ways
 will fall into pits of their
 own making,
 but the blameless will have
 a goodly inheritance.
11 The rich is wise in
 self-esteem,
 but an intelligent poor
 person sees through the
 pose.
12 When the righteous triumph,
 there is great glory,
 but when the wicked
 prevail, people go into
 hiding.
13 No one who conceals
 transgressions will
 prosper,
 but one who confesses and
 forsakes them will
 obtain mercy.
14 Happy is the one who is
 never without fear,
 but one who is
 hard-hearted will fall
 into calamity.
15 Like a roaring lion or a
 charging bear
 is a wicked ruler over a
 poor people.
16 A ruler who lacks
 understanding is a cruel
 oppressor;
 but one who hates unjust
 gain will enjoy a long
 life.
17 If someone is burdened with
 the blood of another,
 let that killer be a fugitive
 until death;
 let no one offer assistance.
18 One who walks in integrity
 will be safe,
 but whoever follows
 crooked ways will fall
 into the Pit.[1]
19 Anyone who tills the land
 will have plenty of
 bread,
 but one who follows
 worthless pursuits will
 have plenty of poverty.
20 The faithful will abound with
 blessings,

28.10
Prov 26.27;
Mt 6.33;
Heb 6.12
28.11
Prov 26.5,
12; 18.17
28.12
Prov 11.10;
Eccl 10.5,6
28.13
Ps 32.3,5
28.14
Ps 16.8;
Rom 2.5
28.15
1 Pet 5.8;
Mt 2.16
28.17
Gen 9.6;
Ex 21.14
28.18
Prov 10.9,
25; v. 6
28.19
Prov 12.11
28.20
Prov 10.6;
v. 22;
1 Tim 6.9

28.21
Prov 18.5;
Ezek 13.19
28.22
Prov 23.6;
v. 20
28.23
Prov 27.5,6
28.24
Prov 19.26;
18.9
28.25
Prov 15.27;
29.25
28.26
Prov 3.5;
v. 18
28.27
Deut 15.7;
Prov 19.17;
21.13
28.28
v. 12
29.1
1 Sam 2.25;
2 Chr 36.16;
Prov 6.15
29.2
Esther 8.15;
Prov 28.15
29.3
Prov 10.1;
5.9,10;
Lk 15.13

 but one who is in a hurry
 to be rich will not go
 unpunished.
21 To show partiality is not
 good—
 yet for a piece of bread a
 person may do wrong.
22 The miser is in a hurry to get
 rich
 and does not know that
 loss is sure to come.
23 Whoever rebukes a person
 will afterward find more
 favor
 than one who flatters with
 the tongue.
24 Anyone who robs father or
 mother
 and says, "That is no
 crime,"
 is partner to a thug.
25 The greedy person stirs up
 strife,
 but whoever trusts in the
 LORD will be enriched.
26 Those who trust in their own
 wits are fools;
 but those who walk in
 wisdom come through
 safely.
27 Whoever gives to the poor
 will lack nothing,
 but one who turns a blind
 eye will get many a
 curse.
28 When the wicked prevail,
 people go into hiding;
 but when they perish, the
 righteous increase.

29 One who is often
 reproved, yet remains
 stubborn,
 will suddenly be broken
 beyond healing.
2 When the righteous are in
 authority, the people
 rejoice;
 but when the wicked rule,
 the people groan.
3 A child who loves wisdom
 makes a parent glad,
 but to keep company with
 prostitutes is to
 squander one's
 substance.

[1] Syr: Heb *fall all at once*

4 By justice a king gives
　　stability to the land,
　but one who makes heavy
　　exactions ruins it.
5 Whoever flatters a neighbor
　　is spreading a net for the
　　neighbor's feet.
6 In the transgression of the
　　evil there is a snare,
　but the righteous sing and
　　rejoice.
7 The righteous know the
　　rights of the poor;
　the wicked have no such
　　understanding.
8 Scoffers set a city aflame,
　but the wise turn away
　　wrath.
9 If the wise go to law with
　　fools,
　there is ranting and
　　ridicule without relief.
10 The bloodthirsty hate the
　　blameless,
　and they seek the life of
　　the upright.
11 A fool gives full vent to
　　anger,
　but the wise quietly holds
　　it back.
12 If a ruler listens to
　　falsehood,
　all his officials will be
　　wicked.
13 The poor and the oppressor
　　have this in common:
　the LORD gives light to the
　　eyes of both.
14 If a king judges the poor
　　with equity,
　his throne will be
　　established forever.
15 The rod and reproof give
　　wisdom,
　but a mother is disgraced
　　by a neglected child.
16 When the wicked are in
　　authority, transgression
　　increases,
　but the righteous will look
　　upon their downfall.
17 Discipline your children, and
　　they will give you rest;
　they will give delight to
　　your heart.

29.5
Ps 5.9
29.6
Prov 22.5;
Ex 15.1
29.7
Job 29.16;
Ps 41.1
29.8
Prov 11.11;
16.14
29.10
1 Jn 3.12
29.11
Prov 12.16;
19.11
29.13
Ps 13.3
29.14
Ps 72.4;
Isa 11.4;
Prov 16.12;
25.5
29.15
Prov 13.24;
10.1
29.16
Ps 37.36;
58.10; 91.8;
92.11
29.17
v. 15;
Prov 10.1

29.18
1 Sam 3.1;
Am 8.11,12;
Jn 13.17
29.20
Jas 1.19;
Prov 26.12
29.22
Prov 15.18;
17.19
29.23
Job 22.29;
Isa 66.2;
Dan 4.30;
Mt 23.12
29.24
Lev 5.1
29.25
Gen 12.12;
Ps 91.1-16
29.26
Isa 49.4
30.1
Prov 31.1

18 Where there is no prophecy,
　　the people cast off
　　restraint,
　but happy are those who
　　keep the law.
19 By mere words servants are
　　not disciplined,
　for though they
　　understand, they will
　　not give heed.
20 Do you see someone who is
　　hasty in speech?
　There is more hope for a
　　fool than for anyone
　　like that.
21 A slave pampered from
　　childhood
　will come to a bad end. m
22 One given to anger stirs up
　　strife,
　and the hothead causes
　　much transgression.
23 A person's pride will bring
　　humiliation,
　but one who is lowly in
　　spirit will obtain honor.
24 To be a partner of a thief is
　　to hate one's own life;
　one hears the victim's
　　curse, but discloses
　　nothing. n
25 The fear of others o lays a
　　snare,
　but one who trusts in the
　　LORD is secure.
26 Many seek the favor of a
　　ruler,
　but it is from the LORD that
　　one gets justice.
27 The unjust are an
　　abomination to the
　　righteous,
　but the upright are an
　　abomination to the
　　wicked.

Sayings of Agur

30 The words of Agur son of
　　Jakeh. An oracle.

　Thus says the man: I am
　　weary, O God,
　I am weary, O God. How
　　can I prevail? p

m Vg: Meaning of Heb uncertain　　　n Meaning
of Heb uncertain　　o Or *human fear*
p Or *I am spent.* Meaning of Heb uncertain

2 Surely I am too stupid to be
human;
I do not have human
understanding.
3 I have not learned wisdom,
nor have I knowledge of
the holy ones. q
4 Who has ascended to heaven
and come down?
Who has gathered the wind
in the hollow of the
hand?
Who has wrapped up the
waters in a garment?
Who has established all the
ends of the earth?
What is the person's name?
And what is the name of
the person's child?
Surely you know!

5 Every word of God proves
true;
he is a shield to those who
take refuge in him.
6 Do not add to his words,
or else he will rebuke you,
and you will be found a
liar.

7 Two things I ask of you;
do not deny them to me
before I die:
8 Remove far from me
falsehood and lying;
give me neither poverty nor
riches;
feed me with the food that
I need,
9 or I shall be full, and deny
you,
and say, "Who is the
LORD?"
or I shall be poor, and steal,
and profane the name of
my God.

10 Do not slander a servant to a
master,
or the servant will curse
you, and you will be
held guilty.

11 There are those who curse
their fathers
and do not bless their
mothers.

30.2
Ps 73.22
30.3
Prov 9.10
30.4
Jn 3.13;
Ps 104.3;
Isa 40.12;
Job 38.8,9;
Isa 45.18
30.5
Ps 12.6;
18.30; 84.11
30.6
Deut 4.2;
12.32;
Rev 22.18
30.8
Mt 6.11
30.9
Deut 8.12;
Neh 9.25;
Job 31.24;
Hos 13.6
30.10
Eccl 7.21
30.11
Prov 20.20

30.12
Lk 18.11
30.13
Ps 131.1;
Prov 6.17
30.14
Job 29.17;
Ps 52.2;
14.4;
Am 8.4
30.16
Prov 27.20
30.17
Gen 9.22;
Prov 23.22;
Deut 28.26
30.20
Prov 5.6

12 There are those who are pure
in their own eyes
yet are not cleansed of
their filthiness.
13 There are those — how lofty
are their eyes,
how high their eyelids lift!
14 There are those whose teeth
are swords,
whose teeth are knives,
to devour the poor from off
the earth,
the needy from among
mortals.

15 The leech r has two
daughters;
"Give, give," they cry.
Three things are never
satisfied;
four never say, "Enough":
16 Sheol, the barren womb,
the earth ever thirsty for
water,
and the fire that never
says, "Enough." r

17 The eye that mocks a father
and scorns to obey a
mother
will be pecked out by the
ravens of the valley
and eaten by the vultures.

18 Three things are too
wonderful for me;
four I do not understand:
19 the way of an eagle in the
sky,
the way of a snake on a
rock,
the way of a ship on the high
seas,
and the way of a man with
a girl.

20 This is the way of an
adulteress:
she eats, and wipes her
mouth,
and says, "I have done no
wrong."

21 Under three things the earth
trembles;

q Or *Holy One* r Meaning of Heb uncertain

under four it cannot bear
up:

22 a slave when he becomes
king,
and a fool when glutted
with food;

23 an unloved woman when she
gets a husband,
and a maid when she
succeeds her mistress.

24 Four things on earth are
small,
yet they are exceedingly
wise:

25 the ants are a people without
strength,
yet they provide their food
in the summer;

26 the badgers are a people
without power,
yet they make their homes
in the rocks;

27 the locusts have no king,
yet all of them march in
rank;

28 the lizard[s] can be grasped in
the hand,
yet it is found in kings'
palaces.

29 Three things are stately in
their stride;
four are stately in their
gait:

30 the lion, which is mightiest
among wild animals
and does not turn back
before any;

31 the strutting rooster,[t] the
he-goat,
and a king striding before[u]
his people.

32 If you have been foolish,
exalting yourself,
or if you have been
devising evil,
put your hand on your
mouth.

33 For as pressing milk
produces curds,
and pressing the nose
produces blood,
so pressing anger produces
strife.

30.22
Prov 19.10
30.25
Prov 6.6-8
30.26
Ps 104.18
30.30
Judg 14.18;
Mic 5.8
30.32
Job 21.5;
40.4;
Mic 7.16
30.33
Prov 10.12;
29.22

31.1
Prov 30.1
31.2
Isa 49.15
31.3
Prov 5.9;
Deut 17.17;
1 Kings 11.1;
Neh 13.26
31.4
Eccl 10.17;
Prov 20.1
31.5
Hos 4.11
31.8
Job 29.12-17
31.9
Lev 19.15;
Deut 1.16
31.10
Prov 12.4;
19.14
31.13
vv. 21-24

The Teaching of King Lemuel's Mother

31 The words of King Lemuel.
An oracle that his mother
taught him:

2 No, my son! No, son of my
womb!
No, son of my vows!

3 Do not give your strength to
women,
your ways to those who
destroy kings.

4 It is not for kings, O Lemuel,
it is not for kings to drink
wine,
or for rulers to desire[v]
strong drink;

5 or else they will drink and
forget what has been
decreed,
and will pervert the rights
of all the afflicted.

6 Give strong drink to one who
is perishing,
and wine to those in bitter
distress;

7 let them drink and forget
their poverty,
and remember their misery
no more.

8 Speak out for those who
cannot speak,
for the rights of all the
destitute.[w]

9 Speak out, judge righteously,
defend the rights of the
poor and needy.

Ode to a Capable Wife

10 A capable wife who can find?
She is far more precious
than jewels.

11 The heart of her husband
trusts in her,
and he will have no lack of
gain.

12 She does him good, and not
harm,
all the days of her life.

13 She seeks wool and flax,

[s] Or *spider* [t] Gk Syr Tg Compare Vg:
Meaning of Heb uncertain [u] Meaning of
Heb uncertain [v] Cn: Heb *where*
[w] Heb *all children of passing away*

and works with willing
 hands.
14 She is like the ships of the
 merchant,
 she brings her food from
 far away.
15 She rises while it is still
 night
 and provides food for her
 household
 and tasks for her servant
 girls.
16 She considers a field and
 buys it;
 with the fruit of her hands
 she plants a vineyard.
17 She girds herself with
 strength,
 and makes her arms strong.
18 She perceives that her
 merchandise is
 profitable.
 Her lamp does not go out
 at night.
19 She puts her hands to the
 distaff,
 and her hands hold the
 spindle.
20 She opens her hand to the
 poor,
 and reaches out her hands
 to the needy.
21 She is not afraid for her
 household when it
 snows,
 for all her household are
 clothed in crimson.
22 She makes herself coverings;

31.15
Rom 12.11;
Lk 12.42
31.20
Eph 4.28;
Heb 13.16
31.21
1 Sam 1.24

31.23
Ruth 4.1,11;
Prov 12.4
31.25
v. 17
31.26
Prov 10.31
31.27
Prov 19.15
31.29
Prov 12.4
31.30
Prov 6.25;
22.4

 her clothing is fine linen
 and purple.
23 Her husband is known in the
 city gates,
 taking his seat among the
 elders of the land.
24 She makes linen garments
 and sells them;
 she supplies the merchant
 with sashes.
25 Strength and dignity are her
 clothing,
 and she laughs at the time
 to come.
26 She opens her mouth with
 wisdom,
 and the teaching of
 kindness is on her
 tongue.
27 She looks well to the ways of
 her household,
 and does not eat the bread
 of idleness.
28 Her children rise up and call
 her happy;
 her husband too, and he
 praises her:
29 "Many women have done
 excellently,
 but you surpass them all."
30 Charm is deceitful, and
 beauty is vain,
 but a woman who fears the
 LORD is to be praised.
31 Give her a share in the fruit
 of her hands,
 and let her works praise
 her in the city gates.

Ecclesiastes

Title and Background

The writer's title ("Teacher") comes from a Hebrew root word related to "assembly" or "congregation." Perhaps the Teacher also held an office in the assembly. The Septuagint word for "Teacher" is *ecclesiastes*, from which most English titles of the book are taken.

Author and Date of Writing

No time period or writer's name is mentioned in the book, but several passages suggest the possibility that Solomon is the author; this would demand a date in the tenth century B.C. Others, however, date the book as late as the third century B.C.

Theme and Message

Life not centered on God is purposeless and meaningless. Without him, nothing can satisfy (2.25). With him, all of life and his other good gifts are to be gratefully received and used and enjoyed to the full (2.26; 11.8). The book contains the philosophical and theological reflections of an old man, most of whose life was meaningless because he had not himself relied on God.

Outline

I. Introduction: The Vanity of Life (1.1-11)
II. Life to Be Enjoyed as a Gift From God (1.12–11.6)
III. Youth as the Time to Begin Enjoying Life (11.7–12.8)
IV. Conclusion: Reverently Trust in and Obey God (12.9-14)

Reflections of a Royal Philosopher

1 The words of the Teacher,[a] the son of David, king in Jerusalem.
2 Vanity of vanities, says the Teacher,[a]
vanity of vanities! All is vanity.
3 What do people gain from all the toil
at which they toil under the sun?
4 A generation goes, and a generation comes,
but the earth remains forever.
5 The sun rises and the sun goes down,
and hurries to the place where it rises.
6 The wind blows to the south,
and goes around to the north;
round and round goes the wind,
and on its circuits the wind returns.
7 All streams run to the sea,
but the sea is not full;
to the place where the streams flow,
there they continue to flow.
8 All things[b] are wearisome;
more than one can express;
the eye is not satisfied with seeing,
or the ear filled with hearing.
9 What has been is what will be,

1.1 v. 12; Eccl 7.27; 12.8-10 **1.2** Ps 39.5,6; 62.9; 144.4; Eccl 12.8 **1.3** Eccl 2.22; 3.9 **1.4** Ps 104.5; 119.90 **1.5** Ps 19.5,6 **1.6** Eccl 11.5; Jn 3.8 **1.8** Prov 27.20 **1.9** Eccl 2.12; 3.15

a Heb *Koheleth*, traditionally rendered *Preacher* b Or *words*

and what has been done is
 what will be done;
there is nothing new under
 the sun.
10 Is there a thing of which it is
 said,
 "See, this is new"?
It has already been,
 in the ages before us.
11 The people of long ago are
 not remembered,
 nor will there be any
 remembrance
of people yet to come
 by those who come after
 them.

The Futility of Seeking Wisdom

12 I, the Teacher,[c] when king
over Israel in Jerusalem, 13 applied
my mind to seek and to search out
by wisdom all that is done under
heaven; it is an unhappy business
that God has given to human be-
ings to be busy with. 14 I saw all the
deeds that are done under the sun;
and see, all is vanity and a chasing
after wind.[d]
15 What is crooked cannot be
 made straight,
 and what is lacking cannot
 be counted.
16 I said to myself, "I have ac-
quired great wisdom, surpassing all
who were over Jerusalem before
me; and my mind has had great ex-
perience of wisdom and knowl-
edge." 17 And I applied my mind to
know wisdom and to know mad-
ness and folly. I perceived that this
also is but a chasing after wind.[d]
18 For in much wisdom is much
 vexation,
 and those who increase
 knowledge increase
 sorrow.

The Futility of Self-Indulgence

2 I said to myself, "Come now, I
will make a test of pleasure;
enjoy yourself." But again, this also
was vanity. 2 I said of laughter, "It is
mad," and of pleasure, "What use
is it?" 3 I searched with my mind
how to cheer my body with wine—
my mind still guiding me with
wisdom—and how to lay hold on

1.11
Eccl 2.16;
9.5
1.12
v. 1
1.13
v. 17;
Eccl 3.10
1.14
Eccl 2.11,17
1.15
Eccl 7.13
1.16
1 Kings 3.12,
13; 4.30;
10.23;
Eccl 2.9
1.17
Eccl 2.3,12;
7.23,25
1.18
Eccl 12.12
2.1
Lk 12.19;
Eccl 1.2
2.2
Prov 14.13;
Eccl 7.6

2.4
1 Kings 7.1-12;
Song 8.10,
11
2.5
Song 4.16;
5.1; Neh 2.8
2.8
1 Kings 9.28;
10.10,14,21;
4.21; 20.14;
2 Sam 19.35
2.9
Eccl 1.16
2.10
Eccl 3.22;
5.18; 9.9
2.11
Eccl 1.3,14
2.12
Eccl 1.17;
7.25
2.13
Eccl 7.11,12
2.14
Prov 17.24;
Ps 49.10;
Eccl 9.2,3,
11
2.15
Eccl 6.8,11

folly, until I might see what was
good for mortals to do under heav-
en during the few days of their life.
4 I made great works; I built houses
and planted vineyards for myself; 5 I
made myself gardens and parks,
and planted in them all kinds of
fruit trees. 6 I made myself pools
from which to water the forest of
growing trees. 7 I bought male and
female slaves, and had slaves who
were born in my house; I also had
great possessions of herds and
flocks, more than any who had
been before me in Jerusalem. 8 I
also gathered for myself silver and
gold and the treasure of kings and
of the provinces; I got singers, both
men and women, and delights of
the flesh, and many concubines.[e]

9 So I became great and sur-
passed all who were before me in
Jerusalem; also my wisdom re-
mained with me. 10 Whatever my
eyes desired I did not keep from
them; I kept my heart from no plea-
sure, for my heart found pleasure
in all my toil, and this was my re-
ward for all my toil. 11 Then I con-
sidered all that my hands had done
and the toil I had spent in doing it,
and again, all was vanity and a
chasing after wind,[d] and there was
nothing to be gained under the
sun.

Wisdom and Joy Given to One Who Pleases God

12 So I turned to consider wis-
dom and madness and folly; for
what can the one do who comes af-
ter the king? Only what has already
been done. 13 Then I saw that wis-
dom excels folly as light excels
darkness.
14 The wise have eyes in their
 head,
 but fools walk in darkness.
Yet I perceived that the same
fate befalls all of them. 15 Then I
said to myself, "What happens to
the fool will happen to me also;
why then have I been so very wise?"

[c] Heb *Koheleth*, traditionally rendered
Preacher [d] Or *a feeding on wind*. See Hos
12.1 [e] Meaning of Heb uncertain

And I said to myself that this also is vanity. 16 For there is no enduring remembrance of the wise or of fools, seeing that in the days to come all will have been long forgotten. How can the wise die just like fools? 17 So I hated life, because what is done under the sun was grievous to me; for all is vanity and a chasing after wind.f

18 I hated all my toil in which I had toiled under the sun, seeing that I must leave it to those who come after me 19 —and who knows whether they will be wise or foolish? Yet they will be master of all for which I toiled and used my wisdom under the sun. This also is vanity. 20 So I turned and gave my heart up to despair concerning all the toil of my labors under the sun, 21 because sometimes one who has toiled with wisdom and knowledge and skill must leave all to be enjoyed by another who did not toil for it. This also is vanity and a great evil. 22 What do mortals get from all the toil and strain with which they toil under the sun? 23 For all their days are full of pain, and their work is a vexation; even at night their minds do not rest. This also is vanity.

24 There is nothing better for mortals than to eat and drink, and find enjoyment in their toil. This also, I saw, is from the hand of God; 25 for apart from himg who can eat or who can have enjoyment? 26 For to the one who pleases him God gives wisdom and knowledge and joy; but to the sinner he gives the work of gathering and heaping, only to give to one who pleases God. This also is vanity and a chasing after wind.f

Everything Has Its Time

3 For everything there is a season, and a time for every matter under heaven:

2 a time to be born, and a
 time to die;
a time to plant, and a time
 to pluck up what is
 planted;

3 a time to kill, and a time to
 heal;
a time to break down, and a
 time to build up;
4 a time to weep, and a time
 to laugh;
a time to mourn, and a time
 to dance;
5 a time to throw away stones,
 and a time to gather
 stones together;
a time to embrace, and a
 time to refrain from
 embracing;
6 a time to seek, and a time to
 lose;
a time to keep, and a time to
 throw away;
7 a time to tear, and a time to
 sew;
a time to keep silence, and a
 time to speak;
8 a time to love, and a time to
 hate;
a time for war, and a time
 for peace.

The God-Given Task

9 What gain have the workers from their toil? 10 I have seen the business that God has given to everyone to be busy with. 11 He has made everything suitable for its time; moreover he has put a sense of past and future into their minds, yet they cannot find out what God has done from the beginning to the end. 12 I know that there is nothing better for them than to be happy and enjoy themselves as long as they live; 13 moreover, it is God's gift that all should eat and drink and take pleasure in all their toil. 14 I know that whatever God does endures forever; nothing can be added to it, nor anything taken from it; God has done this, so that all should stand in awe before him. 15 That which is, already has been; that which is to be, already is; and God seeks out what has gone by.h

2.16 Eccl 1.11; 9.5; v. 14
2.17 Eccl 4.2; vv. 22,23
2.18 v. 11; Ps 39.6; 49.10
2.20 v. 11
2.21 Eccl 4.4; v. 18
2.22 Eccl 1.3; 3.9
2.23 Job 5.7; 14.1; Eccl 1.18; Ps 127.2
2.24 Eccl 3.12, 13,22; 5.18; 8.15
2.26 Job 32.8; 27.16,17; Eccl 1.14
3.1 v. 17; Eccl 8.6
3.2 Heb 9.27

3.4 Rom 12.15; Ps 126.2; Ex 15.20
3.5 1 Cor 7.5
3.7 Am 5.13
3.8 Lk 14.26
3.9 Eccl 1.3
3.10 Eccl 1.13
3.11 Gen 1.31; Eccl 8.17; Rom 11.33
3.13 Eccl 2.24; 5.19
3.14 Jas 1.17; Eccl 5.7; 1.3; 3.9
3.15 Eccl 1.9; 6.10

f Or a feeding on wind. See Hos 12.1
g Gk Syr: Heb apart from me h Heb what is pursued

Judgment and the Future Belong to God

16 Moreover I saw under the sun that in the place of justice, wickedness was there, and in the place of righteousness, wickedness was there as well. 17 I said in my heart, God will judge the righteous and the wicked, for he has appointed a time for every matter, and for every work. 18 I said in my heart with regard to human beings that God is testing them to show that they are but animals. 19 For the fate of humans and the fate of animals is the same; as one dies, so dies the other. They all have the same breath, and humans have no advantage over the animals; for all is vanity. 20 All go to one place; all are from the dust, and all turn to dust again. 21 Who knows whether the human spirit goes upward and the spirit of animals goes downward to the earth? 22 So I saw that there is nothing better than that all should enjoy their work, for that is their lot; who can bring them to see what will be after them?

4 Again I saw all the oppressions that are practiced under the sun. Look, the tears of the oppressed—with no one to comfort them! On the side of their oppressors there was power—with no one to comfort them. 2 And I thought the dead, who have already died, more fortunate than the living, who are still alive; 3 but better than both is the one who has not yet been, and has not seen the evil deeds that are done under the sun.

4 Then I saw that all toil and all skill in work come from one person's envy of another. This also is vanity and a chasing after wind. i

5 Fools fold their hands
 and consume their own
 flesh.
6 Better is a handful with
 quiet
 than two handfuls with
 toil,
 and a chasing after wind. i

7 Again, I saw vanity under the

sun: 8 the case of solitary individuals, without sons or brothers; yet there is no end to all their toil, and their eyes are never satisfied with riches. "For whom am I toiling," they ask, "and depriving myself of pleasure?" This also is vanity and an unhappy business.

The Value of a Friend

9 Two are better than one, because they have a good reward for their toil. 10 For if they fall, one will lift up the other; but woe to one who is alone and falls and does not have another to help. 11 Again, if two lie together, they keep warm; but how can one keep warm alone? 12 And though one might prevail against another, two will withstand one. A threefold cord is not quickly broken.

13 Better is a poor but wise youth than an old but foolish king, who will no longer take advice. 14 One can indeed come out of prison to reign, even though born poor in the kingdom. 15 I saw all the living who, moving about under the sun, follow that j youth who replaced the king; k 16 there was no end to all those people whom he led. Yet those who come later will not rejoice in him. Surely this also is vanity and a chasing after wind. i

Reverence, Humility, and Contentment

5 Guard your steps when you go to the house of God; to draw near to listen is better than the sacrifice offered by fools; for they do not know how to keep from doing evil. m 2 n Never be rash with your mouth, nor let your heart be quick to utter a word before God, for God is in heaven, and you upon earth; therefore let your words be few.

3 For dreams come with many cares, and a fool's voice with many words.

4 When you make a vow to God, do not delay fulfilling it; for he has no pleasure in fools. Fulfill what

3.17
Mt 16.27;
Rom 2.6-8;
2 Cor 5.10;
2 Thes 1.6,
7; v. 1
3.19
Ps 73.22;
Eccl 9.12
3.20
Gen 3.19;
Eccl 12.7
3.21
Eccl 12.7
3.22
Eccl 2.24;
5.18; 6.12;
8.7; 10.14
4.1
Eccl 3.16;
5.8; Isa 5.7;
Lam 1.9
4.2
Job 3.11-26;
Eccl 2.17
4.3
Eccl 6.3
4.4
Eccl 2.21;
1.14
4.5
Prov 6.10;
Isa 9.20
4.6
Prov 15.16,
17; 16.8

4.8
Prov 27.20;
1 Jn 2.16
4.11
1 Kings 1.1
4.13
Eccl 9.15
4.14
Gen 41.14,
41-43
4.16
Eccl 1.14
5.1
Ex 3.5;
Isa 1.12;
1 Sam 15.22;
Prov 15.8;
21-27;
Hos 6.6
5.2
Prov 20.25;
10.19;
Mt 6.7
5.4
Deut 23.21-23;
Ps 50.14;
76.11; 66.13,
14

i Or a feeding on wind. See Hos 12.1
j Heb the second k Heb him l Ch 4.17
in Heb m Cn: Heb they do not know how
to do evil n Ch 5.1 in Heb

you vow. [5] It is better that you should not vow than that you should vow and not fulfill it. [6] Do not let your mouth lead you into sin, and do not say before the messenger that it was a mistake; why should God be angry at your words, and destroy the work of your hands?

7 With many dreams come vanities and a multitude of words; [o] but fear God.

8 If you see in a province the oppression of the poor and the violation of justice and right, do not be amazed at the matter; for the high official is watched by a higher, and there are yet higher ones over them. [9] But all things considered, this is an advantage for a land: a king for a plowed field. [o]

10 The lover of money will not be satisfied with money; nor the lover of wealth, with gain. This also is vanity.

11 When goods increase, those who eat them increase; and what gain has their owner but to see them with his eyes?

12 Sweet is the sleep of laborers, whether they eat little or much; but the surfeit of the rich will not let them sleep.

13 There is a grievous ill that I have seen under the sun: riches were kept by their owners to their hurt, [14] and those riches were lost in a bad venture; though they are parents of children, they have nothing in their hands. [15] As they came from their mother's womb, so they shall go again, naked as they came; they shall take nothing for their toil, which they may carry away with their hands. [16] This also is a grievous ill: just as they came, so shall they go; and what gain do they have from toiling for the wind? [17] Besides, all their days they eat in darkness, in much vexation and sickness and resentment.

18 This is what I have seen to be good: it is fitting to eat and drink and find enjoyment in all the toil with which one toils under the sun the few days of the life God gives us; for this is our lot. [19] Likewise all

to whom God gives wealth and possessions and whom he enables to enjoy them, and to accept their lot and find enjoyment in their toil — this is the gift of God. [20] For they will scarcely brood over the days of their lives, because God keeps them occupied with the joy of their hearts.

The Frustration of Desires

6 There is an evil that I have seen under the sun, and it lies heavy upon humankind: [2] those to whom God gives wealth, possessions, and honor, so that they lack nothing of all that they desire, yet God does not enable them to enjoy these things, but a stranger enjoys them. This is vanity; it is a grievous ill. [3] A man may beget a hundred children, and live many years; but however many are the days of his years, if he does not enjoy life's good things, or has no burial, I say that a stillborn child is better off than he. [4] For it comes into vanity and goes into darkness, and in darkness its name is covered; [5] moreover it has not seen the sun or known anything; yet it finds rest rather than he. [6] Even though he should live a thousand years twice over, yet enjoy no good — do not all go to one place?

7 All human toil is for the mouth, yet the appetite is not satisfied. [8] For what advantage have the wise over fools? And what do the poor have who know how to conduct themselves before the living? [9] Better is the sight of the eyes than the wandering of desire; this also is vanity and a chasing after wind. [p]

10 Whatever has come to be has already been named, and it is known what human beings are, and that they are not able to dispute with those who are stronger. [11] The more words, the more vanity, so how is one the better? [12] For who knows what is good for mortals while they live the few days of their vain life, which they pass like a shadow? For who can tell them

5.5
Prov 20.25;
Acts 5.4
5.7
Eccl 3.14;
12.13
5.8
Eccl 4.1;
Ps 12.5;
58.11; 82.1
5.10
Eccl 2.10,11
5.11
Eccl 2.9
5.12
Prov 3.24
5.13
Eccl 6.1,2
5.15
Job 1.21;
Ps 49.17;
1 Tim 6.7
5.16
Eccl 1.3;
Prov 11.29
5.17
Eccl 2.23
5.18
Eccl 2.10,
24; 3.22
5.19
2 Chr 1.12;
Eccl 2.24;
3.13; 6.2

6.1
Eccl 5.13
6.2
1 Kings 3.13;
Ps 17.14;
73.7
6.3
2 Kings 9.35;
Isa 14.19,
20;
Jer 22.19;
Eccl 4.3
6.7
Prov 16.26
6.8
Eccl 2.15
6.9
Eccl 11.9;
1.14
6.10
Eccl 1.9;
Job 9.32;
Isa 45.9;
Jer 49.19
6.12
Jas 4.14;
Ps 39.6;
Eccl 8.7

o Meaning of Heb uncertain p Or a feeding on wind. See Hos 12.1

what will be after them under the sun?

A Disillusioned View of Life

7 A good name is better than
precious ointment,
and the day of death, than
the day of birth.
2 It is better to go to the
house of mourning
than to go to the house of
feasting;
for this is the end of
everyone,
and the living will lay it to
heart.
3 Sorrow is better than
laughter,
for by sadness of
countenance the heart
is made glad.
4 The heart of the wise is in
the house of mourning;
but the heart of fools is in
the house of mirth.
5 It is better to hear the
rebuke of the wise
than to hear the song of
fools.
6 For like the crackling of
thorns under a pot,
so is the laughter of fools;
this also is vanity.
7 Surely oppression makes the
wise foolish,
and a bribe corrupts the
heart.
8 Better is the end of a thing
than its beginning;
the patient in spirit are
better than the proud in
spirit.
9 Do not be quick to anger,
for anger lodges in the
bosom of fools.
10 Do not say, "Why were the
former days better than
these?"
For it is not from wisdom
that you ask this.
11 Wisdom is as good as an
inheritance,
an advantage to those who
see the sun.
12 For the protection of wisdom
is like the protection of
money,

7.1
Prov 15.30;
22.1;
Eccl 4.2
7.2
Eccl 2.16;
Ps 90.12
7.3
2 Cor 7.10
7.5
Ps 141.5;
Prov 13.18;
15.31,32
7.6
Ps 118.12;
Eccl 2.2
7.7
Ex 23.8;
Deut 16.19
7.8
v. 1;
Prov 14.29;
Gal 5.22;
Eph 4.2
7.9
Prov 14.17;
Jas 1.19
7.11
Prov 8.10,11
7.12
Eccl 9.18;
Prov 3.18;
8.35

7.13
Eccl 3.11;
8.17; 1.15;
Isa 14.27
7.14
Eccl 3.4;
Deut 8.5
7.15
Eccl 6.12;
8.14
7.16
Rom 12.3
7.17
Job 15.32;
Ps 55.23;
Prov 10.27
7.19
Eccl 9.13-18
7.20
1 Kings 8.46;
2 Chr 6.36;
Prov 20.9;
Rom 3.23
7.23
Rom 1.22
7.24
Job 28.12;
Rom 11.33
7.25
Eccl 1.17;
2.12
7.26
Prov 5.3,4;
22.14
7.27
Eccl 1.1,2

and the advantage of
knowledge is that
wisdom gives life to the
one who possesses it.
13 Consider the work of God;
who can make straight
what he has made
crooked?

14 In the day of prosperity be
joyful, and in the day of adversity
consider; God has made the one as
well as the other, so that mortals
may not find out anything that will
come after them.

The Riddles of Life

15 In my vain life I have seen everything; there are righteous people who perish in their righteousness, and there are wicked people who prolong their life in their evildoing. 16 Do not be too righteous, and do not act too wise; why should you destroy yourself? 17 Do not be too wicked, and do not be a fool; why should you die before your time? 18 It is good that you should take hold of the one, without letting go of the other; for the one who fears God shall succeed with both.

19 Wisdom gives strength to the wise more than ten rulers that are in a city.

20 Surely there is no one on earth so righteous as to do good without ever sinning.

21 Do not give heed to everything that people say, or you may hear your servant cursing you; 22 your heart knows that many times you have yourself cursed others.

23 All this I have tested by wisdom; I said, "I will be wise," but it was far from me. 24 That which is, is far off, and deep, very deep; who can find it out? 25 I turned my mind to know and to search out and to seek wisdom and the sum of things, and to know that wickedness is folly and that foolishness is madness. 26 I found more bitter than death the woman who is a trap, whose heart is snares and nets, whose hands are fetters; one who pleases God escapes her, but the sinner is taken by her. 27 See,

this is what I found, says the Teacher,�q adding one thing to another to find the sum, 28 which my mind has sought repeatedly, but I have not found. One man among a thousand I found, but a woman among all these I have not found. 29 See, this alone I found, that God made human beings straightforward, but they have devised many schemes.

•

Obey the King and Enjoy Yourself

8 Who is like the wise man?
And who knows the
 interpretation of a
 thing?
Wisdom makes one's face
 shine,
and the hardness of one's
 countenance is
 changed.

2 Keepʳ the king's command because of your sacred oath. 3 Do not be terrified; go from his presence, do not delay when the matter is unpleasant, for he does whatever he pleases. 4 For the word of the king is powerful, and who can say to him, "What are you doing?" 5 Whoever obeys a command will meet no harm, and the wise mind will know the time and way. 6 For every matter has its time and way, although the troubles of mortals lie heavy upon them. 7 Indeed, they do not know what is to be, for who can tell them how it will be? 8 No one has power over the windˢ to restrain the wind,ˢ or power over the day of death; there is no discharge from the battle, nor does wickedness deliver those who practice it. 9 All this I observed, applying my mind to all that is done under the sun, while one person exercises authority over another to the other's hurt.

God's Ways Are Inscrutable

10 Then I saw the wicked buried; they used to go in and out of the holy place, and were praised in the city where they had done such things.ᵗ This also is vanity. 11 Because sentence against an evil

deed is not executed speedily, the human heart is fully set to do evil. 12 Though sinners do evil a hundred times and prolong their lives, yet I know that it will be well with those who fear God, because they stand in fear before him, 13 but it will not be well with the wicked, neither will they prolong their days like a shadow, because they do not stand in fear before God.

14 There is a vanity that takes place on earth, that there are righteous people who are treated according to the conduct of the wicked, and there are wicked people who are treated according to the conduct of the righteous. I said that this also is vanity. 15 So I commend enjoyment, for there is nothing better for people under the sun than to eat, and drink, and enjoy themselves, for this will go with them in their toil through the days of life that God gives them under the sun.

16 When I applied my mind to know wisdom, and to see the business that is done on earth, how one's eyes see sleep neither day nor night, 17 then I saw all the work of God, that no one can find out what is happening under the sun. However much they may toil in seeking, they will not find it out; even though those who are wise claim to know, they cannot find it out.

Take Life as It Comes

9 All this I laid to heart, examining it all, how the righteous and the wise and their deeds are in the hand of God; whether it is love or hate one does not know. Everything that confronts them 2 is vanity,ᵘ since the same fate comes to all, to the righteous and the wicked, to the good and the evil,ᵛ to the clean and the unclean, to those who sacrifice and those who do not sacrifice. As are the good, so are the sinners; those who swear are like those who shun an oath. 3 This

Cross references

7.29 Gen 1.27; 3.6,7
8.1 Prov 4.8,9; Deut 28.50
8.2 Ezek 17.18
8.4 Job 9.12; Dan 4.35
8.6 Eccl 3.1,17
8.7 Prov 24.22; Eccl 6.12; 9.12; 10.14
8.8 Ps 49.6,7; Deut 20.5-8; v. 13
8.9 Eccl 4.1; 5.8
8.12 Isa 65.20; Ps 37.11,18, 19; Prov 1.32, 33; Isa 3.10, 11
8.13 v. 8; Isa 3.11; Eccl 6.12
8.14 Ps 73.14; Eccl 7.15; Job 21.7; Mal 3.15
8.15 Eccl 2.24; 3.12,13; 5.18; 9.7
8.16 Eccl 1.13, 14; 2.23
8.17 Job 5.9; Eccl 3.11; Rom 11.33; Eccl 8.7; Ps 73.16
9.1 Deut 33.3; Job 12.10; Ps 119.109; v. 6; Eccl 10.14
9.2 Job 9.22; Eccl 6.6; 7.2
9.3 v. 2; Eccl 8.11; 1.17

Footnotes

�q *Koheleth*, traditionally rendered *Preacher* ʳ Heb *I keep* ˢ Or *breath* ᵗ Meaning of Heb uncertain ᵘ Syr Compare Gk: Heb *Everything that confronts them* 2 *is everything* ᵛ Gk Syr Vg: Heb lacks *and the evil*

is an evil in all that happens under the sun, that the same fate comes to everyone. Moreover, the hearts of all are full of evil; madness is in their hearts while they live, and after that they go to the dead. 4 But whoever is joined with all the living has hope, for a living dog is better than a dead lion. 5 The living know that they will die, but the dead know nothing; they have no more reward, and even the memory of them is lost. 6 Their love and their hate and their envy have already perished; never again will they have any share in all that happens under the sun.

7 Go, eat your bread with enjoyment, and drink your wine with a merry heart; for God has long ago approved what you do. 8 Let your garments always be white; do not let oil be lacking on your head. 9 Enjoy life with the wife whom you love, all the days of your vain life that are given you under the sun, because that is your portion in life and in your toil at which you toil under the sun. 10 Whatever your hand finds to do, do with your might; for there is no work or thought or knowledge or wisdom in Sheol, to which you are going.

11 Again I saw that under the sun the race is not to the swift, nor the battle to the strong, nor bread to the wise, nor riches to the intelligent, nor favor to the skillful; but time and chance happen to them all. 12 For no one can anticipate the time of disaster. Like fish taken in a cruel net, and like birds caught in a snare, so mortals are snared at a time of calamity, when it suddenly falls upon them.

Wisdom Superior to Folly

13 I have also seen this example of wisdom under the sun, and it seemed great to me. 14 There was a little city with few people in it. A great king came against it and besieged it, building great siegeworks against it. 15 Now there was found in it a poor wise man, and he by his wisdom delivered the city. Yet no one remembered that poor man.

9.5
Job 14.21;
Eccl 1.11;
2.16;
Ps 88.12;
Isa 26.14
9.6
Eccl 3.22
9.7
Eccl 8.15
9.8
Rev 3.4;
Ps 23.5
9.9
Eccl 6.12;
7.15
9.10
Rom 12.11;
Col 3.23;
Isa 38.10
9.11
Am 2.14,15;
Deut 8.17,
18;
1 Sam 6.9
9.12
Eccl 8.7;
Prov 29.6;
Isa 24.18;
Lk 21.34,35
9.15
Eccl 4.13;
2.16; 8.10

9.16
Prov 21.22;
Eccl 7.19
9.17
Eccl 7.5;
10.12
9.18
v. 16;
Josh 7.1,11,
12
10.3
Prov 13.16;
18.2
10.4
Eccl 8.3;
1 Sam 25.24-
33; Prov 25.15
10.5
Eccl 5.6
10.6
Esther 3.1
10.7
Prov 19.10;
Esther 6.8
10.8
Ps 7.15;
Prov 26.27
10.11
Ps 58.4,5;
Jer 8.17

16 So I said, "Wisdom is better than might; yet the poor man's wisdom is despised, and his words are not heeded."

17 The quiet words of the wise
　　are more to be heeded
than the shouting of a ruler
　　among fools.
18 Wisdom is better than
　　weapons of war,
but one bungler destroys
　　much good.

Miscellaneous Observations

10 Dead flies make the
perfumer's ointment
　　give off a foul odor;
so a little folly outweighs
　　wisdom and honor.
2 The heart of the wise
　　inclines to the right,
but the heart of a fool to
　　the left.
3 Even when fools walk on the
　　road, they lack sense,
and show to everyone that
　　they are fools.
4 If the anger of the ruler rises
　　against you, do not
　　leave your post,
for calmness will undo
　　great offenses.

5 There is an evil that I have seen under the sun, as great an error as if it proceeded from the ruler: 6 folly is set in many high places, and the rich sit in a low place. 7 I have seen slaves on horseback, and princes walking on foot like slaves.

8 Whoever digs a pit will fall
　　into it;
and whoever breaks
　　through a wall will be
　　bitten by a snake.
9 Whoever quarries stones will
　　be hurt by them;
and whoever splits logs will
　　be endangered by them.
10 If the iron is blunt, and one
　　does not whet the edge,
then more strength must
　　be exerted;
but wisdom helps one to
　　succeed.
11 If the snake bites before it is
　　charmed,

there is no advantage in a charmer.

12 Words spoken by the wise
 bring them favor,
 but the lips of fools
 consume them.
13 The words of their mouths
 begin in foolishness,
 and their talk ends in
 wicked madness;
14 yet fools talk on and on.
 No one knows what is to
 happen,
 and who can tell anyone
 what the future holds?
15 The toil of fools wears them
 out,
 for they do not even know
 the way to town.

16 Alas for you, O land, when
 your king is a servant,[w]
 and your princes feast in
 the morning!
17 Happy are you, O land, when
 your king is a
 nobleman,
 and your princes feast at
 the proper time —
 for strength, and not for
 drunkenness!
18 Through sloth the roof sinks
 in,
 and through indolence the
 house leaks.
19 Feasts are made for laughter;
 wine gladdens life,
 and money meets every
 need.
20 Do not curse the king, even
 in your thoughts,
 or curse the rich, even in
 your bedroom;
 for a bird of the air may
 carry your voice,
 or some winged creature
 tell the matter.

The Value of Diligence

11 Send out your bread
 upon the waters,
 for after many days you
 will get it back.
2 Divide your means seven
 ways, or even eight,

10.12
Prov 10.32;
Lk 4.22;
Prov 10.14;
18.7
10.13
Eccl 7.25
10.14
Prov 15.2;
Eccl 3.22;
6.12; 8.7
10.16
Isa 3.4,5,12;
5.11
10.17
Prov 31.4;
Isa 5.11
10.18
Prov 24.30-34
10.19
Ps 104.15;
Eccl 7.12
10.20
Ex 22.28;
Acts 23.5;
2 Kings 6.12;
Lk 12.3
11.1
Isa 32.20;
Deut 15.10;
Prov 19.17;
Mt 10.42;
2 Cor 9.8;
Gal 6.9,10;
Heb 6.10
11.2
Ps 112.9;
Lk 6.30;
1 Tim 6.18,
19;
Eccl 12.1

11.5
Jn 3.8;
Ps 139.14,
15
11.6
Eccl 9.10
11.7
Eccl 7.11
11.8
Eccl 9.7;
12.1
11.9
Eccl 2.10;
Num 15.39;
Eccl 3.17;
12.14;
Rom 14.10
11.10
2 Cor 7.1;
2 Tim 2.22
12.1ff
Ps 63.6;
119.55;
Eccl 11.8;
2 Sam 19.35

for you do not know what
 disaster may happen on
 earth.
3 When clouds are full,
 they empty rain on the earth;
 whether a tree falls to the
 south or to the north,
 in the place where the tree
 falls, there it will lie.
4 Whoever observes the wind
 will not sow;
 and whoever regards the
 clouds will not reap.
5 Just as you do not know how
the breath comes to the bones in
the mother's womb, so you do not
know the work of God, who makes
everything.
6 In the morning sow your seed,
and at evening do not let your
hands be idle; for you do not know
which will prosper, this or that, or
whether both alike will be good.

Youth and Old Age

7 Light is sweet, and it is pleas-
ant for the eyes to see the sun.
8 Even those who live many
years should rejoice in them all; yet
let them remember that the days of
darkness will be many. All that
comes is vanity.
9 Rejoice, young man, while you
are young, and let your heart cheer
you in the days of your youth. Fol-
low the inclination of your heart
and the desire of your eyes, but
know that for all these things God
will bring you into judgment.
10 Banish anxiety from your
mind, and put away pain from your
body; for youth and the dawn of life
are vanity.

12 Remember your creator in
 the days of your youth, be-
fore the days of trouble come, and
the years draw near when you will
say, "I have no pleasure in them";
2 before the sun and the light and
the moon and the stars are dark-
ened and the clouds return with[x]
the rain; 3 in the day when the
guards of the house tremble, and
the strong men are bent, and the
women who grind cease working
because they are few, and those

[w] Or *a child* [x] Or *after*; Heb *'ahar*

who look through the windows see dimly; ⁴when the doors on the street are shut, and the sound of the grinding is low, and one rises up at the sound of a bird, and all the daughters of song are brought low; ⁵when one is afraid of heights, and terrors are in the road; the almond tree blossoms, the grasshopper drags itself along^y and desire fails; because all must go to their eternal home, and the mourners will go about the streets; ⁶before the silver cord is snapped,^z and the golden bowl is broken, and the pitcher is broken at the fountain, and the wheel broken at the cistern, ⁷and the dust returns to the earth as it was, and the breath^a returns to God who gave it. ⁸Vanity of vanities, says the Teacher;^b all is vanity.

Epilogue

9 Besides being wise, the Teacher^b also taught the people knowledge, weighing and studying and arranging many proverbs. ¹⁰The Teacher^b sought to find pleasing words, and he wrote words of truth plainly.

11 The sayings of the wise are like goads, and like nails firmly fixed are the collected sayings that are given by one shepherd.^c ¹²Of anything beyond these, my child, beware. Of making many books there is no end, and much study is a weariness of the flesh.

13 The end of the matter; all has been heard. Fear God, and keep his commandments; for that is the whole duty of everyone. ¹⁴For God will bring every deed into judgment, including^d every secret thing, whether good or evil.

12.4 Jer 25.10; 2 Sam 19.35
12.5 Job 17.13; Jer 9.17
12.7 Gen 3.19; Job 34.15; Ps 90.3; Job 34.14; Isa 57.16; Zech 12.1
12.8 Eccl 1.2
12.9 1 Kings 4.32
12.10 Prov 10.32; 22.20,21
12.11 Eccl 7.5; Acts 2.37; Ezra 9.8; Isa 22.23
12.13 Deut 4.2; Eccl 8.5; Mic 6.8
12.14 Mt 10.26; 12.36; 1 Cor 4.5

^y Or *is a burden* ^z Syr Vg Compare Gk: Heb *is removed* ^a Or *the spirit* ^b *Koheleth*, traditionally rendered *Preacher* ^c Meaning of Heb uncertain ^d Or *into the judgment on*

THE
Song of Solomon

Title and Background

The title in the Hebrew text is "Solomon's Song of Songs," meaning by, for, or about Solomon. The phrase "Song of Songs" means the greatest of songs.

Author and Date of Writing

Verse 1 seems to ascribe authorship to Solomon, and he is referred to seven times in the book. But whether he was the author remains an open question. Consistency of language, style, tone, perspective, and recurring refrains seems to argue for a single author.

If Solomon is the author, the Song must be dated in the tenth century B.C. If he was not the author, it could have been written any time between the tenth and third century.

Theme and Message

In ancient Israel everything human came to expression in words. In the Song, love finds words—inspired words that disclose its exquisite charm and beauty as one of God's choicest gifts. The woman's voice of love in the Song suggests that love and wisdom draw men powerfully with the subtlety and mystery of a woman's allurements. God intends that such love be a normal part of marital life in his good creation.

Outline

 I. Courtship (1.1–3.5)
 II. Wedding Procession (3.6-11)
 III. Expressions of Love (4.1–8.4)
 IV. Homecoming (8.5-14)

1 The Song of Songs, which is Solomon's.

Colloquy of Bride and Friends

2 Let him kiss me with the
 kisses of his mouth!
For your love is better than
 wine,
3 your anointing oils are
 fragrant,
your name is perfume poured
 out;
 therefore the maidens love
 you.
4 Draw me after you, let us
 make haste.
 The king has brought me
 into his chambers.
We will exult and rejoice in
 you;

we will extol your love
 more than wine;
rightly do they love you.

5 I am black and beautiful,
 O daughters of Jerusalem,
like the tents of Kedar,
 like the curtains of
 Solomon.
6 Do not gaze at me because I
 am dark,
 because the sun has gazed
 on me.
My mother's sons were angry
 with me;
 they made me keeper of
 the vineyards,
but my own vineyard I have
 not kept!
7 Tell me, you whom my soul
 loves,

1.1
1 Kings 4.32
1.2
Song 4.10
1.3
Song 4.10;
Eccl 7.1
1.4
Ps 45.14,15

1.5
Song 2.14;
4.3; 2.7; 5.8
1.6
Ps 69.8;
Song 8.11
1.7
Song 3.1-4;
2.16; 8.13

where you pasture your
 flock,
where you make it lie down
 at noon;
for why should I be like one
 who is veiled
beside the flocks of your
 companions?

8 If you do not know,
 O fairest among women,
follow the tracks of the flock,
 and pasture your kids
beside the shepherds'
 tents.

Colloquy of Bridegroom, Friends, and Bride

9 I compare you, my love,
 to a mare among Pharaoh's
 chariots.
10 Your cheeks are comely with
 ornaments,
 your neck with strings of
 jewels.
11 We will make you ornaments
 of gold,
 studded with silver.

12 While the king was on his
 couch,
 my nard gave forth its
 fragrance.
13 My beloved is to me a bag of
 myrrh
 that lies between my
 breasts.
14 My beloved is to me a
 cluster of henna
 blossoms
 in the vineyards of En-gedi.

15 Ah, you are beautiful, my
 love;
 ah, you are beautiful;
 your eyes are doves.
16 Ah, you are beautiful, my
 beloved,
 truly lovely.
Our couch is green;
17 the beams of our house are
 cedar,
 our rafters[a] are pine.

2 I am a rose[b] of Sharon,
 a lily of the valleys.

2 As a lily among brambles,
 so is my love among
 maidens.

3 As an apple tree among the
 trees of the wood,
 so is my beloved among
 young men.
With great delight I sat in his
 shadow,
 and his fruit was sweet to
 my taste.
4 He brought me to the
 banqueting house,
 and his intention toward
 me was love.
5 Sustain me with raisins,
 refresh me with apples;
 for I am faint with love.
6 O that his left hand were
 under my head,
 and that his right hand
 embraced me!
7 I adjure you, O daughters of
 Jerusalem,
 by the gazelles or the wild
 does:
do not stir up or awaken love
 until it is ready!

Springtime Rhapsody

8 The voice of my beloved!
 Look, he comes,
leaping upon the mountains,
 bounding over the hills.
9 My beloved is like a gazelle
 or a young stag.
Look, there he stands
 behind our wall,
gazing in at the windows,
 looking through the lattice.
10 My beloved speaks and says
 to me:
"Arise, my love, my fair one,
 and come away;
11 for now the winter is past,
 the rain is over and gone.
12 The flowers appear on the
 earth;
 the time of singing has
 come,
and the voice of the
 turtledove
 is heard in our land.

1.8
Song 5.9;
6.1
1.9
Song 2.2,10,
13;
2 Chr 1.16
1.10
5.13
1.14
Song 4.13
1.15
Song 4.1;
5.12
1.17
1 Kings 6.9,
10;
2 Chr 3.5
2.1
Isa 35.1,2;
Song 5.13;
7.2

2.3
Song 8.5;
4.13
2.4
Ps 20.5
2.5
Song 7.8;
5.8
2.6
Song 8.3
2.7
Song 3.5;
8.4
2.8
v. 17
2.9
v. 17
2.10
v. 13
2.12
Ps 74.19

a Meaning of Heb uncertain b Heb crocus

13 The fig tree puts forth its
 figs,
 and the vines are in
 blossom;
 they give forth fragrance.
 Arise, my love, my fair one,
 and come away.
14 O my dove, in the clefts of
 the rock,
 in the covert of the cliff,
 let me see your face,
 let me hear your voice;
 for your voice is sweet,
 and your face is lovely.
15 Catch us the foxes,
 the little foxes,
 that ruin the vineyards —
 for our vineyards are in
 blossom."

16 My beloved is mine and I am
 his;
 he pastures his flock
 among the lilies.
17 Until the day breathes
 and the shadows flee,
 turn, my beloved, be like a
 gazelle
 or a young stag on the cleft
 mountains.ᶜ

Love's Dream

3 Upon my bed at night
 I sought him whom my
 soul loves;
 I sought him, but found him
 not;
 I called him, but he gave
 no answer.ᵈ
2 "I will rise now and go about
 the city,
 in the streets and in the
 squares;
 I will seek him whom my
 soul loves."
 I sought him, but found
 him not.
3 The sentinels found me,
 as they went about in the
 city.
 "Have you seen him whom
 my soul loves?"
4 Scarcely had I passed them,
 when I found him whom
 my soul loves.

2.13
Mt 24.32;
Song 7.12;
v. 10
2.14
Song 5.2;
Jer 48.28;
Song 8.13;
1.5
2.15
Ezek 13.4
2.16
Song 6.3;
7.10
2.17
Song 4.6;
vv. 8,9
3.1
Isa 26.9;
Song 1.7;
5.6
3.2
Jer 5.1
3.3
Song 5.7
3.4
Song 8.2

3.5
Song 2.7;
8.4
3.6
Song 8.5;
1.13; 4.6,14
3.8
Jer 50.9;
Ps 45.3;
91.5
3.10
Song 1.5
3.11
Song 3.16,
17

I held him, and would not
 let him go
 until I brought him into my
 mother's house,
 and into the chamber of
 her that conceived me.
5 I adjure you, O daughters of
 Jerusalem,
 by the gazelles or the wild
 does:
 do not stir up or awaken love
 until it is ready!

The Groom and His Party Approach

6 What is that coming up from
 the wilderness,
 like a column of smoke,
 perfumed with myrrh and
 frankincense,
 with all the fragrant
 powders of the
 merchant?
7 Look, it is the litter of
 Solomon!
 Around it are sixty mighty
 men
 of the mighty men of
 Israel,
8 all equipped with swords
 and expert in war,
 each with his sword at his
 thigh
 because of alarms by night.
9 King Solomon made himself
 a palanquin
 from the wood of Lebanon.
10 He made its posts of silver,
 its back of gold, its seat of
 purple;
 its interior was inlaid with
 love.ᵉ
 Daughters of Jerusalem,
11 come out.
 Look, O daughters of Zion,
 at King Solomon,
 at the crown with which his
 mother crowned him
 on the day of his wedding,
 on the day of the gladness
 of his heart.

ᶜ Or *on the mountains of Bether*: meaning of
Heb uncertain ᵈ Gk: Heb lacks this line
ᵉ Meaning of Heb uncertain

The Bride's Beauty Extolled

4 How beautiful you are, my
 love,
 how very beautiful!
Your eyes are doves
 behind your veil.
Your hair is like a flock of
 goats,
 moving down the slopes of
 Gilead.
2 Your teeth are like a flock of
 shorn ewes
 that have come up from
 the washing,
all of which bear twins,
 and not one among them is
 bereaved.
3 Your lips are like a crimson
 thread,
 and your mouth is
 lovely.
Your cheeks are like halves
 of a pomegranate
 behind your veil.
4 Your neck is like the tower
 of David,
 built in courses;
on it hang a thousand
 bucklers,
 all of them shields of
 warriors.
5 Your two breasts are like two
 fawns,
 twins of a gazelle,
 that feed among the
 lilies.
6 Until the day breathes
 and the shadows flee,
I will hasten to the mountain
 of myrrh
 and the hill of
 frankincense.
7 You are altogether beautiful,
 my love;
 there is no flaw in you.
8 Come with me from
 Lebanon, my bride;
 come with me from
 Lebanon.
Depart[f] from the peak of
 Amana,
 from the peak of Senir and
 Hermon,
from the dens of lions,
 from the mountains of
 leopards.

4.1
Song 1.15;
5.12; 6.5,7
4.2
Song 6.6
4.3
Song 6.7
4.4
Song 7.4;
Neh 3.19
4.5
Song 7.3;
2.16; 6.2,3
4.6
Song 2.17;
v. 14
4.7
Song 1.15
4.8
Song 5.1;
Deut 3.9

4.9
vv. 10,12;
Prov 1.9;
Ezek 16.11
4.10
Song 1.2-4
4.11
Prov 5.3;
24.13;
Gen 27.27;
Hos 14.6
4.12
Prov 5.15-18;
Gen 29.3
4.13
Eccl 2.5;
Song 6.11;
7.12; v. 16;
Song 1.14
4.14
Song 1.12;
Ex 30.23;
v. 6;
Song 3.6;
Jn 19.39
4.15
Jn 4.10;
7.38
4.16
Song 5.1;
6.2
5.1
Song 6.2;
4.9,11,14;
Lk 15.7,10;
Jn 3.29

9 You have ravished my heart,
 my sister, my bride,
 you have ravished my heart
 with a glance of your
 eyes,
 with one jewel of your
 necklace.
10 How sweet is your love, my
 sister, my bride!
 how much better is your
 love than wine,
 and the fragrance of your
 oils than any spice!
11 Your lips distill nectar, my
 bride;
 honey and milk are under
 your tongue;
 the scent of your garments
 is like the scent of
 Lebanon.
12 A garden locked is my sister,
 my bride,
 a garden locked, a fountain
 sealed.
13 Your channel[g] is an orchard
 of pomegranates
 with all choicest fruits,
 henna with nard,
14 nard and saffron, calamus
 and cinnamon,
 with all trees of
 frankincense,
 myrrh and aloes,
 with all chief spices—
15 a garden fountain, a well of
 living water,
 and flowing streams from
 Lebanon.

16 Awake, O north wind,
 and come, O south wind!
Blow upon my garden
 that its fragrance may be
 wafted abroad.
Let my beloved come to his
 garden,
 and eat its choicest fruits.

5 I come to my garden, my
 sister, my bride;
 I gather my myrrh with my
 spice,
 I eat my honeycomb with
 my honey,

[f] Or *Look* [g] Meaning of Heb uncertain

I drink my wine with my
milk.

Eat, friends, drink,
and be drunk with love.

Another Dream

2 I slept, but my heart was
awake.
Listen! my beloved is
knocking.
"Open to me, my sister, my
love,
my dove, my perfect one;
for my head is wet with dew,
my locks with the drops of
the night."
3 I had put off my garment;
how could I put it on
again?
I had bathed my feet;
how could I soil them?
4 My beloved thrust his hand
into the opening,
and my inmost being
yearned for him.
5 I arose to open to my
beloved,
and my hands dripped with
myrrh,
my fingers with liquid myrrh,
upon the handles of the
bolt.
6 I opened to my beloved,
but my beloved had turned
and was gone.
My soul failed me when he
spoke.
I sought him, but did not
find him;
I called him, but he gave
no answer.
7 Making their rounds in the
city
the sentinels found me;
they beat me, they wounded
me,
they took away my mantle,
those sentinels of the
walls.
8 I adjure you, O daughters of
Jerusalem,
if you find my beloved,
tell him this:
I am faint with love.

Colloquy of Friends and Bride

9 What is your beloved more
than another beloved,
O fairest among women?
What is your beloved more
than another beloved,
that you thus adjure us?

10 My beloved is all radiant and
ruddy,
distinguished among ten
thousand.
11 His head is the finest gold;
his locks are wavy,
black as a raven.
12 His eyes are like doves
beside springs of water,
bathed in milk,
fitly set. h
13 His cheeks are like beds of
spices,
yielding fragrance.
His lips are lilies,
distilling liquid myrrh.
14 His arms are rounded gold,
set with jewels.
His body is ivory work, h
encrusted with sapphires. i
15 His legs are alabaster
columns,
set upon bases of gold.
His appearance is like
Lebanon,
choice as the cedars.
16 His speech is most sweet,
and he is altogether
desirable.
This is my beloved and this
is my friend,
O daughters of Jerusalem.

6 Where has your beloved
gone,
O fairest among women?
Which way has your beloved
turned,
that we may seek him with
you?

2 My beloved has gone down
to his garden,
to the beds of spices,
to pasture his flock in the
gardens,

5.2
Song 4.9;
6.9; v. 11
5.3
Lk 11.7;
Gen 19.2
5.5
v. 13
5.6
Song 6.1;
3.1;
Prov 1.28
5.7
Song 3.3
5.8
Song 2.7;
3.5; 2.5

5.9
Song 1.8;
6.1
5.12
Song 1.15;
4.1
5.13
Song 6.2;
2.1
5.16
Song 7.9;
2 Sam 1.23
6.1
Song 5.6;
1.8
6.2
Song 4.16;
5.1,13; 1.7;
2.1

h Meaning of Heb uncertain i Heb lapis
lazuli

and to gather lilies.

3 I am my beloved's and my
 beloved is mine;
 he pastures his flock
 among the lilies.

The Bride's Matchless Beauty

4 You are beautiful as Tirzah,
 my love,
 comely as Jerusalem,
 terrible as an army with
 banners.
5 Turn away your eyes from
 me,
 for they overwhelm me!
 Your hair is like a flock of
 goats,
 moving down the slopes of
 Gilead.
6 Your teeth are like a flock of
 ewes,
 that have come up from
 the washing;
 all of them bear twins,
 and not one among them is
 bereaved.
7 Your cheeks are like halves
 of a pomegranate
 behind your veil.
8 There are sixty queens and
 eighty concubines,
 and maidens without
 number.
9 My dove, my perfect one, is
 the only one,
 the darling of her mother,
 flawless to her that bore
 her.
 The maidens saw her and
 called her happy;
 the queens and concubines
 also, and they praised
 her.
10 "Who is this that looks forth
 like the dawn,
 fair as the moon, bright as
 the sun,
 terrible as an army with
 banners?"

11 I went down to the nut
 orchard,
 to look at the blossoms of
 the valley,
 to see whether the vines had
 budded,

whether the pomegranates
 were in bloom.
12 Before I was aware, my fancy
 set me
 in a chariot beside my
 prince.j

13 kReturn, return,
 O Shulammite!
 Return, return, that we
 may look upon you.

Why should you look upon
 the Shulammite,
 as upon a dance before two
 armies?l

Expressions of Praise

7 How graceful are your feet in
 sandals,
 O queenly maiden!
 Your rounded thighs are like
 jewels,
 the work of a master hand.
2 Your navel is a rounded bowl
 that never lacks mixed
 wine.
 Your belly is a heap of
 wheat,
 encircled with lilies.
3 Your two breasts are like two
 fawns,
 twins of a gazelle.
4 Your neck is like an ivory
 tower.
 Your eyes are pools in
 Heshbon,
 by the gate of Bath-rabbim.
 Your nose is like a tower of
 Lebanon,
 overlooking Damascus.
5 Your head crowns you like
 Carmel,
 and your flowing locks are
 like purple;
 a king is held captive in
 the tresses.m

6 How fair and pleasant you
 are,
 O loved one, delectable
 maiden!n

6.3
Song 2.16;
7.10
6.4
Song 1.15;
v. 10
6.5
Song 4.1
6.6
Song 4.2
6.7
Song 4.3
6.8
1 Kings 11.3;
Song 1.3
6.9
Song 2.14;
5.2;
Gen 30.13
6.10
v. 4
6.11
Song 7.12

6.13
Judg 21.21;
Gen 32.2
7.1
Ps 45.13
7.3
Song 4.5
7.4
Song 4.4
7.5
Isa 35.2
7.6
Song 1.15,
16

j Cn: Meaning of Heb uncertain k Ch 7.1
in Heb l Or *dance of Mahanaim*
m Meaning of Heb uncertain n Syr: Heb *in
delights*

7 You are stately° as a palm
tree,
and your breasts are like
its clusters.
8 I say I will climb the palm
tree
and lay hold of its
branches.
Oh, may your breasts be like
clusters of the vine,
and the scent of your
breath like apples,
9 and your kisses ᵖ like the
best wine

that goes down �q smoothly,
gliding over lips and
teeth. ʳ

10 I am my beloved's,
and his desire is for me.
11 Come, my beloved,
let us go forth into the
fields,
and lodge in the villages;
12 let us go out early to the
vineyards,
and see whether the vines
have budded,
whether the grape blossoms
have opened
and the pomegranates are
in bloom.
There I will give you my love.
13 The mandrakes give forth
fragrance,
and over our doors are all
choice fruits,
new as well as old,
which I have laid up for
you, O my beloved.

8 O that you were like a
brother to me,
who nursed at my mother's
breast!
If I met you outside, I would
kiss you,
and no one would despise
me.
2 I would lead you and bring
you
into the house of my
mother,
and into the chamber of
the one who bore me. ˢ
I would give you spiced wine
to drink,

7.8
Song 2.5
7.10
Song 2.16;
6.3;
Ps 45.11
7.12
Song 6.11
7.13
Gen 30.14;
Song 2.3;
4.13,16
8.2
Song 3.4

8.3
Song 2.6
8.4
Song 2.7;
3.5
8.5
Song 3.6;
2.3
8.6
Isa 49.16;
Jer 22.24;
Hag 2.23;
Prov 6.34
8.8
Ezek 16.7

the juice of my
pomegranates.
3 O that his left hand were
under my head,
and that his right hand
embraced me!
4 I adjure you, O daughters of
Jerusalem,
do not stir up or awaken
love
until it is ready!

Homecoming

5 Who is that coming up from
the wilderness,
leaning upon her beloved?

Under the apple tree I
awakened you.
There your mother was in
labor with you;
there she who bore you
was in labor.

6 Set me as a seal upon your
heart,
as a seal upon your arm;
for love is strong as death,
passion fierce as the grave.
Its flashes are flashes of fire,
a raging flame.
7 Many waters cannot quench
love,
neither can floods drown it.
If one offered for love
all the wealth of his house,
it would be utterly scorned.

8 We have a little sister,
and she has no breasts.
What shall we do for our
sister,
on the day when she is
spoken for?
9 If she is a wall,
we will build upon her a
battlement of silver;
but if she is a door,
we will enclose her with
boards of cedar.
10 I was a wall,
and my breasts were like
towers;

° Heb *This your stature is* ᵖ Heb *palate*
�q Heb *down for my lover* ʳ Gk Syr Vg: Heb
lips of sleepers ˢ Gk Syr: Heb *my mother;*
she (or *you*) *will teach me*

then I was in his eyes
as one who brings[t] peace.

11 Solomon had a vineyard at
Baal-hamon;
he entrusted the vineyard
to keepers;
each one was to bring for
its fruit a thousand
pieces of silver.

12 My vineyard, my very own, is
for myself;
you, O Solomon, may have
the thousand,
and the keepers of the fruit
two hundred!

8.11
Eccl 2.4;
Mt 21.33;
Song 1.6;
2.3; Isa 7.23

8.13
Song 1.7;
2.14

8.14
Song 2.17;
4.6

13 O you who dwell in the
gardens,
my companions are
listening for your voice;
let me hear it.

14 Make haste, my beloved,
and be like a gazelle
or a young stag
upon the mountains of
spices!

[t] Or *finds*

Isaiah

Title and Background

This book is named after the prophet whose message it records. Isaiah wrote during the stormy period marking the expansion of the Assyrian empire and the decline of Israel. He warned the people of Judah that their sin would bring captivity at the hands of Babylon. Although the fall of Jerusalem would not take place until 586 B.C., Isaiah assumed its demise and proceeded to predict the restoration of the people from captivity. A decree of Cyrus would allow the Jews to return home, a deliverance that prefigured the greater salvation from sin through Jesus Christ. Significantly, Isaiah's name means "The LORD saves."

Author and Date of Writing

Isaiah son of Amoz was the greatest of the writing prophets and a contemporary of Amos, Hosea, and Micah. Most of the events discussed in chapters 1-39 occurred during Isaiah's ministry, so it is likely they were completed around 700 B.C. He lived until at least 681 and may have written chapters 40-66 during his later years. Some scholars, however, think that these latter chapters were written by a later devoted disciple of Isaiah, rather than by the prophet himself.

Theme and Message

Isaiah unveils the full dimensions of God's judgment and salvation. The awful judgment unleashed on Israel and all who defy God is called "the day of the LORD." The Lord's kingdom on earth, with its righteous Ruler and his righteous subjects, is the goal toward which the book of Isaiah steadily moves. The restored earth and the restored people will then conform to the divine ideal, and all will result in the praise and glory of the Holy God of Israel.

Outline

I. Rebuke and Promise (1.1–6.13)
II. Immanuel and His Kingdom (7.1–12.6)
III. Judgment Against the Nations (13.1–23.18)
IV. Judgment and Promise (24.1–27.13)
V. Six Woes on Israel and Assyria (28.1–33.24)
VI. Judgment and Promise (34.1–35.10)
VII. From the Assyrian Threat to the Babylonian Exile (36.1–39.8)
VIII. Deliverance and Restoration of Israel (40.1–48.22)
IX. The Servant's Ministry and Israel's Restoration (49.1–57.21)
X. Everlasting Deliverance and Judgment (58.1–66.24)

1 The vision of Isaiah son of Amoz, which he saw concerning Judah and Jerusalem in the days of Uzziah, Jotham, Ahaz, and Hezekiah, kings of Judah.

The Wickedness of Judah

2 Hear, O heavens, and listen,
 O earth;
 for the LORD has spoken:

I reared children and brought
 them up,
 but they have rebelled
 against me.
3 The ox knows its owner,
 and the donkey its master's
 crib;
 but Israel does not know,
 my people do not
 understand.

1.1
Num 12.6;
Isa 2.1;
2 Kings 15.1,
13,32; 16.1;
18.1
1.2
Deut 23.1

1.3
Jer 8.7; 9.3,
6

4 Ah, sinful nation,
　　people laden with iniquity,
offspring who do evil,
　　children who deal
　　　corruptly,
who have forsaken the LORD,
　who have despised the
　　Holy One of Israel,
　who are utterly estranged!

5 Why do you seek further
　　beatings?
　Why do you continue to
　　rebel?
The whole head is sick,
　and the whole heart faint.
6 From the sole of the foot
　　even to the head,
　there is no soundness in it,
but bruises and sores
　and bleeding wounds;
they have not been drained,
　or bound up,
　or softened with oil.

7 Your country lies desolate,
　your cities are burned with
　　fire;
in your very presence
　aliens devour your land;
　it is desolate, as
　　overthrown by
　　foreigners.
8 And daughter Zion is left
　like a booth in a vineyard,
like a shelter in a cucumber
　　field,
like a besieged city.
9 If the LORD of hosts
　had not left us a few
　　survivors,
we would have been like
　　Sodom,
　and become like
　　Gomorrah.

10 Hear the word of the LORD,
　you rulers of Sodom!
Listen to the teaching of our
　　God,
　you people of Gomorrah!
11 What to me is the multitude
　　of your sacrifices?
　says the LORD;
I have had enough of burnt
　offerings of rams
　and the fat of fed beasts;

1.4
Isa 14.20;
v. 28;
Isa 5.24
1.5
Isa 31.6;
33.24
1.6
Job 2.7;
Ps 38.3;
Isa 30.26;
Lk 10.34
1.7
Isa 6.11;
Jer 44.6
1.8
Job 27.18
1.9
Rom 9.29;
Isa 10.20-22
1.10
Isa 28.14;
3.9;
Ezek 16.46;
Rev 11.8
1.11
1 Sam 15.22;
Jer 6.20;
Mic 6.7
1.12
Ex 23.17
1.13
Isa 66.3;
1 Chr 23.31;
Ex 12.16;
Jer 7.9,10
1.14
Num 28.11;
Lev 23.2;
Isa 7.13;
43.24
1.15
1 Kings 8.22;
Isa 8.17;
59.2;
Mic 3.4;
Isa 59.3
1.16
Jer 4.14;
Isa 52.11;
55.7;
Jer 25.5
1.17
Jer 22.3;
Isa 58.6;
Ps 82.3
1.18
Isa 43.26;
Ps 51.7;
Rev 7.14

I do not delight in the blood
　of bulls,
　or of lambs, or of goats.

12 When you come to appear
　　before me,[a]
　who asked this from your
　　hand?
　Trample my courts no
　　more;
13 bringing offerings is futile;
　incense is an abomination
　　to me.
New moon and sabbath and
　calling of
　　convocation—
　I cannot endure solemn
　　assemblies with
　　iniquity.
14 Your new moons and your
　　appointed festivals
　my soul hates;
they have become a burden
　　to me,
　I am weary of bearing
　　them.
15 When you stretch out your
　　hands,
　I will hide my eyes from
　　you;
even though you make many
　　prayers,
　I will not listen;
　your hands are full of
　　blood.
16 Wash yourselves; make
　　yourselves clean;
　remove the evil of your
　　doings
　from before my eyes;
cease to do evil,
17 　learn to do good;
seek justice,
　rescue the oppressed,
defend the orphan,
　plead for the widow.

18 Come now, let us argue it
　　out,
　says the LORD:
though your sins are like
　　scarlet,
　they shall be like snow;
though they are red like
　　crimson,

a Or *see my face*

they shall become like
wool.

19 If you are willing and
obedient,
you shall eat the good of
the land;
20 but if you refuse and rebel,
you shall be devoured by
the sword;
for the mouth of the LORD
has spoken.

The Degenerate City

21 How the faithful city
has become a whore!
She that was full of justice,
righteousness lodged in
her —
but now murderers!
22 Your silver has become
dross,
your wine is mixed with
water.
23 Your princes are rebels
and companions of thieves.
Everyone loves a bribe
and runs after gifts.
They do not defend the
orphan,
and the widow's cause
does not come before
them.

24 Therefore says the Sovereign,
the LORD of hosts, the
Mighty One of Israel:
Ah, I will pour out my wrath
on my enemies,
and avenge myself on my
foes!
25 I will turn my hand against
you;
I will smelt away your
dross as with lye
and remove all your alloy.
26 And I will restore your judges
as at the first,
and your counselors as at
the beginning.
Afterward you shall be called
the city of
righteousness,
the faithful city.

27 Zion shall be redeemed by
justice,

and those in her who
repent, by
righteousness.
28 But rebels and sinners shall
be destroyed together,
and those who forsake the
LORD shall be
consumed.
29 For you shall be ashamed of
the oaks
in which you delighted;
and you shall blush for the
gardens
that you have chosen.
30 For you shall be like an oak
whose leaf withers,
and like a garden without
water.
31 The strong shall become like
tinder,
and their work[b] like a
spark;
they and their work shall
burn together,
with no one to quench
them.

The Future House of God

2 The word that Isaiah son of
Amoz saw concerning Judah
and Jerusalem.

2 In days to come
the mountain of the LORD's
house
shall be established as the
highest of the
mountains,
and shall be raised above
the hills;
all the nations shall stream
to it.
3 Many peoples shall come
and say,
"Come, let us go up to the
mountain of the LORD,
to the house of the God of
Jacob;
that he may teach us his
ways
and that we may walk in
his paths."
For out of Zion shall go forth
instruction,

1.19
Deut 30.15,
16
1.20
Isa 3.25;
34.16
1.21
Jer 2.20;
Isa 59.7
1.22
Ezek 22.18
1.23
Hos 9.15;
Ex 23.8;
Mic 7.3;
Jer 5.28;
Zech 7.10
1.24
Isa 49.26;
35.4
1.25
Mal 3.3
1.26
Jer 33.7;
Zech 8.3

1.28
Isa 24.20;
Ps 9.5;
2 Thes 1.8,
9
1.29
Isa 57.5;
65.3
1.31
Isa 5.24;
66.24;
Mt 3.12
2.1ff
Isa 1.1
2.2
Mic 4.1-3;
Isa 27.13;
66.20; 56.7
2.3
Isa 55.5;
66.18;
Zech 8.20-23;
Lk 24.47

[b] Or *its makers*

and the word of the LORD
 from Jerusalem.
4 He shall judge between the
 nations,
 and shall arbitrate for
 many peoples;
 they shall beat their swords
 into plowshares,
 and their spears into
 pruning hooks;
 nation shall not lift up sword
 against nation,
 neither shall they learn war
 any more.

Judgment Pronounced on Arrogance

5 O house of Jacob,
 come, let us walk
 in the light of the LORD!
6 For you have forsaken the
 ways of[c] your people,
 O house of Jacob.
 Indeed they are full of
 diviners[d] from the east
 and of soothsayers like the
 Philistines,
 and they clasp hands with
 foreigners.
7 Their land is filled with silver
 and gold,
 and there is no end to their
 treasures;
 their land is filled with
 horses,
 and there is no end to their
 chariots.
8 Their land is filled with
 idols;
 they bow down to the work
 of their hands,
 to what their own fingers
 have made.
9 And so people are humbled,
 and everyone is brought
 low—
 do not forgive them!
10 Enter into the rock,
 and hide in the dust
 from the terror of the LORD,
 and from the glory of his
 majesty.
11 The haughty eyes of people
 shall be brought low,
 and the pride of everyone
 shall be humbled;

and the LORD alone will be
 exalted
 in that day.
12 For the LORD of hosts has a
 day
 against all that is proud
 and lofty,
 against all that is lifted up
 and high;[e]
13 against all the cedars of
 Lebanon,
 lofty and lifted up;
 and against all the oaks of
 Bashan;
14 against all the high
 mountains,
 and against all the lofty
 hills;
15 against every high tower,
 and against every fortified
 wall;
16 against all the ships of
 Tarshish,
 and against all the
 beautiful craft.[f]
17 The haughtiness of people
 shall be humbled,
 and the pride of everyone
 shall be brought low;
 and the LORD alone will be
 exalted on that day.
18 The idols shall utterly pass
 away.
19 Enter the caves of the rocks
 and the holes of the
 ground,
 from the terror of the LORD,
 and from the glory of his
 majesty,
 when he rises to terrify the
 earth.
20 On that day people will
 throw away
 to the moles and to the
 bats
 their idols of silver and their
 idols of gold,
 which they made for
 themselves to worship,
21 to enter the caverns of the
 rocks
 and the clefts in the crags,
 from the terror of the LORD,

2.4
Isa 32.17, 18;
Hos 2.18
2.5
Isa 58.1; 60.1,2,19; 18.14
2.6
Deut 31.17; 2 Kings 16.7, 8
2.7
Deut 17.16
2.8
Isa 10.11; 17.8
2.9
Isa 5.15; Neh 4.5
2.10
Rev 6.15; 2 Thes 1.9
2.11
Isa 13.11; Zech 9.16

2.12
Isa 24.4,21
2.13
Isa 10.33, 34; Zech 11.2
2.14
Isa 30.25
2.16
1 Kings 10.22
2.17
v. 11
2.18
Isa 21.9
2.19
Hos 10.8; Rev 9.6; 2 Thes 1.9; Heb 12.26
2.20
Isa 30.22
2.21
vv. 10,19

c Heb lacks *the ways of* d Cn: Heb lacks
of diviners e Cn Compare Gk: Heb *low*
f Compare Gk: Meaning of Heb uncertain

and from the glory of his
majesty,
when he rises to terrify the
earth.
22 Turn away from mortals,
who have only breath in
their nostrils,
for of what account are
they?

3 For now the Sovereign, the
Lord of hosts,
is taking away from
Jerusalem and from
Judah
support and staff—
all support of bread,
and all support of water—
2 warrior and soldier,
judge and prophet,
diviner and elder,
3 captain of fifty
and dignitary,
counselor and skillful
magician
and expert enchanter.
4 And I will make boys their
princes,
and babes shall rule over
them.
5 The people will be
oppressed,
everyone by another
and everyone by a
neighbor;
the youth will be insolent to
the elder,
and the base to the
honorable.

6 Someone will even seize a
relative,
a member of the clan,
saying,
"You have a cloak;
you shall be our leader,
and this heap of ruins
shall be under your rule."
7 But the other will cry out on
that day, saying,
"I will not be a healer;
in my house there is
neither bread nor cloak;
you shall not make me
leader of the people."
8 For Jerusalem has stumbled
and Judah has fallen,

2.22
Ps 146.3;
Job 27.3;
Jas 4.14
3.1
Jer 37.21;
Lev 26.26
3.2
2 Kings 24.14
3.4
Eccl 10.16
3.5
Mic 7.3-6;
Isa 9.19
3.6
Isa 4.1
3.7
Ezek 34.4
3.8
Isa 1.7;
6.11; 9.17;
65.3,5

3.9
Isa 1.10;
Gen 13.13
3.10
Deut 28.1-14
3.11
Isa 65.6,7
3.12
v. 4;
Isa 9.16
3.13
Isa 66.16;
Mic 6.2
3.14
Ezek 20.35,
36; Isa 10.1,
2; Jas 2.6
3.15
Ps 94.5
3.16
Isa 4.4

because their speech and
their deeds are against
the Lord,
defying his glorious presence.
9 The look on their faces bears
witness against them;
they proclaim their sin like
Sodom,
they do not hide it.
Woe to them!
For they have brought evil
on themselves.
10 Tell the innocent how
fortunate they are,
for they shall eat the fruit
of their labors.
11 Woe to the guilty! How
unfortunate they are,
for what their hands have
done shall be done to
them.
12 My people—children are
their oppressors,
and women rule over them.
O my people, your leaders
mislead you,
and confuse the course of
your paths.

13 The Lord rises to argue his
case;
he stands to judge the
peoples.
14 The Lord enters into
judgment
with the elders and princes
of his people:
It is you who have devoured
the vineyard;
the spoil of the poor is in
your houses.
15 What do you mean by
crushing my people,
by grinding the face of the
poor? says the Lord God
of hosts.

16 The Lord said:
Because the daughters of
Zion are haughty
and walk with outstretched
necks,
glancing wantonly with
their eyes,
mincing along as they go,
tinkling with their feet;

17 the Lord will afflict with
 scabs
 the heads of the daughters
 of Zion,
 and the LORD will lay bare
 their secret parts.

18 In that day the Lord will take
away the finery of the anklets, the
headbands, and the crescents;
¹⁹the pendants, the bracelets, and
the scarfs; ²⁰the headdresses, the
armlets, the sashes, the perfume
boxes, and the amulets; ²¹the sig-
net rings and nose rings; ²²the fes-
tal robes, the mantles, the cloaks,
and the handbags; ²³the garments
of gauze, the linen garments, the
turbans, and the veils.
24 Instead of perfume there will
 be a stench;
 and instead of a sash, a
 rope;
 and instead of well-set hair,
 baldness;
 and instead of a rich robe,
 a binding of sackcloth;
 instead of beauty, shame.ᵍ
25 Your men shall fall by the
 sword
 and your warriors in battle.
26 And her gates shall lament
 and mourn;
 ravaged, she shall sit upon
 the ground.

4 Seven women shall take hold
 of one man in that day, saying,
"We will eat our own bread
 and wear our own
 clothes;
just let us be called by your
 name;
 take away our disgrace."

The Future Glory of the
Survivors in Zion

2 On that day the branch of the
LORD shall be beautiful and glori-
ous, and the fruit of the land shall
be the pride and glory of the survi-
vors of Israel. ³Whoever is left in
Zion and remains in Jerusalem will
be called holy, everyone who has
been recorded for life in Jerusalem,
⁴once the Lord has washed away
the filth of the daughters of Zion

3.17
Isa 47.3
3.18
Judg 8.21
3.20
Ex 39.28
3.21
Ezek 16.12
3.24
Prov 31.24;
Isa 22.12;
15.3
3.25
Isa 1.20;
65.12
3.26
Jer 14.2;
Lam 2.10
4.1
Isa 13.12;
2 Thes 3.12;
Isa 54.4
4.2
Isa 11.1;
Zech 3.8;
6.12;
Ps 72.16;
Isa 10.20
4.3
Isa 28.5;
60.21; 52.1;
Lk 10.20
4.4
Isa 3.16,24;
1.15; 28.6;
Mal 3.2,3

4.5
Ex 13.21;
Isa 60.1,2
4.6
Isa 25.4
5.1
Ps 80.8;
Mt 21.33;
Mk 12.1;
Lk 20.9
5.2
Jer 2.21;
Mt 21.19;
Mk 11.13;
Lk 13.6
5.3
Mt 21.40
5.4
Mt 23.37
5.5
Ps 89.40;
Isa 6.13;
Ps 80.12;
Isa 10.6;
Lk 21.24;
Rev 11.2
5.6
Isa 24.1,3;
Heb 6.8;
1 Kings 8.35

and cleansed the bloodstains of Je-
rusalem from its midst by a spirit of
judgment and by a spirit of burn-
ing. ⁵Then the LORD will create over
the whole site of Mount Zion and
over its places of assembly a cloud
by day and smoke and the shining
of a flaming fire by night. Indeed
over all the glory there will be a
canopy. ⁶It will serve as a pavilion,
a shade by day from the heat, and
a refuge and a shelter from the
storm and rain.

The Song of the Unfruitful
Vineyard

5 Let me sing for my beloved
 my love-song concerning
 his vineyard:
 My beloved had a vineyard
 on a very fertile hill.
2 He dug it and cleared it of
 stones,
 and planted it with choice
 vines;
 he built a watchtower in the
 midst of it,
 and hewed out a wine vat
 in it;
 he expected it to yield
 grapes,
 but it yielded wild grapes.

3 And now, inhabitants of
 Jerusalem
 and people of Judah,
 judge between me
 and my vineyard.
4 What more was there to do
 for my vineyard
 that I have not done in it?
 When I expected it to yield
 grapes,
 why did it yield wild
 grapes?

5 And now I will tell you
 what I will do to my
 vineyard.
 I will remove its hedge,
 and it shall be devoured;
 I will break down its wall,
 and it shall be trampled
 down.
6 I will make it a waste;

ᵍ Q Ms: MT lacks shame

it shall not be pruned or
 hoed,
and it shall be overgrown
 with briers and thorns;
I will also command the
 clouds
that they rain no rain upon
 it.

7 For the vineyard of the LORD
 of hosts
 is the house of Israel,
and the people of Judah
 are his pleasant planting;
he expected justice,
 but saw bloodshed;
righteousness,
 but heard a cry!

Social Injustice Denounced

8 Ah, you who join house to
 house,
 who add field to field,
until there is room for no
 one but you,
 and you are left to live
 alone
in the midst of the land!
9 The LORD of hosts has sworn
 in my hearing:
 Surely many houses shall be
 desolate,
large and beautiful houses,
 without inhabitant.
10 For ten acres of vineyard
 shall yield but one
 bath,
 and a homer of seed shall
 yield a mere ephah.[h]

11 Ah, you who rise early in the
 morning
 in pursuit of strong drink,
who linger in the evening
 to be inflamed by wine,
12 whose feasts consist of lyre
 and harp,
 tambourine and flute and
 wine,
but who do not regard the
 deeds of the LORD,
 or see the work of his
 hands!
13 Therefore my people go into
 exile without
 knowledge;

their nobles are dying of
 hunger,
 and their multitude is
 parched with thirst.
14 Therefore Sheol has enlarged
 its appetite
 and opened its mouth
 beyond measure;
the nobility of Jerusalem[i]
 and her multitude go
 down,
her throng and all who
 exult in her.
15 People are bowed down,
 everyone is brought
 low,
and the eyes of the
 haughty are humbled.
16 But the LORD of hosts is
 exalted by justice,
 and the Holy God shows
 himself holy by
 righteousness.
17 Then the lambs shall graze
 as in their pasture,
 fatlings and kids[j] shall
 feed among the ruins.

18 Ah, you who drag iniquity
 along with cords of
 falsehood,
 who drag sin along as with
 cart ropes,
19 who say, "Let him make
 haste,
 let him speed his work
 that we may see it;
let the plan of the Holy One
 of Israel hasten to
 fulfillment,
 that we may know it!"
20 Ah, you who call evil good
 and good evil,
 who put darkness for light
 and light for darkness,
who put bitter for sweet
 and sweet for bitter!
21 Ah, you who are wise in your
 own eyes,
 and shrewd in your own
 sight!
22 Ah, you who are heroes in
 drinking wine

5.7
Ps 80.8-11;
Isa 3.14,15
5.8
Mic 2.2
5.9
Isa 22.14;
6.11,12
5.10
Isa 7.23;
Ezek 45.11
5.11
Prov 23.29,
30;
Eccl 10.16
5.12
Am 6.5,6;
Job 34.27;
Ps 28.5
5.13
Hos 4.6;
Isa 1.3; 3.3;
9.14,15

5.14
Prov 30.16;
Num 16.30-34;
Ps 141.7
5.15
Isa 2.9,11
5.16
Isa 2.11,17;
8.13; 29.23
5.18
Isa 59.4-8
5.19
Ezek 12.22;
2 Pet 3.3,4
5.20
Prov 17.15;
Mt 6.22,23;
Lk 11.34,35
5.21
Rom 12.16
5.22
v. 11

h The Heb *bath*, *homer*, and *ephah* are
measures of quantity i Heb *her nobility*
j Cn Compare Gk: Heb *aliens*

and valiant at mixing
drink,

23 who acquit the guilty for a
bribe,
and deprive the innocent of
their rights!

Foreign Invasion Predicted

24 Therefore, as the tongue of
fire devours the stubble,
and as dry grass sinks
down in the flame,
so their root will become
rotten,
and their blossom go up
like dust;
for they have rejected the
instruction of the LORD
of hosts,
and have despised the word
of the Holy One of
Israel.

25 Therefore the anger of the
LORD was kindled
against his people,
and he stretched out his
hand against them and
struck them;
the mountains quaked,
and their corpses were like
refuse
in the streets.
For all this his anger has not
turned away,
and his hand is stretched
out still.

26 He will raise a signal for a
nation far away,
and whistle for a people at
the ends of the earth;
Here they come, swiftly,
speedily!

27 None of them is weary, none
stumbles,
none slumbers or sleeps,
not a loincloth is loose,
not a sandal-thong broken;

28 their arrows are sharp,
all their bows bent,
their horses' hoofs seem like
flint,
and their wheels like the
whirlwind.

29 Their roaring is like a lion,
like young lions they roar;

they growl and seize their
prey,
they carry it off, and no
one can rescue.

30 They will roar over it on that
day,
like the roaring of the sea.
And if one look to the
land—
only darkness and distress;
and the light grows dark with
clouds.

A Vision of God in the Temple

6 In the year that King Uzziah
died, I saw the Lord sitting on
a throne, high and lofty; and the
hem of his robe filled the temple.
2 Seraphs were in attendance above
him; each had six wings: with two
they covered their faces, and with
two they covered their feet, and
with two they flew. 3 And one called
to another and said:
"Holy, holy, holy is the LORD
of hosts;
the whole earth is full of his
glory."
4 The pivots[k] on the thresholds
shook at the voices of those who
called, and the house filled with
smoke. 5 And I said: "Woe is me! I
am lost, for I am a man of unclean
lips, and I live among a people of
unclean lips; yet my eyes have seen
the King, the LORD of hosts!"
6 Then one of the seraphs flew
to me, holding a live coal that had
been taken from the altar with a
pair of tongs. 7 The seraph[l]
touched my mouth with it and said:
"Now that this has touched your
lips, your guilt has departed and
your sin is blotted out." 8 Then I
heard the voice of the Lord saying,
"Whom shall I send, and who will
go for us?" And I said, "Here am I;
send me!" 9 And he said, "Go and
say to this people:
'Keep listening, but do not
comprehend;
keep looking, but do not
understand.'
10 Make the mind of this
people dull,

5.23
Isa 10.1,2;
Ps 94.21
5.24
Isa 9.18,19;
Job 18.16;
Hos 5.12;
Acts 13.41
5.25
2 Kings 22.13;
Jer 4.24;
Isa 14.19;
9.12,17,21;
23.11
5.26
Isa 13.2,3;
7.18;
Deut 28.49;
Isa 13.4,5
5.27
Joel 2.7,8;
Dan 5.6
5.28
Ps 7.12,13;
Jer 4.13
5.29
Jer 51.38;
Isa 10.6;
42.22

5.30
Isa 17.12;
8.22
6.1
Isa 1.1;
2 Kings 15.7;
1 Kings 22.9
6.2
Rev 4.8;
Ezek 1.11
6.3
Rev 4.8;
Ps 72.19
6.5
Ex 33.20;
Jer 9.3-8;
51.57
6.7
Jer 1.9;
Isa 40.2;
1 Jn 1.7
6.8
Ezek 10.5;
Acts 9.4;
26.19
6.9
Ezek 3.11;
Mt 13.14,
15;
Mk 4.12;
Lk 8.10;
Jn 12.40;
Rom 11.8
6.10
Ps 119.70;
Jer 5.21

k Meaning of Heb uncertain l Heb *He*

and stop their ears,
and shut their eyes,
so that they may not look
with their eyes,
and listen with their ears,
and comprehend with their
minds,
and turn and be healed."

11 Then I said, "How long,
O Lord?" And he said:
"Until cities lie waste
without inhabitant,
and houses without people,
and the land is utterly
desolate;
12 until the LORD sends
everyone far away,
and vast is the emptiness
in the midst of the
land.
13 Even if a tenth part remain
in it,
it will be burned again,
like a terebinth or an oak
whose stump remains
standing
when it is felled."[m]
The holy seed is its stump.

Isaiah Reassures King Ahaz

7 In the days of Ahaz son of Jo-
tham son of Uzziah, king of Ju-
dah, King Rezin of Aram and King
Pekah son of Remaliah of Israel
went up to attack Jerusalem, but
could not mount an attack against
it. 2 When the house of David heard
that Aram had allied itself with
Ephraim, the heart of Ahaz[n] and
the heart of his people shook as the
trees of the forest shake before the
wind.

3 Then the LORD said to Isaiah,
Go out to meet Ahaz, you and your
son Shear-jashub,[o] at the end of
the conduit of the upper pool on
the highway to the Fuller's Field,
4 and say to him, Take heed, be qui-
et, do not fear, and do not let your
heart be faint because of these two
smoldering stumps of firebrands,
because of the fierce anger of Rezin
and Aram and the son of Remaliah.
5 Because Aram—with Ephraim
and the son of Remaliah—has
plotted evil against you, saying,

6 Let us go up against Judah and
cut off Jerusalem[p] and conquer it
for ourselves and make the son of
Tabeel king in it; 7 therefore thus
says the Lord GOD:
It shall not stand,
and it shall not come to
pass.
8 For the head of Aram is
Damascus,
and the head of Damascus
is Rezin.
(Within sixty-five years Ephraim
will be shattered, no longer a peo-
ple.)
9 The head of Ephraim is
Samaria,
and the head of Samaria is
the son of Remaliah.
If you do not stand firm in
faith,
you shall not stand at all.

Isaiah Gives Ahaz the Sign of Immanuel

10 Again the LORD spoke to
Ahaz, saying, 11 Ask a sign of the
LORD your God; let it be deep as
Sheol or high as heaven. 12 But
Ahaz said, I will not ask, and I will
not put the LORD to the test. 13 Then
Isaiah[q] said: "Hear then, O house
of David! Is it too little for you to
weary mortals, that you weary my
God also? 14 Therefore the Lord
himself will give you a sign. Look,
the young woman[r] is with child
and shall bear a son, and shall
name him Immanuel.[s] 15 He shall
eat curds and honey by the time he
knows how to refuse the evil and
choose the good. 16 For before the
child knows how to refuse the evil
and choose the good, the land be-
fore whose two kings you are in
dread will be deserted. 17 The LORD
will bring on you and on your peo-
ple and on your ancestral house
such days as have not come since
the day that Ephraim departed
from Judah—the king of Assyria."

18 On that day the LORD will
whistle for the fly that is at the

Cross references (center column)

6.11 Mic 3.12
6.12 Jer 4.29
6.13 Isa 1.9; Job 14.7; Ezra 9.2
7.1 2 Kings 16.1; 15.37; 15.25
7.2 v. 13; Isa 8.12
7.3 Isa 10.21; 2 Kings 18.17
7.4 Isa 30.15; 10.24; 35.4
7.7 Isa 8.10
7.8 Isa 17.1-3
7.9 2 Chr 20.20
7.11 Isa 37.30; 38.7,8;
2 Kings 19.29
7.14 Mt 1.23; Lk 1.31; Isa 9.6; 8.8
7.15 v. 22
7.16 Isa 8.4
7.17 2 Chr 28.19; 1 Kings 12.16
7.18 Isa 5.26

Footnotes

m Meaning of Heb uncertain n Heb his
heart o That is A remnant shall return
p Heb cut it off q Heb he r Gk the
virgin s That is God is with us

sources of the streams of Egypt, and for the bee that is in the land of Assyria. ¹⁹And they will all come and settle in the steep ravines, and in the clefts of the rocks, and on all the thornbushes, and on all the pastures.

20 On that day the Lord will shave with a razor hired beyond the River — with the king of Assyria — the head and the hair of the feet, and it will take off the beard as well.

21 On that day one will keep alive a young cow and two sheep, ²²and will eat curds because of the abundance of milk that they give; for everyone that is left in the land shall eat curds and honey.

23 On that day every place where there used to be a thousand vines, worth a thousand shekels of silver, will become briers and thorns. ²⁴With bow and arrows one will go there, for all the land will be briers and thorns; ²⁵and as for all the hills that used to be hoed with a hoe, you will not go there for fear of briers and thorns; but they will become a place where cattle are let loose and where sheep tread.

Isaiah's Son a Sign of the Assyrian Invasion

8 Then the Lord said to me, Take a large tablet and write on it in common characters, "Belonging to Maher-shalal-hash-baz,"ᵗ ²and have it attestedᵘ for me by reliable witnesses, the priest Uriah and Zechariah son of Jeberechiah. ³And I went to the prophetess, and she conceived and bore a son. Then the Lord said to me, Name him Maher-shalal-hash-baz; ⁴for before the child knows how to call "My father" or "My mother," the wealth of Damascus and the spoil of Samaria will be carried away by the king of Assyria.

5 The Lord spoke to me again: ⁶Because this people has refused the waters of Shiloah that flow gently, and melt in fear beforeᵛ Rezin and the son of Remaliah; ⁷therefore, the Lord is bringing up

against it the mighty flood waters of the River, the king of Assyria and all his glory; it will rise above all its channels and overflow all its banks; ⁸it will sweep on into Judah as a flood, and, pouring over, it will reach up to the neck; and its outspread wings will fill the breadth of your land, O Immanuel.

⁹ Band together, you peoples,
 and be dismayed;
 listen, all you far countries;
 gird yourselves and be
 dismayed;
 gird yourselves and be
 dismayed!
¹⁰ Take counsel together, but it
 shall be brought to
 naught;
 speak a word, but it will
 not stand,
 for God is with us.ʷ

11 For the Lord spoke thus to me while his hand was strong upon me, and warned me not to walk in the way of this people, saying: ¹²Do not call conspiracy all that this people calls conspiracy, and do not fear what it fears, or be in dread. ¹³But the Lord of hosts, him you shall regard as holy; let him be your fear, and let him be your dread. ¹⁴He will become a sanctuary, a stone one strikes against; for both houses of Israel he will become a rock one stumbles over — a trap and a snare for the inhabitants of Jerusalem. ¹⁵And many among them shall stumble; they shall fall and be broken; they shall be snared and taken.

Disciples of Isaiah

16 Bind up the testimony, seal the teaching among my disciples. ¹⁷I will wait for the Lord, who is hiding his face from the house of Jacob, and I will hope in him. ¹⁸See, I and the children whom the Lord has given me are signs and portents in Israel from the Lord of hosts, who dwells on Mount Zion.

ᵗ That is *The spoil speeds, the prey hastens*
ᵘ Q Ms Gk Syr: MT *and I caused to be attested* ᵛ Cn: Meaning of Heb uncertain
ʷ Heb *immanu el*

7.19
Isa 2.19;
Jer 16.16
7.20
Isa 24.1;
Ezek 5.1-4;
Isa 10.5,15;
8.7
7.23
Isa 5.6
7.25
Isa 5.17
8.1
Isa 30.8;
Hab 2.2
8.2
2 Kings 16.10
8.4
Isa 7.16;
7.8,9
8.6
Neh 3.15;
Jn 9.7;
Isa 7.1,2,6
8.7
Isa 17.12,
13; 7.20;
10.5,6

8.8
Isa 10.6;
30.28; 7.14
8.10
Job 5.12;
Isa 7.7;
Rom 8.31
8.11
Ezek 3.14;
2.8
8.12
Isa 7.2;
1 Pet 3.14,
15
8.13
Isa 5.16;
29.23;
Num 20.12
8.14
Ezek 11.16;
Lk 2.34;
Rom 9.33;
1 Pet 2.8
8.15
Isa 28.13;
Mt 21.44;
Lk 20.18;
Rom 9.32
8.16
vv. 1,2;
Dan 12.4
8.17
Isa 54.8;
Hab 2.3
8.18
Heb 2.13;
Ps 71.7;
Zech 3.8

19 Now if people say to you, "Consult the ghosts and the familiar spirits that chirp and mutter; should not a people consult their gods, the dead on behalf of the living, 20 for teaching and for instruction?" Surely, those who speak like this will have no dawn! 21 They will pass through the land,x greatly distressed and hungry; when they are hungry, they will be enraged and will cursey their king and their gods. They will turn their faces upward, 22 or they will look to the earth, but will see only distress and darkness, the gloom of anguish; and they will be thrust into thick darkness. z

The Righteous Reign of the Coming King

9 a But there will be no gloom for those who were in anguish. In the former time he brought into contempt the land of Zebulun and the land of Naphtali, but in the latter time he will make glorious the way of the sea, the land beyond the Jordan, Galilee of the nations.
2 b The people who walked in
 darkness
 have seen a great light;
those who lived in a land of
 deep darkness —
on them light has shined.
3 You have multiplied the
 nation,
 you have increased its joy;
they rejoice before you
 as with joy at the harvest,
 as people exult when
 dividing plunder.
4 For the yoke of their burden,
 and the bar across their
 shoulders,
 the rod of their oppressor,
 you have broken as on the
 day of Midian.
5 For all the boots of the
 tramping warriors
 and all the garments rolled
 in blood
 shall be burned as fuel for
 the fire.
6 For a child has been born for
 us,
 a son given to us;

authority rests upon his
 shoulders;
 and he is named
Wonderful Counselor, Mighty
 God,
 Everlasting Father, Prince
 of Peace.
7 His authority shall grow
 continually,
 and there shall be endless
 peace
for the throne of David and
 his kingdom.
He will establish and
 uphold it
with justice and with
 righteousness
from this time onward and
 forevermore.
The zeal of the LORD of hosts
 will do this.

Judgment on Arrogance and Oppression

8 The Lord sent a word against
 Jacob,
 and it fell on Israel;
9 and all the people knew it —
 Ephraim and the
 inhabitants of
 Samaria —
but in pride and arrogance
 of heart they said:
10 "The bricks have fallen,
 but we will build with
 dressed stones;
the sycamores have been cut
 down,
 but we will put cedars in
 their place."
11 So the LORD raised
 adversariesc against
 them,
 and stirred up their
 enemies,
12 the Arameans on the east
 and the Philistines on
 the west,
 and they devoured Israel
 with open mouth.
For all this his anger has not
 turned away;

8.19
1 Sam 28.8;
Isa 19.3;
30.2; 45.11
8.20
Lk 16.29;
Mic 3.6
8.21
Isa 9.20,21;
Rev 16.11
8.22
Isa 5.30; 9.1
9.1
2 Kings 15.29;
2 Chr 16.4
9.2
Mt 4.15,16
9.3
Isa 26.15;
35.10;
1 Sam 30.16
9.4
Isa 10.27;
14.4; 10.26
9.5
Isa 2.4
9.6
Isa 7.14;
Lk 2.11;
Jn 3.16;
Mt 28.18;
1 Cor 15.25;
Isa 28.29;
10.21; 63.16;
Eph 2.14

9.7
Dan 2.44;
Lk 1.32,33;
Isa 16.15;
11.4,5; 37.32
9.9
Isa 7.8,9;
46.12
9.11
Isa 7.1,8
9.12
2 Kings 16.6;
2 Chr 28.18;
Ps 79.7;
Isa 5.25

x Heb it y Or curse by z Meaning of Heb uncertain a Ch 8.23 in Heb
b Ch 9.1 in Heb c Cn: Heb the adversaries of Rezin

his hand is stretched out
still.

13 The people did not turn to
him who struck them,
or seek the LORD of hosts.
14 So the LORD cut off from
Israel head and tail,
palm branch and reed in
one day—
15 elders and dignitaries are the
head,
and prophets who teach
lies are the tail;
16 for those who led this people
led them astray,
and those who were led by
them were left in
confusion.
17 That is why the Lord did not
have pity on[d] their
young people,
or compassion on their
orphans and widows;
for everyone was godless and
an evildoer,
and every mouth spoke
folly.
For all this his anger has not
turned away,
his hand is stretched out
still.

18 For wickedness burned like a
fire,
consuming briers and
thorns;
it kindled the thickets of the
forest,
and they swirled upward in
a column of smoke.
19 Through the wrath of the
LORD of hosts
the land was burned,
and the people became like
fuel for the fire;
no one spared another.
20 They gorged on the right, but
still were hungry,
and they devoured on the
left, but were not
satisfied;
they devoured the flesh of
their own kindred;[e]
21 Manasseh devoured Ephraim,
and Ephraim Manasseh,

9.13
Jer 5.3;
Hos 7.10;
Isa 31.1
9.14
Isa 19.15;
Rev 18.8
9.15
Isa 3.2,3;
28.15
9.16
Isa 3.12
9.17
Jer 18.21;
Isa 27.11;
10.6;
Mic 7.2;
Isa 5.25
9.18
Isa 10.17;
Mal 4.1
9.19
Isa 10.6;
Joel 2.3;
Isa 1.31;
24.6;
Mic 7.2,6
9.20
Isa 8.21,22;
49.26
9.21
Isa 5.25

10.1
Ps 94.20
10.2
Isa 5.23;
1.23
10.3
Job 31.14;
Hos 9.7;
Lk 19.44;
Isa 5.26;
20.6
10.4
Isa 24.22;
22.2; 5.25
10.5
Jer 51.20
10.6
Isa 9.17,19;
Jer 34.22;
Isa 5.25,29
10.7
Gen 50.20

and together they were
against Judah.
For all this his anger has not
turned away;
his hand is stretched out
still.

10 Ah, you who make
iniquitous decrees,
who write oppressive
statutes,
2 to turn aside the needy from
justice
and to rob the poor of my
people of their right,
that widows may be your
spoil,
and that you may make the
orphans your prey!
3 What will you do on the day
of punishment,
in the calamity that will
come from far away?
To whom will you flee for
help,
and where will you leave
your wealth,
4 so as not to crouch among
the prisoners
or fall among the slain?
For all this his anger has not
turned away;
his hand is stretched out
still.

Arrogant Assyria Also Judged

5 Ah, Assyria, the rod of my
anger—
the club in their hands is
my fury!
6 Against a godless nation I
send him,
and against the people of
my wrath I command
him,
to take spoil and seize
plunder,
and to tread them down
like the mire of the
streets.
7 But this is not what he
intends,
nor does he have this in
mind;

[d] Q Ms: MT *rejoice over* [e] Or *arm*

but it is in his heart to
 destroy,
 and to cut off nations not a
 few.
8 For he says:
 "Are not my commanders all
 kings?
9 Is not Calno like
 Carchemish?
 Is not Hamath like Arpad?
 Is not Samaria like
 Damascus?
10 As my hand has reached to
 the kingdoms of the
 idols
 whose images were greater
 than those of Jerusalem
 and Samaria,
11 shall I not do to Jerusalem
 and her idols
 what I have done to
 Samaria and her
 images?"

12 When the Lord has finished
all his work on Mount Zion and on
Jerusalem, he^f will punish the ar-
rogant boasting of the king of As-
syria and his haughty pride. 13 For
he says:
 "By the strength of my hand
 I have done it,
 and by my wisdom, for I
 have understanding;
 I have removed the
 boundaries of peoples,
 and have plundered their
 treasures;
 like a bull I have brought
 down those who sat on
 thrones.
14 My hand has found, like a
 nest,
 the wealth of the
 peoples;
 and as one gathers eggs that
 have been forsaken,
 so I have gathered all the
 earth;
 and there was none that
 moved a wing,
 or opened its mouth, or
 chirped."

15 Shall the ax vaunt itself over
 the one who wields it,

10.8
2 Kings 18.24,
34; 19.10ff
10.9
Am 6.2;
2 Chr 35.20;
2 Kings 16.9
10.10
2 Kings 19.17,
18
10.12
2 Kings 19.31;
Jer 50.18;
Isa 37.23
10.13
Isa 37.24;
Ezek 28.4;
Dan 4.30
10.14
Job 31.25
10.15
Jer 51.20;
Rom 9.20,
21; v. 5

10.16
Isa 17.4;
Ps 106.15;
v. 18
10.17
Isa 30.33;
37.23; 27.4
10.18
Jer 21.14
10.19
Isa 21.17
10.20
2 Kings 16.7;
2 Chr 28.20;
Isa 17.7,8
10.21
Isa 6.13; 9.6
10.22
Rom 9.27,
28;
Isa 28.22
10.23
Dan 9.27
10.24
Ps 87.5,6;
Isa 37.6;
Ex 5.14-16

or the saw magnify itself
 against the one who
 handles it?
 As if a rod should raise the
 one who lifts it up,
 or as if a staff should lift
 the one who is not
 wood!
16 Therefore the Sovereign, the
 LORD of hosts,
 will send wasting sickness
 among his stout
 warriors,
 and under his glory a
 burning will be kindled,
 like the burning of fire.
17 The light of Israel will
 become a fire,
 and his Holy One a flame;
 and it will burn and devour
 his thorns and briers in one
 day.
18 The glory of his forest and
 his fruitful land
 the LORD will destroy, both
 soul and body,
 and it will be as when an
 invalid wastes away.
19 The remnant of the trees of
 his forest will be so few
 that a child can write them
 down.

The Repentant Remnant of Israel

20 On that day the remnant of
Israel and the survivors of the
house of Jacob will no more lean
on the one who struck them, but
will lean on the LORD, the Holy One
of Israel, in truth. 21 A remnant will
return, the remnant of Jacob, to
the mighty God. 22 For though your
people Israel were like the sand of
the sea, only a remnant of them
will return. Destruction is decreed,
overflowing with righteousness.
23 For the Lord GOD of hosts will
make a full end, as decreed, in all
the earth.^g
24 Therefore thus says the Lord
GOD of hosts: O my people, who
live in Zion, do not be afraid of the

^f Heb I ^g Or land

Assyrians when they beat you with a rod and lift up their staff against you as the Egyptians did. 25 For in a very little while my indignation will come to an end, and my anger will be directed to their destruction. 26 The LORD of hosts will wield a whip against them, as when he struck Midian at the rock of Oreb; his staff will be over the sea, and he will lift it as he did in Egypt. 27 On that day his burden will be removed from your shoulder, and his yoke will be destroyed from your neck.

He has gone up from
 Rimmon, h
28 he has come to Aiath;
he has passed through
 Migron,
 at Michmash he stores his
 baggage;
29 they have crossed over the
 pass,
 at Geba they lodge for the
 night;
Ramah trembles,
 Gibeah of Saul has fled.
30 Cry aloud, O daughter
 Gallim!
 Listen, O Laishah!
 Answer her, O Anathoth!
31 Madmenah is in flight,
 the inhabitants of Gebim
 flee for safety.
32 This very day he will halt at
 Nob,
 he will shake his fist
 at the mount of daughter
 Zion,
 the hill of Jerusalem.

33 Look, the Sovereign, the
 LORD of hosts,
 will lop the boughs with
 terrifying power;
 the tallest trees will be cut
 down,
 and the lofty will be
 brought low.
34 He will hack down the
 thickets of the forest
 with an ax,
 and Lebanon with its
 majestic trees i will fall.

The Peaceful Kingdom

11 A shoot shall come out
 from the stump of
 Jesse,
 and a branch shall grow
 out of his roots.
2 The spirit of the LORD shall
 rest on him,
 the spirit of wisdom and
 understanding,
 the spirit of counsel and
 might,
 the spirit of knowledge and
 the fear of the LORD.
3 His delight shall be in the
 fear of the LORD.

He shall not judge by what
 his eyes see,
 or decide by what his ears
 hear;
4 but with righteousness he
 shall judge the poor,
 and decide with equity for
 the meek of the earth;
 he shall strike the earth with
 the rod of his mouth,
 and with the breath of his
 lips he shall kill the
 wicked.
5 Righteousness shall be the
 belt around his waist,
 and faithfulness the belt
 around his loins.

6 The wolf shall live with the
 lamb,
 the leopard shall lie down
 with the kid,
 the calf and the lion and the
 fatling together,
 and a little child shall lead
 them.
7 The cow and the bear shall
 graze,
 their young shall lie down
 together;
 and the lion shall eat straw
 like the ox.
8 The nursing child shall play
 over the hole of the
 asp,

Cross references (center column)

10.25
Isa 17.14;
v. 5
10.26
Isa 37.36-38;
Judg 7.25;
Ex 14.16,27
10.27
Isa 9.4;
30.23
10.28
1 Sam 14.2;
13.2,5; 17.22
10.29
Josh 21.17;
18.25;
1 Sam 10.26
10.30
1 Sam 25.44;
Josh 21.18
10.31
Josh 15.31
10.32
1 Sam 21.1;
Neh 11.32;
Isa 13.2;
37.22
10.33
Am 2.9

11.1
Zech 6.12;
Rev 5.5;
Acts 13.23;
Isa 4.2
11.2
Isa 61.1;
Mt 3.16;
Jn 1.32
11.3
Jn 2.25;
7.24
11.4
Isa 9.7;
3.14; 29.19;
Mal 4.6;
Job 4.9;
2 Thes 2.8
11.5
Eph 6.14;
Isa 25.1
11.6
Isa 65.25
11.7
Isa 65.25

h Cn: Heb *and his yoke from your neck, and a yoke will be destroyed because of fatness*
i Cn Compare Gk Vg: Heb *with a majestic one*

and the weaned child shall
put its hand on the
adder's den.
9 They will not hurt or destroy
on all my holy mountain;
for the earth will be full of
the knowledge of the
LORD
as the waters cover the sea.

Return of the Remnant of Israel and Judah

10 On that day the root of Jesse shall stand as a signal to the peoples; the nations shall inquire of him, and his dwelling shall be glorious.

11 On that day the Lord will extend his hand yet a second time to recover the remnant that is left of his people, from Assyria, from Egypt, from Pathros, from Ethiopia,[i] from Elam, from Shinar, from Hamath, and from the coastlands of the sea.

12 He will raise a signal for the
nations,
and will assemble the
outcasts of Israel,
and gather the dispersed of
Judah
from the four corners of
the earth.
13 The jealousy of Ephraim
shall depart,
the hostility of Judah shall
be cut off;
Ephraim shall not be jealous
of Judah,
and Judah shall not be
hostile towards
Ephraim.
14 But they shall swoop down
on the backs of the
Philistines in the west,
together they shall plunder
the people of the east.
They shall put forth their
hand against Edom and
Moab,
and the Ammonites shall
obey them.
15 And the LORD will utterly
destroy
the tongue of the sea of
Egypt;

and will wave his hand over
the River
with his scorching wind;
and will split it into seven
channels,
and make a way to cross
on foot;
16 so there shall be a highway
from Assyria
for the remnant that is left
of his people,
as there was for Israel
when they came up from
the land of Egypt.

Thanksgiving and Praise

12 You will say in that day:
I will give thanks to
you, O LORD,
for though you were angry
with me,
your anger turned away,
and you comforted me.

2 Surely God is my salvation;
I will trust, and will not be
afraid,
for the LORD GOD[k] is my
strength and my might;
he has become my
salvation.

3 With joy you will draw water from the wells of salvation. 4And you will say in that day:
Give thanks to the LORD,
call on his name;
make known his deeds
among the nations;
proclaim that his name is
exalted.

5 Sing praises to the LORD, for
he has done gloriously;
let this be known[l] in all
the earth.
6 Shout aloud and sing for joy,
O royal[m] Zion,
for great in your midst is
the Holy One of Israel.

11.9
Job 5.23;
Hab 2.14
11.10
Rom 15.12;
Jn 3.14,15;
Lk 2.32;
Isa 14.3
11.11
Zech 10.10;
Mic 7.12;
Isa 66.19
11.12
v. 10;
Zech 10.6;
Isa 24.16
11.13
Jer 3.18;
Ezek 37.16,
17,22;
Hos 1.11
11.14
Dan 11.41;
Joel 3.19;
Isa 16.14;
25.10
11.15
Isa 43.16;
19.16; 7.20;
8.7

11.16
Isa 19.23;
62.10;
Ex 14.26-29;
Isa 51.10;
63.12,13
12.1
Isa 26.1;
25.1; 40.1,2
12.2
Isa 33.2;
26.3;
Ex 15.2;
Ps 118.14
12.3
Jn 4.10;
7.37,38;
Isa 41.18
12.5
Isa 24.14;
Ex 15.1;
Ps 98.1
12.6
Zeph 3.14;
Isa 49.26

i Or *Nubia;* Heb *Cush* k Heb *for Yah, the*
LORD l Or *this is made known*
m Or *O inhabitant of*

Proclamation against Babylon

13 The oracle concerning Babylon that Isaiah son of Amoz saw.

2 On a bare hill raise a signal,
 cry aloud to them;
 wave the hand for them to
 enter
 the gates of the nobles.
3 I myself have commanded
 my consecrated ones,
 have summoned my
 warriors, my proudly
 exulting ones,
 to execute my anger.

4 Listen, a tumult on the
 mountains
 as of a great multitude!
 Listen, an uproar of
 kingdoms,
 of nations gathering
 together!
 The LORD of hosts is
 mustering
 an army for battle.
5 They come from a distant
 land,
 from the end of the
 heavens,
 the LORD and the weapons of
 his indignation,
 to destroy the whole earth.

6 Wail, for the day of the LORD
 is near;
 it will come like
 destruction from the
 Almighty![n]
7 Therefore all hands will be
 feeble,
 and every human heart will
 melt,
8 and they will be dismayed.
 Pangs and agony will seize
 them;
 they will be in anguish like
 a woman in labor.
 They will look aghast at one
 another;
 their faces will be aflame.
9 See, the day of the LORD
 comes,
 cruel, with wrath and fierce
 anger,

13.1
Jer chs. 50,
51
13.2
Jer 50.2;
51.25;
Isa 10.32
13.3
Joel 3.11;
Ps 149.2
13.4
Isa 5.30
13.5
Isa 5.26;
42.13; 10.5;
24.1
13.6
Zeph 1.7;
Isa 10.25;
Joel 1.15
13.7
Ezek 7.17;
21.7
13.8
Isa 21.3;
26.17
13.9
Isa 66.15,16

13.10
Isa 5.30;
Joel 2.10;
Mt 24.29;
Mk 13.24;
Lk 21.25
13.11
Isa 26.21;
11.4; 2.11;
Jer 48.29
13.12
Isa 4.1;
6.11,12
13.13
Isa 34.4;
51.6;
Jer 10.10;
Am 8.8;
Hag 2.6
13.14
1 Kings 22.17;
Jer 50.16;
51.9
13.15
Isa 14.19
13.16
Ps 137.9;
Nah 3.10;
Zech 14.2
13.17
Isa 21.2;
Jer 51.11;
Dan 5.28
13.18
2 Kings 8.12;
Ezek 9.5,10

 to make the earth a
 desolation,
 and to destroy its sinners
 from it.
10 For the stars of the heavens
 and their constellations
 will not give their light;
 the sun will be dark at its
 rising,
 and the moon will not shed
 its light.
11 I will punish the world for its
 evil,
 and the wicked for their
 iniquity;
 I will put an end to the pride
 of the arrogant,
 and lay low the insolence
 of tyrants.
12 I will make mortals more
 rare than fine gold,
 and humans than the gold
 of Ophir.
13 Therefore I will make the
 heavens tremble,
 and the earth will be
 shaken out of its place,
 at the wrath of the LORD of
 hosts
 in the day of his fierce
 anger.
14 Like a hunted gazelle,
 or like sheep with no one
 to gather them,
 all will turn to their own
 people,
 and all will flee to their
 own lands.
15 Whoever is found will be
 thrust through,
 and whoever is caught will
 fall by the sword.
16 Their infants will be dashed
 to pieces
 before their eyes;
 their houses will be
 plundered,
 and their wives ravished.
17 See, I am stirring up the
 Medes against them,
 who have no regard for
 silver
 and do not delight in gold.
18 Their bows will slaughter the
 young men;

[n] Traditional rendering of Heb *Shaddai*

they will have no mercy on
the fruit of the womb;
their eyes will not pity
children.

19 And Babylon, the glory of
kingdoms,
the splendor and pride of
the Chaldeans,
will be like Sodom and
Gomorrah
when God overthrew them.

20 It will never be inhabited
or lived in for all
generations;
Arabs will not pitch their
tents there,
shepherds will not make
their flocks lie down
there.

21 But wild animals will lie
down there,
and its houses will be full
of howling creatures;
there ostriches will live,
and there goat-demons will
dance.

22 Hyenas will cry in its towers,
and jackals in the pleasant
palaces;
its time is close at hand,
and its days will not be
prolonged.

Restoration of Judah

14 But the LORD will have
compassion on Jacob and
will again choose Israel, and will
set them in their own land; and
aliens will join them and attach
themselves to the house of Jacob.
2 And the nations will take them
and bring them to their place, and
the house of Israel will possess the
nations° as male and female slaves
in the LORD's land; they will take
captive those who were their cap-
tors, and rule over those who op-
pressed them.

Downfall of the King of Babylon

3 When the LORD has given you
rest from your pain and turmoil
and the hard service with which
you were made to serve, 4 you will
take up this taunt against the king
of Babylon:

How the oppressor has
ceased!
How his insolence[p] has
ceased!

5 The LORD has broken the
staff of the wicked,
the scepter of rulers,

6 that struck down the peoples
in wrath
with unceasing blows,
that ruled the nations in
anger
with unrelenting
persecution.

7 The whole earth is at rest
and quiet;
they break forth into
singing.

8 The cypresses exult over you,
the cedars of Lebanon,
saying,
"Since you were laid low,
no one comes to cut us
down."

9 Sheol beneath is stirred up
to meet you when you
come;
it rouses the shades to greet
you,
all who were leaders of the
earth;
it raises from their thrones
all who were kings of the
nations.

10 All of them will speak
and say to you:
"You too have become as
weak as we!
You have become like us!"

11 Your pomp is brought down
to Sheol,
and the sound of your
harps;
maggots are the bed beneath
you,
and worms are your
covering.

12 How you are fallen from
heaven,
O Day Star, son of Dawn!
How you are cut down to the
ground,

Cross references

13.19
Isa 21.9;
Dan 4.30;
Gen 19.24;
Deut 29.23;
Jer 49.18
13.20
Jer 51.37-43
13.21
Isa 34.11-15
13.22
Jer 51.33
14.1
Ps 102.13;
Zech 1.17;
2.12;
Isa 60.4,5,
10;
Eph 2.12-19
14.2
Isa 49.22;
60.9,10;
66.20; 60.14
14.3
Isa 40.2
14.4
Isa 13.19;
Hab 2.6;
Rev 18.6

14.6
Isa 10.14;
47.6
14.8
Isa 55.12
14.9
Ezek 32.21
14.11
Isa 5.14;
Ezek 28.13;
Isa 51.8
14.12
Isa 34.4;
Lk 10.18

° Heb *them*　　　p Q Ms Compare Gk Syr Vg:
Meaning of MT uncertain

you who laid the nations
low!

13 You said in your heart,
"I will ascend to heaven;
I will raise my throne
above the stars of God;
I will sit on the mount of
assembly
on the heights of Zaphon;q

14 I will ascend to the tops of
the clouds,
I will make myself like the
Most High."

15 But you are brought down to
Sheol,
to the depths of the Pit.

16 Those who see you will stare
at you,
and ponder over you:
"Is this the man who made
the earth tremble,
who shook kingdoms,

17 who made the world like a
desert
and overthrew its cities,
who would not let his
prisoners go home?"

18 All the kings of the nations
lie in glory,
each in his own tomb;

19 but you are cast out, away
from your grave,
like loathsome carrion,r
clothed with the dead, those
pierced by the sword,
who go down to the stones
of the Pit,
like a corpse trampled
underfoot.

20 You will not be joined with
them in burial,
because you have destroyed
your land,
you have killed your
people.

May the descendants of
evildoers
nevermore be named!

21 Prepare slaughter for his
sons
because of the guilt of
their father.s
Let them never rise to
possess the earth
or cover the face of the
world with cities.

14.13
Ezek 28.2;
Dan 8.10
14.14
Isa 47.8;
2 Thes 2.4
14.15
Mt 11.23
14.16
Jer 50.23
14.17
Joel 2.3;
Isa 45.13
14.19
Isa 22.16-18;
Jer 41.7,9;
Isa 5.25
14.20
Job 18.19;
Ps 21.10;
37.28;
Isa 31.2
14.21
Ex 20.5;
Isa 13.16;
Mt 23.35;
Isa 27.6

14.22
Isa 26.14;
Prov 10.7;
Isa 47.9
14.23
Isa 34.11-15;
Zeph 2.14;
Isa 13.6
14.24
Isa 45.23;
55.8,9;
Acts 4.28
14.25
Isa 10.12,27
14.26
Isa 23.9;
Ex 15.12
14.27
2 Chr 20.6;
Isa 43.13;
Dan 4.31,35
14.28
2 Kings 16.20
14.29
Jer 47.1-7;
2 Chr 26.6
14.30
Isa 3.14,15;
7.21; 8.21;
Jer 25.16,20

22 I will rise up against them,
says the Lord of hosts, and will cut
off from Babylon name and rem-
nant, offspring and posterity, says
the Lord. 23 And I will make it a
possession of the hedgehog, and
pools of water, and I will sweep it
with the broom of destruction, says
the Lord of hosts.

An Oracle concerning Assyria

24 The Lord of hosts has sworn:
As I have designed,
so shall it be;
and as I have planned,
so shall it come to pass:

25 I will break the Assyrian in
my land,
and on my mountains
trample him under foot;
his yoke shall be removed
from them,
and his burden from their
shoulders.

26 This is the plan that is
planned
concerning the whole
earth;
and this is the hand that is
stretched out
over all the nations.

27 For the Lord of hosts has
planned,
and who will annul it?
His hand is stretched out,
and who will turn it back?

An Oracle concerning Philistia

28 In the year that King Ahaz died
this oracle came:

29 Do not rejoice, all you
Philistines,
that the rod that struck
you is broken,
for from the root of the
snake will come forth
an adder,
and its fruit will be a flying
fiery serpent.

30 The firstborn of the poor will
graze,

q Or assembly in the far north
r Cn Compare Gk: Heb like a loathed branch
s Syr Compare Gk: Heb fathers

and the needy lie down in
 safety;
but I will make your root die
 of famine,
and your remnant I[t] will
 kill.

31 Wail, O gate; cry, O city;
 melt in fear, O Philistia, all
 of you!
For smoke comes out of the
 north,
and there is no straggler in
 its ranks.

32 What will one answer the
 messengers of the
 nation?
"The LORD has founded Zion,
and the needy among his
 people
will find refuge in her."

An Oracle concerning Moab

15 An oracle concerning Mo-
ab.

Because Ar is laid waste in a
 night,
 Moab is undone;
because Kir is laid waste in a
 night,
 Moab is undone.

2 Dibon[u] has gone up to the
 temple,
to the high places to weep;
over Nebo and over Medeba
 Moab wails.
On every head is baldness,
 every beard is shorn;

3 in the streets they bind on
 sackcloth;
on the housetops and in
 the squares
everyone wails and melts in
 tears.

4 Heshbon and Elealeh cry
 out,
 their voices are heard as far
 as Jahaz;
therefore the loins of Moab
 quiver;[v]
 his soul trembles.

5 My heart cries out for Moab;
 his fugitives flee to Zoar,
 to Eglath-shelishiyah.
For at the ascent of Luhith

they go up weeping;
on the road to Horonaim
 they raise a cry of
 destruction;

6 the waters of Nimrim
 are a desolation;
the grass is withered, the
 new growth fails,
 the verdure is no more.

7 Therefore the abundance
 they have gained
and what they have laid up
they carry away
 over the Wadi of the
 Willows.

8 For a cry has gone
 around the land of Moab;
the wailing reaches to
 Eglaim,
the wailing reaches to
 Beer-elim.

9 For the waters of Dibon[w] are
 full of blood;
yet I will bring upon
 Dibon[w] even more —
a lion for those of Moab who
 escape,
for the remnant of the
 land.

16 Send lambs
to the ruler of the land,
from Sela, by way of the
 desert,
to the mount of daughter
 Zion.

2 Like fluttering birds,
 like scattered nestlings,
so are the daughters of Moab
 at the fords of the Arnon.

3 "Give counsel,
 grant justice;
make your shade like night
 at the height of noon;
hide the outcasts,
 do not betray the fugitive;

4 let the outcasts of Moab
 settle among you;
be a refuge to them
 from the destroyer."

When the oppressor is no
 more,
and destruction has ceased,

14.31
Isa 3.26;
v. 29;
Jer 1.14;
Isa 34.16
14.32
Isa 37.9;
Ps 87.1,5;
Zeph 3.12;
Zech 11.11
15.1
Isa 11.14;
Jer 48;
Ezek 25.8-11;
Jer 48.41
15.2
Lev 21.5
15.3
Jon 3.6-8;
Jer 48.38;
Isa 22.4
15.5
Jer 48.5,31,
34; Isa 59.7

15.6
Isa 19.5-7;
Joel 1.10-12
15.7
Isa 30.6
15.9
2 Kings 17.25;
Jer 50.17
16.1
2 Kings 3.4;
14.7;
Isa 10.32
16.2
Num 21.13,
14
16.3
Isa 25.4
16.4
Isa 9.4;
54.14

[t]Q Ms Vg: MT *he* [u]Cn: Heb *the house
and Dibon* [v]Cn Compare Gk Syr: Heb *the
armed men of Moab cry aloud* [w]Q Ms Vg
Compare Syr: MT *Dimon*

and marauders have vanished
from the land,
5 then a throne shall be
established in steadfast
love
in the tent of David,
and on it shall sit in
faithfulness
a ruler who seeks justice
and is swift to do what is
right.

6 We have heard of the pride
of Moab
—how proud he is!—
of his arrogance, his pride,
and his insolence;
his boasts are false.
7 Therefore let Moab wail,
let everyone wail for Moab.
Mourn, utterly stricken,
for the raisin-cakes of
Kir-hareseth.

8 For the fields of Heshbon
languish,
and the vines of Sibmah,
whose clusters once made
drunk
the lords of the nations,
reached to Jazer
and strayed to the desert;
their shoots once spread
abroad
and crossed over the sea.
9 Therefore I weep with the
weeping of Jazer
for the vines of Sibmah;
I drench you with my tears,
O Heshbon and Elealeh;
for the shout over your fruit
harvest
and your grain harvest has
ceased.
10 Joy and gladness are taken
away
from the fruitful field;
and in the vineyards no
songs are sung,
no shouts are raised;
no treader treads out wine in
the presses;
the vintage-shout is
hushed. x
11 Therefore my heart throbs
like a harp for Moab,

16.5
Dan 7.14;
Mic 4.7;
Lk 1.33;
Isa 9.7
16.6
Jer 48.29,
30;
Zeph 2.8,10
16.7
1 Chr 16.3;
2 Kings 3.25;
Jer 48.31
16.8
Isa 15.4;
Num 32.38;
Jer 48.32
16.9
Jer 48.32;
Isa 15.4;
Jer 40.10,12
16.10
Isa 24.7,8;
Jer 48.33;
Job 24.11
16.11
Isa 15.5;
63.15;
Jer 48.36

16.12
Jer 48.35;
1 Kings 18.29;
Isa 15.2;
2 Kings 19.12
16.14
Isa 21.16;
25.10
17.1
2 Kings 16.9;
Jer 49.23;
Am 1.3;
Zech 9.1;
Isa 8.4; 10.9
17.2
Jer 7.33
17.3
Isa 7.16; 8.4
17.4
Isa 10.3,16
17.5
Jer 51.33;
2 Sam 5.18,
22

and my very soul for
Kir-heres.
12 When Moab presents him-
self, when he wearies himself upon
the high place, when he comes to
his sanctuary to pray, he will not
prevail.
13 This was the word that the
LORD spoke concerning Moab in the
past. 14 But now the LORD says, In
three years, like the years of a hired
worker, the glory of Moab will be
brought into contempt, in spite of
all its great multitude; and those
who survive will be very few and
feeble.

An Oracle concerning Damascus

17 An oracle concerning Da-
mascus.

See, Damascus will cease to
be a city,
and will become a heap of
ruins.
2 Her towns will be deserted
forever; y
they will be places for
flocks,
which will lie down, and no
one will make them
afraid.
3 The fortress will disappear
from Ephraim,
and the kingdom from
Damascus;
and the remnant of Aram
will be
like the glory of the
children of Israel,
says the LORD of hosts.

4 On that day
the glory of Jacob will be
brought low,
and the fat of his flesh will
grow lean.
5 And it shall be as when
reapers gather standing
grain
and their arms harvest the
ears,
and as when one gleans the
ears of grain

x Gk: Heb I have hushed y Cn Compare
Gk: Heb the cities of Aroer are deserted

in the Valley of Rephaim.
6 Gleanings will be left in it,
 as when an olive tree is
 beaten —
 two or three berries
 in the top of the highest
 bough,
 four or five
 on the branches of a fruit
 tree,
 says the Lord God
 of Israel.

7 On that day people will regard
their Maker, and their eyes will
look to the Holy One of Israel;
8 they will not have regard for the
altars, the work of their hands, and
they will not look to what their own
fingers have made, either the sa-
cred poles[z] or the altars of in-
cense.

9 On that day their strong cities
will be like the deserted places of
the Hivites and the Amorites,[a]
which they deserted because of the
children of Israel, and there will be
desolation.

10 For you have forgotten the
 God of your salvation,
 and have not remembered
 the Rock of your refuge;
 therefore, though you plant
 pleasant plants
 and set out slips of an
 alien god,
11 though you make them grow
 on the day that you
 plant them,
 and make them blossom in
 the morning that you
 sow;
 yet the harvest will flee away
 in a day of grief and
 incurable pain.

12 Ah, the thunder of many
 peoples,
 they thunder like the
 thundering of the sea!
 Ah, the roar of nations,
 they roar like the roaring of
 mighty waters!
13 The nations roar like the
 roaring of many waters,

17.6
Isa 24.13;
27.12
17.7
Isa 10.20;
Mic 7.7
17.8
Isa 27.9;
30.22; 31.7;
Ex 34.13;
Deut 7.5
17.9
Isa 7.25
17.10
Isa 51.13;
Ps 68.19;
Isa 26.4;
30.29
17.11
Ps 90.6;
Job 4.8
17.12
Jer 6.23;
Ezek 43.2;
Ps 18.4
17.13
Isa 33.3;
Ps 9.5;
Isa 13.14;
29.5; 41.15,
16

17.14
Isa 41.12;
2 Kings 19.35
18.1
Isa 20.3-5;
Ezek 30.4,5,
9;
Zeph 2.12;
3.10
18.2
Ex 2.3;
v. 7;
2 Chr 12.2-4
18.3
Ps 49.1;
Isa 5.26;
26.11
18.4
Isa 26.21;
2 Sam 23.4;
Isa 26.19
18.5
Ezek 17.6-10;
Isa 27.11

but he will rebuke them,
 and they will flee far
 away,
chased like chaff on the
 mountains before the
 wind
and whirling dust before
 the storm.
14 At evening time, lo, terror!
 Before morning, they are
 no more.
This is the fate of those who
 despoil us,
 and the lot of those who
 plunder us.

An Oracle concerning Ethiopia

18 Ah, land of whirring wings
 beyond the rivers of
 Ethiopia,[b]
2 sending ambassadors by the
 Nile
 in vessels of papyrus on the
 waters!
Go, you swift messengers,
 to a nation tall and
 smooth,
 to a people feared near and
 far,
 a nation mighty and
 conquering,
 whose land the rivers
 divide.

3 All you inhabitants of the
 world,
 you who live on the earth,
when a signal is raised on
 the mountains, look!
 When a trumpet is blown,
 listen!
4 For thus the Lord said to me:
 I will quietly look from my
 dwelling
 like clear heat in sunshine,
 like a cloud of dew in the
 heat of harvest.
5 For before the harvest, when
 the blossom is over
 and the flower becomes a
 ripening grape,
 he will cut off the shoots
 with pruning hooks,

z Heb *Asherim* a Cn Compare Gk: Heb
places of the wood and the highest bough
b Or *Nubia*; Heb *Cush*

and the spreading branches
he will hew away.
6 They shall all be left
to the birds of prey of the
mountains
and to the animals of the
earth.
And the birds of prey will
summer on them,
and all the animals of the
earth will winter on
them.

7 At that time gifts will be
brought to the LORD of hosts fromᶜ
a people tall and smooth, from a
people feared near and far, a nation
mighty and conquering, whose
land the rivers divide, to Mount
Zion, the place of the name of the
LORD of hosts.

An Oracle concerning Egypt

19 An oracle concerning
Egypt.

See, the LORD is riding on a
swift cloud
and comes to Egypt;
the idols of Egypt will
tremble at his presence,
and the heart of the
Egyptians will melt
within them.
2 I will stir up Egyptians
against Egyptians,
and they will fight, one
against the other,
neighbor against neighbor,
city against city, kingdom
against kingdom;
3 the spirit of the Egyptians
within them will be
emptied out,
and I will confound their
plans;
they will consult the idols
and the spirits of the
dead
and the ghosts and the
familiar spirits;
4 I will deliver the Egyptians
into the hand of a hard
master;
a fierce king will rule over
them,

says the Sovereign, the
LORD of hosts.

5 The waters of the Nile will
be dried up,
and the river will be
parched and dry;
6 its canals will become foul,
and the branches of
Egypt's Nile will
diminish and dry up,
reeds and rushes will rot
away.
7 There will be bare places by
the Nile,
on the brink of the Nile;
and all that is sown by the
Nile will dry up,
be driven away, and be no
more.
8 Those who fish will mourn;
all who cast hooks in the
Nile will lament,
and those who spread nets
on the water will
languish.
9 The workers in flax will be in
despair,
and the carders and those
at the loom will grow
pale.
10 Its weavers will be dismayed,
and all who work for wages
will be grieved.

11 The princes of Zoan are
utterly foolish;
the wise counselors of
Pharaoh give stupid
counsel.
How can you say to Pharaoh,
"I am one of the sages,
a descendant of ancient
kings"?
12 Where now are your sages?
Let them tell you and
make known
what the LORD of hosts has
planned against Egypt.
13 The princes of Zoan have
become fools,
and the princes of
Memphis are deluded;

18.6
Isa 46.11;
56.9;
Jer 7.33
18.7
Ps 68.31;
Isa 45.14;
Zeph 3.10;
Zech 14.16,
17
19.1
Isa 13.1;
Jer 46.13-26;
Ezek chs.
29,30;
Ps 18.10;
104.3;
Ex 12.12;
Jer 43.12
19.2
Judg 7.22;
1 Sam 14.16,
20;
2 Chr 20.23;
Mt 10.21,36
19.3
vv. 11-14;
Isa 8.19
19.4
Isa 20.4;
Jer 46.26;
Ezek 29.19

19.5
Jer 51.36;
Ezek 30.12
19.6
Ex 7.18;
Isa 37.25;
15.6
19.7
Isa 23.3,10
19.9
Prov 7.16;
Ezek 27.7
19.10
Ps 11.3
19.11
Num 13.22;
1 Kings 4.30;
Acts 7.22
19.12
1 Cor 1.20;
Isa 14.24;
Rom 9.17
19.13
Jer 2.16;
Ezek 30.13;
Zech 10.4

ᶜ Q Ms Gk Vg: MT of

those who are the
 cornerstones of its tribes
have led Egypt astray.
14 The LORD has poured into
 them[d]
a spirit of confusion;
and they have made Egypt
 stagger in all its doings
as a drunkard staggers
 around in vomit.
15 Neither head nor tail, palm
 branch or reed,
will be able to do anything
 for Egypt.

16 On that day the Egyptians
will be like women, and tremble
with fear before the hand that the
LORD of hosts raises against them.
17 And the land of Judah will be-
come a terror to the Egyptians; ev-
eryone to whom it is mentioned
will fear because of the plan that
the LORD of hosts is planning
against them.

Egypt, Assyria, and Israel Blessed

18 On that day there will be five
cities in the land of Egypt that
speak the language of Canaan and
swear allegiance to the LORD of
hosts. One of these will be called
the City of the Sun.
19 On that day there will be an
altar to the LORD in the center of
the land of Egypt, and a pillar to
the LORD at its border. 20 It will be a
sign and a witness to the LORD of
hosts in the land of Egypt; when
they cry to the LORD because of op-
pressors, he will send them a sav-
ior, and will defend and deliver
them. 21 The LORD will make him-
self known to the Egyptians; and
the Egyptians will know the LORD
on that day, and will worship with
sacrifice and burnt offering, and
they will make vows to the LORD
and perform them. 22 The LORD will
strike Egypt, striking and healing;
they will return to the LORD, and he
will listen to their supplications
and heal them.
23 On that day there will be a
highway from Egypt to Assyria, and
the Assyrian will come into Egypt,

and the Egyptian into Assyria, and
the Egyptians will worship with the
Assyrians.
24 On that day Israel will be the
third with Egypt and Assyria, a
blessing in the midst of the earth,
25 whom the LORD of hosts has
blessed, saying, "Blessed be Egypt
my people, and Assyria the work of
my hands, and Israel my heritage."

Isaiah Dramatizes the Conquest of Egypt and Ethiopia

20 In the year that the
commander-in-chief, who
was sent by King Sargon of Assyria,
came to Ashdod and fought against
it and took it — 2 at that time the
LORD had spoken to Isaiah son of
Amoz, saying, "Go, and loose the
sackcloth from your loins and take
your sandals off your feet," and he
had done so, walking naked and
barefoot. 3 Then the LORD said,
"Just as my servant Isaiah has
walked naked and barefoot for
three years as a sign and a portent
against Egypt and Ethiopia,[e] 4 so
shall the king of Assyria lead away
the Egyptians as captives and the
Ethiopians[f] as exiles, both the
young and the old, naked and bare-
foot, with buttocks uncovered, to
the shame of Egypt. 5 And they
shall be dismayed and confounded
because of Ethiopia[e] their hope
and of Egypt their boast. 6 In that
day the inhabitants of this coast-
land will say, 'See, this is what has
happened to those in whom we
hoped and to whom we fled for
help and deliverance from the king
of Assyria! And we, how shall we
escape?' "

Oracles concerning Babylon, Edom, and Arabia

21 The oracle concerning the
wilderness of the sea.

As whirlwinds in the Negeb
 sweep on,
it comes from the desert,
 from a terrible land.

19.14
Isa 29.10;
Mt 17.17;
Isa 3.12;
9.16; 28.7
19.15
Isa 9.14,15
19.16
Jer 51.30;
Isa 2.19;
11.15; 30.32
19.17
Isa 14.24
19.18
Isa 45.23;
65.16
19.19
Isa 56.7;
Gen 28.18;
Ex 24.4;
Josh 22.10,
26,27
19.20
Isa 43.3,11;
49.25
19.21
Isa 11.9;
Mal 1.11;
Isa 44.5
19.22
Isa 30.26;
27.13; 45.14
19.23
Isa 11.16;
27.13

19.25
Isa 45.14;
Hos 2.23;
Eph 2.10
20.1
2 Kings 18.17;
1 Sam 5.1
20.2
Zech 13.4;
Ezek 24.17,
23;
1 Sam 19.24;
Mic 1.8
20.3
Isa 8.18;
37.9; 43.3
20.4
Isa 19.4;
3.17;
Jer 13.22,26
20.5
2 Kings 18.21;
Isa 30.3,5,7;
Ezek 29.6,7
20.6
Isa 10.3;
30.7;
Mt 23.33;
Heb 2.3
21.1
Isa 31.1;
Jer 51.42;
Zech 9.14

d Gk Compare Tg: Heb *it* e Or *Nubia*;
Heb *Cush* f Or *Nubians*; Heb *Cushites*

2 A stern vision is told to me;
the betrayer betrays,
and the destroyer destroys.
Go up, O Elam,
lay siege, O Media;
all the sighing she has
caused
I bring to an end.
3 Therefore my loins are filled
with anguish;
pangs have seized me,
like the pangs of a woman
in labor;
I am bowed down so that I
cannot hear,
I am dismayed so that I
cannot see.
4 My mind reels, horror has
appalled me;
the twilight I longed for
has been turned for me
into trembling.
5 They prepare the table,
they spread the rugs,
they eat, they drink.
Rise up, commanders,
oil the shield!
6 For thus the Lord said to
me:
"Go, post a lookout,
let him announce what he
sees.
7 When he sees riders,
horsemen in pairs,
riders on donkeys, riders
on camels,
let him listen diligently,
very diligently."
8 Then the watcher[g] called
out:
"Upon a watchtower I stand,
O Lord,
continually by day,
and at my post I am
stationed
throughout the night.
9 Look, there they come,
riders,
horsemen in pairs!"
Then he responded,
"Fallen, fallen is Babylon;
and all the images of her
gods
lie shattered on the
ground."
10 O my threshed and
winnowed one,

what I have heard from the
Lord of hosts,
the God of Israel, I
announce to you.

11 The oracle concerning
Dumah.

One is calling to me from
Seir,
"Sentinel, what of the
night?
Sentinel, what of the
night?"
12 The sentinel says:
"Morning comes, and also
the night.
If you will inquire, inquire;
come back again."

13 The oracle concerning the
desert plain.

In the scrub of the desert
plain you will lodge,
O caravans of Dedanites.
14 Bring water to the thirsty,
meet the fugitive with
bread,
O inhabitants of the land
of Tema.
15 For they have fled from the
swords,
from the drawn sword,
from the bent bow,
and from the stress of
battle.
16 For thus the Lord said to me:
Within a year, according to the
years of a hired worker, all the glory
of Kedar will come to an end; 17 and
the remaining bows of Kedar's war-
riors will be few; for the Lord, the
God of Israel, has spoken.

A Warning of Destruction of Jerusalem

22 The oracle concerning the
valley of vision.

What do you mean that you
have gone up,
all of you, to the
housetops,

Cross references

21.2
Isa 33.1;
13.17;
Jer 49.34
21.3
Isa 15.5;
16.11; 13.8
21.4
Deut 28.67
21.5
Jer 51.39,
57;
Dan 5.1-4
21.7
v. 9
21.8
Hab 2.1
21.9
Jer 51.8;
Rev 14.8;
18.2;
Isa 46.1;
Jer 50.2;
51.44
21.10
Jer 51.33

21.11
Gen 25.14;
32.3
21.13
Isa 13.1;
Jer 49.28;
1 Chr 1.9,
32
21.14
Gen 25.15;
Job 6.19
21.15
Isa 13.14,
15; 17.13
21.16
Isa 16.14;
17.4;
Ps 120.5;
Isa 60.7
21.17
Isa 10.19;
Num 23.19;
Zech 1.6
22.1
Isa 13.1;
Joel 3.12,
14; Isa 15.3

g Q Ms: MT *a lion*

2 you that are full of
 shoutings,
 tumultuous city, exultant
 town?
 Your slain are not slain by
 the sword,
 nor are they dead in
 battle.
3 Your rulers have all fled
 together;
 they were captured without
 the use of a bow.[h]
 All of you who were found
 were captured,
 though they had fled far
 away.[i]
4 Therefore I said:
 Look away from me,
 let me weep bitter tears;
 do not try to comfort me
 for the destruction of my
 beloved people.

5 For the Lord GOD of hosts
 has a day
 of tumult and trampling
 and confusion
 in the valley of vision,
 a battering down of walls
 and a cry for help to the
 mountains.
6 Elam bore the quiver
 with chariots and cavalry,[j]
 and Kir uncovered the
 shield.
7 Your choicest valleys were
 full of chariots,
 and the cavalry took their
 stand at the gates.
8 He has taken away the
 covering of Judah.

On that day you looked to the
weapons of the House of the For-
est, 9and you saw that there were
many breaches in the city of David,
and you collected the waters of the
lower pool. 10You counted the
houses of Jerusalem, and you
broke down the houses to fortify
the wall. 11You made a reservoir
between the two walls for the water
of the old pool. But you did not
look to him who did it, or have re-
gard for him who planned it long
ago.

22.2
Isa 32.13;
Jer 14.18;
Lam 2.20
22.3
Isa 21.15
22.4
Isa 15.3;
Jer 4.19; 9.1
22.5
Isa 37.3;
63.3;
Lam 1.5;
2.2; v. 1
22.6
Jer 49.35;
2 Kings 16.9
22.7
2 Chr 32.1
22.8
2 Chr 32.3-5,
30;
1 Kings 7.2;
10.17
22.9
Neh 3.16
22.11
2 Kings 25.4;
20.20;
2 Chr 32.3,
4; Isa 37.26

22.12
Joel 1.13;
Isa 15.2;
Mic 1.16
22.13
Isa 5.11,22;
56.12;
1 Cor 15.32
22.14
Isa 5.9;
65.7,20
22.15
2 Kings 18.37;
Isa 36.3
22.16
2 Sam 18.18;
2 Chr 16.14;
Mt 27.60
22.18
Isa 17.13;
Job 18.18
22.19
Job 40.11,
12;
Ezek 17.24
22.20
2 Kings 18.18;
Isa 36.3
22.22
Rev 3.7;
Isa 7.2,13;
Job 12.14

12 In that day the Lord GOD of
 hosts
 called to weeping and
 mourning,
 to baldness and putting on
 sackcloth;
13 but instead there was joy
 and festivity,
 killing oxen and
 slaughtering sheep,
 eating meat and drinking
 wine.
 "Let us eat and drink,
 for tomorrow we die."
14 The LORD of hosts has
 revealed himself in my
 ears:
 Surely this iniquity will not
 be forgiven you until
 you die,
 says the Lord GOD of hosts.

Denunciation of Self-Seeking Officials

15 Thus says the Lord GOD of
hosts: Come, go to this steward, to
Shebna, who is master of the
household, and say to him: 16What
right do you have here? Who are
your relatives here, that you have
cut out a tomb here for yourself,
cutting a tomb on the height, and
carving a habitation for yourself in
the rock? 17The LORD is about to
hurl you away violently, my fellow.
He will seize firm hold on you,
18whirl you round and round, and
throw you like a ball into a wide
land; there you shall die, and there
your splendid chariots shall lie,
O you disgrace to your master's
house! 19I will thrust you from your
office, and you will be pulled down
from your post.

20 On that day I will call my ser-
vant Eliakim son of Hilkiah, 21and
will clothe him with your robe and
bind your sash on him. I will com-
mit your authority to his hand, and
he shall be a father to the inhabi-
tants of Jerusalem and to the
house of Judah. 22I will place on
his shoulder the key of the house of
David; he shall open, and no one

h Or *without their bows* i Gk Syr Vg: Heb
fled from far away j Meaning of Heb
uncertain

shall shut; he shall shut, and no one shall open. 23 I will fasten him like a peg in a secure place, and he will become a throne of honor to his ancestral house. 24 And they will hang on him the whole weight of his ancestral house, the off-spring and issue, every small ves-sel, from the cups to all the flagons. 25 On that day, says the LORD of hosts, the peg that was fastened in a secure place will give way; it will be cut down and fall, and the load that was on it will perish, for the LORD has spoken.

An Oracle concerning Tyre

23 The oracle concerning Tyre.

Wail, O ships of Tarshish,
 for your fortress is
 destroyed.k
When they came in from
 Cyprus
 they learned of it.
2 Be still, O inhabitants of the
 coast,
 O merchants of Sidon,
your messengers crossed over
 the seal
3 and were on the mighty
 waters;
your revenue was the grain of
 Shihor,
 the harvest of the Nile;
 you were the merchant of
 the nations.
4 Be ashamed, O Sidon, for
 the sea has spoken,
 the fortress of the sea,
 saying:
"I have neither labored nor
 given birth,
 I have neither reared young
 men
 nor brought up young
 women."
5 When the report comes to
 Egypt,
 they will be in anguish over
 the report about Tyre.
6 Cross over to Tarshish—
 wail, O inhabitants of the
 coast!
7 Is this your exultant city

whose origin is from days
 of old,
 whose feet carried her
 to settle far away?
8 Who has planned this
 against Tyre, the bestower
 of crowns, .
 whose merchants were
 princes,
 whose traders were the
 honored of the earth?
9 The LORD of hosts has
 planned it—
 to defile the pride of all
 glory,
 to shame all the honored
 of the earth.
10 Cross over to your own land,
 O ships ofm Tarshish;
 this is a harborn no more.
11 He has stretched out his
 hand over the sea,
 he has shaken the
 kingdoms;
 the LORD has given command
 concerning Canaan
 to destroy its fortresses.
12 He said:
You will exult no longer,
 O oppressed virgin
 daughter Sidon;
 rise, cross over to Cyprus—
 even there you will have no
 rest.

13 Look at the land of the Chal-deans! This is the people; it was not Assyria. They destined Tyre for wild animals. They erected their siege towers, they tore down her palaces, they made her a ruin.o
14 Wail, O ships of Tarshish,
 for your fortress is
 destroyed.
15 From that day Tyre will be forgot-ten for seventy years, the lifetime of one king. At the end of seventy years, it will happen to Tyre as in the song about the prostitute:
16 Take a harp,
 go about the city,

22.23
Ezra 9.8;
Job 36.7
22.25
v. 23;
Isa 46.11;
Mic 4.4
23.1
Jer 25.22;
47.4;
Ezek chs.
26,27,28;
v. 12
23.2
Isa 47.5
23.3
Jer 2.18;
Ezek 27.3-23
23.4
Ezek 28.21,
22
23.7
Isa 22.2;
32.13

23.9
Isa 2.11;
13.11;
Job 40.11,
12; Isa 5.13;
9.15
23.11
Isa 14.26;
50.2; 25.2
23.12
Rev 18.22;
Isa 47.1;
v. 1
23.13
Isa 10.5,7
23.14
v. 1
23.15
Jer 25.11,22

k Cn Compare verse 14: Heb for it is destroyed, without houses l Q Ms: MT crossing over the sea, they replenished you m Cn Compare Gk: Heb like the Nile, daughter n Cn: Heb restraint o Meaning of Heb uncertain

you forgotten prostitute!
Make sweet melody,
 sing many songs,
 that you may be
 remembered.

17 At the end of seventy years, the LORD will visit Tyre, and she will return to her trade, and will prostitute herself with all the kingdoms of the world on the face of the earth. 18 Her merchandise and her wages will be dedicated to the LORD; her profits[p] will not be stored or hoarded, but her merchandise will supply abundant food and fine clothing for those who live in the presence of the LORD.

Impending Judgment on the Earth

24 Now the LORD is about to lay waste the earth
 and make it desolate,
and he will twist its surface
 and scatter its
 inhabitants.
2 And it shall be, as with the
 people, so with the
 priest;
 as with the slave, so with
 his master;
 as with the maid, so with
 her mistress;
as with the buyer, so with
 the seller;
as with the lender, so with
 the borrower;
as with the creditor, so
 with the debtor.
3 The earth shall be utterly
 laid waste and utterly
 despoiled;
for the LORD has spoken
 this word.

4 The earth dries up and
 withers,
 the world languishes and
 withers;
 the heavens languish
 together with the earth.
5 The earth lies polluted
 under its inhabitants;
for they have transgressed
 laws,

violated the statutes,
 broken the everlasting
 covenant.
6 Therefore a curse devours
 the earth,
 and its inhabitants suffer
 for their guilt;
therefore the inhabitants of
 the earth dwindled,
 and few people are left.
7 The wine dries up,
 the vine languishes,
 all the merry-hearted sigh.
8 The mirth of the timbrels is
 stilled,
 the noise of the jubilant
 has ceased,
 the mirth of the lyre is
 stilled.
9 No longer do they drink wine
 with singing;
 strong drink is bitter to
 those who drink it.
10 The city of chaos is broken
 down,
 every house is shut up so
 that no one can enter.
11 There is an outcry in the
 streets for lack of wine;
 all joy has reached its
 eventide;
 the gladness of the earth is
 banished.
12 Desolation is left in the city,
 the gates are battered into
 ruins.
13 For thus it shall be on the
 earth
 and among the nations,
as when an olive tree is
 beaten,
 as at the gleaning when the
 grape harvest is ended.

14 They lift up their voices, they
 sing for joy;
 they shout from the west
 over the majesty of the
 LORD.
15 Therefore in the east give
 glory to the LORD;
 in the coastlands of the sea
 glorify the name of the
 LORD, the God of Israel.

23.17
Rev 17.2
23.18
Isa 60.5-9;
Zech 14.20
24.1
vv. 19,20;
Isa 13.13,14
24.2
Hos 4.9;
Lev 25.36,
37;
Deut 23.19,
20
24.3
Isa 6.11,12
24.4
Isa 33.9;
2.12
24.5
Gen 3.17;
Num 35.33;
Isa 59.12

24.6
Isa 34.5;
Mal 4.6;
Isa 5.24;
9.19
24.7
Isa 16.8-10;
Joel 1.10-12
24.8
Jer 7.34;
16.9; 25.10;
Ezek 26.13;
Hos 2.11;
Rev 18.22
24.9
Isa 5.11,20,
22
24.10
Isa 23.1
24.11
Jer 14.2;
46.12;
Isa 16.10;
32.13
24.12
Isa 14.31;
45.2
24.13
Isa 17.5,6
24.14
Isa 12.6;
42.10
24.15
Isa 25.3;
Mal 1.11;
Isa 66.19

p Heb *it*

16 From the ends of the earth
 we hear songs of praise,
 of glory to the Righteous
 One.
But I say, I pine away,
 I pine away. Woe is me!
For the treacherous deal
 treacherously,
 the treacherous deal very
 treacherously.

17 Terror, and the pit, and the
 snare
 are upon you, O inhabitant
 of the earth!
18 Whoever flees at the sound
 of the terror
 shall fall into the pit;
and whoever climbs out of
 the pit
 shall be caught in the
 snare.
For the windows of heaven
 are opened,
 and the foundations of the
 earth tremble.
19 The earth is utterly broken,
 the earth is torn asunder,
 the earth is violently
 shaken.
20 The earth staggers like a
 drunkard,
 it sways like a hut;
its transgression lies heavy
 upon it,
 and it falls, and will not
 rise again.

21 On that day the Lord will
 punish
 the host of heaven in
 heaven,
 and on earth the kings of
 the earth.
22 They will be gathered
 together
 like prisoners in a pit;
they will be shut up in a
 prison,
 and after many days they
 will be punished.
23 Then the moon will be
 abashed,
 and the sun ashamed;
for the Lord of hosts will
 reign

24.16
Isa 11.12;
28.5;
Jer 5.11
24.17
1 Kings 19.17
24.18
Jer 48.43,
44;
Gen 7.11;
Ps 18.7
24.19
v. 1;
Jer 4.23
24.20
Isa 19.14;
66.24;
Dan 11.19;
Am 8.14
24.21
Isa 10.12;
v. 4;
Ps 76.12
24.22
Isa 10.4;
42.22;
Ezek 38.8;
Zech 9.11,
12
24.23
Isa 13.10;
60.19;
Zech 14.6,7;
Mic 4.7;
Heb 12.22

25.1
Ps 118.28;
98.1;
Num 23.19
25.2
Isa 17.1;
13.22; 32.14
25.4
Isa 14.32;
11.4; 32.2;
49.25
25.5
Jer 51.54-56
25.6
Isa 2.2-4;
Prov 9.2;
Mt 22.4;
Dan 7.14;
Mt 8.11

on Mount Zion and in
 Jerusalem,
and before his elders he will
 manifest his glory.

Praise for Deliverance from Oppression

25 O Lord, you are my God;
 I will exalt you, I will
 praise your name;
for you have done wonderful
 things,
 plans formed of old,
 faithful and sure.
2 For you have made the city a
 heap,
 the fortified city a ruin;
the palace of aliens is a city
 no more,
 it will never be rebuilt.
3 Therefore strong peoples will
 glorify you;
 cities of ruthless nations
 will fear you.
4 For you have been a refuge
 to the poor,
 a refuge to the needy in
 their distress,
 a shelter from the
 rainstorm and a shade
 from the heat.
When the blast of the
 ruthless was like a
 winter rainstorm,
5 the noise of aliens like
 heat in a dry place,
you subdued the heat with
 the shade of clouds;
 the song of the ruthless
 was stilled.

6 On this mountain the Lord
 of hosts will make for
 all peoples
 a feast of rich food, a feast
 of well-aged wines,
 of rich food filled with
 marrow, of well-aged
 wines strained clear.
7 And he will destroy on this
 mountain
 the shroud that is cast over
 all peoples,
 the sheet that is spread
 over all nations;

he will swallow up death
 forever.
8 Then the Lord God will wipe
 away the tears from all
 faces,
 and the disgrace of his
 people he will take
 away from all the earth,
 for the Lord has spoken.
9 It will be said on that day,
 Lo, this is our God; we
 have waited for him, so
 that he might save us.
 This is the Lord for whom
 we have waited;
 let us be glad and rejoice
 in his salvation.
10 For the hand of the Lord will
 rest on this mountain.

 The Moabites shall be
 trodden down in their
 place
 as straw is trodden down in
 a dung-pit.
11 Though they spread out their
 hands in the midst of
 it,
 as swimmers spread out
 their hands to swim,
 their pride will be laid low
 despite the struggle q of
 their hands.
12 The high fortifications of his
 walls will be brought
 down,
 laid low, cast to the
 ground, even to the
 dust.

Judah's Song of Victory

26 On that day this song will
 be sung in the land of
Judah:
 We have a strong city;
 he sets up victory
 like walls and bulwarks.
2 Open the gates,
 so that the righteous
 nation that keeps faith
 may enter in.
3 Those of steadfast mind you
 keep in peace —
 in peace because they trust
 in you.
4 Trust in the Lord forever,

25.8
Hos 13.14;
1 Cor 15.54;
Rev 7.17;
21.4;
Isa 54.4
25.9
Isa 40.9;
30.18; 33.22;
66.10;
Ps 20.5
25.10
Isa 16.14
26.1
Isa 4.2;
12.1; 14.31;
60.18
26.2
Isa 60.11,
18; 61.3;
62.1,2
26.4
Isa 12.2;
17.10

26.5
Isa 25.12;
Job 40.11-13
26.6
Isa 28.3;
3.14,15
26.7
Isa 57.2;
42.16
26.8
Isa 51.4;
56.1; v. 13;
Ex 3.15
26.9
Ps 63.6;
Isa 55.6;
Hos 5.15
26.10
Rom 2.4;
Isa 22.12,
13;
Hos 11.7;
Jn 5.37,38
26.11
Isa 5.12;
9.7; 10.17;
66.15,24
26.12
v. 3;
Isa 64.8

 for in the Lord God r
 you have an everlasting
 rock.
5 For he has brought low
 the inhabitants of the
 height;
 the lofty city he lays low.
 He lays it low to the ground,
 casts it to the dust.
6 The foot tramples it,
 the feet of the poor,
 the steps of the needy.

7 The way of the righteous is
 level;
 O Just One, you make
 smooth the path of the
 righteous.
8 In the path of your
 judgments,
 O Lord, we wait for you;
 your name and your renown
 are the soul's desire.
9 My soul yearns for you in the
 night,
 my spirit within me
 earnestly seeks you.
 For when your judgments are
 in the earth,
 the inhabitants of the
 world learn
 righteousness.
10 If favor is shown to the
 wicked,
 they do not learn
 righteousness;
 in the land of uprightness
 they deal perversely
 and do not see the majesty
 of the Lord.
11 O Lord, your hand is lifted
 up,
 but they do not see it.
 Let them see your zeal for
 your people, and be
 ashamed.
 Let the fire for your
 adversaries consume
 them.
12 O Lord, you will ordain
 peace for us,
 for indeed, all that we have
 done, you have done for
 us.

q Meaning of Heb uncertain r Heb in Yah,
the Lord

¹³ O LORD our God,
 other lords besides you
 have ruled over us,
 but we acknowledge your
 name alone.
¹⁴ The dead do not live;
 shades do not rise—
 because you have punished
 and destroyed them,
 and wiped out all memory
 of them.
¹⁵ But you have increased the
 nation, O LORD,
 you have increased the
 nation; you are
 glorified;
 you have enlarged all the
 borders of the land.

¹⁶ O LORD, in distress they
 sought you,
 they poured out a prayerˢ
 when your chastening was
 on them.
¹⁷ Like a woman with child,
 who writhes and cries out
 in her pangs
 when she is near her time,
 so were we because of you,
 O LORD;
¹⁸ we were with child, we
 writhed,
 but we gave birth only to
 wind.
 We have won no victories on
 earth,
 and no one is born to
 inhabit the world.
¹⁹ Your dead shall live, their
 corpsesᵗ shall rise.
 O dwellers in the dust,
 awake and sing for joy!
 For your dew is a radiant
 dew,
 and the earth will give
 birth to those long
 dead.ᵘ

²⁰ Come, my people, enter your
 chambers,
 and shut your doors behind
 you;
 hide yourselves for a little
 while
 until the wrath is past.
²¹ For the LORD comes out from
 his place

26.13
Isa 2.8;
10.11; 63.7
26.14
Isa 8.19;
Hab 2.19;
Isa 10.3
26.15
Isa 9.3;
33.17
26.16
Hos 5.15
26.17
Isa 13.8;
Jn 16.21
26.18
Isa 33.11;
Ps 17.14
26.19
Ezek 37.1-14;
Dan 12.2
26.20
Ex 12.22,
23; Ps 30.5;
Isa 54.7,8;
2 Cor 4.17
26.21
Mic 1.3;
Jude 14;
Isa 13.11;
Job 16.18

27.1
Isa 34.5,6;
Job 3.8;
Ps 74.14;
Isa 51.9
27.2
Ps 5.7; 80.8;
Jer 2.21
27.3
Isa 58.11;
31.5;
1 Sam 2.9
27.4
2 Sam 23.6;
Isa 33.12
27.5
Isa 25.4;
Job 22.21
27.6
Isa 37.31;
Hos 14.5,6
27.7
Isa 10.12,17
27.8
Job 23.6;
Jer 10.23;
Ps 78.38
27.9
Isa 1.25;
Rom 11.27;
Isa 17.8

to punish the inhabitants
 of the earth for their
 iniquity;
the earth will disclose the
 blood shed on it,
 and will no longer cover its
 slain.

Israel's Redemption

27 On that day the LORD with
 his cruel and great and
strong sword will punish Leviathan
the fleeing serpent, Leviathan the
twisting serpent, and he will kill
the dragon that is in the sea.

² On that day:
 A pleasant vineyard, sing
 about it!
³ I, the LORD, am its keeper;
 every moment I water it.
 I guard it night and day
 so that no one can harm it;
⁴ I have no wrath.
 If it gives me thorns and
 briers,
 I will march to battle
 against it.
 I will burn it up.
⁵ Or else let it cling to me for
 protection,
 let it make peace with me,
 let it make peace with me.

⁶ In days to comeᵛ Jacob shall
 take root,
 Israel shall blossom and
 put forth shoots,
 and fill the whole world
 with fruit.

⁷ Has he struck them down as
 he struck down those
 who struck them?
 Or have they been killed as
 their killers were killed?
⁸ By expulsion,ˢ by exile you
 struggled against them;
 with his fierce blast he
 removed them in the
 day of the east wind.
⁹ Therefore by this the guilt of
 Jacob will be expiated,

ˢ Meaning of Heb uncertain ᵗ Cn Compare
Syr Tg: Heb *my corpse* ᵘ Heb *to the shades*
ᵛ Heb *Those to come*

and this will be the full
 fruit of the removal of
 his sin:
when he makes all the
 stones of the altars
like chalkstones crushed to
 pieces,
no sacred poles^w or
 incense altars will
 remain standing.
10 For the fortified city is
 solitary,
a habitation deserted and
 forsaken, like the
 wilderness;
the calves graze there,
 there they lie down, and
 strip its branches.
11 When its boughs are dry,
 they are broken;
women come and make a
 fire of them.
For this is a people without
 understanding;
therefore he that made
 them will not have
 compassion on them,
he that formed them will
 show them no favor.

12 On that day the LORD will
thresh from the channel of the Eu-
phrates to the Wadi of Egypt, and
you will be gathered one by one,
O people of Israel. 13 And on that
day a great trumpet will be blown,
and those who were lost in the land
of Assyria and those who were driv-
en out to the land of Egypt will
come and worship the LORD on the
holy mountain at Jerusalem.

Judgment on Corrupt Rulers, Priests, and Prophets

28 Ah, the proud garland of
 the drunkards of
 Ephraim,
and the fading flower of its
 glorious beauty,
which is on the head of
 those bloated with rich
 food, of those overcome
 with wine!
2 See, the Lord has one who is
 mighty and strong;

like a storm of hail, a
 destroying tempest,
like a storm of mighty,
 overflowing waters;
with his hand he will hurl
 them down to the
 earth.
3 Trampled under foot will be
 the proud garland of the
 drunkards of Ephraim.
4 And the fading flower of its
 glorious beauty,
which is on the head of
 those bloated with rich
 food,
will be like a first-ripe fig
 before the summer;
whoever sees it, eats it up
 as soon as it comes to
 hand.

5 In that day the LORD of hosts
 will be a garland of
 glory,
and a diadem of beauty, to
 the remnant of his
 people;
6 and a spirit of justice to the
 one who sits in
 judgment,
and strength to those who
 turn back the battle at
 the gate.

7 These also reel with wine
 and stagger with strong
 drink;
the priest and the prophet
 reel with strong drink,
 they are confused with
 wine,
they stagger with strong
 drink;
they err in vision,
 they stumble in giving
 judgment.
8 All tables are covered with
 filthy vomit;
 no place is clean.

9 "Whom will he teach
 knowledge,
and to whom will he
 explain the message?

27.10 Isa 32.13, 14; Jer 26.6, 18
27.11 Deut 32.28; Isa 1.3; Jer 8.7; Deut 32.18; Isa 43.1,7; 44.2,21,24
27.12 Isa 11.11; Gen 15.18; Deut 30.3,4
27.13 Lev 25.9; Mt 24.31; Rev 11.15; Isa 19.23-25
28.1 vv. 3,4,7
28.2 Isa 40.10; 30.30; Ezek 13.11; Isa 29.6; 30.28
28.3 vv. 1,18
28.4 Hos 9.10; Mic 7.1; Nah 3.12
28.5 Isa 41.16; 62.3; 4.2
28.6 Isa 11.2; 32.15; 25.4
28.7 Prov 20.1; Hos 4.11; Isa 56.10,12
28.8 Jer 48.26
28.9 v. 26; Ps 131.2; Heb 5.12,13

^w Heb *Asherim*

Those who are weaned from
milk,
those taken from the
breast?

10 For it is precept upon
precept, precept upon
precept,
line upon line, line upon
line,
here a little, there a
little."ˣ

11 Truly, with stammering lip
and with alien tongue
he will speak to this people,
12 to whom he has said,
"This is rest;
give rest to the weary;
and this is repose";
yet they would not hear.
13 Therefore the word of the
LORD will be to them,
"Precept upon precept,
precept upon precept,
line upon line, line upon
line,
here a little, there a
little;"ˣ
in order that they may go,
and fall backward,
and be broken, and snared,
and taken.

14 Therefore hear the word of
the LORD, you scoffers
who rule this people in
Jerusalem.
15 Because you have said, "We
have made a covenant
with death,
and with Sheol we have an
agreement;
when the overwhelming
scourge passes through
it will not come to us;
for we have made lies our
refuge,
and in falsehood we have
taken shelter";
16 therefore thus says the Lord
GOD,
See, I am laying in Zion a
foundation stone,
a tested stone,
a precious cornerstone, a
sure foundation:

28.10
Neh 9.30
28.11
1 Cor 14.21
28.12
Jer 6.16;
Mt 11.28,29
28.13
Mt 21.44
28.14
v. 22;
Isa 29.20
28.15
vv. 18,2;
Isa 59.3,4;
29.15
28.16
Ps 118.22;
Mt 21.42;
Acts 4.11;
Rom 9.33;
10.11;
Eph 2.20;
1 Pet 2.4-6

28.17
Isa 5.16;
v. 2
28.18
v. 15
28.19
Isa 50.4;
Ps 88.15;
Jer 15.8
28.21
2 Sam 5.20;
1 Chr 14.11;
Josh 10.10,
12;
2 Sam 5.25;
1 Chr 14.16;
Lam 3.33
28.22
v. 14;
Isa 10.22,23

"One who trusts will not
panic."
17 And I will make justice the
line,
and righteousness the
plummet;
hail will sweep away the
refuge of lies,
and waters will overwhelm
the shelter.
18 Then your covenant with
death will be annulled,
and your agreement with
Sheol will not stand;
when the overwhelming
scourge passes through
you will be beaten down by
it.
19 As often as it passes
through, it will take
you;
for morning by morning it
will pass through,
by day and by night;
and it will be sheer terror to
understand the
message.
20 For the bed is too short to
stretch oneself on it,
and the covering too
narrow to wrap oneself
in it.
21 For the LORD will rise up as
on Mount Perazim,
he will rage as in the valley
of Gibeon;
to do his deed—strange is
his deed!
and to work his
work—alien is his
work!
22 Now therefore do not scoff,
or your bonds will be made
stronger;
for I have heard a decree of
destruction
from the Lord GOD of hosts
upon the whole land.

23 Listen, and hear my voice;
Pay attention, and hear my
speech.
24 Do those who plow for
sowing plow
continually?

ˣ Meaning of Heb of this verse uncertain

Do they continually open
and harrow their
ground?
25 When they have leveled its
surface,
do they not scatter dill,
sow cummin,
and plant wheat in rows
and barley in its proper
place,
and spelt as the border?
26 For they are well instructed;
their God teaches them.

27 Dill is not threshed with a
threshing sledge,
nor is a cart wheel rolled
over cummin;
but dill is beaten out with a
stick,
and cummin with a rod.
28 Grain is crushed for bread,
but one does not thresh it
forever;
one drives the cart wheel
and horses over it,
but does not pulverize it.
29 This also comes from the
LORD of hosts;
he is wonderful in counsel,
and excellent in wisdom.

The Siege of Jerusalem

29 Ah, Ariel, Ariel,
the city where David
encamped!
Add year to year;
let the festivals run their
round.
2 Yet I will distress Ariel,
and there shall be moaning
and lamentation,
and Jerusalemʸ shall be to
me like an Ariel.ᶻ
3 And like Davidᵃ I will
encamp against you;
I will besiege you with
towers
and raise siegeworks
against you.
4 Then deep from the earth
you shall speak,
from low in the dust your
words shall come;

your voice shall come from
the ground like the
voice of a ghost,
and your speech shall
whisper out of the dust.

5 But the multitude of your
foesᵇ shall be like
small dust,
and the multitude of
tyrants like flying chaff.
And in an instant, suddenly,
6 you will be visited by the
LORD of hosts
with thunder and earthquake
and great noise,
with whirlwind and
tempest, and the flame
of a devouring fire.
7 And the multitude of all the
nations that fight
against Ariel,
all that fight against her
and her stronghold, and
who distress her,
shall be like a dream, a
vision of the night.
8 Just as when a hungry
person dreams of eating
and wakes up still hungry,
or a thirsty person dreams of
drinking
and wakes up faint, still
thirsty,
so shall the multitude of all
the nations be
that fight against Mount
Zion.

9 Stupefy yourselves and be in
a stupor,
blind yourselves and be
blind!
Be drunk, but not from wine;
stagger, but not from
strong drink!
10 For the LORD has poured out
upon you
a spirit of deep sleep;
he has closed your eyes, you
prophets,
and covered your heads,
you seers.
11 The vision of all this has be-

28.27
Am 1.3
28.29
Isa 9.6;
31.2;
Rom 11.33
29.1
2 Sam 5.9;
vv. 9,13
29.2
Isa 3.26;
Lam 2.5
29.3
Lk 19.43,44
29.4
Isa 8.19;
Lev 20.6;
Deut 18.10,
11;
1 Sam 28.8,
15;
2 Chr 33.6

29.5
Isa 17.13,
14; 25.3-5;
30.13;
1 Thes 5.3
29.6
Isa 28.2;
Mt 24.7;
Mk 13.8;
Lk 21.11;
Rev 11.13,
19; 16.18
29.7
Mic 4.11,12;
Zech 12.9;
Job 20.8;
Ps 73.20
29.8
Isa 54.17
29.9
Isa 51.17,
21,22
29.10
Rom 11.8;
Ps 69.23;
Isa 6.9,10;
Mic 3.6
29.11
Isa 27.7;
8.16;
Dan 12.4,9;
Mt 13.11

ʸ Heb *she* ᶻ Probable meaning, *altar hearth*; compare Ezek 43.15
ᵃ Gk: Meaning of Heb uncertain
ᵇ Cn: Heb *strangers*

come for you like the words of a sealed document. If it is given to those who can read, with the command, "Read this," they say, "We cannot, for it is sealed." [12] And if it is given to those who cannot read, saying, "Read this," they say, "We cannot read."

13 The Lord said:
Because these people draw
near with their mouths
and honor me with their
lips,
while their hearts are far
from me,
and their worship of me is a
human commandment
learned by rote;
14 so I will again do
amazing things with this
people,
shocking and amazing.
The wisdom of their wise
shall perish,
and the discernment of the
discerning shall be
hidden.

15 Ha! You who hide a plan too
deep for the LORD,
whose deeds are in the
dark,
and who say, "Who sees
us? Who knows us?"
16 You turn things upside down!
Shall the potter be
regarded as the clay?
Shall the thing made say of
its maker,
"He did not make me";
or the thing formed say of
the one who formed it,
"He has no
understanding"?

Hope for the Future

17 Shall not Lebanon in a very
little while
become a fruitful field,
and the fruitful field be
regarded as a forest?
18 On that day the deaf shall
hear
the words of a scroll,

and out of their gloom and
darkness
the eyes of the blind shall
see.
19 The meek shall obtain fresh
joy in the LORD,
and the neediest people
shall exult in the
Holy One of Israel.
20 For the tyrant shall be no
more,
and the scoffer shall cease
to be;
all those alert to do evil
shall be cut off—
21 those who cause a person to
lose a lawsuit,
who set a trap for the
arbiter in the gate,
and without grounds deny
justice to the one in the
right.

22 Therefore thus says the LORD,
who redeemed Abraham, concerning the house of Jacob:
No longer shall Jacob be
ashamed,
no longer shall his face
grow pale.
23 For when he sees his
children,
the work of my hands, in
his midst,
they will sanctify my name;
they will sanctify the Holy
One of Jacob,
and will stand in awe of
the God of Israel.
24 And those who err in spirit
will come to
understanding,
and those who grumble will
accept instruction.

The Futility of Reliance on Egypt

30 Oh, rebellious children,
says the LORD,
who carry out a plan, but not
mine;
who make an alliance, but
against my will,
adding sin to sin;
2 who set out to go down to
Egypt

29.13
Ezek 33.31;
Mt 15.8,9;
Mk 7.6,7
29.14
Hab 1.5;
Jer 8.9;
49.7;
1 Cor 1.19
29.15
Isa 30.1;
57.12;
Ps 94.7
29.16
Isa 45.9;
Jer 18.1-6;
Rom 9.19-21
29.17
Isa 32.15
29.18
Isa 35.5;
v. 11

29.19
Isa 61.1;
Mt 11.5;
Jas 2.5
29.20
v. 5;
Isa 28.14,
22; 59.4
29.21
Am 5.10,12;
Prov 28.21
29.22
Isa 41.8;
45.17; 54.4
29.23
Isa 49.20-26;
45.11; 5.16;
8.13
29.24
Isa 28.7
30.1
v. 9;
Isa 29.15;
8.11,12
30.2
Isa 31.1;
Num 27.21;
Josh 9.14;
1 Kings 22.7;
Jer 21.2

without asking for my
 counsel,
to take refuge in the
 protection of Pharaoh,
and to seek shelter in the
 shadow of Egypt;
3 Therefore the protection of
 Pharaoh shall become
 your shame,
and the shelter in the
 shadow of Egypt your
 humiliation.
4 For though his officials are
 at Zoan
and his envoys reach
 Hanes,
5 everyone comes to shame
 through a people that
 cannot profit them,
that brings neither help nor
 profit,
but shame and disgrace.

6 An oracle concerning the ani-
mals of the Negeb.
Through a land of trouble
 and distress,
of lioness and roaring[c] lion,
of viper and flying serpent,
they carry their riches on the
 backs of donkeys,
and their treasures on the
 humps of camels,
to a people that cannot
 profit them.
7 For Egypt's help is worthless
 and empty,
therefore I have called her,
 "Rahab who sits still."[d]

A Rebellious People

8 Go now, write it before them
 on a tablet,
and inscribe it in a book,
so that it may be for the
 time to come
as a witness forever.
9 For they are a rebellious
 people,
faithless children,
children who will not hear
 the instruction of the LORD;
10 who say to the seers, "Do
 not see";
and to the prophets, "Do
 not prophesy to us what
 is right;

30.3
Isa 20.5;
Jer 37.3,5
30.4
Isa 19.11
30.5
Jer 2.36;
v. 7
30.6
Isa 46.1,2;
8.22; 14.29;
15.7
30.7
Jer 37.7;
v. 15
30.8
Isa 8.1;
Hab 2.2
30.9
v. 1;
Isa 28.15;
24.5
30.10
Isa 29.10;
5.20;
1 Kings 22.8,
13

30.11
Job 21.14
30.12
Isa 5.24;
59.13
30.13
Isa 26.21;
Ps 62.3;
Isa 29.5
30.14
Ps 2.9;
Jer 19.10,11
30.15
Isa 7.4;
28.12; 32.17
30.16
Isa 31.1,3
30.17
Lev 26.8;
Deut 28.25;
32.30;
Josh 23.10

speak to us smooth things,
 prophesy illusions,
11 leave the way, turn aside
 from the path,
let us hear no more about
 the Holy One of Israel."
12 Therefore thus says the Holy
 One of Israel:
Because you reject this word,
 and put your trust in
 oppression and deceit,
 and rely on them;
13 therefore this iniquity shall
 become for you
like a break in a high wall,
 bulging out, and about
 to collapse,
whose crash comes
 suddenly, in an instant;
14 its breaking is like that of a
 potter's vessel
that is smashed so
 ruthlessly
that among its fragments not
 a sherd is found
for taking fire from the
 hearth,
or dipping water out of the
 cistern.

15 For thus said the Lord GOD,
 the Holy One of Israel:
In returning and rest you
 shall be saved;
 in quietness and in trust
 shall be your strength.
But you refused 16 and said,
"No! We will flee upon
 horses" —
therefore you shall flee!
and, "We will ride upon swift
 steeds" —
 therefore your pursuers
 shall be swift!
17 A thousand shall flee at the
 threat of one,
 at the threat of five you
 shall flee,
until you are left
like a flagstaff on the top
 of a mountain,
like a signal on a hill.

[c] Cn: Heb *from them* [d] Meaning of Heb
uncertain

God's Promise to Zion

18 Therefore the LORD waits to
be gracious to you;
therefore he will rise up to
show mercy to you.
For the LORD is a God of
justice;
blessed are all those who
wait for him.
19 Truly, O people in Zion, in-
habitants of Jerusalem, you shall
weep no more. He will surely be
gracious to you at the sound of your
cry; when he hears it, he will an-
swer you. 20 Though the Lord may
give you the bread of adversity and
the water of affliction, yet your
Teacher will not hide himself any
more, but your eyes shall see your
Teacher. 21 And when you turn to
the right or when you turn to the
left, your ears shall hear a word be-
hind you, saying, "This is the way;
walk in it." 22 Then you will defile
your silver-covered idols and your
gold-plated images. You will scat-
ter them like filthy rags; you will
say to them, "Away with you!"
23 He will give rain for the seed
with which you sow the ground,
and grain, the produce of the
ground, which will be rich and
plenteous. On that day your cattle
will graze in broad pastures; 24 and
the oxen and donkeys that till the
ground will eat silage, which has
been winnowed with shovel and
fork. 25 On every lofty mountain
and every high hill there will be
brooks running with water — on a
day of the great slaughter, when
the towers fall. 26 Moreover the
light of the moon will be like the
light of the sun, and the light of the
sun will be sevenfold, like the light
of seven days, on the day when the
LORD binds up the injuries of his
people, and heals the wounds in-
flicted by his blow.

Judgment on Assyria

27 See, the name of the LORD
comes from far away,
burning with his anger, and
in thick rising smoke;e

Cross references

30.18 Isa 42.14; 33.5; 5.16; 25.9
30.19 Isa 65.9; 60.20; 61.1-3; Mt 7.7-11
30.20 1 Kings 22.27; Ps 80.5; 74.9; Am 8.11
30.21 Isa 35.8,9; Prov 3.6; Isa 29.24
30.22 Isa 2.20; 31.7; 46.6; Mt 4.10
30.23 Ps 65.9-13; Isa 65.21, 22; 32.20
30.26 Isa 60.19, 20; Rev 21.23; 22.5; Isa 61.1; 1.6; Jer 33.6
30.27 Isa 59.19; 10.5,13,17; 66.15

30.28 Isa 11.4; 2 Thes 2.8; Isa 8.8; 37.29
30.29 Ps 42.4; Isa 2.3; 17.10
30.30 Isa 28.2; 32.19
30.31 Isa 31.8
30.32 Isa 10.24; Jer 31.4; Ezek 32.10
30.33 Jer 7.3; 19.6; vv. 27, 28; Isa 34.9
31.1 Isa 30.2; Ezek 17.15; Isa 2.7; Ps 20.7; Dan 9.13; Isa 10.17
31.2 Isa 28.29; Rom 16.27; Isa 45.7; Num 23.19; Isa 14.20; 22.14

his lips are full of
indignation,
and his tongue is like a
devouring fire;
28 his breath is like an
overflowing stream
that reaches up to the
neck —
to sift the nations with the
sieve of destruction,
and to place on the jaws of
the peoples a bridle
that leads them astray.

29 You shall have a song as in
the night when a holy festival is
kept; and gladness of heart, as
when one sets out to the sound of
the flute to go to the mountain of
the LORD, to the Rock of Israel.
30 And the LORD will cause his ma-
jestic voice to be heard and the de-
scending blow of his arm to be
seen, in furious anger and a flame
of devouring fire, with a cloudburst
and tempest and hailstones. 31 The
Assyrian will be terror-stricken at
the voice of the LORD, when he
strikes with his rod. 32 And every
stroke of the staff of punishment
that the LORD lays upon him will be
to the sound of timbrels and lyres;
battling with brandished arm he
will fight with him. 33 For his burn-
ing placef has long been prepared;
truly it is made ready for the king,g
its pyre made deep and wide, with
fire and wood in abundance; the
breath of the LORD, like a stream of
sulfur, kindles it.

Alliance with Egypt Is Futile

31 Alas for those who go
down to Egypt for help
and who rely on horses,
who trust in chariots because
they are many
and in horsemen because
they are very strong,
but do not look to the Holy
One of Israel
or consult the LORD!
2 Yet he too is wise and brings
disaster;

e Meaning of Heb uncertain f Or Topheth
g Or Molech

he does not call back his
words,
but will rise against the
house of the evildoers,
and against the helpers of
those who work
iniquity.
3 The Egyptians are human,
and not God;
their horses are flesh, and
not spirit.
When the LORD stretches out
his hand,
the helper will stumble,
and the one helped will
fall,
and they will all perish
together.

4 For thus the LORD said to
me,
As a lion or a young lion
growls over its prey,
and—when a band of
shepherds is called out
against it—
is not terrified by their
shouting
or daunted at their noise,
so the LORD of hosts will
come down
to fight upon Mount Zion
and upon its hill.
5 Like birds hovering overhead,
so the LORD of hosts
will protect Jerusalem;
he will protect and deliver it,
he will spare and rescue it.

6 Turn back to him whom you[h]
have deeply betrayed, O people of
Israel. 7 For on that day all of you
shall throw away your idols of silver
and idols of gold, which your hands
have sinfully made for you.
8 "Then the Assyrian shall fall
by a sword, not of
mortals;
and a sword, not of
humans, shall devour
him;
he shall flee from the sword,
and his young men shall be
put to forced labor.
9 His rock shall pass away in
terror,

31.3
Ezek 28.9;
Isa 36.9;
9.17; 30.5,7
31.4
Hos 11.10;
Am 3.8;
Isa 42.13
31.5
Ps 91.4;
Isa 17.13
31.6
Isa 44.22;
1.2,5
31.7
Isa 2.20
31.8
Isa 10.12;
66.16; 21.15;
14.2
31.9
Deut 32.31,
37; Isa 5.26;
10.16

32.1
Isa 9.6,7;
Jer 23.5;
Zech 9.9
32.2
Isa 4.6;
35.6; 41.18;
43.19,20
32.3
Isa 29.18
32.4
Isa 29.24
32.5
1 Sam 25.25
32.6
Isa 59.7,13;
10.6; 9.15,16;
3.15
32.7
Jer 5.26-28;
Isa 11.4;
5.23
32.8
2 Cor 9.6-11

and his officers desert the
standard in panic,"
says the LORD, whose fire is
in Zion,
and whose furnace is in
Jerusalem.

Government with Justice Predicted

32 See, a king will reign in
righteousness,
and princes will rule with
justice.
2 Each will be like a hiding
place from the wind,
a covert from the tempest,
like streams of water in a dry
place,
like the shade of a great
rock in a weary land.
3 Then the eyes of those who
have sight will not be
closed,
and the ears of those who
have hearing will listen.
4 The minds of the rash will
have good judgment,
and the tongues of
stammerers will speak
readily and distinctly.
5 A fool will no longer be
called noble,
nor a villain said to be
honorable.
6 For fools speak folly,
and their minds plot
iniquity:
to practice ungodliness,
to utter error concerning
the LORD,
to leave the craving of the
hungry unsatisfied,
and to deprive the thirsty
of drink.
7 The villainies of villains are
evil;
they devise wicked devices
to ruin the poor with lying
words,
even when the plea of the
needy is right.
8 But those who are noble
plan noble things,
and by noble things they
stand.

h Heb *they*

Complacent Women Warned of Disaster

9 Rise up, you women who are
 at ease, hear my voice;
 you complacent daughters,
 listen to my speech.
10 In little more than a year
 you will shudder, you
 complacent ones;
 for the vintage will fail,
 the fruit harvest will not
 come.
11 Tremble, you women who
 are at ease,
 shudder, you complacent
 ones;
 strip, and make yourselves
 bare,
 and put sackcloth on your
 loins.
12 Beat your breasts for the
 pleasant fields,
 for the fruitful vine,
13 for the soil of my people
 growing up in thorns and
 briers;
 yes, for all the joyous houses
 in the jubilant city.
14 For the palace will be
 forsaken,
 the populous city deserted;
 the hill and the watchtower
 will become dens forever,
 the joy of wild asses,
 a pasture for flocks;
15 until a spirit from on high is
 poured out on us,
 and the wilderness
 becomes a fruitful field,
 and the fruitful field is
 deemed a forest.

The Peace of God's Reign

16 Then justice will dwell in the
 wilderness,
 and righteousness abide in
 the fruitful field.
17 The effect of righteousness
 will be peace,
 and the result of
 righteousness,
 quietness and trust
 forever.
18 My people will abide in a
 peaceful habitation,
 in secure dwellings, and in
 quiet resting places.

32.9
Isa 47.8;
28.23
32.10
Isa 5.5,6
32.11
Isa 22.12;
47.2
32.12
Nah 2.7
32.13
Isa 34.13;
22.2
32.14
Isa 13.22;
6.11; 13.21
32.15
Isa 11.2;
Ezek 39.29;
Joel 2.28;
Isa 29.17;
35.2
32.16
Isa 33.5
32.17
Rom 14.17;
Jas 3.18;
Isa 30.15

32.19
Isa 30.30;
Zech 11.2
32.20
Isa 30.24
33.1
Isa 21.2;
Hab 2.8;
Isa 24.16;
Jer 25.12-14;
Mt 7.2
33.2
Isa 25.9
33.3
Isa 17.13;
Jer 25.30,31
33.5
Ps 97.9
33.6
v. 20;
Isa 45.17;
11.9;
Mt 6.33
33.7
2 Kings 18.18,
37

19 The forest will disappear
 completely,[i]
 and the city will be utterly
 laid low.
20 Happy will you be who sow
 beside every stream,
 who let the ox and the
 donkey range freely.

A Prophecy of Deliverance from Foes

33 Ah, you destroyer,
 who yourself have not
 been destroyed;
 you treacherous one,
 with whom no one has
 dealt treacherously!
 When you have ceased to
 destroy,
 you will be destroyed;
 and when you have stopped
 dealing treacherously,
 you will be dealt with
 treacherously.

2 O LORD, be gracious to us; we
 wait for you.
 Be our arm every morning,
 our salvation in the time of
 trouble.
3 At the sound of tumult,
 peoples fled;
 before your majesty,
 nations scattered.
4 Spoil was gathered as the
 caterpillar gathers;
 as locusts leap, they
 leaped[j] upon it.
5 The LORD is exalted, he
 dwells on high;
 he filled Zion with justice
 and righteousness;
6 he will be the stability of
 your times,
 abundance of salvation,
 wisdom, and
 knowledge;
 the fear of the LORD is
 Zion's treasure.[k]

7 Listen! the valiant[i] cry in
 the streets;

i Cn: Heb *And it will hail when the forest
comes down* j Meaning of Heb uncertain
k Heb *his treasure*; meaning of Heb uncertain

the envoys of peace weep
bitterly.
8 The highways are deserted,
travelers have quit the
road.
The treaty is broken,
its oaths[1] are despised,
its obligation[m] is
disregarded.
9 The land mourns and
languishes;
Lebanon is confounded
and withers away;
Sharon is like a desert;
and Bashan and Carmel
shake off their leaves.

10 "Now I will arise," says the
LORD,
"now I will lift myself up;
now I will be exalted.
11 You conceive chaff, you bring
forth stubble;
your breath is a fire that
will consume you.
12 And the peoples will be as if
burned to lime,
like thorns cut down, that
are burned in the fire."

13 Hear, you who are far away,
what I have done;
and you who are near,
acknowledge my might.
14 The sinners in Zion are
afraid;
trembling has seized the
godless:
"Who among us can live with
the devouring fire?
Who among us can live
with everlasting
flames?"
15 Those who walk righteously
and speak uprightly,
who despise the gain of
oppression,
who wave away a bribe
instead of accepting it,
who stop their ears from
hearing of bloodshed
and shut their eyes from
looking on evil,
16 they will live on the heights;
their refuge will be the
fortresses of rocks;

33.8
Isa 35.8;
24.5
33.9
Isa 24.4;
2.13; 35.2
33.10
Ps 12.5
33.11
Ps 7.14;
Isa 59.4
33.12
Isa 9.18;
10.17
33.13
Isa 49.1
33.14
Isa 32.11;
30.27,30;
9.18,19
33.15
Ps 15.2;
24.4; 119.37
33.16
Isa 25.4;
26.1; 49.10

33.17
vv. 21,22;
Isa 26.15
33.18
Isa 17.14;
1 Cor 1.20
33.19
2 Kings 19.32;
Deut 28.49,
50; Jer 5.15
33.20
Ps 48.12;
46.5; 125.1,2;
Isa 37.33;
54.2
33.21
Isa 41.18
33.22
Isa 2.4;
Jas 4.12;
v. 17;
Zech 9.9;
Isa 35.4
33.23
2 Kings 7.8,
16

their food will be supplied,
their water assured.

The Land of the Majestic King

17 Your eyes will see the king in
his beauty;
they will behold a land that
stretches far away.
18 Your mind will muse on the
terror:
"Where is the one who
counted?
Where is the one who
weighed the tribute?
Where is the one who
counted the towers?"
19 No longer will you see the
insolent people,
the people of an obscure
speech that you cannot
comprehend,
stammering in a language
that you cannot
understand.
20 Look on Zion, the city of our
appointed festivals!
Your eyes will see
Jerusalem,
a quiet habitation, an
immovable tent,
whose stakes will never be
pulled up,
and none of whose ropes
will be broken.
21 But there the LORD in
majesty will be for us
a place of broad rivers and
streams,
where no galley with oars
can go,
nor stately ship can pass.
22 For the LORD is our judge,
the LORD is our ruler,
the LORD is our king; he
will save us.

23 Your rigging hangs loose;
it cannot hold the mast
firm in its place,
or keep the sail spread out.

Then prey and spoil in
abundance will be
divided;

1 Q Ms: MT *cities* m Or *everyone*

even the lame will fall to
plundering.
24 And no inhabitant will say,
"I am sick";
the people who live there
will be forgiven their
iniquity.

Judgment on the Nations

34 Draw near, O nations, to
hear;
O peoples, give heed!
Let the earth hear, and all
that fills it;
the world, and all that
comes from it.
2 For the LORD is enraged
against all the nations,
and furious against all their
hoards;
he has doomed them, has
given them over for
slaughter.
3 Their slain shall be cast out,
and the stench of their
corpses shall rise;
the mountains shall flow
with their blood.
4 All the host of heaven shall
rot away,
and the skies roll up like a
scroll.
All their host shall wither
like a leaf withering on a
vine,
or fruit withering on a fig
tree.

5 When my sword has drunk
its fill in the heavens,
lo, it will descend upon
Edom,
upon the people I have
doomed to judgment.
6 The LORD has a sword; it is
sated with blood,
it is gorged with fat,
with the blood of lambs
and goats,
with the fat of the kidneys
of rams.
For the LORD has a sacrifice
in Bozrah,
a great slaughter in the
land of Edom.
7 Wild oxen shall fall with
them,

and young steers with the
mighty bulls.
Their land shall be soaked
with blood,
and their soil made rich
with fat.

8 For the LORD has a day of
vengeance,
a year of vindication by
Zion's cause. n
9 And the streams of Edom o
shall be turned into
pitch,
and her soil into sulfur;
her land shall become
burning pitch.
10 Night and day it shall not be
quenched;
its smoke shall go up
forever.
From generation to
generation it shall lie
waste;
no one shall pass through
it forever and ever.
11 But the hawk p and the
hedgehog p shall
possess it;
the owl p and the raven
shall live in it.
He shall stretch the line of
confusion over it,
and the plummet of chaos
over q its nobles.
12 They shall name it No
Kingdom There,
and all its princes shall be
nothing.
13 Thorns shall grow over its
strongholds,
nettles and thistles in its
fortresses.
It shall be the haunt of
jackals,
an abode for ostriches.
14 Wildcats shall meet with
hyenas,
goat-demons shall call to
each other;
there too Lilith shall repose,
and find a place to rest.
15 There shall the owl nest

33.24 Jer 30.17; 50.20
34.1 Ps 49.1; Deut 32.1
34.2 Isa 26.20, 21; 13.5; 30.25
34.3 Joel 2.20; Ezek 14.19
34.4 Ezek 32.7,8; Joel 2.31; Mt 24.29; 2 Pet 3.10; Rev 6.13,14
34.5 Jer 46.10; 49.7; Mal 1.4
34.6 Jer 49.13; Isa 63.1
34.7 Ps 22.21; 68.30; Isa 29.9; 49.26
34.8 Isa 63.4
34.9 Deut 29.23
34.10 Isa 66.24; Rev 14.11; 19.3; Mal 1.4; Ezek 29.11
34.11 Isa 14.23; Zeph 2.14; Rev 18.2; 2 Kings 21.13; Lam 2.8
34.13 Isa 13.22; 32.13; Jer 9.11; 10.22
34.14 Isa 13.21
34.15 Deut 14.13

n Or of recompense by Zion's defender
o Heb her streams p Identification
uncertain q Heb lacks over

and lay and hatch and
 brood in its shadow;
there too the buzzards shall
 gather,
 each one with its mate.
16 Seek and read from the book
 of the LORD:
Not one of these shall be
 missing;
none shall be without its
 mate.
For the mouth of the LORD
 has commanded,
and his spirit has gathered
 them.
17 He has cast the lot for
 them,
his hand has portioned it
 out to them with the
 line;
they shall possess it forever,
 from generation to
 generation they shall
 live in it.

The Return of the Redeemed to Zion

35 The wilderness and the
dry land shall be glad,
the desert shall rejoice and
 blossom;
like the crocus 2 it shall
 blossom abundantly,
and rejoice with joy and
 singing.
The glory of Lebanon shall
 be given to it,
the majesty of Carmel and
 Sharon.
They shall see the glory of
 the LORD,
the majesty of our God.

3 Strengthen the weak
 hands,
and make firm the feeble
 knees.
4 Say to those who are of a
 fearful heart,
"Be strong, do not fear!
Here is your God.
He will come with
 vengeance,
with terrible recompense.
He will come and save
 you."

34.16
Isa 30.8;
40.5
34.17
Jer 13.25;
vv. 10,11
35.1f
Isa 55.12;
51.3
35.2
Isa 32.15;
v. 10;
Isa 60.13;
25.9
35.3
Job 4.3,4;
Heb 12.12
35.4
Isa 1.24;
34.8;
Ps 145.19

35.5
Isa 29.18;
Mt 11.5;
Jn 9.6,7
35.6
Mt 15.30;
Jn 5.8,9;
Acts 3.8;
Mt 9.32;
Isa 41.18;
43.19;
Jn 7.38
35.7
Isa 49.10;
34.13
35.8
Isa 62.10;
Mt 7.13,14;
Jer 14.8
35.9
Isa 30.6;
34.14; 62.12
35.10
Isa 51.11;
25.8; 65.19;
Rev 7.17;
21.4
36.1
2 Kings 18.13;
Isa 1.1

5 Then the eyes of the blind
 shall be opened,
and the ears of the deaf
 unstopped;
6 then the lame shall leap like
 a deer,
and the tongue of the
 speechless sing for joy.
For waters shall break forth
 in the wilderness,
and streams in the desert;
7 the burning sand shall
 become a pool,
and the thirsty ground
 springs of water;
the haunt of jackals shall
 become a swamp,r
the grass shall become
 reeds and rushes.

8 A highway shall be there,
and it shall be called the
 Holy Way;
the unclean shall not travel
 on it,s
but it shall be for God's
 people;t
no traveler, not even fools,
 shall go astray.
9 No lion shall be there,
nor shall any ravenous
 beast come up on it;
they shall not be found
 there,
but the redeemed shall
 walk there.
10 And the ransomed of the
 LORD shall return,
and come to Zion with
 singing;
everlasting joy shall be upon
 their heads;
they shall obtain joy and
 gladness,
and sorrow and sighing
 shall flee away.

Sennacherib Threatens Jerusalem

36 In the fourteenth year of
King Hezekiah, King Sen-
nacherib of Assyria came up
against all the fortified cities of Ju-

r Cn: Heb *in the haunt of jackals is her resting
place* s Or *pass it by* t Cn: Heb *for
them*

dah and captured them. ²The king of Assyria sent the Rabshakeh from Lachish to King Hezekiah at Jerusalem, with a great army. He stood by the conduit of the upper pool on the highway to the Fuller's Field. ³And there came out to him Eliakim son of Hilkiah, who was in charge of the palace, and Shebna the secretary, and Joah son of Asaph, the recorder.

4 The Rabshakeh said to them, "Say to Hezekiah: Thus says the great king, the king of Assyria: On what do you base this confidence of yours? ⁵Do you think that mere words are strategy and power for war? On whom do you now rely, that you have rebelled against me? ⁶See, you are relying on Egypt, that broken reed of a staff, which will pierce the hand of anyone who leans on it. Such is Pharaoh king of Egypt to all who rely on him. ⁷But if you say to me, 'We rely on the Lord our God,' is it not he whose high places and altars Hezekiah has removed, saying to Judah and to Jerusalem, 'You shall worship before this altar'? ⁸Come now, make a wager with my master the king of Assyria: I will give you two thousand horses, if you are able on your part to set riders on them. ⁹How then can you repulse a single captain among the least of my master's servants, when you rely on Egypt for chariots and for horsemen? ¹⁰Moreover, is it without the Lord that I have come up against this land to destroy it? The Lord said to me, Go up against this land, and destroy it."

11 Then Eliakim, Shebna, and Joah said to the Rabshakeh, "Please speak to your servants in Aramaic, for we understand it; do not speak to us in the language of Judah within the hearing of the people who are on the wall." ¹²But the Rabshakeh said, "Has my master sent me to speak these words to your master and to you, and not to the people sitting on the wall, who are doomed with you to eat their own dung and drink their own urine?"

36.2
2 Kings 18.17-20;
Isa 7.3
36.3
Isa 22.15,20
36.4
2 Kings 18.19
36.5
2 Kings 18.7
36.6
Ezek 29.6,7;
Isa 30.3,5,7
36.7
2 Kings 18.4,5
36.9
Isa 37.29;
20.5
36.11
Ezra 4.7;
v. 13

36.13
2 Chr 32.18
36.14
Isa 37.10
36.15
v. 18
36.16
Zech 3.10;
Prov 5.15
36.18
v. 15
36.19
Isa 37.11-13;
2 Kings 17.6
36.20
1 Kings 20.23,28; v. 15
36.22
v. 3;
Isa 22.15,20
37.1
2 Kings 19.1-37
37.2
Isa 22.15,20
37.3
Isa 26.16-18

13 Then the Rabshakeh stood and called out in a loud voice in the language of Judah, "Hear the words of the great king, the king of Assyria! ¹⁴Thus says the king: 'Do not let Hezekiah deceive you, for he will not be able to deliver you. ¹⁵Do not let Hezekiah make you rely on the Lord by saying, The Lord will surely deliver us; this city will not be given into the hand of the king of Assyria.' ¹⁶Do not listen to Hezekiah; for thus says the king of Assyria: 'Make your peace with me and come out to me; then everyone of you will eat from your own vine and your own fig tree and drink water from your own cistern, ¹⁷until I come and take you away to a land like your own land, a land of grain and wine, a land of bread and vineyards. ¹⁸Do not let Hezekiah mislead you by saying, The Lord will save us. Has any of the gods of the nations saved their land out of the hand of the king of Assyria? ¹⁹Where are the gods of Hamath and Arpad? Where are the gods of Sepharvaim? Have they delivered Samaria out of my hand? ²⁰Who among all the gods of these countries have saved their countries out of my hand, that the Lord should save Jerusalem out of my hand?' "

21 But they were silent and answered him not a word, for the king's command was, "Do not answer him." ²²Then Eliakim son of Hilkiah, who was in charge of the palace, and Shebna the secretary, and Joah son of Asaph, the recorder, came to Hezekiah with their clothes torn, and told him the words of the Rabshakeh.

Hezekiah Consults Isaiah

37 When King Hezekiah heard it, he tore his clothes, covered himself with sackcloth, and went into the house of the Lord. ²And he sent Eliakim, who was in charge of the palace, and Shebna the secretary, and the senior priests, covered with sackcloth, to the prophet Isaiah son of Amoz. ³They said to him, "Thus says Hezekiah, This day is a day of distress,

of rebuke, and of disgrace; children have come to the birth, and there is no strength to bring them forth. [4] It may be that the LORD your God heard the words of the Rabshakeh, whom his master the king of Assyria has sent to mock the living God, and will rebuke the words that the LORD your God has heard; therefore lift up your prayer for the remnant that is left."

[5] When the servants of King Hezekiah came to Isaiah, [6] Isaiah said to them, "Say to your master, 'Thus says the LORD: Do not be afraid because of the words that you have heard, with which the servants of the king of Assyria have reviled me. [7] I myself will put a spirit in him, so that he shall hear a rumor, and return to his own land; I will cause him to fall by the sword in his own land.'"

[8] The Rabshakeh returned, and found the king of Assyria fighting against Libnah; for he had heard that the king had left Lachish. [9] Now the king[u] heard concerning King Tirhakah of Ethiopia,[v] "He has set out to fight against you." When he heard it, he sent messengers to Hezekiah, saying, [10] "Thus shall you speak to King Hezekiah of Judah: Do not let your God on whom you rely deceive you by promising that Jerusalem will not be given into the hand of the king of Assyria. [11] See, you have heard what the kings of Assyria have done to all lands, destroying them utterly. Shall you be delivered? [12] Have the gods of the nations delivered them, the nations that my predecessors destroyed, Gozan, Haran, Rezeph, and the people of Eden who were in Telassar? [13] Where is the king of Hamath, the king of Arpad, the king of the city of Sepharvaim, the king of Hena, or the king of Ivvah?"

Hezekiah's Prayer

[14] Hezekiah received the letter from the hand of the messengers and read it; then Hezekiah went up to the house of the LORD and spread it before the LORD. [15] And Hezekiah prayed to the LORD, saying: [16] "O LORD of hosts, God of Israel, who are enthroned above the cherubim, you are God, you alone, of all the kingdoms of the earth; you have made heaven and earth. [17] Incline your ear, O LORD, and hear; open your eyes, O LORD, and see; hear all the words of Sennacherib, which he has sent to mock the living God. [18] Truly, O LORD, the kings of Assyria have laid waste all the nations and their lands, [19] and have hurled their gods into the fire, though they were no gods, but the work of human hands — wood and stone — and so they were destroyed. [20] So now, O LORD our God, save us from his hand, so that all the kingdoms of the earth may know that you alone are the LORD."

[21] Then Isaiah son of Amoz sent to Hezekiah, saying: "Thus says the LORD, the God of Israel: Because you have prayed to me concerning King Sennacherib of Assyria, [22] this is the word that the LORD has spoken concerning him:

> She despises you, she scorns
> you —
> virgin daughter Zion;
> she tosses her head — behind
> your back,
> daughter Jerusalem.

[23] Whom have you mocked and
> reviled?
> Against whom have you
> raised your voice
> and haughtily lifted your
> eyes?
> Against the Holy One of
> Israel!
[24] By your servants you have
> mocked the Lord,
> and you have said, 'With
> my many chariots
> I have gone up the heights of
> the mountains,
> to the far recesses of
> Lebanon;
> I felled its tallest cedars,
> its choicest cypresses;
> I came to its remotest
> height,

37.4 Isa 36.15, 18,20
37.6 Isa 7.4; 35.4
37.7 vv. 9,37,38
37.9 v. 7; Isa 18.1; 20.5
37.10 Isa 36.15
37.11 Isa 10.9-11; 36.18-20
37.12 2 Kings 17.6; 18.11; Gen 11.31; 12.1-4; Acts 7.2

37.16 Ex 25.22; Deut 10.17; Isa 42.5; 45.12
37.17 Dan 9.18; Ps 74.22; v. 4
37.18 2 Kings 15.29; 1 Chr 5.26; Nah 2.11,12
37.19 Isa 2.8; 26.14
37.20 Isa 25.9; Ps 46.10; Ezek 36.23
37.21 v. 2
37.22 Jer 14.17; Lam 2.13; Zech 2.10; Job 16.4
37.23 v. 4; Isa 2.11; 5.15,21; Ezek 39.7; Hab 1.12
37.24 Isa 8.7,8; 10.18,33,34; 14.8

u Heb *he* v Or Nubia; Heb *Cush*

its densest forest.

²⁵ I dug wells
 and drank waters,
 I dried up with the sole of
 my foot
 all the streams of Egypt.'

²⁶ Have you not heard
 that I determined it long
 ago?
I planned from days of old
 what now I bring to pass,
that you should make
 fortified cities
 crash into heaps of ruins,
²⁷ while their inhabitants,
 shorn of strength,
 are dismayed and
 confounded;
they have become like plants
 of the field
and like tender grass,
like grass on the housetops,
 blightedʷ before it is
 grown.

²⁸ I know your rising upˣ and
 your sitting down,
your going out and coming
 in,
and your raging against me.
²⁹ Because you have raged
 against me
and your arrogance has
 come to my ears,
I will put my hook in your
 nose
and my bit in your mouth;
I will turn you back on the
 way
 by which you came.

30 "And this shall be the sign for you: This year eat what grows of itself, and in the second year what springs from that; then in the third year sow, reap, plant vineyards, and eat their fruit. ³¹ The surviving remnant of the house of Judah shall again take root downward, and bear fruit upward; ³²for from Jerusalem a remnant shall go out, and from Mount Zion a band of survivors. The zeal of the Lord of hosts will do this.

33 "Therefore thus says the Lord concerning the king of Assyr-

ia: He shall not come into this city, shoot an arrow there, come before it with a shield, or cast up a siege ramp against it. ³⁴ By the way that he came, by the same he shall return; he shall not come into this city, says the Lord. ³⁵ For I will defend this city to save it, for my own sake and for the sake of my servant David."

Sennacherib's Defeat and Death

36 Then the angel of the Lord set out and struck down one hundred eighty-five thousand in the camp of the Assyrians; when morning dawned, they were all dead bodies. ³⁷ Then King Sennacherib of Assyria left, went home, and lived at Nineveh. ³⁸ As he was worshiping in the house of his god Nisroch, his sons Adrammelech and Sharezer killed him with the sword, and they escaped into the land of Ararat. His son Esar-haddon succeeded him.

Hezekiah's Illness

38 In those days Hezekiah became sick and was at the point of death. The prophet Isaiah son of Amoz came to him, and said to him, "Thus says the Lord: Set your house in order, for you shall die; you shall not recover." ² Then Hezekiah turned his face to the wall, and prayed to the Lord: ³ "Remember now, O Lord, I implore you, how I have walked before you in faithfulness with a whole heart, and have done what is good in your sight." And Hezekiah wept bitterly.

4 Then the word of the Lord came to Isaiah: ⁵ "Go and say to Hezekiah, Thus says the Lord, the God of your ancestor David: I have heard your prayer, I have seen your tears; I will add fifteen years to your life. ⁶ I will deliver you and this city out of the hand of the king of Assyria, and defend this city.

7 "This is the sign to you from the Lord, that the Lord will do this thing that he has promised: ⁸ See, I

37.26
Isa 40.21, 28;
Acts 2.23;
4.27,28;
Isa 46.11;
10.6; 17.1
37.27
Isa 40.7;
Ps 129.6
37.28
Ps 139.1
37.29
Isa 10.12;
30.28;
Ezek 38.4;
v. 34
37.30
Lev 25.5,11
37.31
v. 4;
Isa 4.2;
10.20; 27.6
37.32
v. 4;
2 Kings 19.31;
Isa 9.7;
Zech 1.14
37.33
Jer 6.6;
32.24

37.35
2 Kings 20.6;
Isa 38.6;
48.9,11
37.36
2 Kings 19.35;
Isa 10.12,
33,34
37.38
Jer 51.27;
Ezra 4.2
38.1
2 Kings 20.1-
6,9-11;
2 Chr 32.24;
2 Sam 17.23
38.3
Neh 13.14;
2 Kings 18.5,
6;
1 Chr 28.9;
29.19;
Deut 6.18
38.5
2 Kings 18.2,
13
38.6
Isa 37.35
38.7
Isa 7.11
38.8
2 Kings 20.9-
11;
Josh 10.12-14

ʷ With 2 Kings 19.26: Heb *field* ˣ Q Ms
Gk: MT lacks *your rising up*

will make the shadow cast by the
declining sun on the dial of Ahaz
turn back ten steps." So the sun
turned back on the dial the ten
steps by which it had declined.[y]

9 A writing of King Hezekiah of
Judah, after he had been sick and
had recovered from his sickness:
[10] I said: In the noontide of my
 days
 I must depart;
 I am consigned to the gates
 of Sheol
 for the rest of my years.
[11] I said, I shall not see the
 LORD
 in the land of the living;
 I shall look upon mortals no
 more
 among the inhabitants of
 the world.
[12] My dwelling is plucked up
 and removed from me
 like a shepherd's tent;
 like a weaver I have rolled up
 my life;
 he cuts me off from the
 loom;
 from day to night you bring
 me to an end;[y]
[13] I cry for help[z] until
 morning;
 like a lion he breaks all my
 bones;
 from day to night you bring
 me to an end.[y]

[14] Like a swallow or a crane[y] I
 clamor,
 I moan like a dove.
 My eyes are weary with
 looking upward.
 O Lord, I am oppressed; be
 my security!
[15] But what can I say? For he
 has spoken to me,
 and he himself has done it.
 All my sleep has fled[a]
 because of the bitterness of
 my soul.

[16] O Lord, by these things
 people live,
 and in all these is the life
 of my spirit.[y]

Oh, restore me to health
 and make me live!
[17] Surely it was for my welfare
 that I had great bitterness;
 but you have held back[b] my
 life
 from the pit of destruction,
 for you have cast all my sins
 behind your back.
[18] For Sheol cannot thank you,
 death cannot praise you;
 those who go down to the Pit
 cannot hope
 for your faithfulness.
[19] The living, the living, they
 thank you,
 as I do this day;
 fathers make known to
 children
 your faithfulness.

[20] The LORD will save me,
 and we will sing to stringed
 instruments[c]
 all the days of our lives,
 at the house of the LORD.

21 Now Isaiah had said, "Let
them take a lump of figs, and apply
it to the boil, so that he may recov-
er." [22] Hezekiah also had said,
"What is the sign that I shall go up
to the house of the LORD?"

Envoys from Babylon Welcomed

39 At that time King
Merodach-baladan son of
Baladan of Babylon sent envoys
with letters and a present to Heze-
kiah, for he heard that he had been
sick and had recovered. [2] Hezekiah
welcomed them; he showed them
his treasure house, the silver, the
gold, the spices, the precious oil,
his whole armory, all that was
found in his storehouses. There
was nothing in his house or in all
his realm that Hezekiah did not
show them. [3] Then the prophet Isa-
iah came to King Hezekiah and
said to him, "What did these men
say? From where did they come to
you?" Hezekiah answered, "They

38.10
Ps 102.24;
107.18;
Job 17.11,
15;
2 Cor 1.9
38.11
Ps 27.13;
116.9
38.12
2 Cor 5.1,
4; Heb 1.12;
Job 7.6; 6.9;
Ps 73.14
38.13
Job 10.16;
16.12;
Ps 51.8;
32.4
38.14
Isa 59.11;
Ps 119.122,
123
38.15
Ps 39.9;
1 Kings 21.27;
Job 7.11;
10.1
38.16
Ps 119.71,
75; 39.13

38.17
Ps 30.3;
Isa 43.25;
Jer 31.34;
Mic 7.19
38.18
Ps 6.5;
88.11;
115.17;
Eccl 9.10;
Ps 28.1
38.19
Ps 118.17;
Deut 6.7;
Ps 78.5-7
38.20
Ps 86.5;
33.1-3;
104.33;
116.17-19
38.21
2 Kings 20.7,
8
39.1
2 Kings 20.12-
19;
2 Chr 32.31
39.2
2 Chr 32.25,
31;
2 Kings 18.15,
16
39.3
2 Sam 12.1;
2 Chr 16.7;
Jer 5.15

[y] Meaning of Heb uncertain [z] Cn: Meaning
of Heb uncertain [a] Cn Compare Syr: Heb *I
will walk slowly all my years* [b] Cn Compare
Gk Vg: Heb *loved* [c] Heb *my stringed
instruments*

have come to me from a far country, from Babylon." ⁴He said, "What have they seen in your house?" Hezekiah answered, "They have seen all that is in my house; there is nothing in my storehouses that I did not show them."

5 Then Isaiah said to Hezekiah, "Hear the word of the LORD of hosts: ⁶Days are coming when all that is in your house, and that which your ancestors have stored up until this day, shall be carried to Babylon; nothing shall be left, says the LORD. ⁷Some of your own sons who are born to you shall be taken away; they shall be eunuchs in the palace of the king of Babylon." ⁸Then Hezekiah said to Isaiah, "The word of the LORD that you have spoken is good." For he thought, "There will be peace and security in my days."

God's People Are Comforted

40 Comfort, O comfort my people,
 says your God.
² Speak tenderly to Jerusalem,
 and cry to her
 that she has served her
 term,
 that her penalty is paid,
 that she has received from
 the LORD's hand
 double for all her sins.

³ A voice cries out:
 "In the wilderness prepare
 the way of the LORD,
 make straight in the desert
 a highway for our God.
⁴ Every valley shall be lifted
 up,
 and every mountain and
 hill be made low;
 the uneven ground shall
 become level,
 and the rough places a
 plain.
⁵ Then the glory of the LORD
 shall be revealed,
 and all people shall see it
 together,
 for the mouth of the LORD
 has spoken."

⁶ A voice says, "Cry out!"
 And I said, "What shall I
 cry?"
 All people are grass,
 their constancy is like the
 flower of the field.
⁷ The grass withers, the flower
 fades,
 when the breath of the
 LORD blows upon it;
 surely the people are grass.
⁸ The grass withers, the flower
 fades;
 but the word of our God
 will stand forever.

⁹ Get you up to a high
 mountain,
 O Zion, herald of good
 tidings;ᵈ
 lift up your voice with
 strength,
 O Jerusalem, herald of
 good tidings,ᵉ
 lift it up, do not fear;
 say to the cities of Judah,
 "Here is your God!"
¹⁰ See, the Lord GOD comes
 with might,
 and his arm rules for him;
 his reward is with him,
 and his recompense before
 him.
¹¹ He will feed his flock like a
 shepherd;
 he will gather the lambs in
 his arms,
 and carry them in his bosom,
 and gently lead the mother
 sheep.

¹² Who has measured the
 waters in the hollow of
 his hand
 and marked off the heavens
 with a span,
 enclosed the dust of the
 earth in a measure,
 and weighed the mountains
 in scales
 and the hills in a balance?
¹³ Who has directed the spirit
 of the LORD,
 or as his counselor has
 instructed him?

39.5
1 Sam 13.13,
14; 15.16
39.6
Jer 20.5
39.7
Dan 1.2-7
39.8
2 Chr 32.26;
1 Sam 3.18;
2 Chr 34.28
40.1
Isa 12.1
40.2
Isa 35.4;
41.11-13;
33.24;
Jer 16.18
40.3
Mt 3.3;
Mk 1.3;
Lk 3.4-6;
Jn 1.23;
Mal 3.1
40.4
Isa 45.2
40.5
Isa 6.3;
52.10

40.6
Job 14.2;
Ps 102.11;
103.15;
1 Pet 1.24,
25
40.7
Ps 90.5,6;
v. 24
40.8
Isa 55.11;
Mt 5.18;
1 Pet 1.24,
25
40.9
Isa 60.1;
52.7;
Acts 10.36;
Rom 10.15
40.10
Isa 59.16,
18; 62.11;
Rev 22.7,12
40.11
Ezek 34.23;
Mic 5.4;
Jn 10.11;
Heb 13.20
40.12
Isa 48.13;
Job 38.8-11;
Heb 1.10-12
40.13
Rom 11.34;
1 Cor 2.16

ᵈ Or *O herald of good tidings to Zion*
ᵉ Or *O herald of good tidings to Jerusalem*

14 Whom did he consult for his
 enlightenment,
 and who taught him the
 path of justice?
Who taught him knowledge,
 and showed him the way of
 understanding?
15 Even the nations are like a
 drop from a bucket,
 and are accounted as dust
 on the scales;
see, he takes up the isles
 like fine dust.
16 Lebanon would not provide
 fuel enough,
 nor are its animals enough
 for a burnt offering.
17 All the nations are as
 nothing before him;
they are accounted by him
 as less than nothing
 and emptiness.

18 To whom then will you liken
 God,
 or what likeness compare
 with him?
19 An idol? — A workman casts
 it,
 and a goldsmith overlays it
 with gold,
 and casts for it silver
 chains.
20 As a gift one chooses
 mulberry wood[f]
 —wood that will not rot—
then seeks out a skilled
 artisan
 to set up an image that will
 not topple.
21 Have you not known? Have
 you not heard?
Has it not been told you
 from the beginning?
Have you not understood
 from the foundations of
 the earth?
22 It is he who sits above the
 circle of the earth,
 and its inhabitants are like
 grasshoppers;
who stretches out the
 heavens like a curtain,
 and spreads them like a
 tent to live in;

23 who brings princes to
 naught,
 and makes the rulers of the
 earth as nothing.

24 Scarcely are they planted,
 scarcely sown,
 scarcely has their stem
 taken root in the earth,
when he blows upon them,
 and they wither,
 and the tempest carries
 them off like stubble.

25 To whom then will you
 compare me,
 or who is my equal? says
 the Holy One.
26 Lift up your eyes on high
 and see:
 Who created these?
He who brings out their host
 and numbers them,
 calling them all by name;
because he is great in
 strength,
 mighty in power,
 not one is missing.

27 Why do you say, O Jacob,
 and speak, O Israel,
"My way is hidden from the
 LORD,
 and my right is disregarded
 by my God"?
28 Have you not known? Have
 you not heard?
The LORD is the everlasting
 God,
 the Creator of the ends of
 the earth.
He does not faint or grow
 weary;
 his understanding is
 unsearchable.
29 He gives power to the faint,
 and strengthens the
 powerless.
30 Even youths will faint and be
 weary,
 and the young will fall
 exhausted;
31 but those who wait for the
 LORD shall renew their
 strength,

40.14
Job 38.4;
21.22
40.15
Jer 10.10;
Isa 17.13;
29.5
40.17
Isa 29.7;
30.28
40.18
v. 25;
Isa 46.5;
Mic 7.18;
Acts 17.29
40.19
Isa 41.6,7;
44.12;
Jer 10.3
40.20
Isa 41.7;
Jer 10.3-5
40.21
Ps 19.1;
Acts 14.17;
Rom 1.19
40.22
Job 22.14;
Num 13.33;
Isa 42.5;
44.24;
Ps 104.2

40.23
Job 12.21;
Ps 107.40;
Isa 5.21
40.24
Isa 17.10,
11; v. 7;
Isa 17.13;
41.16
40.25
v. 18
40.26
Isa 51.6;
42.5;
Ps 147.4;
89.11-13;
Isa 34.16
40.27
Isa 49.4,14;
54.8;
Lk 18.7,8;
Isa 25.1
40.28
Ps 90.2;
147.5;
Rom 11.33
40.29
Isa 50.4;
Jer 31.25;
Isa 41.10
40.30
Jer 6.11;
Isa 9.17
40.31
Ps 103.5;
2 Cor 4.8-10,
16;
Deut 32.11;
2 Cor 4.1;
Heb 12.3

f Meaning of Heb uncertain

they shall mount up with
 wings like eagles,
they shall run and not be
 weary,
 they shall walk and not
 faint.

Israel Assured of God's Help

41 Listen to me in silence,
 O coastlands;
 let the peoples renew their
 strength;
 let them approach, then let
 them speak;
 let us together draw near
 for judgment.

2 Who has roused a victor from
 the east,
 summoned him to his
 service?
He delivers up nations to
 him,
 and tramples kings under
 foot;
he makes them like dust
 with his sword,
 like driven stubble with his
 bow.
3 He pursues them and passes
 on safely,
 scarcely touching the path
 with his feet.
4 Who has performed and done
 this,
 calling the generations
 from the beginning?
I, the LORD, am first,
 and will be with the last.
5 The coastlands have seen
 and are afraid,
 the ends of the earth
 tremble;
 they have drawn near and
 come.
6 Each one helps the other,
 saying to one another,
 "Take courage!"
7 The artisan encourages the
 goldsmith,
 and the one who smooths
 with the hammer
 encourages the one who
 strikes the anvil,
saying of the soldering, "It is
 good";

41.1
Zech 2.13;
Isa 40.31;
34.1; 43.26
41.2
Isa 45.1-3;
46.11; 42.6;
2 Chr 36.23;
Isa 29.5;
40.24
41.4
Isa 44.7;
46.10; 43.10;
44.6;
Rev 1.17;
22.13
41.5
Ps 67.7
41.6
Isa 40.19
41.7
Isa 40.19,20

41.8
Isa 44.1;
2 Chr 20.7;
Jas 2.23
41.9
Isa 11.11;
43.5-7; 42.1;
Ps 135.4
41.10
Isa 43.5;
Rom 8.31;
Isa 44.2
41.11
Isa 45.24;
17.13
41.12
Isa 17.14;
29.20
41.13
Isa 42.6;
v. 10
41.14
Job 25.6;
Isa 43.14
41.15
Mic 4.13

and they fasten it with
 nails so that it cannot
 be moved.
8 But you, Israel, my servant,
 Jacob, whom I have
 chosen,
 the offspring of Abraham,
 my friend;
9 you whom I took from the
 ends of the earth,
 and called from its farthest
 corners,
saying to you, "You are my
 servant,
 I have chosen you and not
 cast you off";
10 do not fear, for I am with
 you,
 do not be afraid, for I am
 your God;
I will strengthen you, I will
 help you,
 I will uphold you with my
 victorious right hand.

11 Yes, all who are incensed
 against you
 shall be ashamed and
 disgraced;
 those who strive against you
 shall be as nothing and
 shall perish.
12 You shall seek those who
 contend with you,
 but you shall not find
 them;
 those who war against you
 shall be as nothing at all.
13 For I, the LORD your God,
 hold your right hand;
 it is I who say to you, "Do
 not fear,
 I will help you."

14 Do not fear, you worm
 Jacob,
 you insect g Israel!
I will help you, says the
 LORD;
 your Redeemer is the Holy
 One of Israel.
15 Now, I will make of you a
 threshing sledge,
 sharp, new, and having
 teeth;

g Syr: Heb *men of*

you shall thresh the
　　mountains and crush
　　them,
and you shall make the
　　hills like chaff.

16 You shall winnow them and
　　the wind shall carry
　　them away,
and the tempest shall
　　scatter them.
Then you shall rejoice in the
　　Lord;
in the Holy One of Israel
　　you shall glory.

17 When the poor and needy
　　seek water,
and there is none,
and their tongue is parched
　　with thirst,
I the Lord will answer them,
I the God of Israel will not
　　forsake them.

18 I will open rivers on the bare
　　heights,h
and fountains in the midst
　　of the valleys;
I will make the wilderness a
　　pool of water,
and the dry land springs of
　　water.

19 I will put in the wilderness
　　the cedar,
the acacia, the myrtle, and
　　the olive;
I will set in the desert the
　　cypress,
the plane and the pine
　　together,

20 so that all may see and
　　know,
all may consider and
　　understand,
that the hand of the Lord
　　has done this,
the Holy One of Israel has
　　created it.

The Futility of Idols

21 Set forth your case, says the
　　Lord;
bring your proofs, says the
　　King of Jacob.

22 Let them bring them, and
　　tell us
what is to happen.

Tell us the former things,
　　what they are,
so that we may consider
　　them,
and that we may know their
　　outcome;
or declare to us the things
　　to come.

23 Tell us what is to come
　　hereafter,
that we may know that you
　　are gods;
do good, or do harm,
　　that we may be afraid and
　　terrified.

24 You, indeed, are nothing
and your work is nothing at
　　all;
whoever chooses you is an
　　abomination.

25 I stirred up one from the
　　north, and he has
　　come,
from the rising of the sun
　　he was summoned by
　　name.i
He shall tramplei on rulers
　　as on mortar,
as the potter treads clay.

26 Who declared it from the
　　beginning, so that we
　　might know,
and beforehand, so that we
　　might say, "He is
　　right"?
There was no one who
　　declared it, none who
　　proclaimed,
none who heard your
　　words.

27 I first have declared it to
　　Zion,k
and I give to Jerusalem a
　　herald of good tidings.

28 But when I look there is no
　　one;
among these there is no
　　counselor
who, when I ask, gives an
　　answer.

29 No, they are all a delusion;
their works are nothing;

41.16
Jer 51.2;
Isa 45.25
41.17
Isa 43.20;
30.19; 42.16
41.18
Isa 35.6,7;
43.19
41.20
Isa 40.5;
Job 12.9
41.21
v. 1;
Isa 43.15
41.22
Isa 45.21;
43.9

41.23
Isa 42.9;
44.7,8; 45.3;
Jn 13.19;
Jer 10.5
41.24
Ps 115.8;
Isa 44.9;
1 Cor 8.4;
v. 29
41.25
v. 2;
Isa 10.6
41.26
Isa 44.7;
45.21;
Hab 2.18,19
41.27
v. 4;
Isa 40.9
41.28
Isa 63.5;
40.13,14;
46.7
41.29
v. 24;
Isa 44.9;
Jer 5.13

h Or trails　i Cn Compare Q Ms Gk: MT
and he shall call on my name　i Cn: Heb
come　k Cn: Heb First to Zion—Behold,
behold them

their images are empty
wind.

The Servant, a Light to the Nations

42 Here is my servant,
whom I uphold,
my chosen, in whom my
soul delights;
I have put my spirit upon
him;
he will bring forth justice
to the nations.
2 He will not cry or lift up his
voice,
or make it heard in the
street;
3 a bruised reed he will not
break,
and a dimly burning wick
he will not quench;
he will faithfully bring forth
justice.
4 He will not grow faint or be
crushed
until he has established
justice in the earth;
and the coastlands wait for
his teaching.

5 Thus says God, the LORD,
who created the heavens
and stretched them out,
who spread out the earth
and what comes from
it,
who gives breath to the
people upon it
and spirit to those who
walk in it:
6 I am the LORD, I have called
you in righteousness,
I have taken you by the
hand and kept you;
I have given you as a
covenant to the
people,[1]
a light to the nations,
7 to open the eyes that are
blind,
to bring out the prisoners
from the dungeon,
from the prison those who
sit in darkness.
8 I am the LORD, that is my
name;

42.1
Isa 43.10;
53.11;
Mt 12.18-20;
3.16,17; 17.5;
Isa 2.4
42.3
Isa 57.15;
Ps 72.2
42.4
Isa 40.28;
vv. 10,12
42.5
Isa 44.24;
Zech 12.1;
Acts 17.25
42.6
Isa 43.1;
49.6,8;
Lk 2.32;
Acts 13.47
42.7
Isa 35.5;
61.1;
Lk 4.18;
2 Tim 2.26;
Heb 2.14
42.8
Isa 48.11

42.9
Isa 48.3,6
42.10
Isa 33.3;
40.3; 98.1;
107.23
42.12
Isa 24.15;
v. 4
42.13
Isa 9.7;
Ex 15.3;
Hos 11.10;
Isa 66.14-16
42.14
Isa 57.11
42.15
Isa 2.12-16;
44.27
42.16
Isa 29.18;
Lk 1.78,79;
3.5;
Isa 41.17

my glory I give to no other,
nor my praise to idols.
9 See, the former things have
come to pass,
and new things I now
declare;
before they spring forth,
I tell you of them.

A Hymn of Praise

10 Sing to the LORD a new song,
his praise from the end of
the earth!
Let the sea roar[m] and all
that fills it,
the coastlands and their
inhabitants.
11 Let the desert and its towns
lift up their voice,
the villages that Kedar
inhabits;
let the inhabitants of Sela
sing for joy,
let them shout from the
tops of the mountains.
12 Let them give glory to the
LORD,
and declare his praise in
the coastlands.
13 The LORD goes forth like a
soldier,
like a warrior he stirs up
his fury;
he cries out, he shouts
aloud,
he shows himself mighty
against his foes.

14 For a long time I have held
my peace,
I have kept still and
restrained myself;
now I will cry out like a
woman in labor,
I will gasp and pant.
15 I will lay waste mountains
and hills,
and dry up all their
herbage;
I will turn the rivers into
islands,
and dry up the pools.
16 I will lead the blind

[1] Meaning of Heb uncertain m Cn Compare
Ps 96.11; 98.7: Heb *Those who go down to the
sea*

by a road they do not
know,
by paths they have not
known
I will guide them.
I will turn the darkness
before them into light,
the rough places into level
ground.
These are the things I will
do,
and I will not forsake
them.
17 They shall be turned back
and utterly put to
shame —
those who trust in carved
images,
who say to cast images,
"You are our gods."

18 Listen, you that are deaf;
and you that are blind,
look up and see!
19 Who is blind but my servant,
or deaf like my messenger
whom I send?
Who is blind like my
dedicated one,
or blind like the servant of
the LORD?
20 He sees many things, but
does[n] not observe
them;
his ears are open, but he
does not hear.

Israel's Disobedience

21 The LORD was pleased, for
the sake of his
righteousness,
to magnify his teaching
and make it glorious.
22 But this is a people robbed
and plundered,
all of them are trapped in
holes
and hidden in prisons;
they have become a prey
with no one to rescue,
a spoil with no one to say,
"Restore!"
23 Who among you will give
heed to this,
who will attend and listen
for the time to come?

42.17
Ps 97.7;
Isa 1.29;
44.11; 45.16
42.19
Isa 43.8;
Ezek 12.2
42.20
Jer 6.10
42.21
Isa 58.13
42.22
Isa 24.18,
22; 10.6

42.24
Isa 30.15;
48.18
42.25
Isa 5.25;
2 Kings 25.9;
Hos 7.9
43.1
vv. 7,15,21;
Isa 44.2,6,
21
43.2
Ps 66.12;
Deut 31.6,8;
Dan 3.25,27
43.3
Ex 20.2;
v. 11;
Prov 11.8;
21.18
43.4
Isa 63.9

24 Who gave up Jacob to the
spoiler,
and Israel to the robbers?
Was it not the LORD, against
whom we have sinned,
in whose ways they would
not walk,
and whose law they would
not obey?
25 So he poured upon him the
heat of his anger
and the fury of war;
it set him on fire all around,
but he did not
understand;
it burned him, but he did
not take it to heart.

Restoration and Protection Promised

43 But now thus says the
LORD,
he who created you,
O Jacob,
he who formed you,
O Israel:
Do not fear, for I have
redeemed you;
I have called you by name,
you are mine.
2 When you pass through the
waters, I will be with
you;
and through the rivers, they
shall not overwhelm
you;
when you walk through fire
you shall not be
burned,
and the flame shall not
consume you.
3 For I am the LORD your God,
the Holy One of Israel,
your Savior.
I give Egypt as your ransom,
Ethiopia[o] and Seba in
exchange for you.
4 Because you are precious in
my sight,
and honored, and I love
you,
I give people in return for
you,

n Heb *You see many things but do*
o Or *Nubia*; Heb *Cush*

nations in exchange for
your life.
5 Do not fear, for I am with
you;
I will bring your offspring
from the east,
and from the west I will
gather you;
6 I will say to the north, "Give
them up,"
and to the south, "Do not
withhold;
bring my sons from far away
and my daughters from the
end of the earth —
7 everyone who is called by my
name,
whom I created for my
glory,
whom I formed and made."

8 Bring forth the people who
are blind, yet have eyes,
who are deaf, yet have ears!
9 Let all the nations gather
together,
and let the peoples
assemble.
Who among them declared
this,
and foretold to us the
former things?
Let them bring their
witnesses to justify
them,
and let them hear and say,
"It is true."
10 You are my witnesses, says
the LORD,
and my servant whom I
have chosen,
so that you may know and
believe me
and understand that I am
he.
Before me no god was
formed,
nor shall there be any after
me.
11 I, I am the LORD,
and besides me there is no
savior.
12 I declared and saved and
proclaimed,
when there was no strange
god among you;

43.5
Isa 41.10,
14; 44.2;
Jer 30.10,
11; 46.27,28
43.6
Ps 107.3;
Isa 14.2
43.7
Ps 100.3;
Isa 29.23;
Eph 2.10;
v. 1
43.8
Isa 6.9;
42.19;
Ezek 12.2
43.9
Isa 41.21,
22,26
43.10
Isa 44.8;
42.1; 41.4;
44.6
43.11
Isa 45.21
43.12
Deut 32.16;
Ps 81.9;
v. 10;
Isa 44.8

43.13
Ps 90.2;
Job 9.12;
Isa 14.27
43.14
Isa 41.14;
13.14,15
43.16
Ex 14.16;
Ps 77.19;
Isa 51.10;
Josh 3.13
43.17
Ex 14.4-9,
25
43.18
Jer 16.14
43.19
2 Cor 5.17;
Rev 21.5;
Ex 17.6;
Num 20.11;
Isa 35.6
43.20
Isa 48.21

and you are my witnesses,
says the LORD.
13 I am God, and also
henceforth I am He;
there is no one who can
deliver from my hand;
I work and who can hinder
it?

14 Thus says the LORD,
your Redeemer, the Holy
One of Israel:
For your sake I will send to
Babylon
and break down all the
bars,
and the shouting of the
Chaldeans will be
turned to lamentation.p
15 I am the LORD, your Holy
One,
the Creator of Israel, your
King.
16 Thus says the LORD,
who makes a way in the
sea,
a path in the mighty
waters,
17 who brings out chariot and
horse,
army and warrior;
they lie down, they cannot
rise,
they are extinguished,
quenched like a wick:
18 Do not remember the former
things,
or consider the things of
old.
19 I am about to do a new
thing;
now it springs forth, do you
not perceive it?
I will make a way in the
wilderness
and rivers in the desert.
20 The wild animals will honor
me,
the jackals and the
ostriches;
for I give water in the
wilderness,
rivers in the desert,
to give drink to my chosen
people,

p Meaning of Heb uncertain

21 the people whom I formed
 for myself
 so that they might declare
 my praise.

22 Yet you did not call upon
 me, O Jacob;
 but you have been weary of
 me, O Israel!
23 You have not brought me
 your sheep for burnt
 offerings,
 or honored me with your
 sacrifices.
 I have not burdened you with
 offerings,
 or wearied you with
 frankincense.
24 You have not bought me
 sweet cane with money,
 or satisfied me with the fat
 of your sacrifices.
 But you have burdened me
 with your sins;
 you have wearied me with
 your iniquities.

25 I, I am He
 who blots out your
 transgressions for my
 own sake,
 and I will not remember
 your sins.
26 Accuse me, let us go to trial;
 set forth your case, so that
 you may be proved
 right.
27 Your first ancestor sinned,
 and your interpreters
 transgressed against
 me.
28 Therefore I profaned the
 princes of the
 sanctuary,
 I delivered Jacob to utter
 destruction,
 and Israel to reviling.

God's Blessing on Israel

44 But now hear, O Jacob
 my servant,
 Israel whom I have chosen!
2 Thus says the LORD who
 made you,

43.21
v. 1;
Ps 102.18;
Lk 1.74,75
43.22
Isa 30.9-11;
Mal 1.13
43.23
Am 5.25;
Mal 1.6-8
43.24
Ex 30.23;
Isa 1.14;
Mal 2.17
43.25
Isa 44.23;
Ezek 36.22;
Jer 31.34
43.26
Isa 1.18;
v. 9
43.28
Isa 47.6;
Lam 2.2,6;
Zech 8.13
44.1
Isa 41.8;
Jer 30.10;
46.27,28
44.2
Isa 43.1,7;
Deut 32.15

44.3
Isa 35.7;
Joel 2.28;
Jn 7.38;
Acts 2.18
44.5
Isa 19.21;
Zech 8.20-22
44.6
Isa 43.1,14;
41.4; 48.12;
Rev 1.8,17;
22.13
44.7
Isa 41.4,22
44.8
Isa 41.22;
43.10;
Deut 4.35;
1 Sam 2.2;
Isa 26.4
44.9
Isa 41.24;
66.3; 43.9;
42.17

 who formed you in the
 womb and will help
 you:
 Do not fear, O Jacob my
 servant,
 Jeshurun whom I have
 chosen.
3 For I will pour water on the
 thirsty land,
 and streams on the dry
 ground;
 I will pour my spirit upon
 your descendants,
 and my blessing on your
 offspring.
4 They shall spring up like a
 green tamarisk,
 like willows by flowing
 streams.
5 This one will say, "I am the
 LORD's,"
 another will be called by
 the name of Jacob,
 yet another will write on the
 hand, "The LORD's,"
 and adopt the name of
 Israel.

6 Thus says the LORD, the King
 of Israel,
 and his Redeemer, the
 LORD of hosts:
 I am the first and I am the
 last;
 besides me there is no god.
7 Who is like me? Let them
 proclaim it,
 let them declare and set it
 forth before me.
 Who has announced from of
 old the things to
 come?�q
 Let them tell usʳ what is
 yet to be.
8 Do not fear, or be afraid;
 have I not told you from of
 old and declared it?
 You are my witnesses!
 Is there any god besides me?
 There is no other rock; I
 know not one.

The Absurdity of Idol Worship

9 All who make idols are noth-
ing, and the things they delight in

�q Cn: Heb *from my placing an eternal people
and things to come* ʳ Tg: Heb *them*

do not profit; their witnesses neither see nor know. And so they will be put to shame. ¹⁰Who would fashion a god or cast an image that can do no good? ¹¹Look, all its devotees shall be put to shame; the artisans too are merely human. Let them all assemble, let them stand up; they shall be terrified, they shall all be put to shame.

12 The ironsmith fashions itˢ and works it over the coals, shaping it with hammers, and forging it with his strong arm; he becomes hungry and his strength fails, he drinks no water and is faint. ¹³The carpenter stretches a line, marks it out with a stylus, fashions it with planes, and marks it with a compass; he makes it in human form, with human beauty, to be set up in a shrine. ¹⁴He cuts down cedars or chooses a holm tree or an oak and lets it grow strong among the trees of the forest. He plants a cedar and the rain nourishes it. ¹⁵Then it can be used as fuel. Part of it he takes and warms himself; he kindles a fire and bakes bread. Then he makes a god and worships it, makes it a carved image and bows down before it. ¹⁶Half of it he burns in the fire; over this half he roasts meat, eats it and is satisfied. He also warms himself and says, "Ah, I am warm, I can feel the fire!" ¹⁷The rest of it he makes into a god, his idol, bows down to it and worships it; he prays to it and says, "Save me, for you are my god!"

18 They do not know, nor do they comprehend; for their eyes are shut, so that they cannot see, and their minds as well, so that they cannot understand. ¹⁹No one considers, nor is there knowledge or discernment to say, "Half of it I burned in the fire; I also baked bread on its coals, I roasted meat and have eaten. Now shall I make the rest of it an abomination? Shall I fall down before a block of wood?" ²⁰He feeds on ashes; a deluded mind has led him astray, and he cannot save himself or say, "Is not this thing in my right hand a fraud?"

44.10
Jer 10.5;
Hab 2.18
44.11
Isa 1.29;
42.17
44.12
Isa 40.19;
41.6;
Jer 10.3-5
44.13
Isa 41.7;
Ps 115.5-7
44.15
vv. 17,19;
2 Chr 25.14
44.17
v. 15;
Isa 45.20;
1 Kings 18.26,
28
44.18
Isa 1.3; 6.9,
10
44.19
Isa 5.13;
45.20; 27.11;
Deut 27.15
44.20
Ps 102.9;
Job 15.31;
Isa 57.11

44.21
Isa 46.8;
vv. 1,2;
Isa 49.15
44.22
Isa 43.25;
55.7; 43.1;
1 Pet 1.18,
19
44.23
Isa 42.10;
55.12; 43.1;
61.3
44.24
Isa 43.14;
v. 2;
Isa 40.14,22
44.25
Isa 40.14;
29.14;
1 Cor 1.20,
27
44.26
Isa 55.11;
49.7-20;
Jer 32.15,44

Israel Is Not Forgotten

21 Remember these things,
 O Jacob,
 and Israel, for you are my
 servant;
I formed you, you are my
 servant;
 O Israel, you will not be
 forgotten by me.
22 I have swept away your
 transgressions like a
 cloud,
 and your sins like mist;
return to me, for I have
 redeemed you.

23 Sing, O heavens, for the LORD
 has done it;
 shout, O depths of the
 earth;
break forth into singing,
 O mountains,
 O forest, and every tree in
 it!
For the LORD has redeemed
 Jacob,
 and will be glorified in
 Israel.

24 Thus says the LORD, your
 Redeemer,
 who formed you in the
 womb:
I am the LORD, who made all
 things,
 who alone stretched out
 the heavens,
 who by myself spread out
 the earth;
25 who frustrates the omens of
 liars,
 and makes fools of
 diviners;
who turns back the wise,
 and makes their knowledge
 foolish;
26 who confirms the word of his
 servant,
 and fulfills the prediction
 of his messengers;
who says of Jerusalem, "It
 shall be inhabited,"
 and of the cities of Judah,
 "They shall be rebuilt,

ˢ Cn: Heb *an ax*

and I will raise up their
ruins";
27 who says to the deep, "Be
dry—
I will dry up your rivers";
28 who says of Cyrus, "He is my
shepherd,
and he shall carry out all
my purpose";
and who says of Jerusalem,
"It shall be rebuilt,"
and of the temple, "Your
foundation shall be
laid."

Cyrus, God's Instrument

45 Thus says the Lord to
his anointed, to Cyrus,
whose right hand I have
grasped
to subdue nations before
him
and strip kings of their
robes,
to open doors before him—
and the gates shall not be
closed:
2 I will go before you
and level the mountains,[t]
I will break in pieces the
doors of bronze
and cut through the bars of
iron,
3 I will give you the treasures
of darkness
and riches hidden in secret
places,
so that you may know that it
is I, the Lord,
the God of Israel, who call
you by your name.
4 For the sake of my servant
Jacob,
and Israel my chosen,
I call you by your name,
I surname you, though you
do not know me.
5 I am the Lord, and there is
no other;
besides me there is no
god.
I arm you, though you do
not know me,
6 so that they may know, from
the rising of the sun

and from the west, that
there is no one besides
me;
I am the Lord, and there is
no other.
7 I form light and create
darkness,
I make weal and create
woe;
I the Lord do all these
things.

8 Shower, O heavens, from
above,
and let the skies rain down
righteousness;
let the earth open, that
salvation may spring
up,[u]
and let it cause
righteousness to sprout
up also;
I the Lord have created it.

9 Woe to you who strive with
your Maker,
earthen vessels with the
potter![v]
Does the clay say to the one
who fashions it, "What
are you making"?
or "Your work has no
handles"?
10 Woe to anyone who says to a
father, "What are you
begetting?"
or to a woman, "With what
are you in labor?"
11 Thus says the Lord,
the Holy One of Israel, and
its Maker:
Will you question me[w] about
my children,
or command me
concerning the work of
my hands?
12 I made the earth,
and created humankind
upon it;
it was my hands that
stretched out the
heavens,

Cross references

44.27
Isa 43.16;
42.15
44.28
Isa 45.1;
14.32; 45.13
45.1
Isa 44.28;
41.13;
Jer 50.3,35;
v. 5
45.2
Isa 40.4;
Ps 107.16;
Jer 51.30
45.3
Jer 41.8;
Isa 43.1
45.4
Isa 41.8;
43.1;
Acts 17.23
45.5
v. 6;
Isa 44.6,8;
Ps 18.39
45.6
Mal 1.11;
Isa 43.5;
v. 5

45.7
Isa 42.16;
Ps 104.20;
Am 3.6
45.8
Ps 72.6;
85.11;
Isa 12.3;
60.21
45.9
Isa 29.16;
Rom 9.20,
21
45.11
Isa 43.15;
54.5; 8.19;
Jer 31.9;
60.21
45.12
v. 18;
Isa 42.5;
Neh 9.6

[t] Q Ms Gk: MT *the swellings* [u] Q Ms: MT
that they may bring forth salvation
[v] Cn: Heb *with the potsherds*, or *with the
potters* [w] Cn: Heb *Ask me of things to
come*

and I commanded all their
host.

13 I have aroused Cyrus[x] in
righteousness,
and I will make all his
paths straight;
he shall build my city
and set my exiles free,
not for price or reward,
says the LORD of hosts.

14 Thus says the LORD:
The wealth of Egypt and the
merchandise of
Ethiopia,[y]
and the Sabeans, tall of
stature,
shall come over to you and
be yours,
they shall follow you;
they shall come over in
chains and bow down
to you.
They will make supplication
to you, saying,
"God is with you alone,
and there is no other;
there is no god besides
him."

15 Truly, you are a God who
hides himself,
O God of Israel, the Savior.

16 All of them are put to shame
and confounded,
the makers of idols go in
confusion together.

17 But Israel is saved by the
LORD
with everlasting salvation;
you shall not be put to
shame or confounded
to all eternity.

18 For thus says the LORD,
who created the heavens
(he is God!),
who formed the earth and
made it
(he established it;
he did not create it a chaos,
he formed it to be
inhabited!):
I am the LORD, and there is
no other.

19 I did not speak in secret,
in a land of darkness;
I did not say to the offspring
of Jacob,

"Seek me in chaos."
I the LORD speak the truth,
I declare what is right.

Idols Cannot Save Babylon

20 Assemble yourselves and
come together,
draw near, you survivors of
the nations!
They have no knowledge —
those who carry about their
wooden idols,
and keep on praying to a god
that cannot save.

21 Declare and present your
case;
let them take counsel
together!
Who told this long ago?
Who declared it of old?
Was it not I, the LORD?
There is no other god
besides me,
a righteous God and a
Savior;
there is no one besides me.

22 Turn to me and be saved,
all the ends of the earth!
For I am God, and there is
no other.

23 By myself I have sworn,
from my mouth has gone
forth in righteousness
a word that shall not
return:
"To me every knee shall
bow,
every tongue shall swear."

24 Only in the LORD, it shall be
said of me,
are righteousness and
strength;
all who were incensed
against him
shall come to him and be
ashamed.

25 In the LORD all the offspring
of Israel
shall triumph and glory.

46 Bel bows down, Nebo
stoops,

45.13
Isa 41.2;
v. 2;
Isa 44.28;
52.3
45.14
Isa 14.1,2;
Ps 149.8;
Isa 49.23;
Jer 16.19;
1 Cor 14.25;
v. 5
45.15
Isa 8.17;
43.3
45.16
Isa 44.9,11
45.17
Isa 26.4;
Rom 11.26;
Isa 49.23
45.18
Isa 42.5;
v. 12;
Gen 1.2,26;
v. 5
45.19
Isa 48.16;
41.8;
Jer 29.13,
14; Isa 63.1;
44.8

45.20
Isa 43.9;
44.18,19;
Jer 10.5;
Isa 46.6,7
45.21
Isa 41.23,
26; v. 5;
Isa 43.3,11
45.22
Num 21.8,9;
Isa 30.15;
49.6,12
45.23
Isa 62.8;
Rom 14.11;
Isa 55.11;
65.16
45.24
Isa 54.17;
41.11
45.25
Isa 53.11;
60.19
46.1
Jer 50.2-4;
Isa 45.20

their idols are on beasts
and cattle;
these things you carry are
loaded
as burdens on weary
animals.
2 They stoop, they bow down
together;
they cannot save the
burden,
but themselves go into
captivity.

3 Listen to me, O house of
Jacob,
all the remnant of the
house of Israel,
who have been borne by me
from your birth,
carried from the womb;
4 even to your old age I am he,
even when you turn gray I
will carry you.
I have made, and I will bear;
I will carry and will save.

5 To whom will you liken me
and make me equal,
and compare me, as
though we were alike?
6 Those who lavish gold from
the purse,
and weigh out silver in the
scales—
they hire a goldsmith, who
makes it into a god;
then they fall down and
worship!
7 They lift it to their
shoulders, they carry it,
they set it in its place, and
it stands there;
it cannot move from its
place.
If one cries out to it, it does
not answer
or save anyone from
trouble.

8 Remember this and
consider,z
recall it to mind, you
transgressors,
9 remember the former
things of old;
for I am God, and there is no
other;

46.2
Jer 43.12,13
46.3
v. 12;
Isa 45.19;
10.21,22;
63.9
46.4
Isa 43.13;
Ps 71.18
46.5
Isa 40.18,25
46.6
Isa 40.19;
44.15,17
46.7
v. 1;
Isa 40.20;
44.17; 41.26,
28; 45.20
46.8
Isa 44.19,
21; 48.8
46.9
Isa 45.5,21;
41.26,27

46.10
Isa 45.21;
14.24;
Acts 5.39
46.11
Isa 18.6;
41.2,25;
37.26
46.12
v. 3;
Isa 48.4;
Jer 2.5
46.13
Isa 61.11;
43.7; 44.23
47.1
Jer 48.18;
46.11; 51.33
47.3
Ezek 16.37;
Isa 34.8;
63.4
47.4
Isa 41.14

I am God, and there is no
one like me,
10 declaring the end from the
beginning
and from ancient times
things not yet done,
saying, "My purpose shall
stand,
and I will fulfill my
intention,"
11 calling a bird of prey from
the east,
the man for my purpose
from a far country.
I have spoken, and I will
bring it to pass;
I have planned, and I will
do it.

12 Listen to me, you stubborn
of heart,
you who are far from
deliverance:
13 I bring near my deliverance,
it is not far off,
and my salvation will not
tarry;
I will put salvation in Zion,
for Israel my glory.

The Humiliation of Babylon

47 Come down and sit in
the dust,
virgin daughter Babylon!
Sit on the ground without a
throne,
daughter Chaldea!
For you shall no more be
called
tender and delicate.
2 Take the millstones and
grind meal,
remove your veil,
strip off your robe, uncover
your legs,
pass through the rivers.
3 Your nakedness shall be
uncovered,
and your shame shall be
seen.
I will take vengeance,
and I will spare no one.
4 Our Redeemer—the LORD of
hosts is his name—
is the Holy One of Israel.

zMeaning of Heb uncertain

5 Sit in silence, and go into
 darkness,
 daughter Chaldea!
 For you shall no more be
 called
 the mistress of kingdoms.
6 I was angry with my people,
 I profaned my heritage;
 I gave them into your hand,
 you showed them no
 mercy;
 on the aged you made your
 yoke
 exceedingly heavy.
7 You said, "I shall be mistress
 forever,"
 so that you did not lay
 these things to heart
 or remember their end.

8 Now therefore hear this, you
 lover of pleasures,
 who sit securely,
 who say in your heart,
 "I am, and there is no one
 besides me;
 I shall not sit as a widow
 or know the loss of
 children"—
9 both these things shall come
 upon you
 in a moment, in one day:
 the loss of children and
 widowhood
 shall come upon you in full
 measure,
 in spite of your many
 sorceries
 and the great power of your
 enchantments.

10 You felt secure in your
 wickedness;
 you said, "No one sees
 me."
 Your wisdom and your
 knowledge
 led you astray,
 and you said in your heart,
 "I am, and there is no one
 besides me."
11 But evil shall come upon
 you,
 which you cannot charm
 away;
 disaster shall fall upon you,

which you will not be able
 to ward off;
 and ruin shall come on you
 suddenly,
 of which you know
 nothing.

12 Stand fast in your
 enchantments
 and your many sorceries,
 with which you have
 labored from your
 youth;
 perhaps you may be able to
 succeed,
 perhaps you may inspire
 terror.
13 You are wearied with your
 many consultations;
 let those who study[a] the
 heavens
 stand up and save you,
 those who gaze at the
 stars,
 and at each new moon
 predict
 what[b] shall befall you.

14 See, they are like stubble,
 the fire consumes them;
 they cannot deliver
 themselves
 from the power of the
 flame.
 No coal for warming oneself
 is this,
 no fire to sit before!
15 Such to you are those with
 whom you have
 labored,
 who have trafficked with
 you from your youth;
 they all wander about in
 their own paths;
 there is no one to save you.

God the Creator and Redeemer

48 Hear this, O house of
 Jacob,
 who are called by the name
 of Israel,
 and who came forth from
 the loins[c] of Judah;

47.5
Isa 23.2;
13.10;
Isa 13.19;
Dan 2.37
47.6
Zech 1.15;
Isa 43.28;
10.14;
Deut 28.50
47.7
v. 5;
Isa 42.25;
45.21
47.8
Isa 32.9,11;
Zeph 2.15;
Rev 18.7
47.9
Isa 13.16,
18;
1 Thes 5.3;
Nah 3.4
47.10
Ps 52.7;
Isa 29.15;
44.20; v. 8
47.11
Isa 57.1;
1 Thes 5.3;
v. 9

47.12
v. 9
47.13
Isa 57.10;
Dan 2.2
47.14
Nah 1.10;
Mal 4.1
47.15
Rev 18.11;
Isa 43.13;
46.7
48.1
Isa 46.12;
Num 24.7;
Ps 68.26;
Isa 45.23

[a] Meaning of Heb uncertain [b] Gk Syr
Compare Vg: Heb *from what* [c] Cn: Heb
waters

who swear by the name of
the LORD,
and invoke the God of
Israel,
but not in truth or right.
2 For they call themselves
after the holy city,
and lean on the God of
Israel;
the LORD of hosts is his
name.

3 The former things I declared
long ago,
they went out from my
mouth and I made
them known;
then suddenly I did them
and they came to pass.
4 Because I know that you are
obstinate,
and your neck is an iron
sinew
and your forehead brass,
5 I declared them to you from
long ago,
before they came to pass I
announced them to
you,
so that you would not say,
"My idol did them,
my carved image and my
cast image commanded
them."

6 You have heard; now see all
this;
and will you not declare it?
From this time forward I
make you hear new
things,
hidden things that you
have not known.
7 They are created now, not
long ago;
before today you have
never heard of them,
so that you could not say,
"I already knew them."
8 You have never heard, you
have never known,
from of old your ear has
not been opened.
For I knew that you would
deal very treacherously,
and that from birth you
were called a rebel.

48.2
Isa 52.1;
Mic 3.11;
Rom 2.17
48.3
Isa 41.22;
42.9; 43.9;
44.7,8; 45.21;
Josh 21.45
48.4
Ezek 2.4;
Ex 32.9;
Deut 31.27;
Ezek 3.7-9
48.5
Ezek 2.4;
3.7
48.6
Isa 42.9;
43.19
48.8
Isa 42.25;
46.8;
Ps 58.3

48.9
v. 11;
Ps 78.38;
Isa 30.18
48.10
Jer 9.7;
Ezek 22.18-22;
Jer 11.4
48.11
v. 9;
Deut 32.26;
Ezek 20.9;
Isa 42.8
48.12
Deut 32.39;
Isa 41.4;
Rev 1.17;
22.13
48.13
Ps 102.25;
Isa 40.26
48.14
Isa 43.9;
45.21; 46.10,
11;
Jer 50.21-29
48.15
Isa 41.2;
45.1,2
48.16
Isa 41.1;
45.19; 43.13;
Zech 2.9,11
48.17
Isa 43.14;
Ps 32.8

9 For my name's sake I defer
my anger,
for the sake of my praise I
restrain it for you,
so that I may not cut you
off.
10 See, I have refined you, but
not like[d] silver;
I have tested you in the
furnace of adversity.
11 For my own sake, for my
own sake, I do it,
for why should my name[e]
be profaned?
My glory I will not give to
another.

12 Listen to me, O Jacob,
and Israel, whom I called:
I am He; I am the first,
and I am the last.
13 My hand laid the foundation
of the earth,
and my right hand spread
out the heavens;
when I summon them,
they stand at attention.

14 Assemble, all of you, and
hear!
Who among them has
declared these things?
The LORD loves him;
he shall perform his
purpose on Babylon,
and his arm shall be
against the Chaldeans.
15 I, even I, have spoken and
called him,
I have brought him, and he
will prosper in his way.
16 Draw near to me, hear this!
From the beginning I have
not spoken in secret,
from the time it came to
be I have been there.
And now the Lord GOD has
sent me and his spirit.

17 Thus says the LORD,
your Redeemer, the Holy
One of Israel:
I am the LORD your God,

d Cn: Heb *with*　　e Gk Old Latin: Heb *for*
why should it

who teaches you for your
own good,
who leads you in the way
you should go.
18 O that you had paid
attention to my
commandments!
Then your prosperity would
have been like a river,
and your success like the
waves of the sea;
19 your offspring would have
been like the sand,
and your descendants like
its grains;
their name would never be
cut off
or destroyed from before
me.

20 Go out from Babylon, flee
from Chaldea,
declare this with a shout of
joy, proclaim it,
send it forth to the end of
the earth;
say, "The LORD has
redeemed his servant
Jacob!"
21 They did not thirst when he
led them through the
deserts;
he made water flow for
them from the rock;
he split open the rock and
the water gushed out.

22 "There is no peace," says the
LORD, "for the wicked."

The Servant's Mission

49 Listen to me,
O coastlands,
pay attention, you peoples
from far away!
The LORD called me before I
was born,
while I was in my mother's
womb he named me.
2 He made my mouth like a
sharp sword,
in the shadow of his hand
he hid me;
he made me a polished
arrow,

48.18
Deut 32.29;
Ps 119.165;
Isa 61.10,11
48.19
Gen 22.17;
Jer 33.22;
Isa 56.5;
66.22
48.20
Jer 50.8;
Isa 42.10;
62.11; 43.1
48.21
Isa 41.17;
Ex 17.6;
Ps 105.41
48.22
Isa 57.21
49.1
Isa 42.4;
66.19; 44.2,
24; Isa 7.14;
9.6;
Mt 1.20;
Gal 1.15
49.2
Isa 11.4;
Heb 4.12;
Isa 51.16;
Hab 3.11

49.3
Isa 42.1;
44.23
49.4
Isa 65.23
49.5
Isa 44.2,23;
27.12; 43.4;
12.2
49.6
Isa 42.6;
Lk 2.32;
Acts 13.47;
26.23
49.7
Isa 48.17;
53.3;
Ps 22.6-8;
Isa 52.15;
66.23

in his quiver he hid me
away.
3 And he said to me, "You are
my servant,
Israel, in whom I will be
glorified."
4 But I said, "I have labored in
vain,
I have spent my strength
for nothing and vanity;
yet surely my cause is with
the LORD,
and my reward with my
God."

5 And now the LORD says,
who formed me in the
womb to be his servant,
to bring Jacob back to
him,
and that Israel might be
gathered to him,
for I am honored in the sight
of the LORD,
and my God has become
my strength—
6 he says,
"It is too light a thing that
you should be my
servant
to raise up the tribes of
Jacob
and to restore the survivors
of Israel;
I will give you as a light to
the nations,
that my salvation may
reach to the end of the
earth."

7 Thus says the LORD,
the Redeemer of Israel and
his Holy One,
to one deeply despised,
abhorred by the
nations,
the slave of rulers,
"Kings shall see and stand
up,
princes, and they shall
prostrate themselves,
because of the LORD, who is
faithful,
the Holy One of Israel, who
has chosen you."

Zion's Children to Be Brought Home

8 Thus says the LORD:
In a time of favor I have
 answered you,
 on a day of salvation I have
 helped you;
I have kept you and given
 you
 as a covenant to the
 people,[f]
to establish the land,
 to apportion the desolate
 heritages;
9 saying to the prisoners,
 "Come out,"
 to those who are in
 darkness, "Show
 yourselves."
They shall feed along the
 ways,
 on all the bare heights[g]
 shall be their pasture;
10 they shall not hunger or
 thirst,
 neither scorching wind nor
 sun shall strike them
 down,
for he who has pity on them
 will lead them,
 and by springs of water will
 guide them.
11 And I will turn all my
 mountains into a road,
 and my highways shall be
 raised up.
12 Lo, these shall come from far
 away,
 and lo, these from the
 north and from the
 west,
 and these from the land of
 Syene.[h]

13 Sing for joy, O heavens, and
 exult, O earth;
 break forth, O mountains,
 into singing!
For the LORD has comforted
 his people,
 and will have compassion
 on his suffering ones.

14 But Zion said, "The LORD has
 forsaken me,
 my Lord has forgotten me."

15 Can a woman forget her
 nursing child,
 or show no compassion for
 the child of her womb?
Even these may forget,
 yet I will not forget you.
16 See, I have inscribed you on
 the palms of my hands;
 your walls are continually
 before me.
17 Your builders outdo your
 destroyers,[i]
 and those who laid you
 waste go away from
 you.
18 Lift up your eyes all around
 and see;
 they all gather, they come
 to you.
As I live, says the LORD,
 you shall put all of them
 on like an ornament,
 and like a bride you shall
 bind them on.

19 Surely your waste and your
 desolate places
 and your devastated land—
surely now you will be too
 crowded for your
 inhabitants,
 and those who swallowed
 you up will be far away.
20 The children born in the
 time of your
 bereavement
 will yet say in your hearing:
"The place is too crowded
 for me;
 make room for me to
 settle."
21 Then you will say in your
 heart,
 "Who has borne me these?
I was bereaved and barren,
 exiled and put away—
 so who has reared these?
I was left all alone—
 where then have these
 come from?"

22 Thus says the Lord GOD:
I will soon lift up my hand to
 the nations,

Cross references

49.8 Ps 69.13; 2 Cor 6.2; Isa 42.6; 44.26
49.9 Isa 42.7; Lk 4.18; Isa 41.18
49.10 Rev 7.16; Ps 121.6; Isa 14.1; 40.11; 41.17
49.11 Isa 40.4; 62.10
49.12 Isa 43.5,6
49.13 Isa 44.23; 40.1; 54.7,8, 10; Rev 12.12; 18.20
49.14 Isa 40.27
49.15 Isa 44.21
49.16 Song 8.6; Isa 62.6,7
49.17 v. 19
49.18 Isa 60.4; 43.5; 45.23; 52.1
49.19 Isa 51.3; 54.1,2; Zech 10.10; Ps 56.1,2
49.20 Isa 54.1-3
49.21 Isa 54.6,7; 27.10; 5.13; 1.8
49.22 Isa 62.10; 60.4; 66.20

[f] Meaning of Heb uncertain [g] Or the trails
[h] Q Ms: MT Sinim [i] Or Your children
come swiftly; your destroyers

and raise my signal to the
peoples;
and they shall bring your
sons in their bosom,
and your daughters shall be
carried on their
shoulders.
23 Kings shall be your foster
fathers,
and their queens your
nursing mothers.
With their faces to the
ground they shall bow
down to you,
and lick the dust of your
feet.
Then you will know that I
am the LORD;
those who wait for me shall
not be put to shame.

24 Can the prey be taken from
the mighty,
or the captives of a tyrant[j]
be rescued?
25 But thus says the LORD:
Even the captives of the
mighty shall be taken,
and the prey of the tyrant
be rescued;
for I will contend with those
who contend with you,
and I will save your
children.
26 I will make your oppressors
eat their own flesh,
and they shall be drunk
with their own blood as
with wine.
Then all flesh shall know
that I am the LORD your
Savior,
and your Redeemer, the
Mighty One of Jacob.

50 Thus says the LORD:
Where is your mother's
bill of divorce
with which I put her away?
Or which of my creditors is it
to whom I have sold you?
No, because of your sins you
were sold,
and for your transgressions
your mother was put
away.

49.23
Isa 60.16;
45.14;
Ps 72.9;
Mic 7.17;
Isa 43.10;
25.9;
Ps 25.3
49.25
Isa 14.1,2;
25.9
49.26
Isa 9.4,20;
45.6; 43.3;
v. 7
50.1
Deut 24.1,3;
Jer 3.8;
Isa 54.6,7;
Deut 32.30;
Isa 52.3;
48.8

50.2
Isa 65.12;
66.4;
Num 11.23;
Isa 59.1;
Ex 14.21;
Josh 3.16
50.3
Isa 13.10;
Rev 6.12
50.4
Isa 54.13;
Jer 31.25;
Ps 143.8
50.5
Ps 40.6;
Mt 26.39;
Jn 8.29;
14.31;
Phil 2.8
50.6
Isa 53.5;
Mt 26.67;
Lk 22.63
50.7
Isa 49.8;
54.4;
Ezek 3.8,9
50.8
Rom 8.32-34

2 Why was no one there when
I came?
Why did no one answer
when I called?
Is my hand shortened, that it
cannot redeem?
Or have I no power to
deliver?
By my rebuke I dry up the
sea,
I make the rivers a desert;
their fish stink for lack of
water,
and die of thirst.[k]
3 I clothe the heavens with
blackness,
and make sackcloth their
covering.

The Servant's Humiliation and Vindication

4 The Lord GOD has given me
the tongue of a teacher,[l]
that I may know how to
sustain
the weary with a word.
Morning by morning he
wakens—
wakens my ear
to listen as those who are
taught.
5 The Lord GOD has opened my
ear,
and I was not rebellious,
I did not turn backward.
6 I gave my back to those who
struck me,
and my cheeks to those
who pulled out the
beard;
I did not hide my face
from insult and spitting.

7 The Lord GOD helps me;
therefore I have not been
disgraced;
therefore I have set my face
like flint,
and I know that I shall not
be put to shame;
8 he who vindicates me is
near.
Who will contend with me?

j Q Ms Syr Vg: MT *of a righteous person*
k Or *die on the thirsty ground* l Cn: Heb
of those who are taught

Let us stand up together.
Who are my adversaries?
Let them confront me.
9 It is the Lord GoD who helps
 me;
who will declare me guilty?
All of them will wear out like
 a garment;
the moth will eat them up.

10 Who among you fears the
 LORD
and obeys the voice of his
 servant,
who walks in darkness
 and has no light,
yet trusts in the name of the
 LORD
and relies upon his God?
11 But all of you are kindlers of
 fire,
lighters of firebrands.^m
Walk in the flame of your
 fire,
and among the brands that
 you have kindled!
This is what you shall have
 from my hand:
you shall lie down in
 torment.

Blessings in Store for God's People

51 Listen to me, you that
 pursue righteousness,
you that seek the LORD.
Look to the rock from which
 you were hewn,
and to the quarry from
 which you were dug.
2 Look to Abraham your father
 and to Sarah who bore you;
for he was but one when I
 called him,
but I blessed him and
 made him many.
3 For the LORD will comfort
 Zion;
he will comfort all her
 waste places,
and will make her wilderness
 like Eden,
her desert like the garden
 of the LORD;
joy and gladness will be
 found in her,

thanksgiving and the voice
 of song.

4 Listen to me, my people,
 and give heed to me, my
 nation;
for a teaching will go out
 from me,
and my justice for a light
 to the peoples.
5 I will bring near my
 deliverance swiftly,
my salvation has gone out
and my arms will rule the
 peoples;
the coastlands wait for me,
 and for my arm they hope.
6 Lift up your eyes to the
 heavens,
and look at the earth
 beneath;
for the heavens will vanish
 like smoke,
the earth will wear out like
 a garment,
and those who live on it
 will die like gnats;ⁿ
but my salvation will be
 forever,
and my deliverance will
 never be ended.

7 Listen to me, you who know
 righteousness,
you people who have my
 teaching in your hearts;
do not fear the reproach of
 others,
and do not be dismayed
 when they revile you.
8 For the moth will eat them
 up like a garment,
and the worm will eat
 them like wool;
but my deliverance will be
 forever,
and my salvation to all
 generations.

9 Awake, awake, put on
 strength,
O arm of the LORD!
Awake, as in days of old,

50.9
Isa 41.10;
54.17; 5.18
50.10
Isa 49.2,3;
9.2;
Eph 5.8;
Isa 12.2
50.11
Ps 35.8;
Isa 65.13-15
51.1
v. 7;
Ps 94.15
51.2
Rom 4.16;
Heb 11.11,
12;
Gen 12.1;
24.35
51.3
Isa 40.1;
52.9;
Joel 2.3;
Gen 13.10;
Isa 66.10

51.4
Ps 50.7;
Isa 2.3;
42.4,6
51.5
Isa 46.13;
40.10; 42.4;
63.5
51.6
Isa 40.26;
Ps 102.26;
Mt 24.35;
2 Pet 3.10;
Isa 45.17
51.7
v. 1;
Ps 37.31;
Mt 5.11;
Acts 5.41
51.8
Isa 50.9;
v. 6
51.9
Isa 52.1;
Deut 4.34;
Ps 89.10;
74.13;
Ezek 29.3

^m Syr: Heb *you gird yourselves with firebrands*
ⁿ Or *in like manner*

the generations of long
ago!
Was it not you who cut
Rahab in pieces,
who pierced the dragon?
10 Was it not you who dried up
the sea,
the waters of the great
deep;
who made the depths of the
sea a way
for the redeemed to cross
over?
11 So the ransomed of the LORD
shall return,
and come to Zion with
singing;
everlasting joy shall be upon
their heads;
they shall obtain joy and
gladness,
and sorrow and sighing
shall flee away.

12 I, I am he who comforts you;
why then are you afraid of
a mere mortal who
must die,
a human being who fades
like grass?
13 You have forgotten the LORD,
your Maker,
who stretched out the
heavens
and laid the foundations of
the earth.
You fear continually all day
long
because of the fury of the
oppressor,
who is bent on destruction.
But where is the fury of the
oppressor?
14 The oppressed shall speedily
be released;
they shall not die and go
down to the Pit,
nor shall they lack bread.
15 For I am the LORD your God,
who stirs up the sea so
that its waves roar—
the LORD of hosts is his
name.
16 I have put my words in your
mouth,
and hidden you in the
shadow of my hand,

stretching out° the heavens
and laying the foundations
of the earth,
and saying to Zion, "You
are my people."

17 Rouse yourself, rouse
yourself!
Stand up, O Jerusalem,
you who have drunk at the
hand of the LORD
the cup of his wrath,
who have drunk to the dregs
the bowl of staggering.
18 There is no one to guide her
among all the children she
has borne;
there is no one to take her
by the hand
among all the children she
has brought up.
19 These two things have
befallen you
—who will grieve with
you?—
devastation and destruction,
famine and sword—
who will comfort you?ᵖ
20 Your children have fainted,
they lie at the head of
every street
like an antelope in a net;
they are full of the wrath of
the LORD,
the rebuke of your God.

21 Therefore hear this, you who
are wounded,�q
who are drunk, but not
with wine:
22 Thus says your Sovereign,
the LORD,
your God who pleads the
cause of his people:
See, I have taken from your
hand the cup of
staggering;
you shall drink no more
from the bowl of my wrath.
23 And I will put it into the
hand of your
tormentors,
who have said to you,

51.10
Ex 14.21;
Isa 43.16;
63.9,16
51.11
Isa 35.10;
60.19;
Rev 7.17;
22.3
51.12
v. 3;
2 Cor 1.3;
Ps 118.6;
Isa 40.6,7;
1 Pet 1.24
51.13
Isa 17.10;
Job 9.8;
Ps 104.2;
Isa 40.22;
7.4; 49.26
51.14
Isa 52.2;
38.18; 49.10
51.16
Deut 18.18;
Isa 59.21;
49.2; 65.17

51.17
Isa 52.1;
Job 21.20;
Jer 25.15
51.18
Isa 59.21
51.19
Isa 9.20
51.20
Isa 5.25;
42.25; 66.15
51.21
Isa 54.11;
29.9
51.22
Jer 50.34;
v. 17
51.23
Jer 25.15-17,
26,28;
Zech 12.2;
Josh 10.24

° Syr: Heb *planting* ᵖ Q Ms Gk Syr Vg:
MT *how may I comfort you?* q Or *humbled*

"Bow down, that we may
 walk on you";
and you have made your
 back like the ground
and like the street for them
 to walk on.

Let Zion Rejoice

52 Awake, awake,
 put on your strength,
 O Zion!
Put on your beautiful
 garments,
 O Jerusalem, the holy city;
for the uncircumcised and
 the unclean
 shall enter you no more.
² Shake yourself from the dust,
 rise up,
 O captive^r Jerusalem;
loose the bonds from your
 neck,
 O captive daughter Zion!

3 For thus says the Lord: You
were sold for nothing, and you shall
be redeemed without money. ⁴ For
thus says the Lord God: Long ago,
my people went down into Egypt to
reside there as aliens; the Assyrian,
too, has oppressed them without
cause. ⁵ Now therefore what am I
doing here, says the Lord, seeing
that my people are taken away
without cause? Their rulers howl,
says the Lord, and continually, all
day long, my name is despised.
⁶ Therefore my people shall know
my name; therefore in that day
they shall know that it is I who
speak; here am I.

7 How beautiful upon the
 mountains
 are the feet of the
 messenger who
 announces peace,
who brings good news,
 who announces salvation,
 who says to Zion, "Your
 God reigns."
⁸ Listen! Your sentinels lift up
 their voices,
 together they sing for joy;
for in plain sight they see

the return of the Lord to
 Zion.
⁹ Break forth together into
 singing,
 you ruins of Jerusalem;
for the Lord has comforted
 his people,
he has redeemed
 Jerusalem.
¹⁰ The Lord has bared his holy
 arm
 before the eyes of all the
 nations;
and all the ends of the earth
 shall see
 the salvation of our God.

¹¹ Depart, depart, go out from
 there!
 Touch no unclean thing;
go out from the midst of it,
 purify yourselves,
 you who carry the vessels
 of the Lord.
¹² For you shall not go out in
 haste,
 and you shall not go in
 flight;
for the Lord will go before
 you,
 and the God of Israel will
 be your rear guard.

The Suffering Servant

¹³ See, my servant shall
 prosper;
 he shall be exalted and
 lifted up,
 and shall be very high.
¹⁴ Just as there were many who
 were astonished at
 him^s
 — so marred was his
 appearance, beyond
 human semblance,
 and his form beyond that
 of mortals —
¹⁵ so he shall startle^t many
 nations;
 kings shall shut their
 mouths because of him;
for that which had not been
 told them they shall
 see,

52.1
Isa 51.9,17;
Neh 11.1;
Mt 4.5;
Rev 21.2,27
52.2
Isa 29.4;
9.4; 51.14
52.3
Ps 44.12;
Isa 63.4;
45.13
52.4
Gen 46.6
52.5
Ezek 36.20;
Rom 2.24
52.6
Isa 49.23
52.7
Nah 1.15;
Rom 10.15;
Ps 93.1
52.8
Isa 62.6

52.9
Isa 44.23,
26; 48.20
52.10
Ps 98.2,3;
Isa 45.22;
48.20;
Lk 3.6
52.11
Jer 50.8;
2 Cor 6.17;
2 Tim 2.19;
Isa 1.16
52.12
Ex 12.33;
Isa 42.16;
58.8
52.13
Isa 42.1;
Phil 2.9
52.14
Ps 22.6,7;
Isa 53.2,3
52.15
Ezek 36.25;
Rom 15.21

^r Cn: Heb *rise up, sit* ^s Syr Tg: Heb *you*
^t Meaning of Heb uncertain

and that which they had
 not heard they shall
 contemplate.

53 Who has believed what
 we have heard?
And to whom has the arm
 of the Lord been
 revealed?

2 For he grew up before him
 like a young plant,
 and like a root out of dry
 ground;
 he had no form or majesty
 that we should look at
 him,
 nothing in his appearance
 that we should desire
 him.

3 He was despised and
 rejected by others;
 a man of suffering[u] and
 acquainted with
 infirmity;
 and as one from whom
 others hide their faces[v]
 he was despised, and we
 held him of no account.

4 Surely he has borne our
 infirmities
 and carried our diseases;
 yet we accounted him
 stricken,
 struck down by God, and
 afflicted.

5 But he was wounded for our
 transgressions,
 crushed for our iniquities;
 upon him was the
 punishment that made
 us whole,
 and by his bruises we are
 healed.

6 All we like sheep have gone
 astray;
 we have all turned to our
 own way,
 and the Lord has laid on him
 the iniquity of us all.

7 He was oppressed, and he
 was afflicted,
 yet he did not open his
 mouth;
 like a lamb that is led to the
 slaughter,

53.1
Jn 12.38;
Rom 10.16
53.2
Isa 11.1;
52.14
53.3
Ps 22.6;
v. 10;
Jn 1.10,11
53.4
Mt 8.17;
Heb 9.28;
1 Pet 2.24
53.5
Rom 4.25;
1 Cor 15.3;
1 Pet 2.24
53.6
v. 11
53.7
Mt 26.63;
Acts 8.32

53.8
vv. 5,12
53.9
Mt 27.57;
1 Pet 2.22
53.10
vv. 3-6;
Isa 54.3;
46.10
53.11
Jn 10.14-18;
Rom 5.18,
19; vv. 5,6
53.12
Isa 52.13;
Mt 26.38,
39,42;
Lk 22.37;
2 Cor 5.21

and like a sheep that
 before its shearers is
 silent,
 so he did not open his
 mouth.

8 By a perversion of justice he
 was taken away.
 Who could have imagined
 his future?
 For he was cut off from the
 land of the living,
 stricken for the
 transgression of my
 people.

9 They made his grave with the
 wicked
 and his tomb[w] with the
 rich,[x]
 although he had done no
 violence,
 and there was no deceit in
 his mouth.

10 Yet it was the will of the
 Lord to crush him with
 pain.[y]
 When you make his life an
 offering for sin,[z]
 he shall see his offspring,
 and shall prolong his
 days;
 through him the will of the
 Lord shall prosper.

11 Out of his anguish he shall
 see light;[a]
 he shall find satisfaction
 through his knowledge.
 The righteous one,[b] my
 servant, shall make
 many righteous,
 and he shall bear their
 iniquities.

12 Therefore I will allot him a
 portion with the great,
 and he shall divide the
 spoil with the strong;
 because he poured out
 himself to death,
 and was numbered with
 the transgressors;

[u] Or *a man of sorrows* [v] Or *as one who
hides his face from us* [w] Q Ms: MT *and in
his death* [x] Cn: Heb *with a rich person*
[y] Or *by disease*; meaning of Heb uncertain
[z] Meaning of Heb uncertain [a] Q Mss: MT
lacks *light* [b] Or *and he shall find
satisfaction. Through his knowledge, the
righteous one*

yet he bore the sin of many,
and made intercession for
the transgressors.

The Eternal Covenant of Peace

54 Sing, O barren one who
did not bear;
burst into song and shout,
you who have not been in
labor!
For the children of the
desolate woman will be
more
than the children of her
that is married, says the
Lord.
2 Enlarge the site of your tent,
and let the curtains of your
habitations be stretched
out;
do not hold back; lengthen
your cords
and strengthen your stakes.
3 For you will spread out to
the right and to the
left,
and your descendants will
possess the nations
and will settle the desolate
towns.

4 Do not fear, for you will not
be ashamed;
do not be discouraged, for
you will not suffer
disgrace;
for you will forget the shame
of your youth,
and the disgrace of your
widowhood you will
remember no more.
5 For your Maker is your
husband,
the Lord of hosts is his
name;
the Holy One of Israel is
your Redeemer,
the God of the whole earth
he is called.
6 For the Lord has called you
like a wife forsaken and
grieved in spirit,
like the wife of a man's
youth when she is cast
off,
says your God.

54.1
Gal 4.27;
1 Sam 2.5;
Isa 62.4
54.2
Isa 49.19,20
54.3
Isa 43.5,6;
49.19,23
54.4
Isa 45.17;
Jer 31.19;
Isa 4.1; 25.8
54.5
Jer 3.14;
Isa 43.14;
48.17; 6.3
54.6
Isa 62.4

54.7
Isa 26.20;
43.5
54.8
Isa 60.10;
v. 10;
Isa 49.10,
13; v. 5
54.9
Gen 9.11;
Isa 12.1
54.10
Isa 51.6;
Ps 89.33,34;
v. 8
54.11
1 Chr 29.2;
Rev 21.18
54.13
Jer 31.34;
Jn 6.45;
Ps 119.165
54.14
Isa 62.1;
9.4; 14.4;
v. 4

7 For a brief moment I
abandoned you,
but with great compassion
I will gather you.
8 In overflowing wrath for a
moment
I hid my face from you,
but with everlasting love I
will have compassion
on you,
says the Lord, your
Redeemer.

9 This is like the days of Noah
to me:
Just as I swore that the
waters of Noah
would never again go over
the earth,
so I have sworn that I will
not be angry with you
and will not rebuke you.
10 For the mountains may
depart
and the hills be removed,
but my steadfast love shall
not depart from you,
and my covenant of peace
shall not be removed,
says the Lord, who has
compassion on you.

11 O afflicted one,
storm-tossed, and not
comforted,
I am about to set your
stones in antimony,
and lay your foundations
with sapphires. c
12 I will make your pinnacles of
rubies,
your gates of jewels,
and all your wall of
precious stones.
13 All your children shall be
taught by the Lord,
and great shall be the
prosperity of your
children.
14 In righteousness you shall be
established;
you shall be far from
oppression, for you
shall not fear;

c Or lapis lazuli

and from terror, for it shall
not come near you.
¹⁵ If anyone stirs up strife,
it is not from me;
whoever stirs up strife with
you
shall fall because of you.
¹⁶ See it is I who have created
the smith
who blows the fire of coals,
and produces a weapon fit
for its purpose;
I have also created the
ravager to destroy.
¹⁷ No weapon that is
fashioned against you
shall prosper,
and you shall confute every
tongue that rises
against you in
judgment.
This is the heritage of the
servants of the LORD
and their vindication from
me, says the LORD.

An Invitation to Abundant Life

55 Ho, everyone who thirsts,
come to the waters;
and you that have no money,
come, buy and eat!
Come, buy wine and milk
without money and without
price.
² Why do you spend your
money for that which is
not bread,
and your labor for that
which does not satisfy?
Listen carefully to me, and
eat what is good,
and delight yourselves in
rich food.
³ Incline your ear, and come
to me;
listen, so that you may live.
I will make with you an
everlasting covenant,
my steadfast, sure love for
David.
⁴ See, I made him a witness to
the peoples,
a leader and commander
for the peoples.
⁵ See, you shall call nations
that you do not know,

54.15
Isa 41.11-16
54.17
Isa 29.8;
50.8,9; 45.24
55.1
Isa 41.17;
Jn 4.14;
7.37;
Mt 13.44;
Rev 3.18
55.2
Hos 8.7;
Isa 62.8,9;
25.6
55.3
Isa 51.4;
Rom 10.5;
Isa 61.8;
Acts 13.34
55.4
Jer 30.9;
Ezek 34.23,
24;
Dan 9.25
55.5
Isa 49.6,12,
23;
Zech 8.22;
Isa 60.9

55.6
Ps 32.6;
Isa 49.8;
2 Cor 6.1,
2
55.7
Isa 1.16;
59.7; 31.6;
54.8,10;
44.22
55.9
Ps 103.11
55.10
Isa 30.23;
2 Cor 9.10
55.11
Isa 45.23;
59.21; 46.10
55.12
Isa 51.11;
54.10,13;
44.23;
1 Chr 16.33

and nations that do not
know you shall run to
you,
because of the LORD your
God, the Holy One of
Israel,
for he has glorified you.

⁶ Seek the LORD while he may
be found,
call upon him while he is
near;
⁷ let the wicked forsake their
way,
and the unrighteous their
thoughts;
let them return to the LORD,
that he may have mercy
on them,
and to our God, for he will
abundantly pardon.
⁸ For my thoughts are not your
thoughts,
nor are your ways my ways,
says the LORD.
⁹ For as the heavens are
higher than the earth,
so are my ways higher than
your ways
and my thoughts than your
thoughts.

¹⁰ For as the rain and the snow
come down from
heaven,
and do not return there
until they have watered
the earth,
making it bring forth and
sprout,
giving seed to the sower
and bread to the eater,
¹¹ so shall my word be that
goes out from my
mouth;
it shall not return to me
empty,
but it shall accomplish that
which I purpose,
and succeed in the thing
for which I sent it.

¹² For you shall go out in joy,
and be led back in peace;
the mountains and the hills
before you
shall burst into song,

and all the trees of the
 field shall clap their
 hands.
13 Instead of the thorn shall
 come up the cypress;
instead of the brier shall
 come up the myrtle;
and it shall be to the LORD
 for a memorial,
for an everlasting sign that
 shall not be cut off.

The Covenant Extended to All Who Obey

56 Thus says the LORD:
 Maintain justice, and do
 what is right,
for soon my salvation will
 come,
and my deliverance be
 revealed.

2 Happy is the mortal who
 does this,
 the one who holds it fast,
who keeps the sabbath, not
 profaning it,
and refrains from doing any
 evil.

3 Do not let the foreigner
 joined to the LORD say,
"The LORD will surely
 separate me from his
 people";
and do not let the eunuch
 say,
"I am just a dry tree."
4 For thus says the LORD:
To the eunuchs who keep
 my sabbaths,
who choose the things that
 please me
and hold fast my covenant,
5 I will give, in my house and
 within my walls,
a monument and a name
 better than sons and
 daughters;
I will give them an
 everlasting name
that shall not be cut off.

6 And the foreigners who join
 themselves to the LORD,

to minister to him, to love
 the name of the LORD,
and to be his servants,
all who keep the sabbath,
 and do not profane it,
and hold fast my
 covenant —
7 these I will bring to my holy
 mountain,
 and make them joyful in
 my house of prayer;
their burnt offerings and
 their sacrifices
will be accepted on my
 altar;
for my house shall be called
 a house of prayer
 for all peoples.
8 Thus says the Lord GOD,
 who gathers the outcasts of
 Israel,
I will gather others to them
 besides those already
 gathered. d

The Corruption of Israel's Rulers

9 All you wild animals,
 all you wild animals in the
 forest, come to devour!
10 Israel'se sentinels are blind,
 they are all without
 knowledge;
they are all silent dogs
 that cannot bark;
dreaming, lying down,
 loving to slumber.
11 The dogs have a mighty
 appetite;
 they never have enough.
The shepherds also have no
 understanding;
 they have all turned to
 their own way,
to their own gain, one and
 all.
12 "Come," they say, "let us f
 get wine;
let us fill ourselves with
 strong drink.
And tomorrow will be like
 today,
 great beyond measure."

55.13
Isa 41.19;
32.13; 63.12,
14; 19.20
56.1
Isa 61.8;
46.13
56.2
Isa 58.13
56.3
v. 6;
Acts 8.27
56.4
vv. 2,6
56.5
v. 7;
Isa 66.20;
26.1; 62.2;
48.19
56.6
Isa 60.10;
61.5; vv. 2,4

56.7
Isa 11.9;
65.25;
Rom 12.1;
Heb 13.15;
Mt 21.13;
Mk 11.17;
Lk 19.46
56.8
Isa 11.12;
60.3-11;
Jn 10.16
56.9
Jer 12.9
56.10
Isa 29.9-14;
Nah 3.18

d Heb *besides his gathered ones*
e Heb *His* f Q Ms Syr Vg Tg: MT *me*

Israel's Futile Idolatry

57 The righteous perish,
and no one takes it to
heart;
the devout are taken away,
while no one understands.
For the righteous are taken
away from calamity,

2 and they enter into peace;
those who walk uprightly
will rest on their couches.

3 But as for you, come here,
you children of a sorceress,
you offspring of an
adulterer and a whore.g

4 Whom are you mocking?
Against whom do you open
your mouth wide
and stick out your tongue?
Are you not children of
transgression,
the offspring of deceit —

5 you that burn with lust
among the oaks,
under every green tree;
you that slaughter your
children in the valleys,
under the clefts of the
rocks?

6 Among the smooth stones of
the valley is your
portion;
they, they, are your lot;
to them you have poured out
a drink offering,
you have brought a grain
offering.
Shall I be appeased for
these things?

7 Upon a high and lofty
mountain
you have set your bed,
and there you went up to
offer sacrifice.

8 Behind the door and the
doorpost
you have set up your
symbol;
for, in deserting me,h you
have uncovered your
bed,
you have gone up to it,
you have made it wide;
and you have made a bargain
for yourself with them,
you have loved their bed,

you have gazed on their
nakedness.i

9 You journeyed to Molechi
with oil,
and multiplied your
perfumes;
you sent your envoys far
away,
and sent down even to
Sheol.

10 You grew weary from your
many wanderings,
but you did not say, "It is
useless."
You found your desire
rekindled,
and so you did not weaken.

11 Whom did you dread and
fear
so that you lied,
and did not remember me
or give me a thought?
Have I not kept silent and
closed my eyes,k
and so you do not fear me?

12 I will concede your
righteousness and your
works,
but they will not help you.

13 When you cry out, let your
collection of idols
deliver you!
The wind will carry them
off,
a breath will take them
away.
But whoever takes refuge in
me shall possess the
land
and inherit my holy
mountain.

A Promise of Help and Healing

14 It shall be said,
"Build up, build up, prepare
the way,
remove every obstruction
from my people's way."

15 For thus says the high and
lofty one
who inhabits eternity,
whose name is Holy:

57.1
Ps 12.1;
Isa 42.25;
47.7,11
57.2
Isa 26.7
57.3
Mt 16.4;
Isa 1.21
57.4
Isa 48.8
57.5
2 Kings 16.4;
Lev 18.21;
2 Kings 16.3;
Jer 7.31
57.6
Jer 3.9;
7.18; 5.9,29
57.7
Ezek 16.16;
23.41
57.8
Ezek 23.7,
18; 16.26,28

57.9
Ezek 23.16,
40
57.10
Isa 47.13;
Jer 2.25
57.11
Isa 51.12;
Jer 2.32;
v. 1;
Ps 50.21
57.13
Jer 22.20;
Isa 25.4;
60.21; 65.9
57.14
Isa 62.10;
Jer 18.15
57.15
Isa 52.13;
40.28; 66.1;
Ps 34.18;
51.17; 14.2,3;
Isa 61.1

g Heb an adulterer and she plays the whore
h Meaning of Heb uncertain i Or their
phallus; Heb the hand j Or the king
k Gk Vg: Heb silent even for a long time

I dwell in the high and holy
place,
and also with those who
are contrite and humble
in spirit,
to revive the spirit of the
humble,
and to revive the heart of
the contrite.
16 For I will not continually
accuse,
nor will I always be angry;
for then the spirits would
grow faint before me,
even the souls that I have
made.
17 Because of their wicked
covetousness I was
angry;
I struck them, I hid and
was angry;
but they kept turning back
to their own ways.
18 I have seen their ways, but I
will heal them;
I will lead them and repay
them with comfort,
creating for their mourners
the fruit of the lips.[1]
19 Peace, peace, to the far and
the near, says the LORD;
and I will heal them.
20 But the wicked are like the
tossing sea
that cannot keep still;
its waters toss up mire and
mud.
21 There is no peace, says my
God, for the wicked.

False and True Worship

58 Shout out, do not hold
back!
Lift up your voice like a
trumpet!
Announce to my people their
rebellion,
to the house of Jacob their
sins.
2 Yet day after day they seek
me
and delight to know my
ways,
as if they were a nation that
practiced righteousness

and did not forsake the
ordinance of their God;
they ask of me righteous
judgments,
they delight to draw near
to God.
3 "Why do we fast, but you do
not see?
Why humble ourselves, but
you do not notice?"
Look, you serve your own
interest on your fast
day,
and oppress all your
workers.
4 Look, you fast only to
quarrel and to fight
and to strike with a wicked
fist.
Such fasting as you do today
will not make your voice
heard on high.
5 Is such the fast that I
choose,
a day to humble oneself?
Is it to bow down the head
like a bulrush,
and to lie in sackcloth and
ashes?
Will you call this a fast,
a day acceptable to the
LORD?

6 Is not this the fast that I
choose:
to loose the bonds of
injustice,
to undo the thongs of the
yoke,
to let the oppressed go free,
and to break every yoke?
7 Is it not to share your bread
with the hungry,
and bring the homeless
poor into your house;
when you see the naked, to
cover them,
and not to hide yourself
from your own kin?
8 Then your light shall break
forth like the dawn,
and your healing shall
spring up quickly;

57.16
Gen 6.3;
Ps 85.5;
103.9;
Mic 7.18;
Job 34.14;
Isa 42.5
57.17
Jer 6.13;
Isa 1.4
57.18
Isa 53.5;
52.12; 61.1-3
57.19
Heb 13.15;
Acts 2.39;
Eph 2.17
57.20
Job 18.5-14
57.21
Isa 48.22
58.1
Isa 48.8;
50.1; 59.12
58.2
Isa 1.11;
48.1; 59.13;
29.13

58.3
Mal 3.14;
Isa 22.12,13
58.4
1 Kings 21.9,
12,13;
Isa 59.2
58.5
Zech 7.5;
Esther 4.3;
Job 2.8
58.6
Neh 5.10-12;
Jer 34.9
58.7
Ezek 18.7,
16;
Mt 25.35;
Job 31.19;
Gen 29.14;
Neh 5.5
58.8
v. 10;
Isa 30.26;
62.1;
Ex 14.19;
Isa 52.12

[1] Meaning of Heb uncertain

your vindicator[m] shall go
　before you,
　the glory of the LORD shall
　be your rear guard.
9 Then you shall call, and the
　LORD will answer;
　you shall cry for help, and
　he will say, Here I am.

If you remove the yoke from
　among you,
　the pointing of the finger,
　the speaking of evil,
10 if you offer your food to the
　hungry
　and satisfy the needs of the
　afflicted,
　then your light shall rise in
　the darkness
　and your gloom be like the
　noonday.
11 The LORD will guide you
　continually,
　and satisfy your needs in
　parched places,
　and make your bones
　strong;
　and you shall be like a
　watered garden,
　like a spring of water,
　whose waters never fail.
12 Your ancient ruins shall be
　rebuilt;
　you shall raise up the
　foundations of many
　generations;
　you shall be called the
　repairer of the breach,
　the restorer of streets to
　live in.

13 If you refrain from trampling
　the sabbath,
　from pursuing your own
　interests on my holy
　day;
　if you call the sabbath a
　delight
　and the holy day of the
　LORD honorable;
　if you honor it, not going
　your own ways,
　serving your own interests,
　or pursuing your own
　affairs;[n]
14 then you shall take delight
　in the LORD,

and I will make you ride
　upon the heights of the
　earth;
I will feed you with the
　heritage of your
　ancestor Jacob,
　for the mouth of the LORD
　has spoken.

Injustice and Oppression to Be Punished

59 See, the LORD's hand is
　not too short to save,
　nor his ear too dull to hear.
2 Rather, your iniquities have
　been barriers
　between you and your God,
　and your sins have hidden
　his face from you
　so that he does not hear.
3 For your hands are defiled
　with blood,
　and your fingers with
　iniquity;
　your lips have spoken lies,
　your tongue mutters
　wickedness.
4 No one brings suit justly,
　no one goes to law
　honestly;
　they rely on empty pleas,
　they speak lies,
　conceiving mischief and
　begetting iniquity.
5 They hatch adders' eggs,
　and weave the spider's
　web;
　whoever eats their eggs dies,
　and the crushed egg
　hatches out a viper.
6 Their webs cannot serve as
　clothing;
　they cannot cover
　themselves with what
　they make.
Their works are works of
　iniquity,
　and deeds of violence are
　in their hands.
7 Their feet run to evil,
　and they rush to shed
　innocent blood;
　their thoughts are thoughts
　of iniquity,

58.9 Isa 55.6; v. 6; Ps 12.2
58.10 v. 7; Ps 37.6
58.11 Isa 49.10; 41.17; 66.14; Jn 4.14; 7.38
58.12 Isa 49.8; 44.28; 30.13; Am 9.11
58.13 Isa 56.2; Ps 84.2,10; Isa 55.8; 59.13
58.14 Isa 61.10; Deut 32.13; Isa 1.19,20
59.1 Num 11.23; Isa 50.2; 58.9
59.2 Isa 1.15; 58.4
59.3 Isa 1.15; Jer 2.30; v. 13; Isa 28.15
59.4 vv. 14,15; Isa 30.12; Job 15.35; Ps 7.14
59.5 Isa 14.29; Job 8.14
59.6 Isa 28.20; 57.12; 58.4
59.7 Rom 3.15-17; Isa 65.2

[m] Or vindication　[n] Heb or speaking words

desolation and destruction
are in their highways.

8 The way of peace they do
not know,
and there is no justice in
their paths.
Their roads they have made
crooked;
no one who walks in them
knows peace.

9 Therefore justice is far from
us,
and righteousness does not
reach us;
we wait for light, and lo!
there is darkness;
and for brightness, but we
walk in gloom.

10 We grope like the blind
along a wall,
groping like those who
have no eyes;
we stumble at noon as in the
twilight,
among the vigorous° as
though we were dead.

11 We all growl like bears;
like doves we moan
mournfully.
We wait for justice, but there
is none;
for salvation, but it is far
from us.

12 For our transgressions before
you are many,
and our sins testify against
us.
Our transgressions indeed
are with us,
and we know our
iniquities:

13 transgressing, and denying
the LORD,
and turning away from
following our God,
talking oppression and
revolt,
conceiving lying words and
uttering them from the
heart.

14 Justice is turned back,
and righteousness stands at
a distance;
for truth stumbles in the
public square,

59.8
vv. 9,11;
Ps 125.5;
v. 14
59.9
v. 14;
Isa 5.30;
8.21,22
59.10
Deut 28.29;
Job 5.14;
Am 8.9;
Isa 8.14,15
59.11
Isa 38.14;
Ezek 7.16;
vv. 9,14
59.12
Isa 58.1;
Jer 14.7
59.13
Josh 24.27;
Titus 1.16;
Isa 30.12;
vv. 3,4
59.14
Isa 1.21;
46.12; 48.1

59.15
Isa 5.23;
1.21-23
59.16
Isa 63.5;
Ezek 22.30;
Ps 98.1
59.17
Eph 6.14;
1 Thes 5.8;
Isa 63.2,3
59.18
Isa 65.6,7;
66.6
59.19
Ps 113.3;
Isa 66.12
59.20
Rom 11.26,
27;
Ezek 18.30,
31;
Acts 2.38,39
59.21
Jer 31.31-34;
Isa 44.3,26;
54.10;
Jer 32.40

and uprightness cannot
enter.

15 Truth is lacking,
and whoever turns from
evil is despoiled.

The LORD saw it, and it
displeased him
that there was no justice.

16 He saw that there was no
one,
and was appalled that
there was no one to
intervene;
so his own arm brought him
victory,
and his righteousness
upheld him.

17 He put on righteousness like
a breastplate,
and a helmet of salvation
on his head;
he put on garments of
vengeance for clothing,
and wrapped himself in
fury as in a mantle.

18 According to their deeds, so
will he repay;
wrath to his adversaries,
requital to his enemies;
to the coastlands he will
render requital.

19 So those in the west shall
fear the name of the
LORD,
and those in the east, his
glory;
for he will come like a
pent-up stream
that the wind of the LORD
drives on.

20 And he will come to Zion as
Redeemer,
to those in Jacob who turn
from transgression, says
the LORD.

21 And as for me, this is my cove-
nant with them, says the LORD: my
spirit that is upon you, and my
words that I have put in your
mouth, shall not depart out of your
mouth, or out of the mouths of
your children, or out of the mouths

°Meaning of Heb uncertain

of your children's children, says
the LORD, from now on and forever.

The Ingathering of the Dispersed

60 Arise, shine; for your
light has come,
and the glory of the LORD
has risen upon you.
2 For darkness shall cover the
earth,
and thick darkness the
peoples;
but the LORD will arise upon
you,
and his glory will appear
over you.
3 Nations shall come to your
light,
and kings to the brightness
of your dawn.

4 Lift up your eyes and look
around;
they all gather together,
they come to you;
your sons shall come from
far away,
and your daughters shall be
carried on their nurses'
arms.
5 Then you shall see and be
radiant;
your heart shall thrill and
rejoice,P
because the abundance of
the sea shall be brought
to you,
the wealth of the nations
shall come to you.
6 A multitude of camels shall
cover you,
the young camels of
Midian and Ephah;
all those from Sheba shall
come.
They shall bring gold and
frankincense,
and shall proclaim the
praise of the LORD.
7 All the flocks of Kedar shall
be gathered to you,
the rams of Nebaioth shall
minister to you;
they shall be acceptable on
my altar,

and I will glorify my
glorious house.

8 Who are these that fly like a
cloud,
and like doves to their
windows?
9 For the coastlands shall wait
for me,
the ships of Tarshish first,
to bring your children from
far away,
their silver and gold with
them,
for the name of the LORD
your God,
and for the Holy One of
Israel,
because he has glorified
you.
10 Foreigners shall build up
your walls,
and their kings shall
minister to you;
for in my wrath I struck you
down,
but in my favor I have had
mercy on you.
11 Your gates shall always be
open;
day and night they shall
not be shut,
so that nations shall bring
you their wealth,
with their kings led in
procession.
12 For the nation and kingdom
that will not serve you
shall perish;
those nations shall be
utterly laid waste.
13 The glory of Lebanon shall
come to you,
the cypress, the plane, and
the pine,
to beautify the place of my
sanctuary;
and I will glorify where my
feet rest.
14 The descendants of those
who oppressed you
shall come bending low to
you,
and all who despised you

60.1
Eph 5.14;
Mal 4.2
60.2
Col 1.13;
Isa 4.5
60.3
Isa 49.6,23;
v. 11
60.4
Isa 49.18,
20-22
60.5
Ps 34.5;
Isa 23.18;
24.14; 61.6
60.6
Gen 25.4;
Ps 72.10;
Isa 43.23;
42.10
60.7
Gen 25.13;
Isa 56.7;
Hag 2.7,9

60.9
Isa 66.19;
2.16; 49.22;
55.5
60.10
Zech 6.15;
Isa 49.23;
54.8
60.11
vv. 18,5;
Ps 149.8
60.12
Zech 14.17
60.13
Isa 35.2;
41.19;
1 Chr 28.2;
Ps 132.7
60.14
Isa 49.23;
Heb 12.22;
Rev 3.9

P Heb *be enlarged*

shall bow down at your
feet;
they shall call you the City
of the LORD,
the Zion of the Holy One
of Israel.
15 Whereas you have been
forsaken and hated,
with no one passing
through,
I will make you majestic
forever,
a joy from age to age.
16 You shall suck the milk of
nations,
you shall suck the breasts
of kings;
and you shall know that I,
the LORD, am your
Savior
and your Redeemer, the
Mighty One of Jacob.

17 Instead of bronze I will bring
gold,
instead of iron I will bring
silver;
instead of wood, bronze,
instead of stones, iron.
I will appoint Peace as your
overseer
and Righteousness as your
taskmaster.
18 Violence shall no more be
heard in your land,
devastation or destruction
within your borders;
you shall call your walls
Salvation,
and your gates Praise.

God the Glory of Zion

19 The sun shall no longer be
your light by day,
nor for brightness shall the
moon
give light to you by night;q
but the LORD will be your
everlasting light,
and your God will be your
glory.
20 Your sun shall no more go
down,
or your moon withdraw
itself;
for the LORD will be your
everlasting light,

and your days of mourning
shall be ended.
21 Your people shall all be
righteous;
they shall possess the land
forever.
They are the shoot that I
planted, the work of my
hands,
so that I might be glorified.
22 The least of them shall
become a clan,
and the smallest one a
mighty nation;
I am the LORD;
in its time I will
accomplish it quickly.

The Good News of Deliverance

61 The spirit of the Lord
GOD is upon me,
because the LORD has
anointed me;
he has sent me to bring good
news to the oppressed,
to bind up the
brokenhearted,
to proclaim liberty to the
captives,
and release to the
prisoners;
2 to proclaim the year of the
LORD's favor,
and the day of vengeance
of our God;
to comfort all who mourn;
3 to provide for those who
mourn in Zion—
to give them a garland
instead of ashes,
the oil of gladness instead of
mourning,
the mantle of praise
instead of a faint spirit.
They will be called oaks of
righteousness,
the planting of the LORD, to
display his glory.
4 They shall build up the
ancient ruins,
they shall raise up the
former devastations;
they shall repair the ruined
cities,

60.15
Jer 30.17;
Isa 66.5;
33.8,9; 65.18
60.16
Isa 49.23;
66.11; 63.8,
16
60.18
Isa 54.14;
51.19; 26.1;
v. 11
60.19
Rev 21.23;
22.5;
Isa 9.2;
Zech 2.5
60.20
Isa 30.26;
65.19

60.21
Isa 52.1;
Ps 37.11,22;
Isa 29.23;
45.11
60.22
Isa 51.2
61.1f
Isa 11.2;
Lk 4.18;
Ps 45.7;
Isa 57.15;
42.7
61.2
Isa 49.8;
34.8; 57.18;
Mt 5.4
61.3
Isa 60.20;
Ps 45.7;
Isa 60.21
61.4
Isa 49.8;
Ezek 36.33

q Q Ms Gk Old Latin Tg: MT lacks *by night*

the devastations of many
generations.

5 Strangers shall stand and
feed your flocks,
foreigners shall till your
land and dress your
vines;
6 but you shall be called
priests of the Lord,
you shall be named
ministers of our God;
you shall enjoy the wealth of
the nations,
and in their riches you
shall glory.
7 Because their[r] shame was
double,
and dishonor was
proclaimed as their lot,
therefore they shall possess a
double portion;
everlasting joy shall be
theirs.

8 For I the Lord love justice,
I hate robbery and
wrongdoing;[s]
I will faithfully give them
their recompense,
and I will make an
everlasting covenant
with them.
9 Their descendants shall be
known among the
nations,
and their offspring among
the peoples;
all who see them shall
acknowledge
that they are a people
whom the Lord has
blessed.
10 I will greatly rejoice in the
Lord,
my whole being shall exult
in my God;
for he has clothed me with
the garments of
salvation,
he has covered me with the
robe of righteousness,
as a bridegroom decks
himself with a garland,
and as a bride adorns
herself with her jewels.

61.5
Isa 60.10
61.6
Isa 66.21;
60.5,11
61.7
Isa 54.4;
40.2;
Zech 9.12;
Isa 60.15;
Ps 16.11
61.8
Isa 30.18;
55.3
61.9
Isa 54.3;
44.3
61.10
Isa 12.1,2;
49.4,18;
Rev 21.2

61.11
Isa 55.10;
45.23,24;
Ps 72.3;
85.11;
Isa 60.18
62.1
Isa 61.11;
52.10
62.2
Isa 60.3;
vv. 4,12;
Isa 65.15
62.3
Zech 9.16
62.4
Hos 1.10;
Isa 54.6,7;
Jer 32.41;
3.14
62.5
Isa 65.19

11 For as the earth brings forth
its shoots,
and as a garden causes
what is sown in it to
spring up,
so the Lord God will cause
righteousness and
praise
to spring up before all the
nations.

The Vindication and Salvation of Zion

62 For Zion's sake I will not
keep silent,
and for Jerusalem's sake I
will not rest,
until her vindication shines
out like the dawn,
and her salvation like a
burning torch.
2 The nations shall see your
vindication,
and all the kings your
glory;
and you shall be called by a
new name
that the mouth of the Lord
will give.
3 You shall be a crown of
beauty in the hand of
the Lord,
and a royal diadem in the
hand of your God.
4 You shall no more be termed
Forsaken,[t]
and your land shall no
more be termed
Desolate;[u]
but you shall be called My
Delight Is in Her,[v]
and your land Married;[w]
for the Lord delights in you,
and your land shall be
married.
5 For as a young man marries
a young woman,
so shall your builder[x]
marry you,
and as the bridegroom
rejoices over the bride,
so shall your God rejoice
over you.

[r] Heb *your* [s] Or *robbery with a burnt offering* [t] Heb *Azubah*
[u] Heb *Shemamah* [v] Heb *Hephzibah*
[w] Heb *Beulah* [x] Cn: Heb *your sons*

6 Upon your walls,
 O Jerusalem,
 I have posted sentinels;
all day and all night
 they shall never be silent.
You who remind the LORD,
 take no rest,
7 and give him no rest
 until he establishes
 Jerusalem
 and makes it renowned
 throughout the earth.
8 The LORD has sworn by his
 right hand
 and by his mighty arm:
I will not again give your
 grain
 to be food for your
 enemies,
 and foreigners shall not
 drink the wine
 for which you have labored;
9 but those who garner it shall
 eat it
 and praise the LORD,
and those who gather it shall
 drink it
 in my holy courts.

10 Go through, go through the
 gates,
 prepare the way for the
 people;
build up, build up the
 highway,
 clear it of stones,
 lift up an ensign over the
 peoples.
11 The LORD has proclaimed
 to the end of the earth:
Say to daughter Zion,
 "See, your salvation comes;
his reward is with him,
 and his recompense before
 him."
12 They shall be called, "The
 Holy People,
 The Redeemed of the
 LORD";
and you shall be called,
 "Sought Out,
 A City Not Forsaken."

Vengeance on Edom

63 "Who is this that comes
 from Edom,

from Bozrah in garments
 stained crimson?
Who is this so splendidly
 robed,
 marching in his great
 might?"

"It is I, announcing
 vindication,
 mighty to save."

2 "Why are your robes red,
 and your garments like
 theirs who tread the
 winepress?"

3 "I have trodden the
 winepress alone,
 and from the peoples no
 one was with me;
I trod them in my anger
 and trampled them in my
 wrath;
 their juice spattered on my
 garments,
 and stained all my robes.
4 For the day of vengeance was
 in my heart,
 and the year for my
 redeeming work had
 come.
5 I looked, but there was no
 helper;
 I stared, but there was no
 one to sustain me;
so my own arm brought me
 victory,
 and my wrath sustained
 me.
6 I trampled down peoples in
 my anger,
 I crushed them in my
 wrath,
 and I poured out their
 lifeblood on the earth."

God's Mercy Remembered

7 I will recount the gracious
 deeds of the LORD,
 the praiseworthy acts of
 the LORD,
because of all that the LORD
 has done for us,
 and the great favor to the
 house of Israel

62.6
Isa 52.8;
Jer 6.17;
Ezek 3.17;
Ps 74.2
62.7
Mt 15.21-28;
Lk 18.1-8;
Jer 33.9
62.8
Isa 45.23;
Deut 28.31,
33; Jer 5.17
62.9
Isa 65.13,
21-23
62.10
Isa 57.14;
49.11; 11.10,
12
62.11
Isa 49.6;
Zech 9.9;
Mt 21.5;
Isa 51.1;
40.10
62.12
Isa 4.3;
51.10; v. 4
63.1
Isa 34.5,6;
Am 1.12;
Zeph 3.17

63.2
Rev 19.13,
15
63.3
Isa 22.5;
28.3;
Mic 7.10;
Rev 19.15
63.4
Isa 34.8;
61.2
63.5
Isa 59.16;
Ps 98.1;
Isa 52.10
63.6
Isa 65.12;
51.17,21,22;
34.3
63.7
Isa 54.8,10;
1 Kings 8.66;
Ps 51.1

that he has shown them
 according to his mercy,
according to the
 abundance of his
 steadfast love.
8 For he said, "Surely they are
 my people,
children who will not deal
 falsely";
and he became their savior
9 in all their distress.
It was no messenger[y] or
 angel
but his presence that saved
 them;[z]
in his love and in his pity he
 redeemed them;
he lifted them up and
 carried them all the
 days of old.

10 But they rebelled
 and grieved his holy spirit;
therefore he became their
 enemy;
he himself fought against
 them.
11 Then they[a] remembered the
 days of old,
of Moses his servant.[b]
Where is the one who
 brought them up out of
 the sea
with the shepherds of his
 flock?
Where is the one who put
 within them
his holy spirit,
12 who caused his glorious arm
 to march at the right hand
 of Moses,
who divided the waters
 before them
to make for himself an
 everlasting name,
13 who led them through the
 depths?
Like a horse in the desert,
 they did not stumble.
14 Like cattle that go down into
 the valley,
 the spirit of the LORD gave
 them rest.
Thus you led your people,
 to make for yourself a
 glorious name.

A Prayer of Penitence

15 Look down from heaven and
 see,
 from your holy and glorious
 habitation.
Where are your zeal and your
 might?
The yearning of your heart
 and your compassion?
They are withheld from me.
16 For you are our father,
 though Abraham does not
 know us
 and Israel does not
 acknowledge us;
you, O LORD, are our father;
 our Redeemer from of old
 is your name.
17 Why, O LORD, do you make
 us stray from your ways
 and harden our heart, so
 that we do not fear
 you?
Turn back for the sake of
 your servants,
 for the sake of the tribes
 that are your heritage.
18 Your holy people took
 possession for a little
 while;
 but now our adversaries
 have trampled down
 your sanctuary.
19 We have long been like those
 whom you do not rule,
 like those not called by
 your name.

64 O that you would tear
 open the heavens and
 come down,
 so that the mountains
 would quake at your
 presence—
2 [c]as when fire kindles
 brushwood
 and the fire causes water
 to boil—
to make your name known to
 your adversaries,
 so that the nations might
 tremble at your
 presence!

63.9
Judg 10.16;
Ex 23.20-23;
Deut 7.7,8;
Ex 19.4;
Deut 1.31
63.10
Ps 78.40;
Acts 7.51;
Eph 4.30;
Ps 106.40
63.11
Ps 106.44,
45;
Ex 14.30;
Isa 51.9,10;
Num 11.17
63.12
Ex 15.6;
14.21;
Isa 50.10,11
63.13
Ps 106.9
63.14
Deut 32.12

63.15
Deut 26.15;
Ps 80.14;
Jer 31.20;
Hos 11.8
63.16
Isa 64.8;
51.2; 44.6;
60.16
63.17
Ezek 14.7-9;
Isa 29.13,
14;
Num 10.36
63.18
Deut 7.6;
Ps 74.3-7
63.19
Lam 3.43-45
64.1
Ps 144.5;
Judg 5.5
64.2
Jer 5.22

y Gk: Heb anguish z Or savior. 9In all
their distress he was distressed; the angel of his
presence saved them; a Heb he
b Cn: Heb his people c Ch 64.1 in Heb

3 When you did awesome
 deeds that we did not
 expect,
you came down, the
 mountains quaked at
 your presence.
4 From ages past no one has
 heard,
 no ear has perceived,
no eye has seen any God
 besides you,
who works for those who
 wait for him.
5 You meet those who gladly
 do right,
 those who remember you
 in your ways.
But you were angry, and we
 sinned;
because you hid yourself
 we transgressed.d
6 We have all become like one
 who is unclean,
and all our righteous deeds
 are like a filthy cloth.
We all fade like a leaf,
 and our iniquities, like the
 wind, take us away.
7 There is no one who calls on
 your name,
or attempts to take hold of
 you;
for you have hidden your
 face from us,
and have deliverede us
 into the hand of our
 iniquity.
8 Yet, O Lord, you are our
 Father;
we are the clay, and you
 are our potter;
we are all the work of your
 hand.
9 Do not be exceedingly angry,
 O Lord,
and do not remember
 iniquity forever.
Now consider, we are all
 your people.
10 Your holy cities have become
 a wilderness,
Zion has become a
 wilderness,
Jerusalem a desolation.
11 Our holy and beautiful
 house,

64.3
Ps 65.5;
66.3,5;
106.22
64.4
1 Cor 2.9;
Isa 40.31
64.5
Ex 20.24;
Isa 56.1;
63.7,10
64.6
Isa 6.5;
46.12;
Ps 90.5,6;
Isa 50.1
64.7
Isa 59.4;
27.5; 54.8;
9.18
64.8
Isa 63.16;
29.16; 60.21
64.9
Isa 60.10;
43.25; 63.8
64.10
Isa 6.11
64.11
Isa 63.18;
Ps 74.5-7;
Isa 7.23

64.12
Isa 42.14;
Ps 83.1
65.1
Rom 10.20;
Hos 1.10
65.2
Rom 10.21;
Isa 30.1,9;
59.7
65.3
Isa 3.8;
66.3,17
65.4
Lev 11.7;
Isa 66.3,17
65.5
Mt 9.11;
Lk 18.9-12
65.6
Ps 50.3;
79.12;
Jer 16.18

where our ancestors
 praised you,
has been burned by fire,
and all our pleasant places
 have become ruins.
12 After all this, will you
 restrain yourself,
 O Lord?
Will you keep silent, and
 punish us so severely?

The Righteousness of God's Judgment

65 I was ready to be sought
 out by those who did
 not ask,
to be found by those who
 did not seek me.
I said, "Here I am, here I
 am,"
to a nation that did not
 call on my name.
2 I held out my hands all day
 long
to a rebellious people,
who walk in a way that is
 not good,
following their own
 devices;
3 a people who provoke me
 to my face continually,
sacrificing in gardens
 and offering incense on
 bricks;
4 who sit inside tombs,
 and spend the night in
 secret places;
who eat swine's flesh,
 with broth of abominable
 things in their vessels;
5 who say, "Keep to yourself,
 do not come near me, for I
 am too holy for you."
These are a smoke in my
 nostrils,
a fire that burns all day
 long.
6 See, it is written before me:
 I will not keep silent, but I
 will repay;
I will indeed repay into their
 laps

dMeaning of Heb uncertain eGk Syr Old
Latin Tg: Heb *melted*

7 their[f] iniquities and their[f]
　　ancestors' iniquities
　　together,
　　　　　　says the LORD;
because they offered incense
　　on the mountains
and reviled me on the hills,
I will measure into their laps
　　full payment for their
　　actions.
8 Thus says the LORD:
As the wine is found in the
　　cluster,
and they say, "Do not
　　destroy it,
　　for there is a blessing in
　　it,"
so I will do for my servants'
　　sake,
and not destroy them all.
9 I will bring forth
　　descendants[g] from
　　Jacob,
and from Judah inheritors[h]
　　of my mountains;
my chosen shall inherit it,
and my servants shall settle
　　there.
10 Sharon shall become a
　　pasture for flocks,
and the Valley of Achor a
　　place for herds to lie
　　down,
for my people who have
　　sought me.
11 But you who forsake the
　　LORD,
who forget my holy
　　mountain,
who set a table for Fortune
　　and fill cups of mixed wine
　　for Destiny;
12 I will destine you to the
　　sword,
and all of you shall bow
　　down to the slaughter;
because, when I called, you
　　did not answer,
when I spoke, you did not
　　listen,
but you did what was evil in
　　my sight,
and chose what I did not
　　delight in.
13 Therefore thus says the Lord
　　GOD:
My servants shall eat,

65.7
Isa 30.13,
14; 57.7;
Ezek 20.27,
28; Jer 5.29
65.9f
Isa 45.19,
25; 49.8;
57.13; 32.18
65.10
Isa 33.9;
Josh 7.24;
Hos 2.15
65.11
Deut 29.24,
25; Isa 56.7
65.12
Isa 34.5,6;
63.6;
2 Chr 36.15,
16;
Prov 1.24;
Jer 7.13
65.13
Isa 1.19;
8.21; 41.17,
18; 5.13;
66.5,14

65.14
Mt 8.12;
Lk 13.28
65.15
Zech 8.13;
Isa 62.2
65.16
Ps 72.17;
31.5;
Isa 45.23;
Jer 31.12
65.17
2 Pet 3.13;
Isa 43.18
65.18
Isa 61.10
65.19
Isa 62.5;
35.10;
Rev 7.17
65.20
Deut 4.40;
Eccl 8.12,13

but you shall be hungry;
my servants shall drink,
　　but you shall be thirsty;
my servants shall rejoice,
　　but you shall be put to
　　shame;
14 my servants shall sing for
　　gladness of heart,
but you shall cry out for
　　pain of heart,
and shall wail for anguish
　　of spirit.
15 You shall leave your name to
　　my chosen to use as a
　　curse,
and the Lord GOD will put
　　you to death;
but to his servants he will
　　give a different name.
16 Then whoever invokes a
　　blessing in the land
shall bless by the God of
　　faithfulness,
and whoever takes an oath in
　　the land
shall swear by the God of
　　faithfulness;
because the former troubles
　　are forgotten
and are hidden from my
　　sight.

The Glorious New Creation

17 For I am about to create new
　　heavens
　　and a new earth;
the former things shall not
　　be remembered
　　or come to mind.
18 But be glad and rejoice
　　forever
　　in what I am creating;
for I am about to create
　　Jerusalem as a joy,
　　and its people as a delight.
19 I will rejoice in Jerusalem,
　　and delight in my people;
no more shall the sound of
　　weeping be heard in it,
　　or the cry of distress.
20 No more shall there be in it
　　an infant that lives but a
　　few days,
　　or an old person who does
　　not live out a lifetime;

f Gk Syr: Heb *your*　g Or *a descendant*
h Or *an inheritor*

for one who dies at a
　　hundred years will be
　　considered a youth,
　　and one who falls short of
　　a hundred will be
　　considered accursed.
21 They shall build houses and
　　inhabit them;
　　they shall plant vineyards
　　and eat their fruit.
22 They shall not build and
　　another inhabit;
　　they shall not plant and
　　another eat;
　　for like the days of a tree
　　shall the days of my
　　people be,
　　and my chosen shall long
　　enjoy the work of their
　　hands.
23 They shall not labor in vain,
　　or bear children for
　　calamity;[i]
　　for they shall be offspring
　　blessed by the LORD—
　　and their descendants as
　　well.
24 Before they call I will
　　answer,
　　while they are yet speaking
　　I will hear.
25 The wolf and the lamb shall
　　feed together,
　　the lion shall eat straw like
　　the ox;
　　but the serpent—its food
　　shall be dust!
　　They shall not hurt or
　　destroy
　　on all my holy mountain,
　　　　says the LORD.

The Worship God Demands

66 Thus says the LORD:
　　Heaven is my throne
　　and the earth is my
　　footstool;
　　what is the house that you
　　would build for me,
　　and what is my resting
　　place?
2 All these things my hand has
　　made,
　　and so all these things are
　　mine,[i]
　　　　says the LORD.

65.21
Am 9.14;
Isa 37.30
65.22
Isa 62.8,9;
Ps 92.12-14;
Deut 32.46,
47
65.23
Isa 55.2;
61.9
65.24
Dan 9.27
65.25
Isa 11.6,7,9;
Gen 3.14
66.1
1 Kings 8.27;
2 Chr 6.18;
Mt 5.34,35;
Jer 7.4;
Acts 7.49,50
66.2
Isa 40.26;
57.15;
Mt 5.3,4;
v. 5

66.3
Isa 1.11,13;
65.2,4
66.4
Prov 1.24;
Isa 65.12;
Jer 7.13
66.5
v. 2;
Isa 60.15;
Mt 5.10-12;
Lk 13.17
66.6
Isa 6.1,8;
65.6

But this is the one to whom
　　I will look,
　　to the humble and contrite
　　in spirit,
　　who trembles at my word.
3 Whoever slaughters an ox is
　　like one who kills a
　　human being;
　　whoever sacrifices a lamb,
　　like one who breaks a
　　dog's neck;
　　whoever presents a grain
　　offering, like one who
　　offers swine's blood;[k]
　　whoever makes a memorial
　　offering of frankincense,
　　like one who blesses an
　　idol.
　　These have chosen their own
　　ways,
　　and in their abominations
　　they take delight;
4 I also will choose to mock[l]
　　them,
　　and bring upon them what
　　they fear;
　　because, when I called, no
　　one answered,
　　when I spoke, they did not
　　listen;
　　but they did what was evil in
　　my sight,
　　and chose what did not
　　please me.

The LORD Vindicates Zion

5 Hear the word of the LORD,
　　you who tremble at his
　　word:
　　Your own people who hate
　　you
　　and reject you for my
　　name's sake
　　have said, "Let the LORD be
　　glorified,
　　so that we may see your
　　joy";
　　but it is they who shall be
　　put to shame.

6 Listen, an uproar from the
　　city!

i Or *sudden terror*　i Gk Syr: Heb *these*
things came to be　k Meaning of Heb
uncertain　l Or *to punish*

A voice from the temple!
The voice of the LORD,
 dealing retribution to his
 enemies!

7 Before she was in labor
 she gave birth;
before her pain came upon
 her
 she delivered a son.
8 Who has heard of such a
 thing?
 Who has seen such
 things?
Shall a land be born in one
 day?
 Shall a nation be delivered
 in one moment?
Yet as soon as Zion was in
 labor
 she delivered her children.
9 Shall I open the womb and
 not deliver?
 says the LORD;
shall I, the one who delivers,
 shut the womb?
 says your God.

10 Rejoice with Jerusalem, and
 be glad for her,
 all you who love her;
rejoice with her in joy,
 all you who mourn over
 her —
11 that you may nurse and be
 satisfied
 from her consoling
 breast;
that you may drink deeply
 with delight
 from her glorious bosom.

12 For thus says the LORD:
I will extend prosperity to
 her like a river,
 and the wealth of the
 nations like an
 overflowing stream;
and you shall nurse and be
 carried on her arm,
 and dandled on her knees.
13 As a mother comforts her
 child,
 so I will comfort you;
you shall be comforted in
 Jerusalem.

The Reign and Indignation of God

14 You shall see, and your heart
 shall rejoice;
 your bodiesᵐ shall flourish
 like the grass;
and it shall be known that
 the hand of the LORD is
 with his servants,
 and his indignation is
 against his enemies.
15 For the LORD will come in
 fire,
 and his chariots like the
 whirlwind,
to pay back his anger in fury,
 and his rebuke in flames of
 fire.
16 For by fire will the LORD
 execute judgment,
 and by his sword, on all
 flesh;
 and those slain by the LORD
 shall be many.

17 Those who sanctify and purify themselves to go into the gardens, following the one in the center, eating the flesh of pigs, vermin, and rodents, shall come to an end together, says the LORD.

18 For I knowⁿ their works and their thoughts, and I amᵒ coming to gather all nations and tongues; and they shall come and shall see my glory, ¹⁹and I will set a sign among them. From them I will send survivors to the nations, to Tarshish, Put,ᵖ and Lud — which draw the bow — to Tubal and Javan, to the coastlands far away that have not heard of my fame or seen my glory; and they shall declare my glory among the nations. ²⁰They shall bring all your kindred from all the nations as an offering to the LORD, on horses, and in chariots, and in litters, and on mules, and on dromedaries, to my holy mountain Jerusalem, says the LORD, just as the Israelites bring a grain offering in a clean vessel to the house of the

66.7
Isa 37.3
66.8
Isa 64.4
66.10
Isa 65.18;
Ps 26.8;
137.6
66.11
Isa 60.16
66.12
Isa 48.18;
60.4,5
66.13
2 Cor 1.3,
4

66.14
Isa 33.20;
Zech 10.7;
Isa 58.11;
Ezra 7.9;
Isa 34.2
66.15
Isa 31.9;
2 Thes 1.8;
Ps 78.16
66.16
Isa 30.30;
65.12; 34.3
66.17
Isa 65.3,4;
Ps 37.20
66.18
Isa 59.7;
45.22-25
66.19
Isa 62.10;
42.12
66.20
Isa 60.4;
65.11,25;
52.11

ᵐ Heb bones ⁿ Gk Syr: Heb lacks know
ᵒ Gk Syr Vg Tg: Heb it is ᵖ Gk: Heb Pul

LORD. ²¹And I will also take some of them as priests and as Levites, says the LORD.

²² For as the new heavens and
 the new earth,
 which I will make,
 shall remain before me, says
 the LORD;
 so shall your descendants
 and your name remain.
²³ From new moon to new
 moon,

and from sabbath to
 sabbath,
 all flesh shall come to
 worship before me,
 says the LORD.

24 And they shall go out and look at the dead bodies of the people who have rebelled against me; for their worm shall not die, their fire shall not be quenched, and they shall be an abhorrence to all flesh.

66.21
Isa 61.6;
1 Pet 2.5,9
66.22
Isa 65.17;
2 Pet 3.13;
Rev 21.1;
Isa 65.22,
23; 56.5
66.23
Isa 1.13,14;
49.7
66.24
Isa 5.25;
24.20;
Mk 9.48;
Isa 1.31;
Dan 12.2

Jeremiah

Title and Background

This book is named after the prophet whose ministry it records. Jeremiah prophesied in Judah during the reigns of Josiah and succeeding kings, living to see the destruction of Jerusalem and the Babylonian exile. It was a period of storm and stress throughout the entire world. After Josiah's reign, Jeremiah was often in danger from political and religious leaders in Judah who were angry because of his messages. Through all this, God protected Jeremiah so he could continue to warn the wicked and comfort those who trusted in God.

Author and Date of Writing

This book preserves an account of the prophetic ministry of Jeremiah, whose personal life and struggles are known to us in greater depth and detail than those of any other Old Testament prophet. His prophetic ministry began in 626 B.C. and ended sometime after 586.

Theme and Message

Jeremiah was always conscious of his call from the Lord to be a prophet, and as such proclaimed words that were spoken first by God himself and were therefore certain of fulfillment. Judgment is one of his all-pervasive themes. He was careful to point out, however, that repentance, if sincere, would postpone the inevitable.

For Jeremiah God was ultimate. He conceived of God as the Creator of all that exists, and as the all-powerful and everywhere present Lord. At the same time he emphasized that God was very much concerned about individual people who were accountable to God.

Outline

 I. The Call of Jeremiah (1.1-19)
 II. Warnings and Exhortations to Judah (2.1-29.32)
 III. Promises of Restoration (30.1-33.26)
 IV. Historical Insertion (34.1-35.19)
 V. The Sufferings of Jeremiah (36.1-38.28)
 VI. The Fall of Jerusalem and Its Aftermath (39.1-45.5)
 VII. Judgment Against the Nations (46.1-51.64)
 VIII. Historical Appendix (52.1-34)

1 The words of Jeremiah son of Hilkiah, of the priests who were in Anathoth in the land of Benjamin, ² to whom the word of the LORD came in the days of King Josiah son of Amon of Judah, in the thirteenth year of his reign. ³ It came also in the days of King Jehoiakim son of Josiah of Judah, and until the end of the eleventh year of King Zedekiah son of Josiah of Judah, until the captivity of Jerusalem in the fifth month.

1.1
2 Chr 35.25;
1 Chr 6.60;
Isa 32.7-9
1.2
1 Kings 13.2;
2 Kings 21.18,
24
1.3
Jer 25.1;
39.2; 52.12
1.5
Ps 139.15,
16; Isa 49.1,
5
1.6
Ex 4.10;
Isa 6.5

Jeremiah's Call and Commission

4 Now the word of the LORD came to me saying,

5 "Before I formed you in the
 womb I knew you,
and before you were born I
 consecrated you;
I appointed you a prophet to
 the nations."

6 Then I said, "Ah, Lord GOD! Truly I do not know how to speak, for I am only a boy." 7 But the LORD said to me,

"Do not say, 'I am only a
 boy';
for you shall go to all to
 whom I send you,
and you shall speak whatever
 I command you,
8 Do not be afraid of them,
for I am with you to deliver
 you,
 says the LORD."
9 Then the LORD put out his hand
and touched my mouth; and the
LORD said to me,
"Now I have put my words in
 your mouth.
10 See, today I appoint you over
 nations and over
 kingdoms,
to pluck up and to pull
 down,
to destroy and to overthrow,
to build and to plant."

11 The word of the LORD came to
me, saying, "Jeremiah, what do you
see?" And I said, "I see a branch of
an almond tree."a 12 Then the LORD
said to me, "You have seen well, for
I am watchingb over my word to
perform it." 13 The word of the LORD
came to me a second time, saying,
"What do you see?" And I said, "I
see a boiling pot, tilted away from
the north."

14 Then the LORD said to me:
Out of the north disaster shall
break out on all the inhabitants of
the land. 15 For now I am calling all
the tribes of the kingdoms of the
north, says the LORD; and they shall
come and all of them shall set their
thrones at the entrance of the gates
of Jerusalem, against all its sur-
rounding walls and against all the
cities of Judah. 16 And I will utter
my judgments against them, for all
their wickedness in forsaking me;
they have made offerings to other
gods, and worshiped the works of
their own hands. 17 But you, gird up
your loins; stand up and tell them
everything that I command you. Do
not break down before them, or I
will break you before them. 18 And
I for my part have made you today
a fortified city, an iron pillar, and a
bronze wall, against the whole
land—against the kings of Judah,

1.8
Ezek 2.6;
Jer 15.20
1.9
Isa 6.7;
Ex 4.11-16
1.10
Jer 18.7;
2 Cor 10.4,
5
1.11
Jer 24.3
1.13
Zech 4.2;
Ezek 11.3,7;
24.3
1.14
Jer 4.6; 6.1
1.15
Isa 22.7;
Jer 9.11
1.16
Deut 28.20;
Jer 17.13;
7.9; 10.3-5
1.17
1 Kings 18.46;
Ex 3.12;
Ezek 2.6
1.18
Isa 50.7;
Jer 6.27;
15.20
1.19
Jer 11.19;
15.10,11;
v. 8
2.1
Jer 1.2,11
2.2
Jer 7.2;
11.6;
Ezek 16.8;
Deut 2.7
2.3
Ex 19.5,6;
Jer 30.16;
50.7
2.5
Isa 5.4;
Mic 6.3;
Jer 8.19;
2 Kings 17.15
2.6
Ex 20.2;
Isa 63.11;
Hos 13.4;
Deut 8.15;
32.10
2.7
Num 13.27;
Lev 18.25;
Ps 78.58

its princes, its priests, and the peo-
ple of the land. 19 They will fight
against you; but they shall not pre-
vail against you, for I am with you,
says the LORD, to deliver you.

God Pleads with Israel to Repent

2 The word of the LORD came to
me, saying: 2 Go and proclaim
in the hearing of Jerusalem, Thus
says the LORD:
I remember the devotion of
 your youth,
 your love as a bride,
how you followed me in the
 wilderness,
in a land not sown.
3 Israel was holy to the LORD,
 the first fruits of his
 harvest.
All who ate of it were held
 guilty;
disaster came upon them,
 says the LORD.

4 Hear the word of the LORD,
O house of Jacob, and all the fami-
lies of the house of Israel. 5 Thus
says the LORD:
What wrong did your
 ancestors find in me
that they went far from me,
and went after worthless
 things, and became
 worthless themselves?
6 They did not say, "Where is
 the LORD
who brought us up from
 the land of Egypt,
who led us in the wilderness,
in a land of deserts and
 pits,
in a land of drought and
 deep darkness,
in a land that no one
 passes through,
where no one lives?"
7 I brought you into a plentiful
 land
to eat its fruits and its
 good things.
But when you entered you
 defiled my land,

a Heb shaqed b Heb shoqed

and made my heritage an
abomination.

8 The priests did not say,
"Where is the LORD?"
Those who handle the law
did not know me;
the rulers^c transgressed
against me;
the prophets prophesied by
Baal,
and went after things that
do not profit.

9 Therefore once more I
accuse you,
　　　　　says the LORD,
and I accuse your
children's children.

10 Cross to the coasts of Cyprus
and look,
send to Kedar and examine
with care;
see if there has ever been
such a thing.

11 Has a nation changed its
gods,
even though they are no
gods?
But my people have changed
their glory
for something that does
not profit.

12 Be appalled, O heavens, at
this,
be shocked, be utterly
desolate,
　　　　　says the LORD,

13 for my people have
committed two evils:
they have forsaken me,
the fountain of living water,
and dug out cisterns for
themselves,
cracked cisterns
that can hold no water.

14 Is Israel a slave? Is he a
homeborn servant?
Why then has he become
plunder?

15 The lions have roared against
him,
they have roared loudly.
They have made his land a
waste;
his cities are in ruins,
without inhabitant.

2.8
Jer 10.21;
Mal 2.6,7;
Rom 2.20;
Jer 23.13;
16.19
2.9
Ezek 20.35,
36; Mic 6.2
2.10
Isa 23.12;
Jer 49.28
2.11
Mic 4.5;
Ps 106.20;
Rom 1.23
2.13
Ps 36.9;
Jer 17.13;
Jn 4.14;
Jer 14.3
2.14
Ex 4.22;
Jer 5.19
2.15
Jer 50.17;
4.7

2.16
Jer 44.1;
43.7-9; 48.45
2.17
Jer 4.18;
Deut 32.10
2.18
Isa 30.1,2;
Josh 13.3;
Jer 50.17
2.19
Isa 3.9;
Hos 5.5;
11.7;
Jer 5.24;
Ps 36.1
2.20
Lev 26.13;
v. 25;
Deut 12.2;
Isa 57.5,7
2.21
Ex 15.17;
Isa 5.4
2.22
Jer 4.14
2.23
Prov 30.12;
Jer 9.14;
7.31

16 Moreover, the people of
Memphis and
Tahpanhes
have broken the crown of
your head.

17 Have you not brought this
upon yourself
by forsaking the LORD your
God,
while he led you in the
way?

18 What then do you gain by
going to Egypt,
to drink the waters of the
Nile?
Or what do you gain by
going to Assyria,
to drink the waters of the
Euphrates?

19 Your wickedness will punish
you,
and your apostasies will
convict you.
Know and see that it is evil
and bitter
for you to forsake the LORD
your God;
the fear of me is not in
you,
　　　　　says the Lord GOD
of hosts.

20 For long ago you broke your
yoke
and burst your bonds,
and you said, "I will not
serve!"
On every high hill
and under every green tree
you sprawled and played
the whore.

21 Yet I planted you as a choice
vine,
from the purest stock.
How then did you turn
degenerate
and become a wild vine?

22 Though you wash yourself
with lye
and use much soap,
the stain of your guilt is
still before me,
　　　　　says the Lord GOD.

23 How can you say, "I am not
defiled,

^c Heb *shepherds*

I have not gone after the
Baals"?
Look at your way in the
valley;
know what you have
done—
a restive young camel
interlacing her tracks,
24 a wild ass at home in the
wilderness,
in her heat sniffing the wind!
Who can restrain her lust?
None who seek her need
weary themselves;
in her month they will find
her.
25 Keep your feet from going
unshod
and your throat from thirst.
But you said, "It is hopeless,
for I have loved strangers,
and after them I will go."

26 As a thief is shamed when
caught,
so the house of Israel shall
be shamed—
they, their kings, their
officials,
their priests, and their
prophets,
27 who say to a tree, "You are
my father,"
and to a stone, "You gave
me birth."
For they have turned their
backs to me,
and not their faces.
But in the time of their
trouble they say,
"Come and save us!"
28 But where are your gods
that you made for yourself?
Let them come, if they can
save you,
in your time of trouble;
for you have as many gods
as you have towns,
O Judah.

29 Why do you complain against
me?
You have all rebelled
against me,
says the LORD.
30 In vain I have struck down
your children;

they accepted no
correction.
Your own sword devoured
your prophets
like a ravening lion.
31 And you, O generation,
behold the word of the
LORD!d
Have I been a wilderness to
Israel,
or a land of thick
darkness?
Why then do my people say,
"We are free,
we will come to you no
more"?
32 Can a girl forget her
ornaments,
or a bride her attire?
Yet my people have forgotten
me,
days without number.

33 How well you direct your
course
to seek lovers!
So that even to wicked
women
you have taught your ways.
34 Also on your skirts is found
the lifeblood of the
innocent poor,
though you did not catch
them breaking in.
Yet in spite of all these
thingsd
35 you say, "I am innocent;
surely his anger has turned
from me."
Now I am bringing you to
judgment
for saying, "I have not
sinned."
36 How lightly you gad about,
changing your ways!
You shall be put to shame by
Egypt
as you were put to shame
by Assyria.
37 From there also you will
come away
with your hands on your
head;

2.24
Jer 14.6
2.25
Jer 18.12;
14.10;
Deut 32.16
2.26
Jer 48.27
2.27
Jer 3.9;
18.17; 22.23;
Isa 26.16
2.28
Deut 32.37;
Isa 45.20;
Jer 11.13
2.29
Jer 5.1; 6.13
2.30
Isa 1.5;
Jer 26.20-24

2.31
Isa 45.19;
Deut 32.15
2.32
Isa 17.10;
Hos 8.14
2.34
Jer 19.4;
Ex 22.2
2.35
v. 23;
Jer 25.31;
1 Jn 1.8,
10
2.36
v. 23;
Hos 12.1;
Isa 30.3;
2 Chr 28.16,
20,21
2.37
2 Sam 13.19;
Jer 37.7-10

d Meaning of Heb uncertain

for the LORD has rejected
 those in whom you
 trust,
and you will not prosper
 through them.

Unfaithful Israel

3 If[e] a man divorces his wife
 and she goes from him
and becomes another man's
 wife,
 will he return to her?
Would not such a land be
 greatly polluted?
You have played the whore
 with many lovers;
 and would you return to
 me? says the LORD.
2 Look up to the bare
 heights,[f] and see!
 Where have you not been
 lain with?
By the waysides you have sat
 waiting for lovers,
 like a nomad in the
 wilderness.
You have polluted the land
 with your whoring and
 wickedness.
3 Therefore the showers have
 been withheld,
 and the spring rain has not
 come;
yet you have the forehead of
 a whore,
 you refuse to be ashamed.
4 Have you not just now called
 to me,
 "My Father, you are the
 friend of my youth—
5 will he be angry forever,
 will he be indignant to the
 end?"
This is how you have spoken,
 but you have done all the
 evil that you could.

A Call to Repentance

6 The LORD said to me in the
days of King Josiah: Have you seen
what she did, that faithless one, Is-
rael, how she went up on every high
hill and under every green tree, and
played the whore there? 7 And I
thought, "After she has done all
this she will return to me"; but she

did not return, and her false sister
Judah saw it. 8 She[g] saw that for all
the adulteries of that faithless one,
Israel, I had sent her away with a
decree of divorce; yet her false sis-
ter Judah did not fear, but she too
went and played the whore. 9 Be-
cause she took her whoredom so
lightly, she polluted the land, com-
mitting adultery with stone and
tree. 10 Yet for all this her false sis-
ter Judah did not return to me with
her whole heart, but only in pre-
tense, says the LORD.

11 Then the LORD said to me:
Faithless Israel has shown herself
less guilty than false Judah. 12 Go,
and proclaim these words toward
the north, and say:
 Return, faithless Israel,
 says the LORD.
 I will not look on you in
 anger,
 for I am merciful,
 says the LORD;
 I will not be angry forever.
13 Only acknowledge your guilt,
 that you have rebelled
 against the LORD your
 God,
 and scattered your favors
 among strangers under
 every green tree,
 and have not obeyed my
 voice,
 says the LORD.
14 Return, O faithless children,
 says the LORD,
 for I am your master;
 I will take you, one from a
 city and two from a
 family,
 and I will bring you to
 Zion.

15 I will give you shepherds af-
ter my own heart, who will feed you
with knowledge and understand-
ing. 16 And when you have multi-
plied and increased in the land, in
those days, says the LORD, they
shall no longer say, "The ark of the
covenant of the LORD." It shall not
come to mind, or be remembered,

3.1
Deut 24.4;
Jer 2.20;
Ezek 16.26,
28,29;
Zech 1.3
3.2
Deut 12.2;
Jer 2.20;
Prov 23.28;
Jer 2.7
3.3
Lev 26.19;
Jer 6.15;
Ezek 3.7
3.4
v. 19;
Ps 71.17
3.5
v. 12;
Isa 57.16
3.6
Jer 7.24;
17.2
3.7
Ezek 16.46,
47

3.8
2 Kings 17.6;
Isa 50.1;
Ezek 23.11
3.9
Jer 2.7,27
3.10
Hos 7.14
3.11
Ezek 16.51;
v. 7
3.12
2 Kings 17.6;
Ps 86.15
3.13
Deut 30.1-3;
Jer 2.20,25;
Deut 12.2
3.14
Hos 2.19;
Jer 50.4,5
3.15
Jer 23.4;
Acts 20.28
3.16
Isa 65.17

e Q Ms Gk Syr: MT *Saying, If* f Or *the*
trails g Q Ms Gk Mss Syr: MT *I*

or missed; nor shall another one be made. ¹⁷At that time Jerusalem shall be called the throne of the LORD, and all nations shall gather to it, to the presence of the LORD in Jerusalem, and they shall no longer stubbornly follow their own evil will. ¹⁸In those days the house of Judah shall join the house of Israel, and together they shall come from the land of the north to the land that I gave your ancestors for a heritage.

¹⁹ I thought
 how I would set you among
 my children,
and give you a pleasant land,
 the most beautiful heritage
 of all the nations.
And I thought you would call
 me, My Father,
and would not turn from
 following me.
²⁰ Instead, as a faithless wife
 leaves her husband,
so you have been faithless
 to me, O house of
 Israel,
 says the LORD.

²¹ A voice on the bare heights ʰ
 is heard,
the plaintive weeping of
 Israel's children,
because they have perverted
 their way,
they have forgotten the
 LORD their God:
²² Return, O faithless children,
 I will heal your
 faithlessness.

"Here we come to you;
 for you are the LORD our
 God.
²³ Truly the hills are ⁱ a
 delusion,
 the orgies on the
 mountains.
Truly in the LORD our God
 is the salvation of Israel.
24 "But from our youth the shameful thing has devoured all for which our ancestors had labored, their flocks and their herds, their sons and their daughters. ²⁵Let us

lie down in our shame, and let our dishonor cover us; for we have sinned against the LORD our God, we and our ancestors, from our youth even to this day; and we have not obeyed the voice of the LORD our God."

4 If you return, O Israel,
 says the LORD,
 if you return to me,
if you remove your
 abominations from my
 presence,
 and do not waver,
² and if you swear, "As the
 LORD lives!"
in truth, in justice, and in
 uprightness,
then nations shall be
 blessed ʲ by him,
and by him they shall
 boast.

3 For thus says the LORD to the people of Judah and to the inhabitants of Jerusalem:
Break up your fallow ground,
 and do not sow among
 thorns.
⁴ Circumcise yourselves to the
 LORD,
remove the foreskin of your
 hearts,
O people of Judah and
 inhabitants of
 Jerusalem,
or else my wrath will go forth
 like fire,
and burn with no one to
 quench it,
because of the evil of your
 doings.

Invasion and Desolation of Judah Threatened

5 Declare in Judah, and proclaim in Jerusalem, and say:
Blow the trumpet through
 the land;
 shout aloud ᵏ and say,
"Gather together, and let us
 go

3.17
Jer 17.12;
v. 19;
Isa 60.9;
Jer 11.8
3.18
Isa 11.13;
Hos 1.11;
Jer 31.8;
Am 9.15
3.19
Dan 8.9;
Ps 16.6;
Isa 63.16
3.20
vv. 6,7;
Isa 48.8
3.21
Isa 15.2;
Jer 2.32
3.22
v. 14;
Hos 6.1;
14.4;
Jer 31.6
3.23
Ps 121.1,2;
3.8
3.24
Jer 8.16
3.25
Ezra 9.7;
Jer 22.21

4.1
Jer 3.1,22;
Joel 2.12;
Jer 7.3,7
4.2
Deut 10.20;
Gen 22.18;
Gal 3.8;
Isa 45.25;
1 Cor 1.31
4.3
Hos 10.12;
Mt 13.7,22
4.4
Deut 10.16;
30.6;
Jer 9.26;
Rom 2.28,
29;
Jer 21.12;
Mk 9.43,48
4.5
Jer 6.1; 8.14

ʰ Or *the trails* ⁱ Gk Syr Vg: Heb *Truly from the hills is* ʲ Or *shall bless themselves* ᵏ Or *shout, take your weapons*: Heb *shout, fill (your hand)*

into the fortified cities!"

6 Raise a standard toward
 Zion,
 flee for safety, do not
 delay,
 for I am bringing evil from
 the north,
 and a great destruction.
7 A lion has gone up from its
 thicket,
 a destroyer of nations has
 set out;
 he has gone out from his
 place
 to make your land a waste;
 your cities will be ruins
 without inhabitant.
8 Because of this put on
 sackcloth,
 lament and wail:
 "The fierce anger of the LORD
 has not turned away from
 us."

9 On that day, says the LORD, cour-
age shall fail the king and the offi-
cials; the priests shall be appalled
and the prophets astounded.
10 Then I said, "Ah, Lord GOD, how
utterly you have deceived this peo-
ple and Jerusalem, saying, 'It shall
be well with you,' even while the
sword is at the throat!"

11 At that time it will be said to
this people and to Jerusalem: A hot
wind comes from me out of the
bare heights[1] in the desert toward
my poor people, not to winnow or
cleanse— 12 a wind too strong for
that. Now it is I who speak in judg-
ment against them.
13 Look! He comes up like
 clouds,
 his chariots like the
 whirlwind;
 his horses are swifter than
 eagles—
 woe to us, for we are
 ruined!
14 O Jerusalem, wash your
 heart clean of
 wickedness
 so that you may be saved.
 How long shall your evil
 schemes
 lodge within you?

15 For a voice declares from
 Dan
 and proclaims disaster
 from Mount Ephraim.
16 Tell the nations, "Here they
 are!"
 Proclaim against
 Jerusalem,
 "Besiegers come from a
 distant land;
 they shout against the
 cities of Judah.
17 They have closed in around
 her like watchers of a
 field,
 because she has rebelled
 against me,
 says the LORD.
18 Your ways and your doings
 have brought this upon
 you.
 This is your doom; how
 bitter it is!
 It has reached your very
 heart."

Sorrow for a Doomed Nation

19 My anguish, my anguish! I
 writhe in pain!
 Oh, the walls of my heart!
 My heart is beating wildly;
 I cannot keep silent;
 for I[m] hear the sound of the
 trumpet,
 the alarm of war.
20 Disaster overtakes disaster,
 the whole land is laid
 waste.
 Suddenly my tents are
 destroyed,
 my curtains in a moment.
21 How long must I see the
 standard,
 and hear the sound of the
 trumpet?
22 "For my people are foolish,
 they do not know me;
 they are stupid children,
 they have no
 understanding.
 They are skilled in doing
 evil,
 but do not know how to do
 good."

4.6
Jer 1.13-15;
6.1,22
4.7
2 Kings 24.1;
Jer 5.6;
Dan 7.4;
Jer 25.9;
Isa 1.7;
Jer 2.15
4.8
Isa 22.12;
Jer 6.26;
30.24
4.9
Isa 22.3-5;
29.9,10
4.10
Ezek 14.9;
2 Thes 2.11;
Jer 5.12;
14.13
4.11
Jer 51.1;
Ezek 17.10;
Hos 13.15
4.12
Jer 1.16
4.13
Isa 19.1;
5.28;
Deut 28.49;
Lam 4.19;
Isa 3.8
4.14
Isa 1.16;
Jas 4.8;
Jer 6.19;
13.27

4.15
Jer 8.16
4.16
Jer 5.6,15;
Isa 39.3;
Ezek 21.22
4.17
2 Kings 25.1,
4; Jer 5.23
4.18
Ps 107.17;
Isa 50.1;
Jer 2.17,19
4.19
Isa 15.5;
16.11; 21.3;
22.4;
Jer 9.1,10
4.20
Ps 42.7;
Ezek 7.26;
Jer 10.20
4.22
Jer 10.8;
2.8;
Rom 16.19

[1] Or the trails [m] Another reading is for you,
O my soul,

23 I looked on the earth, and lo,
 it was waste and void;
 and to the heavens, and
 they had no light.
24 I looked on the mountains,
 and lo, they were
 quaking,
 and all the hills moved to
 and fro.
25 I looked, and lo, there was
 no one at all,
 and all the birds of the air
 had fled.
26 I looked, and lo, the fruitful
 land was a desert,
 and all its cities were laid
 in ruins
 before the LORD, before his
 fierce anger.
27 For thus says the LORD: The
whole land shall be a desolation;
yet I will not make a full end.
28 Because of this the earth
 shall mourn,
 and the heavens above
 grow black;
 for I have spoken, I have
 purposed;
 I have not relented nor will
 I turn back.

29 At the noise of horseman
 and archer
 every town takes to flight;
 they enter thickets; they
 climb among rocks;
 all the towns are forsaken,
 and no one lives in them.
30 And you, O desolate one,
 what do you mean that you
 dress in crimson,
 that you deck yourself with
 ornaments of gold,
 that you enlarge your eyes
 with paint?
 In vain you beautify yourself.
 Your lovers despise you;
 they seek your life.
31 For I heard a cry as of a
 woman in labor,
 anguish as of one bringing
 forth her first child,
 the cry of daughter Zion
 gasping for breath,
 stretching out her hands,
 "Woe is me! I am fainting
 before killers!"

4.23
Gen 1.2;
Isa 24.19
4.24
Isa 5.25;
Ezek 38.20
4.25
Zeph 1.3
4.26
Jer 9.10
4.27
Jer 12.11,
12; 5.10,18;
30.11; 46.28
4.28
Hos 4.3;
Isa 5.30;
50.3;
Num 23.19;
Jer 7.16
4.29
Jer 6.23;
16.16
4.30
Jer 13.21;
2 Kings 9.30;
Ezek 23.40;
Jer 22.20,22
4.31
Jer 13.21;
Isa 42.14;
1.15;
Lam 1.17

5.1
2 Chr 16.9;
Ezek 22.30;
Gen 18.23,
26,32
5.2
Titus 1.16;
Jer 4.2; 7.9
5.3
Isa 1.5;
9.13;
Jer 2.30;
Zeph 3.2;
Jer 7.26;
19.15
5.4
Jer 4.22; 8.7
5.5
Mic 3.1;
Ps 2.3
5.6
Hab 1.8;
Zeph 3.3;
Hos 13.7;
Jer 30.14,15
5.7
Josh 23.7;
Zeph 1.5;
Deut 32.21;
Gal 4.8;
Jer 7.9;
Num 25.1-3

The Utter Corruption of God's People

5 Run to and fro through the
 streets of Jerusalem,
 look around and take note!
Search its squares and see
 if you can find one person
 who acts justly
 and seeks truth—
 so that I may pardon
 Jerusalem.[n]
2 Although they say, "As the
 LORD lives,"
 yet they swear falsely.
3 O LORD, do your eyes not
 look for truth?
You have struck them,
 but they felt no anguish;
you have consumed them,
 but they refused to take
 correction.
They have made their faces
 harder than rock;
 they have refused to turn
 back.

4 Then I said, "These are only
 the poor,
 they have no sense;
for they do not know the way
 of the LORD,
 the law of their God.
5 Let me go to the rich[o]
 and speak to them;
surely they know the way of
 the LORD,
 the law of their God."
But they all alike had broken
 the yoke,
 they had burst the bonds.

6 Therefore a lion from the
 forest shall kill them,
 a wolf from the desert shall
 destroy them.
A leopard is watching against
 their cities;
 everyone who goes out of
 them shall be torn in
 pieces—
because their transgressions
 are many,
 their apostasies are great.

7 How can I pardon you?

[n] Heb it [o] Or the great

Your children have
　　forsaken me,
and have sworn by those
　　who are no gods.
When I fed them to the full,
　　they committed adultery
and trooped to the houses
　　of prostitutes.
8 They were well-fed lusty
　　stallions,
　　each neighing for his
　　　　neighbor's wife.
9 Shall I not punish them for
　　these things?
　　　　　　　says the LORD;
　　and shall I not bring
　　retribution
　　on a nation such as this?

10 Go up through her vine-rows
　　and destroy,
　　but do not make a full end;
strip away her branches,
　　for they are not the LORD's.
11 For the house of Israel and
　　the house of Judah
have been utterly faithless
　　to me,
　　　　　　　says the LORD.
12 They have spoken falsely of
　　the LORD,
　　and have said, "He will do
　　nothing.
No evil will come upon us,
　　and we shall not see sword
　　or famine."
13 The prophets are nothing but
　　wind,
　　for the word is not in
　　them.
Thus shall it be done to
　　them!

14 Therefore thus says the LORD,
　　the God of hosts:
Because they[p] have spoken
　　this word,
I am now making my words
　　in your mouth a fire,
　　and this people wood, and
　　the fire shall devour
　　them.
15 I am going to bring upon you
　　a nation from far away,
　　O house of Israel,
　　　　　　　says the LORD.
It is an enduring nation,

5.8
Ezek 22.11;
Jer 13.27
5.9
Jer 9.9;
44.22
5.10
Jer 39.8;
v. 18;
Jer 4.27
5.11
Jer 3.20
5.12
2 Chr 36.16;
Isa 28.15;
Jer 23.17;
14.13
5.13
Jer 14.13,15
5.14
Jer 1.9;
23.29
5.15
Deut 28.49;
Isa 5.26;
Jer 1.15;
6.22; 4.16;
Isa 39.3

5.16
Isa 5.28;
13.18
5.17
Lev 26.16;
Deut 28.31,
33; Jer 8.13;
Hos 8.14
5.18
Jer 4.27
5.19
Deut 29.24-26;
1 Kings 9.8,
9;
Jer 16.10-13;
Deut 28.48
5.21
v. 4;
Isa 6.9;
Ezek 12.2;
Mt 13.14;
Jer 6.10
5.22
Jer 2.19;
Job 26.10;
Ps 104.9

it is an ancient nation,
　　a nation whose language you
　　　　do not know,
　　nor can you understand
　　　　what they say.
16 Their quiver is like an open
　　tomb;
　　all of them are mighty
　　　　warriors.
17 They shall eat up your
　　harvest and your food;
　　they shall eat up your sons
　　　　and your daughters;
　　they shall eat up your flocks
　　　　and your herds;
　　they shall eat up your vines
　　　　and your fig trees;
　　they shall destroy with the
　　sword
　　　　your fortified cities in
　　　　which you trust.

18 But even in those days, says
the LORD, I will not make a full end
of you. 19 And when your people
say, "Why has the LORD our God
done all these things to us?" you
shall say to them, "As you have for-
saken me and served foreign gods
in your land, so you shall serve
strangers in a land that is not
yours."

20 Declare this in the house of
　　Jacob,
　　proclaim it in Judah:
21 Hear this, O foolish and
　　senseless people,
　　who have eyes, but do not
　　　　see,
　　who have ears, but do not
　　　　hear.
22 Do you not fear me? says the
　　LORD;
　　Do you not tremble before
　　me?
I placed the sand as a
　　boundary for the sea,
　　a perpetual barrier that it
　　cannot pass;
though the waves toss, they
　　cannot prevail,
　　though they roar, they
　　cannot pass over it.

P Heb *you*

23 But this people has a
 stubborn and rebellious
 heart;
 they have turned aside and
 gone away.
24 They do not say in their
 hearts,
 "Let us fear the LORD our
 God,
 who gives the rain in its
 season,
 the autumn rain and the
 spring rain,
 and keeps for us
 the weeks appointed for
 the harvest."
25 Your iniquities have turned
 these away,
 and your sins have
 deprived you of good.
26 For scoundrels are found
 among my people;
 they take over the goods of
 others.
 Like fowlers they set a trap;q
 they catch human beings.
27 Like a cage full of birds,
 their houses are full of
 treachery;
 therefore they have become
 great and rich,
28 they have grown fat and
 sleek.
 They know no limits in
 deeds of wickedness;
 they do not judge with
 justice
 the cause of the orphan, to
 make it prosper,
 and they do not defend the
 rights of the needy.
29 Shall I not punish them for
 these things?
 says the LORD,
 and shall I not bring
 retribution
 on a nation such as this?

30 An appalling and horrible
 thing
 has happened in the land:
31 the prophets prophesy falsely,
 and the priests rule as the
 prophets direct;r
 my people love to have it so,
 but what will you do when
 the end comes?

**The Imminence and Horror of
 the Invasion**

6 Flee for safety, O children of
 Benjamin,
 from the midst of
 Jerusalem!
 Blow the trumpet in Tekoa,
 and raise a signal on
 Beth-haccherem;
 for evil looms out of the
 north,
 and great destruction.
2 I have likened daughter Zion
 to the loveliest pasture.s
3 Shepherds with their flocks
 shall come against her.
 They shall pitch their tents
 around her;
 they shall pasture, all in
 their places.
4 "Prepare war against her;
 up, and let us attack at
 noon!"
 "Woe to us, for the day
 declines,
 the shadows of evening
 lengthen!"
5 "Up, and let us attack by
 night,
 and destroy her palaces!"
6 For thus says the LORD of
 hosts:
 Cut down her trees;
 cast up a siege ramp
 against Jerusalem.
 This is the city that must be
 punished;t
 there is nothing but
 oppression within her.
7 As a well keeps its water
 fresh,
 so she keeps fresh her
 wickedness;
 violence and destruction are
 heard within her;
 sickness and wounds are
 ever before me.
8 Take warning, O Jerusalem,
 or I shall turn from you in
 disgust,
 and make you a desolation,
 an uninhabited land.

5.23
Jer 4.17;
6.28
5.24
Ps 147.8;
Mt 5.45;
Joel 2.23;
Gen 8.22
5.25
Jer 2.17;
4.18
5.26
Ps 10.9;
Prov 1.11;
Hab 1.15
5.27
Jer 9.6; 12.1
5.28
Deut 32.15;
Isa 1.23;
Zech 7.10;
Jer 2.34
5.29
Mal 3.5
5.30
Hos 6.10
5.31
Jer 14.14;
Ezek 13.6;
Mic 2.11

6.1
2 Chr 11.6;
Neh 3.14;
Jer 1.14; 4.6
6.2
Deut 28.56;
Jer 4.31
6.3
Jer 12.10;
2 Kings 25.1;
Jer 4.17
6.4
Joel 3.9;
Jer 15.8
6.5
Jer 52.13
6.6
Deut 20.19,
20;
Jer 32.24;
22.17
6.7
Isa 57.20;
Ps 55.9-11;
Jer 20.8;
Ezek 7.11,
23
6.8
Jer 7.28;
Ezek 23.18;
Hos 9.12

q Meaning of Heb uncertain r Or rule by
their own authority s Or I will destroy
daughter Zion, the loveliest pasture t Or the
city of license

9 Thus says the LORD of hosts:
 Glean^u thoroughly as a vine
 the remnant of Israel;
 like a grape-gatherer, pass
 your hand again
 over its branches.

10 To whom shall I speak and
 give warning,
 that they may hear?
 See, their ears are closed,^v
 they cannot listen.
 The word of the LORD is to
 them an object of
 scorn;
 they take no pleasure in it.
11 But I am full of the wrath of
 the LORD;
 I am weary of holding it in.

 Pour it out on the children
 in the street,
 and on the gatherings of
 young men as well;
 both husband and wife shall
 be taken,
 the old folk and the very
 aged.
12 Their houses shall be turned
 over to others,
 their fields and wives
 together;
 for I will stretch out my hand
 against the inhabitants of
 the land,
 says the LORD.

13 For from the least to the
 greatest of them,
 everyone is greedy for
 unjust gain;
 and from prophet to priest,
 everyone deals falsely.
14 They have treated the wound
 of my people carelessly,
 saying, "Peace, peace,"
 when there is no peace.
15 They acted shamefully, they
 committed
 abomination;
 yet they were not ashamed,
 they did not know how to
 blush.
 Therefore they shall fall
 among those who fall;
 at the time that I punish

them, they shall be
 overthrown,
 says the LORD.

16 Thus says the LORD:
 Stand at the crossroads, and
 look,
 and ask for the ancient
 paths,
 where the good way lies; and
 walk in it,
 and find rest for your souls.
 But they said, "We will not
 walk in it."
17 Also I raised up sentinels for
 you:
 "Give heed to the sound of
 the trumpet!"
 But they said, "We will not
 give heed."
18 Therefore hear, O nations,
 and know, O congregation,
 what will happen to
 them.
19 Hear, O earth; I am going to
 bring disaster on this
 people,
 the fruit of their schemes,
 because they have not given
 heed to my words;
 and as for my teaching,
 they have rejected it.
20 Of what use to me is
 frankincense that
 comes from Sheba,
 or sweet cane from a
 distant land?
 Your burnt offerings are not
 acceptable,
 nor are your sacrifices
 pleasing to me.
21 Therefore thus says the LORD:
 See, I am laying before this
 people
 stumbling blocks against
 which they shall
 stumble;
 parents and children
 together,
 neighbor and friend shall
 perish.

22 Thus says the LORD:
 See, a people is coming from
 the land of the north,

6.9
Jer 49.9; 8.3
6.10
Jer 7.26;
Acts 7.51;
Jer 20.8
6.11
Job 32.18,
19; Jer 20.9;
9.21
6.12
Deut 28.30;
Jer 8.10;
15.6
6.13
Isa 56.11;
Jer 8.10;
22.17;
Mic 3.5,11
6.14
Jer 8.11;
Ezek 13.10;
Jer 4.10;
23.17
6.15
Jer 3.3; 8.12

6.16
Isa 8.20;
Jer 18.15;
Mal 4.4;
Lk 16.29;
Mt 11.29
6.17
Isa 21.11;
58.1;
Jer 25.4;
Ezek 3.17;
Hab 2.1
6.19
Isa 1.2;
Jer 19.3,15;
Prov 1.31;
Jer 8.9
6.20
Isa 1.11;
Am 5.21;
Mic 6.6;
Isa 60.6;
Jer 7.21
6.21
Isa 8.14;
Jer 13.16;
9.21,22
6.22
Jer 1.15;
5.15; 10.22;
50.41-43;
Neh 1.9

^u Cn: Heb *They shall glean* ^v Heb *are uncircumcised*

a great nation is stirring
from the farthest parts
of the earth.
23 They grasp the bow and the
javelin,
they are cruel and have no
mercy,
their sound is like the
roaring sea;
they ride on horses,
equipped like a warrior for
battle,
against you, O daughter
Zion!

24 "We have heard news of
them,
our hands fall helpless;
anguish has taken hold of us,
pain as of a woman in
labor.
25 Do not go out into the
field,
or walk on the road;
for the enemy has a sword,
terror is on every side."

26 O my poor people, put on
sackcloth,
and roll in ashes;
make mourning as for an
only child,
most bitter lamentation:
for suddenly the destroyer
will come upon us.

27 I have made you a tester and
a refiner[w] among my
people
so that you may know and
test their ways.
28 They are all stubbornly
rebellious,
going about with slanders;
they are bronze and iron,
all of them act corruptly.
29 The bellows blow fiercely,
the lead is consumed by
the fire;
in vain the refining goes on,
for the wicked are not
removed.
30 They are called "rejected
silver,"
for the LORD has rejected
them.

6.23
Jer 4.29;
50.42;
Isa 5.30
6.24
Jer 4.31;
13.21; 49.24;
50.43
6.25
Jer 14.18;
12.12; 20.10
6.26
Jer 4.8;
25.34;
Mic 1.10;
Zech 12.10
6.27
Jer 1.18;
15.20; 9.7
6.28
Jer 5.23;
9.4;
Ezek 22.18
6.29
Jer 15.19
6.30
Jer 7.29

7.1f
Jer 26.1,2
7.2
Jer 17.19;
2.4
7.3
Jer 18.11;
26.13
7.4
Mic 3.11
7.5
Jer 4.1,2;
22.3
7.6
Deut 6.14,
15; 8.19;
Jer 13.10
7.8
Jer 13.25
7.9
Ex 20.3;
Jer 11.13,
17; 19.4
7.10
Ezek 23.39;
Jer 32.34;
2.23,35
7.11
Mt 21.13;
Mk 11.17;
Lk 19.46
7.12
Jer 26.6;
1 Sam 4.10,
11
7.13
2 Chr 36.15;
Jer 35.17;
Isa 65.12
7.14
1 Kings 9.7;
vv. 4,12

Jeremiah Proclaims God's Judgment on the Nation

7 The word that came to Jeremiah from the LORD: [2] Stand in the gate of the LORD's house, and proclaim there this word, and say, Hear the word of the LORD, all you people of Judah, you that enter these gates to worship the LORD. [3] Thus says the LORD of hosts, the God of Israel: Amend your ways and your doings, and let me dwell with you[x] in this place. [4] Do not trust in these deceptive words: "This is[y] the temple of the LORD, the temple of the LORD, the temple of the LORD."

5 For if you truly amend your ways and your doings, if you truly act justly one with another, [6] if you do not oppress the alien, the orphan, and the widow, or shed innocent blood in this place, and if you do not go after other gods to your own hurt, [7] then I will dwell with you in this place, in the land that I gave of old to your ancestors forever and ever.

8 Here you are, trusting in deceptive words to no avail. [9] Will you steal, murder, commit adultery, swear falsely, make offerings to Baal, and go after other gods that you have not known, [10] and then come and stand before me in this house, which is called by my name, and say, "We are safe!" — only to go on doing all these abominations? [11] Has this house, which is called by my name, become a den of robbers in your sight? You know, I too am watching, says the LORD. [12] Go now to my place that was in Shiloh, where I made my name dwell at first, and see what I did to it for the wickedness of my people Israel. [13] And now, because you have done all these things, says the LORD, and when I spoke to you persistently, you did not listen, and when I called you, you did not answer, [14] therefore I will do to the house that is called by my name, in which you trust, and to the place that I

[w] Or *a fortress* [x] Or *and I will let you dwell* [y] Heb *They are*

gave to you and to your ancestors, just what I did to Shiloh. [15] And I will cast you out of my sight, just as I cast out all your kinsfolk, all the offspring of Ephraim.

The People's Disobedience

16 As for you, do not pray for this people, do not raise a cry or prayer on their behalf, and do not intercede with me, for I will not hear you. [17] Do you not see what they are doing in the towns of Judah and in the streets of Jerusalem? [18] The children gather wood, the fathers kindle fire, and the women knead dough, to make cakes for the queen of heaven; and they pour out drink offerings to other gods, to provoke me to anger. [19] Is it I whom they provoke? says the LORD. Is it not themselves, to their own hurt? [20] Therefore thus says the Lord GOD: My anger and my wrath shall be poured out on this place, on human beings and animals, on the trees of the field and the fruit of the ground; it will burn and not be quenched.

21 Thus says the LORD of hosts, the God of Israel: Add your burnt offerings to your sacrifices, and eat the flesh. [22] For in the day that I brought your ancestors out of the land of Egypt, I did not speak to them or command them concerning burnt offerings and sacrifices. [23] But this command I gave them, "Obey my voice, and I will be your God, and you shall be my people; and walk only in the way that I command you, so that it may be well with you." [24] Yet they did not obey or incline their ear, but, in the stubbornness of their evil will, they walked in their own counsels, and looked backward rather than forward. [25] From the day that your ancestors came out of the land of Egypt until this day, I have persistently sent all my servants the prophets to them, day after day; [26] yet they did not listen to me, or pay attention, but they stiffened their necks. They did worse than their ancestors did.

27 So you shall speak all these

words to them, but they will not listen to you. You shall call to them, but they will not answer you. [28] You shall say to them: This is the nation that did not obey the voice of the LORD their God, and did not accept discipline; truth has perished; it is cut off from their lips.

²⁹ Cut off your hair and throw
　　it away;
　raise a lamentation on the
　　bare heights,ᶻ
　for the LORD has rejected and
　　forsaken
　the generation that
　　provoked his wrath.

30 For the people of Judah have done evil in my sight, says the LORD; they have set their abominations in the house that is called by my name, defiling it. [31] And they go on building the high placeᵃ of Topheth, which is in the valley of the son of Hinnom, to burn their sons and their daughters in the fire— which I did not command, nor did it come into my mind. [32] Therefore, the days are surely coming, says the LORD, when it will no more be called Topheth, or the valley of the son of Hinnom, but the valley of Slaughter: for they will bury in Topheth until there is no more room. [33] The corpses of this people will be food for the birds of the air, and for the animals of the earth; and no one will frighten them away. [34] And I will bring to an end the sound of mirth and gladness, the voice of the bride and bridegroom in the cities of Judah and in the streets of Jerusalem; for the land shall become a waste.

8 At that time, says the LORD, the bones of the kings of Judah, the bones of its officials, the bones of the priests, the bones of the prophets, and the bones of the inhabitants of Jerusalem shall be brought out of their tombs; [2] and they shall be spread before the sun and the moon and all the host of heaven, which they have loved and served, which they have followed,

7.15
Jer 15.1;
2 Kings 17.23;
Ps 78.67
7.16
Ex 32.10;
Jer 11.14;
15.1
7.18
Jer 44.17;
19.13; 11.17
7.19
Deut 32.16,
21
7.20
Jer 6.11,12;
8.13; 11.16
7.21
Isa 1.11;
Am 5.21;
Hos 8.13
7.22
1 Sam 15.22;
Ps 51.16;
Hos 6.6
7.23
Ex 15.26;
Lev 26.12;
Isa 3.10
7.24
Ps 81.11,12;
Jer 15.6
7.25
Jer 25.4;
Lk 11.49
7.26
Jer 19.15;
16.12
7.27
Ezek 2.7;
3.7; Isa 50.2

7.28
Jer 6.17;
5.3; 9.5
7.29
Job 1.20;
Isa 15.2;
Jer 16.6;
Mic 1.16;
Jer 3.21;
14.19
7.30
2 Kings 21.4;
2 Chr 33.4,
5,7;
Jer 23.11;
Ezek 7.20;
Dan 9.27
7.31
2 Kings 23.10;
Jer 19.5;
Ps 106.38;
Deut 17.3
7.32
Jer 19.5,7,
11;
2 Kings 23.10
7.34
Isa 24.7,8;
Ezek 26.13;
Hos 2.11;
Rev 18.23;
Isa 1.7
8.1
Ezek 6.5

8.2 Acts 7.42; Jer 22.19

ᶻ Or *the trails*　　ᵃ Gk Tg: Heb *high places*

and which they have inquired of and worshiped; and they shall not be gathered or buried; they shall be like dung on the surface of the ground. ³Death shall be preferred to life by all the remnant that remains of this evil family in all the places where I have driven them, says the LORD of hosts.

The Blind Perversity of the Whole Nation

⁴ You shall say to them, Thus
 says the LORD:
When people fall, do they
 not get up again?
 If they go astray, do they
 not turn back?
⁵ Why then has this people[b]
 turned away
 in perpetual backsliding?
They have held fast to
 deceit,
 they have refused to return.
⁶ I have given heed and
 listened,
 but they do not speak
 honestly;
no one repents of
 wickedness,
 saying, "What have I done!"
All of them turn to their own
 course,
 like a horse plunging
 headlong into battle.
⁷ Even the stork in the
 heavens
 knows its times;
and the turtledove, swallow,
 and crane[c]
 observe the time of their
 coming;
but my people do not know
 the ordinance of the LORD.

⁸ How can you say, "We are
 wise,
 and the law of the LORD is
 with us,"
when, in fact, the false pen
 of the scribes
 has made it into a lie?
⁹ The wise shall be put to
 shame,
 they shall be dismayed and
 taken;

since they have rejected the
 word of the LORD,
 what wisdom is in them?
¹⁰ Therefore I will give their
 wives to others
 and their fields to
 conquerors,
because from the least to the
 greatest
 everyone is greedy for
 unjust gain;
from prophet to priest
 everyone deals falsely.
¹¹ They have treated the wound
 of my people carelessly,
 saying, "Peace, peace,"
 when there is no peace.
¹² They acted shamefully, they
 committed
 abomination;
 yet they were not at all
 ashamed,
 they did not know how to
 blush.
Therefore they shall fall
 among those who fall;
 at the time when I punish
 them, they shall be
 overthrown,
 says the LORD.
¹³ When I wanted to gather
 them, says the LORD,
 there are[d] no grapes on
 the vine,
 nor figs on the fig tree;
even the leaves are withered,
 and what I gave them has
 passed away from
 them.[c]

¹⁴ Why do we sit still?
 Gather together, let us go
 into the fortified cities
 and perish there;
for the LORD our God has
 doomed us to perish,
 and has given us poisoned
 water to drink,
 because we have sinned
 against the LORD.
¹⁵ We look for peace, but find
 no good,
 for a time of healing, but
 there is terror instead.

Cross references (center column)

8.3 Job 3.21; 7.15,16; Rev 9.6; Jer 23.3,8
8.4 Prov 24.16
8.5 Jer 5.6; 7.24; 5.27; 9.6
8.6 Ps 14.2; Ezek 22.30; Rev 9.20; Job 39.21-25
8.7 Isa 1.3; Song 2.12; Jer 5.4,5
8.8 Jer 4.22; Rom 2.17
8.9 Jer 6.15,19
8.10 Deut 28.30; Isa 56.11
8.11 Jer 6.14; Ezek 13.10
8.12 Jer 3.3; 6.21; 10.15
8.13 Jer 14.12; Ezek 22.20, 21; Isa 5.2; Joel 1.7; Mt 21.19
8.14 Jer 4.5; 35.11; 9.15; Mt 27.34; Jer 3.25; 14.20
8.15 Jer 14.19

b One Ms Gk: MT *this people, Jerusalem,*
c Meaning of Heb uncertain d Or *I will make an end of them, says the LORD. There are*

16 The snorting of their horses
 is heard from Dan;
 at the sound of the
 neighing of their
 stallions
 the whole land quakes.
 They come and devour the
 land and all that fills it,
 the city and those who live
 in it.
17 See, I am letting snakes
 loose among you,
 adders that cannot be
 charmed,
 and they shall bite you,
 says the Lord.

The Prophet Mourns for the People

18 My joy is gone, grief is upon
 me,
 my heart is sick.
19 Hark, the cry of my poor
 people
 from far and wide in the
 land:
 "Is the Lord not in Zion?
 Is her King not in her?"
 ("Why have they provoked
 me to anger with their
 images,
 with their foreign idols?")
20 "The harvest is past, the
 summer is ended,
 and we are not saved."
21 For the hurt of my poor
 people I am hurt,
 I mourn, and dismay has
 taken hold of me.
22 Is there no balm in Gilead?
 Is there no physician there?
 Why then has the health of
 my poor people
 not been restored?

9 [e] O that my head were a
 spring of water,
 and my eyes a fountain of
 tears,
 so that I might weep day and
 night
 for the slain of my poor
 people!
2 [f] O that I had in the desert
 a traveler's lodging place,
 that I might leave my people

and go away from them!
 For they are all adulterers,
 a band of traitors.
3 They bend their tongues like
 bows;
 they have grown strong in
 the land for falsehood,
 and not for truth;
 for they proceed from evil to
 evil,
 and they do not know me,
 says the Lord.

4 Beware of your neighbors,
 and put no trust in any of
 your kin;[g]
 for all your kin[h] are
 supplanters,
 and every neighbor goes
 around like a slanderer.
5 They all deceive their
 neighbors,
 and no one speaks the
 truth;
 they have taught their
 tongues to speak lies;
 they commit iniquity and
 are too weary to
 repent.[i]
6 Oppression upon oppression,
 deceit[j] upon deceit!
 They refuse to know me,
 says the Lord.

7 Therefore thus says the Lord
 of hosts:
 I will now refine and test
 them,
 for what else can I do with
 my sinful people?[k]
8 Their tongue is a deadly
 arrow;
 it speaks deceit through
 the mouth.
 They all speak friendly words
 to their neighbors,
 but inwardly are planning
 to lay an ambush.
9 Shall I not punish them for
 these things? says the
 Lord;

8.16
Jer 4.15;
Judg 5.22;
Jer 3.24;
10.25
8.17
Num 21.6;
Ps 58.4,5
8.19
Jer 4.16;
Isa 39.3;
Jer 14.9;
Deut 32.21;
Ps 31.6
8.21
Jer 14.17;
Joel 2.6;
Nah 2.10
8.22
Gen 37.25;
Jer 14.19;
30.13
9.1
Isa 22.4;
Lam 2.11;
Jer 6.26;
8.21,22
9.2
Isa 55.6,7;
Jer 5,7,8,11;
12.1,6

9.3
Ps 64.3;
Isa 59.4;
Jer 4.22;
1 Sam 2.12;
Hos 4.1
9.4
v. 8;
Jer 12.6;
Gen 27.35;
Jer 6.28
9.5
Mic 6.12;
Jer 12.13;
51.58,64
9.6
Jer 5.27;
11.10;
Jn 3.19,20
9.7
Isa 1.25;
Mal 3.3;
Hos 11.8
9.8
Ps 12.2;
28.3;
Jer 5.26
9.9
Jer 5.9,29

[e] Ch 8.23 in Heb [f] Ch 9.1 in Heb
[g] Heb *in a brother* [h] Heb *for every brother*
[i] Cn Compare Gk: Heb *they weary themselves
with iniquity.* [j] *Your dwelling* [j] Cn: Heb
Your dwelling in the midst of deceit
[k] Or *my poor people*

and shall I not bring
retribution
on a nation such as this?

10 Take up[1] weeping and
wailing for the
mountains,
and a lamentation for the
pastures of the
wilderness,
because they are laid waste
so that no one passes
through,
and the lowing of cattle is
not heard;
both the birds of the air and
the animals
have fled and are gone.
11 I will make Jerusalem a heap
of ruins,
a lair of jackals;
and I will make the towns of
Judah a desolation,
without inhabitant.

12 Who is wise enough to un-
derstand this? To whom has the
mouth of the LORD spoken, so that
they may declare it? Why is the
land ruined and laid waste like a
wilderness, so that no one passes
through? 13 And the LORD says: Be-
cause they have forsaken my law
that I set before them, and have not
obeyed my voice, or walked in ac-
cordance with it, 14 but have stub-
bornly followed their own hearts
and have gone after the Baals, as
their ancestors taught them.
15 Therefore thus says the LORD of
hosts, the God of Israel: I am feed-
ing this people with wormwood,
and giving them poisonous water
to drink. 16 I will scatter them
among nations that neither they
nor their ancestors have known;
and I will send the sword after
them, until I have consumed them.

The People Mourn in Judgment

17 Thus says the LORD of hosts:
Consider, and call for the
mourning women to
come;
send for the skilled women
to come;

9.10
Jer 4.24-26;
Hos 4.3;
Ezek 14.15
9.11
Isa 25.2;
13.22; 34.13;
Jer 4.27;
26.9
9.12
Ps 107.43;
Hos 14.9;
Jer 23.10,16
9.13
Jer 5.19;
Ps 89.30
9.14
Rom 1.21-24;
Gal 1.14;
1 Pet 1.18
9.15
Jer 8.14;
23.15
9.16
Lev 26.33;
Deut 28.64;
Jer 44.27;
Ezek 5.2
9.17
2 Chr 35.25;
Eccl 12.5;
Am 5.16

9.18
Jer 14.17
9.19
Jer 4.13;
7.15; 15.1
9.20
Isa 32.9
9.21
Jer 15.7;
18.21; 6.11
9.22
Jer 8.2; 16.4
9.23
Eccl 9.11;
Isa 10.8-12;
Ps 49.6-9
9.24
1 Cor 1.31;
2 Cor 10.17;
Gal 6.14;
Ps 36.5,7;
Mic 7.18
9.25
Rom 2.8,9
9.26
Jer 25.23;
Lev 26.41;
Ezek 44.7;
Rom 2.28

18 let them quickly raise a dirge
over us,
so that our eyes may run
down with tears,
and our eyelids flow with
water.
19 For a sound of wailing is
heard from Zion:
"How we are ruined!
We are utterly shamed,
because we have left the
land,
because they have cast
down our dwellings."

20 Hear, O women, the word of
the LORD,
and let your ears receive
the word of his mouth;
teach to your daughters a
dirge,
and each to her neighbor a
lament.
21 "Death has come up into our
windows,
it has entered our palaces,
to cut off the children from
the streets
and the young men from
the squares."
22 Speak! Thus says the LORD:
"Human corpses shall fall
like dung upon the open
field,
like sheaves behind the
reaper,
and no one shall gather
them."

23 Thus says the LORD: Do not
let the wise boast in their wisdom,
do not let the mighty boast in their
might, do not let the wealthy boast
in their wealth; 24 but let those who
boast boast in this, that they un-
derstand and know me, that I am
the LORD; I act with steadfast love,
justice, and righteousness in the
earth, for in these things I delight,
says the LORD.

25 The days are surely coming,
says the LORD, when I will attend to
all those who are circumcised only
in the foreskin: 26 Egypt, Judah,
Edom, the Ammonites, Moab, and

[1] Gk Syr: Heb *I will take up*

all those with shaven temples who live in the desert. For all these nations are uncircumcised, and all the house of Israel is uncircumcised in heart.

Idolatry Has Brought Ruin on Israel

10 Hear the word that the LORD speaks to you, O house of Israel. ² Thus says the LORD:

Do not learn the way of the
 nations,
 or be dismayed at the signs
 of the heavens;
for the nations are
 dismayed at them.
³ For the customs of the
 peoples are false:
a tree from the forest is cut
 down,
and worked with an ax by
 the hands of an artisan;
⁴ people deck it with silver
 and gold;
they fasten it with hammer
 and nails
so that it cannot move.
⁵ Their idols[m] are like
 scarecrows in a
 cucumber field,
and they cannot speak;
they have to be carried,
 for they cannot walk.
Do not be afraid of them,
 for they cannot do evil,
nor is it in them to do
 good.

⁶ There is none like you,
 O LORD;
you are great, and your
 name is great in might.
⁷ Who would not fear you,
 O King of the nations?
For that is your due;
among all the wise ones of
 the nations
and in all their kingdoms
 there is no one like you.
⁸ They are both stupid and
 foolish;
the instruction given by
 idols
is no better than wood![n]

⁹ Beaten silver is brought from
 Tarshish,
 and gold from Uphaz.
They are the work of the
 artisan and of the
 hands of the goldsmith;
their clothing is blue and
 purple;
they are all the product of
 skilled workers.
¹⁰ But the LORD is the true God;
he is the living God and
 the everlasting King.
At his wrath the earth
 quakes,
and the nations cannot
 endure his indignation.

11 Thus shall you say to them: The gods who did not make the heavens and the earth shall perish from the earth and from under the heavens.[o]

¹² It is he who made the earth
 by his power,
who established the world
 by his wisdom,
and by his understanding
 stretched out the
 heavens.
¹³ When he utters his voice,
 there is a tumult of
 waters in the heavens,
and he makes the mist rise
 from the ends of the
 earth.
He makes lightnings for the
 rain,
and he brings out the wind
 from his storehouses.
¹⁴ Everyone is stupid and
 without knowledge;
goldsmiths are all put to
 shame by their idols;
for their images are false,
 and there is no breath in
 them.
¹⁵ They are worthless, a work of
 delusion;
at the time of their
 punishment they shall
 perish.

10.2 Lev 18.3; Isa 47.12-14
10.3 Isa 40.19; 45.20
10.4 v. 14; Isa 41.7
10.5 Ps 115.5; 1 Cor 12.2; Isa 46.1,7; 41.23
10.6 Deut 33.26; Isa 12.6; Jer 32.18
10.7 Ps 22.28; Dan 2.27, 28; 1 Cor 1.19, 20
10.8 v. 14; Jer 4.22; 2.27
10.9 Isa 40.19; Ps 72.10; Dan 10.5; Ps 115.4
10.10 Isa 65.16; Jer 4.2; 50.46; Ps 76.7
10.11 Ps 96.5; Isa 2.18; Zeph 2.11
10.12 Jer 51.15-19; Ps 78.69; Job 9.8; Isa 40.22
10.13 Ps 29.3-9; Job 36.27-29; Ps 135.7
10.14 Jer 51.17; Isa 42.17; Hab 2.18
10.15 Jer 8.19; 51.18

[m] Heb *They* [n] Meaning of Heb uncertain
[o] This verse is in Aramaic

16 Not like these is the LORD, P
 the portion of Jacob,
for he is the one who
 formed all things,
and Israel is the tribe of his
 inheritance;
the LORD of hosts is his
 name.

The Coming Exile

17 Gather up your bundle from
 the ground,
O you who live under
 siege!
18 For thus says the LORD:
I am going to sling out the
 inhabitants of the land
at this time,
and I will bring distress on
 them,
so that they shall feel it.

19 Woe is me because of my
 hurt!
My wound is severe.
But I said, "Truly this is my
 punishment,
and I must bear it."
20 My tent is destroyed,
and all my cords are
 broken;
my children have gone from
 me,
and they are no more;
there is no one to spread my
 tent again,
and to set up my curtains.
21 For the shepherds are stupid,
and do not inquire of the
 LORD;
therefore they have not
 prospered,
and all their flock is
 scattered.

22 Hear, a noise! Listen, it is
 coming—
a great commotion from
 the land of the north
to make the cities of Judah a
 desolation,
a lair of jackals.

23 I know, O LORD, that the way
 of human beings is not
 in their control,

that mortals as they walk
 cannot direct their
 steps.
24 Correct me, O LORD, but in
 just measure;
not in your anger, or you
 will bring me to
 nothing.

25 Pour out your wrath on the
 nations that do not
 know you,
and on the peoples that do
 not call on your name;
for they have devoured
 Jacob;
they have devoured him
 and consumed him,
and have laid waste his
 habitation.

Israel and Judah Have Broken the Covenant

11 The word that came to Jeremiah from the LORD: 2 Hear the words of this covenant, and speak to the people of Judah and the inhabitants of Jerusalem. 3 You shall say to them, Thus says the LORD, the God of Israel: Cursed be anyone who does not heed the words of this covenant, 4 which I commanded your ancestors when I brought them out of the land of Egypt, from the iron-smelter, saying, Listen to my voice, and do all that I command you. So shall you be my people, and I will be your God, 5 that I may perform the oath that I swore to your ancestors, to give them a land flowing with milk and honey, as at this day. Then I answered, "So be it, LORD."

6 And the LORD said to me: Proclaim all these words in the cities of Judah, and in the streets of Jerusalem: Hear the words of this covenant and do them. 7 For I solemnly warned your ancestors when I brought them up out of the land of Egypt, warning them persistently, even to this day, saying, Obey my voice. 8 Yet they did not obey or incline their ear, but everyone walked in the stubbornness of an

10.16
Ps 73.26;
Jer 51.19;
Isa 45.7;
Deut 32.9;
Jer 31.35
10.17
Ezek 12.3-12
10.18
1 Sam 25.29;
Ezek 6.10
10.19
Jer 4.19,31;
14.17;
Mic 7.9
10.20
Jer 4.20;
31.15;
Isa 51.18
10.21
Jer 2.8; 23.2
10.22
Jer 4.15;
1.14; 9.11
10.23
Prov 20.24;
Isa 26.7

10.24
Ps 6.1
10.25
Ps 79.6,7;
Job 18.21;
Jer 8.16;
50.7,17
11.3
Deut 27.26;
Gal 3.10
11.4
Ex 24.3-8;
Deut 4.20;
1 Kings 8.51;
Jer 7.23;
24.7
11.5
Ex 13.5;
Deut 7.12;
Jer 32.22;
28.6
11.6
Jer 3.12;
v. 2;
Rom 2.13
11.7
1 Sam 8.9;
Jer 7.13,25
11.8
Jer 7.26;
Mic 7.9;
Lev 26.14-43

p Heb lacks the LORD

evil will. So I brought upon them all the words of this covenant, which I commanded them to do, but they did not.

9 And the LORD said to me: Conspiracy exists among the people of Judah and the inhabitants of Jerusalem. ¹⁰ They have turned back to the iniquities of their ancestors of old, who refused to heed my words; they have gone after other gods to serve them; the house of Israel and the house of Judah have broken the covenant that I made with their ancestors. ¹¹ Therefore, thus says the LORD, assuredly I am going to bring disaster upon them that they cannot escape; though they cry out to me, I will not listen to them. ¹² Then the cities of Judah and the inhabitants of Jerusalem will go and cry out to the gods to whom they make offerings, but they will never save them in the time of their trouble. ¹³ For your gods have become as many as your towns, O Judah; and as many as the streets of Jerusalem are the altars you have set up to shame, altars to make offerings to Baal.

14 As for you, do not pray for this people, or lift up a cry or prayer on their behalf, for I will not listen when they call to me in the time of their trouble. ¹⁵ What right has my beloved in my house, when she has done vile deeds? Can vows �q and sacrificial flesh avert your doom? Can you then exult? ¹⁶ The LORD once called you, "A green olive tree, fair with goodly fruit"; but with the roar of a great tempest he will set fire to it, and its branches will be consumed. ¹⁷ The LORD of hosts, who planted you, has pronounced evil against you, because of the evil that the house of Israel and the house of Judah have done, provoking me to anger by making offerings to Baal.

Jeremiah's Life Threatened

¹⁸ It was the LORD who made it
 known to me, and I
 knew;

11.9
Ezek 22.25;
Hos 6.9
11.10
1 Sam 15.11;
Jer 13.10;
Judg 2.11-13;
Jer 3.6-11
11.11
v. 17;
Jer 25.35;
v. 14;
Jer 14.12
11.12
Deut 32.37;
Jer 44.17
11.13
Jer 2.28;
3.24; 7.9
11.14
Ex 32.10;
v. 11;
Ps 66.18
11.15
Jer 12.7;
13.27; 4.22
11.16
Ps 52.8;
83.2;
Jer 21.14
11.17
Jer 12.2;
16.10,11;
32.27
11.18
1 Sam 23.11,
12

11.19
Isa 53.7;
Jer 18.18;
Ps 83.4;
52.5; 109.13
11.20
Jer 20.12;
Ps 7.9
11.21
Jer 12.5,6;
Am 2.12;
Jer 26.8;
38.4
11.22
Jer 21.14;
18.21
11.23
Jer 6.9;
23.12; 48.44
12.1
Jer 11.20;
Job 13.3;
Jer 5.27,28;
20.5,11
12.2
Jer 11.17;
Isa 29.13;
Ezek 33.31
12.3
Ps 139.1-4;
Jer 11.20;
17.18

 then you showed me their
 evil deeds.
¹⁹ But I was like a gentle lamb
 led to the slaughter.
And I did not know it was
 against me
 that they devised schemes,
 saying,
"Let us destroy the tree with
 its fruit,
let us cut him off from the
 land of the living,
so that his name will no
 longer be remembered!"
²⁰ But you, O LORD of hosts,
 who judge righteously,
who try the heart and the
 mind,
let me see your retribution
 upon them,
for to you I have
 committed my cause.

21 Therefore thus says the LORD concerning the people of Anathoth, who seek your life, and say, "You shall not prophesy in the name of the LORD, or you will die by our hand" — ²² therefore thus says the LORD of hosts: I am going to punish them; the young men shall die by the sword; their sons and their daughters shall die by famine; ²³ and not even a remnant shall be left of them. For I will bring disaster upon the people of Anathoth, the year of their punishment.

Jeremiah Complains to God

12 You will be in the right,
 O LORD,
when I lay charges against
 you;
but let me put my case to
 you.
Why does the way of the
 guilty prosper?
Why do all who are
 treacherous thrive?
² You plant them, and they
 take root;
 they grow and bring forth
 fruit;
you are near in their mouths
 yet far from their hearts.
³ But you, O LORD, know me;

�q Gk: Heb *Can many*

You see me and test
me — my heart is with
you.
Pull them out like sheep for
the slaughter,
and set them apart for the
day of slaughter.
4 How long will the land
mourn,
and the grass of every field
wither?
For the wickedness of those
who live in it
the animals and the birds
are swept away,
and because people said,
"He is blind to our
ways."ʳ

God Replies to Jeremiah

5 If you have raced with
foot-runners and they
have wearied you,
how will you compete with
horses?
And if in a safe land you fall
down,
how will you fare in the
thickets of the Jordan?
6 For even your kinsfolk and
your own family,
even they have dealt
treacherously with you;
they are in full cry after
you;
do not believe them,
though they speak friendly
words to you.

7 I have forsaken my house,
I have abandoned my
heritage;
I have given the beloved of
my heart
into the hands of her
enemies.
8 My heritage has become to
me
like a lion in the forest;
she has lifted up her voice
against me —
therefore I hate her.
9 Is the hyena greedyˢ for my
heritage at my
command?

Are the birds of prey all
around her?
Go, assemble all the wild
animals;
bring them to devour her.
10 Many shepherds have
destroyed my vineyard,
they have trampled down
my portion,
they have made my pleasant
portion
a desolate wilderness.
11 They have made it a
desolation;
desolate, it mourns to me.
The whole land is made
desolate,
but no one lays it to heart.
12 Upon all the bare heightsᵗ
in the desert
spoilers have come;
for the sword of the LORD
devours
from one end of the land
to the other;
no one shall be safe.
13 They have sown wheat and
have reaped thorns,
they have tired themselves
out but profit nothing.
They shall be ashamed of
theirᵘ harvests
because of the fierce anger
of the LORD.

14 Thus says the LORD concerning all my evil neighbors who touch the heritage that I have given my people Israel to inherit: I am about to pluck them up from their land, and I will pluck up the house of Judah from among them. 15 And after I have plucked them up, I will again have compassion on them, and I will bring them again to their heritage and to their land, everyone of them. 16 And then, if they will diligently learn the ways of my people, to swear by my name, "As the LORD lives," as they taught my people to swear by Baal, then they shall be built up in the midst of my people. 17 But if any nation will not listen,

12.4
Jer 9.10;
Joel 1.10-17;
Hos 4.3;
Jer 4.25
12.5
Jer 26.8;
38.4-6; 49.19;
50.44
12.6
Jer 9.4;
Ps 12.2;
Prov 26.25
12.7
Jer 7.29;
11.15;
Lam 2.1
12.8
Isa 59.13;
Hos 9.15
12.9
2 Kings 24.2;
Isa 56.9

12.10
Jer 23.1;
Isa 5.1-7;
63.18;
Jer 3.19
12.11
Jer 4.20,27;
Isa 42.25
12.12
Jer 3.2,21;
Isa 34.6;
Jer 16.5;
30.5
12.13
Lev 26.16;
Deut 28.38;
Mic 6.15;
Hag 1.6;
Jer 9.5;
17.10
12.14
Zech 2.8-10;
Deut 30.3;
Isa 11.11-16
12.15
Ezek 28.25;
Jer 48.47;
49.6,39;
Am 9.14
12.16
Isa 42.6;
Jer 4.2; 5.7;
Eph 2.20,21
12.17
Isa 60.12

ʳ Gk: Heb to our future
hyena, the bird of prey
ᵘ Heb your
ˢ Cn: Heb Is the
ᵗ Or the trails

then I will completely uproot it and destroy it, says the LORD.

The Linen Loincloth

13 Thus said the LORD to me, "Go and buy yourself a linen loincloth, and put it on your loins, but do not dip it in water." [2] So I bought a loincloth according to the word of the LORD, and put it on my loins. [3] And the word of the LORD came to me a second time, saying, [4] "Take the loincloth that you bought and are wearing, and go now to the Euphrates,[v] and hide it there in a cleft of the rock." [5] So I went, and hid it by the Euphrates,[w] as the LORD commanded me. [6] And after many days the LORD said to me, "Go now to the Euphrates,[v] and take from there the loincloth that I commanded you to hide there." [7] Then I went to the Euphrates,[v] and dug, and I took the loincloth from the place where I had hidden it. But now the loincloth was ruined; it was good for nothing.

8 Then the word of the LORD came to me: [9] Thus says the LORD: Just so I will ruin the pride of Judah and the great pride of Jerusalem. [10] This evil people, who refuse to hear my words, who stubbornly follow their own will and have gone after other gods to serve them and worship them, shall be like this loincloth, which is good for nothing. [11] For as the loincloth clings to one's loins, so I made the whole house of Israel and the whole house of Judah cling to me, says the LORD, in order that they might be for me a people, a name, a praise, and a glory. But they would not listen.

Symbol of the Wine-Jars

12 You shall speak to them this word: Thus says the LORD, the God of Israel: Every wine-jar should be filled with wine. And they will say to you, "Do you think we do not know that every wine-jar should be filled with wine?" [13] Then you shall say to them: Thus says the LORD: I

am about to fill all the inhabitants of this land—the kings who sit on David's throne, the priests, the prophets, and all the inhabitants of Jerusalem—with drunkenness. [14] And I will dash them one against another, parents and children together, says the LORD. I will not pity or spare or have compassion when I destroy them.

Exile Threatened

15 Hear and give ear; do not be haughty,
for the LORD has spoken.
16 Give glory to the LORD your God
before he brings darkness,
and before your feet stumble
on the mountains at twilight;
while you look for light,
he turns it into gloom
and makes it deep darkness.
17 But if you will not listen,
my soul will weep in secret for your pride;
my eyes will weep bitterly
and run down with tears,
because the LORD's flock
has been taken captive.

18 Say to the king and the queen mother;
"Take a lowly seat,
for your beautiful crown
has come down from your head."[x]
19 The towns of the Negeb are shut up
with no one to open them;
all Judah is taken into exile,
wholly taken into exile.

20 Lift up your eyes and see
those who come from the north.
Where is the flock that was given you,
your beautiful flock?

13.1
v. 11
13.2
Isa 20.2
13.4
Jer 51.63
13.5
Ex 39.42, 43; 40.16
13.9
Lev 26.19; vv. 15-17
13.10
Jer 9.14; 11.8; 16.12
13.11
Ex 19.5,6; Jer 7.23; 32.20; 33.9
13.13
Isa 51.17, 21; 63.6; Jer 25.27; 51.7
13.14
Jer 19.9-11; 6.21; 16.5; Isa 27.11
13.15
Prov 16.5
13.16
Ps 96.8; Isa 59.9; Jer 23.12; 2.6
13.17
Mal 2.2; Jer 9.1; 14.17; 23.1,2
13.18
2 Chr 33.12, 19; Isa 3.20; Ezek 24.17, 23
13.19
Jer 32.44; 20.4; 52.27-30
13.20
Jer 6.22; v. 17

[v] Or to Parah; Heb perath [w] Or by Parah; Heb perath [x] Gk Syr Vg: Meaning of Heb uncertain

²¹ What will you say when they
 set as head over you
 • those whom you have
 trained
 to be your allies?
Will not pangs take hold of
 you,.
like those of a woman in
 labor?
²² And if you say in your heart,
 "Why have these things
 come upon me?"
it is for the greatness of your
 iniquity
 that your skirts are lifted
 up,
and you are violated.
²³ Can Ethiopians^y change
 their skin
 or leopards their spots?
Then also you can do good
 who are accustomed to do
 evil.
²⁴ I will scatter you^z like chaff
 driven by the wind from
 the desert.
²⁵ This is your lot,
 the portion I have
 measured out to you,
 says the LORD,
because you have forgotten
 me
 and trusted in lies.
²⁶ I myself will lift up your
 skirts over your face,
and your shame will be
 seen.
²⁷ I have seen your
 abominations,
 your adulteries and
 neighings, your
 shameless prostitutions
on the hills of the
 countryside.
Woe to you, O Jerusalem!
 How long will it be
before you are made clean?

The Great Drought

14 The word of the LORD that
came to Jeremiah concern-
ing the drought:
² Judah mourns
 and her gates languish;
they lie in gloom on the
 ground,

13.21
Jer 5.31;
2.25; 4.31
13.22
Deut 7.17;
Jer 5.19;
16.10
13.23
Prov 27.22;
Jer 4.22
13.24
Jer 9.16;
4.11; 18.17
13.25
Ps 11.6;
Jer 2.32;
3.21
13.26
Ezek 16.37;
Hos 2.10
13.27
Jer 5.7,8;
11.15; 2.20;
4.14;
Hos 8.5
14.1
Jer 17.8
14.2
Isa 3.26;
Jer 8.21;
11.11; 46.12

14.3
1 Kings 18.5;
2 Kings 18.31;
2 Sam 15.30
14.4
Joel 1.19,
20; Jer 3.3;
Joel 1.11
14.5
Isa 15.6
14.6
Jer 2.24;
Joel 1.18
14.7
Isa 59.12;
Jer 5.6; 8.5
14.8
Jer 17.13;
Isa 43.3;
63.8;
Ps 50.15
14.9
Isa 50.2;
Jer 8.19;
15.16;
Isa 63.19

and the cry of Jerusalem
 goes up.
³ Her nobles send their
 servants for water;
they come to the cisterns,
they find no water,
 they return with their
 vessels empty.
They are ashamed and
 dismayed
and cover their heads,
⁴ because the ground is
 cracked.
Because there has been no
 rain on the land
the farmers are dismayed;
 they cover their heads.
⁵ Even the doe in the field
 forsakes her newborn
 fawn
because there is no grass.
⁶ The wild asses stand on the
 bare heights,^a
 they pant for air like
 jackals;
their eyes fail
 because there is no
 herbage.

⁷ Although our iniquities
 testify against us,
 act, O LORD, for your
 name's sake;
our apostasies indeed are
 many,
 and we have sinned against
 you.
⁸ O hope of Israel,
 its savior in time of
 trouble,
why should you be like a
 stranger in the land,
like a traveler turning aside
 for the night?
⁹ Why should you be like
 someone confused,
like a mighty warrior who
 cannot give help?
Yet you, O LORD, are in the
 midst of us,
and we are called by your
 name;
 do not forsake us!

^y Or *Nubians*; Heb *Cushites* ^z Heb *them*
^a Or *the trails*

10 Thus says the Lord
 concerning this people:
 Truly they have loved to
 wander,
 they have not restrained
 their feet;
 therefore the Lord does not
 accept them,
 now he will remember their
 iniquity
 and punish their sins.

11 The Lord said to me: Do not
pray for the welfare of this people.
12 Although they fast, I do not hear
their cry, and although they offer
burnt offering and grain offering, I
do not accept them; but by the
sword, by famine, and by pesti-
lence I consume them.

Denunciation of Lying Prophets

13 Then I said: "Ah, Lord God!
Here are the prophets saying to
them, 'You shall not see the sword,
nor shall you have famine, but I
will give you true peace in this
place.' " 14 And the Lord said to me:
The prophets are prophesying lies
in my name; I did not send them,
nor did I command them or speak
to them. They are prophesying to
you a lying vision, worthless divina-
tion, and the deceit of their own
minds. 15 Therefore thus says the
Lord concerning the prophets who
prophesy in my name though I did
not send them, and who say,
"Sword and famine shall not come
on this land": By sword and famine
those prophets shall be consumed.
16 And the people to whom they
prophesy shall be thrown out into
the streets of Jerusalem, victims of
famine and sword. There shall be
no one to bury them—themselves,
their wives, their sons, and their
daughters. For I will pour out their
wickedness upon them.

17 You shall say to them this
word:
 Let my eyes run down with
 tears night and day,
 and let them not cease,

for the virgin daughter—my
 people—is struck down
 with a crushing blow,
 with a very grievous wound.
18 If I go out into the field,
 look—those killed by the
 sword!
 And if I enter the city,
 look—those sick with[b]
 famine!
 For both prophet and priest
 ply their trade
 throughout the land,
 and have no knowledge.

The People Plead for Mercy

19 Have you completely rejected
 Judah?
 Does your heart loathe
 Zion?
 Why have you struck us
 down
 so that there is no healing
 for us?
 We look for peace, but find
 no good;
 for a time of healing, but
 there is terror instead.
20 We acknowledge our
 wickedness, O Lord,
 the iniquity of our
 ancestors,
 for we have sinned against
 you.
21 Do not spurn us, for your
 name's sake;
 do not dishonor your
 glorious throne;
 remember and do not
 break your covenant
 with us.
22 Can any idols of the nations
 bring rain?
 Or can the heavens give
 showers?
 Is it not you, O Lord our
 God?
 We set our hope on you,
 for it is you who do all this.

Punishment Is Inevitable

15 Then the Lord said to me:
Though Moses and Samuel
stood before me, yet my heart
would not turn toward this people.

[b] Heb look—the sicknesses of

Send them out of my sight, and let them go! ² And when they say to you, "Where shall we go?" you shall say to them: Thus says the LORD:
Those destined for
pestilence, to
pestilence,
and those destined for the
sword, to the sword;
those destined for famine, to
famine,
and those destined for
captivity, to captivity.
³ And I will appoint over them four kinds of destroyers, says the LORD: the sword to kill, the dogs to drag away, and the birds of the air and the wild animals of the earth to devour and destroy. ⁴ I will make them a horror to all the kingdoms of the earth because of what King Manasseh son of Hezekiah of Judah did in Jerusalem.

⁵ Who will have pity on you,
O Jerusalem,
or who will bemoan you?
Who will turn aside
to ask about your welfare?
⁶ You have rejected me, says
the LORD,
you are going backward;
so I have stretched out my
hand against you and
destroyed you—
I am weary of relenting.
⁷ I have winnowed them with
a winnowing fork
in the gates of the land;
I have bereaved them, I have
destroyed my people;
they did not turn from
their ways.
⁸ Their widows became more
numerous
than the sand of the seas;
I have brought against the
mothers of youths
a destroyer at noonday;
I have made anguish and
terror
fall upon her suddenly.
⁹ She who bore seven has
languished;
she has swooned away;
her sun went down while it
was yet day;

she has been shamed and
disgraced.
And the rest of them I will
give to the sword
before their enemies,
says the LORD.

Jeremiah Complains Again and Is Reassured

10 Woe is me, my mother, that you ever bore me, a man of strife and contention to the whole land! I have not lent, nor have I borrowed, yet all of them curse me. ¹¹ The LORD said: Surely I have intervened in your life[c] for good, surely I have imposed enemies on you in a time of trouble and in a time of distress.[d] ¹² Can iron and bronze break iron from the north?

13 Your wealth and your treasures I will give as plunder, without price, for all your sins, throughout all your territory. ¹⁴ I will make you serve your enemies in a land that you do not know, for in my anger a fire is kindled that shall burn forever.
¹⁵ O LORD, you know;
remember me and visit me,
and bring down retribution
for me on my
persecutors.
In your forbearance do not
take me away;
know that on your account
I suffer insult.
¹⁶ Your words were found, and I
ate them,
and your words became to
me a joy
and the delight of my
heart;
for I am called by your
name,
O LORD, God of hosts.
¹⁷ I did not sit in the company
of merrymakers,
nor did I rejoice;
under the weight of your
hand I sat alone,
for you had filled me with
indignation.
¹⁸ Why is my pain unceasing,

Cross references

15.2
Jer 43.11;
Ezek 5.2,12;
Zech 11.9
15.3
Lev 26.16;
1 Kings 21.23,
24;
Deut 28.26;
Jer 7.33
15.4
Deut 28.25;
2 Kings 21.11ff;
23.26
15.5
Ps 69.20;
Isa 51.19;
Jer 16.5
15.6
Jer 6.19;
7.24; 6.11,12;
7.16
15.7
Jer 51.2;
18.21; 5.3
15.8
Isa 3.25,26;
Jer 22.7; 6.4
15.9
1 Sam 2.5;
Isa 47.9;
Jer 6.4;
Am 8.9;
Jer 50.12;
21.7

15.10
Job 3.1;
Jer 20.14;
Deut 23.19
15.11
Isa 41.10;
Jer 39.11,
12; 40.4,5
15.12
Jer 28.14
15.13
Ps 44.12;
Jer 17.3;
Isa 52.3,5
15.14
Jer 16.13;
17.4;
Deut 32.22
15.15
Jer 12.3;
20.11;
Ps 69.7-9
15.16
Ezek 3.1-3;
Ps 119.72;
Jer 14.9
15.17
Jer 16.8;
Ezek 3.24,
25
15.18
Jer 30.15;
Mic 1.9;
Jer 14.3

c Heb *intervened with you* d Meaning of Heb uncertain

my wound incurable,
 refusing to be healed?
Truly, you are to me like a
 deceitful brook,
 like waters that fail.

19 Therefore thus says the Lord:
 If you turn back, I will take
 you back,
 and you shall stand before
 me.
 If you utter what is precious,
 and not what is
 worthless,
 you shall serve as my
 mouth.
 It is they who will turn to
 you,
 not you who will turn to
 them.
20 And I will make you to this
 people
 a fortified wall of bronze;
 they will fight against you,
 but they shall not prevail
 over you,
 for I am with you
 to save you and deliver
 you,
 says the Lord.
21 I will deliver you out of the
 hand of the wicked,
 and redeem you from the
 grasp of the ruthless.

Jeremiah's Celibacy and Message

16 The word of the Lord came
 to me: 2 You shall not take
a wife, nor shall you have sons or
daughters in this place. 3 For thus
says the Lord concerning the sons
and daughters who are born in this
place, and concerning the mothers
who bear them and the fathers who
beget them in this land: 4 They
shall die of deadly diseases. They
shall not be lamented, nor shall
they be buried; they shall become
like dung on the surface of the
ground. They shall perish by the
sword and by famine, and their
dead bodies shall become food for
the birds of the air and for the wild
animals of the earth.

5 For thus says the Lord: Do not
enter the house of mourning, or go

15.19
Jer 4.1;
Ezek 22.26
15.20
Jer 1.18,19;
20.11;
Isa 41.10
15.21
Jer 20.13;
31.11
16.1
Jer 1.2,4
16.2
1 Cor 7.26
16.3
Jer 6.11;
15.8; 6.21
16.4
Ps 83.10;
Jer 9.22;
15.3; 34.20
16.5
Ezek 24.16-23;
Jer 12.12;
13.14

16.6
Ezek 9.6;
Jer 41.5;
47.5
16.7
Ezek 24.17;
Hos 9.4
16.8
Jer 15.17
16.9
Jer 7.34;
25.10;
Hos 2.11;
Rev 18.23
16.10
Deut 29.24;
1 Kings 9.8,
9; Jer 5.19
16.11
Jer 22.9;
Ezek 11.21;
1 Pet 4.3
16.12
Jer 7.26;
13.10;
Eccl 9.3
16.13
Deut 4.26-28;
28.36;
Jer 15.4;
5.19
16.14
Isa 43.18;
Jer 23.7,8;
Ex 20.2
16.15
Ps 106.47;
Isa 11.11-16;
Jer 24.6

to lament, or bemoan them; for I
have taken away my peace from
this people, says the Lord, my
steadfast love and mercy. 6 Both
great and small shall die in this
land; they shall not be buried, and
no one shall lament for them; there
shall be no gashing, no shaving of
the head for them. 7 No one shall
break bread[e] for the mourner, to
offer comfort for the dead; nor shall
anyone give them the cup of conso-
lation to drink for their fathers or
their mothers. 8 You shall not go
into the house of feasting to sit
with them, to eat and drink. 9 For
thus says the Lord of hosts, the
God of Israel: I am going to banish
from this place, in your days and
before your eyes, the voice of mirth
and the voice of gladness, the voice
of the bridegroom and the voice of
the bride.

10 And when you tell this peo-
ple all these words, and they say to
you, "Why has the Lord pro-
nounced all this great evil against
us? What is our iniquity? What is
the sin that we have committed
against the Lord our God?" 11 then
you shall say to them: It is because
your ancestors have forsaken me,
says the Lord, and have gone after
other gods and have served and
worshiped them, and have forsak-
en me and have not kept my law;
12 and because you have behaved
worse than your ancestors, for here
you are, everyone of you, following
your stubborn evil will, refusing to
listen to me. 13 Therefore I will hurl
you out of this land into a land that
neither you nor your ancestors
have known, and there you shall
serve other gods day and night, for
I will show you no favor.

God Will Restore Israel

14 Therefore, the days are sure-
ly coming, says the Lord, when it
shall no longer be said, "As the
Lord lives who brought the people
of Israel up out of the land of
Egypt," 15 but "As the Lord lives
who brought the people of Israel up
out of the land of the north and out

e Two Mss Gk: MT *break for them*

of all the lands where he had driven them." For I will bring them back to their own land that I gave to their ancestors.

16 I am now sending for many fishermen, says the LORD, and they shall catch them; and afterward I will send for many hunters, and they shall hunt them from every mountain and every hill, and out of the clefts of the rocks. [17] For my eyes are on all their ways; they are not hidden from my presence, nor is their iniquity concealed from my sight. [18] And[f] I will doubly repay their iniquity and their sin, because they have polluted my land with the carcasses of their detestable idols, and have filled my inheritance with their abominations.

[19] O LORD, my strength and my
 stronghold,
 my refuge in the day of
 trouble,
to you shall the nations
 come
 from the ends of the earth
 and say:
Our ancestors have inherited
 nothing but lies,
 worthless things in which
 there is no profit.
[20] Can mortals make for
 themselves gods?
 Such are no gods!

21 "Therefore I am surely going to teach them, this time I am going to teach them my power and my might, and they shall know that my name is the LORD."

Judah's Sin and Punishment

17 The sin of Judah is written with an iron pen; with a diamond point it is engraved on the tablet of their hearts, and on the horns of their altars, [2] while their children remember their altars and their sacred poles,[g] beside every green tree, and on the high hills, [3] on the mountains in the open country. Your wealth and all your treasures I will give for spoil as the price of your sin[h] throughout all

your territory. [4] By your own act you shall lose the heritage that I gave you, and I will make you serve your enemies in a land that you do not know, for in my anger a fire is kindled[i] that shall burn forever.

[5] Thus says the LORD:
Cursed are those who trust
 in mere mortals
 and make mere flesh their
 strength,
 whose hearts turn away
 from the LORD.
[6] They shall be like a shrub in
 the desert,
 and shall not see when
 relief comes.
They shall live in the
 parched places of the
 wilderness,
 in an uninhabited salt
 land.

[7] Blessed are those who trust
 in the LORD,
 whose trust is the LORD.
[8] They shall be like a tree
 planted by water,
 sending out its roots by the
 stream.
It shall not fear when heat
 comes,
 and its leaves shall stay
 green;
in the year of drought it is
 not anxious,
 and it does not cease to
 bear fruit.

[9] The heart is devious above
 all else;
 it is perverse—
 who can understand it?
[10] I the LORD test the mind
 and search the heart,
 to give to all according to
 their ways,
 according to the fruit of
 their doings.

[11] Like the partridge hatching
 what it did not lay,

16.16
Am 4.2;
Hab 1.14,
15; Mic 7.2;
Isa 2.21
16.17
Ps 90.8;
1 Cor 4.5;
Heb 4.13;
Jer 2.22
16.18
Rev 18.6;
Ezek 11.18,
21
16.19
Jer 15.11;
Ps 14.6;
Hab 2.18,19
16.20
Isa 37.19;
Jer 2.11;
Gal 4.8
16.21
Ps 9.16;
Jer 33.2;
Am 5.8
17.1
Jer 2.22;
Job 19.24;
Prov 3.3;
2 Cor 3.3
17.2
Jer 7.18;
Ex 34.13;
Jer 3.6
17.3
Jer 26.18;
15.13
17.4
Jer 12.7;
15.14; 7.20
17.5
Isa 30.1-3;
2 Chr 32.8
17.6
Jer 48.6;
Deut 29.23
17.7
Ps 34.8;
84.12; 40.4;
Prov 16.20
17.8
Ps 1.3;
Jer 14.1-6
17.9
Mk 7.21,22;
Rom 7.11;
Eph 4.22
17.10
1 Sam 16.7;
Jer 11.20;
20.12;
Rom 8.27;
Jer 32.19;
Rom 2.6
17.11
Jer 6.13;
8.10; 22.13,
17

f Gk: Heb And first g Heb Asherim
h Cn: Heb spoil your high places for sin
i Two Mss Theodotion: you kindled

so are all who amass
wealth unjustly;
in mid-life it will leave them,
and at their end they will
prove to be fools.

12 O glorious throne, exalted
from the beginning,
shrine of our sanctuary!
13 O hope of Israel! O LORD!
All who forsake you shall
be put to shame;
those who turn away from
you[j] shall be recorded
in the underworld,[k]
for they have forsaken the
fountain of living water,
the LORD.

Jeremiah Prays for Vindication

14 Heal me, O LORD, and I shall
be healed;
save me, and I shall be
saved;
for you are my praise.
15 See how they say to me,
"Where is the word of the
LORD?
Let it come!"
16 But I have not run away from
being a shepherd[l] in
your service,
nor have I desired the fatal
day.
You know what came from
my lips;
it was before your face.
17 Do not become a terror to
me;
you are my refuge in the
day of disaster;
18 Let my persecutors be
shamed,
but do not let me be
shamed;
let them be dismayed,
but do not let me be
dismayed;
bring on them the day of
disaster;
destroy them with double
destruction!

Hallow the Sabbath Day

19 Thus said the LORD to me: Go
and stand in the People's Gate, by

which the kings of Judah enter and
by which they go out, and in all the
gates of Jerusalem, 20 and say to
them: Hear the word of the LORD,
you kings of Judah, and all Judah,
and all the inhabitants of Jerusa-
lem, who enter by these gates.
21 Thus says the LORD: For the sake
of your lives, take care that you do
not bear a burden on the sabbath
day or bring it in by the gates of
Jerusalem. 22 And do not carry a
burden out of your houses on the
sabbath or do any work, but keep
the sabbath day holy, as I com-
manded your ancestors. 23 Yet they
did not listen or incline their ear;
they stiffened their necks and
would not hear or receive instruc-
tion.

24 But if you listen to me, says
the LORD, and bring in no burden by
the gates of this city on the sabbath
day, but keep the sabbath day holy
and do no work on it, 25 then there
shall enter by the gates of this city
kings[m] who sit on the throne of Da-
vid, riding in chariots and on
horses, they and their officials, the
people of Judah and the inhabi-
tants of Jerusalem; and this city
shall be inhabited forever. 26 And
people shall come from the towns
of Judah and the places around Je-
rusalem, from the land of Benja-
min, from the Shephelah, from the
hill country, and from the Negeb,
bringing burnt offerings and sacri-
fices, grain offerings and frankin-
cense, and bringing thank offerings
to the house of the LORD. 27 But if
you do not listen to me, to keep the
sabbath day holy, and to carry in no
burden through the gates of Jeru-
salem on the sabbath day, then I
will kindle a fire in its gates; it shall
devour the palaces of Jerusalem
and shall not be quenched.

The Potter and the Clay

18 The word that came to Jer-
emiah from the LORD:
2 "Come, go down to the potter's

17.12 Jer 3.17; 14.21
17.13 Jer 14.8; Ps 73.27; Isa 1.28; Jer 2.13,17
17.14 Jer 30.17; Ps 54.1; Deut 10.21; Ps 109.1
17.15 Isa 5.19; Am 5.18
17.16 Jer 1.6; 12.3
17.17 Ps 88.15; Jer 16.19
17.18 Ps 35.4,26; 35.8; Jer 16.18
17.19 Jer 7.2; 26.2
17.20 Jer 19.3; 22.2; Hos 5.1
17.21 Deut 4.9,15, 23; Num 15.32-36; Neh 13.15-21
17.22 Ex 20.8; 23.12; 31.13; Ezek 20.12
17.23 Jer 7.24,26; 11.10; 19.15
17.24 Deut 11.13; Ex 20.8-11; Ezek 20.20
17.25 Jer 22.4; Isa 9.7; Lk 1.32; Heb 12.22
17.26 Zech 7.7; Ps 107.22
17.27 Jer 22.5; Isa 9.18,19; Jer 11.16; Am 2.5; 7.20
18.2 Jer 19.1,2; 23.22

i Heb *me* k Or *in the earth* l Meaning
of Heb uncertain m Cn: Heb *kings and
officials*

house, and there I will let you hear my words." ³ So I went down to the potter's house, and there he was working at his wheel. ⁴ The vessel he was making of clay was spoiled in the potter's hand, and he reworked it into another vessel, as seemed good to him.

5 Then the word of the LORD came to me: ⁶ Can I not do with you, O house of Israel, just as this potter has done? says the LORD. Just like the clay in the potter's hand, so are you in my hand, O house of Israel. ⁷ At one moment I may declare concerning a nation or a kingdom, that I will pluck up and break down and destroy it, ⁸ but if that nation, concerning which I have spoken, turns from its evil, I will change my mind about the disaster that I intended to bring on it. ⁹ And at another moment I may declare concerning a nation or a kingdom that I will build and plant it, ¹⁰ but if it does evil in my sight, not listening to my voice, then I will change my mind about the good that I had intended to do to it. ¹¹ Now, therefore, say to the people of Judah and the inhabitants of Jerusalem: Thus says the LORD: Look, I am a potter shaping evil against you and devising a plan against you. Turn now, all of you from your evil way, and amend your ways and your doings.

Israel's Stubborn Idolatry

12 But they say, "It is no use! We will follow our own plans, and each of us will act according to the stubbornness of our evil will."

13 Therefore thus says the LORD:
Ask among the nations:
 Who has heard the like of
 this?
The virgin Israel has done
 a most horrible thing.
14 Does the snow of Lebanon
 leave
 the crags of Sirion?ⁿ
Do the mountainº waters
 run dry,ᵖ
 the cold flowing streams?

15 But my people have
 forgotten me,
 they burn offerings to a
 delusion;
they have stumbled�q in their
 ways,
 in the ancient roads,
and have gone into bypaths,
 not the highway,
16 making their land a horror,
 a thing to be hissed at
 forever.
All who pass by it are
 horrified
 and shake their heads.
17 Like the wind from the east,
 I will scatter them before
 the enemy.
I will show them my back,
 not my face,
 in the day of their
 calamity.

A Plot against Jeremiah

18 Then they said, "Come, let us make plots against Jeremiah — for instruction shall not perish from the priest, nor counsel from the wise, nor the word from the prophet. Come, let us bring charges against him,ʳ and let us not heed any of his words."

19 Give heed to me, O LORD,
 and listen to what my
 adversaries say!
20 Is evil a recompense for
 good?
 Yet they have dug a pit for
 my life.
Remember how I stood
 before you
 to speak good for them,
 to turn away your wrath
 from them.
21 Therefore give their children
 over to famine;
 hurl them out to the power
 of the sword,
let their wives become
 childless and widowed.
May their men meet death
 by pestilence,

18.6
Isa 45.9;
Mt 20.15;
Rom 9.20,
21
18.7
Jer 1.10
18.8
Ezek 18.21;
Jer 26.3;
Jon 3.10
18.9
Jer 1.10;
31.28
18.10
Jer 7.24-28;
Ezek 33.18
18.11
Jer 4.6;
2 Kings 17.13;
Isa 1.16-19;
Acts 26.20
18.12
Jer 2.25;
7.24; 16.12
18.13
Jer 2.10,11;
14.17; 5.30;
23.14
18.15
Isa 65.7;
Jer 7.9;
6.16;
Isa 57.14;
62.10
18.16
Jer 25.9;
50.13; 48.27
18.17
Job 27.21;
Jer 13.24;
2.27; 46.21
18.18
Jer 11.19;
Mal 2.7;
Jer 8.8;
5.13; 20.10;
43.2
18.20
Ps 35.7;
57.6; 106.23
18.21
Ps 109.9,10;
Isa 13.18;
Jer 15.8;
Ezek 22.25;
Jer 9.21;
11.22

ⁿ Cn: Heb *of the field* º Cn: Heb *foreign*
ᵖ Cn: Heb *Are . . . plucked up?* q Gk Syr
Vg: Heb *they made them stumble*
ʳ Heb *strike him with the tongue*

their youths be slain by the
 sword in battle.
22 May a cry be heard from
 their houses,
 when you bring the
 marauder suddenly
 upon them!
 For they have dug a pit to
 catch me,
 and laid snares for my feet.
23 Yet you, O LORD, know
 all their plotting to kill me.
 Do not forgive their iniquity,
 do not blot out their sin
 from your sight.
 Let them be tripped up
 before you;
 deal with them while you
 are angry.

The Broken Earthenware Jug

19 Thus said the LORD: Go and
 buy a potter's earthenware
jug. Take with you[s] some of the el-
ders of the people and some of the
senior priests, 2 and go out to the
valley of the son of Hinnom at
the entry of the Potsherd Gate, and
proclaim there the words that I tell
you. 3 You shall say: Hear the word
of the LORD, O kings of Judah and
inhabitants of Jerusalem. Thus
says the LORD of hosts, the God of
Israel: I am going to bring such di-
saster upon this place that the ears
of everyone who hears of it will tin-
gle. 4 Because the people have for-
saken me, and have profaned this
place by making offerings in it to
other gods whom neither they nor
their ancestors nor the kings of Ju-
dah have known; and because they
have filled this place with the
blood of the innocent, 5 and gone
on building the high places of Baal
to burn their children in the fire as
burnt offerings to Baal, which I did
not command or decree, nor did it
enter my mind. 6 Therefore the
days are surely coming, says the
LORD, when this place shall no
more be called Topheth, or the val-
ley of the son of Hinnom, but the
valley of Slaughter. 7 And in this
place I will make void the plans of
Judah and Jerusalem, and will
make them fall by the sword before

their enemies, and by the hand of
those who seek their life. I will give
their dead bodies for food to the
birds of the air and to the wild ani-
mals of the earth. 8 And I will make
this city a horror, a thing to be
hissed at; everyone who passes by
it will be horrified and will hiss be-
cause of all its disasters. 9 And I will
make them eat the flesh of their
sons and the flesh of their daugh-
ters, and all shall eat the flesh of
their neighbors in the siege, and in
the distress with which their ene-
mies and those who seek their life
afflict them.

10 Then you shall break the jug
in the sight of those who go with
you, 11 and shall say to them: Thus
says the LORD of hosts: So will I
break this people and this city, as
one breaks a potter's vessel, so that
it can never be mended. In To-
pheth they shall bury until there is
no more room to bury. 12 Thus will
I do to this place, says the LORD,
and to its inhabitants, making this
city like Topheth. 13 And the
houses of Jerusalem and the
houses of the kings of Judah shall
be defiled like the place of
Topheth—all the houses upon
whose roofs offerings have been
made to the whole host of heaven,
and libations have been poured out
to other gods.

14 When Jeremiah came from
Topheth, where the LORD had sent
him to prophesy, he stood in the
court of the LORD's house and said
to all the people: 15 Thus says the
LORD of hosts, the God of Israel: I
am now bringing upon this city and
upon all its towns all the disaster
that I have pronounced against it,
because they have stiffened their
necks, refusing to hear my words.

Jeremiah Persecuted by Pashhur

20 Now the priest Pashhur
 son of Immer, who was
chief officer in the house of the
LORD, heard Jeremiah prophesying
these things. 2 Then Pashhur struck
the prophet Jeremiah, and put him
in the stocks that were in the upper

18.22
Jer 6.26;
Ps 140.5
18.23
Ps 109.14;
Isa 2.9;
Jer 6.15,21;
7.20
19.1
Jer 18.2;
v. 10;
Num 11.16;
2 Kings 19.2
19.2
Josh 15.8;
Jer 7.31
19.3
Jer 17.20;
1 Sam 3.11;
4.18
19.4
Deut 28.20;
Isa 65.11;
2 Kings 21.16;
Jer 2.34
19.5
Jer 32.35;
2 Kings 17.17;
Lev 18.21
19.6
Jer 7.32;
Josh 15.8
19.7
Jer 15.2,9;
Ps 79.2;
Jer 16.4

19.8
Jer 18.16;
49.13;
1 Kings 9.8;
2 Chr 7.21
19.9
Deut 28.53,
55; Isa 9.20;
Lam 4.10
19.10
v. 1
19.11
Ps 2.9;
Isa 30.14;
Rev 2.27;
Jer 7.32
19.13
Jer 52.13;
7.18;
Ezek 20.28;
Acts 7.42
19.14
Jer 26.2
19.15
Jer 7.26;
17.23;
Ps 58.4
20.1
1 Chr 24.14;
2 Kings 25.18
20.2
Jer 1.19;
Job 13.27;
Jer 37.13;
38.7

s Syr Tg Compare Gk: Heb lacks *take with you*

Benjamin Gate of the house of the LORD. ³ The next morning when Pashhur released Jeremiah from the stocks, Jeremiah said to him, The LORD has named you not Pashhur but "Terror-all-around." ⁴ For thus says the LORD: I am making you a terror to yourself and to all your friends; and they shall fall by the sword of their enemies while you look on. And I will give all Judah into the hand of the king of Babylon; he shall carry them captive to Babylon, and shall kill them with the sword. ⁵ I will give all the wealth of this city, all its gains, all its prized belongings, and all the treasures of the kings of Judah into the hand of their enemies, who shall plunder them, and seize them, and carry them to Babylon. ⁶ And you, Pashhur, and all who live in your house, shall go into captivity, and to Babylon you shall go; there you shall die, and there you shall be buried, you and all your friends, to whom you have prophesied falsely.

Jeremiah Denounces His Persecutors

⁷ O LORD, you have enticed
 me,
 and I was enticed;
you have overpowered me,
 and you have prevailed.
I have become a
 laughingstock all day
 long;
 everyone mocks me.
⁸ For whenever I speak, I must
 cry out,
 I must shout, "Violence
 and destruction!"
For the word of the LORD has
 become for me
 a reproach and derision all
 day long.
⁹ If I say, "I will not mention
 him,
 or speak any more in his
 name,"
then within me there is
 something like a
 burning fire
 shut up in my bones;

I am weary with holding it
 in,
 and I cannot.
¹⁰ For I hear many whispering:
 "Terror is all around!
Denounce him! Let us
 denounce him!"
 All my close friends
 are watching for me to
 stumble.
"Perhaps he can be enticed,
 and we can prevail against
 him,
 and take our revenge on
 him."
¹¹ But the LORD is with me like
 a dread warrior;
therefore my persecutors
 will stumble,
 and they will not prevail.
They will be greatly shamed,
 for they will not succeed.
Their eternal dishonor
 will never be forgotten.
¹² O LORD of hosts, you test the
 righteous,
 you see the heart and the
 mind;
let me see your retribution
 upon them,
 for to you I have
 committed my cause.

¹³ Sing to the LORD;
 praise the LORD!
For he has delivered the life
 of the needy
 from the hands of
 evildoers.

¹⁴ Cursed be the day
 on which I was born!
The day when my mother
 bore me,
 let it not be blessed!
¹⁵ Cursed be the man
 who brought the news to
 my father, saying,
"A child is born to you, a
 son,"
 making him very glad.
¹⁶ Let that man be like the
 cities
 that the LORD overthrew
 without pity;
 let him hear a cry in the
 morning

Cross references

20.3
v. 10
20.4
Job 18.11-21;
Jer 29.21;
21.4-10;
52.27
20.5
Jer 15.13;
17.3;
2 Kings 20.17;
2 Chr 36.10;
Jer 3.24
20.6
v. 1;
Jer 28.15-17;
14.13-15;
29.21
20.7
Jer 1.6-8;
Mic 3.8;
Jer 38.19
20.8
Jer 6.7,10;
2 Chr 36.16
20.9
1 Kings 19.3,
4; Ps 39.3;
Job 32.18-20;
Acts 4.20
20.10
Ps 31.13;
41.9;
Lk 11.53,54
20.11
Jer 1.8,19;
15.20; 17.18;
23.40
20.12
Jer 11.20;
17.10;
Ps 54.7;
59.10
20.13
Jer 31.7;
Ps 35.9,10;
Jer 15.21
20.14
Job 3.3;
Jer 15.10
20.15
Gen 21.6,7
20.16
Gen 19.25;
Jer 18.22

and an alarm at noon,
17 because he did not kill me in
 the womb;
 so my mother would have
 been my grave,
 and her womb forever
 great.
18 Why did I come forth from
 the womb
 to see toil and sorrow,
 and spend my days in
 shame?

Jerusalem Will Fall to Nebuchadrezzar

21 This is the word that came to Jeremiah from the LORD, when King Zedekiah sent to him Pashhur son of Malchiah and the priest Zephaniah son of Maaseiah, saying, 2 "Please inquire of the LORD on our behalf, for King Nebuchadrezzar of Babylon is making war against us; perhaps the LORD will perform a wonderful deed for us, as he has often done, and will make him withdraw from us."

3 Then Jeremiah said to them: 4 Thus you shall say to Zedekiah: Thus says the LORD, the God of Israel: I am going to turn back the weapons of war that are in your hands and with which you are fighting against the king of Babylon and against the Chaldeans who are besieging you outside the walls; and I will bring them together into the center of this city. 5 I myself will fight against you with outstretched hand and mighty arm, in anger, in fury, and in great wrath. 6 And I will strike down the inhabitants of this city, both human beings and animals; they shall die of a great pestilence. 7 Afterward, says the LORD, I will give King Zedekiah of Judah, and his servants, and the people in this city — those who survive the pestilence, sword, and famine — into the hands of King Nebuchadrezzar of Babylon, into the hands of their enemies, into the hands of those who seek their lives. He shall strike them down with the edge of the sword; he shall

20.17
Job 3.10,11;
10.18,19
20.18
Job 3.20;
Ps 90.9;
Jer 3.25
21.1
2 Kings 24.17,
18; Jer 38.1;
2 Kings 25.18;
Jer 29.25;
37.3
21.2
Jer 37.3,7
21.4
Zech 14.2
21.5
Isa 63.10;
Jer 32.37
21.6
Jer 7.20;
14.12
21.7
Jer 37.17;
39.5; 52.9;
13.14
21.8
Deut 30.15,
19
21.9
Jer 38.2,17,
18; 14.12;
39.18; 45.5
21.10
Jer 44.11,
27; 39.16;
32.28,29;
38.18,23;
52.13
21.11
Jer 13.18;
17.20
21.12
Isa 7.2,13;
Jer 22.3;
Zech 7.9;
Jer 7.20
21.13
Ezek 13.8;
Jer 49.4
21.14
Isa 3.10,11;
Ezek 20.46,
48;
2 Chr 36.19;
Jer 52.13
22.1
Jer 21.11;
2 Chr 25.15,
16

not pity them, or spare them, or have compassion.

8 And to this people you shall say: Thus says the LORD: See, I am setting before you the way of life and the way of death. 9 Those who stay in this city shall die by the sword, by famine, and by pestilence; but those who go out and surrender to the Chaldeans who are besieging you shall live and shall have their lives as a prize of war. 10 For I have set my face against this city for evil and not for good, says the LORD: it shall be given into the hands of the king of Babylon, and he shall burn it with fire.

Message to the House of David

11 To the house of the king of Judah say: Hear the word of the LORD, 12 O house of David! Thus says the LORD:
 Execute justice in the
 morning,
 and deliver from the hand
 of the oppressor
 anyone who has been
 robbed,
 or else my wrath will go forth
 like fire,
 and burn, with no one to
 quench it,
 because of your evil doings.

13 See, I am against you,
 O inhabitant of the
 valley,
 O rock of the plain,
 says the LORD;
 you who say, "Who can come
 down against us,
 or who can enter our
 places of refuge?"
14 I will punish you according
 to the fruit of your
 doings,
 says the LORD;
 I will kindle a fire in its
 forest,
 and it shall devour all that
 is around it.

Exhortation to Repent

22 Thus says the LORD: Go down to the house of the

king of Judah, and speak there this word, ² and say: Hear the word of the Lord, O King of Judah sitting on the throne of David—you, and your servants, and your people who enter these gates. ³ Thus says the Lord: Act with justice and righteousness, and deliver from the hand of the oppressor anyone who has been robbed. And do no wrong or violence to the alien, the orphan, and the widow, or shed innocent blood in this place. ⁴ For if you will indeed obey this word, then through the gates of this house shall enter kings who sit on the throne of David, riding in chariots and on horses, they, and their servants, and their people. ⁵ But if you will not heed these words, I swear by myself, says the Lord, that this house shall become a desolation. ⁶ For thus says the Lord concerning the house of the king of Judah:

You are like Gilead to me,
　like the summit of
　　Lebanon;
but I swear that I will make
　you a desert,
　an uninhabited city.ᵗ
⁷ I will prepare destroyers
　against you,
　all with their weapons;
they shall cut down your
　choicest cedars
and cast them into the fire.

8 And many nations will pass by this city, and all of them will say one to another, "Why has the Lord dealt in this way with that great city?" ⁹ And they will answer, "Because they abandoned the covenant of the Lord their God, and worshiped other gods and served them."

¹⁰ Do not weep for him who is
　　dead,
　nor bemoan him;
weep rather for him who
　goes away,
　for he shall return no more
　to see his native land.

Message to the Sons of Josiah

11 For thus says the Lord concerning Shallum son of King Josiah

of Judah, who succeeded his father Josiah, and who went away from this place: He shall return here no more, ¹² but in the place where they have carried him captive he shall die, and he shall never see this land again.

¹³ Woe to him who builds his
　　house by
　　unrighteousness,
　and his upper rooms by
　　injustice;
who makes his neighbors
　work for nothing,
　and does not give them
　　their wages;
¹⁴ who says, "I will build myself
　　a spacious house
　with large upper rooms,"
and who cuts out windows
　for it,
　paneling it with cedar,
　and painting it with
　　vermilion.
¹⁵ Are you a king
　because you compete in
　　cedar?
Did not your father eat and
　drink
　and do justice and
　　righteousness?
　Then it was well with him.
¹⁶ He judged the cause of the
　poor and needy;
　then it was well.
Is not this to know me?
　says the Lord.
¹⁷ But your eyes and heart
　are only on your dishonest
　　gain,
　for shedding innocent blood,
　and for practicing
　　oppression and
　　violence.

18 Therefore thus says the Lord concerning King Jehoiakim son of Josiah of Judah:

They shall not lament for
　him, saying,
"Alas, my brother!" or
　"Alas, sister!"
They shall not lament for
　him, saying,

22.2
Jer 19.3;
29.20
22.3
Jer 21.12;
Ps 72.4;
Ex 22.21-24
22.4
Jer 17.25
22.5
Jer 17.27;
26.4;
Heb 6.13;
Jer 7.14;
26.6,9
22.6
Jer 7.34
22.7
Isa 10.3-6;
Jer 4.6,7;
Isa 10.33,34
22.8
Deut 29.24,
25;
1 Kings 9.8,
9; Jer 16.10
22.9
2 Kings 22.17;
2 Chr 34.25
22.10
2 Kings 22.20;
v. 18;
Jer 16.7;
44.14
22.11
2 Kings 23.30,
34

22.13
Mic 3.10;
Hab 2.9;
Jas 5.4
22.14
Isa 5.8,9;
2 Sam 7.2
22.15
2 Kings 23.25;
Jer 7.5; 42.6
22.16
Ps 72.1-4,
12,13;
1 Chr 28.9;
Jer 9.24
22.17
Jer 6.13;
8.10; 6.6
22.18
1 Kings 13.30;
Jer 34.5

ᵗ Cn: Heb *uninhabited cities*

"Alas, lord!" or "Alas, his
majesty!"
19 With the burial of a donkey
he shall be buried—
dragged off and thrown out
beyond the gates of
Jerusalem.

20 Go up to Lebanon, and cry
out,
and lift up your voice in
Bashan;
cry out from Abarim,
for all your lovers are
crushed.
21 I spoke to you in your
prosperity,
but you said, "I will not
listen."
This has been your way from
your youth,
for you have not obeyed my
voice.
22 The wind shall shepherd all
your shepherds,
and your lovers shall go
into captivity;
then you will be ashamed
and dismayed
because of all your
wickedness.
23 O inhabitant of Lebanon,
nested among the cedars,
how you will groan u when
pangs come upon you,
pain as of a woman in
labor!

Judgment on Coniah
(Jehoiachin)

24 As I live, says the LORD, even
if King Coniah son of Jehoiakim of
Judah were the signet ring on my
right hand, even from there I would
tear you off 25 and give you into the
hands of those who seek your life,
into the hands of those of whom
you are afraid, even into the hands
of King Nebuchadrezzar of Babylon
and into the hands of the Chalde-
ans. 26 I will hurl you and the moth-
er who bore you into another coun-
try, where you were not born, and
there you shall die. 27 But they shall
not return to the land to which they
long to return.

22.19
Jer 36.30
22.20
Deut 32.49;
Jer 2.25; 3.1
22.21
Jer 13.10;
19.15; 3.24,
25; 32.30
22.22
Jer 5.13;
30.14;
Isa 65.13;
Jer 20.11
22.23
Jer 4.31;
6.24
22.24
Jer 37.1;
Song 8.6;
Hag 2.23
22.25
2 Kings 24.15,
16;
Jer 34.20
22.26
2 Kings 24.15;
2 Chr 36.10;
2 Kings 24.8

22.28
Ps 31.12;
Jer 48.38;
Hos 8.8;
Jer 15.1;
17.4
22.29
Deut 32.1;
Jer 6.19;
Mic 1.2
22.30
1 Chr 3.16,
17; Mt 1.12
23.1
Ezek 13.3;
Jer 10.21;
50.6;
Ezek 34.31
23.3
Isa 11.11-16;
Jer 32.37;
Ezek 34.13-16
23.4
Jer 3.15;
Ezek 34.23;
Jer 30.10;
Jn 6.39;
10.28
23.5
Isa 4.2;
11.1; 53.2;
Jer 33.14-16;
Zech 3.8;
6.12;
Isa 9.7;
Lk 1.32,33
23.6
Deut 33.28;
Zech 14.11;
Isa 7.14;
9.6;
Mt 1.21-23;
Jer 33.16;
Rom 3.22;
1 Cor 1.30

28 Is this man Coniah a
despised broken pot,
a vessel no one wants?
Why are he and his offspring
hurled out
and cast away in a land
that they do not know?
29 O land, land, land,
hear the word of the LORD!
30 Thus says the LORD:
Record this man as childless,
a man who shall not
succeed in his days;
for none of his offspring shall
succeed
in sitting on the throne of
David,
and ruling again in Judah.

Restoration after Exile

23 Woe to the shepherds who
destroy and scatter the
sheep of my pasture! says the LORD.
2 Therefore thus says the LORD, the
God of Israel, concerning the shep-
herds who shepherd my people: It
is you who have scattered my flock,
and have driven them away, and
you have not attended to them. So
I will attend to you for your evil do-
ings, says the LORD. 3 Then I myself
will gather the remnant of my flock
out of all the lands where I have
driven them, and I will bring them
back to their fold, and they shall be
fruitful and multiply. 4 I will raise
up shepherds over them who will
shepherd them, and they shall not
fear any longer, or be dismayed,
nor shall any be missing, says the
LORD.

The Righteous Branch of David

5 The days are surely coming,
says the LORD, when I will raise up
for David a righteous Branch, and
he shall reign as king and deal
wisely, and shall execute justice
and righteousness in the land. 6 In
his days Judah will be saved and
Israel will live in safety. And this is
the name by which he will be
called: "The LORD is our righteous-
ness."

u Gk Vg Syr: Heb will be pitied

7 Therefore, the days are surely coming, says the LORD, when it shall no longer be said, "As the LORD lives who brought the people of Israel up out of the land of Egypt," 8 but "As the LORD lives who brought out and led the offspring of the house of Israel out of the land of the north and out of all the lands where he v had driven them." Then they shall live in their own land.

False Prophets of Hope Denounced

9 Concerning the prophets:
My heart is crushed within me,
all my bones shake;
I have become like a drunkard,
like one overcome by wine,
because of the LORD
and because of his holy words.
10 For the land is full of adulterers;
because of the curse the land mourns,
and the pastures of the wilderness are dried up.
Their course has been evil,
and their might is not right.
11 Both prophet and priest are ungodly;
even in my house I have found their wickedness,
says the LORD.
12 Therefore their way shall be to them
like slippery paths in the darkness,
into which they shall be driven and fall;
for I will bring disaster upon them
in the year of their punishment,
says the LORD.
13 In the prophets of Samaria
I saw a disgusting thing:
they prophesied by Baal
and led my people Israel astray.
14 But in the prophets of Jerusalem

I have seen a more shocking thing:
they commit adultery and walk in lies;
they strengthen the hands of evildoers,
so that no one turns from wickedness;
all of them have become like Sodom to me,
and its inhabitants like Gomorrah.
15 Therefore thus says the LORD of hosts concerning the prophets:
"I am going to make them eat wormwood,
and give them poisoned water to drink;
for from the prophets of Jerusalem
ungodliness has spread throughout the land."

16 Thus says the LORD of hosts: Do not listen to the words of the prophets who prophesy to you; they are deluding you. They speak visions of their own minds, not from the mouth of the LORD. 17 They keep saying to those who despise the word of the LORD, "It shall be well with you"; and to all who stubbornly follow their own stubborn hearts, they say, "No calamity shall come upon you."

18 For who has stood in the council of the LORD
so as to see and to hear his word?
Who has given heed to his word so as to proclaim it?
19 Look, the storm of the LORD!
Wrath has gone forth,
a whirling tempest;
it will burst upon the head of the wicked.
20 The anger of the LORD will not turn back
until he has executed and accomplished
the intents of his mind.

v Gk: Heb I

In the latter days you will
understand it clearly.

21 I did not send the prophets,
yet they ran;
I did not speak to them,
yet they prophesied.
22 But if they had stood in my
council,
then they would have
proclaimed my words to
my people,
and they would have turned
them from their evil
way,
and from the evil of their
doings.

23 Am I a God near by, says the
LORD, and not a God far off? 24 Who
can hide in secret places so that I
cannot see them? says the LORD. Do
I not fill heaven and earth? says the
LORD. 25 I have heard what the
prophets have said who prophesy
lies in my name, saying, "I have
dreamed, I have dreamed!" 26 How
long? Will the hearts of the proph-
ets ever turn back — those who
prophesy lies, and who prophesy
the deceit of their own heart?
27 They plan to make my people for-
get my name by their dreams that
they tell one another, just as their
ancestors forgot my name for Baal.
28 Let the prophet who has a dream
tell the dream, but let the one who
has my word speak my word faith-
fully. What has straw in common
with wheat? says the LORD. 29 Is not
my word like fire, says the LORD,
and like a hammer that breaks a
rock in pieces? 30 See, therefore, I
am against the prophets, says the
LORD, who steal my words from one
another. 31 See, I am against the
prophets, says the LORD, who use
their own tongues and say, "Says
the LORD." 32 See, I am against
those who prophesy lying dreams,
says the LORD, and who tell them,
and who lead my people astray by
their lies and their recklessness,
when I did not send them or ap-
point them; so they do not profit
this people at all, says the LORD.
33 When this people, or a

23.21
Jer 14.14;
27.15; 29.9
23.22
Jer 9.12;
35.15;
1 Thes 1.9,
10
23.23
Ps 139.1-10;
Jer 50.51
23.24
Ps 139.7-12;
Isa 29.15;
Am 9.2;
1 Kings 8.27
23.25
Jer 8.6;
14.14; 29.8
23.27
Judg 3.7;
8.33,34
23.28
Jer 9.12,20
23.29
Jer 5.14;
20.9;
2 Cor 10.4,
5
23.30
Ezek 13.8
23.31
v. 17
23.32
vv. 25,28
23.33
Isa 13.1;
Hab 1.1;
Mal 1.1;
v. 39

23.34
Lam 2.14;
Zech 13.3
23.35
Jer 33.3;
42.4
23.36
Jer 10.10
23.38
v. 36
23.39
Jer 7.14,15;
Ezek 8.18
23.40
Jer 20.11
24.1
Am 8.1;
2 Kings 24.10-
16;
2 Chr 36.10;
Jer 22.24;
29.2
24.2
Nah 3.12;
Jer 27.19
24.3
Jer 1.11,13

prophet, or a priest asks you,
"What is the burden of the LORD?"
you shall say to them, "You are the
burden,ʷ and I will cast you off,
says the LORD." 34 And as for the
prophet, priest, or the people who
say, "The burden of the LORD," I
will punish them and their house-
holds. 35 Thus shall you say to one
another, among yourselves, "What
has the LORD answered?" or "What
has the LORD spoken?" 36 But "the
burden of the LORD" you shall men-
tion no more, for the burden is ev-
eryone's own word, and so you per-
vert the words of the living God, the
LORD of hosts, our God. 37 Thus you
shall ask the prophet, "What has
the LORD answered you?" or "What
has the LORD spoken?" 38 But if you
say, "the burden of the LORD," thus
says the LORD: Because you have
said these words, "the burden of
the LORD," when I sent to you, say-
ing, You shall not say, "the burden
of the LORD," 39 therefore, I will
surely lift you upˣ and cast you
away from my presence, you and
the city that I gave to you and your
ancestors. 40 And I will bring upon
you everlasting disgrace and per-
petual shame, which shall not be
forgotten.

The Good and the Bad Figs

24 The LORD showed me two
baskets of figs placed be-
fore the temple of the LORD. This
was after King Nebuchadrezzar of
Babylon had taken into exile from
Jerusalem King Jeconiah son of Je-
hoiakim of Judah, together with
the officials of Judah, the artisans,
and the smiths, and had brought
them to Babylon. 2 One basket had
very good figs, like first-ripe figs,
but the other basket had very bad
figs, so bad that they could not be
eaten. 3 And the LORD said to me,
"What do you see, Jeremiah?" I
said, "Figs, the good figs very good,
and the bad figs very bad, so bad
that they cannot be eaten."
4 Then the word of the LORD

ʷ Gk Vg: Heb *What burden* ˣ Heb Mss Gk
Vg: MT *forget you*

came to me: 5 Thus says the LORD, the God of Israel: Like these good figs, so I will regard as good the exiles from Judah, whom I have sent away from this place to the land of the Chaldeans. 6 I will set my eyes upon them for good, and I will bring them back to this land. I will build them up, and not tear them down; I will plant them, and not pluck them up. 7 I will give them a heart to know that I am the LORD; and they shall be my people and I will be their God, for they shall return to me with their whole heart.

8 But thus says the LORD: Like the bad figs that are so bad they cannot be eaten, so will I treat King Zedekiah of Judah, his officials, the remnant of Jerusalem who remain in this land, and those who live in the land of Egypt. 9 I will make them a horror, an evil thing, to all the kingdoms of the earth — a disgrace, a byword, a taunt, and a curse in all the places where I shall drive them. 10 And I will send sword, famine, and pestilence upon them, until they are utterly destroyed from the land that I gave to them and their ancestors.

The Babylonian Captivity Foretold

25 The word that came to Jeremiah concerning all the people of Judah, in the fourth year of King Jehoiakim son of Josiah of Judah (that was the first year of King Nebuchadrezzar of Babylon), 2 which the prophet Jeremiah spoke to all the people of Judah and all the inhabitants of Jerusalem: 3 For twenty-three years, from the thirteenth year of King Josiah son of Amon of Judah, to this day, the word of the LORD has come to me, and I have spoken persistently to you, but you have not listened. 4 And though the LORD persistently sent you all his servants the prophets, you have neither listened nor inclined your ears to hear 5 when they said, "Turn now, everyone of you, from your evil way and wicked doings, and you will remain upon the land that the LORD has given to

24.5
Nah 1.7;
Zech 13.9
24.6
Jer 29.10;
Ezek 11.17;
Jer 33.7;
42.10
24.7
Jer 31.33;
32.40;
Zech 8.8;
Heb 8.10;
Jer 29.13
24.8
Jer 29.17;
39.5,9;
44.26-30
24.9
Jer 15.4;
29.18; 34.17;
1 Kings 9.7;
Ps 44.13,14;
Isa 65.15
24.10
Isa 51.19;
Jer 21.9;
27.8
25.1
Jer 36.1;
2 Kings 24.1,
2
25.2
Jer 18.11
25.3
Jer 1.2;
2 Chr 34.1-3,
8; Jer 36.2;
7.13; 22.21
25.4
Jer 7.13,25;
26.5
25.5
Isa 55.6,7;
Jer 4.1; 7.7
25.6
Deut 6.14;
8.19;
Jer 35.15
25.7
Deut 32.21;
2 Kings 17.17;
21.15;
Jer 7.19
25.9
Jer 1.15;
27.6; 18.16
25.10
Isa 24.7;
Ezek 26.13;
Eccl 12.4;
Isa 47.2
25.11
Jer 4.27;
12.11,12;
Dan 9.2
25.12
Ezra 1.1;
Jer 29.10;
Isa 13.14;
13.19; 14.23
25.14
Jer 50.9;
51.27,28;
50.41; 51.6,
24

you and your ancestors from of old and forever; 6 do not go after other gods to serve and worship them, and do not provoke me to anger with the work of your hands. Then I will do you no harm." 7 Yet you did not listen to me, says the LORD, and so you have provoked me to anger with the work of your hands to your own harm.

8 Therefore thus says the LORD of hosts: Because you have not obeyed my words, 9 I am going to send for all the tribes of the north, says the LORD, even for King Nebuchadrezzar of Babylon, my servant, and I will bring them against this land and its inhabitants, and against all these nations around; I will utterly destroy them, and make them an object of horror and of hissing, and an everlasting disgrace.y 10 And I will banish from them the sound of mirth and the sound of gladness, the voice of the bridegroom and the voice of the bride, the sound of the millstones and the light of the lamp. 11 This whole land shall become a ruin and a waste, and these nations shall serve the king of Babylon seventy years. 12 Then after seventy years are completed, I will punish the king of Babylon and that nation, the land of the Chaldeans, for their iniquity, says the LORD, making the land an everlasting waste. 13 I will bring upon that land all the words that I have uttered against it, everything written in this book, which Jeremiah prophesied against all the nations. 14 For many nations and great kings shall make slaves of them also; and I will repay them according to their deeds and the work of their hands.

The Cup of God's Wrath

15 For thus the LORD, the God of Israel, said to me: Take from my hand this cup of the wine of wrath, and make all the nations to whom I send you drink it. 16 They shall

25.15 Ps 75.8; Isa 51.17 **25.16** Jer 51.7;
Nah 3.11

y Gk Compare Syr: Heb and everlasting
desolations

drink and stagger and go out of their minds because of the sword that I am sending among them.

17 So I took the cup from the LORD's hand, and made all the nations to whom the LORD sent me drink it: 18 Jerusalem and the towns of Judah, its kings and officials, to make them a desolation and a waste, an object of hissing and of cursing, as they are today; 19 Pharaoh king of Egypt, his servants, his officials, and all his people; 20 all the mixed people; z all the kings of the land of Uz; all the kings of the land of the Philistines — Ashkelon, Gaza, Ekron, and the remnant of Ashdod; 21 Edom, Moab, and the Ammonites; 22 all the kings of Tyre, all the kings of Sidon, and the kings of the coastland across the sea; 23 Dedan, Tema, Buz, and all who have shaven temples; 24 all the kings of Arabia and all the kings of the mixed peoples z that live in the desert; 25 all the kings of Zimri, all the kings of Elam, and all the kings of Media; 26 all the kings of the north, far and near, one after another, and all the kingdoms of the world that are on the face of the earth. And after them the king of Sheshach a shall drink.

27 Then you shall say to them, Thus says the LORD of hosts, the God of Israel: Drink, get drunk and vomit, fall and rise no more, because of the sword that I am sending among you.

28 And if they refuse to accept the cup from your hand to drink, then you shall say to them: Thus says the LORD of hosts: You must drink! 29 See, I am beginning to bring disaster on the city that is called by my name, and how can you possibly avoid punishment? You shall not go unpunished, for I am summoning a sword against all the inhabitants of the earth, says the LORD of hosts.

30 You, therefore, shall prophesy against them all these words, and say to them:

The LORD will roar from on high,

and from his holy
 habitation utter his voice;
he will roar mightily against
 his fold,
and shout, like those who
 tread grapes,
against all the inhabitants
 of the earth.
31 The clamor will resound to
 the ends of the earth,
 for the LORD has an
 indictment against the
 nations;
he is entering into judgment
 with all flesh,
 and the guilty he will put
 to the sword,
 says the LORD.

32 Thus says the LORD of hosts:
See, disaster is spreading
 from nation to nation,
and a great tempest is
 stirring
from the farthest parts of
 the earth!

33 Those slain by the LORD on that day shall extend from one end of the earth to the other. They shall not be lamented, or gathered, or buried; they shall become dung on the surface of the ground.

34 Wail, you shepherds, and cry
 out;
 roll in ashes, you lords of
 the flock,
for the days of your slaughter
 have come — and your
 dispersions, z
and you shall fall like a
 choice vessel.
35 Flight shall fail the
 shepherds,
 and there shall be no
 escape for the lords of
 the flock.
36 Hark! the cry of the
 shepherds,
 and the wail of the lords of
 the flock!
For the LORD is despoiling
 their pasture,
37 and the peaceful folds are
 devastated,

25.17
v. 28;
Ezek 43.3
25.18
Isa 51.17;
Jer 24.9;
44.22
25.19
Jer 46.2-28
25.20
Job 1.1;
Jer 47.1-7;
Isa 20.1
25.21
Jer 49.1-22;
48.1-47
25.22
Jer 47.4;
49.23
25.23
Jer 49.7,8;
9.26; 49.32
25.24
2 Chr 9.14
25.26
Jer 50.9
25.27
Hab 2.16;
Ezek 21.4,5
25.29
Ezek 9.6;
1 Pet 4.17;
1 Kings 8.43;
v. 31
25.30
Isa 42.13;
Joel 3.16;
Am 1.2;
Isa 16.9

25.31
Hos 4.1;
Mic 6.2;
Joel 3.2
25.32
Isa 34.2;
Jer 29.19;
30.23
25.33
Isa 66.16;
Ps 79.3;
Jer 16.4;
Isa 5.25
25.34
Jer 6.26;
Ezek 27.30;
Isa 34.7;
Jer 50.27
25.35
Jer 11.11
25.36
v. 34
25.37
Isa 27.10,
11; Jer 5.17;
13.10

z Meaning of Heb uncertain a Sheshach is a cryptogram for Babel, Babylon

because of the fierce anger of the LORD.

38 Like a lion he has left his covert;
for their land has become a waste
because of the cruel sword,
and because of his fierce anger.

Jeremiah's Prophecies in the Temple

26 At the beginning of the reign of King Jehoiakim son of Josiah of Judah, this word came from the LORD: 2 Thus says the LORD: Stand in the court of the LORD's house, and speak to all the cities of Judah that come to worship in the house of the LORD; speak to them all the words that I command you; do not hold back a word. 3 It may be that they will listen, all of them, and will turn from their evil way, that I may change my mind about the disaster that I intend to bring on them because of their evil doings. 4 You shall say to them: Thus says the LORD: If you will not listen to me, to walk in my law that I have set before you, 5 and to heed the words of my servants the prophets whom I send to you urgently—though you have not heeded— 6 then I will make this house like Shiloh, and I will make this city a curse for all the nations of the earth.

7 The priests and the prophets and all the people heard Jeremiah speaking these words in the house of the LORD. 8 And when Jeremiah had finished speaking all that the LORD had commanded him to speak to all the people, then the priests and the prophets and all the people laid hold of him, saying, "You shall die! 9 Why have you prophesied in the name of the LORD, saying, 'This house shall be like Shiloh, and this city shall be desolate, without inhabitant'?" And all the people gathered around Jeremiah in the house of the LORD.

10 When the officials of Judah heard these things, they came up

from the king's house to the house of the LORD and took their seat in the entry of the New Gate of the house of the LORD. 11 Then the priests and the prophets said to the officials and to all the people, "This man deserves the sentence of death because he has prophesied against this city, as you have heard with your own ears."

12 Then Jeremiah spoke to all the officials and all the people, saying, "It is the LORD who sent me to prophesy against this house and this city all the words you have heard. 13 Now therefore amend your ways and your doings, and obey the voice of the LORD your God, and the LORD will change his mind about the disaster that he has pronounced against you. 14 But as for me, here I am in your hands. Do with me as seems good and right to you. 15 Only know for certain that if you put me to death, you will be bringing innocent blood upon yourselves and upon this city and its inhabitants, for in truth the LORD sent me to you to speak all these words in your ears."

16 Then the officials and all the people said to the priests and the prophets, "This man does not deserve the sentence of death, for he has spoken to us in the name of the LORD our God." 17 And some of the elders of the land arose and said to all the assembled people, 18 "Micah of Moresheth, who prophesied during the days of King Hezekiah of Judah, said to all the people of Judah: 'Thus says the LORD of hosts,
Zion shall be plowed as a field;
Jerusalem shall become a heap of ruins,
and the mountain of the house a wooded height.'
19 Did King Hezekiah of Judah and all Judah actually put him to death? Did he not fear the LORD and entreat the favor of the LORD, and did not the LORD change his mind about the disaster that he had pronounced against them? But we are

25.38
Jer 4.7
26.1
2 Kings 23.36;
2 Chr 36.4,
5; Jer 7.1,2
26.2
Jer 19.14;
Lk 19.47,48;
Jer 1.17;
Acts 20.20,
27; Deut 4.2
26.3
Jer 36.3-7;
18.8
26.4
Lev 26.14;
Deut 28.15;
Jer 17.27;
32.23; 44.10,
23
26.5
2 Kings 9.7;
Jer 25.3,4
26.6
1 Sam 4.10,
11;
Isa 65.15;
Jer 24.9
26.8
Jer 20.1,2;
11.19; 18.23
26.9
Jer 9.11;
33.10
26.10
Jer 36.10

26.11
Jer 18.23;
Deut 18.20;
Mt 26.66;
Jer 38.4;
Acts 6.11-14
26.12
Jer 1.17,18;
5.6; 46.16
26.13
Jer 7.3,5;
18.11;
Joel 2.14;
Jon 3.9; 4.2
26.14
Jer 38.5
26.15
Prov 6.16,
17; Jer 7.6
26.16
v. 11;
Acts 5.34-39;
23.9,29;
25.25; 26.31
26.18
Mic 1.1;
Ps 79.1;
Mic 3.12;
Zech 8.3
26.19
2 Chr 29.6-11;
32.26;
2 Sam 24.16;
Acts 5.39

about to bring great disaster on ourselves!"

20 There was another man prophesying in the name of the LORD, Uriah son of Shemaiah from Kiriath-jearim. He prophesied against this city and against this land in words exactly like those of Jeremiah. 21 And when King Jehoiakim, with all his warriors and all the officials, heard his words, the king sought to put him to death; but when Uriah heard of it, he was afraid and fled and escaped to Egypt. 22 Then King Jehoiakim sent[b] Elnathan son of Achbor and men with him to Egypt, 23 and they took Uriah from Egypt and brought him to King Jehoiakim, who struck him down with the sword and threw his dead body into the burial place of the common people.

24 But the hand of Ahikam son of Shaphan was with Jeremiah so that he was not given over into the hands of the people to be put to death.

The Sign of the Yoke

27 In the beginning of the reign of King Zedekiah[c] son of Josiah of Judah, this word came to Jeremiah from the LORD. 2 Thus the LORD said to me: Make yourself a yoke of straps and bars, and put them on your neck. 3 Send word[d] to the king of Edom, the king of Moab, the king of the Ammonites, the king of Tyre, and the king of Sidon by the hand of the envoys who have come to Jerusalem to King Zedekiah of Judah. 4 Give them this charge for their masters: Thus says the LORD of hosts, the God of Israel: This is what you shall say to your masters: 5 It is I who by my great power and my outstretched arm have made the earth, with the people and animals that are on the earth, and I give it to whomever I please. 6 Now I have given all these lands into the hand of King Nebuchadnezzar of Babylon, my servant, and I have given him even the wild animals of the field to serve him. 7 All the na-

tions shall serve him and his son and his grandson, until the time of his own land comes; then many nations and great kings shall make him their slave.

8 But if any nation or kingdom will not serve this king, Nebuchadnezzar of Babylon, and put its neck under the yoke of the king of Babylon, then I will punish that nation with the sword, with famine, and with pestilence, says the LORD, until I have completed its[e] destruction by his hand. 9 You, therefore, must not listen to your prophets, your diviners, your dreamers,[f] your soothsayers, or your sorcerers, who are saying to you, 'You shall not serve the king of Babylon.' 10 For they are prophesying a lie to you, with the result that you will be removed far from your land; I will drive you out, and you will perish. 11 But any nation that will bring its neck under the yoke of the king of Babylon and serve him, I will leave on its own land, says the LORD, to till it and live there.

12 I spoke to King Zedekiah of Judah in the same way: Bring your necks under the yoke of the king of Babylon, and serve him and his people, and live. 13 Why should you and your people die by the sword, by famine, and by pestilence, as the LORD has spoken concerning any nation that will not serve the king of Babylon? 14 Do not listen to the words of the prophets who are telling you not to serve the king of Babylon, for they are prophesying a lie to you. 15 I have not sent them, says the LORD, but they are prophesying falsely in my name, with the result that I will drive you out and you will perish, you and the prophets who are prophesying to you.

16 Then I spoke to the priests and to all this people, saying, Thus says the LORD: Do not listen to the words of your prophets who are prophesying to you, saying, "The vessels of the LORD's house will soon be brought back from Bab-

26.20
Josh 9.17;
1 Sam 6.21;
7.2
26.21
1 Kings 19.2-4;
Mt 10.23,28
26.22
Jer 36.12
26.23
Jer 2.30
26.24
2 Kings 22.12-14; Jer 39.14
27.1
Jer 26.1
27.2
Jer 28.10,13
27.3
Jer 25.21,22
27.5
Jer 10.12;
51.15;
Ps 115.15, 16;
Acts 17.26
27.6
Ezek 29.18-20;
Jer 25.9;
28.14
27.7
Jer 44.30;
46.13; 25.12;
Isa 14.4-6

27.8
Jer 38.17-19;
Ezek 17.19-21;
Jer 29.17, 18;
Ezek 14.21
27.9
Ex 22.18;
Deut 18.10;
Isa 8.19;
Mal 3.5
27.10
Jer 23.25;
8.19; 32.31
27.11
Jer 21.9
27.12
Jer 28.1
27.13
Ezek 18.31
27.14
Jer 14.14;
Ezek 13.22
27.15
Jer 23.21,
25; 6.13-15;
14.15,16
27.16
2 Chr 36.7,
10; Jer 28.3;
Dan 1.2;
v. 10

[b] Heb adds *men to Egypt* [c] Another reading is *Jehoiakim* [d] Cn: Heb *send them* [e] Heb *their* [f] Gk Syr Vg: Heb *dreams*

ylon," for they are prophesying a lie to you. ¹⁷Do not listen to them; serve the king of Babylon and live. Why should this city become a desolation? ¹⁸If indeed they are prophets, and if the word of the LORD is with them, then let them intercede with the LORD of hosts, that the vessels left in the house of the LORD, in the house of the king of Judah, and in Jerusalem may not go to Babylon. ¹⁹For thus says the LORD of hosts concerning the pillars, the sea, the stands, and the rest of the vessels that are left in this city, ²⁰which King Nebuchadnezzar of Babylon did not take away when he took into exile from Jerusalem to Babylon King Jeconiah son of Jehoiakim of Judah, and all the nobles of Judah and Jerusalem— ²¹thus says the LORD of hosts, the God of Israel, concerning the vessels left in the house of the LORD, in the house of the king of Judah, and in Jerusalem: ²²They shall be carried to Babylon, and there they shall stay, until the day when I give attention to them, says the LORD. Then I will bring them up and restore them to this place.

Hananiah Opposes Jeremiah and Dies

28 In that same year, at the beginning of the reign of King Zedekiah of Judah, in the fifth month of the fourth year, the prophet Hananiah son of Azzur, from Gibeon, spoke to me in the house of the LORD, in the presence of the priests and all the people, saying, ²"Thus says the LORD of hosts, the God of Israel: I have broken the yoke of the king of Babylon. ³Within two years I will bring back to this place all the vessels of the LORD's house, which King Nebuchadnezzar of Babylon took away from this place and carried to Babylon. ⁴I will also bring back to this place King Jeconiah son of Jehoiakim of Judah, and all the exiles from Judah who went to Babylon, says the LORD, for I will break the yoke of the king of Babylon."

5 Then the prophet Jeremiah

Cross-references (center column)

27.17
v. 13
27.18
1 Sam 7.8;
12.19,23
27.19
2 Kings 25.13,
17;
Jer 52.17-23
27.20
2 Kings 24.14-
16; Jer 24.1
27.22
2 Kings 25.13;
2 Chr 36.18;
Jer 29.10;
32.5;
Ezra 1.7;
7.19
28.1
Jer 27.1,3,
12;
Josh 9.3;
10.12
28.3
2 Kings 24.13;
2 Chr 36.10;
Jer 27.12
28.4
Jer 22.24,
26,27; 27.8
28.5
v. 1
28.6
1 Kings 1.36;
Jer 11.5
28.7
1 Kings 22.28
28.8
1 Kings 14.15;
Isa 5.5-7;
Joel 1.20;
Am 1.2;
Nah 1.2
28.9
Deut 18.22
28.10
Jer 27.2
28.11
Jer 14.14;
27.10
28.12
Jer 1.2
28.13
Ps 107.16;
Isa 45.2
28.14
Deut 28.48;
Jer 27.6-8;
25.11
28.15
Jer 29.31;
Ezek 13.22
28.16
Deut 6.15;
13.5;
Jer 29.32

spoke to the prophet Hananiah in the presence of the priests and all the people who were standing in the house of the LORD; ⁶and the prophet Jeremiah said, "Amen! May the LORD do so; may the LORD fulfill the words that you have prophesied, and bring back to this place from Babylon the vessels of the house of the LORD, and all the exiles. ⁷But listen now to this word that I speak in your hearing and in the hearing of all the people. ⁸The prophets who preceded you and me from ancient times prophesied war, famine, and pestilence against many countries and great kingdoms. ⁹As for the prophet who prophesies peace, when the word of that prophet comes true, then it will be known that the LORD has truly sent the prophet."

10 Then the prophet Hananiah took the yoke from the neck of the prophet Jeremiah, and broke it. ¹¹And Hananiah spoke in the presence of all the people, saying, "Thus says the LORD: This is how I will break the yoke of King Nebuchadnezzar of Babylon from the neck of all the nations within two years." At this, the prophet Jeremiah went his way.

12 Sometime after the prophet Hananiah had broken the yoke from the neck of the prophet Jeremiah, the word of the LORD came to Jeremiah: ¹³Go, tell Hananiah, Thus says the LORD: You have broken wooden bars only to forge iron bars in place of them! ¹⁴For thus says the LORD of hosts, the God of Israel: I have put an iron yoke on the neck of all these nations so that they may serve King Nebuchadnezzar of Babylon, and they shall indeed serve him; I have even given him the wild animals. ¹⁵And the prophet Jeremiah said to the prophet Hananiah, "Listen, Hananiah, the LORD has not sent you, and you made this people trust in a lie. ¹⁶Therefore thus says the LORD: I am going to send you off the face of the earth. Within this year you will be dead, because you have spoken rebellion against the LORD."

17 In that same year, in the seventh month, the prophet Hananiah died.

Jeremiah's Letter to the Exiles in Babylon

29 These are the words of the letter that the prophet Jeremiah sent from Jerusalem to the remaining elders among the exiles, and to the priests, the prophets, and all the people, whom Nebuchadnezzar had taken into exile from Jerusalem to Babylon. ² This was after King Jeconiah, and the queen mother, the court officials, the leaders of Judah and Jerusalem, the artisans, and the smiths had departed from Jerusalem. ³ The letter was sent by the hand of Elasah son of Shaphan and Gemariah son of Hilkiah, whom King Zedekiah of Judah sent to Babylon to King Nebuchadnezzar of Babylon. It said: ⁴ Thus says the Lord of hosts, the God of Israel, to all the exiles whom I have sent into exile from Jerusalem to Babylon: ⁵ Build houses and live in them; plant gardens and eat what they produce. ⁶ Take wives and have sons and daughters; take wives for your sons, and give your daughters in marriage, that they may bear sons and daughters; multiply there, and do not decrease. ⁷ But seek the welfare of the city where I have sent you into exile, and pray to the Lord on its behalf, for in its welfare you will find your welfare. ⁸ For thus says the Lord of hosts, the God of Israel: Do not let the prophets and the diviners who are among you deceive you, and do not listen to the dreams that they dream,ᵍ ⁹ for it is a lie that they are prophesying to you in my name; I did not send them, says the Lord.

10 For thus says the Lord: Only when Babylon's seventy years are completed will I visit you, and I will fulfill to you my promise and bring you back to this place. ¹¹ For surely I know the plans I have for you, says the Lord, plans for your welfare and not for harm, to give you a future with hope. ¹² Then when you call upon me and come and pray to me, I will hear you. ¹³ When you search for me, you will find me; if you seek me with all your heart, ¹⁴ I will let you find me, says the Lord, and I will restore your fortunes and gather you from all the nations and all the places where I have driven you, says the Lord, and I will bring you back to the place from which I sent you into exile.

15 Because you have said, "The Lord has raised up prophets for us in Babylon," — ¹⁶ Thus says the Lord concerning the king who sits on the throne of David, and concerning all the people who live in this city, your kinsfolk who did not go out with you into exile: ¹⁷ Thus says the Lord of hosts, I am going to let loose on them sword, famine, and pestilence, and I will make them like rotten figs that are so bad they cannot be eaten. ¹⁸ I will pursue them with the sword, with famine, and with pestilence, and will make them a horror to all the kingdoms of the earth, to be an object of cursing, and horror, and hissing, and a derision among all the nations where I have driven them, ¹⁹ because they did not heed my words, says the Lord, when I persistently sent to you my servants the prophets, but theyʰ would not listen, says the Lord. ²⁰ But now, all you exiles whom I sent away from Jerusalem to Babylon, hear the word of the Lord: ²¹ Thus says the Lord of hosts, the God of Israel, concerning Ahab son of Kolaiah and Zedekiah son of Maaseiah, who are prophesying a lie to you in my name: I am going to deliver them into the hand of King Nebuchadrezzar of Babylon, and he shall kill them before your eyes. ²² And on account of them this curse shall be used by all the exiles from Judah in Babylon: "The Lord make you like Zedekiah and Ahab, whom the king of Babylon roasted in the fire," ²³ because they have perpetrated outrage in Israel and have

ᵍ Cn: Heb *your dreams that you cause to dream* ʰ Syr: Heb *you*

29.1
vv. 25,29
29.2
2 Kings 24.12-16;
Jer 22.24-28;
24.1; 28.4
29.4ff
Isa 10.5,6;
Jer 24.5
29.6
Jer 16.2-4
29.7
Ezra 6.10;
Dan 4.19;
1 Tim 2.2
29.8
Jer 27.9;
14.14; 23.21,
25,27
29.9
Jer 27.15;
v. 31
29.10
2 Chr 36.21,
22;
Jer 25.12;
27.22;
Dan 9.2
29.11
Isa 40.9-11;
Jer 30.18-22;
31.17
29.12
Ps 50.15;
Jer 33.3;
Ps 145.19

29.13
1 Chr 22.19;
2 Chr 22.9;
Jer 24.7
29.14
Deut 30.1-10;
Jer 30.3;
Isa 45.5,6;
Jer 3.14
29.16
Jer 38.2,3,
17-23
29.17
Jer 27.8;
32.24; 24.3,
8-10
29.18
Isa 65.15;
Jer 42.18;
25.9
29.19
Jer 6.19;
25.4; 26.5
29.20
Jer 24.5
29.21
vv. 8,9
29.22
Isa 65.15;
Dan 3.6
29.23
2 Sam 13.12;
Prov 5.21;
Jer 16.17

committed adultery with their neighbors' wives, and have spoken in my name lying words that I did not command them; I am the one who knows and bears witness, says the LORD.

The Letter of Shemaiah

24 To Shemaiah of Nehelam you shall say: 25 Thus says the LORD of hosts, the God of Israel: In your own name you sent a letter to all the people who are in Jerusalem, and to the priest Zephaniah son of Maaseiah, and to all the priests, saying, 26 The LORD himself has made you priest instead of the priest Jehoiada, so that there may be officers in the house of the LORD to control any madman who plays the prophet, to put him in the stocks and the collar. 27 So now why have you not rebuked Jeremiah of Anathoth who plays the prophet for you? 28 For he has actually sent to us in Babylon, saying, "It will be a long time; build houses and live in them, and plant gardens and eat what they produce."

29 The priest Zephaniah read this letter in the hearing of the prophet Jeremiah. 30 Then the word of the LORD came to Jeremiah: 31 Send to all the exiles, saying, Thus says the LORD concerning Shemaiah of Nehelam: Because Shemaiah has prophesied to you, though I did not send him, and has led you to trust in a lie, 32 therefore thus says the LORD: I am going to punish Shemaiah of Nehelam and his descendants; he shall not have anyone living among this people to see[i] the good that I am going to do to my people, says the LORD, for he has spoken rebellion against the LORD.

Restoration Promised for Israel and Judah

30 The word that came to Jeremiah from the LORD: 2 Thus says the LORD, the God of Israel: Write in a book all the words that I have spoken to you. 3 For the days are surely coming, says the

LORD, when I will restore the fortunes of my people, Israel and Judah, says the LORD, and I will bring them back to the land that I gave to their ancestors and they shall take possession of it.

4 These are the words that the LORD spoke concerning Israel and Judah:
5 Thus says the LORD:
We have heard a cry of
 panic,
 of terror, and no peace.
6 Ask now, and see,
 can a man bear a child?
Why then do I see every man
 with his hands on his loins
 like a woman in labor?
Why has every face turned
 pale?
7 Alas! that day is so great
 there is none like it;
it is a time of distress for
 Jacob;
 yet he shall be rescued
 from it.

8 On that day, says the LORD of hosts, I will break the yoke from off his[j] neck, and I will burst his[j] bonds, and strangers shall no more make a servant of him. 9 But they shall serve the LORD their God and David their king, whom I will raise up for them.

10 But as for you, have no fear,
 my servant Jacob, says
 the LORD,
 and do not be dismayed,
 O Israel;
for I am going to save you
 from far away,
 and your offspring from the
 land of their captivity.
Jacob shall return and have
 quiet and ease,
 and no one shall make him
 afraid.
11 For I am with you, says the
 LORD, to save you;
I will make an end of all the
 nations
 among which I scattered
 you,

29.24
vv. 31,32
29.25
vv. 1,29;
2 Kings 25.18;
Jer 21.1
29.26
Jer 20.1;
2 Kings 9.11;
Acts 26.24;
Jer 20.2
29.28
vv. 1,5,10
29.29
v. 25
29.31
vv. 20,24;
Jer 14.14,
15; 28.15
29.32
Jer 36.31;
22.30; 17.6;
28.16
30.2
Jer 25.13;
Hab 2.2
30.3
Jer 29.10;
Ps 53.6;
Zeph 3.20;
Jer 16.15;
Ezek 20.42

30.5
Isa 5.30;
Am 5.16-18
30.6
Jer 4.31;
6.24
30.7
Isa 2.12;
Joel 2.11;
Lam 1.12;
Jer 2.27,28;
v. 10
30.8
Isa 9.4;
Jer 27.2;
Ezek 34.27
30.9
Isa 55.3,4;
Ezek 34.23;
37.24;
Hos 3.5;
Lk 1.69;
Acts 2.30;
13.23
30.10
Isa 43.5;
44.2;
Jer 46.27,
28; Isa 60.4;
Jer 33.16;
Mic 4.4
30.11
Jer 46.28;
4.27; 10.24

i Gk: Heb *and he shall not see* j Cn: Heb *your*

but of you I will not make
an end.
I will chastise you in just
measure,
and I will by no means
leave you unpunished.

12 For thus says the Lord:
Your hurt is incurable,
your wound is grievous.
13 There is no one to uphold
your cause,
no medicine for your
wound,
no healing for you.
14 All your lovers have forgotten
you;
they care nothing for you;
for I have dealt you the blow
of an enemy,
the punishment of a
merciless foe,
because your guilt is great,
because your sins are so
numerous.
15 Why do you cry out over your
hurt?
Your pain is incurable.
Because your guilt is great,
because your sins are so
numerous,
I have done these things to
you.
16 Therefore all who devour you
shall be devoured,
and all your foes, everyone
of them, shall go into
captivity;
those who plunder you shall
be plundered,
and all who prey on you I
will make a prey.
17 For I will restore health to
you,
and your wounds I will
heal,
says the Lord,
because they have called you
an outcast:
"It is Zion; no one cares for
her!"

18 Thus says the Lord:
I am going to restore the
fortunes of the tents of
Jacob,

30.12
v. 15;
Jer 15.18
30.13
Jer 14.19;
46.11
30.14
Lam 1.2;
2.4,5;
Jer 5.6;
32.30-35
30.16
Isa 33.1;
41.11;
Jer 10.25;
50.10
30.17
Jer 8.22;
22.33; 33.24
30.18
Jer 31.23;
Ps 102.13;
Jer 31.4,
38-40

30.19
Isa 35.10;
Jer 31.4,12,
13; 33.10,11,
22
30.20
Isa 54.13;
Jer 31.17;
Isa 54.14
30.21
Num 16.5;
Jer 50.44
30.22
Jer 32.38;
Ezek 11.20;
36.28;
Zech 13.9
30.23f
Jer 23.19,
20; 25.32
30.24
Jer 4.8;
23.20
31.1
Jer 30.22,
24;
Isa 41.10;
Rom 11.26-28
31.2
Num 14.20;
Josh 1.13;
Isa 63.14

and have compassion on
his dwellings;
the city shall be rebuilt upon
its mound,
and the citadel set on its
rightful site.
19 Out of them shall come
thanksgiving,
and the sound of
merrymakers.
I will make them many, and
they shall not be few;
I will make them honored,
and they shall not be
disdained.
20 Their children shall be as of
old,
their congregation shall be
established before me;
and I will punish all who
oppress them.
21 Their prince shall be one of
their own,
their ruler shall come from
their midst;
I will bring him near, and he
shall approach me,
for who would otherwise
dare to approach me?
says the Lord.
22 And you shall be my people,
and I will be your God.

23 Look, the storm of the Lord!
Wrath has gone forth,
a whirling[k] tempest;
it will burst upon the head
of the wicked.
24 The fierce anger of the Lord
will not turn back
until he has executed and
accomplished
the intents of his mind.
In the latter days you will
understand this.

The Joyful Return of the Exiles

31 At that time, says the Lord,
I will be the God of all the
families of Israel, and they shall be
my people.
2 Thus says the Lord:
The people who survived the
sword
found grace in the
wilderness;

k One Ms: Meaning of MT uncertain

when Israel sought for rest,
3 the LORD appeared to him[1]
 from far away.[m]
I have loved you with an
 everlasting love;
therefore I have continued
 my faithfulness to you.
4 Again I will build you, and
 you shall be built,
O virgin Israel!
Again you shall take[n] your
 tambourines,
and go forth in the dance
 of the merrymakers.
5 Again you shall plant
 vineyards
on the mountains of
 Samaria;
the planters shall plant,
and shall enjoy the fruit.
6 For there shall be a day
 when sentinels will call
in the hill country of
 Ephraim:
"Come, let us go up to Zion,
to the LORD our God."

7 For thus says the LORD:
Sing aloud with gladness for
 Jacob,
and raise shouts for the
 chief of the nations;
proclaim, give praise, and
 say,
"Save, O LORD, your people,
 the remnant of Israel."
8 See, I am going to bring
 them from the land of
 the north,
and gather them from the
 farthest parts of the
 earth,
among them the blind and
 the lame,
those with child and those
 in labor, together;
a great company, they shall
 return here.
9 With weeping they shall
 come,
and with consolations[o] I
 will lead them back,
I will let them walk by
 brooks of water,
in a straight path in which
 they shall not stumble;

for I have become a father to
 Israel,
and Ephraim is my
 firstborn.

10 Hear the word of the LORD,
 O nations,
and declare it in the
 coastlands far away;
say, "He who scattered Israel
 will gather him,
and will keep him as a
 shepherd a flock."
11 For the LORD has ransomed
 Jacob,
and has redeemed him
 from hands too strong
 for him.
12 They shall come and sing
 aloud on the height of
 Zion,
and they shall be radiant
 over the goodness of
 the LORD,
over the grain, the wine, and
 the oil,
and over the young of the
 flock and the herd;
their life shall become like a
 watered garden,
and they shall never
 languish again.
13 Then shall the young women
 rejoice in the dance,
and the young men and the
 old shall be merry.
I will turn their mourning
 into joy,
I will comfort them, and
 give them gladness for
 sorrow.
14 I will give the priests their
 fill of fatness,
and my people shall be
 satisfied with my
 bounty,
 says the LORD.

15 Thus says the LORD:
A voice is heard in Ramah,
 lamentation and bitter
 weeping.
Rachel is weeping for her
 children;

31.3
Deut 7.8;
Ps 25.6;
Hos 11.4
31.4
Jer 30.19
31.5
Isa 65.21;
Jer 50.19
31.6
Isa 2.3;
Mic 4.2
31.7
Ps 14.7;
Deut 28.13;
Isa 61.9;
Ps 28.9;
Isa 37.31
31.8
Jer 3.18;
23.8;
Isa 43.6;
Ezek 20.34,
41;
Isa 42.16;
40.11
31.9
Isa 43.19;
49.10,11;
64.8;
Jer 3.4,19

31.10
Isa 66.19;
Jer 50.19;
Isa 40.11
31.11
Isa 44.23;
48.20;
Jer 50.34;
Isa 49.24,25
31.12
Ezek 17.23;
Hos 3.5;
Isa 58.11;
35.10; 65.19;
Rev 21.4
31.13
Ps 30.11;
Zech 8.4,5;
Isa 61.3;
51.11
31.14
v. 25;
Jer 50.19
31.15
Mt 2.17,18;
Gen 37.35;
Ps 77.2;
Jer 10.20

[1] Gk: Heb *me* [m] Or *to him long ago*
[n] Or *adorn yourself with* [o] Gk Compare
Vg Tg: Heb *supplications*

she refuses to be comforted
　for her children,
because they are no more.
16 Thus says the LORD:
Keep your voice from
　weeping,
and your eyes from tears;
for there is a reward for your
　work,
　　　　　　says the LORD:
they shall come back from
　the land of the enemy;
17 there is hope for your future,
　　　　　　says the LORD:
your children shall come
　back to their own
　country.

18 Indeed I heard Ephraim
　pleading:
"You disciplined me, and I
　took the discipline;
I was like a calf untrained.
Bring me back, let me come
　back,
for you are the LORD my
　God.
19 For after I had turned away I
　repented;
and after I was discovered,
　I struck my thigh;
I was ashamed, and I was
　dismayed
because I bore the disgrace
　of my youth."
20 Is Ephraim my dear son?
Is he the child I delight in?
As often as I speak against
　him,
I still remember him.
Therefore I am deeply moved
　for him;
I will surely have mercy on
　him,
　　　　　　says the LORD.

21 Set up road markers for
　yourself,
make yourself guideposts;
consider well the highway,
the road by which you
　went.
Return, O virgin Israel,
return to these your cities.
22 How long will you waver,
O faithless daughter?

For the LORD has created a
　new thing on the earth:
　a woman encompasses[p] a
　man.

23 Thus says the LORD of hosts,
the God of Israel: Once more they
shall use these words in the land of
Judah and in its towns when I re-
store their fortunes:
"The LORD bless you,
　O abode of
　　righteousness,
　O holy hill!"
24 And Judah and all its towns shall
live there together, and the farmers
and those who wander[q] with their
flocks.
25 I will satisfy the weary,
and all who are faint I will
　replenish.
26 Thereupon I awoke and
looked, and my sleep was pleasant
to me.

Individual Retribution

27 The days are surely coming,
says the LORD, when I will sow the
house of Israel and the house of Ju-
dah with the seed of humans and
the seed of animals. 28 And just as
I have watched over them to pluck
up and break down, to overthrow,
destroy, and bring evil, so I will
watch over them to build and to
plant, says the LORD. 29 In those
days they shall no longer say:
"The parents have eaten sour
　grapes,
and the children's teeth are
　set on edge."
30 But all shall die for their own
sins; the teeth of everyone who eats
sour grapes shall be set on edge.

A New Covenant

31 The days are surely coming,
says the LORD, when I will make a
new covenant with the house of Is-
rael and the house of Judah. 32 It
will not be like the covenant that I
made with their ancestors when I
took them by the hand to bring
them out of the land of Egypt—a
covenant that they broke, though I

31.16
Isa 25.8;
30.19;
Heb 6.10;
vv. 4,5;
Jer 30.3;
Ezek 11.17
31.17
Jer 29.11
31.18
Job 5.17;
Ps 94.12;
Hos 4.16;
Ps 80.3,7,
19;
Jer 17.14;
Acts 3.26
31.19
Ezek 36.31;
Zech 12.10;
Ezek 21.12;
Jer 3.25;
Ps 25.7;
Jer 22.21
31.20
Hos 11.8;
Gen 43.30;
Isa 63.15;
55.7;
Hos 14.4
31.21
Jer 6.16;
50.5;
Isa 48.20;
v. 4
31.22
Jer 2.18,23,
36; 49.4

31.23
Jer 30.18;
32.44;
Isa 1.26;
Jer 50.7;
Zech 8.3
31.24
Jer 33.12,13
31.25
Mt 5.6
31.27
Ezek 36.9-11;
Hos 2.23
31.28
Jer 44.27;
1.10
31.29
Ezek 18.2
31.30
Deut 24.16;
Ezek 18.4,
20; Gal 6.5,
7
31.31
Jer 32.40;
Ezek 37.26;
Heb 8.8-12
31.32
Ex 19.5;
24.6-8;
Deut 1.31;
Jer 11.7,8;
3.14

p Meaning of Heb uncertain　　q Cn Compare
Syr Vg Tg: Heb and they shall wander

was their husband,ʳ says the LORD. ³³But this is the covenant that I will make with the house of Israel after those days, says the LORD: I will put my law within them, and I will write it on their hearts; and I will be their God, and they shall be my people. ³⁴No longer shall they teach one another, or say to each other, "Know the LORD," for they shall all know me, from the least of them to the greatest, says the LORD; for I will forgive their iniquity, and remember their sin no more.

³⁵ Thus says the LORD,
　who gives the sun for light
　　by day
　and the fixed order of the
　　moon and the stars for
　　light by night,
　who stirs up the sea so that
　　its waves roar—
　the LORD of hosts is his
　　name:
³⁶ If this fixed order were ever
　　to cease
　from my presence, says the
　　LORD,
　then also the offspring of
　　Israel would cease
　to be a nation before me
　　forever.

³⁷ Thus says the LORD:
　If the heavens above can be
　　measured,
　and the foundations of the
　　earth below can be
　　explored,
　then I will reject all the
　　offspring of Israel
　because of all they have
　　done,
　　　　　　　says the LORD.

Jerusalem to Be Enlarged

38 The days are surely coming, says the LORD, when the city shall be rebuilt for the LORD from the tower of Hananel to the Corner Gate. ³⁹And the measuring line shall go out farther, straight to the hill Gareb, and shall then turn to Goah. ⁴⁰The whole valley of the dead bodies and the ashes, and all

31.33
Jer 32.40;
24.7; 32.38
31.34
1 Thes 4.9;
Isa 54.13;
Jn 6.45;
Mic 7.18;
Rom 11.27
31.35
Gen 1.16;
Ps 19.1-6;
Jer 10.16
31.36
Isa 54.9,10;
Jer 33.20;
Am 9.8,9
31.37
Jer 33.22-26
31.38
Neh 3.1;
Zech 14.10;
2 Kings 14.13
31.40
Jer 7.32;
2 Sam 15.23;
2 Kings 23.6;
Joel 3.17

32.1
2 Kings 25.1,
2; Jer 39.1;
25.1
32.2
Neh 3.25;
Jer 37.21;
39.14
32.3
2 Kings 6.31,
32; Jer 26.8,
9; 34.2,3
32.4
Jer 38.18,
23; 39.5
32.5
Jer 39.7;
27.22; 34.4,5;
21.4
32.7
Jer 1.1;
Lev 25.25;
Ruth 4.4
32.8
vv. 2,7,25
32.9
Gen 23.16;
24.22;
Ex 21.32
32.10
Ruth 4.1,9

the fields as far as the Wadi Kidron, to the corner of the Horse Gate toward the east, shall be sacred to the LORD. It shall never again be uprooted or overthrown.

Jeremiah Buys a Field During the Siege

32 The word that came to Jeremiah from the LORD in the tenth year of King Zedekiah of Judah, which was the eighteenth year of Nebuchadrezzar. ²At that time the army of the king of Babylon was besieging Jerusalem, and the prophet Jeremiah was confined in the court of the guard that was in the palace of the king of Judah, ³where King Zedekiah of Judah had confined him. Zedekiah had said, "Why do you prophesy and say: Thus says the LORD: I am going to give this city into the hand of the king of Babylon, and he shall take it; ⁴King Zedekiah of Judah shall not escape out of the hands of the Chaldeans, but shall surely be given into the hands of the king of Babylon, and shall speak with him face to face and see him eye to eye; ⁵and he shall take Zedekiah to Babylon, and there he shall remain until I attend to him, says the LORD; though you fight against the Chaldeans, you shall not succeed?"

6 Jeremiah said, The word of the LORD came to me: ⁷Hanamel son of your uncle Shallum is going to come to you and say, "Buy my field that is at Anathoth, for the right of redemption by purchase is yours." ⁸Then my cousin Hanamel came to me in the court of the guard, in accordance with the word of the LORD, and said to me, "Buy my field that is at Anathoth in the land of Benjamin, for the right of possession and redemption is yours; buy it for yourself." Then I knew that this was the word of the LORD.

9 And I bought the field at Anathoth from my cousin Hanamel, and weighed out the money to him, seventeen shekels of silver. ¹⁰I

ʳ Or *master*

signed the deed, sealed it, got witnesses, and weighed the money on scales. [11] Then I took the sealed deed of purchase, containing the terms and conditions, and the open copy; [12] and I gave the deed of purchase to Baruch son of Neriah son of Mahseiah, in the presence of my cousin Hanamel, in the presence of the witnesses who signed the deed of purchase, and in the presence of all the Judeans who were sitting in the court of the guard. [13] In their presence I charged Baruch, saying, [14] Thus says the LORD of hosts, the God of Israel: Take these deeds, both this sealed deed of purchase and this open deed, and put them in an earthenware jar, in order that they may last for a long time. [15] For thus says the LORD of hosts, the God of Israel: Houses and fields and vineyards shall again be bought in this land.

Jeremiah Prays for Understanding

16 After I had given the deed of purchase to Baruch son of Neriah, I prayed to the LORD, saying: [17] Ah Lord GOD! It is you who made the heavens and the earth by your great power and by your outstretched arm! Nothing is too hard for you. [18] You show steadfast love to the thousandth generation,[s] but repay the guilt of parents into the laps of their children after them, O great and mighty God whose name is the LORD of hosts, [19] great in counsel and mighty in deed; whose eyes are open to all the ways of mortals, rewarding all according to their ways and according to the fruit of their doings. [20] You showed signs and wonders in the land of Egypt, and to this day in Israel and among all humankind, and have made yourself a name that continues to this very day. [21] You brought your people Israel out of the land of Egypt with signs and wonders, with a strong hand and outstretched arm, and with great terror; [22] and you gave them this land, which you swore to their ancestors to give

them, a land flowing with milk and honey; [23] and they entered and took possession of it. But they did not obey your voice or follow your law; of all you commanded them to do, they did nothing. Therefore you have made all these disasters come upon them. [24] See, the siege-ramps have been cast up against the city to take it, and the city, faced with sword, famine, and pestilence, has been given into the hands of the Chaldeans who are fighting against it. What you spoke has happened, as you yourself can see. [25] Yet you, O Lord GOD, have said to me, "Buy the field for money and get witnesses" — though the city has been given into the hands of the Chaldeans.

God's Assurance of the People's Return

26 The word of the LORD came to Jeremiah: [27] See, I am the LORD, the God of all flesh; is anything too hard for me? [28] Therefore, thus says the LORD: I am going to give this city into the hands of the Chaldeans and into the hand of King Nebuchadrezzar of Babylon, and he shall take it. [29] The Chaldeans who are fighting against this city shall come, set it on fire, and burn it, with the houses on whose roofs offerings have been made to Baal and libations have been poured out to other gods, to provoke me to anger. [30] For the people of Israel and the people of Judah have done nothing but evil in my sight from their youth; the people of Israel have done nothing but provoke me to anger by the work of their hands, says the LORD. [31] This city has aroused my anger and wrath, from the day it was built until this day, so that I will remove it from my sight [32] because of all the evil of the people of Israel and the people of Judah that they did to provoke me to anger — they, their kings and their officials, their priests and their prophets, the citizens of Judah and the inhabitants of Jerusalem. [33] They have turned their

32.11
Lk 2.27
32.12
Jer 36.4;
51.59
32.14
vv. 10-12
32.15
Jer 33.12,
13;
Zech 3.10
32.17
Jer 1.6;
4.10;
2 Kings 19.15;
Isa 40.26-28
32.18
Ex 34.7;
Jer 20.11;
10.16
32.19
Isa 28.29;
Jer 16.17;
17.10
32.20
Ex 9.16;
Dan 9.15
32.21
Ex 6.6;
1 Chr 17.21
32.22
Ex 3.8,17;
Jer 11.5

32.23
Jer 2.7;
26.4; 44.10;
Neh 9.26;
Jer 11.8;
Dan 9.10-14
32.24
Jer 33.4;
Ezek 14.21;
Deut 4.26;
Zech 1.6
32.25
vv. 8,24
32.27
Num 16.22
32.28
Jer 34.2,3
32.29
Jer 21.10;
37.8,10;
52.13; 19.13
32.30
Jer 2.7;
22.21; 25.7
32.31
2 Kings 23.27;
24.3
32.32
Isa 1.4-6;
Dan 9.8
32.33
Jer 2.27;
Ezek 8.16;
Jer 35.15

[s] Or to thousands

backs to me, not their faces; though I have taught them persistently, they would not listen and accept correction. 34 They set up their abominations in the house that bears my name, and defiled it. 35 They built the high places of Baal in the valley of the son of Hinnom, to offer up their sons and daughters to Molech, though I did not command them, nor did it enter my mind that they should do this abomination, causing Judah to sin.

36 Now therefore thus says the LORD, the God of Israel, concerning this city of which you say, "It is being given into the hand of the king of Babylon by the sword, by famine, and by pestilence": 37 See, I am going to gather them from all the lands to which I drove them in my anger and my wrath and in great indignation; I will bring them back to this place, and I will settle them in safety. 38 They shall be my people, and I will be their God. 39 I will give them one heart and one way, that they may fear me for all time, for their own good and the good of their children after them. 40 I will make an everlasting covenant with them, never to draw back from doing good to them; and I will put the fear of me in their hearts, so that they may not turn from me. 41 I will rejoice in doing good to them, and I will plant them in this land in faithfulness, with all my heart and all my soul.

42 For thus says the LORD: Just as I have brought all this great disaster upon this people, so I will bring upon them all the good fortune that I now promise them. 43 Fields shall be bought in this land of which you are saying, It is a desolation, without human beings or animals; it has been given into the hands of the Chaldeans. 44 Fields shall be bought for money, and deeds shall be signed and sealed and witnessed, in the land of Benjamin, in the places around Jerusalem, and in the cities of Judah, of the hill country, of the Shephelah, and of the Negeb; for I

32.34
Jer 7.30,31;
Ezek 8.5,6
32.35
Jer 7.31;
19.5;
Lev 18.21;
1 Kings 11.33
32.37
Deut 30.3;
Jer 23.3,6;
Zech 14.11
32.38
Jer 30.22;
31.33
32.39
Jer 24.7;
Ezek 11.19,
20; 37.25
32.40
Isa 55.3;
31.31,33;
Ezek 39.29
32.41
Deut 30.9;
Zeph 3.17;
Am 9.15
32.42
Jer 31.28;
Zech 8.14,
15;
Jer 33.14
32.43
vv. 15,25
32.44
Jer 17.26;
33.7,11,26

33.1
Jer 32.2,3
33.2
Jer 10.16;
51.19;
Ex 15.3
33.3
Ps 50.15;
Jer 29.12;
32.17,27;
Isa 48.6
33.4
Jer 32.13,
14,24
33.5
Isa 8.17;
Jer 21.10
33.6
Isa 66.12;
Gal 5.22,23
33.7
Jer 32.44;
Am 9.14,15
33.8
Mic 7.18;
Zech 13.1;
Heb 9.13,14
33.9
Isa 62.7;
Jer 13.11;
Isa 60.5
33.10
Jer 32.43;
26.9; 34.22
33.11
Isa 35.10;
51.3,11;
1 Chr 16.8,
34;

will restore their fortunes, says the LORD.

Healing after Punishment

33 The word of the LORD came to Jeremiah a second time, while he was still confined in the court of the guard: 2 Thus says the LORD who made the earth,[t] the LORD who formed it to establish it—the LORD is his name: 3 Call to me and I will answer you, and will tell you great and hidden things that you have not known. 4 For thus says the LORD, the God of Israel, concerning the houses of this city and the houses of the kings of Judah that were torn down to make a defense against the siege-ramps and before the sword:[u] 5 The Chaldeans are coming in to fight[v] and to fill them with the dead bodies of those whom I shall strike down in my anger and my wrath, for I have hidden my face from this city because of all their wickedness. 6 I am going to bring it recovery and healing; I will heal them and reveal to them abundance[u] of prosperity and security. 7 I will restore the fortunes of Judah and the fortunes of Israel, and rebuild them as they were at first. 8 I will cleanse them from all the guilt of their sin against me, and I will forgive all the guilt of their sin and rebellion against me. 9 And this city[w] shall be to me a name of joy, a praise and a glory before all the nations of the earth who shall hear of all the good that I do for them; they shall fear and tremble because of all the good and all the prosperity I provide for it.

10 Thus says the LORD: In this place of which you say, "It is a waste without human beings or animals," in the towns of Judah and the streets of Jerusalem that are desolate, without inhabitants, human or animal, there shall once more be heard 11 the voice of mirth and the voice of gladness, the voice

2 Chr 5.13; Lev 7.12

[t] Gk: Heb it [u] Meaning of Heb uncertain
[v] Cn: Heb They are coming in to fight against the Chaldeans [w] Heb And it

of the bridegroom and the voice of the bride, the voices of those who sing, as they bring thank offerings to the house of the LORD:

"Give thanks to the LORD of
hosts,
for the LORD is good,
for his steadfast love
endures forever!"

For I will restore the fortunes of the land as at first, says the LORD.

12 Thus says the LORD of hosts: In this place that is waste, without human beings or animals, and in all its towns there shall again be pasture for shepherds resting their flocks. 13 In the towns of the hill country, of the Shephelah, and of the Negeb, in the land of Benjamin, the places around Jerusalem, and in the towns of Judah, flocks shall again pass under the hands of the one who counts them, says the LORD.

The Righteous Branch and the Covenant with David

14 The days are surely coming, says the LORD, when I will fulfill the promise I made to the house of Israel and the house of Judah. 15 In those days and at that time I will cause a righteous Branch to spring up for David; and he shall execute justice and righteousness in the land. 16 In those days Judah will be saved and Jerusalem will live in safety. And this is the name by which it will be called: "The LORD is our righteousness."

17 For thus says the LORD: David shall never lack a man to sit on the throne of the house of Israel, 18 and the levitical priests shall never lack a man in my presence to offer burnt offerings, to make grain offerings, and to make sacrifices for all time.

19 The word of the LORD came to Jeremiah: 20 Thus says the LORD: If any of you could break my covenant with the day and my covenant with the night, so that day and night would not come at their appointed time, 21 only then could my covenant with my servant David be broken, so that he would not have a son to reign on his throne, and my

covenant with my ministers the Levites. 22 Just as the host of heaven cannot be numbered and the sands of the sea cannot be measured, so I will increase the offspring of my servant David, and the Levites who minister to me.

23 The word of the LORD came to Jeremiah: 24 Have you not observed how these people say, "The two families that the LORD chose have been rejected by him," and how they hold my people in such contempt that they no longer regard them as a nation? 25 Thus says the LORD: Only if I had not established my covenant with day and night and the ordinances of heaven and earth, 26 would I reject the offspring of Jacob and of my servant David and not choose any of his descendants as rulers over the offspring of Abraham, Isaac, and Jacob. For I will restore their fortunes, and will have mercy upon them.

Death in Captivity Predicted for Zedekiah

34 The word that came to Jeremiah from the LORD, when King Nebuchadrezzar of Babylon and all his army and all the kingdoms of the earth and all the peoples under his dominion were fighting against Jerusalem and all its cities: 2 "Thus says the LORD, the God of Israel: Go and speak to King Zedekiah of Judah and say to him: Thus says the LORD: I am going to give this city into the hand of the king of Babylon, and he shall burn it with fire. 3 And you yourself shall not escape from his hand, but shall surely be captured and handed over to him; you shall see the king of Babylon eye to eye and speak with him face to face; and you shall go to Babylon. 4 Yet hear the word of the LORD, O King Zedekiah of Judah! Thus says the LORD concerning you: You shall not die by the sword; 5 you shall die in peace. And as spices were burned[x] for your ancestors, the earlier kings who preceded you, so they shall burn

x Heb as there was burning

Cross-references (center column):

33.12
Isa 65.10;
Ezek 34.12-14
33.13
Jer 17.26;
Lev 27.32;
Lk 15.4
33.14
Jer 23.5;
Ezek 34.23-25
33.15
Isa 4.2;
11.1;
Zech 3.8;
Ps 72.1-5
33.16
Jer 23.6;
Isa 45.24,
25; Phil 3.9
33.17
2 Sam 7.16;
1 Kings 2.4;
Lk 1.32,33
33.18
Deut 18.1;
24.8;
Heb 13.15
33.20
Ps 89.37;
Isa 54.9;
Jer 31.36
33.21
Ps 89.34

33.22
Gen 15.5;
22.17;
Jer 30.19
33.24
Neh 4.2-4;
Ezek 36.2
33.25
Ps 74.16,17;
Jer 31.35,36
33.26
Jer 31.37;
Isa 14.1;
Hos 1.7;
2.23
34.1
2 Kings 25.1ff;
Jer 39.1;
1.15;
Dan 2.37,38
34.2
Jer 22.1,2;
37.1-4;
Jer 32.29
34.3
Jer 32.4;
2 Kings 25.6,
7; Jer 39.6,7
34.5
2 Chr 16.14;
21.19;
Jer 22.18

spices[y] for you and lament for you, saying, "Alas, lord!" For I have spoken the word, says the LORD.

6 Then the prophet Jeremiah spoke all these words to Zedekiah king of Judah, in Jerusalem, [7]when the army of the king of Babylon was fighting against Jerusalem and against all the cities of Judah that were left, Lachish and Azekah; for these were the only fortified cities of Judah that remained.

Treacherous Treatment of Slaves

8 The word that came to Jeremiah from the LORD, after King Zedekiah had made a covenant with all the people in Jerusalem to make a proclamation of liberty to them, [9]that all should set free their Hebrew slaves, male and female, so that no one should hold another Judean in slavery. [10]And they obeyed, all the officials and all the people who had entered into the covenant that all would set free their slaves, male or female, so that they would not be enslaved again; they obeyed and set them free. [11]But afterward they turned around and took back the male and female slaves they had set free, and brought them again into subjection as slaves. [12]The word of the LORD came to Jeremiah from the LORD: [13]Thus says the LORD, the God of Israel: I myself made a covenant with your ancestors when I brought them out of the land of Egypt, out of the house of slavery, saying, [14]"Every seventh year each of you must set free any Hebrews who have been sold to you and have served you six years; you must set them free from your service." But your ancestors did not listen to me or incline their ears to me. [15]You yourselves recently repented and did what was right in my sight by proclaiming liberty to one another, and you made a covenant before me in the house that is called by my name; [16]but then you turned around and profaned my name when each of you took back your male and female slaves, whom you had set free according to their de-

Cross references
34.7 2 Chr 11.9; 2 Kings 18.13; 19.8
34.8 Ex 21.2; Lev 25.10
34.9 Neh 5.11; Lev 25.39-46
34.11 v. 21; Jer 37.5; Hos 6.4
34.13 Ex 24.3,7,8; Deut 15.22
34.14 Ex 21.2; 23.10; Deut 15.12; 1 Sam 8.7, 8; 2 Kings 17.13, 14
34.15 2 Kings 23.3; Neh 10.29; Jer 7.10,11; 32.34
34.16 Ex 20.7; Lev 19.12
34.17 Mt 7.2; Gal 6.7; Deut 28.25, 64
34.18 Deut 17.2; Hos 6.7; Gen 15.10, 17
34.19 v. 10
34.20 Jer 11.21; 7.33; 19.7
34.21 Jer 37.5,11
34.22 Jer 37.8,10; 4.7; 33.10; 44.22
35.1 2 Kings 24.1; Jer 1.3; 27.20
35.2 2 Kings 10.15; 1 Chr 2.55; 1 Kings 6.5
35.4 Deut 33.1; 1 Kings 12.22; 2 Kings 12.9; 25.18; 1 Chr 9.18, 19

sire, and you brought them again into subjection to be your slaves. [17]Therefore, thus says the LORD: You have not obeyed me by granting a release to your neighbors and friends; I am going to grant a release to you, says the LORD—a release to the sword, to pestilence, and to famine. I will make you a horror to all the kingdoms of the earth. [18]And those who transgressed my covenant and did not keep the terms of the covenant that they made before me, I will make like[z] the calf when they cut it in two and passed between its parts: [19]the officials of Judah, the officials of Jerusalem, the eunuchs, the priests, and all the people of the land who passed between the parts of the calf [20]shall be handed over to their enemies and to those who seek their lives. Their corpses shall become food for the birds of the air and the wild animals of the earth. [21]And as for King Zedekiah of Judah and his officials, I will hand them over to their enemies and to those who seek their lives, to the army of the king of Babylon, which has withdrawn from you. [22]I am going to command, says the LORD, and will bring them back to this city; and they will fight against it, and take it, and burn it with fire. The towns of Judah I will make a desolation without inhabitant.

The Rechabites Commended

35 The word that came to Jeremiah from the LORD in the days of King Jehoiakim son of Josiah of Judah: [2]Go to the house of the Rechabites, and speak with them, and bring them to the house of the LORD, into one of the chambers; then offer them wine to drink. [3]So I took Jaazaniah son of Jeremiah son of Habazziniah, and his brothers, and all his sons, and the whole house of the Rechabites. [4]I brought them to the house of the LORD into the chamber of the sons of Hanan son of Igdaliah, the man of God, which was near the cham-

[y] Heb *shall burn* [z] Cn: Heb lacks *like*

ber of the officials, above the chamber of Maaseiah son of Shallum, keeper of the threshold. ⁵Then I set before the Rechabites pitchers full of wine, and cups; and I said to them, "Have some wine." ⁶But they answered, "We will drink no wine, for our ancestor Jonadab son of Rechab commanded us, 'You shall never drink wine, neither you nor your children; ⁷nor shall you ever build a house, or sow seed; nor shall you plant a vineyard, or even own one; but you shall live in tents all your days, that you may live many days in the land where you reside.' ⁸We have obeyed the charge of our ancestor Jonadab son of Rechab in all that he commanded us, to drink no wine all our days, ourselves, our wives, our sons, or our daughters, ⁹and not to build houses to live in. We have no vineyard or field or seed; ¹⁰but we have lived in tents, and have obeyed and done all that our ancestor Jonadab commanded us. ¹¹But when King Nebuchadrezzar of Babylon came up against the land, we said, 'Come, and let us go to Jerusalem for fear of the army of the Chaldeans and the army of the Arameans.' That is why we are living in Jerusalem."

12 Then the word of the LORD came to Jeremiah: ¹³Thus says the LORD of hosts, the God of Israel: Go and say to the people of Judah and the inhabitants of Jerusalem, Can you not learn a lesson and obey my words? says the LORD. ¹⁴The command has been carried out that Jonadab son of Rechab gave to his descendants to drink no wine; and they drink none to this day, for they have obeyed their ancestor's command. But I myself have spoken to you persistently, and you have not obeyed me. ¹⁵I have sent to you all my servants the prophets, sending them persistently, saying, 'Turn now everyone of you from your evil way, and amend your doings, and do not go after other gods to serve them, and then you shall live in the land that I gave to you and your ancestors.' But you did not incline

your ear or obey me. ¹⁶The descendants of Jonadab son of Rechab have carried out the command that their ancestor gave them, but this people has not obeyed me. ¹⁷Therefore, thus says the LORD, the God of hosts, the God of Israel: I am going to bring on Judah and on all the inhabitants of Jerusalem every disaster that I have pronounced against them; because I have spoken to them and they have not listened, I have called to them and they have not answered.

18 But to the house of the Rechabites Jeremiah said: Thus says the LORD of hosts, the God of Israel: Because you have obeyed the command of your ancestor Jonadab, and kept all his precepts, and done all that he commanded you, ¹⁹therefore thus says the LORD of hosts, the God of Israel: Jonadab son of Rechab shall not lack a descendant to stand before me for all time.

The Scroll Read in the Temple

36 In the fourth year of King Jehoiakim son of Josiah of Judah, this word came to Jeremiah from the LORD: ²Take a scroll and write on it all the words that I have spoken to you against Israel and Judah and all the nations, from the day I spoke to you, from the days of Josiah until today. ³It may be that when the house of Judah hears of all the disasters that I intend to do to them, all of them may turn from their evil ways, so that I may forgive their iniquity and their sin.

4 Then Jeremiah called Baruch son of Neriah, and Baruch wrote on a scroll at Jeremiah's dictation all the words of the LORD that he had spoken to him. ⁵And Jeremiah ordered Baruch, saying, "I am prevented from entering the house of the LORD; ⁶so you go yourself, and on a fast day in the hearing of the people in the LORD's house you shall read the words of the LORD from the scroll that you have written at my dictation. You shall read

35.5 Am 2.12
35.6 2 Kings 10.15; 1 Chr 2.55; Lev 10.9; Lk 1.15
35.7 Gen 25.27; Heb 11.9; Ex 20.12; Eph 6.2,3
35.8 Prov 1.8,9; Eph 6.1; Col 3.20
35.9 v. 7
35.10 vv. 6,7
35.11 2 Kings 24.1, 2; Jer 4.5-7; 8.14
35.13 Isa 28.9-12; Jer 32.33
35.14 2 Chr 36.15; Jer 7.13; 25.3; Isa 30.9; 50.2
35.15 Jer 26.5; 32.33; Isa 1.16,17; Jer 4.1; 18.11; 7.6; 13.10; 22.4; 34.14

35.16 v. 14
35.17 Jer 19.3,15; Mic 3.12; Prov 1.24; Isa 65.12; 66.4; Jer 7.13
35.19 Jer 33.17; 15.19
36.1 2 Kings 24.1; Jer 25.1,3
36.2 vv. 6,23,28; Zech 5.1; Jer 1.9,10; 25.9-29; 25.3
36.3 v. 7; Jer 26.3; Isa 55.7; Jer 18.8; Jon 3.8; Mk 4.12; Acts 3.19
36.4 v. 18; Jer 32.12; v. 14; Ezek 2.9
36.5 Jer 32.2; 33.1

them also in the hearing of all the people of Judah who come up from their towns. ⁷It may be that their plea will come before the Lᴏʀᴅ, and that all of them will turn from their evil ways, for great is the anger and wrath that the Lᴏʀᴅ has pronounced against this people." ⁸And Baruch son of Neriah did all that the prophet Jeremiah ordered him about reading from the scroll the words of the Lᴏʀᴅ in the Lᴏʀᴅ's house.

9 In the fifth year of King Jehoiakim son of Josiah of Judah, in the ninth month, all the people in Jerusalem and all the people who came from the towns of Judah to Jerusalem proclaimed a fast before the Lᴏʀᴅ. ¹⁰Then, in the hearing of all the people, Baruch read the words of Jeremiah from the scroll, in the house of the Lᴏʀᴅ, in the chamber of Gemariah son of Shaphan the secretary, which was in the upper court, at the entry of the New Gate of the Lᴏʀᴅ's house.

The Scroll Read in the Palace

11 When Micaiah son of Gemariah son of Shaphan heard all the words of the Lᴏʀᴅ from the scroll, ¹²he went down to the king's house, into the secretary's chamber; and all the officials were sitting there: Elishama the secretary, Delaiah son of Shemaiah, Elnathan son of Achbor, Gemariah son of Shaphan, Zedekiah son of Hananiah, and all the officials. ¹³And Micaiah told them all the words that he had heard, when Baruch read the scroll in the hearing of the people. ¹⁴Then all the officials sent Jehudi son of Nethaniah son of Shelemiah son of Cushi to say to Baruch, "Bring the scroll that you read in the hearing of the people, and come." So Baruch son of Neriah took the scroll in his hand and came to them. ¹⁵And they said to him, "Sit down and read it to us." So Baruch read it to them. ¹⁶When they heard all the words, they turned to one another in alarm, and said to Baruch, "We certainly must report all these words to the

king." ¹⁷Then they questioned Baruch, "Tell us now, how did you write all these words? Was it at his dictation?" ¹⁸Baruch answered them, "He dictated all these words to me, and I wrote them with ink on the scroll." ¹⁹Then the officials said to Baruch, "Go and hide, you and Jeremiah, and let no one know where you are."

Jehoiakim Burns the Scroll

20 Leaving the scroll in the chamber of Elishama the secretary, they went to the court of the king; and they reported all the words to the king. ²¹Then the king sent Jehudi to get the scroll, and he took it from the chamber of Elishama the secretary; and Jehudi read it to the king and all the officials who stood beside the king. ²²Now the king was sitting in his winter apartment (it was the ninth month), and there was a fire burning in the brazier before him. ²³As Jehudi read three or four columns, the kingᵃ would cut them off with a penknife and throw them into the fire in the brazier, until the entire scroll was consumed in the fire that was in the brazier. ²⁴Yet neither the king, nor any of his servants who heard all these words, was alarmed, nor did they tear their garments. ²⁵Even when Elnathan and Delaiah and Gemariah urged the king not to burn the scroll, he would not listen to them. ²⁶And the king commanded Jerahmeel the king's son and Seraiah son of Azriel and Shelemiah son of Abdeel to arrest the secretary Baruch and the prophet Jeremiah. But the Lᴏʀᴅ hid them.

Jeremiah Dictates Another

27 Now, after the king had burned the scroll with the words that Baruch wrote at Jeremiah's dictation, the word of the Lᴏʀᴅ came to Jeremiah: ²⁸Take another scroll and write on it all the former words that were in the first scroll, which King Jehoiakim of Judah has burned. ²⁹And concerning King Jehoiakim of Judah you shall

36.7
2 Kings 22.13;
Jer 4.4; 21.5
36.8
v. 6
36.9
v. 6;
Esther 4.16;
Jon 3.5
36.10
Jer 26.10
36.11
v. 13
36.12
vv. 20,25;
Jer 26.22
36.13
2 Kings 22.10;
36.14; v. 21
36.15
v. 21
36.16
v. 24;
Acts 24.25;
Jer 13.18;
Am 7.10,11

36.18
v. 4
36.19
v. 26;
Jer 26.20-24
36.20
v. 12
36.21
v. 14;
2 Chr 34.18
36.22
Am 3.15
36.23
v. 29
36.24
2 Kings 19.1,
2; 22.11;
Isa 36.22;
37.1
36.25
Acts 5.34-39
36.26
1 Kings 19.1ff;
Jer 15.20,21
36.27
vv. 23,4,18
36.28
Jer 28.13,14
36.29
Job 15.24,
25; Isa 45.9;
30.10;
32.3; 25.9-11

ᵃ Heb *he*

say: Thus says the LORD, You have dared to burn this scroll, saying, Why have you written in it that the king of Babylon will certainly come and destroy this land, and will cut off from it human beings and animals? 30 Therefore thus says the LORD concerning King Jehoiakim of Judah: He shall have no one to sit upon the throne of David, and his dead body shall be cast out to the heat by day and the frost by night. 31 And I will punish him and his offspring and his servants for their iniquity; I will bring on them, and on the inhabitants of Jerusalem, and on the people of Judah, all the disasters with which I have threatened them—but they would not listen.

32 Then Jeremiah took another scroll and gave it to the secretary Baruch son of Neriah, who wrote on it at Jeremiah's dictation all the words of the scroll that King Jehoiakim of Judah had burned in the fire; and many similar words were added to them.

Zedekiah's Vain Hope

37 Zedekiah son of Josiah, whom King Nebuchadrezzar of Babylon made king in the land of Judah, succeeded Coniah son of Jehoiakim. 2 But neither he nor his servants nor the people of the land listened to the words of the LORD that he spoke through the prophet Jeremiah.

3 King Zedekiah sent Jehucal son of Shelemiah and the priest Zephaniah son of Maaseiah to the prophet Jeremiah saying, "Please pray for us to the LORD our God." 4 Now Jeremiah was still going in and out among the people, for he had not yet been put in prison. 5 Meanwhile, the army of Pharaoh had come out of Egypt; and when the Chaldeans who were besieging Jerusalem heard news of them, they withdrew from Jerusalem.

6 Then the word of the LORD came to the prophet Jeremiah: 7 Thus says the LORD, God of Israel: This is what the two of you shall

say to the king of Judah, who sent you to me to inquire of me, Pharaoh's army, which set out to help you, is going to return to its own land, to Egypt. 8 And the Chaldeans shall return and fight against this city; they shall take it and burn it with fire. 9 Thus says the LORD: Do not deceive yourselves, saying, "The Chaldeans will surely go away from us," for they will not go away. 10 Even if you defeated the whole army of Chaldeans who are fighting against you, and there remained of them only wounded men in their tents, they would rise up and burn this city with fire.

Jeremiah Is Imprisoned

11 Now when the Chaldean army had withdrawn from Jerusalem at the approach of Pharaoh's army, 12 Jeremiah set out from Jerusalem to go to the land of Benjamin to receive his share of property[b] among the people there. 13 When he reached the Benjamin Gate, a sentinel there named Irijah son of Shelemiah son of Hananiah arrested the prophet Jeremiah saying, "You are deserting to the Chaldeans." 14 And Jeremiah said, "That is a lie; I am not deserting to the Chaldeans." But Irijah would not listen to him, and arrested Jeremiah and brought him to the officials. 15 The officials were enraged at Jeremiah, and they beat him and imprisoned him in the house of the secretary Jonathan, for it had been made a prison. 16 Thus Jeremiah was put in the cistern house, in the cells, and remained there many days.

17 Then King Zedekiah sent for him, and received him. The king questioned him secretly in his house, and said, "Is there any word from the LORD?" Jeremiah said, "There is!" Then he said, "You shall be handed over to the king of Babylon." 18 Jeremiah also said to King Zedekiah, "What wrong have I done to you or your servants or this people, that you have put me in prison? 19 Where are your prophets

b Meaning of Heb uncertain

Cross references

36.30
2 Kings 24.12-15; Jer 22.30; 22.19
36.31
Jer 23.34; Deut 28.15; Jer 19.15
36.32
vv. 28,4,23
37.1
2 Kings 24.17; 2 Chr 36.10; Jer 22.24; Ezek 17.12-21
37.2
2 Chr 36.12, 14
37.3
Jer 21.1,2; 29.25; 52.24; 1 Kings 13.6; Acts 8.24
37.4
v. 15
37.5
2 Kings 24.7; Ezek 17.15; Jer 34.21
37.7
Jer 21.2; Isa 30.1-3; 31.1-3; Ezek 17.17
37.8
Jer 34.22
37.9
Jer 29.8
37.10
Jer 21.4,5; Joel 2.11
37.11
v. 5
37.13
Jer 38.7; Zech 14.10; Jer 18.18; 20.10; Lk 23.2; Acts 24.5-9, 13
37.14
Jer 40.4-6; Mt 5.11,12
37.15
Jer 18.23; 2 Chr 16.10; 18.26
37.16
Jer 38.6
37.17
Jer 38.5, 14-16,24-27
37.18
Dan 6.22; Jn 10.32; Acts 25.8, 11,25
37.19
Jer 2.28; 6.14; 29.31

who prophesied to you, saying, 'The king of Babylon will not come against you and against this land'? [20] Now please hear me, my lord king: be good enough to listen to my plea, and do not send me back to the house of the secretary Jonathan to die there." [21] So King Zedekiah gave orders, and they committed Jeremiah to the court of the guard; and a loaf of bread was given him daily from the bakers' street, until all the bread of the city was gone. So Jeremiah remained in the court of the guard.

Jeremiah in the Dungeon

38 Now Shephatiah son of Mattan, Gedaliah son of Pashhur, Jucal son of Shelemiah, and Pashhur son of Malchiah heard the words that Jeremiah was saying to all the people, [2] Thus says the LORD, Those who stay in this city shall die by the sword, by famine, and by pestilence; but those who go out to the Chaldeans shall live; they shall have their lives as a prize of war, and live. [3] Thus says the LORD, This city shall surely be handed over to the army of the king of Babylon and be taken. [4] Then the officials said to the king, "This man ought to be put to death, because he is discouraging the soldiers who are left in this city, and all the people, by speaking such words to them. For this man is not seeking the welfare of this people, but their harm." [5] King Zedekiah said, "Here he is; he is in your hands; for the king is powerless against you." [6] So they took Jeremiah and threw him into the cistern of Malchiah, the king's son, which was in the court of the guard, letting Jeremiah down by ropes. Now there was no water in the cistern, but only mud, and Jeremiah sank in the mud.

Jeremiah Is Rescued by Ebed-melech

[7] Ebed-melech the Ethiopian,[c] a eunuch in the king's house, heard that they had put Jeremiah into the cistern. The king happened to be sitting at the Benjamin Gate, [8] So

Ebed-melech left the king's house and spoke to the king, [9] "My lord king, these men have acted wickedly in all they did to the prophet Jeremiah by throwing him into the cistern to die there of hunger, for there is no bread left in the city." [10] Then the king commanded Ebed-melech the Ethiopian,[c] "Take three men with you from here, and pull the prophet Jeremiah up from the cistern before he dies." [11] So Ebed-melech took the men with him and went to the house of the king, to a wardrobe of[d] the storehouse, and took from there old rags and worn-out clothes, which he let down to Jeremiah in the cistern by ropes. [12] Then Ebed-melech the Ethiopian[c] said to Jeremiah, "Just put the rags and clothes between your armpits and the ropes." Jeremiah did so. [13] Then they drew Jeremiah up by the ropes and pulled him out of the cistern. And Jeremiah remained in the court of the guard.

Zedekiah Consults Jeremiah Again

[14] King Zedekiah sent for the prophet Jeremiah and received him at the third entrance of the temple of the LORD. The king said to Jeremiah, "I have something to ask you; do not hide anything from me." [15] Jeremiah said to Zedekiah, "If I tell you, you will put me to death, will you not? And if I give you advice, you will not listen to me." [16] So King Zedekiah swore an oath in secret to Jeremiah, "As the LORD lives, who gave us our lives, I will not put you to death or hand you over to these men who seek your life."

[17] Then Jeremiah said to Zedekiah, "Thus says the LORD, the God of hosts, the God of Israel, If you will only surrender to the officials of the king of Babylon, then your life shall be spared, and this city shall not be burned with fire, and you and your house shall live.

37.20
Jer 36.7;
38.26; 18.23
37.21
Jer 32.3;
38.13,28;
Isa 33.16;
Jer 38.9;
52.6; 39.14,
15
38.1
Jer 37.3;
21.1,8
38.2
Jer 21.9;
42.17; 45.5
38.3
Jer 21.10;
32.3
38.4
Jer 18.23;
26.11;
1 Kings 18.17,
18; 21.20;
Am 7.10;
Acts 16.20;
Jer 29.7
38.5
2 Sam 3.39
38.6
Jer 37.21;
Acts 16.24;
Zech 9.11
38.7
Jer 39.16;
37.13;
Am 5.10

38.9
Jer 37.21;
52.6
38.11
v. 6
38.13
Jer 37.21;
39.14,15
38.14
Jer 21.1,2;
37.17; 15.11;
42.2-5,20
38.15
Lk 22.67,68
38.16
Jer 37.17;
Isa 57.16;
Zech 12.1;
vv. 4-6
38.17
Ps 80.7,14;
1 Chr 17.24;
Ezek 8.4;
2 Kings 24.12;
26.27-30

c Or *Nubian*; Heb *Cushite* d Cn: Heb *to under*

18 But if you do not surrender to the officials of the king of Babylon, then this city shall be handed over to the Chaldeans, and they shall burn it with fire, and you yourself shall not escape from their hand." 19 King Zedekiah said to Jeremiah, "I am afraid of the Judeans who have deserted to the Chaldeans, for I might be handed over to them and they would abuse me." 20 Jeremiah said, "That will not happen. Just obey the voice of the Lord in what I say to you, and it shall go well with you, and your life shall be spared. 21 But if you are determined not to surrender, this is what the Lord has shown me — 22 a vision of all the women remaining in the house of the king of Judah being led out to the officials of the king of Babylon and saying,

'Your trusted friends have
 seduced you
 and have overcome you;
Now that your feet are stuck
 in the mud,
 they desert you.'

23 All your wives and your children shall be led out to the Chaldeans, and you yourself shall not escape from their hand, but shall be seized by the king of Babylon; and this city shall be burned with fire."

24 Then Zedekiah said to Jeremiah, "Do not let anyone else know of this conversation, or you will die. 25 If the officials should hear that I have spoken with you, and they should come and say to you, 'Just tell us what you said to the king; do not conceal it from us, or we will put you to death. What did the king say to you?' 26 then you shall say to them, 'I was presenting my plea to the king not to send me back to the house of Jonathan to die there.' " 27 All the officials did come to Jeremiah and questioned him; and he answered them in the very words the king had commanded. So they stopped questioning him, for the conversation had not been overheard. 28 And Jeremiah remained in the court of the guard until the day that Jerusalem was taken.

38.18
Jer 27.8;
32.4; 34.3
38.19
Isa 51.12,
13;
Jn 12.42;
19,12,13;
Jer 39.9;
2 Chr 30.10;
Neh 4.1
38.20
Jer 11.4,8;
7.23;
Isa 55.3
38.22
Jer 6.12;
8.10; 43.6
38.23
Jer 39.6;
41.10
38.25
vv. 4-6,27
38.26
Jer 37.15,20
38.27
1 Sam 10.15,
16; 16.2-5
38.28
Jer 37.21;
39.14

39.1
2 Kings 25.1-4;
Jer 52.4-7;
Ezek 24.1,2
39.2
2 Kings 25.4;
Jer 52.7
39.3
Jer 38.17
39.4
2 Kings 25.4;
Jer 52.7;
Am 2.14;
2 Chr 32.5
39.5
Jer 32.4;
38.18,23;
Josh 4.13;
2 Kings 23.33
39.6
2 Kings 25.7;
Jer 34.19-21
39.7
2 Kings 25.7;
Jer 52.11;
Ezek 12.13;
Jer 32.5
39.8
2 Kings 25.9,
10;
Jer 38.18;
52.13
39.9
2 Kings 25.11,
20;
Jer 52.12-16;
24.8; 38.19
39.10
2 Kings 25.12;
Jer 52.16

The Fall of Jerusalem

39 In the ninth year of King Zedekiah of Judah, in the tenth month, King Nebuchadrezzar of Babylon and all his army came against Jerusalem and besieged it; 2 in the eleventh year of Zedekiah, in the fourth month, on the ninth day of the month, a breach was made in the city. 3 When Jerusalem was taken,e all the officials of the king of Babylon came and sat in the middle gate: Nergal-sharezer, Samgar-nebo, Sarsechim the Rab-saris, Nergal-sharezer the Rab-mag, with all the rest of the officials of the king of Babylon. 4 When King Zedekiah of Judah and all the soldiers saw them, they fled, going out of the city at night by way of the king's garden through the gate between the two walls; and they went toward the Arabah. 5 But the army of the Chaldeans pursued them, and overtook Zedekiah in the plains of Jericho; and when they had taken him, they brought him up to King Nebuchadrezzar of Babylon, at Riblah, in the land of Hamath; and he passed sentence on him. 6 The king of Babylon slaughtered the sons of Zedekiah at Riblah before his eyes; also the king of Babylon slaughtered all the nobles of Judah. 7 He put out the eyes of Zedekiah, and bound him in fetters to take him to Babylon. 8 The Chaldeans burned the king's house and the houses of the people, and broke down the walls of Jerusalem. 9 Then Nebuzaradan the captain of the guard exiled to Babylon the rest of the people who were left in the city, those who had deserted to him, and the people who remained. 10 Nebuzaradan the captain of the guard left in the land of Judah some of the poor people who owned nothing, and gave them vineyards and fields at the same time.

e This clause has been transposed from 38.28

Jeremiah, Set Free, Remembers Ebed-melech

11 King Nebuchadrezzar of Babylon gave command concerning Jeremiah through Nebuzaradan, the captain of the guard, saying, [12] "Take him, look after him well and do him no harm, but deal with him as he may ask you." [13] So Nebuzaradan the captain of the guard, Nebushazban the Rab-saris, Nergal-sharezer the Rab-mag, and all the chief officers of the king of Babylon sent [14] and took Jeremiah from the court of the guard. They entrusted him to Gedaliah son of Ahikam son of Shaphan to be brought home. So he stayed with his own people.

15 The word of the LORD came to Jeremiah while he was confined in the court of the guard: [16] Go and say to Ebed-melech the Ethiopian:[f] Thus says the LORD of hosts, the God of Israel: I am going to fulfill my words against this city for evil and not for good, and they shall be accomplished in your presence on that day. [17] But I will save you on that day, says the LORD, and you shall not be handed over to those whom you dread. [18] For I will surely save you, and you shall not fall by the sword; but you shall have your life as a prize of war, because you have trusted in me, says the LORD.

Jeremiah with Gedaliah the Governor

40 The word that came to Jeremiah from the LORD after Nebuzaradan the captain of the guard had let him go from Ramah, when he took him bound in fetters along with all the captives of Jerusalem and Judah who were being exiled to Babylon. [2] The captain of the guard took Jeremiah and said to him, "The LORD your God threatened this place with this disaster; [3] and now the LORD has brought it about, and has done as he said, because all of you sinned against the LORD and did not obey his voice. Therefore this thing has come upon you. [4] Now look, I have just

39.11
Jer 1.8;
15.20,21;
Acts 24.23
39.14
Jer 58.28;
40.1-6;
2 Kings 22.12,
14;
2 Chr 34.20
39.16
Jer 58.7,12;
21.10;
Dan 9.12;
Zech 1.6
39.17
Ps 41.1,2;
50.15
39.18
Jer 21.9;
45.5;
Ps 34.22;
Jer 17.7,8
40.1
Jer 39.9,11,
14; 31.15;
Eph 6.20
40.2
Jer 22.8,9;
50.7
40.3
Deut 29.24,
25;
Dan 9.11
40.4
Jer 39.11,
12;
Gen 20.15

40.5
Jer 39.14;
2 Kings 25.23;
v. 4;
Jer 52.34
40.6
Jer 39.14;
Judg 20.1
40.7
2 Kings 25.23,
24;
Jer 39.10;
52.16
40.8
Jer 41.1
40.9
2 Kings 25.24;
Jer 27.11;
38.17-20
40.10
v. 6;
Jer 35.19;
39.10; v. 12;
Jer 48.32
40.11
Isa 16.4;
1 Sam 11.1;
12.12;
Isa 11.14

released you today from the fetters on your hands. If you wish to come with me to Babylon, come, and I will take good care of you; but if you do not wish to come with me to Babylon, you need not come. See, the whole land is before you; go wherever you think it good and right to go. [5] If you remain,[g] then return to Gedaliah son of Ahikam son of Shaphan, whom the king of Babylon appointed governor of the towns of Judah, and stay with him among the people; or go wherever you think it right to go." So the captain of the guard gave him an allowance of food and a present, and let him go. [6] Then Jeremiah went to Gedaliah son of Ahikam at Mizpah, and stayed with him among the people who were left in the land.

7 When all the leaders of the forces in the open country and their troops heard that the king of Babylon had appointed Gedaliah son of Ahikam governor in the land, and had committed to him men, women, and children, those of the poorest of the land who had not been taken into exile to Babylon, [8] they went to Gedaliah at Mizpah—Ishmael son of Nethaniah, Johanan son of Kareah, Seraiah son of Tanhumeth, the sons of Ephai the Netophathite, Jezaniah son of the Maacathite, they and their troops. [9] Gedaliah son of Ahikam son of Shaphan swore to them and their troops, saying, "Do not be afraid to serve the Chaldeans. Stay in the land and serve the king of Babylon, and it shall go well with you. [10] As for me, I am staying at Mizpah to represent you before the Chaldeans who come to us; but as for you, gather wine and summer fruits and oil, and store them in your vessels, and live in the towns that you have taken over." [11] Likewise, when all the Judeans who were in Moab and among the Ammonites and in Edom and in other lands heard that the king of Babylon had left a remnant in Judah

f Or *Nubian*; Heb *Cushite* g Syr: Meaning of Heb uncertain

and had appointed Gedaliah son of Ahikam son of Shaphan as governor over them, 12 then all the Judeans returned from all the places to which they had been scattered and came to the land of Judah, to Gedaliah at Mizpah; and they gathered wine and summer fruits in great abundance.

13 Now Johanan son of Kareah and all the leaders of the forces in the open country came to Gedaliah at Mizpah 14 and said to him, "Are you at all aware that Baalis king of the Ammonites has sent Ishmael son of Nethaniah to take your life?" But Gedaliah son of Ahikam would not believe them. 15 Then Johanan son of Kareah spoke secretly to Gedaliah at Mizpah, "Please let me go and kill Ishmael son of Nethaniah, and no one else will know. Why should he take your life, so that all the Judeans who are gathered around you would be scattered, and the remnant of Judah would perish?" 16 But Gedaliah son of Ahikam said to Johanan son of Kareah, "Do not do such a thing, for you are telling a lie about Ishmael."

Insurrection against Gedaliah

41 In the seventh month, Ishmael son of Nethaniah son of Elishama, of the royal family, one of the chief officers of the king, came with ten men to Gedaliah son of Ahikam, at Mizpah. As they ate bread together there at Mizpah, 2 Ishmael son of Nethaniah and the ten men with him got up and struck down Gedaliah son of Ahikam son of Shaphan with the sword and killed him, because the king of Babylon had appointed him governor in the land. 3 Ishmael also killed all the Judeans who were with Gedaliah at Mizpah, and the Chaldean soldiers who happened to be there.

4 On the day after the murder of Gedaliah, before anyone knew of it, 5 eighty men arrived from Shechem and Shiloh and Samaria, with their beards shaved and their clothes torn, and their bodies gashed, bringing grain offerings and in-

cense to present at the temple of the LORD. 6 And Ishmael son of Nethaniah came out from Mizpah to meet them, weeping as he came. As he met them, he said to them, "Come to Gedaliah son of Ahikam." 7 When they reached the middle of the city, Ishmael son of Nethaniah and the men with him slaughtered them, and threw them h into a cistern. 8 But there were ten men among them who said to Ishmael, "Do not kill us, for we have stores of wheat, barley, oil, and honey hidden in the fields." So he refrained, and did not kill them along with their companions.

9 Now the cistern into which Ishmael had thrown all the bodies of the men whom he had struck down was the large cistern i that King Asa had made for defense against King Baasha of Israel; Ishmael son of Nethaniah filled that cistern with those whom he had killed. 10 Then Ishmael took captive all the rest of the people who were in Mizpah, the king's daughters and all the people who were left at Mizpah, whom Nebuzaradan, the captain of the guard, had committed to Gedaliah son of Ahikam. Ishmael son of Nethaniah took them captive and set out to cross over to the Ammonites.

11 But when Johanan son of Kareah and all the leaders of the forces with him heard of all the crimes that Ishmael son of Nethaniah had done, 12 they took all their men and went to fight against Ishmael son of Nethaniah. They came upon him at the great pool that is in Gibeon. 13 And when all the people who were with Ishmael saw Johanan son of Kareah and all the leaders of the forces with him, they were glad. 14 So all the people whom Ishmael had carried away captive from Mizpah turned around and came back, and went to Johanan son of Kareah. 15 But Ishmael son of Nethaniah escaped from Johanan with eight men, and

40.12 Jer 43.5; v. 10
40.13 v. 8
40.14 Jer 41.10
40.15 1 Sam 26.8; 2 Sam 21.17; Jer 42.2
40.16 Mt 10.16
41.1 2 Kings 25.25; Jer 40.6,8, 14
41.2 2 Kings 25.25; Jer 40.5
41.5 Gen 33.18; Josh 18.1; 1 Kings 16.24, 29; Jer 16.6; 2 Kings 25.9
41.6 Jer 50.4
41.7 Isa 59.7; Ezek 22.27
41.9 1 Kings 15.22; 2 Chr 16.6
41.10 Jer 40.11, 12; 43.6; 40.7,14
41.11 Jer 40.7,8, 13-16
41.12 2 Sam 2.13
41.13 vv. 10,14
41.15 v. 2

h Syr: Heb lacks and threw them; compare verse 9 i Gk: Heb whom he had killed by the hand of Gedaliah

went to the Ammonites. [16] Then Johanan son of Kareah and all the leaders of the forces with him took all the rest of the people whom Ishmael son of Nethaniah had carried away captive[j] from Mizpah after he had slain Gedaliah son of Ahikam — soldiers, women, children, and eunuchs, whom Johanan brought back from Gibeon. [k] [17] And they set out, and stopped at Geruth Chimham near Bethlehem, intending to go to Egypt [18] because of the Chaldeans; for they were afraid of them, because Ishmael son of Nethaniah had killed Gedaliah son of Ahikam, whom the king of Babylon had made governor over the land.

Jeremiah Advises Survivors Not to Migrate

42 Then all the commanders of the forces, and Johanan son of Kareah and Azariah[l] son of Hoshaiah, and all the people from the least to the greatest, approached [2] the prophet Jeremiah and said, "Be good enough to listen to our plea, and pray to the LORD your God for us — for all this remnant. For there are only a few of us left out of many, as your eyes can see. [3] Let the LORD your God show us where we should go and what we should do." [4] The prophet Jeremiah said to them, "Very well: I am going to pray to the LORD your God as you request, and whatever the LORD answers you I will tell you; I will keep nothing back from you." [5] They in their turn said to Jeremiah, "May the LORD be a true and faithful witness against us if we do not act according to everything that the LORD your God sends us through you. [6] Whether it is good or bad, we will obey the voice of the LORD our God to whom we are sending you, in order that it may go well with us when we obey the voice of the LORD our God."

7 At the end of ten days the word of the LORD came to Jeremiah. [8] Then he summoned Johanan son of Kareah and all the commanders of the forces who were with him,

and all the people from the least to the greatest, [9] and said to them, "Thus says the LORD, the God of Israel, to whom you sent me to present your plea before him: [10] If you will only remain in this land, then I will build you up and not pull you down; I will plant you, and not pluck you up; for I am sorry for the disaster that I have brought upon you. [11] Do not be afraid of the king of Babylon, as you have been; do not be afraid of him, says the LORD, for I am with you, to save you and to rescue you from his hand. [12] I will grant you mercy, and he will have mercy on you and restore you to your native soil. [13] But if you continue to say, 'We will not stay in this land,' thus disobeying the voice of the LORD your God [14] and saying, 'No, we will go to the land of Egypt, where we shall not see war, or hear the sound of the trumpet, or be hungry for bread, and there we will stay,' [15] then hear the word of the LORD, O remnant of Judah. Thus says the LORD of hosts, the God of Israel: If you are determined to enter Egypt and go to settle there, [16] then the sword that you fear shall overtake you there, in the land of Egypt; and the famine that you dread shall follow close after you into Egypt; and there you shall die. [17] All the people who have determined to go to Egypt to settle there shall die by the sword, by famine, and by pestilence; they shall have no remnant or survivor from the disaster that I am bringing upon them.

18 "For thus says the LORD of hosts, the God of Israel: Just as my anger and my wrath were poured out on the inhabitants of Jerusalem, so my wrath will be poured out on you when you go to Egypt. You shall become an object of execration and horror, of cursing and ridicule. You shall see this place no more. [19] The LORD has said to you,

Cross references

41.16 Jer 42.8; 43.4-7
41.17 2 Sam 19.37, 38; Jer 42.14
41.18 Jer 42.11, 16; Lk 12.4, 5; Jer 40.5
42.1 Jer 40.8,13; 41.11
42.2 Jer 36.7; 37.20; v. 20; 1 Kings 13.6; Acts 8.24; Deut 28.62; Lam 1.1
42.3 Ps 86.11; Mic 4.2
42.4 1 Sam 12.23; 1 Kings 22.14; Jer 23.28; 1 Sam 3.17, 18; Ps 40.10
42.5 Gen 31.50; Mic 1.2
42.6 Deut 6.3; Jer 7.23
42.8 v. 1
42.9 2 Kings 19.4, 6,20; 22.15
42.10 Jer 24.6; 31.28; Ezek 36.36; Jon 3.10; 4.2
42.11 Jer 41.18; Isa 43.5; Rom 8.31
42.12 Ps 106.45, 46
42.13 Jer 44.16
42.14 Jer 41.17; 4.19,21
42.15 Jer 44.12-14
42.16 Jer 44.13, 27; Ezek 11.8
42.17 Jer 44.13, 14,28
42.18 Jer 7.20; 33.5; Isa 65.15; Jer 29.18; 22.10,27
42.19 Deut 17.16;

Isa 30.1-7; Neh 9.26,29,30

i Cn: Heb *whom he recovered from Ishmael son of Nethaniah* k Meaning of Heb uncertain l Gk: Heb *Jezaniah*

O remnant of Judah, Do not go to Egypt. Be well aware that I have warned you today [20]that you have made a fatal mistake. For you yourselves sent me to the LORD your God, saying, 'Pray for us to the LORD our God, and whatever the LORD our God says, tell us and we will do it.' [21]So I have told you today, but you have not obeyed the voice of the LORD your God in anything that he sent me to tell you. [22]Be well aware, then, that you shall die by the sword, by famine, and by pestilence in the place where you desire to go and settle."

Taken to Egypt, Jeremiah Warns of Judgment

43 When Jeremiah finished speaking to all the people all these words of the LORD their God, with which the LORD their God had sent him to them, [2]Azariah son of Hoshaiah and Johanan son of Kareah and all the other insolent men said to Jeremiah, "You are telling a lie. The LORD our God did not send you to say, 'Do not go to Egypt to settle there'; [3]but Baruch son of Neriah is inciting you against us, to hand us over to the Chaldeans, in order that they may kill us or take us into exile in Babylon." [4]So Johanan son of Kareah and all the commanders of the forces and all the people did not obey the voice of the LORD, to stay in the land of Judah. [5]But Johanan son of Kareah and all the commanders of the forces took all the remnant of Judah who had returned to settle in the land of Judah from all the nations to which they had been driven — [6]the men, the women, the children, the princesses, and everyone whom Nebuzaradan the captain of the guard had left with Gedaliah son of Ahikam son of Shaphan; also the prophet Jeremiah and Baruch son of Neriah. [7]And they came into the land of Egypt, for they did not obey the voice of the LORD. And they arrived at Tahpanhes.

8 Then the word of the LORD came to Jeremiah in Tahpanhes:

[9]Take some large stones in your hands, and bury them in the clay pavement[m] that is at the entrance to Pharaoh's palace in Tahpanhes. Let the Judeans see you do it, [10]and say to them, Thus says the LORD of hosts, the God of Israel: I am going to send and take my servant King Nebuchadrezzar of Babylon, and he[n] will set his throne above these stones that I have buried, and he will spread his royal canopy over them. [11]He shall come and ravage the land of Egypt, giving

those who are destined for
pestilence, to
pestilence,
and those who are destined
for captivity, to
captivity,
and those who are destined
for the sword, to the
sword.

[12]He[o] shall kindle a fire in the temples of the gods of Egypt; and he shall burn them and carry them away captive; and he shall pick clean the land of Egypt, as a shepherd picks his cloak clean of vermin; and he shall depart from there safely. [13]He shall break the obelisks of Heliopolis, which is in the land of Egypt; and the temples of the gods of Egypt he shall burn with fire.

Denunciation of Persistent Idolatry

44 The word that came to Jeremiah for all the Judeans living in the land of Egypt, at Migdol, at Tahpanhes, at Memphis, and in the land of Pathros, [2]Thus says the LORD of hosts, the God of Israel: You yourselves have seen all the disaster that I have brought on Jerusalem and on all the towns of Judah. Look at them; today they are a desolation, without an inhabitant in them, [3]because of the wickedness that they committed, provoking me to anger, in that they went to make offerings and serve other gods that they had not

Cross references (center column)

42.20 v. 2
42.21 Jer 43.1; Ezek 2.7; Jer 43.4
42.22 Jer 43.11; Hos 9.6
43.1 Jer 26.8; 51.63; 42.10-18
43.2 Jer 42.1; 2 Chr 36.13; Jer 42.5
43.3 Jer 38.4
43.4 Jer 42.5,6, 10-12
43.5 Jer 40.11,12
43.6 Jer 41.10; 39.10; 40.7
43.7 Jer 44.1
43.8 Jer 2.16; 44.1; 46.14

43.10 Jer 25.9,11; 27.5,6; 31.20
43.11 Isa 19.1-25; Jer 44.13; 46.13; Ezek 29.19, 20; Jer 15.2
43.12 Isa 19.1; Jer 46.25; Ezek 30.13
44.1 Jer 46.14; 43.7; Isa 19.13
44.2 Jer 9.11; 34.22; Mic 3.12
44.3 Ezek 8.17, 18; Dan 9.5; Isa 3.8; Jer 19.4; Deut 13.6; 32.17

m Meaning of Heb uncertain n Gk Syr:
Heb *I* o Gk Syr Vg: Heb *I*

known, neither they, nor you, nor your ancestors. ⁴Yet I persistently sent to you all my servants the prophets, saying, "I beg you not to do this abominable thing that I hate!" ⁵But they did not listen or incline their ear, to turn from their wickedness and make no offerings to other gods. ⁶So my wrath and my anger were poured out and kindled in the towns of Judah and in the streets of Jerusalem; and they became a waste and a desolation, as they still are today. ⁷And now thus says the Lord God of hosts, the God of Israel: Why are you doing such great harm to yourselves, to cut off man and woman, child and infant, from the midst of Judah, leaving yourselves without a remnant? ⁸Why do you provoke me to anger with the works of your hands, making offerings to other gods in the land of Egypt where you have come to settle? Will you be cut off and become an object of cursing and ridicule among all the nations of the earth? ⁹Have you forgotten the crimes of your ancestors, of the kings of Judah, of theirᵖ wives, your own crimes and those of your wives, which they committed in the land of Judah and in the streets of Jerusalem? ¹⁰They have shown no contrition or fear to this day, nor have they walked in my law and my statutes that I set before you and before your ancestors.

11 Therefore thus says the Lord of hosts, the God of Israel: I am determined to bring disaster on you, to bring all Judah to an end. ¹²I will take the remnant of Judah who are determined to come to the land of Egypt to settle, and they shall perish, everyone; in the land of Egypt they shall fall; by the sword and by famine they shall perish; from the least to the greatest, they shall die by the sword and by famine; and they shall become an object of execration and horror, of cursing and ridicule. ¹³I will punish those who live in the land of Egypt, as I have punished Jerusalem, with the sword, with famine, and with pesti-

lence, ¹⁴so that none of the remnant of Judah who have come to settle in the land of Egypt shall escape or survive or return to the land of Judah. Although they long to go back to live there, they shall not go back, except some fugitives.

15 Then all the men who were aware that their wives had been making offerings to other gods, and all the women who stood by, a great assembly, all the people who lived in Pathros in the land of Egypt, answered Jeremiah: ¹⁶"As for the word that you have spoken to us in the name of the Lord, we are not going to listen to you. ¹⁷Instead, we will do everything that we have vowed, make offerings to the queen of heaven and pour out libations to her, just as we and our ancestors, our kings and our officials, used to do in the towns of Judah and in the streets of Jerusalem. We used to have plenty of food, and prospered, and saw no misfortune. ¹⁸But from the time we stopped making offerings to the queen of heaven and pouring out libations to her, we have lacked everything and have perished by the sword and by famine." ¹⁹And the women said,�q "Indeed we will go on making offerings to the queen of heaven and pouring out libations to her; do you think that we made cakes for her, marked with her image, and poured out libations to her without our husbands' being involved?"

20 Then Jeremiah said to all the people, men and women, all the people who were giving him this answer: ²¹"As for the offerings that you made in the towns of Judah and in the streets of Jerusalem, you and your ancestors, your kings and your officials, and the people of the land, did not the Lord remember them? Did it not come into his mind? ²²The Lord could no longer bear the sight of your evil doings, the abominations that you com-

44.4
2 Chr 36.15;
Jer 7.25;
25.4; 26.5;
Ezek 8.10
44.5
Jer 11.8,10;
13.10
44.6
Jer 42.18
44.7
Jer 26.19;
Ezek 33.11;
Jer 9.21;
51.22
44.8
2 Kings 17.15-17;
Jer 25.6,7;
42.18
44.9
Jer 7.9,10,
17,18
44.10
Jer 6.15;
8.12; 26.4;
32.23
44.11
Lev 26.17;
Jer 21.10;
Am 9.4
44.12
Jer 42.15-18,
22
44.13
Jer 11.22;
21.9; 24.10;
42.17,22

44.14
Jer 22.26,
27; Isa 4.2;
10.20; v. 28;
Rom 9.27
44.15
Jer 5.1-5
44.16
Jer 8.6,12;
13.10
44.17
2 Kings 17.16;
Jer 7.18;
Hos 2.5-9;
Phil 3.19
44.18
Jer 40.12
44.19
Jer 7.18;
Num 30.6,7
44.21
Ezek 8.10,
11; 16.24;
Isa 64.9;
Jer 14.10;
Hos 7.2
44.22
Isa 7.13;
Jer 4.4;
21.12; 25.11,
18,38

ᵖHeb *his* qCompare Syr: Heb lacks *And the women said*

mitted; therefore your land became a desolation and a waste and a curse, without inhabitant, as it is to this day. 23 It is because you burned offerings, and because you sinned against the LORD and did not obey the voice of the LORD or walk in his law and in his statutes and in his decrees, that this disaster has befallen you, as is still evident today."

24 Jeremiah said to all the people and all the women, "Hear the word of the LORD, all you Judeans who are in the land of Egypt, 25 Thus says the LORD of hosts, the God of Israel: You and your wives have accomplished in deeds what you declared in words, saying, 'We are determined to perform the vows that we have made, to make offerings to the queen of heaven and to pour out libations to her.' By all means, keep your vows and make your libations! 26 Therefore hear the word of the LORD, all you Judeans who live in the land of Egypt: Lo, I swear by my great name, says the LORD, that my name shall no longer be pronounced on the lips of any of the people of Judah in all the land of Egypt, saying, 'As the Lord GOD lives.' 27 I am going to watch over them for harm and not for good; all the people of Judah who are in the land of Egypt shall perish by the sword and by famine, until not one is left. 28 And those who escape the sword shall return from the land of Egypt to the land of Judah, few in number; and all the remnant of Judah, who have come to the land of Egypt to settle, shall know whose words will stand, mine or theirs! 29 This shall be the sign to you, says the LORD, that I am going to punish you in this place, in order that you may know that my words against you will surely be carried out: 30 Thus says the LORD, I am going to give Pharaoh Hophra, king of Egypt, into the hands of his enemies, those who seek his life, just as I gave King Zedekiah of Judah into the hand of King Nebuchadrezzar of Babylon, his enemy who sought his life."

44.23
Jer 40.3;
vv. 10,2;
Dan 9.11,12
44.24
Jer 42.15;
v. 15;
Jer 43.7
44.25
Mt 14.9;
Acts 23.12
44.26
Gen 22.16;
Am 6.8;
Heb 6.13, 18;
Ezek 20.39;
Jer 5.2
44.27
Jer 1.10;
31.28;
Ezek 7.6
44.28
Isa 27.13;
vv. 17,25,26
44.29
Isa 7.11,14;
8.18;
Prov 19.21;
Isa 40.8
44.30
Jer 46.25, 26;
Ezek 29.3;
2 Kings 25.4-7;
Jer 39.5

45.1
Jer 36.1,4, 18,32
45.3
Ps 6.6;
2 Cor 4.1, 16
45.4
Isa 5.5;
Jer 11.17;
18.7-10
45.5
1 Kings 3.9, 11; Mt 6.25, 32,33;
Rom 12.16;
Jer 25.31;
21.9; 38.2;
39.18
46.1
Jer 25.15-38
46.2
2 Kings 23.29;
2 Chr 35.20;
Jer 45.1
46.3
Jer 51.11, 12; Nah 2.1;
3.14
46.4
Ezek 21.9-11;
Jer 51.3
46.5
Isa 42.17;
Ezek 39.18;
Jer 6.25;
49.29
46.6
Isa 30.16;
Dan 11.19

A Word of Comfort to Baruch

45 The word that the prophet Jeremiah spoke to Baruch son of Neriah, when he wrote these words in a scroll at the dictation of Jeremiah, in the fourth year of King Jehoiakim son of Josiah of Judah: 2 Thus says the LORD, the God of Israel, to you, O Baruch: 3 You said, "Woe is me! The LORD has added sorrow to my pain; I am weary with my groaning, and I find no rest." 4 Thus you shall say to him, "Thus says the LORD: I am going to break down what I have built, and pluck up what I have planted — that is, the whole land. 5 And you, do you seek great things for yourself? Do not seek them; for I am going to bring disaster upon all flesh, says the LORD; but I will give you your life as a prize of war in every place to which you may go."

Judgment on Egypt

46 The word of the LORD that came to the prophet Jeremiah concerning the nations.

2 Concerning Egypt, about the army of Pharaoh Neco, king of Egypt, which was by the river Euphrates at Carchemish and which King Nebuchadrezzar of Babylon defeated in the fourth year of King Jehoiakim son of Josiah of Judah:

3 Prepare buckler and shield,
 and advance for battle!
4 Harness the horses;
 mount the steeds!
Take your stations with your
 helmets,
 whet your lances,
 put on your coats of mail!
5 Why do I see them terrified?
 They have fallen back;
their warriors are beaten
 down,
 and have fled in haste.
They do not look back —
 terror is all around!
 says the LORD.
6 The swift cannot flee away,
 nor can the warrior escape;
in the north by the river
 Euphrates

they have stumbled and
 fallen.

7 Who is this, rising like the
 Nile,
 like rivers whose waters
 surge?
8 Egypt rises like the Nile,
 like rivers whose waters
 surge.
 It said, Let me rise, let me
 cover the earth,
 let me destroy cities and
 their inhabitants.
9 Advance, O horses,
 and dash madly,
 O chariots!
 Let the warriors go forth:
 Ethiopia[r] and Put who
 carry the shield,
 the Ludim, who draw[s] the
 bow.
10 That day is the day of the
 Lord GOD of hosts,
 a day of retribution,
 to gain vindication from his
 foes.
 The sword shall devour and
 be sated,
 and drink its fill of their
 blood.
 For the Lord GOD of hosts
 holds a sacrifice
 in the land of the north by
 the river Euphrates.
11 Go up to Gilead, and take
 balm,
 O virgin daughter Egypt!
 In vain you have used many
 medicines;
 there is no healing for you.
12 The nations have heard of
 your shame,
 and the earth is full of your
 cry;
 for warrior has stumbled
 against warrior;
 both have fallen together.

Babylonia Will Strike Egypt

13 The word that the LORD
spoke to the prophet Jeremiah
about the coming of King Nebu-
chadrezzar of Babylon to attack the
land of Egypt:

46.7
Jer 47.2
46.8
Isa 37.24;
10.13
46.9
Jer 47.3;
Nah 2.4;
3.9;
Isa 66.19
46.10
Isa 13.6;
Joel 1.15;
2.1;
Jer 50.15,
28; Isa 34.6;
Zeph 1.7
46.11
Jer 8.22;
51.8;
Isa 47.1;
Jer 31.4,21;
30.13;
Ezek 30.21
46.12
Jer 2.36;
Nah 3.8-10;
Jer 14.2
46.13
Isa 19.1;
Jer 43.10,11

46.14
Jer 44.1;
43.8;
Nah 2.13
46.16
Lev 26.36,
37; Jer 51.9;
50.16
46.17
Isa 19.11-16
46.18
Jer 48.15;
Ps 89.12;
1 Kings 18.42
46.19
Jer 48.18;
Isa 20.4;
v. 4;
Ezek 30.13
46.20
Jer 50.11;
v. 24
46.21
v. 5;
Ps 37.13;
Jer 50.27

14 Declare in Egypt, and
 proclaim in Migdol;
 proclaim in Memphis and
 Tahpanhes;
 Say, "Take your stations and
 be ready,
 for the sword shall devour
 those around you."
15 Why has Apis fled?[t]
 Why did your bull not
 stand?
 —because the LORD thrust
 him down.
16 Your multitude stumbled[u]
 and fell,
 and one said to another,[v]
 "Come, let us go back to our
 own people
 and to the land of our
 birth,
 because of the destroying
 sword."
17 Give Pharaoh, king of Egypt,
 the name
 "Braggart who missed his
 chance."

18 As I live, says the King,
 whose name is the LORD of
 hosts,
 one is coming
 like Tabor among the
 mountains,
 and like Carmel by the sea.
19 Pack your bags for exile,
 sheltered daughter Egypt!
 For Memphis shall become a
 waste,
 a ruin, without inhabitant.

20 A beautiful heifer is Egypt —
 a gadfly from the north
 lights upon her.
21 Even her mercenaries in her
 midst
 are like fatted calves;
 they too have turned and
 fled together,
 they did not stand;
 for the day of their calamity
 has come upon them,

[r] Or *Nubia*; Heb *Cush* [s] Cn: Heb *who grasp, who draw* [t] Gk: Heb *Why was it swept away* [u] Gk: Meaning of Heb uncertain [v] Gk: Heb *and fell one to another and they said*

the time of their
punishment.

22 She makes a sound like a
snake gliding away;
for her enemies march in
force,
and come against her with
axes,
like those who fell trees.
23 They shall cut down her
forest,
says the Lord,
though it is impenetrable,
because they are more
numerous
than locusts;
they are without number.
24 Daughter Egypt shall be put
to shame;
she shall be handed over to
a people from the
north.

25 The Lord of hosts, the God of
Israel, said: See, I am bringing pun-
ishment upon Amon of Thebes,
and Pharaoh, and Egypt and her
gods and her kings, upon Pharaoh
and those who trust in him. 26 I will
hand them over to those who seek
their life, to King Nebuchadrezzar
of Babylon and his officers. After-
ward Egypt shall be inhabited as in
the days of old, says the Lord.

God Will Save Israel

27 But as for you, have no fear,
my servant Jacob,
and do not be dismayed,
O Israel;
for I am going to save you
from far away,
and your offspring from the
land of their captivity.
Jacob shall return and have
quiet and ease,
and no one shall make him
afraid.
28 As for you, have no fear, my
servant Jacob,
says the Lord,
for I am with you.
I will make an end of all the
nations

among which I have
banished you,
but I will not make an end
of you!
I will chastise you in just
measure,
and I will by no means
leave you unpunished.

Judgment on the Philistines

47 The word of the Lord that
came to the prophet Jere-
miah concerning the Philistines,
before Pharaoh attacked Gaza:
2 Thus says the Lord:
See, waters are rising out of
the north
and shall become an
overflowing torrent;
they shall overflow the land
and all that fills it,
the city and those who live
in it.
People shall cry out,
and all the inhabitants of
the land shall wail.
3 At the noise of the stamping
of the hoofs of his
stallions,
at the clatter of his
chariots, at the
rumbling of their
wheels,
parents do not turn back for
children,
so feeble are their hands,
4 because of the day that is
coming
to destroy all the
Philistines,
to cut off from Tyre and
Sidon
every helper that remains.
For the Lord is destroying
the Philistines,
the remnant of the
coastland of Caphtor.
5 Baldness has come upon
Gaza,
Ashkelon is silenced.
O remnant of their power!w
How long will you gash
yourselves?
6 Ah, sword of the Lord!

w Gk: Heb *their valley*

46.22
Isa 29.4
46.23
Isa 10.34;
Jer 21.14;
Judg 6.5;
Joel 2.25
46.24
v. 19;
Jer 1.15
46.25
Jer 43.12;
Ezek 30.14-16;
Jer 44.30;
Ezek 30.13;
Isa 20.5
46.26
Jer 44.30;
Ezek 32.11;
29.11-14
46.27
Isa 41.13;
43.5;
Jer 30.10,
11; 23.3,4,6;
50.19
46.28
Isa 8.9,10;
Jer 1.19;
4.27;
Am 9.8,9;
Jer 10.24;
30.11

47.1
Jer 25.17,
20; Am 1.6;
Zeph 2.4
47.2
Isa 14.31;
Jer 46.20,
24; Isa 8.7;
15.2-5;
Jer 46.12
47.3
Jer 8.16;
Nah 3.2
47.4
Isa 14.31;
23.5,6,11;
Joel 3.4;
Zech 9.2-4;
Gen 10.14
47.5
Mic 1.16;
Jer 25.20;
16.6; 41.5
47.6
Jer 12.12;
4.21

How long until you are
 quiet?
Put yourself into your
 scabbard,
rest and be still!
7 How can it[x] be quiet,
 when the LORD has given it
 an order?
Against Ashkelon and against
 the seashore—
there he has appointed it.

Judgment on Moab

48

Concerning Moab.

Thus says the LORD of hosts, the
God of Israel:
 Alas for Nebo, it is laid
 waste!
 Kiriathaim is put to shame,
 it is taken;
 the fortress is put to shame
 and broken down;
2 the renown of Moab is no
 more.
 In Heshbon they planned evil
 against her:
 "Come, let us cut her off
 from being a nation!"
 You also, O Madmen, shall
 be brought to silence;[y]
 the sword shall pursue you.

3 Hark! a cry from Horonaim,
 "Desolation and great
 destruction!"
4 "Moab is destroyed!"
 her little ones cry out.
5 For at the ascent of Luhith
 they go[z] up weeping
 bitterly;
 for at the descent of
 Horonaim
 they have heard the
 distressing cry of
 anguish.
6 Flee! Save yourselves!
 Be like a wild ass[a] in the
 desert!

7 Surely, because you trusted
 in your strongholds[b]
 and your treasures,
 you also shall be taken;
Chemosh shall go out into
 exile,

with his priests and his
 attendants.
8 The destroyer shall come
 upon every town,
 and no town shall escape;
the valley shall perish,
 and the plain shall be
 destroyed,
 as the LORD has spoken.

9 Set aside salt for Moab,
 for she will surely fall;
 her towns shall become a
 desolation,
 with no inhabitant in them.

10 Accursed is the one who is
slack in doing the work of the LORD;
and accursed is the one who keeps
back the sword from bloodshed.

11 Moab has been at ease from
 his youth,
 settled like wine[c] on its
 dregs;
 he has not been emptied
 from vessel to vessel,
 nor has he gone into exile;
 therefore his flavor has
 remained
 and his aroma is unspoiled.
12 Therefore, the time is surely
coming, says the LORD, when I shall
send to him decanters to decant
him, and empty his vessels, and
break his[d] jars in pieces. 13 Then
Moab shall be ashamed of Che-
mosh, as the house of Israel was
ashamed of Bethel, their confi-
dence.

14 How can you say, "We are
 heroes
 and mighty warriors"?
15 The destroyer of Moab and
 his towns has come up,
 and the choicest of his
 young men have gone
 down to slaughter,
 says the King, whose name
 is the LORD of hosts.

Cross references (center column)

47.7 Ezek 14.17; Mic 6.9
48.1 Isa 15.2; vv. 22,23; Num 32.37
48.2 Isa 16.14; 15.4; Jer 49.3
48.3 Isa 15.5; vv. 5,34
48.5 Isa 15.5
48.6 Jer 51.6; 17.6
48.7 Jer 9.23; Num 21.29; 1 Kings 11.33; Jer 49.3
48.8 Jer 6.26
48.9 Isa 16.2; Jer 44.22
48.10 Jer 11.3; 1 Sam 15.3, 9; 1 Kings 20.42; Jer 47.6,7
48.11 Jer 22.21; Zech 1.15; Zeph 1.12; Nah 2.2
48.13 Isa 45.16; v. 39; Hos 10.6; 1 Kings 12.29
48.14 Isa 10.13-16
48.15 Jer 50.27; 46.18

[x] Gk Vg: Heb *you* [y] The place-name
Madmen sounds like the Hebrew verb *to be
silent* [z] Cn: Heb *he goes* [a] Gk Aquila:
Heb *like Aroer* [b] Gk: Heb *works*
[c] Heb lacks *like wine* [d] Gk Aquila: Heb
their

¹⁶ The calamity of Moab is near
at hand
and his doom approaches
swiftly.
¹⁷ Mourn over him, all you his
neighbors,
and all who know his
name;
say, "How the mighty scepter
is broken,
the glorious staff!"

¹⁸ Come down from glory,
and sit on the parched
ground,
enthroned daughter Dibon!
For the destroyer of Moab
has come up against
you;
he has destroyed your
strongholds.
¹⁹ Stand by the road and watch,
you inhabitant of Aroer!
Ask the man fleeing and the
woman escaping;
say, "What has happened?"
²⁰ Moab is put to shame, for it
is broken down;
wail and cry!
Tell it by the Arnon,
that Moab is laid waste.

21 Judgment has come upon
the tableland, upon Holon, and
Jahzah, and Mephaath, ²²and Di-
bon, and Nebo, and Beth-
diblathaim, ²³and Kiriathaim, and
Beth-gamul, and Beth-meon,
²⁴and Kerioth, and Bozrah, and all
the towns of the land of Moab, far
and near. ²⁵The horn of Moab is
cut off, and his arm is broken, says
the LORD.

26 Make him drunk, because he
magnified himself against the
LORD; let Moab wallow in his vomit;
he too shall become a laughing-
stock. ²⁷Israel was a laughingstock
for you, though he was not caught
among thieves; but whenever you
spoke of him you shook your head!

²⁸ Leave the towns, and live on
the rock,
O inhabitants of Moab!
Be like the dove that nests

48.16
Isa 13.22
48.17
Jer 9.17-20;
Isa 14.5
48.18
Isa 47.1;
Jer 46.19;
v. 8
48.19
Deut 2.36;
1 Sam 4.13,
16
48.20
Isa 16.7;
Num 21.13
48.21
vv. 8,34;
Josh 13.18
48.24
Am 2.2
48.25
Ps 75.10;
Ezek 30.21
48.26
Jer 25.15,27
48.27
Zeph 2.8;
Jer 2.26;
18.16
48.28
Jer 49.16;
Ps 55.6,7;
Song 2.14

48.29
Isa 16.6;
Zeph 2.8;
Ps 138.6
48.30
Isa 37.28;
16.6
48.31
Isa 15.5;
16.7,11
48.32
Isa 16.8,9;
Num 21.32
48.33
Isa 16.10;
Joel 1.12;
Isa 5.10;
Hag 2.16
48.34
Isa 15.4-6
48.35
Isa 15.2;
16.12;
Jer 7.9;
11.13
48.36
Isa 16.11;
15.7
48.37
Isa 15.2,3;
Jer 47.5

on the sides of the mouth
of a gorge.
²⁹ We have heard of the pride
of Moab—
he is very proud—
of his loftiness, his pride,
and his arrogance,
and the haughtiness of his
heart.
³⁰ I myself know his insolence,
says the LORD;
his boasts are false,
his deeds are false.
³¹ Therefore I wail for Moab;
I cry out for all Moab;
for the people of Kir-heres
I mourn.
³² More than for Jazer I weep
for you,
O vine of Sibmah!
Your branches crossed over
the sea,
reached as far as Jazer;ᵉ
upon your summer fruits and
your vintage
the destroyer has fallen.
³³ Gladness and joy have been
taken away
from the fruitful land of
Moab;
I have stopped the wine from
the wine presses;
no one treads them with
shouts of joy;
the shouting is not the
shout of joy.

34 Heshbon and Elealeh cry
out;ᶠ as far as Jahaz they utter
their voice, from Zoar to Horonaim
and Eglath-shelishiyah. For even
the waters of Nimrim have become
desolate. ³⁵And I will bring to an
end in Moab, says the LORD, those
who offer sacrifice at a high place
and make offerings to their gods.
³⁶Therefore my heart moans for
Moab like a flute, and my heart
moans like a flute for the people of
Kir-heres; for the riches they
gained have perished.

37 For every head is shaved and
every beard cut off; on all the hands
there are gashes, and on the loins

ᵉ Two Mss and Isa 16.8: MT *the sea of Jazer*
ᶠ Cn: Heb *From the cry of Heshbon to Elealeh*

sackcloth. 38 On all the housetops of Moab and in the squares there is nothing but lamentation; for I have broken Moab like a vessel that no one wants, says the LORD. 39 How it is broken! How they wail! How Moab has turned his back in shame! So Moab has become a derision and a horror to all his neighbors.

40 For thus says the LORD:
Look, he shall swoop down
 like an eagle,
and spread his wings
 against Moab;
41 the towns[g] shall be taken
 and the strongholds seized.
The hearts of the warriors of
 Moab, on that day,
shall be like the heart of a
 woman in labor.
42 Moab shall be destroyed as a
 people,
because he magnified
 himself against the
 LORD.
43 Terror, pit, and trap
 are before you,
 O inhabitants of Moab!
 says the LORD.
44 Everyone who flees from the
 terror
shall fall into the pit,
and everyone who climbs out
 of the pit
shall be caught in the trap.
For I will bring these things[h]
 upon Moab
in the year of their
 punishment,
 says the LORD.

45 In the shadow of Heshbon
 fugitives stop exhausted;
for a fire has gone out from
 Heshbon,
a flame from the house of
 Sihon;
it has destroyed the forehead
 of Moab,
 the scalp of the people of
 tumult.[i]
46 Woe to you, O Moab!
 The people of Chemosh
 have perished,
for your sons have been
 taken captive,

and your daughters into
 captivity.
47 Yet I will restore the fortunes
 of Moab
 in the latter days, says the
 LORD.
Thus far is the judgment on
 Moab.

Judgment on the Ammonites

49 Concerning the Ammonites.

Thus says the LORD:
 Has Israel no sons?
 Has he no heir?
Why then has Milcom
 dispossessed Gad,
 and his people settled in
 its towns?
2 Therefore, the time is surely
 coming,
 says the LORD,
when I will sound the battle
 alarm
 against Rabbah of the
 Ammonites;
it shall become a desolate
 mound,
 and its villages shall be
 burned with fire;
then Israel shall dispossess
 those who dispossessed
 him,
 says the LORD.

3 Wail, O Heshbon, for Ai is
 laid waste!
 Cry out, O daughters[i] of
 Rabbah!
Put on sackcloth,
 lament, and slash
 yourselves with whips![k]
For Milcom shall go into
 exile,
 with his priests and his
 attendants.
4 Why do you boast in your
 strength?
 Your strength is ebbing,
 O faithless daughter.
You trusted in your
 treasures, saying,

48.38
Jer 22.28;
25.34
48.39
Ezek 26.16
48.40
Jer 49.22;
Dan 7.4;
Hos 8.1;
Isa 8.8
48.41
Isa 21.3;
Jer 30.6;
49.22,24;
Mic 4.9
48.42
v. 2;
Ps 83.4;
v. 26;
Isa 37.23
48.43
Isa 24.17,
18;
Lam 3.47
48.44
1 Kings 19.17;
Jer 11.23;
46.21
48.45
v. 2;
Num 21.21,
26,28,29;
24.17
48.46
Num 21.29;
v. 7

48.47
Jer 49.6,39
49.1
Ezek 21.28;
25.2;
Am 1.13;
Zeph 2.8,9
49.2
Jer 4.19;
Ezek 21.20;
Isa 14.2
49.3
Jer 48.2;
Josh 7.2-5;
8.1-29;
Isa 32.11;
Jer 4.8; 48.7
49.4
Jer 9.23;
31.22;
Ps 62.10;
Ezek 28.4,5

g Or *Kerioth* h Gk Syr: Heb *bring upon it*
i Or *of Shaon* j Or *villages*
k Cn: Meaning of Heb uncertain

"Who will attack me?"
5 I am going to bring terror
 upon you,
 says the Lord GOD of hosts,
 from all your neighbors,
and you will be scattered,
 each headlong,
 with no one to gather the
 fugitives.
6 But afterward I will restore the
fortunes of the Ammonites, says
the LORD.

Judgment on Edom

7 Concerning Edom.

Thus says the LORD of hosts:
 Is there no longer wisdom in
 Teman?
 Has counsel perished from
 the prudent?
 Has their wisdom
 vanished?
8 Flee, turn back, get down
 low,
 inhabitants of Dedan!
For I will bring the calamity
 of Esau upon him,
 the time when I punish
 him.
9 If grape-gatherers came to
 you,
 would they not leave
 gleanings?
If thieves came by night,
 even they would pillage
 only what they wanted.
10 But as for me, I have
 stripped Esau bare,
I have uncovered his hiding
 places,
 and he is not able to
 conceal himself.
His offspring are destroyed,
 his kinsfolk
 and his neighbors; and he
 is no more.
11 Leave your orphans, I will
 keep them alive;
 and let your widows trust
 in me.
12 For thus says the LORD: If
those who do not deserve to drink
the cup still have to drink it, shall
you be the one to go unpunished?
You shall not go unpunished; you

must drink it. 13 For by myself I
have sworn, says the LORD, that
Bozrah shall become an object of
horror and ridicule, a waste, and an
object of cursing; and all her towns
shall be perpetual wastes.
14 I have heard tidings from the
 LORD,
 and a messenger has been
 sent among the nations:
 "Gather yourselves together
 and come against her,
 and rise up for battle!"
15 For I will make you least
 among the nations,
 despised by humankind.
16 The terror you inspire
 and the pride of your heart
 have deceived you,
 you who live in the clefts of
 the rock,[1]
 who hold the height of the
 hill.
 Although you make your nest
 as high as the eagle's,
 from there I will bring you
 down,
 says the LORD.
17 Edom shall become an ob-
ject of horror; everyone who passes
by it will be horrified and will hiss
because of all its disasters. 18 As
when Sodom and Gomorrah and
their neighbors were overthrown,
says the LORD, no one shall live
there, nor shall anyone settle in it.
19 Like a lion coming up from the
thickets of the Jordan against a pe-
rennial pasture, I will suddenly
chase Edom[m] away from it; and I
will appoint over it whomever I
choose.[n] For who is like me? Who
can summon me? Who is the shep-
herd who can stand before me?
20 Therefore hear the plan that the
LORD has made against Edom and
the purposes that he has formed
against the inhabitants of Teman:
Surely the little ones of the flock
shall be dragged away; surely their
fold shall be appalled at their fate.
21 At the sound of their fall the
earth shall tremble; the sound of
their cry shall be heard at the Red

49.5
Jer 48.43,
44; 16.16;
46.5;
Lam 4.15
49.6
v. 39;
Jer 48.47
49.7
Isa 34.5,6;
Ezek 25.12;
Am 1.11,12;
Jer 8.9;
v. 20
49.8
v. 30;
Jer 25.23;
46.21
49.9
Ob 5
49.10
Jer 13.26;
Mal 1.3;
Isa 17.14
49.11
Ps 68.5
49.12
Jer 25.28,
29;
1 Pet 4.17

49.13
Jer 44.26;
Isa 34.6;
34.9-15
49.14
Ob 1-4;
Isa 18.2;
30.4;
Jer 50.14
49.16
Isa 25.5;
14.13-15;
Am 9.2
49.17
Jer 50.13;
1 Kings 9.8;
Jer 51.37
49.18
Gen 19.25;
Deut 29.23;
Am 4.11
49.19
Jer 50.44;
12.5;
Isa 46.9
49.20
Jer 50.45;
Mal 1.3,4
49.21
Jer 50.46;
Ezek 26.15,
18

[1] Or of Sela m Heb him n Or and I
will single out the choicest of his rams:
Meaning of Heb uncertain

Sea.ᵒ ²²Look, he shall mount up
and swoop down like an eagle, and
spread his wings against Bozrah,
and the heart of the warriors of
Edom in that day shall be like the
heart of a woman in labor.

Judgment on Damascus

23 Concerning Damascus.

Hamath and Arpad are
 confounded,
 for they have heard bad
 news;
they melt in fear, they are
 troubled like the seaᵖ
 that cannot be quiet.
²⁴ Damascus has become
 feeble, she turned to
 flee,
 and panic seized her;
anguish and sorrows have
 taken hold of her,
 as of a woman in labor.
²⁵ How the famous city is
 forsaken,�q
 the joyful town!ʳ
²⁶ Therefore her young men
 shall fall in her squares,
 and all her soldiers shall be
 destroyed in that day,
 says the LORD of hosts.
²⁷ And I will kindle a fire at the
 wall of Damascus,
 and it shall devour the
 strongholds of
 Ben-hadad.

Judgment on Kedar and Hazor

28 Concerning Kedar and the
kingdoms of Hazor that King Neb-
uchadrezzar of Babylon defeated.

Thus says the LORD:
Rise up, advance against
 Kedar!
 Destroy the people of the
 east!
²⁹ Take their tents and their
 flocks,
 their curtains and all their
 goods;
carry off their camels for
 yourselves,
 and a cry shall go up:
 "Terror is all around!"

³⁰ Flee, wander far away, hide
 in deep places,
 O inhabitants of Hazor!
 says the LORD.
For King Nebuchadrezzar of
 Babylon
 has made a plan against
 you
 and formed a purpose
 against you.

³¹ Rise up, advance against a
 nation at ease,
 that lives secure,
 says the LORD,
that has no gates or bars,
 that lives alone.
³² Their camels shall become
 booty,
 their herds of cattle a spoil.
I will scatter to every wind
 those who have shaven
 temples,
and I will bring calamity
 against them from every
 side,
 says the LORD.
³³ Hazor shall become a lair of
 jackals,
 an everlasting waste;
no one shall live there,
 nor shall anyone settle in
 it.

Judgment on Elam

34 The word of the LORD that
came to the prophet Jeremiah con-
cerning Elam, at the beginning of
the reign of King Zedekiah of Ju-
dah.

35 Thus says the LORD of hosts:
I am going to break the bow of
Elam, the mainstay of their might;
³⁶and I will bring upon Elam the
four winds from the four quarters
of heaven; and I will scatter them
to all these winds, and there shall
be no nation to which the exiles
from Elam shall not come. ³⁷I will
terrify Elam before their enemies,
and before those who seek their
life; I will bring disaster upon

49.22
Jer 4.13;
48.40,41
49.23
2 Chr 16.2;
Jer 39.5;
Isa 10.9;
57.20
49.24
v. 22;
Jer 6.24;
30.6; 48.41
49.25
Jer 33.9;
51.41
49.26
Jer 50.30;
51.4;
Am 4.10
49.27
Jer 43.12;
Am 1.3-5;
1 Kings 15.18-
20
49.28
Isa 21.16,
17; Jer 2.10;
Ezek 27.21;
Isa 11.14
49.29
Jer 6.25;
20.3,10; 46.5

49.30
Jer 25.9
49.31
Isa 47.8;
Ezek 38.11;
Deut 33.28
49.32
Ezek 12.14,
15; Jer 9.26;
25.23
49.33
Jer 10.22;
Zeph 2.9,
13-15
49.34
Ezek 32.24;
2 Kings 24.17,
18; Jer 28.1
49.35
Isa 22.6;
Jer 51.56
49.36
Rev 7.1;
Ezek 5.10;
Am 9.9
49.37
Jer 8.9;
17.18; 6.19;
30.24; 9.16

ᵒ Or *Sea of Reeds* ᵖ Cn: Heb *there is
trouble in the sea* q Vg: Heb *is not forsaken*
ʳ Syr Vg Tg: Heb *the town of my joy*

them, my fierce anger, says the
LORD. I will send the sword after
them, until I have consumed them;
[38] and I will set my throne in Elam,
and destroy their king and officials,
says the LORD.

39 But in the latter days I will
restore the fortunes of Elam, says
the LORD.

Judgment on Babylon

50 The word that the LORD
spoke concerning Babylon,
concerning the land of the Chalde-
ans, by the prophet Jeremiah:
² Declare among the nations
and proclaim,
set up a banner and
proclaim,
do not conceal it, say:
Babylon is taken,
Bel is put to shame,
Merodach is dismayed.
Her images are put to
shame,
her idols are dismayed.
3 For out of the north a nation
has come up against her; it shall
make her land a desolation, and no
one shall live in it; both human be-
ings and animals shall flee away.

4 In those days and in that time,
says the LORD, the people of Israel
shall come, they and the people of
Judah together; they shall come
weeping as they seek the LORD their
God. ⁵They shall ask the way to
Zion, with faces turned toward it,
and they shall come and join[s]
themselves to the LORD by an ever-
lasting covenant that will never be
forgotten.

6 My people have been lost
sheep; their shepherds have led
them astray, turning them away on
the mountains; from mountain to
hill they have gone, they have for-
gotten their fold. ⁷All who found
them have devoured them, and
their enemies have said, "We are
not guilty, because they have
sinned against the LORD, the true
pasture, the LORD, the hope of their
ancestors."

8 Flee from Babylon, and go out
of the land of the Chaldeans, and
be like male goats leading the
flock. ⁹For I am going to stir up and
bring against Babylon a company
of great nations from the land of
the north; and they shall array
themselves against her; from there
she shall be taken. Their arrows are
like the arrows of a skilled warrior
who does not return empty-
handed. ¹⁰Chaldea shall be plun-
dered; all who plunder her shall be
sated, says the LORD.

¹¹ Though you rejoice, though
you exult,
O plunderers of my
heritage,
though you frisk about like a
heifer on the grass,
and neigh like stallions,
¹² your mother shall be utterly
shamed,
and she who bore you shall
be disgraced.
Lo, she shall be the last of
the nations,
a wilderness, dry land, and
a desert.
¹³ Because of the wrath of the
LORD she shall not be
inhabited,
but shall be an utter
desolation;
everyone who passes by
Babylon shall be
appalled
and hiss because of all her
wounds.
¹⁴ Take up your positions
around Babylon,
all you that bend the bow;
shoot at her, spare no
arrows,
for she has sinned against
the LORD.
¹⁵ Raise a shout against her
from all sides,
"She has surrendered;
her bulwarks have fallen,
her walls are thrown
down."
For this is the vengeance of
the LORD:

49.39 Jer 48.47 **50.1** Isa 13.1; Rev 14.8 **50.2** Jer 51.27, 31; Isa 46.1; Jer 51.44,47 **50.3** Jer 51.48; 9.10; Zeph 1.3 **50.4** Hos 1.11; Ezra 3.12, 13; Jer 31.9; Zech 12.10; Hos 3.5 **50.6** Isa 53.6; Ezek 34.15, 16; Jer 23.11-14; 2.20; 3.6,23; 33.12 **50.7** Jer 40.2,3; 31.23; 14.8; 17.13 **50.8** Jer 51.6,45; Rev 18.4 **50.9** Jer 51.1,2 **50.10** Jer 51.24, 35; Rev 17.16 **50.11** Jer 12.14; 46.20 **50.12** Jer 22.6; 51.43 **50.13** Jer 25.12; 49.17 **50.14** Jer 49.35; Hab 2.8,17 **50.15** Jer 51.14; 1 Chr 29.24; Ezek 17.18; Jer 51.44, 58; 46.10

ˢ Gk: Heb *toward it. Come! They shall join*

take vengeance on her,
 do to her as she has done.
16 Cut off from Babylon the
 sower,
 and the wielder of the
 sickle in time of
 harvest;
 because of the destroying
 sword
 all of them shall return to
 their own people,
 and all of them shall flee
 to their own land.

17 Israel is a hunted sheep driven away by lions. First the king of Assyria devoured it, and now at the end King Nebuchadrezzar of Babylon has gnawed its bones. 18 Therefore, thus says the LORD of hosts, the God of Israel: I am going to punish the king of Babylon and his land, as I punished the king of Assyria. 19 I will restore Israel to its pasture, and it shall feed on Carmel and in Bashan, and on the hills of Ephraim and in Gilead its hunger shall be satisfied. 20 In those days and at that time, says the LORD, the iniquity of Israel shall be sought, and there shall be none; and the sins of Judah, and none shall be found; for I will pardon the remnant that I have spared.

21 Go up to the land of
 Merathaim; [t]
 go up against her,
 and attack the inhabitants of
 Pekod [u]
 and utterly destroy the last
 of them, [v]
 says the LORD;
 do all that I have
 commanded you.
22 The noise of battle is in the
 land,
 and great destruction!
23 How the hammer of the
 whole earth
 is cut down and broken!
 How Babylon has become
 a horror among the
 nations!
24 You set a snare for yourself
 and you were caught,
 O Babylon,

but you did not know it;
 you were discovered and
 seized,
 because you challenged the
 LORD.
25 The LORD has opened his
 armory,
 and brought out the
 weapons of his wrath,
 for the Lord GOD of hosts has
 a task to do
 in the land of the
 Chaldeans.
26 Come against her from every
 quarter;
 open her granaries;
 pile her up like heaps of
 grain, and destroy her
 utterly;
 let nothing be left of her.
27 Kill all her bulls,
 let them go down to the
 slaughter.
 Alas for them, their day has
 come,
 the time of their
 punishment!

28 Listen! Fugitives and refugees from the land of Babylon are coming to declare in Zion the vengeance of the LORD our God, vengeance for his temple.

29 Summon archers against Babylon, all who bend the bow. Encamp all around her; let no one escape. Repay her according to her deeds; just as she has done, do to her—for she has arrogantly defied the LORD, the Holy One of Israel. 30 Therefore her young men shall fall in her squares, and all her soldiers shall be destroyed on that day, says the LORD.

31 I am against you, O arrogant
 one,
 says the Lord GOD of hosts;
 for your day has come,
 the time when I will punish
 you.
32 The arrogant one shall
 stumble and fall,

50.16
Joel 1.11;
Jer 51.9
50.17
Jer 2.15;
2 Kings 17.6;
24.10,14
50.18
Isa 10.12;
Ezek 31.3,
11,12
50.19
Jer 31.10;
33.12; 31.5
50.20
Jer 31.34;
Mic 7.19;
Isa 1.9;
Jer 33.8
50.21
Ezek 23.23;
Isa 10.6;
44.28; 48.14;
Jer 34.22
50.22
Jer 51.54-56
50.23
Isa 14.6;
Jer 51.20-24
50.24
Jer 48.43,
44; 51.8,31,
39,57;
Dan 5.30,31

50.25
Isa 13.5;
Jer 51.12,
25,55
50.26
v. 41;
Isa 14.23
50.27
Isa 34.7;
Ezek 7.7;
Jer 48.44
50.28
Isa 48.20;
Jer 51.6;
51.10,11
50.29
Jer 51.56;
Rev 18.6;
Isa 47.10
50.30
Isa 13.17,
18;
Jer 49.26;
51.56,57
50.31
Jer 21.13;
Nah 2.13
50.32
Isa 10.12-15;
Jer 21.14;
49.27

t Or of Double Rebellion u Or of
Punishment v Tg: Heb destroy after them

with no one to raise him
 up,
and I will kindle a fire in his
 cities,
 and it will devour
 everything around him.

33 Thus says the LORD of hosts:
The people of Israel are oppressed,
and so too are the people of Judah;
all their captors have held them
fast and refuse to let them go.
34 Their Redeemer is strong; the
LORD of hosts is his name. He will
surely plead their cause, that he
may give rest to the earth, but un-
rest to the inhabitants of Babylon.

35 A sword against the
 Chaldeans, says the
 LORD,
 and against the inhabitants
 of Babylon,
 and against her officials
 and her sages!
36 A sword against the diviners,
 so that they may become
 fools!
A sword against her warriors,
 so that they may be
 destroyed!
37 A sword against her[w] horses
 and against her[w]
 chariots,
 and against all the foreign
 troops in her midst,
 so that they may become
 women!
A sword against all her
 treasures,
 that they may be
 plundered!
38 A drought[x] against her
 waters,
 that they may be dried up!
For it is a land of images,
 and they go mad over idols.

39 Therefore wild animals shall
live with hyenas in Babylon,[y] and
ostriches shall inhabit her; she
shall never again be peopled, or in-
habited for all generations. 40 As
when God overthrew Sodom and
Gomorrah and their neighbors,
says the LORD, so no one shall live

there, nor shall anyone settle in
her.

41 Look, a people is coming
 from the north;
 a mighty nation and many
 kings
are stirring from the
 farthest parts of the
 earth.
42 They wield bow and spear,
 they are cruel and have no
 mercy.
The sound of them is like
 the roaring sea;
 they ride upon horses,
set in array as a warrior for
 battle,
 against you, O daughter
 Babylon!

43 The king of Babylon heard
 news of them,
 and his hands fell helpless;
anguish seized him,
 pain like that of a woman
 in labor.

44 Like a lion coming up from
the thickets of the Jordan against a
perennial pasture, I will suddenly
chase them away from her; and I
will appoint over her whomever I
choose.[z] For who is like me? Who
can summon me? Who is the shep-
herd who can stand before me?
45 Therefore hear the plan that the
LORD has made against Babylon,
and the purposes that he has
formed against the land of the
Chaldeans: Surely the little ones of
the flock shall be dragged away;
surely their[a] fold shall be appalled
at their fate. 46 At the sound of the
capture of Babylon the earth shall
tremble, and her cry shall be heard
among the nations.

51 Thus says the LORD:
I am going to stir up a
 destructive wind[b]

50.33
Isa 14.17;
58.6
50.34
Isa 43.14;
Jer 15.21;
31.11; 32.18;
51.19,36;
Isa 14.3-7
50.35
Dan 5.1,2,7,
8,30
50.36
Isa 44.25;
Jer 49.22
50.37
Jer 51.21,
22; 25.30;
Ezek 30.5;
Jer 51.30;
Nah 3.13
50.38
Jer 51.32,
36,42,47,52
50.39
Isa 13.21,
22;
Jer 51.37;
Isa 13.20
50.40
Gen 19.25;
Jer 49.18;
Lk 17.28-30
50.41
cf. v. 3;
Jer 6.22;
Rev 17.16
50.42
Jer 6.23;
Isa 13.18;
5.30
50.43
Jer 51.31;
49.24
50.44
Jer 49.19-21;
Isa 46.9;
Job 41.10;
Jer 49.19
50.45
Isa 14.24;
Jer 51.11;
49.20
50.46
Rev 18.9;
Ezek 27.28
51.1
Jer 4.11;
Hos 13.15

[w] Cn: Heb *his* [x] Another reading is *A
sword* [y] Heb lacks *in Babylon* [z] Or *and
I will single out the choicest of her rams:
Meaning of Heb uncertain* [a] Syr Gk Tg
Compare 49.20: Heb lacks *their* [b] Or *stir
up the spirit of a destroyer*

against Babylon
and against the inhabitants
of Leb-qamai;^c

2 and I will send winnowers to
Babylon,
and they shall winnow her.
They shall empty her land
when they come against
her from every side
on the day of trouble.

3 Let not the archer bend his
bow,
and let him not array
himself in his coat of
mail.
Do not spare her young men;
utterly destroy her entire
army.

4 They shall fall down slain in
the land of the
Chaldeans,
and wounded in her
streets.

5 Israel and Judah have not
been forsaken
by their God, the LORD of
hosts,
though their land is full of
guilt
before the Holy One of
Israel.

6 Flee from the midst of
Babylon,
save your lives, each of
you!
Do not perish because of her
guilt,
for this is the time of the
LORD's vengeance;
he is repaying her what is
due.

7 Babylon was a golden cup in
the LORD's hand,
making all the earth
drunken;
the nations drank of her
wine,
and so the nations went
mad.

8 Suddenly Babylon has fallen
and is shattered;
wail for her!
Bring balm for her wound;
perhaps she may be healed.

9 We tried to heal Babylon,

but she could not be
healed.
Forsake her, and let each of
us go
to our own country;
for her judgment has reached
up to heaven
and has been lifted up
even to the skies.

10 The LORD has brought forth
our vindication;
come, let us declare in
Zion
the work of the LORD our
God.

11 Sharpen the arrows!
Fill the quivers!
The LORD has stirred up the spirit of
the kings of the Medes, because his
purpose concerning Babylon is to
destroy it, for that is the vengeance
of the LORD, vengeance for his tem-
ple.

12 Raise a standard against the
walls of Babylon;
make the watch strong;
post sentinels;
prepare the ambushes;
for the LORD has both
planned and done
what he spoke concerning
the inhabitants of
Babylon.

13 You who live by mighty
waters,
rich in treasures,
your end has come,
the thread of your life is
cut.

14 The LORD of hosts has sworn
by himself:
Surely I will fill you with
troops like a swarm of
locusts,
and they shall raise a shout
of victory over you.

15 It is he who made the earth
by his power,
who established the world
by his wisdom,

51.2
Isa 41.16;
Jer 15.7;
Mt 3.12
51.3
Jer 50.14;
46.4; 50.21
51.4
Jer 49.26;
50.30,37
51.5
Isa 54.7,8;
Jer 33.24-26
51.6
Jer 50.8;
Rev 18.4;
Num 16.26;
Jer 50.15;
25.14
51.7
Rev 17.4;
Jer 25.15;
Rev 14.8;
18.3;
Jer 25.16
51.8
Isa 21.9;
Rev 14.8;
18.2;
Jer 48.20;
Rev 18.9,11,
19
51.9
Isa 13.14;
Jer 50.16;
Rev 18.5

51.10
Ps 37.6;
Mic 7.9;
Isa 40.2;
Jer 50.28
51.11
Jer 46.4;
Joel 3.9,10;
Jer 50.3,9,
28
51.12
Isa 13.2;
Jer 50.2
51.13
Rev 17.1,15
51.14
Jer 49.13;
Am 6.8;
Nah 3.15;
Jer 50.15
51.15ff
Gen 1.1,6;
Jer 10.12-16;
Acts 14.15;
Rom 1.20;
Job 9.8;
Ps 104.2;
Isa 40.22

^c *Leb-qamai* is a cryptogram for *Kasdim*,
Chaldea

and by his understanding
 stretched out the
 heavens.
16 When he utters his voice
 there is a tumult of
 waters in the heavens,
 and he makes the mist rise
 from the ends of the
 earth.
He makes lightnings for the
 rain,
 and he brings out the wind
 from his storehouses.
17 Everyone is stupid and
 without knowledge;
 goldsmiths are all put to
 shame by their idols;
 for their images are false,
 and there is no breath in
 them.
18 They are worthless, a work of
 delusion;
 at the time of their
 punishment they shall
 perish.
19 Not like these is the LORD, d
 the portion of Jacob,
 for he is the one who
 formed all things,
 and Israel is the tribe of his
 inheritance;
 the LORD of hosts is his
 name.

Israel the Creator's Instrument

20 You are my war club, my
 weapon of battle:
with you I smash nations;
 with you I destroy
 kingdoms;
21 with you I smash the horse
 and its rider;
 with you I smash the
 chariot and the
 charioteer;
22 with you I smash man and
 woman;
 with you I smash the old
 man and the boy;
 with you I smash the young
 man and the girl;
23 with you I smash
 shepherds and their
 flocks;
with you I smash farmers
 and their teams;

with you I smash governors
 and deputies.

The Doom of Babylon

24 I will repay Babylon and all
the inhabitants of Chaldea before
your very eyes for all the wrong that
they have done in Zion, says the
LORD.

25 I am against you,
 O destroying mountain,
 says the LORD,
 that destroys the whole
 earth;
I will stretch out my hand
 against you,
 and roll you down from the
 crags,
 and make you a burned-out
 mountain.
26 No stone shall be taken from
 you for a corner
 and no stone for a
 foundation,
but you shall be a perpetual
 waste,
 says the LORD.

27 Raise a standard in the land,
 blow the trumpet among
 the nations;
prepare the nations for war
 against her,
 summon against her the
 kingdoms,
 Ararat, Minni, and
 Ashkenaz;
appoint a marshal against
 her,
 bring up horses like
 bristling locusts.
28 Prepare the nations for war
 against her,
 the kings of the Medes,
 with their governors
 and deputies,
 and every land under their
 dominion.
29 The land trembles and
 writhes,
 for the LORD's purposes
 against Babylon stand,
 to make the land of Babylon
 a desolation,

51.16
Ps 18.13;
Jer 10.13;
Ps 135.7
51.17
Jer 10.14;
50.2;
Hab 2.18,19
51.18
Jer 10.15
51.19
Jer 10.16;
50.34
51.20
Isa 10.5,15;
Jer 50.23;
Isa 41.15,
16;
Mic 4.12,13
51.22
2 Chr 36.17
51.23
v. 57

51.24
Jer 50.10,
15,29
51.25
Jer 50.31;
Zech 4.7;
Rev 8.8
51.26
v. 29;
Jer 50.13
51.27
Isa 13.2;
Jer 50.2;
25.14; 50.41,
42
51.28
v. 11
51.29
Jer 8.16;
10.10; 50.46;
Am 8.8;
Isa 13.19,
20; 47.11

d Heb lacks the LORD

without inhabitant.

30 The warriors of Babylon have
 given up fighting,
 they remain in their
 strongholds;
 their strength has failed,
 they have become women;
 her buildings are set on fire,
 her bars are broken.
31 One runner runs to meet
 another,
 and one messenger to meet
 another,
 to tell the king of Babylon
 that his city is taken from
 end to end:
32 the fords have been seized,
 the marshes have been
 burned with fire,
 and the soldiers are in
 panic.
33 For thus says the LORD of
 hosts, the God of Israel:
 Daughter Babylon is like a
 threshing floor
 at the time when it is
 trodden;
 yet a little while
 and the time of her harvest
 will come.

34 "King Nebuchadrezzar of
 Babylon has devoured
 me,
 he has crushed me;
 he has made me an empty
 vessel,
 he has swallowed me like a
 monster;
 he has filled his belly with
 my delicacies,
 he has spewed me out.
35 May my torn flesh be
 avenged on Babylon,"
 the inhabitants of Zion
 shall say.
 "May my blood be avenged
 on the inhabitants of
 Chaldea,"
 Jerusalem shall say.
36 Therefore thus says the LORD:
 I am going to defend your
 cause
 and take vengeance for
 you.
 I will dry up her sea
 and make her fountain dry;

37 and Babylon shall become a
 heap of ruins,
 a den of jackals,
 an object of horror and of
 hissing,
 without inhabitant.
38 Like lions they shall roar
 together;
 they shall growl like lions'
 whelps.
39 When they are inflamed, I
 will set out their drink
 and make them drunk,
 until they become
 merry
 and then sleep a perpetual
 sleep
 and never wake, says the
 LORD.
40 I will bring them down like
 lambs to the slaughter,
 like rams and goats.

41 How Sheshach[e] is taken,
 the pride of the whole
 earth seized!
 How Babylon has become
 an object of horror among
 the nations!
42 The sea has risen over
 Babylon;
 she has been covered by its
 tumultuous waves.
43 Her cities have become an
 object of horror,
 a land of drought and a
 desert,
 a land in which no one lives,
 and through which no
 mortal passes.
44 I will punish Bel in Babylon,
 and make him disgorge
 what he has swallowed.
 The nations shall no longer
 stream to him;
 the wall of Babylon has
 fallen.

45 Come out of her, my people!
 Save your lives, each of
 you,
 from the fierce anger of the
 LORD!

51.30
Ps 76.5;
Jer 50.36,
37; Isa 13.7,
8; Lam 2.9;
Am 1.5;
Nah 3.13
51.31
2 Chr 30.6;
2 Sam 18.19-
31; Jer 50.24
51.32
Jer 50.37,38
51.33
Isa 21.10;
41.15;
Hab 3.12;
Isa 17.5-7;
Hos 6.11;
Joel 3.13
51.34
Jer 50.17;
Isa 24.1-3;
Am 8.4
51.35
Ps 137.8;
v. 24
51.36
Ps 140.12;
Jer 50.34;
Rom 12.19;
Jer 50.38

51.37
Isa 13.22;
Jer 50.39;
Rev 18.2
Jer 49.33;
50.13
51.39
Jer 25.27
51.40
Jer 50.27
51.41
Jer 25.26;
Isa 13.19;
Jer 49.25
51.42
Isa 8.7,8;
Dan 9.26
51.43
Jer 50.12;
Isa 13.20
51.44
Isa 46.1;
Jer 50.2;
vv. 34,58
51.45
v. 6;
Jer 50.8;
Rev 18.4;
Acts 2.40

e *Sheshach* is a cryptogram for *Babel*, Babylon

46 Do not be faint-hearted or
 fearful
 at the rumors heard in the
 land—
one year one rumor comes,
 the next year another,
rumors of violence in the
 land
 and of ruler against ruler.

47 Assuredly, the days are
 coming
 when I will punish the
 images of Babylon;
her whole land shall be put
 to shame,
 and all her slain shall fall
 in her midst.
48 Then the heavens and the
 earth,
 and all that is in them,
shall shout for joy over
 Babylon;
 for the destroyers shall
 come against them out
 of the north,
 says the LORD.
49 Babylon must fall for the
 slain of Israel,
 as the slain of all the earth
 have fallen because of
 Babylon.

50 You survivors of the sword,
 go, do not linger!
Remember the LORD in a
 distant land,
 and let Jerusalem come
 into your mind:
51 We are put to shame, for we
 have heard insults;
dishonor has covered our
 face,
for aliens have come
 into the holy places of the
 LORD's house.

52 Therefore the time is surely
 coming, says the LORD,
 when I will punish her
 idols,
and through all her land
 the wounded shall groan.
53 Though Babylon should
 mount up to heaven,

and though she should
 fortify her strong height,
from me destroyers would
 come upon her,
 says the LORD.

54 Listen!—a cry from Babylon!
 A great crashing from the
 land of the Chaldeans!
55 For the LORD is laying
 Babylon waste,
 and stilling her loud
 clamor.
Their waves roar like mighty
 waters,
 the sound of their clamor
 resounds;
56 for a destroyer has come
 against her,
 against Babylon;
her warriors are taken,
 their bows are broken;
for the LORD is a God of
 recompense,
 he will repay in full.
57 I will make her officials and
 her sages drunk,
 also her governors, her
 deputies, and her
 warriors;
they shall sleep a perpetual
 sleep and never wake,
 says the King, whose name
 is the LORD of hosts.

58 Thus says the LORD of hosts:
The broad wall of Babylon
 shall be leveled to the
 ground,
and her high gates
 shall be burned with fire.
The peoples exhaust
 themselves for nothing,
 and the nations weary
 themselves only for
 fire.[f]

Jeremiah's Command to Seraiah

59 The word that the prophet
Jeremiah commanded Seraiah son
of Neriah son of Mahseiah, when
he went with King Zedekiah of Ju-
dah to Babylon, in the fourth year
of his reign. Seraiah was the quar-

Center reference column:

51.46
Jer 46.27,
28;
2 Kings 19.7;
Isa 13.3-5;
19.2
51.47
Isa 46.1,2;
v. 52;
Jer 50.2;
50.12,35-37
51.48
Isa 44.23;
49.13;
Rev 12.12;
18.20;
vv. 11,27
51.49
Jer 50.29
51.50
v. 45;
Ps 137.6
51.51
Ps 79.4
51.52
v. 47;
Jer 50.38
51.53
Isa 14.12,
13;
Jer 49.16;
Isa 13.3

51.54
Jer 50.46
51.55
v. 42
51.56
v. 48;
Hab 2.8;
Ps 94.1,2;
vv. 6,24
51.57
v. 39;
Ps 76.5,6;
Jer 46.18;
48.15
51.58
v. 44;
Jer 50.15;
Hab 2.13;
v. 64
51.59
Jer 32.12;
28.1

[f] Gk Syr Compare Hab 2.13: Heb *and the
nations for fire, and they are weary*

termaster. [60] Jeremiah wrote in a [g] scroll all the disasters that would come on Babylon, all these words that are written concerning Babylon. [61] And Jeremiah said to Seraiah: "When you come to Babylon, see that you read all these words, [62] and say, 'O LORD, you yourself threatened to destroy this place so that neither human beings nor animals shall live in it, and it shall be desolate forever.' [63] When you finish reading this scroll, tie a stone to it, and throw it into the middle of the Euphrates, [64] and say, 'Thus shall Babylon sink, to rise no more, because of the disasters that I am bringing on her.'" [h]

Thus far are the words of Jeremiah.

The Destruction of Jerusalem Reviewed

52 Zedekiah was twenty-one years old when he began to reign; he reigned eleven years in Jerusalem. His mother's name was Hamutal daughter of Jeremiah of Libnah. [2] He did what was evil in the sight of the LORD, just as Jehoiakim had done. [3] Indeed, Jerusalem and Judah so angered the LORD that he expelled them from his presence.

Zedekiah rebelled against the king of Babylon. [4] And in the ninth year of his reign, in the tenth month, on the tenth day of the month, King Nebuchadrezzar of Babylon came with all his army against Jerusalem, and they laid siege to it; they built siegeworks against it all around. [5] So the city was besieged until the eleventh year of King Zedekiah. [6] On the ninth day of the fourth month the famine became so severe in the city that there was no food for the people of the land. [7] Then a breach was made in the city wall; [i] and all the soldiers fled and went out from the city by night by the way of the gate between the two walls, by the king's garden, though the Chaldeans were all around the city. They went in the direction of the Ara-

bah. [8] But the army of the Chaldeans pursued the king, and overtook Zedekiah in the plains of Jericho; and all his army was scattered, deserting him. [9] Then they captured the king, and brought him up to the king of Babylon at Riblah in the land of Hamath, and he passed sentence on him. [10] The king of Babylon killed the sons of Zedekiah before his eyes, and also killed all the officers of Judah at Riblah. [11] He put out the eyes of Zedekiah, and bound him in fetters, and the king of Babylon took him to Babylon, and put him in prison until the day of his death.

12 In the fifth month, on the tenth day of the month—which was the nineteenth year of King Nebuchadrezzar, king of Babylon—Nebuzaradan the captain of the bodyguard who served the king of Babylon, entered Jerusalem. [13] He burned the house of the LORD, the king's house, and all the houses of Jerusalem; every great house he burned down. [14] All the army of the Chaldeans, who were with the captain of the guard, broke down all the walls around Jerusalem. [15] Nebuzaradan the captain of the guard carried into exile some of the poorest of the people and the rest of the people who were left in the city and the deserters who had defected to the king of Babylon, together with the rest of the artisans. [16] But Nebuzaradan the captain of the guard left some of the poorest people of the land to be vinedressers and tillers of the soil.

17 The pillars of bronze that were in the house of the LORD, and the stands and the bronze sea that were in the house of the LORD, the Chaldeans broke in pieces, and carried all the bronze to Babylon. [18] They took away the pots, the shovels, the snuffers, the basins, the ladles, and all the vessels of bronze used in the temple service. [19] The captain of the guard took

Center reference column

51.60
Jer 30.2,3;
36.2,4,32
51.62
Jer 25.12;
50.3,39;
v. 43;
Ezek 35.9
51.63
Rev 18.21
51.64
Nah 1.8,9;
v. 58
52.1
2 Kings 24.18;
2 Chr 36.11-13
52.2
Jer 36.30,31
52.3
Isa 3.1,4,5;
2 Chr 36.13
52.4
2 Kings 25.1-7;
Jer 39.1;
Ezek 24.1,2;
Jer 32.24
52.6
Jer 38.9
52.7
Jer 39.2;
39.4-7

52.8
Jer 21.7;
32.4; 34.21;
37.17; 38.23
52.9
Jer 32.4;
2 Kings 25.6;
Jer 39.5
52.10
Jer 39.6
52.11
Jer 39.7;
Ezek 12.13
52.12
2 Kings 25.8-21;
Jer 39.9
52.13
2 Chr 36.19;
Lam 2.7;
Mic 3.12;
Jer 39.8
52.14
2 Kings 25.10
52.15
2 Kings 25.11;
Jer 39.9
52.16
2 Kings 25.12;
Jer 39.10;
40.2-6
52.17
1 Kings 7.15-36;
Jer 27.19-22
52.18
1 Kings 7.40,45
52.19
1 Kings 7.49,50

g Or one h Gk: Heb on her. And they shall weary themselves i Heb lacks wall

away the small bowls also, the fire-pans, the basins, the pots, the lampstands, the ladles, and the bowls for libation, both those of gold and those of silver. ²⁰As for the two pillars, the one sea, the twelve bronze bulls that were under the sea, and the stands,ⁱ which King Solomon had made for the house of the LORD, the bronze of all these vessels was beyond weighing. ²¹As for the pillars, the height of the one pillar was eighteen cubits, its circumference was twelve cubits; it was hollow and its thickness was four fingers. ²²Upon it was a capital of bronze; the height of the one capital was five cubits; latticework and pomegranates, all of bronze, encircled the top of the capital. And the second pillar had the same, with pomegranates. ²³There were ninety-six pomegranates on the sides; all the pomegranates encircling the latticework numbered one hundred.

24 The captain of the guard took the chief priest Seraiah, the second priest Zephaniah, and the three guardians of the threshold; ²⁵and from the city he took an officer who had been in command of the soldiers, and seven men of the king's council who were found in the city; the secretary of the commander of the army who mustered the people of the land; and sixty men of the people of the land who were found inside the city. ²⁶Then Nebuzaradan the captain of the guard took them, and brought

them to the king of Babylon at Riblah. ²⁷And the king of Babylon struck them down, and put them to death at Riblah in the land of Hamath. So Judah went into exile out of its land.

28 This is the number of the people whom Nebuchadrezzar took into exile: in the seventh year, three thousand twenty-three Judeans; ²⁹in the eighteenth year of Nebuchadrezzar he took into exile from Jerusalem eight hundred thirty-two persons; ³⁰in the twenty-third year of Nebuchadrezzar, Nebuzaradan the captain of the guard took into exile of the Judeans seven hundred forty-five persons; all the persons were four thousand six hundred.

Jehoiachin Favored in Captivity

31 In the thirty-seventh year of the exile of King Jehoiachin of Judah, in the twelfth month, on the twenty-fifth day of the month, King Evil-merodach of Babylon, in the year he began to reign, showed favor to King Jehoiachin of Judah and brought him out of prison; ³²he spoke kindly to him, and gave him a seat above the seats of the other kings who were with him in Babylon. ³³So Jehoiachin put aside his prison clothes, and every day of his life he dined regularly at the king's table. ³⁴For his allowance, a regular daily allowance was given him by the king of Babylon, as long as he lived, up to the day of his death.

i Cn: Heb *that were under the stands*

52.20
1 Kings 7.47
52.21
1 Kings 7.15
52.22
1 Kings 7.16, 20,42
52.24
2 Kings 25.18; Jer 21.1; 29.25; 37.3; 35.4
52.26
vv. 12,15, 16;
2 Kings 25.20, 21; v. 9

52.27
Isa 6.11,12; Jer 13.19; Ezek 33.28; Mic 4.10
52.28
2 Kings 24.2, 3,12-16; Neh 7.6; Dan 1.1-3
52.30
2 Kings 25.11; Jer 39.9
52.31
2 Kings 25.27-30; Gen 40.13
52.33
Gen 41.14, 42;
2 Sam 9.13; 1 Kings 2.7
52.34
2 Sam 9.10

Lamentations

Title and Background

Because of its subject matter, this book is referred to in Jewish tradition as "Lamentations." It was written as an expression of the people's feelings after Jerusalem was destroyed and the temple burned to the ground.

Author and Date of Writing

Although the writer of Lamentations is anonymous, ancient Jewish and Christian tradition ascribes it to Jeremiah. Since he was an eyewitness to the divine judgment on Jerusalem in 586 B.C., it is reasonable to assume he was the author. The book was probably written shortly after 586.

Theme and Message

Lamentations is the only Old Testament book that consists solely of laments. Jeremiah recognizes that the judgment on Jerusalem and the temple is the judgment of a righteous God. The book that begins with a lament (1.1-2) rightly ends in repentance (5.21-22). Knowing that God is merciful, he appeals for mercy in prayer to God. In the middle of the book, the theology of Lamentations reaches its apex as it focuses on the goodness of God. In spite of all evidence to the contrary, "his mercies never come to an end" (3.22).

Outline

 I. Jerusalem's Misery and Desolation (1.1-22)
 II. The Lord's Anger Against His People (2.1-22)
 III. Judah's Complaint and the Basis for Consolation (3.1-66)
 IV. The Contrast Between Zion's Past and Present (4.1-22)
 V. Judah's Appeal for God's Forgiveness (5.1-22)

The Deserted City

1 How lonely sits the city
 that once was full of
 people!
How like a widow she has
 become,
 she that was great among
 the nations!
She that was a princess
 among the provinces
has become a vassal.

2 She weeps bitterly in the
 night,
 with tears on her cheeks;
among all her lovers
 she has no one to comfort
 her;
all her friends have dealt
 treacherously with her,

 they have become her
 enemies.

3 Judah has gone into exile
 with suffering
 and hard servitude;
she lives now among the
 nations,
 and finds no resting place;
her pursuers have all
 overtaken her
 in the midst of her distress.

4 The roads to Zion mourn,
 for no one comes to the
 festivals;
all her gates are desolate,
 her priests groan;
her young girls grieve,[a]
 and her lot is bitter.

1.1 Isa 3.26; 54.4; Ezra 4.20; Jer 40.9
1.2 Ps 6.6; Jer 2.25; 4.30
1.3 Jer 13.19; Deut 28.64, 65; 2 Kings 25.4, 5
1.4 Jer 9.11; 10.22; Joel 1.8-13

[a] Meaning of Heb uncertain

5 Her foes have become the
masters,
her enemies prosper,
because the LORD has made
her suffer
for the multitude of her
transgressions;
her children have gone away,
captives before the foe.

6 From daughter Zion has
departed
all her majesty.
Her princes have become
like stags
that find no pasture;
they fled without strength
before the pursuer.

7 Jerusalem remembers,
in the days of her affliction
and wandering,
all the precious things
that were hers in days of
old.
When her people fell into the
hand of the foe,
and there was no one to
help her,
the foe looked on mocking
over her downfall.

8 Jerusalem sinned grievously,
so she has become a
mockery;
all who honored her despise
her,
for they have seen her
nakedness;
she herself groans,
and turns her face away.

9 Her uncleanness was in her
skirts;
she took no thought of her
future;
her downfall was appalling,
with none to comfort her.
"O LORD, look at my
affliction,
for the enemy has
triumphed!"

10 Enemies have stretched out
their hands
over all her precious
things;

1.5
Deut 28.43,
44;
Jer 30.14,
15; 39.9;
52.28
1.6
Jer 13.18;
2 Kings 25.4,
5
1.7
Ps 42.4;
Isa 5.1-4;
Jer 37.7;
Lam 4.17;
Jer 48.27
1.8
1 Kings 8.46;
vv. 5,20,17;
Jer 13.22,
26; vv. 4,11,
21,22
1.9
Ezek 24.13;
Deut 32.29;
Isa 47.7;
Jer 13.17,
18; 16.7
1.10
Isa 64.10,
11;
Jer 51.51;
Deut 23.3

1.11
Jer 38.9;
52.6;
1 Sam 30.12
1.12
Jer 18.16;
48.27; v. 18;
Jer 30.23,
24; 4.8
1.13
Job 30.30;
Hab 3.16;
Job 19.6;
Jer 44.6
1.14
Deut 28.48;
Isa 47.6;
Jer 28.13,
14; 32.3,5;
Ezek 25.4,7
1.15
Isa 41.2;
Jer 13.24;
18.21;
Isa 28.18;
Mic 7.10;
Rev 14.19

she has even seen the
nations
invade her sanctuary,
those whom you forbade
to enter your congregation.

11 All her people groan
as they search for bread;
they trade their treasures for
food
to revive their strength.
Look, O LORD, and see
how worthless I have
become.

12 Is it nothing to you,b all you
who pass by?
Look and see
if there is any sorrow like my
sorrow,
which was brought upon
me,
which the LORD inflicted
on the day of his fierce
anger.

13 From on high he sent fire;
it went deep into my
bones;
he spread a net for my feet;
he turned me back;
he has left me stunned,
faint all day long.

14 My transgressions were
boundb into a yoke;
by his hand they were
fastened together;
they weigh on my neck,
sapping my strength;
the Lord handed me over
to those whom I cannot
withstand.

15 The LORD has rejected
all my warriors in the midst
of me;
he proclaimed a time against
me
to crush my young men;
the Lord has trodden as in a
wine press
the virgin daughter Judah.

b Meaning of Heb uncertain

16 For these things I weep;
 my eyes flow with tears;
for a comforter is far from
 me,
 one to revive my courage;
my children are desolate,
 for the enemy has
 prevailed.

17 Zion stretches out her hands,
 but there is no one to
 comfort her;
the LORD has commanded
 against Jacob
 that his neighbors should
 become his foes;
Jerusalem has become
 a filthy thing among them.

18 The LORD is in the right,
 for I have rebelled against
 his word;
but hear, all you peoples,
 and behold my suffering;
my young women and young
 men
 have gone into captivity.

19 I called to my lovers
 but they deceived me;
my priests and elders
 perished in the city
while seeking food
 to revive their strength.

20 See, O LORD, how distressed I
 am;
 my stomach churns,
my heart is wrung within me,
 because I have been very
 rebellious.
In the street the sword
 bereaves;
 in the house it is like
 death.

21 They heard how I was
 groaning,
 with no one to comfort me.
All my enemies heard of my
 trouble;
 they are glad that you have
 done it.
Bring on the day you have
 announced,
 and let them be as I am.

22 Let all their evil doing come
 before you;
 and deal with them
as you have dealt with me
 because of all my
 transgressions;
for my groans are many
 and my heart is faint.

God's Warnings Fulfilled

2 How the Lord in his anger
 has humiliated[c] daughter
 Zion!
He has thrown down from
 heaven to earth
 the splendor of Israel;
he has not remembered his
 footstool
 in the day of his anger.

2 The Lord has destroyed
 without mercy
 all the dwellings of Jacob;
in his wrath he has broken
 down
 the strongholds of daughter
 Judah;
he has brought down to the
 ground in dishonor
 the kingdom and its rulers.

3 He has cut down in fierce
 anger
 all the might of Israel;
he has withdrawn his right
 hand from them
 in the face of the enemy;
he has burned like a flaming
 fire in Jacob,
 consuming all around.

4 He has bent his bow like an
 enemy,
 with his right hand set like
 a foe;
he has killed all in whom we
 took pride
 in the tent of daughter
 Zion;
he has poured out his fury
 like fire.

5 The Lord has become like an
 enemy;
 he has destroyed Israel;

1.16
Jer 13.17;
14.17;
Lam 2.18;
vv. 2,9
1.17
Jer 4.31;
2 Kings 24.2-
4; v. 8
1.18
Jer 12.1;
1 Sam 12.14;
v. 12;
Deut 28.32,
41
1.19
Jer 30.14;
14.15;
Lam 2.20
1.20
Isa 16.11;
Jer 4.19;
Lam 2.11;
Deut 32.29;
Ezek 7.15
1.21
Lam 2.15;
Isa 14.5,6;
Jer 30.16

1.22
Neh 4.4,5;
Ps 137.7,8
2.1
Lam 3.43,
44;
Ezek 28.14-
16;
Isa 64.11;
Ps 99.5;
132.7
2.2
Ps 21.9;
Lam 3.43;
Mic 5.11,14;
Isa 25.12;
Ps 89.39
2.3
Ps 75.5,10;
74.11;
Jer 21.4,5;
21.14
2.4
Lam 3.12,
13;
Ezek 24.25;
Isa 42.25;
Jer 7.20
2.5
Jer 30.14;
6.26; 9.17-20

c Meaning of Heb uncertain

He has destroyed all its
palaces,
laid in ruins its
strongholds,
and multiplied in daughter
Judah
mourning and lamentation.

6 He has broken down his
booth like a garden,
he has destroyed his
tabernacle;
the Lord has abolished in
Zion
festival and sabbath,
and in his fierce indignation
has spurned
king and priest.

7 The Lord has scorned his
altar,
disowned his sanctuary;
he has delivered into the
hand of the enemy
the walls of her palaces;
a clamor was raised in the
house of the Lord
as on a day of festival.

8 The Lord determined to lay
in ruins
the wall of daughter Zion;
he stretched the line;
he did not withhold his
hand from destroying;
he caused rampart and wall
to lament;
they languish together.

9 Her gates have sunk into the
ground;
he has ruined and broken
her bars;
her king and princes are
among the nations;
guidance is no more,
and her prophets obtain
no vision from the Lord.

10 The elders of daughter Zion
sit on the ground in
silence;
they have thrown dust on
their heads
and put on sackcloth;
the young girls of Jerusalem

2.6
Jer 7.14;
52.13;
Lam 1.4;
Zeph 3.18;
Lam 4.16,
20; 5.12
2.7
Isa 64.11;
Ezek 7.20-22;
Jer 33.4,5;
Ps 74.4
2.8
Jer 5.10;
2 Kings 21.13;
Isa 34.11;
3.26;
Jer 14.2
2.9
Neh 1.3;
Jer 51.30;
Deut 28.36;
2 Kings 24.15;
2 Chr 15.3;
Jer 14.14;
23.16;
Ezek 7.26
2.10
Job 2.13;
Isa 3.26;
Am 8.3;
Job 2.12;
Ezek 27.30,
31; Isa 15.3;
Lam 1.4

2.11
Ps 6.7;
Lam 3.48;
1.20;
Job 16.13;
Ps 22.14;
Lam 4.4
2.12
Jer 5.17;
Lam 4.4;
Job 30.16
2.13
Lam 1.12;
Isa 37.22;
Jer 14.17;
8.22;
30.12-15
2.14
Jer 2.8;
29.8,9;
Isa 58.1;
Jer 23.36;
Ezek 22.25,
28
2.15
Jer 19.8;
Zeph 2.15;
Isa 37.22;
Ps 48.2;
50.2
2.16
Ps 22.13;
Lam 3.46;
Ps 37.12;
56.2;
Ob 12-15

have bowed their heads to
the ground.

11 My eyes are spent with
weeping;
my stomach churns;
my bile is poured out on the
ground
because of the destruction
of my people,
because infants and babes
faint
in the streets of the city.

12 They cry to their mothers,
"Where is bread and
wine?"
as they faint like the
wounded
in the streets of the city,
as their life is poured out
on their mothers' bosom.

13 What can I say for you, to
what compare you,
O daughter Jerusalem?
To what can I liken you, that
I may comfort you,
O virgin daughter Zion?
For vast as the sea is your
ruin;
who can heal you?

14 Your prophets have seen for
you
false and deceptive visions;
they have not exposed your
iniquity
to restore your fortunes,
but have seen oracles for you
that are false and
misleading.

15 All who pass along the way
clap their hands at you;
they hiss and wag their
heads
at daughter Jerusalem;
"Is this the city that was
called
the perfection of beauty,
the joy of all the earth?"

16 All your enemies
open their mouths against
you;

they hiss, they gnash their
teeth,
they cry: "We have
devoured her!
Ah, this is the day we longed
for;
at last we have seen it!"

17 The LORD has done what he
purposed,
he has carried out his
threat;
as he ordained long ago,
he has demolished without
pity;
he has made the enemy
rejoice over you,
and exalted the might of
your foes.

18 Cry aloud[d] to the Lord!
O wall of daughter Zion!
Let tears stream down like a
torrent
day and night!
Give yourself no rest,
your eyes no respite!

19 Arise, cry out in the night,
at the beginning of the
watches!
Pour out your heart like
water
before the presence of the
Lord!
Lift your hands to him
for the lives of your
children,
who faint for hunger
at the head of every street.

20 Look, O LORD, and consider!
To whom have you done
this?
Should women eat their
offspring,
the children they have
borne?
Should priest and prophet be
killed
in the sanctuary of the
Lord?

21 The young and the old are
lying
on the ground in the
streets;

2.17
Deut 28.15;
Jer 18.11;
vv. 1,2;
Ps 35.24,26;
Lam 1.5
2.18
Hos 7.14;
Jer 9.1;
Lam 1.2,16
2.19
Ps 42.3;
Isa 26.9;
Ps 62.8;
Isa 51.20
2.20
Jer 19.9;
14.15;
Lam 4.13,16
2.21
2 Chr 36.17;
Jer 6.11;
Ps 78.62,63;
Jer 13.14;
Zech 11.6

2.22
Ps 31.13;
Jer 6.25;
Hos 9.12,13
3.1
Job 19.21;
Jer 15.17,18
3.2
Isa 59.9;
Jer 4.23
3.3
Isa 5.25
3.4
Job 16.8;
Ps 51.8;
Isa 38.13;
Jer 50.17
3.5
Job 19.8;
Jer 23.15
3.6
Ps 88.5,6
3.7
Job 3.23;
Jer 40.4
3.8
Job 30.20;
Ps 22.2
3.9
Hos 2.6;
Isa 63.17

my young women and my
young men
have fallen by the sword;
in the day of your anger you
have killed them,
slaughtering without
mercy.

22 You invited my enemies from
all around
as if for a day of festival;
and on the day of the anger
of the LORD
no one escaped or survived;
those whom I bore and
reared
my enemy has destroyed.

God's Steadfast Love Endures

3 I am one who has seen
affliction
under the rod of God's[e]
wrath;
2 he has driven and brought
me
into darkness without any
light;
3 against me alone he turns
his hand,
again and again, all day
long.

4 He has made my flesh and
my skin waste away,
and broken my bones;
5 he has besieged and
enveloped me
with bitterness and
tribulation;
6 he has made me sit in
darkness
like the dead of long ago.

7 He has walled me about so
that I cannot escape;
he has put heavy chains on
me;
8 though I call and cry for
help,
he shuts out my prayer;
9 he has blocked my ways with
hewn stones,
he has made my paths
crooked.

[d] Cn: Heb *Their heart cried* [e] Heb *his*

10 He is a bear lying in wait for
 me,
 a lion in hiding;
11 he led me off my way and
 tore me to pieces;
 he has made me desolate;
12 he bent his bow and set me
 as a mark for his arrow.

13 He shot into my vitals
 the arrows of his quiver;
14 I have become the
 laughingstock of all my
 people,
 the object of their
 taunt-songs all day
 long.
15 He has filled me with
 bitterness,
 he has sated me with
 wormwood.

16 He has made my teeth grind
 on gravel,
 and made me cower in
 ashes;
17 my soul is bereft of peace;
 I have forgotten what
 happiness is;
18 so I say, "Gone is my glory,
 and all that I had hoped
 for from the LORD."

19 The thought of my affliction
 and my homelessness
 is wormwood and gall!
20 My soul continually thinks of
 it
 and is bowed down within
 me.
21 But this I call to mind,
 and therefore I have hope:

22 The steadfast love of the
 LORD never ceases,f
 his mercies never come to
 an end;
23 they are new every morning;
 great is your faithfulness.
24 "The LORD is my portion,"
 says my soul,
 "therefore I will hope in
 him."

25 The LORD is good to those
 who wait for him,
 to the soul that seeks him.

26 It is good that one should
 wait quietly
 for the salvation of the
 LORD.
27 It is good for one to bear
 the yoke in youth,
28 to sit alone in silence
 when the Lord has imposed
 it,
29 to put one's mouth to the
 dust
 (there may yet be hope),
30 to give one's cheek to the
 smiter,
 and be filled with insults.

31 For the Lord will not
 reject forever.
32 Although he causes grief, he
 will have compassion
 according to the
 abundance of his
 steadfast love;
33 for he does not willingly
 afflict
 or grieve anyone.

34 When all the prisoners of the
 land
 are crushed under foot,
35 when human rights are
 perverted
 in the presence of the Most
 High,
36 when one's case is subverted
 —does the Lord not see it?

37 Who can command and have
 it done,
 if the Lord has not
 ordained it?
38 Is it not from the mouth of
 the Most High
 that good and bad come?
39 Why should any who draw
 breath complain
 about the punishment of
 their sins?

40 Let us test and examine our
 ways,
 and return to the LORD.
41 Let us lift up our hearts as
 well as our hands

3.10
Job 10.16;
Isa 38.13
3.11
Hos 6.1
3.12
Ps 7.12,13;
Job 7.20
3.13
Job 6.4
3.14
Jer 20.7;
Job 30.9
3.15
Jer 9.15
3.16
Prov 20.17;
Jer 6.26
3.17
Jer 12.12
3.18
Ps 31.22
3.19
Jer 9.15
3.20
Ps 42.5,6,11
3.21
Ps 130.7
3.22
Mal 3.6
3.23
Zeph 3.5
3.24
Ps 16.5;
33.18
3.25
Isa 25.9;
30.18; 26.9
3.26
Ps 37.7;
40.1;
Isa 30.15
3.27
Ps 94.12
3.28
Jer 15.17
3.29
Job 16.15;
Jer 31.17
3.30
Isa 50.6;
Mt 5.39
3.31
Ps 94.14
3.32
Ps 78.38;
Hos 11.8
3.33
Ezek 33.11;
Heb 12.10
3.35
Ps 140.12
3.36
Hab 1.13
3.37
Ps 33.9
3.38
Job 2.10;
Isa 45.7;
Jer 32.42
3.39
Mic 7.9;
Heb 12.5,6
3.40
Ps 119.59;
2 Cor 13.5
3.41 Ps 25.1; 28.2

f Syr Tg: Heb *LORD, we are not cut off*

to God in heaven.

42 We have transgressed and
 rebelled,
 and you have not forgiven.

43 You have wrapped yourself
 with·anger and pursued
 us,
 killing without pity;
44 you have wrapped yourself
 with a cloud
 so that no prayer can pass
 through.
45 You have made us filth and
 rubbish
 among the peoples.

46 All our enemies
 have opened their mouths
 against us;
47 panic and pitfall have come
 upon us,
 devastation and
 destruction.
48 My eyes flow with rivers of
 tears
 because of the destruction
 of my people.

49 My eyes will flow without
 ceasing,
 without respite,
50 until the LORD from heaven
 looks down and sees.
51 My eyes cause me grief
 at the fate of all the young
 women in my city.

52 Those who were my enemies
 without cause
 have hunted me like a bird;
53 they flung me alive into a pit
 and hurled stones on me;
54 water closed over my head;
 I said, "I am lost."

55 I called on your name,
 O LORD,
 from the depths of the pit;
56 you heard my plea, "Do not
 close your ear
 to my cry for help, but give
 me relief!"
57 You came near when I called
 on you;
 you said, "Do not fear!"

58 You have taken up my cause,
 O Lord,
 you have redeemed my life.
59 You have seen the wrong
 done to me, O LORD;
 judge my cause.
60 You have seen all their
 malice,
 all their plots against me.

61 You have heard their taunts,
 O LORD,
 all their plots against me.
62 The whispers and murmurs
 of my assailants
 are against me all day long.
63 Whether they sit or
 rise — see,
 I am the object of their
 taunt-songs.

64 Pay them back for their
 deeds, O LORD,
 according to the work of
 their hands!
65 Give them anguish of heart;
 your curse be on them!
66 Pursue them in anger and
 destroy them
 from under the LORD's
 heavens.

The Punishment of Zion

4 How the gold has grown dim,
 how the pure gold is
 changed!
 The sacred stones lie
 scattered
 at the head of every street.

2 The precious children of
 Zion,
 worth their weight in fine
 gold —
 how they are reckoned as
 earthen pots,
 the work of a potter's
 hands!

3 Even the jackals offer the
 breast
 and nurse their young,
 but my people has become
 cruel,
 like the ostriches in the
 wilderness.

3.42
Dan 9.5;
Jer 5.7,9
3.43
Lam 2.21;
Ps 83.15
3.44
Ps 97.2;
v. 8
3.45
1 Cor 4.13
3.46
Lam 2.16
3.47
Isa 24.17;
Jer 48.43;
Isa 51.19
3.48
Lam 1.16;
2.11,18
3.49
Ps 77.2
3.50
Isa 63.15
3.52
Ps 35.7
3.53
Jer 37.16
3.54
Ps 69.2;
Isa 38.10
3.55
Jon 2.2
3.56
Ps 116.1,2
3.57
Ps 145.18;
Isa 41.10,14

3.58
Jer 51.36;
Ps 71.23
3.59
Jer 18.19,
20; Ps 35.23
3.60
Jer 11.19,
20; 18.18
3.61
Lam 5.1
3.62
Ezek 36.3
3.63
Ps 139.2
3.64
Ps 28.4
3.65
Isa 6.10
3.66
Ps 8.3
4.1
Ezek 7.19-22;
Jer 52.13,14
4.2
Isa 51.18;
30.14;
Jer 19.11
4.3
Isa 34.13;
49.15;
Job 39.14,
16

4 The tongue of the infant
 sticks
 to the roof of its mouth for
 thirst;
the children beg for food,
 but no one gives them
 anything.

5 Those who feasted on
 delicacies
 perish in the streets;
those who were brought up
 in purple
 cling to ash heaps.

6 For the chastisement^g of my
 people has been greater
 than the punishment^h of
 Sodom,
which was overthrown in a
 moment,
 though no hand was laid
 on it.ⁱ

7 Her princes were purer than
 snow,
 whiter than milk;
their bodies were more ruddy
 than coral,
 their hairⁱ like sapphire.ⁱ

8 Now their visage is blacker
 than soot;
 they are not recognized in
 the streets.
Their skin has shriveled on
 their bones;
 it has become as dry as
 wood.

9 Happier were those pierced
 by the sword
 than those pierced by
 hunger,
whose life drains away,
 deprived
 of the produce of the field.

10 The hands of compassionate
 women
 have boiled their own
 children;
they became their food
 in the destruction of my
 people.

4.4
Jer 14.3;
Lam 2.12
4.5
Jer 6.2;
Am 6.3-7;
Ps 113.7
4.6
Ezek 16.48;
Gen 19.23;
Jer 20.16
4.7
Ps 51.7
4.8
Job 30.30;
Lam 5.10;
Ps 102.5
4.9
Jer 15.2;
Ezek 24.23
4.10
Lam 2.20;
2 Kings 6.29;
Deut 28.57

4.11
Jer 7.20;
v. 22;
Deut 32.22;
Jer 21.14
4.12
1 Kings 9.8,
9; Jer 21.13
4.13
Jer 5.31;
6.13;
Ezek 22.26;
Mic 3.11,12;
Mt 23.31
4.14
Isa 56.10;
59.9,10;
Jer 19.4;
2.34
4.15
Lev 13.45;
Jer 49.5
4.16
Lam 5.12
4.17
2 Kings 24.7;
Isa 20.5;
Jer 37.7;
Ezek 29.16

11 The LORD gave full vent to
 his wrath;
 he poured out his hot
 anger,
and kindled a fire in Zion
 that consumed its
 foundations.

12 The kings of the earth did
 not believe,
 nor did any of the
 inhabitants of the
 world,
that foe or enemy could
 enter
 the gates of Jerusalem.

13 It was for the sins of her
 prophets
 and the iniquities of her
 priests,
who shed the blood of the
 righteous
 in the midst of her.

14 Blindly they wandered
 through the streets,
 so defiled with blood
that no one was able
 to touch their garments.

15 "Away! Unclean!" people
 shouted at them;
 "Away! Away! Do not
 touch!"
So they became fugitives and
 wanderers;
 it was said among the
 nations,
"They shall stay here no
 longer."

16 The LORD himself has
 scattered them,
 he will regard them no
 more;
no honor was shown to the
 priests,
 no favor to the elders.

17 Our eyes failed, ever
 watching
 vainly for help;
we were watching eagerly

g Or *iniquity* h Or *sin* i Meaning of
Heb uncertain i Or *lapis lazuli*

for a nation that could not
 save.

18 They dogged our steps
 so that we could not walk
 in our streets;
our end drew near; our days
 were numbered;
for our end had come.

19 Our pursuers were swifter
 than the eagles in the
 heavens;
they chased us on the
 mountains,
 they lay in wait for us in
 the wilderness.

20 The LORD's anointed, the
 breath of our life,
was taken in their pits —
the one of whom we said,
 "Under his shadow
we shall live among the
 nations."

21 Rejoice and be glad,
 O daughter Edom,
you that live in the land of
 Uz;
but to you also the cup shall
 pass;
 you shall become drunk
 and strip yourself bare.

22 The punishment of your
 iniquity, O daughter
 Zion, is accomplished,
he will keep you in exile
 no longer;
but your iniquity, O daughter
 Edom, he will punish,
he will uncover your sins.

A Plea for Mercy

5 Remember, O LORD, what
 has befallen us;
look, and see our disgrace!
2 Our inheritance has been
 turned over to
 strangers,
 our homes to aliens.
3 We have become orphans,
 fatherless;
 our mothers are like
 widows.

4 We must pay for the water
 we drink;
 the wood we get must be
 bought.
5 With a yoke[k] on our necks
 we are hard driven;
we are weary, we are given
 no rest.
6 We have made a pact with[l]
 Egypt and Assyria,
to get enough bread.
7 Our ancestors sinned; they
 are no more,
and we bear their
 iniquities.
8 Slaves rule over us;
 there is no one to deliver
 us from their hand.
9 We get our bread at the peril
 of our lives,
because of the sword in the
 wilderness.
10 Our skin is black as an oven
 from the scorching heat of
 famine.
11 Women are raped in Zion,
 virgins in the towns of
 Judah.
12 Princes are hung up by their
 hands;
 no respect is shown to the
 elders.
13 Young men are compelled to
 grind,
 and boys stagger under
 loads of wood.
14 The old men have left the
 city gate,
 the young men their music.
15 The joy of our hearts has
 ceased;
 our dancing has been
 turned to mourning.
16 The crown has fallen from
 our head;
 woe to us, for we have
 sinned!
17 Because of this our hearts
 are sick,
 because of these things our
 eyes have grown dim:
18 because of Mount Zion,
 which lies desolate;
 jackals prowl over it.

k Symmachus: Heb lacks *With a yoke*
l Heb *have given the hand to*

Cross references (center column):

4.18: 2 Kings 25.4; Ezek 7.2,3; Am 8.2
4.19: Deut 28.49; Jer 4.13; Hab 1.8
4.20: 2 Sam 1.14; 19.21; Ezek 12.13; 19.4,8
4.21: Isa 34.7; Am 1.11,12; Ob 1,16
4.22: Isa 40.2; Mal 1.3,4
5.1: Ps 89.50; 44.13-16
5.2: Ps 79.1; Zeph 1.13
5.3: Jer 15.8; 18.21
5.4: Isa 3.1
5.5: Jer 28.14; Neh 9.36,37
5.6: Jer 2.36; Hos 5.13; 7.11; 9.3
5.7: Jer 14.20; 16.12
5.8: Neh 5.15; Zech 11.6
5.10: Lam 4.8
5.11: Isa 13.16; Zech 14.2
5.12: Lam 4.16
5.13: Jer 7.18
5.14: Lam 4.8; Jer 7.34
5.15: Jer 25.10
5.16: Ps 89.39; Isa 3.9-11
5.17: Isa 1.5; Ps 6.7
5.18: Ps 74.2,3; Neh 4.3

19 But you, O Lord, reign
 forever;
 your throne endures to all
 generations.
20 Why have you forgotten us
 completely?
 Why have you forsaken us
 these many days?

21 Restore us to yourself,
 O Lord, that we may be
 restored;
 renew our days as of old—
22 unless you have utterly
 rejected us,
 and are angry with us
 beyond measure.

5.19
Ps 9.7;
102.12,25-27;
45.6
5.20
Ps 13.1
5.21
Jer 31.18
5.22
Jer 7.29;
Isa 64.9

Ezekiel

Title and Background

This book is named after the prophet Ezekiel, whose name means "God is strong." The Babylonians laid siege to Jerusalem in 588 B.C., and in 586 the city and temple were burned. Israel's monarchy was ended; the City of David and the Lord's temple were no more.

Author and Date of Writing

Ezekiel was among the more than 3,000 Jews exiled to Babylon by Nebuchadnezzar in 597 B.C., and there among the exiles he received his call to become a prophet. As a priest-prophet called to minister to the exiles, his message had much to do with the temple and its ritual.

Since the book of Ezekiel contains many dates, its prophecies can be dated with considerable precision. Ezekiel's period of activity coincides with Jerusalem's darkest hour. His messages are to be dated between 593 and 571 B.C.

Theme and Message

Nowhere in the Bible are God's initiative and control over all creation expressed more clearly and pervasively than in Ezekiel. This sovereign God must be known and acknowledged by everyone, for at least 65 times we read the clause (or variations): "Then they will know that I am the LORD."

God's total sovereignty is also evident in his mobility. He is not limited to the temple or even to the city of Jerusalem; he can respond to his people anywhere and under any circumstance.

Outline

I. Ezekiel's Call and Commission (1.1–3.27)
II. Judgment Against Judah and Jerusalem (4.1–24.27)
III. Judgment Against the Nations (25.1–32.32)
IV. Preparation for Restoration (33.1–39.29)
V. Renewed Worship (40.1–48.35)

The Vision of the Chariot

1 In the thirtieth year, in the fourth month, on the fifth day of the month, as I was among the exiles by the river Chebar, the heavens were opened, and I saw visions of God. ² On the fifth day of the month (it was the fifth year of the exile of King Jehoiachin), ³ the word of the LORD came to the priest Ezekiel son of Buzi, in the land of the Chaldeans by the river Chebar; and the hand of the LORD was on him there.

4 As I looked, a stormy wind came out of the north: a great cloud with brightness around it and fire flashing forth continually, and in the middle of the fire, something like gleaming amber. ⁵ In the middle of it was something like four living creatures. This was their appearance: they were of human form. ⁶ Each had four faces, and each of them had four wings. ⁷ Their legs were straight, and the soles of their feet were like the sole of a calf's foot; and they sparkled like burnished bronze. ⁸ Under their wings on their four sides they had human hands. And the four

1.1 Ezek 3.15, 23; Mt 3.16; Acts 7.56
1.2 2 Kings 24.12
1.3 1 Kings 18.46; 2 Kings 3.15
1.4 Isa 21.1
1.5 Rev 4.6; Ezek 10.8, 14
1.6 vv. 10,23
1.7 Rev 1.15; 2.18
1.8 Ezek 10.8,21

had their faces and their wings thus: [9]their wings touched one another; each of them moved straight ahead, without turning as they moved. [10]As for the appearance of their faces: the four had the face of a human being, the face of a lion on the right side, the face of an ox on the left side, and the face of an eagle; [11]such were their faces. Their wings were spread out above; each creature had two wings, each of which touched the wing of another, while two covered their bodies. [12]Each moved straight ahead; wherever the spirit would go, they went, without turning as they went. [13]In the middle of[a] the living creatures there was something that looked like burning coals of fire, like torches moving to and fro among the living creatures; the fire was bright, and lightning issued from the fire. [14]The living creatures darted to and fro, like a flash of lightning.

15 As I looked at the living creatures, I saw a wheel on the earth beside the living creatures, one for each of the four of them.[b] [16]As for the appearance of the wheels and their construction: their appearance was like the gleaming of beryl; and the four had the same form, their construction being something like a wheel within a wheel. [17]When they moved, they moved in any of the four directions without veering as they moved. [18]Their rims were tall and awesome, for the rims of all four were full of eyes all around. [19]When the living creatures moved, the wheels moved beside them; and when the living creatures rose from the earth, the wheels rose. [20]Wherever the spirit would go, they went, and the wheels rose along with them; for the spirit of the living creatures was in the wheels. [21]When they moved, the others moved; when they stopped, the others stopped; and when they rose from the earth, the wheels rose along with them; for the spirit of the living creatures was in the wheels.

22 Over the heads of the living

creatures there was something like a dome, shining like crystal,[c] spread out above their heads. [23]Under the dome their wings were stretched out straight, one toward another; and each of the creatures had two wings covering its body. [24]When they moved, I heard the sound of their wings like the sound of mighty waters, like the thunder of the Almighty,[d] a sound of tumult like the sound of an army; when they stopped, they let down their wings. [25]And there came a voice from above the dome over their heads; when they stopped, they let down their wings.

26 And above the dome over their heads there was something like a throne, in appearance like sapphire;[e] and seated above the likeness of a throne was something that seemed like a human form. [27]Upward from what appeared like the loins I saw something like gleaming amber, something that looked like fire enclosed all around; and downward from what looked like the loins I saw something that looked like fire, and there was a splendor all around. [28]Like the bow in a cloud on a rainy day, such was the appearance of the splendor all around. This was the appearance of the likeness of the glory of the LORD.

When I saw it, I fell on my face, and I heard the voice of someone speaking.

The Vision of the Scroll

2 He said to me: O mortal,[f] stand up on your feet, and I will speak with you. [2]And when he spoke to me, a spirit entered into me and set me on my feet; and I heard him speaking to me. [3]He said to me, Mortal, I am sending you to the people of Israel, to a nation[g] of rebels who have rebelled against me; they and their ances-

Cross references
1.9
vv. 17,12
1.10
Rev 4.7;
Ezek 10.14
1.11
Ezek 10.16,
19; Isa 6.2
1.12
vv. 9,20
1.13
Ps 104.4;
Rev 4.5
1.14
Mt 24.27
1.15
vv. 19-21
1.16
Ezek 10.9-11;
Dan 10.6
1.17
v. 12
1.18
Ezek 10.12;
Rev 4.6,8
1.19
Ezek 10.16,
17,19
1.20
v. 12;
Ezek 10.17
1.21
Ezek 10.17
1.22
Ezek 10.1
1.23
vv. 6,4
1.24
Ezek 10.5;
43.2;
Rev 1.15;
19.6;
2 Kings 7.6
1.25
v. 22
1.26
Ezek 10.1;
Ex 24.10;
Ezek 43.6,7;
Rev 1.13
1.27
v. 4;
Ezek 8.2
1.28
Rev 4.3;
10.1;
Ezek 3.23;
8.4;
Dan 8.17;
Rev 1.17
2.1
Dan 10.11
2.2
Dan 8.18;
Ezek 3.24
2.3
Jer 3.25;
Ezek 20.18,
30

[a] Gk OL: Heb *And the appearance of*
[b] Heb *of their faces*　　[c] Gk: Heb *like the awesome crystal*　　[d] Traditional rendering of Heb *Shaddai*　　[e] Or *lapis lazuli*　　[f] Or *son of man*; Heb *ben adam* (and so throughout the book when Ezekiel is addressed)
[g] Syr: Heb *to nations*

tors have transgressed against me to this very day. [4] The descendants are impudent and stubborn. I am sending you to them, and you shall say to them, "Thus says the Lord GOD." [5] Whether they hear or refuse to hear (for they are a rebellious house), they shall know that there has been a prophet among them. [6] And you, O mortal, do not be afraid of them, and do not be afraid of their words, though briers and thorns surround you and you live among scorpions; do not be afraid of their words, and do not be dismayed at their looks, for they are a rebellious house. [7] You shall speak my words to them, whether they hear or refuse to hear; for they are a rebellious house.

8 But you, mortal, hear what I say to you; do not be rebellious like that rebellious house; open your mouth and eat what I give you. [9] I looked, and a hand was stretched out to me, and a written scroll was in it. [10] He spread it before me; it had writing on the front and on the back, and written on it were words of lamentation and mourning and woe.

3 He said to me, O mortal, eat what is offered to you; eat this scroll, and go, speak to the house of Israel. [2] So I opened my mouth, and he gave me the scroll to eat. [3] He said to me, Mortal, eat this scroll that I give you and fill your stomach with it. Then I ate it; and in my mouth it was as sweet as honey.

4 He said to me: Mortal, go to the house of Israel and speak my very words to them. [5] For you are not sent to a people of obscure speech and difficult language, but to the house of Israel— [6] not to many peoples of obscure speech and difficult language, whose words you cannot understand. Surely, if I sent you to them, they would listen to you. [7] But the house of Israel will not listen to you, for they are not willing to listen to me; because all the house of Israel have a hard forehead and a stubborn heart. [8] See, I have made your face

hard against their faces, and your forehead hard against their foreheads. [9] Like the hardest stone, harder than flint, I have made your forehead; do not fear them or be dismayed at their looks, for they are a rebellious house. [10] He said to me: Mortal, all my words that I shall speak to you receive in your heart and hear with your ears; [11] then go to the exiles, to your people, and speak to them. Say to them, "Thus says the Lord GOD"; whether they hear or refuse to hear.

Ezekiel at the River Chebar

12 Then the spirit lifted me up, and as the glory of the LORD rose[h] from its place, I heard behind me the sound of loud rumbling; [13] it was the sound of the wings of the living creatures brushing against one another, and the sound of the wheels beside them, that sounded like a loud rumbling. [14] The spirit lifted me up and bore me away; I went in bitterness in the heat of my spirit, the hand of the LORD being strong upon me. [15] I came to the exiles at Tel-abib, who lived by the river Chebar.[i] And I sat there among them, stunned, for seven days.

16 At the end of seven days, the word of the LORD came to me: [17] Mortal, I have made you a sentinel for the house of Israel; whenever you hear a word from my mouth, you shall give them warning from me. [18] If I say to the wicked, "You shall surely die," and you give them no warning, or speak to warn the wicked from their wicked way, in order to save their life, those wicked persons shall die for their iniquity; but their blood I will require at your hand. [19] But if you warn the wicked, and they do not turn from their wickedness, or from their wicked way, they shall die for their iniquity; but you will have saved

3.19 Ezek 33.3,9; Acts 18.6; 20.26

h Cn: Heb *and blessed be the glory of the* LORD
i Two Mss Syr: Heb *Chebar, and to where they lived.* Another reading is *Chebar, and I sat where they sat*

2.4
Jer 5.3;
Ezek 3.7
2.5
Ezek 3.11,
26,27; 33.33
2.6
Jer 1.8,17;
Isa 9.18;
Mic 7.4;
Ezek 3.9
2.7
Jer 1.7,17
2.8
Isa 50.5;
Rev 10.9
2.9
Ezek 8.3;
3.1
2.10
Rev 8.13
3.1
Ezek 2.8,9
3.3
Rev 10.9,10;
Jer 15.16;
Ps 19.10;
119.103
3.4
v. 11
3.5
Jon 1.2;
Isa 28.11;
33.19
3.6
Mt 11.21,
23;
Acts 13.46-48
3.7
Jn 15.20;
Ezek 2.4
3.8
Jer 1.18;
15.20

3.9
Isa 50.7;
Mic 3.8;
Ezek 2.6
3.10
vv. 1-3
3.11
Ezek 2.5,7
3.12
Ezek 8.3;
Acts 8.39;
2.2
3.13
Ezek 1.24;
10.5,16,17
3.14
Jer 6.11;
Ezek 1.3;
8.1
3.15
Ezek 1.1;
Job 2.13
3.17
Ezek 33.7-9;
Isa 52.8;
56.10;
Jer 6.17
3.18
Gen 2.17;
Ezek 33.6;
Jn 8.21,24

your life. ²⁰Again, if the righteous turn from their righteousness and commit iniquity, and I lay a stumbling block before them, they shall die; because you have not warned them, they shall die for their sin, and their righteous deeds that they have done shall not be remembered; but their blood I will require at your hand. ²¹If, however, you warn the righteous not to sin, and they do not sin, they shall surely live, because they took warning; and you will have saved your life.

Ezekiel Isolated and Silenced

22 Then the hand of the LORD was upon me there; and he said to me, Rise up, go out into the valley, and there I will speak with you. ²³So I rose up and went out into the valley; and the glory of the LORD stood there, like the glory that I had seen by the river Chebar; and I fell on my face. ²⁴The spirit entered into me, and set me on my feet; and he spoke with me and said to me: Go, shut yourself inside your house. ²⁵As for you, mortal, cords shall be placed on you, and you shall be bound with them, so that you cannot go out among the people; ²⁶and I will make your tongue cling to the roof of your mouth, so that you shall be speechless and unable to reprove them; for they are a rebellious house. ²⁷But when I speak with you, I will open your mouth, and you shall say to them, "Thus says the Lord GOD"; let those who will hear, hear; and let those who refuse to hear, refuse; for they are a rebellious house.

The Siege of Jerusalem Portrayed

4 And you, O mortal, take a brick and set it before you. On it portray a city, Jerusalem; ²and put siegeworks against it, and build a siege-wall against it, and cast up a ramp against it; set camps also against it, and plant battering rams against it all around. ³Then take an iron plate and place it as an iron wall between you and the city; set

your face toward it, and let it be in a state of siege, and press the siege against it. This is a sign for the house of Israel.

4 Then lie on your left side, and place the punishment of the house of Israel upon it; you shall bear their punishment for the number of the days that you lie there. ⁵For I assign to you a number of days, three hundred ninety days, equal to the number of the years of their punishment; and so you shall bear the punishment of the house of Israel. ⁶When you have completed these, you shall lie down a second time, but on your right side, and bear the punishment of the house of Judah; forty days I assign you, one day for each year. ⁷You shall set your face toward the siege of Jerusalem, and with your arm bared you shall prophesy against it. ⁸See, I am putting cords on you so that you cannot turn from one side to the other until you have completed the days of your siege.

9 And you, take wheat and barley, beans and lentils, millet and spelt; put them into one vessel, and make bread for yourself. During the number of days that you lie on your side, three hundred ninety days, you shall eat it. ¹⁰The food that you eat shall be twenty shekels a day by weight; at fixed times you shall eat it. ¹¹And you shall drink water by measure, one-sixth of a hin; at fixed times you shall drink. ¹²You shall eat it as a barley-cake, baking it in their sight on human dung. ¹³The LORD said, "Thus shall the people of Israel eat their bread, unclean, among the nations to which I will drive them." ¹⁴Then I said, "Ah Lord GOD! I have never defiled myself; from my youth up until now I have never eaten what died of itself or was torn by animals, nor has carrion flesh come into my mouth." ¹⁵Then he said to me, "See, I will let you have cow's dung instead of human dung, on which you may prepare your bread." 16 Then he said to me, Mortal, I am going to break the staff of bread in Jerusalem; they shall eat bread

by weight and with fearfulness; and they shall drink water by measure and in dismay. [17]Lacking bread and water, they will look at one another in dismay, and waste away under their punishment.

A Sword against Jerusalem

5 And you, O mortal, take a sharp sword; use it as a barber's razor and run it over your head and your beard; then take balances for weighing, and divide the hair. [2]One third of the hair you shall burn in the fire inside the city, when the days of the siege are completed; one third you shall take and strike with the sword all around the city;[j] and one third you shall scatter to the wind, and I will unsheathe the sword after them. [3]Then you shall take from these a small number, and bind them in the skirts of your robe. [4]From these, again, you shall take some, throw them into the fire and burn them up; from there a fire will come out against all the house of Israel.

5 Thus says the Lord God: This is Jerusalem; I have set her in the center of the nations, with countries all around her. [6]But she has rebelled against my ordinances and my statutes, becoming more wicked than the nations and the countries all around her, rejecting my ordinances and not following my statutes. [7]Therefore thus says the Lord God: Because you are more turbulent than the nations that are all around you, and have not followed my statutes or kept my ordinances, but have acted according to the ordinances of the nations that are all around you; [8]therefore thus says the Lord God: I, I myself, am coming against you; I will execute judgments among you in the sight of the nations. [9]And because of all your abominations, I will do to you what I have never yet done, and the like of which I will never do again. [10]Surely, parents shall eat their children in your midst, and children shall eat their parents; I will execute

judgments on you, and any of you who survive I will scatter to every wind. [11]Therefore, as I live, says the Lord God, surely, because you have defiled my sanctuary with all your detestable things and with all your abominations — therefore I will cut you down;[k] my eye will not spare, and I will have no pity. [12]One third of you shall die of pestilence or be consumed by famine among you; one third shall fall by the sword around you; and one third I will scatter to every wind and will unsheathe the sword after them.

13 My anger shall spend itself, and I will vent my fury on them and satisfy myself; and they shall know that I, the Lord, have spoken in my jealousy, when I spend my fury on them. [14]Moreover I will make you a desolation and an object of mocking among the nations around you, in the sight of all that pass by. [15]You shall be[l] a mockery and a taunt, a warning and a horror, to the nations around you, when I execute judgments on you in anger and fury, and with furious punishments — I, the Lord, have spoken — [16]when I loose against you[m] my deadly arrows of famine, arrows for destruction, which I will let loose to destroy you, and when I bring more and more famine upon you, and break your staff of bread. [17]I will send famine and wild animals against you, and they will rob you of your children; pestilence and bloodshed shall pass through you; and I will bring the sword upon you. I, the Lord, have spoken.

Judgment on Idolatrous Israel

6 The word of the Lord came to me: [2]O mortal, set your face toward the mountains of Israel, and prophesy against them, [3]and say, You mountains of Israel, hear the word of the Lord God! Thus says the Lord God to the mountains and the hills, to the ravines and the valleys: I, I myself will bring a

4.17
Lev 26.39;
Ezek 24.23
5.1
Lev 21.5;
Isa 7.20;
Ezek 44.20
5.2
v. 12;
Ezek 4.2-8;
Lev 26.33
5.3
Jer 39.10
5.4
Jer 41.1,2;
44.14
5.5
Ezek 4.1;
Lam 1.1
5.6
Ezek 16.47,
48,51;
Jer 11.10;
Zech 7.11
5.7
2 Chr 33.9;
Ezek 16.47
5.8
Ezek 15.7
5.9
Dan 9.12;
Mt 24.21
5.10
Lev 26.29;
Ezek 12.14;
Zech 2.6

5.11
2 Chr 36.14;
Ezek 7.4,9;
8.18
5.12
Jer 43.10,
11;
Ezek 12.14
5.13
Lam 4.11;
Ezek 21.17;
36.6
5.14
Lev 26.31,
32;
Neh 2.17
5.15
Deut 28.37;
1 Kings 9.7;
Jer 24.9;
Ezek 25.17
5.16
Deut 32.23,
24;
Ezek 4.16
5.17
Ezek 14.21;
28.23
6.2
Ezek 36.1
6.3
Ezek 36.4,6

j Heb it k Another reading is I will
withdraw l Gk Syr Vg Tg: Heb It shall be
m Heb them

sword upon you, and I will destroy your high places. 4 Your altars shall become desolate, and your incense stands shall be broken; and I will throw down your slain in front of your idols. 5 I will lay the corpses of the people of Israel in front of their idols; and I will scatter your bones around your altars. 6 Wherever you live, your towns shall be waste and your high places ruined, so that your altars will be waste and ruined,[n] your idols broken and destroyed, your incense stands cut down, and your works wiped out. 7 The slain shall fall in your midst; then you shall know that I am the LORD.

8 But I will spare some. Some of you shall escape the sword among the nations and be scattered through the countries. 9 Those of you who escape shall remember me among the nations where they are carried captive, how I was crushed by their wanton heart that turned away from me, and their wanton eyes that turned after their idols. Then they will be loathsome in their own sight for the evils that they have committed, for all their abominations. 10 And they shall know that I am the LORD; I did not threaten in vain to bring this disaster upon them.

11 Thus says the Lord GOD: Clap your hands and stamp your foot, and say, Alas for all the vile abominations of the house of Israel! For they shall fall by the sword, by famine, and by pestilence. 12 Those far off shall die of pestilence; those nearby shall fall by the sword; and any who are left and are spared shall die of famine. Thus I will spend my fury upon them. 13 And you shall know that I am the LORD, when their slain lie among their idols around their altars, on every high hill, on all the mountain tops, under every green tree, and under every leafy oak, wherever they offered pleasing odor to all their idols. 14 I will stretch out my hand against them, and make the land desolate and waste, throughout all their settlements, from the wilder-

6.4
Lev 26.30
6.5
Jer 8.1,2
6.6
Lev 26.31;
Zech 13.2
6.7
Ezek 11.10,
12
6.8
Jer 44.28;
Ezek 5.2,12;
12.16; 14.22
6.9
Jer 51.50;
Ps 78.40;
Isa 7.13;
Ezek 43.24;
20.7,24;
20.43
6.10
v. 7
6.11
Ezek 21.14;
25.6; 5.12;
7.15
6.12
Dan 9.7;
Ezek 5.13
6.13
v. 7;
Jer 2.20;
Hos 4.13;
Isa 57.5
6.14
Isa 5.25;
Ezek 14.13;
Num 33.46

7.2
Am 8.2;
Ezek 11.13;
Rev 7.1;
20.8
7.3
vv. 8,9,27
7.4
Ezek 5.11;
8.18; 11.21;
6.7
7.5
2 Kings 21.12,
13
7.6
vv. 2,10
7.7
v. 12;
Isa 22.5
7.8
Ezek 20.8,
21; 6.12;
v. 3

ness to Riblah.[o] Then they shall know that I am the LORD.

Impending Disaster

7 The word of the LORD came to me: 2 You, O mortal, thus says the Lord GOD to the land of Israel:
An end! The end has come
upon the four corners of
the land.
3 Now the end is upon you,
I will let loose my anger
upon you;
I will judge you according to
your ways,
I will punish you for all
your abominations.
4 My eye will not spare you, I
will have no pity.
I will punish you for your
ways,
while your abominations
are among you.
Then you shall know that I am the
LORD.

5 Thus says the Lord GOD:
Disaster after disaster! See, it
comes.
6 An end has come, the end
has come.
It has awakened against you;
see, it comes!
7 Your doom[p] has come to
you,
O inhabitant of the land.
The time has come, the day
is near—
of tumult, not of reveling
on the mountains.
8 Soon now I will pour out my
wrath upon you;
I will spend my anger
against you.
I will judge you according to
your ways,
and punish you for all your
abominations.
9 My eye will not spare; I will
have no pity.
I will punish you according
to your ways,
while your abominations
are among you.

[n] Syr Vg Tg: Heb and be made guilty
[o] Another reading is Diblah [p] Meaning of Heb uncertain

Then you shall know that it is I the LORD who strike.

10 See, the day! See, it comes!
 Your doom^q has gone out.
 The rod has blossomed,
 pride has budded.
11 Violence has grown into a
 rod of wickedness.
 None of them shall remain,
 not their abundance, not
 their wealth;
 no pre-eminence among
 them.^q
12 The time has come, the day
 draws near;
 let not the buyer rejoice,
 nor the seller mourn,
 for wrath is upon all their
 multitude.
13 For the sellers shall not return to what has been sold as long as they remain alive. For the vision concerns all their multitude; it shall not be revoked. Because of their iniquity, they cannot maintain their lives.^q
14 They have blown the horn
 and made everything
 ready;
 but no one goes to battle,
 for my wrath is upon all
 their multitude.
15 The sword is outside,
 pestilence and famine
 are inside;
 those in the field die by
 the sword;
 those in the city—famine
 and pestilence devour
 them.
16 If any survivors escape,
 they shall be found on the
 mountains
 like doves of the valleys,
 all of them moaning over
 their iniquity.
17 All hands shall grow feeble,
 all knees turn to water.
18 They shall put on sackcloth,
 horror shall cover them.
 Shame shall be on all faces,
 baldness on all their heads.
19 They shall fling their silver
 into the streets,
 their gold shall be treated
 as unclean.
 Their silver and gold cannot save

them on the day of the wrath of the LORD. They shall not satisfy their hunger or fill their stomachs with it. For it was the stumbling block of their iniquity. 20 From their^r beautiful ornament, in which they took pride, they made their abominable images, their detestable things; therefore I will make of it an unclean thing to them.
21 I will hand it over to
 strangers as booty,
 to the wicked of the earth
 as plunder;
 they shall profane it.
22 I will avert my face from
 them,
 so that they may profane
 my treasured^s place;
 the violent shall enter it,
 they shall profane it.
23 Make a chain!^q
 For the land is full of bloody
 crimes;
 the city is full of violence.
24 I will bring the worst of the
 nations
 to take possession of their
 houses.
 I will put an end to the
 arrogance of the strong,
 and their holy places shall
 be profaned.
25 When anguish comes, they
 will seek peace,
 but there shall be
 none.
26 Disaster comes upon
 disaster,
 rumor follows rumor;
 they shall keep seeking a
 vision from the prophet;
 instruction shall perish
 from the priest,
 and counsel from the
 elders.
27 The king shall mourn,
 the prince shall be
 wrapped in despair,
 and the hands of the
 people of the land shall
 tremble.
 According to their way I will
 deal with them;

7.10 v. 7; Isa 10.5
7.11 Jer 6.7; 16.5,6; Ezek 24.16, 22
7.12 vv. 5-7,10; 1 Cor 7.30; v. 14
7.14 Jer 4.5; v. 12
7.15 Deut 32.25; Ezek 5.12
7.16 Ezek 6.8; 14.22; Isa 38.14; 59.11
7.17 Isa 13.7; Ezek 21.7; Heb 12.12
7.18 Isa 15.2,3; Am 8.10; Ezek 27.31
7.19 Isa 30.22; Prov 11.4; Zeph 1.18; Ezek 13.5; 14.3,4
7.20 Jer 7.30
7.21 Ps 74.2-8
7.22 Ezek 39.23, 24
7.23 2 Kings 21.16; Ezek 9.9; 8.17
7.24 Ezek 21.31; 33.28; 24.21
7.25 Ezek 13.10, 16
7.26 Deut 32.23; Jer 4.20; Ezek 21.7; Ps 74.9; Ezek 20.1,3
7.27 Ps 35.26; Ezek 26.16; vv. 3,4,8; Ezek 18.20

^q Meaning of Heb uncertain ^r Syr Symmachus: Heb its ^s Or secret

according to their own judgments I will judge them.

And they shall know that I am the LORD.

Abominations in the Temple

8 In the sixth year, in the sixth month, on the fifth day of the month, as I sat in my house, with the elders of Judah sitting before me, the hand of the Lord GOD fell upon me there. 2 I looked, and there was a figure that looked like a human being;[t] below what appeared to be its loins it was fire, and above the loins it was like the appearance of brightness, like gleaming amber. 3 It stretched out the form of a hand, and took me by a lock of my head; and the spirit lifted me up between earth and heaven, and brought me in visions of God to Jerusalem, to the entrance of the gateway of the inner court that faces north, to the seat of the image of jealousy, which provokes to jealousy. 4 And the glory of the God of Israel was there, like the vision that I had seen in the valley.

5 Then God[u] said to me, "O mortal, lift up your eyes now in the direction of the north." So I lifted up my eyes toward the north, and there, north of the altar gate, in the entrance, was this image of jealousy. 6 He said to me, "Mortal, do you see what they are doing, the great abominations that the house of Israel are committing here, to drive me far from my sanctuary? Yet you will see still greater abominations."

7 And he brought me to the entrance of the court; I looked, and there was a hole in the wall. 8 Then he said to me, "Mortal, dig through the wall"; and when I dug through the wall, there was an entrance. 9 He said to me, "Go in, and see the vile abominations that they are committing here." 10 So I went in and looked; there, portrayed on the wall all around, were all kinds of creeping things, and loathsome animals, and all the idols of the house of Israel. 11 Before them stood sev-

enty of the elders of the house of Israel, with Jaazaniah son of Shaphan standing among them. Each had his censer in his hand, and the fragrant cloud of incense was ascending. 12 Then he said to me, "Mortal, have you seen what the elders of the house of Israel are doing in the dark, each in his room of images? For they say, 'The LORD does not see us, the LORD has forsaken the land.' " 13 He said also to me, "You will see still greater abominations that they are committing."

14 Then he brought me to the entrance of the north gate of the house of the LORD; women were sitting there weeping for Tammuz. 15 Then he said to me, "Have you seen this, O mortal? You will see still greater abominations than these."

16 And he brought me into the inner court of the house of the LORD; there, at the entrance of the temple of the LORD, between the porch and the altar, were about twenty-five men, with their backs to the temple of the LORD, and their faces toward the east, prostrating themselves to the sun toward the east. 17 Then he said to me, "Have you seen this, O mortal? Is it not bad enough that the house of Judah commits the abominations done here? Must they fill the land with violence, and provoke my anger still further? See, they are putting the branch to their nose! 18 Therefore I will act in wrath; my eye will not spare, nor will I have pity; and though they cry in my hearing with a loud voice, I will not listen to them."

The Slaughter of the Idolaters

9 Then he cried in my hearing with a loud voice, saying, "Draw near, you executioners of the city, each with his destroying weapon in his hand." 2 And six men came from the direction of the upper gate, which faces north, each with his weapon for slaughter in his hand; among them was a man clothed in linen, with a writing

8.1 Ezek 14.1; 20.1; 33.31; 1.3; 3.22
8.2 Ezek 1.4,27
8.3 Dan 5.5; Ezek 3.12, 14; 11.1; Jer 32.34; Ezek 5.11
8.4 Ezek 1.28
8.5 Zech 5.5; v. 3
8.6 vv. 9,17; Ezek 5.11; 7.22,24; vv. 11,14,16
8.10 Ex 20.4; Ezek 14.3
8.11 Jer 19.1; Num 16.17, 35; Ezek 16.18; 23.41

8.12 Ezek 9.9
8.13 Ezek 9.3
8.14 Ezek 44.4; 46.9
8.16 Ezek 11.1; Jer 2.27; Deut 4.19; Job 31.26; Jer 44.17
8.17 Ezek 9.9; Mic 2.2; Jer 7.18,19; Ezek 16.26
8.18 Ezek 5.13; 7.4; 9.5,10; Isa 1.15; Jer 11.11; Mic 3.4; Zech 7.13
9.2 Ezek 10.2; Rev 15.6

t Gk: Heb *like fire* u Heb *he*

case at his side. They went in and stood beside the bronze altar.

3 Now the glory of the God of Israel had gone up from the cherub on which it rested to the threshold of the house. The LORD called to the man clothed in linen, who had the writing case at his side; ⁴and said to him, "Go through the city, through Jerusalem, and put a mark on the foreheads of those who sigh and groan over all the abominations that are committed in it." ⁵To the others he said in my hearing, "Pass through the city after him, and kill; your eye shall not spare, and you shall show no pity. ⁶Cut down old men, young men and young women, little children and women, but touch no one who has the mark. And begin at my sanctuary." So they began with the elders who were in front of the house. ⁷Then he said to them, "Defile the house, and fill the courts with the slain. Go!" So they went out and killed in the city. ⁸While they were killing, and I was left alone, I fell prostrate on my face and cried out, "Ah Lord GOD! will you destroy all who remain of Israel as you pour out your wrath upon Jerusalem?" ⁹He said to me, "The guilt of the house of Israel and Judah is exceedingly great; the land is full of bloodshed and the city full of perversity; for they say, 'The LORD has forsaken the land, and the LORD does not see.' ¹⁰As for me, my eye will not spare, nor will I have pity, but I will bring down their deeds upon their heads."

11 Then the man clothed in linen, with the writing case at his side, brought back word, saying, "I have done as you commanded me."

God's Glory Leaves Jerusalem

10 Then I looked, and above the dome that was over the heads of the cherubim there appeared above them something like a sapphire,ᵛ in form resembling a throne. ²He said to the man clothed in linen, "Go within the wheelwork underneath the cherubim; fill your hands with burning

coals from among the cherubim, and scatter them over the city." He went in as I looked on. ³Now the cherubim were standing on the south side of the house when the man went in; and a cloud filled the inner court. ⁴Then the glory of the LORD rose up from the cherub to the threshold of the house; the house was filled with the cloud, and the court was full of the brightness of the glory of the LORD. ⁵The sound of the wings of the cherubim was heard as far as the outer court, like the voice of God Almightyʷ when he speaks.

6 When he commanded the man clothed in linen, "Take fire from within the wheelwork, from among the cherubim," he went in and stood beside a wheel. ⁷And a cherub stretched out his hand from among the cherubim to the fire that was among the cherubim, took some of it and put it into the hands of the man clothed in linen, who took it and went out. ⁸The cherubim appeared to have the form of a human hand under their wings.

9 I looked, and there were four wheels beside the cherubim, one beside each cherub; and the appearance of the wheels was like gleaming beryl. ¹⁰And as for their appearance, the four looked alike, something like a wheel within a wheel. ¹¹When they moved, they moved in any of the four directions without veering as they moved; but in whatever direction the front wheel faced, the others followed without veering as they moved. ¹²Their entire body, their rims, their spokes, their wings, and the wheels—the wheels of the four of them—were full of eyes all around. ¹³As for the wheels, they were called in my hearing "the wheelwork." ¹⁴Each one had four faces: the first face was that of the cherub, the second face was that of a human being, the third that of a lion, and the fourth that of an eagle.

Cross references

9.3 Ezek 8.4; 10.4,18; 11.22,23
9.4 Ex 12.7; 1 Pet 4.17; Rev 7.3; 9.4; Ps 119.53, 136; Jer 13.17
9.5 Ezek 5.11; 7.4,9
9.6 2 Chr 36.17; Rev 9.4; Jer 25.29; Am 3.2; Ezek 8.11, 12,16
9.7 2 Chr 36.17; Ezek 7.20-22; 6.4
9.8 1 Chr 21.16; Josh 7.6; Ezek 11.13
9.9 Ezek 7.23; 22.29; 8.12
9.10 Isa 65.6; Ezek 8.18; 7.4; 11.21
10.1 Ezek 1.22, 26; Rev 4.2
10.2 Ezek 9.2,3; v. 13; Isa 6.6; Rev 8.5
10.3 Ezek 8.3,16
10.4 Ezek 1.28; 9.3; Ex 40.34, 35; 1 Kings 8.10, 11
10.5 Ezek 1.24
10.6 v. 2
10.7 Ezek 1.13
10.8 Ezek 1.8
10.9 Ezek 1.15, 16
10.11 Ezek 1.17; v. 22
10.12 Rev 4.6,8; Ezek 1.18
10.13 v. 2
10.14 Ezek 1.6,10; Rev 4.7

ᵛ Or lapis lazuli ʷ Traditional rendering of Heb El Shaddai

15 The cherubim rose up. These were the living creatures that I saw by the river Chebar. ¹⁶When the cherubim moved, the wheels moved beside them; and when the cherubim lifted up their wings to rise up from the earth, the wheels at their side did not veer. ¹⁷When they stopped, the others stopped, and when they rose up, the others rose up with them; for the spirit of the living creatures was in them.

18 Then the glory of the LORD went out from the threshold of the house and stopped above the cherubim. ¹⁹The cherubim lifted up their wings and rose up from the earth in my sight as they went out with the wheels beside them. They stopped at the entrance of the east gate of the house of the LORD; and the glory of the God of Israel was above them.

20 These were the living creatures that I saw underneath the God of Israel by the river Chebar; and I knew that they were cherubim. ²¹Each had four faces, each four wings, and underneath their wings something like human hands. ²²As for what their faces were like, they were the same faces whose appearance I had seen by the river Chebar. Each one moved straight ahead.

Judgment on Wicked Counselors

11 The spirit lifted me up and brought me to the east gate of the house of the LORD, which faces east. There, at the entrance of the gateway, were twenty-five men; among them I saw Jaazaniah son of Azzur, and Pelatiah son of Benaiah, officials of the people. ²He said to me, "Mortal, these are the men who devise iniquity and who give wicked counsel in this city; ³they say, 'The time is not near to build houses; this city is the pot, and we are the meat.' ⁴Therefore prophesy against them; prophesy, O mortal."

5 Then the spirit of the LORD fell upon me, and he said to me, "Say, Thus says the LORD: This is what you think, O house of Israel; I

know the things that come into your mind. ⁶You have killed many in this city, and have filled its streets with the slain. ⁷Therefore thus says the Lord GOD: The slain whom you have placed within it are the meat, and this city is the pot; but you shall be taken out of it. ⁸You have feared the sword; and I will bring the sword upon you, says the Lord GOD. ⁹I will take you out of it and give you over to the hands of foreigners, and execute judgments upon you. ¹⁰You shall fall by the sword; I will judge you at the border of Israel. And you shall know that I am the LORD. ¹¹This city shall not be your pot, and you shall not be the meat inside it; I will judge you at the border of Israel. ¹²Then you shall know that I am the LORD, whose statutes you have not followed, and whose ordinances you have not kept, but you have acted according to the ordinances of the nations that are around you."

13 Now, while I was prophesying, Pelatiah son of Benaiah died. Then I fell down on my face, cried with a loud voice, and said, "Ah Lord GOD! will you make a full end of the remnant of Israel?"

God Will Restore Israel

14 Then the word of the LORD came to me: ¹⁵Mortal, your kinsfolk, your own kin, your fellow exiles,ˣ the whole house of Israel, all of them, are those of whom the inhabitants of Jerusalem have said, "They have gone far from the LORD; to us this land is given for a possession." ¹⁶Therefore say: Thus says the Lord GOD: Though I removed them far away among the nations, and though I scattered them among the countries, yet I have been a sanctuary to them for a little whileʸ in the countries where they have gone. ¹⁷Therefore say: Thus says the Lord GOD: I will gather you from the peoples, and assemble you out of the countries where you have been scattered, and I will give you the land of Israel. ¹⁸When they

ˣ Gk Syr: Heb *people of your kindred*
ʸ Or *to some extent*

10.15 Ezek 1.3,5
10.16 Ezek 1.19
10.17 Ezek 1.12, 20,21
10.18 v. 4
10.19 11.1,22
10.20 v. 15; Ezek 1.22; 1.1
10.21 Ezek 1.6,8
10.22 Ezek 1.10, 12
11.1 Ezek 3.12, 14; 8.3; 10.19; 8.16
11.2 Isa 30.1; Mic 2.1
11.3 Ezek 12.22, 27; 2 Pet 3.4; Jer 1.13; Ezek 24.3,6
11.4 Ezek 3.4,17
11.5 Ezek 2.2; 3.24; Jer 11.20; Ezek 38.10
11.6 Ezek 7.23; 22.3,4
11.7 Ezek 24.3,6, 10,11; Mic 3.3; v. 9
11.9 Ps 106.41; Ezek 5.8
11.10 2 Kings 25.19-21; Jer 52.10; 2 Kings 14.25; Ezek 6.7
11.11 v. 3
11.12 v. 10; Ezek 18.8,9; 8.10,14,16
11.13 v. 1; Ezek 9.8
11.15 Ezek 33.24
11.16 Isa 8.14
11.17 Jer 24.5; Ezek 28.25; 34.13
11.18 Ezek 37.23; 5.11

come there, they will remove from it all its detestable things and all its abominations. [19] I will give them one[z] heart, and put a new spirit within them; I will remove the heart of stone from their flesh and give them a heart of flesh, [20] so that they may follow my statutes and keep my ordinances and obey them. Then they shall be my people, and I will be their God. [21] But as for those whose heart goes after their detestable things and their abominations,[a] I will bring their deeds upon their own heads, says the Lord God.

22 Then the cherubim lifted up their wings, with the wheels beside them; and the glory of the God of Israel was above them. [23] And the glory of the Lord ascended from the middle of the city, and stopped on the mountain east of the city. [24] The spirit lifted me up and brought me in a vision by the spirit of God into Chaldea, to the exiles. Then the vision that I had seen left me. [25] And I told the exiles all the things that the Lord had shown me.

Judah's Captivity Portrayed

12 The word of the Lord came to me: [2] Mortal, you are living in the midst of a rebellious house, who have eyes to see but do not see, who have ears to hear but do not hear; [3] for they are a rebellious house. Therefore, mortal, prepare for yourself an exile's baggage, and go into exile by day in their sight; you shall go like an exile from your place to another place in their sight. Perhaps they will understand, though they are a rebellious house. [4] You shall bring out your baggage by day in their sight, as baggage for exile; and you shall go out yourself at evening in their sight, as those do who go into exile. [5] Dig through the wall in their sight, and carry the baggage through it. [6] In their sight you shall lift the baggage on your shoulder, and carry it out in the dark; you shall cover your face, so that you may not see

the land; for I have made you a sign for the house of Israel.

7 I did just as I was commanded. I brought out my baggage by day, as baggage for exile, and in the evening I dug through the wall with my own hands; I brought it out in the dark, carrying it on my shoulder in their sight.

8 In the morning the word of the Lord came to me: [9] Mortal, has not the house of Israel, the rebellious house, said to you, "What are you doing?" [10] Say to them, "Thus says the Lord God: This oracle concerns the prince in Jerusalem and all the house of Israel in it." [11] Say, "I am a sign for you: as I have done, so shall it be done to them; they shall go into exile, into captivity." [12] And the prince who is among them shall lift his baggage on his shoulder in the dark, and shall go out; he[b] shall dig through the wall and carry it through; he shall cover his face, so that he may not see the land with his eyes. [13] I will spread my net over him, and he shall be caught in my snare; and I will bring him to Babylon, the land of the Chaldeans, yet he shall not see it; and he shall die there. [14] I will scatter to every wind all who are around him, his helpers and all his troops; and I will unsheathe the sword behind them. [15] And they shall know that I am the Lord, when I disperse them among the nations and scatter them through the countries. [16] But I will let a few of them escape from the sword, from famine and pestilence, so that they may tell of all their abominations among the nations where they go; then they shall know that I am the Lord.

Judgment Not Postponed

17 The word of the Lord came to me: [18] Mortal, eat your bread with quaking, and drink your water with trembling and with fearfulness; [19] and say to the people of the land, Thus says the Lord God concerning

Cross-references

11.19 Jer 32.39; Ezek 36.26, 27; 18.31; Zech 7.12; 2 Cor 3.3
11.20 Ps 105.45; Ezek 14.11
11.21 Ezek 9.10
11.22 Ezek 1.19; 10.19
11.23 Ezek 8.4; 9.3; Zech 14.4
11.24 Ezek 8.3; 1.1,3
11.25 Ezek 2.7
12.2 Ezek 2.6-8; Jer 5.21; Mt 13.13,14
12.3 Jer 26.3; 36.3,7; 2 Tim 2.25
12.4 Jer 39.4; v. 12
12.6 vv. 12,13; Isa 8.18; Ezek 4.3; 24.24
12.7 Ezek 24.18; vv. 3-6
12.9 Ezek 2.5; 17.12; 24.19
12.10 Mal 1.1
12.11 v. 6; 2 Kings 25.4-7
12.12 Jer 39.4
12.13 Isa 24.17, 18; Hos 7.12; Jer 52.11; Ezek 17.16
12.14 2 Kings 25.4, 5; Ezek 5.2, 12
12.15 Ezek 6.7,14
12.16 Ezek 6.8-10; 14.22; Jer 22.8,9
12.18 Ezek 4.16
12.19 Ezek 4.16; 23.33; Zech 7.14

z Another reading is *a new* a Cn: Heb *And to the heart of their detestable things and their abominations their heart goes* b Gk Syr: Heb *they*

the inhabitants of Jerusalem in the land of Israel: They shall eat their bread with fearfulness, and drink their water in dismay, because their land shall be stripped of all it contains, on account of the violence of all those who live in it. 20 The inhabited cities shall be laid waste, and the land shall become a desolation; and you shall know that I am the LORD.

21 The word of the LORD came to me: 22 Mortal, what is this proverb of yours about the land of Israel, which says, "The days are prolonged, and every vision comes to nothing"? 23 Tell them therefore, "Thus says the Lord GOD: I will put an end to this proverb, and they shall use it no more as a proverb in Israel." But say to them, The days are near, and the fulfillment of every vision. 24 For there shall no longer be any false vision or flattering divination within the house of Israel. 25 But I the LORD will speak the word that I speak, and it will be fulfilled. It will no longer be delayed; but in your days, O rebellious house, I will speak the word and fulfill it, says the Lord GOD.

26 The word of the LORD came to me: 27 Mortal, the house of Israel is saying, "The vision that he sees is for many years ahead; he prophesies for distant times." 28 Therefore say to them, Thus says the Lord GOD: None of my words will be delayed any longer, but the word that I speak will be fulfilled, says the Lord GOD.

False Prophets Condemned

13 The word of the LORD came to me: 2 Mortal, prophesy against the prophets of Israel who are prophesying; say to those who prophesy out of their own imagination: "Hear the word of the LORD!" 3 Thus says the Lord GOD, Alas for the senseless prophets who follow their own spirit, and have seen nothing! 4 Your prophets have been like jackals among ruins, O Israel. 5 You have not gone up into the breaches, or repaired a wall for the house of Israel, so that it might

stand in battle on the day of the LORD. 6 They have envisioned falsehood and lying divination; they say, "Says the LORD," when the LORD has not sent them, and yet they wait for the fulfillment of their word! 7 Have you not seen a false vision or uttered a lying divination, when you have said, "Says the LORD," even though I did not speak?

8 Therefore thus says the Lord GOD: Because you have uttered falsehood and envisioned lies, I am against you, says the Lord GOD. 9 My hand will be against the prophets who see false visions and utter lying divinations; they shall not be in the council of my people, nor be enrolled in the register of the house of Israel, nor shall they enter the land of Israel; and you shall know that I am the Lord GOD. 10 Because, in truth, because they have misled my people, saying, "Peace," when there is no peace; and because, when the people build a wall, these prophets[c] smear whitewash on it. 11 Say to those who smear whitewash on it that it shall fall. There will be a deluge of rain,[d] great hailstones will fall, and a stormy wind will break out. 12 When the wall falls, will it not be said to you, "Where is the whitewash you smeared on it?" 13 Therefore thus says the Lord GOD: In my wrath I will make a stormy wind break out, and in my anger there shall be a deluge of rain, and hailstones in wrath to destroy it. 14 I will break down the wall that you have smeared with whitewash, and bring it to the ground, so that its foundation will be laid bare; when it falls, you shall perish within it; and you shall know that I am the LORD. 15 Thus I will spend my wrath upon the wall, and upon those who have smeared it with whitewash; and I will say to you, The wall is no more, nor those who smeared it — 16 the prophets of Israel who prophesied concerning Jerusalem and saw visions of

Cross references

12.20
Ezek 5.14;
36.3
12.22
Ezek 16.44;
11.3; v. 27;
Am 6.3;
2 Pet 3.4
12.23
Joel 2.1;
Zeph 1.14
12.24
Ezek 13.23;
Zech 13.2-4
12.25
v. 28;
Isa 55.11;
Dan 9.12;
Hab 1.5;
v. 2
12.27
v. 22;
Dan 10.14;
2 Pet 3.4
12.28
v. 25;
Mt 24.48-50
13.2
Jer 37.19;
v. 17;
Jer 14.14;
23.16,26;
Am 7.16
13.3
Lam 2.14;
Jer 23.28-32
13.5
Ps 106.23,
30;
Ezek 22.30;
Isa 58.12;
Ezek 7.19

13.6
v. 22;
Ezek 22.28;
Jer 28.15
13.7
Ezek 22.28
13.8
Ezek 21.29;
5.8
13.9
Ezra 2.59,
62; Neh 7.5;
Ps 69.28;
Ezek 11.10,
12
13.10
Jer 50.6;
8.11; v. 16;
Ezek 22.28
13.11
Ezek 38.22
13.13
v. 11;
Isa 30.30;
Rev 11.19;
16.21
13.14
Mic 1.6;
v. 9;
Ezek 14.8
13.16
Ezek 6.14;
Isa 57.21

c Heb *they* d Heb *rain and you*

peace for it, when there was no peace, says the Lord God.

17 As for you, mortal, set your face against the daughters of your people, who prophesy out of their own imagination; prophesy against them [18] and say, Thus says the Lord God: Woe to the women who sew bands on all wrists, and make veils for the heads of persons of every height, in the hunt for human lives! Will you hunt down lives among my people, and maintain your own lives? [19] You have profaned me among my people for handfuls of barley and for pieces of bread, putting to death persons who should not die and keeping alive persons who should not live, by your lies to my people, who listen to lies.

20 Therefore thus says the Lord God: I am against your bands with which you hunt lives;[e] I will tear them from your arms, and let the lives go free, the lives that you hunt down like birds. [21] I will tear off your veils, and save my people from your hands; they shall no longer be prey in your hands; and you shall know that I am the Lord. [22] Because you have disheartened the righteous falsely, although I have not disheartened them, and you have encouraged the wicked not to turn from their wicked way and save their lives; [23] therefore you shall no longer see false visions or practice divination; I will save my people from your hand. Then you will know that I am the Lord.

God's Judgments Justified

14 Certain elders of Israel came to me and sat down before me. [2] And the word of the Lord came to me: [3] Mortal, these men have taken their idols into their hearts, and placed their iniquity as a stumbling block before them; shall I let myself be consulted by them? [4] Therefore speak to them, and say to them, Thus says the Lord God: Any of those of the house of Israel who take their idols into their hearts and place their iniquity as a stumbling block before them, and yet come to the

prophet—I the Lord will answer those who come with the multitude of their idols, [5] in order that I may take hold of the hearts of the house of Israel, all of whom are estranged from me through their idols.

6 Therefore say to the house of Israel, Thus says the Lord God: Repent and turn away from your idols; and turn away your faces from all your abominations. [7] For any of those of the house of Israel, or of the aliens who reside in Israel, who separate themselves from me, taking their idols into their hearts and placing their iniquity as a stumbling block before them, and yet come to a prophet to inquire of me by him, I the Lord will answer them myself. [8] I will set my face against them; I will make them a sign and a byword and cut them off from the midst of my people; and you shall know that I am the Lord.

9 If a prophet is deceived and speaks a word, I, the Lord, have deceived that prophet, and I will stretch out my hand against him, and will destroy him from the midst of my people Israel. [10] And they shall bear their punishment—the punishment of the inquirer and the punishment of the prophet shall be the same— [11] so that the house of Israel may no longer go astray from me, nor defile themselves any more with all their transgressions. Then they shall be my people, and I will be their God, says the Lord God.

12 The word of the Lord came to me: [13] Mortal, when a land sins against me by acting faithlessly, and I stretch out my hand against it, and break its staff of bread and send famine upon it, and cut off from it human beings and animals, [14] even if Noah, Daniel,[f] and Job, these three, were in it, they would save only their own lives by their righteousness, says the Lord God. [15] If I send wild animals through

13.17 Ezek 20.46; 21.2; v. 2
13.18 Ezek 22.25; 2 Pet 2.14
13.19 Ezek 20.39; Prov 28.21; Mic 3.5; Jer 23.14,17
13.20 v. 17
13.21 Ps 124.7; v. 9
13.22 Am 5.12; Jer 23.14; Ezek 33.14-16
13.23 v. 6; Ezek 12.24; Mic 3.6; v. 9; Ezek 14.8
14.1 Ezek 8.1; 20.1; 33.31
14.3 Ezek 20.16; 7.19; Jer 11.11; Ezek 20.3, 31
14.4 v. 7

14.5 Isa 1.4; Jer 2.11; Zech 11.8
14.6 Isa 2.20; 30.22; Ezek 18.30; 8.6
14.7 Ex 12.48; 20.10; v. 4
14.8 Jer 44.11; Ezek 15.7; Isa 65.15; Ezek 5.15; 6.7
14.9 1 Kings 22.23; Job 12.16; Jer 4.10; 2 Thes 2.11; Jer 14.15
14.11 Ezek 44.10, 15; 11.20; 37.27
14.13 Ezek 15.8; 6.14; 5.16; vv. 17,19,21
14.14 Jer 15.1; Gen 6.8; Dan 1.6; Job 1.1,5; vv. 16,18,20

14.15 Ezek 5.17

e Gk Syr: Heb *lives for birds* f Or, as otherwise read, *Danel*

the land to ravage it, so that it is made desolate, and no one may pass through because of the animals; [16] even if these three men were in it, as I live, says the Lord God, they would save neither sons nor daughters; they alone would be saved, but the land would be desolate. [17] Or if I bring a sword upon that land and say, 'Let a sword pass through the land,' and I cut off human beings and animals from it; [18] though these three men were in it, as I live, says the Lord God, they would save neither sons nor daughters, but they alone would be saved. [19] Or if I send a pestilence into that land, and pour out my wrath upon it with blood, to cut off humans and animals from it; [20] even if Noah, Daniel,[g] and Job were in it, as I live, says the Lord God, they would save neither son nor daughter; they would save only their own lives by their righteousness.

21 For thus says the Lord God: How much more when I send upon Jerusalem my four deadly acts of judgment, sword, famine, wild animals, and pestilence, to cut off humans and animals from it! [22] Yet, survivors shall be left in it, sons and daughters who will be brought out; they will come out to you. When you see their ways and their deeds, you will be consoled for the evil that I have brought upon Jerusalem, for all that I have brought upon it. [23] They shall console you, when you see their ways and their deeds; and you shall know that it was not without cause that I did all that I have done in it, says the Lord God.

The Useless Vine

15 The word of the Lord came to me:
[2] O mortal, how does the wood of the vine surpass all other wood —
the vine branch that is among the trees of the forest?

[3] Is wood taken from it to make anything?
Does one take a peg from it on which to hang any object?
[4] It is put in the fire for fuel;
when the fire has consumed both ends of it
and the middle of it is charred,
is it useful for anything?
[5] When it was whole it was used for nothing;
how much less — when the fire has consumed it,
and it is charred —
can it ever be used for anything!

6 Therefore thus says the Lord God: Like the wood of the vine among the trees of the forest, which I have given to the fire for fuel, so I will give up the inhabitants of Jerusalem. [7] I will set my face against them; although they escape from the fire, the fire shall still consume them; and you shall know that I am the Lord, when I set my face against them. [8] And I will make the land desolate, because they have acted faithlessly, says the Lord God.

God's Faithless Bride

16 The word of the Lord came to me: [2] Mortal, make known to Jerusalem her abominations, [3] and say, Thus says the Lord God to Jerusalem: Your origin and your birth were in the land of the Canaanites; your father was an Amorite, and your mother a Hittite. [4] As for your birth, on the day you were born your navel cord was not cut, nor were you washed with water to cleanse you, nor rubbed with salt, nor wrapped in cloths. [5] No eye pitied you, to do any of these things for you out of compassion for you; but you were thrown out in the open field, for you were abhorred on the day you were born.

6 I passed by you, and saw you flailing about in your blood. As you lay in your blood, I said to you,

14.16
vv. 14,18, 20;
Ezek 18.20
14.17
Ezek 5.12;
21.3,4; 25.13;
Zeph 1.3
14.18
v. 14
14.19
v. 21;
Ezek 38.22;
7.8
14.20
v. 14
14.21
Ezek 5.17;
Jer 15.2,3;
Rev 6.8
14.22
Ezek 12.16;
7.16; 20.43;
16.54
14.23
Jer 22.8,9
15.2
Isa 5.1-7;
Jer 2.21;
Hos 10.1

15.4
v. 6;
Ezek 19.14;
Jn 15.6
15.6
v. 2;
Ezek 17.3-10
15.7
Lev 17.10;
Ezek 14.8;
Isa 24.18;
Ezek 6.7;
7.4; 14.8
15.8
Ezek 14.13
16.2
Ezek 20.4;
22.2; 8.9-17
16.3
Ezek 21.30;
v. 45
16.4
Hos 2.3
16.5
Deut 32.10
16.6
v. 22;
Ex 19.4

g Or, as otherwise read, *Danel*

"Live! [7] and grow up[h] like a plant of the field." You grew up and became tall and arrived at full womanhood;[i] your breasts were formed, and your hair had grown; yet you were naked and bare.

8 I passed by you again and looked on you; you were at the age for love. I spread the edge of my cloak over you, and covered your nakedness: I pledged myself to you and entered into a covenant with you, says the Lord GOD, and you became mine. [9] Then I bathed you with water and washed off the blood from you, and anointed you with oil. [10] I clothed you with embroidered cloth and with sandals of fine leather; I bound you in fine linen and covered you with rich fabric.[j] [11] I adorned you with ornaments: I put bracelets on your arms, a chain on your neck, [12] a ring on your nose, earrings in your ears, and a beautiful crown upon your head. [13] You were adorned with gold and silver, while your clothing was of fine linen, rich fabric,[j] and embroidered cloth. You had choice flour and honey and oil for food. You grew exceedingly beautiful, fit to be a queen. [14] Your fame spread among the nations on account of your beauty, for it was perfect because of my splendor that I had bestowed on you, says the Lord GOD.

15 But you trusted in your beauty, and played the whore because of your fame, and lavished your whorings on any passer-by.[k] [16] You took some of your garments, and made for yourself colorful shrines, and on them played the whore; nothing like this has ever been or ever shall be.[j] [17] You also took your beautiful jewels of my gold and my silver that I had given you, and made for yourself male images, and with them played the whore; [18] and you took your embroidered garments to cover them, and set my oil and my incense before them. [19] Also my bread that I gave you — I fed you with choice flour and oil and honey — you set it before them as a pleasing odor; and so it was, says the Lord GOD. [20] You took your

sons and your daughters, whom you had borne to me, and these you sacrificed to them to be devoured. As if your whorings were not enough! [21] You slaughtered my children and delivered them up as an offering to them. [22] And in all your abominations and your whorings you did not remember the days of your youth, when you were naked and bare, flailing about in your blood.

23 After all your wickedness (woe, woe to you! says the Lord GOD), [24] you built yourself a platform and made yourself a lofty place in every square; [25] at the head of every street you built your lofty place and prostituted your beauty, offering yourself to every passer-by, and multiplying your whoring. [26] You played the whore with the Egyptians, your lustful neighbors, multiplying your whoring, to provoke me to anger. [27] Therefore I stretched out my hand against you, reduced your rations, and gave you up to the will of your enemies, the daughters of the Philistines, who were ashamed of your lewd behavior. [28] You played the whore with the Assyrians, because you were insatiable; you played the whore with them, and still you were not satisfied. [29] You multiplied your whoring with Chaldea, the land of merchants; and even with this you were not satisfied.

30 How sick is your heart, says the Lord GOD, that you did all these things, the deeds of a brazen whore; [31] building your platform at the head of every street, and making your lofty place in every square! Yet you were not like a whore, because you scorned payment. [32] Adulterous wife, who receives strangers instead of her husband! [33] Gifts are given to all whores; but you gave your gifts to all your lovers, bribing them to come to you from all around for your whorings. [34] So you were different from other

Cross-references (center column):

16.7
Ex 1.7;
v. 22
16.8
Ruth 3.9;
Gen 22.16-18;
Ex 24.7,8;
19.5; Jer 2.2
16.10
v. 13
16.11
Ezek 23.40;
Gen 24.22,
47; Prov 1.9
16.13
Deut 32.13,
14;
1 Sam 10.1
16.14
Ps 50.2;
Lam 2.15
16.15
Isa 57.8;
Jer 2.20;
Ezek 23.3,8,
11,12
16.16
v. 10;
Ezek 6.3,6;
Hos 2.8
16.17
Ezek 7.20
16.18
v. 10
16.19
Hos 2.8
16.20
2 Kings 16.3;
Isa 57.5

16.21
2 Kings 17.17;
Jer 19.5
16.22
Hos 11.1;
vv. 4-6
16.24
Isa 57.5,7;
Jer 2.20; 3.2
16.25
Prov 9.14;
v. 15
16.26
Ezek 8.17;
20.7,8;
23.19-21
16.27
Ezek 14.13;
20.33,34;
2 Chr 28.18,
19
16.28
2 Kings 16.7,
10;
2 Chr 28.23
16.29
Ezek 23.14-17
16.30
Jer 3.3
16.31
v. 24;
Isa 52.3
16.33
Isa 30.6;
Hos 8.9,10

h Gk Syr: Heb *Live! I made you a myriad*
i Cn: Heb *ornament of ornaments*
j Meaning of Heb uncertain k Heb adds *let it be his*

women in your whorings: no one solicited you to play the whore; and you gave payment, while no payment was given to you; you were different.

35 Therefore, O whore, hear the word of the LORD: [36] Thus says the Lord GOD, Because your lust was poured out and your nakedness uncovered in your whoring with your lovers, and because of all your abominable idols, and because of the blood of your children that you gave to them, [37] therefore, I will gather all your lovers, with whom you took pleasure, all those you loved and all those you hated; I will gather them against you from all around, and will uncover your nakedness to them, so that they may see all your nakedness. [38] I will judge you as women who commit adultery and shed blood are judged, and bring blood upon you in wrath and jealousy. [39] I will deliver you into their hands, and they shall throw down your platform and break down your lofty places; they shall strip you of your clothes and take your beautiful objects and leave you naked and bare. [40] They shall bring up a mob against you, and they shall stone you and cut you to pieces with their swords. [41] They shall burn your houses and execute judgments on you in the sight of many women; I will stop you from playing the whore, and you shall also make no more payments. [42] So I will satisfy my fury on you, and my jealousy shall turn away from you; I will be calm, and will be angry no longer. [43] Because you have not remembered the days of your youth, but have enraged me with all these things; therefore, I have returned your deeds upon your head, says the Lord GOD.

Have you not committed lewdness beyond all your abominations? [44] See, everyone who uses proverbs will use this proverb about you, "Like mother, like daughter." [45] You are the daughter of your mother, who loathed her husband and her children; and you

are the sister of your sisters, who loathed their husbands and their children. Your mother was a Hittite and your father an Amorite. [46] Your elder sister is Samaria, who lived with her daughters to the north of you; and your younger sister, who lived to the south of you, is Sodom with her daughters. [47] You not only followed their ways, and acted according to their abominations; within a very little time you were more corrupt than they in all your ways. [48] As I live, says the Lord GOD, your sister Sodom and her daughters have not done as you and your daughters have done. [49] This was the guilt of your sister Sodom: she and her daughters had pride, excess of food, and prosperous ease, but did not aid the poor and needy. [50] They were haughty, and did abominable things before me; therefore I removed them when I saw it. [51] Samaria has not committed half your sins; you have committed more abominations than they, and have made your sisters appear righteous by all the abominations that you have committed. [52] Bear your disgrace, you also, for you have brought about for your sisters a more favorable judgment; because of your sins in which you acted more abominably than they, they are more in the right than you. So be ashamed, you also, and bear your disgrace, for you have made your sisters appear righteous.

53 I will restore their fortunes, the fortunes of Sodom and her daughters and the fortunes of Samaria and her daughters, and I will restore your own fortunes along with theirs, [54] in order that you may bear your disgrace and be ashamed of all that you have done, becoming a consolation to them. [55] As for your sisters, Sodom and her daughters shall return to their former state, Samaria and her daughters shall return to their former state, and you and your daughters shall return to your former state. [56] Was not your sister Sodom a byword in your mouth in the day of your

pride, 57 before your wickedness was uncovered? Now you are a mockery to the daughters of Aram[1] and all her neighbors, and to the daughters of the Philistines, those all around who despise you. 58 You must bear the penalty of your lewdness and your abominations, says the LORD.

An Everlasting Covenant

59 Yes, thus says the Lord GOD: I will deal with you as you have done, you who have despised the oath, breaking the covenant; 60 yet I will remember my covenant with you in the days of your youth, and I will establish with you an everlasting covenant. 61 Then you will remember your ways, and be ashamed when I[m] take your sisters, both your elder and your younger, and give them to you as daughters, but not on account of my[n] covenant with you. 62 I will establish my covenant with you, and you shall know that I am the LORD, 63 in order that you may remember and be confounded, and never open your mouth again because of your shame, when I forgive you all that you have done, says the Lord GOD.

The Two Eagles and the Vine

17 The word of the LORD came to me: 2 O mortal, propound a riddle, and speak an allegory to the house of Israel. 3 Say: Thus says the Lord GOD:
A great eagle, with great
 wings and long pinions,
rich in plumage of many
 colors,
came to the Lebanon.
He took the top of the cedar,
4 broke off its topmost shoot;
He carried it to a land of
 trade,
 set it in a city of
 merchants.
5 Then he took a seed from
 the land,
 placed it in fertile soil;
A plant[o] by abundant
 waters,
he set it like a willow twig.

6 It sprouted and became a
 vine
spreading out, but low;
Its branches turned toward
 him,
 its roots remained where it
 stood.
So it became a vine;
 it brought forth branches,
 put forth foliage.

7 There was another great
 eagle,
 with great wings and much
 plumage.
And see! This vine stretched
 out
 its roots toward him;
It shot out its branches
 toward him,
 so that he might water it.
From the bed where it was
 planted
8 it was transplanted
to good soil by abundant
 waters,
 so that it might produce
 branches
 and bear fruit
 and become a noble vine.
9 Say: Thus says the Lord GOD:
Will it prosper?
Will it not pull up its roots,
 cause its fruit to rot[o] and
 wither,
 its fresh sprouting leaves to
 fade?
No strong arm or mighty
 army will be needed
 to pull it from its roots.
10 When it is transplanted, will
 it thrive?
When the east wind strikes
 it,
 will it not utterly wither,
 wither on the bed where it
 grew?

11 Then the word of the LORD came to me: 12 Say now to the rebellious house: Do you not know what these things mean? Tell them: The king of Babylon came to Jerusalem, took its king and its officials, and brought them back with

Cross references (center column)

16.57
2 Kings 16.5;
2 Chr 28.18;
Ezek 5.14
16.58
Ezek 23.49
16.59
Ezek 17.13;
Deut 29.12
16.60
Jer 2.2;
Hos 2.15;
Jer 32.40;
Ezek 37.26
16.61
Ezek 20.43;
Isa 54.1;
60.4;
Jer 31.31
16.62
Ezek 20.37;
Hos 2.19,
20;
Ezek 20.43,
44
16.63
v. 61;
Rom 3.19
17.2
Ezek 20.49;
24.3
17.3
Jer 22.23
17.5
Deut 8.7-9;
Isa 44.4

17.6
v. 14
17.7
v. 15
17.8
v. 5
17.9
vv. 10,15-21
17.10
v. 15;
Ezek 19.14;
Hos 13.15
17.12
Ezek 2.5;
12.9; v. 3;
2 Kings 24.11-
16

[l] Another reading is *Edom* [m] Syr: Heb *you* [n] Heb lacks *my* [o] Meaning of Heb uncertain

him to Babylon. [13] He took one of the royal offspring and made a covenant with him, putting him under oath (he had taken away the chief men of the land), [14] so that the kingdom might be humble and not lift itself up, and that by keeping his covenant it might stand. [15] But he rebelled against him by sending ambassadors to Egypt, in order that they might give him horses and a large army. Will he succeed? Can one escape who does such things? Can he break the covenant and yet escape? [16] As I live, says the Lord God, surely in the place where the king resides who made him king, whose oath he despised, and whose covenant with him he broke—in Babylon he shall die. [17] Pharaoh with his mighty army and great company will not help him in war, when ramps are cast up and siege-walls built to cut off many lives. [18] Because he despised the oath and broke the covenant, because he gave his hand and yet did all these things, he shall not escape. [19] Therefore thus says the Lord God: As I live, I will surely return upon his head my oath that he despised, and my covenant that he broke. [20] I will spread my net over him, and he shall be caught in my snare; I will bring him to Babylon and enter into judgment with him there for the treason he has committed against me. [21] All the pick[p] of his troops shall fall by the sword, and the survivors shall be scattered to every wind; and you shall know that I, the Lord, have spoken.

Israel Exalted at Last

22 Thus says the Lord God:
I myself will take a sprig
 from the lofty top of a
 cedar;
I will set it out.
I will break off a tender one
 from the topmost of its
 young twigs;
I myself will plant it
on a high and lofty
 mountain.
23 On the mountain height of
 Israel

I will plant it,
 in order that it may produce
 boughs and bear fruit,
 and become a noble cedar.
Under it every kind of bird
 will live;
 in the shade of its
 branches will nest
 winged creatures of every
 kind.
24 All the trees of the field shall
 know
 that I am the Lord.
I bring low the high tree,
 I make high the low tree;
I dry up the green tree
 and make the dry tree
 flourish.
I the Lord have spoken;
 I will accomplish it.

Individual Retribution

18 The word of the Lord came to me: [2] What do you mean by repeating this proverb concerning the land of Israel, "The parents have eaten sour grapes, and the children's teeth are set on edge"? [3] As I live, says the Lord God, this proverb shall no more be used by you in Israel. [4] Know that all lives are mine; the life of the parent as well as the life of the child is mine: it is only the person who sins that shall die.

5 If a man is righteous and does what is lawful and right— [6] if he does not eat upon the mountains or lift up his eyes to the idols of the house of Israel, does not defile his neighbor's wife or approach a woman during her menstrual period, [7] does not oppress anyone, but restores to the debtor his pledge, commits no robbery, gives his bread to the hungry and covers the naked with a garment, [8] does not take advance or accrued interest, withholds his hand from iniquity, executes true justice between contending parties, [9] follows my statutes, and is careful to observe my ordinances, acting faithfully—

17.13
2 Kings 24.15-17;
2 Chr 36.13
17.14
v. 6;
Ezek 29.14
17.15
2 Kings 24.20;
2 Chr 36.13
17.16
vv. 13,18, 19;
Jer 52.11;
Ezek 12.13
17.17
Jer 37.7;
Ezek 29.6,7;
4.2
17.18
Lam 5.6
17.19
Ezek 16.59
17.20
Ezek 12.13;
32.3; 20.36
17.21
2 Kings 25.5, 11;
Ezek 12.14;
6.7,10
17.22
Isa 11.1;
Jer 23.5;
Zech 3.8;
Ezek 36.36;
20.40
17.23
Isa 2.2,3;
Ezek 20.40;
Hos 14.5-7;
Mt 13.31,32
17.24
Ps 96.12;
Ezek 21.26;
19.12; 22.14;
24.14
18.2
Jer 31.29;
Lam 5.7
18.3
vv. 11,20,30
18.4
Isa 42.5;
v. 20;
Rom 6.23
18.6
Ezek 22.9;
vv. 12,15;
Lev 18.19;
20.18;
Ezek 22.10
18.7
Ex 22.21;
Lev 19.15;
Deut 24.12, 13;
Lev 19.13
18.8
Ex 22.25;
Lev 25.36, 37;
Deut 23.19;
1.16;
Zech 8.16
18.9
Ezek 20.11;
Am 5.4

p Another reading is *fugitives*

such a one is righteous; he shall surely live, says the Lord GOD.

10 If he has a son who is violent, a shedder of blood, [11] who does any of these things (though his father[q] does none of them), who eats upon the mountains, defiles his neighbor's wife, [12] oppresses the poor and needy, commits robbery, does not restore the pledge, lifts up his eyes to the idols, commits abomination, [13] takes advance or accrued interest; shall he then live? He shall not. He has done all these abominable things; he shall surely die; his blood shall be upon himself.

14 But if this man has a son who sees all the sins that his father has done, considers, and does not do likewise, [15] who does not eat upon the mountains or lift up his eyes to the idols of the house of Israel, does not defile his neighbor's wife, [16] does not wrong anyone, exacts no pledge, commits no robbery, but gives his bread to the hungry and covers the naked with a garment, [17] withholds his hand from iniquity,[r] takes no advance or accrued interest, observes my ordinances, and follows my statutes; he shall not die for his father's iniquity; he shall surely live. [18] As for his father, because he practiced extortion, robbed his brother, and did what is not good among his people, he dies for his iniquity.

19 Yet you say, "Why should not the son suffer for the iniquity of the father?" When the son has done what is lawful and right, and has been careful to observe all my statutes, he shall surely live. [20] The person who sins shall die. A child shall not suffer for the iniquity of a parent, nor a parent suffer for the iniquity of a child; the righteousness of the righteous shall be his own, and the wickedness of the wicked shall be his own.

21 But if the wicked turn away from all their sins that they have committed and keep all my statutes and do what is lawful and right, they shall surely live; they shall not die. [22] None of the trans-

gressions that they have committed shall be remembered against them; for the righteousness that they have done they shall live. [23] Have I any pleasure in the death of the wicked, says the Lord GOD, and not rather that they should turn from their ways and live? [24] But when the righteous turn away from their righteousness and commit iniquity and do the same abominable things that the wicked do, shall they live? None of the righteous deeds that they have done shall be remembered; for the treachery of which they are guilty and the sin they have committed, they shall die.

25 Yet you say, "The way of the Lord is unfair." Hear now, O house of Israel: Is my way unfair? Is it not your ways that are unfair? [26] When the righteous turn away from their righteousness and commit iniquity, they shall die for it; for the iniquity that they have committed they shall die. [27] Again, when the wicked turn away from the wickedness they have committed and do what is lawful and right, they shall save their life. [28] Because they considered and turned away from all the transgressions that they had committed, they shall surely live; they shall not die. [29] Yet the house of Israel says, "The way of the Lord is unfair." O house of Israel, are my ways unfair? Is it not your ways that are unfair?

30 Therefore I will judge you, O house of Israel, all of you according to your ways, says the Lord GOD. Repent and turn from all your transgressions; otherwise iniquity will be your ruin.[s] [31] Cast away from you all the transgressions that you have committed against me, and get yourselves a new heart and a new spirit! Why will you die, O house of Israel? [32] For I have no pleasure in the death of anyone, says the Lord GOD. Turn, then, and live.

18.10
Ex 21.12;
Num 35.31
18.11
vv. 6,15
18.12
Am 4.1;
Isa 59.6,7;
Ezek 8.6,17
18.13
vv. 8,17;
Ezek 33.4,5
18.14
Prov 23.24
18.15
vv. 6,11,12
18.16
Ps 41.1
18.17
vv. 8,9,13,
19,20
18.18
vv. 10-13;
Ezek 3.18
18.19
Ex 20.5;
Deut 5.9;
2 Kings 23.26
18.20
Deut 24.16;
Isa 3.10,11;
Rom 2.9
18.21
Ezek 33.12,
19; 3.21
18.22
Ezek 33.16;
Mic 7.19;
Ps 18.20-24

18.23
Ezek 33.11;
1 Tim 2.4;
2 Pet 3.9
18.24
Ezek 3.20;
33.12,13,18;
2 Pet 2.20
18.25
v. 29;
Ezek 33.17,
20; Zeph 3.5
18.26
v. 24
18.27
v. 21
18.28
vv. 22,30,31
18.29
v. 25
18.30
Ezek 7.3;
33.20;
Mt 3.2;
Rev 2.5
18.31
Isa 1.16,17;
55.7;
Ezek 11.19;
36.26
18.32
Ezek 33.11;
2 Pet 3.9

q Heb *he* r Gk: Heb *the poor* s Or *so that they shall not be a stumbling block of iniquity to you*

Israel Degraded

19 As for you, raise up a lamentation for the princes of Israel, ² and say:

What a lioness was your
 mother
among lions!
She lay down among young
 lions,
 rearing her cubs.
³ She raised up one of her
 cubs;
 he became a young lion,
and he learned to catch prey;
 he devoured humans.
⁴ The nations sounded an
 alarm against him;
 he was caught in their pit;
and they brought him with
 hooks
 to the land of Egypt.
⁵ When she saw that she was
 thwarted,
 that her hope was lost,
she took another of her cubs
 and made him a young
 lion.
⁶ He prowled among the lions;
 he became a young lion,
and he learned to catch prey;
 he devoured people.
⁷ And he ravaged their
 strongholds,ᵗ
 and laid waste their towns;
the land was appalled, and
 all in it,
 at the sound of his roaring.
⁸ The nations set upon him
 from the provinces all
 around;
they spread their net over
 him;
 he was caught in their pit.
⁹ With hooks they put him in
 a cage,
 and brought him to the
 king of Babylon;
they brought him into
 custody,
so that his voice should be
 heard no more
 on the mountains of Israel.
¹⁰ Your mother was like a vine
 in a vineyardᵘ
 transplanted by the water,
fruitful and full of branches

from abundant water.
¹¹ Its strongest stem became
 a ruler's scepter;ᵛ
 it towered aloft
 among the thick boughs;
 it stood out in its height
 with its mass of branches.
¹² But it was plucked up in
 fury,
 cast down to the ground;
the east wind dried it up;
 its fruit was stripped off,
its strong stem was withered;
 the fire consumed it.
¹³ Now it is transplanted into
 the wilderness,
 into a dry and thirsty land.
¹⁴ And fire has gone out from
 its stem,
 has consumed its branches
 and fruit,
so that there remains in it no
 strong stem,
 no scepter for ruling.

This is a lamentation, and it is
used as a lamentation.

Israel's Continuing Rebellion

20 In the seventh year, in the fifth month, on the tenth day of the month, certain elders of Israel came to consult the LORD, and sat down before me. ² And the word of the LORD came to me: ³ Mortal, speak to the elders of Israel, and say to them: Thus says the Lord GOD: Why are you coming? To consult me? As I live, says the Lord GOD, I will not be consulted by you. ⁴ Will you judge them, mortal, will you judge them? Then let them know the abominations of their ancestors, ⁵ and say to them: Thus says the Lord GOD: On the day when I chose Israel, I swore to the offspring of the house of Jacob — making myself known to them in the land of Egypt — I swore to them, saying, I am the LORD your God. ⁶ On that day I swore to them that I would bring them out of the land of Egypt into a land that I had searched out for them, a land flow-

Cross references

19.1 Ezek 26.17; 27.2
19.2 Nah 2.11, 12; Isa 5.29; Zech 11.3
19.3 2 Kings 23.31, 32; v. 6
19.4 2 Kings 23.33; 2 Chr 36.4
19.5 2 Kings 23.34
19.6 2 Kings 24.9; v. 3
19.7 Ezek 12.19; 30.12
19.8 2 Kings 24.2; v. 4
19.9 2 Chr 36.6; Jer 22.18; Ezek 6.2
19.10 Ps 80.8-11
19.11 Ezek 31.3; Dan 4.11
19.12 Jer 31.28; Ezek 28.17; 17.10; Hos 13.15
19.13 Hos 2.3
19.14 Ezek 15.4; Lam 4.20
20.1 Ezek 8.1,11, 12; 9.6
20.3 v. 31; Ezek 14.3; Mic 3.7
20.4 Ezek 16.2; 22.2
20.5 Ex 6.7; Deut 7.6; Ex 6.2,3; 20.2
20.6 Ex 3.8,17; Deut 8.7-9; Jer 32.22; Ps 48.2; Dan 8.9

ᵗ Heb *his widows* ᵘ Cn: Heb *in your blood*
ᵛ Heb *Its strongest stems became rulers' scepters*

ing with milk and honey, the most glorious of all lands. ⁷And I said to them, Cast away the detestable things your eyes feast on, every one of you, and do not defile yourselves with the idols of Egypt; I am the LORD your God. ⁸But they rebelled against me and would not listen to me; not one of them cast away the detestable things their eyes feasted on, nor did they forsake the idols of Egypt.

Then I thought I would pour out my wrath upon them and spend my anger against them in the midst of the land of Egypt. ⁹But I acted for the sake of my name, that it should not be profaned in the sight of the nations among whom they lived, in whose sight I made myself known to them in bringing them out of the land of Egypt. ¹⁰So I led them out of the land of Egypt and brought them into the wilderness. ¹¹I gave them my statutes and showed them my ordinances, by whose observance everyone shall live. ¹²Moreover I gave them my sabbaths, as a sign between me and them, so that they might know that I the LORD sanctify them. ¹³But the house of Israel rebelled against me in the wilderness; they did not observe my statutes but rejected my ordinances, by whose observance everyone shall live; and my sabbaths they greatly profaned.

Then I thought I would pour out my wrath upon them in the wilderness, to make an end of them. ¹⁴But I acted for the sake of my name, so that it should not be profaned in the sight of the nations, in whose sight I had brought them out. ¹⁵Moreover I swore to them in the wilderness that I would not bring them into the land that I had given them, a land flowing with milk and honey, the most glorious of all lands, ¹⁶because they rejected my ordinances and did not observe my statutes, and profaned my sabbaths; for their heart went after their idols. ¹⁷Nevertheless my eye spared them, and I did not destroy them or make an end of them in the wilderness.

18 I said to their children in the wilderness, Do not follow the statutes of your parents, nor observe their ordinances, nor defile yourselves with their idols. ¹⁹I the LORD am your God; follow my statutes, and be careful to observe my ordinances, ²⁰and hallow my sabbaths that they may be a sign between me and you, so that you may know that I the LORD am your God. ²¹But the children rebelled against me; they did not follow my statutes, and were not careful to observe my ordinances, by whose observance everyone shall live; they profaned my sabbaths.

Then I thought I would pour out my wrath upon them and spend my anger against them in the wilderness. ²²But I withheld my hand, and acted for the sake of my name, so that it should not be profaned in the sight of the nations, in whose sight I had brought them out. ²³Moreover I swore to them in the wilderness that I would scatter them among the nations and disperse them through the countries, ²⁴because they had not executed my ordinances, but had rejected my statutes and profaned my sabbaths, and their eyes were set on their ancestors' idols. ²⁵Moreover I gave them statutes that were not good and ordinances by which they could not live. ²⁶I defiled them through their very gifts, in their offering up all their firstborn, in order that I might horrify them, so that they might know that I am the LORD.

27 Therefore, mortal, speak to the house of Israel and say to them, Thus says the Lord GOD: In this again your ancestors blasphemed me, by dealing treacherously with me. ²⁸For when I had brought them into the land that I swore to give them, then wherever they saw any high hill or any leafy tree, there they offered their sacrifices and presented the provocation of their offering; there they sent up their

20.7 Ezek 18.31; Deut 29.16, 18; Ex 20.2 **20.8** Isa 63.10; Ezek 7.8 **20.9** Ex 32.12; Num 14.13ff; Ezek 36.21; 39.7 **20.10** Ex 13.18 **20.11** Deut 4.8; Lev 18.5; Rom 10.5; Gal 3.12 **20.12** Ex 31.13, 17; v. 20 **20.13** Num 14.22; Ps 78.40; 95.8-10; Prov 1.25; Num 14.29; Ps 106.23 **20.14** vv. 9,22; Ezek 36.22, 23 **20.15** Num 14.28; Ps 95.11; v. 6 **20.16** Num 15.39; Ps 78.37; Am 5.25

20.18 Deut 4.3-6; Zech 1.4; v. 7 **20.19** Ex 6.7; 20.2; Deut 5.32 **20.20** v. 12 **20.21** Num 25.1; vv. 8,13,16 **20.22** v. 17; Ps 78.38; vv. 9,14 **20.23** Lev 26.33; Deut 28.64; Ps 106.27; Jer 15.4 **20.24** vv. 13,16; Ezek 6.9 **20.25** Ps 81.12; Rom 1.24; 2 Thes 2.11 **20.26** v. 30; 2 Kings 17.17; 2 Chr 28.3; Ezek 16.20, 21; 6.7

20.27 Ezek 2.7; Rom 2.24; Ezek 18.24; 39.23,26 **20.28** Isa 57.5-7; Ezek 6.13; 16.19

pleasing odors, and there they poured out their drink offerings. ²⁹(I said to them, What is the high place to which you go? So it is called Bamahʷ to this day.) ³⁰Therefore say to the house of Israel, Thus says the Lord God: Will you defile yourselves after the manner of your ancestors and go astray after their detestable things? ³¹When you offer your gifts and make your children pass through the fire, you defile yourselves with all your idols to this day. And shall I be consulted by you, O house of Israel? As I live, says the Lord God, I will not be consulted by you.

32 What is in your mind shall never happen—the thought, "Let us be like the nations, like the tribes of the countries, and worship wood and stone."

God Will Restore Israel

33 As I live, says the Lord God, surely with a mighty hand and an outstretched arm, and with wrath poured out, I will be king over you. ³⁴I will bring you out from the peoples and gather you out of the countries where you are scattered, with a mighty hand and an outstretched arm, and with wrath poured out; ³⁵and I will bring you into the wilderness of the peoples, and there I will enter into judgment with you face to face. ³⁶As I entered into judgment with your ancestors in the wilderness of the land of Egypt, so I will enter into judgment with you, says the Lord God. ³⁷I will make you pass under the staff, and will bring you within the bond of the covenant. ³⁸I will purge out the rebels among you, and those who transgress against me; I will bring them out of the land where they reside as aliens, but they shall not enter the land of Israel. Then you shall know that I am the Lord.

39 As for you, O house of Israel, thus says the Lord God: Go serve your idols, everyone of you now and hereafter, if you will not listen to me; but my holy name you shall no more profane with your gifts and your idols.

40 For on my holy mountain, the mountain height of Israel, says the Lord God, there all the house of Israel, all of them, shall serve me in the land; there I will accept them, and there I will require your contributions and the choicest of your gifts, with all your sacred things. ⁴¹As a pleasing odor I will accept you, when I bring you out from the peoples, and gather you out of the countries where you have been scattered; and I will manifest my holiness among you in the sight of the nations. ⁴²You shall know that I am the Lord, when I bring you into the land of Israel, the country that I swore to give to your ancestors. ⁴³There you shall remember your ways and all the deeds by which you have polluted yourselves; and you shall loathe yourselves for all the evils that you have committed. ⁴⁴And you shall know that I am the Lord, when I deal with you for my name's sake, not according to your evil ways, or corrupt deeds, O house of Israel, says the Lord God.

A Prophecy against the Negeb

45ˣThe word of the Lord came to me: ⁴⁶Mortal, set your face toward the south, preach against the south, and prophesy against the forest land in the Negeb; ⁴⁷say to the forest of the Negeb, Hear the word of the Lord: Thus says the Lord God, I will kindle a fire in you, and it shall devour every green tree in you and every dry tree; the blazing flame shall not be quenched, and all faces from south to north shall be scorched by it. ⁴⁸All flesh shall see that I the Lord have kindled it; it shall not be quenched. ⁴⁹Then I said, "Ah Lord God! they are saying of me, 'Is he not a maker of allegories?' "

The Drawn Sword of God

21ʸ The word of the Lord came to me: ²Mortal, set your face toward Jerusalem and preach

20.30
v. 43;
Jer 7.26;
16.12
20.31
Ps 106.37-39;
Jer 7.31;
Ezek 16.20
20.32
Ezek 11.5;
16.16;
Jer 2.25;
44.17
20.33
Jer 21.5
20.34
v. 38;
Jer 42.18;
44.6;
Lam 2.4
20.35
Ezek 17.20
20.36
vv. 13,21;
1 Cor 10.5-10;
Deut 32.10
20.37
Lam 27.32;
Jer 33.13;
Ezek 16.60,
62
20.38
Ezek 34.17,
20; Am 9.9,
10;
Jer 44.14;
Ezek 6.7
20.39
Jer 44.25,
26; Am 4.4;
Isa 1.13;
Ezek 23.38,
39
20.40
Ezek 17.23;
Mic 4.1;
Ezek 37.22,
24; Isa 56.7;
60.7;
Mal 3.4
20.41
Eph 5.2;
Phil 4.18
20.42
Ezek 34.13;
36.24
20.43
Ezek 16.61;
Hos 5.15;
Ezek 36.31;
Zech 12.10
20.44
Ezek 24.44;
36.22
20.46
Ezek 6.2;
21.2
20.47
Jer 21.14;
17.24; 21.4
20.48
Jer 7.20;
17.27
20.49
Ezek 17.2;
Mt 13.13,14

21.2 Ezek 20.46; Am 7.16

ʷThat is *High Place* ˣCh 21.1 in Heb
ʸCh 21.6 in Heb

against the sanctuaries; prophesy against the land of Israel ³and say to the land of Israel, Thus says the LORD: I am coming against you, and will draw my sword out of its sheath, and will cut off from you both righteous and wicked. ⁴Because I will cut off from you both righteous and wicked, therefore my sword shall go out of its sheath against all flesh from south to north; ⁵and all flesh shall know that I the LORD have drawn my sword out of its sheath; it shall not be sheathed again. ⁶Moan therefore, mortal; moan with breaking heart and bitter grief before their eyes. ⁷And when they say to you, "Why do you moan?" you shall say, "Because of the news that has come. Every heart will melt and all hands will be feeble, every spirit will faint and all knees will turn to water. See, it comes and it will be fulfilled," says the Lord GOD.

8 And the word of the LORD came to me: ⁹Mortal, prophesy and say: Thus says the Lord; Say:

A sword, a sword is
 sharpened,
 it is also polished;
¹⁰ It is sharpened for slaughter,
 honed to flash like
 lightning!
How can we make merry?
 You have despised the rod,
 and all discipline.ᶻ
¹¹ The swordᵃ is given to be
 polished,
 to be grasped in the hand;
It is sharpened, the sword is
 polished,
 to be placed in the slayer's
 hand.
¹² Cry and wail, O mortal,
 for it is against my people;
it is against all Israel's
 princes;
they are thrown to the
 sword,
 together with my people.
Ah! Strike the thigh!
¹³For consider: What! If you despise the rod, will it not happen?ᶻ says the Lord GOD.
¹⁴ And you, mortal, prophesy;
 Strike hand to hand.

Let the sword fall twice,
 thrice;
 it is a sword for killing.
A sword for great slaughter—
 it surrounds them;
¹⁵ therefore hearts melt
 and many stumble.
At all their gates I have
 set
 the pointᶻ of the sword.
Ah! It is made for flashing,
 it is polishedᵇ for
 slaughter.
¹⁶ Attack to the right!
 Engage to the left!
Wherever your edge is
 directed.
¹⁷ I too will strike hand to
 hand,
 I will satisfy my fury;
 I the LORD have spoken.

18 The word of the LORD came to me: ¹⁹Mortal, mark out two roads for the sword of the king of Babylon to come; both of them shall issue from the same land. And make a signpost, make it for a fork in the road leading to a city; ²⁰mark out the road for the sword to come to Rabbah of the Ammonites or to Judah and toᶜ Jerusalem the fortified. ²¹For the king of Babylon stands at the parting of the way, at the fork in the two roads, to use divination; he shakes the arrows, he consults the teraphim,ᵈ he inspects the liver. ²²Into his right hand comes the lot for Jerusalem, to set battering rams, to call out for slaughter, for raising the battle cry, to set battering rams against the gates, to cast up ramps, to build siege-towers. ²³But to them it will seem like a false divination; they have sworn solemn oaths; but he brings their guilt to remembrance, bringing about their capture.

24 Therefore thus says the Lord GOD: Because you have brought your guilt to remembrance, in that your transgressions are uncovered, so that in all your deeds your sins

21.3
Jer 21.13;
Ezek 5.8;
vv. 9-11,19;
Job 9.22
21.4
Ezek 20.47
21.5
Ezek 20.48;
Jer 23.20;
Nah 1.9
21.6
Isa 22.4
21.7
Ezek 7.26;
Isa 13.7;
Ezek 7.17;
22.14
21.9
Deut 32.41
21.10
Isa 34.5,6;
v. 15
21.11
vv. 15,19
21.12
Jer 31.19
21.14
Num 24.10;
Ezek 6.11;
Lev 26.21,
24;
Ezek 30.24

21.15
vv. 7,10
21.17
v. 14;
Ezek 22.13;
5.13
21.19
Ezek 4.1-3;
v. 15
21.20
Jer 49.2;
Ezek 25.5;
Am 1.14
21.21
Num 23.23;
Prov 16.33;
Judg 17.5
21.22
Jer 51.14;
Ezek 4.2
21.23
Ezek 17.13,
15,16,18;
29.16

ᶻMeaning of Heb uncertain ᵃHeb *It*
ᵇTg: Heb *wrapped up* ᶜGk Syr: Heb *Judah in* ᵈOr *the household gods*

appear—because you have come
to remembrance, you shall be tak-
en in hand.ᵉ

²⁵ As for you, vile, wicked
 prince of Israel,
 you whose day has come,
 the time of final
 punishment,
²⁶ thus says the Lord GOD:
 Remove the turban, take off
 the crown;
 things shall not remain as
 they are.
 Exalt that which is low,
 abase that which is
 high.
²⁷ A ruin, a ruin, a ruin—
 I will make it!
 (Such has never occurred.)
 Until he comes whose right
 it is;
 to him I will give it.
28 As for you, mortal, prophesy,
and say, Thus says the Lord GOD
concerning the Ammonites, and
concerning their reproach; say:
 A sword, a sword! Drawn for
 slaughter
 Polished to consume,ᶠ to
 flash like lightning.
²⁹ Offering false visions for you,
 divining lies for you,
 they place you over the
 necks
 of the vile, wicked ones—
 those whose day has come,
 the time of final
 punishment.
³⁰ Return it to its sheath!
 In the place where you were
 created,
 in the land of your origin,
 I will judge you.
³¹ I will pour out my
 indignation upon you,
 with the fire of my wrath
 I will blow upon you.
 I will deliver you into brutish
 hands,
 those skillful to destroy.
³² You shall be fuel for the fire,
 your blood shall enter the
 earth;
 You shall be remembered no
 more,
 for I the LORD have spoken.

21.25
Ezek 7.2,3,
7; 35.5
21.26
Jer 13.18;
Ezek 16.12;
17.24;
Lk 1.52
21.27
Hag 2.21,
22; Ps 2.6;
Jer 23.5,6;
Ezek 34.24;
37.24
21.28
Jer 49.1;
Ezek 25.2,3;
Zeph 2.8;
Isa 31.8;
Jer 12.12
21.29
Ezek 13.6-9;
22.28; v. 25;
Ezek 35.5
21.30
Jer 47.6,7;
Ezek 16.3
21.31
Ezek 7.8;
14.19; 22.20,
21; Jer 6.22,
23; 51.20,21
21.32
Mal 4.1;
Ezek 25.10

22.2
Ezek 20.4;
24.6-9;
Nah 3.1;
Ezek 16.2;
20.4
22.3
vv. 6,27;
Ezek 23.37,
45
22.4
2 Kings 21.16;
Ezek 24.7,8;
21.25; 5.14,
15; 16.57
22.5
Isa 22.5
22.6
Isa 1.23
22.7
Deut 27.16;
Ex 22.21,22
22.8
v. 26;
Lev 19.30;
Ezek 23.38,
39
22.9
Ezek 18.6,
11,15
22.10
Lev 18.8,19;
Ezek 18.6
22.11
Ezek 18.11;
Lev 18.15;
18.9
22.12
Mic 7.2,3;
Lev 25.36;
19.13;

The Bloody City

22 The word of the LORD came
to me: ²You, mortal, will
you judge, will you judge the
bloody city? Then declare to it all
its abominable deeds. ³You shall
say, Thus says the Lord GOD: A city!
Shedding blood within itself; its
time has come; making its idols,
defiling itself. ⁴You have become
guilty by the blood that you have
shed, and defiled by the idols that
you have made; you have brought
your day near, the appointed time
of your years has come. Therefore I
have made you a disgrace before
the nations, and a mockery to all
the countries. ⁵Those who are near
and those who are far from you will
mock you, you infamous one, full
of tumult.

6 The princes of Israel in you,
everyone according to his power,
have been bent on shedding blood.
⁷Father and mother are treated
with contempt in you; the alien re-
siding within you suffers extortion;
the orphan and the widow are
wronged in you. ⁸You have de-
spised my holy things, and pro-
faned my sabbaths. ⁹In you are
those who slander to shed blood,
those in you who eat upon the
mountains, who commit lewdness
in your midst. ¹⁰In you they uncov-
er their fathers' nakedness; in you
they violate women in their men-
strual periods. ¹¹One commits
abomination with his neighbor's
wife; another lewdly defiles his
daughter-in-law; another in you
defiles his sister, his father's
daughter. ¹²In you, they take
bribes to shed blood; you take both
advance interest and accrued inter-
est, and make gain of your neigh-
bors by extortion; and you have for-
gotten me, says the Lord GOD.

13 See, I strike my hands to-
gether at the dishonest gain you
have made, and at the blood that
has been shed within you. ¹⁴Can

Jer 3.21 **22.13** Ezek 21.17; Isa 33.15;
v. 3 **22.14** Ezek 21.7; 24.14

ᵉ Or be taken captive ᶠ Cn: Heb to
contain

your courage endure, or can your hands remain strong in the days when I shall deal with you? I the LORD have spoken, and I will do it. [15]I will scatter you among the nations and disperse you through the countries, and I will purge your filthiness out of you. [16]And I[g] shall be profaned through you in the sight of the nations; and you shall know that I am the LORD.

17 The word of the LORD came to me: [18]Mortal, the house of Israel has become dross to me; all of them, silver,[h] bronze, tin, iron, and lead. In the smelter they have become dross. [19]Therefore thus says the Lord GOD: Because you have all become dross, I will gather you into the midst of Jerusalem. [20]As one gathers silver, bronze, iron, lead, and tin into a smelter, to blow the fire upon them in order to melt them; so I will gather you in my anger and in my wrath, and I will put you in and melt you. [21]I will gather you and blow upon you with the fire of my wrath, and you shall be melted within it. [22]As silver is melted in a smelter, so you shall be melted in it; and you shall know that I the LORD have poured out my wrath upon you.

23 The word of the LORD came to me: [24]Mortal, say to it: You are a land that is not cleansed, not rained upon in the day of indignation. [25]Its princes[i] within it are like a roaring lion tearing the prey; they have devoured human lives; they have taken treasure and precious things; they have made many widows within it. [26]Its priests have done violence to my teaching and have profaned my holy things; they have made no distinction between the holy and the common, neither have they taught the difference between the unclean and the clean, and they have disregarded my sabbaths, so that I am profaned among them. [27]Its officials within it are like wolves tearing the prey, shedding blood, destroying lives to get dishonest gain. [28]Its prophets have smeared whitewash on their behalf, seeing false visions and divin-

ing lies for them, saying, "Thus says the Lord GOD," when the LORD has not spoken. [29]The people of the land have practiced extortion and committed robbery; they have oppressed the poor and needy, and have extorted from the alien without redress. [30]And I sought for anyone among them who would repair the wall and stand in the breach before me on behalf of the land, so that I would not destroy it; but I found no one. [31]Therefore I have poured out my indignation upon them; I have consumed them with the fire of my wrath; I have returned their conduct upon their heads, says the Lord GOD.

Oholah and Oholibah

23 The word of the LORD came to me: [2]Mortal, there were two women, the daughters of one mother; [3]they played the whore in Egypt; they played the whore in their youth; their breasts were caressed there, and their virgin bosoms were fondled. [4]Oholah was the name of the elder and Oholibah the name of her sister. They became mine, and they bore sons and daughters. As for their names, Oholah is Samaria, and Oholibah is Jerusalem.

5 Oholah played the whore while she was mine; she lusted after her lovers the Assyrians, warriors[i] [6]clothed in blue, governors and commanders, all of them handsome young men, mounted horsemen. [7]She bestowed her favors upon them, the choicest men of Assyria all of them; and she defiled herself with all the idols of everyone for whom she lusted. [8]She did not give up her whorings that she had practiced since Egypt; for in her youth men had lain with her and fondled her virgin bosom and poured out their lust upon her. [9]Therefore I delivered her into the hands of her lovers, into the hands

2 Kings 18.9-11; Hos 11.5

Cross-references (center column):

22.15 Deut 4.27; Zech 4.17; Ezek 23.27
22.18 Isa 1.22; Jer 6.28
22.20 v. 21; Mal 3.2
22.22 Ezek 21.7; 20.8,33
22.24 Ezek 24.13; v. 31
22.25 Hos 6.9; Ps 10.9; Jer 15.8
22.26 Mal 2.8; Lev 10.10; Ezek 44.23; Hag 2.11-14; Ezek 20.12, 13; 36.20
22.27 Isa 1.23
22.28 Ezek 13.10-16; 13.6,7
22.29 Isa 5.7; Am 3.10; Ex 22.21; 23.9
22.30 Jer 5.1; Ezek 13.5; Ps 106.23
22.31 Isa 13.5; Ezek 9.10; 11.21; 16.43
23.2 Jer 3.7,8; Ezek 16.44, 46; 16.3,45
23.3 Josh 24.14; Ezek 20.8; 16.22
23.4 Ezek 16.8, 20
23.5 1 Kings 12.28-30; Ezek 16.28; Hos 8.9,10
23.6 vv. 12,23
23.7 v. 30; Ezek 16.15; 20.7; Hos 5.3; 6.10
23.8 Ex 32.4; v. 3; Ezek 16.15
23.9 v. 22; Ezek 16.37;

g Gk Syr Vg: Heb you h Transposed from the end of the verse; compare verse 20 i Gk: Heb indignation. 25A conspiracy of its prophets j Meaning of Heb uncertain

of the Assyrians, for whom she lusted. [10] These uncovered her nakedness; they seized her sons and her daughters; and they killed her with the sword. Judgment was executed upon her, and she became a byword among women.

11 Her sister Oholibah saw this, yet she was more corrupt than she in her lusting and in her whorings, which were worse than those of her sister. [12] She lusted after the Assyrians, governors and commanders, warriors[k] clothed in full armor, mounted horsemen, all of them handsome young men. [13] And I saw that she was defiled; they both took the same way. [14] But she carried her whorings further; she saw male figures carved on the wall, images of the Chaldeans portrayed in vermilion, [15] with belts around their waists, with flowing turbans on their heads, all of them looking like officers — a picture of Babylonians whose native land was Chaldea. [16] When she saw them she lusted after them, and sent messengers to them in Chaldea. [17] And the Babylonians came to her into the bed of love, and they defiled her with their lust; and after she defiled herself with them, she turned from them in disgust. [18] When she carried on her whorings so openly and flaunted her nakedness, I turned in disgust from her, as I had turned from her sister. [19] Yet she increased her whorings, remembering the days of her youth, when she played the whore in the land of Egypt [20] and lusted after her paramours there, whose members were like those of donkeys, and whose emission was like that of stallions. [21] Thus you longed for the lewdness of your youth, when the Egyptians[l] fondled your bosom and caressed[m] your young breasts.

22 Therefore, O Oholibah, thus says the Lord GOD: I will rouse against you your lovers from whom you turned in disgust, and I will bring them against you from every side: [23] the Babylonians and all the Chaldeans, Pekod and Shoa and

Koa, and all the Assyrians with them, handsome young men, governors and commanders all of them, officers and warriors,[n] all of them riding on horses. [24] They shall come against you from the north[o] with chariots and wagons and a host of peoples; they shall set themselves against you on every side with buckler, shield, and helmet, and I will commit the judgment to them, and they shall judge you according to their ordinances. [25] I will direct my indignation against you, in order that they may deal with you in fury. They shall cut off your nose and your ears, and your survivors shall fall by the sword. They shall seize your sons and your daughters, and your survivors shall be devoured by fire. [26] They shall also strip you of your clothes and take away your fine jewels. [27] So I will put an end to your lewdness and your whoring brought from the land of Egypt; you shall not long for them, or remember Egypt any more. [28] For thus says the Lord GOD: I will deliver you into the hands of those whom you hate, into the hands of those from whom you turned in disgust; [29] and they shall deal with you in hatred, and take away all the fruit of your labor, and leave you naked and bare, and the nakedness of your whorings shall be exposed. Your lewdness and your whorings [30] have brought this upon you, because you played the whore with the nations, and polluted yourself with their idols. [31] You have gone the way of your sister; therefore I will give her cup into your hand. [32] Thus says the Lord GOD:

> You shall drink your sister's cup,
>> deep and wide;
> you shall be scorned and derided,
>> it holds so much.

23.10
Ezek 16.37;
Hos 2.10;
v. 47;
Ezek 16.57
23.11
Jer 3.8-11;
Ezek 16.47
23.12
2 Kings 16.7-10;
2 Chr 28.16-23; v. 6,23
23.14
Ezek 8.10;
16.29;
Jer 22.14
23.15
Isa 22.21
23.16
v. 20
23.17
vv. 28,30
23.18
v. 10;
Jer 6.8
23.19
vv. 14,3
23.20
Ezek 16.26
23.21
v. 3
23.22
v. 28;
Ezek 16.37
23.23
Ezek 21.19;
2 Kings 24.2;
Jer 50.21;
vv. 6,12

23.24
Ezek 21.15,
19; Jer 47.3;
Ezek 16.40;
Jer 39.5,6
23.25
Ezek 8.17,
18;
Zeph 1.18;
v. 47;
Ezek 20.47,
48; 22.20,21
23.26
Ezek 16.39
23.27
Ezek 16.41;
22.15; vv. 3,
19
23.28
Ezek 16.37
23.29
v. 26;
Ezek 16.39
23.30
vv. 7,17;
Jer 2.18-20;
Ezek 6.9
23.32
Isa 51.17;
Jer 25.15;
Ezek 22.4,5

k Meaning of Heb uncertain l Two Mss: MT *from Egypt* m Cn: Heb *for the sake of* n Compare verses 6 and 12: Heb *officers and called ones* o Gk: Meaning of Heb uncertain

33 You shall be filled with
　　　drunkenness and
　　　sorrow.
　　A cup of horror and
　　　desolation
　　is the cup of your sister
　　　Samaria;
34 you shall drink it and drain
　　　it out,
　　and gnaw its sherds,
　　and tear out your breasts;
for I have spoken, says the Lord
GOD. 35 Therefore thus says the
Lord GOD: Because you have forgotten me and cast me behind your
back, therefore bear the consequences of your lewdness and
whorings.

36 The LORD said to me: Mortal,
will you judge Oholah and Oholibah? Then declare to them their
abominable deeds. 37 For they have
committed adultery, and blood is
on their hands; with their idols
they have committed adultery; and
they have even offered up to them
for food the children whom they
had borne to me. 38 Moreover this
they have done to me: they have
defiled my sanctuary on the same
day and profaned my sabbaths.
39 For when they had slaughtered
their children for their idols, on the
same day they came into my sanctuary to profane it. This is what
they did in my house.

40 They even sent for men to
come from far away, to whom a
messenger was sent, and they
came. For them you bathed yourself, painted your eyes, and decked
yourself with ornaments; 41 you sat
on a stately couch, with a table
spread before it on which you had
placed my incense and my oil.
42 The sound of a raucous multitude was around her, with many of
the rabble brought in drunken from
the wilderness; and they put bracelets on the arms[p] of the women,
and beautiful crowns upon their
heads.

43 Then I said, Ah, she is worn
out with adulteries, but they carry
on their sexual acts with her. 44 For
they have gone in to her, as one
goes in to a whore. Thus they went

in to Oholah and to Oholibah, wanton women. 45 But righteous judges
shall declare them guilty of adultery and of bloodshed; because
they are adulteresses and blood is
on their hands.

46 For thus says the Lord GOD:
Bring up an assembly against
them, and make them an object of
terror and of plunder. 47 The assembly shall stone them and with their
swords they shall cut them down;
they shall kill their sons and their
daughters, and burn up their
houses. 48 Thus will I put an end to
lewdness in the land, so that all
women may take warning and not
commit lewdness as you have
done. 49 They shall repay you for
your lewdness, and you shall bear
the penalty for your sinful idolatry;
and you shall know that I am the
Lord GOD.

The Boiling Pot

24 In the ninth year, in the
tenth month, on the tenth
day of the month, the word of the
LORD came to me: 2 Mortal, write
down the name of this day, this
very day. The king of Babylon has
laid siege to Jerusalem this very
day. 3 And utter an allegory to the
rebellious house and say to them,
Thus says the Lord GOD:
　　Set on the pot, set it on,
　　　pour in water also;
4 put in it the pieces,
　　all the good pieces, the
　　　thigh and the shoulder;
　　fill it with choice bones.
5 Take the choicest one of the
　　　flock,
　　pile the logs[q] under it;
　　boil its pieces,[r]
　　seethe[s] also its bones in
　　　it.

6 Therefore thus says the Lord
GOD:
　　Woe to the bloody city,
　　　the pot whose rust is in it,

23.33
Jer 25.15,
16,27;
Ezek 4.16
23.34
Ps 75.8;
Isa 51.17
23.35
Jer 3.21;
Hos 8.14;
1 Kings 14.9;
Neh 9.26
23.36
Ezek 20.4;
22.2;
Isa 58.1
23.37
vv. 3,45;
Ezek 16.20,
21,36,45
23.38
Ezek 5.11;
7.20; 22.8
23.39
2 Kings 21.4
23.40
Isa 57.9;
2 Kings 9.30;
Jer 4.30;
Ezek 16.13-16
23.41
Esther 1.6;
Am 6.4;
Prov 7.17;
Hos 2.8
23.42
Ezek 16.49;
Jer 51.7;
Ezek 16.11,
12
23.45
Ezek 16.38;
Hos 6.5;
Lev 20.10
23.46
v. 24;
Ezek 16.40;
Jer 15.4;
24.9; 29.18
23.47
Ezek 16.40;
2 Chr 36.17,
19;
Ezek 24.21;
Jer 39.8
23.48
v. 27;
Ezek 22.15;
2 Pet 2.6
23.49
v. 35;
Ezek 6.7;
20.38,42,44
24.1
Ezek 1.2;
8.1; 20.1;
26.1
24.2
Isa 8.1;
2 Kings 25.1;
Jer 39.1;
52.4
24.3
Ezek 17.2;
Jer 1.13;
Ezek 11.3

24.4 Ezek 22.19-22; Mic 3.2,3　24.5 v. 10
24.6 v. 9; Ezek 22.3; Mic 7.2; Joel 3.3;
Nah 3.10

p Heb hands　q Compare verse 10: Heb the
bones　r Two Mss: Heb its boilings
s Cn: Heb its bones seethe

whose rust has not gone
 out of it!
Empty it piece by piece,
 making no choice at all.ᵗ
⁷ For the blood she shed is
 inside it;
 she placed it on a bare
 rock;
 she did not pour it out on
 the ground,
 to cover it with earth.
⁸ To rouse my wrath, to take
 vengeance,
 I have placed the blood she
 shed
 on a bare rock,
 so that it may not be
 covered.
⁹ Therefore thus says the Lord GOD:
 Woe to the bloody city!
 I will even make the pile
 great.
¹⁰ Heap up the logs, kindle the
 fire;
 boil the meat well, mix in
 the spices,
 let the bones be burned.
¹¹ Stand it empty upon the
 coals,
 so that it may become hot,
 its copper glow,
 its filth melt in it, its rust
 be consumed.
¹² In vain I have wearied
 myself;ᵘ
 its thick rust does not
 depart.
 To the fire with its rust!ᵛ
¹³ Yet, when I cleansed you in
 your filthy lewdness,
 you did not become clean
 from your filth;
 you shall not again be
 cleansed
 until I have satisfied my
 fury upon you.
¹⁴ I the LORD have spoken; the time
is coming, I will act. I will not re-
frain, I will not spare, I will not re-
lent. According to your ways and
your doings I will judge you, says
the Lord GOD.

Ezekiel's Bereavement

15 The word of the LORD came to
me: ¹⁶ Mortal, with one blow I am
about to take away from you the
delight of your eyes; yet you shall
not mourn or weep, nor shall your
tears run down. ¹⁷ Sigh, but not
aloud; make no mourning for the
dead. Bind on your turban, and put
your sandals on your feet; do not
cover your upper lip or eat the
bread of mourners.ʷ ¹⁸ So I spoke
to the people in the morning, and
at evening my wife died. And on the
next morning I did as I was com-
manded.

19 Then the people said to me,
"Will you not tell us what these
things mean for us, that you are
acting this way?" ²⁰ Then I said to
them: The word of the LORD came
to me: ²¹ Say to the house of Israel,
Thus says the Lord GOD: I will pro-
fane my sanctuary, the pride of
your power, the delight of your
eyes, and your heart's desire; and
your sons and your daughters
whom you left behind shall fall by
the sword. ²² And you shall do as I
have done; you shall not cover your
upper lip or eat the bread of
mourners.ʷ ²³ Your turbans shall
be on your heads and your sandals
on your feet; you shall not mourn
or weep, but you shall pine away in
your iniquities and groan to one
another. ²⁴ Thus Ezekiel shall be a
sign to you; you shall do just as he
has done. When this comes, then
you shall know that I am the Lord
GOD.

25 And you, mortal, on the day
when I take from them their strong-
hold, their joy and glory, the de-
light of their eyes and their heart's
affection, and alsoˣ their sons and
their daughters, ²⁶ on that day, one
who has escaped will come to you
to report to you the news. ²⁷ On
that day your mouth shall be
opened to the one who has es-
caped, and you shall speak and no
longer be silent. So you shall be a
sign to them; and they shall know
that I am the LORD.

24.7
Ezek 23.37,
45;
Lev 17.13;
Deut 12.16
24.8
Mt 7.2
24.9
v. 6;
Nah 3.1;
Hab 2.12
24.10
v. 5
24.11
Ezek 21.10;
22.15
24.13
Jer 6.28-30;
Ezek 22.24;
5.13; 8.18;
16.42
24.14
1 Sam 15.29;
Isa 55.11;
Ezek 9.10;
18.30; 36.19
24.16
Job 23.2;
Jer 16.5;
22.10; 13.17
24.17
Jer 16.5-7;
2 Sam 15.30;
Mic 3.7
24.19
Ezek 12.9;
37.18
24.21
Jer 7.14;
Ps 27.4;
Jer 6.11;
Ezek 23.47
24.22
Jer 16.6,7;
v. 17
24.23
Job 27.15;
Ps 78.64;
Ezek 33.10
24.24
Ezek 4.3;
12.6,11;
Jer 17.15;
Ezek 6.7;
25.5
24.25
Jer 11.22
24.26
Ezek 33.21f
24.27
Ezek 3.26,
27; 33.22;
v. 24

ᵗ Heb *piece, no lot has fallen on it*
ᵘ Cn: Meaning of Heb uncertain ᵛ Meaning
of Heb uncertain ʷ Vg Tg: Heb *of men*
ˣ Heb lacks *and also*

Proclamation against Ammon

25 The word of the LORD came to me: [2] Mortal, set your face toward the Ammonites and prophesy against them. [3] Say to the Ammonites, Hear the word of the Lord GOD: Thus says the Lord GOD, Because you said, "Aha!" over my sanctuary when it was profaned, and over the land of Israel when it was made desolate, and over the house of Judah when it went into exile; [4] therefore I am handing you over to the people of the East for a possession. They shall set their encampments among you and pitch their tents in your midst; they shall eat your fruit, and they shall drink your milk. [5] I will make Rabbah a pasture for camels and Ammon a fold for flocks. Then you shall know that I am the LORD. [6] For thus says the Lord GOD: Because you have clapped your hands and stamped your feet and rejoiced with all the malice within you against the land of Israel, [7] therefore I have stretched out my hand against you, and will hand you over as plunder to the nations. I will cut you off from the peoples and will make you perish out of the countries; I will destroy you. Then you shall know that I am the LORD.

Proclamation against Moab

8 Thus says the Lord GOD: Because Moab[y] said, The house of Judah is like all the other nations, [9] therefore I will lay open the flank of Moab from the towns[z] on its frontier, the glory of the country, Beth-jeshimoth, Baal-meon, and Kiriathaim. [10] I will give it along with Ammon to the people of the East as a possession. Thus Ammon shall be remembered no more among the nations, [11] and I will execute judgments upon Moab. Then they shall know that I am the LORD.

Proclamation against Edom

12 Thus says the Lord GOD: Because Edom acted revengefully against the house of Judah and has grievously offended in taking vengeance upon them, [13] therefore

thus says the Lord GOD, I will stretch out my hand against Edom, and cut off from it humans and animals, and I will make it desolate; from Teman even to Dedan they shall fall by the sword. [14] I will lay my vengeance upon Edom by the hand of my people Israel; and they shall act in Edom according to my anger and according to my wrath; and they shall know my vengeance, says the Lord GOD.

Proclamation against Philistia

15 Thus says the Lord GOD: Because with unending hostilities the Philistines acted in vengeance, and with malice of heart took revenge in destruction; [16] therefore thus says the Lord GOD, I will stretch out my hand against the Philistines, cut off the Cherethites, and destroy the rest of the seacoast. [17] I will execute great vengeance on them with wrathful punishments. Then they shall know that I am the LORD, when I lay my vengeance on them.

Proclamation against Tyre

26 In the eleventh year, on the first day of the month, the word of the LORD came to me: [2] Mortal, because Tyre said concerning Jerusalem,
"Aha, broken is the gateway
 of the peoples;
 it has swung open to me;
I shall be replenished,
 now that it is wasted."
[3] Therefore, thus says the Lord GOD:
See, I am against you,
 O Tyre!
I will hurl many nations
 against you,
 as the sea hurls its waves.
[4] They shall destroy the walls
 of Tyre
 and break down its towers.
I will scrape its soil from it
 and make it a bare rock.
[5] It shall become, in the midst
 of the sea,
 a place for spreading nets.
I have spoken, says the Lord GOD.

Cross-references (center column):

25.2
Jer 27.3;
Ezek 21.28;
Am 1.13;
Zeph 2.8,9
25.3
Prov 17.5;
Ezek 26.2
25.4
Ezek 21.31
25.5
Ezek 21.20;
Isa 17.2;
Zeph 2.14
25.6
Job 27.23;
Lam 2.15;
Zeph 2.8,10
25.7
Ezek 26.5;
Am 1.14,15;
Ezek 6.14
25.8
Isa chs. 15,
16; Jer 48.1;
Am 2.1;
Ezek 35.2,5
25.9
Num 33.49;
32.3,38;
32.37
25.10
v. 4;
Ezek 21.32
25.11
Ezek 5.15;
11.9
25.12
Lam 4.21,
22;
Ezek 35.2;
Am 1.11;
Ob 10-16
25.13
Am 1.12;
Jer 25.23

25.14
Isa 11.14;
Jer 49.2
25.15
Jer 25.20;
Isa 14.29-31;
Joel 3.4;
2 Chr 28.18
25.16
Zeph 2.4,5;
1 Sam 30.14;
Jer 47.1-7
25.17
Ezek 5.15;
Ps 9.16
26.2
Isa ch. 23;
Jer 25.22;
Ezek 25.3;
36.2
26.3
Mic 4.11;
Isa 5.30;
Jer 50.42
26.4
Am 1.10
26.5
Ezek 27.32;
29.19

It shall become plunder for
 the nations,
6 and its daughter-towns in
 the country
shall be killed by the
 sword.
Then they shall know that I am the
Lord.

7 For thus says the Lord God: I
will bring against Tyre from the
north King Nebuchadrezzar of Babylon, king of kings, together with
horses, chariots, cavalry, and a
great and powerful army.
8 Your daughter-towns in the
 country
 he shall put to the sword.
He shall set up a siege-wall
 against you,
 cast up a ramp against you,
and raise a roof of shields
 against you.
9 He shall direct the shock of
 his battering rams
 against your walls
and break down your
 towers with his axes.
10 His horses shall be so many
 that their dust shall cover
 you.
At the noise of cavalry,
 wheels, and chariots
your very walls shall shake,
when he enters your gates
 like those entering a
 breached city.
11 With the hoofs of his horses
 he shall trample all your
 streets.
He shall put your people to
 the sword,
 and your strong pillars
shall fall to the ground.
12 They will plunder your riches
 and loot your merchandise.
they shall break down your
 walls
and destroy your fine
 houses.
Your stones and timber and
 soil
 they shall cast into the
 water.
13 I will silence the music of
 your songs;
the sound of your lyres
 shall be heard no more.

14 I will make you a bare rock;
 you shall be a place for
 spreading nets.
You shall never again be
 rebuilt,
for I the Lord have spoken,
 says the Lord God.

15 Thus says the Lord God to
Tyre: Shall not the coastlands
shake at the sound of your fall,
when the wounded groan, when
slaughter goes on within you?
16 Then all the princes of the sea
shall step down from their thrones;
they shall remove their robes and
strip off their embroidered garments. They shall clothe themselves with trembling, and shall sit
on the ground; they shall tremble
every moment, and be appalled at
you. 17 And they shall raise a lamentation over you, and say to you:
 How you have vanished[a]
 from the seas,
 O city renowned,
once mighty on the sea,
 you and your inhabitants,[b]
who imposed your[c] terror
 on all the mainland![d]
18 Now the coastlands tremble
 on the day of your fall;
the coastlands by the sea
 are dismayed at your
 passing.

19 For thus says the Lord God:
When I make you a city laid waste,
like cities that are not inhabited,
when I bring up the deep over you,
and the great waters cover you,
20 then I will thrust you down with
those who descend into the Pit, to
the people of long ago, and I will
make you live in the world below,
among primeval ruins, with those
who go down to the Pit, so that you
will not be inhabited or have a
place[e] in the land of the living. 21 I
will bring you to a dreadful end,
and you shall be no more; though
sought for, you will never be found
again, says the Lord God.

[a] Gk OL Aquila: Heb *have vanished,
O inhabited one,* [b] Heb *it and its
inhabitants* [c] Heb *their* [d] Cn: Heb *its
inhabitants* [e] Gk: Heb *I will give beauty*

26.6
Ezek 25.5
26.7
Jer 27.3-6;
Ezra 7.12;
Dan 2.37;
Ezek 23.24
26.8
v. 6;
Ezek 21.22;
Jer 6.6;
32.24
26.9
Ezek 21.22
26.10
Jer 4.13;
39.3;
Ezek 27.28
26.11
Hab 1.8;
Isa 26.5;
Jer 43.13
26.12
v. 5
26.13
Isa 14.11;
25.10;
Isa 23.16;
Rev 18.22

26.14
vv. 4,5;
Mal 1.4;
Isa 14.27
26.15
v. 18;
Ezek 31.16
26.16
Ezek 27.35;
Jon 3.6;
Job 2.13
26.17
Ezek 27.32;
Rev 18.9;
Isa 23.4;
Ezek 28.2
26.18
v. 15
26.20
Ezek 32.18,
24; Am 9.2;
Jer 33.9
26.21
Ezek 27.36;
28.19; v. 14

Lamentation over Tyre

27 The word of the LORD came to me: [2] Now you, mortal, raise a lamentation over Tyre, [3] and say to Tyre, which sits at the entrance to the sea, merchant of the peoples on many coastlands, Thus says the Lord GOD:

O Tyre, you have said,
"I am perfect in beauty."
[4] Your borders are in the heart
of the seas;
your builders made perfect
your beauty.
[5] They made all your planks
of fir trees from Senir;
they took a cedar from
Lebanon
to make a mast for you.
[6] From oaks of Bashan
they made your oars;
they made your deck of
pines[f]
from the coasts of Cyprus,
inlaid with ivory.
[7] Of fine embroidered linen
from Egypt
was your sail,
serving as your ensign;
blue and purple from the
coasts of Elishah
was your awning.
[8] The inhabitants of Sidon and
Arvad
were your rowers;
skilled men of Zemer[g] were
within you,
they were your pilots.
[9] The elders of Gebal and its
artisans were within
you,
caulking your seams;
all the ships of the sea with
their mariners were
within you,
to barter for your wares.
[10] Paras[h] and Lud and Put
were in your army,
your mighty warriors;
they hung shield and helmet
in you;
they gave you splendor.
[11] Men of Arvad and Helech[i]
were on your walls all
around;

men of Gamad were at
your towers.
They hung their quivers all
around your walls;
they made perfect your
beauty.
[12] Tarshish did business with you out of the abundance of your great wealth; silver, iron, tin, and lead they exchanged for your wares. [13] Javan, Tubal, and Meshech traded with you; they exchanged human beings and vessels of bronze for your merchandise. [14] Beth-togarmah exchanged for your wares horses, war horses, and mules. [15] The Rhodians[j] traded with you; many coastlands were your own special markets; they brought you in payment ivory tusks and ebony. [16] Edom[k] did business with you because of your abundant goods; they exchanged for your wares turquoise, purple, embroidered work, fine linen, coral, and rubies. [17] Judah and the land of Israel traded with you; they exchanged for your merchandise wheat from Minneth, millet,[l] honey, oil, and balm. [18] Damascus traded with you for your abundant goods — because of your great wealth of every kind — wine of Helbon, and white wool. [19] Vedan and Javan from Uzal[l] entered into trade for your wares; wrought iron, cassia, and sweet cane were bartered for your merchandise. [20] Dedan traded with you in saddlecloths for riding. [21] Arabia and all the princes of Kedar were your favored dealers in lambs, rams, and goats; in these they did business with you. [22] The merchants of Sheba and Raamah traded with you; they exchanged for your wares the best of all kinds of spices, and all precious stones, and gold. [23] Haran, Canneh, Eden, the merchants of Sheba, Asshur, and Chilmad traded with you. [24] These traded with you in choice garments, in clothes of

27.2 Ezek 28.12
27.3 Ezek 28.2; v. 33;
Ezek 28.12
27.4 vv. 25-27
27.5 Deut 3.9
27.6 Zech 11.2; Isa 2.13; Jer 2.10
27.8 1 Kings 9.27
27.9 1 Kings 5.18; v. 27
27.10 Ezek 30.5; 38.5; v. 11
27.11 vv. 3,8,10
27.12 2 Chr 20.36; Isa 23.6,10; vv. 18,33
27.13 Gen 10.2; Isa 66.19; Ezek 38.2; Joel 3.3; Rev 18.13
27.14 Gen 10.3; Ezek 38.6
27.15 Gen 10.7; Rev 18.12
27.16 Ezek 28.13; 16.13,18
27.17 Judg 11.33; Jer 8.22
27.18 Jer 49.23; Ezek 47.16-18; vv. 12,33
27.20 v. 15
27.21 Jer 25.24; 49.28; Isa 60.7
27.22 Gen 10.7; 1 Kings 10.1, 2; Isa 60.6
27.23 Gen 11.31; 2 Kings 19.12; Am 1.5

f Or boxwood g Cn Compare Gen 10.18: Heb your skilled men, O Tyre h Or Persia i Or and your army j Gk: Heb The Dedanites k Another reading is Aram l Meaning of Heb uncertain

blue and embroidered work, and in carpets of colored material, bound with cords and made secure; in these they traded with you. ^m 25 The ships of Tarshish traveled for you in your trade.

So you were filled and
 heavily laden
in the heart of the seas.
26 Your rowers have brought
 you
 into the high seas.
The east wind has wrecked
 you
 in the heart of the seas.
27 Your riches, your wares, your
 merchandise,
 your mariners and your
 pilots,
 your caulkers, your dealers in
 merchandise,
 and all your warriors within
 you,
with all the company
 that is with you,
sink into the heart of the
 seas
 on the day of your ruin.
28 At the sound of the cry of
 your pilots
 the countryside shakes,
29 and down from their ships
 come all that handle the
 oar.
The mariners and all the
 pilots of the sea
 stand on the shore
30 and wail aloud over you,
 and cry bitterly.
They throw dust on their
 heads
 and wallow in ashes;
31 they make themselves bald
 for you,
 and put on sackcloth,
and they weep over you in
 bitterness of soul,
 with bitter mourning.
32 In their wailing they raise a
 lamentation for you,
 and lament over you:
"Who was ever destroyed^n
 like Tyre
 in the midst of the sea?
33 When your wares came from
 the seas,
 you satisfied many peoples;

with your abundant wealth
 and merchandise
 you enriched the kings of
 the earth.
34 Now you are wrecked by the
 seas,
 in the depths of the waters;
your merchandise and all
 your crew
 have sunk with you.
35 All the inhabitants of the
 coastlands
 are appalled at you;
and their kings are horribly
 afraid,
 their faces are convulsed.
36 The merchants among the
 peoples hiss at you;
you have come to a
 dreadful end
and shall be no more
 forever.

Proclamation against the King of Tyre

28 The word of the Lord came
 to me: 2 Mortal, say to the
prince of Tyre, Thus says the Lord
God:
 Because your heart is proud
 and you have said, "I am a
 god;
 I sit in the seat of the gods,
 in the heart of the seas,"
 yet you are but a mortal, and
 no god,
 though you compare your
 mind
 with the mind of a god.
3 You are indeed wiser than
 Daniel;^o
 no secret is hidden from
 you;
4 by your wisdom and your
 understanding
 you have amassed wealth
 for yourself,
 and have gathered gold and
 silver
 into your treasuries.
5 By your great wisdom in
 trade
 you have increased your
 wealth,

27.25 Isa 2.16; 23.14; v. 4
27.26 Ezek 26.19; Ps 48.7; vv. 4,25,27
27.27 Prov 11.4; Rev 18.9-19
27.28 Ezek 26.15
27.29 Rev 18.17-19
27.30 Job 2.12; Rev 18.19; Esther 4.1, 3; Jer 6.26
27.31 Jer 16.6; Ezek 29.18; Isa 22.12; 16.9
27.32 v. 2; Ezek 26.17; Rev 18.18
27.33 Rev 18.19

27.34 vv. 26,27; Ezek 26.19; Zech 9.3,4
27.35 Ezek 26.15, 16; 32.10
27.36 Jer 18.16; Zeph 2.15; Ezek 26.21; Ps 37.10,36
28.2 Ezek 27.25-27; Isa 31.3; v. 6
28.3 Dan 1.20
28.4 Ezek 27.33
28.5 Ps 62.10; Zech 9.3; Hos 13.6

^m Cn: Heb *in your market* ^n Tg Vg: Heb *like silence* ^o Or, as otherwise read, *Danel*

and your heart has become
 proud in your wealth.
6 Therefore thus says the Lord
 GOD:
 Because you compare your
 mind
 with the mind of a god,
7 therefore, I will bring
 strangers against you,
 the most terrible of the
 nations;
 they shall draw their swords
 against the beauty of
 your wisdom
 and defile your splendor.
8 They shall thrust you down
 to the Pit,
 and you shall die a violent
 death
 in the heart of the seas.
9 Will you still say, "I am a
 god,"
 in the presence of those
 who kill you,
 though you are but a mortal,
 and no god,
 in the hands of those who
 wound you?
10 You shall die the death of
 the uncircumcised
 by the hand of foreigners;
 for I have spoken, says the
 Lord GOD.

Lamentation over the King of Tyre

11 Moreover the word of the
LORD came to me: 12 Mortal, raise a
lamentation over the king of Tyre,
and say to him, Thus says the Lord
GOD:
 You were the signet of
 perfection, P
 full of wisdom
 and perfect in beauty.
13 You were in Eden, the
 garden of God;
 every precious stone was
 your covering,
 carnelian, chrysolite, and
 moonstone,
 beryl, onyx, and jasper,
 sapphire, q turquoise, and
 emerald;
 and worked in gold were
 your settings
 and your engravings. P

Cross references (center column)

28.6
v. 2
28.7
Ezek 26.7;
30.11; 31.12;
32.12; v. 17
28.8
Ezek 32.30;
27.26,27,34
28.9
v. 2
28.10
Ezek 31.18;
32.19,21,25,
27
28.12
Ezek 27.2;
v. 3;
Ezek 27.3
28.13
Ezek 31.8,9;
36.35

28.14
Ex 25.20;
v. 16;
Ezek 20.40;
Rev 18.16
28.15
Ezek 27.3,4;
Isa 14.12;
vv. 17,18
28.16
Ezek 27.12ff;
8.17;
Gen 3.24;
v. 14
28.17
vv. 2,5;
Ezek 31.10;
27.3,4; 26.16
28.18
v. 16;
Am 1.9,10;
Mal 4.3
28.19
Ezek 26.21;
27.36;
Jer 51.64

 On the day that you were
 created
 they were prepared.
14 With an anointed cherub as
 guardian I placed you; P
 you were on the holy
 mountain of God;
 you walked among the
 stones of fire.
15 You were blameless in your
 ways
 from the day that you were
 created,
 until iniquity was found in
 you.
16 In the abundance of your
 trade
 you were filled with
 violence, and you
 sinned;
 so I cast you as a profane
 thing from the
 mountain of God,
 and the guardian cherub
 drove you out
 from among the stones of
 fire.
17 Your heart was proud
 because of your beauty;
 you corrupted your wisdom
 for the sake of your
 splendor.
 I cast you to the ground;
 I exposed you before kings,
 to feast their eyes on
 you
18 By the multitude of your
 iniquities,
 in the unrighteousness of
 your trade,
 you profaned your
 sanctuaries.
 So I brought out fire from
 within you;
 it consumed you,
 and I turned you to ashes on
 the earth
 in the sight of all who saw
 you.
19 All who know you among the
 peoples
 are appalled at you;
 you have come to a dreadful
 end

P Meaning of Heb uncertain q Or lapis
lazuli

and shall be no more forever.

Proclamation against Sidon

20 The word of the LORD came to me: 21 Mortal, set your face toward Sidon, and prophesy against it, 22 and say, Thus says the Lord GOD:

I am against you, O Sidon,
 and I will gain glory in your midst.
They shall know that I am the LORD
 when I execute judgments in it,
 and manifest my holiness in it;
23 for I will send pestilence into it,
 and bloodshed into its streets;
 and the dead shall fall in its midst,
 by the sword that is against it on every side.
And they shall know that I am the LORD.

24 The house of Israel shall no longer find a pricking brier or a piercing thorn among all their neighbors who have treated them with contempt. And they shall know that I am the Lord GOD.

Future Blessing for Israel

25 Thus says the Lord GOD: When I gather the house of Israel from the peoples among whom they are scattered, and manifest my holiness in them in the sight of the nations, then they shall settle on their own soil that I gave to my servant Jacob. 26 They shall live in safety in it, and shall build houses and plant vineyards. They shall live in safety, when I execute judgments upon all their neighbors who have treated them with contempt. And they shall know that I am the LORD their God.

Proclamation against Egypt

29 In the tenth year, in the tenth month, on the twelfth day of the month, the word of the LORD came to me: 2 Mortal, set your face against Pharaoh king of Egypt, and prophesy against him

and against all Egypt; 3 speak, and say, Thus says the Lord GOD:

I am against you,
 Pharaoh king of Egypt,
the great dragon sprawling
 in the midst of its channels,
saying, "My Nile is my own;
 I made it for myself."
4 I will put hooks in your jaws,
 and make the fish of your channels stick to your scales.
I will draw you up from your channels,
 with all the fish of your channels
 sticking to your scales.
5 I will fling you into the wilderness,
 you and all the fish of your channels;
you shall fall in the open field,
 and not be gathered and buried.
To the animals of the earth
 and to the birds of the air
I have given you as food.
6 Then all the inhabitants of Egypt shall know
 that I am the LORD
because you[r] were a staff of reed
 to the house of Israel;
7 when they grasped you with the hand, you broke,
 and tore all their shoulders;
and when they leaned on you, you broke,
 and made all their legs unsteady.[s]

8 Therefore, thus says the Lord GOD: I will bring a sword upon you, and will cut off from you human being and animal; 9 and the land of Egypt shall be a desolation and a waste. Then they shall know that I am the LORD.

Because you[t] said, "The Nile is mine, and I made it," 10 therefore, I am against you, and against your

28.21 Ezek 6.2; 25.2; Isa 23.4,12; Ezek 32.30
28.22 Ezek 26.3; 39.13; Ps 9.16; v. 26; Ezek 38.16
28.23 Ezek 38.22; Jer 51.52; vv. 24,26
28.24 Num 33.55; Josh 23.13; Isa 55.13; Ezek 25.6; 36.5
28.25 Isa 11.12; Jer 32.37; Ezek 20.41; Jer 23.8; 27.11; Ezek 37.25
28.26 Jer 23.6; Isa 65.21; Am 9.13,14
29.2 Ezek 28.21; Jer 44.30; Isa 19.1; Jer 25.19; 46.2,25

29.3 Jer 44.30; Ezek 28.22; Isa 27.1; 51.9; Ezek 32.2
29.4 2 Kings 19.28; Isa 37.29; Ezek 38.4
29.5 Ezek 32.4-6; Jer 7.33; 34.20; Ezek 39.4
29.6 Isa 36.6
29.7 Jer 37.5-11; Ezek 17.17
29.8 Ezek 14.17; 32.11-13
29.9 vv. 10-12,6, 3
29.10 Ezek 30.12, 6

[r] Gk Syr Vg: Heb *they* [s] Syr: Heb *stand*
[t] Gk Syr Vg: Heb *he*

channels, and I will make the land of Egypt an utter waste and desolation, from Migdol to Syene, as far as the border of Ethiopia.ᵘ ¹¹No human foot shall pass through it, and no animal foot shall pass through it; it shall be uninhabited forty years. ¹²I will make the land of Egypt a desolation among desolated countries; and her cities shall be a desolation forty years among cities that are laid waste. I will scatter the Egyptians among the nations, and disperse them among the countries.

13 Further, thus says the Lord GOD: At the end of forty years I will gather the Egyptians from the peoples among whom they were scattered; ¹⁴and I will restore the fortunes of Egypt, and bring them back to the land of Pathros, the land of their origin; and there they shall be a lowly kingdom. ¹⁵It shall be the most lowly of the kingdoms, and never again exalt itself above the nations; and I will make them so small that they will never again rule over the nations. ¹⁶The Egyptiansᵛ shall never again be the reliance of the house of Israel; they will recall their iniquity, when they turned to them for aid. Then they shall know that I am the Lord GOD.

Babylonia Will Plunder Egypt

17 In the twenty-seventh year, in the first month, on the first day of the month, the word of the LORD came to me: ¹⁸Mortal, King Nebuchadrezzar of Babylon made his army labor hard against Tyre; every head was made bald and every shoulder was rubbed bare; yet neither he nor his army got anything from Tyre to pay for the labor that he had expended against it. ¹⁹Therefore thus says the Lord GOD: I will give the land of Egypt to King Nebuchadrezzar of Babylon; and he shall carry off its wealth and despoil it and plunder it; and it shall be the wages for his army. ²⁰I have given him the land of Egypt as his payment for which he labored, because they worked for me, says the Lord GOD.

29.11
Jer 43.11,
12;
Ezek 32.13
29.12
Ezek 30.7,
26
29.13
Isa 19.22,
23;
Jer 46.26
29.14
Ezek 30.14;
17.6,14
29.15
v. 14;
Zech 10.11
29.16
Isa 30.2,3;
36.4,6;
Jer 14.10;
Hos 8.13;
vv. 6,9,21
29.18
Jer 27.6;
Ezek 26.7,8;
27.31
29.19
Ezek 30.10;
Jer 43.10-13;
Ezek 30.4
29.20
Isa 45.1-3;
Jer 25.9

29.21
Ps 132.17;
Ezek 24.27;
33.22;
Lk 21.15;
Ezek 6.7;
v. 6
30.2
Isa 13.6;
Ezek 21.12;
Joel 1.5,11,
13
30.3
Ezek 7.7,12;
Joel 2.1;
Ob 15;
Zeph 1.7;
v. 18
30.4
vv. 11,5,9;
Ezek 29.19
30.5
Jer 25.20,24
30.6
Isa 20.3-6;
Ezek 29.10
30.7
Ezek 29.12
30.8
Ezek 29.6;
9.16; vv. 14,
16,5,6
30.9
Isa 18.1,2;
Ezek 38.11;
32.9,10

21 On that day I will cause a horn to sprout up for the house of Israel, and I will open your lips among them. Then they shall know that I am the LORD.

Lamentation for Egypt

30 The word of the LORD came to me: ²Mortal, prophesy, and say, Thus says the Lord GOD:
Wail, "Alas for the day!"
³ For a day is near,
 the day of the LORD is near;
 it will be a day of clouds,
 a time of doomʷ for the
 nations.
⁴ A sword shall come upon
 Egypt,
 and anguish shall be in
 Ethiopia,ᵘ
 when the slain fall in Egypt,
 and its wealth is carried
 away,
 and its foundations are
 torn down.
⁵Ethiopia,ᵘ and Put, and Lud, and all Arabia, and Libya,ˣ and the people of the allied landʸ shall fall with them by the sword.

⁶ Thus says the LORD:
 Those who support Egypt
 shall fall,
 and its proud might shall
 come down;
 from Migdol to Syene
 they shall fall within it by
 the sword,
 says the Lord GOD.
⁷ They shall be desolated
 among other desolated
 countries,
 and their cities shall lie
 among cities laid waste.
⁸ Then they shall know that I
 am the LORD,
 when I have set fire to
 Egypt,
 and all who help it are
 broken.
9 On that day, messengers shall go out from me in ships to terrify the unsuspecting Ethiopians;ᶻ and

ᵘOr Nubia; Heb Cush ᵛHeb It
ʷHeb lacks of doom ˣCompare Gk Syr Vg:
Heb Cub ʸMeaning of Heb uncertain
ᶻOr Nubians; Heb Cush

anguish shall come upon them on the day of Egypt's doom;[a] for it is coming!

10 Thus says the Lord GOD:
I will put an end to the
hordes of Egypt,
by the hand of King
Nebuchadrezzar of
Babylon.
[11] He and his people with him,
the most terrible of the
nations,
shall be brought in to
destroy the land;
and they shall draw their
swords against Egypt,
and fill the land with the
slain.
[12] I will dry up the channels,
and will sell the land into
the hand of evildoers;
I will bring desolation upon
the land and everything
in it
by the hand of foreigners;
I the LORD have spoken.

13 Thus says the Lord GOD:
I will destroy the idols
and put an end to the
images in Memphis;
there shall no longer be a
prince in the land of
Egypt;
so I will put fear in the
land of Egypt.
[14] I will make Pathros a
desolation,
and will set fire to Zoan,
and will execute acts of
judgment on Thebes.
[15] I will pour my wrath upon
Pelusium,
the stronghold of Egypt,
and cut off the hordes of
Thebes.
[16] I will set fire to Egypt;
Pelusium shall be in great
agony;
Thebes shall be breached,
and Memphis face
adversaries by day.
[17] The young men of On and of
Pi-beseth shall fall by
the sword;

and the cities themselves[b]
shall go into captivity.
[18] At Tehaphnehes the day
shall be dark,
when I break there the
dominion of Egypt,
and its proud might shall
come to an end;
the city[c] shall be covered
by a cloud,
and its daughter-towns
shall go into captivity.
[19] Thus I will execute acts of
judgment on Egypt.
Then they shall know that I
am the LORD.

Proclamation against Pharaoh

20 In the eleventh year, in the first month, on the seventh day of the month, the word of the LORD came to me: [21] Mortal, I have broken the arm of Pharaoh king of Egypt; it has not been bound up for healing or wrapped with a bandage, so that it may become strong to wield the sword. [22] Therefore thus says the Lord GOD: I am against Pharaoh king of Egypt, and will break his arms, both the strong arm and the one that was broken; and I will make the sword fall from his hand. [23] I will scatter the Egyptians among the nations, and disperse them throughout the lands. [24] I will strengthen the arms of the king of Babylon, and put my sword in his hand; but I will break the arms of Pharaoh, and he will groan before him with the groans of one mortally wounded. [25] I will strengthen the arms of the king of Babylon, but the arms of Pharaoh shall fall. And they shall know that I am the LORD, when I put my sword into the hand of the king of Babylon. He shall stretch it out against the land of Egypt, [26] and I will scatter the Egyptians among the nations and disperse them throughout the countries. Then they shall know that I am the LORD.

30.10
Ezek 29.19
30.11
Ezek 28.7;
v. 4
30.12
Isa 19.5,6;
Ezek 29.3,9
30.13
Isa 19.1;
Zech 13.2;
v. 16;
Zech 10.11;
Isa 19.16
30.14
Ezek 29.14;
Ps 78.12,43;
vv. 15,16
30.15
Jer 46.25;
v. 16
30.16
vv. 8,13-15

30.18
Jer 43.8-13;
Ezek 34.27;
v. 3
30.19
vv. 14,25,26
30.21
Ps 10.15;
Jer 46.11
30.22
Ezek 29.3;
Ps 37.17
30.23
Ezek 29.12;
v. 26
30.24
vv. 10,25;
Zech 10.12;
Zeph 2.12;
Ezek 26.15;
21.14,25
30.25
vv. 24,22,
11; Isa 5.25
30.26
Ezek 29.12

[a] Heb *the day of Egypt* [b] Heb *and they*
[c] Heb *she*

The Lofty Cedar

31 In the eleventh year, in the third month, on the first day of the month, the word of the LORD came to me: ² Mortal, say to Pharaoh king of Egypt and to his hordes:

Whom are you like in your
 greatness?
³ Consider Assyria, a cedar of
 Lebanon,
with fair branches and forest
 shade,
 and of great height,
 its top among the clouds.ᵈ
⁴ The waters nourished it,
 the deep made it grow tall,
making its rivers floweᵉ
 around the place it was
 planted,
sending forth its streams
 to all the trees of the field.
⁵ So it towered high
 above all the trees of the
 field;
its boughs grew large
 and its branches long,
from abundant water in its
 shoots.
⁶ All the birds of the air
 made their nests in its
 boughs;
under its branches all the
 animals of the field
gave birth to their young;
and in its shade
 all great nations lived.
⁷ It was beautiful in its
 greatness,
 in the length of its
 branches;
for its roots went down
 to abundant water.
⁸ The cedars in the garden of
 God could not rival it,
 nor the fir trees equal its
 boughs;
the plane trees were as
 nothing
 compared with its
 branches;
no tree in the garden of God
 was like it in beauty.
⁹ I made it beautiful
 with its mass of branches,

31.2
Ezek 29.19;
30.10; v. 18
31.3
Nah 3.1ff;
Ezek 17.23;
vv. 5,10
31.4
Ezek 17.5,8;
Rev 17.1,15
31.5
Ps 37.35;
Ezek 17.5
31.6
Ezek 17.23;
Dan 4.12;
Mt 13.32;
Mk 4.32;
Lk 13.19
31.7
vv. 2,9
31.8
Gen 2.8;
13.10;
Ezek 28.13;
vv. 16,18
31.9
Ezek 16.14

31.10
Isa 14.13,
14;
Ezek 28.17;
Dan 5.20
31.11
Ezek 30.10,
11;
Nah 3.18
31.12
Ezek 28.7;
Hab 1.6;
Ezek 32.5;
35.8;
Nah 3.17,18
31.13
Isa 18.6;
Ezek 32.4
31.14
vv. 16,17;
Ps 63.9;
v. 18;
Ezek 32.24
31.15
Ezek 32.7;
Nah 2.10
31.16
Ezek 26.15;
Isa 14.15;
Ezek 32.18;
Isa 14.8;
Ezek 32.31
31.17
Ps 9.17;
Ezek 32.18-20

the envy of all the trees of
 Eden
that were in the garden of
 God.
10 Therefore thus says the Lord GOD: Because itᶠ towered high and set its top among the clouds,ᵈ and its heart was proud of its height, ¹¹ I gave it into the hand of the prince of the nations; he has dealt with it as its wickedness deserves. I have cast it out. ¹² Foreigners from the most terrible of the nations have cut it down and left it. On the mountains and in all the valleys its branches have fallen, and its boughs lie broken in all the water-courses of the land; and all the peoples of the earth went away from its shade and left it.
13 On its fallen trunk settle
 all the birds of the air,
 and among its boughs lodge
 all the wild animals.
¹⁴ All this is in order that no trees by the waters may grow to lofty height or set their tops among the clouds,ᵈ and that no trees that drink water may reach up to them in height.
For all of them are handed
 over to death,
 to the world below;
along with all mortals,
 with those who go down to
 the Pit.
15 Thus says the Lord GOD: On the day it went down to Sheol I closed the deep over it and covered it; I restrained its rivers, and its mighty waters were checked. I clothed Lebanon in gloom for it, and all the trees of the field fainted because of it. ¹⁶ I made the nations quake at the sound of its fall, when I cast it down to Sheol with those who go down to the Pit; and all the trees of Eden, the choice and best of Lebanon, all that were well watered, were consoled in the world below. ¹⁷ They also went down to Sheol with it, to those killed by the sword, along with its allies,ᵍ those

ᵈ Gk: Heb *thick boughs* ᵉ Gk: Heb *rivers*
going ᶠ Syr Vg: Heb *you* ᵍ Heb *its arms*

who lived in its shade among the nations.

18 Which among the trees of Eden was like you in glory and in greatness? Now you shall be brought down with the trees of Eden to the world below; you shall lie among the uncircumcised, with those who are killed by the sword. This is Pharaoh and all his horde, says the Lord God.

Lamentation over Pharaoh and Egypt

32 In the twelfth year, in the twelfth month, on the first day of the month, the word of the Lord came to me: 2 Mortal, raise a lamentation over Pharaoh king of Egypt, and say to him:

You consider yourself a lion
 among the nations,
but you are like a dragon
 in the seas;
you thrash about in your
 streams,
trouble the water with your
 feet,
and foul your[h] streams.
3 Thus says the Lord God:
In an assembly of many
 peoples
I will throw my net over
 you;
and I[i] will haul you up in
 my dragnet.
4 I will throw you on the
 ground,
on the open field I will
 fling you,
and will cause all the birds
 of the air to settle on
 you,
and I will let the wild
 animals of the whole
 earth gorge themselves
 with you.
5 I will strew your flesh on the
 mountains,
and fill the valleys with
 your carcass.[j]
6 I will drench the land with
 your flowing blood
up to the mountains,
and the watercourses will
 be filled with you.

7 When I blot you out, I will
 cover the heavens,
 and make their stars dark;
I will cover the sun with a
 cloud,
 and the moon shall not
 give its light.
8 All the shining lights of the
 heavens
 I will darken above you,
 and put darkness on your
 land,
 says the Lord God.
9 I will trouble the hearts of
 many peoples,
 as I carry you captive[k]
 among the nations,
 into countries you have not
 known.
10 I will make many peoples
 appalled at you;
 their kings shall shudder
 because of you.
When I brandish my sword
 before them,
 they shall tremble every
 moment
 for their lives, each one of
 them,
 on the day of your
 downfall.
11 For thus says the Lord God:
The sword of the king of
 Babylon shall come
 against you.
12 I will cause your hordes to
 fall
 by the swords of mighty
 ones,
 all of them most terrible
 among the nations.
They shall bring to ruin the
 pride of Egypt,
 and all its hordes shall
 perish.
13 I will destroy all its livestock
 from beside abundant
 waters;
and no human foot shall
 trouble them any more,
 nor shall the hoofs of cattle
 trouble them.
14 Then I will make their
 waters clear,

Cross references

31.18
Ezek 32.19;
vv. 8,9,14;
Ezek 28.10;
32.19,21
32.2
Ezek 27.2;
19.3,6; 38.13;
34.18
32.3
Ezek 12.13;
17.20;
Hos 7.12
32.4
Ezek 29.5;
31.13;
Isa 18.6
32.5
Ezek 35.8
32.6
Ezek 35.6;
Rev 14.20

32.7
Prov 13.9;
Isa 34.4;
13.10;
Joel 2.31;
3.15;
Am 8.9;
Mt 24.29;
Rev 6.12,13
32.9
Ezek 28.19;
Rev 18.10-15;
Ex 15.14-16
32.10
Ezek 27.35;
26.16;
Jer 46.10
32.11
Jer 46.26;
Ezek 30.4
32.12
Ezek 28.7;
31.12; 30.18
32.13
Ezek 29.8,
11

h Heb their i Gk Vg: Heb they
j Symmachus Syr Vg: Heb your height
k Gk: Heb bring your destruction

and cause their streams to
　　run like oil, says the
　　Lord God.
15 When I make the land of
　　Egypt desolate
　and when the land is
　　stripped of all that fills
　　it,
　when I strike down all who
　　live in it,
　then they shall know that I
　　am the Lord.
16 This is a lamentation; it
　　shall be chanted.
　The women of the nations
　　shall chant it.
　Over Egypt and all its hordes
　　they shall chant it,
　says the Lord God.

Dirge over Egypt

17 In the twelfth year, in the
first month,[1] on the fifteenth day
of the month, the word of the Lord
came to me:
18 Mortal, wail over the hordes
　　of Egypt,
　and send them down,
　with Egypt[m] and the
　　daughters of majestic
　　nations,
　to the world below,
　with those who go down to
　　the Pit.
19 "Whom do you surpass in
　　beauty?
　Go down! Be laid to rest
　　with the
　　uncircumcised!"
20 They shall fall among those who
are killed by the sword. Egypt[n] has
been handed over to the sword;
carry away both it and its hordes.
21 The mighty chiefs shall speak of
them, with their helpers, out of the
midst of Sheol: "They have come
down, they lie still, the uncircum-
cised, killed by the sword."

22 Assyria is there, and all its
company, their graves all around it,
all of them killed, fallen by the
sword. 23 Their graves are set in the
uttermost parts of the Pit. Its com-
pany is all around its grave, all of
them killed, fallen by the sword,
who spread terror in the land of the
living.

24 Elam is there, and all its
hordes around its grave; all of them
killed, fallen by the sword, who
went down uncircumcised into the
world below, who spread terror in
the land of the living. They bear
their shame with those who go
down to the Pit. 25 They have made
Elam[m] a bed among the slain with
all its hordes, their graves all
around it, all of them uncircum-
cised, killed by the sword; for terror
of them was spread in the land of
the living, and they bear their
shame with those who go down to
the Pit; they are placed among the
slain.

26 Meshech and Tubal are
there, and all their multitude, their
graves all around them, all of them
uncircumcised, killed by the
sword; for they spread terror in the
land of the living. 27 And they do
not lie with the fallen warriors of
long ago[o] who went down to Sheol
with their weapons of war, whose
swords were laid under their heads,
and whose shields[p] are upon their
bones; for the terror of the warriors
was in the land of the living. 28 So
you shall be broken and lie among
the uncircumcised, with those who
are killed by the sword.

29 Edom is there, its kings and
all its princes, who for all their
might are laid with those who are
killed by the sword; they lie with
the uncircumcised, with those who
go down to the Pit.

30 The princes of the north are
there, all of them, and all the Sido-
nians, who have gone down in
shame with the slain, for all the ter-
ror that they caused by their might;
they lie uncircumcised with those
who are killed by the sword, and
bear their shame with those who go
down to the Pit.

31 When Pharaoh sees them, he
will be consoled for all his
hordes — Pharaoh and all his army,
killed by the sword, says the Lord
God. 32 For he[q] spread terror in the

32.15
Ezek 29.12,
19,20;
Ps 9.16;
Ezek 6.7
32.16
2 Sam 1.17;
2 Chr 35.25;
Ezek 26.17
32.18
vv. 2,16;
Mic 1.8;
Ezek 26.20;
31.14; v. 24
32.19
Ezek 31.2,
18; 28.10;
vv. 21,24,29
32.21
Isa 1.31;
14.9,10;
vv. 27,31,32
32.22
Ezek 31.3,
16
32.23
Isa 14.15;
vv. 24-27,32

32.24
Jer 49.34-39;
Ps 27.13;
Isa 38.11;
Jer 11.19;
vv. 25,30
32.25
Ps 139.8;
vv. 19,23,24
32.26
Gen 10.2;
Ezek 27.13;
38.2; vv. 19,
32
32.27
Isa 14.18,
19,21,23
32.28
v. 19
32.29
Isa 34.5-15;
Jer 49.7-22;
Ezek 25.13
32.30
Ezek 38.6,
15; 39.2;
28.21
32.31
vv. 18,21;
Ezek 31.16
32.32
vv. 19-24

[1]Gk: Heb lacks in the first month
[m]Heb it　　[n]Heb It　　[o]Gk Old Latin:
Heb of the uncircumcised　　[p]Cn: Heb
iniquities　　[q]Cn: Heb I

land of the living; therefore he shall be laid to rest among the uncircumcised, with those who are slain by the sword — Pharaoh and all his multitude, says the Lord God.

Ezekiel Israel's Sentry

33 The word of the Lord came to me: ²O Mortal, speak to your people and say to them, If I bring the sword upon a land, and the people of the land take one of their number as their sentinel; ³and if the sentinel sees the sword coming upon the land and blows the trumpet and warns the people; ⁴then if any who hear the sound of the trumpet do not take warning, and the sword comes and takes them away, their blood shall be upon their own heads. ⁵They heard the sound of the trumpet and did not take warning; their blood shall be upon themselves. But if they had taken warning, they would have saved their lives. ⁶But if the sentinel sees the sword coming and does not blow the trumpet, so that the people are not warned, and the sword comes and takes any of them, they are taken away in their iniquity, but their blood I will require at the sentinel's hand.

7 So you, mortal, I have made a sentinel for the house of Israel; whenever you hear a word from my mouth, you shall give them warning from me. ⁸If I say to the wicked, "O wicked ones, you shall surely die," and you do not speak to warn the wicked to turn from their ways, the wicked shall die in their iniquity, but their blood I will require at your hand. ⁹But if you warn the wicked to turn from their ways, and they do not turn from their ways, the wicked shall die in their iniquity, but you will have saved your life.

God's Justice and Mercy

10 Now you, mortal, say to the house of Israel, Thus you have said: "Our transgressions and our sins weigh upon us, and we waste away because of them; how then can we live?" ¹¹Say to them, As I live, says the Lord God, I have no pleasure in the death of the wicked, but that the wicked turn from their ways and live; turn back, turn back from your evil ways; for why will you die, O house of Israel? ¹²And you, mortal, say to your people, The righteousness of the righteous shall not save them when they transgress; and as for the wickedness of the wicked, it shall not make them stumble when they turn from their wickedness; and the righteous shall not be able to live by their righteousness ʳ when they sin. ¹³Though I say to the righteous that they shall surely live, yet if they trust in their righteousness and commit iniquity, none of their righteous deeds shall be remembered; but in the iniquity that they have committed they shall die. ¹⁴Again, though I say to the wicked, "You shall surely die," yet if they turn from their sin and do what is lawful and right — ¹⁵if the wicked restore the pledge, give back what they have taken by robbery, and walk in the statutes of life, committing no iniquity — they shall surely live, they shall not die. ¹⁶None of the sins that they have committed shall be remembered against them; they have done what is lawful and right, they shall surely live.

17 Yet your people say, "The way of the Lord is not just," when it is their own way that is not just. ¹⁸When the righteous turn from their righteousness, and commit iniquity, they shall die for it.ˢ ¹⁹And when the wicked turn from their wickedness, and do what is lawful and right, they shall live by it. ˢ ²⁰Yet you say, "The way of the Lord is not just." O house of Israel, I will judge all of you according to your ways!

The Fall of Jerusalem

21 In the twelfth year of our exile, in the tenth month, on the fifth day of the month, someone who had escaped from Jerusalem came to me and said, "The city has fall-

33.2 Ezek 3.11; Jer 12.12; Zech 13.7; 2 Sam 18.24, 25; 2 Kings 9.17
33.3 Hos 8.1; Joel 2.1
33.4 Jer 6.17; Zech 1.4; Ezek 18.13; Acts 18.6
33.5 Heb 11.7
33.6 Isa 56.10, 11; v. 8; Ezek 3.18, 20
33.7 Ezek 3.17-21; Jer 26.2; Acts 5.20
33.8 vv. 14,6
33.9 Acts 13.40, 41,46; Ezek 3.19, 21
33.10 Ezek 18.2; 24.23; 37.11
33.11 2 Sam 14.14; Ezek 18.23, 32; 2 Pet 3.9; Ezek 18.30, 31
33.12 Ezek 3.20; 2 Chr 7.14
33.13 Ezek 3.20; 18.24; 2 Pet 2.20, 21
33.14 Ezek 3.18, 19; 18.27
33.15 Lev 6.2,4,5; Num 5.6,7; Lk 19.8; Ezek 20.11
33.16 Ezek 18.22
33.17 Ezek 18.25, 29; v. 20
33.18 Ezek 18.26
33.19 vv. 12,14
33.20 Ezek 18.25; v. 17
33.21 Ezek 1.2; 24.26; 2 Kings 25.4

ʳ Heb *by it* ˢ Heb *them*

en." 22 Now the hand of the LORD had been upon me the evening before the fugitive came; but he had opened my mouth by the time the fugitive came to me in the morning; so my mouth was opened, and I was no longer unable to speak.

The Survivors in Judah

23 The word of the LORD came to me: 24 Mortal, the inhabitants of these waste places in the land of Israel keep saying, "Abraham was only one man, yet he got possession of the land; but we are many; the land is surely given us to possess." 25 Therefore say to them, Thus says the Lord GOD: You eat flesh with the blood, and lift up your eyes to your idols, and shed blood; shall you then possess the land? 26 You depend on your swords, you commit abominations, and each of you defiles his neighbor's wife; shall you then possess the land? 27 Say this to them, Thus says the Lord GOD: As I live, surely those who are in the waste places shall fall by the sword; and those who are in the open field I will give to the wild animals to be devoured; and those who are in strongholds and in caves shall die by pestilence. 28 I will make the land a desolation and a waste, and its proud might shall come to an end; and the mountains of Israel shall be so desolate that no one will pass through. 29 Then they shall know that I am the LORD, when I have made the land a desolation and a waste because of all their abominations that they have committed.

30 As for you, mortal, your people who talk together about you by the walls, and at the doors of the houses, say to one another, each to a neighbor, "Come and hear what the word is that comes from the LORD." 31 They come to you as people come, and they sit before you as my people, and they hear your words, but they will not obey them. For flattery is on their lips, but their heart is set on their gain. 32 To them you are like a singer of love songs,[t] one who has a beautiful

voice and plays well on an instrument; they hear what you say, but they will not do it. 33 When this comes—and come it will!—then they shall know that a prophet has been among them.

Israel's False Shepherds

34 The word of the LORD came to me: 2 Mortal, prophesy against the shepherds of Israel: prophesy, and say to them—to the shepherds: Thus says the Lord GOD: Ah, you shepherds of Israel who have been feeding yourselves! Should not shepherds feed the sheep? 3 You eat the fat, you clothe yourselves with the wool, you slaughter the fatlings; but you do not feed the sheep. 4 You have not strengthened the weak, you have not healed the sick, you have not bound up the injured, you have not brought back the strayed, you have not sought the lost, but with force and harshness you have ruled them. 5 So they were scattered, because there was no shepherd; and scattered, they became food for all the wild animals. 6 My sheep were scattered, they wandered over all the mountains and on every high hill; my sheep were scattered over all the face of the earth, with no one to search or seek for them.

7 Therefore, you shepherds, hear the word of the LORD: 8 As I live, says the Lord GOD, because my sheep have become a prey, and my sheep have become food for all the wild animals, since there was no shepherd; and because my shepherds have not searched for my sheep, but the shepherds have fed themselves, and have not fed my sheep; 9 therefore, you shepherds, hear the word of the LORD: 10 Thus says the Lord GOD, I am against the shepherds; and I will demand my sheep at their hand, and put a stop to their feeding the sheep; no longer shall the shepherds feed themselves. I will rescue my sheep from their mouths, so that they may not be food for them.

t Cn: Heb *like a love song*

33.22
Ezek 1.3;
24.27;
Lk 1.64
33.24
Ezek 36.4;
Isa 51.2;
Acts 7.5
33.25
Deut 12.16;
Ezek 20.24;
22.6,9
33.26
Ezek 18.6;
22.11
33.27
Ezek 39.4;
1 Sam 13.6;
Isa 2.19
33.28
Jer 44.2,6,
22;
Ezek 7.24;
36.34,35
33.29
Ezek 23.33,
35
33.30
vv. 2,17;
Isa 29.13;
58.2
33.31
Ezek 14.1;
20.1; 8.1;
Ps 78.36,37;
Isa 29.13;
Mt 13.22

33.33
1 Sam 3.20;
Ezek 2.5
34.2
Jer 10.21;
vv. 8-10,14,
15;
Jn 10.11;
21.15-17
34.3
Isa 56.11;
Zech 11.16;
Ezek 22.25,
27
34.4
Zech 11.16;
Mt 9.36;
Lk 15.4;
1 Pet 5.3
34.5
Jer 10.21;
50.6,7;
Jer 23.2;
Mt 9.36
34.8
Acts 20.29;
vv. 5,6,2
34.10
Ezek 3.18;
Heb 13.17;
vv. 2,8

God, the True Shepherd

11 For thus says the Lord God: I myself will search for my sheep, and will seek them out. 12 As shepherds seek out their flocks when they are among their scattered sheep, so I will seek out my sheep. I will rescue them from all the places to which they have been scattered on a day of clouds and thick darkness. 13 I will bring them out from the peoples and gather them from the countries, and will bring them into their own land; and I will feed them on the mountains of Israel, by the watercourses, and in all the inhabited parts of the land. 14 I will feed them with good pasture, and the mountain heights of Israel shall be their pasture; there they shall lie down in good grazing land, and they shall feed on rich pasture on the mountains of Israel. 15 I myself will be the shepherd of my sheep, and I will make them lie down, says the Lord God. 16 I will seek the lost, and I will bring back the strayed, and I will bind up the injured, and I will strengthen the weak, but the fat and the strong I will destroy. I will feed them with justice.

17 As for you, my flock, thus says the Lord God: I shall judge between sheep and sheep, between rams and goats: 18 Is it not enough for you to feed on the good pasture, but you must tread down with your feet the rest of your pasture? When you drink of clear water, must you foul the rest with your feet? 19 And must my sheep eat what you have trodden with your feet, and drink what you have fouled with your feet?

20 Therefore, thus says the Lord God to them: I myself will judge between the fat sheep and the lean sheep. 21 Because you pushed with flank and shoulder, and butted at all the weak animals with your horns until you scattered them far and wide, 22 I will save my flock, and they shall no longer be ravaged; and I will judge between sheep and sheep.

23 I will set up over them one shepherd, my servant David, and he shall feed them: he shall feed them and be their shepherd. 24 And I, the Lord, will be their God, and my servant David shall be prince among them; I, the Lord, have spoken.

25 I will make with them a covenant of peace and banish wild animals from the land, so that they may live in the wild and sleep in the woods securely. 26 I will make them and the region around my hill a blessing; and I will send down the showers in their season; they shall be showers of blessing. 27 The trees of the field shall yield their fruit, and the earth shall yield its increase. They shall be secure on their soil; and they shall know that I am the Lord, when I break the bars of their yoke, and save them from the hands of those who enslaved them. 28 They shall no more be plunder for the nations, nor shall the animals of the land devour them; they shall live in safety, and no one shall make them afraid. 29 I will provide for them a splendid vegetation so that they shall no more be consumed with hunger in the land, and no longer suffer the insults of the nations. 30 They shall know that I, the Lord their God, am with them, and that they, the house of Israel, are my people, says the Lord God. 31 You are my sheep, the sheep of my pasture u and I am your God, says the Lord God.

Judgment on Mount Seir

35 The word of the Lord came to me: 2 Mortal, set your face against Mount Seir, and prophesy against it, 3 and say to it, Thus says the Lord God:

I am against you, Mount
 Seir;
I stretch out my hand
 against you
to make you a desolation
 and a waste.

u Gk OL: Heb *pasture, you are people*

34.11
Ezek 11.17;
20.41
34.12
Jn 10.16;
Ezek 30.3;
Joel 2.2
34.13
Isa 65.9,10;
Jer 23.3;
Ezek 37.22;
Isa 30.25
34.14
Ps 23.1,2;
Ezek 20.40;
28.25,26
34.16
Mt 18.11;
Lk 5.32;
Isa 49.26
34.17
Ezek 20.37,
38;
Zech 10.3;
Mt 25.32,33
34.18
2 Sam 7.19
34.20
v. 17
34.21
Deut 33.17;
Dan 8.4
34.22
vv. 5,8,10,
17

34.23
Isa 40.11;
Jer 23.4,5;
30.9;
Hos 3.5
34.24
Ezek 36.28;
37.27; 37.24,
25; Hos 3.5
34.25
Isa 11.6-9;
Hos 2.18;
Jer 23.6
34.26
Isa 56.7;
Zech 8.13
34.27
Ps 85.12;
Isa 4.2;
Jer 2.20
34.28
Jer 30.10
34.29
Isa 60.21;
Ezek 36.29,
3,6
34.30
Ezek 36.28;
37.27
34.31
Ps 100.3;
Jn 10.11
35.2
Jer 49.7,8
35.3
Ezek 21.3;
Jer 6.12;
15.6;
Ezek 25.13;
v. 7

4 I lay your towns in ruins;
 you shall become a
 desolation,
and you shall know that I
 am the LORD.

5 Because you cherished an ancient enmity, and gave over the people of Israel to the power of the sword at the time of their calamity, at the time of their final punishment; 6 therefore, as I live, says the Lord GOD, I will prepare you for blood, and blood shall pursue you; since you did not hate bloodshed, bloodshed shall pursue you. 7 I will make Mount Seir a waste and a desolation; and I will cut off from it all who come and go. 8 I will fill its mountains with the slain; on your hills and in your valleys and in all your watercourses those killed with the sword shall fall. 9 I will make you a perpetual desolation, and your cities shall never be inhabited. Then you shall know that I am the LORD.

10 Because you said, "These two nations and these two countries shall be mine, and we will take possession of them," — although the LORD was there — 11 therefore, as I live, says the Lord GOD, I will deal with you according to the anger and envy that you showed because of your hatred against them; and I will make myself known among you,[v] when I judge you. 12 You shall know that I, the LORD, have heard all the abusive speech that you uttered against the mountains of Israel, saying, "They are laid desolate, they are given us to devour." 13 And you magnified yourselves against me with your mouth, and multiplied your words against me; I heard it. 14 Thus says the Lord GOD: As the whole earth rejoices, I will make you desolate. 15 As you rejoiced over the inheritance of the house of Israel, because it was desolate, so I will deal with you; you shall be desolate, Mount Seir, and all Edom, all of it. Then they shall know that I am the LORD.

Blessing on Israel

36 And you, mortal, prophesy to the mountains of Israel, and say: O mountains of Israel, hear the word of the LORD. 2 Thus says the Lord GOD: Because the enemy said of you, "Aha!" and, "The ancient heights have become our possession," 3 therefore prophesy, and say: Thus says the Lord GOD: Because they made you desolate indeed, and crushed you from all sides, so that you became the possession of the rest of the nations, and you became an object of gossip and slander among the people; 4 therefore, O mountains of Israel, hear the word of the Lord GOD: Thus says the Lord GOD to the mountains and the hills, the watercourses and the valleys, the desolate wastes and the deserted towns, which have become a source of plunder and an object of derision to the rest of the nations all around; 5 therefore thus says the Lord GOD: I am speaking in my hot jealousy against the rest of the nations, and against all Edom, who, with wholehearted joy and utter contempt, took my land as their possession, because of its pasture, to plunder it. 6 Therefore prophesy concerning the land of Israel, and say to the mountains and hills, to the watercourses and valleys, Thus says the Lord GOD: I am speaking in my jealous wrath, because you have suffered the insults of the nations; 7 therefore thus says the Lord GOD: I swear that the nations that are all around you shall themselves suffer insults.

8 But you, O mountains of Israel, shall shoot out your branches, and yield your fruit to my people Israel; for they shall soon come home. 9 See now, I am for you; I will turn to you, and you shall be tilled and sown; 10 and I will multiply your population, the whole house of Israel, all of it; the towns shall be inhabited and the waste places re-

35.4
v. 9;
Mal 1.3,4
35.5
Ezek 25.12;
Ob 10;
Ezek 7.2;
21.25,29
35.6
Ezek 16.38;
32.6
35.7
Ezek 25.13;
29.11
35.8
Isa 34.5,6;
Ezek 31.12;
32.4,5
35.9
Jer 49.13;
Ezek 6.7;
36.11
35.10
Ezek 36.2,5;
Ps 48.1,3;
Ezek 48.35
35.11
Am 1.11;
Mt 7.2;
Ps 9.16
35.13
Ezek 36.3;
Jer 7.11;
29.23
35.14
Isa 49.13;
Jer 51.48
35.15
Jer 50.11;
Ob 4,21;
Ezek 6.7

36.1
Ezek 6.2,3
36.2
Ezek 25.3;
Hab 3.19;
Ezek 35.10
36.3
Jer 2.15;
51.34; 18.16;
Ezek 35.13
36.4
Ezek 6.3;
34.28;
Ps 79.4;
Jer 48.27
36.5
Ezek 38.19;
25.12-14;
35.10,12;
Jer 50.11;
Mic 7.8
36.6
Ps 123.3,4;
Ezek 34.29
36.7
Ezek 20.6,
15,23;
Jer 25.9,15,
29
36.8
v. 4;
Isa 27.6;
Ezek 17.23

36.10 Isa 27.6; Ezek 37.21, 22; v. 33

[v] Gk: Heb *them*

built; [11] and I will multiply human beings and animals upon you. They shall increase and be fruitful; and I will cause you to be inhabited as in your former times, and will do more good to you than ever before. Then you shall know that I am the LORD. [12] I will lead people upon you—my people Israel—and they shall possess you, and you shall be their inheritance. No longer shall you bereave them of children.

13 Thus says the Lord GOD: Because they say to you, "You devour people, and you bereave your nation of children," [14] therefore you shall no longer devour people and no longer bereave your nation of children, says the Lord GOD; [15] and no longer will I let you hear the insults of the nations, no longer shall you bear the disgrace of the peoples; and no longer shall you cause your nation to stumble, says the Lord GOD.

The Renewal of Israel

16 The word of the LORD came to me: [17] Mortal, when the house of Israel lived on their own soil, they defiled it with their ways and their deeds; their conduct in my sight was like the uncleanness of a woman in her menstrual period. [18] So I poured out my wrath upon them for the blood that they had shed upon the land, and for the idols with which they had defiled it. [19] I scattered them among the nations, and they were dispersed through the countries; in accordance with their conduct and their deeds I judged them. [20] But when they came to the nations, wherever they came, they profaned my holy name, in that it was said of them, "These are the people of the LORD, and yet they had to go out of his land." [21] But I had concern for my holy name, which the house of Israel had profaned among the nations to which they came.

22 Therefore say to the house of Israel, Thus says the Lord GOD: It is not for your sake, O house of Israel, that I am about to act, but for the sake of my holy name, which

you have profaned among the nations to which you came. [23] I will sanctify my great name, which has been profaned among the nations, and which you have profaned among them; and the nations shall know that I am the LORD, says the Lord GOD, when through you I display my holiness before their eyes. [24] I will take you from the nations, and gather you from all the countries, and bring you into your own land. [25] I will sprinkle clean water upon you, and you shall be clean from all your uncleannesses, and from all your idols I will cleanse you. [26] A new heart I will give you, and a new spirit I will put within you; and I will remove from your body the heart of stone and give you a heart of flesh. [27] I will put my spirit within you, and make you follow my statutes and be careful to observe my ordinances. [28] Then you shall live in the land that I gave to your ancestors; and you shall be my people, and I will be your God. [29] I will save you from all your uncleannesses, and I will summon the grain and make it abundant and lay no famine upon you. [30] I will make the fruit of the tree and the produce of the field abundant, so that you may never again suffer the disgrace of famine among the nations. [31] Then you shall remember your evil ways, and your dealings that were not good; and you shall loathe yourselves for your iniquities and your abominable deeds. [32] It is not for your sake that I will act, says the Lord GOD; let that be known to you. Be ashamed and dismayed for your ways, O house of Israel.

33 Thus says the Lord GOD: On the day that I cleanse you from all your iniquities, I will cause the towns to be inhabited, and the waste places shall be rebuilt. [34] The land that was desolate shall be tilled, instead of being the desolation that it was in the sight of all who passed by. [35] And they will say, "This land that was desolate has become like the garden of Eden;

36.11
Jer 30.18;
Ezek 16.55;
35.9
36.13
Num 13.32
36.15
Ezek 34.29;
22.4;
Jer 13.16;
18.15
36.17
Lev 18.25,
27,28;
Jer 2.7
36.18
Ezek 22.20;
16.36,38;
23.37
36.19
Am 9.9;
Ezek 39.24;
Rom 2.6
36.20
Isa 52.5;
Rom 2.24;
Jer 33.24
36.21
Ps 74.18;
Isa 48.9;
Ezek 20.44
36.22
Ps 106.8

36.23
Ezek 20.41;
Ps 126.2;
Ezek 28.25;
39.27
36.24
Ezek 34.13;
37.21
36.25
Isa 52.15;
Heb 10.22;
Zech 13.1
36.26
Ps 51.10;
Ezek 11.19
36.27
Ezek 11.19;
37.14
36.28
Jer 30.22;
Ezek 11.20;
37.27
36.29
Zech 13.1
36.30
Ezek 34.27,
29;
Hos 2.21-23
36.31
Ezek 16.61-63;
20.43; 6.9
36.32
Ezek 20.44;
v. 22
36.33
v. 25;
Zech 8.7,8;
Isa 58.12;
v. 10
36.34
v. 9
36.35
Isa 51.3;

Ezek 31.9; Joel 2.3

and the waste and desolate and ruined towns are now inhabited and fortified." [36] Then the nations that are left all around you shall know that I, the LORD, have rebuilt the ruined places, and replanted that which was desolate; I, the LORD, have spoken, and I will do it.

37 Thus says the Lord GOD: I will also let the house of Israel ask me to do this for them: to increase their population like a flock. [38] Like the flock for sacrifices,[w] like the flock at Jerusalem during her appointed festivals, so shall the ruined towns be filled with flocks of people. Then they shall know that I am the LORD.

The Valley of Dry Bones

37 The hand of the LORD came upon me, and he brought me out by the spirit of the LORD and set me down in the middle of a valley; it was full of bones. [2] He led me all around them; there were very many lying in the valley, and they were very dry. [3] He said to me, "Mortal, can these bones live?" I answered, "O Lord GOD, you know." [4] Then he said to me, "Prophesy to these bones, and say to them: O dry bones, hear the word of the LORD. [5] Thus says the Lord GOD to these bones: I will cause breath[x] to enter you, and you shall live. [6] I will lay sinews on you, and will cause flesh to come upon you, and cover you with skin, and put breath[x] in you, and you shall live; and you shall know that I am the LORD."

[7] So I prophesied as I had been commanded; and as I prophesied, suddenly there was a noise, a rattling, and the bones came together, bone to its bone. [8] I looked, and there were sinews on them, and flesh had come upon them, and skin had covered them; but there was no breath in them. [9] Then he said to me, "Prophesy to the breath, prophesy, mortal, and say to the breath:[y] Thus says the Lord GOD: Come from the four winds, O breath,[y] and breathe upon these slain, that they may live." [10] I

prophesied as he commanded me, and the breath came into them, and they lived, and stood on their feet, a vast multitude.

11 Then he said to me, "Mortal, these bones are the whole house of Israel. They say, 'Our bones are dried up, and our hope is lost; we are cut off completely.' [12] Therefore prophesy, and say to them, Thus says the Lord GOD: I am going to open your graves, and bring you up from your graves, O my people; and I will bring you back to the land of Israel. [13] And you shall know that I am the LORD, when I open your graves, and bring you up from your graves, O my people. [14] I will put my spirit within you, and you shall live, and I will place you on your own soil; then you shall know that I, the LORD, have spoken and will act," says the LORD.

The Two Sticks

15 The word of the LORD came to me: [16] Mortal, take a stick and write on it, "For Judah, and the Israelites associated with it"; then take another stick and write on it, "For Joseph (the stick of Ephraim) and all the house of Israel associated with it"; [17] and join them together into one stick, so that they may become one in your hand. [18] And when your people say to you, "Will you not show us what you mean by these?" [19] say to them, Thus says the Lord GOD: I am about to take the stick of Joseph (which is in the hand of Ephraim) and the tribes of Israel associated with it; and I will put the stick of Judah upon it,[z] and make them one stick, in order that they may be one in my hand. [20] When the sticks on which you write are in your hand before their eyes, [21] then say to them, Thus says the Lord GOD: I will take the people of Israel from the nations among which they have gone, and will gather them from every quarter, and bring them to their own land.

Cross references

36.36
Ezek 39.27, 28; 22.14; 37.14
36.38
1 Kings 8.63; vv. 33-35; Zech 11.17
37.1
Ezek 1.3; 8.3; 11.24; Lk 4.1; Acts 8.39
37.2
v. 11
37.3
Isa 26.19; Deut 32.39; 1 Sam 2.6
37.4
vv. 9,12; Isa 42.18; Ezek 36.1
37.5
Ps 104.29, 30; vv. 9,10
37.6
vv. 8-10; Ezek 6.7; 35.12; Joel 2.27; 3.17
37.7
Jer 13.5-7; Ezek 38.19
37.9
Ps 104.30; v. 5; Hos 13.14
37.10
vv. 5,6; Rev 11.11
37.11
Ezek 36.10; 39.25; Ps 141.7; Isa 49.14
37.12
Isa 26.19; Hos 13.14; v. 25; Ezek 36.24; Am 9.14,15
37.13
Ezek 6.7; vv. 6,12
37.14
Ezek 36.27; 39.29; 36.36
37.16
Num 17.2; 2 Chr 11.11-17; 15.9
37.17
vv. 22-24
37.18
Ezek 12.9; 24.19
37.19
Zech 10.6; vv. 16,17
37.21
Ezek 36.24; 39.27

[w] Heb *flock of holy things* [x] Or *spirit*
[y] Or *wind* or *spirit* [z] Heb *I will put them upon it*

22 I will make them one nation in the land, on the mountains of Israel; and one king shall be king over them all. Never again shall they be two nations, and never again shall they be divided into two kingdoms. 23 They shall never again defile themselves with their idols and their detestable things, or with any of their transgressions. I will save them from all the apostasies into which they have fallen,[a] and will cleanse them. Then they shall be my people, and I will be their GOD.

24 My servant David shall be king over them; and they shall all have one shepherd. They shall follow my ordinances and be careful to observe my statutes. 25 They shall live in the land that I gave to my servant Jacob, in which your ancestors lived; they and their children and their children's children shall live there forever; and my servant David shall be their prince forever. 26 I will make a covenant of peace with them; it shall be an everlasting covenant with them; and I will bless[b] them and multiply them, and will set my sanctuary among them forevermore. 27 My dwelling place shall be with them; and I will be their God, and they shall be my people. 28 Then the nations shall know that I the LORD sanctify Israel, when my sanctuary is among them forevermore.

Invasion by Gog

38 The word of the LORD came to me: 2 Mortal, set your face toward Gog, of the land of Magog, the chief prince of Meshech and Tubal. Prophesy against him 3 and say: Thus says the Lord GOD: I am against you, O Gog, chief prince of Meshech and Tubal; 4 I will turn you around and put hooks into your jaws, and I will lead you out with all your army, horses and horsemen, all of them clothed in full armor, a great company, all of them with shield and buckler, wielding swords. 5 Persia, Ethiopia,[c] and Put are with them, all of them with buckler and helmet; 6 Gomer and all its troops; Beth-

togarmah from the remotest parts of the north with all its troops — many peoples are with you.

7 Be ready and keep ready, you and all the companies that are assembled around you, and hold yourselves in reserve for them. 8 After many days you shall be mustered; in the latter years you shall go against a land restored from war, a land where people were gathered from many nations on the mountains of Israel, which had long lain waste; its people were brought out from the nations and now are living in safety, all of them. 9 You shall advance, coming on like a storm; you shall be like a cloud covering the land, you and all your troops, and many peoples with you.

10 Thus says the Lord GOD: On that day thoughts will come into your mind, and you will devise an evil scheme. 11 You will say, "I will go up against the land of unwalled villages; I will fall upon the quiet people who live in safety, all of them living without walls, and having no bars or gates"; 12 to seize spoil and carry off plunder; to assail the waste places that are now inhabited, and the people who were gathered from the nations, who are acquiring cattle and goods, who live at the center[d] of the earth. 13 Sheba and Dedan and the merchants of Tarshish and all its young warriors[e] will say to you, "Have you come to seize spoil? Have you assembled your horde to carry off plunder, to carry away silver and gold, to take away cattle and goods, to seize a great amount of booty?"

14 Therefore, mortal, prophesy, and say to Gog: Thus says the Lord GOD: On that day when my people Israel are living securely, you will rouse yourself[f] 15 and come from your place out of the remotest parts of the north, you and many peoples with you, all of them riding

37.22
Isa 11.13;
Jer 3.18;
Hos 1.11;
Ezek 34.23
37.23
Ezek 11.18;
43.7; 36.25;
36.28
37.24
Jer 30.9;
Isa 40.11;
Hos 3.5;
Ezek 36.27
37.25
Ezek 28.25;
36.28;
Zech 6.12
37.26
Isa 55.3;
Ezek 36.10;
20.40; 43.7
37.27
Lev 26.11;
Jn 1.14
37.28
Ezek 36.23;
20.12
38.2
Ezek 39.1;
Rev 20.8
38.3
Ezek 39.1
38.4
2 Kings 19.28;
Ezek 39.2
38.5
Ezek 27.10;
30.4,5
38.6
Gen 10.2;
Ezek 27.14

38.7
Jer 46.3;
51.12
38.8
Isa 24.22;
Ezek 36.24
38.9
Isa 28.2;
Joel 2.2
38.10
Mic 2.1
38.11
Zech 2.4;
Jer 49.31;
v. 8
38.12
Isa 10.6;
Ezek 29.19;
v. 8
38.13
Ezek 27.22;
27.15;
Nah 2.11-13
38.14
Jer 23.6;
Zech 2.5,8
38.15
v. 6;
Ezek 39.2

a Another reading is *from all the settlements in which they have sinned* b Tg: Heb *give* c Or *Nubia*; Heb *Cush* d Heb *navel* e Heb *young lions* f Gk: Heb *will you not know?*

on horses, a great horde, a mighty army; ¹⁶you will come up against my people Israel, like a cloud covering the earth. In the latter days I will bring you against my land, so that the nations may know me, when through you, O Gog, I display my holiness before their eyes.

Judgment on Gog

17 Thus says the Lord GOD: Are you he of whom I spoke in former days by my servants the prophets of Israel, who in those days prophesied for years that I would bring you against them? ¹⁸On that day, when Gog comes against the land of Israel, says the Lord GOD, my wrath shall be aroused. ¹⁹For in my jealousy and in my blazing wrath I declare: On that day there shall be a great shaking in the land of Israel; ²⁰the fish of the sea, and the birds of the air, and the animals of the field, and all creeping things that creep on the ground, and all human beings that are on the face of the earth, shall quake at my presence, and the mountains shall be thrown down, and the cliffs shall fall, and every wall shall tumble to the ground. ²¹I will summon the sword against Gogᵍ inʰ all my mountains, says the Lord GOD; the swords of all will be against their comrades. ²²With pestilence and bloodshed I will enter into judgment with him; and I will pour down torrential rains and hailstones, fire and sulfur, upon him and his troops and the many peoples that are with him. ²³So I will display my greatness and my holiness and make myself known in the eyes of many nations. Then they shall know that I am the LORD.

Gog's Armies Destroyed

39 And you, mortal, prophesy against Gog, and say: Thus says the Lord GOD: I am against you, O Gog, chief prince of Meshech and Tubal! ²I will turn you around and drive you forward, and bring you up from the remotest parts of the north, and lead you against the mountains of Israel. ³I

will strike your bow from your left hand, and will make your arrows drop out of your right hand. ⁴You shall fall upon the mountains of Israel, you and all your troops and the peoples that are with you; I will give you to birds of prey of every kind and to the wild animals to be devoured. ⁵You shall fall in the open field; for I have spoken, says the Lord GOD. ⁶I will send fire on Magog and on those who live securely in the coastlands; and they shall know that I am the LORD.

7 My holy name I will make known among my people Israel; and I will not let my holy name be profaned any more; and the nations shall know that I am the LORD, the Holy One in Israel. ⁸It has come! It has happened, says the Lord GOD. This is the day of which I have spoken.

9 Then those who live in the towns of Israel will go out and make fires of the weapons and burn them — bucklers and shields, bows and arrows, handpikes and spears — and they will make fires of them for seven years. ¹⁰They will not need to take wood out of the field or cut down any trees in the forests, for they will make their fires of the weapons; they will despoil those who despoiled them, and plunder those who plundered them, says the Lord GOD.

The Burial of Gog

11 On that day I will give to Gog a place for burial in Israel, the Valley of the Travelersⁱ east of the sea; it shall block the path of the travelers, for there Gog and all his horde will be buried; it shall be called the Valley of Hamon-gog.ʲ ¹²Seven months the house of Israel shall spend burying them, in order to cleanse the land. ¹³All the people of the land shall bury them; and it will bring them honor on the day that I show my glory, says the Lord GOD. ¹⁴They will set apart men to pass through the land regularly and

38.16
Ezek 36.23;
39.21
38.17
Isa 34.1-6
38.18
v. 2;
Ps 18.8,15
38.19
Ezek 36.5,6;
Nah 1.2;
Hag 2.6,7;
Rev 16.18
38.20
Jer 4.24;
Hos 4.3;
Nah 1.5,6;
Zech 14.4
38.21
Ezek 14.17;
Judg 7.22;
1 Sam 14.20;
2 Chr 20.23
38.22
Isa 66.16;
Jer 25.31;
Rev 16.21;
Ps 11.6
38.23
Ezek 36.23;
Ps 9.16;
Ezek 37.28
39.1
Ezek 38.2-4
39.2
Ezek 38.15
39.3
Ezek 30.21-24;
Hos 1.5

39.4
Ezek 38.21;
33.37
39.6
Ezek 38.22;
Am 1.4;
Ps 72.10;
Jer 25.22
39.7
Ezek 36.20-22;
v. 25;
Ezek 20.39;
38.16;
Isa 60.9,14
39.8
Ezek 38.17
39.9
Ps 46.9
39.10
Isa 14.2;
Hab 2.8
39.11
Ezek 38.2;
vv. 1,15
39.12
v. 14,16
39.13
Jer 33.9;
Ezek 28.22
39.14
Jer 14.16;
v. 12

ᵍHeb him ʰHeb to or for ⁱOr of the Abarim ʲThat is, the Horde of Gog

bury any invaders[k] who remain on the face of the land, so as to cleanse it; for seven months they shall make their search. [15]As the searchers[k] pass through the land, anyone who sees a human bone shall set up a sign by it, until the buriers have buried it in the Valley of Hamon-gog.[l] [16](A city Hamonah[m] is there also.) Thus they shall cleanse the land.

17 As for you, mortal, thus says the Lord God: Speak to the birds of every kind and to all the wild animals: Assemble and come, gather from all around to the sacrificial feast that I am preparing for you, a great sacrificial feast on the mountains of Israel, and you shall eat flesh and drink blood. [18]You shall eat the flesh of the mighty, and drink the blood of the princes of the earth — of rams, of lambs, and of goats, of bulls, all of them fatlings of Bashan. [19]You shall eat fat until you are filled, and drink blood until you are drunk, at the sacrificial feast that I am preparing for you. [20]And you shall be filled at my table with horses and charioteers,[n] with warriors and all kinds of soldiers, says the Lord God.

Israel Restored to the Land

21 I will display my glory among the nations; and all the nations shall see my judgment that I have executed, and my hand that I have laid on them. [22]The house of Israel shall know that I am the Lord their God, from that day forward. [23]And the nations shall know that the house of Israel went into captivity for their iniquity, because they dealt treacherously with me. So I hid my face from them and gave them into the hand of their adversaries, and they all fell by the sword. [24]I dealt with them according to their uncleanness and their transgressions, and hid my face from them.

25 Therefore thus says the Lord God: Now I will restore the fortunes of Jacob, and have mercy on the whole house of Israel; and I will be jealous for my holy name. [26]They shall forget[o] their shame, and all the treachery they have practiced against me, when they live securely in their land with no one to make them afraid, [27]when I have brought them back from the peoples and gathered them from their enemies' lands, and through them have displayed my holiness in the sight of many nations. [28]Then they shall know that I am the Lord their God because I sent them into exile among the nations, and then gathered them into their own land. I will leave none of them behind; [29]and I will never again hide my face from them, when I pour out my spirit upon the house of Israel, says the Lord God.

The Vision of the New Temple

40 In the twenty-fifth year of our exile, at the beginning of the year, on the tenth day of the month, in the fourteenth year after the city was struck down, on that very day, the hand of the Lord was upon me, and he brought me there. [2]He brought me, in visions of God, to the land of Israel, and set me down upon a very high mountain, on which was a structure like a city to the south. [3]When he brought me there, a man was there, whose appearance shone like bronze, with a linen cord and a measuring reed in his hand; and he was standing in the gateway. [4]The man said to me, "Mortal, look closely and listen attentively, and set your mind upon all that I shall show you, for you were brought here in order that I might show it to you; declare all that you see to the house of Israel."

5 Now there was a wall all around the outside of the temple area. The length of the measuring reed in the man's hand was six long cubits, each being a cubit and a handbreadth in length; so he measured the thickness of the wall, one reed; and the height, one reed.

Cross references:

39.15 v. 11
39.16 v. 12
39.17 v. 4; Rev 19.17; Isa 34.6,7; Jer 46.10; Zeph 1.7
39.18 Rev 19.18; Deut 32.14; Ps 22.12; Am 4.1
39.20 Ps 76.6; Ezek 38.4; Rev 19.18
39.21 Ezek 38.16, 23; v. 13
39.22 vv. 7,28
39.23 Ezek 36.18-20, 23; 20.27; v. 26; Isa 59.2; v. 29
39.24 Ezek 36.19; v. 23
39.25 Jer 30.3,18; Ezek 34.13; 36.24; 20.40; Hos 1.11
39.26 Ezek 34.25-28; Isa 17.2; Mic 4.4
39.27 Ezek 28.25, 26; 36.23,24; 38.16
39.28 Ezek 34.30; v. 22
39.29 Isa 32.15; Ezek 36.27; 37.14; Joel 2.28; Acts 2.17
40.1 Ezek 33.21; 1.2,3
40.2 Ezek 8.3; Dan 7.1,7; Ezek 17.23; Rev 21.10
40.3 Ezek 1.7; Dan 10.6; Ezek 47.3; Rev 11.1; 21.15
40.4 Ezek 44.5; 43.10; Jer 26.2; Acts 20.27
40.5 Ezek 42.20; v. 3

[k] Heb travelers　[l] That is, the Horde of Gog　[m] That is The Horde　[n] Heb chariots　[o] Another reading is They shall bear

⁶Then he went into the gateway facing east, going up its steps, and measured the threshold of the gate, one reed deep.ᴾ There were ⁷recesses, and each recess was one reed wide and one reed deep; and the space between the recesses, five cubits; and the threshold of the gate by the vestibule of the gate at the inner end was one reed deep. ⁸Then he measured the inner vestibule of the gateway, one cubit. ⁹Then he measured the vestibule of the gateway, eight cubits; and its pilasters, two cubits; and the vestibule of the gate was at the inner end. ¹⁰There were three recesses on either side of the east gate; the three were of the same size; and the pilasters on either side were of the same size. ¹¹Then he measured the width of the opening of the gateway, ten cubits; and the width of the gateway, thirteen cubits. ¹²There was a barrier before the recesses, one cubit on either side; and the recesses were six cubits on either side. ¹³Then he measured the gate from the back�q of the one recess to the back�q of the other, a width of twenty-five cubits, from wall to wall.ʳ ¹⁴He measuredˢ also the vestibule, twenty cubits; and the gate next to the pilaster on every side of the court.ᵗ ¹⁵From the front of the gate at the entrance to the end of the inner vestibule of the gate was fifty cubits. ¹⁶The recesses and their pilasters had windows, with shuttersᵗ on the inside of the gateway all around, and the vestibules also had windows on the inside all around; and on the pilasters were palm trees.

17 Then he brought me into the outer court; there were chambers there, and a pavement, all around the court; thirty chambers fronted on the pavement. ¹⁸The pavement ran along the side of the gates, corresponding to the length of the gates; this was the lower pavement. ¹⁹Then he measured the distance from the inner front ofᵘ the lower gate to the outer front of the inner court, one hundred cubits.ᵛ

20 Then he measured the gate of the outer court that faced north—its depth and width. ²¹Its recesses, three on either side, and its pilasters and its vestibule were of the same size as those of the first gate; its depth was fifty cubits, and its width twenty-five cubits. ²²Its windows, its vestibule, and its palm trees were of the same size as those of the gate that faced toward the east. Seven steps led up to it; and its vestibule was on the inside.ʷ ²³Opposite the gate on the north, as on the east, was a gate to the inner court; he measured from gate to gate, one hundred cubits.

24 Then he led me toward the south, and there was a gate on the south; and he measured its pilasters and its vestibule; they had the same dimensions as the others. ²⁵There were windows all around in it and in its vestibule, like the windows of the others; its depth was fifty cubits, and its width twenty-five cubits. ²⁶There were seven steps leading up to it; its vestibule was on the inside.ʷ It had palm trees on its pilasters, one on either side. ²⁷There was a gate on the south of the inner court; and he measured from gate to gate toward the south, one hundred cubits.

28 Then he brought me to the inner court by the south gate, and he measured the south gate; it was of the same dimensions as the others. ²⁹Its recesses, its pilasters, and its vestibule were of the same size as the others; and there were windows all around in it and in its vestibule; its depth was fifty cubits, and its width twenty-five cubits. ³⁰There were vestibules all around, twenty-five cubits deep and five cubits wide. ³¹Its vestibule faced the outer court, and palm trees were on its pilasters, and its stairway had eight steps.

32 Then he brought me to the inner court on the east side, and he

Cross references

40.6
vv. 20,26
40.7
vv. 10-16, 21,29,33,36
40.10
v. 7
40.14
vv. 9,16;
1 Chr 28.6;
Isa 62.9;
Ezek 42.1
40.16
1 Kings 6.4;
vv. 21,22, 26,31,34,37
40.17
Rev 11.2;
1 Chr 9.26;
2 Chr 31.11;
Ezek 41.6;
45.5
40.19
vv. 23,27
40.20
v. 6

40.21
vv. 7,16,30, 15,13
40.22
vv. 16,6,26, 31,34,37,49
40.23
vv. 19,27
40.24
v. 21
40.25
vv. 16,22, 21,33
40.26
vv. 6,22,16
40.27
vv. 23,32,19
40.28
vv. 32,35
40.29
vv. 7,10,21, 16,22,25
40.30
vv. 16,21,25
40.31
vv. 16,22, 26,34,37
40.32
vv. 28-31,35

Footnotes

ᵖ Heb deep, and one threshold, one reed deep �q Gk: Heb roof ʳ Heb opening facing opening ˢ Heb made ᵗ Meaning of Heb uncertain ᵘ Compare Gk: Heb from before ᵛ Heb adds the east and the north ʷ Gk: Heb before them

measured the gate; it was of the same size as the others. [33] Its recesses, its pilasters, and its vestibule were of the same dimensions as the others; and there were windows all around in it and in its vestibule; its depth was fifty cubits, and its width twenty-five cubits. [34] Its vestibule faced the outer court, and it had palm trees on its pilasters, on either side; and its stairway had eight steps.

35 Then he brought me to the north gate, and he measured it; it had the same dimensions as the others. [36] Its recesses, its pilasters, and its vestibule were of the same size as the others;[x] and it had windows all around. Its depth was fifty cubits, and its width twenty-five cubits. [37] Its vestibule[y] faced the outer court, and it had palm trees on its pilasters, on either side; and its stairway had eight steps.

38 There was a chamber with its door in the vestibule of the gate,[z] where the burnt offering was to be washed. [39] And in the vestibule of the gate were two tables on either side, on which the burnt offering and the sin offering and the guilt offering were to be slaughtered. [40] On the outside of the vestibule[a] at the entrance of the north gate were two tables; and on the other side of the vestibule of the gate were two tables. [41] Four tables were on the inside, and four tables on the outside of the side of the gate, eight tables, on which the sacrifices were to be slaughtered. [42] There were also four tables of hewn stone for the burnt offering, a cubit and a half long, and one cubit and a half wide, and one cubit high, on which the instruments were to be laid with which the burnt offerings and the sacrifices were slaughtered. [43] There were pegs, one handbreadth long, fastened all around the inside. And on the tables the flesh of the offering was to be laid.

44 On the outside of the inner gateway there were chambers for the singers in the inner court, one[b] at the side of the north gate facing

south, the other at the side of the east gate facing north. [45] He said to me, "This chamber that faces south is for the priests who have charge of the temple, [46] and the chamber that faces north is for the priests who have charge of the altar; these are the descendants of Zadok, who alone among the descendants of Levi may come near to the LORD to minister to him." [47] He measured the court, one hundred cubits deep, and one hundred cubits wide, a square; and the altar was in front of the temple.

The Temple

48 Then he brought me to the vestibule of the temple and measured the pilasters of the vestibule, five cubits on either side; and the width of the gate was fourteen cubits; and the sidewalls of the gate were three cubits[c] on either side. [49] The depth of the vestibule was twenty cubits, and the width twelve[d] cubits; ten steps led up[e] to it; and there were pillars beside the pilasters on either side.

41 Then he brought me to the nave, and measured the pilasters; on each side six cubits was the width of the pilasters.[f] [2] The width of the entrance was ten cubits; and the sidewalls of the entrance were five cubits on either side. He measured the length of the nave, forty cubits, and its width, twenty cubits. [3] Then he went into the inner room and measured the pilasters of the entrance, two cubits; and the width of the entrance, six cubits; and the sidewalls[g] of the entrance, seven cubits. [4] He measured the depth of the room, twenty cubits, and its width, twenty cubits, beyond the nave. And he said to me, This is the most holy place.

5 Then he measured the wall of

Cross references (center column):

40.33 : vv. 29,16,21
40.34 : vv. 16,22,37
40.35 : Ezek 44.4; 47.2
40.36 : vv. 7,29,16, 21
40.37 : vv. 16,35
40.38 : Ezek 41.10; 42.13; 2 Chr 4.6
40.39 : Lev 4.2,3; 5.6; 6.6; 7.1
40.41 : vv. 39,40
40.42 : v. 39; Ex 20.25
40.44 : vv. 23,27, 17,38; 1 Chr 6.31; 25.1-7
40.45 : vv. 17,38; Lev 8.35; 1 Chr 9.23; 2 Chr 13.11
40.46 : vv. 17,38; Num 18.5; Ezek 44.15; 43.19; 1 Kings 2.35
40.47 : vv. 19,23,27
40.49 : 1 Kings 6.3; 2 Kings 7.21; Jer 52.17-23; Rev 3.12
41.1 : Ezek 40.2,3, 17; vv. 21, 23; Ezek 40.9
41.2 : 1 Kings 6.2, 17; 2 Chr 3.3
41.3 : Ezek 40.16; v. 1
41.4 : 1 Kings 6.20; 2 Chr 3.8
41.5 : vv. 6-11

Footnotes:

[x] One Ms: Compare verses 29 and 33: MT lacks *were of the same size as the others*
[y] Gk Vg Compare verses 26, 31, 34: Heb *pilasters* [z] Cn: Heb *at the pilasters of the gates* [a] Cn: Heb *to him who goes up*
[b] Heb lacks *one* [c] Gk: Heb *and the width of the gate was three cubits* [d] Gk: Heb *eleven* [e] Gk: Heb *and by steps that went up*
[f] Compare Gk: Heb *tent* [g] Gk: Heb *width*

the temple, six cubits thick; and the width of the side chambers, four cubits, all around the temple. [6] The side chambers were in three stories, one over another, thirty in each story. There were offsets[h] all around the wall of the temple to serve as supports for the side chambers, so that they should not be supported by the wall of the temple. [7] The passageway[i] of the side chambers widened from story to story; for the structure was supplied with a stairway all around the temple. For this reason the structure became wider from story to story. One ascended from the bottom story to the uppermost story by way of the middle one. [8] I saw also that the temple had a raised platform all around; the foundations of the side chambers measured a full reed of six long cubits. [9] The thickness of the outer wall of the side chambers was five cubits; and the free space between the side chambers of the temple [10] and the chambers of the court was a width of twenty cubits all around the temple on every side. [11] The side chambers opened onto the area left free, one door toward the north, and another door toward the south; and the width of the part that was left free was five cubits all around.

12 The building that was facing the temple yard on the west side was seventy cubits wide; and the wall of the building was five cubits thick all around, and its depth ninety cubits.

13 Then he measured the temple, one hundred cubits deep; and the yard and the building with its walls, one hundred cubits deep; [14] also the width of the east front of the temple and the yard, one hundred cubits.

15 Then he measured the depth of the building facing the yard at the west, together with its galleries[j] on either side, one hundred cubits.

The nave of the temple and the inner room and the outer[k] vestibule [16] were paneled,[l] and, all around, all three had windows with

41.6
1 Kings 6.5, 6
41.7
1 Kings 6.8
41.8
Ezek 40.5
41.9
v. 11
41.10
Ezek 40.17
41.11
v. 9
41.12
vv. 13-15;
Ezek 42.1
41.13
Ezek 40.47;
vv. 13-15
41.14
Ezek 40.47
41.15
Ezek 42.1,
10,13; 40.6;
v. 25
41.16
vv. 25,26;
Ezek 40.16;
v. 15;
Ezek 42.3;
1 Kings 6.15

41.18
1 Kings 6.29;
7.36;
Ezek 40.16;
2 Chr 3.5
41.19
Ezek 1.10;
10.14
41.20
v. 18
41.21
v. 1;
1 Kings 6.33;
Ezek 40.9,
14,16
41.22
Ex 30.1;
Rev 8.3;
Ezek 44.16;
Mal 1.7,12;
Ex 30.8
41.23
1 Kings 6.31-35;
vv. 1,4
41.25
v. 16
41.26
v. 16;
Ezek 40.9,
16,48
42.1
Ezek 40.17,
28; 41.1,12;
vv. 10,13

recessed[m] frames. Facing the threshold the temple was paneled with wood all around, from the floor up to the windows (now the windows were covered), [17] to the space above the door, even to the inner room, and on the outside. And on all the walls all around in the inner room and the nave there was a pattern.[n] [18] It was formed of cherubim and palm trees, a palm tree between cherub and cherub. Each cherub had two faces: [19] a human face turned toward the palm tree on the one side, and the face of a young lion turned toward the palm tree on the other side. They were carved on the whole temple all around; [20] from the floor to the area above the door, cherubim and palm trees were carved on the wall.[o]

21 The doorposts of the nave were square. In front of the holy place was something resembling [22] an altar of wood, three cubits high, two cubits long, and two cubits wide;[p] its corners, its base,[q] and its walls were of wood. He said to me, "This is the table that stands before the LORD." [23] The nave and the holy place had each a double door. [24] The doors had two leaves apiece, two swinging leaves for each door. [25] On the doors of the nave were carved cherubim and palm trees, such as were carved on the walls; and there was a canopy of wood in front of the vestibule outside. [26] And there were recessed windows and palm trees on either side, on the sidewalls of the vestibule.[r]

The Holy Chambers and the Outer Wall

42 Then he led me out into the outer court, toward the

h Gk Compare 1 Kings 6.6: Heb *they entered*
i Cn: Heb *it was surrounded*
j Cn: Meaning of Heb uncertain
k Gk: Heb *of the court* l Gk: Heb *the thresholds* m Cn Compare Gk 1 Kings 6.4: Meaning of Heb uncertain n Heb *measures*
o Cn Compare verse 25: Heb *and the wall*
p Gk: Heb lacks *two cubits wide*
q Gk: Heb *length* r Cn: Heb *vestibule. And the side chambers of the temple and the canopies*

north, and he brought me to the chambers that were opposite the temple yard and opposite the building on the north. [2]The length of the building that was on the north side[s] was[t] one hundred cubits, and the width fifty cubits. [3]Across the twenty cubits that belonged to the inner court, and facing the pavement that belonged to the outer court, the chambers rose[u] gallery[v] by gallery[v] in three stories. [4]In front of the chambers was a passage on the inner side, ten cubits wide and one hundred cubits deep,[w] and its[x] entrances were on the north. [5]Now the upper chambers were narrower, for the galleries[v] took more away from them than from the lower and middle chambers in the building. [6]For they were in three stories, and they had no pillars like the pillars of the outer[y] court; for this reason the upper chambers were set back from the ground more than the lower and the middle ones. [7]There was a wall outside parallel to the chambers, toward the outer court, opposite the chambers, fifty cubits long. [8]For the chambers on the outer court were fifty cubits long, while those opposite the temple were one hundred cubits long. [9]At the foot of these chambers ran a passage that one entered from the east in order to enter them from the outer court. [10]The width of the passage[z] is fixed by the wall of the court.

On the south[a] also, opposite the vacant area and opposite the building, there were chambers [11]with a passage in front of them; they were similar to the chambers on the north, of the same length and width, with the same exits[b] and arrangements and doors. [12]So the entrances of the chambers to the south were entered through the entrance at the head of the corresponding passage, from the east, along the matching wall.[v]

13 Then he said to me, "The north chambers and the south chambers opposite the vacant area are the holy chambers, where the priests who approach the LORD shall eat the most holy offerings; there they shall deposit the most holy offerings — the grain offering, the sin offering, and the guilt offering, for the place is holy. [14]When the priests enter the holy place, they shall not go out of it into the outer court without laying there the vestments in which they minister, for these are holy; they shall put on other garments before they go near to the area open to the people."

15 When he had finished measuring the interior of the temple area, he led me out by the gate that faces east, and measured the temple area all around. [16]He measured the east side with the measuring reed, five hundred cubits by the measuring reed. [17]Then he turned and measured[c] the north side, five hundred cubits by the measuring reed. [18]Then he turned and measured[c] the south side, five hundred cubits by the measuring reed. [19]Then he turned to the west side and measured, five hundred cubits by the measuring reed. [20]He measured it on the four sides. It had a wall around it, five hundred cubits long and five hundred cubits wide, to make a separation between the holy and the common.

The Divine Glory Returns to the Temple

43 Then he brought me to the gate, the gate facing east. [2]And there, the glory of the God of Israel was coming from the east; the sound was like the sound of mighty waters; and the earth shone with his glory. [3]The[d] vision I saw was like the vision that I had seen when he came to destroy the city, and[e] like the vision that I had seen by the river Chebar; and I fell upon my face. [4]As the glory of the LORD

42.2 Ezek 41.13
42.3 Ezek 41.10, 16
42.4 Ezek 46.19
42.5 v. 3
42.6 Ezek 41.6
42.7 vv. 10,12
42.8 Ezek 41.13, 14
42.9 Ezek 44.5; 46.19
42.10 vv. 7,1,13; Ezek 40.17
42.11 v. 4
42.13 Lev 7.6; 10.13,14,17; Lev 6.25,29; Num 18.9, 10
42.14 Ezek 44.19; Ex 29.4-9; Zech 3.4,5
42.15 Ezek 40.6; 43.1
42.16 Ezek 40.3
42.20 Ezek 40.5; Zech 2.5; Ezek 45.2
43.1 Ezek 10.19; 44.1; 46.1
43.2 Ezek 11.23; 1.24; Rev 1.15; 18.1; Ezek 10.4
43.3 Ezek 1.4,28; Jer 1.10; Ezek 1.3; 3.23
43.4 Ezek 10.19; 44.2

s Gk: Heb door t Gk: Heb *before the length* u Heb lacks *the chambers rose* v Meaning of Heb uncertain w Gk Syr: Heb *a way of one cubit* x Heb *their* y Gk: Heb lacks *outer* z Heb lacks *of the passage* a Gk: Heb *east* b Heb *and all their exits* c Gk: Heb *measuring reed all around. He measured* d Gk: Heb *Like the vision* e Syr: Heb *and the visions*

entered the temple by the gate facing east, [5] the spirit lifted me up, and brought me into the inner court; and the glory of the Lord filled the temple.

6 While the man was standing beside me, I heard someone speaking to me out of the temple. [7] He said to me: Mortal, this is the place of my throne and the place for the soles of my feet, where I will reside among the people of Israel forever. The house of Israel shall no more defile my holy name, neither they nor their kings, by their whoring, and by the corpses of their kings at their death.[f] [8] When they placed their threshold by my threshold and their doorposts beside my doorposts, with only a wall between me and them, they were defiling my holy name by their abominations that they committed; therefore I have consumed them in my anger. [9] Now let them put away their idolatry and the corpses of their kings far from me, and I will reside among them forever.

10 As for you, mortal, describe the temple to the house of Israel, and let them measure the pattern; and let them be ashamed of their iniquities. [11] When they are ashamed of all that they have done, make known to them the plan of the temple, its arrangement, its exits and its entrances, and its whole form — all its ordinances and its entire plan and all its laws; and write it down in their sight, so that they may observe and follow the entire plan and all its ordinances. [12] This is the law of the temple: the whole territory on the top of the mountain all around shall be most holy. This is the law of the temple.

The Altar

13 These are the dimensions of the altar by cubits (the cubit being one cubit and a handbreadth): its base shall be one cubit high,[g] and one cubit wide, with a rim of one span around its edge. This shall be the height of the altar: [14] From the base on the ground to the lower ledge, two cubits, with a width of

one cubit; and from the smaller ledge to the larger ledge, four cubits, with a width of one cubit; [15] and the altar hearth, four cubits; and from the altar hearth projecting upward, four horns. [16] The altar hearth shall be square, twelve cubits long by twelve wide. [17] The ledge also shall be square, fourteen cubits long by fourteen wide, with a rim around it half a cubit wide, and its surrounding base, one cubit. Its steps shall face east.

18 Then he said to me: Mortal, thus says the Lord God: These are the ordinances for the altar: On the day when it is erected for offering burnt offerings upon it and for dashing blood against it, [19] you shall give to the levitical priests of the family of Zadok, who draw near to me to minister to me, says the Lord God, a bull for a sin offering. [20] And you shall take some of its blood, and put it on the four horns of the altar, and on the four corners of the ledge, and upon the rim all around; thus you shall purify it and make atonement for it. [21] You shall also take the bull of the sin offering, and it shall be burnt in the appointed place belonging to the temple, outside the sacred area.

22 On the second day you shall offer a male goat without blemish for a sin offering; and the altar shall be purified, as it was purified with the bull. [23] When you have finished purifying it, you shall offer a bull without blemish and a ram from the flock without blemish. [24] You shall present them before the Lord, and the priests shall throw salt on them and offer them up as a burnt offering to the Lord. [25] For seven days you shall provide daily a goat for a sin offering; also a bull and a ram from the flock, without blemish, shall be provided. [26] Seven days shall they make atonement for the altar and cleanse it, and so consecrate it. [27] When these days are over, then from the eighth day onward the priests shall offer upon

Cross references

43.5
Ezek 3.14;
8.3;
1 Kings 8.10,
11;
Ezek 44.4
43.6
Ezek 1.26;
40.3
43.7
Ps 47.8;
Ezek 1.26;
37.26,28;
Jer 16.18;
Ezek 6.5,13
43.8
Ezek 8.3;
23.39; 44.7
43.9
Ezek 18.30,
31
43.10
Ezek 40.4;
v. 11
43.11
Ezek 44.5;
12.3; 11.20;
36.27
43.12
Ezek 40.2
43.13
Ezek 40.5;
41.8
43.14
vv. 17,20;
Ezek 45.19
43.15
Ex 27.2;
Lev 9.9;
1 Kings 1.50
43.16
Ex 27.1
43.17
Ex 20.26;
Ezek 40.6
43.18
Ezek 2.1;
Ex 40.29;
Lev 1.5
43.19
1 Kings 2.35;
Ezek 44.15;
Num 16.5,
40; v. 23;
Ezek 45.18,
19
43.21
Ex 29.14;
Heb 13.11
43.22
vv. 25,20,26
43.23
Ex 29.1
43.24
Lev 2.13;
Mk 9.49,50;
Col 4.6
43.25
Ex 29.35,
36; Lev 8.33
43.27
Lev 9.1; 3.1;
17.5;
Ezek 20.40

f Or on their high places g Gk: Heb lacks high

the altar your burnt offerings and your offerings of well-being; and I will accept you, says the Lord God.

The Closed Gate

44 Then he brought me back to the outer gate of the sanctuary, which faces east; and it was shut. [2] The Lord said to me: This gate shall remain shut; it shall not be opened, and no one shall enter by it; for the Lord, the God of Israel, has entered by it; therefore it shall remain shut. [3] Only the prince, because he is a prince, may sit in it to eat food before the Lord; he shall enter by way of the vestibule of the gate, and shall go out by the same way.

Admission to the Temple

4 Then he brought me by way of the north gate to the front of the temple; and I looked, and lo! the glory of the Lord filled the temple of the Lord; and I fell upon my face. [5] The Lord said to me: Mortal, mark well, look closely, and listen attentively to all that I shall tell you concerning all the ordinances of the temple of the Lord and all its laws; and mark well those who may be admitted to[h] the temple and all those who are to be excluded from the sanctuary. [6] Say to the rebellious house,[i] to the house of Israel, Thus says the Lord God: O house of Israel, let there be an end to all your abominations [7] in admitting foreigners, uncircumcised in heart and flesh, to be in my sanctuary, profaning my temple when you offer to me my food, the fat and the blood. You[j] have broken my covenant with all your abominations. [8] And you have not kept charge of my sacred offerings; but you have appointed foreigners[k] to act for you in keeping my charge in my sanctuary.

9 Thus says the Lord God: No foreigner, uncircumcised in heart and flesh, of all the foreigners who are among the people of Israel, shall enter my sanctuary. [10] But the Levites who went far from me, going astray from me after their idols

when Israel went astray, shall bear their punishment. [11] They shall be ministers in my sanctuary, having oversight at the gates of the temple, and serving in the temple; they shall slaughter the burnt offering and the sacrifice for the people, and they shall attend on them and serve them. [12] Because they ministered to them before their idols and made the house of Israel stumble into iniquity, therefore I have sworn concerning them, says the Lord God, that they shall bear their punishment. [13] They shall not come near to me, to serve me as priest, nor come near any of my sacred offerings, the things that are most sacred; but they shall bear their shame, and the consequences of the abominations that they have committed. [14] Yet I will appoint them to keep charge of the temple, to do all its chores, all that is to be done in it.

The Levitical Priests

15 But the levitical priests, the descendants of Zadok, who kept the charge of my sanctuary when the people of Israel went astray from me, shall come near to me to minister to me; and they shall attend me to offer me the fat and the blood, says the Lord God. [16] It is they who shall enter my sanctuary, it is they who shall approach my table, to minister to me, and they shall keep my charge. [17] When they enter the gates of the inner court, they shall wear linen vestments; they shall have nothing of wool on them, while they minister at the gates of the inner court, and within. [18] They shall have linen turbans on their heads, and linen undergarments on their loins; they shall not bind themselves with anything that causes sweat. [19] When they go out into the outer court to the people, they shall remove the vestments in which they have been ministering, and lay them in the holy chambers; and they shall put on other gar-

44.1
Ezek 42.14;
43.1
44.2
Ezek 43.4
44.3
Ezek 37.25;
Gen 31.54;
1 Cor 10.18;
Ezek 46.2,8
44.4
Ezek 40.20,
40; 3.23;
43.5; 1.28;
Rev 15.8
44.5
Ezek 40.4;
43.10,11
44.6
Ezek 2.5;
3.9; 45.9;
1 Pet 4.3
44.7
Ex 12.43-49;
Lev 26.41;
Deut 10.16;
Jer 4.4;
9.26;
Lev 22.25;
Gen 17.14
44.8
Num 18.7
44.9
v. 7;
Zech 14.21
44.10
2 Kings 23.8,
9;
Ezek 22.26;
Num 18.23

44.11
1 Chr 26.1;
2 Chr 29.34;
Num 16.9
44.12
2 Kings 16.10-
16;
Ezek 14.3,4;
Ps 106.26
44.13
Num 18.3;
2 Kings 23.9;
Ezek 32.30;
39.26
44.14
Num 18.4;
v. 11
44.15
Ezek 40.46;
48.11;
Deut 10.8
44.16
Ezek 41.22;
Mal 1.7,12
44.17
Ex 28.39,
40,43; 39.27,
28
44.18
Ex 28.40,
42; Isa 3.20
44.19
Ezek 42.14;
46.20

h Cn: Heb *the entrance of* i Gk: Heb lacks *house* j Gk Syr Vg: Heb *They* k Heb lacks *foreigners*

ments, so that they may not communicate holiness to the people with their vestments. 20 They shall not shave their heads or let their locks grow long; they shall only trim the hair of their heads. 21 No priest shall drink wine when he enters the inner court. 22 They shall not marry a widow, or a divorced woman, but only a virgin of the stock of the house of Israel, or a widow who is the widow of a priest. 23 They shall teach my people the difference between the holy and the common, and show them how to distinguish between the unclean and the clean. 24 In a controversy they shall act as judges, and they shall decide it according to my judgments. They shall keep my laws and my statutes regarding all my appointed festivals, and they shall keep my sabbaths holy. 25 They shall not defile themselves by going near to a dead person; for father or mother, however, and for son or daughter, and for brother or unmarried sister they may defile themselves. 26 After he has become clean, they shall count seven days for him. 27 On the day that he goes into the holy place, into the inner court, to minister in the holy place, he shall offer his sin offering, says the Lord God.

28 This shall be their inheritance: I am their inheritance; and you shall give them no holding in Israel; I am their holding. 29 They shall eat the grain offering, the sin offering, and the guilt offering; and every devoted thing in Israel shall be theirs. 30 The first of all the first fruits of all kinds, and every offering of all kinds from all your offerings, shall belong to the priests; you shall also give to the priests the first of your dough, in order that a blessing may rest on your house. 31 The priests shall not eat of anything, whether bird or animal, that died of itself or was torn by animals.

The Holy District

45 When you allot the land as an inheritance, you shall set aside for the Lord a portion of the land as a holy district, twenty-five thousand cubits long and twenty[1] thousand cubits wide; it shall be holy throughout its entire extent. 2 Of this, a square plot of five hundred by five hundred cubits shall be for the sanctuary, with fifty cubits for an open space around it. 3 In the holy district you shall measure off a section twenty-five thousand cubits long and ten thousand wide, in which shall be the sanctuary, the most holy place. 4 It shall be a holy portion of the land; it shall be for the priests, who minister in the sanctuary and approach the Lord to minister to him; and it shall be both a place for their houses and a holy place for the sanctuary. 5 Another section, twenty-five thousand cubits long and ten thousand cubits wide, shall be for the Levites who minister at the temple, as their holding for cities to live in.[m]

6 Alongside the portion set apart as the holy district you shall assign as a holding for the city an area five thousand cubits wide, and twenty-five thousand cubits long; it shall belong to the whole house of Israel.

7 And to the prince shall belong the land on both sides of the holy district and the holding of the city, alongside the holy district and the holding of the city, on the west and on the east, corresponding in length to one of the tribal portions, and extending from the western to the eastern boundary 8 of the land. It is to be his property in Israel. And my princes shall no longer oppress my people; but they shall let the house of Israel have the land according to their tribes.

9 Thus says the Lord God: Enough, O princes of Israel! Put away violence and oppression, and do what is just and right. Cease your evictions of my people, says the Lord God.

Cross references (center column):

44.20
Lev 21.5;
Num 6.5
44.21
Lev 10.9
44.22
Lev 21.7,13, 14
44.23
Lev 10.10;
Mal 2.7
44.24
Deut 17.8,9;
Ezek 20.12, 20
44.25
Lev 21.1-3
44.26
Num 19.13-19
44.28
Num 18.20;
Deut 10.9;
Josh 13.14, 33
44.29
Num 18.9, 14;
Lev 27.21, 28
44.30
Ex 29.19;
Num 3.13;
15.20;
Neh 10.37;
Mal 3.10
44.31
Ex 22.31;
Lev 22.8
45.1
Ezek 47.21, 22; 48.8
45.2
Ezek 42.20
45.3
Ezek 48.10
45.4
v. 1;
Ezek 48.10, 11
45.5
Ezek 48.13
45.6
Ezek 48.15
45.7
Ezek 46.16-18; 48.21
45.8
Isa 11.3-5;
Jer 23.5;
Ezek 22.27; 46.18;
Josh 11.23
45.9
Ezek 44.6;
Jer 6.7;
22.3;
Neh 5.1-5

[1] Gk: Heb ten [m] Gk: Heb as their holding, twenty chambers

Weights and Measures

10 You shall have honest balances, an honest ephah, and an honest bath.[n] 11 The ephah and the bath shall be of the same measure, the bath containing one-tenth of a homer, and the ephah one-tenth of a homer; the homer shall be the standard measure. 12 The shekel shall be twenty gerahs. Twenty shekels, twenty-five shekels, and fifteen shekels shall make a mina for you.

Offerings

13 This is the offering that you shall make: one-sixth of an ephah from each homer of wheat, and one-sixth of an ephah from each homer of barley, 14 and as the fixed portion of oil,[o] one-tenth of a bath from each cor (the cor,[p] like the homer, contains ten baths); 15 and one sheep from every flock of two hundred, from the pastures of Israel. This is the offering for grain offerings, burnt offerings, and offerings of well-being, to make atonement for them, says the Lord God. 16 All the people of the land shall join with the prince in Israel in making this offering. 17 But this shall be the obligation of the prince regarding the burnt offerings, grain offerings, and drink offerings, at the festivals, the new moons, and the sabbaths, all the appointed festivals of the house of Israel: he shall provide the sin offerings, grain offerings, the burnt offerings, and the offerings of well-being, to make atonement for the house of Israel.

Festivals

18 Thus says the Lord God: In the first month, on the first day of the month, you shall take a young bull without blemish, and purify the sanctuary. 19 The priest shall take some of the blood of the sin offering and put it on the doorposts of the temple, the four corners of the ledge of the altar, and the posts of the gate of the inner court. 20 You shall do the same on the seventh day of the month for anyone who

has sinned through error or ignorance; so you shall make atonement for the temple.

21 In the first month, on the fourteenth day of the month, you shall celebrate the festival of the passover, and for seven days unleavened bread shall be eaten. 22 On that day the prince shall provide for himself and all the people of the land a young bull for a sin offering. 23 And during the seven days of the festival he shall provide as a burnt offering to the Lord seven young bulls and seven rams without blemish, on each of the seven days; and a male goat daily for a sin offering. 24 He shall provide as a grain offering an ephah for each bull, an ephah for each ram, and a hin of oil to each ephah. 25 In the seventh month, on the fifteenth day of the month and for the seven days of the festival, he shall make the same provision for sin offerings, burnt offerings, and grain offerings, and for the oil.

Miscellaneous Regulations

46 Thus says the Lord God: The gate of the inner court that faces east shall remain closed on the six working days; but on the sabbath day it shall be opened and on the day of the new moon it shall be opened. 2 The prince shall enter by the vestibule of the gate from outside, and shall take his stand by the post of the gate. The priests shall offer his burnt offering and his offerings of well-being, and he shall bow down at the threshold of the gate. Then he shall go out, but the gate shall not be closed until evening. 3 The people of the land shall bow down at the entrance of that gate before the Lord on the sabbaths and on the new moons. 4 The burnt offering that the prince offers to the Lord on the sabbath day shall be six lambs without blemish and a ram without blemish; 5 and the grain offering with the ram shall be an ephah, and the grain offering with the lambs shall

45.10
Lev 19.35, 36;
Prov 11.1
45.11
Isa 5.10
45.12
Ex 30.13;
Lev 27.25;
Num 3.47
45.15
v. 17;
Lev 1.4;
6.30
45.17
Ezek 46.4-12;
1 Kings 8.64;
2 Chr 31.3;
Lev 23.1-44;
Ezek 43.27
45.18
Ezek 46.1,3, 6; Lev 16.16
45.19
Ezek 43.20
45.20
Lev 4.27;
16.20;
vv. 15,18
45.21
Ex 12.18;
Lev 23.5,6;
Num 9.2,3;
28.16,17
45.22
Lev 4.14
45.23
Lev 23.8;
Num 28.16-25;
Job 42.8
45.25
Lev 23.34;
Num 29.12;
Deut 16.13
46.1
Ezek 45.17-19
46.2
v. 8;
Ezek 44.3;
45.9; v. 12
46.3
Lk 1.10;
v. 1
46.4
Ezek 45.17
46.5
Ezek 45.24;
vv. 7,11

[n] A Heb measure of volume [o] Cn: Heb oil, the bath the oil [p] Vg: Heb homer

be as much as he wishes to give, together with a hin of oil to each ephah. 6 On the day of the new moon he shall offer a young bull without blemish, and six lambs and a ram, which shall be without blemish; 7 as a grain offering he shall provide an ephah with the bull and an ephah with the ram, and with the lambs as much as he wishes, together with a hin of oil to each ephah. 8 When the prince enters, he shall come in by the vestibule of the gate, and he shall go out by the same way.

9 When the people of the land come before the LORD at the appointed festivals, whoever enters by the north gate to worship shall go out by the south gate; and whoever enters by the south gate shall go out by the north gate: they shall not return by way of the gate by which they entered, but shall go out straight ahead. 10 When they come in, the prince shall come in with them; and when they go out, he shall go out.

11 At the festivals and the appointed seasons the grain offering with a young bull shall be an ephah, and with a ram an ephah, and with the lambs as much as one wishes to give, together with a hin of oil to an ephah. 12 When the prince provides a freewill offering, either a burnt offering or offerings of well-being as a freewill offering to the LORD, the gate facing east shall be opened for him; and he shall offer his burnt offering or his offerings of well-being as he does on the sabbath day. Then he shall go out, and after he has gone out the gate shall be closed.

13 He shall provide a lamb, a yearling, without blemish, for a burnt offering to the LORD daily; morning by morning he shall provide it. 14 And he shall provide a grain offering with it morning by morning regularly, one-sixth of an ephah, and one-third of a hin of oil to moisten the choice flour, as a grain offering to the LORD; this is the ordinance for all time. 15 Thus the lamb and the grain offering and

the oil shall be provided, morning by morning, as a regular burnt offering.

16 Thus says the Lord GOD: If the prince makes a gift to any of his sons out of his inheritance,q it shall belong to his sons, it is their holding by inheritance. 17 But if he makes a gift out of his inheritance to one of his servants, it shall be his to the year of liberty; then it shall revert to the prince; only his sons may keep a gift from his inheritance. 18 The prince shall not take any of the inheritance of the people, thrusting them out of their holding; he shall give his sons their inheritance out of his own holding, so that none of my people shall be dispossessed of their holding.

19 Then he brought me through the entrance, which was at the side of the gate, to the north row of the holy chambers for the priests; and there I saw a place at the extreme western end of them. 20 He said to me, "This is the place where the priests shall boil the guilt offering and the sin offering, and where they shall bake the grain offering, in order not to bring them out into the outer court and so communicate holiness to the people."

21 Then he brought me out to the outer court, and led me past the four corners of the court; and in each corner of the court there was a court— 22 in the four corners of the court were small r courts, forty cubits long and thirty wide; the four were of the same size. 23 On the inside, around each of the four courts s was a row of masonry, with hearths made at the bottom of the rows all around. 24 Then he said to me, "These are the kitchens where those who serve at the temple shall boil the sacrifices of the people."

Water Flowing from the Temple

47 Then he brought me back to the entrance of the temple; there, water was flowing from

Cross references

46.6
v. 1
46.7
v. 5
46.8
Ezek 44.3;
v. 2
46.9
Ex 23.14-17;
Deut 16.16
46.11
Ezek 45.17;
vv. 5,7
46.12
2 Chr 29.31;
Ezek 44.3;
v. 2;
Ezek 45.17
46.13
Ex 29.38;
Num 28.3;
Isa 50.4
46.14
Num 28.5
46.15
Ex 29.42;
Num 28.6

46.16
2 Chr 21.3
46.17
Lev 27.10
46.18
Ezek 45.8;
Mic 2.1,2;
Ezek 34.3-6,
21
46.19
Ezek 42.9,
13
46.20
2 Chr 35.13;
Lev 2.4,5,7;
Ezek 44.19
46.24
Ezek 44.11;
v. 20
47.1
Jer 2.13;
Joel 3.18;
Zech 13.1;
14.8;
Rev 22.1

q Gk: Heb it is his inheritance r Gk Syr Vg: Meaning of Heb uncertain s Heb the four of them

below the threshold of the temple toward the east (for the temple faced east); and the water was flowing down from below the south end of the threshold of the temple, south of the altar. ² Then he brought me out by way of the north gate, and led me around on the outside to the outer gate that faces toward the east;ᵗ and the water was coming out on the south side.

3 Going on eastward with a cord in his hand, the man measured one thousand cubits, and then led me through the water; and it was ankle-deep. ⁴ Again he measured one thousand, and led me through the water; and it was knee-deep. Again he measured one thousand, and led me through the water; and it was up to the waist. ⁵ Again he measured one thousand, and it was a river that I could not cross, for the water had risen; it was deep enough to swim in, a river that could not be crossed. ⁶ He said to me, "Mortal, have you seen this?"

Then he led me back along the bank of the river. ⁷ As I came back, I saw on the bank of the river a great many trees on the one side and on the other. ⁸ He said to me, "This water flows toward the eastern region and goes down into the Arabah; and when it enters the sea, the sea of stagnant waters, the water will become fresh. ⁹ Wherever the river goes,ᵘ every living creature that swarms will live, and there will be very many fish, once these waters reach there. It will become fresh; and everything will live where the river goes. ¹⁰ People will stand fishing beside the seaᵛ from En-gedi to En-eglaim; it will be a place for the spreading of nets; its fish will be of a great many kinds, like the fish of the Great Sea. ¹¹ But its swamps and marshes will not become fresh; they are to be left for salt. ¹² On the banks, on both sides of the river, there will grow all kinds of trees for food. Their leaves will not wither nor their fruit fail, but they will bear fresh fruit every month, because the water for them flows from the sanctuary. Their

fruit will be for food, and their leaves for healing."

The New Boundaries of the Land

13 Thus says the Lord GOD: These are the boundaries by which you shall divide the land for inheritance among the twelve tribes of Israel. Joseph shall have two portions. ¹⁴ You shall divide it equally; I swore to give it to your ancestors, and this land shall fall to you as your inheritance.

15 This shall be the boundary of the land: On the north side, from the Great Sea by way of Hethlon to Lebo-hamath, and on to Zedad,ʷ ¹⁶ Berothah, Sibraim (which lies between the border of Damascus and the border of Hamath), as far as Hazer-hatticon, which is on the border of Hauran. ¹⁷ So the boundary shall run from the sea to Hazarenon, which is north of the border of Damascus, with the border of Hamath to the north.ᵗ This shall be the north side.

18 On the east side, between Hauran and Damascus; along the Jordan between Gilead and the land of Israel; to the eastern sea and as far as Tamar.ˣ This shall be the east side.

19 On the south side, it shall run from Tamar as far as the waters of Meribath-kadesh, from there along the Wadi of Egyptʸ to the Great Sea. This shall be the south side.

20 On the west side, the Great Sea shall be the boundary to a point opposite Lebo-hamath. This shall be the west side.

21 So you shall divide this land among you according to the tribes of Israel. ²² You shall allot it as an inheritance for yourselves and for the aliens who reside among you and have begotten children among you. They shall be to you as citi-

Cross references

47.2
Ezek 44.1,2, 4
47.3
Ezek 40.3
47.5
Isa 11.9; Hab 2.14
47.6
Ezek 2.1; 8.6; 40.4; 44.5
47.7
v. 12; Rev 22.2
47.8
Deut 3.17; Isa 35.6,7; Josh 3.16
47.9
Jn 4.14; 7.37,38; Rev 21.7
47.10
Gen 14.7; 2 Chr 20.2; Ezek 26.5, 14; Num 34.6; Josh 23.4; Ezek 48.28
47.12
v. 7; Job 8.16; Ps 1.3; Jer 17.8; Rev 22.2

47.13
Num 34.2-12; Gen 48.5; 1 Chr 5.1; Ezek 48.4
47.14
Gen 12.7; Deut 1.8; Ezek 20.5,6
47.15
Num 34.8; Ezek 48.1
47.16
vv. 17,20; Ezek 48.1; v. 18
47.17
Num 34.9; Ezek 48.1; v. 16
47.18
v. 16; Jer 50.19; Gen 13.10, 11
47.19
Ezek 48.28; Deut 32.51; Isa 27.12
47.20
Num 34.6; vv. 10,15; Ezek 48.1; Am 6.14
47.22
Num 26.55, 56; Isa 56.6, 7; Rom 10.12;

Eph 2.12-14; 3.6; Col 3.11

ᵗ Meaning of Heb uncertain　ᵘ Gk Syr Vg Tg: Heb *the two rivers go*　ᵛ Heb *it* ʷ Gk: Heb *Lebo-zedad*, ¹⁶ Hamath ˣ Compare Syr: Heb *you shall measure* ʸ Heb lacks *of Egypt*

zens of Israel; with you they shall be allotted an inheritance among the tribes of Israel. [23] In whatever tribe aliens reside, there you shall assign them their inheritance, says the Lord GOD.

The Tribal Portions

48 These are the names of the tribes: Beginning at the northern border, on the Hethlon road,[z] from Lebo-hamath, as far as Hazar-enon (which is on the border of Damascus, with Hamath to the north), and[a] extending from the east side to the west,[b] Dan, one portion. [2] Adjoining the territory of Dan, from the east side to the west, Asher, one portion. [3] Adjoining the territory of Asher, from the east side to the west, Naphtali, one portion. [4] Adjoining the territory of Naphtali, from the east side to the west, Manasseh, one portion. [5] Adjoining the territory of Manasseh, from the east side to the west, Ephraim, one portion. [6] Adjoining the territory of Ephraim, from the east side to the west, Reuben, one portion. [7] Adjoining the territory of Reuben, from the east side to the west, Judah, one portion.

8 Adjoining the territory of Judah, from the east side to the west, shall be the portion that you shall set apart, twenty-five thousand cubits in width, and in length equal to one of the tribal portions, from the east side to the west, with the sanctuary in the middle of it. [9] The portion that you shall set apart for the LORD shall be twenty-five thousand cubits in length, and twenty[c] thousand in width. [10] These shall be the allotments of the holy portion: the priests shall have an allotment measuring twenty-five thousand cubits on the northern side, ten thousand cubits in width on the western side, ten thousand in width on the eastern side, and twenty-five thousand in length on the southern side, with the sanctuary of the LORD in the middle of it. [11] This shall be for the consecrated priests, the descendants[d] of Zadok, who kept my charge, who did

not go astray when the people of Israel went astray, as the Levites did. [12] It shall belong to them as a special portion from the holy portion of the land, a most holy place, adjoining the territory of the Levites. [13] Alongside the territory of the priests, the Levites shall have an allotment twenty-five thousand cubits in length and ten thousand in width. The whole length shall be twenty-five thousand cubits and the width twenty[e] thousand. [14] They shall not sell or exchange any of it; they shall not transfer this choice portion of the land, for it is holy to the LORD.

15 The remainder, five thousand cubits in width and twenty-five thousand in length, shall be for ordinary use for the city, for dwellings and for open country. In the middle of it shall be the city; [16] and these shall be its dimensions: the north side four thousand five hundred cubits, the south side four thousand five hundred, the east side four thousand five hundred, and the west side four thousand and five hundred. [17] The city shall have open land: on the north two hundred fifty cubits, on the south two hundred fifty, on the east two hundred fifty, on the west two hundred fifty. [18] The remainder of the length alongside the holy portion shall be ten thousand cubits to the east, and ten thousand to the west, and it shall be alongside the holy portion. Its produce shall be food for the workers of the city. [19] The workers of the city, from all the tribes of Israel, shall cultivate it. [20] The whole portion that you shall set apart shall be twenty-five thousand cubits square, that is, the holy portion together with the property of the city.

21 What remains on both sides of the holy portion and of the property of the city shall belong to the

48.1 Ezek 47.15-17, 20; Josh 19.40-48
48.2 Josh 19.24-31
48.3 Josh 19.32-39
48.4 Josh 13.29-31; 17.1-11
48.5 Josh 16.5-9; 17.8-10,14-18
48.6 Josh 13.15-21
48.7 Josh 15.1-63
48.8 Ezek 45.1-6
48.10 Ezek 44.28; 45.4; v. 8
48.11 Ezek 44.15, 10,12

48.12 Ezek 45.4
48.13 Ezek 45.3
48.14 Lev 25.32-34
48.15 Ezek 42.20; 45.6
48.16 Rev 21.16
48.17 Ezek 45.2
48.18 v. 8
48.19 Ezek 45.6
48.20 v. 16
48.21 Ezek 34.24; 45.7; vv. 22, 8,10

z Compare 47.15: Heb *by the side of the way*
a Cn: Heb *and they shall be his*
b Gk Compare verses 2-8: Heb *the east side the west* c Compare 45.1: Heb *ten* d One Ms Gk: Heb *of the descendants* e Gk: Heb *ten*

prince. Extending from the twenty-five thousand cubits of the holy portion to the east border, and westward from the twenty-five thousand cubits to the west border, parallel to the tribal portions, it shall belong to the prince. The holy portion with the sanctuary of the temple in the middle of it, 22 and the property of the Levites and of the city, shall be in the middle of that which belongs to the prince. The portion of the prince shall lie between the territory of Judah and the territory of Benjamin.

23 As for the rest of the tribes: from the east side to the west, Benjamin, one portion. 24 Adjoining the territory of Benjamin, from the east side to the west, Simeon, one portion. 25 Adjoining the territory of Simeon, from the east side to the west, Issachar, one portion. 26 Adjoining the territory of Issachar, from the east side to the west, Zebulun, one portion. 27 Adjoining the territory of Zebulun, from the east side to the west, Gad, one portion. 28 And adjoining the territory of Gad to the south, the boundary shall run from Tamar to the waters of Meribath-kadesh, from there along the Wadi of Egypt[f] to the Great Sea. 29 This is the land that you shall allot as an inheritance among the tribes of Israel, and these are their portions, says the Lord God.

30 These shall be the exits of the city: On the north side, which is to be four thousand five hundred cubits by measure, 31 three gates, the gate of Reuben, the gate of Judah, and the gate of Levi, the gates of the city being named after the tribes of Israel. 32 On the east side, which is to be four thousand five hundred cubits, three gates, the gate of Joseph, the gate of Benjamin, and the gate of Dan. 33 On the south side, which is to be four thousand five hundred cubits by measure, three gates, the gate of Simeon, the gate of Issachar, and the gate of Zebulun. 34 On the west side, which is to be four thousand five hundred cubits, three gates,[g] the gate of Gad, the gate of Asher, and the gate of Naphtali. 35 The circumference of the city shall be eighteen thousand cubits. And the name of the city from that time on shall be, The Lord is There.

48.23
vv. 1-7;
Josh 18.21-28
48.24
Josh 19.1-9
48.25
Josh 19.17-23
48.26
Josh 19.10-16
48.27
Josh 13.24-28
48.28
Ezek 47.19,
20

48.29
Ezek 47.13-20
48.30
vv. 31-34
48.31
Rev 21.12,
13
48.35
Jer 23.6;
33.16; 3.17;
Joel 3.21;
Zech 2.10;
Rev 21.3;
22.3

[f] Heb lacks *of Egypt* [g] One Ms Gk Syr: MT *their gates three*

Daniel

Title and Background

This book is named after the prophet whose ministry it records. Daniel recounts events that took place during Israel's captivity in Babylon.

Author and Date of Writing

In several passages, such as 9.2 and 10.2, the book itself mentions Daniel as the author. Jesus himself referred to Daniel as the author (Mt 24.15). This would indicate that the book was written about 530 B.C., shortly after the capture of Babylon by Cyrus in 539. Not all scholars agree with this date, however.

Theme and Message

The theological theme of the book is God's sovereignty: "the Most High God has sovereignty over the kingdom of mortals" (5.21). Daniel's visions always show God as triumphant. The prophet encourages the people to trust in the God who controls all history; by depending on him they would experience victory over their enemies.

Outline

Four Young Israelites at the Babylonian Court

1 In the third year of the reign of King Jehoiakim of Judah, King Nebuchadnezzar of Babylon came to Jerusalem and besieged it. ²The Lord let King Jehoiakim of Judah fall into his power, as well as some of the vessels of the house of God. These he brought to the land of Shinar,ᵃ and placed the vessels in the treasury of his gods.

3 Then the king commanded his palace master Ashpenaz to bring some of the Israelites of the royal family and of the nobility, ⁴young men without physical defect and handsome, versed in every branch of wisdom, endowed with knowledge and insight, and competent to serve in the king's palace; they were to be taught the literature and language of the Chaldeans. ⁵The king assigned them a daily portion of the royal rations of food and wine. They were to be educated for three years, so that at the end of that time they could be stationed in the king's court. ⁶Among them were Daniel, Hananiah, Mishael, and Azariah, from the tribe of Judah. ⁷The palace master gave them other names: Daniel he called Belteshazzar, Hananiah he called Shadrach, Mishael he called Meshach, and Azariah he called Abednego.

8 But Daniel resolved that he would not defile himself with the

1.1 2 Kings 24.1; 2 Chr 36.6
1.2 Jer 27.19, 20; Isa 11.11; Zech 5.11
1.3 2 Kings 20.17, 18; Isa 39.7
1.4 2 Sam 14.25; Dan 2.4

1.5ff vv. 8,18; 1 Kings 10.8; v. 19
1.6 Ezek 14.14, 20; 28.3
1.7 Dan 4.8; 5.12; 2.49; 3.12

1.8 Deut 32.38; Ezek 4.13; Hos 9.3

ᵃ Gk Theodotion: Heb adds *to the house of his own gods*

royal rations of food and wine; so he asked the palace master to allow him not to defile himself. [9]Now God allowed Daniel to receive favor and compassion from the palace master. [10]The palace master said to Daniel, "I am afraid of my lord the king; he has appointed your food and your drink. If he should see you in poorer condition than the other young men of your own age, you would endanger my head with the king." [11]Then Daniel asked the guard whom the palace master had appointed over Daniel, Hananiah, Mishael, and Azariah: [12]"Please test your servants for ten days. Let us be given vegetables to eat and water to drink. [13]You can then compare our appearance with the appearance of the young men who eat the royal rations, and deal with your servants according to what you observe." [14]So he agreed to this proposal and tested them for ten days. [15]At the end of ten days it was observed that they appeared better and fatter than all the young men who had been eating the royal rations. [16]So the guard continued to withdraw their royal rations and the wine they were to drink, and gave them vegetables. [17]To these four young men God gave knowledge and skill in every aspect of literature and wisdom; Daniel also had insight into all visions and dreams.

18 At the end of the time that the king had set for them to be brought in, the palace master brought them into the presence of Nebuchadnezzar, [19]and the king spoke with them. And among them all, no one was found to compare with Daniel, Hananiah, Mishael, and Azariah; therefore they were stationed in the king's court. [20]In every matter of wisdom and understanding concerning which the king inquired of them, he found them ten times better than all the magicians and enchanters in his whole kingdom. [21]And Daniel continued there until the first year of King Cyrus.

Nebuchadnezzar's Dream

2 In the second year of Nebuchadnezzar's reign, Nebuchadnezzar dreamed such dreams that his spirit was troubled and his sleep left him. [2]So the king commanded that the magicians, the enchanters, the sorcerers, and the Chaldeans be summoned to tell the king his dreams. When they came in and stood before the king, [3]he said to them, "I have had such a dream that my spirit is troubled by the desire to understand it." [4]The Chaldeans said to the king (in Aramaic),[b] "O king, live forever! Tell your servants the dream, and we will reveal the interpretation." [5]The king answered the Chaldeans, "This is a public decree: if you do not tell me both the dream and its interpretation, you shall be torn limb from limb, and your houses shall be laid in ruins. [6]But if you do tell me the dream and its interpretation, you shall receive from me gifts and rewards and great honor. Therefore tell me the dream and its interpretation." [7]They answered a second time, "Let the king first tell his servants the dream, then we can give its interpretation." [8]The king answered, "I know with certainty that you are trying to gain time, because you see I have firmly decreed: [9]if you do not tell me the dream, there is but one verdict for you. You have agreed to speak lying and misleading words to me until things take a turn. Therefore, tell me the dream, and I shall know that you can give me its interpretation." [10]The Chaldeans answered the king, "There is no one on earth who can reveal what the king demands! In fact no king, however great and powerful, has ever asked such a thing of any magician or enchanter or Chaldean. [11]The thing that the king is asking is too difficult, and no one can reveal it to the king except the gods, whose dwelling is not with mortals."

12 Because of this the king flew

Cross references

1.9
Job 5.15,16;
Ps 106.46;
Prov 16.7
1.10
v. 7
1.12
v. 16
1.15
Ex 23.25;
Prov 10.22
1.16
v. 12
1.17
1 Kings 3.12;
Jas 1.5,17;
Dan 2.19;
7.1; 8.1
1.18
vv. 5,3,7
Gen 41.46;
1 Kings 10.8;
Jer 15.1
1.20
Dan 2.27,
28,46,48; 2.2
1.21
Dan 6.28;
10.1

2.1
Gen 41.8;
Dan 4.5;
Esther 6.1;
Dan 6.18
2.2
Gen 41.8;
Ex 7.11;
vv. 10,27;
Dan 5.7
2.3
Gen 40.8;
41.15;
Dan 4.5
2.4
Isa 36.11;
1 Kings 1.31;
Dan 3.9;
5.10; 6.6,21
2.5
Ezra 6.11;
v. 12;
Dan 3.29
2.6
Dan 5.7,16,
29
2.7
v. 4
2.9
Esther 4.11;
Isa 41.23
2.10
v. 27
2.11
Dan 5.11;
Isa 57.15
2.12
v. 5

b The text from this point to the end of chapter 7 is in Aramaic

into a violent rage and commanded that all the wise men of Babylon be destroyed. ¹³ The decree was issued, and the wise men were about to be executed; and they looked for Daniel and his companions, to execute them. ¹⁴ Then Daniel responded with prudence and discretion to Arioch, the king's chief executioner, who had gone out to execute the wise men of Babylon; ¹⁵ he asked Arioch, the royal official, "Why is the decree of the king so urgent?" Arioch then explained the matter to Daniel. ¹⁶ So Daniel went in and requested that the king give him time and he would tell the king the interpretation.

God Reveals Nebuchadnezzar's Dream

17 Then Daniel went to his home and informed his companions, Hananiah, Mishael, and Azariah, ¹⁸ and told them to seek mercy from the God of heaven concerning this mystery, so that Daniel and his companions with the rest of the wise men of Babylon might not perish. ¹⁹ Then the mystery was revealed to Daniel in a vision of the night, and Daniel blessed the God of heaven.

20 Daniel said:

"Blessed be the name of God
 from age to age,
 for wisdom and power are
 his.

21 He changes times and
 seasons,
 deposes kings and sets up
 kings;
 he gives wisdom to the wise
 and knowledge to those
 who have
 understanding.

22 He reveals deep and hidden
 things;
 he knows what is in the
 darkness,
 and light dwells with him.

23 To you, O God of my
 ancestors,
 I give thanks and praise,
 for you have given me
 wisdom and power,

2.13
Dan 1.19,20
2.14
v. 24;
Jer 52.12,14
2.15
Dan 3.22;
vv. 1-12
2.16
Dan 1.19
2.18
Isa 37.4;
Jer 33.3;
Dan 9.9
2.19
vv. 22,
27-29;
Num 12.6;
Job 33.15,
16
2.20
Ps 113.2;
Jer 32.19;
vv. 21-23
2.21
Esther 1.13;
Dan 7.25;
Job 12.18;
Ps 75.6,7;
Jas 1.5
2.22
Job 12.22;
Ps 25.14;
139.11,12;
Isa 45.7;
Jer 23.24;
Dan 5.11,
14; Jas 1.17
2.23
Gen 31.42;
v. 21;
Dan 1.17;
vv. 18,29,30
2.24
vv. 12-14
2.25
Gen 41.14;
Dan 1.6;
5.13; 6.13
2.26
Dan 1.7;
vv. 3-7
2.27
vv. 2,10
2.28
Gen 40.8;
41.16; 49.1;
Isa 2.2;
Mic 4.1;
Dan 4.5
2.29
vv. 22,28
2.30
Gen 41.16;
Isa 45.3;
Ps 139.2
2.31
Dan 7.7;
Hab 1.7
2.32
vv. 38,39
2.33
vv. 40-43
2.34
Dan 8.25;
Zech 4.6;

and have now revealed to
 me what we asked of you,
 for you have revealed to us
 what the king ordered."

Daniel Interprets the Dream

24 Therefore Daniel went to Arioch, whom the king had appointed to destroy the wise men of Babylon, and said to him, "Do not destroy the wise men of Babylon; bring me in before the king, and I will give the king the interpretation."

25 Then Arioch quickly brought Daniel before the king and said to him: "I have found among the exiles from Judah a man who can tell the king the interpretation." ²⁶ The king said to Daniel, whose name was Belteshazzar, "Are you able to tell me the dream that I have seen and its interpretation?" ²⁷ Daniel answered the king, "No wise men, enchanters, magicians, or diviners can show to the king the mystery that the king is asking, ²⁸ but there is a God in heaven who reveals mysteries, and he has disclosed to King Nebuchadnezzar what will happen at the end of days. Your dream and the visions of your head as you lay in bed were these: ²⁹ To you, O king, as you lay in bed, came thoughts of what would be hereafter, and the revealer of mysteries disclosed to you what is to be. ³⁰ But as for me, this mystery has not been revealed to me because of any wisdom that I have more than any other living being, but in order that the interpretation may be known to the king and that you may understand the thoughts of your mind.

31 "You were looking, O king, and lo! there was a great statue. This statue was huge, its brilliance extraordinary; it was standing before you, and its appearance was frightening. ³² The head of that statue was of fine gold, its chest and arms of silver, its middle and thighs of bronze, ³³ its legs of iron, its feet partly of iron and partly of clay. ³⁴ As you looked on, a stone

Isa 2.9; 60.12

was cut out, not by human hands, and it struck the statue on its feet of iron and clay and broke them in pieces. ³⁵ Then the iron, the clay, the bronze, the silver, and the gold, were all broken in pieces and became like the chaff of the summer threshing floors; and the wind carried them away, so that not a trace of them could be found. But the stone that struck the statue became a great mountain and filled the whole earth.

36 "This was the dream; now we will tell the king its interpretation. ³⁷ You, O king, the king of kings — to whom the God of heaven has given the kingdom, the power, the might, and the glory, ³⁸ into whose hand he has given human beings, wherever they live, the wild animals of the field, and the birds of the air, and whom he has established as ruler over them all — you are the head of gold. ³⁹ After you shall arise another kingdom inferior to yours, and yet a third kingdom of bronze, which shall rule over the whole earth. ⁴⁰ And there shall be a fourth kingdom, strong as iron; just as iron crushes and smashes everything,ᶜ it shall crush and shatter all these. ⁴¹ As you saw the feet and toes partly of potter's clay and partly of iron, it shall be a divided kingdom; but some of the strength of iron shall be in it, as you saw the iron mixed with the clay. ⁴² As the toes of the feet were part iron and part clay, so the kingdom shall be partly strong and partly brittle. ⁴³ As you saw the iron mixed with clay, so will they mix with one another in marriage,ᵈ but they will not hold together, just as iron does not mix with clay. ⁴⁴ And in the days of those kings the God of heaven will set up a kingdom that shall never be destroyed, nor shall this kingdom be left to another people. It shall crush all these kingdoms and bring them to an end, and it shall stand forever; ⁴⁵ just as you saw that a stone was cut from the mountain not by hands, and that it crushed the iron, the bronze, the clay, the silver, and

the gold. The great God has informed the king what shall be hereafter. The dream is certain, and its interpretation trustworthy."

Daniel and His Friends Promoted

46 Then King Nebuchadnezzar fell on his face, worshiped Daniel, and commanded that a grain offering and incense be offered to him. ⁴⁷ The king said to Daniel, "Truly, your God is God of gods and Lord of kings and a revealer of mysteries, for you have been able to reveal this mystery!" ⁴⁸ Then the king promoted Daniel, gave him many great gifts, and made him ruler over the whole province of Babylon and chief prefect over all the wise men of Babylon. ⁴⁹ Daniel made a request of the king, and he appointed Shadrach, Meshach, and Abednego over the affairs of the province of Babylon. But Daniel remained at the king's court.

The Golden Image

3 King Nebuchadnezzar made a golden statue whose height was sixty cubits and whose width was six cubits; he set it up on the plain of Dura in the province of Babylon. ² Then King Nebuchadnezzar sent for the satraps, the prefects, and the governors, the counselors, the treasurers, the justices, the magistrates, and all the officials of the provinces to assemble and come to the dedication of the statue that King Nebuchadnezzar had set up. ³ So the satraps, the prefects, and the governors, the counselors, the treasurers, the justices, the magistrates, and all the officials of the provinces, assembled for the dedication of the statue that King Nebuchadnezzar had set up. When they were standing before the statue that Nebuchadnezzar had set up, ⁴ the herald proclaimed aloud, "You are commanded, O peoples, nations, and languages, ⁵ that when you hear the sound of the horn, pipe, lyre, tri-

2.35
Ps 1.4;
Hos 13.3;
Ps 37.10,36;
Isa 2.2,3
2.36
v. 24
2.37
Isa 47.5;
Jer 27.6,7;
Ezek 26.7;
Ezra 1.2;
Ps 62.11
2.38
Jer 27.6;
Dan 4.21,
22; v. 32
2.39
v. 32
2.40
Dan 7.7,23
2.41
v. 33
2.44
Ps 2.9;
Isa 60.12;
1 Cor 15.24
2.45
Isa 28.16;
v. 35;
Dan 8.25;
v. 29;
Mal 1.11;
Gen 41.28,
32

2.46
Dan 8.17;
Acts 10.25;
14.13; 28.6;
Rev 19.10
2.47
Dan 11.36;
vv. 22,28
2.48
v. 6;
Dan 4.9;
5.11
2.49
Dan 3.12;
Esther 2.19,
21; Dan 3.2
3.1
Isa 46.6;
Hab 2.19;
v. 30;
Dan 2.48
3.2
vv. 3,27
3.4
Isa 40.9;
58.1;
Rev 18.2;
Dan 4.1;
6.25
3.5
vv. 7,10,15

ᶜ Gk Theodotion Syr Vg: Aram adds *and like iron that crushes* ᵈ Aram *by human seed*

gon, harp, drum, and entire musical ensemble, you are to fall down and worship the golden statue that King Nebuchadnezzar has set up. [6]Whoever does not fall down and worship shall immediately be thrown into a furnace of blazing fire." [7]Therefore, as soon as all the peoples heard the sound of the horn, pipe, lyre, trigon, harp, drum, and entire musical ensemble, all the peoples, nations, and languages fell down and worshiped the golden statue that King Nebuchadnezzar had set up.

[8] Accordingly, at this time certain Chaldeans came forward and denounced the Jews. [9]They said to King Nebuchadnezzar, "O king, live forever! [10]You, O king, have made a decree, that everyone who hears the sound of the horn, pipe, lyre, trigon, harp, drum, and entire musical ensemble, shall fall down and worship the golden statue, [11]and whoever does not fall down and worship shall be thrown into a furnace of blazing fire. [12]There are certain Jews whom you have appointed over the affairs of the province of Babylon: Shadrach, Meshach, and Abednego. These pay no heed to you, O King. They do not serve your gods and they do not worship the golden statue that you have set up."

[13] Then Nebuchadnezzar in furious rage commanded that Shadrach, Meshach, and Abednego be brought in; so they brought those men before the king. [14]Nebuchadnezzar said to them, "Is it true, O Shadrach, Meshach, and Abednego, that you do not serve my gods and you do not worship the golden statue that I have set up? [15]Now if you are ready when you hear the sound of the horn, pipe, lyre, trigon, harp, drum, and entire musical ensemble to fall down and worship the statue that I have made, well and good.[e] But if you do not worship, you shall immediately be thrown into a furnace of blazing fire, and who is the god that will deliver you out of my hands?"

[16] Shadrach, Meshach, and

Abednego answered the king, "O Nebuchadnezzar, we have no need to present a defense to you in this matter. [17]If our God whom we serve is able to deliver us from the furnace of blazing fire and out of your hand, O king, let him deliver us.[f] [18]But if not, be it known to you, O king, that we will not serve your gods and we will not worship the golden statue that you have set up."

The Fiery Furnace

[19] Then Nebuchadnezzar was so filled with rage against Shadrach, Meshach, and Abednego that his face was distorted. He ordered the furnace heated up seven times more than was customary, [20]and ordered some of the strongest guards in his army to bind Shadrach, Meshach, and Abednego and to throw them into the furnace of blazing fire. [21]So the men were bound, still wearing their tunics,[g] their trousers,[g] their hats, and their other garments, and they were thrown into the furnace of blazing fire. [22]Because the king's command was urgent and the furnace was so overheated, the raging flames killed the men who lifted Shadrach, Meshach, and Abednego. [23]But the three men, Shadrach, Meshach, and Abednego, fell down, bound, into the furnace of blazing fire.

[24] Then King Nebuchadnezzar was astonished and rose up quickly. He said to his counselors, "Was it not three men that we threw bound into the fire?" They answered the king, "True, O king." [25]He replied, "But I see four men unbound, walking in the middle of the fire, and they are not hurt; and the fourth has the appearance of a god."[h] [26]Nebuchadnezzar then approached the door of the furnace of blazing fire and said, "Shadrach, Meshach, and Abednego, servants

Center reference column:

3.6
vv. 11,15, 21;
Jer 29.22;
Rev 14.11
3.7
vv. 4,5
3.8
Dan 4.7; 6.12
3.9
Dan 2.4; 5.10
3.10
vv. 4-6;
Dan 6.2;
vv. 5,7,15
3.12
Dan 2.49;
1.7; 6.13
3.13
Dan 2.12;
v. 19
3.14
Isa 46.1;
Jer 50.2;
v. 1
3.15
vv. 5,6;
Ex 5.2;
Isa 36.18-20;
Dan 2.47
3.16
v. 12

3.17
Ps 27.1,2;
Isa 26.3,4;
Jer 15.20,21
3.18
v. 28
3.19
v. 13;
Dan 5.6;
v. 12
3.20
vv. 23-25
3.21
v. 27
3.22
Ex 12.33;
Dan 2.15
3.23
v. 21
3.25
Isa 43.2;
v. 28
3.26
v. 17;
Dan 4.2

[e]Aram lacks *well and good* [f]Or *If our God whom we serve is able to deliver us, he will deliver us from the furnace of blazing fire and out of your hand, O king.* [g]Meaning of Aram word uncertain [h]Aram *a son of the gods*

of the Most High God, come out! Come here!" So Shadrach, Meshach, and Abednego came out from the fire. ²⁷And the satraps, the prefects, the governors, and the king's counselors gathered together and saw that the fire had not had any power over the bodies of those men; the hair of their heads was not singed, their tunicsⁱ were not harmed, and not even the smell of fire came from them. ²⁸Nebuchadnezzar said, "Blessed be the God of Shadrach, Meshach, and Abednego, who has sent his angel and delivered his servants who trusted in him. They disobeyed the king's command and yielded up their bodies rather than serve and worship any god except their own God. ²⁹Therefore I make a decree: Any people, nation, or language that utters blasphemy against the God of Shadrach, Meshach, and Abednego shall be torn limb from limb, and their houses laid in ruins; for there is no other god who is able to deliver in this way." ³⁰Then the king promoted Shadrach, Meshach, and Abednego in the province of Babylon.

Nebuchadnezzar's Second Dream

4 ʲ King Nebuchadnezzar to all peoples, nations, and languages that live throughout the earth: May you have abundant prosperity! ²The signs and wonders that the Most High God has worked for me I am pleased to recount.

³ How great are his signs,
 how mighty his wonders!
 His kingdom is an
 everlasting kingdom,
 and his sovereignty is from
 generation to
 generation.

4 ᵏI, Nebuchadnezzar, was living at ease in my home and prospering in my palace. ⁵I saw a dream that frightened me; my fantasies in bed and the visions of my head terrified me. ⁶So I made a decree that all the wise men of Babylon should be brought before me, in order that they might tell me the interpreta-

tion of the dream. ⁷Then the magicians, the enchanters, the Chaldeans, and the diviners came in, and I told them the dream, but they could not tell me its interpretation. ⁸At last Daniel came in before me—he who was named Belteshazzar after the name of my god, and who is endowed with a spirit of the holy godsˡ—and I told him the dream: ⁹"O Belteshazzar, chief of the magicians, I know that you are endowed with a spirit of the holy godsˡ and that no mystery is too difficult for you. Hearᵐ the dream that I saw; tell me its interpretation.

¹⁰ⁿUpon my bed this is what I
 saw;
 there was a tree at the
 center of the earth,
 and its height was great.
¹¹ The tree grew great and
 strong,
 its top reached to heaven,
 and it was visible to the
 ends of the whole
 earth.
¹² Its foliage was beautiful,
 its fruit abundant,
 and it provided food for all.
 The animals of the field
 found shade under it,
 the birds of the air nested
 in its branches,
 and from it all living beings
 were fed.

¹³I continued looking, in the visions of my head as I lay in bed, and there was a holy watcher, coming down from heaven. ¹⁴He cried aloud and said:
 'Cut down the tree and chop
 off its branches,
 strip off its foliage and
 scatter its fruit.
 Let the animals flee from
 beneath it
 and the birds from its
 branches.

Cross references

3.27 v. 2; Isa 43.2; Heb 11.34; v. 21
3.28 vv. 15,25; Acts 5.19; 12.7; Ps 34.7,8; Jer 17.7; v. 18
3.29 Dan 6.26; v. 12; Dan 2.5; 2.47; 6.27
3.30 Dan 2.49
4.1 Dan 6.25
4.2 Dan 3.26
4.3 Dan 6.27; v. 34; Dan 2.44; 6.26
4.4 Isa 47.7,8
4.5 Dan 2.28, 29; 2.1
4.6 Dan 2.2
4.7 Dan 2.2
4.8 Dan 1.7; 2.26; Dan 5.11,14
4.9 Dan 2.48; 5.11; 2.47; 2.4,5
4.10 vv. 5,20; Ezek 31.3-6
4.11 vv. 20,22
4.12 Ezek 31.6,7; Lam 4.20; Mt 13.32; Lk 13.19
4.13 Dan 7.1; vv. 17,23; Dan 8.13; Zech 14.5
4.14 Ezek 31.10-14; Mt 3.10; Ezek 31.12, 13

ⁱMeaning of Aram word uncertain ʲCh 3.31 in Aram ᵏCh 4.1 in Aram ˡOr *a holy, divine spirit* ᵐTheodotion: Aram *The visions of* ⁿTheodotion Syr Compare Gk: Aram adds *The visions of my head*

15 But leave its stump and
 roots in the ground,
 with a band of iron and
 bronze,
 in the tender grass of the
 field.
 Let him be bathed with the
 dew of heaven.
 and let his lot be with the
 animals of the field
 in the grass of the earth.
16 Let his mind be changed
 from that of a human,
 and let the mind of an
 animal be given to him.
 And let seven times pass
 over him.
17 The sentence is rendered by
 decree of the watchers,
 the decision is given by
 order of the holy ones,
 in order that all who live
 may know
 that the Most High is
 sovereign over the
 kingdom of mortals;
 he gives it to whom he will
 and sets over it the lowliest
 of human beings.'

18 This is the dream that I, King
Nebuchadnezzar, saw. Now you,
Belteshazzar, declare the interpre-
tation, since all the wise men of my
kingdom are unable to tell me the
interpretation. You are able, how-
ever, for you are endowed with a
spirit of the holy gods."o

Daniel Interprets the Second
Dream

19 Then Daniel, who was called
Belteshazzar, was severely dis-
tressed for a while. His thoughts
terrified him. The king said, "Bel-
teshazzar, do not let the dream or
the interpretation terrify you." Bel-
teshazzar answered, "My lord, may
the dream be for those who hate
you, and its interpretation for your
enemies! 20 The tree that you saw,
which grew great and strong, so
that its top reached to heaven and
was visible to the end of the whole
earth, 21 whose foliage was beauti-
ful and its fruit abundant, and
which provided food for all, under

4.15
Job 14.7-9;
v. 32
4.16
Dan 7.25;
11.13; 12.7
4.17
Ps 9.16;
vv. 2,25;
Dan 5.18,
19;
Dan 11.21
4.18
Gen 41.8,
15; Dan 5.8,
15; vv. 7-9
4.19
Dan 7.15,
28;
2 Sam 18.32;
Jer 29.7
4.20
vv. 10-12
4.21
see v. 12

4.22
2 Sam 12.7;
Dan 2.37,
38; 5.18,19;
Jer 27.6-8
4.23
vv. 13-17;
Dan 5.21
4.24
vv. 17,2;
Job 40.11,
12;
Ps 107.40
4.25
Dan 5.21;
Ps 83.18;
Jer 27.5
4.26
Mt 21.25;
Lk 15.18
4.27
Isa 55.6,7;
Ezek 18.21,
22;
Ps 41.1-3;
1 Kings 21.29
4.28ff
Zech 1.6
4.30
Hab 2.4;
v. 25;
Dan 5.20,
21;
Isa 37.24,25
4.31
Dan 5.5;
vv. 13,14,23

which animals of the field lived,
and in whose branches the birds of
the air had nests— 22 it is you,
O king! You have grown great and
strong. Your greatness has in-
creased and reaches to heaven, and
your sovereignty to the ends of the
earth. 23 And whereas the king saw
a holy watcher coming down from
heaven and saying, 'Cut down the
tree and destroy it, but leave its
stump and roots in the ground,
with a band of iron and bronze, in
the grass of the field; and let him
be bathed with the dew of heaven,
and let his lot be with the animals
of the field, until seven times pass
over him'— 24 this is the interpre-
tation, O king, and it is a decree of
the Most High that has come upon
my lord the king: 25 You shall be
driven away from human society,
and your dwelling shall be with the
wild animals. You shall be made to
eat grass like oxen, you shall be
bathed with the dew of heaven, and
seven times shall pass over you, un-
til you have learned that the Most
High has sovereignty over the king-
dom of mortals, and gives it to
whom he will. 26 As it was com-
manded to leave the stump and
roots of the tree, your kingdom
shall be reestablished for you from
the time that you learn that Heav-
en is sovereign. 27 Therefore,
O king, may my counsel be accept-
able to you: atone forp your sins
with righteousness, and your iniq-
uities with mercy to the oppressed,
so that your prosperity may be pro-
longed."

Nebuchadnezzar's Humiliation

28 All this came upon King
Nebuchadnezzar. 29 At the end of
twelve months he was walking on
the roof of the royal palace of Bab-
ylon, 30 and the king said, "Is this
not magnificent Babylon, which I
have built as a royal capital by my
mighty power and for my glorious
majesty?" 31 While the words were
still in the king's mouth, a voice
came from heaven: "O King Nebu-
chadnezzar, to you it is declared:

o Or *a holy, divine spirit* p Aram *break off*

THE NEO-BABYLONIAN EMPIRE 626-539 B.C.

Babylon boasted one of the world's seven wonders, the famed Hanging Gardens, as well as a staged temple-tower 295 feet high and, according to Herodotus, several colossal gold statues weighing many tons.

The kingdom has departed from you! 32 You shall be driven away from human society, and your dwelling shall be with the animals of the field. You shall be made to eat grass like oxen, and seven times shall pass over you, until you have learned that the Most High has sovereignty over the kingdom of mortals and gives it to whom he will." 33 Immediately the sentence was fulfilled against Nebuchadnezzar. He was driven away from human society, ate grass like oxen, and his body was bathed with the dew of heaven, until his hair grew as long as eagles' feathers and his nails became like birds' claws.

Nebuchadnezzar Praises God

34 When that period was over, I, Nebuchadnezzar, lifted my eyes to heaven, and my reason returned to me.

I blessed the Most High,
 and praised and honored
 the one who lives
 forever.
For his sovereignty is an
 everlasting sovereignty,
 and his kingdom endures
 from generation to
 generation.
35 All the inhabitants of the
 earth are accounted as
 nothing,
 and he does what he wills
 with the host of heaven
 and the inhabitants of the
 earth.
There is no one who can stay
 his hand
 or say to him, "What are
 you doing?"

36 At that time my reason returned to me; and my majesty and splendor were restored to me for the glory of my kingdom. My counselors and my lords sought me out, I was reestablished over my kingdom, and still more greatness was added to me. 37 Now I, Nebuchadnezzar, praise and extol and honor the King of heaven,

for all his works are truth,
 and his ways are justice;

and he is able to bring low
 those who walk in pride.

Belshazzar's Feast

5 King Belshazzar made a great festival for a thousand of his lords, and he was drinking wine in the presence of the thousand.

2 Under the influence of the wine, Belshazzar commanded that they bring in the vessels of gold and silver that his father Nebuchadnezzar had taken out of the temple in Jerusalem, so that the king and his lords, his wives, and his concubines might drink from them. 3 So they brought in the vessels of gold and silver q that had been taken out of the temple, the house of God in Jerusalem, and the king and his lords, his wives, and his concubines drank from them. 4 They drank the wine and praised the gods of gold and silver, bronze, iron, wood, and stone.

The Writing on the Wall

5 Immediately the fingers of a human hand appeared and began writing on the plaster of the wall of the royal palace, next to the lampstand. The king was watching the hand as it wrote. 6 Then the king's face turned pale, and his thoughts terrified him. His limbs gave way, and his knees knocked together. 7 The king cried aloud to bring in the enchanters, the Chaldeans, and the diviners; and the king said to the wise men of Babylon, "Whoever can read this writing and tell me its interpretation shall be clothed in purple, have a chain of gold around his neck, and rank third in the kingdom." 8 Then all the king's wise men came in, but they could not read the writing or tell the king the interpretation. 9 Then King Belshazzar became greatly terrified and his face turned pale, and his lords were perplexed.

10 The queen, when she heard the discussion of the king and his lords, came into the banqueting hall. The queen said, "O king, live forever! Do not let your thoughts

Cross references (center column):

4.32
v. 25
4.33
Dan 5.21
4.34
vv. 16,25,
32,36,2;
Dan 5.18,
21; 12.7;
Rev 4.10;
Lk 1.33
4.35
Isa 40.15,
17;
Ps 135.6;
Isa 43.13;
45.9;
Rom 9.20
4.36
vv. 34,30;
Dan 2.31;
v. 26
4.37
Ps 33.4,5;
Ex 18.11;
Dan 5.20

5.1
Esther 1.3
5.2
Dan 1.2;
Jer 52.19;
v.23
5.4
v. 23;
Rev 9.20
5.5
Dan 4.31;
v. 24
5.6
Dan 4.5,19;
Nah 2.10;
Ezek 7.17;
21.7
5.7
Isa 47.13;
Dan 2.6;
Ezek 16.11;
Dan 6.2,3
5.8
Dan 2.10,
27; 4.7
5.9
Isa 21.2-4;
Jer 6.24;
v. 6
5.10
Dan 2.4; 3.9

q Theodotion Vg: Aram lacks *and silver*

terrify you or your face grow pale. ¹¹There is a man in your kingdom who is endowed with a spirit of the holy gods.ʳ In the days of your father he was found to have enlightenment, understanding, and wisdom like the wisdom of the gods. Your father, King Nebuchadnezzar, made him chief of the magicians, enchanters, Chaldeans, and diviners,ˢ ¹²because an excellent spirit, knowledge, and understanding to interpret dreams, explain riddles, and solve problems were found in this Daniel, whom the king named Belteshazzar. Now let Daniel be called, and he will give the interpretation."

The Writing on the Wall Interpreted

13 Then Daniel was brought in before the king. The king said to Daniel, "So you are Daniel, one of the exiles of Judah, whom my father the king brought from Judah? ¹⁴I have heard of you that a spirit of the godsᵗ is in you, and that enlightenment, understanding, and excellent wisdom are found in you. ¹⁵Now the wise men, the enchanters, have been brought in before me to read this writing and tell me its interpretation, but they were not able to give the interpretation of the matter. ¹⁶But I have heard that you can give interpretations and solve problems. Now if you are able to read the writing and tell me its interpretation, you shall be clothed in purple, have a chain of gold around your neck, and rank third in the kingdom."

17 Then Daniel answered in the presence of the king, "Let your gifts be for yourself, or give your rewards to someone else! Nevertheless I will read the writing to the king and let him know the interpretation. ¹⁸O king, the Most High God gave your father Nebuchadnezzar kingship, greatness, glory, and majesty. ¹⁹And because of the greatness that he gave him, all peoples, nations, and languages trembled and feared before him. He killed those he wanted to kill, kept alive those

5.11 Dan 2.47, 48; 4.8,9,18; 1.17
5.12 Dan 6.3; 1.7
5.13 Dan 2.25; 6.13; 1.1,2
5.14 vv. 11,12
5.16 Gen 40.8; vv.7,29
5.17 2 Kings 5.16
5.18 v. 21;
Dan 2.37, 38; 4.17; Jer 27.5-7
5.19 Dan 3.4; 2.12,13

5.20 Dan 4.30, 37; 2 Kings 17.14; 2 Chr 36.13; Jer 13.18
5.21 Dan 4.32-34; 4.16; Ezek 17.24; Dan 4.34,35
5.22 2 Chr 33.23; 36.12
5.23 Jer 50.29; vv. 3,4; Ps 115.5,6; Hab 2.18, 19; Job 12.10; 31.4; Jer 10.23
5.24 v. 5
5.26 Isa 13.6,17; Jer 27.7; 50.41-43
5.27 Job 31.6; Ps 62.9
5.29 vv. 7,16
5.30 Isa 21.4-9; Jer 51.31, 39,57

he wanted to keep alive, honored those he wanted to honor, and degraded those he wanted to degrade. ²⁰But when his heart was lifted up and his spirit was hardened so that he acted proudly, he was deposed from his kingly throne, and his glory was stripped from him. ²¹He was driven from human society, and his mind was made like that of an animal. His dwelling was with the wild asses, he was fed grass like oxen, and his body was bathed with the dew of heaven, until he learned that the Most High God has sovereignty over the kingdom of mortals, and sets over it whomever he will. ²²And you, Belshazzar his son, have not humbled your heart, even though you knew all this! ²³You have exalted yourself against the Lord of heaven! The vessels of his temple have been brought in before you, and you and your lords, your wives and your concubines have been drinking wine from them. You have praised the gods of silver and gold, of bronze, iron, wood, and stone, which do not see or hear or know; but the God in whose power is your very breath, and to whom belong all your ways, you have not honored.

24 "So from his presence the hand was sent and this writing was inscribed. ²⁵And this is the writing that was inscribed: MENE, MENE, TEKEL, and PARSIN. ²⁶This is the interpretation of the matter: MENE, God has numbered the days ofᵘ your kingdom and brought it to an end; ²⁷TEKEL, you have been weighed on the scales and found wanting; ²⁸PERES,ᵛ your kingdom is divided and given to the Medes and Persians."

29 Then Belshazzar gave the command, and Daniel was clothed in purple, a chain of gold was put around his neck, and a proclamation was made concerning him that he should rank third in the kingdom.

30 That very night Belshazzar,

ʳ Or *a holy, divine spirit* ˢ Aram adds *the king your father* ᵗ Or *a divine spirit* ᵘ Aram lacks *the days of* ᵛ The singular of *Parsin*

the Chaldean king, was killed. ³¹ᵂ And Darius the Mede received the kingdom, being about sixty-two years old.

The Plot against Daniel

6 It pleased Darius to set over the kingdom one hundred twenty satraps, stationed throughout the whole kingdom, ² and over them three presidents, including Daniel; to these the satraps gave account, so that the king might suffer no loss. ³ Soon Daniel distinguished himself above all the other presidents and satraps because an excellent spirit was in him, and the king planned to appoint him over the whole kingdom. ⁴ So the presidents and the satraps tried to find grounds for complaint against Daniel in connection with the kingdom. But they could find no grounds for complaint or any corruption, because he was faithful, and no negligence or corruption could be found in him. ⁵ The men said, "We shall not find any ground for complaint against this Daniel unless we find it in connection with the law of his God."

6 So the presidents and satraps conspired and came to the king and said to him, "O King Darius, live forever! ⁷ All the presidents of the kingdom, the prefects and the satraps, the counselors and the governors are agreed that the king should establish an ordinance and enforce an interdict, that whoever prays to anyone, divine or human, for thirty days, except to you, O king, shall be thrown into a den of lions. ⁸ Now, O king, establish the interdict and sign the document, so that it cannot be changed, according to the law of the Medes and the Persians, which cannot be revoked." ⁹ Therefore King Darius signed the document and interdict.

Daniel in the Lions' Den

10 Although Daniel knew that the document had been signed, he continued to go to his house, which had windows in its upper room open toward Jerusalem, and

to get down on his knees three times a day to pray to his God and praise him, just as he had done previously. ¹¹ The conspirators came and found Daniel praying and seeking mercy before his God. ¹² Then they approached the king and said concerning the interdict, "O king! Did you not sign an interdict, that anyone who prays to anyone, divine or human, within thirty days except to you, O king, shall be thrown into a den of lions?" The king answered, "The thing stands fast, according to the law of the Medes and Persians, which cannot be revoked." ¹³ Then they responded to the king, "Daniel, one of the exiles from Judah, pays no attention to you, O king, or to the interdict you have signed, but he is saying his prayers three times a day."

14 When the king heard the charge, he was very much distressed. He was determined to save Daniel, and until the sun went down he made every effort to rescue him. ¹⁵ Then the conspirators came to the king and said to him, "Know, O king, that it is a law of the Medes and Persians that no interdict or ordinance that the king establishes can be changed."

16 Then the king gave the command, and Daniel was brought and thrown into the den of lions. The king said to Daniel, "May your God, whom you faithfully serve, deliver you!" ¹⁷ A stone was brought and laid on the mouth of the den, and the king sealed it with his own signet and with the signet of his lords, so that nothing might be changed concerning Daniel. ¹⁸ Then the king went to his palace and spent the night fasting; no food was brought to him, and sleep fled from him.

Daniel Saved from the Lions

19 Then, at break of day, the king got up and hurried to the den of lions. ²⁰ When he came near the den where Daniel was, he cried out anxiously to Daniel, "O Daniel, servant of the living God, has your

ʷCh 6.1 in Aram

Cross-references:

5.31 Dan 6.1; 9.1
6.1 Esther 1.1; Dan 5.31
6.2 Dan 2.48, 49;
6.3 Dan 1.20; 5.12,14; Esther 10.3
6.4 Gen 43.18; v.22
6.6 v. 21; Neh 2.3; Dan 2.4
6.7 Dan 3.2,27; Ps 59.3; Dan 3.6; v. 16
6.8 vv. 12,15; Esther 1.19; 8.8
6.9 Ps 118.9; 146.3
6.10 1 Kings 8.48, 49; Ps 95.6; 55.17; 1 Thes 5.17, 18

6.11 v.6
6.12 Dan 3.8; Acts 16.19-21
6.13 Dan 1.6; 5.13; Esther 3.8; Dan 3.12; Acts 5.29
6.14 Mk 6.26
6.15 Esther 8.8; v.8
6.16 Jer 38.5; vv. 7,20; Ps 37.39,40
6.17 Lam 3.55; Mt 27.66
6.18 2 Sam 12.16, 17; Esther 6.1; Dan 2.1
6.20 vv. 26,27; Jer 32.17; Dan 3.17

God whom you faithfully serve been able to deliver you from the lions?" ²¹Daniel then said to the king, "O king, live forever! ²²My God sent his angel and shut the lions' mouths so that they would not hurt me, because I was found blameless before him; and also before you, O king, I have done no wrong." ²³Then the king was exceedingly glad and commanded that Daniel be taken up out of the den. So Daniel was taken up out of the den, and no kind of harm was found on him, because he had trusted in his God. ²⁴The king gave a command, and those who had accused Daniel were brought and thrown into the den of lions — they, their children, and their wives. Before they reached the bottom of the den the lions overpowered them and broke all their bones in pieces.

25 Then King Darius wrote to all peoples and nations of every language throughout the whole world: "May you have abundant prosperity! ²⁶I make a decree, that in all my royal dominion people should tremble and fear before the God of Daniel:

For he is the living God,
　enduring forever.
His kingdom shall never be
　　destroyed,
　and his dominion has no
　　end.
²⁷ He delivers and rescues,
　he works signs and
　　wonders in heaven and
　　on earth;
　for he has saved Daniel
　from the power of the
　　lions."

²⁸So this Daniel prospered during the reign of Darius and the reign of Cyrus the Persian.

Visions of the Four Beasts

7 In the first year of King Belshazzar of Babylon, Daniel had a dream and visions of his head as he lay in bed. Then he wrote down the dream.ˣ ²I,ʸ Daniel, saw in my vision by night the four winds of heaven stirring up the great sea, ³and four great beasts came up out

of the sea, different from one another. ⁴The first was like a lion and had eagles' wings. Then, as I watched, its wings were plucked off, and it was lifted up from the ground and made to stand on two feet like a human being; and a human mind was given to it. ⁵Another beast appeared, a second one, that looked like a bear. It was raised up on one side, had three tusksᶻ in its mouth among its teeth and was told, "Arise, devour many bodies!" ⁶After this, as I watched, another appeared, like a leopard. The beast had four wings of a bird on its back and four heads; and dominion was given to it. ⁷After this I saw in the visions by night a fourth beast, terrifying and dreadful and exceedingly strong. It had great iron teeth and was devouring, breaking in pieces, and stamping what was left with its feet. It was different from all the beasts that preceded it, and it had ten horns. ⁸I was considering the horns, when another horn appeared, a little one coming up among them; to make room for it, three of the earlier horns were plucked up by the roots. There were eyes like human eyes in this horn, and a mouth speaking arrogantly.

Judgment before the Ancient One

⁹ As I watched,
　thrones were set in place,
　　and an Ancient Oneᵃ took
　　　his throne,
　his clothing was white as
　　　snow,
　　and the hair of his head
　　　like pure wool;
　his throne was fiery flames,
　　and its wheels were
　　　burning fire.
¹⁰ A stream of fire issued
　and flowed out from his
　　　presence.
　A thousand thousands served
　　　him,

6.21
Dan 2.4;
v. 6
6.22
Acts 12.11;
2 Tim 4.17;
Heb 11.33;
1 Sam 24.10
6.23
vv. 14,18;
Dan 3.25,
27; Isa 26.3;
Heb 11.33
6.24
2 Kings 14.6;
Ps 54.5;
Isa 38.13
6.25
Ezra 1.1,2;
Esther 3.12;
8.9;
Dan 4.1;
1 Pet 1.2
6.26
Dan 3.29;
Ps 99.1;
Dan 4.34;
Ps 93.1,2;
Dan 4.3;
7.14,27
6.27
v. 22;
Dan 4.3
6.28
Ezra 1.1,2;
Dan 1.21;
10.1
7.1
Dan 5.1,22,
30; 1.17;
vv. 7,13,15;
Jer 36.4,32
7.3
v. 17;
Rev 13.1

7.4
Jer 48.40;
Ezek 17.3;
Hab 1.8
7.5
Dan 2.39
7.6
v. 12
7.7
Rev 12.3;
13.1; 17.3
7.8
vv. 20,21;
Rev 9.7;
vv. 11,25
7.9
Mk 9.3;
Rev 1.14;
Ezek 1.13,
26; 10.2,6
7.10
Ps 50.3;
97.3;
Isa 30.33;
Rev 5.11;
20.12

ˣQ Ms Theodotion: MT adds *the beginning of the words; he said* ʸTheodotion: Aram *Daniel answered and said, "I* ᶻOr *ribs* ᵃAram *an Ancient of Days*

and ten thousand times ten
 thousand stood
 attending him.
The court sat in judgment,
 and the books were
 opened.

11 I watched then because of the noise of the arrogant words that the horn was speaking. And as I watched, the beast was put to death, and its body destroyed and given over to be burned with fire. 12 As for the rest of the beasts, their dominion was taken away, but their lives were prolonged for a season and a time. 13 As I watched in the night visions,

I saw one like a human
 being[b]
coming with the clouds of
 heaven.
And he came to the Ancient
 One[c]
and was presented before
 him.
14 To him was given dominion
 and glory and kingship,
that all peoples, nations, and
 languages
should serve him.
His dominion is an
 everlasting dominion
that shall not pass away,
and his kingship is one
 that shall never be
 destroyed.

Daniel's Visions Interpreted

15 As for me, Daniel, my spirit was troubled within me,[d] and the visions of my head terrified me. 16 I approached one of the attendants to ask him the truth concerning all this. So he said that he would disclose to me the interpretation of the matter: 17 "As for these four great beasts, four kings shall arise out of the earth. 18 But the holy ones of the Most High shall receive the kingdom and possess the kingdom forever—forever and ever."

19 Then I desired to know the truth concerning the fourth beast, which was different from all the rest, exceedingly terrifying, with its teeth of iron and claws of bronze, and which devoured and broke in

pieces, and stamped what was left with its feet; 20 and concerning the ten horns that were on its head, and concerning the other horn, which came up and to make room for which three of them fell out—the horn that had eyes and a mouth that spoke arrogantly, and that seemed greater than the others. 21 As I looked, this horn made war with the holy ones and was prevailing over them, 22 until the Ancient One[c] came; then judgment was given for the holy ones of the Most High, and the time arrived when the holy ones gained possession of the kingdom.

23 This is what he said: "As for the fourth beast,
there shall be a fourth
 kingdom on earth
that shall be different from
 all the other kingdoms;
it shall devour the whole
 earth,
and trample it down, and
 break it to pieces.
24 As for the ten horns,
out of this kingdom ten
 kings shall arise,
and another shall arise
 after them.
This one shall be different
 from the former ones,
and shall put down three
 kings.
25 He shall speak words against
 the Most High,
shall wear out the holy
 ones of the Most High,
and shall attempt to
 change the sacred
 seasons and the law;
and they shall be given into
 his power
for a time, two times,[e] and
 half a time.
26 Then the court shall sit in
 judgment,
and his dominion shall be
 taken away,
to be consumed and totally
 destroyed.
27 The kingship and dominion

7.11
vv. 7,8;
Rev 19.20
7.12
vv. 3-6
7.13
Ezek 1.26;
Mt 24.30;
26.64;
Mk 13.26;
Lk 21.27;
Rev 1.7,13
7.14
Ps 2.6-8;
1 Cor 15.27;
Eph 1.22;
Phil 2.9-11;
Ps 72.11;
102.22;
Dan 2.44;
Mic 4.7;
Heb 12.28
7.15
vv. 1,28
7.16
Rev 5.5;
7.13,14;
Dan 8.16,17
7.17
v. 3
7.18
Isa 60.12-14;
Rev 2.26;
20.4
7.19
vv. 7,8
7.21
Rev 13.7
7.22
vv. 9,13;
1 Cor 6.2,
3; v. 18
7.23
vv. 7,19
7.24
vv. 7,8;
Rev 17.12
7.25
Isa 37.23;
Dan 8.24,
25;
Rev 13.5;
17.6; 18.24;
Dan 2.21;
12.7;
Rev 12.14
7.26
vv. 10,22
7.27
vv. 14,18,
22; Lk 1.33;
Jn 12.34;
Rev 11.15;
Ps 2.6-12;
Isa 60.12

b Aram *one like a son of man* c Aram *the Ancient of Days* d Aram *troubled in its sheath* e Aram *a time, times*

and the greatness of the
　　kingdoms under the
　　whole heaven
shall be given to the people
　　of the holy ones of the
　　Most High;
　their kingdom shall be an
　　everlasting kingdom,
and all dominions shall
　　serve and obey them."

28 Here the account ends. As
for me, Daniel, my thoughts greatly
terrified me, and my face turned
pale; but I kept the matter in my
mind.

Vision of a Ram and a Goat

8 In the third year of the reign of
King Belshazzar a vision ap-
peared to me, Daniel, after the one
that had appeared to me at first.
[2] In the vision I was looking and
saw myself in Susa the capital, in
the province of Elam,[f] and I was
by the river Ulai.[g] [3] I looked up and
saw a ram standing beside the riv-
er.[h] It had two horns. Both horns
were long, but one was longer than
the other, and the longer one came
up second. [4] I saw the ram charging
westward and northward and
southward. All beasts were power-
less to withstand it, and no one
could rescue from its power; it did
as it pleased and became strong.

5 As I was watching, a male goat
appeared from the west, coming
across the face of the whole earth
without touching the ground. The
goat had a horn[i] between its eyes.
[6] It came toward the ram with the
two horns that I had seen standing
beside the river,[h] and it ran at it
with savage force. [7] I saw it ap-
proaching the ram. It was enraged
against it and struck the ram,
breaking its two horns. The ram did
not have power to withstand it; it
threw the ram down to the ground
and trampled upon it, and there
was no one who could rescue the
ram from its power. [8] Then the
male goat grew exceedingly great;
but at the height of its power, the
great horn was broken, and in its
place there came up four promi-

7.28
v. 15;
Dan 8.27;
Lk 2.19
8.1
Dan 7.1,15,
28
8.2
Dan 7.2,15;
Esther 1.2;
Ezek 32.24;
v. 16
8.3
Dan 10.5;
v. 20
8.4
v. 7
8.5
v. 21
8.6
v. 3
8.7
Dan 11.11;
7.7
8.8
2 Chr 26.16;
Dan 5.20;
v. 22;
Dan 7.2;
Rev 7.1

8.9
v. 23;
Dan 11.16,
41
8.10
Rev 12.4
8.11
Dan 11.36,
37;
Josh 5.14;
Dan 11.31;
12.11;
Ezek 46.13,
14
8.13
Dan 4.13,
23; 12.6,8;
Rev 11.2
8.15
v. 1;
Dan 7.13
8.16
Dan 9.21;
Lk 1.19,26
8.17
Ezek 1.28;
Rev 1.17
8.18
Dan 10.9,
16,18;
Ezek 2.2
8.19
Hab 2.3

nent horns toward the four winds
of heaven.

9 Out of one of them came an-
other[j] horn, a little one, which
grew exceedingly great toward the
south, toward the east, and toward
the beautiful land. [10] It grew as high
as the host of heaven. It threw
down to the earth some of the host
and some of the stars, and tram-
pled on them. [11] Even against the
prince of the host it acted arrogant-
ly; it took the regular burnt offering
away from him and overthrew the
place of his sanctuary. [12] Because
of wickedness, the host was given
over to it together with the regular
burnt offering;[k] it cast truth to the
ground, and kept prospering in
what it did. [13] Then I heard a holy
one speaking, and another holy
one said to the one that spoke,
"For how long is this vision con-
cerning the regular burnt offering,
the transgression that makes deso-
late, and the giving over of the
sanctuary and host to be tram-
pled?"[k] [14] And he answered him,[l]
"For two thousand three hundred
evenings and mornings; then the
sanctuary shall be restored to its
rightful state."

Gabriel Interprets the Vision

15 When I, Daniel, had seen the
vision, I tried to understand it.
Then someone appeared standing
before me, having the appearance
of a man, [16] and I heard a human
voice by the Ulai, calling, "Gabriel,
help this man understand the vi-
sion." [17] So he came near where I
stood; and when he came, I be-
came frightened and fell prostrate.
But he said to me, "Understand,
O mortal,[m] that the vision is for
the time of the end."

18 As he was speaking to me, I
fell into a trance, face to the
ground; then he touched me and
set me on my feet. [19] He said, "Lis-

[f] Gk Theodotion: MT Q Ms repeat *in the
vision I was looking*　　[g] Or *the Ulai Gate*
[h] Or *gate*　　[i] Theodotion: Gk *one horn*; Heb
a horn of vision　　[j] Cn Compare 7.8: Heb
one　　[k] Meaning of Heb uncertain
[l] Gk Theodotion Syr Vg: Heb *me*
[m] Heb *son of man*

ten, and I will tell you what will take place later in the period of wrath; for it refers to the appointed time of the end. 20 As for the ram that you saw with the two horns, these are the kings of Media and Persia. 21 The male goat n is the king of Greece, and the great horn between its eyes is the first king. 22 As for the horn that was broken, in place of which four others arose, four kingdoms shall arise from his o nation, but not with his power.

23 At the end of their rule,
when the transgressions
have reached their full
measure,
a king of bold countenance
shall arise,
skilled in intrigue.
24 He shall grow strong in
power, p
shall cause fearful
destruction,
and shall succeed in what
he does.
He shall destroy the powerful
and the people of the holy
ones.
25 By his cunning
he shall make deceit
prosper under his hand,
and in his own mind he
shall be great.
Without warning he shall
destroy many
and shall even rise up
against the Prince of
princes.
But he shall be broken, and
not by human hands.
26 The vision of the evenings and the mornings that has been told is true. As for you, seal up the vision, for it refers to many days from now."

27 So I, Daniel, was overcome and lay sick for some days; then I arose and went about the king's business. But I was dismayed by the vision and did not understand it.

Daniel's Prayer for the People

9 In the first year of Darius son of Ahasuerus, by birth a Mede, who became king over the realm of the Chaldeans — 2 in the first year of his reign, I, Daniel, perceived in the books the number of years that, according to the word of the LORD to the prophet Jeremiah, must be fulfilled for the devastation of Jerusalem, namely, seventy years.

3 Then I turned to the Lord God, to seek an answer by prayer and supplication with fasting and sackcloth and ashes. 4 I prayed to the LORD my God and made confession, saying,

"Ah, Lord, great and awesome God, keeping covenant and steadfast love with those who love you and keep your commandments, 5 we have sinned and done wrong, acted wickedly and rebelled, turning aside from your commandments and ordinances. 6 We have not listened to your servants the prophets, who spoke in your name to our kings, our princes, and our ancestors, and to all the people of the land.

7 "Righteousness is on your side, O Lord, but open shame, as at this day, falls on us, the people of Judah, the inhabitants of Jerusalem, and all Israel, those who are near and those who are far away, in all the lands to which you have driven them, because of the treachery that they have committed against you. 8 Open shame, O LORD, falls on us, our kings, our officials, and our ancestors, because we have sinned against you. 9 To the Lord our God belong mercy and forgiveness, for we have rebelled against him, 10 and have not obeyed the voice of the LORD our God by following his laws, which he set before us by his servants the prophets.

11 "All Israel has transgressed your law and turned aside, refusing to obey your voice. So the curse and the oath written in the law of Moses, the servant of God, have been poured out upon us, because we have sinned against you. 12 He

Cross-references (center column):

8.21 v. 5; Dan 10.20
8.22 v. 8
8.24 Dan 11.36
8.25 Dan 11.21; v. 11; Dan 2.34,45
8.26 Dan 10.1; 12.4,9; 10.14
8.27 Dan 7.28; Hab 3.16
9.1 Dan 5.31; 11.1
9.2 2 Chr 36.21; Jer 29.10; Zech 7.5
9.3 Neh 1.4; Jer 29.12; Jas 4.8
9.4 Deut 7.21; Neh 9.32; Deut 7.9
9.5 Ps 106.6; Lam 1.18, 20; v. 11
9.6 2 Chr 36.15, 16; v. 8
9.7 Jer 23.6; 33.16; Am 9.9
9.8 vv. 6,5
9.9 Neh 9.17; Ps 130.4
9.10 2 Kings 17.13-15; 18.12
9.11 Isa 1.4-6; Jer 8.5,10; Deut 27.15
9.12 Isa 44.26; Zech 1.6; Ezek 5.9

n Or shaggy male goat o Gk Theodotion
Vg: Heb the p Theodotion and one Gk Ms:
Heb repeats (from 8.22) but not with his power

has confirmed his words, which he spoke against us and against our rulers, by bringing upon us a calamity so great that what has been done against Jerusalem has never before been done under the whole heaven. [13] Just as it is written in the law of Moses, all this calamity has come upon us. We did not entreat the favor of the LORD our God, turning from our iniquities and reflecting on his[q] fidelity. [14] So the LORD kept watch over this calamity until he brought it upon us. Indeed, the LORD our God is right in all that he has done; for we have disobeyed his voice.

15 "And now, O Lord our God, who brought your people out of the land of Egypt with a mighty hand and made your name renowned even to this day — we have sinned, we have done wickedly. [16] O Lord, in view of all your righteous acts, let your anger and wrath, we pray, turn away from your city Jerusalem, your holy mountain; because of our sins and the iniquities of our ancestors, Jerusalem and your people have become a disgrace among all our neighbors. [17] Now therefore, O our God, listen to the prayer of your servant and to his supplication, and for your own sake, Lord,[r] let your face shine upon your desolated sanctuary. [18] Incline your ear, O my God, and hear. Open your eyes and look at our desolation and the city that bears your name. We do not present our supplication before you on the ground of our righteousness, but on the ground of your great mercies. [19] O Lord, hear; O Lord, forgive; O Lord, listen and act and do not delay! For your own sake, O my God, because your city and your people bear your name!"

The Seventy Weeks

20 While I was speaking, and was praying and confessing my sin and the sin of my people Israel, and presenting my supplication before the LORD my God on behalf of the holy mountain of my God — [21] while I was speaking in prayer, the man Gabriel, whom I had seen

9.13
Isa 9.13;
Jer 2.30
9.14
Jer 31.28;
44.27; vv. 7,
10
9.15
Ex 6.1,6;
Jer 32.21;
Neh 9.10;
Jer 32.20
9.16
1 Sam 12.7;
Ps 31.1;
Zech 8.3
9.17
Num 6.25;
Lam 5.18
9.18
Isa 37.17;
Jer 25.29;
36.7
9.19
Ps 44.23;
74.10,11
9.20
v. 3;
Isa 58.9; 6.5
9.21
Dan 8.16;
Isa 6.2;
Dan 8.18;
10.10,16,18

9.23
Dan 10.12;
Lk 1.28;
Mt 24.15
9.24
Isa 55.10;
Rom 5.10;
Acts 3.14
9.25
Ezra 4.24;
Neh 2.1-8;
3.1; Jn 1.41;
4.25; Isa 9.6
9.26
Isa 53.8;
Mk 9.12;
Lk 19.43,44;
Nah 1.8
9.27
Dan 11.31;
Mt 24.15;
Lk 21.20;
Isa 10.23
10.1
Dan 6.28;
1.7; 8.26;
2.21
10.2
Ezra 9.4,5;
Neh 1.4

before in a vision, came to me in swift flight at the time of the evening sacrifice. [22] He came[s] and said to me, "Daniel, I have now come out to give you wisdom and understanding. [23] At the beginning of your supplications a word went out, and I have come to declare it, for you are greatly beloved. So consider the word and understand the vision:

24 "Seventy weeks are decreed for your people and your holy city: to finish the transgression, to put an end to sin, and to atone for iniquity, to bring in everlasting righteousness, to seal both vision and prophet, and to anoint a most holy place.[t] [25] Know therefore and understand: from the time that the word went out to restore and rebuild Jerusalem until the time of an anointed prince, there shall be seven weeks; and for sixty-two weeks it shall be built again with streets and moat, but in a troubled time. [26] After the sixty-two weeks, an anointed one shall be cut off and shall have nothing, and the troops of the prince who is to come shall destroy the city and the sanctuary. Its[u] end shall come with a flood, and to the end there shall be war. Desolations are decreed. [27] He shall make a strong covenant with many for one week, and for half of the week he shall make sacrifice and offering cease; and in their place[v] shall be an abomination that desolates, until the decreed end is poured out upon the desolator."

Conflict of Nations and Heavenly Powers

10 In the third year of King Cyrus of Persia a word was revealed to Daniel, who was named Belteshazzar. The word was true, and it concerned a great conflict. He understood the word, having received understanding in the vision.

2 At that time I, Daniel, had

[q] Heb *your* [r] Theodotion Vg Compare Syr:
Heb *for the Lord's sake* [s] Gk Syr: Heb *He
made to understand* [t] Or *thing* or *one*
[u] Or *His* [v] Cn: Meaning of Heb uncertain

been mourning for three weeks. ³ I had eaten no rich food, no meat or wine had entered my mouth, and I had not anointed myself at all, for the full three weeks. ⁴ On the twenty-fourth day of the first month, as I was standing on the bank of the great river (that is, the Tigris), ⁵ I looked up and saw a man clothed in linen, with a belt of gold from Uphaz around his waist. ⁶ His body was like beryl, his face like lightning, his eyes like flaming torches, his arms and legs like the gleam of burnished bronze, and the sound of his words like the roar of a multitude. ⁷ I, Daniel, alone saw the vision; the people who were with me did not see the vision, though a great trembling fell upon them, and they fled and hid themselves. ⁸ So I was left alone to see this great vision. My strength left me, and my complexion grew deathly pale, and I retained no strength. ⁹ Then I heard the sound of his words; and when I heard the sound of his words, I fell into a trance, face to the ground.

10 But then a hand touched me and roused me to my hands and knees. ¹¹ He said to me, "Daniel, greatly beloved, pay attention to the words that I am going to speak to you. Stand on your feet, for I have now been sent to you." So while he was speaking this word to me, I stood up trembling. ¹² He said to me, "Do not fear, Daniel, for from the first day that you set your mind to gain understanding and to humble yourself before your God, your words have been heard, and I have come because of your words. ¹³ But the prince of the kingdom of Persia opposed me twenty-one days. So Michael, one of the chief princes, came to help me, and I left him there with the prince of the kingdom of Persia,ʷ ¹⁴ and have come to help you understand what is to happen to your people at the end of days. For there is a further vision for those days."

15 While he was speaking these words to me, I turned my face toward the ground and was speech-less. ¹⁶ Then one in human form touched my lips, and I opened my mouth to speak, and said to the one who stood before me, "My lord, because of the vision such pains have come upon me that I retain no strength. ¹⁷ How can my lord's servant talk with my lord? For I am shaking,ˣ no strength remains in me, and no breath is left in me."

18 Again one in human form touched me and strengthened me. ¹⁹ He said, "Do not fear, greatly beloved, you are safe. Be strong and courageous!" When he spoke to me, I was strengthened and said, "Let my lord speak, for you have strengthened me." ²⁰ Then he said, "Do you know why I have come to you? Now I must return to fight against the prince of Persia, and when I am through with him, the prince of Greece will come. ²¹ But I am to tell you what is inscribed in the book of truth. There is no one with me who contends against these princes except Michael, your

11 prince. ¹ As for me, in the first year of Darius the Mede, I stood up to support and strengthen him.

2 "Now I will announce the truth to you. Three more kings shall arise in Persia. The fourth shall be far richer than all of them, and when he has become strong through his riches, he shall stir up all against the kingdom of Greece. ³ Then a warrior king shall arise, who shall rule with great dominion and take action as he pleases. ⁴ And while still rising in power, his kingdom shall be broken and divided toward the four winds of heaven, but not to his posterity, nor according to the dominion with which he ruled; for his kingdom shall be uprooted and go to others besides these.

5 "Then the king of the south shall grow strong, but one of his officers shall grow stronger than he

10.4
Dan 8.2;
Gen 2.14
10.5
Dan 12.6,7;
Rev 1.13;
Jer 10.9
10.6
Mt 17.2;
Rev 1.16,14;
1.15; 2.18
10.7
2 Kings 6.17;
Acts 9.7;
Ezek 12.18
10.8
Gen 32.24;
Dan 7.28;
8.27
10.9
Dan 8.18
10.10
Jer 1.9;
Dan 9.21;
Rev 1.17
10.11
Dan 9.23
10.12
Rev 1.17;
Dan 9.3,
20-23
10.13
vv. 20,21;
Dan 12.1;
Jude 9;
Rev 12.7
10.14
Dan 2.28;
8.26;
Hab 2.3
10.15
Ezek 24.27;
Lk 1.20

10.16
Dan 8.15;
v. 10;
Jer 1.9;
v. 8
10.17
Isa 6.1-5;
v. 8
10.18
v. 16;
Isa 35.3,4
10.19
vv. 11,12;
Judg 6.23
10.20
v. 13;
Dan 8.21;
11.2
10.21
Dan 11.2;
v. 13
11.1ff
Dan 9.1;
5.31
11.2
Dan 8.26;
8.21
11.3
Dan 8.4,5,
21
11.4
Dan 8.8,22;
Ezek 37.9;

Zech 2.6; Rev 7.1 **11.5** vv. 9,11,14,25,40

ʷ Gk Theodotion: Heb *I was left there with the kings of Persia* ˣ Gk: Heb *from now*

and shall rule a realm greater than his own realm. ⁶After some years they shall make an alliance, and the daughter of the king of the south shall come to the king of the north to ratify the agreement. But she shall not retain her power, and his offspring shall not endure. She shall be given up, she and her attendants and her child and the one who supported her.

"In those times ⁷a branch from her roots shall rise up in his place. He shall come against the army and enter the fortress of the king of the north, and he shall take action against them and prevail. ⁸Even their gods, with their idols and with their precious vessels of silver and gold, he shall carry off to Egypt as spoils of war. For some years he shall refrain from attacking the king of the north; ⁹then the latter shall invade the realm of the king of the south, but will return to his own land.

10 "His sons shall wage war and assemble a multitude of great forces, which shall advance like a flood and pass through, and again shall carry the war as far as his fortress. ¹¹Moved with rage, the king of the south shall go out and do battle against the king of the north, who shall muster a great multitude, which shall, however, be defeated by his enemy. ¹²When the multitude has been carried off, his heart shall be exalted, and he shall overthrow tens of thousands, but he shall not prevail. ¹³For the king of the north shall again raise a multitude, larger than the former, and after some yearsʸ he shall advance with a great army and abundant supplies.

14 "In those times many shall rise against the king of the south. The lawless among your own people shall lift themselves up in order to fulfill the vision, but they shall fail. ¹⁵Then the king of the north shall come and throw up siegeworks, and take a well-fortified city. And the forces of the south shall not stand, not even his picked troops, for there shall be no

strength to resist. ¹⁶But he who comes against him shall take the actions he pleases, and no one shall withstand him. He shall take a position in the beautiful land, and all of it shall be in his power. ¹⁷He shall set his mind to come with the strength of his whole kingdom, and he shall bring terms of peaceᶻ and perform them. In order to destroy the kingdom,ᵃ he shall give him a woman in marriage; but it shall not succeed or be to his advantage. ¹⁸Afterward he shall turn to the coastlands, and shall capture many. But a commander shall put an end to his insolence; indeed,ᵇ he shall turn his insolence back upon him. ¹⁹Then he shall turn back toward the fortresses of his own land, but he shall stumble and fall, and shall not be found.

20 "Then shall arise in his place one who shall send an official for the glory of the kingdom; but within a few days he shall be broken, though not in anger or in battle. ²¹In his place shall arise a contemptible person on whom royal majesty had not been conferred; he shall come in without warning and obtain the kingdom through intrigue. ²²Armies shall be utterly swept away and broken before him, and the prince of the covenant as well. ²³And after an alliance is made with him, he shall act deceitfully and become strong with a small party. ²⁴Without warning he shall come into the richest partsᶜ of the province and do what none of his predecessors had ever done, lavishing plunder, spoil, and wealth on them. He shall devise plans against strongholds, but only for a time. ²⁵He shall stir up his power and determination against the king of the south with a great army, and the king of the south shall wage war with a much greater and stronger army. But he shall not succeed, for plots shall be devised against him ²⁶by those who eat of

11.6
vv. 13,15,40
11.7
vv. 19,38,39
11.8
Isa 37.19;
46.1,2;
Jer 43.12,13
11.10
Isa 8.8;
Jer 46.7,8;
Dan 9.26;
v. 7
11.11
v. 5;
Dan 8.7;
vv. 13,10
11.13
Dan 4.16;
12.7
11.15
Jer 6.6;
Ezek 4.2;
17.17

11.16
Dan 8.4,7;
vv. 3,36;
Josh 1.5;
vv. 41,45
11.17
2 Kings 12.17;
Ezek 4.3,7
11.18
Isa 66.19;
Jer 31.10;
Hos 12.14
11.19
Ps 27.2;
Job 20.8;
Ezek 26.21
11.20
Isa 60.17
11.21
vv. 24,32,34
11.22
v. 10;
Dan 8.10,11
11.23
Dan 8.25
11.24
v. 21;
Ezek 34,14
11.26
vv. 10,40

ʸ Heb *and at the end of the times years*
ᶻ Gk: Heb *kingdom, and upright ones with him*
ᵃ Heb *it* ᵇ Meaning of Heb uncertain
ᶜ Or *among the richest men*

the royal rations. They shall break him, his army shall be swept away, and many shall fall slain. [27] The two kings, their minds bent on evil, shall sit at one table and exchange lies. But it shall not succeed, for there remains an end at the time appointed. [28] He shall return to his land with great wealth, but his heart shall be set against the holy covenant. He shall work his will, and return to his own land.

29 "At the time appointed he shall return and come into the south, but this time it shall not be as it was before. [30] For ships of Kittim shall come against him, and he shall lose heart and withdraw. He shall be enraged and take action against the holy covenant. He shall turn back and pay heed to those who forsake the holy covenant. [31] Forces sent by him shall occupy and profane the temple and fortress. They shall abolish the regular burnt offering and set up the abomination that makes desolate. [32] He shall seduce with intrigue those who violate the covenant; but the people who are loyal to their God shall stand firm and take action. [33] The wise among the people shall give understanding to many; for some days, however, they shall fall by sword and flame, and suffer captivity and plunder. [34] When they fall victim, they shall receive a little help, and many shall join them insincerely. [35] Some of the wise shall fall, so that they may be refined, purified, and cleansed,[d] until the time of the end, for there is still an interval until the time appointed.

36 "The king shall act as he pleases. He shall exalt himself and consider himself greater than any god, and shall speak horrendous things against the God of gods. He shall prosper until the period of wrath is completed, for what is determined shall be done. [37] He shall pay no respect to the gods of his ancestors, or to the one beloved by women; he shall pay no respect to any other god, for he shall consider himself greater than all. [38] He shall

honor the god of fortresses instead of these; a god whom his ancestors did not know he shall honor with gold and silver, with precious stones and costly gifts. [39] He shall deal with the strongest fortresses by the help of a foreign god. Those who acknowledge him he shall make more wealthy, and shall appoint them as rulers over many, and shall distribute the land for a price.

The Time of the End

40 "At the time of the end the king of the south shall attack him. But the king of the north shall rush upon him like a whirlwind, with chariots and horsemen, and with many ships. He shall advance against countries and pass through like a flood. [41] He shall come into the beautiful land, and tens of thousands shall fall victim, but Edom and Moab and the main part of the Ammonites shall escape from his power. [42] He shall stretch out his hand against the countries, and the land of Egypt shall not escape. [43] He shall become ruler of the treasures of gold and of silver, and all the riches of Egypt; and the Libyans and the Ethiopians[e] shall follow in his train. [44] But reports from the east and the north shall alarm him, and he shall go out with great fury to bring ruin and complete destruction to many. [45] He shall pitch his palatial tents between the sea and the beautiful holy mountain. Yet he shall come to his end, with no one to help him.

The Resurrection of the Dead

12 "At that time Michael, the great prince, the protector of your people, shall arise. There shall be a time of anguish, such as has never occurred since nations first came into existence. But at that time your people shall be delivered, everyone who is found written in the book. [2] Many of those who sleep in the dust of the earth[f] shall awake, some to everlasting

Cross references

11.27 Ps 52.1; 64.6; Jer 9.3-5; vv. 35,40; Hab 2.3
11.30 Gen 10.4; Num 24.24; Jer 2.10
11.31 Dan 8.11; 9.27; Mt 24.15; Mk 13.14
11.32 vv. 21,34; Mic 5.7-9
11.33 Mt 24.9; Jn 16.2; Heb 11.36-38
11.34 Mt 7.15; Rom 16.18
11.35 Zech 13.9; Jn 15.2; vv. 27,40
11.36 2 Thes 2.4; Rev 13.5,6; Dan 2.47; 8.12; 8.19; 9.27
11.37 v. 36
11.40 vv. 10,13, 15,26; Isa 5.28
11.41 Jer 48.47; 49.6
11.43 2 Chr 12.3; Ezek 30.4,5; Nah 3.9
11.45 vv. 16,41; Isa 65.25; 66.20; Dan 9.16,20
12.1 Dan 10.13, 21; 9.12; Mt 24.21; Rev 16.18; v. 4
12.2 Isa 26.19; Mt 25.46; Jn 5.28; Acts 24.15

d Heb made them white e Or Nubians; Heb Cushites f Or the land of dust

life, and some to shame and everlasting contempt. ³Those who are wise shall shine like the brightness of the sky,ᵍ and those who lead many to righteousness, like the stars forever and ever. ⁴But you, Daniel, keep the words secret and the book sealed until the time of the end. Many shall be running back and forth, and evilʰ shall increase."

5 Then I, Daniel, looked, and two others appeared, one standing on this bank of the stream and one on the other. ⁶One of them said to the man clothed in linen, who was upstream, "How long shall it be until the end of these wonders?" ⁷The man clothed in linen, who was upstream, raised his right hand and his left hand toward heaven. And I heard him swear by the one who lives forever that it would be for a time, two times, and half a time,ⁱ and that when the shattering of the power of the holy people comes to

an end, all these things would be accomplished. ⁸I heard but could not understand; so I said, "My lord, what shall be the outcome of these things?" ⁹He said, "Go your way, Daniel, for the words are to remain secret and sealed until the time of the end. ¹⁰Many shall be purified, cleansed, and refined, but the wicked shall continue to act wickedly. None of the wicked shall understand, but those who are wise shall understand. ¹¹From the time that the regular burnt offering is taken away and the abomination that desolates is set up, there shall be one thousand two hundred ninety days. ¹²Happy are those who persevere and attain the thousand three hundred thirty-five days. ¹³But you, go your way,ⁱ and rest; you shall rise for your reward at the end of the days."

12.3
Mt 13.43;
Dan 11.33
12.4
Rev 22.10;
Dan 11.33
12.5
Dan 10.4ff
12.7
Rev 10.5,6;
Dan 4.34;
7.25;
Rev 12.14;
Lk 21.24;
Rev 10.7

12.8
v. 6
12.9
vv. 13,4
12.10
Dan 11.35;
Isa 32.6,7
12.11f
Dan 8.11-14;
9.27; 11.31;
Mt 24.15
12.12
Isa 30.18;
Rev 11.2;
12.6; 13.5
12.13
vv. 9,4;
Rev 14.13

ᵍ Or *dome* ʰ Cn Compare Gk: Heb
knowledge ⁱ Heb *a time, times, and a half*
ⁱ Gk Theodotion: Heb adds *to the end*

Hosea

Title and Background

This book is named after the prophet whose message it preserves. Hosea lived during the tragic last days of the northern kingdom, when six kings reigned in twenty-five years. Assyria was expanding westward and in about 733 B.C. they dismembered Israel. Twelve years later, in 722-721 B.C., Samaria was captured and its people exiled. The northern kingdom was at an end.

Author and Date of Writing

Hosea prophesied about the middle of the eighth century B.C., shortly after the ministry of Amos. Amos had threatened God's judgment on Israel at the hands of an unnamed enemy; Hosea identified that enemy as Assyria. Hosea stands first in the division of the Bible called the Minor Prophets (Hosea through Malachi).

Theme and Message

In the first half of the book Hosea's family life is made a symbolic action to convey God's message for his people. The Lord loved his covenant people and would take them back, however often they would wander. The second half of the book gives the details of Israel's involvement in Canaanite religion. Like other prophetic books, Hosea is a call to repentance. The alternative to futility is to forsake idols and return to the Lord.

Outline

 I. The Unfaithful Wife and the Faithful Husband (1.1–3.5)
 II. The Unfaithful Nation and the Faithful God (4.1–14.9)
 A. Israel's Unfaithfulness (4.1–6.3)
 B. Israel's Punishment (6.4–10.15)
 C. The Lord's Compassion and Faithful Love (11.1–14.9)

1 The word of the LORD that came to Hosea son of Beeri, in the days of Kings Uzziah, Jotham, Ahaz, and Hezekiah of Judah, and in the days of King Jeroboam son of Joash of Israel.

The Family of Hosea

2 When the LORD first spoke through Hosea, the LORD said to Hosea, "Go, take for yourself a wife of whoredom and have children of whoredom, for the land commits great whoredom by forsaking the LORD." ³So he went and took Gomer daughter of Diblaim, and she conceived and bore him a son.

4 And the LORD said to him, "Name him Jezreel;[a] for in a little while I will punish the house of Jehu for the blood of Jezreel, and I will put an end to the kingdom of the house of Israel. ⁵On that day I will break the bow of Israel in the valley of Jezreel."

6 She conceived again and bore a daughter. Then the LORD said to him, "Name her Lo-ruhamah,[b] for I will no longer have pity on the house of Israel or forgive them. ⁷But I will have pity on the house of Judah, and I will save them by the LORD their God; I will not save them by bow, or by sword, or by war, or by horses, or by horsemen."

8 When she had weaned Lo-ruhamah, she conceived and bore a son. ⁹Then the LORD said, "Name

1.1 Rom 9.25; 2 Kings 5.1-7; 2 Chr 27.1-9; 2 Kings 16.1-20; 2 Chr 28.1-27; 2 Kings 18.1-20; 2 Chr 29.1-32; 2 Kings 13.13; 14.23-29
1.2 Hos 3.1; Jer 3.1,12, 14; Hos 2.5; 3.5
1.4 2 Kings 10.1-14; 15.10
1.5 2 Kings 15.29
1.6 vv. 3,9; Hos 2.4

1.7 Isa 30.18; Jer 25.5,6; Zech 9.9,10 **1.9** v. 6

a That is *God sows* b That is *Not pitied*

him Lo-ammi,[c] for you are not my people and I am not your God."[d]

The Restoration of Israel

10[e] Yet the number of the people of Israel shall be like the sand of the sea, which can be neither measured nor numbered; and in the place where it was said to them, "You are not my people," it shall be said to them, "Children of the living God." 11 The people of Judah and the people of Israel shall be gathered together, and they shall appoint for themselves one head; and they shall take possession of[f] the land, for great shall be the day of Jezreel.

2 [g] Say to your brother,[h] Ammi,[i] and to your sister,[i] Ruhamah.[k]

Israel's Infidelity, Punishment, and Redemption

2 Plead with your mother, plead—
for she is not my wife,
and I am not her
husband—
that she put away her
whoring from her face,
and her adultery from
between her breasts,
3 or I will strip her naked
and expose her as in the
day she was born,
and make her like a
wilderness,
and turn her into a parched
land,
and kill her with thirst.
4 Upon her children also I will
have no pity,
because they are children
of whoredom.
5 For their mother has played
the whore;
she who conceived them
has acted shamefully.
For she said, "I will go after
my lovers;
they give me my bread and
my water,
my wool and my flax, my
oil and my drink."
6 Therefore I will hedge up
her[l] way with thorns;

and I will build a wall
against her,
so that she cannot find her
paths.
7 She shall pursue her lovers,
but not overtake them;
and she shall seek them,
but shall not find them.
Then she shall say, "I will go
and return to my first
husband,
for it was better with me
then than now."
8 She did not know
that it was I who gave her
the grain, the wine, and
the oil,
and who lavished upon her
silver
and gold that they used for
Baal.
9 Therefore I will take back
my grain in its time,
and my wine in its season;
and I will take away my wool
and my flax,
which were to cover her
nakedness.
10 Now I will uncover her
shame
in the sight of her lovers,
and no one shall rescue her
out of my hand.
11 I will put an end to all her
mirth,
her festivals, her new
moons, her sabbaths,
and all her appointed
festivals.
12 I will lay waste her vines and
her fig trees,
of which she said,
"These are my pay,
which my lovers have given
me."
I will make them a forest,
and the wild animals shall
devour them.
13 I will punish her for the
festival days of the
Baals,

1.10
Gen 32.12;
Jer 33.22;
Rom 9.25-27;
v. 9;
Isa 63.16;
64.8
1.11
Isa 11.12;
Jer 23.5,6;
Ezek 37.21-24;
Hos 3.5
2.1
v. 23
2.2
v. 5;
Hos 4.5;
Isa 50.1;
Hos 1.2
2.3
Ezek 16.7,
22,39;
Isa 32.13,
14; Am 8.11
2.4
Jer 13.14;
Ezek 8.18
2.5
Isa 1.21;
Jer 3.1,2,6;
44.17,18
2.6
Job 3.23;
19.8;
Hos 9.6;
10.8

2.7
Jer 2.2; 3.1;
Ezek 16.8;
Hos 13.6
2.8
Isa 1.3;
Ezek 16.19;
Hos 8.4
2.9
Hos 8.7; 9.2
2.10
Ezek 16.37
2.11
Jer 7.34;
16.9;
Am 8.10;
Isa 1.13,14
2.12
v. 5;
Isa 5.5;
Hos 13.8
2.13
Ezek 16.12,
17; Hos 4.6;
8.14; 13.6

[c] That is *Not my people* [d] Heb *I am not yours* [e] Ch 2.1 in Heb [f] Heb *rise up from* [g] Ch 2.3 in Heb [h] Gk: Heb *brothers* [i] That is *My People* [i] Gk Vg: Heb *sisters* [k] That is *Pitied* [l] Gk Syr: Heb *your*

when she offered incense
 to them
and decked herself with her
 ring and jewelry,
and went after her lovers,
and forgot me, says the
 LORD.

14 Therefore, I will now allure
 her,
and bring her into the
 wilderness,
and speak tenderly to her.
15 From there I will give her
 her vineyards,
and make the Valley of
 Achor a door of hope.
There she shall respond as in
 the days of her youth,
as at the time when she
 came out of the land of
 Egypt.

16 On that day, says the LORD, you
will call me, "My husband," and no
longer will you call me, "My
Baal."[m] 17 For I will remove the
names of the Baals from her
mouth, and they shall be men-
tioned by name no more. 18 I will
make for you[n] a covenant on that
day with the wild animals, the
birds of the air, and the creeping
things of the ground; and I will
abolish[o] the bow, the sword, and
war from the land; and I will make
you lie down in safety. 19 And I will
take you for my wife forever; I will
take you for my wife in righteous-
ness and in justice, in steadfast
love, and in mercy. 20 I will take you
for my wife in faithfulness; and you
shall know the LORD.
21 On that day I will answer,
 says the LORD,
I will answer the heavens
and they shall answer the
 earth;
22 and the earth shall answer
 the grain, the wine, and
 the oil,
and they shall answer
 Jezreel;[p]
23 and I will sow him[q] for
 myself in the land.
And I will have pity on
 Lo-ruhamah,[r]

2.14
Ezek 20.33-38
2.15
Ezek 28.25,
26;
Josh 7.26;
Jer 2.2;
Ex 15.1,2;
Hos 11.1
2.17
Ex 23.13;
Josh 23.7;
Ps 16.4;
Zech 13.2;
v. 13
2.18
Job 5.23;
Isa 11.6-9;
Ps 46.9;
Ezek 34.25
2.19
Isa 62.4,5;
Jer 3.14;
Isa 1.27
2.20
Hos 6.6;
13.4
2.21
Isa 55.10;
Zech 8.12
2.22
Jer 31.12;
Joel 2.19
2.23
Jer 31.27;
Hos 1.6;
1.9,10;
Zech 13.9;
Rom 9.25,
26

3.1
Hos 1.2;
2 Sam 6.19;
1 Chr 16.3
3.2
Ruth 4.10
3.4
Hos 13.10,
11; 2.11;
Ex 28.6;
Judg 17.5;
Zech 10.2
3.5
Jer 50.4,5;
Ezek 34.23,
24; Jer 31.9;
Mic 4.1
4.1
Hos 5.1;
12.2;
Mic 6.2;
Isa 59.4;
Jer 7.28;
Hos 6.6; 5.4
4.2
Hos 10.4;
7.3; 6.9; 7.1,
4; 6.8
4.3
Jer 4.28;
Zeph 1.3;
Jer 4.25

and I will say to
 Lo-ammi,[s] "You are my
 people";
and he shall say, "You are
 my God."

Further Assurances of God's Redeeming Love

3 The LORD said to me again,
"Go, love a woman who has a
lover and is an adulteress, just as
the LORD loves the people of Israel,
though they turn to other gods and
love raisin cakes." 2 So I bought her
for fifteen shekels of silver and a
homer of barley and a measure of
wine.[t] 3 And I said to her, "You
must remain as mine for many
days; you shall not play the whore,
you shall not have intercourse with
a man, nor I with you." 4 For the Is-
raelites shall remain many days
without king or prince, without
sacrifice or pillar, without ephod or
teraphim. 5 Afterward the Israelites
shall return and seek the LORD their
God, and David their king; they
shall come in awe to the LORD and
to his goodness in the latter days.

God Accuses Israel

4 Hear the word of the LORD,
 O people of Israel;
for the LORD has an
 indictment against the
 inhabitants of the land.
There is no faithfulness or
 loyalty,
and no knowledge of God
 in the land.
2 Swearing, lying, and murder,
and stealing and adultery
 break out;
bloodshed follows
 bloodshed.
3 Therefore the land mourns,
and all who live in it
 languish;
together with the wild
 animals
and the birds of the air,
even the fish of the sea are
 perishing.

[m] That is, *"My master"* [n] Heb *them*
[o] Heb *break* [p] That is *God sows*
[q] Cn: Heb *her* [r] That is *Not pitied*
[s] That is *Not my people* [t] Gk: Heb *a homer of barley and a lethech of barley*

4 Yet let no one contend,
 and let none accuse,
for with you is my
 contention, O priest. u
5 You shall stumble by day;
 the prophet also shall
 stumble with you by
 night,
and I will destroy your
 mother.
6 My people are destroyed for
 lack of knowledge;
because you have rejected
 knowledge,
I reject you from being a
 priest to me.
And since you have forgotten
 the law of your God,
I also will forget your
 children.

7 The more they increased,
 the more they sinned
 against me;
they changed v their glory
 into shame.
8 They feed on the sin of my
 people;
they are greedy for their
 iniquity.
9 And it shall be like people,
 like priest;
I will punish them for their
 ways,
and repay them for their
 deeds.
10 They shall eat, but not be
 satisfied;
they shall play the whore,
 but not multiply;
because they have forsaken
 the LORD
to devote themselves to
 11whoredom.

The Idolatry of Israel

Wine and new wine
 take away the
 understanding.
12 My people consult a piece of
 wood,
and their divining rod gives
 them oracles.
For a spirit of whoredom has
 led them astray,

and they have played the
 whore, forsaking their
 God.
13 They sacrifice on the tops of
 the mountains,
 and make offerings upon
 the hills,
under oak, poplar, and
 terebinth,
 because their shade is
 good.

Therefore your daughters
 play the whore,
 and your daughters-in-law
 commit adultery.
14 I will not punish your
 daughters when they
 play the whore,
 nor your daughters-in-law
 when they commit
 adultery;
for the men themselves go
 aside with whores,
 and sacrifice with temple
 prostitutes;
thus a people without
 understanding comes to
 ruin.

15 Though you play the whore,
 O Israel,
do not let Judah become
 guilty.
Do not enter into Gilgal,
 or go up to Beth-aven,
and do not swear, "As the
 LORD lives."
16 Like a stubborn heifer,
 Israel is stubborn;
can the LORD now feed them
 like a lamb in a broad
 pasture?

17 Ephraim is joined to idols—
 let him alone.
18 When their drinking is
 ended, they indulge in
 sexual orgies;
they love lewdness more
 than their glory. w
19 A wind has wrapped them x
 in its wings,

4.4
Ezek 3.26;
Deut 17.12
4.5
Hos 5.5;
Ezek 14.3,7;
Hos 2.2,5
4.6
v. 1;
Mal 2.7,8;
Hos 2.13;
8.1,12
4.7
Hos 10.1;
13.6;
Hab 2.16;
Mal 2.9
4.8
Hos 10.13;
Isa 56.11
4.9
Isa 24.2;
Jer 5.31;
Hos 9.9
4.10
Lev 26.26;
Mic 6.14;
Hos 7.14;
9.17
4.11
Hos 5.4;
Isa 28.7
4.12
Jer 2.27;
Hab 2.19;
Hos 5.4; 9.1

4.13
Jer 3.6;
Ezek 6.13;
Hos 2.13;
11.2;
Am 7.17;
Rom 1.28
4.14
v. 18;
Deut 23.17;
vv. 6,11
4.15
Am 4.4;
1 Kings 12.28,
29
4.16
Ps 78.8;
Isa 5.17;
7.25
4.17
Ps 81.12;
v. 4
4.18
vv. 14,7
4.19
Hos 12.1;
13.15;
Isa 1.29

u Cn: Meaning of Heb uncertain v Ancient
Heb tradition: MT *I will change*
w Cn Compare Gk: Meaning of Heb uncertain
x Heb *her*

and they shall be ashamed
because of their
altars.y

Impending Judgment on Israel and Judah

5 Hear this, O priests!
Give heed, O house of
Israel!
Listen, O house of the king!
For the judgment pertains
to you;
for you have been a snare at
Mizpah,
and a net spread upon
Tabor,
2 and a pit dug deep in
Shittim;z
but I will punish all of
them.

3 I know Ephraim,
and Israel is not hidden
from me;
for now, O Ephraim, you
have played the whore;
Israel is defiled.
4 Their deeds do not permit
them
to return to their God.
For the spirit of whoredom is
within them,
and they do not know the
LORD.

5 Israel's pride testifies against
him;
Ephraima stumbles in his
guilt;
Judah also stumbles with
them.
6 With their flocks and herds
they shall go
to seek the LORD,
but they will not find him;
he has withdrawn from
them.
7 They have dealt faithlessly
with the LORD;
for they have borne
illegitimate children.
Now the new moon shall
devour them along with
their fields.

8 Blow the horn in Gibeah,
the trumpet in Ramah.

Sound the alarm at
Beth-aven;
look behind you, Benjamin!
9 Ephraim shall become a
desolation
in the day of punishment;
among the tribes of Israel
I declare what is sure.
10 The princes of Judah have
become
like those who remove the
landmark;
on them I will pour out
my wrath like water.
11 Ephraim is oppressed,
crushed in judgment,
because he was determined
to go after vanity.b
12 Therefore I am like maggots
to Ephraim,
and like rottenness to the
house of Judah.
13 When Ephraim saw his
sickness,
and Judah his wound,
then Ephraim went to
Assyria,
and sent to the great
king.c
But he is not able to cure
you
or heal your wound.
14 For I will be like a lion to
Ephraim,
and like a young lion to
the house of Judah.
I myself will tear and go
away;
I will carry off, and no one
shall rescue.
15 I will return again to my
place
until they acknowledge
their guilt and seek my
face.
In their distress they will
beg my favor:

A Call to Repentance

6 "Come, let us return to the
LORD;
for it is he who has torn,
and he will heal us;

Cross references

5.1
Hos 4.1; 6.9
5.3
Am 3.2;
Hos 6.10
5.4
Hos 4.11,12
5.5
Hos 7.10;
4.5;
Ezek 23.31-35
5.6
Mic 6.6,7;
Isa 1.15;
Ezek 8.6
5.7
Isa 48.8;
Hos 6.7;
2.4,11,12
5.8
Hos 9.9;
10.9;
Isa 10.29,
30;
Hos 4.15

5.9
Isa 37.3;
46.10;
Zech 1.6
5.10
Deut 19.14;
Ezek 7.8;
Ps 93.3,4
5.11
Hos 9.16
5.12
Ps 39.11;
Prov 12.4
5.13
Jer 30.12;
Hos 7.11;
8.9; 10.6;
14.3
5.14
Hos 13.7,8;
Ps 50.22;
Mic 5.8
5.15
Isa 64.7-9;
Jer 2.27;
Hos 3.5
6.1
Jer 50.4,5;
Hos 5.14;
14.4;
Isa 30.26

y Gk Syr: Heb *sacrifices* z Cn: Meaning of
Heb uncertain a Heb *Israel and Ephraim*
b Gk: Meaning of Heb uncertain
c Cn: Heb *to a king who will contend*

he has struck down, and he
 will bind us up.
2 After two days he will revive
 us;
 on the third day he will
 raise us up,
 that we may live before
 him.
3 Let us know, let us press on
 to know the LORD;
 his appearing is as sure as
 the dawn;
 he will come to us like the
 showers,
 like the spring rains that
 water the earth."

Impenitence of Israel and Judah

4 What shall I do with you,
 O Ephraim?
 What shall I do with you,
 O Judah?
 Your love is like a morning
 cloud,
 like the dew that goes away
 early.
5 Therefore I have hewn them
 by the prophets,
 I have killed them by the
 words of my mouth,
 and my[d] judgment goes
 forth as the light.
6 For I desire steadfast love
 and not sacrifice,
 the knowledge of God
 rather than burnt
 offerings.

7 But at[e] Adam they
 transgressed the
 covenant;
 there they dealt faithlessly
 with me.
8 Gilead is a city of evildoers,
 tracked with blood.
9 As robbers lie in wait[f] for
 someone,
 so the priests are banded
 together;[g]
 they murder on the road to
 Shechem,
 they commit a monstrous
 crime.
10 In the house of Israel I have
 seen a horrible thing;
 Ephraim's whoredom is
 there, Israel is defiled.

6.2
Ps 30.5
6.3
Isa 2.3;
Mic 4.2;
Ps 19.6;
Mic 5.2;
Joel 2.23
6.4
Hos 7.1;
11.8; 13.3
6.5
Jer 1.10,18;
Heb 4.12;
v. 3
6.6
Mt 9.13;
Ps 50.8,9;
Hos 2.20
6.7
Hos 8.1; 5.7
6.8
Hos 4.2
6.9
Hos 7.1;
Jer 7.9,10;
Ezek 22.9;
23.27
6.10
Jer 5.30,31;
Hos 5.3

6.11
Joel 3.13;
Zeph 2.7
7.1
v. 13;
Hos 6.4;
11.8; 4.2; 6.9
7.2
Hos 8.13;
9.9; Am 8.7;
Jer 2.19;
Hos 4.9
7.3
v. 5;
Mic 7.3;
Hos 4.2;
11.12;
Rom 1.32
7.4
Jer 9.2;
23.10
7.5
Isa 28.1,7,8
7.7
Ps 21.9;
v. 16;
Isa 64.7

11 For you also, O Judah, a
 harvest is appointed.

When I would restore the
 fortunes of my people,
7 [1]when I would heal Israel,
 the corruption of Ephraim
 is revealed,
 and the wicked deeds of
 Samaria;
 for they deal falsely,
 the thief breaks in,
 and the bandits raid
 outside.
2 But they do not consider
 that I remember all their
 wickedness.
 Now their deeds surround
 them,
 they are before my face.
3 By their wickedness they
 make the king glad,
 and the officials by their
 treachery.
4 They are all adulterers;
 they are like a heated oven,
 whose baker does not need
 to stir the fire,
 from the kneading of the
 dough until it is
 leavened.
5 On the day of our king the
 officials
 became sick with the heat
 of wine;
 he stretched out his hand
 with mockers.
6 For they are kindled[h] like an
 oven, their heart burns
 within them;
 all night their anger
 smolders;
 in the morning it blazes
 like a flaming fire.
7 All of them are hot as an
 oven,
 and they devour their
 rulers.
 All their kings have fallen;
 none of them calls upon
 me.

[d] Gk Syr: Heb *your* [e] Cn: Heb *like*
[f] Cn: Meaning of Heb uncertain
[g] Syr: Heb *are a company* [h] Gk Syr: Heb
brought near

8 Ephraim mixes himself with
the peoples;
Ephraim is a cake not
turned.
9 Foreigners devour his
strength,
but he does not know it;
gray hairs are sprinkled upon
him,
but he does not know it.
10 Israel's pride testifies
against[i] him;
yet they do not return to
the LORD their God,
or seek him, for all this.

Futile Reliance on the Nations

11 Ephraim has become like a
dove,
silly and without sense;
they call upon Egypt, they
go to Assyria.
12 As they go, I will cast my net
over them;
I will bring them down like
birds of the air;
I will discipline them
according to the report
made to their
assembly.[i]
13 Woe to them, for they have
strayed from me!
Destruction to them, for
they have rebelled
against me!
I would redeem them,
but they speak lies against
me.

14 They do not cry to me from
the heart,
but they wail upon their
beds;
they gash themselves for
grain and wine;
they rebel against me.
15 It was I who trained and
strengthened their
arms,
yet they plot evil against
me.
16 They turn to that which does
not profit;[k]
they have become like a
defective bow;

7.8
Ps 106.35;
v. 11;
Hos 5.13
7.9
Isa 1.7;
Hos 4.6
7.10
Hos 5.5;
vv. 7,14;
Hos 5.4
7.11
Hos 11.11;
4.6,11,14;
v. 16;
Hos 5.13;
8.9; 12.1
7.12
Ezek 12.13
7.13
Hos 9.12,
17;
Jer 14.10;
Ezek 34.6;
v. 1;
Mt 23.37
7.14
Jer 3.10;
Am 2.8;
Mic 2.11;
Hos 13.16
7.15
Hos 11.13;
Nah 1.9
7.16
Ps 78.57;
v. 7;
Ezek 23.32

8.1
Hos 5.8;
Hab 1.8;
Hos 6.7; 4.6
8.2
Hos 7.14
8.4
Hos 13.10,
11; 2.8
8.5
v. 6;
Hos 10.5;
13.2;
Jer 13.27
8.6
Hos 13.2
8.7
Hos 10.12,
13;
Isa 66.15;
Nah 1.3
8.8
Jer 51.34;
Hos 13.15

their officials shall fall by the
sword
because of the rage of their
tongue.
So much for their babbling
in the land of Egypt.

Israel's Apostasy

8 Set the trumpet to your lips!
One like a vulture[i] is over
the house of the LORD,
because they have broken my
covenant,
and transgressed my law.
2 Israel cries to me,
"My God,
we — Israel — know
you!"
3 Israel has spurned the good;
the enemy shall pursue
him.

4 They made kings, but not
through me;
they set up princes, but
without my knowledge.
With their silver and gold
they made idols
for their own destruction.
5 Your calf is rejected,
O Samaria.
My anger burns against
them.
How long will they be
incapable of innocence?
6 For it is from Israel,
an artisan made it;
it is not God.
The calf of Samaria
shall be broken to pieces.[l]

7 For they sow the wind,
and they shall reap the
whirlwind.
The standing grain has no
heads,
it shall yield no meal;
if it were to yield,
foreigners would devour it.
8 Israel is swallowed up;
now they are among the
nations
as a useless vessel.

i Or *humbles* j Meaning of Heb uncertain
k Cn: Meaning of Heb uncertain
l Or *shall go up in flames*

9 For they have gone up to
 Assyria,
 a wild ass wandering alone;
 Ephraim has bargained for
 lovers.
10 Though they bargain with
 the nations,
 I will now gather them up.
 They shall soon writhe
 under the burden of kings
 and princes.

11 When Ephraim multiplied
 altars to expiate sin,
 they became to him altars
 for sinning.
12 Though I write for him the
 multitude of my
 instructions,
 they are regarded as a
 strange thing.
13 Though they offer choice
 sacrifices,[m]
 though they eat flesh,
 the LORD does not accept
 them.
 Now he will remember their
 iniquity,
 and punish their sins;
 they shall return to Egypt.
14 Israel has forgotten his
 Maker,
 and built palaces;
 and Judah has multiplied
 fortified cities;
 but I will send a fire upon
 his cities,
 and it shall devour his
 strongholds.

Punishment for Israel's Sin

9 Do not rejoice, O Israel!
 Do not exult[n] as other
 nations do;
 for you have played the
 whore, departing from
 your God.
 You have loved a
 prostitute's pay
 on all threshing floors.
2 Threshing floor and winevat
 shall not feed them,
 and the new wine shall fail
 them.
3 They shall not remain in the
 land of the LORD;

but Ephraim shall return to
 Egypt,
 and in Assyria they shall
 eat unclean food.
4 They shall not pour drink
 offerings of wine to the
 LORD,
 and their sacrifices shall
 not please him.
 Such sacrifices shall be like
 mourners' bread;
 all who eat of it shall be
 defiled;
 for their bread shall be for
 their hunger only;
 it shall not come to the
 house of the LORD.

5 What will you do on the day
 of appointed festival,
 and on the day of the
 festival of the LORD?
6 For even if they escape
 destruction,
 Egypt shall gather them,
 Memphis shall bury them.
 Nettles shall possess their
 precious things of
 silver;[o]
 thorns shall be in their
 tents.

7 The days of punishment have
 come,
 the days of recompense
 have come;
 Israel cries,[p]
 "The prophet is a fool,
 the man of the spirit is
 mad!"
 Because of your great
 iniquity,
 your hostility is great.
8 The prophet is a sentinel for
 my God over Ephraim,
 yet a fowler's snare is on all
 his ways,
 and hostility in the house
 of his God.
9 They have deeply corrupted
 themselves
 as in the days of Gibeah;

8.9 Hos 7.11; Jer 2.24; Ezek 16.3 8.10 Ezek 16.37; 22.40; Jer 42.2 8.11 Hos 10.1; 12.11 8.12 v. 1; Hos 4.6 8.13 Jer 7.21; Hos 7.2; 1 Cor 4.5; Hos 4.9; 9.7; 9.3,6 8.14 Hos 2.13; 13.6; Jer 17.27 9.1 Isa 22.12, 13; Hos 10.5; 4.12; Jer 44.17 9.2 Hos 2.9 9.3 Jer 2.7; Hos 8.13; Ezek 4.13; Hos 7.11
9.4 Jer 6.20; Hos 5.6; 8.13; Hag 2.14 9.5 Isa 10.3; Jer 5.31; Joel 1.13 9.6 v. 3; Jer 2.16; Ezek 30.13, 16; Isa 5.6; Hos 10.8 9.7 Jer 10.15; Mic 7.4; Isa 34.8; Jer 16.18; Ezek 14.9, 10 9.8 Hos 5.1 9.9 Isa 31.6; Judg 19.12; Hos 5.8; 10.9; 7.2; 8.13

m Cn: Meaning of Heb uncertain
n Gk: Heb *To exultation* o Meaning of Heb uncertain p Cn Compare Gk: Heb *shall know*

he will remember their
iniquity,
he will punish their sins.

10 Like grapes in the
wilderness,
I found Israel.
Like the first fruit on the fig
tree,
in its first season,
I saw your ancestors.
But they came to Baal-peor,
and consecrated
themselves to a thing of
shame,
and became detestable like
the thing they loved.
11 Ephraim's glory shall fly
away like a bird—
no birth, no pregnancy, no
conception!
12 Even if they bring up
children,
I will bereave them until
no one is left.
Woe to them indeed
when I depart from them!
13 Once I saw Ephraim as a
young palm planted in
a lovely meadow, q
but now Ephraim must
lead out his children for
slaughter.
14 Give them, O LORD—
what will you give?
Give them a miscarrying
womb
and dry breasts.

15 Every evil of theirs began at
Gilgal;
there I came to hate them.
Because of the wickedness of
their deeds
I will drive them out of my
house.
I will love them no more;
all their officials are rebels.

16 Ephraim is stricken,
their root is dried up,
they shall bear no fruit.
Even though they give birth,
I will kill the cherished
offspring of their womb.
17 Because they have not
listened to him,

my God will reject them;
they shall become
wanderers among the
nations.

Israel's Sin and Captivity

10 Israel is a luxuriant vine
that yields its fruit.
The more his fruit increased
the more altars he built;
as his country improved,
he improved his pillars.
2 Their heart is false;
now they must bear their
guilt.
The LORD r will break down
their altars,
and destroy their pillars.

3 For now they will say:
"We have no king,
for we do not fear the LORD,
and a king—what could he
do for us?"
4 They utter mere words;
with empty oaths they
make covenants;
so litigation springs up like
poisonous weeds
in the furrows of the field.
5 The inhabitants of Samaria
tremble
for the calf s of Beth-aven.
Its people shall mourn for it,
and its idolatrous priests
shall wail t over it,
over its glory that has
departed from it.
6 The thing itself shall be
carried to Assyria
as tribute to the great
king. u
Ephraim shall be put to
shame,
and Israel shall be
ashamed of his idol. v

7 Samaria's king shall perish
like a chip on the face of
the waters.
8 The high places of Aven, the
sin of Israel,
shall be destroyed.

9.10
Mic 7.1;
Jer 24.2;
Num 25.3;
Hos 4.14;
Jer 11.13
9.11
Hos 4.7;
10.5; v. 14
9.12
v. 16;
Hos 7.13
9.13
Ezek 27.3,4
9.14
v. 11;
Lk 23.29
9.15
Hos 4.9;
7.2; 12.2;
Isa 1.23
9.16
Hos 5.11;
8.7; v. 12
9.17
Hos 4.10;
Deut 28.65

10.1
Ezek 15.1-5;
Hos 8.11;
3.4
10.2
1 Kings 18.21;
Mt 6.24;
Hos 13.16;
v. 8
10.3
Ps 12.4
10.4
Ezek 17.13-19;
Hos 4.2;
Deut 31.16,
17
10.5
Hos 8.5,6;
9.11
10.6
Hos 11.5;
5.13; 4.7;
Isa 30.5;
Jer 7.24
10.7
Hos 13.11
10.8
v. 5;
1 Kings 12.30;
v. 2;
Hos 9.6;
Lk 23.30;
Rev 6.16

q Meaning of Heb uncertain　　r Heb he
s Gk Syr: Heb calves　　t Cn: Heb exult
u Cn: Heb to a king who will contend
v Cn: Heb counsel

Thorn and thistle shall grow
 up
on their altars.
They shall say to the
 mountains, Cover us,
and to the hills, Fall on us.

9 Since the days of Gibeah you
 have sinned, O Israel;
there they have continued.
Shall not war overtake
 them in Gibeah?
10 I will come[w] against the
 wayward people to
 punish them;
and nations shall be
 gathered against them
when they are punished[x]
 for their double
 iniquity.

11 Ephraim was a trained heifer
 that loved to thresh,
and I spared her fair neck;
but I will make Ephraim
 break the ground;
Judah must plow;
Jacob must harrow for
 himself.
12 Sow for yourselves
 righteousness;
reap steadfast love;
break up your fallow
 ground;
for it is time to seek the
 LORD,
that he may come and rain
 righteousness upon you.

13 You have plowed wickedness,
 you have reaped injustice,
you have eaten the fruit of
 lies.
Because you have trusted in
 your power
and in the multitude of
 your warriors,
14 therefore the tumult of war
 shall rise against your
 people,
and all your fortresses shall
 be destroyed,
as Shalman destroyed
 Beth-arbel on the day
 of battle

10.9
Hos 5.8; 9.9
10.10
Ezek 5.13;
Hos 4.9
10.11
Jer 50.11;
Hos 4.16;
Jer 28.14;
Ps 66.12
10.12
Prov 11.18;
Jer 4.3;
Hos 12.6;
6.3;
Isa 44.3;
45.8
10.13
Job 4.8;
Gal 6.7,8;
Hos 4.2; 7.3
10.14
Isa 17.3;
Hos 13.16

10.15
v. 7
11.1
Hos 2.15;
12.9,13; 13.4;
Mt 2.15
11.2
2 Kings 17.13-
15;
Hos 2.13;
Isa 65.7;
Jer 18.15
11.3
Hos 7.15;
Deut 1.31;
Jer 30.17
11.4
Jer 31.2,3;
Lev 26.13;
Ex 16.32;
Ps 78.25
11.5
Hos 10.6;
7.16
11.6
Hos 13.16;
4.16,17
11.7
Jer 8.5;
v. 2

when mothers were dashed
 in pieces with their
 children.
15 Thus it shall be done to you,
 O Bethel,
because of your great
 wickedness.
At dawn the king of Israel
 shall be utterly cut off.

God's Compassion Despite Israel's Ingratitude

11 When Israel was a child, I
 loved him,
and out of Egypt I called
 my son.
2 The more I[y] called them,
 the more they went from
 me;[z]
they kept sacrificing to the
 Baals,
and offering incense to
 idols.

3 Yet it was I who taught
 Ephraim to walk,
I took them up in my[a]
 arms;
but they did not know that
 I healed them.
4 I led them with cords of
 human kindness,
with bands of love.
I was to them like those
 who lift infants to their
 cheeks.[b]
I bent down to them and
 fed them.

5 They shall return to the land
 of Egypt,
and Assyria shall be their
 king,
because they have refused
 to return to me.
6 The sword rages in their
 cities,
it consumes their
 oracle-priests,
and devours because of
 their schemes.
7 My people are bent on
 turning away from me.

w Cn Compare Gk: Heb *In my desire*
x Gk: Heb *bound* y Gk: Heb *they*
z Gk: Heb *them* a Gk Syr Vg: Heb *his*
b Or *who ease the yoke on their jaws*

To the Most High they call,
but he does not raise them
up at all.[c]

8 How can I give you up,
 Ephraim?
How can I hand you over,
 O Israel?
How can I make you like
 Admah?
How can I treat you like
 Zeboiim?
My heart recoils within
 me;
 my compassion grows
 warm and tender.
9 I will not execute my fierce
 anger;
I will not again destroy
 Ephraim;
for I am God and no mortal,
 the Holy One in your
 midst,
and I will not come in
 wrath.[c]

10 They shall go after the LORD,
 who roars like a lion;
when he roars,
 his children shall come
 trembling from the
 west.
11 They shall come trembling
 like birds from Egypt,
and like doves from the
 land of Assyria;
and I will return them to
 their homes, says the
 LORD.

12 [d]Ephraim has surrounded me
 with lies,
and the house of Israel
 with deceit;
but Judah still walks[e] with
 God,
and is faithful to the Holy
 One.

12 Ephraim herds the wind,
 and pursues the east
 wind all day long;
they multiply falsehood and
 violence;
they make a treaty with
 Assyria,
and oil is carried to Egypt.

11.8
Hos 6.4;
Gen 14.8;
Isa 63.15
11.9
Deut 13.17;
Jer 26.3;
Isa 41.14,
16; 55.8,9;
Mal 3.6
11.10
Hos 6.1-3;
Joel 3.16;
Isa 66.2,5
11.11
Isa 11.11;
60.8;
Ezek 28.25,
26
11.12
Hos 4.2; 7.3
12.1
2 Kings 17.4;
Isa 30.6

12.2
Mic 6.2;
Hos 4.9
12.3
Gen 25.26;
32.24,28
12.4
Gen 32.26;
28.12-15
12.5
Ex 3.15
12.6
Mic 6.8;
Hos 6.6;
Mic 7.7
12.7
Am 8.5;
Mic 6.11
12.8
Hos 13.6;
Rev 3.17;
Hos 4.8;
14.1
12.9
Hos 11.1;
13.4;
Lev 23.42;
Neh 8.17
12.10
2 Kings 17.13;
Jer 7.25;
Ezek 17.2;
20.49
12.11
Hos 6.8;
4.15; 9.15;
10.1,2

The Long History of Rebellion

2 The LORD has an indictment
 against Judah,
and will punish Jacob
 according to his ways,
and repay him according to
 his deeds.
3 In the womb he tried to
 supplant his brother,
and in his manhood he
 strove with God.
4 He strove with the angel and
 prevailed,
he wept and sought his
 favor;
he met him at Bethel,
and there he spoke with
 him.[f]
5 The LORD the God of hosts,
 the LORD is his name!
6 But as for you, return to your
 God,
hold fast to love and
 justice,
and wait continually for
 your God.

7 A trader, in whose hands are
 false balances,
he loves to oppress.
8 Ephraim has said, "Ah, I am
 rich,
I have gained wealth for
 myself;
in all of my gain
 no offense has been found
 in me
that would be sin."[c]
9 I am the LORD your God
 from the land of Egypt;
I will make you live in tents
 again,
as in the days of the
 appointed festival.

10 I spoke to the prophets;
 it was I who multiplied
 visions,
and through the prophets I
 will bring destruction.
11 In Gilead[g] there is iniquity,
they shall surely come to
 nothing.

c Meaning of Heb uncertain d Ch 12.1 in
Heb e Heb *roams* or *rules* f Gk Syr:
Heb *us* g Compare Syr: Heb *Gilead*

In Gilgal they sacrifice bulls,
so their altars shall be like
stone heaps
on the furrows of the field.
12 Jacob fled to the land of
Aram,
there Israel served for a
wife,
and for a wife he guarded
sheep. h
13 By a prophet the LORD
brought Israel up from
Egypt,
and by a prophet he was
guarded.
14 Ephraim has given bitter
offense,
so his Lord will bring his
crimes down on him
and pay him back for his
insults.

Relentless Judgment on Israel

13 When Ephraim spoke,
there was trembling;
he was exalted in Israel;
but he incurred guilt
through Baal and died.
2 And now they keep on
sinning
and make a cast image for
themselves,
idols of silver made
according to their
understanding,
all of them the work of
artisans.
"Sacrifice to these," they
say. i
People are kissing calves!
3 Therefore they shall be like
the morning mist
or like the dew that goes
away early,
like chaff that swirls from
the threshing floor
or like smoke from a
window.

4 Yet I have been the LORD
your God
ever since the land of
Egypt;
you know no God but me,
and besides me there is no
savior.

5 It was I who fed j you in the
wilderness,
in the land of drought.
6 When I fed k them, they were
satisfied;
they were satisfied, and
their heart was proud;
therefore they forgot me.
7 So I will become like a lion
to them,
like a leopard I will lurk
beside the way.
8 I will fall upon them like a
bear robbed of her
cubs,
and will tear open the
covering of their heart;
there I will devour them like
a lion,
as a wild animal would
mangle them.

9 I will destroy you, O Israel;
who can help you? l
10 Where now is m your king,
that he may save you?
Where in all your cities are
your rulers,
of whom you said,
"Give me a king and
rulers"?
11 I gave you a king in my
anger,
and I took him away in my
wrath.

12 Ephraim's iniquity is bound
up;
his sin is kept in store.
13 The pangs of childbirth come
for him,
but he is an unwise son;
for at the proper time he
does not present
himself
at the mouth of the womb.

14 Shall I ransom them from
the power of Sheol?
Shall I redeem them from
Death?

Cross references

12.12 Gen 28.5; 29.20
12.13 Ex 13.3
12.14 Ezek 18.10-13; Dan 11.18; Mic 6.16
13.1 Judg 8.1; 12.1; Hos 2.8-17
13.2 Isa 46.6; Hos 8.6
13.3 Hos 6.4; Dan 2.35; Ps 68.2
13.4 Hos 12.9; Isa 43.11
13.5 Deut 2.7; 8.15; 32.10
13.6 Deut 8.12, 14; 32.15; Hos 2.13; 4.6; 8.14
13.7 Lam 3.10; Jer 5.6
13.8 2 Sam 17.8; Ps 50.22
13.10 2 Kings 17.4; Hos 8.4
13.11 1 Sam 8.7; 1 Kings 14.7-10
13.12 Deut 32.34; Rom 2.5
13.13 Mic 4.9,10; Isa 37.3; 66.9
13.14 Ezek 37.12, 13; 1 Cor 15.54, 55; Rom 11.29

h Heb lacks *sheep*　i Cn Compare Gk: Heb
To these they say sacrifices of people
j Gk Syr: Heb *knew*　k Cn: Heb *according
to their pasture*　l Gk Syr: Heb *for in me is
your help*　m Gk Syr Vg: Heb *I will be*

O Death, where are[n] your
plagues?
O Sheol, where is[n] your
destruction?
Compassion is hidden from
my eyes.

15 Although he may flourish
among rushes,[o]
the east wind shall come, a
blast from the LORD,
rising from the wilderness;
and his fountain shall dry
up,
his spring shall be parched.
It shall strip his treasury
of every precious thing.
16p Samaria shall bear her guilt,
because she has rebelled
against her God;
they shall fall by the sword,
their little ones shall be
dashed in pieces,
and their pregnant women
ripped open.

A Plea for Repentance

14 Return, O Israel, to the
LORD your God,
for you have stumbled
because of your
iniquity.
2 Take words with you
and return to the LORD;
say to him,
"Take away all guilt;
accept that which is good,
and we will offer
the fruit[q] of our lips.
3 Assyria shall not save us;
we will not ride upon
horses;
we will say no more, 'Our
God,'
to the work of our hands.
In you the orphan finds
mercy."

13.15
Hos 10.1;
Ezek 17.10;
19.12;
Jer 51.36;
20.5
13.16
Hos 10.2;
7.14;
Isa 13.16;
Hos 10.14;
2 Kings 15.16
14.1
Hos 10.12;
14.6;
Joel 2.13
14.2
Mic 7.18,19;
Heb 13.15
14.3
Hos 5.13;
Isa 31.1;
Hos 8.6;
13.2;
Ps 10.14

14.4
Zeph 3.17;
Isa 12.1
14.5
Job 29.19;
Mt 6.28;
Isa 35.2
14.6
Ps 52.8;
Song 4.11
14.7
Ps 91.4;
Ezek 17.23;
Hos 2.21,22
14.8
v. 3;
Isa 41.19;
Ezek 17.23
14.9
Ps 107.43;
Acts 13.10;
Isa 26.7;
1.28

Assurance of Forgiveness

4 I will heal their disloyalty;
I will love them freely,
for my anger has turned
from them.
5 I will be like the dew to
Israel;
he shall blossom like the
lily,
he shall strike root like the
forests of Lebanon.[r]
6 His shoots shall spread out;
his beauty shall be like the
olive tree,
and his fragrance like that
of Lebanon.
7 They shall again live beneath
my[s] shadow,
they shall flourish as a
garden;[t]
they shall blossom like the
vine,
their fragrance shall be like
the wine of Lebanon.

8 O Ephraim, what have I[u] to
do with idols?
It is I who answer and look
after you.[v]
I am like an evergreen
cypress;
your faithfulness[w] comes
from me.
9 Those who are wise
understand these
things;
those who are discerning
know them.
For the ways of the LORD are
right,
and the upright walk in
them,
but transgressors stumble
in them.

[n] Gk Syr: Heb *I will be* [o] Or *among*
brothers [p] Ch 14.1 in Heb [q] Gk Syr:
Heb *bulls* [r] Cn: Heb *like Lebanon*
[s] Heb *his* [t] Cn: Heb *they shall grow grain*
[u] Or *What more has Ephraim* [v] Heb *him*
[w] Heb *your fruit*

Joel

Title and Background

Joel was a common Old Testament name, meaning "The LORD is God." This prophet ministered during a time of a severe plague of locusts. Such plagues occur frequently in the Near East; Joel sees this one as a judgment from God on the nation of Israel.

Author and Date of Writing

This book contains no references to datable historical events, but a good case can be made for its being written about 830 B.C. during the reign of King Joash, when Jehoiada the high priest was regent in Judah.

Theme and Message

Joel sees in the massive locust plague and severe drought devastating Judah a harbinger of "the great and terrible day of the LORD" (2.31). Confronted with this crisis, he calls on everyone to repent. He sees this day as a day of punishment for the unfaithful Israelites as well as their neighbors. Restoration and blessing will come only after judgment and repentance.

Outline

I. A Foretaste of the Day of the Lord (1.1–2.17)
 A. A Call to Lament and Prayer (1.2-14)
 B. The Announcement of the Day of the Lord (1.15–2.11)
 C. A Call to Repentance (2.12-17)
II. Salvation in the Day of the Lord (2.18–3.21)
 A. The Lord's Restoration of Judah (2.18-27)
 B. The Lord's Renewal of His People (2.28-32)
 C. The Coming of the Day of the Lord (3.1-21)

1 The word of the LORD that came to Joel son of Pethuel:

Lament over the Ruin of the Country

2 Hear this, O elders,
 give ear, all inhabitants of
 the land!
Has such a thing happened
 in your days,
 or in the days of your
 ancestors?
3 Tell your children of it,
 and let your children tell
 their children,
 and their children another
 generation.

4 What the cutting locust left,

1.1
Jer 1.2;
Ezek 1.3;
Hos 1.1;
Acts 2.16
1.2
Hos 4.1;
5.1; v. 14;
Joel 2.2
1.3
Ps 78.4
1.4
Deut 28.38;
Joel 2.25;
Nah 3.15,
16; Isa 33.4

1.5
Joel 3.3;
Isa 32.10
1.6
Joel 2.2,11;
Rev 9.8

the swarming locust has
 eaten.
What the swarming locust
 left,
 the hopping locust has
 eaten,
and what the hopping locust
 left,
 the destroying locust has
 eaten.

5 Wake up, you drunkards, and
 weep;
 and wail, all you
 wine-drinkers,
over the sweet wine,
 for it is cut off from your
 mouth.
6 For a nation has invaded my
 land,
 powerful and innumerable;

its teeth are lions' teeth,
and it has the fangs of a
lioness.

7 It has laid waste my vines,
and splintered my fig trees;
it has stripped off their bark
and thrown it down;
their branches have turned
white.

8 Lament like a virgin dressed
in sackcloth
for the husband of her
youth.

9 The grain offering and the
drink offering are cut
off
from the house of the LORD.
The priests mourn,
the ministers of the LORD.

10 The fields are devastated,
the ground mourns;
for the grain is destroyed,
the wine dries up,
the oil fails.

11 Be dismayed, you farmers,
wail, you vinedressers,
over the wheat and the
barley;
for the crops of the field
are ruined.

12 The vine withers,
the fig tree droops.
Pomegranate, palm, and
apple —
all the trees of the field are
dried up;
surely, joy withers away
among the people.

A Call to Repentance and Prayer

13 Put on sackcloth and lament,
you priests;
wail, you ministers of the
altar.
Come, pass the night in
sackcloth,
you ministers of my God!
Grain offering and drink
offering
are withheld from the
house of your God.

14 Sanctify a fast,
call a solemn assembly.

1.7
Isa 5.6;
Am 4.9
1.8
v. 13;
Am 8.10
1.9
Joel 2.14,17
1.10
Isa 24.4,7;
Hos 9.2
1.11
Jer 14.3,4;
Isa 17.11;
Jer 9.12
1.12
Hab 3.17,
18;
Isa 16.10;
24.11;
Jer 48.33
1.13
v. 8;
Jer 4.8;
v. 9;
Joel 2.17;
1 Kings 21.27
1.14
2 Chr 20.3,
4; Joel 2.15,
16; v. 2;
Jon 3.8
1.15
Jer 30.7;
Isa 13.6,9;
Joel 2.1,11,
31
1.16
Isa 3.7;
Deut 12.6,7;
Ps 43.4
1.17
Isa 17.10,11
1.18
1 Kings 18.5;
Jer 14.5,6;
Hos 4.3
1.19
Ps 50.15;
Jer 9.10;
Joel 2.3
1.20
Job 38.41;
Ps 104.21;
1 Kings 17.7;
18.5
2.1
Jer 4.5;
Num 10.9;
Zeph 1.14-16;
vv. 11,31;
Joel 1.15
2.2
Am 5.18;
Joel 1.6;
Lam 1.12;
Joel 1.2

Gather the elders
and all the inhabitants of
the land
to the house of the LORD
your God,
and cry out to the LORD.

15 Alas for the day!
For the day of the LORD is
near,
and as destruction from the
Almighty[a] it comes.

16 Is not the food cut off
before our eyes,
joy and gladness
from the house of our God?

17 The seed shrivels under the
clods,[b]
the storehouses are
desolate;
the granaries are ruined
because the grain has
failed.

18 How the animals groan!
The herds of cattle wander
about
because there is no pasture
for them;
even the flocks of sheep
are dazed.[c]

19 To you, O LORD, I cry.
For fire has devoured
the pastures of the
wilderness,
and flames have burned
all the trees of the field.

20 Even the wild animals cry to
you
because the watercourses
are dried up,
and fire has devoured
the pastures of the
wilderness.

2 Blow the trumpet in Zion;
sound the alarm on my
holy mountain!
Let all the inhabitants of the
land tremble,
for the day of the LORD is
coming, it is near —

2 a day of darkness and gloom,

a Traditional rendering of Heb *Shaddai*
b Meaning of Heb uncertain c Compare Gk
Syr Vg: Meaning of Heb uncertain

a day of clouds and thick
 darkness!
Like blackness spread upon
 the mountains
a great and powerful army
 comes;
their like has never been
 from of old,
nor will be again after
 them
in ages to come.

3 Fire devours in front of
 them,
 and behind them a flame
 burns.
Before them the land is like
 the garden of Eden,
but after them a desolate
 wilderness,
and nothing escapes them.

4 They have the appearance of
 horses,
 and like war-horses they
 charge.
5 As with the rumbling of
 chariots,
 they leap on the tops of
 the mountains,
like the crackling of a flame
 of fire
devouring the stubble,
like a powerful army
 drawn up for battle.

6 Before them peoples are in
 anguish,
 all faces grow pale.d
7 Like warriors they charge,
 like soldiers they scale the
 wall.
Each keeps to its own
 course,
 they do not swerve frome
 their paths.
8 They do not jostle one
 another,
 each keeps to its own
 track;
they burst through the
 weapons
and are not halted.
9 They leap upon the city,
 they run upon the walls;
they climb up into the
 houses,

2.3
Joel 1.19,
20; Gen 2.8;
Isa 51.3;
Ps 105.34,
35
2.4
Rev 9.7
2.5
Rev 9.9;
Isa 5.24;
30.30
2.6
Isa 13.8;
Nah 2.10;
Jer 30.6
2.7
Isa 5.26,27;
v. 9
2.9
v. 7;
Jer 9.21;
Jn 10.1

2.10
Ps 18.7;
Isa 13.10;
Joel 3.15;
Mt 24.29
2.11
Joel 3.16;
Am 1.2;
vv. 2,25;
Jer 50.34;
Rev 18.8;
Joel 3.14;
Ezek 22.14
2.12
Jer 4.1;
Hos 12.6
2.13
Ps 34.18;
Isa 57.15;
2 Sam 1.11;
Jon 4.2;
Jer 18.8;
42.10
2.14
Jer 26.3;
Hag 2.19;
Joel 1.9,13
2.15
Num 10.3;
v. 1;
Jer 36.9;
Joel 1.14
2.16
Ex 19.10,
22; Ps 19.5

they enter through the
 windows like a thief.

10 The earth quakes before
 them,
 the heavens tremble.
The sun and the moon are
 darkened,
 and the stars withdraw
 their shining.
11 The Lord utters his voice
 at the head of his army;
how vast is his host!
 Numberless are those who
 obey his command.
Truly the day of the Lord is
 great;
 terrible indeed—who can
 endure it?

12 Yet even now, says the Lord,
 return to me with all your
 heart,
with fasting, with weeping,
 and with mourning;
13 rend your hearts and not
 your clothing.
Return to the Lord, your
 God,
 for he is gracious and
 merciful,
slow to anger, and abounding
 in steadfast love,
 and relents from punishing.
14 Who knows whether he will
 not turn and relent,
 and leave a blessing behind
 him,
a grain offering and a drink
 offering
 for the Lord, your God?

15 Blow the trumpet in Zion;
 sanctify a fast;
call a solemn assembly;
16 gather the people.
Sanctify the congregation;
 assemble the aged;
gather the children,
 even infants at the breast.
Let the bridegroom leave his
 room,
 and the bride her canopy.

d Meaning of Heb uncertain e Gk Syr Vg:
Heb *they do not take a pledge along*

17 Between the vestibule and
 the altar
 let the priests, the
 ministers of the LORD,
 weep.
Let them say, "Spare your
 people, O LORD,
and do not make your
 heritage a mockery,
a byword among the
 nations.
Why should it be said among
 the peoples,
'Where is their God?' "

God's Response and Promise

18 Then the LORD became
 jealous for his land,
 and had pity on his people.
19 In response to his people the
 LORD said:
I am sending you
 grain, wine, and oil,
 and you will be satisfied;
and I will no more make you
 a mockery among the
 nations.

20 I will remove the northern
 army far from you,
 and drive it into a parched
 and desolate land,
its front into the eastern sea,
 and its rear into the
 western sea;
its stench and foul smell will
 rise up.
Surely he has done great
 things!

21 Do not fear, O soil;
 be glad and rejoice,
 for the LORD has done great
 things!
22 Do not fear, you animals of
 the field,
 for the pastures of the
 wilderness are green;
the tree bears its fruit,
 the fig tree and vine give
 their full yield.

23 O children of Zion, be glad
 and rejoice in the LORD
 your God;

2.17
Ezek 8.16;
Mt 23.35;
Joel 1.9;
Deut 9.26-29;
Isa 37.20;
Ps 44.13;
42.10
2.18
Zech 1.14;
Isa 60.10
2.19
Hos 2.21,
22;
Ezek 34.29;
36.15
2.20
Jer 1.14,15;
Zech 14.8;
Deut 11.24;
Isa 34.3;
Am 4.10
2.21
Jer 30.10;
v. 26
2.22
Ps 65.12,13
2.23
Ps 149.2;
Isa 41.16;
Deut 11.14;
Jer 5.24;
Hos 6.3

2.24
Am 9.13;
Mal 3.10
2.25
Joel 1.4
2.26
Isa 62.9;
Ps 67.5-7;
Isa 25.1;
45.17
2.27
Joel 3.17,
21; Isa 45.1,
21; 49.23
2.28
Acts 2.17-21;
Ezek 39.29;
Isa 40.5
2.29
1 Cor 12.13;
Gal 3.28
2.30
Mt 24.29;
Lk 21.11,25;
Acts 2.19
2.31
Isa 13.9,10;
Mt 24.29;
Mal 4.1,5;
Rev 6.12

for he has given the early
 rain^f for your vindication,
he has poured down for
 you abundant rain,
the early and the later rain,
 as before.
24 The threshing floors shall be
 full of grain,
 the vats shall overflow with
 wine and oil.

25 I will repay you for the years
 that the swarming locust
 has eaten,
the hopper, the destroyer,
 and the cutter,
my great army, which I
 sent against you.

26 You shall eat in plenty and
 be satisfied,
 and praise the name of the
 LORD your God,
 who has dealt wondrously
 with you.
And my people shall never
 again be put to shame.
27 You shall know that I am in
 the midst of Israel,
 and that I, the LORD, am
 your God and there is
 no other.
And my people shall never
 again
 be put to shame.

God's Spirit Poured Out

28 gThen afterward
 I will pour out my spirit on
 all flesh;
 your sons and your daughters
 shall prophesy,
 your old men shall dream
 dreams,
 and your young men shall
 see visions.
29 Even on the male and female
 slaves,
 in those days, I will pour
 out my spirit.

30 I will show portents in the
heavens and on the earth, blood
and fire and columns of smoke.
31 The sun shall be turned to dark-

f Meaning of Heb uncertain g Ch 3.1 in Heb

ness, and the moon to blood, before the great and terrible day of the LORD comes. ³²Then everyone who calls on the name of the LORD shall be saved; for in Mount Zion and in Jerusalem there shall be those who escape, as the LORD has said, and among the survivors shall be those whom the LORD calls.

3 ʰ For then, in those days and at that time, when I restore the fortunes of Judah and Jerusalem, ²I will gather all the nations and bring them down to the valley of Jehoshaphat, and I will enter into judgment with them there, on account of my people and my heritage Israel, because they have scattered them among the nations. They have divided my land, ³and cast lots for my people, and traded boys for prostitutes, and sold girls for wine, and drunk it down.

4 What are you to me, O Tyre and Sidon, and all the regions of Philistia? Are you paying me back for something? If you are paying me back, I will turn your deeds back upon your own heads swiftly and speedily. ⁵For you have taken my silver and my gold, and have carried my rich treasures into your temples.ⁱ ⁶You have sold the people of Judah and Jerusalem to the Greeks, removing them far from their own border. ⁷But now I will rouse them to leave the places to which you have sold them, and I will turn your deeds back upon your own heads. ⁸I will sell your sons and your daughters into the hand of the people of Judah, and they will sell them to the Sabeans, to a nation far away; for the LORD has spoken.

Judgment in the Valley of Jehoshaphat

⁹ Proclaim this among the nations:
Prepare war,ʲ
stir up the warriors.
Let all the soldiers draw near,
let them come up.

2.32
Isa 46.13;
Mic 4.7;
Rom 9.27
3.1
Jer 30.3;
Ezek 38.14
3.2
Isa 66.16;
Ezek 34.6;
35.10; 36.1-5
3.3
Ob 11;
Nah 3.10
3.4
Am 1.9,10;
Ezek 25.12,
17
3.5
2 Kings 12.18;
2 Chr 21.16,
17
3.7
Isa 43.5,6;
Jer 23.8
3.8
Isa 14.2;
60.14;
Ezek 23.42;
Jer 6.20
3.9
Isa 8.9,10;
Jer 51.27,
28; 6.4; 46.3,
4;
Zech 14.2,3

3.10
Isa 2.4;
Mic 4.3;
Zech 12.8
3.11
Ezek 38.15,
16; Isa 13.3
3.12
Isa 2.4; 3.13
3.13
Mt 13.39;
Rev 14.15;
Isa 63.3;
Rev 14.19
3.14
Isa 34.2-8;
Joel 1.15;
2.1
3.15
Joel 2.10,31
3.16
Am 1.2;
Joel 2.11;
Hag 2.6;
Jer 17.17
3.17
v. 21;
Ezek 20.40;
Ob 17;
Isa 52.1;
Nah 1.15

¹⁰ Beat your plowshares into swords,
and your pruning hooks into spears;
let the weakling say, "I am a warrior."

¹¹ Come quickly,ᵏ
all you nations all around,
gather yourselves there.
Bring down your warriors,
O LORD.
¹² Let the nations rouse themselves,
and come up to the valley of Jehoshaphat;
for there I will sit to judge all the neighboring nations.

¹³ Put in the sickle,
for the harvest is ripe.
Go in, tread,
for the wine press is full.
The vats overflow,
for their wickedness is great.

¹⁴ Multitudes, multitudes,
in the valley of decision!
For the day of the LORD is near
in the valley of decision.
¹⁵ The sun and the moon are darkened,
and the stars withdraw their shining.

¹⁶ The LORD roars from Zion,
and utters his voice from Jerusalem,
and the heavens and the earth shake.
But the LORD is a refuge for his people,
a stronghold for the people of Israel.

The Glorious Future of Judah

¹⁷ So you shall know that I, the LORD your God,
dwell in Zion, my holy mountain.

ʰ Ch 4.1 in Heb ⁱ Or *palaces*
ʲ Heb *sanctify war* ᵏ Meaning of Heb uncertain

And Jerusalem shall be holy,
and strangers shall never
again pass through it.

18 In that day
the mountains shall drip
sweet wine,
the hills shall flow with
milk,
and all the stream beds of
Judah
shall flow with water;
a fountain shall come forth
from the house of the
LORD
and water the Wadi
Shittim.

19 Egypt shall become a
desolation
and Edom a desolate
wilderness,
because of the violence done
to the people of Judah,
in whose land they have
shed innocent blood.
20 But Judah shall be inhabited
forever,
and Jerusalem to all
generations.
21 I will avenge their blood, and
I will not clear the
guilty,[1]
for the LORD dwells in Zion.

3.18
Am 9.13;
Isa 30.25;
35.6;
Ezek 47.1-12;
Rev 22.1

3.19
Ob 10
3.20
Ezek 37.25;
Am 9.15
3.21
Ezek 36.25;
v. 17

[1] Gk Syr: Heb *I will hold innocent their blood
that I have not held innocent*

Amos

Title and Background

The concurrent reigns of Uzziah of Judah and Jeroboam II of Israel were marked by a period of peace and prosperity. But such prosperity was accompanied by an almost unprecedented degree of social corruption, and it is to this that the book of Amos is addressed.

Author and Date of Writing

Amos was a herdsman from the small town of Tekoa; he was not a man of the court like Isaiah or a priest like Jeremiah. Though he lived in Judah, God sent him to announce judgment on the northern kingdom (Israel). The main part of his ministry was probably carried out about 760-750 B.C., and this book can be dated during that time.

Theme and Message

The dominant theme is clearly stated in 5.24, which calls for social justice as the indispensable expression of true piety. In other words, Amos was a vigorous spokesman for God's justice and righteousness. He condemns all who make themselves powerful or rich at the expense of others.

Outline

1 The words of Amos, who was among the shepherds of Tekoa, which he saw concerning Israel in the days of King Uzziah of Judah and in the days of King Jeroboam son of Joash of Israel, two years[a] before the earthquake.

Judgment on Israel's Neighbors

2 And he said:

The LORD roars from Zion,
 and utters his voice from
 Jerusalem;
the pastures of the
 shepherds wither,
 and the top of Carmel dries
 up.

3 Thus says the LORD:
For three transgressions of
 Damascus,

and for four, I will not
 revoke the
 punishment;[b]
because they have threshed
 Gilead
 with threshing sledges of
 iron.
4 So I will send a fire on the
 house of Hazael,
 and it shall devour the
 strongholds of
 Ben-hadad.
5 I will break the gate bars of
 Damascus,
 and cut off the inhabitants
 from the Valley of Aven,
 and the one who holds the
 scepter from Beth-eden;

1.1 2 Sam 14.2; 2 Kings 14.23-29; Zech 14.5
1.2 Jer 25.30; Joel 3.16; 1.18,19; Am 9.3
1.3 Isa 7.8; 8.4; v. 13
1.4 Jer 49.27; 1 Kings 20.1; 2 Kings 6.24
1.5 Jer 51.30; 2 Kings 16.9; Am 9.7

a Or *during two years* b Heb *cause it to return*

and the people of Aram
　　shall go into exile to
　　Kir,
　　　　　says the LORD.

6 Thus says the LORD:
　For three transgressions of
　　Gaza,
　and for four, I will not
　　revoke the
　　punishment;c
　because they carried into
　　exile entire
　　communities,
　to hand them over to
　　Edom.
7 So I will send a fire on the
　　wall of Gaza,
　fire that shall devour its
　　strongholds.
8 I will cut off the inhabitants
　　from Ashdod,
　and the one who holds the
　　scepter from Ashkelon;
　I will turn my hand against
　　Ekron,
　and the remnant of the
　　Philistines shall perish,
　　　　　says the Lord GOD.

9 Thus says the LORD:
　For three transgressions of
　　Tyre,
　and for four, I will not
　　revoke the
　　punishment;c
　because they delivered entire
　　communities over to
　　Edom,
　and did not remember the
　　covenant of kinship.
10 So I will send a fire on the
　　wall of Tyre,
　fire that shall devour its
　　strongholds.

11 Thus says the LORD:
　For three transgressions of
　　Edom,
　and for four, I will not
　　revoke the
　　punishment;c
　because he pursued his
　　brother with the sword
　and cast off all pity;
　he maintained his anger
　　perpetually,d

1.6
1 Sam 6.17;
Jer 47.1,5;
v. 9;
Ob 11
1.7
Jer 47.1;
v. 6
1.8
Zeph 2.4;
Zech 9.6;
Ps 81.14;
Ezek 25.16
1.9
Isa 23.1-18;
Ezek 26.2-4;
1 Kings 5.1;
9.11-14
1.10
Zech 9.4
1.11
Isa 34.5,6;
63.1-6;
Jer 49.7-22;
Ob 10-12;
Isa 57.16;
Mic 7.18

1.12
Jer 49.7,20;
Ob 9,10
1.13
Jer 49.1-6;
Ezek 25.2-7;
2 Kings 15.16
1.14
Jer 49.2;
Am 2.2;
Ezek 21.22;
Isa 29.6;
30.30
1.15
Jer 49.3
2.1
Isa chs. 15,
16; Jer ch.
48;
Zeph 2.8,9
2.2
Jer 48.41,45
2.3
Am 5.7,12;
6.12;
Ps 2.10;
Isa 40.23;
Jer 48.7

　and kept his wrathe
　　forever.
12 So I will send a fire on
　　Teman,
　and it shall devour the
　　strongholds of Bozrah.

13 Thus says the LORD:
　For three transgressions of
　　the Ammonites,
　and for four, I will not
　　revoke the
　　punishment;c
　because they have ripped
　　open pregnant women
　　in Gilead
　in order to enlarge their
　　territory.
14 So I will kindle a fire against
　　the wall of Rabbah,
　fire that shall devour its
　　strongholds,
　with shouting on the day of
　　battle,
　with a storm on the day of
　　the whirlwind;
15 then their king shall go into
　　exile,
　he and his officials
　　together,
　　　　　says the LORD.

2 Thus says the LORD:
　For three transgressions of
　　Moab,
　and for four, I will not
　　revoke the
　　punishment;c
　because he burned to lime
　　the bones of the king of
　　Edom.
2 So I will send a fire on
　　Moab,
　and it shall devour the
　　strongholds of Kerioth,
　and Moab shall die amid
　　uproar,
　amid shouting and the
　　sound of the trumpet;
3 I will cut off the ruler from
　　its midst,
　and will kill all its officials
　　with him,
　　　　　says the LORD.

c Heb cause it to return d Syr Vg: Heb and
his anger tore perpetually e Gk Syr Vg: Heb
and his wrath kept

Judgment on Judah

4 Thus says the LORD:
For three transgressions of
 Judah,
and for four, I will not
 revoke the
 punishment;[f]
because they have rejected
 the law of the LORD,
and have not kept his
 statutes,
but they have been led astray
 by the same lies
after which their ancestors
 walked.
5 So I will send a fire on
 Judah,
and it shall devour the
 strongholds of
 Jerusalem.

Judgment on Israel

6 Thus says the LORD:
For three transgressions of
 Israel,
and for four, I will not
 revoke the
 punishment;[f]
because they sell the
 righteous for silver,
and the needy for a pair of
 sandals —
7 they who trample the head
 of the poor into the
 dust of the earth,
and push the afflicted out
 of the way;
father and son go in to the
 same girl,
so that my holy name is
 profaned;
8 they lay themselves down
 beside every altar
on garments taken in
 pledge;
and in the house of their
 God they drink
wine bought with fines
 they imposed.

9 Yet I destroyed the Amorite
 before them,
whose height was like the
 height of cedars,
and who was as strong as
 oaks;

2.4
2 Kings 17.19;
Joel 3.2;
Jer 6.19;
8.9;
Dan 9.11;
Isa 28.15;
Jer 16.19;
Ezek 20.13,
16,18
2.5
Jer 17.27;
Hos 8.14
2.6
2 Kings 18.12;
Joel 3.3;
Am 5.11,12;
8.6
2.7
Am 8.4;
5.12;
Lev 20.3;
Hos 4.14
2.8
1 Cor 8.10;
Ex 22.26;
Am 4.1; 6.6
2.9
Deut 2.31;
Num 13.33;
Isa 5.24;
Mal 4.1

2.10
Ex 12.51;
Deut 2.7;
Ex 3.8
2.11
Jer 7.25;
Num 6.2,3
2.12
Isa 30.10;
Jer 11.21;
Am 7.12,13;
Mic 2.6
2.13
Joel 3.13
2.14
Isa 30.16,
17; Jer 9.23;
Ps 33.16
2.15
Jer 51.56;
Ezek 39.3;
Isa 31.3
2.16
Jer 48.41
3.1
Jer 8.3;
13.11;
Am 2.10;
9.7
3.2
Deut 7.6;
Jer 14.20;
Ezek 20.36;
Lk 12.47;
Rom 2.9

I destroyed his fruit above,
 and his roots beneath.
10 Also I brought you up out of
 the land of Egypt,
and led you forty years in
 the wilderness,
to possess the land of the
 Amorite.
11 And I raised up some of your
 children to be prophets
and some of your youths to
 be nazirites.[g]
Is it not indeed so,
 O people of Israel?
 says the LORD.

12 But you made the nazirites[g]
 drink wine,
and commanded the
 prophets,
saying, "You shall not
 prophesy."

13 So, I will press you down in
 your place,
just as a cart presses down
 when it is full of sheaves.[h]
14 Flight shall perish from the
 swift,
and the strong shall not
 retain their strength,
nor shall the mighty save
 their lives;
15 those who handle the bow
 shall not stand,
and those who are swift of
 foot shall not save
 themselves,
nor shall those who ride
 horses save their lives;
16 and those who are stout of
 heart among the mighty
shall flee away naked in
 that day,
 says the LORD.

Israel's Guilt and Punishment

3 Hear this word that the LORD
 has spoken against you,
O people of Israel, against the
whole family that I brought up out
of the land of Egypt:
2 You only have I known

[f] Heb *cause it to return* [g] That is, *those
separated* or *those consecrated* [h] Meaning of
Heb uncertain

of all the families of the
earth;
therefore I will punish you
for all your iniquities.

3 Do two walk together
unless they have made an
appointment?
4 Does a lion roar in the
forest,
when it has no prey?
Does a young lion cry out
from its den,
if it has caught nothing?
5 Does a bird fall into a snare
on the earth,
when there is no trap for
it?
Does a snare spring up from
the ground,
when it has taken nothing?
6 Is a trumpet blown in a city,
and the people are not
afraid?
Does disaster befall a city,
unless the LORD has done
it?
7 Surely the Lord GOD does
nothing,
without revealing his secret
to his servants the
prophets.
8 The lion has roared;
who will not fear?
The Lord GOD has spoken;
who can but prophesy?

9 Proclaim to the strongholds
in Ashdod,
and to the strongholds in
the land of Egypt,
and say, "Assemble
yourselves on Mountⁱ
Samaria,
and see what great tumults
are within it,
and what oppressions are
in its midst."
10 They do not know how to do
right, says the LORD,
those who store up
violence and robbery in
their strongholds.
11 Therefore thus says the Lord
GOD:
An adversary shall surround
the land,

3.3
Lev 26.23,
24
3.4
Hos 11.10
3.6
Jer 6.1;
Hos 5.8;
Isa 14.24-27;
45.7
3.7
Gen 18.17;
Jn 15.15;
Rev 10.7
3.8
Am 1.2;
Jon 1.1; 3.1;
Jer 20.9;
Acts 4.20
3.9
Am 1.8; 4.1;
6.1; 8.6
3.10
Jer 4.22;
Am 5.7;
6.12;
Hab 2.8-11;
Zeph 1.9;
Zech 5.3,4
3.11
Am 6.14;
2.14; 2.5

3.12
1 Sam 17.34-
37; Am 6.4;
Ps 132.3
3.13
Ezek 2.7
3.14
v.2; Am 4.4;
5.5,6
3.15
Jer 36.22;
Judg 3.20;
1 Kings 22.39
4.1
Ps 22.12;
Ezek 39.18;
Am 3.9; 6.1;
5.11; 8.6; 2.8;
6.6
4.2
Ps 89.25;
Am 6.8; 8.7;
Isa 37.29;
Ezek 58.4;
29.4
4.3
Jer 52.7;
Ezek 12.5

and strip you of your
defense;
and your strongholds shall
be plundered.

12 Thus says the LORD: As the
shepherd rescues from the mouth
of the lion two legs, or a piece of an
ear, so shall the people of Israel
who live in Samaria be rescued,
with the corner of a couch and
part^j of a bed.

13 Hear, and testify against the
house of Jacob,
says the Lord GOD, the God
of hosts:
14 On the day I punish Israel
for its transgressions,
I will punish the altars of
Bethel,
and the horns of the altar
shall be cut off
and fall to the ground.
15 I will tear down the winter
house as well as the
summer house;
and the houses of ivory
shall perish,
and the great houses^k shall
come to an end,
says the LORD.

4 Hear this word, you cows of
Bashan
who are on Mount Samaria,
who oppress the poor, who
crush the needy,
who say to their husbands,
"Bring something to
drink!"
2 The Lord GOD has sworn by
his holiness:
The time is surely coming
upon you,
when they shall take you
away with hooks,
even the last of you with
fishhooks.
3 Through breaches in the wall
you shall leave,
each one straight ahead;

ⁱ Gk Syr: Heb the mountains of ^j Meaning
of Heb uncertain ^k Or many houses

and you shall be flung out
 into Harmon,[1]
 says the LORD.
4 Come to Bethel — and
 transgress;
 to Gilgal — and multiply
 transgression;
 bring your sacrifices every
 morning,
 your tithes every three
 days;
5 bring a thank-offering of
 leavened bread,
 and proclaim freewill
 offerings, publish them;
 for so you love to do,
 O people of Israel!
 says the Lord GOD.

Israel Rejects Correction

6 I gave you cleanness of teeth
 in all your cities,
 and lack of bread in all
 your places,
 yet you did not return to me,
 says the LORD.

7 And I also withheld the rain
 from you
 when there were still three
 months to the harvest;
 I would send rain on one
 city,
 and send no rain on
 another city;
 one field would be rained
 upon,
 and the field on which it
 did not rain withered;
8 so two or three towns
 wandered to one town
 to drink water, and were
 not satisfied;
 yet you did not return to me,
 says the LORD.

9 I struck you with blight and
 mildew;
 I laid waste[m] your gardens
 and your vineyards;
 the locust devoured your
 fig trees and your olive
 trees;
 yet you did not return to me,
 says the LORD.

4.4
Am 3.14;
5.5;
Hos 4.15;
Num 28.3,4;
Deut 14.28
4.5
Lev 7.13;
22.18,21;
Hos 9.1,10
4.6
Isa 3.1;
Jer 14.18;
5.3;
Hag 2.17
4.7
Deut 11.17;
2 Chr 7.13;
Ex 9.4,26;
10.22,23
4.8
Jer 14.4;
Ezek 4.16;
Jer 3.7
4.9
Deut 28.22;
Hag 2.17;
Joel 1.4;
2.25;
Jer 3.10

4.10
Ex 9.3,6;
Deut 28.27,
60;
Jer 11.22;
18.21; 48.15;
Joel 2.20;
Isa 9.13
4.11
Isa 13.19;
Zech 3.2;
Jer 23.14
4.12
v. 2;
Ezek 13.5
4.13
Jer 10.13;
Ps 139.2;
Dan 2.28;
Jer 13.16;
Mic 1.3;
Am 5.8,27;
9.6
5.1
Ezek 19.1
5.2
Jer 14.17;
Am 8.14;
Isa 51.18;
Jer 50.32
5.3
Isa 6.13;
Am 6.9

10 I sent among you a
 pestilence after the
 manner of Egypt;
 I killed your young men
 with the sword;
 I carried away your horses;[n]
 and I made the stench of
 your camp go up into
 your nostrils;
 yet you did not return to me,
 says the LORD.

11 I overthrew some of you,
 as when God overthrew
 Sodom and Gomorrah,
 and you were like a brand
 snatched from the fire;
 yet you did not return to me,
 says the LORD.

12 Therefore thus I will do to
 you, O Israel;
 because I will do this to
 you,
 prepare to meet your God,
 O Israel!

13 For lo, the one who forms
 the mountains, creates
 the wind,
 reveals his thoughts to
 mortals,
 makes the morning darkness,
 and treads on the heights
 of the earth —
 the LORD, the God of hosts,
 is his name!

A Lament for Israel's Sin

5 Hear this word that I take up
 over you in lamentation,
O house of Israel:
2 Fallen, no more to rise,
 is maiden Israel;
 forsaken on her land,
 with no one to raise her
 up.

3 For thus says the Lord GOD:
 The city that marched out a
 thousand
 shall have a hundred left,
 and that which marched out
 a hundred

[1]Meaning of Heb uncertain [m]Cn: Heb the
multitude of [n]Heb with the captivity of
your horses

shall have ten left. °

4 For thus says the LORD to the
house of Israel:
Seek me and live;
5 but do not seek Bethel,
and do not enter into Gilgal
or cross over to Beer-sheba;
for Gilgal shall surely go into
exile,
and Bethel shall come to
nothing.

6 Seek the LORD and live,
or he will break out against
the house of Joseph
like fire,
and it will devour Bethel,
with no one to quench
it.
7 Ah, you that turn justice to
wormwood,
and bring righteousness to
the ground!

8 The one who made the
Pleiades and Orion,
and turns deep darkness
into the morning,
and darkens the day into
night,
who calls for the waters of
the sea,
and pours them out on the
surface of the earth,
the LORD is his name,
9 who makes destruction flash
out against the strong,
so that destruction comes
upon the fortress.

10 They hate the one who
reproves in the gate,
and they abhor the one
who speaks the truth.
11 Therefore because you
trample on the poor
and take from them levies
of grain,
you have built houses of
hewn stone,
but you shall not live in
them;
you have planted pleasant
vineyards,
but you shall not drink
their wine.

5.4
Jer 29.3;
Isa 55.3
5.5
Am 4.4;
1 Sam 7.16;
11.14;
Am 8.14
5.6
Isa 55.3,6,7;
v. 14;
Deut 4.24;
Am 3.14
5.7
Am 6.12
5.8
Job 9.9;
12.22;
Isa 42.16;
Am 8.9;
Ps 104.6-9;
Am 9.6;
4.13
5.9
Isa 29.5;
Mic 5.11
5.10
Isa 29.21;
1 Kings 22.8;
Isa 59.15
5.11
Am 3.9; 8.6;
3.15; 6.11;
Mic 6.15

5.12
Am 2.6,7;
Isa 29.21
5.13
Eccl 3.7
5.14
v. 6;
Mic 3.11
5.15
Ps 97.10;
Rom 12.9;
Joel 2.14;
Mic 5.3,7,8
5.16
Jer 9.17;
Joel 1.11;
2 Chr 35.25
5.17
Isa 16.10;
Jer 48.33;
Nah 1.2
5.18
Isa 5.19;
Joel 1.15;
2.1,11,31;
2 Pet 3.4;
Jer 30.7
5.19
Jer 48.44

12 For I know how many are
your transgressions,
and how great are your
sins —
you who afflict the righteous,
who take a bribe,
and push aside the needy
in the gate.
13 Therefore the prudent will
keep silent in such a
time;
for it is an evil time.

14 Seek good and not evil,
that you may live;
and so the LORD, the God of
hosts, will be with you,
just as you have said.
15 Hate evil and love good,
and establish justice in the
gate;
it may be that the LORD, the
God of hosts,
will be gracious to the
remnant of Joseph.

16 Therefore thus says the LORD,
the God of hosts, the
Lord:
In all the squares there shall
be wailing;
and in all the streets they
shall say, "Alas! alas!"
They shall call the farmers to
mourning,
and those skilled in
lamentation, to wailing;
17 in all the vineyards there
shall be wailing,
for I will pass through the
midst of you,
says the LORD.

The Day of the LORD a Dark Day

18 Alas for you who desire the
day of the LORD!
Why do you want the day
of the LORD?
It is darkness, not light;
19 as if someone fled from a
lion,
and was met by a bear;
or went into the house and
rested a hand against
the wall,

° Heb adds to the house of Israel

and was bitten by a snake.

20 Is not the day of the LORD
darkness, not light,
and gloom with no
brightness in it?

21 I hate, I despise your
festivals,
and I take no delight in
your solemn
assemblies.

22 Even though you offer me
your burnt offerings and
grain offerings,
I will not accept them;
and the offerings of
well-being of your
fatted animals
I will not look upon.

23 Take away from me the
noise of your songs;
I will not listen to the
melody of your harps.

24 But let justice roll down like
waters,
and righteousness like an
everflowing stream.

25 Did you bring to me sacrifices and offerings the forty years in the wilderness, O house of Israel? 26 You shall take up Sakkuth your king, and Kaiwan your star-god, your images,p which you made for yourselves; 27 therefore I will take you into exile beyond Damascus, says the LORD, whose name is the God of hosts.

Complacent Self-Indulgence Will Be Punished

6 Alas for those who are at
ease in Zion,
and for those who feel
secure on Mount
Samaria,
the notables of the first of
the nations,
to whom the house of
Israel resorts!

2 Cross over to Calneh, and
see;
from there go to Hamath
the great;
then go down to Gath of
the Philistines.

Are you betterq than these
kingdoms?
Or is yourr territory greater
than theirss territory,

3 O you that put far away the
evil day,
and bring near a reign of
violence?

4 Alas for those who lie on
beds of ivory,
and lounge on their
couches,
and eat lambs from the
flock,
and calves from the stall;

5 who sing idle songs to the
sound of the harp,
and like David improvise
on instruments of
music;

6 who drink wine from bowls,
and anoint themselves with
the finest oils,
but are not grieved over the
ruin of Joseph!

7 Therefore they shall now be
the first to go into
exile,
and the revelry of the
loungers shall pass
away.

8 The Lord GOD has sworn by
himself
(says the LORD, the God of
hosts):
I abhor the pride of Jacob
and hate his strongholds;
and I will deliver up the
city and all that is in it.

9 If ten people remain in one house, they shall die. 10 And if a relative, one who burns the dead,t shall take up the body to bring it out of the house, and shall say to someone in the innermost parts of the house, "Is anyone else with you?" the answer will come, "No." Then the relativeu shall say, "Hush! We must not mention the name of the LORD."

5.20
Isa 13.10;
Zeph 1.15
5.21
Isa 1.11-16;
Lev 26.31
5.22
Isa 66.3;
Mic 6.6,7;
Am 4.5
5.23
Am 6.4,5;
8.10
5.24
Jer 22.3;
Ezek 45.9;
Mic 6.8
5.25
Deut 32.17;
Ezek 20.8,
16,24;
Acts 7.42
5.27
2 Kings 17.6;
Am 4.13
6.1
Isa 32.9-11;
Lk 6.24;
Ex 19.5;
Am 3.2
6.2
Jer 2.10;
Isa 10.9;
2 Kings 18.34;
2 Chr 26.6;
Nah 3.8

6.3
Isa 56.12;
Am 9.10
6.4
Am 3.15;
3.12;
Ezek 34.2,3
6.5
Isa 5.12;
Am 5.23;
1 Chr 23.5
6.6
Am 2.8; 4.1;
Gen 37.25;
Ezek 9.4
6.7
Am 7.11,17;
Dan 5.4-6,
30; v. 4
6.8
Jer 51.14;
Heb 6.13;
Deut 32.19;
Ps 106.40;
Am 3.10,11;
Hos 11.6
6.9
Am 5.3
6.10
Am 5.13;
8.3

p Heb your images, your star-god q Or Are
they better r Heb their s Heb your
t Or who makes a burning for him
u Heb he

11 See, the LORD commands,
 and the great house shall
 be shattered to bits,
 and the little house to
 pieces.
12 Do horses run on rocks?
 Does one plow the sea with
 oxen?ᵛ
 But you have turned justice
 into poison
 and the fruit of
 righteousness into
 wormwood—
13 you who rejoice in
 Lo-debar,ʷ
 who say, "Have we not by
 our own strength
 taken Karnaimˣ for
 ourselves?"
14 Indeed, I am raising up
 against you a nation,
 O house of Israel, says the
 LORD, the God of hosts,
 and they shall oppress you
 from Lebo-hamath
 to the Wadi Arabah.

Locusts, Fire, and a Plumb Line

7 This is what the Lord GOD
 showed me: he was forming
locusts at the time the latter
growth began to sprout (it was the
latter growth after the king's mow-
ings). 2 When they had finished eat-
ing the grass of the land, I said,
"O Lord GOD, forgive, I beg
 you!
 How can Jacob stand?
 He is so small!"
3 The LORD relented
 concerning this;
 "It shall not be," said the
 LORD.

4 This is what the Lord GOD
showed me: the Lord GOD was call-
ing for a shower of fire,ʸ and it de-
voured the great deep and was eat-
ing up the land. 5 Then I said,
"O Lord GOD, cease, I beg
 you!
 How can Jacob stand?
 He is so small!"
6 The LORD relented
 concerning this;

6.11
Isa 55.11;
Am 3.15
6.12
Isa 59.13,
14;
Hos 10.4;
Am 5.7
6.13
Ps 75.4,5
6.14
Jer 5.15;
Am 3.11;
Num 34.8;
1 Kings 8.65
7.1
vv. 4,7;
Am 8.1;
Joel 1.4;
Am 4.9;
Nah 3.15
7.2
Ex 10.14,
15;
Ezek 9.8;
11.13;
Isa 37.4;
Jer 42.2
7.3
Deut 32.36;
Jer 26.19;
Jon 3.10
7.4
Isa 66.15,
16; Am 2.5
7.5
v. 2
7.6
v. 3
7.8
Am 8.2;
Isa 28.17;
34.11;
Lam 2.8;
Mic 7.18
7.9
Hos 10.8;
Mic 1.5;
Isa 63.18;
2 Kings 15.10
7.10
1 Kings 12.32;
2 Kings 14.23;
Jer 26.8-11
7.11
vv. 9,17
7.13
Am 2.12;
1 Kings 12.32;
13.1
7.14
1 Kings 20.35;
2 Kings 2.5;
4.38;
2 Chr 19.2;
Am 1.1
7.15
2 Sam 7.8;
Am 3.8;
Jer 7.1;
Ezek 2.3,4

"This also shall not be,"
 said the Lord GOD.

7 This is what he showed me:
the Lord was standing beside a wall
built with a plumb line, with a
plumb line in his hand. 8 And the
LORD said to me, "Amos, what do
you see?" And I said, "A plumb
line." Then the Lord said,
"See, I am setting a plumb
 line
 in the midst of my people
 Israel;
 I will never again pass
 them by;
9 the high places of Isaac shall
 be made desolate,
 and the sanctuaries of
 Israel shall be laid
 waste,
 and I will rise against the
 house of Jeroboam with
 the sword."

Amaziah Complains to the King

10 Then Amaziah, the priest of
Bethel, sent to King Jeroboam of
Israel, saying, "Amos has conspired
against you in the very center of the
house of Israel; the land is not able
to bear all his words. 11 For thus
Amos has said,
 'Jeroboam shall die by the
 sword,
 and Israel must go into
 exile
 away from his land.' "
12 And Amaziah said to Amos,
"O seer, go, flee away to the land of
Judah, earn your bread there, and
prophesy there; 13 but never again
prophesy at Bethel, for it is the
king's sanctuary, and it is a temple
of the kingdom."

14 Then Amos answered Amazi-
ah, "I amᶻ no prophet, nor a
prophet's son; but I amᶻ a herds-
man, and a dresser of sycamore
trees, 15 and the LORD took me from
following the flock, and the LORD
said to me, 'Go, prophesy to my
people Israel.'

ᵛ Or *Does one plow them with oxen*
ʷ Or *in a thing of nothingness* ˣ Or *horns*
ʸ Or *for a judgment by fire* ᶻ Or *was*

16 "Now therefore hear the
 word of the LORD.
You say, 'Do not prophesy
 against Israel,
and do not preach against
 the house of Isaac.'
17 Therefore thus says the LORD:
 'Your wife shall become a
 prostitute in the city,
and your sons and your
 daughters shall fall by
 the sword,
and your land shall be
 parceled out by line;
you yourself shall die in an
 unclean land,
and Israel shall surely go
 into exile away from its
 land.' "

The Basket of Fruit

8 This is what the Lord GOD
 showed me—a basket of sum-
mer fruit.[a] 2 He said, "Amos, what
do you see?" And I said, "A basket
of summer fruit."[a] Then the LORD
said to me,
 The end[b] has come upon my
 people Israel;
 I will never again pass
 them by.
3 The songs of the temple[c]
 shall become wailings
 in that day,"
 says the Lord GOD;
"the dead bodies shall be
 many,
 cast out in every place. Be
 silent!"

4 Hear this, you that trample
 on the needy,
and bring to ruin the poor
 of the land,
5 saying, "When will the new
 moon be over
 so that we may sell grain;
and the sabbath,
 so that we may offer wheat
 for sale?
We will make the ephah
 small and the shekel
 great,
and practice deceit with
 false balances,
6 buying the poor for silver

7.16
Am 2.12;
Ezek 21.2;
Mic 2.6
7.17
Jer 29.21;
Hos 4.13,
14;
Jer 14.16;
Ezek 4.13;
Hos 9.3
8.2
Am 7.8;
Jer 24.3;
Ezek 7.2
8.3
Am 5.23;
6.9,10
8.4
Ps 14.4;
Am 5.11,12
8.5
2 Kings 4.23;
Neh 13.15,
16;
Mic 6.10,11
8.6
Am 2.6

8.7
Am 6.8;
Deut 33.26,
29;
Hos 8.13;
9.9
8.8
Isa 5.25;
Hos 4.3;
Am 9.5
8.9
Isa 13.10;
Jer 15.9;
Mic 3.6;
Am 4.13;
5.8
8.10
Am 5.21;
6.4,5;
Jer 48.37;
Ezek 7.18;
Jer 6.26;
Zech 12.10
8.11
1 Sam 3.1;
2 Chr 15.3;
Ezek 7.26;
Mic 3.6
8.12
Ezek 20.3,
31

and the needy for a pair of
 sandals,
and selling the sweepings
 of the wheat."

7 The LORD has sworn by the
 pride of Jacob:
Surely I will never forget any
 of their deeds.
8 Shall not the land tremble
 on this account,
and everyone mourn who
 lives in it,
and all of it rise like the
 Nile,
and be tossed about and
 sink again, like the Nile
 of Egypt?

9 On that day, says the Lord
 GOD,
I will make the sun go
 down at noon,
and darken the earth in
 broad daylight.
10 I will turn your feasts into
 mourning,
and all your songs into
 lamentation;
I will bring sackcloth on all
 loins,
and baldness on every
 head;
I will make it like the
 mourning for an only
 son,
and the end of it like a
 bitter day.

11 The time is surely coming,
 says the Lord GOD,
when I will send a famine
 on the land;
not a famine of bread, or a
 thirst for water,
but of hearing the words of
 the LORD.
12 They shall wander from sea
 to sea,
and from north to east;
they shall run to and fro,
 seeking the word of the
 LORD,
but they shall not find it.

a Heb *qayits* b Heb *qets* c Or *palace*

13 In that day the beautiful
 young women and the
 young men
 shall faint for thirst.
14 Those who swear by
 Ashimah of Samaria,
 and say, "As your god lives,
 O Dan,"
 and, "As the way of
 Beer-sheba lives" —
 they shall fall, and never
 rise again.

The Destruction of Israel

9 I saw the Lord standing be-
 side[d] the altar, and he said:
Strike the capitals until the
 thresholds shake,
 and shatter them on the
 heads of all the
 people;[e]
and those who are left I will
 kill with the sword;
 not one of them shall flee
 away,
 not one of them shall
 escape.

2 Though they dig into Sheol,
 from there shall my hand
 take them;
though they climb up to
 heaven,
 from there I will bring
 them down.
3 Though they hide themselves
 on the top of Carmel,
 from there I will search out
 and take them;
and though they hide from
 my sight at the bottom
 of the sea,
 there I will command the
 sea-serpent, and it shall
 bite them.
4 And though they go into
 captivity in front of
 their enemies,
 there I will command the
 sword, and it shall kill
 them;
and I will fix my eyes on
 them
 for harm and not for good.

5 The Lord, God of hosts,

8.13
Lam 1.18;
Isa 41.17;
Hos 2.3
8.14
Hos 4.15;
1 Kings 12.28,
29; Am 5.5
9.1
Am 3.14;
Zeph 2.14;
Hab 3.13;
v. 4;
Am 2.14
9.2
Ps 139.8;
Jer 51.53;
Ob 4
9.3
Am 1.2;
Jer 16.16,
17; Isa 27.1
9.4
Lev 26.33;
Ezek 5.12;
Jer 44.11
9.5
Mic 1.4;
Am 8.8

9.6
Ps 104.3;
Am 5.8;
4.13
9.7
Isa 43.3;
Am 2.10;
3.1;
Deut 2.23;
Jer 47.4;
Am 1.5
9.8
Jer 44.27;
vv. 4,10;
Jer 30.11;
Joel 2.32
9.9
Isa 30.28
9.10
Am 8.14;
6.3
9.11
Acts 15.16,
17;
Ps 80.12;
Isa 63.11;
Jer 46.26

he who touches the earth
 and it melts,
 and all who live in it
 mourn,
and all of it rises like the
 Nile,
 and sinks again, like the
 Nile of Egypt;
6 who builds his upper
 chambers in the
 heavens,
 and founds his vault upon
 the earth;
who calls for the waters of
 the sea,
 and pours them out upon
 the surface of the
 earth —
the Lord is his name.

7 Are you not like the
 Ethiopians[f] to me,
 O people of Israel? says the
 Lord.
Did I not bring Israel up
 from the land of Egypt,
 and the Philistines from
 Caphtor and the
 Arameans from Kir?
8 The eyes of the Lord God are
 upon the sinful
 kingdom,
 and I will destroy it from
 the face of the earth
 — except that I will not
 utterly destroy the
 house of Jacob,
 says the Lord.

9 For lo, I will command,
 and shake the house of
 Israel among all the
 nations
as one shakes with a sieve,
 but no pebble shall fall to
 the ground.
10 All the sinners of my people
 shall die by the sword,
 who say, "Evil shall not
 overtake or meet us."

The Restoration of David's Kingdom

11 On that day I will raise up

d Or on e Heb all of them
f Or Nubians; Heb Cushites

the booth of David that is
 fallen,
and repair its^g breaches,
and raise up its^h ruins,
and rebuild it as in the
 days of old;
12 in order that they may
 possess the remnant of
 Edom
and all the nations who are
 called by my name,
says the LORD who does
 this.

13 The time is surely coming,
 says the LORD,
when the one who plows
 shall overtake the one
 who reaps,
and the treader of grapes
 the one who sows the
 seed;

9.12
Ob 19;
Isa 11.14;
43.7
9.13
Lev 26.5;
Joel 3.18

9.14
Isa 60.4;
Jer 30.18;
Isa 61.4;
Ezek 36.35;
28.26
9.15
Jer 24.6;
31.28;
Isa 60.21;
Jer 32.41;
Ezek 34.28

the mountains shall drip
 sweet wine,
and all the hills shall flow
 with it.
14 I will restore the fortunes of
 my people Israel,
and they shall rebuild the
 ruined cities and
 inhabit them;
they shall plant vineyards
 and drink their wine,
and they shall make
 gardens and eat their
 fruit.
15 I will plant them upon their
 land,
and they shall never again
 be plucked up
out of the land that I have
 given them,
 says the LORD your God.

g Gk: Heb *their* h Gk: Heb *his*

Obadiah

Title and Background

Obadiah's name means "servant of the LORD." His prophecy centers around an ancient feud between Edom and Israel. The Edomites were descendants of Esau, and had always held a grudge against Israel because Jacob had cheated their ancestor out of his birthright.

Author and Date of Writing

The author is Obadiah. The date and place of composition are uncertain. A date between 853 and 841 B.C. is suggested by relating verses 11-14 to the invasion of Jerusalem by Philistines and Arabians during Jehoram's reign (2 Kings 8.20-22). An exilic date is also possible by relating those verses to the Babylonian attacks on Jerusalem.

Theme and Message

Obadiah's theme is that Edomites are proud of their own security and have gloated when Israel was devastated by foreign powers. But their participation in that disaster will bring on God's wrath; the Edomites themselves will be destroyed, while Mount Zion and Israel will be delivered and God's kingdom will triumph.

Outline

I. The Doom of Edom (1-14)
II. Edom in the Day of the Lord (15-21)

Proud Edom Will Be Brought Low

1 The vision of Obadiah.

Thus says the Lord GOD
 concerning Edom:
We have heard a report from
 the LORD,
 and a messenger has been
 sent among the nations:
"Rise up! Let us rise against
 it for battle!"
2 I will surely make you least
 among the nations;
 you shall be utterly
 despised.
3 Your proud heart has
 deceived you,
 you that live in the clefts
 of the rock,[a]
 whose dwelling is in the
 heights.
You say in your heart,
 "Who will bring me down
 to the ground?"

4 Though you soar aloft like
 the eagle,
 though your nest is set
 among the stars,
 from there I will bring you
 down,
 says the LORD.

Pillage and Slaughter Will Repay Edom's Cruelty

5 If thieves came to you,
 if plunderers by night
 —how you have been
 destroyed!—
 would they not steal only
 what they wanted?
If grape-gatherers came to
 you,
 would they not leave
 gleanings?
6 How Esau has been pillaged,
 his treasures searched out!
7 All your allies have deceived
 you,

1
Isa 34.5;
Ezek 25.12;
Joel 3.19;
Jer 49.14;
Isa 30.4;
Jer 6.4,5
3
Isa 16.6;
Jer 49.16;
2 Kings 14.7;
Isa 14.13-15;
Rev 18.7

4
Job 20.6;
Hab 2.9;
Isa 14.13-15
5
Jer 49.9;
vv. 9,10;
Isa 17.6
6
Jer 49.10
7
Jer 30.14;
38.22;
Ps 41.9;
Jer 49.7

a Or clefts of Sela

they have driven you to the
border;
your confederates have
prevailed against you;
those who ate[b] your bread
have set a trap for
you —
there is no understanding
of it.
8 On that day, says the Lord,
I will destroy the wise out
of Edom,
and understanding out of
Mount Esau.
9 Your warriors shall be
shattered, O Teman,
so that everyone from
Mount Esau will be cut
off.

Edom Mistreated His Brother

10 For the slaughter and
violence done to your
brother Jacob,
shame shall cover you,
and you shall be cut off
forever.
11 On the day that you stood
aside,
on the day that strangers
carried off his wealth,
and foreigners entered his
gates
and cast lots for Jerusalem,
you too were like one of
them.
12 But you should not have
gloated[c] over[d] your
brother
on the day of his
misfortune;
you should not have rejoiced
over the people of
Judah
on the day of their ruin;
you should not have boasted
on the day of distress.
13 You should not have entered
the gate of my people
on the day of their
calamity;
you should not have joined
in the gloating over
Judah's[e] disaster
on the day of his calamity;
you should not have looted
his goods

8
Job 5.12;
Isa 29.14
9
Jer 49.22;
Am 1.12;
Hab 3.3;
v. 5
10
Ps 137.7;
Joel 3.19;
Am 1.11
11
Ps 137.7;
Joel 3.3;
Nah 3.10
12
Mic 4.11;
Ezek 35.15;
36.5;
Ps 31.18
13
Ezek 35.5,
10; 36.2,3

15
Ezek 30.3;
Joel 1.15;
Jer 50.29;
Hab 2.8;
Ezek 35.11
16
Jer 49.12,
13; 25.15,16
17
Isa 4.2,3;
Am 9.11-15
18
Isa 10.17;
Jer 11.23;
Am 1.8
19
Am 9.12;
Isa 11.14;
Zeph 2.7;
Jer 31.5;
32.44

on the day of his calamity.
14 You should not have stood at
the crossings
to cut off his fugitives;
you should not have handed
over his survivors
on the day of distress.

15 For the day of the Lord is
near against all the
nations.
As you have done, it shall be
done to you;
your deeds shall return on
your own head.
16 For as you have drunk on my
holy mountain,
all the nations around you
shall drink;
they shall drink and gulp
down,[f]
and shall be as though they
had never been.

Israel's Final Triumph

17 But on Mount Zion there
shall be those that
escape,
and it shall be holy;
and the house of Jacob shall
take possession of
those who dispossessed
them.
18 The house of Jacob shall be
a fire,
the house of Joseph a
flame,
and the house of Esau
stubble;
they shall burn them and
consume them,
and there shall be no
survivor of the house of
Esau;
for the Lord has
spoken.
19 Those of the Negeb shall
possess Mount Esau,
and those of the Shephelah
the land of the
Philistines;

b Cn: Heb lacks *those who ate* c Heb *But
do not gloat* (and similarly through verse 14)
d Heb *on the day of* e Heb *his*
f Meaning of Heb uncertain

they shall possess the land of
Ephraim and the land
of Samaria,
and Benjamin shall possess
Gilead.
20 The exiles of the Israelites
who are in Halah[g]
shall possess[h] Phoenicia as
far as Zarephath;
and the exiles of Jerusalem
who are in Sepharad

shall possess the towns of
the Negeb.
21 Those who have been saved[i]
shall go up to Mount
Zion
to rule Mount Esau;
and the kingdom shall be
the LORD's.

20
1 Kings 17.9;
Jer 32.44;
33.13

21
Neh 9.27;
Ps 22.28;
67.4;
Dan 2.44;
Zech 14.9

g Cn: Heb *in this army* h Cn: Meaning of
Heb uncertain i Or *Saviors*

Jonah

Title and Background

The book is named after its principal character, whose name means "dove." The events in the book probably took place during the eighth century, when the Assyrians were a feared and despised enemy.

Author and Date of Writing

Traditionally, the book has been ascribed to Jonah son of Amittai (see 2 Kings 14.25), though nowhere in the book is that plainly stated. Acceptance of the book's authorship by Jonah would necessitate a date no later than the third quarter of the eighth century B.C.

Theme and Message

The theme that runs throughout the four chapters of this book is that God's great mercy extends equally to Gentile nations if they repent. In addition, the book depicts the larger scope of God's purpose for his people: they must rediscover God's concern for the whole creation and understand their own role in carrying out that concern.

Outline

Jonah Tries to Run Away from God

1 Now the word of the LORD came to Jonah son of Amittai, saying, ² "Go at once to Nineveh, that great city, and cry out against it; for their wickedness has come up before me." ³ But Jonah set out to flee to Tarshish from the presence of the LORD. He went down to Joppa and found a ship going to Tarshish; so he paid his fare and went on board, to go with them to Tarshish, away from the presence of the LORD.

4 But the LORD hurled a great wind upon the sea, and such a mighty storm came upon the sea that the ship threatened to break up. ⁵ Then the mariners were afraid, and each cried to his god. They threw the cargo that was in the ship into the sea, to lighten it for them. Jonah, meanwhile, had gone down into the hold of the ship and had lain down, and was fast asleep. ⁶ The captain came and said to him, "What are you doing sound asleep? Get up, call on your god! Perhaps the god will spare us a thought so that we do not perish."

7 The sailors[a] said to one another, "Come, let us cast lots, so that we may know on whose account this calamity has come upon us." So they cast lots, and the lot

1.1
2 Kings 14.25;
Mt 12.39
1.2
Jon 3.2,3;
4.1;
Ezra 9.6
1.3
Ps 139.7,9,
10;
Acts 9.36
1.4
Ps 107.25

1.5
Acts 27.18;
1 Sam 24.3
1.6
Ps 107.28;
Jon 3.9
1.7
Josh 7.14;
1 Sam 10.20;
14.41,42;
Acts 1.26

[a] Heb *They*

fell on Jonah. [8] Then they said to him, "Tell us why this calamity has come upon us. What is your occupation? Where do you come from? What is your country? And of what people are you?" [9] "I am a Hebrew," he replied. "I worship the LORD, the God of heaven, who made the sea and the dry land." [10] Then the men were even more afraid, and said to him, "What is this that you have done!" For the men knew that he was fleeing from the presence of the LORD, because he had told them so.

11 Then they said to him, "What shall we do to you, that the sea may quiet down for us?" For the sea was growing more and more tempestuous. [12] He said to them, "Pick me up and throw me into the sea; then the sea will quiet down for you; for I know it is because of me that this great storm has come upon you." [13] Nevertheless the men rowed hard to bring the ship back to land, but they could not, for the sea grew more and more stormy against them. [14] Then they cried out to the LORD, "Please, O LORD, we pray, do not let us perish on account of this man's life. Do not make us guilty of innocent blood; for you, O LORD, have done as it pleased you." [15] So they picked Jonah up and threw him into the sea; and the sea ceased from its raging. [16] Then the men feared the LORD even more, and they offered a sacrifice to the LORD and made vows.

17 [b] But the LORD provided a large fish to swallow up Jonah; and Jonah was in the belly of the fish three days and three nights.

A Psalm of Thanksgiving

2 Then Jonah prayed to the LORD his God from the belly of the fish, [2] saying,

"I called to the LORD out of
 my distress,
and he answered me;
out of the belly of Sheol I
 cried,
and you heard my voice.
[3] You cast me into the deep,
 into the heart of the seas,

1.8
Josh 7.19;
1 Sam 14.43
1.9
Ps 146.6;
Acts 17.24
1.10
Job 27.22
1.12
2 Sam 24.17;
Jn 11.50;
1 Chr 21.17
1.13
Prov 21.30
1.14
v. 16;
Deut 21.8;
Ps 115.3
1.15
Ps 89.9;
107.29;
Lk 8.24
1.16
1 Sam 6.2-5;
Mk 4.41
1.17
Jon 4.6;
Mt 12.40;
16.4;
Lk 11.30
2.1
Ps 130.1
2.2
Ps 18.4-6
2.3
Ps 88.6;
42.7

2.4
Ps 31.22;
1 Kings 8.38
2.5
Ps 69.1;
Lam 3.54
2.6
Ps 16.10
2.7
Ps 142.3;
77.10,11;
18.6
2.8
2 Kings 17.15;
Ps 31.6;
Jer 10.8;
16.19
2.9
Ps 50.14;
Hos 14.2;
Heb 13.15;
Job 22.27;
Ps 3.8
2.10
Jon 1.17
3.1
Jon 1.1,2
3.5
Dan 9.3;
Joel 1.14;
Jer 31.34

and the flood surrounded
 me;
all your waves and your
 billows
passed over me.
[4] Then I said, 'I am driven
 away
from your sight;
how [c] shall I look again
 upon your holy temple?'
[5] The waters closed in over
 me;
the deep surrounded me;
weeds were wrapped around
 my head
[6] at the roots of the
 mountains.
I went down to the land
 whose bars closed upon me
 forever;
yet you brought up my life
 from the Pit,
O LORD my God.
[7] As my life was ebbing away,
 I remembered the LORD;
and my prayer came to you,
 into your holy temple.
[8] Those who worship vain
 idols
forsake their true loyalty.
[9] But I with the voice of
 thanksgiving
will sacrifice to you;
what I have vowed I will pay.
Deliverance belongs to the
 LORD!"

[10] Then the LORD spoke to the fish, and it spewed Jonah out upon the dry land.

Conversion of Nineveh

3 The word of the LORD came to Jonah a second time, saying, [2] "Get up, go to Nineveh, that great city, and proclaim to it the message that I tell you." [3] So Jonah set out and went to Nineveh, according to the word of the LORD. Now Nineveh was an exceedingly large city, a three days' walk across. [4] Jonah began to go into the city, going a day's walk. And he cried out, "Forty days more, and Nineveh shall be overthrown!" [5] And the people of Nineveh believed God; they proclaimed

b Ch 2.1 in Heb c Theodotion: Heb *surely*

a fast, and everyone, great and small, put on sackcloth.

6 When the news reached the king of Nineveh, he rose from his throne, removed his robe, covered himself with sackcloth, and sat in ashes. 7 Then he had a proclamation made in Nineveh: "By the decree of the king and his nobles: No human being or animal, no herd or flock, shall taste anything. They shall not feed, nor shall they drink water. 8 Human beings and animals shall be covered with sackcloth, and they shall cry mightily to God. All shall turn from their evil ways and from the violence that is in their hands. 9 Who knows? God may relent and change his mind; he may turn from his fierce anger, so that we do not perish."

10 When God saw what they did, how they turned from their evil ways, God changed his mind about the calamity that he had said he would bring upon them; and he did not do it.

Jonah's Anger

4 But this was very displeasing to Jonah, and he became angry. 2 He prayed to the LORD and said, "O LORD! Is not this what I said while I was still in my own country? That is why I fled to Tarshish at the beginning; for I knew that you are a gracious God and merciful, slow to anger, and abounding in steadfast love, and ready to relent from punishing. 3 And now, O LORD, please take my life from me, for it is better for me

to die than to live." 4 And the LORD said, "Is it right for you to be angry?" 5 Then Jonah went out of the city and sat down east of the city, and made a booth for himself there. He sat under it in the shade, waiting to see what would become of the city.

6 The LORD God appointed a bush,[d] and made it come up over Jonah, to give shade over his head, to save him from his discomfort; so Jonah was very happy about the bush. 7 But when dawn came up the next day, God appointed a worm that attacked the bush, so that it withered. 8 When the sun rose, God prepared a sultry east wind, and the sun beat down on the head of Jonah so that he was faint and asked that he might die. He said, "It is better for me to die than to live."

Jonah Is Reproved

9 But God said to Jonah, "Is it right for you to be angry about the bush?" And he said, "Yes, angry enough to die." 10 Then the LORD said, "You are concerned about the bush, for which you did not labor and which you did not grow; it came into being in a night and perished in a night. 11 And should I not be concerned about Nineveh, that great city, in which there are more than a hundred and twenty thousand persons who do not know their right hand from their left, and also many animals?"

d Heb qiqayon, possibly the castor bean plant

3.6
Job 2.8;
Jer 6.25;
Dan 9.3
3.7
v. 5;
2 Chr 20.3
3.8
Ps 130.1;
Jon 1.6,14;
Isa 55.6,7;
Jer 18.11
3.9
2 Sam 12.22;
Joel 2.14
3.10
Jer 31.18;
Ex 32.14;
Jer 18.8;
Am 7.3,6
4.1
vv. 4,9;
Mt 20.15;
Lk 15.28
4.2
Jon 1.3;
Ex 34.6;
Ps 86.5;
Joel 2.13
4.3
1 Kings 19.4;
v. 8;
Job 7.15,16

4.4
v. 9;
Mt 20.11,15
4.5
1 Kings 19.9,13
4.7
Joel 1.12
4.9
v. 4
4.11
Jon 1.2; 3.2,3;
Deut 1.39;
Ps 36.6

Micah

Title and Background

The book is named after Micah, a shortened form of Micaiah, meaning "Who is like the LORD?" Judah had enjoyed comparative economic prosperity when Micah came on the scene. This prosperity placed wealth and power in the hands of a few and brought with it social injustice.

Author and Date of Writing

Little is known about Micah beyond what can be learned from the book itself. He was deeply sensitive to the social ills of his day, especially as they affected the small towns and villages of his homeland. Micah prophesied sometime after 750 B.C. and prior to 686 B.C..

Theme and Message

Micah's message alternated between oracles of doom and oracles of hope. The theme is judgment and deliverance by God. Micah also stressed that God hates idolatry, injustice, rebellion, and empty ritualism, but he delights in pardoning the penitent.

Outline

I. Judgment Against Israel and Judah (1.1–3.12)
II. Hope for Israel and Judah (4.1–5.15)
III. The Lord's Case Against Israel (6.1-16)
IV. Gloom Turns to Triumph (7.1-20)

1 The word of the LORD that came to Micah of Moresheth in the days of Kings Jotham, Ahaz, and Hezekiah of Judah, which he saw concerning Samaria and Jerusalem.

Judgment Pronounced against Samaria

2 Hear, you peoples, all of you;
 listen, O earth, and all that
 is in it;
and let the Lord GOD be a
 witness against you,
 the Lord from his holy
 temple.
3 For lo, the LORD is coming
 out of his place,
 and will come down and
 tread upon the high
 places of the earth.
4 Then the mountains will
 melt under him

and the valleys will burst
 open,
 like wax near the fire,
 like waters poured down a
 steep place.
5 All this is for the
 transgression of Jacob
 and for the sins of the
 house of Israel.
What is the transgression of
 Jacob?
 Is it not Samaria?
And what is the high place[a]
 of Judah?
 Is it not Jerusalem?
6 Therefore I will make
 Samaria a heap in the
 open country,
 a place for planting
 vineyards.
I will pour down her stones
 into the valley,

1.1 Jer 26.18; 2 Kings 15.5, 7,32-38; 16.1-20; 18.1-21
1.2 Jer 6.19; 22.29; Ps 50.7; 11.4
1.3 Isa 26.21; Am 4.13
1.4 Isa 64.1,2; Nah 1.5
1.5 Isa 28.1; Am 8.14; 2 Chr 34.3, 4
1.6 Jer 31.5; Am 5.11; Ezek 13.14

a Heb *what are the high places*

and uncover her
 foundations.
⁷ All her images shall be
 beaten to pieces,
 all her wages shall be
 burned with fire,
 and all her idols I will lay
 waste;
 for as the wages of a
 prostitute she gathered
 them,
 and as the wages of a
 prostitute they shall
 again be used.

The Doom of the Cities of Judah

⁸ For this I will lament and
 wail;
 I will go barefoot and
 naked;
 I will make lamentation like
 the jackals,
 and mourning like the
 ostriches.
⁹ For her wound ᵇ is incurable.
 It has come to Judah;
 it has reached to the gate of
 my people,
 to Jerusalem.

¹⁰ Tell it not in Gath,
 weep not at all;
 in Beth-leaphrah
 roll yourselves in the dust.
¹¹ Pass on your way,
 inhabitants of Shaphir,
 in nakedness and shame;
 the inhabitants of Zaanan
 do not come forth;
 Beth-ezel is wailing
 and shall remove its
 support from you.
¹² For the inhabitants of
 Maroth
 wait anxiously for good,
 yet disaster has come down
 from the LORD
 to the gate of Jerusalem.
¹³ Harness the steeds to the
 chariots,
 inhabitants of Lachish;
 it was the beginning of sin
 to daughter Zion,
 for in you were found
 the transgressions of Israel.

1.7
Deut 9.21;
2 Chr 34.7;
Isa 23.17
1.8
Isa 22.4;
32.11; 13.21,
22
1.9
Jer 30.12,
15;
2 Kings 18.13;
v. 12
1.10
2 Sam 1.20
1.11
Ezek 23.29
1.12
Isa 59.9-11;
Jer 14.19
1.13
2 Kings 14.19;
Isa 36.2

1.14
2 Kings 16.8;
Josh 15.44;
Jer 15.18
1.15
Josh 15.44;
Mic 5.2;
Josh 12.15;
2 Sam 23.13
1.16
Isa 15.2;
22.12;
Lam 4.5;
Am 7.11,17
2.1
Isa 32.7;
Nah 1.11;
Hos 7.6,7;
Prov 3.27
2.2
Am 8.4;
Isa 5.8;
1 Kings 21.1-
15
2.3
Am 3.1,2;
Deut 28.48;
Jer 18.11;
Isa 2.11,12;
Am 5.13
2.4
Hab 2.6;
Mic 1.8;
Isa 24.3;
Jer 4.13;
6.12; 8.10

¹⁴ Therefore you shall give
 parting gifts
 to Moresheth-gath;
 the houses of Achzib shall be
 a deception
 to the kings of Israel.
¹⁵ I will again bring a
 conqueror upon you,
 inhabitants of Mareshah;
 the glory of Israel
 shall come to Adullam.
¹⁶ Make yourselves bald and
 cut off your hair
 for your pampered
 children;
 make yourselves as bald as
 the eagle,
 for they have gone from
 you into exile.

Social Evils Denounced

2 Alas for those who devise
 wickedness
 and evil deeds ᶜ on their
 beds!
 When the morning dawns,
 they perform it,
 because it is in their
 power.
² They covet fields, and seize
 them;
 houses, and take them
 away;
 they oppress householder
 and house,
 people and their
 inheritance.

³ Therefore thus says the LORD:
 Now, I am devising against
 this family an evil
 from which you cannot
 remove your necks;
 and you shall not walk
 haughtily,
 for it will be an evil time.
⁴ On that day they shall take
 up a taunt song against
 you,
 and wail with bitter
 lamentation,
 and say, "We are utterly
 ruined;

ᵇ Gk Syr Vg: Heb *wounds* ᶜ Cn: Heb *work*
evil

the LORD[d] alters the
inheritance of my
people;
how he removes it from
me!
Among our captors[e] he
parcels out our fields."

5 Therefore you will have no
one to cast the line by
lot
in the assembly of the
LORD.

6 "Do not preach"—thus they
preach—
"one should not preach of
such things;
disgrace will not overtake
us."

7 Should this be said, O house
of Jacob?
Is the LORD's patience
exhausted?
Are these his doings?
Do not my words do good
to one who walks
uprightly?

8 But you rise up against my
people[f] as an enemy;
you strip the robe from the
peaceful,[g]
from those who pass by
trustingly
with no thought of war.

9 The women of my people
you drive out
from their pleasant
houses;
from their young children
you take away
my glory forever.

10 Arise and go;
for this is no place to rest,
because of uncleanness that
destroys
with a grievous
destruction.[h]

11 If someone were to go about
uttering empty
falsehoods,
saying, "I will preach to
you of wine and strong
drink,"
such a one would be the
preacher for this
people!

2.5
Josh 18.4,
10
2.6
Isa 30.10;
Am 2.12;
7.16;
Mic 3.6;
6.16
2.7
Isa 50.2;
59.1;
Jer 15.16;
Ps 15.2;
84.11
2.8
Jer 12.8;
Mic 3.2,3;
7.2,3;
Ps 120.6,7
2.9
Jer 10.20
2.10
Lev 18.25,
28,29;
Deut 12.9;
Ps 106.38
2.11
Jer 5.13,31;
Isa 28.7;
30.10,11

2.12
Mic 4.6,7;
5.7,8; 7.18;
Jer 33.22
2.13
Hos 3.5;
Isa 52.12
3.1
Jer 5.4,5
3.2
Mic 2.8;
7.2,3;
Ezek 22.27
3.3
Ps 14.4;
Zeph 3.3;
Ezek 34.2,3;
11.3
3.4
Ps 18.41;
Prov 1.28;
Isa 1.15;
Zech 7.13;
Isa 59.2;
Mic 7.13
3.5
Isa 56.10;
Ezek 13.10;
Jer 14.14,
15;
Mic 2.11;
Jer 6.14;
Ezek 13.18,
19

A Promise for the Remnant of Israel

12 I will surely gather all of you,
O Jacob,
I will gather the survivors
of Israel;
I will set them together
like sheep in a fold,
like a flock in its pasture;
it will resound with people.

13 The one who breaks out will
go up before them;
they will break through and
pass the gate,
going out by it.
Their king will pass on
before them,
the LORD at their head.

Wicked Rulers and Prophets

3 And I said:
Listen, you heads of Jacob
and rulers of the house of
Israel!
Should you not know
justice?—

2 you who hate the good and
love the evil,
who tear the skin off my
people,[i]
and the flesh off their
bones;

3 who eat the flesh of my
people,
flay their skin off them,
break their bones in pieces,
and chop them up like
meat[j] in a kettle,
like flesh in a caldron.

4 Then they will cry to the
LORD,
but he will not answer
them;
he will hide his face from
them at that time,
because they have acted
wickedly.

5 Thus says the LORD
concerning the prophets

who lead my people astray,
who cry "Peace"
 when they have something
 to eat,
 but declare war against
 those
 who put nothing into their
 mouths.
6 Therefore it shall be night to
 you, without vision,
 and darkness to you,
 without revelation.
 The sun shall go down upon
 the prophets,
 and the day shall be black
 over them;
7 the seers shall be disgraced,
 and the diviners put to
 shame;
 they shall all cover their
 lips,
 for there is no answer from
 God.
8 But as for me, I am filled
 with power,
 with the spirit of the
 LORD,
 and with justice and might,
 to declare to Jacob his
 transgression
 and to Israel his sin.

9 Hear this, you rulers of the
 house of Jacob
 and chiefs of the house of
 Israel,
 who abhor justice
 and pervert all equity,
10 who build Zion with blood
 and Jerusalem with wrong!
11 Its rulers give judgment for a
 bribe,
 its priests teach for a price,
 its prophets give oracles for
 money;
 yet they lean upon the LORD
 and say,
 "Surely the LORD is with us!
 No harm shall come upon
 us."
12 Therefore because of you
 Zion shall be plowed as a
 field;
 Jerusalem shall become a
 heap of ruins,
 and the mountain of the
 house a wooded height.

3.6
Isa 8.20,22;
Ezek 13.23;
Am 8.9
3.7
Zech 13.4;
Isa 44.25;
Mic 7.16;
1 Sam 28.6;
v. 4
3.8
Isa 61.1,2;
58.1
3.9
v. 1;
Isa 1.23
3.10
Jer 22.13;
Ezek 22.27;
Hab 2.12
3.11
Isa 1.23;
Hos 4.18;
Jer 6.13;
Isa 48.2;
Jer 7.4
3.12
Jer 26.18;
Mic 4.1,2

4.1
Isa 2.2-4;
Ezek 17.22;
43.12;
Jer 3.17
4.2
Zech 2.11;
14.16;
Jer 31.6;
Isa 54.13;
42.1-4;
Zech 14.8,9
4.3
Isa 2.4;
Joel 3.10;
Ps 72.7
4.4
1 Kings 4.25;
Zech 3.10;
Isa 1.20;
40.5
4.5
2 Kings 17.29;
Isa 26.8,13;
Zech 10.12
4.6
Ezek 34.16;
Zeph 3.19;
Ps 147.2;
Ezek 34.13

Peace and Security through Obedience

4 In days to come
 the mountain of the LORD's
 house
 shall be established as the
 highest of the
 mountains,
 and shall be raised up
 above the hills.
 Peoples shall stream to it,
2 and many nations shall
 come and say:
 "Come, let us go up to the
 mountain of the LORD,
 to the house of the God of
 Jacob;
 that he may teach us his
 ways
 and that we may walk in
 his paths."
 For out of Zion shall go forth
 instruction,
 and the word of the LORD
 from Jerusalem.
3 He shall judge between many
 peoples,
 and shall arbitrate between
 strong nations far away;
 they shall beat their swords
 into plowshares,
 and their spears into
 pruning hooks;
 nation shall not lift up sword
 against nation,
 neither shall they learn war
 any more;
4 but they shall all sit under
 their own vines and
 under their own fig
 trees,
 and no one shall make
 them afraid;
 for the mouth of the LORD
 of hosts has spoken.

5 For all the peoples walk,
 each in the name of its
 god,
 but we will walk in the name
 of the LORD our God
 forever and ever.

Restoration Promised after Exile

6 In that day, says the LORD,
 I will assemble the lame

and gather those who have
 been driven away,
and those whom I have
 afflicted.
7 The lame I will make the
 remnant,
and those who were cast
 off, a strong nation;
and the LORD will reign over
 them in Mount Zion
now and forevermore.

8 And you, O tower of the
 flock,
 hill of daughter Zion,
to you it shall come,
 the former dominion shall
 come,
 the sovereignty of daughter
 Jerusalem.

9 Now why do you cry aloud?
 Is there no king in you?
Has your counselor perished,
 that pangs have seized you
 like a woman in labor?
10 Writhe and groan,ᵏ
 O daughter Zion,
 like a woman in labor;
for now you shall go forth
 from the city
 and camp in the open
 country;
 you shall go to Babylon.
There you shall be rescued,
 there the LORD will redeem
 you
 from the hands of your
 enemies.

11 Now many nations
 are assembled against you,
saying, "Let her be profaned,
 and let our eyes gaze upon
 Zion."
12 But they do not know
 the thoughts of the LORD;
they do not understand his
 plan,
 that he has gathered them
 as sheaves to the
 threshing floor.
13 Arise and thresh,
 O daughter Zion,
for I will make your horn
 iron
 and your hoofs bronze;

you shall beat in pieces
 many peoples,
 and shallˡ devote their
 gain to the LORD,
 their wealth to the Lord of
 the whole earth.

5ᵐNow you are walled
 around with a wall;ⁿ
 siege is laid against us;
with a rod they strike the
 ruler of Israel
 upon the cheek.

The Ruler from Bethlehem

2 ᵒBut you, O Bethlehem of
 Ephrathah,
 who are one of the little
 clans of Judah,
from you shall come forth for
 me
 one who is to rule in Israel,
whose origin is from of old,
 from ancient days.
3 Therefore he shall give them
 up until the time
 when she who is in labor
 has brought forth;
then the rest of his kindred
 shall return
 to the people of Israel.
4 And he shall stand and feed
 his flock in the strength
 of the LORD,
 in the majesty of the name
 of the LORD his God.
And they shall live secure,
 for now he shall be
 great
 to the ends of the earth;
5 and he shall be the one of
 peace.

If the Assyrians come into
 our land
 and tread upon our soil,ᵖ
we will raise against them
 seven shepherds
 and eight installed as
 rulers.
6 They shall rule the land of
 Assyria with the sword,

4.7
Mic 2.12;
5.7,8; 7.18;
Isa 9.6;
Dan 7.14;
Lk 1.33;
Rev 11.15
4.8
Mic 2.12;
Isa 1.26;
Zech 9.10
4.9
Jer 8.19;
Isa 13.8;
Jer 30.6
4.10
Hos 2.14;
Isa 45.13;
Mic 7.8-12;
Isa 48.20;
52.9-12
4.11
Lam 2.16;
Ob 12;
Mic 7.10
4.12
Isa 55.8;
Rom 11.33;
Isa 21.10
4.13
Isa 41.15;
Dan 2.44;
Zech 4.14

5.1
Jer 5.7;
1 Kings 22.24;
Lam 3.30
5.2
Mt 2.6;
1 Sam 17.12;
23.23;
Lk 2.4;
Isa 9.6
5.3
Mic 4.10;
Hos 11.8;
Isa 10.20-22
5.4
Isa 40.11;
Ezek 34.23;
Isa 52.13;
Lk 1.32
5.5
Isa 9.6;
Rev 11.15;
Isa 8.7,8
5.6
Nah 2.11-13;
Zeph 2.13;
Gen 10.8;
Isa 37.36,37

ᵏMeaning of Heb uncertain ˡGk Syr Tg:
Heb *and I will* ᵐCh 4.14 in Heb
ⁿCn Compare Gk: Meaning of Heb uncertain
ᵒCh 5.1 in Heb ᵖGk: Heb *in our palaces*

and the land of Nimrod
 with the drawn sword;q
they[r] shall rescue us from
 the Assyrians
if they come into our land
or tread within our border.

The Future Role of the Remnant

7 Then the remnant of Jacob,
 surrounded by many
 peoples,
 shall be like dew from the
 Lord,
 like showers on the grass,
 which do not depend upon
 people
 or wait for any mortal.
8 And among the nations the
 remnant of Jacob,
 surrounded by many
 peoples,
 shall be like a lion among
 the animals of the
 forest,
 like a young lion among
 the flocks of sheep,
 which, when it goes through,
 treads down
 and tears in pieces, with no
 one to deliver.
9 Your hand shall be lifted up
 over your adversaries,
 and all your enemies shall
 be cut off.

10 In that day, says the Lord,
 I will cut off your horses
 from among you
 and will destroy your
 chariots;
11 and I will cut off the cities of
 your land
 and throw down all your
 strongholds;
12 and I will cut off sorceries
 from your hand,
 and you shall have no more
 soothsayers;
13 and I will cut off your images
 and your pillars from
 among you,
 and you shall bow down no
 more
 to the work of your hands;
14 and I will uproot your sacred
 poless from among you

5.7
Mic 2.12;
Deut 32.2;
Hos 14.5
5.8
Mic 4.13;
Zech 10.5;
Hos 5.14;
Ps 50.22
5.9
Ps 10.12;
21.8;
Isa 26.11
5.10
Isa 2.7;
Hos 14.3;
Zech 9.10
5.11
Isa 1.7;
Hos 10.14;
Am 5.9
5.12
Deut 18.10-12;
Isa 2.6
5.13
Zech 13.2;
Isa 2.8
5.14
Ex 34.13;
Isa 17.8;
27.9

5.15
Ps 149.7;
Isa 65.12
6.1
Ps 50.1;
Ezek 6.2,3
6.2
Deut 32.1;
Hos 12.2;
Isa 1.8;
Hos 4.1
6.3
Ps 50.7;
Jer 2.5;
Isa 43.22,23
6.4
Ex 12.51;
Deut 4.20;
7.8;
Ps 77.20;
Ex 15.20
6.5
Num 22.5,6;
Rev 2.14;
Num 25.1;
Josh 4.19;
5.9,10;
Judg 5.11;
1 Sam 12.7
6.6
Ps 40.6-8;
51.16,17
6.7
2 Kings 16.3;
21.6;
Jer 7.31

and destroy your towns.
15 And in anger and wrath I will
 execute vengeance
 on the nations that did not
 obey.

God Challenges Israel

6 Hear what the Lord says:
 Rise, plead your case
 before the mountains,
 and let the hills hear your
 voice.
2 Hear, you mountains, the
 controversy of the Lord,
 and you enduring
 foundations of the
 earth;
 for the Lord has a
 controversy with his
 people,
 and he will contend with
 Israel.

3 "O my people, what have I
 done to you?
 In what have I wearied
 you? Answer me!
4 For I brought you up from
 the land of Egypt,
 and redeemed you from the
 house of slavery;
 and I sent before you Moses,
 Aaron, and Miriam.
5 O my people, remember now
 what King Balak of
 Moab devised,
 what Balaam son of Beor
 answered him,
 and what happened from
 Shittim to Gilgal,
 that you may know the
 saving acts of the
 Lord."

What God Requires

6 "With what shall I come
 before the Lord,
 and bow myself before God
 on high?
 Shall I come before him with
 burnt offerings,
 with calves a year old?
7 Will the Lord be pleased
 with thousands of rams,

q Cn: Heb *in its entrances* r Heb *he*
s Heb *Asherim*

with ten thousands of
rivers of oil?
Shall I give my firstborn for
my transgression,
the fruit of my body for the
sin of my soul?"

8 He has told you, O mortal,
what is good;
and what does the LORD
require of you
but to do justice, and to love
kindness,
and to walk humbly with
your God?

Cheating and Violence to Be Punished

9 The voice of the LORD cries
to the city
(it is sound wisdom to fear
your name):
Hear, O tribe and assembly
of the city!ᵗ

10 Can I forgetᵘ the treasures
of wickedness in the
house of the wicked,
and the scant measure that
is accursed?

11 Can I tolerate wicked scales
and a bag of dishonest
weights?

12 Yourᵛ wealthy are full of
violence;
yourʷ inhabitants speak
lies,
with tongues of deceit in
their mouths.

13 Therefore I have begunˣ to
strike you down,
making you desolate
because of your sins.

14 You shall eat, but not be
satisfied,
and there shall be a
gnawing hunger within
you;
you shall put away, but not
save,
and what you save, I will
hand over to the sword.

15 You shall sow, but not reap;
you shall tread olives, but
not anoint yourselves
with oil;
you shall tread grapes, but
not drink wine.

16 For you have kept the
statutes of Omriʸ
and all the works of the
house of Ahab,
and you have followed their
counsels.
Therefore I will make you a
desolation, and yourᶻ
inhabitants an object of
hissing;
so you shall bear the scorn
of my people.

The Total Corruption of the People

7 Woe is me! For I have
become like one who,
after the summer fruit has
been gathered,
after the vintage has been
gleaned,
finds no cluster to eat;
there is no first-ripe fig for
which I hunger.

2 The faithful have
disappeared from the
land,
and there is no one left
who is upright;
they all lie in wait for blood,
and they hunt each other
with nets.

3 Their hands are skilled to do
evil;
the official and the judge
ask for a bribe,
and the powerful dictate
what they desire;
thus they pervert justice.ᵃ

4 The best of them is like a
brier,
the most upright of them a
thorn hedge.
The day of theirᵇ sentinels,
of theirᵇ punishment,
has come;
now their confusion is at
hand.

5 Put no trust in a friend,

6.8
Deut 10.12;
1 Sam 15.22;
Hos 6.6;
12.6;
Isa 56.1;
57.15; 66.2
6.10
Jer 5.26,27;
Am 3.10;
8.5
6.11
Hos 12.7
6.12
Am 6.3,4;
Mic 2.1,2;
Jer 9.3,5;
Hos 7.13;
Am 2.4;
Isa 3.8
6.13
Mic 1.9;
Isa 1.7; 6.11
6.14
Lev 26.26;
Isa 9.20;
30.6
6.15
Deut 28.38;
Jer 12.13;
Am 5.11;
Zeph 1.13

6.16
1 Kings 16.25-
33; Jer 7.24;
19.8; 29.18;
51.51
7.1
Isa 24.13;
28.4;
Hos 9.10
7.2
Ps 12.1;
Isa 57.1;
59.7;
Jer 5.26;
Hos 5.1
7.3
Prov 4.16,
17;
Am 5.12;
Mic 3.11
7.4
Ezek 2.6;
28.24;
Nah 1.10;
Isa 10.3;
Hos 9.7;
Isa 22.5
7.5
Jer 9.4

ᵗ Cn Compare Gk: Heb *tribe, and who has
appointed it yet?* ᵘ Cn: Meaning of Heb
uncertain ᵛ Heb *Whose* ʷ Heb *whose*
ˣ Gk Syr Vg: Heb *have made sick*
ʸ Gk Syr Vg Tg: Heb *the statutes of Omri are
kept* ᶻ Heb *its* ᵃ Cn: Heb *they weave it*
ᵇ Heb *your*

have no confidence in a
loved one;
guard the doors of your
mouth
from her who lies in your
embrace;
6 for the son treats the father
with contempt,
the daughter rises up
against her mother,
the daughter-in-law against
her mother-in-law;
your enemies are members
of your own household.
7 But as for me, I will look to
the Lord,
I will wait for the God of
my salvation;
my God will hear me.

Penitence and Trust in God

8 Do not rejoice over me,
O my enemy;
when I fall, I shall rise;
when I sit in darkness,
the Lord will be a light to
me.
9 I must bear the indignation
of the Lord,
because I have sinned
against him,
until he takes my side
and executes judgment for
me.
He will bring me out to the
light;
I shall see his vindication.
10 Then my enemy will see,
and shame will cover her
who said to me,
"Where is the Lord your
God?"
My eyes will see her
downfall;c
now she will be trodden
down
like the mire of the streets.

A Prophecy of Restoration

11 A day for the building of
your walls!
In that day the boundary
shall be far extended.
12 In that day they will come to
you
from Assyria tod Egypt,

and from Egypt to the River,
from sea to sea and from
mountain to mountain.
13 But the earth will be
desolate
because of its inhabitants,
for the fruit of their doings.

14 Shepherd your people with
your staff,
the flock that belongs to
you,
which lives alone in a forest
in the midst of a garden
land;
let them feed in Bashan and
Gilead
as in the days of old.
15 As in the days when you
came out of the land of
Egypt,
show use marvelous
things.
16 The nations shall see and be
ashamed
of all their might;
they shall lay their hands on
their mouths;
their ears shall be deaf;
17 they shall lick dust like a
snake,
like the crawling things of
the earth;
they shall come trembling
out of their fortresses;
they shall turn in dread to
the Lord our God,
and they shall stand in fear
of you.

God's Compassion and Steadfast Love

18 Who is a God like you,
pardoning iniquity
and passing over the
transgression
of the remnant of yourf
possession?
He does not retain his anger
forever,
because he delights in
showing clemency.

7.6
Ezek 22.7;
Mt 10.21,
35.36;
Lk 12.53
7.7
Hab 2.1;
Ps 130.5;
4.3
7.8
Prov 24.17;
Lam 4.21;
Ps 37.24;
Isa 9.2
7.9
Lam 3.29,
40; Isa 42.7,
16; 56.1
7.10
Ps 35.26;
Isa 51.23;
Zech 10.5
7.11
Isa 54.11;
Zeph 2.2
7.12
Isa 11.16;
19.23-25

7.13
Jer 25.11;
Mic 6.13;
Isa 3.10,11;
Mic 3.4
7.14
Mic 5.4;
Ps 23.4;
Jer 50.19;
Am 9.11
7.15
Ex 3.20;
20.34;
Ps 78.12
7.16
Job 21.5;
Mic 3.7
7.17
Ps 72.9;
Isa 49.23;
Deut 32.24;
Ps 18.45;
Isa 59.19
7.18
Ex 34.7,9;
Isa 43.25;
Jer 32.41

c Heb lacks *downfall* d One Ms: MT
Assyria and cities of e Cn: Heb *I will show*
him f Heb *his*

¹⁹ He will again have
 compassion upon us;
 he will tread our iniquities
 under foot.
 You will cast all our[g] sins
 into the depths of the sea.
²⁰ You will show faithfulness to
 Jacob

and unswerving loyalty to
 Abraham,
as you have sworn to our
 ancestors
from the days of old.

7.19
Jer 50.20;
Isa 38.17;
43.25;
Jer 31.34
7.20
Lk 1.55,72;
Deut 7.8,12

[g] Gk Syr Vg Tg: Heb *their*

Nahum

Title and Background

The name Nahum means "comfort" or "consolation." During Jonah's time Nineveh repented and their destruction was temporarily averted. Not long after that, however, Nineveh reverted to its extreme wickedness, brutality, and pride.

Author and Date of Writing

Nothing is known about Nahum except his hometown (Elkosh), but even its precise location is uncertain. In all three chapters Nahum prophesied Nineveh's fall, which was fulfilled in 612 B.C. Nahum therefore uttered this oracle between 663 and 612, perhaps near the middle of this period.

Theme and Message

The focal point of this whole book is the Lord's judgment on the Ninevites for their oppression, cruelty, idolatry, and wickedness. God's righteous and just kingdom will ultimately triumph, while kingdoms built on wickedness and tyranny must eventually fall. In addition, Nahum declares the universal sovereignty of God. God is Lord of history and all nations; as such he controls their destinies.

Outline

1 An oracle concerning Nineveh. The book of the vision of Nahum of Elkosh.

The Consuming Wrath of God

2 A jealous and avenging God
 is the LORD,
 the LORD is avenging and
 wrathful;
 the LORD takes vengeance on
 his adversaries
 and rages against his
 enemies.
3 The LORD is slow to anger
 but great in power,
 and the LORD will by no
 means clear the guilty.

His way is in whirlwind and
 storm,
 and the clouds are the dust
 of his feet.
4 He rebukes the sea and
 makes it dry,

1.1 Isa 13.1; Hab 1.1; Nah 2.8; 3.7; Zeph 2.13
1.2 Ex 20.5; Deut 4.24; 32.35,41; Ps 94.1
1.3 Ex 34.6,7; Ps 103.8; Isa 29.6; Ps 104.3
1.4 Ps 106.9; Isa 33.9
1.5 Ex 19.18; Mic 1.4; Isa 24.1,20
1.6 Jer 10.10; Mal 3.2; Isa 66.15; 1 Kings 19.11
1.7 1 Chr 16.34; Ps 28.8
1.8 Isa 28.2,18; 13.9,10

 and he dries up all the
 rivers;
 Bashan and Carmel wither,
 and the bloom of Lebanon
 fades.
5 The mountains quake before
 him,
 and the hills melt;
 the earth heaves before him,
 the world and all who live
 in it.

6 Who can stand before his
 indignation?
 Who can endure the heat
 of his anger?
 His wrath is poured out like
 fire,
 and by him the rocks are
 broken in pieces.
7 The LORD is good,
 a stronghold in a day of
 trouble;
 he protects those who take
 refuge in him,
8 even in a rushing flood.

He will make a full end of
his adversaries,[a]
and will pursue his
enemies into darkness.
9 Why do you plot against the
LORD?
He will make an end;
no adversary will rise up
twice.
10 Like thorns they are
entangled,
like drunkards they are
drunk;
they are consumed like dry
straw.
11 From you one has gone
out
who plots evil against the
LORD,
who counsels wickedness.

Good News for Judah

12 Thus says the LORD,
"Though they are at full
strength and many,[b]
they will be cut off and
pass away.
Though I have afflicted
you,
I will afflict you no more.
13 And now I will break off his
yoke from you
and snap the bonds that
bind you."

14 The LORD has commanded
concerning you:
"Your name shall be
perpetuated no longer;
from the house of your gods
I will cut off
the carved image and the
cast image.
I will make your grave, for
you are worthless."

15c Look! On the mountains the
feet of one
who brings good tidings,
who proclaims peace!
Celebrate your festivals,
O Judah,
fulfill your vows,
for never again shall the
wicked invade you;
they are utterly cut off.

1.9
Ps 2.1;
Isa 28.22
1.10
2 Sam 23.6;
Mal 4.1
1.11
v. 9;
Ezek 11.2
1.12
Isa 10.16-19,
33,34; 54.7,8
1.13
Isa 9.4;
Jer 2.20
1.14
Isa 46.1,2;
Mic 5.13,14;
Ezek 32.22,
23
1.15
Isa 40.9;
Ps 52.7;
Rom 10.15;
Lev 23.2,4;
Isa 52.1;
Joel 3.17;
Isa 29.7,8

2.1
Jer 51.20-23;
Nah 3.12,14
2.2
Isa 60.15;
Ezek 37.21-23
2.3
Ezek 23.14,
15;
Job 39.23
2.4
Ezek 26.10;
Jer 4.13
2.5
Nah 3.18;
Jer 46.12
2.6
Nah 3.18
2.7
Isa 59.11;
32.12
2.8
Nah 3.7;
Jer 46.5;
47.3

The Destruction of the Wicked City

2 A shatterer[d] has come up
against you.
Guard the ramparts;
watch the road;
gird your loins;
collect all your strength.

2 (For the LORD is restoring the
majesty of Jacob,
as well as the majesty of
Israel,
though ravagers have ravaged
them
and ruined their branches.)

3 The shields of his warriors
are red;
his soldiers are clothed in
crimson.
The metal on the chariots
flashes
on the day when he
musters them;
the chargers[e] prance.
4 The chariots race madly
through the streets,
they rush to and fro
through the squares;
their appearance is like
torches,
they dart like lightning.
5 He calls his officers;
they stumble as they come
forward;
they hasten to the wall,
and the mantelet[b] is set
up.
6 The river gates are opened,
the palace trembles.
7 It is decreed[b] that the city[f]
be exiled,
its slave women led away,
moaning like doves
and beating their breasts.
8 Nineveh is like a pool
whose waters[g] run away.
"Halt! Halt!" —
but no one turns back.
9 "Plunder the silver,

a Gk: Heb *of her place* b Meaning of Heb
uncertain c Ch 2.1 in Heb d Cn: Heb
scatterer e Cn Compare Gk Syr: Heb
cypresses f Heb *it* g Cn Compare Gk:
Heb *a pool, from the days that she has become,
and they*

plunder the gold!
There is no end of treasure!
An abundance of every
 precious thing!"

¹⁰ Devastation, desolation, and
 destruction!
Hearts faint and knees
 tremble,
all loins quake,
all faces grow pale!
¹¹ What became of the lions'
 den,
the cave[h] of the young
 lions,
where the lion goes,
and the lion's cubs, with
 no one to disturb them?
¹² The lion has torn enough for
 his whelps
and strangled prey for his
 lionesses;
he has filled his caves with
 prey
and his dens with torn
 flesh.

13 See, I am against you, says
the LORD of hosts, and I will burn
your[i] chariots in smoke, and the
sword shall devour your young li-
ons; I will cut off your prey from the
earth, and the voice of your mes-
sengers shall be heard no more.

Ruin Imminent and Inevitable

3 Ah! City of bloodshed,
 utterly deceitful, full of
 booty—
no end to the plunder!
² The crack of whip and
 rumble of wheel,
galloping horse and
 bounding chariot!
³ Horsemen charging,
 flashing sword and
 glittering spear,
piles of dead,
 heaps of corpses,
dead bodies without end—
 they stumble over the
 bodies!
⁴ Because of the countless
 debaucheries of the
 prostitute,
gracefully alluring, mistress
 of sorcery,

2.10
Ps 22.14;
Isa 13.7,8;
Joel 2.6
2.11
Isa 5.29;
Jer 4.7;
Nah 3.1
2.12
Isa 10.6-14;
Jer 51.34
2.13
Nah 3.5;
Ps 46.9;
Isa 49.24,25
3.1
Ezek 24.6,9
3.2
Nah 2.3,4;
Jer 47.3
3.3
Hab 3.11;
Isa 34.3;
66.16;
2 Kings 19.35
3.4
Isa 23.17;
Rev 17.1,2;
Isa 47.9;
Rev 18.3

3.5
Nah 2.13;
Isa 47.2,3;
Jer 13.22;
Ezek 16.37
3.6
Job 9.31;
Mal 2.9;
Isa 14.16;
Jer 51.37
3.7
Jer 51.9;
Nah 2.8;
Zeph 2.13;
Isa 51.19;
Jer 15.5
3.8
Jer 46.25;
Ezek 30.14-16;
Isa 19.6-8
3.9
Isa 20.5;
Ezek 27.10;
30.5; 38.5;
2 Chr 12.3;
16.8
3.10
Isa 20.4;
13.16;
Hos 13.16;
Lam 2.19;
Joel 3.3;
Ob 11
3.11
Jer 25.27;
Isa 2.10,19
3.12
Isa 28.4;
Rev 6.13

who enslaves[j] nations
 through her
 debaucheries,
and peoples through her
 sorcery,
⁵ I am against you,
 says the LORD of hosts,
 and will lift up your skirts
 over your face;
and I will let nations look on
 your nakedness
and kingdoms on your
 shame.
⁶ I will throw filth at you
 and treat you with
 contempt,
 and make you a spectacle.
⁷ Then all who see you will
 shrink from you and
 say,
"Nineveh is devastated; who
 will bemoan her?"
 Where shall I seek
 comforters for you?

⁸ Are you better than Thebes[k]
 that sat by the Nile,
with water around her,
 her rampart a sea,
 water her wall?
⁹ Ethiopia[l] was her strength,
 Egypt too, and that without
 limit;
Put and the Libyans were
 her[m] helpers.

¹⁰ Yet she became an exile,
 she went into captivity;
even her infants were dashed
 in pieces
 at the head of every street;
lots were cast for her nobles,
 all her dignitaries were
 bound in fetters.
¹¹ You also will be drunken,
 you will go into hiding;[n]
you will seek
 a refuge from the enemy.
¹² All your fortresses are like fig
 trees
 with first-ripe figs—
 if shaken they fall

h Cn: Heb *pasture* i Heb *her*
i Heb *sells* k Heb *No-amon*
l Or *Nubia*; Heb *Cush* m Gk: Heb *your*
n Meaning of Heb uncertain

into the mouth of the
eater.

13 Look at your troops:
they are women in your
midst.
The gates of your land
are wide open to your foes;
fire has devoured the bars
of your gates.

14 Draw water for the siege,
strengthen your forts;
trample the clay,
tread the mortar,
take hold of the brick
mold!
15 There the fire will devour
you,
the sword will cut you off.
It will devour you like the
locust.

Multiply yourselves like the
locust,
multiply like the
grasshopper!
16 You increased your
merchants
more than the stars of the
heavens.

3.13
Jer 50.37;
51.30;
Ps 147.13
3.14
2 Chr 32.3,
4,11;
Nah 2.1
3.15
v. 13;
Joel 1.4
3.16
Isa 23.8
3.17
Jer 51.27;
Rev 9.7
3.18
Ps 76.5,6;
Isa 56.10;
Jer 51.57;
Nah 2.5;
1 Kings 22.17
3.19
Mic 1.9;
Lam 2.15;
Zeph 2.15

The locust sheds its skin
and flies away.
17 Your guards are like
grasshoppers,
your scribes like swarms°
of locusts
settling on the fences
on a cold day—
when the sun rises, they fly
away;
no one knows where they
have gone.

18 Your shepherds are asleep,
O king of Assyria;
your nobles slumber.
Your people are scattered on
the mountains
with no one to gather
them.
19 There is no assuaging your
hurt,
your wound is mortal.
All who hear the news about
you
clap their hands over you.
For who has ever escaped
your endless cruelty?

° Meaning of Heb uncertain

Habakkuk

Title and Background

The title of this book is the author's name and apparently comes from a Hebrew root meaning "to clasp" or "to embrace." Habakkuk prayed and prophesied in a time of impending crisis. Externally the nation of Babylon was increasing in power and influence. Internally the people of God were caught up in religious and moral bewilderment.

Author and Date of Writing

Little is known about the author except his name and that he was a contemporary of Jeremiah. He was a man of vigorous faith, a faith rooted deeply in the religious traditions of Israel. The prophecy is generally dated a little before or after the battle of Carchemish (605 B.C.).

Theme and Message

Habakkuk was written as a dialogue or conversation between God and the prophet. Habakkuk saw that the leaders were oppressing the poor, so he asked why God allowed the wicked to prosper. After God replied to him, Habakkuk responds with a beautiful confession of faith. His confession appears to have been used as a psalm.

Outline

I. Habakkuk's First Question and God's Answer (1.1-11)
II. Habakkuk's Second Question and God's Answer (1.12–2.20)
III. Habakkuk's Prayer (3.1-19)

1 The oracle that the prophet Habakkuk saw.

The Prophet's Complaint

2 O LORD, how long shall I cry
 for help,
 and you will not listen?
 Or cry to you "Violence!"
 and you will not save?
3 Why do you make me see
 wrong-doing
 and look at trouble?
 Destruction and violence are
 before me;
 strife and contention arise.
4 So the law becomes slack
 and justice never prevails.
 The wicked surround the
 righteous—
 therefore judgment comes
 forth perverted.

5 Look at the nations, and see!
 Be astonished! Be
 astounded!
 For a work is being done in
 your days
 that you would not believe
 if you were told.
6 For I am rousing the
 Chaldeans,
 that fierce and impetuous
 nation,
 who march through the
 breadth of the earth
 to seize dwellings not their
 own.
7 Dread and fearsome are they;
 their justice and dignity
 proceed from
 themselves.
8 Their horses are swifter than
 leopards,
 more menacing than
 wolves at dusk;
 their horses charge.
 Their horsemen come from
 far away;
 they fly like an eagle swift
 to devour.
9 They all come for violence,

1.1
Isa 13.1;
Nah 1.1
1.2
Ps 13.1,2;
22.1,2
1.3
v. 13;
Jer 20.8
1.4
Ps 119.126;
22.12;
Isa 5.20
1.5
Acts 13.41;
Isa 29.9,14

1.6
2 Kings 24.2;
Jer 4.11-13;
5.15; 8.10
1.7
Isa 18.2,7;
Jer 39.5-9
1.8
Jer 4.13;
5.6;
Ezek 17.3;
Hos 8.1
1.9
Hab 2.5

with faces pressing[a]
 forward;
they gather captives like
 sand.

10 At kings they scoff,
 and of rulers they make
 sport.
They laugh at every fortress,
 and heap up earth to take
 it.

11 Then they sweep by like the
 wind;
they transgress and become
 guilty;
their own might is their
 god!

12 Are you not from of old,
 O Lord my God, my Holy
 One?
You[b] shall not die.
O Lord, you have marked
 them for judgment;
and you, O Rock, have
 established them for
 punishment.

13 Your eyes are too pure to
 behold evil,
and you cannot look on
 wrongdoing;
why do you look on the
 treacherous,
and are silent when the
 wicked swallow
those more righteous than
 they?

14 You have made people like
 the fish of the sea,
like crawling things that
 have no ruler.

15 The enemy[c] brings all of
 them up with a hook,
he drags them out with his
 net,
he gathers them in his seine;
 so he rejoices and exults.

16 Therefore he sacrifices to his
 net
and makes offerings to his
 seine;
for by them his portion is
 lavish,
and his food is rich.

17 Is he then to keep on
 emptying his net,

1.10
2 Chr 36.6,
10; Isa 10.9;
14.16;
Jer 32.24;
Ezek 26.8
1.11
Jer 4.11,12;
2.3;
Dan 4.30
1.12
Deut 33.27;
Ps 90.2;
Isa 10.5-7;
Deut 32.4
1.13
Jer 12.1,2;
Isa 24.16;
Ps 50.21;
56.1,2
1.14
Eccl 9.12
1.15
Jer 16.16;
Am 4.2;
Ps 10.9
1.17
Isa 19.8;
14.5,6

2.1
Isa 21.8,11;
Ps 5.3; 85.8
2.2
Deut 27.8;
Isa 8.1;
Rev 1.19
2.3
Dan 8.17,
19; 10.14;
Ezek 12.25;
Heb 10.37,
38
2.4
Rom 1.17;
Gal 3.11;
Heb 10.38,
39
2.5
Prov 20.1;
21.24;
2 Kings 14.10;
Jer 25.9
2.6ff
Jer 50.13;
v. 12;
Ezek 18.12;
Am 2.8

and destroying nations
 without mercy?

God's Reply to the Prophet's Complaint

2 I will stand at my watchpost,
 and station myself on the
 rampart;
I will keep watch to see what
 he will say to me,
and what he[d] will answer
 concerning my
 complaint.

2 Then the Lord answered me
 and said:
Write the vision;
 make it plain on tablets,
so that a runner may read
 it.

3 For there is still a vision for
 the appointed time;
it speaks of the end, and
 does not lie.
If it seems to tarry, wait for
 it;
it will surely come, it will
 not delay.

4 Look at the proud!
 Their spirit is not right in
 them,
but the righteous live by
 their faith.[e]

5 Moreover, wealth[f] is
 treacherous;
the arrogant do not endure.
They open their throats wide
 as Sheol;
like Death they never have
 enough.
They gather all nations for
 themselves,
and collect all peoples as
 their own.

The Woes of the Wicked

6 Shall not everyone taunt such people and, with mocking riddles, say about them,
"Alas for you who heap up
 what is not your own!"

a Meaning of Heb uncertain b Ancient Heb
tradition: MT *We* c Heb *He* d Syr:
Heb *I* e Or *faithfulness* f Other Heb Mss
read *wine*

How long will you load
yourselves with goods
taken in pledge?
7 Will not your own creditors
suddenly rise,
and those who make you
tremble wake up?
Then you will be booty for
them.
8 Because you have plundered
many nations,
all that survive of the
peoples shall plunder
you —
because of human
bloodshed, and violence
to the earth,
to cities and all who live in
them.

9 "Alas for you who get evil
gain for your houses,
setting your nest on high
to be safe from the reach
of harm!"
10 You have devised shame for
your house
by cutting off many
peoples;
you have forfeited your life.
11 The very stones will cry out
from the wall,
and the plasterg will
respond from the
woodwork.

12 "Alas for you who build a
town by bloodshed,
and found a city on
iniquity!"
13 Is it not from the Lord of
hosts
that peoples labor only to
feed the flames,
and nations weary
themselves for nothing?
14 But the earth will be filled
with the knowledge of the
glory of the Lord,
as the waters cover the sea.

15 "Alas for you who make your
neighbors drink,
pouring out your wrathh
until they are drunk,
in order to gaze on their
nakedness!"

2.7
Prov 29.1
2.8
Isa 33.1;
Zech 2.8;
v. 17
2.9
Jer 22.13;
Ezek 22.27;
Jer 49.16
2.10
2 Kings 9.26;
v. 16;
Prov 1.18;
Jer 26.29
2.11
Josh 24.27;
Lk 19.40
2.12
Mic 3.10;
Nah 3.1
2.13
Isa 50.11;
Jer 51.58
2.14
Isa 11.9;
Zech 14.8,9
2.15
Isa 28.7,8;
Hos 7.5

2.16
v. 10;
Lam 4.21;
Jer 25.15,
27; Nah 3.6
2.17
Zech 11.1;
v. 8;
Jer 51.35
2.18
Isa 42.17;
Jer 2.27,28;
10.8,14;
Zech 10.2;
Ps 115.4,8
2.19
Jer 2.27,28;
1 Kings 18.26-
29;
Jer 10.9,14;
Ps 135.17
2.20
Mic 1.2;
Zeph 1.7;
Zech 2.13
3.2
Job 42.5,6;
Ps 119.120;
Jer 10.7;
Ps 85.6;
Isa 54.8

16 You will be sated with
contempt instead of
glory.
Drink, you yourself, and
stagger!i
The cup in the Lord's right
hand
will come around to you,
and shame will come upon
your glory!
17 For the violence done to
Lebanon will
overwhelm you;
the destruction of the
animals will terrify
you — i
because of human bloodshed
and violence to the
earth,
to cities and all who live in
them.

18 What use is an idol
once its maker has shaped
it —
a cast image, a teacher of
lies?
For its maker trusts in what
has been made,
though the product is only
an idol that cannot
speak!
19 Alas for you who say to the
wood, "Wake up!"
to silent stone, "Rouse
yourself!"
Can it teach?
See, it is gold and silver
plated,
and there is no breath in it
at all.

20 But the Lord is in his holy
temple;
let all the earth keep
silence before him!

3 A prayer of the prophet Ha-
bakkuk according to Shigio-
noth.

The Prophet's Prayer

2 O Lord, I have heard of your
renown,

g Or beam h Or poison i Q Ms Gk:
MT be uncircumcised i Gk Syr: Meaning of
Heb uncertain

and I stand in awe, O Lord,
of your work.
In our own time revive it;
in our own time make it
known;
in wrath may you
remember mercy.

3 God came from Teman,
the Holy One from Mount
Paran. *Selah*
His glory covered the
heavens,
and the earth was full of
his praise.

4 The brightness was like the
sun;
rays came forth from his
hand,
where his power lay
hidden.

5 Before him went pestilence,
and plague followed close
behind.

6 He stopped and shook the
earth;
he looked and made the
nations tremble.
The eternal mountains were
shattered;
along his ancient pathways
the everlasting hills sank
low.

7 I saw the tents of Cushan
under affliction;
the tent-curtains of the
land of Midian
trembled.

8 Was your wrath against the
rivers,k O Lord?
Or your anger against the
rivers,k
or your rage against the
sea,l
when you drove your horses,
your chariots to victory?

9 You brandished your naked
bow,
satedm were the arrows at
your command.n *Selah*
You split the earth with
rivers.

10 The mountains saw you, and
writhed;
a torrent of water swept by;
the deep gave forth its voice.
The suno raised high its
hands;

3.3
Am 1.12;
Deut 33.2;
Ps 113.4;
48.10
3.4
Ps 18.12;
Job 26.14
3.5
Ex 12.29,
30;
Num 16.46-49
3.6
Ps 35.5;
114.1-6;
Mic 5.2
3.7
Ex 15.14-16;
Judg 7.24,
25
3.8
Ex 7.19,20;
14.16,21;
Deut 33.26;
Ps 68.17
3.9
Gen 26.3;
Deut 7.8;
Ps 78.16;
105.41
3.10
Ps 114.1-6;
98.7,8;
Ex 14.22

3.11
Josh 10.12-14;
Ps 18.9,11,
14
3.12
Ps 68.7;
Isa 41.15;
Jer 51.33
3.13
Ex 15.2;
Ps 68.19,20;
110.6;
Ezek 13.14
3.14
Judg 7.22;
Dan 11.40;
Zech 9.14;
Ps 10.8;
64.2-5
3.15
Ps 77.19;
Ex 15.8
3.16
Jer 23.9;
5.15
3.17ff
Joel 1.18;
Jer 5.17

11 the moonp stood still in its
exalted place,
at the light of your arrows
speeding by,
at the gleam of your
flashing spear.

12 In fury you trod the earth,
in anger you trampled
nations.

13 You came forth to save your
people,
to save your anointed.
You crushed the head of the
wicked house,
laying it bare from
foundation to roof.n
Selah

14 You pierced with his own
arrows the headq of his
warriors,r
who came like a whirlwind
to scatter us,s
gloating as if ready to
devour the poor who
were in hiding.

15 You trampled the sea with
your horses,
churning the mighty
waters.

16 I hear, and I tremble within;
my lips quiver at the
sound.
Rottenness enters into my
bones,
and my steps tremblet
beneath me.
I wait quietly for the day of
calamity
to come upon the people
who attack us.

Trust and Joy in the Midst of Trouble

17 Though the fig tree does not
blossom,
and no fruit is on the
vines;
though the produce of the
olive fails

k Or *against River* l Or *against Sea*
m Cn: Heb *oaths* n Meaning of Heb
uncertain o Heb *It* p Heb *sun, moon*
q Or *leader* r Vg Compare Gk Syr:
Meaning of Heb uncertain s Heb *me*
t Cn Compare Gk: Meaning of Heb uncertain

and the fields yield no
food;
though the flock is cut off
from the fold
and there is no herd in the
stalls,
18 yet I will rejoice in the
LORD;
I will exult in the God of
my salvation.

3.18
Isa 61.10;
Ps 46.1-5;
Isa 12.2

3.19
2 Sam 22.34;
Ps 18.33;
Deut 33.29

19 GOD, the Lord, is my
strength;
he makes my feet like the
feet of a deer,
and makes me tread upon
the heights. u

To the choirmaster: with
stringedv instruments.

u Heb *my heights* v Heb *my stringed*

Zephaniah

Title and Background

The name Zephaniah means "The LORD hides (or protects)." The religious state of Judah declined markedly following the death of Hezekiah, but Josiah launched a sweeping reform. He was backed by Jeremiah and Nahum, but their calls for repentance fell on deaf ears. Judah became ripe for judgment.

Author and Date of Writing

Zephaniah, a fourth generation descendant of King Hezekiah, was evidently a person of considerable social standing in Judah. The prophet shows great familiarity with court circles and current political issues. According to 1.1, he prophesied during the reign of King Josiah (640-609 B.C.), so this prophecy could have been written about 630.

Theme and Message

The intent of the author was to announce to Judah God's approaching judgment. His main theme was the coming of the day of the Lord when God would severely punish the nations. He portrayed the stark horror of that ordeal, but also made it clear that God would yet be merciful toward his people.

Outline

 I. Introduction (1.1-3)
 II. The Day of the Lord Coming on Judah and the Nations (1.4-18)
 III. God's Judgment on the Nations (2.1–3.8)
 IV. Redemption of the Remnant (3.9-20)

1 The word of the LORD that came to Zephaniah son of Cushi son of Gedaliah son of Amariah son of Hezekiah, in the days of King Josiah son of Amon of Judah.

The Coming Judgment on Judah

2 I will utterly sweep away everything
 from the face of the earth,
 says the LORD.
3 I will sweep away humans and animals;
 I will sweep away the birds of the air
 and the fish of the sea.
I will make the wicked stumble.[a]
I will cut off humanity
 from the face of the earth,
 says the LORD.
4 I will stretch out my hand against Judah,
and against all the inhabitants of Jerusalem;
and I will cut off from this place every remnant of Baal
and the name of the idolatrous priests;[b]
5 those who bow down on the roofs
 to the host of the heavens;
those who bow down and swear to the LORD,
 but also swear by Milcom;[c]
6 those who have turned back from following the LORD,

1.1 2 Kings 22.1-23, 34; 21.18-26
1.2 Ezek 33.27
1.3 Isa 6.11,12; Jer 9.10; Ezek 7.19
1.4 Ezek 6.14; Mic 5.13; Hos 10.5
1.5 Jer 19.13; 5.2,7; 49.1
1.6 Isa 1.4; Jer 2.13; Isa 9.13; Hos 7.7

a Cn: Heb *sea, and those who cause the wicked to stumble* b Compare Gk: Heb *the idolatrous priests with the priests* c Gk Mss Syr Vg: Heb *Malcam* (or, *their king*)

who have not sought the
LORD or inquired of him.

7 Be silent before the Lord GOD!
For the day of the LORD is
at hand;
the LORD has prepared a
sacrifice,
he has consecrated his
guests.
8 And on the day of the LORD's
sacrifice
I will punish the officials and
the king's sons
and all who dress
themselves in foreign
attire.
9 On that day I will punish
all who leap over the
threshold,
who fill their master's
house
with violence and fraud.

10 On that day, says the LORD,
a cry will be heard from
the Fish Gate,
a wail from the Second
Quarter,
a loud crash from the
hills.
11 The inhabitants of the
Mortar wail,
for all the traders have
perished;
all who weigh out silver are
cut off.
12 At that time I will search
Jerusalem with lamps,
and I will punish the
people
who rest complacently[d] on
their dregs,
those who say in their
hearts,
"The LORD will not do good,
nor will he do harm."
13 Their wealth shall be
plundered,
and their houses laid
waste.
Though they build houses,
they shall not inhabit
them;
though they plant vineyards,
they shall not drink wine
from them.

1.7
Hab 2.20;
Zech 2.13;
Isa 13.6;
v. 14;
Isa 34.6;
Jer 46.10
1.8
Isa 24.21;
Jer 39.6;
Isa 2.6
1.9
Jer 5.27;
Am 3.10
1.10
Am 8.3;
2 Chr 33.14;
34.22;
Ezek 6.13
1.11
Jas 5.1;
Zeph 2.5;
Hos 9.6
1.12
Jer 16.16,
17;
Jer 48.11;
Am 6.1;
Ezek 8.12;
9.9
1.13
Deut 28.30,
39;
Am 5.11;
Mic 6.15

1.14
Joel 2.1,11
1.15
Isa 22.5;
Jer 30.7;
Am 5.18-20
1.16
Jer 4.19;
Isa 2.12-15
1.17
Jer 10.18;
Isa 59.10;
Ps 79.3;
Jer 9.22
1.18
Prov 11.4;
Zeph 3.8;
vv. 2,3
2.1
Joel 1.14;
Jer 3.3; 6.15
2.2
Isa 17.13;
Hos 13.3;
Nah 1.6;
Zeph 1.18

The Great Day of the LORD

14 The great day of the LORD is
near,
near and hastening fast;
the sound of the day of the
LORD is bitter,
the warrior cries aloud
there.
15 That day will be a day of
wrath,
a day of distress and
anguish,
a day of ruin and
devastation,
a day of darkness and
gloom,
a day of clouds and thick
darkness,
16 a day of trumpet blast and
battle cry
against the fortified cities
and against the lofty
battlements.

17 I will bring such distress
upon people
that they shall walk like
the blind;
because they have sinned
against the LORD,
their blood shall be poured
out like dust,
and their flesh like dung.
18 Neither their silver nor their
gold
will be able to save them
on the day of the LORD's
wrath;
in the fire of his passion
the whole earth shall be
consumed;
for a full, a terrible end
he will make of all the
inhabitants of the
earth.

Judgment on Israel's Enemies

2 Gather together, gather,
O shameless nation,
2 before you are driven away
like the drifting chaff,[e]
before there comes upon you

d Heb *who thicken* e Cn Compare Gk Syr:
Heb *before a decree is born; like chaff a day
has passed away*

the fierce anger of the
LORD,
before there comes upon you
the day of the LORD's
wrath.
3 Seek the LORD, all you
humble of the land,
who do his commands;
seek righteousness, seek
humility;
perhaps you may be hidden
on the day of the LORD's
wrath.
4 For Gaza shall be deserted,
and Ashkelon shall become
a desolation;
Ashdod's people shall be
driven out at noon,
and Ekron shall be
uprooted.

5 Ah, inhabitants of the
seacoast,
you nation of the
Cherethites!
The word of the LORD is
against you,
O Canaan, land of the
Philistines;
and I will destroy you until
no inhabitant is left.
6 And you, O seacoast, shall
be pastures,
meadows for shepherds
and folds for flocks.
7 The seacoast shall become
the possession
of the remnant of the
house of Judah,
on which they shall
pasture,
and in the houses of
Ashkelon
they shall lie down at
evening.
For the LORD their God will
be mindful of them
and restore their fortunes.

8 I have heard the taunts of
Moab
and the revilings of the
Ammonites,
how they have taunted my
people
and made boasts against
their territory.

2.3
Am 5.6;
Ps 76.9;
Am 5.14,15;
Ps 57.1
2.4
Am 1.7,8;
Zech 9.5-7
2.5
Ezek 25.16;
Am 3.1;
Isa 14.29-31;
Zeph 3.6
2.6
Isa 17.2
2.7
Mic 4.7;
Isa 32.14;
Ps 80.14;
Lk 1.68;
Ps 126.1,4
2.8
Ezek 25.3,6,
8; Jer 49.1

2.9
Isa 15.1-16,
14;
Am 1.13;
Deut 29.23;
Isa 11.14
2.10
Isa 16.6;
Jer 48.29;
v. 8
2.11
Joel 2.11;
Zeph 1;4;
3.9;
Mal 1.11;
Isa 24.15
2.12
Isa 18.1
2.13
Isa 14.26;
10.12;
Nah 3.7
2.14
v. 6;
Isa 13.21;
34.11,14;
Jer 22.14
2.15
Isa 22.2;
47.8; 32.14;
Jer 18.16;
19.8

9 Therefore, as I live, says the
LORD of hosts,
the God of Israel,
Moab shall become like
Sodom
and the Ammonites like
Gomorrah,
a land possessed by nettles
and salt pits,
and a waste forever.
The remnant of my people
shall plunder them,
and the survivors of my
nation shall possess
them.
10 This shall be their lot in
return for their pride,
because they scoffed and
boasted
against the people of the
LORD of hosts.
11 The LORD will be terrible
against them;
he will shrivel all the gods
of the earth,
and to him shall bow down,
each in its place,
all the coasts and islands
of the nations.

12 You also, O Ethiopians,f
shall be killed by my
sword.

13 And he will stretch out his
hand against the north,
and destroy Assyria;
and he will make Nineveh a
desolation,
a dry waste like the desert.
14 Herds shall lie down in it,
every wild animal;g
the desert owlh and the
screech owlh
shall lodge on its capitals;
the owli shall hoot at the
window,
the raveni croak on the
threshold;
for its cedar work will be
laid bare.
15 Is this the exultant city
that lived secure,
that said to itself,

f Or *Nubians*; Heb *Cushites* g Tg Compare
Gk: Heb *nation* h Meaning of Heb uncertain
i Cn: Heb *a voice* j Gk Vg: Heb *desolation*

"I am, and there is no one
 else"?
What a desolation it has
 become,
 a lair for wild animals!
Everyone who passes by it
 hisses and shakes the fist.

The Wickedness of Jerusalem

3 Ah, soiled, defiled,
 oppressing city!
2 It has listened to no voice;
 it has accepted no
 correction.
 It has not trusted in the
 LORD;
 it has not drawn near to its
 God.

3 The officials within it
 are roaring lions;
 its judges are evening wolves
 that leave nothing until the
 morning.
4 Its prophets are reckless,
 faithless persons;
 its priests have profaned
 what is sacred,
 they have done violence to
 the law.
5 The LORD within it is
 righteous;
 he does no wrong.
 Every morning he renders his
 judgment,
 each dawn without fail;
 but the unjust knows no
 shame.

6 I have cut off nations;
 their battlements are in
 ruins;
 I have laid waste their streets
 so that no one walks in
 them;
 their cities have been made
 desolate,
 without people, without
 inhabitants.
7 I said, "Surely the city[k] will
 fear me,
 it will accept correction;
 it will not lose sight[l]
 of all that I have brought
 upon it."

But they were the more
 eager
 to make all their deeds
 corrupt.

Punishment and Conversion of
the Nations

8 Therefore wait for me, says
 the LORD,
 for the day when I arise as
 a witness.
 For my decision is to gather
 nations,
 to assemble kingdoms,
 to pour out upon them my
 indignation,
 all the heat of my anger;
 for in the fire of my passion
 all the earth shall be
 consumed.

9 At that time I will change
 the speech of the
 peoples
 to a pure speech,
 that all of them may call on
 the name of the LORD
 and serve him with one
 accord.
10 From beyond the rivers of
 Ethiopia[m]
 my suppliants, my
 scattered ones,
 shall bring my offering.

11 On that day you shall not be
 put to shame
 because of all the deeds by
 which you have rebelled
 against me;
 for then I will remove from
 your midst
 your proudly exultant ones,
 and you shall no longer be
 haughty
 in my holy mountain.
12 For I will leave in the midst
 of you
 a people humble and lowly.
 They shall seek refuge in the
 name of the LORD—
13 the remnant of Israel;
 they shall do no wrong
 and utter no lies,

Cross references

3.1 Jer 5.23; Ezek 23.30; Jer 6.6
3.2 Jer 22.21; 5.3; Ps 78.22; 73.28
3.3 Ezek 22.27; Hab 1.8
3.4 Hos 9.7; Ezek 22.26
3.5 vv. 15,17; Deut 32.4; Jer 3.3
3.6 Zeph 1.16; Isa 6.11; Zeph 2.5
3.7 v. 2; Jer 7.7; Hos 9.9
3.8 Ps 27.14; Zeph 2.2; Joel 3.2; Zeph 1.18
3.9 Isa 19.18; Ps 22.27; Zeph 2.11
3.10 Ps 68.31; Isa 18.1,7; 60.6,7
3.11 Isa 45.17; Joel 2.26, 27; Isa 2.12; 5.15; Ezek 20.40
3.12 Isa 14.32; Nah 1.7
3.13 Mic 4.7; Isa 60.21; Zech 8.3,16; Rev 14.5; Ezek 34.28; Mic 4.4

k Heb it l Gk Syr: Heb its dwelling will not be cut off m Or Nubia; Heb Cush

nor shall a deceitful tongue
 be found in their mouths.
Then they will pasture and
 lie down,
and no one shall make
 them afraid.

A Song of Joy

14 Sing aloud, O daughter Zion;
 shout, O Israel!
Rejoice and exult with all
 your heart,
 O daughter Jerusalem!
15 The LORD has taken away the
 judgments against you,
he has turned away your
 enemies.
The king of Israel, the LORD,
 is in your midst;
you shall fear disaster no
 more.
16 On that day it shall be said
 to Jerusalem:
Do not fear, O Zion;
 do not let your hands grow
 weak.
17 The LORD, your God, is in
 your midst,
a warrior who gives victory;
he will rejoice over you with
 gladness,

he will renew you[n] in his
 love;
he will exult over you with
 loud singing
18 as on a day of festival.[o]
I will remove disaster from
 you,[p]
so that you will not bear
 reproach for it.
19 I will deal with all your
 oppressors
 at that time.
And I will save the lame
 and gather the outcast,
and I will change their
 shame into praise
 and renown in all the
 earth.
20 At that time I will bring you
 home,
 at the time when I gather
 you;
for I will make you renowned
 and praised
 among all the peoples of
 the earth,
when I restore your fortunes
 before your eyes, says the
 LORD.

3.14
Isa 12.6;
Zech 2.10
3.15
Ezek 37.26-28;
v. 5;
Isa 54.14
3.16
Isa 35.3,4;
Heb 12.12
3.17
vv. 5,15;
Isa 63.1;
62.5

3.19
Isa 60.14;
Ezek 34.16;
Mic 4.6,7
3.20
Ezek 37.12,
21; Isa 56.5;
66.22;
Zeph 2.7

n Gk Syr: Heb *he will be silent* o Gk Syr:
Meaning of Heb uncertain p Cn: Heb *I will
remove from you; they were*

Haggai

Title and Background

This book is named for its author, and the name means "festal" or "festival." In 538 B.C. Cyrus issued a decree allowing the Jews to return to Jerusalem and rebuild the temple. Samaritans and other neighbors opposed the project vigorously and managed to halt work until Darius the Great became king. Haggai began to preach in Darius's second year.

Author and Date of Writing

Haggai was a prophet who, along with Zechariah, encouraged the returned exiles to rebuild the temple. Based on 2.3, Haggai may have witnessed the destruction of Solomon's temple. If so, he was about 80 years old during his ministry recorded in this book. The messages of Haggai were given during a four-month period in 520 B.C.

Theme and Message

Haggai clearly shows the consequences of disobedience and the blessings of obedience. When the people give priority to God and his house, they will be blessed. Obedience brings the encouragement and strength of the Spirit of God.

Outline

 I. First Message: The Call to Rebuild the Temple (1.1-11)
 II. The Response of Zerubbabel and the People (1.12-15)
 III. Second Message: The Temple to Be Filled With Glory (2.1-9)
 IV. Third Message: A Defiled People Purified and Blessed (2.10-19)
 V. Fourth Message: The Promise to Zerubbabel (2.20-23)

The Command to Rebuild the Temple

1 In the second year of King Darius, in the sixth month, on the first day of the month, the word of the LORD came by the prophet Haggai to Zerubbabel son of Shealtiel, governor of Judah, and to Joshua son of Jehozadak, the high priest: ²Thus says the LORD of hosts: These people say the time has not yet come to rebuild the LORD's house. ³Then the word of the LORD came by the prophet Haggai, saying: ⁴Is it a time for you yourselves to live in your paneled houses, while this house lies in ruins? ⁵Now therefore thus says the LORD of hosts: Consider how you have fared. ⁶You have sown much, and harvested little; you eat, but you never have enough; you drink, but you never have your fill; you clothe yourselves, but no one is warm; and you that earn wages earn wages to put them into a bag with holes.

7 Thus says the LORD of hosts: Consider how you have fared. ⁸Go up to the hills and bring wood and build the house, so that I may take pleasure in it and be honored, says the LORD. ⁹You have looked for much, and, lo, it came to little; and when you brought it home, I blew it away. Why? says the LORD of hosts. Because my house lies in ruins, while all of you hurry off to your own houses. ¹⁰Therefore the heavens above you have withheld the dew, and the earth has withheld its produce. ¹¹And I have called for a drought on the land and the hills,

1.1 Zech 1.1; 1 Chr 3.17; Ezra 3.2; Zech 6.11
1.2 v. 15
1.4 2 Sam 7.2; v. 9
1.5 Lam 3.40
1.6 Deut 28.38; Mic 6.14; Zech 8.10
1.7 v. 1
1.8 Ezra 3.7; Ps 132.13, 14; Hag 2.7, 9
1.9 v. 6; Isa 40.7
1.10 Lev 26.19; Deut 28.23; 1 Kings 8.35
1.11 Mal 3.9-11; Deut 28.22; Hag 2.17

on the grain, the new wine, the oil, on what the soil produces, on human beings and animals, and on all their labors.

12 Then Zerubbabel son of Shealtiel, and Joshua son of Jehozadak, the high priest, with all the remnant of the people, obeyed the voice of the LORD their God, and the words of the prophet Haggai, as the LORD their God had sent him; and the people feared the LORD. 13 Then Haggai, the messenger of the LORD, spoke to the people with the LORD's message, saying, I am with you, says the LORD. 14 And the LORD stirred up the spirit of Zerubbabel son of Shealtiel, governor of Judah, and the spirit of Joshua son of Jehozadak, the high priest, and the spirit of all the remnant of the people; and they came and worked on the house of the LORD of hosts, their God, 15 on the twenty-fourth day of the month, in the sixth month.

The Future Glory of the Temple

2 In the second year of King Darius, 1 in the seventh month, on the twenty-first day of the month, the word of the LORD came by the prophet Haggai, saying: 2 Speak now to Zerubbabel son of Shealtiel, governor of Judah, and to Joshua son of Jehozadak, the high priest, and to the remnant of the people, and say, 3 Who is left among you that saw this house in its former glory? How does it look to you now? Is it not in your sight as nothing? 4 Yet now take courage, O Zerubbabel, says the LORD; take courage, O Joshua, son of Jehozadak, the high priest; take courage, all you people of the land, says the LORD; work, for I am with you, says the LORD of hosts, 5 according to the promise that I made you when you came out of Egypt. My spirit abides among you; do not fear. 6 For thus says the LORD of hosts: Once again, in a little while, I will shake the heavens and the earth and the sea and the dry land; 7 and I will shake all the nations, so that the treasure of all nations shall come, and I will

fill this house with splendor, says the LORD of hosts. 8 The silver is mine, and the gold is mine, says the LORD of hosts. 9 The latter splendor of this house shall be greater than the former, says the LORD of hosts; and in this place I will give prosperity, says the LORD of hosts.

A Rebuke and a Promise

10 On the twenty-fourth day of the ninth month, in the second year of Darius, the word of the LORD came by the prophet Haggai, saying: 11 Thus says the LORD of hosts: Ask the priests for a ruling: 12 If one carries consecrated meat in the fold of one's garment, and with the fold touches bread, or stew, or wine, or oil, or any kind of food, does it become holy? The priests answered, "No." 13 Then Haggai said, "If one who is unclean by contact with a dead body touches any of these, does it become unclean?" The priests answered, "Yes, it becomes unclean." 14 Haggai then said, So is it with this people, and with this nation before me, says the LORD; and so with every work of their hands; and what they offer there is unclean. 15 But now, consider what will come to pass from this day on. Before a stone was placed upon a stone in the LORD's temple, 16 how did you fare?[a] When one came to a heap of twenty measures, there were but ten; when one came to the winevat to draw fifty measures, there were but twenty. 17 I struck you and all the products of your toil with blight and mildew and hail; yet you did not return to me, says the LORD. 18 Consider from this day on, from the twenty-fourth day of the ninth month. Since the day that the foundation of the LORD's temple was laid, consider: 19 Is there any seed left in the barn? Do the vine, the fig tree, the pomegranate, and the olive tree still yield nothing? From this day on I will bless you.

Cross-references (center column)

1.12
Hag 2.2;
Isa 1.19;
50.10
1.13
Mal 2.7;
3.1;
Mt 28.30;
Rom 8.31
1.14
2 Chr 36.22;
Ezra 1.1;
5.2,8
2.3
Ezra 3.12;
Zech 4.10
2.4
Zech 8.9;
Acts 7.9
2.5
Ex 29.45,
46;
Neh 9.20;
Isa 63.11,14
2.6
Heb 12.26;
Isa 10.25;
29.17; v. 21
2.7
Dan 2.44;
Isa 60.4-9

2.9
Isa 66.12;
Zech 2.5
2.10
vv. 1,20
2.11
Lev 10.10;
Deut 33.10;
Mal 2.7
2.12
Ezek 44.19;
Mt 23.19
2.13
Num 19.11,
22
2.14
Prov 15.8;
Isa 1.11-15
2.15
Hag 1.5;
Ezra 3.10;
4.24
2.16
Hag 1.6,9;
Zech 8.10
2.17
1 Kings 8.37;
Am 4.9;
Isa 9.13
2.18
Zech 8.9
2.19
Zech 8.12

a Gk: Heb since they were

God's Promise to Zerubbabel

20 The word of the LORD came a second time to Haggai on the twenty-fourth day of the month: 21 Speak to Zerubbabel, governor of Judah, saying, I am about to shake the heavens and the earth, 22 and to overthrow the throne of kingdoms; I am about to destroy the strength of the kingdoms of the nations, and overthrow the chariots and their riders; and the horses and their riders shall fall, every one by the sword of a comrade. 23 On that day, says the LORD of hosts, I will take you, O Zerubbabel my servant, son of Shealtiel, says the LORD, and make you like a signet ring; for I have chosen you, says the LORD of hosts.

2.20ff
v. 10
2.21
Hag 1.14;
Zech 4.6-10;
Heb 12.26
2.22
Dan 2.44;
Mic 5.10;
Zech 4.6;
2 Chr 20.23

2.23
Song 8.6;
Jer 22.24;
Isa 42.1; 43.10

Zechariah

Title and Background

The book is named after its author, and the title means "The LORD remembers." Zechariah's prophetic ministry took place in the postexilic period, the time when the Jews returned from Babylon to the land of Judah. His prophecies began two months after Haggai's first message.

Author and Date of Writing

Zechariah was not only a prophet but also a priest. He was among those who returned to Judah in 538 B.C. He was a contemporary of Haggai but continued his ministry long after him. The book of Zechariah was probably written sometime before 480 B.C.

Theme and Message

Zechariah was concerned about the rebuilding of the temple, and in his first message he warned the people they ought to listen to God's message through the prophets. He was also interested in their spiritual renewal.

Zechariah contains many Messianic passages: he predicted Christ's coming in lowliness (9.9), his humanity (6.12; 13.7), his rejection and betrayal for thirty shekels of silver (11.12-13), his being struck by the sword of the Lord (13.7), his priesthood (6.13), his kingship (6.13; 9.9; 14.9,16), his coming in power (14.4), his building of the Lord's temple (6.12-13), his reign (9.10,14) and his establishment of enduring peace and prosperity (3.10; 9.9-10).

Outline

I. A Call to Repentance (1.1-6)
II. Eight Visions (1.7–6.8)
III. The Coronation of Joshua the High Priest (6.9-15)
IV. Fasting and the Future (7.1–8.23)
V. The Advent and Rejection of the Messiah (9.1–11.17)
VI. The Advent and Redemption of the Messiah (12.1–14.21)

Israel Urged to Repent

1 In the eighth month, in the second year of Darius, the word of the LORD came to the prophet Zechariah son of Berechiah son of Iddo, saying: ² The LORD was very angry with your ancestors. ³ Therefore say to them, Thus says the LORD of hosts: Return to me, says the LORD of hosts, and I will return to you, says the LORD of hosts. ⁴ Do not be like your ancestors, to whom the former prophets proclaimed, "Thus says the LORD of hosts, Return from your evil ways and from your evil deeds." But they did not hear or heed me, says the LORD. ⁵ Your ancestors, where are they? And the prophets, do they live forever? ⁶ But my words and my statutes, which I commanded my servants the prophets, did they not overtake your ancestors? So they repented and said, "The LORD of hosts has dealt with us according to our ways and deeds, just as he planned to do."

First Vision: The Horsemen

7 On the twenty-fourth day of the eleventh month, the month of Shebat, in the second year of Darius, the word of the LORD came to the prophet Zechariah son of Bere-

1.1 Ezra 4.24; Hag 1.1; Neh 12.4,16
1.3 Isa 31.6; Mal 3.7; Jas 4.8
1.4 2 Chr 36.15; Hos 14.1; Jer 6.17; 11.7,8
1.6 Jer 12.16, 17; Lam 2.17

chiah son of Iddo; and Zechariah[a] said, [8] In the night I saw a man riding on a red horse! He was standing among the myrtle trees in the glen; and behind him were red, sorrel, and white horses. [9] Then I said, "What are these, my lord?" The angel who talked with me said to me, "I will show you what they are." [10] So the man who was standing among the myrtle trees answered, "They are those whom the LORD has sent to patrol the earth." [11] Then they spoke to the angel of the LORD who was standing among the myrtle trees, "We have patrolled the earth, and lo, the whole earth remains at peace." [12] Then the angel of the LORD said, "O LORD of hosts, how long will you withhold mercy from Jerusalem and the cities of Judah, with which you have been angry these seventy years?" [13] Then the LORD replied with gracious and comforting words to the angel who talked with me. [14] So the angel who talked with me said to me, Proclaim this message: Thus says the LORD of hosts; I am very jealous for Jerusalem and for Zion. [15] And I am extremely angry with the nations that are at ease; for while I was only a little angry, they made the disaster worse. [16] Therefore, thus says the LORD, I have returned to Jerusalem with compassion; my house shall be built in it, says the LORD of hosts, and the measuring line shall be stretched out over Jerusalem. [17] Proclaim further: Thus says the LORD of hosts: My cities shall again overflow with prosperity; the LORD will again comfort Zion and again choose Jerusalem.

Second Vision: The Horns and the Smiths

18 [b] And I looked up and saw four horns. [19] I asked the angel who talked with me, "What are these?" And he answered me, "These are the horns that have scattered Judah, Israel, and Jerusalem." [20] Then the LORD showed me four blacksmiths. [21] And I asked, "What are they coming to do?" He answered, "These are the horns that

scattered Judah, so that no head could be raised; but these have come to terrify them, to strike down the horns of the nations that lifted up their horns against the land of Judah to scatter its people."[c]

Third Vision: The Man with a Measuring Line

2 [d] I looked up and saw a man with a measuring line in his hand. [2] Then I asked, "Where are you going?" He answered me, "To measure Jerusalem, to see what is its width and what is its length." [3] Then the angel who talked with me came forward, and another angel came forward to meet him, [4] and said to him, "Run, say to that young man: Jerusalem shall be inhabited like villages without walls, because of the multitude of people and animals in it. [5] For I will be a wall of fire all around it, says the LORD, and I will be the glory within it."

Interlude: An Appeal to the Exiles

6 Up, up! Flee from the land of the north, says the LORD; for I have spread you abroad like the four winds of heaven, says the LORD. [7] Up! Escape to Zion, you that live with daughter Babylon. [8] For thus said the LORD of hosts (after his glory[e] sent me) regarding the nations that plundered you: Truly, one who touches you touches the apple of my eye.[f] [9] See now, I am going to raise[g] my hand against them, and they shall become plunder for their own slaves. Then you will know that the LORD of hosts has sent me. [10] Sing and rejoice, O daughter Zion! For lo, I will come and dwell in your midst, says the LORD. [11] Many nations shall join themselves to the LORD on that day, and shall be my people; and I will dwell in your midst. And you shall know that the LORD of hosts has sent me to you. [12] The LORD will inherit Ju-

1.8
Josh 5.13;
Rev 6.4;
Zech 6.2-7
1.9
Zech 2.3;
4.5
1.10
Heb 1.14
1.11
Isa 14.7
1.12
Hab 1.2;
Dan 9.2
1.13
Zech 4.1;
Isa 40.1,2
1.14
Zech 8.2
1.15
Ps 123.4;
Am 1.11
1.16
Isa 54.8;
Zech 2.1,2,
10
1.17
Isa 44.26;
51.3;
Zech 2.12;
3.2
1.20
Isa 44.12;
54.16
1.21
Ps 75.10

2.1
Zech 1.18;
Ezek 40.3
2.2
Ezek 40.3;
Rev 21.15-17
2.4
Ezek 38.11;
Jer 30.19
2.5
Isa 26.1;
Zech 9.8;
Rev 21.23
2.6
Isa 48.20;
Jer 1.14;
Ezek 17.21
2.8
Isa 60.7-9;
Deut 32.10
2.9
Isa 11.15;
Zech 4.9
2.10
Isa 12.6;
Zeph 3.14;
Lev 26.12;
Ezek 37.27
2.12
Deut 32.9;
Zech 1.17

a Heb *and he*　　b Ch 2.1 in Heb　　c Heb *it*
d Ch 2.5 in Heb　　e Cn: Heb *after glory he*
f Heb *his eye*　　g Or *wave*

dah as his portion in the holy land, and will again choose Jerusalem.

13 Be silent, all people, before the LORD; for he has roused himself from his holy dwelling.

Fourth Vision: Joshua and Satan

3 Then he showed me the high priest Joshua standing before the angel of the LORD, and Satan[h] standing at his right hand to accuse him. [2] And the LORD said to Satan,[h] "The LORD rebuke you, O Satan![h] The LORD who has chosen Jerusalem rebuke you! Is not this man a brand plucked from the fire?" [3] Now Joshua was dressed with filthy clothes as he stood before the angel. [4] The angel said to those who were standing before him, "Take off his filthy clothes." And to him he said, "See, I have taken your guilt away from you, and I will clothe you with festal apparel." [5] And I said, "Let them put a clean turban on his head." So they put a clean turban on his head and clothed him with the apparel; and the angel of the LORD was standing by.

6 Then the angel of the LORD assured Joshua, saying [7] "Thus says the LORD of hosts: If you will walk in my ways and keep my requirements, then you shall rule my house and have charge of my courts, and I will give you the right of access among those who are standing here. [8] Now listen, Joshua, high priest, you and your colleagues who sit before you! For they are an omen of things to come: I am going to bring my servant the Branch. [9] For on the stone that I have set before Joshua, on a single stone with seven facets, I will engrave its inscription, says the LORD of hosts, and I will remove the guilt of this land in a single day. [10] On that day, says the LORD of hosts, you shall invite each other to come under your vine and fig tree."

Fifth Vision: The Lampstand and Olive Trees

4 The angel who talked with me came again, and wakened me,

as one is wakened from sleep. [2] He said to me, "What do you see?" And I said, "I see a lampstand all of gold, with a bowl on the top of it; there are seven lamps on it, with seven lips on each of the lamps that are on the top of it. [3] And by it there are two olive trees, one on the right of the bowl and the other on its left." [4] I said to the angel who talked with me, "What are these, my lord?" [5] Then the angel who talked with me answered me, "Do you not know what these are?" I said, "No, my lord." [6] He said to me, "This is the word of the LORD to Zerubbabel: Not by might, nor by power, but by my spirit, says the LORD of hosts. [7] What are you, O great mountain? Before Zerubbabel you shall become a plain; and he shall bring out the top stone amid shouts of 'Grace, grace to it!'"

8 Moreover the word of the LORD came to me, saying, [9] "The hands of Zerubbabel have laid the foundation of this house; his hands shall also complete it. Then you will know that the LORD of hosts has sent me to you. [10] For whoever has despised the day of small things shall rejoice, and shall see the plummet in the hand of Zerubbabel.

"These seven are the eyes of the LORD, which range through the whole earth." [11] Then I said to him, "What are these two olive trees on the right and the left of the lampstand?" [12] And a second time I said to him, "What are these two branches of the olive trees, which pour out the oil[i] through the two golden pipes?" [13] He said to me, "Do you not know what these are?" I said, "No, my lord." [14] Then he said, "These are the two anointed ones who stand by the Lord of the whole earth."

Sixth Vision: The Flying Scroll

5 Again I looked up and saw a flying scroll. [2] And he said to me, "What do you see?" I an-

h Or the Accuser; Heb the Adversary
i Cn: Heb gold

2.13
Hab 2.20;
Ps 78.65;
Isa 51.9
3.1
Hag 1.1;
Ps 109.6
3.2
Jude 9,23;
Am 4.11
3.4
Isa 43.25;
Rev 19.8
3.5
Ex 29.6
3.7
1 Kings 3.14;
Ezek 44.16;
Deut 17.9;
Zech 4.14
3.8
Isa 20.3;
Ezek 12.11;
Isa 4.2;
53.2;
Jer 33.15
3.9
Isa 28.16;
Zech 4.10;
Jer 31.34;
Mic 7.18
3.10
1 Kings 4.25;
Isa 36.16
4.1
Zech 1.9;
2.3;
Dan 8.18

4.2
Ex 25.31;
Rev 1.12;
Ex 25.37;
Rev 4.5
4.3
Rev 11.4
4.5
Zech 1.9
4.6
Hag 2.4,5;
Hos 1.7;
Eph 6.17
4.7
Jer 51.25;
Ps 118.22;
Ezra 3.10,11
4.9
Ezra 3.10;
6.15;
Zech 2.9,11;
6.15;
Isa 48.16;
Zech 2.8
4.10
Hag 2.3;
Zech 3.9;
Rev 8.2;
Zech 1.10
4.11
v. 3
4.14
Rev 11.4;
Zech 3.1-7;
Mic 4.13
5.1
Ezek 2.9

swered, "I see a flying scroll; its length is twenty cubits, and its width ten cubits." ³Then he said to me, "This is the curse that goes out over the face of the whole land; for everyone who steals shall be cut off according to the writing on one side, and everyone who swears falsely[j] shall be cut off according to the writing on the other side. ⁴I have sent it out, says the LORD of hosts, and it shall enter the house of the thief, and the house of anyone who swears falsely by my name; and it shall abide in that house and consume it, both timber and stones."

Seventh Vision: The Woman in a Basket

5 Then the angel who talked with me came forward and said to me, "Look up and see what this is that is coming out." ⁶I said, "What is it?" He said, "This is a basket[k] coming out." And he said, "This is their iniquity[l] in all the land." ⁷Then a leaden cover was lifted, and there was a woman sitting in the basket![k] ⁸And he said, "This is Wickedness." So he thrust her back into the basket,[k] and pressed the leaden weight down on its mouth. ⁹Then I looked up and saw two women coming forward. The wind was in their wings; they had wings like the wings of a stork, and they lifted up the basket[k] between earth and sky. ¹⁰Then I said to the angel who talked with me, "Where are they taking the basket?"[k] ¹¹He said to me, "To the land of Shinar, to build a house for it; and when this is prepared, they will set the basket[k] down there on its base."

Eighth Vision: Four Chariots

6 And again I looked up and saw four chariots coming out from between two mountains — mountains of bronze. ²The first chariot had red horses, the second chariot black horses, ³the third chariot white horses, and the fourth chariot dappled gray[m] horses. ⁴Then I said to the angel who talked with me, "What are

these, my lord?" ⁵The angel answered me, "These are the four winds[n] of heaven going out, after presenting themselves before the LORD of all the earth. ⁶The chariot with the black horses goes toward the north country, the white ones go toward the west country,[o] and the dappled ones go toward the south country." ⁷When the steeds came out, they were impatient to get off and patrol the earth. And he said, "Go, patrol the earth." So they patrolled the earth. ⁸Then he cried out to me, "Lo, those who go toward the north country have set my spirit at rest in the north country."

The Coronation of the Branch

9 The word of the LORD came to me: ¹⁰Collect silver and gold[p] from the exiles — from Heldai, Tobijah, and Jedaiah — who have arrived from Babylon; and go the same day to the house of Josiah son of Zephaniah. ¹¹Take the silver and gold and make a crown,[q] and set it on the head of the high priest Joshua son of Jehozadak; ¹²say to him: Thus says the LORD of hosts: Here is a man whose name is Branch: for he shall branch out in his place, and he shall build the temple of the LORD. ¹³It is he that shall build the temple of the LORD; he shall bear royal honor, and shall sit and rule on his throne. There shall be a priest by his throne, with peaceful understanding between the two of them. ¹⁴And the crown[r] shall be in the care of Heldai,[s] Tobijah, Jedaiah, and Josiah[t] son of Zephaniah, as a memorial in the temple of the LORD.

15 Those who are far off shall come and help to build the temple of the LORD; and you shall know that the LORD of hosts has sent me to you. This will happen if you dili-

Cross-references (center column)

5.3 Jer 26.6; Ex 20.15; Mal 3.8,9; v. 4
5.4 Mal 3.5; Hos 4.2,3; Lev 14.45; Hab 2.9-11
5.5 Zech 1.9,18
5.6 Lev 19.36; Am 8.5
5.8 Hos 12.7; Am 8.5; Mic 6.11
5.9 v. 5; Jer 8.7
5.11 Jer 29.5,28; Gen 10.10
6.1 Zech 1.18; 5.9; v. 5
6.2 Rev 6.4,5
6.3 Rev 6.2
6.4 Zech 5.10
6.5 Jer 49.36; Ezek 37.9; Mt 24.31; Rev 7.1
6.6 Jer 1.14; Ezek 1.4; Dan 11.5
6.7 Zech 1.10
6.8 Ezek 5.13
6.9 Zech 1.1; 7.1; 8.1
6.10 Jer 28.6
6.11 Ezra 3.2; Hag 1.1
6.12 Isa 11.1; Zech 3.8; Isa 53.2
6.13 Isa 9.6; 22.24; 9.7; Ps 110.1,4
6.14 v. 11
6.15 Isa 57.19; 60.10; Zech 4.9; 3.7

[j] The word *falsely* added from verse 4 [k] Heb *ephah* [l] Gk Compare Syr: Heb *their eye* [m] Compare Gk: Meaning of Heb uncertain [n] Or *spirits* [o] Cn: Heb *go after them* [p] Cn Compare verse 11: Heb lacks *silver and gold* [q] Gk Mss Syr Tg: Heb *crowns* [r] Gk Syr: Heb *crowns* [s] Syr Compare verse 10: Heb *Helem* [t] Syr Compare verse 10: Heb *Hen*

gently obey the voice of the Lord your God.

Hypocritical Fasting Condemned

7 In the fourth year of King Darius, the word of the Lord came to Zechariah on the fourth day of the ninth month, which is Chislev. 2 Now the people of Bethel had sent Sharezer and Regem-melech and their men, to entreat the favor of the Lord, 3 and to ask the priests of the house of the Lord of hosts and the prophets, "Should I mourn and practice abstinence in the fifth month, as I have done for so many years?" 4 Then the word of the Lord of hosts came to me: 5 Say to all the people of the land and the priests: When you fasted and lamented in the fifth month and in the seventh, for these seventy years, was it for me that you fasted? 6 And when you eat and when you drink, do you not eat and drink only for yourselves? 7 Were not these the words that the Lord proclaimed by the former prophets, when Jerusalem was inhabited and in prosperity, along with the towns around it, and when the Negeb and the Shephelah were inhabited?

Punishment for Rejecting God's Demands

8 The word of the Lord came to Zechariah, saying: 9 Thus says the Lord of hosts: Render true judgments, show kindness and mercy to one another; 10 do not oppress the widow, the orphan, the alien, or the poor; and do not devise evil in your hearts against one another. 11 But they refused to listen, and turned a stubborn shoulder, and stopped their ears in order not to hear. 12 They made their hearts adamant in order not to hear the law and the words that the Lord of hosts had sent by his spirit through the former prophets. Therefore great wrath came from the Lord of hosts. 13 Just as, when I[u] called, they would not hear, so, when they called, I would not hear, says the Lord of hosts, 14 and I scattered them with a whirlwind among all

the nations that they had not known. Thus the land they left was desolate, so that no one went to and fro, and a pleasant land was made desolate.

God's Promises to Zion

8 The word of the Lord of hosts came to me, saying: 2 Thus says the Lord of hosts: I am jealous for Zion with great jealousy, and I am jealous for her with great wrath. 3 Thus says the Lord: I will return to Zion, and will dwell in the midst of Jerusalem; Jerusalem shall be called the faithful city, and the mountain of the Lord of hosts shall be called the holy mountain. 4 Thus says the Lord of hosts: Old men and old women shall again sit in the streets of Jerusalem, each with staff in hand because of their great age. 5 And the streets of the city shall be full of boys and girls playing in its streets. 6 Thus says the Lord of hosts: Even though it seems impossible to the remnant of this people in these days, should it also seem impossible to me, says the Lord of hosts? 7 Thus says the Lord of hosts: I will save my people from the east country and from the west country; 8 and I will bring them to live in Jerusalem. They shall be my people and I will be their God, in faithfulness and in righteousness.

9 Thus says the Lord of hosts: Let your hands be strong—you that have recently been hearing these words from the mouths of the prophets who were present when the foundation was laid for the rebuilding of the temple, the house of the Lord of hosts. 10 For before those days there were no wages for people or for animals, nor was there any safety from the foe for those who went out or came in, and I set them all against one other. 11 But now I will not deal with the remnant of this people as in the former days, says the Lord of hosts. 12 For there shall be a sowing of

8.12 Joel 2.22; Hag 1.10; Isa 61.7

u Heb *he*

Cross references

7.1 Zech 1.1,7; Neh 1.1
7.2 Jer 26.19; Zech 8.21
7.3 Jer 52.12; Zech 8.19; 12.12-14
7.5 Isa 58.5; Zech 8.19; Jer 41.1; Rom 14.6
7.7 Zech 1.4; Jer 22.21; 17.26
7.9 Ezek 18.8; Zech 8.16; Mic 6.8
7.10 Deut 24.17; Jer 7.6; Mic 2.1
7.11 Jer 11.10; 17.23; 5.21; Acts 7.57
7.12 Ezek 11.19; 36.26; Neh 9.29, 30; Dan 9.11
7.13 Prov 1.24; Isa 1.15; Mic 3.4
7.14 Deut 4.27; Jer 23.19; 44.6; Isa 60.15

8.2 Zech 1.14
8.3 Zech 1.16; 2.10,11; Jer 31.23
8.4 Isa 65.20
8.5 Jer 30.19,20
8.6 Ps 118.23; Jer 32.17,27
8.7 Isa 11.11; 43.5,6; Am 9.14
8.8 Zech 10.10; Ezek 37.25; Zech 2.11
8.9 Hag 2.4; Ezra 5.1
8.10 Hag 1.6
8.11 Ps 103.9; Isa 12.1

peace; the vine shall yield its fruit, the ground shall give its produce, and the skies shall give their dew; and I will cause the remnant of this people to possess all these things. [13] Just as you have been a cursing among the nations, O house of Judah and house of Israel, so I will save you and you shall be a blessing. Do not be afraid, but let your hands be strong.

14 For thus says the LORD of hosts: Just as I purposed to bring disaster upon you, when your ancestors provoked me to wrath, and I did not relent, says the LORD of hosts, [15] so again I have purposed in these days to do good to Jerusalem and to the house of Judah; do not be afraid. [16] These are the things that you shall do: Speak the truth to one another, render in your gates judgments that are true and make for peace, [17] do not devise evil in your hearts against one another, and love no false oath; for all these are things that I hate, says the LORD.

Joyful Fasting

18 The word of the LORD of hosts came to me, saying: [19] Thus says the LORD of hosts: The fast of the fourth month, and the fast of the fifth, and the fast of the seventh, and the fast of the tenth, shall be seasons of joy and gladness, and cheerful festivals for the house of Judah: therefore love truth and peace.

Many Peoples Drawn to Jerusalem

20 Thus says the LORD of hosts: Peoples shall yet come, the inhabitants of many cities; [21] the inhabitants of one city shall go to another, saying, "Come, let us go to entreat the favor of the LORD, and to seek the LORD of hosts; I myself am going." [22] Many peoples and strong nations shall come to seek the LORD of hosts in Jerusalem, and to entreat the favor of the LORD. [23] Thus says the LORD of hosts: In those days ten men from nations of every language shall take hold of a Jew,

grasping his garment and saying, "Let us go with you, for we have heard that God is with you."

Judgment on Israel's Enemies

9 An Oracle.

The word of the LORD is
 against the land of
 Hadrach
and will rest upon
 Damascus.
For to the LORD belongs the
 capital[v] of Aram,[w]
as do all the tribes of
 Israel;
[2] Hamath also, which borders
 on it,
Tyre and Sidon, though
 they are very wise.
[3] Tyre has built itself a
 rampart,
and heaped up silver like
 dust,
and gold like the dirt of
 the streets.
[4] But now, the Lord will strip
 it of its possessions
and hurl its wealth into the
 sea,
and it shall be devoured by
 fire.

[5] Ashkelon shall see it and be
 afraid;
Gaza too, and shall writhe
 in anguish;
Ekron also, because its
 hopes are withered.
The king shall perish from
 Gaza;
Ashkelon shall be
 uninhabited;
[6] a mongrel people shall settle
 in Ashdod,
and I will make an end of
 the pride of Philistia.
[7] I will take away its blood
 from its mouth,
and its abominations from
 between its teeth;
it too shall be a remnant for
 our God;

8.13 Jer 42.18; Gen 12.2; Ruth 4.11
8.14 Jer 31.28; Ezek 24.14
8.15 Jer 29.11; v. 13
8.16 Zech 7.9; Eph 4.25
8.17 Prov 3.29; Zech 7.10; 5.4; Hab 1.13
8.19 Zech 7.3,5; Jer 39.2; 52.4; Isa 12.1; v. 16
8.21 Mic 4.1,2
8.22 Isa 60.3; 66.23; v. 21
8.23 Isa 45.14, 24; 60.14; 1 Cor 14.25; 2 Chr 15.5; Isa 19.2

9.2 Jer 49.23; Ezek 28.3-5, 12,21
9.3 2 Sam 24.7; Ezek 27.33; 1 Kings 10.21, 27
9.4 Isa 23.1; Ezek 28.18
9.5 Am 1.6-8
9.6 Am 1.6-8
9.7 Ezek 25.15-17

[v] Heb *eye* [w] Cn: Heb *of Adam* (or *of humankind*)

it shall be like a clan in
Judah,
and Ekron shall be like the
Jebusites.
8 Then I will encamp at my
house as a guard,
so that no one shall march
to and fro;
no oppressor shall again
overrun them,
for now I have seen with
my own eyes.

The Coming Ruler of God's People

9 Rejoice greatly, O daughter
Zion!
Shout aloud, O daughter
Jerusalem!
Lo, your king comes to you;
triumphant and victorious
is he,
humble and riding on a
donkey,
on a colt, the foal of a
donkey.
10 He[x] will cut off the chariot
from Ephraim
and the war horse from
Jerusalem;
and the battle bow shall be
cut off,
and he shall command
peace to the nations;
his dominion shall be from
sea to sea,
and from the River to the
ends of the earth.

11 As for you also, because of
the blood of my
covenant with you,
I will set your prisoners
free from the waterless
pit.
12 Return to your stronghold,
O prisoners of hope;
today I declare that I will
restore to you double.
13 For I have bent Judah as my
bow;
I have made Ephraim its
arrow.
I will arouse your sons,
O Zion,

against your sons,
O Greece,
and wield you like a
warrior's sword.

14 Then the LORD will appear
over them,
and his arrow go forth like
lightning;
the Lord GOD will sound the
trumpet
and march forth in the
whirlwinds of the south.
15 The LORD of hosts will
protect them,
and they shall devour and
tread down the
slingers;[y]
they shall drink their blood[z]
like wine,
and be full like a bowl,
drenched like the corners
of the altar.

16 On that day the LORD their
God will save them
for they are the flock of his
people;
for like the jewels of a crown
they shall shine on his
land.
17 For what goodness and
beauty are his!
Grain shall make the young
men flourish,
and new wine the young
women.

Restoration of Judah and Israel

10 Ask rain from the LORD
in the season of the
spring rain,
from the LORD who makes
the storm clouds,
who gives showers of rain
to you,[a]
the vegetation in the field
to everyone.
2 For the teraphim[b] utter
nonsense,
and the diviners see lies;
the dreamers tell false
dreams,

9.8
Zech 2.5;
Isa 52.1;
54.14; 60.18
9.9
Zeph 3.14,
15; Isa 9.6,
7; Mt 21.5;
Jn 12.15;
Isa 43.3,11;
57.15
9.10
Hos 1.7;
2.18;
Hag 2.22;
Isa 57.19;
Ps 72.8;
Isa 60.12
9.11
Ex 24.8;
Heb 10.29;
Isa 51.14
9.12
Jer 16.19;
17.13;
Isa 61.7
9.13
Jer 51.20;
Joel 3.6;
Ps 45.3;
Isa 49.2

9.14
Isa 31.5;
Ps 18.14;
Isa 27.13;
21.1; 66.15
9.15
Isa 37.35;
Zech 12.6;
Job 41.28;
Ps 78.65;
Ex 27.2
9.16
Jer 31.10,
11; Isa 62.3
9.17
Jer 31.12,14
10.1
Jer 14.22;
10.13;
Isa 30.23
10.2
Ezek 21.21;
Hos 3.4;
Jer 27.9;
Job 13.4;
Ezek 34.5

x Gk: Heb I y Cn: Heb the slingstones
z Gk: Heb shall drink a Heb them
b Or household gods

and give empty
consolation.
Therefore the people wander
like sheep;
they suffer for lack of a
shepherd.

3 My anger is hot against the
shepherds,
and I will punish the
leaders;^c
for the Lord of hosts cares
for his flock, the house
of Judah,
and will make them like
his proud war horse.
4 Out of them shall come the
cornerstone,
out of them the tent peg,
out of them the battle bow,
out of them every
commander.
5 Together they shall be like
warriors in battle,
trampling the foe in the
mud of the streets;
they shall fight, for the Lord
is with them,
and they shall put to
shame the riders on
horses.

6 I will strengthen the house
of Judah,
and I will save the house of
Joseph.
I will bring them back
because I have
compassion on them,
and they shall be as though
I had not rejected
them;
for I am the Lord their God
and I will answer them.
7 Then the people of Ephraim
shall become like
warriors,
and their hearts shall be
glad as with wine.
Their children shall see it
and rejoice,
their hearts shall exult in
the Lord.

8 I will signal for them and
gather them in,
for I have redeemed them,

and they shall be as
numerous as they were
before.
9 Though I scattered them
among the nations,
yet in far countries they
shall remember me,
and they shall rear their
children and return.
10 I will bring them home from
the land of Egypt,
and gather them from
Assyria;
I will bring them to the land
of Gilead and to
Lebanon,
until there is no room for
them.
11 They^d shall pass through the
sea of distress,
and the waves of the sea
shall be struck down,
and all the depths of the
Nile dried up.
The pride of Assyria shall be
laid low,
and the scepter of Egypt
shall depart.
12 I will make them strong in
the Lord,
and they shall walk in his
name,
　　　　says the Lord.

11

Open your doors,
O Lebanon,
so that fire may devour
your cedars!
2 Wail, O cypress, for the
cedar has fallen,
for the glorious trees are
ruined!
Wail, oaks of Bashan,
for the thick forest has
been felled!
3 Listen, the wail of the
shepherds,
for their glory is despoiled!
Listen, the roar of the lions,
for the thickets of the
Jordan are destroyed!

Two Kinds of Shepherds

4 Thus said the Lord my God: Be
a shepherd of the flock doomed to

10.3
Jer 25.34-36;
Ezek 34.12,
17
10.4
Zech 9.10
10.5
2 Sam 22.43;
Hag 2.22
10.6
v. 12;
Zech 9.16;
8.8; 1.1,6;
13.9
10.7
Zech 9.13,
15;
Isa 54.13
10.8
Isa 5.26;
Jer 33.22;
Ezek 36.11

10.9
Ezek 6.9
10.10
Isa 11.11;
Jer 50.19;
Isa 49.19,20
10.11
Isa 51.9,10;
19.5-7;
Zeph 2.13;
Ezek 30.13
10.12
Mic 4.5
11.1
Jer 22.6,7;
Ezek 31.3
11.2
Isa 32.19
11.3
Jer 25.34-36;
50.44
11.4
v. 7

^c Or *male goats*　^d Gk: Heb *He*

slaughter. ⁵Those who buy them kill them and go unpunished; and those who sell them say, "Blessed be the Lord, for I have become rich"; and their own shepherds have no pity on them. ⁶For I will no longer have pity on the inhabitants of the earth, says the Lord. I will cause them, every one, to fall each into the hand of a neighbor, and each into the hand of the king; and they shall devastate the earth, and I will deliver no one from their hand.

7 So, on behalf of the sheep merchants, I became the shepherd of the flock doomed to slaughter. I took two staffs; one I named Favor, the other I named Unity, and I tended the sheep. ⁸In one month I disposed of the three shepherds, for I had become impatient with them, and they also detested me. ⁹So I said, "I will not be your shepherd. What is to die, let it die; what is to be destroyed, let it be destroyed; and let those that are left devour the flesh of one another!" ¹⁰I took my staff Favor and broke it, annulling the covenant that I had made with all the peoples. ¹¹So it was annulled on that day, and the sheep merchants, who were watching me, knew that it was the word of the Lord. ¹²I then said to them, "If it seems right to you, give me my wages; but if not, keep them." So they weighed out as my wages thirty shekels of silver. ¹³Then the Lord said to me, "Throw it into the treasury"ᵉ—this lordly price at which I was valued by them. So I took the thirty shekels of silver and threw them into the treasuryᵉ in the house of the Lord. ¹⁴Then I broke my second staff Unity, annulling the family ties between Judah and Israel.

15 Then the Lord said to me: Take once more the implements of a worthless shepherd. ¹⁶For I am now raising up in the land a shepherd who does not care for the perishing, or seek the wandering,ᶠ or heal the maimed, or nourish the healthy,ᵍ but devours the flesh of

the fat ones, tearing off even their hoofs.
¹⁷ Oh, my worthless shepherd,
 who deserts the flock!
May the sword strike his arm
 and his right eye!
Let his arm be completely
 withered,
 his right eye utterly
 blinded!

Jerusalem's Victory

12 An Oracle.

The word of the Lord concerning Israel: Thus says the Lord, who stretched out the heavens and founded the earth and formed the human spirit within: ²See, I am about to make Jerusalem a cup of reeling for all the surrounding peoples; it will be against Judah also in the siege against Jerusalem. ³On that day I will make Jerusalem a heavy stone for all the peoples; all who lift it shall grievously hurt themselves. And all the nations of the earth shall come together against it. ⁴On that day, says the Lord, I will strike every horse with panic, and its rider with madness. But on the house of Judah I will keep a watchful eye, when I strike every horse of the peoples with blindness. ⁵Then the clans of Judah shall say to themselves, "The inhabitants of Jerusalem have strength through the Lord of hosts, their God."

6 On that day I will make the clans of Judah like a blazing pot on a pile of wood, like a flaming torch among sheaves; and they shall devour to the right and to the left all the surrounding peoples, while Jerusalem shall again be inhabited in its place, in Jerusalem.

7 And the Lord will give victory to the tents of Judah first, that the glory of the house of David and the glory of the inhabitants of Jerusalem may not be exalted over that of

11.5
Jer 50.7;
Hos 12.8
11.6
Jer 13.14;
Zech 14.13;
Mic 5.8
11.7
Zeph 3.12;
Ezek 37.16;
vv. 10,14
11.8
Hos 5.7
11.9
Jer 15.2;
43.11
11.10
v. 7;
Jer 14.21
11.11
Zeph 3.12
11.12
1 Kings 5.6;
Gen 37.28;
Ex 21.32;
Mt 26.15;
27.9,10
11.13
Mt 27.9
11.15
Ezek 34.2-4
11.16
Jer 23.2;
Ezek 34.2-6

11.17
Jer 23.1;
Jn 10.12;
Ezek 30.21,
22; Mic 3.6,
7
12.1
Isa 42.5;
57.16;
Heb 12.9
12.2
Isa 51.22,
23;
Zech 14.14
12.3
Dan 2.34,
35,44,45;
Mt 21.44;
Zech 14.2
12.4
Ps 76.6;
Ezek 38.4;
Zech 9.10
12.5
Zech 10.6,
12
12.6
Isa 10.17,
18; Ob 18;
Zech 2.4;
8 3-5
12.7
Jer 30.18;
Am 9.11

ᵉ Syr: Heb it to the potter ᶠ Syr Compare Gk Vg: Heb the youth ᵍ Meaning of Heb uncertain

Judah. ⁸On that day the Lᴏʀᴅ will shield the inhabitants of Jerusalem so that the feeblest among them on that day shall be like David, and the house of David shall be like God, like the angel of the Lᴏʀᴅ, at their head. ⁹And on that day I will seek to destroy all the nations that come against Jerusalem.

Mourning for the Pierced One

10 And I will pour out a spirit of compassion and supplication on the house of David and the inhabitants of Jerusalem, so that, when they look on the oneʰ whom they have pierced, they shall mourn for him, as one mourns for an only child, and weep bitterly over him, as one weeps over a firstborn. ¹¹On that day the mourning in Jerusalem will be as great as the mourning for Hadad-rimmon in the plain of Megiddo. ¹²The land shall mourn, each family by itself; the family of the house of David by itself, and their wives by themselves; the family of the house of Nathan by itself, and their wives by themselves; ¹³the family of the house of Levi by itself, and their wives by themselves; the family of the Shimeites by itself, and their wives by themselves; ¹⁴and all the families that are left, each by itself, and their wives by themselves.

13 On that day a fountain shall be opened for the house of David and the inhabitants of Jerusalem, to cleanse them from sin and impurity.

Idolatry Cut Off

2 On that day, says the Lᴏʀᴅ of hosts, I will cut off the names of the idols from the land, so that they shall be remembered no more; and also I will remove from the land the prophets and the unclean spirit. ³And if any prophets appear again, their fathers and mothers who bore them will say to them, "You shall not live, for you speak lies in the name of the Lᴏʀᴅ"; and their fathers and their mothers who bore them shall pierce them through when they prophesy. ⁴On that day

the prophets will be ashamed, every one, of their visions when they prophesy; they will not put on a hairy mantle in order to deceive, ⁵but each of them will say, "I am no prophet, I am a tiller of the soil; for the land has been my possessionⁱ since my youth." ⁶And if anyone asks them, "What are these wounds on your chest?"ⁱ the answer will be "The wounds I received in the house of my friends."

The Shepherd Struck, the Flock Scattered

⁷ "Awake, O sword, against my
 shepherd,
 against the man who is my
 associate,"
 says the Lᴏʀᴅ of hosts.
Strike the shepherd, that the
 sheep may be scattered;
 I will turn my hand against
 the little ones.
⁸ In the whole land, says the
 Lᴏʀᴅ,
 two-thirds shall be cut off
 and perish,
 and one-third shall be left
 alive.
⁹ And I will put this third into
 the fire,
 refine them as one refines
 silver,
 and test them as gold is
 tested.
They will call on my name,
 and I will answer them.
I will say, "They are my
 people";
 and they will say, "The
 Lᴏʀᴅ is our God."

Future Warfare and Final Victory

14 See, a day is coming for the Lᴏʀᴅ, when the plunder taken from you will be divided in your midst. ²For I will gather all the nations against Jerusalem to battle, and the city shall be taken and the houses looted and the women raped; half the city shall go into exile, but the rest of the peo-

12.8
Zech 9.14,
15; Mic 7.8;
Ps 8.5; 82.6
12.9
v. 3;
Zech 14.2,3
12.10
Isa 44.3;
Ezek 39.29;
Joel 2.28;
Jn 19.34;
Rev 1.7;
Jer 6.26;
Am 8.10
12.11
2 Kings 23.29
12.12
Mt 24.30;
Rev 1.7
13.1
Jer 2.13;
Heb 9.14;
Ps 51.2,7;
Ezek 36.25
13.2
Ex 23.13;
Hos 2.17;
Jer 23.14,
15;
Ezek 36.25,
29
13.3
Jer 23.34;
Deut 18.20;
13.6-11
13.4
Mic 3.6,7;
2 Kings 1.8;
Mt 3.4

13.5
Am 7.14
13.6
2 Kings 9.24
13.7
Jer 47.6;
Mic 5.2,4;
Jer 23.5,6;
Isa 53.4,5,
10;
Mt 26.31;
Isa 1.25
13.8
Isa 6.13
13.9
Isa 48.10;
1 Pet 1.6;
Zech 10.6;
Jer 30.22;
Hos 2.23
14.1
Isa 13.9;
Joel 2.1;
Mal 4.1;
v. 14
14.2
Zech 12.2,3;
Isa 13.6;
Zech 13.8

ʰ Heb *on me* ⁱ Cn: Heb *for humankind has caused me to possess* ⁱ Heb *wounds between your hands*

ple shall not be cut off from the city. [3] Then the LORD will go forth and fight against those nations as when he fights on a day of battle. [4] On that day his feet shall stand on the Mount of Olives, which lies before Jerusalem on the east; and the Mount of Olives shall be split in two from east to west by a very wide valley; so that one half of the Mount shall withdraw northward, and the other half southward. [5] And you shall flee by the valley of the LORD's mountain,[k] for the valley between the mountains shall reach to Azal;[l] and you shall flee as you fled from the earthquake in the days of King Uzziah of Judah. Then the LORD my God will come, and all the holy ones with him.

[6] On that day there shall not be[m] either cold or frost.[n] [7] And there shall be continuous day (it is known to the LORD), not day and not night, for at evening time there shall be light.

[8] On that day living waters shall flow out from Jerusalem, half of them to the eastern sea and half of them to the western sea; it shall continue in summer as in winter.

[9] And the LORD will become king over all the earth; on that day the LORD will be one and his name one.

[10] The whole land shall be turned into a plain from Geba to Rimmon south of Jerusalem. But Jerusalem shall remain aloft on its site from the Gate of Benjamin to the place of the former gate, to the Corner Gate, and from the Tower of Hananel to the king's wine presses. [11] And it shall be inhabited, for never again shall it be doomed to destruction; Jerusalem shall abide in security.

[12] This shall be the plague with which the LORD will strike all the peoples that wage war against Jerusalem: their flesh shall rot while they are still on their feet; their eyes shall rot in their sockets, and their tongues shall rot in their

mouths. [13] On that day a great panic from the LORD shall fall on them, so that each will seize the hand of a neighbor, and the hand of the one will be raised against the hand of the other; [14] even Judah will fight at Jerusalem. And the wealth of all the surrounding nations shall be collected — gold, silver, and garments in great abundance. [15] And a plague like this plague shall fall on the horses, the mules, the camels, the donkeys, and whatever animals may be in those camps.

[16] Then all who survive of the nations that have come against Jerusalem shall go up year after year to worship the King, the LORD of hosts, and to keep the festival of booths.[o] [17] If any of the families of the earth do not go up to Jerusalem to worship the King, the LORD of hosts, there will be no rain upon them. [18] And if the family of Egypt do not go up and present themselves, then on them shall[p] come the plague that the LORD inflicts on the nations that do not go up to keep the festival of booths.[o] [19] Such shall be the punishment of Egypt and the punishment of all the nations that do not go up to keep the festival of booths.[o]

[20] On that day there shall be inscribed on the bells of the horses, "Holy to the LORD." And the cooking pots in the house of the LORD shall be as holy as[q] the bowls in front of the altar; [21] and every cooking pot in Jerusalem and Judah shall be sacred to the LORD of hosts, so that all who sacrifice may come and use them to boil the flesh of the sacrifice. And there shall no longer be traders[r] in the house of the LORD of hosts on that day.

14.3 Zech 9.14, 15
14.4 Ezek 11.23; Mic 1.3,4; Hab 3.6
14.5 Am 1.1; Isa 66.15, 16; Mt 25.31; Jude 14
14.7 Isa 30.26; Rev 21.23
14.8 Ezek 47.1; Joel 3.18; Rev 22.1
14.9 Rev 11.15; Isa 45.21-24; Eph 4.5,6
14.10 Am 9.11; Zech 12.6; Jer 37.13; 38.7; 31.38
14.11 Zech 2.4; Rev 22.3; Jer 23.5,6
14.12 Deut 28.21, 22
14.13 1 Sam 14.15, 20; Zech 11.6; Ezek 38.21
14.14 Zech 12.2,5; Isa 23.18
14.15 v. 12
14.16 Isa 60.6,7,9; 66.23; v. 9
14.17 vv. 9,16; Am 4.7
14.18 v. 12
14.19 v. 12
14.20 Ex 28.36-38; Zech 9.15
14.21 Neh 8.10; 1 Cor 10.31; Ezek 44.9; Zech 9.8

[k] Heb my mountains [l] Meaning of Heb uncertain [m] Cn: Heb there shall not be light [n] Compare Gk Syr Vg Tg: Meaning of Heb uncertain [o] Or tabernacles; Heb succoth [p] Gk Syr: Heb shall not [q] Heb shall be like [r] Or Canaanites

Malachi

Title and Background

The temple had been rebuilt, but times of prosperity had not come. The people were suffering drought, famine, and blighted crops, and they met these conditions with indifference and spiritual lethargy. They had forgotten God and treated him with dishonor. They had also married foreign women. Against such a background Malachi (meaning "my messenger") was written.

Author and Date of Writing

Since the term "my messenger" occurs in 3.1, and since both prophets and priests were called messengers of the Lord, some have thought "Malachi" is only a title. There is no certainty about this, however, and it seems probable that Malachi was in fact the author's name. The book was probably written 433-430 B.C.

Theme and Message

Malachi's message was filled with indictments and warnings. He rebuked the Jews for doubting God's love (1.2-5) and for the faithlessness of both priests (1.6–2.9) and people (2.10-16). How quickly the nation had forgotten! Only through repentance and reformation would the people again experience God's blessing (3.6-12). That "great and terrible day of the LORD" (4.5) was coming, and Malachi both reassured and warned his people.

Outline

I. God's Covenant Love for Israel (1.1-5)
II. Israel's Unfaithfulness (1.6–2.16)
 A. The Unfaithfulness of the Priests (1.6–2.9)
 B. The Unfaithfulness of the People (2.10-16)
III. The Lord's Coming (2.17–4.6)

1 An oracle. The word of the LORD to Israel by Malachi.[a]

Israel Preferred to Edom

2 I have loved you, says the LORD. But you say, "How have you loved us?" Is not Esau Jacob's brother? says the LORD. Yet I have loved Jacob ³but I have hated Esau; I have made his hill country a desolation and his heritage a desert for jackals. ⁴If Edom says, "We are shattered but we will rebuild the ruins," the LORD of hosts says: They may build, but I will tear down, until they are called the wicked country, the people with whom the LORD is angry forever. ⁵Your own eyes shall see this, and

you shall say, "Great is the LORD beyond the borders of Israel!"

Corruption of the Priesthood

6 A son honors his father, and servants their master. If then I am a father, where is the honor due me? And if I am a master, where is the respect due me? says the LORD of hosts to you, O priests, who despise my name. You say, "How have we despised your name?" ⁷By offering polluted food on my altar. And you say, "How have we polluted it?"[b] By thinking that the LORD's table may be despised. ⁸When you offer blind animals in sacrifice, is that not wrong? And when you offer those that are lame or sick, is that not wrong? Try presenting that

1.1 Nah 1.1; Hab 1.1
1.2 Isa 41.8,9; Jer 31.3; Rom 9.13
1.3 Jer 49.18; Ezek 35.3-9
1.5 Ps 35.27; Job 42.8
1.6 Ex 20.12; Mal 2.10; Lk 6.46; Mal 3.5; 2.1-9
1.7 Lev 21.6,8; v. 12
1.8 Lev 22.22

a Or by my messenger b Gk: Heb you

to your governor; will he be pleased with you or show you favor? says the LORD of hosts. ⁹And now implore the favor of God, that he may be gracious to us. The fault is yours. Will he show favor to any of you? says the LORD of hosts. ¹⁰Oh, that someone among you would shut the temple^c doors, so that you would not kindle fire on my altar in vain! I have no pleasure in you, says the LORD of hosts, and I will not accept an offering from your hands. ¹¹For from the rising of the sun to its setting my name is great among the nations, and in every place incense is offered to my name, and a pure offering; for my name is great among the nations, says the LORD of hosts. ¹²But you profane it when you say that the Lord's table is polluted, and the food for it^d may be despised. ¹³"What a weariness this is," you say, and you sniff at me,^e says the LORD of hosts. You bring what has been taken by violence or is lame or sick, and this you bring as your offering! Shall I accept that from your hand? says the LORD. ¹⁴Cursed be the cheat who has a male in the flock and vows to give it, and yet sacrifices to the Lord what is blemished; for I am a great King, says the LORD of hosts, and my name is reverenced among the nations.

2 And now, O priests, this command is for you. ²If you will not listen, if you will not lay it to heart to give glory to my name, says the LORD of hosts, then I will send the curse on you and I will curse your blessings; indeed I have already cursed them,^f because you do not lay it to heart. ³I will rebuke your offspring, and spread dung on your faces, the dung of your offerings, and I will put you out of my presence.^g

4 Know, then, that I have sent this command to you, that my covenant with Levi may hold, says the LORD of hosts. ⁵My covenant with him was a covenant of life and wellbeing, which I gave him; this called for reverence, and he revered me and stood in awe of my name.

⁶True instruction was in his mouth, and no wrong was found on his lips. He walked with me in integrity and uprightness, and he turned many from iniquity. ⁷For the lips of a priest should guard knowledge, and people should seek instruction from his mouth, for he is the messenger of the LORD of hosts. ⁸But you have turned aside from the way; you have caused many to stumble by your instruction; you have corrupted the covenant of Levi, says the LORD of hosts, ⁹and so I make you despised and abased before all the people, inasmuch as you have not kept my ways but have shown partiality in your instruction.

The Covenant Profaned by Judah

10 Have we not all one father? Has not one God created us? Why then are we faithless to one another, profaning the covenant of our ancestors? ¹¹Judah has been faithless, and abomination has been committed in Israel and in Jerusalem; for Judah has profaned the sanctuary of the LORD, which he loves, and has married the daughter of a foreign god. ¹²May the LORD cut off from the tents of Jacob anyone who does this—any to witness^h or answer, or to bring an offering to the LORD of hosts.

13 And this you do as well: You cover the Lord's altar with tears, with weeping and groaning because he no longer regards the offering or accepts it with favor at your hand. ¹⁴You ask, "Why does he not?" Because the LORD was a witness between you and the wife of your youth, to whom you have been faithless, though she is your companion and your wife by covenant. ¹⁵Did not one God make her?ⁱ Both flesh and spirit are

1.9
Am 5.22;
Lev 23.34-44
1.10
Isa 1.13;
Jer 14.10-12;
Hos 5.6
1.11
Isa 45.6;
60.3,5,6;
Rev 8.3;
Jer 10.6,7
1.12
Deut 28.15;
v. 7
1.13
Isa 43.22;
61.8;
Lev 22.20
1.14
Lev 22.18-20;
Zech 14.9;
Zeph 2.11
2.1
vv. 7,8
2.2
Lev 26.14;
Deut 28.15-20
2.3
Nah 3.6;
Ex 29.14
2.4
Num 3.45;
18.21
2.5
Num 25.12;
Ezek 34.25;
Deut 33.9
2.6
Deut 33.8-10;
Jer 23.22;
Jas 5.20
2.7
Lev 10.11;
Jer 18.18;
Num 27.21
2.8
Mal 3.7;
Jer 18.15;
Ezek 44.10
2.9
1 Sam 2.30;
Deut 1.17;
Mic 3.11
2.10
Isa 63.16;
1 Cor 8.6;
Jer 9.4,5;
Ex 19.4-6
2.11
Jer 3.7-9;
Ezra 9.1;
Neh 13.23
2.12
Hos 9.12;
Mal 1.10,13
2.13
Jer 11.14;
14.12
2.14
Prov 5.18;
2.17
2.15
Gen 2.24;
Mt 19.4;
Ex 20.14;

Lev 20.10

^c Heb lacks temple ^d Compare Syr Tg: Heb its fruit, its food ^e Another reading is at it ^f Heb it ^g Cn Compare Gk Syr: Heb and he shall bear you to it ^h Cn Compare Gk: Heb arouse ⁱ Or Has he not made one?

his.[j] And what does the one God[k] desire? Godly offspring. So look to yourselves, and do not let anyone be faithless to the wife of his youth. [16]For I hate[l] divorce, says the Lord, the God of Israel, and covering one's garment with violence, says the Lord of hosts. So take heed to yourselves and do not be faithless.

17 You have wearied the Lord with your words. Yet you say, "How have we wearied him?" By saying, "All who do evil are good in the sight of the Lord, and he delights in them." Or by asking, "Where is the God of justice?"

The Coming Messenger

3 See, I am sending my messenger to prepare the way before me, and the Lord whom you seek will suddenly come to his temple. The messenger of the covenant in whom you delight—indeed, he is coming, says the Lord of hosts. [2]But who can endure the day of his coming, and who can stand when he appears?

For he is like a refiner's fire and like fullers' soap; [3]he will sit as a refiner and purifier of silver, and he will purify the descendants of Levi and refine them like gold and silver, until they present offerings to the Lord in righteousness.[m] [4]Then the offering of Judah and Jerusalem will be pleasing to the Lord as in the days of old and as in former years.

5 Then I will draw near to you for judgment; I will be swift to bear witness against the sorcerers, against the adulterers, against those who swear falsely, against those who oppress the hired workers in their wages, the widow and the orphan, against those who thrust aside the alien, and do not fear me, says the Lord of hosts.

6 For I the Lord do not change; therefore you, O children of Jacob, have not perished. [7]Ever since the days of your ancestors you have turned aside from my statutes and have not kept them. Return to me, and I will return to you, says the

2.16
Deut 24.1;
Mt 5.31,32;
Ps 73.6;
Isa 59.6
2.17
Isa 43.24;
5.19,20
3.1
Mt 11.10;
Mk 1.2;
Lk 1.76;
7.27
3.2
Ezek 22.14;
Zech 13.9;
Mt 3.10-12;
1 Cor 3.13-15
3.3
Isa 1.25;
Zech 13.9
3.4
Mal 1.11
3.5
Deut 18.10;
Ezek 22.9-11;
Zech 5.4;
Lev 19.13
3.6
Num 23.19;
Jas 1.17
3.7
Acts 7.51;
Zech 1.3

3.8
Neh 13.10-12
3.9
Mal 2.2
3.10
Prov 3.9,10;
Ps 78.23-29;
2 Chr 31.10
3.11
Joel 1.4;
2.25
3.12
Isa 61.9;
62.4
3.13
Mal 2.17
3.14
Ps 73.13;
Jer 2.25;
18.12;
Isa 58.3
3.15
Mal 4.1;
Jer 7.10
3.16
Ps 34.15;
56.8;
Rev 20.12
3.17
1 Pet 2.9;
Isa 26.20
3.18
Gen 18.25;
Am 5.15

Lord of hosts. But you say, "How shall we return?"

Do Not Rob God

8 Will anyone rob God? Yet you are robbing me! But you say, "How are we robbing you?" In your tithes and offerings! [9]You are cursed with a curse, for you are robbing me—the whole nation of you! [10]Bring the full tithe into the storehouse, so that there may be food in my house, and thus put me to the test, says the Lord of hosts; see if I will not open the windows of heaven for you and pour down for you an overflowing blessing. [11]I will rebuke the locust[n] for you, so that it will not destroy the produce of your soil; and your vine in the field shall not be barren, says the Lord of hosts. [12]Then all nations will count you happy, for you will be a land of delight, says the Lord of hosts.

13 You have spoken harsh words against me, says the Lord. Yet you say, "How have we spoken against you?" [14]You have said, "It is vain to serve God. What do we profit by keeping his command or by going about as mourners before the Lord of hosts? [15]Now we count the arrogant happy; evildoers not only prosper, but when they put God to the test they escape."

The Reward of the Faithful

16 Then those who revered the Lord spoke with one another. The Lord took note and listened, and a book of remembrance was written before him of those who revered the Lord and thought on his name. [17]They shall be mine, says the Lord of hosts, my special possession on the day when I act, and I will spare them as parents spare their children who serve them. [18]Then once more you shall see the difference between the righteous and the wicked, between one who serves God and one who does not serve him.

j Cn: Heb *and a remnant of spirit was his*
k Heb *he* l Cn: Heb *he hates*
m Or *right offerings to the Lord*
n Heb *devourer*

The Great Day of the LORD

4 ° See, the day is coming, burning like an oven, when all the arrogant and all evildoers will be stubble; the day that comes shall burn them up, says the LORD of hosts, so that it will leave them neither root nor branch. [2] But for you who revere my name the sun of righteousness shall rise, with healing in its wings. You shall go out leaping like calves from the stall. [3] And you shall tread down the wicked, for they will be ashes under the soles of your feet, on the day when I act, says the LORD of hosts.

[4] Remember the teaching of my servant Moses, the statutes and ordinances that I commanded him at Horeb for all Israel.

[5] Lo, I will send you the prophet Elijah before the great and terrible day of the LORD comes. [6] He will turn the hearts of parents to their children and the hearts of children to their parents, so that I will not come and strike the land with a curse. P

° Ch 4.1-6 are Ch 3.19-24 in Heb P Or a ban of utter destruction

4.1 Joel 2.31; Ob 18; Am 2.9
4.2 Mal 3.16; Lk 1.78; Eph 5.14
4.3 Mic 7.10; Zech 10.5
4.4 Ex 20.3
4.5 Mt 11.14; Mk 9.11; Lk 1.17

FROM MALACHI TO CHRIST

THE PERSIAN PERIOD
450-330 B.C.

For about 200 years after Nehemiah's time the Persians controlled Judah, but the Jews were allowed to carry on their religious observances and were not interfered with. During this time Judah was ruled by high priests who were responsible to the Jewish government.

THE HELLENISTIC PERIOD
330-166 B.C.

In 333 B.C. the Persian armies stationed in Macedonia were defeated by Alexander the Great. He was convinced that Greek culture was the one force that could unify the world. Alexander permitted the Jews to observe their laws and even granted them exemption from tribute or tax during their sabbath years. The Greek conquest prepared the way for the translation of the OT into Greek (Septuagint version) c. 250 B.C.

Malachi c. 430 B.C.

Year	Event
410	
400 B.C.	
390	
380	
370	
360	
350	
340	
330	334-323 Alexander the Great conquers the East
320	330-328 Alexander's years of power
310	320 Ptolemy (I) Soter conquers Jerusalem; Seleucid dynasty begins
300	311 Seleucus conquers Babylon; Seleucid dynasty begins
290	
280	
270	
260	
250	
240	
230	226 Antiochus III (the Great) of Syria overpowers Palestine
220	223-187 Antiochus becomes Seleucid ruler of Syria
210	
200	198 Antiochus defeats Egypt and gains control of Palestine
190	

Rule of Alexander the Great

Rule of the Ptolemies of Egypt

(Continued)

(Continued)

THE HASMONEAN PERIOD 166-63 B.C.

When this historical period began, the Jews were being greatly oppressed. The Ptolemies had been tolerant of the Jews and their religious practices but the Seleucid rulers were determined to force Hellenism on them. Copies of the Scriptures were ordered destroyed and laws were enforced with extreme cruelty. The oppressed Jews revolted, led by Judas the Maccabee.

THE ROMAN PERIOD 63 B.C.

In the year 63 B.C. Pompey, the Roman general, captured Jerusalem, and the provinces of Palestine became subject to Rome. The local government was entrusted part of the time to princes and the rest of the time to procurators who were appointed by the emperors. Herod the Great was ruler of all Palestine at the time of Christ's birth.

		Events
Rule of the Seleucids of Syria	180	
	170	175-164 Antiochus (IV) Epiphanes rules Syria; Judaism is prohibited
	160	167 Mattathias and his sons rebel against Antiochus; Maccabean revolt begins
	150	166-160 Judas Maccabeus's leadership
	140	143 Jonathan is high priest
	130	142 Tower of Jerusalem cleansed
	120	142-134 Simon becomes high priest; establishes Hasmonean dynasty
Hasmonean Dynasty	110	134-104 John Hyrcanus enlarges the independent Jewish state
	100	103 Aristobulus's rule
	90	102-76 Alexander Janneus's rule
	80	75-67 Rule of Salome Alexandra with Hyrcanus II as high priest
	70	
	60	66-63 Battle between Aristobulus II and Hyrcanus II
		63 Pompey invades Palestine; Roman rule begins
	50	63-40 Hyrcanus II rules but is subject to Rome
	40	40-37 Parthians conquer Jerusalem
Herod the Great rules as king; subject to Rome	30	37 Jerusalem besieged for six months
	20	32 Herod defeated
	10	19 Herod's temple begun
		16 Herod visits Agrippa
	10	4 Herod dies; Archelaus succeeds
	20	
	A.D. 30	

THE NEW COVENANT
commonly called

THE NEW TESTAMENT

OF OUR LORD AND SAVIOR JESUS CHRIST

NEW
REVISED
STANDARD
VERSION

THE GOSPEL ACCORDING TO
Matthew

Title and Background

The Gospel of Matthew was so named to distinguish it from the other Gospel accounts. There is only one gospel message, but four accounts of it. So we have here Matthew's version of the "good news" from God. Matthew's name means "gift of the LORD."

Author and Date of Writing

All four of the canonical Gospels are anonymous, but the early church fathers were unanimous in holding that Matthew was the author of this Gospel. Also known as Levi, he was a tax collector. The Gospel was most likely written shortly after the destruction of Jerusalem in A.D. 70.

Theme and Message

Matthew's main purpose is to demonstrate to his Jewish readers that Jesus is their Messiah. He quotes the Old Testament often and uses the phrase "kingdom of heaven" frequently. The whole Gospel is woven around five great discourses: (1) chapters 5-7; (2) chapter 10; (3) chapter 13; (4) chapter 18; (5) chapters 24-25.

Outline

 I. The Birth and Early Years of Jesus (1.1–2.23)
 II. The Beginnings of Jesus' Ministry (3.1–4.11)
 III. Jesus' Ministry in Galilee (4.12–14.12)
 IV. Jesus' Withdrawals From Galilee (14.13–17.20)
 V. Jesus' Last Ministry in Galilee (17.22–18.35)
 VI. Jesus' Ministry in Judea and Perea (19.1–20.34)
VII. Passion Week (21:1–27.66)
VIII. The Resurrection (28.1-20)

The Genealogy of Jesus the Messiah

1 An account of the genealogy[a] of Jesus the Messiah,[b] the son of David, the son of Abraham.

2 Abraham was the father of Isaac, and Isaac the father of Jacob, and Jacob the father of Judah and his brothers, 3 and Judah the father of Perez and Zerah by Tamar, and Perez the father of Hezron, and Hezron the father of Aram, 4 and Aram the father of Aminadab, and Aminadab the father of Nahshon, and Nahshon the father of Salmon, 5 and Salmon the father of Boaz by Rahab, and Boaz the father of Obed by Ruth, and Obed the father of Jesse, 6 and Jesse the father of King David.

And David was the father of Solomon by the wife of Uriah, 7 and Solomon the father of Rehoboam, and Rehoboam the father of Abijah, and Abijah the father of Asaph,[c] 8 and Asaph[c] the father of Jehoshaphat, and Jehoshaphat the father of Joram, and Joram the father of Uzziah, 9 and Uzziah the father of Jotham, and Jotham the father of Ahaz, and Ahaz the father of Hezekiah, 10 and Hezekiah the father of Manasseh, and Manasseh the father of Amos,[d] and Amos[d] the father of Josiah, 11 and Josiah

1.1 Ps 132.11; Isa 11.1; Lk 1.32; Jn 7.42; Acts 2.30; 13.23; Rom 1.3; Gen 12.3; 22.18; Gal 3.16 **1.2** Gen 21.2,3; 25.26; 29.35 **1.3** Gen 38.27ff; Ruth 4.18ff; 1 Chr 2.5, 9ff **1.6** 1 Sam 16.1; 17.1; 2 Sam 12.24 **1.7** 1 Chr 3.10 **1.10** 2 Kings 20.21; 1 Chr 3.13 **1.11** 2 Kings 24.14-16; Jer 27.20; 39.9; Dan 1.2

a Or *birth* b Or *Jesus Christ* c Other ancient authorities read *Asa* d Other ancient authorities read *Amon*

the father of Jechoniah and his brothers, at the time of the deportation to Babylon.

12 And after the deportation to Babylon: Jechoniah was the father of Salathiel, and Salathiel the father of Zerubbabel, 13 and Zerubbabel the father of Abiud, and Abiud the father of Eliakim, and Eliakim the father of Azor, 14 and Azor the father of Zadok, and Zadok the father of Achim, and Achim the father of Eliud, 15 and Eliud the father of Eleazar, and Eleazar the father of Matthan, and Matthan the father of Jacob, 16 and Jacob the father of Joseph the husband of Mary, of whom Jesus was born, who is called the Messiah. e

17 So all the generations from Abraham to David are fourteen generations; and from David to the deportation to Babylon, fourteen generations; and from the deportation to Babylon to the Messiah, e fourteen generations.

The Birth of Jesus the Messiah

18 Now the birth of Jesus the Messiah f took place in this way. When his mother Mary had been engaged to Joseph, but before they lived together, she was found to be with child from the Holy Spirit. 19 Her husband Joseph, being a righteous man and unwilling to expose her to public disgrace, planned to dismiss her quietly. 20 But just when he had resolved to do this, an angel of the Lord appeared to him in a dream and said, "Joseph, son of David, do not be afraid to take Mary as your wife, for the child conceived in her is from the Holy Spirit. 21 She will bear a son, and you are to name him Jesus, for he will save his people from their sins." 22 All this took place to fulfill what had been spoken by the Lord through the prophet:

23 "Look, the virgin shall
 conceive and bear a
 son,
 and they shall name him
 Emmanuel,"

which means, "God is with us." 24 When Joseph awoke from sleep, he did as the angel of the Lord commanded him; he took her as his wife, 25 but had no marital relations with her until she had borne a son; g and he named him Jesus.

The Visit of the Wise Men

2 In the time of King Herod, after Jesus was born in Bethlehem of Judea, wise men h from the East came to Jerusalem, 2 asking, "Where is the child who has been born king of the Jews? For we observed his star at its rising, i and have come to pay him homage." 3 When King Herod heard this, he was frightened, and all Jerusalem with him; 4 and calling together all the chief priests and scribes of the people, he inquired of them where the Messiah e was to be born. 5 They told him, "In Bethlehem of Judea; for so it has been written by the prophet:

6 'And you, Bethlehem, in the
 land of Judah,
 are by no means least
 among the rulers of
 Judah;
 for from you shall come a
 ruler
 who is to shepherd j my
 people Israel.' "

7 Then Herod secretly called for the wise men h and learned from them the exact time when the star had appeared. 8 Then he sent them to Bethlehem, saying, "Go and search diligently for the child; and when you have found him, bring me word so that I may also go and pay him homage." 9 When they had heard the king, they set out; and there, ahead of them, went the star that they had seen at its rising, i until it stopped over the place where the child was. 10 When they saw that the star had stopped, k they were overwhelmed with joy. 11 On entering the house, they saw the child with Mary his mother;

1.12
1 Chr 3.17,
19
1.16
Lk 1.27
1.17
vv. 11,12
1.19
Deut 24.1
1.21
Lk 2.21;
2.11;
Jn 1.29;
Acts 4.12;
13.3,38
1.23
Isa 7.14

1.25
Ex 13.2;
Lk 2.21
2.1
Lk 2.4-7;
1.5
2.2
Jer 23.5;
Zech 9.9;
Mk 15.2;
Jn 1.49
2.5
Jn 7.42
2.6
Mic 5.2;
Jn 21.16
2.11
Mt 1.18;
12.46;
Ps 72.10;
Isa 60.2

e Or the Christ f Or Jesus Christ
g Other ancient authorities read her firstborn
son h Or astrologers; Gk magi i Or in
the East j Or rule k Gk saw the star

and they knelt down and paid him homage. Then, opening their treasure chests, they offered him gifts of gold, frankincense, and myrrh. [12] And having been warned in a dream not to return to Herod, they left for their own country by another road.

The Escape to Egypt

13 Now after they had left, an angel of the Lord appeared to Joseph in a dream and said, "Get up, take the child and his mother, and flee to Egypt, and remain there until I tell you; for Herod is about to search for the child, to destroy him." [14] Then Joseph[1] got up, took the child and his mother by night, and went to Egypt, [15] and remained there until the death of Herod. This was to fulfill what had been spoken by the Lord through the prophet, "Out of Egypt I have called my son."

The Massacre of the Infants

16 When Herod saw that he had been tricked by the wise men,[m] he was infuriated, and he sent and killed all the children in and around Bethlehem who were two years old or under, according to the time that he had learned from the wise men.[m] [17] Then was fulfilled what had been spoken through the prophet Jeremiah:
[18] "A voice was heard in
　　Ramah,
　wailing and loud
　　lamentation,
Rachel weeping for her
　　children;
　she refused to be consoled,
　　because they are no
　　more."

The Return from Egypt

19 When Herod died, an angel of the Lord suddenly appeared in a dream to Joseph in Egypt and said, [20] "Get up, take the child and his mother, and go to the land of Israel, for those who were seeking the child's life are dead." [21] Then Joseph[1] got up, took the child and his mother, and went to the land of Israel. [22] But when he heard that

Archelaus was ruling over Judea in place of his father Herod, he was afraid to go there. And after being warned in a dream, he went away to the district of Galilee. [23] There he made his home in a town called Nazareth, so that what had been spoken through the prophets might be fulfilled, "He will be called a Nazorean."

The Proclamation of John the Baptist

3 In those days John the Baptist appeared in the wilderness of Judea, proclaiming, [2] "Repent, for the kingdom of heaven has come near."[n] [3] This is the one of whom the prophet Isaiah spoke when he said,
　"The voice of one crying out
　　in the wilderness:
　'Prepare the way of the Lord,
　　make his paths straight.' "
[4] Now John wore clothing of camel's hair with a leather belt around his waist, and his food was locusts and wild honey. [5] Then the people of Jerusalem and all Judea were going out to him, and all the region along the Jordan, [6] and they were baptized by him in the river Jordan, confessing their sins.

7 But when he saw many Pharisees and Sadducees coming for baptism, he said to them, "You brood of vipers! Who warned you to flee from the wrath to come? [8] Bear fruit worthy of repentance. [9] Do not presume to say to yourselves, 'We have Abraham as our ancestor'; for I tell you, God is able from these stones to raise up children to Abraham. [10] Even now the ax is lying at the root of the trees; every tree therefore that does not bear good fruit is cut down and thrown into the fire.

11 "I baptize you with[o] water for repentance, but one who is more powerful than I is coming after me; I am not worthy to carry his sandals. He will baptize you with[o] the Holy Spirit and fire. [12] His win-

2.12
Mt 2.22;
Acts 10.22;
Heb 11.7
2.13
v. 19
2.14
Hos 11.1;
Ex 4.22
2.18
Jer 31.15
2.19
Mt 1.20;
v. 13
2.22
v. 12;
Mt 3.13;
Lk 2.39

2.23
Lk 1.26;
Isa 11.1;
Mk 1.24
3.2
Dan 2.44;
Mk 4.7; 10.7
3.3
Isa 40.3;
Mk 1.3;
Lk 3.4;
Jn 1.23;
Lk 1.76
3.4
2 Kings 1.8;
Zech 13.4;
Lev 11.22
3.6
Acts 19.4,18
3.7
Mt 12.34;
23.33;
Rom 5.9;
1 Thes 1.10
3.8
Acts 26.20
3.9
Jn 8.33,39;
Acts 13.26;
Rom 4.1,11,16
3.10
Mt 7.19
3.11
Acts 1.5;
11.16; 19.4;
Isa 4.4;
Acts 2.3,4
3.12
Mal 3.3;
Mt 13.30

[1] Gk he 　[m] Or astrologers; Gk magi
[n] Or is at hand 　[o] Or in

nowing fork is in his hand, and he will clear his threshing floor and will gather his wheat into the granary; but the chaff he will burn with unquenchable fire."

The Baptism of Jesus

13 Then Jesus came from Galilee to John at the Jordan, to be baptized by him. [14] John would have prevented him, saying, "I need to be baptized by you, and do you come to me?" [15] But Jesus answered him, "Let it be so now; for it is proper for us in this way to fulfill all righteousness." Then he consented. [16] And when Jesus had been baptized, just as he came up from the water, suddenly the heavens were opened to him and he saw the Spirit of God descending like a dove and alighting on him. [17] And a voice from heaven said, "This is my Son, the Beloved,[p] with whom I am well pleased."

The Temptation of Jesus

4 Then Jesus was led up by the Spirit into the wilderness to be tempted by the devil. [2] He fasted forty days and forty nights, and afterwards he was famished. [3] The tempter came and said to him, "If you are the Son of God, command these stones to become loaves of bread." [4] But he answered, "It is written,

'One does not live by bread
 alone,
but by every word that
 comes from the mouth
 of God.' "

5 Then the devil took him to the holy city and placed him on the pinnacle of the temple, [6] saying to him, "If you are the Son of God, throw yourself down; for it is written,

'He will command his angels
 concerning you,'
and 'On their hands they
 will bear you up,
so that you will not dash
 your foot against a
 stone.' "

[7] Jesus said to him, "Again it is

written, 'Do not put the Lord your God to the test.' "

8 Again, the devil took him to a very high mountain and showed him all the kingdoms of the world and their splendor; [9] and he said to him, "All these I will give you, if you will fall down and worship me." [10] Jesus said to him, "Away with you, Satan! for it is written,

'Worship the Lord your God,
 and serve only him.' "

[11] Then the devil left him, and suddenly angels came and waited on him.

Jesus Begins His Ministry in Galilee

12 Now when Jesus[q] heard that John had been arrested, he withdrew to Galilee. [13] He left Nazareth and made his home in Capernaum by the sea, in the territory of Zebulun and Naphtali, [14] so that what had been spoken through the prophet Isaiah might be fulfilled:

[15] "Land of Zebulun, land of
 Naphtali,
on the road by the sea,
 across the Jordan,
 Galilee of the
 Gentiles—
[16] the people who sat in
 darkness
have seen a great light,
and for those who sat in the
 region and shadow of
 death
light has dawned."

[17] From that time Jesus began to proclaim, "Repent, for the kingdom of heaven has come near."[r]

Jesus Calls the First Disciples

18 As he walked by the Sea of Galilee, he saw two brothers, Simon, who is called Peter, and Andrew his brother, casting a net into the sea—for they were fishermen. [19] And he said to them, "Follow me, and I will make you fish for people." [20] Immediately they left their nets and followed him. [21] As he went from there, he saw two other

3.13
Jn 1.31-34
3.16
Isa 11.2;
42.1;
Jn 1.32
3.17
Ps 2.7;
Mt 12.18;
17.5;
Mk 9.7;
Lk 9.35
4.2
Ex 34.28;
1 Kings 19.8
4.3
1 Thes 3.5
4.4
Deut 8.3
4.5
Neh 11.1;
Dan 9.24;
Mt 27.53;
Rev 21.10
4.6
Ps 91.11,12
4.7
Deut 6.16

4.10
1 Chr 21.1;
Deut 6.13
4.11
Mt 26.53;
Lk 22.43;
Heb 1.14
4.15
Isa 9.1,2
4.16
Isa 42.7;
Lk 2.32
4.17
Mt 3.2; 10.7
4.18
Jn 1.35-42
4.20
Mt 10.28;
Lk 18.28

p Or *my beloved Son* q Gk *he* r Or *is at hand*

brothers, James son of Zebedee and his brother John, in the boat with their father Zebedee, mending their nets, and he called them. [22] Immediately they left the boat and their father, and followed him.

Jesus Ministers to Crowds of People

23 Jesus[s] went throughout Galilee, teaching in their synagogues and proclaiming the good news[t] of the kingdom and curing every disease and every sickness among the people. [24] So his fame spread throughout all Syria, and they brought to him all the sick, those who were afflicted with various diseases and pains, demoniacs, epileptics, and paralytics, and he cured them. [25] And great crowds followed him from Galilee, the Decapolis, Jerusalem, Judea, and from beyond the Jordan.

The Beatitudes

5 When Jesus[u] saw the crowds, he went up the mountain; and after he sat down, his disciples came to him. [2] Then he began to speak, and taught them, saying:

3 "Blessed are the poor in spirit, for theirs is the kingdom of heaven.

4 "Blessed are those who mourn, for they will be comforted.

5 "Blessed are the meek, for they will inherit the earth.

6 "Blessed are those who hunger and thirst for righteousness, for they will be filled.

7 "Blessed are the merciful, for they will receive mercy.

8 "Blessed are the pure in heart, for they will see God.

9 "Blessed are the peacemakers, for they will be called children of God.

10 "Blessed are those who are persecuted for righteousness' sake, for theirs is the kingdom of heaven.

11 "Blessed are you when people revile you and persecute you and utter all kinds of evil against you falsely[v] on my account. [12] Rejoice and be glad, for your reward is great in heaven, for in the same way they persecuted the prophets who were before you.

Salt and Light

13 "You are the salt of the earth; but if salt has lost its taste, how can its saltiness be restored? It is no longer good for anything, but is thrown out and trampled under foot.

14 "You are the light of the world. A city built on a hill cannot be hid. [15] No one after lighting a lamp puts it under the bushel basket, but on the lampstand, and it gives light to all in the house. [16] In the same way, let your light shine before others, so that they may see your good works and give glory to your Father in heaven.

The Law and the Prophets

17 "Do not think that I have come to abolish the law or the prophets; I have come not to abolish but to fulfill. [18] For truly I tell you, until heaven and earth pass away, not one letter,[w] not one stroke of a letter, will pass from the law until all is accomplished. [19] Therefore, whoever breaks[x] one of the least of these commandments, and teaches others to do the same, will be called least in the kingdom of heaven; but whoever does them and teaches them will be called great in the kingdom of heaven. [20] For I tell you, unless your righteousness exceeds that of the scribes and Pharisees, you will never enter the kingdom of heaven.

Concerning Anger

21 "You have heard that it was said to those of ancient times, 'You shall not murder'; and 'whoever murders shall be liable to judgment.' [22] But I say to you that if you are angry with a brother or sister,[y] you will be liable to judgment; and if you insult[z] a brother or sister,[a] you will be liable to the council; and if you say, 'You fool,' you will

Cross references (center column)

4.23
Mk 1.39;
Lk 4.15,44;
Mt 9.35;
13.54;
Mk 1.21;
1.34
4.24
Lk 2.2;
Mt 8.16,28, 33;
Mk 1.32;
Lk 8.36;
Mt 17.15;
8.6; 9.2,6
4.25
Mk 3.7,8;
Lk 6.17
5.1
Mk 3.13;
Jn 6.3
5.3
Mk 10.14;
Lk 22.29
5.4
Isa 61.2,3
5.6
Isa 55.1,2
5.8
Heb 12.14;
1 Jn 3.2
5.9
Rom 8.14
5.10
1 Pet 3.14
5.11
1 Pet 4.14
5.12
Acts 7.52;
1 Thes 2.15;
Jas 5.10
5.13
Mk 9.50;
Lk 14.34,35
5.14
Phil 2.15
5.15
Mk 4.21;
Lk 8.16
5.16
1 Pet 2.12
5.17
Rom 3.31;
Gal 3.24
5.18
Lk 16.17
5.19
Jas 2.10
5.21f
Ex 20.13;
Deut 5.17
5.22
1 Jn 3.15;
Jas 2.20

Footnotes

[s] Gk *He*　[t] Gk *gospel*　[u] Gk *he*
[v] Other ancient authorities lack *falsely*
[w] Gk *one iota*　[x] Or *annuls*　[y] Gk *a brother*; other ancient authorities add *without cause*　[z] Gk *say Raca to* (an obscure term of abuse)　[a] Gk *a brother*

be liable to the hell[b] of fire. 23 So when you are offering your gift at the altar, if you remember that your brother or sister[c] has something against you, 24 leave your gift there before the altar and go; first be reconciled to your brother or sister,[c] and then come and offer your gift. 25 Come to terms quickly with your accuser while you are on the way to court[d] with him, or your accuser may hand you over to the judge, and the judge to the guard, and you will be thrown into prison. 26 Truly I tell you, you will never get out until you have paid the last penny.

Concerning Adultery

27 "You have heard that it was said, 'You shall not commit adultery.' 28 But I say to you that everyone who looks at a woman with lust has already committed adultery with her in his heart. 29 If your right eye causes you to sin, tear it out and throw it away; it is better for you to lose one of your members than for your whole body to be thrown into hell.[b] 30 And if your right hand causes you to sin, cut it off and throw it away; it is better for you to lose one of your members than for your whole body to go into hell.[b]

Concerning Divorce

31 "It was also said, 'Whoever divorces his wife, let him give her a certificate of divorce.' 32 But I say to you that anyone who divorces his wife, except on the ground of unchastity, causes her to commit adultery; and whoever marries a divorced woman commits adultery.

Concerning Oaths

33 "Again, you have heard that it was said to those of ancient times, 'You shall not swear falsely, but carry out the vows you have made to the Lord.' 34 But I say to you, Do not swear at all, either by heaven, for it is the throne of God, 35 or by the earth, for it is his footstool, or by Jerusalem, for it is the city of the great King. 36 And do not swear by your head, for you cannot

make one hair white or black. 37 Let your word be 'Yes, Yes' or 'No, No'; anything more than this comes from the evil one.[e]

Concerning Retaliation

38 "You have heard that it was said, 'An eye for an eye and a tooth for a tooth.' 39 But I say to you, Do not resist an evildoer. But if anyone strikes you on the right cheek, turn the other also; 40 and if anyone wants to sue you and take your coat, give your cloak as well; 41 and if anyone forces you to go one mile, go also the second mile. 42 Give to everyone who begs from you, and do not refuse anyone who wants to borrow from you.

Love for Enemies

43 "You have heard that it was said, 'You shall love your neighbor and hate your enemy.' 44 But I say to you, Love your enemies and pray for those who persecute you, 45 so that you may be children of your Father in heaven; for he makes his sun rise on the evil and on the good, and sends rain on the righteous and on the unrighteous. 46 For if you love those who love you, what reward do you have? Do not even the tax collectors do the same? 47 And if you greet only your brothers and sisters,[f] what more are you doing than others? Do not even the Gentiles do the same? 48 Be perfect, therefore, as your heavenly Father is perfect.

Concerning Almsgiving

6 "Beware of practicing your piety before others in order to be seen by them; for then you have no reward from your Father in heaven.

2 "So whenever you give alms, do not sound a trumpet before you, as the hypocrites do in the synagogues and in the streets, so that they may be praised by others. Truly I tell you, they have received their reward. 3 But when you give alms, do not let your left hand know what your right hand is do-

5.23
Mt 8.4;
23.19
5.25
Prov 25.8;
Lk 12.57-59
5.27
Ex 20.14;
Deut 5.18
5.28
Job 31.1;
Prov 6.25
5.29
Mt 18.9;
Mk 9.43-47
5.31
Deut 24.1-4;
Mk 10.11,
12;
Lk 16.18
5.33
Lev 19.12;
Num 30.2;
Deut 23.21;
Mt 23.16
5.34
Jas 5.12;
Isa 66.1

5.38
Ex 21.24;
Lev 24.20;
Deut 19.21
5.39
Prov 24.29;
Lk 6.29;
Rom 12.17,
19;
1 Cor 6.7;
1 Pet 3.9
5.42
Deut 15.8;
Lk 6.30
5.43
Lev 19.18;
Deut 23.6;
Ps 41.10
5.44
Rom 12.14;
Acts 7.60;
1 Cor 4.12;
1 Pet 2.23
5.45
Job 25.3
5.48
Lev 19.2;
Col 1.28;
Jas 1.4
6.1
Mt 23.5
6.2
Rom 12.8

[b] Gk *Gehenna* [c] Gk *your brother* [d] Gk lacks *to court* [e] Or *evil* [f] Gk *your brothers*

ing, [4]so that your alms may be done in secret; and your Father who sees in secret will reward you. [g]

Concerning Prayer

5 "And whenever you pray, do not be like the hypocrites; for they love to stand and pray in the synagogues and at the street corners, so that they may be seen by others. Truly I tell you, they have received their reward. [6]But whenever you pray, go into your room and shut the door and pray to your Father who is in secret; and your Father who sees in secret will reward you. [g]

7 "When you are praying, do not heap up empty phrases as the Gentiles do; for they think that they will be heard because of their many words. [8]Do not be like them, for your Father knows what you need before you ask him.

9 "Pray then in this way:
 Our Father in heaven,
 hallowed be your name.
[10] Your kingdom come.
 Your will be done,
 on earth as it is in
 heaven.
[11] Give us this day our daily
 bread. [h]
[12] And forgive us our debts,
 as we also have forgiven
 our debtors.
[13] And do not bring us to the
 time of trial, [i]
 but rescue us from the
 evil one. [j]
[14]For if you forgive others their trespasses, your heavenly Father will also forgive you; [15]but if you do not forgive others, neither will your Father forgive your trespasses.

Concerning Fasting

16 "And whenever you fast, do not look dismal, like the hypocrites, for they disfigure their faces so as to show others that they are fasting. Truly I tell you, they have received their reward. [17]But when you fast, put oil on your head and wash your face, [18]so that your fasting may be seen not by others but

by your Father who is in secret; and your Father who sees in secret will reward you. [g]

Concerning Treasures

19 "Do not store up for yourselves treasures on earth, where moth and rust [k] consume and where thieves break in and steal; [20]but store up for yourselves treasures in heaven, where neither moth nor rust [k] consumes and where thieves do not break in and steal. [21]For where your treasure is, there your heart will be also.

The Sound Eye

22 "The eye is the lamp of the body. So, if your eye is healthy, your whole body will be full of light; [23]but if your eye is unhealthy, your whole body will be full of darkness. If then the light in you is darkness, how great is the darkness!

Serving Two Masters

24 "No one can serve two masters; for a slave will either hate the one and love the other, or be devoted to the one and despise the other. You cannot serve God and wealth. [l]

Do Not Worry

25 "Therefore I tell you, do not worry about your life, what you will eat or what you will drink, [m] or about your body, what you will wear. Is not life more than food, and the body more than clothing? [26]Look at the birds of the air; they neither sow nor reap nor gather into barns, and yet your heavenly Father feeds them. Are you not of more value than they? [27]And can any of you by worrying add a single hour to your span of life? [n] [28]And why do you worry about clothing? Consider the lilies of the field, how they grow; they neither toil nor

6.4
Col 3.23,24
6.5
Mk 11.25;
Lk 18.10-14
6.6
2 Kings 4.33
6.7
Eccl 5.2;
1 Kings 18.26, 29
6.10
Mt 26.39,42
6.11
Prov 30.8
6.12
Mt 18.21
6.13
Jn 17.15;
2 Thes 3.3;
Jas 1.13
6.14
Mk 11.25, 26;
Eph 4.32;
Col 3.13
6.15
Mt 18.35
6.16
Isa 58.5
6.18
vv. 4,6

6.19
Prov 23.4;
1 Tim 6.17
Heb 13.5;
Jas 5.1
6.20
Lk 12.33,34;
18.22;
1 Tim 6.19;
1 Pet 1.4
6.22
Mt 20.15;
Mk 7.22;
Lk 11.34-36
6.24
Lk 16.13
6.25
Ps 55.22;
Phil 4.6;
1 Pet 5.7
6.26
Job 38.41;
Ps 147.9;
Lk 12.24
6.27
Ps 39.5

g Other ancient authorities add *openly* h Or *our bread for tomorrow* i Or *us into temptation* j Or *from evil.* Other ancient authorities add, in some form, *For the kingdom and the power and the glory are yours forever. Amen.* k Gk *eating* l Gk *mammon* m Other ancient authorities lack *or what you will drink* n Or *add one cubit to your height*

spin, [29] yet I tell you, even Solomon in all his glory was not clothed like one of these. [30] But if God so clothes the grass of the field, which is alive today and tomorrow is thrown into the oven, will he not much more clothe you — you of little faith? [31] Therefore do not worry, saying, 'What will we eat?' or 'What will we drink?' or 'What will we wear?' [32] For it is the Gentiles who strive for all these things; and indeed your heavenly Father knows that you need all these things. [33] But strive first for the kingdom of God[o] and his[p] righteousness, and all these things will be given to you as well.

34 "So do not worry about tomorrow, for tomorrow will bring worries of its own. Today's trouble is enough for today.

Judging Others

7 "Do not judge, so that you may not be judged. [2] For with the judgment you make you will be judged, and the measure you give will be the measure you get. [3] Why do you see the speck in your neighbor's[q] eye, but do not notice the log in your own eye? [4] Or how can you say to your neighbor,[r] 'Let me take the speck out of your eye,' while the log is in your own eye? [5] You hypocrite, first take the log out of your own eye, and then you will see clearly to take the speck out of your neighbor's[q] eye.

Profaning the Holy

6 "Do not give what is holy to dogs; and do not throw your pearls before swine, or they will trample them under foot and turn and maul you.

Ask, Search, Knock

7 "Ask, and it will be given you; search, and you will find; knock, and the door will be opened for you. [8] For everyone who asks receives, and everyone who searches finds, and for everyone who knocks, the door will be opened. [9] Is there anyone among you who, if your child asks for bread, will give a stone? [10] Or if the child asks for a

6.29
1 Kings 10.4-7
6.30
Mt 8.26;
14.31; 16.8
6.32
v. 8
6.33
Mt 19.28;
Mk 10.29,
30;
Lk 18.29,30
7.1
Mk 4.24;
Rom 2.1;
14.10;
1 Cor 4.3
7.6
Prov 9.7,8;
Acts 13.45
7.7
Mk 11.24;
Jn 15.7;
16.23,24;
Jas 4.3;
1 Jn 3.22;
5.14,15
7.8
Jer 29.12,13

7.12
Lk 6.31;
Rom 13.8-10;
Gal 5.14
7.13
Lk 13.24
7.15
Jer 23.16;
Mt 24.11,
24;
Mk 13.22;
2 Pet 2.1;
1 Jn 4.1;
Rev 16.13;
19.20; 20.10;
Acts 20.29
7.16
Mt 12.33;
Mk 3.10;
Jas 3.12
7.19
Mt 3.10;
Lk 3.9;
Jn 15.2,6
7.21
Hos 8.2
Mt 25.11,
12;
Acts 19.13;
Rom 2.13;
Jas 1.22
7.22
Mt 25.12;
Lk 13.25-27
7.23
Ps 6.8;
Mt 25.12;
Lk 13.25,27
7.24
Lk 6.47-49;
Jas 1.22-25

fish, will give a snake? [11] If you then, who are evil, know how to give good gifts to your children, how much more will your Father in heaven give good things to those who ask him!

The Golden Rule

12 "In everything do to others as you would have them do to you; for this is the law and the prophets.

The Narrow Gate

13 "Enter through the narrow gate; for the gate is wide and the road is easy[s] that leads to destruction, and there are many who take it. [14] For the gate is narrow and the road is hard that leads to life, and there are few who find it.

A Tree and Its Fruit

15 "Beware of false prophets, who come to you in sheep's clothing but inwardly are ravenous wolves. [16] You will know them by their fruits. Are grapes gathered from thorns, or figs from thistles? [17] In the same way, every good tree bears good fruit, but the bad tree bears bad fruit. [18] A good tree cannot bear bad fruit, nor can a bad tree bear good fruit. [19] Every tree that does not bear good fruit is cut down and thrown into the fire. [20] Thus you will know them by their fruits.

Concerning Self-Deception

21 "Not everyone who says to me, 'Lord, Lord,' will enter the kingdom of heaven, but only the one who does the will of my Father in heaven. [22] On that day many will say to me, 'Lord, Lord, did we not prophesy in your name, and cast out demons in your name, and do many deeds of power in your name?' [23] Then I will declare to them, 'I never knew you; go away from me, you evildoers.'

Hearers and Doers

24 "Everyone then who hears these words of mine and acts on

o Other ancient authorities lack *of God*
p Or *its* q Gk *brother's* r Gk *brother*
s Other ancient authorities read *for the road is wide and easy*

them will be like a wise man who built his house on rock. 25 The rain fell, the floods came, and the winds blew and beat on that house, but it did not fall, because it had been founded on rock. 26 And everyone who hears these words of mine and does not act on them will be like a foolish man who built his house on sand. 27 The rain fell, and the floods came, and the winds blew and beat against that house, and it fell — and great was its fall!"

28 Now when Jesus had finished saying these things, the crowds were astounded at his teaching, 29 for he taught them as one having authority, and not as their scribes.

Jesus Cleanses a Leper

8 When Jesus^t had come down from the mountain, great crowds followed him; 2 and there was a leper^u who came to him and knelt before him, saying, "Lord, if you choose, you can make me clean." 3 He stretched out his hand and touched him, saying, "I do choose. Be made clean!" Immediately his leprosy^u was cleansed. 4 Then Jesus said to him, "See that you say nothing to anyone; but go, show yourself to the priest, and offer the gift that Moses commanded, as a testimony to them."

Jesus Heals a Centurion's Servant

5 When he entered Capernaum, a centurion came to him, appealing to him 6 and saying, "Lord, my servant is lying at home paralyzed, in terrible distress." 7 And he said to him, "I will come and cure him." 8 The centurion answered, "Lord, I am not worthy to have you come under my roof; but only speak the word, and my servant will be healed. 9 For I also am a man under authority, with soldiers under me; and I say to one, 'Go,' and he goes, and to another, 'Come,' and he comes, and to my slave, 'Do this,' and the slave does it." 10 When Jesus heard him, he was amazed and said to those who followed

him, "Truly I tell you, in no one^v in Israel have I found such faith. 11 I tell you, many will come from east and west and will eat with Abraham and Isaac and Jacob in the kingdom of heaven, 12 while the heirs of the kingdom will be thrown into the outer darkness, where there will be weeping and gnashing of teeth." 13 And to the centurion Jesus said, "Go; let it be done for you according to your faith." And the servant was healed in that hour.

Jesus Heals Many at Peter's House

14 When Jesus entered Peter's house, he saw his mother-in-law lying in bed with a fever; 15 he touched her hand, and the fever left her, and she got up and began to serve him. 16 That evening they brought to him many who were possessed with demons; and he cast out the spirits with a word, and cured all who were sick. 17 This was to fulfill what had been spoken through the prophet Isaiah, "He took our infirmities and bore our diseases."

Would-Be Followers of Jesus

18 Now when Jesus saw great crowds around him, he gave orders to go over to the other side. 19 A scribe then approached and said, "Teacher, I will follow you wherever you go." 20 And Jesus said to him, "Foxes have holes, and birds of the air have nests; but the Son of Man has nowhere to lay his head." 21 Another of his disciples said to him, "Lord, first let me go and bury my father." 22 But Jesus said to him, "Follow me, and let the dead bury their own dead."

Jesus Stills the Storm

23 And when he got into the boat, his disciples followed him. 24 A windstorm arose on the sea, so great that the boat was being swamped by the waves; but he was asleep. 25 And they went and woke

7.28
Mt 11.1;
13.53; 19.1;
26.1; 13.54;
Mk 1.22;
6.2;
Lk 4.32;
Jn 7.46
8.2
Mt 9.18;
15.25; 18.26;
20.20;
Jn 9.38
8.4
Lev 14.3,4,
10;
Mk 3.12;
5.43; 7.36;
8.30; 9.9
8.8
Ps 107.20

8.11
Isa 49.12;
59.19;
Mal 1.11;
Lk 13.29;
Acts 10.45
8.12
Mt 13.42,
50; 22.13;
25.30;
Lk 13.28
8.14
1 Cor 9.5
8.17
Isa 53.4
8.18
Mk 4.35;
Lk 8.22
8.22
Mt 9.9;
Jn 1.43;
21.19

^t Gk he ^u The terms *leper* and *leprosy* can refer to several diseases ^v Other ancient authorities read *Truly I tell you, not even*

him up, saying, "Lord, save us! We are perishing!" 26 And he said to them, "Why are you afraid, you of little faith?" Then he got up and rebuked the winds and the sea; and there was a dead calm. 27 They were amazed, saying, "What sort of man is this, that even the winds and the sea obey him?"

Jesus Heals the Gadarene Demoniacs

28 When he came to the other side, to the country of the Gadarenes,^w two demoniacs coming out of the tombs met him. They were so fierce that no one could pass that way. 29 Suddenly they shouted, "What have you to do with us, Son of God? Have you come here to torment us before the time?" 30 Now a large herd of swine was feeding at some distance from them. 31 The demons begged him, "If you cast us out, send us into the herd of swine." 32 And he said to them, "Go!" So they came out and entered the swine; and suddenly, the whole herd rushed down the steep bank into the sea and perished in the water. 33 The swineherds ran off, and on going into the town, they told the whole story about what had happened to the demoniacs. 34 Then the whole town came out to meet Jesus; and when they saw him, they begged him to leave their neighborhood. 1 And after getting into a boat he crossed the sea and came to his own town.

Jesus Heals a Paralytic

2 And just then some people were carrying a paralyzed man lying on a bed. When Jesus saw their faith, he said to the paralytic, "Take heart, son; your sins are forgiven." 3 Then some of the scribes said to themselves, "This man is blaspheming." 4 But Jesus, perceiving their thoughts, said, "Why do you think evil in your hearts? 5 For which is easier, to say, 'Your sins are forgiven,' or to say, 'Stand up and walk'? 6 But so that you may know that the Son of Man has au-

8.26
Mt. 6.30;
14.31; 16.8;
Ps 65.7;
89.9; 107.29
8.29
Judg 11.12;
2 Sam 16.10;
Mk 1.24;
Jn 2.4
8.34
see
1 Kings 17.18;
Lk 5.8;
Acts 16.39
9.1
Mt 4.13
9.2
Mt 9.22;
Mk 6.50;
10.49;
Acts 23.11
9.4
Mt 12.25;
Lk 6.8;
9.47; 11.17

9.8
Mt 5.16;
15.31;
Lk 7.16;
13.13; 17.15;
23.47;
Jn 15.8;
Acts 4.21;
11.18; 21.20
9.11
Mt 11.19;
Gal 2.15
9.13
Hos 6.6;
Mic 6.6-8;
Mt 12.7;
1 Tim 1.15
9.14
Lk 18.12
9.15
Jn 3.29;
Acts 13.2,3;
14.23
9.16
Lk 5.36

thority on earth to forgive sins"— he then said to the paralytic— "Stand up, take your bed and go to your home." 7 And he stood up and went to his home. 8 When the crowds saw it, they were filled with awe, and they glorified God, who had given such authority to human beings.

The Call of Matthew

9 As Jesus was walking along, he saw a man called Matthew sitting at the tax booth; and he said to him, "Follow me." And he got up and followed him.

10 And as he sat at dinner^x in the house, many tax collectors and sinners came and were sitting^y with him and his disciples. 11 When the Pharisees saw this, they said to his disciples, "Why does your teacher eat with tax collectors and sinners?" 12 But when he heard this, he said, "Those who are well have no need of a physician, but those who are sick. 13 Go and learn what this means, 'I desire mercy, not sacrifice.' For I have come to call not the righteous but sinners."

The Question about Fasting

14 Then the disciples of John came to him, saying, "Why do we and the Pharisees fast often,^z but your disciples do not fast?" 15 And Jesus said to them, "The wedding guests cannot mourn as long as the bridegroom is with them, can they? The days will come when the bridegroom is taken away from them, and then they will fast. 16 No one sews a piece of unshrunk cloth on an old cloak, for the patch pulls away from the cloak, and a worse tear is made. 17 Neither is new wine put into old wineskins; otherwise, the skins burst, and the wine is spilled, and the skins are destroyed; but new wine is put into fresh wineskins, and so both are preserved."

^w Other ancient authorities read *Gergesenes*; others, *Gerasenes* ^x Gk *reclined*
^y Gk *were reclining* ^z Other ancient authorities lack *often*

A Girl Restored to Life and a Woman Healed

18 While he was saying these things to them, suddenly a leader of the synagogue[a] came in and knelt before him, saying, "My daughter has just died; but come and lay your hand on her, and she will live." 19 And Jesus got up and followed him, with his disciples. 20 Then suddenly a woman who had been suffering from hemorrhages for twelve years came up behind him, and touched the fringe of his cloak, 21 for she said to herself, "If I only touch his cloak, I will be made well." 22 Jesus turned, and seeing her he said, "Take heart, daughter; your faith has made you well." And instantly the woman was made well. 23 When Jesus came to the leader's house and saw the flute players and the crowd making a commotion, 24 he said, "Go away; for the girl is not dead but sleeping." And they laughed at him. 25 But when the crowd had been put outside, he went in and took her by the hand, and the girl got up. 26 And the report of this spread throughout that district.

Jesus Heals Two Blind Men

27 As Jesus went on from there, two blind men followed him, crying loudly, "Have mercy on us, Son of David!" 28 When he entered the house, the blind men came to him; and Jesus said to them, "Do you believe that I am able to do this?" They said to him, "Yes, Lord." 29 Then he touched their eyes and said, "According to your faith let it be done to you." 30 And their eyes were opened. Then Jesus sternly ordered them, "See that no one knows of this." 31 But they went away and spread the news about him throughout that district.

Jesus Heals One Who Was Mute

32 After they had gone away, a demoniac who was mute was brought to him. 33 And when the demon had been cast out, the one who had been mute spoke; and the crowds were amazed and said,

"Never has anything like this been seen in Israel." 34 But the Pharisees said, "By the ruler of the demons he casts out the demons."[b]

The Harvest Is Great, the Laborers Few

35 Then Jesus went about all the cities and villages, teaching in their synagogues, and proclaiming the good news of the kingdom, and curing every disease and every sickness. 36 When he saw the crowds, he had compassion for them, because they were harassed and helpless, like sheep without a shepherd. 37 Then he said to his disciples, "The harvest is plentiful, but the laborers are few; 38 therefore ask the Lord of the harvest to send out laborers into his harvest."

The Twelve Apostles

10 Then Jesus[c] summoned his twelve disciples and gave them authority over unclean spirits, to cast them out, and to cure every disease and every sickness. 2 These are the names of the twelve apostles: first, Simon, also known as Peter, and his brother Andrew; James son of Zebedee, and his brother John; 3 Philip and Bartholomew; Thomas and Matthew the tax collector; James son of Alphaeus, and Thaddaeus;[d] 4 Simon the Cananaean, and Judas Iscariot, the one who betrayed him.

The Mission of the Twelve

5 These twelve Jesus sent out with the following instructions: "Go nowhere among the Gentiles, and enter no town of the Samaritans, 6 but go rather to the lost sheep of the house of Israel. 7 As you go, proclaim the good news, 'The kingdom of heaven has come near.'[e] 8 Cure the sick, raise the dead, cleanse the lepers,[f] cast out demons. You received without payment; give without payment. 9 Take

9.18 Mt 8.2; Jn 9.38
9.20 Mt 14.36; Mk 3.10
9.21 see Lk 6.19
9.22 Mk 10.52; Lk 7.50; 17.19; 18.42; Mt 9.9; 15.28
9.23 see 2 Chr 35.25; Jer 9.17; 16.6; Ezek 24.17
9.24 Jn 11.13; Acts 20.10
9.27 Mt 15.22; Mk 10.47, 48; Lk 18.38,39
9.29 see v. 22; Mt 8.13
9.30 Mt 8.4; 17.9
9.31 Mk 7.36
9.32 Mt 12.22-24; Lk 11.14
9.34 Mt 12.24; Mk 3.22; Lk 11.15
9.35 Mk 6.6; Lk 13.22
9.36 Mk 6.34; Ezek 34.5; Zech 10.2
9.37 Lk 10.2; Jn 4.35
10.1 Mk 3.13-15; Lk 6.14-16; Acts 1.13
10.4 Lk 6.15; Acts 1.13; Jn 13.26
10.5 Lk 9.52; Acts 8.5,25
10.6 Mt 15.24; Ezek 34.5
10.7 Mt 3.2; Lk 10.9

a Gk lacks *of the synagogue*　b Other ancient authorities lack this verse　c Gk *he*　d Other ancient authorities read *Lebbaeus*, or *Lebbaeus called Thaddaeus*　e *Or is at hand*　f The terms *leper* and *leprosy* can refer to several diseases

no gold, or silver, or copper in your belts, 10 no bag for your journey, or two tunics, or sandals, or a staff; for laborers deserve their food. 11 Whatever town or village you enter, find out who in it is worthy, and stay there until you leave. 12 As you enter the house, greet it. 13 If the house is worthy, let your peace come upon it; but if it is not worthy, let your peace return to you. 14 If anyone will not welcome you or listen to your words, shake off the dust from your feet as you leave that house or town. 15 Truly I tell you, it will be more tolerable for the land of Sodom and Gomorrah on the day of judgment than for that town.

Coming Persecutions

16 "See, I am sending you out like sheep into the midst of wolves; so be wise as serpents and innocent as doves. 17 Beware of them, for they will hand you over to councils and flog you in their synagogues; 18 and you will be dragged before governors and kings because of me, as a testimony to them and the Gentiles. 19 When they hand you over, do not worry about how you are to speak or what you are to say; for what you are to say will be given to you at that time; 20 for it is not you who speak, but the Spirit of your Father speaking through you. 21 Brother will betray brother to death, and a father his child, and children will rise against parents and have them put to death; 22 and you will be hated by all because of my name. But the one who endures to the end will be saved. 23 When they persecute you in one town, flee to the next; for truly I tell you, you will not have gone through all the towns of Israel before the Son of Man comes.

24 "A disciple is not above the teacher, nor a slave above the master; 25 it is enough for the disciple to be like the teacher, and the slave like the master. If they have called the master of the house Beelzebul, how much more will they malign those of his household!

10.10
1 Cor 9.7;
1 Tim 5.18
10.14
Lk 10.10,11;
Acts 13.51;
18.6
10.15
Mt 11.22
10.16
Lk 10.3;
Rom 16.19
10.18
Acts 25.24-26
10.20
2 Sam 23.2;
Jn 16.7-11;
Acts 4.8
10.22
Lk 21.17;
Dan 12.12;
Mt 24.13;
Mk 13.13
10.24
Lk 6.40;
Jn 13.16;
15.20
10.25
Mt 12.24;
Mk 3.22;
Lk 11.15

10.26
Mk 4.22;
Lk 8.17;
12.2,3
10.28
Isa 8.12,13;
Heb 10.31
10.30
Lk 21.18;
Acts 27.34
10.32
Rom 10.9;
2 Tim 2.12;
Rev 3.5
10.34
Lk 12.51-53;
Mk 13.12
10.35
Mic 7.6
10.36
Mic 7.6
10.37
Lk 14.26
10.38
Mt 16.24
10.39
Mt 16.25;
Lk 17.33;
Jn 12.25
10.40
Lk 9.48;
Jn 12.44;
Gal 4.14

Whom to Fear

26 "So have no fear of them; for nothing is covered up that will not be uncovered, and nothing secret that will not become known. 27 What I say to you in the dark, tell in the light; and what you hear whispered, proclaim from the housetops. 28 Do not fear those who kill the body but cannot kill the soul; rather fear him who can destroy both soul and body in hell. g 29 Are not two sparrows sold for a penny? Yet not one of them will fall to the ground apart from your Father. 30 And even the hairs of your head are all counted. 31 So do not be afraid; you are of more value than many sparrows.

32 "Everyone therefore who acknowledges me before others, I also will acknowledge before my Father in heaven; 33 but whoever denies me before others, I also will deny before my Father in heaven.

Not Peace, but a Sword

34 "Do not think that I have come to bring peace to the earth; I have not come to bring peace, but a sword.
35 For I have come to set a
man against his father,
and a daughter against her
mother,
and a daughter-in-law
against her
mother-in-law;
36 and one's foes will be
members of one's own
household.
37 Whoever loves father or mother more than me is not worthy of me; and whoever loves son or daughter more than me is not worthy of me; 38 and whoever does not take up the cross and follow me is not worthy of me. 39 Those who find their life will lose it, and those who lose their life for my sake will find it.

Rewards

40 "Whoever welcomes you welcomes me, and whoever welcomes me welcomes the one who sent me. 41 Whoever welcomes a prophet in

g Gk *Gehenna*

the name of a prophet will receive a prophet's reward; and whoever welcomes a righteous person in the name of a righteous person will receive the reward of the righteous; [42] and whoever gives even a cup of cold water to one of these little ones in the name of a disciple — truly I tell you, none of these will lose their reward."

11 Now when Jesus had finished instructing his twelve disciples, he went on from there to teach and proclaim his message in their cities.

Messengers from John the Baptist

2 When John heard in prison what the Messiah[h] was doing, he sent word by his[i] disciples [3] and said to him, "Are you the one who is to come, or are we to wait for another?" [4] Jesus answered them, "Go and tell John what you hear and see: [5] the blind receive their sight, the lame walk, the lepers[j] are cleansed, the deaf hear, the dead are raised, and the poor have good news brought to them. [6] And blessed is anyone who takes no offense at me."

Jesus Praises John the Baptist

7 As they went away, Jesus began to speak to the crowds about John: "What did you go out into the wilderness to look at? A reed shaken by the wind? [8] What then did you go out to see? Someone[k] dressed in soft robes? Look, those who wear soft robes are in royal palaces. [9] What then did you go out to see? A prophet?[l] Yes, I tell you, and more than a prophet. [10] This is the one about whom it is written,

'See, I am sending my
 messenger ahead of
 you,
who will prepare your way
 before you.'

[11] Truly I tell you, among those born of women no one has arisen greater than John the Baptist; yet the least in the kingdom of heaven is greater than he. [12] From the days

of John the Baptist until now the kingdom of heaven has suffered violence,[m] and the violent take it by force. [13] For all the prophets and the law prophesied until John came; [14] and if you are willing to accept it, he is Elijah who is to come. [15] Let anyone with ears[n] listen!

16 "But to what will I compare this generation? It is like children sitting in the marketplaces and calling to one another,

[17] 'We played the flute for you,
 and you did not dance;
we wailed, and you did not
 mourn.'

[18] For John came neither eating nor drinking, and they say, 'He has a demon'; [19] the Son of Man came eating and drinking, and they say, 'Look, a glutton and a drunkard, a friend of tax collectors and sinners!' Yet wisdom is vindicated by her deeds."[o]

Woes to Unrepentant Cities

20 Then he began to reproach the cities in which most of his deeds of power had been done, because they did not repent. [21] "Woe to you, Chorazin! Woe to you, Bethsaida! For if the deeds of power done in you had been done in Tyre and Sidon, they would have repented long ago in sackcloth and ashes. [22] But I tell you, on the day of judgment it will be more tolerable for Tyre and Sidon than for you. [23] And you, Capernaum,

will you be exalted to
 heaven?
No, you will be brought
 down to Hades.

For if the deeds of power done in you had been done in Sodom, it would have remained until this day. [24] But I tell you that on the day of judgment it will be more tolerable for the land of Sodom than for you."

h Or *the Christ* i Other ancient authorities read *two of his* j The terms *leper* and *leprosy* can refer to several diseases k Or *Why then did you go out? To see someone* l Other ancient authorities read *Why then did you go out? To see a prophet?* m Or *has been coming violently* n Other ancient authorities add *to hear* o Other ancient authorities read *children*

Cross references (center column):

10.42
Mt 25.40;
Heb 6.10
11.2
Mt 14.3;
Mk 6.17;
Lk 9.7ff
11.3
Jn 11.27
11.5
Isa 35.4-6;
61.1;
Lk 4.18,19
11.6
Isa 8.14,15;
Rom 9.32;
1 Pet 2.8
11.7
Mt 3.1
11.9
Lk 1.76
11.10
Mal 3.1;
Mk 1.2

11.14
Mal 4.5;
Mt 17.12;
Lk 1.17
11.15
Mt 13.9,43;
Mk 4.23;
Rev 13.9
11.19
Mt 9.11;
Lk 15.2
11.21
Jon 3.7,8
11.22
v. 24;
Mt 10.15
11.23
Isa 14.13;
Lam 2.1
11.24
Mt 10.15

Jesus Thanks His Father

25 At that time Jesus said, "I thank[p] you, Father, Lord of heaven and earth, because you have hidden these things from the wise and the intelligent and have revealed them to infants; [26]yes, Father, for such was your gracious will.[q] [27]All things have been handed over to me by my Father; and no one knows the Son except the Father, and no one knows the Father except the Son and anyone to whom the Son chooses to reveal him.

28 "Come to me, all you that are weary and are carrying heavy burdens, and I will give you rest. [29]Take my yoke upon you, and learn from me; for I am gentle and humble in heart, and you will find rest for your souls. [30]For my yoke is easy, and my burden is light."

Plucking Grain on the Sabbath

12 At that time Jesus went through the grainfields on the sabbath; his disciples were hungry, and they began to pluck heads of grain and to eat. [2]When the Pharisees saw it, they said to him, "Look, your disciples are doing what is not lawful to do on the sabbath." [3]He said to them, "Have you not read what David did when he and his companions were hungry? [4]He entered the house of God and ate the bread of the Presence, which it was not lawful for him or his companions to eat, but only for the priests. [5]Or have you not read in the law that on the sabbath the priests in the temple break the sabbath and yet are guiltless? [6]I tell you, something greater than the temple is here. [7]But if you had known what this means, 'I desire mercy and not sacrifice,' you would not have condemned the guiltless. [8]For the Son of Man is lord of the sabbath."

The Man with a Withered Hand

9 He left that place and entered their synagogue; [10]a man was there with a withered hand, and they asked him, "Is it lawful to cure on the sabbath?" so that they might

accuse him. [11]He said to them, "Suppose one of you has only one sheep and it falls into a pit on the sabbath; will you not lay hold of it and lift it out? [12]How much more valuable is a human being than a sheep! So it is lawful to do good on the sabbath." [13]Then he said to the man, "Stretch out your hand." He stretched it out, and it was restored, as sound as the other. [14]But the Pharisees went out and conspired against him, how to destroy him.

God's Chosen Servant

15 When Jesus became aware of this, he departed. Many crowds[r] followed him, and he cured all of them, [16]and he ordered them not to make him known. [17]This was to fulfill what had been spoken through the prophet Isaiah:

18 "Here is my servant, whom I
 have chosen,
 my beloved, with whom my
 soul is well pleased.
 I will put my Spirit upon
 him,
 and he will proclaim
 justice to the Gentiles.
19 He will not wrangle or cry
 aloud,
 nor will anyone hear his
 voice in the streets.
20 He will not break a bruised
 reed
 or quench a smoldering
 wick
 until he brings justice to
 victory.
21 And in his name the
 Gentiles will hope."

Jesus and Beelzebul

22 Then they brought to him a demoniac who was blind and mute; and he cured him, so that the one who had been mute could speak and see. [23]All the crowds were amazed and said, "Can this be the Son of David?" [24]But when the Pharisees heard it, they said, "It is only by Beelzebul, the ruler of the

Cross-references (center column)

11.25
1 Cor 1.26-29
11.27
Mt 28.18;
Jn 3.35;
13.3; 17.2
11.28
see
Jer 31.25;
Jn 7.37
11.29
Jn 13.15;
Phil 2.5;
1 Pet 2.21;
1 Jn 2.6;
Jer 6.16
12.1
Deut 23.25
12.2
v. 10;
Lk 13.14;
14.3;
Jn 5.10;
7.23; 9.16
12.3
1 Sam 21.6
12.4
Ex 25.30;
Lev 24.5,9
12.5
Num 28.9,
10
12.6
vv. 41,42
12.7
Hos 6.6;
Mt 9.13
12.10
Lk 13.14;
14.3;
Jn 9.16

12.11
Lk 14.5
12.12
Mt 10.31
12.14
Mt 27.1;
Mk 3.6;
Lk 6.11;
Jn 5.18;
11.53
12.15
Mt 10.23;
19.2
12.16
Mt 9.30
12.18
Isa 42.1-4
12.22
Mt 9.32,33
12.23
Mt 9.27
12.24
Mt 9.34;
10.25;
Jn 7.20;
8.52; 10.20

p Or praise q Or for so it was well-pleasing in your sight r Other ancient authorities lack crowds

demons, that this fellow casts out the demons." 25 He knew what they were thinking and said to them, "Every kingdom divided against itself is laid waste, and no city or house divided against itself will stand. 26 If Satan casts out Satan, he is divided against himself; how then will his kingdom stand? 27 If I cast out demons by Beelzebul, by whom do your own exorcists s cast them out? Therefore they will be your judges. 28 But if it is by the Spirit of God that I cast out demons, then the kingdom of God has come to you. 29 Or how can one enter a strong man's house and plunder his property, without first tying up the strong man? Then indeed the house can be plundered. 30 Whoever is not with me is against me, and whoever does not gather with me scatters. 31 Therefore I tell you, people will be forgiven for every sin and blasphemy, but blasphemy against the Spirit will not be forgiven. 32 Whoever speaks a word against the Son of Man will be forgiven, but whoever speaks against the Holy Spirit will not be forgiven, either in this age or in the age to come.

A Tree and Its Fruit

33 "Either make the tree good, and its fruit good; or make the tree bad, and its fruit bad; for the tree is known by its fruit. 34 You brood of vipers! How can you speak good things, when you are evil? For out of the abundance of the heart the mouth speaks. 35 The good person brings good things out of a good treasure, and the evil person brings evil things out of an evil treasure. 36 I tell you, on the day of judgment you will have to give an account for every careless word you utter; 37 for by your words you will be justified, and by your words you will be condemned."

The Sign of Jonah

38 Then some of the scribes and Pharisees said to him, "Teacher, we wish to see a sign from you." 39 But he answered them, "An evil

12.25
Mt 9.4
12.27
Mt 9.34;
10.25;
Acts 19.13
12.28
Dan 2.44;
7.14;
Lk 1.33;
17.20,21
12.30
Mk 9.40;
Lk 9.50
12.31
Lk 12.10
12.32
Mt 11.19;
13.55;
Jn 7.12,52
12.33
Mt 7.17;
Lk 6.43,44
12.34
Mt 3.7;
23.33;
Lk 6.45
12.38
Mt 16.1;
Mk 8.11,12;
Jn 2.18;
6.30;
1 Cor 1.22
12.39
Mt 16.4

12.40
Jon 1.17
12.41
Jon 1.2; 3.5
12.42
1 Kings 10.2;
2 Chr 9.1
12.45
2 Pet 2.20
12.46
Mt 13.55;
Mk 6.3;
Jn 2.12; 7.3,
5; Acts 1.4;
1 Cor 9.5;
Gal 1.9
12.50
Jn 15.14

and adulterous generation asks for a sign, but no sign will be given to it except the sign of the prophet Jonah. 40 For just as Jonah was three days and three nights in the belly of the sea monster, so for three days and three nights the Son of Man will be in the heart of the earth. 41 The people of Nineveh will rise up at the judgment with this generation and condemn it, because they repented at the proclamation of Jonah, and see, something greater than Jonah is here! 42 The queen of the South will rise up at the judgment with this generation and condemn it, because she came from the ends of the earth to listen to the wisdom of Solomon, and see, something greater than Solomon is here!

The Return of the Unclean Spirit

43 "When the unclean spirit has gone out of a person, it wanders through waterless regions looking for a resting place, but it finds none. 44 Then it says, 'I will return to my house from which I came.' When it comes, it finds it empty, swept, and put in order. 45 Then it goes and brings along seven other spirits more evil than itself, and they enter and live there; and the last state of that person is worse than the first. So will it be also with this evil generation."

The True Kindred of Jesus

46 While he was still speaking to the crowds, his mother and his brothers were standing outside, wanting to speak to him. 47 Someone told him, "Look, your mother and your brothers are standing outside, wanting to speak to you." t 48 But to the one who had told him this, Jesus u replied, "Who is my mother, and who are my brothers?" 49 And pointing to his disciples, he said, "Here are my mother and my brothers! 50 For whoever does the will of my Father in heaven is my brother and sister and mother."

s Gk *sons* t Other ancient authorities lack verse 47 u Gk *he*

The Parable of the Sower

13 That same day Jesus went out of the house and sat beside the sea. [2] Such great crowds gathered around him that he got into a boat and sat there, while the whole crowd stood on the beach. [3] And he told them many things in parables, saying: "Listen! A sower went out to sow. [4] And as he sowed, some seeds fell on the path, and the birds came and ate them up. [5] Other seeds fell on rocky ground, where they did not have much soil, and they sprang up quickly, since they had no depth of soil. [6] But when the sun rose, they were scorched; and since they had no root, they withered away. [7] Other seeds fell among thorns, and the thorns grew up and choked them. [8] Other seeds fell on good soil and brought forth grain, some a hundredfold, some sixty, some thirty. [9] Let anyone with ears[v] listen!"

The Purpose of the Parables

10 Then the disciples came and asked him, "Why do you speak to them in parables?" [11] He answered, "To you it has been given to know the secrets[w] of the kingdom of heaven, but to them it has not been given. [12] For to those who have, more will be given, and they will have an abundance; but from those who have nothing, even what they have will be taken away. [13] The reason I speak to them in parables is that 'seeing they do not perceive, and hearing they do not listen, nor do they understand.' [14] With them indeed is fulfilled the prophecy of Isaiah that says:

'You will indeed listen, but
 never understand,
and you will indeed look,
 but never perceive.
15 For this people's heart has
 grown dull,
and their ears are hard of
 hearing,
and they have shut their
 eyes;
so that they might not
 look with their eyes,
and listen with their ears,

and understand with their
 heart and turn —
and I would heal them.'
16 But blessed are your eyes, for they see, and your ears, for they hear. [17] Truly I tell you, many prophets and righteous people longed to see what you see, but did not see it, and to hear what you hear, but did not hear it.

The Parable of the Sower Explained

18 "Hear then the parable of the sower. [19] When anyone hears the word of the kingdom and does not understand it, the evil one comes and snatches away what is sown in the heart; this is what was sown on the path. [20] As for what was sown on rocky ground, this is the one who hears the word and immediately receives it with joy; [21] yet such a person has no root, but endures only for a while, and when trouble or persecution arises on account of the word, that person immediately falls away.[x] [22] As for what was sown among thorns, this is the one who hears the word, but the cares of the world and the lure of wealth choke the word, and it yields nothing. [23] But as for what was sown on good soil, this is the one who hears the word and understands it, who indeed bears fruit and yields, in one case a hundredfold, in another sixty, and in another thirty."

The Parable of Weeds among the Wheat

24 He put before them another parable: "The kingdom of heaven may be compared to someone who sowed good seed in his field; [25] but while everybody was asleep, an enemy came and sowed weeds among the wheat, and then went away. [26] So when the plants came up and bore grain, then the weeds appeared as well. [27] And the slaves of the householder came and said to him, 'Master, did you not sow good seed in your field? Where, then, did these weeds come from?' [28] He an-

Cross references (center column)

13.2 Lk 5.3
13.8 Gen 26.12
13.9 Mt 11.15
13.11 Mt 11.25; 19.11; Jn 6.65; 1 Cor 2.10; 1 Jn 2.27
13.12 Mt 25.29; Lk 19.26
13.13 Jer 5.21; Ezek 12.2
13.14 Isa 6.9,10; Ezek 12.2; Jn 12.40; Acts 28.26, 27; Rom 11.8
13.15 Heb 5.11
13.16 Mt 16.17; Lk 10.23,24; Jn 20.29
13.17 Heb 11.13; 1 Pet 1.10, 11
13.19 Mt 4.23
13.21 Mt 11.6
13.22 Rom 12.2; 1 Cor 1.20; 2 Cor 4.4; Gal 1.4; Eph 2.2; Mt 19.23; 1 Tim 6.9, 10,17
13.23 v. 8
13.24 Lk 13.18,20

v Other ancient authorities add *to hear*
w Or *mysteries* x Gk *stumbles*

swered, 'An enemy has done this.' The slaves said to him, 'Then do you want us to go and gather them?' [29] But he replied, 'No; for in gathering the weeds you would uproot the wheat along with them. [30] Let both of them grow together until the harvest; and at harvest time I will tell the reapers, Collect the weeds first and bind them in bundles to be burned, but gather the wheat into my barn.' "

The Parable of the Mustard Seed

31 He put before them another parable: "The kingdom of heaven is like a mustard seed that someone took and sowed in his field; [32] it is the smallest of all the seeds, but when it has grown it is the greatest of shrubs and becomes a tree, so that the birds of the air come and make nests in its branches."

The Parable of the Yeast

33 He told them another parable: "The kingdom of heaven is like yeast that a woman took and mixed in with[y] three measures of flour until all of it was leavened."

The Use of Parables

34 Jesus told the crowds all these things in parables; without a parable he told them nothing. [35] This was to fulfill what had been spoken through the prophet:[z]
"I will open my mouth to
 speak in parables;
I will proclaim what has
 been hidden from the
 foundation of the
 world."[a]

Jesus Explains the Parable of the Weeds

36 Then he left the crowds and went into the house. And his disciples approached him, saying, "Explain to us the parable of the weeds of the field." [37] He answered, "The one who sows the good seed is the Son of Man; [38] the field is the world, and the good seed are the children of the kingdom; the weeds are the children of the evil one, [39] and the enemy who sowed them is the devil; the harvest is the end

13.30
Mt 3.12
13.31
Isa 2.2,
3; Mic 4.1
13.32
Ps 104.12;
Ezek 17.23;
31.6;
Dan 4.12
13.33
Gen 18.6;
Gal 5.9
13.34
Mk 4.33,34
13.35
Ps 78.2;
Rom 16.25,
26;
1 Cor 2.7;
Eph 3.9;
Col 1.26
13.38
Mt 24.14;
28.19;
Lk 24.47;
Jn 8.44;
1 Jn 3.10
13.39
Joel 3.13;
Mt 24.3;
28.20;
Rev 14.15

13.40
1 Cor 10.11;
Heb 9.26
13.41
Mt 24.31
13.42
Mt 8.12;
v. 50;
Mt 24.51;
25.30;
Lk 13.28
13.43
Dan 12.3;
Mt 11.15
13.44
see Phil 3.7,
8; Isa 55.1
13.47
Mt 22.10
13.49
Mt 25.32
13.50
v. 42
13.53
Mt 7.28;
11.1; 19.1;
26.1
13.54
Mt 4.23;
7.28

of the age, and the reapers are angels. [40] Just as the weeds are collected and burned up with fire, so will it be at the end of the age. [41] The Son of Man will send his angels, and they will collect out of his kingdom all causes of sin and all evildoers, [42] and they will throw them into the furnace of fire, where there will be weeping and gnashing of teeth. [43] Then the righteous will shine like the sun in the kingdom of their Father. Let anyone with ears[b] listen!

Three Parables

44 "The kingdom of heaven is like treasure hidden in a field, which someone found and hid; then in his joy he goes and sells all that he has and buys that field.

45 "Again, the kingdom of heaven is like a merchant in search of fine pearls; [46] on finding one pearl of great value, he went and sold all that he had and bought it.

47 "Again, the kingdom of heaven is like a net that was thrown into the sea and caught fish of every kind; [48] when it was full, they drew it ashore, sat down, and put the good into baskets but threw out the bad. [49] So it will be at the end of the age. The angels will come out and separate the evil from the righteous [50] and throw them into the furnace of fire, where there will be weeping and gnashing of teeth.

Treasures New and Old

51 "Have you understood all this?" They answered, "Yes." [52] And he said to them, "Therefore every scribe who has been trained for the kingdom of heaven is like the master of a household who brings out of his treasure what is new and what is old." [53] When Jesus had finished these parables, he left that place.

The Rejection of Jesus at Nazareth

54 He came to his hometown

y Gk hid in z Other ancient authorities read *the prophet Isaiah* a Other ancient authorities lack *of the world* b Other ancient authorities add *to hear*

and began to teach the people[c] in their synagogue, so that they were astounded and said, "Where did this man get this wisdom and these deeds of power? 55 Is not this the carpenter's son? Is not his mother called Mary? And are not his brothers James and Joseph and Simon and Judas? 56 And are not all his sisters with us? Where then did this man get all this?" 57 And they took offense at him. But Jesus said to them, "Prophets are not without honor except in their own country and in their own house." 58 And he did not do many deeds of power there, because of their unbelief.

The Death of John the Baptist

14 At that time Herod the ruler[d] heard reports about Jesus; 2 and he said to his servants, "This is John the Baptist; he has been raised from the dead, and for this reason these powers are at work in him." 3 For Herod had arrested John, bound him, and put him in prison on account of Herodias, his brother Philip's wife,[e] 4 because John had been telling him, "It is not lawful for you to have her." 5 Though Herod[f] wanted to put him to death, he feared the crowd, because they regarded him as a prophet. 6 But when Herod's birthday came, the daughter of Herodias danced before the company, and she pleased Herod 7 so much that he promised on oath to grant her whatever she might ask. 8 Prompted by her mother, she said, "Give me the head of John the Baptist here on a platter." 9 The king was grieved, yet out of regard for his oaths and for the guests, he commanded it to be given; 10 he sent and had John beheaded in the prison. 11 The head was brought on a platter and given to the girl, who brought it to her mother. 12 His disciples came and took the body and buried it; then they went and told Jesus.

Feeding the Five Thousand

13 Now when Jesus heard this, he withdrew from there in a boat to

13.55
Lk 3.23;
Jn 6.42
13.57
Jn 4.44
14.1
Mk 8.15;
Lk 5.1,19;
8.3; 13.31;
23.7,8;
Acts 4.27;
12.1
14.3
Lk 3.19,20
14.4
Lev 18.16;
20.21
14.5
Mt 21.26;
Lk 20.6

14.14
Mt 9.36
14.17
Mt 16.9
14.19
1 Sam 9.13;
Mt 15.36;
Mk 14.22;
Lk 24.30
14.23
Lk 6.12;
9.28
14.26
see
Lk 24.37
14.27
Mt 9.2;
17.7; 28.10;
Rev 1.17

a deserted place by himself. But when the crowds heard it, they followed him on foot from the towns. 14 When he went ashore, he saw a great crowd; and he had compassion for them and cured their sick. 15 When it was evening, the disciples came to him and said, "This is a deserted place, and the hour is now late; send the crowds away so that they may go into the villages and buy food for themselves." 16 Jesus said to them, "They need not go away; you give them something to eat." 17 They replied, "We have nothing here but five loaves and two fish." 18 And he said, "Bring them here to me." 19 Then he ordered the crowds to sit down on the grass. Taking the five loaves and the two fish, he looked up to heaven, and blessed and broke the loaves, and gave them to the disciples, and the disciples gave them to the crowds. 20 And all ate and were filled; and they took up what was left over of the broken pieces, twelve baskets full. 21 And those who ate were about five thousand men, besides women and children.

Jesus Walks on the Water

22 Immediately he made the disciples get into the boat and go on ahead to the other side, while he dismissed the crowds. 23 And after he had dismissed the crowds, he went up the mountain by himself to pray. When evening came, he was there alone, 24 but by this time the boat, battered by the waves, was far from the land,[g] for the wind was against them. 25 And early in the morning he came walking toward them on the sea. 26 But when the disciples saw him walking on the sea, they were terrified, saying, "It is a ghost!" And they cried out in fear. 27 But immediately Jesus spoke to them and said, "Take heart, it is I; do not be afraid."

28 Peter answered him, "Lord, if

c Gk them d Gk tetrarch e Other ancient authorities read his brother's wife f Gk he g Other ancient authorities read was out on the sea

it is you, command me to come to you on the water." [29] He said, "Come." So Peter got out of the boat, started walking on the water, and came toward Jesus. [30] But when he noticed the strong wind,[h] he became frightened, and beginning to sink, he cried out, "Lord, save me!" [31] Jesus immediately reached out his hand and caught him, saying to him, "You of little faith, why did you doubt?" [32] When they got into the boat, the wind ceased. [33] And those in the boat worshiped him, saying, "Truly you are the Son of God."

Jesus Heals the Sick in Gennesaret

[34] When they had crossed over, they came to land at Gennesaret. [35] After the people of that place recognized him, they sent word throughout the region and brought all who were sick to him, [36] and begged him that they might touch even the fringe of his cloak; and all who touched it were healed.

The Tradition of the Elders

15 Then Pharisees and scribes came to Jesus from Jerusalem and said, [2] "Why do your disciples break the tradition of the elders? For they do not wash their hands before they eat." [3] He answered them, "And why do you break the commandment of God for the sake of your tradition? [4] For God said,[i] 'Honor your father and your mother,' and, 'Whoever speaks evil of father or mother must surely die.' [5] But you say that whoever tells father or mother, 'Whatever support you might have had from me is given to God,'[j] then that person need not honor the father.[k] [6] So, for the sake of your tradition, you make void the word[l] of God. [7] You hypocrites! Isaiah prophesied rightly about you when he said:

[8] 'This people honors me with
 their lips,
 but their hearts are far
 from me;
[9] in vain do they worship me,

14.31
Mt 6.30;
8.26; 16.8
14.33
Ps 2.7;
Mt 16.16;
26.63;
Lk 4.41;
Jn 11.27;
Acts 8.37;
Rom 1.4
14.36
Mt 9.20;
Mk 3.10
15.2
Lk 11.38
15.4
Ex 20.12;
Deut 5.16;
Eph 6.2
15.5
Ex 21.17;
Lev 20.9;
Deut 27.16
15.9
Col 2.18-22

15.11
Acts 10.14,
15;
1 Tim 4.3
15.13
Isa 60.21;
Jn 15.2;
1 Cor 3.9ff
15.14
Mt 23.16;
Lk 6.39;
Rom 2.19
15.15
Mt 13.36
15.16
Mt 16.9
15.18
Mt 12.34;
Jas 3.6
15.19
Gal 5.19-21;
1 Cor 6.9,
10;
Rom 14.14
15.22
Mt 9.27;
4.24
15.24
Mt 10.6,23
15.25
Mt 8.2;
18.26; 20.20;
Jn 9.38

teaching human precepts as doctrines.' "

Things That Defile

[10] Then he called the crowd to him and said to them, "Listen and understand: [11] it is not what goes into the mouth that defiles a person, but it is what comes out of the mouth that defiles." [12] Then the disciples approached and said to him, "Do you know that the Pharisees took offense when they heard what you said?" [13] He answered, "Every plant that my heavenly Father has not planted will be uprooted. [14] Let them alone; they are blind guides of the blind.[m] And if one blind person guides another, both will fall into a pit." [15] But Peter said to him, "Explain this parable to us." [16] Then he said, "Are you also still without understanding? [17] Do you not see that whatever goes into the mouth enters the stomach, and goes out into the sewer? [18] But what comes out of the mouth proceeds from the heart, and this is what defiles. [19] For out of the heart come evil intentions, murder, adultery, fornication, theft, false witness, slander. [20] These are what defile a person, but to eat with unwashed hands does not defile."

The Canaanite Woman's Faith

[21] Jesus left that place and went away to the district of Tyre and Sidon. [22] Just then a Canaanite woman from that region came out and started shouting, "Have mercy on me, Lord, Son of David; my daughter is tormented by a demon." [23] But he did not answer her at all. And his disciples came and urged him, saying, "Send her away, for she keeps shouting after us." [24] He answered, "I was sent only to the lost sheep of the house of Israel." [25] But she came and knelt be-

[h] Other ancient authorities read *the wind*
[i] Other ancient authorities read *commanded, saying* [j] Or *is an offering* [k] Other ancient authorities add *or the mother*
[l] Other ancient authorities read *law*; others, *commandment* [m] Other ancient authorities lack *of the blind*

fore him, saying, "Lord, help me."
26 He answered, "It is not fair to take the children's food and throw it to the dogs." 27 She said, "Yes, Lord, yet even the dogs eat the crumbs that fall from their masters' table." 28 Then Jesus answered her, "Woman, great is your faith! Let it be done for you as you wish." And her daughter was healed instantly.

Jesus Cures Many People

29 After Jesus had left that place, he passed along the Sea of Galilee, and he went up the mountain, where he sat down. 30 Great crowds came to him, bringing with them the lame, the maimed, the blind, the mute, and many others. They put them at his feet, and he cured them, 31 so that the crowd was amazed when they saw the mute speaking, the maimed whole, the lame walking, and the blind seeing. And they praised the God of Israel.

Feeding the Four Thousand

32 Then Jesus called his disciples to him and said, "I have compassion for the crowd, because they have been with me now for three days and have nothing to eat; and I do not want to send them away hungry, for they might faint on the way." 33 The disciples said to him, "Where are we to get enough bread in the desert to feed so great a crowd?" 34 Jesus asked them, "How many loaves have you?" They said, "Seven, and a few small fish." 35 Then ordering the crowd to sit down on the ground, 36 he took the seven loaves and the fish; and after giving thanks he broke them and gave them to the disciples, and the disciples gave them to the crowds. 37 And all of them ate and were filled; and they took up the broken pieces left over, seven baskets full. 38 Those who had eaten were four thousand men, besides women and children. 39 After sending away the crowds, he got into the boat and went to the region of Magadan. n

15.28
Mt 9.22,28;
Mk 10.52;
Lk 7.50;
17.19
15.30
Lk 7.22
15.31
Mt 9.8
15.32
Mt 9.36
15.36
Mt 14.19;
1 Sam 9.13

16.1
Mt 12.38;
Lk 11.16,29;
12.54-56
16.4
Jon 3.4,5;
Mt 12.39
16.6
Lk 12.1
16.8
Mt 6.30;
8.26; 14.31
16.9
Mt 14.17-21
16.10
Mt 15.34-38
16.14
Mt 14.2;
Jn 1.21

The Demand for a Sign

16 The Pharisees and Sadducees came, and to test Jesus o they asked him to show them a sign from heaven. 2 He answered them, "When it is evening, you say, 'It will be fair weather, for the sky is red.' 3 And in the morning, 'It will be stormy today, for the sky is red and threatening.' You know how to interpret the appearance of the sky, but you cannot interpret the signs of the times. p 4 An evil and adulterous generation asks for a sign, but no sign will be given to it except the sign of Jonah." Then he left them and went away.

The Yeast of the Pharisees and Sadducees

5 When the disciples reached the other side, they had forgotten to bring any bread. 6 Jesus said to them, "Watch out, and beware of the yeast of the Pharisees and Sadducees." 7 They said to one another, "It is because we have brought no bread." 8 And becoming aware of it, Jesus said, "You of little faith, why are you talking about having no bread? 9 Do you still not perceive? Do you not remember the five loaves for the five thousand, and how many baskets you gathered? 10 Or the seven loaves for the four thousand, and how many baskets you gathered? 11 How could you fail to perceive that I was not speaking about bread? Beware of the yeast of the Pharisees and Sadducees!" 12 Then they understood that he had not told them to beware of the yeast of bread, but of the teaching of the Pharisees and Sadducees.

Peter's Declaration about Jesus

13 Now when Jesus came into the district of Caesarea Philippi, he asked his disciples, "Who do people say that the Son of Man is?" 14 And they said, "Some say John the Baptist, but others Elijah, and

n Other ancient authorities read *Magdala* or *Magdalan* o Gk *him* p Other ancient authorities lack 2 *When it is . . . of the times*

still others Jeremiah or one of the prophets." [15] He said to them, "But who do you say that I am?" [16] Simon Peter answered, "You are the Messiah,q the Son of the living God." [17] And Jesus answered him, "Blessed are you, Simon son of Jonah! For flesh and blood has not revealed this to you, but my Father in heaven. [18] And I tell you, you are Peter,r and on this rocks I will build my church, and the gates of Hades will not prevail against it. [19] I will give you the keys of the kingdom of heaven, and whatever you bind on earth will be bound in heaven, and whatever you loose on earth will be loosed in heaven." [20] Then he sternly ordered the disciples not to tell anyone that he wast the Messiah.q

Jesus Foretells His Death and Resurrection

[21] From that time on, Jesus began to show his disciples that he must go to Jerusalem and undergo great suffering at the hands of the elders and chief priests and scribes, and be killed, and on the third day be raised. [22] And Peter took him aside and began to rebuke him, saying, "God forbid it, Lord! This must never happen to you." [23] But he turned and said to Peter, "Get behind me, Satan! You are a stumbling block to me; for you are setting your mind not on divine things but on human things."

The Cross and Self-Denial

[24] Then Jesus told his disciples, "If any want to become my followers, let them deny themselves and take up their cross and follow me. [25] For those who want to save their life will lose it, and those who lose their life for my sake will find it. [26] For what will it profit them if they gain the whole world but forfeit their life? Or what will they give in return for their life?

[27] "For the Son of Man is to come with his angels in the glory of his Father, and then he will repay everyone for what has been done.

[28] Truly I tell you, there are some standing here who will not taste death before they see the Son of Man coming in his kingdom."

The Transfiguration

17 Six days later, Jesus took with him Peter and James and his brother John and led them up a high mountain, by themselves. [2] And he was transfigured before them, and his face shone like the sun, and his clothes became dazzling white. [3] Suddenly there appeared to them Moses and Elijah, talking with him. [4] Then Peter said to Jesus, "Lord, it is good for us to be here; if you wish, I u will make three dwellingsv here, one for you, one for Moses, and one for Elijah." [5] While he was still speaking, suddenly a bright cloud overshadowed them, and from the cloud a voice said, "This is my Son, the Beloved;w with him I am well pleased; listen to him!" [6] When the disciples heard this, they fell to the ground and were overcome by fear. [7] But Jesus came and touched them, saying, "Get up and do not be afraid." [8] And when they looked up, they saw no one except Jesus himself alone.

[9] As they were coming down the mountain, Jesus ordered them, "Tell no one about the vision until after the Son of Man has been raised from the dead." [10] And the disciples asked him, "Why, then, do the scribes say that Elijah must come first?" [11] He replied, "Elijah is indeed coming and will restore all things; [12] but I tell you that Elijah has already come, and they did not recognize him, but they did to him whatever they pleased. So also the Son of Man is about to suffer at their hands." [13] Then the disciples understood that he was speaking to them about John the Baptist.

Jesus Cures a Boy with a Demon

[14] When they came to the crowd, a man came to him, knelt

16.16
Mt 14.33;
Jn 6.69;
11.27
16.17
1 Cor 15.50;
Gal 1.6;
Eph 6.12
16.18
Jn 1.42
16.19
Mt 18.18;
Jn 20.23
16.20
Mk 3.12;
5.43; 7.36;
9.9
16.21
Mt 17.22,
23; 20.17-19;
Lk 17.25
16.24
Mt 10.38,
39;
Lk 14.27;
17.33;
Jn 12.25
16.27
Mt 10.33;
Lk 12.9;
1 Jn 2.18;
Rom 2.6;
Rev 22.12

16.28
Mt 10.23;
1 Cor 16.22;
1 Thes 4.15-
18; Rev 1.7;
Jas 5.7
17.1
Mt 26.37;
Mk 5.37;
13.2
17.5
2 Pet 1.17;
Mt 3.17;
Isa 42.1;
Acts 3.22,23
17.7
Mt 14.27
17.9
Mt 8.4;
16.20;
Mk 3.12;
5.43; 7.36
17.10
Mal 4.5;
Mt 11.14
17.11
Mal 4.6;
Lk 1.16,17
17.12
Mt 11.14;
14.3,10;
16.21

q Or the Christ　　r Gk Petros　　s Gk petra
t Other ancient authorities add Jesus
u Other ancient authorities read we
v Or tents　　w Or my beloved Son

before him, [15]and said, "Lord, have mercy on my son, for he is an epileptic and he suffers terribly; he often falls into the fire and often into the water. [16]And I brought him to your disciples, but they could not cure him." [17]Jesus answered, "You faithless and perverse generation, how much longer must I be with you? How much longer must I put up with you? Bring him here to me." [18]And Jesus rebuked the demon,[x] and it[y] came out of him, and the boy was cured instantly. [19]Then the disciples came to Jesus privately and said, "Why could we not cast it out?" [20]He said to them, "Because of your little faith. For truly I tell you, if you have faith the size of a[z] mustard seed, you will say to this mountain, 'Move from here to there,' and it will move; and nothing will be impossible for you."[a]

Jesus Again Foretells His Death and Resurrection

22 As they were gathering[b] in Galilee, Jesus said to them, "The Son of Man is going to be betrayed into human hands, [23]and they will kill him, and on the third day he will be raised." And they were greatly distressed.

Jesus and the Temple Tax

24 When they reached Capernaum, the collectors of the temple tax[c] came to Peter and said, "Does your teacher not pay the temple tax?"[c] [25]He said, "Yes, he does." And when he came home, Jesus spoke of it first, asking, "What do you think, Simon? From whom do kings of the earth take toll or tribute? From their children or from others?" [26]When Peter[d] said, "From others," Jesus said to him, "Then the children are free. [27]However, so that we do not give offense to them, go to the sea and cast a hook; take the first fish that comes up; and when you open its mouth, you will find a coin;[e] take that and give it to them for you and me."

17.15
Mt 4.24
17.20
Mt 21.21;
Mk 11.23;
Lk 17.6;
1 Cor 12.9
17.22
Mt 16.21;
20.17;
Lk 18.31;
24.6,7
17.24
Ex 30.13;
38.26
17.25
Rom 13.7;
Mt 22.17,19
17.27
Mt 5.29,30;
18.6,8;
Lk 17.2;
Jn 6.61;
1 Cor 8.13

18.3
Mt 19.14;
Mk 10.15;
Lk 18.17;
1 Pet 2.2
18.4
Mt 20.27;
23.11
18.5
Mt 10.40;
Lk 18.17
18.6
Lk 17.1,2
18.7
Lk 17.1;
1 Cor 11.19
18.8
Mt 5.29,30;
Mk 9.43,45
18.9
Mt 5.29;
Mk 9.47;
Mt 17.27
18.10
Ps 34.7;
Acts 12.11;
Heb 1.14

True Greatness

18 At that time the disciples came to Jesus and asked, "Who is the greatest in the kingdom of heaven?" [2]He called a child, whom he put among them, [3]and said, "Truly I tell you, unless you change and become like children, you will never enter the kingdom of heaven. [4]Whoever becomes humble like this child is the greatest in the kingdom of heaven. [5]Whoever welcomes one such child in my name welcomes me.

Temptations to Sin

6 "If any of you put a stumbling block before one of these little ones who believe in me, it would be better for you if a great millstone were fastened around your neck and you were drowned in the depth of the sea. [7]Woe to the world because of stumbling blocks! Occasions for stumbling are bound to come, but woe to the one by whom the stumbling block comes!

8 "If your hand or your foot causes you to stumble, cut it off and throw it away; it is better for you to enter life maimed or lame than to have two hands or two feet and to be thrown into the eternal fire. [9]And if your eye causes you to stumble, tear it out and throw it away; it is better for you to enter life with one eye than to have two eyes and to be thrown into the hell[f] of fire.

The Parable of the Lost Sheep

10 "Take care that you do not despise one of these little ones; for, I tell you, in heaven their angels continually see the face of my Father in heaven.[g] [12]What do you think? If a shepherd has a hundred sheep, and one of them has gone astray, does he not leave the

[x] Gk it or him [y] Gk the demon
[z] Gk faith as a grain of [a] Other ancient authorities add verse 21, But this kind does not come out except by prayer and fasting
[b] Other ancient authorities read living
[c] Gk didrachma [d] Gk he [e] Gk stater; the stater was worth two didrachmas
[f] Gk Gehenna [g] Other ancient authorities add verse 11, For the Son of Man came to save the lost

ninety-nine on the mountains and go in search of the one that went astray? [13] And if he finds it, truly I tell you, he rejoices over it more than over the ninety-nine that never went astray. [14] So it is not the will of your[h] Father in heaven that one of these little ones should be lost.

Reproving Another Who Sins

15 "If another member of the church[i] sins against you,[j] go and point out the fault when the two of you are alone. If the member listens to you, you have regained that one.[k] [16] But if you are not listened to, take one or two others along with you, so that every word may be confirmed by the evidence of two or three witnesses. [17] If the member refuses to listen to them, tell it to the church; and if the offender refuses to listen even to the church, let such a one be to you as a Gentile and a tax collector. [18] Truly I tell you, whatever you bind on earth will be bound in heaven, and whatever you loose on earth will be loosed in heaven. [19] Again, truly I tell you, if two of you agree on earth about anything you ask, it will be done for you by my Father in heaven. [20] For where two or three are gathered in my name, I am there among them."

Forgiveness

21 Then Peter came and said to him, "Lord, if another member of the church[l] sins against me, how often should I forgive? As many as seven times?" [22] Jesus said to him, "Not seven times, but, I tell you, seventy-seven[m] times.

The Parable of the Unforgiving Servant

23 "For this reason the kingdom of heaven may be compared to a king who wished to settle accounts with his slaves. [24] When he began the reckoning, one who owed him ten thousand talents[n] was brought to him; [25] and, as he could not pay, his lord ordered him to be sold, together with his wife and children and all his possessions, and pay-

ment to be made. [26] So the slave fell on his knees before him, saying, 'Have patience with me, and I will pay you everything.' [27] And out of pity for him, the lord of that slave released him and forgave him the debt. [28] But that same slave, as he went out, came upon one of his fellow slaves who owed him a hundred denarii;[o] and seizing him by the throat, he said, 'Pay what you owe.' [29] Then his fellow slave fell down and pleaded with him, 'Have patience with me, and I will pay you.' [30] But he refused; then he went and threw him into prison until he would pay the debt. [31] When his fellow slaves saw what had happened, they were greatly distressed, and they went and reported to their lord all that had taken place. [32] Then his lord summoned him and said to him, 'You wicked slave! I forgave you all that debt because you pleaded with me. [33] Should you not have had mercy on your fellow slave, as I had mercy on you?' [34] And in anger his lord handed him over to be tortured until he would pay his entire debt. [35] So my heavenly Father will also do to every one of you, if you do not forgive your brother or sister[p] from your heart."

Teaching about Divorce

19 When Jesus had finished saying these things, he left Galilee and went to the region of Judea beyond the Jordan. [2] Large crowds followed him, and he cured them there.

3 Some Pharisees came to him, and to test him they asked, "Is it lawful for a man to divorce his wife for any cause?" [4] He answered, "Have you not read that the one who made them at the beginning 'made them male and female,' [5] and said, 'For this reason a man

18.15
Lev 19.17;
Lk 17.3;
Gal 6.1;
Jas 5.19,20
18.16
Deut 19.15;
Jn 8.17;
2 Cor 13.1;
Heb 10.28
18.17
1 Cor 6.1-6;
2 Thes 3.6,
14
18.18
Mt 16.19;
Jn 20.23
18.19
Mt 5.24;
1 Jn 5.14
18.21
Gen 4.24;
Lk 17.4
18.22
Mt 6.14;
Mk 11.25;
Col 3.13
18.23
Mt 25.19
18.25
Lk 7.42;
2 Kings 4.1;
Neh 5.5,8

18.26
Mt 8.2
18.35
Mt 6.14;
Mk 11.26;
Jas 2.13
19.1
Mk 10.1;
Jn 10.40
19.2
Mt 4.23
19.3
Mt 5.31
19.4
Gen 1.27;
5.2
19.5
Gen 2.24;
1 Cor 6.16;
Eph 5.31

h Other ancient authorities read *my* i Gk *If your brother* i Other ancient authorities lack *against you* k Gk *the brother* l Gk *if my brother* m Or *seventy times seven* n A talent was worth more than fifteen years' wages of a laborer o The denarius was the usual day's wage for a laborer p Gk *brother*

shall leave his father and mother and be joined to his wife, and the two shall become one flesh'? 6 So they are no longer two, but one flesh. Therefore what God has joined together, let no one separate." 7 They said to him, "Why then did Moses command us to give a certificate of dismissal and to divorce her?" 8 He said to them, "It was because you were so hardhearted that Moses allowed you to divorce your wives, but from the beginning it was not so. 9 And I say to you, whoever divorces his wife, except for unchastity, and marries another commits adultery."q

10 His disciples said to him, "If such is the case of a man with his wife, it is better not to marry." 11 But he said to them, "Not everyone can accept this teaching, but only those to whom it is given. 12 For there are eunuchs who have been so from birth, and there are eunuchs who have been made eunuchs by others, and there are eunuchs who have made themselves eunuchs for the sake of the kingdom of heaven. Let anyone accept this who can."

Jesus Blesses Little Children

13 Then little children were being brought to him in order that he might lay his hands on them and pray. The disciples spoke sternly to those who brought them; 14 but Jesus said, "Let the little children come to me, and do not stop them; for it is to such as these that the kingdom of heaven belongs." 15 And he laid his hands on them and went on his way.

The Rich Young Man

16 Then someone came to him and said, "Teacher, what good deed must I do to have eternal life?" 17 And he said to him, "Why do you ask me about what is good? There is only one who is good. If you wish to enter into life, keep the commandments." 18 He said to him, "Which ones?" And Jesus said, "You shall not murder; You shall not commit adultery; You

19.7
Deut 24.1-4;
Mt 5.31
19.9
Mk 5.32;
Lk 16.18;
1 Cor 7.10-13
19.11
1 Cor 7.7-9
19.14
Mt 18.3;
1 Cor 14.20;
1 Pet 2.2
19.16
Lev 18.5;
Lk 10.25
19.18
Ex 20.13;
Deut 5.17;
Rom 13.9;
Jas 2.11

19.19
Lev 19.18;
Mt 22.39;
Rom 13.9;
Gal 5.14
19.21
Mt 6.20;
Lk 12.33;
16.9;
Acts 2.45;
4.34,35
19.23
Mt 13.22;
1 Cor 1.26;
1 Tim 6.9,
10
19.26
Gen 18.14;
Job 42.2;
Jer 32.17;
Zech 8.6
19.27
Mt 4.20;
Lk 5.11
19.28
Mt 20.21;
Lk 22.28-30;
Rev 3.21
19.30
Mt 20.16;
Lk 13.30
20.1
Mt 13.24;
21.28,33

shall not steal; You shall not bear false witness; 19 Honor your father and mother; also, You shall love your neighbor as yourself." 20 The young man said to him, "I have kept all these;r what do I still lack?" 21 Jesus said to him, "If you wish to be perfect, go, sell your possessions, and give the moneys to the poor, and you will have treasure in heaven; then come, follow me." 22 When the young man heard this word, he went away grieving, for he had many possessions.

23 Then Jesus said to his disciples, "Truly I tell you, it will be hard for a rich person to enter the kingdom of heaven. 24 Again I tell you, it is easier for a camel to go through the eye of a needle than for someone who is rich to enter the kingdom of God." 25 When the disciples heard this, they were greatly astounded and said, "Then who can be saved?" 26 But Jesus looked at them and said, "For mortals it is impossible, but for God all things are possible."

27 Then Peter said in reply, "Look, we have left everything and followed you. What then will we have?" 28 Jesus said to them, "Truly I tell you, at the renewal of all things, when the Son of Man is seated on the throne of his glory, you who have followed me will also sit on twelve thrones, judging the twelve tribes of Israel. 29 And everyone who has left houses or brothers or sisters or father or mother or children or fields, for my name's sake, will receive a hundredfold,t and will inherit eternal life. 30 But many who are first will be last, and the last will be first.

The Laborers in the Vineyard

20 "For the kingdom of heaven is like a landowner who went out early in the morning to hire laborers for his vineyard. 2 Af-

q Other ancient authorities read *except on the ground of unchastity, causes her to commit adultery*; others add at the end of the verse *and he who marries a divorced woman commits adultery* r Other ancient authorities add *from my youth* s Gk lacks *the money* t Other ancient authorities read *manifold*

ter agreeing with the laborers for the usual daily wage,ᵘ he sent them into his vineyard. ³When he went out about nine o'clock, he saw others standing idle in the marketplace; ⁴and he said to them, 'You also go into the vineyard, and I will pay you whatever is right.' So they went. ⁵When he went out again about noon and about three o'clock, he did the same. ⁶And about five o'clock he went out and found others standing around; and he said to them, 'Why are you standing here idle all day?' ⁷They said to him, 'Because no one has hired us.' He said to them, 'You also go into the vineyard.' ⁸When evening came, the owner of the vineyard said to his manager, 'Call the laborers and give them their pay, beginning with the last and then going to the first.' ⁹When those hired about five o'clock came, each of them received the usual daily wage.ᵘ ¹⁰Now when the first came, they thought they would receive more; but each of them also received the usual daily wage.ᵘ ¹¹And when they received it, they grumbled against the landowner, ¹²saying, 'These last worked only one hour, and you have made them equal to us who have borne the burden of the day and the scorching heat.' ¹³But he replied to one of them, 'Friend, I am doing you no wrong; did you not agree with me for the usual daily wage?ᵘ ¹⁴Take what belongs to you and go; I choose to give to this last the same as I give to you. ¹⁵Am I not allowed to do what I choose with what belongs to me? Or are you envious because I am generous?'ᵛ ¹⁶So the last will be first, and the first will be last."ʷ

A Third Time Jesus Foretells His Death and Resurrection

17 While Jesus was going up to Jerusalem, he took the twelve disciples aside by themselves, and said to them on the way, ¹⁸"See, we are going up to Jerusalem, and the Son of Man will be handed over to

the chief priests and scribes, and they will condemn him to death; ¹⁹then they will hand him over to the Gentiles, to be mocked and flogged and crucified; and on the third day he will be raised."

The Request of the Mother of James and John

20 Then the mother of the sons of Zebedee came to him with her sons, and kneeling before him, she asked a favor of him. ²¹And he said to her, "What do you want?" She said to him, "Declare that these two sons of mine will sit, one at your right hand and one at your left, in your kingdom." ²²But Jesus answered, "You do not know what you are asking. Are you able to drink the cup that I am about to drink?"ˣ They said to him, "We are able." ²³He said to them, "You will indeed drink my cup, but to sit at my right hand and at my left, this is not mine to grant, but it is for those for whom it has been prepared by my Father."

24 When the ten heard it, they were angry with the two brothers. ²⁵But Jesus called them to him and said, "You know that the rulers of the Gentiles lord it over them, and their great ones are tyrants over them. ²⁶It will not be so among you; but whoever wishes to be great among you must be your servant, ²⁷and whoever wishes to be first among you must be your slave; ²⁸just as the Son of Man came not to be served but to serve, and to give his life a ransom for many."

Jesus Heals Two Blind Men

29 As they were leaving Jericho, a large crowd followed him. ³⁰There were two blind men sitting by the roadside. When they heard that Jesus was passing by, they shouted, "Lord,ʸ have mercy on us, Son of David!" ³¹The crowd sternly ordered them to be quiet;

20.8
Lev 19.3;
Deut 24.15
20.12
Jon 4.8;
Lk 12.55;
Jas 1.11
20.13
Mt 22.12;
26.50
20.15
Deut 15.9;
Mt 6.23;
Mk 7.22
20.16
Mt 19.30
20.18
Mt 16.21

20.19
Mt 16.21;
27.2;
Acts 2.23;
3.13
20.20
Mt 4.21;
8.2; 9.18;
Jn 9.38
20.21
Mt 19.28
20.22
Mt 26.39,
42;
Lk 22.42;
Jn 18.11
20.23
Acts 12.2;
Rev 1.9;
Mt 25.34
20.24
Lk 22.24,25
20.25
Lk 22.25-27
20.26
Mt 23.11;
Mk 9.35;
Lk 9.48
20.28
Jn 13.4;
Phil 2.7;
Jn 13.14;
Isa 53.10;
1 Tim 2.6;
Titus 2.14;
1 Pet 1.19;
Mt 26.28;
Heb 9.28
20.30
Mt 9.27

ᵘ Gk *a denarius* ᵛ Gk *is your eye evil because I am good?* ʷ Other ancient authorities add *for many are called but few are chosen* ˣ Other ancient authorities add *or to be baptized with the baptism that I am baptized with?* ʸ Other ancient authorities lack *Lord*

but they shouted even more loudly, "Have mercy on us, Lord, Son of David!" ³²Jesus stood still and called them, saying, "What do you want me to do for you?" ³³They said to him, "Lord, let our eyes be opened." ³⁴Moved with compassion, Jesus touched their eyes. Immediately they regained their sight and followed him.

Jesus' Triumphal Entry into Jerusalem

21 When they had come near Jerusalem and had reached Bethphage, at the Mount of Olives, Jesus sent two disciples, ²saying to them, "Go into the village ahead of you, and immediately you will find a donkey tied, and a colt with her; untie them and bring them to me. ³If anyone says anything to you, just say this, 'The Lord needs them.' And he will send them immediately.ᶻ" ⁴This took place to fulfill what had been spoken through the prophet, saying,

⁵ "Tell the daughter of Zion,
Look, your king is coming to you,
 humble, and mounted on a donkey,
 and on a colt, the foal of a donkey."

⁶The disciples went and did as Jesus had directed them; ⁷they brought the donkey and the colt, and put their cloaks on them, and he sat on them. ⁸A very large crowdᵃ spread their cloaks on the road, and others cut branches from the trees and spread them on the road. ⁹The crowds that went ahead of him and that followed were shouting,

"Hosanna to the Son of David!
Blessed is the one who comes in the name of the Lord!
Hosanna in the highest heaven!"

¹⁰When he entered Jerusalem, the whole city was in turmoil, asking, "Who is this?" ¹¹The crowds were

saying, "This is the prophet Jesus from Nazareth in Galilee."

Jesus Cleanses the Temple

12 Then Jesus entered the templeᵇ and drove out all who were selling and buying in the temple, and he overturned the tables of the money changers and the seats of those who sold doves. ¹³He said to them, "It is written,

'My house shall be called a house of prayer';

but you are making it a den of robbers."

14 The blind and the lame came to him in the temple, and he cured them. ¹⁵But when the chief priests and the scribes saw the amazing things that he did, and heardᶜ the children crying out in the temple, "Hosanna to the Son of David," they became angry ¹⁶and said to him, "Do you hear what these are saying?" Jesus said to them, "Yes; have you never read,

'Out of the mouths of infants and nursing babies
you have prepared praise for yourself'?"

¹⁷He left them, went out of the city to Bethany, and spent the night there.

Jesus Curses the Fig Tree

18 In the morning, when he returned to the city, he was hungry. ¹⁹And seeing a fig tree by the side of the road, he went to it and found nothing at all on it but leaves. Then he said to it, "May no fruit ever come from you again!" And the fig tree withered at once. ²⁰When the disciples saw it, they were amazed, saying, "How did the fig tree wither at once?" ²¹Jesus answered them, "Truly I tell you, if you have faith and do not doubt, not only will you do what has been done to the fig tree, but even if you say to this mountain, 'Be lifted up and thrown into the sea,' it will be done. ²²Whatever you ask for in prayer with faith, you will receive."

21.5
Isa 62.11;
Zech 9.9
21.8
2 Kings 9.13
21.9
Ps 118.26;
v. 15;
Mt 23.39
21.11
Jn 6.14;
7.40;
Acts 3.22;
Mk 6.15;
Lk 13.33

21.12
Ex 30.13;
Deut 14.25
21.13
Isa 56.7;
Jer 7.11
21.15
v. 9;
Lk 19.39
21.16
Ps 8.2
21.21
Mt 17.20;
Lk 17.6;
Jas 1.6
21.22
Mt 7.7;
Jn 14.13,14;
16.23;
Jas 5.16

ᶻ Or *'The Lord needs them and will send them back immediately.'* ᵃ Or *Most of the crowd* ᵇ Other ancient authorities add *of God* ᶜ Gk lacks *heard*

The Authority of Jesus Questioned

23 When he entered the temple, the chief priests and the elders of the people came to him as he was teaching, and said, "By what authority are you doing these things, and who gave you this authority?" 24 Jesus said to them, "I will also ask you one question; if you tell me the answer, then I will also tell you by what authority I do these things. 25 Did the baptism of John come from heaven, or was it of human origin?" And they argued with one another, "If we say, 'From heaven,' he will say to us, 'Why then did you not believe him?' 26 But if we say, 'Of human origin,' we are afraid of the crowd; for all regard John as a prophet." 27 So they answered Jesus, "We do not know." And he said to them, "Neither will I tell you by what authority I am doing these things.

The Parable of the Two Sons

28 "What do you think? A man had two sons; he went to the first and said, 'Son, go and work in the vineyard today.' 29 He answered, 'I will not'; but later he changed his mind and went. 30 The father[d] went to the second and said the same; and he answered, 'I go, sir'; but he did not go. 31 Which of the two did the will of his father?" They said, "The first." Jesus said to them, "Truly I tell you, the tax collectors and the prostitutes are going into the kingdom of God ahead of you. 32 For John came to you in the way of righteousness and you did not believe him, but the tax collectors and the prostitutes believed him; and even after you saw it, you did not change your minds and believe him.

The Parable of the Wicked Tenants

33 "Listen to another parable. There was a landowner who planted a vineyard, put a fence around it, dug a wine press in it, and built a watchtower. Then he leased it to tenants and went to another coun-

try. 34 When the harvest time had come, he sent his slaves to the tenants to collect his produce. 35 But the tenants seized his slaves and beat one, killed another, and stoned another. 36 Again he sent other slaves, more than the first; and they treated them in the same way. 37 Finally he sent his son to them, saying, 'They will respect my son.' 38 But when the tenants saw the son, they said to themselves, 'This is the heir; come, let us kill him and get his inheritance.' 39 So they seized him, threw him out of the vineyard, and killed him. 40 Now when the owner of the vineyard comes, what will he do to those tenants?" 41 They said to him, "He will put those wretches to a miserable death, and lease the vineyard to other tenants who will give him the produce at the harvest time."

42 Jesus said to them, "Have you never read in the scriptures:

'The stone that the builders rejected
 has become the
 cornerstone;[e]
 this was the Lord's doing,
 and it is amazing in our
 eyes'?

43 Therefore I tell you, the kingdom of God will be taken away from you and given to a people that produces the fruits of the kingdom.[f] 44 The one who falls on this stone will be broken to pieces; and it will crush anyone on whom it falls."[g]

45 When the chief priests and the Pharisees heard his parables, they realized that he was speaking about them. 46 They wanted to arrest him, but they feared the crowds, because they regarded him as a prophet.

The Parable of the Wedding Banquet

22 Once more Jesus spoke to them in parables, saying: 2 "The kingdom of heaven may be compared to a king who gave a

21.23
Acts 4.7;
7.27
21.26
Mt 14.5;
Mk 6.20
21.28
v. 33;
Mt 20.21
21.31
Lk 7.29,50
21.32
Mt 3.1ff;
Lk 7.29,30;
3.12,13
21.33
Ps 80.8;
Isa 5.1-7;
Mt 25.14,15
21.34
Mt 22.3
21.35
2 Chr 24.21;
Mt 23.34,
37;
Heb 11.36,
37
21.38
Ps 2.8;
Heb 1.2;
Mt 26.3;
27.1
21.41
Mt 8.11;
Acts 13.46;
18.6; 28.28
21.42
Ps 118.22,
23;
Acts 4.11;
1 Pet 2.7
21.43
Mt 8.12
21.46
vv. 26,11
22.2
Mt 13.24

d Gk He e Or keystone f Gk the fruits of it g Other ancient authorities lack verse 44

wedding banquet for his son. ³He sent his slaves to call those who had been invited to the wedding banquet, but they would not come. ⁴Again he sent other slaves, saying, 'Tell those who have been invited: Look, I have prepared my dinner, my oxen and my fat calves have been slaughtered, and everything is ready; come to the wedding banquet.' ⁵But they made light of it and went away, one to his farm, another to his business, ⁶while the rest seized his slaves, mistreated them, and killed them. ⁷The king was enraged. He sent his troops, destroyed those murderers, and burned their city. ⁸Then he said to his slaves, 'The wedding is ready, but those invited were not worthy. ⁹Go therefore into the main streets, and invite everyone you find to the wedding banquet.' ¹⁰Those slaves went out into the streets and gathered all whom they found, both good and bad; so the wedding hall was filled with guests.

11 "But when the king came in to see the guests, he noticed a man there who was not wearing a wedding robe, ¹²and he said to him, 'Friend, how did you get in here without a wedding robe?' And he was speechless. ¹³Then the king said to the attendants, 'Bind him hand and foot, and throw him into the outer darkness, where there will be weeping and gnashing of teeth.' ¹⁴For many are called, but few are chosen."

The Question about Paying Taxes

15 Then the Pharisees went and plotted to entrap him in what he said. ¹⁶So they sent their disciples to him, along with the Herodians, saying, "Teacher, we know that you are sincere, and teach the way of God in accordance with truth, and show deference to no one; for you do not regard people with partiality. ¹⁷Tell us, then, what you think. Is it lawful to pay taxes to the emperor, or not?" ¹⁸But Jesus, aware of their malice, said, "Why are you putting me to the test, you hypo-

22.3
Mt 21.34
22.4
Mt 21.36
22.7
Lk 19.27
22.8
Mt 10.11,13
22.10
Mt 13.47
22.11
2 Cor 5.3;
Eph 4.24;
Col 3.10,12;
Rev 3.4;
16.15; 19.8
22.12
Mt 20.13;
26.50
22.13
Mt 8.12;
Lk 13.28
22.16
Mk 3.6;
8.15
22.17
Mt 17.25

22.21
Rom 13.7
22.23
Acts 23.8
22.24
Deut 25.5
22.29
Jn 20.9
22.32
Ex 3.6,16;
Acts 7.32;
Heb 11.16
22.33
Mt 7.28
22.35
Lk 7.30;
10.25; 11.45;
14.3

crites? ¹⁹Show me the coin used for the tax." And they brought him a denarius. ²⁰Then he said to them, "Whose head is this, and whose title?" ²¹They answered, "The emperor's." Then he said to them, "Give therefore to the emperor the things that are the emperor's, and to God the things that are God's." ²²When they heard this, they were amazed; and they left him and went away.

The Question about the Resurrection

23 The same day some Sadducees came to him, saying there is no resurrection;ʰ and they asked him a question, saying, ²⁴"Teacher, Moses said, 'If a man dies childless, his brother shall marry the widow, and raise up children for his brother.' ²⁵Now there were seven brothers among us; the first married, and died childless, leaving the widow to his brother. ²⁶The second did the same, so also the third, down to the seventh. ²⁷Last of all, the woman herself died. ²⁸In the resurrection, then, whose wife of the seven will she be? For all of them had married her."

29 Jesus answered them, "You are wrong, because you know neither the scriptures nor the power of God. ³⁰For in the resurrection they neither marry nor are given in marriage, but are like angelsⁱ in heaven. ³¹And as for the resurrection of the dead, have you not read what was said to you by God, ³²'I am the God of Abraham, the God of Isaac, and the God of Jacob'? He is God not of the dead, but of the living." ³³And when the crowd heard it, they were astounded at his teaching.

The Greatest Commandment

34 When the Pharisees heard that he had silenced the Sadducees, they gathered together, ³⁵and one of them, a lawyer, asked him a question to test him. ³⁶"Teacher,

ʰ Other ancient authorities read *who say that there is no resurrection* ⁱ Other ancient authorities add *of God*

JEWISH SECTS

PHARISEES

Their roots can be traced to the second century B.C. — to the Hasidim.
1. Along with the Torah, they accepted as equally inspired and authoritative, all material contained within the oral tradition.
2. On free will and determination, they held to a mediating view that made it impossible for either free will or the sovereignty of God to cancel out the other.
3. They accepted a rather developed hierarchy of angels and demons.
4. They taught that there was a future for the dead.
5. They believed in the immortality of the soul and in reward and retribution after death.
6. They were champions of human equality.
7. The emphasis of their teaching was ethical rather than theological.

SADDUCEES

They probably had their beginning during the Hasmonean period (166-63 B.C.). Their demise occurred c. A.D. 70 with the fall of Jerusalem.
1. They denied that the oral law was authoritative and binding.
2. They interpreted Mosaic law more literally than did the Pharisees.
3. They were very exacting in Levitical purity.
4. They attributed all to free will.
5. They argued there is neither resurrection of the dead nor a future life.
6. They rejected a belief in angels and demons.
7. They rejected the idea of a spiritual world.
8. Only the books of Moses were canonical Scripture.

ESSENES

They probably originated among the Hasidim, along with the Pharisees, from whom they later separated (I Maccabees 2:42; 7:13). They were a group of very strict and zealous Jews who took part with the Maccabeans in a revolt against the Syrians, c. 165-155 B.C.
1. They followed a strict observance of the purity laws of the Torah.
2. They were notable for their communal ownership of property.
3. They had a strong sense of mutual responsibility.
4. Daily worship was an important feature along with a daily study of their sacred scriptures.
5. Solemn oaths of piety and obedience had to be taken.
6. Sacrifices were offered on holy days and during sacred seasons.
7. Marriage was not condemned in principle but was avoided.
8. They attributed all that happened to fate.

ZEALOTS

They originated during the reign of Herod the Great c. 6 B.C. and ceased to exist in A.D. 73 at Masada.
1. They opposed payment of tribute for taxes to a pagan emperor, saying that allegiance was due only to God.
2. They held a fierce loyalty to the Jewish traditions.
3. They were opposed to the use of the Greek language in Palestine.
4. They prophesied the coming of the time of salvation.

which commandment in the law is the greatest?" [37] He said to him, " 'You shall love the Lord your God with all your heart, and with all your soul, and with all your mind.' [38] This is the greatest and first commandment. [39] And a second is like it: 'You shall love your neighbor as yourself.' [40] On these two commandments hang all the law and the prophets."

The Question about David's Son

41 Now while the Pharisees were gathered together, Jesus asked them this question: [42] "What do you think of the Messiah?[i] Whose son is he?" They said to him, "The son of David." [43] He said to them, "How is it then that David by the Spirit[k] calls him Lord, saying,

[44] 'The Lord said to my Lord,
 "Sit at my right hand,
 until I put your enemies
 under your feet" '?
[45] If David thus calls him Lord, how can he be his son?" [46] No one was able to give him an answer, nor from that day did anyone dare to ask him any more questions.

Jesus Denounces Scribes and Pharisees

23 Then Jesus said to the crowds and to his disciples, [2] "The scribes and the Pharisees sit on Moses' seat; [3] therefore, do whatever they teach you and follow it; but do not do as they do, for they do not practice what they teach. [4] They tie up heavy burdens, hard to bear,[l] and lay them on the shoulders of others; but they themselves are unwilling to lift a finger to move them. [5] They do all their deeds to be seen by others; for they make their phylacteries broad and their fringes long. [6] They love to have the place of honor at banquets and the best seats in the synagogues, [7] and to be greeted with respect in the marketplaces, and to have people call them rabbi. [8] But you are not to be called rabbi, for you have one teacher, and you are all students. [m] [9] And call no one

22.37
Deut 6.5
22.39
Lev 19.18;
Mt 19.19;
Rom 13.9;
Gal 5.14;
Jas 2.8
22.40
Mt 7.12
22.42
Mt 9.27
22.44
Ps 110.1;
Acts 2.34;
Heb 1.13;
10.13
22.46
Mk 12.34;
Lk 20.40
23.2
Ezra 7.6,25;
Neh 8.4
23.4
Lk 11.46;
Acts 15.10;
Gal 6.13
23.5
Mt 6.1,2,5,
16; Deut 6.8
23.6
Lk 11.43;
14.7; 20.46
23.8
Jas 3.1
23.9
Mal 1.6

23.11
Mt 20.26
23.12
Lk 14.11;
18.14;
Jas 4.6;
1 Pet 5.5
23.13
Lk 11.52
23.16
v. 24;
Mt 15.14;
5.33-35
23.17
Ex 30.29
23.19
Ex 29.37
23.22
Ps 11.4;
Mt 5.34
23.23
Mt 11.42;
Lev 27.30;
Mic 6.8

your father on earth, for you have one Father—the one in heaven. [10] Nor are you to be called instructors, for you have one instructor, the Messiah. [n] [11] The greatest among you will be your servant. [12] All who exalt themselves will be humbled, and all who humble themselves will be exalted.

13 "But woe to you, scribes and Pharisees, hypocrites! For you lock people out of the kingdom of heaven. For you do not go in yourselves, and when others are going in, you stop them. [o] [15] Woe to you, scribes and Pharisees, hypocrites! For you cross sea and land to make a single convert, and you make the new convert twice as much a child of hell[p] as yourselves.

16 "Woe to you, blind guides, who say, 'Whoever swears by the sanctuary is bound by nothing, but whoever swears by the gold of the sanctuary is bound by the oath.' [17] You blind fools! For which is greater, the gold or the sanctuary that has made the gold sacred? [18] And you say, 'Whoever swears by the altar is bound by nothing, but whoever swears by the gift that is on the altar is bound by the oath.' [19] How blind you are! For which is greater, the gift or the altar that makes the gift sacred? [20] So whoever swears by the altar, swears by it and by everything on it; [21] and whoever swears by the sanctuary, swears by it and by the one who dwells in it; [22] and whoever swears by heaven, swears by the throne of God and by the one who is seated upon it.

23 "Woe to you, scribes and Pharisees, hypocrites! For you tithe mint, dill, and cummin, and have neglected the weightier matters of the law: justice and mercy and faith. It is these you ought to have

i Or Christ k Gk in spirit l Other ancient authorities lack hard to bear
m Gk brothers n Or the Christ o Other authorities add here (or after verse 12) verse 14, Woe to you, scribes and Pharisees, hypocrites! For you devour widows' houses and for the sake of appearance you make long prayers; therefore you will receive the greater condemnation p Gk Gehenna

practiced without neglecting the others. 24 You blind guides! You strain out a gnat but swallow a camel!

25 "Woe to you, scribes and Pharisees, hypocrites! For you clean the outside of the cup and of the plate, but inside they are full of greed and self-indulgence. 26 You blind Pharisee! First clean the inside of the cup, q so that the outside also may become clean.

27 "Woe to you, scribes and Pharisees, hypocrites! For you are like whitewashed tombs, which on the outside look beautiful, but inside they are full of the bones of the dead and of all kinds of filth. 28 So you also on the outside look righteous to others, but inside you are full of hypocrisy and lawlessness.

29 "Woe to you, scribes and Pharisees, hypocrites! For you build the tombs of the prophets and decorate the graves of the righteous, 30 and you say, 'If we had lived in the days of our ancestors, we would not have taken part with them in shedding the blood of the prophets.' 31 Thus you testify against yourselves that you are descendants of those who murdered the prophets. 32 Fill up, then, the measure of your ancestors. 33 You snakes, you brood of vipers! How can you escape being sentenced to hell?r 34 Therefore I send you prophets, sages, and scribes, some of whom you will kill and crucify, and some you will flog in your synagogues and pursue from town to town, 35 so that upon you may come all the righteous blood shed on earth, from the blood of righteous Abel to the blood of Zechariah son of Barachiah, whom you murdered between the sanctuary and the altar. 36 Truly I tell you, all this will come upon this generation.

The Lament over Jerusalem

37 "Jerusalem, Jerusalem, the city that kills the prophets and stones those who are sent to it! How often have I desired to gather your children together as a hen gathers her brood under her wings,

23.24
v. 16
23.25
Mk 7.4;
Lk 11.39
23.27
Lk 11.44;
Acts 23.3
23.29
Lk 11.47,48
23.31
Acts 7.51,52
23.32
1 Thes 2.16
23.33
Mt 3.7; 5.22
23.34
Lk 11.49;
2 Chr 36.15,
16
23.35
Gen 4.8;
Heb 11.4;
Zech 1.1;
2 Chr 24.21
23.36
Mt 10.23;
24.34
23.37
2 Chr 24.21

23.39
Ps 118.26;
Mt 21.9
24.1
Mk 13.1
24.2
Mt 26.61;
27.39,40;
Lk 19.44;
Jn 2.19
24.4
Jer 29.8;
2 Thes 2.3
24.5
vv. 11,23,
24;
1 Jn 2.18
24.7
Isa 19.2;
Hag 2.22;
Zech 14.13
24.9
Mt 10.17,
22;
Jn 15.18;
16.2
24.10
Mt 11.6
24.11
Mt 7.15;
Acts 20.29;
1 Tim 4.1
24.13
Mt 10.22;
Rev 2.7

and you were not willing! 38 See, your house is left to you, desolate. s 39 For I tell you, you will not see me again until you say, 'Blessed is the one who comes in the name of the Lord.' "

The Destruction of the Temple Foretold

24 As Jesus came out of the temple and was going away, his disciples came to point out to him the buildings of the temple. 2 Then he asked them, "You see all these, do you not? Truly I tell you, not one stone will be left here upon another; all will be thrown down."

Signs of the End of the Age

3 When he was sitting on the Mount of Olives, the disciples came to him privately, saying, "Tell us, when will this be, and what will be the sign of your coming and of the end of the age?" 4 Jesus answered them, "Beware that no one leads you astray. 5 For many will come in my name, saying, 'I am the Messiah!' t and they will lead many astray. 6 And you will hear of wars and rumors of wars; see that you are not alarmed; for this must take place, but the end is not yet. 7 For nation will rise against nation, and kingdom against kingdom, and there will be famines u and earthquakes in various places: 8 all this is but the beginning of the birthpangs.

Persecutions Foretold

9 "Then they will hand you over to be tortured and will put you to death, and you will be hated by all nations because of my name. 10 Then many will fall away, v and they will betray one another and hate one another. 11 And many false prophets will arise and lead many astray. 12 And because of the increase of lawlessness, the love of many will grow cold. 13 But the one

q Other ancient authorities add and of the plate r Gk Gehenna s Other ancient authorities lack desolate t Or the Christ u Other ancient authorities add and pestilences v Or stumble

who endures to the end will be saved. [14]And this good news[w] of the kingdom will be proclaimed throughout the world, as a testimony to all the nations; and then the end will come.

The Desolating Sacrilege

15 "So when you see the desolating sacrilege standing in the holy place, as was spoken of by the prophet Daniel (let the reader understand), [16]then those in Judea must flee to the mountains; [17]the one on the housetop must not go down to take what is in the house; [18]the one in the field must not turn back to get a coat. [19]Woe to those who are pregnant and to those who are nursing infants in those days! [20]Pray that your flight may not be in winter or on a sabbath. [21]For at that time there will be great suffering, such as has not been from the beginning of the world until now, no, and never will be. [22]And if those days had not been cut short, no one would be saved; but for the sake of the elect those days will be cut short. [23]Then if anyone says to you, 'Look! Here is the Messiah!'[x] or 'There he is!' — do not believe it. [24]For false messiahs[y] and false prophets will appear and produce great signs and omens, to lead astray, if possible, even the elect. [25]Take note, I have told you beforehand. [26]So, if they say to you, 'Look! He is in the wilderness,' do not go out. If they say, 'Look! He is in the inner rooms,' do not believe it. [27]For as the lightning comes from the east and flashes as far as the west, so will be the coming of the Son of Man. [28]Wherever the corpse is, there the vultures will gather.

The Coming of the Son of Man

29 "Immediately after the suffering of those days
 the sun will be darkened,
 and the moon will not give
 its light;
 the stars will fall from
 heaven,

24.14
Rom 10.18;
Col 1.6,23
24.15
Dan 9.27;
11.31; 12.11;
Acts 21.28;
1 Cor 15.52;
1 Thes 4.16
24.21
Dan 12.1;
Joel 2.2
24.22
Isa 65.8,9
24.23
Lk 17.23;
21.8
24.24
2 Thes 2.9-11;
Rev 13.13
24.27
Lk 17.24
24.29
Isa 13.10;
Ezek 32.7;
Joel 2.10;
Rev 8.12

24.30
Dan 7.13;
Mt 16.27;
Rev 1.7
24.31
Isa 27.13;
Zech 9.14
24.33
Jas 5.9
24.34
Mt 16.28;
23.36
24.35
Mt 5.18
24.37
Gen 6.5;
7.6-23;
Lk 17.26,27
24.40
Lk 17.34,35
24.42
Mt 25.13;
Lk 12.40
24.43
1 Thes 5.2;
2 Pet 3.10;
Rev 3.3;
16.15

 and the powers of heaven
 will be shaken.
[30]Then the sign of the Son of Man will appear in heaven, and then all the tribes of the earth will mourn, and they will see 'the Son of Man coming on the clouds of heaven' with power and great glory. [31]And he will send out his angels with a loud trumpet call, and they will gather his elect from the four winds, from one end of heaven to the other.

The Lesson of the Fig Tree

32 "From the fig tree learn its lesson: as soon as its branch becomes tender and puts forth its leaves, you know that summer is near. [33]So also, when you see all these things, you know that he[z] is near, at the very gates. [34]Truly I tell you, this generation will not pass away until all these things have taken place. [35]Heaven and earth will pass away, but my words will not pass away.

The Necessity for Watchfulness

36 "But about that day and hour no one knows, neither the angels of heaven, nor the Son,[a] but only the Father. [37]For as the days of Noah were, so will be the coming of the Son of Man. [38]For as in those days before the flood they were eating and drinking, marrying and giving in marriage, until the day Noah entered the ark, [39]and they knew nothing until the flood came and swept them all away, so too will be the coming of the Son of Man. [40]Then two will be in the field; one will be taken and one will be left. [41]Two women will be grinding meal together; one will be taken and one will be left. [42]Keep awake therefore, for you do not know on what day[b] your Lord is coming. [43]But understand this: if the owner of the house had known in what part of the night the thief was coming, he would have stayed awake and would not have let his house

[w] Or *gospel* [x] Or *the Christ* [y] Or *christs* [z] Or *it* [a] Other ancient authorities lack *nor the Son* [b] Other ancient authorities read *at what hour*

be broken into. ⁴⁴Therefore you also must be ready, for the Son of Man is coming at an unexpected hour.

The Faithful or the Unfaithful Slave

45 "Who then is the faithful and wise slave, whom his master has put in charge of his household, to give the other slaves ᶜ their allowance of food at the proper time? ⁴⁶Blessed is that slave whom his master will find at work when he arrives. ⁴⁷Truly I tell you, he will put that one in charge of all his possessions. ⁴⁸But if that wicked slave says to himself, 'My master is delayed,' ⁴⁹and he begins to beat his fellow slaves, and eats and drinks with drunkards, ⁵⁰the master of that slave will come on a day when he does not expect him and at an hour that he does not know. ⁵¹He will cut him in pieces ᵈ and put him with the hypocrites, where there will be weeping and gnashing of teeth.

The Parable of the Ten Bridesmaids

25 "Then the kingdom of heaven will be like this. Ten bridesmaids ᵉ took their lamps and went to meet the bridegroom.ᶠ ²Five of them were foolish, and five were wise. ³When the foolish took their lamps, they took no oil with them; ⁴but the wise took flasks of oil with their lamps. ⁵As the bridegroom was delayed, all of them became drowsy and slept. ⁶But at midnight there was a shout, 'Look! Here is the bridegroom! Come out to meet him.' ⁷Then all those bridesmaids ᵉ got up and trimmed their lamps. ⁸The foolish said to the wise, 'Give us some of your oil, for our lamps are going out.' ⁹But the wise replied, 'No! there will not be enough for you and for us; you had better go to the dealers and buy some for yourselves.' ¹⁰And while they went to buy it, the bridegroom came, and those who were ready went with him into the wedding banquet; and

the door was shut. ¹¹Later the other bridesmaids ᵉ came also, saying, 'Lord, lord, open to us.' ¹²But he replied, 'Truly I tell you, I do not know you.' ¹³Keep awake therefore, for you know neither the day nor the hour.ᵍ

The Parable of the Talents

14 "For it is as if a man, going on a journey, summoned his slaves and entrusted his property to them; ¹⁵to one he gave five talents,ʰ to another two, to another one, to each according to his ability. Then he went away. ¹⁶The one who had received the five talents went off at once and traded with them, and made five more talents. ¹⁷In the same way, the one who had the two talents made two more talents. ¹⁸But the one who had received the one talent went off and dug a hole in the ground and hid his master's money. ¹⁹After a long time the master of those slaves came and settled accounts with them. ²⁰Then the one who had received the five talents came forward, bringing five more talents, saying, 'Master, you handed over to me five talents; see, I have made five more talents.' ²¹His master said to him, 'Well done, good and trustworthy slave; you have been trustworthy in a few things, I will put you in charge of many things; enter into the joy of your master.' ²²And the one with the two talents also came forward, saying, 'Master, you handed over to me two talents; see, I have made two more talents.' ²³His master said to him, 'Well done, good and trustworthy slave; you have been trustworthy in a few things, I will put you in charge of many things; enter into the joy of your master.' ²⁴Then the one who had received the one talent also came forward, saying, 'Master, I knew that you were a harsh man, reaping where you did not sow, and

24.44
1 Thes 5.6
24.45
Mt 25.21,23
24.46
Rev 16.15
24.49
Lk 21.34
24.51
Mt 8.12;
13.42,50;
25.30
25.1
Mt 13.24;
Lk 12.35-38;
Rev 19.7;
21.2,9
25.2
Mt 7.24;
10.16; 24.45
25.5
1 Thes 5.6
25.7
Lk 12.35
25.10
Lk 13.25;
Rev 19.9

25.11
Mt 7.21-23
25.13
Mt 24.42,
44;
Mk 13.35;
Lk 12.40;
1 Thes 5.6
25.14
Lk 19.12;
Mt 21.33
25.15
Mt 18.23,
24;
Lk 19.13
25.19
Mt 18.23
25.21
Mt 24.45,
47;
Lk 16.10
25.23
v. 21
25.24
Jn 10.28,29;
2 Thes 2.9-11;
2 Tim 2.19;
Rev 13.13

ᶜ Gk *to give them* ᵈ Or *cut him off*
ᵉ Gk *virgins* ᶠ Other ancient authorities add *and the bride* ᵍ Other ancient authorities add *in which the Son of Man is coming* ʰ A talent was worth more than fifteen years' wages of a laborer

gathering where you did not scatter seed; 25 so I was afraid, and I went and hid your talent in the ground. Here you have what is yours.' 26 But his master replied, 'You wicked and lazy slave! You knew, did you, that I reap where I did not sow, and gather where I did not scatter? 27 Then you ought to have invested my money with the bankers, and on my return I would have received what was my own with interest. 28 So take the talent from him, and give it to the one with the ten talents. 29 For to all those who have, more will be given, and they will have an abundance; but from those who have nothing, even what they have will be taken away.' 30 As for this worthless slave, throw him into the outer darkness, where there will be weeping and gnashing of teeth.'

The Judgment of the Nations

31 "When the Son of Man comes in his glory, and all the angels with him, then he will sit on the throne of his glory. 32 All the nations will be gathered before him, and he will separate people one from another as a shepherd separates the sheep from the goats, 33 and he will put the sheep at his right hand and the goats at the left. 34 Then the king will say to those at his right hand, 'Come, you that are blessed by my Father, inherit the kingdom prepared for you from the foundation of the world; 35 for I was hungry and you gave me food, I was thirsty and you gave me something to drink, I was a stranger and you welcomed me, 36 I was naked and you gave me clothing, I was sick and you took care of me, I was in prison and you visited me.' 37 Then the righteous will answer him, 'Lord, when was it that we saw you hungry and gave you food, or thirsty and gave you something to drink? 38 And when was it that we saw you a stranger and welcomed you, or naked and gave you clothing? 39 And when was it that we saw you sick or in prison and visited you?' 40 And the king will answer

them, 'Truly I tell you, just as you did it to one of the least of these who are members of my family,i you did it to me.' 41 Then he will say to those at his left hand, 'You that are accursed, depart from me into the eternal fire prepared for the devil and his angels; 42 for I was hungry and you gave me no food, I was thirsty and you gave me nothing to drink, 43 I was a stranger and you did not welcome me, naked and you did not give me clothing, sick and in prison and you did not visit me.' 44 Then they also will answer, 'Lord, when was it that we saw you hungry or thirsty or a stranger or naked or sick or in prison, and did not take care of you?' 45 Then he will answer them, 'Truly I tell you, just as you did not do it to one of the least of these, you did not do it to me.' 46 And these will go away into eternal punishment, but the righteous into eternal life."

The Plot to Kill Jesus

26 When Jesus had finished saying all these things, he said to his disciples, 2 "You know that after two days the Passover is coming, and the Son of Man will be handed over to be crucified."

3 Then the chief priests and the elders of the people gathered in the palace of the high priest, who was called Caiaphas, 4 and they conspired to arrest Jesus by stealth and kill him. 5 But they said, "Not during the festival, or there may be a riot among the people."

The Anointing at Bethany

6 Now while Jesus was at Bethany in the house of Simon the leper,j 7 a woman came to him with an alabaster jar of very costly ointment, and she poured it on his head as he sat at the table. 8 But when the disciples saw it, they were angry and said, "Why this waste? 9 For this ointment could have been sold for a large sum, and the money given to the poor."

Cross-references

25.27 Lk 17.24
25.29 Mt 13.12; Mk 4.25; Lk 8.18
25.30 Mt 8.12; 3.42,50; 22.13; Lk 13.28
25.31 Mt 16.27; 19.28
25.32 Ezek 34.17, 20
25.34 Lk 12.32; 1 Cor 6.9; 15.50; Gal 5.21; Rev 13.8; 17.8
25.35 Isa 58.7; Ezek 18.7; Jas 1.27; Heb 13.2
25.36 Jas 2.15,16; 2 Tim 1.16
25.40 Prov 14.31; 19.17; Mt 10.42; Heb 6.10
25.41 Mt 7.23; Mk 9.48; Lk 16.24; Jude 7; 2 Pet 2.4
25.45 Prov 14.31; 17.5
25.46 Dan 12.2; Jn 5.29; Rom 2.7; Gal 6.8
26.1 Mt 7.28; 11.1; 13.53; 19.1
26.2 Jn 13.1
26.3 Ps 2.2; Jn 11.47-53
26.4 Mt 12.14
26.5 Mt 27.24
26.6 Mt 21.17

i Gk these my brothers j The terms leper and leprosy can refer to several diseases

10 But Jesus, aware of this, said to them, "Why do you trouble the woman? She has performed a good service for me. 11 For you always have the poor with you, but you will not always have me. 12 By pouring this ointment on my body she has prepared me for burial. 13 Truly I tell you, wherever this good news^k is proclaimed in the whole world, what she has done will be told in remembrance of her."

Judas Agrees to Betray Jesus

14 Then one of the twelve, who was called Judas Iscariot, went to the chief priests 15 and said, "What will you give me if I betray him to you?" They paid him thirty pieces of silver. 16 And from that moment he began to look for an opportunity to betray him.

The Passover with the Disciples

17 On the first day of Unleavened Bread the disciples came to Jesus, saying, "Where do you want us to make the preparations for you to eat the Passover?" 18 He said, "Go into the city to a certain man, and say to him, 'The Teacher says, My time is near; I will keep the Passover at your house with my disciples.'" 19 So the disciples did as Jesus had directed them, and they prepared the Passover meal.

20 When it was evening, he took his place with the twelve;^l 21 and while they were eating, he said, "Truly I tell you, one of you will betray me." 22 And they became greatly distressed and began to say to him one after another, "Surely not I, Lord?" 23 He answered, "The one who has dipped his hand into the bowl with me will betray me. 24 The Son of Man goes as it is written of him, but woe to that one by whom the Son of Man is betrayed! It would have been better for that one not to have been born." 25 Judas, who betrayed him, said, "Surely not I, Rabbi?" He replied, "You have said so."

The Institution of the Lord's Supper

26 While they were eating,

Jesus took a loaf of bread, and after blessing it he broke it, gave it to the disciples, and said, "Take, eat; this is my body." 27 Then he took a cup, and after giving thanks he gave it to them, saying, "Drink from it, all of you; 28 for this is my blood of the^m covenant, which is poured out for many for the forgiveness of sins. 29 I tell you, I will never again drink of this fruit of the vine until that day when I drink it new with you in my Father's kingdom."

30 When they had sung the hymn, they went out to the Mount of Olives.

Peter's Denial Foretold

31 Then Jesus said to them, "You will all become deserters because of me this night; for it is written,

'I will strike the shepherd,
 and the sheep of the flock
 will be scattered.'

32 But after I am raised up, I will go ahead of you to Galilee." 33 Peter said to him, "Though all become deserters because of you, I will never desert you." 34 Jesus said to him, "Truly I tell you, this very night, before the cock crows, you will deny me three times." 35 Peter said to him, "Even though I must die with you, I will not deny you." And so said all the disciples.

Jesus Prays in Gethsemane

36 Then Jesus went with them to a place called Gethsemane; and he said to his disciples, "Sit here while I go over there and pray." 37 He took with him Peter and the two sons of Zebedee, and began to be grieved and agitated. 38 Then he said to them, "I am deeply grieved, even to death; remain here, and stay awake with me." 39 And going a little farther, he threw himself on the ground and prayed, "My Father, if it is possible, let this cup pass from me; yet not what I want but what you want." 40 Then he came to the disciples and found

Cross references (center column):
26.11 Deut 15.11
26.12
26.15 Jn 19.40
Ex 21.32; Zech 11.12
26.18 Jn 7.6,8; 12.23; 13.1; 17.1
26.19 Deut 16.5-8
26.23 Ps 41.9; Lk 22.21; Jn 13.18; Isa 53; Dan 9.26; Lk 24.25; Acts 17.2,3; 1 Cor 15.3
26.26 1 Cor 10.16; 11.23-25
26.28 Ex 24.6-8; Mt 20.28; Mk 1.4; Heb 9.20
26.30 Mk 14.26
26.31 Jn 16.32; Mt 11.6; Zech 13.7
26.32 Mt 28.7,10,16
26.34 Jn 13.38
26.35 Jn 13.37
26.37 Mt 4.21
26.38 Jn 12.27
26.39 Jn 12.27; Mt 20.22; Jn 6.38; Phil 2.8
26.40 v. 38

^k Or gospel ^l Other ancient authorities add disciples ^m Other ancient authorities add new

them sleeping; and he said to Peter, "So, could you not stay awake with me one hour? [41] Stay awake and pray that you may not come into the time of trial;[n] the spirit indeed is willing, but the flesh is weak." [42] Again he went away for the second time and prayed, "My Father, if this cannot pass unless I drink it, your will be done." [43] Again he came and found them sleeping, for their eyes were heavy. [44] So leaving them again, he went away and prayed for the third time, saying the same words. [45] Then he came to the disciples and said to them, "Are you still sleeping and taking your rest? See, the hour is at hand, and the Son of Man is betrayed into the hands of sinners. [46] Get up, let us be going. See, my betrayer is at hand."

The Betrayal and Arrest of Jesus

47 While he was still speaking, Judas, one of the twelve, arrived; with him was a large crowd with swords and clubs, from the chief priests and the elders of the people. [48] Now the betrayer had given them a sign, saying, "The one I will kiss is the man; arrest him." [49] At once he came up to Jesus and said, "Greetings, Rabbi!" and kissed him. [50] Jesus said to him, "Friend, do what you are here to do." Then they came and laid hands on Jesus and arrested him. [51] Suddenly, one of those with Jesus put his hand on his sword, drew it, and struck the slave of the high priest, cutting off his ear. [52] Then Jesus said to him, "Put your sword back into its place; for all who take the sword will perish by the sword. [53] Do you think that I cannot appeal to my Father, and he will at once send me more than twelve legions of angels? [54] But how then would the scriptures be fulfilled, which say it must happen in this way?" [55] At that hour Jesus said to the crowds, "Have you come out with swords and clubs to arrest me as though I were a bandit? Day after day I sat in the temple teaching, and you did not arrest me. [56] But all this has taken

place, so that the scriptures of the prophets may be fulfilled." Then all the disciples deserted him and fled.

Jesus before the High Priest

57 Those who had arrested Jesus took him to Caiaphas the high priest, in whose house the scribes and the elders had gathered. [58] But Peter was following him at a distance, as far as the courtyard of the high priest; and going inside, he sat with the guards in order to see how this would end. [59] Now the chief priests and the whole council were looking for false testimony against Jesus so that they might put him to death, [60] but they found none, though many false witnesses came forward. At last two came forward [61] and said, "This fellow said, 'I am able to destroy the temple of God and to build it in three days.' " [62] The high priest stood up and said, "Have you no answer? What is it that they testify against you?" [63] But Jesus was silent. Then the high priest said to him, "I put you under oath before the living God, tell us if you are the Messiah,[o] the Son of God." [64] Jesus said to him, "You have said so. But I tell you,

From now on you will see
 the Son of Man
seated at the right hand of
 Power
and coming on the clouds
 of heaven."

[65] Then the high priest tore his clothes and said, "He has blasphemed! Why do we still need witnesses? You have now heard his blasphemy. [66] What is your verdict?" They answered, "He deserves death." [67] Then they spat in his face and struck him; and some slapped him, [68] saying, "Prophesy to us, you Messiah![o] Who is it that struck you?"

Peter's Denial of Jesus

69 Now Peter was sitting outside in the courtyard. A servant-girl came to him and said, "You also

n Or *into temptation* o Or *Christ*

were with Jesus the Galilean."
⁷⁰ But he denied it before all of
them, saying, "I do not know what
you are talking about." ⁷¹ When he
went out to the porch, another
servant-girl saw him, and she said
to the bystanders, "This man was
with Jesus of Nazareth."ᴾ ⁷² Again
he denied it with an oath, "I do not
know the man." ⁷³ After a little
while the bystanders came up and
said to Peter, "Certainly you are
also one of them, for your accent
betrays you." ⁷⁴ Then he began to
curse, and he swore an oath, "I do
not know the man!" At that mo-
ment the cock crowed. ⁷⁵ Then Pe-
ter remembered what Jesus had
said: "Before the cock crows, you
will deny me three times." And he
went out and wept bitterly.

Jesus Brought before Pilate

27 When morning came, all
the chief priests and the el-
ders of the people conferred to-
gether against Jesus in order to
bring about his death. ² They
bound him, led him away, and
handed him over to Pilate the gov-
ernor.

The Suicide of Judas

3 When Judas, his betrayer, saw
that Jesus�q was condemned, he re-
pented and brought back the thirty
pieces of silver to the chief priests
and the elders. ⁴ He said, "I have
sinned by betraying innocentʳ
blood." But they said, "What is that
to us? See to it yourself." ⁵ Throw-
ing down the pieces of silver in the
temple, he departed; and he went
and hanged himself. ⁶ But the chief
priests, taking the pieces of silver,
said, "It is not lawful to put them
into the treasury, since they are
blood money." ⁷ After conferring
together, they used them to buy
the potter's field as a place to bury
foreigners. ⁸ For this reason that
field has been called the Field of
Blood to this day. ⁹ Then was ful-
filled what had been spoken
through the prophet Jeremiah,ˢ
"And they tookᵗ the thirty pieces
of silver, the price of the one on

26.75
v. 34;
Jn 13.38
27.2
Mt 20.19;
Acts 3.13
27.3
Mt 26.14,15
27.4
v. 24
27.5
Acts 1.18
27.8
Acts 1.19
27.9f
Zech 11.12,
13

whom a price had been set,ᵘ on
whom some of the people of Israel
had set a price, ¹⁰ and they gaveᵛ
them for the potter's field, as the
Lord commanded me."

Pilate Questions Jesus

11 Now Jesus stood before the
governor; and the governor asked
him, "Are you the King of the
Jews?" Jesus said, "You say so."
¹² But when he was accused by the
chief priests and elders, he did not
answer. ¹³ Then Pilate said to him,
"Do you not hear how many accu-
sations they make against you?"
¹⁴ But he gave him no answer, not
even to a single charge, so that the
governor was greatly amazed.

Barabbas or Jesus?

15 Now at the festival the gover-
nor was accustomed to release a
prisoner for the crowd, anyone
whom they wanted. ¹⁶ At that time
they had a notorious prisoner,
called Jesusʷ Barabbas. ¹⁷ So after
they had gathered, Pilate said to
them, "Whom do you want me to
release for you, Jesusʷ Barabbas or
Jesus who is called the Messiah?"ˣ
¹⁸ For he realized that it was out of
jealousy that they had handed him
over. ¹⁹ While he was sitting on the
judgment seat, his wife sent word
to him, "Have nothing to do with
that innocent man, for today I have
suffered a great deal because of a
dream about him." ²⁰ Now the chief
priests and the elders persuaded
the crowds to ask for Barabbas and
to have Jesus killed. ²¹ The gover-
nor again said to them, "Which of
the two do you want me to release
for you?" And they said, "Barab-
bas." ²² Pilate said to them, "Then
what should I do with Jesus who is
called the Messiah?"ˣ All of them
said, "Let him be crucified!"
²³ Then he asked, "Why, what evil
has he done?" But they shouted all

27.12
Mt 26.63;
Jn 19.9
27.13
Mt 26.62;
Jn 19.10
27.14
1 Tim 6.13
27.19
Acts 12.21;
v. 24
27.20
Acts 3.14

ᴾ Gk the Nazorean q Gk he ʳ Other
ancient authorities read righteous ˢ Other
ancient authorities read Zechariah or Isaiah
ᵗ Or I took ᵘ Or the price of the precious
One ᵛ Other ancient authorities read I gave
ʷ Other ancient authorities lack Jesus
ˣ Or the Christ

the more, "Let him be crucified!"

Pilate Hands Jesus over to Be Crucified

24 So when Pilate saw that he could do nothing, but rather that a riot was beginning, he took some water and washed his hands before the crowd, saying, "I am innocent of this man's blood;[y] see to it yourselves." 25 Then the people as a whole answered, "His blood be on us and on our children!" 26 So he released Barabbas for them; and after flogging Jesus, he handed him over to be crucified.

The Soldiers Mock Jesus

27 Then the soldiers of the governor took Jesus into the governor's headquarters,[z] and they gathered the whole cohort around him. 28 They stripped him and put a scarlet robe on him, 29 and after twisting some thorns into a crown, they put it on his head. They put a reed in his right hand and knelt before him and mocked him, saying, "Hail, King of the Jews!" 30 They spat on him, and took the reed and struck him on the head. 31 After mocking him, they stripped him of the robe and put his own clothes on him. Then they led him away to crucify him.

The Crucifixion of Jesus

32 As they went out, they came upon a man from Cyrene named Simon; they compelled this man to carry his cross. 33 And when they came to a place called Golgotha (which means Place of a Skull), 34 they offered him wine to drink, mixed with gall; but when he tasted it, he would not drink it. 35 And when they had crucified him, they divided his clothes among themselves by casting lots;[a] 36 then they sat down there and kept watch over him. 37 Over his head they put the charge against him, which read, "This is Jesus, the King of the Jews."

38 Then two bandits were crucified with him, one on his right and one on his left. 39 Those who passed by derided[b] him, shaking their heads 40 and saying, "You who would destroy the temple and build it in three days, save yourself! If you are the Son of God, come down from the cross." 41 In the same way the chief priests also, along with the scribes and elders, were mocking him, saying, 42 "He saved others; he cannot save himself.[c] He is the King of Israel; let him come down from the cross now, and we will believe in him. 43 He trusts in God; let God deliver him now, if he wants to; for he said, 'I am God's Son.' " 44 The bandits who were crucified with him also taunted him in the same way.

The Death of Jesus

45 From noon on, darkness came over the whole land[d] until three in the afternoon. 46 And about three o'clock Jesus cried with a loud voice, "Eli, Eli, lema sabachthani?" that is, "My God, my God, why have you forsaken me?" 47 When some of the bystanders heard it, they said, "This man is calling for Elijah." 48 At once one of them ran and got a sponge, filled it with sour wine, put it on a stick, and gave it to him to drink. 49 But the others said, "Wait, let us see whether Elijah will come to save him."[e] 50 Then Jesus cried again with a loud voice and breathed his last.[f] 51 At that moment the curtain of the temple was torn in two, from top to bottom. The earth shook, and the rocks were split. 52 The tombs also were opened, and many bodies of the saints who had fallen asleep were raised. 53 After his resurrection they came out of the tombs and entered the holy city and appeared to many. 54 Now when the centurion and those with

Cross references

27.24 Mt 26.5; Deut 21.6-8; Ps 26.6; v. 19
27.25 Josh 2.19; Acts 5.28
27.26 Isa 53.5
27.27 Jn 18.28,33; Acts 10.1
27.29 Ps 69.19; Isa 53.3
27.30 Mt 26.67; Mk 10.34; 14.65
27.31 Isa 53.7
27.32 Heb 13.12
27.34 Ps 69.21
27.35 Ps 22.18
27.36 v. 54
27.38 Isa 53.12
27.39 Ps 22.7; 109.25
27.40 Mt 26.61; Acts 6.14; Jn 2.19
27.42 Jn 1.49; 12.13
27.43 Ps 22.8
27.45 Am 8.9
27.46 Ps 22.1
27.48 Ps 69.21
27.51 Ex 26.31; Heb 9.3; v. 54
27.54 Mt 3.17; 17.5

Footnotes

y Other ancient authorities read *this righteous blood*, or *this righteous man's blood*
z Gk *the praetorium* a Other ancient authorities add *in order that what had been spoken through the prophet might be fulfilled, "They divided my clothes among themselves, and for my clothing they cast lots."*
b Or *blasphemed* c Or *is he unable to save himself?* d Or *earth* e Other ancient authorities add *And another took a spear and pierced his side, and out came water and blood*
f Or *gave up his spirit*

him, who were keeping watch over Jesus, saw the earthquake and what took place, they were terrified and said, "Truly this man was God's Son!" [g]

55 Many women were also there, looking on from a distance; they had followed Jesus from Galilee and had provided for him. [56] Among them were Mary Magdalene, and Mary the mother of James and Joseph, and the mother of the sons of Zebedee.

The Burial of Jesus

57 When it was evening, there came a rich man from Arimathea, named Joseph, who was also a disciple of Jesus. [58] He went to Pilate and asked for the body of Jesus; then Pilate ordered it to be given to him. [59] So Joseph took the body and wrapped it in a clean linen cloth [60] and laid it in his own new tomb, which he had hewn in the rock. He then rolled a great stone to the door of the tomb and went away. [61] Mary Magdalene and the other Mary were there, sitting opposite the tomb.

The Guard at the Tomb

62 The next day, that is, after the day of Preparation, the chief priests and the Pharisees gathered before Pilate [63] and said, "Sir, we remember what that impostor said while he was still alive, 'After three days I will rise again.' [64] Therefore command the tomb to be made secure until the third day; otherwise his disciples may go and steal him away, and tell the people, 'He has been raised from the dead,' and the last deception would be worse than the first." [65] Pilate said to them, "You have a guard [h] of soldiers; go, make it as secure as you can." [i] [66] So they went with the guard and made the tomb secure by sealing the stone.

The Resurrection of Jesus

28 After the sabbath, as the first day of the week was dawning, Mary Magdalene and the other Mary went to see the tomb. [2] And suddenly there was a great

earthquake; for an angel of the Lord, descending from heaven, came and rolled back the stone and sat on it. [3] His appearance was like lightning, and his clothing white as snow. [4] For fear of him the guards shook and became like dead men. [5] But the angel said to the women, "Do not be afraid; I know that you are looking for Jesus who was crucified. [6] He is not here; for he has been raised, as he said. Come, see the place where he [j] lay. [7] Then go quickly and tell his disciples, 'He has been raised from the dead, [k] and indeed he is going ahead of you to Galilee; there you will see him.' This is my message for you." [8] So they left the tomb quickly with fear and great joy, and ran to tell his disciples. [9] Suddenly Jesus met them and said, "Greetings!" And they came to him, took hold of his feet, and worshiped him. [10] Then Jesus said to them, "Do not be afraid; go and tell my brothers to go to Galilee; there they will see me."

The Report of the Guard

11 While they were going, some of the guard went into the city and told the chief priests everything that had happened. [12] After the priests [l] had assembled with the elders, they devised a plan to give a large sum of money to the soldiers, [13] telling them, "You must say, 'His disciples came by night and stole him away while we were asleep.' [14] If this comes to the governor's ears, we will satisfy him and keep you out of trouble." [15] So they took the money and did as they were directed. And this story is still told among the Jews to this day.

The Commissioning of the Disciples

16 Now the eleven disciples went to Galilee, to the mountain to which Jesus had directed them. [17] When they saw him, they worshiped him; but some doubted. [18] And Jesus came and said to

27.55
Lk 8.2,3
27.56
Mk 15.40, 47;
Lk 24.10
27.57
Acts 13.29
27.60
Mt 28.2;
Mk 16.4
27.63
Mt 16.21;
17.23; 20.19;
Mk 8.31;
10.34;
Lk 9.22;
18.33; 24.6,7;
Jn 2.19
27.66
v. 60;
Mt 28.11-15
28.1
Lk 8.2;
Mt 27.56
28.2
Mt 27.51,60

28.3
Dan 7.9;
10.6;
Mk 9.3;
Jn 20.12;
Acts 1.10
28.5
v. 10;
Mt 14.27
28.6
Mt 12.40;
16.21; 17.23;
20.19
28.7
Mt 26.32;
v. 16
28.9
Jn 20.14-18
28.10
Rom 8.29;
Heb 2.11
28.11
Mt 27.65,66
28.14
Mt 27.2
28.16
v. 7;
Mt 26.32
28.18
Dan 7.13, 14;
Lk 10.22;
Phil 2.9,10;
1 Pet 3.22

g Or *a son of God* h Or *Take a guard*
i Gk *you know how* j Other ancient
authorities read *the Lord* k Other ancient
authorities lack *from the dead* l Gk *they*

them, "All authority in heaven and on earth has been given to me. [19] Go therefore and make disciples of all nations, baptizing them in the name of the Father and of the Son and of the Holy Spirit, [20] and

teaching them to obey everything that I have commanded you. And remember, I am with you always, to the end of the age."[m]

28.19
Lk 24.47;
Acts 1.8
28.20
Acts 2.42;
Mt 18.20;
Acts 18.10

[m] Other ancient authorities add *Amen*

THE GOSPEL ACCORDING TO
Mark

Title and Background

The early church fathers agreed that Mark's Gospel reproduces the preaching of Peter. Peter's personality can be found on almost every page, and the main characteristic of this Gospel is action.

Author and Date of Writing

John Mark was the son of Mary (Acts 12.12) and the cousin of Barnabas (Col 4.10). He accompanied Paul and Barnabas on their first missionary journey (Acts 13.5). Paul spoke of him as his companion in Rome and paid high tribute to his service (2 Tim 4.11). It is believed that Mark is the first of the Gospels to be written, possibly when Christians were beginning to suffer persecution under Emperor Nero. It would therefore be dated about A.D. 65.

Theme and Message

The book of Mark stresses the facts and actions of Jesus rather than his words or sayings. Although it is the shortest of the four Gospels, it is often the most detailed. Jewish customs are carefully explained for Roman readers. One of Mark's purposes was to demonstrate the deity of Christ. He tells the stories of Christ's ministry, especially his miracles. Mark spends one-third of the book telling the events of Christ's last week on earth, ending with his death and resurrection.

Outline

 I. The Beginnings of Jesus' Ministry (1.1-13)
 II. Jesus' Ministry in Galilee (1.14–6.29)
 III. Withdrawals From Galilee (6.30–9.32)
 IV. Final Ministry in Galilee (9.33-50)
 V. Jesus' Ministry in Judea and Perea (10.1-52)
 VI. The Passion of Jesus (11.1–15.47)
 VII. The Resurrection of Jesus (16.1-20)

The Proclamation of John the Baptist

1 The beginning of the good news[a] of Jesus Christ, the Son of God.[b]

2 As it is written in the prophet Isaiah,[c]

"See, I am sending my
 messenger ahead of
 you,[d]
who will prepare your way;
3 the voice of one crying out in
 the wilderness:
'Prepare the way of the
 Lord,
make his paths straight,' "

4 John the baptizer appeared[e] in the wilderness, proclaiming a baptism of repentance for the forgiveness of sins. 5 And people from the whole Judean countryside and all the people of Jerusalem were going out to him, and were baptized by him in the river Jordan, confessing their sins. 6 Now John was clothed with camel's hair, with a leather belt around his waist, and he ate locusts and wild honey. 7 He proclaimed, "The one who is more powerful than I is coming after me; I am not worthy to stoop down and untie the thong of his sandals. 8 I

Cross references:
1.1 Mt 4.3
1.2 Mal 3.1; Mt 11.10; Lk 7.27
1.3 Isa 40.3
1.4 Acts 13.24; Lk 1.77
1.6 Lev 11.22
1.7 Acts 13.25
1.8 Acts 1.5; Isa 44.3; Joel 2.28

a Or *gospel* b Other ancient authorities lack *the Son of God* c Other ancient authorities read *in the prophets* d Gk *before your face* e Other ancient authorities read *John was baptizing*

have baptized you with[f] water; but he will baptize you with[f] the Holy Spirit."

The Baptism of Jesus

9 In those days Jesus came from Nazareth of Galilee and was baptized by John in the Jordan. [10]And just as he was coming up out of the water, he saw the heavens torn apart and the Spirit descending like a dove on him. [11]And a voice came from heaven, "You are my Son, the Beloved;[g] with you I am well pleased."

The Temptation of Jesus

12 And the Spirit immediately drove him out into the wilderness. [13]He was in the wilderness forty days, tempted by Satan; and he was with the wild beasts; and the angels waited on him.

The Beginning of the Galilean Ministry

14 Now after John was arrested, Jesus came to Galilee, proclaiming the good news[h] of God,[i] [15]and saying, "The time is fulfilled, and the kingdom of God has come near;[j] repent, and believe in the good news."[h]

Jesus Calls the First Disciples

16 As Jesus passed along the Sea of Galilee, he saw Simon and his brother Andrew casting a net into the sea—for they were fishermen. [17]And Jesus said to them, "Follow me and I will make you fish for people." [18]And immediately they left their nets and followed him. [19]As he went a little farther, he saw James son of Zebedee and his brother John, who were in their boat mending the nets. [20]Immediately he called them; and they left their father Zebedee in the boat with the hired men, and followed him.

The Man with an Unclean Spirit

21 They went to Capernaum; and when the sabbath came, he entered the synagogue and taught. [22]They were astounded at his teaching, for he taught them as one

1.9
Mt 2.23
1.10
Jn 1.32
1.11
Ps 2.7;
Isa 42.1
1.14
Mt 4.23
1.15
Gal 4.4;
Eph 1.10;
Acts 20.21
1.18
Mt 19.27
1.21
Mt 4.23
1.22
Mt 7.28

1.24
Mt 8.29;
Mk 10.47;
14.67;
Jn 6.69;
Acts 3.14
1.25
v. 34
1.27
Mk 10.24,
32
1.29
vv. 21,23
1.32
Mk 4.24
1.34
Mt 4.23;
Mk 3.12;
Acts 16.17,
18
1.35
Mt 14.23;
Lk 5.16
1.38
Isa 61.1

having authority, and not as the scribes. [23]Just then there was in their synagogue a man with an unclean spirit, [24]and he cried out, "What have you to do with us, Jesus of Nazareth? Have you come to destroy us? I know who you are, the Holy One of God." [25]But Jesus rebuked him, saying, "Be silent, and come out of him!" [26]And the unclean spirit, convulsing him and crying with a loud voice, came out of him. [27]They were all amazed, and they kept on asking one another, "What is this? A new teaching—with authority! He[k] commands even the unclean spirits, and they obey him." [28]At once his fame began to spread throughout the surrounding region of Galilee.

Jesus Heals Many at Simon's House

29 As soon as they[l] left the synagogue, they entered the house of Simon and Andrew, with James and John. [30]Now Simon's mother-in-law was in bed with a fever, and they told him about her at once. [31]He came and took her by the hand and lifted her up. Then the fever left her, and she began to serve them.

32 That evening, at sundown, they brought to him all who were sick or possessed with demons. [33]And the whole city was gathered around the door. [34]And he cured many who were sick with various diseases, and cast out many demons; and he would not permit the demons to speak, because they knew him.

A Preaching Tour in Galilee

35 In the morning, while it was still very dark, he got up and went out to a deserted place, and there he prayed. [36]And Simon and his companions hunted for him. [37]When they found him, they said to him, "Everyone is searching for you." [38]He answered, "Let us go on

[f] Or in [g] Or my beloved Son
[h] Or gospel [i] Other ancient authorities read of the kingdom [j] Or is at hand
[k] Or A new teaching! With authority he
[l] Other ancient authorities read he

to the neighboring towns, so that I may proclaim the message there also; for that is what I came out to do." [39] And he went throughout Galilee, proclaiming the message in their synagogues and casting out demons.

Jesus Cleanses a Leper

40 A leper[m] came to him begging him, and kneeling[n] he said to him, "If you choose, you can make me clean." [41] Moved with pity,[o] Jesus[p] stretched out his hand and touched him, and said to him, "I do choose. Be made clean!" [42] Immediately the leprosy[m] left him, and he was made clean. [43] After sternly warning him he sent him away at once, [44] saying to him, "See that you say nothing to anyone; but go, show yourself to the priest, and offer for your cleansing what Moses commanded, as a testimony to them." [45] But he went out and began to proclaim it freely, and to spread the word, so that Jesus[p] could no longer go into a town openly, but stayed out in the country; and people came to him from every quarter.

Jesus Heals a Paralytic

2 When he returned to Capernaum after some days, it was reported that he was at home. [2] So many gathered around that there was no longer room for them, not even in front of the door; and he was speaking the word to them. [3] Then some people[q] came, bringing to him a paralyzed man, carried by four of them. [4] And when they could not bring him to Jesus because of the crowd, they removed the roof above him; and after having dug through it, they let down the mat on which the paralytic lay. [5] When Jesus saw their faith, he said to the paralytic, "Son, your sins are forgiven." [6] Now some of the scribes were sitting there, questioning in their hearts, [7] "Why does this fellow speak in this way? It is blasphemy! Who can forgive sins but God alone?" [8] At once Jesus perceived in his spirit that

they were discussing these questions among themselves; and he said to them, "Why do you raise such questions in your hearts? [9] Which is easier, to say to the paralytic, 'Your sins are forgiven,' or to say, 'Stand up and take your mat and walk'? [10] But so that you may know that the Son of Man has authority on earth to forgive sins" — he said to the paralytic — [11] "I say to you, stand up, take your mat and go to your home." [12] And he stood up, and immediately took the mat and went out before all of them; so that they were all amazed and glorified God, saying, "We have never seen anything like this!"

Jesus Calls Levi

13 Jesus[r] went out again beside the sea; the whole crowd gathered around him, and he taught them. [14] As he was walking along, he saw Levi son of Alphaeus sitting at the tax booth, and he said to him, "Follow me." And he got up and followed him.

15 And as he sat at dinner[s] in Levi's[t] house, many tax collectors and sinners were also sitting[u] with Jesus and his disciples — for there were many who followed him. [16] When the scribes of[v] the Pharisees saw that he was eating with sinners and tax collectors, they said to his disciples, "Why does he eat[w] with tax collectors and sinners?" [17] When Jesus heard this, he said to them, "Those who are well have no need of a physician, but those who are sick; I have come to call not the righteous but sinners."

The Question about Fasting

18 Now John's disciples and the Pharisees were fasting; and people[q] came and said to him, "Why do John's disciples and the disciples of the Pharisees fast, but your

1.39
Mt 4.23-25
1.40
Mk 10.17
1.44
Lev 13.49;
14.2-32
1.45
Lk 5.15;
Mt 28.15;
Mk 2.13;
Lk 5.17;
Jn 6.2
2.2
v. 13
2.3
Mt 4.24
2.7
Isa 43.25

2.12
Mt 9.33
2.13
Mk 1.45
2.14
Mt 8.22
2.16
Acts 23.9
2.17
Lk 19.10;
1 Tim 1.15

m The terms *leper* and *leprosy* can refer to several diseases n Other ancient authorities lack *kneeling* o Other ancient authorities read *anger* p Gk *he* q Gk *they* r Gk *He* s Gk *reclined* t Gk *his* u Gk *reclining* v Other ancient authorities read *and* w Other ancient authorities add *and drink*

disciples do not fast?" ¹⁹Jesus said to them, "The wedding guests cannot fast while the bridegroom is with them, can they? As long as they have the bridegroom with them, they cannot fast. ²⁰The days will come when the bridegroom is taken away from them, and then they will fast on that day.

21 "No one sews a piece of unshrunk cloth on an old cloak; otherwise, the patch pulls away from it, the new from the old, and a worse tear is made. ²²And no one puts new wine into old wineskins; otherwise, the wine will burst the skins, and the wine is lost, and so are the skins; but one puts new wine into fresh wineskins."ˣ

Pronouncement about the Sabbath

23 One sabbath he was going through the grainfields; and as they made their way his disciples began to pluck heads of grain. ²⁴The Pharisees said to him, "Look, why are they doing what is not lawful on the sabbath?" ²⁵And he said to them, "Have you never read what David did when he and his companions were hungry and in need of food? ²⁶He entered the house of God, when Abiathar was high priest, and ate the bread of the Presence, which it is not lawful for any but the priests to eat, and he gave some to his companions." ²⁷Then he said to them, "The sabbath was made for humankind, and not humankind for the sabbath; ²⁸so the Son of Man is lord even of the sabbath."

The Man with a Withered Hand

3 Again he entered the synagogue, and a man was there who had a withered hand. ²They watched him to see whether he would cure him on the sabbath, so that they might accuse him. ³And he said to the man who had the withered hand, "Come forward." ⁴Then he said to them, "Is it lawful to do good or to do harm on the sabbath, to save life or to kill?" But they were silent. ⁵He looked

around at them with anger; he was grieved at their hardness of heart and said to the man, "Stretch out your hand." He stretched it out, and his hand was restored. ⁶The Pharisees went out and immediately conspired with the Herodians against him, how to destroy him.

A Multitude at the Seaside

7 Jesus departed with his disciples to the sea, and a great multitude from Galilee followed him; ⁸hearing all that he was doing, they came to him in great numbers from Judea, Jerusalem, Idumea, beyond the Jordan, and the region around Tyre and Sidon. ⁹He told his disciples to have a boat ready for him because of the crowd, so that they would not crush him; ¹⁰for he had cured many, so that all who had diseases pressed upon him to touch him. ¹¹Whenever the unclean spirits saw him, they fell down before him and shouted, "You are the Son of God!" ¹²But he sternly ordered them not to make him known.

Jesus Appoints the Twelve

13 He went up the mountain and called to him those whom he wanted, and they came to him. ¹⁴And he appointed twelve, whom he also named apostles,ʸ to be with him, and to be sent out to proclaim the message, ¹⁵and to have authority to cast out demons. ¹⁶So he appointed the twelve:ᶻ Simon (to whom he gave the name Peter); ¹⁷James son of Zebedee and John the brother of James (to whom he gave the name Boanerges, that is, Sons of Thunder); ¹⁸and Andrew, and Philip, and Bartholomew, and Matthew, and Thomas, and James son of Alphaeus, and Thaddaeus, and Simon the Cananaean, ¹⁹and Judas Iscariot, who betrayed him.

Jesus and Beelzebul

Then he went home; ²⁰and the

ˣ Other ancient authorities lack *but one puts new wine into fresh wineskins* ʸ Other ancient authorities lack *whom he also named apostles* ᶻ Other ancient authorities lack *So he appointed the twelve*

crowd came together again, so that they could not even eat. ²¹When his family heard it, they went out to restrain him, for people were saying, "He has gone out of his mind." ²²And the scribes who came down from Jerusalem said, "He has Beelzebul, and by the ruler of the demons he casts out demons." ²³And he called them to him, and spoke to them in parables, "How can Satan cast out Satan? ²⁴If a kingdom is divided against itself, that kingdom cannot stand. ²⁵And if a house is divided against itself, that house will not be able to stand. ²⁶And if Satan has risen up against himself and is divided, he cannot stand, but his end has come. ²⁷But no one can enter a strong man's house and plunder his property without first tying up the strong man; then indeed the house can be plundered. ²⁸ "Truly I tell you, people will be forgiven for their sins and whatever blasphemies they utter; ²⁹but whoever blasphemes against the Holy Spirit can never have forgiveness, but is guilty of an eternal sin" — ³⁰for they had said, "He has an unclean spirit."

The True Kindred of Jesus

31 Then his mother and his brothers came; and standing outside, they sent to him and called him. ³²A crowd was sitting around him; and they said to him, "Your mother and your brothers and sisters[a] are outside, asking for you." ³³And he replied, "Who are my mother and my brothers?" ³⁴And looking at those who sat around him, he said, "Here are my mother and my brothers! ³⁵Whoever does the will of God is my brother and sister and mother."

The Parable of the Sower

4 Again he began to teach beside the sea. Such a very large crowd gathered around him that he got into a boat on the sea and sat there, while the whole crowd was beside the sea on the land. ²He began to teach them many things in parables, and in his teaching he

said to them: ³ "Listen! A sower went out to sow. ⁴And as he sowed, some seed fell on the path, and the birds came and ate it up. ⁵Other seed fell on rocky ground, where it did not have much soil, and it sprang up quickly, since it had no depth of soil. ⁶And when the sun rose, it was scorched; and since it had no root, it withered away. ⁷Other seed fell among thorns, and the thorns grew up and choked it, and it yielded no grain. ⁸Other seed fell into good soil and brought forth grain, growing up and increasing and yielding thirty and sixty and a hundredfold." ⁹And he said, "Let anyone with ears to hear listen!"

The Purpose of the Parables

10 When he was alone, those who were around him along with the twelve asked him about the parables. ¹¹And he said to them, "To you has been given the secret[b] of the kingdom of God, but for those outside, everything comes in parables; ¹²in order that

'they may indeed look, but
 not perceive,
 and may indeed listen, but
 not understand;
so that they may not turn
 again and be forgiven.' "

13 And he said to them, "Do you not understand this parable? Then how will you understand all the parables? ¹⁴The sower sows the word. ¹⁵These are the ones on the path where the word is sown: when they hear, Satan immediately comes and takes away the word that is sown in them. ¹⁶And these are the ones sown on rocky ground: when they hear the word, they immediately receive it with joy. ¹⁷But they have no root, and endure only for a while; then, when trouble or persecution arises on account of the word, immediately they fall away.[c] ¹⁸And others are those sown among the thorns: these are the ones who hear the word, ¹⁹but the cares of the world, and the lure of wealth, and the desire for other

3.21
Jn 10.20;
Acts 26.24
3.22
Mt 9.34;
10.25;
Jn 7.20;
8.48,52
3.23
Mk 4.2ff
3.27
Isa 49.24,25
3.28
Lk 12.10
3.31
Mt 12.46;
Lk 8.19
4.1
Mk 2.13;
3.7
4.2
Mk 3.23

4.8
Jn 15.5;
Col 1.6
4.9
Mt 11.15
4.11
1 Cor 5.12;
Col 4.5;
1 Thes 4.12;
1 Tim 3.7
4.12
Isa 6.9;
Jn 12.40;
Acts 28.26;
Rom 11.8
4.15
Mk 2.23,26

a Other ancient authorities lack *and sisters*
b Or *mystery* c Or *stumble*

things come in and choke the word, and it yields nothing. 20 And these are the ones sown on the good soil: they hear the word and accept it and bear fruit, thirty and sixty and a hundredfold."

A Lamp under a Bushel Basket

21 He said to them, "Is a lamp brought in to be put under the bushel basket, or under the bed, and not on the lampstand? 22 For there is nothing hidden, except to be disclosed; nor is anything secret, except to come to light. 23 Let anyone with ears to hear listen!" 24 And he said to them, "Pay attention to what you hear; the measure you give will be the measure you get, and still more will be given you. 25 For to those who have, more will be given; and from those who have nothing, even what they have will be taken away."

The Parable of the Growing Seed

26 He also said, "The kingdom of God is as if someone would scatter seed on the ground, 27 and would sleep and rise night and day, and the seed would sprout and grow, he does not know how. 28 The earth produces of itself, first the stalk, then the head, then the full grain in the head. 29 But when the grain is ripe, at once he goes in with his sickle, because the harvest has come."

The Parable of the Mustard Seed

30 He also said, "With what can we compare the kingdom of God, or what parable will we use for it? 31 It is like a mustard seed, which, when sown upon the ground, is the smallest of all the seeds on earth; 32 yet when it is sown it grows up and becomes the greatest of all shrubs, and puts forth large branches, so that the birds of the air can make nests in its shade."

The Use of Parables

33 With many such parables he spoke the word to them, as they were able to hear it; 34 he did not speak to them except in parables,

4.22
Mt 10.26;
Lk 8.17;
12.2
4.23
Mt 11.15
4.24
Mt 7.2;
Lk 6.38
4.25
Mt 13.12;
25.29;
Lk 8.18;
19.26
4.26
Mt 13.24
4.29
Rev 14.15
4.30
Mt 13.24
4.33
Jn 16.12
4.34
Mt 13.34;
Jn 16.25

4.36
Mk 5.2,21
4.40
Mt 14.31,
32;
Mk 16.14
5.2
Mt 4.1; 1.23
5.6
Mt 4.9;
18.26
5.7
Mt 8.29;
4.3;
Lk 8.28;
Acts 16.17;
Heb 7.1

but he explained everything in private to his disciples.

Jesus Stills a Storm

35 On that day, when evening had come, he said to them, "Let us go across to the other side." 36 And leaving the crowd behind, they took him with them in the boat, just as he was. Other boats were with him. 37 A great windstorm arose, and the waves beat into the boat, so that the boat was already being swamped. 38 But he was in the stern, asleep on the cushion; and they woke him up and said to him, "Teacher, do you not care that we are perishing?" 39 He woke up and rebuked the wind, and said to the sea, "Peace! Be still!" Then the wind ceased, and there was a dead calm. 40 He said to them, "Why are you afraid? Have you still no faith?" 41 And they were filled with great awe and said to one another, "Who then is this, that even the wind and the sea obey him?"

Jesus Heals the Gerasene Demoniac

5 They came to the other side of the sea, to the country of the Gerasenes.ᵈ 2 And when he had stepped out of the boat, immediately a man out of the tombs with an unclean spirit met him. 3 He lived among the tombs; and no one could restrain him any more, even with a chain; 4 for he had often been restrained with shackles and chains, but the chains he wrenched apart, and the shackles he broke in pieces; and no one had the strength to subdue him. 5 Night and day among the tombs and on the mountains he was always howling and bruising himself with stones. 6 When he saw Jesus from a distance, he ran and bowed down before him; 7 and he shouted at the top of his voice, "What have you to do with me, Jesus, Son of the Most High God? I adjure you by God, do not torment me." 8 For he had said

ᵈ Other ancient authorities read *Gergesenes*; others, *Gadarenes*

to him, "Come out of the man, you unclean spirit!" ⁹Then Jesus*e* asked him, "What is your name?" He replied, "My name is Legion; for we are many." ¹⁰He begged him earnestly not to send them out of the country. ¹¹Now there on the hillside a great herd of swine was feeding; ¹²and the unclean spirits*f* begged him, "Send us into the swine; let us enter them." ¹³So he gave them permission. And the unclean spirits came out and entered the swine; and the herd, numbering about two thousand, rushed down the steep bank into the sea, and were drowned in the sea.

14 The swineherds ran off and told it in the city and in the country. Then people came to see what it was that had happened. ¹⁵They came to Jesus and saw the demoniac sitting there, clothed and in his right mind, the very man who had had the legion; and they were afraid. ¹⁶Those who had seen what had happened to the demoniac and to the swine reported it. ¹⁷Then they began to beg Jesus*g* to leave their neighborhood. ¹⁸As he was getting into the boat, the man who had been possessed by demons begged him that he might be with him. ¹⁹But Jesus*e* refused, and said to him, "Go home to your friends, and tell them how much the Lord has done for you, and what mercy he has shown you." ²⁰And he went away and began to proclaim in the Decapolis how much Jesus had done for him; and everyone was amazed.

A Girl Restored to Life and a Woman Healed

21 When Jesus had crossed again in the boat*h* to the other side, a great crowd gathered around him; and he was by the sea. ²²Then one of the leaders of the synagogue named Jairus came and, when he saw him, fell at his feet ²³and begged him repeatedly, "My little daughter is at the point of death. Come and lay your hands on her, so that she may be made well, and live." ²⁴So he went with him.

And a large crowd followed him and pressed in on him. ²⁵Now there was a woman who had been suffering from hemorrhages for twelve years. ²⁶She had endured much under many physicians, and had spent all that she had; and she was no better, but rather grew worse. ²⁷She had heard about Jesus, and came up behind him in the crowd and touched his cloak, ²⁸for she said, "If I but touch his clothes, I will be made well." ²⁹Immediately her hemorrhage stopped; and she felt in her body that she was healed of her disease. ³⁰Immediately aware that power had gone forth from him, Jesus turned about in the crowd and said, "Who touched my clothes?" ³¹And his disciples said to him, "You see the crowd pressing in on you; how can you say, 'Who touched me?' " ³²He looked all around to see who had done it. ³³But the woman, knowing what had happened to her, came in fear and trembling, fell down before him, and told him the whole truth. ³⁴He said to her, "Daughter, your faith has made you well; go in peace, and be healed of your disease."

35 While he was still speaking, some people came from the leader's house to say, "Your daughter is dead. Why trouble the teacher any further?" ³⁶But overhearing*i* what they said, Jesus said to the leader of the synagogue, "Do not fear, only believe." ³⁷He allowed no one to follow him except Peter, James, and John, the brother of James. ³⁸When they came to the house of the leader of the synagogue, he saw a commotion, people weeping and wailing loudly. ³⁹When he had entered, he said to them, "Why do you make a commotion and weep? The child is not dead but sleeping." ⁴⁰And they laughed at him. Then he put them all outside, and took the child's father and mother and those who were with him, and went

5.15
vv. 16,18;
Mt 4.24;
v. 9
5.18
Acts 16.39
5.20
Mk 7.31;
Mt 4.25
5.21
Mt 9.1
5.22
Lk 8.49;
13.14;
Acts 13.15;
18.8,17
5.23
Mk 6.5;
7.32; 8.23;
Acts 9.17;
28.8

5.25
Lev 15.25
5.29
v. 34
5.30
Lk 5.17
5.34
Lk 7.50;
8.48;
Acts 16.36;
Jas 2.16
5.35
v. 22
5.36
Lk 8.50
5.37
Mt 17.1;
26.37
5.38
v. 22
5.39
Jn 11.11

e Gk he *f* Gk they *g* Gk him
h Other ancient authorities lack *in the boat*
i Or *ignoring*; other ancient authorities read *hearing*

in where the child was. 41 He took her by the hand and said to her, "Talitha cum," which means, "Little girl, get up!" 42 And immediately the girl got up and began to walk about (she was twelve years of age). At this they were overcome with amazement. 43 He strictly ordered them that no one should know this, and told them to give her something to eat.

The Rejection of Jesus at Nazareth

6 He left that place and came to his hometown, and his disciples followed him. 2 On the sabbath he began to teach in the synagogue, and many who heard him were astounded. They said, "Where did this man get all this? What is this wisdom that has been given to him? What deeds of power are being done by his hands! 3 Is not this the carpenter, the son of Maryi and brother of James and Joses and Judas and Simon, and are not his sisters here with us?" And they took offensek at him. 4 Then Jesus said to them, "Prophets are not without honor, except in their hometown, and among their own kin, and in their own house." 5 And he could do no deed of power there, except that he laid his hands on a few sick people and cured them. 6 And he was amazed at their unbelief.

The Mission of the Twelve

Then he went about among the villages teaching. 7 He called the twelve and began to send them out two by two, and gave them authority over the unclean spirits. 8 He ordered them to take nothing for their journey except a staff; no bread, no bag, no money in their belts; 9 but to wear sandals and not to put on two tunics. 10 He said to them, "Wherever you enter a house, stay there until you leave the place. 11 If any place will not welcome you and they refuse to hear you, as you leave, shake off the dust that is on your feet as a testimony against them." 12 So they

went out and proclaimed that all should repent. 13 They cast out many demons, and anointed with oil many who were sick and cured them.

The Death of John the Baptist

14 King Herod heard of it, for Jesus'l name had become known. Some werem saying, "John the baptizer has been raised from the dead; and for this reason these powers are at work in him." 15 But others said, "It is Elijah." And others said, "It is a prophet, like one of the prophets of old." 16 But when Herod heard of it, he said, "John, whom I beheaded, has been raised."

17 For Herod himself had sent men who arrested John, bound him, and put him in prison on account of Herodias, his brother Philip's wife, because Herodn had married her. 18 For John had been telling Herod, "It is not lawful for you to have your brother's wife." 19 And Herodias had a grudge against him, and wanted to kill him. But she could not, 20 for Herod feared John, knowing that he was a righteous and holy man, and he protected him. When he heard him, he was greatly perplexed;o and yet he liked to listen to him. 21 But an opportunity came when Herod on his birthday gave a banquet for his courtiers and officers and for the leaders of Galilee. 22 When his daughter Herodiasp came in and danced, she pleased Herod and his guests; and the king said to the girl, "Ask me for whatever you wish, and I will give it." 23 And he solemnly swore to her, "Whatever you ask me, I will give you, even half of my kingdom." 24 She went out and said to her mother, "What should I ask for?" She replied, "The head of John the baptizer." 25 Immediately she

5.41
Lk 7.14;
Acts 9.40
5.43
Mt 8.4
6.2
Mt 4.23;
7.28;
Mk 1.21
6.3
Mt 12.46;
11.6
6.4
Jn 4.44
6.5
Mt 5.23;
7.32; 8.23
6.6
Mt 9.35;
Lk 13.22
6.7
Mk 3.13;
Lk 10.1
6.12
Mt 11.1;
Lk 9.6

Lk 9/10

6.13
Jas 5.14
6.15
Mt 16.14;
Mk 8.28;
Mt 21.11
6.16
Lk 3.19
6.18
Lev 18.16;
20.21
6.20
Mt 21.26
6.21
Esther 1.3;
2.18
6.23
Esther 5.3,
6; 7.2

i Other ancient authorities read son of the carpenter and of Mary k Or stumbled
l Gk his m Other ancient authorities read He was n Gk he o Other ancient authorities read he did many things p Other ancient authorities read the daughter of Herodias herself

rushed back to the king and requested, "I want you to give me at once the head of John the Baptist on a platter." 26 The king was deeply grieved; yet out of regard for his oaths and for the guests, he did not want to refuse her. 27 Immediately the king sent a soldier of the guard with orders to bring John's q head. He went and beheaded him in the prison, 28 brought his head on a platter, and gave it to the girl. Then the girl gave it to her mother. 29 When his disciples heard about it, they came and took his body, and laid it in a tomb.

Feeding the Five Thousand

30 The apostles gathered around Jesus, and told him all that they had done and taught. 31 He said to them, "Come away to a deserted place all by yourselves and rest a while." For many were coming and going, and they had no leisure even to eat. 32 And they went away in the boat to a deserted place by themselves. 33 Now many saw them going and recognized them, and they hurried there on foot from all the towns and arrived ahead of them. 34 As he went ashore, he saw a great crowd; and he had compassion for them, because they were like sheep without a shepherd; and he began to teach them many things. 35 When it grew late, his disciples came to him and said, "This is a deserted place, and the hour is now very late; 36 send them away so that they may go into the surrounding country and villages and buy something for themselves to eat." 37 But he answered them, "You give them something to eat." They said to him, "Are we to go and buy two hundred denarii r worth of bread, and give it to them to eat?" 38 And he said to them, "How many loaves have you? Go and see." When they had found out, they said, "Five, and two fish." 39 Then he ordered them to get all the people to sit down in groups on the green grass. 40 So they sat down in groups of hundreds and of fifties.

41 Taking the five loaves and the two fish, he looked up to heaven, and blessed and broke the loaves, and gave them to his disciples to set before the people; and he divided the two fish among them all. 42 And all ate and were filled; 43 and they took up twelve baskets full of broken pieces and of the fish. 44 Those who had eaten the loaves numbered five thousand men.

Jesus Walks on the Water

45 Immediately he made his disciples get into the boat and go on ahead to the other side, to Bethsaida, while he dismissed the crowd. 46 After saying farewell to them, he went up on the mountain to pray.

47 When evening came, the boat was out on the sea, and he was alone on the land. 48 When he saw that they were straining at the oars against an adverse wind, he came towards them early in the morning, walking on the sea. He intended to pass them by. 49 But when they saw him walking on the sea, they thought it was a ghost and cried out; 50 for they all saw him and were terrified. But immediately he spoke to them and said, "Take heart, it is I; do not be afraid." 51 Then he got into the boat with them and the wind ceased. And they were utterly astounded, 52 for they did not understand about the loaves, but their hearts were hardened.

Healing the Sick in Gennesaret

53 When they had crossed over, they came to land at Gennesaret and moored the boat. 54 When they got out of the boat, people at once recognized him, 55 and rushed about that whole region and began to bring the sick on mats to wherever they heard he was. 56 And wherever he went, into villages or cities or farms, they laid the sick in the marketplaces, and begged him that they might touch even the fringe of

6.31
Mk 3.20
6.32
v. 45
6.34
Mt 9.36
6.37
2 Kings 4.42-44
6.38
Mt 15.34;
Mk 8.5

6.41
Mt 26.26;
Mk 14.22;
Lk 24.30,31
6.45
v. 32;
Mt 11.21;
Mk 8.22
6.48
Mt 13.35;
24.43
6.50
Mt 9.2
6.51
v. 32
6.52
Mk 8.17,18;
3.5
6.53
Jn 6.24,25
6.56
Mk 3.10;
Mt 9.20

q Gk *his* r The denarius was the usual day's wage for a laborer

his cloak; and all who touched it were healed.

The Tradition of the Elders

7 Now when the Pharisees and some of the scribes who had come from Jerusalem gathered around him, [2]they noticed that some of his disciples were eating with defiled hands, that is, without washing them. [3](For the Pharisees, and all the Jews, do not eat unless they thoroughly wash their hands,[s] thus observing the tradition of the elders; [4]and they do not eat anything from the market unless they wash it;[t] and there are also many other traditions that they observe, the washing of cups, pots, and bronze kettles.[u]) [5]So the Pharisees and the scribes asked him, "Why do your disciples not live[v] according to the tradition of the elders, but eat with defiled hands?" [6]He said to them, "Isaiah prophesied rightly about you hypocrites, as it is written,

'This people honors me with
 their lips,
but their hearts are far
 from me;
[7] in vain do they worship me,
 teaching human precepts
 as doctrines.'

[8]You abandon the commandment of God and hold to human tradition."

9 Then he said to them, "You have a fine way of rejecting the commandment of God in order to keep your tradition! [10]For Moses said, 'Honor your father and your mother'; and, 'Whoever speaks evil of father or mother must surely die.' [11]But you say that if anyone tells father or mother, 'Whatever support you might have had from me is Corban' (that is, an offering to God[w])— [12]then you no longer permit doing anything for a father or mother, [13]thus making void the word of God through your tradition that you have handed on. And you do many things like this."

14 Then he called the crowd again and said to them, "Listen to me, all of you, and understand:

[15]there is nothing outside a person that by going in can defile, but the things that come out are what defile."[x]

17 When he had left the crowd and entered the house, his disciples asked him about the parable. [18]He said to them, "Then do you also fail to understand? Do you not see that whatever goes into a person from outside cannot defile, [19]since it enters, not the heart but the stomach, and goes out into the sewer?" (Thus he declared all foods clean.) [20]And he said, "It is what comes out of a person that defiles. [21]For it is from within, from the human heart, that evil intentions come: fornication, theft, murder, [22]adultery, avarice, wickedness, deceit, licentiousness, envy, slander, pride, folly. [23]All these evil things come from within, and they defile a person."

The Syrophoenician Woman's Faith

24 From there he set out and went away to the region of Tyre.[y] He entered a house and did not want anyone to know he was there. Yet he could not escape notice, [25]but a woman whose little daughter had an unclean spirit immediately heard about him, and she came and bowed down at his feet. [26]Now the woman was a Gentile, of Syrophoenician origin. She begged him to cast the demon out of her daughter. [27]He said to her, "Let the children be fed first, for it is not fair to take the children's food and throw it to the dogs." [28]But she answered him, "Sir,[z] even the dogs under the table eat the children's crumbs." [29]Then he said to her, "For saying that, you may go—the demon has left your daughter." [30]So she went home, found the

Cross-references (center column)

7.3 v. 5; Acts 10.14, 28; 11.8
7.4 Mt 23.25; Lk 11.39
7.5 vv. 3,8,9,13; Gal 1.14
7.6 Isa 29.13
7.8 vv. 5,9,13
7.9 vv. 5,8,13
7.10 Ex 20.12; Deut 5.6; Ex 21.17; Lev 20.9
7.11 Mt 23.18
7.13 vv. 5,8,9
7.17 Mk 9.28
7.19 Rom 14.1-12; Col 2.16; Lk 11.41; Acts 10.15; 11.9
7.22 Mt 6.23; 20.15
7.24 Mt 11.21

[s] Meaning of Gk uncertain [t] Other ancient authorities read *and when they come from the marketplace, they do not eat unless they purify themselves* [u] Other ancient authorities add *and beds* [v] Gk *walk* [w] Gk lacks *to God* [x] Other ancient authorities add verse 16, *"Let anyone with ears to hear listen"* [y] Other ancient authorities add *and Sidon* [z] Or *Lord;* other ancient authorities prefix *Yes*

child lying on the bed, and the demon gone.

Jesus Cures a Deaf Man

31 Then he returned from the region of Tyre, and went by way of Sidon towards the Sea of Galilee, in the region of the Decapolis. [32] They brought to him a deaf man who had an impediment in his speech; and they begged him to lay his hand on him. [33] He took him aside in private, away from the crowd, and put his fingers into his ears, and spat and touched his tongue. [34] Then looking up to heaven, he sighed and said to him, "Ephphatha," that is, "Be opened." [35] And immediately his ears were opened, his tongue was released, and he spoke plainly. [36] Then Jesus[a] ordered them to tell no one; but the more he ordered them, the more zealously they proclaimed it. [37] They were astounded beyond measure, saying, "He has done everything well; he even makes the deaf to hear and the mute to speak."

Feeding the Four Thousand

8 In those days when there was again a great crowd without anything to eat, he called his disciples and said to them, [2] "I have compassion for the crowd, because they have been with me now for three days and have nothing to eat. [3] If I send them away hungry to their homes, they will faint on the way—and some of them have come from a great distance." [4] His disciples replied, "How can one feed these people with bread here in the desert?" [5] He asked them, "How many loaves do you have?" They said, "Seven." [6] Then he ordered the crowd to sit down on the ground; and he took the seven loaves, and after giving thanks he broke them and gave them to his disciples to distribute; and they distributed them to the crowd. [7] They had also a few small fish; and after blessing them, he ordered that these too should be distributed. [8] They ate and were filled; and

they took up the broken pieces left over, seven baskets full. [9] Now there were about four thousand people. And he set them away. [10] And immediately he got into the boat with his disciples and went to the district of Dalmanutha.[b]

The Demand for a Sign

11 The Pharisees came and began to argue with him, asking him for a sign from heaven, to test him. [12] And he sighed deeply in his spirit and said, "Why does this generation ask for a sign? Truly I tell you, no sign will be given to this generation." [13] And he left them, and getting into the boat again, he went across to the other side.

The Yeast of the Pharisees and of Herod

14 Now the disciples[c] had forgotten to bring any bread; and they had only one loaf with them in the boat. [15] And he cautioned them, saying, "Watch out—beware of the yeast of the Pharisees and the yeast of Herod."[d] [16] They said to one another, "It is because we have no bread." [17] And becoming aware of it, Jesus said to them, "Why are you talking about having no bread? Do you still not perceive or understand? Are your hearts hardened? [18] Do you have eyes, and fail to see? Do you have ears, and fail to hear? And do you not remember? [19] When I broke the five loaves for the five thousand, how many baskets full of broken pieces did you collect?" They said to him, "Twelve." [20] "And the seven for the four thousand, how many baskets full of broken pieces did you collect?" And they said to him, "Seven." [21] Then he said to them, "Do you not yet understand?"

Jesus Cures a Blind Man at Bethsaida

22 They came to Bethsaida. Some people[e] brought a blind man

Cross references (center column)

7.32
Mk 5.23;
Mt 9.32;
Lk 11.14
7.33
Mk 8.23
7.34
Mk 6.41;
8.12
7.35
Isa 35.5,6
7.36
Mk 1.44;
5.43
8.2
Mt 9.36
8.5
Mk 6.38
8.7
Mt 14.19;
Mk 6.41

8.11
Mt 12.38,
39;
Lk 11.29;
Jn 6.30
8.12
Mk 7.34
8.15
Lk 12.1;
Mk 16.4;
12.13
8.17
Mk 6.52;
Isa 6.9,10
8.19
Mt 14.20;
Mk 6.43;
Lk 9.17;
Jn 6.13
8.20
vv. 6-9;
Mt 15.37
8.21
Mk 6.52
8.22
Mt 11.21;
Mk 6.45;
Lk 9.10

[a] Gk *he* [b] Other ancient authorities read *Mageda* or *Magdala* [c] Gk *they* [d] Other ancient authorities read *the Herodians* [e] Gk *They*

to him and begged him to touch him. 23 He took the blind man by the hand and led him out of the village; and when he had put saliva on his eyes and laid his hands on him, he asked him, "Can you see anything?" 24 And the man[f] looked up and said, "I can see people, but they look like trees, walking." 25 Then Jesus[f] laid his hands on his eyes again; and he looked intently and his sight was restored, and he saw everything clearly. 26 Then he sent him away to his home, saying, "Do not even go into the village."[g]

Peter's Declaration about Jesus

27 Jesus went on with his disciples to the villages of Caesarea Philippi; and on the way he asked his disciples, "Who do people say that I am?" 28 And they answered him, "John the Baptist; and others, Elijah; and still others, one of the prophets." 29 He asked them, "But who do you say that I am?" Peter answered him, "You are the Messiah."[h] 30 And he sternly ordered them not to tell anyone about him.

Jesus Foretells His Death and Resurrection

31 Then he began to teach them that the Son of Man must undergo great suffering, and be rejected by the elders, the chief priests, and the scribes, and be killed, and after three days rise again. 32 He said all this quite openly. And Peter took him aside and began to rebuke him. 33 But turning and looking at his disciples, he rebuked Peter and said, "Get behind me, Satan! For you are setting your mind not on divine things but on human things."

34 He called the crowd with his disciples, and said to them, "If any want to become my followers, let them deny themselves and take up their cross and follow me. 35 For those who want to save their life will lose it, and those who lose their life for my sake, and for the sake of the gospel,[i] will save it. 36 For what will it profit them to

gain the whole world and forfeit their life? 37 Indeed, what can they give in return for their life? 38 Those who are ashamed of me and of my words[j] in this adulterous and sinful generation, of them the Son of Man will also be ashamed when he comes in the glory of his Father with the holy angels." 1 And he said to them, "Truly I tell you, there are some standing here who will not taste death until they see that the kingdom of God has come with[k] power."

The Transfiguration

2 Six days later, Jesus took with him Peter and James and John, and led them up a high mountain apart, by themselves. And he was transfigured before them, 3 and his clothes became dazzling white, such as no one[l] on earth could bleach them. 4 And there appeared to them Elijah with Moses, who were talking with Jesus. 5 Then Peter said to Jesus, "Rabbi, it is good for us to be here; let us make three dwellings,[m] one for you, one for Moses, and one for Elijah." 6 He did not know what to say, for they were terrified. 7 Then a cloud overshadowed them, and from the cloud there came a voice, "This is my Son, the Beloved;[n] listen to him!" 8 Suddenly when they looked around, they saw no one with them any more, but only Jesus.

The Coming of Elijah

9 As they were coming down the mountain, he ordered them to tell no one about what they had seen, until after the Son of Man had risen from the dead. 10 So they kept the matter to themselves, questioning what this rising from the dead could mean. 11 Then they asked him, "Why do the scribes say that Elijah must come first?" 12 He said to them, "Elijah is indeed coming

Cross references (center column)

8.23 Mk 7.33; 5.23
8.26 Mt 8.4
8.27 Jn 6.66-69
8.28 Mk 6.14
8.29 Jn 6.69; 11.27
8.30 Mk 9.9
8.32 Jn 18.20
8.33 Mt 4.10
8.34 Mt 10.38; Lk 14.27
8.35 Mt 10.39; Lk 17.33; Jn 12.25

8.38 Mt 10.33; Lk 12.9; Mt 8.20; Mk 13.26
9.1 Mt 24.30; 25.31; Mk 13.30; Lk 22.18
9.2 Mk 5.37; 13.3
9.3 Mt 28.3
9.5 Mt 23.7
9.7 2 Pet 1.17, 18; Mk 1.11
9.9 Mk 5.43; 7.36; 8.30
9.11 Mt 11.14
9.12 Ps 22.6; Lk 23.11; Phil 2.7

[f] Gk he　　[g] Other ancient authorities add or tell anyone in the village　　[h] Or the Christ
[i] Other ancient authorities read lose their life for the sake of the gospel　　[j] Other ancient authorities read and of mine　　[k] Or in
[l] Gk no fuller　　[m] Or tents　　[n] Or my beloved Son

first to restore all things. How then is it written about the Son of Man, that he is to go through many sufferings and be treated with contempt? [13] But I tell you that Elijah has come, and they did to him whatever they pleased, as it is written about him."

The Healing of a Boy with a Spirit

14 When they came to the disciples, they saw a great crowd around them, and some scribes arguing with them. [15] When the whole crowd saw him, they were immediately overcome with awe, and they ran forward to greet him. [16] He asked them, "What are you arguing about with them?" [17] Someone from the crowd answered him, "Teacher, I brought you my son; he has a spirit that makes him unable to speak; [18] and whenever it seizes him, it dashes him down; and he foams and grinds his teeth and becomes rigid; and I asked your disciples to cast it out, but they could not do so." [19] He answered them, "You faithless generation, how much longer must I be among you? How much longer must I put up with you? Bring him to me." [20] And they brought the boy[o] to him. When the spirit saw him, immediately it convulsed the boy,[o] and he fell on the ground and rolled about, foaming at the mouth. [21] Jesus[p] asked the father, "How long has this been happening to him?" And he said, "From childhood. [22] It has often cast him into the fire and into the water, to destroy him; but if you are able to do anything, have pity on us and help us." [23] Jesus said to him, "If you are able! — All things can be done for the one who believes." [24] Immediately the father of the child cried out,[q] "I believe; help my unbelief!" [25] When Jesus saw that a crowd came running together, he rebuked the unclean spirit, saying to it, "You spirit that keeps this boy from speaking and hearing, I command you, come out of him, and never enter him again!" [26] After crying out and convulsing

him terribly, it came out, and the boy was like a corpse, so that most of them said, "He is dead." [27] But Jesus took him by the hand and lifted him up, and he was able to stand. [28] When he had entered the house, his disciples asked him privately, "Why could we not cast it out?" [29] He said to them, "This kind can come out only through prayer."[r]

Jesus Again Foretells His Death and Resurrection

30 They went on from there and passed through Galilee. He did not want anyone to know it; [31] for he was teaching his disciples, saying to them, "The Son of Man is to be betrayed into human hands, and they will kill him, and three days after being killed, he will rise again." [32] But they did not understand what he was saying and were afraid to ask him.

Who Is the Greatest?

33 Then they came to Capernaum; and when he was in the house he asked them, "What were you arguing about on the way?" [34] But they were silent, for on the way they had argued with one another who was the greatest. [35] He sat down, called the twelve, and said to them, "Whoever wants to be first must be last of all and servant of all." [36] Then he took a little child and put it among them; and taking it in his arms, he said to them, [37] "Whoever welcomes one such child in my name welcomes me, and whoever welcomes me welcomes not me but the one who sent me."

Another Exorcist

38 John said to him, "Teacher, we saw someone[s] casting out demons in your name, and we tried to stop him, because he was not following us." [39] But Jesus said, "Do not stop him; for no one who does

9.13
Mt 11.14;
Lk 1.17
9.15
Mk 14.33;
16.5,6
9.20
Mk 1.26
9.23
Mk 11.23;
Lk 17.6;
Jn 11.40
9.25
v. 15

9.28
Mk 7.17
9.31
Mt 16.21;
Mk 8.31
9.32
Jn 12.16
9.34
Lk 22.24
9.35
Mt 20.26,
27;
Mk 10.43;
Lk 22.26
9.36
Mk 10.16
9.37
Mt 10.40;
Jn 12.44;
13.20
9.38
Num 11.27-29

o Gk *him* p Gk *He* q Other ancient authorities add *with tears* r Other ancient authorities add *and fasting* s Other ancient authorities add *who does not follow us*

a deed of power in my name will be able soon afterward to speak evil of me. [40] Whoever is not against us is for us. [41] For truly I tell you, whoever gives you a cup of water to drink because you bear the name of Christ will by no means lose the reward.

Temptations to Sin

42 "If any of you put a stumbling block before one of these little ones who believe in me,[t] it would be better for you if a great millstone were hung around your neck and you were thrown into the sea. [43] If your hand causes you to stumble, cut it off; it is better for you to enter life maimed than to have two hands and to go to hell,[u] to the unquenchable fire.[v] [45] And if your foot causes you to stumble, cut it off; it is better for you to enter life lame than to have two feet and to be thrown into hell.[u,v] [47] And if your eye causes you to stumble, tear it out; it is better for you to enter the kingdom of God with one eye than to have two eyes and to be thrown into hell,[u] [48] where their worm never dies, and the fire is never quenched.

49 "For everyone will be salted with fire.[w] [50] Salt is good; but if salt has lost its saltiness, how can you season it?[x] Have salt in yourselves, and be at peace with one another."

Teaching about Divorce

10 He left that place and went to the region of Judea and[y] beyond the Jordan. And crowds again gathered around him; and, as was his custom, he again taught them.

2 Some Pharisees came, and to test him they asked, "Is it lawful for a man to divorce his wife?" [3] He answered them, "What did Moses command you?" [4] They said, "Moses allowed a man to write a certificate of dismissal and to divorce her." [5] But Jesus said to them, "Because of your hardness of heart he wrote this commandment for you. [6] But from the beginning of creation, 'God made them male and

female.' [7] 'For this reason a man shall leave his father and mother and be joined to his wife,[z] [8] and the two shall become one flesh.' So they are no longer two, but one flesh. [9] Therefore what God has joined together, let no one separate."

10 Then in the house the disciples asked him again about this matter. [11] He said to them, "Whoever divorces his wife and marries another commits adultery against her; [12] and if she divorces her husband and marries another, she commits adultery."

Jesus Blesses Little Children

13 People were bringing little children to him in order that he might touch them; and the disciples spoke sternly to them. [14] But when Jesus saw this, he was indignant and said to them, "Let the little children come to me; do not stop them; for it is to such as these that the kingdom of God belongs. [15] Truly I tell you, whoever does not receive the kingdom of God as a little child will never enter it." [16] And he took them up in his arms, laid his hands on them, and blessed them.

The Rich Man

17 As he was setting out on a journey, a man ran up and knelt before him, and asked him, "Good Teacher, what must I do to inherit eternal life?" [18] Jesus said to him, "Why do you call me good? No one is good but God alone. [19] You know the commandments: 'You shall not murder; You shall not commit adultery; You shall not steal; You shall not bear false witness; You shall not defraud; Honor your father and mother.'" [20] He said to him, "Teacher, I have kept all these since my youth." [21] Jesus, looking

Cross-references (center column)

9.40 Mt 12.30
9.41 Mt 10.42
9.42 Lk 17.1,2; 1 Cor 8.12
9.43 Mt 5.29,30; 5.22; 25.41
9.45 Mt 5.22
9.47 Mt 5.29
9.48 Isa 66.24
9.49 Lev 2.13
9.50 Mt 5.13; Lk 14.34,35; Col 4.6; Rom 12.18; 2 Cor 13.11; 1 Thes 5.13
10.1 Mt 19.1; Jn 10.40; 11.7
10.4 Deut 24.1-4; Mt 5.31; 19.7
10.6 Gen 1.27; 5.2
10.7 Gen 2.24; 1 Cor 6.16
10.11 Mt 5.32; Lk 16.18; Rom 7.3; 1 Cor 7.10, 11
10.15 Mt 18.3; 1 Cor 14.20; 1 Pet 2.2
10.16 Mk 9.36
10.17 Mk 1.40; Lk 10.25; Eph 1.18
10.19 Ex 20.12-16; Deut 5.16-20
10.21 Mt 6.20; Lk 12.33; Acts 2.35; 4.34,35

[t] Other ancient authorities lack *in me* [u] Gk *Gehenna* [v] Verses 44 and 46 (which are identical with verse 48) are lacking in the best ancient authorities [w] Other ancient authorities either add or substitute *and every sacrifice will be salted with salt* [x] Or *how can you restore its saltiness?* [y] Other ancient authorities lack *and* [z] Other ancient authorities lack *and be joined to his wife*

at him, loved him and said, "You lack one thing; go, sell what you own, and give the money[a] to the poor, and you will have treasure in heaven; then come, follow me." [22]When he heard this, he was shocked and went away grieving, for he had many possessions.

23 Then Jesus looked around and said to his disciples, "How hard it will be for those who have wealth to enter the kingdom of God!" [24]And the disciples were perplexed at these words. But Jesus said to them again, "Children, how hard it is[b] to enter the kingdom of God! [25]It is easier for a camel to go through the eye of a needle than for someone who is rich to enter the kingdom of God." [26]They were greatly astounded and said to one another,[c] "Then who can be saved?" [27]Jesus looked at them and said, "For mortals it is impossible, but not for God; for God all things are possible."

28 Peter began to say to him, "Look, we have left everything and followed you." [29]Jesus said, "Truly I tell you, there is no one who has left house or brothers or sisters or mother or father or children or fields, for my sake and for the sake of the good news,[d] [30]who will not receive a hundredfold now in this age — houses, brothers and sisters, mothers and children, and fields with persecutions — and in the age to come eternal life. [31]But many who are first will be last, and the last will be first."

A Third Time Jesus Foretells His Death and Resurrection

32 They were on the road, going up to Jerusalem, and Jesus was walking ahead of them; they were amazed, and those who followed were afraid. He took the twelve aside again and began to tell them what was to happen to him, [33]saying, "See, we are going up to Jerusalem, and the Son of Man will be handed over to the chief priests and the scribes, and they will condemn him to death; then they will

hand him over to the Gentiles; [34]they will mock him, and spit upon him, and flog him, and kill him; and after three days he will rise again."

The Request of James and John

35 James and John, the sons of Zebedee, came forward to him and said to him, "Teacher, we want you to do for us whatever we ask of you." [36]And he said to them, "What is it you want me to do for you?" [37]And they said to him, "Grant us to sit, one at your right hand and one at your left, in your glory." [38]But Jesus said to them, "You do not know what you are asking. Are you able to drink the cup that I drink, or be baptized with the baptism that I am baptized with?" [39]They replied, "We are able." Then Jesus said to them, "The cup that I drink you will drink; and with the baptism with which I am baptized, you will be baptized; [40]but to sit at my right hand or at my left is not mine to grant, but it is for those for whom it has been prepared."

41 When the ten heard this, they began to be angry with James and John. [42]So Jesus called them and said to them, "You know that among the Gentiles those whom they recognize as their rulers lord it over them, and their great ones are tyrants over them. [43]But it is not so among you; but whoever wishes to become great among you must be your servant, [44]and whoever wishes to be first among you must be slave of all. [45]For the Son of Man came not to be served but to serve, and to give his life a ransom for many."

The Healing of Blind Bartimaeus

46 They came to Jericho. As he and his disciples and a large crowd were leaving Jericho, Bartimaeus son of Timaeus, a blind beggar, was sitting by the roadside. [47]When he heard that it was Jesus of Nazareth, he began to shout out and say,

10.23
Mt 19.23;
Lk 18.24
10.24
Ps 52.7;
62.10;
1 Tim 6.17
10.27
Jer 32.17
10.28
Mt 4.20-22
10.29
Mt 6.33
10.31
Mt 20.16;
Lk 13.30
10.32
Mk 8.31;
9.31;
Lk 9.22

10.34
Mt 26.67;
27.30;
Mk 14.65
10.37
Mt 19.28;
Lk 22.30
10.38
Lk 12.50;
Jn 18.11
10.39
Acts 12.2;
Rev 1.9;
10.41;
Lk 22.25-27
10.43
Mt 9.35
10.45
Jn 13.14;
1 Tim 2.5,
6
10.47
Mt 9.27

a Gk lacks the money b Other ancient authorities add for those who trust in riches c Other ancient authorities read to him d Or gospel

"Jesus, Son of David, have mercy on me!" ⁴⁸Many sternly ordered him to be quiet, but he cried out even more loudly, "Son of David, have mercy on me!" ⁴⁹Jesus stood still and said, "Call him here." And they called the blind man, saying to him, "Take heart; get up, he is calling you." ⁵⁰So throwing off his cloak, he sprang up and came to Jesus. ⁵¹Then Jesus said to him, "What do you want me to do for you?" The blind man said to him, "My teacher,^e let me see again." ⁵²Jesus said to him, "Go; your faith has made you well." Immediately he regained his sight and followed him on the way.

Jesus' Triumphal Entry into Jerusalem

11 When they were approaching Jerusalem, at Bethphage and Bethany, near the Mount of Olives, he sent two of his disciples ²and said to them, "Go into the village ahead of you, and immediately as you enter it, you will find tied there a colt that has never been ridden; untie it and bring it. ³If anyone says to you, 'Why are you doing this?' just say this, 'The Lord needs it and will send it back here immediately.' " ⁴They went away and found a colt tied near a door, outside in the street. As they were untying it, ⁵some of the bystanders said to them, "What are you doing, untying the colt?" ⁶They told them what Jesus had said; and they allowed them to take it. ⁷Then they brought the colt to Jesus and threw their cloaks on it; and he sat on it. ⁸Many people spread their cloaks on the road, and others spread leafy branches that they had cut in the fields. ⁹Then those who went ahead and those who followed were shouting,

"Hosanna!
Blessed is the one who comes in the name of the Lord!
¹⁰ Blessed is the coming kingdom of our ancestor David!

Hosanna in the highest heaven!"

11 Then he entered Jerusalem and went into the temple; and when he had looked around at everything, as it was already late, he went out to Bethany with the twelve.

Jesus Curses the Fig Tree

12 On the following day, when they came from Bethany, he was hungry. ¹³Seeing in the distance a fig tree in leaf, he went to see whether perhaps he would find anything on it. When he came to it, he found nothing but leaves, for it was not the season for figs. ¹⁴He said to it, "May no one ever eat fruit from you again." And his disciples heard it.

Jesus Cleanses the Temple

15 Then they came to Jerusalem. And he entered the temple and began to drive out those who were selling and those who were buying in the temple, and he overturned the tables of the money changers and the seats of those who sold doves; ¹⁶and he would not allow anyone to carry anything through the temple. ¹⁷He was teaching and saying, "Is it not written,

'My house shall be called a house of prayer for all the nations'?
But you have made it a den of robbers."

¹⁸And when the chief priests and the scribes heard it, they kept looking for a way to kill him; for they were afraid of him, because the whole crowd was spellbound by his teaching. ¹⁹And when evening came, Jesus and his disciples^f went out of the city.

The Lesson from the Withered Fig Tree

20 In the morning as they passed by, they saw the fig tree withered away to its roots. ²¹Then Peter remembered and said to him, "Rabbi, look! The fig tree that you

10.51
Jn 20.16;
Mt 23.7
10.52
Mt 9.22;
Mk 5.34;
Lk 7.50;
8.48; 17.19
11.1
Mt 21.17
11.4
Mk 14.16
11.9
Ps 118.26;
Mt 23.39

11.11
Mt 21.10,
11,17
11.12
Lk 13.6-9
11.17
Isa 56.7;
Jer 7.11
11.18
Mt 21.46;
7.28;
Mk 1.22;
Lk 4.32
11.20
Mt 21.19
11.21
Mt 23.7

^eAramaic *Rabbouni* ^fGk *they:* other ancient authorities read *he*

cursed has withered." ²²Jesus answered them, "Have g faith in God. ²³Truly I tell you, if you say to this mountain, 'Be taken up and thrown into the sea,' and if you do not doubt in your heart, but believe that what you say will come to pass, it will be done for you. ²⁴So I tell you, whatever you ask for in prayer, believe that you have received h it, and it will be yours.

25 "Whenever you stand praying, forgive, if you have anything against anyone; so that your Father in heaven may also forgive you your trespasses."ⁱ

Jesus' Authority Is Questioned

27 Again they came to Jerusalem. As he was walking in the temple, the chief priests, the scribes, and the elders came to him ²⁸and said, "By what authority are you doing these things? Who gave you this authority to do them?" ²⁹Jesus said to them, "I will ask you one question; answer me, and I will tell you by what authority I do these things. ³⁰Did the baptism of John come from heaven, or was it of human origin? Answer me." ³¹They argued with one another, "If we say, 'From heaven,' he will say, 'Why then did you not believe him?' ³²But shall we say, 'Of human origin'?"— they were afraid of the crowd, for all regarded John as truly a prophet. ³³So they answered Jesus, "We do not know." And Jesus said to them, "Neither will I tell you by what authority I am doing these things."

The Parable of the Wicked Tenants

12 Then he began to speak to them in parables. "A man planted a vineyard, put a fence around it, dug a pit for the wine press, and built a watchtower; then he leased it to tenants and went to another country. ²When the season came, he sent a slave to the tenants to collect from them his share of the produce of the vineyard. ³But they seized him, and beat him, and sent him away empty-handed.

11.22
Mt 17.20
11.23
Mt 21.21;
Lk 17.6
11.24
Mt 7.7;
Jn 14.13,14;
15.7; 16.23,
24; Jas 1.5,
6
11.25
Mt 6.14,15;
Col 3.13
11.32
Mt 14.5
12.1
Isa 5.1-7

12.6
cf.
Heb 1.1-3
12.10
Ps 118.22,
23;
Acts 4.11;
1 Pet 2.7
12.12
Mt 21.45,
46;
Mk 11.18;
Mt 22.22
12.13
Mk 3.6;
Lk 11.54

⁴And again he sent another slave to them; this one they beat over the head and insulted. ⁵Then he sent another, and that one they killed. And so it was with many others; some they beat, and others they killed. ⁶He had still one other, a beloved son. Finally he sent him to them, saying, 'They will respect my son.' ⁷But those tenants said to one another, 'This is the heir; come, let us kill him, and the inheritance will be ours.' ⁸So they seized him, killed him, and threw him out of the vineyard. ⁹What then will the owner of the vineyard do? He will come and destroy the tenants and give the vineyard to others. ¹⁰Have you not read this scripture:

'The stone that the builders
 rejected
has become the
 cornerstone;ʲ
¹¹ this was the Lord's doing,
 and it is amazing in our
 eyes'?"

12 When they realized that he had told this parable against them, they wanted to arrest him, but they feared the crowd. So they left him and went away.

The Question about Paying Taxes

13 Then they sent to him some Pharisees and some Herodians to trap him in what he said. ¹⁴And they came and said to him, "Teacher, we know that you are sincere, and show deference to no one; for you do not regard people with partiality, but teach the way of God in accordance with truth. Is it lawful to pay taxes to the emperor, or not? ¹⁵Should we pay them, or should we not?" But knowing their hypocrisy, he said to them, "Why are you putting me to the test? Bring me a denarius and let me see it." ¹⁶And they brought one. Then he said to them, "Whose head is this, and

g Other ancient authorities read "If you have
h Other ancient authorities read are receiving
i Other ancient authorities add verse 26, "But
if you do not forgive, neither will your Father in
heaven forgive your trespasses."
j Or keystone

whose title?" They answered, "The emperor's." [17] Jesus said to them, "Give to the emperor the things that are the emperor's, and to God the things that are God's." And they were utterly amazed at him.

The Question about the Resurrection

18 Some Sadducees, who say there is no resurrection, came to him and asked him a question, saying, [19] "Teacher, Moses wrote for us that 'if a man's brother dies, leaving a wife but no child, the man[k] shall marry the widow and raise up children for his brother.' [20] There were seven brothers; the first married and, when he died, left no children; [21] and the second married her and died, leaving no children; and the third likewise; [22] none of the seven left children. Last of all the woman herself died. [23] In the resurrection[l] whose wife will she be? For the seven had married her."

24 Jesus said to them, "Is not this the reason you are wrong, that you know neither the scriptures nor the power of God? [25] For when they rise from the dead, they neither marry nor are given in marriage, but are like angels in heaven. [26] And as for the dead being raised, have you not read in the book of Moses, in the story about the bush, how God said to him, 'I am the God of Abraham, the God of Isaac, and the God of Jacob'? [27] He is God not of the dead, but of the living; you are quite wrong."

The First Commandment

28 One of the scribes came near and heard them disputing with one another, and seeing that he answered them well, he asked him, "Which commandment is the first of all?" [29] Jesus answered, "The first is, 'Hear, O Israel: the Lord our God, the Lord is one; [30] you shall love the Lord your God with all your heart, and with all your soul, and with all your mind, and with all your strength.' [31] The second is this, 'You shall love your neighbor as yourself.' There is no

12.17
Rom 13.7
12.19
Deut 25.5
12.25
1 Cor 15.42,
49,52
12.26
Ex 3.6
12.28
Lk 10.25-28;
20.39
12.29
Deut 6.4
12.31
Lev 19.18;
Rom 13.9;
Gal 5.14;
Jas 2.8

12.32
Deut 4.39;
Isa 45.6,14;
46.9
12.33
1 Sam 15.22;
Hos 6.6;
Mic 6.6-8
12.34
Mt 22.46
12.35
Mt 26.55;
9.27
12.36
Ps 110.1;
Acts 2.34,
35;
Heb 1.13
12.37
Jn 12.9
12.38
Lk 11.43
12.41
Jn 8.20;
2 Kings 12.9
12.43
2 Cor 8.12

other commandment greater than these." [32] Then the scribe said to him, "You are right, Teacher; you have truly said that 'he is one, and besides him there is no other'; [33] and 'to love him with all the heart, and with all the understanding, and with all the strength', and 'to love one's neighbor as oneself,' — this is much more important than all whole burnt offerings and sacrifices." [34] When Jesus saw that he answered wisely, he said to him, "You are not far from the kingdom of God." After that no one dared to ask him any question.

The Question about David's Son

35 While Jesus was teaching in the temple, he said, "How can the scribes say that the Messiah[m] is the son of David? [36] David himself, by the Holy Spirit, declared,

'The Lord said to my Lord,
　"Sit at my right hand,
　　until I put your enemies
　　　under your feet." '
[37] David himself calls him Lord; so how can he be his son?" And the large crowd was listening to him with delight.

Jesus Denounces the Scribes

38 As he taught, he said, "Beware of the scribes, who like to walk around in long robes, and to be greeted with respect in the marketplaces, [39] and to have the best seats in the synagogues and places of honor at banquets! [40] They devour widows' houses and for the sake of appearance say long prayers. They will receive the greater condemnation."

The Widow's Offering

41 He sat down opposite the treasury, and watched the crowd putting money into the treasury. Many rich people put in large sums. [42] A poor widow came and put in two small copper coins, which are worth a penny. [43] Then he called his disciples and said to them, "Truly I tell you, this poor widow has put in more than all

[k] Gk his brother　　[l] Other ancient authorities add when they rise　　[m] Or the Christ

those who are contributing to the treasury. [44] For all of them have contributed out of their abundance; but she out of her poverty has put in everything she had, all she had to live on."

The Destruction of the Temple Foretold

13 As he came out of the temple, one of his disciples said to him, "Look, Teacher, what large stones and what large buildings!" [2] Then Jesus asked him, "Do you see these great buildings? Not one stone will be left here upon another; all will be thrown down."

3 When he was sitting on the Mount of Olives opposite the temple, Peter, James, John, and Andrew asked him privately, [4] "Tell us, when will this be, and what will be the sign that all these things are about to be accomplished?" [5] Then Jesus began to say to them, "Beware that no one leads you astray. [6] Many will come in my name and say, 'I am he!'[n] and they will lead many astray. [7] When you hear of wars and rumors of wars, do not be alarmed; this must take place, but the end is still to come. [8] For nation will rise against nation, and kingdom against kingdom; there will be earthquakes in various places; there will be famines. This is but the beginning of the birthpangs.

Persecution Foretold

9 "As for yourselves, beware; for they will hand you over to councils; and you will be beaten in synagogues; and you will stand before governors and kings because of me, as a testimony to them. [10] And the good news[o] must first be proclaimed to all nations. [11] When they bring you to trial and hand you over, do not worry beforehand about what you are to say; but say whatever is given you at that time, for it is not you who speak, but the Holy Spirit. [12] Brother will betray brother to death, and a father his child, and children will rise against parents and have them put to death; [13] and you will be hated by

13.2
Lk 19.44;
Mk 14.58;
15.29;
Acts 6.14
13.3
Mk 5.37;
9.2
13.5
Eph 5.6;
1 Thes 2.3
13.6
Jn 8.24
13.9
Mt 10.17
13.11
Mt 10.19;
Lk 12.11
13.12
Mic 7.6;
Mt 10.21
13.13
Jn 15.21;
Mt 10.22;
Rev 2.10

13.14
Dan 9.27;
11.31; 12.11
13.17
Lk 23.29
13.19
Dan 9.26;
12.1;
Joel 2.2
13.21
Lk 17.23;
21.8
13.22
Mt 7.15;
Jn 4.48
13.23
2 Pet 3.17
13.24
Zeph 1.15
13.26
Dan 7.13;
Mt 16.27;
Mk 14.62;
1 Thes 4.16;
2 Thes 1.7,
10

all because of my name. But the one who endures to the end will be saved.

The Desolating Sacrilege

14 "But when you see the desolating sacrilege set up where it ought not to be (let the reader understand), then those in Judea must flee to the mountains; [15] the one on the housetop must not go down or enter the house to take anything away; [16] the one in the field must not turn back to get a coat. [17] Woe to those who are pregnant and to those who are nursing infants in those days! [18] Pray that it may not be in winter. [19] For in those days there will be suffering, such as has not been from the beginning of the creation that God created until now, no, and never will be. [20] And if the Lord had not cut short those days, no one would be saved; but for the sake of the elect, whom he chose, he has cut short those days. [21] And if anyone says to you at that time, 'Look! Here is the Messiah!'[p] or 'Look! There he is!' — do not believe it. [22] False messiahs[q] and false prophets will appear and produce signs and omens, to lead astray, if possible, the elect. [23] But be alert; I have already told you everything.

The Coming of the Son of Man

24 "But in those days, after that suffering,

the sun will be darkened,
 and the moon will not give
 its light,
[25] and the stars will be falling
 from heaven,
 and the powers in the
 heavens will be shaken.

[26] Then they will see 'the Son of Man coming in clouds' with great power and glory. [27] Then he will send out the angels, and gather his elect from the four winds, from the ends of the earth to the ends of heaven.

The Lesson of the Fig Tree

28 "From the fig tree learn its

n Gk I am o Gk gospel p Or the Christ q Or christs

lesson: as soon as its branch be-comes tender and puts forth its leaves, you know that summer is near. ²⁹ So also, when you see these things taking place, you know that he^r is near, at the very gates. ³⁰ Truly I tell you, this generation will not pass away until all these things have taken place. ³¹ Heaven and earth will pass away, but my words will not pass away.

The Necessity for Watchfulness

32 "But about that day or hour no one knows, neither the angels in heaven, nor the Son, but only the Father. ³³ Beware, keep alert;^s for you do not know when the time will come. ³⁴ It is like a man going on a journey, when he leaves home and puts his slaves in charge, each with his work, and commands the door-keeper to be on the watch. ³⁵ There-fore, keep awake — for you do not know when the master of the house will come, in the evening, or at midnight, or at cockcrow, or at dawn, ³⁶ or else he may find you asleep when he comes suddenly. ³⁷ And what I say to you I say to all: Keep awake."

The Plot to Kill Jesus

14 It was two days before the Passover and the festival of Unleavened Bread. The chief priests and the scribes were look-ing for a way to arrest Jesus^t by stealth and kill him; ² for they said, "Not during the festival, or there may be a riot among the people."

The Anointing at Bethany

3 While he was at Bethany in the house of Simon the leper,^u as he sat at the table, a woman came with an alabaster jar of very costly ointment of nard, and she broke open the jar and poured the oint-ment on his head. ⁴ But some were there who said to one another in anger, "Why was the ointment wasted in this way? ⁵ For this oint-ment could have been sold for more than three hundred denarii,^v and the money given to the poor." And they scolded her. ⁶ But Jesus

said, "Let her alone; why do you trouble her? She has performed a good service for me. ⁷ For you al-ways have the poor with you, and you can show kindness to them whenever you wish; but you will not always have me. ⁸ She has done what she could; she has anointed my body beforehand for its burial. ⁹ Truly I tell you, wherever the good news^w is proclaimed in the whole world, what she has done will be told in remembrance of her."

Judas Agrees to Betray Jesus

10 Then Judas Iscariot, who was one of the twelve, went to the chief priests in order to betray him to them. ¹¹ When they heard it, they were greatly pleased, and promised to give him money. So he began to look for an opportunity to betray him.

The Passover with the Disciples

12 On the first day of Unleav-ened Bread, when the Passover lamb is sacrificed, his disciples said to him, "Where do you want us to go and make the preparations for you to eat the Passover?" ¹³ So he sent two of his disciples, saying to them, "Go into the city, and a man carrying a jar of water will meet you; follow him, ¹⁴ and wher-ever he enters, say to the owner of the house, 'The Teacher asks, Where is my guest room where I may eat the Passover with my disci-ples?' ¹⁵ He will show you a large room upstairs, furnished and ready. Make preparations for us there." ¹⁶ So the disciples set out and went to the city, and found ev-erything as he had told them; and they prepared the Passover meal.

17 When it was evening, he came with the twelve. ¹⁸ And when they had taken their places and were eating, Jesus said, "Truly I tell you, one of you will betray me, one who is eating with me." ¹⁹ They be-gan to be distressed and to say to

Center reference column:

13.30 Mk 9.1
13.31 Mt 5.18; Lk 16.17
13.32 Acts 1.7
13.33 Eph 6.18; Col 4.2; 1 Thes 5.6
13.34 Mt 25.14
13.35 Lk 12.35-40
14.1 Jn 11.55; 13.1; Mt 12.14
14.3 Lk 7.37-39; Mt 21.17

14.7 Deut 15.11
14.8 Jn 19.20
14.10 Lk 22.3,4; Jn 6.71
14.12 Ex 12.11
14.18 vv. 44,45

^r Or it ^s Other ancient authorities add *and pray* ^t Gk *him* ^u The terms *leper* and *leprosy* can refer to several diseases
^v The denarius was the usual day's wage for a laborer ^w Or *gospel*

him one after another, "Surely, not I?" 20 He said to them, "It is one of the twelve, one who is dipping bread[x] into the bowl[y] with me. 21 For the Son of Man goes as it is written of him, but woe to that one by whom the Son of Man is betrayed! It would have been better for that one not to have been born."

The Institution of the Lord's Supper

22 While they were eating, he took a loaf of bread, and after blessing it he broke it, gave it to them, and said, "Take; this is my body." 23 Then he took a cup, and after giving thanks he gave it to them, and all of them drank from it. 24 He said to them, "This is my blood of the[z] covenant, which is poured out for many. 25 Truly I tell you, I will never again drink of the fruit of the vine until that day when I drink it new in the kingdom of God."

Peter's Denial Foretold

26 When they had sung the hymn, they went out to the Mount of Olives. 27 And Jesus said to them, "You will all become deserters; for it is written,
'I will strike the shepherd,
 and the sheep will be
 scattered.'
28 But after I am raised up, I will go before you to Galilee." 29 Peter said to him, "Even though all become deserters, I will not." 30 Jesus said to him, "Truly I tell you, this day, this very night, before the cock crows twice, you will deny me three times." 31 But he said vehemently, "Even though I must die with you, I will not deny you." And all of them said the same.

Jesus Prays in Gethsemane

32 They went to a place called Gethsemane; and he said to his disciples, "Sit here while I pray." 33 He took with him Peter and James and John, and began to be distressed and agitated. 34 And said to them, "I am deeply grieved, even to death; remain here, and keep awake." 35 And going a little far-

ther, he threw himself on the ground and prayed that, if it were possible, the hour might pass from him. 36 He said, "Abba,[a] Father, for you all things are possible; remove this cup from me; yet, not what I want, but what you want." 37 He came and found them sleeping; and he said to Peter, "Simon, are you asleep? Could you not keep awake one hour? 38 Keep awake and pray that you may not come into the time of trial;[b] the spirit indeed is willing, but the flesh is weak." 39 And again he went away and prayed, saying the same words. 40 And once more he came and found them sleeping, for their eyes were very heavy; and they did not know what to say to him. 41 He came a third time and said to them, "Are you still sleeping and taking your rest? Enough! The hour has come; the Son of Man is betrayed into the hands of sinners. 42 Get up, let us be going. See, my betrayer is at hand."

The Betrayal and Arrest of Jesus

43 Immediately, while he was still speaking, Judas, one of the twelve, arrived; and with him there was a crowd with swords and clubs, from the chief priests, the scribes, and the elders. 44 Now the betrayer had given them a sign, saying, "The one I will kiss is the man; arrest him and lead him away under guard." 45 So when he came, he went up to him at once and said, "Rabbi!" and kissed him. 46 Then they laid hands on him and arrested him. 47 But one of those who stood near drew his sword and struck the slave of the high priest, cutting off his ear. 48 Then Jesus said to them, "Have you come out with swords and clubs to arrest me as though I were a bandit? 49 Day after day I was with you in the temple teaching, and you did not arrest me. But let the scriptures be ful-

Cross references

14.22 Mk 6.41; 8.6; Lk 24.30; 1 Cor 11.23-25
14.23 1 Cor 10.16
14.24 Ex 24.8; Heb 9.20
14.26 Mt 21.1
14.27 Zech 13.7
14.28 Mk 16.7
14.29 Jn 13.37,38
14.30 vv. 66-72; Jn 13.38
14.34 Jn 12.27
14.35 v. 41
14.36 Rom 8.15; Gal 4.6; Jn 5.30; 6.38
14.38 Mt 6.13; Lk 11.4; Rom 7.23; Gal 5.17
14.41 v. 35; Jn 13.1
14.45 Mt 23.7
14.49 Mk 12.35; Isa 53.7ff; Lk 19.47; Jn 18.19-21

x Gk lacks *bread* y Other ancient authorities read *same bowl* z Other ancient authorities add *new* a Aramaic for *Father* b Or *into temptation*

filled." [50]All of them deserted him and fled.

[51] A certain young man was following him, wearing nothing but a linen cloth. They caught hold of him, [52]but he left the linen cloth and ran off naked.

Jesus before the Council

[53] They took Jesus to the high priest; and all the chief priests, the elders, and the scribes were assembled. [54]Peter had followed him at a distance, right into the courtyard of the high priest; and he was sitting with the guards, warming himself at the fire. [55]Now the chief priests and the whole council were looking for testimony against Jesus to put him to death; but they found none. [56]For many gave false testimony against him, and their testimony did not agree. [57]Some stood up and gave false testimony against him, saying, [58]"We heard him say, 'I will destroy this temple that is made with hands, and in three days I will build another, not made with hands.' " [59]But even on this point their testimony did not agree. [60]Then the high priest stood up before them and asked Jesus, "Have you no answer? What is it that they testify against you?" [61]But he was silent and did not answer. Again the high priest asked him, "Are you the Messiah,[c] the Son of the Blessed One?" [62]Jesus said, "I am; and

'you will see the Son of Man
seated at the right hand of
the Power,'
and 'coming with the clouds
of heaven.' "

[63]Then the high priest tore his clothes and said, "Why do we still need witnesses? [64]You have heard his blasphemy! What is your decision?" All of them condemned him as deserving death. [65]Some began to spit on him, to blindfold him, and to strike him, saying to him, "Prophesy!" The guards also took him over and beat him.

Peter Denies Jesus

[66] While Peter was below in the courtyard, one of the servant-girls of the high priest came by. [67]When she saw Peter warming himself, she stared at him and said, "You also were with Jesus, the man from Nazareth." [68]But he denied it, saying, "I do not know or understand what you are talking about." And he went out into the forecourt.[d] Then the cock crowed.[e] [69]And the servant-girl, on seeing him, began again to say to the bystanders, "This man is one of them." [70]But again he denied it. Then after a little while the bystanders again said to Peter, "Certainly you are one of them; for you are a Galilean." [71]But he began to curse, and he swore an oath, "I do not know this man you are talking about." [72]At that moment the cock crowed for the second time. Then Peter remembered that Jesus had said to him, "Before the cock crows twice, you will deny me three times." And he broke down and wept.

Jesus before Pilate

15 As soon as it was morning, the chief priests held a consultation with the elders and scribes and the whole council. They bound Jesus, led him away, and handed him over to Pilate. [2]Pilate asked him, "Are you the King of the Jews?" He answered him, "You say so." [3]Then the chief priests accused him of many things. [4]Pilate asked him again, "Have you no answer? See how many charges they bring against you." [5]But Jesus made no further reply, so that Pilate was amazed.

Pilate Hands Jesus over to Be Crucified

[6] Now at the festival he used to release a prisoner for them, anyone for whom they asked. [7]Now a man called Barabbas was in prison with the rebels who had committed murder during the insurrection. [8]So the crowd came and began to ask Pilate to do for them according to his custom. [9]Then he answered

[c] Or the Christ [d] Or gateway [e] Other ancient authorities lack Then the cock crowed

14.50
Ps 88.8;
v. 27
14.54
v. 68;
Mt 26.3;
Jn 18.18
14.58
Mk 15.29;
Jn 2.19;
Acts 6.14
14.61
Isa 53.7
14.62
Dan 7.13;
Mt 24.30;
Mk 13.26
14.63
Num 14.6;
Acts 14.14
14.64
Lev 24.16
14.65
Mk 10.34;
Esther 7.8;
Lk 22.64
14.66
vv. 30,54

14.67
v. 54;
Mk 1.24
14.68
v. 54
14.70
v. 68;
Acts 2.7
14.72
v. 30
15.1
Mt 5.22;
Lk 22.66;
23.1;
Jn 18.28
15.5
Isa 53.7
15.6
Mt 27.15;
Lk 23.17;
Jn 18.39

them, "Do you want me to release for you the King of the Jews?" [10] For he realized that it was out of jealousy that the chief priests had handed him over. [11] But the chief priests stirred up the crowd to have him release Barabbas for them instead. [12] Pilate spoke to them again, "Then what do you wish me to do[f] with the man you call[g] the King of the Jews?" [13] They shouted back, "Crucify him!" [14] Pilate asked them, "Why, what evil has he done?" But they shouted all the more, "Crucify him!" [15] So Pilate, wishing to satisfy the crowd, released Barabbas for them; and after flogging Jesus, he handed him over to be crucified.

The Soldiers Mock Jesus

16 Then the soldiers led him into the courtyard of the palace (that is, the governor's headquarters[h]); and they called together the whole cohort. [17] And they clothed him in a purple cloak; and after twisting some thorns into a crown, they put it on him. [18] And they began saluting him, "Hail, King of the Jews!" [19] They struck his head with a reed, spat upon him, and knelt down in homage to him. [20] After mocking him, they stripped him of the purple cloak and put his own clothes on him. Then they led him out to crucify him.

The Crucifixion of Jesus

21 They compelled a passer-by, who was coming in from the country, to carry his cross; it was Simon of Cyrene, the father of Alexander and Rufus. [22] Then they brought Jesus[i] to the place called Golgotha (which means the place of a skull). [23] And they offered him wine mixed with myrrh; but he did not take it. [24] And they crucified him, and divided his clothes among them, casting lots to decide what each should take.

25 It was nine o'clock in the morning when they crucified him. [26] The inscription of the charge against him read, "The King of the Jews." [27] And with him they cruci-

15.11
Acts 3.14
15.15
Jn 19.1,16
15.16
Acts 10.1
15.21
Lk 23.26;
Rom 16.13
15.24
Ps 22.18

15.29
Ps 22.7;
Mk 13.2;
14.58;
Jn 2.19
15.31
Ps 22.8
15.32
vv. 26,27
15.34
Ps 22.1
15.36
Ps 69.21
15.38
Heb 10.19,
20
15.39
Mk 1.11;
9.7
15.40
Ps 38.11;
Jn 19.25;
Mk 16.1
15.41
Lk 8.1-3

fied two bandits, one on his right and one on his left.[j] [29] Those who passed by derided[k] him, shaking their heads and saying, "Aha! You who would destroy the temple and build it in three days, [30] save yourself, and come down from the cross!" [31] In the same way the chief priests, along with the scribes, were also mocking him among themselves and saying, "He saved others; he cannot save himself. [32] Let the Messiah,[l] the King of Israel, come down from the cross now, so that we may see and believe." Those who were crucified with him also taunted him.

The Death of Jesus

33 When it was noon, darkness came over the whole land[m] until three in the afternoon. [34] At three o'clock Jesus cried out with a loud voice, "Eloi, Eloi, lema sabachthani?" which means, "My God, my God, why have you forsaken me?"[n] [35] When some of the bystanders heard it, they said, "Listen, he is calling for Elijah." [36] And someone ran, filled a sponge with sour wine, put it on a stick, and gave it to him to drink, saying, "Wait, let us see whether Elijah will come to take him down." [37] Then Jesus gave a loud cry and breathed his last. [38] And the curtain of the temple was torn in two, from top to bottom. [39] Now when the centurion, who stood facing him, saw that in this way he[o] breathed his last, he said, "Truly this man was God's Son!"[p]

40 There were also women looking on from a distance; among them were Mary Magdalene, and Mary the mother of James the younger and of Joses, and Salome. [41] These used to follow him and

f Other ancient authorities read *what should I do*　g Other ancient authorities lack *the man you call*　h Gk *the praetorium*　i Gk *him*　j Other ancient authorities add verse 28, *And the scripture was fulfilled that says, "And he was counted among the lawless."*　k Or *blasphemed*　l Or *the Christ*　m Or *earth*　n Other ancient authorities read *made me a reproach*　o Other ancient authorities add *cried out and*　p Or *a son of God*

provided for him when he was in Galilee; and there were many other women who had come up with him to Jerusalem.

The Burial of Jesus

42 When evening had come, and since it was the day of Preparation, that is, the day before the sabbath, 43 Joseph of Arimathea, a respected member of the council, who was also himself waiting expectantly for the kingdom of God, went boldly to Pilate and asked for the body of Jesus. 44 Then Pilate wondered if he were already dead; and summoning the centurion, he asked him whether he had been dead for some time. 45 When he learned from the centurion that he was dead, he granted the body to Joseph. 46 Then Joseph q bought a linen cloth, and taking down the body, r wrapped it in the linen cloth, and laid it in a tomb that had been hewn out of the rock. He then rolled a stone against the door of the tomb. 47 Mary Magdalene and Mary the mother of Joses saw where the body r was laid.

The Resurrection of Jesus

16 When the sabbath was over, Mary Magdalene, and Mary the mother of James, and Salome bought spices, so that they might go and anoint him. 2 And very early on the first day of the week, when the sun had risen, they went to the tomb. 3 They had been saying to one another, "Who will roll away the stone for us from the entrance to the tomb?" 4 When they looked up, they saw that the stone, which was very large, had already been rolled back. 5 As they entered the tomb, they saw a young man, dressed in a white robe, sitting on the right side; and they were alarmed. 6 But he said to them, "Do not be alarmed; you are looking for Jesus of Nazareth, who was crucified. He has been raised; he is not here. Look, there is the place they laid him. 7 But go, tell his disciples and Peter that he is going ahead of you to Galilee; there

15.42
Deut 21.22, 23;
Mt 27.62
15.43
Acts 13.50;
17.12;
Lk 2.25,38
15.45
v. 39
16.1
Lk 23.56;
Jn 19.39
16.3
Mk 15.46
16.5
Mk 9.15
16.6
v. 5;
Mk 1.24
16.7
Mk 14.28;
Jn 21.1-23

you will see him, just as he told you." 8 So they went out and fled from the tomb, for terror and amazement had seized them; and they said nothing to anyone, for they were afraid. s

THE SHORTER ENDING OF MARK

⟦And all that had been commanded them they told briefly to those around Peter. And afterward Jesus himself sent out through them, from east to west, the sacred and imperishable proclamation of eternal salvation. t⟧

THE LONGER ENDING OF MARK

Jesus Appears to Mary Magdalene

9 ⟦Now after he rose early on the first day of the week, he appeared first to Mary Magdalene, from whom he had cast out seven demons. 10 She went out and told those who had been with him, while they were mourning and weeping. 11 But when they heard that he was alive and had been seen by her, they would not believe it.

Jesus Appears to Two Disciples

12 After this he appeared in another form to two of them, as they were walking into the country. 13 And they went back and told the rest, but they did not believe them.

Jesus Commissions the Disciples

14 Later he appeared to the eleven themselves as they were sitting at the table; and he upbraided them for their lack of faith and stubbornness, because they had not believed those who saw him af-

q Gk *he* r Gk *it* s Some of the most ancient authorities bring the book to a close at the end of verse 8. One authority concludes the book with the shorter ending; others include the shorter ending and then continue with verses 9-20. In most authorities verses 9-20 follow immediately after verse 8, though in some of these authorities the passage is marked as being doubtful. t Other ancient authorities add *Amen*

16.9
Jn 20.11-18
16.12
Lk 24.13-35
16.14
Lk 24.36-38;
Jn 20.26

ter he had risen.[u] 15 And he said to them, "Go into all the world and proclaim the good news[v] to the whole creation. 16 The one who believes and is baptized will be saved; but the one who does not believe will be condemned. 17 And these signs will accompany those who believe: by using my name they will cast out demons; they will speak in new tongues; 18 they will pick up snakes in their hands,[w] and if they drink any deadly thing, it will not hurt them; they will lay their hands on the sick, and they will recover."

The Ascension of Jesus

19 So then the Lord Jesus, after he had spoken to them, was taken up into heaven and sat down at the

16.15
Mt 28.18-20;
Lk 24.47,48
16.19
Lk 24.50,51;
Acts 1.9-11

right hand of God. 20 And they went out and proclaimed the good news everywhere, while the Lord worked with them and confirmed the message by the signs that accompanied it. [x]⟧

[u] Other ancient authorities add, in whole or in part, *And they excused themselves, saying, "This age of lawlessness and unbelief is under Satan, who does not allow the truth and power of God to prevail over the unclean things of the spirits. Therefore reveal your righteousness now"—thus they spoke to Christ. And Christ replied to them, "The term of years of Satan's power has been fulfilled, but other terrible things draw near. And for those who have sinned I was handed over to death, that they may return to the truth and sin no more, that they may inherit the spiritual and imperishable glory of righteousness that is in heaven."*
[v] Or *gospel* [w] Other ancient authorities lack *in their hands* [x] Other ancient authorities add *Amen*

THE GOSPEL ACCORDING TO
Luke

Title and Background

The Gospel of Luke has been called the most beautiful book ever written. Luke's writing shows him to be a highly educated man, one who wrote from a Greek background and viewpoint. He wrote especially with Gentiles in mind, for he explained Jewish customs and traced the genealogy of Jesus back to Adam.

Author and Date of Writing

Though the author's name does not appear in the book, early church tradition ascribes this Gospel to Luke, "the beloved physician" (Col 4.14). It is a companion volume to the book of Acts, and the language and structure of these books indicate that both were written by the same person.

Luke was probably a Gentile by birth, well educated in Greek culture, a physician by profession and a companion of Paul at various times. Since Luke probably used Mark as one of his sources (cf. Lk 1.1-4), he likely wrote this book shortly after A.D. 70.

Theme and Message

Luke tells us in the first four verses that he wrote this Gospel to give Theophilus (likely a government official) the true and complete story of Jesus' life. One of his interests in writing this book was to show that Jesus loved all kinds of people. In the parables especially, he wrote about the poor and oppressed. The theme of joy is felt throughout the book, as Christ's coming brought joy and the hope of salvation to a sinful world.

Outline

Dedication to Theophilus

1 Since many have undertaken to set down an orderly account of the events that have been fulfilled among us, [2] just as they were handed on to us by those who from the beginning were eyewitnesses and servants of the word, [3] I too decided, after investigating everything carefully from the very first,[a] to write an orderly account for you, most excellent Theophilus, [4] so that you may know the truth concerning the things about which you have been instructed.

The Birth of John the Baptist Foretold

5 In the days of King Herod of Judea, there was a priest named Zechariah, who belonged to the priestly order of Abijah. His wife was a descendant of Aaron, and her name was Elizabeth. [6] Both of them were righteous before God, living blamelessly according to all the

1.2
Heb 2.3;
1 Pet 5.1;
2 Pet 1.16;
1 Jn 1.1;
Mk 1.1;
Jn 15.27
1.3
Acts 11.4;
18.23; 1.1
1.4
Jn 20.31
1.5
Mt 2.1;
1 Chr 24.10
1.6
Gen 7.1;
1 Kings 9.4;
2 Kings 20.3

a Or *for a long time*

commandments and regulations of the Lord. ⁷But they had no children, because Elizabeth was barren, and both were getting on in years.

8 Once when he was serving as priest before God and his section was on duty, ⁹he was chosen by lot, according to the custom of the priesthood, to enter the sanctuary of the Lord and offer incense. ¹⁰Now at the time of the incense offering, the whole assembly of the people was praying outside. ¹¹Then there appeared to him an angel of the Lord, standing at the right side of the altar of incense. ¹²When Zechariah saw him, he was terrified; and fear overwhelmed him. ¹³But the angel said to him, "Do not be afraid, Zechariah, for your prayer has been heard. Your wife Elizabeth will bear you a son, and you will name him John. ¹⁴You will have joy and gladness, and many will rejoice at his birth, ¹⁵for he will be great in the sight of the Lord. He must never drink wine or strong drink; even before his birth he will be filled with the Holy Spirit. ¹⁶He will turn many of the people of Israel to the Lord their God. ¹⁷With the spirit and power of Elijah he will go before him, to turn the hearts of parents to their children, and the disobedient to the wisdom of the righteous, to make ready a people prepared for the Lord." ¹⁸Zechariah said to the angel, "How will I know that this is so? For I am an old man, and my wife is getting on in years." ¹⁹The angel replied, "I am Gabriel. I stand in the presence of God, and I have been sent to speak to you and to bring you this good news. ²⁰But now, because you did not believe my words, which will be fulfilled in their time, you will become mute, unable to speak, until the day these things occur."

21 Meanwhile the people were waiting for Zechariah, and wondered at his delay in the sanctuary. ²²When he did come out, he could not speak to them, and they realized that he had seen a vision in the sanctuary. He kept motioning to them and remained unable to speak. ²³When his time of service was ended, he went to his home.

24 After those days his wife Elizabeth conceived, and for five months she remained in seclusion. She said, ²⁵"This is what the Lord has done for me when he looked favorably on me and took away the disgrace I have endured among my people."

The Birth of Jesus Foretold

26 In the sixth month the angel Gabriel was sent by God to a town in Galilee called Nazareth, ²⁷to a virgin engaged to a man whose name was Joseph, of the house of David. The virgin's name was Mary. ²⁸And he came to her and said, "Greetings, favored one! The Lord is with you."^b ²⁹But she was much perplexed by his words and pondered what sort of greeting this might be. ³⁰The angel said to her, "Do not be afraid, Mary, for you have found favor with God. ³¹And now, you will conceive in your womb and bear a son, and you will name him Jesus. ³²He will be great, and will be called the Son of the Most High, and the Lord God will give to him the throne of his ancestor David. ³³He will reign over the house of Jacob forever, and of his kingdom there will be no end." ³⁴Mary said to the angel, "How can this be, since I am a virgin?"^c ³⁵The angel said to her, "The Holy Spirit will come upon you, and the power of the Most High will overshadow you; therefore the child to be born^d will be holy; he will be called Son of God. ³⁶And now, your relative Elizabeth in her old age has also conceived a son; and this is the sixth month for her who was said to be barren. ³⁷For nothing will be impossible with God." ³⁸Then Mary said, "Here am I, the servant of the Lord; let it be with me according to your word." Then the angel departed from her.

^b Other ancient authorities add *Blessed are you among women* ^c Gk *I do not know a man* ^d Other ancient authorities add *of you*

1.8
1 Chr 24.19;
2 Chr 8.14
1.9
Ex 30.7,8;
1 Chr 23.13;
2 Chr 29.11
1.10
Lev 16.17
1.13
vv. 30,60,63
1.14
v. 58
1.15
Num 6.3;
Judg 13.4;
Lk 7.33;
Jer 1.5;
Gal 1.15
1.16
Mal 4.5,6
1.17
Mt 11.14;
17.13
1.18
Gen 17.17;
v. 34
1.19
Dan 8.16;
9.21-23;
Mt 18.10
1.20
Ezek 3.26;
24.27
1.22
v. 62

1.25
Gen 30.23;
Isa 4.1
1.26
Mt 2.23
1.27
Mt 1.16;
v. 19
1.28
Dan 9.23;
10.19
1.31
Isa 7.14;
Lk 2.21
1.32
Mk 5.7;
Isa 9.6,7;
Jer 23.5;
Rev 3.7
1.33
Dan 2.44;
7.14,27;
Mt 28.18;
Heb 1.8
1.35
v. 32;
Mk 1.24;
Mt 4.3
1.37
Gen 18.14;
Jer 32.17;
Mt 19.26;
Mk 10.27;
Lk 18.27;
Rom 4.21

Mary Visits Elizabeth

39 In those days Mary set out and went with haste to a Judean town in the hill country, 40 where she entered the house of Zechariah and greeted Elizabeth. 41 When Elizabeth heard Mary's greeting, the child leaped in her womb. And Elizabeth was filled with the Holy Spirit 42 and exclaimed with a loud cry, "Blessed are you among women, and blessed is the fruit of your womb. 43 And why has this happened to me, that the mother of my Lord comes to me? 44 For as soon as I heard the sound of your greeting, the child in my womb leaped for joy. 45 And blessed is she who believed that there would be e a fulfillment of what was spoken to her by the Lord."

Mary's Song of Praise

46 And Mary f said,

47 "My soul magnifies the Lord,
 and my spirit rejoices in
 God my Savior,
48 for he has looked with favor
 on the lowliness of his
 servant.
 Surely, from now on all
 generations will call me
 blessed;
49 for the Mighty One has done
 great things for me,
 and holy is his name.
50 His mercy is for those who
 fear him
 from generation to
 generation.
51 He has shown strength with
 his arm;
 he has scattered the proud
 in the thoughts of their
 hearts.
52 He has brought down the
 powerful from their
 thrones,
 and lifted up the lowly;
53 he has filled the hungry with
 good things,
 and sent the rich away
 empty.
54 He has helped his servant
 Israel,
 in remembrance of his
 mercy,

55 according to the promise he
 made to our ancestors,
 to Abraham and to his
 descendants forever."

56 And Mary remained with her about three months and then returned to her home.

The Birth of John the Baptist

57 Now the time came for Elizabeth to give birth, and she bore a son. 58 Her neighbors and relatives heard that the Lord had shown his great mercy to her, and they rejoiced with her.

59 On the eighth day they came to circumcise the child, and they were going to name him Zechariah after his father. 60 But his mother said, "No; he is to be called John." 61 They said to her, "None of your relatives has this name." 62 Then they began motioning to his father to find out what name he wanted to give him. 63 He asked for a writing tablet and wrote, "His name is John." And all of them were amazed. 64 Immediately his mouth was opened and his tongue freed, and he began to speak, praising God. 65 Fear came over all their neighbors, and all these things were talked about throughout the entire hill country of Judea. 66 All who heard them pondered them and said, "What then will this child become?" For, indeed, the hand of the Lord was with him.

Zechariah's Prophecy

67 Then his father Zechariah was filled with the Holy Spirit and spoke this prophecy:

68 "Blessed be the Lord God of
 Israel,
 for he has looked favorably
 on his people and
 redeemed them.
69 He has raised up a mighty
 savior g for us
 in the house of his servant
 David,

e Or believed, for there will be f Other ancient authorities read Elizabeth g Gk a horn of salvation

Cross-references (center column):

1.39
v. 65
1.41
v. 67
1.42
Judg 5.24;
Lk 11.27,28
1.43
Lk 2.11
1.46
1 Sam 2.1-10;
Ps 34.2,3
1.47
Ps 35.9;
1 Tim 1.1;
2.3;
Titus 2.10;
Jude 25
1.48
Ps 138.6;
Lk 11.27
1.49
Ps 71.19;
111.9
1.50
Ps 103.17
1.51
Ps 98.1;
Isa 40.10;
Ps 33.10;
1 Pet 5.5
1.52
Job 5.11
1.53
Ps 34.10
1.54
Ps 98.3
1.55
Gen 17.19;
Ps 132.11;
Gal 3.16
1.58
Gen 19.19
1.59
Gen 17.12;
Lev 12.3
1.62
v. 22
1.63
v. 13
1.64
v. 20
1.66
Lk 2.19,51;
Gen 39.2;
Acts 11.21
1.67
v. 41;
Joel 2.28
1.68
Ps 72.18;
111.9;
Lk 1.16
1.69
Ps 18.2;
89.17;
132.17;
Ezek 29.21

70 as he spoke through the
 mouth of his holy
 prophets from of old,
71 that we would be saved
 from our enemies and
 from the hand of all
 who hate us.
72 Thus he has shown the
 mercy promised to our
 ancestors,
 and has remembered his
 holy covenant,
73 the oath that he swore to our
 ancestor Abraham,
 to grant us 74 that we, being
 rescued from the hands
 of our enemies,
 might serve him without
 fear, 75 in holiness and
 righteousness
 before him all our days.
76 And you, child, will be called
 the prophet of the Most
 High;
 for you will go before the
 Lord to prepare his ways,
77 to give knowledge of
 salvation to his people
 by the forgiveness of their
 sins.
78 By the tender mercy of our
 God,
 the dawn from on high will
 break upon h us,
79 to give light to those who sit
 in darkness and in the
 shadow of death,
 to guide our feet into the
 way of peace."

80 The child grew and became strong in spirit, and he was in the wilderness until the day he appeared publicly to Israel.

The Birth of Jesus

2 In those days a decree went out from Emperor Augustus that all the world should be registered. 2 This was the first registration and was taken while Quirinius was governor of Syria. 3 All went to their own towns to be registered. 4 Joseph also went from the town of Nazareth in Galilee to Judea, to the city of David called Bethlehem, because he was descended from the

1.70
Jer 23.5;
Dan 9.24;
Acts 3.21;
Rom 1.2;
Mic 7.20;
Ps 105.8,9;
106.45;
Ezek 16.60
1.74
Rom 6.18;
Heb 9.14
1.75
Eph 4.24;
Titus 2.12
1.76
Mal 3.1;
4.5;
Mt 11.9,10
1.77
Mk 1.4
1.79
Mt 9.2;
Mk 4.16;
Acts 26.18
1.80
Lk 2.40,52
2.1
Lk 3.1
2.4
Lk 1.27

2.9
Lk 1.11;
Acts 5.19
2.10
Mt 14.27
2.11
Jn 4.42;
Mt 1.16;
16.16;
Lk 1.43;
Acts 2.36
2.12
1 Sam 2.34;
2 Kings 19.29;
Isa 7.14
2.13
Dan 7.10;
Rev 5.11
2.14
Isa 57.19;
Lk 1.79;
Rom 5.1;
Eph 1.9;
Phil 2.13
2.19
v. 51
2.20
Mt 9.8

house and family of David. 5 He went to be registered with Mary, to whom he was engaged and who was expecting a child. 6 While they were there, the time came for her to deliver her child. 7 And she gave birth to her firstborn son and wrapped him in bands of cloth, and laid him in a manger, because there was no place for them in the inn.

The Shepherds and the Angels

8 In that region there were shepherds living in the fields, keeping watch over their flock by night. 9 Then an angel of the Lord stood before them, and the glory of the Lord shone around them, and they were terrified. 10 But the angel said to them, "Do not be afraid; for see — I am bringing you good news of great joy for all the people: 11 to you is born this day in the city of David a Savior, who is the Messiah, i the Lord. 12 This will be a sign for you: you will find a child wrapped in bands of cloth and lying in a manger." 13 And suddenly there was with the angel a multitude of the heavenly host, j praising God and saying,

14 "Glory to God in the highest
 heaven,
 and on earth peace among
 those whom he
 favors!" k

15 When the angels had left them and gone into heaven, the shepherds said to one another, "Let us go now to Bethlehem and see this thing that has taken place, which the Lord has made known to us." 16 So they went with haste and found Mary and Joseph, and the child lying in the manger. 17 When they saw this, they made known what had been told them about this child; 18 and all who heard it were amazed at what the shepherds told them. 19 But Mary treasured all these words and pondered them in her heart. 20 The shepherds returned, glorifying and praising

h Other ancient authorities read *has broken upon* i Or *the Christ* j Gk *army*
k Other ancient authorities read *peace, good will among people*

God for all they had heard and seen, as it had been told them.

Jesus Is Named

21 After eight days had passed, it was time to circumcise the child; and he was called Jesus, the name given by the angel before he was conceived in the womb.

Jesus Is Presented in the Temple

22 When the time came for their purification according to the law of Moses, they brought him up to Jerusalem to present him to the Lord [23] (as it is written in the law of the Lord, "Every firstborn male shall be designated as holy to the Lord"), [24] and they offered a sacrifice according to what is stated in the law of the Lord, "a pair of turtledoves or two young pigeons."

25 Now there was a man in Jerusalem whose name was Simeon;[l] this man was righteous and devout, looking forward to the consolation of Israel, and the Holy Spirit rested on him. [26] It had been revealed to him by the Holy Spirit that he would not see death before he had seen the Lord's Messiah.[m] [27] Guided by the Spirit, Simeon[n] came into the temple; and when the parents brought in the child Jesus, to do for him what was customary under the law, [28] Simeon[o] took him in his arms and praised God, saying,

29 "Master, now you are
dismissing your
servant[p] in peace,
according to your word;
30 for my eyes have seen your
salvation,
31 which you have prepared in
the presence of all
peoples,
32 a light for revelation to the
Gentiles
and for glory to your
people Israel."

33 And the child's father and mother were amazed at what was being said about him. [34] Then Simeon[l] blessed them and said to his mother Mary, "This child is des-

tined for the falling and the rising of many in Israel, and to be a sign that will be opposed [35] so that the inner thoughts of many will be revealed — and a sword will pierce your own soul too."

36 There was also a prophet, Anna[q] the daughter of Phanuel, of the tribe of Asher. She was of a great age, having lived with her husband seven years after her marriage, [37] then as a widow to the age of eighty-four. She never left the temple but worshiped there with fasting and prayer night and day. [38] At that moment she came, and began to praise God and to speak about the child[r] to all who were looking for the redemption of Jerusalem.

The Return to Nazareth

39 When they had finished everything required by the law of the Lord, they returned to Galilee, to their own town of Nazareth. [40] The child grew and became strong, filled with wisdom; and the favor of God was upon him.

The Boy Jesus in the Temple

41 Now every year his parents went to Jerusalem for the festival of the Passover. [42] And when he was twelve years old, they went up as usual for the festival. [43] When the festival was ended and they started to return, the boy Jesus stayed behind in Jerusalem, but his parents did not know it. [44] Assuming that he was in the group of travelers, they went a day's journey. Then they started to look for him among their relatives and friends. [45] When they did not find him, they returned to Jerusalem to search for him. [46] After three days they found him in the temple, sitting among the teachers, listening to them and asking them questions. [47] And all who heard him were amazed at his understanding and his answers. [48] When his parents[s] saw him they were astonished; and his mother

said to him, "Child, why have you treated us like this? Look, your father and I have been searching for you in great anxiety." ⁴⁹ He said to them, "Why were you searching for me? Did you not know that I must be in my Father's house?"^{t 50} But they did not understand what he said to them. ⁵¹ Then he went down with them and came to Nazareth, and was obedient to them. His mother treasured all these things in her heart.

52 And Jesus increased in wisdom and in years,^u and in divine and human favor.

The Proclamation of John the Baptist

3 In the fifteenth year of the reign of Emperor Tiberius, when Pontius Pilate was governor of Judea, and Herod was ruler^v of Galilee, and his brother Philip ruler^v of the region of Ituraea and Trachonitis, and Lysanias ruler^v of Abilene, ² during the high priesthood of Annas and Caiaphas, the word of God came to John son of Zechariah in the wilderness. ³ He went into all the region around the Jordan, proclaiming a baptism of repentance for the forgiveness of sins, ⁴ as it is written in the book of the words of the prophet Isaiah,
 "The voice of one crying out
 in the wilderness:
 'Prepare the way of the Lord,
 make his paths straight.
⁵ Every valley shall be filled,
 and every mountain and
 hill shall be made low,
 and the crooked shall be
 made straight,
 and the rough ways made
 smooth;
⁶ and all flesh shall see the
 salvation of God.'"

⁷ John said to the crowds that came out to be baptized by him, "You brood of vipers! Who warned you to flee from the wrath to come? ⁸ Bear fruits worthy of repentance. Do not begin to say to yourselves, 'We have Abraham as our ancestor'; for I tell you, God is able from

these stones to raise up children to Abraham. ⁹ Even now the ax is lying at the root of the trees; every tree therefore that does not bear good fruit is cut down and thrown into the fire."

10 And the crowds asked him, "What then should we do?" ¹¹ In reply he said to them, "Whoever has two coats must share with anyone who has none; and whoever has food must do likewise." ¹² Even tax collectors came to be baptized, and they asked him, "Teacher, what should we do?" ¹³ He said to them, "Collect no more than the amount prescribed for you." ¹⁴ Soldiers also asked him, "And we, what should we do?" He said to them, "Do not extort money from anyone by threats or false accusation, and be satisfied with your wages."

15 As the people were filled with expectation, and all were questioning in their hearts concerning John, whether he might be the Messiah,^{w 16} John answered all of them by saying, "I baptize you with water; but one who is more powerful than I is coming; I am not worthy to untie the thong of his sandals. He will baptize you with^x the Holy Spirit and fire. ¹⁷ His winnowing fork is in his hand, to clear his threshing floor and to gather the wheat into his granary; but the chaff he will burn with unquenchable fire."

18 So, with many other exhortations, he proclaimed the good news to the people. ¹⁹ But Herod the ruler,^v who had been rebuked by him because of Herodias, his brother's wife, and because of all the evil things that Herod had done, ²⁰ added to them all by shutting up John in prison.

The Baptism of Jesus

21 Now when all the people were baptized, and when Jesus also had been baptized and was praying, the heaven was opened, ²² and the Holy Spirit descended upon

2.49 Jn 2.16
2.50 Mk 9.32; Lk 9.45
2.51 vv. 19,39
2.52 v. 40; 1 Sam 2.26
3.1 Mt 27.2; 14.1
3.2 Jn 11.49; 18.13; Acts 4.6; Mt 26.3
3.4 Isa 40.3-5
3.6 Ps 98.2; Isa 52.10; Lk 2.30
3.7 Mt 12.34; 23.33
3.8 Jn 8.33,39
3.9 Mt 7.19; Heb 6.7,8
3.10 Acts 2.37
3.11 Jas 2.15,16
3.12 Lk 7.29
3.13 Lk 19.8
3.14 Ex 23.1; Lev 19.11
3.15 Acts 13.25
3.16 Acts 1.5; 11.16; 19.4
3.17 Isa 30.24; Mic 4.12; Mt 13.30
3.19 Mt 14.3,4; Mk 6.17,18
3.21 Lk 5.16; 6.12; 9.18,28; 11.1
3.22 Ps 2.7; Isa 42.1; Lk 9.35; Acts 10.38; 2 Pet 1.17

^t Or be about my Father's interests?
^u Or in stature ^v Gk tetrarch ^w Or the Christ ^x Or in

him in bodily form like a dove. And a voice came from heaven, "You are my Son, the Beloved;[y] with you I am well pleased."[z]

The Ancestors of Jesus

23 Jesus was about thirty years old when he began his work. He was the son (as was thought) of Joseph son of Heli, 24 son of Matthat, son of Levi, son of Melchi, son of Jannai, son of Joseph, 25 son of Mattathias, son of Amos, son of Nahum, son of Esli, son of Naggai, 26 son of Maath, son of Mattathias, son of Semein, son of Josech, son of Joda, 27 son of Joanan, son of Rhesa, son of Zerubbabel, son of Shealtiel,[a] son of Neri, 28 son of Melchi, son of Addi, son of Cosam, son of Elmadam, son of Er, 29 son of Joshua, son of Eliezer, son of Jorim, son of Matthat, son of Levi, 30 son of Simeon, son of Judah, son of Joseph, son of Jonam, son of Eliakim, 31 son of Melea, son of Menna, son of Mattatha, son of Nathan, son of David, 32 son of Jesse, son of Obed, son of Boaz, son of Sala,[b] son of Nahshon, 33 son of Amminadab, son of Admin, son of Arni,[c] son of Hezron, son of Perez, son of Judah, 34 son of Jacob, son of Isaac, son of Abraham, son of Terah, son of Nahor, 35 son of Serug, son of Reu, son of Peleg, son of Eber, son of Shelah, 36 son of Cainan, son of Arphaxad, son of Shem, son of Noah, son of Lamech, 37 son of Methuselah, son of Enoch, son of Jared, son of Mahalaleel, son of Cainan, 38 son of Enos, son of Seth, son of Adam, son of God.

The Temptation of Jesus

4 Jesus, full of the Holy Spirit, returned from the Jordan and was led by the Spirit in the wilderness, 2 where for forty days he was tempted by the devil. He ate nothing at all during those days, and when they were over, he was famished. 3 The devil said to him, "If you are the Son of God, command this stone to become a loaf of bread." 4 Jesus answered him, "It is

written, 'One does not live by bread alone.' "

5 Then the devil[d] led him up and showed him in an instant all the kingdoms of the world. 6 And the devil[d] said to him, "To you I will give their glory and all this authority; for it has been given over to me, and I give it to anyone I please. 7 If you, then, will worship me, it will all be yours." 8 Jesus answered him, "It is written,

'Worship the Lord your God,
　and serve only him.' "

9 Then the devil[d] took him to Jerusalem, and placed him on the pinnacle of the temple, saying to him, "If you are the Son of God, throw yourself down from here, 10 for it is written,

'He will command his angels
　　concerning you,
　to protect you,'
11 and

'On their hands they will
　　bear you up,
　so that you will not dash
　　your foot against a
　　stone.' "

12 Jesus answered him, "It is said, 'Do not put the Lord your God to the test.' " 13 When the devil had finished every test, he departed from him until an opportune time.

The Beginning of the Galilean Ministry

14 Then Jesus, filled with the power of the Spirit, returned to Galilee, and a report about him spread through all the surrounding country. 15 He began to teach in their synagogues and was praised by everyone.

The Rejection of Jesus at Nazareth

16 When he came to Nazareth, where he had been brought up, he went to the synagogue on the sabbath day, as was his custom. He stood up to read, 17 and the scroll of

3.23
Mt 4.17;
Acts 1.1;
Jn 8.57;
Lk 1.27
3.27
Mt 1.12
3.31
2 Sam 5.14;
1 Chr 3.5
3.32
Ruth 4.18ff;
1 Chr 2.10ff
3.34
Gen 11.24,
26
3.36
Gen 11.12;
5.6ff
3.38
Gen 5.1,2
4.1
v. 14;
Lk 2.27
4.2
Ex 34.28;
1 Kings 19.8
4.4
Deut 8.3

4.6
Jn 12.31;
14.30;
1 Jn 5.19
4.8
Deut 6.13
4.10
Ps 91.11,12
4.12
Deut 6.16
4.13
Jn 14.30;
Heb 4.15
4.14
Mt 9.26
4.15
Mt 9.35;
11.1
4.16
Mt 13.54;
Mk 6.1;
Acts 13.14-16

y Or *my beloved Son*　z Other ancient authorities read *You are my Son, today I have begotten you*　a Gk *Salathiel*　b Other ancient authorities read *Salmon*　c Other ancient authorities read *Amminadab, son of Aram*; others vary widely　d Gk *he*

the prophet Isaiah was given to him. He unrolled the scroll and found the place where it was written:

18 "The Spirit of the Lord is
 upon me,
because he has anointed
 me
 to bring good news to the
 poor.
He has sent me to proclaim
 release to the captives
and recovery of sight to the
 blind,
 to let the oppressed go
 free,
19 to proclaim the year of the
 Lord's favor."

20 And he rolled up the scroll, gave it back to the attendant, and sat down. The eyes of all in the synagogue were fixed on him. 21 Then he began to say to them, "Today this scripture has been fulfilled in your hearing." 22 All spoke well of him and were amazed at the gracious words that came from his mouth. They said, "Is not this Joseph's son?" 23 He said to them, "Doubtless you will quote to me this proverb, 'Doctor, cure yourself!' And you will say, 'Do here also in your hometown the things that we have heard you did at Capernaum.' " 24 And he said, "Truly I tell you, no prophet is accepted in the prophet's hometown. 25 But the truth is, there were many widows in Israel in the time of Elijah, when the heaven was shut up three years and six months, and there was a severe famine over all the land; 26 yet Elijah was sent to none of them except to a widow at Zarephath in Sidon. 27 There were also many lepers[e] in Israel in the time of the prophet Elisha, and none of them was cleansed except Naaman the Syrian." 28 When they heard this, all in the synagogue were filled with rage. 29 They got up, drove him out of the town, and led him to the brow of the hill on which their town was built, so that they might hurl him off the cliff. 30 But he passed through the midst of them and went on his way.

4.18
Isa 61.1,2;
Mt 12.18
4.19
Lev 25.10
4.20
v. 17
4.22
Ps 45.2;
Mt 13.54,
55; Mk 6.2,
3; Jn 6.42;
7.15
4.23
Mk 1.21ff;
2.1ff; v. 16
4.24
Mt 13.57;
Mk 6.4;
Jn 4.44
4.25
1 Kings 17.1,
8-16; 18.1;
Jas 5.17,18
4.27
2 Kings 5.1-14
4.29
Num 15.35;
Acts 7.58;
Heb 13.12
4.30
Jn 8.49;
10.39

4.31
Mt 4.13
4.32
Mt 7.28;
Mk 11.18;
Jn 7.46
4.34
v. 41;
Ps 16.10;
Dan 9.24
4.35
vv. 39,41;
Mt 8.26;
Mk 4.39;
Lk 8.24
4.36
v. 32
4.37
v. 14
4.39
vv. 35,41
4.40
Mk 5.23;
Mt 4.23
4.41
Mt 4.3; 8.4
4.42
Mk 1.35-38

The Man with an Unclean Spirit

31 He went down to Capernaum, a city in Galilee, and was teaching them on the sabbath. 32 They were astounded at his teaching, because he spoke with authority. 33 In the synagogue there was a man who had the spirit of an unclean demon, and he cried out with a loud voice, 34 "Let us alone! What have you to do with us, Jesus of Nazareth? Have you come to destroy us? I know who you are, the Holy One of God." 35 But Jesus rebuked him, saying, "Be silent, and come out of him!" When the demon had thrown him down before them, he came out of him without having done him any harm. 36 They were all amazed and kept saying to one another, "What kind of utterance is this? For with authority and power he commands the unclean spirits, and out they come!" 37 And a report about him began to reach every place in the region.

Healings at Simon's House

38 After leaving the synagogue he entered Simon's house. Now Simon's mother-in-law was suffering from a high fever, and they asked him about her. 39 Then he stood over her and rebuked the fever, and it left her. Immediately she got up and began to serve them.

40 As the sun was setting, all those who had any who were sick with various kinds of diseases brought them to him; and he laid his hands on each of them and cured them. 41 Demons also came out of many, shouting, "You are the Son of God!" But he rebuked them and would not allow them to speak, because they knew that he was the Messiah.[f]

Jesus Preaches in the Synagogues

42 At daybreak he departed and went into a deserted place. And the crowds were looking for him; and when they reached him, they wanted to prevent him from leaving

e The terms *leper* and *leprosy* can refer to several diseases f Or *the Christ*

them. [43]But he said to them, "I must proclaim the good news of the kingdom of God to the other cities also; for I was sent for this purpose." [44]So he continued proclaiming the message in the synagogues of Judea.[g]

Jesus Calls the First Disciples

5 Once while Jesus[h] was standing beside the lake of Gennesaret, and the crowd was pressing in on him to hear the word of God, [2]he saw two boats there at the shore of the lake; the fishermen had gone out of them and were washing their nets. [3]He got into one of the boats, the one belonging to Simon, and asked him to put out a little way from the shore. Then he sat down and taught the crowds from the boat. [4]When he had finished speaking, he said to Simon, "Put out into the deep water and let down your nets for a catch." [5]Simon answered, "Master, we have worked all night long but have caught nothing. Yet if you say so, I will let down the nets." [6]When they had done this, they caught so many fish that their nets were beginning to break. [7]So they signaled their partners in the other boat to come and help them. And they came and filled both boats, so that they began to sink. [8]But when Simon Peter saw it, he fell down at Jesus' knees, saying, "Go away from me, Lord, for I am a sinful man!" [9]For he and all who were with him were amazed at the catch of fish that they had taken; [10]and so also were James and John, sons of Zebedee, who were partners with Simon. Then Jesus said to Simon, "Do not be afraid; from now on you will be catching people." [11]When they had brought their boats to shore, they left everything and followed him.

Jesus Cleanses a Leper

[12]Once, when he was in one of the cities, there was a man covered with leprosy.[i] When he saw Jesus, he bowed with his face to the ground and begged him, "Lord, if you choose, you can make me

clean." [13]Then Jesus[h] stretched out his hand, touched him, and said, "I do choose. Be made clean." Immediately the leprosy[i] left him. [14]And he ordered him to tell no one. "Go," he said, "and show yourself to the priest, and, as Moses commanded, make an offering for your cleansing, for a testimony to them." [15]But now more than ever the word about Jesus[i] spread abroad; many crowds would gather to hear him and to be cured of their diseases. [16]But he would withdraw to deserted places and pray.

Jesus Heals a Paralytic

[17]One day, while he was teaching, Pharisees and teachers of the law were sitting near by (they had come from every village of Galilee and Judea and from Jerusalem); and the power of the Lord was with him to heal.[k] [18]Just then some men came, carrying a paralyzed man on a bed. They were trying to bring him in and lay him before Jesus;[i] [19]but finding no way to bring him in because of the crowd, they went up on the roof and let him down with his bed through the tiles into the middle of the crowd[l] in front of Jesus. [20]When he saw their faith, he said, "Friend,[m] your sins are forgiven you." [21]Then the scribes and the Pharisees began to question, "Who is this who is speaking blasphemies? Who can forgive sins but God alone?" [22]When Jesus perceived their questionings, he answered them, "Why do you raise such questions in your hearts? [23]Which is easier, to say, 'Your sins are forgiven you,' or to say, 'Stand up and walk'? [24]But so that you may know that the Son of Man has authority on earth to forgive sins"—he said to the one who was paralyzed—"I say to you, stand up and take your bed and go to your home." [25]Immediately he stood up before them, took what he had

Cross references (center column)

4.44 Mt 4.18-22; Mk 1.16-20; Jn 1.40-42
5.3 Mt 13.1,2; Mk 4.1
5.4 Jn 21.6
5.5 Lk 8.24,45; 9.33,49; 17.13
5.10 Mt 14.27
5.11 v. 28; Mt 19.29
5.12 Lk 17.11-19
5.15 Mt 9.26; Lk 4.14,37
5.16 Mt 14.23; Mk 6.46; Lk 3.21; 6.12; 9.18,28; 11.1
5.17 Mt 15.1; Mk 5.30; Lk 6.19
5.19 Mt 24.17
5.20 Lk 7.48,49
5.21 Isa 43.25

[g] Other ancient authorities read *Galilee*
[h] Gk *he* [i] The terms *leper* and *leprosy* can refer to several diseases [i] Gk *him*
[k] Other ancient authorities read *was present to heal them* [l] Gk *into the midst*
[m] Gk *Man*

been lying on, and went to his home, glorifying God. [26] Amazement seized all of them, and they glorified God and were filled with awe, saying, "We have seen strange things today."

Jesus Calls Levi

27 After this he went out and saw a tax collector named Levi, sitting at the tax booth; and he said to him, "Follow me." [28] And he got up, left everything, and followed him.

29 Then Levi gave a great banquet for him in his house; and there was a large crowd of tax collectors and others sitting at the table[n] with them. [30] The Pharisees and their scribes were complaining to his disciples, saying, "Why do you eat and drink with tax collectors and sinners?" [31] Jesus answered, "Those who are well have no need of a physician, but those who are sick; [32] I have come to call not the righteous but sinners to repentance."

The Question about Fasting

33 Then they said to him, "John's disciples, like the disciples of the Pharisees, frequently fast and pray, but your disciples eat and drink. [34] Jesus said to them, "You cannot make wedding guests fast while the bridegroom is with them, can you? [35] The days will come when the bridegroom will be taken away from them, and then they will fast in those days." [36] He also told them a parable: "No one tears a piece from a new garment and sews it on an old garment; otherwise the new will be torn, and the piece from the new will not match the old. [37] And no one puts new wine into old wineskins; otherwise the new wine will burst the skins and will be spilled, and the skins will be destroyed. [38] But new wine must be put into fresh wineskins. [39] And no one after drinking old wine desires new wine, but says, 'The old is good.' "[o]

The Question about the Sabbath

6 One sabbath[p] while Jesus[q] was going through the grain-

fields, his disciples plucked some heads of grain, rubbed them in their hands, and ate them. [2] But some of the Pharisees said, "Why are you doing what is not lawful[r] on the sabbath?" [3] Jesus answered, "Have you not read what David did when he and his companions were hungry? [4] He entered the house of God and took and ate the bread of the Presence, which it is not lawful for any but the priests to eat, and gave some to his companions?" [5] Then he said to them, "The Son of Man is lord of the sabbath."

The Man with a Withered Hand

6 On another sabbath he entered the synagogue and taught, and there was a man there whose right hand was withered. [7] The scribes and the Pharisees watched him to see whether he would cure on the sabbath, so that they might find an accusation against him. [8] Even though he knew what they were thinking, he said to the man who had the withered hand, "Come and stand here." He got up and stood there. [9] Then Jesus said to them, "I ask you, is it lawful to do good or to do harm on the sabbath, to save life or to destroy it?" [10] After looking around at all of them, he said to him, "Stretch out your hand." He did so, and his hand was restored. [11] But they were filled with fury and discussed with one another what they might do to Jesus.

Jesus Chooses the Twelve Apostles

12 Now during those days he went out to the mountain to pray; and he spent the night in prayer to God. [13] And when day came, he called his disciples and chose twelve of them, whom he also named apostles: [14] Simon, whom he named Peter, and his brother Andrew, and James, and John, and Philip, and Bartholomew, [15] and

Cross references (center column):

5.26
Lk 7.16
5.28
v. 11
5.29
Lk 15.1
5.30
Acts 23.9
5.32
1 Tim 1.15
5.33
Lk 7.18;
Jn 3.25,26
5.35
Lk 9.22;
17.22
6.1
Deut 23.25

6.2
Ex 20.10;
23.12;
Deut 5.14
6.3
1 Sam 21.6
6.4
Lev 24.9
6.6
Lk 13.14;
14.3;
Jn 9.16
6.8
Mt 9.4
6.12
Mt 14.23;
Lk 9.28
6.13
Mk 6.30

[n] Gk *reclining* [o] Other ancient authorities read *better*; others lack verse 39 [p] Other ancient authorities read *On the second first sabbath* [q] Gk *he* [r] Other ancient authorities add *to do*

Matthew, and Thomas, and James son of Alphaeus, and Simon, who was called the Zealot, [16] and Judas son of James, and Judas Iscariot, who became a traitor.

Jesus Teaches and Heals

17 He came down with them and stood on a level place, with a great crowd of his disciples and a great multitude of people from all Judea, Jerusalem, and the coast of Tyre and Sidon. [18] They had come to hear him and to be healed of their diseases; and those who were troubled with unclean spirits were cured. [19] And all in the crowd were trying to touch him, for power came out from him and healed all of them.

Blessings and Woes

20 Then he looked up at his disciples and said:
"Blessed are you who are
 poor,
 for yours is the kingdom of
 God.
[21] "Blessed are you who are
 hungry now,
 for you will be filled.
"Blessed are you who weep
 now,
 for you will laugh.
22 "Blessed are you when people hate you, and when they exclude you, revile you, and defame you[s] on account of the Son of Man. [23] Rejoice in that day and leap for joy, for surely your reward is great in heaven; for that is what their ancestors did to the prophets.
24 "But woe to you who are rich,
 for you have received your
 consolation.
25 "Woe to you who are full
 now,
 for you will be hungry.
"Woe to you who are
 laughing now,
 for you will mourn and
 weep.
26 "Woe to you when all speak well of you, for that is what their ancestors did to the false prophets.

Love for Enemies

27 "But I say to you that listen,

Love your enemies, do good to those who hate you, [28] bless those who curse you, pray for those who abuse you. [29] If anyone strikes you on the cheek, offer the other also; and from anyone who takes away your coat do not withhold even your shirt. [30] Give to everyone who begs from you; and if anyone takes away your goods, do not ask for them again. [31] Do to others as you would have them do to you.

32 "If you love those who love you, what credit is that to you? For even sinners love those who love them. [33] If you do good to those who do good to you, what credit is that to you? For even sinners do the same. [34] If you lend to those from whom you hope to receive, what credit is that to you? Even sinners lend to sinners, to receive as much again. [35] But love your enemies, do good, and lend, expecting nothing in return.[t] Your reward will be great, and you will be children of the Most High; for he is kind to the ungrateful and the wicked. [36] Be merciful, just as your Father is merciful.

Judging Others

37 "Do not judge, and you will not be judged; do not condemn, and you will not be condemned. Forgive, and you will be forgiven; [38] give, and it will be given to you. A good measure, pressed down, shaken together, running over, will be put into your lap; for the measure you give will be the measure you get back."

39 He also told them a parable: "Can a blind person guide a blind person? Will not both fall into a pit? [40] A disciple is not above the teacher, but everyone who is fully qualified will be like the teacher. [41] Why do you see the speck in your neighbor's[u] eye, but do not notice the log in your own eye? [42] Or how can you say to your neighbor,[v] 'Friend,[v] let me take out the speck in your eye,' when you yourself do

Cross references (center column)

6.16 Jude 1
6.17 Mt 4.25; Mk 3.7,8
6.19 Mt 9.21; 14.36; Mk 3.10; Lk 5.17
6.21 Isa 61.3
6.22 1 Pet 4.14; Jn 9.22; 16.2
6.23 Acts 5.41; Col 1.24; Mal 4.2; Acts 7.51
6.24 Jas 5.1; Lk 16.25
6.25 Isa 65.13; Prov 14.13
6.26 Jn 15.19
6.27 v. 35; Rom 12.20
6.28 Lk 23.34; Acts 7.60
6.30 Deut 15.7,8, 10; Prov 21.26
6.31 Mt 7.12
6.35 vv. 27,30
6.37 Rom 2.1
6.38 Mk 4.24; Jas 2.13
6.39 Mt 15.4
6.40 Mt 10.24; Jn 13.16; 15.20

s Gk *cast out your name as evil* t Other ancient authorities read *despairing of no one*
u Gk *brother's* v Gk *brother*

not see the log in your own eye? You hypocrite, first take the log out of your own eye, and then you will see clearly to take the speck out of your neighbor's^w eye.

A Tree and Its Fruit

43 "No good tree bears bad fruit, nor again does a bad tree bear good fruit; 44 for each tree is known by its own fruit. Figs are not gathered from thorns, nor are grapes picked from a bramble bush. 45 The good person out of the good treasure of the heart produces good, and the evil person out of evil treasure produces evil; for it is out of the abundance of the heart that the mouth speaks.

The Two Foundations

46 "Why do you call me 'Lord, Lord,' and do not do what I tell you? 47 I will show you what someone is like who comes to me, hears my words, and acts on them. 48 That one is like a man building a house, who dug deeply and laid the foundation on rock; when a flood arose, the river burst against that house but could not shake it, because it had been well built.^x 49 But the one who hears and does not act is like a man who built a house on the ground without a foundation. When the river burst against it, immediately it fell, and great was the ruin of that house."

Jesus Heals a Centurion's Servant

7 After Jesus^y had finished all his sayings in the hearing of the people, he entered Capernaum. 2 A centurion there had a slave whom he valued highly, and who was ill and close to death. 3 When he heard about Jesus, he sent some Jewish elders to him, asking him to come and heal his slave. 4 When they came to Jesus, they appealed to him earnestly, saying, "He is worthy of having you do this for him, 5 for he loves our people, and it is he who built our synagogue for us." 6 And Jesus went with them, but when he was not far from the

house, the centurion sent friends to say to him, "Lord, do not trouble yourself, for I am not worthy to have you come under my roof; 7 therefore I did not presume to come to you. But only speak the word, and let my servant be healed. 8 For I also am a man set under authority, with soldiers under me; and I say to one, 'Go,' and he goes, and to another, 'Come,' and he comes, and to my slave, 'Do this,' and the slave does it." 9 When Jesus heard this he was amazed at him, and turning to the crowd that followed him, he said, "I tell you, not even in Israel have I found such faith." 10 When those who had been sent returned to the house, they found the slave in good health.

Jesus Raises the Widow's Son at Nain

11 Soon afterwards^z he went to a town called Nain, and his disciples and a large crowd went with him. 12 As he approached the gate of the town, a man who had died was being carried out. He was his mother's only son, and she was a widow; and with her was a large crowd from the town. 13 When the Lord saw her, he had compassion for her and said to her, "Do not weep." 14 Then he came forward and touched the bier, and the bearers stood still. And he said, "Young man, I say to you, rise!" 15 The dead man sat up and began to speak, and Jesus^y gave him to his mother. 16 Fear seized all of them; and they glorified God, saying, "A great prophet has risen among us!" and "God has looked favorably on his people!" 17 This word about him spread throughout Judea and all the surrounding country.

Messengers from John the Baptist

18 The disciples of John reported all these things to him. So John summoned two of his disciples 19 and sent them to the Lord to ask,

6.43
Mt 7.16,18, 20
6.44
Mt 12.33
6.45
Mt 12.34, 35; Mk 7.20
6.46
Mt 7.21
6.47
Jas 1.22-25
7.1
Mt 7.28

7.9
v. 50
7.11
1 Kings 17.17-24;
2 Kings 4.32-37;
Mk 5.21-24, 35-43;
Jn 11.1-44
7.13
v. 19;
Lk 10.1;
11.1,39;
12.42; 13.15;
17.5,6; 18.6;
19.8; 22.61;
24.34
7.14
Lk 8.54;
Jn 11.43;
Acts 9.40
7.16
Lk 1.65;
Jn 6.14;
Lk 1.68

w Gk brother's　x Other ancient authorities read founded upon the rock　y Gk he
z Other ancient authorities read Next day

"Are you the one who is to come, or are we to wait for another?" [20] When the men had come to him, they said, "John the Baptist has sent us to you to ask, 'Are you the one who is to come, or are we to wait for another?' " [21] Jesus[a] had just then cured many people of diseases, plagues, and evil spirits, and had given sight to many who were blind. [22] And he answered them, "Go and tell John what you have seen and heard: the blind receive their sight, the lame walk, the lepers[b] are cleansed, the deaf hear, the dead are raised, the poor have good news brought to them. [23] And blessed is anyone who takes no offense at me."

[24] When John's messengers had gone, Jesus[c] began to speak to the crowds about John:[d] "What did you go out into the wilderness to look at? A reed shaken by the wind? [25] What then did you go out to see? Someone[e] dressed in soft robes? Look, those who put on fine clothing and live in luxury are in royal palaces. [26] What then did you go out to see? A prophet? Yes, I tell you, and more than a prophet. [27] This is the one about whom it is written,

'See, I am sending my
 messenger ahead of
 you,
who will prepare your way
 before you.'

[28] I tell you, among those born of women no one is greater than John; yet the least in the kingdom of God is greater than he." [29] (And all the people who heard this, including the tax collectors, acknowledged the justice of God,[f] because they had been baptized with John's baptism. [30] But by refusing to be baptized by him, the Pharisees and the lawyers rejected God's purpose for themselves.)

[31] "To what then will I compare the people of this generation, and what are they like? [32] They are like children sitting in the marketplace and calling to one another,

'We played the flute for you,
 and you did not dance;

we wailed, and you did not
 weep.'

[33] For John the Baptist has come eating no bread and drinking no wine, and you say, 'He has a demon'; [34] the Son of Man has come eating and drinking, and you say, 'Look, a glutton and a drunkard, a friend of tax collectors and sinners!' [35] Nevertheless, wisdom is vindicated by all her children."

A Sinful Woman Forgiven

[36] One of the Pharisees asked Jesus[d] to eat with him, and he went into the Pharisee's house and took his place at the table. [37] And a woman in the city, who was a sinner, having learned that he was eating in the Pharisee's house, brought an alabaster jar of ointment. [38] She stood behind him at his feet, weeping, and began to bathe his feet with her tears and to dry them with her hair. Then she continued kissing his feet and anointing them with the ointment. [39] Now when the Pharisee who had invited him saw it, he said to himself, "If this man were a prophet, he would have known who and what kind of woman this is who is touching him—that she is a sinner." [40] Jesus spoke up and said to him, "Simon, I have something to say to you." "Teacher," he replied, "Speak." [41] "A certain creditor had two debtors; one owed five hundred denarii,[g] and the other fifty. [42] When they could not pay, he canceled the debts for both of them. Now which of them will love him more?" [43] Simon answered, "I suppose the one for whom he canceled the greater debt." And Jesus[c] said to him, "You have judged rightly." [44] Then turning toward the woman, he said to Simon, "Do you see this woman? I entered your house; you gave me no water for my feet, but she has bathed my feet with her tears and dried them with her hair.

7.21 Mt 4.23; Mk 3.10
7.22 Isa 29.18, 19; 35.5,6; Lk 4.18
7.27 Mal 3.1; Mk 1.2
7.29 Mt 21.32; Lk 3.12
7.30 Mt 22.35; Acts 20.27
7.33 Lk 1.15
7.34 Lk 5.29; 15.1,2
7.36ff Mt 26.6-13; Mk 14.3-9; Jn 12.1-8
7.39 v. 16; Lk 24.19; Jn 6.14
7.41 Mt 18.28
7.44 Gen 18.4; 19.2; 43.24; Judg 19.21; 1 Tim 5.10

a Gk He b The terms *leper* and *leprosy* can refer to several diseases c Gk *he* d Gk *him* e Or *Why then did you go out? To see someone* f Or *praised God* g The denarius was the usual day's wage for a laborer

45 You gave me no kiss, but from the time I came in she has not stopped kissing my feet. 46 You did not anoint my head with oil, but she has anointed my feet with ointment. 47 Therefore, I tell you, her sins, which were many, have been forgiven; hence she has shown great love. But the one to whom little is forgiven, loves little." 48 Then he said to her, "Your sins are forgiven." 49 But those who were at the table with him began to say among themselves, "Who is this who even forgives sins?" 50 And he said to the woman, "Your faith has saved you; go in peace."

Some Women Accompany Jesus

8 Soon afterwards he went on through cities and villages, proclaiming and bringing the good news of the kingdom of God. The twelve were with him, 2 as well as some women who had been cured of evil spirits and infirmities: Mary, called Magdalene, from whom seven demons had gone out, 3 and Joanna, the wife of Herod's steward Chuza, and Susanna, and many others, who provided for them[h] out of their resources.

The Parable of the Sower

4 When a great crowd gathered and people from town after town came to him, he said in a parable: 5 "A sower went out to sow his seed; and as he sowed, some fell on the path and was trampled on, and the birds of the air ate it up. 6 Some fell on the rock; and as it grew up, it withered for lack of moisture. 7 Some fell among thorns, and the thorns grew with it and choked it. 8 Some fell into good soil, and when it grew, it produced a hundredfold." As he said this, he called out, "Let anyone with ears to hear listen!"

The Purpose of the Parables

9 Then his disciples asked him what this parable meant. 10 He said, "To you it has been given to know the secrets[i] of the kingdom of God; but to others I speak[j] in parables, so that

'looking they may not
 perceive,
and listening they may not
 understand.'

The Parable of the Sower Explained

11 "Now the parable is this: The seed is the word of God. 12 The ones on the path are those who have heard; then the devil comes and takes away the word from their hearts, so that they may not believe and be saved. 13 The ones on the rock are those who, when they hear the word, receive it with joy. But these have no root; they believe only for a while and in a time of testing fall away. 14 As for what fell among the thorns, these are the ones who hear; but as they go on their way, they are choked by the cares and riches and pleasures of life, and their fruit does not mature. 15 But as for that in the good soil, these are the ones who, when they hear the word, hold it fast in an honest and good heart, and bear fruit with patient endurance.

A Lamp under a Jar

16 "No one after lighting a lamp hides it under a jar, or puts it under a bed, but puts it on a lampstand, so that those who enter may see the light. 17 For nothing is hidden that will not be disclosed, nor is anything secret that will not become known and come to light. 18 Then pay attention to how you listen; for to those who have, more will be given; and from those who do not have, even what they seem to have will be taken away."

The True Kindred of Jesus

19 Then his mother and his brothers came to him, but they could not reach him because of the crowd. 20 And he was told, "Your mother and your brothers are standing outside, wanting to see you." 21 But he said to them, "My mother and my brothers are those who hear the word of God and do it."

h Other ancient authorities read *him*
i Or *mysteries* j Gk lacks *I speak*

7.46
Ps 23.5
7.48
Mt 9.2;
Mk 2.5;
Lk 5.20
7.50
Mt 9.22;
Mk 5.34;
Lk 8.48
8.1
Mt 4.23
8.2
Mt 27.55,56
8.8
Mt 11.15
8.10
Isa 6.9,10;
Jer 5.21;
Ezek 12.2

8.11
1 Thes 2.13;
1 Pet 1.23
8.16
Mt 5.15;
Mk 4.21;
Lk 11.33
8.17
Mt 10.26;
Mk 4.22;
Lk 12.2
8.18
Mt 13.12;
25.29;
Lk 19.26
8.21
Lk 11.28;
Jn 15.14

Jesus Calms a Storm

22 One day he got into a boat with his disciples, and he said to them, "Let us go across to the other side of the lake." So they put out, 23 and while they were sailing he fell asleep. A windstorm swept down on the lake, and the boat was filling with water, and they were in danger. 24 They went to him and woke him up, shouting, "Master, Master, we are perishing!" And he woke up and rebuked the wind and the raging waves; they ceased, and there was a calm. 25 He said to them, "Where is your faith?" They were afraid and amazed, and said to one another, "Who then is this, that he commands even the winds and the water, and they obey him?"

Jesus Heals the Gerasene Demoniac

26 Then they arrived at the country of the Gerasenes,k which is opposite Galilee. 27 As he stepped out on land, a man of the city who had demons met him. For a long time he had worn1 no clothes, and he did not live in a house but in the tombs. 28 When he saw Jesus, he fell down before him and shouted at the top of his voice, "What have you to do with me, Jesus, Son of the Most High God? I beg you, do not torment me" — 29 for Jesusm had commanded the unclean spirit to come out of the man. (For many times it had seized him; he was kept under guard and bound with chains and shackles, but he would break the bonds and be driven by the demon into the wilds.) 30 Jesus then asked him, "What is your name?" He said, "Legion"; for many demons had entered him. 31 They begged him not to order them to go back into the abyss.

32 Now there on the hillside a large herd of swine was feeding; and the demonsn begged Jesuso to let them enter these. So he gave them permission. 33 Then the demons came out of the man and entered the swine, and the herd rushed down the steep bank into the lake and was drowned.

34 When the swineherds saw what had happened, they ran off and told it in the city and in the country. 35 Then people came out to see what had happened, and when they came to Jesus, they found the man from whom the demons had gone sitting at the feet of Jesus, clothed and in his right mind. And they were afraid. 36 Those who had seen it told them how the one who had been possessed by demons had been healed. 37 Then all the people of the surrounding country of the Gerasenesk asked Jesuso to leave them; for they were seized with great fear. So he got into the boat and returned. 38 The man from whom the demons had gone begged that he might be with him; but Jesusm sent him away, saying, 39 "Return to your home, and declare how much God has done for you." So he went away, proclaiming throughout the city how much Jesus had done for him.

A Girl Restored to Life and a Woman Healed

40 Now when Jesus returned, the crowd welcomed him, for they were all waiting for him. 41 Just then there came a man named Jairus, a leader of the synagogue. He fell at Jesus' feet and begged him to come to his house, 42 for he had an only daughter, about twelve years old, who was dying.

As he went, the crowds pressed in on him. 43 Now there was a woman who had been suffering from hemorrhages for twelve years; and though she had spent all she had on physicians,p no one could cure her. 44 She came up behind him and touched the fringe of his clothes, and immediately her hemorrhage stopped. 45 Then Jesus

8.22
Mk 6.47-52;
Jn 6.16-21
8.24
Lk 5.5; 4.39
8.28
Mk 1.24
8.31
Rom 10.7;
Rev 20.1,3
8.33
vv. 22,23

8.35
Lk 10.39
8.36
Mt 4.24
8.37
Acts 16.39
8.45
Lk 5.5

k Other ancient authorities read *Gadarenes*; others, *Gergesenes* l Other ancient authorities read *a man of the city who had had demons for a long time met him. He wore* m Gk *he* n Gk *they* o Gk *him*
p Other ancient authorities lack *and had spent all she had on physicians*

asked, "Who touched me?" When all denied it, Peter[q] said, "Master, the crowds surround you and press in on you." [46]But Jesus said, "Someone touched me; for I noticed that power had gone out from me." [47]When the woman saw that she could not remain hidden, she came trembling; and falling down before him, she declared in the presence of all the people why she had touched him, and how she had been immediately healed. [48]He said to her, "Daughter, your faith has made you well; go in peace."

[49] While he was still speaking, someone came from the leader's house to say, "Your daughter is dead; do not trouble the teacher any longer." [50]When Jesus heard this, he replied, "Do not fear. Only believe, and she will be saved." [51]When he came to the house, he did not allow anyone to enter with him, except Peter, John, and James, and the child's father and mother. [52]They were all weeping and wailing for her; but he said, "Do not weep; for she is not dead but sleeping." [53]And they laughed at him, knowing that she was dead. [54]But he took her by the hand and called out, "Child, get up!" [55]Her spirit returned, and she got up at once. Then he directed them to give her something to eat. [56]Her parents were astounded; but he ordered them to tell no one what had happened.

The Mission of the Twelve

9 Then Jesus[r] called the twelve together and gave them power and authority over all demons and to cure diseases, [2]and he sent them out to proclaim the kingdom of God and to heal. [3]He said to them, "Take nothing for your journey, no staff, nor bag, nor bread, nor money — not even an extra tunic. [4]Whatever house you enter, stay there, and leave from there. [5]Wherever they do not welcome you, as you are leaving that town shake the dust off your feet as a testimony against them." [6]They departed and

8.46
Lk 5.17;
6.19
8.48
Lk 7.50;
17.19; 18.42
8.49
v. 41
8.52
Lk 23.27;
Jn 11.11,13
8.54
Lk 7.14;
Jn 11.43
8.56
Mt 8.4;
Mk 3.12;
7.36;
Lk 9.21
9.1
Mk 3.13,14
9.2
Lk 10.1,9
9.3
Lk 10.4;
22.35
9.5
Acts 13.51

9.7
v. 19
9.8
Mt 16.14
9.9
Lk 23.8
9.10
v. 17
9.13
2 Kings 4.42-44
9.16
Lk 22.19;
24.30,31;
Acts 2.42;
20.11; 27.35

went through the villages, bringing the good news and curing diseases everywhere.

Herod's Perplexity

[7] Now Herod the ruler[s] heard about all that had taken place, and he was perplexed, because it was said by some that John had been raised from the dead, [8]by some that Elijah had appeared, and by others that one of the ancient prophets had arisen. [9]Herod said, "John I beheaded; but who is this about whom I hear such things?" And he tried to see him.

Feeding the Five Thousand

[10] On their return the apostles told Jesus[t] all they had done. He took them with him and withdrew privately to a city called Bethsaida. [11]When the crowds found out about it, they followed him; and he welcomed them, and spoke to them about the kingdom of God, and healed those who needed to be cured.

[12] The day was drawing to a close, and the twelve came to him and said, "Send the crowd away, so that they may go into the surrounding villages and countryside, to lodge and get provisions; for we are here in a deserted place." [13]But he said to them, "You give them something to eat." They said, "We have no more than five loaves and two fish — unless we are to go and buy food for all these people." [14]For there were about five thousand men. And he said to his disciples, "Make them sit down in groups of about fifty each." [15]They did so and made them all sit down. [16]And taking the five loaves and the two fish, he looked up to heaven, and blessed and broke them, and gave them to the disciples to set before the crowd. [17]And all ate and were filled. What was left over was gathered up, twelve baskets of broken pieces.

q Other ancient authorities add *and those who were with him* r Gk *he* s Gk *tetrarch*
t Gk *him*

Peter's Declaration about Jesus

18 Once when Jesus[u] was praying alone, with only the disciples near him, he asked them, "Who do the crowds say that I am?" 19 They answered, "John the Baptist; but others, Elijah; and still others, that one of the ancient prophets has arisen." 20 He said to them, "But who do you say that I am?" Peter answered, "The Messiah[v] of God."

Jesus Foretells His Death and Resurrection

21 He sternly ordered and commanded them not to tell anyone, 22 saying, "The Son of Man must undergo great suffering, and be rejected by the elders, chief priests, and scribes, and be killed, and on the third day be raised."

23 Then he said to them all, "If any want to become my followers, let them deny themselves and take up their cross daily and follow me. 24 For those who want to save their life will lose it, and those who lose their life for my sake will save it. 25 What does it profit them if they gain the whole world, but lose or forfeit themselves? 26 Those who are ashamed of me and of my words, of them the Son of Man will be ashamed when he comes in his glory and the glory of the Father and of the holy angels. 27 But truly I tell you, there are some standing here who will not taste death before they see the kingdom of God."

The Transfiguration

28 Now about eight days after these sayings Jesus[u] took with him Peter and John and James, and went up on the mountain to pray. 29 And while he was praying, the appearance of his face changed, and his clothes became dazzling white. 30 Suddenly they saw two men, Moses and Elijah, talking to him. 31 They appeared in glory and were speaking of his departure, which he was about to accomplish at Jerusalem. 32 Now Peter and his companions were weighed down with sleep; but since they had stayed awake,[w] they saw his glory and the

two men who stood with him. 33 Just as they were leaving him, Peter said to Jesus, "Master, it is good for us to be here; let us make three dwellings,[x] one for you, one for Moses, and one for Elijah" — not knowing what he said. 34 While he was saying this, a cloud came and overshadowed them; and they were terrified as they entered the cloud. 35 Then from the cloud came a voice that said, "This is my Son, my Chosen;[y] listen to him!" 36 When the voice had spoken, Jesus was found alone. And they kept silent and in those days told no one any of the things they had seen.

Jesus Heals a Boy with a Demon

37 On the next day, when they had come down from the mountain, a great crowd met him. 38 Just then a man from the crowd shouted, "Teacher, I beg you to look at my son; he is my only child. 39 Suddenly a spirit seizes him, and all at once he[z] shrieks. It convulses him until he foams at the mouth; it mauls him and will scarcely leave him. 40 I begged your disciples to cast it out, but they could not." 41 Jesus answered, "You faithless and perverse generation, how much longer must I be with you and bear with you? Bring your son here." 42 While he was coming, the demon dashed him to the ground in convulsions. But Jesus rebuked the unclean spirit, healed the boy, and gave him back to his father. 43 And all were astounded at the greatness of God.

Jesus Again Foretells His Death

While everyone was amazed at all that he was doing, he said to his disciples, 44 "Let these words sink into your ears: The Son of Man is going to be betrayed into human hands." 45 But they did not understand this saying; its meaning was concealed from them, so that they could not perceive it. And they

Cross references

9.18 Jn 1.49; 6.66-69; 11.27
9.19 vv. 7,8; Mk 9.11-13
9.20 Jn 6.69
9.21 Mt 16.20
9.22 vv. 43-45; Lk 18.31-34
9.23 Mt 10.38; Lk 14.27
9.24 Mt 10.39
9.25 Jn 12.25
9.26 Mt 10.33; Lk 12.9; 2 Tim 2.12; 1 Jn 2.28
9.27 Lk 22.18; Jn 21.22
9.28 Lk 3.21; 5.16; 6.12
9.31 2 Pet 1.15
9.32 Mt 26.43; Mk 14.40
9.33 Lk 5.8; 8.24,45; 17.13
9.35 2 Pet 1.17, 18; Mt 3.17
9.36 Mt 17.9
9.43 2 Pet 1.16
9.44 v. 22
9.45 Lk 2.50; 18.34

Footnotes

u Gk he v Or The Christ w Or but when they were fully awake x Or tents
y Other ancient authorities read my Beloved
z Or it

were afraid to ask him about this saying.

True Greatness

46 An argument arose among them as to which one of them was the greatest. 47 But Jesus, aware of their inner thoughts, took a little child and put it by his side, 48 and said to them, "Whoever welcomes this child in my name welcomes me, and whoever welcomes me welcomes the one who sent me; for the least among all of you is the greatest."

Another Exorcist

49 John answered, "Master, we saw someone casting out demons in your name, and we tried to stop him, because he does not follow with us." 50 But Jesus said to him, "Do not stop him; for whoever is not against you is for you."

A Samaritan Village Refuses to Receive Jesus

51 When the days drew near for him to be taken up, he set his face to go to Jerusalem. 52 And he sent messengers ahead of him. On their way they entered a village of the Samaritans to make ready for him; 53 but they did not receive him, because his face was set toward Jerusalem. 54 When his disciples James and John saw it, they said, "Lord, do you want us to command fire to come down from heaven and consume them?"a 55 But he turned and rebuked them. 56 Thenb they went on to another village.

Would-Be Followers of Jesus

57 As they were going along the road, someone said to him, "I will follow you wherever you go." 58 And Jesus said to him, "Foxes have holes, and birds of the air have nests; but the Son of Man has nowhere to lay his head." 59 To another he said, "Follow me." But he said, "Lord, first let me go and bury my father." 60 But Jesusc said to him, "Let the dead bury their own dead; but as for you, go and proclaim the kingdom of God." 61 An-

other said, "I will follow you, Lord; but let me first say farewell to those at my home." 62 Jesus said to him, "No one who puts a hand to the plow and looks back is fit for the kingdom of God."

The Mission of the Seventy

10 After this the Lord appointed seventyd others and sent them on ahead of him in pairs to every town and place where he himself intended to go. 2 He said to them, "The harvest is plentiful, but the laborers are few; therefore ask the Lord of the harvest to send out laborers into his harvest. 3 Go on your way. See, I am sending you out like lambs into the midst of wolves. 4 Carry no purse, no bag, no sandals; and greet no one on the road. 5 Whatever house you enter, first say, 'Peace to this house!' 6 And if anyone is there who shares in peace, your peace will rest on that person; but if not, it will return to you. 7 Remain in the same house, eating and drinking whatever they provide, for the laborer deserves to be paid. Do not move about from house to house. 8 Whenever you enter a town and its people welcome you, eat what is set before you; 9 cure the sick who are there, and say to them, 'The kingdom of God has come near to you.'e 10 But whenever you enter a town and they do not welcome you, go out into its streets and say, 11 'Even the dust of your town that clings to our feet, we wipe off in protest against you. Yet know this: the kingdom of God has come near.'f 12 I tell you, on that day it will be more tolerable for Sodom than for that town.

Woes to Unrepentant Cities

13 "Woe to you, Chorazin! Woe to you, Bethsaida! For if the deeds of power done in you had been done in Tyre and Sidon, they would

9.48 Mt 10.40; Jn 12.44; 13.20; Mt 23.11,12
9.49 Mk 9.38
9.50 Mt 12.30
9.51 Lk 13.22; 17.11; 18.31; 19.11,28
9.52 Mt 10.5; Jn 4.4
9.54 Mk 3.17; 1 Kings 1.10,12
9.59 Mt 8.21,22

10.1 Mt 10.1; Mk 6.7; Lk 9.1,2,51,52
10.2 Mt 9.37,38; Jn 4.35
10.3 Mt 10.16
10.4 Mt 10.9,10; Mk 6.8; Lk 9.3
10.5 Mk 10.12
10.7 Mt 10.10; 1 Cor 9.14; 1 Tim 5.18
10.9 Mt 3.2; 10.7
10.11 Mt 10.14;
10.12 Mt 10.15; 11.24
10.13 Mt 11.21; Lk 6.24-26

a Other ancient authorities add as Elijah did b Other ancient authorities read rebuked them, and said, "You do not know what spirit you are of, 56for the Son of Man has not come to destroy the lives of human beings but to save them." Then c Gk he d Other ancient authorities read seventy-two e Or is at hand for you f Or is at hand

have repented long ago, sitting in sackcloth and ashes. 14 But at the judgment it will be more tolerable for Tyre and Sidon than for you. 15 And you, Capernaum,

will you be exalted to
heaven?

No, you will be brought
down to Hades.

16 "Whoever listens to you listens to me, and whoever rejects you rejects me, and whoever rejects me rejects the one who sent me."

The Return of the Seventy

17 The seventy[g] returned with joy, saying, "Lord, in your name even the demons submit to us!" 18 He said to them, "I watched Satan fall from heaven like a flash of lightning. 19 See, I have given you authority to tread on snakes and scorpions, and over all the power of the enemy; and nothing will hurt you. 20 Nevertheless, do not rejoice at this, that the spirits submit to you, but rejoice that your names are written in heaven."

Jesus Rejoices

21 At that same hour Jesus[h] rejoiced in the Holy Spirit[i] and said, "I thank[j] you, Father, Lord of heaven and earth, because you have hidden these things from the wise and the intelligent and have revealed them to infants; yes, Father, for such was your gracious will.[k] 22 All things have been handed over to me by my Father; and no one knows who the Son is except the Father, or who the Father is except the Son and anyone to whom the Son chooses to reveal him."

23 Then turning to the disciples, Jesus[h] said to them privately, "Blessed are the eyes that see what you see! 24 For I tell you that many prophets and kings desired to see what you see, but did not see it, and to hear what you hear, but did not hear it."

The Parable of the Good Samaritan

25 Just then a lawyer stood up to test Jesus.[l] "Teacher," he said, "what must I do to inherit eternal

life?" 26 He said to him, "What is written in the law? What do you read there?" 27 He answered, "You shall love the Lord your God with all your heart, and with all your soul, and with all your strength, and with all your mind; and your neighbor as yourself." 28 And he said to him, "You have given the right answer; do this, and you will live."

29 But wanting to justify himself, he asked Jesus, "And who is my neighbor?" 30 Jesus replied, "A man was going down from Jerusalem to Jericho, and fell into the hands of robbers, who stripped him, beat him, and went away, leaving him half dead. 31 Now by chance a priest was going down that road; and when he saw him, he passed by on the other side. 32 So likewise a Levite, when he came to the place and saw him, passed by on the other side. 33 But a Samaritan while traveling came near him; and when he saw him, he was moved with pity. 34 He went to him and bandaged his wounds, having poured oil and wine on them. Then he put him on his own animal, brought him to an inn, and took care of him. 35 The next day he took out two denarii,[m] gave them to the innkeeper, and said, 'Take care of him; and when I come back, I will repay you whatever more you spend.' 36 Which of these three, do you think, was a neighbor to the man who fell into the hands of the robbers?" 37 He said, "The one who showed him mercy." Jesus said to him, "Go and do likewise."

Jesus Visits Martha and Mary

38 Now as they went on their way, he entered a certain village, where a woman named Martha welcomed him into her home. 39 She had a sister named Mary, who sat at the Lord's feet and listened to what he was saying. 40 But

10.15	Mt 11.23
10.16	Mt 10.40; Mk 9.37; Lk 9.48; Jn 13.20
10.17	v. 1
10.18	Jn 12.31; Rev 9.1; 12.8,9
10.19	Acts 28.5
10.20	Ex 32.32; Ps 69.28; Dan 12.1; Phil 4.3; Heb 12.23; Rev 13.8; 21.27
10.21	Mt 11.25; 1 Cor 1.26-29
10.22	Mt 28.18; Jn 3.35; 17.2
10.23	Mt 13.16
10.24	1 Pet 1.10
10.25	Mt 19.16; Mk 10.17; Lk 18.18
10.27	Deut 6.5; Lev 19.18; Rom 13.9; Gal 5.14; Jas 2.8
10.28	Lev 18.5; Mt 19.17
10.29	Lk 16.15
10.33	Lk 9.52; Jn 4.9
10.38	Jn 11.1; 12.2,3
10.39	Lk 8.35; Acts 22.3

g Other ancient authorities read *seventy-two*
h Gk *he* i Other authorities read *in the spirit* j Or *praise* k Or *for so it was well-pleasing in your sight* l Gk *him*
m The denarius was the usual day's wage for a laborer

Martha was distracted by her many tasks; so she came to him and asked, "Lord, do you not care that my sister has left me to do all the work by myself? Tell her then to help me." [41] But the Lord answered her, "Martha, Martha, you are worried and distracted by many things; [42] there is need of only one thing.[n] Mary has chosen the better part, which will not be taken away from her."

The Lord's Prayer

11 He was praying in a certain place, and after he had finished, one of his disciples said to him, "Lord, teach us to pray, as John taught his disciples." [2] He said to them, "When you pray, say:

"Father,[o] hallowed be your name.
Your kingdom come.[p]
[3] Give us each day our daily bread.[q]
[4] And forgive us our sins,
 for we ourselves forgive everyone indebted to us.
 And do not bring us to the time of trial."[r]

Perseverance in Prayer

[5] And he said to them, "Suppose one of you has a friend, and you go to him at midnight and say to him, 'Friend, lend me three loaves of bread; [6] for a friend of mine has arrived, and I have nothing to set before him.' [7] And he answers from within, 'Do not bother me; the door has already been locked, and my children are with me in bed; I cannot get up and give you anything.' [8] I tell you, even though he will not get up and give him anything because he is his friend, at least because of his persistence he will get up and give him whatever he needs.

[9] "So I say to you, Ask, and it will be given you; search, and you will find; knock, and the door will be opened for you. [10] For everyone who asks receives, and everyone who searches finds, and for everyone who knocks, the door will be opened. [11] Is there anyone among you who, if your child asks for[s] a fish, will give a snake instead of a fish? [12] Or if the child asks for an egg, will give a scorpion? [13] If you then, who are evil, know how to give good gifts to your children, how much more will the heavenly Father give the Holy Spirit[t] to those who ask him!"

Jesus and Beelzebul

[14] Now he was casting out a demon that was mute; when the demon had gone out, the one who had been mute spoke, and the crowds were amazed. [15] But some of them said, "He casts out demons by Beelzebul, the ruler of the demons." [16] Others, to test him, kept demanding from him a sign from heaven. [17] But he knew what they were thinking and said to them, "Every kingdom divided against itself becomes a desert, and house falls on house. [18] If Satan also is divided against himself, how will his kingdom stand? —for you say that I cast out the demons by Beelzebul. [19] Now if I cast out the demons by Beelzebul, by whom do your exorcists[u] cast them out? Therefore they will be your judges. [20] But if it is by the finger of God that I cast out the demons, then the kingdom of God has come to you. [21] When a strong man, fully armed, guards his castle, his property is safe. [22] But when one stronger than he attacks him and overpowers him, he takes away his armor in which he trusted and divides his plunder. [23] Whoever is not with me is against me, and whoever does not gather with me scatters.

[10.42] Ps 27.4
[11.1] Mk 1.35; Lk 3.21
[11.4] Mt 18.35; Mk 11.25
[11.8] Lk 18.1-6
[11.9] Mt 7.7-11; 18.19; 21.22; Mk 11.24; Jas 1.5-8; 1 Jn 5.14, 15

[11.14] Mt 9.32-34
[11.16] Mt 16.1; Mk 8.11
[11.17] Jn 2.25
[11.20] Ex 8.19
[11.23] Lk 9.50

n Other ancient authorities read *few things are necessary, or only one* o Other ancient authorities read *Our Father in heaven* p A few ancient authorities read *Your Holy Spirit come upon us and cleanse us.* Other ancient authorities add *Your will be done, on earth as in heaven* q Or *our bread for tomorrow* r Or *us into temptation.* Other ancient authorities add *but rescue us from the evil one* (or *from evil*) s Other ancient authorities add *bread, will give a stone; or if your child asks for* t Other ancient authorities read *the Father give the Holy Spirit from heaven* u Gk *sons*

The Return of the Unclean Spirit

24 "When the unclean spirit has gone out of a person, it wanders through waterless regions looking for a resting place, but not finding any, it says, 'I will return to my house from which I came.' 25 When it comes, it finds it swept and put in order. 26 Then it goes and brings seven other spirits more evil than itself, and they enter and live there; and the last state of that person is worse than the first."

True Blessedness

27 While he was saying this, a woman in the crowd raised her voice and said to him, "Blessed is the womb that bore you and the breasts that nursed you!" 28 But he said, "Blessed rather are those who hear the word of God and obey it!"

The Sign of Jonah

29 When the crowds were increasing, he began to say, "This generation is an evil generation; it asks for a sign, but no sign will be given to it except the sign of Jonah. 30 For just as Jonah became a sign to the people of Nineveh, so the Son of Man will be to this generation. 31 The queen of the South will rise at the judgment with the people of this generation and condemn them, because she came from the ends of the earth to listen to the wisdom of Solomon, and see, something greater than Solomon is here! 32 The people of Nineveh will rise up at the judgment with this generation and condemn it, because they repented at the proclamation of Jonah, and see, something greater than Jonah is here!

The Light of the Body

33 "No one after lighting a lamp puts it in a cellar,ᵛ but on the lampstand so that those who enter may see the light. 34 Your eye is the lamp of your body. If your eye is healthy, your whole body is full of light; but if it is not healthy, your body is full of darkness. 35 Therefore consider whether the light in you is not darkness. 36 If then your

whole body is full of light, with no part of it in darkness, it will be as full of light as when a lamp gives you light with its rays."

Jesus Denounces Pharisees and Lawyers

37 While he was speaking, a Pharisee invited him to dine with him; so he went in and took his place at the table. 38 The Pharisee was amazed to see that he did not first wash before dinner. 39 Then the Lord said to him, "Now you Pharisees clean the outside of the cup and of the dish, but inside you are full of greed and wickedness. 40 You fools! Did not the one who made the outside make the inside also? 41 So give for alms those things that are within; and see, everything will be clean for you.

42 "But woe to you Pharisees! For you tithe mint and rue and herbs of all kinds, and neglect justice and the love of God; it is these you ought to have practiced, without neglecting the others. 43 Woe to you Pharisees! For you love to have the seat of honor in the synagogues and to be greeted with respect in the marketplaces. 44 Woe to you! For you are like unmarked graves, and people walk over them without realizing it."

45 One of the lawyers answered him, "Teacher, when you say these things, you insult us too." 46 And he said, "Woe also to you lawyers! For you load people with burdens hard to bear, and you yourselves do not lift a finger to ease them. 47 Woe to you! For you build the tombs of the prophets whom your ancestors killed. 48 So you are witnesses and approve of the deeds of your ancestors; for they killed them, and you build their tombs. 49 Therefore also the Wisdom of God said, 'I will send them prophets and apostles, some of whom they will kill and persecute,' 50 so that this generation may be charged with the blood of all the prophets shed since the foundation of the world, 51 from the

Cross references (center column)

11.26 Heb 10.26; 2 Pet 2.20
11.27 Lk 23.29
11.28 Lk 8.21; Jn 15.14
11.29 Mt 16.4; Mk 8.12; v. 16
11.31 1 Kings 10.1; 2 Chr 9.1
11.32 Jon 3.5
11.33 Mt 5.15; Mk 4.21; Lk 8.16
11.34 Mt 6.22,23
11.37 Lk 7.36; 14.1
11.38 Mk 7.3,4
11.39 Mt 23.25,26
11.41 Lk 12.33;
11.41 Mk 7.19; Titus 1.15
11.42 Mt 23.23; Lk 18.12
11.43 Mt 23.6,7; Mk 12.38, 39; Lk 20.46
11.44 Mt 23.27
11.46 Mt 23.4
11.47 Mt 23.29-32; Acts 7.51-53
11.49 Mt 23.34-36; 1 Cor 1.24; Col 2.3
11.51 Gen 4.8; 2 Chr 24.20, 21

ᵛ Other ancient authorities add *or under the bushel basket*

blood of Abel to the blood of Zechariah, who perished between the altar and the sanctuary. Yes, I tell you, it will be charged against this generation. [52] Woe to you lawyers! For you have taken away the key of knowledge; you did not enter yourselves, and you hindered those who were entering."

53 When he went outside, the scribes and the Pharisees began to be very hostile toward him and to cross-examine him about many things, [54] lying in wait for him, to catch him in something he might say.

A Warning against Hypocrisy

12 Meanwhile, when the crowd gathered by the thousands, so that they trampled on one another, he began to speak first to his disciples, "Beware of the yeast of the Pharisees, that is, their hypocrisy. [2] Nothing is covered up that will not be uncovered, and nothing secret that will not become known. [3] Therefore whatever you have said in the dark will be heard in the light, and what you have whispered behind closed doors will be proclaimed from the housetops.

Exhortation to Fearless Confession

4 "I tell you, my friends, do not fear those who kill the body, and after that can do nothing more. [5] But I will warn you whom to fear: fear him who, after he has killed, has authority[w] to cast into hell.[x] Yes, I tell you, fear him! [6] Are not five sparrows sold for two pennies? Yet not one of them is forgotten in God's sight. [7] But even the hairs of your head are all counted. Do not be afraid; you are of more value than many sparrows.

8 "And I tell you, everyone who acknowledges me before others, the Son of Man also will acknowledge before the angels of God; [9] but whoever denies me before others will be denied before the angels of God. [10] And everyone who speaks a word against the Son of Man will be

11.52
Mt 23.13
11.54
Mk 12.13
12.1
Mt 16.6;
Mk 8.15;
Mt 16.12
12.2
Mt 10.26,
27;
Mk 4.22;
Lk 8.17;
Eph 5.13
12.4
Mt 10.28-33;
Jn 15.14,15
12.5
Heb 10.31
12.7
Mt 12.12;
Lk 21.18;
Acts 27.34
12.8
Mk 8.38;
2 Tim 2.12;
1 Jn 2.23
12.10
Mt 12.31,
32;
Mk 3.28,29

12.11
Mt 10.19;
Mk 13.11;
Lk 21.14
12.14
Mic 6.8;
Rom 2.1,3
12.19
Eccl 11.9;
Jas 5.5
12.20
Jer 17.11;
Job 27.8;
Ps 39.6
12.21
v. 33
12.24
Job 38.41
12.25
Ps 39.5

forgiven; but whoever blasphemes against the Holy Spirit will not be forgiven. [11] When they bring you before the synagogues, the rulers, and the authorities, do not worry about how[y] you are to defend yourselves or what you are to say; [12] for the Holy Spirit will teach you at that very hour what you ought to say."

The Parable of the Rich Fool

13 Someone in the crowd said to him, "Teacher, tell my brother to divide the family inheritance with me." [14] But he said to him, "Friend, who set me to be a judge or arbitrator over you?" [15] And he said to them, "Take care! Be on your guard against all kinds of greed; for one's life does not consist in the abundance of possessions." [16] Then he told them a parable: "The land of a rich man produced abundantly. [17] And he thought to himself, 'What should I do, for I have no place to store my crops?' [18] Then he said, 'I will do this: I will pull down my barns and build larger ones, and there I will store all my grain and my goods. [19] And I will say to my soul, 'Soul, you have ample goods laid up for many years; relax, eat, drink, be merry.' [20] But God said to him, 'You fool! This very night your life is being demanded of you. And the things you have prepared, whose will they be?' [21] So it is with those who store up treasures for themselves but are not rich toward God."

Do Not Worry

22 He said to his disciples, "Therefore I tell you, do not worry about your life, what you will eat, or about your body, what you will wear. [23] For life is more than food, and the body more than clothing. [24] Consider the ravens: they neither sow nor reap, they have neither storehouse nor barn, and yet God feeds them. Of how much more value are you than the birds! [25] And can any of you by worrying add a

[w] Or *power* [x] Gk *Gehenna* [y] Other ancient authorities add *or what*

single hour to your span of life?[z]
[26] If then you are not able to do so
small a thing as that, why do you
worry about the rest? [27] Consider
the lilies, how they grow: they nei-
ther toil nor spin;[a] yet I tell you,
even Solomon in all his glory was
not clothed like one of these. [28] But
if God so clothes the grass of the
field, which is alive today and to-
morrow is thrown into the oven,
how much more will he clothe
you—you of little faith! [29] And do
not keep striving for what you are
to eat and what you are to drink,
and do not keep worrying. [30] For it
is the nations of the world that
strive after all these things, and
your Father knows that you need
them. [31] Instead, strive for his[b]
kingdom, and these things will be
given to you as well.

[32] "Do not be afraid, little flock,
for it is your Father's good pleasure
to give you the kingdom. [33] Sell
your possessions, and give alms.
Make purses for yourselves that do
not wear out, an unfailing treasure
in heaven, where no thief comes
near and no moth destroys. [34] For
where your treasure is, there your
heart will be also.

Watchful Slaves

[35] "Be dressed for action and
have your lamps lit; [36] be like those
who are waiting for their master to
return from the wedding banquet,
so that they may open the door for
him as soon as he comes and
knocks. [37] Blessed are those slaves
whom the master finds alert when
he comes; truly I tell you, he will
fasten his belt and have them sit
down to eat, and he will come and
serve them. [38] If he comes during
the middle of the night, or near
dawn, and finds them so, blessed
are those slaves.

[39] But know this: if the owner of
the house had known at what hour
the thief was coming, he[c] would
not have let his house be broken
into. [40] You also must be ready, for
the Son of Man is coming at an un-
expected hour."

12.27
1 Kings 10.4-7
12.30
Mt 6.8
12.32
Jn 21.15-17
12.33
Mt 19.21;
Mk 6.20
12.34
Mt 6.21
12.35
Mt 25.1-13;
Mk 13.33-37;
Eph 6.14
12.37
Mt 24.42,
46; Lk 17.8;
Jn 13.4
12.39
Mt 24.43;
1 Thes 5.2;
2 Pet 3.10;
Rev 3.3;
16.15
12.40
Mt 24.44;
Mk 13.33;
Lk 21.36

12.42
Lk 7.13
12.47
Num 15.30;
Deut 25.2
12.48
Lev 5.17
12.50
Mk 10.38;
Jn 12.27
12.51
Mt 10.34-36;
v. 49
12.53
Mic 7.6;
Mt 10.21

The Faithful or the Unfaithful Slave

[41] Peter said, "Lord, are you
telling this parable for us or for ev-
eryone?" [42] And the Lord said,
"Who then is the faithful and pru-
dent manager whom his master
will put in charge of his slaves, to
give them their allowance of food
at the proper time? [43] Blessed is
that slave whom his master will
find at work when he arrives. [44] Tru-
ly I tell you, he will put that one in
charge of all his possessions. [45] But
if that slave says to himself, 'My
master is delayed in coming,' and if
he begins to beat the other slaves,
men and women, and to eat and
drink and get drunk, [46] the master
of that slave will come on a day
when he does not expect him and
at an hour that he does not know,
and will cut him in pieces,[d] and
put him with the unfaithful. [47] That
slave who knew what his master
wanted, but did not prepare him-
self or do what was wanted, will re-
ceive a severe beating. [48] But the
one who did not know and did what
deserved a beating will receive a
light beating. From everyone to
whom much has been given, much
will be required; and from the one
to whom much has been entrusted,
even more will be demanded.

Jesus the Cause of Division

[49] "I came to bring fire to the
earth, and how I wish it were al-
ready kindled! [50] I have a baptism
with which to be baptized, and
what stress I am under until it is
completed! [51] Do you think that I
have come to bring peace to the
earth? No, I tell you, but rather di-
vision! [52] From now on five in one
household will be divided, three
against two and two against three;
[53] they will be divided:
 father against son
 and son against father,
 mother against daughter

[z] Or add a cubit to your stature [a] Other
ancient authorities read Consider the lilies;
they neither spin nor weave [b] Other ancient
authorities read God's [c] Other ancient
authorities add would have watched and
[d] Or cut him off

and daughter against
mother,
mother-in-law against her
daughter-in-law
and daughter-in-law against
mother-in-law."

Interpreting the Time

54 He also said to the crowds, "When you see a cloud rising in the west, you immediately say, 'It is going to rain'; and so it happens. 55 And when you see the south wind blowing, you say, 'There will be scorching heat'; and it happens. 56 You hypocrites! You know how to interpret the appearance of earth and sky, but why do you not know how to interpret the present time?

Settling with Your Opponent

57 "And why do you not judge for yourselves what is right? 58 Thus, when you go with your accuser before a magistrate, on the way make an effort to settle the case,e or you may be dragged before the judge, and the judge hand you over to the officer, and the officer throw you in prison. 59 I tell you, you will never get out until you have paid the very last penny."

Repent or Perish

13 At that very time there were some present who told him about the Galileans whose blood Pilate had mingled with their sacrifices. 2 He asked them, "Do you think that because these Galileans suffered in this way they were worse sinners than all other Galileans? 3 No, I tell you; but unless you repent, you will all perish as they did. 4 Or those eighteen who were killed when the tower of Siloam fell on them— do you think that they were worse offenders than all the others living in Jerusalem? 5 No, I tell you; but unless you repent, you will all perish just as they did."

The Parable of the Barren Fig Tree

6 Then he told this parable: "A man had a fig tree planted in his vineyard; and he came looking for

12.54
Mt 16.2
12.55
Mt 20.12
12.56
Mt 16.3
12.58
Mt 5.25,26
12.59
Mk 12.42
13.1
Mt 27.2
13.2
Jn 9.2,3
13.4
Lk 11.4
13.6
Mt 21.19

13.7
Mt 3.10;
7.19; Lk 3.9
13.11
v. 16
13.13
Mk 5.23
13.14
Ex 20.9;
Lk 6.7; 14.3
13.15
Lk 7.13;
14.5
13.16
Lk 19.9

fruit on it and found none. 7 So he said to the gardener, 'See here! For three years I have come looking for fruit on this fig tree, and still I find none. Cut it down! Why should it be wasting the soil?' 8 He replied, 'Sir, let it alone for one more year, until I dig around it and put manure on it. 9 If it bears fruit next year, well and good; but if not, you can cut it down.' "

Jesus Heals a Crippled Woman

10 Now he was teaching in one of the synagogues on the sabbath. 11 And just then there appeared a woman with a spirit that had crippled her for eighteen years. She was bent over and was quite unable to stand up straight. 12 When Jesus saw her, he called her over and said, "Woman, you are set free from your ailment." 13 When he laid his hands on her, immediately she stood up straight and began praising God. 14 But the leader of the synagogue, indignant because Jesus had cured on the sabbath, kept saying to the crowd, "There are six days on which work ought to be done; come on those days and be cured, and not on the sabbath day." 15 But the Lord answered him and said, "You hypocrites! Does not each of you on the sabbath untie his ox or his donkey from the manger, and lead it away to give it water? 16 And ought not this woman, a daughter of Abraham whom Satan bound for eighteen long years, be set free from this bondage on the sabbath day?" 17 When he said this, all his opponents were put to shame; and the entire crowd was rejoicing at all the wonderful things that he was doing.

The Parable of the Mustard Seed

18 He said therefore, "What is the kingdom of God like? And to what should I compare it? 19 It is like a mustard seed that someone took and sowed in the garden; it grew and became a tree, and the birds of the air made nests in its branches."

e Gk settle with him

The Parable of the Yeast

20 And again he said, "To what should I compare the kingdom of God? 21 It is like yeast that a woman took and mixed in with[f] three measures of flour until all of it was leavened."

The Narrow Door

22 Jesus[g] went through one town and village after another, teaching as he made his way to Jerusalem. 23 Someone asked him, "Lord, will only a few be saved?" He said to them, 24 "Strive to enter through the narrow door; for many, I tell you, will try to enter and will not be able. 25 When once the owner of the house has got up and shut the door, and you begin to stand outside and to knock at the door, saying, 'Lord, open to us,' then in reply he will say to you, 'I do not know where you come from.' 26 Then you will begin to say, 'We ate and drank with you, and you taught in our streets.' 27 But he will say, 'I do not know where you come from; go away from me, all you evildoers!' 28 There will be weeping and gnashing of teeth when you see Abraham and Isaac and Jacob and all the prophets in the kingdom of God, and you yourselves thrown out. 29 Then people will come from east and west, from north and south, and will eat in the kingdom of God. 30 Indeed, some are last who will be first, and some are first who will be last."

The Lament over Jerusalem

31 At that very hour some Pharisees came and said to him, "Get away from here, for Herod wants to kill you." 32 He said to them, "Go and tell that fox for me, [h] 'Listen, I am casting out demons and performing cures today and tomorrow, and on the third day I finish my work. 33 Yet today, tomorrow, and the next day I must be on my way, because it is impossible for a prophet to be killed outside of Jerusalem.' 34 Jerusalem, Jerusalem, the city that kills the prophets and stones those who are sent to it!

13.22
Lk 9.51
13.24
Mt 7.13
13.25
Mt 25.10-12;
7.23
13.27
Mt 7.23;
25.41
13.28
Mt 8.11,12
13.30
Mt 19.30;
Mk 10.31
13.32
Heb 2.10;
7.28
13.34
Mt 23.37-39;
Lk 19.41

13.35
Ps 118.26;
Mt 21.9;
Lk 19.38
14.1
Mk 3.2
14.3
Mt 12.10;
Mk 3.4;
Lk 6.9
14.5
Ex 23.5;
Lk 13.15
14.7
Mt 23.6
14.8
Prov 25.6,7
14.10
Prov 25.6,7
14.11
Mt 23.12;
LK 18.14;
Jas 4.6;
1 Pet 5.5,6

How often have I desired to gather your children together as a hen gathers her brood under her wings, and you were not willing! 35 See, your house is left to you. And I tell you, you will not see me until the time comes when[i] you say, 'Blessed is the one who comes in the name of the Lord.' "

Jesus Heals the Man with Dropsy

14 On one occasion when Jesus[j] was going to the house of a leader of the Pharisees to eat a meal on the sabbath, they were watching him closely. 2 Just then, in front of him, there was a man who had dropsy. 3 And Jesus asked the lawyers and Pharisees, "Is it lawful to cure people on the sabbath, or not?" 4 But they were silent. So Jesus[j] took him and healed him, and sent him away. 5 Then he said to them, "If one of you has a child[k] or an ox that has fallen into a well, will you not immediately pull it out on a sabbath day?" 6 And they could not reply to this.

Humility and Hospitality

7 When he noticed how the guests chose the places of honor, he told them a parable. 8 "When you are invited by someone to a wedding banquet, do not sit down at the place of honor, in case someone more distinguished than you has been invited by your host; 9 and the host who invited both of you may come and say to you, 'Give this person your place,' and then in disgrace you would start to take the lowest place. 10 But when you are invited, go and sit down at the lowest place, so that when your host comes, he may say to you, 'Friend, move up higher'; then you will be honored in the presence of all who sit at the table with you. 11 For all who exalt themselves will be humbled, and those who humble themselves will be exalted."

f Gk hid in g Gk He h Gk lacks for me i Other ancient authorities lack the time comes when j Gk he k Other ancient authorities read a donkey

12 He said also to the one who had invited him, "When you give a luncheon or a dinner, do not invite your friends or your brothers or your relatives or rich neighbors, in case they may invite you in return, and you would be repaid. 13 But when you give a banquet, invite the poor, the crippled, the lame, and the blind. 14 And you will be blessed, because they cannot repay you, for you will be repaid at the resurrection of the righteous."

The Parable of the Great Dinner

15 One of the dinner guests, on hearing this, said to him, "Blessed is anyone who will eat bread in the kingdom of God!" 16 Then Jesus[1] said to him, "Someone gave a great dinner and invited many. 17 At the time for the dinner he sent his slave to say to those who had been invited, 'Come; for everything is ready now.' 18 But they all alike began to make excuses. The first said to him, 'I have bought a piece of land, and I must go out and see it; please accept my regrets.' 19 Another said, 'I have bought five yoke of oxen, and I am going to try them out; please accept my regrets.' 20 Another said, 'I have just been married, and therefore I cannot come.' 21 So the slave returned and reported this to his master. Then the owner of the house became angry and said to his slave, 'Go out at once into the streets and lanes of the town and bring in the poor, the crippled, the blind, and the lame.' 22 And the slave said, 'Sir, what you ordered has been done, and there is still room.' 23 Then the master said to the slave, 'Go out into the roads and lanes, and compel people to come in, so that my house may be filled. 24 For I tell you,[m] none of those who were invited will taste my dinner.' "

The Cost of Discipleship

25 Now large crowds were traveling with him; and he turned and said to them, 26 "Whoever comes to me and does not hate father and mother, wife and children, broth-

ers and sisters, yes, and even life itself, cannot be my disciple. 27 Whoever does not carry the cross and follow me cannot be my disciple. 28 For which of you, intending to build a tower, does not first sit down and estimate the cost, to see whether he has enough to complete it? 29 Otherwise, when he has laid a foundation and is not able to finish, all who see it will begin to ridicule him, 30 saying, 'This fellow began to build and was not able to finish.' 31 Or what king, going out to wage war against another king, will not sit down first and consider whether he is able with ten thousand to oppose the one who comes against him with twenty thousand? 32 If he cannot, then, while the other is still far away, he sends a delegation and asks for the terms of peace. 33 So therefore, none of you can become my disciple if you do not give up all your possessions.

About Salt

34 "Salt is good; but if salt has lost its taste, how can its saltiness be restored?[n] 35 It is fit neither for the soil nor for the manure pile; they throw it away. Let anyone with ears to hear listen!"

The Parable of the Lost Sheep

15 Now all the tax collectors and sinners were coming near to listen to him. 2 And the Pharisees and the scribes were grumbling and saying, "This fellow welcomes sinners and eats with them."

3 So he told them this parable: 4 "Which one of you, having a hundred sheep and losing one of them, does not leave the ninety-nine in the wilderness and go after the one that is lost until he finds it? 5 When he has found it, he lays it on his shoulders and rejoices. 6 And when he comes home, he calls together his friends and neighbors, saying to them, 'Rejoice with me, for I have found my sheep that was lost.'

14.13
v. 21
14.15
Rev 19.9
14.17
Prov 9.2,5
14.20
Deut 24.5;
1 Cor 7.33
14.21
v. 13
14.24
Mt 21.43;
Acts 13.46
14.25
Mt 10.37,38

14.27
Mt 16.24;
Mk 8.34;
Lk 9.23
14.33
Lk 18.29,30;
Phil 3.7;
Heb 11.26
14.34
Mt 5.13;
Mk 9.50
14.35
Mt 11.15
15.1
Lk 5.29
15.2
Mt 9.11

[1] Gk *he*　　[m] The Greek word for *you* here is plural　　[n] Or *how can it be used for seasoning?*

7 Just so, I tell you, there will be more joy in heaven over one sinner who repents than over ninety-nine righteous persons who need no repentance.

The Parable of the Lost Coin

8 "Or what woman having ten silver coins,o if she loses one of them, does not light a lamp, sweep the house, and search carefully until she finds it? 9 When she has found it, she calls together her friends and neighbors, saying, 'Rejoice with me, for I have found the coin that I had lost.' 10 Just so, I tell you, there is joy in the presence of the angels of God over one sinner who repents."

The Parable of the Prodigal and His Brother

11 Then Jesusp said, "There was a man who had two sons. 12 The younger of them said to his father, 'Father, give me the share of the property that will belong to me.' So he divided his property between them. 13 A few days later the younger son gathered all he had and traveled to a distant country, and there he squandered his property in dissolute living. 14 When he had spent everything, a severe famine took place throughout that country, and he began to be in need. 15 So he went and hired himself out to one of the citizens of that country, who sent him to his fields to feed the pigs. 16 He would gladly have filled himself withq the pods that the pigs were eating; and no one gave him anything. 17 But when he came to himself he said, 'How many of my father's hired hands have bread enough and to spare, but here I am dying of hunger! 18 I will get up and go to my father, and I will say to him, "Father, I have sinned against heaven and before you; 19 I am no longer worthy to be called your son; treat me like one of your hired hands." ' 20 So he set off and went to his father. But while he was still far off, his father saw him and was filled with compassion; he ran and put his arms

around him and kissed him. 21 Then the son said to him, 'Father, I have sinned against heaven and before you; I am no longer worthy to be called your son.'r 22 But the father said to his slaves, 'Quickly, bring out a robe — the best one — and put it on him; put a ring on his finger and sandals on his feet. 23 And get the fatted calf and kill it, and let us eat and celebrate; 24 for this son of mine was dead and is alive again; he was lost and is found!' And they began to celebrate.

25 "Now his elder son was in the field; and when he came and approached the house, he heard music and dancing. 26 He called one of the slaves and asked what was going on. 27 He replied, 'Your brother has come, and your father has killed the fatted calf, because he has got him back safe and sound.' 28 Then he became angry and refused to go in. His father came out and began to plead with him. 29 But he answered his father, 'Listen! For all these years I have been working like a slave for you, and I have never disobeyed your command; yet you have never given me even a young goat so that I might celebrate with my friends. 30 But when this son of yours came back, who has devoured your property with prostitutes, you killed the fatted calf for him!' 31 Then the fatherp said to him, 'Son, you are always with me, and all that is mine is yours. 32 But we had to celebrate and rejoice, because this brother of yours was dead and has come to life; he was lost and has been found.' "

The Parable of the Dishonest Manager

16 Then Jesusp said to the disciples, "There was a rich man who had a manager, and charges were brought to him that this man was squandering his prop-

Cross-references (center column)

15.7
v. 10;
Lk 19.10;
Jas 5.20
15.10
v. 7
15.11
Mt 21.28
15.12
Deut 21.17
15.20
Gen 45.14;
46.29;
Acts 20.37

15.21
Ps 51.4
15.22
Zech 3.4;
Gen 41.42
15.24
v. 32;
1 Tim 5.6;
Eph 2.1;
5.14
15.30
v. 12
15.32
v. 24
16.1
Lk 15.13

Footnotes

o Gk drachmas, each worth about a day's wage for a laborer p Gk he q Other ancient authorities read filled his stomach with r Other ancient authorities add treat me as one of your hired servants

erty. ²So he summoned him and said to him, 'What is this that I hear about you? Give me an accounting of your management, because you cannot be my manager any longer.' ³Then the manager said to himself, 'What will I do, now that my master is taking the position away from me? I am not strong enough to dig, and I am ashamed to beg. ⁴I have decided what to do so that, when I am dismissed as manager, people may welcome me into their homes.' ⁵So, summoning his master's debtors one by one, he asked the first, 'How much do you owe my master?' ⁶He answered, 'A hundred jugs of olive oil.' He said to him, 'Take your bill, sit down quickly, and make it fifty.' ⁷Then he asked another, 'And how much do you owe?' He replied, 'A hundred containers of wheat.' He said to him, 'Take your bill and make it eighty.' ⁸And his master commended the dishonest manager because he had acted shrewdly; for the children of this age are more shrewd in dealing with their own generation than are the children of light. ⁹And I tell you, make friends for yourselves by means of dishonest wealth ˢ so that when it is gone, they may welcome you into the eternal homes. ᵗ

10 "Whoever is faithful in a very little is faithful also in much; and whoever is dishonest in a very little is dishonest also in much. ¹¹If then you have not been faithful with the dishonest wealth, ˢ who will entrust to you the true riches? ¹²And if you have not been faithful with what belongs to another, who will give you what is your own? ¹³No slave can serve two masters; for a slave will either hate the one and love the other, or be devoted to the one and despise the other. You cannot serve God and wealth." ˢ

The Law and the Kingdom of God

14 The Pharisees, who were lovers of money, heard all this, and they ridiculed him. ¹⁵So he said to them, "You are those who justify

yourselves in the sight of others; but God knows your hearts; for what is prized by human beings is an abomination in the sight of God.

16 "The law and the prophets were in effect until John came; since then the good news of the kingdom of God is proclaimed, and everyone tries to enter it by force. ᵘ ¹⁷But it is easier for heaven and earth to pass away, than for one stroke of a letter in the law to be dropped.

18 "Anyone who divorces his wife and marries another commits adultery, and whoever marries a woman divorced from her husband commits adultery.

The Rich Man and Lazarus

19 "There was a rich man who was dressed in purple and fine linen and who feasted sumptuously every day. ²⁰And at his gate lay a poor man named Lazarus, covered with sores, ²¹who longed to satisfy his hunger with what fell from the rich man's table; even the dogs would come and lick his sores. ²²The poor man died and was carried away by the angels to be with Abraham. ᵛ The rich man also died and was buried. ²³In Hades, where he was being tormented, he looked up and saw Abraham far away with Lazarus by his side. ʷ ²⁴He called out, 'Father Abraham, have mercy on me, and send Lazarus to dip the tip of his finger in water and cool my tongue; for I am in agony in these flames.' ²⁵But Abraham said, 'Child, remember that during your lifetime you received your good things, and Lazarus in like manner evil things; but now he is comforted here, and you are in agony. ²⁶Besides all this, between you and us a great chasm has been fixed, so that those who might want to pass from here to you cannot do so, and no one can cross from there to us.' ²⁷He said, 'Then, father, I beg you

16.8
Jn 12.36;
Eph 5.8;
1 Thes 5.5
16.9
Mt 6.19,24;
19.21;
Lk 11.41;
12.33
16.10
Mt 25.21;
Lk 19.17
16.11
v. 9
16.13
Mt 6.24
16.14
2 Tim 3.2;
Lk 23.35
16.15
Lk 10.29;
1 Sam 16.7;
Prov 21.2;
Acts 1.24

16.16
Mt 11.12,
13; 4.23
16.17
Isa 40.8;
Mt 5.17,18;
Lk 21.33
16.18
Mt 5.31,32;
19.19;
Mk 10.11;
1 Cor 7.10,
11
16.20
Acts 3.2
16.22
Jn 13.23
16.23
Mt 11.23
16.24
v. 30;
Mt 25.41
16.25
Lk 6.24

ˢ Gk *mammon* ᵗ Gk *tents*
ᵘ Or *everyone is strongly urged to enter it*
ᵛ Gk *to Abraham's bosom* ʷ Gk *in his bosom*

to send him to my father's house — [28]for I have five brothers — that he may warn them, so that they will not also come into this place of torment.' [29]Abraham replied, 'They have Moses and the prophets; they should listen to them.' [30]He said, 'No, father Abraham; but if someone goes to them from the dead, they will repent.' [31]He said to him, 'If they do not listen to Moses and the prophets, neither will they be convinced even if someone rises from the dead.' "

Some Sayings of Jesus

17 Jesus[x] said to his disciples, "Occasions for stumbling are bound to come, but woe to anyone by whom they come! [2]It would be better for you if a millstone were hung around your neck and you were thrown into the sea than for you to cause one of these little ones to stumble. [3]Be on your guard! If another disciple[y] sins, you must rebuke the offender, and if there is repentance, you must forgive. [4]And if the same person sins against you seven times a day, and turns back to you seven times and says, 'I repent,' you must forgive."

[5]The apostles said to the Lord, "Increase our faith!" [6]The Lord replied, "If you had faith the size of a[z] mustard seed, you could say to this mulberry tree, 'Be uprooted and planted in the sea,' and it would obey you.

[7]"Who among you would say to your slave who has just come in from plowing or tending sheep in the field, 'Come here at once and take your place at the table'? [8]Would you not rather say to him, 'Prepare supper for me, put on your apron and serve me while I eat and drink; later you may eat and drink'? [9]Do you thank the slave for doing what was commanded? [10]So you also, when you have done all that you were ordered to do, say, 'We are worthless slaves; we have done only what we ought to have done!' "

16.29
Lk 4.17;
Jn 5.45-47;
Acts 15.21
16.30
Lk 3.8; 19.9
17.1
Mt 18.6,7;
Mk 9.42;
1 Cor 11.19
17.2
1 Cor 8.12
17.3
Mt 18.15
17.4
Mt 18.21,22
17.5
Mk 6.30
17.6
Mt 17.20;
21.21;
Mk 9.23;
Lk 7.13
17.8
Lk 12.37

17.11
Lk 9.51,52;
Jn 4.3,4
17.12
Lev 13.46
17.14
Lev 13.2;
14.2; Mt 8.4
17.15
Mt 9.8
17.16
Mt 10.5
17.19
Mt 9.22;
Mk 5.34;
Lk 7.50;
8.48; 18.42
17.20
Lk 19.11;
Acts 1.6
17.21
v. 23
17.22
Mt 9.15;
Mk 2.20;
Lk 5.35
17.23
Mt 24.23;
Mk 13.21;
Lk 21.8
17.24
Mt 24.27
17.25
Mt 16.21;
Lk 9.22
17.26
Mt 24.37-39;
Gen ch. 7

Jesus Cleanses Ten Lepers

11 On the way to Jerusalem Jesus[a] was going through the region between Samaria and Galilee. [12]As he entered a village, ten lepers[b] approached him. Keeping their distance, [13]they called out, saying, "Jesus, Master, have mercy on us!" [14]When he saw them, he said to them, "Go and show yourselves to the priests." And as they went, they were made clean. [15]Then one of them, when he saw that he was healed, turned back, praising God with a loud voice. [16]He prostrated himself at Jesus'[c] feet and thanked him. And he was a Samaritan. [17]Then Jesus asked, "Were not ten made clean? But the other nine, where are they? [18]Was none of them found to return and give praise to God except this foreigner?" [19]Then he said to him, "Get up and go on your way; your faith has made you well."

The Coming of the Kingdom

20 Once Jesus[a] was asked by the Pharisees when the kingdom of God was coming, and he answered, "The kingdom of God is not coming with things that can be observed; [21]nor will they say, 'Look, here it is!' or 'There it is!' For, in fact, the kingdom of God is among[d] you."

22 Then he said to the disciples, "The days are coming when you will long to see one of the days of the Son of Man, and you will not see it. [23]They will say to you, 'Look there!' or 'Look here!' Do not go, do not set off in pursuit. [24]For as the lightning flashes and lights up the sky from one side to the other, so will the Son of Man be in his day.[e] [25]But first he must endure much suffering and be rejected by this generation. [26]Just as it was in the days of Noah, so too it will be in the days of the Son of Man. [27]They were eating and drinking, and mar-

x Gk He　　y Gk your brother　　z Gk faith
as a grain of　　a Gk he　　b The terms
leper and leprosy can refer to several diseases
c Gk his　　d Or within　　e Other ancient
authorities lack in his day

rying and being given in marriage, until the day Noah entered the ark, and the flood came and destroyed all of them. 28 Likewise, just as it was in the days of Lot: they were eating and drinking, buying and selling, planting and building, 29 but on the day that Lot left Sodom, it rained fire and sulfur from heaven and destroyed all of them 30 — it will be like that on the day that the Son of Man is revealed. 31 On that day, anyone on the housetop who has belongings in the house must not come down to take them away; and likewise anyone in the field must not turn back. 32 Remember Lot's wife. 33 Those who try to make their life secure will lose it, but those who lose their life will keep it. 34 I tell you, on that night there will be two in one bed; one will be taken and the other left. 35 There will be two women grinding meal together; one will be taken and the other left." f 37 Then they asked him, "Where, Lord?" He said to them, "Where the corpse is, there the vultures will gather."

The Parable of the Widow and the Unjust Judge

18 Then Jesus g told them a parable about their need to pray always and not to lose heart. 2 He said, "In a certain city there was a judge who neither feared God nor had respect for people. 3 In that city there was a widow who kept coming to him and saying, 'Grant me justice against my opponent.' 4 For a while he refused; but later he said to himself, 'Though I have no fear of God and no respect for anyone, 5 yet because this widow keeps bothering me, I will grant her justice, so that she may not wear me out by continually coming.' " h 6 And the Lord said, "Listen to what the unjust judge says. 7 And will not God grant justice to his chosen ones who cry to him day and night? Will he delay long in helping them? 8 I tell you, he will quickly grant justice to them. And yet, when the Son of Man comes, will he find faith on earth?"

The Parable of the Pharisee and the Tax Collector

9 He also told this parable to some who trusted in themselves that they were righteous and regarded others with contempt: 10 "Two men went up to the temple to pray, one a Pharisee and the other a tax collector. 11 The Pharisee, standing by himself, was praying thus, 'God, I thank you that I am not like other people: thieves, rogues, adulterers, or even like this tax collector. 12 I fast twice a week; I give a tenth of all my income.' 13 But the tax collector, standing far off, would not even look up to heaven, but was beating his breast and saying, 'God, be merciful to me, a sinner!' 14 I tell you, this man went down to his home justified rather than the other; for all who exalt themselves will be humbled, but all who humble themselves will be exalted."

Jesus Blesses Little Children

15 People were bringing even infants to him that he might touch them; and when the disciples saw it, they sternly ordered them not to do it. 16 But Jesus called for them and said, "Let the little children come to me, and do not stop them; for it is to such as these that the kingdom of God belongs. 17 Truly I tell you, whoever does not receive the kingdom of God as a little child will never enter it."

The Rich Ruler

18 A certain ruler asked him, "Good Teacher, what must I do to inherit eternal life?" 19 Jesus said to him, "Why do you call me good? No one is good but God alone. 20 You know the commandments: 'You shall not commit adultery; You shall not murder; You shall not steal; You shall not bear false witness; Honor your father and mother.' " 21 He replied, "I have kept all these since my youth." 22 When

17.28
Gen 18.20-33;
19.24,25
17.30
2 Thes 1.7
17.31
Mt 24.17,
18;
Mk 13.15,
16
17.32
Gen 19.26
17.33
Mt 10.39;
16.25;
Mk 8.35;
Lk 9.24
17.34
Mt 24.40,41
17.37
Mt 24.28
18.1
Lk 11.5-8;
Rom 12.12;
Eph 6.18;
Col 4.2;
1 Thes 5.17
18.5
Lk 11.8
18.6
Lk 7.13
18.7
Rev 6.10;
Rom 8.33;
Col 3.12;
2 Tim 2.10

18.9
Lk 16.15
18.11
Mt 6.5;
Mk 11.25
18.12
Mt 9.14;
Lk 11.42
18.13
Lk 23.48
18.14
Mt 23.12;
Lk 14.11;
1 Pet 5.6
18.17
Mt 18.3
18.18
Lk 10.25
18.20
Ex 20.12-16;
Deut 5.16-20;
Rom 13.9
18.22
Lk 12.33;
Mt 19.21

f Other ancient authorities add verse 36, *"Two will be in the field; one will be taken and the other left."* g Gk he h Or *so that she may not finally come and slap me in the face*

Jesus heard this, he said to him, "There is still one thing lacking. Sell all that you own and distribute the money[i] to the poor, and you will have treasure in heaven; then come, follow me." 23 But when he heard this, he became sad; for he was very rich. 24 Jesus looked at him and said, "How hard it is for those who have wealth to enter the kingdom of God! 25 Indeed, it is easier for a camel to go through the eye of a needle than for someone who is rich to enter the kingdom of God."

26 Those who heard it said, "Then who can be saved?" 27 He replied, "What is impossible for mortals is possible for God."

28 Then Peter said, "Look, we have left our homes and followed you." 29 And he said to them, "Truly I tell you, there is no one who has left house or wife or brothers or parents or children, for the sake of the kingdom of God, 30 who will not get back very much more in this age, and in the age to come eternal life."

A Third Time Jesus Foretells His Death and Resurrection

31 Then he took the twelve aside and said to them, "See, we are going up to Jerusalem, and everything that is written about the Son of Man by the prophets will be accomplished. 32 For he will be handed over to the Gentiles; and he will be mocked and insulted and spat upon. 33 After they have flogged him, they will kill him, and on the third day he will rise again." 34 But they understood nothing about all these things; in fact, what he said was hidden from them, and they did not grasp what was said.

Jesus Heals a Blind Beggar Near Jericho

35 As he approached Jericho, a blind man was sitting by the roadside begging. 36 When he heard a crowd going by, he asked what was happening. 37 They told him, "Jesus of Nazareth[j] is passing by." 38 Then he shouted, "Jesus, Son of

David, have mercy on me!" 39 Those who were in front sternly ordered him to be quiet; but he shouted even more loudly, "Son of David, have mercy on me!" 40 Jesus stood still and ordered the man to be brought to him; and when he came near, he asked him, 41 "What do you want me to do for you?" He said, "Lord, let me see again." 42 Jesus said to him, "Receive your sight; your faith has saved you." 43 Immediately he regained his sight and followed him, glorifying God; and all the people, when they saw it, praised God.

Jesus and Zacchaeus

19 He entered Jericho and was passing through it. 2 A man was there named Zacchaeus; he was a chief tax collector and was rich. 3 He was trying to see who Jesus was, but on account of the crowd he could not, because he was short in stature. 4 So he ran ahead and climbed a sycamore tree to see him, because he was going to pass that way. 5 When Jesus came to the place, he looked up and said to him, "Zacchaeus, hurry and come down; for I must stay at your house today." 6 So he hurried down and was happy to welcome him. 7 All who saw it began to grumble and said, "He has gone to be the guest of one who is a sinner." 8 Zacchaeus stood there and said to the Lord, "Look, half of my possessions, Lord, I will give to the poor; and if I have defrauded anyone of anything, I will pay back four times as much." 9 Then Jesus said to him, "Today salvation has come to this house, because he too is a son of Abraham. 10 For the Son of Man came to seek out and to save the lost."

The Parable of the Ten Pounds

11 As they were listening to this, he went on to tell a parable, because he was near Jerusalem, and because they supposed that the kingdom of God was to appear immediately. 12 So he said, "A no-

Cross references (center column)

18.24 Prov 11.28
18.27 Gen 18.14; Job 42.2; Jer 32.17; Lk 1.37
18.28 Lk 5.11
18.30 Mt 12.32
18.31 Lk 9.51; Ps 22
18.32 Mt 16.21; 27.2; Lk 23.1
18.34 Mk 9.32; Lk 9.45
18.38 Mt 9.27
18.39 v. 38
18.42 Mt 9.22; Mk 5.34; Lk 17.19
18.43 Mt 9.8; Lk 13.17
19.1 Lk 18.35
19.4 1 Kings 10.27; 1 Chr 27.28; Isa 9.10
19.7 Mt 9.11; Lk 5.30
19.8 Lk 7.13; 3.14; Ex 22.1; Lev 6.5; Num 5.7; 2 Sam 12.6
19.9 Lk 3.8; 13.16; Rom 4.16; Gal 3.7
19.10 Mt 18.11
19.11 Acts 1.6
19.12 Mt 25.14-30; Mk 13.34

i Gk lacks *the money* j Gk *the Nazorean*

bleman went to a distant country to get royal power for himself and then return. 13 He summoned ten of his slaves, and gave them ten pounds,k and said to them, 'Do business with these until I come back.' 14 But the citizens of his country hated him and sent a delegation after him, saying, 'We do not want this man to rule over us.' 15 When he returned, having received royal power, he ordered these slaves, to whom he had given the money, to be summoned so that he might find out what they had gained by trading. 16 The first came forward and said, 'Lord, your pound has made ten more pounds.' 17 He said to him, 'Well done, good slave! Because you have been trustworthy in a very small thing, take charge of ten cities.' 18 Then the second came, saying, 'Lord, your pound has made five pounds.' 19 He said to him, 'And you, rule over five cities.' 20 Then the other came, saying, 'Lord, here is your pound. I wrapped it up in a piece of cloth, 21 for I was afraid of you, because you are a harsh man; you take what you did not deposit, and reap what you did not sow.' 22 He said to him, 'I will judge you by your own words, you wicked slave! You knew, did you, that I was a harsh man, taking what I did not deposit and reaping what I did not sow? 23 Why then did you not put my money into the bank? Then when I returned, I could have collected it with interest.' 24 He said to the bystanders, 'Take the pound from him and give it to the one who has ten pounds.' 25 (And they said to him, 'Lord, he has ten pounds!') 26 'I tell you, to all those who have, more will be given; but from those who have nothing, even what they have will be taken away. 27 But as for these enemies of mine who did not want me to be king over them—bring them here and slaughter them in my presence.' "

Jesus' Triumphal Entry into Jerusalem

28 After he had said this, he went on ahead, going up to Jerusalem.

29 When he had come near Bethphage and Bethany, at the place called the Mount of Olives, he sent two of the disciples, 30 saying, "Go into the village ahead of you, and as you enter it you will find tied there a colt that has never been ridden. Untie it and bring it here. 31 If anyone asks you, 'Why are you untying it?' just say this, 'The Lord needs it.' " 32 So those who were sent departed and found it as he had told them. 33 As they were untying the colt, its owners asked them, "Why are you untying the colt?" 34 They said, "The Lord needs it." 35 Then they brought it to Jesus; and after throwing their cloaks on the colt, they set Jesus on it. 36 As he rode along, people kept spreading their cloaks on the road. 37 As he was now approaching the path down from the Mount of Olives, the whole multitude of the disciples began to praise God joyfully with a loud voice for all the deeds of power that they had seen, 38 saying,

"Blessed is the king
　who comes in the name of
　　the Lord!
Peace in heaven,
　and glory in the highest
　　heaven!"

39 Some of the Pharisees in the crowd said to him, "Teacher, order your disciples to stop." 40 He answered, "I tell you, if these were silent, the stones would shout out."

Jesus Weeps over Jerusalem

41 As he came near and saw the city, he wept over it, 42 saying, "If you, even you, had only recognized on this day the things that make for peace! But now they are hidden from your eyes. 43 Indeed, the days will come upon you, when your enemies will set up ramparts around you and surround you, and hem you in on every side. 44 They will crush you to the ground, you and your children within you, and they

19.17
Lk 16.10
19.21
Mt 25.24
19.22
2 Sam 1.16;
Job 15.6;
Mt 25.26
19.26
Mt 13.12;
Lk 8.18
19.28
Mk 10.32;
Mt 21.17;
Lk 21.37

19.32
Lk 22.13
19.36
2 Kings 9.13
19.38
Ps 118.26;
Lk 13.35;
2.14
19.39
Mt 21.15,16
19.40
Hab 2.11
19.41
Lk 13.34,35
19.43
Isa 29.3;
Jer 6.6;
Ezek 4.2;
Lk 21.20
19.44
Mt 24.2;
Mk 13.2;
Lk 21.6;
1 Pet 2.12

k The mina, rendered here by *pound*, was about three months' wages for a laborer

will not leave within you one stone upon another; because you did not recognize the time of your visitation from God."[1]

Jesus Cleanses the Temple

45 Then he entered the temple and began to drive out those who were selling things there; [46]and he said, "It is written,

'My house shall be a house
　　of prayer';
but you have made it a den
　　of robbers."

47 Every day he was teaching in the temple. The chief priests, the scribes, and the leaders of the people kept looking for a way to kill him; [48]but they did not find anything they could do, for all the people were spellbound by what they heard.

The Authority of Jesus Questioned

20 One day, as he was teaching the people in the temple and telling the good news, the chief priests and the scribes came with the elders [2]and said to him, "Tell us, by what authority are you doing these things? Who is it who gave you this authority?" [3]He answered them, "I will also ask you a question, and you tell me: [4]Did the baptism of John come from heaven, or was it of human origin?" [5]They discussed it with one another, saying, "If we say, 'From heaven,' he will say, 'Why did you not believe him?' [6]But if we say, 'Of human origin,' all the people will stone us; for they are convinced that John was a prophet." [7]So they answered that they did not know where it came from. [8]Then Jesus said to them, "Neither will I tell you by what authority I am doing these things."

The Parable of the Wicked Tenants

9 He began to tell the people this parable: "A man planted a vineyard, and leased it to tenants, and went to another country for a long time. [10]When the season came, he sent a slave to the tenants

19.46
Isa 56.7
19.47
Mt 26.55;
Mk 11.18;
Jn 7.19
20.1
Mt 26.55;
Lk 8.1
20.2
Jn 2.18;
Acts 4.7;
7.27
20.6
Mt 14.5;
Lk 7.29
20.9
Isa 5.1-7;
Mt 25.14

20.16
Lk 19.27;
Rom 3.4,6,
31
20.17
Ps 118.22,
23;
1 Pet 2.6
20.18
Isa 8.14,15
20.19
Lk 19.47
20.21
Jn 3.2

in order that they might give him his share of the produce of the vineyard; but the tenants beat him and sent him away empty-handed. [11]Next he sent another slave; that one also they beat and insulted and sent away empty-handed. [12]And he sent still a third; this one also they wounded and threw out. [13]Then the owner of the vineyard said, 'What shall I do? I will send my beloved son; perhaps they will respect him.' [14]But when the tenants saw him, they discussed it among themselves and said, 'This is the heir; let us kill him so that the inheritance may be ours.' [15]So they threw him out of the vineyard and killed him. What then will the owner of the vineyard do to them? [16]He will come and destroy those tenants and give the vineyard to others." When they heard this, they said, "Heaven forbid!" [17]But he looked at them and said, "What then does this text mean:

'The stone that the builders
　　rejected
has become the
　　cornerstone'?[m]
[18]Everyone who falls on that stone will be broken to pieces; and it will crush anyone on whom it falls." [19]When the scribes and chief priests realized that he had told this parable against them, they wanted to lay hands on him at that very hour, but they feared the people.

The Question about Paying Taxes

20 So they watched him and sent spies who pretended to be honest, in order to trap him by what he said, so as to hand him over to the jurisdiction and authority of the governor. [21]So they asked him, "Teacher, we know that you are right in what you say and teach, and you show deference to no one, but teach the way of God in accordance with truth. [22]Is it lawful for us to pay taxes to the emperor, or not?" [23]But he perceived their craftiness and said to them,

[1]Gk lacks from God　　[m]Or keystone

24"Show me a denarius. Whose head and whose title does it bear?" They said, "The emperor's." 25 He said to them, "Then give to the emperor the things that are the emperor's, and to God the things that are God's." 26 And they were not able in the presence of the people to trap him by what he said; and being amazed by his answer, they became silent.

The Question about the Resurrection

27 Some Sadducees, those who say there is no resurrection, came to him 28 and asked him a question, "Teacher, Moses wrote for us that if a man's brother dies, leaving a wife but no children, the man n shall marry the widow and raise up children for his brother. 29 Now there were seven brothers; the first married, and died childless; 30 then the second 31 and the third married her, and so in the same way all seven died childless. 32 Finally the woman also died. 33 In the resurrection, therefore, whose wife will the woman be? For the seven had married her."

34 Jesus said to them, "Those who belong to this age marry and are given in marriage; 35 but those who are considered worthy of a place in that age and in the resurrection from the dead neither marry nor are given in marriage. 36 Indeed they cannot die anymore, because they are like angels and are children of God, being children of the resurrection. 37 And the fact that the dead are raised Moses himself showed, in the story about the bush, where he speaks of the Lord as the God of Abraham, the God of Isaac, and the God of Jacob. 38 Now he is God not of the dead, but of the living; for to him all of them are alive." 39 Then some of the scribes answered, "Teacher, you have spoken well." 40 For they no longer dared to ask him another question.

The Question about David's Son

41 Then he said to them, "How

can they say that the Messiah o is David's son? 42 For David himself says in the book of Psalms,

'The Lord said to my Lord,
"Sit at my right hand,
43 until I make your enemies
 your footstool" '

44 David thus calls him Lord; so how can he be his son?"

Jesus Denounces the Scribes

45 In the hearing of all the people he said to the p disciples, 46 "Beware of the scribes, who like to walk around in long robes, and love to be greeted with respect in the marketplaces, and to have the best seats in the synagogues and places of honor at banquets. 47 They devour widows' houses and for the sake of appearance say long prayers. They will receive the greater condemnation."

The Widow's Offering

21 He looked up and saw rich people putting their gifts into the treasury; 2 he also saw a poor widow put in two small copper coins. 3 He said, "Truly I tell you, this poor widow has put in more than all of them; 4 for all of them have contributed out of their abundance, but she out of her poverty has put in all she had to live on."

The Destruction of the Temple Foretold

5 When some were speaking about the temple, how it was adorned with beautiful stones and gifts dedicated to God, he said, 6 "As for these things that you see, the days will come when not one stone will be left upon another; all will be thrown down."

Signs and Persecutions

7 They asked him, "Teacher, when will this be, and what will be the sign that this is about to take place?" 8 And he said, "Beware that you are not led astray; for many will come in my name and say, 'I am

20.25
Rom 13.7;
Lk 23.2
20.27
Acts 23.6,8
20.28
Deut 25.5
20.36
Rom 8.16,
17;
1 Jn 3.1,2
20.37
Ex 3.6
20.38
Rom 6.10,
11
20.40
Mt 22.46;
Mk 12.34

20.42
Ps 110.1;
Acts 2.34
20.46
Lk 11.43
21.1
Mk 12.41-44
21.2
Mk 12.42
21.5
Mk 13.1
21.6
Lk 19.44
21.8
Mk 13.21;
Lk 17.23

n Gk his brother o Or the Christ
p Other ancient authorities read his

he!'q and, 'The time is near!'r Do not go after them.

9 "When you hear of wars and insurrections, do not be terrified; for these things must take place first, but the end will not follow immediately." 10 Then he said to them, "Nation will rise against nation, and kingdom against kingdom; 11 there will be great earthquakes, and in various places famines and plagues; and there will be dreadful portents and great signs from heaven.

12 "But before all this occurs, they will arrest you and persecute you; they will hand you over to synagogues and prisons, and you will be brought before kings and governors because of my name. 13 This will give you an opportunity to testify. 14 So make up your minds not to prepare your defense in advance; 15 for I will give you words s and a wisdom that none of your opponents will be able to withstand or contradict. 16 You will be betrayed even by parents and brothers, by relatives and friends; and they will put some of you to death. 17 You will be hated by all because of my name. 18 But not a hair of your head will perish. 19 By your endurance you will gain your souls.

The Destruction of Jerusalem Foretold

20 "When you see Jerusalem surrounded by armies, then know that its desolation has come near.t 21 Then those in Judea must flee to the mountains, and those inside the city must leave it, and those out in the country must not enter it; 22 for these are days of vengeance, as a fulfillment of all that is written. 23 Woe to those who are pregnant and to those who are nursing infants in those days! For there will be great distress on the earth and wrath against this people; 24 they will fall by the edge of the sword and be taken away as captives among all nations; and Jerusalem will be trampled on by the Gentiles, until the times of the Gentiles are fulfilled.

21.10
2 Chr 15.6;
Isa 19.2
21.12
Jn 16.2
21.13
Phil 1.12
21.14
Lk 12.11,12
21.15
Lk 12.12
21.16
Lk 12.52,53
21.17
Mt 10.22
21.18
Mt 10.30;
Lk 12.7
21.19
Rev 2.7
21.20
Lk 19.43
21.21
Lk 17.31
21.22
Isa 63.4;
Dan 9.24-27;
Zech 11.1
21.24
Isa 63.18;
Dan 8.13;
9.27; 12.7;
Rom 11.25;
Rev 11.2

21.25
2 Pet 3.10,
12
21.27
Rev 1.7;
14.14
21.28
Lk 18.7
21.31
Mt 3.2
21.33
Lk 16.17
21.34
Mk 4.19;
Lk 12.45;
1 Thes 5.6,
7
21.36
Lk 18.1
21.37
Lk 19.47;
Mk 11.19

The Coming of the Son of Man

25 "There will be signs in the sun, the moon, and the stars, and on the earth distress among nations confused by the roaring of the sea and the waves. 26 People will faint from fear and foreboding of what is coming upon the world, for the powers of the heavens will be shaken. 27 Then they will see 'the Son of Man coming in a cloud' with power and great glory. 28 Now when these things begin to take place, stand up and raise your heads, because your redemption is drawing near."

The Lesson of the Fig Tree

29 Then he told them a parable: "Look at the fig tree and all the trees; 30 as soon as they sprout leaves you can see for yourselves and know that summer is already near. 31 So also, when you see these things taking place, you know that the kingdom of God is near. 32 Truly I tell you, this generation will not pass away until all things have taken place. 33 Heaven and earth will pass away, but my words will not pass away.

Exhortation to Watch

34 "Be on guard so that your hearts are not weighed down with dissipation and drunkenness and the worries of this life, and that day catch you unexpectedly, 35 like a trap. For it will come upon all who live on the face of the whole earth. 36 Be alert at all times, praying that you may have the strength to escape all these things that will take place, and to stand before the Son of Man."

37 Every day he was teaching in the temple, and at night he would go out and spend the night on the Mount of Olives, as it was called. 38 And all the people would get up early in the morning to listen to him in the temple.

q Gk I am r Or at hand s Gk a mouth
t Or is at hand

The Plot to Kill Jesus

22 Now the festival of Unleavened Bread, which is called the Passover, was near. ² The chief priests and the scribes were looking for a way to put Jesusᵘ to death, for they were afraid of the people.

3 Then Satan entered into Judas called Iscariot, who was one of the twelve; ⁴ he went away and conferred with the chief priests and officers of the temple police about how he might betray him to them. ⁵ They were greatly pleased and agreed to give him money. ⁶ So he consented and began to look for an opportunity to betray him to them when no crowd was present.

The Preparation of the Passover

7 Then came the day of Unleavened Bread, on which the Passover lamb had to be sacrificed. ⁸ So Jesusᵛ sent Peter and John, saying, "Go and prepare the Passover meal for us that we may eat it." ⁹ They asked him, "Where do you want us to make preparations for it?" ¹⁰ "Listen," he said to them, "when you have entered the city, a man carrying a jar of water will meet you; follow him into the house he enters ¹¹ and say to the owner of the house, 'The teacher asks you, "Where is the guest room, where I may eat the Passover with my disciples?" ' ¹² He will show you a large room upstairs, already furnished. Make preparations for us there." ¹³ So they went and found everything as he had told them; and they prepared the Passover meal.

The Institution of the Lord's Supper

14 When the hour came, he took his place at the table, and the apostles with him. ¹⁵ He said to them, "I have eagerly desired to eat this Passover with you before I suffer; ¹⁶ for I tell you, I will not eat itʷ until it is fulfilled in the kingdom of God." ¹⁷ Then he took a cup, and after giving thanks he said, "Take this and divide it among your-

selves; ¹⁸ for I tell you that from now on I will not drink of the fruit of the vine until the kingdom of God comes." ¹⁹ Then he took a loaf of bread, and when he had given thanks, he broke it and gave it to them, saying, "This is my body, which is given for you. Do this in remembrance of me." ²⁰ And he did the same with the cup after supper, saying, "This cup that is poured out for you is the new covenant in my blood. ˣ ²¹ But see, the one who betrays me is with me, and his hand is on the table. ²² For the Son of Man is going as it has been determined, but woe to that one by whom he is betrayed!" ²³ Then they began to ask one another, which one of them it could be who would do this.

The Dispute about Greatness

24 A dispute also arose among them as to which one of them was to be regarded as the greatest. ²⁵ But he said to them, "The kings of the Gentiles lord it over them; and those in authority over them are called benefactors. ²⁶ But not so with you; rather the greatest among you must become like the youngest, and the leader like one who serves. ²⁷ For who is greater, the one who is at the table or the one who serves? Is it not the one at the table? But I am among you as one who serves.

28 "You are those who have stood by me in my trials; ²⁹ and I confer on you, just as my Father has conferred on me, a kingdom, ³⁰ so that you may eat and drink at my table in my kingdom, and you will sit on thrones judging the twelve tribes of Israel.

Jesus Predicts Peter's Denial

31 "Simon, Simon, listen! Satan has demandedʸ to sift all of you like wheat, ³² but I have prayed for you that your own faith may not fail; and you, when once you have

22.1
Jn 11.47-53
22.2
Mt 12.14
22.3
Jn 13.2
22.5
Zech 11.12
22.7
Ex 12.18-20;
Deut 16.5-8
22.8
Lk 19.29;
Acts 3.1
22.16
Lk 14.15;
Rev 19.9

22.21
Mt 26.21-24;
Mk 14.18-21;
Jn 13.21-30
22.22
Acts 2.23;
4.28
22.24
Mk 9.34;
Lk 9.46
22.25
Mt 20.25-28;
Mk 10.42-45
22.26
Lk 9.48;
1 Pet 5.5
22.27
Lk 12.37
22.28
Heb 2.18;
4.15
22.29
Lk 12.32;
2 Tim 2.12
22.30
Lk 14.15;
Rev 19.9;
Mt 19.28;
Rev 3.21
22.31
Job 1.6-12;
Am 9.9
22.32
Jn 17.9,15;
21.15-17

ᵘ Gk him ᵛ Gk he ʷ Other ancient authorities read *never eat it again* ˣ Other ancient authorities lack, in whole or in part, verses 19b-20 (*which is given . . . in my blood*) ʸ Or *has obtained permission*

turned back, strengthen your brothers." ³³And he said to him, "Lord, I am ready to go with you to prison and to death!" ³⁴Jesus[z] said, "I tell you, Peter, the cock will not crow this day, until you have denied three times that you know me."

Purse, Bag, and Sword

35 He said to them, "When I sent you out without a purse, bag, or sandals, did you lack anything?" They said, "No, not a thing." ³⁶He said to them, "But now, the one who has a purse must take it, and likewise a bag. And the one who has no sword must sell his cloak and buy one. ³⁷For I tell you, this scripture must be fulfilled in me, 'And he was counted among the lawless'; and indeed what is written about me is being fulfilled." ³⁸They said, "Lord, look, here are two swords." He replied, "It is enough."

Jesus Prays on the Mount of Olives

39 He came out and went, as was his custom, to the Mount of Olives; and the disciples followed him. ⁴⁰When he reached the place, he said to them, "Pray that you may not come into the time of trial."[a] ⁴¹Then he withdrew from them about a stone's throw, knelt down, and prayed, ⁴²"Father, if you are willing, remove this cup from me; yet, not my will but yours be done." ⟦⁴³Then an angel from heaven appeared to him and gave him strength. ⁴⁴In his anguish he prayed more earnestly, and his sweat became like great drops of blood falling down on the ground.⟧[b] ⁴⁵When he got up from prayer, he came to the disciples and found them sleeping because of grief, ⁴⁶and he said to them, "Why are you sleeping? Get up and pray that you may not come into the time of trial."[a]

The Betrayal and Arrest of Jesus

47 While he was still speaking, suddenly a crowd came, and the one called Judas, one of the twelve, was leading them. He approached Jesus to kiss him; ⁴⁸but Jesus said to him, "Judas, is it with a kiss that you are betraying the Son of Man?" ⁴⁹When those who were around him saw what was coming, they asked, "Lord, should we strike with the sword?" ⁵⁰Then one of them struck the slave of the high priest and cut off his right ear. ⁵¹But Jesus said, "No more of this!" And he touched his ear and healed him. ⁵²Then Jesus said to the chief priests, the officers of the temple police, and the elders who had come for him, "Have you come out with swords and clubs as if I were a bandit? ⁵³When I was with you day after day in the temple, you did not lay hands on me. But this is your hour, and the power of darkness!"

Peter Denies Jesus

54 Then they seized him and led him away, bringing him into the high priest's house. But Peter was following at a distance. ⁵⁵When they had kindled a fire in the middle of the courtyard and sat down together, Peter sat among them. ⁵⁶Then a servant-girl, seeing him in the firelight, stared at him and said, "This man also was with him." ⁵⁷But he denied it, saying, "Woman, I do not know him." ⁵⁸A little later someone else, on seeing him, said, "You also are one of them." But Peter said, "Man, I am not!" ⁵⁹Then about an hour later still another kept insisting, "Surely this man also was with him; for he is a Galilean." ⁶⁰But Peter said, "Man, I do not know what you are talking about!" At that moment, while he was still speaking, the cock crowed. ⁶¹The Lord turned and looked at Peter. Then Peter remembered the word of the Lord, how he had said to him, "Before the cock crows today, you will deny me three times." ⁶²And he went out and wept bitterly.

22.35
Mt 10.9;
Lk 9.3; 10.4
22.37
Isa 53.12;
Mk 15.28
22.39
Lk 21.37
22.40
Mt 6.13
22.42
Mk 10.38;
Jn 5.30;
18.11
22.46
v. 40

22.49
v. 38
22.52
vv. 4, 37
22.53
Jn 12.27
22.54
Mt 26.58;
Mk 14.54
22.61
v. 34

[z] Gk *He*　　[a] Or *into temptation*　　[b] Other ancient authorities lack verses 43 and 44

The Mocking and Beating of Jesus

63 Now the men who were holding Jesus began to mock him and beat him; [64]they also blindfolded him and kept asking him, "Prophesy! Who is it that struck you?" [65]They kept heaping many other insults on him.

Jesus before the Council

66 When day came, the assembly of the elders of the people, both chief priests and scribes, gathered together, and they brought him to their council. [67]They said, "If you are the Messiah,[c] tell us." He replied, "If I tell you, you will not believe; [68]and if I question you, you will not answer. [69]But from now on the Son of Man will be seated at the right hand of the power of God." [70]All of them asked, "Are you, then, the Son of God?" He said to them, "You say that I am." [71]Then they said, "What further testimony do we need? We have heard it ourselves from his own lips!"

Jesus before Pilate

23 Then the assembly rose as a body and brought Jesus[d] before Pilate. [2]They began to accuse him, saying, "We found this man perverting our nation, forbidding us to pay taxes to the emperor, and saying that he himself is the Messiah, a king."[e] [3]Then Pilate asked him, "Are you the king of the Jews?" He answered, "You say so." [4]Then Pilate said to the chief priests and the crowds, "I find no basis for an accusation against this man." [5]But they were insistent and said, "He stirs up the people by teaching throughout all Judea, from Galilee where he began even to this place."

Jesus before Herod

6 When Pilate heard this, he asked whether the man was a Galilean. [7]And when he learned that he was under Herod's jurisdiction, he sent him off to Herod, who was himself in Jerusalem at that time. [8]When Herod saw Jesus, he was

very glad, for he had been wanting to see him for a long time, because he had heard about him and was hoping to see him perform some sign. [9]He questioned him at some length, but Jesus[f] gave him no answer. [10]The chief priests and the scribes stood by, vehemently accusing him. [11]Even Herod with his soldiers treated him with contempt and mocked him; then he put an elegant robe on him, and sent him back to Pilate. [12]That same day Herod and Pilate became friends with each other; before this they had been enemies.

Jesus Sentenced to Death

13 Pilate then called together the chief priests, the leaders, and the people, [14]and said to them, "You brought me this man as one who was perverting the people; and here I have examined him in your presence and have not found this man guilty of any of your charges against him. [15]Neither has Herod, for he sent him back to us. Indeed, he has done nothing to deserve death. [16]I will therefore have him flogged and release him."[g]

18 Then they all shouted out together, "Away with this fellow! Release Barabbas for us!" [19](This was a man who had been put in prison for an insurrection that had taken place in the city, and for murder.) [20]Pilate, wanting to release Jesus, addressed them again; [21]but they kept shouting, "Crucify, crucify him!" [22]A third time he said to them, "Why, what evil has he done? I have found in him no ground for the sentence of death; I will therefore have him flogged and then release him." [23]But they kept urgently demanding with loud shouts that he should be crucified; and their voices prevailed. [24]So Pilate gave his verdict that their demand should be granted. [25]He released the man they asked for, the one who had been put in prison for

Cross references

22.63: Mt 26.67, 68; Mk 14.65; Jn 18.22,23
22.66: Mt 27.1; Mk 15.1
22.67: Mt 26.63-66; Mk 14.61-63; Jn 18.19-21
22.70: Mt 27.11; Lk 23.3
23.1: Mt 27.2; Mk 15.1; Jn 18.28
23.2: Lk 20.22; Jn 19.12
23.3: Lk 22.70; 1 Tim 6.13
23.4: 1 Pet 2.22
23.7: Lk 3.1
23.8: Lk 9.9; Mt 14.1; Mk 6.14

23.11: Mk 15.17-19; Jn 19.2,3
23.12: Acts 4.27
23.14: vv. 2,4
23.16: Mt 27.26; Mk 15.15; Jn 19.1
23.18: Mt 27.20-23; Mk 15.11-14; Jn 18.38-40; 19.14,15; Acts 3.13,14
23.22: v. 16

c Or the Christ d Gk him e Or is an anointed king f Gk he g Here, or after verse 19, other ancient authorities add verse 17, *Now he was obliged to release someone for them at the festival*

insurrection and murder, and he handed Jesus over as they wished.

The Crucifixion of Jesus

26 As they led him away, they seized a man, Simon of Cyrene, who was coming from the country, and they laid the cross on him, and made him carry it behind Jesus. [27] A great number of the people followed him, and among them were women who were beating their breasts and wailing for him. [28] But Jesus turned to them and said, "Daughters of Jerusalem, do not weep for me, but weep for yourselves and for your children. [29] For the days are surely coming when they will say, 'Blessed are the barren, and the wombs that never bore, and the breasts that never nursed.' [30] Then they will begin to say to the mountains, 'Fall on us'; and to the hills, 'Cover us.' [31] For if they do this when the wood is green, what will happen when it is dry?"

32 Two others also, who were criminals, were led away to be put to death with him. [33] When they came to the place that is called The Skull, they crucified Jesus[h] there with the criminals, one on his right and one on his left. [[[34] Then Jesus said, "Father, forgive them; for they do not know what they are doing."]][i] And they cast lots to divide his clothing. [35] And the people stood by, watching; but the leaders scoffed at him, saying, "He saved others; let him save himself if he is the Messiah[j] of God, his chosen one!" [36] The soldiers also mocked him, coming up and offering him sour wine, [37] and saying, "If you are the King of the Jews, save yourself!" [38] There was also an inscription over him,[k] "This is the King of the Jews."

39 One of the criminals who were hanged there kept deriding[l] him and saying, "Are you not the Messiah?[j] Save yourself and us!" [40] But the other rebuked him, saying, "Do you not fear God, since you are under the same sentence of condemnation? [41] And we indeed

have been condemned justly, for we are getting what we deserve for our deeds, but this man has done nothing wrong." [42] Then he said, "Jesus, remember me when you come into[m] your kingdom." [43] He replied, "Truly I tell you, today you will be with me in Paradise."

The Death of Jesus

44 It was now about noon, and darkness came over the whole land[n] until three in the afternoon, [45] while the sun's light failed;[o] and the curtain of the temple was torn in two. [46] Then Jesus, crying with a loud voice, said, "Father, into your hands I commend my spirit." Having said this, he breathed his last. [47] When the centurion saw what had taken place, he praised God and said, "Certainly this man was innocent."[p] [48] And when all the crowds who had gathered there for this spectacle saw what had taken place, they returned home, beating their breasts. [49] But all his acquaintances, including the women who had followed him from Galilee, stood at a distance, watching these things.

The Burial of Jesus

50 Now there was a good and righteous man named Joseph, who, though a member of the council, [51] had not agreed to their plan and action. He came from the Jewish town of Arimathea, and he was waiting expectantly for the kingdom of God. [52] This man went to Pilate and asked for the body of Jesus. [53] Then he took it down, wrapped it in a linen cloth, and laid it in a rock-hewn tomb where no one had ever been laid. [54] It was the day of Preparation, and the sabbath was beginning.[q] [55] The women who had come with him from

[h] Gk him [i] Other ancient authorities lack the sentence *Then Jesus . . . what they are doing* [j] Or *the Christ* [k] Other ancient authorities add *written in Greek and Latin and Hebrew* (that is, *Aramaic*) [l] Or *blaspheming* [m] Other ancient authorities read *in* [n] Or *earth* [o] Or *the sun was eclipsed.* Other ancient authorities read *the sun was darkened* [p] Or *righteous* [q] Gk *was dawning*

Cross references:

23.26 Jn 19.17
23.27 Lk 8.52
23.28 Lk 19.41-44; 21.23,24
23.30 Isa 2.19; Hos 10.8; Rev 6.16
23.31 Ezek 20.47
23.32 Isa 53.12
23.34 Ps 22.18; Acts 7.60
23.35 Ps 22.17
23.36 Ps 69.21; Mt 27.48
23.39 vv. 35,37
23.41 vv. 4,14,22
23.43 2 Cor 12.3, 4; Rev 2.7
23.45 Ex 26.31-35; Heb 9.8; 10.19
23.46 Ps 31.5; 1 Pet 2.23
23.47 Mt 27.54
23.49 Ps 38.11; Lk 8.2
23.51 Lk 2.25
23.54 Mt 27.62
23.55 v. 49

Galilee followed, and they saw the tomb and how his body was laid. [56] Then they returned, and prepared spices and ointments.

On the sabbath they rested according to the commandment.

The Resurrection of Jesus

24 But on the first day of the week, at early dawn, they came to the tomb, taking the spices that they had prepared. [2] They found the stone rolled away from the tomb, [3] but when they went in, they did not find the body.[r] [4] While they were perplexed about this, suddenly two men in dazzling clothes stood beside them. [5] The women[s] were terrified and bowed their faces to the ground, but the men[t] said to them, "Why do you look for the living among the dead? He is not here, but has risen.[u] [6] Remember how he told you, while he was still in Galilee, [7] that the Son of Man must be handed over to sinners, and be crucified, and on the third day rise again." [8] Then they remembered his words, [9] and returning from the tomb, they told all this to the eleven and to all the rest. [10] Now it was Mary Magdalene, Joanna, Mary the mother of James, and the other women with them who told this to the apostles. [11] But these words seemed to them an idle tale, and they did not believe them. [12] But Peter got up and ran to the tomb; stooping and looking in, he saw the linen cloths by themselves; then he went home, amazed at what had happened.[v]

The Walk to Emmaus

13 Now on that same day two of them were going to a village called Emmaus, about seven miles[w] from Jerusalem, [14] and talking with each other about all these things that had happened. [15] While they were talking and discussing, Jesus himself came near and went with them, [16] but their eyes were kept from recognizing him. [17] And he said to them, "What are you discussing with each other while you walk

along?" They stood still, looking sad.[x] [18] Then one of them, whose name was Cleopas, answered him, "Are you the only stranger in Jerusalem who does not know the things that have taken place there in these days?" [19] He asked them, "What things?" They replied, "The things about Jesus of Nazareth,[y] who was a prophet mighty in deed and word before God and all the people, [20] and how our chief priests and leaders handed him over to be condemned to death and crucified him. [21] But we had hoped that he was the one to redeem Israel.[z] Yes, and besides all this, it is now the third day since these things took place. [22] Moreover, some women of our group astounded us. They were at the tomb early this morning, [23] and when they did not find his body there, they came back and told us that they had indeed seen a vision of angels who said that he was alive. [24] Some of those who were with us went to the tomb and found it just as the women had said; but they did not see him." [25] Then he said to them, "Oh, how foolish you are, and how slow of heart to believe all that the prophets have declared! [26] Was it not necessary that the Messiah[a] should suffer these things and then enter into his glory?" [27] Then beginning with Moses and all the prophets, he interpreted to them the things about himself in all the scriptures.

28 As they came near the village to which they were going, he walked ahead as if he were going on. [29] But they urged him strongly, saying, "Stay with us, because it is almost evening and the day is now nearly over." So he went in to stay with them. [30] When he was at the table with them, he took bread, blessed and broke it, and gave it to

Cross references (center column)

23.56
Mk 16.1;
Ex 12.16;
20.10
24.1
Lk 23.56
24.4
Acts 1.10;
12.7
24.6
Mt 17.22,
23;
Mk 9.30,31;
Lk 9.22
24.8
Jn 2.22
24.9
v. 46
24.10
Lk 8.1-3
24.11
v. 35
24.15
v. 36
24.16
Jn 21.4

24.18
Jn 19.25
24.19
Mt 21.11;
Lk 7.16;
13.33;
Acts 3.22
24.20
Lk 23.13
24.21
Lk 1.68
24.22
vv. 9,10
24.24
v. 12
24.26
Heb 2.10;
1 Pet 1.11
24.27
Gen 3.15;
Num 21.9;
Deut 18.15;
Isa 7.14;
9.6; 40.10,11;
ch. 53;
Ezek 34.23;
Dan 9.24;
Mic 7.20;
Mal 3.1
24.28
Mk 6.48
24.30
Mt 14.19

Footnotes

[r] Other ancient authorities add *of the Lord Jesus* [s] Gk *They* [t] Gk *but they*
[u] Other ancient authorities lack *He is not here, but has risen* [v] Other ancient authorities lack verse 12 [w] Gk *sixty stadia;* other ancient authorities read *a hundred sixty stadia* [x] Other ancient authorities read *walk along, looking sad?"* [y] Other ancient authorities read *Jesus the Nazorean* [z] Or *to set Israel free* [a] Or *the Christ*

RESURRECTION APPEARANCES

Event	Date	Matthew	Mark	Luke	John	Acts	I Corinthians
At the empty tomb outside Jerusalem	Early Sunday morning	28:1-10	16:1-8	24:1-12	20:1-9		
To Mary Magdalene at the tomb	Early Sunday morning		16:9-11		20:11-18		
To two travelers on the road to Emmaus	Sunday at midday			24:13-32			
To Peter in Jerusalem	During the day on Sunday			24:34			15:5
To the ten disciples in the upper room	Sunday evening		16:14	24:36-43	20:19-25		
To the eleven disciples in the upper room	One week later				20:26-31		15:5
To seven disciples fishing on the Sea of Galilee	One day at daybreak				21:1-23		
To the eleven disciples on the mountain in Galilee	Some time later	28:16-20	16:15-18				
To more than 500	Some time later						15:6
To James	Some time later						15:7
At the Ascension on the Mt. of Olives	Forty days after the resurrection			24:44-51		1:3-8	

them. [31] Then their eyes were opened, and they recognized him; and he vanished from their sight. [32] They said to each other, "Were not our hearts burning within us[b] while he was talking to us on the road, while he was opening the scriptures to us?" [33] That same hour they got up and returned to Jerusalem; and they found the eleven and their companions gathered together. [34] They were saying, "The Lord has risen indeed, and he has appeared to Simon!" [35] Then they told what had happened on the road, and how he had been made known to them in the breaking of the bread.

Jesus Appears to His Disciples

[36] While they were talking about this, Jesus himself stood among them and said to them, "Peace be with you."[c] [37] They were startled and terrified, and thought that they were seeing a ghost. [38] He said to them, "Why are you frightened, and why do doubts arise in your hearts? [39] Look at my hands and my feet; see that it is I myself. Touch me and see; for a ghost does not have flesh and bones as you see that I have." [40] And when he had said this, he showed them his hands and his feet.[d] [41] While in their joy they were disbelieving and still wondering, he said to them, "Have you anything here to eat?" [42] They gave him a piece of broiled fish, [43] and he took it and ate in their presence.

[44] Then he said to them, "These are my words that I spoke to you while I was still with you—that everything written about me in the law of Moses, the prophets, and the psalms must be fulfilled." [45] Then he opened their minds to understand the scriptures, [46] and he said to them, "Thus it is written, that the Messiah[e] is to suffer and to rise from the dead on the third day, [47] and that repentance and forgiveness of sins is to be proclaimed in his name to all nations,[f] beginning from Jerusalem. [48] You are witnesses of these things. [49] And see, I am sending upon you what my Father promised; so stay here in the city until you have been clothed with power from on high."

The Ascension of Jesus

[50] Then he led them out as far as Bethany, and, lifting up his hands, he blessed them. [51] While he was blessing them, he withdrew from them and was carried up into heaven.[g] [52] And they worshiped him, and[h] returned to Jerusalem with great joy; [53] and they were continually in the temple blessing God.[i]

24.33
Acts 1.14
24.34
1 Cor 15.5
24.37
Mk 6.49
24.39
Jn 20.27
24.41
Jn 21.5
24.43
Acts 10.41

24.44
Mt 16.21;
Mk 8.31;
Lk 9.22;
18.31
24.46
Isa 50.6;
Hos 6.2;
1 Cor 15.3,
4
24.47
Acts 5.31;
13.38;
Mt 28.19
24.48
Acts 1.8
24.49
Jn 14.16;
Acts 1.4
24.50
Acts 1.12
24.51
2 Kings 2.11
24.53
Acts 2.46

[b] Other ancient authorities lack *within us*
[c] Other ancient authorities lack *and said to them, "Peace be with you."* [d] Other ancient authorities lack verse 40 [e] Or *the Christ* [f] Or *nations. Beginning from Jerusalem you are witnesses* [g] Other ancient authorities lack *and was carried up into heaven* [h] Other ancient authorities lack *worshiped him, and* [i] Other ancient authorities add *Amen*

THE GOSPEL ACCORDING TO
John

Title and Background

The Gospel of John gets its name from the person who undoubtedly wrote it—the apostle John. His name means "The LORD is gracious." He was greatly influenced by the Old Testament. The prologue, for example, with its account of the origin of light and life, reminds us of the Genesis account of creation.

Author and Date of Writing

The apostle John is "the disciple whom Jesus loved" (13.23; 19.26; 20.2; 21.7,20,24). He knew Jewish life well and referred often to Jewish customs. John's account has many touches that were based on the recollections of an eyewitness. The date of writing was probably about A.D. 85 or a little later.

Theme and Message

The writer states his main goal clearly in 20.31: "so that you may come to believe that Jesus is the Messiah." He may have had Greek readers in mind. Along with this evangelistic purpose, John wanted to make clear to his readers both that Jesus was God and that Jesus had come in the flesh.

Outline

- I. Prologue (1.1-18)
- II. Beginnings of Jesus' Ministry (1.19-51)
- III. Jesus' Ministry: Signs and Discourses (2.1–11.57)
- IV. Passion Week (12.1–19.42)
- V. The Resurrection (20.1-29)
- VI. Statement of Purpose (20.30-31)
- VII. Epilogue (21.1-25)

The Word Became Flesh

1 In the beginning was the Word, and the Word was with God, and the Word was God. [2] He was in the beginning with God. [3] All things came into being through him, and without him not one thing came into being. What has come into being [4] in him was life,[a] and the life was the light of all people. [5] The light shines in the darkness, and the darkness did not overcome it.

6 There was a man sent from God, whose name was John. [7] He came as a witness to testify to the light, so that all might believe through him. [8] He himself was not the light, but he came to testify to the light. [9] The true light, which enlightens everyone, was coming into the world.[b]

10 He was in the world, and the world came into being through him; yet the world did not know him. [11] He came to what was his own,[c] and his own people did not accept him. [12] But to all who received him, who believed in his name, he gave power to become children of God, [13] who were born, not of blood or of the will of the flesh or of the will of man, but of God.

Cross-references

1.1 Col 1.17; 1 Jn 1.1; Phil 2.6
1.3 Col 1.16; Heb 1.2
1.4 Jn 5.26; 11.25; 14.6
1.5 Jn 3.19; 9.5; 12.46
1.7 Acts 19.4
1.8 v. 20
1.9 Isa 49.6; 1 Jn 2.8
1.10 Col 1.16; Heb 1.2
1.12 Gal 3.26; Jn 3.18; 1 Jn 5.13
1.13 Jn 3.5,6; Jas 1.18; 1 Pet 1.23

a Or 3through him. And without him not one thing came into being that has come into being. 4In him was life b Or He was the true light that enlightens everyone coming into the world c Or to his own home

14 And the Word became flesh and lived among us, and we have seen his glory, the glory as of a father's only son,[d] full of grace and truth. [15] (John testified to him and cried out, "This was he of whom I said, 'He who comes after me ranks ahead of me because he was before me.' ") [16] From his fullness we have all received, grace upon grace. [17] The law indeed was given through Moses; grace and truth came through Jesus Christ. [18] No one has ever seen God. It is God the only Son,[e] who is close to the Father's heart,[f] who has made him known.

The Testimony of John the Baptist

19 This is the testimony given by John when the Jews sent priests and Levites from Jerusalem to ask him, "Who are you?" [20] He confessed and did not deny it, but confessed, "I am not the Messiah."[g] [21] And they asked him, "What then? Are you Elijah?" He said, "I am not." "Are you the prophet?" He answered, "No." [22] Then they said to him, "Who are you? Let us have an answer for those who sent us. What do you say about yourself?" [23] He said,

"I am the voice of one crying
　　out in the wilderness,
'Make straight the way of the
　　Lord,' "

as the prophet Isaiah said.

24 Now they had been sent from the Pharisees. [25] They asked him, "Why then are you baptizing if you are neither the Messiah, nor Elijah, nor the prophet?" [26] John answered them, "I baptize with water. Among you stands one whom you do not know, [27] the one who is coming after me; I am not worthy to untie the thong of his sandal." [28] This took place in Bethany across the Jordan where John was baptizing.

The Lamb of God

29 The next day he saw Jesus coming toward him and declared, "Here is the Lamb of God who takes away the sin of the world!

1.14
Rom 1.3;
Gal 4.4;
1 Tim 3.16;
Heb 2.14
1.15
v. 30
1.16
Eph 1.23;
Col 1.19
1.17
Rom 3.24
1.18
Ex 33.20;
Jn 6.46;
1 Jn 4.9
1.20
Jn 3.28;
Lk 3.15,16
1.21
Mt 11.14;
16.14;
Deut 18.15
1.23
Mt 3.1;
Mk 1.3;
Lk 3.4;
Isa 40.3
1.26
Acts 1.5
1.27
vv. 15,30
1.28
Jn 3.26;
10.40
1.29
Isa 53.7;
1 Pet 1.19

1.30
vv. 15,27
1.32
Mt 3.16;
Mk 1.10;
Lk 3.22
1.33
Mt 3.11;
Acts 1.5
1.34
v. 49
1.35
v. 29
1.36
v. 29
1.38
v. 49
1.40
Mt 4.18-22;
Mk 1.16-20;
Lk 5.2-11
1.41
Dan 9.25;
Jn 4.25
1.42
Jn 21.15-17;
1 Cor 15.5;
Mt 16.18
1.43
Mt 10.3;
Jn 6.5,7;
12.21,22;
14.8,9

[30] This is he of whom I said, 'After me comes a man who ranks ahead of me because he was before me.' [31] I myself did not know him; but I came baptizing with water for this reason, that he might be revealed to Israel." [32] And John testified, "I saw the Spirit descending from heaven like a dove, and it remained on him. [33] I myself did not know him, but the one who sent me to baptize with water said to me, 'He on whom you see the Spirit descend and remain is the one who baptizes with the Holy Spirit.' [34] And I myself have seen and have testified that this is the Son of God."[h]

The First Disciples of Jesus

35 The next day John again was standing with two of his disciples, [36] and as he watched Jesus walk by, he exclaimed, "Look, here is the Lamb of God!" [37] The two disciples heard him say this, and they followed Jesus. [38] When Jesus turned and saw them following, he said to them, "What are you looking for?" They said to him, "Rabbi" (which translated means Teacher), "where are you staying?" [39] He said to them, "Come and see." They came and saw where he was staying, and they remained with him that day. It was about four o'clock in the afternoon. [40] One of the two who heard John speak and followed him was Andrew, Simon Peter's brother. [41] He first found his brother Simon and said to him, "We have found the Messiah" (which is translated Anointed[i]). [42] He brought Simon to Jesus, who looked at him and said, "You are Simon son of John. You are to be called Cephas" (which is translated Peter[k]).

Jesus Calls Philip and Nathanael

43 The next day Jesus decided

[d] Or *the Father's only Son*　　[e] Other ancient authorities read *It is an only Son, God,* or *It is the only Son*　　[f] Gk *bosom*　　[g] Or *the Christ*　　[h] Other ancient authorities read *is God's chosen one*　　[i] Or *Christ*　　[j] Gk *him*　　[k] From the word for *rock* in Aramaic (*kepha*) and Greek (*petra*), respectively

to go to Galilee. He found Philip and said to him, "Follow me." 44 Now Philip was from Bethsaida, the city of Andrew and Peter. 45 Philip found Nathanael and said to him, "We have found him about whom Moses in the law and also the prophets wrote, Jesus son of Joseph from Nazareth." 46 Nathanael said to him, "Can anything good come out of Nazareth?" Philip said to him, "Come and see." 47 When Jesus saw Nathanael coming toward him, he said of him, "Here is truly an Israelite in whom there is no deceit!" 48 Nathanael asked him, "Where did you get to know me?" Jesus answered, "I saw you under the fig tree before Philip called you." 49 Nathanael replied, "Rabbi, you are the Son of God! You are the King of Israel!" 50 Jesus answered, "Do you believe because I told you that I saw you under the fig tree? You will see greater things than these." 51 And he said to him, "Very truly, I tell you,[1] you will see heaven opened and the angels of God ascending and descending upon the Son of Man."

The Wedding at Cana

2 On the third day there was a wedding in Cana of Galilee, and the mother of Jesus was there. 2 Jesus and his disciples had also been invited to the wedding. 3 When the wine gave out, the mother of Jesus said to him, "They have no wine." 4 And Jesus said to her, "Woman, what concern is that to you and to me? My hour has not yet come." 5 His mother said to the servants, "Do whatever he tells you." 6 Now standing there were six stone water jars for the Jewish rites of purification, each holding twenty or thirty gallons. 7 Jesus said to them, "Fill the jars with water." And they filled them up to the brim. 8 He said to them, "Now draw some out, and take it to the chief steward." So they took it. 9 When the steward tasted the water that had become wine, and did not know where it came from (though the servants who had drawn the

water knew), the steward called the bridegroom 10 and said to him, "Everyone serves the good wine first, and then the inferior wine after the guests have become drunk. But you have kept the good wine until now." 11 Jesus did this, the first of his signs, in Cana of Galilee, and revealed his glory; and his disciples believed in him.

12 After this he went down to Capernaum with his mother, his brothers, and his disciples; and they remained there a few days.

Jesus Cleanses the Temple

13 The Passover of the Jews was near, and Jesus went up to Jerusalem. 14 In the temple he found people selling cattle, sheep, and doves, and the money changers seated at their tables. 15 Making a whip of cords, he drove all of them out of the temple, both the sheep and the cattle. He also poured out the coins of the money changers and overturned their tables. 16 He told those who were selling the doves, "Take these things out of here! Stop making my Father's house a marketplace!" 17 His disciples remembered that it was written, "Zeal for your house will consume me." 18 The Jews then said to him, "What sign can you show us for doing this?" 19 Jesus answered them, "Destroy this temple, and in three days I will raise it up." 20 The Jews then said, "This temple has been under construction for forty-six years, and will you raise it up in three days?" 21 But he was speaking of the temple of his body. 22 After he was raised from the dead, his disciples remembered that he had said this; and they believed the scripture and the word that Jesus had spoken.

23 When he was in Jerusalem during the Passover festival, many believed in his name because they saw the signs that he was doing. 24 But Jesus on his part would not entrust himself to them, because he knew all people 25 and needed

1.44
Jn 12.21
1.45
Jn 21.2;
Lk 24.27;
Mt 2.23;
Lk 2.4
1.46
Jn 7.41,42
1.47
Ps 32.2;
73.1;
Rom 9.4,6
1.49
vv. 38,34;
Mt 2.2;
Mk 15.32;
Jn 12.13
1.51
Gen 28.12;
Mt 3.16;
Lk 3.21;
Mt 8.20
2.1
Jn 4.46;
21.2
2.4
Jn 19.26;
7.6,30; 8.20
2.6
Mk 7.3,4;
Jn 3.25
2.9
Jn 4.46

2.11
Jn 1.14
2.12
Mt 4.13;
12.46
2.13
Jn 6.4;
11.55;
Deut 16.1-6;
Lk 2.41
2.16
Lk 2.49
2.17
Ps 69.9
2.18
Mt 12.38
2.19
Mt 26.61;
27.40;
Mk 14.58
2.21
1 Cor 6.19
2.22
Lk 24.8;
Jn 12.16;
14.26
2.23
v. 13
2.25
Jn 6.61,64;
13.11 2

[1] Both instances of the Greek word for *you* in this verse are plural

no one to testify about anyone; for he himself knew what was in everyone.

Nicodemus Visits Jesus

3 Now there was a Pharisee named Nicodemus, a leader of the Jews. ²He came to Jesus[m] by night and said to him, "Rabbi, we know that you are a teacher who has come from God; for no one can do these signs that you do apart from the presence of God." ³Jesus answered him, "Very truly, I tell you, no one can see the kingdom of God without being born from above."[n] ⁴Nicodemus said to him, "How can anyone be born after having grown old? Can one enter a second time into the mother's womb and be born?" ⁵Jesus answered, "Very truly, I tell you, no one can enter the kingdom of God without being born of water and Spirit. ⁶What is born of the flesh is flesh, and what is born of the Spirit is spirit.[o] ⁷Do not be astonished that I said to you, 'You[p] must be born from above.'[q] ⁸The wind[o] blows where it chooses, and you hear the sound of it, but you do not know where it comes from or where it goes. So it is with everyone who is born of the Spirit." ⁹Nicodemus said to him, "How can these things be?" ¹⁰Jesus answered him, "Are you a teacher of Israel, and yet you do not understand these things?

11 "Very truly, I tell you, we speak of what we know and testify to what we have seen; yet you[r] do not receive our testimony. ¹²If I have told you about earthly things and you do not believe, how can you believe if I tell you about heavenly things? ¹³No one has ascended into heaven except the one who descended from heaven, the Son of Man.[s] ¹⁴And just as Moses lifted up the serpent in the wilderness, so must the Son of Man be lifted up, ¹⁵that whoever believes in him may have eternal life.[t]

16 "For God so loved the world that he gave his only Son, so that everyone who believes in him may

not perish but may have eternal life.

17 "Indeed, God did not send the Son into the world to condemn the world, but in order that the world might be saved through him. ¹⁸Those who believe in him are not condemned; but those who do not believe are condemned already, because they have not believed in the name of the only Son of God. ¹⁹And this is the judgment, that the light has come into the world, and people loved darkness rather than light because their deeds were evil. ²⁰For all who do evil hate the light and do not come to the light, so that their deeds may not be exposed. ²¹But those who do what is true come to the light, so that it may be clearly seen that their deeds have been done in God."[t]

Jesus and John the Baptist

22 After this Jesus and his disciples went into the Judean countryside, and he spent some time there with them and baptized. ²³John also was baptizing at Aenon near Salim because water was abundant there; and people kept coming and were being baptized ²⁴—John, of course, had not yet been thrown into prison.

25 Now a discussion about purification arose between John's disciples and a Jew.[u] ²⁶They came to John and said to him, "Rabbi, the one who was with you across the Jordan, to whom you testified, here he is baptizing, and all are going to him." ²⁷John answered, "No one can receive anything except what has been given from heaven. ²⁸You yourselves are my witnesses that I said, 'I am not the Messiah,[v] but I have been sent ahead of him.' ²⁹He who has the bride is the bridegroom. The friend of the bride-

3.1
Jn 7.50;
19.39;
Lk 23.13;
Jn 7.26
3.2
Jn 9.16,33;
Acts 2.22;
10.38
3.3
Titus 3.5;
Jas 1.18;
1 Pet 1.23;
1 Jn 3.9
3.5
Eph 5.26;
Titus 3.5
3.6
Jn 1.13;
1 Cor 15.50
3.8
1 Cor 2.11
3.9
Jn 6.52,60
3.10
Lk 2.46
3.11
Jn 7.16,17
3.13
Prov 30.4;
Acts 2.34;
Rom 10.6;
Eph 4.9
3.14
Num 21.9;
Jn 8.28;
12.34
3.15
v. 36;
Jn 20.21;
1 Jn 5.11-13
3.16
Rom 5.8;
1 Jn 4.9
3.17
Jn 5.36,38;
8.15; 12.47;
1 Jn 4.14
3.18
Jn 5.24;
1 Jn 4.9
3.19
Jn 1.4; 8.12
3.20
Eph 5.11,13
3.21
1 Jn 1.6
3.22
Jn 4.2
3.24
Mt 4.12;
14.3
3.25
Jn 2.6
3.26
Jn 1.7,28
3.27
1 Cor 4.7;
Heb 5.4
3.28
Jn 1.20,23
3.29
Mk 2.19,20;
Mt 25.1;
Jn 15.11;
16.24

[m] Gk him [n] Or born anew
[o] The same Greek word means both wind and spirit [p] The Greek word for you here is plural [q] Or anew [r] The Greek word for you here and in verse 12 is plural [s] Other ancient authorities add who is in heaven
[t] Some interpreters hold that the quotation concludes with verse 15 [u] Other ancient authorities read the Jews [v] Or the Christ

groom, who stands and hears him, rejoices greatly at the bridegroom's voice. For this reason my joy has been fulfilled. [30] He must increase, but I must decrease."[w]

The One Who Comes from Heaven

31 The one who comes from above is above all; the one who is of the earth belongs to the earth and speaks about earthly things. The one who comes from heaven is above all. [32] He testifies to what he has seen and heard, yet no one accepts his testimony. [33] Whoever has accepted his testimony has certified[x] this, that God is true. [34] He whom God has sent speaks the words of God, for he gives the Spirit without measure. [35] The Father loves the Son and has placed all things in his hands. [36] Whoever believes in the Son has eternal life; whoever disobeys the Son will not see life, but must endure God's wrath.

Jesus and the Woman of Samaria

4 Now when Jesus[y] learned that the Pharisees had heard, "Jesus is making and baptizing more disciples than John" [2] — although it was not Jesus himself but his disciples who baptized — [3] he left Judea and started back to Galilee. [4] But he had to go through Samaria. [5] So he came to a Samaritan city called Sychar, near the plot of ground that Jacob had given to his son Joseph. [6] Jacob's well was there, and Jesus, tired out by his journey, was sitting by the well. It was about noon.

7 A Samaritan woman came to draw water, and Jesus said to her, "Give me a drink." [8] (His disciples had gone to the city to buy food.) [9] The Samaritan woman said to him, "How is it that you, a Jew, ask a drink of me, a woman of Samaria?" (Jews do not share things in common with Samaritans.)[z] [10] Jesus answered her, "If you knew the gift of God, and who it is that is saying to you, 'Give me a drink,'

3.31	Jn 8.23; 1 Jn 4.5
3.32	v. 11; Jn 8.26; 15.15
3.33	Rom 4.11; 15.28; Eph 1.13; 4.30
3.34	Mt 12.18; Lk 4.18
3.35	Mt 28.18; Jn 5.20,22; 17.2
3.36	Jn 5.24; 6.47
4.1	Jn 3.22,26
4.3	Jn 3.22
4.4	Lk 9.52
4.5	Gen 33.19; 48.22; Josh 24.32
4.8	w. 5,39
4.9	Mt 10.5; Lk 9.52,53; Jn 8.48
4.10	Isa 44.3; Jn 7.37; Rev 21.6; 22.17
4.12	v. 6
4.14	Jn 6.35; 7.38
4.15	Jn 6.34
4.19	Lk 7.39
4.20	Deut 11.29; Josh 8.33; Lk 9.53
4.21	Mal 1.11; 1 Tim 2.8
4.22	2 Kings 17.28-41; Isa 2.3; Rom 3.1,2; 9.4,5
4.23	Jn 5.25; Phil 3.3
4.24	Phil 3.3
4.25	Jn 1.41; Mt 1.16

you would have asked him, and he would have given you living water." [11] The woman said to him, "Sir, you have no bucket, and the well is deep. Where do you get that living water? [12] Are you greater than our ancestor Jacob, who gave us the well, and with his sons and his flocks drank from it?" [13] Jesus said to her, "Everyone who drinks of this water will be thirsty again, [14] but those who drink of the water that I will give them will never be thirsty. The water that I will give will become in them a spring of water gushing up to eternal life." [15] The woman said to him, "Sir, give me this water, so that I may never be thirsty or have to keep coming here to draw water."

16 Jesus said to her, "Go, call your husband, and come back." [17] The woman answered him, "I have no husband." Jesus said to her, "You are right in saying, 'I have no husband'; [18] for you have had five husbands, and the one you have now is not your husband. What you have said is true!" [19] The woman said to him, "Sir, I see that you are a prophet. [20] Our ancestors worshiped on this mountain, but you[a] say that the place where people must worship is in Jerusalem." [21] Jesus said to her, "Woman, believe me, the hour is coming when you will worship the Father neither on this mountain nor in Jerusalem. [22] You worship what you do not know; we worship what we know, for salvation is from the Jews. [23] But the hour is coming, and is now here, when the true worshipers will worship the Father in spirit and truth, for the Father seeks such as these to worship him. [24] God is spirit, and those who worship him must worship in spirit and truth." [25] The woman said to him, "I know that Messiah is coming" (who is called Christ). "When he

[w] Some interpreters hold that the quotation continues through verse 36　[x] Gk *set a seal to*　[y] Other ancient authorities read *the Lord*　[z] Other ancient authorities lack this sentence　[a] The Greek word for *you* here and in verses 21 and 22 is plural

comes, he will proclaim all things to us." 26 Jesus said to her, "I am he,[b] the one who is speaking to you."

27 Just then his disciples came. They were astonished that he was speaking with a woman, but no one said, "What do you want?" or, "Why are you speaking with her?" 28 Then the woman left her water jar and went back to the city. She said to the people, 29 "Come and see a man who told me everything I have ever done! He cannot be the Messiah,[c] can he?" 30 They left the city and were on their way to him.

31 Meanwhile the disciples were urging him, "Rabbi, eat something." 32 But he said to them, "I have food to eat that you do not know about." 33 So the disciples said to one another, "Surely no one has brought him something to eat?" 34 Jesus said to them, "My food is to do the will of him who sent me and to complete his work. 35 Do you not say, 'Four months more, then comes the harvest'? But I tell you, look around you, and see how the fields are ripe for harvesting. 36 The reaper is already receiving[d] wages and is gathering fruit for eternal life, so that sower and reaper may rejoice together. 37 For here the saying holds true, 'One sows and another reaps.' 38 I sent you to reap that for which you did not labor. Others have labored, and you have entered into their labor."

39 Many Samaritans from that city believed in him because of the woman's testimony, "He told me everything I have ever done." 40 So when the Samaritans came to him, they asked him to stay with them; and he stayed there two days. 41 And many more believed because of his word. 42 They said to the woman, "It is no longer because of what you said that we believe, for we have heard for ourselves, and we know that this is truly the Savior of the world."

Jesus Returns to Galilee

43 When the two days were over, he went from that place to Galilee 44 (for Jesus himself had testified that a prophet has no honor in the prophet's own country). 45 When he came to Galilee, the Galileans welcomed him, since they had seen all that he had done in Jerusalem at the festival; for they too had gone to the festival.

Jesus Heals an Official's Son

46 Then he came again to Cana in Galilee where he had changed the water into wine. Now there was a royal official whose son lay ill in Capernaum. 47 When he heard that Jesus had come from Judea to Galilee, he went and begged him to come down and heal his son, for he was at the point of death. 48 Then Jesus said to him, "Unless you[e] see signs and wonders you will not believe." 49 The official said to him, "Sir, come down before my little boy dies." 50 Jesus said to him, "Go; your son will live." The man believed the word that Jesus spoke to him and started on his way. 51 As he was going down, his slaves met him and told him that his child was alive. 52 So he asked them the hour when he began to recover, and they said to him, "Yesterday at one in the afternoon the fever left him." 53 The father realized that this was the hour when Jesus had said to him, "Your son will live." So he himself believed, along with his whole household. 54 Now this was the second sign that Jesus did after coming from Judea to Galilee.

Jesus Heals on the Sabbath

5 After this there was a festival of the Jews, and Jesus went up to Jerusalem.

2 Now in Jerusalem by the Sheep Gate there is a pool, called in Hebrew[f] Beth-zatha,[g] which has five porticoes. 3 In these lay many invalids—blind, lame, and

4.26
Mt 26.63, 64;
Mk 14.61, 62; Jn 8.24
4.27
v. 8
4.29
vv. 17,18;
Jn 7.26,31
4.32
Mt 4.4
4.34
Jn 5.30;
6.38; 17.4;
19.30
4.35
Mt 9.37;
Lk 10.2
4.36
Rom 1.13;
v. 14
4.37
Job 31.8;
Mic 6.15 2
4.39
v. 29
4.42
1 Jn 4.14;
1 Tim 4.10;
2 Tim 1.10
4.43
v. 40

4.44
Mt 13.57;
Mk 6.4;
Lk 4.24
4.45
Jn 2.23
4.46
Jn 2.1-11
4.47
vv. 3,54
4.48
Dan 4.2;
Mk 13.22;
Acts 2.19,
22,43; 4.30;
Rom 15.19;
Heb 2.4
4.53
Acts 11.14
4.54
Jn 2.11
5.2
Neh 3.1;
12.39

[b] Gk *I am* [c] Or *the Christ*
[d] Or *35. . . . the fields are already ripe for harvesting. 36The reaper is receiving* [e] Both instances of the Greek word for *you* in this verse are plural [f] That is, *Aramaic*
[g] Other ancient authorities read *Bethesda*, others *Bethsaida*

paralyzed.[h] [5]One man was there who had been ill for thirty-eight years. [6]When Jesus saw him lying there and knew that he had been there a long time, he said to him, "Do you want to be made well?" [7]The sick man answered him, "Sir, I have no one to put me into the pool when the water is stirred up; and while I am making my way, someone else steps down ahead of me." [8]Jesus said to him, "Stand up, take your mat and walk." [9]At once the man was made well, and he took up his mat and began to walk.

Now that day was a sabbath. [10]So the Jews said to the man who had been cured, "It is the sabbath; it is not lawful for you to carry your mat." [11]But he answered them, "The man who made me well said to me, 'Take up your mat and walk.' " [12]They asked him, "Who is the man who said to you, 'Take it up and walk'?" [13]Now the man who had been healed did not know who it was, for Jesus had disappeared in[i] the crowd that was there. [14]Later Jesus found him in the temple and said to him, "See, you have been made well! Do not sin any more, so that nothing worse happens to you." [15]The man went away and told the Jews that it was Jesus who had made him well. [16]Therefore the Jews started persecuting Jesus, because he was doing such things on the sabbath. [17]But Jesus answered them, "My Father is still working, and I also am working." [18]For this reason the Jews were seeking all the more to kill him, because he was not only breaking the sabbath, but was also calling God his own Father, thereby making himself equal to God.

The Authority of the Son

[19] Jesus said to them, "Very truly, I tell you, the Son can do nothing on his own, but only what he sees the Father doing; for whatever the Father[j] does, the Son does likewise. [20]The Father loves the Son and shows him all that he himself is doing; and he will show him greater works than these, so that

you will be astonished. [21]Indeed, just as the Father raises the dead and gives them life, so also the Son gives life to whomever he wishes. [22]The Father judges no one but has given all judgment to the Son, [23]so that all may honor the Son just as they honor the Father. Anyone who does not honor the Son does not honor the Father who sent him. [24]Very truly, I tell you, anyone who hears my word and believes him who sent me has eternal life, and does not come under judgment, but has passed from death to life.

[25] "Very truly, I tell you, the hour is coming, and is now here, when the dead will hear the voice of the Son of God, and those who hear will live. [26]For just as the Father has life in himself, so he has granted the Son also to have life in himself; [27]and he has given him authority to execute judgment, because he is the Son of Man. [28]Do not be astonished at this; for the hour is coming when all who are in their graves will hear his voice [29]and will come out—those who have done good, to the resurrection of life, and those who have done evil, to the resurrection of condemnation.

Witnesses to Jesus

[30] "I can do nothing on my own. As I hear, I judge; and my judgment is just, because I seek to do not my own will but the will of him who sent me.

[31] "If I testify about myself, my testimony is not true. [32]There is another who testifies on my behalf, and I know that his testimony to me is true. [33]You sent messengers to John, and he testified to the truth. [34]Not that I accept such human testimony, but I say these things so that you may be saved. [35]He was a burning and shining

5.8
Mt 9.6;
Mk 2.11;
Lk 5.24
5.9
Jn 9.14
5.10
vv. 15,16;
Neh 13.19;
Jer 17.21;
Mt 12.2;
Mk 2.24;
Jn 7.23;
9.16
5.14
Mk 2.5;
Jn 8.11
5.17
Jn 9.4;
14.10
5.18
Jn 7.1,19;
10.30,33
5.19
Jn 8.28;
12.49; 14.10
5.20
Jn 3.35;
14.12

5.21
Rom 4.17;
8.11;
Jn 11.25
5.22
Jn 9.39;
Acts 17.31
5.23
Lk 10.16;
1 Jn 2.23
5.24
Jn 3.18;
12.44; 20.31;
1 Jn 5.13;
3.14
5.25
Jn 4.21;
6.60; 8.43,47
5.26
Jn 6.57
5.27
Acts 10.42;
17.31
5.29
Dan 12.2;
Acts 24.15;
Mt 25.46
5.30
Jn 8.16;
4.34; 6.38
5.31
Jn 8.14
5.32
Jn 8.18
5.33
Jn 1.7,15,
19,27,32
5.34
1 Jn 5.9
5.35
2 Pet 1.19;
Mt 21.26

[h] Other ancient authorities add, wholly or in part, *waiting for the stirring of the water;* [4]*for an angel of the Lord went down at certain seasons into the pool, and stirred up the water; whoever stepped in first after the stirring of the water was made well from whatever disease that person had.* [i] Or *had left because of* [j] Gk *that one*

lamp, and you were willing to rejoice for a while in his light. [36] But I have a testimony greater than John's. The works that the Father has given me to complete, the very works that I am doing, testify on my behalf that the Father has sent me. [37] And the Father who sent me has himself testified on my behalf. You have never heard his voice or seen his form, [38] and you do not have his word abiding in you, because you do not believe him whom he has sent.

[39] "You search the scriptures because you think that in them you have eternal life; and it is they that testify on my behalf. [40] Yet you refuse to come to me to have life. [41] I do not accept glory from human beings. [42] But I know that you do not have the love of God in[k] you. [43] I have come in my Father's name, and you do not accept me; if another comes in his own name, you will accept him. [44] How can you believe when you accept glory from one another and do not seek the glory that comes from the one who alone is God? [45] Do not think that I will accuse you before the Father; your accuser is Moses, on whom you have set your hope. [46] If you believed Moses, you would believe me, for he wrote about me. [47] But if you do not believe what he wrote, how will you believe what I say?"

Feeding the Five Thousand

6 After this Jesus went to the other side of the Sea of Galilee, also called the Sea of Tiberias.[1] [2] A large crowd kept following him, because they saw the signs that he was doing for the sick. [3] Jesus went up the mountain and sat down there with his disciples. [4] Now the Passover, the festival of the Jews, was near. [5] When he looked up and saw a large crowd coming toward him, Jesus said to Philip, "Where are we to buy bread for these people to eat?" [6] He said this to test him, for he himself knew what he was going to do. [7] Philip answered him, "Six

months' wages[m] would not buy enough bread for each of them to get a little." [8] One of his disciples, Andrew, Simon Peter's brother, said to him, [9] "There is a boy here who has five barley loaves and two fish. But what are they among so many people?" [10] Jesus said, "Make the people sit down." Now there was a great deal of grass in the place; so they[n] sat down, about five thousand in all. [11] Then Jesus took the loaves, and when he had given thanks, he distributed them to those who were seated; so also the fish, as much as they wanted. [12] When they were satisfied, he told his disciples, "Gather up the fragments left over, so that nothing may be lost." [13] So they gathered them up, and from the fragments of the five barley loaves, left by those who had eaten, they filled twelve baskets. [14] When the people saw the sign that he had done, they began to say, "This is indeed the prophet who is to come into the world."

[15] When Jesus realized that they were about to come and take him by force to make him king, he withdrew again to the mountain by himself.

Jesus Walks on the Water

[16] When evening came, his disciples went down to the sea, [17] got into a boat, and started across the sea to Capernaum. It was now dark, and Jesus had not yet come to them. [18] The sea became rough because a strong wind was blowing. [19] When they had rowed about three or four miles,[o] they saw Jesus walking on the sea and coming near the boat, and they were terrified. [20] But he said to them, "It is I;[p] do not be afraid." [21] Then they wanted to take him into the boat, and immediately the boat reached the land toward which they were going.

Cross references (center column):

5.36 1 Jn 5.9; Jn 10.25; 14.11; 15.24
5.37 Jn 8.18; Deut 4.12; 1 Tim 1.17
5.38 Jn 3.17
5.39 Lk 24.25,27; Acts 13.27
5.41 v. 44
5.43 Mt 24.5
5.44 Rom 2.29
5.45 Jn 9.28; Rom 2.17
5.46 Gen 3.15; Lk 24.27; Acts 26.22
5.47 Jn 16.29,31
6.2 Jn 2.11
6.3 v. 15
6.4 Jn 2.13
6.5 Jn 1.43
6.6 2 Cor 13.5
6.8 Jn 1.40
6.9 2 Kings 4.43
6.11 v. 23; Mt 15.36
6.14 Gen 49.10; Deut 18.15, 18; Mt 11.3; 21.11
6.15 Jn 18.36

[k] Or *among* [l] Gk *of Galilee of Tiberius*
[m] Gk *Two hundred denarii*; the denarius was the usual day's wage for a laborer
[n] Gk *the men* [o] Gk *about twenty-five or thirty stadia* [p] Gk *I am*

The Bread from Heaven

22 The next day the crowd that had stayed on the other side of the sea saw that there had been only one boat there. They also saw that Jesus had not got into the boat with his disciples, but that his disciples had gone away alone. 23 Then some boats from Tiberias came near the place where they had eaten the bread after the Lord had given thanks.q 24 So when the crowd saw that neither Jesus nor his disciples were there, they themselves got into the boats and went to Capernaum looking for Jesus.

25 When they found him on the other side of the sea, they said to him, "Rabbi, when did you come here?" 26 Jesus answered them, "Very truly, I tell you, you are looking for me, not because you saw signs, but because you ate your fill of the loaves. 27 Do not work for the food that perishes, but for the food that endures for eternal life, which the Son of Man will give you. For it is on him that God the Father has set his seal." 28 Then they said to him, "What must we do to perform the works of God?" 29 Jesus answered them, "This is the work of God, that you believe in him whom he has sent." 30 So they said to him, "What sign are you going to give us then, so that we may see it and believe you? What work are you performing? 31 Our ancestors ate the manna in the wilderness; as it is written, 'He gave them bread from heaven to eat.' " 32 Then Jesus said to them, "Very truly, I tell you, it was not Moses who gave you the bread from heaven, but it is my Father who gives you the true bread from heaven. 33 For the bread of God is that whichr comes down from heaven and gives life to the world." 34 They said to him, "Sir, give us this bread always."

35 Jesus said to them, "I am the bread of life. Whoever comes to me will never be hungry, and whoever believes in me will never be thirsty. 36 But I said to you that you have

seen me and yet do not believe. 37 Everything that the Father gives me will come to me, and anyone who comes to me I will never drive away; 38 for I have come down from heaven, not to do my own will, but the will of him who sent me. 39 And this is the will of him who sent me, that I should lose nothing of all that he has given me, but raise it up on the last day. 40 This is indeed the will of my Father, that all who see the Son and believe in him may have eternal life; and I will raise them up on the last day."

41 Then the Jews began to complain about him because he said, "I am the bread that came down from heaven." 42 They were saying, "Is not this Jesus, the son of Joseph, whose father and mother we know? How can he now say, 'I have come down from heaven'?" 43 Jesus answered them, "Do not complain among yourselves. 44 No one can come to me unless drawn by the Father who sent me; and I will raise that person up on the last day. 45 It is written in the prophets, 'And they shall all be taught by God.' Everyone who has heard and learned from the Father comes to me. 46 Not that anyone has seen the Father except the one who is from God; he has seen the Father. 47 Very truly, I tell you, whoever believes has eternal life. 48 I am the bread of life. 49 Your ancestors ate the manna in the wilderness, and they died. 50 This is the bread that comes down from heaven, so that one may eat of it and not die. 51 I am the living bread that came down from heaven. Whoever eats of this bread will live forever; and the bread that I will give for the life of the world is my flesh."

52 The Jews then disputed among themselves, saying, "How can this man give us his flesh to eat?" 53 So Jesus said to them, "Very truly, I tell you, unless you eat the flesh of the Son of Man and

6.22 v. 2,16ff
6.23 v. 1,11
6.24 Mt 14.34; Mk 6.53
6.26 vv. 24,30
6.27 Isa 55.2; v. 54; Jn 4.14; 3.35
6.29 1 Jn 3.23; Jn 3.17
6.30 Mt 12.38; Mk 8.11
6.31 Ex 16.15; Num 11.8; Neh 9.15; Ps 78.24
6.33 v. 50
6.34 Jn 4.15
6.35 vv. 48,51; Jn 4.14
6.36 v. 26
6.37 v. 39; Jn 17.2
6.38 Jn 4.34; 5.30
6.39 Jn 10.28; 17.12; 18.9
6.40 vv. 27,47, 54; Jn 3.15, 16
6.42 Lk 4.22; Jn 7.27,28; vv. 38,62
6.44 Jer 31.3; Hos 11.4; Jn 12.32
6.45 Isa 54.13; Jer 31.34; Heb 8.10; 10.16
6.46 Jn 1.18; 5.37; 7.29; 8.19
6.47 Jn 3.16,18, 36; 5.24; 11.26
6.48 vv. 35,51
6.49 v. 31
6.50 v. 33
6.51 Heb 10.10

6.52 Jn 9.16; 10.19 **6.53** Mt 26.26,28

q Other ancient authorities lack *after the Lord had given thanks* r Or *he who*

drink his blood, you have no life in you. ⁵⁴ Those who eat my flesh and drink my blood have eternal life, and I will raise them up on the last day; ⁵⁵ for my flesh is true food and my blood is true drink. ⁵⁶ Those who eat my flesh and drink my blood abide in me, and I in them. ⁵⁷ Just as the living Father sent me, and I live because of the Father, so whoever eats me will live because of me. ⁵⁸ This is the bread that came down from heaven, not like that which your ancestors ate, and they died. But the one who eats this bread will live forever." ⁵⁹ He said these things while he was teaching in the synagogue at Capernaum.

The Words of Eternal Life

60 When many of his disciples heard it, they said, "This teaching is difficult; who can accept it?" ⁶¹ But Jesus, being aware that his disciples were complaining about it, said to them, "Does this offend you? ⁶² Then what if you were to see the Son of Man ascending to where he was before? ⁶³ It is the spirit that gives life; the flesh is useless. The words that I have spoken to you are spirit and life. ⁶⁴ But among you there are some who do not believe." For Jesus knew from the first who were the ones that did not believe, and who was the one that would betray him. ⁶⁵ And he said, "For this reason I have told you that no one can come to me unless it is granted by the Father."

66 Because of this many of his disciples turned back and no longer went about with him. ⁶⁷ So Jesus asked the twelve, "Do you also wish to go away?" ⁶⁸ Simon Peter answered him, "Lord, to whom can we go? You have the words of eternal life. ⁶⁹ We have come to believe and know that you are the Holy One of God."ˢ ⁷⁰ Jesus answered them, "Did I not choose you, the twelve? Yet one of you is a devil." ⁷¹ He was speaking of Judas son of Simon Iscariot,ᵗ for he, though one of the twelve, was going to betray him.

The Unbelief of Jesus' Brothers

7 After this Jesus went about in Galilee. He did not wishᵘ to go about in Judea because the Jews were looking for an opportunity to kill him. ² Now the Jewish festival of Boothsᵛ was near. ³ So his brothers said to him, "Leave here and go to Judea so that your disciples also may see the works you are doing; ⁴ for no one who wantsʷ to be widely known acts in secret. If you do these things, show yourself to the world." ⁵ (For not even his brothers believed in him.) ⁶ Jesus said to them, "My time has not yet come, but your time is always here. ⁷ The world cannot hate you, but it hates me because I testify against it that its works are evil. ⁸ Go to the festival yourselves. I am notˣ going to this festival, for my time has not yet fully come." ⁹ After saying this, he remained in Galilee.

Jesus at the Festival of Booths

10 But after his brothers had gone to the festival, then he also went, not publicly but as it wereʸ in secret. ¹¹ The Jews were looking for him at the festival and saying, "Where is he?" ¹² And there was considerable complaining about him among the crowds. While some were saying, "He is a good man," others were saying, "No, he is deceiving the crowd." ¹³ Yet no one would speak openly about him for fear of the Jews.

14 About the middle of the festival Jesus went up into the temple and began to teach. ¹⁵ The Jews were astonished at it, saying, "How does this man have such learning,ᶻ when he has never been taught?" ¹⁶ Then Jesus answered them, "My teaching is not mine but his who sent me. ¹⁷ Anyone who resolves to do the will of God will know wheth-

6.54
Jn 4.14
6.56
Jn 15.4;
1 Jn 3.24;
4.15,16
6.57
Jn 3.17
6.58
vv. 49-51
6.60
v. 66
6.61
Mt 11.6
6.62
Jn 3.13;
17.5
6.63
2 Cor 3.6
6.64
Jn 2.25
6.65
vv. 37,44;
Jn 3.27
6.66
v. 60
6.67
Mt 10.2
6.68
Mt 16.16;
Acts 5.20
6.69
Mk 8.29;
Lk 9.20
6.70
Jn 15.16,19;
13.27
6.71
Jn 13.26;
Mk 14.10

7.1
Jn 5.18
7.2
Lev 23.34;
Deut 16.16
7.3
Mt 12.46;
Mk 3.31
7.5
Mk 3.21
7.6
Mt 26.18;
vv. 8,30
7.7
Jn 15.18,19;
3.19,20
7.8
v. 6
7.11
Jn 11.56
7.12
vv. 40-43
7.13
Jn 9.22;
12.42; 19.38
7.14
v. 28
7.15
Mt 13.54;
Mk 6.2;
Lk 4.22
7.16
Jn 3.11;
8.28; 12.49
7.17
Jn 8.43

ˢ Other ancient authorities read *the Christ, the Son of the living God* ᵗ Other ancient authorities read *Judas Iscariot son of Simon;* others, *Judas son of Simon from Karyot* (Kerioth) ᵘ Other ancient authorities read *was not at liberty* ᵛ Or *Tabernacles* ʷ Other ancient authorities read *wants it* ˣ Other ancient authorities add *yet* ʸ Other ancient authorities lack *as it were* ᶻ Or *this man know his letters*

er the teaching is from God or whether I am speaking on my own. 18 Those who speak on their own seek their own glory; but the one who seeks the glory of him who sent him is true, and there is nothing false in him.

19 "Did not Moses give you the law? Yet none of you keeps the law. Why are you looking for an opportunity to kill me?" 20 The crowd answered, "You have a demon! Who is trying to kill you?" 21 Jesus answered them, "I performed one work, and all of you are astonished. 22 Moses gave you circumcision (it is, of course, not from Moses, but from the patriarchs), and you circumcise a man on the sabbath. 23 If a man receives circumcision on the sabbath in order that the law of Moses may not be broken, are you angry with me because I healed a man's whole body on the sabbath? 24 Do not judge by appearances, but judge with right judgment."

Is This the Christ?

25 Now some of the people of Jerusalem were saying, "Is not this the man whom they are trying to kill? 26 And here he is, speaking openly, but they say nothing to him! Can it be that the authorities really know that this is the Messiah?a 27 Yet we know where this man is from; but when the Messiaha comes, no one will know where he is from." 28 Then Jesus cried out as he was teaching in the temple, "You know me, and you know where I am from. I have not come on my own. But the one who sent me is true, and you do not know him. 29 I know him, because I am from him, and he sent me." 30 Then they tried to arrest him, but no one laid hands on him, because his hour had not yet come. 31 Yet many in the crowd believed in him and were saying, "When the Messiaha comes, will he do more signs than this man has done?"b

Officers Are Sent to Arrest Jesus

32 The Pharisees heard the crowd muttering such things about

7.18
Jn 5.41;
8.50
7.19
Ex 24.3;
Jn 1.17;
11.53
7.20
Jn 8.48;
10.20
7.22
Lev 12.3;
Gen 17.10
7.23
Mk 3.5
7.24
Lev 19.15;
Jn 8.15
7.26
v. 48
7.27
Mt 13.55;
Mk 6.3;
Lk 4.22
7.28
Jn 8.14;
8.26; 1.18
7.29
Mt 11.27;
Jn 10.15
7.30
Mt 21.46;
Jn 8.20
7.31
Jn 8.30;
Mt 12.23

7.33
Jn 13.33;
16.16-19
7.34
Jn 8.21;
13.33
7.35
Jas 1.1;
1 Pet 1.1
7.37
Lev 23.36;
Isa 55.1;
Rev 22.17
7.38
Isa 12.3;
Jn 4.10,14
7.39
Joel 2.28;
Acts 2.17,
33;
Jn 20.22;
12.23
7.40
Mt 21.11;
Jn 1.21
7.41
Jn 1.46
7.42
Jer 23.5;
Mic 5.2;
Mt 2.5;
Lk 2.4
7.43
Jn 9.16;
10.19
7.44
v. 30

him, and the chief priests and Pharisees sent temple police to arrest him. 33 Jesus then said, "I will be with you a little while longer, and then I am going to him who sent me. 34 You will search for me, but you will not find me; and where I am, you cannot come." 35 The Jews said to one another, "Where does this man intend to go that we will not find him? Does he intend to go to the Dispersion among the Greeks and teach the Greeks? 36 What does he mean by saying, 'You will search for me and you will not find me' and 'Where I am, you cannot come'?"

Rivers of Living Water

37 On the last day of the festival, the great day, while Jesus was standing there, he cried out, "Let anyone who is thirsty come to me, 38 and let the one who believes in me drink. Asc the scripture has said, 'Out of the believer's heartd shall flow rivers of living water.' " 39 Now he said this about the Spirit, which believers in him were to receive; for as yet there was no Spirit,e because Jesus was not yet glorified.

Division among the People

40 When they heard these words, some in the crowd said, "This is really the prophet." 41 Others said, "This is the Messiah."a But some asked, "Surely the Messiaha does not come from Galilee, does he? 42 Has not the scripture said that the Messiaha is descended from David and comes from Bethlehem, the village where David lived?" 43 So there was a division in the crowd because of him. 44 Some of them wanted to arrest him, but no one laid hands on him.

The Unbelief of Those in Authority

45 Then the temple police went back to the chief priests and Phari-

a Or the Christ　b Other ancient authorities read is doing　c Or come to me and drink. 38 The one who believes in me, as　d Gk out of his belly　e Other ancient authorities read for as yet the Spirit (others, Holy Spirit) had not been given

sees, who asked them, "Why did you not arrest him?" ⁴⁶The police answered, "Never has anyone spoken like this!" ⁴⁷Then the Pharisees replied, "Surely you have not been deceived too, have you? ⁴⁸Has any one of the authorities or of the Pharisees believed in him? ⁴⁹But this crowd, which does not know the law—they are accursed." ⁵⁰Nicodemus, who had gone to Jesusᶠ before, and who was one of them, asked, ⁵¹"Our law does not judge people without first giving them a hearing to find out what they are doing, does it?" ⁵²They replied, "Surely you are not also from Galilee, are you? Search and you will see that no prophet is to arise from Galilee."

The Woman Caught in Adultery

⟦⁵³Then each of them went home, **8** ¹while Jesus went to the Mount of Olives. ²Early in the morning he came again to the temple. All the people came to him and he sat down and began to teach them. ³The scribes and the Pharisees brought a woman who had been caught in adultery; and making her stand before all of them, ⁴they said to him, "Teacher, this woman was caught in the very act of committing adultery. ⁵Now in the law Moses commanded us to stone such women. Now what do you say?" ⁶They said this to test him, so that they might have some charge to bring against him. Jesus bent down and wrote with his finger on the ground. ⁷When they kept on questioning him, he straightened up and said to them, "Let anyone among you who is without sin be the first to throw a stone at her." ⁸And once again he bent down and wrote on the ground. ᵍ ⁹When they heard it, they went away, one by one, beginning with the elders; and Jesus was left alone with the woman standing before him. ¹⁰Jesus straightened up and said to her, "Woman, where are they? Has no one condemned you?" ¹¹She said, "No one, sir."ʰ

And Jesus said, "Neither do I condemn you. Go your way, and from now on do not sin again."⟧ᶦ

Jesus the Light of the World

12 Again Jesus spoke to them, saying, "I am the light of the world. Whoever follows me will never walk in darkness but will have the light of life." ¹³Then the Pharisees said to him, "You are testifying on your own behalf; your testimony is not valid." ¹⁴Jesus answered, "Even if I testify on my own behalf, my testimony is valid because I know where I have come from and where I am going, but you do not know where I come from or where I am going. ¹⁵You judge by human standards;ᶦ I judge no one. ¹⁶Yet even if I do judge, my judgment is valid; for it is not I alone who judge, but I and the Fatherᵏ who sent me. ¹⁷In your law it is written that the testimony of two witnesses is valid. ¹⁸I testify on my own behalf, and the Father who sent me testifies on my behalf." ¹⁹Then they said to him, "Where is your Father?" Jesus answered, "You know neither me nor my Father. If you knew me, you would know my Father also." ²⁰He spoke these words while he was teaching in the treasury of the temple, but no one arrested him, because his hour had not yet come.

Jesus Foretells His Death

21 Again he said to them, "I am going away, and you will search for me, but you will die in your sin. Where I am going, you cannot come." ²²Then the Jews said, "Is he going to kill himself? Is that what he means by saying, 'Where I am going, you cannot come'?" ²³He said to them, "You are from below, I am from above; you are of this world, I am not of this world. ²⁴I told you that you would die in

Cross-reference column:

7.46 Mt 7.28,29
7.47 v. 12
7.48 Jn 12.42
7.51 Deut 17.6; 19.15
8.5 Lev 20.10; Deut 22.22
8.7 Deut 17.7; Rom 2.1
8.9 Rom 2.22
8.11 Jn 3.18; 5.14
8.12 Jn 1.4; 9.5; 12.35
8.13 Jn 5.31
8.14 Jn 18.37; 13.3; 16.28; 7.28; 9.29
8.15 Jn 7.24; 3.17
8.16 Jn 5.30
8.17 Deut 17.6; Mt 18.16
8.18 Jn 5.37
8.19 Jn 14.7; 16.3
8.20 Mk 12.41; Jn 7.30
8.21 Jn 7.34
8.23 Jn 3.31; 17.14
8.24 Mk 13.6; Jn 4.26; 13.19

ᶠGk *him* ᵍOther ancient authorities add *the sins of each of them* ʰOr *Lord* ᶦThe most ancient authorities lack 7.53–8.11; other authorities add the passage here or after 7.36 or after 21.25 or after Luke 21.38, with variations of text; some mark the passage as doubtful. ᶦGk *according to the flesh* ᵏOther ancient authorities read *he*

your sins, for you will die in your sins unless you believe that I am he."[1] 25 They said to him, "Who are you?" Jesus said to them, "Why do I speak to you at all?[m] 26 I have much to say about you and much to condemn; but the one who sent me is true, and I declare to the world what I have heard from him." 27 They did not understand that he was speaking to them about the Father. 28 So Jesus said, "When you have lifted up the Son of Man, then you will realize that I am he,[1] and that I do nothing on my own, but I speak these things as the Father instructed me. 29 And the one who sent me is with me; he has not left me alone, for I always do what is pleasing to him." 30 As he was saying these things, many believed in him.

True Disciples

31 Then Jesus said to the Jews who had believed in him, "If you continue in my word, you are truly my disciples; 32 and you will know the truth, and the truth will make you free." 33 They answered him, "We are descendants of Abraham and have never been slaves to anyone. What do you mean by saying, 'You will be made free'?"

34 Jesus answered them, "Very truly, I tell you, everyone who commits sin is a slave to sin. 35 The slave does not have a permanent place in the household; the son has a place there forever. 36 So if the Son makes you free, you will be free indeed. 37 I know that you are descendants of Abraham; yet you look for an opportunity to kill me, because there is no place in you for my word. 38 I declare what I have seen in the Father's presence; as for you, you should do what you have heard from the Father."[n]

Jesus and Abraham

39 They answered him, "Abraham is our father." Jesus said to them, "If you were Abraham's children, you would be doing[o] what Abraham did, 40 but now you are trying to kill me, a man who has

8.26
Jn 7.28;
3.32; 15.15
8.28
Jn 3.14;
12.32; 5.19;
3.11
8.29
Jn 4.34;
5.30; 6.38
8.30
Jn 7.31;
10.42; 11.45
8.31
Jn 15.7;
2 Jn 9
8.32
Rom 8.2;
Jas 2.12
8.33
Mt 3.9
8.34
Rom 6.16;
2 Pet 2.19
8.35
Gal 4.30
8.37
vv. 39,40
8.38
Jn 5.19,30;
14.10,24
8.39
Rom 9.7;
Gal 3.7
8.40
v. 26

8.41
Isa 63.16;
64.8
8.42
1 Jn 5.1;
Jn 16.27,28;
17.8; 7.28
8.44
1 Jn 3.8;
vv. 38,41;
1 Jn 2.4;
Mt 12.34
8.47
1 Jn 4.6
8.48
v. 52;
Jn 7.20;
10.20
8.50
Jn 5.41
8.51
Jn 14.23;
15.20; 17.6;
Mt 16.28;
Heb 11.5
8.52
Jn 7.20;
14.23; 15.20;
17.6
8.53
Jn 4.12
8.54
v. 50;
Jn 16.14
8.55
Jn 7.28,29;
15.10

told you the truth that I heard from God. This is not what Abraham did. 41 You are indeed doing what your father does." They said to him, "We are not illegitimate children; we have one father, God himself." 42 Jesus said to them, "If God were your Father, you would love me, for I came from God and now I am here. I did not come on my own, but he sent me. 43 Why do you not understand what I say? It is because you cannot accept my word. 44 You are from your father the devil, and you choose to do your father's desires. He was a murderer from the beginning and does not stand in the truth, because there is no truth in him. When he lies, he speaks according to his own nature, for he is a liar and the father of lies. 45 But because I tell the truth, you do not believe me. 46 Which of you convicts me of sin? If I tell the truth, why do you not believe me? 47 Whoever is from God hears the words of God. The reason you do not hear them is that you are not from God."

48 The Jews answered him, "Are we not right in saying that you are a Samaritan and have a demon?" 49 Jesus answered, "I do not have a demon; but I honor my Father, and you dishonor me. 50 Yet I do not seek my own glory; there is one who seeks it and he is the judge. 51 Very truly, I tell you, whoever keeps my word will never see death." 52 The Jews said to him, "Now we know that you have a demon. Abraham died, and so did the prophets; yet you say, 'Whoever keeps my word will never taste death.' 53 Are you greater than our father Abraham, who died? The prophets also died. Who do you claim to be?" 54 Jesus answered, "If I glorify myself, my glory is nothing. It is my Father who glorifies me, he of whom you say, 'He is our God,' 55 though you do not know him. But

[1] Gk I am [m] Or What I have told you from the beginning [n] Other ancient authorities read you do what you have heard from your father [o] Other ancient authorities read If you are Abraham's children, then do

I know him; if I would say that I do not know him, I would be a liar like you. But I do know him and I keep his word. [56] Your ancestor Abraham rejoiced that he would see my day; he saw it and was glad." [57] Then the Jews said to him, "You are not yet fifty years old, and have you seen Abraham?"[p] [58] Jesus said to them, "Very truly, I tell you, before Abraham was, I am." [59] So they picked up stones to throw at him, but Jesus hid himself and went out of the temple.

A Man Born Blind Receives Sight

9 As he walked along, he saw a man blind from birth. [2] His disciples asked him, "Rabbi, who sinned, this man or his parents, that he was born blind?" [3] Jesus answered, "Neither this man nor his parents sinned; he was born blind so that God's works might be revealed in him. [4] We[q] must work the works of him who sent me[r] while it is day; night is coming when no one can work. [5] As long as I am in the world, I am the light of the world." [6] When he had said this, he spat on the ground and made mud with the saliva and spread the mud on the man's eyes, [7] saying to him, "Go, wash in the pool of Siloam" (which means Sent). Then he went and washed and came back able to see. [8] The neighbors and those who had seen him before as a beggar began to ask, "Is this not the man who used to sit and beg?" [9] Some were saying, "It is he." Others were saying, "No, but it is someone like him." He kept saying, "I am the man." [10] But they kept asking him, "Then how were your eyes opened?" [11] He answered, "The man called Jesus made mud, spread it on my eyes, and said to me, 'Go to Siloam and wash.' Then I went and washed and received my sight." [12] They said to him, "Where is he?" He said, "I do not know."

The Pharisees Investigate the Healing

[13] They brought to the Phari-

sees the man who had formerly been blind. [14] Now it was a sabbath day when Jesus made the mud and opened his eyes. [15] Then the Pharisees also began to ask him how he had received his sight. He said to them, "He put mud on my eyes. Then I washed, and now I see." [16] Some of the Pharisees said, "This man is not from God, for he does not observe the sabbath." But others said, "How can a man who is a sinner perform such signs?" And they were divided. [17] So they said again to the blind man, "What do you say about him? It was your eyes he opened." He said, "He is a prophet."

18 The Jews did not believe that he had been blind and had received his sight until they called the parents of the man who had received his sight [19] and asked them, "Is this your son, who you say was born blind? How then does he now see?" [20] His parents answered, "We know that this is our son, and that he was born blind; [21] but we do not know how it is that now he sees, nor do we know who opened his eyes. Ask him; he is of age. He will speak for himself." [22] His parents said this because they were afraid of the Jews; for the Jews had already agreed that anyone who confessed Jesus[s] to be the Messiah[t] would be put out of the synagogue. [23] Therefore his parents said, "He is of age; ask him."

24 So for the second time they called the man who had been blind, and they said to him, "Give glory to God! We know that this man is a sinner." [25] He answered, "I do not know whether he is a sinner. One thing I do know, that though I was blind, now I see." [26] They said to him, "What did he do to you? How did he open your eyes?" [27] He answered them, "I have told you already, and you would not listen. Why do you want to hear it again? Do you also want to become his

8.56
Mt 13.17;
Heb 11.13
8.58
Jn 1.1; 17.5,
24; Rev 1.8
8.59
Jn 10.31;
11.8; 12.36
9.2
v. 34;
Lk 13.2;
Ex 20.5;
Ezek 18.20
9.3
Jn 11.4
9.4
Jn 11.9;
12.35
9.5
Jn 1.4; 8.12;
12.46
9.6
Mk 7.33;
8.23
9.7
v. 11;
Lk 13.4;
Jn 11.37
9.11
v. 7

9.14
Jn 5.9
9.15
v. 10
9.16
Mt 12.2;
Jn 7.43;
10.19
9.17
v. 15;
Mt 21.11
9.18
v. 22
9.22
Jn 7.13;
12.42; v. 34;
Lk 6.22
9.23
v. 21
9.24
Josh 7.19;
1 Sam 6.5;
v. 16
9.27
v. 15;
Jn 5.25

p Other ancient authorities read *has Abraham seen you?* q Other ancient authorities read *I* r Other ancient authorities read *us* s Gk *him* t Or *the Christ*

disciples?" 28 Then they reviled him, saying, "You are his disciple, but we are disciples of Moses. 29 We know that God has spoken to Moses, but as for this man, we do not know where he comes from." 30 The man answered, "Here is an astonishing thing! You do not know where he comes from, and yet he opened my eyes. 31 We know that God does not listen to sinners, but he does listen to one who worships him and obeys his will. 32 Never since the world began has it been heard that anyone opened the eyes of a person born blind. 33 If this man were not from God, he could do nothing." 34 They answered him, "You were born entirely in sins, and are you trying to teach us?" And they drove him out.

Spiritual Blindness

35 Jesus heard that they had driven him out, and when he found him, he said, "Do you believe in the Son of Man?"u 36 He answered, "And who is he, sir?v Tell me, so that I may believe in him." 37 Jesus said to him, "You have seen him, and the one speaking with you is he." 38 He said, "Lord,v I believe." And he worshiped him. 39 Jesus said, "I came into this world for judgment so that those who do not see may see, and those who do see may become blind." 40 Some of the Pharisees near him heard this and said to him, "Surely we are not blind, are we?" 41 Jesus said to them, "If you were blind, you would not have sin. But now that you say, 'We see,' your sin remains.

Jesus the Good Shepherd

10 "Very truly, I tell you, anyone who does not enter the sheepfold by the gate but climbs in by another way is a thief and a bandit. 2 The one who enters by the gate is the shepherd of the sheep. 3 The gatekeeper opens the gate for him, and the sheep hear his voice. He calls his own sheep by name and leads them out. 4 When he has brought out all his own, he goes ahead of them, and the sheep fol-

low him because they know his voice. 5 They will not follow a stranger, but they will run from him because they do not know the voice of strangers." 6 Jesus used this figure of speech with them, but they did not understand what he was saying to them.

7 So again Jesus said to them, "Very truly, I tell you, I am the gate for the sheep. 8 All who came before me are thieves and bandits; but the sheep did not listen to them. 9 I am the gate. Whoever enters by me will be saved, and will come in and go out and find pasture. 10 The thief comes only to steal and kill and destroy. I came that they may have life, and have it abundantly.

11 "I am the good shepherd. The good shepherd lays down his life for the sheep. 12 The hired hand, who is not the shepherd and does not own the sheep, sees the wolf coming and leaves the sheep and runs away—and the wolf snatches them and scatters them. 13 The hired hand runs away because a hired hand does not care for the sheep. 14 I am the good shepherd. I know my own and my own know me, 15 just as the Father knows me and I know the Father. And I lay down my life for the sheep. 16 I have other sheep that do not belong to this fold. I must bring them also, and they will listen to my voice. So there will be one flock, one shepherd. 17 For this reason the Father loves me, because I lay down my life in order to take it up again. 18 No one takesw it from me, but I lay it down of my own accord. I have power to lay it down, and I have power to take it up again. I have received this command from my Father."

19 Again the Jews were divided because of these words. 20 Many of them were saying, "He has a de-

Cross references (center column)

9.28 Jn 5.45
9.29 Jn 8.14
9.31 Job 27.8,9; Ps 34.15; 66.18; Prov 15.29; 28.9; Isa 1.15; Jer 11.11; Zech 7.13
9.33 v. 16
9.34 v. 2
9.35 Mt 14.33; 16.16; Mk 1.1; Jn 10.36
9.36 Rom 10.14
9.37 Jn 4.26
9.38 Mt 28.9
9.39 Jn 5.22,27; 3.19; Mt 13.13; 15.14
9.40 Rom 2.19
9.41 Jn 15.22,24
10.2 Mk 6.34; vv. 11,12
10.3 vv. 16,27,9
10.4 v. 3
10.6 Jn 16.25
10.7 Jer 23.1,2; Ezek 34.2
10.10 Jn 5.40
10.11 Isa 40.11; Ezek 34.11-16; 23; Heb 13.20; 1 Pet 5.4; Rev 7.17; 1 Jn 3.16; Jn 15.13
10.12 Zech 11.16, 17
10.14 vv. 11,27
10.15 Mt 11.27
10.16 Isa 56.8; Jn 11.52; Eph 2.14; 1 Pet 2.25
10.17 Isa 53.7,8, 12

10.18 Jn 2.19; 15.10; Heb 5.8 10.19 Jn 7.43; 9.16 10.20 Jn 7.20; 8.48; Mk 3.21

u Other ancient authorities read *the Son of God*
v *Sir* and *Lord* translate the same Greek word
w Other ancient authorities read *has taken*

mon and is out of his mind. Why listen to him?" [21] Others were saying, "These are not the words of one who has a demon. Can a demon open the eyes of the blind?"

Jesus Is Rejected by the Jews

22 At that time the festival of the Dedication took place in Jerusalem. It was winter, [23] and Jesus was walking in the temple, in the portico of Solomon. [24] So the Jews gathered around him and said to him, "How long will you keep us in suspense? If you are the Messiah,[x] tell us plainly." [25] Jesus answered, "I have told you, and you do not believe. The works that I do in my Father's name testify to me; [26] but you do not believe, because you do not belong to my sheep. [27] My sheep hear my voice. I know them, and they follow me. [28] I give them eternal life, and they will never perish. No one will snatch them out of my hand. [29] What my Father has given me is greater than all else, and no one can snatch it out of the Father's hand.[y] [30] The Father and I are one."

31 The Jews took up stones again to stone him. [32] Jesus replied, "I have shown you many good works from the Father. For which of these are you going to stone me?" [33] The Jews answered, "It is not for a good work that we are going to stone you, but for blasphemy, because you, though only a human being, are making yourself God." [34] Jesus answered, "Is it not written in your law,[z] 'I said, you are gods'? [35] If those to whom the word of God came were called 'gods'—and the scripture cannot be annulled— [36] can you say that the one whom the Father has sanctified and sent into the world is blaspheming because I said, 'I am God's Son'? [37] If I am not doing the works of my Father, then do not believe me. [38] But if I do them, even though you do not believe me, believe the works, so that you may know and understand[a] that the Father is in me and I am in the Father." [39] Then they tried to arrest

him again, but he escaped from their hands.

40 He went away again across the Jordan to the place where John had been baptizing earlier, and he remained there. [41] Many came to him, and they were saying, "John performed no sign, but everything that John said about this man was true." [42] And many believed in him there.

The Death of Lazarus

11 Now a certain man was ill, Lazarus of Bethany, the village of Mary and her sister Martha. [2] Mary was the one who anointed the Lord with perfume and wiped his feet with her hair; her brother Lazarus was ill. [3] So the sisters sent a message to Jesus,[b] "Lord, he whom you love is ill." [4] But when Jesus heard it, he said, "This illness does not lead to death; rather it is for God's glory, so that the Son of God may be glorified through it." [5] Accordingly, though Jesus loved Martha and her sister and Lazarus, [6] after having heard that Lazarus[c] was ill, he stayed two days longer in the place where he was.

7 Then after this he said to the disciples, "Let us go to Judea again." [8] The disciples said to him, "Rabbi, the Jews were just now trying to stone you, and are you going there again?" [9] Jesus answered, "Are there not twelve hours of daylight? Those who walk during the day do not stumble, because they see the light of this world. [10] But those who walk at night stumble, because the light is not in them." [11] After saying this, he told them, "Our friend Lazarus has fallen asleep, but I am going there to awaken him." [12] The disciples said to him, "Lord, if he has fallen asleep, he will be all right." [13] Jesus, however, had been speaking about his death, but they

Cross-references (center column)

10.21 Jn 9.32,33; Ex 4.11
10.23 Acts 3.11; 5.12
10.25 Jn 5.36
10.26 Jn 8.47
10.27 vv. 4,14
10.28 Jn 17.2,3; 1 Jn 2.25; Jn 6.37,39
10.29 Jn 14.28; 17.2,6ff
10.30 Jn 17.21ff
10.31 Jn 8.59
10.33 Jn 5.18
10.34 Ps 82.6
10.36 Jn 6.69; 3.17; Jn 5.17,18
10.37 Jn 15.24
10.38 Jn 14.10,11; 17.21
10.39 Jn 7.30; 8.59

10.40 Jn 1.28
10.41 Jn 2.11; 3.30
10.42 Jn 7.31; 11.45
11.1 Mk 11.1; Lk 10.38
11.2 Mk 14.3; Lk 7.38; Jn 12.3
11.3 Lk 7.13
11.4 v. 40; Jn 9.3
11.7 Jn 10.40
11.8 Jn 10.31
11.9 Lk 13.33; Jn 9.4; 12.35
11.11 v. 3; Mt 27.52; Mk 5.39; Acts 7.60
11.13 Mt 9.24; Lk 8.52

x Or the Christ y Other ancient authorities read My Father who has given them to me is greater than all, and no one can snatch them out of the Father's hand z Other ancient authorities read in the law a Other ancient authorities lack and understand; others read and believe b Gk him c Gk he

thought that he was referring merely to sleep. [14] Then Jesus told them plainly, "Lazarus is dead. [15] For your sake I am glad I was not there, so that you may believe. But let us go to him." [16] Thomas, who was called the Twin,[d] said to his fellow disciples, "Let us also go, that we may die with him."

Jesus the Resurrection and the Life

17 When Jesus arrived, he found that Lazarus[e] had already been in the tomb four days. [18] Now Bethany was near Jerusalem, some two miles[f] away, [19] and many of the Jews had come to Martha and Mary to console them about their brother. [20] When Martha heard that Jesus was coming, she went and met him, while Mary stayed at home. [21] Martha said to Jesus, "Lord, if you had been here, my brother would not have died. [22] But even now I know that God will give you whatever you ask of him." [23] Jesus said to her, "Your brother will rise again." [24] Martha said to him, "I know that he will rise again in the resurrection on the last day." [25] Jesus said to her, "I am the resurrection and the life.[g] Those who believe in me, even though they die, will live, [26] and everyone who lives and believes in me will never die. Do you believe this?" [27] She said to him, "Yes, Lord, I believe that you are the Messiah,[h] the Son of God, the one coming into the world."

Jesus Weeps

28 When she had said this, she went back and called her sister Mary, and told her privately, "The Teacher is here and is calling for you." [29] And when she heard it, she got up quickly and went to him. [30] Now Jesus had not yet come to the village, but was still at the place where Martha had met him. [31] The Jews who were with her in the house, consoling her, saw Mary get up quickly and go out. They followed her because they thought that she was going to the tomb to

weep there. [32] When Mary came where Jesus was and saw him, she knelt at his feet and said to him, "Lord, if you had been here, my brother would not have died." [33] When Jesus saw her weeping, and the Jews who came with her also weeping, he was greatly disturbed in spirit and deeply moved. [34] He said, "Where have you laid him?" They said to him, "Lord, come and see." [35] Jesus began to weep. [36] So the Jews said, "See how he loved him!" [37] But some of them said, "Could not he who opened the eyes of the blind man have kept this man from dying?"

Jesus Raises Lazarus to Life

38 Then Jesus, again greatly disturbed, came to the tomb. It was a cave, and a stone was lying against it. [39] Jesus said, "Take away the stone." Martha, the sister of the dead man, said to him, "Lord, already there is a stench because he has been dead four days." [40] Jesus said to her, "Did I not tell you that if you believed, you would see the glory of God?" [41] So they took away the stone. And Jesus looked upward and said, "Father, I thank you for having heard me. [42] I knew that you always hear me, but I have said this for the sake of the crowd standing here, so that they may believe that you sent me." [43] When he had said this, he cried with a loud voice, "Lazarus, come out!" [44] The dead man came out, his hands and feet bound with strips of cloth, and his face wrapped in a cloth. Jesus said to them, "Unbind him, and let him go."

The Plot to Kill Jesus

45 Many of the Jews therefore, who had come with Mary and had seen what Jesus did, believed in him. [46] But some of them went to the Pharisees and told them what he had done. [47] So the chief priests and the Pharisees called a meeting

11.16
Mt 10.3;
Jn 20.24-28
11.17
v. 39
11.18
v. 1
11.19
Job 2.11
11.21
vv. 2,32
11.22
Jn 9.31
11.24
Dan 12.2;
Jn 5.28,29;
Acts 24.15
11.25
Jn 1.4; 5.26;
14.6; 3.36
11.26
Jn 6.47;
8.51
11.27
Mt 16.16;
Jn 6.14
11.28
Mt 26.18;
Lk 22.11
11.30
v. 20
11.31
v. 19

11.32
v. 21
11.33
v. 38;
Jn 12.27;
13.21
11.35
Lk 19.41
11.37
Jn 9.6,7
11.38
v. 33;
Mt 27.60;
Mk 15.46;
Lk 24.2;
Jn 20.1
11.39
v. 17
11.40
vv. 4,23
11.41
Jn 17.1;
Mt 11.25
11.42
Jn 12.30;
3.17
11.44
Jn 19.40;
20.7
11.45
v. 19;
Jn 2.23
11.47
v. 57;
Mt 26.3

d Gk Didymus e Gk he f Gk fifteen
stadia g Other ancient authorities lack and
the life h Or the Christ

of the council, and said, "What are we to do? This man is performing many signs. ⁴⁸If we let him go on like this, everyone will believe in him, and the Romans will come and destroy both our holy placeⁱ and our nation." ⁴⁹But one of them, Caiaphas, who was high priest that year, said to them, "You know nothing at all! ⁵⁰You do not understand that it is better for you to have one man die for the people than to have the whole nation destroyed." ⁵¹He did not say this on his own, but being high priest that year he prophesied that Jesus was about to die for the nation, ⁵²and not for the nation only, but to gather into one the dispersed children of God. ⁵³So from that day on they planned to put him to death.

54 Jesus therefore no longer walked about openly among the Jews, but went from there to a town called Ephraim in the region near the wilderness; and he remained there with the disciples.

55 Now the Passover of the Jews was near, and many went up from the country to Jerusalem before the Passover to purify themselves. ⁵⁶They were looking for Jesus and were asking one another as they stood in the temple, "What do you think? Surely he will not come to the festival, will he?" ⁵⁷Now the chief priests and the Pharisees had given orders that anyone who knew where Jesusⁱ was should let them know, so that they might arrest him.

Mary Anoints Jesus

12 Six days before the Passover Jesus came to Bethany, the home of Lazarus, whom he had raised from the dead. ²There they gave a dinner for him. Martha served, and Lazarus was one of those at the table with him. ³Mary took a pound of costly perfume made of pure nard, anointed Jesus' feet, and wiped themᵏ with her hair. The house was filled with the fragrance of the perfume. ⁴But Judas Iscariot, one of his disciples (the one who was about to betray

11.49
Mt 26.3;
Jn 18.13,14
11.50
Jn 18.14
11.52
Isa 49.6;
Jn 10.16
11.53
Mt 26.4
11.54
Jn 7.1;
2 Chr 13.19
11.55
Mt 26.1,2;
Mk 14.1;
Lk 22.1;
Jn 12.1;
Num 9.10;
2 Chr 30.17,
18
11.56
Jn 7.11
12.1
Lk 7.37-39;
Jn 11.55
12.2
Lk 10.38
12.3
Jn 11.2;
Mk 14.3
12.4
Jn 6.71

12.6
Jn 13.29;
Lk 8.3
12.7
Jn 19.40
12.8
Mt 26.11;
Mk 14.7
12.9
Mk 12.37;
Mt 11.43,44
12.11
v. 18;
Jn 11.45
12.13
Ps 118.25,
26; Jn 1.49
12.15
Zech 9.9
12.16
Mk 9.32;
Jn 2.22;
14.26; 7.39

him), said, ⁵"Why was this perfume not sold for three hundred denariiˡ and the money given to the poor?" ⁶(He said this not because he cared about the poor, but because he was a thief; he kept the common purse and used to steal what was put into it.) ⁷Jesus said, "Leave her alone. She bought itᵐ so that she might keep it for the day of my burial. ⁸You always have the poor with you, but you do not always have me."

The Plot to Kill Lazarus

9 When the great crowd of the Jews learned that he was there, they came not only because of Jesus but also to see Lazarus, whom he had raised from the dead. ¹⁰So the chief priests planned to put Lazarus to death as well, ¹¹since it was on account of him that many of the Jews were deserting and were believing in Jesus.

Jesus' Triumphal Entry into Jerusalem

12 The next day the great crowd that had come to the festival heard that Jesus was coming to Jerusalem. ¹³So they took branches of palm trees and went out to meet him, shouting,

"Hosanna!
Blessed is the one who
 comes in the name of
 the Lord—
the King of Israel!"

¹⁴Jesus found a young donkey and sat on it; as it is written:
¹⁵ "Do not be afraid, daughter
 of Zion.
Look, your king is coming,
 sitting on a donkey's colt!"

¹⁶His disciples did not understand these things at first; but when Jesus was glorified, then they remembered that these things had been written of him and had been done to him. ¹⁷So the crowd that had been with him when he called Lazarus out of the tomb and raised him from the dead continued to

ⁱOr *our temple*; Greek *our place* ⁱGk *he*
ᵏGk *his feet* ˡThree hundred denarii
would be nearly a year's wages for a laborer
ᵐGk lacks *She bought it*

testify.ⁿ ¹⁸It was also because they heard that he had performed this sign that the crowd went to meet him. ¹⁹The Pharisees then said to one another, "You see, you can do nothing. Look, the world has gone after him!"

Some Greeks Wish to See Jesus

20 Now among those who went up to worship at the festival were some Greeks. ²¹They came to Philip, who was from Bethsaida in Galilee, and said to him, "Sir, we wish to see Jesus." ²²Philip went and told Andrew; then Andrew and Philip went and told Jesus. ²³Jesus answered them, "The hour has come for the Son of Man to be glorified. ²⁴Very truly, I tell you, unless a grain of wheat falls into the earth and dies, it remains just a single grain; but if it dies, it bears much fruit. ²⁵Those who love their life lose it, and those who hate their life in this world will keep it for eternal life. ²⁶Whoever serves me must follow me, and where I am, there will my servant be also. Whoever serves me, the Father will honor.

Jesus Speaks about His Death

27 "Now my soul is troubled. And what should I say—'Father, save me from this hour'? No, it is for this reason that I have come to this hour. ²⁸Father, glorify your name." Then a voice came from heaven, "I have glorified it, and I will glorify it again." ²⁹The crowd standing there heard it and said that it was thunder. Others said, "An angel has spoken to him." ³⁰Jesus answered, "This voice has come for your sake, not for mine. ³¹Now is the judgment of this world; now the ruler of this world will be driven out. ³²And I, when I am lifted up from the earth, will draw all peopleᵒ to myself." ³³He said this to indicate the kind of death he was to die. ³⁴The crowd answered him, "We have heard from the law that the Messiahᵖ remains forever. How can you say that the Son of Man must be lifted up? Who is this Son of Man?" ³⁵Jesus said to them, "The light is with you for a little longer. Walk while you have the light, so that the darkness may not overtake you. If you walk in the darkness, you do not know where you are going. ³⁶While you have the light, believe in the light, so that you may become children of light."

The Unbelief of the People

After Jesus had said this, he departed and hid from them. ³⁷Although he had performed so many signs in their presence, they did not believe in him. ³⁸This was to fulfill the word spoken by the prophet Isaiah:

"Lord, who has believed our message,
and to whom has the arm of the Lord been revealed?"

³⁹And so they could not believe, because Isaiah also said,

⁴⁰ "He has blinded their eyes and hardened their heart,
so that they might not look with their eyes,
and understand with their heart and turn—
and I would heal them."

⁴¹Isaiah said this because�q he saw his glory and spoke about him. ⁴²Nevertheless many, even of the authorities, believed in him. But because of the Pharisees they did not confess it, for fear that they would be put out of the synagogue; ⁴³for they loved human glory more than the glory that comes from God.

Summary of Jesus' Teaching

44 Then Jesus cried aloud: "Whoever believes in me believes not in me but in him who sent me. ⁴⁵And whoever sees me sees him who sent me. ⁴⁶I have come as light

12.18 v. 11
12.19 Jn 11.47,48
12.20 Jn 7.35; Acts 11.20
12.21 Jn 1.44
12.23 Jn 13.1,32; 17.1; Mk 14.35, 41
12.24 1 Cor 15.36
12.25 Mt 10.39; Mk 8.35; Lk 9.24; 14.26
12.26 Jn 14.3; 17.24; 1 Thes 4.17
12.27 Mt 26.38, 39; Mk 14.34; Jn 11.33
12.28 Mt 3.17; 17.5; Mk 1.11; 9.7; Lk 3.22; 9.35
12.30 Jn 11.42
12.31 Jn 16.11; 14.30; 2 Cor 4.4; Eph 2.2
12.32 Jn 3.14; 8.28; 6.44
12.33 Jn 18.32
12.34 Ps 110.4; Isa 9.7; Ezek 37.25; Dan 7.14
12.35 Eph 5.8
12.36 Lk 16.8; Jn 8.59
12.37 Jn 2.11
12.38 Isa 53.1; Rom 10.16
12.40 Isa 6.9,10; Mt 13.14
12.41 Isa 6.1
12.42 Jn 7.48,13; 9.22
12.43 Jn 5.44
12.44 Mt 10.40;

Jn 5.24 **12.45** Jn 14.9 **12.46** Jn 1.4; 3.19; 8.12; 9.5

ⁿ Other ancient authorities read *with him began to testify that he had called. . .from the dead* ᵒ Other ancient authorities read *all things* ᵖ Or *the Christ* q Other ancient witnesses read *when*

into the world, so that everyone who believes in me should not remain in the darkness. 47 I do not judge anyone who hears my words and does not keep them, for I came not to judge the world, but to save the world. 48 The one who rejects me and does not receive my word has a judge; on the last day the word that I have spoken will serve as judge, 49 for I have not spoken on my own, but the Father who sent me has himself given me a commandment about what to say and what to speak. 50 And I know that his commandment is eternal life. What I speak, therefore, I speak just as the Father has told me."

Jesus Washes the Disciples' Feet

13 Now before the festival of the Passover, Jesus knew that his hour had come to depart from this world and go to the Father. Having loved his own who were in the world, he loved them to the end. 2 The devil had already put it into the heart of Judas son of Simon Iscariot to betray him. And during supper 3 Jesus, knowing that the Father had given all things into his hands, and that he had come from God and was going to God, 4 got up from the table,r took off his outer robe, and tied a towel around himself. 5 Then he poured water into a basin and began to wash the disciples' feet and to wipe them with the towel that was tied around him. 6 He came to Simon Peter, who said to him, "Lord, are you going to wash my feet?" 7 Jesus answered, "You do not know now what I am doing, but later you will understand." 8 Peter said to him, "You will never wash my feet." Jesus answered, "Unless I wash you, you have no share with me." 9 Simon Peter said to him, "Lord, not my feet only but also my hands and my head!" 10 Jesus said to him, "One who has bathed does not need to wash, except for the feet,s but is entirely clean. And yout are clean, though not all of you." 11 For he knew who was to betray him; for

this reason he said, "Not all of you are clean."

12 After he had washed their feet, had put on his robe, and had returned to the table, he said to them, "Do you know what I have done to you? 13 You call me Teacher and Lord—and you are right, for that is what I am. 14 So if I, your Lord and Teacher, have washed your feet, you also ought to wash one another's feet. 15 For I have set you an example, that you also should do as I have done to you. 16 Very truly, I tell you, servantsu are not greater than their master, nor are messengers greater than the one who sent them. 17 If you know these things, you are blessed if you do them. 18 I am not speaking of all of you; I know whom I have chosen. But it is to fulfill the scripture, 'The one who ate my breadv has lifted his heel against me.' 19 I tell you this now, before it occurs, so that when it does occur, you may believe that I am he.w 20 Very truly, I tell you, whoever receives one whom I send receives me; and whoever receives me receives him who sent me."

Jesus Foretells His Betrayal

21 After saying this Jesus was troubled in spirit, and declared, "Very truly, I tell you, one of you will betray me." 22 The disciples looked at one another, uncertain of whom he was speaking. 23 One of his disciples—the one whom Jesus loved—was reclining next to him; 24 Simon Peter therefore motioned to him to ask Jesus of whom he was speaking. 25 So while reclining next to Jesus, he asked him, "Lord, who is it?" 26 Jesus answered, "It is the one to whom I give this piece of bread when I have dipped it in the dish."x So when he had dipped the piece of bread, he gave it to Judas

12.47 Jn 3.17
12.48 Lk 10.16; Mt 10.15
12.49 Jn 14.31
12.50 Jn 8.28
13.1 Jn 11.55; 12.23; 16.28
13.2 Jn 6.70,71; Mk 14.10
13.3 Mt 28.18; Heb 2.8; Jn 8.42; 16.28
13.4 Lk 22.27
13.5 Lk 7.44
13.8 Jn 3.5; 9.7
13.10 Jn 15.3
13.11 Jn 6.64

13.13 Lk 6.46; Phil 2.11
13.14 1 Pet 5.5
13.15 1 Pet 2.21
13.16 Mt 10.24; Lk 6.40; Jn 15.20
13.17 Lk 11.28; Jas 1.25
13.18 Ps 41.9; Mt 26.23
13.19 Jn 14.29; 16.4; 8.24
13.20 Mt 10.40; Lk 10.16
13.21 Jn 12.27
13.23 Jn 19.26; 20.2; 21.7,20
13.25 Jn 21.20
13.26 Jn 6.71

r Gk *from supper* s Other ancient authorities lack *except for the feet*
t The Greek word for *you* here is plural
u Gk *slaves* v Other ancient authorities read *ate bread with me* w Gk *I am*
x Gk *dipped it*

son of Simon Iscariot.ʸ ²⁷After he received the piece of bread,ᶻ Satan entered into him. Jesus said to him, "Do quickly what you are going to do." ²⁸Now no one at the table knew why he said this to him. ²⁹Some thought that, because Judas had the common purse, Jesus was telling him, "Buy what we need for the festival"; or, that he should give something to the poor. ³⁰So, after receiving the piece of bread, he immediately went out. And it was night.

The New Commandment

31 When he had gone out, Jesus said, "Now the Son of Man has been glorified, and God has been glorified in him. ³²If God has been glorified in him,ᵃ God will also glorify him in himself and will glorify him at once. ³³Little children, I am with you only a little longer. You will look for me; and as I said to the Jews so now I say to you, 'Where I am going, you cannot come.' ³⁴I give you a new commandment, that you love one another. Just as I have loved you, you also should love one another. ³⁵By this everyone will know that you are my disciples, if you have love for one another."

Jesus Foretells Peter's Denial

36 Simon Peter said to him, "Lord, where are you going?" Jesus answered, "Where I am going, you cannot follow me now; but you will follow afterward." ³⁷Peter said to him, "Lord, why can I not follow you now? I will lay down my life for you." ³⁸Jesus answered, "Will you lay down your life for me? Very truly, I tell you, before the cock crows, you will have denied me three times.

Jesus the Way to the Father

14 "Do not let your hearts be troubled. Believeᵇ in God, believe also in me. ²In my Father's house there are many dwelling places. If it were not so, would I have told you that I go to prepare a place for you?ᶜ ³And if I go and

prepare a place for you, I will come again and will take you to myself, so that where I am, there you may be also. ⁴And you know the way to the place where I am going."ᵈ ⁵Thomas said to him, "Lord, we do not know where you are going. How can we know the way?" ⁶Jesus said to him, "I am the way, and the truth, and the life. No one comes to the Father except through me. ⁷If you know me, you will knowᵉ my Father also. From now on you do know him and have seen him."

8 Philip said to him, "Lord, show us the Father, and we will be satisfied." ⁹Jesus said to him, "Have I been with you all this time, Philip, and you still do not know me? Whoever has seen me has seen the Father. How can you say, 'Show us the Father'? ¹⁰Do you not believe that I am in the Father and the Father is in me? The words that I say to you I do not speak on my own; but the Father who dwells in me does his works. ¹¹Believe me that I am in the Father and the Father is in me; but if you do not, then believe me because of the works themselves. ¹²"Very truly, I tell you, the one who believes in me will also do the works that I do and, in fact, will do greater works than these, because I am going to the Father. ¹³I will do whatever you ask in my name, so that the Father may be glorified in the Son. ¹⁴If in my name you ask meᶠ for anything, I will do it.

The Promise of the Holy Spirit

15 "If you love me, you will keepᵍ my commandments. ¹⁶And I will ask the Father, and he will give you another Advocate,ʰ to be with

Cross references (center column)

13.27
Lk 22.3
13.29
Jn 12.5,6
13.31
Jn 7.39;
14.13;
1 Pet 4.11
13.32
Jn 17.1
13.33
Jn 7.33,34
13.34
Lev 19.18;
Jn 15.12;
1 Pet 1.22;
1 Jn 2.7;
3.11; 4.10
13.35
1 Jn 3.14;
4.20
13.36
Jn 21.18;
2 Pet 1.14
13.37
Mt 26.33-35;
Mk 14.29-31;
Lk 22.33,34
13.38
Jn 18.27
14.1
Jn 16.23,24
14.2
Jn 13.33
14.3
Jn 12.26

14.5
Jn 11.16
14.6
Jn 10.9;
8.32; 1.4;
11.25
14.7
Jn 8.19
14.9
Jn 12.45
14.10
Jn 10.38;
5.19; 12.49
14.11
Jn 5.36;
10.38
14.12
Mt 21.21;
Lk 10.17
14.13
Jn 15.7,16;
16.23;
Jas 1.5
14.15
Jn 15.10;
1 Jn 5.3
14.16
Jn 15.26;
16.7;
1 Jn 2.1

Footnotes

ʸ Other ancient authorities read *Judas Iscariot son of Simon*; others, *Judas son of Simon from Karyot (Kerioth)*　ᶻ Gk *After the piece of bread*　ᵃ Other ancient authorities lack *If God has been glorified in him*　ᵇ Or *You believe*　ᶜ Or *If it were not so, I would have told you; for I go to prepare a place for you*　ᵈ Other ancient authorities read *Where I am going you know, and the way you know*　ᵉ Other ancient authorities read *If you had known me, you would have known*　ᶠ Other ancient authorities lack *me*　ᵍ Other ancient authorities read *me, keep*　ʰ Or *Helper*

you forever. [17] This is the Spirit of truth, whom the world cannot receive, because it neither sees him nor knows him. You know him, because he abides with you, and he will be in[i] you.

18 "I will not leave you orphaned; I am coming to you. [19] In a little while the world will no longer see me, but you will see me; because I live, you also will live. [20] On that day you will know that I am in my Father, and you in me, and I in you. [21] They who have my commandments and keep them are those who love me; and those who love me will be loved by my Father, and I will love them and reveal myself to them." [22] Judas (not Iscariot) said to him, "Lord, how is it that you will reveal yourself to us, and not to the world?" [23] Jesus answered him, "Those who love me will keep my word, and my Father will love them, and we will come to them and make our home with them. [24] Whoever does not love me does not keep my words; and the word that you hear is not mine, but is from the Father who sent me.

25 "I have said these things to you while I am still with you. [26] But the Advocate,[j] the Holy Spirit, whom the Father will send in my name, will teach you everything, and remind you of all that I have said to you. [27] Peace I leave with you; my peace I give to you. I do not give to you as the world gives. Do not let your hearts be troubled, and do not let them be afraid. [28] You heard me say to you, 'I am going away, and I am coming to you.' If you loved me, you would rejoice that I am going to the Father, because the Father is greater than I. [29] And now I have told you this before it occurs, so that when it does occur, you may believe. [30] I will no longer talk much with you, for the ruler of this world is coming. He has no power over me; [31] but I do as the Father has commanded me, so that the world may know that I love the Father. Rise, let us be on our way.

14.17
Jn 16.13;
1 Jn 4.6;
1 Cor 2.14
14.18
vv. 3,28
14.19
Jn 7.33;
16.16; 6.57
14.20
Jn 10.38
14.21
1 Jn 2.5;
5.3
14.22
Acts 1.13;
10.14,41
14.23
1 Jn 2.24;
Rev 3.20
14.24
Jn 7.16;
8.28; 12.49
14.26
Jn 15.26;
16.7,13;
1 Jn 2.20,
27
14.27
Jn 16.33;
Phil 4.7;
Col 3.15
14.28
vv. 3,18;
Jn 5.18;
10.29,30;
Phil 2.6
14.29
Jn 13.19
14.30
Jn 12.31
14.31
Jn 10.18;
12.49; 18.1

15.1
Isa 5.1-7;
Ezek 19.10
15.3
Jn 13.10;
17.17;
Eph 5.26
15.4
1 Jn 2.6
15.5
v. 16
15.6
v. 2
15.7
Jn 14.13;
16.23
15.8
Mt 5.16;
Jn 8.31
15.10
Jn 14.15,23
15.11
Jn 17.13
15.12
Jn 13.34
15.13
Rom 5.7,8;
Jn 10.11
15.14
Mt 12.50
15.15
Jn 8.26

Jesus the True Vine

15 "I am the true vine, and my Father is the vinegrower. [2] He removes every branch in me that bears no fruit. Every branch that bears fruit he prunes[k] to make it bear more fruit. [3] You have already been cleansed[k] by the word that I have spoken to you. [4] Abide in me as I abide in you. Just as the branch cannot bear fruit by itself unless it abides in the vine, neither can you unless you abide in me. [5] I am the vine, you are the branches. Those who abide in me and I in them bear much fruit, because apart from me you can do nothing. [6] Whoever does not abide in me is thrown away like a branch and withers; such branches are gathered, thrown into the fire, and burned. [7] If you abide in me, and my words abide in you, ask for whatever you wish, and it will be done for you. [8] My Father is glorified by this, that you bear much fruit and become[l] my disciples. [9] As the Father has loved me, so I have loved you; abide in my love. [10] If you keep my commandments, you will abide in my love, just as I have kept my Father's commandments and abide in his love. [11] I have said these things to you so that my joy may be in you, and that your joy may be complete.

12 "This is my commandment, that you love one another as I have loved you. [13] No one has greater love than this, to lay down one's life for one's friends. [14] You are my friends if you do what I command you. [15] I do not call you servants[m] any longer, because the servant[n] does not know what the master is doing; but I have called you friends, because I have made known to you everything that I have heard from my Father. [16] You did not choose me but I chose you. And I appointed you to go and bear fruit, fruit that will last, so that the Father will give you whatever you

15.16 Jn 6.70; 14.13

[i] Or *among* [j] Or *Helper* [k] The same Greek root refers to pruning and cleansing [l] Or *be* [m] Gk *slaves* [n] Gk *slave*

ask him in my name. [17] I am giving you these commands so that you may love one another.

The World's Hatred

18 "If the world hates you, be aware that it hated me before it hated you. [19] If you belonged to the world,[o] the world would love you as its own. Because you do not belong to the world, but I have chosen you out of the world — therefore the world hates you. [20] Remember the word that I said to you, 'Servants[p] are not greater than their master.' If they persecuted me, they will persecute you; if they kept my word, they will keep yours also. [21] But they will do all these things to you on account of my name, because they do not know him who sent me. [22] If I had not come and spoken to them, they would not have sin; but now they have no excuse for their sin. [23] Whoever hates me hates my Father also. [24] If I had not done among them the works that no one else did, they would not have sin. But now they have seen and hated both me and my Father. [25] It was to fulfill the word that is written in their law, 'They hated me without a cause.'

26 "When the Advocate[q] comes, whom I will send to you from the Father, the Spirit of truth who comes from the Father, he will testify on my behalf. [27] You also are to testify because you have been with me from the beginning.

16 "I have said these things to you to keep you from stumbling. [2] They will put you out of the synagogues. Indeed, an hour is coming when those who kill you will think that by doing so they are offering worship to God. [3] And they will do this because they have not known the Father or me. [4] But I have said these things to you so that when their hour comes you may remember that I told you about them.

The Work of the Spirit

"I did not say these things to you from the beginning, because I was

with you. [5] But now I am going to him who sent me; yet none of you asks me, 'Where are you going?' [6] But because I have said these things to you, sorrow has filled your hearts. [7] Nevertheless I tell you the truth: it is to your advantage that I go away, for if I do not go away, the Advocate[q] will not come to you; but if I go, I will send him to you. [8] And when he comes, he will prove the world wrong about[r] sin and righteousness and judgment: [9] about sin, because they do not believe in me; [10] about righteousness, because I am going to the Father and you will see me no longer; [11] about judgment, because the ruler of this world has been condemned.

12 "I still have many things to say to you, but you cannot bear them now. [13] When the Spirit of truth comes, he will guide you into all the truth; for he will not speak on his own, but will speak whatever he hears, and he will declare to you the things that are to come. [14] He will glorify me, because he will take what is mine and declare it to you. [15] All that the Father has is mine. For this reason I said that he will take what is mine and declare it to you.

Sorrow Will Turn into Joy

16 "A little while, and you will no longer see me, and again a little while, and you will see me." [17] Then some of his disciples said to one another, "What does he mean by saying to us, 'A little while, and you will no longer see me, and again a little while, and you will see me'; and 'Because I am going to the Father'?" [18] They said, "What does he mean by this 'a little while'? We do not know what he is talking about." [19] Jesus knew that they wanted to ask him, so he said to them, "Are you discussing among yourselves what I meant when I said, 'A little while, and you

will no longer see me, and again a little while, and you will see me'? ²⁰Very truly, I tell you, you will weep and mourn, but the world will rejoice; you will have pain, but your pain will turn into joy. ²¹When a woman is in labor, she has pain, because her hour has come. But when her child is born, she no longer remembers the anguish because of the joy of having brought a human being into the world. ²²So you have pain now; but I will see you again, and your hearts will rejoice, and no one will take your joy from you. ²³On that day you will ask nothing of me.^s Very truly, I tell you, if you ask anything of the Father in my name, he will give it to you.^t ²⁴Until now you have not asked for anything in my name. Ask and you will receive, so that your joy may be complete.

Peace for the Disciples

25 "I have said these things to you in figures of speech. The hour is coming when I will no longer speak to you in figures, but will tell you plainly of the Father. ²⁶On that day you will ask in my name. I do not say to you that I will ask the Father on your behalf; ²⁷for the Father himself loves you, because you have loved me and have believed that I came from God.^u ²⁸I came from the Father and have come into the world; again, I am leaving the world and am going to the Father."

29 His disciples said, "Yes, now you are speaking plainly, not in any figure of speech! ³⁰Now we know that you know all things, and do not need to have anyone question you; by this we believe that you came from God." ³¹Jesus answered them, "Do you now believe? ³²The hour is coming, indeed it has come, when you will be scattered, each one to his home, and you will leave me alone. Yet I am not alone because the Father is with me. ³³I have said this to you, so that in me you may have peace. In the world you face persecution. But take

16.20
Lk 23.27;
Jn 20.20
16.21
1 Thes 5.3
16.22
vv. 6,16
16.23
Mt 7.7;
Jn 14.13;
15.16
16.24
Jn 15.11
16.25
Jn 10.6;
Mt 13.34
16.27
Jn 14.21,23
16.28
Jn 13.3
16.29
v. 25
16.30
Jn 8.42
16.32
Mt 26.31;
Mk 14.27
16.33
Jn 14.27;
Col 1.20;
Rom 8.37;
Rev 3.21

17.1
Jn 12.23;
13.32
17.2
Dan 7.14;
Heb 2.8;
Jn 6.37
17.3
Jn 5.44;
3.34; 6.29,57
17.4
Jn 13.31;
4.34; 14.31
17.5
Jn 1.1;
Phil 2.6
17.6
Jn 6.37,39
17.8
Jn 8.28;
16.27
17.9
Lk 22.32;
Jn 14.16
17.10
Jn 16.15
17.11
Jn 13.1;
7.33;
Rev 19.12;
Jn 10.30
17.12
Heb 2.13;
Jn 6.39;
18.9; 6.70

courage; I have conquered the world!"

Jesus Prays for His Disciples

17 After Jesus had spoken these words, he looked up to heaven and said, "Father, the hour has come; glorify your Son so that the Son may glorify you, ²since you have given him authority over all people,^v to give eternal life to all whom you have given him. ³And this is eternal life, that they may know you, the only true God, and Jesus Christ whom you have sent. ⁴I glorified you on earth by finishing the work that you gave me to do. ⁵So now, Father, glorify me in your own presence with the glory that I had in your presence before the world existed.

6 "I have made your name known to those whom you gave me from the world. They were yours, and you gave them to me, and they have kept your word. ⁷Now they know that everything you have given me is from you; ⁸for the words that you gave to me I have given to them, and they have received them and know in truth that I came from you; and they have believed that you sent me. ⁹I am asking on their behalf; I am not asking on behalf of the world, but on behalf of those whom you gave me, because they are yours. ¹⁰All mine are yours, and yours are mine; and I have been glorified in them. ¹¹And now I am no longer in the world, but they are in the world, and I am coming to you. Holy Father, protect them in your name that^w you have given me, so that they may be one, as we are one. ¹²While I was with them, I protected them in your name that^w you have given me. I guarded them, and not one of them was lost except the one destined to be lost,^x so that the scripture might be fulfilled. ¹³But now I am coming to

^s Or *will ask me no question* ^t Other ancient authorities read *Father, he will give it to you in my name* ^u Other ancient authorities read *the Father* ^v Gk *flesh*
^w Other ancient authorities read *protected in your name those whom* ^x Gk *except the son of destruction*

you, and I speak these things in the world so that they may have my joy made complete in themselves.ʸ ¹⁴ I have given them your word, and the world has hated them because they do not belong to the world, just as I do not belong to the world. ¹⁵ I am not asking you to take them out of the world, but I ask you to protect them from the evil one.ᶻ ¹⁶ They do not belong to the world, just as I do not belong to the world. ¹⁷ Sanctify them in the truth; your word is truth. ¹⁸ As you have sent me into the world, so I have sent them into the world. ¹⁹ And for their sakes I sanctify myself, so that they also may be sanctified in truth.

20 "I ask not only on behalf of these, but also on behalf of those who will believe in me through their word, ²¹ that they may all be one. As you, Father, are in me and I am in you, may they also be in us,ᵃ so that the world may believe that you have sent me. ²² The glory that you have given me I have given them, so that they may be one, as we are one, ²³ I in them and you in me, that they may become completely one, so that the world may know that you have sent me and have loved them even as you have loved me. ²⁴ Father, I desire that those also, whom you have given me, may be with me where I am, to see my glory, which you have given me because you loved me before the foundation of the world.

25 "Righteous Father, the world does not know you, but I know you; and these know that you have sent me. ²⁶ I made your name known to them, and I will make it known, so that the love with which you have loved me may be in them, and I in them."

The Betrayal and Arrest of Jesus

18 After Jesus had spoken these words, he went out with his disciples across the Kidron valley to a place where there was a garden, which he and his disciples entered. ² Now Judas, who betrayed him, also knew the place,

because Jesus often met there with his disciples. ³ So Judas brought a detachment of soldiers together with police from the chief priests and the Pharisees, and they came there with lanterns and torches and weapons. ⁴ Then Jesus, knowing all that was to happen to him, came forward and asked them, "Whom are you looking for?" ⁵ They answered, "Jesus of Nazareth."ᵇ Jesus replied, "I am he."ᶜ Judas, who betrayed him, was standing with them. ⁶ When Jesusᵈ said to them, "I am he,"ᶜ they stepped back and fell to the ground. ⁷ Again he asked them, "Whom are you looking for?" And they said, "Jesus of Nazareth."ᵇ ⁸ Jesus answered, "I told you that I am he.ᶜ So if you are looking for me, let these men go." ⁹ This was to fulfill the word that he had spoken, "I did not lose a single one of those whom you gave me." ¹⁰ Then Simon Peter, who had a sword, drew it, struck the high priest's slave, and cut off his right ear. The slave's name was Malchus. ¹¹ Jesus said to Peter, "Put your sword back into its sheath. Am I not to drink the cup that the Father has given me?"

Jesus before the High Priest

12 So the soldiers, their officer, and the Jewish police arrested Jesus and bound him. ¹³ First they took him to Annas, who was the father-in-law of Caiaphas, the high priest that year. ¹⁴ Caiaphas was the one who had advised the Jews that it was better to have one person die for the people.

Peter Denies Jesus

15 Simon Peter and another disciple followed Jesus. Since that disciple was known to the high priest, he went with Jesus into the courtyard of the high priest, ¹⁶ but Peter was standing outside at the gate. So the other disciple, who was known to the high priest, went out, spoke to the woman who

17.14
Jn 15.19;
8.23
17.15
Mt 6.13
17.16
v. 14
17.17
Jn 15.3
17.18
Jn 20.21
17.19
Jn 15.13
17.21
Jn 10.38
17.22
Jn 14.20
17.24
Jn 12.26;
Mt 25.34;
v. 5
17.25
Jn 15.21;
16.3; 7.29;
Jn 16.27
17.26
v. 6;
Jn 15.9
18.1
2 Sam 15.23
18.2
Lk 21.37;
22.39

18.3
Acts 1.16
18.4
Jn 6.64;
13.1,11; v. 7
18.7
v. 4
18.9
Jn 17.12
18.11
Mt 20.22
18.13
Mt 26.57;
Mk 14.53;
Lk 22.54
18.14
Jn 11.49-51
18.15
Mt 26.58;
Mk 14.54;
Lk 22.54

ʸ Or *among themselves* ᶻ Or *from evil*
ᵃ Other ancient authorities read *be one in us*
ᵇ Gk *the Nazorean* ᶜ Gk *I am* ᵈ Gk *he*

guarded the gate, and brought Peter in. [17] The woman said to Peter, "You are not also one of this man's disciples, are you?" He said, "I am not." [18] Now the slaves and the police had made a charcoal fire because it was cold, and they were standing around it and warming themselves. Peter also was standing with them and warming himself.

The High Priest Questions Jesus

19 Then the high priest questioned Jesus about his disciples and about his teaching. [20] Jesus answered, "I have spoken openly to the world; I have always taught in synagogues and in the temple, where all the Jews come together. I have said nothing in secret. [21] Why do you ask me? Ask those who heard what I said to them; they know what I said." [22] When he had said this, one of the police standing nearby struck Jesus on the face, saying, "Is that how you answer the high priest?" [23] Jesus answered, "If I have spoken wrongly, testify to the wrong. But if I have spoken rightly, why do you strike me?" [24] Then Annas sent him bound to Caiaphas the high priest.

Peter Denies Jesus Again

25 Now Simon Peter was standing and warming himself. They asked him, "You are not also one of his disciples, are you?" He denied it and said, "I am not." [26] One of the slaves of the high priest, a relative of the man whose ear Peter had cut off, asked, "Did I not see you in the garden with him?" [27] Again Peter denied it, and at that moment the cock crowed.

Jesus before Pilate

28 Then they took Jesus from Caiaphas to Pilate's headquarters.[e] It was early in the morning. They themselves did not enter the headquarters,[e] so as to avoid ritual defilement and to be able to eat the Passover. [29] So Pilate went out to them and said, "What accusation do you bring against this man?" [30] They answered, "If this man were

not a criminal, we would not have handed him over to you." [31] Pilate said to them, "Take him yourselves and judge him according to your law." The Jews replied, "We are not permitted to put anyone to death." [32] (This was to fulfill what Jesus had said when he indicated the kind of death he was to die.)

33 Then Pilate entered the headquarters[e] again, summoned Jesus, and asked him, "Are you the King of the Jews?" [34] Jesus answered, "Do you ask this on your own, or did others tell you about me?" [35] Pilate replied, "I am not a Jew, am I? Your own nation and the chief priests have handed you over to me. What have you done?" [36] Jesus answered, "My kingdom is not from this world. If my kingdom were from this world, my followers would be fighting to keep me from being handed over to the Jews. But as it is, my kingdom is not from here." [37] Pilate asked him, "So you are a king?" Jesus answered, "You say that I am a king. For this I was born, and for this I came into the world, to testify to the truth. Everyone who belongs to the truth listens to my voice." [38] Pilate asked him, "What is truth?"

Jesus Sentenced to Death

After he had said this, he went out to the Jews again and told them, "I find no case against him. [39] But you have a custom that I release someone for you at the Passover. Do you want me to release for you the King of the Jews?" [40] They shouted in reply, "Not this man, but Barabbas!" Now Barabbas was a bandit.

19 Then Pilate took Jesus and had him flogged. [2] And the soldiers wove a crown of thorns and put it on his head, and they dressed him in a purple robe. [3] They kept coming up to him, saying, "Hail, King of the Jews!" and striking him on the face. [4] Pilate went out again and said to them, "Look, I am bringing him out to you to let you know that I find no case against

18.17
v. 25
18.18
Mk 14.54,
67; Jn 21.9
18.19
Mt 26.59-68;
Mk 14.55-65;
Lk 22.63-71
18.20
Mt 26.55;
Jn 7.26
18.22
v. 3;
Jn 19.3
18.23
Mt 5.39;
Acts 23.2-5
18.24
v. 13
18.25
v. 18
18.26
v. 10
18.27
Jn 13.38
18.28
Mt 27.1,2;
Mk 15.1;
Lk 23.1;
Jn 11.55;
Acts 11.3

18.32
Mt 20.19;
Jn 12.32,33
18.33
vv. 28,29;
Jn 19.9;
Lk 23.3
18.36
Mt 26.53;
Lk 17.21;
Jn 6.15
18.37
Jn 8.47;
1 Jn 3.19;
4.6
18.38
Jn 19.4,6
18.39
Mt 27.15-18,
20-23;
Mk 15.6-15;
Lk 23.18-25
18.40
Acts 3.14
19.1
Mt 27.26
19.2
Mt 27.27-30;
Mk 15.16-19
19.3
Jn 18.22
19.4
v. 6;
Jn 18.38

e Gk the praetorium

him." ⁵So Jesus came out, wearing the crown of thorns and the purple robe. Pilate said to them, "Here is the man!" ⁶When the chief priests and the police saw him, they shouted, "Crucify him! Crucify him!" Pilate said to them, "Take him yourselves and crucify him; I find no case against him." ⁷The Jews answered him, "We have a law, and according to that law he ought to die because he has claimed to be the Son of God."

8 Now when Pilate heard this, he was more afraid than ever. ⁹He entered his headquarters[f] again and asked Jesus, "Where are you from?" But Jesus gave him no answer. ¹⁰Pilate therefore said to him, "Do you refuse to speak to me? Do you not know that I have power to release you, and power to crucify you?" ¹¹Jesus answered him, "You would have no power over me unless it had been given you from above; therefore the one who handed me over to you is guilty of a greater sin." ¹²From then on Pilate tried to release him, but the Jews cried out, "If you release this man, you are no friend of the emperor. Everyone who claims to be a king sets himself against the emperor."

13 When Pilate heard these words, he brought Jesus outside and sat[g] on the judge's bench at a place called The Stone Pavement, or in Hebrew[h] Gabbatha. ¹⁴Now it was the day of Preparation for the Passover; and it was about noon. He said to the Jews, "Here is your King!" ¹⁵They cried out, "Away with him! Away with him! Crucify him!" Pilate asked them, "Shall I crucify your King?" The chief priests answered, "We have no king but the emperor." ¹⁶Then he handed him over to them to be crucified.

The Crucifixion of Jesus

So they took Jesus; ¹⁷and carrying the cross by himself, he went out to what is called The Place of the Skull, which in Hebrew[h] is called Golgotha. ¹⁸There they crucified him, and with him two oth-

ers, one on either side, with Jesus between them. ¹⁹Pilate also had an inscription written and put on the cross. It read, "Jesus of Nazareth,[i] the King of the Jews." ²⁰Many of the Jews read this inscription, because the place where Jesus was crucified was near the city; and it was written in Hebrew,[h] in Latin, and in Greek. ²¹Then the chief priests of the Jews said to Pilate, "Do not write, 'The King of the Jews,' but, 'This man said, I am King of the Jews.' " ²²Pilate answered, "What I have written I have written." ²³When the soldiers had crucified Jesus, they took his clothes and divided them into four parts, one for each soldier. They also took his tunic; now the tunic was seamless, woven in one piece from the top. ²⁴So they said to one another, "Let us not tear it, but cast lots for it to see who will get it." This was to fulfill what the scripture says,

> "They divided my clothes
>> among themselves,
>> and for my clothing they
>> cast lots."

²⁵And that is what the soldiers did.

Meanwhile, standing near the cross of Jesus were his mother, and his mother's sister, Mary the wife of Clopas, and Mary Magdalene. ²⁶When Jesus saw his mother and the disciple whom he loved standing beside her, he said to his mother, "Woman, here is your son." ²⁷Then he said to the disciple, "Here is your mother." And from that hour the disciple took her into his own home.

28 After this, when Jesus knew that all was now finished, he said (in order to fulfill the scripture), "I am thirsty." ²⁹A jar full of sour wine was standing there. So they put a sponge full of the wine on a branch of hyssop and held it to his mouth. ³⁰When Jesus had received the wine, he said, "It is finished." Then he bowed his head and gave up his spirit.

Cross-references (center column):

19.5 v. 2
19.6 Acts 3.13
19.7 Lev 24.16; Mt 26.63-66; Jn 5.18; 10.33
19.9 Isa 53.7; Mt 27.12,14
19.11 Rom 13.11; Jn 18.28ff
19.12 Lk 23.2
19.13 Mt 27.19
19.14 Mt 27.62; Mk 15.25; vv. 19,21
19.16 Mt 27.26; Mk 15.15; Lk 23.25
19.17 Lk 23.26
19.21 v. 14
19.24 Ex 28.32; Ps 22.18
19.25 Mt 27.55, 56; Mk 15.40, 41; Lk 23.49; 24.18; Jn 20.1,18
19.26 Jn 13.23; 20.2; 21.20; 2.4
19.28 Jn 13.1; 17.4; Ps 69.21
19.30 Jn 17.4

[f] Gk *the praetorium* [g] Or *seated him*
[h] That is, *Aramaic* [i] Gk *the Nazorean*

Jesus' Side Is Pierced

31 Since it was the day of Preparation, the Jews did not want the bodies left on the cross during the sabbath, especially because that sabbath was a day of great solemnity. So they asked Pilate to have the legs of the crucified men broken and the bodies removed. 32 Then the soldiers came and broke the legs of the first and of the other who had been crucified with him. 33 But when they came to Jesus and saw that he was already dead, they did not break his legs. 34 Instead, one of the soldiers pierced his side with a spear, and at once blood and water came out. 35 (He who saw this has testified so that you also may believe. His testimony is true, and he knows^i that he tells the truth.) 36 These things occurred so that the scripture might be fulfilled, "None of his bones shall be broken." 37 And again another passage of scripture says, "They will look on the one whom they have pierced."

The Burial of Jesus

38 After these things, Joseph of Arimathea, who was a disciple of Jesus, though a secret one because of his fear of the Jews, asked Pilate to let him take away the body of Jesus. Pilate gave him permission; so he came and removed his body. 39 Nicodemus, who had at first come to Jesus by night, also came, bringing a mixture of myrrh and aloes, weighing about a hundred pounds. 40 They took the body of Jesus and wrapped it with the spices in linen cloths, according to the burial custom of the Jews. 41 Now there was a garden in the place where he was crucified, and in the garden there was a new tomb in which no one had ever been laid. 42 And so, because it was the Jewish day of Preparation, and the tomb was nearby, they laid Jesus there.

The Resurrection of Jesus

20 Early on the first day of the week, while it was still

19.31
Deut 21.23;
Ex 12.16
19.32
v. 18
19.34
1 Jn 5.6,8
19.35
Jn 15.27;
21.24
19.36
Ex 12.46;
Num 9.12;
Ps 34.20
19.37
Zech 12.10
19.39
Jn 3.1; 7.50
19.40
Jn 11.44;
Mt 26.12;
Jn 20.5,7;
Lk 24.12
19.42
vv. 14,31,
20,41
20.1
Mt 27.60,66

20.2
Jn 13.23;
19.26; 21.7,
20,24
20.3
Lk 24.12
20.5
Jn 19.40
20.8
v. 4
20.9
Mt 22.29;
Lk 24.26,46
20.11
Mk 16.5;
20.12
Mt 28.2,3;
Mk 16.5;
Lk 24.4
20.13
v. 2
20.14
Mt 28.9;
Jn 21.4
20.15
v. 13

dark, Mary Magdalene came to the tomb and saw that the stone had been removed from the tomb. 2 So she ran and went to Simon Peter and the other disciple, the one whom Jesus loved, and said to them, "They have taken the Lord out of the tomb, and we do not know where they have laid him." 3 Then Peter and the other disciple set out and went toward the tomb. 4 The two were running together, but the other disciple outran Peter and reached the tomb first. 5 He bent down to look in and saw the linen wrappings lying there, but he did not go in. 6 Then Simon Peter came, following him, and went into the tomb. He saw the linen wrappings lying there, 7 and the cloth that had been on Jesus' head, not lying with the linen wrappings but rolled up in a place by itself. 8 Then the other disciple, who reached the tomb first, also went in, and he saw and believed; 9 for as yet they did not understand the scripture, that he must rise from the dead. 10 Then the disciples returned to their homes.

Jesus Appears to Mary Magdalene

11 But Mary stood weeping outside the tomb. As she wept, she bent over to look^k into the tomb; 12 and she saw two angels in white, sitting where the body of Jesus had been lying, one at the head and the other at the feet. 13 They said to her, "Woman, why are you weeping?" She said to them, "They have taken away my Lord, and I do not know where they have laid him." 14 When she had said this, she turned around and saw Jesus standing there, but she did not know that it was Jesus. 15 Jesus said to her, "Woman, why are you weeping? Whom are you looking for?" Supposing him to be the gardener, she said to him, "Sir, if you have carried him away, tell me where you have laid him, and I will take him away." 16 Jesus said to

i Or *there is one who knows* k Gk lacks *to look*

her, "Mary!" She turned and said to him, in Hebrew,[1] "Rabbouni!" (which means Teacher). [17] Jesus said to her, "Do not hold on to me, because I have not yet ascended to the Father. But go to my brothers and say to them, 'I am ascending to my Father and your Father, to my God and your God.'" [18] Mary Magdalene went and announced to the disciples, "I have seen the Lord"; and she told them that he had said these things to her.

Jesus Appears to the Disciples

19 When it was evening on that day, the first day of the week, and the doors of the house where the disciples had met were locked for fear of the Jews, Jesus came and stood among them and said, "Peace be with you." [20] After he said this, he showed them his hands and his side. Then the disciples rejoiced when they saw the Lord. [21] Jesus said to them again, "Peace be with you. As the Father has sent me, so I send you." [22] When he had said this, he breathed on them and said to them, "Receive the Holy Spirit. [23] If you forgive the sins of any, they are forgiven them; if you retain the sins of any, they are retained."

Jesus and Thomas

24 But Thomas (who was called the Twin[m]), one of the twelve, was not with them when Jesus came. [25] So the other disciples told him, "We have seen the Lord." But he said to them, "Unless I see the mark of the nails in his hands, and put my finger in the mark of the nails and my hand in his side, I will not believe."

26 A week later his disciples were again in the house, and Thomas was with them. Although the doors were shut, Jesus came and stood among them and said, "Peace be with you." [27] Then he said to Thomas, "Put your finger here and see my hands. Reach out your hand and put it in my side. Do not doubt but believe." [28] Thomas answered him, "My Lord and my

God!" [29] Jesus said to him, "Have you believed because you have seen me? Blessed are those who have not seen and yet have come to believe."

The Purpose of This Book

30 Now Jesus did many other signs in the presence of his disciples, which are not written in this book. [31] But these are written so that you may come to believe[n] that Jesus is the Messiah,[o] the Son of God, and that through believing you may have life in his name.

Jesus Appears to Seven Disciples

21 After these things Jesus showed himself again to the disciples by the Sea of Tiberias; and he showed himself in this way. [2] Gathered there together were Simon Peter, Thomas called the Twin,[m] Nathanael of Cana in Galilee, the sons of Zebedee, and two others of his disciples. [3] Simon Peter said to them, "I am going fishing." They said to him, "We will go with you." They went out and got into the boat, but that night they caught nothing.

4 Just after daybreak, Jesus stood on the beach; but the disciples did not know that it was Jesus. [5] Jesus said to them, "Children, you have no fish, have you?" They answered him, "No." [6] He said to them, "Cast the net to the right side of the boat, and you will find some." So they cast it, and now they were not able to haul it in because there were so many fish. [7] That disciple whom Jesus loved said to Peter, "It is the Lord!" When Simon Peter heard that it was the Lord, he put on some clothes, for he was naked, and jumped into the sea. [8] But the other disciples came in the boat, dragging the net full of fish, for they were not far from the land, only about a hundred yards[p] off.

[1] That is, *Aramaic* [m] Gk *Didymus*
[n] Other ancient authorities read *may continue to believe* [o] Or *the Christ* [p] Gk *two hundred cubits*

Cross-references (center column):

20.17 Mt 28.10; v. 27; Jn 7.33
20.18 Lk 24.10,13
20.19 Lk 24.36-39; vv. 21,26
20.20 Lk 24.39,40; Jn 16.20,22
20.21 Mt 28.19; Jn 17.18,19
20.23 Mt 16.19; 18.18
20.24 Jn 11.16
20.25 v. 20
20.26 v. 21
20.27 v. 25; Lk 24.40

20.29 1 Pet 1.8
20.30 Jn 21.25
20.31 Jn 19.35; 3.15
21.1 Jn 20.19,26; 6.1
21.2 Jn 11.16; 1.45; Mt 4.21; Mk 1.19; Lk 5.10
21.3 Lk 5.5
21.4 Jn 20.14
21.5 Lk 24.41
21.6 Lk 5.4,6,7
21.7 Jn 13.23; 20.2; v. 20

9 When they had gone ashore, they saw a charcoal fire there, with fish on it, and bread. 10 Jesus said to them, "Bring some of the fish that you have just caught." 11 So Simon Peter went aboard and hauled the net ashore, full of large fish, a hundred fifty-three of them; and though there were so many, the net was not torn. 12 Jesus said to them, "Come and have breakfast." Now none of the disciples dared to ask him, "Who are you?" because they knew it was the Lord. 13 Jesus came and took the bread and gave it to them, and did the same with the fish. 14 This was now the third time that Jesus appeared to the disciples after he was raised from the dead.

Jesus and Peter

15 When they had finished breakfast, Jesus said to Simon Peter, "Simon son of John, do you love me more than these?" He said to him, "Yes, Lord; you know that I love you." Jesus said to him, "Feed my lambs." 16 A second time he said to him, "Simon son of John, do you love me?" He said to him, "Yes, Lord; you know that I love you." Jesus said to him, "Tend my sheep." 17 He said to him the third time, "Simon son of John, do you love me?" Peter felt hurt because he said to him the third time, "Do you love me?" And he said to him, "Lord, you know everything; you know that I love you." Jesus said to him, "Feed my sheep. 18 Very truly, I tell you, when you were younger,

you used to fasten your own belt and to go wherever you wished. But when you grow old, you will stretch out your hands, and someone else will fasten a belt around you and take you where you do not wish to go." 19 (He said this to indicate the kind of death by which he would glorify God.) After this he said to him, "Follow me."

Jesus and the Beloved Disciple

20 Peter turned and saw the disciple whom Jesus loved following them; he was the one who had reclined next to Jesus at the supper and had said, "Lord, who is it that is going to betray you?" 21 When Peter saw him, he said to Jesus, "Lord, what about him?" 22 Jesus said to him, "If it is my will that he remain until I come, what is that to you? Follow me!" 23 So the rumor spread in the community q that this disciple would not die. Yet Jesus did not say to him that he would not die, but, "If it is my will that he remain until I come, what is that to you?" r

24 This is the disciple who is testifying to these things and has written them, and we know that his testimony is true. 25 But there are also many other things that Jesus did; if every one of them were written down, I suppose that the world itself could not contain the books that would be written.

q Gk *among the brothers*　r Other ancient authorities lack *what is that to you*

21.9
vv. 10,13
21.13
v. 9
21.14
Jn 20.19,26
21.15
Jn 13.37;
Mt 26.33;
Mk 14.29
21.16
Mt 2.6;
Acts 20.28;
1 Pet 5.2;
Rev 7.17
21.17
Jn 16.30;
v. 16

21.19
2 Pet 1.14
21.20
v. 7;
Jn 13.25
21.22
Mt 16.27,
28; 25.31;
1 Cor 4.5;
11.26;
Rev 2.25;
3.11; 22.7,20
21.23
Acts 1.15
21.24
Jn 15.27;
19.35
21.25
Jn 20.30

THE
Acts
OF THE APOSTLES

Title and Background

The book of Acts provides the basic history of the spread of Christianity during the thirty years immediately following the death and resurrection of Jesus Christ. It serves as a link between the Gospels and the letters. It can be called "The Acts of the Holy Spirit," because it teaches about the coming and the work of the Spirit.

Author and Date of Writing

Although the author does not name himself, evidence outside the Scriptures and inferences from the book itself lead to the conclusion that the author was Luke. It is a companion volume to the Gospel of Luke (cf. Lk 1.1-4 and Acts 1.1-2), and it was written after that book (that is, shortly after A.D. 70).

Theme and Message

The theme of the work is best summarized in 1.8. Luke weaves together different interests and emphases as he relates the beginnings and expansion of the church. The design of the book revolves around (1) key persons: Peter and Paul; (2) important topics and events: the role of the Holy Spirit, pioneer missionary outreach to new fields, conversions, the growth of the church, and life in the Christian community; (3) significant problems: conflict between Jewish and Gentile Christians, persecution of the church by some Jewish elements, trials before Jews and Romans, confrontations with Gentiles, and other hardships in the ministry; (4) geographical advances: from Jerusalem to Rome.

Outline

The Promise of the Holy Spirit

1 In the first book, Theophilus, I wrote about all that Jesus did and taught from the beginning [1.1 Lk 1.1-4] [1.2 Mt 28.19] [1.3 Mt 28.17; Lk 24.34,36; 1 Cor 15.5-7] [1.4 Lk 24.49; Jn 14.16] ²until the day when he was taken up to heaven, after giving instructions through the Holy Spirit to the apostles whom he had chosen. ³After his suffering he presented himself alive to them by many convincing proofs, appearing to them during forty days and speaking about the kingdom of God. [1.5 Acts 11.16] [1.6 Mt 24.3] [1.7 Mt 24.36; Mk 13.32] ⁴While staying[a] with them, he ordered them not to leave Jerusalem, but to wait there for the promise of the Father. "This," he said, "is what you have heard from me; ⁵for John baptized with water, but you will be baptized with[b] the Holy Spirit not many days from now."

The Ascension of Jesus

6 So when they had come together, they asked him, "Lord, is this the time when you will restore the kingdom to Israel?" ⁷He replied, "It is not for you to know the times or periods that the Father

a Or *eating* b Or *by*

has set by his own authority. [8]But you will receive power when the Holy Spirit has come upon you; and you will be my witnesses in Jerusalem, in all Judea and Samaria, and to the ends of the earth." [9]When he had said this, as they were watching, he was lifted up, and a cloud took him out of their sight. [10]While he was going and they were gazing up toward heaven, suddenly two men in white robes stood by them. [11]They said, "Men of Galilee, why do you stand looking up toward heaven? This Jesus, who has been taken up from you into heaven, will come in the same way as you saw him go into heaven."

Matthias Chosen to Replace Judas

12 Then they returned to Jerusalem from the mount called Olivet, which is near Jerusalem, a sabbath day's journey away. [13]When they had entered the city, they went to the room upstairs where they were staying, Peter, and John, and James, and Andrew, Philip and Thomas, Bartholomew and Matthew, James son of Alphaeus, and Simon the Zealot, and Judas son of[c] James. [14]All these were constantly devoting themselves to prayer, together with certain women, including Mary the mother of Jesus, as well as his brothers.

15 In those days Peter stood up among the believers[d] (together the crowd numbered about one hundred twenty persons) and said, [16]"Friends,[e] the scripture had to be fulfilled, which the Holy Spirit through David foretold concerning Judas, who became a guide for those who arrested Jesus— [17]for he was numbered among us and was allotted his share in this ministry." [18](Now this man acquired a field with the reward of his wickedness; and falling headlong,[f] he burst open in the middle and all his bowels gushed out. [19]This became known to all the residents of Jerusalem, so that the field was called in their language Hakeldama, that

is, Field of Blood.) [20]"For it is written in the book of Psalms,

'Let his homestead become
　　desolate,
　　and let there be no one to
　　　live in it';
and
'Let another take his
　　position of overseer.'
[21]So one of the men who have accompanied us during all the time that the Lord Jesus went in and out among us, [22]beginning from the baptism of John until the day when he was taken up from us—one of these must become a witness with us to his resurrection." [23]So they proposed two, Joseph called Barsabbas, who was also known as Justus, and Matthias. [24]Then they prayed and said, "Lord, you know everyone's heart. Show us which one of these two you have chosen [25]to take the place[g] in this ministry and apostleship from which Judas turned aside to go to his own place." [26]And they cast lots for them, and the lot fell on Matthias; and he was added to the eleven apostles.

The Coming of the Holy Spirit

2 When the day of Pentecost had come, they were all together in one place. [2]And suddenly from heaven there came a sound like the rush of a violent wind, and it filled the entire house where they were sitting. [3]Divided tongues, as of fire, appeared among them, and a tongue rested on each of them. [4]All of them were filled with the Holy Spirit and began to speak in other languages, as the Spirit gave them ability.

5 Now there were devout Jews from every nation under heaven living in Jerusalem. [6]And at this sound the crowd gathered and was bewildered, because each one heard them speaking in the native language of each. [7]Amazed and astonished, they asked, "Are not all these who are speaking Galileans?

1.8
Acts 2.1-4;
Lk 24.48;
Jn 15.27
1.9
Lk 24.51;
v. 2
1.10
Lk 24.4;
Jn 20.12
1.11
Mt 24.30;
Mk 13.26;
Jn 14.3
1.13
Acts 9.37,
39; 20.8;
Mt 10.2-4;
Mk 3.16-19;
Lk 6.14-16
1.14
Acts 2.1,46;
Lk 23.49,55;
Mt 12.46
1.15
Jn 21.23;
Acts 6.3;
9.30
1.16
Jn 13.18
1.17
Jn 6.70,71;
v. 25;
Acts 20.24;
21.19
1.18
Mt 27.3-10;
26.14,15

1.20
Ps 69.25;
109.8
1.21
Lk 24.3
1.22
Mk 1.1;
v. 8;
Acts 2.32
1.24
1 Sam 16.7;
Jer 17.10;
Acts 15.8;
Rom 8.27
1.26
Lev 16.8
2.1
Lev 23.15;
Deut 16.9;
Acts 1.14
2.2
Acts 4.31
2.4
Acts 4.8,31;
9.17; 13.9,52;
1 Cor 12.10,
11; 14.21
2.5
Acts 8.2
2.7
v. 12;
Acts 1.11

c Or *the brother of*　　d Gk *brothers*
e Gk *Men, brothers*　　f Or *swelling up*
g Other ancient authorities read *the share*

8 And how is it that we hear, each of us, in our own native language? 9 Parthians, Medes, Elamites, and residents of Mesopotamia, Judea and Cappadocia, Pontus and Asia, 10 Phrygia and Pamphylia, Egypt and the parts of Libya belonging to Cyrene, and visitors from Rome, both Jews and proselytes, 11 Cretans and Arabs—in our own languages we hear them speaking about God's deeds of power." 12 All were amazed and perplexed, saying to one another, "What does this mean?" 13 But others sneered and said, "They are filled with new wine."

Peter Addresses the Crowd

14 But Peter, standing with the eleven, raised his voice and addressed them, "Men of Judea and all who live in Jerusalem, let this be known to you, and listen to what I say. 15 Indeed, these are not drunk, as you suppose, for it is only nine o'clock in the morning. 16 No, this is what was spoken through the prophet Joel:

17 'In the last days it will be,
God declares,
that I will pour out my Spirit
upon all flesh,
and your sons and your
daughters shall
prophesy,
and your young men shall
see visions,
and your old men shall
dream dreams.
18 Even upon my slaves, both
men and women,
in those days I will pour
out my Spirit;
and they shall prophesy.
19 And I will show portents in
the heaven above
and signs on the earth
below,
blood, and fire, and
smoky mist.
20 The sun shall be turned to
darkness
and the moon to blood,
before the coming of the
Lord's great and
glorious day.

21 Then everyone who calls on
the name of the Lord
shall be saved.'

22 "You that are Israelites,[h] listen to what I have to say: Jesus of Nazareth,[i] a man attested to you by God with deeds of power, wonders, and signs that God did through him among you, as you yourselves know— 23 this man, handed over to you according to the definite plan and foreknowledge of God, you crucified and killed by the hands of those outside the law. 24 But God raised him up, having freed him from death,[j] because it was impossible for him to be held in its power. 25 For David says concerning him,

'I saw the Lord always before
me,
for he is at my right hand
so that I will not be
shaken;
26 therefore my heart was glad,
and my tongue rejoiced;
moreover my flesh will live
in hope.
27 For you will not abandon my
soul to Hades,
or let your Holy One
experience corruption.
28 You have made known to me
the ways of life;
you will make me full of
gladness with your
presence.'

29 "Fellow Israelites,[k] I may say to you confidently of our ancestor David that he both died and was buried, and his tomb is with us to this day. 30 Since he was a prophet, he knew that God had sworn with an oath to him that he would put one of his descendants on his throne. 31 Foreseeing this, David[l] spoke of the resurrection of the Messiah,[m] saying,

'He was not abandoned to
Hades,
nor did his flesh
experience corruption.'

32 This Jesus God raised up, and of that all of us are witnesses. 33 Being

Cross references (center column)

2.9
1 Pet 1.1;
Acts 6.9;
16.6;
Rom 16.5;
1 Cor 16.19;
2 Cor 1.8
2.12
v. 7
2.13
1 Cor 14.23
2.15
1 Thes 5.7
2.17
Joel 2.28-32;
Zech 12.10;
Jn 7.38;
Acts 10.45;
21.9
2.18
Acts 21.4,9,
10
2.20
Mt 24.29;
Mk 13.24;
Lk 21.25

2.21
Rom 10.13
2.22
Jn 3.2;
Acts 10.38;
Jn 4.48
2.23
Mt 26.24;
Lk 22.22;
Acts 3.18;
4.28; 3.13
2.24
Acts 3.15;
Rom 4.24;
2 Cor 4.14;
Eph 1.20;
Col 2.12;
Heb 13.20;
1 Pet 1.21
2.25
Ps 16.8-11
2.27
Mt 11.23;
Acts 13.35
2.29
Acts 7.8,9;
13.36;
1 Kings 2.10;
Neh 3.16
2.30
2 Sam 7.12,
13;
Ps 132.11;
Rom 1.3
2.31
Ps 16.10
2.32
v. 24;
Acts 1.8
2.33
Acts 5.31;
1.4; Jn 7.39;
14.26; 15.26;
Acts 10.45

h Gk Men, Israelites i Gk the Nazorean
j Gk the pains of death k Gk Men,
brothers l Gk he m Or the Christ

COUNTRIES OF PEOPLE MENTIONED AT PENTECOST

ASIA—Provinces of the Roman empire
Media—Provinces of the Parthian empire
Rome —Cities
CRETE—Island

(1) (2) (3) etc.—Numbers indicate sequence listed in Ac 2:9-11

Caspian Sea

Parthian empire (1)

Ecbatana •
Media (2)

Susa •
Elam (3)

Meso-
potamia (4)

• Jerusalem

JUDEA (5)

Red Sea

ARABIA (15)

Black Sea

PONTUS (7)

CAPPA-
DOCIA (6)

ASIA (8)

PHRYGIA (9)

PAMPHYLIA (10)

EGYPT (11)

CRETE (14)

Cyrene

CYRENE (12)

Mediterranean Sea

Rome (13)

| Miles | 0 | 200 | 400 | 600 | 800 | 1000 |
| Kms | 0 | 300 | 600 | 900 | 1200 | 1500 |

therefore exalted at[n] the right hand of God, and having received from the Father the promise of the Holy Spirit, he has poured out this that you both see and hear. [34]For David did not ascend into the heavens, but he himself says,

'The Lord said to my Lord,
 "Sit at my right hand,
[35] until I make your enemies
 your footstool." '

[36]Therefore let the entire house of Israel know with certainty that God has made him both Lord and Messiah,[o] this Jesus whom you crucified."

The First Converts

[37] Now when they heard this, they were cut to the heart and said to Peter and to the other apostles, "Brothers,[p] what should we do?" [38]Peter said to them, "Repent, and be baptized every one of you in the name of Jesus Christ so that your sins may be forgiven; and you will receive the gift of the Holy Spirit. [39]For the promise is for you, for your children, and for all who are far away, everyone whom the Lord our God calls to him." [40]And he testified with many other arguments and exhorted them, saying, "Save yourselves from this corrupt generation." [41]So those who welcomed his message were baptized, and that day about three thousand persons were added. [42]They devoted themselves to the apostles' teaching and fellowship, to the breaking of bread and the prayers.

Life among the Believers

[43] Awe came upon everyone, because many wonders and signs were being done by the apostles. [44]All who believed were together and had all things in common; [45]they would sell their possessions and goods and distribute the proceeds[q] to all, as any had need. [46]Day by day, as they spent much time together in the temple, they broke bread at home[r] and ate their food with glad and generous[s] hearts, [47]praising God and having the goodwill of all the people. And

day by day the Lord added to their number those who were being saved.

Peter Heals a Crippled Beggar

3 One day Peter and John were going up to the temple at the hour of prayer, at three o'clock in the afternoon. [2]And a man lame from birth was being carried in. People would lay him daily at the gate of the temple called the Beautiful Gate so that he could ask for alms from those entering the temple. [3]When he saw Peter and John about to go into the temple, he asked them for alms. [4]Peter looked intently at him, as did John, and said, "Look at us." [5]And he fixed his attention on them, expecting to receive something from them. [6]But Peter said, "I have no silver or gold, but what I have I give you; in the name of Jesus Christ of Nazareth,[t] stand up and walk." [7]And he took him by the right hand and raised him up; and immediately his feet and ankles were made strong. [8]Jumping up, he stood and began to walk, and he entered the temple with them, walking and leaping and praising God. [9]All the people saw him walking and praising God, [10]and they recognized him as the one who used to sit and ask for alms at the Beautiful Gate of the temple; and they were filled with wonder and amazement at what had happened to him.

Peter Speaks in Solomon's Portico

[11] While he clung to Peter and John, all the people ran together to them in the portico called Solomon's Portico, utterly astonished. [12]When Peter saw it, he addressed the people, "You Israelites,[u] why do you wonder at this, or why do you stare at us, as though by our own power or piety we had made him walk? [13]The God of Abraham, the God of Isaac, and the God of Jacob, the God of our ancestors has

2.34
Ps 110.1;
Mt 22.44
2.37
Lk 3.10;
Acts 9.6;
16.30
2.38
Lk 24.47;
Acts 3.19;
5.31; 8.12,16;
22.16
2.39
Isa 57.19;
Joel 2.32;
Acts 10.45;
Eph 2.13
2.43
Acts 5.12
2.44
Acts 4.32,34
2.46
Acts 5.42;
20.7;
1 Cor 10.16
2.47
Acts 4.33;
Rom 14.18;
Acts 5.14;
11.24

3.1
Acts 2.46;
Ps 55.17
3.2
Acts 14.8;
Lk 16.20;
v. 10
3.4
Acts 10.4
3.6
Acts 4.10
3.9
Acts 4.16,21
3.10
Jn 9.8
3.11
Lk 22.8;
Jn 10.23;
Acts 5.12
3.13
Isa 52.13;
Acts 5.30;
Mt 27.2;
Acts 2.23;
Lk 23.4

n Or by o Or Christ p Gk Men,
brothers q Gk them r Or from house to
house s Or sincere t Gk the Nazorean
u Gk Men, Israelites

glorified his servant[v] Jesus, whom you handed over and rejected in the presence of Pilate, though he had decided to release him. [14]But you rejected the Holy and Righteous One and asked to have a murderer given to you, [15]and you killed the Author of life, whom God raised from the dead. To this we are witnesses. [16]And by faith in his name, his name itself has made this man strong, whom you see and know; and the faith that is through Jesus[w] has given him this perfect health in the presence of all of you.

[17] "And now, friends,[x] I know that you acted in ignorance, as did also your rulers. [18]In this way God fulfilled what he had foretold through all the prophets, that his Messiah[y] would suffer. [19]Repent therefore, and turn to God so that your sins may be wiped out, [20]so that times of refreshing may come from the presence of the Lord, and that he may send the Messiah[z] appointed for you, that is, Jesus, [21]who must remain in heaven until the time of universal restoration that God announced long ago through his holy prophets. [22]Moses said, 'The Lord your God will raise up for you from your own people[x] a prophet like me. You must listen to whatever he tells you. [23]And it will be that everyone who does not listen to that prophet will be utterly rooted out of the people.' [24]And all the prophets, as many as have spoken, from Samuel and those after him, also predicted these days. [25]You are the descendants of the prophets and of the covenant that God gave to your ancestors, saying to Abraham, 'And in your descendants all the families of the earth shall be blessed.' [26]When God raised up his servant,[v] he sent him first to you, to bless you by turning each of you from your wicked ways."

Peter and John before the Council

4 While Peter and John[a] were speaking to the people, the priests, the captain of the temple,

and the Sadducees came to them, [2]much annoyed because they were teaching the people and proclaiming that in Jesus there is the resurrection of the dead. [3]So they arrested them and put them in custody until the next day, for it was already evening. [4]But many of those who heard the word believed; and they numbered about five thousand.

[5] The next day their rulers, elders, and scribes assembled in Jerusalem, [6]with Annas the high priest, Caiaphas, John,[b] and Alexander, and all who were of the high-priestly family. [7]When they had made the prisoners[c] stand in their midst, they inquired, "By what power or by what name did you do this?" [8]Then Peter, filled with the Holy Spirit, said to them, "Rulers of the people and elders, [9]if we are questioned today because of a good deed done to someone who was sick and are asked how this man has been healed, [10]let it be known to all of you, and to all the people of Israel, that this man is standing before you in good health by the name of Jesus Christ of Nazareth,[d] whom you crucified, whom God raised from the dead. [11]This Jesus[e] is

'the stone that was rejected
 by you, the builders;
it has become the
 cornerstone.'[f]

[12]There is salvation in no one else, for there is no other name under heaven given among mortals by which we must be saved."

[13] Now when they saw the boldness of Peter and John and realized that they were uneducated and ordinary men, they were amazed and recognized them as companions of Jesus. [14]When they saw the man who had been cured standing beside them, they had nothing to say in opposition. [15]So they ordered

3.14
Mk 1.24;
Acts 4.27;
7.52;
Mk 15.11;
Lk 23.18-25
3.15
Acts 5.31;
2.24,32
3.17
Lk 23.34;
Acts 13.27
3.18
Acts 2.23;
Lk 24.27;
Acts 17.3;
26.23
3.21
Acts 1.11;
Mt 17.11;
Lk 1.70
3.22
Deut 18.15;
Acts 7.37
3.23
Deut 18.19
3.25
Acts 2.39;
Rom 9.4,8;
Gen 12.3;
28.14
3.26
Acts 13.46;
2.24; v. 22
4.1
Lk 22.4;
Mt 3.7;
Acts 6.12

4.2
Acts 17.18;
23.8
4.3
Acts 5.18
4.4
Acts 2.41
4.5
Lk 23.13
4.6
Lk 3.2;
Mt 26.3
4.8
Acts 13.9;
Lk 23.13;
v. 5
4.10
Acts 3.6;
2.24
4.11
Ps 118.22;
Isa 28.16;
Mt 21.42
4.12
Mt 1.21;
Acts 10.43;
1 Tim 2.5,
6
4.13
v. 31;
Mt 11.25;
1 Cor 1.27
4.15
Mt 5.22

v Or *child* w Gk *him* x Gk *brothers*
y Or *his Christ* z Or *the Christ*
a Gk *While they* b Other ancient
authorities read *Jonathan* c Gk *them*
d Gk *the Nazorean* e Gk *This*
f Or *keystone*

them to leave the council while they discussed the matter with one another. [16] They said, "What will we do with them? For it is obvious to all who live in Jerusalem that a notable sign has been done through them; we cannot deny it. [17] But to keep it from spreading further among the people, let us warn them to speak no more to anyone in this name." [18] So they called them and ordered them not to speak or teach at all in the name of Jesus. [19] But Peter and John answered them, "Whether it is right in God's sight to listen to you rather than to God, you must judge; [20] for we cannot keep from speaking about what we have seen and heard." [21] After threatening them again, they let them go, finding no way to punish them because of the people, for all of them praised God for what had happened. [22] For the man on whom this sign of healing had been performed was more than forty years old.

The Believers Pray for Boldness

23 After they were released, they went to their friends[g] and reported what the chief priests and the elders had said to them. [24] When they heard it, they raised their voices together to God and said, "Sovereign Lord, who made the heaven and the earth, the sea, and everything in them, [25] it is you who said by the Holy Spirit through our ancestor David, your servant:[h]
'Why did the Gentiles rage,
 and the peoples imagine
 vain things?
[26] The kings of the earth took
 their stand,
 and the rulers have
 gathered together
 against the Lord and
 against his Messiah.'[i]
[27] For in this city, in fact, both Herod and Pontius Pilate, with the Gentiles and the peoples of Israel, gathered together against your holy servant[h] Jesus, whom you anointed, [28] to do whatever your hand and your plan had predestined to take place. [29] And now, Lord, look at

their threats, and grant to your servants[j] to speak your word with all boldness, [30] while you stretch out your hand to heal, and signs and wonders are performed through the name of your holy servant[h] Jesus." [31] When they had prayed, the place in which they were gathered together was shaken; and they were all filled with the Holy Spirit and spoke the word of God with boldness.

The Believers Share Their Possessions

32 Now the whole group of those who believed were of one heart and soul, and no one claimed private ownership of any possessions, but everything they owned was held in common. [33] With great power the apostles gave their testimony to the resurrection of the Lord Jesus, and great grace was upon them all. [34] There was not a needy person among them, for as many as owned lands or houses sold them and brought the proceeds of what was sold. [35] They laid it at the apostles' feet, and it was distributed to each as any had need. [36] There was a Levite, a native of Cyprus, Joseph, to whom the apostles gave the name Barnabas (which means "son of encouragement"). [37] He sold a field that belonged to him, then brought the money, and laid it at the apostles' feet.

Ananias and Sapphira

5 But a man named Ananias, with the consent of his wife Sapphira, sold a piece of property; [2] with his wife's knowledge, he kept back some of the proceeds, and brought only a part and laid it at the apostles' feet. [3] "Ananias," Peter asked, "why has Satan filled your heart to lie to the Holy Spirit and to keep back part of the proceeds of the land? [4] While it remained unsold, did it not remain your own? And after it was sold, were not the proceeds at your dis-

4.16
Jn 11.47;
Acts 3.7-10
4.18
Acts 5.40
4.19
Acts 5.28,29
4.20
Acts 1.8;
2.32
4.24
2 Kings 19.15
4.25
Ps 2.1;
Acts 1.16
4.26
Heb 1.9
4.27
v. 30;
Lk 4.18;
Jn 10.36;
Mt 14.1;
Lk 23.12
4.28
Acts 2.23
4.29
vv. 13,31;
Acts 9.27;
13.46; 28.31
4.30
Acts 2.43;
5.12; 3.6,16;
v. 27
4.31
Acts 2.2,4;
v. 29
4.32
Acts 5.12;
2.44
4.33
Acts 1.8;
1.22
4.34
Acts 2.45
4.35
v. 37;
Acts 5.2;
2.45; 6.1
4.37
v. 35;
Acts 5.2
5.2
Acts 4.37
5.3
Deut 23.21;
Lk 22.3;
Jn 13.2,7;
v. 9

g Gk their own h Or child i Or his Christ j Gk slaves

posal? How is it that you have contrived this deed in your heart? You did not lie to us[k] but to God!" [5]Now when Ananias heard these words, he fell down and died. And great fear seized all who heard of it. [6]The young men came and wrapped up his body,[l] then carried him out and buried him.

7 After an interval of about three hours his wife came in, not knowing what had happened. [8]Peter said to her, "Tell me whether you and your husband sold the land for such and such a price." And she said, "Yes, that was the price." [9]Then Peter said to her, "How is it that you have agreed together to put the Spirit of the Lord to the test? Look, the feet of those who have buried your husband are at the door, and they will carry you out." [10]Immediately she fell down at his feet and died. When the young men came in they found her dead, so they carried her out and buried her beside her husband. [11]And great fear seized the whole church and all who heard of these things.

The Apostles Heal Many

12 Now many signs and wonders were done among the people through the apostles. And they were all together in Solomon's Portico. [13]None of the rest dared to join them, but the people held them in high esteem. [14]Yet more than ever believers were added to the Lord, great numbers of both men and women, [15]so that they even carried out the sick into the streets, and laid them on cots and mats, in order that Peter's shadow might fall on some of them as he came by. [16]A great number of people would also gather from the towns around Jerusalem, bringing the sick and those tormented by unclean spirits, and they were all cured.

The Apostles Are Persecuted

17 Then the high priest took action; he and all who were with him (that is, the sect of the Sadducees),

being filled with jealousy, [18]arrested the apostles and put them in the public prison. [19]But during the night an angel of the Lord opened the prison doors, brought them out, and said, [20]"Go, stand in the temple and tell the people the whole message about this life." [21]When they heard this, they entered the temple at daybreak and went on with their teaching.

When the high priest and those with him arrived, they called together the council and the whole body of the elders of Israel, and sent to the prison to have them brought. [22]But when the temple police went there, they did not find them in the prison; so they returned and reported, [23]"We found the prison securely locked and the guards standing at the doors, but when we opened them, we found no one inside." [24]Now when the captain of the temple and the chief priests heard these words, they were perplexed about them, wondering what might be going on. [25]Then someone arrived and announced, "Look, the men whom you put in prison are standing in the temple and teaching the people!" [26]Then the captain went with the temple police and brought them, but without violence, for they were afraid of being stoned by the people.

27 When they had brought them, they had them stand before the council. The high priest questioned them, [28]saying, "We gave you strict orders not to teach in this name,[m] yet here you have filled Jerusalem with your teaching and you are determined to bring this man's blood on us." [29]But Peter and the apostles answered, "We must obey God rather than any human authority.[n] [30]The God of our ancestors raised up Jesus, whom you had killed by hanging him on a tree. [31]God exalted him at his right hand as Leader and Savior that he

Cross references (center column):

5.5
vv. 10,11
5.6
Jn 19.40
5.8
v. 2
5.9
v. 3
5.10
v. 5
5.11
v. 5;
Acts 19.17
5.12
Acts 2.43;
3.11; 4.32
5.13
Acts 2.47;
4.21
5.14
Acts 2.47;
11.24
5.15
Mt 9.21;
14.36;
Acts 19.12 2
5.17
Acts 15.5;
4.1

5.18
Acts 4.3
5.19
Acts 12.7;
16.26
5.20
Jn 6.63,68
5.21
Acts 4.5,6;
vv. 27,34,41
5.24
Acts 4.1
5.26
Acts 4.21
5.28
Acts 4.18;
2.33,36; 3.15;
7.52;
Mt 23.35;
27.25
5.29
Acts 4.19
5.30
Acts 3.13,
15; 22.14;
10.39; 13.29;
Gal 3.13;
1 Pet 2.24
5.31
Acts 2.33;
Heb 2.10;
Acts 3.15

[k] Gk to men [l] Meaning of Gk uncertain
[m] Other ancient authorities read Did we not give you strict orders not to teach in this name?
[n] Gk than men

might give repentance to Israel and forgiveness of sins. 32 And we are witnesses to these things, and so is the Holy Spirit whom God has given to those who obey him."

33 When they heard this, they were enraged and wanted to kill them. 34 But a Pharisee in the council named Gamaliel, a teacher of the law, respected by all the people, stood up and ordered the men to be put outside for a short time. 35 Then he said to them, "Fellow Israelites, o consider carefully what you propose to do to these men. 36 For some time ago Theudas rose up, claiming to be somebody, and a number of men, about four hundred, joined him; but he was killed, and all who followed him were dispersed and disappeared. 37 After him Judas the Galilean rose up at the time of the census and got people to follow him; he also perished, and all who followed him were scattered. 38 So in the present case, I tell you, keep away from these men and let them alone; because if this plan or this undertaking is of human origin, it will fail; 39 but if it is of God, you will not be able to overthrow them — in that case you may even be found fighting against God!"

They were convinced by him, 40 and when they had called in the apostles, they had them flogged. Then they ordered them not to speak in the name of Jesus, and let them go. 41 As they left the council, they rejoiced that they were considered worthy to suffer dishonor for the sake of the name. 42 And every day in the temple and at home p they did not cease to teach and proclaim Jesus as the Messiah. q

Seven Chosen to Serve

6 Now during those days, when the disciples were increasing in number, the Hellenists complained against the Hebrews because their widows were being neglected in the daily distribution of food. 2 And the twelve called together the whole community of the

5.32
Lk 24.48;
Jn 15.26;
Rom 8.16
5.33
Acts 2.37;
7.54
5.38
Mt 15.13
5.39
Acts 7.51;
9.5; 11.17
5.40
Mt 10.17;
Mk 13.9
5.41
1 Pet 4.13,
16; Jn 15.21
5.42
Acts 2.46;
8.35; 11.20;
17.18;
Gal 1.16
6.1
Acts 2.41,
47; 9.29;
11.20; 4.35

6.3
Jn 21.23;
Acts 1.15
6.5
Acts 11.19,
24; 8.5,26;
21.8
6.6
Acts 1.24;
8.17; 9.17;
13.3;
1 Tim 4.14;
5.22;
2 Tim 1.6
6.7
Acts 12.24;
19.20;
Acts 13.8;
14.22;
Gal 1.23;
6.10
6.10
Lk 21.15;
Acts 5.39
6.11
Mt 26.59,60
6.13
Acts 7.58;
21.28
6.14
Mt 26.61;
15.1; 21.21;
26.3; 28.17

disciples and said, "It is not right that we should neglect the word of God in order to wait on tables. r 3 Therefore, friends, s select from among yourselves seven men of good standing, full of the Spirit and of wisdom, whom we may appoint to this task, 4 while we, for our part, will devote ourselves to prayer and to serving the word." 5 What they said pleased the whole community, and they chose Stephen, a man full of faith and the Holy Spirit, together with Philip, Prochorus, Nicanor, Timon, Parmenas, and Nicolaus, a proselyte of Antioch. 6 They had these men stand before the apostles, who prayed and laid their hands on them.

7 The word of God continued to spread; the number of the disciples increased greatly in Jerusalem, and a great many of the priests became obedient to the faith.

The Arrest of Stephen

8 Stephen, full of grace and power, did great wonders and signs among the people. 9 Then some of those who belonged to the synagogue of the Freedmen (as it was called), Cyrenians, Alexandrians, and others of those from Cilicia and Asia, stood up and argued with Stephen. 10 But they could not withstand the wisdom and the Spirit t with which he spoke. 11 Then they secretly instigated some men to say, "We have heard him speak blasphemous words against Moses and God." 12 They stirred up the people as well as the elders and the scribes; then they suddenly confronted him, seized him, and brought him before the council. 13 They set up false witnesses who said, "This man never stops saying things against this holy place and the law; 14 for we have heard him say that this Jesus of Nazareth u will destroy this place and will change the customs that Moses handed on to us."

o Gk Men, Israelites　　p Or from house to house　　q Or the Christ　　r Or keep accounts　　s Gk brothers　　t Or spirit
u Gk the Nazorean

[15] And all who sat in the council looked intently at him, and they saw that his face was like the face of an angel.

Stephen's Speech to the Council

7 Then the high priest asked him, "Are these things so?" [2] And Stephen replied:

"Brothers[v] and fathers, listen to me. The God of glory appeared to our ancestor Abraham when he was in Mesopotamia, before he lived in Haran, [3] and said to him, 'Leave your country and your relatives and go to the land that I will show you.' [4] Then he left the country of the Chaldeans and settled in Haran. After his father died, God had him move from there to this country in which you are now living. [5] He did not give him any of it as a heritage, not even a foot's length, but promised to give it to him as his possession and to his descendants after him, even though he had no child. [6] And God spoke in these terms, that his descendants would be resident aliens in a country belonging to others, who would enslave them and mistreat them during four hundred years. [7] 'But I will judge the nation that they serve,' said God, 'and after that they shall come out and worship me in this place.' [8] Then he gave him the covenant of circumcision. And so Abraham[w] became the father of Isaac and circumcised him on the eighth day; and Isaac became the father of Jacob, and Jacob of the twelve patriarchs.

[9] "The patriarchs, jealous of Joseph, sold him into Egypt; but God was with him, [10] and rescued him from all his afflictions, and enabled him to win favor and to show wisdom when he stood before Pharaoh, king of Egypt, who appointed him ruler over Egypt and over all his household. [11] Now there came a famine throughout Egypt and Canaan, and great suffering, and our ancestors could find no food. [12] But when Jacob heard that there was grain in Egypt, he sent our ancestors there on their first visit. [13] On the second visit Joseph made himself known to his brothers, and Joseph's family became known to Pharaoh. [14] Then Joseph sent and invited his father Jacob and all his relatives to come to him, seventy-five in all; [15] so Jacob went down to Egypt. He himself died there as well as our ancestors, [16] and their bodies[x] were brought back to Shechem and laid in the tomb that Abraham had bought for a sum of silver from the sons of Hamor in Shechem.

[17] "But as the time drew near for the fulfillment of the promise that God had made to Abraham, our people in Egypt increased and multiplied [18] until another king who had not known Joseph ruled over Egypt. [19] He dealt craftily with our race and forced our ancestors to abandon their infants so that they would die. [20] At this time Moses was born, and he was beautiful before God. For three months he was brought up in his father's house; [21] and when he was abandoned, Pharaoh's daughter adopted him and brought him up as her own son. [22] So Moses was instructed in all the wisdom of the Egyptians and was powerful in his words and deeds.

[23] "When he was forty years old, it came into his heart to visit his relatives, the Israelites.[y] [24] When he saw one of them being wronged, he defended the oppressed man and avenged him by striking down the Egyptian. [25] He supposed that his kinsfolk would understand that God through him was rescuing them, but they did not understand. [26] The next day he came to some of them as they were quarreling and tried to reconcile them, saying, 'Men, you are brothers; why do you wrong each other?' [27] But the man who was wronging his neighbor pushed Moses[z] aside, saying, 'Who made you a ruler and a judge over us? [28] Do you want to kill me as you killed the Egyptian yester-

Cross references

7.2 Acts 22.1; Ps 29.3; Gen 11.31; 15.7
7.3 Gen 12.1
7.4 Gen 12.5
7.5 Gen 12.7; 17.8; 26.3
7.6 Gen 15.13, 14; Ex 12.40
7.7 Ex 3.12
7.8 Gen 17.9-11; 21.2-4; 25.26; 29.31ff
7.9 Gen 37.4, 11,28; 39.2, 21,23
7.10 Gen 41.37; 42.6
7.11 Gen 41.54
7.12 Gen 42.1,2
7.13 Gen 45.1-4

7.14 Gen 45.9, 10; 46.26,27; Deut 10.22
7.15 Gen 46.5; 49.33; Ex 1.6
7.16 Gen 23.16; 33.19; Josh 24.32
7.17 Ex 1.7-9; Ps 105.24, 25
7.19 Ex 1.10,11, 15-22
7.22 1 Kings 4.30; Isa 19.11
7.23 Ex 2.11,12

[v] Gk *Men, brothers* [w] Gk *he*
[x] Gk *they* [y] Gk *his brothers, the sons of Israel* [z] Gk *him*

day?' ²⁹When he heard this, Moses fled and became a resident alien in the land of Midian. There he became the father of two sons.

30 "Now when forty years had passed, an angel appeared to him in the wilderness of Mount Sinai, in the flame of a burning bush. ³¹When Moses saw it, he was amazed at the sight; and as he approached to look, there came the voice of the Lord: ³²'I am the God of your ancestors, the God of Abraham, Isaac, and Jacob.' Moses began to tremble and did not dare to look. ³³Then the Lord said to him, 'Take off the sandals from your feet, for the place where you are standing is holy ground. ³⁴I have surely seen the mistreatment of my people who are in Egypt and have heard their groaning, and I have come down to rescue them. Come now, I will send you to Egypt.'

35 "It was this Moses whom they rejected when they said, 'Who made you a ruler and a judge?' and whom God now sent as both ruler and liberator through the angel who appeared to him in the bush. ³⁶He led them out, having performed wonders and signs in Egypt, at the Red Sea, and in the wilderness for forty years. ³⁷This is the Moses who said to the Israelites, 'God will raise up a prophet for you from your own people[a] as he raised me up.' ³⁸He is the one who was in the congregation in the wilderness with the angel who spoke to him at Mount Sinai, and with our ancestors; and he received living oracles to give to us. ³⁹Our ancestors were unwilling to obey him; instead, they pushed him aside, and in their hearts they turned back to Egypt, ⁴⁰saying to Aaron, 'Make gods for us who will lead the way for us; as for this Moses who led us out from the land of Egypt, we do not know what has happened to him.' ⁴¹At that time they made a calf, offered a sacrifice to the idol, and reveled in the works of their hands. ⁴²But God turned away from them and handed them over to worship the host of

7.30 Ex 3.1,2
7.32 Ex 3.6
7.33 Ex 3.5; Josh 5.15
7.34 Ex 3.7
7.35 Ex 14.19
7.36 Ex 12.41; 14.21
7.37 Deut 18.15, 18; Acts 3.22
7.38 Ex 19.17; Isa 63.9; Rom 3.2; Heb 5.12; 1 Pet 4.11
7.40 Ex 32.1,23
7.41 Ex 32.4,6; Ps 106.19
7.42 Ezek 20.25, 39; Am 5.25,26

7.44 Ex 25.9,40
7.45 Josh 3.14-17; Ps 44.2
7.46 2 Sam 7.8-16; Ps 132.1-5
7.48 1 Kings 8.27; 2 Chr 2.6
7.49 Isa 66.1,2; Mt 5.34,35
7.51 Lev 26.41; Jer 6.10; 9.26
7.52 2 Chr 36.16; Mt 23.31, 37; Acts 3.14
7.53 Ex 20.1; Heb 2.2

heaven, as it is written in the book of the prophets:

'Did you offer to me slain
 victims and sacrifices
forty years in the
 wilderness, O house of
 Israel?
⁴³ No; you took along the tent
 of Moloch,
and the star of your god
 Rephan,
 the images that you made
 to worship;
so I will remove you beyond
 Babylon.'

44 "Our ancestors had the tent of testimony in the wilderness, as God[b] directed when he spoke to Moses, ordering him to make it according to the pattern he had seen. ⁴⁵Our ancestors in turn brought it in with Joshua when they dispossessed the nations that God drove out before our ancestors. And it was there until the time of David, ⁴⁶who found favor with God and asked that he might find a dwelling place for the house of Jacob.[c] ⁴⁷But it was Solomon who built a house for him. ⁴⁸Yet the Most High does not dwell in houses made with human hands;[d] as the prophet says,

⁴⁹ 'Heaven is my throne,
 and the earth is my
 footstool.
 What kind of house will you
 build for me, says the
 Lord,
 or what is the place of my
 rest?
⁵⁰ Did not my hand make all
 these things?'

51 "You stiff-necked people, uncircumcised in heart and ears, you are forever opposing the Holy Spirit, just as your ancestors used to do. ⁵²Which of the prophets did your ancestors not persecute? They killed those who foretold the coming of the Righteous One, and now you have become his betrayers and murderers. ⁵³You are the ones that

a Gk *your brothers* b Gk *he* c Other ancient authorities read *for the God of Jacob* d Gk *with hands*

received the law as ordained by angels, and yet you have not kept it."

The Stoning of Stephen

54 When they heard these things, they became enraged and ground their teeth at Stephen.e 55 But filled with the Holy Spirit, he gazed into heaven and saw the glory of God and Jesus standing at the right hand of God. 56 "Look," he said, "I see the heavens opened and the Son of Man standing at the right hand of God!" 57 But they covered their ears, and with a loud shout all rushed together against him. 58 Then they dragged him out of the city and began to stone him; and the witnesses laid their coats at the feet of a young man named Saul. 59 While they were stoning Stephen, he prayed, "Lord Jesus, receive my spirit." 60 Then he knelt down and cried out in a loud voice, "Lord, do not hold this sin against them." When he had said this, he died.f 8 1 And Saul approved of their killing him.

Saul Persecutes the Church

That day a severe persecution began against the church in Jerusalem, and all except the apostles were scattered throughout the countryside of Judea and Samaria. 2 Devout men buried Stephen and made loud lamentation over him. 3 But Saul was ravaging the church by entering house after house; dragging off both men and women, he committed them to prison.

Philip Preaches in Samaria

4 Now those who were scattered went from place to place, proclaiming the word. 5 Philip went down to the cityg of Samaria and proclaimed the Messiahh to them. 6 The crowds with one accord listened eagerly to what was said by Philip, hearing and seeing the signs that he did, 7 for unclean spirits, crying with loud shrieks, came out of many who were possessed; and many others who were paralyzed or lame were cured. 8 So there was great joy in that city.

9 Now a certain man named Si-

mon had previously practiced magic in the city and amazed the people of Samaria, saying that he was someone great. 10 All of them, from the least to the greatest, listened to him eagerly, saying, "This man is the power of God that is called Great." 11 And they listened eagerly to him because for a long time he had amazed them with his magic. 12 But when they believed Philip, who was proclaiming the good news about the kingdom of God and the name of Jesus Christ, they were baptized, both men and women. 13 Even Simon himself believed. After being baptized, he stayed constantly with Philip and was amazed when he saw the signs and great miracles that took place.

14 Now when the apostles at Jerusalem heard that Samaria had accepted the word of God, they sent Peter and John to them. 15 The two went down and prayed for them that they might receive the Holy Spirit 16 (for as yet the Spirit had not comei upon any of them; they had only been baptized in the name of the Lord Jesus). 17 Then Peter and Johnj laid their hands on them, and they received the Holy Spirit. 18 Now when Simon saw that the Spirit was given through the laying on of the apostles' hands, he offered them money, 19 saying, "Give me also this power so that anyone on whom I lay my hands may receive the Holy Spirit." 20 But Peter said to him, "May your silver perish with you, because you thought you could obtain God's gift with money! 21 You have no part or share in this, for your heart is not right before God. 22 Repent therefore of this wickedness of yours, and pray to the Lord that, if possible, the intent of your heart may be forgiven you. 23 For I see that you are in the gall of bitterness and the chains of wickedness." 24 Simon answered, "Pray for me to the Lord, that nothing of

Center column cross-references:

7.55 Acts 6.5
7.56 Mt 3.16; Dan 7.13
7.58 Lk 4.29; Lev 24.16; Deut 13.9, 10
7.59 Acts 9.14
7.60 Acts 9.40
8.1 Acts 7.58; 11.19
8.2 Gen 23.2; 50.10; 2 Sam 3.31
8.3 Acts 7.58; 22.4; 25.10, 11; 1 Cor 15.9; Gal 1.13; Phil 3.6; 1 Tim 1.13
8.4 v. 1; Acts 15.35
8.5 Acts 6.5
8.7 Mt 4.24
8.9 Acts 13.6; 5.36
8.10 Acts 14.11; 28.6
8.12 Acts 1.3; 2.38
8.13 v. 6; Acts 19.11
8.14 v. 1
8.15 Acts 2.38
8.16 Acts 19.2; Mt 28.19; Acts 10.48; 19.5
8.17 Acts 6.6; 2.4
8.20 Acts 2.38; Mt 10.8; 2 Kings 5.16
8.21 Ps 78.37
8.23 Isa 58.6; Heb 12.15

e Gk him f Gk fell asleep g Other ancient authorities read a city h Or the Christ i Gk fallen j Gk they

what you[k] have said may happen to me."

25 Now after Peter and John[l] had testified and spoken the word of the Lord, they returned to Jerusalem, proclaiming the good news to many villages of the Samaritans.

Philip and the Ethiopian Eunuch

26 Then an angel of the Lord said to Philip, "Get up and go toward the south[m] to the road that goes down from Jerusalem to Gaza." (This is a wilderness road.) [27] So he got up and went. Now there was an Ethiopian eunuch, a court official of the Candace, queen of the Ethiopians, in charge of her entire treasury. He had come to Jerusalem to worship [28] and was returning home; seated in his chariot, he was reading the prophet Isaiah. [29] Then the Spirit said to Philip, "Go over to this chariot and join it." [30] So Philip ran up to it and heard him reading the prophet Isaiah. He asked, "Do you understand what you are reading?" [31] He replied, "How can I, unless someone guides me?" And he invited Philip to get in and sit beside him. [32] Now the passage of the scripture that he was reading was this:

"Like a sheep he was led to
 the slaughter,
and like a lamb silent
 before its shearer,
so he does not open his
 mouth.
[33] In his humiliation justice
 was denied him.
Who can describe his
 generation?
For his life is taken away
 from the earth."

[34] The eunuch asked Philip, "About whom, may I ask you, does the prophet say this, about himself or about someone else?" [35] Then Philip began to speak, and starting with this scripture, he proclaimed to him the good news about Jesus. [36] As they were going along the road, they came to some water; and the eunuch said, "Look, here is water! What is to prevent me from be-

ing baptized?"[n] [38] He commanded the chariot to stop, and both of them, Philip and the eunuch, went down into the water, and Philip[o] baptized him. [39] When they came up out of the water, the Spirit of the Lord snatched Philip away; the eunuch saw him no more, and went on his way rejoicing. [40] But Philip found himself at Azotus, and as he was passing through the region, he proclaimed the good news to all the towns until he came to Caesarea.

The Conversion of Saul

9 Meanwhile Saul, still breathing threats and murder against the disciples of the Lord, went to the high priest [2] and asked him for letters to the synagogues at Damascus, so that if he found any who belonged to the Way, men or women, he might bring them bound to Jerusalem. [3] Now as he was going along and approaching Damascus, suddenly a light from heaven flashed around him. [4] He fell to the ground and heard a voice saying to him, "Saul, Saul, why do you persecute me?" [5] He asked, "Who are you, Lord?" The reply came, "I am Jesus, whom you are persecuting. [6] But get up and enter the city, and you will be told what you are to do." [7] The men who were traveling with him stood speechless because they heard the voice but saw no one. [8] Saul got up from the ground, and though his eyes were open, he could see nothing; so they led him by the hand and brought him into Damascus. [9] For three days he was without sight, and neither ate nor drank.

10 Now there was a disciple in Damascus named Ananias. The Lord said to him in a vision, "Ananias." He answered, "Here I am, Lord." [11] The Lord said to him,

Cross-references (center column)

8.25 Lk 16.28; v. 40
8.26 Acts 5.19; v. 5
8.27 Ps 68.31; Zeph 3.10; Jn 12.20
8.29 Acts 10.19; 11.12; 13.2; 20.23; 21.11
8.32 Isa 53.7,8
8.35 Mt 5.2; Lk 24.27; Acts 17.2; 18.28; 5.42
8.36 Acts 10.47

8.39 1 Kings 18.12; 2 Kings 2.16; Ezek 3.12, 14
9.1 Acts 8.3; 22.4-16; 26.9-18
9.3 Acts 22.6; 26.12; 1 Cor 15.8
9.4 Acts 22.7; 26.14
9.7 Acts 22.9; 26.13,14
9.8 Acts 22.11; Gal 1.17
9.10 Acts 22.12
9.11 Acts 21.39; 22.3

[k] The Greek word for *you* and the verb *pray* are plural [l] Gk *after they* [m] Or *go at noon* [n] Other ancient authorities add all or most of verse 37, *And Philip said, "If you believe with all your heart, you may." And he replied, "I believe that Jesus Christ is the Son of God."* [o] Gk *he*

"Get up and go to the street called Straight, and at the house of Judas look for a man of Tarsus named Saul. At this moment he is praying, [12] and he has seen in a vision[p] a man named Ananias come in and lay his hands on him so that he might regain his sight." [13] But Ananias answered, "Lord, I have heard from many about this man, how much evil he has done to your saints in Jerusalem; [14] and here he has authority from the chief priests to bind all who invoke your name." [15] But the Lord said to him, "Go, for he is an instrument whom I have chosen to bring my name before Gentiles and kings and before the people of Israel; [16] I myself will show him how much he must suffer for the sake of my name." [17] So Ananias went and entered the house. He laid his hands on Saul[q] and said, "Brother Saul, the Lord Jesus, who appeared to you on your way here, has sent me so that you may regain your sight and be filled with the Holy Spirit." [18] And immediately something like scales fell from his eyes, and his sight was restored. Then he got up and was baptized, [19] and after taking some food, he regained his strength.

Saul Preaches in Damascus

For several days he was with the disciples in Damascus, [20] and immediately he began to proclaim Jesus in the synagogues, saying, "He is the Son of God." [21] All who heard him were amazed and said, "Is not this the man who made havoc in Jerusalem among those who invoked this name? And has he not come here for the purpose of bringing them bound before the chief priests?" [22] Saul became increasingly more powerful and confounded the Jews who lived in Damascus by proving that Jesus[r] was the Messiah.[s]

Saul Escapes from the Jews

23 After some time had passed, the Jews plotted to kill him, [24] but their plot became known to Saul. They were watching the gates day

and night so that they might kill him; [25] but his disciples took him by night and let him down through an opening in the wall,[t] lowering him in a basket.

Saul in Jerusalem

26 When he had come to Jerusalem, he attempted to join the disciples; and they were all afraid of him, for they did not believe that he was a disciple. [27] But Barnabas took him, brought him to the apostles, and described for them how on the road he had seen the Lord, who had spoken to him, and how in Damascus he had spoken boldly in the name of Jesus. [28] So he went in and out among them in Jerusalem, speaking boldly in the name of the Lord. [29] He spoke and argued with the Hellenists; but they were attempting to kill him. [30] When the believers[u] learned of it, they brought him down to Caesarea and sent him off to Tarsus.

31 Meanwhile the church throughout Judea, Galilee, and Samaria had peace and was built up. Living in the fear of the Lord and in the comfort of the Holy Spirit, it increased in numbers.

The Healing of Aeneas

32 Now as Peter went here and there among all the believers,[v] he came down also to the saints living in Lydda. [33] There he found a man named Aeneas, who had been bedridden for eight years, for he was paralyzed. [34] Peter said to him, "Aeneas, Jesus Christ heals you; get up and make your bed!" And immediately he got up. [35] And all the residents of Lydda and Sharon saw him and turned to the Lord.

Peter in Lydda and Joppa

36 Now in Joppa there was a disciple whose name was Tabitha, which in Greek is Dorcas.[w] She was devoted to good works and acts

Center cross-reference column

9.14
v. 21;
Acts 7.59;
1 Cor 1.2;
2 Tim 2.22
9.15
Acts 13.2;
Eph 3.7,8;
Gal 2.7,8;
Acts 25.22,
23; 26.1
9.16
Acts 20.23;
21.11;
2 Cor 11.23
9.17
Acts 22.12,
13; 8.17; 2.4;
4.31
9.19
Acts 26.20
9.21
Acts 8.3;
Gal 1.13,23
9.22
Acts 18.28
9.23
Acts 23.12;
25.3
9.24
2 Cor 11.32,
33

9.26
Acts 22.17;
Gal 1.17,18
9.27
Acts 4.36;
vv. 20,22
9.29
Acts 6.1;
11.20;
2 Cor 11.26
9.31
Acts 8.1
9.32
v. 13
9.34
Acts 3.6,16;
4.10
9.35
1 Chr 5.16;
Acts 11.21
9.36
Jn 1.5;
1 Tim 2.10;
Titus 3.8

Footnotes

p Other ancient authorities lack *in a vision*
q Gk *him* r Gk *that this* s Or the Christ t Gk *through the wall*
u Gk *brothers* v Gk *all of them*
w The name Tabitha in Aramaic and the name Dorcas in Greek mean *a gazelle*

of charity. [37] At that time she became ill and died. When they had washed her, they laid her in a room upstairs. [38] Since Lydda was near Joppa, the disciples, who heard that Peter was there, sent two men to him with the request, "Please come to us without delay." [39] So Peter got up and went with them; and when he arrived, they took him to the room upstairs. All the widows stood beside him, weeping and showing tunics and other clothing that Dorcas had made while she was with them. [40] Peter put all of them outside, and then he knelt down and prayed. He turned to the body and said, "Tabitha, get up." Then she opened her eyes, and seeing Peter, she sat up. [41] He gave her his hand and helped her up. Then calling the saints and widows, he showed her to be alive. [42] This became known throughout Joppa, and many believed in the Lord. [43] Meanwhile he stayed in Joppa for some time with a certain Simon, a tanner.

Peter and Cornelius

10 In Caesarea there was a man named Cornelius, a centurion of the Italian Cohort, as it was called. [2] He was a devout man who feared God with all his household; he gave alms generously to the people and prayed constantly to God. [3] One afternoon at about three o'clock he had a vision in which he clearly saw an angel of God coming in and saying to him, "Cornelius." [4] He stared at him in terror and said, "What is it, Lord?" He answered, "Your prayers and your alms have ascended as a memorial before God. [5] Now send men to Joppa for a certain Simon who is called Peter; [6] he is lodging with Simon, a tanner, whose house is by the seaside." [7] When the angel who spoke to him had left, he called two of his slaves and a devout soldier from the ranks of those who served him, [8] and after telling them everything, he sent them to Joppa.

[9] About noon the next day, as they were on their journey and ap-

9.37
Acts 1.13
9.38
Acts 11.26
9.39
Acts 6.1
9.40
Mt 9.25;
Acts 7.60;
Mk 5.41,42
9.41
v. 13
9.43
Acts 10.6
10.2
vv. 22,35
10.3
Acts 9.10;
3.1; 5.19
10.4
Acts 3.4;
Rev 8.4;
Mt 26.13
10.6
Acts 9.43
10.9
Acts 11.5-14;
Mt 24.17

10.10
Acts 22.17
10.11
Acts 7.56;
Rev 19.11
10.14
Acts 9.5;
Lev 11.4;
20.25;
Deut 14.3,7;
Ezek 4.14
10.15
v. 28;
Mt 15.11;
Rom 14.14,
17,20;
1 Cor 10.25;
1 Tim 4.4;
Titus 1.15
10.17
v. 3
10.19
Acts 11.12
10.20
Acts 15.7
10.22
v. 2;
Acts 11.14
10.23
v. 45;
Acts 11.12

proaching the city, Peter went up on the roof to pray. [10] He became hungry and wanted something to eat; and while it was being prepared, he fell into a trance. [11] He saw the heaven opened and something like a large sheet coming down, being lowered to the ground by its four corners. [12] In it were all kinds of four-footed creatures and reptiles and birds of the air. [13] Then he heard a voice saying, "Get up, Peter; kill and eat." [14] But Peter said, "By no means, Lord; for I have never eaten anything that is profane or unclean." [15] The voice said to him again, a second time, "What God has made clean, you must not call profane." [16] This happened three times, and the thing was suddenly taken up to heaven.

[17] Now while Peter was greatly puzzled about what to make of the vision that he had seen, suddenly the men sent by Cornelius appeared. They were asking for Simon's house and were standing by the gate. [18] They called out to ask whether Simon, who was called Peter, was staying there. [19] While Peter was still thinking about the vision, the Spirit said to him, "Look, three[x] men are searching for you. [20] Now get up, go down, and go with them without hesitation; for I have sent them." [21] So Peter went down to the men and said, "I am the one you are looking for; what is the reason for your coming?" [22] They answered, "Cornelius, a centurion, an upright and God-fearing man, who is well spoken of by the whole Jewish nation, was directed by a holy angel to send for you to come to his house and to hear what you have to say." [23] So Peter[y] invited them in and gave them lodging.

The next day he got up and went with them, and some of the believers[z] from Joppa accompanied him. [24] The following day they came to Caesarea. Cornelius was expecting them and had called together his relatives and close

[x] One ancient authority reads *two*; others lack the word [y] Gk *he* [z] Gk *brothers*

friends. 25On Peter's arrival Cornelius met him, and falling at his feet, worshiped him. 26But Peter made him get up, saying, "Stand up; I am only a mortal." 27And as he talked with him, he went in and found that many had assembled; 28and he said to them, "You yourselves know that it is unlawful for a Jew to associate with or to visit a Gentile; but God has shown me that I should not call anyone profane or unclean. 29So when I was sent for, I came without objection. Now may I ask why you sent for me?"

30 Cornelius replied, "Four days ago at this very hour, at three o'clock, I was praying in my house when suddenly a man in dazzling clothes stood before me. 31He said, 'Cornelius, your prayer has been heard and your alms have been remembered before God. 32Send therefore to Joppa and ask for Simon, who is called Peter; he is staying in the home of Simon, a tanner, by the sea.' 33Therefore I sent for you immediately, and you have been kind enough to come. So now all of us are here in the presence of God to listen to all that the Lord has commanded you to say."

Gentiles Hear the Good News

34 Then Peter began to speak to them: "I truly understand that God shows no partiality, 35but in every nation anyone who fears him and does what is right is acceptable to him. 36You know the message he sent to the people of Israel, preaching peace by Jesus Christ—he is Lord of all. 37That message spread throughout Judea, beginning in Galilee after the baptism that John announced: 38how God anointed Jesus of Nazareth with the Holy Spirit and with power; how he went about doing good and healing all who were oppressed by the devil, for God was with him. 39We are witnesses to all that he did both in Judea and in Jerusalem. They put him to death by hanging him on a tree; 40but God raised him on the third day and allowed him to ap-

pear, 41not to all the people but to us who were chosen by God as witnesses, and who ate and drank with him after he rose from the dead. 42He commanded us to preach to the people and to testify that he is the one ordained by God as judge of the living and the dead. 43All the prophets testify about him that everyone who believes in him receives forgiveness of sins through his name."

Gentiles Receive the Holy Spirit

44 While Peter was still speaking, the Holy Spirit fell upon all who heard the word. 45The circumcised believers who had come with Peter were astounded that the gift of the Holy Spirit had been poured out even on the Gentiles, 46for they heard them speaking in tongues and extolling God. Then Peter said, 47"Can anyone withhold the water for baptizing these people who have received the Holy Spirit just as we have?" 48So he ordered them to be baptized in the name of Jesus Christ. Then they invited him to stay for several days.

Peter's Report to the Church at Jerusalem

11 Now the apostles and the believers[a] who were in Judea heard that the Gentiles had also accepted the word of God. 2So when Peter went up to Jerusalem, the circumcised believers[b] criticized him, 3saying, "Why did you go to uncircumcised men and eat with them?" 4Then Peter began to explain it to them, step by step, saying, 5"I was in the city of Joppa praying, and in a trance I saw a vision. There was something like a large sheet coming down from heaven, being lowered by its four corners; and it came close to me. 6As I looked at it closely I saw four-footed animals, beasts of prey, reptiles, and birds of the air. 7I also heard a voice saying to me, 'Get up, Peter; kill and eat.' 8But I replied, 'By no means, Lord; for nothing profane or unclean has ever en-

10.26
Acts 24.14, 15;
Rev 19.10
10.28
Jn 4.9;
18.28;
Acts 11.3;
15.8,9
10.30
Acts 1.10;
Mt 28.3;
Mk 16.5;
Lk 24.4
10.34
Deut 10.17;
Rom 2.11;
Eph 6.9;
Col 3.25;
1 Pet 1.17
10.35
Acts 15.9
10.36
Isa 57.19;
Mt 28.18;
Rom 10.12;
Eph 1.20,22
10.38
Acts 2.22;
Jn 3.2
10.39
Lk 24.48;
Acts 5.30
10.40
Acts 2.24

10.41
Jn 14.17,22;
21.13
10.42
Mt 28.19, 20;
Rom 14.9;
2 Cor 5.10;
1 Pet 4.5
10.43
Isa 53.11;
Acts 26.22;
15.9;
Rom 10.11;
Gal 3.22
10.44
Acts 4.31;
8.15,16;
11.15; 15.8
10.45
v. 23;
Acts 11.18
10.47
Acts 8.36;
11.17
10.48
1 Cor 1.17;
Acts 2.38;
8.16; 19.5
11.2
Acts 10.45
11.3
Acts 10.28;
Gal 2.12
11.4
Lk 1.3
11.5
Acts 10.9-32

a Gk brothers b Gk lacks believers

tered my mouth.' ⁹But a second time the voice answered from heaven, 'What God has made clean, you must not call profane.' ¹⁰This happened three times; then everything was pulled up again to heaven. ¹¹At that very moment three men, sent to me from Caesarea, arrived at the house where we were. ¹²The Spirit told me to go with them and not to make a distinction between them and us.ᶜ These six brothers also accompanied me, and we entered the man's house. ¹³He told us how he had seen the angel standing in his house and saying, 'Send to Joppa and bring Simon, who is called Peter; ¹⁴he will give you a message by which you and your entire household will be saved.' ¹⁵And as I began to speak, the Holy Spirit fell upon them just as it had upon us at the beginning. ¹⁶And I remembered the word of the Lord, how he had said, 'John baptized with water, but you will be baptized with the Holy Spirit.' ¹⁷If then God gave them the same gift that he gave us when we believed in the Lord Jesus Christ, who was I that I could hinder God?" ¹⁸When they heard this, they were silenced. And they praised God, saying, "Then God has given even to the Gentiles the repentance that leads to life."

The Church in Antioch

19 Now those who were scattered because of the persecution that took place over Stephen traveled as far as Phoenicia, Cyprus, and Antioch, and they spoke the word to no one except Jews. ²⁰But among them were some men of Cyprus and Cyrene who, on coming to Antioch, spoke to the Hellenistsᵈ also, proclaiming the Lord Jesus. ²¹The hand of the Lord was with them, and a great number became believers and turned to the Lord. ²²News of this came to the ears of the church in Jerusalem, and they sent Barnabas to Antioch. ²³When he came and saw the grace of God, he rejoiced, and he exhorted them all to remain faithful to the Lord

with steadfast devotion; ²⁴for he was a good man, full of the Holy Spirit and of faith. And a great many people were brought to the Lord. ²⁵Then Barnabas went to Tarsus to look for Saul, ²⁶and when he had found him, he brought him to Antioch. So it was that for an entire year they met withᵉ the church and taught a great many people, and it was in Antioch that the disciples were first called "Christians."

27 At that time prophets came down from Jerusalem to Antioch. ²⁸One of them named Agabus stood up and predicted by the Spirit that there would be a severe famine over all the world; and this took place during the reign of Claudius. ²⁹The disciples determined that according to their ability, each would send relief to the believersᶠ living in Judea; ³⁰this they did, sending it to the elders by Barnabas and Saul.

James Killed and Peter Imprisoned

12 About that time King Herod laid violent hands upon some who belonged to the church. ²He had James, the brother of John, killed with the sword. ³After he saw that it pleased the Jews, he proceeded to arrest Peter also. (This was during the festival of Unleavened Bread.) ⁴When he had seized him, he put him in prison and handed him over to four squads of soldiers to guard him, intending to bring him out to the people after the Passover. ⁵While Peter was kept in prison, the church prayed fervently to God for him.

Peter Delivered from Prison

6 The very night before Herod was going to bring him out, Peter, bound with two chains, was sleeping between two soldiers, while guards in front of the door were keeping watch over the prison. ⁷Suddenly an angel of the Lord ap-

11.9 Acts 10.15
11.12 Acts 8.29; 15.9; 10.23
11.13 Acts 10.30
11.15 Acts 10.44; 2.4
11.16 Mt 3.11; Jn 1.26,33; Acts 1.5; Joel 2.28; 3.18
11.17 Acts 10.45, 47
11.18 Rom 10.12, 13; 2 Cor 7.10
11.19 Acts 8.1,4
11.20 Acts 4.36; 6.5; 13.1; 5.42
11.21 Lk 1.66; Acts 2.47; 9.35
11.23 Acts 13.43; 14.22

11.24 Acts 6.5; v. 21; Acts 5.14
11.25 Acts 9.11,30
11.26 Acts 26.28
11.27 Acts 18.22; 1 Cor 12.28
11.28 Acts 21.10
11.29 Rom 15.26; 1 Cor 16.1; 2 Cor 9.1
11.30 Acts 12.25; 14.23
12.2 Mt 4.21; 20.23
12.3 Acts 24.27; Ex 12.15; 23.15
12.5 Eph 6.18; 1 Thes 5.17
12.6 Acts 21.33
12.7 Acts 5.19; 16.26

ᶜ Or not to hesitate ᵈ Other ancient authorities read Greeks ᵉ Or were guests of ᶠ Gk brothers

peared and a light shone in the cell. He tapped Peter on the side and woke him, saying, "Get up quickly." And the chains fell off his wrists. 8 The angel said to him, "Fasten your belt and put on your sandals." He did so. Then he said to him, "Wrap your cloak around you and follow me." 9 Peter[g] went out and followed him; he did not realize that what was happening with the angel's help was real; he thought he was seeing a vision. 10 After they had passed the first and the second guard, they came before the iron gate leading into the city. It opened for them of its own accord, and they went outside and walked along a lane, when suddenly the angel left him. 11 Then Peter came to himself and said, "Now I am sure that the Lord has sent his angel and rescued me from the hands of Herod and from all that the Jewish people were expecting."

12 As soon as he realized this, he went to the house of Mary, the mother of John whose other name was Mark, where many had gathered and were praying. 13 When he knocked at the outer gate, a maid named Rhoda came to answer. 14 On recognizing Peter's voice, she was so overjoyed that, instead of opening the gate, she ran in and announced that Peter was standing at the gate. 15 They said to her, "You are out of your mind!" But she insisted that it was so. They said, "It is his angel." 16 Meanwhile Peter continued knocking; and when they opened the gate, they saw him and were amazed. 17 He motioned to them with his hand to be silent, and described for them how the Lord had brought him out of the prison. And he added, "Tell this to James and to the believers."[h] Then he left and went to another place.

18 When morning came, there was no small commotion among the soldiers over what had become of Peter. 19 When Herod had searched for him and could not find him, he examined the guards

and ordered them to be put to death. Then Peter[i] went down from Judea to Caesarea and stayed there.

The Death of Herod

20 Now Herod was angry with the people of Tyre and Sidon. So they came to him in a body; and after winning over Blastus, the king's chamberlain, they asked for a reconciliation, because their country depended on the king's country for food. 21 On an appointed day Herod put on his royal robes, took his seat on the platform, and delivered a public address to them. 22 The people kept shouting, "The voice of a god, and not of a mortal!" 23 And immediately, because he had not given the glory to God, an angel of the Lord struck him down, and he was eaten by worms and died.

24 But the word of God continued to advance and gain adherents. 25 Then after completing their mission Barnabas and Saul returned to[j] Jerusalem and brought with them John, whose other name was Mark.

Barnabas and Saul Commissioned

13 Now in the church at Antioch there were prophets and teachers: Barnabas, Simeon who was called Niger, Lucius of Cyrene, Manaen a member of the court of Herod the ruler,[k] and Saul. 2 While they were worshiping the Lord and fasting, the Holy Spirit said, "Set apart for me Barnabas and Saul for the work to which I have called them." 3 Then after fasting and praying they laid their hands on them and sent them off.

The Apostles Preach in Cyprus

4 So, being sent out by the Holy Spirit, they went down to Seleucia; and from there they sailed to Cyprus. 5 When they arrived at Salamis, they proclaimed the word of

12.9
Acts 9.10
12.10
Acts 16.26
12.11
Lk 15.17;
Dan 3.28;
6.22;
2 Cor 1.10;
2 Pet 2.9
12.12
Acts 15.37;
v. 5
12.13
Jn 18.16,17
12.14
Lk 24.41
12.15
Gen 48.16;
Mt 18.10
12.17
Acts 13.16;
19.33; 21.40
12.19
Acts 16.27;
27.42

12.20
Mt 11.21;
1 Kings 5.9,
11;
Ezek 27.17
12.23
1 Sam 25.38;
2 Sam 24.17
12.24
Acts 6.7;
19.20
12.25
Acts 13.5,
13; 15.37
13.1
Acts 11.22-26
13.2
Acts 9.15;
22.21; 14.26
13.3
Acts 6.65;
14.26
13.4
vv. 2,3;
Acts 4.36
13.5
Acts 9.20

g Gk He h Gk brothers i Gk he
j Other ancient authorities read from
k Gk tetrarch

God in the synagogues of the Jews. And they had John also to assist them. [6]When they had gone through the whole island as far as Paphos, they met a certain magician, a Jewish false prophet, named Bar-Jesus. [7]He was with the proconsul, Sergius Paulus, an intelligent man, who summoned Barnabas and Saul and wanted to hear the word of God. [8]But the magician Elymas (for that is the translation of his name) opposed them and tried to turn the proconsul away from the faith. [9]But Saul, also known as Paul, filled with the Holy Spirit, looked intently at him [10]and said, "You son of the devil, you enemy of all righteousness, full of all deceit and villainy, will you not stop making crooked the straight paths of the Lord? [11]And now listen—the hand of the Lord is against you, and you will be blind for a while, unable to see the sun." Immediately mist and darkness came over him, and he went about groping for someone to lead him by the hand. [12]When the proconsul saw what had happened, he believed, for he was astonished at the teaching about the Lord.

Paul and Barnabas in Antioch of Pisidia

13 Then Paul and his companions set sail from Paphos and came to Perga in Pamphylia. John, however, left them and returned to Jerusalem; [14]but they went on from Perga and came to Antioch in Pisidia. And on the sabbath day they went into the synagogue and sat down. [15]After the reading of the law and the prophets, the officials of the synagogue sent them a message, saying, "Brothers, if you have any word of exhortation for the people, give it." [16]So Paul stood up and with a gesture began to speak:

"You Israelites,[1] and others who fear God, listen. [17]The God of this people Israel chose our ancestors and made the people great during their stay in the land of Egypt, and with uplifted arm he led them out of it. [18]For about forty years he put

up with[m] them in the wilderness. [19]After he had destroyed seven nations in the land of Canaan, he gave them their land as an inheritance [20]for about four hundred fifty years. After that he gave them judges until the time of the prophet Samuel. [21]Then they asked for a king; and God gave them Saul son of Kish, a man of the tribe of Benjamin, who reigned for forty years. [22]When he had removed him, he made David their king. In his testimony about him he said, 'I have found David, son of Jesse, to be a man after my heart, who will carry out all my wishes.' [23]Of this man's posterity God has brought to Israel a Savior, Jesus, as he promised; [24]before his coming John had already proclaimed a baptism of repentance to all the people of Israel. [25]And as John was finishing his work, he said, 'What do you suppose that I am? I am not he. No, but one is coming after me; I am not worthy to untie the thong of the sandals[n] on his feet.'

26 "My brothers, you descendants of Abraham's family, and others who fear God, to us[o] the message of this salvation has been sent. [27]Because the residents of Jerusalem and their leaders did not recognize him or understand the words of the prophets that are read every sabbath, they fulfilled those words by condemning him. [28]Even though they found no cause for a sentence of death, they asked Pilate to have him killed. [29]When they had carried out everything that was written about him, they took him down from the tree and laid him in a tomb. [30]But God raised him from the dead; [31]and for many days he appeared to those who came up with him from Galilee to Jerusalem, and they are now his witnesses to the people. [32]And we bring you the good news that what God promised to our ancestors [33]he has fulfilled for us, their

Cross references (center column)

13.6 Acts 8.9
13.7 vv. 8,12
13.8 Acts 8.9; vv. 7,12; Acts 6.7
13.9 Acts 4.8
13.10 Mt 13.38; Jn 8.44; Hos 14.9
13.11 Ex 9.3
13.12 vv. 7,8; Acts 8.25
13.13 Acts 15.38
13.14 Acts 14.19, 21; 16.13
13.17 Deut 7.6-8
13.18 Ex 16.35; Deut 1.31
13.19 Deut 7.1; Josh 19.51
13.20 Judg 2.16; 1 Sam 3.20
13.21 1 Sam 8.5; 10.1
13.22 1 Sam 13.14; 15.23,26
13.23 Isa 11.1; Mt 1.21; Rom 11.26
13.24 Mt 3.1; Lk 3.3
13.25 Mt 3.11; Lk 3.16
13.27 Lk 23.13; Acts 3.17; Lk 24.27
13.28 Mt 27.22
13.29 Lk 18.31; Mt 27.59
13.30 Mt 28.6
13.31 Mt 28.16; Lk 24.48
13.32 Gen 3.15; Rom 4.13
13.33 Ps 2.7

[1]Gk Men, Israelites　[m]Other ancient authorities read cared for　[n]Gk untie the sandals　[o]Other ancient authorities read you

children, by raising Jesus; as also it is written in the second psalm,

'You are my Son;
today I have begotten you.'

34 As to his raising him from the dead, no more to return to corruption, he has spoken in this way,

'I will give you the holy
promises made to
David.'

35 Therefore he has also said in another psalm,

'You will not let your Holy
One experience
corruption.'

36 For David, after he had served the purpose of God in his own generation, died,[p] was laid beside his ancestors, and experienced corruption; 37 but he whom God raised up experienced no corruption. 38 Let it be known to you therefore, my brothers, that through this man forgiveness of sins is proclaimed to you; 39 by this Jesus[q] everyone who believes is set free from all those sins[r] from which you could not be freed by the law of Moses. 40 Beware, therefore, that what the prophets said does not happen to you:

41 'Look, you scoffers!
Be amazed and perish,
for in your days I am doing a
work,
a work that you will never
believe, even if
someone tells you.' "

42 As Paul and Barnabas[s] were going out, the people urged them to speak about these things again the next sabbath. 43 When the meeting of the synagogue broke up, many Jews and devout converts to Judaism followed Paul and Barnabas, who spoke to them and urged them to continue in the grace of God.

44 The next sabbath almost the whole city gathered to hear the word of the Lord.[t] 45 But when the Jews saw the crowds, they were filled with jealousy; and blaspheming, they contradicted what was spoken by Paul. 46 Then both Paul and Barnabas spoke out boldly, saying, "It was necessary that the

word of God should be spoken first to you. Since you reject it and judge yourselves to be unworthy of eternal life, we are now turning to the Gentiles. 47 For so the Lord has commanded us, saying,

'I have set you to be a light
for the Gentiles,
so that you may bring
salvation to the ends of
the earth.' "

48 When the Gentiles heard this, they were glad and praised the word of the Lord; and as many as had been destined for eternal life became believers. 49 Thus the word of the Lord spread throughout the region. 50 But the Jews incited the devout women of high standing and the leading men of the city, and stirred up persecution against Paul and Barnabas, and drove them out of their region. 51 So they shook the dust off their feet in protest against them, and went to Iconium. 52 And the disciples were filled with joy and with the Holy Spirit.

Paul and Barnabas in Iconium

14 The same thing occurred in Iconium, where Paul and Barnabas[s] went into the Jewish synagogue and spoke in such a way that a great number of both Jews and Greeks became believers. 2 But the unbelieving Jews stirred up the Gentiles and poisoned their minds against the brothers. 3 So they remained for a long time, speaking boldly for the Lord, who testified to the word of his grace by granting signs and wonders to be done through them. 4 But the residents of the city were divided; some sided with the Jews, and some with the apostles. 5 And when an attempt was made by both Gentiles and Jews, with their rulers, to mistreat them and to stone them, 6 the apostles[s] learned of it and fled to Lystra and Derbe, cities of Lycaonia, and to the surrounding country; 7 and there they continued proclaiming the good news.

Reference column
13.34 Isa 55.3
13.35 Ps 16.10; Acts 2.27
13.36 Acts 2.29; 1 Kings 2.10
13.38 Lk 24.47
13.39 Rom 3.28; Acts 10.43
13.40 Jn 6.45
13.41 Hab 1.5
13.42 v. 14
13.43 Acts 11.23; 14.22
13.45 Acts 18.6; 1 Pet 4.4; Jude 10
13.46 v. 26; Acts 3.26; 18.6; 28.28
13.47 Isa 49.6; Lk 2.32
13.48 Acts 2.47; Rom 3.28ff
13.51 Mt 10.14; Mk 6.11; Lk 9.5; Acts 18.6
13.52 Acts 2.4
14.1 Acts 13.51; 13.5; 2.47; 18.4
14.3 Heb 2.4; Jn 4.48
14.4 Acts 17.4,5; v. 14
14.5 2 Tim 3.11
14.6 Mt 10.23

p Gk *fell asleep* q Gk *this* r Gk *all*
s Gk *they* t Other ancient authorities read *God*

Paul and Barnabas in Lystra and Derbe

8 In Lystra there was a man sitting who could not use his feet and had never walked, for he had been crippled from birth. [9] He listened to Paul as he was speaking. And Paul, looking at him intently and seeing that he had faith to be healed, [10] said in a loud voice, "Stand upright on your feet." And the man[u] sprang up and began to walk. [11] When the crowds saw what Paul had done, they shouted in the Lycaonian language, "The gods have come down to us in human form!" [12] Barnabas they called Zeus, and Paul they called Hermes, because he was the chief speaker. [13] The priest of Zeus, whose temple was just outside the city,[v] brought oxen and garlands to the gates; he and the crowds wanted to offer sacrifice. [14] When the apostles Barnabas and Paul heard of it, they tore their clothes and rushed out into the crowd, shouting, [15] "Friends,[w] why are you doing this? We are mortals just like you, and we bring you good news, that you should turn from these worthless things to the living God, who made the heaven and the earth and the sea and all that is in them. [16] In past generations he allowed all the nations to follow their own ways; [17] yet he has not left himself without a witness in doing good—giving you rains from heaven and fruitful seasons, and filling you with food and your hearts with joy." [18] Even with these words, they scarcely restrained the crowds from offering sacrifice to them.

19 But Jews came there from Antioch and Iconium and won over the crowds. Then they stoned Paul and dragged him out of the city, supposing that he was dead. [20] But when the disciples surrounded him, he got up and went into the city. The next day he went on with Barnabas to Derbe.

The Return to Antioch in Syria

21 After they had proclaimed the good news to that city and had made many disciples, they returned to Lystra, then on to Iconium and Antioch. [22] There they strengthened the souls of the disciples and encouraged them to continue in the faith, saying, "It is through many persecutions that we must enter the kingdom of God." [23] And after they had appointed elders for them in each church, with prayer and fasting they entrusted them to the Lord in whom they had come to believe.

24 Then they passed through Pisidia and came to Pamphylia. [25] When they had spoken the word in Perga, they went down to Attalia. [26] From there they sailed back to Antioch, where they had been commended to the grace of God for the work[x] that they had completed. [27] When they arrived, they called the church together and related all that God had done with them, and how he had opened a door of faith for the Gentiles. [28] And they stayed there with the disciples for some time.

The Council at Jerusalem

15 Then certain individuals came down from Judea and were teaching the brothers, "Unless you are circumcised according to the custom of Moses, you cannot be saved." [2] And after Paul and Barnabas had no small dissension and debate with them, Paul and Barnabas and some of the others were appointed to go up to Jerusalem to discuss this question with the apostles and the elders. [3] So they were sent on their way by the church, and as they passed through both Phoenicia and Samaria, they reported the conversion of the Gentiles, and brought great joy to all the believers.[y] [4] When they came to Jerusalem, they were welcomed by the church and the apostles and the elders, and they reported all that God had done with them. [5] But some believers who be-

u Gk he v Or The priest of Zeus-Outside-the-City w Gk Men x Or committed in the grace of God to the work y Gk brothers

longed to the sect of the Pharisees stood up and said, "It is necessary for them to be circumcised and ordered to keep the law of Moses."

6 The apostles and the elders met together to consider this matter. [7] After there had been much debate, Peter stood up and said to them, "My brothers,[z] you know that in the early days God made a choice among you, that I should be the one through whom the Gentiles would hear the message of the good news and become believers. [8] And God, who knows the human heart, testified to them by giving them the Holy Spirit, just as he did to us; [9] and in cleansing their hearts by faith he has made no distinction between them and us. [10] Now therefore why are you putting God to the test by placing on the neck of the disciples a yoke that neither our ancestors nor we have been able to bear? [11] On the contrary, we believe that we will be saved through the grace of the Lord Jesus, just as they will."

12 The whole assembly kept silence, and listened to Barnabas and Paul as they told of all the signs and wonders that God had done through them among the Gentiles. [13] After they finished speaking, James replied, "My brothers,[z] listen to me. [14] Simeon has related how God first looked favorably on the Gentiles, to take from among them a people for his name. [15] This agrees with the words of the prophets, as it is written,
[16] 'After this I will return,
 and I will rebuild the
 dwelling of David,
 which has fallen;
 from its ruins I will rebuild
 it,
 and I will set it up,
[17] so that all other peoples may
 seek the Lord—
 even all the Gentiles over
 whom my name has
 been called.
 Thus says the Lord, who
 has been making these
 things [18] known from
 long ago.'[a]

15.7
Acts 10.19,
20; 20.24
15.8
Acts 1.24;
10.44,47
15.9
Acts 10.28,
34,43; 11.12
15.10
Mt 23.4;
Gal 5.1
15.11
Rom 3.24;
Eph 2.5-8;
Titus 2.11;
3.4,5
15.12
Jn 4.48;
Acts 14.27
15.13
Acts 12.17
15.15
Acts 13.40
15.16
Am 9.11,12;
Jer 12.15

15.20
v. 29;
1 Cor 8.7-13;
10.7,8,14-28;
Rev 2.14,20;
Gen 9.4;
Lev 3.17;
Deut 12.16,
23
15.21
Acts 13.15;
2 Cor 3.14,
15
15.22
Acts 11.20;
vv. 27,32,40
15.23
vv. 1,41;
Acts 23.26;
Jas 1.1
15.24
v. 1;
Gal 1.7;
5.10
15.26
Acts 14.19;
1 Cor 15.30
15.29
v. 20;
Acts 21.25;
Lev 17.14

[19] Therefore I have reached the decision that we should not trouble those Gentiles who are turning to God, [20] but we should write to them to abstain only from things polluted by idols and from fornication and from whatever has been strangled[b] and from blood. [21] For in every city, for generations past, Moses has had those who proclaim him, for he has been read aloud every sabbath in the synagogues."

The Council's Letter to Gentile Believers

22 Then the apostles and the elders, with the consent of the whole church, decided to choose men from among their members[c] and to send them to Antioch with Paul and Barnabas. They sent Judas called Barsabbas, and Silas, leaders among the brothers, [23] with the following letter: "The brothers, both the apostles and the elders, to the believers[d] of Gentile origin in Antioch and Syria and Cilicia, greetings. [24] Since we have heard that certain persons who have gone out from us, though with no instructions from us, have said things to disturb you and have unsettled your minds,[e] [25] we have decided unanimously to choose representatives[f] and send them to you, along with our beloved Barnabas and Paul, [26] who have risked their lives for the sake of our Lord Jesus Christ. [27] We have therefore sent Judas and Silas, who themselves will tell you the same things by word of mouth. [28] For it has seemed good to the Holy Spirit and to us to impose on you no further burden than these essentials: [29] that you abstain from what has been sacrificed to idols and from blood and from what is strangled[g] and from fornication. If you keep yourselves

z Gk Men, brothers a Other ancient
authorities read things. [18] Known to God from
of old are all his works.' b Other ancient
authorities lack and from whatever has been
strangled c Gk from among them
d Gk brothers e Other ancient authorities
add saying, 'You must be circumcised and keep
the law,' f Gk men g Other ancient
authorities lack and from what is strangled

from these, you will do well. Farewell."

30 So they were sent off and went down to Antioch. When they gathered the congregation together, they delivered the letter. [31] When its members[h] read it, they rejoiced at the exhortation. [32] Judas and Silas, who were themselves prophets, said much to encourage and strengthen the believers.[i] [33] After they had been there for some time, they were sent off in peace by the believers[i] to those who had sent them.[i] [35] But Paul and Barnabas remained in Antioch, and there, with many others, they taught and proclaimed the word of the Lord.

Paul and Barnabas Separate

36 After some days Paul said to Barnabas, "Come, let us return and visit the believers[i] in every city where we proclaimed the word of the Lord and see how they are doing." [37] Barnabas wanted to take with them John called Mark. [38] But Paul decided not to take with them one who had deserted them in Pamphylia and had not accompanied them in the work. [39] The disagreement became so sharp that they parted company; Barnabas took Mark with him and sailed away to Cyprus. [40] But Paul chose Silas and set out, the believers[i] commending him to the grace of the Lord. [41] He went through Syria and Cilicia, strengthening the churches.

Timothy Joins Paul and Silas

16 Paul[k] went on also to Derbe and to Lystra, where there was a disciple named Timothy, the son of a Jewish woman who was a believer; but his father was a Greek. [2] He was well spoken of by the believers[i] in Lystra and Iconium. [3] Paul wanted Timothy to accompany him; and he took him and had him circumcised because of the Jews who were in those places, for they all knew that his father was a Greek. [4] As they went from town to town, they delivered

to them for observance the decisions that had been reached by the apostles and elders who were in Jerusalem. [5] So the churches were strengthened in the faith and increased in numbers daily.

Paul's Vision of the Man of Macedonia

6 They went through the region of Phrygia and Galatia, having been forbidden by the Holy Spirit to speak the word in Asia. [7] When they had come opposite Mysia, they attempted to go into Bithynia, but the Spirit of Jesus did not allow them; [8] so, passing by Mysia, they went down to Troas. [9] During the night Paul had a vision: there stood a man of Macedonia pleading with him and saying, "Come over to Macedonia and help us." [10] When he had seen the vision, we immediately tried to cross over to Macedonia, being convinced that God had called us to proclaim the good news to them.

The Conversion of Lydia

11 We set sail from Troas and took a straight course to Samothrace, the following day to Neapolis, [12] and from there to Philippi, which is a leading city of the district[l] of Macedonia and a Roman colony. We remained in this city for some days. [13] On the sabbath day we went outside the gate by the river, where we supposed there was a place of prayer; and we sat down and spoke to the women who had gathered there. [14] A certain woman named Lydia, a worshiper of God, was listening to us; she was from the city of Thyatira and a dealer in purple cloth. The Lord opened her heart to listen eagerly to what was said by Paul. [15] When she and her household were baptized, she urged us, saying, "If you have judged me to be faithful to the Lord, come and stay at my home." And she prevailed upon us.

h Gk When they i Gk brothers j Other ancient authorities add verse 34, But it seemed good to Silas to remain there k Gk He
l Other authorities read a city of the first district

Cross references (center column)

15.33
Acts 16.36;
1 Cor 16.11;
Heb 11.31
15.36ff
Acts 13.4,
13,14,51;
14.1,6,24,25
15.37
Acts 12.12
15.38
Acts 13.13
15.41
Acts 16.5
16.1
Acts 14.6;
19.22;
Rom 16.21;
1 Cor 4.17;
2 Tim 1.2;
1.5
16.3
Gal 2.3
16.4
Acts 15.28,
29; 15.2;
11.30

16.5
Acts 15.41
16.6
Acts 18.23;
2.9
16.7
v. 8;
Lk 24.49;
Rom 8.9;
Gal 4.6
16.8
v. 11;
2 Cor 2.12;
2 Tim 4.13
16.9
Acts 9.10;
18.5; 20.1,3;
27.2
16.10
2 Cor 2.13
16.11
v. 8;
2 Tim 4.13
16.12
Phil 1.1;
Acts 18.5;
19.21,22,29;
20.1,3; 27.2
16.13
Acts 13.14
16.14
Lk 24.45
16.15
Acts 11.14;
Lk 24.29

Paul and Silas in Prison

16 One day, as we were going to the place of prayer, we met a slave girl who had a spirit of divination and brought her owners a great deal of money by fortune-telling. [17] While she followed Paul and us, she would cry out, "These men are slaves of the Most High God, who proclaim to you[m] a way of salvation." [18] She kept doing this for many days. But Paul, very much annoyed, turned and said to the spirit, "I order you in the name of Jesus Christ to come out of her." And it came out that very hour.

19 But when her owners saw that their hope of making money was gone, they seized Paul and Silas and dragged them into the marketplace before the authorities. [20] When they had brought them before the magistrates, they said, "These men are disturbing our city; they are Jews [21] and are advocating customs that are not lawful for us as Romans to adopt or observe." [22] The crowd joined in attacking them, and the magistrates had them stripped of their clothing and ordered them to be beaten with rods. [23] After they had given them a severe flogging, they threw them into prison and ordered the jailer to keep them securely. [24] Following these instructions, he put them in the innermost cell and fastened their feet in the stocks.

25 About midnight Paul and Silas were praying and singing hymns to God, and the prisoners were listening to them. [26] Suddenly there was an earthquake, so violent that the foundations of the prison were shaken; and immediately all the doors were opened and everyone's chains were unfastened. [27] When the jailer woke up and saw the prison doors wide open, he drew his sword and was about to kill himself, since he supposed that the prisoners had escaped. [28] But Paul shouted in a loud voice, "Do not harm yourself, for we are all here." [29] The jailer[n] called for lights, and rushing in, he fell down trembling

before Paul and Silas. [30] Then he brought them outside and said, "Sirs, what must I do to be saved?" [31] They answered, "Believe on the Lord Jesus, and you will be saved, you and your household." [32] They spoke the word of the Lord[o] to him and to all who were in his house. [33] At the same hour of the night he took them and washed their wounds; then he and his entire family were baptized without delay. [34] He brought them up into the house and set food before them; and he and his entire household rejoiced that he had become a believer in God.

35 When morning came, the magistrates sent the police, saying, "Let those men go." [36] And the jailer reported the message to Paul, saying, "The magistrates sent word to let you go; therefore come out now and go in peace." [37] But Paul replied, "They have beaten us in public, uncondemned, men who are Roman citizens, and have thrown us into prison; and now are they going to discharge us in secret? Certainly not! Let them come and take us out themselves." [38] The police reported these words to the magistrates, and they were afraid when they heard that they were Roman citizens; [39] so they came and apologized to them. And they took them out and asked them to leave the city. [40] After leaving the prison they went to Lydia's home; and when they had seen and encouraged the brothers and sisters[p] there, they departed.

The Uproar in Thessalonica

17 After Paul and Silas[q] had passed through Amphipolis and Apollonia, they came to Thessalonica, where there was a synagogue of the Jews. [2] And Paul went in, as was his custom, and on three sabbath days argued with them from the scriptures, [3] explaining and proving that it was neces-

16.16
Deut 18.11;
1 Sam 28.3,
7
16.17
Mk 5.7
16.19
Acts 19.25,
26; 15.40;
17.6,7;
Jas 2.6
16.20
Acts 17.6
16.22
2 Cor 11.23,
25;
1 Thes 2.2
16.23
vv. 27,36
16.24
Jer 20.2,3
16.25
Eph 5.19
16.26
Acts 4.31;
5.19; 12.7,10
16.27
Acts 12.19

16.30
Acts 2.37;
9.6; 22.10
16.31
Jn 3.16,36;
6.47;
1 Jn 5.10
16.33
v. 25
16.34
Acts 11.14
16.36
vv. 23,27
16.37
Acts 22.25-27
16.38
Acts 22.29
16.39
Mt 8.34
16.40
v. 14
17.1
Acts 27.2;
1 Thes 1.1;
2 Thes 1.1
17.2
Acts 9.20;
13.14; 16.13;
19.8
17.3
Lk 24.26,46;
Acts 18.28;
Gal 3.1

m Other ancient authorities read *to us*
n Gk *He*　o Other ancient authorities read *word of God*　p Gk *brothers*　q Gk *they*

sary for the Messiah[r] to suffer and to rise from the dead, and saying, "This is the Messiah,[r] Jesus whom I am proclaiming to you." [4] Some of them were persuaded and joined Paul and Silas, as did a great many of the devout Greeks and not a few of the leading women. [5] But the Jews became jealous, and with the help of some ruffians in the marketplaces they formed a mob and set the city in an uproar. While they were searching for Paul and Silas to bring them out to the assembly, they attacked Jason's house. [6] When they could not find them, they dragged Jason and some believers[s] before the city authorities,[t] shouting, "These people who have been turning the world upside down have come here also, [7] and Jason has entertained them as guests. They are all acting contrary to the decrees of the emperor, saying that there is another king named Jesus." [8] The people and the city officials were disturbed when they heard this, [9] and after they had taken bail from Jason and the others, they let them go.

Paul and Silas in Beroea

[10] That very night the believers[s] sent Paul and Silas off to Beroea; and when they arrived, they went to the Jewish synagogue. [11] These Jews were more receptive than those in Thessalonica, for they welcomed the message very eagerly and examined the scriptures every day to see whether these things were so. [12] Many of them therefore believed, including not a few Greek women and men of high standing. [13] But when the Jews of Thessalonica learned that the word of God had been proclaimed by Paul in Beroea as well, they came there too, to stir up and incite the crowds. [14] Then the believers[s] immediately sent Paul away to the coast, but Silas and Timothy remained behind. [15] Those who conducted Paul brought him as far as Athens; and after receiving instructions to have

Silas and Timothy join him as soon as possible, they left him.

Paul in Athens

[16] While Paul was waiting for them in Athens, he was deeply distressed to see that the city was full of idols. [17] So he argued in the synagogue with the Jews and the devout persons, and also in the marketplace[u] every day with those who happened to be there. [18] Also some Epicurean and Stoic philosophers debated with him. Some said, "What does this babbler want to say?" Others said, "He seems to be a proclaimer of foreign divinities." (This was because he was telling the good news about Jesus and the resurrection.) [19] So they took him and brought him to the Areopagus and asked him, "May we know what this new teaching is that you are presenting? [20] It sounds rather strange to us, so we would like to know what it means." [21] Now all the Athenians and the foreigners living there would spend their time in nothing but telling or hearing something new.

[22] Then Paul stood in front of the Areopagus and said, "Athenians, I see how extremely religious you are in every way. [23] For as I went through the city and looked carefully at the objects of your worship, I found among them an altar with the inscription, 'To an unknown god.' What therefore you worship as unknown, this I proclaim to you. [24] The God who made the world and everything in it, he who is Lord of heaven and earth, does not live in shrines made by human hands, [25] nor is he served by human hands, as though he needed anything, since he himself gives to all mortals life and breath and all things. [26] From one ancestor[v] he made all nations to inhabit the whole earth, and he allotted the times of their existence and the boundaries of the places where

17.4
Acts 15.22,
27,32,40
17.5
v. 13;
Rom 16.21
17.6
Acts 16.19,
20
17.7
Lk 23.2;
Jn 19.12
17.9
v. 5
17.10
v. 14;
Acts 20.4;
v. 2
17.11
Isa 34.16;
Lk 16.29;
Jn 5.39
17.14
vv. 6,10;
Acts 16.1
17.15
Acts 15.3;
vv. 16,21,
22;
Acts 18.5

17.16
2 Pet 2.8
17.18
1 Cor 4.10;
Acts 4.2
17.19
Acts 23.19;
v. 22
17.24
Isa 42.5;
Acts 14.15;
Mt 11.25;
Acts 7.48
17.25
Ps 50.10-12;
Isa 42.5;
57.16;
Zech 12.1
17.26
Mal 2.10;
Deut 32.8

[r] Or *the Christ* [s] Gk *brothers*
[t] Gk *politarchs* [u] Or *civic center;* Gk
agora [v] Gk *From one;* other ancient
authorities read *From one blood*

they would live, [27] so that they would search for God[w] and perhaps grope for him and find him — though indeed he is not far from each one of us. [28] For 'In him we live and move and have our being'; as even some of your own poets have said,

'For we too are his offspring.'

[29] Since we are God's offspring, we ought not to think that the deity is like gold, or silver, or stone, an image formed by the art and imagination of mortals. [30] While God has overlooked the times of human ignorance, now he commands all people everywhere to repent, [31] because he has fixed a day on which he will have the world judged in righteousness by a man whom he has appointed, and of this he has given assurance to all by raising him from the dead."

[32] When they heard of the resurrection of the dead, some scoffed; but others said, "We will hear you again about this." [33] At that point Paul left them. [34] But some of them joined him and became believers, including Dionysius the Areopagite and a woman named Damaris, and others with them.

Paul in Corinth

18 After this Paul[x] left Athens and went to Corinth. [2] There he found a Jew named Aquila, a native of Pontus, who had recently come from Italy with his wife Priscilla, because Claudius had ordered all Jews to leave Rome. Paul[y] went to see them, [3] and, because he was of the same trade, he stayed with them, and they worked together — by trade they were tentmakers. [4] Every sabbath he would argue in the synagogue and would try to convince Jews and Greeks.

[5] When Silas and Timothy arrived from Macedonia, Paul was occupied with proclaiming the word,[z] testifying to the Jews that the Messiah[a] was Jesus. [6] When they opposed and reviled him, in protest he shook the dust from his

17.27
Rom 1.20;
Acts 14.17
17.28
Col 1.17;
Heb 1.3,5
17.29
Isa 40.18ff
17.30
v. 23;
Acts 14.16;
Rom 3.25;
Lk 24.47;
Titus 2.11,
12;
1 Pet 1.14
17.31
Mt 10.15;
Acts 10.42;
Lk 22.22;
Acts 22.4
17.34
vv. 19,22
18.1
Acts 17.15;
1 Cor 1.2
18.2
Rom 16.3;
1 Cor 16.19;
2 Tim 4.19;
Acts 11.28
18.3
Acts 20.34;
1 Cor 4.12;
1 Thes 2.9;
2 Thes 3.8
18.4
Acts 17.2
18.5
Acts 17.14,
15; 16.9;
20.21; v. 28;
Acts 17.3
18.6
Acts 13.45,
51;
2 Sam 1.16;
Ezek 18.13;
Acts 20.26;
13.46

18.7
Acts 16.14
18.8
1 Cor 1.14
18.9
Acts 23.11
18.10
Mt 28.20
18.14
Acts 23.29;
25.11,19
18.17
1 Cor 1.1
18.18
Num 6.18;
Acts 21.24;
Rom 16.1

clothes[b] and said to them, "Your blood be on your own heads! I am innocent. From now on I will go to the Gentiles." [7] Then he left the synagogue[c] and went to the house of a man named Titius[d] Justus, a worshiper of God; his house was next door to the synagogue. [8] Crispus, the official of the synagogue, became a believer in the Lord, together with all his household; and many of the Corinthians who heard Paul became believers and were baptized. [9] One night the Lord said to Paul in a vision, "Do not be afraid, but speak and do not be silent; [10] for I am with you, and no one will lay a hand on you to harm you, for there are many in this city who are my people." [11] He stayed there a year and six months, teaching the word of God among them.

[12] But when Gallio was proconsul of Achaia, the Jews made a united attack on Paul and brought him before the tribunal. [13] They said, "This man is persuading people to worship God in ways that are contrary to the law." [14] Just as Paul was about to speak, Gallio said to the Jews, "If it were a matter of crime or serious villainy, I would be justified in accepting the complaint of you Jews; [15] but since it is a matter of questions about words and names and your own law, see to it yourselves; I do not wish to be a judge of these matters." [16] And he dismissed them from the tribunal. [17] Then all of them[e] seized Sosthenes, the official of the synagogue, and beat him in front of the tribunal. But Gallio paid no attention to any of these things.

Paul's Return to Antioch

[18] After staying there for a considerable time, Paul said farewell to the believers[f] and sailed for Syria, accompanied by Priscilla and Aquila. At Cenchreae he had his

w Other ancient authorities read *the Lord*
x Gk *he* y Gk *He* z Gk *with the word*
a Or *the Christ* b Gk *reviled him, he shook out his clothes* c Gk *left there* d Other ancient authorities read *Titus* e Other ancient authorities read *all the Greeks*
f Gk *brothers*

hair cut, for he was under a vow. [19] When they reached Ephesus, he left them there, but first he himself went into the synagogue and had a discussion with the Jews. [20] When they asked him to stay longer, he declined; [21] but on taking leave of them, he said, "I[g] will return to you, if God wills." Then he set sail from Ephesus.

22 When he had landed at Caesarea, he went up to Jerusalem[h] and greeted the church, and then went down to Antioch. [23] After spending some time there he departed and went from place to place through the region of Galatia[i] and Phrygia, strengthening all the disciples.

Ministry of Apollos

24 Now there came to Ephesus a Jew named Apollos, a native of Alexandria. He was an eloquent man, well-versed in the scriptures. [25] He had been instructed in the Way of the Lord; and he spoke with burning enthusiasm and taught accurately the things concerning Jesus, though he knew only the baptism of John. [26] He began to speak boldly in the synagogue; but when Priscilla and Aquila heard him, they took him aside and explained the Way of God to him more accurately. [27] And when he wished to cross over to Achaia, the believers[j] encouraged him and wrote to the disciples to welcome him. On his arrival he greatly helped those who through grace had become believers, [28] for he powerfully refuted the Jews in public, showing by the scriptures that the Messiah[k] is Jesus.

Paul in Ephesus

19 While Apollos was in Corinth, Paul passed through the interior regions and came to Ephesus, where he found some disciples. [2] He said to them, "Did you receive the Holy Spirit when you became believers?" They replied, "No, we have not even heard that there is a Holy Spirit." [3] Then he said, "Into what then were you bap-

tized?" They answered, "Into John's baptism." [4] Paul said, "John baptized with the baptism of repentance, telling the people to believe in the one who was to come after him, that is, in Jesus." [5] On hearing this, they were baptized in the name of the Lord Jesus. [6] When Paul had laid his hands on them, the Holy Spirit came upon them, and they spoke in tongues and prophesied — [7] altogether there were about twelve of them.

8 He entered the synagogue and for three months spoke out boldly, and argued persuasively about the kingdom of God. [9] When some stubbornly refused to believe and spoke evil of the Way before the congregation, he left them, taking the disciples with him, and argued daily in the lecture hall of Tyrannus.[l] [10] This continued for two years, so that all the residents of Asia, both Jews and Greeks, heard the word of the Lord.

The Sons of Sceva

11 God did extraordinary miracles through Paul, [12] so that when the handkerchiefs or aprons that had touched his skin were brought to the sick, their diseases left them, and the evil spirits came out of them. [13] Then some itinerant Jewish exorcists tried to use the name of the Lord Jesus over those who had evil spirits, saying, "I adjure you by the Jesus whom Paul proclaims." [14] Seven sons of a Jewish high priest named Sceva were doing this. [15] But the evil spirit said to them in reply, "Jesus I know, and Paul I know; but who are you?" [16] Then the man with the evil spirit leaped on them, mastered them all, and so overpowered them that they fled out of the house naked and wounded. [17] When this became known to all residents of Ephesus, both Jews and Greeks, everyone

g Other ancient authorities read *I must at all costs keep the approaching festival in Jerusalem, but I* h Gk went up i Gk the Galatian region j Gk brothers k Or *the Christ* l Other ancient authorities read *of a certain Tyrannus, from eleven o'clock in the morning to four in the afternoon*

Cross references (center column):

18.21 1 Cor 4.19
18.22 Acts 11.19
18.23 Acts 16.6; 14.22; 15.32, 41
18.24 Acts 19.1; 1 Cor 1.12; 3.5,6; 4.6; Titus 3.13
18.25 Rom 12.11; Acts 19.3
18.27 vv. 12,18
18.28 Acts 9.22; 17.3; v. 5
19.1 1 Cor 1.12; 3.5,6; Acts 18.1, 19-24
19.3 Acts 18.25
19.4 Mt 3.11; Acts 13.24, 25
19.6 Acts 6.6; 8.17; 2.4; 10.46
19.8 Acts 17.2; 18.4; 1.3; 28.23
19.9 Acts 14.4; 2 Tim 1.15; Acts 9.2; v. 30
19.10 Acts 20.31; vv. 22,26, 27;
19.11 Acts 13.12
19.11 Acts 8.13
19.12 Acts 5.15
19.13 Mt 12.27; Mk 9.38; Lk 9.49
19.17 Acts 2.43; 5.5,11

was awestruck; and the name of the Lord Jesus was praised. [18] Also many of those who became believers confessed and disclosed their practices. [19] A number of those who practiced magic collected their books and burned them publicly; when the value of these books[m] was calculated, it was found to come to fifty thousand silver coins. [20] So the word of the Lord grew mightily and prevailed.

The Riot in Ephesus

21 Now after these things had been accomplished, Paul resolved in the Spirit to go through Macedonia and Achaia, and then to go on to Jerusalem. He said, "After I have gone there, I must also see Rome." [22] So he sent two of his helpers, Timothy and Erastus, to Macedonia, while he himself stayed for some time longer in Asia.

23 About that time no little disturbance broke out concerning the Way. [24] A man named Demetrius, a silversmith who made silver shrines of Artemis, brought no little business to the artisans. [25] These he gathered together, with the workers of the same trade, and said, "Men, you know that we get our wealth from this business. [26] You also see and hear that not only in Ephesus but in almost the whole of Asia this Paul has persuaded and drawn away a considerable number of people by saying that gods made with hands are not gods. [27] And there is danger not only that this trade of ours may come into disrepute but also that the temple of the great goddess Artemis will be scorned, and she will be deprived of her majesty that brought all Asia and the world to worship her."

28 When they heard this, they were enraged and shouted, "Great is Artemis of the Ephesians!" [29] The city was filled with the confusion; and people[n] rushed together to the theater, dragging with them Gaius and Aristarchus, Macedonians who were Paul's travel companions.

[30] Paul wished to go into the crowd, but the disciples would not let him; [31] even some officials of the province of Asia,[o] who were friendly to him, sent him a message urging him not to venture into the theater. [32] Meanwhile, some were shouting one thing, some another; for the assembly was in confusion, and most of them did not know why they had come together. [33] Some of the crowd gave instructions to Alexander, whom the Jews had pushed forward. And Alexander motioned for silence and tried to make a defense before the people. [34] But when they recognized that he was a Jew, for about two hours all of them shouted in unison, "Great is Artemis of the Ephesians!" [35] But when the town clerk had quieted the crowd, he said, "Citizens of Ephesus, who is there that does not know that the city of the Ephesians is the temple keeper of the great Artemis and of the statue that fell from heaven?[p] [36] Since these things cannot be denied, you ought to be quiet and do nothing rash. [37] You have brought these men here who are neither temple robbers nor blasphemers of our[q] goddess. [38] If therefore Demetrius and the artisans with him have a complaint against anyone, the courts are open, and there are proconsuls; let them bring charges there against one another. [39] If there is anything further[r] you want to know, it must be settled in the regular assembly. [40] For we are in danger of being charged with rioting today, since there is no cause that we can give to justify this commotion." [41] When he had said this, he dismissed the assembly.

Paul Goes to Macedonia and Greece

20 After the uproar had ceased, Paul sent for the disciples; and after encouraging them and saying farewell, he left

Cross-references (center column):

19.20 Acts 6.7; 12.24
19.21 Rom 15.24-28
19.22 Acts 13.5; Rom 16.23; 2 Tim 4.20; v. 10
19.23 v. 9
19.24 Acts 16.16, 19
19.26 Ps 115.4; Isa 44.10-20; Jer 10.3; Acts 17.29
19.28 Acts 18.19
19.29 Rom 16.23; 1 Cor 1.4; Acts 20.4; 27.2; Col 4.10; Philem 24

19.32 Acts 21.34
19.33 1 Tim 1.20; 2 Tim 4.14; Acts 12.17
19.35 Acts 18.19
19.37 Rom 2.22
19.38 Acts 13.7
20.1 Acts 11.26; 1 Cor 16.5; 1 Tim 1.3

Footnotes:

m Gk them n Gk they o Gk some of the Asiarchs p Meaning of Gk uncertain
q Other ancient authorities read your
r Other ancient authorities read about other matters

for Macedonia. [2] When he had gone through those regions and had given the believers[s] much encouragement, he came to Greece, [3] where he stayed for three months. He was about to set sail for Syria when a plot was made against him by the Jews, and so he decided to return through Macedonia. [4] He was accompanied by Sopater son of Pyrrhus from Beroea, by Aristarchus and Secundus from Thessalonica, by Gaius from Derbe, and by Timothy, as well as by Tychicus and Trophimus from Asia. [5] They went ahead and were waiting for us in Troas; [6] but we sailed from Philippi after the days of Unleavened Bread, and in five days we joined them in Troas, where we stayed for seven days.

Paul's Farewell Visit to Troas

[7] On the first day of the week, when we met to break bread, Paul was holding a discussion with them; since he intended to leave the next day, he continued speaking until midnight. [8] There were many lamps in the room upstairs where we were meeting. [9] A young man named Eutychus, who was sitting in the window, began to sink off into a deep sleep while Paul talked still longer. Overcome by sleep, he fell to the ground three floors below and was picked up dead. [10] But Paul went down, and bending over him took him in his arms, and said, "Do not be alarmed, for his life is in him." [11] Then Paul went upstairs, and after he had broken bread and eaten, he continued to converse with them until dawn; then he left. [12] Meanwhile they had taken the boy away alive and were not a little comforted.

The Voyage from Troas to Miletus

13 We went ahead to the ship and set sail for Assos, intending to take Paul on board there; for he had made this arrangement, intending to go by land himself. [14] When he met us in Assos, we

20.3
v. 19;
Acts 23.12;
25.3;
2 Cor 11.26
20.4
Acts 19.29;
27.2; 16.1;
Eph 6.21;
Col 4.7;
2 Tim 4.12;
Titus 3.12;
Acts 21.29;
2 Tim 4.20
20.6
Acts 16.8;
2 Cor 2.12;
2 Tim 4.13
20.7
1 Cor 16.2;
Rev 1.10
20.8
Acts 1.13
20.10
1 Kings 17.21;
Mt 9.23,24

20.15
v. 17;
2 Tim 4.20
20.16
Acts 18.19;
21.4,12;
19.21; 2.1;
1 Cor 16.8
20.17
Acts 11.30
20.18
Acts 18.19;
19.1,10
20.20
v. 27
20.21
Acts 18.5;
2.38; 24.24;
26.18
20.22
v. 16
20.23
Acts 21.4,11
20.24
Acts 21.13;
2 Cor 4.16;
Acts 1.17;
2 Cor 4.1;
Gal 1.1;
Titus 1.3
20.25
v. 38
20.26
Acts 18.6;
2 Cor 7.2
20.27
v. 20;
Acts 13.36
20.28
1 Tim 4.16;
1 Pet 5.2;
1 Cor 12.28;
1 Pet 1.19;
20.29;
Mt 7.15

took him on board and went to Mitylene. [15] We sailed from there, and on the following day we arrived opposite Chios. The next day we touched at Samos, and[t] the day after that we came to Miletus. [16] For Paul had decided to sail past Ephesus, so that he might not have to spend time in Asia, for he was eager to be in Jerusalem, if possible, on the day of Pentecost.

Paul Speaks to the Ephesian Elders

17 From Miletus he sent a message to Ephesus, asking the elders of the church to meet him. [18] When they came to him, he said to them:

"You yourselves know how I lived among you the entire time from the first day that I set foot in Asia, [19] serving the Lord with all humility and with tears, enduring the trials that came to me through the plots of the Jews. [20] I did not shrink from doing anything helpful, proclaiming the message to you and teaching you publicly and from house to house, [21] as I testified to both Jews and Greeks about repentance toward God and faith toward our Lord Jesus. [22] And now, as a captive to the Spirit,[u] I am on my way to Jerusalem, not knowing what will happen to me there, [23] except that the Holy Spirit testifies to me in every city that imprisonment and persecutions are waiting for me. [24] But I do not count my life of any value to myself, if only I may finish my course and the ministry that I received from the Lord Jesus, to testify to the good news of God's grace.

25 "And now I know that none of you, among whom I have gone about proclaiming the kingdom, will ever see my face again. [26] Therefore I declare to you this day that I am not responsible for the blood of any of you, [27] for I did not shrink from declaring to you the whole purpose of God. [28] Keep watch over yourselves and over all

[s] Gk *given them* [t] Other ancient authorities add *after remaining at Trogyllium* [u] Or *And now, bound in the spirit*

the flock, of which the Holy Spirit has made you overseers, to shepherd the church of God[v] that he obtained with the blood of his own Son.[w] [29]I know that after I have gone, savage wolves will come in among you, not sparing the flock. [30]Some even from your own group will come distorting the truth in order to entice the disciples to follow them. [31]Therefore be alert, remembering that for three years I did not cease night or day to warn everyone with tears. [32]And now I commend you to God and to the message of his grace, a message that is able to build you up and to give you the inheritance among all who are sanctified. [33]I coveted no one's silver or gold or clothing. [34]You know for yourselves that I worked with my own hands to support myself and my companions. [35]In all this I have given you an example that by such work we must support the weak, remembering the words of the Lord Jesus, for he himself said, 'It is more blessed to give than to receive.'"

36 When he had finished speaking, he knelt down with them all and prayed. [37]There was much weeping among them all; they embraced Paul and kissed him, [38]grieving especially because of what he had said, that they would not see him again. Then they brought him to the ship.

Paul's Journey to Jerusalem

21 When we had parted from them and set sail, we came by a straight course to Cos, and the next day to Rhodes, and from there to Patara.[x] [2]When we found a ship bound for Phoenicia, we went on board and set sail. [3]We came in sight of Cyprus; and leaving it on our left, we sailed to Syria and landed at Tyre, because the ship was to unload its cargo there. [4]We looked up the disciples and stayed there for seven days. Through the Spirit they told Paul not to go on to Jerusalem. [5]When our days there were ended, we left and proceeded on our journey; and all of them,

with wives and children, escorted us outside the city. There we knelt down on the beach and prayed [6]and said farewell to one another. Then we went on board the ship, and they returned home.

7 When we had finished[y] the voyage from Tyre, we arrived at Ptolemais; and we greeted the believers[z] and stayed with them for one day. [8]The next day we left and came to Caesarea; and we went into the house of Philip the evangelist, one of the seven, and stayed with him. [9]He had four unmarried daughters[a] who had the gift of prophecy. [10]While we were staying there for several days, a prophet named Agabus came down from Judea. [11]He came to us and took Paul's belt, bound his own feet and hands with it, and said, "Thus says the Holy Spirit, 'This is the way the Jews in Jerusalem will bind the man who owns this belt and will hand him over to the Gentiles.'" [12]When we heard this, we and the people there urged him not to go up to Jerusalem. [13]Then Paul answered, "What are you doing, weeping and breaking my heart? For I am ready not only to be bound but even to die in Jerusalem for the name of the Lord Jesus." [14]Since he would not be persuaded, we remained silent except to say, "The Lord's will be done."

15 After these days we got ready and started to go up to Jerusalem. [16]Some of the disciples from Caesarea also came along and brought us to the house of Mnason of Cyprus, an early disciple, with whom we were to stay.

Paul Visits James at Jerusalem

17 When we arrived in Jerusalem, the brothers welcomed us warmly. [18]The next day Paul went with us to visit James; and all the elders were present. [19]After greeting them, he related one by one the things that God had done among

Cross references (center column)

20.31 Acts 19.10
20.32 Acts 14.23; 9.31; 26.18; Eph 1.18; Col 1.12; 3.24; 1 Pet 1.4
20.33 1 Cor 9.12; 2 Cor 7.2; 11.9; 12.17
20.34 Acts 18.3
20.35 Rom 15.1
20.36 Acts 9.40; 21.5
20.37 Gen 45.14
20.38 v. 25; Acts 15.3
21.2 Acts 11.19
21.4 v. 11; Acts 20.23
21.5 Acts 20.36

21.7 Acts 12.20; 1.15
21.8 Eph 4.11; 2 Tim 4.5; Acts 6.5; 8.26,40
21.9 Acts 2.17; Lk 2.36
21.10 Acts 11.28
21.11 v. 33; Acts 20.23
21.13 Acts 20.24
21.14 Mt 26.42; Lk 22.42
21.16 vv. 3,4
21.17 Acts 15.4
21.18 Acts 12.17; 15.13
21.19 Acts 14.27; 1.17; 20.24

Footnotes

v Other ancient authorities read *of the Lord*　w Or *with his own blood*; Gk *with the blood of his Own*　x Other ancient authorities add *and Myra*　y Or *continued*　z Gk *brothers*　a Gk *four daughters, virgins,*

the Gentiles through his ministry. ²⁰When they heard it, they praised God. Then they said to him, "You see, brother, how many thousands of believers there are among the Jews, and they are all zealous for the law. ²¹They have been told about you that you teach all the Jews living among the Gentiles to forsake Moses, and that you tell them not to circumcise their children or observe the customs. ²²What then is to be done? They will certainly hear that you have come. ²³So do what we tell you. We have four men who are under a vow. ²⁴Join these men, go through the rite of purification with them, and pay for the shaving of their heads. Thus all will know that there is nothing in what they have been told about you, but that you yourself observe and guard the law. ²⁵But as for the Gentiles who have become believers, we have sent a letter with our judgment that they should abstain from what has been sacrificed to idols and from blood and from what is strangledᵇ and from fornication." ²⁶Then Paul took the men, and the next day, having purified himself, he entered the temple with them, making public the completion of the days of purification when the sacrifice would be made for each of them.

Paul Arrested in the Temple

27 When the seven days were almost completed, the Jews from Asia, who had seen him in the temple, stirred up the whole crowd. They seized him, ²⁸shouting, "Fellow Israelites, help! This is the man who is teaching everyone everywhere against our people, our law, and this place; more than that, he has actually brought Greeks into the temple and has defiled this holy place." ²⁹For they had previously seen Trophimus the Ephesian with him in the city, and they supposed that Paul had brought him into the temple. ³⁰Then all the city was aroused, and the people rushed together. They seized Paul and dragged him out of the temple,

and immediately the doors were shut. ³¹While they were trying to kill him, word came to the tribune of the cohort that all Jerusalem was in an uproar. ³²Immediately he took soldiers and centurions and ran down to them. When they saw the tribune and the soldiers, they stopped beating Paul. ³³Then the tribune came, arrested him, and ordered him to be bound with two chains; he inquired who he was and what he had done. ³⁴Some in the crowd shouted one thing, some another; and as he could not learn the facts because of the uproar, he ordered him to be brought into the barracks. ³⁵When Paulᶜ came to the steps, the violence of the mob was so great that he had to be carried by the soldiers. ³⁶The crowd that followed kept shouting, "Away with him!"

Paul Defends Himself

37 Just as Paul was about to be brought into the barracks, he said to the tribune, "May I say something to you?" The tribuneᵈ replied, "Do you know Greek? ³⁸Then you are not the Egyptian who recently stirred up a revolt and led the four thousand assassins out into the wilderness?" ³⁹Paul replied, "I am a Jew, from Tarsus in Cilicia, a citizen of an important city; I beg you, let me speak to the people." ⁴⁰When he had given him permission, Paul stood on the steps and motioned to the people for silence; and when there was a great hush, he addressed them in the Hebrewᵉ language, saying:

22 "Brothers and fathers, listen to the defense that I now make before you."

2 When they heard him addressing them in Hebrew,ᵉ they became even more quiet. Then he said:

3 "I am a Jew, born in Tarsus in Cilicia, but brought up in this city at the feet of Gamaliel, educated strictly according to our ancestral law, being zealous for God, just as

21.20
Acts 22.3;
Rom 10.2;
Gal 1.14
21.21
v. 28;
1 Cor 7.18,
19
21.23
Acts 18.18
21.24
v. 26;
Acts 24.18
21.25
Acts 15.20,
29
21.26
Num 6.13;
Acts 24.18
21.27
Acts 24.18;
26.21
21.28
Acts 24.5,6
21.29
Acts 20.4;
18.19
21.30
Acts 26.21;
16.19

21.32
Acts 23.27
21.33
Acts 20.23;
v. 11
21.34
Acts 19.32;
v. 37
21.36
Lk 23.18;
Jn 19.15;
Acts 22.22
21.37
v. 34
21.38
Acts 5.36;
Mt 24.26
21.39
Acts 9.11;
22.3
21.40
Acts 12.17;
22.2; 26.14
22.1
Acts 7.2
22.2
Acts 21.40
22.3
Acts 21.39;
20.4;
Lk 10.39;
Acts 26.5;
21.20

ᵇOther ancient authorities lack *and from what is strangled* ᶜGk *he* ᵈGk *He* ᵉThat is, *Aramaic*

all of you are today. ⁴I persecuted this Way up to the point of death by binding both men and women and putting them in prison, ⁵as the high priest and the whole council of elders can testify about me. From them I also received letters to the brothers in Damascus, and I went there in order to bind those who were there and to bring them back to Jerusalem for punishment.

Paul Tells of His Conversion

6 "While I was on my way and approaching Damascus, about noon a great light from heaven suddenly shone about me. ⁷I fell to the ground and heard a voice saying to me, 'Saul, Saul, why are you persecuting me?' ⁸I answered, 'Who are you, Lord?' Then he said to me, 'I am Jesus of Nazareth ᶠ whom you are persecuting.' ⁹Now those who were with me saw the light but did not hear the voice of the one who was speaking to me. ¹⁰I asked, 'What am I to do, Lord?' The Lord said to me, 'Get up and go to Damascus; there you will be told everything that has been assigned to you to do.' ¹¹Since I could not see because of the brightness of that light, those who were with me took my hand and led me to Damascus. 12 "A certain Ananias, who was a devout man according to the law and well spoken of by all the Jews living there, ¹³came to me; and standing beside me, he said, 'Brother Saul, regain your sight!' In that very hour I regained my sight and saw him. ¹⁴Then he said, 'The God of our ancestors has chosen you to know his will, to see the Righteous One and to hear his own voice; ¹⁵for you will be his witness to all the world of what you have seen and heard. ¹⁶And now why do you delay? Get up, be baptized, and have your sins washed away, calling on his name.'

Paul Sent to the Gentiles

17 "After I had returned to Jerusalem and while I was praying in the temple, I fell into a trance ¹⁸and saw Jesus ᵍ saying to me,

'Hurry and get out of Jerusalem quickly, because they will not accept your testimony about me.' ¹⁹And I said, 'Lord, they themselves know that in every synagogue I imprisoned and beat those who believed in you. ²⁰And while the blood of your witness Stephen was shed, I myself was standing by, approving and keeping the coats of those who killed him.' ²¹Then he said to me, 'Go, for I will send you far away to the Gentiles.' "

Paul and the Roman Tribune

22 Up to this point they listened to him, but then they shouted, "Away with such a fellow from the earth! For he should not be allowed to live." ²³And while they were shouting, throwing off their cloaks, and tossing dust into the air, ²⁴the tribune directed that he was to be brought into the barracks, and ordered him to be examined by flogging, to find out the reason for this outcry against him. ²⁵But when they had tied him up with thongs, ʰ Paul said to the centurion who was standing by, "Is it legal for you to flog a Roman citizen who is uncondemned?" ²⁶When the centurion heard that, he went to the tribune and said to him, "What are you about to do? This man is a Roman citizen." ²⁷The tribune came and asked Paul, ᵍ "Tell me, are you a Roman citizen?" And he said, "Yes." ²⁸The tribune answered, "It cost me a large sum of money to get my citizenship." Paul said, "But I was born a citizen." ²⁹Immediately those who were about to examine him drew back from him; and the tribune also was afraid, for he realized that Paul was a Roman citizen and that he had bound him.

Paul before the Council

30 Since he wanted to find out what Paul ⁱ was being accused of by the Jews, the next day he released him and ordered the chief priests and the entire council to

22.4	Acts 8.3; 26.9-11; Phil 3.6; 1 Tim 1.13
22.5	Lk 22.66; Acts 4.5; 9.2; 26.10,12
22.6	Acts 9.3; 26.12,13
22.9	Acts 9.7; 26.13
22.10	Acts 16.30
22.11	Acts 9.8
22.12	Acts 9.17; 10.22
22.14	Acts 3.13; 5.30; 9.15; 26.16; 1 Cor 9.1; 15.8; Acts 7.52
22.15	Acts 23.11; 26.16
22.16	Acts 2.38; Heb 10.22; Acts 9.14; Rom 10.13
22.17	Acts 9.26; 10.10
22.19	v. 4; Acts 8.3; 26.11; Mt 10.17
22.20	Lk 11.48; Acts 8.1; Rom 1.32
22.21	Acts 9.15
22.22	Acts 21.36; 25.24
22.23	Acts 7.58; 2 Sam 16.13
22.24	Acts 21.34
22.25	Acts 16.37
22.29	vv. 24,25
22.30	Acts 23.28; 21.33

ᶠ Gk the Nazorean ᵍ Gk him ʰ Or up for the lashes ⁱ Gk he

meet. He brought Paul down and had him stand before them.

23 While Paul was looking intently at the council he said, "Brothers,ⁱ up to this day I have lived my life with a clear conscience before God." ² Then the high priest Ananias ordered those standing near him to strike him on the mouth. ³ At this Paul said to him, "God will strike you, you whitewashed wall! Are you sitting there to judge me according to the law, and yet in violation of the law you order me to be struck?" ⁴ Those standing nearby said, "Do you dare to insult God's high priest?" ⁵ And Paul said, "I did not realize, brothers, that he was high priest; for it is written, 'You shall not speak evil of a leader of your people.' "

6 When Paul noticed that some were Sadducees and others were Pharisees, he called out in the council, "Brothers, I am a Pharisee, a son of Pharisees. I am on trial concerning the hope of the resurrectionᵏ of the dead." ⁷ When he said this, a dissension began between the Pharisees and the Sadducees, and the assembly was divided. ⁸ (The Sadducees say that there is no resurrection, or angel, or spirit; but the Pharisees acknowledge all three.) ⁹ Then a great clamor arose, and certain scribes of the Pharisees' group stood up and contended, "We find nothing wrong with this man. What if a spirit or an angel has spoken to him?" ¹⁰ When the dissension became violent, the tribune, fearing that they would tear Paul to pieces, ordered the soldiers to go down, take him by force, and bring him into the barracks.

11 That night the Lord stood near him and said, "Keep up your courage! For just as you have testified for me in Jerusalem, so you must bear witness also in Rome."

The Plot to Kill Paul

12 In the morning the Jews joined in a conspiracy and bound themselves by an oath neither to eat nor drink until they had killed

Paul. ¹³ There were more than forty who joined in this conspiracy. ¹⁴ They went to the chief priests and elders and said, "We have strictly bound ourselves by an oath to taste no food until we have killed Paul. ¹⁵ Now then, you and the council must notify the tribune to bring him down to you, on the pretext that you want to make a more thorough examination of his case. And we are ready to do away with him before he arrives."

16 Now the son of Paul's sister heard about the ambush; so he went and gained entrance to the barracks and told Paul. ¹⁷ Paul called one of the centurions and said, "Take this young man to the tribune, for he has something to report to him." ¹⁸ So he took him, brought him to the tribune, and said, "The prisoner Paul called me and asked me to bring this young man to you; he has something to tell you." ¹⁹ The tribune took him by the hand, drew him aside privately, and asked, "What is it that you have to report to me?" ²⁰ He answered, "The Jews have agreed to ask you to bring Paul down to the council tomorrow, as though they were going to inquire more thoroughly into his case. ²¹ But do not be persuaded by them, for more than forty of their men are lying in ambush for him. They have bound themselves by an oath neither to eat nor drink until they kill him. They are ready now and are waiting for your consent." ²² So the tribune dismissed the young man, ordering him, "Tell no one that you have informed me of this."

Paul Sent to Felix the Governor

23 Then he summoned two of the centurions and said, "Get ready to leave by nine o'clock tonight for Caesarea with two hundred soldiers, seventy horsemen, and two hundred spearmen. ²⁴ Also provide mounts for Paul to ride, and take him safely to Felix the governor." ²⁵ He wrote a letter to this effect:

Cross references (center column):

23.1 Acts 22.30; 24.16; 2 Cor 1.12; 2 Tim 1.3
23.2 Jn 18.22
23.3 Mt 23.27; Lev 19.35; Deut 25.1,2; Jn 7.51
23.5 Ex 22.28
23.6 Acts 26.5; Phil 3.5; Acts 24.15, 16; 26.8
23.8 Mt 22.23; Mk 12.18; Lk 20.27
23.9 Acts 25.25; 26.31; 22.7, 17,18
23.10 Acts 21.34
23.11 Acts 18.9; 19.21; 28.23
23.12 vv. 21,30; Acts 25.3
23.14 v. 21
23.15 Acts 22.30
23.16 Acts 21.34; v. 10
23.18 Eph 3.1
23.20 vv. 14,15
23.21 vv.12,14
23.23 v. 33
23.24 Acts 24.1,3; 10; 25.14

26 "Claudius Lysias to his Excellency the governor Felix, greetings. 27 This man was seized by the Jews and was about to be killed by them, but when I had learned that he was a Roman citizen, I came with the guard and rescued him. 28 Since I wanted to know the charge for which they accused him, I had him brought to their council. 29 I found that he was accused concerning questions of their law, but was charged with nothing deserving death or imprisonment. 30 When I was informed that there would be a plot against the man, I sent him to you at once, ordering his accusers also to state before you what they have against him.1"

31 So the soldiers, according to their instructions, took Paul and brought him during the night to Antipatris. 32 The next day they let the horsemen go on with him, while they returned to the barracks. 33 When they came to Caesarea and delivered the letter to the governor, they presented Paul also before him. 34 On reading the letter, he asked what province he belonged to, and when he learned that he was from Cilicia, 35 he said, "I will give you a hearing when your accusers arrive." Then he ordered that he be kept under guard in Herod's headquarters.m

Paul before Felix at Caesarea

24 Five days later the high priest Ananias came down with some elders and an attorney, a certain Tertullus, and they reported their case against Paul to the governor. 2 When Pauln had been summoned, Tertullus began to accuse him, saying:

"Your Excellency,o because of you we have long enjoyed peace, and reforms have been made for this people because of your foresight. 3 We welcome this in every way and everywhere with utmost gratitude. 4 But, to detain you no further, I beg you to hear us briefly with your customary graciousness. 5 We have, in fact, found this man a pestilent fellow, an agitator among

all the Jews throughout the world, and a ringleader of the sect of the Nazarenes.p 6 He even tried to profane the temple, and so we seized him.q 8 By examining him yourself you will be able to learn from him concerning everything of which we accuse him."

9 The Jews also joined in the charge by asserting that all this was true.

Paul's Defense before Felix

10 When the governor motioned to him to speak, Paul replied:

"I cheerfully make my defense, knowing that for many years you have been a judge over this nation. 11 As you can find out, it is not more than twelve days since I went up to worship in Jerusalem. 12 They did not find me disputing with anyone in the temple or stirring up a crowd either in the synagogues or throughout the city. 13 Neither can they prove to you the charge that they now bring against me. 14 But this I admit to you, that according to the Way, which they call a sect, I worship the God of our ancestors, believing everything laid down according to the law or written in the prophets. 15 I have a hope in God — a hope that they themselves also accept — that there will be a resurrection of bothr the righteous and the unrighteous. 16 Therefore I do my best always to have a clear conscience toward God and all people. 17 Now after some years I came to bring alms to my nation and to offer sacrifices. 18 While I was doing this, they found me in the temple, completing the rite of purification, without any crowd or disturbance. 19 But there were some Jews from Asia — they ought to be here before you to make an accusation, if they have anything against me. 20 Or let these men here tell what crime

23.26
Acts 24.3;
15.23
23.27
Acts 21.32,
33; 22.25-29
23.28
Acts 22.30
23.29
Acts 18.15;
25.19; 26.31
23.30
vv. 20,21;
Acts 24.19;
25.16
23.32
v. 23
23.33
vv. 23,24,26
23.34
Acts 21.39
23.35
Acts 24.19;
25.16; 24.27
24.1
Acts 23.2,
30,35
24.3
Acts 23.26;
26.25
24.5
Acts 16.20;
17.6; 21.28

24.6
Acts 21.28
24.9
1 Thes 2.16
24.10
Acts 23.24
24.11
Acts 21.26
24.12
Acts 25.8;
28.17
24.13
Acts 25.7
24.14
Acts 9.2;
v. 5;
Acts 3.13;
26.22; 28.23
24.15
Acts 23.6;
28.20;
Dan 12.2;
Jn 5.28,29
24.16
Acts 23.1
24.17
Acts 11.29,
30;
Rom 15.25-28;
2 Cor 8.1-4;
Gal 2.10
24.18
Acts 21.26,
27
24.19
Acts 23.30

1 Other ancient authorities add *Farewell* m Gk *praetorium* n Gk *he* o Gk lacks *Your Excellency* p Gk *Nazoreans* q Other ancient authorities add *and we would have judged him according to our law.* 7 *But the chief captain Lysias came and with great violence took him out of our hands,* 8 *commanding his accusers to come before you.* r Other ancient authorities read *of the dead, both of*

they had found when I stood before the council, [21]unless it was this one sentence that I called out while standing before them, 'It is about the resurrection of the dead that I am on trial before you today.' "

22 But Felix, who was rather well informed about the Way, adjourned the hearing with the comment, "When Lysias the tribune comes down, I will decide your case." [23]Then he ordered the centurion to keep him in custody, but to let him have some liberty and not to prevent any of his friends from taking care of his needs.

Paul Held in Custody

24 Some days later when Felix came with his wife Drusilla, who was Jewish, he sent for Paul and heard him speak concerning faith in Christ Jesus. [25]And as he discussed justice, self-control, and the coming judgment, Felix became frightened and said, "Go away for the present; when I have an opportunity, I will send for you." [26]At the same time he hoped that money would be given him by Paul, and for that reason he used to send for him very often and converse with him.

27 After two years had passed, Felix was succeeded by Porcius Festus; and since he wanted to grant the Jews a favor, Felix left Paul in prison.

Paul Appeals to Caesar

25 Three days after Festus had arrived in the province, he went up from Caesarea to Jerusalem [2]where the chief priests and the leaders of the Jews gave him a report against Paul. They appealed to him [3]and requested, as a favor to them against Paul,[s] to have him transferred to Jerusalem. They were, in fact, planning an ambush to kill him along the way. [4]Festus replied that Paul was being kept at Caesarea, and that he himself intended to go there shortly. [5]"So,"

24.21
Acts 23.6
24.23
Acts 23.35;
28.16; 23.16;
27.3
24.25
Gal 5.23;
Acts 10.42
24.27
Acts 25.1,4,
9,14; 12.3;
23.35
25.2
Acts 24.1;
v. 15
25.3
Acts 23.12,
15
25.4
Acts 24.23

25.7
Mk 15.3;
Lk 23.2,10;
Acts 24.5,13
25.8
Acts 6.13;
24.12; 28.17
25.9
Acts 24.27;
v. 20
25.11
v. 25;
Acts 26.32;
28.19
25.14
Acts 24.27
25.15
Acts 24.1;
v. 2
25.16
vv. 4,5

he said, "let those of you who have the authority come down with me, and if there is anything wrong about the man, let them accuse him."

6 After he had stayed among them not more than eight or ten days, he went down to Caesarea; the next day he took his seat on the tribunal and ordered Paul to be brought. [7]When he arrived, the Jews who had gone down from Jerusalem surrounded him, bringing many serious charges against him, which they could not prove. [8]Paul said in his defense, "I have in no way committed an offense against the law of the Jews, or against the temple, or against the emperor." [9]But Festus, wishing to do the Jews a favor, asked Paul, "Do you wish to go up to Jerusalem and be tried there before me on these charges?" [10]Paul said, "I am appealing to the emperor's tribunal; this is where I should be tried. I have done no wrong to the Jews, as you very well know. [11]Now if I am in the wrong and have committed something for which I deserve to die, I am not trying to escape death; but if there is nothing to their charges against me, no one can turn me over to them. I appeal to the emperor." [12]Then Festus, after he had conferred with his council, replied, "You have appealed to the emperor; to the emperor you will go."

Festus Consults King Agrippa

13 After several days had passed, King Agrippa and Bernice arrived at Caesarea to welcome Festus. [14]Since they were staying there several days, Festus laid Paul's case before the king, saying, "There is a man here who was left in prison by Felix. [15]When I was in Jerusalem, the chief priests and the elders of the Jews informed me about him and asked for a sentence against him. [16]I told them that it was not the custom of the Romans to hand over anyone before the ac-

[s] Gk *him*

cused had met the accusers face to face and had been given an opportunity to make a defense against the charge. ¹⁷So when they met here, I lost no time, but on the next day took my seat on the tribunal and ordered the man to be brought. ¹⁸When the accusers stood up, they did not charge him with any of the crimest that I was expecting. ¹⁹Instead they had certain points of disagreement with him about their own religion and about a certain Jesus, who had died, but whom Paul asserted to be alive. ²⁰Since I was at a loss how to investigate these questions, I asked whether they wished to go to Jerusalem and be tried there on these charges.u ²¹But when Paul had appealed to be kept in custody for the decision of his Imperial Majesty, I ordered him to be held until I could send him to the emperor." ²²Agrippa said to Festus, "I would like to hear the man myself." "Tomorrow," he said, "you will hear him."

Paul Brought before Agrippa

23 So on the next day Agrippa and Bernice came with great pomp, and they entered the audience hall with the military tribunes and the prominent men of the city. Then Festus gave the order and Paul was brought in. ²⁴And Festus said, "King Agrippa and all here present with us, you see this man about whom the whole Jewish community petitioned me, both in Jerusalem and here, shouting that he ought not to live any longer. ²⁵But I found that he had done nothing deserving death; and when he appealed to his Imperial Majesty, I decided to send him. ²⁶But I have nothing definite to write to our sovereign about him. Therefore I have brought him before all of you, and especially before you, King Agrippa, so that, after we have examined him, I may have something to write — ²⁷for it seems to me unreasonable to send a prisoner without indicating the charges against him."

25.17
vv. 6,10
25.19
Acts 18.15;
23.29
25.20
v. 9
25.21
vv. 11,12
25.22
Acts 9.15
25.23
v. 13;
Acts 26.30
25.24
vv. 2,3,7;
Acts 22.22
25.25
Acts 23.9,
29; 26.31,32

26.1
Acts 9.15;
25.22
26.3
Acts 6.14;
25.19; v. 7
26.4
Gal 1.13,14;
Phil 3.5
26.5
Acts 22.3;
23.6;
Phil 3.5
26.6
Acts 23.6;
13.32;
Rom 15.8;
Titus 2.13
26.7
Jas 1.1;
1 Thes 3.10;
1 Tim 5.5
26.9
Jn 16.2;
1 Tim 1.13;
Jn 15.21
26.10
Acts 8.3;
Gal 1.13;
Acts 9.14,21
26.12
Acts 9.3;
22.6

Paul Defends Himself before Agrippa

26 Agrippa said to Paul, "You have permission to speak for yourself." Then Paul stretched out his hand and began to defend himself:

2 "I consider myself fortunate that it is before you, King Agrippa, I am to make my defense today against all the accusations of the Jews, ³because you are especially familiar with all the customs and controversies of the Jews; therefore I beg of you to listen to me patiently.

4 "All the Jews know my way of life from my youth, a life spent from the beginning among my own people and in Jerusalem. ⁵They have known for a long time, if they are willing to testify, that I have belonged to the strictest sect of our religion and lived as a Pharisee. ⁶And now I stand here on trial on account of my hope in the promise made by God to our ancestors, ⁷a promise that our twelve tribes hope to attain, as they earnestly worship day and night. It is for this hope, your Excellency,v that I am accused by Jews! ⁸Why is it thought incredible by any of you that God raises the dead?

9 "Indeed, I myself was convinced that I ought to do many things against the name of Jesus of Nazareth.w ¹⁰And that is what I did in Jerusalem; with authority received from the chief priests, I not only locked up many of the saints in prison, but I also cast my vote against them when they were being condemned to death. ¹¹By punishing them often in all the synagogues I tried to force them to blaspheme; and since I was so furiously enraged at them, I pursued them even to foreign cities.

Paul Tells of His Conversion

12 "With this in mind, I was traveling to Damascus with the authority and commission of the

t Other ancient authorities read *with anything*
u Gk *on them* v Gk *O king* w Gk *the Nazorean*

chief priests, [13]when at midday along the road, your Excellency,[x] I saw a light from heaven, brighter than the sun, shining around me and my companions. [14]When we had all fallen to the ground, I heard a voice saying to me in the Hebrew[y] language, 'Saul, Saul, why are you persecuting me? It hurts you to kick against the goads.' [15]I asked, 'Who are you, Lord?' The Lord answered, 'I am Jesus whom you are persecuting. [16]But get up and stand on your feet; for I have appeared to you for this purpose, to appoint you to serve and testify to the things in which you have seen me[z] and to those in which I will appear to you. [17]I will rescue you from your people and from the Gentiles—to whom I am sending you [18]to open their eyes so that they may turn from darkness to light and from the power of Satan to God, so that they may receive forgiveness of sins and a place among those who are sanctified by faith in me.'

Paul Tells of His Preaching

19 "After that, King Agrippa, I was not disobedient to the heavenly vision, [20]but declared first to those in Damascus, then in Jerusalem and throughout the countryside of Judea, and also to the Gentiles, that they should repent and turn to God and do deeds consistent with repentance. [21]For this reason the Jews seized me in the temple and tried to kill me. [22]To this day I have had help from God, and so I stand here, testifying to both small and great, saying nothing but what the prophets and Moses said would take place: [23]that the Messiah[a] must suffer, and that, by being the first to rise from the dead, he would proclaim light both to our people and to the Gentiles."

Paul Appeals to Agrippa to Believe

24 While he was making this defense, Festus exclaimed, "You are out of your mind, Paul! Too much learning is driving you insane!"

[25]But Paul said, "I am not out of my mind, most excellent Festus, but I am speaking the sober truth. [26]Indeed the king knows about these things, and to him I speak freely; for I am certain that none of these things has escaped his notice, for this was not done in a corner. [27]King Agrippa, do you believe the prophets? I know that you believe." [28]Agrippa said to Paul, "Are you so quickly persuading me to become a Christian?"[b] [29]Paul replied, "Whether quickly or not, I pray to God that not only you but also all who are listening to me today might become such as I am— except for these chains."

30 Then the king got up, and with him the governor and Bernice and those who had been seated with them; [31]and as they were leaving, they said to one another, "This man is doing nothing to deserve death or imprisonment." [32]Agrippa said to Festus, "This man could have been set free if he had not appealed to the emperor."

Paul Sails for Rome

27 When it was decided that we were to sail for Italy, they transferred Paul and some other prisoners to a centurion of the Augustan Cohort, named Julius. [2]Embarking on a ship of Adramyttium that was about to set sail to the ports along the coast of Asia, we put to sea, accompanied by Aristarchus, a Macedonian from Thessalonica. [3]The next day we put in at Sidon; and Julius treated Paul kindly, and allowed him to go to his friends to be cared for. [4]Putting out to sea from there, we sailed under the lee of Cyprus, because the winds were against us. [5]After we had sailed across the sea that is off Cilicia and Pamphylia, we came to Myra in Lycia. [6]There the centurion found an Alexandrian ship bound for Italy and put us on board. [7]We sailed slowly for

Center column cross-references

26.14
Acts 9.7;
21.40
26.16
Ezek 2.1;
Dan 10.11;
Acts 22.14,
15
26.17
Jer 1.8,19;
Acts 22.21
26.18
Isa 35.5;
42.7;
Eph 5.8;
Col 1.13;
1 Pet 2.9;
Lk 24.47;
Acts 2.38;
20.32
26.20
Acts 9.19-29;
22.17-20;
13.46; 9.15;
3.19;
Mt 3.8;
Lk 3.8
26.21
Acts 21.30,
31
26.22
Lk 24.27,44;
Acts 24.14
26.23
Mt 26.24;
1 Cor 15.20;
Col 1.18;
Rev 1.5;
Lk 2.32
26.24
2 Kings 9.11;
Jn 10.20;
1 Corr 1.23

26.25
Acts 23.26;
24.3
26.30
Acts 25.33
26.31
Acts 23.29
26.32
Acts 28.18;
25.11
27.1
Acts 25.12,
25; 10.1
27.2
Acts 19.29;
16.9; 17.1
27.3
Acts 24.23;
28.16
27.4
v. 7
27.5
Acts 6.9;
13.13
27.6
Acts 28.11;
v. 1
27.7
vv. 4,12,13

x Gk O king y That is, Aramaic z Other ancient authorities read the things that you have seen a Or the Christ b Or Quickly you will persuade me to play the Christian

a number of days and arrived with difficulty off Cnidus, and as the wind was against us, we sailed under the lee of Crete off Salmone. [8]Sailing past it with difficulty, we came to a place called Fair Havens, near the city of Lasea.

9 Since much time had been lost and sailing was now dangerous, because even the Fast had already gone by, Paul advised them, [10]saying, "Sirs, I can see that the voyage will be with danger and much heavy loss, not only of the cargo and the ship, but also of our lives." [11]But the centurion paid more attention to the pilot and to the owner of the ship than to what Paul said. [12]Since the harbor was not suitable for spending the winter, the majority was in favor of putting to sea from there, on the chance that somehow they could reach Phoenix, where they could spend the winter. It was a harbor of Crete, facing southwest and northwest.

The Storm at Sea

13 When a moderate south wind began to blow, they thought they could achieve their purpose; so they weighed anchor and began to sail past Crete, close to the shore. [14]But soon a violent wind, called the northeaster, rushed down from Crete.[c] [15]Since the ship was caught and could not be turned head-on into the wind, we gave way to it and were driven. [16]By running under the lee of a small island called Cauda[d] we were scarcely able to get the ship's boat under control. [17]After hoisting it up they took measures[e] to undergird the ship; then, fearing that they would run on the Syrtis, they lowered the sea anchor and so were driven. [18]We were being pounded by the storm so violently that on the next day they began to throw the cargo overboard, [19]and on the third day with their own hands they threw the ship's tackle overboard. [20]When neither sun nor stars appeared for many days, and no small

tempest raged, all hope of our being saved was at last abandoned.

21 Since they had been without food for a long time, Paul then stood up among them and said, "Men, you should have listened to me and not have set sail from Crete and thereby avoided this damage and loss. [22]I urge you now to keep up your courage, for there will be no loss of life among you, but only of the ship. [23]For last night there stood by me an angel of the God to whom I belong and whom I worship, [24]and he said, 'Do not be afraid, Paul; you must stand before the emperor; and indeed, God has granted safety to all those who are sailing with you.' [25]So keep up your courage, men, for I have faith in God that it will be exactly as I have been told. [26]But we will have to run aground on some island."

27 When the fourteenth night had come, as we were drifting across the sea of Adria, about midnight the sailors suspected that they were nearing land. [28]So they took soundings and found twenty fathoms; a little farther on they took soundings again and found fifteen fathoms. [29]Fearing that we might run on the rocks, they let down four anchors from the stern and prayed for day to come. [30]But when the sailors tried to escape from the ship and had lowered the boat into the sea, on the pretext of putting out anchors from the bow, [31]Paul said to the centurion and the soldiers, "Unless these men stay in the ship, you cannot be saved." [32]Then the soldiers cut away the ropes of the boat and set it adrift.

33 Just before daybreak, Paul urged all of them to take some food, saying, "Today is the fourteenth day that you have been in suspense and remaining without food, having eaten nothing. [34]Therefore I urge you to take some food, for it will help you survive; for none of you will lose a hair from

27.9
Lev 23.27-29
27.10
v. 21
27.13
vv. 7,12
27.14
Mk 4.37
27.17
vv. 26,29
27.18
Jon 1.5;
v. 38

27.21
vv. 10,7,12,
13
27.22
vv. 25,36
27.23
Acts 23.11;
5.19;
Rom 1.9
27.24
Acts 23.11;
v. 44
27.25
vv. 22,36;
Rom 4.20,
21
27.26
Acts 28.1
27.30
v. 16
27.34
1 Kings 1.52;
Mt 10.30;
Lk 12.7;
21.18

[c] Gk *it Clauda* [d] Other ancient authorities read
 [e] Gk *helps*

your heads." 35After he had said this, he took bread; and giving thanks to God in the presence of all, he broke it and began to eat. 36Then all of them were encouraged and took food for themselves. 37(We were in all two hundred seventy-six[f] persons in the ship.) 38After they had satisfied their hunger, they lightened the ship by throwing the wheat into the sea.

The Shipwreck

39 In the morning they did not recognize the land, but they noticed a bay with a beach, on which they planned to run the ship ashore, if they could. 40So they cast off the anchors and left them in the sea. At the same time they loosened the ropes that tied the steering-oars; then hoisting the foresail to the wind, they made for the beach. 41But striking a reef,[g] they ran the ship aground; the bow stuck and remained immovable, but the stern was being broken up by the force of the waves. 42The soldiers' plan was to kill the prisoners, so that none might swim away and escape; 43but the centurion, wishing to save Paul, kept them from carrying out their plan. He ordered those who could swim to jump overboard first and make for the land, 44and the rest to follow, some on planks and others on pieces of the ship. And so it was that all were brought safely to land.

Paul on the Island of Malta

28 After we had reached safety, we then learned that the island was called Malta. 2The natives showed us unusual kindness. Since it had begun to rain and was cold, they kindled a fire and welcomed all of us around it. 3Paul had gathered a bundle of brushwood and was putting it on the fire, when a viper, driven out by the heat, fastened itself on his hand. 4When the natives saw the creature hanging from his hand, they said to one another, "This man must be a murderer; though he has escaped

27.35
1 Sam 9.13;
Mt 15.36;
Mk 8.6;
Jn 6.11;
1 Tim 4.3,
4
27.36
vv. 22,25
27.38
v. 18
27.39
Acts 28.1
27.40
v. 29
27.41
2 Cor 11.25
27.42
Acts 12.19
27.43
v. 3
27.44
vv. 22,31
28.1
Acts 27.26,
39
28.2
Rom 1.14;
1 Cor 14.11;
Col 3.11
28.4
Lk 13.2,4

28.5
Lk 10.19
28.6
Acts 14.11
28.8
Jas 5.14,15;
Mk 5.23
28.11
Acts 27.6
28.14
Acts 1.15
28.16
Acts 24.23;
27.3

from the sea, justice has not allowed him to live." 5He, however, shook off the creature into the fire and suffered no harm. 6They were expecting him to swell up or drop dead, but after they had waited a long time and saw that nothing unusual had happened to him, they changed their minds and began to say that he was a god.

7 Now in the neighborhood of that place were lands belonging to the leading man of the island, named Publius, who received us and entertained us hospitably for three days. 8It so happened that the father of Publius lay sick in bed with fever and dysentery. Paul visited him and cured him by praying and putting his hands on him. 9After this happened, the rest of the people on the island who had diseases also came and were cured. 10They bestowed many honors on us, and when we were about to sail, they put on board all the provisions we needed.

Paul Arrives at Rome

11 Three months later we set sail on a ship that had wintered at the island, an Alexandrian ship with the Twin Brothers as its figurehead. 12We put in at Syracuse and stayed there for three days; 13then we weighed anchor and came to Rhegium. After one day there a south wind sprang up, and on the second day we came to Puteoli. 14There we found believers[h] and were invited to stay with them for seven days. And so we came to Rome. 15The believers[h] from there, when they heard of us, came as far as the Forum of Appius and Three Taverns to meet us. On seeing them, Paul thanked God and took courage.

16 When we came into Rome, Paul was allowed to live by himself, with the soldier who was guarding him.

[f] Other ancient authorities read seventy-six; others, about seventy-six [g] Gk place of two seas [h] Gk brothers

Paul and Jewish Leaders in Rome

17 Three days later he called together the local leaders of the Jews. When they had assembled, he said to them, "Brothers, though I had done nothing against our people or the customs of our ancestors, yet I was arrested in Jerusalem and handed over to the Romans. 18 When they had examined me, the Romans[i] wanted to release me, because there was no reason for the death penalty in my case. 19 But when the Jews objected, I was compelled to appeal to the emperor — even though I had no charge to bring against my nation. 20 For this reason therefore I have asked to see you and speak with you,[j] since it is for the sake of the hope of Israel that I am bound with this chain." 21 They replied, "We have received no letters from Judea about you, and none of the brothers coming here has reported or spoken anything evil about you. 22 But we would like to hear from you what you think, for with regard to this sect we know that everywhere it is spoken against."

Paul Preaches in Rome

23 After they had set a day to meet with him, they came to him at his lodgings in great numbers. From morning until evening he explained the matter to them, testifying to the kingdom of God and trying to convince them about Jesus both from the law of Moses and from the prophets. 24 Some were convinced by what he had said, while others refused to believe. 25 So they disagreed with each other; and as they were leaving, Paul made one further statement: "The Holy Spirit was right in saying to your ancestors through the prophet Isaiah,

26 'Go to this people and say,
 You will indeed listen, but
 never understand,
 and you will indeed look,
 but never perceive.
27 For this people's heart has
 grown dull,
 and their ears are hard of
 hearing,
 and they have shut their
 eyes;
 so that they might not
 look with their eyes,
 and listen with their ears,
 and understand with their
 heart and turn —
 and I would heal them.'
28 Let it be known to you then that this salvation of God has been sent to the Gentiles; they will listen."[k]

30 He lived there two whole years at his own expense[l] and welcomed all who came to him, 31 proclaiming the kingdom of God and teaching about the Lord Jesus Christ with all boldness and without hindrance.

28.17
Acts 13.50;
25.8; 6.14
28.18
Acts 22.24;
26.31,32;
23.29
28.19
Acts 25.11
28.20
Acts 26.6,7,
29; Eph 3.1;
4.1; 6.20;
2 Tim 1.16
28.21
Acts 22.5
28.22
Acts 24.14;
1 Pet 2.12;
4.14
28.23
Acts 17.3;
19.8
28.24
Acts 14.4

28.26
Isa 6.9,10;
Mt 13.14,
15;
Rom 11.8
28.28
Mt 21.41,
43;
Acts 13.46,
47;
Rom 11.11
28.31
v. 23;
Eph 6.19;
2 Tim 2.9

[i] Gk they [j] Or I have asked you to see me and speak with me [k] Other ancient authorities add verse 29, And when he had said these words, the Jews departed, arguing vigorously among themselves [l] Or in his own hired dwelling

THE LETTER OF PAUL TO THE
Romans

Title and Background

When Paul wrote this letter, he was probably in Corinth on his third missionary journey. His work in the eastern Mediterranean was almost finished, and he greatly desired to visit the church in Rome. At this time, however, he could not go to Rome, so he sent a letter there, intending to visit Rome while en route on a mission to Spain. This letter served as a theological introduction to that hoped-for personal ministry.

Author and Date of Writing

The writer of this letter was the apostle Paul; it was probably written in the early spring of A.D. 57.

Theme and Message

Paul's primary theme in Romans is the basic gospel—God's plan of salvation and righteousness for the whole human race, Jew and Gentile alike (see 1.16-17). "The gospel of God" (1.1) includes justification by faith, but it also embraces such related ideas as guilt, sanctification, and security. Romans is the most comprehensive and systematic statement of the Christian faith in the Bible.

Outline

Salutation

1 Paul, a servant[a] of Jesus Christ, called to be an apostle, set apart for the gospel of God, [2]which he promised beforehand through his prophets in the holy scriptures, [3]the gospel concerning his Son, who was descended from David according to the flesh [4]and was declared to be Son of God with power according to the spirit[b] of holiness by resurrection from the dead, Jesus Christ our Lord, [5]through whom we have received grace and apostleship to bring about the obedience of faith among all the Gentiles for the sake of his name, [6]including yourselves who are called to belong to Jesus Christ,

7 To all God's beloved in Rome, who are called to be saints:

Grace to you and peace from God our Father and the Lord Jesus Christ.

Prayer of Thanksgiving

8 First, I thank my God through Jesus Christ for all of you, because your faith is proclaimed throughout the world. [9]For God, whom I

1.1 1 Cor 1.1; Acts 9.15; 2 Cor 11.7
1.2 Acts 26.6; Gal 3.8
1.3 Jn 1.14
1.4 Acts 13.33; Heb 9.14
1.5 Gal 1.16; Acts 6.7; 9.15
1.7 1 Cor 1.2, 3; Gal 1.3; Eph 1.2
1.8 Phil 1.3; Acts 16.19
1.9 Phil 1.8; Acts 24.14; Eph 1.16

a Gk slave b Or Spirit

serve with my spirit by announcing the gospel[c] of his Son, is my witness that without ceasing I remember you always in my prayers, [10] asking that by God's will I may somehow at last succeed in coming to you. [11] For I am longing to see you so that I may share with you some spiritual gift to strengthen you — [12] or rather so that we may be mutually encouraged by each other's faith, both yours and mine. [13] I want you to know, brothers and sisters,[d] that I have often intended to come to you (but thus far have been prevented), in order that I may reap some harvest among you as I have among the rest of the Gentiles. [14] I am a debtor both to Greeks and to barbarians, both to the wise and to the foolish [15] — hence my eagerness to proclaim the gospel to you also who are in Rome.

The Power of the Gospel

16 For I am not ashamed of the gospel; it is the power of God for salvation to everyone who has faith, to the Jew first and also to the Greek. [17] For in it the righteousness of God is revealed through faith for faith; as it is written, "The one who is righteous will live by faith."[e]

The Guilt of Humankind

18 For the wrath of God is revealed from heaven against all ungodliness and wickedness of those who by their wickedness suppress the truth. [19] For what can be known about God is plain to them, because God has shown it to them. [20] Ever since the creation of the world his eternal power and divine nature, invisible though they are, have been understood and seen through the things he has made. So they are without excuse; [21] for though they knew God, they did not honor him as God or give thanks to him, but they became futile in their thinking, and their senseless minds were darkened. [22] Claiming to be wise, they became fools; [23] and they exchanged the

glory of the immortal God for images resembling a mortal human being or birds or four-footed animals or reptiles.

24 Therefore God gave them up in the lusts of their hearts to impurity, to the degrading of their bodies among themselves, [25] because they exchanged the truth about God for a lie and worshiped and served the creature rather than the Creator, who is blessed forever! Amen.

26 For this reason God gave them up to degrading passions. Their women exchanged natural intercourse for unnatural, [27] and in the same way also the men, giving up natural intercourse with women, were consumed with passion for one another. Men committed shameless acts with men and received in their own persons the due penalty for their error.

28 And since they did not see fit to acknowledge God, God gave them up to a debased mind and to things that should not be done. [29] They were filled with every kind of wickedness, evil, covetousness, malice. Full of envy, murder, strife, deceit, craftiness, they are gossips, [30] slanderers, God-haters,[f] insolent, haughty, boastful, inventors of evil, rebellious toward parents, [31] foolish, faithless, heartless, ruthless. [32] They know God's decree, that those who practice such things deserve to die — yet they not only do them but even applaud others who practice them.

The Righteous Judgment of God

2 Therefore you have no excuse, whoever you are, when you judge others; for in passing judgment on another you condemn yourself, because you, the judge, are doing the very same things. [2] You say,[g] "We know that God's judgment on those who do such things is in accordance with truth." [3] Do you imagine, whoever you are,

1.10
Rom 15.32
1.11
Rom 15.23
1.13
Rom 15.22
1.14
1 Cor 9.16;
Acts 28.2
1.15
Rom 12.18;
15.20
1.16
2 Tim 1.8;
1 Cor 1.18;
Acts 3.26;
Rom 2.9
1.17
Rom 3.21;
Gal 3.11;
Heb 10.38
1.18ff
Eph 5.6;
Col 3.6
1.19
Acts 14.17
1.20
Ps 19.1-6
1.21
Jer 2.5;
Eph 4.17,18
1.22
Jer 10.14
1.23
Ps 106.20;
Jer 2.11;
Acts 17.29

1.24
Eph 4.18,
19;
1 Pet 4.3
1.25
Isa 44.20;
Jer 10.14;
Rom 9.5
1.26
Lev 18.22;
Eph 4.19;
1 Thes 4.5
1.27
Lev 18.22;
20.13
1.28
Eph 4.19
1.30
Ps 5.5;
2 Tim 3.2
1.31
2 Tim 3.3
1.32
Rom 6.21;
Acts 8.1;
22.20
2.1
Rom 1.20;
2 Sam 12.5-7;
Mt 7.1,2

[c] Gk *my spirit in the gospel* [d] Gk *brothers*
[e] Or *The one who is righteous through faith will live* [f] Or *God-hated* [g] Gk *lacks You say*

that when you judge those who do such things and yet do them yourself, you will escape the judgment of God? [4] Or do you despise the riches of his kindness and forbearance and patience? Do you not realize that God's kindness is meant to lead you to repentance? [5] But by your hard and impenitent heart you are storing up wrath for yourself on the day of wrath, when God's righteous judgment will be revealed. [6] For he will repay according to each one's deeds: [7] to those who by patiently doing good seek for glory and honor and immortality, he will give eternal life; [8] while for those who are self-seeking and who obey not the truth but wickedness, there will be wrath and fury. [9] There will be anguish and distress for everyone who does evil, the Jew first and also the Greek, [10] but glory and honor and peace for everyone who does good, the Jew first and also the Greek. [11] For God shows no partiality.

12 All who have sinned apart from the law will also perish apart from the law, and all who have sinned under the law will be judged by the law. [13] For it is not the hearers of the law who are righteous in God's sight, but the doers of the law who will be justified. [14] When Gentiles, who do not possess the law, do instinctively what the law requires, these, though not having the law, are a law to themselves. [15] They show that what the law requires is written on their hearts, to which their own conscience also bears witness; and their conflicting thoughts will accuse or perhaps excuse them [16] on the day when, according to my gospel, God, through Jesus Christ, will judge the secret thoughts of all.

The Jews and the Law

17 But if you call yourself a Jew and rely on the law and boast of your relation to God [18] and know his will and determine what is best because you are instructed in the law, [19] and if you are sure that you are a guide to the blind, a light to

those who are in darkness, [20] a corrector of the foolish, a teacher of children, having in the law the embodiment of knowledge and truth, [21] you, then, that teach others, will you not teach yourself? While you preach against stealing, do you steal? [22] You that forbid adultery, do you commit adultery? You that abhor idols, do you rob temples? [23] You that boast in the law, do you dishonor God by breaking the law? [24] For, as it is written, "The name of God is blasphemed among the Gentiles because of you."

25 Circumcision indeed is of value if you obey the law; but if you break the law, your circumcision has become uncircumcision. [26] So, if those who are uncircumcised keep the requirements of the law, will not their uncircumcision be regarded as circumcision? [27] Then those who are physically uncircumcised but keep the law will condemn you that have the written code and circumcision but break the law. [28] For a person is not a Jew who is one outwardly, nor is true circumcision something external and physical. [29] Rather, a person is a Jew who is one inwardly, and real circumcision is a matter of the heart — it is spiritual and not literal. Such a person receives praise not from others but from God.

3 Then what advantage has the Jew? Or what is the value of circumcision? [2] Much, in every way. For in the first place the Jews[h] were entrusted with the oracles of God. [3] What if some were unfaithful? Will their faithlessness nullify the faithfulness of God? [4] By no means! Although everyone is a liar, let God be proved true, as it is written,

"So that you may be justified
　　in your words,
　and prevail in your
　　judging."[i]

[5] But if our injustice serves to con-

2.4
Eph 1.7;
2.7;
Rom 11.22;
3.25;
Ex 34.6;
2 Pet 3.9
2.5
Deut 32.34;
Jude 6
2.6
Mt 16.27;
1 Cor 3.8;
2 Cor 5.10
2.8
Gal 5.20;
2 Thes 2.12
2.9
1 Pet 4.17
2.10
1 Pet 1.7;
v. 9
2.11
Deut 10.17;
Gal 2.6;
Eph 6.9
2.12
Rom 3.19;
1 Cor 9.21
2.13
Jas 1.22,23,
25
2.14ff
v. 15
2.15
vv. 14,27
2.16
Eccl 12.14;
1 Cor 4.5;
Acts 10.42;
1 Tim 1.11
2.17
v. 23;
Mic 3.11;
Rom 9.4
2.18
Phil 1.10

2.20
Rom 6.17;
2 Tim 1.13
2.21
Mt 23.3,4
2.22
Acts 19.37
2.23
v. 17
2.24
Isa 52.5
2.25
Gal 5.3
2.26
1 Cor 7.19;
Eph 2.11;
Rom 8.4
2.27
Mt 12.41
2.28
Mt 3.9;
Jn 8.39;
Rom 9.6;
Gal 6.15
2.29
Col 2.11;
2 Cor 10.18;
1 Pet 3.4

3.2 Deut 4.8; Ps 147.19 **3.3** Heb 4.2;
2 Tim 2.13 **3.4** Jn 3.33; Ps 116.11; 51.4
3.5 Rom 6.19; Gal 3.15

[h] Gk *they*　　[i] Gk *when you are being judged*

firm the justice of God, what should we say? That God is unjust to inflict wrath on us? (I speak in a human way.) 6 By no means! For then how could God judge the world? 7 But if through my false-hood God's truthfulness abounds to his glory, why am I still being condemned as a sinner? 8 And why not say (as some people slander us by saying that we say), "Let us do evil so that good may come"? Their condemnation is deserved!

None Is Righteous

9 What then? Are we any better off?j No, not at all; for we have al-ready charged that all, both Jews and Greeks, are under the power of sin, 10 as it is written:
"There is no one who is
 righteous, not even one;
11 there is no one who has
 understanding,
 there is no one who seeks
 God.
12 All have turned aside,
 together they have
 become worthless;
 there is no one who shows
 kindness,
 there is not even one."
13 "Their throats are opened
 graves;
 they use their tongues to
 deceive."
"The venom of vipers is
 under their lips."
14 "Their mouths are full of
 cursing and bitterness."
15 "Their feet are swift to shed
 blood;
16 ruin and misery are in their
 paths,
17 and the way of peace they
 have not known."
18 "There is no fear of God
 before their eyes."
19 Now we know that whatever the law says, it speaks to those who are under the law, so that every mouth may be silenced, and the whole world may be held account-able to God. 20 For "no human be-ing will be justified in his sight" by deeds prescribed by the law, for

through the law comes the knowl-edge of sin.

Righteousness through Faith

21 But now, apart from law, the righteousness of God has been dis-closed, and is attested by the law and the prophets, 22 the righteous-ness of God through faith in Jesus Christk for all who believe. For there is no distinction, 23 since all have sinned and fall short of the glory of God; 24 they are now justi-fied by his grace as a gift, through the redemption that is in Christ Jesus, 25 whom God put forward as a sacrifice of atonement1 by his blood, effective through faith. He did this to show his righteousness, because in his divine forbearance he had passed over the sins previ-ously committed; 26 it was to prove at the present time that he himself is righteous and that he justifies the one who has faith in Jesus.m

27 Then what becomes of boast-ing? It is excluded. By what law? By that of works? No, but by the law of faith. 28 For we hold that a person is justified by faith apart from works prescribed by the law. 29 Or is God the God of Jews only? Is he not the God of Gentiles also? Yes, of Gen-tiles also, 30 since God is one; and he will justify the circumcised on the ground of faith and the uncir-cumcised through that same faith. 31 Do we then overthrow the law by this faith? By no means! On the contrary, we uphold the law.

The Example of Abraham

4 What then are we to say was gained byn Abraham, our an-cestor according to the flesh? 2 For if Abraham was justified by works, he has something to boast about, but not before God. 3 For what does the scripture say? "Abraham be-lieved God, and it was reckoned to him as righteousness." 4 Now to one who works, wages are not reck-oned as a gift but as something

3.6 Gen 18.25
3.7 v. 4
3.8 Rom 6.1
3.9 Gal 3.22
3.10 Ps 14.1-3
3.13 Ps 5.9
3.14 Ps 10.7; 140.3
3.15 Isa 59.7,8
3.18 Ps 36.1
3.19 Jn 10.34; Rom 2.12
3.20 Ps 143.2; Acts 13.39; Gal 2.16; Rom 7.7

3.21 Rom 1.17; 9.30; 1.2; Acts 10.43
3.22 Rom 10.12; Gal 3.28; Col 3.11
3.23 Gal 3.22
3.24 Rom 4.16; Eph 1.7; 2.8; Col 1.14; Heb 9.12,15
3.25 1 Jn 2.2; Heb 9.14, 28; 1 Pet 1.19
3.27 Rom 2.17, 23; 4.2; 1 Cor 1.29-31; Eph 2.9
3.28 Acts 13.39; Eph 2.9
3.29 Rom 9.24; Acts 10.34, 35
3.30 Gal 3.8
4.2 1 Cor 1.31
4.3 Gen 15.6; Gal 3.6; Jas 2.23
4.4 Rom 11.6

j Or at any disadvantage? k Or through the faith of Jesus Christ l Or a place of atonement m Or who has the faith of Jesus n Other ancient authorities read say about

due. [5] But to one who without works trusts him who justifies the ungodly, such faith is reckoned as righteousness. [6] So also David speaks of the blessedness of those to whom God reckons righteousness apart from works:

[7] "Blessed are those whose
　　iniquities are forgiven,
　　and whose sins are
　　covered;
[8] blessed is the one against
　　whom the Lord will not
　　reckon sin."

[9] Is this blessedness, then, pronounced only on the circumcised, or also on the uncircumcised? We say, "Faith was reckoned to Abraham as righteousness." [10] How then was it reckoned to him? Was it before or after he had been circumcised? It was not after, but before he was circumcised. [11] He received the sign of circumcision as a seal of the righteousness that he had by faith while he was still uncircumcised. The purpose was to make him the ancestor of all who believe without being circumcised and who thus have righteousness reckoned to them, [12] and likewise the ancestor of the circumcised who are not only circumcised but who also follow the example of the faith that our ancestor Abraham had before he was circumcised.

God's Promise Realized through Faith

[13] For the promise that he would inherit the world did not come to Abraham or to his descendants through the law but through the righteousness of faith. [14] If it is the adherents of the law who are to be the heirs, faith is null and the promise is void. [15] For the law brings wrath; but where there is no law, neither is there violation.

[16] For this reason it depends on faith, in order that the promise may rest on grace and be guaranteed to all his descendants, not only to the adherents of the law but also to those who share the faith of Abraham (for he is the father of all of us, [17] as it is written, "I have made you

4.7
Ps 32.1,2
4.8
2 Cor 5.19
4.9
Rom 3.30;
v. 3
4.11
Gen 17.10;
Lk 19.9
4.13
Gen 17.4-6;
Gal 3.29
4.14
Gal 3.18
4.15
Rom 3.20;
7.8,10,11;
Gal 3.10
4.16
Rom 3.24;
9.8; 15.8
4.17
Gen 17.5;
1 Cor 1.28

4.18
Gen 15.5
4.19
Gen 17.17;
Heb 11.11
4.21
Gen 18.14;
Heb 11.19
4.23
Rom 15.4;
1 Cor 9.10;
10.11
4.24
Rom 10.9;
Acts 2.24
4.25
Isa 53.5,6;
2 Cor 5.21;
1 Cor 15.17
5.1
Rom 3.28
5.2
Eph 2.18;
1 Cor 15.1;
Heb 3.6
5.3
2 Cor 12.10;
Jas 1.2,3
5.5
Phil 1.20;
Eph 1.13
5.6
Gal 4.4;
Rom 4.25

the father of many nations")—in the presence of the God in whom he believed, who gives life to the dead and calls into existence the things that do not exist. [18] Hoping against hope, he believed that he would become "the father of many nations," according to what was said, "So numerous shall your descendants be." [19] He did not weaken in faith when he considered his own body, which was already[o] as good as dead (for he was about a hundred years old), or when he considered the barrenness of Sarah's womb. [20] No distrust made him waver concerning the promise of God, but he grew strong in his faith as he gave glory to God, [21] being fully convinced that God was able to do what he had promised. [22] Therefore his faith[p] "was reckoned to him as righteousness." [23] Now the words, "it was reckoned to him," were written not for his sake alone, [24] but for ours also. It will be reckoned to us who believe in him who raised Jesus our Lord from the dead, [25] who was handed over to death for our trespasses and was raised for our justification.

Results of Justification

[5] Therefore, since we are justified by faith, we[q] have peace with God through our Lord Jesus Christ, [2] through whom we have obtained access[r] to this grace in which we stand; and we[s] boast in our hope of sharing the glory of God. [3] And not only that, but we[s] also boast in our sufferings, knowing that suffering produces endurance, [4] and endurance produces character, and character produces hope, [5] and hope does not disappoint us, because God's love has been poured into our hearts through the Holy Spirit that has been given to us.

[6] For while we were still weak, at the right time Christ died for the ungodly. [7] Indeed, rarely will any-

o Other ancient authorities lack *already*
p Gk *Therefore it*　　q Other ancient
authorities read *let us*　　r Other ancient
authorities add *by faith*　　s Or *let us*

one die for a righteous person — though perhaps for a good person someone might actually dare to die. ⁸ But God proves his love for us in that while we still were sinners Christ died for us. ⁹ Much more surely then, now that we have been justified by his blood, will we be saved through him from the wrath of God.ᵗ ¹⁰ For if while we were enemies, we were reconciled to God through the death of his Son, much more surely, having been reconciled, will we be saved by his life. ¹¹ But more than that, we even boast in God through our Lord Jesus Christ, through whom we have now received reconciliation.

Adam and Christ

12 Therefore, just as sin came into the world through one man, and death came through sin, and so death spread to all because all have sinned — ¹³ sin was indeed in the world before the law, but sin is not reckoned when there is no law. ¹⁴ Yet death exercised dominion from Adam to Moses, even over those whose sins were not like the transgression of Adam, who is a type of the one who was to come.

15 But the free gift is not like the trespass. For if the many died through the one man's trespass, much more surely have the grace of God and the free gift in the grace of the one man, Jesus Christ, abounded for the many. ¹⁶ And the free gift is not like the effect of the one man's sin. For the judgment following one trespass brought condemnation, but the free gift following many trespasses brings justification. ¹⁷ If, because of the one man's trespass, death exercised dominion through that one, much more surely will those who receive the abundance of grace and the free gift of righteousness exercise dominion in life through the one man, Jesus Christ.

18 Therefore just as one man's trespass led to condemnation for all, so one man's act of righteousness leads to justification and life for all. ¹⁹ For just as by the one

man's disobedience the many were made sinners, so by the one man's obedience the many will be made righteous. ²⁰ But law came in, with the result that the trespass multiplied; but where sin increased, grace abounded all the more, ²¹ so that, just as sin exercised dominion in death, so grace might also exercise dominion through justificationᵘ leading to eternal life through Jesus Christ our Lord.

Dying and Rising with Christ

6 What then are we to say? Should we continue in sin in order that grace may abound? ² By no means! How can we who died to sin go on living in it? ³ Do you not know that all of us who have been baptized into Christ Jesus were baptized into his death? ⁴ Therefore we have been buried with him by baptism into death, so that, just as Christ was raised from the dead by the glory of the Father, so we too might walk in newness of life.

5 For if we have been united with him in a death like his, we will certainly be united with him in a resurrection like his. ⁶ We know that our old self was crucified with him so that the body of sin might be destroyed, and we might no longer be enslaved to sin. ⁷ For whoever has died is freed from sin. ⁸ But if we have died with Christ, we believe that we will also live with him. ⁹ We know that Christ, being raised from the dead, will never die again; death no longer has dominion over him. ¹⁰ The death he died, he died to sin, once for all; but the life he lives, he lives to God. ¹¹ So you also must consider yourselves dead to sin and alive to God in Christ Jesus.

12 Therefore, do not let sin exercise dominion in your mortal bodies, to make you obey their passions. ¹³ No longer present your members to sin as instrumentsᵛ of wickedness, but present yourselves to God as those who have been

5.8
Jn 15.13;
1 Pet 3.18;
1 Jn 3.16
5.9
Rom 3.5,25;
Heb 9.14;
1 Thes 1.10
5.10
Rom 11.28;
Col 1.21,22;
2 Cor 5.18;
Rom 8.34
5.12
Gen 2.17;
3.6,19;
1 Cor 15.21;
Rom 6.23
5.13
Rom 4.15
5.14
1 Cor 15.22,
45
5.15
vv. 12,18,
19;
Isa 53.11;
Acts 15.11
5.17
2 Tim 2.12;
Rev 22.5
5.18
v. 12;
Rom 4.25
5.19
v. 12;
Rom 11.32;
Phil 2.8

5.20
Rom 7.7,8;
Gal 3.19;
1 Tim 1.14
5.21
vv. 12,14;
Jn 1.17;
Rom 6.23
6.1
Rom 3.5,8;
v. 15
6.2
Rom 7.4,6;
Gal 2.19;
Col 3.3;
1 Pet 2.24
6.3
Acts 2.38;
8.16; 19.5
6.4
Col 2.12;
Gal 6.15;
Eph 4.22-24;
Col 3.10
6.6
Eph 4.22;
Col 3.9;
Gal 2.20;
Rom 7.24
6.9
Rev 1.18
6.10
Heb 7.27
6.11
v. 2;
Gal 2.19
6.12
v. 14

6.13 Rom 7.5; Col 3.5; Rom 12.1

ᵗ Gk *the wrath* ᵘ Or *righteousness*
ᵛ Or *weapons*

brought from death to life, and present your members to God as instruments[w] of righteousness. [14]For sin will have no dominion over you, since you are not under law but under grace.

Slaves of Righteousness

15 What then? Should we sin because we are not under law but under grace? By no means! [16]Do you not know that if you present yourselves to anyone as obedient slaves, you are slaves of the one whom you obey, either of sin, which leads to death, or of obedience, which leads to righteousness? [17]But thanks be to God that you, having once been slaves of sin, have become obedient from the heart to the form of teaching to which you were entrusted, [18]and that you, having been set free from sin, have become slaves of righteousness. [19]I am speaking in human terms because of your natural limitations.[x] For just as you once presented your members as slaves to impurity and to greater and greater iniquity, so now present your members as slaves to righteousness for sanctification.

20 When you were slaves of sin, you were free in regard to righteousness. [21]So what advantage did you then get from the things of which you now are ashamed? The end of those things is death. [22]But now that you have been freed from sin and enslaved to God, the advantage you get is sanctification. The end is eternal life. [23]For the wages of sin is death, but the free gift of God is eternal life in Christ Jesus our Lord.

An Analogy from Marriage

7 Do you not know, brothers and sisters[y] — for I am speaking to those who know the law — that the law is binding on a person only during that person's lifetime? [2]Thus a married woman is bound by the law to her husband as long as he lives; but if her husband dies, she is discharged from the law concerning the husband. [3]According-

ly, she will be called an adulteress if she lives with another man while her husband is alive. But if her husband dies, she is free from that law, and if she marries another man, she is not an adulteress.

4 In the same way, my friends,[y] you have died to the law through the body of Christ, so that you may belong to another, to him who has been raised from the dead in order that we may bear fruit for God. [5]While we were living in the flesh, our sinful passions, aroused by the law, were at work in our members to bear fruit for death. [6]But now we are discharged from the law, dead to that which held us captive, so that we are slaves not under the old written code but in the new life of the Spirit.

The Law and Sin

7 What then should we say? That the law is sin? By no means! Yet, if it had not been for the law, I would not have known sin. I would not have known what it is to covet if the law had not said, "You shall not covet." [8]But sin, seizing an opportunity in the commandment, produced in me all kinds of covetousness. Apart from the law sin lies dead. [9]I was once alive apart from the law, but when the commandment came, sin revived [10]and I died, and the very commandment that promised life proved to be death to me. [11]For sin, seizing an opportunity in the commandment, deceived me and through it killed me. [12]So the law is holy, and the commandment is holy and just and good.

13 Did what is good, then, bring death to me? By no means! It was sin, working death in me through what is good, in order that sin might be shown to be sin, and through the commandment might become sinful beyond measure.

The Inner Conflict

14 For we know that the law is spiritual; but I am of the flesh, sold

6.14	Rom 8.2; Gal 5.18
6.16	Rom 11.2; Mt 6.24; Jn 8.34; 2 Pet 2.19
6.17	Rom 1.8; 2 Tim 1.13
6.18	Jn 8.32; Rom 8.2
6.19	Rom 3.5; 6.13; 12.1
6.20	Mt 6.24; Jn 8.34
6.21	Rom 7.5; 8.6,13,21
6.22	Jn 8.32; 1 Cor 7.22; 1 Pet 2.16
6.23	Rom 5.12; 5.21; Gal 6.7,8
7.2	1 Cor 7.39
7.3	Mt 5.32
7.4	Rom 6.2,11; Gal 2.19; Col 1.22
7.5	Rom 6.13, 21; Gal 5.19; Jas 1.15
7.6	Rom 2.29; 2 Cor 3.6
7.7	Ex 20.17; Deut 5.21; Rom 3.20; 5.20
7.8	v. 11; 1 Cor 15.56
7.10	Lev 18.5; Rom 10.5; Gal 3.12
7.12	1 Tim 1.8

w Or *weapons* x Gk *the weakness of your flesh* y Gk *brothers*

into slavery under sin.[z] [15]I do not understand my own actions. For I do not do what I want, but I do the very thing I hate. [16]Now if I do what I do not want, I agree that the law is good. [17]But in fact it is no longer I that do it, but sin that dwells within me. [18]For I know that nothing good dwells within me, that is, in my flesh. I can will what is right, but I cannot do it. [19]For I do not do the good I want, but the evil I do not want is what I do. [20]Now if I do what I do not want, it is no longer I that do it, but sin that dwells within me.

[21] So I find it to be a law that when I want to do what is good, evil lies close at hand. [22]For I delight in the law of God in my inmost self, [23]but I see in my members another law at war with the law of my mind, making me captive to the law of sin that dwells in my members. [24]Wretched man that I am! Who will rescue me from this body of death? [25]Thanks be to God through Jesus Christ our Lord!

So then, with my mind I am a slave to the law of God, but with my flesh I am a slave to the law of sin.

Life in the Spirit

8 There is therefore now no condemnation for those who are in Christ Jesus. [2]For the law of the Spirit[a] of life in Christ Jesus has set you[b] free from the law of sin and of death. [3]For God has done what the law, weakened by the flesh, could not do: by sending his own Son in the likeness of sinful flesh, and to deal with sin,[c] he condemned sin in the flesh, [4]so that the just requirement of the law might be fulfilled in us, who walk not according to the flesh but according to the Spirit.[a] [5]For those who live according to the flesh set their minds on the things of the flesh, but those who live according to the Spirit[a] set their minds on the things of the Spirit.[a] [6]To set the mind on the flesh is death, but to set the mind on the Spirit[a] is life and peace. [7]For this reason the

mind that is set on the flesh is hostile to God; it does not submit to God's law—indeed it cannot, [8]and those who are in the flesh cannot please God.

[9] But you are not in the flesh; you are in the Spirit,[a] since the Spirit of God dwells in you. Anyone who does not have the Spirit of Christ does not belong to him. [10]But if Christ is in you, though the body is dead because of sin, the Spirit[a] is life because of righteousness. [11]If the Spirit of him who raised Jesus from the dead dwells in you, he who raised Christ[d] from the dead will give life to your mortal bodies also through[e] his Spirit that dwells in you.

[12] So then, brothers and sisters,[f] we are debtors, not to the flesh, to live according to the flesh—[13]for if you live according to the flesh, you will die; but if by the Spirit you put to death the deeds of the body, you will live. [14]For all who are led by the Spirit of God are children of God. [15]For you did not receive a spirit of slavery to fall back into fear, but you have received a spirit of adoption. When we cry, "Abba![g] Father!" [16]it is that very Spirit bearing witness[h] with our spirit that we are children of God, [17]and if children, then heirs, heirs of God and joint heirs with Christ—if, in fact, we suffer with him so that we may also be glorified with him.

Future Glory

[18] I consider that the sufferings of this present time are not worth comparing with the glory about to be revealed to us. [19]For the creation waits with eager longing for the revealing of the children of

8.18 2 Cor 4.17; Col 3.4; 1 Pet 5.1
8.19 Col 3.4; 1 Pet 1.7,13; 1 Jn 3.2

[z]Gk *sold under sin* [a]Or *spirit* [b]Here the Greek word *you* is singular number; other ancient authorities read *me* or *us* [c]Or *and as a sin offering* [d]Other ancient authorities read *the Christ* or *Christ Jesus* or *Jesus Christ* [e]Other ancient authorities read *on account of* [f]Gk *brothers* [g]Aramaic for *Father* [h]Or *15a spirit of adoption, by which we cry, "Abba! Father!" 16The Spirit itself bears witness*

7.15 Gal 5.17
7.16 v. 12
7.17 v. 20
7.18 v. 25
7.19 v. 15
7.20 v. 17
7.21 vv. 23,25
7.22 Ps 1.2; 2 Cor 4.16; Eph 3.16
7.23 Gal 5.17
7.24 Rom 6.6; 8.2
7.25 1 Cor 15.57
8.1 Rom 5.16
8.2 1 Cor 15.45; Rom 6.14, 18; Jn 8.32, 36
8.3 Acts 13.39; Heb 7.18; Ph 2.7; Heb 2.14
8.4 Gal 5.16,25
8.5 Gal 5.19-25
8.6 Rom 6.21; Gal 6.8
8.7 Jas 4.4
8.8 Rom 7.5
8.9 1 Cor 3.16; Gal 4.6; Phil 1.19; 1 Jn 4.13
8.10 Gal 2.20; Eph 3.17
8.11 Acts 2.24; Jn 5.21; 1 Cor 6.14
8.13 Gal 6.8; Col 3.5
8.14 Gal 5.18
8.15 2 Tim 1.7; Heb 2.15; Gal 4.5,6
8.16 2 Cor 1.22; Eph 1.13
8.17 Gal 4.7; 2 Tim 2.12; 1 Pet 4.13

God; [20] for the creation was subjected to futility, not of its own will but by the will of the one who subjected it, in hope [21] that the creation itself will be set free from its bondage to decay and will obtain the freedom of the glory of the children of God. [22] We know that the whole creation has been groaning in labor pains until now; [23] and not only the creation, but we ourselves, who have the first fruits of the Spirit, groan inwardly while we wait for adoption, the redemption of our bodies. [24] For in[i] hope we were saved. Now hope that is seen is not hope. For who hopes[i] for what is seen? [25] But if we hope for what we do not see, we wait for it with patience.

[26] Likewise the Spirit helps us in our weakness; for we do not know how to pray as we ought, but that very Spirit intercedes[k] with sighs too deep for words. [27] And God,[l] who searches the heart, knows what is the mind of the Spirit, because the Spirit[m] intercedes for the saints according to the will of God.[n]

[28] We know that all things work together for good[o] for those who love God, who are called according to his purpose. [29] For those whom he foreknew he also predestined to be conformed to the image of his Son, in order that he might be the firstborn within a large family.[p] [30] And those whom he predestined he also called; and those whom he called he also justified; and those whom he justified he also glorified.

God's Love in Christ Jesus

[31] What then are we to say about these things? If God is for us, who is against us? [32] He who did not withhold his own Son, but gave him up for all of us, will he not with him also give us everything else? [33] Who will bring any charge against God's elect? It is God who justifies. [34] Who is to condemn? It is Christ Jesus, who died, yes, who was raised, who is at the right hand of God, who indeed intercedes for us.[q] [35] Who will separate us from the love of Christ? Will hardship, or distress, or persecution, or famine, or nakedness, or peril, or sword? [36] As it is written,

"For your sake we are being
 killed all day long;
we are accounted as sheep
 to be slaughtered."

[37] No, in all these things we are more than conquerors through him who loved us. [38] For I am convinced that neither death, nor life, nor angels, nor rulers, nor things present, nor things to come, nor powers, [39] nor height, nor depth, nor anything else in all creation, will be able to separate us from the love of God in Christ Jesus our Lord.

God's Election of Israel

9 I am speaking the truth in Christ—I am not lying; my conscience confirms it by the Holy Spirit— [2] I have great sorrow and unceasing anguish in my heart. [3] For I could wish that I myself were accursed and cut off from Christ for the sake of my own people,[r] my kindred according to the flesh. [4] They are Israelites, and to them belong the adoption, the glory, the covenants, the giving of the law, the worship, and the promises; [5] to them belong the patriarchs, and from them, according to the flesh, comes the Messiah,[s] who is over all, God blessed forever.[t] Amen.

[6] It is not as though the word of God had failed. For not all Israelites truly belong to Israel, [7] and not all of Abraham's children are his true descendants; but "It is through Isaac that descendants shall be named for you." [8] This means that it is not the children of

Cross references (center column)

8.20 Gen 3.17-19; Eccl 1.2
8.21 Acts 3.21; Rom 6.21; 2 Pet 3.13; Rev 21.1
8.23 2 Cor 1.22; 5.2,4; Gal 5.5
8.26 Mt 20.22; Eph 6.18
8.27 Ps 139.1,2; Lk 16.15; Rev 2.23
8.28 v. 32
8.29 Rom 11.2; 1 Pet 1.2, 20; Eph 1.5, 11; Phil 3.21; Heb 1.6
8.30 Eph 1.5,11; Rom 9.24; 1 Cor 6.11
8.31 Rom 4.1; Ps 118.6
8.32 Jn 3.16; Rom 5.8; 4.25
8.33 Lk 18.7; Isa 50.8,9
8.34 Col 3.1; Heb 1.3; 7.25; 9.24; 1 Jn 2.1
8.36 Ps 44.22; 2 Cor 4.11
8.37 1 Cor 15.57; Rev 1.5
8.38 Eph 1.21; 1 Pet 3.22
9.1 2 Cor 1.23; 11.10; 1 Tim 2.7
9.3 Ex 32.32
9.4 Acts 3.25; Ps 147.19; Heb 9.1
9.5 Col 1.16-19; Jn 1.1; Rom 1.25
9.6 Num 23.19; Rom 2.28, 29; Gal 6.16
9.7 Gal 4.23;

Heb 11.18 **9.8** Rom 8.14; Gal 3.29; 4.28

i Or by j Other ancient authorities read *awaits* k Other ancient authorities add *for us* l Gk *the one* m Gk *he* or *it* n Gk *according to God* o Other ancient authorities read *God makes all things work together for good*, or in all things God works for good p Gk *among many brothers* q Or *Is it Christ Jesus . . . for us?* r Gk *my brothers* s Or *the Christ* t Or *Messiah, who is God over all, blessed forever*; or *Messiah. May he who is God over all be blessed forever*

the flesh who are the children of God, but the children of the promise are counted as descendants. ⁹For this is what the promise said, "About this time I will return and Sarah shall have a son." ¹⁰Nor is that all; something similar happened to Rebecca when she had conceived children by one husband, our ancestor Isaac. ¹¹Even before they had been born or had done anything good or bad (so that God's purpose of election might continue, ¹²not by works but by his call) she was told, "The elder shall serve the younger." ¹³As it is written,

"I have loved Jacob,
 but I have hated Esau."

14 What then are we to say? Is there injustice on God's part? By no means! ¹⁵For he says to Moses, "I will have mercy on whom
 I have mercy,
and I will have compassion
 on whom I have
 compassion."
¹⁶So it depends not on human will or exertion, but on God who shows mercy. ¹⁷For the scripture says to Pharaoh, "I have raised you up for the very purpose of showing my power in you, so that my name may be proclaimed in all the earth." ¹⁸So then he has mercy on whomever he chooses, and he hardens the heart of whomever he chooses.

God's Wrath and Mercy

19 You will say to me then, "Why then does he still find fault? For who can resist his will?" ²⁰But who indeed are you, a human being, to argue with God? Will what is molded say to the one who molds it, "Why have you made me like this?" ²¹Has the potter no right over the clay, to make out of the same lump one object for special use and another for ordinary use? ²²What if God, desiring to show his wrath and to make known his power, has endured with much patience the objects of wrath that are made for destruction; ²³and what if he has done so in order to make known the riches of his glory for

the objects of mercy, which he has prepared beforehand for glory— ²⁴including us whom he has called, not from the Jews only but also from the Gentiles? ²⁵As indeed he says in Hosea,

"Those who were not my
 people I will call 'my
 people,'
and her who was not
 beloved I will call
 'beloved.'"
²⁶"And in the very place where
 it was said to them,
 'You are not my
 people,'
there they shall be called
 children of the living
 God."

27 And Isaiah cries out concerning Israel, "Though the number of the children of Israel were like the sand of the sea, only a remnant of them will be saved; ²⁸for the Lord will execute his sentence on the earth quickly and decisively."ᵘ ²⁹And as Isaiah predicted,

"If the Lord of hosts had not
 left survivorsᵛ to us,
we would have fared like
 Sodom
and been made like
 Gomorrah."

Israel's Unbelief

30 What then are we to say? Gentiles, who did not strive for righteousness, have attained it, that is, righteousness through faith; ³¹but Israel, who did strive for the righteousness that is based on the law, did not succeed in fulfilling that law. ³²Why not? Because they did not strive for it on the basis of faith, but as if it were based on works. They have stumbled over the stumbling stone, ³³as it is written,

"See, I am laying in Zion a
 stone that will make
 people stumble, a rock
 that will make them
 fall,

ᵘ Other ancient authorities read *for he will finish his work and cut it short in righteousness, because the Lord will make the sentence shortened on the earth* ᵛ Or *descendants*; Gk *seed*

Cross references (center column)

9.9 Gen 18.10
9.10 Gen 25.21
9.11 Rom 4.17; 8.28
9.12 Gen 25.23
9.13 Mal 1.2,3
9.14 2 Chr 19.7
9.15 Ex 33.19
9.16 Eph 2.8
9.17 Ex 9.16
9.19 2 Chr 20.6; Job 23.13; Dan 4.35
9.20 Isa 29.16; 64.8
9.21 2 Tim 2.20
9.22 Rom 2.4
9.23 Eph 3.16; Rom 8.29, 30
9.24 Rom 3.29
9.25 Hos 2.23; 1 Pet 2.10
9.26 Hos 1.10
9.27 Isa 10.22, 23; Gen 22.17; Hos 1.10
9.29 Isa 1.4; 13.19; Jer 50.40
9.30 Rom 10.6; Gal 2.16; Heb 11.7
9.31 Rom 10.2,3; Gal 5.4
9.32 1 Pet 2.6,8
9.33 Isa 28.16; Mt 21.42; Rom 10.11

and whoever believes in him[w] will not be put to shame."

10 Brothers and sisters,[x] my heart's desire and prayer to God for them is that they may be saved. [2] I can testify that they have a zeal for God, but it is not enlightened. [3] For, being ignorant of the righteousness that comes from God, and seeking to establish their own, they have not submitted to God's righteousness. [4] For Christ is the end of the law so that there may be righteousness for everyone who believes.

Salvation Is for All

[5] Moses writes concerning the righteousness that comes from the law, that "the person who does these things will live by them." [6] But the righteousness that comes from faith says, "Do not say in your heart, 'Who will ascend into heaven?' " (that is, to bring Christ down) [7] "or 'Who will descend into the abyss?' " (that is, to bring Christ up from the dead). [8] But what does it say?

"The word is near you,
on your lips and in your heart"

(that is, the word of faith that we proclaim); [9] because[y] if you confess with your lips that Jesus is Lord and believe in your heart that God raised him from the dead, you will be saved. [10] For one believes with the heart and so is justified, and one confesses with the mouth and so is saved. [11] The scripture says, "No one who believes in him will be put to shame." [12] For there is no distinction between Jew and Greek; the same Lord is Lord of all and is generous to all who call on him. [13] For, "Everyone who calls on the name of the Lord shall be saved."

[14] But how are they to call on one in whom they have not believed? And how are they to believe in one of whom they have never heard? And how are they to hear without someone to proclaim him? [15] And how are they to proclaim

him unless they are sent? As it is written, "How beautiful are the feet of those who bring good news!" [16] But not all have obeyed the good news;[z] for Isaiah says, "Lord, who has believed our message?" [17] So faith comes from what is heard, and what is heard comes through the word of Christ.[a]

[18] But I ask, have they not heard? Indeed they have; for
"Their voice has gone out to all the earth,
and their words to the ends of the world."
[19] Again I ask, did Israel not understand? First Moses says,
"I will make you jealous of those who are not a nation;
with a foolish nation I will make you angry."
[20] Then Isaiah is so bold as to say,
"I have been found by those who did not seek me;
I have shown myself to those who did not ask for me."
[21] But of Israel he says, "All day long I have held out my hands to a disobedient and contrary people."

Israel's Rejection Is Not Final

11 I ask, then, has God rejected his people? By no means! I myself am an Israelite, a descendant of Abraham, a member of the tribe of Benjamin. [2] God has not rejected his people whom he foreknew. Do you not know what the scripture says of Elijah, how he pleads with God against Israel? [3] "Lord, they have killed your prophets, they have demolished your altars; I alone am left, and they are seeking my life." [4] But what is the divine reply to him? "I have kept for myself seven thousand who have not bowed the knee to Baal." [5] So too at the present time there is a remnant, chosen by grace. [6] But if it is by grace, it is no longer on the basis of works, other-

10.2
Acts 21.20
10.3
Rom 1.17;
Phil 3.9
10.4
Gal 3.24;
Rom 7.1-4
10.5
Neh 9.29;
Ezek 20.11,
13,21;
Rom 7.10
10.7
Heb 13.20
10.8
Deut 30.14
10.9
Mt 10.32;
Lk 12.8;
Acts 16.31
10.11
Isa 28.16;
Rom 9.33
10.12
Rom 3.22,
29;
Gal 3.28;
Acts 10.36
10.13
Joel 2.32;
Acts 2.21
10.15
Isa 52.7

10.16
Heb 4.2;
Isa 53.1;
Jn 12.38
10.17
Gal 3.2,5;
Col 3.16
10.18
Ps 19.4;
Col 1.6,23;
1 Thes 1.8
10.19
Deut 32.21;
Rom 11.11
10.20
Isa 65.1;
Rom 9.30
10.21
Isa 65.2
11.1
1 Sam 12.22;
Jer 31.37;
2 Cor 11.22;
Phil 3.5
11.2
Ps 94.19;
1 Kings 19.10;
Rom 8.29
11.4
1 Kings 19.18
11.5
2 Kings 19.4;
Rom 9.27
11.6
Rom 4.4

[w] Or *trusts in it* [x] Gk *Brothers*
[y] Or *namely, that* [z] Or *gospel*
[a] Or *about Christ*; other ancient authorities read *of God*

wise grace would no longer be grace.[b]

7 What then? Israel failed to obtain what it was seeking. The elect obtained it, but the rest were hardened, [8]as it is written,

"God gave them a sluggish
 spirit,
 eyes that would not see
 and ears that would not
 hear,
 down to this very day."
[9]And David says,

"Let their table become a
 snare and a trap,
 a stumbling block and a
 retribution for them;
[10] let their eyes be darkened so
 that they cannot see,
 and keep their backs
 forever bent."

The Salvation of the Gentiles

11 So I ask, have they stumbled so as to fall? By no means! But through their stumbling[c] salvation has come to the Gentiles, so as to make Israel[d] jealous. [12]Now if their stumbling[c] means riches for the world, and if their defeat means riches for Gentiles, how much more will their full inclusion mean!

13 Now I am speaking to you Gentiles. Inasmuch then as I am an apostle to the Gentiles, I glorify my ministry [14]in order to make my own people[e] jealous, and thus save some of them. [15]For if their rejection is the reconciliation of the world, what will their acceptance be but life from the dead! [16]If the part of the dough offered as first fruits is holy, then the whole batch is holy; and if the root is holy, then the branches also are holy.

17 But if some of the branches were broken off, and you, a wild olive shoot, were grafted in their place to share the rich root[f] of the olive tree, [18]do not boast over the branches. If you do boast, remember that it is not you that support the root, but the root that supports you. [19]You will say, "Branches were broken off so that I might be grafted in." [20]That is true. They were broken off because of their unbe-

lief, but you stand only through faith. So do not become proud, but stand in awe. [21]For if God did not spare the natural branches, perhaps he will not spare you.[g] [22]Note then the kindness and the severity of God: severity toward those who have fallen, but God's kindness toward you, provided you continue in his kindness; otherwise you also will be cut off. [23]And even those of Israel,[h] if they do not persist in unbelief, will be grafted in, for God has the power to graft them in again. [24]For if you have been cut from what is by nature a wild olive tree and grafted, contrary to nature, into a cultivated olive tree, how much more will these natural branches be grafted back into their own olive tree.

All Israel Will Be Saved

25 So that you may not claim to be wiser than you are, brothers and sisters,[i] I want you to understand this mystery: a hardening has come upon part of Israel, until the full number of the Gentiles has come in. [26]And so all Israel will be saved; as it is written,

"Out of Zion will come the
 Deliverer;
 he will banish ungodliness
 from Jacob."
[27] "And this is my covenant
 with them,
 when I take away their
 sins."

[28]As regards the gospel they are enemies of God[j] for your sake; but as regards election they are beloved, for the sake of their ancestors; [29]for the gifts and the calling of God are irrevocable. [30]Just as you were once disobedient to God but have now received mercy because of their disobedience, [31]so they have now been disobedient in order that, by the mercy shown to you,

Cross-references (center column):

11.7
Rom 9.18, 31
11.8
Isa 29.10; Deut 29.4; Mt 13.13,14
11.9
Ps 69.22,23
11.11
Acts 13.46; Rom 10.19
11.12
v. 25
11.13
Acts 9.15; Rom 15.16
11.14
Rom 10.19; 1 Cor 7.16; 9.22
11.15
Lk 15.24,32
11.16
Lev 23.10; Num 15.18
11.17
Jer 11.17; Acts 2.39; Eph 2.11,12
11.20
Rom 12.16; 2 Cor 1.24

11.22
1 Cor 15.2; Heb 3.6; Jn 15.2
11.23
2 Cor 3.16
11.25
1 Cor 2.7-10; Eph 3.3-5,9; Rom 9.18
11.26
Isa 59.20,21
11.27
Isa 27.9
11.28
Deut 7.8; 10.15; Rom 5.10; 9.5
11.29
Num 23.19
11.30
Eph 2.2

[b] Other ancient authorities add *But if it is by works, it is no longer on the basis of grace, otherwise work would no longer be work* [c] Gk *transgression* [d] Gk *them* [e] Gk *my flesh* [f] Other ancient authorities read *the richness* [g] Other ancient authorities read *neither will he spare you* [h] Gk lacks *of Israel* [i] Gk *brothers* [j] Gk lacks *of God*

they too may now[k] receive mercy. [32]For God has imprisoned all in disobedience so that he may be merciful to all.

33 O the depth of the riches and wisdom and knowledge of God! How unsearchable are his judgments and how inscrutable his ways! [34] "For who has known the
 mind of the Lord?
 Or who has been his
 counselor?"
[35] "Or who has given a gift to
 him,
 to receive a gift in return?"
[36]For from him and through him and to him are all things. To him be the glory forever. Amen.

The New Life in Christ

12 I appeal to you therefore, brothers and sisters,[l] by the mercies of God, to present your bodies as a living sacrifice, holy and acceptable to God, which is your spiritual[m] worship. [2]Do not be conformed to this world,[n] but be transformed by the renewing of your minds, so that you may discern what is the will of God—what is good and acceptable and perfect.[o]

3 For by the grace given to me I say to everyone among you not to think of yourself more highly than you ought to think, but to think with sober judgment, each according to the measure of faith that God has assigned. [4]For as in one body we have many members, and not all the members have the same function, [5]so we, who are many, are one body in Christ, and individually we are members one of another. [6]We have gifts that differ according to the grace given to us: prophecy, in proportion to faith; [7]ministry, in ministering; the teacher, in teaching; [8]the exhorter, in exhortation; the giver, in generosity; the leader, in diligence; the compassionate, in cheerfulness.

Marks of the True Christian

9 Let love be genuine; hate what is evil, hold fast to what is good;

[10]love one another with mutual affection; outdo one another in showing honor. [11]Do not lag in zeal, be ardent in spirit, serve the Lord.[p] [12]Rejoice in hope, be patient in suffering, persevere in prayer. [13]Contribute to the needs of the saints; extend hospitality to strangers.

14 Bless those who persecute you; bless and do not curse them. [15]Rejoice with those who rejoice, weep with those who weep. [16]Live in harmony with one another; do not be haughty, but associate with the lowly;[q] do not claim to be wiser than you are. [17]Do not repay anyone evil for evil, but take thought for what is noble in the sight of all. [18]If it is possible, so far as it depends on you, live peaceably with all. [19]Beloved, never avenge yourselves, but leave room for the wrath of God;[r] for it is written, "Vengeance is mine, I will repay, says the Lord." [20]No, "if your enemies are hungry, feed them; if they are thirsty, give them something to drink; for by doing this you will heap burning coals on their heads." [21]Do not be overcome by evil, but overcome evil with good.

Being Subject to Authorities

13 Let every person be subject to the governing authorities; for there is no authority except from God, and those authorities that exist have been instituted by God. [2]Therefore whoever resists authority resists what God has appointed, and those who resist will incur judgment. [3]For rulers are not a terror to good conduct, but to bad. Do you wish to have no fear of the authority? Then do what is good, and you will receive its approval; [4]for it is God's servant for your good. But if you do what is

11.32
Rom 3.9;
Gal 3.22,23
11.33
Eph 3.8;
Ps 92.5
11.34
Isa 40.13,
14;
1 Cor 2.16;
Job 36.22
11.36
1 Cor 8.6;
Heb 2.10,
Rom 16.27;
Heb 13.21
12.1
2 Cor 10.1,2
Rom 6.13,
16,19;
1 Pet 2.5
12.2
1 Pet 1.14;
1 Jn 2.15;
Eph 4.23;
5.10
12.3
Rom 15.15;
2 Cor 10.13;
Eph 4.7
12.4
1 Cor 12.12-
14; Eph 4.4,16
12.6
1 Cor 7.7;
12.4,10;
1 Pet 4.10,
11
12.7
1 Cor 12.28;
14.26
12.8
Acts 15.32;
Mt 6.1-3;
1 Tim 5.17;
2 Cor 9.7

12.12
Heb 10.32,
36;
Acts 1.14
12.13
Rom 15.25;
Heb 13.2
12.14
Mt 5.44;
Lk 6.28
12.16
Rom 15.5;
11.25
12.17
Prov 20.22;
2 Cor 8.21
12.18
Mk 9.50;
Rom 14.19
12.19
Lev 19.18;
Heb 10.30
12.20
Prov 25.21,
22; Mt 5.44;
Lk 6.27
13.1
Titus 3.1;
1 Pet 2.13;

Jn 19.11; Dan 2.21 **13.2** Titus 3.1 **13.3**
1 Pet 2.14 **13.4** 1 Thes 4.6

k Other ancient authorities lack *now*
l Gk *brothers* m Or *reasonable*
n Gk *age* o Or *what is the good and acceptable and perfect will of God* p Other ancient authorities read *serve the opportune time* q Or *give yourselves to humble tasks*
r Gk *the wrath*

wrong, you should be afraid, for the authority[s] does not bear the sword in vain! It is the servant of God to execute wrath on the wrongdoer. [5]Therefore one must be subject, not only because of wrath but also because of conscience. [6]For the same reason you also pay taxes, for the authorities are God's servants, busy with this very thing. [7]Pay to all what is due them—taxes to whom taxes are due, revenue to whom revenue is due, respect to whom respect is due, honor to whom honor is due.

Love for One Another

[8]Owe no one anything, except to love one another; for the one who loves another has fulfilled the law. [9]The commandments, "You shall not commit adultery; You shall not murder; You shall not steal; You shall not covet"; and any other commandment, are summed up in this word, "Love your neighbor as yourself." [10]Love does no wrong to a neighbor; therefore, love is the fulfilling of the law.

An Urgent Appeal

[11]Besides this, you know what time it is, how it is now the moment for you to wake from sleep. For salvation is nearer to us now than when we became believers; [12]the night is far gone, the day is near. Let us then lay aside the works of darkness and put on the armor of light; [13]let us live honorably as in the day, not in reveling and drunkenness, not in debauchery and licentiousness, not in quarreling and jealousy. [14]Instead, put on the Lord Jesus Christ, and make no provision for the flesh, to gratify its desires.

Do Not Judge Another

14 Welcome those who are weak in faith,[t] but not for the purpose of quarreling over opinions. [2]Some believe in eating anything, while the weak eat only vegetables. [3]Those who eat must not despise those who abstain, and those who abstain must not pass judgment on those who eat; for God has welcomed them. [4]Who are you to pass judgment on servants of another? It is before their own lord that they stand or fall. And they will be upheld, for the Lord[u] is able to make them stand.

5 Some judge one day to be better than another, while others judge all days to be alike. Let all be fully convinced in their own minds. [6]Those who observe the day, observe it in honor of the Lord. Also those who eat, eat in honor of the Lord, since they give thanks to God; while those who abstain, abstain in honor of the Lord and give thanks to God.

7 We do not live to ourselves, and we do not die to ourselves. [8]If we live, we live to the Lord, and if we die, we die to the Lord; so then, whether we live or whether we die, we are the Lord's. [9]For to this end Christ died and lived again, so that he might be Lord of both the dead and the living.

10 Why do you pass judgment on your brother or sister?[v] Or you, why do you despise your brother or sister?[v] For we will all stand before the judgment seat of God.[w] [11]For it is written,

"As I live, says the Lord,
　　every knee shall bow to
　　　me,
　　and every tongue shall give
　　　praise to[x] God."
[12]So then, each of us will be accountable to God.[y]

Do Not Make Another Stumble

13 Let us therefore no longer pass judgment on one another, but resolve instead never to put a stumbling block or hindrance in the way of another.[z] [14]I know and am persuaded in the Lord Jesus that nothing is unclean in itself; but it is unclean for anyone who thinks it unclean. [15]If your brother or sister[v] is being injured by what you eat, you are no longer walking in

Cross references (center column):

13.5 Eccl 8.2; 1 Pet 2.19
13.7 Mt 22.21; Mk 12.17; Lk 20.25
13.8 Gal 5.14; Col 3.14; Jas 2.8
13.9 Ex 20.13, 14; Mt 19.19
13.10 Mt 22.39,40
13.11ff 1 Cor 7.29, 30; 15.34; Eph 5.14; 1 Thes 5.5, 6
13.12 1 Jn 2.8; Eph 5.11; 1 Thes 5.8
13.13 1 Thes 4.12; Gal 5.21; Eph 5.18
13.14 Gal 3.27; Eph 4.24; Gal 5.16
14.1 1 Cor 8.9; 9.22
14.2 1 Tim 4.4; Titus 1.15
14.3 Col 2.16
14.4 Jas 4.12
14.5 Gal 4.10
14.6 1 Cor 10.31; 1 Tim 4.3
14.7 2 Cor 5.15; Gal 2.20; Phil 1.20,21
14.8 Phil 1.20
14.9 2 Cor 5.15; Acts 10.36
14.10 2 Cor 5.10
14.11 Isa 45.23; Phil 2.10,11
14.12 Mt 12.36; 1 Pet 4.5
14.13 Mt 7.1; 1 Cor 8.13
14.14 Acts 10.15; 1 Cor 8.7
14.15 Eph 5.2; 1 Cor 8.11

[s] Gk it　[t] Or conviction　[u] Other ancient authorities read for God　[v] Gk brother　[w] Other ancient authorities read of Christ　[x] Or confess　[y] Other ancient authorities lack to God　[z] Gk of a brother

love. Do not let what you eat cause the ruin of one for whom Christ died. [16] So do not let your good be spoken of as evil. [17] For the kingdom of God is not food and drink but righteousness and peace and joy in the Holy Spirit. [18] The one who thus serves Christ is acceptable to God and has human approval. [19] Let us then pursue what makes for peace and for mutual upbuilding. [20] Do not, for the sake of food, destroy the work of God. Everything is indeed clean, but it is wrong for you to make others fall by what you eat; [21] it is good not to eat meat or drink wine or do anything that makes your brother or sister[a] stumble.[b] [22] The faith that you have, have as your own conviction before God. Blessed are those who have no reason to condemn themselves because of what they approve. [23] But those who have doubts are condemned if they eat, because they do not act from faith;[c] for whatever does not proceed from faith[c] is sin.[d]

Please Others, Not Yourselves

15 We who are strong ought to put up with the failings of the weak, and not to please ourselves. [2] Each of us must please our neighbor for the good purpose of building up the neighbor. [3] For Christ did not please himself; but, as it is written, "The insults of those who insult you have fallen on me." [4] For whatever was written in former days was written for our instruction, so that by steadfastness and by the encouragement of the scriptures we might have hope. [5] May the God of steadfastness and encouragement grant you to live in harmony with one another, in accordance with Christ Jesus, [6] so that together you may with one voice glorify the God and Father of our Lord Jesus Christ.

The Gospel for Jews and Gentiles Alike

7 Welcome one another, therefore, just as Christ has welcomed you, for the glory of God. [8] For I tell you that Christ has become a servant of the circumcised on behalf of the truth of God in order that he might confirm the promises given to the patriarchs, [9] and in order that the Gentiles might glorify God for his mercy. As it is written,

"Therefore I will confess[e]
you among the
Gentiles,
and sing praises to your
name";

[10] and again he says,

"Rejoice, O Gentiles, with
his people";

[11] and again,

"Praise the Lord, all you
Gentiles,
and let all the peoples
praise him";

[12] and again Isaiah says,

"The root of Jesse shall
come,
the one who rises to rule
the Gentiles;
in him the Gentiles shall
hope."

[13] May the God of hope fill you with all joy and peace in believing, so that you may abound in hope by the power of the Holy Spirit.

Paul's Reason for Writing So Boldly

14 I myself feel confident about you, my brothers and sisters,[f] that you yourselves are full of goodness, filled with all knowledge, and able to instruct one another. [15] Nevertheless on some points I have written to you rather boldly by way of reminder, because of the grace given me by God [16] to be a minister of Christ Jesus to the Gentiles in the priestly service of the gospel of God, so that the offering of the Gentiles may be acceptable, sanctified by the Holy Spirit. [17] In Christ Jesus, then, I have reason to boast of my work for God. [18] For I will not

15.18 Acts 15.12; 21.19; Rom 1.5; 16.26

Cross references (center column):

14.16 1 Cor 10.30
14.17 1 Cor 8.8; Rom 15.13
14.18 2 Cor 8.21
14.19 Ps 34.14; Heb 12.14; Rom 15.2
14.20 v. 15; 1 Cor 8.9-12
14.21 1 Cor 8.13
14.22 1 Jn 3.21
15.1 Rom 14.1; Gal 6.1,2
15.2 1 Cor 10.33; Rom 14.19
15.3 Ps 69.9; 2 Cor 8.9
15.4 Rom 4.23, 24; 2 Tim 3.16, 17
15.5 Rom 12.16; 1 Cor 1.10
15.6 Rev 1.6
15.7 Rom 14.1
15.8 Mt 15.24; Acts 3.25, 26; Rom 3.3; 2 Cor 1.20
15.9 Ps 18.49; 2 Sam 22.50
15.10 Deut 32.43
15.11 Ps 117.1
15.12 Isa 11.10; Mt 12.21; Rev 5.5; 22.16
15.13 Rom 14.17; 1 Thes 1.5
15.14 2 Pet 1.12; 1 Cor 8.1, 7,10
15.15 Rom 12.3; Eph 3.7,8
15.16 Acts 9.15; Rom 11.13; Phil 2.17
15.17 Phil 3.3; Heb 2.17; 5.1

a Gk brother b Other ancient authorities add *or be upset or be weakened*
c Or conviction d Other authorities, some ancient, add here 16.25-27 e Or thank
f Gk brothers

venture to speak of anything except what Christ has accomplished[g] through me to win obedience from the Gentiles, by word and deed, [19] by the power of signs and wonders, by the power of the Spirit of God,[h] so that from Jerusalem and as far around as Illyricum I have fully proclaimed the good news[i] of Christ. [20] Thus I make it my ambition to proclaim the good news,[i] not where Christ has already been named, so that I do not build on someone else's foundation, [21] but as it is written,

"Those who have never been
 told of him shall see,
and those who have never
 heard of him shall
 understand."

Paul's Plan to Visit Rome

22 This is the reason that I have so often been hindered from coming to you. [23] But now, with no further place for me in these regions, I desire, as I have for many years, to come to you [24] when I go to Spain. For I do hope to see you on my journey and to be sent on by you, once I have enjoyed your company for a little while. [25] At present, however, I am going to Jerusalem in a ministry to the saints; [26] for Macedonia and Achaia have been pleased to share their resources with the poor among the saints at Jerusalem. [27] They were pleased to do this, and indeed they owe it to them; for if the Gentiles have come to share in their spiritual blessings, they ought also to be of service to them in material things. [28] So, when I have completed this, and have delivered to them what has been collected,[j] I will set out by way of you to Spain; [29] and I know that when I come to you, I will come in the fullness of the blessing[k] of Christ.

30 I appeal to you, brothers and sisters,[l] by our Lord Jesus Christ and by the love of the Spirit, to join me in earnest prayer to God on my behalf, [31] that I may be rescued from the unbelievers in Judea, and that my ministry[m] to Jerusalem may be acceptable to the saints,

15.19
Acts 19.11;
2 Cor 12.12
15.20
2 Cor 10.15,
16
15.21
Isa 52.15
15.22
Rom 1.13
15.23
Acts 19.21;
Rom 1.11
15.24
v. 28;
Acts 15.3
15.25
Acts 19.21;
24.27
15.26
2 Cor 8.1;
9.2;
1 Thes 1.7,
8
15.27
1 Cor 9.11
15.30
Gal 5.22;
2 Cor 1.11;
Col 4.12

15.32
Rom 1.10;
Acts 18.21;
1 Cor 16.18
15.33
Rom 16.20;
2 Cor 13.11;
Phil 4.9;
Heb 13.20
16.1
Acts 18.18
16.2
Phil 2.29;
Rom 15.15,
31
16.3
Acts 18.2;
2 Tim 4.19
16.5
1 Cor 16.15,
19; Col 4.15
16.9
2 Cor 5.17
16.10
2 Cor 5.17
16.11
vv. 7,21;
1 Cor 1.11

[32] so that by God's will I may come to you with joy and be refreshed in your company. [33] The God of peace be with all of you.[n] Amen.

Personal Greetings

16 I commend to you our sister Phoebe, a deacon[o] of the church at Cenchreae, [2] so that you may welcome her in the Lord as is fitting for the saints, and help her in whatever she may require from you, for she has been a benefactor of many and of myself as well.

3 Greet Prisca and Aquila, who work with me in Christ Jesus, [4] and who risked their necks for my life, to whom not only I give thanks, but also all the churches of the Gentiles. [5] Greet also the church in their house. Greet my beloved Epaenetus, who was the first convert[p] in Asia for Christ. [6] Greet Mary, who has worked very hard among you. [7] Greet Andronicus and Junia,[q] my relatives[r] who were in prison with me; they are prominent among the apostles, and they were in Christ before I was. [8] Greet Ampliatus, my beloved in the Lord. [9] Greet Urbanus, our co-worker in Christ, and my beloved Stachys. [10] Greet Apelles, who is approved in Christ. Greet those who belong to the family of Aristobulus. [11] Greet my relative[s] Herodion. Greet those in the Lord who belong to the family of Narcissus. [12] Greet those workers in the Lord, Tryphaena and Tryphosa. Greet the beloved Persis, who has worked hard in the Lord. [13] Greet Rufus, chosen in the Lord; and greet his mother—a mother to me also. [14] Greet Asyncritus, Phlegon, Hermes, Patrobas, Hermas, and the brothers and sis-

g Gk *speak of those things that Christ has not accomplished* h Other ancient authorities read *of the Spirit* or *of the Holy Spirit* i Or *gospel* j Gk *have sealed to them this fruit* k Other ancient authorities add *of the gospel* l Gk *brothers* m Other ancient authorities read *my bringing of a gift* n One ancient authority adds 16.25-27 here o Or *minister* p Gk *first fruits* q Or *Junias*; other ancient authorities read *Julia* r Or *compatriots* s Or *compatriot*

ters[t] who are with them. [15] Greet Philologus, Julia, Nereus and his sister, and Olympas, and all the saints who are with them. [16] Greet one another with a holy kiss. All the churches of Christ greet you.

Final Instructions

[17] I urge you, brothers and sisters,[t] to keep an eye on those who cause dissensions and offenses, in opposition to the teaching that you have learned; avoid them. [18] For such people do not serve our Lord Christ, but their own appetites,[u] and by smooth talk and flattery they deceive the hearts of the simple-minded. [19] For while your obedience is known to all, so that I rejoice over you, I want you to be wise in what is good and guileless in what is evil. [20] The God of peace will shortly crush Satan under your feet. The grace of our Lord Jesus Christ be with you.[v]

[21] Timothy, my co-worker, greets you; so do Lucius and Jason and Sosipater, my relatives.[w]

[22] I Tertius, the writer of this letter, greet you in the Lord.[x]

[23] Gaius, who is host to me and

to the whole church, greets you. Erastus, the city treasurer, and our brother Quartus, greet you.[y]

Final Doxology

[25] Now to God[z] who is able to strengthen you according to my gospel and the proclamation of Jesus Christ, according to the revelation of the mystery that was kept secret for long ages [26] but is now disclosed, and through the prophetic writings is made known to all the Gentiles, according to the command of the eternal God, to bring about the obedience of faith— [27] to the only wise God, through Jesus Christ, to whom[a] be the glory forever! Amen.[b]

16.15
vv. 2,14
16.16
1 Cor 16.20;
2 Cor 13.12;
1 Thes 5.26
16.17
1 Tim 1.3;
6.3; Gal 1.8,
9;
2 Thes 3.6,
14;
2 Jn 10
16.18
Phil 3.19;
Col 2.4
16.19
Rom 1.8;
Mt 10.16;
1 Cor 14.20
16.20
Rom 15.33;
Gen 3.15;
1 Cor 16.23;
1 Thes 5.28
16.21
Acts 16.1;
13.1; 17.5;
20.4; vv. 7,
11

[t] Gk brothers　　[u] Gk their own belly
[v] Other ancient authorities lack this sentence
[w] Or compatriots　　[x] Or I Tertius, writing this letter in the Lord, greet you　　[y] Other ancient authorities add verse 24, The grace of our Lord Jesus Christ be with all of you. Amen.
[z] Gk the one　　[a] Other ancient authorities lack to whom. The verse then reads, to the only wise God be the glory through Jesus Christ forever. Amen.　　[b] Other ancient authorities lack 16.25-27 or include it after 14.23 or 15.33; others put verse 24 after verse 27

THE FIRST LETTER OF PAUL TO THE
Corinthians

Title and Background

Located between the Corinthian Gulf and the Saronic Gulf, the city of Corinth was a wealthy trading center. It was also a wicked city, known for its vice throughout the Roman world. Because the church in Corinth was new, it was hard for the Christians there not to act like their neighbors. Consequently, they were facing some serious problems.

Author and Date of Writing

Few question Paul's authorship of this letter (see 1.1). It was written about A.D. 55, toward the close of Paul's three-year residency in Ephesus.

Theme and Message

The letter revolves around a series of problems in Christian conduct permeating the church at Corinth. Thus it deals with progressive sanctification, the continuing development of holiness of character. Obviously Paul was personally concerned with the Corinthians' problems, revealing a true pastor's (shepherd's) heart. In spite of the concentration on problems, the book contains some of the most familiar and beloved chapters in the entire Bible—e.g., ch. 13 (on love) and ch. 15 (on the resurrection).

Outline

Salutation

1 Paul, called to be an apostle of Christ Jesus by the will of God, and our brother Sosthenes,

2 To the church of God that is in Corinth, to those who are sanctified in Christ Jesus, called to be saints, together with all those who in every place call on the name of our Lord Jesus Christ, both their Lord[a] and ours:

3 Grace to you and peace from God our Father and the Lord Jesus Christ.

4 I give thanks to my[b] God always for you because of the grace of God that has been given you in Christ Jesus, 5 for in every way you have been enriched in him, in speech and knowledge of every kind— 6 just as the testimony of[c] Christ has been strengthened among you— 7 so that you are not lacking in any spiritual gift as you wait for the revealing of our Lord Jesus Christ. 8 He will also

1.7 Phil 3.20; Titus 2.13; 2 Pet 3.12

a Gk *theirs* b Other ancient authorities lack *my* c Or *to*

1.1
Rom 1.1;
2 Cor 1.1;
Eph 1.1;
Col 1.1;
Acts 18.17
1.2
Acts 18.1;
Rom 1.7;
Acts 7.59
1.3
Rom 1.7
1.4
Rom 1.8
1.5
2 Cor 9.11;
8.7
1.6
2 Tim 1.8;
Rev 1.2

strengthen you to the end, so that you may be blameless on the day of our Lord Jesus Christ. [9] God is faithful; by him you were called into the fellowship of his Son, Jesus Christ our Lord.

Divisions in the Church

10 Now I appeal to you, brothers and sisters, [d] by the name of our Lord Jesus Christ, that all of you be in agreement and that there be no divisions among you, but that you be united in the same mind and the same purpose. [11] For it has been reported to me by Chloe's people that there are quarrels among you, my brothers and sisters. [e] [12] What I mean is that each of you says, "I belong to Paul," or "I belong to Apollos," or "I belong to Cephas," or "I belong to Christ." [13] Has Christ been divided? Was Paul crucified for you? Or were you baptized in the name of Paul? [14] I thank God [f] that I baptized none of you except Crispus and Gaius, [15] so that no one can say that you were baptized in my name. [16] (I did baptize also the household of Stephanas; beyond that, I do not know whether I baptized anyone else.) [17] For Christ did not send me to baptize but to proclaim the gospel, and not with eloquent wisdom, so that the cross of Christ might not be emptied of its power.

Christ the Power and Wisdom of God

18 For the message about the cross is foolishness to those who are perishing, but to us who are being saved it is the power of God. [19] For it is written,

"I will destroy the wisdom of
 the wise,
and the discernment of the
 discerning I will
 thwart."

[20] Where is the one who is wise? Where is the scribe? Where is the debater of this age? Has not God made foolish the wisdom of the world? [21] For since, in the wisdom of God, the world did not know God through wisdom, God decided,

through the foolishness of our proclamation, to save those who believe. [22] For Jews demand signs and Greeks desire wisdom, [23] but we proclaim Christ crucified, a stumbling block to Jews and foolishness to Gentiles, [24] but to those who are the called, both Jews and Greeks, Christ the power of God and the wisdom of God. [25] For God's foolishness is wiser than human wisdom, and God's weakness is stronger than human strength.

26 Consider your own call, brothers and sisters: [d] not many of you were wise by human standards, [g] not many were powerful, not many were of noble birth. [27] But God chose what is foolish in the world to shame the wise; God chose what is weak in the world to shame the strong; [28] God chose what is low and despised in the world, things that are not, to reduce to nothing things that are, [29] so that no one [h] might boast in the presence of God. [30] He is the source of your life in Christ Jesus, who became for us wisdom from God, and righteousness and sanctification and redemption, [31] in order that, as it is written, "Let the one who boasts, boast in [i] the Lord."

Proclaiming Christ Crucified

2 When I came to you, brothers and sisters, [d] I did not come proclaiming the mystery [j] of God to you in lofty words or wisdom. [2] For I decided to know nothing among you except Jesus Christ, and him crucified. [3] And I came to you in weakness and in fear and in much trembling. [4] My speech and my proclamation were not with plausible words of wisdom, [k] but with a demonstration of the Spirit and of power, [5] so that your faith might rest not on human wisdom but on the power of God.

Cross references

1.9 Isa 49.7; 1 Jn 1.3
1.10 2 Cor 13.11; Rom 12.16
1.13 2 Cor 11.4; Mt 28.19; Acts 2.38
1.14 Acts 18.8; Rom 16.23
1.16 1 Cor 16.15
1.17 Jn 4.2; Acts 10.48; 1 Cor 2.1, 4,13
1.18 Acts 17.18; 1 Cor 15.2; Rom 1.16
1.19 Isa 29.14
1.20 Isa 33.18; Rom 1.22
1.21 Gal 1.15; 1 Tim 4.16; Heb 7.25

1.22 Mt 12.38
1.23 Gal 5.11; 1 Cor 2.14
1.24 Rom 1.4; Col 2.3
1.26 Rom 11.29
1.27 Jas 2.5
1.29 Eph 2.9
1.30 1 Cor 6.11; 1 Thes 5.23; Eph 1.7,14; Rom 3.24
1.31 Jer 9.23,24; 2 Cor 10.17
2.1 1 Cor 1.17
2.2 Gal 6.14; 1 Cor 1.23
2.4 Rom 15.19; 1 Cor 4.20
2.5 2 Cor 4.7; 6.7

d Gk *brothers* e Gk *my brothers* f Other ancient authorities read *I am thankful* g Gk *according to the flesh* h Gk *no flesh* i Or *of* j Other ancient authorities read *testimony* k Other ancient authorities read *the persuasiveness of wisdom*

The True Wisdom of God

6 Yet among the mature we do speak wisdom, though it is not a wisdom of this age or of the rulers of this age, who are doomed to perish. [7] But we speak God's wisdom, secret and hidden, which God decreed before the ages for our glory. [8] None of the rulers of this age understood this; for if they had, they would not have crucified the Lord of glory. [9] But, as it is written,
"What no eye has seen, nor
 ear heard,
 nor the human heart
 conceived,
what God has prepared for
 those who love him"—
[10] these things God has revealed to us through the Spirit; for the Spirit searches everything, even the depths of God. [11] For what human being knows what is truly human except the human spirit that is within? So also no one comprehends what is truly God's except the Spirit of God. [12] Now we have received not the spirit of the world, but the Spirit that is from God, so that we may understand the gifts bestowed on us by God. [13] And we speak of these things in words not taught by human wisdom but taught by the Spirit, interpreting spiritual things to those who are spiritual.[1]

14 Those who are unspiritual[m] do not receive the gifts of God's Spirit, for they are foolishness to them, and they are unable to understand them because they are spiritually discerned. [15] Those who are spiritual discern all things, and they are themselves subject to no one else's scrutiny.
[16] "For who has known the
 mind of the Lord
 so as to instruct him?"
But we have the mind of Christ.

On Divisions in the Corinthian Church

3 And so, brothers and sisters,[n] I could not speak to you as spiritual people, but rather as people of the flesh, as infants in Christ. [2] I fed you with milk, not solid food,

for you were not ready for solid food. Even now you are still not ready, [3] for you are still of the flesh. For as long as there is jealousy and quarreling among you, are you not of the flesh, and behaving according to human inclinations? [4] For when one says, "I belong to Paul," and another, "I belong to Apollos," are you not merely human?

5 What then is Apollos? What is Paul? Servants through whom you came to believe, as the Lord assigned to each. [6] I planted, Apollos watered, but God gave the growth. [7] So neither the one who plants nor the one who waters is anything, but only God who gives the growth. [8] The one who plants and the one who waters have a common purpose, and each will receive wages according to the labor of each. [9] For we are God's servants, working together; you are God's field, God's building.

10 According to the grace of God given to me, like a skilled master builder I laid a foundation, and someone else is building on it. Each builder must choose with care how to build on it. [11] For no one can lay any foundation other than the one that has been laid; that foundation is Jesus Christ. [12] Now if anyone builds on the foundation with gold, silver, precious stones, wood, hay, straw— [13] the work of each builder will become visible, for the Day will disclose it, because it will be revealed with fire, and the fire will test what sort of work each has done. [14] If what has been built on the foundation survives, the builder will receive a reward. [15] If the work is burned up, the builder will suffer loss; the builder will be saved, but only as through fire.

16 Do you not know that you are God's temple and that God's Spirit dwells in you?[o] [17] If anyone destroys God's temple, God will de-

2.6
Eph 4.13;
Phil 3.15;
1 Cor 1.20;
1.28
2.8
Acts 7.2;
Jas 2.1
2.9
Isa 64.4;
65.17
2.10
Mt 16.17;
Eph 3.3,5;
Jn 14.26
2.11
Prov 20.27;
Jer 17.9
2.12
Rom 8.15;
1 Cor 1.27
2.13
1 Cor 1.17
2.14
1 Cor 1.18;
Jas 3.15
2.16
Isa 40.13;
Jn 15.15
3.1
1 Cor 2.15;
Rom 7.14;
1 Cor 2.14;
Heb 5.13
3.2
Heb 5.12,
13;
1 Pet 2.2

3.3
1 Cor 1.11;
Gal 5.20;
Jas 3.16
3.4
1 Cor 1.12
3.8
Ps 62.12;
Gal 6.4,5
3.9
2 Cor 6.1;
Isa 61.3;
1 Pet 2.5
3.10
Rom 12.3;
15.20;
1 Cor 15.10
3.11
Isa 28.6;
Eph 2.20
3.13
1 Cor 4.5;
2 Thes 1.7-10
3.14
1 Cor 4.5;
9.17
3.15
Job 23.10;
Jude 23
3.16
1 Cor 6.19;
2 Cor 6.16

[1] Or interpreting spiritual things in spiritual language, or comparing spiritual things with spiritual [m] Or natural [n] Gk brothers [o] In verses 16 and 17 the Greek word for you is plural

stroy that person. For God's temple is holy, and you are that temple.

18 Do not deceive yourselves. If you think that you are wise in this age, you should become fools so that you may become wise. ¹⁹For the wisdom of this world is foolishness with God. For it is written,

"He catches the wise in their
 craftiness,"

²⁰and again,

"The Lord knows the
 thoughts of the wise,
 that they are futile."

²¹So let no one boast about human leaders. For all things are yours, ²²whether Paul or Apollos or Cephas or the world or life or death or the present or the future—all belong to you, ²³and you belong to Christ, and Christ belongs to God.

The Ministry of the Apostles

4 Think of us in this way, as servants of Christ and stewards of God's mysteries. ²Moreover, it is required of stewards that they be found trustworthy. ³But with me it is a very small thing that I should be judged by you or by any human court. I do not even judge myself. ⁴I am not aware of anything against myself, but I am not thereby acquitted. It is the Lord who judges me. ⁵Therefore do not pronounce judgment before the time, before the Lord comes, who will bring to light the things now hidden in darkness and will disclose the purposes of the heart. Then each one will receive commendation from God.

6 I have applied all this to Apollos and myself for your benefit, brothers and sisters,ᴾ so that you may learn through us the meaning of the saying, "Nothing beyond what is written," so that none of you will be puffed up in favor of one against another. ⁷For who sees anything different in you?�q What do you have that you did not receive? And if you received it, why do you boast as if it were not a gift? 8 Already you have all you want!

Already you have become rich! Quite apart from us you have become kings! Indeed, I wish that you had become kings, so that we might be kings with you! ⁹For I think that God has exhibited us apostles as last of all, as though sentenced to death, because we have become a spectacle to the world, to angels and to mortals. ¹⁰We are fools for the sake of Christ, but you are wise in Christ. We are weak, but you are strong. You are held in honor, but we in disrepute. ¹¹To the present hour we are hungry and thirsty, we are poorly clothed and beaten and homeless, ¹²and we grow weary from the work of our own hands. When reviled, we bless; when persecuted, we endure; ¹³when slandered, we speak kindly. We have become like the rubbish of the world, the dregs of all things, to this very day.

Fatherly Admonition

14 I am not writing this to make you ashamed, but to admonish you as my beloved children. ¹⁵For though you might have ten thousand guardians in Christ, you do not have many fathers. Indeed, in Christ Jesus I became your father through the gospel. ¹⁶I appeal to you, then, be imitators of me. ¹⁷For this reason I sentʳ you Timothy, who is my beloved and faithful child in the Lord, to remind you of my ways in Christ Jesus, as I teach them everywhere in every church. ¹⁸But some of you, thinking that I am not coming to you, have become arrogant. ¹⁹But I will come to you soon, if the Lord wills, and I will find out not the talk of these arrogant people but their power. ²⁰For the kingdom of God depends not on talk but on power. ²¹What would you prefer? Am I to come to you with a stick, or with love in a spirit of gentleness?

3.18
Isa 5.21;
1 Cor 8.2
3.19
Job 5.13;
1 Cor 1.20
3.20
Ps 94.11
3.21
1 Cor 4.6;
Rom 8.32
3.23
1 Cor 15.23;
2 Cor 10.7;
Gal 3.29
4.1
2 Cor 6.4;
1 Cor 9.17;
Rom 11.25;
16.25
4.4
2 Cor 1.12;
Rom 2.13
4.5
Rom 2.1;
2 Cor 10.18;
Rom 2.29
4.6
1 Cor 1.19,
31; 3.19,20;
1.12; 3.4
4.7
Rom 12.3,6
4.8
Rev 3.17,18

4.9
1 Cor 15.31;
2 Cor 11.23;
Rom 8.36;
Heb 10.33
4.10
1 Cor 1.18;
Acts 17.18;
1 Cor 3.18
4.11
Rom 8.35;
2 Cor 11.23-27
4.12
Acts 18.3;
1 Pet 3.9;
Jn 15.20;
Rom 8.35
4.14
1 Thes 2.11
4.15
1 Cor 1.30;
Philem 10
4.16
Phil 3.17;
1 Thes 1.6;
2 Thes 3.9
4.19
Acts 19.21;
2 Cor 1.15;
Rom 15.32
4.20
1 Thes 1.5
4.21
2 Cor 1.23;
13.10

ᴾ Gk brothers qOr Who makes you different from another? ʳOr am sending

Sexual Immorality Defiles the Church

5 It is actually reported that there is sexual immorality among you, and of a kind that is not found even among pagans; for a man is living with his father's wife. ²And you are arrogant! Should you not rather have mourned, so that he who has done this would have been removed from among you?

3 For though absent in body, I am present in spirit; and as if present I have already pronounced judgment ⁴in the name of the Lord Jesus on the man who has done such a thing.ˢ When you are assembled, and my spirit is present with the power of our Lord Jesus, ⁵you are to hand this man over to Satan for the destruction of the flesh, so that his spirit may be saved in the day of the Lord.ᵗ

6 Your boasting is not a good thing. Do you not know that a little yeast leavens the whole batch of dough? ⁷Clean out the old yeast so that you may be a new batch, as you really are unleavened. For our paschal lamb, Christ, has been sacrificed. ⁸Therefore, let us celebrate the festival, not with the old yeast, the yeast of malice and evil, but with the unleavened bread of sincerity and truth.

Sexual Immorality Must Be Judged

9 I wrote to you in my letter not to associate with sexually immoral persons — ¹⁰not at all meaning the immoral of this world, or the greedy and robbers, or idolaters, since you would then need to go out of the world. ¹¹But now I am writing to you not to associate with anyone who bears the name of brother or sisterᵘ who is sexually immoral or greedy, or is an idolater, reviler, drunkard, or robber. Do not even eat with such a one. ¹²For what have I to do with judging those outside? Is it not those who are inside that you are to judge? ¹³God will judge those outside.

5.1
Lev 18.8;
Deut 22.30;
2 Cor 7.12
5.2
1 Cor 4.18;
2 Cor 7.7
5.3
Col 2.5
5.4
2 Thes 3.6;
2 Cor 2.10
5.5
1 Tim 1.20
5.6
Jas 4.16;
Gal 5.9
5.7
1 Pet 1.19
5.8
Deut 16.3;
Mk 8.15
5.9
2 Cor 6.14;
Eph 5.11;
2 Thes 3.14
5.10
1 Cor 10.27
5.11
2 Thes 3.6;
1 Cor 10.7,
14,20,21
5.12
Mk 4.11;
1 Cor 6.1-4
5.13
Deut 13.5;
21.21

6.1
Mt 18.17
6.2
Dan 7.22;
Mt 19.28;
Lk 22.30
6.4
1 Cor 5.12
6.5
1 Cor 15.34;
Acts 1.15
6.6
2 Cor 6.14,
15
6.7
Mt 5.39,40;
Rom 12.17
6.8
1 Thes 4.6
6.9
Gal 5.21;
1 Tim 1.10;
Rev 22.15
6.11
Eph 2.2;
Col 3.7;
Titus 3.3
6.12
1 Cor 10.23
6.13
Mt 15.17;
Eph 5.23

"Drive out the wicked person from among you."

Lawsuits among Believers

6 When any of you has a grievance against another, do you dare to take it to court before the unrighteous, instead of taking it before the saints? ²Do you not know that the saints will judge the world? And if the world is to be judged by you, are you incompetent to try trivial cases? ³Do you not know that we are to judge angels — to say nothing of ordinary matters? ⁴If you have ordinary cases, then, do you appoint as judges those who have no standing in the church? ⁵I say this to your shame. Can it be that there is no one among you wise enough to decide between one believerᵘ and another, ⁶but a believerᵘ goes to court against a believerᵘ — and before unbelievers at that?

7 In fact, to have lawsuits at all with one another is already a defeat for you. Why not rather be wronged? Why not rather be defrauded? ⁸But you yourselves wrong and defraud — and believersᵛ at that.

9 Do you not know that wrongdoers will not inherit the kingdom of God? Do not be deceived! Fornicators, idolaters, adulterers, male prostitutes, sodomites, ¹⁰thieves, the greedy, drunkards, revilers, robbers — none of these will inherit the kingdom of God. ¹¹And this is what some of you used to be. But you were washed, you were sanctified, you were justified in the name of the Lord Jesus Christ and in the Spirit of our God.

Glorify God in Body and Spirit

12 "All things are lawful for me," but not all things are beneficial. "All things are lawful for me," but I will not be dominated by anything. ¹³"Food is meant for the stomach and the stomach for

ˢ Or on the man who has done such a thing in the name of the Lord Jesus ᵗ Other ancient authorities add Jesus ᵘ Gk brother ᵛ Gk brothers

food,"ʷ and God will destroy both one and the other. The body is meant not for fornication but for the Lord, and the Lord for the body. 14 And God raised the Lord and will also raise us by his power. 15 Do you not know that your bodies are members of Christ? Should I therefore take the members of Christ and make them members of a prostitute? Never! 16 Do you not know that whoever is united to a prostitute becomes one body with her? For it is said, "The two shall be one flesh." 17 But anyone united to the Lord becomes one spirit with him. 18 Shun fornication! Every sin that a person commits is outside the body; but the fornicator sins against the body itself. 19 Or do you not know that your body is a templeˣ of the Holy Spirit within you, which you have from God, and that you are not your own? 20 For you were bought with a price; therefore glorify God in your body.

Directions concerning Marriage

7 Now concerning the matters about which you wrote: "It is well for a man not to touch a woman." 2 But because of cases of sexual immorality, each man should have his own wife and each woman her own husband. 3 The husband should give to his wife her conjugal rights, and likewise the wife to her husband. 4 For the wife does not have authority over her own body, but the husband does; likewise the husband does not have authority over his own body, but the wife does. 5 Do not deprive one another except perhaps by agreement for a set time, to devote yourselves to prayer, and then come together again, so that Satan may not tempt you because of your lack of self-control. 6 This I say by way of concession, not of command. 7 I wish that all were as I myself am. But each has a particular gift from God, one having one kind and another a different kind.

8 To the unmarried and the widows I say that it is well for them to

remain unmarried as I am. 9 But if they are not practicing self-control, they should marry. For it is better to marry than to be aflame with passion.

10 To the married I give this command—not I but the Lord—that the wife should not separate from her husband 11 (but if she does separate, let her remain unmarried or else be reconciled to her husband), and that the husband should not divorce his wife.

12 To the rest I say—I and not the Lord—that if any believerʸ has a wife who is an unbeliever, and she consents to live with him, he should not divorce her. 13 And if any woman has a husband who is an unbeliever, and he consents to live with her, she should not divorce him. 14 For the unbelieving husband is made holy through his wife, and the unbelieving wife is made holy through her husband. Otherwise, your children would be unclean, but as it is, they are holy. 15 But if the unbelieving partner separates, let it be so; in such a case the brother or sister is not bound. It is to peace that God has called you.ᶻ 16 Wife, for all you know, you might save your husband. Husband, for all you know, you might save your wife.

The Life That the Lord Has Assigned

17 However that may be, let each of you lead the life that the Lord has assigned, to which God called you. This is my rule in all the churches. 18 Was anyone at the time of his call already circumcised? Let him not seek to remove the marks of circumcision. Was anyone at the time of his call uncircumcised? Let him not seek circumcision. 19 Circumcision is nothing, and uncircumcision is nothing; but obeying the commandments of God is everything. 20 Let each of you remain in the

Cross references

6.14
Rom 6.5,8;
8.11;
2 Cor 4.14;
Eph 1.19
6.15
Rom 12.5;
1 Cor 12.27
6.16
Gen 2.4;
Mt 19.5;
Eph 5.31
6.17
Jn 17.21-23;
Gal 2.20
6.18
Rom 6.12;
Heb 13.4;
1 Thes 4.4
6.19
Jn 2.21;
Rom 14.7,8
6.20
1 Cor 7.23;
1 Pet 1.18,
19; Rev 5.9
7.1
vv. 8,26
7.3
1 Pet 3.7
7.5
Ex 19.15;
1 Sam 21.4,
5;
1 Thes 3.5
7.6
2 Cor 8.8
7.7
v. 8;
1 Cor 9.5;
12.11;
Mt 19.12
7.8
vv. 1,26
7.9
1 Tim 5.14
7.10
Mal 2.14;
Mt 5.32;
19.3-9;
Mk 10.11;
Lk 16.18
7.12
v. 6;
2 Cor 11.17
7.14
Mal 2.15
7.15
Rom 14.19;
1 Cor 14.33
7.16
1 Pet 3.1
7.17
Rom 12.3;
1 Cor 4.17;
14.33;
2 Cor 8.18;
11.28
7.18
Acts 15.1,2
7.19
Gal 5.6;
6.15;
Rom 2.25
7.20
v. 24

ʷ The quotation may extend to the word other ˣ Or sanctuary ʸ Gk brother
ᶻ Other ancient authorities read us

condition in which you were called.

21 Were you a slave when called? Do not be concerned about it. Even if you can gain your freedom, make use of your present condition now more than ever.[a] [22] For whoever was called in the Lord as a slave is a freed person belonging to the Lord, just as whoever was free when called is a slave of Christ. [23] You were bought with a price; do not become slaves of human masters. [24] In whatever condition you were called, brothers and sisters,[b] there remain with God.

The Unmarried and the Widows

25 Now concerning virgins, I have no command of the Lord, but I give my opinion as one who by the Lord's mercy is trustworthy. [26] I think that, in view of the impending[c] crisis, it is well for you to remain as you are. [27] Are you bound to a wife? Do not seek to be free. Are you free from a wife? Do not seek a wife. [28] But if you marry, you do not sin, and if a virgin marries, she does not sin. Yet those who marry will experience distress in this life,[d] and I would spare you that. [29] I mean, brothers and sisters,[b] the appointed time has grown short; from now on, let even those who have wives be as though they had none, [30] and those who mourn as though they were not mourning, and those who rejoice as though they were not rejoicing, and those who buy as though they had no possessions, [31] and those who deal with the world as though they had no dealings with it. For the present form of this world is passing away.

32 I want you to be free from anxieties. The unmarried man is anxious about the affairs of the Lord, how to please the Lord; [33] but the married man is anxious about the affairs of the world, how to please his wife, [34] and his interests are divided. And the unmarried woman and the virgin are anxious about the affairs of the Lord, so that they may be holy in body and

spirit; but the married woman is anxious about the affairs of the world, how to please her husband. [35] I say this for your own benefit, not to put any restraint upon you, but to promote good order and unhindered devotion to the Lord.

36 If anyone thinks that he is not behaving properly toward his fiancé,[e] if his passions are strong, and so it has to be, let him marry as he wishes; it is no sin. Let them marry. [37] But if someone stands firm in his resolve, being under no necessity but having his own desire under control, and has determined in his own mind to keep her as his fiancé,[e] he will do well. [38] So then, he who marries his fiancé[e] does well; and he who refrains from marriage will do better.

39 A wife is bound as long as her husband lives. But if the husband dies,[f] she is free to marry anyone she wishes, only in the Lord. [40] But in my judgment she is more blessed if she remains as she is. And I think that I too have the Spirit of God.

Food Offered to Idols

8 Now concerning food sacrificed to idols: we know that "all of us possess knowledge." Knowledge puffs up, but love builds up. [2] Anyone who claims to know something does not yet have the necessary knowledge; [3] but anyone who loves God is known by him.

4 Hence, as to the eating of food offered to idols, we know that "no idol in the world really exists," and that "there is no God but one." [5] Indeed, even though there may be so-called gods in heaven or on earth — as in fact there are many gods and many lords — [6] yet for us there is one God, the Father, from whom are all things and for whom we exist, and one Lord, Jesus Christ, through whom are all things and through whom we exist.

7.22
Jn 8.32,36;
Philem 16;
Eph 6.6
7.23
1 Cor 6.20
7.25
2 Cor 8.8,
10;
1 Tim 1.13,
16
7.26
vv. 1,8
7.29
Rom 13.11,
12; v. 31
7.31
1 Cor 9.18;
1 Jn 2.17
7.32
1 Tim 5.5
7.34
Lk 10.40

7.38
Heb 13.4
7.39
Rom 7.2;
2 Cor 6.14
7.40
v. 25
8.1
Acts 15.20;
Rom 15.14;
14.3,10
8.2
1 Cor 3.18;
13.8,9,12;
1 Tim 6.4
8.3
Gal 4.9;
Rom 8.29
8.4
1 Cor 10.19;
Deut 6.4;
Eph 4.6
8.6
Mal 2.10;
Rom 11.36;
Phil 2.11

[a] Or avail yourself of the opportunity [b] Gk brothers [c] Or present [d] Gk in the flesh [e] Gk virgin [f] Gk falls asleep

7 It is not everyone, however, who has this knowledge. Since some have become so accustomed to idols until now, they still think of the food they eat as food offered to an idol; and their conscience, being weak, is defiled. 8 "Food will not bring us close to God."g We are no worse off if we do not eat, and no better off if we do. 9 But take care that this liberty of yours does not somehow become a stumbling block to the weak. 10 For if others see you, who possess knowledge, eating in the temple of an idol, might they not, since their conscience is weak, be encouraged to the point of eating food sacrificed to idols? 11 So by your knowledge those weak believers for whom Christ died are destroyed.h 12 But when you thus sin against members of your family,i and wound their conscience when it is weak, you sin against Christ. 13 Therefore, if food is a cause of their falling,j I will never eat meat, so that I may not cause one of themk to fall.

The Rights of an Apostle

9 Am I not free? Am I not an apostle? Have I not seen Jesus our Lord? Are you not my work in the Lord? 2 If I am not an apostle to others, at least I am to you; for you are the seal of my apostleship in the Lord.

3 This is my defense to those who would examine me. 4 Do we not have the right to our food and drink? 5 Do we not have the right to be accompanied by a believing wife,l as do the other apostles and the brothers of the Lord and Cephas? 6 Or is it only Barnabas and I who have no right to refrain from working for a living? 7 Who at any time pays the expenses for doing military service? Who plants a vineyard and does not eat any of its fruit? Or who tends a flock and does not get any of its milk?

8 Do I say this on human authority? Does not the law also say the same? 9 For it is written in the law of Moses, "You shall not muz-

zle an ox while it is treading out the grain." Is it for oxen that God is concerned? 10 Or does he not speak entirely for our sake? It was indeed written for our sake, for whoever plows should plow in hope and whoever threshes should thresh in hope of a share in the crop. 11 If we have sown spiritual good among you, is it too much if we reap your material benefits? 12 If others share this rightful claim on you, do not we still more?

Nevertheless, we have not made use of this right, but we endure anything rather than put an obstacle in the way of the gospel of Christ. 13 Do you not know that those who are employed in the temple service get their food from the temple, and those who serve at the altar share in what is sacrificed on the altar? 14 In the same way, the Lord commanded that those who proclaim the gospel should get their living by the gospel.

15 But I have made no use of any of these rights, nor am I writing this so that they may be applied in my case. Indeed, I would rather die than that—no one will deprive me of my ground for boasting! 16 If I proclaim the gospel, this gives me no ground for boasting, for an obligation is laid on me, and woe to me if I do not proclaim the gospel! 17 For if I do this of my own will, I have a reward; but if not of my own will, I am entrusted with a commission. 18 What then is my reward? Just this: that in my proclamation I may make the gospel free of charge, so as not to make full use of my rights in the gospel.

19 For though I am free with respect to all, I have made myself a slave to all, so that I might win more of them. 20 To the Jews I became as a Jew, in order to win Jews. To those under the law I be-

8.7
1 Cor 10.28;
Rom 14.14
8.8
Rom 14.17
8.9
Gal 5.13;
Rom 14.1,
13,20
8.10
1 Cor 10.28,
32
8.11
Rom 14.15,
20
8.13
Rom 14.21;
2 Cor 11.29
9.1
2 Cor 12.12;
Acts 9.3,17;
18.9; 22.14,
18; 23.11;
1 Cor 3.6;
4.15
9.2
2 Cor 3.2,
3
9.4
1 Thes 2.6;
2 Thes 3.8,
9
9.5
1 Cor 7.7,
8; Mt 12.46;
8.14
9.6
Acts 4.36
9.7
2 Cor 10.4;
1 Tim 1.18;
Deut 20.6;
Prov 27.18
9.9
Deut 25.4;
1 Tim 5.18

9.11
Rom 15.27
9.12
2 Cor 6.3;
11,12
9.13
Lev 6.16;
Deut 18.1
9.14
Mt 10.10;
Lk 10.7
9.15
Acts 18.3;
2 Cor 11.10
9.16
Rom 1.14;
Acts 9.15
9.17
1 Cor 3.8,
14; Gal 2.7;
Phil 1.16,
17; Col 1.25
9.18
2 Cor 11.7;
12.13;
1 Cor 7.31
9.19
Gal 5.13;
Mt 18.15;
1 Pet 3.1

9.20 Acts 16.3; 21.23; Rom 11.14;
Gal 2.19

g The quotation may extend to the end of the verse h Gk the weak brother . . . is destroyed i Gk against the brothers j Gk my brother's falling k Gk cause my brother l Gk a sister as wife

came as one under the law (though I myself am not under the law) so that I might win those under the law. 21 To those outside the law I became as one outside the law (though I am not free from God's law but am under Christ's law) so that I might win those outside the law. 22 To the weak I became weak, so that I might win the weak. I have become all things to all people, that I might by all means save some. 23 I do it all for the sake of the gospel, so that I may share in its blessings.

24 Do you not know that in a race the runners all compete, but only one receives the prize? Run in such a way that you may win it. 25 Athletes exercise self-control in all things; they do it to receive a perishable wreath, but we an imperishable one. 26 So I do not run aimlessly, nor do I box as though beating the air; 27 but I punish my body and enslave it, so that after proclaiming to others I myself should not be disqualified.

Warnings from Israel's History

10 I do not want you to be unaware, brothers and sisters,[m] that our ancestors were all under the cloud, and all passed through the sea, 2 and all were baptized into Moses in the cloud and in the sea, 3 and all ate the same spiritual food, 4 and all drank the same spiritual drink. For they drank from the spiritual rock that followed them, and the rock was Christ. 5 Nevertheless, God was not pleased with most of them, and they were struck down in the wilderness.

6 Now these things occurred as examples for us, so that we might not desire evil as they did. 7 Do not become idolaters as some of them did; as it is written, "The people sat down to eat and drink, and they rose up to play." 8 We must not indulge in sexual immorality as some of them did, and twenty-three thousand fell in a single day. 9 We must not put Christ[n] to the test, as

some of them did, and were destroyed by serpents. 10 And do not complain as some of them did, and were destroyed by the destroyer. 11 These things happened to them to serve as an example, and they were written down to instruct us, on whom the ends of the ages have come. 12 So if you think you are standing, watch out that you do not fall. 13 No testing has overtaken you that is not common to everyone. God is faithful, and he will not let you be tested beyond your strength, but with the testing he will also provide the way out so that you may be able to endure it.

14 Therefore, my dear friends,[o] flee from the worship of idols. 15 I speak as to sensible people; judge for yourselves what I say. 16 The cup of blessing that we bless, is it not a sharing in the blood of Christ? The bread that we break, is it not a sharing in the body of Christ? 17 Because there is one bread, we who are many are one body, for we all partake of the one bread. 18 Consider the people of Israel;[p] are not those who eat the sacrifices partners in the altar? 19 What do I imply then? That food sacrificed to idols is anything, or that an idol is anything? 20 No, I imply that what pagans sacrifice, they sacrifice to demons and not to God. I do not want you to be partners with demons. 21 You cannot drink the cup of the Lord and the cup of demons. You cannot partake of the table of the Lord and the table of demons. 22 Or are we provoking the Lord to jealousy? Are we stronger than he?

Do All to the Glory of God

23 "All things are lawful," but not all things are beneficial. "All things are lawful," but not all things build up. 24 Do not seek your own advantage, but that of the other. 25 Eat whatever is sold in the meat market without raising any question on the ground of con-

9.21
Rom 2.12, 14; Gal 3.2; 1 Cor 7.22
9.24
2 Tim 4.7; Heb 12.1
9.25
Eph 6.12; 1 Tim 6.12
9.27
Rom 8.13; Col 3.5; Rom 6.18
10.1
Ex 13.21; 14.22,29; Rom 1.13
10.3
Ex 16.4,35
10.4
Ex 17.6; Num 20.11
10.5
Num 14.29, 30; Heb 3.17
10.6
Num 11.4, 34; Ps 106.14
10.7
Ex 32.4,6
10.8
Num 25.1ff
10.9
Num 21.5,6
10.10
Num 16.41, 49; Ex 12.23
10.11
Rom 13.11; Phil 4.5
10.12
Rom 11.20
10.13
2 Pet 2.9
10.14
2 Cor 6.17
10.16
Mt 26.26; Acts 2.42
10.17
Rom 12.5; 1 Cor 12.27
10.18
Lev 7.6
10.20
Deut 32.17; Ps 106.37; Rev 9.20
10.21
2 Cor 6.15, 16
10.22
Deut 32.21; Eccl 6.10; Isa 45.9
10.23
1 Cor 6.12; Rom 14.19
10.24
v. 33; Rom 15.1,2; Phil 2.4,21

10.25 1 Cor 8.7

m Gk brothers n Other ancient authorities read the Lord o Gk my beloved
p Gk Israel according to the flesh

science, 26for "the earth and its fullness are the Lord's." 27If an unbeliever invites you to a meal and you are disposed to go, eat whatever is set before you without raising any question on the ground of conscience. 28But if someone says to you, "This has been offered in sacrifice," then do not eat it, out of consideration for the one who informed you, and for the sake of conscience — 29I mean the other's conscience, not your own. For why should my liberty be subject to the judgment of someone else's conscience? 30If I partake with thankfulness, why should I be denounced because of that for which I give thanks?

31 So, whether you eat or drink, or whatever you do, do everything for the glory of God. 32Give no offense to Jews or to Greeks or to the church of God, 33just as I try to please everyone in everything I do, not seeking my own advantage, but that of many, so that they may be saved. 1Be imitators of me, as I am of Christ.

Head Coverings

2 I commend you because you remember me in everything and maintain the traditions just as I handed them on to you. 3But I want you to understand that Christ is the head of every man, and the husband[q] is the head of his wife,[r] and God is the head of Christ. 4Any man who prays or prophesies with something on his head disgraces his head, 5but any woman who prays or prophesies with her head unveiled disgraces her head — it is one and the same thing as having her head shaved. 6For if a woman will not veil herself, then she should cut off her hair; but if it is disgraceful for a woman to have her hair cut off or to be shaved, she should wear a veil. 7For a man ought not to have his head veiled, since he is the image and reflection[s] of God; but woman is the reflection[s] of man. 8Indeed, man was not made from woman, but

woman from man. 9Neither was man created for the sake of woman, but woman for the sake of man. 10For this reason a woman ought to have a symbol of[t] authority on her head,[u] because of the angels. 11Nevertheless, in the Lord woman is not independent of man or man independent of woman. 12For just as woman came from man, so man comes through woman; but all things come from God. 13Judge for yourselves: is it proper for a woman to pray to God with her head unveiled? 14Does not nature itself teach you that if a man wears long hair, it is degrading to him, 15but if a woman has long hair, it is her glory? For her hair is given to her for a covering. 16But if anyone is disposed to be contentious — we have no such custom, nor do the churches of God.

Abuses at the Lord's Supper

17 Now in the following instructions I do not commend you, because when you come together it is not for the better but for the worse. 18For, to begin with, when you come together as a church, I hear that there are divisions among you; and to some extent I believe it. 19Indeed, there have to be factions among you, for only so will it become clear who among you are genuine. 20When you come together, it is not really to eat the Lord's supper. 21For when the time comes to eat, each of you goes ahead with your own supper, and one goes hungry and another becomes drunk. 22What! Do you not have homes to eat and drink in? Or do you show contempt for the church of God and humiliate those who have nothing? What should I say to you? Should I commend you? In this matter I do not commend you!

The Institution of the Lord's Supper

23 For I received from the Lord

10.26
Ps 24.1
10.29
Rom 14.16
10.30
Rom 14.6;
1 Tim 4.3,
4
10.31
Col 3.17;
1 Pet 4.11
10.32
1 Cor 8.13
10.33
Rom 15.2;
1 Cor 9.22;
13.5
11.1
1 Cor 4.16
11.2
1 Cor 4.17;
2 Thes 2.15
11.3
Eph 1.22;
4.15; 5.23;
1 Cor 3.23
11.4
Acts 13.1;
1 Thes 5.20
11.5
Acts 21.9;
Deut 21.12
11.7
Gen 1.26
11.8
Gen 2.21-23

11.9
Gen 2.18
11.10
Gen 24.65
11.12
2 Cor 5.18;
Rom 11.36
11.13
Lk 12.57
11.16
1 Cor 7.17
11.17
vv. 2,22
11.18
1 Cor 1.10-12
11.19
Mt 18.7;
Lk 17.1;
1 Tim 4.1;
Deut 13.5;
1 Jn 2.19
11.21
2 Pet 2.13;
Jude 12
11.22
1 Cor 10.32;
Jas 2.6
11.23
1 Cor 15.3;
Mt 26.26-28;
Mk 14.22-24;
Lk 22.17-20

q The same Greek word means *man* or *husband* r Or *head of the woman* s Or *glory* t Gk lacks *a symbol of* u Or *have freedom of choice regarding her head*

what I also handed on to you, that the Lord Jesus on the night when he was betrayed took a loaf of bread, [24] and when he had given thanks, he broke it and said, "This is my body that is for[v] you. Do this in remembrance of me." [25] In the same way he took the cup also, after supper, saying, "This cup is the new covenant in my blood. Do this, as often as you drink it, in remembrance of me." [26] For as often as you eat this bread and drink the cup, you proclaim the Lord's death until he comes.

Partaking of the Supper Unworthily

27 Whoever, therefore, eats the bread or drinks the cup of the Lord in an unworthy manner will be answerable for the body and blood of the Lord. [28] Examine yourselves, and only then eat of the bread and drink of the cup. [29] For all who eat and drink[w] without discerning the body,[x] eat and drink judgment against themselves. [30] For this reason many of you are weak and ill, and some have died.[y] [31] But if we judged ourselves, we would not be judged. [32] But when we are judged by the Lord, we are disciplined[z] so that we may not be condemned along with the world.

33 So then, my brothers and sisters,[a] when you come together to eat, wait for one another. [34] If you are hungry, eat at home, so that when you come together, it will not be for your condemnation. About the other things I will give instructions when I come.

Spiritual Gifts

12 Now concerning spiritual gifts,[b] brothers and sisters,[a] I do not want you to be uninformed. [2] You know that when you were pagans, you were enticed and led astray to idols that could not speak. [3] Therefore I want you to understand that no one speaking by the Spirit of God ever says "Let Jesus be cursed!" and no one can say "Jesus is Lord" except by the Holy Spirit.

4 Now there are varieties of gifts, but the same Spirit; [5] and there are varieties of services, but the same Lord; [6] and there are varieties of activities, but it is the same God who activates all of them in everyone. [7] To each is given the manifestation of the Spirit for the common good. [8] To one is given through the Spirit the utterance of wisdom, and to another the utterance of knowledge according to the same Spirit, [9] to another faith by the same Spirit, to another gifts of healing by the one Spirit, [10] to another the working of miracles, to another prophecy, to another the discernment of spirits, to another various kinds of tongues, to another the interpretation of tongues. [11] All these are activated by one and the same Spirit, who allots to each one individually just as the Spirit chooses.

One Body with Many Members

12 For just as the body is one and has many members, and all the members of the body, though many, are one body, so it is with Christ. [13] For in the one Spirit we were all baptized into one body — Jews or Greeks, slaves or free — and we were all made to drink of one Spirit.

14 Indeed, the body does not consist of one member but of many. [15] If the foot would say, "Because I am not a hand, I do not belong to the body," that would not make it any less a part of the body. [16] And if the ear would say, "Because I am not an eye, I do not belong to the body," that would not make it any less a part of the body. [17] If the whole body were an eye, where would the hearing be? If the whole body were hearing, where would the sense of smell be? [18] But as it is, God arranged the members in the body, each one of them, as

11.25
2 Cor 3.6;
Lk 22.20
11.26
1 Cor 4.5;
Jn 14.3;
Acts 1.11;
Rev 1.7
11.27
Heb 10.29
11.28
2 Cor 13.5
11.31
Ps 32.5;
1 Jn 1.9
11.32
Ps 94.12;
Heb 12.7-10;
1 Cor 1.20
11.34
vv. 21,22;
1 Cor 4.19
12.1
1 Cor 14.1,
37;
Rom 1.13
12.2
Eph 2.11,
12;
1 Pet 4.3;
1 Thes 1.9;
Ps 115.5
12.3
1 Jn 4.2,3;
Rom 9.3;
10.9

12.4
Rom 12.4-7;
Heb 2.4
12.5
Eph 4.11
12.7
Eph 4.7
12.8
1 Cor 2.6,
7;
Rom 15.4;
2 Cor 8.7
12.9
Mt 17.19,
20;
2 Cor 4.13;
vv. 28,30
12.10
Gal 3.5;
Rom 12.6;
1 Jn 4.1;
Acts 2.4;
1 Cor 13.1
12.11
2 Cor 10.13;
Heb 2.4
12.12
Rom 12.4;
Gal 3.16
12.13
Eph 2.18;
Gal 3.28;
Col 3.11;
Jn 7.37-39
12.18
vv. 28,11

v Other ancient authorities read *is broken for*
w Other ancient authorities add *in an unworthy manner.* x Other ancient authorities read *the Lord's body* y Gk *fallen asleep* z Or *When we are judged, we are being disciplined by the Lord* a Gk *brothers* b Or *spiritual persons*

he chose. ¹⁹If all were a single member, where would the body be? ²⁰As it is, there are many members, yet one body. ²¹The eye cannot say to the hand, "I have no need of you," nor again the head to the feet, "I have no need of you." ²²On the contrary, the members of the body that seem to be weaker are indispensable, ²³and those members of the body that we think less honorable we clothe with greater honor, and our less respectable members are treated with greater respect; ²⁴whereas our more respectable members do not need this. But God has so arranged the body, giving the greater honor to the inferior member, ²⁵that there may be no dissension within the body, but the members may have the same care for one another. ²⁶If one member suffers, all suffer together with it; if one member is honored, all rejoice together with it.

27 Now you are the body of Christ and individually members of it. ²⁸And God has appointed in the church first apostles, second prophets, third teachers; then deeds of power, then gifts of healing, forms of assistance, forms of leadership, various kinds of tongues. ²⁹Are all apostles? Are all prophets? Are all teachers? Do all work miracles? ³⁰Do all possess gifts of healing? Do all speak in tongues? Do all interpret? ³¹But strive for the greater gifts. And I will show you a still more excellent way.

The Gift of Love

13 If I speak in the tongues of mortals and of angels, but do not have love, I am a noisy gong or a clanging cymbal. ²And if I have prophetic powers, and understand all mysteries and all knowledge, and if I have all faith, so as to remove mountains, but do not have love, I am nothing. ³If I give away all my possessions, and if I hand over my body so that I may boast, c but do not have love, I gain nothing.

4 Love is patient; love is kind; love is not envious or boastful or arrogant ⁵or rude. It does not insist on its own way; it is not irritable or resentful; ⁶it does not rejoice in wrongdoing, but rejoices in the truth. ⁷It bears all things, believes all things, hopes all things, endures all things.

8 Love never ends. But as for prophecies, they will come to an end; as for tongues, they will cease; as for knowledge, it will come to an end. ⁹For we know only in part, and we prophesy only in part; ¹⁰but when the complete comes, the partial will come to an end. ¹¹When I was a child, I spoke like a child, I thought like a child, I reasoned like a child; when I became an adult, I put an end to childish ways. ¹²For now we see in a mirror, dimly, d but then we will see face to face. Now I know only in part; then I will know fully, even as I have been fully known. ¹³And now faith, hope, and love abide, these three; and the greatest of these is love.

Gifts of Prophecy and Tongues

14 Pursue love and strive for the spiritual gifts, and especially that you may prophesy. ²For those who speak in a tongue do not speak to other people but to God; for nobody understands them, since they are speaking mysteries in the Spirit. ³On the other hand, those who prophesy speak to other people for their upbuilding and encouragement and consolation. ⁴Those who speak in a tongue build up themselves, but those who prophesy build up the church. ⁵Now I would like all of you to speak in tongues, but even more to prophesy. One who prophesies is greater than one who speaks in tongues, unless someone interprets, so that the church may be built up.

6 Now, brothers and sisters, e if I come to you speaking in tongues, how will I benefit you unless I speak to you in some revelation or

c Other ancient authorities read *body to be burned*　d Gk *in a riddle*　e Gk *brothers*

Cross references

12.20 v. 14
12.27 Eph 1.23; 4.12; Col 1.18,24; Eph 5.30; Rom 12.5
12.28 Eph 4.11; 2.30; 3.5; Rom 12.6,8; vv. 9,10
12.30 v. 10
12.31 1 Cor 14.1, 39
13.2 Acts 13.1; 1 Cor 14.1; Mt 7.22; 1 Cor 12.9; Mt 17.20; 21.21
13.3 Mt 6.2
13.4 Prov 10.12; 1 Pet 4.8
13.5 1 Cor 10.24; 2 Cor 5.19
13.6 2 Jn 4
13.7 Rom 15.1; 1 Cor 9.12
13.8 vv. 1,2
13.9 1 Cor 8.2
13.12 2 Cor 5.7; Phil 3.12; 1 Jn 3.2; 1 Cor 8.3
13.13 1 Cor 16.14
14.1 1 Cor 16.14; 12.31; 12.1; 13.2
14.2 Acts 10.46; 1 Cor 12.10, 28,30; 13.1
14.3 vv. 5,12,17, 26; Acts 4.36
14.5 Num 11.29
14.6 v. 26; 1 Cor 12.8; Rom 6.17

knowledge or prophecy or teaching? [7] It is the same way with lifeless instruments that produce sound, such as the flute or the harp. If they do not give distinct notes, how will anyone know what is being played? [8] And if the bugle gives an indistinct sound, who will get ready for battle? [9] So with yourselves; if in a tongue you utter speech that is not intelligible, how will anyone know what is being said? For you will be speaking into the air. [10] There are doubtless many different kinds of sounds in the world, and nothing is without sound. [11] If then I do not know the meaning of a sound, I will be a foreigner to the speaker and the speaker a foreigner to me. [12] So with yourselves; since you are eager for spiritual gifts, strive to excel in them for building up the church.

13 Therefore, one who speaks in a tongue should pray for the power to interpret. [14] For if I pray in a tongue, my spirit prays but my mind is unproductive. [15] What should I do then? I will pray with the spirit, but I will pray with the mind also; I will sing praise with the spirit, but I will sing praise with the mind also. [16] Otherwise, if you say a blessing with the spirit, how can anyone in the position of an outsider say the "Amen" to your thanksgiving, since the outsider does not know what you are saying? [17] For you may give thanks well enough, but the other person is not built up. [18] I thank God that I speak in tongues more than all of you; [19] nevertheless, in church I would rather speak five words with my mind, in order to instruct others also, than ten thousand words in a tongue.

20 Brothers and sisters, [f] do not be children in your thinking; rather, be infants in evil, but in thinking be adults. [21] In the law it is written,

"By people of strange
 tongues
 and by the lips of
 foreigners
I will speak to this people;

yet even then they will not
 listen to me,"

says the Lord. [22] Tongues, then, are a sign not for believers but for unbelievers, while prophecy is not for unbelievers but for believers. [23] If, therefore, the whole church comes together and all speak in tongues, and outsiders or unbelievers enter, will they not say that you are out of your mind? [24] But if all prophesy, an unbeliever or outsider who enters is reproved by all and called to account by all. [25] After the secrets of the unbeliever's heart are disclosed, that person will bow down before God and worship him, declaring, "God is really among you."

Orderly Worship

26 What should be done then, my friends? [f] When you come together, each one has a hymn, a lesson, a revelation, a tongue, or an interpretation. Let all things be done for building up. [27] If anyone speaks in a tongue, let there be only two or at most three, and each in turn; and let one interpret. [28] But if there is no one to interpret, let them be silent in church and speak to themselves and to God. [29] Let two or three prophets speak, and let the others weigh what is said. [30] If a revelation is made to someone else sitting nearby, let the first person be silent. [31] For you can all prophesy one by one, so that all may learn and all be encouraged. [32] And the spirits of prophets are subject to the prophets, [33] for God is a God not of disorder but of peace.

(As in all the churches of the saints, [34] women should be silent in the churches. For they are not permitted to speak, but should be subordinate, as the law also says. [35] If there is anything they desire to know, let them ask their husbands at home. For it is shameful for a woman to speak in church. [g] [36] Or did the word of God originate with you? Or are you the only ones it has reached?)

14.8
Num 10.9
14.9
1 Cor 9.26
14.11
Acts 28.2
14.12
vv. 4,5,17,
26
14.15
Eph 5.19;
Col 3.16
14.16
1 Chr 16.36;
Ps 106.48;
Mt 15.36;
1 Cor 11.24
14.17
Rom 14.19
14.20
Eph 4.14;
Heb 5.12,
13;
Ps 131.2;
Rom 16.19;
1 Pet 2.2
14.21
Jn 10.34;
Isa 28.11,12

14.22
v. 1
14.23
Acts 2.13
14.25
Jn 4.19;
Lk 17.16;
Isa 45.14;
Zech 8.23
14.26
1 Cor 12.7-10;
2 Cor 12.19;
Eph 4.12
14.29
1 Cor 12.10
14.32
1 Jn 4.1
14.33
v. 40;
1 Cor 4.17;
11.16
14.34
1 Tim 2.11,
12;
1 Pet 3.1;
Gen 3.16

[f] Gk *brothers* [g] Other ancient authorities put verses 34-35 after verse 40

37 Anyone who claims to be a prophet, or to have spiritual powers, must acknowledge that what I am writing to you is a command of the Lord. 38 Anyone who does not recognize this is not to be recognized. 39 So, my friends, h be eager to prophesy, and do not forbid speaking in tongues; 40 but all things should be done decently and in order.

The Resurrection of Christ

15 Now I would remind you, brothers and sisters, i of the good news j that I proclaimed to you, which you in turn received, in which also you stand, 2 through which also you are being saved, if you hold firmly to the message that I proclaimed to you—unless you have come to believe in vain.

3 For I handed on to you as of first importance what I in turn had received: that Christ died for our sins in accordance with the scriptures, 4 and that he was buried, and that he was raised on the third day in accordance with the scriptures, 5 and that he appeared to Cephas, then to the twelve. 6 Then he appeared to more than five hundred brothers and sisters i at one time, most of whom are still alive, though some have died. k 7 Then he appeared to James, then to all the apostles. 8 Last of all, as to one untimely born, he appeared also to me. 9 For I am the least of the apostles, unfit to be called an apostle, because I persecuted the church of God. 10 But by the grace of God I am what I am, and his grace toward me has not been in vain. On the contrary, I worked harder than any of them—though it was not I, but the grace of God that is with me. 11 Whether then it was I or they, so we proclaim and so you have come to believe.

The Resurrection of the Dead

12 Now if Christ is proclaimed as raised from the dead, how can some of you say there is no resurrection of the dead? 13 If there is no resurrection of the dead, then

Christ has not been raised; 14 and if Christ has not been raised, then our proclamation has been in vain and your faith has been in vain. 15 We are even found to be misrepresenting God, because we testified of God that he raised Christ—whom he did not raise if it is true that the dead are not raised. 16 For if the dead are not raised, then Christ has not been raised. 17 If Christ has not been raised, your faith is futile and you are still in your sins. 18 Then those also who have died k in Christ have perished. 19 If for this life only we have hoped in Christ, we are of all people most to be pitied.

20 But in fact Christ has been raised from the dead, the first fruits of those who have died. k 21 For since death came through a human being, the resurrection of the dead has also come through a human being; 22 for as all die in Adam, so all will be made alive in Christ. 23 But each in his own order: Christ the first fruits, then at his coming those who belong to Christ. 24 Then comes the end, l when he hands over the kingdom to God the Father, after he has destroyed every ruler and every authority and power. 25 For he must reign until he has put all his enemies under his feet. 26 The last enemy to be destroyed is death. 27 For "God m has put all things in subjection under his feet." But when it says, "All things are put in subjection," it is plain that this does not include the one who put all things in subjection under him. 28 When all things are subjected to him, then the Son himself will also be subjected to the one who put all things in subjection under him, so that God may be all in all.

29 Otherwise, what will those people do who receive baptism on behalf of the dead? If the dead are

14.37
2 Cor 10.7;
1 Jn 4.6
14.39
1 Cor 12.31
14.40
v. 33
15.1
Gal 1.11;
Rom 2.16;
5.2
15.2
Rom 1.16;
11.22;
Gal 3.4
15.3
1 Cor 11.23;
1 Pet 2.24;
Isa 53.5-12;
Lk 24.25-27;
Acts 26.22,
23
15.4
Mt 16.21;
Ps 16.8-10;
Acts 2.24,25
15.5
Lk 24.34;
1 Cor 1.12;
Mt 28.17
15.7
Lk 24.33,36,
37; Acts 1.3,
4
15.8
Acts 9.3-8;
1 Cor 9.1;
Gal 1.16
15.9
Eph 3.8;
1 Tim 1.15;
Acts 8.3
15.10
Eph 3.7,8;
2 Cor 11.23;
3.5; Gal 2.8;
Phil 2.13
15.12
Acts 17.32;
23.8;
2 Tim 2.18

15.14
1 Thes 4.14
15.15
Acts 2.24
15.17
Rom 4.25
15.18
1 Thes 4.16
15.19
2 Tim 3.12
15.20
1 Pet 1.3;
v. 23;
Acts 26.23;
Rev 1.5
15.21
Rom 5.12
15.24
Dan 7.14,27
15.25
Ps 110.1
15.26
2 Tim 1.10;
Rev 20.14

15.27 Ps 8.6; Mt 28.18; Heb 2.8 **15.28**
Phil 3.21; 1 Cor 3.23

h Gk my brothers i Gk brothers
j Or gospel k Gk fallen asleep
l Or Then come the rest m Gk he

not raised at all, why are people baptized on their behalf?

30 And why are we putting ourselves in danger every hour? ³¹I die every day! That is as certain, brothers and sisters,ⁿ as my boasting of you—a boast that I make in Christ Jesus our Lord. ³²If with merely human hopes I fought with wild animals at Ephesus, what would I have gained by it? If the dead are not raised,

"Let us eat and drink,
 for tomorrow we die."

³³Do not be deceived:

"Bad company ruins good
 morals."

³⁴Come to a sober and right mind, and sin no more; for some people have no knowledge of God. I say this to your shame.

The Resurrection Body

35 But someone will ask, "How are the dead raised? With what kind of body do they come?" ³⁶Fool! What you sow does not come to life unless it dies. ³⁷And as for what you sow, you do not sow the body that is to be, but a bare seed, perhaps of wheat or of some other grain. ³⁸But God gives it a body as he has chosen, and to each kind of seed its own body. ³⁹Not all flesh is alike, but there is one flesh for human beings, another for animals, another for birds, and another for fish. ⁴⁰There are both heavenly bodies and earthly bodies, but the glory of the heavenly is one thing, and that of the earthly is another. ⁴¹There is one glory of the sun, and another glory of the moon, and another glory of the stars; indeed, star differs from star in glory.

42 So it is with the resurrection of the dead. What is sown is perishable, what is raised is imperishable. ⁴³It is sown in dishonor, it is raised in glory. It is sown in weakness, it is raised in power. ⁴⁴It is sown a physical body, it is raised a spiritual body. If there is a physical body, there is also a spiritual body. ⁴⁵Thus it is written, "The first man, Adam, became a living being"; the

last Adam became a life-giving spirit. ⁴⁶But it is not the spiritual that is first, but the physical, and then the spiritual. ⁴⁷The first man was from the earth, a man of dust; the second man isᵒ from heaven. ⁴⁸As was the man of dust, so are those who are of the dust; and as is the man of heaven, so are those who are of heaven. ⁴⁹Just as we have borne the image of the man of dust, we willᵖ also bear the image of the man of heaven.

50 What I am saying, brothers and sisters,ⁿ is this: flesh and blood cannot inherit the kingdom of God, nor does the perishable inherit the imperishable. ⁵¹Listen, I will tell you a mystery! We will not all die,ᑫ but we will all be changed, ⁵²in a moment, in the twinkling of an eye, at the last trumpet. For the trumpet will sound, and the dead will be raised imperishable, and we will be changed. ⁵³For this perishable body must put on imperishability, and this mortal body must put on immortality. ⁵⁴When this perishable body puts on imperishability, and this mortal body puts on immortality, then the saying that is written will be fulfilled:

"Death has been swallowed
 up in victory."

⁵⁵ "Where, O death, is your
 victory?
 Where, O death, is your
 sting?"

⁵⁶The sting of death is sin, and the power of sin is the law. ⁵⁷But thanks be to God, who gives us the victory through our Lord Jesus Christ.

58 Therefore, my beloved,ʳ be steadfast, immovable, always excelling in the work of the Lord, because you know that in the Lord your labor is not in vain.

The Collection for the Saints

16 Now concerning the collection for the saints: you should follow the directions I gave

15.30
2 Cor 11.26
15.31
Rom 8.36;
2 Cor 4.10;
11.23
15.32
2 Cor 1.8;
Lk 12.19
15.34
1 Thes 4.5;
1 Cor 6.5
15.35
Rom 9.19;
Ezek 37.3
15.36
Jn 12.24
15.38
Gen 1.11
15.42
Dan 12.3;
Mt 13.43
15.43
Phil 3.21
15.45
Gen 2.7;
Rom 5.14;
8.2

15.47
Jn 3.31;
Gen 2.7;
3.19
15.49
Gen 5.3;
Rom 8.29;
1 Jn 3.2
15.50
Mt 16.17;
Jn 3.3,5
15.51
1 Thes 4.15-
17; Phil 3.21
15.52
Mt 24.31;
Jn 5.25;
1 Thes 4.16
15.53
2 Cor 5.4
15.54
Isa 25.8;
Heb 2.14;
Rev 20.14
15.55
Hos 13.14
15.56
Rom 5.12;
4.15; 5.13
2 Pet 3.14;
1 Cor 16.10
16.1
Acts 24.17;
9.13; 16.6

ⁿ Gk *brothers* ᵒ Other ancient authorities
add *the Lord* ᵖ Other ancient authorities
read *let us* ᑫ Gk *fall asleep*
ʳ Gk *beloved brothers*

to the churches of Galatia. ² On the first day of every week, each of you is to put aside and save whatever extra you earn, so that collections need not be taken when I come. ³ And when I arrive, I will send any whom you approve with letters to take your gift to Jerusalem. ⁴ If it seems advisable that I should go also, they will accompany me.

Plans for Travel

5 I will visit you after passing through Macedonia — for I intend to pass through Macedonia — ⁶ and perhaps I will stay with you or even spend the winter, so that you may send me on my way, wherever I go. ⁷ I do not want to see you now just in passing, for I hope to spend some time with you, if the Lord permits. ⁸ But I will stay in Ephesus until Pentecost, ⁹ for a wide door for effective work has opened to me, and there are many adversaries.

10 If Timothy comes, see that he has nothing to fear among you, for he is doing the work of the Lord just as I am; ¹¹ therefore let no one despise him. Send him on his way in peace, so that he may come to me; for I am expecting him with the brothers.

12 Now concerning our brother Apollos, I strongly urged him to visit you with the other brothers, but he was not at all willingˢ to come now. He will come when he has the opportunity.

16.2
Acts 20.7;
2 Cor 9.4,
5
16.3
2 Cor 8.18,
19
16.5
Acts 19.21
16.6
Acts 15.3
16.7
Acts 18.21
16.10
Acts 16.1;
19.22;
1 Cor 15.58
16.11
1 Tim 4.12;
Acts 15.33
16.12
Acts 18.24;
1 Cor 1.12;
3.5,6

16.13
Phil 1.27;
2 Thes 2.15;
Eph 6.10
16.14
1 Cor 14.1
16.15
Rom 16.5;
2 Cor 8.4;
Heb 6.10
16.16
Heb 13.1
16.17
2 Cor 7.6,
7; 11.9
16.18
2 Cor 7.13;
Phil 2.29
16.19
Acts 16.6;
Rom 16.5
16.22
Eph 6.24;
Rom 9.3
16.23
Rom 16.20

Final Messages and Greetings

13 Keep alert, stand firm in your faith, be courageous, be strong. ¹⁴ Let all that you do be done in love.

15 Now, brothers and sisters,ᵗ you know that members of the household of Stephanas were the first converts in Achaia, and they have devoted themselves to the service of the saints; ¹⁶ I urge you to put yourselves at the service of such people, and of everyone who works and toils with them. ¹⁷ I rejoice at the coming of Stephanas and Fortunatus and Achaicus, because they have made up for your absence; ¹⁸ for they refreshed my spirit as well as yours. So give recognition to such persons.

19 The churches of Asia send greetings. Aquila and Prisca, together with the church in their house, greet you warmly in the Lord. ²⁰ All the brothers and sistersᵗ send greetings. Greet one another with a holy kiss.

21 I, Paul, write this greeting with my own hand. ²² Let anyone be accursed who has no love for the Lord. Our Lord, come!ᵘ ²³ The grace of the Lord Jesus be with you. ²⁴ My love be with all of you in Christ Jesus.ᵛ

ˢ Or *it was not at all God's will for him* ᵗ Gk *brothers* ᵘ Gk *Marana tha*. These Aramaic words can also be read *Maran atha*, meaning *Our Lord has come* ᵛ Other ancient authorities add *Amen*

THE SECOND LETTER OF PAUL TO THE
Corinthians

Title and Background

This letter was probably written from Macedonia a few months after the first letter. The divisions and problems spoken of in 1 Corinthians were still present in the church at Corinth. False teachers were challenging both Paul's personal integrity and his authority as an apostle. They insisted that he was not a genuine apostle and that he was putting into his own pocket the money they had collected for the poverty-stricken believers in Jerusalem.

Author and Date of Writing

The apostle Paul wrote this letter. It is stamped with his style and contains more autobiographical material than any of his other writings. The available evidence indicates that 2 Corinthians was written in the fall of A.D. 55.

Theme and Message

Paul shows his feelings in this letter more than in any other, going from despair to ecstatic joy. It falls naturally into three sections: (1) Paul explains the reasons for the change of his itinerary (chs. 1-7); (2) he encourages the Corinthians to complete the collection in preparation for his arrival (chs. 8-9); (3) he stresses the certainty of his coming, his authenticity as an apostle, and his readiness as an apostle to excercise discipline if necessary (chs. 10-13).

Outline

Salutation

1 Paul, an apostle of Christ Jesus by the will of God, and Timothy our brother,

To the church of God that is in Corinth, including all the saints throughout Achaia:

2 Grace to you and peace from God our Father and the Lord Jesus Christ.

Paul's Thanksgiving after Affliction

3 Blessed be the God and Father of our Lord Jesus Christ, the Father of mercies and the God of all consolation, ⁴who consoles us in all our affliction, so that we may be able to console those who are in any affliction with the consolation with which we ourselves are consoled by God. ⁵For just as the sufferings of Christ are abundant for us, so also our consolation is abundant through Christ. ⁶If we are being afflicted, it is for your consolation and salvation; if we are being consoled, it is for your consolation, which you experience when you patiently endure the same sufferings that we are also suffering. ⁷Our hope for you is unshaken; for we know that as you share in our sufferings, so also you share in our consolation.

8 We do not want you to be unaware, brothers and sisters,ᵃ of the affliction we experienced in Asia; for we were so utterly, unbearably

1.1
Col 1.1;
1 Tim 1.1;
1 Cor 1.1
1.2
Rom 1.7;
1 Cor 1.3;
Gal 1.3
1.3
Eph 1.3;
1 Pet 1.3;
Rom 15.5
1.4
2 Cor 7.6,
7,13
1.5
2 Cor 4.10;
Col 1.24
1.6
2 Cor 4.15
1.7
2 Tim 2.12
1.8
Acts 19.23;
1 Cor 15.32

ᵃ Gk *brothers*

crushed that we despaired of life itself. [9]Indeed, we felt that we had received the sentence of death so that we would rely not on ourselves but on God who raises the dead. [10]He who rescued us from so deadly a peril will continue to rescue us; on him we have set our hope that he will rescue us again, [11]as you also join in helping us by your prayers, so that many will give thanks on our[b] behalf for the blessing granted us through the prayers of many.

The Postponement of Paul's Visit

12 Indeed, this is our boast, the testimony of our conscience: we have behaved in the world with frankness[c] and godly sincerity, not by earthly wisdom but by the grace of God—and all the more toward you. [13]For we write you nothing other than what you can read and also understand; I hope you will understand until the end— [14]as you have already understood us in part—that on the day of the Lord Jesus we are your boast even as you are our boast.

15 Since I was sure of this, I wanted to come to you first, so that you might have a double favor;[d] [16]I wanted to visit you on my way to Macedonia, and to come back to you from Macedonia and have you send me on to Judea. [17]Was I vacillating when I wanted to do this? Do I make my plans according to ordinary human standards,[e] ready to say "Yes, yes" and "No, no" at the same time? [18]As surely as God is faithful, our word to you has not been "Yes and No." [19]For the Son of God, Jesus Christ, whom we proclaimed among you, Silvanus and Timothy and I, was not "Yes and No"; but in him it is always "Yes." [20]For in him every one of God's promises is a "Yes." For this reason it is through him that we say the "Amen," to the glory of God. [21]But it is God who establishes us with you in Christ and has anointed us, [22]by putting his seal on us and giv-

ing us his Spirit in our hearts as a first installment.

23 But I call on God as witness against me: it was to spare you that I did not come again to Corinth. [24]I do not mean to imply that we lord it over your faith; rather, we are workers with you for your joy, because you stand firm in the faith. 2 [1]So I made up my mind not to make you another painful visit. [2]For if I cause you pain, who is there to make me glad but the one whom I have pained? [3]And I wrote as I did, so that when I came, I might not suffer pain from those who should have made me rejoice; for I am confident about all of you, that my joy would be the joy of all of you. [4]For I wrote you out of much distress and anguish of heart and with many tears, not to cause you pain, but to let you know the abundant love that I have for you.

Forgiveness for the Offender

5 But if anyone has caused pain, he has caused it not to me, but to some extent—not to exaggerate it—to all of you. [6]This punishment by the majority is enough for such a person; [7]so now instead you should forgive and console him, so that he may not be overwhelmed by excessive sorrow. [8]So I urge you to reaffirm your love for him. [9]I wrote for this reason: to test you and to know whether you are obedient in everything. [10]Anyone whom you forgive, I also forgive. What I have forgiven, if I have forgiven anything, has been for your sake in the presence of Christ. [11]And we do this so that we may not be outwitted by Satan; for we are not ignorant of his designs.

Paul's Anxiety in Troas

12 When I came to Troas to proclaim the good news of Christ, a door was opened for me in the

Cross references (center column)

1.9
Jer 17.5,7
1.10
2 Pet 2.9
1.11
Rom 15.30;
Phil 1.19;
2 Cor 4.15
1.12
2 Cor 2.17;
1 Cor 2.4,
13
1.14
1 Cor 1.8
1.15
1 Cor 4.19;
Rom 1.11;
15.29
1.16
1 Cor 16.5-7
1.17
2 Cor 10.2,
3
1.18
1 Cor 1.9;
2 Cor 2.17
1.19
Mt 16.16;
1 Thes 1.1;
Heb 13.8
1.20
Rom 15.8,9;
1 Cor 14.16
1.21
1 Cor 1.8;
1 Jn 2.20,
27
1.22
Eph 1.13
1.23
Gal 1.20;
1 Cor 4.21;
2 Cor 2.3
1.24
1 Pet 5.3;
Rom 11.20;
1 Cor 15.1
2.1
2 Cor 1.23
2.2
2 Cor 7.8
2.3
2 Cor 12.21;
7.16; 8.22
2.4
2 Cor 7.8,
9,12
2.5
1 Cor 5.1,
2
2.6
1 Cor 5.4,
5
2.7
Gal 6.1;
Eph 4.32
2.9
Phil 2.22;
2 Cor 7.15;
10.6
2.11
Mt 4.10;
Lk 22.31;
2 Cor 4.4;
1 Pet 5.8

2.12 Acts 16.8; 1 Cor 16.9

b Other ancient authorities read *your*
c Other ancient authorities read *holiness*
d Other ancient authorities read *pleasure*
e Gk *according to the flesh*

Lord; [13] but my mind could not rest because I did not find my brother Titus there. So I said farewell to them and went on to Macedonia.

14 But thanks be to God, who in Christ always leads us in triumphal procession, and through us spreads in every place the fragrance that comes from knowing him. [15] For we are the aroma of Christ to God among those who are being saved and among those who are perishing; [16] to the one a fragrance from death to death, to the other a fragrance from life to life. Who is sufficient for these things? [17] For we are not peddlers of God's word like so many;[f] but in Christ we speak as persons of sincerity, as persons sent from God and standing in his presence.

Ministers of the New Covenant

3 Are we beginning to commend ourselves again? Surely we do not need, as some do, letters of recommendation to you or from you, do we? [2] You yourselves are our letter, written on our[g] hearts, to be known and read by all; [3] and you show that you are a letter of Christ, prepared by us, written not with ink but with the Spirit of the living God, not on tablets of stone but on tablets of human hearts.

4 Such is the confidence that we have through Christ toward God. [5] Not that we are competent of ourselves to claim anything as coming from us; our competence is from God, [6] who has made us competent to be ministers of a new covenant, not of letter but of spirit; for the letter kills, but the Spirit gives life.

7 Now if the ministry of death, chiseled in letters on stone tablets,[h] came in glory so that the people of Israel could not gaze at Moses' face because of the glory of his face, a glory now set aside, [8] how much more will the ministry of the Spirit come in glory? [9] For if there was glory in the ministry of condemnation, much more does the ministry of justification abound in glory! [10] Indeed, what once had glory has lost its glory be-

cause of the greater glory; [11] for if what was set aside came through glory, much more has the permanent come in glory!

12 Since, then, we have such a hope, we act with great boldness, [13] not like Moses, who put a veil over his face to keep the people of Israel from gazing at the end of the glory that[i] was being set aside. [14] But their minds were hardened. Indeed, to this very day, when they hear the reading of the old covenant, that same veil is still there, since only in Christ is it set aside. [15] Indeed, to this very day whenever Moses is read, a veil lies over their minds; [16] but when one turns to the Lord, the veil is removed. [17] Now the Lord is the Spirit, and where the Spirit of the Lord is, there is freedom. [18] And all of us, with unveiled faces, seeing the glory of the Lord as though reflected in a mirror, are being transformed into the same image from one degree of glory to another; for this comes from the Lord, the Spirit.

Treasure in Clay Jars

4 Therefore, since it is by God's mercy that we are engaged in this ministry, we do not lose heart. [2] We have renounced the shameful things that one hides; we refuse to practice cunning or to falsify God's word; but by the open statement of the truth we commend ourselves to the conscience of everyone in the sight of God. [3] And even if our gospel is veiled, it is veiled to those who are perishing. [4] In their case the god of this world has blinded the minds of the unbelievers, to keep them from seeing the light of the gospel of the glory of Christ, who is the image of God. [5] For we do not proclaim ourselves; we proclaim Jesus Christ as Lord and ourselves as your slaves for Jesus' sake. [6] For it is the God who said, "Let light shine out of darkness,"

2.13 2 Cor 7.5, 6; Mk 6.46; Rom 15.26
2.14 Rom 6.17; Eph 5.2; Phil 4.18; 1 Cor 12.8
2.15 Eph 5.2; Phil 4.18; 2 Cor 4.3
2.16 Jn 9.39; 1 Pet 2.7
2.17 2 Cor 4.2; 1.12; 12.19
3.1 2 Cor 5.12; 12.11; Acts 18.27
3.2 1 Cor 9.2
3.3 Jer 31.33; Ezek 11.19
3.4 Eph 3.12
3.5 2 Cor 2.16; 1 Cor 15.10
3.6 Heb 8.6,8; Gal 3.10; Jn 6.63
3.7 Ex 34.29-35
3.9 v. 7; Rom 1.17; 3.21
3.12 2 Cor 7.4; Eph 6.19
3.13 v. 7; Ex 34.33
3.14 Rom 11.7; Acts 13.15; v. 6
3.16 Rom 11.23
3.17 1 Cor 15.45; Isa 61.1,2; Jn 8.32
3.18 1 Cor 13.12; 2 Cor 4.4, 6; Rom 8.29
4.1 2 Cor 3.6; 1 Cor 7.25
4.2 2 Cor 2.17
4.3 2 Cor 2.12; 3.14; 1 Cor 1.18
4.4 Jn 12.31; Col 1.15; Jn 1.18

4.5 1 Cor 1.13,23; 9.19 **4.6** Gen 1.3; 2 Pet 1.19

f Other ancient authorities read *like the others*
g Other ancient authorities read *your*
h Gk *on stones* i Gk *of what*

who has shone in our hearts to give the light of the knowledge of the glory of God in the face of Jesus Christ.

7 But we have this treasure in clay jars, so that it may be made clear that this extraordinary power belongs to God and does not come from us. ⁸We are afflicted in every way, but not crushed; perplexed, but not driven to despair; ⁹persecuted, but not forsaken; struck down, but not destroyed; ¹⁰always carrying in the body the death of Jesus, so that the life of Jesus may also be made visible in our bodies. ¹¹For while we live, we are always being given up to death for Jesus' sake, so that the life of Jesus may be made visible in our mortal flesh. ¹²So death is at work in us, but life in you.

13 But just as we have the same spirit of faith that is in accordance with scripture—"I believed, and so I spoke"—we also believe, and so we speak, ¹⁴because we know that the one who raised the Lord Jesus will raise us also with Jesus, and will bring us with you into his presence. ¹⁵Yes, everything is for your sake, so that grace, as it extends to more and more people, may increase thanksgiving, to the glory of God.

Living by Faith

16 So we do not lose heart. Even though our outer nature is wasting away, our inner nature is being renewed day by day. ¹⁷For this slight momentary affliction is preparing us for an eternal weight of glory beyond all measure, ¹⁸because we look not at what can be seen but at what cannot be seen; for what can be seen is temporary, but what cannot be seen is eternal.

5 For we know that if the earthly tent we live in is destroyed, we have a building from God, a house not made with hands, eternal in the heavens. ²For in this tent we groan, longing to be clothed with our heavenly dwelling— ³if indeed, when we have taken it offⁱ we will not be found naked. ⁴For

4.7
2 Cor 5.1;
1 Cor 2.5
4.8
2 Cor 7.5;
6.12
4.9
Jn 15.20;
Heb 13.5;
Ps 37.24
4.10
Gal 6.17;
Rom 8.17
4.11
Rom 8.36
4.12
2 Cor 13.9
4.13
Ps 116.10
4.14
1 Thes 4.14
4.16
Rom 7.22;
Col 3.10
4.17
Rom 8.18;
1 Pet 1.6
4.18
Rom 8.24;
Heb 11.1
5.1
2 Pet 1.13,
14
5.2
Rom 8.23;
v. 4
5.4
1 Cor 15.53,
54
5.5
Rom 8.23;
2 Cor 1.22
5.6
Heb 11.13,
14
5.7
1 Cor 13.12
5.8
Phil 1.23
5.10
Rom 14.10;
Eph 6.8
5.11
Heb 10.31;
Jude 23;
2 Cor 4.2
5.12
2 Cor 3.1;
1.14
5.13
2 Cor 11.1,
16,17
5.14
Acts 18.5;
Rom 5.15;
Gal 2.20
5.15
Rom 14.7-9
5.16
2 Cor 11.18;
Phil 3.4;
Jn 8.15
5.17
Rom 16.7;
Gal 5.6;
Rev 21.4,5

while we are still in this tent, we groan under our burden, because we wish not to be unclothed but to be further clothed, so that what is mortal may be swallowed up by life. ⁵He who has prepared us for this very thing is God, who has given us the Spirit as a guarantee.

6 So we are always confident; even though we know that while we are at home in the body we are away from the Lord— ⁷for we walk by faith, not by sight. ⁸Yes, we do have confidence, and we would rather be away from the body and at home with the Lord. ⁹So whether we are at home or away, we make it our aim to please him. ¹⁰For all of us must appear before the judgment seat of Christ, so that each may receive recompense for what has been done in the body, whether good or evil.

The Ministry of Reconciliation

11 Therefore, knowing the fear of the Lord, we try to persuade others; but we ourselves are well known to God, and I hope that we are also well known to your consciences. ¹²We are not commending ourselves to you again, but giving you an opportunity to boast about us, so that you may be able to answer those who boast in outward appearance and not in the heart. ¹³For if we are beside ourselves, it is for God; if we are in our right mind, it is for you. ¹⁴For the love of Christ urges us on, because we are convinced that one has died for all; therefore all have died. ¹⁵And he died for all, so that those who live might live no longer for themselves, but for him who died and was raised for them.

16 From now on, therefore, we regard no one from a human point of view;ᵏ even though we once knew Christ from a human point of view,ᵏ we know him no longer in that way. ¹⁷So if anyone is in Christ, there is a new creation: everything old has passed away; see,

ⁱOther ancient authorities read *put it on*
ᵏGk *according to the flesh*

everything has become new! [18]All this is from God, who reconciled us to himself through Christ, and has given us the ministry of reconciliation; [19]that is, in Christ God was reconciling the world to himself,[1] not counting their trespasses against them, and entrusting the message of reconciliation to us. [20]So we are ambassadors for Christ, since God is making his appeal through us; we entreat you on behalf of Christ, be reconciled to God. [21]For our sake he made him to be sin who knew no sin, so that in him we might become the righteousness of God.

6 As we work together with him,[m] we urge you also not to accept the grace of God in vain. [2]For he says,

"At an acceptable time I
　　have listened to you,
and on a day of salvation I
　　have helped you."

See, now is the acceptable time; see, now is the day of salvation! [3]We are putting no obstacle in anyone's way, so that no fault may be found with our ministry, [4]but as servants of God we have commended ourselves in every way: through great endurance, in afflictions, hardships, calamities, [5]beatings, imprisonments, riots, labors, sleepless nights, hunger; [6]by purity, knowledge, patience, kindness, holiness of spirit, genuine love, [7]truthful speech, and the power of God; with the weapons of righteousness for the right hand and for the left; [8]in honor and dishonor, in ill repute and good repute. We are treated as impostors, and yet are true; [9]as unknown, and yet are well known; as dying, and see—we are alive; as punished, and yet not killed; [10]as sorrowful, yet always rejoicing; as poor, yet making many rich; as having nothing, and yet possessing everything.

11 We have spoken frankly to you Corinthians; our heart is wide open to you. [12]There is no restriction in our affections, but only in yours. [13]In return—I speak as to

children—open wide your hearts also.

The Temple of the Living God

14 Do not be mismatched with unbelievers. For what partnership is there between righteousness and lawlessness? Or what fellowship is there between light and darkness? [15]What agreement does Christ have with Beliar? Or what does a believer share with an unbeliever? [16]What agreement has the temple of God with idols? For we[n] are the temple of the living God; as God said,

"I will live in them and walk
　　among them,
and I will be their God,
　　and they shall be my
　　　　people.
[17] Therefore come out from
　　them,
　　and be separate from them,
　　　　says the Lord,
and touch nothing unclean;
　　then I will welcome you,
[18] and I will be your father,
　　and you shall be my sons
　　　　and daughters,
　　says the Lord Almighty."

7 Since we have these promises, beloved, let us cleanse ourselves from every defilement of body and of spirit, making holiness perfect in the fear of God.

Paul's Joy at the Church's Repentance

2 Make room in your hearts[o] for us; we have wronged no one, we have corrupted no one, we have taken advantage of no one. [3]I do not say this to condemn you, for I said before that you are in our hearts, to die together and to live together. [4]I often boast about you; I have great pride in you; I am filled with consolation; I am overjoyed in all our affliction.

5 For even when we came into Macedonia, our bodies had no rest,

Cross references (center column):

5.18 Col 1.20; Rom 5.10
5.20 2 Cor 3.6; Eph 6.20; 2 Cor 6.1
5.21 1 Pet 2.22; 1 Jn 3.5; Gal 3.13
6.1 1 Cor 3.9; 2 Cor 5.20; Heb 12.15
6.2 Isa 49.8
6.3 Rom 14.13; 1 Cor 9.12; 10.32
6.5 2 Cor 11.23
6.7 2 Cor 4.2; 10.4; Eph 6.11,13
6.9 Rom 8.36; 2 Cor 1.8-10; 4.10,11
6.10 Rom 8.32; 1 Cor 3.21
6.11 Ezek 33.22; 2 Cor 7.3; Isa 60.5
6.13 1 Cor 4.14
6.14 Deut 7.2,3; 1 Cor 5.9, 10; Eph 5.7, 11; 1 Jn 1.6
6.16 1 Cor 3.16; Jer 31.1; Ezek 37.27
6.17 Isa 52.11; Rev 18.4
6.18 Hos 1.10; Isa 43.6
7.1 2 Cor 6.17, 18
7.2 2 Cor 6.12, 13
7.3 2 Cor 6.11, 12
7.4 2 Cor 1.4, 14; 3.12
7.5 2 Cor 2.13; 4.8; Deut 32.25

[1]Or *God was in Christ reconciling the world to himself*　[m]Gk *As we work together*
[n]Other ancient authorities read *you*
[o]Gk lacks *in your hearts*

but we were afflicted in every way — disputes without and fears within. [6] But God, who consoles the downcast, consoled us by the arrival of Titus, [7] and not only by his coming, but also by the consolation with which he was consoled about you, as he told us of your longing, your mourning, your zeal for me, so that I rejoiced still more. [8] For even if I made you sorry with my letter, I do not regret it (though I did regret it, for I see that I grieved you with that letter, though only briefly). [9] Now I rejoice, not because you were grieved, but because your grief led to repentance; for you felt a godly grief, so that you were not harmed in any way by us. [10] For godly grief produces a repentance that leads to salvation and brings no regret, but worldly grief produces death. [11] For see what earnestness this godly grief has produced in you, what eagerness to clear yourselves, what indignation, what alarm, what longing, what zeal, what punishment! At every point you have proved yourselves guiltless in the matter. [12] So although I wrote to you, it was not on account of the one who did the wrong, nor on account of the one who was wronged, but in order that your zeal for us might be made known to you before God. [13] In this we find comfort.

In addition to our own consolation, we rejoiced still more at the joy of Titus, because his mind has been set at rest by all of you. [14] For if I have been somewhat boastful about you to him, I was not disgraced; but just as everything we said to you was true, so our boasting to Titus has proved true as well. [15] And his heart goes out all the more to you, as he remembers the obedience of all of you, and how you welcomed him with fear and trembling. [16] I rejoice, because I have complete confidence in you.

Encouragement to Be Generous

8 We want you to know, brothers and sisters,[p] about the grace of God that has been granted to the churches of Macedonia; [2] for during a severe ordeal of affliction, their abundant joy and their extreme poverty have overflowed in a wealth of generosity on their part. [3] For, as I can testify, they voluntarily gave according to their means, and even beyond their means, [4] begging us earnestly for the privilege[q] of sharing in this ministry to the saints — [5] and this, not merely as we expected; they gave themselves first to the Lord and, by the will of God, to us, [6] so that we might urge Titus that, as he had already made a beginning, so he should also complete this generous undertaking[r] among you. [7] Now as you excel in everything — in faith, in speech, in knowledge, in utmost eagerness, and in our love for you[s] — so we want you to excel also in this generous undertaking.[r]

8 I do not say this as a command, but I am testing the genuineness of your love against the earnestness of others. [9] For you know the generous act[t] of our Lord Jesus Christ, that though he was rich, yet for your sakes he became poor, so that by his poverty you might become rich. [10] And in this matter I am giving my advice: it is appropriate for you who began last year not only to do something but even to desire to do something — [11] now finish doing it, so that your eagerness may be matched by completing it according to your means. [12] For if the eagerness is there, the gift is acceptable according to what one has — not according to what one does not have. [13] I do not mean that there should be relief for others and pressure on you, but it is a question of a fair balance between [14] your present abundance and their need, so that their abundance may be for your need, in order that there may be a fair balance. [15] As it is written,

7.6
2 Cor 1.3,
4; v. 13;
2 Cor 2.13
7.8
2 Cor 2.2,
4
7.10
Acts 11.18
7.11
2 Cor 2.6;
Rom 3.5
7.12
v. 8;
2 Cor 2.3,
9;
1 Cor 5.1,
2
7.13
v. 6;
1 Cor 16.18
7.14
vv. 4,6
7.15
2 Cor 2.9;
Phil 2.12
7.16
2 Thes 3.4
8.1
Acts 16.9

8.2
2 Cor 9.11
8.3
1 Cor 16.2
8.4
Acts 24.17;
Rom 15.25,
26,31;
2 Cor 9.1
8.6
v. 17;
2 Cor 12.18;
vv. 16,23,10
8.7
2 Cor 9.8;
1 Cor 1.5;
12.13
8.8
1 Cor 7.6
8.9
2 Cor 13.14;
Phil 2.6,7
8.10
1 Cor 7.25;
2 Cor 9.2;
1 Cor 16.2,
3
8.11
2 Cor 9.2
8.12
Mk 12.43,
44; Lk 21.3
8.14
2 Cor 9.12
8.15
Ex 16.18

p Gk brothers q Gk grace r Gk this grace s Other ancient authorities read your love for us t Gk the grace

"The one who had much did
 not have too much,
and the one who had little
 did not have too little."

Commendation of Titus

16 But thanks be to God who
put in the heart of Titus the same
eagerness for you that I myself
have. [17] For he not only accepted
our appeal, but since he is more eager
than ever, he is going to you of
his own accord. [18] With him we are
sending the brother who is famous
among all the churches for his proclaiming the good news;[u] [19] and
not only that, but he has also been
appointed by the churches to travel
with us while we are administering
this generous undertaking[v] for the
glory of the Lord himself[w] and to
show our goodwill. [20] We intend
that no one should blame us about
this generous gift that we are administering, [21] for we intend to do
what is right not only in the Lord's
sight but also in the sight of others.
[22] And with them we are sending
our brother whom we have often
tested and found eager in many
matters, but who is now more eager
than ever because of his great confidence in you. [23] As for Titus, he is
my partner and co-worker in your
service; as for our brothers, they are
messengers[x] of the churches, the
glory of Christ. [24] Therefore openly
before the churches, show them
the proof of your love and of our
reason for boasting about you.

The Collection for Christians at Jerusalem

9 Now it is not necessary for me
to write you about the ministry to the saints, [2] for I know your
eagerness, which is the subject of
my boasting about you to the people of Macedonia, saying that
Achaia has been ready since last
year; and your zeal has stirred up
most of them. [3] But I am sending
the brothers in order that our
boasting about you may not prove
to have been empty in this case, so
that you may be ready, as I said you
would be; [4] otherwise, if some Mac-

edonians come with me and find
that you are not ready, we would be
humiliated—to say nothing of
you—in this undertaking.[y] [5] So I
thought it necessary to urge the
brothers to go on ahead to you, and
arrange in advance for this bountiful gift that you have promised, so
that it may be ready as a voluntary
gift and not as an extortion.

6 The point is this: the one who
sows sparingly will also reap sparingly, and the one who sows bountifully will also reap bountifully.
[7] Each of you must give as you have
made up your mind, not reluctantly
or under compulsion, for God loves
a cheerful giver. [8] And God is able
to provide you with every blessing
in abundance, so that by always
having enough of everything, you
may share abundantly in every
good work. [9] As it is written,

"He scatters abroad, he gives
 to the poor;
his righteousness[z] endures
 forever."

[10] He who supplies seed to the sower and bread for food will supply
and multiply your seed for sowing
and increase the harvest of your
righteousness.[z] [11] You will be enriched in every way for your great
generosity, which will produce
thanksgiving to God through us;
[12] for the rendering of this ministry
not only supplies the needs of the
saints but also overflows with
many thanksgivings to God.
[13] Through the testing of this ministry you glorify God by your obedience to the confession of the gospel of Christ and by the generosity
of your sharing with them and with
all others, [14] while they long for you
and pray for you because of the surpassing grace of God that he has
given you. [15] Thanks be to God for
his indescribable gift!

Paul Defends His Ministry

10 I myself, Paul, appeal to
you by the meekness and

8.17
v. 6
8.18
2 Cor 12.18
8.19
1 Cor 16.3,
4; vv. 4,6,11
8.21
Rom 12.17;
14.18
8.23
Phil 2.25
8.24
2 Cor 7.14;
9.2
9.1
2 Cor 8.4
9.2
2 Cor 7.4;
Rom 15.26;
Acts 18.12;
2 Cor 8.10
9.3
1 Cor 16.2
9.4
Rom 15.26

9.5
Gen 33.11;
1 Sam 25.27;
Phil 4.17;
2 Cor 12.17,
18
9.6
Gal 6.7,9
9.7
Deut 15.7,
10; Ex 25.2;
Rom 12.8;
2 Cor 8.12
9.8
Eph 3.20;
Phil 4.19
9.9
Ps 112.9
9.10
Isa 55.10;
Hos 10.12
9.11
1 Cor 1.5,
11
9.12
2 Cor 8.14
9.13
2 Cor 8.4;
Rom 15.31;
Mt 9.8;
2 Cor 2.12
9.15
2 Cor 2.14;
Rom 5.15,
16
10.1
Gal 5.2;
Rom 12.1

u Or *the gospel* v Gk *this grace* w Other
ancient authorities lack *himself*
x Gk *apostles* y Other ancient authorities
add *of boasting* z Or *benevolence*

gentleness of Christ—I who am humble when face to face with you, but bold toward you when I am away!— [2] I ask that when I am present I need not show boldness by daring to oppose those who think we are acting according to human standards.[a] [3] Indeed, we live as human beings,[b] but we do not wage war according to human standards;[a] [4] for the weapons of our warfare are not merely human,[c] but they have divine power to destroy strongholds. We destroy arguments [5] and every proud obstacle raised up against the knowledge of God, and we take every thought captive to obey Christ. [6] We are ready to punish every disobedience when your obedience is complete.

7 Look at what is before your eyes. If you are confident that you belong to Christ, remind yourself of this, that just as you belong to Christ, so also do we. [8] Now, even if I boast a little too much of our authority, which the Lord gave for building you up and not for tearing you down, I will not be ashamed of it. [9] I do not want to seem as though I am trying to frighten you with my letters. [10] For they say, "His letters are weighty and strong, but his bodily presence is weak, and his speech contemptible." [11] Let such people understand that what we say by letter when absent, we will also do when present.

12 We do not dare to classify or compare ourselves with some of those who commend themselves. But when they measure themselves by one another, and compare themselves with one another, they do not show good sense. [13] We, however, will not boast beyond limits, but will keep within the field that God has assigned to us, to reach out even as far as you. [14] For we were not overstepping our limits when we reached you; we were the first to come all the way to you with the good news[d] of Christ. [15] We do not boast beyond limits, that is, in the labors of others; but our hope is that, as your faith in-

creases, our sphere of action among you may be greatly enlarged, [16] so that we may proclaim the good news[d] in lands beyond you, without boasting of work already done in someone else's sphere of action. [17] "Let the one who boasts, boast in the Lord." [18] For it is not those who commend themselves that are approved, but those whom the Lord commends.

Paul and the False Apostles

11 I wish you would bear with me in a little foolishness. Do bear with me! [2] I feel a divine jealousy for you, for I promised you in marriage to one husband, to present you as a chaste virgin to Christ. [3] But I am afraid that as the serpent deceived Eve by its cunning, your thoughts will be led astray from a sincere and pure[e] devotion to Christ. [4] For if someone comes and proclaims another Jesus than the one we proclaimed, or if you receive a different spirit from the one you received, or a different gospel from the one you accepted, you submit to it readily enough. [5] I think that I am not in the least inferior to these superapostles. [6] I may be untrained in speech, but not in knowledge; certainly in every way and in all things we have made this evident to you.

7 Did I commit a sin by humbling myself so that you might be exalted, because I proclaimed God's good news[f] to you free of charge? [8] I robbed other churches by accepting support from them in order to serve you. [9] And when I was with you and was in need, I did not burden anyone, for my needs were supplied by the friends[g] who came from Macedonia. So I refrained and will continue to refrain from burdening you in any way. [10] As the truth of Christ is in me, this boast of mine will not be silenced in the

Cross references

10.2
1 Cor 4.21;
2 Cor 13.2,
10
10.3
v. 2
10.4
1 Tim 1.18;
2 Tim 2.3;
Acts 7.22;
1 Cor 2.5;
Jer 1.10
10.5
1 Cor 1.19;
Isa 2.11,12;
2 Cor 9.13
10.6
2 Cor 2.9
10.7
Jn 7.24;
1 Cor 1.12;
14.37
10.8
2 Cor 7.4;
13.10
10.10
1 Cor 2.3;
Gal 4.13,14;
1 Cor 1.17
10.12
2 Cor 3.1;
5.12
10.13
v. 15
10.14
2 Cor 2.12
10.15
Rom 15.20;
2 Thes 1.3
10.17
Jer 9.24;
1 Cor 1.31
10.18
Rom 2.29;
1 Cor 4.5
11.1
vv. 16,17,
21;
2 Cor 5.13
11.2
Hos 2.19;
Eph 5.26,
27;
2 Cor 4.14
11.3
Gen 3.4;
Jn 8.44
11.4
1 Cor 3.11;
Rom 8.15;
Gal 1.6-8
11.5
2 Cor 12.11;
Gal 2.6
11.6
1 Cor 1.17;
Eph 3.4;
2 Cor 4.2
11.7
2 Cor 12.13;
1 Cor 9.18
11.8
Phil 4.15,18
11.9
2 Cor 12.13,
14

11.10 Rom 9.1; 1 Cor 9.15; Acts 18.12

a Gk *according to the flesh* ・ b Gk *in the flesh* ・ c Gk *fleshly* ・ d Or *the gospel* ・ e Other ancient authorities lack *and pure* ・ f Gk *the gospel of God* ・ g Gk *brothers*

regions of Achaia. [11] And why? Because I do not love you? God knows I do!

12 And what I do I will also continue to do, in order to deny an opportunity to those who want an opportunity to be recognized as our equals in what they boast about. [13] For such boasters are false apostles, deceitful workers, disguising themselves as apostles of Christ. [14] And no wonder! Even Satan disguises himself as an angel of light. [15] So it is not strange if his ministers also disguise themselves as ministers of righteousness. Their end will match their deeds.

Paul's Sufferings as an Apostle

16 I repeat, let no one think that I am a fool; but if you do, then accept me as a fool, so that I too may boast a little. [17] What I am saying in regard to this boastful confidence, I am saying not with the Lord's authority, but as a fool; [18] since many boast according to human standards, [h] I will also boast. [19] For you gladly put up with fools, being wise yourselves! [20] For you put up with it when someone makes slaves of you, or preys upon you, or takes advantage of you, or puts on airs, or gives you a slap in the face. [21] To my shame, I must say, we were too weak for that!

But whatever anyone dares to boast of—I am speaking as a fool—I also dare to boast of that. [22] Are they Hebrews? So am I. Are they Israelites? So am I. Are they descendants of Abraham? So am I. [23] Are they ministers of Christ? I am talking like a madman—I am a better one: with far greater labors, far more imprisonments, with countless floggings, and often near death. [24] Five times I have received from the Jews the forty lashes minus one. [25] Three times I was beaten with rods. Once I received a stoning. Three times I was shipwrecked; for a night and a day I was adrift at sea; [26] on frequent journeys, in danger from rivers, danger from bandits, danger from my own people, danger from Gentiles, dan-

ger in the city, danger in the wilderness, danger at sea, danger from false brothers and sisters; [i] [27] in toil and hardship, through many a sleepless night, hungry and thirsty, often without food, cold and naked. [28] And, besides other things, I am under daily pressure because of my anxiety for all the churches. [29] Who is weak, and I am not weak? Who is made to stumble, and I am not indignant?

30 If I must boast, I will boast of the things that show my weakness. [31] The God and Father of the Lord Jesus (blessed be he forever!) knows that I do not lie. [32] In Damascus, the governor[j] under King Aretas guarded the city of Damascus in order to[k] seize me, [33] but I was let down in a basket through a window in the wall,[l] and escaped from his hands.

Paul's Visions and Revelations

12 It is necessary to boast; nothing is to be gained by it, but I will go on to visions and revelations of the Lord. [2] I know a person in Christ who fourteen years ago was caught up to the third heaven—whether in the body or out of the body I do not know; God knows. [3] And I know that such a person—whether in the body or out of the body I do not know; God knows— [4] was caught up into Paradise and heard things that are not to be told, that no mortal is permitted to repeat. [5] On behalf of such a one I will boast, but on my own behalf I will not boast, except of my weaknesses. [6] But if I wish to boast, I will not be a fool, for I will be speaking the truth. But I refrain from it, so that no one may think better of me than what is seen in me or heard from me, [7] even considering the exceptional character of the revelations. Therefore, to keep[m] me from being too elated, a thorn was given me in the flesh, a messenger of Satan to torment me,

11.11
2 Cor 12.15
11.12
1 Cor 9.12
11.13
Gal 1.7;
2 Pet 2.1;
Phil 3.2
11.15
Phil 3.19
11.16
v. 1
11.17
1 Cor 7.6,
12,25;
Acts 9.24,25
11.18
Phil 3.3,4
11.21
2 Cor 10.10;
Phil 3.4
11.22
Acts 6.1;
Phil 3.5;
Rom 9.4
11.23
1 Cor 15.10;
Acts 16.23;
2 Cor 6.5
11.24
Deut 25.3
11.25
Acts 16.22;
14.19
11.26
Acts 9.23;
14.5; 21.31;
Gal 2.4

11.27
1 Thes 2.9;
1 Cor 4.11;
2 Cor 6.5
11.29
1 Cor 9.22
11.30
1 Cor 2.3
11.31
Gal 1.20;
Rom 9.5
11.32
Acts 9.24,25
12.1
Co 11.30;
v. 7;
Gal 1.12;
2.2
12.2
Rom 16.7;
Eph 4.10;
2 Cor 11.11
12.4
Lk 23.43
12.6
2 Cor 10.8;
11.16

h Gk *according to the flesh* i Gk *brothers*
i Gk *ethnarch* k Other ancient authorities
read *and wanted to* l Gk *through the wall*
m Other ancient authorities read *To keep*

to keep me from being too elated.[n] [8]Three times I appealed to the Lord about this, that it would leave me, [9]but he said to me, "My grace is sufficient for you, for power[o] is made perfect in weakness." So, I will boast all the more gladly of my weaknesses, so that the power of Christ may dwell in me. [10]Therefore I am content with weaknesses, insults, hardships, persecutions, and calamities for the sake of Christ; for whenever I am weak, then I am strong.

Paul's Concern for the Corinthian Church

[11] I have been a fool! You forced me to it. Indeed you should have been the ones commending me, for I am not at all inferior to these super-apostles, even though I am nothing. [12]The signs of a true apostle were performed among you with utmost patience, signs and wonders and mighty works. [13]How have you been worse off than the other churches, except that I myself did not burden you? Forgive me this wrong!

[14] Here I am, ready to come to you this third time. And I will not be a burden, because I do not want what is yours but you; for children ought not to lay up for their parents, but parents for their children. [15]I will most gladly spend and be spent for you. If I love you more, am I to be loved less? [16]Let it be assumed that I did not burden you. Nevertheless (you say) since I was crafty, I took you in by deceit. [17]Did I take advantage of you through any of those whom I sent to you? [18]I urged Titus to go, and sent the brother with him. Titus did not take advantage of you, did he? Did we not conduct ourselves with the same spirit? Did we not take the same steps?

[19] Have you been thinking all along that we have been defending ourselves before you? We are speaking in Christ before God. Everything we do, beloved, is for the sake of building you up. [20]For I fear that when I come, I may find you

not as I wish, and that you may find me not as you wish; I fear that there may perhaps be quarreling, jealousy, anger, selfishness, slander, gossip, conceit, and disorder. [21]I fear that when I come again, my God may humble me before you, and that I may have to mourn over many who previously sinned and have not repented of the impurity, sexual immorality, and licentiousness that they have practiced.

Further Warning

13 This is the third time I am coming to you. "Any charge must be sustained by the evidence of two or three witnesses." [2]I warned those who sinned previously and all the others, and I warn them now while absent, as I did when present on my second visit, that if I come again, I will not be lenient— [3]since you desire proof that Christ is speaking in me. He is not weak in dealing with you, but is powerful in you. [4]For he was crucified in weakness, but lives by the power of God. For we are weak in him,[p] but in dealing with you we will live with him by the power of God.

[5] Examine yourselves to see whether you are living in the faith. Test yourselves. Do you not realize that Jesus Christ is in you?— unless, indeed, you fail to meet the test! [6]I hope you will find out that we have not failed. [7]But we pray to God that you may not do anything wrong—not that we may appear to have met the test, but that you may do what is right, though we may seem to have failed. [8]For we cannot do anything against the truth, but only for the truth. [9]For we rejoice when we are weak and you are strong. This is what we pray for, that you may become perfect. [10]So I write these things while I am away from you, so that when I come, I may not have to be severe in using the authority that the Lord has giv-

Cross references (center column)

12.8
Mt 26.44
12.9
Phil 4.13;
2 Cor 11.30;
1 Pet 4.14
12.10
Rom 5.3;
2 Cor 6.4;
2 Thes 1.4
12.11
2 Cor 11.1,
5
12.12
Rom 15.18,
19
12.13
1 Cor 9.12,
18;
2 Cor 11.7
12.14
2 Cor 13.1;
1 Cor 10.24,
33; 4.14,15;
Prov 19.14
12.15
Phil 2.17;
1 Thes 2.8
12.18
2 Cor 8.6,
16,18
12.19
Rom 9.1;
2 Cor 10.8
12.20
2 Cor 2.1-4;
1 Cor 1.11;
3.3
12.21
2 Cor 2.1,
4; 13.2;
Gal 5.19
13.1
2 Cor 12.14;
Deut 19.15;
Mt 18.16
13.3
Mt 10.20;
1 Cor 5.4;
2 Cor 9.8;
10.4
13.4
Phil 2.7,8;
1 Pet 3.18;
Rom 6.4,8;
v. 9
13.5
Jn 6.6;
1 Cor 11.28;
9.27
13.9
2 Cor 11.30;
12.10
13.10
2 Cor 2.3;
Titus 1.13;
2 Cor 10.8

n Other ancient authorities lack *to keep me from being too elated* o Other ancient authorities read *my power* p Other ancient authorities read *with him*

en me for building up and not for tearing down.

Final Greetings and Benediction

11 Finally, brothers and sisters,q farewell.r Put things in order, listen to my appeal,s agree with one another, live in peace; and the God of love and peace will be with you. 12 Greet one another with a holy kiss. All the saints greet you.

13 The grace of the Lord Jesus Christ, the love of God, and the communion oft the Holy Spirit be with all of you.

q Gk *brothers* r Or *rejoice*
s Or *encourage one another* t Or *and the sharing in*

13.11
Rom 15.33;
Eph 6.23

13.13
Phil 4.22

THE LETTER OF PAUL TO THE
Galatians

Title and Background

Judaizers were Jewish Christians who believed, among other things, that a number of the ceremonial practices of the Old Testament were still binding on the New Testament church. Following Paul's successful campaign in Galatia, they insisted that Gentile converts to Christianity abide by certain Old Testament practices, especially circumcision. The Judaizers argued that Paul was not an authentic apostle and that out of a desire to make the message more appealing to Gentiles, he had removed from the gospel certain legal requirements. Paul responds by writing this letter.

Author and Date of Writing

The opening verse identifies the author as the apostle Paul. Various dates have been given for the writing of this letter, but it was probably one of his earliest letters, written near A.D. 50.

Theme and Message

Galatians stands as an eloquent and vigorous defense for the essential New Testament truth that we are justified by faith in Jesus Christ—by nothing less and nothing more. Furthermore, we are sanctified by depending on the grace of Christ and by experiencing the power of the Holy Spirit working within us. Some have called this letter the *Magna Charta* of Christian liberty.

Outline

 I. Introduction: Greetings and Denunciation (1.1-9)
 II. Authentication of the Apostle of Liberty and Faith (1.10–2.21)
III. Justification of the Doctrine of Liberty and Faith (3.1–4.31)
 IV. Practice of the Life of Liberty and Faith (5.1–6.10)
 V. Conclusion (6.11-18)

Salutation

1 Paul an apostle — sent neither by human commission nor from human authorities, but through Jesus Christ and God the Father, who raised him from the dead — 2 and all the members of God's family[a] who are with me,

To the churches of Galatia:

3 Grace to you and peace from God our Father and the Lord Jesus Christ, 4 who gave himself for our sins to set us free from the present evil age, according to the will of our God and Father, 5 to whom be the glory forever and ever. Amen.

There Is No Other Gospel

6 I am astonished that you are so quickly deserting the one who called you in the grace of Christ and are turning to a different gospel — 7 not that there is another gospel, but there are some who are confusing you and want to pervert the gospel of Christ. 8 But even if we or an angel[b] from heaven should proclaim to you a gospel contrary to what we proclaimed to you, let that one be accursed! 9 As we have said before, so now I repeat, if anyone proclaims to you a gospel contrary to what you received, let that one be accursed!

10 Am I now seeking human approval, or God's approval? Or am I

1.1 2 Cor 1.1; vv. 11,12; Acts 9.6; 2.24
1.2 Phil 4.21; 1 Cor 16.1
1.3 Rom 1.7
1.4 Rom 4.25; Gal 2.20; 2 Cor 4.4
1.5 Rom 16.27
1.6 Gal 5.8; 2 Cor 11.4
1.7 Acts 15.24; Gal 5.10
1.8 2 Cor 11.4, 14; Rom 9.3
1.9 Rom 16.17 **1.10** 1 Thes 2.4

a Gk *all the brothers* b Or *a messenger*

trying to please people? If I were still pleasing people, I would not be a servant[c] of Christ.

Paul's Vindication of His Apostleship

11 For I want you to know, brothers and sisters,[d] that the gospel that was proclaimed by me is not of human origin; 12 for I did not receive it from a human source, nor was I taught it, but I received it through a revelation of Jesus Christ.

13 You have heard, no doubt, of my earlier life in Judaism. I was violently persecuting the church of God and was trying to destroy it. 14 I advanced in Judaism beyond many among my people of the same age, for I was far more zealous for the traditions of my ancestors. 15 But when God, who had set me apart before I was born and called me through his grace, was pleased 16 to reveal his Son to me,[e] so that I might proclaim him among the Gentiles, I did not confer with any human being, 17 nor did I go up to Jerusalem to those who were already apostles before me, but I went away at once into Arabia, and afterwards I returned to Damascus.

18 Then after three years I did go up to Jerusalem to visit Cephas and stayed with him fifteen days; 19 but I did not see any other apostle except James the Lord's brother. 20 In what I am writing to you, before God, I do not lie! 21 Then I went into the regions of Syria and Cilicia, 22 and I was still unknown by sight to the churches of Judea that are in Christ; 23 they only heard it said, "The one who formerly was persecuting us is now proclaiming the faith he once tried to destroy." 24 And they glorified God because of me.

Paul and the Other Apostles

2 Then after fourteen years I went up again to Jerusalem with Barnabas, taking Titus along with me. 2 I went up in response to a revelation. Then I laid before them (though only in a private

meeting with the acknowledged leaders) the gospel that I proclaim among the Gentiles, in order to make sure that I was not running, or had not run, in vain. 3 But even Titus, who was with me, was not compelled to be circumcised, though he was a Greek. 4 But because of false believers[f] secretly brought in, who slipped in to spy on the freedom we have in Christ Jesus, so that they might enslave us — 5 we did not submit to them even for a moment, so that the truth of the gospel might always remain with you. 6 And from those who were supposed to be acknowledged leaders (what they actually were makes no difference to me; God shows no partiality) — those leaders contributed nothing to me. 7 On the contrary, when they saw that I had been entrusted with the gospel for the uncircumcised, just as Peter had been entrusted with the gospel for the circumcised 8 (for he who worked through Peter making him an apostle to the circumcised also worked through me in sending me to the Gentiles), 9 and when James and Cephas and John, who were acknowledged pillars, recognized the grace that had been given to me, they gave to Barnabas and me the right hand of fellowship, agreeing that we should go to the Gentiles and they to the circumcised. 10 They asked only one thing, that we remember the poor, which was actually what I was[g] eager to do.

Paul Rebukes Peter at Antioch

11 But when Cephas came to Antioch, I opposed him to his face, because he stood self-condemned; 12 for until certain people came from James, he used to eat with the Gentiles. But after they came, he drew back and kept himself separate for fear of the circumcision faction. 13 And the other Jews joined him in this hypocrisy, so that even Barnabas was led astray by their hypocrisy. 14 But when I

Cross references

1.11 1 Cor 15.1
1.12 vv. 1,16; Eph 3.3
1.13 Acts 8.3; 9.21
1.14 Acts 22.3; Col 2.8
1.15 Isa 49.1,5; Jer 1.5; Acts 9.15; Rom 1.1
1.16 Acts 9.20; Eph 6.12
1.18 Acts 9.22, 23,26,27
1.19 Mt 13.55
1.21 Acts 9.30
1.22 1 Thes 2.14; Rom 16.7
2.1 Acts 15.2
2.2 Acts 15.12; Gal 1.6; Phil 2.16
2.3 2 Cor 2.13; Acts 16.3; 1 Cor 9.21
2.4 Acts 15.1; 2 Cor 11.26
2.5 v. 14; Col 1.5
2.6 Gal 6.3; Rom 2.11; 2 Cor 12.11
2.7 1 Thes 2.4; Acts 13.46
2.9 Rom 12.3; Gal 1.16
2.10 Acts 11.29, 30; 24.17
2.11 Acts 11.10
2.12 Acts 11.2,3
2.13 v. 1
2.14 vv. 5,9,11

Footnotes

c Gk slave d Gk brothers e Gk in me
f Gk false brothers g Or had been

saw that they were not acting consistently with the truth of the gospel, I said to Cephas before them all, "If you, though a Jew, live like a Gentile and not like a Jew, how can you compel the Gentiles to live like Jews?"[h]

Jews and Gentiles Are Saved by Faith

15 We ourselves are Jews by birth and not Gentile sinners; [16]yet we know that a person is justified[i] not by the works of the law but through faith in Jesus Christ.[j] And we have come to believe in Christ Jesus, so that we might be justified by faith in Christ,[k] and not by doing the works of the law, because no one will be justified by the works of the law. [17]But if, in our effort to be justified in Christ, we ourselves have been found to be sinners, is Christ then a servant of sin? Certainly not! [18]But if I build up again the very things that I once tore down, then I demonstrate that I am a transgressor. [19]For through the law I died to the law, so that I might live to God. I have been crucified with Christ; [20]and it is no longer I who live, but it is Christ who lives in me. And the life I now live in the flesh I live by faith in the Son of God,[l] who loved me and gave himself for me. [21]I do not nullify the grace of God; for if justification[m] comes through the law, then Christ died for nothing.

Law or Faith

3 You foolish Galatians! Who has bewitched you? It was before your eyes that Jesus Christ was publicly exhibited as crucified! [2]The only thing I want to learn from you is this: Did you receive the Spirit by doing the works of the law or by believing what you heard? [3]Are you so foolish? Having started with the Spirit, are you now ending with the flesh? [4]Did you experience so much for nothing? — if it really was for nothing. [5]Well then, does God[n] supply you with the Spirit and work miracles among you by your doing the works of the

law, or by your believing what you heard?

6 Just as Abraham "believed God, and it was reckoned to him as righteousness," [7]so, you see, those who believe are the descendants of Abraham. [8]And the scripture, foreseeing that God would justify the Gentiles by faith, declared the gospel beforehand to Abraham, saying, "All the Gentiles shall be blessed in you." [9]For this reason, those who believe are blessed with Abraham who believed.

10 For all who rely on the works of the law are under a curse; for it is written, "Cursed is everyone who does not observe and obey all the things written in the book of the law." [11]Now it is evident that no one is justified before God by the law; for "The one who is righteous will live by faith."[o] [12]But the law does not rest on faith; on the contrary, "Whoever does the works of the law[p] will live by them." [13]Christ redeemed us from the curse of the law by becoming a curse for us — for it is written, "Cursed is everyone who hangs on a tree" — [14]in order that in Christ Jesus the blessing of Abraham might come to the Gentiles, so that we might receive the promise of the Spirit through faith.

The Promise to Abraham

15 Brothers and sisters,[q] I give an example from daily life: once a person's will[r] has been ratified, no one adds to it or annuls it. [16]Now the promises were made to Abraham and to his offspring;[s] it does not say, "And to offsprings,"[t] as of many; but it says, "And to your offspring,"[s] that is, to one person, who is Christ. [17]My point is this: the law, which came four hundred thirty years later, does not annul a

2.15
Phil 3.4,5;
Mt 9.11
2.16
Acts 13.39;
Rom 1.17;
3.20
2.17
v. 15;
Gal 3.21
2.19
Rom 8.2;
6.14;
2 Cor 5.15;
1 Thes 5.10
2.20
1 Pet 4.2;
Eph 5.2;
Titus 2.14
2.21
Gal 3.21
3.1
Gal 1.2; 5.7;
1 Cor 1.23
3.2
Acts 2.38;
Rom 10.16,
17
3.3
Gal 4.9;
Heb 7.16
3.4
1 Cor 15.2
3.5
Phil 1.19;
1 Cor 12.10;
Rom 10.17

3.6
Gen 15.6;
Rom 4.3;
Jas 2.23
3.7
v. 9
3.8
Gen 12.3;
Acts 3.25
3.9
Rom 4.16;
v. 7
3.10
Deut 27.26
3.11
Gal 2.16;
Hab 2.4;
Heb 10.38
3.12
Lev 18.5;
Rom 10.5
3.13
Gal 4.5;
Acts 5.30;
Deut 21.23
3.14
Rom 4.9;
Joel 2.28;
Acts 2.33
3.15
Heb 9.17
3.16
Gen 12.3;
13.15;
Acts 3.25
3.17
Ex 12.40;
Rom 4.13

h Some interpreters hold that the quotation extends into the following paragraph
i Or reckoned as righteous; and so elsewhere
j Or the faith of Jesus Christ k Or the faith of Christ l Or by the faith of the Son of God m Or righteousness n Gk he
o Or The one who is righteous through faith will live p Gk does them q Gk Brothers
r Or covenant (as in verse 17) s Gk seed
t Gk seeds

covenant previously ratified by God, so as to nullify the promise. [18]For if the inheritance comes from the law, it no longer comes from the promise; but God granted it to Abraham through the promise.

The Purpose of the Law

19 Why then the law? It was added because of transgressions, until the offspring[u] would come to whom the promise had been made; and it was ordained through angels by a mediator. [20]Now a mediator involves more than one party; but God is one.

21 Is the law then opposed to the promises of God? Certainly not! For if a law had been given that could make alive, then righteousness would indeed come through the law. [22]But the scripture has imprisoned all things under the power of sin, so that what was promised through faith in Jesus Christ[v] might be given to those who believe.

23 Now before faith came, we were imprisoned and guarded under the law until faith would be revealed. [24]Therefore the law was our disciplinarian until Christ came, so that we might be justified by faith. [25]But now that faith has come, we are no longer subject to a disciplinarian, [26]for in Christ Jesus you are all children of God through faith. [27]As many of you as were baptized into Christ have clothed yourselves with Christ. [28]There is no longer Jew or Greek, there is no longer slave or free, there is no longer male and female; for all of you are one in Christ Jesus. [29]And if you belong to Christ, then you are Abraham's offspring,[u] heirs according to the promise.

4 My point is this: heirs, as long as they are minors, are no better than slaves, though they are the owners of all the property; [2]but they remain under guardians and trustees until the date set by the father. [3]So with us; while we were minors, we were enslaved to the elemental spirits[w] of the world. [4]But

when the fullness of time had come, God sent his Son, born of a woman, born under the law, [5]in order to redeem those who were under the law, so that we might receive adoption as children. [6]And because you are children, God has sent the Spirit of his Son into our[x] hearts, crying, "Abba![y] Father!" [7]So you are no longer a slave but a child, and if a child then also an heir, through God.[z]

Paul Reproves the Galatians

8 Formerly, when you did not know God, you were enslaved to beings that by nature are not gods. [9]Now, however, that you have come to know God, or rather to be known by God, how can you turn back again to the weak and beggarly elemental spirits?[a] How can you want to be enslaved to them again? [10]You are observing special days, and months, and seasons, and years. [11]I am afraid that my work for you may have been wasted.

12 Friends,[b] I beg you, become as I am, for I also have become as you are. You have done me no wrong. [13]You know that it was because of a physical infirmity that I first announced the gospel to you; [14]though my condition put you to the test, you did not scorn or despise me, but welcomed me as an angel of God, as Christ Jesus. [15]What has become of the good will you felt? For I testify that, had it been possible, you would have torn out your eyes and given them to me. [16]Have I now become your enemy by telling you the truth? [17]They make much of you, but for no good purpose; they want to exclude you, so that you may make much of them. [18]It is good to be made much of for a good purpose at all times, and not only when I am present with you. [19]My little children, for whom I am again in the

3.18
Rom 4.14;
8.17
3.19
Acts 7.53;
Deut 5.5
3.20
Heb 8.6;
9.15; 12.24
3.21
Gal 2.17,21
3.22
Rom 3.9-19;
11.32
3.23
Rom 11.32
3.24
Rom 10.4;
1 Cor 4.15;
Gal 2.16
3.26
Jn 1.12;
Rom 8.14
3.27
Rom 6.3;
13.14
3.28
Col 3.11;
Jn 10.16;
Eph 2.14,15
3.29
1 Cor 3.23;
Gal 4.28
4.3
Col 2.8,20;
Heb 5.12
4.4
Eph 1.10;
Mt 5.17

4.5
Eph 1.7;
Jn 1.12;
Eph 1.5
4.6
Rom 5.5;
8.15
4.8
Eph 2.12;
1 Thes 4.5;
Rom 1.25;
1 Cor 12.2
4.9
1 Cor 8.3;
Col 2.20
4.10
Rom 14.5
4.11
1 Thes 3.5
4.12
Gal 6.18
4.13
1 Cor 2.3
4.14
Mt 10.40;
Lk 10.16
4.16
Am 5.10
4.18
vv. 13,14
4.19
1 Jn 2.1;
1 Cor 4.15;
Eph 4.13

u Gk *seed* v Or *through the faith of Jesus Christ* w Or *the rudiments* x Other ancient authorities read *your* y Aramaic for *Father* z Other ancient authorities read *an heir of God through Christ* a Or *beggarly rudiments* b Gk *Brothers*

pain of childbirth until Christ is formed in you, 20 I wish I were present with you now and could change my tone, for I am perplexed about you.

The Allegory of Hagar and Sarah

21 Tell me, you who desire to be subject to the law, will you not listen to the law? 22 For it is written that Abraham had two sons, one by a slave woman and the other by a free woman. 23 One, the child of the slave, was born according to the flesh; the other, the child of the free woman, was born through the promise. 24 Now this is an allegory: these women are two covenants. One woman, in fact, is Hagar, from Mount Sinai, bearing children for slavery. 25 Now Hagar is Mount Sinai in Arabia[c] and corresponds to the present Jerusalem, for she is in slavery with her children. 26 But the other woman corresponds to the Jerusalem above; she is free, and she is our mother. 27 For it is written,

"Rejoice, you childless one,
 you who bear no
 children,
 burst into song and shout,
 you who endure no
 birthpangs;
for the children of the
 desolate woman are
 more numerous
 than the children of the
 one who is married."

28 Now you,[d] my friends,[e] are children of the promise, like Isaac. 29 But just as at that time the child who was born according to the flesh persecuted the child who was born according to the Spirit, so it is now also. 30 But what does the scripture say? "Drive out the slave and her child; for the child of the slave will not share the inheritance with the child of the free woman." 31 So then, friends,[e] we are children, not of the slave but of the free woman. 5 1 For freedom Christ has set us free. Stand firm, therefore, and do not submit again to a yoke of slavery.

4.21 Lk 16.29
4.22 Gen 16.15; 21.2,9
4.23 Rom 9.7; Gen 18.10; Heb 11.11
4.24 Deut 33.2
4.26 Isa 2.2;
Heb 12.22; Rev 3.12
4.27 Isa 54.1
4.28 Acts 3.25; Rom 9.8
4.29 Gen 21.9
4.30 Gen 21.10-12
5.1 Jn 8.32; Acts 15.10

5.2 Acts 15.1
5.3 Gal 3.10
5.4 Heb 12.15; 2 Pet 3.17
5.5 Rom 8.23, 24; 2 Tim 4.8
5.6 1 Cor 7.19; Jas 2.18
5.7 1 Cor 9.24; Gal 3.1
5.8 Gal 1.6
5.9 1 Cor 5.6
5.10 2 Cor 2.3; Gal 1.7
5.11 Gal 4.29; 6.12; 1 Cor 1.23
5.13 1 Cor 8.9; 1 Pet 2.16; 1 Cor 9.19
5.14 Lev 19.18; Mt 7.12; 22.39; Rom 13.8
5.16 Rom 8.4; vv. 24,25; Eph 2.3
5.17 Rom 7.15-23

The Nature of Christian Freedom

2 Listen! I, Paul, am telling you that if you let yourselves be circumcised, Christ will be of no benefit to you. 3 Once again I testify to every man who lets himself be circumcised that he is obliged to obey the entire law. 4 You who want to be justified by the law have cut yourselves off from Christ; you have fallen away from grace. 5 For through the Spirit, by faith, we eagerly wait for the hope of righteousness. 6 For in Christ Jesus neither circumcision nor uncircumcision counts for anything; the only thing that counts is faith working[f] through love.

7 You were running well; who prevented you from obeying the truth? 8 Such persuasion does not come from the one who calls you. 9 A little yeast leavens the whole batch of dough. 10 I am confident about you in the Lord that you will not think otherwise. But whoever it is that is confusing you will pay the penalty. 11 But my friends,[e] why am I still being persecuted if I am still preaching circumcision? In that case the offense of the cross has been removed. 12 I wish those who unsettle you would castrate themselves!

13 For you were called to freedom, brothers and sisters;[e] only do not use your freedom as an opportunity for self-indulgence,[g] but through love become slaves to one another. 14 For the whole law is summed up in a single commandment, "You shall love your neighbor as yourself." 15 If, however, you bite and devour one another, take care that you are not consumed by one another.

The Works of the Flesh

16 Live by the Spirit, I say, and do not gratify the desires of the flesh. 17 For what the flesh desires is opposed to the Spirit, and what

c Other ancient authorities read *For Sinai is a mountain in Arabia* d Other ancient authorities read *we* e Gk *brothers* f Or *made effective* g Gk *the flesh*

the Spirit desires is opposed to the flesh; for these are opposed to each other, to prevent you from doing what you want. [18] But if you are led by the Spirit, you are not subject to the law. [19] Now the works of the flesh are obvious: fornication, impurity, licentiousness, [20] idolatry, sorcery, enmities, strife, jealousy, anger, quarrels, dissensions, factions, [21] envy,[h] drunkenness, carousing, and things like these. I am warning you, as I warned you before: those who do such things will not inherit the kingdom of God.

The Fruit of the Spirit

[22] By contrast, the fruit of the Spirit is love, joy, peace, patience, kindness, generosity, faithfulness, [23] gentleness, and self-control. There is no law against such things. [24] And those who belong to Christ Jesus have crucified the flesh with its passions and desires. [25] If we live by the Spirit, let us also be guided by the Spirit. [26] Let us not become conceited, competing against one another, envying one another.

Bear One Another's Burdens

6 My friends,[i] if anyone is detected in a transgression, you who have received the Spirit should restore such a one in a spirit of gentleness. Take care that you yourselves are not tempted. [2] Bear one another's burdens, and in this way you will fulfill[j] the law of Christ. [3] For if those who are nothing think they are something, they deceive themselves. [4] All must test their own work; then that work, rather than their neighbor's work, will become a cause for pride. [5] For all must carry their own loads.

[6] Those who are taught the word must share in all good things with their teacher.

[7] Do not be deceived; God is not

mocked, for you reap whatever you sow. [8] If you sow to your own flesh, you will reap corruption from the flesh; but if you sow to the Spirit, you will reap eternal life from the Spirit. [9] So let us not grow weary in doing what is right, for we will reap at harvest-time, if we do not give up. [10] So then, whenever we have an opportunity, let us work for the good of all, and especially for those of the family of faith.

Final Admonitions and Benediction

[11] See what large letters I make when I am writing in my own hand! [12] It is those who want to make a good showing in the flesh that try to compel you to be circumcised — only that they may not be persecuted for the cross of Christ. [13] Even the circumcised do not themselves obey the law, but they want you to be circumcised so that they may boast about your flesh. [14] May I never boast of anything except the cross of our Lord Jesus Christ, by which[k] the world has been crucified to me, and I to the world. [15] For[l] neither circumcision nor uncircumcision is anything; but a new creation is everything! [16] As for those who will follow this rule — peace be upon them, and mercy, and upon the Israel of God.

[17] From now on, let no one make trouble for me; for I carry the marks of Jesus branded on my body.

[18] May the grace of our Lord Jesus Christ be with your spirit, brothers and sisters.[m] Amen.

h Other ancient authorities add *murder*
i Gk *Brothers* i Other ancient authorities
read *in this way fulfill* k Or *through whom*
l Other ancient authorities add *in Christ Jesus*
m Gk *brothers*

5.18
Rom 6.14
5.19
Eph 5.3;
Col 3.5
5.21
1 Cor 6.9
5.22
Eph 5.9;
Col 3.12-15;
1 Cor 13.7
5.24
Rom 6.6
5.25
Rom 8.4
5.26
Phil 2.3
6.2
Rom 15.1;
Jas 2.8
6.3
Rom 12.3;
1 Cor 8.2;
2 Cor 3.5
6.4
1 Cor 11.28;
Phil 1.26
6.6
1 Cor 9.11
6.7
1 Cor 6.9;
Job 13.9

6.8
Hos 8.7;
Jas 3.18
6.9
1 Cor 15.58;
Heb 3.6;
Rev 2.10
6.10
Jn 9.4;
Titus 3.8;
Eph 2.19
6.12
Mt 23.27,
28;
Acts 15.1;
Gal 5.11
6.13
Rom 2.25;
Phil 3.3
6.14
Gal 2.20;
Rom 6.2,6
6.15
2 Cor 5.17
6.17
2 Cor 1.5

THE LETTER OF PAUL TO THE
Ephesians

Title and Background

Ephesus was the most important city in western Asia Minor (now Turkey). Because it was at an intersection of major trade routes, it became a commercial center. It also boasted a pagan temple dedicated to the Roman goddess Diana (Greek name: Artemis). Paul made Ephesus a center for evangelism for about three years. This letter was probably not sent merely to the church at Ephesus but also to the various churches in the province of Asia, where Paul conducted his third missionary journey.

Author and Date of Writing

Most scholars believe that Paul wrote this letter about A.D. 60, during his two-year imprisonment in Rome.

Theme and Message

Unlike several of Paul's other letters, Ephesians does not address any particular error or heresy. Paul wrote so that his readers might better understand the dimensions of God's eternal purpose and grace and come to appreciate the high goals God has for the church.

One of Paul's themes is that of unity, that all Christians are one family in Jesus and they should act with love toward each other. He also writes about the church—not a church building, but the church that is made up of all Christians throughout the ages.

Outline

I. Greetings (1.1-2)
II. The Glory and Headship of Christ (1.3-14)
III. Prayer That Christians May Realize God's Purpose and Power (1.15-23)
IV. Steps Toward the Fulfillment of God's Purpose (2.1–3.21)
V. Ways to Fulfill God's Purpose in the Church (4.1–6.20)
VI. Conclusion (6.21-24)

Salutation

1 Paul, an apostle of Christ Jesus by the will of God,
To the saints who are in Ephesus and are faithful[a] in Christ Jesus:

2 Grace to you and peace from God our Father and the Lord Jesus Christ.

Spiritual Blessings in Christ

3 Blessed be the God and Father of our Lord Jesus Christ, who has blessed us in Christ with every spiritual blessing in the heavenly places, 4 just as he chose us in Christ[b] before the foundation of the world to be holy and blameless before him in love. 5 He destined us for adoption as his children through Jesus Christ, according to the good pleasure of his will, 6 to the praise of his glorious grace that he freely bestowed on us in the Beloved. 7 In him we have redemption through his blood, the forgiveness of our trespasses, according to the riches of his grace 8 that he lavished on us. With all wisdom and insight 9 he has made known to us the mystery of his will, according to his good pleasure that he set forth in

1.1
2 Cor 1.1;
1 Cor 1.1;
Phil 1.1;
Col 1.1,2
1.2
Rom 1.7
1.3
2 Cor 1.3;
Eph 2.6;
3.10; 6.12
1.4
Eph 5.27;
Col 1.22;
Eph 4.2,15,
16
1.5
Rom 8.29f
1.7
Col 1.14
1.9
Rom 16.25

a Other ancient authorities lack *in Ephesus*, reading *saints who are also faithful* b Gk *in him*

Christ, [10]as a plan for the fullness of time, to gather up all things in him, things in heaven and things on earth. [11]In Christ we have also obtained an inheritance,[c] having been destined according to the purpose of him who accomplishes all things according to his counsel and will, [12]so that we, who were the first to set our hope on Christ, might live for the praise of his glory. [13]In him you also, when you had heard the word of truth, the gospel of your salvation, and had believed in him, were marked with the seal of the promised Holy Spirit; [14]this[d] is the pledge of our inheritance toward redemption as God's own people, to the praise of his glory.

Paul's Prayer

15 I have heard of your faith in the Lord Jesus and your love[e] toward all the saints, and for this reason [16]I do not cease to give thanks for you as I remember you in my prayers. [17]I pray that the God of our Lord Jesus Christ, the Father of glory, may give you a spirit of wisdom and revelation as you come to know him, [18]so that, with the eyes of your heart enlightened, you may know what is the hope to which he has called you, what are the riches of his glorious inheritance among the saints, [19]and what is the immeasurable greatness of his power for us who believe, according to the working of his great power. [20]God[f] put this power to work in Christ when he raised him from the dead and seated him at his right hand in the heavenly places, [21]far above all rule and authority and power and dominion, and above every name that is named, not only in this age but also in the age to come. [22]And he has put all things under his feet and has made him the head over all things for the church, [23]which is his body, the fullness of him who fills all in all.

From Death to Life

2 You were dead through the trespasses and sins [2]in which

you once lived, following the course of this world, following the ruler of the power of the air, the spirit that is now at work among those who are disobedient. [3]All of us once lived among them in the passions of our flesh, following the desires of flesh and senses, and we were by nature children of wrath, like everyone else. [4]But God, who is rich in mercy, out of the great love with which he loved us [5]even when we were dead through our trespasses, made us alive together with Christ[g] — by grace you have been saved — [6]and raised us up with him and seated us with him in the heavenly places in Christ Jesus, [7]so that in the ages to come he might show the immeasurable riches of his grace in kindness toward us in Christ Jesus. [8]For by grace you have been saved through faith, and this is not your own doing; it is the gift of God — [9]not the result of works, so that no one may boast. [10]For we are what he has made us, created in Christ Jesus for good works, which God prepared beforehand to be our way of life.

One in Christ

11 So then, remember that at one time you Gentiles by birth,[h] called "the uncircumcision" by those who are called "the circumcision" — a physical circumcision made in the flesh by human hands — [12]remember that you were at that time without Christ, being aliens from the commonwealth of Israel, and strangers to the covenants of promise, having no hope and without God in the world. [13]But now in Christ Jesus you who once were far off have been brought near by the blood of Christ. [14]For he is our peace; in his flesh he has made both groups into one and has broken down the di-

1.10
Gal 4.4;
Col 1.16,20
1.11
Eph 3.11;
Rom 9.11;
Heb 6.17
1.12
vv. 6,14
1.13
Col 1.5;
Eph 4.30
1.14
2 Cor 1.22;
Acts 20.32
1.15
Col 1.4;
Eph 3.18
1.16
Rom 1.8,9;
Col 1.3,9
1.17
Jn 20.17;
Col 1.9
1.18
Acts 26.18;
Eph 4.4
1.19
Col 1.29;
Eph 6.10
1.20
Acts 2.24;
Heb 1.3
1.21
Phil 2.9,10
1.22
Mt 28.18;
Eph 4.15;
5.23
1.23
Rom 12.5;
Col 2.17
2.1
v. 5;
Jn 5.24
2.2
Eph 6.12;
5.6
2.3
Gal 5.16,17;
Rom 2.14;
5.10
2.4
Rom 10.12
2.5
vv. 1,8
2.6
Eph 1.20
2.7
Titus 3.4
2.8
Gal 2.16;
v. 5
2.9
Rom 3.20,
28;
2 Tim 1.9
2.10
Eph 4.24;
Titus 2.14
2.11
Rom 2.28;
Col 2.11
2.12
1 Thes 4.5;
Gal 4.8

2.13 Acts 2.39; Col 1.20 **2.14** Col 3.15;
1 Cor 12.13

[c] Or *been made a heritage* [d] Other ancient authorities read *who* [e] Other ancient authorities lack *and your love* [f] Gk *He* [g] Other ancient authorities read *in Christ* [h] Gk *in the flesh*

viding wall, that is, the hostility between us. [15] He has abolished the law with its commandments and ordinances, that he might create in himself one new humanity in place of the two, thus making peace, [16] and might reconcile both groups to God in one body[i] through the cross, thus putting to death that hostility through it.[j] [17] So he came and proclaimed peace to you who were far off and peace to those who were near; [18] for through him both of us have access in one Spirit to the Father. [19] So then you are no longer strangers and aliens, but you are citizens with the saints and also members of the household of God, [20] built upon the foundation of the apostles and prophets, with Christ Jesus himself as the cornerstone.[k] [21] In him the whole structure is joined together and grows into a holy temple in the Lord; [22] in whom you also are built together spiritually[l] into a dwelling place for God.

Paul's Ministry to the Gentiles

3 This is the reason that I Paul am a prisoner for[m] Christ Jesus for the sake of you Gentiles— [2] for surely you have already heard of the commission of God's grace that was given me for you, [3] and how the mystery was made known to me by revelation, as I wrote above in a few words, [4] a reading of which will enable you to perceive my understanding of the mystery of Christ. [5] In former generations this mystery[n] was not made known to humankind, as it has now been revealed to his holy apostles and prophets by the Spirit: [6] that is, the Gentiles have become fellow heirs, members of the same body, and sharers in the promise in Christ Jesus through the gospel.

[7] Of this gospel I have become a servant according to the gift of God's grace that was given me by the working of his power. [8] Although I am the very least of all the saints, this grace was given to me to bring to the Gentiles the news of the boundless riches of Christ,

[9] and to make everyone see[o] what is the plan of the mystery hidden for ages in[p] God who created all things; [10] so that through the church the wisdom of God in its rich variety might now be made known to the rulers and authorities in the heavenly places. [11] This was in accordance with the eternal purpose that he has carried out in Christ Jesus our Lord, [12] in whom we have access to God in boldness and confidence through faith in him.[q] [13] I pray therefore that you[r] may not lose heart over my sufferings for you; they are your glory.

Prayer for the Readers

[14] For this reason I bow my knees before the Father,[s] [15] from whom every family[t] in heaven and on earth takes its name. [16] I pray that, according to the riches of his glory, he may grant that you may be strengthened in your inner being with power through his Spirit, [17] and that Christ may dwell in your hearts through faith, as you are being rooted and grounded in love. [18] I pray that you may have the power to comprehend, with all the saints, what is the breadth and length and height and depth, [19] and to know the love of Christ that surpasses knowledge, so that you may be filled with all the fullness of God.

[20] Now to him who by the power at work within us is able to accomplish abundantly far more than all we can ask or imagine, [21] to him be glory in the church and in Christ Jesus to all generations, forever and ever. Amen.

Unity in the Body of Christ

4 I therefore, the prisoner in the Lord, beg you to lead a life worthy of the calling to which you

Cross references (center column)

2.15 Col 1.21,22; Gal 6.15
2.16 Col 1.20,22
2.17 Isa 57.19; Ps 148.14
2.18 Eph 3.12; 1 Cor 12.13; Col 1.12
2.19 Phil 3.20; Gal 6.10
2.20 Mt 16.18; Rev 21.14
2.21 1 Cor 3.16, 17
3.1 Acts 23.18; Eph 4.1
3.2 Col 1.25; 1 Tim 1.4
3.3 Acts 22.17; Gal 1.12; Rom 16.25
3.4 1 Cor 4.1
3.5 Rom 16.26
3.6 Gal 3.29; Eph 2.15,16
3.8 1 Cor 15.9; Gal 1.16; Col 1.27
3.9 Col 1.26,27
3.10 1 Pet 1.12; 1 Cor 2.7; Eph 1.21
3.12 Heb 4.16; Eph 2.18
3.13 2 Cor 4.1
3.14 Phil 2.10
3.16 Eph 1.18; Col 1.11; Rom 7.22
3.17 Jn 14.23; Col 1.23
3.18 Eph 1.18; Job 11.8,9
3.19 Col 2.10; Eph 1.23
3.20 Rom 16.25
3.21 Rom 11.36
4.1 Eph 3.1; Col 1.10

i Or reconcile both of us in one body for God j Or in him, or in himself k Or keystone l Gk in the Spirit m Or of n Gk it o Other ancient authorities read to bring to light p Or by q Or the faith of him r Or I s Other ancient authorities add of our Lord Jesus Christ t Gk fatherhood

have been called, ²with all humility and gentleness, with patience, bearing with one another in love, ³making every effort to maintain the unity of the Spirit in the bond of peace. ⁴There is one body and one Spirit, just as you were called to the one hope of your calling, ⁵one Lord, one faith, one baptism, ⁶one God and Father of all, who is above all and through all and in all.

7 But each of us was given grace according to the measure of Christ's gift. ⁸Therefore it is said,

"When he ascended on high
 he made captivity itself
 a captive;
 he gave gifts to his
 people."

⁹(When it says, "He ascended," what does it mean but that he had also descendedᵘ into the lower parts of the earth? ¹⁰He who descended is the same one who ascended far above all the heavens, so that he might fill all things.) ¹¹The gifts he gave were that some would be apostles, some prophets, some evangelists, some pastors and teachers, ¹²to equip the saints for the work of ministry, for building up the body of Christ, ¹³until all of us come to the unity of the faith and of the knowledge of the Son of God, to maturity, to the measure of the full stature of Christ. ¹⁴We must no longer be children, tossed to and fro and blown about by every wind of doctrine, by people's trickery, by their craftiness in deceitful scheming. ¹⁵But speaking the truth in love, we must grow up in every way into him who is the head, into Christ, ¹⁶from whom the whole body, joined and knit together by every ligament with which it is equipped, as each part is working properly, promotes the body's growth in building itself up in love.

The Old Life and the New

17 Now this I affirm and insist on in the Lord: you must no longer live as the Gentiles live, in the futility of their minds. ¹⁸They are darkened in their understanding, alienated from the life of God because of their ignorance and hardness of heart. ¹⁹They have lost all sensitivity and have abandoned themselves to licentiousness, greedy to practice every kind of impurity. ²⁰That is not the way you learned Christ! ²¹For surely you have heard about him and were taught in him, as truth is in Jesus. ²²You were taught to put away your former way of life, your old self, corrupt and deluded by its lusts, ²³and to be renewed in the spirit of your minds, ²⁴and to clothe yourselves with the new self, created according to the likeness of God in true righteousness and holiness.

Rules for the New Life

25 So then, putting away falsehood, let all of us speak the truth to our neighbors, for we are members of one another. ²⁶Be angry but do not sin; do not let the sun go down on your anger, ²⁷and do not make room for the devil. ²⁸Thieves must give up stealing; rather let them labor and work honestly with their own hands, so as to have something to share with the needy. ²⁹Let no evil talk come out of your mouths, but only what is useful for building up,ᵛ as there is need, so that your words may give grace to those who hear. ³⁰And do not grieve the Holy Spirit of God, with which you were marked with a seal for the day of redemption. ³¹Put away from you all bitterness and wrath and anger and wrangling and slander, together with all malice, ³²and be kind to one another, tenderhearted, forgiving one another, as God in Christ has forgiven you.ʷ

5 ¹Therefore be imitators of God, as beloved children, ²and live in love, as Christ loved usˣ and gave himself up for us, a fragrant offering and sacrifice to God.

4.2
Col 3.12;
Eph 1.4
4.3
Col 3.14
4.4
1 Cor 12.12;
Eph 2.16;
1.18
4.6
Rom 11.36
4.7
Rom 12.3
4.8
Ps 68.18;
Judg 5.12;
Col 2.15
4.9
Jn 3.13
4.11
1 Cor 12.28
4.12
2 Cor 13.9;
Eph 1.23;
1 Cor 12.27
4.13
Col 2.2;
1 Cor 14.20;
Col 1.28
4.14
1 Cor 14.20;
Jas 1.6;
Eph 6.11
4.15
2 Cor 4.2;
Eph 1.22;
Col 1.18
4.17
Col 3.7;
1 Pet 4.3;
Rom 1.21
4.18
Eph 2.1,12;
2 Cor 3.14
4.19
1 Tim 4.2;
Rom 1.24;
Col 3.5
4.22
1 Pet 2.1;
Rom 6.6
4.23
Col 3.10
4.24
Rom 6.4;
2 Cor 5.17
4.25
Zech 8.16;
Rom 12.5
4.26
Ps 37.8
4.27
2 Cor 2.10,
11
4.28
Acts 20.35;
Lk 3.11
4.30
1 Thes 5.19;
Rom 8.23
4.31
Col 3.8;
Titus 3.3
4.32
2 Cor 2.10;
Mt 6.14,15

5.1 Lk 6.36 **5.2** 1 Thes 4.9; Gal 1.4;
2 Cor 2.15

ᵘ Other ancient authorities add *first* ᵛ Other
ancient authorities read *building up faith*
ʷ Other ancient authorities read *us* ˣ Other
ancient authorities read *you*

Renounce Pagan Ways

3 But fornication and impurity of any kind, or greed, must not even be mentioned among you, as is proper among saints. [4] Entirely out of place is obscene, silly, and vulgar talk; but instead, let there be thanksgiving. [5] Be sure of this, that no fornicator or impure person, or one who is greedy (that is, an idolater), has any inheritance in the kingdom of Christ and of God.

6 Let no one deceive you with empty words, for because of these things the wrath of God comes on those who are disobedient. [7] Therefore do not be associated with them. [8] For once you were darkness, but now in the Lord you are light. Live as children of light— [9] for the fruit of the light is found in all that is good and right and true. [10] Try to find out what is pleasing to the Lord. [11] Take no part in the unfruitful works of darkness, but instead expose them. [12] For it is shameful even to mention what such people do secretly; [13] but everything exposed by the light becomes visible, [14] for everything that becomes visible is light. Therefore it says,

"Sleeper, awake!
 Rise from the dead,
and Christ will shine on
 you."

15 Be careful then how you live, not as unwise people but as wise, [16] making the most of the time, because the days are evil. [17] So do not be foolish, but understand what the will of the Lord is. [18] Do not get drunk with wine, for that is debauchery; but be filled with the Spirit, [19] as you sing psalms and hymns and spiritual songs among yourselves, singing and making melody to the Lord in your hearts, [20] giving thanks to God the Father at all times and for everything in the name of our Lord Jesus Christ.

The Christian Household

21 Be subject to one another out of reverence for Christ.

22 Wives, be subject to your husbands as you are to the Lord.

[23] For the husband is the head of the wife just as Christ is the head of the church, the body of which he is the Savior. [24] Just as the church is subject to Christ, so also wives ought to be, in everything, to their husbands.

25 Husbands, love your wives, just as Christ loved the church and gave himself up for her, [26] in order to make her holy by cleansing her with the washing of water by the word, [27] so as to present the church to himself in splendor, without a spot or wrinkle or anything of the kind—yes, so that she may be holy and without blemish. [28] In the same way, husbands should love their wives as they do their own bodies. He who loves his wife loves himself. [29] For no one ever hates his own body, but he nourishes and tenderly cares for it, just as Christ does for the church, [30] because we are members of his body.[y] [31] "For this reason a man will leave his father and mother and be joined to his wife, and the two will become one flesh." [32] This is a great mystery, and I am applying it to Christ and the church. [33] Each of you, however, should love his wife as himself, and a wife should respect her husband.

Children and Parents

6 Children, obey your parents in the Lord,[z] for this is right. [2] "Honor your father and mother"—this is the first commandment with a promise: [3] "so that it may be well with you and you may live long on the earth."

4 And, fathers, do not provoke your children to anger, but bring them up in the discipline and instruction of the Lord.

Slaves and Masters

5 Slaves, obey your earthly masters with fear and trembling, in singleness of heart, as you obey Christ; [6] not only while being

Phil 2.12; 1 Chr 29.17

y Other ancient authorities add *of his flesh and of his bones* z Other ancient authorities lack *in the Lord*

Cross-references (center column):

5.3 Rom 6.13; Col 3.5; 1 Cor 5.1
5.5 1 Cor 6.9; Col 3.5
5.6 Jer 29.8; Rom 1.18
5.8 Jn 8.12; Lk 16.8
5.9 Gal 5.22
5.11 1 Cor 5.9; Rom 6.21
5.12 Rom 1.24
5.14 Isa 60.1; Jn 5.25
5.16 Col 4.5; Eph 6.13
5.17 Rom 12.2; 1 Thes 4.3
5.18 Prov 20.1; Lk 1.15
5.19 Col 3.16; Acts 16.25
5.20 Ps 34.1; Heb 13.15
5.22 Gen 3.16; Eph 6.5
5.23 1 Cor 11.3; Col 1.18; Eph 1.23
5.24 Col 3.18
5.25 Col 3.19
5.26 Titus 3.5
5.27 Col 1.22; Eph 1.4
5.28 v. 25
5.30 1 Cor 6.15; Eph 1.23
5.31 Gen 2.24; Mt 19.5; 1 Cor 6.16
5.32 Col 3.19; 1 Pet 3.6
6.1 Col 3.20
6.2 Deut 5.16
6.4 Col 3.21; Gen 18.19
6.5 Col 3.22; 1 Tim 6.1;

watched, and in order to please them, but as slaves of Christ, doing the will of God from the heart. [7]Render service with enthusiasm, as to the Lord and not to men and women, [8]knowing that whatever good we do, we will receive the same again from the Lord, whether we are slaves or free.

9 And, masters, do the same to them. Stop threatening them, for you know that both of you have the same Master in heaven, and with him there is no partiality.

The Whole Armor of God

10 Finally, be strong in the Lord and in the strength of his power. [11]Put on the whole armor of God, so that you may be able to stand against the wiles of the devil. [12]For our[a] struggle is not against enemies of blood and flesh, but against the rulers, against the authorities, against the cosmic powers of this present darkness, against the spiritual forces of evil in the heavenly places. [13]Therefore take up the whole armor of God, so that you may be able to withstand on that evil day, and having done everything, to stand firm. [14]Stand therefore, and fasten the belt of truth around your waist, and put on the breastplate of righteousness. [15]As shoes for your feet put on whatever will make you ready to proclaim the gospel of peace. [16]With all of these,[b] take the shield of faith,

with which you will be able to quench all the flaming arrows of the evil one. [17]Take the helmet of salvation, and the sword of the Spirit, which is the word of God.

18 Pray in the Spirit at all times in every prayer and supplication. To that end keep alert and always persevere in supplication for all the saints. [19]Pray also for me, so that when I speak, a message may be given to me to make known with boldness the mystery of the gospel,[c] [20]for which I am an ambassador in chains. Pray that I may declare it boldly, as I must speak.

Personal Matters and Benediction

21 So that you also may know how I am and what I am doing, Tychicus will tell you everything. He is a dear brother and a faithful minister in the Lord. [22]I am sending him to you for this very purpose, to let you know how we are, and to encourage your hearts.

23 Peace be to the whole community,[d] and love with faith, from God the Father and the Lord Jesus Christ. [24]Grace be with all who have an undying love for our Lord Jesus Christ.[e]

6.7
Col 3.23
6.9
Lev 25.43;
Jn 13.13;
Col 3.25
6.10
1 Cor 16.13;
Eph 1.19
6.11
1 Cor 16.21
6.12
1 Cor 9.25;
Rom 8.38
6.13
2 Cor 10.4;
Eph 5.16
6.14
Isa 11.5;
59.17
6.15
Isa 52.7
6.16
1 Jn 5.4

6.17
Isa 59.17;
Heb 4.12
6.18
Lk 18.1;
Mt 26.41;
Phil 1.4
6.19
Acts 4.29;
2 Cor 3.12
6.20
2 Cor 5.20;
Phil 1.20
6.21
Acts 20.4
6.23
1 Pet 5.14;
Gal 5.6

[a] Other ancient authorities read *your*
[b] Or *In all circumstances* [c] Other ancient authorities lack *of the gospel* [d] Gk *to the brothers* [e] Other ancient authorities add *Amen*

THE LETTER OF PAUL TO THE
Philippians

Title and Background

Philippians was written by Paul while he was in prison. The church at Philippi had sent Paul a gift by way of Epaphroditus, their messenger. Epaphroditus became sick, and the Philippian Christians were concerned about him. This made Epaphroditus all the more eager to return home. Paul therefore wrote this letter to his Christian friends in Philippi, expressing his gratitude for their love and help.

Author and Date of Writing

The first verse of Philippians tells us that Paul was the author, and the writing itself reveals the stamp of genuineness. The many personal references of the author fit what we know of Paul from other New Testament books. The most widely accepted date for the writing of the letter is about A.D. 61, during Paul's Roman imprisonment.

Theme and Message

The theme of the book is "joy" or "rejoicing in the Lord." The word "joy" in its various forms occurs sixteen times. There were also perils to watch out for because the church had many enemies, both inside and outside. Paul warns the Philippians of the present dangers of a self-seeking attitude and of pride, both of which could lead to harmful divisions. In Philippians can also be found the most profound statement of the meaning of the incarnation (2.5-11).

Outline

- I. Greetings, Thanksgiving, and Prayer (1.1-11)
- II. Paul's Personal Circumstances (1.12-26)
- III. Exhortations (1.27-2.18)
 - A. Live a Life Worthy of the Gospel (1.27-30)
 - B. Follow the Servant Attitude of Christ (2.1-18)
- IV. Paul's Associates in the Gospel (2.19-30)
- V. Warnings Against Judaizers and Libertines (3.1-4.1)
- VI. Final Exhortations, Thanks, and Conclusion (4.2-23)

Salutation

1 Paul and Timothy, servants[a] of Christ Jesus,

To all the saints in Christ Jesus who are in Philippi, with the bishops[b] and deacons:[c]

2 Grace to you and peace from God our Father and the Lord Jesus Christ.

Paul's Prayer for the Philippians

3 I thank my God every time I remember you, 4 constantly praying with joy in every one of my prayers for all of you, 5 because of your sharing in the gospel from the first day until now. 6 I am confident of this, that the one who began a good work among you will bring it to completion by the day of Jesus Christ. 7 It is right for me to think this way about all of you, because you hold me in your heart,[d] for all of you share in God's grace[e] with me, both in my imprisonment and in the defense and confirmation of the gospel. 8 For God is my witness, how I long for all of you with the

1.1	2 Cor 1.1; Acts 16.1; 1 Cor 1.2
1.2	1 Pet 1.2
1.3	1 Cor 1.4
1.4	Rom 1.9
1.5	Acts 2.42; 16.17
1.6	v. 10
1.7	2 Pet 1.13; 2 Cor 7.3; vv. 13,14,17
1.8	Rom 1.9; Gal 1.20

a Gk *slaves* b Or *overseers*
c Or *overseers and helpers* d Or *because I hold you in my heart* e Gk *in grace*

compassion of Christ Jesus. 9 And this is my prayer, that your love may overflow more and more with knowledge and full insight 10 to help you to determine what is best, so that in the day of Christ you may be pure and blameless, 11 having produced the harvest of righteousness that comes through Jesus Christ for the glory and praise of God.

Paul's Present Circumstances

12 I want you to know, beloved[f] that what has happened to me has actually helped to spread the gospel, 13 so that it has become known throughout the whole imperial guard[g] and to everyone else that my imprisonment is for Christ; 14 and most of the brothers and sisters,[f] having been made confident in the Lord by my imprisonment, dare to speak the word[h] with greater boldness and without fear.

15 Some proclaim Christ from envy and rivalry, but others from goodwill. 16 These proclaim Christ out of love, knowing that I have been put here for the defense of the gospel; 17 the others proclaim Christ out of selfish ambition, not sincerely but intending to increase my suffering in my imprisonment. 18 What does it matter? Just this, that Christ is proclaimed in every way, whether out of false motives or true; and in that I rejoice.

Yes, and I will continue to rejoice, 19 for I know that through your prayers and the help of the Spirit of Jesus Christ this will turn out for my deliverance. 20 It is my eager expectation and hope that I will not be put to shame in any way, but that by my speaking with all boldness, Christ will be exalted now as always in my body, whether by life or by death. 21 For to me, living is Christ and dying is gain. 22 If I am to live in the flesh, that means fruitful labor for me; and I do not know which I prefer. 23 I am hard pressed between the two: my desire is to depart and be with Christ, for that is far better; 24 but to remain in the flesh is more necessary

for you. 25 Since I am convinced of this, I know that I will remain and continue with all of you for your progress and joy in faith, 26 so that I may share abundantly in your boasting in Christ Jesus when I come to you again.

27 Only, live your life in a manner worthy of the gospel of Christ, so that, whether I come and see you or am absent and hear about you, I will know that you are standing firm in one spirit, striving side by side with one mind for the faith of the gospel, 28 and are in no way intimidated by your opponents. For them this is evidence of their destruction, but of your salvation. And this is God's doing. 29 For he has graciously granted you the privilege not only of believing in Christ, but of suffering for him as well — 30 since you are having the same struggle that you saw I had and now hear that I still have.

Imitating Christ's Humility

2 If then there is any encouragement in Christ, any consolation from love, any sharing in the Spirit, any compassion and sympathy, 2 make my joy complete: be of the same mind, having the same love, being in full accord and of one mind. 3 Do nothing from selfish ambition or conceit, but in humility regard others as better than yourselves. 4 Let each of you look not to your own interests, but to the interests of others. 5 Let the same mind be in you that was[i] in Christ Jesus,

6 who, though he was in the
　　form of God,
　did not regard equality
　　with God
　as something to be
　　exploited,
7 but emptied himself,
　taking the form of a slave,
　being born in human
　　likeness.
　And being found in human
　　form,

Cross-references (center column)

1.9
1 Thes 3.12;
Col 1.9
1.13
Phil 4.22
1.14
v. 7
1.15
Phil 2.3
1.16
1 Cor 9.17;
v. 12
1.17
Phil 2.3
1.19
2 Cor 1.11
1.20
Rom 8.19;
5.5;
Eph 6.19
1.23
2 Cor 5.8;
2 Tim 4.6

1.26
2 Cor 1.14;
5.12
1.28
2 Thes 1.5;
Rom 8.17
1.29
Mt 5.12;
Acts 14.22
1.30
1 Thes 2.2;
Col 2.1;
Acts 16.19
2.1
2 Cor 13.14;
Col 3.12
2.2
Jn 3.29;
Rom 12.16;
1 Pet 3.8
2.3
Gal 5.26;
Rom 12.10;
1 Pet 5.5
2.4
Rom 15.1,2
2.5
Mt 11.29;
1 Pet 2.21
2.6
Jn 1.1;
2 Cor 4.4;
Jn 5.18
2.7
Jn 1.14;
Gal 4.4;
Heb 2.17

[f] Gk brothers　[g] Gk whole praetorium
[h] Other ancient authorities read word of God
[i] Or that you have

8 he humbled himself
and became obedient to
the point of death —
even death on a cross.

9 Therefore God also highly
exalted him
and gave him the name
that is above every name,
10 so that at the name of Jesus
every knee should bend,
in heaven and on earth and
under the earth,
11 and every tongue should
confess
that Jesus Christ is Lord,
to the glory of God the
Father.

Shining as Lights in the World

12 Therefore, my beloved, just
as you have always obeyed me, not
only in my presence, but much
more now in my absence, work out
your own salvation with fear and
trembling; 13 for it is God who is at
work in you, enabling you both to
will and to work for his good plea-
sure.

14 Do all things without mur-
muring and arguing, 15 so that you
may be blameless and innocent,
children of God without blemish in
the midst of a crooked and perverse
generation, in which you shine like
stars in the world. 16 It is by your
holding fast to the word of life that
I can boast on the day of Christ that
I did not run in vain or labor in vain.
17 But even if I am being poured out
as a libation over the sacrifice and
the offering of your faith, I am glad
and rejoice with all of you — 18 and
in the same way you also must be
glad and rejoice with me.

Timothy and Epaphroditus

19 I hope in the Lord Jesus to
send Timothy to you soon, so that
I may be cheered by news of you.
20 I have no one like him who will
be genuinely concerned for your
welfare. 21 All of them are seeking
their own interests, not those of
Jesus Christ. 22 But Timothy's[i]
worth you know, how like a son
with a father he has served with me

2.8
Mt 26.39;
Jn 10.18;
Heb 5.8
2.9
Acts 2.33;
Heb 2.9;
Eph 1.20,21
2.10
Mt 28.18;
Rom 14.11
2.11
Jn 13.13;
Acts 2.36
2.12f
Phil 1.5;
Eph 6.5
2.13
2 Cor 3.5
2.14
1 Cor 10.10;
Rom 14.1
2.15
Mt 5.45;
Eph 5.1; 5.8
2.16
2 Cor 1.14;
1 Thes 2.19
2.17
2 Tim 4.6;
Rom 15.16;
Col 1.24
2.19
Rom 16.21
2.20
1 Cor 16.10
2.21
1 Cor 10.24;
13.5
2.22
1 Cor 4.17;
1 Tim 1.2

2.24
Phil 1.25
2.25
Phil 4.18;
Philem 2
2.26
Phil 1.8
2.29
1 Cor 16.18;
1 Tim 5.17
2.30
1 Cor 16.17
3.1
Phil 4.4
3.2
Gal 5.15;
2 Cor 11.13
3.3
Rom 2.28,
29;
Gal 6.14,15
3.5
Rom 11.1;
2 Cor 11.22
3.6
Acts 22.3;
Rom 10.5;
Lk 1.6

in the work of the gospel. 23 I hope
therefore to send him as soon as I
see how things go with me; 24 and I
trust in the Lord that I will also
come soon.

25 Still, I think it necessary to
send to you Epaphroditus — my
brother and co-worker and fellow
soldier, your messenger[k] and min-
ister to my need; 26 for he has been
longing for[l] all of you, and has
been distressed because you heard
that he was ill. 27 He was indeed so
ill that he nearly died. But God had
mercy on him, and not only on him
but on me also, so that I would not
have one sorrow after another. 28 I
am the more eager to send him,
therefore, in order that you may re-
joice at seeing him again, and that
I may be less anxious. 29 Welcome
him then in the Lord with all joy,
and honor such people, 30 because
he came close to death for the work
of Christ,[m] risking his life to make
up for those services that you could
not give me.

3 Finally, my brothers and sis-
ters,[n] rejoice[o] in the Lord.

Breaking with the Past

To write the same things to you
is not troublesome to me, and for
you it is a safeguard.

2 Beware of the dogs, beware of
the evil workers, beware of those
who mutilate the flesh![p] 3 For it is
we who are the circumcision, who
worship in the Spirit of God[q] and
boast in Christ Jesus and have no
confidence in the flesh — 4 even
though I, too, have reason for con-
fidence in the flesh.

If anyone else has reason to be
confident in the flesh, I have more:
5 circumcised on the eighth day, a
member of the people of Israel, of
the tribe of Benjamin, a Hebrew
born of Hebrews; as to the law, a
Pharisee; 6 as to zeal, a persecutor

i Gk his k Gk apostle l Other ancient
authorities read longing to see m Other
ancient authorities read of the Lord
n Gk my brothers o Or farewell
p Gk the mutilation q Other ancient
authorities read worship God in spirit

of the church; as to righteousness under the law, blameless.

7 Yet whatever gains I had, these I have come to regard as loss because of Christ. [8] More than that, I regard everything as loss because of the surpassing value of knowing Christ Jesus my Lord. For his sake I have suffered the loss of all things, and I regard them as rubbish, in order that I may gain Christ [9] and be found in him, not having a righteousness of my own that comes from the law, but one that comes through faith in Christ,[r] the righteousness from God based on faith. [10] I want to know Christ[s] and the power of his resurrection and the sharing of his sufferings by becoming like him in his death, [11] if somehow I may attain the resurrection from the dead.

Pressing toward the Goal

12 Not that I have already obtained this or have already reached the goal;[t] but I press on to make it my own, because Christ Jesus has made me his own. [13] Beloved,[u] I do not consider that I have made it my own;[v] but this one thing I do: forgetting what lies behind and straining forward to what lies ahead, [14] I press on toward the goal for the prize of the heavenly[w] call of God in Christ Jesus. [15] Let those of us then who are mature be of the same mind; and if you think differently about anything, this too God will reveal to you. [16] Only let us hold fast to what we have attained.

17 Brothers and sisters,[u] join in imitating me, and observe those who live according to the example you have in us. [18] For many live as enemies of the cross of Christ; I have often told you of them, and now I tell you even with tears. [19] Their end is destruction; their god is the belly; and their glory is in their shame; their minds are set on earthly things. [20] But our citizenship[x] is in heaven, and it is from there that we are expecting a Savior, the Lord Jesus Christ. [21] He will transform the body of our humiliation[y] that it may be conformed to

the body of his glory,[z] by the power that also enables him to make all things subject to himself.

4 [1] Therefore, my brothers and sisters,[a] whom I love and long for, my joy and crown, stand firm in the Lord in this way, my beloved.

Exhortations

2 I urge Euodia and I urge Syntyche to be of the same mind in the Lord. [3] Yes, and I ask you also, my loyal companion,[b] help these women, for they have struggled beside me in the work of the gospel, together with Clement and the rest of my co-workers, whose names are in the book of life.

4 Rejoice[c] in the Lord always; again I will say, Rejoice.[c] [5] Let your gentleness be known to everyone. The Lord is near. [6] Do not worry about anything, but in everything by prayer and supplication with thanksgiving let your requests be made known to God. [7] And the peace of God, which surpasses all understanding, will guard your hearts and your minds in Christ Jesus.

8 Finally, beloved,[d] whatever is true, whatever is honorable, whatever is just, whatever is pure, whatever is pleasing, whatever is commendable, if there is any excellence and if there is anything worthy of praise, think about[e] these things. [9] Keep on doing the things that you have learned and received and heard and seen in me, and the God of peace will be with you.

Acknowledgment of the Philippians' Gift

10 I rejoice[f] in the Lord greatly that now at last you have revived your concern for me; indeed, you

Cross references (center column):

3.7 Mt 13.44; Lk 14.33
3.8 Eph 4.13; 2 Pet 1.3
3.9 Rom 10.5; 9.30
3.10 Rom 6.3-5; 8.17
3.11 Acts 26.7
3.12 1 Tim 6.12; 1 Cor 13.10; Acts 9.5,6
3.13 Lk 9.62; 1 Cor 9.24
3.14 Heb 6.1; 2 Tim 1.9
3.15 1 Cor 2.6; Gal 5.10
3.16 Rom 12.16; Gal 6.16
3.17 1 Cor 4.16; 1 Pet 5.3
3.18 Acts 20.31; Gal 6.14
3.19 2 Cor 11.15; Rom 16.18; 6.21; 8.5,6
3.20 Eph 2.19; Col 3.1; 1 Cor 1.7
3.21 1 Cor 15.43; Col 3.4; Eph 1.19

4.1 Phil 1.8; 1 Cor 16.13; Phil 1.27
4.2 Phil 2.2
4.3 Rom 16.3; Lk 10.20; Rev 3.5
4.4 Rom 12.12; Phil 3.1
4.5 Heb 10.37; Jas 5.8,9
4.6 Mt 6.25; Eph 6.18
4.7 Jn 14.27; Col 3.15; 1 Pet 1.5
4.8 1 Pet 2.12; 1 Thes 5.22

4.9 Phil 3.17; Rom 15.33

r Or *through the faith of Christ* s Gk *him*
t Or *have already been made perfect*
u Gk *Brothers* v Other ancient authorities read *my own yet* w Gk *upward*
x Or *commonwealth* y Or *our humble bodies* z Or *his glorious body* a Gk *my brothers* b Or *loyal Syzygus*
c Or *Farewell* d Gk *brothers*
e Gk *take account of* f Gk *I rejoiced*

were concerned for me, but had no opportunity to show it.^g ¹¹Not that I am referring to being in need; for I have learned to be content with whatever I have. ¹²I know what it is to have little, and I know what it is to have plenty. In any and all circumstances I have learned the secret of being well-fed and of going hungry, of having plenty and of being in need. ¹³I can do all things through him who strengthens me. ¹⁴In any case, it was kind of you to share my distress.

15 You Philippians indeed know that in the early days of the gospel, when I left Macedonia, no church shared with me in the matter of giving and receiving, except you alone. ¹⁶For even when I was in Thessalonica, you sent me help for my needs more than once. ¹⁷Not that I seek the gift, but I seek the profit that accumulates to your ac-

count. ¹⁸I have been paid in full and have more than enough; I am fully satisfied, now that I have received from Epaphroditus the gifts you sent, a fragrant offering, a sacrifice acceptable and pleasing to God. ¹⁹And my God will fully satisfy every need of yours according to his riches in glory in Christ Jesus. ²⁰To our God and Father be glory forever and ever. Amen.

Final Greetings and Benediction

21 Greet every saint in Christ Jesus. The friends^h who are with me greet you. ²²All the saints greet you, especially those of the emperor's household.

23 The grace of the Lord Jesus Christ be with your spirit.ⁱ

g Gk lacks *to show it*　h Gk *brothers*
i Other ancient authorities add *Amen*

4.11
1 Tim 6.6
4.12
1 Cor 4.11;
2 Cor 11.9
4.13
Jn 15.5;
2 Cor 12.9
4.14
Phil 1.7
4.15
2 Cor 11.8,
9
4.16
Acts 17.1;
1 Thes 2.9
4.17
Titus 3.14

4.18
Phil 2.25;
2 Cor 2.14
4.19
Ps 23.1;
2 Cor 9.8;
Eph 1.7
4.20
Gal 1.4;
Rom 11.36

THE LETTER OF PAUL TO THE
Colossians

Title and Background

During Paul's three-year ministry in Ephesus, Epaphras had been converted and had carried the gospel to Colosse. The young church that resulted then became the target of a heretical attack (the Colossian heresy), which led to Epaphras's visit to Paul in Rome and ultimately to the writing of this letter.

Author and Date of Writing

Because of the many parallels between Ephesians and Colossians, it seems likely that Paul wrote Colossians at the same time as Ephesians and from the same place, that is, from Rome. It should be dated about A.D. 60, during Paul's first Roman imprisonment.

Theme and Message

Paul's purpose is to refute the Colossian heresy. To accomplish this goal he exalts Christ and states that he is the supreme Lord of all. His theme, in other words, is the complete adequacy of Christ as contrasted with the emptiness of mere human philosophy. For "in him the whole fullness of diety dwells bodily," and we "have come to fullness in him" (2.9-10).

Outline

Salutation

1 Paul, an apostle of Christ Jesus by the will of God, and Timothy our brother,

2 To the saints and faithful brothers and sisters[a] in Christ in Colossae:

Grace to you and peace from God our Father.

Paul Thanks God for the Colossians

3 In our prayers for you we always thank God, the Father of our Lord Jesus Christ, 4 for we have heard of your faith in Christ Jesus and of the love that you have for all the saints, 5 because of the hope laid up for you in heaven. You have heard of this hope before in the word of the truth, the gospel 6 that has come to you. Just as it is bearing fruit and growing in the whole world, so it has been bearing fruit among yourselves from the day you heard it and truly comprehended the grace of God. 7 This you learned from Epaphras, our beloved fellow servant.[b] He is a faithful minister of Christ on your[c] behalf, 8 and he has made known to us your love in the Spirit.

9 For this reason, since the day we heard it, we have not ceased praying for you and asking that you may be filled with the knowledge of God's[d] will in all spiritual wisdom and understanding, 10 so that you may lead lives worthy of the Lord, fully pleasing to him, as you bear

1.1
Eph 1.1
1.2
Rom 1.7
1.3
Eph 1.16
1.4
Eph 1.15;
Gal 5.6
1.5
1 Thes 5.8;
1 Pet 1.4
1.6
Mt 24.14;
Jn 15.16
1.7
Philem 23;
Col 4.7
1.8
Rom 15.30
1.9
Eph 1.15-17;
Rom 12.2
1.10
Eph 4.1;
1 Thes 4.1;
Rom 1.13

[a] Gk *brothers* [b] Gk *slave* [c] Other ancient authorities read *our* [d] Gk *his*

fruit in every good work and as you grow in the knowledge of God. [11] May you be made strong with all the strength that comes from his glorious power, and may you be prepared to endure everything with patience, while joyfully [12] giving thanks to the Father, who has enabled[e] you[f] to share in the inheritance of the saints in the light. [13] He has rescued us from the power of darkness and transferred us into the kingdom of his beloved Son, [14] in whom we have redemption, the forgiveness of sins.[g]

The Supremacy of Christ

15 He is the image of the invisible God, the firstborn of all creation; [16] for in[h] him all things in heaven and on earth were created, things visible and invisible, whether thrones or dominions or rulers or powers — all things have been created through him and for him. [17] He himself is before all things, and in[h] him all things hold together. [18] He is the head of the body, the church; he is the beginning, the firstborn from the dead, so that he might come to have first place in everything. [19] For in him all the fullness of God was pleased to dwell, [20] and through him God was pleased to reconcile to himself all things, whether on earth or in heaven, by making peace through the blood of his cross.

21 And you who were once estranged and hostile in mind, doing evil deeds, [22] he has now reconciled[i] in his fleshly body[j] through death, so as to present you holy and blameless and irreproachable before him — [23] provided that you continue securely established and steadfast in the faith, without shifting from the hope promised by the gospel that you heard, which has been proclaimed to every creature under heaven. I, Paul, became a servant of this gospel.

Paul's Interest in the Colossians

24 I am now rejoicing in my sufferings for your sake, and in my flesh I am completing what is lack-

1.11 Eph 3.16; 4.2;
Acts 5.41
1.12 Eph 5.20; 1.11
1.13 Eph 6.12; 2 Pet 1.11
1.15 2 Cor 4.4; Rev 3.14
1.16 Heb 1.2; Eph 1.20, 21; Heb 2.10
1.17 Jn 1.1; 8.58
1.18 Eph 1.22, 23; Rev 1.5
1.19 Jn 1.16
1.20 2 Cor 5.18; Eph 2.13,14
1.21 Rom 5.10; Eph 2.3
1.22 Rom 7.4; Eph 2.15; 5.27
1.23 Eph 3.17; Rom 10.18

1.25 Eph 3.2
1.26 Eph 3.3,4
1.27 2 Cor 2.14; Rom 9.23; 1 Tim 1.1
1.28 Col 3.16; 1 Cor 2.6, 7
1.29 1 Cor 15.10; Col 2.1; Eph 1.19
2.1 Col 1.29; 4.12
2.2 Phil 3.8
2.3 Isa 45.3; Rom 11.33
2.5 1 Thes 2.17; 1 Cor 14.40; 1 Pet 5.9
2.6 1 Thes 4.1
2.7 Eph 2.21
2.8 1 Cor 8.9; 1 Tim 6.20; Gal 4.3

ing in Christ's afflictions for the sake of his body, that is, the church. [25] I became its servant according to God's commission that was given to me for you, to make the word of God fully known, [26] the mystery that has been hidden throughout the ages and generations but has now been revealed to his saints. [27] To them God chose to make known how great among the Gentiles are the riches of the glory of this mystery, which is Christ in you, the hope of glory. [28] It is he whom we proclaim, warning everyone and teaching everyone in all wisdom, so that we may present everyone mature in Christ. [29] For this I toil and struggle with all the energy that he powerfully inspires within me.

2 For I want you to know how much I am struggling for you, and for those in Laodicea, and for all who have not seen me face to face. [2] I want their hearts to be encouraged and united in love, so that they may have all the riches of assured understanding and have the knowledge of God's mystery, that is, Christ himself,[k] [3] in whom are hidden all the treasures of wisdom and knowledge. [4] I am saying this so that no one may deceive you with plausible arguments. [5] For though I am absent in body, yet I am with you in spirit, and I rejoice to see your morale and the firmness of your faith in Christ.

Fullness of Life in Christ

6 As you therefore have received Christ Jesus the Lord, continue to live your lives[l] in him, [7] rooted and built up in him and established in the faith, just as you were taught, abounding in thanksgiving.

8 See to it that no one takes you captive through philosophy and

[e] Other ancient authorities read *called* [f] Other ancient authorities read *us* [g] Other ancient authorities add *through his blood* [h] Or *by* [i] Other ancient authorities read *you have now been reconciled* [j] Gk *in the body of his flesh* [k] Other ancient authorities read *of the mystery of God, both of the Father and of Christ* [l] Gk *to walk*

empty deceit, according to human tradition, according to the elemental spirits of the universe, [m] and not according to Christ. [9] For in him the whole fullness of deity dwells bodily, [10] and you have come to fullness in him, who is the head of every ruler and authority. [11] In him also you were circumcised with a spiritual circumcision, [n] by putting off the body of the flesh in the circumcision of Christ; [12] when you were buried with him in baptism, you were also raised with him through faith in the power of God, who raised him from the dead. [13] And when you were dead in trespasses and the uncircumcision of your flesh, God [o] made you [p] alive together with him, when he forgave us all our trespasses, [14] erasing the record that stood against us with its legal demands. He set this aside, nailing it to the cross. [15] He disarmed [q] the rulers and authorities and made a public example of them, triumphing over them in it.

[16] Therefore do not let anyone condemn you in matters of food and drink or of observing festivals, new moons, or sabbaths. [17] These are only a shadow of what is to come, but the substance belongs to Christ. [18] Do not let anyone disqualify you, insisting on self-abasement and worship of angels, dwelling [r] on visions, [s] puffed up without cause by a human way of thinking, [t] [19] and not holding fast to the head, from whom the whole body, nourished and held together by its ligaments and sinews, grows with a growth that is from God.

Warnings against False Teachers

20 If with Christ you died to the elemental spirits of the universe, [m] why do you live as if you still belonged to the world? Why do you submit to regulations, [21] "Do not handle, Do not taste, Do not touch"? [22] All these regulations refer to things that perish with use; they are simply human commands and teachings. [23] These have indeed an appearance of wisdom in promoting self-imposed piety, hu-

mility, and severe treatment of the body, but they are of no value in checking self-indulgence. [u]

The New Life in Christ

3 So if you have been raised with Christ, seek the things that are above, where Christ is, seated at the right hand of God. [2] Set your minds on things that are above, not on things that are on earth, [3] for you have died, and your life is hidden with Christ in God. [4] When Christ who is your [v] life is revealed, then you also will be revealed with him in glory.

5 Put to death, therefore, whatever in you is earthly: fornication, impurity, passion, evil desire, and greed (which is idolatry). [6] On account of these the wrath of God is coming on those who are disobedient. [w] [7] These are the ways you also once followed, when you were living that life. [x] [8] But now you must get rid of all such things — anger, wrath, malice, slander, and abusive [y] language from your mouth. [9] Do not lie to one another, seeing that you have stripped off the old self with its practices [10] and have clothed yourselves with the new self, which is being renewed in knowledge according to the image of its creator. [11] In that renewal [z] there is no longer Greek and Jew, circumcised and uncircumcised, barbarian, Scythian, slave and free; but Christ is all and in all!

12 As God's chosen ones, holy and beloved, clothe yourselves with compassion, kindness, humility, meekness, and patience. [13] Bear with one another and, if

2.9
Jn 1.14;
Col 1.19
2.10
Eph 1.21,22
2.11f
Rom 2.29;
Phil 3.3;
Rom 6.6;
Gal 5.24
2.12
Rom 6.4,5;
Acts 2.24
2.13
Eph 2.1
2.14
Eph 2.15
2.15
Gen 3.15;
Isa 53.12;
Eph 6.12
2.16
Rom 14.3;
14.17; 14.5;
Gal 4.10,11
2.17
Heb 8.5
2.18
Phil 3.14;
v. 23
2.19
Eph 1.22;
4.16
2.20
Rom 6.3,5;
Gal 4.3,9
2.22
1 Cor 6.13;
Isa 29.13;
Titus 1.14
2.23
Rom 13.14;
1 Tim 4.8

3.1
Ps 110.1;
Rom 8.34
3.2
Phil 3.19,20
3.3
Rom 6.2;
2 Cor 5.14
3.4
1 Jn 3.2;
Jn 14.6
3.5
Rom 6.13;
Eph 5.3,5
3.6
Rom 1.18;
Eph 5.6
3.8
Eph 4.22,29
3.9
Eph 4.25;
4.22
3.10
Rom 12.2;
Eph 4.23;
2.10
3.11
Gal 3.28;
Eph 1.23
3.12
Gal 5.22,23;

Phil 2.3; 2 Cor 6.6 **3.13** Eph 4.2,32

[m] Or *the rudiments of the world* [n] Gk *a circumcision made without hands* [o] Gk *he*
[p] Other ancient authorities read *made us*; others, *made* [q] Or *divested himself of*
[r] Other ancient authorities read *not dwelling*
[s] Meaning of Gk uncertain [t] Gk *by the mind of his flesh* [u] Or *are of no value, serving only to indulge the flesh* [v] Other authorities read *our* [w] Other ancient authorities lack *on those who are disobedient* (Gk *the children of disobedience*)
[x] Or *living among such people* [y] Or *filthy*
[z] Gk *its creator*, [11] *where*

anyone has a complaint against another, forgive each other; just as the Lord[a] has forgiven you, so you also must forgive. [14] Above all, clothe yourselves with love, which binds everything together in perfect harmony. [15] And let the peace of Christ rule in your hearts, to which indeed you were called in the one body. And be thankful. [16] Let the word of Christ[b] dwell in you richly; teach and admonish one another in all wisdom; and with gratitude in your hearts sing psalms, hymns, and spiritual songs to God. [c] [17] And whatever you do, in word or deed, do everything in the name of the Lord Jesus, giving thanks to God the Father through him.

Rules for Christian Households

18 Wives, be subject to your husbands, as is fitting in the Lord. [19] Husbands, love your wives and never treat them harshly.

20 Children, obey your parents in everything, for this is your acceptable duty in the Lord. [21] Fathers, do not provoke your children, or they may lose heart. [22] Slaves, obey your earthly masters[d] in everything, not only while being watched and in order to please them, but wholeheartedly, fearing the Lord. [d] [23] Whatever your task, put yourselves into it, as done for the Lord and not for your masters, [e] [24] since you know that from the Lord you will receive the inheritance as your reward; you serve[f] the Lord Christ. [25] For the wrongdoer will be paid back for whatever wrong has been done, and there is no partiality. [1] Masters, treat your slaves justly and fairly, for you know that you also have a Master in heaven.

Further Instructions

2 Devote yourselves to prayer, keeping alert in it with thanksgiving. [3] At the same time pray for us as well that God will open to us a door for the word, that we may declare the mystery of Christ, for

which I am in prison, [4] so that I may reveal it clearly, as I should.

5 Conduct yourselves wisely toward outsiders, making the most of the time. [g] [6] Let your speech always be gracious, seasoned with salt, so that you may know how you ought to answer everyone.

Final Greetings and Benediction

7 Tychicus will tell you all the news about me; he is a beloved brother, a faithful minister, and a fellow servant[h] in the Lord. [8] I have sent him to you for this very purpose, so that you may know how we are[i] and that he may encourage your hearts; [9] he is coming with Onesimus, the faithful and beloved brother, who is one of you. They will tell you about everything here.

10 Aristarchus my fellow prisoner greets you, as does Mark the cousin of Barnabas, concerning whom you have received instructions—if he comes to you, welcome him. [11] And Jesus who is called Justus greets you. These are the only ones of the circumcision among my co-workers for the kingdom of God, and they have been a comfort to me. [12] Epaphras, who is one of you, a servant[h] of Christ Jesus, greets you. He is always wrestling in his prayers on your behalf, so that you may stand mature and fully assured in everything that God wills. [13] For I testify for him that he has worked hard for you and for those in Laodicea and in Hierapolis. [14] Luke, the beloved physician, and Demas greet you. [15] Give my greetings to the brothers and sisters[j] in Laodicea, and to Nympha and the church in her house. [16] And when this letter has been read among you, have it read also in the church of the Laodice-

a Other ancient authorities read *just as Christ*
b Other ancient authorities read *of God*, or *of the Lord* c Other ancient authorities read *to the Lord* d In Greek the same word is used for *master* and *Lord* e Gk *not for men*
f Or *you are slaves of*, or *be slaves of*
g Or *opportunity* h Gk *slave* i Other authorities read *that I may know how you are*
j Gk *brothers*

3.14
Eph 4.3
3.15
Phil 4.7;
1 Cor 7.15;
Eph 4.4
3.16
Eph 5.19
3.17
1 Cor 10.31;
Eph 5.20
3.18
Eph 5.22-6.9
3.19
Eph 5.25
3.20
Eph 6.1
3.21
Eph 6.4
3.22
Eph 6.5,6;
Philem 16
3.24
Eph 6.8;
1 Cor 7.22
3.25
Eph 6.8,9;
Acts 10.34
4.1
Lev 25.43,
53; Eph 6.9
4.2
Rom 12.12;
Eph 6.18;
Phil 2.7
4.3
Eph 6.19;
1 Cor 16.9;
Eph 6.20

4.5
Eph 5.15,16
4.6
Eph 4.29;
Mk 9.50;
1 Pet 3.15
4.7
Eph 6.21,22
4.9
Philem 10
4.10
Acts 19.29;
15.37; 4.36
4.11
Acts 11.2;
Rom 16.3
4.12
Col 1.7;
Rom 15.30;
Phil 3.15
4.13
Col 2.1
4.14
2 Tim 4.10,
11;
Philem 24
4.15
Rom 16.5

ans; and see that you read also the letter from Laodicea. [17] And say to Archippus, "See that you complete the task that you have received in the Lord."

4.17
Philem 2;
2 Tim 4.5
4.18
1 Cor 16.21;
Heb 13.3;
13.25

[18] I, Paul, write this greeting with my own hand. Remember my chains. Grace be with you. [k]

[k] Other ancient authorities add *Amen*

THE FIRST LETTER OF PAUL TO THE
Thessalonians

Title and Background

Paul founded the church at Thessalonica during his second missionary journey. He had taught there just three weeks when he had to leave suddenly because of the opposition of the Jews. Recent converts from paganism were thus left with little pastoral support in the midst of persecution. Paul wrote to give encouragement to them.

Author and Date of Writing

Both external and internal evidence support the view that Paul wrote 1 Thessalonians. It is generally dated about A.D. 51. Except for the possibility of an early date for Galatians (A.D. 48-49), 1 Thessalonians is Paul's earliest canonical letter.

Theme and Message

Although the thrust of each letter is varied, the subject of what happens at the return of Christ is predominant in both Thessalonian letters. Every chapter of 1 Thessalonians ends with a reference to the second coming of Christ, with chapter 4 giving it major consideration. Christians are encouraged to eagerly await that day of days.

Outline

 I. Greetings and Thanksgiving (1.1-10)
 II. Paul's Defense of His Actions and Absence (2.1–3.13)
III. Exhortations (4.1–5.22)
 A. About One's Personal Life (4.1-12)
 B. About Christ's Coming (4.13–5.11)
 C. About Church Life (5.12-22)
 IV. Concluding Prayer, Greetings, and Benediction (5.23-28)

Salutation

1 Paul, Silvanus, and Timothy,
To the church of the Thessalonians in God the Father and the Lord Jesus Christ:
Grace to you and peace.

The Thessalonians' Faith and Example

2 We always give thanks to God for all of you and mention you in our prayers, constantly ³remembering before our God and Father your work of faith and labor of love and steadfastness of hope in our Lord Jesus Christ. ⁴For we know, brothers and sisters[a] beloved by God, that he has chosen you, ⁵because our message of the gospel came to you not in word only, but also in power and in the Holy Spirit and with full conviction; just as you know what kind of persons we proved to be among you for your sake. ⁶And you became imitators of us and of the Lord, for in spite of persecution you received the word with joy inspired by the Holy Spirit, ⁷so that you became an example to all the believers in Macedonia and in Achaia. ⁸For the word of the Lord has sounded forth from you not only in Macedonia and Achaia, but in every place your faith in God has become known, so that we have no need to speak about it.

1.1
2 Thes 1.1;
2 Cor 1.19;
Acts 16.1;
17.1;
Rom 1.7
1.2
2 Thes 1.3;
Rom 1.8,9
1.3
2 Thes 1.11;
1.3
1.5
2 Thes 2.14;
Col 2.2;
2 Thes 3.7

1.6
1 Cor 4.16;
11.1;
Acts 17.5-10;
13.52
1.8
Rom 10.18;
1.8;
2 Thes 1.4

[a] Gk *brothers*

9 For the people of those regions[b] report about us what kind of welcome we had among you, and how you turned to God from idols, to serve a living and true God, 10 and to wait for his Son from heaven, whom he raised from the dead — Jesus, who rescues us from the wrath that is coming.

Paul's Ministry in Thessalonica

2 You yourselves know, brothers and sisters,[c] that our coming to you was not in vain, 2 but though we had already suffered and been shamefully mistreated at Philippi, as you know, we had courage in our God to declare to you the gospel of God in spite of great opposition. 3 For our appeal does not spring from deceit or impure motives or trickery, 4 but just as we have been approved by God to be entrusted with the message of the gospel, even so we speak, not to please mortals, but to please God who tests our hearts. 5 As you know and as God is our witness, we never came with words of flattery or with a pretext for greed; 6 nor did we seek praise from mortals, whether from you or from others, 7 though we might have made demands as apostles of Christ. But we were gentle[d] among you, like a nurse tenderly caring for her own children. 8 So deeply do we care for you that we are determined to share with you not only the gospel of God but also our own selves, because you have become very dear to us.

9 You remember our labor and toil, brothers and sisters;[c] we worked night and day, so that we might not burden any of you while we proclaimed to you the gospel of God. 10 You are witnesses, and God also, how pure, upright, and blameless our conduct was toward you believers. 11 As you know, we dealt with each one of you like a father with his children, 12 urging and encouraging you and pleading that you lead a life worthy of God, who calls you into his own kingdom and glory.

13 We also constantly give

1.9
1 Cor 12.2;
Gal 4.8
1.10
2 Pet 3.12;
Acts 2.24;
Rom 5.9
2.1
1 Thes 1.5,
9
2.2
Acts 16.22;
1 Thes 1.5;
Phil 1.30
2.3
2 Cor 7.2
2.4
2 Cor 2.17;
Gal 2.7;
1.10
2.5
Acts 20.33;
Rom 1.9
2.6
2 Cor 4.5;
1 Cor 9.1,
2
2.7
v. 11;
Gal 4.19
2.8
2 Cor 12.15;
1 Jn 3.16
2.9
Acts 20.34;
2 Thes 3.8;
2 Cor 12.13
2.10
1 Thes 1.5.
2 Cor 1.12
2.11
1 Cor 4.14;
v. 7
2.12
Eph 4.1;
1 Pet 5.10
2.13
1 Thes 1.2;
Gal 4.14
2.14
Acts 17.5;
2 Thes 1.4
2.15
Acts 2.23;
7.52
2.16
Acts 9.23;
13.45,50ff;
Mt 23.32
2.17
1 Cor 5.3;
1 Thes 3.10
2.18
Rom 15.22;
1.13
2.19
2 Cor 1.14;
Phil 4.1;
1 Thes 3.13
2.20
2 Cor 1.14
3.1
v. 5;
Acts 17.15
3.2
2 Cor 1.1;

thanks to God for this, that when you received the word of God that you heard from us, you accepted it not as a human word but as what it really is, God's word, which is also at work in you believers. 14 For you, brothers and sisters,[c] became imitators of the churches of God in Christ Jesus that are in Judea, for you suffered the same things from your own compatriots as they did from the Jews, 15 who killed both the Lord Jesus and the prophets,[e] and drove us out; they displease God and oppose everyone 16 by hindering us from speaking to the Gentiles so that they may be saved. Thus they have constantly been filling up the measure of their sins; but God's wrath has overtaken them at last.[f]

Paul's Desire to Visit the Thessalonians Again

17 As for us, brothers and sisters,[c] when, for a short time, we were made orphans by being separated from you — in person, not in heart — we longed with great eagerness to see you face to face. 18 For we wanted to come to you — certainly I, Paul, wanted to again and again — but Satan blocked our way. 19 For what is our hope or joy or crown of boasting before our Lord Jesus at his coming? Is it not you? 20 Yes, you are our glory and joy!

3 Therefore when we could bear it no longer, we decided to be left alone in Athens; 2 and we sent Timothy, our brother and coworker for God in proclaiming[g] the gospel of Christ, to strengthen and encourage you for the sake of your faith, 3 so that no one would be shaken by these persecutions. Indeed, you yourselves know that this is what we are destined for. 4 In fact, when we were with you, we

Col 1.1 **3.3** Acts 9.16; 14.22 **3.4**
Acts 20.24; 1 Thes 2.14

b Gk For they c Gk brothers d Other
ancient authorities read infants e Other
ancient authorities read their own prophets
f Or completely or forever g Gk lacks
proclaiming

told you beforehand that we were to suffer persecution; so it turned out, as you know. [5]For this reason, when I could bear it no longer, I sent to find out about your faith; I was afraid that somehow the tempter had tempted you and that our labor had been in vain.

Timothy's Encouraging Report

6 But Timothy has just now come to us from you, and has brought us the good news of your faith and love. He has told us also that you always remember us kindly and long to see us — just as we long to see you. [7]For this reason, brothers and sisters,[h] during all our distress and persecution we have been encouraged about you through your faith. [8]For we now live, if you continue to stand firm in the Lord. [9]How can we thank God enough for you in return for all the joy that we feel before our God because of you? [10]Night and day we pray most earnestly that we may see you face to face and restore whatever is lacking in your faith.

11 Now may our God and Father himself and our Lord Jesus direct our way to you. [12]And may the Lord make you increase and abound in love for one another and for all, just as we abound in love for you. [13]And may he so strengthen your hearts in holiness that you may be blameless before our God and Father at the coming of our Lord Jesus with all his saints.

A Life Pleasing to God

4 Finally, brothers and sisters,[h] we ask and urge you in the Lord Jesus that, as you learned from us how you ought to live and to please God (as, in fact, you are doing), you should do so more and more. [2]For you know what instructions we gave you through the Lord Jesus. [3]For this is the will of God, your sanctification: that you abstain from fornication; [4]that each one of you know how to control your own body[i] in holiness and honor, [5]not with lustful passion, like the Gentiles who do not know

God; [6]that no one wrong or exploit a brother or sister[j] in this matter, because the Lord is an avenger in all these things, just as we have already told you beforehand and solemnly warned you. [7]For God did not call us to impurity but in holiness. [8]Therefore whoever rejects this rejects not human authority but God, who also gives his Holy Spirit to you.

9 Now concerning love of the brothers and sisters,[h] you do not need to have anyone write to you, for you yourselves have been taught by God to love one another; [10]and indeed you do love all the brothers and sisters[h] throughout Macedonia. But we urge you, beloved,[h] to do so more and more, [11]to aspire to live quietly, to mind your own affairs, and to work with your hands, as we directed you, [12]so that you may behave properly toward outsiders and be dependent on no one.

The Coming of the Lord

13 But we do not want you to be uninformed, brothers and sisters,[h] about those who have died,[k] so that you may not grieve as others do who have no hope. [14]For since we believe that Jesus died and rose again, even so, through Jesus, God will bring with him those who have died.[k] [15]For this we declare to you by the word of the Lord, that we who are alive, who are left until the coming of the Lord, will by no means precede those who have died.[k] [16]For the Lord himself, with a cry of command, with the archangel's call and with the sound of God's trumpet, will descend from heaven, and the dead in Christ will rise first. [17]Then we who are alive, who are left, will be caught up in the clouds together with them to meet the Lord in the air; and so we will be with the Lord forever. [18]Therefore encourage one another with these words.

Jn 12.26

3.5
1 Cor 11.3;
Gal 2.2
3.6
Acts 18.5;
1 Thes 1.3
3.7
2 Cor 1.4
3.8
Phil 4.1
3.9
1 Thes 1.2
3.10
2 Tim 1.3;
2 Cor 13.9
3.11
2 Thes 3.5
3.12
1 Thes 4.1,
10
3.13
1 Cor 1.8;
1 Thes 2.19;
4.17
4.1
Phil 1.27;
1 Thes 2.12;
Col 1.10
4.3
1 Cor 6.18;
Col 3.5
4.4
1 Cor 7.2;
1 Pet 3.7
4.5
Col 3.5;
Eph 4.17;
1 Cor 15.34
4.6
1 Cor 6.8;
Heb 13.4
4.7
Lev 11.44;
1 Pet 1.15;
1 Thes 2.3
4.8
Rom 5.5
4.9
Rom 12.10;
1 Thes 5.1
4.10
1 Thes 1.7;
3.12
4.11
Eph 4.28;
2 Thes 3.10-12
4.12
Rom 13.13
4.13
Eph 2.12
4.14
1 Cor 15.13,
23
4.15
1 Kings 13.17;
20.35;
1 Cor 15.51,
52
4.16
Mt 24.31;
1 Cor 15.23;
2 Thes 2.1
4.17
1 Cor 15.52;
Acts 1.9;
Rev 11.12;

[h] Gk brothers [i] Or how to take a wife for himself [j] Gk brother [k] Gk fallen asleep

5 Now concerning the times and the seasons, brothers and sisters,[1] you do not need to have anything written to you. [2] For you yourselves know very well that the day of the Lord will come like a thief in the night. [3] When they say, "There is peace and security," then sudden destruction will come upon them, as labor pains come upon a pregnant woman, and there will be no escape! [4] But you, beloved,[1] are not in darkness, for that day to surprise you like a thief; [5] for you are all children of light and children of the day; we are not of the night or of darkness. [6] So then let us not fall asleep as others do, but let us keep awake and be sober; [7] for those who sleep sleep at night, and those who are drunk get drunk at night. [8] But since we belong to the day, let us be sober, and put on the breastplate of faith and love, and for a helmet the hope of salvation. [9] For God has destined us not for wrath but for obtaining salvation through our Lord Jesus Christ, [10] who died for us, so that whether we are awake or asleep we may live with him. [11] Therefore encourage one another and build up each other, as indeed you are doing.

Final Exhortations, Greetings, and Benediction

[12] But we appeal to you, brothers and sisters,[1] to respect those who labor among you, and have

charge of you in the Lord and admonish you; [13] esteem them very highly in love because of their work. Be at peace among yourselves. [14] And we urge you, beloved[1] to admonish the idlers, encourage the faint hearted, help the weak, be patient with all of them. [15] See that none of you repays evil for evil, but always seek to do good to one another and to all. [16] Rejoice always, [17] pray without ceasing, [18] give thanks in all circumstances; for this is the will of God in Christ Jesus for you. [19] Do not quench the Spirit. [20] Do not despise the words of prophets,[m] [21] but test everything; hold fast to what is good; [22] abstain from every form of evil.

23 May the God of peace himself sanctify you entirely; and may your spirit and soul and body be kept sound[n] and blameless at the coming of our Lord Jesus Christ. [24] The one who calls you is faithful, and he will do this.

25 Beloved,[o] pray for us.

26 Greet all the brothers and sisters[1] with a holy kiss. [27] I solemnly command you by the Lord that this letter be read to all of them.[p]

28 The grace of our Lord Jesus Christ be with you.[q]

5.1
Acts 1.7;
1 Thes 4.9
5.2
1 Cor 1.8;
2 Pet 3.10
5.3
Hos 13.13
5.4
Acts 26.18;
1 Jn 2.8
5.6
Rom 13.11;
1 Pet 1.13
5.7
Acts 2.15;
2 Pet 2.13
5.8
Eph 6.14,
23,17
5.9
2 Thes 2.13,
14;
Rom 14.9
5.10
2 Cor 5.15
5.12
1 Tim 5.17;
Heb 13.17

5.14
2 Thes 3.11;
Rom 14.1
5.15
Rom 12.17;
1 Pet 3.9;
Gal 6.10;
2.13,14;
Rom 14.9
5.16
Phil 4.4
5.19
Eph 4.30
5.21
1 Cor 14.29;
1 Jn 4.1
5.23
Rom 15.33
5.24
1 Cor 1.9
5.25
Eph 6.19

5.27 Col 4.16

[1] Gk brothers [m] Gk despise prophecies [n] Or complete [o] Gk Brothers [p] Gk to all the brothers [q] Other ancient authorities add Amen

THE SECOND LETTER OF PAUL TO
Thessalonians

Title and Background

See Introduction to 1 Thessalonians.

Author and Date of Writing

Because of its similarity to 1 Thessalonians, this letter must have been written not long after the first one, about A.D. 51 or 52.

Theme and Message

Like 1 Thessalonians, this letter deals extensively with the doctrine of the last things. In fact, 18 of the 47 verses in 2 Thessalonians deal with this subject. Some people had misunderstood Paul and were sure Jesus was coming very soon. They had even stopped working and were just waiting for his return. Paul writes to correct this misunderstanding.

Outline

 I. Greetings, Thanksgiving, and Prayer (1.1-12)
 II. Instruction on Christ's Coming and Christian Conduct (2.1-17)
 III. Request for Prayer and Warning against Idleness (3.1-15)
 IV. Final Greetings and Benediction (3.16-18)

Salutation

1 Paul, Silvanus, and Timothy,
To the church of the Thessalonians in God our Father and the Lord Jesus Christ:

2 Grace to you and peace from God our[a] Father and the Lord Jesus Christ.

Thanksgiving

3 We must always give thanks to God for you, brothers and sisters,[b] as is right, because your faith is growing abundantly, and the love of everyone of you for one another is increasing. 4 Therefore we ourselves boast of you among the churches of God for your steadfastness and faith during all your persecutions and the afflictions that you are enduring.

The Judgment at Christ's Coming

5 This is evidence of the righteous judgment of God, and is intended to make you worthy of the kingdom of God, for which you are also suffering. 6 For it is indeed just of God to repay with affliction those who afflict you, 7 and to give relief to the afflicted as well as to us, when the Lord Jesus is revealed from heaven with his mighty angels 8 in flaming fire, inflicting vengeance on those who do not know God and on those who do not obey the gospel of our Lord Jesus. 9 These will suffer the punishment of eternal destruction, separated from the presence of the Lord and from the glory of his might, 10 when he comes to be glorified by his saints and to be marveled at on that day among all who have believed, because our testimony to you was believed. 11 To this end we always pray for you, asking that our God will make you worthy of his call and will fulfill by his power every good resolve and work of faith, 12 so that the name of our Lord Jesus may be glorified in you, and you in him, according to the grace

1.1 1 Thes 1.1; 2 Cor 1.19; Acts 16.1
1.2 Rom 1.7; 1 Cor 1.3
1.3 1 Thes 1.2; 3.12
1.4 2 Cor 7.14; 1 Thes 1.3; 2.14
1.5 Phil 1.28; 1 Thes 2.14
1.6 Col 3.25; Rev 6.10
1.7 1 Thes 4.16; Jude 14
1.8 Gal 4.8; Rom 2.8
1.9 Phil 3.19; 2 Pet 3.7; 2 Thes 2.8
1.10 Jn 17.10; 1 Cor 3.13; 1.6
1.11 v. 5; 1 Thes 1.3

1.12 Phil 2.9ff

a Other ancient authorities read *the*
b Gk *brothers*

of our God and the Lord Jesus Christ.

The Man of Lawlessness

2 As to the coming of our Lord Jesus Christ and our being gathered together to him, we beg you, brothers and sisters,[c] [2]not to be quickly shaken in mind or alarmed, either by spirit or by word or by letter, as though from us, to the effect that the day of the Lord is already here. [3]Let no one deceive you in any way; for that day will not come unless the rebellion comes first and the lawless one[d] is revealed, the one destined for destruction.[e] [4]He opposes and exalts himself above every so-called god or object of worship, so that he takes his seat in the temple of God, declaring himself to be God. [5]Do you not remember that I told you these things when I was still with you? [6]And you know what is now restraining him, so that he may be revealed when his time comes. [7]For the mystery of lawlessness is already at work, but only until the one who now restrains it is removed. [8]And then the lawless one will be revealed, whom the Lord Jesus[f] will destroy[g] with the breath of his mouth, annihilating him by the manifestation of his coming. [9]The coming of the lawless one is apparent in the working of Satan, who uses all power, signs, lying wonders, [10]and every kind of wicked deception for those who are perishing, because they refused to love the truth and so be saved. [11]For this reason God sends them a powerful delusion, leading them to believe what is false, [12]so that all who have not believed the truth but took pleasure in unrighteousness will be condemned.

Chosen for Salvation

13 But we must always give thanks to God for you, brothers and sisters[c] beloved by the Lord, because God chose you as the first fruits[h] for salvation through sanctification by the Spirit and through belief in the truth. [14]For this pur-

pose he called you through our proclamation of the good news,[i] so that you may obtain the glory of our Lord Jesus Christ. [15]So then, brothers and sisters,[c] stand firm and hold fast to the traditions that you were taught by us, either by word of mouth or by our letter.

16 Now may our Lord Jesus Christ himself and God our Father, who loved us and through grace gave us eternal comfort and good hope, [17]comfort your hearts and strengthen them in every good work and word.

Request for Prayer

3 Finally, brothers and sisters,[c] pray for us, so that the word of the Lord may spread rapidly and be glorified everywhere, just as it is among you, [2]and that we may be rescued from wicked and evil people; for not all have faith. [3]But the Lord is faithful; he will strengthen you and guard you from the evil one.[j] [4]And we have confidence in the Lord concerning you, that you are doing and will go on doing the things that we command. [5]May the Lord direct your hearts to the love of God and to the steadfastness of Christ.

Warning against Idleness

6 Now we command you, beloved,[c] in the name of our Lord Jesus Christ, to keep away from believers who are[k] living in idleness and not according to the tradition that they[l] received from us. [7]For you yourselves know how you ought to imitate us; we were not idle when we were with you, [8]and we did not eat anyone's bread without paying for it; but with toil and labor we worked night and day, so that we might not burden any of you. [9]This was not because we do

2.1
1 Thes 4.15-17; Mk 13.27
2.2
Eph 5.6; 2 Thes 3.17; 1 Cor 1.8
2.3
Eph 5.6-8; Dan 7.25; 8.25; 11.36; Rev 13.5ff; Jn 17.12
2.4
1 Cor 8.5; Isa 14.13, 14; Ezek 28.2
2.7
Rev 17.5,7
2.8
Dan 7.10; Rev 19.15
2.9
Mt 24.24; Jn 4.48
2.10
1 Cor 1.18
2.11
Rom 1.28;
Mt 24.5;
1 Tim 4.1
2.12
Rom 1.32
2.13
Eph 1.4;
1 Pet 1.2
2.14
1 Pet 5.10

2.15
1 Cor 16.13; 11.2
2.16
1 Thes 3.11; Jn 3.16
2.17
1 Thes 3.2; 2 Thes 3.3
3.1
1 Thes 4.1; 5.25; 1.8
3.2
Rom 15.31
3.3
1 Cor 1.9;
1 Thes 5.24;
2 Pet 2.9
3.4
2 Cor 2.3;
Gal 5.10
3.5
1 Chr 29.18
3.6
1 Cor 5.4, 11;
2 Thes 2.15
3.7
1 Thes 1.6
3.8
1 Thes 2.9;
Acts 18.3;
Eph 4.28
3.9
1 Cor 9.4ff

[c] Gk brothers [d] Gk the man of lawlessness; other ancient authorities read the man of sin [e] Gk the son of destruction [f] Other ancient authorities lack Jesus [g] Other ancient authorities read consume [h] Other ancient authorities read from the beginning [i] Or through our gospel [j] Or from evil [k] Gk from every brother who is [l] Other ancient authorities read you

not have that right, but in order to give you an example to imitate. [10] For even when we were with you, we gave you this command: Anyone unwilling to work should not eat. [11] For we hear that some of you are living in idleness, mere busybodies, not doing any work. [12] Now such persons we command and exhort in the Lord Jesus Christ to do their work quietly and to earn their own living. [13] Brothers and sisters,[m] do not be weary in doing what is right.

14 Take note of those who do not obey what we say in this letter; have nothing to do with them, so

that they may be ashamed. [15] Do not regard them as enemies, but warn them as believers.[n]

Final Greetings and Benediction

16 Now may the Lord of peace himself give you peace at all times in all ways. The Lord be with all of you.

17 I, Paul, write this greeting with my own hand. This is the mark in every letter of mine; it is the way I write. [18] The grace of our Lord Jesus Christ be with all of you.[o]

1 Thes 5.28

3.10
1 Thes 4.11
3.11
1 Tim 5.13
3.12
1 Thes 4.1, 11;
Eph 4.28
3.13
Gal 6.9
3.14
Mt 18.17

3.15
Gal 6.1;
1 Thes 5.14
3.16
Rom 15.33;
Ruth 2.4
3.17
1 Cor 16.21
3.18
Rom 16.20;

m Gk *Brothers* n Gk *a brother* o Other ancient authorities add *Amen*

THE FIRST LETTER OF PAUL TO
Timothy

Title and Background

During his (assumed) fourth missionary journey, Paul had instructed Timothy to care for the church at Ephesus while he went on to Macedonia (1 Tim 1.3). When Paul realized he might not return to Ephesus in the near future, he wrote this first letter to Timothy, to encourage the young pastor in the tasks that awaited him.

Author and Date of Writing

Both early church tradition and the salutations of the Pastoral Letters testify that Paul wrote this letter, though not all scholars are convinced of his authorship today. It was probably written about A.D. 64, at least eight years after Paul's three-year stay in Ephesus.

Theme and Message

The letter was written to Timothy to give him instructions regarding the church. The two main responsibilities Paul had given his young assistant were to refute false teachings and to supervise the affairs of the growing Ephesian church. A major problem in this church was a heresy that combined Gnosticism, decadent Judaism, and false asceticism.

Outline

Salutation

1 Paul, an apostle of Christ Jesus by the command of God our Savior and of Christ Jesus our hope,

2 To Timothy, my loyal child in the faith:

Grace, mercy, and peace from God the Father and Christ Jesus our Lord.

Warning against False Teachers

3 I urge you, as I did when I was on my way to Macedonia, to remain in Ephesus so that you may instruct certain people not to teach any different doctrine, 4 and not to occupy themselves with myths and endless genealogies that promote speculations rather than the divine training[a] that is known by faith. 5 But the aim of such instruction is love that comes from a pure heart, a good conscience, and sincere faith. 6 Some people have deviated from these and turned to meaningless talk, 7 desiring to be teachers of the law, without understanding either what they are saying or the things about which they make assertions.

8 Now we know that the law is good, if one uses it legitimately. 9 This means understanding that the law is laid down not for the innocent but for the lawless and disobedient, for the godless and sinful, for the unholy and profane, for those who kill their father or moth-

1.1
Acts 9.15;
Col 1.27
1.2
Acts 16.1;
2 Tim 1.2
1.3
Acts 20.1;
Gal 1.6,7
1.4
Titus 1.14;
1 Tim 6.4
1.5
2 Tim 2.22
1.6
Titus 1.10
1.7
Jas 3.1;
1 Tim 6.4
1.8
Rom 7.12
1.9
Gal 3.19;
1 Pet 4.18

a Or *plan*

er, for murderers, [10] fornicators, sodomites, slave traders, liars, perjurers, and whatever else is contrary to the sound teaching [11] that conforms to the glorious gospel of the blessed God, which he entrusted to me.

Gratitude for Mercy

12 I am grateful to Christ Jesus our Lord, who has strengthened me, because he judged me faithful and appointed me to his service, [13] even though I was formerly a blasphemer, a persecutor, and a man of violence. But I received mercy because I had acted ignorantly in unbelief, [14] and the grace of our Lord overflowed for me with the faith and love that are in Christ Jesus. [15] The saying is sure and worthy of full acceptance, that Christ Jesus came into the world to save sinners—of whom I am the foremost. [16] But for that very reason I received mercy, so that in me, as the foremost, Jesus Christ might display the utmost patience, making me an example to those who would come to believe in him for eternal life. [17] To the King of the ages, immortal, invisible, the only God, be honor and glory forever and ever.[b] Amen.

18 I am giving you these instructions, Timothy, my child, in accordance with the prophecies made earlier about you, so that by following them you may fight the good fight, [19] having faith and a good conscience. By rejecting conscience, certain persons have suffered shipwreck in the faith; [20] among them are Hymenaeus and Alexander, whom I have turned over to Satan, so that they may learn not to blaspheme.

Instructions concerning Prayer

2 First of all, then, I urge that supplications, prayers, intercessions, and thanksgivings be made for everyone, [2] for kings and all who are in high positions, so that we may lead a quiet and peaceable life in all godliness and dignity. [3] This is right and is accept-

able in the sight of God our Savior, [4] who desires everyone to be saved and to come to the knowledge of the truth. [5] For

there is one God;
 there is also one mediator
 between God and
 humankind,
 Christ Jesus, himself human,
6 who gave himself a ransom
 for all

—this was attested at the right time. [7] For this I was appointed a herald and an apostle (I am telling the truth,[c] I am not lying), a teacher of the Gentiles in faith and truth.

8 I desire, then, that in every place the men should pray, lifting up holy hands without anger or argument; [9] also that the women should dress themselves modestly and decently in suitable clothing, not with their hair braided, or with gold, pearls, or expensive clothes, [10] but with good works, as is proper for women who profess reverence for God. [11] Let a woman[d] learn in silence with full submission. [12] I permit no woman[d] to teach or to have authority over a man;[e] she is to keep silent. [13] For Adam was formed first, then Eve; [14] and Adam was not deceived, but the woman was deceived and became a transgressor. [15] Yet she will be saved through childbearing, provided they continue in faith and love and holiness, with modesty.

Qualifications of Bishops

3 The saying is sure:[f] whoever aspires to the office of bishop[g] desires a noble task. [2] Now a bishop[h] must be above reproach, married only once,[i] temperate, sensible, respectable, hospitable, an apt teacher, [3] not a drunkard, not violent but gentle, not quarrelsome, and not a lover of money. [4] He must manage his own house-

1.10
2 Tim 4.3;
Titus 1.9
1.11
Gal 2.7
1.12
2 Cor 12.9;
Col 1.25
1.13
Acts 8.3
1.14
Rom 5.20;
2 Tim 1.13
1.15
2 Tim 2.11;
Titus 3.8
1.16
v. 13;
Eph 2.7
1.17
Col 1.15;
Rom 11.36
1.18
1 Tim 4.14;
2 Tim 2.2,
3
1.19
1 Tim 6.12,
21
1.20
2 Tim 2.17;
4.14
2.2
Ezra 6.10;
Rom 13.1
2.3
Rom 12.2;
1 Tim 4.10
2.4
Jn 3.16;
2 Tim 2.25
2.5
Gal 3.20;
Heb 9.15
2.6
Mk 10.45;
1 Cor 1.6;
Gal 4.4
2.7
Eph 3.7,8;
Gal 1.16
2.8
Ps 134.2
2.9
1 Pet 3.3
2.11
1 Cor 14.34
2.13
Gen 1.27;
1 Cor 11.8
2.14
Gen 3.6;
2 Cor 11.3
2.15
1 Tim 1.14
3.1
1 Tim 1.15;
Acts 20.28
3.2
Titus 1.6-8;
2 Tim 2.24
3.3
2 Tim 2.24;
1 Pet 5.2
3.4
Titus 1.6

[b] Gk *to the ages of the ages* [c] Other ancient authorities add *in Christ* [d] Or *wife* [e] Or *her husband* [f] Some interpreters place these words at the end of the previous paragraph. Other ancient authorities read *The saying is commonly accepted* [g] Or *overseer* [h] Or *an overseer* [i] Gk *the husband of one wife*

hold well, keeping his children submissive and respectful in every way— ⁵for if someone does not know how to manage his own household, how can he take care of God's church? ⁶He must not be a recent convert, or he may be puffed up with conceit and fall into the condemnation of the devil. ⁷Moreover, he must be well thought of by outsiders, so that he may not fall into disgrace and the snare of the devil.

Qualifications of Deacons

8 Deacons likewise must be serious, not double-tongued, not indulging in much wine, not greedy for money; ⁹they must hold fast to the mystery of the faith with a clear conscience. ¹⁰And let them first be tested; then, if they prove themselves blameless, let them serve as deacons. ¹¹Womenʲ likewise must be serious, not slanderers, but temperate, faithful in all things. ¹²Let deacons be married only once,ᵏ and let them manage their children and their households well; ¹³for those who serve well as deacons gain a good standing for themselves and great boldness in the faith that is in Christ Jesus.

The Mystery of Our Religion

14 I hope to come to you soon, but I am writing these instructions to you so that, ¹⁵if I am delayed, you may know how one ought to behave in the household of God, which is the church of the living God, the pillar and bulwark of the truth. ¹⁶Without any doubt, the mystery of our religion is great:

He¹ was revealed in flesh,
 vindicatedᵐ in spirit,ⁿ
 seen by angels,
proclaimed among Gentiles,
 believed in throughout the
 world,
 taken up in glory.

False Asceticism

4 Now the Spirit expressly says that in laterᵒ times some will renounce the faith by paying attention to deceitful spirits and teach-

ings of demons, ²through the hypocrisy of liars whose consciences are seared with a hot iron. ³They forbid marriage and demand abstinence from foods, which God created to be received with thanksgiving by those who believe and know the truth. ⁴For everything created by God is good, and nothing is to be rejected, provided it is received with thanksgiving; ⁵for it is sanctified by God's word and by prayer.

A Good Minister of Jesus Christ

6 If you put these instructions before the brothers and sisters,ᵖ you will be a good servant�q of Christ Jesus, nourished on the words of the faith and of the sound teaching that you have followed. ⁷Have nothing to do with profane myths and old wives' tales. Train yourself in godliness, ⁸for, while physical training is of some value, godliness is valuable in every way, holding promise for both the present life and the life to come. ⁹The saying is sure and worthy of full acceptance. ¹⁰For to this end we toil and struggle,ʳ because we have our hope set on the living God, who is the Savior of all people, especially of those who believe.

11 These are the things you must insist on and teach. ¹²Let no one despise your youth, but set the believers an example in speech and conduct, in love, in faith, in purity. ¹³Until I arrive, give attention to the public reading of scripture,ˢ to exhorting, to teaching. ¹⁴Do not neglect the gift that is in you, which was given to you through prophecy with the laying on of hands by the council of elders.ᵗ ¹⁵Put these things into practice, devote yourself to them, so that all may see your progress. ¹⁶Pay close attention to yourself and to your

3.5
v. 15
3.6
1 Tim 6.4
3.7
1 Cor 5.12;
2 Tim 2.26
3.8
Acts 6.3;
Titus 2.3
3.9
1 Tim 1.19
3.11
2 Tim 3.3;
Titus 2.3
3.13
Mt 25.21
3.15
Eph 2.21;
v. 5;
1 Tim 4.10;
Gal 2.9
3.16
Jn 1.14;
1 Pet 3.18;
Acts 1.9
4.1
Jn 16.13;
2 Thes 2.3;
2 Tim 3.1;
3.13;
Rev 9.20

4.2
Eph 4.19
4.3
1 Cor 7.28;
Heb 13.4;
Gen 1.29;
Rom 14.6
4.4
Rom 14.14
4.6
2 Cor 11.23;
1 Tim 1.10;
2 Tim 3.10
4.7
2 Tim 2.16;
Heb 5.14
4.8
1 Tim 6.6;
Ps 37.4;
Rom 8.28
4.10
1 Cor 4.11;
1 Tim 2.4
4.11
1 Tim 5.7;
6.2
4.12
Titus 2.7;
1 Pet 5.3;
1 Tim 1.14
4.14
2 Tim 1.6;
1 Tim 1.18;
5.22;
Acts 6.6
4.16
Acts 20.28;
Ezek 33.9

ⁱ Or *Their wives*, or *Women deacons*
ᵏ Gk *be husbands of one wife* ¹ Gk *Who*;
other ancient authorities read *God*; others,
Which ᵐ Or *justified* ⁿ Or *by the Spirit*
ᵒ Or *the last* ᵖ Gk *brothers*
q Or *deacon* ʳ Other ancient authorities
read *suffer reproach* ˢ Gk *to the reading*
ᵗ Gk *by the presbytery*

teaching; continue in these things, for in doing this you will save both yourself and your hearers.

Duties toward Believers

5 Do not speak harshly to an older man,[u] but speak to him as to a father, to younger men as brothers, [2] to older women as mothers, to younger women as sisters — with absolute purity.

3 Honor widows who are really widows. [4] If a widow has children or grandchildren, they should first learn their religious duty to their own family and make some repayment to their parents; for this is pleasing in God's sight. [5] The real widow, left alone, has set her hope on God and continues in supplications and prayers night and day; [6] but the widow[v] who lives for pleasure is dead even while she lives. [7] Give these commands as well, so that they may be above reproach. [8] And whoever does not provide for relatives, and especially for family members, has denied the faith and is worse than an unbeliever.

9 Let a widow be put on the list if she is not less than sixty years old and has been married only once;[w] [10] she must be well attested for her good works, as one who has brought up children, shown hospitality, washed the saints' feet, helped the afflicted, and devoted herself to doing good in every way. [11] But refuse to put younger widows on the list; for when their sensual desires alienate them from Christ, they want to marry, [12] and so they incur condemnation for having violated their first pledge. [13] Besides that, they learn to be idle, gadding about from house to house; and they are not merely idle, but also gossips and busybodies, saying what they should not say. [14] So I would have younger widows marry, bear children, and manage their households, so as to give the adversary no occasion to revile us. [15] For some have already turned away to follow Satan. [16] If any believing woman[x] has relatives who are real-

ly widows, let her assist them; let the church not be burdened, so that it can assist those who are real widows.

17 Let the elders who rule well be considered worthy of double honor,[y] especially those who labor in preaching and teaching; [18] for the scripture says, "You shall not muzzle an ox while it is treading out the grain," and, "The laborer deserves to be paid." [19] Never accept any accusation against an elder except on the evidence of two or three witnesses. [20] As for those who persist in sin, rebuke them in the presence of all, so that the rest also may stand in fear. [21] In the presence of God and of Christ Jesus and of the elect angels, I warn you to keep these instructions without prejudice, doing nothing on the basis of partiality. [22] Do not ordain[z] anyone hastily, and do not participate in the sins of others; keep yourself pure.

23 No longer drink only water, but take a little wine for the sake of your stomach and your frequent ailments.

24 The sins of some people are conspicuous and precede them to judgment, while the sins of others follow them there. [25] So also good works are conspicuous; and even when they are not, they cannot remain hidden.

6 Let all who are under the yoke of slavery regard their masters as worthy of all honor, so that the name of God and the teaching may not be blasphemed. [2] Those who have believing masters must not be disrespectful to them on the ground that they are members of the church;[a] rather they must serve them all the more, since those who benefit by their service are believers and beloved.[b]

5.1 Lev 19.32
5.3 vv. 5,16
5.4 Eph 6.1,2
5.5 vv. 3,16; 1 Cor 7.32; Lk 2.37
5.6 Jas 5.5
5.7 1 Tim 4.11
5.8 Gal 6.10; Titus 1.16
5.10 Acts 16.15; Heb 13.2; Lk 7.44; v. 16
5.13 2 Thes 3.11; Titus 1.11
5.14 1 Cor 7.9; Titus 2.5
5.16 vv. 3,5

5.17 Phil 2.29; Rom 12.8; Acts 28.10
5.18 1 Cor 9.9; Lev 19.13; Deut 24.14,15; Mt 10.10
5.19 Deut 19.15
5.20 Titus 1.13; Deut 13.11
5.21 1 Tim 6.13; 2 Tim 2.14
5.22 Acts 6.6; 2 Tim 1.6; Eph 5.11
5.23 1 Tim 3.8
6.1 Titus 2.9; 1 Pet 2.18; Titus 2.5,8
6.2 Gal 3.28; Philem 16; 1 Tim 4.11

[u] Or *an elder*, or *a presbyter* [v] Gk *she* [w] Gk *the wife of one husband* [x] Other ancient authorities read *believing man or woman*; others, *believing man* [y] Or *compensation* [z] Gk *Do not lay hands on* [a] Gk *are brothers* [b] Or *since they are believers and beloved, who devote themselves to good deeds*

False Teaching and True Riches

Teach and urge these duties. [3] Whoever teaches otherwise and does not agree with the sound words of our Lord Jesus Christ and the teaching that is in accordance with godliness, [4] is conceited, understanding nothing, and has a morbid craving for controversy and for disputes about words. From these come envy, dissension, slander, base suspicions, [5] and wrangling among those who are depraved in mind and bereft of the truth, imagining that godliness is a means of gain.[c] [6] Of course, there is great gain in godliness combined with contentment; [7] for we brought nothing into the world, so that[d] we can take nothing out of it; [8] but if we have food and clothing, we will be content with these. [9] But those who want to be rich fall into temptation and are trapped by many senseless and harmful desires that plunge people into ruin and destruction. [10] For the love of money is a root of all kinds of evil, and in their eagerness to be rich some have wandered away from the faith and pierced themselves with many pains.

The Good Fight of Faith

11 But as for you, man of God, shun all this; pursue righteousness, godliness, faith, love, endurance, gentleness. [12] Fight the good fight of the faith; take hold of the eternal life, to which you were called and for which you made[e] the good confession in the presence of many witnesses. [13] In the presence of God, who gives life to all things, and of Christ Jesus, who in his testimony before Pontius Pilate made the good confession, I charge you [14] to keep the commandment without spot or blame until the manifestation of our Lord Jesus Christ, [15] which he will bring about at the right time — he who is the blessed and only Sovereign, the King of kings and Lord of lords. [16] It is he alone who has immortality and dwells in unapproachable light, whom no one has ever seen or can see; to him be honor and eternal dominion. Amen.

17 As for those who in the present age are rich, command them not to be haughty, or to set their hopes on the uncertainty of riches, but rather on God who richly provides us with everything for our enjoyment. [18] They are to do good, to be rich in good works, generous, and ready to share, [19] thus storing up for themselves the treasure of a good foundation for the future, so that they may take hold of the life that really is life.

Personal Instructions and Benediction

20 Timothy, guard what has been entrusted to you. Avoid the profane chatter and contradictions of what is falsely called knowledge; [21] by professing it some have missed the mark as regards the faith.

Grace be with you.[f]

c Other ancient authorities add *Withdraw yourself from such people* d Other ancient authorities read *world — it is certain that* e Gk *confessed* f The Greek word for *you* here is plural; in other ancient authorities it is singular. Other ancient authorities add *Amen*

Cross-references:

6.3 2 Tim 1.13; Titus 1.1
6.4 1 Cor 8.2; 2 Tim 2.14
6.5 1 Cor 11.16; Titus 1.11; 2 Pet 2.3
6.6 Phil 4.11; Heb 13.5
6.7 Job 1.21
6.8 Heb 13.5
6.9 1 Tim 3.7; 1.19
6.10 1 Tim 3.3; Jas 5.19
6.12 1 Cor 9.25, 26; 1 Tim 1.18; Heb 13.23
6.13 1 Tim 5.21; Jn 18.37
6.14 Phil 1.6; 2 Thes 2.8
6.15 1 Tim 1.11, 17; Rev 17.14; 19.16
6.16 1 Tim 1.17; Jn 1.18; Eph 3.21
6.17 Lk 12.20,21; 1 Tim 4.10; Acts 14.17
6.18 1 Tim 5.10; Rom 12.8, 13
6.20 2 Tim 1.14; 2.16

THE SECOND LETTER OF PAUL TO
Timothy

Title and Background

After Paul's release from prison in Rome in A.D. 62-63 and after his (assumed) fourth missionary journey, during which he wrote 1 Timothy and Titus, he was again imprisoned in Rome under Emperor Nero about 66-67. He was languishing in a cold dungeon, chained like a common criminal. Paul knew that his work was done and that his life was nearly at an end.

Author and Date of Writing

The first verse states that the author is Paul, and numerous references in the letter confirm this, though like 1 Timothy, Paul's authorship is disputed. It was probably written about A.D. 66.

Theme and Message

Paul had three reasons for writing to Timothy at this time: (1) Paul was lonely because many of his friends had deserted him. He wanted very much for Timothy to join him. (2) He was concerned about the welfare of the churches during this time of persecution under Nero, and he admonished Timothy to guard the gospel and, if necessary, to suffer for it. (3) He wanted to write to the Ephesian church through Timothy.

Outline

Salutation

1 Paul, an apostle of Christ Jesus by the will of God, for the sake of the promise of life that is in Christ Jesus,

2 To Timothy, my beloved child: Grace, mercy, and peace from God the Father and Christ Jesus our Lord.

Thanksgiving and Encouragement

3 I am grateful to God—whom I worship with a clear conscience, as my ancestors did—when I remember you constantly in my prayers night and day. 4Recalling your tears, I long to see you so that I may be filled with joy. 5I am reminded of your sincere faith, a faith that lived first in your grandmother Lois

and your mother Eunice and now, I am sure, lives in you. 6For this reason I remind you to rekindle the gift of God that is within you through the laying on of my hands; 7for God did not give us a spirit of cowardice, but rather a spirit of power and of love and of self-discipline.

8 Do not be ashamed, then, of the testimony about our Lord or of me his prisoner, but join with me in suffering for the gospel, relying on the power of God, 9who saved us and called us with a holy calling, not according to our works but according to his own purpose and grace. This grace was given to us in Christ Jesus before the ages began, 10but it has now been revealed

1.1
2 Cor 1.1;
Eph 3.6;
Titus 1.2
1.2
1 Tim 1.2
1.3
Rom 1.8,9;
1 Thes 1.2,
21;
Acts 20.37
1.4
2 Tim 4.9
1.5
1 Tim 1.5;
Acts 16.1

1.6
1 Tim 4.14
1.7
Rom 8.15;
Jn 14.27
1.8
Rom 1.16;
Eph 3.1;
2 Tim 2.3,
9; 4.5
1.9
Heb 3.1;

Rom 16.25 **1.10** Eph 1.9; 1 Cor 15.54

through the appearing of our Savior Christ Jesus, who abolished death and brought life and immortality to light through the gospel. [11] For this gospel I was appointed a herald and an apostle and a teacher,[a] [12] and for this reason I suffer as I do. But I am not ashamed, for I know the one in whom I have put my trust, and I am sure that he is able to guard until that day what I have entrusted to him.[b] [13] Hold to the standard of sound teaching that you have heard from me, in the faith and love that are in Christ Jesus. [14] Guard the good treasure entrusted to you, with the help of the Holy Spirit living in us.

15 You are aware that all who are in Asia have turned away from me, including Phygelus and Hermogenes. [16] May the Lord grant mercy to the household of Onesiphorus, because he often refreshed me and was not ashamed of my chain; [17] when he arrived in Rome, he eagerly[c] searched for me and found me [18] —may the Lord grant that he will find mercy from the Lord on that day! And you know very well how much service he rendered in Ephesus.

A Good Soldier of Christ Jesus

2 You then, my child, be strong in the grace that is in Christ Jesus; [2] and what you have heard from me through many witnesses entrust to faithful people who will be able to teach others as well. [3] Share in suffering like a good soldier of Christ Jesus. [4] No one serving in the army gets entangled in everyday affairs; the soldier's aim is to please the enlisting officer. [5] And in the case of an athlete, no one is crowned without competing according to the rules. [6] It is the farmer who does the work who ought to have the first share of the crops. [7] Think over what I say, for the Lord will give you understanding in all things.

8 Remember Jesus Christ, raised from the dead, a descendant of David—that is my gospel, [9] for

which I suffer hardship, even to the point of being chained like a criminal. But the word of God is not chained. [10] Therefore I endure everything for the sake of the elect, so that they may also obtain the salvation that is in Christ Jesus, with eternal glory. [11] The saying is sure:

If we have died with him, we
　　will also live with him;
[12] if we endure, we will also
　　reign with him;
if we deny him, he will also
　　deny us;
[13] if we are faithless, he
　　remains faithful—
for he cannot deny himself.

A Worker Approved by God

14 Remind them of this, and warn them before God[d] that they are to avoid wrangling over words, which does no good but only ruins those who are listening. [15] Do your best to present yourself to God as one approved by him, a worker who has no need to be ashamed, rightly explaining the word of truth. [16] Avoid profane chatter, for it will lead people into more and more impiety, [17] and their talk will spread like gangrene. Among them are Hymenaeus and Philetus, [18] who have swerved from the truth by claiming that the resurrection has already taken place. They are upsetting the faith of some. [19] But God's firm foundation stands, bearing this inscription: "The Lord knows those who are his," and, "Let everyone who calls on the name of the Lord turn away from wickedness."

20 In a large house there are utensils not only of gold and silver but also of wood and clay, some for special use, some for ordinary. [21] All who cleanse themselves of the things I have mentioned[e] will become special utensils, dedicated and useful to the owner of the house, ready for every good work. [22] Shun youthful passions and pur-

1.11
1 Tim 2.7
1.12
Titus 3.8;
1 Tim 6.20
1.13
Titus 1.9;
Rom 2.20;
1 Tim 1.14
1.14
Rom 8.9,11
1.15
Acts 19.10;
2 Tim 4.10,
11,16
1.16
2 Tim 4.19
1.18
2 Thes 1.10;
Heb 6.10
2.1
2 Tim 1.2;
Eph 6.10
2.2
2 Tim 1.13;
1 Tim 6.12;
1.18; 1.12
2.3
1 Tim 1.18
2.4
2 Pet 2.20
2.5
1 Cor 9.25
2.8
Acts 2.24;
Mt 1.1;
Rom 2.16
2.9
Acts 9.16;
Phil 1.7;
Acts 28.31

2.10
Eph 3.13;
2 Cor 1.6
2.12
1 Pet 4.13;
Mt 10.33
2.13
Rom 3.3;
Num 23.19
2.14
1 Tim 5.21;
6.4
2.15
Jas 1.12
2.16
1 Tim 4.7
2.17
1 Tim 1.20
2.18
1 Cor 15.12
2.19
Isa 28.16,
17;
1 Tim 3.15;
Jn 10.14;
1 Cor 1.2
2.20
Rom 9.21
2.21
Isa 52.11;
2 Tim 3.17
2.22
1 Tim 6.11;
1.14; 1.5

a Other ancient authorities add *of the Gentiles*
b Or *what has been entrusted to me*
c Or *promptly*　d Other ancient authorities read *the Lord*　e Gk *of these things*

sue righteousness, faith, love, and peace, along with those who call on the Lord from a pure heart. [23] Have nothing to do with stupid and senseless controversies; you know that they breed quarrels. [24] And the Lord's servant[f] must not be quarrelsome but kindly to everyone, an apt teacher, patient, [25] correcting opponents with gentleness. God may perhaps grant that they will repent and come to know the truth, [26] and that they may escape from the snare of the devil, having been held captive by him to do his will. [g]

Godlessness in the Last Days

3 You must understand this, that in the last days distressing times will come. [2] For people will be lovers of themselves, lovers of money, boasters, arrogant, abusive, disobedient to their parents, ungrateful, unholy, [3] inhuman, implacable, slanderers, profligates, brutes, haters of good, [4] treacherous, reckless, swollen with conceit, lovers of pleasure rather than lovers of God, [5] holding to the outward form of godliness but denying its power. Avoid them! [6] For among them are those who make their way into households and captivate silly women, overwhelmed by their sins and swayed by all kinds of desires, [7] who are always being instructed and can never arrive at a knowledge of the truth. [8] As Jannes and Jambres opposed Moses, so these people, of corrupt mind and counterfeit faith, also oppose the truth. [9] But they will not make much progress, because, as in the case of those two men,[h] their folly will become plain to everyone.

Paul's Charge to Timothy

10 Now you have observed my teaching, my conduct, my aim in life, my faith, my patience, my love, my steadfastness, [11] my persecutions and suffering the things that happened to me in Antioch, Iconium, and Lystra. What persecutions I endured! Yet the Lord rescued me from all of them. [12] Indeed, all who want to live a godly life in Christ

Jesus will be persecuted. [13] But wicked people and impostors will go from bad to worse, deceiving others and being deceived. [14] But as for you, continue in what you have learned and firmly believed, knowing from whom you learned it, [15] and how from childhood you have known the sacred writings that are able to instruct you for salvation through faith in Christ Jesus. [16] All scripture is inspired by God and is[i] useful for teaching, for reproof, for correction, and for training in righteousness, [17] so that everyone who belongs to God may be proficient, equipped for every good work.

4 In the presence of God and of Christ Jesus, who is to judge the living and the dead, and in view of his appearing and his kingdom, I solemnly urge you: [2] proclaim the message; be persistent whether the time is favorable or unfavorable; convince, rebuke, and encourage, with the utmost patience in teaching. [3] For the time is coming when people will not put up with sound doctrine, but having itching ears, they will accumulate for themselves teachers to suit their own desires, [4] and will turn away from listening to the truth and wander away to myths. [5] As for you, always be sober, endure suffering, do the work of an evangelist, carry out your ministry fully.

6 As for me, I am already being poured out as a libation, and the time of my departure has come. [7] I have fought the good fight, I have finished the race, I have kept the faith. [8] From now on there is reserved for me the crown of righteousness, which the Lord, the righteous judge, will give me on that day, and not only to me but also to all who have longed for his appearing.

2.23
1 Tim 6.4;
Titus 3.9
2.24
1 Tim 3.3;
Titus 1.7;
1 Tim 3.2
2.25
Gal 6.1;
1 Pet 3.15
2.26
1 Tim 3.7
3.1
1 Tim 4.1
3.2
2 Pet 2.3;
Rom 1.30
3.3
Rom 1.31;
Titus 1.8
3.4
2 Pet 2.10;
Phil 3.19
3.5
2 Thes 3.6
3.6
Titus 1.11
3.7
2 Tim 2.25
3.8
Ex 7.11;
Acts 13.8;
1 Tim 6.5
3.9
Ex 7.12
3.10
1 Tim 4.6;
Phil 2.22
3.11
Acts 13.45;
14.2,19
3.12
Ps 34.19;
Mt 16.24;
1 Thes 3.3
3.13
2 Tim 2.16;
Titus 3.3
3.14
2 Tim 1.13
3.15
2 Tim 1.5;
Jn 5.39
3.16
Rom 15.4;
2 Pet 1.20,
21
3.17
1 Tim 6.11;
2 Tim 2.21
4.1
1 Tim 5.21;
Acts 10.42
4.2
1 Tim 5.20;
Titus 1.13;
1 Tim 4.13
4.3
2 Tim 3.1,
6;
1 Tim 1.10
4.5
Acts 21.8
4.6
Phil 2.17;
1.23

4.7 Phil 3.14; 1 Tim 6.12 **4.8** Jas 1.12;
1 Pet 5.4; 2 Tim 1.12

[f] Gk slave [g] Or by him, to do his (that is,
God's) will [h] Gk lacks two men
[i] Or Every scripture inspired by God is also

Personal Instructions

9 Do your best to come to me soon, [10] for Demas, in love with this present world, has deserted me and gone to Thessalonica; Crescens has gone to Galatia,ⁱ Titus to Dalmatia. [11] Only Luke is with me. Get Mark and bring him with you, for he is useful in my ministry. [12] I have sent Tychicus to Ephesus. [13] When you come, bring the cloak that I left with Carpus at Troas, also the books, and above all the parchments. [14] Alexander the coppersmith did me great harm; the Lord will pay him back for his deeds. [15] You also must beware of him, for he strongly opposed our message.

16 At my first defense no one came to my support, but all deserted me. May it not be counted against them! [17] But the Lord stood by me and gave me strength, so that through me the message might be fully proclaimed and all the Gentiles might hear it. So I was rescued from the lion's mouth. [18] The Lord will rescue me from every evil attack and save me for his heavenly kingdom. To him be the glory forever and ever. Amen.

Final Greetings and Benediction

19 Greet Prisca and Aquila, and the household of Onesiphorus. [20] Erastus remained in Corinth; Trophimus I left ill in Miletus. [21] Do your best to come before winter. Eubulus sends greetings to you, as do Pudens and Linus and Claudia and all the brothers and sisters.ᵏ

22 The Lord be with your spirit. Grace be with you.ˡ

ⁱ Other ancient authorities read *Gaul*
ᵏ Gk *all the brothers* ˡ The Greek word for *you* here is plural. Other ancient authorities add *Amen*

4.10
Col 4.14;
1 Jn 2.15
4.11
2 Tim 1.15;
Col 4.14;
Acts 12.12
4.14
Acts 19.33;
Rom 12.19;
Ps 119.98,
99
4.16
Acts 7.60
4.17
Acts 23.11;
2 Pet 2.9

4.18
Ps 121.7;
Rom 11.36
4.19
Acts 18.2
4.20
Acts 19.22
4.21
v. 9
4.22
Gal 6.18;
Philem 25

THE LETTER OF PAUL TO
Titus

Title and Background

When Paul left Antioch to discuss "his" gospel with the Jerusalem leaders, he took Titus with him (Gal 2.1-3). Presumably Titus, who is not referred to in Acts, worked with Paul at Ephesus during the third missionary journey. From there the apostle sent him to Corinth, to help that church with its work (2 Cor 7.6-7; 8.17). Following Paul's release from his first Roman imprisonment, he and Titus worked briefly in Crete (Titus 1.5), after which he commissioned Titus to remain there as his representative and to complete some needed work.

Author and Date of Writing

Paul probably wrote this letter to Titus from Corinth about A.D. 64. See also the Introduction to 1 Timothy.

Theme and Message

Paul wrote Titus to give him personal authorization and guidance in meeting opposition, instructions about faith and conduct, and warnings about false teachers. He also informed Titus of his future plans for him.

Outline

I. Concerning Elders (1.1-9)
II. Concerning False Teachers (1.10-16)
III. Concerning Various Groups (2.1-15)
IV. Concerning Believers in General (3.1-8)
V. Concerning Response to Spiritual Error (3.9-15)

Salutation

1 Paul, a servant[a] of God and an apostle of Jesus Christ, for the sake of the faith of God's elect and the knowledge of the truth that is in accordance with godliness, [2] in the hope of eternal life that God, who never lies, promised before the ages began — [3] in due time he revealed his word through the proclamation with which I have been entrusted by the command of God our Savior,

4 To Titus, my loyal child in the faith we share:

Grace[b] and peace from God the Father and Christ Jesus our Savior.

Titus in Crete

5 I left you behind in Crete for this reason, so that you should put in order what remained to be done, and should appoint elders in every town, as I directed you: [6] someone who is blameless, married only once,[c] whose children are believers, not accused of debauchery and not rebellious. [7] For a bishop,[d] as God's steward, must be blameless; he must not be arrogant or quick-tempered or addicted to wine or violent or greedy for gain; [8] but he must be hospitable, a lover of goodness, prudent, upright, devout, and self-controlled. [9] He must have a firm grasp of the word that is trustworthy in accordance with the teaching, so that he may be able both to preach with sound doctrine and to refute those who contradict it.

10 There are also many rebel-

1.1
Rom 1.1;
2 Cor 1.1;
1 Tim 2.4;
6.3
1.2
2 Tim 1.1;
Rom 16.25
1.3
2 Tim 1.10;
1 Thes 2.4
1.4
2 Cor 2.13;
Eph 1.2;
1 Tim 1.2
1.5
Acts 27.7;
14.23; 11.30
1.6
1 Tim 3.2-4
1.7
1 Cor 4.1;
Eph 5.18
1.8
1 Tim 3.2;
2 Tim 3.3
1.9
1 Tim 1.19;
1.10
1.10
1 Tim 1.6;

Acts 11.2

a Gk *slave* b Other ancient authorities read *Grace, mercy,* c Gk *husband of one wife*
d Or *an overseer*

lious people, idle talkers and deceivers, especially those of the circumcision; [11]they must be silenced, since they are upsetting whole families by teaching for sordid gain what it is not right to teach. [12]It was one of them, their very own prophet, who said,

"Cretans are always liars,
vicious brutes, lazy
gluttons."

[13]That testimony is true. For this reason rebuke them sharply, so that they may become sound in the faith, [14]not paying attention to Jewish myths or to commandments of those who reject the truth. [15]To the pure all things are pure, but to the corrupt and unbelieving nothing is pure. Their very minds and consciences are corrupted. [16]They profess to know God, but they deny him by their actions. They are detestable, disobedient, unfit for any good work.

Teach Sound Doctrine

2 But as for you, teach what is consistent with sound doctrine. [2]Tell the older men to be temperate, serious, prudent, and sound in faith, in love, and in endurance.

[3]Likewise, tell the older women to be reverent in behavior, not to be slanderers or slaves to drink; they are to teach what is good, [4]so that they may encourage the young women to love their husbands, to love their children, [5]to be self-controlled, chaste, good managers of the household, kind, being submissive to their husbands, so that the word of God may not be discredited.

[6]Likewise, urge the younger men to be self-controlled. [7]Show yourself in all respects a model of good works, and in your teaching show integrity, gravity, [8]and sound speech that cannot be censured; then any opponent will be put to shame, having nothing evil to say of us.

[9]Tell slaves to be submissive to their masters and to give satisfac-

tion in every respect; they are not to talk back, [10]not to pilfer, but to show complete and perfect fidelity, so that in everything they may be an ornament to the doctrine of God our Savior.

11 For the grace of God has appeared, bringing salvation to all,[e] [12]training us to renounce impiety and worldly passions, and in the present age to live lives that are self-controlled, upright, and godly, [13]while we wait for the blessed hope and the manifestation of the glory of our great God and Savior,[f] Jesus Christ. [14]He it is who gave himself for us that he might redeem us from all iniquity and purify for himself a people of his own who are zealous for good deeds.

15 Declare these things; exhort and reprove with all authority.[g] Let no one look down on you.

Maintain Good Deeds

3 Remind them to be subject to rulers and authorities, to be obedient, to be ready for every good work, [2]to speak evil of no one, to avoid quarreling, to be gentle, and to show every courtesy to everyone. [3]For we ourselves were once foolish, disobedient, led astray, slaves to various passions and pleasures, passing our days in malice and envy, despicable, hating one another. [4]But when the goodness and loving kindness of God our Savior appeared, [5]he saved us, not because of any works of righteousness that we had done, but according to his mercy, through the water[h] of rebirth and renewal by the Holy Spirit. [6]This Spirit he poured out on us richly through Jesus Christ our Savior, [7]so that, having been justified by his grace, we might become heirs according to the hope of eternal life. [8]The saying is sure.

I desire that you insist on these things, so that those who have come to believe in God may be careful to devote themselves to

Cross references

1.11
2 Tim 3.6;
1 Tim 6.5
1.12
Acts 17.28
1.13
2 Cor 13.10;
Titus 2.2
1.14
1 Tim 1.4;
Isa 29.13
1.15
Lk 11.39,41;
Rom 14.23
1.16
1 Jn 2.4;
2 Tim 3.5,
8
2.1
Titus 1.9
2.2
Titus 1.13
2.3
1 Tim 3.8
2.5
1 Cor 14.34;
Eph 5.22;
1 Tim 6.1
2.7
1 Tim 4.12
2.8
1 Tim 6.3
2.9
Eph 6.5
2.10
Mt 5.16
2.11
Rom 5.15;
1 Tim 2.4
2.12
Titus 3.3;
2 Tim 3.12
2.13
2 Thes 2.8;
2 Pet 1.1
2.14
1 Tim 2.6;
Heb 9.14;
Ex 19.5;
Eph 2.10
3.1
Rom 13.1;
2 Tim 2.21
3.2
Eph 4.31;
2 Tim 2.24,
25
3.3
1 Cor 6.11;
1 Pet 4.3
3.4
Titus 2.11;
1 Tim 2.3
3.5
Rom 3.20;
Eph 5.26;
Rom 12.2
3.6
Rom 5.5
3.7
Rom 3.24;
8.17,24
3.8
1 Tim 1.15;
Titus 2.14

[e] Or *has appeared to all, bringing salvation*
[f] Or *of the great God and our Savior* [g] Gk *commandment* [h] Gk *washing*

good works; these things are excellent and profitable to everyone. [9]But avoid stupid controversies, genealogies, dissensions, and quarrels about the law, for they are unprofitable and worthless. [10]After a first and second admonition, have nothing more to do with anyone who causes divisions, [11]since you know that such a person is perverted and sinful, being self-condemned.

Final Messages and Benediction

[12]When I send Artemas to you, or Tychicus, do your best to come to me at Nicopolis, for I have decided to spend the winter there. [13]Make every effort to send Zenas the lawyer and Apollos on their way, and see that they lack nothing. [14]And let people learn to devote themselves to good works in order to meet urgent needs, so that they may not be unproductive.

[15]All who are with me send greetings to you. Greet those who love us in the faith.

Grace be with all of you.[i]

[i]Other ancient authorities add *Amen*

3.9
1 Tim 1.4;
2 Tim 2.14
3.10
Rom 16.17
3.12
Acts 20.4;
2 Tim 4.9,
10

3.13
Acts 18.24
3.14
v. 8
3.15
Col 4.18

THE LETTER OF PAUL TO
Philemon

Title and Background

Philemon was a believer in Colosse who, along with other Christians, was a slave owner. One of his slaves, Onesimus, had apparently stolen from him and then run away, which under Roman law was punishable by death. But Onesimus met Paul and through his ministry became a Christian. Now he was willing to return to his master.

Author and Date of Writing

Paul wrote this short letter about A.D. 60 from prison in Rome and sent it to Colosse with Onesimus and Tychicus.

Theme and Message

Paul wrote this personal appeal to ask Philemon to welcome Onesimus as a Christian brother, not as a slave. Now that Onesimus (whose name means "useful") was a believer, he was really useful.

Outline

 I. Greetings (1-3)
 II. Thanksgiving and Prayer (4-7)
 III. Paul's Plea for Onesimus (8-21)
 IV. Conclusion (22-25)

Salutation

1 Paul, a prisoner of Christ Jesus, and Timothy our brother,[a]

To Philemon our dear friend and co-worker, 2 to Apphia our sister,[b] to Archippus our fellow soldier, and to the church in your house: 3 Grace to you and peace from God our Father and the Lord Jesus Christ.

Philemon's Love and Faith

4 When I remember you[c] in my prayers, I always thank my God 5 because I hear of your love for all the saints and your faith toward the Lord Jesus. 6 I pray that the sharing of your faith may become effective when you perceive all the good that we[d] may do for Christ. 7 I have indeed received much joy and encouragement from your love, because the hearts of the saints have been refreshed through you, my brother.

Paul's Plea for Onesimus

8 For this reason, though I am bold enough in Christ to command you to do your duty, 9 yet I would rather appeal to you on the basis of love — and I, Paul, do this as an old man, and now also as a prisoner of Christ Jesus.[e] 10 I am appealing to you for my child, Onesimus, whose father I have become during my imprisonment. 11 Formerly he was useless to you, but now he is indeed useful[f] both to you and to me. 12 I am sending him, that is, my own heart, back to you. 13 I wanted to keep him with me, so that he might be of service to me in your place during my imprisonment for the gospel; 14 but I preferred to do nothing without your consent, in

1 Eph 3.1; 2 Cor 1.1; Phil 2.25
2 Col 4.17; Phil 2.25; Rom 16.5
4 Rom 1.8,9
5 Eph 1.15; Col 1.4
v. 20; 2 Cor 7.13
10 Col 4.9; 1 Cor 4.14, 15
13 Phil 1.7
14 1 Pet 5.2; 2 Cor 9.7

a Gk *the brother* b Gk *the sister* c From verse 4 through verse 21, *you* is singular d Other ancient authorities read *you* (plural) e Or *as an ambassador of Christ Jesus, and now also his prisoner* f The name Onesimus means *useful* or (compare verse 20) *beneficial*

order that your good deed might be voluntary and not something forced. ¹⁵ Perhaps this is the reason he was separated from you for a while, so that you might have him back forever, ¹⁶ no longer as a slave but more than a slave, a beloved brother—especially to me but how much more to you, both in the flesh and in the Lord.

17 So if you consider me your partner, welcome him as you would welcome me. ¹⁸ If he has wronged you in any way, or owes you anything, charge that to my account. ¹⁹ I, Paul, am writing this with my own hand: I will repay it. I say nothing about your owing me even your own self. ²⁰ Yes, brother, let me have this benefit from you in the

16
Mt 23.8;
1 Tim 6.2;
Col 3.22
17
2 Cor 8.23

21
2 Cor 2.3
22
Acts 28.23;
Phil 1.25;
2.24;
2 Cor 1.11
23
Col 1.7
24
Acts 12.12;
Col 4.10
25
2 Tim 4.22

Lord! Refresh my heart in Christ. ²¹ Confident of your obedience, I am writing to you, knowing that you will do even more than I say.

22 One thing more—prepare a guest room for me, for I am hoping through your prayers to be restored to you.

Final Greetings and Benediction

23 Epaphras, my fellow prisoner in Christ Jesus, sends greetings to you,ᵍ ²⁴ and so do Mark, Aristarchus, Demas, and Luke, my fellow workers.

25 The grace of the Lord Jesus Christ be with your spirit. ʰ

ᵍ Here *you* is singular ʰ Other ancient
authorities add *Amen*

THE LETTER TO THE
Hebrews

Title and Background

The first-century church underwent much persecution, and this letter was written in that setting. The persecution had not yet resulted in martyrdom, but it was severe. The intended readers seem to have been Jewish Christians who were thinking of abandoning their faith and of lapsing back into Judaism. So the author exhorts them to hold fast to their confession of Christ as Savior and Lord.

Author and Date of Writing

The author of this letter does not identify himself, but he was obviously well known to the original recipients. For many years Paul was considered to be the author, but since the Reformation it has been widely recognized that Paul could not have been the author. Apollos and Barnabas are those most often suggested. The book was written prior to the fall of Jerusalem in A.D. 70.

Theme and Message

The theme of Hebrews is the absolute supremacy and sufficiency of Jesus Christ as revealer and as mediator of God's grace. The prologue presents Christ as God's full and final revelation. Hebrews could be called "the book of better things," since the two Greek words for "better" and "superior" occur fifteen times in the letter. Practical applications of this theme are given throughout the book.

Outline

God Has Spoken by His Son

1 Long ago God spoke to our ancestors in many and various ways by the prophets, [2] but in these last days he has spoken to us by a Son,[a] whom he appointed heir of all things, through whom he also created the worlds. [3] He is the reflection of God's glory and the exact imprint of God's very being, and he sustains[b] all things by his powerful word. When he had made purification for sins, he sat down at the right hand of the Majesty on high, [4] having become as much superior to angels as the name he has inherited is more excellent than theirs.

1.2
Gal 4.4;
Heb 2.3;
Ps 2.8;
Jn 1.3;
1 Cor 8.6
1.3
Jn 1.14;
Col 1.17;
Heb 7.27;
8.1
1.4
Eph 1.21;
Phil 2.9,10

1.5
Ps 2.7
1.6
Heb 10.5;
Deut 32.43
1.7
Ps 104.4

The Son Is Superior to Angels

5 For to which of the angels did God ever say,

"You are my Son;
today I have begotten
you?"

Or again,

"I will be his Father,
and he will be my Son"?

[6] And again, when he brings the firstborn into the world, he says,

"Let all God's angels worship
him."

[7] Of the angels he says,

"He makes his angels winds,
and his servants flames of
fire."

[a] Or *the Son* [b] Or *bears along*

8 But of the Son he says,
"Your throne, O God,[c] is
forever and ever,
and the righteous scepter is
the scepter of your[d]
kingdom.
9 You have loved righteousness
and hated wickedness;
therefore God, your God, has
anointed you
with the oil of gladness
beyond your
companions."
10 And,
"In the beginning, Lord, you
founded the earth,
and the heavens are the
work of your hands;
11 they will perish, but you
remain;
they will all wear out like
clothing;
12 like a cloak you will roll
them up,
and like clothing[e] they will
be changed.
But you are the same,
and your years will never
end."
13 But to which of the angels has he
ever said,
"Sit at my right hand
until I make your enemies
a footstool for your
feet"?
14 Are not all angels[f] spirits in the
divine service, sent to serve for the
sake of those who are to inherit sal-
vation?

Warning to Pay Attention

2 Therefore we must pay greater
attention to what we have
heard, so that we do not drift away
from it. 2 For if the message de-
clared through angels was valid,
and every transgression or disobe-
dience received a just penalty,
3 how can we escape if we neglect
so great a salvation? It was de-
clared at first through the Lord,
and it was attested to us by those
who heard him, 4 while God added
his testimony by signs and wonders
and various miracles, and by gifts
of the Holy Spirit, distributed ac-
cording to his will.

1.8
Ps 45.6,7
1.9
Phil 2.9;
Isa 61.1,3
1.10
Ps 102.25
1.11
Isa 34.4
1.12
Heb 13.8
1.13
Ps 110.1;
Heb 10.13
1.14
Ps 103.20;
Heb 5.9
2.2
Heb 1.1;
Acts 7.53;
Heb 10.28,
35
2.3
Heb 10.29;
1.1; Lk 1.2
2.4
Jn 4.48;
1 Cor 12.4;
Eph 1.5

2.5
Heb 6.5
2.6
Ps 8.4-6
2.8
Mt 28.18;
1 Cor 15.27;
15.25
2.9
Phil 2.7-9;
Acts 2.33;
Jn 3.16;
1 Jn 2.2
2.10
Lk 24.46;
Rom 11.36;
Acts 3.15;
5.31;
Lk 13.32
2.11
Heb 10.10;
Acts 17.26;
Jn 20.17
2.12
Ps 22.22
2.13
Isa 8.17,18;
Jn 10.29

Exaltation through Abasement

5 Now God[g] did not subject the
coming world, about which we are
speaking, to angels. 6 But someone
has testified somewhere,
"What are human beings that
you are mindful of
them,[h]
or mortals, that you care
for them?[i]
7 You have made them for a
little while lower[j] than
the angels;
you have crowned them
with glory and honor,[k]
8 subjecting all things under
their feet."
Now in subjecting all things to
them, God[g] left nothing outside
their control. As it is, we do not yet
see everything in subjection to
them, 9 but we do see Jesus, who
for a little while was made lower[l]
than the angels, now crowned with
glory and honor because of the suf-
fering of death, so that by the grace
of God[m] he might taste death for
everyone.
10 It was fitting that God,[g] for
whom and through whom all things
exist, in bringing many children to
glory, should make the pioneer of
their salvation perfect through suf-
ferings. 11 For the one who sancti-
fies and those who are sanctified
all have one Father.[n] For this rea-
son Jesus[g] is not ashamed to call
them brothers and sisters,[o] 12 say-
ing,
"I will proclaim your name
to my brothers and
sisters,[o]
in the midst of the
congregation I will
praise you."
13 And again,

[c] Or God is your throne　　[d] Other ancient
authorities read his　　[e] Other ancient
authorities lack like clothing　　[f] Gk all of
them　　[g] Gk he　　[h] Gk What is man that
you are mindful of him?　　[i] Gk or the son of
man that you care for him? In the Hebrew of
Psalm 8.4-6 both man and son of man refer to
all humankind　　[j] Or them only a little lower
[k] Other ancient authorities add and set them
over the works of your hands　　[l] Or who was
made a little lower　　[m] Other ancient
authorities read apart from God　　[n] Gk are
all of one　　[o] Gk brothers

"I will put my trust in him."
And again,
> "Here am I and the children
> whom God has given
> me."

14 Since, therefore, the children share flesh and blood, he himself likewise shared the same things, so that through death he might destroy the one who has the power of death, that is, the devil, [15] and free those who all their lives were held in slavery by the fear of death. [16] For it is clear that he did not come to help angels, but the descendants of Abraham. [17] Therefore he had to become like his brothers and sisters[p] in every respect, so that he might be a merciful and faithful high priest in the service of God, to make a sacrifice of atonement for the sins of the people. [18] Because he himself was tested by what he suffered, he is able to help those who are being tested.

Moses a Servant, Christ a Son

3 Therefore, brothers and sisters,[p] holy partners in a heavenly calling, consider that Jesus, the apostle and high priest of our confession, [2] was faithful to the one who appointed him, just as Moses also "was faithful in all[q] God's[r] house." [3] Yet Jesus[s] is worthy of more glory than Moses, just as the builder of a house has more honor than the house itself. [4] (For every house is built by someone, but the builder of all things is God.) [5] Now Moses was faithful in all God's[r] house as a servant, to testify to the things that would be spoken later. [6] Christ, however, was faithful over God's[r] house as a son, and we are his house if we hold firm[t] the confidence and the pride that belong to hope.

Warning against Unbelief

7 Therefore, as the Holy Spirit says,
> "Today, if you hear his voice,
> [8] do not harden your hearts as
> in the rebellion,

2.14
Mt 16.17;
Jn 1.14;
1 Cor 15.54-
57; 1 Jn 3.8
2.15
Rom 8.15;
2 Tim 1.7
2.17
Phil 2.7;
Heb 4.15;
5.1,2;
1 Jn 2.2;
4.10
2.18
Heb 4.15
3.1
Heb 2.11;
Phil 3.14;
Rom 15.8;
Heb 10.21
3.3
2 Cor 3.7-11
3.4
Eph 2.10;
Heb 1.2
3.5
Num 12.7;
Ex 14.31;
Deut 18.18,
19
3.6
Heb 1.2;
1 Cor 3.16;
Rom 5.2;
Col 1.23
3.7
Heb 9.8;
Ps 95.7

3.9
Acts 7.36
3.11
Heb 4.3,5
3.12
Heb 12.25;
9.14
3.13
Heb 10.24,
25;
Eph 4.22
3.14
v. 6
3.15
v. 7
3.16
Num 14.2
3.17
Num 14.29;
Ps 106.26
3.18
Num 14.23;
Heb 4.6
3.19
Jn 3.36
4.1
Heb 12.15
4.2
1 Thes 2.13
4.3
Ps 95.11;
Heb 3.11

> as on the day of testing in
> the wilderness,
> [9] where your ancestors put me
> to the test,
> though they had seen my
> works [10] for forty years.
> Therefore I was angry with
> that generation,
> and I said, 'They always go
> astray in their hearts,
> and they have not known
> my ways.'
> [11] As in my anger I swore,
> 'They will not enter my
> rest.' "

[12] Take care, brothers and sisters,[p] that none of you may have an evil, unbelieving heart that turns away from the living God. [13] But exhort one another every day, as long as it is called "today," so that none of you may be hardened by the deceitfulness of sin. [14] For we have become partners of Christ, if only we hold our first confidence firm to the end. [15] As it is said,
> "Today, if you hear his voice,
> do not harden your hearts as
> in the rebellion."

[16] Now who were they who heard and yet were rebellious? Was it not all those who left Egypt under the leadership of Moses? [17] But with whom was he angry forty years? Was it not those who sinned, whose bodies fell in the wilderness? [18] And to whom did he swear that they would not enter his rest, if not to those who were disobedient? [19] So we see that they were unable to enter because of unbelief.

The Rest That God Promised

4 Therefore, while the promise of entering his rest is still open, let us take care that none of you should seem to have failed to reach it. [2] For indeed the good news came to us just as to them; but the message they heard did not benefit them, because they were not united by faith with those who listened.[u] [3] For we who have believed

p Gk *brothers* q Other ancient authorities
lack *all* r Gk *his* s Gk *this one*
t Other ancient authorities add *to the end*
u Other ancient authorities read *it did not meet
with faith in those who listened*

enter that rest, just as God[v] has said,

"As in my anger I swore,
'They shall not enter my
 rest,' "

though his works were finished at the foundation of the world. [4] For in one place it speaks about the seventh day as follows, "And God rested on the seventh day from all his works." [5] And again in this place it says, "They shall not enter my rest." [6] Since therefore it remains open for some to enter it, and those who formerly received the good news failed to enter because of disobedience, [7] again he sets a certain day — "today" — saying through David much later, in the words already quoted,

"Today, if you hear his voice,
 do not harden your hearts."

[8] For if Joshua had given them rest, God[v] would not speak later about another day. [9] So then, a sabbath rest still remains for the people of God; [10] for those who enter God's rest also cease from their labors as God did from his. [11] Let us therefore make every effort to enter that rest, so that no one may fall through such disobedience as theirs.

[12] Indeed, the word of God is living and active, sharper than any two-edged sword, piercing until it divides soul from spirit, joints from marrow; it is able to judge the thoughts and intentions of the heart. [13] And before him no creature is hidden, but all are naked and laid bare to the eyes of the one to whom we must render an account.

Jesus the Great High Priest

[14] Since, then, we have a great high priest who has passed through the heavens, Jesus, the Son of God, let us hold fast to our confession. [15] For we do not have a high priest who is unable to sympathize with our weaknesses, but we have one who in every respect has been tested[w] as we are, yet without sin. [16] Let us therefore approach the

4.4
Gen 2.2;
Ex 20.11
4.5
Ps 95.11;
Heb 3.11
4.6
Heb 3.18,19
4.7
Ps 95.7,8;
Heb 3.7,8
4.8
Josh 22.4;
Heb 1.1
4.10
v. 4
4.11
Heb 3.18
4.12
Jer 23.29;
Eph 6.17;
1 Cor 14.24,
25
4.13
Ps 33.13-15;
Job 26.6
4.14
Heb 3.1;
7.26; 10.23
4.15
Heb 2.18;
2 Cor 5.21;
1 Pet 2.22
4.16
Eph 2.18
5.1
Heb 8.3,4;
7.27
5.2
Heb 2.18;
Jas 5.19;
Heb 7.28
5.3
Heb 7.27;
9.7
5.4
2 Chr 26.18;
Ex 28.1
5.5
Jn 8.54;
Ps 2.7;
Heb 1.1,5
5.6
Ps 110.4;
Heb 7.17
5.7
Mt 26.39,
53; 27.46;
Mk 14.36;
15.34
5.8
Heb 3.6;
Phil 2.8
5.9
Heb 2.10
5.10
vv. 5,6
5.12
Gal 4.3;
Heb 6.1;
Acts 7.38;
1 Cor 3.2
5.13
1 Cor 3.1
5.14
Isa 7.15

throne of grace with boldness, so that we may receive mercy and find grace to help in time of need.

5 Every high priest chosen from among mortals is put in charge of things pertaining to God on their behalf, to offer gifts and sacrifices for sins. [2] He is able to deal gently with the ignorant and wayward, since he himself is subject to weakness; [3] and because of this he must offer sacrifice for his own sins as well as for those of the people. [4] And one does not presume to take this honor, but takes it only when called by God, just as Aaron was.

[5] So also Christ did not glorify himself in becoming a high priest, but was appointed by the one who said to him,

"You are my Son,
 today I have begotten you";

[6] as he says also in another place,

"You are a priest forever,
 according to the order of
 Melchizedek."

[7] In the days of his flesh, Jesus[v] offered up prayers and supplications, with loud cries and tears, to the one who was able to save him from death, and he was heard because of his reverent submission. [8] Although he was a Son, he learned obedience through what he suffered; [9] and having been made perfect, he became the source of eternal salvation for all who obey him, [10] having been designated by God a high priest according to the order of Melchizedek.

Warning against Falling Away

[11] About this[x] we have much to say that is hard to explain, since you have become dull in understanding. [12] For though by this time you ought to be teachers, you need someone to teach you again the basic elements of the oracles of God. You need milk, not solid food; [13] for everyone who lives on milk, being still an infant, is unskilled in the word of righteousness. [14] But solid food is for the mature, for those whose faculties have been trained

[v] Gk he [w] Or tempted [x] Or him

by practice to distinguish good from evil.

The Peril of Falling Away

6 Therefore let us go on toward perfection,[y] leaving behind the basic teaching about Christ, and not laying again the foundation: repentance from dead works and faith toward God, [2] instruction about baptisms, laying on of hands, resurrection of the dead, and eternal judgment. [3] And we will do[z] this, if God permits. [4] For it is impossible to restore again to repentance those who have once been enlightened, and have tasted the heavenly gift, and have shared in the Holy Spirit, [5] and have tasted the goodness of the word of God and the powers of the age to come, [6] and then have fallen away, since on their own they are crucifying again the Son of God and are holding him up to contempt. [7] Ground that drinks up the rain falling on it repeatedly, and that produces a crop useful to those for whom it is cultivated, receives a blessing from God. [8] But if it produces thorns and thistles, it is worthless and on the verge of being cursed; its end is to be burned over.

[9] Even though we speak in this way, beloved, we are confident of better things in your case, things that belong to salvation. [10] For God is not unjust; he will not overlook your work and the love that you showed for his sake[a] in serving the saints, as you still do. [11] And we want each one of you to show the same diligence so as to realize the full assurance of hope to the very end, [12] so that you may not become sluggish, but imitators of those who through faith and patience inherit the promises.

The Certainty of God's Promise

[13] When God made a promise to Abraham, because he had no one greater by whom to swear, he swore by himself, [14] saying, "I will surely bless you and multiply you." [15] And thus Abraham,[b] having patiently endured, obtained

the promise. [16] Human beings, of course, swear by someone greater than themselves, and an oath given as confirmation puts an end to all dispute. [17] In the same way, when God desired to show even more clearly to the heirs of the promise the unchangeable character of his purpose, he guaranteed it by an oath, [18] so that through two unchangeable things, in which it is impossible that God would prove false, we who have taken refuge might be strongly encouraged to seize the hope set before us. [19] We have this hope, a sure and steadfast anchor of the soul, a hope that enters the inner shrine behind the curtain, [20] where Jesus, a forerunner on our behalf, has entered, having become a high priest forever according to the order of Melchizedek.

The Priestly Order of Melchizedek

7 This "King Melchizedek of Salem, priest of the Most High God, met Abraham as he was returning from defeating the kings and blessed him"; [2] and to him Abraham apportioned "one-tenth of everything." His name, in the first place, means "king of righteousness"; next he is also king of Salem, that is, "king of peace." [3] Without father, without mother, without genealogy, having neither beginning of days nor end of life, but resembling the Son of God, he remains a priest forever.

[4] See how great he is! Even[c] Abraham the patriarch gave him a tenth of the spoils. [5] And those descendants of Levi who receive the priestly office have a commandment in the law to collect tithes[d] from the people, that is, from their kindred,[e] though these also are descended from Abraham. [6] But this man, who does not belong to their ancestry, collected tithes[d] from Abraham and blessed him

6.1 Phil 3.12-14; Heb 5.12; 9.14
6.2 Acts 19.3,4; 6.6; 17.31,32
6.3 Acts 18.21
6.4ff Heb 10.26, 32; Eph 2.8; Gal 3.2,5
6.5 Heb 2.5
6.6 Heb 10.26-29
6.7 Ps 65.10
6.8 Gen 3.17,18
6.10 Mt 10.42; 25.40; 2 Thes 1.6, 7; 1 Thes 1.3; Rom 15.25
6.11 Heb 3.6,14; Col 2.2
6.12 Heb 10.36
6.13 Gen 22.16, 17; Lk 1.73

6.16 Gal 3.15; Ex 22.11
6.17 Heb 11.9; Ps 110.4
6.18 Titus 1.2; Heb 7.19
6.19 Lev 16.2; Heb 9.7
6.20 Heb 4.14; 5.6
7.1 Gen 14.18-20
7.3 vv. 6,28
7.4 Gen 14.20
7.5 Num 18.21, 26
7.6 Gen 14.19; Rom 4.13

[y] Or *toward maturity* [z] Other ancient authorities read *let us do* [a] Gk *for his name* [b] Gk *he* [c] Other ancient authorities lack *Even* [d] Or *a tenth* [e] Gk *brothers*

who had received the promises. ⁷It is beyond dispute that the inferior is blessed by the superior. ⁸In the one case, tithes are received by those who are mortal; in the other, by one of whom it is testified that he lives. ⁹One might even say that Levi himself, who receives tithes, paid tithes through Abraham, ¹⁰for he was still in the loins of his ancestor when Melchizedek met him.

Another Priest, Like Melchizedek

11 Now if perfection had been attainable through the levitical priesthood — for the people received the law under this priesthood — what further need would there have been to speak of another priest arising according to the order of Melchizedek, rather than one according to the order of Aaron? ¹²For when there is a change in the priesthood, there is necessarily a change in the law as well. ¹³Now the one of whom these things are spoken belonged to another tribe, from which no one has ever served at the altar. ¹⁴For it is evident that our Lord was descended from Judah, and in connection with that tribe Moses said nothing about priests.

15 It is even more obvious when another priest arises, resembling Melchizedek, ¹⁶one who has become a priest, not through a legal requirement concerning physical descent, but through the power of an indestructible life. ¹⁷For it is attested of him,

"You are a priest forever, according to the order of Melchizedek."

¹⁸There is, on the one hand, the abrogation of an earlier commandment because it was weak and ineffectual ¹⁹(for the law made nothing perfect); there is, on the other hand, the introduction of a better hope, through which we approach God.

20 This was confirmed with an oath; for others who became priests took their office without an oath, ²¹but this one became a

7.8
Heb 5.6;
6.20
7.11
vv. 18,19;
Heb 8.7;
10.1; v. 17
7.13
vv. 14,11
7.14
Isa 11.1;
Mt 1.3;
Lk 3.33;
Rom 1.3;
Rev 5.5
7.16
Heb 9.10,14
7.17
Ps 110.4;
Heb 5.6;
6.20; v.21
7.18
Rom 8.3;
Gal 4.9
7.19
Acts 13.39;
Rom 3.20;
Gal 2.16;
Heb 9.9;
6.18; 8.6;
4.16
7.21
Ps 110.4

7.22
Heb 8.6;
9.15; 12.24
7.24
v. 28
7.25
v. 19;
Rom 8.34;
Heb 9.24
7.26
Heb 4.15;
8.1
7.27
Heb 5.1,3;
9.12;
Eph 5.2;
Heb 9.14,28
7.28
Heb 5.2;
1.2; 2.10
8.1
Heb 2.17;
1.3
8.2
Heb 9.11,24
8.3
Heb 5.1;
9.14
8.4
Heb 5.1
8.5
Col 2.17;
Heb 9.23;
10.1;
Ex 25.40;
Heb 11.7;
12.25

priest with an oath, because of the one who said to him,

"The Lord has sworn and will not change his mind,

'You are a priest forever' " — ²²accordingly Jesus has also become the guarantee of a better covenant.

23 Furthermore, the former priests were many in number, because they were prevented by death from continuing in office; ²⁴but he holds his priesthood permanently, because he continues forever. ²⁵Consequently he is able for all time to save[f] those who approach God through him, since he always lives to make intercession for them.

26 For it was fitting that we should have such a high priest, holy, blameless, undefiled, separated from sinners, and exalted above the heavens. ²⁷Unlike the other[g] high priests, he has no need to offer sacrifices day after day, first for his own sins, and then for those of the people; this he did once for all when he offered himself. ²⁸For the law appoints as high priests those who are subject to weakness, but the word of the oath, which came later than the law, appoints a Son who has been made perfect forever.

Mediator of a Better Covenant

8 Now the main point in what we are saying is this: we have such a high priest, one who is seated at the right hand of the throne of the Majesty in the heavens, ²a minister in the sanctuary and the true tent[h] that the Lord, and not any mortal, has set up. ³For every high priest is appointed to offer gifts and sacrifices; hence it is necessary for this priest also to have something to offer. ⁴Now if he were on earth, he would not be a priest at all, since there are priests who offer gifts according to the law. ⁵They offer worship in a sanctuary that is a

[f] Or *able to save completely* [g] Gk lacks *other* [h] Or *tabernacle*

sketch and shadow of the heavenly one; for Moses, when he was about to erect the tent,[i] was warned, "See that you make everything according to the pattern that was shown you on the mountain." [6] But Jesus[j] has now obtained a more excellent ministry, and to that degree he is the mediator of a better covenant, which has been enacted through better promises. [7] For if that first covenant had been faultless, there would have been no need to look for a second one.

[8] God[k] finds fault with them when he says:

"The days are surely coming,
 says the Lord,
 when I will establish a new
 covenant with the
 house of Israel
 and with the house of
 Judah;
[9] not like the covenant that I
 made with their
 ancestors,
 on the day when I took
 them by the hand to
 lead them out of the
 land of Egypt;
 for they did not continue in
 my covenant,
 and so I had no concern for
 them, says the Lord.
[10] This is the covenant that I
 will make with the
 house of Israel
 after those days, says the
 Lord:
 I will put my laws in their
 minds,
 and write them on their
 hearts,
 and I will be their God,
 and they shall be my
 people.
[11] And they shall not teach one
 another
 or say to each other, 'Know
 the Lord,'
 for they shall all know me,
 from the least of them to
 the greatest.
[12] For I will be merciful toward
 their iniquities,
 and I will remember their
 sins no more."

[13] In speaking of "a new covenant," he has made the first one obsolete. And what is obsolete and growing old will soon disappear.

The Earthly and the Heavenly Sanctuaries

9 Now even the first covenant had regulations for worship and an earthly sanctuary. [2] For a tent[i] was constructed, the first one, in which were the lampstand, the table, and the bread of the Presence;[l] this is called the Holy Place. [3] Behind the second curtain was a tent[i] called the Holy of Holies. [4] In it stood the golden altar of incense and the ark of the covenant overlaid on all sides with gold, in which there were a golden urn holding the manna, and Aaron's rod that budded, and the tablets of the covenant; [5] above it were the cherubim of glory overshadowing the mercy seat.[m] Of these things we cannot speak now in detail.

[6] Such preparations having been made, the priests go continually into the first tent[i] to carry out their ritual duties; [7] but only the high priest goes into the second, and he but once a year, and not without taking the blood that he offers for himself and for the sins committed unintentionally by the people. [8] By this the Holy Spirit indicates that the way into the sanctuary has not yet been disclosed as long as the first tent[i] is still standing. [9] This is a symbol[n] of the present time, during which gifts and sacrifices are offered that cannot perfect the conscience of the worshiper, [10] but deal only with food and drink and various baptisms, regulations for the body imposed until the time comes to set things right.

[11] But when Christ came as a high priest of the good things that have come,[o] then through the greater and perfect[p] tent[i] (not made with hands, that is, not of

8.6
1 Tim 2.5;
Heb 7.22
8.7
Heb 7.11,18
8.8
Jer 31.31-34
8.9
Ex 19.5,6
8.10
Heb 10.16;
2 Cor 3.3;
Zech 8.8
8.11
Isa 54.13;
Jn 6.45;
1 Jn 2.27
8.12
Heb 10.17

8.13
2 Cor 5.17
9.1
Ex 25.8
9.2
Ex 25.8,9,
23-39
9.3
Ex 26.31-33
9.4
Ex 30.1-5;
25.10ff;
16.32,33;
Num 17.10
9.5
Ex 25.17ff
9.6
Num 28.3
9.7
Lev 16.11ff;
Ex 30.10;
Heb 5.2,3
9.8
Heb 10.19,
20; Jn 14.6
9.9
Heb 11.19;
5.1;
Gal 3.21
9.10
Lev 11.2ff;
Col 2.16;
Heb 7.16
9.11ff
Heb 2.17;
10.1; 8.2

[i] Or tabernacle [j] Gk he [k] Gk He
[l] Gk the presentation of the loaves
[m] Or the place of atonement [n] Gk parable
[o] Other ancient authorities read good things to
come [p] Gk more perfect

this creation), [12]he entered once for all into the Holy Place, not with the blood of goats and calves, but with his own blood, thus obtaining eternal redemption. [13]For if the blood of goats and bulls, with the sprinkling of the ashes of a heifer, sanctifies those who have been defiled so that their flesh is purified, [14]how much more will the blood of Christ, who through the eternal Spirit[q] offered himself without blemish to God, purify our[r] conscience from dead works to worship the living God!

[15]For this reason he is the mediator of a new covenant, so that those who are called may receive the promised eternal inheritance, because a death has occurred that redeems them from the transgressions under the first covenant.[s] [16]Where a will[s] is involved, the death of the one who made it must be established. [17]For a will[s] takes effect only at death, since it is not in force as long as the one who made it is alive. [18]Hence not even the first covenant was inaugurated without blood. [19]For when every commandment had been told to all the people by Moses in accordance with the law, he took the blood of calves and goats,[t] with water and scarlet wool and hyssop, and sprinkled both the scroll itself and all the people, [20]saying, "This is the blood of the covenant that God has ordained for you." [21]And in the same way he sprinkled with the blood both the tent[u] and all the vessels used in worship. [22]Indeed, under the law almost everything is purified with blood, and without the shedding of blood there is no forgiveness of sins.

Christ's Sacrifice Takes Away Sin

23 Thus it was necessary for the sketches of the heavenly things to be purified with these rites, but the heavenly things themselves need better sacrifices than these. [24]For Christ did not enter a sanctuary made by human hands, a mere copy of the true one, but he en-

tered into heaven itself, now to appear in the presence of God on our behalf. [25]Nor was it to offer himself again and again, as the high priest enters the Holy Place year after year with blood that is not his own; [26]for then he would have had to suffer again and again since the foundation of the world. But as it is, he has appeared once for all at the end of the age to remove sin by the sacrifice of himself. [27]And just as it is appointed for mortals to die once, and after that the judgment, [28]so Christ, having been offered once to bear the sins of many, will appear a second time, not to deal with sin, but to save those who are eagerly waiting for him.

Christ's Sacrifice Once for All

10 Since the law has only a shadow of the good things to come and not the true form of these realities, it[v] can never, by the same sacrifices that are continually offered year after year, make perfect those who approach. [2]Otherwise, would they not have ceased being offered, since the worshipers, cleansed once for all, would no longer have any consciousness of sin? [3]But in these sacrifices there is a reminder of sin year after year. [4]For it is impossible for the blood of bulls and goats to take away sins. [5]Consequently, when Christ[w] came into the world, he said,

"Sacrifices and offerings you
　　have not desired,
　　but a body you have
　　　prepared for me;
[6] in burnt offerings and sin
　　　offerings
　　you have taken no
　　　pleasure.
[7] Then I said, 'See, God, I
　　　have come to do your
　　　will, O God'
　　(in the scroll of the book[x]
　　　it is written of me)."

[q] Other ancient authorities read *Holy Spirit*
[r] Other ancient authorities read *your*
[s] The Greek word used here means both *covenant* and *will*　[t] Other ancient authorities lack *and goats*　[u] Or *tabernacle*
[v] Other ancient authorities read *they*
[w] Gk *he*　[x] Meaning of Gk uncertain

Cross-references:

9.12 Heb 7.27; 10.4
9.13 Num 19.9, 17,18
9.14 1 Jn 1.7; 1 Pet 3.18; Titus 2.14
9.15 1 Tim 2.5; Heb 3.1; 7.22
9.17 Gal 3.15
9.18 Ex 24.6
9.19 Ex 24.65ff; Lev 14.4,7
9.20 Ex 24.8; Mt 26.28
9.21 Lev 8.15
9.22 Lev 17.11
9.23 Heb 8.5
9.24 Heb 6.20; 8.2; 7.25; 1 Jn 2.1
9.25 v. 7; Heb 10.19
9.26 Heb 4.3; 7.27; 1.2
9.27 Gen 3.19; 2 Cor 5.10
9.28 Rom 6.10; 1 Pet 2.24; Titus 2.13
10.1 Heb 9.9,11, 23
10.3 Heb 9.7
10.4 Mic 6.6,7
10.5 Ps 40.6-8; Heb 1.6; 1 Pet 2.24
10.7 Jer 36.2

8 When he said above, "You have neither desired nor taken pleasure in sacrifices and offerings and burnt offerings and sin offerings" (these are offered according to the law), 9 then he added, "See, I have come to do your will." He abolishes the first in order to establish the second. 10 And it is by God's will[y] that we have been sanctified through the offering of the body of Jesus Christ once for all.

11 And every priest stands day after day at his service, offering again and again the same sacrifices that can never take away sins. 12 But when Christ[z] had offered for all time a single sacrifice for sins, "he sat down at the right hand of God," 13 and since then has been waiting "until his enemies would be made a footstool for his feet." 14 For by a single offering he has perfected for all time those who are sanctified. 15 And the Holy Spirit also testifies to us, for after saying,

16 "This is the covenant that I
　　will make with them
　　after those days, says the
　　　Lord:
I will put my laws in their
　　hearts,
and I will write them on
　　their minds,"

17 he also adds,

"I will remember[a] their sins
　　and their lawless deeds
　　no more."

18 Where there is forgiveness of these, there is no longer any offering for sin.

A Call to Persevere

19 Therefore, my friends,[b] since we have confidence to enter the sanctuary by the blood of Jesus, 20 by the new and living way that he opened for us through the curtain (that is, through his flesh), 21 and since we have a great priest over the house of God, 22 let us approach with a true heart in full assurance of faith, with our hearts sprinkled clean from an evil conscience and our bodies washed with pure water. 23 Let us hold fast to the confession of our hope with-

out wavering, for he who has promised is faithful. 24 And let us consider how to provoke one another to love and good deeds, 25 not neglecting to meet together, as is the habit of some, but encouraging one another, and all the more as you see the Day approaching.

26 For if we willfully persist in sin after having received the knowledge of the truth, there no longer remains a sacrifice for sins, 27 but a fearful prospect of judgment, and a fury of fire that will consume the adversaries. 28 Anyone who has violated the law of Moses dies without mercy "on the testimony of two or three witnesses." 29 How much worse punishment do you think will be deserved by those who have spurned the Son of God, profaned the blood of the covenant by which they were sanctified, and outraged the Spirit of grace? 30 For we know the one who said, "Vengeance is mine, I will repay." And again, "The Lord will judge his people." 31 It is a fearful thing to fall into the hands of the living God.

32 But recall those earlier days when, after you had been enlightened, you endured a hard struggle with sufferings, 33 sometimes being publicly exposed to abuse and persecution, and sometimes being partners with those so treated. 34 For you had compassion for those who were in prison, and you cheerfully accepted the plundering of your possessions, knowing that you yourselves possessed something better and more lasting. 35 Do not, therefore, abandon that confidence of yours; it brings a great reward. 36 For you need endurance, so that when you have done the will of God, you may receive what was promised.

37 For yet "in a very little
　　while,

10.8 vv. 5,6; Mk 12.33
10.9 v. 7
10.10 Jn 17.19; Heb 7.27; 1 Pet 2.24
10.11 Heb 5.1; v. 4
10.12 Heb 1.3
10.13 Ps 110.1; Heb 1.13
10.14 v. 1
10.15 Heb 3.7
10.16 Jer 31.33,34
10.17 Heb 8.12
10.19 Eph 2.18; Heb 9.8,12
10.20 Heb 9.8,3
10.21 Heb 2.17; 1 Tim 3.15
10.22 Heb 4.16; Eph 3.12; Heb 9.14; Ezek 36.25
10.23 Heb 4.14; 1 Cor 1.9

10.24 Heb 13.1; Titus 3.8
10.25 Acts 2.42; Heb 3.13; Phil 4.5
10.26 Num 15.30; 2 Pet 2.20
10.27 Heb 9.27; Isa 26.11
10.28 Deut 17.2-6; Heb 2.2
10.29 Heb 2.3; 6.6; 13.20; Eph 4.30; Heb 6.4
10.30 Deut 32.35, 36; Rom 12.19
10.32 Heb 6.4; Phil 1.29,30
10.33 1 Cor 4.9; 1 Thes 2.14
10.34 Heb 9.15
10.35 Heb 2.2

10.36 Lk 21.19; Col 3.24 **10.37** Hab 2.3, 4; Lk 18.8

y Gk by that will　z Gk this one
a Gk on their minds and I will remember
b Gk Therefore, brothers

the one who is coming will
 come and will not
 delay;
38 but my righteous one will
 live by faith.
My soul takes no pleasure
 in anyone who shrinks
 back."
39 But we are not among those who
shrink back and so are lost, but
among those who have faith and so
are saved.

The Meaning of Faith

11 Now faith is the assurance
of things hoped for, the
conviction of things not seen. 2 In-
deed, by faith[c] our ancestors re-
ceived approval. 3 By faith we un-
derstand that the worlds were
prepared by the word of God, so
that what is seen was made from
things that are not visible.[d]

The Examples of Abel, Enoch, and Noah

4 By faith Abel offered to God a
more acceptable[e] sacrifice than
Cain's. Through this he received
approval as righteous, God himself
giving approval to his gifts; he died,
but through his faith[f] he still
speaks. 5 By faith Enoch was taken
so that he did not experience
death; and "he was not found, be-
cause God had taken him." For it
was attested before he was taken
away that "he had pleased God."
6 And without faith it is impossible
to please God, for whoever would
approach him must believe that he
exists and that he rewards those
who seek him. 7 By faith Noah,
warned by God about events as yet
unseen, respected the warning and
built an ark to save his household;
by this he condemned the world
and became an heir to the righ-
teousness that is in accordance
with faith.

The Faith of Abraham

8 By faith Abraham obeyed
when he was called to set out for a
place that he was to receive as an
inheritance; and he set out, not
knowing where he was going. 9 By

10.38
Rom 1.17;
Gal 3.11
10.39
2 Pet 2.20;
Acts 16.30
11.1
Rom 8.24;
2 Cor 4.18;
5.7
11.2
vv. 4,39
11.3
Gen 1.1;
Jn 1.3;
Heb 6.5
11.4
Gen 4.4,10;
1 Jn 3.12;
Heb 12.24
11.5
Gen 5.21-24
11.6
Heb 7.19
11.7
Gen 6.13-22
11.8
Gen 12.1-4;
Acts 7.2-4
11.9
Gen 12.8;
18.1,9;
Heb 6.17

11.10
Heb 12.22;
13.14;
Rev 21.2
11.11
Gen 17.19;
18.11-14;
21.2
11.12
Rom 4.19;
Gen 22.17;
32.12
11.13
Gen 23.4;
Ps 39.12
11.16
Ex 3.6,15;
Phil 3.20;
Heb 13.14
11.17
Gen 22.1-10;
Jas 2.21
11.18
Gen 21.12;
Rom 9.7
11.19
Rom 4.21
11.21
Gen 48.5,
16,20
11.22
Gen 50.24,
25;
Ex 13.19

faith he stayed for a time in the
land he had been promised, as in a
foreign land, living in tents, as did
Isaac and Jacob, who were heirs
with him of the same promise.
10 For he looked forward to the city
that has foundations, whose archi-
tect and builder is God. 11 By faith
he received power of procreation,
even though he was too old—and
Sarah herself was barren—because
he considered him faithful who
had promised.[g] 12 Therefore from
one person, and this one as good as
dead, descendants were born, "as
many as the stars of heaven and as
the innumerable grains of sand by
the seashore."

13 All of these died in faith
without having received the prom-
ises, but from a distance they saw
and greeted them. They confessed
that they were strangers and for-
eigners on the earth, 14 for people
who speak in this way make it clear
that they are seeking a homeland.
15 If they had been thinking of the
land that they had left behind, they
would have had opportunity to re-
turn. 16 But as it is, they desire a
better country, that is, a heavenly
one. Therefore God is not ashamed
to be called their God; indeed, he
has prepared a city for them.

17 By faith Abraham, when put
to the test, offered up Isaac. He
who had received the promises was
ready to offer up his only son, 18 of
whom he had been told, "It is
through Isaac that descendants
shall be named for you." 19 He con-
sidered the fact that God is able
even to raise someone from the
dead—and figuratively speaking,
he did receive him back. 20 By faith
Isaac invoked blessings for the fu-
ture on Jacob and Esau. 21 By faith
Jacob, when dying, blessed each of
the sons of Joseph, "bowing in wor-
ship over the top of his staff." 22 By
faith Joseph, at the end of his life,

c Gk by this d Or was not made out of
visible things e Gk greater
f Gk through it g Other ancient authorities
read By faith Sarah herself, though barren,
received power to conceive, even when she was
too old, because she considered him faithful
who had promised.

made mention of the exodus of the Israelites and gave instructions about his burial.[h]

The Faith of Moses

23 By faith Moses was hidden by his parents for three months after his birth, because they saw that the child was beautiful; and they were not afraid of the king's edict.[i] 24 By faith Moses, when he was grown up, refused to be called a son of Pharaoh's daughter, 25 choosing rather to share ill-treatment with the people of God than to enjoy the fleeting pleasures of sin. 26 He considered abuse suffered for the Christ[j] to be greater wealth than the treasures of Egypt, for he was looking ahead to the reward. 27 By faith he left Egypt, unafraid of the king's anger; for he persevered as though[k] he saw him who is invisible. 28 By faith he kept the Passover and the sprinkling of blood, so that the destroyer of the firstborn would not touch the firstborn of Israel.[l]

The Faith of Other Israelite Heroes

29 By faith the people passed through the Red Sea as if it were dry land, but when the Egyptians attempted to do so they were drowned. 30 By faith the walls of Jericho fell after they had been encircled for seven days. 31 By faith Rahab the prostitute did not perish with those who were disobedient,[m] because she had received the spies in peace.

32 And what more should I say? For time would fail me to tell of Gideon, Barak, Samson, Jephthah, of David and Samuel and the prophets— 33 who through faith conquered kingdoms, administered justice, obtained promises, shut the mouths of lions, 34 quenched raging fire, escaped the edge of the sword, won strength out of weakness, became mighty in war, put foreign armies to flight. 35 Women received their dead by resurrection. Others were tortured, refusing to accept release, in order

to obtain a better resurrection. 36 Others suffered mocking and flogging, and even chains and imprisonment. 37 They were stoned to death, they were sawn in two,[n] they were killed by the sword; they went about in skins of sheep and goats, destitute, persecuted, tormented— 38 of whom the world was not worthy. They wandered in deserts and mountains, and in caves and holes in the ground.

39 Yet all these, though they were commended for their faith, did not receive what was promised, 40 since God had provided something better so that they would not, apart from us, be made perfect.

The Example of Jesus

12 Therefore, since we are surrounded by so great a cloud of witnesses, let us also lay aside every weight and the sin that clings so closely,[o] and let us run with perseverance the race that is set before us, 2 looking to Jesus the pioneer and perfecter of our faith, who for the sake of[p] the joy that was set before him endured the cross, disregarding its shame, and has taken his seat at the right hand of the throne of God.

3 Consider him who endured such hostility against himself from sinners,[q] so that you may not grow weary or lose heart. 4 In your struggle against sin you have not yet resisted to the point of shedding your blood. 5 And you have forgotten the exhortation that addresses you as children—

"My child, do not regard
 lightly the discipline of
 the Lord,
or lose heart when you are
 punished by him;

Cross-references (center column):

11.23 Ex 2.2; 1.16
11.24 Ex 2.10
11.25 v. 37
11.26 Heb 13.13; 2.2
11.27 Ex 12.50, 51; v. 13
11.28 Ex 12.21
11.29 Ex 14.21-31
11.30 Josh 6.12-21
11.31 Josh 2.9ff; 6.23; Jas 2.25
11.33 2 Sam 7.11; Judg 14.5; 1 Sam 17.34; Dan 6.22
11.34 2 Kings 20.7; Judg 15.8
11.35 1 Kings 17.22; Acts 22.25
11.36 Jer 20.2
11.37 1 Kings 21.13; Acts 7.58
11.38 2 Kings 1.8
11.38 1 Kings 18.4
11.40 Heb 5.9
12.1 1 Cor 9.24; Heb 10.36
12.2 Phil 2.8,9; Heb 1.3,13; 1 Pet 3.22
12.3 Mt 10.24; Gal 6.9
12.4 Heb 10.32-34; 1 Cor 10.13
12.5 Prov 3.11,12

Footnotes:

h Gk his bones i Other ancient authorities add By faith Moses, when he was grown up, killed the Egyptian, because he observed the humiliation of his people (Gk brothers) j Or the Messiah k Or because l Gk would not touch them m Or unbelieving n Other ancient authorities add they were tempted o Other ancient authorities read sin that easily distracts p Or who instead of q Other ancient authorities read such hostility from sinners against themselves

6 for the Lord disciplines those
whom he loves,
and chastises every child
whom he accepts."
7 Endure trials for the sake of discipline. God is treating you as children; for what child is there whom a parent does not discipline? 8 If you do not have that discipline in which all children share, then you are illegitimate and not his children. 9 Moreover, we had human parents to discipline us, and we respected them. Should we not be even more willing to be subject to the Father of spirits and live? 10 For they disciplined us for a short time as seemed best to them, but he disciplines us for our good, in order that we may share his holiness. 11 Now, discipline always seems painful rather than pleasant at the time, but later it yields the peaceful fruit of righteousness to those who have been trained by it.

12 Therefore lift your drooping hands and strengthen your weak knees, 13 and make straight paths for your feet, so that what is lame may not be put out of joint, but rather be healed.

Warnings against Rejecting God's Grace

14 Pursue peace with everyone, and the holiness without which no one will see the Lord. 15 See to it that no one fails to obtain the grace of God; that no root of bitterness springs up and causes trouble, and through it many become defiled. 16 See to it that no one becomes like Esau, an immoral and godless person, who sold his birthright for a single meal. 17 You know that later, when he wanted to inherit the blessing, he was rejected, for he found no chance to repent,[r] even though he sought the blessing[s] with tears.

18 You have not come to something[t] that can be touched, a blazing fire, and darkness, and gloom, and a tempest, 19 and the sound of a trumpet, and a voice whose words made the hearers beg that not another word be spoken to them.

20 (For they could not endure the order that was given, "If even an animal touches the mountain, it shall be stoned to death." 21 Indeed, so terrifying was the sight that Moses said, "I tremble with fear.") 22 But you have come to Mount Zion and to the city of the living God, the heavenly Jerusalem, and to innumerable angels in festal gathering, 23 and to the assembly[u] of the firstborn who are enrolled in heaven, and to God the judge of all, and to the spirits of the righteous made perfect, 24 and to Jesus, the mediator of a new covenant, and to the sprinkled blood that speaks a better word than the blood of Abel.

25 See that you do not refuse the one who is speaking; for if they did not escape when they refused the one who warned them on earth, how much less will we escape if we reject the one who warns from heaven! 26 At that time his voice shook the earth; but now he has promised, "Yet once more I will shake not only the earth but also the heaven." 27 This phrase, "Yet once more," indicates the removal of what is shaken — that is, created things — so that what cannot be shaken may remain. 28 Therefore, since we are receiving a kingdom that cannot be shaken, let us give thanks, by which we offer to God an acceptable worship with reverence and awe; 29 for indeed our God is a consuming fire.

Service Well-Pleasing to God

13 Let mutual love continue. 2 Do not neglect to show hospitality to strangers, for by doing that some have entertained angels without knowing it. 3 Remember those who are in prison, as though you were in prison with them; those who are being tortured, as though you yourselves

12.6	Ps 94.12; Jas 1.12
12.7	Deut 8.5
12.8	1 Pet 5.9
12.9	Lk 18.2; Num 16.22; Isa 38.16
12.10	2 Pet 1.4
12.11	1 Pet 1.6; Jas 3.17,18
12.12	Isa 35.3
12.13	Prov 4.26; Gal 6.1
12.14	Rom 14.19; 6.22; Mt 5.8
12.15	Gal 5.4; Deut 29.18; Heb 3.12
12.16	Gen 25.33
12.17	Gen 27.30-40
12.18	Ex 19.12-22; Deut 4.11
12.19	Ex 20.19; Deut 5.5
12.20	Ex 19.12,13
12.21	Ex 19.16
12.22	Phil 3.20; Gal 4.26
12.23	Lk 10.20; Phil 3.12
12.24	1 Tim 2.5; Gen 4.10; Heb 11.4
12.25	Heb 2.2,3; 8.5; 11.7
12.26	Ex 19.18; Hag 2.6
12.27	1 Cor 7.31; 2 Pet 3.10
12.28	Dan 2.44; Heb 13.15
12.29	Deut 4.24
13.1	Rom 12.10; 1 Thes 4.9; 1 Pet 1.22
13.2	1 Pet 4.9; Gen 18.3
13.3	Mt 25.36; Col 4.18

r Or no chance to change his father's mind s Gk it t Other ancient authorities read a mountain u Or angels, and to the festal gathering 23 and assembly

were being tortured.[v] [4]Let marriage be held in honor by all, and let the marriage bed be kept undefiled; for God will judge fornicators and adulterers. [5]Keep your lives free from the love of money, and be content with what you have; for he has said, "I will never leave you or forsake you." [6]So we can say with confidence,

"The Lord is my helper;
 I will not be afraid.
What can anyone do to me?"

[7] Remember your leaders, those who spoke the word of God to you; consider the outcome of their way of life, and imitate their faith. [8]Jesus Christ is the same yesterday and today and forever. [9]Do not be carried away by all kinds of strange teachings; for it is well for the heart to be strengthened by grace, not by regulations about food,[w] which have not benefited those who observe them. [10]We have an altar from which those who officiate in the tent[x] have no right to eat. [11]For the bodies of those animals whose blood is brought into the sanctuary by the high priest as a sacrifice for sin are burned outside the camp. [12]Therefore Jesus also suffered outside the city gate in order to sanctify the people by his own blood. [13]Let us then go to him outside the camp and bear the abuse he endured. [14]For here we have no lasting city, but we are looking for the city that is to come. [15]Through him, then, let us continually offer a sacrifice of praise to God, that is, the fruit of lips that confess his name. [16]Do not neglect to do good and to share what you

have, for such sacrifices are pleasing to God.

[17] Obey your leaders and submit to them, for they are keeping watch over your souls and will give an account. Let them do this with joy and not with sighing—for that would be harmful to you.

[18] Pray for us; we are sure that we have a clear conscience, desiring to act honorably in all things. [19]I urge you all the more to do this, so that I may be restored to you very soon.

Benediction

[20] Now may the God of peace, who brought back from the dead our Lord Jesus, the great shepherd of the sheep, by the blood of the eternal covenant, [21]make you complete in everything good so that you may do his will, working among us[y] that which is pleasing in his sight, through Jesus Christ, to whom be the glory forever and ever. Amen.

Final Exhortation and Greetings

[22] I appeal to you, brothers and sisters,[z] bear with my word of exhortation, for I have written to you briefly. [23]I want you to know that our brother Timothy has been set free; and if he comes in time, he will be with me when I see you. [24]Greet all your leaders and all the saints. Those from Italy send you greetings. [25]Grace be with all of you.[a]

[v] Gk *were in the body* [w] Gk *not by foods*
[x] Or *tabernacle* [y] Other ancient authorities read *you* [z] Gk *brothers* [a] Other ancient authorities add *Amen*

13.4 1 Cor 6.9; Rev 22.15
13.5 Phil 4.11; Deut 31.6,8; Josh 1.5
13.7 v. 17; Heb 6.12
13.8 Heb 1.12
13.9 Eph 4.14; Col 2.7,16
13.10 1 Cor 9.13; 10.18
13.11 Ex 29.14; Lev 16.27
13.12 Jn 19.17
13.13 Heb 11.26
13.14 Phil 3.20; Heb 10.34; 12.22
13.15 1 Pet 2.5; Isa 57.9; Hos 14.2
13.17 Isa 62.6; Acts 20.28
13.18 1 Thes 5.25; Acts 24.16
13.19 Philem 22
13.20 Rom 15.33; Zech 9.11
13.21 1 Pet 5.10; Phil 2.13
13.23 1 Thes 3.2; 1 Tim 6.12
13.24 v. 7
13.25 Col 4.18; Titus 3.15

THE LETTER OF
James

Title and Background

The book of James has a distinctively Jewish nature that suggests it was composed when the church was still predominantly Jewish. It reflects a simple church order, and no reference is made to the controversy over Gentile circumcision. The seven New Testament letters from James through the book of Jude are called the General Letters because they are addressed to Christians in general and not to a particular church.

Author and Date of Writing

The author identifies himself as James, and he was probably the brother of Jesus and the leader of the Jerusalem council. At first James did not believe in Jesus and even challenged him and misunderstood his mission. Later he became very prominent in the church. The book of James was written about A.D. 48, and certainly before 50.

Theme and Message

As the pastor and leader of the Jerusalem church, James wrote to instruct and encourage his dispersed people in the face of their difficulties. The letter is concerned mainly with the practical aspects of the Christian faith, consisting of maxims and counsel for everyday conduct. Many of his statements bear similarity to Jesus' Sermon on the Mount (Mt 5-7). The letter discusses true religion, true faith, and true wisdom.

Outline

Salutation

1 James, a servant[a] of God and of the Lord Jesus Christ,

To the twelve tribes in the Dispersion:

Greetings.

Faith and Wisdom

2 My brothers and sisters,[b] whenever you face trials of any kind, consider it nothing but joy, ³because you know that the testing of your faith produces endurance; ⁴and let endurance have its full effect, so that you may be mature and complete, lacking in nothing.

5 If any of you is lacking in wisdom, ask God, who gives to all generously and ungrudgingly, and it will be given you. ⁶But ask in faith, never doubting, for the one who doubts is like a wave of the sea, driven and tossed by the wind; ⁷, ⁸for the doubter, being double-minded and unstable in every way,

1.1 Acts 12.17; Titus 1.1; Acts 26.7; Deut 32.26; Jn 7.35; 1 Pet 1.1
1.2 Mt 5.12; Heb 10.34; 1 Pet 1.6
1.3 Rom 5.3
1.4 Col 4.12; 1 Thes 5.23
1.5 1 Kings 3.9; Prov 2.3;

1 Jn 5.14 **1.6** Mk 11.24 **1.7** Jas 4.8

a Gk *slave* b Gk *brothers*

must not expect to receive anything from the Lord.

Poverty and Riches

9 Let the believer[c] who is lowly boast in being raised up, [10] and the rich in being brought low, because the rich will disappear like a flower in the field. [11] For the sun rises with its scorching heat and withers the field; its flower falls, and its beauty perishes. It is the same way with the rich; in the midst of a busy life, they will wither away.

Trial and Temptation

12 Blessed is anyone who endures temptation. Such a one has stood the test and will receive the crown of life that the Lord[d] has promised to those who love him. [13] No one, when tempted, should say, "I am being tempted by God"; for God cannot be tempted by evil and he himself tempts no one. [14] But one is tempted by one's own desire, being lured and enticed by it; [15] then, when that desire has conceived, it gives birth to sin, and that sin, when it is fully grown, gives birth to death. [16] Do not be deceived, my beloved.[e]

17 Every generous act of giving, with every perfect gift, is from above, coming down from the Father of lights, with whom there is no variation or shadow due to change.[f] [18] In fulfillment of his own purpose he gave us birth by the word of truth, so that we would become a kind of first fruits of his creatures.

Hearing and Doing the Word

19 You must understand this, my beloved:[e] let everyone be quick to listen, slow to speak, slow to anger; [20] for your anger does not produce God's righteousness. [21] Therefore rid yourselves of all sordidness and rank growth of wickedness, and welcome with meekness the implanted word that has the power to save your souls.

22 But be doers of the word, and not merely hearers who deceive themselves. [23] For if any are hearers of the word and not doers, they are

like those who look at themselves[g] in a mirror; [24] for they look at themselves and, on going away, immediately forget what they were like. [25] But those who look into the perfect law, the law of liberty, and persevere, being not hearers who forget but doers who act—they will be blessed in their doing.

26 If any think they are religious, and do not bridle their tongues but deceive their hearts, their religion is worthless. [27] Religion that is pure and undefiled before God, the Father, is this: to care for orphans and widows in their distress, and to keep oneself unstained by the world.

Warning against Partiality

2 My brothers and sisters,[h] do you with your acts of favoritism really believe in our glorious Lord Jesus Christ?[i] [2] For if a person with gold rings and in fine clothes comes into your assembly, and if a poor person in dirty clothes also comes in, [3] and if you take notice of the one wearing the fine clothes and say, "Have a seat here, please," while to the one who is poor you say, "Stand there," or, "Sit at my feet,"[i] [4] have you not made distinctions among yourselves, and become judges with evil thoughts? [5] Listen, my beloved brothers and sisters.[k] Has not God chosen the poor in the world to be rich in faith and to be heirs of the kingdom that he has promised to those who love him? [6] But you have dishonored the poor. Is it not the rich who oppress you? Is it not they who drag you into court? [7] Is it not they who blaspheme the excellent name that was invoked over you?

8 You do well if you really fulfill the royal law according to the scripture, "You shall love your neighbor as yourself." [9] But if you

Cross-references (center column):

1.10 1 Cor 7.31; 1 Pet 1.24
1.11 Isa 40.6-8; Ps 102.4,11
1.12 Heb 12.5; Jas 2.5
1.15 Job 15.35; Ps 7.14; Rom 6.21, 23
1.16 1 Cor 6.9; v. 19
1.17 Jn 3.27; Mal 3.6
1.18 Jn 1.13; Eph 1.12; Rev 14.4
1.19 Prov 5.1,2; 10.19
1.21 Eph 4.22; 1 Pet 2.1; Eph 1.13; Titus 2.11
1.22 Mt 7.21; Rom 2.13; 1 Jn 3.7
1.23 Lk 6.47; 1 Cor 13.12
1.25 2 Cor 3.18; Jas 2.12; Jn 13.17
1.26 Ps 34.13; 1 Pet 3.10
1.27 Mt 25.36; Rom 12.2; 1 Jn 5.18
2.1 Prov 24.23; Mt 22.16; 1 Cor 2.8
2.2 v. 3
2.3 v. 2
2.4 Jn 7.24
2.5 1 Cor 1.26-28; Lk 12.21; Jas 1.12
2.6 1 Cor 11.22; Acts 8.3
2.8 Lev 19.18; Mt 22.39

[c] Gk brother　[d] Gk he; other ancient authorities read God　[e] Gk my beloved brothers　[f] Other ancient authorities read variation due to a shadow of turning　[g] Gk at the face of his birth　[h] Gk My brothers　[i] Or hold the faith of our glorious Lord Jesus Christ without acts of favoritism　[i] Gk Sit under my footstool　[k] Gk brothers

show partiality, you commit sin and are convicted by the law as transgressors. [10] For whoever keeps the whole law but fails in one point has become accountable for all of it. [11] For the one who said, "You shall not commit adultery," also said, "You shall not murder." Now if you do not commit adultery but if you murder, you have become a transgressor of the law. [12] So speak and so act as those who are to be judged by the law of liberty. [13] For judgment will be without mercy to anyone who has shown no mercy; mercy triumphs over judgment.

Faith without Works Is Dead

14 What good is it, my brothers and sisters,[1] if you say you have faith but do not have works? Can faith save you? [15] If a brother or sister is naked and lacks daily food, [16] and one of you says to them, "Go in peace; keep warm and eat your fill," and yet you do not supply their bodily needs, what is the good of that? [17] So faith by itself, if it has no works, is dead.

18 But someone will say, "You have faith and I have works." Show me your faith apart from your works, and I by my works will show you my faith. [19] You believe that God is one; you do well. Even the demons believe—and shudder. [20] Do you want to be shown, you senseless person, that faith apart from works is barren? [21] Was not our ancestor Abraham justified by works when he offered his son Isaac on the altar? [22] You see that faith was active along with his works, and faith was brought to completion by the works. [23] Thus the scripture was fulfilled that says, "Abraham believed God, and it was reckoned to him as righteousness," and he was called the friend of God. [24] You see that a person is justified by works and not by faith alone. [25] Likewise, was not Rahab the prostitute also justified by works when she welcomed the messengers and sent them out by another road? [26] For just as the

body without the spirit is dead, so faith without works is also dead.

Taming the Tongue

3 Not many of you should become teachers, my brothers and sisters,[1] for you know that we who teach will be judged with greater strictness. [2] For all of us make many mistakes. Anyone who makes no mistakes in speaking is perfect, able to keep the whole body in check with a bridle. [3] If we put bits into the mouths of horses to make them obey us, we guide their whole bodies. [4] Or look at ships: though they are so large that it takes strong winds to drive them, yet they are guided by a very small rudder wherever the will of the pilot directs. [5] So also the tongue is a small member, yet it boasts of great exploits.

How great a forest is set ablaze by a small fire! [6] And the tongue is a fire. The tongue is placed among our members as a world of iniquity; it stains the whole body, sets on fire the cycle of nature,[m] and is itself set on fire by hell.[n] [7] For every species of beast and bird, of reptile and sea creature, can be tamed and has been tamed by the human species, [8] but no one can tame the tongue—a restless evil, full of deadly poison. [9] With it we bless the Lord and Father, and with it we curse those who are made in the likeness of God. [10] From the same mouth come blessing and cursing. My brothers and sisters,[o] this ought not to be so. [11] Does a spring pour forth from the same opening both fresh and brackish water? [12] Can a fig tree, my brothers and sisters,[p] yield olives, or a grapevine figs? No more can salt water yield fresh.

Two Kinds of Wisdom

13 Who is wise and understanding among you? Show by your good life that your works are done with gentleness born of wisdom. [14] But if

2.10	
Mt 5.19;	
Gal 3.10	
2.11	
Ex 20.13,	
14;	
Deut 5.17,	
18	
2.12	
Jas 1.25	
2.13	
Mt 5.7;	
18.32-35	
2.14	
Mt 7.26;	
Jas 1.22ff	
2.15	
Lk 3.11	
2.16	
1 Jn 3.17,	
18	
2.18	
Jas 3.13	
2.19	
Deut 6.4;	
Mt 8.29;	
Lk 4.34	
2.20	
v. 17	
2.21	
Gen 22.9	
2.22	
Heb 11.17	
2.23	
Gen 15.6;	
Rom 4.3;	
2 Chr 20.7;	
Isa 41.8	
2.25	
Josh 2.1ff;	
Heb 11.31	
2.26	
v. 20	
3.1	
Mt 23.8;	
Lk 6.37	
3.2	
1 Kings 8.46;	
1 Pet 3.10;	
Mt 12.37;	
Jas 1.26	
3.3	
Ps 32.9	
3.5	
Prov 12.18;	
Ps 12.3	
3.6	
Prov 16.27;	
Mt 15.11,	
18,19	
3.8	
Ps 140.3;	
Rom 3.13	
3.9	
Gen 1.26	
3.12	
Mt 7.16	
3.13	
Gal 6.4;	
Jas 2.18	
3.14	
Rom 2.8;	
v. 16;	
1 Tim 2.4;	
Jas 5.19	

[1] Gk brothers [m] Or wheel of birth
[n] Gk Gehenna [o] Gk My brothers
[p] Gk my brothers

you have bitter envy and selfish ambition in your hearts, do not be boastful and false to the truth. [15]Such wisdom does not come down from above, but is earthly, unspiritual, devilish. [16]For where there is envy and selfish ambition, there will also be disorder and wickedness of every kind. [17]But the wisdom from above is first pure, then peaceable, gentle, willing to yield, full of mercy and good fruits, without a trace of partiality or hypocrisy. [18]And a harvest of righteousness is sown in peace for[q] those who make peace.

Friendship with the World

4 Those conflicts and disputes among you, where do they come from? Do they not come from your cravings that are at war within you? [2]You want something and do not have it; so you commit murder. And you covet[r] something and cannot obtain it; so you engage in disputes and conflicts. You do not have, because you do not ask. [3]You ask and do not receive, because you ask wrongly, in order to spend what you get on your pleasures. [4]Adulterers! Do you not know that friendship with the world is enmity with God? Therefore whoever wishes to be a friend of the world becomes an enemy of God. [5]Or do you suppose that it is for nothing that the scripture says, "God[s] yearns jealously for the spirit that he has made to dwell in us"? [6]But he gives all the more grace; therefore it says,

"God opposes the proud,
 but gives grace to the
 humble."

[7]Submit yourselves therefore to God. Resist the devil, and he will flee from you. [8]Draw near to God, and he will draw near to you. Cleanse your hands, you sinners, and purify your hearts, you double-minded. [9]Lament and mourn and weep. Let your laughter be turned into mourning and your joy into dejection. [10]Humble yourselves before the Lord, and he will exalt you.

3.15
Jas 1.17;
1 Tim 4.1
3.16
Gal 5.20
3.17
1 Cor 2.6;
Rom 12.9;
1 Pet 1.22
3.18
Prov 11.18;
Isa 32.17
4.1
Titus 3.9;
Rom 7.23
4.3
Ps 18.41;
1 Jn 3.22;
5.14
4.4
Jas 1.27;
1 Jn 2.15;
Jn 15.19
4.5
Gen 6.5;
Num 11.29
4.6
Ps 138.6;
Prov 3.34
4.7
1 Pet 5.6-9
4.8
2 Chr 15.2;
Isa 1.16;
Jas 1.8
4.9
Lk 6.25
4.10
Mt 23.12

4.11
1 Pet 2.1
4.12
Mt 10.28;
Rom 14.4
4.13
Prov 27.1
4.14
Job 7.7;
Ps 102.3
4.15
Acts 18.21
4.16
1 Cor 5.6
4.17
Lk 12.47;
Jn 9.41
5.1
Lk 6.24
5.2
Job 13.28;
Mt 6.20
5.3
vv. 7,8
5.4
Lev 19.13;
Deut 24.15;
Rom 9.29
5.5
Am 6.1;
Jer 12.3;
25.34

Warning against Judging Another

11 Do not speak evil against one another, brothers and sisters.[t] Whoever speaks evil against another or judges another, speaks evil against the law and judges the law; but if you judge the law, you are not a doer of the law but a judge. [12]There is one lawgiver and judge who is able to save and to destroy. So who, then, are you to judge your neighbor?

Boasting about Tomorrow

13 Come now, you who say, "Today or tomorrow we will go to such and such a town and spend a year there, doing business and making money." [14]Yet you do not even know what tomorrow will bring. What is your life? For you are a mist that appears for a little while and then vanishes. [15]Instead you ought to say, "If the Lord wishes, we will live and do this or that." [16]As it is, you boast in your arrogance; all such boasting is evil. [17]Anyone, then, who knows the right thing to do and fails to do it, commits sin.

Warning to Rich Oppressors

5 Come now, you rich people, weep and wail for the miseries that are coming to you. [2]Your riches have rotted, and your clothes are moth-eaten. [3]Your gold and silver have rusted, and their rust will be evidence against you, and it will eat your flesh like fire. You have laid up treasure[u] for the last days. [4]Listen! The wages of the laborers who mowed your fields, which you kept back by fraud, cry out, and the cries of the harvesters have reached the ears of the Lord of hosts. [5]You have lived on the earth in luxury and in pleasure; you have fattened your hearts in a day of slaughter. [6]You have condemned and murdered the righteous one, who does not resist you.

q Or by r Or you murder and you covet
s Gk He t Gk brothers u Or will eat
your flesh, since you have stored up fire

Patience in Suffering

7 Be patient, therefore, beloved,[v] until the coming of the Lord. The farmer waits for the precious crop from the earth, being patient with it until it receives the early and the late rains. [8]You also must be patient. Strengthen your hearts, for the coming of the Lord is near.[w] [9]Beloved,[x] do not grumble against one another, so that you may not be judged. See, the Judge is standing at the doors! [10]As an example of suffering and patience, beloved,[v] take the prophets who spoke in the name of the Lord. [11]Indeed we call blessed those who showed endurance. You have heard of the endurance of Job, and you have seen the purpose of the Lord, how the Lord is compassionate and merciful.

12 Above all, my beloved,[v] do not swear, either by heaven or by earth or by any other oath, but let your "Yes" be yes and your "No" be no, so that you may not fall under condemnation.

The Prayer of Faith

13 Are any among you suffering? They should pray. Are any cheerful? They should sing songs of praise. [14]Are any among you sick? They should call for the elders of the church and have them pray over them, anointing them with oil in the name of the Lord. [15]The prayer of faith will save the sick, and the Lord will raise them up; and anyone who has committed sins will be forgiven. [16]Therefore confess your sins to one another, and pray for one another, so that you may be healed. The prayer of the righteous is powerful and effective. [17]Elijah was a human being like us, and he prayed fervently that it might not rain, and for three years and six months it did not rain on the earth. [18]Then he prayed again, and the heaven gave rain and the earth yielded its harvest.

19 My brothers and sisters,[y] if anyone among you wanders from the truth and is brought back by another, [20]you should know that whoever brings back a sinner from wandering will save the sinner's[z] soul from death and will cover a multitude of sins.

[v] Gk brothers [w] Or is at hand
[x] Gk Brothers [y] Gk My brothers
[z] Gk his

Cross references

5.7 Deut 11.14; Jer 5.24
5.8 1 Pet 4.7
5.9 Jas 4.11,12; Mt 24.33
5.10 Mt 5.12
5.11 Mt 5.10; Job 1.21,22; 42.10; Num 14.18
5.12 Mt 5.34-37
5.13 v. 10; Ps 50.15; Col 3.16
5.14 Mk 6.13
5.16 Mt 3.6; 1 Pet 2.24; Jn 9.31
5.17 Acts 14.15; 1 Kings 17.1; Lk 4.25
5.18 1 Kings 18.42, 45
5.19 Mt 18.15
5.20 Rom 11.14; 1 Pet 4.8

THE FIRST LETTER OF
Peter

Title and Background

The recipients of this letter had been suffering various trials and afflictions, and the possibility of greater and more severe difficulties was very real. This letter was addressed to Christians who were scattered throughout the Roman world.

Author and Date of Writing

The author identifies himself as the apostle Peter, and the contents and character of the letter tend to support his authorship. Moreover, the letter reflects the history and terminology of the Gospels and Acts, notably Peter's speeches. It was written about A.D. 64.

Theme and Message

1 Peter touches on various doctrines and has much to say about Christian life and duties. It has been characterized as a letter of separation, of suffering and persecution, of suffering and glory, of hope, of pilgrimage, of courage, and as a letter dealing with the true grace of God. It contains numerous exhortations.

Outline

 I. Greetings (1.1-2)
 II. Praise for God's Grace and Salvation (1.3-12)
 III. Holy Living (1.13–5.11)
 IV. The Purpose of the Letter (5.12)
 V. Closing Greetings (5.13-14)

Salutation

1 Peter, an apostle of Jesus Christ,
 To the exiles of the Dispersion in Pontus, Galatia, Cappadocia, Asia, and Bithynia, ² who have been chosen and destined by God the Father and sanctified by the Spirit to be obedient to Jesus Christ and to be sprinkled with his blood:
 May grace and peace be yours in abundance.

A Living Hope

3 Blessed be the God and Father of our Lord Jesus Christ! By his great mercy he has given us a new birth into a living hope through the resurrection of Jesus Christ from the dead, ⁴ and into an inheritance that is imperishable, undefiled, and unfading, kept in heaven for you, ⁵ who are being protected by the power of God through faith for a salvation ready to be revealed in

the last time. ⁶ In this you rejoice,[a] even if now for a little while you have had to suffer various trials, ⁷ so that the genuineness of your faith — being more precious than gold that, though perishable, is tested by fire — may be found to result in praise and glory and honor when Jesus Christ is revealed. ⁸ Although you have not seen[b] him, you love him; and even though you do not see him now, you believe in him and rejoice with an indescribable and glorious joy, ⁹ for you are receiving the outcome of your faith, the salvation of your souls.

10 Concerning this salvation, the prophets who prophesied of the grace that was to be yours made careful search and inquiry, ¹¹ inquiring about the person or time

1.1 2 Pet 2.1; Acts 2.5,9
1.2 2 Thes 2.13; Heb 10.22; 2 Pet 1.2
1.3 2 Cor 1.3; Jas 1.18; 1 Cor 15.20
1.4 Col 3.24
1.5 Jn 10.28

1.6 Rom 5.2; 1 Pet 5.10; Jas 1.2
1.7 Jas 1.3; Ps 66.10; Rom 2.7
1.8 1 Jn 4.20; Jn 20.29
1.9 Rom 6.22
1.10 Mt 13.17; 26.24

1.11 2 Pet 1.21; Isa ch. 53

[a] Or *Rejoice in this* [b] Other ancient authorities read *known*

that the Spirit of Christ within them indicated when it testified in advance to the sufferings destined for Christ and the subsequent glory. [12] It was revealed to them that they were serving not themselves but you, in regard to the things that have now been announced to you through those who brought you good news by the Holy Spirit sent from heaven — things into which angels long to look!

A Call to Holy Living

13 Therefore prepare your minds for action;[c] discipline yourselves; set all your hope on the grace that Jesus Christ will bring you when he is revealed. [14] Like obedient children, do not be conformed to the desires that you formerly had in ignorance. [15] Instead, as he who called you is holy, be holy yourselves in all your conduct; [16] for it is written, "You shall be holy, for I am holy."

17 If you invoke as Father the one who judges all people impartially according to their deeds, live in reverent fear during the time of your exile. [18] You know that you were ransomed from the futile ways inherited from your ancestors, not with perishable things like silver or gold, [19] but with the precious blood of Christ, like that of a lamb without defect or blemish. [20] He was destined before the foundation of the world, but was revealed at the end of the ages for your sake. [21] Through him you have come to trust in God, who raised him from the dead and gave him glory, so that your faith and hope are set on God.

22 Now that you have purified your souls by your obedience to the truth[d] so that you have genuine mutual love, love one another deeply[e] from the heart.[f] [23] You have been born anew, not of perishable but of imperishable seed, through the living and enduring word of God.[g] [24] For

"All flesh is like grass
 and all its glory like the
 flower of grass.

The grass withers,
 and the flower falls,
25 but the word of the Lord
 endures forever."
That word is the good news that was announced to you.

The Living Stone and a Chosen People

2 Rid yourselves, therefore, of all malice, and all guile, insincerity, envy, and all slander. [2] Like newborn infants, long for the pure, spiritual milk, so that by it you may grow into salvation — [3] if indeed you have tasted that the Lord is good.

4 Come to him, a living stone, though rejected by mortals yet chosen and precious in God's sight, and [5] like living stones, let yourselves be built[h] into a spiritual house, to be a holy priesthood, to offer spiritual sacrifices acceptable to God through Jesus Christ. [6] For it stands in scripture:

"See, I am laying in Zion a
 stone,
a cornerstone chosen and
 precious;
and whoever believes in
 him[i] will not be put to
 shame."

[7] To you then who believe, he is precious; but for those who do not believe,

"The stone that the builders
 rejected
has become the very head
 of the corner,"

[8] and

"A stone that makes them
 stumble,
and a rock that makes
 them fall."

They stumble because they disobey the word, as they were destined to do.

9 But you are a chosen race, a royal priesthood, a holy nation, God's own people,[j] in order that

Cross references

1.12 Dan 9.24; Eph 3.10
1.13 Eph 6.14; 1 Thes 5.6
1.14 Rom 12.2; Eph 4.18
1.15 2 Cor 7.1
1.16 Lev 11.44
1.17 Deut 10.17; Heb 12.28
1.18 1 Cor 6.20; Ezek 20.18
1.19 Ex 12.5
1.20 Eph 1.4; Heb 9.26
1.22 Jas 4.8; Heb 13.1
1.23 Jn 3.3; 1.13; Heb 4.12
1.24 Isa 40.6-9; Jas 1.10,11

1.25 Jn 1.1
2.1 Eph 4.22; Jas 1.21; 4.11
2.2 Mk 10.15; 1 Cor 3.2
2.3 Heb 6.5; Titus 3.4
2.4 v. 7
2.5 Heb 13.15; Phil 4.18
2.6 Isa 28.16; Eph 2.20
2.7 Ps 118.22; Mt 21.42
2.8 Isa 8.14; 1 Cor 1.23; Rom 9.22
2.9 Deut 10.15; Acts 26.18

c Gk *gird up the loins of your mind* d Other ancient authorities add *through the Spirit* e Or *constantly* f Other ancient authorities read *a pure heart* g Or *through the word of the living and enduring God* h Or *you yourselves are being built* i Or *it* j Gk *a people for his possession*

you may proclaim the mighty acts of him who called you out of darkness into his marvelous light. [10] Once you were not a people, but now you are God's people; once you had not received mercy, but now you have received mercy.

Live as Servants of God

11 Beloved, I urge you as aliens and exiles to abstain from the desires of the flesh that wage war against the soul. [12] Conduct yourselves honorably among the Gentiles, so that, though they malign you as evildoers, they may see your honorable deeds and glorify God when he comes to judge.[k]

13 For the Lord's sake accept the authority of every human institution,[l] whether of the emperor as supreme, [14] or of governors, as sent by him to punish those who do wrong and to praise those who do right. [15] For it is God's will that by doing right you should silence the ignorance of the foolish. [16] As servants[m] of God, live as free people, yet do not use your freedom as a pretext for evil. [17] Honor everyone. Love the family of believers.[n] Fear God. Honor the emperor.

The Example of Christ's Suffering

18 Slaves, accept the authority of your masters with all deference, not only those who are kind and gentle but also those who are harsh. [19] For it is a credit to you if, being aware of God, you endure pain while suffering unjustly. [20] If you endure when you are beaten for doing wrong, what credit is that? But if you endure when you do right and suffer for it, you have God's approval. [21] For to this you have been called, because Christ also suffered for you, leaving you an example, so that you should follow in his steps.

22 "He committed no sin, and no deceit was found in his mouth."

23 When he was abused, he did not return abuse; when he suffered, he did not threaten; but he entrusted himself to the one who judges justly. [24] He himself bore our sins in his body on the cross,[o] so that, free from sins, we might live for righteousness; by his wounds[p] you have been healed. [25] For you were going astray like sheep, but now you have returned to the shepherd and guardian of your souls.

Wives and Husbands

3 Wives, in the same way, accept the authority of your husbands, so that, even if some of them do not obey the word, they may be won over without a word by their wives' conduct, [2] when they see the purity and reverence of your lives. [3] Do not adorn yourselves outwardly by braiding your hair, and by wearing gold ornaments or fine clothing; [4] rather, let your adornment be the inner self with the lasting beauty of a gentle and quiet spirit, which is very precious in God's sight. [5] It was in this way long ago that the holy women who hoped in God used to adorn themselves by accepting the authority of their husbands. [6] Thus Sarah obeyed Abraham and called him lord. You have become her daughters as long as you do what is good and never let fears alarm you.

7 Husbands, in the same way, show consideration for your wives in your life together, paying honor to the woman as the weaker sex,[q] since they too are also heirs of the gracious gift of life — so that nothing may hinder your prayers.

Suffering for Doing Right

8 Finally, all of you, have unity of spirit, sympathy, love for one another, a tender heart, and a humble mind. [9] Do not repay evil for evil or abuse for abuse; but, on the contrary, repay with a blessing. It is for

2.10
Hos 1.9,10
2.11
Rom 12.1;
Ps 39.12;
Gal 5.16;
Jas 4.1
2.12
Phil 2.15;
1 Pet 3.16;
Mt 5.16
2.13
Rom 13.1
2.14
Rom 13.4,3
2.15
1 Pet 3.17;
Titus 2.8
2.16
Gal 5.1;
1 Cor 7.22
2.17
Rom 12.10;
Heb 13.1
2.18
Eph 6.5
2.19
Rom 13.5
2.20
1 Pet 3.17
2.21
Mt 16.24;
Acts 14.22
2.22
Isa 53.9

2.23
Isa 53.7;
Heb 12.3;
Lk 23.46
2.24
Heb 9.28;
Rom 6.2;
Isa 53.5
2.25
Isa 53.6;
1 Pet 5.4
3.1
Eph 5.22;
1 Cor 7.16
3.3
1 Tim 2.9;
Isa 3.18-23
3.4
Rom 7.22
3.5
1 Tim 5.5
3.6
Gen 18.12
3.7
Eph 5.25;
1 Thes 4.4;
Mt 5.23ff
3.8
Phil 2.3;
1 Pet 5.5
3.9
Rom 12.17;
Heb 6.14

k Gk *God on the day of visitation*
l Or *every institution ordained for human beings* m Gk *slaves* n Gk *Love the brotherhood* o Or *carried up our sins in his body to the tree* p Gk *bruise*
q Gk *vessel*

this that you were called—that you might inherit a blessing. 10 For

"Those who desire life
 and desire to see good
 days,
let them keep their tongues
 from evil
and their lips from
 speaking deceit;
11 let them turn away from evil
 and do good;
let them seek peace and
 pursue it.
12 For the eyes of the Lord are
 on the righteous,
and his ears are open to
 their prayer.
But the face of the Lord is
 against those who do
 evil."

13 Now who will harm you if you are eager to do what is good? 14 But even if you do suffer for doing what is right, you are blessed. Do not fear what they fear,r and do not be intimidated, 15 but in your hearts sanctify Christ as Lord. Always be ready to make your defense to anyone who demands from you an accounting for the hope that is in you; 16 yet do it with gentleness and reverence.s Keep your conscience clear, so that, when you are maligned, those who abuse you for your good conduct in Christ may be put to shame. 17 For it is better to suffer for doing good, if suffering should be God's will, than to suffer for doing evil. 18 For Christ also sufferedt for sins once for all, the righteous for the unrighteous, in order to bring youu to God. He was put to death in the flesh, but made alive in the spirit, 19 in which also he went and made a proclamation to the spirits in prison, 20 who in former times did not obey, when God waited patiently in the days of Noah, during the building of the ark, in which a few, that is, eight persons, were saved through water. 21 And baptism, which this prefigured, now saves you—not as a removal of dirt from the body, but as an appeal to God forv a good conscience, through the resurrection of Jesus

Christ, 22 who has gone into heaven and is at the right hand of God, with angels, authorities, and powers made subject to him.

Good Stewards of God's Grace

4 Since therefore Christ suffered in the flesh,w arm yourselves also with the same intention (for whoever has suffered in the flesh has finished with sin), 2 so as to live for the rest of your earthly lifex no longer by human desires but by the will of God. 3 You have already spent enough time in doing what the Gentiles like to do, living in licentiousness, passions, drunkenness, revels, carousing, and lawless idolatry. 4 They are surprised that you no longer join them in the same excesses of dissipation, and so they blaspheme.y 5 But they will have to give an accounting to him who stands ready to judge the living and the dead. 6 For this is the reason the gospel was proclaimed even to the dead, so that, though they had been judged in the flesh as everyone is judged, they might live in the spirit as God does.

7 The end of all things is near;z therefore be serious and discipline yourselves for the sake of your prayers. 8 Above all, maintain constant love for one another, for love covers a multitude of sins. 9 Be hospitable to one another without complaining. 10 Like good stewards of the manifold grace of God, serve one another with whatever gift each of you has received. 11 Whoever speaks must do so as one speaking the very words of God; whoever serves must do so with the strength that God supplies, so that God may be glorified in all things through Jesus Christ. To him belong the glory and the power forever and ever. Amen.

Cross references

3.10
Ps 34.12-16;
Jas 1.26;
1 Pet 2.1,
22
3.13
Prov 16.7
3.14
1 Pet 2.19ff;
Isa 8.12,13
3.15
Col 4.6;
1 Pet 1.3;
1.17
3.16
Heb 13.18;
1 Pet 2.12,
15
3.17
1 Pet 2.20,
15
3.18
1 Pet 2.21;
2 Cor 13.4;
Eph 3.12;
1 Pet 4.1,6
3.19
1 Pet 4.6
3.20
Gen 6.3,5;
Heb 11.7;
Gen 8.18
3.21
Titus 3.5;
Heb 9.14;
1 Pet 1.3

3.22
Rom 8.34,
38
4.1
1 Pet 3.18;
Gal 5.24
4.2
Gal 2.20;
Rom 6.11
4.3
Eph 4.17
4.4
1 Pet 3.16
4.5
Acts 10.42;
2 Tim 4.1
4.6
1 Pet 3.19
4.7
Rom 13.11;
1 Pet 1.13
4.8
Heb 13.1;
1 Cor 13.7
4.9
Heb 13.2;
2 Cor 9.7
4.10
Rom 12.6,7;
1 Cor 4.1
4.11
Eph 6.10;
5.20;
1 Tim 6.16

r Gk their fear s Or respect t Other ancient authorities read died u Other ancient authorities read us v Or a pledge to God from w Other ancient authorities add for us; others, for you x Gk rest of the time in the flesh y Or they malign you z Or is at hand

Suffering as a Christian

12 Beloved, do not be surprised at the fiery ordeal that is taking place among you to test you, as though something strange were happening to you. 13 But rejoice insofar as you are sharing Christ's sufferings, so that you may also be glad and shout for joy when his glory is revealed. 14 If you are reviled for the name of Christ, you are blessed, because the spirit of glory,[a] which is the Spirit of God, is resting on you.[b] 15 But let none of you suffer as a murderer, a thief, a criminal, or even as a mischief maker. 16 Yet if any of you suffers as a Christian, do not consider it a disgrace, but glorify God because you bear this name. 17 For the time has come for judgment to begin with the household of God; if it begins with us, what will be the end for those who do not obey the gospel of God? 18 And

"If it is hard for the
 righteous to be saved,
 what will become of the
 ungodly and the
 sinners?"

19 Therefore, let those suffering in accordance with God's will entrust themselves to a faithful Creator, while continuing to do good.

Tending the Flock of God

5 Now as an elder myself and a witness of the sufferings of Christ, as well as one who shares in the glory to be revealed, I exhort the elders among you 2 to tend the flock of God that is in your charge, exercising the oversight,[c] not under compulsion but willingly, as God would have you do it[d]—not for sordid gain but eagerly. 3 Do not lord it over those in your charge, but be examples to the flock. 4 And when the chief shepherd appears, you will win the crown of glory that never fades away. 5 In the same

way, you who are younger must accept the authority of the elders.[e] And all of you must clothe yourselves with humility in your dealings with one another, for

 "God opposes the proud,
 but gives grace to the
 humble."

6 Humble yourselves therefore under the mighty hand of God, so that he may exalt you in due time. 7 Cast all your anxiety on him, because he cares for you. 8 Discipline yourselves, keep alert.[f] Like a roaring lion your adversary the devil prowls around, looking for someone to devour. 9 Resist him, steadfast in your faith, for you know that your brothers and sisters[g] in all the world are undergoing the same kinds of suffering. 10 And after you have suffered for a little while, the God of all grace, who has called you to his eternal glory in Christ, will himself restore, support, strengthen, and establish you. 11 To him be the power forever and ever. Amen.

Final Greetings and Benediction

12 Through Silvanus, whom I consider a faithful brother, I have written this short letter to encourage you and to testify that this is the true grace of God. Stand fast in it. 13 Your sister church[h] in Babylon, chosen together with you, sends you greetings; and so does my son Mark. 14 Greet one another with a kiss of love.

Peace to all of you who are in Christ.[i]

a Other ancient authorities add *and of power*
b Other ancient authorities add *On their part he is blasphemed, but on your part he is glorified* c Other ancient authorities lack *exercising the oversight* d Other ancient authorities lack *as God would have you do it*
e Or *of those who are older* f Or *be vigilant* g Gk *your brotherhood*
h Gk *She who is* i Other ancient authorities add *Amen*

Cross references (center column)

4.12
1 Pet 1.6,7
4.13
Phil 3.10;
Rom 8.17
4.14
Mt 5.11
4.15
1 Thes 4.11
4.16
Acts 5.41
4.17
Jer 25.29;
Mal 3.5
4.18
Prov 11.31;
Lk 23.31
4.19
2 Tim 1.12
5.1
Lk 24.48;
1 Pet 1.5,
7; Rev 1.9
5.2
Jn 21.16;
1 Cor 9.17;
1 Tim 3.3,
8; Titus 1.7
5.3
Ezek 34.4;
Phil 3.17
5.4
Heb 13.20;
2 Tim 4.8
5.5
Jas 4.6;
Isa 57.15
5.6
Jas 4.10
5.7
Ps 37.5;
Mt 6.25;
Heb 13.5
5.8
Lk 21.34;
Job 1.7
5.9
Jas 4.7;
Col 2.5;
Acts 14.22
5.10
Heb 13.21;
2 Thes 2.17
5.12
2 Cor 1.19;
Heb 13.22
5.13
Acts 12.12
5.14
Rom 16.16;
Eph 6.23

THE SECOND LETTER OF
Peter

Title and Background

The recipients of this letter were probably the same group of Christians addressed in Peter's first letter. They were in danger of being confused by false teachers.

Author and Date of Writing

The author identifies himself as Simon Peter. He asserts that this is his second letter to the readers (3.1) and refers to Paul as "our beloved brother" (3.15). The character of the letter is compatible with the claim that it was written by Peter. If this is so, it was written about A.D. 66. Some, however, maintain that it is a much later work.

Theme and Message

Peter as a "shepherd" of Christ's sheep is particularly concerned about the false teachers and evildoers who have come into the church. He teaches the church how to deal with these false teachers, but he also recommends to his readers a wholesome combination of Christian faith and practice. The Lord is certain to return, so the believers are to be watchful!

Outline

I. Introduction (1.1-2)
II. Growth in Christian Virtues (1.3-11)
III. Peter's Message (1.12-21)
IV. Warning Against False Teachers (2.1-22)
V. Christ's Return (3.1-16)
VI. Conclusion (3.17-18)

Salutation

1 Simeon[a] Peter, a servant[b] and apostle of Jesus Christ,
To those who have received a faith as precious as ours through the righteousness of our God and Savior Jesus Christ:[c]

2 May grace and peace be yours in abundance in the knowledge of God and of Jesus our Lord.

The Christian's Call and Election

3 His divine power has given us everything needed for life and godliness, through the knowledge of him who called us by[d] his own glory and goodness. 4 Thus he has given us, through these things, his precious and very great promises, so that through them you may escape from the corruption that is in the world because of lust, and may become participants of the divine nature. 5 For this very reason, you must make every effort to support your faith with goodness, and goodness with knowledge, 6 and knowledge with self-control, and self-control with endurance, and endurance with godliness, 7 and godliness with mutual[e] affection, and mutual[e] affection with love. 8 For if these things are yours and are increasing among you, they keep you from being ineffective and unfruitful in the knowledge of our Lord Jesus Christ. 9 For anyone who lacks these things is nearsighted and blind, and is forgetful of the

1.1 Rom 1.1; 1 Pet 1.1; Rom 1.12; 3.21-26; Titus 2.13
1.2 1 Pet 1.2; vv. 3,8
1.3 1 Pet 1.5; 1 Thes 2.12
1.4 2 Cor 7.1; Eph 4.24; 1 Jn 3.2; 2 Pet 2.18-20
1.5 2 Pet 3.18; Col 2.3
1.6 Acts 24.26; Lk 21.19; v. 3
1.7 1 Thes 3.12
1.8 Jn 15.2; Titus 3.14

1.9 1 Jn 2.11; Eph 5.26; 1 Jn 1.7

a Other ancient authorities read *Simon*
b Gk *slave* c Or *of our God and the Savior Jesus Christ* d Other ancient authorities read *through* e Gk *brotherly*

cleansing of past sins. [10] Therefore, brothers and sisters,[f] be all the more eager to confirm your call and election, for if you do this, you will never stumble. [11] For in this way, entry into the eternal kingdom of our Lord and Savior Jesus Christ will be richly provided for you.

12 Therefore I intend to keep on reminding you of these things, though you know them already and are established in the truth that has come to you. [13] I think it right, as long as I am in this body,[g] to refresh your memory, [14] since I know that my death[h] will come soon, as indeed our Lord Jesus Christ has made clear to me. [15] And I will make every effort so that after my departure you may be able at any time to recall these things.

Eyewitnesses of Christ's Glory

16 For we did not follow cleverly devised myths when we made known to you the power and coming of our Lord Jesus Christ, but we had been eyewitnesses of his majesty. [17] For he received honor and glory from God the Father when that voice was conveyed to him by the Majestic Glory, saying, "This is my Son, my Beloved,[i] with whom I am well pleased." [18] We ourselves heard this voice come from heaven, while we were with him on the holy mountain.

19 So we have the prophetic message more fully confirmed. You will do well to be attentive to this as to a lamp shining in a dark place, until the day dawns and the morning star rises in your hearts. [20] First of all you must understand this, that no prophecy of scripture is a matter of one's own interpretation, [21] because no prophecy ever came by human will, but men and women moved by the Holy Spirit spoke from God.[j]

False Prophets and Their Punishment

2 But false prophets also arose among the people, just as there will be false teachers among you, who will secretly bring in de-structive opinions. They will even deny the Master who bought them — bringing swift destruction on themselves. [2] Even so, many will follow their licentious ways, and because of these teachers[k] the way of truth will be maligned. [3] And in their greed they will exploit you with deceptive words. Their condemnation, pronounced against them long ago, has not been idle, and their destruction is not asleep.

4 For if God did not spare the angels when they sinned, but cast them into hell[l] and committed them to chains[m] of deepest darkness to be kept until the judgment; [5] and if he did not spare the ancient world, even though he saved Noah, a herald of righteousness, with seven others, when he brought a flood on a world of the ungodly; [6] and if by turning the cities of Sodom and Gomorrah to ashes he condemned them to extinction[n] and made them an example of what is coming to the ungodly;[o] [7] and if he rescued Lot, a righteous man greatly distressed by the licentiousness of the lawless [8] (for that righteous man, living among them day after day, was tormented in his righteous soul by their lawless deeds that he saw and heard), [9] then the Lord knows how to rescue the godly from trial, and to keep the unrighteous under punishment until the day of judgment [10] — especially those who indulge their flesh in depraved lust, and who despise authority.

Bold and willful, they are not afraid to slander the glorious ones,[p] [11] whereas angels, though greater in might and power, do not bring against them a slanderous judgment from the Lord.[q] [12] These

1.12
1 Jn 2.21
1.13
2 Cor 5.1
1.14
2 Tim 4.6;
Jn 21.18,19
1.16
1 Tim 1.4;
Mt 17.1;
Mk 9.2
1.17
Mt 3.17;
Lk 9.35
1.18
Mt 17.6
1.19
1 Pet 1.10,
11;
Ps 119.105;
Rev 22.16
1.20f
Rom 12.6
1.21
2 Tim 3.16;
1 Pet 1.11;
Acts 1.16
2.1
1 Tim 4.1;
Jude 18;
1 Cor 6.20
2.3
1 Tim 6.5;
2 Cor 2.17;
Deut 32.35
2.4
Jude 6;
Jn 8.44;
Rev 20.1,2
2.5
Gen 7.1;
Heb 11.7;
1 Pet 3.20
2.6
Gen 19.24;
Jude 7;
Num 26.10
2.7
Gen 19.16;
2 Pet 3.17
2.9
1 Cor 10.13;
Jude 6
2.10
2 Pet 3.3;
Jude 8;
Titus 1.7
2.11
Jude 9
2.12
Jude 10

[f] Gk brothers [g] Gk tent [h] Gk the putting off of my tent [i] Other ancient authorities read my beloved Son [j] Other ancient authorities read but moved by the Holy Spirit saints of God spoke [k] Gk because of them [l] Gk Tartaros [m] Other ancient authorities read pits [n] Other ancient authorities lack to extinction [o] Other ancient authorities read an example to those who were to be ungodly [p] Or angels; Gk glories [q] Other ancient authorities read before the Lord; others lack the phrase

people, however, are like irrational animals, mere creatures of instinct, born to be caught and killed. They slander what they do not understand, and when those creatures are destroyed,ʳ they also will be destroyed, ¹³ sufferingˢ the penalty for doing wrong. They count it a pleasure to revel in the daytime. They are blots and blemishes, reveling in their dissipationᵗ while they feast with you. ¹⁴ They have eyes full of adultery, insatiable for sin. They entice unsteady souls. They have hearts trained in greed. Accursed children! ¹⁵ They have left the straight road and have gone astray, following the road of Balaam son of Bosor,ᵘ who loved the wages of doing wrong, ¹⁶ but was rebuked for his own transgression; a speechless donkey spoke with a human voice and restrained the prophet's madness.

17 These are waterless springs and mists driven by a storm; for them the deepest darkness has been reserved. ¹⁸ For they speak bombastic nonsense, and with licentious desires of the flesh they entice people who have justᵛ escaped from those who live in error. ¹⁹ They promise them freedom, but they themselves are slaves of corruption; for people are slaves to whatever masters them. ²⁰ For if, after they have escaped the defilements of the world through the knowledge of our Lord and Savior Jesus Christ, they are again entangled in them and overpowered, the last state has become worse for them than the first. ²¹ For it would have been better for them never to have known the way of righteousness than, after knowing it, to turn back from the holy commandment that was passed on to them. ²² It has happened to them according to the true proverb,
 "The dog turns back to its
 own vomit,"
and,
 "The sow is washed only to
 wallow in the mud."

2.13
Rom 13.13;
Jude 12;
1 Cor 11.20,
21
2.14
v. 18;
Jude 11;
v. 3;
Eph 2.3
2.15
Num 22.5,7;
Jude 11
2.16
Num 22.21,
23,28,30,31
2.17
Jude 12,13
2.18
Jude 16
2.19f
Jn 8.34;
Rom 6.16
2.20
Mt 12.45;
Lk 11.26;
2 Pet 1.2
2.21
Heb 6.4ff;
2 Pet 3.2;
Jude 3
2.22
Prov 26.11

3.3
1 Tim 4.1;
Jude 18;
2 Pet 2.10
3.4
Isa 5.9;
Jer 17.15;
Ezek 12.22;
Mt 24.48;
Acts 7.60;
Mt 10.6
3.5
Gen 1.6,9;
Heb 11.3;
Ps 24.2;
Col 1.17
3.6
Gen 7.21,22
3.7
v. 10;
2 Thes 1.7;
1 Cor 3.13
3.8
Ps 90.4
3.9
Heb 10.37;
Isa 30.18;
1 Pet 3.20;
Rom 2.4
3.10
Mt 24.43;
1 Thes 5.2;
Mt 24.35;
Rev 21.1

The Promise of the Lord's Coming

3 This is now, beloved, the second letter I am writing to you; in them I am trying to arouse your sincere intention by reminding you ² that you should remember the words spoken in the past by the holy prophets, and the commandment of the Lord and Savior spoken through your apostles. ³ First of all you must understand this, that in the last days scoffers will come, scoffing and indulging their own lusts ⁴ and saying, "Where is the promise of his coming? For ever since our ancestors died,ʷ all things continue as they were from the beginning of creation!" ⁵ They deliberately ignore this fact, that by the word of God heavens existed long ago and an earth was formed out of water and by means of water, ⁶ through which the world of that time was deluged with water and perished. ⁷ But by the same word the present heavens and earth have been reserved for fire, being kept until the day of judgment and destruction of the godless.

8 But do not ignore this one fact, beloved, that with the Lord one day is like a thousand years, and a thousand years are like one day. ⁹ The Lord is not slow about his promise, as some think of slowness, but is patient with you,ˣ not wanting any to perish, but all to come to repentance. ¹⁰ But the day of the Lord will come like a thief, and then the heavens will pass away with a loud noise, and the elements will be dissolved with fire, and the earth and everything that is done on it will be disclosed.ʸ

11 Since all these things are to be dissolved in this way, what sort of persons ought you to be in leading lives of holiness and godliness,

ʳ Gk *in their destruction* ˢ Other ancient authorities read *receiving* ᵗ Other ancient authorities read *love feasts* ᵘ Other ancient authorities read *Beor* ᵛ Other ancient authorities read *actually* ʷ Gk *our fathers fell asleep* ˣ Other ancient authorities read *on your account* ʸ Other ancient authorities read *will be burned up*

12 waiting for and hastening[z] the coming of the day of God, because of which the heavens will be set ablaze and dissolved, and the elements will melt with fire? 13 But, in accordance with his promise, we wait for new heavens and a new earth, where righteousness is at home.

Final Exhortation and Doxology

14 Therefore, beloved, while you are waiting for these things, strive to be found by him at peace, without spot or blemish; 15 and regard the patience of our Lord as salvation. So also our beloved brother Paul wrote to you according to the wisdom given him,

16 speaking of this as he does in all his letters. There are some things in them hard to understand, which the ignorant and unstable twist to their own destruction, as they do the other scriptures. 17 You therefore, beloved, since you are forewarned, beware that you are not carried away with the error of the lawless and lose your own stability. 18 But grow in the grace and knowledge of our Lord and Savior Jesus Christ. To him be the glory both now and to the day of eternity. Amen.[a]

3.12 1 Cor 1.7; Titus 2.13; Ps 50.3; Isa 34.4; v. 10 **3.13** Isa 65.17; 66.22; Rev 21.1 **3.14** 2 Pet 1.10; 1 Cor 15.58; Phil 2.15 **3.15** v. 9; 1 Cor 3.10; Eph 3.3 **3.16** v. 14; v. 2 **3.17** 1 Cor 10.12; 2 Pet 2.18; Rev 2.5

[z] Or *earnestly desiring* [a] Other ancient authorities lack *Amen*

THE FIRST LETTER OF
John

Title and Background

False teachers were trying to mislead first-century Christians by denying, among other things, the true humanity of Christ. This view came to be called Gnosticism and is the background of much of 1 John.

Author and Date of Writing

The author is John son of Zebedee–the apostle and the author of the Gospel of John. He was a first cousin of Jesus. The letter is difficult to date with precision, but many factors indicate that it was written near the end of the first century, probably around A.D. 90.

Theme and Message

John had two basic purposes in mind in this letter: (1) to expose false teachers, and (2) to give believers assurance of salvation. In keeping with his intention to combat Gnostic teachers, John specifically struck at their total lack of morality; and by giving eyewitness testimony to the human nature of the Son of God, he sought to confirm his readers' belief in the incarnate Christ. He tells his readers that if he is successful in doing this, it would give him great joy.

Outline

I. The Reality of the Incarnation (1.1-4)
II. Fellowship With the Father and the Son (1.5–2.28)
III. Divine Sonship (2.29–4.6)
IV. Ethics and Christ (4.7–5.12)
V. Great Christian Certainties (5.13-21)

The Word of Life

1 We declare to you what was from the beginning, what we have heard, what we have seen with our eyes, what we have looked at and touched with our hands, concerning the word of life — ²this life was revealed, and we have seen it and testify to it, and declare to you the eternal life that was with the Father and was revealed to us — ³we declare to you what we have seen and heard so that you also may have fellowship with us; and truly our fellowship is with the Father and with his Son Jesus Christ. ⁴We are writing these things so that our[a] joy may be complete.

God Is Light

5 This is the message we have heard from him and proclaim to you, that God is light and in him there is no darkness at all. ⁶If we say that we have fellowship with him while we are walking in darkness, we lie and do not do what is true; ⁷but if we walk in the light as he himself is in the light, we have fellowship with one another, and the blood of Jesus his Son cleanses us from all sin. ⁸If we say that we have no sin, we deceive ourselves, and the truth is not in us. ⁹If we confess our sins, he who is faithful and just will forgive us our sins and cleanse us from all unrighteousness. ¹⁰If we say that we have not sinned, we make him a liar, and his word is not in us.

1.1 Jn 1.1,14; 2 Pet 1.16; Jn 20.27 **1.2** Jn 1.1-4; Rom 16.26; Jn 21.24 **1.3** Acts 4.20; 1 Cor 1.9 **1.4** 1 Jn 2.1; Jn 3.29 **1.5** 1 Jn 3.11 **1.6** 2 Cor 6.14; Jn 8.55; 3.21 **1.7** Heb 9.14; 1 Pet 1.19; Rev 1.5 **1.8** Job 15.14; Prov 20.9; Jas 3.2; 1 Jn 2.4 **1.9** Ps 51.2 **1.10** 1 Jn 5.10; 2.14

a Other ancient authorities read *your*

Christ Our Advocate

2 My little children, I am writing these things to you so that you may not sin. But if anyone does sin, we have an advocate with the Father, Jesus Christ the righteous; ² and he is the atoning sacrifice for our sins, and not for ours only but also for the sins of the whole world.

3 Now by this we may be sure that we know him, if we obey his commandments. ⁴ Whoever says, "I have come to know him," but does not obey his commandments, is a liar, and in such a person the truth does not exist; ⁵ but whoever obeys his word, truly in this person the love of God has reached perfection. By this we may be sure that we are in him: ⁶ whoever says, "I abide in him," ought to walk just as he walked.

A New Commandment

7 Beloved, I am writing you no new commandment, but an old commandment that you have had from the beginning; the old commandment is the word that you have heard. ⁸ Yet I am writing you a new commandment that is true in him and in you, because ᵇ the darkness is passing away and the true light is already shining. ⁹ Whoever says, "I am in the light," while hating a brother or sister, ᶜ is still in the darkness. ¹⁰ Whoever loves a brother or sister ᵈ lives in the light, and in such a person ᵉ there is no cause for stumbling. ¹¹ But whoever hates another believer ᶠ is in the darkness, walks in the darkness, and does not know the way to go, because the darkness has brought on blindness.

¹² I am writing to you, little
 children,
because your sins are
 forgiven on account of
 his name.
¹³ I am writing to you, fathers,
because you know him who
 is from the beginning.
I am writing to you, young
 people,
because you have
 conquered the evil one.

¹⁴ I write to you, children,
because you know the
 Father.
I write to you, fathers,
because you know him who
 is from the beginning.
I write to you, young people,
because you are strong
and the word of God abides
 in you,
 and you have overcome
 the evil one.

15 Do not love the world or the things in the world. The love of the Father is not in those who love the world; ¹⁶ for all that is in the world — the desire of the flesh, the desire of the eyes, the pride in riches — comes not from the Father but from the world. ¹⁷ And the world and its desire ᵍ are passing away, but those who do the will of God live forever.

Warning against Antichrists

18 Children, it is the last hour! As you have heard that antichrist is coming, so now many antichrists have come. From this we know that it is the last hour. ¹⁹ They went out from us, but they did not belong to us; for if they had belonged to us, they would have remained with us. But by going out they made it plain that none of them belongs to us. ²⁰ But you have been anointed by the Holy One, and all of you have knowledge. ʰ ²¹ I write to you, not because you do not know the truth, but because you know it, and you know that no lie comes from the truth. ²² Who is the liar but the one who denies that Jesus is the Christ? ⁱ This is the antichrist, the one who denies the Father and the Son. ²³ No one who denies the Son has the Father; everyone who confesses the Son has the Father also. ²⁴ Let what you heard from the beginning abide in you. If what you heard from the beginning abides in you, then you will abide in the Son and in the Father. ²⁵ And this is

2.1
Rom 8.34;
Heb 7.25
2.2
Rom 3.25;
Jn 1.29
2.5
Jn 14.23;
1 Jn 4.12,
13
2.6
Jn 15.4;
1 Pet 2.21
2.7
1 Jn 3.2;
2 Jn 5;
1 Jn 3.11
2.8
Eph 5.8;
1 Thes 5.5;
Jn 1.9
2.9
2 Pet 1.9
2.10
1 Jn 3.14;
v. 11
2.11
Jn 12.35
2.12
Lk 24.47
2.13
1 Jn 1.1;
v. 14

2.14
1 Jn 1.1;
Eph 6.10;
Jn 5.38
2.15
Rom 12.2;
Mt 6.24;
Jas 4.4
2.16
Rom 13.14;
Prov 27.20;
Jas 4.16
2.17
1 Cor 7.31
2.18
1 Pet 4.7;
1 Jn 4.1,3
2.19
Acts 20.30;
Mt 24.24;
1 Cor 11.19
2.20
2 Cor 1.21;
Acts 3.14;
Jn 14.26
2.21
2 Pet 1.12;
1 Jn 3.19
2.23
Jn 14.7
2.24
2 Jn 6;
Jn 14.23
2.25
Jn 17.3

ᵇ Or that ᶜ Gk hating a brother
ᵈ Gk loves a brother ᵉ Or in it
ᶠ Gk hates a brother ᵍ Or the desire for it
ʰ Other ancient authorities read you know all
things ⁱ Or the Messiah

what he has promised us,[i] eternal life.

26 I write these things to you concerning those who would deceive you. [27]As for you, the anointing that you received from him abides in you, and so you do not need anyone to teach you. But as his anointing teaches you about all things, and is true and is not a lie, and just as it has taught you, abide in him.[k]

28 And now, little children, abide in him, so that when he is revealed we may have confidence and not be put to shame before him at his coming.

Children of God

29 If you know that he is righteous, you may be sure that everyone who does right has been born of him. [1]See what love the Father has given us, that we should be called children of God; and that is what we are. The reason the world does not know us is that it did not know him. [2]Beloved, we are God's children now; what we will be has not yet been revealed. What we do know is this: when he[k] is revealed, we will be like him, for we will see him as he is. [3]And all who have this hope in him purify themselves, just as he is pure.

4 Everyone who commits sin is guilty of lawlessness; sin is lawlessness. [5]You know that he was revealed to take away sins, and in him there is no sin. [6]No one who abides in him sins; no one who sins has either seen him or known him. [7]Little children, let no one deceive you. Everyone who does what is right is righteous, just as he is righteous. [8]Everyone who commits sin is a child of the devil; for the devil has been sinning from the beginning. The Son of God was revealed for this purpose, to destroy the works of the devil. [9]Those who have been born of God do not sin, because God's seed abides in them;[l] they cannot sin, because they have been born of God. [10]The children of God and the children of the devil are revealed in this way:

all who do not do what is right are not from God, nor are those who do not love their brothers and sisters.[m]

Love One Another

11 For this is the message you have heard from the beginning, that we should love one another. [12]We must not be like Cain who was from the evil one and murdered his brother. And why did he murder him? Because his own deeds were evil and his brother's righteous. [13]Do not be astonished, brothers and sisters,[n] that the world hates you. [14]We know that we have passed from death to life because we love one another. Whoever does not love abides in death. [15]All who hate a brother or sister[m] are murderers, and you know that murderers do not have eternal life abiding in them. [16]We know love by this, that he laid down his life for us — and we ought to lay down our lives for one another. [17]How does God's love abide in anyone who has the world's goods and sees a brother or sister[o] in need and yet refuses help?

18 Little children, let us love, not in word or speech, but in truth and action. [19]And by this we will know that we are from the truth and will reassure our hearts before him [20]whenever our hearts condemn us; for God is greater than our hearts, and he knows everything. [21]Beloved, if our hearts do not condemn us, we have boldness before God; [22]and we receive from him whatever we ask, because we obey his commandments and do what pleases him.

23 And this is his commandment, that we should believe in the name of his Son Jesus Christ and love one another, just as he has commanded us. [24]All who obey his commandments abide in him, and he abides in them. And by this we

2.26
2 Jn 7
2.27
Jn 14.26,17
2.28
1 Jn 3.2,
21; 4.17;
Mk 8.38;
1 Thes 2.19
2.29
1 Jn 3.7,9;
4.7
3.1
Jn 1.12;
16.3
3.2
Rom 8.15;
2 Cor 4.17;
Rom 8.29;
2 Pet 1.4;
2 Cor 3.18
3.4
Rom 4.15;
1 Jn 5.17
3.5
Isa 53.5,6;
2 Cor 5.21
3.7
1 Jn 2.1,
26,29
3.8
Jn 8.44;
16.11;
Heb 2.14
3.9
1 Jn 5.18;
1 Pet 1.23
3.10
1 Jn 2.29

3.11
1 Jn 1.5;
Jn 13.34,35;
2 Jn 5
3.13
Jn 15.18
3.14
Jn 5.24;
1 Jn 2.9,
11
3.15
Mt 5.21,22;
Jn 8.44;
Gal 5.20,21
3.16
Jn 3.16;
13.1; 15.13
3.17
Deut 15.7;
1 Jn 4.20
3.18
Rom 12.9;
Jas 1.22
3.19
1 Jn 2.21
3.20
1 Cor 4.4
3.21
1 Jn 5.14
3.22
Mt 7.7;
21.22;
1 Jn 2.3
3.23
1 Jn 2.8

3.24 Rom 8.9; 1 Jn 4.13

i Other ancient authorities read you k Or it
l Or because the children of God abide in him
m Gk his brother n Gk brothers
o Gk brother

know that he abides in us, by the Spirit that he has given us.

Testing the Spirits

4 Beloved, do not believe every spirit, but test the spirits to see whether they are from God; for many false prophets have gone out into the world. [2] By this you know the Spirit of God: every spirit that confesses that Jesus Christ has come in the flesh is from God, [3] and every spirit that does not confess Jesus[p] is not from God. And this is the spirit of the antichrist, of which you have heard that it is coming; and now it is already in the world. [4] Little children, you are from God, and have conquered them; for the one who is in you is greater than the one who is in the world. [5] They are from the world; therefore what they say is from the world, and the world listens to them. [6] We are from God. Whoever knows God listens to us, and whoever is not from God does not listen to us. From this we know the spirit of truth and the spirit of error.

God Is Love

7 Beloved, let us love one another, because love is from God; everyone who loves is born of God and knows God. [8] Whoever does not love does not know God, for God is love. [9] God's love was revealed among us in this way: God sent his only Son into the world so that we might live through him. [10] In this is love, not that we loved God but that he loved us and sent his Son to be the atoning sacrifice for our sins. [11] Beloved, since God loved us so much, we also ought to love one another. [12] No one has ever seen God; if we love one another, God lives in us, and his love is perfected in us.

13 By this we know that we abide in him and he in us, because he has given us of his Spirit. [14] And we have seen and do testify that the Father has sent his Son as the Savior of the world. [15] God abides in those who confess that Jesus is the

Son of God, and they abide in God. [16] So we have known and believe the love that God has for us.

God is love, and those who abide in love abide in God, and God abides in them. [17] Love has been perfected among us in this: that we may have boldness on the day of judgment, because as he is, so are we in this world. [18] There is no fear in love, but perfect love casts out fear; for fear has to do with punishment, and whoever fears has not reached perfection in love. [19] We love[q] because he first loved us. [20] Those who say, "I love God," and hate their brothers or sisters,[r] are liars; for those who do not love a brother or sister[s] whom they have seen, cannot love God whom they have not seen. [21] The commandment we have from him is this: those who love God must love their brothers and sisters[r] also.

Faith Conquers the World

5 Everyone who believes that Jesus is the Christ[t] has been born of God, and everyone who loves the parent loves the child. [2] By this we know that we love the children of God, when we love God and obey his commandments. [3] For the love of God is this, that we obey his commandments. And his commandments are not burdensome, [4] for whatever is born of God conquers the world. And this is the victory that conquers the world, our faith. [5] Who is it that conquers the world but the one who believes that Jesus is the Son of God?

Testimony concerning the Son of God

6 This is the one who came by water and blood, Jesus Christ, not with the water only but with the water and the blood. And the Spirit is the one that testifies, for the Spirit is the truth. [7] There are three

4.1
Mt 24.4;
2 Pet 2.1;
1 Jn 2.18
4.2
1 Cor 12.3;
1 Jn 2.23
4.3
2 Jn 7;
1 Jn 2.22;
2 Thes 2.7
4.4
1 Jn 5.4
4.5
Jn 3.31;
15.19
4.6
Jn 8.47;
1 Cor 14.37;
Jn 14.17;
1 Tim 4.1
4.7
1 Jn 3.10,
11
4.8
v. 16
4.9
Jn 3.16;
1 Jn 5.11
4.10
Rom 5.8,10;
1 Jn 2.2
4.11
Jn 3.16;
15.12
4.12
Jn 1.18;
1 Tim 6.16;
1 Jn 2.5
4.13
1 Jn 3.24
4.15
Rom 10.9

4.16
v. 8;
1 Jn 3.24
4.17
1 Jn 2.28
4.18
Rom 8.15;
v. 12
4.19
v. 10
4.20
1 Jn 2.4;
1.6; 3.17
5.1
Jn 1.12;
1 Jn 2.22,
23; Jn 1.13;
8.42
5.2
1 Jn 2.5
5.3
Jn 14.15;
1 Jn 2.5;
2 Jn 6
5.4
Jn 16.33
5.5
1 Jn 4.15
5.6
Jn 19.34
5.7
Jn 15.26

p Other ancient authorities read *does away with Jesus* (Gk *dissolves Jesus*) q Other ancient authorities add *him*; others add *God* r Gk *brothers* s Gk *brother* t Or *the Messiah*

that testify:[u] 8 the Spirit and the water and the blood, and these three agree. 9 If we receive human testimony, the testimony of God is greater; for this is the testimony of God that he has testified to his Son. 10 Those who believe in the Son of God have the testimony in their hearts. Those who do not believe in God[v] have made him a liar by not believing in the testimony that God has given concerning his Son. 11 And this is the testimony: God gave us eternal life, and this life is in his Son. 12 Whoever has the Son has life; whoever does not have the Son of God does not have life.

Epilogue

13 I write these things to you who believe in the name of the Son of God, so that you may know that you have eternal life.

14 And this is the boldness we have in him, that if we ask anything according to his will, he hears us. 15 And if we know that he hears us in whatever we ask, we know that we have obtained the requests made of him. 16 If you see your brother or sister[w] committing what

is not a mortal sin, you will ask, and God[x] will give life to such a one—to those whose sin is not mortal. There is sin that is mortal; I do not say that you should pray about that. 17 All wrongdoing is sin, but there is sin that is not mortal.

18 We know that those who are born of God do not sin, but the one who was born of God protects them, and the evil one does not touch them. 19 We know that we are God's children, and that the whole world lies under the power of the evil one. 20 And we know that the Son of God has come and has given us understanding so that we may know him who is true;[y] and we are in him who is true, in his Son Jesus Christ. He is the true God and eternal life.

21 Little children, keep yourselves from idols.[z]

5.8
Mt 18.16
5.9
Jn 8.17,18;
Mt 3.16,17
5.10
Rom 8.16;
Gal 4.6;
Jn 3.33
5.11
1 Jn 2.25;
Jn 1.4
5.12
Jn 3.36
5.13
Jn 20.31;
1 Jn 1.1,2
5.14
1 Jn 3.21,
22; Mt 7.7
5.16
Jas 5.15;
Heb 6.4,6

5.17
1 Jn 3.4
5.18
1 Jn 3.9;
Jn 14.30
5.19
1 Jn 4.6;
Gal 1.4
5.20
Lk 24.45;
Jn 17.3;
Rev 3.7
5.21
1 Cor 10.14

[u] A few other authorities read (with variations) 7 *There are three that testify in heaven, the Father, the Word, and the Holy Spirit, and these three are one.* 8 *And there are three that testify on earth:* [v] Other ancient authorities read *in the Son* [w] Gk *your brother* [x] Gk *he* [y] Other ancient authorities read *know the true God* [z] Other ancient authorities add *Amen*

THE SECOND LETTER OF
John

Title and Background

During the first two centuries A.D. the gospel was taken from place to place by traveling evangelists and teachers. Believers customarily took these missionaries into their homes and gave them provisions for their journey when they left. Since Gnostic teachers also relied on this practice, 2 John was written to urge discernment in supporting traveling teachers.

Author and Date of Writing

John wrote this letter shortly after his first letter, about A.D. 90.

Theme and Message

John writes of how important it is for Christians to love one another. To love means to obey God's commandments, and God's commandments in turn tell us to live lives of love. John again emphasizes the importance of the doctrine that Jesus is God's Son—both God and man. Christians should separate themselves from those who teach otherwise.

Outline

Salutation

1 The elder to the elect lady and her children, whom I love in the truth, and not only I but also all who know the truth, 2 because of the truth that abides in us and will be with us forever:

3 Grace, mercy, and peace will be with us from God the Father and from[a] Jesus Christ, the Father's Son, in truth and love.

Truth and Love

4 I was overjoyed to find some of your children walking in the truth, just as we have been commanded by the Father. 5 But now, dear lady, I ask you, not as though I were writing you a new commandment, but one we have had from the beginning, let us love one another. 6 And this is love, that we walk according to his commandments; this is the commandment just as you have heard it from the beginning—you must walk in it.

7 Many deceivers have gone out into the world, those who do not confess that Jesus Christ has come in the flesh; any such person is the deceiver and the antichrist! 8 Be on your guard, so that you do not lose what we[b] have worked for, but may receive a full reward. 9 Everyone who does not abide in the teaching of Christ, but goes beyond it, does not have God; whoever abides in the teaching has both the Father and the Son. 10 Do not receive into the house or welcome anyone who comes to you and does not bring this teaching; 11 for to welcome is to participate in the evil deeds of such a person.

1
3 Jn 1;
1 Jn 3.18;
Jn 8.32
2
2 Pet 1.12;
1 Jn 1.8
3
1 Tim 1.2
4
3 Jn 3,4
5
1 Jn 2.7;
3.11
6
1 Jn 2.5;
2.24
7
1 Jn 4.1-3;
2.22
8
Mk 13.9;
1 Cor 3.8;
Heb 10.32
9
1 Jn 2.23
10
Rom 16.17
11
1 Tim 5.22

a Other ancient authorities add *the Lord*
b Other ancient authorities read *you*

Final Greetings

12 Although I have much to write to you, I would rather not use paper and ink; instead I hope to come to you and talk with you face to face, so that our joy may be complete.

13 The children of your elect sister send you their greetings. [c]

12
3 Jn 13, 14;
1 Jn 1.4

13
v. 1

[c] Other ancient authorities add *Amen*

THE THIRD LETTER OF
John

Title and Background

Itinerant teachers sent out by John were rejected by Diotrephes, a dictatorial leader in one of the churches in the province of Asia. This man had gone so far as to excommunicate members who showed hospitality to John's messengers.

Author and Date of Writing

The letter was probably written about the same time as 1 and 2 John, around A.D. 90. The apostle John is the author.

Theme and Message

John writes to Gaius, his personal friend and a leader in the church. He wants to praise and thank him for his help and to encourage him. He also reproves Diotrephes for not cooperating and for rebelling against John's leadership. In a later visit John will deal with him personally.

Outline

Salutation

1 The elder to the beloved Gaius, whom I love in truth.

Gaius Commended for His Hospitality

2 Beloved, I pray that all may go well with you and that you may be in good health, just as it is well with your soul. 3 I was overjoyed when some of the friends[a] arrived and testified to your faithfulness to the truth, namely how you walk in the truth. 4 I have no greater joy than this, to hear that my children are walking in the truth.

5 Beloved, you do faithfully whatever you do for the friends,[a] even though they are strangers to you; 6 they have testified to your love before the church. You will do well to send them on in a manner worthy of God; 7 for they began their journey for the sake of Christ,[b] accepting no support from non-believers.[c] 8 Therefore we ought to support such people, so that we may become co-workers with the truth.

Diotrephes and Demetrius

9 I have written something to the church; but Diotrephes, who likes to put himself first, does not acknowledge our authority. 10 So if I come, I will call attention to what he is doing in spreading false charges against us. And not content with those charges, he refuses to welcome the friends,[a] and even prevents those who want to do so and expels them from the church.

11 Beloved, do not imitate what is evil but imitate what is good. Whoever does good is from God; whoever does evil has not seen God. 12 Everyone has testified favorably about Demetrius, and so has the truth itself. We also testify

a Gk *brothers* b Gk *for the sake of the name* c Gk *the Gentiles*

1
2 Jn 1
3
2 Jn 4;
vv. 5,10
4
1 Cor 4.15;
Philem 10
5
Rom 12.13;
Heb 13.2
6
Acts 15.3;
Titus 3.13
7
Acts 5.41;
20.33,35
9
2 Jn 9
10
2 Jn 12;
v. 5;
Jn 9.34
11
Ps 37.27;
1 Jn 2.29;
3.6,9
12
1 Tim 3.7;
Jn 21.24

for him,[d] and you know that our testimony is true.

Final Greetings

13 I have much to write to you, but I would rather not write with pen and ink; [14] instead I hope to see you soon, and we will talk together face to face.

15 Peace to you. The friends send you their greetings. Greet the friends there, each by name.

13
2 Jn 12
14
1 Pet 5.14

[d] Gk lacks *for him*

THE LETTER OF
Jude

Title and Background

Jude originated as a personal letter from a leader in the apostolic church to one or more of the congregations dispersed throughout the Roman Empire. The dangers facing the church at this time were not those of outright persecution and extinction but of heresy and distortion of the faith.

Author and Date of Writing

The author identifies himself as Jude, another form of the Hebrew name Judah. He was most likely Judas, the brother of our Lord Jesus. The letter was probably written about A.D. 65.

Theme and Message

Although Jude was eager to write to his readers about salvation, he thought he must instead warn them about certain immoral, false teachers circulating among them, who were perverting the grace of God. They were apparently trying to convince believers that being saved by grace gave them license to sin, since their sins would no longer be held against them. It has been thought that these false teachers were Gnostics, probably forerunners of second-century, fully developed Gnosticism.

Outline

Salutation

1 Jude,[a] a servant[b] of Jesus Christ and brother of James,

To those who are called, who are beloved[c] in[d] God the Father and kept safe for[d] Jesus Christ:

2 May mercy, peace, and love be yours in abundance.

Occasion of the Letter

3 Beloved, while eagerly preparing to write to you about the salvation we share, I find it necessary to write and appeal to you to contend for the faith that was once for all entrusted to the saints. 4 For certain intruders have stolen in among you, people who long ago were designated for this condemnation as ungodly, who pervert the grace of our God into licentiousness and deny our only Master and Lord, Jesus Christ.[e]

Judgment on False Teachers

5 Now I desire to remind you, though you are fully informed, that the Lord, who once for all saved[f] a people out of the land of Egypt, afterward destroyed those who did not believe. 6 And the angels who did not keep their own position, but left their proper dwelling, he has kept in eternal chains in deepest darkness for the judgment of the great Day. 7 Likewise, Sodom and Gomorrah and the surrounding cities, which, in the same manner as they, indulged in sexual immorality and pursued unnatural lust,[g]

1 Acts 1.13; 1 Pet 1.5
2 1 Pet 1.2; 2 Pet 1.2
3 Titus 1.4; 1 Tim 6.12
4 Gal 2.4; 2 Pet 2.1; Rom 9.22; 2 Pet 2.1
5 Num 14.29; Ps 106.26
6 Jn 8.44; 2 Pet 2.4; Rev 20.10
7 2 Pet 2.6; Gen 19.24

a Gk *Judas* b Gk *slave* c Other ancient authorities read *sanctified* d Or *by* e Or *the only Master and our Lord Jesus Christ* f Other ancient authorities read *though you were once for all fully informed, that Jesus* (or *Joshua*) *who saved* g Gk *went after other flesh*

serve as an example by undergoing a punishment of eternal fire.

8 Yet in the same way these dreamers also defile the flesh, reject authority, and slander the glorious ones.[h] 9 But when the archangel Michael contended with the devil and disputed about the body of Moses, he did not dare to bring a condemnation of slander[i] against him, but said, "The Lord rebuke you!" 10 But these people slander whatever they do not understand, and they are destroyed by those things that, like irrational animals, they know by instinct. 11 Woe to them! For they go the way of Cain, and abandon themselves to Balaam's error for the sake of gain, and perish in Korah's rebellion. 12 These are blemishes[j] on your love-feasts, while they feast with you without fear, feeding themselves.[k] They are waterless clouds carried along by the winds; autumn trees without fruit, twice dead, uprooted; 13 wild waves of the sea, casting up the foam of their own shame; wandering stars, for whom the deepest darkness has been reserved forever.

14 It was also about these that Enoch, in the seventh generation from Adam, prophesied, saying, "See, the Lord is coming[l] with ten thousands of his holy ones, 15 to execute judgment on all, and to convict everyone of all the deeds of ungodliness that they have committed in such an ungodly way, and of all the harsh things that ungodly sinners have spoken against him." 16 These are grumblers and malcontents; they indulge their own lusts; they are bombastic in speech, flattering people to their own advantage.

Warnings and Exhortations

17 But you, beloved, must remember the predictions of the apostles of our Lord Jesus Christ; 18 for they said to you, "In the last time there will be scoffers, indulging their own ungodly lusts." 19 It is these worldly people, devoid of the Spirit, who are causing divisions. 20 But you, beloved, build yourselves up on your most holy faith; pray in the Holy Spirit; 21 keep yourselves in the love of God; look forward to the mercy of our Lord Jesus Christ that leads to[m] eternal life. 22 And have mercy on some who are wavering; 23 save others by snatching them out of the fire; and have mercy on still others with fear, hating even the tunic defiled by their bodies.[n]

Benediction

24 Now to him who is able to keep you from falling, and to make you stand without blemish in the presence of his glory with rejoicing, 25 to the only God our Savior, through Jesus Christ our Lord, be glory, majesty, power, and authority, before all time and now and forever. Amen.

[h] Or angels; Gk glories [i] Or condemnation for blasphemy [j] Or reefs [k] Or without fear. They are shepherds who care only for themselves [l] Gk came [m] Gk Christ to [n] Gk by the flesh. The Greek text of verses 22-23 is uncertain at several points

8
2 Pet 2.10
9
Dan 10.13;
Zech 3.2
10
2 Pet 2.12;
Phil 3.19
11
Gen 4.3-8;
1 Jn 3.12;
Num 22.7;
2 Pet 2.15;
Num 16.1-3,
31-35
12
2 Pet 2.13;
1 Cor 11.20ff;
Eph 4.14;
Mt 15.13
13
Isa 57.20;
Phil 3.19;
2 Pet 2.17
14
Gen 5.18;
Deut 33.2;
Dan 7.10
15
2 Pet 2.6ff;
1 Tim 1.9
16
2 Pet 2.18
17
2 Pet 3.2
18
1 Tim 4.1;
2 Pet 2.1
19
1 Cor 2.14,
15; Jas 3.15
20
Col 2.7;
Eph 6.18
21
Titus 2.13;
2 Pet 3.12
23
Am 4.11;
Zech 3.2-5
24
Rom 16.25;
Eph 3.20;
Col 1.22
25
1 Tim 1.17;
Rom 11.36

THE
Revelation
TO JOHN

Title and Background

Since Roman authorities at this time were beginning to enforce the cult of emperor worship, Christians—who held that Christ, not the emperor, was Lord—were facing increasing hostility. Some in the church were advocating a policy of compromise; this had to be corrected lest its subtle influence undermine believers' determination to stand fast in the perilous days that lay ahead.

Author and Date of Writing

Four times the author identifies himself as John, and John was held to be the author from as early as the second century. Whether or not this was the same John as the one who wrote the Gospel cannot be determined for certain. Most scholars hold that the book was written about A.D. 95.

Theme and Message

John writes to encourage the faithful to resist staunchly the demands that they worship the emperor. He informs his readers that the final showdown between God and Satan is imminent. Satan will increase his persecution of believers, but they must stand fast, even to death. They are sealed against any spiritual harm and will soon be vindicated when Christ returns, when the wicked are forever destroyed, and when God's people enter an eternity of glory and blessedness.

Outline

Introduction and Salutation

1 The revelation of Jesus Christ, which God gave him to show his servants[a] what must soon take place; he made[b] it known by sending his angel to his servant[c] John, [2] who testified to the word of God and to the testimony of Jesus Christ, even to all that he saw.

1.1
Jn 12.49;
Rev 22.16
1.2
1 Cor 1.6;
Rev 12.17

1.3
Lk 11.28;
Rev 22.10

[3] Blessed is the one who reads aloud the words of the prophecy, and blessed are those who hear and who keep what is written in it; for the time is near.

[a] Gk *slaves* [b] Gk *and he made*
[c] Gk *slave*

4 John to the seven churches that are in Asia:

Grace to you and peace from him who is and who was and who is to come, and from the seven spirits who are before his throne, [5] and from Jesus Christ, the faithful witness, the firstborn of the dead, and the ruler of the kings of the earth.

To him who loves us and freed[d] us from our sins by his blood, [6] and made[e] us to be a kingdom, priests serving[f] his God and Father, to him be glory and dominion forever and ever. Amen.

[7] Look! He is coming with the
 clouds;
 every eye will see him,
 even those who pierced him;
 and on his account all the
 tribes of the earth will
 wail.
So it is to be. Amen.

[8] "I am the Alpha and the Omega," says the Lord God, who is and who was and who is to come, the Almighty.

A Vision of Christ

[9] I, John, your brother who share with you in Jesus the persecution and the kingdom and the patient endurance, was on the island called Patmos because of the word of God and the testimony of Jesus.[g] [10] I was in the spirit[h] on the Lord's day, and I heard behind me a loud voice like a trumpet [11] saying, "Write in a book what you see and send it to the seven churches, to Ephesus, to Smyrna, to Pergamum, to Thyatira, to Sardis, to Philadelphia, and to Laodicea."

[12] Then I turned to see whose voice it was that spoke to me, and on turning I saw seven golden lampstands, [13] and in the midst of the lampstands I saw one like the Son of Man, clothed with a long robe and with a golden sash across his chest. [14] His head and his hair were white as white wool, white as snow; his eyes were like a flame of fire, [15] his feet were like burnished bronze, refined as in a furnace, and

his voice was like the sound of many waters. [16] In his right hand he held seven stars, and from his mouth came a sharp, two-edged sword, and his face was like the sun shining with full force.

[17] When I saw him, I fell at his feet as though dead. But he placed his right hand on me, saying, "Do not be afraid; I am the first and the last, [18] and the living one. I was dead, and see, I am alive forever and ever; and I have the keys of Death and of Hades. [19] Now write what you have seen, what is, and what is to take place after this. [20] As for the mystery of the seven stars that you saw in my right hand, and the seven golden lampstands: the seven stars are the angels of the seven churches, and the seven lampstands are the seven churches.

The Message to Ephesus

2 "To the angel of the church in Ephesus write: These are the words of him who holds the seven stars in his right hand, who walks among the seven golden lampstands:

[2] "I know your works, your toil and your patient endurance. I know that you cannot tolerate evildoers; you have tested those who claim to be apostles but are not, and have found them to be false. [3] I also know that you are enduring patiently and bearing up for the sake of my name, and that you have not grown weary. [4] But I have this against you, that you have abandoned the love you had at first. [5] Remember then from what you have fallen; repent, and do the works you did at first. If not, I will come to you and remove your lampstand from its place, unless you repent. [6] Yet this is to your credit: you hate the works of the Nicolaitans, which I also hate. [7] Let anyone who has an ear listen to what the Spirit is saying to the

1.4
Jn 1.1;
Rev 3.1; 4.5
1.5
Rev 3.14;
Col 1.18;
Ps 89.27;
Rev 17.14;
Jn 13.34;
Heb 9.14
1.6
1 Pet 2.5;
Rev 5.10;
Rom 11.36
1.7
Zech 12.10
1.8
Rev 21.6;
4.8; 16.7
1.9
Phil 4.14;
2 Tim 2.12
1.10
Rev 4.1,2
1.11
vv. 8,17
1.12
Ex 25.27;
Zech 4.2
1.13
Ezek 1.26;
Dan 7.13;
10.5
1.14
Dan 7.9;
10.6;
Rev 19.12
1.15
Dan 10.6;
Ezek 43.2
1.16
Rev 2.1; 3.1;
Heb 4.12;
Rev 2.12,16
1.17
Ezek 1.28;
Dan 8.18;
10.10;
Isa 41.4
1.18
Rom 6.9;
Rev 4.9;
20.1
1.20
Zech 4.2
2.1
Rev 1.16;
1.13
2.2
Rev 3.1,8;
1 Jn 4.1;
2 Cor 11.13
2.3
Jn 15.21
2.4
Mt 24.12
2.5
vv. 16,22,2;
Rev 1.20
2.6
v. 15
2.7
Mt 11.15;
Rev 3.6,13;
22.2,14;
Gen 2.9

[d] Other ancient authorities read *washed*
[e] Gk *and he made* [f] Gk *priests to*
[g] Or *testimony to Jesus* [h] Or *in the Spirit*

churches. To everyone who conquers, I will give permission to eat from the tree of life that is in the paradise of God.

The Message to Smyrna

8 "And to the angel of the church in Smyrna write: These are the words of the first and the last, who was dead and came to life:

9 "I know your affliction and your poverty, even though you are rich. I know the slander on the part of those who say that they are Jews and are not, but are a synagogue of Satan. [10] Do not fear what you are about to suffer. Beware, the devil is about to throw some of you into prison so that you may be tested, and for ten days you will have affliction. Be faithful until death, and I will give you the crown of life. [11] Let anyone who has an ear listen to what the Spirit is saying to the churches. Whoever conquers will not be harmed by the second death.

The Message to Pergamum

12 "And to the angel of the church in Pergamum write: These are the words of him who has the sharp two-edged sword:

13 "I know where you are living, where Satan's throne is. Yet you are holding fast to my name, and you did not deny your faith in me[i] even in the days of Antipas my witness, my faithful one, who was killed among you, where Satan lives. [14] But I have a few things against you: you have some there who hold to the teaching of Balaam, who taught Balak to put a stumbling block before the people of Israel, so that they would eat food sacrificed to idols and practice fornication. [15] So you also have some who hold to the teaching of the Nicolaitans. [16] Repent then. If not, I will come to you soon and make war against them with the sword of my mouth. [17] Let anyone who has an ear listen to what the Spirit is saying to the churches. To everyone who conquers I will give

some of the hidden manna, and I will give a white stone, and on the white stone is written a new name that no one knows except the one who receives it.

The Message to Thyatira

18 "And to the angel of the church in Thyatira write: These are the words of the Son of God, who has eyes like a flame of fire, and whose feet are like burnished bronze:

19 "I know your works—your love, faith, service, and patient endurance. I know that your last works are greater than the first. [20] But I have this against you: you tolerate that woman Jezebel, who calls herself a prophet and is teaching and beguiling my servants[j] to practice fornication and to eat food sacrificed to idols. [21] I gave her time to repent, but she refuses to repent of her fornication. [22] Beware, I am throwing her on a bed, and those who commit adultery with her I am throwing into great distress, unless they repent of her doings; [23] and I will strike her children dead. And all the churches will know that I am the one who searches minds and hearts, and I will give to each of you as your works deserve. [24] But to the rest of you in Thyatira, who do not hold this teaching, who have not learned what some call 'the deep things of Satan,' to you I say, I do not lay on you any other burden; [25] only hold fast to what you have until I come. [26] To everyone who conquers and continues to do my works to the end,

I will give authority over the
 nations;
[27] to rule[k] them with an iron
 rod,
 as when clay pots are
 shattered—
[28] even as I also received authority from my Father. To the one who conquers I will also give the morning star. [29] Let anyone who has an

2.8
Rev 1.11,17, 18
2.9
Rev 1.9;
Jas 2.5;
Rev 3.9
2.10
Rev 3.10;
Dan 1.12
2.11
Rev 20.14;
21.8
2.12
Rev 1.11,16
2.13
Rev 14.12;
v. 9
2.14
Num 24.14;
2 Pet 2.15;
Jude 11;
1 Cor 8.9;
10.19,20;
6.13
2.15
v. 6
2.16
2 Thes 2.8;
Rev 1.16
2.17
Jn 6.49,50;
Isa 62.2;
Rev 19.12

2.18
Rev 1.11,14, 15
2.19
v. 2
2.20
1 Kings 16.31;
21.25;
2 Kings 9.7;
Acts 15.20
2.21
Rom 2.4;
Rev 9.20
2.22
Rev 17.2;
18.9
2.23
Jer 11.20;
Acts 1.24;
Rom 8.27;
Ps 62.12
2.24
Acts 15.28
2.26
Heb 3.6;
Ps 2.8;
Rev 3.21
2.27
Rev 12.5;
Isa 30.14;
Jer 19.11
2.28
Rev 22.16

i Or deny my faith j Gk slaves k Or to shepherd

ear listen to what the Spirit is saying to the churches.

The Message to Sardis

3 "And to the angel of the church in Sardis write: These are the words of him who has the seven spirits of God and the seven stars:

"I know your works; you have a name of being alive, but you are dead. ²Wake up, and strengthen what remains and is on the point of death, for I have not found your works perfect in the sight of my God. ³Remember then what you received and heard; obey it, and repent. If you do not wake up, I will come like a thief, and you will not know at what hour I will come to you. ⁴Yet you have still a few persons in Sardis who have not soiled their clothes; they will walk with me, dressed in white, for they are worthy. ⁵If you conquer, you will be clothed like them in white robes, and I will not blot your name out of the book of life; I will confess your name before my Father and before his angels. ⁶Let anyone who has an ear listen to what the Spirit is saying to the churches.

The Message to Philadelphia

7 "And to the angel of the church in Philadelphia write:
These are the words of the
 holy one, the true one,
 who has the key of David,
 who opens and no one will
 shut,
 who shuts and no one
 opens:
8 "I know your works. Look, I have set before you an open door, which no one is able to shut. I know that you have but little power, and yet you have kept my word and have not denied my name. ⁹I will make those of the synagogue of Satan who say that they are Jews and are not, but are lying — I will make them come and bow down before your feet, and they will learn that I have loved you. ¹⁰Because you have kept my word of patient

3.1
Rev 1.4,16;
2.2;
1 Tim 5.6
3.3
1 Thes 5.2,
6;
2 Pet 3.10
3.4
Acts 1.15;
Jude 23;
Rev 6.11;
7.9,13
3.5
Mt 10.32
3.6
Rev 2.7
3.7
Acts 3.14;
1 Jn 5.20;
Isa 22.22
3.8
Acts 14.27;
Rev 2.13
3.9
Rev 2.9;
Isa 49.23;
43.4
3.10
2 Pet 2.9;
Rev 16.14;
6.10; 17.8

3.11
Rev 22.7,12,
20; 2.25,10
3.12
Gal 2.9;
Rev 22.4;
21.2
3.13
v. 6
3.14
Isa 65.16
3.15
v. 1
3.17
Hos 12.8;
Zech 11.5;
1 Cor 4.8
3.18
Isa 55.1;
Mt 13.44;
Rev 7.13
3.19
Prov 3.11;
Heb 12.5,6;
Rev 2.5
3.20
Mt 24.33;
Lk 12.36;
Jn 14.23
3.21
Rev 2.7;
Mt 19.28;
Rev 5.5
3.22
Rev 2.7

endurance, I will keep you from the hour of trial that is coming on the whole world to test the inhabitants of the earth. ¹¹I am coming soon; hold fast to what you have, so that no one may seize your crown. ¹²If you conquer, I will make you a pillar in the temple of my God; you will never go out of it. I will write on you the name of my God, and the name of the city of my God, the new Jerusalem that comes down from my God out of heaven, and my own new name. ¹³Let anyone who has an ear listen to what the Spirit is saying to the churches.

The Message to Laodicea

14 "And to the angel of the church in Laodicea write: The words of the Amen, the faithful and true witness, the origin[1] of God's creation:

15 "I know your works; you are neither cold nor hot. I wish that you were either cold or hot. ¹⁶So, because you are lukewarm, and neither cold nor hot, I am about to spit you out of my mouth. ¹⁷For you say, 'I am rich, I have prospered, and I need nothing.' You do not realize that you are wretched, pitiable, poor, blind, and naked. ¹⁸Therefore I counsel you to buy from me gold refined by fire so that you may be rich; and white robes to clothe you and to keep the shame of your nakedness from being seen; and salve to anoint your eyes so that you may see. ¹⁹I reprove and discipline those whom I love. Be earnest, therefore, and repent. ²⁰Listen! I am standing at the door, knocking; if you hear my voice and open the door, I will come in to you and eat with you, and you with me. ²¹To the one who conquers I will give a place with me on my throne, just as I myself conquered and sat down with my Father on his throne. ²²Let anyone who has an ear listen to what the Spirit is saying to the churches."

[1]Or *beginning*

The Heavenly Worship

4 After this I looked, and there in heaven a door stood open! And the first voice, which I had heard speaking to me like a trumpet, said, "Come up here, and I will show you what must take place after this." [2] At once I was in the spirit,[m] and there in heaven stood a throne, with one seated on the throne! [3] And the one seated there looks like jasper and carnelian, and around the throne is a rainbow that looks like an emerald. [4] Around the throne are twenty-four thrones, and seated on the thrones are twenty-four elders, dressed in white robes, with golden crowns on their heads. [5] Coming from the throne are flashes of lightning, and rumblings and peals of thunder, and in front of the throne burn seven flaming torches, which are the seven spirits of God; [6] and in front of the throne there is something like a sea of glass, like crystal.

Around the throne, and on each side of the throne, are four living creatures, full of eyes in front and behind: [7] the first living creature like a lion, the second living creature like an ox, the third living creature with a face like a human face, and the fourth living creature like a flying eagle. [8] And the four living creatures, each of them with six wings, are full of eyes all around and inside. Day and night without ceasing they sing,

"Holy, holy, holy,
 the Lord God the Almighty,
 who was and is and is to
 come."

[9] And whenever the living creatures give glory and honor and thanks to the one who is seated on the throne, who lives forever and ever, [10] the twenty-four elders fall before the one who is seated on the throne and worship the one who lives forever and ever; they cast their crowns before the throne, singing,

[11] "You are worthy, our Lord
 and God,
 to receive glory and honor
 and power,

for you created all things,
 and by your will they
 existed and were
 created."

The Scroll and the Lamb

5 Then I saw in the right hand of the one seated on the throne a scroll written on the inside and on the back, sealed[n] with seven seals; [2] and I saw a mighty angel proclaiming with a loud voice, "Who is worthy to open the scroll and break its seals?" [3] And no one in heaven or on earth or under the earth was able to open the scroll or to look into it. [4] And I began to weep bitterly because no one was found worthy to open the scroll or to look into it. [5] Then one of the elders said to me, "Do not weep. See, the Lion of the tribe of Judah, the Root of David, has conquered, so that he can open the scroll and its seven seals."

[6] Then I saw between the throne and the four living creatures and among the elders a Lamb standing as if it had been slaughtered, having seven horns and seven eyes, which are the seven spirits of God sent out into all the earth. [7] He went and took the scroll from the right hand of the one who was seated on the throne. [8] When he had taken the scroll, the four living creatures and the twenty-four elders fell before the Lamb, each holding a harp and golden bowls full of incense, which are the prayers of the saints. [9] They sing a new song:

"You are worthy to take the
 scroll
 and to open its seals,
for you were slaughtered and
 by your blood you
 ransomed for God
 saints from[o] every tribe
 and language and
 people and nation;

4.1
Rev 1.10;
11.12; 1.19
4.2
Rev 1.10;
Isa 6.1;
Ezek 1.26-28;
Dan 7.9
4.4
Rev 11.16;
3.4,5
4.5
Rev 8.5;
16.18; 1.4;
Zech 4.2
4.6
Rev 15.2;
Ezek 1.5
4.7
Ezek 1.10;
10.14
4.8
Isa 6.2,3;
Rev 1.8,4
4.9
Ps 47.8;
Rev 10.6;
15.7
4.10
Rev 5.8,14;
vv. 2,9,4
4.11
Rev 5.12;
Gen 1.1;
Eph 3.9;
Rev 10.6

5.1
vv. 7,13;
Ezek 2.9,10;
Isa 29.11;
Dan 12.4
5.2
Rev 10.1
5.5
Gen 49.9;
Heb 7.14;
Isa 11.1,10;
Rom 15.12;
Rev 22.16
5.6
Rev 4.6;
Isa 53.7;
Rev 13.8;
Zech 3.9;
4.10;
Rev 4.5
5.7
v. 1
5.8
Rev 14.2;
Ps 141.2
5.9
Ps 40.3;
Rev 4.11;
1 Cor 6.20;
Heb 9.12

m Or *in the Spirit* n Or *written on the inside, and sealed on the back*
o Gk *ransomed for God from*

10 you have made them to be a
 kingdom and priests
 serving[p] our God,
 and they will reign on
 earth."

11 Then I looked, and I heard the voice of many angels surrounding the throne and the living creatures and the elders; they numbered myriads of myriads and thousands of thousands, 12 singing with full voice,

"Worthy is the Lamb that
 was slaughtered
to receive power and wealth
 and wisdom and might
and honor and glory and
 blessing!"

13 Then I heard every creature in heaven and on earth and under the earth and in the sea, and all that is in them, singing,

"To the one seated on the
 throne and to the Lamb
be blessing and honor and
 glory and might
forever and ever!"

14 And the four living creatures said, "Amen!" And the elders fell down and worshiped.

The Seven Seals

6 Then I saw the Lamb open one of the seven seals, and I heard one of the four living creatures call out, as with a voice of thunder, "Come!"[q] 2 I looked, and there was a white horse! Its rider had a bow; a crown was given to him, and he came out conquering and to conquer.

3 When he opened the second seal, I heard the second living creature call out, "Come!"[q] 4 And out came[r] another horse, bright red; its rider was permitted to take peace from the earth, so that people would slaughter one another; and he was given a great sword.

5 When he opened the third seal, I heard the third living creature call out, "Come!"[q] I looked, and there was a black horse! Its rider held a pair of scales in his hand, 6 and I heard what seemed to be a voice in the midst of the four living creatures saying, "A quart of wheat

5.10
Ex 19.6;
Isa 61.6
5.11
Dan 7.10;
Heb 12.22
5.12
Rev 4.11
5.13
Phil 2.10;
v. 3;
1 Tim 6.16;
Rev 1.6;
6.16; 7.10
5.14
Rev 19.4;
4.9,10
6.1
Rev 5.5-7,1;
14.2; 19.6
6.2
Zech 6.3;
Rev 19.11;
Zech 6.11;
Rev 14.14
6.3
Rev 4.7
6.4
Zech 6.2
6.5
Rev 4.7;
Zech 6.2
6.6
Rev 4.6,7;
9.4
6.7
Rev 4.7
6.8
Zech 6.3;
Hos 13.14;
Ezek 5.12
6.9
Rev 14.18;
16.7; 20.4;
1.9; 12.17
6.10
Zech 1.12;
Ps 79.5;
Rev 3.7;
19.2
6.11
Rev 3.5; 7.9;
14.13;
Heb 11.40
6.12
Rev 16.18;
Mt 24.29;
Joel 2.31;
Acts 2.20
6.13
Rev 8.10;
9.1; Isa 34.4
6.14
Isa 34.4;
Jer 3.23;
4.24;
Rev 16.10
6.15
Isa 2.10,19
6.16
Hos 10.8;
Lk 23.30;
Rev 9.6
6.17
Zeph 1.14;
Rev 16.14;
Ps 76.7

for a day's pay,[s] and three quarts of barley for a day's pay,[s] but do not damage the olive oil and the wine!"

7 When he opened the fourth seal, I heard the voice of the fourth living creature call out, "Come!"[q] 8 I looked and there was a pale green horse! Its rider's name was Death, and Hades followed with him; they were given authority over a fourth of the earth, to kill with sword, famine, and pestilence, and by the wild animals of the earth.

9 When he opened the fifth seal, I saw under the altar the souls of those who had been slaughtered for the word of God and for the testimony they had given; 10 they cried out with a loud voice, "Sovereign Lord, holy and true, how long will it be before you judge and avenge our blood on the inhabitants of the earth?" 11 They were each given a white robe and told to rest a little longer, until the number would be complete both of their fellow servants[t] and of their brothers and sisters,[u] who were soon to be killed as they themselves had been killed.

12 When he opened the sixth seal, I looked, and there came a great earthquake; the sun became black as sackcloth, the full moon became like blood, 13 and the stars of the sky fell to the earth as the fig tree drops its winter fruit when shaken by a gale. 14 The sky vanished like a scroll rolling itself up, and every mountain and island was removed from its place. 15 Then the kings of the earth and the magnates and the generals and the rich and the powerful, and everyone, slave and free, hid in the caves and among the rocks of the mountains, 16 calling to the mountains and rocks, "Fall on us and hide us from the face of the one seated on the throne and from the wrath of the Lamb; 17 for the great day of their wrath has come, and who is able to stand?"

p Gk priests to q Or "Go!" r Or went
s Gk a denarius t Gk slaves
u Gk brothers

The 144,000 of Israel Sealed

7 After this I saw four angels standing at the four corners of the earth, holding back the four winds of the earth so that no wind could blow on earth or sea or against any tree. [2] I saw another angel ascending from the rising of the sun, having the seal of the living God, and he called with a loud voice to the four angels who had been given power to damage earth and sea, [3] saying, "Do not damage the earth or the sea or the trees, until we have marked the servants[v] of our God with a seal on their foreheads."

4 And I heard the number of those who were sealed, one hundred forty-four thousand, sealed out of every tribe of the people of Israel:

5 From the tribe of Judah twelve thousand sealed,

from the tribe of Reuben twelve thousand,

from the tribe of Gad twelve thousand,

6 from the tribe of Asher twelve thousand,

from the tribe of Naphtali twelve thousand,

from the tribe of Manasseh twelve thousand,

7 from the tribe of Simeon twelve thousand,

from the tribe of Levi twelve thousand,

from the tribe of Issachar twelve thousand,

8 from the tribe of Zebulun twelve thousand,

from the tribe of Joseph twelve thousand,

from the tribe of Benjamin twelve thousand sealed.

The Multitude from Every Nation

9 After this I looked, and there was a great multitude that no one could count, from every nation, from all tribes and peoples and languages, standing before the throne and before the Lamb, robed in white, with palm branches in their hands. [10] They cried out in a loud voice, saying,

"Salvation belongs to our
God who is seated on
the throne, and to the
Lamb!"

[11] And all the angels stood around the throne and around the elders and the four living creatures, and they fell on their faces before the throne and worshiped God, [12] singing,

"Amen! Blessing and glory
and wisdom
and thanksgiving and honor
and power and might
be to our God forever and
ever! Amen."

13 Then one of the elders addressed me, saying, "Who are these, robed in white, and where have they come from?" [14] I said to him, "Sir, you are the one that knows." Then he said to me, "These are they who have come out of the great ordeal; they have washed their robes and made them white in the blood of the Lamb.

[15] For this reason they are
before the throne of
God,
and worship him day and
night within his temple,
and the one who is seated
on the throne will
shelter them.
[16] They will hunger no more,
and thirst no more;
the sun will not strike
them,
nor any scorching heat;
[17] for the Lamb at the center of
the throne will be their
shepherd,
and he will guide them to
springs of the water of
life,
and God will wipe away
every tear from their
eyes."

The Seventh Seal and the Golden Censer

8 When the Lamb opened the seventh seal, there was silence in heaven for about half an hour.

Cross references (center column)

7.1 Rev 9.4
7.3 Rev 6.6; Ezek 9.4; Rev 22.4
7.4ff Rev 9.16; 14.1
7.9 Rom 11.25; Rev 5.9; 3.5, 18; 4.4; 6.11
7.10 Ps 3.8; Rev 12.10; 19.1; 5.13
7.11 Rev 4.6
7.12 Rev 5.12-14
7.13 v. 9
7.14 Mt 24.21; Zech 3.3-5; Heb 9.14; 1 Jn 1.7
7.15 Isa 4.5,6; Rev 21.3
7.16 Isa 49.10; Ps 121.5,6; Rev 21.4
7.17 Ps 23.1; Jn 10.11,14; Isa 25.8
8.1 Rev 6.1

v Gk slaves

2 And I saw the seven angels who stand before God, and seven trumpets were given to them.

3 Another angel with a golden censer came and stood at the altar; he was given a great quantity of incense to offer with the prayers of all the saints on the golden altar that is before the throne. 4 And the smoke of the incense, with the prayers of the saints, rose before God from the hand of the angel. 5 Then the angel took the censer and filled it with fire from the altar and threw it on the earth; and there were peals of thunder, rumblings, flashes of lightning, and an earthquake.

The Seven Trumpets

6 Now the seven angels who had the seven trumpets made ready to blow them.

7 The first angel blew his trumpet, and there came hail and fire, mixed with blood, and they were hurled to the earth; and a third of the earth was burned up, and a third of the trees were burned up, and all green grass was burned up.

8 The second angel blew his trumpet, and something like a great mountain, burning with fire, was thrown into the sea. 9 A third of the sea became blood, a third of the living creatures in the sea died, and a third of the ships were destroyed.

10 The third angel blew his trumpet, and a great star fell from heaven, blazing like a torch, and it fell on a third of the rivers and on the springs of water. 11 The name of the star is Wormwood. A third of the waters became wormwood, and many died from the water, because it was made bitter.

12 The fourth angel blew his trumpet, and a third of the sun was struck, and a third of the moon, and a third of the stars, so that a third of their light was darkened; a third of the day was kept from shining, and likewise the night.

13 Then I looked, and I heard an eagle crying with a loud voice as it flew in midheaven, "Woe, woe, woe

to the inhabitants of the earth, at the blasts of the other trumpets that the three angels are about to blow!"

9 And the fifth angel blew his trumpet, and I saw a star that had fallen from heaven to earth, and he was given the key to the shaft of the bottomless pit; 2 he opened the shaft of the bottomless pit, and from the shaft rose smoke like the smoke of a great furnace, and the sun and the air were darkened with the smoke from the shaft. 3 Then from the smoke came locusts on the earth, and they were given authority like the authority of scorpions of the earth. 4 They were told not to damage the grass of the earth or any green growth or any tree, but only those people who do not have the seal of God on their foreheads. 5 They were allowed to torture them for five months, but not to kill them, and their torture was like the torture of a scorpion when it stings someone. 6 And in those days people will seek death but will not find it; they will long to die, but death will flee from them.

7 In appearance the locusts were like horses equipped for battle. On their heads were what looked like crowns of gold; their faces were like human faces, 8 their hair like women's hair, and their teeth like lions' teeth; 9 they had scales like iron breastplates, and the noise of their wings was like the noise of many chariots with horses rushing into battle. 10 They have tails like scorpions, with stingers, and in their tails is their power to harm people for five months; 11 They have as king over them the angel of the bottomless pit; his name in Hebrew is Abaddon,w and in Greek he is called Apollyon.x

12 The first woe has passed. There are still two woes to come.

13 Then the sixth angel blew his trumpet, and I heard a voice from the foury horns of the golden altar before God, 14 saying to the sixth

w That is, *Destruction* x That is, *Destroyer*
y Other ancient authorities lack *four*

angel who had the trumpet, "Release the four angels who are bound at the great river Euphrates." [15] So the four angels were released, who had been held ready for the hour, the day, the month, and the year, to kill a third of humankind. [16] The number of the troops of cavalry was two hundred million; I heard their number. [17] And this was how I saw the horses in my vision: the riders wore breastplates the color of fire and of sapphire[z] and of sulfur; the heads of the horses were like lions' heads, and fire and smoke and sulfur came out of their mouths. [18] By these three plagues a third of humankind was killed, by the fire and smoke and sulfur coming out of their mouths. [19] For the power of the horses is in their mouths and in their tails; their tails are like serpents, having heads; and with them they inflict harm.

20 The rest of humankind, who were not killed by these plagues, did not repent of the works of their hands or give up worshiping demons and idols of gold and silver and bronze and stone and wood, which cannot see or hear or walk. [21] And they did not repent of their murders or their sorceries or their fornication or their thefts.

The Angel with the Little Scroll

10 And I saw another mighty angel coming down from heaven, wrapped in a cloud, with a rainbow over his head; his face was like the sun, and his legs like pillars of fire. [2] He held a little scroll open in his hand. Setting his right foot on the sea and his left foot on the land, [3] he gave a great shout, like a lion roaring. And when he shouted, the seven thunders sounded. [4] And when the seven thunders had sounded, I was about to write, but I heard a voice from heaven saying, "Seal up what the seven thunders have said, and do not write it down." [5] Then the angel whom I saw standing on the sea and the land

raised his right hand to heaven
6 and swore by him who lives forever and ever,
who created heaven and what is in it, the earth and what is in it, and the sea and what is in it: "There will be no more delay, [7] but in the days when the seventh angel is to blow his trumpet, the mystery of God will be fulfilled, as he announced to his servants[a] the prophets."

8 Then the voice that I had heard from heaven spoke to me again, saying, "Go, take the scroll that is open in the hand of the angel who is standing on the sea and on the land." [9] So I went to the angel and told him to give me the little scroll; and he said to me, "Take it, and eat; it will be bitter to your stomach, but sweet as honey in your mouth." [10] So I took the little scroll from the hand of the angel and ate it; it was sweet as honey in my mouth, but when I had eaten it, my stomach was made bitter.

11 Then they said to me, "You must prophesy again about many peoples and nations and languages and kings."

The Two Witnesses

11 Then I was given a measuring rod like a staff, and I was told, "Come and measure the temple of God and the altar and those who worship there, [2] but do not measure the court outside the temple; leave that out, for it is given over to the nations, and they will trample over the holy city for forty-two months. [3] And I will grant my two witnesses authority to prophesy for one thousand two hundred sixty days, wearing sackcloth."

4 These are the two olive trees and the two lampstands that stand before the Lord of the earth. [5] And if anyone wants to harm them, fire pours from their mouth and consumes their foes; anyone who wants to harm them must be killed

9.15
v. 18
9.16
Rev 5.11;
7.4
9.17
v. 18;
Rev 11.5
9.18
vv. 15,17
9.20
Deut 31.29;
1 Cor 10.20;
Ps 115.4;
135.15;
Dan 5.23
9.21
Rev 2.21;
18.23; 17.2,5
10.1
Rev 5.2;
Mt 17.2;
Rev 1.16,15
10.3
Isa 31.4;
Rev 4.5
10.4
Dan 8.26;
12.4,9;
Rev 22.10
10.5
Ex 6.8;
Dan 12.7

10.6
Rev 4.11;
14.7; 16.17
10.7
Rev 11.15;
Rom 16.25
10.8
v. 4
10.9
Jer 15.16;
Ezek 2.8
10.10
Ezek 3.3
10.11
Rev 11.1;
Ezek 37.4,9
11.1
Ezek 40.3;
Rev 21.15
11.2
Ezek 40.17;
Lk 21.24;
Rev 13.5
11.3
Rev 19.10;
12.6
11.4
Ps 52.8;
Jer 11.16;
Zech 4.3;
Mt 11.14
11.5
2 Kings 1.10;
Jer 5.14;
Num 16.29

z Gk *hyacinth* a Gk *slaves*

in this manner. [6] They have authority to shut the sky, so that no rain may fall during the days of their prophesying, and they have authority over the waters to turn them into blood, and to strike the earth with every kind of plague, as often as they desire.

7 When they have finished their testimony, the beast that comes up from the bottomless pit will make war on them and conquer them and kill them, [8] and their dead bodies will lie in the street of the great city that is prophetically[b] called Sodom and Egypt, where also their Lord was crucified. [9] For three and a half days members of the peoples and tribes and languages and nations will gaze at their dead bodies and refuse to let them be placed in a tomb; [10] and the inhabitants of the earth will gloat over them and celebrate and exchange presents, because these two prophets had been a torment to the inhabitants of the earth.

11 But after the three and a half days, the breath[c] of life from God entered them, and they stood on their feet, and those who saw them were terrified. [12] Then they[d] heard a loud voice from heaven saying to them, "Come up here!" And they went up to heaven in a cloud while their enemies watched them. [13] At that moment there was a great earthquake, and a tenth of the city fell; seven thousand people were killed in the earthquake, and the rest were terrified and gave glory to the God of heaven.

14 The second woe has passed. The third woe is coming very soon.

The Seventh Trumpet

15 Then the seventh angel blew his trumpet, and there were loud voices in heaven, saying,

"The kingdom of the world
 has become the
 kingdom of our Lord
and of his Messiah,[e]
and he will reign forever and
 ever."

16 Then the twenty-four elders who sit on their thrones before God

11.6
1 Kings 17.1;
Ex 7.17,19
11.7
Rev 13.1;
9.1,2;
Dan 7.21
11.8
Rev 14.8;
Isa 1.9;
Heb 13.12
11.10
Rev 3.10;
Esther 9.19,
22
11.11
Ezek 37.5,9,
10,14
11.12
Rev 4.1;
2 Kings 2.11;
Acts 1.9
11.13
Rev 6.12;
14.7; 16.11
11.14
Rev 9.12
11.15
Rev 10.7;
16.17; 19.1;
12.10;
Dan 2.44;
7.14,27
11.16
Rev 4.4; 5.8

11.17
Rev 1.8;
19.6
11.18
Ps 2.1;
Dan 7.9,10;
Rev 10.7;
19.5
11.19
Rev 15.5,8;
8.5; 16.21
12.2
Isa 66.7;
Gal 4.19
12.3
Rev 13.1;
Dan 7.7;
Rev 19.12
12.4
Rev 8.7,12;
Dan 8.10
12.5
Ps 2.9;
Rev 2.27;
2 Cor 12.2
12.6
Rev 11.3

fell on their faces and worshiped God, [17] singing,

"We give you thanks, Lord
 God Almighty,
 who are and who were,
 for you have taken your great
 power
 and begun to reign.
[18] The nations raged,
 but your wrath has come,
 and the time for judging
 the dead,
 for rewarding your servants,[f]
 the prophets
 and saints and all who fear
 your name,
 both small and great,
 and for destroying those who
 destroy the earth."

19 Then God's temple in heaven was opened, and the ark of his covenant was seen within his temple; and there were flashes of lightning, rumblings, peals of thunder, an earthquake, and heavy hail.

The Woman and the Dragon

12 A great portent appeared in heaven: a woman clothed with the sun, with the moon under her feet, and on her head a crown of twelve stars. [2] She was pregnant and was crying out in birthpangs, in the agony of giving birth. [3] Then another portent appeared in heaven: a great red dragon, with seven heads and ten horns, and seven diadems on his heads. [4] His tail swept down a third of the stars of heaven and threw them to the earth. Then the dragon stood before the woman who was about to bear a child, so that he might devour her child as soon as it was born. [5] And she gave birth to a son, a male child, who is to rule[g] all the nations with a rod of iron. But her child was snatched away and taken to God and to his throne; [6] and the woman fled into the wilderness, where she has a place prepared by God, so that there she can be nourished for one thousand two hundred sixty days.

b Or *allegorically*; Gk *spiritually* c Or *the
spirit* d Other ancient authorities read *I*
e Gk *Christ* f Gk *slaves* g Or *to
shepherd*

Michael Defeats the Dragon

7 And war broke out in heaven; Michael and his angels fought against the dragon. The dragon and his angels fought back, 8 but they were defeated, and there was no longer any place for them in heaven. 9 The great dragon was thrown down, that ancient serpent, who is called the Devil and Satan, the deceiver of the whole world — he was thrown down to the earth, and his angels were thrown down with him. 10 Then I heard a loud voice in heaven, proclaiming,

"Now have come the
 salvation and the power
and the kingdom of our
 God
and the authority of his
 Messiah,[h]
for the accuser of our
 comrades[i] has been
 thrown down,
who accuses them day and
 night before our God.
11 But they have conquered
 him by the blood of the
 Lamb
and by the word of their
 testimony,
for they did not cling to life
 even in the face of
 death.
12 Rejoice then, you heavens
 and those who dwell in
 them!
But woe to the earth and the
 sea,
for the devil has come
 down to you
with great wrath,
 because he knows that his
 time is short!"

The Dragon Fights Again on Earth

13 So when the dragon saw that he had been thrown down to the earth, he pursued[j] the woman who had given birth to the male child. 14 But the woman was given the two wings of the great eagle, so that she could fly from the serpent into the wilderness, to her place where she is nourished for a time, and times, and half a time. 15 Then

from his mouth the serpent poured water like a river after the woman, to sweep her away with the flood. 16 But the earth came to the help of the woman; it opened its mouth and swallowed the river that the dragon had poured from his mouth. 17 Then the dragon was angry with the woman, and went off to make war on the rest of her children, those who keep the commandments of God and hold the testimony of Jesus.

The First Beast

18 Then the dragon[k] took his stand on the sand of the seashore.

13 ¹And I saw a beast rising out of the sea; and on its horns were ten diadems, and on its heads were blasphemous names. ²And the beast that I saw was like a leopard, its feet were like a bear's, and its mouth was like a lion's mouth. And the dragon gave it his power and his throne and great authority. ³One of its heads seemed to have received a death-blow, but its mortal wound[l] had been healed. In amazement the whole earth followed the beast. ⁴They worshiped the dragon, for he had given his authority to the beast, and they worshiped the beast, saying, "Who is like the beast, and who can fight against it?"

5 The beast was given a mouth uttering haughty and blasphemous words, and it was allowed to exercise authority for forty-two months. ⁶It opened its mouth to utter blasphemies against God, blaspheming his name and his dwelling, that is, those who dwell in heaven. ⁷Also it was allowed to make war on the saints and to conquer them.[m] It was given authority over every tribe and people and language and nation, ⁸and all the inhabitants of the earth will worship it, everyone whose name has not been written from the founda-

12.7
Dan 10.13;
Rev 20.2
12.9
Gen 3.1,4;
Rev 20.2,3,
8,10;
Jn 12.31
12.10
Rev 11.15;
Job 1.9-11;
Zech 3.1
12.11
Rom 16.20;
Lk 14.26
12.12
Ps 96.11;
Isa 49.13;
Rev 18.20;
8.13; 10.6
12.13
vv. 3,5
12.14
Ex 19.4;
Dan 7.25;
12.7
12.15
Isa 59.19

12.17
Gen 3.15;
Rev 11.7;
14.12; 1.2,9
13.1
Dan 7.1-6;
Rev 17.3
13.2
Rev 16.10
13.3
Rev 17.8
13.4
Rev 18.18
13.5
Dan 7.8,11,
25; Rev 11.2
13.6
Rev 12.12
13.7
Dan 7.21;
Rev 11.7;
5.9
13.8
Phil 4.3;
Rev 3.5;
17.8; 5.6

h Gk *Christ* i Gk *brothers*
j Or *persecuted* k Gk *Then he;* other ancient authorities read *Then I stood*
l Gk *the plague of its death* m Other ancient authorities lack this sentence

tion of the world in the book of life of the Lamb that was slaughtered.[n]

9 Let anyone who has an ear listen:

10 If you are to be taken
captive,
into captivity you go;
if you kill with the sword,
with the sword you must
be killed.

Here is a call for the endurance and faith of the saints.

The Second Beast

11 Then I saw another beast that rose out of the earth; it had two horns like a lamb and it spoke like a dragon. 12 It exercises all the authority of the first beast on its behalf, and it makes the earth and its inhabitants worship the first beast, whose mortal wound[o] had been healed. 13 It performs great signs, even making fire come down from heaven to earth in the sight of all; 14 and by the signs that it is allowed to perform on behalf of the beast, it deceives the inhabitants of earth, telling them to make an image for the beast that had been wounded by the sword[p] and yet lived; 15 and it was allowed to give breath[q] to the image of the beast so that the image of the beast could even speak and cause those who would not worship the image of the beast to be killed. 16 Also it causes all, both small and great, both rich and poor, both free and slave, to be marked on the right hand or the forehead, 17 so that no one can buy or sell who does not have the mark, that is, the name of the beast or the number of its name. 18 This calls for wisdom: let anyone with understanding calculate the number of the beast, for it is the number of a person. Its number is six hundred sixty-six.[r]

The Lamb and the 144,000

14 Then I looked, and there was the Lamb, standing on Mount Zion! And with him were one hundred forty-four thousand who had his name and his Father's

13.9
Mk 4.23;
Rev 2.7
13.10
Isa 33.1;
Mt 26.52;
Rev 14.12
13.11
Rev 11.7
13.12
vv. 4,14;
Rev 14.9,11;
v. 3
13.13
Mt 24.24;
Rev 16.14;
1 Kings 18.38;
Rev 20.9
13.14
Rev 12.9;
2 Thes 2.9,
10
13.15
Dan 3.5;
Rev 16.2
13.16
Rev 11.18;
19.5,18; 14.9
13.17
Rev 14.9,11;
15.2
13.18
Rev 17.9;
15.2; 21.17
14.1
Rev 5.6;
Ps 2.6;
Rev 3.12;
7.3
14.2
Rev 1.15;
5.8
14.3
Rev 5.9;
v. 1
14.4
2 Cor 11.2;
Rev 3.4; 5.9;
Jas 1.18
14.5
Ps 32.2;
Zeph 3.13;
Eph 5.27
14.6
Rev 8.13;
3.10; 5.9
14.7
Rev 15.4;
11.13; 4.11;
8.10
14.8
Isa 21.9;
Jer 51.8;
Rev 18.2;
17.5; 18.10
14.9
Rev 13.14-16
14.10
Isa 51.17;
Jer 25.15;
Rev 18.6;
20.10; 19.20
14.11
Isa 34.10;
Rev 19.3;
4.8; 13.17

name written on their foreheads. 2 And I heard a voice from heaven like the sound of many waters and like the sound of loud thunder; the voice I heard was like the sound of harpists playing on their harps, 3 and they sing a new song before the throne and before the four living creatures and before the elders. No one could learn that song except the one hundred forty-four thousand who have been redeemed from the earth. 4 It is these who have not defiled themselves with women, for they are virgins; these follow the Lamb wherever he goes. They have been redeemed from humankind as first fruits for God and the Lamb, 5 and in their mouth no lie was found; they are blameless.

The Messages of the Three Angels

6 Then I saw another angel flying in midheaven, with an eternal gospel to proclaim to those who live[s] on the earth — to every nation and tribe and language and people. 7 He said in a loud voice, "Fear God and give him glory, for the hour of his judgment has come; and worship him who made heaven and earth, the sea and the springs of water."

8 Then another angel, a second, followed, saying, "Fallen, fallen is Babylon the great! She has made all nations drink of the wine of the wrath of her fornication."

9 Then another angel, a third, followed them, crying with a loud voice, "Those who worship the beast and its image, and receive a mark on their foreheads or on their hands, 10 they will also drink the wine of God's wrath, poured unmixed into the cup of his anger, and they will be tormented with fire and sulfur in the presence of the holy angels and in the presence of the Lamb. 11 And the smoke of their torment goes up forever and

[n] Or *written in the book of life of the Lamb that was slaughtered from the foundation of the world* [o] Gk *whose plague of its death* [p] Or *that had received the plague of the sword* [q] Or *spirit* [r] Other ancient authorities read *six hundred sixteen* [s] Gk *sit*

ever. There is no rest day or night for those who worship the beast and its image and for anyone who receives the mark of its name."

12 Here is a call for the endurance of the saints, those who keep the commandments of God and hold fast to the faith of[t] Jesus.

13 And I heard a voice from heaven saying, "Write this: Blessed are the dead who from now on die in the Lord." "Yes," says the Spirit, "they will rest from their labors, for their deeds follow them."

Reaping the Earth's Harvest

14 Then I looked, and there was a white cloud, and seated on the cloud was one like the Son of Man, with a golden crown on his head, and a sharp sickle in his hand! [15] Another angel came out of the temple, calling in a loud voice to the one who sat on the cloud, "Use your sickle and reap, for the hour to reap has come, because the harvest of the earth is fully ripe." [16] So the one who sat on the cloud swung his sickle over the earth, and the earth was reaped.

17 Then another angel came out of the temple in heaven, and he too had a sharp sickle. [18] Then another angel came out from the altar, the angel who has authority over fire, and he called with a loud voice to him who had the sharp sickle, "Use your sharp sickle and gather the clusters of the vine of the earth, for its grapes are ripe." [19] So the angel swung his sickle over the earth and gathered the vintage of the earth, and he threw it into the great wine press of the wrath of God. [20] And the wine press was trodden outside the city, and blood flowed from the wine press, as high as a horse's bridle, for a distance of about two hundred miles.[u]

The Angels with the Seven Last Plagues

15 Then I saw another portent in heaven, great and amazing: seven angels with seven plagues, which are the last, for with them the wrath of God is ended.

2 And I saw what appeared to be a sea of glass mixed with fire, and those who had conquered the beast and its image and the number of its name, standing beside the sea of glass with harps of God in their hands. [3] And they sing the song of Moses, the servant[v] of God, and the song of the Lamb:

"Great and amazing are your
 deeds,
 Lord God the Almighty!
Just and true are your ways,
 King of the nations![w]
4 Lord, who will not fear
 and glorify your name?
For you alone are holy.
 All nations will come
 and worship before you,
for your judgments have
 been revealed."

5 After this I looked, and the temple of the tent[x] of witness in heaven was opened, [6] and out of the temple came the seven angels with the seven plagues, robed in pure bright linen,[y] with golden sashes across their chests. [7] Then one of the four living creatures gave the seven angels seven golden bowls full of the wrath of God, who lives forever and ever; [8] and the temple was filled with smoke from the glory of God and from his power, and no one could enter the temple until the seven plagues of the seven angels were ended.

The Bowls of God's Wrath

16 Then I heard a loud voice from the temple telling the seven angels, "Go and pour out on the earth the seven bowls of the wrath of God."

2 So the first angel went and poured his bowl on the earth, and a foul and painful sore came on those who had the mark of the beast and who worshiped its image.

3 The second angel poured his

14.12
Rev 13.10;
12.17
14.13
Rev 20.6;
1 Cor 15.18;
1 Thes 4.16
14.14
Dan 7.13;
Rev 1.13;
6.2
14.15
Joel 3.13;
Jer 51.33;
Rev 13.12
14.18
Rev 16.8;
Joel 3.13
14.19
Rev 19.15
14.20
Isa 63.3;
Heb 13.12;
Rev 11.8
15.1
Rev 12.1,3;
16.1;
Lev 26.21;
Rev 14.10

15.2
Rev 4.6;
13.14,15; 5.8
15.3
Deut 32.3,4;
Ps 111.2;
145.17;
Hos 14.9
15.4
Jer 10.7;
Isa 66.23
15.5
Rev 11.19;
Num 1.50
15.6
Rev 14.15;
v. 1;
Rev 1.13
15.7
Rev 4.6,9;
10.6
15.8
Ex 40.34;
1 Kings 8.10;
Isa 6.4
16.1
Rev 15.1
16.2
Rev 8.7;
Ex 9.9-11;
Rev 13.15-17
16.3
Rev 8.8,9;
Ex 17.17-21

t Or to their faith in u Gk one thousand six hundred stadia v Gk slave w Other ancient authorities read the ages x Or tabernacle y Other ancient authorities read stone

bowl into the sea, and it became like the blood of a corpse, and every living thing in the sea died.

4 The third angel poured his bowl into the rivers and the springs of water, and they became blood. 5 And I heard the angel of the waters say,

"You are just, O Holy One,
 who are and were,
 for you have judged these
 things;
6 because they shed the blood
 of saints and prophets,
 you have given them blood
 to drink.
It is what they deserve!"
7 And I heard the altar respond,
"Yes, O Lord God, the
 Almighty,
 your judgments are true
 and just!"

8 The fourth angel poured his bowl on the sun, and it was allowed to scorch them with fire; 9 they were scorched by the fierce heat, but they cursed the name of God, who had authority over these plagues, and they did not repent and give him glory.

10 The fifth angel poured his bowl on the throne of the beast, and its kingdom was plunged into darkness; people gnawed their tongues in agony, 11 and cursed the God of heaven because of their pains and sores, and they did not repent of their deeds.

12 The sixth angel poured his bowl on the great river Euphrates, and its water was dried up in order to prepare the way for the kings from the east. 13 And I saw three foul spirits like frogs coming from the mouth of the dragon, from the mouth of the beast, and from the mouth of the false prophet. 14 These are demonic spirits, performing signs, who go abroad to the kings of the whole world, to assemble them for battle on the great day of God the Almighty. 15 ("See, I am coming like a thief! Blessed is the one who stays awake and is clothed,ᶻ not going about naked and exposed to shame.") 16 And they assembled them at the place

that in Hebrew is called Harmagedon.

17 The seventh angel poured his bowl into the air, and a loud voice came out of the temple, from the throne, saying, "It is done!" 18 And there came flashes of lightning, rumblings, peals of thunder, and a violent earthquake, such as had not occurred since people were upon the earth, so violent was that earthquake. 19 The great city was split into three parts, and the cities of the nations fell. God remembered great Babylon and gave her the wine-cup of the fury of his wrath. 20 And every island fled away, and no mountains were to be found; 21 and huge hailstones, each weighing about a hundred pounds,ª dropped from heaven on people, until they cursed God for the plague of the hail, so fearful was that plague.

The Great Whore and the Beast

17 Then one of the seven angels who had the seven bowls came and said to me, "Come, I will show you the judgment of the great whore who is seated on many waters, 2 with whom the kings of the earth have committed fornication, and with the wine of whose fornication the inhabitants of the earth have become drunk." 3 So he carried me away in the spiritᵇ into a wilderness, and I saw a woman sitting on a scarlet beast that was full of blasphemous names, and it had seven heads and ten horns. 4 The woman was clothed in purple and scarlet, and adorned with gold and jewels and pearls, holding in her hand a golden cup full of abominations and the impurities of her fornication; 5 and on her forehead was written a name, a mystery: "Babylon the great, mother of whores and of earth's abominations."

16.4
Rev 8.10;
Ex 7.17-21
16.5
Rev 15.3;
11.17; 15.4
16.6
Rev 17.6;
18.24;
Isa 49.26
16.7
Rev 6.9;
14.18; 15.3;
19.2
16.8
Rev 8.12;
14.18
16.9
Rev 2.21;
11.13
16.10
Rev 13.2;
9.2; 11.10
16.11
vv. 9,21;
Rev 11.13;
2.21
16.12
Rev 9.14;
Isa 41.2
16.13
Rev 12.3;
13.1; 19.20
16.14
1 Tim 4.1;
Rev 13.13;
3.10; 17.14
16.15
1 Thes 5.2;
2 Cor 5.3
16.16
Rev 19.19;
9.11;
2 Kings 23.29,
30
16.17
Eph 2.2;
Rev 11.15;
14.15; 21.6
16.18
Rev 4.5;
6.12;
Dan 12.1
16.19
Rev 17.18;
14.8; 18.5;
14.10
16.20
Rev 6.14
16.21
Rev 11.19;
Ex 9.23
17.1
Rev 21.9;
16.19; 19.2;
Jer 51.13
17.2
Rev 18.3;
14.8
17.3
Rev 12.3,6,
14
17.4
Jer 51.7;
Rev 18.16;
18.6

17.5 2 Thes 2.7; Rev 14.8; 16.19; 18.9
17.6 Rev 18.24; 13.15; 12.11

ᶻ Gk and keeps his robes ª Gk weighing about a talent ᵇ Or in the Spirit

6 And I saw that the woman was drunk with the blood of the saints and the blood of the witnesses to Jesus.

When I saw her, I was greatly amazed. 7 But the angel said to me, "Why are you so amazed? I will tell you the mystery of the woman, and of the beast with seven heads and ten horns that carries her. 8 The beast that you saw was, and is not, and is about to ascend from the bottomless pit and go to destruction. And the inhabitants of the earth, whose names have not been written in the book of life from the foundation of the world, will be amazed when they see the beast, because it was and is not and is to come.

9 "This calls for a mind that has wisdom: the seven heads are seven mountains on which the woman is seated; also, they are seven kings, 10 of whom five have fallen, one is living, and the other has not yet come; and when he comes, he must remain only a little while. 11 As for the beast that was and is not, it is an eighth but it belongs to the seven, and it goes to destruction. 12 And the ten horns that you saw are ten kings who have not yet received a kingdom, but they are to receive authority as kings for one hour, together with the beast. 13 These are united in yielding their power and authority to the beast; 14 they will make war on the Lamb, and the Lamb will conquer them, for he is Lord of lords and King of kings, and those with him are called and chosen and faithful."

15 And he said to me, "The waters that you saw, where the whore is seated, are peoples and multitudes and nations and languages. 16 And the ten horns that you saw, they and the beast will hate the whore; they will make her desolate and naked; they will devour her flesh and burn her up with fire. 17 For God has put it into their hearts to carry out his purpose by agreeing to give their kingdom to the beast, until the words of God will be fulfilled. 18 The woman you saw is the great city that rules over the kings of the earth."

The Fall of Babylon

18 After this I saw another angel coming down from heaven, having great authority; and the earth was made bright with his splendor. 2 He called out with a mighty voice,

"Fallen, fallen is Babylon the great!
It has become a dwelling place of demons,
a haunt of every foul and hateful bird,
a haunt of every foul and hateful beast.[c]
3 For all the nations have drunk[d]
of the wine of the wrath of her fornication,
and the kings of the earth have committed fornication with her,
and the merchants of the earth have grown rich from the power[e] of her luxury."

4 Then I heard another voice from heaven saying,

"Come out of her, my people,
so that you do not take part in her sins,
and so that you do not share in her plagues;
5 for her sins are heaped high as heaven,
and God has remembered her iniquities.
6 Render to her as she herself has rendered,
and repay her double for her deeds;
mix a double draught for her in the cup she mixed.
7 As she glorified herself and lived luxuriously,
so give her a like measure of torment and grief.
Since in her heart she says,

17.7
vv. 5,3,9
17.8
Rev 11.7;
13.10; 3.10;
13.3,8
17.9
Rev 13.18
17.11
v. 8
17.12
Dan 7.20;
Rev 13.1;
18.10,17,19
17.13
v. 17
17.14
Rev 16.14;
1 Tim 6.15;
Rev 19.16;
Mt 22.14
17.15
Isa 8.7;
Rev 5.9;
13.7
17.16
Rev 18.17,
19;
Ezek 16.37,
39;
Rev 19.18;
18.8
17.17
2 Thes 2.11;
Rev 10.7
17.18
Rev 16.19

18.1
Rev 17.1;
10.1;
Ezek 43.2
18.2
Rev 14.8;
Isa 13.21,
22;
Jer 50.39
18.3
Rev 14.8;
Jer 25.15,27
18.4
Isa 48.20;
Jer 50.8;
2 Cor 6.17
18.5
Jer 51.9;
Rev 16.19
18.6
Ps 137.8;
Jer 50.15;
Rev 14.10;
16.19
18.7
Ezek 28.2-8;
Isa 47.7,8;
Zeph 2.15

c Some ancient authorities lack *a haunt of every foul and hateful beast* d Other ancient authorities read *she has made all nations drink* e Or *resources*

'I rule as a queen;
I am no widow,
and I will never see grief,'
8 therefore her plagues will
come in a single day—
pestilence and mourning
and famine—
and she will be burned with
fire;
for mighty is the Lord God
who judges her."

9 And the kings of the earth,
who committed fornication and
lived in luxury with her, will weep
and wail over her when they see the
smoke of her burning; 10 they will
stand far off, in fear of her torment,
and say,

"Alas, alas, the great city,
Babylon, the mighty city!
For in one hour your
judgment has come."

11 And the merchants of the
earth weep and mourn for her,
since no one buys their cargo any-
more, 12 cargo of gold, silver, jewels
and pearls, fine linen, purple, silk
and scarlet, all kinds of scented
wood, all articles of ivory, all arti-
cles of costly wood, bronze, iron,
and marble, 13 cinnamon, spice, in-
cense, myrrh, frankincense, wine,
olive oil, choice flour and wheat,
cattle and sheep, horses and chari-
ots, slaves—and human lives. f
14 "The fruit for which your
soul longed
has gone from you,
and all your dainties and
your splendor
are lost to you,
never to be found again!"
15 The merchants of these wares,
who gained wealth from her, will
stand far off, in fear of her torment,
weeping and mourning aloud,
16 "Alas, alas, the great city,
clothed in fine linen,
in purple and scarlet,
adorned with gold,
with jewels, and with
pearls!
17 For in one hour all this
wealth has been laid
waste!"

And all shipmasters and seafar-
ers, sailors and all whose trade is

on the sea, stood far off 18 and cried
out as they saw the smoke of her
burning,

"What city was like the great
city?"

19 And they threw dust on their
heads, as they wept and mourned,
crying out,

"Alas, alas, the great city,
where all who had ships at
sea
grew rich by her wealth!
For in one hour she has been
laid waste.
20 Rejoice over her, O heaven,
you saints and apostles and
prophets!
For God has given judgment
for you against her."

21 Then a mighty angel took up
a stone like a great millstone and
threw it into the sea, saying,

"With such violence Babylon
the great city
will be thrown down,
and will be found no more;
22 and the sound of harpists
and minstrels and of
flutists and trumpeters
will be heard in you no
more;
and an artisan of any trade
will be found in you no
more;
and the sound of the
millstone
will be heard in you no
more;
23 and the light of a lamp
will shine in you no more;
and the voice of bridegroom
and bride
will be heard in you no
more;
for your merchants were the
magnates of the earth,
and all nations were
deceived by your
sorcery.
24 And in you g was found the
blood of prophets and
of saints,
and of all who have been
slaughtered on earth."

18.8
Isa 47.9;
Rev 17.16;
Jer 50.34;
Rev 11.17
18.9
Rev 17.2;
Jer 50.46;
v. 18;
Rev 19.3
18.10
vv. 15,17,
16,19
18.11
v. 3;
Ezek 27.27
18.12
Rev 17.4
18.13
Ezek 27.13
18.15
Ezek 27.36,
31
18.16
Rev 17.4
18.17
Rev 17.16;
Isa 23.14;
Ezek 27.29

18.18
Ezek 27.30;
Rev 13.4
18.19
Josh 7.6;
Job 2.12;
Ezek 27.30
18.20
Isa 44.23;
Jer 51.48;
Rev 19.2
18.21
Jer 51.63;
Rev 12.8
18.22
Isa 24.8;
Ezek 26.13;
Jer 25.10
18.23
Jer 25.10;
7.34; 16.9;
Isa 23.8;
Nah 3.4
18.24
Rev 17.6;
Jer 51.49

f Or *chariots, and human bodies and souls*
g Gk *her*

The Rejoicing in Heaven

19 After this I heard what seemed to be the loud voice of a great multitude in heaven, saying,

"Hallelujah!
Salvation and glory and
 power to our God,
2 for his judgments are true
 and just;
he has judged the great
 whore
who corrupted the earth
 with her fornication,
and he has avenged on her
 the blood of his
 servants."[h]

3 Once more they said,

"Hallelujah!
The smoke goes up from her
 forever and ever."

4 And the twenty-four elders and the four living creatures fell down and worshiped God who is seated on the throne, saying,

"Amen. Hallelujah!"

5 And from the throne came a voice saying,

"Praise our God,
 all you his servants,[h]
and all who fear him,
 small and great."

6 Then I heard what seemed to be the voice of a great multitude, like the sound of many waters and like the sound of mighty thunderpeals, crying out,

"Hallelujah!
For the Lord our God
 the Almighty reigns.
7 Let us rejoice and exult
 and give him the glory,
for the marriage of the Lamb
 has come,
and his bride has made
 herself ready;
8 to her it has been granted to
 be clothed
with fine linen, bright and
 pure"—

for the fine linen is the righteous deeds of the saints.

9 And the angel said[i] to me, "Write this: Blessed are those who are invited to the marriage supper of the Lamb." And he said to me,

"These are true words of God." 10 Then I fell down at his feet to worship him, but he said to me, "You must not do that! I am a fellow servant[j] with you and your comrades[k] who hold the testimony of Jesus.[l] Worship God! For the testimony of Jesus[l] is the spirit of prophecy."

The Rider on the White Horse

11 Then I saw heaven opened, and there was a white horse! Its rider is called Faithful and True, and in righteousness he judges and makes war. 12 His eyes are like a flame of fire, and on his head are many diadems; and he has a name inscribed that no one knows but himself. 13 He is clothed in a robe dipped in[m] blood, and his name is called The Word of God. 14 And the armies of heaven, wearing fine linen, white and pure, were following him on white horses. 15 From his mouth comes a sharp sword with which to strike down the nations, and he will rule[n] them with a rod of iron; he will tread the winepress of the fury of the wrath of God the Almighty. 16 On his robe and on his thigh he has a name inscribed, "King of kings and Lord of lords."

The Beast and Its Armies Defeated

17 Then I saw an angel standing in the sun, and with a loud voice he called to all the birds that fly in midheaven, "Come, gather for the great supper of God, 18 to eat the flesh of kings, the flesh of captains, the flesh of the mighty, the flesh of horses and their riders—flesh of all, both free and slave, both small and great." 19 Then I saw the beast and the kings of the earth with their armies gathered to make war against the rider on the horse and against his army. 20 And the beast was captured, and with it the false prophet who had performed in its presence the signs by which he de-

19.1
Rev 11.15;
4.11; 7.10,12;
12.10
19.2
Deut 32.43;
Rev 6.10
19.3
Isa 34.10;
Rev 14.11
19.4
Rev 4.4,6;
5.14
19.5
Ps 134.1;
Rev 11.18;
20.12
19.6
Rev 11.15,
17; 14.2
19.7
Mt 22.2;
25.10;
2 Cor 11.2;
Eph 5.32;
Rev 21.2,9
19.8
Rev 15.4
19.9
v. 10;
Rev 1.19;
Lk 14.15;
Rev 21.5

19.10
Rev 22.8;
Acts 10.26;
Rev 22.9;
12.17
19.11
Rev 15.5;
6.2; 3.14;
Isa 11.4
19.12
Rev 1.14;
6.2; 2.17
19.13
Isa 63.2,3;
Jn 1.1
19.14
v. 8
19.15
Isa 11.4;
2 Thes 2.8;
Ps 2.9;
Rev 2.27;
14.19,20
19.16
Dan 2.47;
Rev 17.14
19.17
Rev 8.13;
Ezek 39.17
19.18
Ezek 39.18-20;
Rev 11.18
19.19
Rev 11.7;
16.14,16
19.20
Rev 16.13;
13.12ff;
Dan 7.11;
Rev 20.10;
14.10; 21.8

h Gk *slaves* i Gk *he said* j Gk *slave*
k Gk *brothers* l Or *to Jesus* m Other
ancient authorities read *sprinkled with*
n Or *will shepherd*

ceived those who had received the mark of the beast and those who worshiped its image. These two were thrown alive into the lake of fire that burns with sulfur. ²¹And the rest were killed by the sword of the rider on the horse, the sword that came from his mouth; and all the birds were gorged with their flesh.

The Thousand Years

20 Then I saw an angel coming down from heaven, holding in his hand the key to the bottomless pit and a great chain. ²He seized the dragon, that ancient serpent, who is the Devil and Satan, and bound him for a thousand years, ³and threw him into the pit, and locked and sealed it over him, so that he would deceive the nations no more, until the thousand years were ended. After that he must be let out for a little while.

4 Then I saw thrones, and those seated on them were given authority to judge. I also saw the souls of those who had been beheaded for their testimony to Jesusᵒ and for the word of God. They had not worshiped the beast or its image and had not received its mark on their foreheads or their hands. They came to life and reigned with Christ a thousand years. ⁵(The rest of the dead did not come to life until the thousand years were ended.) This is the first resurrection. ⁶Blessed and holy are those who share in the first resurrection. Over these the second death has no power, but they will be priests of God and of Christ, and they will reign with him a thousand years.

Satan's Doom

7 When the thousand years are ended, Satan will be released from his prison ⁸and will come out to deceive the nations at the four corners of the earth, Gog and Magog, in order to gather them for battle; they are as numerous as the sands of the sea. ⁹They marched up over the breadth of the earth and surrounded the camp of the saints and

19.21
vv. 11,19,
15,17
20.1
Rev 10.1;
1.18; 9.1
20.2
2 Pet 2.4;
Jude 6;
Rev 12.9
20.3
Dan 6.17;
Rev 12.9
20.4
Dan 7.9,22,
27; Rev 6.9;
13.12,15,16
20.5
Lk 14.14;
Phil 3.11;
1 Thes 4.16
20.6
Rev 14.13;
2.11; 21.8;
1.6
20.7
v. 2
20.8
Ezek 38.2;
39.1;
Rev 16.14;
Heb 11.12
20.9
Ezek 38.9,
22; 39.6

20.10
vv. 3,8
20.11f
Rev 4.2;
21.1;
Dan 2.35;
Rev 12.8
20.12
Mt 16.27;
Rev 2.3;
22.12
20.13
Rev 6.8;
Isa 26.19;
Rev 2.23
20.14
1 Cor 15.26;
Rev 6.8
21.1
Isa 65.17;
2 Pet 3.13;
Rev 20.11
21.2
Heb 11.10;
12.22;
Rev 3.12
21.3
Ezek 37.27;
2 Cor 6.16;
Rev 7.15

the beloved city. And fire came down from heavenᵖ and consumed them. ¹⁰And the devil who had deceived them was thrown into the lake of fire and sulfur, where the beast and the false prophet were, and they will be tormented day and night forever and ever.

The Dead Are Judged

11 Then I saw a great white throne and the one who sat on it; the earth and the heaven fled from his presence, and no place was found for them. ¹²And I saw the dead, great and small, standing before the throne, and books were opened. Also another book was opened, the book of life. And the dead were judged according to their works, as recorded in the books. ¹³And the sea gave up the dead that were in it, Death and Hades gave up the dead that were in them, and all were judged according to what they had done. ¹⁴Then Death and Hades were thrown into the lake of fire. This is the second death, the lake of fire; ¹⁵and anyone whose name was not found written in the book of life was thrown into the lake of fire.

The New Heaven and the New Earth

21 Then I saw a new heaven and a new earth; for the first heaven and the first earth had passed away, and the sea was no more. ²And I saw the holy city, the new Jerusalem, coming down out of heaven from God, prepared as a bride adorned for her husband. ³And I heard a loud voice from the throne saying,

"See, the home�q of God is
 among mortals.
He will dwellq with them as
 their God;ʳ
they will be his peoples,ˢ

ᵒOr *for the testimony of Jesus* ᵖOther ancient authorities read *from God, out of heaven,* or *out of heaven from God*
qGk *tabernacle* ʳOther ancient authorities lack *as their God* ˢOther ancient authorities read *people*

and God himself will be with them;[t]

4 he will wipe every tear from their eyes.

Death will be no more;
mourning and crying and pain will be no more,
for the first things have passed away."

5 And the one who was seated on the throne said, "See, I am making all things new." Also he said, "Write this, for these words are trustworthy and true." 6 Then he said to me, "It is done! I am the Alpha and the Omega, the beginning and the end. To the thirsty I will give water as a gift from the spring of the water of life. 7 Those who conquer will inherit these things, and I will be their God and they will be my children. 8 But as for the cowardly, the faithless,[u] the polluted, the murderers, the fornicators, the sorcerers, the idolaters, and all liars, their place will be in the lake that burns with fire and sulfur, which is the second death."

Vision of the New Jerusalem

9 Then one of the seven angels who had the seven bowls full of the seven last plagues came and said to me, "Come, I will show you the bride, the wife of the Lamb." 10 And in the spirit[v] he carried me away to a great, high mountain and showed me the holy city Jerusalem coming down out of heaven from God. 11 It has the glory of God and a radiance like a very rare jewel, like jasper, clear as crystal. 12 It has a great, high wall with twelve gates, and at the gates twelve angels, and on the gates are inscribed the names of the twelve tribes of the Israelites; 13 on the east three gates, on the north three gates, on the south three gates, and on the west three gates. 14 And the wall of the city has twelve foundations, and on them are the twelve names of the twelve apostles of the Lamb.

15 The angel[w] who talked to me had a measuring rod of gold to measure the city and its gates and walls. 16 The city lies foursquare, its

length the same as its width; and he measured the city with his rod, fifteen hundred miles;[x] its length and width and height are equal. 17 He also measured its wall, one hundred forty-four cubits[y] by human measurement, which the angel was using. 18 The wall is built of jasper, while the city is pure gold, clear as glass. 19 The foundations of the wall of the city are adorned with every jewel; the first was jasper, the second sapphire, the third agate, the fourth emerald, 20 the fifth onyx, the sixth carnelian, the seventh chrysolite, the eighth beryl, the ninth topaz, the tenth chrysoprase, the eleventh jacinth, the twelfth amethyst. 21 And the twelve gates are twelve pearls, each of the gates is a single pearl, and the street of the city is pure gold, transparent as glass.

22 I saw no temple in the city, for its temple is the Lord God the Almighty and the Lamb. 23 And the city has no need of sun or moon to shine on it, for the glory of God is its light, and its lamp is the Lamb. 24 The nations will walk by its light, and the kings of the earth will bring their glory into it. 25 Its gates will never be shut by day—and there will be no night there. 26 People will bring into it the glory and the honor of the nations. 27 But nothing unclean will enter it, nor anyone who practices abomination or falsehood, but only those who are written in the Lamb's book of life.

The River of Life

22 Then the angel[z] showed me the river of the water of life, bright as crystal, flowing from the throne of God and of the Lamb 2 through the middle of the street of the city. On either side of the river, is the tree of life[a] with its twelve kinds of fruit, producing its fruit each month; and the leaves of the

21.4
Rev 7.17;
1 Cor 15.26;
Rev 20.14;
Isa 35.10;
65.19
21.5
Rev 4.9;
20.11;
Isa 43.19;
Rev 19.9
21.6
Rev 16.17;
1.8; 22.13;
Jn 4.10
21.7
Rev 2.7;
v. 3
21.8
Heb 12.14;
Rev 22.15;
19.20; 2.11
21.9
Rev 15.1,6,
7; 20.14ff
21.10
Rev 1.10;
Ezek 40.2;
Rev 17.3
21.11
Rev 15.8;
22.5; 4.6
21.12
Ezek 48.31-34
21.14
Mt 16.18;
Eph 2.20
21.15
Rev 11.1

21.18
vv. 11,19,
21; Rev 4.6
21.19
Isa 54.11,
12; vv. 11,
18; Rev 4.3
21.20
Rev 4.3
21.21
vv. 15,25,18
21.22
Jn 4.21,23;
Rev 1.8; 5.6
21.23
Isa 24.23;
60.19,20;
Rev 22.5
21.24
Isa 60.3,5
21.25
Isa 60.11;
Zech 14.7;
Rev 22.5
21.27
Isa 52.1;
Joel 3.17;
Rev 22.14;
3.5
22.1
Ezek 47.1;
Zech 14.8;
Rev 4.6
22.2
Gen 2.9;
Rev 2.7;
Ezek 47.12

t Other ancient authorities add *and be their God* u Or *the unbelieving* v Or *in the Spirit* w Gk *He* x Gk *twelve thousand stadia* y That is, almost seventy-five yards z Gk *he* a Or *the Lamb.* 2 *In the middle of the street of the city, and on either side of the river, is the tree of life*

tree are for the healing of the nations. ³ Nothing accursed will be found there any more. But the throne of God and of the Lamb will be in it, and his servants ᵇ will worship him; ⁴ they will see his face, and his name will be on their foreheads. ⁵ And there will be no more night; they need no light of lamp or sun, for the Lord God will be their light, and they will reign forever and ever.

6 And he said to me, "These words are trustworthy and true, for the Lord, the God of the spirits of the prophets, has sent his angel to show his servants ᵇ what must soon take place."

7 "See, I am coming soon! Blessed is the one who keeps the words of the prophecy of this book."

Epilogue and Benediction

8 I, John, am the one who heard and saw these things. And when I heard and saw them, I fell down to worship at the feet of the angel who showed them to me; ⁹ but he said to me, "You must not do that! I am a fellow servant ᶜ with you and your comrades ᵈ the prophets, and with those who keep the words of this book. Worship God!"

10 And he said to me, "Do not seal up the words of the prophecy of this book, for the time is near. ¹¹ Let the evildoer still do evil, and the filthy still be filthy, and the righteous still do right, and the holy still be holy."

12 "See, I am coming soon; my reward is with me, to repay according to everyone's work. ¹³ I am the Alpha and the Omega, the first and

the last, the beginning and the end."

14 Blessed are those who wash their robes, ᵉ so that they will have the right to the tree of life and may enter the city by the gates. ¹⁵ Outside are the dogs and sorcerers and fornicators and murderers and idolaters, and everyone who loves and practices falsehood.

16 "It is I, Jesus, who sent my angel to you with this testimony for the churches. I am the root and the descendant of David, the bright morning star."

17 The Spirit and the bride say, "Come."

And let everyone who hears say, "Come."
And let everyone who is thirsty come.
Let anyone who wishes take the water of life as a gift.

18 I warn everyone who hears the words of the prophecy of this book: if anyone adds to them, God will add to that person the plagues described in this book; ¹⁹ if anyone takes away from the words of the book of this prophecy, God will take away that person's share in the tree of life and in the holy city, which are described in this book.

20 The one who testifies to these things says, "Surely I am coming soon."

Amen. Come, Lord Jesus!

21 The grace of the Lord Jesus be with all the saints. Amen. ᶠ

22.3 Zech 14.11; Rev 7.15
22.4 Mt 5.8; Rev 14.1
22.5 Rev 21.25, 23; Dan 7.27
22.6 Rev 1.1; 19.19; 21.5
22.7 Rev 3.11; 1.3
22.8 Rev 1.1; 19.10
22.9 Rev 19.10; 1.1; vv. 10, 18,19; Rev 21.2
22.10 Dan 8.26; Rev 1.3
22.11 Dan 12.10; Ezek 3.27
22.12 Isa 40.10; Jer 17.10; Rev 2.23
22.13 Rev 1.8,17; 21.6
22.15 Gal 5.19ff; Col 3.6; Phil 3.2
22.16 Rev 1.1; 5.5; Zech 6.12; 2 Pet 1.19; Rev 2.28
22.17 Rev 2.7; 21.2; Isa 55.1; Rev 21.6
22.18 Deut 4.2; Prov 30.6; Rev 15.6; 16.21
22.20 Rev 1.2; 2 Tim 4.8; Rom 16.20; 2 Thes 3.18

ᵇ Gk *slaves* ᶜ Gk *slave* ᵈ Gk *brothers*
ᵉ Other ancient authorities read *do his commandments* ᶠ Other ancient authorities lack *all;* others lack *the saints;* others lack *Amen*

STUDY HELPS

PARABLES OF THE BIBLE

PARABLES OF THE OLD TESTAMENT

Parable	Reference
The trees	Judg 9.7–15
The ewe lamb	2 Sam 12.1–4
Two sons	2 Sam 14.1–24
Thorn bush and cedar	2 Kings 14.8–14
The vineyard	Isa 5.1–7
Almond branch and boiling pot	Jer 1.11–19
Linen loincloth	Jer 13.1–11
Wine-jars	Jer 13.12–14
Potter and clay	Jer 18.1–10
Two baskets of figs	Jer 24.1–10
Cup of God's wrath	Jer 25.15–38
Useless vine	Ezek 15.1–8
Boiling pot	Ezek 24.1–4
Valley of dry bones	Ezek 37.1–14
Measuring line	Zech 2.1–13
Golden lampstand and two olive trees	Zech 4.1–14
Flying scroll	Zech 5.1–4

THE PARABLES OF JESUS

Parable	Matthew	Mark	Luke
Lamp under a bushel basket	5.14–15	4.21–22	8.16; 11.33
Wise and foolish builders	7.24–27		6.47–49
Unshrunk cloth on an old cloak	9.16	2.21	5.36
New wine in old wineskins	9.17	2.22	5.37–38
Sower and the soils	13.3–8,18–23	4.3–8,14–20	8.5–8,11–15
Weeds	13.24–30,36–43		
Mustard seed	13.31–32	4.30–32	13.18–19
Yeast	13.33		13.20–21
Hidden treasure	13.44		
Valuable pearl	13.45–46		
Net	13.47–50		
Master of a household	13.52		
Lost sheep	18.12–14		15.4–7
Unforgiving servant	18.23–34		
Laborers in the vineyard	20.1–16		
Two sons	21.28–32		
Tenants	21.33–44	12.1–11	20.9–18
Wedding banquet	22.2–14		
Fig tree	24.32–35	13.28–29	21.29–31
Faithful and wise slave	24.45–51		12.42–48

THE PARABLES OF JESUS *(cont.)*

Parable	Matthew	Mark	Luke
Ten bridesmaids	25.1–13		
Talents (pounds)	25.14–30		19.12–27
Sheep and goats	25.31–46		
Growing seed		4.26–29	
Watchful slaves		13.35–37	12.35–40
Creditor			7.41–43
Good Samaritan			10.30–37
Friend in need			11.5–8
Rich fool			12.16–21
Barren fig tree			13.6–9
Lowest seat at the banquet			14.7–14
Great dinner			14.16–24
Cost of discipleship			14.28–33
Lost coin			15.8–10
Prodigal son			15.11–32
Dishonest manager			16.1–8
Rich man and Lazarus			16.19–31
Master and his slave			17.7–10
Persistent widow			18.2–8
Pharisee and tax collector			18.10–14

MIRACLES OF THE BIBLE

MIRACLES OF THE OLD TESTAMENT

Miracle	Reference
Burning bush	Ex 3.1–14
Staff becoming a snake	Ex 4.1–5; 7.8–13
Leprous hand	Ex 4.6–12
Ten plagues	Ex 8.14—12.30
Dividing of the Red Sea	Ex 14.21–31
Water from the rock	Ex 17.1–9
Destruction of Korah	Num 16.31–35
Aaron's staff budding	Num 17.1–19
Water from the rock in Kadesh	Num 20.9–11
Bronze serpent	Num 21.4–9
Balaam's donkey	Num 22.20–35
Jordan divided	Josh 3.7–17
Fall of Jericho	Josh 6.1–20
Sun standing still	Josh 10.1–14
Slain lion	Judg 14.5–10
Dagon's temple pulled down	Judg 16.23–30
Thunder and rain	1 Sam 12.16–18
Jeroboam's hand withered and restored	1 Kings 13.6
Elijah fed by ravens	1 Kings 17.1–6
Widow's meal and oil	1 Kings 17.8–16
Widow's son raised from the dead	1 Kings 17.17–24
Sacrifice consumed by fire	1 Kings 18.30–39
Rain in answer to prayer	1 Kings 18.41–45
Jordan divided	2 Kings 2.1–8
Water made wholesome	2 Kings 2.19–22
Widow's oil multiplied	2 Kings 4.1–7
Shunammite's son restored to life	2 Kings 4.8–37
Poison stew rendered harmless	2 Kings 4.38–41
Feeding of one hundred men	2 Kings 4.42–44
Naaman healed of leprosy	2 Kings 5.1–19
Floating ax head	2 Kings 6.1–7
Blinded eyes	2 Kings 6.8–23
Dead man restored to life	2 Kings 13.21
Hezekiah healed	2 Kings 20.1–7
Three men delivered from blazing furnace	Dan 3.23–27
Daniel delivered from the den of lions	Dan 6.10–23
Sea stilled when Jonah cast in	Jon 1.15
Jonah delivered from fish's mouth	Jon 2.10
Withering of the bush	Jon 4.6–7

THE MIRACLES OF JESUS

	Matthew	Mark	Luke	John
Healing Miracles				
Man with leprosy	8.2–4	1.40–42	5.12–13	
Roman centurion's servant	8.5–13		7.1–10	
Peter's mother-in-law	8.14–15	1.30–31	4.38–39	
Two Gadarena demoniacs	8.28–34	5.1–15	8.27–35	
Paralyzed man	9.2–7	2.3–12	5.18–25	
Woman with hemorrhages	9.20–22	5.25–29	8.43–48	
Two blind men	9.27–31			
Mute, demon-possessed man	9.32–33			
Man with a withered hand	12.10–13	3.1–5	6.6–10	
Blind, mute, demon-possessed man	12.22		11.14	
Canaanite woman's daughter	15.21–28	7.24–30		
Boy with a demon	17.14–18	9.17–29	9.38–43	
Two blind men (including Bartimaeus)	20.29–34	10.46–52	18.35–43	
Deaf man with speech impediment		7.31–37		
Possessed man in synagogue		1.23–26	4.33–35	
Blind man at Bethsaida		8.22–26		
Crippled woman			13.11–13	
Man with dropsy			14.1–4	
Ten men with leprosy			17.11–19	
The high priest's slave			22.50–51	
Official's son at Capernaum				4.46–54
Sick man at pool of Beth-zatha				5.1–9
Man born blind				9.1–7
Miracles showing power over nature				
Calming the storm	8.23–27	4.37–41	8.22–25	
Walking on water	14.25	6.48–51		6.19–21
Feeding of the 5000	14.15–21	6.35–44	9.12–17	6.5–13
Feeding of the 4000	15.32–38	8.1–9		
Coin in fish	17.24–27			
Fig tree withered	21.18–22	11.12–14, 20–25		
Large catch of fish			5.4–11	
Water turned into wine				2.1–11
Another large catch of fish				21.1–11
Miracles of raising the dead				
Jairus's daughter	9.18–19, 23–25	5.22–24, 38–42	8.41–42, 49–56	
Widow's son at Nain			7.11–15	
Lazarus				11.1–44

MIRACLES OF THE APOSTLES

Miracle	Acts
Crippled beggar healed (by Peter)	3.6–9
Death of Ananias and Sapphira	5.1–10
Saul's sight restored	9.17–18
Healing of Aeneas	9.33–35
Raising of Dorcas	9.36–41
Elymas blinded	13.8–11
Crippled man healed (by Paul)	14.8–10
Demon cast out of a girl	16.16–18
Raising of Eutychus	20.9–10
Unharmed by viper	28.3–5
Healing of Publius's father	28.7–9

MINISTRY OF JESUS

THE YEAR OF INAUGURATION

Event	Place	Matthew	Mark	Luke	John
Jesus baptized	Jordan River	3.13–17	1.9–11	3.21–23	1.29–39
Jesus tempted by Satan	Wilderness	4.1–11	1.12–13	4.1–13	
Jesus' first miracle	Cana				2.1–11
Jesus and Nicodemus	Judea				3.1–21
Jesus talks to a Samaritan woman	Samaria				4.5–42
Jesus heals an official's son	Cana				4.46–54
The people of Nazareth try to kill Jesus	Nazareth			4.16–31	

THE YEAR OF POPULARITY

Event	Place	Matthew	Mark	Luke	John
Jesus calls four fishermen	Sea of Galilee	4.18–22	1.16–20	5.1–11	
Jesus heals Peter's mother-in-law	Capernaum	8.14–17	1.29–34	4.38–41	
Jesus begins preaching in Galilee	Galilee	4.23–25	1.35–39	4.42–44	
Matthew decides to follow Jesus	Capernaum	9.9–13	2.13–17	5.27–32	
Jesus chooses twelve disciples	Galilee	10.2–4	3.13–19	6.12–15	
Jesus preaches the Sermon on the Mount	Galilee	5.1—7.29		6.20–49	
A sinful woman anoints Jesus	Capernaum			7.36–50	
Jesus travels again through Galilee	Galilee			8.1–3	
Jesus tells parables about the kingdom	Galilee	13.1–52	4.1–34	8.4–18	
Jesus quiets the storm	Sea of Galilee	8.23–27	4.35–41	8.22–25	
Jairus's daughter raised to life by Jesus	Capernaum	9.18–26	5.21–43	8.40–56	
Jesus sends out the twelve	Galilee	9.35—11.1	6.6–13	9.1–6	

THE YEAR OF OPPOSITION

Event	Place	Matthew	Mark	Luke	John
John the Baptist killed by Herod	Machaerus in Judea	14.1–12	6.14–29	9.7–9	
Jesus feeds the 5000	Near Bethsaida	14.13–21	6.30–44	9.10–17	6.1–14
Jesus walks on water	Sea of Galilee	14.22–23	6.45–52		6.16–21
Jesus feeds the 4000	Sea of Galilee	15.32–39	8.1–9		
Peter confesses Jesus as the Son of God	Caesarea Philippi	16.13–20	8.27–30	9.18–21	
Jesus predicts his death	Caesarea Philippi	16.21–26	8.31–37	9.22–25	
Jesus is transfigured	Mount Hermon	17.1–13	9.2–13	9.28–36	

THE YEAR OF OPPOSITION *(cont.)*

Event	Place	Matthew	Mark	Luke	John
Jesus pays his temple taxes	Capernaum	17.24–27			
Jesus attends the Feast of Tabernacles	Jerusalem				7.11–52
Jesus heals a man born blind	Jerusalem				9.1–41
Jesus visits Mary and Martha	Bethany			10.38–42	
Jesus raises Lazarus from the dead	Bethany				11.1–44
Jesus begins his last trip to Jerusalem	Border road			17.11	
Jesus blesses the little children	Transjordan	19.13–15	10.13–16	18.15–17	
Jesus talks to the rich young man	Transjordan	19.16–30	10.17–31	18.18–30	
Jesus again predicts his death	Near the Jordan	20.17–19	10.32–34	18.31–34	
Jesus heals blind Bartimaeus	Jericho	20.29–34	10.46–52	18.35–43	
Jesus talks to Zacchaeus	Jericho			19.1–10	
Jesus visits Mary and Martha again	Bethany				11.55—12.1

THE LAST WEEK

Event	Place	Day of week	Matthew	Mark	Luke	John
The triumphal entry	Jerusalem	Sunday	21.1–11	11.1–10	19.29–44	12.12–19
Jesus curses the fig tree	Jerusalem	Monday	21.18–19	11.12–14		
Jesus cleanses the temple	Jerusalem	Monday	21.12–13	11.15–18	19.45–48	
The authority of Jesus questioned	Jerusalem	Tuesday	21.23–27	11.27–33	20.1–8	
Jesus teaches in the temple	Jerusalem	Tuesday	21.28—23.29	12.1–44	20.9—21.4	
Jesus' feet anointed	Bethany	Tuesday	26.6–13	14.3–9		12.2–11
The plot against Jesus	Jerusalem	Wednesday	26.14–16	14.10–11	22.3–6	
The Last Supper	Jerusalem	Thursday	26.17–29	14.12–25	22.7–20	13.1–38
Jesus comforts his disciples	Jerusalem	Thursday				14.1—16.33
Jesus' high priestly prayer	Jerusalem	Thursday				17.1–26
Gethsemane	Jerusalem	Thursday	26.36–46	14.32–42	22.40–46	
Jesus' arrest and trial	Jerusalem	Friday	26.47—27.26	14.43—15.15	22.47—23.25	18.2—19.16
Jesus' crucifixion and death	Golgotha	Friday	27.27–56	15.16–41	23.26–49	19.17–30
The burial of Jesus	Garden tomb	Friday	27.57–66	15.42–47	23.50–56	19.31–42

PROMISES
AND
PERSPECTIVES
FROM THE BIBLE

PROMISES FROM THE BIBLE

GOD'S PROMISE OF:

Love—Matthew 10.30-31; John 3.16; John 15.9,13; 1 John 4.9
Forgiveness—Luke 15.3-7; Acts 10.43; Ephesians 1.7; 1 John 1.9
Salvation—Matthew 1.21; Acts 16.31; Ephesians 2.8; Hebrews 7.25
the Holy Spirit—Luke 11.13; John 14.16-17; Acts 2.38; Romans 8.11
Everlasting Life—John 6.40; John 10.28; 1 Corinthians 15.51-52; 1 Thessalonians 4.17
Peace—John 14.27; Romans 5.1-2; Ephesians 2.14; 2 Thessalonians 3.16
Joy—John 15.10-11; John 16.22; Romans 16.13; 1 Peter 1.8
Freedom—John 8.34-36; Romans 6.6,14,20-22; 2 Corinthians 3.17; Revelation 1.5
Growth—Philippians 1.6; 2 Corinthians 3.18; Ephesians 4.14-15; 2 Peter 1.3-4
Encouragement—1 Thessalonians 5.23; 2 Thessalonians 2.16-17; Hebrews 6.10;
 1 Peter 2.9
Excellence—Matthew 20.26-28; John 14.12; John 15.15-16; 2 Corinthians 3.5-6
Strength—1 Corinthians 1.8; Ephesians 3.20; 2 Thessalonians 3.3; 1 Peter 5.10
Blessing—John 1.16; John 10.10; Romans 8.28; Ephesians 1.3
His Presence—Matthew 18.20; Matthew 28.20; John 6.37; Romans 8.38-39
Answered Prayer—Matthew 7.7-11; Matthew 21.22; 1 Peter 3.12; 1 John 5.14-15
Christ's Return—John 14.2-3; Acts 1.11; 1 Thessalonians 4.16-17; Revelation 1.7

GOD'S PROMISE WHEN YOU:

Feel Guilty—Romans 8.1-2; 1 Corinthians 6.11; Ephesians 3.12; Hebrews 10.22-23
Feel Dejected—Matthew 11.28-30; Romans 8.26-27; Hebrews 4.16; James 4.8,10
Are Disappointed—Matthew 19.25-26; Mark 9.21-24; John 15.7; Ephesians 3.20
Are Persecuted—Matthew 5.10-12; 2 Corinthians 4.8-12; 2 Timothy 1.11-12; 1 Peter
 3.13-14
Are Anxious—Matthew 6.25; Matthew 11.28-29; Philippians 4.6-7; 1 Peter 5.7
Are Sick—Matthew 8.16-17; John 16.33; Romans 8.37-39; James 5.14-15
Are Impatient—Romans 2.7; 1 Timothy 1.16; Hebrews 6.12; 1 Peter 3.9
Are Confused—John 8.12; John 14.27; 1 Corinthians 2.15-16; James 1.5
Are Tempted—1 Corinthians 10.13; Hebrews 2.18; Hebrews 4.15-16; 1 Peter 5.8-10
Are Weak—Romans 8.26; 1 Corinthians 1.7-9; 2 Corinthians 4.7-9; 2 Corinthians
 12.9-10
Are Afraid—Romans 8.37-39; 2 Corinthians 1.10; 2 Timothy 1.7; Hebrews 13.6
Obey—Matthew 16.27; John 8.31-32; John 14.21, 23; James 1.25
Are In Need—John 6.35; 2 Corinthians 9.10-11; Ephesians 3.20-21; Philippians 4.19
Grieve—Matthew 5.4; John 16.20-22; 1 Thessalonians 4.13-14; Revelation 21.3-4
Suffer—John 16.33; Romans 8.16-17; 1 Peter 2.20-21; 1 Peter 4.12-13
Fail—Romans 3.23-24; Romans 5.8; Hebrews 10.36; 1 John 1.8-9
Doubt—John 3.18; John 11.25-26; Romans 4.5; 1 John 4.15-16

PERSPECTIVES FROM THE BIBLE

WHAT THE BIBLE SAYS ABOUT:

Adultery—Matthew 5.27-32; Galatians 5.13-26; Ephesians 4.17–5.3
Ambition—Matthew 16.21-27; Mark 9.33-37; Mark 10.35-45; Philippians 2.1-4
Anger—Matthew 5.21-26; Ephesians 4.25–5.2; James 1.19-27
Anxiety—Luke 12.22-34; Philippians 4.4-9; Hebrews 13.5-6
Atonement—Romans 3.21-26; 2 Corinthians 5.14-21; Hebrews 9; 1 Peter 2.22-25
Baptism—Matthew 3.1-12; Matthew 28.16-20; Romans 6.1-5
Bible Reading—2 Timothy 3.14-17; Hebrews 4.12; James 1.19-27
Blood of Christ—Matthew 26.27-29; Hebrews 9.11-28
Body of Christ—Mark 14.22-24; 1 Corinthians 12.12-31; Hebrews 2.14-18
Celibacy—Matthew 19.4-12; 1 Corinthians 7.32-40; 1 Timothy 4.1-5
Children—Matthew 18.1-9; Mark 10.13-16; Ephesians 6.1-4
Compassion—John 11.17-44; 2 Corinthians 1.3-7; 1 John 3.11-24
Conversion—John 3.1-21; 2 Corinthians 5.17-19; Ephesians 2.1-10
Creation—Romans 1.18-23; Romans 8.18-27; Colossians 1.15-17
Cross—Mark 8.31–9.1; Luke 23.26-49
Death—John 12.23-26; Romans 6.1-23; 1 Corinthians 15
Discipleship—Luke 14.25-34; John 15.1-17; John 21.15-19
Discipline—1 Corinthians 11.27-32; Hebrews 12.1-13; Revelation 3.19
Divorce—Matthew 19.1-12; Mark 10.2-12; 1 Corinthians 7.10-16
Eternal Life—Matthew 19.16-30; John 3.1-21; Romans 6.15-23
Faith—Matthew 6.25-34; Romans 3.21–5.11; Hebrews 11
Freedom—John 8.31-41; Romans 8.1-17; Galatians 4.21–5.26
Friendship—John 14.23–15.17; Colossians 3.12-17; 1 John 1.1-7
Giving—Matthew 6.1-4; 2 Corinthians 8–9
Grace—Luke 15.11-31; Romans 5; Ephesians 2
Greed—Luke 12.13-21; 1 Timothy 6.3-10; James 5.1-6
Happiness—Matthew 5.1-12; John 13.1-17; Philippians 4.4-9
Heaven—Matthew 6.19-24; Matthew 25.31-46; Philippians 3.12–4.1
Holy Spirit—John 14.15-31; John 16.5-16; Acts 2; Romans 8.1-17
Homosexuality—Romans 1.18-32; 1 Corinthians 6.9-11; 1 Timothy 1.9-11
Hope—Romans 5.1-11; Colossians 1.3-27; 1 Peter 1.3-9
Hospitality—Luke 14.12-14; Romans 12.13; 1 Peter 4.9
Hypocrisy—Matthew 6.1-24; Matthew 23; James 1.22-27
Joy—Luke 15; James 1.2-18; 1 Peter 4.12-19
Justification—Romans 3.21-31; Romans 4.1–5.11; Galatians 2.15-21
Loneliness—Matthew 26.36-46; 2 Timothy 4.16-18
Lord's Supper—Luke 22.7-23; John 13; 1 Corinthians 11.17-34
Love—Mark 12.28-34; 1 Corinthians 13; 1 John 4.7-21
Marriage—Matthew 19.1-12; 1 Corinthians 7; Ephesians 5.22-33
Peace—John 14.25-27; Romans 5.1-11; Ephesians 2.14-18; Philippians 4.4-9
Poor—Matthew 25.31-46; Luke 1.39-56; James 2.1-13
Profanity—Ephesians 4.29-32; James 3.1-12
Reconciliation—Matthew 5.23-26; 2 Corinthians 5.11–6.2; Ephesians 2.11-22
Repentance—Matthew 4.12-17; Luke 18.9-14; Acts 2.38-41
Resurrection—Matthew 27.57–28.20; 1 Corinthians 15
Revenge—Matthew 5.38-47; Romans 12.17-21
Reward—Matthew 5.3-12; Mark 10.29-31; 1 Corinthians 3.10-15
Salvation—Luke 19.1-10; Acts 16.16-34; Ephesians 2.1-10
Sanctification—2 Corinthians 7.1; 1 Thessalonians 5.23; 2 Peter 1.3-11

Second Coming—Matthew 24; John 14.1-4; 1 Corinthians 15.12-28; 1 Thessalonians 4.13–5.11
Stewardship—Matthew 25.14-30; Luke 12.35-48
Suffering—Romans 8.12-17; 1 Peter 3.8-22; 1 Peter 4.12-19
Unity—John 17; Ephesians 4.1-16

WHAT TO READ WHEN:

The Future Seems Hopeless—1 Corinthians 15.20-28; 1 Peter 1.1-9; 1 Peter 5.10-11; Revelation 11.15-19

Seeking God's Direction—Romans 12.1-3; Ephesians 5.15-17; Colossians 1.9-14; James 1.5-8

You Need Comfort—2 Corinthians 1.3-7; 2 Corinthians 7.6-13

Others Disagree With You—Matthew 7.1-5; Romans 12.9-21; Romans 14.1–15.7; 2 Corinthians 5.11-21

The World Seems Enticing—2 Corinthians 6.14–7.1; James 1.26-27; James 4.4-10; 1 John 2.15-17

You Need Assurance of Salvation—John 3.14-21; John 11.25-26; Acts 16.31-34; 1 John 5.9-13

Others Have Sinned Against You—Matthew 6.14-15; Matthew 18.21-35; Colossians 3.12-14; James 2.12-13

You Are Tempted to be Bitter—1 Corinthians 13; Ephesians 4.29–5.2; Hebrews 12.14-15

You Are Tempted to Neglect Public Worship—Acts 2.42-47; Hebrews 10.19-25

Your Faith Needs Strengthening—Romans 5.1-11; 1 Corinthians 9.24-27; Hebrews 10.19-25,35-39; Hebrews 11.1–12.13

You Need to Control Your Tongue—Matthew 15.1-20; James 3.1-12

You Are Prone to Judge Others—Matthew 7.1-5; 1 Corinthians 4.1-5; James 2.1-13; James 4.11-12

You Have Been Cheated—Matthew 18.15-17; 1 Corinthians 6.1-8; James 5.1-8

Things Are Going Well—Luke 12.13-21; 1 Timothy 6.3-19; Hebrews 13.5; James 2.1-17

You Wonder About Your Spiritual Gifts—Romans 12.3-8; 1 Corinthians 1.4-9; 1 Corinthians 12.1–14.25; 1 Peter 4.7-11

You Are Starting a New Job—Matthew 5.13-16; Romans 12.1-2; Galatians 5.13-26; Ephesians 1.3-14

You Are in a Position of Responsibility—Mark 10.35-45; Luke 7.1-10; 1 Corinthians 16.13-14; Galatians 6.9-10

You Are Establishing a New Home—Ephesians 5.22–6.4; Colossians 3.18-21; 1 Peter 3.1-7

You Have Been Quarreling—1 Corinthians 3; Ephesians 4.1-6, 4.15–5.2; 2 Timothy 2.14-26; James 4.1-12

You Are Challenged by Dark Forces—Romans 8.38-39; 2 Corinthians 4.7-18; Ephesians 6.10-18; 2 Timothy 4.6-7

You Are Jealous—Galatians 5.13-15,19-21; James 3.13-18

You Struggle With Laziness—Ephesians 5.15-16; Philippians 2.12-13; 1 Thessalonians 4.1-12; 2 Thessalonians 3.6-15

You Struggle With Lust—Matthew 5.27-30; Romans 7.7-25; Romans 13.8-14; James 1.13-18

You Are Angry—Matthew 5.21-22; Matthew 18.21-35; Ephesians 4.25–5.2; James 1.19-21

You Desire Revenge—Matthew 5.38-42; Romans 12.17-21; 1 Thessalonians 5.12-15; 1 Peter 3.8-14

You Are Proud—Matthew 25.34-40; Mark 10.35-45; Romans 12.3; Philippians 2.1-11

You Struggle With Addiction—Romans 6.1-23; Romans 12.1-2; 1 Corinthians 6.12-20; Philippians 3.17–4.1

You Are Greedy—Luke 12.13-21; 2 Corinthians 9.6-15; Ephesians 5.3-7; 1 John 3.16-18

You Desire to Learn How to Pray—Matthew 6.5-15; Mark 11.22-25; Luke 18.9-14; Philippians 4.4-7

You Struggle With Apathy—Matthew 25.1-13; Luke 12.35-48; 1 Thessalonians 5.1-11; Revelation 3.1-6,14-22

CONCORDANCE

NEW
REVISED
STANDARD
VERSION

CONCORDANCE

INTRODUCTION TO THE
NEW REVISED STANDARD VERSION
CONCORDANCE

This concordance to the New Revised Standard Version of the Bible began with the one found in the RSV Harper Study Bible. Each verse used in that earlier concordance was examined for changes that scholars made in the NRSV text, and these changes have been incorporated in this concordance.

The RSV Harper Study Bible concordance was the product of extensive research. Incorporated into it were (a) Bible verses relating to approximately three hundred carefully selected doctrinal and practical topics (such as *grace*, *justify*, *redemption*, *faith*, *hope*, *love*, etc.), and (b) the favorite Bible verses and golden texts from several Sunday School curriculum courses. In other words, almost any verse that the average user might want to look up should be found within this concordance.

Note the following features of this concordance:

1. For each verse quoted, an italicized single letter is used to designate the word entry.

2. The texts chosen for each word entry have been placed in Bible book order.

3. Occasionally the verses under a word entry contain different forms of that entry (for example, under the word ABIDE, they contain "abide," "abides," or "abode"); the alternative forms have been placed in parentheses after the key word entry. The context given in each verse will clue the reader which form of the word entry fits the italicized letter.

4. Many Bible names have been placed in a paragraph style, giving the most important references to events in that person's life.

5. Sometimes a verse is taken from a footnote reading rather than the main text of the NRSV. When this is the case, the verse reference has an "n" after it.

A concordance of this type is naturally limited and cannot be expected to meet the needs of every user. Nevertheless, in the extent of coverage, relevance of inclusion, and objectivity of selection, it should prove to be a valuable tool for Bible reading, study, and comprehension.

AARON

Brother of Moses, Ex 4.14; 7.1; commended for his eloquence, Ex 4.14; chosen to assist Moses, Ex 4.16,27-28; co-leader with Moses, Ex 5.1; 8.25; supported Moses' arms, Ex 17.12; set apart as priest, Ex 28; Heb 5.4; made a golden calf, Ex 32; Acts 7.40-41; found fault with Moses, Num 12; his rod budded, Num 17; Heb 9.4; with Moses disobedient at Meribah, Num 20.10-53; died on Mount Hor, Num 20.26-29.

ABANDON (ABANDONED)

Deut	4.31	a merciful God, he will neither *a* you
	29.25	they *a* the covenant of the LORD, the
	32.15	He *a* God who made him, and scoffed
2 Kings	22.17	Because they have *a* me and have made
2 Chr	12. 1	he *a* the law of the LORD, he and all
	13.10	the LORD is our God, and we have not *a*
Ps	37.33	The LORD will not *a* them to their
Isa	54. 7	For a brief moment I *a* you, but with
Jer	22. 9	"Because they *a* the covenant of the
Acts	2.27	you will not *a* my soul to Hades, or let
Rev	2. 4	you, that you have *a* the love you had

ABASE

Job	40.11	look on all who are proud, and *a* them.
Ezek	21.26	that which is low, *a* that which is high.

ABEL

Gen	4. 2	Now *A* was a keeper of sheep, and Cain
	4. 8	Cain said to his brother *A*, "Let us go
	4.25	for me another child instead of *A*,
Mt	23.35	from the blood of righteous *A* to the
Heb	11. 4	By faith *A* offered to God a more
	12.24	a better word than the blood of *A*.

ABHOR

Job	19.19	All my intimate friends *a* me, and those
	30.10	They *a* me, they keep aloof from me;

ABHORRENT

Deut	12.31	every *a* thing that the LORD hates
	17. 1	for that is *a* to the LORD your God.
1 Sam	27.12	"He has made himself utterly *a* to his

ABIATHAR

1 Sam	22.20	Ahitub, *A*, escaped and fled after David.
	23. 6	When *A* ... fled to David at Keilah, he

1 Sam	30. 7 David said to the priest *A* son of
2 Sam	15.29 So Zadok and *A* carried the ark of God
	20.25 was secretary; Zadok and *A* were priests;
Mk	2.26 when *A* was high priest, and ate the

ABIDE (ABIDES ABODE)

Gen	6. 3 My spirit shall not *a* in mortals forever,
Ps	15. 1 O LORD, who may *a* in your tent? Who
	68.16 at the mount that God desired for his *a*,
	91. 1 who *a* in the shadow of the Almighty,
Prov	3.33 but he blesses the *a* of the righteous.
Hag	2. 5 My spirit *a* among you; do not fear. For
Jn	15. 4 *A* in me, as I *a* in you. Just as the
1 Cor	13.13 So faith, hope, and love *a*, these three;
1 Jn	2.24 *a* in you, then you will *a* in the Son
	3. 6 No one who *a* in him sins; no one who
2 Jn	2 because of the truth that *a* in us and

ABILITY

Ex	31. 3 I have filled him . . . with *a*,
Mt	25.15 another one, to each according to his *a*.

ABIMELECH

Gen	20. 2 King *A* of Gerar sent and took Sarah.

ABISHAI

Sought to kill Saul, 1 Sam 26.5-9; pursued Abner, 2 Sam 2.18,24; desired to kill Shimei, 2 Sam 16.9-11; 19.21; one of David's key warriors, 2 Sam 23.18-19; slew the Edomites, 1 Chr 18.12.

ABLE

Num	13.30 it, for we are well *a* to overcome it."
	14.16 is because the LORD was not *a* to bring
Josh	23. 9 no one has been *a* to withstand you to
1 Sam	6.20 "Who is *a* to stand before the LORD, this
2 Chr	25. 9 "The LORD is *a* to give you much more
Dan	3.17 is *a* to deliver us from the furnace of
	6.20 been *a* to deliver you from the lions?
Mt	3. 9 God is *a* from these stones to raise up
	9.28 "Do you believe that I am *a* to do this?"
	20.22 Are you *a* to drink the cup that I am
Lk	12.26 you are not *a* to do so small a thing
2 Cor	9. 8 And God is *a* to provide you with every
Eph	3.20 within us is *a* to accomplish abundantly
Heb	2.18 suffered, he is *a* to help those who are

ABNER

Captain of Saul's host, 1 Sam 14.50; made Ish-bosheth king, 2 Sam 2.8-11; fought David's forces, 2 Sam 2.12-32; made a league with David, 2 Sam 3.6-21; slain by Joab, 2 Sam 3.22-30; mourned by David, 2 Sam 3.31-39.

ABOLISH (ABOLISHED)

Hos	2.18 I will *a* the bow, the sword, and war
2 Tim	1.10 Jesus, who *a* death and brought life and

ABOMINABLE

Ps	14. 1 They are corrupt, they do *a* deeds; there

ABOMINATION (ABOMINATIONS)

Lev	18.30 my charge not to commit any of these *a*
Prov	6.16 seven that are an *a* to him: haughty
	11. 1 A false balance is an *a* to the LORD, but
	17.15 are both alike an *a* to the LORD.
	20.23 Differing weights are an *a* to the LORD,
	28. 9 to the law, even one's prayer are an *a*.
Isa	1.13 offerings is futile; incense is an *a* to me.
Ezek	8. 9 "Go in, and see the vile *a* that they are
	11.18 it all its detestable things and all its *a*.
	16. 2 make known to Jerusalem her *a*,
Dan	9.27 in their place shall be an *a* that
	11.31 and set up the *a* that makes desolate.
Mal	2.11 *a* has been committed in Israel and in
Rev	17. 4 a golden cup full of *a* and the

ABOUND (ABOUNDED ABOUNDS)

Ps	72. 7 may righteousness flourish and peace *a*,
Prov	28.20 The faithful will *a* with blessings, but

Rom	3. 7 God's truthfulness *a* to his glory,
	5.20 where sin increased, grace *a* all the

ABRAHAM

Born, Gen 11.26; married Sarai, Gen 11.29; migrated from Ur to Haran, Gen 11.31; called by God, Gen 12.1-5; Heb 11.8; went to Egypt, Gen 12.10-20; separated from Lot, Gen 13.7-11; rescued Lot, Gen 14.13-16; God's covenant with him, Gen 15.18; 17.1-21; Ishmael is born to him, Gen 16.15-16; entertained angels, Gen 18.1-21; interceded for Sodom, Gen 18.22-33; banished Hagar and Ishmael, Gen 21.9-21; offered up Isaac, Gen 22.1-14; buried Sarah, Gen 23; married Keturah, Gen 25.1; death and burial, Gen 25.8-10.

Gen	17. 5 your name shall be *A*; for I have made
	20. 1 *A* journeyed toward . . . the Negeb,
	22. 1 God tested *A*. He said to him, "*A*!" And
Mt	3. 9 'We have *A* as our ancestor'; for I tell
Lk	16.22 carried away by the angels to be with *A*.
Jn	8.58 truly, I tell you, before *A* was, I am."
Heb	11. 8 By faith *A* obeyed when he was called

ABSALOM

Third son of David, 2 Sam 3.3; avenged Tamar and fled, 2 Sam 13.20-39; returned to Jerusalem, 2 Sam 14.23-33; conspired against David, 2 Sam 15.1-12; slain by Joab, 2 Sam 18.9-17; mourned by David, 2 Sam 18.33.

ABSENT

1 Cor	5. 3 though *a* in body, I am present in spirit;
Col	2. 5 though I am *a* in body, yet I am with

ABSTAIN

Acts	15.20 write to them to *a* only from things
1 Thess	5.22 what is good; *a* from every form of evil.

ABUNDANCE

Ps	37.16 one has than the *a* of many wicked.
	105. 40 and gave them food from heaven in *a*.
Mt	12.34 For out of the *a* of the heart the mouth
Mk	12.15 life does not consist in the *a* of
Lk	21. 4 have contributed out of their *a*, but she
2 Cor	9. 8 to provide you with every blessing in *a*,

ABUNDANT (ABUNDANTLY)

Gen	30.30 before I came, and it has increased *a*;
Jn	10.10 that they may have life, and have it *a*.
2 Cor	8. 2 their *a* joy and their extreme poverty

ABUSE

Ex	22.22 You shall not *a* any widow or orphan.

ACCEPT (ACCEPTED)

Gen	4. 7 If you do well, will you not be *a*? But if
Deut	33.11 substance, and *a* the work of his hands;
2 Kings	5.26 Is this a time to *a* money and to *a*
Job	42. 8 I will *a* his prayer not to deal with you
Prov	2. 1 child, if you *a* my words and treasure
Jer	14.12 and grain offering, I do not *a* them;
Ezek	43.27 offerings of well-being; and I will *a* you,
Hos	14. 2 away all guilt; *a* that which is good,
Am	5.22 and grain offerings, I will not *a* them;
Mt	19.12 of heaven. Let anyone *a* this who can.
Lk	4.24 no prophet is *a* in the prophet's
Jn	5.43 my Father's name and you do not *a* me;
Acts	22.18 they will not *a* your testimony about
1 Pet	2.13 For the Lord's sake *a* the authority of
	3. 1 *a* the authority of your husbands, so

ACCEPTABLE

Lev	22.20 a blemish, for it will not be *a* for you.
2 Cor	6. 2 "At an *a* time I have listened to you,

ACCESS

Rom	5. 2 through whom we have obtained *a* to
Eph	2.18 him both of us have *a* in one Spirit
	3.12 in whom we have *a* to God in boldness

ACCORD

Zeph	3.	9 of the LORD and serve him with one *a*.
Acts	8.	6 with one *a* listened eagerly to what was

ACCOUNT (ACCOUNTS ACCOUNTING)

Mt	1.	1 An *a* of the genealogy of Jesus the
	12.	36 you will have to give an *a* for every
	18.	23 who wished to settle *a* with his slaves.
Lk	16.	2 Give me an *a* of your management,
Philem		18 owes you anything, charge that to my *a*.

ACCOUNTABLE

Rom	14.	12 So then, each of us will be *a* to God.

ACCURSED

Isa	65.	20 short of a hundred will be considered *a*.
Jer	48.	10 *A* is the one who is slack in doing the
Rom	9.	3 For I could wish that I myself were *a*
1 Cor	16.	22 Let anyone be *a* who has no love for
Gal	1.	8 to what you received, let that one be *a*!

ACCUSATION (ACCUSATIONS)

Mt	27.	13 how many *a* they make against you?"
Lk	23.	4 crowds, "I find no basis for an *a* against
Jn	18.	29 them and said, "What *a* do you bring

ACCUSE (ACCUSED)

Jer	2.	9 *a* you, and I *a* your children's children.
Hos	4.	4 Yet let no one contend, and let none *a*,
Zech	3.	1 standing at his right hand to *a* him.
Mt	12.	10 the sabbath?" so that they might *a* him.
	27.	12 when he was *a* by the chief priests and
Mk	15.	3 the chief priests *a* him of many things.
Acts	23.	28 charge for which they had *a* him, I had

ACCUSER

Mt	5.	25 Come to terms quickly with your *a*
Lk	12.	58 when you go with your *a* before the

ACHAIA

Acts	18.	12 Gallio was proconsul of *A*, the Jews
	19.	21 Spirit to go through Macedonia and *A*,
Rom	15.	26 Macedonia and *A* have been pleased to
2 Cor	9.	2 saying that *A* has been ready since last
1 Thess	1.	7 all the believers in Macedonia and in *A*.

ACKNOWLEDGE (ACKNOWLEDGED ACKNOWLEDGES)

Deut	4.	35 that you would *a* that the LORD is God;
	4.	39 So *a* today and take to heart that the
Job	40.	14 Then I will also *a* to you that your own
Ps	32.	5 Then I *a* my sin to you , and I did not
Prov	3.	6 In all your ways *a* him, and he will
Jer	3.	13 Only *a* your guilt, that you have
	14.	20 We *a* our wickedness, O LORD, the
Dan	11.	39 who *a* him he shall make more wealthy,
Hos	5.	15 until they *a* their guilt and seek my
Mt	10.	32 who *a* me before others, I will also *a*
Lk	12.	8 who *a* me before others, the Son of

ACQUIRED

Ex	15.	16 until the people whom you *a* passed by.
Ruth	4.	9 I have *a* from the hand of Naomi all
	4.	10 I have *a* Ruth the Moabite . . . to be my
Eccl	1.	16 "I have *a* great wisdom, surpassing all

ACQUIT (ACQUITTED)

Deut	5.	11 not *a* anyone who misuses his name.
Isa	5.	23 who *a* the guilty for a bribe, and deprive
1 Cor	4.	4 against myself, but I am not thereby *a*.

ACQUITTAL

Ps	69.	27 guilt; may they have no *a* from you.

ACT (ACTED ACTING ACTS)

Ps	119.	126 It is time for the LORD to *a*, for your law
Jer	22.	3 Thus says the LORD: *A* with justice and
Ezek	20.	14 But I *a* for the sake of my name, so
Mic	3.	4 time, because they have *a* wickedly.

Lk	6.	47 to me, hears my words and *a* on them.
2 Cor	10.	2 to oppose those who think we are *a*
Jas	2.	12 so *a* as those who are to be judged by

ACTION (ACTIONS)

1 Sam	2.	3 knowledge, and by him *a* are weighed.
Dan	11.	32 their God shall stand firm and take *a*.
1 Jn	3.	18 in word or speech, but in truth and *a*.

ACTIVATES

1 Cor	12.	6 is the the same God who *a* all of them

ACTS (n)

Ps	103.	7 to Moses, his *a* to the people of Israel.
Prov	20.	11 make themselves known by their *a*,

ADAM

Gen	3.	21 God made garments of skins for *A* and
	5.	1 This is a list of the descendants of *A*.
	5.	3 When *A* had lived one hundred thirty
Lk	3.	38 Enos, son of Seth, son of *A*, son of God.
Rom	5.	14 death exercised dominion from *A* to
1 Cor	15.	22 as all die in *A*, so all will be made alive
	15.	45 "The first man, *A*, became a living
1 Tim	2.	13 For *A* was formed first, then Eve; and *A*

ADD (ADDED ADDS)

Gen	30.	24 "May the LORD *a* to me another son!"
Deut	4.	2 You must neither *a* anything to what I
	12.	32 I command you; do not *a* to it
Prov	30.	6 Do not *a* to his words, or else he will
Heb	2.	4 God *a* his testimony by signs and
Rev	22.	18 this book: if any one *a* to them, God

ADMIRED

Esth	2.	15 Now Esther was *a* by all who saw her.

ADMITTED

Deut	23.	1 is cut off shall be *a* to the assembly

ADMONISH

1 Cor	4.	14 ashamed, but to *a* you as my beloved
1 Thess	5.	14 we urge you, beloved to *a* the idlers,

ADMONITION

Prov	15.	31 The ear that heeds wholesome *a* will

ADOPTION

Rom	8.	23 groan inwardly while we wait for *a* , the
	8.	15 fear, but you have received a spirit of *a*.
	9.	4 Israelites, and to them belong the *a*, the
Gal	4.	5 so that we might receive *a* as children.

ADORNED

Prov	14.	18 The simple are *a* with folly, but the
Rev	21.	2 prepared as a bride *a* for her husband.

ADULTERERS

Hos	7.	4 They are all *a*; they are like a heated
Mal	3.	5 against the sorcerers, against the *a*,
Jas	4.	4 *A*! Do you not know that friendship

ADULTERESS

Hos	3.	1 a woman who has a lover and is an *a*,
Rom	7.	3 an *a* if she lives with another man

ADULTERY (ADULTERIES)

Ex	20.	14 You shall not commit *a*.
Lev	20.	10 If a man commits *a* with a wife of his
Deut	5.	18 Neither shall you commit *a*.
Prov	6.	32 But he who commits *a* has no sense; he
Jer	3.	8 for all the *a* of that faithless one, Israel,
	5.	7 I fed them to the full, they committed *a*
	13.	27 your abominations, your *a* and your
Mt	5.	27 it was said, 'You shall not commit *a*.'
	5.	28 committed *a* with her in his heart.
	19.	9 and marries another, commits *a*.
Mk	7.	21 come fornication, theft, murder, *a*,
	10.	11 marries another, commits *a* against her;
Lk	16.	18 his wife and marries another commits *a*,

Jn	8. 3 a woman who had been caught in *a*;
2 Pet	2.14 They have eyes full of *a*, insatiable for

ADVANCE (ADVANCED)

Esth	2. 9 and *a* her and her maids to the best
Acts	12.24 But the word of God continued to *a* and

ADVANTAGE

Job	35. 3 If you ask, "What *a* have I? How am I
Eccl	3.19 humans have no *a* over the animals; for
	5. 9 this is an *a* for a land: a king for a
	7.11 an *a* to those who see the sun.
Rom	3. 1 Then what *a* has the Jew? Or what is
1 Cor	10.33 everything I do, not seeking my own *a*,

ADVERSARY (ADVERSARIES)

Ezra	4. 1 When the *a* of Judah and Benjamin
Ps	27.12 Do not give me up to the will of my *a*;
Am	3. 1 An *a* shall surround the land, and strip

ADVERSITY

Ps	10. 6 all generations we shall not meet *a*."
Prov	24.10 If you faint in the day of *a*, your
Isa	48.10 I have tested you in the furnace of *a*.

ADVICE

Num	31.16 These women here, on Balaam's *a*,
1 Kings	12. 8 But he disregarded the *a* that the older
2 Chr	10. 8 he rejected the *a* that the older men
Ps	1. 1 who do not follow the *a* of the wicked,
Prov	8.14 I have good *a* and sound wisdom; I have
	12. 5 just; the *a* of the wicked is treacherous.
	19.20 Listen to *a* and accept instruction, that
Eccl	4.13 foolish king, who will no longer take *a*.
2 Cor	8.10 in this matter I am giving my *a*: it is

ADVOCATE

Jn	14.16 and he will give you another *A*, to be
	15.26 "When the *A* comes, whom I will send
	16. 7 go away, the *A* will not come to you;
1 Jn	2. 1 we have an *a* with the Father, Jesus

AFFLICT (AFFLICTED)

Deut	28.27 Lord will *a* you with the boils of Egypt,
Job	34.28 to him, and he heard the cry of the *a*—
	36. 6 wicked alive, but gives the *a* their right.
Ps	9.12 he does not forget the cry of the *a*.
	34. 2 in the Lord; let the *a* hear and be glad.
	94. 5 people, O Lord, and *a* your heritage.
Isa	53. 7 *a*, yet he did not open his mouth; like a
	58.10 hungry and satisfy the needs of the *a*,
Mic	4. 6 driven away, and those whom I have *a*.
Nah	1.12 I have *a* you, I will *a* you no more.
2 Cor	1. 6 If we are being *a*, it is for your
	4. 8 We are *a* in every way, but not crushed;

AFFLICTION (AFFLICTIONS)

Gen	16.11 for the Lord has given heed to your *a*.
	29.32 the Lord has looked upon my *a*;
	31.42 God saw my *a* and the labor of my
Deut	16. 3 the bread of *a*—because you came out
	28.59 your offspring with severe and lasting *a*
Job	30.16 within me; days of *a* have taken hold
Ps	22.24 For he did not despise or abhor the *a* of
	34.19 Many are the *a* of the righteous; but the
Isa	30.20 bread of adversity and the water of *a*,
Lam	3. 1 I am one who has seen *a* under the rod
2 Cor	1. 4 who consoles us in all our *a*, so that we
	6. 4 way: through great endurance, in *a*,
	7. 4 consolation; I am overjoyed in all our *a*.
Col	1.24 completing what is lacking in Christ's *a*
Rev	2. 9 "I know your *a* and your poverty, even

AFFORD

Lev	27. 8 to what each one making a vow can *a*.

AFRAID

Gen	3.10 I was *a*, because I was naked; and I hid
	32. 7 Then Jacob was greatly *a* and

Gen	43.18 Now the men were *a* because they were
Ex	2.14 Then Moses was *a* and thought, "Surely
	3. 6 his face, for he was *a* to look at God.
	14.13 "Do not be *a*, stand firm, and see the
Num	12. 8 Why then were you not *a* to speak
Deut	13.11 Then all Israel shall hear and be *a*, and
	17.13 All the people shall hear and be *a*, and
1 Sam	18.12 Saul was *a* of David, because the Lord
2 Sam	1.14 "Were you not *a* to lift your hand to
2 Kings	25.24 Do not be *a* because of the Chaldean
1 Chr	13.12 David was *a* of God that day; he said,
2 Chr	20. 3 Jehoshaphat was *a*; he set himself to
Ezra	4. 4 of Judah, and made them *a* to build,
Ps	3. 6 I am not *a* of ten thousands of people
	27. 1 of my life; of whom shall I be *a*?
	56. 3 when I am *a*, I put my trust in you.
	119.120 of you, and I am *a* of your judgments.
Isa	10.24 do not be *a* of the Assyrians when they
	12. 2 salvation; I will trust, and will not be *a*,
	41.10 do not be *a*, for I am your God; I will
Jer	36.24 was *a*, nor did they tear their garments.
Zeph	3.13 down, and no one shall make them *a*.
Zech	8.13 Do not be *a*, but let your hands be
Mt	1.20 do not be *a* to take Mary as your wife,
	10.31 So do not be *a*; you are of more value
	28. 5 angel said to the women, "Do not be *a*;
Mk	6.50 said, "Take heart, it is I; do not be *a*."
	11.18 to kill him; for they were *a* of him,
Lk	19.21 for I was *a* of you, because you are a
Jn	9.22 this because they were *a* of the Jews;
	12.15 "Do not be *a*, daughter of Zion. Look,
	14.27 be troubled, and do not let them be *a*.
	19. 8 when Pilate heard this, he was more *a*
Acts	9.26 disciples; and they were all *a* of him,
	27.24 'Do not be *a*, Paul; you must stand
Heb	11.23 and they were not *a* of the king's edict.

AFFRONT

Prov	17. 9 who forgives an *a* fosters friendship,

AGE (AGES)

Prov	8.23 *A* ago I was set up, at the first, before
Mt	13.40 fire, so it will be at the end of the *a*.

AGED

Job	12.12 Is wisdom with the *a*, and
	15.10 gray-haired and the *a* are on our side,
	29. 8 withdrew, and the *a* rose up and stood;

AGITATED

Mk	14.33 John, and began to be distressed and *a*

AGONY

Isa	13. 8 Pangs and *a* will seize them; they will

AGREE (AGREED)

Gen	23.16 Abraham *a* with Ephron; and Abraham
Dan	1.14 So he *a* to this proposal and tested
Mt	18.19 if two of you *a* on earth about anything
	20.13 did you not *a* with me for the usual
Mk	14.56 him, and their testimony did not *a*.
Acts	5. 9 you have *a* together to put the Spirit of
Rom	7.16 I do not want, I *a* that the law is good.

AGREEABLE

Lev	10.19 would it have been *a* to the Lord?

AGREEMENT

Isa	28.15 death, and with Sheol we have an *a*;
2 Cor	6.15 What *a* does Christ have with Belial? Or
	6.16 What *a* has the temple of God with

AGRIPPA

Acts	25.13 King *A* and Bernice arrived at Caesarea
	26. 1 *A* said to Paul, "You have permission to
	26.27 King *A*, do you believe the prophets? I

AH

Isa	5. 8 *A*, you who join house to house, who

Isa 5.11 *A*, you who rise early in the morning in

AHAB

1 Kings 16.28 in Samaria; his son *A* succeeded him.
 17. 1 Elijah . . . said to *A*, "As the LORD the
 18.17 When *A* saw Elijah, *A* said to him, "Is it
 21. 2 And *A* said to Naboth, "Give me your
 21.29 you seen how *A* has humbled himself
Jer 29.22 make you like Zedekiah and *A*, whom

AI

Gen 12. 8 tent, with Bethel on the west and *A* on
 13. 3 at the beginning, between Bethel and *A*,
Josh 7. 2 sent men from Jericho to *A*, which is
 8. 1 go up now to *A*. See, I have handed

AID

Ps 22.19 away! O my help, come quickly to my *a*!

AILMENT

Lk 13.12 "Woman, you are set free from your *a*."

AIM

2 Tim 3.10 my teaching, my conduct, my *a* in life,

ALARM (ALARMED)

Num 10. 5 When you blow an *a*, the camps on the
Ps 31.22 I had said in my *a*, "I am driven far
Mk 13. 7 wars and rumors of wars, do not be *a*;

ALERT

Lk 12.37 the master finds *a* when he comes;
 21.36 Be *a* at all times, praying that you may
1 Cor 16.13 Keep *a*, stand firm in your faith, be
Col 4. 2 yourselves to prayer, keeping *a* in it

ALEXANDRIA (ALEXANRIAN)

Acts 18.24 a Jew named Apollos, a native of *A*,
 27. 6 *A* ship bound for Italy, and put us on
 28.11 an *A* ship with the Twin Brothers as its

ALIEN (ALIENS)

Gen 12.10 down to Egypt to reside there as an *a*,
 19. 9 " This fellow came here as an *a*, and he
Ex 23. 9 You shall not oppress a resident *a*; you
Lev 19.10 shall leave them for the poor and the *a*:
 19.34 You shall love the *a* as yourself, for you
 23.22 shall leave them for the poor and the *a*:
 24.22 one law for the *a* and for the citizen;
Num 15.16 You and the *a* who resides with you
Deut 24.17 You shall not deprive a resident *a* or an
1 Chr 29.15 we are *a* and transients before you, as
Ps 39.12 I am your passing guest, an *a*, like all
 105. 23 Jacob lived as an *a* in the land of Ham.
 119. 19 I live as an *a* in the land; do not hide
Isa 1. 7 your very presence *a* devour your land;
Jer 51.51 *a* have come into the holy places of the
Zech 7.10 oppress the widow, the orphan, the *a*,
1 Pet 2.11 Beloved, I urge you as *a* and exiles to

ALIVE

Deut 4. 4 to the LORD your God are all *a* today.
Lk 15.24 son of mine was dead and is *a* again;
Acts 25.19 died, but whom Paul asserted to be *a*.
Rom 6.11 dead to sin and *a* to God in Christ
1 Cor 15.22 Adam, so all will be made *a* in Christ.
Eph 2. 5 made us *a* together with Christ—

ALL

1 Chr 29.14 For *a* things come from you, and of
1 Cor 13. 3 If I give away *a* my possessions, and if I
Heb 7.25 he is able for *a* time to save those

ALLEGORY (ALLEGORIES)

Ezek 17. 2 propound a riddle, and speak an *a* to
 20.49 saying of me, 'Is he not a maker of *a*?' "
 24. 3 And utter an *a* to the rebellious house
Gal 4.24 this is an *a*; these women are two

ALLIANCE

1 Kings 15.19 "Let there be an *a* between me and you,

ALLIED

Isa 7. 2 that Aram had *a* itself with Ephraim,

ALLOTMENT

Num 18.20 Aaron: You shall have no *a* in their

ALLY

Prov 18.19 An *a* offended is stronger than a city;

ALMIGHTY

Gen 17. 1 "I am God *A*; walk before me, and be
 48. 3 "God *A* appeared to me at Luz in the
Isa 13. 6 it will come like destruction from the *A*!
Rev 19. 6 For the Lord our God the *A* reigns.

ALMOND (ALMONDS)

Num 17. 8 produced blossoms, and bore ripe *a*.
Eccl 12. 5 the *a* tree blossoms, the grasshopper
Jer 1.11 And I said, "I see a branch of an *a* tree."

ALMS

Mt 6. 2 So whenever you give *a*, do not sound a
Lk 11.41 give for *a* those things that are within;
Acts 10. 4 your *a* have ascended as a memorial

ALONE

Gen 2.18 not good that the man should be *a*; I
Job 7.19 me for a while, let me *a* till I swallow
Lk 18.19 me good? No one is good but God *a*.
Jn 16.32 will leave me *a*. Yet I am not *a* because
Jas 2.24 is justified by works and not by faith *a*.

ALTAR (ALTARS)

Gen 8.20 Then Noah built an *a* to the LORD, and
 12. 7 So he built there an *a* to the LORD, who
 13.18 and there he built an *a* to the LORD.
 22. 9 Abraham built an *a* there and laid the
 26.25 So he built an *a* there, called on the
 33.20 There he erected an *a* and called it
 35. 1 Make an *a* there to the God who
Ex 17.15 And Moses built an *a* and called it, The
 27. 1 You shall make the *a* of acacia wood,
 30. 1 make an *a* on which to offer incense;
 38. 1 He made the *a* of burnt offering also of
Deut 7. 5 deal with them: break down their *a*,
 12. 3 Break down their *a*, smash their pillars,
 12.27 and the blood, on the *a* of the LORD
 27. 5 you shall build an *a* there to the LORD
Josh 8.30 Joshua built on Mount Ebal an *a* to the
 22.11 had built an *a* at the frontier of the
 22.23 building an *a* to turn away from
1 Sam 14.35 Saul built an *a* to the LORD; it was the
1 Kings 1.50 and went to grasp the horns of the *a*.
 18.30 he repaired the *a* of the LORD that had
2 Kings 16.10 he saw the *a* that was at Damascus.
 21. 3 he erected *a* for Baal, made a sacred
2 Chr 4. 1 He made an *a* of bronze, twenty cubits
Ps 43. 4 Then I will go to the *a* of God, to God
Isa 6. 6 coal that had been taken from the *a*
 19.19 an *a* to the LORD in the center of the
Ezek 43.13 are the dimensions of the *a* by cubits
Am 9. 1 I saw the LORD standing beside the *a*,
Mt 5.23 when you are offering your gift at the *a*,
Acts 17.23 an *a* with the inscription, 'To an
Heb 13.10 We have an *a* from which those who

AMALEK (AMALEKITES)

Ex 17.13 And Joshua defeated *A* and his people
Num 24.20 "First among the nations was *A*, but its
1 Sam 15. 2 "I will punish the *A* for what they did in
 15.32 "Bring Agag king of the *A* here to me."
1 Chr 4.43 they destroyed the remnant of the *A*

AMAZED (AMAZING)

Isa 29.14 will again do *a* things with this people,
Mt 8.10 When Jesus heard him, he was *a* and

Mt	8.27 they were *a*, saying, "What sort of man
	9.33 mute spoke; and the crowds were *a* and
	22.22 When they heard this, they were *a*; and
Mk	5.20 had done for him; and everyone was *a*.
	6. 6 And he was *a* at their unbelief. Then he
	12.17 God's." And they were utterly *a* at him.
	15. 5 no further reply, so that Pilate was *a*.
Lk	2.18 all who heard it were *a* at what the
	7. 9 When Jesus heard this he was *a* at him,
Acts	2.12 All were *a* and perplexed, saying to one
	4.13 they were *a* and they recognized them
	8.13 Philip and was *a* when he saw the signs
Rev	15. 3 "Great and *a* are your deeds, Lord God
	17. 7 angel said to me, "Why are you so *a*?

AMAZEMENT

| Gen | 43.33 the men looked at one another in *a*. |
| Mk | 5.42 At this they were overcome with *a*. |

AMBASSADOR (AMBASSADORS)

Isa	18. 2 sending *a* by the Nile in vessels of
Ezek	17.15 against him by sending *a* to Egypt,
2 Cor	5.20 So we are *a* for Christ, since God is
Eph	6.20 of the gospel, I am an *a* in chains.

AMBUSH

| Josh | 8. 9 they went to the place of *a*, and lay |
| 2 Chr | 20.22 the Lord set an *a* against the |

AMEN

Ps	41.13 from everlasting to everlasting. *A* and *A*.
1 Cor	14.16 in the position of an outsider say the "*A*"
Rev	3.14 "The words of the *A*, the faithful and

AMEND

| Jer | 7. 3 *A* your ways and your doings, and let |
| | 26.13 Now therefore *a* your ways and your |

AMMONITES

Gen	19.38 Ben-ammi; he is the ancestor of the *A*
Deut	2.19 you approach the frontier of the *A*,
1 Sam	11.11 and cut down the *A* until the heat of
2 Chr	26. 8 *A* paid tribute to Uzziah, and his fame
Isa	11.14 and Moab, and the *A* shall obey them.

AMOS

Am	1. 1 The words of *A*, who was among the
	7.10 "*A* has conspired against you in the very
	7.14 *A* answered Amaziah, "I am no prophet,
	8. 2 fruit. He said, "*A*, what do you see?"

ANATHOTH

Josh	21.18 *A* with its pasture lands, and Almon
1 Kings	2.26 "Go to *A*, to your estate; for you deserve
Isa	10.30 Listen, O Laishah! Answer her, O *A*!
Jer	1. 1 of the priests who were in *A* in the land
	29.27 have you not rebuked Jeremiah of *A*
	32. 7 "Buy my field that is at *A*, for the right

ANCESTOR (ANCESTORS)

Gen	17. 5 you the *a* of a multitude of nations.
1 Chr	5.25 transgressed against the God of their *a*,
Ps	44. 1 our *a* have told us, what deeds you
Rom	4.11 was to make him the *a* of all who

ANCESTRAL

| 1 Kings | 21. 3 that I should give you my *a* inheritance." |

ANDREW

Mt	4.18 Peter, and *A* his brother, casting a net
	10. 2 also known as Peter, and his brother *A*;
Mk	13. 3 James, John and *A* asked him privately,
Jn	1.40 speak and followed him, was *A*, Simon
	6. 8 disciples, *A*, Simon Peter's brother, said
	12.22 and told *A*; then *A* and Philip went
Acts	1.13 Peter, and John, and James, and *A*,

ANGEL

| Gen | 21.17 the *a* of God called to Hagar from |

Gen	24. 7 he will send his *a* before you, and you
Ex	23.20 I am going to send an *a* in front of you,
	33. 2 I will send an *a* before you, and I will
Num	20.16 voice, and sent an *a* and brought us out
1 Sam	29. 9 blameless in my sight as an *a* of God;
2 Sam	14.17 my lord the king is like the *a* of God,
	19.27 my lord the king is like the *a* of God;
1 Kings	13.18 an *a* spoke to me by the word of the
	19. 5 an *a* touched him, and said to him,
Dan	3.28 who has sent his *a* and delivered his
	6.22 sent his *a* and shut the lions' mouths
Hos	12. 4 He strove with the *a* and prevailed, he
Zech	1. 9 a who talked with me said to me, "I will
Lk	1.30 The *a* said to her, "Do not be afraid,
	22.43 an *a* from heaven appeared to him and
Jn	12.29 Others said, "An *a* has spoken to him."
Acts	6.15 that his face was like the face of an *a*.
	7.30 an *a* appeared to him in the wilderness
	10. 3 in which he clearly saw an *a* of God
	23. 8 there is no resurrection, or *a*, or spirit;
	27.23 stood by me an *a* of the God to whom I
2 Cor	11.14 wonder! Satan disguises himself as an *a*
Gal	1. 8 even if we or an *a* from heaven should
Rev	3. 7 to the *a* of the church in Philadelphia
	10. 1 another mighty *a* coming down from
	18.21 a mighty *a* took up a stone like a great
	19.17 I saw an *a* standing in the sun, and
	22.16 "It is I, Jesus, who sent my *a* to you

ANGELS

Gen	19. 1 The two *a* came to Sodom in the
	19.15 the *a* urged Lot, saying, "Get up, take
	28.12 the *a* of God were ascending and
	32. 1 on his way and the *a* of God met him;
Ps	78.25 Mortals ate of the bread of *a*; he sent
	91.11 he will command his *a* concerning you
	103. 20 Bless the Lord, O you his *a*, you mighty
	148. 2 Praise him, all his *a*; praise him, all his
Mt	4. 6 'He will command his *a* concerning
	4.11 suddenly *a* came and waited on him.
	13.39 end of the age, and the reapers are *a*.
	18.10 in heaven their *a* continually see the
	24.31 he will send out his *a* with a loud
Mk	1.13 wild beasts; and the *a* waited on him.
Lk	4.10 will command his *a* concerning you,
	9.26 glory of the Father and of the holy *a*.
	12. 9 others will be denied before the *a*
	15.10 joy in the presence of the *a* of God over
Jn	1.51 opened and the *a* of God ascending
	20.12 the tomb and she saw two *a* in white,
Acts	7.53 law as ordained by *a*, and yet you have
Rom	8.38 death, nor life, nor *a*, nor rulers, nor
1 Cor	4. 9 become a spectacle to the world, to *a*
	6. 3 Do you not know that we are to judge *a*
	11.10 authority on her head, because of the *a*.
	13. 1 in the tongues of mortals and of *a*,
Col	2.18 on self-abasement and worship of *a*,
Heb	2. 7 them for a little while lower than the *a*;
1 Pet	1.12 into which a long to look!
2 Pet	2. 4 if God did not spare the *a* when they
Jude	6 the *a* who did not keep their own
Rev	7. 1 I saw four *a* standing at the four corners
	9.14 "Release the four *a* who are bound at

ANGEL OF THE LORD

Gen	16. 7 The *a* found her by a spring of water in
	22.11 the *a* called to him from heaven, and
Ex	3. 2 There the *a* appeared to him in a flame
Num	22.23 The donkey saw the *a* standing in the
	22.31 of Balaam, and he saw the *a* standing
Judg	6.11 *a* came and sat under the oak at
	13. 3 the *a* appeared to the woman and said
2 Kings	1. 3 the *a* said to Elijah the Tishbite, "Get
	19.35 That very night the *a* set out and struck
1 Chr	21.16 The *a* was then standing by the
Ps	34. 7 The *a* encamps around those who fear
Isa	37.36 Then the *a* set out and struck down one

Mt	1.20 an *a* appeared to him in a dream,
	28. 2 for an *a*, descending from heaven, came
Lk	1.11 there appeared to him an *a*, standing at
	2. 9 an *a* stood before them, and the glory
Jn	5. 4 for an *a* went down at certain seasons
Acts	5.19 the night an *a* opened the prison doors,
	8.26 an *a* said to Philip, "Get up and go
	12. 7 *a* appeared and a light shone in the

ANGER (ANGERED)

Gen	27.45 until your brother's *a* against you turns
Ex	4.14 Then the *a* of the Lord was kindled
	32.19 dancing, Moses' *a* burned hot, and he
Num	11. 1 the Lord heard it and his *a* was kindled.
	12. 9 the *a* of the Lord was kindled against
	22.22 God's *a* was kindled because he was
	25. 4 in order that the fierce *a* of the Lord
	32.14 the Lord's fierce *a* against Israel!
Judg	8. 3 said this, their *a* against him subsided.
	10. 7 *a* of the Lord was kindled against Israel,
1 Sam	20.30 Then Saul's *a* was kindled against
2 Sam	24. 1 the *a* of the Lord was kindled against
1 Kings	15.30 because of the *a* to which he provoked
1 Chr	13.10 *a* of the Lord was kindled against
Ezra	5.12 because our ancestors had *a* the God
Job	20.23 God will send his fierce *a* into them,
Ps	69.24 and let your burning *a* overtake them.
	78.31 the *a* of God rose against them and he
	103. 8 and gracious, slow to *a* and abounding
	106. 32 They *a* the Lord at the waters of
Prov	14.29 is slow to *a* has great understanding,
	15.18 who are slow to *a* a calm contention.
	16.32 One who is slow to *a* is better than the
	19.12 A king's *a* is like the growling of a lion,
	20. 2 dread *a* of a king is like the growling
	21.14 A gift in secret averts *a*; and a
Eccl	7. 9 Do not be quick to *a*, for *a* lodges in
Isa	5.25 the *a* of the Lord was kindled against
	9.21 his *a* has not turned away; and his hand
	10. 5 Ah, Assyria, the rod of my *a* — the club
	42.25 poured upon him the heat of his *a* and
Jer	4. 8 "The fierce *a* of the Lord has not turned
	23.20 *a* of the Lord will not turn back until
Lam	2. 1 How the Lord in his *a* has humiliated
	2.22 and on the day of the *a* of the Lord no
Dan	9.16 let your *a* and wrath, we pray, turn
Hos	8. 5 rejected, O Samaria. My *a* burns against
	11. 9 I will not execute my fierce *a*; I will not
Nah	1. 3 The Lord is slow to *a* but great in
	1. 6 Who can endure the heat of his *a*? His
Mk	3. 5 He looked around at them with *a*, he

ANGRY

Gen	30. 2 Jacob became very *a* with Rachel and
	44.18 do not be *a* with your servant; for you
Lev	10.16 He was *a* with Eleazar and Ithamar,
Deut	1.37 Even with me the Lord was *a* on your
2 Sam	19.42 Why then are you *a* over this matter?
2 Kings	5.11 Naaman became *a* and went away,
2 Chr	16.10 Asa was *a* with the seer, and put him in
	25.15 Lord was *a* with Amaziah and sent him
Ps	4. 4 When you are *a*, do not sin; ponder it
	60. 1 defenses; you have been *a*; now restore
	112. 10 The wicked see it and are *a*; they gnash
Prov	22.14 pit; he with whom the Lord is *a* falls
	25.23 rain, and a backbiting tongue, *a* looks.
Song	1. 6 My mother's sons were *a* with me; they
Jer	3. 5 will he be *a* for ever, will he be
Jon	4. 4 Lord said, "Is it right for you to be *a*?"
Zech	1. 2 Lord was very *a* with your ancestors.
Mt	5.22 if you are *a* with a brother or sister, you
	26. 8 when the disciples saw it, they were *a*
Mk	10.41 began to be *a* with James and John.
Lk	15.28 he became *a* and refused to go in. His
Rom	10.19 with a foolish nation I will make you *a*."
Eph	4.26 Be *a* but do not sin; do not let the sun
Heb	3.10 I was *a* with that generation, and I said,

ANGUISH

Gen	42.21 not listen. That is why this *a* has come
Ps	119.143 Trouble and *a* have come upon me, but
Isa	53.11 his *a* he shall see light; he shall find
Dan	12. 1 There shall be a time of *a*, such as has
Zeph	1.15 a day of wrath, a day of distress and *a*,
Rom	2. 9 There will be *a* and distress for
Lk	22.44 in his *a* he prayed more earnestly, and

ANIMAL (ANIMALS)

Gen	1.25 God made the wild *a* of the earth of
Ex	22.19 "Whoever lies with an *a* shall be put to
Lev	11. 2 all the land *a*, these . . . you may eat.
Deut	7.22 the wild *a* would become too numerous
Job	5.23 field, and the wild *a* shall be at peace
	12. 7 ask the *a*, and they will teach you; the
Ps	49.12 pomp; they are like the *a* that perish.
	104. 20 night, when all the *a* of the forest come
Eccl	3.18 them to show that they are but *a*.
Dan	4.25 your dwelling shall be with the wild *a*.
1 Cor	15.32 hopes I fought with wild *a* at Ephesus?

ANNIHILATE

Deut	20.17 You shall *a* them — the Hittites and the

ANNOUNCED

Gal	4.13 infirmity that I first *a* the gospel to you;

ANNUL (ANNULLED)

Jn	10.35 — and the scripture cannot be *a* —
Gal	3.17 does not *a* a covenant previously

ANOINT (ANOINTED) (v)

Gen	31.13 the God of Bethel, where you *a* a pillar
Ex	28.41 and shall *a* them and ordain them and
	30.26 With it you shall *a* the tent of meeting
	30.30 You shall *a* Aaron and his sons, and
Lev	8.12 oil on Aaron's head, and *a* him, to
Ruth	3. 3 Wash and *a* yourself, and put on your
1 Sam	9.16 you shall *a* him to be ruler over my
	10. 1 "The Lord has *a* you ruler over his
	16. 3 you shall *a* for me the one whom I
	16.12 Lord said, "Rise and *a* him; for this is
1 Kings	1.39 *a* Solomon. Then they blew the
2 Kings	9. 3 says the Lord: I *a* you king over Israel.'
	11.12 proclaimed him king, and *a* him; they
1 Chr	14. 8 Philistines heard that David had been *a*
	29.22 they *a* him as Lord's prince, and Zadok
Ps	23. 5 you *a* my head with oil, my cup
	45. 7 your God, has *a* you with the oil of
	89.20 servant David; with my holy oil I have *a*
Isa	61. 1 is upon me, because the Lord has *a* me;
Dan	9.24 prophet, and to *a* a most holy place.
Mk	6.13 and *a* with oil many who were sick and
	14. 8 she has *a* my body beforehand for its
	16. 1 spices, so that they might go and *a* him.
Lk	4.18 because he has *a* me to bring good
	7.38 his feet and *a* them with the ointment.
Jn	11. 2 Mary was the one who *a* the Lord with
	12. 3 pure nard, *a* Jesus' feet and wiped them
Acts	4.27 your holy servant Jesus, whom you *a*,
	10.38 how God *a* Jesus of Nazareth with the
2 Cor	1.21 in Christ and has *a* us, by putting his
1 Jn	2.20 But you have been *a* by the Holy One,
Rev	3.18 and salve to *a* your eyes so that you

ANOINTED (ANOINTING) (n and adj)

1 Sam	2.35 go in and out before my *a* one forever.
	16. 6 "Surely the Lord's *a* is now before the
	24.10 against my lord; for he is the Lord's *a*.'
	26. 9 can raise his hand against the Lord's *a*,
	26.16 kept watch over your lord, the Lord's *a*.
2 Sam	1.14 lift your hand to destroy the Lord's *a*?"
	22.51 and shows steadfast love to his *a*, to
1 Chr	16.22 "Do not touch my *a* ones; do my
Ps	2. 2 together, against the Lord and his *a*,
	18.50 king, and shows steadfast love to his *a*,
	28. 8 people; he is the saving refuge of his *a*.

Ps	84.	9 O God; look on the face of your *a*.
	105.	15 saying, "Do not touch my *a* ones; do my
	132.	10 not turn away the face of your *a* one.
Isa	45.	1 Thus says the LORD to his *a*, to Cyrus,
Ezek	28.	14 With an *a* cherub as guardian I placed
Dan	9.	25 Jerusalem until the time of an *a* prince,
Hab	3.	13 to save your people, to save your *a*.
Zech	4.	14 the two *a* ones who stand by the Lord
1 Jn	2.	27 the *a* that you received from him abides

ANSWER (n)

Gen	41.	16 I; God will give Pharaoh a favorable *a*."
Job	32.	3 friends because they had found no *a*,
Ps	119.	42 shall have an *a* for those who taunt me,
Prov	15.	1 A soft *a* turns away wrath, but a harsh
	16.	1 the *a* of the tongue is from the LORD.
	18.	13 If one gives *a* before hearing, it is folly
Song	5.	6 him; I called him, but he gave no *a*.
Lk	23.	9 some length, but Jesus gave him no *a*.

ANSWER (ANSWERED ANSWERS)

Gen	35.	3 an altar there to the God who *a* me in
1 Sam	28.	6 of the LORD, the LORD did not *a* him,
1 Kings	18.	24 the god who *a* by fire is indeed God."
2 Kings	18.	36 king's command was, "Do not *a* him."
Job	9.	14 How then can I *a* him, choosing my
	30.	20 I cry to you and you do not *a* me; I
	31.	35 is my signature! let the Almighty *a* me!)
	33.	13 saying 'He will *a* none of my words'?
	38.	1 the LORD *a* Job out of the whirlwind:
	42.	1 Then Job *a* the LORD; "I know that you
Ps	4.	1 A me when I call, O God of my right!
	20.	1 The LORD *a* you in the day of trouble!
	27.	7 cry aloud, be gracious to me and *a* me!
	81.	7 I *a* you in the secret place of thunder; I
	91.	15 When they call to me, I will *a* them; I
Prov	1.	28 they will call upon me, but I will not *a*;
	26.	4 Do not *a* fools according to their folly,
Isa	30.	19 of your cry; when he hears it, he will *a*
	65.	24 Before they call I will *a*, while they are
Jer	7.	13 and when I called you, you did not *a*,
	33.	3 Call to me and I will *a* you, and will tell
Hos	2.	21 I will *a* the heavens and they shall *a* the
Mic	6.	3 you? In what have I wearied you? *A* me!

ANSWERABLE

1 Cor	11.	27 will be *a* for the body and blood

ANTICHRIST

1 Jn	2.	18 As you have heard that *a* is coming, so
	2.	22 This is the *a*, the who denies the Father
	4.	3 this is the spirit of the *a*, of which you
2 Jn		7 such person is the deceiver and the *a*.

ANTIOCH

Acts	11.	19 Phoenicia and Cyprus and *A*, and they
	11.	26 in *A* the disciples were first called
	13.	1 the church at *A* there were prophets
	13.	14 on from Perga and came to *A* of Pisidia.
	14.	19 Jews came there from *A* and Iconium
	14.	26 From there they sailed to *A*, where they
	15.	35 Paul and Barnabas remained in *A*, and
	18.	22 the church, and then went down to *A*.
Gal	2.	11 But when Cephas came to *A*, I opposed
2 Tim	3.	11 the things that happened to me at *A*,

ANXIETY

Prov	12.	25 *A* weighs down the human heart, but a
2 Cor	11.	28 because of my *a* for all the churches.
1 Pet	5.	7 Cast all your *a* on him, because he

ANXIOUS

1 Cor	7.	32 The unmarried man is *a* about the Lord,

APOLLOS

Acts	18.	24 came to Ephesus a Jew named *A*, a
	19.	1 While *A* was in Corinth, Paul passed
1 Cor	1.	12 "I belong to Paul," or "I belong to *A*,"

1 Cor	3.	4 to Paul," and another, "I belong to *A*,"
	16.	12 concerning our brother *A*, I strongly
Titus	3.	13 Zenas the lawyer and *A* on their way,

APOSTASIES

Jer	2.	19 punish you, and your *a* will convict you.
	14.	7 our *a* indeed are many, and we have

APOSTLE (APOSTLES)

Mk	6.	30 The *a* gathered around Jesus, and told
Lk	9.	10 On their return the *a* told Jesus all they
	22.	14 place at the table, and the *a* with him.
Acts	1.	2 through the Holy Spirit to the *a*
	11.	1 the *a* and the believers who were in
Rom	11.	13 then as I am an *a* to the Gentiles,
1 Cor	1.	1 Paul, called to be an *a* of Christ Jesus
	9.	1 Am I not free? Am I not an *a*? Have I
	12.	28 God has appointed in the church first *a*,
2 Cor	11.	5 in the least inferior to these super-*a*,
Gal	1.	1 Paul an *a* — neither sent by human
Eph	3.	5 now been revealed to his holy *a* and
	4.	11 gave were that some should be *a*, some
1 Tim	1.	1 Paul, an *a* of Christ Jesus by the
2 Tim	1.	11 I was appointed a herald and an *a*
2 Pet	3.	2 Lord and Savior spoken through your *a*.
Jude		17 remember the predictions of the *a* of
Rev	2.	2 who claim to be *a* but are not, and have
	21.	14 names of the twelve *a* of the Lamb.

APOSTLESHIP

Acts	1.	25 ministry and *a* from which Judas turned
Rom	1.	5 whom we have received grace and *a*

APPALLED

Ezra	9.	3 hair from my head and beard, and sat *a*.
Job	17.	8 The upright are *a* at this, and the
Ps	40.	15 Let those be *a* because of their shame

APPEAL (APPEALING)

Mt	26.	53 you think that I cannot *a* to my Father,
Acts	25.	11 me over to them. I *a* to the emperor."
Rom	12.	1 I *a* to you, therefore, brothers and
1 Cor	4.	16 I *a* to you, then, be imitators of me.
2 Cor	5.	20 since God making his *a* through us;
	13.	11 Put things in order, listen to my *a*,
1 Pet	3.	21 as an *a* to God for a good conscience,
2 Cor	10.	1 I myself, Paul, *a* to you by the
Philem		10 I am an *a* to you for my child, Onesimus,

APPEAR (APPEARED)

Gen	18.	1 The LORD *a* to Abraham by the oaks of
	26.	2 The LORD *a* to Isaac and said, "Do not
	48.	3 "God Almighty *a* to me at Luz in the
Ex	3.	2 There the angel of the LORD *a* to him in
	16.	10 the glory of the LORD *a* in the cloud.
	23.	17 all your males shall *a* before the Lord
Num	16.	19 the glory of the LORD *a* to the whole
Deut	31.	15 the LORD *a* at the tent in a pillar of
Judg	6.	12 angel of the LORD *a* to him and said to
2 Chr	1.	7 God *a* to Solomon, and said to him,
	7.	12 the LORD *a* to Solomon in the night and
Isa	1.	12 When you come to *a* before me, who
Jer	31.	3 the LORD *a* to him from far away. I have
Mt	24.	30 sign of the Son of Man will *a* in heaven,
Mk	16.	9n the week, he *a* first to Mary Magdalene,
Lk	9.	31 They *a* in glory and were speaking of
	19.	11 kingdom of God was to *a* immediately.
Acts	7.	2 God of glory *a* to our father Abraham
2 Cor	5.	10 all of us must *a* before the judgment
Heb	9.	24 itself, now to *a* in the presence of God
	9.	26 he has *a* once for all at the end of the
	9.	28 the sins of many, will *a* a second time,

APPEARANCE

Mt	23.	14n for the sake of *a* you make long prayers;
Mk	12.	40 and for the sake of *a* say long prayers.

APPEARING

2 Tim 4. 8 also to all who have longed for his *a*.

APPLAUD

Rom 1.32 but even *a* others who practice them.

APPLE (APPLES)

Deut 32.10 him, guarded him as the *a* of his eye.
Ps 17. 8 Guard me as the *a* of the eye; hide me
Prov 7. 2 keep my teachings as the *a* of your eye;
25.11 A word fitly spoken is like *a* of gold in a
Song 2. 3 As an *a* tree among the trees of the
Zech 2. 8 touches you touches the *a* of my eye.

APPLY

Prov 23.12 *A* your mind to instruction and your ear

APPOINT (APPOINTED)

2 Sam 7.10 I will *a* a place for my people Israel and
2 Chr 11.15 and had *a* his own priests for the high
Neh 5.14 I was *a* to be their governor in the land
Job 30.23 death, and to the house *a* for all living.
Ps 7. 6 O my God; you have *a* a judgment.
Jon 4. 6 The LORD God *a* a bush, and made it
4. 7 God *a* a worm that attacked the bush,
Mk 3.14 he *a* twelve, whom he also named
Lk 10. 1 this the Lord *a* seventy others and sent
Jn 15.16 I chose you. And I *a* you to go and bear
Acts 3.20 may send the Messiah *a* for you, that is,
2 Tim 1.11 For this gospel I was *a* a herald and an
Heb 1. 2 us by a Son, whom he *a* the heir of all

APPROACH

Jer 30.21 for who would otherwise dare to *a* me?
Ezek 42.13 where the priests who *a* the LORD shall
Heb 10.22 let us *a* with a true heart in full

APPROVAL

Rom 13. 3 what is good, and you will receive its *a*;
Heb 11. 2 by faith our ancestors received *a*.

APPROVED (APPROVING)

1 Sam 18. 5 the people, even the servants of Saul, *a*.
Eccl 9. 7 for God has long ago *a* what you do.
Acts 8. 1 Saul *a* of their killing him. That day a
22.20 I myself was standing by, *a* and keeping
2 Tim 2.15 yourself to God as one *a* by him,

AQUILA

Acts 18. 2 There he found a Jew named *A*, a
18.18 Syria, accompanied by Priscilla and *A*.
18.26 when Priscilla and *A* heard him, they
Rom 16. 3 Greet Prisca and *A*, who work with me
1 Cor 16.19 *A* and Prisca, together with the church
2 Tim 4.19 Greet Prisca and *A*, and the household

ARABIA

1 Kings 10.15 and from all the kings of *A* and the
Gal 1.17 but I went away at once into *A*; and
4.25 Hagar is Mount Sinai in *A* and

ARAM (ARAMEANS)

2 Kings 5. 1 of the army of the king of *A*,
6.23 the *A* no longer came raiding into the
Isa 7. 8 the head of *A* is Damascus, and the
Am 9. 7 from Caphtor and the *A* from Kir?

ARARAT

Gen 8. 4 ark came to rest on the mountains of *A*.

ARBITRATE

Mic 4. 3 and shall *a* between strong nations

ARCHANGEL (ARCHANGEL'S)

1 Thess 4.16 with the *a* call, and with the sound of
Jude 9 when the *a* Michael contended with the

ARGUE (ARGUED ARGUES ARGUING)

Isa 3.13 The LORD rises to *a* his case; he stands

Job 13. 3 and I desire to *a* my case with God.
40. 2 Anyone who *a* with God must respond."
Prov 25. 9 *A* your case with your neighbor directly,
Mk 9.33 "What were you *a* about on the way?"
11.31 They *a* with one another, "If we say,
Acts 9.29 He spoke and *a* with the Hellenists; but
17. 2 on three sabbath days *a* with them from
17.17 he *a* in the synagogue with the Jews
18. 4 sabbath he would *a* in the synagogue

ARGUMENT (ARGUMENTS)

2 Cor 10. 4 We destroy *a* and every proud obstacle
Col 2. 4 one may deceive you with plausable *a*.
1 Tim 2. 8 up holy hands without anger or *a*;

ARIMATHEA

Mt 27.57 came a rich man from *A*, named
Jn 19.38 things, Joseph of *A*, who was a disciple

ARISE

Num 10.35 Moses would say, "*A*, O LORD, let your
Isa 60. 1 *A*, shine; for your light has come, and

ARK

Gen 6.14 Make yourself an *a* of cypress wood;
8. 4 the *a* came to rest on the mountains of
Ex 25.10 They shall make an *a* of acacia wood;
37. 1 Bezalel made the *a* of acacia wood; it
Num 10.33 with the *a* of the covenant of the LORD
Josh 3. 3 "When you see the *a* of the covenant of
6.11 the *a* of the LORD went around the city,
Judg 20.27 (for the *a* of the covenant of God was
1 Sam 4. 3 Let us bring the *a* of the covenant of
4.11 The *a* of God was captured; and the two
5. 2 Philistines took the *a* of God and
6.13 they looked up and saw the *a*, they
6.19 when they greeted the *a* of the LORD;
14.18 to Ahijah, "Bring the *a* of God here."
2 Sam 6. 2 to bring up from there the *a* of God,
15.24 Levites, carrying the *a* of the covenant
1 Chr 13. 3 let us bring again the *a* of our God to
16. 1 They brought in the *a* of God, and set it
2 Chr 5. 4 came, and the Levites carried the *a*.
Jer 3.16 no more say, "The *a* of the covenant of
Heb 9. 4 of incense and the *a* of the covenant
Rev 11.19 *a* of his covenant was seen within his

ARM (ARMS)

2 Chr 32. 8 With him is an *a* of flesh; but with us is
Job 40. 9 Have you an *a* like God, and can you
Ps 44. 3 nor did their own *a* give them victory;
98. 1 and his holy *a* have gotten him victory;
Isa 40.10 with might, and his *a* rules for him;
Mk 9.36 them; and taking it in his *a*, he said
10.16 he took them up in his *a*, laid his
Jn 12.38 and to whom has the *a* of the Lord

ARMOR

1 Sam 17.38 Saul clothed David with his *a*; he put a
Eph 6.11 Put on the whole *a* of God, so that you

ARMY (ARMIES)

Josh 5.14 as commander of the *a* of the LORD I
2 Kings 25. 5 the *a* of the Chaldeans pursued the
1 Chr 12.22 there was a great *a*, like an *a* of God.
Ps 27. 3 Though an *a* encamp against me, my
44. 9 us, and have not gone out with our *a*.
Joel 2.25 my great *a*, which I sent against you.

AROMA

2 Cor 2.15 we are the *a* of Christ to God among

AROUSED

Jer 32.31 This city has *a* my anger and wrath,

ARRESTED

Mt 4.12 Jesus heard that John had been *a*,
Mk 1.14 after John was *a*, Jesus came to Galilee,

ARROGANCE

Jas	4.16 you boast in your *a*; all such boasting is

ARROGANT

Ps	36.11 Do not let the foot of the *a* tread on me,
	119.51 The *a* utterly deride me, but I do not
	119.78 Let the *a* be put to shame, because
Prov	16. 5 All those who are *a* are an abomination
Mal	3.15 Now we count the *a* happy; evildoers
1 Cor	4.18 am not coming to you, have become *a*,
	5. 2 And you are *a*! Should you not rather

ARROGANTLY

Dan	8.11 against the prince of the host it acted *a*;

ARROW (ARROWS)

1 Sam	20.20 I will shoot three *a* to the side of it, as
2 Kings	13.17 "The LORD's *a* of victory, the *a* of victory
Job	6. 4 For the *a* of the Almighty are in me; my
Ps	7.13 weapons, making his *a* fiery shafts.
	18.14 he sent out his *a*, and scattered them;
	38. 2 your *a* have sunk into me, and your
	45. 5 Your *a* are sharp in the heart of the
Prov	7.23 the trap until an *a* pierces its entrails,
Isa	5.28 their *a* are sharp, all their bows bent,
Ezek	5.16 deadly *a* of famine, *a* for destruction,

ARTISAN (ARTISANS)

Isa	41. 7 The *a* encourages the goldsmith, and
	44.11 and the *a* too are merely human.

ASCEND (ASCENDED ASCENDING)

Judg	13.20 angel of the LORD *a* in the flame of the
Ps	24. 3 Who shall *a* the hill of the LORD? And
	68.18 You *a* the high mount, leading captives
	139. 8 If I *a* to heaven, you are there; if I make
Prov	30. 4 Who has *a* to heaven and come down?
Isa	14.13 "I will *a* to heaven; I will raise my
Jn	3.13 No one has *a* into heaven except the
	6.62 were to see the Son of man *a* to where
	20.17 because I have not yet *a* to the Father.
Rom	10. 6 in your heart, 'Who will *a* into heaven?' "
Eph	4. 9 "He *a*," what does it mean but that he

ASHAMED

Gen	2.25 wife were both naked, and were not *a*.
Ezra	9. 6 "O my God, I am too *a* and embarrassed
Ps	25. 3 be *a* who are wantonly treacherous.
	34. 5 radiant; so your faces shall never be *a*.
Jer	6.15 yet they were not *a*, they did not know
	8.12 they were not at all *a*, they did not
	12.13 shall be *a* of their harvests because of
Mk	8.38 Those who are *a* of me and of my words
Lk	9.26 Those who are *a* of me and of my
Rom	1.16 I am not *a* of the gospel; it is the power
1 Cor	4.14 I am not writing this to make you *a*,
2 Tim	1. 8 Do not be *a*, then, of the testimony
	1.12 But I am not *a*, for I know the one in

ASHER

Gen	30.13 call me happy"; so she named him *A*.
Num	1.13 from *A*, Pagiel son of Ochran;
Deut	33.24 And of *A* he said, Most blessed of sons
Judg	5.17 *A* sat still at the coast of the sea,

ASHES

Gen	18.27 to the Lord, I who am but dust and *a*.
Job	13.12 Your maxims are proverbs of *a*, your
	30.19 and I have become like dust and *a*.

ASIA

Acts	2. 9 Judea and Cappadocia, Pontus and *A*,
	6. 9 those from Cilicia and *A*, stood up and
	16. 6 the Holy Spirit to speak the word in *A*.
	19.10 all the residents of *A*, both Jews and
	19.27 her majesty that brought all *A* and the
Rom	16. 5 was the first convert in *A* for Christ.
1 Cor	16.19 The churches of *A* send greetings.

1 Pet	1. 1 Galatia, Cappadocia, *A*, and Bithynia,
Rev	1. 4 to the seven churches that are in *A*:

ASK (ASKED ASKING)

Ex	11. 2 that every man is to *a* his neighbor
	12.35 They had *a* the Egyptians for jewelry of
1 Sam	1.20 for she said, "I have *a* him of the LORD."
1 Kings	3. 5 God said, "*A* what I should give you."
2 Chr	1. 7 said to him, "*A* what I should give you."
Ps	2. 8 *A* of me, and I will make the nations
	27. 4 One thing I *a* of the LORD, that will I
	106. 15 he gave them what they *a*, but sent a
Prov	30. 7 Two things I *a* of you; do not deny
Isa	1.12 who *a* this from your hand? Trample my
	7.11 to Ahaz, saying, *A* a sign of the LORD
	65. 1 be sought out by those who did not *a*,
Jer	50. 5 They shall *a* the way to Zion, with faces
Zech	10. 1 *A* rain from the LORD in the season of
Mt	6. 8 knows what you need before you *a* him.
	7. 7 "*A*, and it will be given you; search, and
	9.38 *a* the Lord of the harvest to send out
	21.22 Whatever you *a* for in prayer with faith,
	27.58 to Pilate and *a* for the body of Jesus;
Mk	6.22 the girl, "*A* me for whatever you wish,
	10.35 you to do for us whatever we *a* of you."
Lk	10. 2 laborers are few; therefore *a* the Lord
	11. 9 I say to you, *A*, and it will be given you;
	11.13 give the Holy Spirit to those who *a*
	23.52 to Pilate and *a* for the body of Jesus.
Jn	14.13 I will do whatever you *a* in my name, so
	14.16 And I will *a* the Father, and he will give
	15. 7 and my words abide in you, *a* for
	16.24 *A* and you will receive, so that your joy
	17. 9 I am *a* on their behalf; I am not *a* on
	17.15 world, but I *a* that you protect them
	17.20 "I *a* not only on behalf of these, but
Eph	3.20 far more than all that we *a* or
Jas	1. 5 any of you is lacking wisdom, *a* God,
	4. 2 You do not have, because you do not *a*.
1 Jn	3.22 we receive from him whatever we *a*,
	5.14 if we *a* anything according to his will,
	5.16 not a mortal sin, you will *a*, and God

ASLEEP

1 Kings	18.27 or perhaps he is *a* and must be
Mt	8.24 swamped by the waves; but he was *a*.
Mk	4.38 he was in the stern, *a* on the cushion;
	13.36 else he may find you *a* when he comes
Lk	8.23 and while they were sailing he fell *a*.
Jn	11.11 "Our friend Lazarus has fallen *a*, but I
1 Thess	5. 6 then let us not fall *a* as others do, but

ASSEMBLE (ASSEMBLED)

Gen	49. 2 *A* and hear, O sons of Jacob, listen to
Lev	8. 3 *a* the whole congregation at the
Num	1.18 they *a* the whole congregation together.
1 Kings	8. 1 Solomon *a* the elders of Israel and all
2 Chr	5. 2 Solomon *a* the elders of Israel and all
Neh	9. 1 people of Israel were *a* with fasting and
Isa	45.20 *A* yourselves and come together, draw
Ezek	11.17 and *a* you out of the countries where
	39. 1 to all the wild animals: *A* and come,
1 Cor	5. 4 When you are *a*, and my spirit is

ASSEMBLY

Lev	23.36 it is a solemn *a*; you shall not work at
1 Chr	29.20 David said to the whole *a*, "Bless the
2 Chr	23. 3 the whole *a* made a covenant with the
Ps	7. 1 Let the *a* of the peoples be gathered
	149. 1 song, his praise in the *a* of the faithful.
Joel	2.15 fast; call a solemn *a*; gather the people.
Acts	19.39 it must be settled in the regular *a*.
Heb	12.23 to the *a* of the firstborn who are
Jas	2. 2 and in fine clothes comes into your *a*,

ASSURANCE

Acts	17.31 he has given *a* to all by raising him
Heb	6.11 to realize the full *a* of hope to the very

Heb 11. 1 faith is the *a* of things hoped for, the

ASSYRIA

Gen 2.14 river is Tigris, which flows east of *A*.
2 Kings 15.29 King Tiglath-pileser of *A* came and
19.20 to me about King Sennacherib of *A*.
Isa 7.18 and for the bee that is in the land of *A*.
Hos 7.11 they call upon Egypt, they go to *A*.
14. 3 *A* shall not save us; we will not ride

ASTONISHED

2 Chr 7.21 exalted, everyone passing by will be *a*,
Dan 3.24 King Nebuchadnezzar was *a* and rose
Mt 7.28 the crowds were *a* at his teaching.

ASTOUNDED

Lk 4.32 They were *a* at his teaching, because he

ASTRAY

Ps 58. 3 The wicked go *a* from the womb; they
95.10 "They are a people whose hearts go *a*,
119. 67 Before I was humbled when I went *a*;
Isa 9.16 those who lead this people led them *a*,
Hos 4.12 a spirit of whoredom has led them *a*,
Mt 24. 5 Messiah,' and they will lead many *a*.
Mk 13. 5 "Beware that no one leads you *a*. Many
Lk 21. 8 "Beware that you are not led *a*; for

ASUNDER

Ps 2. 3 "Let us burst their bonds *a*, and cast

ATHENS (ATHENIANS)

Acts 17.15 conducted Paul brought him as far as *A*;
17.22 "*A*, I see how extremely religious you
18. 1 After this Paul left *A* and went to
1 Thess 3. 1 longer, we decided to be left alone in *A*;

ATONE (ATONED)

Prov 16. 6 loyalty and faithfulness iniquity is *a* for,
Dan 9.24 to put an end to sin, and to *a* for

ATONEMENT

Ex 29.36 shall offer a bull as a sin offering for *a*.
32.30 perhaps I can make *a* for your sin."
Lev 1. 4 shall be acceptable in your behalf as *a*
8.15 he consecrated it, to make *a* for it.
9. 7 make *a* for yourself and for the people;
14.18 priest shall make *a* on his behalf before
16.34 everlasting statute for you, to make *a*
17.11 for, as life, it is the blood that makes *a*.
23.27 of this seventh month is the day of *a*.
Num 16.46 the congregation and make *a* for them.
31.50 to make *a* for ourselves before the LORD.
2 Chr 29.24 at the altar, to make *a* for all Israel.
Ezek 45.20 so you shall make *a* for the temple.

ATTACK

Isa 7. 1 of Israel went up to *a* Jerusalem,

ATTEND

Jer 9.25 when I will *a* to all those who are

ATTENTION

Acts 18.17 But Gallio paid no *a* to these things.
27.11 centurion paid more *a* to the pilot and
Heb 2. 1 pay greater *a* to what we have heard,

ATTENTIVE

Neh 1.11 Lord, let your ear be *a* to the prayer of
Prov 4.20 My child, be *a* to my words; incline
5. 1 My child, be *a* to my wisdom; incline

ATTESTED

Acts 2.22 of Nazareth, a man *a* to you by God
Rom 3.21 been disclosed, and is *a* by the law and
Heb 11. 5 it was *a* before he was taken away that

ATTORNEY

Acts 24. 1 elders and an *a*, a certain Tertullus,

AUTHORITIES

Rom 13. 1 every person be subject to governing *a*;
Titus 3. 1 them to be be subject to rulers and *a*,

AUTHORITY

Isa 9. 6 given to us; *a* rests upon his shoulders;
22.21 I will commit your *a* to his hand, and
Mt 7.29 taught them as one having *a*, and not
8. 9 I also am a man under *a*, with soldiers
9. 6 Son of man has *a* on earth to forgive
21.23 "By what *a* are you doing these things,
28.18 "All *a* in heaven and on earth has been
Mk 1.22 he taught them as one having *a*, and
2.10 Son of Man has *a* on earth to forgive
3.15 and to have *a* to cast out demons.
11.28 "By what *a* are you doing these things?
Lk 4. 6 you I will give their glory and all this *a*;
4.36 with *a* and power he commands the
5.24 that the Son of Man has *a* on earth
10.19 I have given you *a* to tread on snakes
20. 2 by what *a* are you doing these things?
Jn 5.27 has given him *a* to execute judgment,
Acts 9.14 he has *a* from the chief priests to bind
Rom 13. 1 there is no *a* except from God, and
2 Cor 10. 8 if I boast a little too much of our *a*,
Rev 2.26 the end, I will give *a* over the nations,
12.10 of our God and the *a* of his Messiah,
13. 2 it his power and his throne and great *a*.

AVARICE

Mk 7.22 adultery, *a*, wickedness, deceit,

AVENGE (AVENGED)

2 Kings 9. 7 that I may *a* on Jezebel the blood
Isa 1.24 my enemies, and *a* myself on my foes!
Joel 3.21 I will *a* their blood, and I will not clear
Rom 12.19 never *a* yourselves, but leave room for
Rev 19. 2 and he has *a* on her the blood of his

AVENGER

Num 35.12 shall be for you a refuge from the *a*,
1 Thess 4. 6 because the Lord is an *a* in all these

AVOID

Prov 4.15 not walk in the way of evildoers. *A* it;
14.27 so that one may *a* the snares of death.
2 Tim 2.16 *A* such profane chatter, for it will lead
Titus 3. 2 of no one, to *a* quarreling, to be gentle,

AWAKE (AWAKES)

Ps 57. 8 *A*, my soul! *A*, O harp and lyre! I will *a*
73.20 They are like a dream when one *a*, an
Isa 52. 1 *A*, *a*, put on your strength, O Zion! Put
Mt 24.42 Keep *a* therefore, for you do not know
25.13 Keep *a* therefore, for you know neither
26.38 remain here, and stay *a* with me."
26.42 Stay *a* and pray that you may not come
Mk 14.34 even to death; remain here, and keep *a*."
Rev 16.15 Blessed is the one who stays *a* and is

AWAKEN

Song 8. 4 do not stir up or *a* love until it is ready!
Jn 11.11 asleep, but I am going there to *a* him."

AWARE

1 Pet 2.19 if, being *a* of God, you endure pain

AWE

Ps 33. 8 of the world stand in *a* of him.
119.161 but my heart stands in *a* of your words.
Mt 9. 8 crowds saw it, they were filled with *a*,

AX (AXES)

2 Kings 6. 5 a log, his *a* head fell into the water;
1 Chr 20. 3 to work with saws and iron picks and *a*.
Ps 74. 5 they hacked the wooden trellis with *a*.
Isa 10.15 Shall the *a* vaunt itself over the one
Mt 3.10 now the *a* is lying at the root of the
Lk 3. 9 Even now the *a* is lying at the root of

AZAZEL

Lev 16. 8 lot for the LORD and the other lot for A.

B

BAAL (BAALS)

Judg 2.13 abandoned the LORD, and worshiped *B*
 6.31 "Will you contend for *B*? Or will you
 10.13 our God and have worshiped the *B*."
1 Kings 16.31 and went and served *B*, and worshiped
2 Kings 17.16 all the host of heaven, and served *B*.
Jer 2. 8 the prophets prophesied by *B*, and went
Hos 2. 8 her silver and gold that they used for *B*.

BABEL

Gen 11. 9 Therefore it was called *B*, because there

BABES (BABIES)

Ps 8. 2 Out of the mouths of *b* and infants you
Isa 3. 4 princes, and *b* shall rule over them.
Mt 21.16 of the mouth of infants and nursing *b*

BABYLON (BABYLONIA)

2 Kings 17.24 king of Assyria brought people from *B*,
1 Chr 9. 1 Judah was taken into exile in *B* because
Ezra 1.11 were brought up from *B* to Jerusalem.
Ps 137. 1 By the rivers of *B* — there we sat down
Isa 48.20 Go out from *B*, flee from Chaldea,
Mt 1.11 at the time of the deportation to *B*.
1 Pet 5.13 Your sister church in *B*, chosen together
Rev 14. 8 fallen is *B* the great! She has made all

BACK (BACKS)

Ps 18.40 You have made my enemies turn their *b*
Isa 38.17 you have cast all my sins behind your *b*.

BACKSLIDING

Jer 8. 5 away turned away in perpetual *b*?

BALAAM

Num 22. 5 He sent messengers to *B* son of Beor at
 23. 1 Then *B* said to Balak, "Build me seven
 24. 1 Now *B* saw that it pleased the LORD to
 31. 8 they also slew *B* the son of Beor with
Mic 6. 5 what *B* the son of Beor answered him,
2 Pet 2.15 gone astray, following the road of *B*, son
Rev 2.14 who hold to the teaching of *B*, who

BALANCE (BALANCES)

Job 6. 2 and all my calamity laid in the *b*!
Prov 11. 1 A false *b* is an abomination to the LORD,
Isa 40.12 in scales and the hills in a *b*?
Ezek 5. 1 and your beard; then take *b* for
Hos 12. 7 A trader, in whose hands are false *b*, he

BALDHEAD

2 Kings 2.23 at him, saying, "Go away, *b*! Go away, *b*!"

BAND

Jer 9. 2 they are all adulterers, a *b* of traitors.

BANDIT (BANDITS)

Mk 14.48 clubs to arrest me as though I were a *b*?
 15.27 with him they crucified two *b*, one of
Jn 18.40 but Barabbas!" Now Barabbas was a *b*.
2 Cor 11.26 from rivers, danger from *b*, danger from

BANDS

Lk 2. 7 wrapped him in *b* of cloth, and laid him

BANISH

Eccl 11.10 *B* anxiety from your mind, and put away

BANQUET (BANQUETING)

Song 2. 4 He brought me to the *b* house, and his
Dan 5.10 lords, came into the *b* hall. The queen
Lk 5.29 Levi gave a great *b* for him in his house;

BAPTISM (BAPTISMS)

Mt 21.25 Did the *b* of John come from heaven, or

Mk 10.38 with the *b* that I am baptized with?"
 11.30 Did the *b* of John come from heaven, or
Lk 3. 3 proclaiming a *b* of repentance for the
 12.50 I have a *b* with which to be baptized,
 20. 4 Did the *b* of John come from heaven, or
1 Cor 15.29 do who receive *b* on behalf of the dead?
Eph 4. 5 one Lord, one faith, one *b*, one God and
Col 2.12 when you were buried with him in *b*,
Heb 6. 2 toward God, with instruction about *b*,
 9.10 only with food and drink and various *b*,
1 Pet 3.21 *b*, which this prefigured, now saves

BAPTIZE (BAPTIZED BAPTIZING)

Mt 3. 6 they were *b* by him in the river Jordan,
 3.11 "I *b* you with water for repentance, but
 28.19 *b* them in the name of the Father
Mk 16.16 The one who believes and is *b* will be
Lk 3.16 "I *b* you with water; but one who is
 7.29 justice of God, because they had been *b*
Jn 1.26 John answered them, "I *b* with water.
 3.23 John also was *b* at Aenon near Salim
 4. 1 "Jesus is making and *b* more disciples
Acts 1. 5 you will be *b* with the Holy Spirit not
 8.12 they were *b*, both men and women.
 8.38 down into the water, and Philip *b* him.
 9.18 restored. Then he got up and was *b*,
 16.15 When she and her household were *b*,
 22.16 Get up and be *b*, and have your sins
Rom 6. 3 have been *b* into Christ Jesus were *b*
1 Cor 1.13 Or were you *b* in the name of Paul?
 1.17 Christ did not send me to *b* but to
 10. 2 all were *b* into Moses in the cloud and
 12.13 Spirit we were all *b* into one body—
Gal 3.27 *b* into Christ have clothed yourselves

BAPTIZER

Mk 1. 4 John the *b* appeared in the wilderness,
 6.14 saying, "John the *b* has been raised

BARABBAS

Mt 27.21 to release for you?" And they said, "*B*."
Mk 15. 7 a man called *B* was in prison with the
 15.11 to have him release *B* for them instead.
 15.15 satisfy the crowd, released *B* for them;
Jn 18.40 in reply, "Not this man, but *B*!" Now *B*

BAREFOOT

2 Sam 15.30 with his head covered and walking *b*;
Isa 20. 3 Isaiah has walked naked and *b* for three

BARNABAS

Benevolent, Acts 4.36-37; introduced Paul to the apostles, Acts 9.26-27; preached at Antioch, Acts 11.22-24; ministered with Paul at Antioch, Acts 11.25-26; took relief offerings to Judea, Acts 11.29-30; accompanied Paul on his first missionary journey, Acts 13.1–14.28; attended the Council of Jerusalem, Acts 15.1-31; separated from Paul, Acts 15.36-41.

BARNS

Prov 3.10 then your *b* will be filled with plenty,
Mt 6.26 neither sow nor reap nor gather into *b*,
Lk 12.18 I will pull down my *b*, and build larger

BARREN

Gen 11.30 Now Sarai was *b*; she had no child.
 29.31 he opened her womb; but Rachel was *b*.
Judg 13. 2 Manoah; and his wife was *b*, having
Ps 113. 9 He gives the *b* woman a home, making
Isa 54. 1 Sing, O *b* one who did not bear; burst
Lk 1. 7 Elizabeth was *b*, and both were getting

BARRIERS

Isa 59. 2 your iniquities have been *b* between you

BARTHOLOMEW

Mt 10. 3 Philip and *B*; Thomas and Matthew the
Lk 6.14 and John, and Philip, and *B*, and
Acts 1.13 Philip and Thomas, *B* and Matthew,

BARUCH

Jer	32.12 I gave the deed of purchase to *B* son of
	36. 4 and *B* wrote on a scroll at Jeremiah's
	36.18 *B* answered them, "He dictated all these
	43. 3 but *B* son of Neraiah is inciting you
	45. 1 the prophet Jeremiah spoke to *B* son of

BASIN

| Ex | 30.18 You shall make a bronze *b* with a |
| | 38. 8 He made the bronze *b* with its stand of |

BASKET (BASKETS)

Ex	2. 3 she got a papyrus *b* for him, and
Jer	24. 1 two *b* of figs placed before the temple
Am	8. 1 GOD showed me —a *b* of summer fruit.
Mt	13.48 put the good into *b* but threw out the
	14.20 over of the broken pieces, twelve *b* full.
	15.37 the broken pieces left over, seven *b* full.
Mk	8.19 how many *b* full of broken pieces did
Acts	9.25 in the wall, lowering him in a *b*.
2 Cor	11.33 I was let down in a *b* through a window

BATHED (BATHING)

| 2 Sam | 11. 2 that he saw from the roof a woman *b*; |
| Ezek | 16. 9 Then I *b* you with water and washed off |

BATHSHEBA

Taken by David, 2 Sam 11.1-5; gave birth to Solomon, 2 Sam 12.24; interceded for Solomon's succession on the throne, 1 Kings 1.15-31; petitioned for Adonijah, 1 Kings 2.12-25.

BATTLE

Num	31. 7 They did *b* against Midian, as the LORD
1 Sam	4.16 "I have just come from the *b*; I fled
1 Kings	8.44 "If you people go out to *b* against their
2 Chr	20.15 for the *b* is not yours but God's.
1 Cor	14. 8 sound, who will get ready for *b*?
Rev	16.14 to assemble them for *b* on the great day

BEAR (BEARS) (n)

1 Sam	17.34 whenever a lion or a *b* came, and took a
2 Kings	2.24 Then two she-*b* came out of the woods
Dan	7. 5 a second one, that looked like a *b*.

BEAR (BEARS BORE) (v)

Gen	4.13 "My punishment is greater than I can *b*!
	43. 9 you, then let me *b* the blame forever.
	44.32 then I shall *b* the blame in the sight of
Ex	28.12 Aaron shall *b* their names before the
	28.30 Aaron shall *b* the judgment of the
Num	18. 1 shall *b* responsibility for the offenses
Esth	8. 6 how can I *b* to see the calamity that is
Ps	55.12 enemies who taunt me—I could *b* that;
	68.19 Blessed be the Lord, who daily *b* us up;
Isa	53.11 and he shall *b* their iniquities.
Jer	44.22 longer *b* the sight of your evil doings,
Gal	6. 2 *B* one another's burdens, and in this
1 Pet	2.24 He himself *b* our sins in his body on

BEAST

| Rev | 13.11 Then I saw another *b* that rose out of |
| | 17. 8 *b* that you saw was, and is not, and is |

BEATINGS

| Isa | 1. 5 Why do you seek further *b*? Why do you |

BEATINGS

BEAUTIFUL

Gen	12.11 that you are a woman *b* in appearance;
2 Sam	11. 2 woman bathing; the woman was very *b*.
Esth	2. 7 the girl was fair and *b*, and when her
Ps	48. 2 His holy mountain, *b* in elevation, is
Song	1. 5 I am black and *b*, O daughters of
	6. 4 you are *b* as Tirzah, my love, comely as
Isa	4. 2 day the branch of the LORD shall be *b*
Jer	13.20 flock that was given you, your *b* flock?
Ezek	16.13 You grew exceedingly *b*, fit to be a

BEAUTIFY

| Jer | 4.30 In vain you *b* yourself. Your lovers |

BEAUTY

Ps	27. 4 to behold the *b* of the LORD, and to
	45.11 house, and the king will desire your *b*.
Prov	6.25 Do not desire her *b* in your heart, and
	31.30 Charm is deceitful, and *b* is vain, but a
Ezek	27. 3 Tyre, you have said, "I am perfect in *b*."
	28.17 Your heart was proud because of your *b*;
1 Pet	3. 4 lasting *b* of a gentle and quiet spirit,

BED (BEDS)

Job	7.13 When I say, "My *b* will comfort me, my
Isa	28.20 the *b* is too short to stretch oneself on
Am	6. 4 Alas for those who lie upon *b* of ivory,
Mt	9. 6 "Stand up, take your *b* and go to your
Lk	5.19 him down with his *b* through the tiles

BEE (BEES)

Deut	1.44 out against you and chased you as *b* do.
Judg	14. 8 a swarm of *b* in the body of the lion,
Isa	7.18 for the *b* that is in the land of Assyria.

BEELZEBUL

| Mt | 12.24 "It is only by *B*, the ruler of demons, |
| Mk | 3.22 "He has *B*, and by the ruler of the |

BEER-SHEBA

Gen	21.14 wandered about in the wilderness of *B*.
	21.32 When they had made a covenant at *B*,
	22.19 together to *B*; and Abraham lived at *B*.
	46. 1 and came to *B*, he offered sacrifices to
1 Sam	3.20 all Israel from Dan to *B* knew that
1 Chr	21. 2 number Israel, from *B* to Dan, and bring
Am	5. 5 not enter into Gilgal or cross over to *B*;

BEFITS

| Ps | 33. 1 O you righteous. Praise *b* the upright. |

BEG

| Gal | 4.12 Friends, I *b* you, become as I am, for I |

BEGGAR

| Mk | 10.46 a blind *b*, was sitting by the roadside. |
| Jn | 9. 8 those who had seen him before as a *b*, |

BEGINNING

Gen	1. 1 In the *b* when God created the heavens
Ex	12. 2 shall mark for you the *b* of months;
Ps	111. 10 The fear of the LORD is the *b* of wisdom;
Prov	1. 7 The fear of the LORD is the *b* of
	4. 7 The *b* of wisdom is this: Get wisdom,
Mt	24. 8 all this is but the *b* of the birthpangs.
Mk	1. 1 The *b* of the good news of Jesus Christ,
Jn	1. 1 In the *b* was the Word, and the Word

BEGUILING

| Rev | 2.20 and is teaching and *b* my servants |

BEHAVE (BEHAVED BEHAVING)

1 Cor	3. 3 and *b* according to human inclinations?
	7.36 he is not *b* properly toward his fiancee,
2 Cor	1.12 we have *b* in the world with frankness
1 Tim	3.15 ought to *b* in the household of God,

BEHAVIOR

| 1 Sam | 21.13 he changed his *b* before them; he |

BEHEADED

| Mt | 14.10 he sent and had John *b* in the prison. |
| Mk | 6.16 it, he said, "John, whom I *b*, has been |

BEHEMOTH

| Job | 40.15 "Look at *B*, which I made just as I |

BEHOLD

Ps	17.15 As for me, I shall *b* your face in
	46. 8 Come, *b* the works of the LORD; see
	97. 6 and all the peoples *b* his glory.

BEINGS

Job	1.	6 One day the heavenly *b* came to present
	38.	7 and all the heavenly *b* shouted for joy?

BELIEVE

Gen	45.26	He was stunned; he could not *b* them.
Ex	4.	5 "so that they may *b* that the LORD, the
2 Chr	20.20	you will be established; *b* his prophets,"
Job	9.16	I do not *b* that he would listen to my
Ps	27.13	I *b* that I shall see the goodness of the
	119.	66 for I *b* in your commandments.
Prov	14.15	The simple *b* everything, but the clever
	26.25	an enemy speaks graciously, do not *b*
Isa	43.10	that you may know and *b* me and
Jer	12.	6 do not *b* them, though they speak
Hab	1.	5 that you would not *b* if you were told.
Mt	9.28	"Do you *b* that I am able to do this?"
	21.25	to us, 'Why then did you not *b* him?'
	27.42	the cross now, and we will *b* in him.
Mk	1.15	near; repent, and *b* in the good news."
	5.36	of the synagogue, "Do not fear, only *b*."
	11.24	ask for in prayer, *b* that you receive it,
	13.21	or 'Look! There he is!'—do not *b* it.
	16.11	had been seen by her, they would not *b*
Lk	1.20	because you did not *b* my words, which
	8.13	no root, they *b* for a while and in a
	8.50	not fear. Only *b*, and she shall be saved."
	20.	5 he will say, 'Why did you not *b* him?'
	22.67	He replied, "If I tell you, you will not *b*;
	24.25	how slow of heart to *b* all that the
Jn	1.	7 light, so that all might *b* through him.
	3.18	who in him are not condemned;
	4.42	we *b*, for we have heard for ourselves,
	5.46	If you believed Moses, you would *b* me,
	6.69	We have come to *b* and know that you
	9.35	he said, "Do you *b* in the Son of man?"
	10.26	but you do not *b*, because you do not
	10.38	though you do not *b* me, *b* the works,
	11.15	glad I was not there, so that you may *b*.
	12.37	in their presence, they did not *b* in him.
	14.	1 be troubled. *B* in God, *b* also in me
	17.20	on behalf of those who will *b* in me
	19.35	has testified so that you also may *b*."
	20.25	and my hand in his side, I will not *b*."
	20.29	have not seen and yet have come to *b*."
Acts	8.37n	Philip said, "If you *b* with all your heart,
	15.11	we *b* that we will be saved through the
	16.31	"*B* in the Lord Jesus, and you will be
	26.27	King Agrippa, do you *b* the prophets? I
Rom	3.22	faith in Jesus Christ for all who *b*.
	10.	9 and *b* in your heart that God raised him
1 Cor	1.21	our proclamation, to save those who *b*.
Heb	11.	6 approach him must *b* that he exists
1 Jn	5.10	Those who *b* in the Son of God have

BELIEVED (BELIEVES BELIEVING)

Gen	15.	6 And he *b* the LORD; and the LORD
Ex	4.31	The people *b*; and when they heard that
	14.31	*b* in the LORD and in his servant Moses.
Ps	106.	12 Then they *b* his words; they sang his
Isa	53.	1 Who has *b* what we have heard? And to
Mk	9.23	things can be done for the one who *b*."
	16.16n	The one who *b* and is baptized will be
Lk	1.45	blessed is she who *b* that there would
Jn	2.22	they *b* the scripture and the word that
	3.15	up, that whoever *b* in him may have
	4.39	Many Samaritans from that city *b* in
	4.50	The man *b* the word that Jesus spoke to
	4.53	will live." So he himself *b*, along with his
	5.24	anyone who hears my word and *b* him
	7.	5 (For not even his brothers *b* in him.)
	7.31	Yet many in the crowd *b* in him and
	11.45	and had seen what Jesus did, *b* in him.
	20.	8 first, also went in, and he saw and *b*;
Acts	4.	4 many of those who heard the word *b*;
	9.42	throughout Joppa, and many *b* in the
	10.43	everyone who *b* in him receives

Acts	13.12	saw what had happened, he *b*,
	17.12	Many of them therefore *b*, including not
Rom	9.33	whoever *b* in him will not be put to
	10.11	one who *b* in him will be put to shame."
1 Cor	13.	7 It bears all things, *b* all things, hopes
Gal	3.	6 Just as Abraham "*b* God, and it was
Phil	1.29	not only of *b* in Christ, but of suffering
Titus	3.	8 so that those who have *b* in God may
1 Jn	5.	1 who *b* that Jesus is the Christ has been

BELIEVER (BELIEVERS)

Acts	5.14	more than ever *b* were added to the
	9.30	when the *b* learned of it, they brought
	11.21	a great number became *b* and turned to
	11.29	send relief to the *b* living in Judea;
	14.	1 of both Jews and Greeks became *b*.
	15.	3 and brought great joy to all the *b*.
	16.	1 son of a Jewish woman who was a *b*;
	17.34	him and became *b*, including Dionysius
	18.	8 official of the synagogue, became a *b*
1 Cor	6.	6 but a *b* goes to court against a *b*
	8.11	So by your knowledge those weak *b* for
1 Thess	2.13	word, which is also at work in you *b*.
2 Thess	3.15	them as enemies, but warn them as *b*.
1 Jn	2.11	Whoever hates another *b* is in the

BELLY

Gen	3.14	upon your *b* you shall go, and dust shall
Jon	2.	2 me; out of the *b* of Sheol I cried,

BELONG (BELONGED BELONGS)

Ps	82.	8 the earth; for all the nations *b* to you!
Mic	7.14	with your staff, the flock that *b* to you,
Rom	7.	4 you may *b* to another, to him who has
Col	2.20	you live as if you still *b* to the world?

BELOVED

Deut	33.12	The *b* of the LORD rests in safety—the
Neh	13.26	he was *b* by his God, and God made
Ps	127.	2 anxious toil; for he gives sleep to his *b*.
Song	1.14	My *b* is to me a cluster of henna
	2.16	My *b* is mine and I am his; he pastures
	5.	9 What is your *b* more than another *b*, O
	6.	3 I am my beloved's and my *b* is mine; he
	8.	5 the wilderness, leaning upon her *b*?
Dan	10.11	He said to me, "Daniel, greatly *b*, pay
Mt	3.17	"This is my Son, the *B*, with whom I am
	17.	5 "This is my Son, the *B*; with him I am
Mk	1.11	"You are my Son, the *B*; with you I am
	9.	7 "This is my Son, the *B*; listen to him."
	12.	6 still one other, a *b* son. Finally he sent
Lk	3.22	"You are my Son, the *B*; with you I am
Rom	9.25	and her who was not *b* I will call '*b*.'"
	11.28	as regards election they are *b*, for the
	16.	8 Greet Ampliatus, my *b* in the Lord.
Eph	1.	6 that he freely bestowed on us in the *B*.
1 Tim	6.	2 by their service are believers and *b*.
2 Pet	1.17	"This is my Son, my *B*, with whom I am
Jude		20 you, *b*, build yourselves up on your

BELTS

Job	12.21	princes, and looses the *b* of the strong.
Isa	11.	5 Righteousness shall be the *b* around his
Mt	3.	4 hair with a leather *b* around his waist,
Mk	6.	8 no bread, no bag, no money in their *b*;
Acts	21.11	us and took Paul's *b*, and bound his

BEND

Phil	2.10	the name of Jesus every knee should *b*,

BENEFICIAL

1 Cor	6.12	lawful for me," but not all things are *b*.
	10.23	are lawful," but not all things are *b*.

BENEFIT (BENEFITS)

Ps	103.	2 my soul, and do not forget all his *b*—
1 Cor	7.35	I say this for your own *b*, not to put any
Gal	5.	2 Christ will be of no *b* to you.

BEN-HADAD I

King of Syria, 1 Kings 15.18; made alliance with Asa, 1 Kings 15.19; ravaged cities in northern Israel, 1 Kings 15.20-21. (See also 2 Chr 16.4.)

BEN-HADAD II

King of Syria, 1 Kings 20.1; besieged Samaria, 1 Kings 20.1; defeated twice by Ahab, 1 Kings 20.2-30; granted conditions of peace, 1 Kings 20.31-34.

BEN-HADAD III

King of Syria, 2 Kings 13.3,24; oppressed cities of Israel, 2 Kings 13.3-13; defeated by Jehoahaz, king of Israel, 2 Kings 13.22-25.

BENJAMIN

Born, Gen 35.16-18; brought to Egypt, Gen 43; accused of theft but interceded for by Judah, Gen 44; blessed by Jacob, Gen 49.27.

Tribe of Benjamin: blessed by Moses, Deut 33.12; allotted its territory, Josh 18.11-28; decimated almost to extinction, Judg 20; rebuilt through new wives and families, Judg 21; Saul, the first king of Israel, and Paul, the apostle, from this tribe, 1 Sam 9.1; Phil 3.5.

BEREAVE (BEREAVED)

Gen	42.36	"I am the one you have *b* of children:
Jer	15.	7 have *b* them, I have destroyed my
Hos	9.12	I will *b* them until no one is left.

BESET

Ps	109.	3 They *b* me with words of hate, and

BESIDE

Ps	23.	2 pastures; he leads me *b* still waters;

BESIEGE (BESIEGED)

Deut	20.12	war against you, then you shall *b* it;
	28.52	It shall *b* you in all your towns until
2 Chr	6.28	if their enemies *b* them in any of the
Eccl	9.14	it. A great king came against it and *b* it,
Isa	1.	8 in a cucumber field, like a *b* city.
Jer	52.	5 city was *b* untill the eleventh year of

BEST

Phil	1.10	insight to help you determine what is *b*,

BESTIR

Ps	35.23	Wake up! *B* yourself for my defense, for

BESTOWED

Acts	28.10	They *b* many honors on us, and when
1 Cor	2.12	we may understand the gifts *b* on us
Eph	1.	6 glorious grace which he freely *b* on us

BETHANY

Mt	21.17	out of the city to *B* and lodged there.
	26.	6 while Jesus was at *B* in the house of
Lk	19.29	come near Bethphage and *B*, at the
	24.50	led them out as far as *B*, and lifting up
Jn	11.	1 a certain man was ill, Lazarus of *B*, the
	12.	1 Jesus came to *B*, the home of Lazarus,

BETHEL

Gen	12.	8 east of *B*, and pitched his tent, with *B*
	28.19	He called that place *B*; but the name of
	31.13	I am the God of *B*, where you anointed
Josh	8.	9 ambush, and lay between *B* and Ai, to
1 Sam	7.16	He went on a circuit year by year to *B*,
1 Kings	12.29	He set one in *B*, and the other he put
	13.11	there lived an old prophet in *B*. One of
Ezra	2.28	Of *B* and Ai, two hundred twenty-three.
Am	4.	4 Come to *B*—and transgress; to
	7.10	Then Amaziah, the priest of *B*, sent to
	7.13	never again prophesy at *B*, for it is the

BETHLEHEM

Gen	35.19	on the way to Ephrath (that is, *B*),
Ruth	1.19	until they came to *B*. When they came

1 Sam	16.	4 the LORD commanded, and came to *B*.
	17.15	from Saul to his father's sheep at *B*.
2 Sam	23.16	drew water from the well of *B* that was
Mic	5.	2 But you, O *B* of Ephrathah, who are
Mt	2.	1 after Jesus was born in *B* of Judea, wise
	2.	6 'And you, *B*, in the land of Judah, are
Lk	2.	4 to the city of David called *B*, because
Jn	7.42	comes from *B*, the village where David

BETHSAIDA

Mt	11.21	Woe to you, *B*! For if the deeds of
Mk	6.45	and go on ahead to the other side, to *B*,
	8.22	They came to *B*. Some people brought a
Lk	9.10	withdrew privately to a city called *B*.

BETRAY (BETRAYED BETRAYING)

Mt	17.22	"The Son of Man is going to be *b* into
	26.16	to look for an opportunity to *b* him.
	26.24	that one by whom the Son of man is *b*!
	26.45	the Son of Man is *b* into the hands of
	27.	4 "I have sinned in *b* innocent blood." But
Mk	3.19	and Judas Iscariot, who *b* him.
	13.12	Brother will *b* brother to death, and a
	14.11	to look for an opportunity to *b* him.
	14.18	"Truly I tell you, one of you will *b* me,
	14.41	the Son of Man is *b* into the hands of
Lk	21.16	You will be *b* even by parents and
	22.	4 about how he might *b* him to them.
Jn	13.11	For he knew who was to *b* him; for this
	18.	2 Judas, who *b* him, also knew the place,
1 Cor	11.23	on the night when he was *b* took a

BETTER

Job	35.	3 How am I *b* off than if I had sinned?
Eccl	3.12	nothing *b* for them than to be happy
Phil	2.	3 but in humility regard others *b* than
Heb	8.	6 he is the mediator of a *b* covenant,
	9.23	themselves need *b* sacrifices than these.

BEWARE

Eccl	12.12	Of anything beyond these, my child, *b*.
Mt	7.15	"*B* of false prophets, who come to you
	16.	6 out, and *b* of the yeast of the Pharisees
Mk	8.15	out—*b* of the yeast of the Pharisees
	12.38	"*B* of the scribes, who like to walk

BIND (BINDS BOUND)

Gen	44.30	then, as his life is *b* up in the boy's life,
Job	26.	8 He *b* up the waters in his thick clouds,
Ps	147.	3 bokenhearted, and *b* up their wounds.
Prov	6.21	*B* them upon your heart always; tie
Ezek	34.16	the strayed, and I will *b* up the injured,
Mt	16.19	whatever you *b* on earth will be bound
	18.18	whatever you *b* on earth will be bound
1 Cor	7.27	Are you *b* to a wife? Do not seek to be

BIRD (BIRDS BIRD'S)

Gen	1.20	let *b* fly above the earth across the
Deut	22.	6 If you come on a *b* nest, in any tree or
Ps	11.	1 to me, "Flee like a *b* to the mountains;
	102.	7 I lie awake; I am like a lonely *b* on the
	124.	7 have escaped like a *b* from the snare
Prov	1.17	the net baited while the *b* is looking on;
Isa	31.	5 Like *b* hovering overhead, so the LORD
Jer	12.	9 Are the *b* of prey all around her? Go,
Am	3.	5 Does a *b* fall into a snare on the earth,
Mt	8.20	have holes, and *b* of the air have nests;
	13.32	*b* of the air come and make nests in its
Mk	4.32	so that the *b* of the air can make nests
Lk	9.58	and *b* of the air have nests; but the Son
	13.19	the *b* of the air made nests in its

BIRTH

Deut	32.18	you forgot the God who gave you *b*.
Ezek	16.	3 Your origin and your *b* were in the land
Mt	1.18	Now the *b* of Jesus the Messiah took

BIRTHRIGHT

Gen	25.31 Jacob said, "First sell me your *b*."
	27.36 He took away my *b*; and look, now he
	43.33 the firstborn according to his *b* and the

BISHOP (BISHOPS)

Phil	1. 1 who are in in Philippi, with the *b* and
1 Tim	3. 1 whoever aspires to the office of *b*
Titus	1. 7 a *b*, as God's steward, must be

BIT

2 Kings	19.28 in your nose and my *b* in your mouth,
Isa	37.29 in your nose and my *b* in your mouth;

BITTER

Gen	26.35 they made life *b* for Isaac and Rebekah.
Jer	4.18 This is your doom; how *b* it is! It has
Rev	10. 9 it will be *b* to your stomach, but sweet

BITTERNESS

Num	5.18 shall have the water of *b* that brings the
Job	10. 1 I will speak in the *b* of my soul.
	21.25 Another dies in *b* of soul, never having
Prov	14.10 The heart knows its own *b*, and no

BLACK

Song	1. 5 I am *b* and beautiful, O daughters of

BLAME

Gen	43. 9 you, then let me bear the *b* forever.
	44.32 then I will bear the *b* in the sight of my
2 Cor	8.20 no one should *b* us about this generous

BLAMELESS (BLAMELESSLY)

Gen	6. 9 a righteous man, *b* in his generation;
	17. 1 Almighty; walk before me, and be *b*.
Job	1. 1 That man was *b* and upright, one who
	8.20 God will not reject a *b* person, nor take
	9.20 me; though I am *b*, he would prove
Ps	18.25 loyal; with the *b* you show yourself *b*;
	37.37 Mark the *b*, and behold the upright, for
	119. 1 Happy are those whose way is *b*, who
	119. 80 May my heart be *b* in your statutes, so
Ezek	28.15 You were *b* in your ways from the day
Lk	1. 6 living *b* according to all the
1 Cor	1. 8 that you may be *b* on the day of our
Phil	3. 6 as to righteousness under the law, *b*.

BLASPHEME (BLASPHEMED BLASPHEMES BLASPHEMING)

Lev	24.11 Israelite woman's son *b* the Name in a
Ezek	20.27 In this again your fathers *b* me, by
Mt	9. 3 said to themselves, "This man is *b*."
Mk	3.29 whoever *b* against the Holy Spirit can
Acts	26.11 synagogues I tried to force them to *b*;
Rom	2.24 "The name of God is *b* among the
Rev	13. 6 God, *b* his name and his dwelling,

BLASPHEMER

1 Tim	1.13 though I was formerly a *b*, a persecutor,

BLASPHEMOUS

Acts	6.11 "We have heard him speak *b* words
Rev	13. 1 and on its heads were *b* names.

BLASPHEMY (BLASPHEMIES)

Mt	12.31 every sin and *b*, but *b* against the Spirit
	26.65 witnesses? You have now heard his *b*.
Mk	14.64 You have heard his *b*! What is your
Lk	5.21 "Who is this who is speaking *b*? Who
Jn	10.33 we are going to stone you, but for *b*;

BLAZING

Deut	4.11 while the mountain was *b* up to the

BLEMISH

Lev	21.18 no one who has a *b* shall draw near,
Num	19. 2 without defect, in which there is no *b*
	28. 3 two male lambs a year old without *b*,

2 Sam	14.25 of his head there was no *b* in him.

BLESS (BLESSING) (v)

Gen	12. 2 and I will *b* you, and make your name
	22.17 I will indeed *b* you, and I will make you
	27. 4 to eat, so that I may *b* you before I die."
	32.26 I will not let you go, unless you *b* me."
	49.25 by the Almighty who will *b* you with
Num	6.24 The LORD *b* you and keep you;
Deut	7.13 he will love you, *b* you, and multiply
Judg	5. 2 offer themselves willingly — *b* the LORD!
Ruth	2. 4 you." They answered, "The LORD *b* you."
1 Chr	4.10 "Oh that you would *b* me and enlarge
	17.27 please you to *b* the house of your
Neh	9. 5 "Stand up and *b* the LORD your God
Ps	29.11 May the LORD *b* his people with peace!
	34. 1 I will *b* the LORD at all times; his praise
	66. 8 B our God, O peoples, let the sound of
	103. 1 B the LORD, O my soul; and all that is
Hag	2.19 nothing? From this day on I will *b* you.
Lk	24.53 were continually in the temple *b* God.
Rom	12.14 B those who persecute you; *b* and do
1 Cor	4.12 When reviled, we *b*; when persecuted,
Heb	6.14 himself, saying, "I will surely *b* you and

BLESSED (v and adj)

Gen	1.22 And God *b* them, saying, "Be fruitful
	9. 1 God *b* Noah and his sons, and said to
	18.18 nations of the earth shall be *b* in him?
	24. 1 and the LORD had *b* Abraham in all
	24.27 he said, "B be the LORD, the God of my
	27.29 and *b* be everyone who blesses you!"
	39. 5 the LORD *b* the Egyptian's house for
	47. 7 before Pharaoh, and Jacob *b* Pharaoh.
Num	22.12 not curse the people, for they are *b*."
	23.20 a command to bless; he has *b*, and I
	24. 9 B is everyone who blesses you, and
Deut	33. 1 which Moses the man of God *b* the
Josh	17.14 people, whom all along the LORD *b*?"
Judg	5.24 "Most *b* of women be Jael, the wife of
	13.24 The boy grew, and the LORD *b* him.
Ruth	2. 19 B be the man who took notice of you."
2 Sam	6.11 the LORD *b* Obed-edom and all his
1 Kings	8.56 "B be the LORD, who has given rest to
1 Chr	13.14 *b* the household of Obed-edom and all
	16.36 B be the LORD, the God of Isreal, from
2 Chr	20.26 of Beracah, for there they *b* the LORD;
Job	1.21 taken away; *b* be the name of the LORD."
	42.12 LORD *b* the latter days of Job more than
Isa	30.18 God of justice; *b* are all those who wait
	61. 9 they are a people whom the LORD has *b*.
Jer	17. 7 B are those who trust in the LORD,
Dan	2.19 night, and Daniel *b* the God of heaven.
Mt	5. 3 "B are the poor in spirit, for theirs is
	13.16 *b* are your eyes, for they see, and your
	14.19 and *b* and broke the loaves, and gave
	21. 9 B is the one who comes in the name of
	24.46 B is that slave whom his master will
	25.34 "Come, you that are *b* of my Father,
Mk	10.16 laid his hands on them, and *b* them.
	11. 9 "Hosanna! B is the one who comes in
	14.61 you the Messiah, the Son of the B One?"
Lk	1.42 "B are you among women, and *b* is the
	1.68 "B be the Lord God of Israel, for he has
	6.20 "B are you who are poor, for yours is
	10.23 "B are the eyes that see what you see!
	11.27 B is the womb that bore you and the
	12.38 and finds them so, *b* are those slaves!
	13.35 'B is the one who comes in the name
	19.38 "B is the King who comes in the name
	24.50 and, lifting up his hands, he *b* them.
Jn	13.17 you are *b* if you do them.
	20.29 B are those who have not seen and yet
Acts	20.35 said, 'It is more *b* to give than to
Rom	9. 5 Messiah, who is over all, God *b* forever.
1 Cor	7.40 she is more *b* if she remains as she is.
Gal	3. 8 "All the Gentiles shall be *b* in you."

Eph	1. 3 who has *b* us in Christ with every
Jas	5.11 we call *b* those who showed endurance.
1 Pet	3.14 suffer for doing what is right, you are *b*.
Rev	14.13 "Write this: *B* are the dead who from
	22. 7 *B* is the one who keeps the words of
	22.14 *B* are those who wash their robes, so

BLESSING (BLESSINGS)

Gen	22.18 of the earth gain *b* for themselves,
Lev	25.21 I will order my *b* upon you in the sixth
Deut	11.26 I am setting before you today a *b* and a
	23. 5 God turned the curse into a *b* for you,
	27.12 shall stand on Mount Gerizim for the *b*
	28. 2 all these *b* shall come upon you and
Josh	8.34 all the words of the law, *b* and curses,
Ps	21. 3 For you meet him with rich *b*; you set a
Prov	10.22 The *b* of the LORD makes rich, and he
	11.11 By the *b* of the upright a city is exalted,
Isa	19.24 Assyria, a *b* in the midst of the earth,
	65.16 whoever invokes a *b* in the land shall
Ezek	34.26 their season; they shall be showers of *b*.
	44.30 order that a *b* may rest on your house.
Mal	3.10 pour down for you an overflowing *b*.
Rom	15.29 come in the fullness of the *b* of Christ.
1 Cor	10.16 The cup of *b* which we bless, is it not a
Jas	3.10 the same mouth come *b* and cursing.

BLIND (n and adj)

Deut	28.29 at noon as *b* people grope in darkness,
2 Sam	5. 8 to attack the lame and the *b*, those
Job	29.15 I was eyes to the *b*, and feet to the
Ps	146. 8 LORD opens the eyes of the *b*. The LORD
Isa	29.18 darkness the eyes of the *b* shall see.
	35. 5 Then the eyes of the *b* shall be opened,
	42. 7 the nations, to open the eyes that are *b*,
	42.16 I will lead the *b* by a road they do not
	42.19 Who is *b* but my servant, or deaf like
	43. 8 the people who are *b*, yet have eyes,
	56.10 Israel's sentinels are *b*, they are all
	59.10 We grope like the *b* along a wall,
Mal	1. 8 When you offer *b* animals in sacrifice, is
Mt	9.27 two *b* men followed him, crying loudly,
	11. 5 the *b* receive their sight, the lame walk,
	12.22 brought to him a demoniac who was *b*
	15.14 them alone; they are *b* guides of the *b*.
	15.30 the lame, the maimed, the *b*, the mute,
	20.30 two *b* men sitting by the roadside.
	23.16 "Woe to you, *b* guides, who say,
Mk	8.22 Some people brought a *b* man to him
	10.51 And the *b* man said to him, "My
Lk	4.18 and recovering of sight to the *b*,
	6.39 "Can a *b* person guide a *b* person? Will
	7.21 had given sight to many who were *b*.
	14.13 poor, the crippled, the lame, and the *b*,
	18.35 Jericho, a *b* man was sitting by the
Jn	9. 1 along, he saw a man *b* from birth.
	9.20 this is our son, and that he was born *b*;
	9.25 know, that though I was *b*, now I see."
	9.39 and those who do see may become *b*."
	10.21 Can a demon open the eyes of the *b*?"
Rom	2.19 you are a guide to the *b*, a light to
2 Pet	1. 9 lacks these things is nearsighted and *b*,
Rev	3.17 wretched, pitiable, poor, *b*, and naked.

BLIND (BLINDED BLINDS) (v)

Deut	16.19 for a bribe *b* the eyes of the wise and
1 Sam	12. 3 I taken a bribe to *b* my eyes with it?
2 Cor	4. 4 god of this world has *b* the minds of the

BLINDLY

Lam	4.14 *b* they wandered through the streets, so

BLINDNESS

Gen	19.11 they struck with *b* the men who were at
2 Kings	6.18 said, "Strike this people, please, with *b*."
Zech	12. 4 horse with panic, and its rider with *b*.
1 Jn	2.11 because the darkness has brought on *b*.

BLOOD

Gen	4.10 your brother's *b* is crying out to me
	9. 4 not eat flesh with its life, that is, its *b*.
	9. 6 Whoever sheds the *b* of a human, by a
	42.22 now there comes a reckoning for his *b*."
Ex	7.17 in the Nile, and it shall be turned to *b*.
	24. 8 "See the *b* of the covenant that the
	29.12 shall take some of the *b* of the bull and
Lev	16.14 He shall take some of the *b* of the bull,
	17.11 life, it is the *b* that makes atonement.
Deut	12.16 The *b*, however, you must not eat; you
1 Sam	14.32 and the troops ate them with the *b*.
Ps	105. 29 He turned their waters into *b*, and
Ezek	3.18 but their *b* I will require at your hand.
Mt	23.30 in shedding the *b* of the prophets.'
	23.35 from the *b* of righteous Abel to the *b* of
	26.28 this is my *b* of the covenant, which is
	27.24 saying, "I am innocent of this man's *b*;
Mk	14.24 "This is my *b* of the covenant, which is
Lk	11.51 from the *b* of Abel to the *b* of
	22.20 out for you is the new covenant in my *b*
Jn	6.53 of Man and drink his *b*, you have no life
Acts	1.19 Hakeldama, that is, Field of *B*.)
	18. 6 "Your *b* be upon your heads! I am
Rom	5. 9 we have been justified by his *b*, will we
1 Cor	15.50 flesh and *b* cannot inherit the kingdom
Eph	1. 7 we have redemption through his *b*, the
	2.13 been brought near by the *b* of Christ.
Heb	9. 7 and not without taking the *b* that he
	9.12 but his own *b*, thus obtaining eternal
	10.19 to enter the sanctuary by the *b* of Jesus,
	10.29 profaned the *b* of the covenant by
1 Pet	1.19 with the precious *b* of Christ, like that
1 Jn	1. 7 the *b* of Jesus his Son cleanses us from
	5. 6 only but with the water and the *b*.
Rev	7.14 made them white in the *b* of the Lamb.
	11. 6 over the waters to turn them into *b*,
	12.11 conquered him by the *b* of the Lamb
	19. 2 and he has avenged on her the *b* of his

BLOODSHED

Isa	5. 7 he expected justice, but saw *b*;
Jer	48.10 one who keeps back the sword from *b*.

BLOT (BLOTS BLOTTED)

Ex	32.32 if not, *b* me out of the book that you
Deut	9.14 and *b* out their name from under
	25.19 shall *b* out the remembrance of Amalek
	29.20 LORD will *b* out their names from under
2 Kings	14.27 had not said he would *b* out the name
Ps	51. 1 mercy *b* out my transgressions.
	109. 14 not let the sin of his mother be *b* out.
Isa	6. 7 guilt has departed and your sin is *b* out."
	43.25 I am He who *b* out your transgressions
Jer	18.23 do not *b* out their sin from your sight.

BLOW

Num	10. 5 When you *b* an alarm, the camp on the
Song	4.16 O south wind! *B* upon my garden,

BOAST (BOASTING) (n)

Ps	34. 2 My soul makes its *b* in the LORD; let the
Rom	3.27 Then what becomes of *b*? It is
2 Cor	7.14 true, so our *b* to Titus has proved true
	8.24 of your love and of our reason for *b*
	11.10 this *b* of mine shall not be silenced in

BOAST (BOASTED BOASTS) (v)

Ps	10. 3 the wicked *b* of the desires of their
	38.16 rejoice over me, those who *b* against
	44. 8 In God we have *b* continually, and we
Prov	20.14 says the buyer, then goes away and *b*.
	25.14 rain is one who *b* of a gift never given.
	27. 1 Do not *b* about tomorrow, for you do
Jer	9.24 let those who *b* *b* in this, that they
Rom	2.17 the law and *b* of your relation to God
	2.23 You that *b* in the law, do you dishonor

Rom	5. 2 and we *b* in our hope of sharing the
	5.11 we even *b* in God through our Lord
	11.18 do not *b* over the branches. If you do *b*,
1 Cor	1.31 written, "Let one who *b*, *b* in the Lord."
	3.21 So let no one *b* about human leaders.
2 Cor	7. 4 I often *b* about you; I have great pride
	10.17 "Let the one who *b*, *b* in the Lord." For
	11.21 as a fool— I also dare to *b* of that.
Gal	6.14 I never *b* of anything except the cross
Eph	2. 9 result of works, so that no one may *b*.
Jas	1. 9 Let the believer who is lowly *b* in being

BOAT

Mt	4.22 they left the *b* and their father, and
Mk	3. 9 He told his disciples to have a *b* ready
Lk	8.22 day he got into a *b* with his disciples,
Jn	6.21 and immediately the *b* reached the land

BODILY

Lk	3.22 Spirit descended on him in *b* form like
Col	2. 9 the whole fullness of deity dwells *b*,

BODY (BODIES)

Gen	47.18 of my lord but our *b* and our lands.
1 Sam	31.12 took the *b* of Saul and the *b* of his sons
Isa	37.36 morning dawned, they were all dead *b*.
Mt	10.28 Do not fear those who can kill the *b*
	26.26 and said, "Take, eat; this is my *b*."
	27.58 to Pilate and asked for the *b* of Jesus;
Mk	6.29 about it, they came and took his *b*,
	14.22 to them, and said, "Take; this is my *b*."
	15.43 to Pilate and asked for the *b* of Jesus.
Lk	22.19 saying, "This is my *b*, which is given for
Jn	2.21 he was speaking of the temple of his *b*.
Rom	12. 4 as in one *b* we have many members,
1 Cor	6.13 *b* is meant not for fornication but for
	6.15 that your *b* are members of Christ?
	6.19 your *b* is a temple of the Holy Spirit
	12.12 For just as the *b* is one and has many
	12.24 God has so arranged the *b*, giving the
	12.27 Now you are the *b* of Christ and
	15.35 With what kind of *b* do they come?"
Gal	6.17 the marks of Jesus branded on my *b*.
Eph	1.23 the church, which is his *b*, the fullness
	4. 4 There is one *b* and one Spirit, just as
	4.16 the whole *b*, joined and knit together by
	5.30 because we are members of his *b*.
Phil	3.21 transform the *b* of our humiliation that
Col	1.18 He is the head of the *b*, the church; he
	2.19 head, from whom the whole *b*,
Heb	10. 5 but a *b* you have prepared for me;
Jude	9 disputed about the *b* of Moses, he did
Rev	11. 8 dead *b* will lie in the street of the great

BOG

Ps	40. 2 from the desolate pit, out of the miry *b*,

BOIL (v)

Deut	14.21 shall not *b* a kid in its mother's milk.

BOILS (n)

Ex	9. 9 shall cause festering *b* on humans and
Deut	28.27 LORD will afflict you with the *b* of Egypt,

BOLD

Prov	21.29 The wicked put on a *b* face, but the

BOLDNESS

Acts	4.13 when they saw the *b* of Peter and John
	4.29 servants to speak thy word with all *b*,
	28.31 about the Lord Jesus Christ with all *b*
2 Cor	3.12 have such a hope, we act with great *b*,
Eph	3.12 have access to God in *b* and confidence
Phil	1.14 dare to speak the word with greater *b*
1 Jn	4.17 we may have *b* on the day of judgment,
	5.14 this is the *b* we have in him, that if we

BOND (BONDS)

Ps	69.33 does not despise his own that are in *b*.

Isa	58. 6 to loose the *b* of injustice, to undo the
Eph	4. 3 the unity of the Spirit in the *b* of peace.

BONE (BONES)

Gen	50.25 comes to you, you shall carry up my *b*
Ex	13.19 Moses took with him the *b* of Joseph
Num	9.12 of it until morning, nor break a *b* of it;
Josh	24.32 The *b* of Joseph, which the Israelites
2 Kings	13.21 man touched the *b* of Elisha, he came
1 Chr	11. 1 and said, "See, we are your *b* and flesh.
Ps	22.17 I can count all my *b*. They stare and
	34.20 He keeps all their *b*; not one of them
Jer	8. 1 the *b* of the kings of Judah, the *b* of its
Ezek	37. 7 a rattling, and the *b* came together,
Jn	19.36 fulfilled, "None of his *b* shall be broken."

BOOK (BOOKS)

Ex	24. 7 took the *b* of the covenant, and read it
Num	21.14 is said in the *B* of the Wars of the Lord,
Deut	31.26 "Take this *b* of the law and put it
Josh	1. 8 This *b* of the law shall not depart out of
	8.31 is written in the *b* of the law of Moses,
2 Kings	22. 8 I have found the *b* of the law in the
	23. 2 all the words of the *b* of the covenant
2 Chr	34.16 Shaphan brought the *b* to the king, and
Neh	7. 5 I found the *b* of the genealogy of those
	8. 1 Ezra to bring the *b* of the law of Moses
Job	19.23 down! O that they were inscribed in a *b*!
Ps	139. 16 In your *b* were written, all the days that
Eccl	12.12 Of making many *b* there is no end, and
Isa	30. 8 them on a tablet, inscribe it in a *b*,
	34.16 Seek and read from the *b* of the LORD:
Jer	25.13 everything written in this *b*, which
Dan	7.10 in judgment, and the *b* were opened.
	9. 2 perceived in the *b* the number of years
	10.21 you what is inscribed in the *b* of truth.
	12. 1 everyone who is found written in the *b*.
Mal	3.16 a *b* of remembrance was written before
Jn	20.30 are not written in this *b*. But these
	21.25 itself could not contain the *b* that
Acts	19.19 magic collected their *b* and burned
Phil	4. 3 whose names are in the *b* of life.
2 Tim	4.13 also the *b*, and above all the
Rev	1.11 "Write in a *b* what you see and send it
	3. 5 I will not blot your name out of the *b* of
	13. 8 of the world in the *b* of life of the Lamb
	20.12 Also another *b* was opened, the *b* of
	21.27 who are written in the Lamb's *b* of life.

BOOTH (BOOTHS)

Gen	33.17 a house, and made *b* for his cattle;
Lev	23.34 there shall be the festival of *b* to the
	23.42 You shall live in *b* for seven days; all
Deut	16.13 You shall keep the festival of *b* for
Neh	8.14 Israel should live in *b* during the festival
Am	9.11 I will raise up the *b* of David that has
Jon	4. 5 city, and made a *b* for himself there.
Jn	7. 2 Now the Jewish festival of *B* was near

BOOTY

Num	31.32 The *b* remaining from the spoil that the

BORN

1 Kings	13. 2 'A son shall be *b* to the house of David,
Job	14. 1 "A mortal *b* of woman, few of days, and
	25. 4 How can one *b* of woman be pure?
Eccl	3. 2 time to be *b*, and a time to die, a time
Isa	9. 6 For a child has been *b* for us, a son is
Jer	1. 5 before you were *b* I consecrated you;
Mt	1.16 husband of Mary, of whom Jesus was *b*,
	2. 1 after Jesus was *b* in Bethlehem of
	11.11 among those *b* of women no one has
Lk	1.35 child to be *b* will be holy; he will be
Jn	1.13 of God, who were *b*, not of blood or
	3. 3 of God without being *b* from above.
	9.34 "You were *b* entirely in sins, and you
	16.21 her child is *b*, she no longer remembers
1 Pet	1.23 You have been *b* anew, not of

BORROW (cont.)

| 1 Jn | 3. 9 Those who have been *b* of God do not |
| | 5.18 know that those *b* of God do not sin, |

BORROW

2 Kings	4. 3 "Go outside, *b* vessels from all your
Ps	37.21 The wicked *b*, and do not pay back, but
Mt	5.42 do not refuse anyone who wants to *b*

BORROWER

| Prov | 22. 7 and the *b* is the slave of the lender. |
| Isa | 24. 2 as with the lender, so with the *b*; as |

BOSOM

Prov	6.27 Can fire be carried in the *b* without
Isa	40.11 in his arms, and carry them in his *b*,
	66.11 deeply with delight from her glorious *b*.

BOTHER (BOTHERING)

| Lk | 11. 7 "Do not *b* me; the door has already |
| | 18. 5 because this widow keeps *b* me, I will |

BOTTLE

| Ps | 33. 7 gathered the waters of the sea as in a *b*; |
| | 56. 8 of my tossings; put my tears in your *b*. |

BOUGH (BOUGHS)

| Gen | 49.22 Joseph is a fruitful *b*, a fruitful *b* by a |
| Ezek | 31.12 have fallen, and its *b* lie broken in all |

BOUNDARY (BOUNDARIES)

| Deut | 19.14 not remove your neighbor's *b* marker, |
| | 32. 8 he fixed the *b* of the peoples according |

BOUNDLESS

| Eph | 3. 8 to the Gentiles the news of the *b* riches |

BOUNDS

| Ps | 74.17 You have fixed all the *b* of the earth; |

BOUNTY

| Ps | 65.11 You crown the year with your *b*; your |
| | 116. 12 I return to the Lord for all his *b* to me? |

BOW (n)

Gen	9.13 I set my *b* in the cloud, and it shall be
	21.20 and became an expert with the *b*.
Ps	44. 6 For not in my *b* do I trust, nor can my
	46. 9 he breaks the *b*, and shatters the spear;
Hos	1. 5 On that day I will break the *b* of Israel

BOW (BOWED BOWING)

Gen	33. 6 they and their children, and *b* down;
	42. 6 Joseph's brothers came and *b*
	43.28 And they bent their heads and did
	49. 8 your father's sons shall *b* down before
Ex	23.24 you shall not *b* down to their gods, or
Deut	5. 9 You shall not *b* down to them or
	26.10 and *b* down before the Lord your God.
1 Kings	19.18 all the knees that have not *b* to Baal,
2 Kings	4.37 and fell at his feet, *b* to the ground;
Ps	5. 7 I will *b* down toward your holy temple
	81. 9 you shall not *b* down to a foreign god.
	86. 9 you have made shall come and *b* down
Zeph	1. 5 who *b* down on the roofs to the host of
Jn	19.30 Then he *b* his head and gave up his
Rev	3. 9 and *b* down before your feet, and they

BOWL (BOWLS)

2 Kings	2.20 "Bring me a new *b*, and put salt in it."
Mt	26.23 has dipped his hand in the *b* with me,
Rev	16. 1 earth the seven *b* of the wrath of God."

BOY (BOYS)

Gen	44.34 to my father if the *b* is not with me?
	48.16 bless the *b*; and in them let my name
1 Sam	20.21 Then I will send the *b*, saying, 'Go, find
	17.33 to fight against him; for you are just a *b*
2 Kings	5.14 was restored like the flesh of a young *b*,
2 Chr	34. 3 while he was still a *b*, he began to seek
Prov	22.15 Folly is bound up in the heart of a *b*,

Isa	3. 4 I will make *b* their princes, and babes
Jer	1. 6 know how to speak, for I am only a *b*."
Zech	8. 5 city shall be of *b* and girls playing in its
Jn	6. 9 is a *b* here who has five barley loaves

BRANCH (BRANCHES)

Isa	4. 2 day the *b* of the Lord shall be beautiful
	11. 1 and a *b* shall grow out of his roots.
Jer	23. 5 I will raise up for David a righteous *B*,
	33.15 I will cause a righteous *B* to spring up
Zech	3. 8 I am going to bring my servant the *B*.
Mk	11. 8 and others spread leafy *b* that they had
Jn	12.13 So they took *b* of palm trees and went
	15. 2 He removes every *b* in me that bears no
Rom	11.18 do not boast over the *b*. If you do boast,

BREACH

| Ps | 106. 23 Moses, his chosen one, stood in the *b* |
| Ezek | 22.30 stand in the *b* before me on behalf of |

BREAD

Ex	16. 4 I am going to rain *b* from heaven for
Deut	8. 3 one does not live by *b* alone, but by
1 Sam	21. 6 no *b* there except the *b* of the Presence,
Prov	4.17 For they eat the *b* of wickedness and
	22. 9 are blessed, for they share their *b* with
Eccl	11. 1 Send out your *b* upon the waters, for
Isa	3. 1 all support of *b*, and all support of
Jer	37.21 loaf of *b* was given him daily from the
Ezek	4.17 Lacking *b* and water, they will look at
Mt	4. 3 these stones to become loaves of *b*."
	12. 4 of God and ate the *b* of the Presence,
	15.33 "Where are we to get enough *b* in the
	26.26 Jesus took a loaf of *b*, and after
Mk	8. 4 can one feed these people with *b* here
	14.22 he took a loaf of *b*, and after blessing it
Lk	4. 3 this stone to become a loaf of *b*."
	22.19 he took a loaf of *b*, and when he had
	24.30 he took *b*, blessed and broke it, and
Jn	6.32 not Moses who gave you the *b* from
	6.35 "I am the *b* of life; Whoever comes to
	13.26 the one to whom I give this piece of *b*
	21.13 Jesus came and took the *b* and gave it
Acts	20. 7 of the week, when we met to break *b*,
1 Cor	10.16 The *b* that we break, is it not a sharing
	11.23 when he was betrayed took a loaf of *b*,

BREAK (BREAKING BROKE BROKEN)

Gen	17.14 from his people; he has *b* my covenant."
Num	9.12 of it until morning, nor *b* a bone of it;
Deut	7. 5 *b* down their altars, smash their pillars,
Ezra	9.14 shall we *b* your commandments again
Job	16.12 at ease, and he *b* me in two; he seized
	17.11 My days are past, my plans are *b* off,
Ps	34.20 their bones; not one of them will be *b*.
	102. 23 He has *b* my strength in midcourse; he
	119.126 Lord to act, for your law has been *b*.
Prov	18.14 sickness; a *b* spirit—who can bear?
Jer	19.11 So will I *b* this people and this city, as
	33.20 If any of you could *b* my covenant with
Hos	8. 1 have *b* my covenant, and transgressed
Jn	19.33 already dead, they did not *b* his legs.
Acts	21.13 are you doing, weeping and *b* my heart?
Rom	2.27 code and circumcision but *b* the law.

BREASTPLATE

Isa	59.17 He put on righteousness like a *b*, and a
Eph	6.14 and put on the *b* of righteousness.
1 Thess	5. 8 and put on the *b* of faith and love,

BREASTS

| Song | 4. 5 Your two *b* are like two fawns, twins of |
| Isa | 32.12 Beat upon your *b* for the present fields, |

BREATH

Job	32. 8 the *b* of the Almighty, that makes for
Ps	18.15 rebuke, O Lord, at the blast of the *b* of
	33. 6 and all their host by the *b* of his mouth.

Ps 62. 9 Those of low estate are but a *b*, those
94.11 thoughts, that they are but an empty *b*.
144. 4 They are like a *b*; their days are like a
146. 4 their *b* departs they return to the earth;
Eccl 3.19 They all have the same *b*, and humans
11. 5 as you do not know how the *b* comes
12. 7 and the *b* returns to God who gave it.
Isa 11. 4 and with the *b* of his lips he shall kill
40. 7 fades, when the *b* of the LORD blows
Ezek 37. 5 to these bones: I will cause *b* to enter
37. 9 "Prophesy to the *b*, prophesy, mortal,
Rev 13.15 to give *b* to the image of the beast

BREATHE (BREATHED BREATHES BREATHING)

Gen 2. 7 *b* into his nostrils the breath of life; and
Ps 27.12 against me, and they are *b* out violence.
150. 6 Let everything that *b* praise the LORD!
Acts 9. 1 Saul, still *b* threats and murder against

BREEZE

Gen 3. 8 the garden at the time of the evening *b*,

BRIBE (BRIBES)

Ex 23. 8 take no *b*, for a *b* blinds the officials,
Deut 16.19 not accept *b*, for a *b* blinds the eyes
1 Sam 8. 3 gain; they took *b* and perverted justice.
12. 3 from whose hand have I taken a *b* to
Ps 26.10 and whose right hands are full of *b*.
Prov 15.27 but those who hate *b* will live.
17. 8 A *b* is like a magic stone in the eyes of
Am 5.12 who take a *b*, and push aside the needy
Mic 3.11 Its rulers give judgment for a *b*, its
7. 3 the official and the judge ask for a *b*,

BRIBERY

Job 15.34 and fire consumes the tents of *b*.

BRICK (BRICKS)

Gen 11. 3 "Come, let us make *b*, and burn them
Ex 5. 7 longer give the people straw to make *b*,
Isa 9.10 "The *b* have fallen, but we will build
Ezek 4. 1 take a *b* and set it before you. On it

BRIDE

Song 4. 9 sister, my *b*, you have ravished my heart
Isa 61.10 garland, and as a *b* adorns herself with
Jer 2.32 forget her ornaments, or a *b* her attire?
7.34 mirth and gladness, the voice of the *b*
Rev 21. 2 from God, prepared as a *b* adorned for
21. 9 I will show you the *b*, the wife of the

BRIDEGROOM

Ex 4.26 "Truly you are a *b* of blood to me!"
Ps 19. 5 which comes out like a *b* from his
Mt 9.15 mourn as long as the *b* is with them,
Mk 2.19 cannot fast while the *b* is with them
Lk 5.34 wedding guests fast while the *b* is with
Jn 3.29 The friend of the *b*, who stands and

BRIDESMAIDS

Mt 25. 1 Ten *b* took their lamps and went to

BRIDLE

Ps 32. 9 temper must be curbed with bit and *b*,
Jas 1.26 are religious, and do not *b* their tongues
3. 2 keep the whole body in check with a *b*.

BRIGHT (BRIGHTER)

Job 11.17 your life will be *b* than the noonday; its
Acts 26.13 a light from heaven, *b* than the sun,
Rev 22.16 of David, the *b* morning star."

BRING (BRINGING BRINGS BROUGHT)

Gen 28.15 will *b* you back to this land; for I will
45.19 wives, and *b* your father, and come.
Ex 13.11 "When the LORD has *b* you into the land
Num 24. 8 God *b* him out of Egypt, is like the
27. 5 Moses *b* their case before the LORD.
Job 33.30 to *b* back their soul from the Pit, so

Ps 64. 9 they will tell what God has *b* about,
Isa 49.22 they shall *b* your sons in their bosom,
52. 7 announces peace, who *b* good news,
60. 5 abundance of the sea shall be *b* to you,
61. 1 he has sent me to *b* good news to the
Jer 21. 4 I will *b* them together into the center of
Am 5.25 Did you *b* to me sacrifices and offerings
Nah 1.15 the feet of one who *b* good tidings,
Mal 3.10 *B* the full tithe into the storehouse, so
Mt 6.13 And do not *b* us to the time of trial, but
10.34 the earth; I have not come to *b* peace,
Lk 2.10 —I am *b* you good news of great joy for
4.18 me to *b* good news to the poor.
Jn 1.42 He *b* Simon to Jesus, who looked at
Jas 5.19 from the truth and is *b* back by another,

BROKENHEARTED

Ps 34.18 The LORD is near to the *b*, and saves the
Isa 61. 1 to the oppressed, to bind up the *b*, to

BRONZE

Gen 4.22 who made all kinds of *b* and iron tools.
Num 21. 9 Moses made a serpent of *b*, and put it
Jer 15.20 you to this people a fortified wall of *b*;
Dan 2.32 of silver, its middle and thighs of *b*,

BROOD

Mt 23.37 as a hen gathers her *b* under her wings,
Lk 3. 7 "You *b* of vipers! Who warned you to

BROOKS

Jer 31. 9 I will let them walk by *b* of water, in a

BROTHER (BROTHERS BROTHER'S)

Gen 4. 8 Cain rose up against his *b* Abel, and
20.16 I have given your *b* a thousand pieces of
27.45 until your *b* anger against you turns
37.11 So his *b* were jealous of him, but his
37.27 lay our hands on him, for he is our *b*,
45. 4 "I am your *b*, Joseph, whom you sold
49. 8 Judah, your *b* shall praise you; your
Num 20.14 "Thus says your *b* Israel: You know all
Deut 25. 5 Her husband's *b* shall go in to her,
Judg 9. 5 house at Ophrah, and killed his *b*
1 Sam 17.22 the ranks, and went and greeted his *b*.
1 Kings 2.15 has turned about and become my *b*,
13.30 mourned over him, saying, "Alas, my *b*!"
20.32 he said, "Is he still live? He is my *b*."
1 Chr 5. 2 Judah became prominent among his *b*
Ps 22.22 will tell of your name to my *b* and
Mal 1. 2 you loved us?" Is not Esau Jacob's *b*?
Mt 5.22 if you are angry with a *b* or sister, you
10.21 *B* will betray *b* to death, and a father
12.46 his mother and his *b* were standing
12.50 the will of my Father in heaven is my *b*,
13.55 are not his *b* James and Joseph and
20.24 it, they were angry with the two *b*.
28.10 go and tell my *b* to go to Galilee; there
Mk 3.35 does the will of God is my *b* and sister
12.19 widow and raise up children for his *b*.
13.12 *B* will betray *b* to death, and a father
Lk 8.20 mother and your *b* are standing outside,
Jn 7. 5 (For not even his *b* believed in him.)
Acts 7.13 Joseph made himself known to his *b*,
7.26 you are *b*; why do you wrong each
9.17 hands on Saul and said, "*B* Saul, the
Rom 14.10 Why do you pass judgment on your *b* or
14.21 that makes your *b* or sister stumble.
1 Cor 5.11 with anyone who bears the name of *b* or
2 Cor 8.18 we are sending the *b* who is famous
Gal 1.19 apostle except James the Lord's *b*.
1 Thess 4. 6 that no one wrong or exploit a *b* or
Philem 16 but more than a slave, a beloved *b*
1 Jn 3.17 sees a *b* or sister in need, yet refuses to
4.20 "I love God," and hates their *b* or sisters,

BRUISED

Isa 42. 3 a *b* reed he will not break, and a dimly

BUCKET

Isa	40.15 the nations are like a drop from a *b*,

BUILD (BUILDING BUILDS BUILT)

1 Kings	6. 1 he began to *b* the house of the LORD.
1 Chr	17.12 He shall *b* a house for me, and I will
	22.19 Go and *b* the sanctuary of the LORD God
2 Chr	2. 6 who is able to *b* him a house, since
Neh	2.18 to me. Then they said, "Let us start *b*!"
Ps	127. 1 Unless the LORD *b* the house, those who
Prov	9. 1 Wisdom has *b* her house, she has hewn
	14. 1 The wise woman *b* her house, but the
	24. 3 By wisdom a house is *b*, and by
Eccl	2. 4 works; I *b* houses and planted vineyards
Isa	61. 4 They shall *b* up the ancient ruins, they
Jer	29. 5 *B* houses and live in them; plant
Dan	4.30 magnificent Babylon, which I have *b* as
Hab	2.12 for you who *b* a town by bloodshed,
Hag	1. 8 hills and bring wood and *b* the house,
Mal	1. 4 They may *b*, but I will tear down, until
Mt	16.18 on this rock I will *b* my church, and the
Lk	6.48 like a man *b* a house, who dug deeply
	14.30 fellow began to *b*, and was not able
Acts	20.32 a message that is able to *b* you up and
1 Cor	10.23 are lawful," but not all things *b* up.
	14.12 to excel in them for *b* up the church.
	14.26 Let all things be done for *b* up. If
2 Cor	10. 8 which the Lord gave for *b* you up
	12.19 do, beloved, is for the sake of *b* you up.
Eph	2.20 household of God, *b* upon the
1 Thess	5.11 one another and *b* up each other,
Jude	20 beloved, *b* yourselves up on most holy

BUILDERS

Ps	118. 22 The stone that the *b* rejected has
Lk	20.17 stone that the *b* rejected has become

BUILDING (BUILDINGS)

Mk	13. 1 what large stones and what large *b*!"
1 Cor	3. 9 together; you are God's field, God's *b*.

BULWARK (BULWARKS)

Ps	8. 2 you have founded a *b* because of your
Isa	26. 1 city; he sets up victory like walls and *b*.
Jer	50.15 surrendered; her *b* have fallen, her walls

BURDEN (BURDENS) (n)

Num	11.11 that you lay the *b* of all this people on
Ps	38. 4 my head; they weigh like a *b* too heavy
	55.22 Cast your *b* on the LORD, and he will
	66.11 us into the net; you laid *b* on our backs;
Isa	9. 4 the yoke of their *b*, and the bar across
	10.27 On that day his *b* will be removed from
Jer	17.21 that you do not bear a *b* on the sabbath
	23.33 asks you, "What is the *b* of the LORD?"
	23.36 the *b* is everyone's own word, and so
Mt	11.30 For my yoke is easy, and my *b* is light."
	20.12 equal to us who have borne the *b* of the
	23. 4 They tie up heavy *b*, hard to bear, and
Lk	11.46 you load people with *b* hard to bear,
Acts	15.28 impose on you no further *b* than these
Gal	6. 2 Bear one another's *b*, and in this way
Rev	2.24 I say, I do not lay upon you any other *b*;

BURDEN (BURDENED BURDENING)

Isa	43.24 But you have *b* me with your sins; you
2 Cor	11. 9 and will continue to refrain from *b* you
	12.13 except that I myself did not *b* you?
2 Thess	3. 8 day, so that we might not *b* any of you.

BURIAL

Mk	14. 8 anointed my body beforehand for its *b*.

BURN (BURNED BURNING)

Josh	11.11 who breathed, and he *b* Hazor with fire.
Ps	38. 7 my loins are filled with *b*, and there is
	39. 3 While I mused, the fire *b*; then I spoke
Jer	20. 9 like a *b* fire shut up in my bones,

Jer	36.25 urged the king not to *b* the scroll, he
	39. 8 Chaldeans *b* the king's house and the
	52.13 He *b* the house of the LORD, the king's
Lam	2. 3 he has *b* like a flaming fire in Jacob,
Mt	13.30 first and bind them in bundles to be *b*,
Lk	24.32 "Were not our hearts *b* within us while
Acts	19.19 their books and *b* them publicly;
1 Cor	3.15 If the work is *b* up, the builder will

BURNT OFFERING (BURNT OFFERINGS)

Gen	8.20 clean bird, and offered *b* on the altar.
	22. 7 are here, but where is the lamb for a *b*?"
Ex	29.18 it is a *b* to the LORD; it is a pleasing
Lev	1. 3 If the offering is a *b* from the herd, you
	1.17 the wood that is on the fire; it is a *b*,
	6. 9 This is the ritual of the *b*. The *b* itself
Judg	13.16 if you want to prepare a *b*, then offer it
1 Sam	7. 9 lamb and offered it as a whole *b*
	13.12 so I forced myself, and offered the *b*."
	15.22 Has the LORD as great delight in *b* and
2 Sam	24.24 I will not offer *b* to the LORD my God
2 Kings	3.27 succeed him, and offered him as a *b*
1 Chr	16.40 to offer *b* to the LORD on the altar of *b*
	21.26 and presented *b* and offerings of
Ezra	3. 4 and offered the daily *b* by number
Ps	40. 6 ear. *B* and sin offering you have not
	50. 8 you; your *b* are continually before me.
	51.16 if I were to give a *b*, you would not be
Isa	1.11 I have had enough of *b* of rams and the
Jer	7.21 Add your *b* to your sacrifices, and eat
Ezek	46.12 provides a freewill offering, either a *b*
Dan	8.11 it took the regular *b* away from him and
Mic	6. 6 Shall I come before him with *b*, with

BURY (BURIED)

Gen	23.19 Abraham *b* Sarah his wife in the cave of
	35.29 and his sons Esau and Jacob *b* him.
	47.29 truly with me. Do not *b* me in Egypt.
Deut	34. 6 He was *b* in a valley in the land of
Mt	8.21 "Lord, first let me go and *b* my father."
Lk	9.59 "Lord, first let me go and *b* my father."
Rom	6. 4 we have been *b* with him by baptism
1 Cor	15. 4 he was *b*, and that he was raised on the
Col	2.12 when you were *b* with him in baptism,

BUSH

Ex	3. 2 to him in a flame of fire out of a *b*;
Jon	4. 6 God appointed a *b*, and made it come
Lk	20.37 showed, in the story about the *b*,
Acts	7.30 Sinai, in the flame of a burning *b*.

BUSHEL

Mt	5.15 lighting a lamp puts it under a *b* basket,
Mk	4.21 brought in to be put under a *b* basket,

BUSY

1 Kings	20.40 While your servant was *b* here and
Ps	141. 4 to *b* myself with wicked deeds in

BUSYBODIES

2 Thess	3.11 in idleness, mere *b*, not doing any work.
1 Tim	5.13 not merely idle, but also gossips and *b*,

BUY (BOUGHT)

Ex	21. 2 When you *b* a male Hebrew slave, he
2 Sam	24.24 "No, but I will *b* them from you for a
1 Chr	21.24 "No; I will *b* them for the full price. I
Neh	5. 8 have *b* back our Jewish kindred who
Hos	3. 2 I *b* her for fifteen shekels of silver and a
1 Cor	6.20 you were *b* with a price; therefore
	7.23 You were *b* with a price; do not become
2 Pet	2. 1 even deny the Master who *b* them—

BUYER

Deut	28.68 female slaves, but there will be no *b*.

BYWORD

Deut	28.37 and a *b* among all the peoples where
2 Chr	7.20 make it a proverb and a *b* among all

Job	17.	6 "He has made me a *b* of the peoples,
Ps	44.	14 have made us a *b* among the nations,

C

CAESAREA

Mt	16.	13 came into the district of *C* Philippi,
Mk	8.	27 disciples to the villages of *C* Philippi;
Acts	8.	40 to all the towns until he came to *C*.
	10.	1 In *C* there was a man named Cornelius,
	11.	11 three men, sent to me from *C*, arrived
	18.	22 When he had landed at *C*, he went up
	23.	33 When they came to *C* and delivered the
	25.	4 replied that Paul was being kept at *C*,

CAIAPHAS

High priest, Mt 26.3, 57; Lk 3.2; Jn 18.13; prophesied that Jesus should die, 11.49-53; 18.14; took part in the trial of Jesus, Mt 26.62-66 (Mk 14.60-64; Jn 18.19-24,28); present at examination of Peter and John, Acts 4.6-21.

CAIN (CAIN'S)

Gen	4.	1 Eve, and she conceived and bore *C*,
	4.	3 *C* brought to the LORD an offering of the
	4.	8 *C* rose up against his brother Abel, and
	4.	16 *C* went away from the presence of the
	4.	25 instead of Abel, for *C* had killed him."
Heb	11.	4 God a more acceptable sacrifice than *C*.
1 Jn	3.	12 not be like *C* who was from the evil one
Jude		11 they go the way of *C*, and abandon

CAKE (CAKES)

Gen	18.	6 of choice flour, knead it, and make *c*."
Hos	7.	8 the peoples; Ephraim is a *c* not turned.

CALAMITY

Job	6.	30 my tongue? Cannot my taste discern *c*?
Ps	18.	18 They confronted me in the day of my *c*;
Prov	1.	26 I also will laugh at your *c*; I will mock
Jer	48.	16 The *c* of Moab is near at hand and his
Dan	9.	14 So the LORD kept watch over this *c* until
Ob		13 gate of my people on the day of their *c*;

CALEB

Sent with the spies, Num 13.16; exhorted the people, Num 13.30; 14.6-10; was promised entrance into Canaan, Num 14.22-38 (32.10-12; Deut 1.34-36); Num 26.65; received Hebron as an inheritance, Josh 14.6-15; 15.13-19; Judg 1.20.

CALF (CALVES)

Gen	18.	7 herd, and took a *c*, tender and good,
Ex	32.	4 it in a mold, and cast an image of a *c*;
	32.	24 it into the fire, and out came this *c*!"
1 Kings	12.	28 took counsel, and made two *c* of gold.
Ps	106.	19 They made a *c* at Horeb and worshiped
Hos	13.	2 to these," they say. People are kissing *c*!
Lk	15.	23 get the fatted *c* and kill it, and let us
Acts	7.	41 they made a *c*, offered a sacrifice to the

CALL (CALLING CALLS)

Job	13.	22 Then *c*, and I will answer; or let me
	14.	15 You would *c*, and I would answer you;
Ps	50.	4 He *c* to the heavens above and to the
	53.	4 they eat bread, and do not *c* upon God?
	55.	16 But I *c* upon God; and the LORD will
	80.	18 us life, and we will *c* on your name.
	91.	15 When they *c* to me, I will answer them;
	102.	2 answer me speedily in the day when I *c*.
	105.	1 give thanks to the LORD, *c* on his name,
	116.	2 I will *c* on him as long as I live.
	145.	18 the LORD is near to all who *c* on him, to
Prov	8.	1 Does not wisdom *c*, does not
Isa	45.	1 I *c* you by your name, I surname you,
	55.	6 be found, *c* upon him while he is near;
	64.	7 There is no one who *c* upon your name,
	65.	24 Before they *c* I will answer, while they

Jer	3.	19 I thought you would *c* me, My Father,
	33.	3 *C* to me and I will answer you, and will
Joel	2.	15 sanctify a fast; *c* a solemn assembly;
	2.	32 who *c* on the name of the LORD
Mk	10.	49 to him, "Take heart; get up, he is *c* you.
	15.	35 it, they said "Listen, he is *c* for Elijah.
Lk	15.	6 he *c* together his friends and neighbors,
Jn	10.	3 his voice. He *c* his own sheep by name
Acts	2.	21 who *c* on the name of the Lord
Rom	10.	12 all and is generous to all who *c* on him.
	10.	14 how are they to *c* on one in whom they
	11.	29 gifts and the *c* of God are irrevocable.
1 Cor	1.	26 Consider your own *c*, brothers and
2 Tim	2.	22 who *c* upon the Lord from a pure heart.
2 Pet	1.	10 eager to confirm your *c* and election,

CALLED

Gen	13.	4 there Abram *c* on the name of the LORD.
	22.	14 So Abraham *c* that place "The LORD will
Ex	3.	4 God *c* to him out of the bush, "Moses,
Judg	16.	28 Then Samson *c* to the LORD and said,
1 Sam	3.	4 the Lord *c*, "Samuel! Samuel!" and he
Prov	1.	24 Because I have *c* and you refused, have
Song	5.	6 him; I *c* him, but he gave no answer.
Isa	41.	9 earth, and *c* from its farthest corners,
	42.	6 the LORD, I have *c* you in righteousness,
	49.	1 The LORD *c* me before I was born, while
Jer	35.	17 I have *c* to them and they have not
Mt	2.	15 prophet, "Out of Egypt have I *c* my son."
Mk	3.	13 the hills, and *c* to him those whom he
	6.	7 He *c* the twelve and began to send
Lk	1.	32 and will be *c* the Son of the Most High,
	9.	1 Jesus *c* the twelve together and gave
Acts	11.	26 the disciples were first *c* "Christians."
	28.	17 he *c* together the local leaders of the
Rom	1.	6 yourselves who are *c* to belong to Jesus
	8.	30 whom he predestined he also *c*; and
1 Cor	1.	24 to those who are *c*, both Jews and
	7.	15 It is to peace that God has *c* you.
Gal	1.	6 quickly deserting the one who *c* you in
	5.	13 you were *c* to freedom, brothers and
Heb	5.	4 it only when *c* by God, just as Aaron
	11.	8 faith Abraham obeyed when he was *c*
Jas	2.	23 and he was *c* the friend of God.
Jude		1 To those who are *c*, who are beloved in

CALM

Mt	8.	26 and the sea; and there was a dead *c*.
Mk	4.	39 wind ceased, and there was a dead *c*.
Lk	8.	24 waves; they ceased, and there was a *c*.

CAMEL (CAMELS CAMEL'S)

Gen	24.	10 the servant took ten of his master's *c*
Mt	3.	4 John wore clothing of *c* hair with a
	19.	24 easier for a *c* to go through the eye of a
	23.	24 You strain out a gnat but swallow a *c*!
Mk	10.	25 It is easier for a *c* to go through the eye
Lk	18.	25 easier for a *c* to go through the eye of a

CAMP

Num	2.	2 The Israelites shall *c* each in their
	4.	5 When the *c* is to set out, Aaron and his
	5.	2 put out of the *c* everyone who is

CANA

Jn	2.	1 there was a wedding in *C* in Galilee.
	4.	46 he came again to *C* in Galilee where he
	21.	2 the Twin, Nathanael of *C* in Galilee,

CANAAN (CANAANITE)

Gen	9.	22 Ham, the father of *C*, saw the
	9.	25 "Cursed be *C*; lowest of slaves shall he
	11.	31 the Chaldeans to go into the land of *C*;
	12.	5 they set forth to go to the land of *C*.
	42.	5 the famine had reached the land of *C*.
Ex	6.	4 with them, to give them the land of *C*,
Deut	32.	49 view the land of *C*, which I am giving to
Ps	106.	38 whom they sacrificed to the idols of *C*;

Mt 15.22 a *C* woman from that region came out

CANCELED

Lk 7.42 they could not pay, he *c* the debts

CAPABLE

Prov 31.10 A *c* wife who can find? She is far more

CAPERNAUM

Mt 4.13 left Nazareth and made his home in *C*
8. 5 When he entered *C*, a centurion came
11.23 and you *C*, will you be exalted to
17.24 When they reaced *C*, the collectors of
Mk 2. 1 When he returned to *C* after some days,
Lk 7. 1 the hearing of the people, he entered *C*.
10.15 you *C*, will you be exalted to heaven?
Jn 4.46 a royal official whose son lay ill in *C*.
6.59 he was teaching in the synagogue at *C*.

CAPTIVE (CAPTIVES)

Gen 14.14 that his nephew had been taken *c*,
Deut 21.11 you see among the *c* a beautiful woman
Ezra 2. 1 province who came from those *c* exiles
Ps 68.18 the high mount, leading *c* in thy train,
Isa 20. 4 of Assyria lead away the Egyptians as *c*
52. 2 from your neck, O *c* daughter Zion!
Jer 13.17 the LORD's flock has been taken *c*.
20. 4 he shall carry them *c* to Babylon, and
Lk 21.24 be taken away as *c* among all nations;
Rom 7.23 making me *c* to the law of sin that
2 Cor 10. 5 and we take every thought *c* to obey
Eph 4. 8 on high he made captivity itself a *c*;
Rev 13.10 If you are to be taken *c*, into captivity

CAPTIVITY

Isa 46. 2 the burden, but themselves go into *c*.
Jer 15. 2 famine, and those destined for *c*, to *c*.
22.22 and your lovers shall go into *c*;
Ezek 39.23 Israel went into *c* for their iniquity,

CAPTORS

Ps 137. 3 our *c* asked us for songs, and our
Isa 14. 2 will take captive those who were their *c*,

CARE (CARED CARES)

Deut 32.10 *c* for him, guarded him as the apple of
Ps 8. 4 of them, mortals that you *c* for them?
142. 4 refuge remains to me; no one *c* for me.
Jer 30.17 an outcast: "It is Zion, no one *c* for her!"
Mk 4.38 do you not *c* that we are perishing?"
4.19 but the *c* of the world, and the lure of
Lk 8.14 they are choked by the *c* and riches and
10.34 him to an inn, and took *c* of him.
1 Cor 3.10 must choose with *c* how to build it.
12.25 but the members may have the same *c*
Heb 2. 6 them, or mortals, that you *c* for them?

CAREFUL

Deut 5.32 You must therefore be *c* to do as the
2 Kings 10.31 Jehu was not *c* to follow the law of the

CARELESS

Prov 14.16 the fool throws off restraint and is *c*.
Mt 12.36 have to give an account for every *c* word

CARMEL

Josh 12.22 one; the king of Jokneam in *C*, one;
1 Sam 15.12 "Saul went to *C*, where he set up a
25. 5 "Go up to *C*, and go to Nabal, and greet
1 Kings 18.19 all Israel assemble for me at Mount *C*,
Song 7. 5 Your head crowns you like *C*, and your
Isa 35. 2 to it, the majesty of *C* and Sharon.

CARPENTER (CARPENTER'S)

Isa 44.13 The *c* stretches a line, marks it out with
Mt 13.55 Is not this the *c* son? Is not his mother
Mk 6. 3 Is not this the *c*, the son of Mary and

CARRY (CARRIED CARRIES CARRYING)

Gen 50.25 comes to you, you shall *c* up my bones
Deut 1.31 your God *c* you, just as one *c* a child,
2 Kings 24.14 He *c* away all Jerusalem, all the
2 Chr 36. 7 Nebuchadnezzar also *c* some of the
Ps 49.17 when they die they will *c* nothing away;
Eccl 5.15 for their toil, which they may *c* away
Isa 46. 4 even when you turn gray I will *c* you.
63. 9 he lifted them up and *c* them all the
Jer 20. 5 and seize them, and *c* them to Babylon.
Mk 15.21 to *c* his cross; it was Simon of Cyrene,
Lk 14.27 Whoever does not *c* the cross and follow
24.51 from them and was *c* up into heaven.
Jn 19.17 *c* the cross by himself, he went out to
Acts 13.29 they had *c* out all that was written
2 Cor 4.10 always *c* in the body the death of Jesus,
Rev 17.17 to *c* out his purpose by agreeing to give

CASE

Num 27. 5 Moses brought their *c* before the LORD.
Job 13.18 I have indeed prepared my *c*; I know
23. 4 I would lay my *c* before him, and fill my
Prov 18.17 one who first states a *c* seems right,
25. 9 Argue your *c* with your neighbor
Isa 41.21 Set forth your *c*, says the LORD; bring
Jn 18.38 and told them, "I find no *c* against him.
19. 4 you know that I find no *c* against him."
19. 6 crucify him; I find no *c* against him."
Acts 25.14 Festus laid Paul's *c* before the king,

CAST (CASTING CASTS)

Gen 21.10 "C out this slave woman with her son;
2 Kings 21.14 I will *c* off the remnant of my heritage,
Ps 42. 5 Why are you *c* down, O my soul, and
43. 5 Why are you *c* down, O my soul, and
55.22 *C* your burden on the LORD, and he will
Prov 21.12 wicked; he *c* the wicked down to ruin.
Jer 7.15 I will *c* you out of my sight, just as I *c*
Mk 3.15 and to have authority to *c* out demons.
3.22 and by the ruler of the demons he *c* out
9.28 privately, "Why could we not *c* it out?"
Lk 9.49 we saw a man *c* out demons in your
11.15 "He *c* out demons by Beelzebul, the
Jn 21. 6 "C the net to the right side of the boat,

CASTLE

Lk 11.21 a strong man, fully armed, guards his *c*,

CATCH (CATCHES CATCHING CAUGHT)

Jer 5.26 they set a trap; they *c* human beings.
Lk 5.10 from now on you will be *c* people."
1 Cor 3.19 "He *c* the wise in their craftiness,
2 Cor 12. 2 ago was *c* up to the third heaven—
1 Thess 4.17 will be *c* up in the clouds together with

CATTLE

Gen 1.25 God made . . . the *c* of every kind, and
Job 18. 3 Why are we counted as *c*? Why are we

CAUSE

Job 5. 8 seek God, to God I would commit my *c*.
Ps 35. 7 without *c* they hid their net for me;
69. 4 my head those who hate me without *c*;
119.154 Plead my *c* and redeem me; give me life
140. 12 LORD maintains the *c* of the needy, and
Prov 23.11 strong; he will plead their *c* against you.
Isa 51.22 God who pleads the *c* of his people:
Jer 5.28 they do not judge with justice the *c* of
Jn 15.25 their law, 'They hated me without a *c*.'

CAVE (CAVES)

Gen 19.30 Zoar; so he lived in a *c* with his two
23.19 buried Sarah his wife in the *c* of the
25. 9 buried him in the *c* of Machpelah, in
49.29 Bury me with my ancestors—in the *c*
50.13 buried him in the *c* of the field at
1 Sam 13. 6 people hid themselves in *c* and in holes
22. 1 there and escaped to the *c* of Adullam;

1 Kings 18. 4 hundred prophets, hid them fifty to a *c*,
 19. 9 At that place he came to a *c*, and spent
Isa 2.19 Enter the *c* of the rocks and the holes

CEASE (CEASED CEASES CEASING)
1 Sam 7. 8 "Do not *c* to cry out to the LORD our
 12.23 against the LORD by *c* to pray for you;
Ezra 4.23 and by fear and power made them *c*.
Job 3.17 There the wicked *c* from troubling, and
Ps 46. 9 He makes wars *c* to the end of the
Prov 22.10 goes out; quarreling and abuse will *c*.
Isa 1.16 *c* to do evil, learn to do good; seek
Lam 3.22 The steadfast love of the LORD never *c*,
Dan 9.27 he shall make sacrifice and offering *c*;
Jon 1.15 the sea; and the sea *c* from its raging.
Mk 6.51 into the boat with them and the wind *c*.
Rev 4. 8 Day and night without *c* they sing,

CEDAR (CEDARS)
Judg 9.15 bramble and devour the *c* of Lebanon.'
Ps 29. 5 voice of the LORD breaks the *c*; the LORD
Song 1.17 the beams of our house are *c*, our
Isa 2.13 against all the *c* of Lebanon, lofty and
 9.10 down, but we will put *c* in their place."
Ezek 31. 3 Consider Assyria, a *c* of Lebanon, with

CELLAR
Lk 11.33 lighting a lamp puts it in a *c*, but on

CENSUS
Num 1. 2 Take a *c* of the whole congregation of
 26. 2 Take a *c* of the whole congregation of
Acts 5.37 rose up at the time of the *c* and got

CENTURION
Mt 8. 5 a *c* came to him, appealing to him and
 27.54 and those with him, who were
Mk 15.39 Now when the *c*, who stood facing him,
Lk 7. 2 A *c* there had a slave whom he valued
 23.47 When the *c* saw what had taken place,

CEPHAS
1 Cor 15. 5 that he appeared to *C*, then to the

CERTIFIED
Jn 3.33 testimony has *c* this, that God is true.

CHAFF
Job 21.18 wind, and like *c* that the storm carries
Ps 1. 4 are not so but are like *c* which the wind
 35. 5 them be like *c* before the wind, with
Isa 17.13 they will flee far away, chased like *c* on
 29. 5 the multitude of tyrants like flying *c*.
 33.11 You conceive *c*, you bring forth stubble;
 41.15 and you shall make the hills like *c*.
Dan 2.35 broken in pieces and became like the *c*
Hos 13. 3 like *c* that swirls from the threshing
Mt 3.12 but the *c* he will burn with . . . fire.
Lk 3.17 but the *c* he will burn with . . . fire.

CHAIN (CHAINS)
Mk 5. 3 restrain him anymore, even with a *c*;
Acts 26.29 become as I am—except for these *c*."
 28.20 of Israel that I am bound with this *c*."
2 Tim 1.16 me and was not ashamed of my *c*;

CHANGE (CHANGED)
Gen 31.41 and you have *c* my wages ten times.
 35. 2 purify yourselves, and *c* your clothes;
Ex 13.17 they may *c* their minds and return to
 32.12 *c* your mind and do not bring disaster
Num 23.19 or a mortal, that he should *c* his mind.
Esth 9. 1 which had been *c* to a day when the
Ps 102.26 a garment. You *c* them like clothing,
Jer 2.11 Has a nation *c* its gods, even though
 13.23 Can Ethiopians *c* their skin or leopards
 18. 8 turns from its evil, I will *c* my mind
 26.13 the LORD will *c* his mind about the
 26.19 did not the LORD *c* his mind about the

Dan 4.16 his mind be *c* from that of a human,
Hos 4. 7 me; they *c* their glory into shame.
Mal 3. 6 For I the LORD do not *c*; therefore you,
Mt 18. 3 unless you *c* and become like children,
 21.29 not'; but later he *c* his mind and went.
1 Cor 15.51 We will not all die, but we will all be *c*,
Heb 7.21 Lord has sworn and will not *c* his mind,

CHANNELS
Job 28.10 They cut out *c* in the rocks, and their
Ps 18.15 the *c* of the sea were seen, and the

CHARACTER
Rom 5. 4 endurance produces *c*, and *c* produces
Heb 6.17 the unchangeable *c* of his purpose,

CHARGE (CHARGED CHARGES)
Gen 28. 1 Jacob and blessed him, and *c* him,
Deut 3.28 But *c* Joshua, and encourage and
 33. 4 Moses *c* us with the law, as a
1 Kings 2. 1 to die drew near, he *c* Solomon his son,
Neh 5. 7 I brought *c* against the nobles and the
Ezra 1. 2 he has *c* me to build him a house at
Mt 27.37 over his head they put the *c* against
Mk 13.34 he leaves home and puts his slaves in *c*,
Lk 11.50 may be *c* with the blood of all
Acts 25. 7 bringing many serious *c* against him,
 25.18 they did not *c* him with any of the
 25.27 without indicating the *c* against
Rom 3. 9 for we have already *c* that all, both Jews
 8.33 will bring any *c* against God's elect?

CHARIOT (CHARIOTS)
Josh 17.16 who live in the plain have *c* of iron,
2 Kings 2.11 a *c* of fire and horses of fire separated
 6.17 of horses and *c* of fire round all Elisha.
Ps 20. 7 Some take pride in *c*, and some in
Isa 31. 1 who rely on horses, who trust in *c*
Joel 2. 5 As with the rumbling of *c*, they leap on
Nah 2. 4 The *c* race madly through the streets,
Hab 3. 8 you drove your horses, your *c* to victory?
Zech 6. 1 up and saw four *c* came out from

CHARM
Isa 47.11 upon you, which you cannot *c* away;

CHARMER (CHARMERS)
Ps 58. 5 it does not hear the voice of *c* or of the
Eccl 10.11 charmed, there is no advantage in a *c*.

CHASE (CHASED)
Lev 26. 7 You shall give *c* to your enemies, and
Deut 1.44 out against you and *c* you as bees do.
Neh 13.28 the Horonite; I *c* him away from me.

CHASTENING
Isa 26.16 poured out a prayer when your *c* was on

CHASTISE
Ps 39.11 You *c* mortals in punishment for sin,
Jer 30.11 I will *c* you in just measure, and I will
 46.28 I will *c* you in just measure, and I will

CHEAT
Lev 25.17 You shall not *c* one another, but you

CHEDORLAOMER
Gen 14. 1 King Arioch of Ellasar, King *C* of Elam,

CHEEK (CHEEKS)
1 Kings 22.24 up to Micaiah, slapped him on the *c*,
2 Chr 18.23 up to Micaiah, slapped him on the *c*,
Song 1.10 Your *c* are comely with ornaments, your
Isa 50. 6 my *c* to those who pulled out the beard;
Lam 3.30 to give one's *c* to the smiter, and be
Mt 5.39 if anyone strikes you on the right *c*,

CHEER
Job 9.27 my sad countenance and be of good *c*,'

CHEERFUL

Prov	15.13 A glad heart makes a *c* countenance,
	17.22 A *c* heart is a good medicine, but a
2 Cor	9. 7 compulsion, for God loves a *c* giver.

CHEERFULNESS

| Rom | 12. 8 in diligence; the compassionate, in *c*. |

CHERISHED

| Ps | 66.18 If I had *c* iniquity in my heart, the Lord |
| Ezek | 35. 5 Because you *c* an ancient enmity, and |

CHERUB (CHERUBIM)

Gen	3.24 of the garden of Eden he placed the *c*,
Ex	25.18 You shall make two *c* of gold; you shall
	26. 1 make them with *c* skillfully worked
2 Sam	22.11 He rode on a *c*, and flew; he was seen
1 Kings	6.23 he made two *c* of olivewood, each ten
Isa	37.16 Israel, who are enthroned above the *c*,
Ezek	9. 3 God of Israel had gone up from the *c*
	10. 3 Now the *c* were standing on the south
	28.14 With an anointed *c* as guardian I placed
Heb	9. 5 above it were the *c* of glory

CHEST

| Zech | 13. 6 "What are these wounds on your *c*?" the |

CHEW (CHEWS)

| Lev | 11.26 or does not *c* the cud is unclean |
| Deut | 14. 6 and *c* the cud, among the animals, you |

CHILD

Ruth	4.16 Naomi took the *c* and laid him in her
1 Kings	3. 7 although I am only a little *c*; I do not
Ps	131. 2 like a weaned *c* with its mother; my
Prov	2. 1 My *c*, if you accept my words and
	10. 1 A wise *c* makes a glad father but a
	23.19 Hear, my *c*, and be wise, and direct
	23.26 My *c*, give me your heart, and let your
	27.11 Be wise, my *c*, and make my heart glad,
	29.15 a mother is disgraced by a neglected *c*.
Isa	9. 6 For a *c* has been born for us, a son is
	11. 6 together, and a little *c* shall lead them.
Ezek	18.20 A *c* shall not suffer for the iniquity of a
Hos	11. 1 Israel was a *c*, I loved him, and out of
Mt	1.18 found to be with *c* from the Holy Spirit.
	2. 8 "Go and search diligently for the *c*; and
	7. 9 who if your *c* asks for bread, will give a
	18. 2 He called a *c*, whom he put among
Mk	9.36 he took a little *c* and put it among
	13.12 brother to death, and a father his *c*,
Lk	1.41 greeting, the *c* leaped in her womb.
	1.66 said, "What then will this *c* become?"
	1.76 you, *c*, will be called the prophet of the
	1.80 the *c* grew and became strong in spirit,
	2.40 the *c* grew and became strong, filled
	2.48 his mother said to him, "*C*, why have
	11.11 if your *c* asks for a fish, will give a
	8.54 by the hand and called out, "*C*, get up!"
	9.47 thoughts, took a little *c* and put it by
1 Cor	13.11 I was a *c*, I spoke like a *c*, I thought
Gal	4. 7 but a *c*, and if a *c* then also an heir,
1 Tim	1. 2 To Timothy, my loyal *c* in the faith:
2 Tim	1. 2 To Timothy, my beloved *c*: Grace,
Heb	12. 5 "My *c*, do not regard lightly the
1 Jn	5. 1 who loves the parent loves the *c*.
Rev	12. 4 that he might devour her *c* as soon as it

CHILDBEARING

| 1 Tim | 2.15 she will be saved through *c*, provided |

CHILDHOOD

| 2 Tim | 3.15 how from *c* you have known the sacred |

CHILDLESS

| Gen | 15. 2 what will you give me, for I continue *c*, |
| Gal | 4.27 "Rejoice, you *c* one, you who bear no |

CHILDREN (CHILDREN'S)

Gen	18.19 chosen him, that he may charge his *c*
	33. 5 "The *c* whom God has graciously given
Ex	12.26 when your *c* ask you, "What do you
Num	14.18 the iniquity of the parents upon the *c*
Deut	1.39 your *c*, who today do not yet know right
	4.10 on the earth, and may teach their *c* so";
	6. 7 Recite them to your *c* and talk about
	11. 2 Remember today that it was not your *c*
	12.25 go well with you and your *c* after you,
	32.46 give them as a command to your *c*,
1 Kings	9. 6 you or your *c*, do not keep my
2 Kings	14. 6 nor *c* be put to death for the parents;
2 Chr	6.16 if only your *c* keep to their way, to walk
	25. 4 he did not put their *c* to death,
Job	8. 4 If your *c* sinned against him, he
Ps	89.30 If his *c* forsake my law and and do not
	103. 17 fear him, and his righteousness to *c c*,
	128. 3 your *c* will be like olive shoots around
	128. 6 May you see your *c c*! Peace be upon
Prov	4. 1 Listen, *c*, to a father's instruction, and
	13.22 good leave an inheritance to their *c c*,
	13.24 Those who spare the rod hate their *c*,
	17.25 Foolish *c* are a grief to their father and
	19.26 their mother are *c* who cause shame
	20.11 Even *c* make themselves known by their
	22. 6 Train *c* in the right way, and when old,
	29.17 Discipline your *c*, and they will give you
	31.28 Her *c* rise up and call her happy; her
Isa	1. 2 I reared *c* and brought them up, but
	8.18 I and the *c* whom the Lord has given
	30. 9 rebellious people, faithless *c*, *c* who will
	49.20 The *c* born in the time of your
	54.13 All your *c* shall be taught by the Lord,
	66. 8 as Zion was in labor she delivered her *c*.
Jer	31.29 grapes, and the *c* teeth are set on edge."
Ezek	5.10 midst, and *c* shall eat their parents;
	18. 2 grapes, and the *c* teeth are set on edge"?
	23.39 they had slaughtered their *c* for their
Hos	1.10 be said to them, "*C* of the living God."
Joel	1. 3 Tell your *c* of it, and let your *c* tell their
Mal	4. 6 will turn the hearts of parents to their *c*
Mt	2.16 and he sent and killed all the *c*
	3. 9 these stones to raise up *c* to Abraham.
	5. 9 for they will be called *c* of God.
	7.11 know how to give good gifts to your *c*,
	17.26 Jesus said to him, "Then the *c* are free.
	19.13 Then little *c* were being brought to him
	19.14 "Let the little *c* come to me, and do not
	21.15 heard the *c* crying out in the temple,
Mk	7.27 said to her, "Let the *c* be fed first, for it
	10.14 "Let the little *c* come to me; do not
Lk	1.17 to turn the hearts of parents to their *c*,
	3. 8 is able from these stones to raise up *c*
	6.35 and you will be *c* of the Most High;
	7.32 like *c* sitting in the marketplace and
	16. 8 the *c* of this age are more shrewd in
	18.16 "Let the little *c* come to me, and do not
Jn	1.12 he gave power to become *c* of God,
	8.39 "If you were Abraham's *c*, you would be
	12.36 so that you may become *c* of light."
	13.33 Little *c*, I am with you only a little
Acts	2.39 promise is for you, for your *c*, and for
Rom	8.14 led by the Spirit of God are *c* of God.
	8.16 we are *c* of God, and if *c*, then heirs,
	9. 8 but the *c* of the promise are counted
1 Cor	7.14 Otherwise, your *c* would be unclean,
	14.20 do not be *c* in your thinking; rather, be
2 Cor	12.14 *c* ought not to lay up for their parents,
Gal	3.26 Jesus you are all *c* of God through faith.
	4.28 my friends, are *c* of promise, like Isaac.
Eph	1. 5 adoption as his *c* through Jesus Christ,
	2. 3 and we were by nature *c* of wrath,
	4.14 We must no longer be *c*, tossed to and
	6. 1 *C*, obey your parents in the Lord, for
Phil	2.15 *c* of God without blemish in the midst

Col	3.20 *C*, obey your parents in everything, for
1 Thess	5. 5 you are all *c* of light and *c* of the day;
1 Pet	1.14 Like obedient *c*, do not be conformed
1 Jn	2.18 *C*, it is the last hour! As you have heard
	3. 1 us, that we should be called *c* of God;
2 Jn	4 some of your *c* walking in the truth,

CHOKE (CHOKED)

Mt	13.22 lure of wealth *c* the word, and it yields
Mk	4. 7 thorns, the thorns grew up and *c* it,
	4.19 other things come in and *c* the word,
Lk	8. 7 and the thorns grew with it and *c* it.
	8.14 their way, they are *c* by the cares and

CHOOSE (CHOOSES CHOOSING)

Num	16. 7 man whom the LORD *c* shall be the holy
	17. 5 staff of the man whom I *c* shall sprout;
Deut	12. 5 God will *c* out of all your tribes as his
	14.24 LORD your God will *c* to set his name
	17.15 a king whom the LORD your God will *c*.
	30.19 *C* life so that you and your descendants
Josh	24.15 *c* this day whom you will serve, whether
1 Sam	17. 8 *C* a man for yourselves, and let him
2 Sam	24.12 Three things I offer you; *c* one of them,
1 Chr	21.10 Three things I offer you; *c* one of them,
Ps	16. 4 who *c* another god multiply their
	25.12 will teach them the way they should *c*.
	65. 4 Happy are those whom you *c* and bring
Prov	1.29 and did not *c* the fear of the LORD,
Isa	7.15 how to refuse the evil and *c* the good.
	58. 5 Is such the fast that I *c*, a day to
Zech	1.17 comfort Zion and again *c* Jerusalem.
Mt	20.15 to do what I *c* with what belongs
Mk	1.40 he said to him, "If you *c*, you can make
Jn	15.16 You did not *c* me, but I chose you. And
Acts	15.25 to *c* representatives and send them to
Heb	11.25 daughter, *c* rather to share ill-treatment

CHORAZIN

Mt	11.21 "Woe to you, *C*! Woe to you, Bethsaida!
Lk	10.13 "Woe to you, *C*! Woe to you, Bethsaida!

CHOSE (CHOSEN) (v)

Gen	13.11 So Lot *c* for himself all the plain of the
	18.19 No, for I have *c* him, that he may
Ex	18.25 Moses *c* able men from all Israel and
Num	1.16 were the ones *c* from the congregation,
Deut	4.37 your ancestors, he *c* their descendants
	7. 7 the LORD set his heart on you and *c* you,
	18. 5 LORD your God has *c* Levi out of all your
1 Sam	2.28 I *c* him out of all the tribes of Israel to
	10.24 see the one one whom the LORD has *c*?
1 Kings	3. 8 midst of the people whom you have *c*,
	11.13 the sake of Jerusalem, which I have *c*."
2 Kings	23.27 I will reject this city that I have *c*,
1 Chr	28.10 LORD has *c* you to build a house as the
2 Chr	29.11 for the LORD has *c* you to stand in his
Ps	47. 4 He *c* our heritage for us, the pride of
	78.68 But he *c* the tribe of Judah, Mount
	119. 30 I have *c* the way of faithfulness; I set
	119.173 to help me, for I have *c* your precepts.
Prov	22. 1 A good name is to be *c* rather than
Isa	41. 8 my servant, Jacob, whom I have *c*,
	43.10 my servant whom I have *c*, so that you
	49. 7 the Holy One of Israel, who has *c*."
	66. 3 These have *c* their own ways, and in
Jer	33.24 "The two families that the LORD *c* have
Hag	2.23 you like a signet ring; for I have *c* you,
Mt	12.18 Here is my servant, whom I have *c*, my
	22.14 For many are called, but few are *c*."
Lk	6.13 and *c* twelve of them, whom he also
	14. 7 how the guests *c* the places of honor,
Jn	13.18 I know whom I have *c*. But it is to
Acts	6. 5 they *c* Stephen, a man full of faith and
	9.15 instrument whom I have *c* to bring my
	22.14 ancestors has *c* you to know his will,
1 Cor	1.27 God *c* what is foolish in the world to

1 Cor	12.18 members in the body, each one as he *c*.
Eph	1. 4 just as he *c* us in Christ before the
1 Thess	1. 4 beloved by God, that he has *c* you,
2 Thess	2.13 God *c* you as the first fruits for
1 Pet	1. 2 who have been *c* and destined by God

CHOSEN (n and adj)

1 Chr	16.13 Israel, children of Jacob, his *c* ones.
Ps	89. 3 "I have made a covenant with my *c* one,
	105. 43 out with joy, his *c* ones with singing.
	106. 23 had not Moses, his *c* one, stood in the
Isa	42. 1 my *c*, in whom my soul delights;
	45. 4 Jacob, and Israel my *c*, I call you
	65. 9 my *c* shall inherit it, and my servants
	65.22 my *c* shall long enjoy the work of their
Lk	9.35 said, "This is my Son, my *C*; listen to
Col	3.12 As God's *c* ones, holy and beloved,
1 Pet	2. 9 you are a *c* race, a royal priesthood, a

CHRISTIAN (CHRISTIANS)

Acts	11.26 that the disciples were first called "*C*."
	26.28 quickly persuading me to become a *C*?"
1 Pet	4.16 Yet if any of you suffers as a *C*, do not

CHURCH (CHURCHES)

Mt	16.18 on this rock I will build my *c*, and the
	18.17 to listen to them, tell it to the *c*;
Acts	9.31 the *c* throughout Judea, Galilee, and
	11.22 News of this came to the ears of the *c*
	12. 1 upon some who belonged to the *c*.
	12. 5 Peter was kept in prison, the *c* prayed
	16. 5 So the *c* were strengthened in the faith
Rom	16. 5 Greet also the *c* in their house.
1 Cor	10.32 to Jews or to Greeks or to the *c* of God,
	12.28 God has appointed in the *c* first
	14. 4 but those who prophesy build up the *c*.
	15. 9 an apostle, because I persecuted the *c*
2 Cor	8. 1 has been granted to the *c* of Macedonia;
Eph	1.22 head over all things for the *c*, which is
	3.21 to him be glory in the *c* and in Christ
	5.24 Just as the *c* is subject to Christ, so
1 Tim	3. 5 how can he take care of God's *c*?
	5.16 let the *c* not be burdened, so that it can
Philem	2 soldier, and to the *c* in your house:
3 Jn	10 to do so and expels them from the *c*.
Rev	1. 4 John to the seven *c* that are in Asia:
	2.23 all the *c* will know that I am the one

CIRCLE

Prov	8.27 there, when he drew a *c* on the face of
Isa	40.22 is he who sits above the *c* of the earth,

CIRCUMCISE (CIRCUMCISED)

Gen	17.10 you: Every male among you shall be *c*.
	34.24 and every male was *c*, all who went out
Deut	10.16 *C*, then, the foreskin of your heart, and
	30. 6 God will *c* your heart and the heart of
Josh	5. 3 made flint knives and *c* the Israelites
Jer	4. 4 *C* yourselves to the LORD, remove the
Jn	7.22 and you *c* a man on the sabbath.
Acts	11. 2 the *c* believers criticized him,
	15. 1 "Unless you are *c* according to the
Gal	2. 3 with me, was not compelled to be *c*,
Col	2.11 were *c* with a spiritual circumcision,

CIRCUMCISION

Ex	4.26 she said, "A bridegroom of blood by *c*."
Rom	2.26 their uncircumcision be regarded as *c*?
	4.11 He received the sign of *c* as a seal of
1 Cor	7.19 *C* is nothing, and uncircumcision is
Gal	5. 6 in Christ Jesus neither *c* nor
Eph	2.11 by those who are called "the *c*"—

CISTERN (CISTERNS)

Prov	5.15 Drink water from your own *c*, flowing
Jer	2.13 water, and dug out *c* for themselves,
	38. 6 and threw him into the *c* of Malchiah,

CITIZENSHIP

Phil 3.20 But our c is in heaven, and it is from

CITY (CITIES)

Num	35.	6 the Levites shall include six c of refuge,
Deut	19.	2 you shall set apart three c in the land
Josh	6.	3 You shall march around the c, all the
	20.	2 'Appoint the c of refuge, of which I
2 Kings	25.	4 a breach was made in the c wall; the
Ps	46.	4 whose streams make glad the c of God,
	48.	1 to be praised in the c of our God.
Prov	11.10	blessing of the upright c is exalted,
Eccl	9.14	a little c with few people in it. A great
Isa	1.26	shall be called the c of righteousness,
Jer	39.	2 the month, a breach was made in the c.
Lam	1.	1 How lonely sits the c that once was full
Ezek	33.21	came to me and said, "The c has fallen."
Dan	9.19	because your c and your people bear
Zech	8.	3 Jerusalem shall be called the faithful c,
Mt	5.14	world. A c built on a hill cannot be hid.
Mk	1.33	the whole c was gathered around the
Lk	19.19	said to him, 'And you, rule over five c.'
Acts	17.16	to see that the c was full of idols.
Heb	11.10	he looked forward to the c that has
Rev	3.12	God, and the name of the c of my God,
	21.	2 the holy c, new Jerusalem, coming
	21.15	of gold to measure the c and its gates

CLAIMS

1 Cor 14.37 Anyone who c to be a prophet, or to

CLAN

Num 27. 4 of our father be taken away from his c

CLAY

Job	10.	9 that you have fashioned me like c;
	13.12	ashes, your defenses are defenses of c.
	33.	6 are; I too was formed from a piece of c.
Isa	29.16	Shall the potter be regarded as the c?
	45.	9 Does the c say to the one who fashions
	64.	8 we are the c, and you are our potter; we
Jer	18.	6 Just like the c in the potter's hand, so

CLEAN

Gen	7.	2 with you seven pairs of all c animals,
Deut	14.11	You may eat any c birds.
2 Kings	5.14	the flesh of a young boy, and he was c.
Job	14.	4 Who can bring a c thing out of an
	15.14	What are mortals that they can be c? Or
	25.	4 How can one born of woman be c?
	33.	9 You say, "I am c, without transgression;
Ps	24.	4 Those who have c hands and pure
	73.13	in vain I have kept my heart c and
Prov	20.	9 Who can say, "I have made my heart c;
Isa	1.16	Wash yourselves; make yourselves c;
Jer	13.27	long will it be before you are made c?
Mt	8.	2 if you choose, you can make me c."
	23.25	you c the outside of the cup and of the
Mk	1.40	"If you choose, you can make me c."
Lk	5.12	if you choose, you can make me c."
	11.41	and see, everything will be c for you.
	17.14	And as they went they were made c
Acts	10.15	"What God has made c, you must not
	11.	9 'What God has made c, you must not
Rom	14.20	Everything is indeed c, but it is wrong

CLEANNESS

Ps 18.20 according to the c of my hands he

CLEANSE (CLEANSED CLEANSES CLEANSING)

Lev	14.11	The priest who c shall set the person to
Num	8.	6 from among the Israelites and c them.
Deut	32.43	hate him, and c the land for his people.
2 Chr	29.16	part of the house of the LORD to c it,
Job	9.30	with soap and c my hands with lye,
Ps	51.	2 my iniquity, and c me from my sin.
Prov	20.30	Blows that wound c away evil; beatings
Isa	4.	4 and c the bloodstains of Jerusalem from

Jer	33.	8 I will c them from all the guilt of their
Ezek	22.24	You are a land that is not c, not rained
	36.25	from all your idols I will c you. A new
	37.23	and will c them. Then they shall be my
Dan	11.35	they may be refined, purified, and c,
Mt	10.	8 the sick, raise the dead, c the lepers,
Lk	4.27	none of them was c, except Naaman
Jn	15.	3 You have already been c by the word
2 Cor	7.	1 let us c ourselves from every defilement
Eph	5.26	to make her holy by c her with the
Jas	4.	8 C your hands, you sinners, and purify

CLEAR (CLEARED)

Gen	44.16	can we speak? How can we c ourselves?
Ps	19.12	their errors? C me from hidden faults.
	80.	9 You c the ground for it; it took deep
Lk	3.17	to c his threshing floor, and to gather

CLEFT-FOOTED

Lev 11. 3 and is c and chews the cud —such you

CLING (CLINGS)

Gen	2.24	his father and mother and c to his wife,
Job	19.20	My bones c to my skin and flesh, and I
Ps	119.25	My soul c to the dust; revive me
	119.31	I c to your decrees, O LORD; let me not
Rev	12.11	for they did not c to life even in the

CLOAK (CLOAKS)

Ruth	3.	9 spread your c over your servant, for you
1 Sam	24.	4 stealthily cut off a corner of Saul's c.
Ezek	16.	8 and I spread the edge of my c over you,
Mt	5.40	and take your coat, give your c as well;
	21.	8 A very large crowd spread their c on the
Mk	2.21	a pice of unshrunk cloth on an old c;
	5.27	him in the crowd and touched his c.
	6.56	might touch even the fringe of his c;
	11.	8 Many people spread their c on the road,
Lk	19.36	kept spreading their c on the road.
2 Tim	4.13	When you come, bring the c that I left

CLOTH

Isa	64.	6 our righteous deeds are like a filthy c.
Mt	9.16	a piece of unshrunk c on an old cloak,
Lk	2.	7 son and wrapped him in bands of c,

CLOTHE (CLOTHED CLOTHES)

Gen	3.21	for the man and his wife, and c them.
2 Chr	28.15	with the booty they c all that were
Job	29.14	I put on righteousness, and it c me; my
Ps	30.11	off my sackcloth and c me with joy,
Isa	22.21	will c him with your robe and bind your
Zech	3.	5 a clean turban on his head and c him
Mt	6.30	if God so c the grass of the field, which
	6.29	all his glory was not c like one of these.
Mk	5.15	saw the demoniac sitting there, c and in
	15.17	they c him in a purple cloak; and after
Lk	8.35	feet of Jesus, c and in his right mind;
	12.27	all his glory was not c like one of these.
	12.28	if God so c the grass of the field, which
2 Cor	5.	2 to be c with our heavenly dwelling—
Eph	4.24	and to c yourselves with a new self,
Col	3.12	c yourselves with compassion, kindness,
Rev	16.15	is the one who stays awake and is c,

CLOTHES (CLOTHING)

Deut	8.	4 The c on your back did not wear out
Job	31.19	I have seen anyone perish for lack of c,
Ps	22.18	they divide my c among themselves, and
Prov	25.20	Like a moth in c or a worm in wood,
	27.26	lambs will provide your c, and the goats
Mt	6.25	than food, and the body more than c?
	7.15	prophets, who come to you in sheep's c
	17.	2 sun, and his c became dazzling white.
	27.35	they divided his c among themselves by
Mk	15.24	divided his c among them, casting lots
Lk	8.44	touched the fringe of his c, and
	23.34	doing. And they cast lots to divide his c.

Jn	19.24 themselves, and for my *c* they cast lots."
Acts	9.39 and other *c* that Dorcas had made
1 Pet	3. 3 by wearing gold ornaments or fine *c*;

CLOUD (CLOUDS)

Gen	9.13 I set my bow in the *c*, and it shall be a
Ex	13.21 a pillar of *c* by day, to lead them along
	40.34 Then the *c* covered the tent of meeting,
Num	9.15 the *c* covered the tabernacle, the tent of
	12. 5 LORD came down in a pillar of *c*, and
Deut	31.15 the pillar of *c* stood at the entrance to
Isa	4. 5 over its places of assembly a *c* by day
Mt	17. 5 suddenly a bright *c* overshadowed them,
Mk	9. 7 Then a *c* overshadowed them, and from
Acts	1. 9 up, and a *c* took him out of their sight.
1 Cor	10. 2 all were baptized into Moses in the *c*

COAL (COALS)

Ps	18. 8 glowing *c* flamed forth from him.
	140. 10 Let burning *c* fall on them! Let them be
Prov	25.22 you will heap *c* of fire on their heads,
Isa	6. 6 seraphs flew to me, holding a live *c* that
Rom	12.20 you will heap burning *c* on their heads."

COAT (COATS)

Mt	5.40 sue you and take your *c*, give your cloak
Lk	3.11 "Whoever has two *c* must share with
	6.29 takes away your *c* do not withhold even
Acts	22.20 and keeping the *c* of those who killed

COAX

Judg	14.15 said to Samson's wife, "C your husband
	16. 5 "C him, and find out what makes his

COCK

Mt	26.74 the man!" At that moment the *c* crowed.
Mk	14.30 before the *c* crows twice, you will deny
	14.68 into the forecourt. Then the *c* crowed.
Lk	22.34 Peter, the *c* will not crow this day, until
	22.60 he was still speaking, the *c* crowed.
Jn	13.38 before the *c* crows, you will have denied

COIN (COINS)

Mt	17.27 you open its mouth you will find a *c*;
Mk	12.42 came and put in two small copper *c*,
Lk	21. 2 a poor widow put in two small copper *c*.

COLD

Mt	24.12 the love of many will grow *c*.
Rev	3.16 are lukewarm, and neither *c* nor hot,

COLLECT (COLLECTED)

Gen	47.14 Joseph *c* all the money to be found in
Mt	13.41 they will *c* out of his kingdom all

COLLECTION

1 Cor	16. 1 concerning the *c* for the saints: you

COLT

Zech	9. 9 and riding on a donkey, on a *c*, the foal
Mk	11. 2 you will find tied there a *c* that has
Lk	19.30 will find tied there a *c* that has never

COME

Gen	24.31 "C in, O blessed of the LORD. Why do
Num	10.29 *c* with us, and we will treat you well;
Ps	66.16 C and hear, all you who fear God, and I
	100. 2 C into his presence with singing.
Prov	2.19 those who go to her never *c* back, nor
	25. 7 for it is better to be told, "C up here,"
Song	7.11 C, my beloved, let us go forth into the
Isa	1.18 C now, let us argue it out, says the
	2. 3 C, let us go up to the mountain of the
	2. 5 of Jacob, *c*, let us walk in the light
	26.20 C, my people, enter your chambers, and
	35. 4 recompense. He will *c* and save you."
	55. 1 you that have no money, *c*, buy and eat!
Jer	2.27 their trouble they say, "C and save us!"
Hos	6. 1 "C, let us return to the LORD; for it is he

Mic	4. 2 "C, let us go up to the mountain of the
Mal	3. 1 you seek will suddenly *c* to his temple;
Mt	6.10 Your kingdom *c*, Your will be done, on
	8. 9 to another, 'C,' and he *c*, and to my
	11. 3 "Are you the one who is to *c*, or are we
	11.28 C to me, all you that are weary and are
	24. 5 For many will *c* in my name, saying, 'I
Mk	6.31 "C away to a deserted place all by
	13. 6 Many will *c* in my name and say, 'I am
Jn	1.39 He said to them, "C and see." They came
	4.29 "C and see a man who told me
	7.28 I am from. I have not *c* on my own.
	7.37 "Let anyone who is thirsty *c* to me, and
	11.43 cried with a loud voice, "Lazarus, *c* out!"
Acts	1.11 will *c* in the same way as you saw him
	16. 9 "C over to Macedonia and help us."
Rom	15.23 years, to *c* to you when I go to Spain.
1 Cor	16.22 has no love for the Lord. Our Lord, *c*!
2 Tim	4. 9 Do your best to *c* to me soon, for
Heb	12.22 But you have *c* to Mount Zion and to
Rev	18. 4 "C out of her, my people, so that you
	22.17 Spirit and the Bride say, "C." And let

COMES (CAME COMING)

1 Sam	28.13 a divine being *c* up out of the ground."
2 Sam	19.15 king *c* back to the Jordan; and Judah *c*
Ps	50. 3 God *c*, and does not keep silence,
	96.13 for he is *c*, he is *c* to judge the earth.
	118. 26 Blessed is the one who *c* in the name of
Isa	63. 1 "Who is this that *c* from Edom, from
Dan	6. 6 and satraps conspired and *c* to the king
Mal	4. 1 the day is *c*, burning like an oven, when
	4. 5 the great and terrible day of the LORD *c*.
Mt	21. 9 Blessed is the one who *c* in the name of
	23.39 'Blessed is the one who *c* in the name
	24.42 not know on what day your Lord is *c*.
	25.31 "When the Son of Man *c* in his glory,
	26.64 of Power and *c* on the clouds of heaven."
Mk	3.13 whom he wanted, and they *c* to him.
	8.38 also be ashamed when he *c* in the glory
	10.45 Son of Man *c* not to be served but to
	13.26 they will see the Son of man *c* in clouds
	14.62 and '*c* with the clouds of heaven.' "
Lk	12.40 Son of Man is *c* at an unexpected hour."
	13.35 the one who *c* in the name of the Lord!' "
	21.27 'Son of Man *c* in a cloud' with power
Jn	6.35 "Whoever *c* to me will never be hungry,
	6.37 who *c* to me I will never drive away;
	12.13 Blessed is the one who *c* in the name of
	14.18 not leave you orphaned; I am *c* to you.
1 Cor	11.26 proclaim the Lord's death until he *c*.
2 Cor	13. 1 This is the third time I am *c* to you.
Heb	10.37 the one who is *c* one will come and
Jude	14 "See, the Lord is *c* with ten thousands
Rev	1. 7 Look! he is *c* with the clouds; every eye
	3.11 I am *c* soon; hold fast to what you have,
	22.12 I am *c* soon, my reward is with me, to
	22.20 these things says, "Surely I am *c* soon."

COMELY

Song	6. 4 my love, *c* as Jerusalem, terrible as an

COMFORT (n)

Ps	119. 50 This is my *c* in my distress, that your
2 Cor	7.13 to you before God. In this we find *c*.
2 Thess	2.16 grace gave us eternal *c* and good hope,

COMFORT (COMFORTED COMFORTS)

Gen	24.67 So Isaac was *c* after his mother's death.
	37.35 sought to *c* him; but he refused to be *c*,
Job	2.11 together to go and console and *c* him.
	21.34 will you *c* me with empty nothings?
Ps	23. 4 your rod and your staff—they *c* me.
	77. 2 wearying; my soul refuses to be *c*.
	86.17 you, LORD, have helped me and *c* me.
Isa	12. 1 your anger turned away, and you *c* me.
	40. 1 C, O *c* my people, says your God. Speak

Isa	49.13 For the LORD has c his people, and will
	51. 3 For the LORD will c Zion; he will c all
	51.12 I am he who c you; why then are you
	52. 9 for the LORD has c his people, he has
	61. 2 of our God; to c all who mourn;
	66.13 As a mother c her child, so I will c you;
Lam	1. 2 all her lovers she has no one to c her;
Lk	16.25 but now he is c here, and you are in

COMFORTERS

Job	16. 2 such things; miserable c are you all.
Ps	69.20 was none; and for c, but I found none.
Nah	3. 7 her? Where shall I seek c for you?

COMING (n)

Mt	24. 3 what will be the sign of your c and of
	24.27 so will be the c of the Son of Man.
	24.37 so will be the c of the Son of Man.
Lk	12.45 'My master is delayed in c.' and if he
1 Cor	15.23 fruits, then at his c those who belong to
1 Thess	2.19 boasting before our Lord Jesus at his c?
	3.13 at the c of our Lord Jesus with all his
	4.15 who are alive, who are left until the c of
	5.23 and blameless at the c of our Lord
2 Thess	2. 1 As to the c of our Lord Jesus Christ and
Jas	5. 7 beloved, until the c of the Lord.
2 Pet	1.16 to you the power and c of our Lord
	3. 4 "Where is the promise of his c? For ever
1 Jn	2.28 be put to shame before him at his c.

COMMAND (n)

Num	9.18 At the c of the LORD the Israelites would
	20.24 you rebelled against my c at the waters
	22.18 I could not go beyond the c of the LORD
Ps	68.11 The Lord gives the c; great is the
Eccl	8. 2 Keep the king's c because of your
1 Cor	7.10 To the married I give c — not I but the
	14.37 what I am writing to you is a c of the

COMMAND (COMMANDED COMMANDS)

Gen	2.16 God c the man, "You may freely eat of
	6.22 did this; he did all that God c him.
Ex	7. 2 You shall speak all that I c you, and
	39.32 just as the LORD had c Moses.
Lev	8.36 did all the things that the LORD c
Deut	4.13 his covenant, which he c you to
	28. 8 LORD will c the blessing upon you in
Josh	1. 9 I hereby c you: Be strong and
	11.15 As the LORD c . . . Moses, so Moses c
Ps	33. 9 it came to be; he c, and it stood firm.
	148. 5 LORD, for he c and they were created.
Jer	1. 7 and you shall speak whatever I c you.
	11. 4 to my voice, and do all that I c you.
	26. 2 to them all the words that I c you;
Mt	4. 6 'He will c his angels concerning you,'
	28.20 them to obey everything I have c you.
Lk	8.25 this, that he c even the winds and the
	9.54 do you want us to c fire to come down
Jn	15.14 You are my friends if you do what I c
1 Cor	9.14 Lord c that those who proclaim the
1 Tim	6.17 age are rich, c them not to be haughty,

COMMANDER (COMMANDERS COMMANDER'S)

Gen	21.22 with Phicol the c of his army, said to
Deut	20. 9 then the c shall take charge of them.
	33.21 for there a c allotment was reserved; he
Josh	5.14 as c of the army of the LORD have I now

COMMANDMENT (COMMANDMENTS)

Ex	34.28 the words of the covenant, the ten c.
Lev	27.34 These are the c that the LORD gave to
Deut	4.13 you to observe, that is, the ten c;
1 Kings	2. 3 keeping his statutes, his c, his
Ezra	9.14 shall we break your c again and
Ps	119.151 near, O LORD, and all your c are true.
Prov	4. 4 fast to my words; keep my c, and live;
	13.13 who respect the c will be rewarded.
Eccl	12.13 Fear God, and keep his c; for that is the

Mt	19.17 you wish to enter into life, keep the c."
Jn	13.34 I give you a new c, that you love one
Rom	7.12 law is holy, and the c is holy and just
1 Jn	2. 7 no new c, but an old c that you have
	5. 3 his c. And his c are not burdensome,
2 Jn	5 though I were writing you a new c, but

COMMEND (COMMENDED COMMENDS)

Prov	12. 8 One is c for good sense, but a perverse
Eccl	8.15 I c enjoyment, for there is nothing
Lk	16. 8 his master c the dishonest manager
	23.46 "Father, into your hands I c my spirit!"
Acts	20.32 now I c you to God and to the message
Rom	16. 1 I c to you our sister Phoebe, a deacon
2 Cor	3. 1 Are we beginning to c ourselves again?
	10.12 with some of those who c themselves.
	10.18 approved, but those whom the Lord c.

COMMISSION

1 Cor	9.17 of my own will, I am entrusted with a c.
Eph	3. 2 of the c of God's grace that was given
Col	1.25 became its servant according to God's c

COMMIT (COMMITTED)

Josh	22.31 you have not c this treachery against
1 Kings	15. 3 he c all the sins that his father did
Neh	2.18 they c themselves to the common good.
Job	5. 8 God, and to God I would c my cause.
Ps	31. 5 Into your hand I c my spirit; you have
	37. 5 C your way to the LORD; trust in him
Prov	16. 3 C your work to the LORD, and your plans
Jer	20.12 them, for to you have I c my cause.
Ezek	17.20 for the treason he has c against me.
Dan	9. 7 of the treachery that they have c

COMMON

Acts	2.44 were together and had all things in c;
	4.32 everything they owned was held in c.
1 Cor	10.13 overtaken you that is not c to everyone.

COMMONWEALTH

Eph	2.12 Christ, being aliens from the c of Israel,

COMMUNE

Ps	77. 6 I c with my heart in the night; I

COMMUNION

2 Cor	13.13 and the c of the Holy Spirit be with all

COMMUNITY

Jn	21.23 rumor spread in the c that this disciple

COMPANION (COMPANIONS)

Josh	14. 8 my c who went up with me made the
Judg	14.20 Samson's wife was given to his c, who
Job	6.15 My c are treacherous like a torrent-bed,
Ps	119. 63 I am a c of all who fear you, of those
Prov	13.20 wise, but the c of fools suffers harm.
	28. 7 but c of gluttons shame their parents.
Song	8.13 my c are listening for your voice;
Mal	2.14 though she is your c and your wife by
Phil	4. 3 Yes, and I ask you, my loyal c, help

COMPANY

Ps	50.18 see one, and you keep c with adulterers.
	111. 1 in the c of the upright, in the
Jer	15.17 I did not sit in the c of merrymakers,
1 Cor	15.33 be deceived: "Bad c ruins good morals."

COMPARE (COMPARED)

Ps	40. 5 none can c with you. Were I to proclaim
	89. 6 who in the skies can be c to the LORD?
Isa	46. 5 and c me, as though we were alike?
Mt	11.16 to what will I c this generation? It is
2 Cor	10.12 We do not dare to classify or c ourselves

COMPASSION

Deut	13.17 show you c, and in his c multiply you,
Judg	21. 6 Israelites had c for Benjamin their kin,

COMPASSIONATE (continued)

Judg	21.15 people had c on Benjamin because the
2 Kings	13.23 gracious to them and had c on them;
2 Chr	30. 9 kindred and your children will find c
	36.15 he had c on his people and on his
Ps	103. 13 As a father has c on his children, so the
	135. 14 his people, and have c on his servants.
Isa	14. 1 the LORD will have c on Jacob and will
	54. 7 you, but with great c I will gather you.
Jer	12.15 them up, I will again have c on them,
Dan	1. 9 allowed Daniel to receive favor and c
Mic	7.19 He will again have c upon us; he will
Zech	12.10 I will pour out a spirit of c and
Mt	9.36 he saw the crowds, he had c for them,
	14.14 and he had c for them and cured their
	15.32 "I have c for the crowd, because they
	20.34 Moved with c, Jesus touched their eyes.
Mk	6.34 he saw a great crowd; and he had c on
	8. 2 "I have c for the crowd, because they
Lk	7.13 he had c for her and said to her, and
	15.20 father saw him and was filled with c;
Heb	10.34 For you had c for those who were in

COMPASSIONATE

Ex	22.27 cries out to me, I will listen, for I am c.
Ps	78.38 he, being c, forgave their iniquity, and
Jas	5.11 Lord, how the Lord is c and merciful.

COMPEL (COMPELLED)

Mt	27.32 they c this man to carry his cross.
Lk	14.23 and lanes, and c the people to come in,
Gal	2. 3 with me, was not c to be circumcised,
	2.14 Jew, how can you c the Gentiles to live

COMPETE

Jer	12. 5 you, how will you c with horses?
1 Cor	9.24 in a race the runners all c, but only one

COMPETENT

2 Cor	3. 5 Not that we are c of ourselves to claim

COMPLAIN (COMPLAINED)

Gen	21.25 Abraham c to Abimelech about a well
Ex	16. 2 the Israelites c against Moses and Aaron
Num	11. 1 people c in the hearing of the LORD
	14. 2 Israelites c against Moses and Aaron;
	14.27 long shall this wicked congregation c
Job	7.11 of my spirit; I will c in the bitterness of
Jn	6.41 the Jews began to c about him because
Acts	6. 1 Hellenists c against the Hebrews
1 Cor	10.10 do not c as some of them did, and were

COMPLAINT

Job	23. 2 "Today also my c is bitter; his hand is
Ps	55.17 and at noon I utter my c and moan, and
	142. 2 I pour out my c before him; I tell my
Dan	6. 4 to find grounds for c against Daniel
Hab	2. 1 what he will answer concerning my c.

COMPLETE (COMPLETED COMPLETING)

Gen	15.16 the iniquity of the Amorites is not yet c."
Jn	5.36 that the Father has given me to c,
Rom	15.28 when I have c this, and have delievered
2 Cor	8.11 by c it according to your means.
Jas	1. 4 so that you may be mature and c,

COMPLETELY

Jn	17.23 that they may become c one, so that

COMPLETION

Jas	2.22 faith was brought to c by the works,

COMPREHEND

Job	37. 5 he does great things that we cannot c.
Eph	3.18 I pray that you may have power to c,

COMPUTE

Lev	25.50 They shall c with the purchaser the

CONCEAL (CONCEALED CONCEALS)

Job	31.33 if I have c my transgressions as others
Prov	12.23 One who is clever c knowledge, but the
	25. 2 It is the glory of God to c things, but
	28.13 No one who c transgressions will

CONCEIT

Job	37.24 regard any who are wise in their own c."

CONCEITED

1 Tim	6. 4 is c, understanding nothing, and has a

CONCEIVE (CONCEIVED)

Gen	4. 1 his wife Eve, and she c and bore Cain,
Ps	35.20 they c deceitful words against those

CONCERNED

Jon	4.10 LORD said, "You are c about the bush,
Phil	2.20 will be genuinely c for your welfare.

CONCOCT

Prov	16.27 Scoundrels c evil, and their speech is

CONCUBINE (CONCUBINES)

Judg	19. 2 his c became angry with him, and she
2 Sam	16.22 Absalom went in to his father's c in the

CONDEMN (CONDEMNED CONDEMNS)

Job	34.29 When he is quiet, who can c? When he
	40. 8 you c me that you may be justified?
Ps	34.22 those who take refuge in him will be c.
	37.33 or let them be c when they are brought
	94.21 righteous, and c the innocent to death.
	109. 31 to save them from those who would c
Prov	12. 2 LORD, but those who devise evil he c.
Mt	20.18 scribes, and they will c him to death;
Mk	10.33 scribes, and they will c him to death,
Lk	11.32 judgment with this generation and c it;
Jn	3.17 not to c the world, but in order that
	8.10 where are they? Has no one c you?"
Rom	8.34 Who is to c? Is it Christ Jesus, who
Col	2.16 do not let anyone c you in the matters
1 Jn	3.21 if our hearts do not c us, we have

CONDEMNATION

Rom	5.18 as one man's trespass led to c for all,
	8. 1 is now no c for those who are in Christ

CONDITION

1 Cor	7.20 you remain in the c in which you were

CONDUCT

Job	11. 4 you say, "My c is pure, and I am clean
Ps	112. 5 lend, who c their affairs with justice.
Prov	10.23 wise c is a pleasure to a person of
Col	4. 5 C yourselves wisely toward outsiders,
1 Pet	2.12 C yourselves honorably among the
	3.16 those who abuse you for your good c in

CONDUIT

2 Kings	18.17 and stood by the c of the upper pool,
	20.20 how he made the pool and the c and
Isa	36. 2 He stood by the c of the upper pool on

CONFERRED

Mt	27. 1 and elders of the people c together
Lk	22.29 on you just as my Father has c on me,

CONFESS (CONFESSED CONFESSES CONFESSING)

Lev	5. 5 you shall c the sin that you have
	26.40 But if they c their iniquity and the
Num	5. 7 c the sin that has been committed. The
1 Kings	8.33 turn again to you, c your name, pray
Ps	32. 5 "I will c my transgressions to the LORD,"
Prov	28.13 but one who c and forsakes them will
Mt	3. 6 by him in the river Jordan, c their sins.
Mk	1. 5 by him in the river Jordan, c their sins.
Jn	1.20 He c and did not deny it, but c, "I am

Jn	9.22	anyone who *c* Jesus to be the Messiah
Acts	19.18	many of those who became believers *c*
Rom	10. 9	if you *c* with your lips that Jesus is
	10.10	one *c* with the mouth and is so saved.
	15. 9	I will *c* you among the Gentiles,
Phil	2.11	every tongue should *c* that Jesus Christ
Heb	11.13	They *c* that they were strangers and
Jas	5.16	*c* your sins to one another, and pray for
1 Jn	1. 9	we *c* our sins, he who is faithful and
	4.15	abides in those who *c* that Jesus is the
Rev	3. 5	I will *c* your name before my Father and

CONFESSION

Ezra	10. 1	Ezra prayed and made *c*, weeping and
	10.11	Now make *c* to the LORD the God of
Dan	9. 4	made *c*, saying, "Ah, Lord, great and
1 Tim	6.13	made the good *c*, I charge you to keep
Heb	4.14	Son of God, let us hold fast to our *c*.

CONFIDENCE

2 Kings	18.19	of Assyria: On what do you base this *c*
Prov	3.26	the LORD will be your *c* and will keep
	11.13	who is trustworthy in spirit keeps a *c*.
Isa	36. 4	On what do you base this *c* of yours?
Mic	7. 5	in a friend, have no *c* in a loved one;
Phil	3. 4	I, too, have reason for *c* in the flesh,
2 Thess	3. 4	we have *c* in the Lord concerning you,

CONFIDENT

Ps	27. 3	war rise up against me, yet I will be *c*.
2 Cor	5. 6	So we are always *c*; even though we
	10. 7	If you are *c* that you belong to Christ,
Gal	5.10	I am *c* about you in the Lord that you
Phil	1. 6	I am *c* of this, that the one who began
Heb	6. 9	beloved, we are *c* of better things in

CONFIRMS (CONFIRMED)

Ps	119.106	I have sworn an oath and *c* it, to
Isa	44.26	who *c* the word of his servant, and
Mt	18.16	every word may be *c* by the evidence of
Mk	16.20n	*c* the message by the signs that

CONFLICTS

Jas	4. 1	Those *c* and disputes among you, where

CONFORMED

Rom	12. 2	Do not be *c* to this world but be
Phil	3.21	it may be *c* to the body of his glory,
1 Pet	1.14	do not be *c* to the desires that you

CONFRONT

Deut	31.21	this song shall *c* them as a witness,
Ps	17.13	Rise up, O LORD, *c* them, overthrow

CONFUSING

Gal	1. 7	but there are some who are *c* you and

CONFUSION

Ex	23.27	will throw into *c* all the people against
Esth	3.15	but the city of Susa was thrown into *c*.

CONFUTED

Job	32.12	there was in fact no one that *c* Job, no

CONGREGATION

Lev	4.13	If the whole *c* of Israel errs
Num	1. 2	Take a census of the whole *c* of
	35.24	the *c* shall judge between the slayer and
Ps	22.22	and sisters; in the midst of the *c* I will
	26.12	level ground; in the great *c* I will bless
	40.10	and your faithfulness from the great *c*.
	107. 32	Let them extol him in the *c* of the
Acts	7.38	in the *c* in the wilderness with the
Heb	2.12	in the midst of the *c* I will praise

CONQUER (CONQUERED CONQUERING CONQUERS)

Jn	16.33	But take courage; I have *c* the world!"
Heb	11.33	who through faith *c* kingdoms,

1 Jn	4. 4	you are from God, and have *c* them; for
	5. 4	And this is the victory that *c* the world,
Rev	2.17	To everyone who *c* I will give some of
	3. 5	If you *c* you will be clothed like them in
	3.21	one who *c*, I will give a place with me
	5. 5	Judah, the Root of David, has *c*, so that
	6. 2	to him, and he came out *c* and to *c*.
	12.11	have *c* him by the blood of the Lamb
	15. 2	those who had *c* the beast and its
	17.14	the Lamb will *c* them, for he is Lord of
	21. 7	who *c* will inherit these things, and I

CONQUERORS

Rom	8.37	we are more than *c* through him who

CONSCIENCE

Acts	23. 1	I have lived my life with a clear *c* before
	24.16	I do my best always to have a clear *c*
Rom	2.15	to which their own *c* also bears witness;
	9. 1	—I am not lying; my *c* confirms it by
	13. 5	because of wrath but also because of *c*.
1 Cor	8.10	since their *c* is weak, be encouraged to
	10.29	I mean the other's *c*, not your own. For
1 Tim	1.19	good fight, having faith and a good *c*.
2 Tim	1. 3	God— whom I worship with a clear *c*,
Heb	9. 9	cannot perfect the *c* of the worshiper,
1 Pet	3.16	Keep your *c* clear, so that, when you
	3.21	but as an appeal to God for a good *c*,

CONSCIENTIOUS

2 Chr	29.34	—for the Levites were more *c* than the

CONSECRATE (CONSECRATED CONSECRATES CONSECRATING)

Ex	13. 2	"*C* to me all the firstborn; whatever is
	19.10	"Go to the people and *c* them today and
	28.41	ordain them and *c* them, so that they
	29. 1	is what you shall do to them to *c* them,
Lev	8.10	and all that was in it, and *c* them.
	20. 7	*C* yourselves therefore, and be holy; for
	27.14	If a person *c* a house to the LORD, the
Num	8.17	in the land of Egypt I *c* them for myself,
Deut	15.19	herd and flock you shall *c* to the LORD
1 Chr	29. 5	will offer willingly, *c* themselves today
Jer	1. 5	you, and before you were born I *c* you;

CONSECRATION

Num	6. 7	their *c* to God is upon the head.

CONSENT (CONSENTED CONSENTS)

Prov	1.10	child, if sinners entice you, do not *c*.
Lk	22. 6	he *c* and began to look for a way to
Acts	15.22	elders, with the *c* of the whole church,
1 Cor	7.12	and she *c* to live with him, he should

CONSIDER (CONSIDERED CONSIDERS)

Judg	19.30	until this day? *C* it, take counsel, and
Ruth	1. 6	the LORD had *c* his people and given
1 Sam	12.24	for *c* what great things he has done for
Job	1. 8	to Satan, "Have you *c* my servant Job?
	37.14	stop and *c* the wondrous works of God.
Ps	41. 1	Happy are those who *c* the poor; The
	90.11	Who *c* the power of your anger? Your
	119. 95	to destroy me, but I *c* your decrees.
Prov	6. 6	you lazybones; *c* its ways, and be wise.
	24.32	Then I saw and *c* it; I looked and
Isa	44.19	No one *c*, nor is there knowledge or
Hag	1. 5	*C* how you have fared. You have sown
	2.15	But now, *c* what will come to pass from
Mt	6.28	*C* the lilies of the field, how they grow;
Lk	12.24	*C* the ravens: they neither sow nor reap,
Acts	20.24	I do not *c* my life of any value to
Rom	6.11	you also must *c* yourselves dead to sin
Heb	3. 1	*c* that Jesus, the apostle and high priest
	10.24	let us *c* how to provoke one another to
	11.11	barren— because he *c* him faithful who
	11.19	He *c* the fact that God is able even to
	12. 3	*C* him who endured such hostility

Jas　　1. 2 trials of any kind, *c* it nothing but joy,

CONSIGNED

Isa　　38.10 I am *c* to the gates of Sheol for the

CONSISTENT (CONSISTENTLY)

Gal　　2.14 they were not acting *c* with the truth
Titus　2. 1 teach what is *c* with sound doctrine.

CONSOLATION (CONSOLATIONS)

Job　　15.11 Are the *c* of God too small for you, or
　　　　21. 2 to my words, and let this be your *c*.
Jer　　16. 7 anyone give them the cup of *c* to drink
Ezek　16.54 you have done, becoming a *c* to them.
Zech　10. 2 tell false dreams, and give empty *c*.
Lk　　2.25 looking forward to the *c* of Israel,
2 Cor　1. 3 Father of of mercies and God of all *c*,

CONSOLE (CONSOLED)

Ezek　14.22 you will be *c* for the evil that I have
Jn　　11.19 to Martha and Mary to *c* them about
2 Cor　7. 6 downcast, *c* us by the arrival of Titus,

CONSPIRACY

2 Sam　15.12 The *c* grew in strength, and the people
Isa　　8.12 Do not call *c* all that this people call *c*,
Acts　23.13 more than forty who joined in this *c*.

CONSPIRE (CONSPIRED)

Gen　　37.18 came near to them, they *c* to kill him.
1 Kings 16. 9 his his servant Zimri *c* against him.
Ps　　2. 1 Why do the nations *c*, and the peoples
Am　　7.10 "Amos has *c* against you in the very

CONSTRAINS

Job　　32.18 full of words; the spirit within me *c* me.

CONSULT (CONSULTED CONSULTS)

1 Chr　13. 1 David *c* with the commanders of the
Isa　　8.19 if the people say to you, "*C* the ghosts
　　　　31. 1 to the Holy One of Israel or *c* the LORD!
Ezek　14. 3 them; shall I let myself be *c* by them?
　　　　20. 3 Why are you coming? To *c* me? As I
　　　　21.21 shakes the arrows, he *c* the teraphim,
Hos　　4.12 My people *c* a piece of wood, and their

CONSUME (CONSUMED CONSUMES CONSUMING)

Num　　16.21 so that I may *c* them in a moment.
Job　　1.16 the sheep and the servants, and *c* them;
　　　　20.26 them; what is left in their tent will be *c*.
Ps　　59.13 *c* them in wrath, *c* them until they are
　　　　90. 7 For we are *c* by your anger; by your
Mt　　6.20 where neither moth nor rust *c* and
Heb　　12.29 and awe; for indeed our God is a *c* fire.

CONTAIN

1 Kings 8.27 and the highest heaven cannot *c* you,
Jn　　21.25 world itself could not *c* the books that

CONTEMPLATE

Isa　　52.15 which they had not heard they shall *c*.

CONTEMPT

Gen　　16. 4 she looked with *c* on her mistress.
Esth　　1.17 to look with *c* upon their husbands,
Job　　12. 5 Those at ease have *c* for misfortune, but
Isa　　9. 1 he brought into *c* the land of Zebulun
Lk　　18. 9 righteous and regarded others with *c*:
1 Cor　11.22 Or do you show *c* for the church of God

CONTEND

Judg　　6.31 "Will you *c* for Baal? Or will you defend
Job　　10. 2 me; let me know why you *c* against me.
　　　　13.19 Who is there that will *c* with me? For
Ps　　35. 1 *C*, O LORD, with those who *c* with me;
Isa　　49.25 I will *c* with those who *c* with you, and
Hos　　4. 4 Yet let no one *c*, and let none accuse,
Jude　　3 appeal to you to *c* for the faith that was

CONTENT

Josh　　7. 7 Would that we had been *c* to settle
2 Cor　12.10 Therefore I am *c* with weaknesses,
Phil　　4.11 need; for I have learned to be *c* with
1 Tim　6. 8 and clothing, we will be *c* with these.

CONTENTIOUS

Prov　21.19 land than with a *c* and fretful wife.
　　　　27.15 on a rainy day and a *c* wife are alike;

CONTINUALLY

Ps　　34. 1 his praise shall *c* be in my mouth.

CONTINUE (CONTINUED)

Ps　　36.10 O *c* your steadfast love to those who
Jer　　31. 3 I have *c* my faithfulness to you.
Jn　　8.31 "If you *c* in my word, you are truly my
Acts　13.43 them and urged them to *c* in the grace
Rom　　6. 1 we *c* in sin that grace may abound?
Phil　　1.25 I will remain and *c* with all of you for
2 Tim　3.14 for you, *c* in what you have learned and

CONTRIBUTIONS

2 Chr　31.12 Faithfully brought in the *c*, the tithes

CONTRITE

Ps　　51.17 a broken and *c* heart, O God, you will
Isa　　66. 2 to the humble and *c* in spirit, who

CONTRITION

Jer　　44.10 They have shown no *c* or fear to this

CONTROL (CONTROLLED)

Gen　　45. 1 Joseph could no longer *c* himself before
Prov　16.32 one whose temper is *c* than one who
1 Cor　7.37 necessity but having his desire under *c*,
1 Thess 4. 4 you know how to *c* your body in
Heb　　2. 8 them, God left nothing outside their *c*.

CONTROVERSY

Mic　　6. 2 Hear, you mountains, the *c* of the LORD,

CONVERT (CONVERTS)

Mt　　23.15 cross sea and land to make a single *c*,
Rom　16. 5 Epaenetus, who was the first *c* in Asia
1 Cor　16.15 were the first *c* in Achaia, and
1 Tim　3. 6 He must not be a recent *c*, or he may

CONVICT (CONVICTS)

Jer　　2.19 you, and your apostasies will *c* you.
Jn　　8.46 Which of you *c* me of sin? If I tell the
Jude　　15 to *c* everyone of all the deeds of

CONVINCE (CONVINCED)

Acts　18. 4 and would try to *c* Jews and Greeks.
Rom　　4.21 fully *c* that God was able to do what he
　　　　8.38 I am *c* that neither death, nor life, nor
　　　　14. 5 Let all be fully *c* in their own minds.

CONVOCATION

Lev　　23. 3 is a sabbath of complete rest, a holy *c*;
Num　　28.26 of weeks, you shall have a holy *c*;

COOKED

2 Kings 6.29 we *c* my son and ate him. The next day

COOL

Prov　17.27 who is *c* in spirit has understanding.

COPY

Josh　　8.32 wrote on the stones a *c* of the law
Esth　　4. 8 Mordecai also gave him a *c* of the

CORBAN

Mk　　7.11 might have had from me is C' (that is,

CORD (CORDS)

Ps　　18. 4 The *c* of death encompassed me, the
　　　　129. 4 he has cut the *c* of the wicked.
Eccl　　4.12 A threefold *c* is not quickly broken.

CORINTH

Eccl	12.	6 before the silver *c* is snapped, and the
Hos	11.	4 I led them with *c* of human kindness,

CORINTH

Acts	18.	1 this Paul left Athens and went to *C*.
	19.	1 While Apollos was at *C*, Paul passed
1 Cor	1.	2 church of God that is in *C*, to those

CORNELIUS

Acts	10.	1 there was a man named *C*, a centurion
	10.	3 of God coming in and saying to him, "*C*."
	10.24	*C* was expecting them and had called
	10.31	'*C*, your prayer has been heard and

CORNER

Acts	26.26	his notice, for this was not done in a *c*.
1 Pet	2.	7 has become the very head of the *c*,"

CORNERSTONE

Eph	2.20	with Christ Jesus himself as the *c*,
1 Pet	2.	6 Zion a stone, a *c* chosen and precious;

CORPSE

Mt	24.28	Wherever the *c* is, there the vultures

CORRECT

Jer	10.24	*C* me, O LORD, but in just measure; not

CORRECTION

Jer	2.30	down your children; they accepted no *c*.
	5.	3 them, but they refused to take *c*.
Zeph	3.	2 to no voice; it has accepted no *c*.
	3.	7 the city will fear me, it will accept *c*;

CORRUPT (CORRUPTED)

Gen	6.11	Now the earth was *c* in God's sight, and
Hos	9.	9 They have deeply *c* themselves as in the
Mal	2.	8 you have *c* the covenant of Levi,

CORRUPTION

Dan	6.	4 find no grounds for complaint or any *c*,
Acts	2.27	or let your Holy One experience *c*.
	13.35	not let your Holy One experience *c*.'

CORRUPTLY

Deut	4.16	do not act *c* by making an idol for

COST

2 Sam	24.24	to the LORD my God that *c* me nothing."
1 Chr	21.24	offer burnt offerings that *c* me nothing."
Ezra	6.	4 timber; let the *c* be paid from the royal
Lk	14.28	not first sit down and estimate the *c*,

COUNCIL (COUNCILS)

Job	15.	8 Have you listened in the *c* of God? And
Ps	82.	1 God has taken his place in the divine *c*;
	89.	7 a God feared in the *c* of the holy ones,
Jer	23.18	For who has stood in the *c* of the LORD
Mt	10.17	they will hand you over to *c* and flog
Lk	23.50	though a member of the *c*, had not

COUNSEL (COUNSELED COUNSELS)

Ex	18.19	Now listen to me. I will give you *c*, and
2 Sam	17.	7 time the *c* which Ahithophel has given
Job	26.	2 you have *c* one who has no wisdom,
	38.	2 "Who is this that darkens *c* by words
Ps	2.	2 the rulers take *c* together, against the
	33.10	brings the *c* of the nations to nothing;
	33.11	*c* of the LORD stands forever, the
	73.24	You guide me with your *c*, and
	106.	13 his works; they did not wait for his *c*.
Prov	15.22	Without *c*, plans go wrong, but with
Isa	11.	2 the spirit of *c* and might, the spirit of
	28.29	LORD of hosts; he is wonderful in *c*, and
Jer	7.24	evil will they walked in their own *c*,
	18.18	from the priest, nor *c* from the wise,
	32.19	of hosts, great in *c* and mighty in deed;
Dan	4.27	O king, let my *c* be acceptable to you:
Eph	1.11	all things according to his *c* and will,

COUNSELOR (COUNSELORS)

2 Chr	22.	3 his mother was his *c* in doing wickedly.
	25.16	"Have we made you a royal *c*? Stop!
Ps	119.	24 decrees are my delight, they are my *c*.
Isa	1.26	at the first, your *c* as at the beginning.
	3.	3 dignitary, *c* and the skillful magician
	9.	6 and he is named Wonderful *C*, Mighty
	40.13	LORD, or as his *c* has instructed him?
	41.28	among these there is no *c* who, when I
Mic	4.	9 Has your *c* perished, that pangs have

COUNT (COUNTED COUNTING)

Gen	15.	5 *c* the stars, if you are able to *c* them."
Num	23.10	Who can *c* the dust of Jacob, or number
2 Sam	24.	1 "Go, *c* the people of Israel and Judah."
Ps	90.12	So teach us to *c* our days that we may
	139.	18 I try to *c* them—they are more than
Mk	15.28	says, "And he was *c* among the lawless."
Lk	22.37	'And he was *c* among the lawless'; and
2 Cor	5.19	world to himself, not *c* their trespasses

COUNTENANCE

Gen	4.	5 So Cain was very angry, and his *c* fell.
Job	29.24	light of my *c* they did not extinguish.
Prov	15.13	A glad heart makes a cheerful *c*, but by

COUNTRY

Heb	11.16	they desire a better *c*, that is, a

COURAGE

1 Sam	4.	9 Take *c*, and be men, O Philistines, in
1 Chr	28.20	"Be strong and of good *c*, and act. Do
2 Chr	15.	8 he took *c*, and put away the abominable
Ps	27.14	be strong, and let your heart take *c*;
	31.24	Be strong, and let your heart take *c*, all
Ezek	22.14	Can your *c* endure, or can your hands
Jn	16.33	But take *c*; I have conquered
Acts	23.11	"Keep up your *c*! For just as you have
	27.22	I urge you now to keep up your *c*, for
	27.25	So keep up your *c*, men, for I have faith
	28.15	them, Paul thanked God and took *c*.

COURAGEOUS (COURAGEOUSLY)

Josh	1.	6 Be strong and *c*; for you shall put this
	1.	9 Be strong and *c*; do not be frightened or
	10.25	Be strong and *c*; for thus the LORD will
2 Sam	10.12	Be strong, and let us be *c* for the sake
2 Chr	19.11	Deal *c*, and may the LORD be with you
1 Cor	16.13	stand firm in your faith, be *c*, be strong.

COURSE

Ps	19.	5 like a strong man runs its *c* with joy.
Acts	20.24	if only I may finish my *c* and the

COURT

Ex	27.	9 You shall make the *c* of the tabernacle.
1 Cor	4.	3 be judged by you or by any human *c*.
	6.	1 do you dare to take it to *c* before the

COVENANT

Gen	6.18	I will establish my *c* with you; and you
	9.	9 I am establishing my *c* with you and
	17.	2 I will make my *c* between me and you,
	21.27	Abimelech, and the two men made a *c*.
	26.28	and us, and let us make a *c* with you,
	31.44	Come now, let us make a *c*, you and I;
Ex	2.24	God remembered his *c* with Abraham,
	6.	4 I also established my *c* with them, to
	23.32	You shall make no *c* with them and
	24.	8 "See the blood of the *c* that the LORD
	25.16	You shall put into the ark the *c* that I
	34.28	wrote . . . the words of the *c*, the ten
Lev	26.	9 you; and I will maintain my *c* with you.
	26.25	you, executing vengeance for the *c*;
	26.42	I will remember also my *c* with Isaac,
Num	25.12	say, 'I hereby grant him my *c* of peace.
Deut	4.31	he will not forget the *c* with your
	5.	3 our ancestors did the LORD make this *c*,

Deut	7.	2 Make no c with them and show them
	7.	9 the faithful God who maintains c loyalty
	7.12	God will maintain with you the c loyalty
	17.	2 the LORD your God, and transgress his c
	29.	1 These are the words of the c that the
	29.12	to enter into the c of the LORD your
	29.25	it is because they abandoned the c of
	33.	9 observed your word, and kept your c.
Josh	24.25	So Joshua made a c with the people
Judg	2.	1 I said, 'I will never break my c with
	2.	2 do not make a c with the inhabitants of
1 Sam	18.	3 Jonathan made a c with David, because
	20.	8 brought your servant into a sacred c
2 Sam	3.21	they may make a c with you, and that
	5.	3 David made a c with them at Hebron
	23.	5 he has made with me an everlasting c,
1 Kings	8.23	keeping c and showing steadfast love for
	19.10	Israelites have forsaken your c, thrown
2 Kings	11.	4 He made a c with them and put them
	11.17	Jehoiada made a c between the LORD
	23.	2 book of the c that had been found in
	23.	3 book. All the people joined in the c.
1 Chr	16.15	Remember his c forever, the word that
2 Chr	6.14	keeping c in steadfast love with your
	15.12	They entered into a c to seek the LORD,
	21.	7 of the c that he had made with David,
	34.31	his place and made a c before the LORD,
Ezra	10.	3 let us make a c with our God to send
Ps	25.10	for those who keep his c and
	25.14	and he makes his c known to them.
	44.17	not forgotten you, or be false to your c.
	50.	5 faithful ones, who made a c with me by
	55.20	on a friend and violated a c with me.
	74.20	Have regard for your c, for the dark
	78.37	toward him; they were not true to his c.
	83.	5 accord; against thee they make a c—
	89.	3 "I have made a c with my chosen one,
	103.	18 to those who keep his c and remember
	105.	10 a statute, to Israel as an everlasting c,
	106.	45 their sake he remembered his c,
	132.	12 If your sons keep my c and my decrees
Prov	2.17	of her youth and forgets her sacred c;
Isa	28.18	your c with death will be annulled,
	42.	6 I have given you as a c to the people, a
	59.21	as for me, this is my c with them, says
	61.	8 I will make an everlasting c with them.
Jer	11.10	the house of Judah have broken the c
	14.21	and do not break your c with us.
	22.	9 "Because they abandoned the c of the
	31.31	when I will make a new c with the
	32.40	I will make an everlasting c with them,
	33.21	then could my c with my servant David
	50.	5 c that will never be forgotten.
Ezek	16.60	yet I will remember my c with you in
	17.14	that by keeping his c it might stand.
	37.26	I will make a c of peace with them; it
Dan	9.27	He shall make a strong c with many for
	11.28	his heart shall be set against the holy c.
Hos	6.	7 But at Adam they transgressed the c;
Mal	2.	4 to you, that my c with Levi may hold,
	2.14	is your companion and your wife by c.
Mt	26.28	this is my blood of the c, which is
Mk	14.24	"This is my blood of the c, which is
Lk	1.72	and has remembered his holy c,
Acts	3.25	of the prophets and of the c
	7.	8 Then he gave him the c of circumcision.
Rom	11.27	"And this is my c with them, when I
1 Cor	11.25	"This cup is the new c in my blood. Do
2 Cor	3.	6 competent to be ministers of a new c,
	3.14	when they hear the reading of the old c,
Gal	3.17	does not annul a c previously ratified by
Heb	7.22	also become the guarantee of a better c.
	8.	8 when I will establish a new c with the
	9.15	reason he is the mediator of a new c,
	10.16	is the c that I will make with them
Rev	11.19	the ark of his c was seen within his

COVENANTS

Hos	10.	4 words; with empty oaths they make c;
Eph	2.12	strangers to the c of promise, having no

COVER (COVERED COVERING COVERS)

Gen	7.20	mountains, c them fifteen cubits deep.
	24.65	So she took her veil and c herself.
Ex	33.22	I will c you with my hand until I have
Num	9.15	the cloud c the tabernacle, the tent of
	16.42	the cloud had c it, and the glory of the
Ps	5.12	LORD; you c them with favor as a shield.
	91.	4 he will c you with his pinions, and
Prov	10.12	stirs up strife, but love c all offenses.
Isa	6.	2 with two they c their faces, and with
	11.	9 of the LORD as the waters c the sea.
Hos	10.	8 They shall say to the mountains, C us,
Mt	10.26	nothing is c up that will not be
Lk	12.	2 Nothing is c up that will not be
	23.30	'Fall on us'; and to the hills, 'C us.'

COVERING (n)

Ps	18.11	He made darkness his c around him, his
Isa	28.20	on it, and the c too narrow to wrap

COVET (COVETED)

Ex	20.17	You shall not c your neighbor's house;
Deut	5.21	Neither shall you c your neighbor's
Josh	7.21	fifty shekels, then I c them and took
Mic	2.	2 They c fields, and seize them; houses,
Acts	20.33	I c no one's silver or gold or clothing.
Rom	7.	7 the law had not said, "You shall not c."
	13.	9 You shall not steal, You shall not c,"

COVETOUSNESS

Isa	57.17	Because of their wicked c I was angry; I
Rom	1.29	kind of wickedness, evil, c, malice.
	7.	8 produced in me all kinds of c.

CO-WORKERS

Col	4.11	among my c for the kingdom of God,
3 Jn		8 that we may become c with the truth.

CRAFT

Isa	2.16	Tarshish, and against all the beautiful c.

CRAFTINESS

Job	5.13	He takes the wise in their own c; and
1 Cor	3.19	written, "He catches the wise in their c,"
Eph	4.14	by their c in deceitful scheming.

CRAFTY

Job	5.12	He frustrates the devices of the c, so
	15.	5 and you choose the tongue of the c.

CRAVING (CRAVINGS)

Prov	21.25	The c of the lazy person is fatal, for lazy
Jas	4.	1 they come from your c that are at war

CREATE (CREATED CREATES)

Gen	1.	1 when God c the heavens and the earth,
	1.21	God c the great sea monsters and every
	1.27	God c humankind in his own image, in
Deut	32.	6 Is not he your father, who c you, who
Ps	51.10	C in me a clean heart, O God, and put
	104.	30 you send forth your Spirit, they are c;
	148.	5 for he commanded and they were c.
Prov	8.22	The LORD c me at the beginning of his
Isa	4.	5 Then the LORD will c over the whole site
	40.26	your eyes on high and see: who c these?
	41.20	this, the Holy One of Israel has c it.
	42.	5 says God, the LORD, who c the heavens
	43.	7 whom I c for my glory, whom I formed
	45.	7 I form light and c darkness, I make
	45.18	thus says the LORD, who c the heavens
	65.17	For I am about to c new heavens and a
Jer	31.22	For the LORD has c a new thing on the
Am	4.13	c the wind, and reveals his thoughts to
Eph	2.10	us, c in Christ Jesus for good works,
Col	1.16	—all things have been c through him

1 Tim	4. 4 For everything *c* by God is good, and		
Rev	4.11 for you *c* all things, and by your will		
	10. 6 who *c* heaven and what is in it, the		

CREATION

Mk	13.19 not been from the beginning of the *c*
Rom	8.21 the *c* itself will be set free from its
	8.22 the whole *c* has been groaning in labor
2 Cor	5.17 if anyone is in Christ, there is a new *c*:
Gal	6.15 is anything; but a new *c* is everything!
2 Pet	3. 4 as they were from the beginning of *c*!"

CREATOR

Eccl	12. 1 Remember your *C* in the days of your
Isa	40.28 God, *C* of the ends of the earth.
	43.15 Holy One, the *C* of Israel, your King.
Rom	1.25 served the creature rather than the *C*,

CREATURES

Gen	1.20 waters bring forth swarms of living *c*,
Ezek	10.17 for the spirit of the living *c* was in
Rev	4. 6 four living *c*, full of eyes in front and

CREDIT

Deut	24.13 it will be to your *c* before the LORD your

CREDITOR (CREDITORS)

Deut	15. 2 every *c* shall remit the claim that is
Isa	50. 1 Or which of my *c* is it to whom I have
Lk	7.41 "A certain *c* had two debtors; one owed

CREEPING

Gen	1.24 cattle and *c* things and wild animals of

CRETE

Acts	27.12 It was a harbor of *C*, facing southwest
Titus	1. 5 I left you behind in *C* for this reason, so

CRIME (CRIMES)

Gen	50.17 I beg you, forgive the *c* of your brothers
Deut	24.16 only for their own *c* may persons be put
Judg	9.56 God repaid Abimelech for the *c* he
Ezek	7.23 the land is full of bloody *c*; the city is

CRIMINAL

Judg	20. 3 us, how did this *c* act come about?"

CRIMSON

Josh	2.18 tie this *c* cord in the window through

CRINGE (CRINGING)

Ps	18.44 obeyed me; foreigners came *c* to me.
	66. 3 great power, your enemies *c* before you.

CRIPPLED

Acts	14. 8 walked, for he had been *c* from birth.
2 Sam	4. 4 Jonathan had a son who was *c* in his
	9. 3 a son of Jonathan; he is *c* in his feet."

CRISIS

1 Cor	7.26 in view of the impending *c*, it is well for

CROOKED

Prov	2.15 those whose paths are *c*, and who are
Eccl	1.15 What is *c* cannot be made straight, and
	7.13 can make straight what he has made *c*?
Isa	59. 8 Their roads they have made *c*; no one

CROPS

Lk	12.17 I do, for I have no place to store my *c*?'
2 Tim	2. 6 ought to have the first share of the *c*.

CROSS

Mt	10.38 whoever does not take the *c* and follow
	16.24 and take up their *c* and follow me.
	27.32 they compelled this man to carry his *c*.
Mk	8.34 deny themselves and take up their *c*
	15.21 to carry his *c*; it was Simon of Cyrene,
	15.30 yourself, and come down from the *c*!"
Lk	9.23 themselves and take up their *c* daily

Lk	14.27 does not carry the *c* and follow me
	23.26 laid the *c* on him, and made him carry
Jn	19.17 and carrying the *c* by himself, he went
1 Cor	1.17 so that the *c* of Christ be emptied of its
Gal	5.11 the offense of the *c* has been removed.
	6.12 they may not be persecuted for the *c*
	6.14 I never boast of anything except the *c*
Phil	2. 8 the point of death—even death on a *c*.
	3.18 many live as enemies of the *c* of Christ;
Col	2.14 He set this aside, nailing it to the *c*.
Heb	12. 2 endured the *c*, disregarding its shame,
1 Pet	2.24 bore our sins in his body on the *c*,

CROSS-EXAMINE

Lk	11.53 to *c* him about many things, lying in

CROSSING

Josh	3.17 entire nation finished *c* over the Jordan.

CROWD (CROWDS)

Mt	4.25 And great *c* followed him from Galilee,
Mk	8. 2 "I have compassion on the *c*, because
	12.37 the large *c* was listening to him with

CROWN (CROWNED)

2 Chr	23.11 out the king's son, put the *c* on him,
Ps	8. 5 God, and *c* them with glory and honor.
	21. 3 rich blessings; you set a *c* of fine gold
	65.11 You *c* the year with your bounty; your
Prov	4. 9 she will bestow on you a beautiful *c*."
	12. 4 A good wife is the *c* of her husband, but
	16.31 Gray hair is a *c* of glory; it is gained in
Isa	62. 3 You shall be a *c* of beauty in the hand
Lam	5.16 *c* has fallen from our head; woe to us,
Ezek	16.12 ears, and a beautiful *c* upon your head.
Zech	6.11 make a *c*, and set it on the head of the
2 Tim	4. 8 reserved for me the *c* of righteousness,
Rev	3.11 have so that no one may seize your *c*.
	14.14 Son of Man, with a golden *c* on his

CROWS

Mk	14.30 very night, before the cock *c* twice, you

CRUCIBLE

Prov	17. 3 The *c* is for silver, and the furnace is for

CRUCIFY (CRUCIFIED)

Mt	20.19 to be mocked and flogged and *c*;
	23.34 some of whom you will kill and *c*, and
	27.22 All of them said, "Let him be *c*."
	27.35 when they had *c* him, they divided his
	28. 5 you are looking for Jesus who was *c*.
Mk	15.13 They shouted back, "*C* him!
	15.20 him. Then they led him out to *c* him.
	16. 6 for Jesus of Nazareth, who was *c*.
Lk	23.21 but they kept shouting, "*C*, *c*, him!"
	23.33 The Skull, they *c* Jesus there with the
Jn	19. 6 saw him, they shouted, "*C* him, *c* him!"
	19.10 to release you, and power to *c* you?"
	19.18 There they *c* him, and with him two
Acts	2.23 you *c* and killed by the hands of those
Rom	6. 6 our old self was *c* with him so that the
1 Cor	1.13 been divided? Was Paul *c* for you?
	2. 2 you except Jesus Christ and him *c*.
	2. 8 had, they would not have *c* the Lord
2 Cor	13. 4 For he was *c* in weakness, but lives by
Gal	2.19 I have been *c* with Christ; and it is no
	3. 1 Jesus Christ was publicly exhibited as *c*!
	6.14 by which the world has been *c* to me,
Rev	11. 8 and Egypt, where also their Lord was *c*.

CRUEL (CRUELLY)

Job	30.21 You have turned to me; with the
	39.16 It deals *c* with its young, as if they were
Prov	11.17 but the *c* do themselves harm.

CRUMBS

Mt	15.27 yet even the dogs eat the *c* that fall
Mk	7.28 under the table eat the children's *c*."

CRUSH (CRUSHED)

Job	20.19 they have c and abandoned the poor,
Ps	18.29 By you I can c a troop; and by my God I
Lam	1.15 a time against me to c my young men;
Mk	3. 9 crowd, so that they would not c him;
Lk	20.18 and it will c anyone on whom it falls."
Rom	16.20 The God of peace will shortly c Satan

CRY (CRIED CRYING)

Gen	4.10 Listen, your brother's blood is c out to
	27.34 Esau heard his father's words, he c out
Ex	2. 6 the child. He was c, and she took pity
	22.23 c out to me, I will surely heed their c;
Lev	13.45 upper lip and c out, "Unclean, unclean."
1 Sam	7. 9 Samuel c out to the LORD for Israel, and
	5.11 Samuel was angry; and he c out to the
Job	19. 7 Even when I c out, 'Violence!' I am not
Ps	5. 2 Listen to the sound of my c, my King
	18. 6 to my God I c for help. From his temple
	88. 1 when, at night, I c out in your presence,
	99. 6 his name. They c to the LORD, and he
	102. 1 prayer, O LORD; let my c come to you.
	107. 28 they c to the LORD in their trouble,
	119.145 With my whole heart I c; answer me, O
	120. 1 In my distress I c to the LORD, that he
	130. 1 Out of the depths I c to you, O LORD.
Isa	42. 2 He will not c or lift up his voice, or
Jon	1. 2 that great city, and c against it;
Mt	12.19 He will not wrangle or c aloud, nor will

CUNNING

2 Cor	4. 2 we refuse to practice c or to falsify

CUP

Gen	44. 2 Put my c, the silver c, in the top of the
Ps	11. 6 wind shall be the portion of their c.
	16. 5 LORD is my chosen portion and my c;
	23. 5 anoint head with oil; my c overflows.
	75. 8 For in the hand of the LORD there is a c
	116. 13 I will lift up the c of salvation and call
Isa	51.17 the c of his wrath, who have drunk to
Jer	25.28 And if they refuse to accept the c from
Hab	2.16 The c in the LORD's right hand will
Mt	10.42 whoever gives even a c of cold water to
	20.22 Are you able to drink the c that I am
	23.25 you clean the outside of the c and of
	26.27 Then he took a c, and after giving
	26.39 if it is possible, let this c pass from me;
Mk	9.41 whoever gives you a c of water to drink
	10.38 Are you able to drink the c that I drink,
	14.23 Then he took a c, and after giving
	14.36 are possible; remove this c from me;
Lk	11.39 you Pharisees clean the outside of the c
	22.17 he took a c, and after giving thanks he
	22.42 you are willing, remove this c from me;
Jn	18.11 the c that the Father has given me?"
1 Cor	10.16 The c of blessing which we bless, is it
	11.25 "This c is the new covenant in my
Rev	16.19 her the wine-c of the fury of his wrath.

CUPBEARER

Gen	40. 9 So the chief c told his dream to Joseph,

CURDS

Gen	18. 8 he took c and milk and the calf that he
Isa	7.15 He shall eat c and honey by the time he

CURE (CURED CURING)

Mt	4.23 c every disease and every sickness
	8.16 with a word, and c all who were sick.
	10. 8 C the sick, raise the dead, cleanse the
	12.15 followed him, and he c all of them.
	14.14 compassion for them and c their sick.
	17.16 disciples, but they could not c him."
Lk	4.23 to me this proverb, 'Doctor, c yourself!'
	4.40 his hands on each of them and c them.
	7.21 Jesus had just then c many people of
	8. 2 as some women who had been c of evil

Lk	13.14 come on those days and be c, and not
	14. 3 "Is it lawful to c people on the sabbath,
Acts	28. 8 him and c him by praying and putting
	28. 9 who had diseases also came and were c.

CURSE (CURSES CURSING CURSINGS) (n)

Deut	11.26 before you today a blessing and a c:
	21.23 anyone hung on a tree is under God's c.
	27.13 shall stand on Mount Ebal for the c:
Josh	8.34 the words of the law, blessings and c,
Prov	3.33 The LORD's c is on the house of the
Jer	25.18 a waste, an object of hissing and a c,
Zech	5. 3 "This is the c that goes out over the
	8.13 you have been a c among the nations,
Mal	2. 2 then I will send the c on you and I will
Rom	3.14 "Their mouths are full of c and
Gal	3.10 on the works of the law are under a c;
Jas	3.10 the same mouth come blessing and c.

CURSE (CURSED CURSES CURSING) (v)

Gen	3.14 c are you among all animals and among
	4.11 you are c from the ground, which has
	12. 3 and the one who c you I will c; and in
	49. 7 C be their anger, for it is fierce, and
Ex	21.17 Whoever c father or mother shall be put
Num	22. 6 Come now, c this people for me, since
	23. 8 How can I c whom God has not c? How
Josh	6.26 "C before the LORD be anyone who tries
1 Sam	14.24 "C be anyone who eats food before I
2 Sam	16. 5 was Shimei son of Gera; he came out c.
1 Kings	21.13 saying, "Naboth c God and the king."
2 Kings	2.24 and saw them, he c them in the name
Job	1.11 he has, and he will c you to your face."
	2. 9 in your integrity? C God, and die."
	3. 1 his mouth and c the day of his birth.
Ps	109. 17 He loved to c; let curses come on him.
Prov	20.20 If you c father or mother, your lamp will
Eccl	10.20 Do not c the king, even in your thought,
Jer	17. 5 C are those who trust in mere mortals
	20.14 C be the day on which I was born! The
Mk	11.21 "Rabbi, look! The fig tree that you c has
Lk	6.28 bless those who c you, pray for those
1 Cor	12. 3 Spirit of God ever says "Let Jesus be c!"
Gal	3.13 "C is everyone who hangs on a tree"
Rev	16. 9 they c the name of God, who had

CURTAIN (CURTAINS)

Ex	26. 1 make the tabernacle with ten c of fine
Lev	16. 2 into the sanctuary inside the c before
Mt	27.51 the c of the temple was torn in two,
Mk	15.38 the c of the temple was torn in two,
Lk	23.45 failed; and the c of the temple was torn
Heb	9. 3 Behind the second c was a tent called
	10.20 the c (that is, through his flesh),

CUSH

Gen	2.13 that flows around the whole land of C.

CUSTOM (CUSTOMS)

Ezra	7.24 shall not be lawful to impose tribute, c,
Jer	10. 3 For the c of the peoples are false: a tree
Lk	4.16 on the sabbath day, as was his c.

CUT

1 Kings	18.28 aloud, and c themselves with swords
Isa	14.22 will c off from Babylon name and
Dan	9.26 an anointed one shall be c off and shall
Mk	9.43 If your hand causes you to sin, c it off;
Acts	2.37 they heard this, they were c to the heart

CYMBALS (CYMBALS)

Ps	150. 5 Praise him with clanging c; praise him
1 Cor	13. 1 love, I am a noisy gong or a clanging c.

CYPRUS

Acts	4.36 a Levite, a native of C, Joseph, to whom
	11.19 Stephen traveled as far as Phoenicia, C
	13. 4 and from there they sailed to C.

CYRUS

Acts	15.39 Mark with him and sailed away to C.
	27. 4 sailed under the lee of C, because the

CYRUS

Ezra	1. 1 In the first year of King C of Persia, in
	4. 3 as King C of Persia has commanded
	5.13 King C of Babylon, in the first year of
Isa	44.28 who says of C, "He is my shepherd, and
	45. 1 says the LORD to his anointed, to C,
Dan	1.21 there until the first year of King C.

D

DAILY

Lk	9.23 and take up their cross d and follow
	11. 3 Give us each day our d bread.

DAMASCUS

Gen	14.15 pursued them to Hobah, north of D.
2 Sam	8. 6 put garrisons among the Arameans of D;
Isa	7. 8 For the head of Aram is D, and the
Zech	9. 1 land of Hadrach and will rest upon D.
Acts	9. 2 him for letters to the synagogues at D,
	22.10 'Get up and go to D; there you will be
2 Cor	11.32 under King Aretas guarded the city of D
Gal	1.17 Arabia, and afterwards I returned to D.

DAN (Son of Jacob)

Born, Gen 30.6; blessed by Jacob, Gen 49.16-17.

Tribe of Dan: blessed by Moses, Deut 33.22; allotted territory, Josh 19.40-48; migrated north, Judg 18; became center of idolatry, 1 Kings 12.28-30.

DAN (the city)

Gen	14.14 them, and went in pursuit as far as D.
Judg	18.29 They named the city D, after their
	20. 1 came out, from D to Beersheba,
1 Sam	3.20 all Israel from D to Beersheba knew

DANCE (DANCED DANCING)

Ex	32.19 and the d, Moses' anger burned hot,
Judg	21.21 young women of Shiloh come out to d
2 Sam	6.14 David d before the LORD with all his
Ps	30.11 You have turned my mourning into d;
Lam	5.15 our d has been turned to mourning.
Mt	11.17 the flute for you and you did not d;
	14. 6 the daughter of Herodias d before the
Mk	6.22 his daughter Herodias came in and d,
Lk	7.32 the flute for you, and you did not d;

DANGER

1 Cor	15.30 we putting ourselves in d every hour?

DANIEL (BELTESHAZZAR)

Trained in the king's palace, Dan 1.1-7; abstained from the king's food, Dan 1.8-16; interpreted Nebuchadnezzar's dreams, Dan 2; 4; interpreted the handwriting on the wall, Dan 5.10-29; delivered from the lion's den, Dan 6; visions and dreams, Dan 7—8; 10—12; prayed for his people, Dan 9.

DARE

Rom	5. 7 person someone might actually d to die.
1 Cor	6. 1 do you d take it to court before the

DARIUS

Ezra	4. 5 of Persia and until the reign of King D
	6. 1 Then King D made a decree, and they
Dan	5.31 D the Mede received the kingdom,
	6.28 Daniel prospered during the reign of D
Hag	1. 1 In the second year of King D, in the
Zech	1. 1 eighth month, in the second year of D,

DARK

Job	24.16 In the d they dig through houses; by
Mt	10.27 What I say to you in the d, tell in the
2 Pet	1.19 to this as a lamp shining in a d place,

DARKEN (DARKENED DARKENS)

Job	38. 2 "Who is this that d counsel by words
Eccl	12. 2 the stars are d and the clouds return
Am	8. 9 noon, and d the earth in broad daylight.
Mk	13.24 the sun will be d, and the moon will

DARKEST

Ps	23. 4 though I walk through the d valley,

DARKNESS

Gen	1. 5 light Day, and the d he called Night.
	15.12 and terrifying d descended upon him.
Ex	10.21 may be d over the land of Egypt, a d
Job	10.21 return, to the land of gloom and deep d,
	24.17 are friends with the terrors of deep d.
Ps	44.19 of jackals, and covered us with deep d.
	139. 12 even the d is not dark to you; the night
Isa	8.22 earth, but will see only distress and d,
Jer	13.16 the LORD your God before he brings d,
Joel	2. 2 it is near — a day of d and gloom, a day
Mt	6.23 If then the light in you is d, how great
	22.13 throw him into the outer d, where there
	25.30 throw him into the outer d, where there
	27.45 noon on, d came over the whole land
Mk	15.33 was noon, d came over the whole land
Lk	23.44 noon, and d came over the whole land
1 Pet	2. 9 called you out of d into his marvelous

DAUGHTER (DAUGHTERS)

Gen	20.12 the d of my father but not the d of my
Ruth	1.12 Turn back, my d, go your way, for I am
Esth	2. 7 Mordecai adopted her as his own d.
Ps	144. 12 our d like corner pillars, cut for the
Isa	3.17 with scabs the heads of the d of Zion,
Zech	9. 9 greatly, O d Zion! Shout aloud, O d
Mt	9.18 "My d has just died; but come and lay
	21. 5 "Tell the d of Zion, Look, your king is
Mk	5.23 "My little d is at the point of death.
	7.29 may go — the demon has left your d."
Lk	8.42 he had an only d, about twelve years
Acts	7.21 abandoned, Pharaoh's d adopted him
Heb	11.24 to be called the son of Pharaoh's d,

DAVID

Anointed by Samuel, 1 Sam 16.1-13; played the harp for Saul, 1 Sam 16.14-23; killed Goliath, 1 Sam 17; won Jonathan's friendship, 1 Sam 18.1-4; incurred Saul's jealousy, 1 Sam 18.5-9; married Michal, 1 Sam 18.20-29; fled from Saul, 1 Sam 19—22; fought the Philistines, 1 Sam 23; spared Saul at En-gedi, 1 Sam 24; David and Abigail, 1 Sam 25; spared Saul at Ziph, 1 Sam 26; lived among the Philistines, 1 Sam 27.1—28.2; 29; defeated the Amalekites, 1 Sam 30; made king over Judah, 2 Sam 2.1-7; made king over Israel, 2 Sam 5.1-16; brought the ark to Jerusalem, 2 Sam 6; God's covenant with David, 2 Sam 7; extended his kingdom, 2 Sam 8; David and Bath-sheba, 2 Sam 11.1—12.25; fled Absalom's revolt, 2 Sam 15—16; returned to Jerusalem, 2 Sam 19; David's song, 2 Sam 22.1—23.7; numbered Israel and Judah, 2 Sam 24; charged Solomon, 1 Kings 2.1-9; died, 1 Kings 2.10-12. (See also 1 Chr 11—29.)

Ps	78.70 He chose his servant D, and took him
Jer	23. 5 when I will raise up for D a righteous
Ezek	34.23 over them one shepherd, my servant D,
Mt	12. 3 Have you not read what D did when he
Mk	2.25 "Have you never read what D did when
Lk	1.32 will give him the throne of his father D,
Acts	2.25 For D says concerning him, 'I saw the
Rom	1. 3 who was descended from D according to
Rev	5. 5 of Judah, the Root of D, has conquered,

DAWN

Ps	119.147 I rise before d and cry for help; I put
Isa	58. 8 light shall break forth like the d, and
Lk	1.78 our God, the d from on high will break

DAWNING

Mt	28.	1 as the first day of the week was *d*, Mary

DAY (DAYS)

Gen	1.	5 God called the light *D*, and the
	2.	3 God blessed the seventh *d* and hallowed
Deut	33.25	and as your *d*, so is your strength.
Josh	10.14	There has been no *d* like it before or
2 Kings	7.	9 This is a *d* of good news; if we are
Job	15.23	They know that a *d* of darkness is ready
Ps	19.	2 *D* to *d* pours forth speech, and night to
	42.	8 By *d* the LORD commands his steadfast
	74.16	Yours is the *d*, yours also the night; you
	90.12	So teach us to count our *d* that we may
	102.	11 My *d* are like an evening shadow;
	118.	24 This is the *d* that the LORD has made;
	145.	2 Every *d* I will bless you, and praise your
Isa	2.12	LORD of hosts has a *d* against all that is
	11.10	On that *d* the root of Jesse shall stand
	12.	1 You will say in that *d*: "I will give
	13.	6 Wail, for the *d* of the LORD is near; it
	34.	8 the LORD has a *d* of vengeance, a year of
	37.	3 "This *d* is a *d* of distress, of rebuke, and
Jer	46.10	That *d* is the *d* of the Lord GOD of
Ezek	30.	3 a *d* is near, the *d* of the LORD is near;
Joel	1.15	for the *d*! For the *d* of the LORD is near,
	2.11	the *d* of the LORD is great; terrible
Am	5.18	Why do you want the *d* of the LORD? It
Zeph	1.14	great *d* of the LORD is near, near and
Zech	14.	1 a *d* is coming for the LORD, when the
Mal	3.	2 who can endure the *d* of his coming,
	4.	1 the *d* is coming, burning like an oven,
Mk	13.32	"But about that *d* or hour no one
Jn	8.56	rejoiced that he would see my *d*;
Acts	5.42	every *d* in the temple and at home they
Rom	13.13	let us live honorably as in the *d*, not in
1 Cor	15.31	in danger every hour? I die every *d*!
	16.	2 On the first *d* of every week, each of
2 Cor	1.14	on the *d* of the Lord Jesus were your
	6.	2 you, on a *d* of salvation I have helped
Phil	1.	6 bring it to completion by the *d* of Jesus
1 Thess	5.	2 the *d* of the Lord will come like a thief
Heb	10.25	the more as you see the *D* approaching.
2 Pet	3.10	the *d* of the Lord will come like a thief,

DEACONS

Phil	1.	1 are in Philippi, with the bishops' and *d*:
1 Tim	3.	8 *D* likewise must be serious, not

DEAD

Num	14.29	your *d* bodies shall fall in this very
	16.48	He stood between the *d* and the living;
2 Kings	19.35	dawned, they were all *d* bodies.
Eccl	9.	5 live, and after that they go to the *d*.
Mt	8.22	me, and let the *d* bury their own *d*."
	9.24	away; for the girl is not *d* but sleeping."
	11.	5 the deaf hear, the *d* are raised, and the
	22.32	He is not God of the *d*, but of the
Mk	5.39	weep? The child is not *d* but sleeping."
	15.44	Pilate wondered if he were already *d*;
Lk	8.49	"Your daughter is *d*; do not trouble the
	9.60	"Let the *d* bury their own *d*; but as for
	15.24	son of mine was *d*, and is alive again;
Acts	14.19	out of the city, supposing that he was *d*.
	20.	9 below and was picked up *d*. But Paul
Rom	8.10	though the body is *d* because of sin, the
1 Cor	15.29	who receive baptism on behalf of the *d*?
Eph	2.	1 You were *d* through the trespasses and
Jude		12 autumn trees without fruit, twice *d*,
Rev	3.	1 a name of being alive, but you are *d*.
	14.13	Blessed are the *d* who from now on die
	20.12	I saw the *d*, great and small, standing

DEAF

Lev	19.14	You shall not revile the *d* or put a
Isa	29.18	In that day the *d* shall hear the words
Mk	7.32	They brought to him a *d* man who had

Mk	7.37	makes the *d* hear and the dumb speak."

DEAL (DEALT)

Gen	12.16	for her sake he *d* well with Abram; and
	21.	1 The LORD *d* with Sarah as he had said,
Ps	103.	10 not *d* with us according to our sins,
	147.	20 has not *d* thus with any other nation;

DEAR

Ps	39.11	sin, consuming like a moth what is *d*
	102.	14 For your servants hold its stones *d*, and

DEATH

Num	11.15	going to treat me, put me to *d* at once
	23.10	Let me die the *d* of the upright, and let
Deut	30.15	life and prosperity, *d* and adversity.
2 Sam	15.21	whether for *d* or for life, there also your
	22.	6 me, the snares of *d* confronted me.
Job	38.17	Have the gates of *d* been revealed to
Ps	116.	3 The snares of *d* encompassed me; the
	116.	15 of the LORD is the *d* of his faithful ones.
Prov	14.12	to a person, but its end is the way to *d*.
Jer	21.	8 you the way of life and the way of *d*.
Ezek	18.32	I have no pleasure in the *d* of anyone,
Hos	13.14	from *D*? O *D*, where are your plagues?
Mk	5.23	daughter is at the point of *d*. Come and
	14.55	testimony against Jesus to put him to *d*;
Lk	1.79	sit darkness and in the shadow of *d*,
	9.27	some standing here who will not taste *d*
	22.	2 looking for a way to put Jesus to *d*,
Jn	12.33	to indicate the kind of *d* he was to die.
	21.19	to indicate the kind of *d* by which he
Rom	5.14	*d* excercised dominion from Adam to
	8.13	you put to *d* the deeds of the body,
	8.38	I am sure that neither *d*, nor life, nor
1 Cor	15.54	be fulfilled: "*D* has been swallowed up
	15.55	"Where, O *d*, is your victory? Where, O
2 Cor	2.16	to the one a fragrance from *d* to *d*, to
Col	3.	5 Put to *d*, therefore, whatever in you is
2 Tim	1.10	Christ Jesus, who abolished *d* and
2 Pet	1.14	since I know that my *d* will come soon,
Rev	2.11	will not be harmed by the second *d*.

DEBORAH

Judg	4.	4 *D*, a prophetess, the wife of Lappidoth,
	4.14	*D* said to Barak, "Up! For this is the day
	5.	1 Then *D* and Barak . . . sang on that day,

DEBT (DEBTS)

1 Sam	22.	2 in distress, and everyone who was in *d*,
2 Kings	4.	7 "Go sell the oil and pay your *d*, and you
Neh	10.31	year and the exaction of every *d*.
Mt	18.27	released him and forgave him the *d*.

DEBTORS

Lk	7.41	"A certain creditor had two *d*; one owed
	16.	5 summoning his master's *d* one by one,
Rom	8.12	we are *d*, not to the flesh, to live

DECEIT

Job	15.35	forth evil and their heart prepares *d*."
	27.	4 and my tongue will not utter *d*.
Ps	10.	7 mouths are filled with cursing and *d*
	17.	1 give ear to my prayer from lips free of *d*.
	32.	2 and in whose spirit there is no *d*.
	34.13	evil, and your lips from speaking *d*.
	50.19	rein for evil, and your tongue frames *d*.
Prov	12.20	*D* is in the mind of those who plan evil,
Isa	53.	9 and there was no *d* in his mouth.
Jer	14.14	and the *d* of their own minds.
Am	8.	5 and practice *d* with false balances,
Mk	7.22	wickedness, *d*, licentiousness, envy,
Jn	1.47	truly an Israelite in whom there is no *d*!"
Rom	1.29	Full of envy, murder, strife, *d*, craftiness
2 Cor	12.16	since I was crafty, I took you in by *d*.
1 Thess	2.	3 our appeal does not spring from *d* or

DECEITFUL

Ps	5. 6 the Lord abhors the bloodthirsty and *d*.
	52. 4 love all words that devour, O *d* tongue.
Prov	31.30 Charm is *d*, and beauty is vain, but a
Nah	3. 1 City of bloodsheds, utterly *d*, full of
2 Cor	11.13 boasters are false apostles, *d* workers,
Eph	4.14 by their craftiness in *d* scheming.

DECEITFULNESS

Heb	3.13 of you may be hardened by the *d* of sin.

DECEIVE (DECEIVED DECEIVES DECEIVING)

Gen	29.25 for Rachel? Why then have you *d* me?"
Lev	6. 2 trespass against the Lord by *d* a
Josh	9.22 "Why did you *d* us, saying, 'We are very
1 Sam	19.17 "Why have you *d* me like this, and let
1 Kings	13.18 and drink water." But he was *d* him.
2 Kings	18.29 'Do not let Hezekiah *d* you, for he will
Job	12.16 wisdom; the *d* and the deceiver are his.
	13. 9 you *d* him, as one person *d* another?
Prov	26.19 one who *d* his neighbor and says, "I am
Jer	4.10 God, how utterly you have *d* this people
	9. 5 They all *d* their neighbors, and no one
	37. 9 Do not *d* yourselves, saying, "The
Lam	1.19 I called to my lovers but they *d* me; my
Jn	7.12 were saying, "No, he is *d* the crowd."
	7.47 "Surely, you have not been *d* too, have
Rom	16.18 by smooth talk and flattery they will *d*
1 Cor	6. 9 Do not be *d*! Fornicators, idolaters,
	15.33 Do not be *d*: "Bad company ruins good
2 Cor	11. 3 afraid that as the serpent *d* Eve by its
Gal	6. 7 Do not be *d*; God is not mocked, for
Eph	5. 6 Let no one *d* you with empty words, for
Col	2. 4 may *d* you with plausible arguments.
2 Thess	2. 3 Let no one *d* you in any way; for that
1 Tim	2.14 Adam was not *d*, but the woman was *d*
Rev	18.23 and all nations were *d* by your sorcery.

DECEIVER (DECEIVERS)

Titus	1.10 rebellious people, idle talkers and *d*,
2 Jn	7 such person is the *d* and the antichrist.
Rev	12. 9 and Satan, the *d* of the whole world

DECENTLY

1 Cor	14.40 but all things should be done *d* and in

DECIDE (DECIDED)

1 Chr	21.12 Now *d* what answer I shall return to the
2 Chr	2. 1 Solomon *d* to build a temple for the
Isa	11. 4 and *d* with equity for the meek of the
1 Cor	2. 2 I *d* to know nothing among you except

DECISION (DECISIONS)

Deut	17. . 8 If any judicial *d* is too difficult for you
	17. 9 they shall announce to you the *d* in the
Prov	16.10 Inspired *d* are on the lips of a king; his
Joel	3.14 multitudes, in the valley of *d*! For the
Acts	16. 4 the *d* that had been reached by the

DECLARE (DECLARED)

1 Chr	16.24 *D* his glory among the nations, his
Ps	96. 3 *D* his glory among the nations his
	145. 6 proclaimed, and I will *d* your greatness.
Isa	48. 3 "The former things I *d* long ago, they
	66.19 shall *d* my glory among the nations.
Mt	7.23 Then I will *d* to them, 'I never knew
Jn	16.13 and he will *d* to you the things that are
Rom	1. 4 and was *d* to be Son of God with power

DECREE (DECREED DECREES)

Ezra	6. 8 I make a *d* regarding what you shall do
Job	20.29 God, the heritage *d* for him by God."
Ps	2. 7 I will tell of the *d* of the Lord: He said
	19. 7 the *d* of the Lord are sure, making wise
	78. 5 He established a *d* in Jacob, and
	93. 5 Your *d* are very sure; holiness befits
	99. 7 they kept his *d*, and the statutes that he
Isa	10. 1 Ah, you who make iniquitous *d*, who

DEDICATE (DEDICATED)

Dan	4.24 O king, and it is a *d* of the Most High
	6.26 I make a *d*, that in all my royal
	9.24 "Seventy weeks are *d* for your people
Lk	2. 1 *d* went out from Emperor Augustus that
Acts	17. 7 acting contrary to the *d* of the emperor,
1 Cor	2. 7 hidden, which God *d* before the ages

DEDICATE (DEDICATED)

2 Sam	8.11 these also King David *d* to the Lord,
1 Kings	7.51 the things that David his father had *d*,
	8.63 of Israel *d* the house of the Lord.
1 Chr	26.27 From booty won in battles they *d* gifts
2 Chr	2. 4 my God and *d* it to him for offering

DEDICATION

Num	7.10 presented offerings for the *d* of the altar
Ezra	6.17 They offered at the *d* of this house of
Neh	12.27 at the *d* of the wall of Jerusalem they
Dan	3. 2 and come to the *d* of the statue
Jn	10.22 time the festival of the *D* took place

DEED (DEEDS)

Deut	11. 7 seen every great *d* that the Lord did.
Judg	6.13 where are all his wonderful *d* that our
Job	34.11 and according to their *d* he will repay
Ps	150. 2 Praise him for his mighty *d*; praise him
Eccl	12.14 God will bring every *d* into judgment,
Jer	25.14 I will repay them according to their *d*
Lk	23.41 are getting what we deserve for our *d*,
Jn	3.19 than light because their *d* were evil.
Rom	3.20 in his sight" by *d* prescribed by the law,
	8.13 you put to death the *d* of the body
Rev	14.13 their labors, for their *d* follow them."

DEEP

Job	11. 7 "Can you find out the *d* things of God?
Ps	42. 7 *D* calls to *d* at the thunder of your
	92. 5 O Lord! Your thoughts are very *d*!
	104. 6 You cover it with the *d* as a garment;
Prov	8.28 he established the fountains of the *d*,
Dan	2.22 He reveals *d* and hidden things; he
Lk	5. 4 into the *d* water and let down your nets
Rev	2.24 what some call 'the *d* things of Satan,'

DEFEAT

1 Cor	6. 7 at all with one another is already a *d*

DEFECT

Dan	1. 4 young men without physical *d* and

DEFEND

2 Kings	19.34 For I will *d* this city to save it, for my
	20. 6 I will *d* this city for my own sake and
Ps	45. 4 for the cause of truth and to *d* the right;
Prov	31. 9 righteously, *d* the rights of the poor
Isa	37.35 I will *d* this city to save it, for my own
Lk	12.11 worry about how you are to *d* yourselves

DEFENSE

Acts	22. 1 fathers, listen to the *d* that I now make
Phil	1. 7 in the *d* and confirmation of the gospel.

DEFENSELESS

Ps	141. 8 in you I seek refuge; leave me not *d*.

DEFER (DEFERRED)

Lev	19.32 rise before the aged, and *d* to the old;
Prov	13.12 Hope *d* makes the heart sick, but a
Isa	48. 9 For my name's sake I *d* my anger, for

DEFILE (DEFILED DEFILES DEFILING)

Lev	15.31 in their uncleanness by *d* my tabernacle
	18.24 Do not *d* yourselves in any of these
Num	19.13 not purify themselves, *d* the tabernacle
	19.20 they have *d* the sanctuary of the Lord.
	35.34 You shall not *d* the land in which you
Neh	13.29 they have *d* the priesthood, the
Ps	79. 1 they have *d* your holy temple; they have
Jer	2. 7 But when you entered you *d* my land,

Ezek 5.11 you have *d* my sanctuary with all your
 20.31 you *d* yourselves with all your idols to
 23.38 they have *d* my sanctuary on the same
 37.23 They shall never again *d* themselves
 43. 8 they were *d* my holy name by their
Dan 1. 8 not *d* himself with the royal rations of
Hos 5. 3 you have played the whore; Israel is *d.*
Mt 15.18 from the heart, and this is what *d.*
Mk 7.15 *d*, the things that come out are what *d.*"
 7.20 is what comes out of a person that *d.*
1 Cor 8. 7 and their conscience, being weak, is *d.*

DEFRAUD (DEFRAUDED)

Lev 6. 2 robbery, or if you have *d* his neighbor,
 19.13 You shall not *d* your neighbor; you shall
Lk 19. 8 if I have *d* anyone of anything I will pay
1 Cor 6. 7 be wronged? Why not rather be *d?*

DEFY

1 Sam 17.10 "Today I *d* the ranks of Israel! Give me

DEGRADING

Rom 1.24 to impurity, to the *d* of their bodies

DELAY

Hab 2. 3 for it; it will surely come, it will not *d.*

DELIGHT (DELIGHTS) (n)

Gen 3. 6 for food, and that it was a *d* to the eyes,
Deut 28.63 as the Lᴏʀᴅ took *d* in making you
 30. 9 will again take *d* in prospering you,
1 Sam 19. 1 son Jonathan took great *d* in David.
 15.22 "Has the Lᴏʀᴅ as great *d* in burnt
Job 27.10 Will they take *d* in the Almighty? Will
 34. 9 profits one nothing to take *d* in God.'
Ps 1. 2 but their *d* is in the law of the Lᴏʀᴅ,
 36. 8 give them drink from the river of your *d.*
 37. 4 Take *d* in the Lᴏʀᴅ, and he will give you
 51.16 For you have no *d* in sacrifice; if I were
 119. 77 that I may live; for your law is my *d.*
Prov 8.30 I was daily his *d*, rejoicing before him
 11.20 but those of blameless ways are his *d.*
 15. 8 but the prayer of the upright is his *d.*
 16.13 Righteous lips are the *d* of a king, and
Song 2. 3 With great *d* I sat in his shadow, and
Ezek 24.16 take away from you the *d* of your eyes;

DELIGHT (DELIGHTED DELIGHTS) (v)

2 Sam 22.20 he delivered me, because he *d* in me.
1 Kings 10. 9 be the Lᴏʀᴅ your God, who has *d* in you
Job 22.26 you will *d* yourself in the Almighty,
Ps 5. 4 you are not a God who *d* in wickedness;
 37.23 firm by the Lᴏʀᴅ, when he *d* in our way;
 40. 8 I *d* to do your will, O my God; your law
 44. 3 of your countenance, for you *d* in them.
 51.19 then you will *d* in right sacrifices, in
 112. 1 who greatly *d* in his commandmants.
Prov 1.22 How long will scoffers *d* in their
 3.12 loves, as a father the son in whom he *d.*
Isa 1.11 I do not *d* in the blood of bulls, or of
 55. 2 is good, and *d* yourselves in rich food.
 58. 2 they seek me and *d* to know my ways,
 62. 4 for the Lᴏʀᴅ *d* in you, and your land
Mic 7.18 because he *d* in showing clemency.
Mal 3. 1 the covenant in whom you *d*—indeed,
Rom 7.22 I *d* in the law of God, in my inmost

DELIVER

Gen 32.11 *D* me, please, from the hand of my
Ex 3. 8 I have come down to *d* them from the
 5.23 done nothing at all to *d* your people."
 25.22 I will *d* to you all my commands for the
Josh 2.13 to them, and *d* our lives from death."
Judg 7. 7 hundred men that lapped I will *d* you,
Ps 3. 7 Rise up, O Lᴏʀᴅ! *D* me, O my God! For
 6. 4 Turn, O Lᴏʀᴅ, save my life; *d* me for the
 33.19 to *d* their soul from death, and to keep
 59. 1 *D* me from my enemies, O my God;

Eccl 8. 8 wickedness *d* those who practice it.
Isa 43.13 is no one who can *d* from my hand;
 50. 2 redeem? Or have I no power to *d?*
Jer 1. 8 of them, for I am with you to *d* you,
Dan 3.17 serve is able to *d* us from the furnace
 6.16 God, whom you faithfully serve, *d* you!"

DELIVERS (DELIVERED DELIVERING)

Gen 14.20 Most High, who has *d* your enemies
Ex 18. 9 to Israel, in *d* them from the Egyptians.
Judg 2.18 he *d* them from the hand of their
 6. 9 I *d* you from the hand of the Egyptians,
 7. 2 me, saying, 'My own hand has *d* me.'
2 Sam 19. 9 "The king *d* us from the hands of our
 22.18 He *d* me from my strong enemy, from
 22.20 place; he *d* me, because he delighted
Job 29.12 because I *d* the poor who cried, and the
Ps 18.17 He *d* me from my strong enemy, and
 33.16 a warrior is not *d* by his great strength.
 34. 4 me, and *d* me from all my fears.
 54. 7 For he has *d* me from every trouble,
 106. 10 of the foe, and *d* them from the hand of
 107. 6 and he *d* them from their distress;
 116. 8 For you have *d* my soul from death, my
 138. 7 your hand, and your right hand *d* me.
Prov 11. 4 wrath, but righteousness *d* from death.
 11. 8 The righteous are *d* from trouble, and
Eccl 9.15 man, and he by his wisdom *d* the city.
Dan 12. 1 But at that time your people shall be *d*,
Rom 15.28 *d* to them what has been collected,

DELIVERANCE

Ex 14.13 stand firm, and see the *d* that the Lᴏʀᴅ
1 Sam 11. 9 time the sun is hot, you shall have *d*.'"
 11.13 today the Lᴏʀᴅ has brought *d* to Israel."
Ps 3. 8 *D* belongs to the Lᴏʀᴅ; may your
 9.14 of daughter Zion, rejoice in your *d.*
 22.31 proclaim his *d* to a people yet unborn,
 32. 7 you surround me with glad cries of *d.*
 53. 6 O that *d* for Israel would come from
Isa 46.13 I bring near my *d*, it is not far off, and
 51. 5 I will bring near my *d* swiftly, my
Jon 2. 9 vowed I will pay. *D* belongs to the Lᴏʀᴅ!"
Phil 1.19 Jesus Christ this will turn out for my *d.*

DELIVERER

Judg 3. 9 Lᴏʀᴅ raised up a *d* for the Israelites,
2 Sam 22. 2 Lᴏʀᴅ is my rock, my fortress, and my *d*,
Ps 18. 2 Lᴏʀᴅ is my rock, my fortress, and my *d*,
 140. 7 O Lᴏʀᴅ, my Lᴏʀᴅ, my strong *d*, you have

DELUDED

Isa 44.20 a *d* mind has led him astray, and he

DELUSION

Isa 41.29 No, they are all a *d*; their works are
2 Thess 2.11 reason God sends them a powerful *d*,

DEMANDED

Lk 12.20 very night your life is being *d* of you.
 12.48 been entrusted, even more will be *d.*

DEMON (DEMONS)

Mt 15.22 David, my daughter is tormented by a *d.*"
Mk 1.34 various diseases, and cast out many *d*;
 3.22 and by the ruler of the *d* he casts out *d.*"
 9.38 someone casting out *d* in your name,
Lk 7.33 no wine, and you say, 'He has a *d*';
 11.14 casting out a *d* that was mute; when
Jn 7.20 crowd answered, "You have a *d*! Who is
1 Cor 10.20 pagans sacrifice, they sacrifice to *d* and
1 Tim 4. 1 to deceitful spirits and teachings of *d*,
Jas 2.19 well. Even the *d* believe—and shudder.
Rev 9.20 or give up worshiping *d* and idols of
 18. 2 It has become a dwelling place of *d*,

DEMONSTRATION

1 Cor 2. 4 but with a *d* of the Spirit and of power,

DEN

Jer	7.11	become a *d* of robbers in your sight?
Mt	21.13	but you are making it a *d* of robbers."

DENARIUS

Mk	12.15	to the test? Bring me a *d*, and let me
Lk	20.24	"Show me a *d*. Whose head and whose

DENOUNCED

Dan	3. 8	came forward and *d* the Jews.

DENY (DENIED DENIES)

Ezra	8.21	that we might *d* ourselves before our
Mt	10.33	others, I also will *d* before my Father
	16.24	let them *d* themselves and take up their
	26.34	cock crows, you will *d* me three times."
	26.70	he *d* it before all of them, saying, "I do
Mk	8.34	let them *d* themselves and take up their
	14.30	crows twice, you will *d* me three times."
	14.68	he *d* it, saying, "I do not know or
Lk	12. 9	whoever *d* me before others will be
	22.34	have *d* three times that you know me."
	22.57	But he *d* it, saying, "Woman, I do not
Jn	18.25	are you?" He *d* it and said, "I am not."
1 Tim	5. 8	has *d* the faith and is worse than an
2 Tim	2.12	with him; if we *d* him, he also will *d*
Titus	1.16	God, but they *d* him by their actions.
2 Pet	2. 1	They will even *d* the Master who bought
1 Jn	2.22	antichrist, the one who *d* the Father
Rev	2.13	my name, and you did not *d* your faith

DEPART (DEPARTED)

Ps	18.21	and have not wickedly *d* from my God.
	34.14	*D* from evil, and do good; seek peace,
Isa	52.11	*D*, *d*, go out from there! Touch no
Mt	25.41	*d* from me into the eternal fire prepared

DEPARTURE

Lk	9.31	in glory and were speaking of his *d*,
2 Pet	1.15	after my *d* you may be able at any time

DEPRAVED

1 Tim	6. 5	among those who are *d* in mind

DEPRIVE

Isa	5.23	and *d* the innocent of their rights!
1 Cor	7. 5	Do not *d* one another except perhaps by
	9.15	—no one will *d* me of my ground for

DEPTHS

Ps	130. 1	Out of the *d* I cry to you, O Lord. Lord,
1 Cor	2.10	searches everything, even the *d* of God.

DERBE

Acts	14. 6	of it and fled to Lystra and *D*, cities
	16. 1	Paul went on also to *D* and to Lystra,
	20. 4	by Gaius of *D*, and by Timothy, as well

DERIDED

Mt	27.39	Those who passed by *d* him, shaking
Mk	15.29	Those who passed by *d* him, shaking

DESCEND (DESCENDED)

Ex	34. 5	The Lord *d* in the cloud and stood with
Lk	3.22	the Holy Spirit *d* upon him in bodily
1 Thess	4.16	will *d* from heaven, and the dead in
Heb	7.14	evident that our Lord was *d* from Judah,

DESCENDANTS

Gen	5. 1	This is a list of the *d* of Adam. When
	10. 1	These are the *d* of Noah's sons, Shem,
Deut	4.40	well-being and that of your *d* after you,
Ps	89. 4	'I will establish your *d* forever, and
Rom	4.18	was said, "So numerous shall your *d* be."
	9. 7	is through Isaac that *d* shall be named
Gal	3. 7	who believe are the *d* of Abraham.

DESERT

Ps	107. 4	Some wandered in *d* wastes, finding no

Isa	21.13	the scrub of the *d* plain you will lodge,
	35. 6	in the wilderness, and streams in the *d*;
	41.19	I will set in the *d* the cyprus, the plane
	42.11	*d* and the towns lift up their voice, the
	51. 3	her *d* like the garden of the Lord; joy

DESERTED (DESERTING)

Mt	14.13	from there in a boat to a *d* place
	26.56	Then all the disciples *d* him and fled.
Mk	6.31	"Come away to a *d* place all by
	14.50	All of them *d* him and fled.
Gal	1. 6	are so quickly *d* him the one called you
2 Tim	4.10	has *d* me and gone to Thessalonica;

DESERTERS

Mt	26.31	"You will all become *d* because of me

DESERVE (DESERVED DESERVES DESERVING)

Deut	19. 6	although a death sentence was not *d*,
Mt	10.10	or a staff; for laborers *d* their food.
	26.66	verdict?" They answered, "He *d* death."
Mk	14.64	All of them condemned him as *d* death.
1 Tim	5.18	"The laborer *d* to be paid." Never accept
Rev	16. 6	them blood to drink. It is what they *d*!"

DESIGNATED

Heb	5.10	having been *d* by God a high priest

DESIGNS

2 Cor	2.11	Satan; for we are not ignorant of his *d*.

DESIRE (DESIRES) (n)

Gen	3.16	your *d* shall be for your husband, and
Deut	12. 8	today, all of us according to our own *d*,
1 Sam	9.20	And on whom is all Israel's *d* fixed, if
2 Sam	23. 5	cause to prosper all my help and my *d*?
2 Chr	9.12	granted the queen of Sheba every *d* that
Job	17.11	plans are broken off, the *d* of my heart.
Ps	10.17	Lord, you will hear the *d* of the meek;
	37. 4	and he will give you the *d* of your heart.
	140. 8	Grant not, O Lord, the *d* of the wicked;
	145. 16	your hand, satisfying the *d* of every
	145. 19	He fulfills the *d* of all who fear him; he
Prov	10.24	the *d* of the righteous will be granted.
	11.23	The *d* of the righteous ends only in
	13.12	sick, but a *d* fulfilled is a tree of life.
	13.19	A *d* realized is sweet to the soul, but to
Eccl	6. 9	sight of eyes than the wandering of *d*;
	12. 5	and *d* fails; because all must go to their
Song	7.10	I am my beloved's, and his *d* is for me.
Isa	26. 8	name and your renown are the soul's *d*.
Rom	10. 1	and sisters, my heart's *d* and prayer
Eph	2. 3	following the *d* of flesh and senses, and
1 Jn	2.16	the *d* of the flesh, the *d* of the eyes, the

DESIRE (DESIRED DESIRES) (v)

Esth	1. 8	of his palace to do as each one *d*.
Job	21.14	'Leave us alone! We do not *d* to know
Ps	19.10	More to be *d* are they than gold, even
	40. 6	Sacrifice and offering you do not *d*; but
	45.11	house, and the king will *d* your beauty.
	51. 6	You *d* truth in the inward being;
	73.25	And there is nothing on earth that I *d*
Prov	6.25	Do not *d* her beauty in your heart, and
	21.10	The souls of the wicked *d* evil; their
Isa	53. 2	in his appearance that we should *d* him.
Lk	10.24	and kings *d* to see what you see!
	22.15	eagerly *d* to eat this passover with you
Gal	4.21	me, you who *d* to be subject to the law,
	5.17	the flesh *d* is opposed to the Spirit,

DESOLATE

Ps	68. 6	God gives the *d* a home to live in; he
Isa	1. 7	aliens devour your land; it is, as
	24. 1	to lay waste the earth and make it *d*,
Mt	23.38	See, your house is left to you, *d*.

DESOLATION

Jer	4.27	The whole land shall be a *d*; yet I will

Lk 21.20 armies, know that its *d* has come near.

DESPERATE

Ps 88.15 youth up. I suffer your terrors; I am *d*.

DESPISE (DESPISED DESPISING)

Gen 25.34 his way. Thus Esau *d* his birthright.
Num 6.16 the LORD; and she *d* him in her heart.
14.11 How long will this people *d* me? And
15.31 Because of having *d* the word of the
16.30 know that these men have *d* the LORD."
2 Kings 17.15 They *d* his statutes, and his covenant
2 Chr 36.16 the messengers of God, *d* his words,
Neh 4. 4 Hear, O our God, for we are *d*; turn
Job 5.17 therefore do not *d* the discipline of the
19.18 Even young children *d* me; when I rise,
42. 6 therefore I *d* myself, and repent in dust
Ps 22. 6 not human; scorned by others, and *d*
106. 24 Then they *d* the pleasant land, having
119.141 I am small and *d*, yet I do not forget
Prov 1. 7 fools *d* wisdom and instruction.
3.11 My child, do not *d* the LORD's discipline
13.13 Those who *d* the word bring destruction
Isa 1. 4 who have *d* the Holy One of Israel, who
5.24 and have *d* the word of the Holy One
49. 7 to one deeply *d*, abhorred by the
52. 5 continually, all day long my name is *d*.
53. 3 He was *d* and rejected by others; a man
Jer 4.30 you beautify yourself. Your lovers *d* you;
49.15 among the nations, *d* by humankind.
Am 5.21 I hate, I *d* your festivals, and I take no
Zech 4.10 whoever has *d* the day of small things
Mt 6.24 be devoted to the one and *d* the other.
18.10 you do not *d* one of these little ones;
Lk 16.13 be devoted to the one and *d* the other.
1 Cor 1.28 God chose what is low and *d* in the
16.11 let no one *d* him. Send him on his way
Gal 4.14 you did not scorn or *d* me, but
2 Pet 2.10 in depraved lust, and who *d* authority.

DESPOILED

Ps 12. 5 "Because the poor are *d*, because the

DESTINE (DESTINED)

Isa 65.12 I will *d* you to the sword, and all of you
Acts 13.48 many as had been *d* for eternal life
Eph 1. 5 He *d* us for adoption as his children
1 Thess 5. 9 For God has *d* us not for wrath but for
1 Pet 1.20 He was *d* before the foundation of the

DESTITUTE

Ps 102. 17 He will regard the prayer of the *d*, and
Heb 11.37 and goats, *d*, persecuted, tormented —

DESTROY (DESTROYED DESTROYING DESTROYS)

Gen 20. 4 "Lord, will you *d* an innocent people?
Num 33.52 *d* all their figured stones, *d* all their
Deut 7. 2 them, then you must utterly *d* them.
Josh 11.20 that they might be utterly *d*, and might
1 Sam 15. 3 and utterly *d* all that they have;
2 Kings 8.19 LORD would not *d* Judah, for the sake of
Ps 57. 1 take refuge, until the *d* storms pass by.
101. 8 by morning I will *d* all the wicked
Prov 1.32 and the complacency of fools *d* them;
14.11 The house of the wicked is *d*, but the
Jer 5.17 they shall *d* with the sword your
Lam 2. 2 The Lord has *d* without mercy all the
Ezek 9. 8 will you *d* all who remain of Israel as
Hos 4. 6 My people are *d* for lack of knowledge;
Mt 26.61 'I am able to *d* the temple of God and
Mk 12. 9 He will come and *d* the tenants, and
14.58 "We heard him say, 'I will *d* this temple
Lk 12.33 no thief comes near and no moth *d*.
Jn 2.19 "*D* this temple, and in three days I will
1 Cor 3.17 If anyone *d* God's temple, God will *d*
2 Thess 2. 8 whom the Lord Jesus will *d* with the
Heb 2.14 through death he might *d* the one who

2 Pet 2.12 creatures are *d*, they also will be *d*,
Rev 11.18 great, and for *d* those who *d* the earth."

DESTROYERS

Jer 22. 7 I will prepare *d* against you, all with

DESTRUCTION

Prov 16.18 Pride goes before *d*, and a haughty
Isa 28.22 have heard a decree of *d* from the Lord
Lam 2.11 ground because of the *d* of my people,
1 Cor 5. 5 man over to Satan for the *d* of the flesh,

DETERMINE (DETERMINED)

1 Sam 20. 7 angry, then know that evil is *d* by him.
2 Chr 25.16 "I know that God has *d* to destroy you,
Esth 7. 7 saw that the king had *d* to destroy him.
Job 14. 5 Since their days are *d*, and the number
Dan 11.36 completed, for what is *d* shall be done.
Lk 22.22 Son of Man is going as it has been *d*,
Rom 2.18 know his will and *d* what is best
1 Cor 7.37 and has *d* in his own mind to keep her
Phil 1.10 full insight to help you *d* what is best,

DETEST

Num 21. 5 no water, and we *d* this miserable food."

DETESTABLE

Lev 11.10 that are in the waters, they are *d* to you
Ezek 20. 7 Cast away the *d* things your eyes feast
Hos 9.10 and become *d* like the thing they loved.

DEVIL

Mt 4. 1 the wilderness to be tempted by the *d*.
13.39 enemy who sowed them is the *d*; the
Lk 8.12 the *d* comes and takes away the word
Jn 8.44 You are from your father the *d*, and you
13. 2 The *d* had already put it into the heart
Eph 4.27 and do not make room for the *d*.
Jas 4. 7 to God. Resist the *d*, and he will flee
1 Pet 5. 8 roaring lion your adversary the *d* prowls
1 Jn 3. 8 *d* has been sinning from the beginning.
3. 8 purpose, to destroy the works of the *d*.
Rev 2.10 Beware, the *d* is about to throw some of
12.12 the *d* has come down to you with great
20.10 the *d* who had deceived them was

DEVIOUS

Jer 17. 9 The heart is *d* above all else; it is

DEVISE

Prov 24. 2 for their minds *d* violence, and their
Ezek 11. 2 these are the men who *d* iniquity and
Mic 2. 1 Alas for those who *d* wickedness and

DEVOTE (DEVOTED)

Lev 27.28 every *d* thing is most holy to the LORD.
Num 18.14 Every *d* thing in Israel shall be yours.
Josh 6.18 to covet and take any of the *d* things
7. 1 broke faith in regard to the *d* things;
Ezek 44.29 and every *d* thing in Israel shall be
Mic 4.13 and shall *d* their gain to the LORD,
Titus 3. 8 may be careful to *d* themselves to good

DEVOTION

1 Chr 29. 3 because of my *d* to the house of my
Acts 11.23 faithful to the Lord with steadfast *d*;
2 Cor 11. 3 from a sincere and pure *d* to Christ.

DEVOUR (DEVOURED DEVOURING DEVOURS)

2 Sam 2.26 "Is the sword to keep *d* forever? Do you
Prov 21.20 the house of the wise, but the fool *d* it.
Isa 1.20 and rebel, you shall be *d* by the sword;
9.20 satisfied; they *d* the flesh of their own
Jer 30.16 Therefore all who *d* you shall be *d*, and
Hos 7. 7 are as an oven, and they *d* their rulers.
Mt 23.14n For you *d* widows' houses and for the

DEVOUT

Lk 2.25 Simeon, this man was righteous and *d*,

Acts	2. 5	there were *d* Jews from every nation
	10. 2	He was a *d* man who feared God with
	22.12	certain Ananias, who was a *d* man

DEW

Judg	6.37	if there is *d* on the fleece alone, and it
Ps	133. 3	It is like the *d* of Hermon, which falls
Prov	3.20	open, and the clouds drop down the *d*.
	19.12	but his favor is like *d* on the grass.
Hos	6. 4	cloud, like the *d* that goes away early.
	13. 3	mist or like the *d* that goes away early,
	14. 5	I will be as the *d* to Israel; he shall

DIE (DIES DYING)

Gen	2.17	in the day that you eat of it you shall *d*."
Num	16.29	If these people *d* a natural death, or if a
	26.65	them, "They shall *d* in the wilderness."
Deut	4.22	I am going to *d* in this land without
	32.50	you shall *d* there on the mountain
Judg	16.30	said, "Let me *d* with the Philistines."
Job	3.11	"Why did I not *d* at birth, come forth
	12. 2	the people, and wisdom will *d* with you.
	14.10	But mortals *d*, and are laid low; humans
	21.23	One *d* in full prosperity, being wholly at
Ps	41. 5	wonder in malice when I will *d*,
	118. 17	I shall not *d*, but I shall live, and
Prov	10.21	feed many, but fools *d* for lack of sense.
	19.16	who are heedless of their ways will *d*.
Eccl	2.16	How can the wise *d* just like fools?
Ezek	33.11	evil ways; why will you *d*, O house of
Mk	14.31	"Even though I must *d* with you, I will
Jn	8.24	for you will *d* in your sins unless you
	11.16	us also go, that we may *d* with him."
	12.24	grain; but if it *d*, it bears much fruit.
	21.23	that this disciple would not *d*.
Rom	6. 9	raised from the dead, will never *d* again;
	14. 8	if we *d*, we *d* to the Lord; so then,
1 Cor	15.31	in danger every hour? I *d* every day!
2 Cor	6. 9	as *d*, and see—we are alive; as
Phil	1.21	to me, living is Christ, and *d* is gain.

DIED

Gen	7.21	all flesh *d* that moved on the earth,
	25. 8	Abraham . . . *d* in a good old age, an old
	35.29	Isaac . . . *d* and was gathered to his
Ex	2.23	After a long time the king of Egypt *d*.
Deut	34. 5	Then Moses . . . *d* there in the land of
Josh	24.29	Joshua son of Nun . . . *d*, being one
1 Sam	31. 6	Saul and his three sons . . . *d* together
2 Sam	18.33	Would that I had *d* instead of you, O
1 Kings	22.37	So the king *d*, and was brought to
2 Kings	4.20	child sat on her lap till noon, and he *d*.
1 Chr	10.13	Saul *d* for his unfaithfulness; he was
Ezek	24.18	the morning, and at evening my wife *d*.
Lk	7.12	a man who had *d* was being carried out.
Acts	7.60	them." When he had said this, he *d*.
Rom	5. 6	the right time Christ *d* for the ungodly.
	6. 2	can we who *d* to sin go on living in it?
	7. 4	you have *d* to the law through the body
	7.10	and I *d*, and the very commandment
1 Cor	8.11	for whom Christ *d* are destroyed.
	11.30	you are weak and ill, and some have *d*.
	15. 3	that Christ *d* for our sins in accordance
	15. 6	are still alive, though some have *d*.
2 Cor	5.14	that one has *d* for all; therefore all have
Gal	2.19	through the law I *d* to the law, so that I
1 Thess	4.13	about those who have *d*, so that you
Rev	16. 3	and every living thing in the sea *d*.

DIFFERENCE

Ezek	44.23	people the *d* between the holy and the

DIFFERENT

1 Cor	4. 7	who sees anything *d* in you? What do
Gal	1. 6	Christ and are turning to a *d* gospel—

DIG (DIGS DUG)

Gen	26.22	moved from there and *d* another well,

Prov	26.27	Whoever *d* a pit will fall into it, and a
Eccl	10. 8	Whoever *d* a pit will fall into it; and
Mt	25.18	went off and *d* a hole in the ground
Lk	16. 3	I am not strong enough to *d*, and I am

DILIGENT (DILEGENTLY)

Deut	11.22	If you will *d* observe this entire
	28.58	If you do not *d* observe all the words of
Prov	12.24	The hand of the *d* will rule, while the
	13. 4	while the appetite of the *d* is richly
	21. 5	The plans of the *d* lead surely to

DIM

Ps	69. 3	is parched. My eyes grow *d* with waiting

DINE

Gen	43.16	ready, for the men are to *d* with me
Lk	11.37	a Pharisee asked him to *d* with him; so

DINNER

Prov	15.17	Better is a *d* of vegetables where love is
Mt	22. 4	I have prepared my *d*, my oxen and my
Lk	14.12	or *d*, do not invite your friends or your
	14.16	gave a great *d*, and invited many.

DIPPED

Mt	26.23	"The one who has *d* his hand into the
Jn	13.26	of bread when I have *d* it in the dish."

DIRECT (DIRECTED DIRECTS)

1 Sam	7. 3	*D* your heart to the Lord, and serve him
1 Chr	29.18	people, and *d* their hearts toward you.
Ps	119.128	I *d* my steps by all your precepts; I hate
Prov	16. 9	plans the way, but the Lord *d* the steps.
Isa	40.13	Who has *d* the Spirit of the Lord, or as
Mt	28.16	mountain to which Jesus had *d* them.
Acts	10.22	was *d* by a holy angel to send for you to

DIRECTION

Josh	9.14	and did not ask *d* from the Lord.

DISAPPOINTED

Job	41. 9	Any hope of capturing it will be *d*; were

DISASTER

Prov	24.22	for *d* comes from them suddenly, and
Jer	17.18	bring on them the day of *d*; destroy
	44.11	I am determined to bring *d* on you, to
Am	3. 6	Does *d* befall a city, unless the Lord has
Zeph	3.15	in your midst; you shall fear *d* no more.

DISCERN (DISCERNED DISCERNING)

1 Kings	3. 9	able to *d* between good and evil;
Ps	139. 2	I rise up; you *d* my thoughts from far
Rom	12. 2	you may *d* what is the will of God—
1 Cor	1.19	the discernment of the *d* I will thwart."
	2.14	them because they are spiritually *d*.
	11.29	who eat and drink without *d* the body,

DISCERNMENT

1 Cor	1.19	wise, and the *d* of the discerning I will

DISCHARGED

Rom	7. 2	her husband dies she is *d* from the law
	7. 6	But now we are *d* from the law, dead to

DISCIPLE (DISCIPLES)

Isa	8.16	seal the teaching among my *d*.
Mt	10. 1	Jesus summoned his twelve *d* and gave
	10.24	"A is not above the teacher, nor a
	14.19	*d*, and the *d* gave them to the crowds.
	15. 2	"Why do your *d* break the tradition of
	17.16	I brought him to your *d*, but they could
	21. 1	the Mount of Olives, Jesus sent two *d*,
	28. 7	tell his *d*, 'He has been raised from the
	28.19	Go therefore and make *d* of all nations,
Mk	3. 7	Jesus departed with his *d* to the sea,
	6.45	he made his *d* get into the boat and go
	8. 6	gave them to his *d* to distribute and

Mk	9.31 he was teaching his *d*, saying to them,
	10.13 them, and the *d* spoke sternly to them.
Lk	6.40 A *d* is not above the teacher, but
	7.18 John summoned two of his *d* and sent
	9.16 broke them, and gave them to the *d* to
	14.33 cannot become my *d* if you do not give
	17. 3 your guard! If another *d* sins, rebuke the
	19.29 he sent two of the *d*, saying, "Go into
	22.39 of Olives; and the *d* followed him.
Jn	2:11 his glory; and his *d* believed in him.
	3.25 arose between John's *d* and a Jew.
	6.66 many of his *d* turned back and no
	8.31 in my word, you are truly my *d*;
	9.28 are his *d*, but we are *d* of Moses.
	13.35 that you are my *d*, if you have love for
	15. 8 you bear much fruit and become my *d*.
	19.26 Jesus saw his mother and the *d* whom
	19.38 Joseph of Arimathea, who was a *d* of
	20. 2 went to Simon Peter and the other *d*,
	20.19 where the *d* had met were locked for
	21. 4 the *d* did not know that it was Jesus.
Acts	9.10 was a *d* at Damascus named Ananias.

DISCIPLINARIAN

Gal	3.24 the law was our *d* until Christ came, so
	3.25 come, we are no longer subject to a *d*,

DISCIPLINE (n)

Job	5.17 do not despise the *d* of the Almighty.
Ps	50.17 For you hate *d*, and you cast my words
Prov	3.11 do not despise the LORD's *d* or be weary
	15.10 There is severe *d* for one who forsakes
	23.13 Do not withhold *d* from your children; if
Heb	12. 5 do not regard lightly the *d* of the Lord,
	12.11 *d* always seems painful rather than

DISCIPLINE (DISCIPLINED DISCIPLINES)

Deut	4.36 he made you hear his voice to *d* you.
	8. 5 as a parent *d* a child so the LORD your
1 Kings	12.11 My father *d* you with whips, but I will *d*
Ps	6. 1 in your anger, nor *d* me in your wrath.
	38. 1 in your anger, nor *d* me in your wrath!
	94.10 He who *d* the nations, he teaches
	94.12 Happy are those whom you *d*, O LORD,
Prov	19.18 *D* your children while there is hope; do
	29.17 *D* your children, and they will give you
Jer	31.18 "You *d* me, and I took the *d*; I was like
Hos	7.12 I will *d* them according to the report
1 Cor	11.32 we are *d* so that we may not be
Heb	12. 9 we had human parents to *d* us, and we
1 Pet	1.13 your minds for action; *d* yourselves;
Rev	3.19 I reprove and *d* those whom I love. Be

DISCLOSED

Mk	4.22 there is nothing hidden, except to be *d*;

DISCORD

Prov	6.19 falsely, and one who sows *d* in a family.

DISCOURAGE

Num	32. 7 Why will you *d* the hearts of the

DISCOVER

Ps	44.21 to a strange god, would not God *d* this?

DISCRETION

1 Chr	22.12 may the LORD grant you *d* and

DISEASE (DISEASED DISEASES)

Ex	15.26 I will not bring upon you any of the *d*
Deut	7.15 all the dread *d* of Egypt that you
1 Kings	15.23 But in his old age he was *d* in his feet.
2 Chr	16.12 yet even in his *d* he did not seek the
	21.18 him in his bowels with an incurable *d*.
Ps	106. 15 but sent a wasting *d* among them.
Mt	4.23 curing every *d* and every sickness
	8.17 "He took our infirmities and bore our *d*."
Mk	3.10 so that all who had *d* pressed upon him
	5.29 her body that she was healed of her *d*.

Lk	6.18 to hear him and to be healed of their *d*;

DISGRACE

Josh	5. 9 rolled away from you the *d* of Egypt."
2 Kings	19. 3 is a day of distress, of rebuke, and of *d*;
Job	10.15 for I am filled with *d* and look upon my
Ps	44.15 All day long my *d* is before me, and
Prov	3.35 will inherit honor, but stubborn fools, *d*.
	18. 3 comes also; and with dishonor comes *d*.
Jer	31.19 because I bore the *d* of my youth."
Ezek	22. 4 I have made you a *d* to the nations,
Mt	1.19 and unwilling to expose her to public *d*,
Lk	1.25 me and took away the *d* I have endured

DISGRACEFUL

Deut	22.21 she committed a *d* act in Israel by
1 Cor	11. 6 if it is *d* for a woman to have her hair

DISGUISE (DISGUISED DISGUISING)

1 Kings	14. 2 said to his wife, "Go, *d* yourself,
	20.38 the road, *d* himself with a bandage over
2 Chr	18.29 "I will *d* myself and go into battle, but
	35.22 him, but *d* himself in order to fight
2 Cor	11.13 workers, *d* themselves as apostles

DISH

Lk	11.39 the *d*, but inside you are full of greed

DISHONEST

Ex	18.21 God, are trustworthy, and hate *d* gain;
Jer	22.17 eyes and heart are only on your *d* gain,
Ezek	22.13 together at the *d* gain you have made,
Lk	16. 8 master commended the *d* manager
	16.11 not been faithful with the *d* wealth,

DISHONOR

Ps	109. 29 May my accusers be clothed with *d*;
Jer	2.25 in our shame, and let our *d* cover us;
	14.21 sake; do not *d* your glorious throne;

DISINHERIT

Num	14.12 strike them with pestilence and *d* them,

DISLOYALTY

Hos	14. 4 I will heal their *d*; I will love them

DISMAYED

Job	21. 6 When I think of it I am *d*, and
Dan	8.27 But I was *d* by the vision and did not

DISOBEDIENCE

Rom	5.19 just as by one man's *d* many were made

DISOBEDIENT

Lk	1.17 the *d* to the wisdom of the righteous, to
Acts	26.19 that, King Agrippa, I was not *d* to the
Rom	10.21 long I have held out my hands to a *d*
Eph	2. 2 is now at work among those who are *d*.
Titus	3. 3 For we ourselves were once foolish, *d*,
Heb	3.18 his rest, if not to those who were *d*?

DISOBEY (DISOBEYED)

Deut	17.12 anyone who presumes to *d* the priest
1 Kings	13.21 "Because you have *d* the word of the
	13.26 "It is the man of God who *d* the word of
Prov	24.21 the king, and do not *d* either of them;
Lk	15.29 and I never *d* your command; yet you

DISORDER

1 Cor	14.33 God is a God not of *d* but of peace.

DISPLAYED

Ps	77.14 have *d* your might among the peoples.

DISPERSE (DISPERSED)

Isa	11.12 of Israel, and gather the *d* of Judah
Ezek	22.15 and *d* you through the countries,
	36.19 and they were *d* through the countries;

DISPERSION

Jn	7.35	intend to go to the *D* among the Greeks
1 Pet	1. 1	To the exiles of the *D* in Pontus,

DISPLEASE (DISPLEASED DISPLEASING)

Gen	38.10	he did was *d* in the sight of the LORD,
	48.17	hand on the head of Ephraim, it *d* him;
Num	22.34	if it is *d* to you, I will return home."
1 Sam	8. 6	But the thing that Samuel when they said,
2 Sam	11.27	things that David had done *d* the LORD.
1 Kings	1. 6	had never at any time *d* him by asking,
1 Chr	21. 7	God was *d* with this thing, and he
Prov	24.18	or else the LORD will see it and be *d*,
Isa	59.15	The LORD saw it, and it *d* him that there
Jon	4. 1	very *d* to Jonah, and he became angry.
1 Thess	2.15	they *d* God and oppose everyone by

DISPLEASURE

Num	14.34	forty years, and you shall know my *d*."

DISPOSSESS (DISPOSSESSED)

Deut	9. 1	go in and *d* nations larger and mightier
Acts	7.45	with Joshua when they *d* the nations

DISPUTE (DISPUTES)

Deut	19.17	then both parties to the *d* shall appear
Eccl	6.10	they are not able to *d* with those who
Lk	22.24	A *d* also arose among them as to which
2 Cor	7. 5	every way —*d* without and fear within.

DISQUALIFY (DISQUALIFIED)

1 Cor	9.27	to others I myself should not be *d*.
Col	2.18	Do not let anyone *d* you, insisting on

DISREPUTE

Acts	19.27	that this trade of ours may come into *d*
1 Cor	4.10	You are held in honor, but we in *d*. To

DISSENSION (DISSENSIONS)

Rom	16.17	keep an eye on those who cause *d* and
1 Cor	12.25	there may be no *d* within the body, but
Titus	3. 9	genealogies, *d*, and quarrels

DISSOLVED

2 Pet	3.10	elements will be *d* with fire, and the
	3.11	all these things are to be *d* in this way,

DISTANCE

Lk	22.54	house. But Peter was following at a *d*.

DISTINCT

Ex	33.16	way, we shall be *d*, I and your people,

DISTINCTION (DISTINCTIONS)

Ex	8.23	I will make a *d* between my people and
	11. 7	know that the LORD makes a *d* between
Lev	11.47	to make a *d* between the unclean and
	20.25	make a *d* between the clean animal and
Ezek	22.26	have made no *d* between the holy and
Acts	15. 9	has made no *d* between them and us.
Rom	3.22	for all who believe. For there is no *d*,
	10.12	there is no *d* between Jew and Greek;
Jas	2. 4	have you not made *d* among yourselves,

DISTINGUISH (DISTINGUISHED)

Lev	10.10	You are to *d* between the holy and the
Song	5.10	and ruddy, *d* among ten thousand.
Ezek	44.23	how to *d* between the unclean and
Dan	6. 3	Daniel *d* himself above all the other
Heb	5.14	trained by practice to *d* good from evil.

DISTRACTED

Lk	10.41	Martha, you are worried and *d* by many

DISTRESS

Deut	4.30	In your *d*, when all these things have
Judg	10.14	them deliver you in the time of your *d*."
1 Sam	22. 2	Everyone who was in *d*, and everyone
2 Sam	16.12	be that the LORD will look upon my *d*,

2 Kings	14.26	LORD saw that the *d* of Israel was very
2 Chr	15. 4	but when in their *d* they turned to the
	28.22	of his *d* he became yet more faithless
	33.12	he was in *d* he entreated the favor
Neh	9. 9	saw the *d* of our ancestors in Egypt and
Ps	4. 1	You gave me room when I was in *d*. Be
	107. 6	and he delivered them from their *d*;
	116. 3	hold on me; I suffered *d* and anguish.
	120. 1	In my *d* I cry to the LORD, that he may
Prov	1.27	when *d* and anguish come upon you.
Isa	8.22	earth, but will see only *d* and darkness.
	26.16	LORD, in *d* they sought you, they poured
	63. 9	he became their savior in all their *d*.
Jer	30. 7	none like it; it is a time of *d* for Jacob;
Jon	2. 2	I called to the LORD out of my *d*, and he
Lk	21.23	For there will be great *d* on the earth
1 Cor	7.28	who marry will experience *d* in this life,
2 Cor	2. 4	I wrote you out of much *d* and anguish
Rev	2.22	I am throwing into great *d*, unless they

DISTRESSED (DISTRESSING)

Gen	21.11	The matter was very *d* to Abraham on
	45. 5	And now do not be *d*, or angry with
1 Sam	1.10	She was deeply *d* and prayed to the
Dan	4.19	was called Beltashazzar, was severely *d*
	6.14	heard the charge, he was very much *d*.
Mt	17.23	will be raised." And they were greatly *d*.
2 Pet	2. 7	Lot, a righteous man greatly *d* by the

DISTRIBUTED

Josh	13.32	the inheritances that Moses in the
Heb	2. 4	by gifts of the Holy Spirit, *d* according

DISTURBED

1 Sam	28.15	said to Saul, "Why have you *d* me by
Jn	11.38	Then Jesus, again greatly *d*, came to the
Acts	17. 8	and the city officials were *d* when they

DIVIDE (DIVIDED DIVIDES DIVIDING)

Ex	14.21	into dry land; and the waters were *d*.
Num	31.27	*D* the booty into two parts, between the
Josh	19.51	of meeting. So they finished *d* the land.
2 Sam	1.23	In life and in death they were not *d*;
1 Kings	3.25	"*D* the living boy in two; then give half
Neh	9.11	you *d* the sea before them, so that they
Isa	53.12	and he shall *d* the spoil with the strong;
Ezek	37.22	and never again shall they be *d* into two
Mt	12.25	every kingdom *d* against itself is laid
Mk	3.24	If a kingdom is *d* against itself, that
	15.24	him, and *d* his clothes among them.
Lk	11.17	every kingdom *d* against itself becomes
	12.13	"Teacher, tell my brother to *d* the
	12.53	one household will be *d*, father against
	22.17	"Take this, and *d* it among yourselves;
Jn	10.19	Again the Jews were *d* because of these
	19.24	"They *d* my clothes among themselves,
1 Cor	1.13	Has Christ been *d*? Was Paul crucified
Heb	4.12	piercing until it *d* soul from spirit,

DIVINATION

Gen	30.27	I have learned by *d* that the LORD has
Num	22. 7	departed with fees for *d* in their hand;
Ezek	12.24	longer be any false vision or flattering *d*
Acts	16.16	slave girl who had a spirit of *d* and

DIVINE

2 Pet	1. 4	become participants of the *d* nature.

DIVISION (DIVISIONS)

1 Chr	24. 1	The *d* of the sons of Aaron were these.
Lk	12.51	the earth? No, I tell you, but rather *d*;
1 Cor	1.10	and that there be no *d* among you,
	11.18	I hear that there are *d* among you;

DIVORCE (DIVORCES)

Deut	24. 1	he writes her a certificate of *d*, puts it
Jer	3. 8	I had sent her away with a decree of *d*;
Mt	19. 7	whoever *d* his wife, except for

Mk	10. 4 a certificate of dismissal and to *d* her."
1 Cor	7.13 to live with her, she should not *d* him.

DO (DONE)

Gen	2. 3 rested from all the work that he had *d*
2 Chr	29.36 of what God had *d* for the people;
Eccl	9. 7 God has long ago approved what you *d*.
Isa	63. 7 because of all that the LORD has *d* for
Zeph	2. 3 of the land, who *d* his commands;
Mt	7.12 as you would have them *d* to you;
	16.27 will repay everyone for what has been *d*.
Acts	21.19 that God had *d* among the Gentiles

DOCTOR

Lk	4.23 to me this proverb, '*D*, cure yourself!'

DOCTRINE (DOCTRINES)

Mk	7. 7 me, teaching human precepts as *d*.'
Eph	4.14 fro and blown about by every wind of *d*,
1 Tim	1. 3 people not to teach any different *d*,
Titus	1. 9 to preach with sound *d* and to refute
	2.10 may be an ornament to the *d* of God

DOCUMENT

Isa	29.11 for you like the words of a sealed *d*.

DOERS

Rom	2.13 the *d* of the law who will be justified.
Jas	1.22 But be *d* of the word, and not merely

DOG (DOGS)

Judg	7. 5 who lap with their tongues, as a *d* laps,
2 Sam	9. 8 should look upon a dead *d* such as I?"
1 Kings	21.19 Naboth, *d* will also lick up your blood."
2 Kings	8.13 "What is your servant, who is a mere *d*,
Ps	59. 6 evening they come back, howling like *d*
Prov	26.17 who takes a passing *d* by the ears.
Eccl	9. 4 for a living *d* is better than a dead
Isa	56.10 they are all silent *d* that cannot bark;
Mt	7. 6 "Do not give what is holy to *d*; and do
	15.26 children's food and throw it to the *d*."
Mk	7.28 even the *d* under the table eat the
Lk	16.21 the *d* would come and lick his sores.
Phil	3. 2 Beware of the *d*, beware of the evil
2 Pet	2.22 "The *d* turns back to its own vomit,"

DOME

Gen	1. 6 "Let there be a *d* in the midst of the

DOMINATED

1 Cor	6.12 for me," but I will not be *d* by anything.

DOMINION

Ps	22.28 For *d* belongs to the LORD, and he rules
	72. 8 May he have *d* from sea to sea, and
	103. 22 all his works, in all places of his *d*.
Ezek	30.18 dark, when I break there the *d* of Egypt,
Dan	6.26 be destroyed, and his *d* has no end.
Zech	9.10 nations; his *d* shall be from sea to sea,
Rom	5.21 grace also might exercise *d* through
	6. 9 again; death no longer has *d* over him.
	6.12 Do not let sin exercise *d* in your mortal

DONKEY (DONKEY'S)

Num	22.23 The *d* saw the angel of the LORD
	22.28 mouth of the *d*, and it said to Balaam,
Mt	21. 5 humble, and mounted on an *d*, and on
Jn	12.15 your king is coming, sitting on a *d* colt!"
2 Pet	2.16 a speechless *d* spoke with human voice

DOOR (DOORS)

Ps	24. 7 O gates! and be lifted up, O ancient *d*!
Prov	18.16 A gift opens *d*; it gives access to the
Isa	45. 2 I will break in pieces the *d* of bronze
Hos	2.15 make the Valley of Achor a *d* of hope.
Lk	12. 3 have whispered behind closed *d* will be
	13.24 "Strive to enter through the narrow *d*;
	13.25 knock at the *d*, saying, 'Lord, open to
Acts	14.27 opened a *d* of faith for the Gentiles.

1 Cor	16. 9 a wide *d* for effective work has opened
Col	4. 3 God will open to us a *d* for the word,
Rev	3. 8 Look, I have set before you an open *d*,
	3.20 I am standing at the *d*, knocking; if you
	4. 1 and there in heaven a *d* stood open!

DOORKEEPER

Ps	84.10 I would rather be a *d* in the house of

DOORPOSTS

Ex	12. 7 blood and put it on the two *d* and the

DORCAS

Acts	9.36 name was Tabitha, which in Greek is *D*.
	9.39 other clothing that *D* had made while

DOUBLE

Gen	43.15 they took *d* the money with them, as
2 Kings	2. 9 let me inherit a *d* share of your spirit."
Ps	12. 2 with flattering lips and a *d* heart they
Isa	40. 2 from the LORD's hand *d* for all her sins.
Zech	9.12 I declare that I will restore to you *d*.

DOUBT (DOUBTS)

Deut	28.66 Your life shall hang in *d* before you;
Mt	21.21 if you have faith and do not *d*, not only
Mk	11.23 sea and if you do not *d* in your heart,
Jn	20.27 put it in my side. Do not *d* but believe."
Rom	14.23 those who have *d* are condemned if

DOVE (DOVES)

Gen	8. 8 he sent out a *d* from him, to see if the
Ps	55. 6 "O that I had wings like a *d*! I would fly
Song	5.12 His eyes are like *d* beside springs of
Hos	7.11 Ephraim has become like a *d*, silly and
Mt	3.16 the Spirit of God descending like a *d*
Lk	3.22 upon him in bodily form like a *d*,
Jn	1.32 Spirit descending from heaven like a *d*,

DOWNFALL

Prov	29.16 but the righteous will look upon their *d*.
Ezek	32.10 each one of them, on the day of your *d*.

DOWNTRODDEN

Ps	74.21 Do not let the *d* be put to shame; let
	147. 6 The LORD lifts up the *d*, he casts the

DRAGON

Ezek	32. 2 but you are like a *d* in the seas;
Rev	12. 3 a great red *d*, with seven heads and ten

DRAW (DRAWN DREW)

Gen	24.11 time when women go out to *d* water.
	24.19 "I will *d* for your camels also, until they
Ps	18.16 took me; he *d* me out of mighty waters.
	30. 1 you, O LORD, for you have *d* me up,
	69.18 *D* near to me, redeem me, set me free
Song	1. 4 *D* me after you, let us make haste. The
Isa	34. 1 draw near, O nations, to hear, O peoples,
Acts	7.17 as the time *d* near for the fulfillment of
Jas	4. 8 *D* near to God and he will *d* near to

DRAWERS

Josh	9.21 hewers of wood and *d* of water for all

DREAD

Isa	7.16 before whose two kings you are in *d*
	8.12 and do not fear what it fears or be in *d*.

DREAM (DREAMED DREAMS)

Gen	28.12 he *d* that there was a ladder set up on
	31.24 God came to Laban . . . in a *d* by night,
	37. 5 Joseph had a *d*, and when he told it to
	40. 5 One night they both *d* —the cupbearer
	41. 8 Pharaoh told them his *d*, but there was
	42. 9 Joseph also remembered the *d* that he
Num	12. 6 them in visions; I speak to them in *d*.
Deut	13. 1 or those who divine by *d* appear among
Judg	7.13 "I had a *d*; and in it a cake of barley

1 Kings	3.	5 the Lord appeared to Solomon in a *d*
Eccl	5.	7 With many *d* come vanities and a
Isa	29.	8 a hungry person *d* of eating and wakes
Jer	23.28	Let the prophet who has a *d* tell the *d*,
Dan	2.	1 Nebuchadnezzar *d* such *d* that his spirit
Joel	2.28	your old men shall *d d*, and your young
Mt	1.20	of the Lord appeared to him in a *d*
	27.19	a great deal because of a *d* about him."
Acts	2.17	see visions, and your old men shall *d d*.

DREAMER

Gen	37.19	said to one another, "Here comes this *d*.

DRENCH

Ezek	32.	6 I will *d* the land with your flowing

DRINK (n)

Ps	36.	8 and you give them *d* from the river of
Prov	31.	6 Give strong *d* to one who is perishing,
Lk	1.15	He must never drink wine or strong *d*,
Jn	4.	7 and Jesus said to her, "Give me a *d*."
Titus	2.	3 not to be slanderers or slaves to *d*;

DRINK (DRANK DRINKING)

Gen	19.32	Come, let us make our father *d* wine,
	24.14	say, '*D*, and I will water your camels'
Lev	10.	8 *D* no wine nor strong drink, neither you
2 Sam	23.15	that someone would give me water to *d*
Ps	60.	3 given us wine to *d* that made us reel.
	110.	7 He will *d* from the stream by the path;
Prov	5.15	*D* water from your own cistern, flowing
	25.21	if they are thirsty, give them water to *d*;
Song	5.	1 Eat, friends, *d*, and be drunk with love.
Jer	25.17	nations to whom the Lord sent me *d* it:
	35.	6 But they answered, "We will *d* no wine,
Hab	2.15	for you who make your neighbors *d*,
Mt	11.18	John came neither eating nor *d*, and
	24.38	before the flood they were eating and *d*,
	27.34	they offered him wine to *d*, mixed with
Mk	14.23	it to them, and all of them *d* from it.
Lk	7.33	*d* no wine; and you say, 'He has a
	12.29	eat and what you are to *d*, and do not
Jn	4.14	those who *d* of the water that I will give
1 Cor	10.	4 they *d* from the spiritual rock that
	10.31	So, whether you eat or *d*, or whatever
	11.26	this bread and *d* the cup, you proclaim
	12.13	we were all made to *d* of one Spirit.
1 Tim	5.23	No longer *d* only water, but take a little

DRIVE (DRIVES DRIVING DROVE)

Gen	31.18	and he *d* away all his livestock, all the
Ex	14.21	The Lord *d* the sea back by a strong
Judg	1.27	Manasseh did not *d* out the inhabitants
2 Kings	9.20	son of Nimshi; for he *d* like a maniac."
Ps	35.	5 with the angel of the Lord *d* them on.
	44.	2 with your own hand *d* out the nations,
Isa	59.19	stream that the wind of the Lord *d* on.
Mt	21.12	and *d* out all who were selling and
Jn	9.34	trying to teach us?" And they *d* him out.

DROSS

Ps	119.119	the wicked of the earth you count as *d*;
Prov	25.	4 Take away the *d* from the silver, and
Isa	1.22	Your silver has become *d*, your wine is
	1.25	I will smelt away your *d* as with lye and

DROUGHT

Hag	1.11	I have called for a *d* on the land and

DROWNED

Mt	18.	6 your neck and you were *d* in the depth
Mk	5.13	into the sea, and were *d* in the sea.
Lk	8.33	the steep bank into the lake and was *d*.

DRUNK

Gen	9.21	wine and became *d*, and he lay
2 Sam	11.13	in his presence and he made him *d*;
Isa	29.	9 Be *d*, but not with wine; stagger, but
	51.17	wrath, who have *d* to the dregs the bowl

Acts	2.15	Indeed, these men are not *d*, as you

DRUNKARD (DRUNKARDS)

Ps	69.12	gate, and the *d* make songs about me.
Isa	19.14	Egypt stagger in all its doings as a *d*
	28.	1 the proud garland of the *d* of Ephraim,
Mt	11.19	a glutton and a *d*, a friend of tax
	24.49	slaves, and eats and drinks with *d*,
Lk	7.34	'Look, a glutton and a *d*, a friend of tax
1 Cor	5.11	or is an idolater, reviler, *d*, or robber.

DRUNKENNESS

Eccl	10.17	time—for strength, and not for *d*!
Ezek	23.33	You shall be filled with *d* and sorrow. A

DRY (DRIED DRYING)

Gen	8.13	saw that the face of the ground was *d*.
Josh	2.10	heard how the Lord *d* up the water of
	3.17	the priests . . . stood on *d* ground in the
Isa	44.27	deep, "Be *d*—I will *d* up your rivers";
Joel	1.12	the trees of the field are *d* up;

DUE

Rom	4.	4 reckoned as a gift but as something *d*.

DULL

Acts	28.27	For this people's heart has grown *d*,
Heb	5.11	you have become *d* in understanding.

DUST

Gen	2.	7 Lord God formed man from the *d* of the
	3.14	and *d* you shall eat all the days of your
	3.19	you are *d*, and to *d* you shall return."
	13.16	your offspring like the *d* of the earth;
	18.27	to the Lord, I who am but *d* and ashes.
Job	34.15	together, and all mortals return to *d*.
	38.38	when the *d* runs into a mass and the
Ps	90.	3 You turn us back to *d*, and say, "Turn
	103.	14 made; he remembers that we are *d*.
	104.	29 breath, they die and return to their *d*.
Eccl	3.20	all are from the *d*, and all turn to *d*
	12.	7 the *d* returns to the earth as it was, and
Mt	10.14	shake off the *d* from your feet as you
Lk	10.11	*d* of your town that clings to our feet,

DUTY

Deut	25.	5 performing the *d* of a husband's brother
1 Tim	5.	4 first learn their religious *d* to their own

DWELL (DWELLS)

Ex	29.45	I will *d* among the Israelites, and I will
1 Kings	6.13	I will *d* among the children of Israel,
	8.27	will God indeed *d* on the earth? Even
Ps	23.	6 I shall *d* in the house of the Lord my
Isa	33.	5 The Lord is exalted, he *d* on high; he
Jn	14.10	own; but the Father who *d* in me does
Rom	7.17	I that do it, but sin that *d* within me.
1 Cor	3.16	temple and that God's Spirit *d* in you?
Eph	3.17	Christ may *d* in your hearts through
Jas	4.	5 for the spirit that he has made to *d*
Rev	21.	3 He will *d* with them as their God; they

DWELLING (DWELLINGS)

Job	23.	3 him, that I might come even to his *d*!
Ps	43.	3 me to your holy hill and to your *d*!
	78.60	He abandoned his *d* at Shiloh, the tent
Isa	11.10	of him, and his *d* shall be glorious.
Mt	17.	4 I will make three *d* here, one for you,
Mk	9.	5 let us make three *d*, one for you, one
Lk	9.33	let us make three *d*, one for you, one
Acts	28.30n	in his own hired *d* and welcome all who

DWELLING PLACE

Deut	33.27n	The eternal God is a *d*, he shatters
Ps	84.	1 How lovely is your *d*, O Lord of hosts!
	90.	1 Lord, you have been our *d* in all
	132.	5 for the Lord, a *d* for the Mighty One
	132.	7 "Let us go to his *d*; let us worship at his
Ezek	37.27	My *d* shall be with them; and I will be

DWINDLED

Isa 24. 6 inhabitants of the earth *d*, and few

E

EAGER (EAGERNESS)

Rom 1.15 — hence my *e* to proclaim the gospel to
1 Cor 14.39 friends, be *e* to prophesy, and do not
2 Cor 8.16 heart of Titus the same *e* for you that I

EAGLE (EAGLES)

Lev 11.13 they are an abomination: the *e*, the
Job 39.27 it at your command that the *e* mounts
Prov 30.19 I do not understand: the way of an *e* in
Isa 40.31 they shall mount up with wings like *e*,
Ezek 10.14 of a lion, and the fourth that of an *e*.
 17. 2 A great *e*, with great wings and long

EAR (EARS)

Ex 21. 6 his master shall pierce his *e* with an
Job 42. 5 heard of you by the hearing of the *e*,
Ps 34.15 and his *e* are open to their cry.
 40. 6 but you have given me an open *e*.
 94. 9 who planted the *e*, does he not hear?
 135. 17 they have *e*, but they do not hear, and
Prov 2. 2 making your *e* attentive to wisdom and
Jer 5.21 not see, who have *e*, but do not hear.
Ezek 12. 2 who have *e* to hear but do not hear;
Mt 13. 9 Let anyone with *e*, listen!"
 26.51 of the high priest, cutting off his *e*.
Mk 4. 9 said, Let anyone with *e* to hear listen!
 4.23 Let anyone with *e* to hear listen!"
 14.47 of the high priest, cutting off his *e*.
Lk 14.35 away. Let anyone with *e* to hear listen!
 22.50 of the high priest and cut off his right *e*.
Jn 18.10 priest's slave, and cut off his right *e*.
1 Cor 2. 9 "What no eye has seen, nor *e* heard, nor
 12.16 And if the *e* would say, "Because I am
Rev 2.29 Let anyone who had an *e* listen to what

EARN

1 Cor 16. 2 aside and save whatever extra you *e*,

EARTH

Gen 1. 1 God created the heavens and the *e*,
 1.10 God called the dry land *E*, and the
Josh 3.11 Lord of all the *e* is going to pass before
Job 26. 7 the void, and hangs the *e* upon nothing.
Ps 24. 1 The *e* is the LORD's and all that is in it,
 33. 5 the *e* is full of the steadfast love of the
 65. 9 You visit the *e* and water it, you greatly
Isa 6. 3 of hosts; the whole *e* is full of his glory."
Jer 4.27 Because of this the *e* shall mourn, and
Ezek 34.27 fruit, and the *e* shall yield its increase.
Hab 2.20 holy temple; let all the *e* keep silence
 3.12 In fury you trod the *e*, in anger you
Zeph 3. 8 my passion all the *e* shall be consumed.
Mt 27.51 The *e* shook, and the rocks were split.
Mk 4.28 The *e* produces of itself, first the stalk,
1 Cor 10.26 for "the *e* and its fullness are the
 15.47 first man was from the *e*, a man of dust;
2 Pet 3.13 wait for a new heavens and a new *e*,
Rev 6. 4 was permitted to take peace from the *e*,

EARTHLY

2 Cor 1.12 not by *e* wisdom but by the grace of
 5. 1 if the *e* tent we live in is destroyed, we

EARTHQUAKE (EARTHQUAKES)

1 Kings 19.11 after the wind an *e*, but the LORD was
Isa 29. 6 with thunder and *e* and great noise,
Am 1. 1 Joash of Israel, two years before the *e*.
Mt 28. 2 suddenly there was a great *e*; for an
Mk 13. 8 there will be *e* in various places; there
Lk 21.11 there will be great *e*, and in various
Acts 16.26 there was an *e*, so violent that the
Rev 16.18 of thunder, and a violent *e*, such as

EASE

Job 3.26 I am not at *e*, nor am I quiet; I have no
Ps 73.12 are the wicked; always at *e*, they
Am 6. 1 Alas for those who are at *e* in Zion, and

EAST

Mt 2. 1 wise men from the *E* came to
 8.11 many will come from *e* and west and
Lk 13.29 people will come from *e* and west,

EASY (EASIER)

Mt 7.13 the road is *e* that leads to destruction,
 9. 5 which is *e*, to say, 'Your sins are
 11.30 For my yoke is *e*, and my burden is

EAT (ATE EATEN EATING)

Gen 2.17 tree of knowledge . . . you shall not *e*,
 43.32 the Egyptians could not *e* with the
Ex 12.15 days you shall *e* unleavened bread;
 32. 6 the people sat down to *e* and drink, and
Lev 7.26 You must not *e* any blood whatever,
 19.26 You shall not *e* anything with its blood
Deut 12. 7 you shall *e* in the presence of the LORD
1 Sam 9.24 guests." So Saul *a* with Samuel that day.
 14.32 and the troops *a* them with the blood.
Ps 14. 4 all the evildoers who *e* up my people as
Prov 23. 1 you sit down to *e* with a ruler, observe
Isa 1.19 you shall *e* the good of the land;
 22.13 wine. "Let us *e* and drink, for tomorrow
Jer 15.16 Your words were found, and I *a* them,
Ezek 2. 8 open your mouth and *e* what I give you.
 3. 1 *e* this scroll, and go, speak to the house
Dan 4.33 from human society, *a* grass like oxen,
Mt 9.11 "Why does your teacher *e* with tax
 15.38 Those who had *e* were four thousand
 24.38 before the flood they were *e* and
 26.26 and said, "Take, *e*; this is my body."
Mk 14.14 guest room where I may *e* the Passover
Lk 5.30 "Why do you *e* and drink with tax
 12.19 many years; relax, *e*, drink, be merry.'
 17.27 They were *e* and drinking, and marrying
 24.43 and he took it and *a* in their presence.
Jn 4.31 were urging him, "Rabbi, *e* something."
Acts 10.13 voice saying, "Get up, Peter; kill and *e*.
 11. 7 to me, 'Get up, Peter; kill and *e*.'
Rom 14. 3 Those who *e* must not despise those
1 Cor 10.27 *e* whatever is set before you without
 10.31 So, whether you *e* or drink, or whatever
 15.32 "Let us *e* and drink, for tomorrow we
2 Thess 3.10 anyone unwilling to work should not *e*.
Rev 3.20 I will come in to you and *e* with you,

EBENEZER

1 Sam 7.12 and named it *E*; for he said, "Thus far

EDEN

Gen 2. 8 God planted a garden in *E*, in the east;
Isa 51. 3 and will make her wilderness like *E*,
Ezek 28.13 You were in *E*, the garden of God; every
Joel 2. 3 them the land is like the garden of *E*,

EDOM (EDOMITES)

Gen 25.30 famished!" (Therefore he was called *E*.)
 36. 9 descendants of Esau, ancestor of the *E*,
Num 20.21 *E* refused to give Israel passage through
2 Sam 8.14 He put garrisons in *E*; throughout all *E*
Ps 108. 9 is my washbasin; on *E* I hurl my shoe;
Isa 63. 1 "Who is this that comes from *E*, from
Am 9.12 that they may possess the remnant of *E*

EGYPT

Gen 12.10 Abram went down to *E* to reside there
 37.28 of silver. And they took Joseph to *E*.
 41.33 wise, and set him over the land of *E*.
 45.13 father how greatly I am honored in *E*,
Ex 7. 4 I will lay my hand upon *E* and bring my
 13.14 of hand the LORD brought us out of *E*,
1 Kings 3. 1 alliance with Pharaoh king of *E*;

Hos	11. 1 him, and out of *E* I called my son.
Mt	2.13 and flee to *E*, and remain there until I
	2.15 "Out of *E* have I called my son."
Heb	11.26 greater wealth than the treasures of *E*,

ELDER (ELDERS)

Gen	25.23 the other, the *e* shall serve the younger."
Lev	4.15 The *e* of the congregation shall lay their
Num	11.16 "Gather for me seventy of the *e* of
Ruth	4. 2 Boaz took ten men of the *e* of the city,
Prov	31.23 city gates, taking his seat among the *e*
Mt	16.21 great suffering at the hands of the *e*
Lk	7. 3 sent some Jewish *e* to him, asking him
Acts	20.17 asking the *e* of the church to meet him.
Rom	9.12 was told, "The *e* will serve the younger."
1 Tim	4.14 laying on of hands by the council of *e*.
	5.17 Let the *e* who rule well be considered
Titus	1. 5 and should appoint *e* in every town, as I
Jas	5.14 sick? They should call for the *e* of the
1 Pet	5. 1 I exhort the *e* among you to tend the
2 Jn	1 The *e* to the elect lady and her
3 Jn	1 The *e* to the beloved Garius, whom I
Rev	4. 4 on the thrones were twenty-four *e*,
	19. 4 the twenty-four *e* and the four living

ELECT

Mt	24.22 for the sake of the *e* those days will be
	24.31 they will gather his *e* from the four
Mk	13.20 but for the sake of the *e*, whom he
	13.27 gather his *e* from the four winds, from
Rom	8.33 will bring any charge against God's *e*?
	11. 7 The *e* obtained it, but the rest were
2 Tim	2.10 endure everything for the sake of the *e*,

ELECTION

Rom	9.11 that God's purpose of *e* might continue,
	11.28 as regards *e* they are beloved, for the
2 Pet	1.10 more eager to confirm your call and *e*,

ELEMENTS

2 Pet	3.10 the *e* will be dissolved with fire, and the
	3.12 dissolved, and the *e* will melt with fire!

ELEVEN

Mk	16.14 Later he appeared to the *e* themselves
Lk	24.33 found the *e* and their companions

ELI

1 Sam	1. 3 where two sons of *E* . . . were priests of
	1. 9 Now *E* the priest was sitting on the seat
	1.25 bull, and they brought the child to *E*.
	2.11 LORD, in the presence of the priest *E*.
	3. 1 was ministering to the LORD under *E*.
	4.11 and the two sons of *E* . . . died.
	4.15 *E* was ninety-eight years old and his

ELIJAH

Predicted the drought, 1 Kings 17.1; fed by ravens, 1 Kings 17.2-7; fed by the widow of Zarephath, 1 Ki 17.8-16; revived the son of the widow, 1 Kings 17.17-24; met Ahab, 1 Kings 18.1-19; triumphed over the prophets of Baal, 1 Kings 18.20-40; prayed for rain, 1 Kings 18.41-46; fled to Mount Horeb, 1 Kings 19.1-8; heard the still small voice, 1 Kings 19.9-18; chose Elisha, 1 Kings 19.19-21; reproved Ahab, 1 Kings 21.17-29; called fire from heaven, 2 Kings 1.3-16; taken up into heaven, 2 Kings 2.1-11.

Mal	4. 5 I will send you the prophet *E* before the
Mt	11.14 to accept it, he is *E* who is to come.
	17. 3 appeared to them Moses and *E*, talking
Mk	9.13 I tell you that *E* has come, and they did
	15.35 it, they said, "Listen, he is calling for *E*."
Lk	1.17 With the spirit and power of *E* he will
	9.54n heaven and consume them as *E* did?"
Jn	1.21 "What then? Are you *E*?" He said, "I am
Jas	5.17 *E* was a human being like us, and he

ELISHA

Called, 1 Kings 19.19-21; succeeded Elijah, 2 Kings 2.1-15; purified the water, 2 Kings 2.19-22; cursed the children, 2 Kings 2.23-25; prophesied victory over the Moabites, 2 Kings 3; increased the widow's oil, 2 Kings 4.1-7; restored the life of the Shunammite's son, 2 Kings 4.8-37; purified the pot of stew, 2 Kings 4.38-41; fed a multitude, 2 Kings 4.42-44; healed Naaman's leprosy, 2 Kings 5; caused Syrians' blindness, 2 Kings 6.8-23; promised food in time of famine, 2 Kings 6.24—7.2; prophesied Hazael's cruelty, 2 Kings 8.7-15; anointed Jehu, 2 Kings 9.1-10; prophesied victory over Syria, 2 Kings 13.14-19; death and burial, 2 Kings 13.20; bones of Elisha, 2 Kings 13.21.

ELIZABETH

Lk	1. 5 of Aaron, and her name was *E*.
	1.13 your wife *E* will bear you a son, and you
	1.40 the house of Zechariah and greeted *E*.

ELOQUENT

Ex	4.10 O my Lord, I have never been *e*, neither
1 Cor	1.17 the gospel, and not with *e* wisdom,

EMBLEMS

Ps	74. 7 holy place; they set up their *e* there.

EMBRACED

Gen	48.10 him; and he kissed them and *e* them.
Song	2. 6 my head, and that his right hand *e* me!

EMMANUEL (see IMMANUEL)

EMMAUS

Lk	24.13 of them were going to a village called *E*,

EMPEROR (EMPEROR'S)

Mt	22.21 "Give therefore to the *e* the things that
Jn	19.12 to be a king sets himself against the *e*."
Acts	25.10 "I am appealing to the *e* tribunal; this is
Phil	4.22 you especially those of the *e* household.

EMPTY

Job	35.13 God does not hear an *e* cry, nor does
Mt	6. 7 do not heap up *e* phrases as the

ENABLE

Eccl	6. 2 yet God does not *e* them to enjoy these

ENCAMP (ENCAMPS)

Job	19.12 against me, and *e* round about my tent.
Ps	27. 3 Though an army *e* against me, my heart
	34. 7 The angel of the LORD *e* around those
Isa	29. 3 like David I will *e* against you; I will

ENCOMPASSES

Jer	31.22 thing on the earth: a woman *e* a man.

ENCOURAGE (ENCOURAGED)

Deut	1.38 *e* him, for he is the one who will secure
	3.28 charge Joshua, and *e* and strengthen
2 Chr	32. 8 were *e* by the words of King Hezekiah
Job	16. 5 I could *e* you with my mouth, and the
Ezek	13.22 you have *e* the wicked not to turn from
Eph	6.22 know how we are, and to *e* your hearts.
Col	2. 2 I want their hearts to be *e* and united
1 Thess	4.18 *e* one another with these words.
Titus	2. 4 *e* the young women to love their

ENCOURAGEMENT

Acts	4.36 Barnabas (which means "son of *e*").
Phil	2. 1 If then there is any *e* in Christ, any

END (ENDS) (n)

Gen	6.13 determined to make an *e* of all flesh,
Ps	2. 8 and the *e* of the earth your possession.
	19. 4 and their words to the *e* of the world.
	39. 4 "LORD, let me know my *e*, and what is
	90. 9 our years come to an *e* like a sigh.
Eccl	4. 8 yet there is no *e* to all their toil, and
	12.13 The *e* of the matter; all has been heard.
Lam	4.18 our *e* drew near; our days were

Ezek	7.	2 An *e*! The *e* has come upon the four
Dan	11.45	shall come to his *e*, with no one to help
Am	8.	2 The *e* has come upon my people Israel;
Mt	24.	3 of your coming and of the *e* of the age?"
	24.14	the nations; and then the *e* will come.
	28.20	am with you always, to the *e* of the age."
Jn	13.	1 in the world, he loved them to the *e*.
Acts	1.	8 and Samaria, and to the *e* of the earth."
Rom	10.	4 For Christ is the *e* of the law so that
1 Cor	13.	8 as for knowledge, it will come to an *e*.
Heb	6.16	as confirmation puts an *e* to all dispute.
1 Pet	4.	7 The *e* of all things is near; therefore be
	4.17	what will be the *e* for those who do not

END (ENDS) (v)

Mt	26.58	guards in order to see how this would *e*.
1 Cor	13.	8 Love never *e*; But as for prophesies,
Heb	1.12	the same, and your years will never *e*."

ENDURANCE

Lk	21.19	By your *e* you will gain your souls.
Rom	5.	4 produces *e*, and *e* produces character,
2 Cor	6.	4 every way: through great *e*, in
Heb	10.36	For you need *e*, so that when you have
Jas	1.	3 the testing of your faith produces *e*.
2 Pet	1.	6 and self-control with *e*, and *e* with
Rev	14.12	Here is a call for the *e* of the saints,

ENDURE (ENDURED ENDURES)

Job	8.15	if one lays hold of it, it will not *e*.
Ps	72.17	May his name *e* forever, his fame
	100.	5 his steadfast love *e* forever, and his
	102.26	They will perish, but you *e*; they will all
	111.	3 work, and his righteousness *e* forever.
	118.	2 Israel say, "His steadfast love *e* forever."
	136.	2 of gods, for his steadfast love *e* forever.
Ezek	22.14	Can your courage *e*, or can your hands
Nah	1.	6 Who can *e* the heat of his anger? His
Mal	3.	2 who can *e* the day of his coming, and
Mt	10.22	But the one who *e* to the end will be
	24.13	But the one who *e* to the end will be
Mk	4.17	have no root and *e* only for a while;
	13.13	the one who *e* to the end will be saved.
Jn	6.27	for the food that *e* for eternal life,
1 Cor	13.	7 all things, hopes all things, *e* all things.
	10.13	way out so that you may be able to *e* it.
2 Tim	2.12	if we *e*, we will also reign with him; if
Heb	12.	2 *e* the cross, disregarding its shame, and
Jas	1.12	Blessed is anyone who *e* temptation.
1 Pet	2.20	If you *e* when you are beaten for doing

ENEMY (ENEMIES)

Lev	26.32	devastate the land, so that your *e* who
Deut	28.25	cause you to be defeated before your *e*;
Judg	5.31	"So perish all your *e*, O LORD! But may
1 Kings	21.20	to Elijah, "Have you found me, O my *e*?"
Esth	9.22	the Jews gained relief from their *e*,
Job	13.24	hide your face, and count me as your *e*?
Ps	72.	9 before him, and his *e* lick the dust.
	92.	9 your *e*, O LORD, for your *e* shall perish;
Prov	16.	7 he causes even their *e* to be at peace
	24.17	Do not rejoice when your *e* fall, and do
	25.21	If your *e* are hungry, give them bread to
Mt	5.43	love your neighbor and hate your *e*.'
	22.44	until I put your *e* under your feet" '?
Lk	6.27	Love your *e*, do good to those who hate
Rom	12.20	"if your *e* are hungry, feed them; if they
1 Cor	15.26	The last *e* to be destroyed is death. For
Gal	4.16	become your *e* by telling you the truth?
Phil	3.18	many live as *e* of the cross; I have often

ENGAGE (ENGAGED)

Ex	22.16	a man seduces a virgin who is not *e*
Deut	2.	5 not to *e* in battle with them, for I will
	20.	7 Has anyone become *e* to a woman but
Mt	1.18	Mary had been *e* to Joseph, but before
Lk	1.27	to a virgin *e* to a man whose name was
	2.	5 registered with Mary, to whom he was *e*

ENGRAVE

Ex	28.11	you shall *e* the two stones with the
Zech	3.	9 seven facets, I will *e* its inscription,

ENJOY

Isa	65.22	and my chosen shall long *e* the work of
Heb	11.25	of God than to *e* the fleeting pleasures

ENJOYMENT

Eccl	2.24	to eat and drink and find *e* in their toil.
	5.18	fitting is to eat and drink and find *e* in

ENLARGE (ENLARGED)

Ps	119.32	for you *e* my understanding.
Isa	54.	2 *E* the sight of your tent, and let the
2 Cor	10.15	of action among you may be greatly *e*,

ENLIGHTENED

Rom	10.	2 they have a zeal for God, but it is not *e*.
Heb	10.32	after you had been *e*, you endured a

ENLIGHTENING

Ps	19.	8 of the LORD is clear, *e* the eyes;

ENOCH

Gen	4.18	To *E* was born Irad; and Irad was the
	5.18	years he became the father of *E*.
	5.22	*E* walked with God after the birth of
	5.24	*E* walked with God; then he was no
Lk	3.37	of Methuselah, son of *E*, son of Jared,
Heb	11.	5 By faith *E* was taken so that he did not
Jude		14 It was also about these that *E*, in the

ENRAGED

Isa	8.21	when they are hungry, they will be *e*
	34.	2 LORD is *e* against all the nations, and

ENRICH (ENRICHED)

1 Sam	17.25	the king will greatly *e* the man who kills
1 Cor	1.	5 in every way you have been *e* in him, in
2 Cor	9.11	You will be *e* in every way for your great

ENROLLED

Num	1.19	So he *e* them in the wilderness of Sinai.
	2.33	the Levites were not *e* among the other
Heb	12.23	of the firstborn who are *e* in heaven,

ENSIGNS

Num	2.	2 under *e* by their ancestral houses; they

ENSLAVED

Rom	6.	6 and we might no longer be *e* to sin.
Gal	4.	3 while we were minors, we were *e* to the

ENTANGLED

2 Sam	22.	6 the cords of Sheol *e* me, the snares of
Ps	18.	5 the cords of Sheol *e* me; the snares of

ENTER (ENTERED)

Gen	7.13	day Noah with his sons . . . *e* the ark,
Ex	40.35	Moses was not able to *e* the tent of
Num	20.24	For he shall not *e* the land that I have
Deut	29.12	to *e* into the covenant of the LORD your
Ps	95.11	anger I swore, "They shall not *e* my rest."
	100.	4 *E* his gates with thanksgiving, and his
Isa	26.20	Come, my people, *e* your chambers, and
Mt	5.20	you will never *e* the kingdom of
	7.13	"*E* through the narrow gate; for the gate
	7.21	to me, 'Lord, Lord,' will *e* the kingdom
	19.24	hard for a rich person to *e* the kingdom
Mk	3.27	no one can *e* a strong man's house and
	10.23	who have wealth to *e* the kingdom
Lk	11.52	you did not *e* yourselves, and you
Jn	3.	5 no one can *e* the kingdom of God

ENTHRONED

Ps	9.	7 But the LORD sits *e* forever, he has
	80.	1 You who are *e* upon the cherubim,
	123.	1 eyes, O you who are *e* in the heavens!

ENTICE (ENTICED)

1 Kings	22.20	LORD said, 'Who will e Ahab, so that he
2 Chr	18.21	LORD said, "You are to e him, and you
Job	31. 9	"If my heart has been e by a woman,
Prov	1.10	child, if sinners e you, do not consent.
	16.29	The violent e their neighbors, and lead
Jer	20. 7	O LORD, you have e me, and I was e;

ENTREAT (ENTREATED)

Judg	13. 8	Manoah e the LORD, and said, "O LORD, I
Zech	7. 2	to e the favor of the LORD, and to ask
2 Cor	5.20	we e you on behalf of Christ, be

ENTREATY

2 Chr	33.19	His prayer, and how God received his e,
Ezra	8.23	God for this, and he listened to our e.

ENTRUST (ENTRUSTED ENTRUSTING)

Num	12. 7	Moses; he is e with all my house.
Lk	16.11	who will e to you the true riches?
Jn	2.24	his part would not e himself to them,
Rom	3. 2	place the Jews were e with the oracles
1 Cor	9.17	my own will, I am e with a commission.
2 Cor	5.19	and e to us the message of
1 Tim	6.20	Timothy, guard what has been e to you.
2 Tim	1.12	to guard until that day what I e to him.
	2. 2	many witnesses e to faithful people
1 Pet	4.19	will e themselves to a faithful Creator,

ENVIOUS

Ps	37. 1	do not be e of wrongdoers, for they will
	73. 3	For I was e of the arrogant; I saw how
1 Cor	13. 4	love is kind; love is not e or boastful or

ENVOY (ENVOYS)

2 Chr	32.31	of the e of the officials of Babylon,
Prov	13.17	brings trouble, but a faithful e, healing.
Isa	33. 7	the streets; the e of peace weep bitterly.

ENVY (ENVIED)

Gen	26.14	so that the Philistines e him.
	30. 1	bore Jacob no children, she e her sister;
Prov	3.31	Do not e the violent and do not choose
	23.17	Do not let your heart e sinners, but
	24. 1	Do not e the wicked, nor desire to be

EPHESUS

Acts	18.19	When they reached E, he left them
	19. 1	to E, where he found some disciples.
	20.16	For Paul had decided to sail past E, so
1 Cor	15.32	hopes I fought with wild animals at E,
1 Tim	1. 3	remain in E so that you may instruct
Rev	2. 1	"To the angel of the church in E write:

EPHRAIM (EPHRAIMITES)

Gen	41.52	The second he named E, "For God has
	48. 1	him his two sons, Manasseh and E.
Num	7.48	son of Ammihud, the leader of the E:
Judg	1.29	E did not drive out the Canaanites who
Ps	78.67	he did not choose the tribe of E;
Hos	4.17	E is joined to idols— let him alone.
	7. 8	E mixes himself with the peoples; E is
	11. 8	How can I give you up, E? How can I

EPILEPTIC (EPILEPTICS)

Mt	4.24	demoniacs, e, and paralytics, and he
	17.15	have mercy on my son, for he is an e

EQUAL

Jn	5.18	thereby making himself e with God.

EQUITY

Ps	98. 9	righteousness, and the peoples with e.
	99. 4	lover of justice, you have established e;

ERECT (ERECTED)

Gen	33.20	There he e an altar and called it
Lev	26. 1	idols and e no carved images or pillars,

ERR

Prov	14.22	Do they not e that plan evil? Those who

ERROR (ERRORS)

Lev	5.18	atonement on your behalf for the e that
Num	15.25	sin offering before the LORD, for their e.
Job	19. 4	I have erred, my e remains with me.
Ps	19.12	But who can detect their e? Clear me
Eccl	10. 5	sun, as great an e as if it proceeded
Rom	1.27	own persons the due penalty for their e.

ESAU

Born, Gen 25.24-26; sold his birthright, Gen 25.29-34; married Hittite women, Gen 26.34; lost Isaac's blessing, Gen 27.30-40; hated Jacob, Gen 27.41; married Mahalath, Gen 28.9; reconciled with Jacob, Gen 33.1-15.

ESCAPE (ESCAPED ESCAPES)

1 Sam	22.20	named Abiathar, e and fled after David.
Esth	4.13	palace you will e any more than all the
Ps	124. 7	We have e like a bird from the snare of
Eccl	7.26	one who pleases God e her, but the
Jer	44.14	to settle in the land of Egypt shall e
Ezek	24.26	on that day, one who has e will come to
	33.21	someone who had e from Jerusalem
Ob	17	be those that e, and it shall be holy;
1 Thess	5. 3	woman, and there will be no e!
Heb	2. 3	how can we e if we neglect so great a
2 Pet	2.20	they have e the defilements of the world

ESTABLISH (ESTABLISHED ESTABLISHES)

Gen	17. 7	I will e my covenant between me and
	17.21	my covenant I will e with Isaac, whom
Deut	28. 9	LORD will e you as his holy people, as he
	29.13	that he may e you today as his people,
	32. 6	created you, who made you and e you?
2 Sam	5.12	perceived that the LORD had e him king
	7.12	your body, and I will e his kingdom.
1 Kings	2.12	David, and his kingdom was firmly e.
	9. 5	I will e your royal throne over Israel
1 Chr	17.14	and his throne shall be e forever.
Ps	8. 3	the moon and the stars that you have e;
	74.16	night; you e the luminaries and the sun.
	99. 4	King, lover of justice, you have e equity;
Prov	3.19	by understanding he e the heavens;
Isa	2. 2	LORD's house shall be e as the highest
	9. 7	his kingdom. He will e and uphold it
	16. 5	throne shall be e in steadfast love in
Jer	10.12	power, who e the world by his wisdom,
	51.15	power, who e the world by his wisdom,
2 Cor	1.21	it is God who e us with you in Christ
1 Pet	5.10	restore, support, strengthen, and e you.

ESTATE

Prov	20.21	An e quickly acquired in the beginning

ESTEEM

1 Thess	5.13	e them very highly in love because of

ESTHER

Esth	2. 7	is E, his cousin, for she had neither
	9.32	The command of Queen E fixed these

ETERNAL

Mt	18. 8	feet and to be thrown into the e fire.
	19.16	good deed must I do to have e life?"
	19.29	a hundredfold, and will inherit e life.
	25.41	depart from me into the e fire prepared
Mk	3.29	have forgiveness, but is guilty of an e sin"
	10.17	what must I do to inherit e life?
Lk	10.25	said, "what must I do to inherit e life?"
	16. 9	may welcome you into the e homes.
Jn	3.16	him may not perish but may have e life.
	12.25	life in this world will keep it for e life.
	12.50	I know that his commandment is e life.
	17. 2	people, to give e life to all whom you
Acts	13.46	to be unworthy of e life, we are now
	13.48	as had been destined for e life became

Rom 2. 7 and immortality, he will give *e* life;
　　5.21 justification leading to *e* life through
2 Cor 4.18 but what cannot be seen is *e*.
Titus 1. 2 in hope of *e* life that God, who never
1 Jn 2.25 this is what he has promised us, *e* life.
　　5.13 that you may know that you have *e* life.
　　5.20 Christ. He is the true God and *e* life.

ETERNITY
Isa 57.15 the high and lofty one who inhabits *e*,

ETHIOPIA (ETHIOPIAN)
Ps 68.31 Egypt; let *E* hasten to stretch out its
Isa 43. 3 *E* and Seba in exchange for you.
Acts 8.27 an *E* eunuch, a court official of the

EUNUCH (EUNUCHS)
Mt 19.12 *e* who have made themselves *e* for the
Acts 8.27 an Ethiopian *e*, a court official of the

EUPHRATES
Gen 2.14 of Assyria. And the fourth river is the *E*.
　　15.18 the river of Egypt to . . . the river *E*,
Josh 1. 4 the river *E*, all the land of the Hittites,
　　24. 2 lived beyond the *E* and served other
Jer 13. 4 go now to the *E*, and hide it there in a
Rev 16.12 poured his bowl on the great river *E*,

EVANGELIST (EVANGELISTS)
Acts 21. 8 we went into the house of Philip the *e*,
Eph 4.11 some prophets, some *e*, some pastors
2 Tim 4. 5 do the work of an *e*, carry out your

EVE
Gen 3.20 The man named his wife *E*, because she
　　4. 1 Now the man knew his wife *E*, and she
2 Cor 11. 3 afraid that as the serpent deceived *E*
1 Tim 2.13 For Adam was formed first, then *E*; and

EVENING
Mt 8.16 That *e* they brought to him many who
Mk 1.32 That *e*, at sundown, they brought to
　　14.17 When it was *e*, he came with the

EVERLASTING
Gen 9.16 remember the *e* covenant between God
　　17. 7 for an *e* covenant, to be God to you and
　　21.33 on the name of the Lord, the *E* God.
Ps 139. 24 way in me, and lead me in the way *e*.
　　145. 13 Your kingdom is an *e* kingdom, and
Isa 9. 6 Mighty God, *E* Father, Prince
　　26. 4 for in the Lord God you have an *e* rock.
　　60.19 Lord will be your *e* light, and your God
Ezek 16.60 I will establish with you an *e* covenant.
Dan 12. 2 of the earth shall awake, some to *e* life,
Hab 1.12 Are you not from of *e*, O Lord my God,

EVIL
Deut 13. 5 you shall purge the *e* from your midst.
Judg 4. 1 Israelites again did what was *e* in the
　　10. 6 Israelites again did what was *e* in the
1 Sam 20. 7 that *e* has been determined by him.
1 Kings 11. 6 Solomon did what was *e* in the sight of
　　16.25 Omri did what was *e* in the sight of the
2 Chr 33. 6 He did much *e* in the sight of the Lord,
　　33. 9 that they did more *e* than the nations
Neh 9.28 had rest, they again did *e* before you,
Ps 7.14 See how they conceive *e*, and are
　　28. 4 and according to the *e* of their deeds;
　　35. 4 confounded who devise *e* against me.
　　91.10 no *e* shall befall you, no scourge come
　　140. 11 in the land; let *e* speedily hunt down
Prov 6.18 plans, feet that hurry to run to *e*,
Eccl 8.11 the human heart is fully set to do *e*.
Isa 5.20 Ah, you who call *e* good and good *e*,
Jer 9. 3 for they proceed from *e* to *e*, and they
　　16.10 pronounced all this great *e* against us?
Ezek 33.11 turn back, turn back from your *e* ways;
Dan 12. 4 back and forth, and *e* shall increase."

Nah 1.11 gone out who plots *e* against the Lord,
Mt 7.11 If you then, who are *e*, know how to
　　12.45 brings along seven other spirits more *e*
　　13.49 and separate the *e* from the righteous
　　15.19 out of the heart come *e* intentions,
　　27.23 he asked, "Why, what *e* has he done?"
Mk 15.14 asked them, "Why, what *e* has he done?"
Lk 11.13 who are *e*, know how to give good gifts
　　11.26 seven other spirits more *e* than itself,
Jn 7. 7 I testify against it that its works are *e*.
　　17.15 ask you to protect them from the *e* one.
Acts 23. 5 'You shall not speak *e* of a leader of
Rom 2. 9 and distress for everyone who does *e*,
　　3. 8 "Let us do *e* so that good may come?"
　　7.19 but the *e* I do not want is what I do.
1 Cor 5. 8 the old yeast, the yeast of malice and *e*,
Eph 4.29 Let no *e* talk come out of your mouths,
1 Thess 5.15 See that none of you repays *e* for *e*, but
1 Tim 6.10 of money is the root of all kinds of *e*,
Titus 3. 2 every good work, to speak *e* of no one,
1 Jn 2.13 because you have conquered the *e* one.

EVILDOER (EVILDOERS)
Prov 4.14 and do not walk in the way of *e*.
Mt 7.23 knew you; go away from me, you *e*.'
Lk 13.27 come from; go away from me, all you *e*!'
Rev 22.11 Let the *e* still do evil, and the filthy still

EXALT (EXALTED EXALTING EXALTS)
Ex 9.17 You are still *e* yourself against my
Josh 3. 7 "This day I will begin to *e* you in the
　　4.14 On that day the Lord *e* Joshua in the
1 Kings 1. 5 Now Adonijah son of Haggith *e* himself,
1 Chr 29.25 The Lord highly *e* Solomon in the sight
Job 36.22 See, God is *e* in his power; who is a
Ps 18.46 rock, and *e* be the God of my salvation,
　　35.26 let those who *e* themselves against me
　　46.10 among the nations, I am *e* in the earth."
　　57. 5 Be *e*, O God, above the heavens. Let
　　108. 5 Be *e*, O God, above the heavens, and let
　　138. 2 for you have *e* your name and your word
　　148. 13 for his name alone is *e*; his glory is
Prov 4. 8 Prize her highly, and she will *e* you; she
　　14.34 Righteousness *e* a nation, but sin is a
Isa 2.11 humbled; and the Lord alone will be *e*
Ezek 21.26 *E* that which is low, abase that which is
Lk 14.11 all who *e* themselves will be humbled,
Acts 5.31 God *e* him at his right hand as Leader
Phil 1.20 Christ will be *e* now as always in my
　　2. 9 Therefore God also highly *e* him and

EXAMINE (EXAMINED EXAMINES)
Ezra 10.16 month they sat down to *e* the matter.
Prov 5.21 of the Lord, and he *e* all their paths.
Lam 3.40 Let us test and *e* our ways, and return
Lk 23.14 I have *e* him in your presence and have
Acts 12.19 find him, he *e* the guards and ordered
　　17.11 eagerly and *e* the scriptures every day
　　22.24 and ordered him to be *e* by flogging,
1 Cor 9. 3 is my defense to those who would *e* me.
　　11.28 *E* yourselves, and then only eat of the
2 Cor 13. 5 *E* yourselves to see whether you are

EXAMPLE (EXAMPLES)
Jn 13.15 I have set you an *e*, that you also
1 Cor 10. 6 these things occurred as *e* for us, so
　　10.11 happened to them to serve as an *e*,
1 Thess 1. 7 so that you became an *e* to all the
2 Thess 3. 9 but in order to give you an *e* to imitate.
1 Tim 1.16 the utmost patience, making me an *e* to
　　4.12 but set the believers an *e* in speech and
1 Pet 2.21 also suffered for you, leaving you an *e*,
　　5. 3 in your charge, but be *e* to the flock.

EXCEEDS
Mt 5.20 unless your righteousness *e* that of the

EXCELLENCY

Acts 26. 7 for this hope, your *E*, that I am accused

EXCELLENT

Isa 28.29 wonderful in counsel, and *e* in wisdom.
Dan 5.12 an *e* spirit, knowledge, and
1 Cor 12.31 And I will show you a still more *e* way.
Jas 2. 7 they who blaspheme that *e* name that

EXCHANGED

Ps 106. 20 They *e* the glory of God for the image of
Rom 1.26 Their women *e* natural intercourse for

EXCUSE (EXCUSES)

Lk 14.18 they all alike began to make *e*. The first
Jn 15.22 but now they have no *e* for their sin.
Rom 1.20 they are without *e*; for though they

EXECUTE

Isa 66.16 by fire will the LORD *e* judgment, and by
Mic 5.15 wrath I will *e* vengeance on the nations

EXHORTATION

Acts 15.31 members read it, they rejoiced at the *e*.
Rom 12. 8 the exhorter, in *e*; the giver, in
Heb 13.22 bear with my word of *e*, for I have

EXILE (EXILED)

2 Kings 17.23 Israel was *e* from their own land to
Isa 5.13 my people go into *e* without knowledge;
Jer 40. 1 Judah who were being *e* to Babylon.
52.30 of the guard took into *e* of the Judeans
Ezek 12. 4 their sight, as those do who go into *e*.

EXPECTATION

Prov 11.23 in good; the *e* of the wicked in wrath.
Lk 3.15 people were filled with *e*, and all were

EXPECTED (EXPECTING)

Isa 5. 7 he *e* justice, but saw bloodshed;
Phil 3.20 it is from there that we are *e* a Savior,

EXPERIENCE

Gal 3. 4 Did you *e* so much for nothing?— if it

EXPIATION

2 Sam 21. 3 How shall I make *e*, that you may bless

EXPLAIN (EXPLAINED)

Gen 41.24 there was no one who could *e* it to me."
Mk 4.34 he *e* everything in private to his
Acts 18.26 him aside and *e* the way of God to him
28.23 to evening he *e* the matter to them,

EXPOSE (EXPOSED)

Jn 3.20 light, so that their deeds may not be *e*.
Eph 5.11 works of darkness, but instead *e* them.

EXPOUND

Deut 1. 5 Moses undertook to *e* this law as

EXTEND (EXTENDS)

Isa 11.11 the Lord will *e* his hand yet a second
2 Cor 4.15 so that grace, as it *e* to more and more

EXTERNAL

Rom 2.28 nor is true circumcision something *e* or

EXTOL

Ps 99. 5 *E* the LORD our God; worship at his
Song 1. 4 we will *e* your love more than wine;

EXULT

Ps 94. 3 wicked, how long shall the wicked *e*?
Jer 11.15 flesh avert your doom? Can you then *e*?
Zeph 3.14 Rejoice and *e* with all your heart, O
Zech 10. 7 rejoice, their hearts shall *e* in the LORD.

EXULTANT

Ps 68. 4 name is the LORD—be *e* before him.

EYE

Ex 21.24 *e* for *e*, tooth for tooth, hand for hand,
Lev 24.20 *e* for *e*, tooth for tooth; the injury
Deut 19.21 life for life, *e* for *e*, tooth for tooth,
Job 42. 5 of the ear, but now my *e* sees you;
Ps 32. 8 I will counsel you with my *e* upon you.
33.18 the *e* of the LORD is on those who fear
Isa 64. 4 no *e* has seen any God besides you,
Mt 5.29 If your right *e* causes you to sin, tear it
5.38 it was said, 'An *e* for an *e* and a tooth
6.22 if your *e* is healthy, your whole body
7. 3 you see the speck in your neighbor's *e*,
18. 9 if your *e* causes you to stumble, tear it
Mk 9.47 if your *e* causes you to stumble, tear it
Lk 11.34 Your *e* is the lamp of your body. If your
1 Cor 2. 9 "What no *e* has seen, nor ear heard, nor

EYES

Num 10.31 and you will serve as *e* for us.
Deut 11.12 The *e* of the LORD your God are always
29. 4 understand, or *e* to see, or ears to hear.
Judg 17. 6 did what was right in their own *e*.
21.25 did what was right in their own *e*.
1 Kings 1.20 the *e* of all Israel are on you to tell
8.29 that your *e* may be open night and day
2 Kings 6.17 he may see." So the LORD opened the *e*
2 Chr 6.20 May your *e* may be open day and night
16. 9 the *e* of the LORD range throughout the
20.12 know what to do, but our *e* are on you."
Job 28.10 in the rocks, their *e* see every precious
32. 1 because he was righteous in his own *e*.
Ps 6. 7 My *e* waste away because of grief; they
11. 4 His *e* behold, his gaze examines
115. 5 but do not speak; *e*, but do not see.
119. 18 Open my *e*, so that I may behold
119.136 My *e* shed streams of tears because
121. 1 I lift up my *e* to the hills— from where
123. 1 To you I lift up my *e*, O you who are
135. 16 speak; they have *e*, but they do not see;
139. 16 Your *e* beheld my unformed substance.
145. 15 The *e* of all look to you, and you give
Prov 4.25 Let your *e* look directly forward, and
15. 3 The *e* of the LORD are in every place,
22.12 The *e* of the LORD keep watch over
30.12 are those who are pure in their own *e*
Isa 6.10 and shut their *e*, so that they may not
29.10 he has closed your *e*, you prophets, and
32. 3 Then the *e* of those who have sight will
33.17 Your *e* will see the king in his beauty;
37.17 and hear; open your *e*, O LORD, and see;
49.18 Lift up your *e* all around and see; they
Jer 5.21 people, who have *e*, but do not see,
9. 1 of water, and my *e* a fountain of tears,
24. 6 I will set my *e* upon them for good, and
Am 9. 8 *e* of the Lord GOD are upon the sinful
Hab 1.13 Your *e* are too pure to behold evil, and
Lk 10.23 are the *e* that see what you see!
24.31 their *e* were opened, and they
Rom 11. 8 *e* that would not see and ears that
2 Cor 10. 7 Look at what is before your *e*. If you are
Gal 4.15 have torn out your *e* and given them
Heb 4.13 laid bare to the *e* of the one to whom
1 Pet 3.12 the *e* of the Lord are on the righteous,
Rev 3.18 and salve to anoint your *e* so that you

EYEWITNESSES

Lk 1. 2 who from the beginning were *e* and
2 Pet 1.16 but we had been *e* of his majesty.

EZEKIEL

Called, Ezek 2—3. Visions: cherubim, Ezek 1; 10; abominations in Jerusalem, Ezek 8—9; valley of dry bones, Ezek 37; the temple, Ezek 40.1—47.12; division of land, 47.13—48.35. Prophecies: against Israel, Ezek 4—7; 11—12; 14—24; 33; against false prophets, Ezek 13; 34; against other nations, Ezek 25—32; 35; 38—39; of restoration, Ezek 11.14-20; 34; 36; 39.23-29.

EZRA

Ezra	7.	6 *E* went up from Babylonia. He was a
	7.10	For *E* had set his heart to study the law
	10.	1 While *E* prayed and made confession,
Neh	8.	1 They told *E* the scribe to bring the book

F

FACE (FACES)

Ex	33.11	the Lord used to speak to Moses *f* to *f*,
	33.23	my back; but my *f* shall not be seen."
	34.29	the skin of his *f* shone because he has
Num	6.25	the Lord make his *f* to shine upon you,
Deut	5.	4 Lord spoke with you *f* to *f* at the
	34.10	like Moses, whom the Lord knew *f* to *f*.
2 Kings	14.	8 "Come, let us look one another in the *f*."
Ezra	9.15	though no one can *f* you because of
Ps	4.	6 Let the light of your *f* shine on us,
	24.	6 who seek the *f* of the God of Jacob.
	27.	8 Your *f*, Lord, do I seek. Do not hide
	31.16	Let your *f* shine on your servant; save
	34.16	The *f* of the Lord is against evildoers, to
	67.	1 us and make his *f* to shine upon us,
	119.135	Make your *f* shine upon your servant,
Song	2.14	let me see your *f*, let me hear your
Mt	6.16	hypocrites, for they disfigure their *f* so
2 Cor	3.	7 Israel could not gaze at Moses' *f*

FACTIONS

1 Cor	11.19	there have to be *f* among you, so it will

FAIL (FAILED)

Josh	23.14	not one thing has *f* of all the good
1 Sam	17.32	"Let no one's heart *f* because of him;
1 Kings	2.	4 not *f* you a successor on the throne
Job	19.14	and my close friends have *f* me;

FAINT

Song	5.	8 beloved, tell him this: I am *f* with love.
Isa	7.	4 and do not let your heart be *f* because
	40.29	He gives power to the *f*, and strengthens
	42.	4 He will not *f* or be crushed until he has
Lam	1.13	me back; he has left me stunned, *f*
Mt	15.32	hungry, for they might *f* on the way.
Mk	8.	3 to their homes, they will *f* on the way;

FAIR (FAIREST)

Prov	1.	9 for they are a *f* garland for your head,
Song	1.	8 If you do not know, O *f* among women,

FAITH

Deut	32.51	because both of you broke *f* with me
Josh	7.	1 Israelites broke *f* in regard to the
Ps	78.22	Israel, because they had no *f* in God,
Isa	7.	9 If you do not stand firm in *f*, you shall
Hab	2.	4 them, but the righteous live by their *f*.
Mt	8.10	in no one in Israel have I found such *f*.
	8.13	it be done for you according to your *f*."
	8.26	"Why are you afraid, you of little *f*?"
	15.28	"Woman, great is your *f*! Let it be done
	17.20	said to them, "Because of your little *f*.
	21.21	if you have *f* and do not doubt, not only
Mk	2.	5 when Jesus saw their *f*, he said to the
	4.40	are you afraid? Have you still no *f*?"
	5.34	"Daughter, your *f* has made you well; go
	11.22	Jesus answered them, "Have *f* in God.
Lk	5.20	When he saw their *f* he said, "Friend,
	7.	9 not even in Israel have I found such *f*."
	8.48	"Daughter, your *f* has made you well; go
	12.28	will he clothe you—you of little *f*?
	17.	5 said to the Lord, "Increase our *f*!"
	17.19	on your way; your *f* has made you well."
	18.	8 of Man comes, will he find *f* on earth?"
	18.42	your sight; your *f* has saved you."
	22.32	prayed for you that your own *f* may not
Acts	14.	9 and seeing that he had *f* to be healed,
	14.27	had opened a door of *f* for the Gentiles.
	20.21	God and *f* toward our Lord Jesus.

Acts	26.18	those who are sanctified by *f* in me.'
	27.25	for I have *f* in God that it will be
Rom	1.	8 because your *f* is proclaimed throughout
	1.16	God for salvation to everyone who has *f*
	3.31	Do we then overthrow the law by this *f*?
	4.16	For this reason it depends on *f*, in order
	4.19	He did not weaken in *f* when he
	5.	1 since we are justified by *f*, we have
	12.	3 according to the measure of *f* that God
	14.	1 Welcome those who are weak in *f*, but
	14.23	whatever does not proceed from *f* is sin.
1 Cor	12.	9 to another *f* by the same Spirit, to
2 Cor	4.13	we have the same spirit of *f* that is in
Gal	1.23	the *f* he once tried to destroy."
	2.16	that we may be justified by *f* in Christ,
	5.	6 the only thing that counts is *f* working
	6.10	especially for those of the family of *f*.
Eph	1.15	I have heard of your *f* in the Lord Jesus
	2.	8 by grace you have been saved through *f*,
	6.16	take the shield of *f*, with which you will
Col	1.	4 we have heard of your *f* in Christ Jesus
1 Thess	1.	3 your work of *f* and labor of love and
	3.	7 encouraged about you through your *f*.
1 Tim	3.13	themselves and great boldness in the *f*
	5.	8 has denied the *f* and is worse than an
	6.12	Fight the good fight of the *f*; take hold
2 Tim	1.	5 I am reminded of your sincere *f*, a *f* that
Philem		6 sharing of your *f* may become effective
Heb	4.	2 not united in *f* with those who listened.
	10.38	but my righteous one will live by *f*.
	11.	1 Now *f* is the assurance of things hoped
	11.33	who through *f* conquered kingdoms,
	13.	7 of their way of life, and imitate their *f*.
Jas	2.18	and I by my works will show you my *f*.
	2.22	You see that *f* was active along with his
1 Pet	1.	7 the genuineness of your *f*— being more
Jude		3 you to contend for the *f* that was once
Rev	14.12	of God and hold fast to the *f* of Jesus.

FAITHFUL

1 Sam	2.35	I will raise up for myself a *f* priest, who
	22.14	among your servants is so *f* as David?
2 Chr	31.20	he did what was good and right and *f*
Neh	7.	2 —for he was a *f* man and feared God
	9.	8 you found his heart *f* before you, and
Ps	4.	3 the Lord has set apart the *f* for himself;
	16.10	up to Sheol, or let the *f* one see the Pit.
	30.	4 O you his *f* ones, and give thanks to his
	31.23	The Lord preserves the *f*, but
	32.	6 let all who are *f* offer prayer to you;
	37.28	justice; he will not forsake his *f* ones.
	50.	5 "Gather to me my *f* ones, who made a
	78.	8 steadfast, whose spirit was not *f* to God.
	79.	2 the flesh of your *f* to the wild animals
	101.	6 I will look with favor on the *f* in the
	116.15	of the Lord is the death of his *f* ones.
Prov	2.	8 and preserving the way of his *f* ones.
Isa	1.21	How the *f* city has become a whore! She
	25.	1 things, plans formed of old, *f* and sure.
Dan	6.	4 he was *f*, and no negligence or
Hos	11.12	Judah still walks with God, and is *f* to
Mt	24.45	"Who then is the *f* and wise slave,
Lk	12.42	is the *f* and prudent manager whom his
	16.10	whoever is *f* in a very little is *f* also in
Acts	11.23	them all to remain *f* to the Lord
1 Cor	1.	9 God is *f*; by him you were called into
	10.13	God is *f*, and he will not let you be
Col	1.	7 He is a *f* minister of Christ on your
1 Thess	5.24	The one who calls you is *f*, and he will
2 Thess	3.	3 But the Lord is *f*; he will strengthen you
2 Tim	2.	2 entrust to *f* people who will be able to
Heb	11.11	barren— because he considered him *f*
Rev	2.10	Be *f* until death, and I will give you the
	19.11	horse! Its rider is called *F* and True,

FAITHFULNESS

Ps	36.	5 to the heavens, your *f* to the clouds.

FAITHLESS

Ps	40.10	I have spoken of your *f* and your
	57.10	heavens; your *f* extends to the clouds.
	85.11	*F* will spring up from the ground, and
	88.11	in the grave, or your *f* in Abaddon?
	89. 2	forever; your *f* is as firm as the heavens.
	89.33	my steadfast love, or be false to my *f*.
	92. 2	in the morning, and your *f* by night,
	117. 2	us, and the *f* of the LORD endures
	119. 90	Your *f* endures to all generations; you
	119.138	decrees in righteousnsss and in all *f*.
	143. 1	give ear to my supplications in your *f*;
Jer	31. 3	therefore I have continued my *f* to you.
Lam	3.23	are new every morning; great is your *f*.
Hos	4. 1	There is no *f* or loyalty, and no

FAITHLESS (FAITHLESSLY)

Ezek	15. 8	desolate, because they have acted *f*,
Prov	13.15	favor, but the way of the *f* is their ruin.
Jer	3. 6	seen what she did, that *f* one, Israel,
Mt	17.17	"You *f* and perverse generation, how
Lk	9.41	"You *f* and perverse generation, how
Rev	21. 8	as for the cowardly, the *f*, the polluted,

FAITHLESSNESS

Ezra	9. 2	in this *f* the officials and leaders have
Rom	3. 3	Will their *f* nullify the faithfulness of

FALL (FALLEN FELL)

Num	14. 5	Moses and Aaron *f* on their faces before
	16. 4	When Moses heard it, he *f* on his face.
	16.22	They *f* on their faces, and said, "O God,
	16.45	in a moment." And they *f* on their faces.
1 Sam	3.19	let none of his words *f* to the ground.
	25.23	*f* before David on her face, bowing to
2 Sam	1.25	How the mighty have *f* in the midst of
Ps	37.24	we stumble, we shall not *f* headlong,
	53. 3	They have all *f* away, they are all alike
	106. 26	would make them *f* in the wilderness,
	141. 10	Let the wicked *f* into their own nets,
Prov	24.17	Do not rejoice when your enemies *f*,
Isa	14.12	How you are *f* from heaven, O Day Star,
	21. 9	"*F*, *f* is Babylon; and all the images of
Jer	51. 8	Suddenly Babylon has *f* and is
Hos	10. 8	Cover us, and to the hills, *F* on us.
Mic	7. 8	when I *f*, I shall rise; when I sit in
Mt	24.10	Then many will *f* away, and they will
Mk	4.17	of the word, immediately they *f* away.
Rom	11.11	So I ask, have they stumbled so as to *f*?
Gal	5. 4	from Christ; you have *f* away from grace.
Heb	4.11	one may *f* through such disobedience
	6. 6	the age to come, and then have *f* away,
1 Pet	2. 8	stumble, and a rock that makes them *f*."
Rev	1.17	saw him, I *f* at his feet as though dead.
	14. 8	"*F*, *f* is Babylon the great! She has made

FALLING (n)

Lk	2.34	this child is set for the *f* and the rising
1 Cor	8.13	if food is a cause of their *f*, I will never

FALSE (FALSELY)

Gen	21.23	swear . . . that you will not deal *f* with
Deut	32. 5	his degenerate children have dealt *f*
2 Chr	26.16	he was *f* to the LORD his God, and
Job	31.28	judges, for I should have been *f* to God
Ps	119. 29	Put *f* ways far from me; and graciously
	119.104	therefore I hate every *f* way.
Prov	6.19	lying witness who testifies *f*, and one
Jer	51.17	for their images are *f*; and there is no
Hos	10. 2	Their heart is *f*; now they must bear
Mt	7.15	"Beware of *f* prophets, who come to you
	24.24	For *f* messiahs and *f* prophets will
Phil	1.18	way, whether out of *f* motives or true;
2 Thess	2.11	leading them to believe what is *f*,

FALSEHOOD

Job	21.34	is nothing left of your answers but *f*."
Ps	62. 4	They take pleasure in *f*; they bless with
	119.163	I hate and abhor *f*, but I love your law.

Prov	30. 8	Remove far from me *f* and lying; give
Isa	5.18	who drag iniquity along with cords of *f*,
Ezek	13. 6	They have envisioned *f* and lying
Eph	4.25	putting away *f*, let all of us speak the

FALSIFY

2 Cor	4. 2	to practice cunning or to *f* God's word;

FAME

Mk	1.28	At once his *f* began to spread

FAMILY (FAMILIES)

Gen	12. 3	in you all the *f* of the earth shall be
Job	19.13	"He has put my *f* far from me, and my
	22. 6	pledges from your *f* for no reason,
Ps	107. 41	distress, and makes their *f* like flocks.
Jer	31. 1	I will be the God of all the *f* of Israel,
Am	3. 2	have I known of all the *f* of the earth;
Mt	25.40	of these who are members of my *f*, you
Gal	6.10	all, especially for those of the *f* of faith.

FAMINE

Gen	12.10	there was a *f* in the land. So Abram
	41.30	them there will arise seven years of *f*,
	47.20	fields, because *f* was severe upon them;
Ruth	1. 1	judges ruled there was a *f* in the land,
2 Sam	21. 1	a *f* in the days of David for three years,
1 Kings	18. 2	to Ahab. The *f* was severe in Samaria.
2 Kings	6.25	continued, *f* in Samaria became so great
	25. 3	the *f* became so severe in the city that
1 Chr	21.12	either three years of *f*; or three months
Job	5.20	In *f* he will redeem you from death, and
Ps	105. 16	When he summoned *f* against the land,
Jer	14.15	"Sword and *f* shall not come on this
	24.10	I will send sword, *f*, and pestilence
Lam	5.10	as an oven from the scorching heat of *f*.
Am	8.11	not a *f* of bread, or a thirst for water,
Acts	11.28	would be a severe *f* over all the world;

FAR

Lk	15.20	while he was still *f* off, his father saw

FAST (FASTING) (n)

2 Chr	20. 3	proclaimed a *f* throughout all Judah.
Ezra	8.21	I proclaimed a *f* there, at the river
Neh	9. 1	people of Israel were assembled with *f*
Esth	4. 3	mourning among the Jews, with *f* and
	4.16	hold a *f* on my behalf, and neither eat
Ps	109. 24	My knees are weak through *f*; my body
Joel	2.12	return to me with all your heart, with *f*,
Jon	3. 5	believed God; they proclaimed a *f*,
Zech	8.19	The *f* of the fourth month, and the *f* of
Mt	17.21n	not come out except by prayer and *f*."
Mk	9.29n	can come out only through prayer and *f*."

FAST (FASTED FASTING) (v)

1 Sam	7. 6	They *f* that day, and said, "We have
Neh	1. 4	for days, *f* and praying before the God
Isa	58. 3	"Why do we *f*, but you do not see? Why
Zech	7. 5	seventy years, was it for me that you *f*?
Mt	4. 2	He *f* forty days and forty nights, and
	6.16	so as to show others that they are *f*.
	9.14	*f* often, but your disciples do not *f*?"
Mk	2.18	Pharisees *f*, but your disciples do not *f*?"
Lk	5.33	frequently *f* and pray, but your disciples

FATAL

Jer	17.16	service, nor have I desired the *f* day.

FATE

Eccl	3.19	the *f* of humans and the *f* of animals is
	9. 2	since the same *f* comes to all. to the

FATHER (FATHERS FATHER'S)

Gen	2.24	Therefore a man leaves his *f* and his
	5. 3	Adam . . . became the *f* of a son in his
	50. 5	let me go up, so that I may bury my *f*;
Deut	32. 6	Is not he your *f*, who created you, who
1 Sam	2.25	would not listen to the voice of their *f*;

1 Sam	22.	3 "Pray let my *f* and my mother come to
2 Sam	7.	14 I will be his *f*, and he shall be a son to
1 Kings	1.	6 His *f* had never at any time displeased
1 Chr	17.	13 I will be a *f* to him, and he shall be a
Job	29.	16 I was a *f* to the needy, and I
	38.	28 "Has the rain a *f*, or who has begotten
Ps	27.	10 If my *f* and my mother forsake me, the
	68.	5 *F* of the orphans and protector of
	103.	13 As a *f* has compassion for his children,
Prov	1.	8 Hear, my child, your *f* instruction, and
	10.	1 A wise child makes a glad *f*, but a
	23.	22 Listen to your *f* who begot you, and do
	28.	24 Anyone who robs *f* or mother and says,
Isa	64.	8 Yet, O LORD, you are our *f*; we are the
Mal	2.	10 Have we not all one *f*? Has not one God
Mt	5.	45 that you may be children of your *F* in
	5.	48 therefore, as your heavenly *F* is perfect.
	6.	9 in this way: Our *F* in heaven, hallowed
	7.	21 only the one who does the will of my *F*
	10.	32 I also will acknowledge before my *F* in
	10.	37 Whoever loves *f* or mother more than
	19.	5 a man shall leave his *f* and mother and
	23.	9 call no man your *f* on earth, for you
Mk	7.	11 you say that if anyone tells *f* or mother,
	10.	7 leave his *f* and mother and be joined
Lk	2.	49 know that I must be in my *F* house?"
	9.	59 "Lord, first let me go and bury my *f*."
	11.	13 heavenly *F* give the Holy Spirit to those
	12.	53 will be divided, *f* against son and son
	14.	26 to me and does not hate *f* and mother,
Jn	12.	49 but the *F* who sent me has himself
1 Cor	4.	15 I became your *f* through the gospel.
2 Cor	6.	18 I will be your *f*, and you will be my sons
Eph	6.	4 *F*, do not provoke your children to
Col	3.	21 *F*, do not provoke your children, or they
Heb	7.	3 Without *f*, without mother, without
Jas	1.	17 coming down from the *F* of lights, with
1 Jn	2.	13 I am writing to you, *f*, because you

FAULT

1 Sam	29.	3 to me I have found no *f* in him to this
Rom	9.	19 "Why then does he still find *f*? For who
2 Cor	6.	3 so that no *f* may be found with our
Heb	8.	8 God finds *f* with them when he says:

FAVOR

Gen	6.	8 But Noah found *f* in the sight of the
	18.	3 if I find *f* with you, do not pass by your
	32.	5 in order that I may find *f* in your sight.' "
	33.	8 answered, "To find *f* with my lord."
Ex	3.	21 I will bring this people into such *f* with
	11.	3 The LORD gave the people *f* in the sight
	12.	36 The LORD had given the people *f* in the
	33.	12 and you have also found *f* in my sight.'
Lev	26.	9 I will look with *f* upon you and make
Num	11.	15 if I have found *f* in your sight—and do
Judg	6.	17 If now I have found *f* with you, then
Ruth	2.	10 "Why have I found *f* in your sight, that
2 Sam	14.	22 knows that I have found *f* in your sight,
	15.	25 If I find *f* in the eyes of the LORD, he
Ezra	9.	8 for a brief moment *f* has been shown by
Esth	5.	8 If I have won the king's *f*, and if it
Job	20.	10 children will seek the *f* of the poor,
Ps	84.	11 sun and shield; he bestows *f* and honor.
	90.	17 Let the *f* of the Lord our God be upon
	115.	12 the people of Tyre will seek your *f* with
Prov	3.	4 So you will find *f* and good repute in
	3.	34 scornful, but to the humble he shows *f*.
	11.	27 Whoever diligently seeks good seeks *f*,
	16.	15 his *f* is like the clouds that bring the
	18.	22 good thing, and obtains *f* from the LORD.
Eccl	10.	12 words spoken by the wise bring them *f*,
Isa	60.	10 you down, but in my *f* I have had mercy
Jer	16.	13 day and night, for I will show you no *f*.
Lk	1.	30 Mary, for you have found *f* with God.
	2.	40 and the *f* of God was upon him.
	2.	52 in years, and in divine and human *f*.

Acts	7.	46 David, who found *f* with God and asked
	24.	27 to grant the Jews a *f*, Felix left Paul in
2 Cor	1.	15 first, so that you might have a double *f*;

FAVORABLE

1 Kings	22.	8 he never prophesies anything *f* about
	22.	13 with one accord are *f* to the king;
Ps	85.	1 LORD, you were *f* to your land; you

FAVORED

Lk	1.	28 "Greetings, *f* one! The Lord is with you."

FEAR (FEARS) (n)

Ex	14.	10 In great *f* the Israelites cried out to the
Deut	2.	25 to put the dread and *f* of you upon the
2 Chr	20.	29 The *f* of God came on all the kingdoms
	26.	5 who instructed him in the *f* of God;
Esth	8.	17 because the *f* of the Jews had fallen
Job	28.	28 the *f* of the Lord, that is wisdom;
Ps	2.	11 Serve the LORD with *f*, with trembling
	19.	9 the *f* of the LORD is pure, enduring
	36.	1 there is no *f* of God before their eyes.
Prov	1.	7 The *f* of the LORD is the beginning of
	9.	10 The *f* of the LORD is the beginning of
	14.	27 The *f* of the LORD is a fountain of life,
	19.	23 The *f* of the LORD is life indeed; filled
	29.	25 The *f* of others lays a snare, but one
Isa	8.	13 let him be your *f*, and let him be your
Mt	14.	26 "It is a ghost!" And they cried out for *f*.
Jn	20.	19 had met were locked for *f* of the Jews,
Rom	3.	18 "There is no *f* of God before their eyes."
	13.	3 you wish to have no *f* of the authority?
1 Cor	2.	3 and in *f* and in much trembling.
2 Cor	5.	11 knowing the *f* of the Lord, we try to
	7.	5 way—disputes without and *f* within.
	7.	15 welcomed him with *f* and trembling.
1 Jn	4.	18 There is no *f* in love, but perfect love

FEAR (FEARED FEARS) (v)

Gen	42.	18 "Do this and you will live, for I *f* God:
Ex	1.	17 because the midwives *f* God, he gave
	1.	20 of Pharaoh who *f* the word of the LORD
	18.	21 among all the people, men who *f* God,
Num	14.	9 and the LORD is with us; do not *f* them.
Deut	1.	21 promised you; do not *f* or be dismayed."
	5.	29 to *f* me and to keep all my
	6.	2 may *f* the LORD your God all the days of
	31.	8 or forsake you. Do not *f* or be dismayed."
Josh	8.	1 the LORD said to Joshua, "Do not *f* or be
1 Sam	15.	24 because I *f* the people and obeyed their
2 Chr	20.	15 says the LORD to you: 'Do not *f* or be
Ps	25.	14 of the LORD is for those who *f* him,
	46.	2 we will not *f*, though the earth
	102.	15 The nations will *f* the name of the LORD,
	111.	5 He provides food for those who *f* him;
	119.	38 your promise, which is for those who *f*
Prov	3.	7 own eyes; *f* the LORD, and turn away
	24.	21 My child, *f* the LORD and the king, and
	31.	30 but a woman who *f* the LORD is to be
Eccl	5.	7 and a multitude of words; but *f* God.
	8.	12 it will be well with those who *f* God,
	12.	13 *F* God, and keep his commandments;
Isa	41.	10 do not *f*, for I am with you, do not be
	50.	10 Who among you *f* the LORD and obeys
Jer	5.	24 say in their hearts, "Let us *f* the LORD
	33.	9 they shall *f* and tremble because of all
	46.	27 have no *f*, my servant Jacob, and do not
Dan	6.	26 tremble and *f* before the God of Daniel:
Mt	14.	5 he *f* the crowd, because they regarded
Mk	6.	20 Herod *f* John, knowing he was a
Lk	1.	50 His mercy is for those who *f* him from
	12.	5 I will warn you whom to *f*: *f* him who,
Acts	10.	2 He was a devout man who *f* God with
Rev	15.	4 Lord, who will not *f* and glorify your

FEAST (FEASTED FEASTING FEASTS)

Esth	9.	17 they rested and made that a day of *f*
Ps	36.	8 They *f* on the abundance of your house,

FEEBLE (continued)

Ps	63.	5 My soul is satisfied with a rich *f*, and
Isa	25.	6 for all peoples a *f* of rich food, a *f* of
Lam	4.	5 Those who *f* on delicacies perish in the
Am	8.10	I will turn your *f* into mourning, and all

FEEBLE

Neh	4.	2 "What are these *f* Jews doing? Will they
Isa	13.	7 Therefore all hands will be *f*, and every

FEED (FED)

Ex	16.32	may see the food with which I *f* you
Deut	8.16	and *f* you in the wilderness with manna
1 Kings	17.	9 commanded a widow there to *f* you."
Prov	10.21	The lips of the righteous *f* many, but
Isa	40.11	He will *f* his flock like a shepherd; he
	58.14	I will *f* you with the heritage of your
	61.	5 Strangers shall stand and *f* your flocks,
Jer	50.19	and it shall *f* on Camel and in Bashan,
Ezek	34.	2 Should not shepherds *f* the sheep? You
Hos	13.	5 I who *f* you in the wilderness, in the
Mic	5.	4 he shall stand and *f* his flock in the
Mk	8.	4 "How can one *f* these people with bread
Jn	21.17	you." Jesus said to him, "*F* my sheep.

FELLOW

Gen	19.	9 "This *f* came here as an alien, and he
Ex	2.13	"Why do you strike your *f* Hebrew?"
Acts	22.22	then they shouted, "Away with such a *f*
Eph	3.	6 the Gentiles are *f* heirs, members of the
Phil	2.25	co-worker and *f* soldier, your messenger

FELLOWSHIP

Acts	2.42	the apostles' teaching and *f*, to the
1 Cor	1.	9 by him you were called into the *f* of his
Gal	2.	9 to Barnabas and me the right hand of *f*,
1 Jn	1.	3 that you also may have *f* with us; and

FESTIVAL (FESTIVALS)

Ex	23.14	in a year you shall hold a *f* for me.
Lev	23.	2 These are the appointed *f* of the LORD
	23.41	You shall keep it as a *f* to the LORD
Num	29.39	offer to the LORD at your appointed *f*,
1 Kings	8.65	Solomon held the *f* at that time, and all
Dan	5.	1 King Belshazzar made a great *f* for a
Mt	26.	5 "Not during the *f*, or there may be a riot
	27.15	Now at the *f* the governor was
Mk	15.	6 Now at the *f* he used to release a
Lk	2.41	to Jerusalem for the *f* of the Passover.
	22.	1 the *f* of Unleavened Bread which is

FEVER

Mk	1.30	mother-in-law was in bed with a *f*,
Lk	4.38	was suffering from a high *f*,
Jn	4.52	at one in the afternoon the *f* left him."
Acts	28.	8 father of Publius lay sick in bed with *f*

FEW

Eccl	5.	2 earth; therefore let your words be *f*.
Mt	7.14	leads to life, and there are *f* who find it.
Lk	13.23	him, "Lord, will only a *f* be saved?"

FIELD

Isa	5.	8 who add *f* to *f*, until there is room for
Jer	32.	7 "Buy my *f* that is at Anathoth, for the
Mt	13.44	of heaven is like treasure hidden in a *f*,
Acts	1.19	the *f* was called in their language
1 Cor	3.	9 you are God's *f*, God's building.

FIERCE

Song	8.	6 strong as death, passion *f* as the grave.

FIG TREE (FIG TREES)

Song	2.13	The *f* puts forth its figs, and the vines
Isa	34.	4 on a vine, or fruit withering on a *f*.
Joel	1.	7 waste my vines, and splintered my *f*;
Hab	3.17	Though the *f* does not blossom, and no
Mic	4.	4 their own vines and under their own *f*,
Mt	21.19	you again!" And the *f* withered at once.
Mk	11.13	Seeing in the distance a *f* in leaf, he

FIG TREE (continued)

Mk	13.28	"From the *f* learn its lesson: as soon as
Lk	13.	6 A man had a *f* planted in his vineyard;
	21.29	"Look at the *f* and all the trees; as soon
Jn	1.48	"I saw you under the *f* before Philip
Jas	3.12	Can a *f*, my brothers and sister, yield

FIGHT (FIGHTING)

Ex	14.14	The LORD will *f* for you, and you have
Deut	1.30	God . . . is the one who will *f* for you,
	20.	4 God who goes before you, to *f* for you
2 Chr	11.	4 LORD: You shall not go up or *f* against
Isa	31.	4 the LORD of hosts will come down to *f*
	58.	4 Look, you fast only to quarrel and to *f*
Jer	1.19	They will *f* against you; but they shall
	21.	5 I myself will *f* against you with
Zech	14.14	other; even Judah will *f* at Jerusalem.
Jn	18.36	my followers would be *f*, to keep me
Acts	5.39	you may even be found *f* against God!"
1 Tim	1.19	following them, you may *f* the good *f*.
	6.12	*F* the good *f* of the faith; take hold of

FIGS

Jer	8.13	grapes on the vine, nor *f* on the fig tree;
	24.	1 The LORD showed me two baskets of *f*

FILL (FILLED)

Gen	1.22	multiply and *f* the waters in the seas,
	1.28	multiply, and *f* the earth and subdue it;
Ex	40.35	the glory of the LORD *f* the tabernacle.
Num	14.21	all the earth shall be *f* with the glory of
Deut	14.29	in your towns, may come and eat their *f*
1 Kings	8.11	for the glory of the LORD *f* the house of
2 Kings	24.	4 he *f* Jerusalem with innocent blood, and
2 Chr	5.14	glory of the LORD *f* the house of God.
Prov	7.18	Come, let us take our *f* of love until
Isa	27.	6 shoots, and *f* the whole world with fruit.
Ezek	43.	5 and the glory of the LORD *f* the temple.
	44.	4 lo! the glory of the LORD *f* the temple
Hab	2.14	the earth will be *f* with the knowledge
Lk	1.53	he has *f* the hungry with good things,
	3.	5 Every valley shall be *f*, and every
Jn	2.	7 said to them, "*F* the jars with water."
	6.26	because you ate your *f* of the loaves.
Acts	2.	4 All of them were *f* with the Holy Spirit
	5.28	you have *f* Jerusalem with your teaching
Eph	5.18	is debauchery; but be *f* with the Spirit,

FINAL

Ezek	21.25	come, the time of your *f* punishment,

FIND (FINDS FOUND)

Num	32.23	and be sure your sin will *f* you out.
Deut	4.29	you will *f* him if you search after him
	32.10n	He *f* him in a desert land, in a howling
1 Sam	25.28	evil shall not be *f* in you so long as you
2 Chr	34.15	Shaphan, "I have *f* the book of the law
Neh	8.14	they *f* it written in the law, which the
Job	23.	3 Oh, that I knew where I might *f* him,
	33.24	down into the Pit; I have *f* a ransom;
Prov	8.35	For whoever *f* me *f* life and obtains
	18.22	He who *f* a wife *f* a good thing, and
Song	3.	4 when I *f* him whom my soul loves.
Jer	15.16	Your words were *f*, and I ate them, and
	29.14	I will let you *f* me, says the LORD, and I
Lk	15.	9 Rejoice with me, for I have *f* the coin
	15.24	and is alive again; he was lost, and is *f*.
Jn	1.41	said to him. "We have *f* the Messiah"
	1.45	"We have *f* him about whom Moses in
	9.35	had driven him out, and when he *f* him,
Rev	20.15	not *f* written in the book of life was

FINE

Ex	2.	2 that he was a *f* child, she hid him three

FINGER (FINGERS)

Ex	8.19	said to Pharaoh, "This is the *f* of God!"
	31.18	of stone, written with the *f* of God.
Deut	9.10	stone tablets written with the *f* of God;

Ps	8. 3 at your heavens, the work of your *f*,
Dan	5. 5 the *f* of a human hand appeared and
Mt	23. 4 are unwilling to lift a *f* to move them.
Lk	11.20 if it is by the *f* of God that I cast out
	11.46 do not lift one *f* to ease them.

FINISH (FINISHED FINISHING)

Gen	2. 1 Thus the heavens and the earth were *f*,
1 Kings	6.14 So Solomon built the house, and *f* it.
1 Chr	28.20 the service of the house of the LORD is *f*.
Ezra	6.15 and this house was *f* on the third day of
Neh	6.15 So the wall was *f* on the twenty-fifth
Dan	9.24 to *f* the transgression, to put an end to
Lk	13.32 and on the third day I *f* my work.
Jn	17. 4 on earth by *f* the work that you gave
	19.30 he said, "It is *f*." Then he bowed his
Acts	20.24 if only I may *f* my course and the
2 Tim	4. 7 good fight, I have *f* the race, I have kept
1 Pet	4. 1 has suffered in the flesh has *f* with sin),

FIRE

Gen	19.24 and Gomorrah sulfur and *f* from the
Lev	9.24 *F* came out from the LORD and
	10. 1 they offered unholy *f* before the LORD,
Deut	4.12 the LORD spoke to you out of the *f*.
	4.24 the LORD your God is a devouring *f*, a
	5. 4 to face at the mountain, out of the *f*.
Josh	8.19 took it, and at once set the city on *f*.
Judg	1. 8 put it to the sword and set the city on *f*.
1 Kings	18.38 Then the *f* of the LORD fell and
	19.12 a *f*, but the LORD was not in the *f*;
2 Kings	2.11 a chariot of *f* and horses of *f* separated
2 Chr	7. 1 Solomon had ended his prayer, *f* came
Ps	66.12 we went through *f* and through water;
	83.14 As *f* consumes the forest, as the flame
Prov	26.20 For lack of wood the *f* goes out, and
Isa	43. 2 when you walk through *f* you shall not
	66.24 not die, their *f* shall not be quenched,
Jer	20. 9 like a burning *f* shut up in my bones;
	23.29 Is not my word like *f*, says the LORD,
	36.23 the entire scroll was consumed in the *f*
Lam	1.13 "From on high he sent *f*; it went deep
Dan	3.25 walking in the middle of the *f*,
Mt	3.10 fruit is cut down and thrown into the *f*.
	3.11 baptize you with the Holy Spirit and *f*.
	25.41 depart from me into the eternal *f*
Lk	3.16 baptize you with the Holy Spirit and *f*.
	9.54 do you want us to command *f* to come
	12.49 "I came to bring *f* to the earth, and how
Jn	21. 9 ashore, they saw a charcoal *f* there,
Acts	28. 5 shook off the creature into the *f* and
1 Cor	3.13 be revealed with *f*, and the *f* will test
	3.15 will be saved, but only as through *f*.
2 Thess	1. 8 with his mighty angels in flaming *f*,
Heb	12.29 for indeed our God is a consuming *f*.
Jas	3. 6 And the tongue is a *f*. The tongue is
Jude	7 undergoing a punishment of eternal *f*.
	23 others by snatching them out of the *f*;
Rev	21. 8 will be in the lake that burns with *f*

FIRMAMENT

Ps	19. 1 God; and the *f* proclaims his handiwork.

FIRST

Isa	41. 4 I, the LORD, am *f*, and will be with the
Mt	6.33 strive *f* for the kingdom of God and his
	19.30 many who are *f* will be last, and the last
Mk	9.35 "Whoever wants to be *f* must be last of
Lk	9.59 "Lord, *f* let me go and bury my father."
Rom	16. 5 who was the *f* convert in Asia
1 Cor	15.47 The *f* man was from the earth, a man of
	16.15 were the *f* converts in Achaia,
2 Cor	8. 5 they gave themselves *f* to the Lord and,
3 Jn	9 Diotrephes, who likes to put himself *f*,
Rev	1.17 not be afraid; I am the *f* and the last,
	20. 5 were ended.) This is the *f* resurrection.

FIRST FRUITS

Ex	34.26 the *f* of your ground you shall bring to
Lev	2.14 a grain offering of *f* to the LORD, you
	23.10 shall bring the sheaf of the *f* of your
Num	28.26 On the day of the *f*, when you offer a
Prov	3. 9 and with the *f* of all your produce.
Rom	11.16 dough offered as *f* is holy, then the
1 Cor	15.20 the dead, the *f* of those who have died.
2 Thess	3.13 God chose you as the *f* for salvation
Jas	1.18 we would become a kind of *f* of his

FIRSTBORN

Ex	11. 5 Every *f* in the land of Egypt shall die,
Num	3.45 the Levites as substitutes for all the *f*
	8.17 For all the *f* among the Israelites are
Ps	78.51 He struck all the *f* in Egypt, the first
	89.27 I will make him the *f*, the highest of the
Col	1.15 the invisible God, the *f* of all creation;

FIRSTLING

Lev	27.26 A *f* of animals . . . which as a *f* belongs

FISH

Gen	1.26 let them have dominion over the *f* of
Ex	7.21 the *f* in the river died. The river stank
Isa	19. 8 Those who *f* will mourn; all who cast
Jon	1.17 provided a large *f* to swallow up Jonah;
	2.10 spoke to the *f*, and it spewed Jonah out
Mt	7.10 Or if the child asks for a *f*, will give a
	14.17 nothing here but five loaves and two *f*."
	15.34 They said, "Seven, and a few small *f*."
	17.27 take the first *f* that comes up; and when
Mk	1.17 me, and I will make you *f* for people."
	6.38 found out, they said, "Five, and two *f*."
	8. 7 They had also a few small *f*; and after
Lk	11.11 if your child asks for a *f*, will give a
Jn	6. 9 who has five barley loaves and two *f*,
	21. 6 haul it in because there were so many *f*.

FISHERMEN

Jer	16.16 I am now sending for many *f*, says the
Mk	1.16 a net in the sea — for they were *f*.

FIVE

Mt	16. 9 you not remember the *f* loaves for the *f*
Mk	6.38 found out, they said, "*F*, and two fish."
	6.44 loaves were numbered *f* thousand men.
Lk	9.13 "We have no more than *f* loaves and two
Jn	4.18 for you have had *f* husbands, and the

FIXED

Lk	4.20 of all in the synagogue were *f* on him.
Acts	17.31 because he has *f* a day on which he will

FLAME

Isa	10.17 become a fire, and his Holy One a *f*;
	43. 2 and the *f* shall not consume you.

FLASHES

Song	8. 6 as the grave. Its *f* are *f* of fire, a raging
Rev	4. 5 from the throne are *f* of lightning,

FLATTER (FLATTERING FLATTERS)

Job	32.22 For I do not know how to *f* — or my
Ps	12. 2 other; with *f* lips and a double heart
	36. 2 For they *f* themselves in their own eyes
Prov	26.28 its victims, and a *f* mouth works ruin.
	28.23 favor than one who *f* with the tongue.
	29. 5 Whoever *f* a neighbor is spreading a net

FLAVOR

Job	6. 6 is there any *f* in the juice of mallows?

FLEE (FLED)

Ex	2.15 But Moses *f* from Pharaoh. He settled
Deut	19. 5 the killer may *f* to one of these cities
1 Kings	2.29 "Joab has *f* to the tent of the LORD and
Ps	11. 1 how can you say to me, "*F* like a bird to
	143. 9 my enemies; I have *f* to you for refuge.

FLEECE

Prov	28.	1 The wicked *f* when no one pursues, but
Jer	6.	1 *F* for safety, O children of Benjamin,
Jon	1.	3 Jonah set out to *f* to Tarshish from the
Zech	14.	5 you shall *f* as you *f* from the earthquake
Mt		2.13 child and his mother, and *f* to Egypt,
		10.23 you in one town, *f* to the next;
Lk		3. 7 Who warned you to *f* from the wrath
		21.21 those in Judea must *f* to the mountains,
1 Cor		10.14 dear friends, *f* from the worship of idols.

FLEECE

Judg		6.37 I am going to lay a *f* of wool on the

FLEET

1 Kings		9.26 Solomon built a *f* of ships at
		10.11 Moreover, the *f* of Hiram, which carried

FLEETING

Ps		39. 4 my days; let me know how *f* my life is.
Heb		11.25 God than to enjoy the *f* pleasures of sin.

FLESH

1 Chr		11. 1 and said, "See, we are your bone and *f*.
2 Chr		32. 8 With him is an arm of *f*; but with us is
Job		19.26 destroyed, then in my *f* I shall see God,
Ps		145. 21 and all *f* will bless his holy name
Mt		26.41 indeed is willing, but the *f* is weak."
Mk		14.38 indeed is willing, but the *f* is weak."
Lk		3. 6 and all *f* shall see the salvation of God.' "
Jn		1.14 the Word became *f* and lived among us,
		6.51 give for the life of the world is my *f*."
		6.63 the spirit that gives life; the *f* is useless.
Rom		7.14 but I am of the *f*, sold into slavery
		7.18 good dwells within me, that is, in my *f*.
		8. 3 his own Son in the likeness of sinful *f*,
		8. 6 To set the mind on the *f* is death, but
		8. 9 But you are not in the *f*, you are in the
		9. 5 according to the *f*, comes the Messiah,
1 Cor		3. 1 but rather as people of the *f*, as infants
		5. 5 to Satan for the destruction of the *f*,
		15.39 Not all *f* is alike, but there is one *f* for
		15.50 *f* and blood cannot inherit the kingdom
2 Cor		12. 7 a thorn was given me in the *f*, a
Gal		5.17 the *f* desires is opposed to the Spirit,
Phil		3. 4 too, have reason for confidence in the *f*.

FLESHPOTS

Ex		16. 3 when we sat by the *f* and ate our fill of

FLOAT (FLOATED)

Gen		7.18 and the ark *f* on the face of the waters.
2 Kings		6. 6 threw it in there, and made the iron *f*.

FLOCK

Gen		30.41 the stronger of the *f* were breeding,
Ps		68.10 your *f* found a dwelling in it; in your
		77.20 You lead your people like a *f* by the
		79.13 Then we your people, the *f* of your
Isa		40.11 He will feed his *f* like a shepherd; he
Ezek		36.38 Like the *f* for sacrifices, like the *f* at
Lk		12.32 "Do not be afraid, little *f*, for it is the
1 Pet		5. 2 among you to tend to the *f* of God

FLOGGED (FLOGGING)

Mt		20.19 to be mocked and *f* and crucified;
		27.26 and after *f* Jesus, he handed him over
Lk		18.33 After they have *f* him, they will kill him,
		23.16 therefore have him *f* and release him."
Jn		19. 1 Then Pilate took Jesus and had him *f*
Acts		22.24 ordered him to be examined by *f*, to

FLOOD (FLOODS)

Gen		6.17 I am going to bring a *f* of waters on the
		9.11 never again shall there be a *f* to destroy
Ps		6. 6 every night I *f* my bed with my tears.
		29.10 The Lord sits enthroned over the *f*; the
Mt		7.27 The rain fell, and the *f* came, and the
Lk		17.27 ark, and the *f* came and destroyed all

FLOWING

Rev		22. 1 as crystal, *f* from the throne of God

FLOWER (FLOWERS)

Job		14. 2 comes up like a *f* and withers, flees like
Song		2.12 The *f* appear on the earth, the time of
Isa		40. 7 The grass withers, the *f* fades, when the

FLY (FLIES)

Ex		8.21 I will send swarms of *f* on you, your
Eccl		10. 1 Dead *f* make the perfumer's ointment
Isa		7.18 that day the Lord will whistle for the *f*

FOES

2 Sam		24.13 will you flee three months before your *f*
Ps		3. 1 O Lord, how many are my *f*! Many are
		108. 13 it is he who will tread down our *f*.
Mt		10.36 and one's *f* will be members of one's

FOLD

Jer		50. 6 have gone, they have forgotten their *f*.
Jn		10.16 sheep, that do not belong to this *f*.

FOLLOW

Lev		20.23 You shall not *f* the practices of the
		26. 3 If you *f* my statues and keep my
Deut		5.33 You must *f* exactly the path that the
		13. 4 your God you shall *f*, him alone you
1 Sam		8. 3 his sons did not *f* in his ways, but
1 Kings		18.21 If the Lord is God, *f* him; but if Baal,
2 Kings		10.31 Jehu was not careful to *f* the law of the
Ps		38.20 my adversaries because I *f* after good.
Eccl		11. 9 *F* the inclination of your heart and the
Ezek		11.20 they may *f* my statutes and keep my
		20.19 your God; *f* my statutes, and be careful
		37.24 They shall *f* my ordinances and be
Mt		4.19 "*F* me, and I will make you fish for
		8.19 "Teacher, I will *f* you wherever you go."
		8.22 "*F* me, and let the dead bury their own
		9. 9 tax booth; and he said to him, "*F* me.
Mk		2.14 tax booth; and he said to him, "*F* me.
		5.37 allowed no one to *f* him except Peter,
		15.41 These used to *f* him and provided for
Lk		5.27 tax booth; and he said to him, "*F* me.
		9.23 and take up their cross daily and *f*
		9.49 him, because he does not *f* with us."
		9.57 to him, "I will *f* you wherever you go."
		18.22 treasure in heaven; then come, *f* me."
Jn		1.43 He found Philip and said to him, "*F* me."
		10. 4 the sheep *f* him, because they know his
		10.27 my voice. I know them, and they *f* me.
		12.26 Whoever serves me, must *f* me, and
		13.37 "Lord, why can I not *f* you now? I will
		21.19 God.) After this he said to him, "*F* me."
Rom		4.12 who also *f* the example of the faith that

FOLLOWED (FOLLOWING)

Num		32.12 for they have unreservedly *f* the Lord.'
Josh		14. 8 yet I wholeheartedly *f* the Lord my God.
2 Kings		17.15 they *f* the nations that were around
Jer		9.14 but have stubbornly *f* their own hearts
Ezek		11.12 whose statutes you have not *f*, and
Mic		6.16 of Ahab, and you have *f* their counsels.
Mt		26.58 Peter was *f* him at a distance, as far as
Mk		1.18 they left their nets and *f* him.
		10.28 we have left everything and *f* you."
		14.54 Peter had *f* him at a distance, right into
Lk		18.28 we have left our homes and *f* you."
		22.54 house. But Peter was *f* at a distance.
Jn		1.40 John speak, and *f* him was Andrew,
		18.15 Peter and another disciple *f* Jesus.

FOLLOWERS

Mt		16.24 "If any want to become my *f*, let them
Mk		8.34 "If any want to become my *f*, let them

FOLLY (FOLLIES)

1 Sam		25.25 Nabal is his name, and *f* is with him;

Ps 73. 7 fatness; their hearts overflow with *f.*
Prov 24. 9 The devising of *f* is sin, and the scoffer
26.11 his vomit is a fool who reverts to his *f.*

FOOD (FOODS)

Gen 1.29 in its fruit; you shall have them for *f.*
3. 6 woman saw that the tree was good for *f,*
Num 21. 5 no *f* and no water, and we detest this
Lam 4. 4 children beg for *f,* but no one gives
Mt 15.26 It is not fair to take the children's *f* and
Mk 7.27 not fair to take the children's *f* and
Lk 12.23 For life is more than *f,* and the body
Jn 4.32 "I have *f* to eat that you do not know
1 Cor 6.13 "*F* is meant for the stomach and the
9. 4 not have the right to our *f* and drink?
1 Tim 4. 3 marriage and demand abstinence from *f,*
6. 8 have *f* and clothing, we will be content

FOOL (FOOLS)

1 Sam 26.21 I have been a *f,* and have made a great
2 Sam 3.33 saying, "Should Abner die as a *f* dies?
Job 5. 2 Surely vexation kills the *f,* and jealousy
Ps 14. 1 *F* say in their hearts, "There is no God."
49.10 *f* and dolt perish together and leave
53. 1 *F* say in their hearts, "There is no God."
Prov 10. 8 but a babbling *f* will come to ruin.
13.16 intelligently, but the *f* displays folly.
14. 7 Leave the presence of a *f,* for there you
14. 9 *F* mock at the guilt offering, but the
16.22 has it, but folly is the punishment of *f.*
17.12 of its cubs than to confront a *f* in folly.
24. 7 Wisdom is too high for *f;* in the gate
26. 1 in harvest, so honor is not fitting for a *f.*
26. 5 Answer *f* according to their folly, or they
Eccl 2.15 happens to the *f* will happen to me
4. 5 *F* fold their hands, and consume their
7.17 not be too wicked, and do not be a *f;*
Isa 35. 8 no traveler, not even *f,* shall go astray.
Mt 5.22 if you say, 'You *f!*' you will be liable to
Lk 11.40 You *f!* Did not the one who made the
12.20 'you *f!* This very night your life is being
Rom 1.22 Claiming to be wise, they became *f,* and
1 Cor 4.10 We are *f* for the sake of Christ, but you

FOOLISH

Isa 44.25 the wise, and makes their knowledge *f;*
Jer 4.22 "For my people are *f,* they do not know
Mt 7.26 will be like a *f* man who built his house
Lk 24.25 "Oh, how *f* you are, and how slow of

FOOLISHNESS

1 Cor 1.21 through the *f* of our proclamation,
2.14 of God's Spirit, for they are *f* to them,

FOOT (FEET)

Ps 2.12 with trembling kiss his *f,* or he will be
8. 6 you have put all things under their *f,*
119. 59 of your ways, turn my *f* to your decrees;
119.105 Your word is a lamp to my *f* and a light
121. 3 He will not let your *f* be moved, he who
Song 7. 1 How graceful are your *f* in sandals, O
Nah 1.15 mountains the *f* of one who brings good
Mt 22.44 until I put your enemies under your *f*" '?
28. 9 him, took hold of his *f,* and worshiped
Mk 9.45 if your *f* causes you to stumble, cut it
12.36 until I put your enemies under your *f.*" '
Lk 7.38 to bathe his *f* with her tears and to dry
10.39 Mary, who sat at the Lord's *f* and
24.39 Look at my hands and my *f;* see that it
Jn 12. 3 anointed Jesus' *f* and wiped them with
13. 5 began to wash the disciples' *f* and to
Rom 3.15 Their *f* are swift to shed blood, ruin and
1 Cor 12.15 If the *f* would say, "Because I am not a
15.25 he has put all his enemies under his *f.*

FOOT-RUNNERS

Jer 12. 5 If you have raced *f* and they have

FOOTSTOOL

Ps 110. 1 hand until I make your enemies your *f.*"
Isa 66. 1 is my throne and the earth is my *f;*
Lk 20.43 hand, until I make your enemies a *f.*" '
Acts 2.35 hand, until I make your enemies your *f.*" '
Heb 10.13 "until his enemies would be made a *f*

FORBEARANCE

Rom 3.25 in his divine *f* he passed over the sins

FORBID (FORBIDDEN)

1 Cor 14.39 and do not *f* speaking in tongues;
Acts 16. 6 been *f* by the Holy Spirit to speak the

FORCE (FORCED FORCES)

Deut 33.27 the ancient gods, shatters the *f* of old;
1 Sam 13.12 so I *f* myself, and offered the burnt
Prov 12.24 while the lazy will be put to *f* labor.
Mt 11.12 violence, and the violent take it by *f.*
Jn 6.15 and take him by *f* to make him king,
2 Cor 12.11 I have been a fool! You *f* me to it.

FOREHEAD (FOREHEADS)

Ezek 3. 7 have a hard *f* and a stubborn heart.
9. 4 and put a mark on the *f* of the those
Rev 13.16 to be marked on the right hand or the *f,*

FOREIGN

Ezra 10.11 have trespassed and married *f* women,
Ps 137. 4 we sing the LORD's song in a *f* land?

FOREIGNER (FOREIGNERS)

Deut 23.20 On loans to a *f* you may charge interest,
1 Kings 8.41 "Likewise when a *f,* who is not of your
Ezek 44. 7 to all your abominations in admitting *f,*
Lk 17.18 and give praise to God except this *f?*"
1 Cor 14.11 of a sound, I will be a *f* to the speaker

FOREKNEW

Rom 8.29 those whom he *f* he also predestined to
11. 2 has not rejected his people whom he *f.*

FOREKNOWLEDGE

Acts 2.23 definite plan and *f* of God, you crucified

FORFEIT (FORFEITED)

Deut 22. 9 the whole yield will have to be *f,* both
Mk 8.36 to gain the whole world and *f* their life?

FORGET (FORGETS FORGETTING FORGOT FORGOTTEN)

Gen 40.23 did not remember Joseph, but *f* him.
Deut 4.31 he will not *f* the covenant with your
6.12 take care that you do not *f* the LORD,
8.11 Take care that you do not *f* the LORD, by
Judg 3. 7 *f* the LORD their God, and worshiping
1 Sam 12. 9 they *f* the LORD their God; and he sold
Ps 10.11 They think in their heart, "God has *f,* he
42. 9 to God, my rock, "Why have you *f* me?
44.24 Why do you *f* our affliction and
44.17 come upon us, yet we have not *f* you
45.10 *f* your people and your father's house,
74.19 animals; do not *f* the life of your poor
77. 9 Has God *f* to be gracious? Has he in
103. 2 my soul, and do not *f* all his benefits —
106. 13 But they soon *f* his works; they did not
119. 16 in your statutes; I will not *f* your word.
137. 5 If I *f* you, O Jerusalem, let my right
Prov 2.17 of her youth and *f* her sacred covenant;
3. 1 My child, do not *f* my teaching, but let
31. 7 let them drink and *f* their poverty, and
Isa 17.10 you have *f* the God of your salvation,
44.21 my servant; O Israel, you will not be *f*
49.14 has forsaken me, my Lord has *f* me."
51.13 You have *f* the LORD, your Maker, who
65.11 the LORD, who *f* my holy mountain,
Jer 2.32 Yet my people have *f* me, days without
13.25 because you have *f* me and trusted
18.15 But my people have *f* me, they burn

Jer	23.27	plan to make my people *f* my name
	30.14	All your lovers have *f* you; they care
	50. 6	they have gone, they have *f* their fold.
Lam	5.20	Why have you *f* us completely? Why
Hos	4. 6	you have *f* the law of your God, I also
Mk	8.14	the disciples had *f* to bring bread; and
Lk	12. 6	Yet not one of them is *f* in God's sight.
Phil	3.13	I do; *f* what lies behind and straining

FORGIVE

Gen	50.17	I beg you, *f* the crime of your brothers
Ex	32.32	if you will only *f* their sin—but if not,
Num	14.19	*F* the iniquity of this people according
	14.20	said, "I do *f*, just as you have asked;
	30. 8	bound herself; and the LORD will *f* her.
Josh	24.19	God; he will not *f* your transgressions
1 Sam	25.28	Please *f* the trespass of your servant; for
1 Kings	8.30	heaven your dwelling place; heed and *f*.
	8.39	*f*, and act, and render to all whose
2 Chr	6.21	heaven your dwelling place; hear and *f*.
	7.14	and will *f* their sin and heal their land.
Ps	25.18	and my trouble, and *f* all my sins.
	79. 9	deliver us, and *f* our sins, for your
	85. 2	You *f* the iniquity of your people; you
Isa	2. 9	is brought low—-do not *f* them!
Jer	31.34	for I will *f* their iniquity, and remember
	33. 8	I will *f* all the guilt of their sin and
	36. 3	so that I may *f* their iniquity and their
Mt	6.12	And *f* us our debts, as we also have
	6.15	not *f* others, neither will your Father *f*
	18.35	one of you, if you do not *f* your brother
Mk	2. 7	Who can *f* sins but God alone?"
	11.25	Whenever you stand praying, *f*, if you
Lk	6.37	condemned. *F*, and you will be forgiven;
	11. 4	And *f* us our sins, for we ourselves *f*
	17. 3	and if there is repentance you must *f*.
	23.34	Jesus said, "Father, *f* them; for they do
Jn	20.23	If you *f* the sins of any, they are
2 Cor	2. 7	instead you should *f* and console him,
1 Jn	1. 9	and just will *f* us our sins and cleanse

FORGIVES (FORGAVE FORGIVEN FORGIVING)

Ex	34. 7	*f* iniquity and transgression and sin, yet
Lev	4.20	for them, and they shall be *f*.
	19.22	the sin he committed shall be *f* him.
Num	14.18	love, *f* iniquity and transgression,
	15.25	of the Israelites, and they shall be *f*;
Ps	32. 1	are those whose transgression is *f*,
	78.38	being compassionate, *f* their iniquity,
	99. 8	you were a *f* God to them, but an
	103. 3	who *f* all your iniquity, who heals all
Prov	17. 9	One who *f* an affront fosters friendship,
Isa	33.24	the people who live there will be *f* their
Lam	3.42	and rebelled, and you have not *f*.
Mt	9. 2	"Take heart, son; your sins are *f*."
	12.31	will be *f* for every sin and blasphemy,
	18.27	slave released him and *f* him the debt.
	18.32	You wicked slave! I *f* you all that debt
Mk	2. 5	to the paralytic, "Son, your sins are *f*."
	3.28	people will be *f* for their sins and
Lk	5.20	he said, "Friend, your sins are *f* you."
	12.10	a word against the Son of Man will be *f*;
Acts	2.38	Jesus Christ so that your sins may be *f*;
	8.22	the intent of your heart may be *f*
Rom	4. 7	are those whose iniquities are *f*,
Eph	4.32	one another, as God in Christ has *f* you.
Col	2.13	when he *f* us all our trespasses, erasing
1 Jn	2.12	your sins are *f* on account of his name.

FORGIVENESS

Ps	130. 4	But there is *f* with you, so that you may
Dan	9. 9	the Lord our God belong mercy and *f*,
Acts	10.43	everyone who believes in him receives *f*
	13.38	that through this man *f* of sins is
	26.18	so that they may receive *f* of sins and a
Col	1.14	we have redemption, the *f* of sins.
Heb	9.22	the shedding of blood there is no *f*

FORK

Jer	15. 7	winnowed them with a winnowing *f*
Lk	3.17	winnowing *f* is in his hand, to clear his

FORM (FORMED FORMS)

Gen	2. 7	God *f* man from the dust of the ground,
	2.19	God *f* every animal of the field and
Job	33. 6	are; I too was *f* from a piece of clay.
Isa	43. 1	you, O Jacob, he who *f* you, O Israel:
	44. 2	who made you, who *f* you in the womb
Jer	1. 5	"Before I *f* you in the womb I knew you,
Am	4.13	lo, the one who *f* the mountains,
Gal	4.19	of childbirth until Christ be *f* in you,
Acts	14.11	gods have come down to us in human *f*!"
1 Cor	7.31	the present *f* of this world is passing
Phil	2. 6	though he was in the *f* of God, did not
2 Tim	3. 5	holding to the outward *f* of godliness

FORMER

Isa	41.22	Tell us the *f* things, what they are, so
	48. 3	The *f* things I declared long ago, they

FORNICATION

Acts	15.20	to abstain only from . . . *f* and from

FORNICATORS

1 Cor	6. 9	Do not be deceived! *F*, idolaters,

FORSAKE (FORSAKEN FORSAKING)

Deut	31. 8	with you; he will not fail you or *f* you.
Josh	1. 5	be with you; I will not fail you or *f* you.
1 Sam	8. 8	*f* me and serving other gods, so also
1 Kings	9. 9	'Because they have *f* the LORD their
	11.33	because he has *f* me, worshiped Astarte
	18.18	because you have *f* the commandments
1 Chr	28. 9	but if you *f* him, he will abandon you
2 Chr	7.19	if you turn aside and *f* my statutes and
Ps	9.10	O LORD, have not *f* those who seek you.
	22. 1	My God, my God, why have you *f* me?
	27. 9	Do not cast me off, do not *f* me, O God
	37.25	yet I have not seen the righteous for *f*
	37.28	justice; he will not *f* his faithful ones.
	71.11	and seize that person whom God has *f*,
	94.14	For the LORD will not *f* his people; he
	119. 8	your statutes; do not utterly *f* me.
Prov	3. 3	not let loyalty and faithfulness *f* you;
	6.20	and do not *f* your mother's teaching.
Isa	1. 4	deal corruptly, who have *f* the LORD,
	1.28	who *f* the LORD shall be consumed.
	2. 6	you have *f* the ways of your people, O
	55. 7	let the wicked *f* their way, and the
Jer	1.16	them, for all their wickedness in *f* me;
	2.17	brought this upon yourself by *f* the LORD
	5.19	you have *f* me and served foreign gods
	16.11	It is because your ancestors have *f* me,
Ezek	8.12	not see us, the LORD has *f* the land.' "
Am	5. 2	maiden Israel; *f* on her land, with no
Mt	27.46	"My God, my God, why have you *f* me?"
Mk	15.34	"My God, my God, why have you *f* me?"
2 Cor	4. 9	persecuted, but not *f*; struck down, but

FORTRESS

Ps	31. 2	of refuge for me, a strong *f* to save me.
	31. 3	You are indeed my rock and my *f*; for
	59. 9	watch for you; for you, O God, are my *f*.
	144. 2	my rock and my *f*, my stronghold and
Prov	10.15	The wealth of the rich is their *f*; the
Dan	11.38	strongest *f* by the help of a foreign god.

FORTUNES

Deut	30. 3	God will restore your *f* and have
Job	42.10	LORD restored the *f* of Job, when he had
Ps	14. 7	When the LORD restores the *f* of his
	53. 6	When God restores the *f* of his people,
	85. 1	your land; you restored the *f* of Jacob.
	126. 1	When the LORD restored the *f* of Zion,
Jer	31.23	and in its towns when I restore their *f*:
	33. 7	I will restore the *f* of Judah and the *f* of

Am	9.14 I will restore the *f* of my people Israel,
Zeph	2. 7 be mindful of them and restore their *f*.
	3.20 when I restore your *f* before your eyes,

FORTY

Gen	7. 4 rain upon the earth *f* days and *f* nights;
Ex	24.18 on the mountain *f* days and *f* nights.
Num	14.33 shepherds in the wilderness for *f* years,
Deut	2. 7 These *f* years the LORD your God has
	9.11 At the end of *f* days and *f* nights the
	25. 3 *F* lashes may be given but not more; if
	29. 5 I have led you *f* years in the wilderness.

FOUNDATION (FOUNDATIONS)

Ezra	3. 6 But the *f* of the temple of the LORD was
	3.11 because the *f* of the house of the LORD
Job	38. 4 were you when I laid the *f* of the earth?
Ps	11. 3 If the *f* are destroyed, what can the
	18. 7 the earth reeled and rocked; the *f* also
	102. 25 Long ago you laid the *f* of the earth,
Isa	24.18 opened, and the *f* of the earth tremble.
	28.16 See, I am laying in Zion a *f* stone, a
	40.21 not understood from the *f* of the earth?
	54.11 antimony, and lay your *f* with sapphires.
Hag	2.18 the day that the *f* of the LORD's temple
Mt	13.35 been hidden from the *f* of the world."
Rom	15.20 that I do not build on someone else's *f*,
1 Cor	3.11 no one can lay any *f* other than the one
2 Tim	2.19 But God's firm *f* stands, bearing this

FOUNDED

Ps	24. 2 he has *f* it upon the seas, and
Prov	3.19 The LORD by wisdom *f* the earth; by

FOUNTAIN (FOUNTAINS)

Gen	7.11 all the *f* of the great deep burst forth,
Ps	36. 9 with you is the *f* of life; in your light we
Prov	14.27 The fear of the LORD is a *f* of life, so
	16.22 Wisdom is a *f* of life to one who has it,
	18. 4 waters; the *f* of wisdom is a gushing
	25.26 Like a muddied spring or a polluted *f*
Eccl	12. 6 pitcher is broken at the *f*, and the
Song	4.12 my bride, a garden locked, a *f* sealed.
Jer	2.13 they have forsaken me, the *f* of living
	9. 1 of water, and my eyes a *f* of tears,
	17.13 forsaken you the *f* of living water, the LORD.
Joel	3.18 a *f* shall come forth from the house of
Zech	13. 1 that day a *f* shall be opened for the

FOX (FOXES)

Judg	15. 4 and caught three hundred *f*, and took
Neh	4. 3 *f* going up on it would break
Song	2.15 Catch us the *f*, the little *f*, that spoil the
Mt	8.20 "*F* have holes, and birds of the air have
Lk	9.58 "*F* have holes, and birds of the air have
	13.32 "Go and tell that *f* for me, 'Listen, I am

FRAGRANCE

Song	7.13 The mandrakes give forth *f*, and over
2 Cor	2.14 the *f* that comes from knowing him.

FRANKINCENSE

Isa	60. 6 They shall bring gold and *f*, and shall
Mt	2.11 they offered him gifts of gold, *f*, and

FREE (FREED)

Gen	44.10 my slave, but the rest of you shall go *f*.
Ex	21. 5 children; I will not go out a *f* person,"
Num	32.22 and be *f* of obligation to the LORD and
Deut	15.13 a male slave out from you a *f* person
Ps	146. 7 The LORD sets the prisoners *f*; the LORD
Ezek	13.20 and the lives go *f*, the lives that you
Lk	1.64 his tongue *f*, and he began to speak,
Jn	8.32 the truth and the truth will make you *f*.'
	8.36 So if the Son makes you *f*, you will be *f*
Acts	13.39 you could not be *f* by the law of Moses.
Rom	5.15 But the *f* gift is not like the trespass.
	6. 7 For whoever has died is *f* from sin. But

Rom	6.18 you, having been set *f* from sin, have
1 Cor	7.39 the husband dies, she is *f* to marry
2 Cor	11. 7 God's good news to you *f* of charge?
Gal	1. 4 our sins to set us *f* from the present evil
	3.28 or Greek, there is no longer slave or *f*,
Heb	2.15 *f* those who all their lives were held in
Rev	1. 5 us and *f* us from our sins by his blood,

FREEDOM

Rom	8.21 and will obtain the *f* of glory of the
1 Cor	7.21 Even if you can gain your *f*, make use
2 Cor	3.17 the Spirit of the Lord is, there is *f*.
Gal	2. 4 in to spy on the *f* we have in Christ
	5. 1 For *f* Christ has set us free. Stand firm,
	5.13 you were called to *f*, brothers and
1 Pet	2.16 yet do not use your *f* as pretext for evil.
2 Pet	2.19 They promise them *f*, but they

FREELY

Gen	2.16 "You may *f* eat of every tree of the
Prov	11.24 Some give *f*, yet grow all the richer;

FREEWILL OFFERING (FREEWILL OFFERINGS)

Lev	7.16 or a *f*, it shall be eaten on the day that
Deut	16.10 contributing a *f* in proportion to the
Ezra	1. 4 animals, besides *f* for the house of God
	2.68 of families made *f* for the house of God,

FRIEND (FRIENDS)

Ex	33.11 face to face, as one speaks to a *f*.
Judg	5.31 may your *f* be like the sun as it rises in
2 Chr	20. 7 to the descendants of your *f* Abraham?
Job	6.14 "Those who withhold kindness from a *f*
	6.27 the orphan, and bargain over your *f*.
	16.20 My *f* scorn me; my eye pours out tears
	19.14 relatives and my close *f* have failed me;
	42.10 of Job when he had prayed for his *f*;
Ps	35.14 my bosom, as though I grieved for my *f*
	41. 9 Even my bosom *f* in whom I trusted,
	55.13 my equal, my companion, my familiar *f*,
	88.18 have caused *f* and neighbor to shun me;
Prov	16.28 strife, and a whisperer separates close *f*.
	17.17 A *f* loves at all times, and kinsfolk are
	18.24 Some *f* play at friendship but a true *f*
	19. 4 Wealth brings many *f*, but the poor are
	19. 6 generous, and everyone is a *f* to a giver
	22.24 Make no *f* with those given to anger,
	27. 6 Well meant are the wounds a *f* inflicts,
Jer	3. 4 "My father, you are the *f* of my
Mic	7. 5 Put no trust in a *f*, have no confidence
Mt	11.19 a *f* of tax collectors and sinners!'
	20.13 '*F*, I am doing you no wrong; did you
	26.50 to him, "*F*, do what you are here to do."
Mk	5.19 "Go home to your *f*, and tell them how
Lk	7.34 and a drunkard, a *f* of tax collectors and
	11. 5 '*F*, lend me three loaves of bread; for a
	12. 4 my *f*, do not fear those who kill the
	14.10 say to you, '*F*, move up higher'; then
	16. 9 make *f* by means of dishonest wealth so
Jn	11.11 "Our *f* Lazarus has fallen asleep, but I
	15.13 this, to lay down one's life for one's *f*.
	19.12 this man, you are no *f* of the emperor.
2 Cor	11. 9 needs were supplied by the *f* who came
Jas	2.23 and he was called the *f* of God.

FRIENDSHIP

Job	29. 4 when the *f* of God was upon my tent;
Ps	25.14 The *f* of the LORD is for those who fear
Jas	4. 4 know that *f* with the world is enmity

FRIGHTENED

Dan	4. 5 I saw a dream that *f* me. My fantasies
Mt	2. 3 When king Herod heard this, he was *f*,
Lk	24.38 "Why are you *f*, and why do doubts arise

FRINGE

Mt	9.20 him and touched the *f* of his cloak,

Mt 14.36 might touch even the *f* of his cloak;

FROGS

Ex 8. 2 I will plague your whole country with *f*.
Ps 105. 30 Their land swarmed with *f*, even in the

FRUIT (FRUITS)

Num 13.26 and showed them the *f* of the land.
Deut 30. 9 in the *f* of your body, in the *f* of your
Ps 1. 3 water, which yield their *f* in its season,
Prov 1.31 they shall eat the *f* of their way
8.19 My *f* is better than gold, even fine gold,
11.30 The *f* of the righteous is a tree of life,
Song 4.13 of pomegranates with all choicest *f*,
Jer 21.14 you according to the *f* of your doings,
Mic 6. 7 the *f* of my body for the sin of my soul?"
Hab 3.17 not blossom, and no *f* is on the vines;
Mt 7.16 You will know them by their *f*. Are
21.43 that produces the *f* of the kingdom."
Mk 4.20 hear the word and accept it and bear *f*,
11.14 "May no one ever eat *f* from you again."
Lk 1.42 and blessed is the *f* of your womb!
3. 9 not bear good *f* is cut down and thrown
6.43 "No good tree bears bad *f*, nor again
8.15 and bear *f* with patient endurance.
Jn 12.24 grain; but if it dies, it bears much *f*.
15. 5 abide in me and I in them bear much *f*,
Gal 5.22 the *f* of the Spirit is love, joy, peace,
Col 1.10 as you bear *f* in every good work and as
Heb 12.11 it yields the peaceful *f* of righteousness
Rev 18.14 *f* for which your soul longed has gone
22. 2 twelve kinds of *f*, producing its *f* each

FRUSTRATE (FRUSTRATES)

Ezra 4. 5 they bribed officials to *f* their plan
Job 5.12 He *f* the devices of the crafty, so that

FUGITIVE

Gen 4.12 you will be a *f* and a wanderer on the

FULFILL (FULFILLED FULFILLING FULFILLS)

Gen 26. 3 I will *f* the oath that I swore to your
Deut 9. 5 to *f* the promise which the LORD made
1 Kings 2.27 thus *f* the word of the LORD that he had
2 Chr 6.10 the LORD has *f* his promise that he
36.21 to *f* the word of the LORD by the mouth
Ps 20. 5 May the LORD *f* all your petitions.
138. 8 The LORD will *f* his purpose for me; your
145. 19 He *f* the desire of all who fear him; he
Jer 28. 6 may the LORD *f* the words that you have
33.14 I will *f* the promise I made to the house
Mt 3.15 for us in this way to *f* all righteousness."
5.17 I have come not to abolish but to *f*.
8.17 *f* what had been spoken through the
21. 4 took place to *f* what had been spoken
26.56 scriptures of the prophets might be *f*."
Mk 1.15 "The time is *f*, and the kingdom of God
14.49 arrest me. But let the scriptures be *f*."
15.28n the scripture was *f* that says, "And he
Lk 1. 1 the events that have been *f* among us,
4.21 "Today this scripture has been *f* in your
22.16 I will not eat it until it is *f* in the
24.44 the prophets, and the psalms must be *f*."
Jn 3.29 For this reason my joy has been *f*.
17.12 be lost, so that the scripture might be *f*.
19.24 get it." This was to *f* what the scripture
Rom 9.31 the law, did not succeed in *f* that law.
13. 8 who loves one another has *f* the law.

FULL

Isa 6. 3 hosts; the whole earth is *f* of his glory."
Rom 11.25 until the *f* number of the Gentiles
Jas 1. 4 let endurance have its *f* effect, so that

FULLY

Lk 6.40 everyone who is *f* qualified will be like

FULLERS'

Mal 3. 2 he is like refiner's fire and like *f* soap;

FULLNESS

Jn 1.16 From his *f* have we all received, grace
Rom 15.29 you, I will come in the *f* of the blessing
Gal 4. 4 But when the *f* of time had come, God
Eph 3.19 you may be filled with all the *f* of God.
Col 2. 9 in him the whole *f* of deity dwells
2.10 you have come to *f* in him, who is the

FURNACE

Ps 12. 6 that are pure, silver refined in a *f*
21. 9 You will make them like a fiery *f* when
Prov 27.21 is for silver, and the *f* is for gold,
Isa 31. 9 is in Zion, and whose *f* is in Jerusalem.
48.10 I have tested you in the *f* of adversity.
Dan 3.19 He ordered the *f* heated up seven times
Mt 13.42 they will throw them into the *f* of fire,

FURY

Isa 42.13 a soldier, like a warrior he stirs up his *f*;
Ezek 21.17 strike hand to hand, I will satisfy my *f*;
Lk 6.11 they were filled with *f* and discussed

FUTILE

Isa 1.13 courts no more; bringing offerings is *f*;
Rom 1.21 they became *f* in their thinking, and
1 Cor 15.17 your faith is *f* and you are still in your

FUTILITY

Rom 8.20 creation was subjected to *f*, not of its
Eph 4.17 Gentiles live, in the *f* of their minds.

G

GABRIEL

Dan 8.16 "*G*, help this man understand the
9.21 in prayer, the man *G*, whom I had seen
Lk 1.19 "I am *G*. I stand in the presence of God,
1.26 In the sixth month the angel *G* was

GAD

Gen 30.11 "Good fortune!" so she named him *G*.
46.16 The children of *G*: Ziphion, Haggi,
Deut 33.20 he said: Blessed be the enlargement of *G*!

GADITES

Num 32.33 Moses gave to them—to the *G* and to

GAIN (GAINED GAINING)

Ps 119. 36 my heart to your decrees, and not to *g*.
Prov 1. 3 for *g* instruction in wise dealing,
9. 9 righteous and they will *g* in learning.
Eccl 1. 3 What do people *g* from all the toil at
2.11 was nothing to be *g* under the sun.
5.16 go and what *g* do they have for toiling
Mic 4.13 devote their *g* to the LORD, their wealth
Hab 2. 9 Alas for you who get evil *g* for your
Mt 16.26 it profit them if they *g* the whole world
Lk 9.25 find out what that had *g* by trading.
19.15 find out what that had *g* by trading.
2 Cor 12. 1 to boast; nothing is to be *g* by it, but I
Phil 1.21 to me, living is Christ and dying is *g*.
3. 8 as rubbish, in order that I may *g* Christ

GALATIA

Acts 16. 6 through the region of Phrygia and *G*,
18.23 through the region of *G* and Phrygia,
1 Cor 16. 1 directions I gave to the churches of *G*.
Gal 1. 2 To the churches of *G*: Grace to you and
1 Pet 1. 1 exiles of the Dispersion in Pontus, *G*,

GALILEAN

Mt 26.69 said, "You also were with Jesus the *G*."
Mk 14.70 you are one of them; for you are a *G*.
Lk 23. 6 he asked whether the man was a *G*.

GALILEE

Josh	20.	7 they set apart Kedesh in *G* in the hill
Isa	9.	1 the land beyond the Jordan, *G* of the
Mt	2.22	he went away to the district of *G*.
	4.12	has been arrested, he withdrew to *G*.
	4.15	across the Jordan, *G* of the Gentiles —
Mk	3.	7 a great multitude from *G* followed him;
	16.	7 he is going ahead of you to *G*; there you
Lk	2.	4 went up from the town of Nazareth in *G*
Jn	2.	1 there was a wedding in Cana in *G*, and
	4.	3 he left Judea and started back to *G*.
	7.52	you not also from *G*, are you? Search
Acts	1.11	"Men of *G*, why do you stand looking

GALLIO

Acts	18.12	But when *G* was proconsul of Achaia,
	18.17	But *G* paid no attention to any of these

GALLOWS

Esth	5.14	"Let a *g* fifty cubits high be made, and

GAMALIEL

Acts	5.34	Pharisee in the council named *G*, a
	22.	3 brought up in this city at the feet of *G*,

GAME

Gen	27.	3 go out to the field, and hunt *g* for me.

GAP

Neh	6.	1 the wall and there was no *g* left in it

GARDEN

Gen	2.	8 God planted a *g* in Eden, in the east;
	13.10	everywhere like the *g* of the LORD,
Song	4.12	A *g* locked is my sister, my bride, a *g*
Isa	1.30	leaf withers, and like a *g* without water.
Ezek	28.13	You were in Eden, the *g* of God; every
	31.	8 The cedars in the *g* of God could not
	36.35	desolate has become like the *g* of Eden;
Joel	2.	3 them the land is like the *g* of Eden,
Jn	19.41	where he was crucified, and in the *g*

GARDENER

Jn	20.15	Supposing him to be the *g*, she said to

GARLAND

Isa	28.	1 the proud *g* of the drunkards of
	28.	5 the LORD of hosts will be a *g* of glory,

GARLIC

Num	11.	5 the leeks, the onions, and the *g*;

GARMENT (GARMENTS)

Gen	3.21	God made *g* of skins for the man and
	39.13	saw that he had left his *g* in her hand,
Deut	22.	5 nor shall a man put on a woman's *g*;
Job	13.28	rotten thing, like a *g* that is moth-eaten.
Prov	20.16	Take the *g* of the one who has given
Eccl	9.	8 Let your *g* be always white; do not let
Song	5.	3 I had put off my *g*, how could I put it
Lk	5.36	"No one tears a piece from a new *g* and

GATE (GATES)

Neh	2.13	down and its *g* that had been destroyed
Job	38.17	Have the *g* of death been revealed to
Ps	24.	7 Lift up your heads, O *g*! and be lifted
	122.	7 standing within your *g*, O Jerusalem!
Isa	26.	2 Open the *g*, so that the righteous nation
Mk	13.29	you know that he is near, at the very *g*.
Jn	10.	7 I tell you, I am the *g* for the sheep.
	10.	9 I am the *g*; whoever enters by me will
Heb	13.12	Jesus also suffered outside the city *g* in

GATEWAY

Gen	19.	1 Lot was sitting in the *g* of Sodom.

GATHER (GATHERED GATHERING GATHERS)

Gen	1.	9 "Let the waters . . . be *g* together into
	41.35	Let them *g* all the food of these good

Ex	16.16	"*G* as much of it as each of you needs,
Num	15.32	found a man *g* sticks on the sabbath
Deut	30.	4 there the LORD your God will *g* you,
Ps	106.	47 God, and *g* us from among the nations,
	107.	3 and *g* in from the lands, from the east
Prov	10.	5 A child who *g* in summer is prudent,
Eccl	2.	8 I also *g* for myself silver and gold and
Isa	49.	5 him, and that Israel might be *g* to him,
	56.	8 who *g* the outcasts of Israel, I will
Jer	4.	5 and say, "*G* together, and let us go
	9.22	the reaper, and no one shall *g* them."
	23.	3 I myself will *g* the remnant of my flock
	29.14	*g* you from all the nations and all the
	31.10	who scattered Israel will *g* him, and will
	32.37	I am going to *g* them from all the lands
Ezek	22.19	dross, I will *g* you into the midst of
Joel	3.11	nations all around, *g* yourselves there.
Mic	7.	1 who, after the summer fruit has been *g*,
Zeph	3.19	I will save the lame and *g* the outcast,
Mt	12.30	whoever does not *g* with me scatters.
	18.20	two or three are *g* in my name, I am
Mk	13.27	and *g* his elect from the four winds,
Lk	11.23	whoever does not *g* with me scatters.
	13.34	I have *g* your children together as a hen
Jn	6.12	"*G* up the fragments left over, so that
	11.52	to *g* into one the dispersed children of
Eph	1.10	of time, to *g* up all things in him,

GAZA

Gen	10.19	extended from Sidon . . . as far as *G*,
Judg	1.18	Judah took *G* with its territory,
	16.	1 Samson went to *G*, where he saw a
Zech	9.	5 shall see it and be afraid; *G* too,
Acts	8.26	that goes down from Jerusalem to *G*."

GENEALOGY (GENEALOGIES)

Mt	1.	1 An account of the *g* of Jesus the
1 Tim	1.	4 with myths and endless *g* that promote
Heb	7.	3 father, without mother, without *g*,

GENERATION (GENERATIONS)

Gen	2.	4 are the *g* of the heavens and the earth
Ps	100.	5 forever, and his faithfulness to all *g*.
Eccl	1.	4 A *g* goes, and a *g* comes, but the earth
Mt	12.39	evil and adulterous *g* asks for a sign,
Mk	8.38	words in this adulterous and sinful *g*,

GENEROUS (GENEROUSLY)

Ps	112.	5 It is well with those who deal *g* and
Acts	2.46	ate their food with glad and *g* hearts,
2 Cor	8.	9 For you know the *g* act of our Lord
1 Tim	6.18	good, to be rich in good works, *g*, and

GENTILE (GENTILES)

Mt	10.	5 "Go nowhere among the *G*, and enter
Mk	7.26	the woman was a *G*, of Syrophoenician
Acts	4.25	'Why did the *G* rage, and the peoples
	11.18	even to the *G* the repentance that leads
Gal	3.	8 that God would justify the *G* by faith,

GENTLE

Mt	11.29	I am *g* and humble in heart, and you
1 Thess	2.	7 we were *g* among you, like a nurse
Titus	3.	2 avoid quarrelling, to be *g*, and to show
1 Pet	3.	4 lasting beauty of a *g* and quiet spirit,

GENTLENESS

1 Cor	4.21	a stick, or with love in a spirit of *g*?
2 Cor	10.	1 you by the meekness and *g* of Christ —
Gal	6.	1 restore such a one in a spirit of *g*.
Eph	4.	2 called, with all humility and *g*, with

GENUINENESS

1 Pet	1.	7 so that the *g* of your faith, — being more

GET (GETTING GOT)

Lk	15.27	he has *g* him back safe and sound.'
	18.30	who will not *g* back very much more in
	23.41	we are *g* what we deserve for our deeds,

GETHSEMANE

Mt	26.36 went with them to a place called *G*;
Mk	14.32 They went a place which was called *G*;

GHOST

Mt	14.26 they were terrified, saying, "It is a *g*!"
Mk	6.49 on the sea, they thought it was a *g*,
Lk	24.37 and thought that they were seeing a *g*.

GIBEAH

Judg	19.12 of Israel; but we will continue on to *G*."
1 Sam	10.26 Saul also went to his home at *G*, and
	14.16 Saul's lookouts in *G* of Benjamin were
Isa	10.29 Ramah trembles, *G* of Saul has fled.

GIDEON

Judg	6.11 as his son *G* was beating out wheat in
	7. 1 (that is, *G*) and all the troops that were
	7.19 *G* and the hundred who were with him
	8. 4 Then *G* came to the Jordan and crossed
	8.23 *G* said to them, "I will not rule over
	8.32 *G* the son of Joash died at a good old
Heb	11.32 time would fail me to tell of *G*, Barak,

GIFT (GIFTS)

Gen	33.11 Please accept my *g* that I brought you,
Num	8.19 I have given the Levites as a *g* to Aaron
1 Sam	2.20 by this woman for the *g* that she made
Ps	45.12 of Tyre will seek your favor with *g*,
	68.18 receiving *g* among the people, even
	68.29 at Jerusalem kings bear *g* to you.
	72.10 the kings of Sheba and Seba bring *g*.
Prov	18.16 A *g* opens doors; it gives access to the
	21.14 A *g* in secret averts anger; and a
Eccl	3.13 God's *g* that all should eat and drink
Isa	1.23 Everyone loves a bribe and runs after *g*.
Mt	7.11 If you . . . know how to give good *g* to
Lk	11.13 who are evil, know how to give good *g*
	21. 1 people putting their *g* in the treasury;
Acts	2.38 you will receive the *g* of the Holy Spirit.
	8.20 you could obtain *g* of God with money!
	11.17 then God gave them the same *g* that he
Rom	4. 4 wages are not reckoned as a *g* but as
	6.23 but the free *g* of God is eternal life in
	12. 6 We have *g* that differ according to the
1 Cor	7. 7 each has a particular *g* from God, one
	12. 4 there are varieties of *g*, but the same
	14. 1 love and strive for the spiritual *g*,
	16. 3 with letters to take your *g* to Jerusalem.
2 Cor	9.15 be to God for his indescribable *g*!
Eph	3. 7 according to the *g* of God's grace
	4. 7 according to the measure of Christ's *g*.
Phil	4.17 Not that I seek the *g*; but I seek the
1 Tim	4.14 Do not neglect the *g* that is in you,
Heb	2. 4 and by *g* of the Holy Spirit, distributed
1 Pet	4.10 serve one another with whatever *g* each

GILEAD

Gen	31.21 his face toward the hill country of *G*.
Deut	3.15 To Machir I gave *G*.
	34. 1 him the whole land: *G* as far as Dan,
Josh	12. 2 of the Ammonites, that is, half of *G*,
Ps	60. 7 *G* is mine, and Manasseh is mine;
Jer	8.22 Is there no balm in *G*? Is there no

GILGAL

Josh	4.19 they camped in *G* on the east border of
	10. 9 having marched up all night from *G*.
1 Sam	7.16 on a circuit year by year to Bethel, *G*,
	13. 4 were called out to join Saul at *G*.
Am	4. 4 to *G*—and multiply transgression;

GIRD (GIRDED)

Ex	29. 5 and *g* him with the decorated band of
2 Sam	22.40 For you *g* me with strength for the
Ps	45. 3 *G* your sword on your thigh, O mighty

GIRL (GIRLS GIRL'S)

Judg	19. 4 the *g* father, made him stay, and he
2 Kings	5. 2 had taken a young *g* captive from the
Prov	30.19 seas, and the way of a man with a *g*.
Zech	8. 5 city shall be of boys and *g* playing in its
Mt	9.24 away; for the *g* is not dead but sleeping."

GIVE

Gen	13.15 all the land that you see I will *g* to you
Ex	22.29 firstborn of your sons you shall *g* to me.
	30.15 *g* more, and the poor shall not *g* less,
Deut	1.35 the good land which I swore to *g* to
	6.10 to Jacob, to *g* you—a land with fine,
	28.65 LORD will *g* you a trembling heart,
Judg	8. 5 "Please *g* some loaves of bread to my
1 Sam	28.19 the LORD will *g* Israel along with you
2 Kings	12.11 They would *g* the money that was
Ps	16.10 you do not *g* me up to Sheol, or let
	105. 11 "To you I will *g* the land of Canaan as
	119. 34 *G* me understanding, that I may keep
Prov	21.26 covet, but the righteous *g* and do not
	23.26 My child, *g* me your heart, and let your
Hos	11. 8 How can I *g* you up, Ephraim? How can
Mt	6.11 *G* us this day our daily bread.
	14.16 go away; you *g* them something to eat."
	16.19 I *g* you the keys of the kingdom of
	22.21 "*G* therefore to the emperor the things
Mk	6.37 them, "You *g* them something to eat."
	12.17 them, "*G* to the emperor the things that
Lk	6.38 *g*, and it will be given to you. A good
	14.33 my disciple if you do not *g* up all of
	20.25 "Then *g* to the emperor the things that
Jn	4. 7 and Jesus said to her, "*G* me a drink."
	6.34 said to him, "Sir, *g* us this bread always."
	10.28 I *g* them eternal life, and they will never
	14.16 he will *g* you another Advocate, to be
Acts	20.35 said, 'It is more blessed to *g* than to
Rom	8.32 will he not with him also *g* us
1 Cor	7. 3 husband should *g* to his wife her
Eph	1.17 of glory, may *g* you a spirit of wisdom

GIVES (GAVE GIVEN GIVING)

Num	21.34 of him, for I have *g* him into your hand,
Deut	2.33 our God *g* him over to us; and we
2 Chr	13.16 and God *g* them into their hands.
Judg	16.23 "Our god has *g* Samson our enemy into
Job	1.21 the LORD *g*, and the LORD has taken
	35.10 is God my Maker, who *g* strength
Ps	37.21 the righteous are generous and keep *g*;
	68.11 The Lord *g* the command; great is the
	136. 25 who *g* food to all flesh, for his steadfast
Prov	2. 6 For the LORD *g* wisdom; from his mouth
	12.26 The righteous *g* good advice to friends,
	28.27 Whoever *g* to the poor lack nothing, but
Eccl	2.26 the one who pleases him God *g* wisdom
	12. 7 and the breath returns to God who *g* it.
Mt	13.12 For to those who have, more will be *g*,
	15. 5 might have had from me is *g* to God,'
Mk	4.25 For those who have, more will be *g*; and
Lk	8.18 to those who have, more will be *g*; and
	12.48 whom much has been *g*, much will be
Jn	5.22 one but has *g* all judgment to the Son,
2 Cor	9. 9 "He scatters abroad, he *g* to the poor;
Gal	1. 4 Christ, who *g* himself for our sins to set
	2.20 who loved me and *g* himself for me.
Phil	4.15 shared with me in the matter of *g*
1 Jn	3.24 in us, by the Spirit that he has *g* us.

GLAD

Ps	9. 2 I will be *g* and exult in you; I will sing
	40.16 may all who seek you rejoice and be *g*
	46. 4 a river whose streams make *g* the city of
	105. 38 Egypt was *g* when they departed, for
	122. 1 I was glad when they said to me, "Let us
Prov	15.13 A *g* heart makes a cheerful
Isa	25. 9 let us be *g* and rejoice in his salvation.

Isa 65.18 But be g and rejoice forever in what I
Phil 2.17 of your faith, I am g and rejoice with all

GLADNESS

Esth 9.19 of Adar as a day of g and feasting,
Ps 4. 7 You have put more g in my heart more
100. 2 Worship the LORD with g; come into his
Isa 16.10 Joy and g are taken away from the
61. 3 ashes, the oil of g instead of mourning,
Jer 7.34 to an end the sound of mirth and g,

GLORIFY (GLORIFIED)

Ezra 7.27 of the king to g the house of the LORD
Ps 50.15 I will deliver you, and you shall g me."
Isa 44.23 redeemed Jacob, and will be g in Israel.
49. 3 my servant, Israel, in whom I will be g."
55. 5 the Holy One of Israel, for he has g you.
60. 7 my altar, and I will g my glorious house.
Lk 5.26 they g God and were filled with awe,
7.16 they g God, saying, "A great prophet has
Jn 7.39 no Spirit, because Jesus was not yet g.
12.28 Father, g your name." Then a voice came
13.31 said, "Now the Son of Man has been g
14.13 so that the Father may be g in the Son.
15. 8 Father is g by this, that you bear much
17. 1 the hour has come; g your Son so that
Rom 11.13 apostle to the Gentiles. I g my ministry
1 Cor 6.20 a price; therefore g God in your body.
Rev 15. 4 who will not fear and g your name?

GLORIOUS (GLORIOUSLY)

Ps 87. 3 G things are spoken of you, O city of
Isa 12. 5 praises to the LORD, for he has done g;

GLORY

Ex 16. 7 you shall see the g of the LORD, because
24.16 The g of the LORD settled on Mount
40.34 the g of the LORD filled the tabernacle.
Num 14.21 shall be filled with the g of the LORD
16.19 the g of the LORD appeared to the whole
Deut 5.24 God has shown us his g and greatness,
Josh 7.19 give g to the LORD God of Israel and
1 Sam 4.21 "The g has departed from Israel,"
15.29 the G of Israel will not recant or change
1 Kings 8.11 for the g of the LORD filled the house of
1 Chr 16.24 Declare his g among the nations, his
29.11 are the greatness, the power, the g,
2 Chr 5.14 for the g of the LORD filled the house of
Ps 8. 1 You have set your g above the heavens.
19. 1 heavens are telling the g of God; and
21. 5 His g is great through your help;
29. 1 beings, ascribe to the LORD g and
97. 6 and all the peoples behold his g.
106. 47 to your holy name and g in your praise.
115. 1 but to your name give g, for the sake of
Isa 24.15 Therefore in the east give g to the LORD;
35. 2 The g of Lebanon shall be given to it,
35. 2 They shall see the g of the LORD, the
40. 5 the g of the LORD shall be revealed,
42. 8 my g I give to no other, nor my praise
Jer 33. 9 a g before all the nations of the earth
Ezek 1.28 of the likeness of the g of the LORD.
3.12 me up, and as the g of the LORD rose
3.23 and the g of the LORD stood there, like
9. 3 the g of the God of Israel had gone up
10.18 the g of the LORD went out from the
28.22 O Sidon, and I will gain g in your midst
39.21 I will display my g among the nations;
43. 2 And there, the g of the God of Israel
Dan 7.14 was given dominion and g and kingship,
Hab 2.14 the knowledge of the g of the LORD,
Mt 24.30 of heaven' with power and great g.
Lk 2.14 "G to God in the highest heaven , and
Jn 5.41 I do accept g from human beings.
7.18 speak on their own seek their own g;
8.50 Yet I do not seek my own g; there is
11. 4 lead to death; rather it is for God's g,

Jn 12.43 for they loved human g more than the g
17. 5 with the g that I had in your presence
17.24 to see my g which you have given me
Rom 1.23 exchanged the g of the immortal God
3.23 sinned and fall short of the g of God;
8.18 not worth comparing with the g about
11.36 things. To him be the g forever. Amen.
1 Cor 15.43 It is sown in dishonor, it is raised in g.
2 Cor 3.11 more has the permanent come in g.
Phil 3.21 may be conformed to the body of his g,
Col 1.27 which is Christ in you, the hope of g.
2 Thess 1. 9 of the Lord and from the g of his might,
2.14 that you may obtain the g of our Lord
2 Pet 1. 3 of him who called by his own g
Rev 7.12 "Amen! Blessing and g and wisdom and
14. 7 "Fear God and give him g, for the hour

GNASH (GNASHED GNASHING)

Job 16. 9 and hated me; he has g his teeth at me;
Ps 35.16 and more, g at me with their teeth.
Lam 2.16 they hiss, they g their teeth, they cry:
Mt 24.51 there will be weeping and g of teeth.

GNAT (GNATS)

Ex 8.16 become g throughout the whole land
Mt 23.24 guides, You strain out a g but swallow

GO (GOING)

Gen 7. 1 "G into the ark, you and all your
24.58 "Will you g with this man?" She said, "I
Ex 5. 1 'Let my people g, so that they may
9.13 'Let my people g, so that they may
Num 14. 4 choose a captain, and g back to Egypt."
2 Kings 5.10 "G, wash in the Jordan seven times, and
Ps 143. 8 Teach me the way I should g, for to you
Eccl 5.15 they shall g again, naked as they came,
Isa 2. 3 "Come, let us g up to the mountain of
6. 9 "G, and say to this people: 'Keep
48.20 G out from Babylon, flee from Chaldea,
Jer 42. 3 show us where we should g and what
Hos 11.10 They shall g after the LORD, who roars
Am 7.15 LORD said to me, 'G, prophesy to my
Mic 4. 2 "Come, let us g up to the mountain of
Mal 3.14 or by g about as mourners before the
Mt 6. 6 whenever you pray, g into your room
28. 7 Then g quickly and tell his disciples,
28.19 G therefore and make disciples of all
Mk 5.19 "G home to your friends, and tell them
16. 7 But g, tell his disciples and Peter that
16.15n "G into all the world and proclaim the
Lk 9.60 as for you, g and proclaim the kingdom
Jn 6.68 "Lord, to whom can we g? You have the

GOADS

Eccl 12.11 sayings of the wise are like g, and like
Acts 26.14 me? It hurts you to kick against the g.'

GOAL

Phil 3.12 this or have already reached the g;

GOAT-DEMONS

Lev 17. 7 no longer offer their sacrifices for g,
2 Chr 11.15 for the high places, and for the g,
Isa 34.14 with hyenas, g shall call to each other;

GOD

Gen 1. 1 when G created the heavens and
3. 5 and you will be like G, knowing good
8. 1 G remembered Noah and all the wild
50.25 "When G comes to you, you shall carry
Ex 2.24 G heard their groaning, and G
13.17 G did not lead them by way of the land
Josh 10.42 the LORD God of Israel fought for Israel.
2 Sam 7.23 on earth whose G went to redeem it as
1 Kings 8.28 O LORD my G, heeding the cry and the
11.23 G raised up another adversary against
2 Chr 36.15 The LORD, the G of their ancestors, sent
36.16 they kept mocking the messengers of G,

Ps	8.	5 have made them a little lower than *G*,
	22.	1 *G*, my *G*, why have you forsaken me?
Isa	12.	2 the LORD *G* is my strength and my
	26.	4 LORD *G* you have an everlasting rock.
	40.	1 O comfort my people, says your *G*.
Dan	3.25	the fourth has the appearance of a *g*."
Hag	1.14	the house of the LORD of hosts, their *G*,
Mal	3.	8 Will anyone rob *G*? Yet you are robbing
Mk	15.34	"My *G*, my *G*, why have you forsaken
Jn	20.28	answered him. "My Lord and my *G*!"
Acts	2.32	This Jesus *G* raised up, and of that all
	28.	6 minds and began to say that he was a *g*.
1 Cor	14.33	for *G* is not a *G* of disorder but of
2 Cor	4.	4 case the *g* of this world has blinded
Eph	2.	4 But *G*, who is rich in mercy, out of the
	2.	8 your own doing; it is the gift of *G*—
	4.24	created according to the likeness of *G*
	5.	1 be imitators of *G*, as beloved children,
Titus	2.11	the grace of *G* has appeared, bringing
	2.13	the glory of our great *G* and Savior
Rev	21.22	its temple is the Lord *G* the Almighty
	22.	1 as crystal, flowing from the throne of *G*

GODLESS

Job	8.13	forget God; hope of the *g* shall perish.
	13.16	that the *g* shall not come before him.
	20.	5 the joy of the *g* is but for a moment?
	27.	8 For what is the hope of the *g* when God
	36.13	"The *g* in heart cherish anger; they do
Prov	11.	9 the *g* would destroy their neighbors,
Isa	9.17	for everyone was *g* and an evildoer, and
	10.	6 Against a *g* nation I send him, and
	33.14	are afraid; trembling has seized the *g*:

GODLINESS

1 Tim	6.	3 teaching that is in accordance with *g*,
	6.	5 imagining that *g* is a means of gain.
2 Tim	3.	5 holding the outward form of *g* but
2 Pet	1.	7 *g* with mutual affection, and mutual

GODLY

Ps	12.	1 there is no longer anyone who is *g*; the
	52.	1 one, of mischief done against the *g*?
2 Tim	3.12	all who want to live a *g* life in Christ

GODS

Gen	31.19	Rachel stole her father's household *g*.
	31.30	father's house, why did you steal my *g*?"
	31.34	Rachel had taken the household *g* and
1 Kings	20.23	"Their *g* are *g* of the hills, and so they
Ps	82.	6 "You are *g*, children of the Most High,
Isa	37.19	have hurled their *g* into the fire; though
Jer	5.19	served foreign *g* in your land, so you
	16.20	Can mortals make for themselves *g*?
Dan	4.	8 is endowed with a spirit of the holy *g*—
Acts	7.40	saying to Aaron, "Make *g* for us who
1 Cor	8.	5 though there may be so-called *g* in

GOLD

Gen	2.11	whole land of Havilah, where there is *g*;
Num	31.52	all the *g* of the offering that they
Job	22.25	if the Almighty is your *g* and your
	31.24	"If I have made *g* my trust, or called
Ps	19.10	More to be desired are they than *g*,
Prov	8.10	and knowledge rather than choice *g*;
	25.11	spoken is like apples of *g* in a setting of
Isa	60.	6 They shall bring *g* and frankincense,
Lam	4.	1 How the *g* has grown dim, how the pure
Dan	2.32	head of that statue was of fine *g*, its
Acts	3.	6 "I have no silver and *g*, but what I have
Rev	21.18	while the city is pure *g*, clear as glass.

GOLGOTHA

Mt	27.33	they came to a place called *G* (which
Mk	15.22	brought Jesus to the place called *G*
Jn	19.17	the Skull, which in Hebrew is called *G*.

GOLIATH

1 Sam	17.	4 of the Philistines, a champion named *G*,
	17.23	the Philistine of Gath, *G* by name, came
	21.	9 "The sword of *G* the Philistine, whom

GOMORRAH

Gen	13.10	before the LORD had destroyed . . . *G*.
	14.10	as kings of Sodom and *G* fled, some fell
	19.24	the LORD rained on . . . *G* sulfur and fire
Deut	29.23	like the destruction of Sodom and *G*,
Isa	1.	9 been like Sodom, and become like *G*.
Mt	10.15	of Sodom and *G* than for that town.
Jude		6 Likewise, Sodom and *G* and the

GOOD

Gen	1.	4 God saw that the light was *g*; and God
	1.31	he had made, and indeed, it was very *g*.
Deut	1.23	The plan seemed *g* to me, and I
1 Chr	19.13	may the LORD do what seems *g* to him."
Ps	14.	3 perverse; there is no one that does *g*,
	16.	2 my Lord; I have no *g* apart from you."
	25.	8 *G* and upright is the LORD; therefore he
	37.27	Depart from evil, and do *g*; so you shall
	92.	1 It is *g* to give thanks to the LORD, to
	133.	1 *g* and pleasant it is when kindred live
Prov	31.12	She does him *g*, and not harm, all the
Eccl	7.	1 *g* name is better than precious
Isa	5.20	you who call evil *g* and *g* evil, who put
	48.17	God, who teaches you for your own *g*,
Hos	14.	2 accept that which is *g*, and we will offer
Am	5.15	Hate evil, and love *g*, and establish
Mic	3.	2 you who hate the *g* and love the evil,
Mt	13.	8 Other seeds fell on *g* soil and brought
	13.48	put the *g* into baskets but threw out the
	25.21	"Well done, *g* and trustworthy slave; you
Mk	4.	8 Other seed fell into *g* soil and brought
	10.18	call me *g*? No one is *g* but God alone.
Lk	6.	9 is it lawful to do *g* or to do harm on the
	8.	8 Some fell into *g* soil, and when it grew,
	9.33	"Master, it is *g* for us to be here; let us
Jn	1.46	"Can anything *g* come out of Nazareth?"
Rom	3.	8 "Let us do evil so that *g* may come?"
	7.18	I know that nothing *g* dwells within me,
	8.28	all things work together for *g* for those
	14.16	do not let your *g* be spoken of as evil.
	16.19	I want you to be wise in what is *g* and
1 Pet	2.	3 you have tasted that the Lord is *g*.

GOOD NEWS

Mt	26.13	wherever this *g* is proclaimed in the
Mk	1.	1 The beginning of the *g* of Jesus Christ,
	1.14	into Galilee, proclaiming the *g* of God,
	13.10	the *g* must first be preached to all
Acts	14.	7 there they continued proclaiming the *g*.
	20.24	Jesus, to testify to the *g* of God's grace.
1 Cor	15.	1 of the *g* that I proclaimed to you, which
2 Cor	10.14	all the way to you with the *g* of Christ.

GOODNESS

Ps	23.	6 Surely *g* and mercy shall follow me all
	31.19	O how abundant is your *g*, that you
Zech	9.17	what *g* and beauty are his! Grain shall
2 Pet	1.	5 support your faith with *g*, and *g* with

GOSPEL

Mt	24.14n	this *g* of the kingdom will be
	26.13n	wherever this *g* is proclaimed in the
Mk	1.	1n The beginning of the *g* of Jesus Christ,
	1.14n	into Galilee, proclaiming the *g* of God,
	13.10n	the *g* must first be preached to all
	14.	9n wherever the *g* is proclaimed in the
	16.15n	world and proclaim the *g* to the whole
Rom	1.	1 an apostle, set apart for the *g* of God,
	1.16	I am not ashamed of the *g*; it is the
	2.16	day when, according to my *g*, God,
	16.25	to strengthen you according to my *g*
2 Cor	9.13	to the confession of the *g* of Christ

Gal	1.	6 and are turning to a different *g* —
	1.11	the *g* that was proclaimed by me is not
	2.	7 with the *g* for the uncircumcised,
Eph	1.13	word of truth, the *g* of your salvation,
	6.15	you ready to proclaim the *g* of peace;
Phil	1.27	your life in a manner worthy of the *g*
Col	1.23	from the hope promised by the *g*
1 Thess	1.	5 of the *g* came to you not in word only,
1 Tim	1.11	teaching that conforms to the glorious *g*
2 Tim	1.	8 but join with me in suffering for the *g*,
1 Pet	4.	6 *g* was proclaimed even to the dead, so
Rev	14.	6 angel . . . with an eternal *g* to proclaim

GOSSIP (GOSSIPS)

Prov	11.13	A *g* goes about telling secrets, but on
	20.19	A *g* reveals secrets; therefore do not
Rom	1.29	strife, deceit, craftiness, they are *g*,
1 Tim	5.13	they are not merely idle, but also *g* and

GOVERNOR (GOVERNORS)

Gen	42.	6 Joseph was *g* over the land; it was he
Neh	5.14	I was appointed to be their *g* in the
Jer	40.	7 Gedaliah son of Ahikam *g* in the
Mal	1.	8 wrong? Try presenting that to your *g*;
Mk	13.	9 you will stand before *g* and kings

GRACE

Ps	45.	2 of men; *g* is poured upon your lips;
Jer	31.	2 found *g* in the wilderness; when Israel
Zech	4.	7 top stone amid shouts of '*G*, *g* to it!' "
Jn	1.14	a father's only son, full of *g* and truth.
Acts	4.33	Jesus, and great *g* was upon them all.
	13.43	urged them to continue in the *g* of God.
	14.	3 testified to the word of his *g*, by
	14.26	commended to the *g* of God for the
	15.40	commending him to the *g* of the Lord.
Rom	1.	5 through whom we have received *g* and
	3.24	they are now justified by his *g* as a gift,
	4.16	in order that the promise may rest on *g*
	5.	2 access to this *g* in which we stand,
	5.15	much more surely have the *g* of God
	5.20	but where sin increased, *g* abounded all
	6.	1 we continue in sin in order that *g*
	15.15	because of the *g* given me by God
1 Cor	3.10	According to the *g* of God given to me,
	15.10	by the *g* of God I am what I am, and
2 Cor	4.15	so that *g*, as it extends to more and
	12.	9 "My *g* is sufficient for you, for power is
	13.13	The *g* of the Lord Jesus Christ, the love
Gal	1.	6 the one who called you in the *g*
	5.	4 Christ; you have fallen away from *g*.
Eph	1.	7 according to the riches of his *g*
	2.	7 show the immeasurable riches of his *g*
2 Thess	2.16	and through *g* gave us eternal comfort
1 Tim	1.14	the *g* of our Lord overflowed for me
Titus	2.11	For the *g* of God has appeared, bringing
	3.	7 so that, having been justified by his *g*,
Heb	4.16	approach the throne of *g* with boldness,
	13.	9 for the heart to be strengthened by *g*,
Jas	4.	6 But he gives all the more *g*; therefore it
1 Pet	4.10	Like good stewards of the manifold *g* of
	5.	5 the proud, but gives *g* to the humble."
	5.10	God of all *g*, who has called you to his
2 Pet	3.18	grow in the *g* and knowledge of our
Jude		4 who pervert the *g* of our God into

GRACEFUL

Song	7.	1 How *g* are your feet in sandals, O

GRACIOUS

Num	6.25	face shine upon you, and be *g* to you;
2 Kings	13.23	the Lord was *g* to them and had
Ps	67.	1 May God be *g* to us and bless us and
	103.	8 The Lord is merciful and *g*, slow to
	145.	8 The Lord is *g* and merciful, slow to
	147.	1 praises to our God; for he is *g*, and a
Prov	22.11	love a pure heart and are *g* in speech
Isa	33.	2 O Lord, be *g* to us; we wait for you. Be

Joel	2.13	your God, for he is *g* and merciful,
Lk	4.22	were amazed at the *g* words that came
Col	4.	6 Let your speech always be *g*, seasoned

GRAIN

Prov	14.	4 Where there are no oxen, there is no *g*;
Mk	4.28	the head, then the full *g* in the head.
Lk	6.	1 his disciples plucked some heads of *g*,
Acts	7.12	Jacob heard that there was *g* in Egypt,
1 Cor	15.37	perhaps of wheat or of some other *g*.

GRAIN OFFERING

Lev	2.	1 When anyone brings a *g* to the Lord,
	6.14	This is the ritual of the *g*: The sons of

GRAINFIELDS

Mt	12.	1 Jesus through the *g* on the sabbath; his

GRANT (GRANTED)

1 Sam	1.17	God of Israel *g* your petition you have
2 Chr	9.12	Solomon *g* to the queen of Sheba every
Prov	10.24	but the desire of the righteous will be *g*.
Acts	27.24	God has *g* safety to all those who are

GRAPES

Num	13.23	a branch with a single cluster of *g*,
Isa	5.	2 he expected it to yield *g*, but it yielded
Jer	31.29	say: "The parents have eaten sour *g*,
Ezek	18.	2 parents have eaten sour *g*, and the
Hos	9.10	Like *g* in the wilderness, I found Israel.
Am	9.13	reaps, and the treader of *g* the one who

GRASS

Ps	37.	2 they will soon fade like the *g*, and
	103.	15 As for mortals, their days are like *g*;
Isa	5.24	as dry *g* sinks down in the flame, so
	40.	6 All people are *g*, and their constancy is
Dan	4.33	from human society, ate *g* like oxen,
Lk	12.28	if God so clothes the *g* of the field,
1 Pet	1.24	"All flesh is like *g* and all its glory like
Rev	8.	7 up, and all green *g* was burnt up.

GRASSHOPPERS

Num	13.33	to ourselves we seemed like *g*, and so
Isa	40.22	the earth, and its inhabitants are like *g*;
Nah	3.17	Your guards are like *g*, your scribes like

GRAVE (GRAVES)

Ps	49.14	straight to the *g* they descend, and their
Ezek	32.23	Its company is all around it, all of
	37.12	your *g*, and bring you up from your *g*,
Lk	11.44	you are like unmarked *g*, and people
Jn	5.28	all who are in their *g* will hear his voice

GREAT (GREATER GREATEST)

2 Sam	5.10	David became *g* and *g*, for the Lord, the
	7.22	you are *g*, O Lord God; for there is no
1 Chr	11.	9 David became *g* and *g*, for the Lord of
	17.19	you have done all these *g* deeds,
Job	37.23	find him; he is *g* in power and justice,
Ps	40.16	say continually, "*G* is the Lord!"
	70.	4 your salvation say evermore, "God is *g*!"
Eccl	2.	9 So I became *g* and surpassed all who
Jer	45.	5 you, do you seek *g* things for yourself?
Joel	2.21	rejoice, for the Lord has done *g* things!
Mal	1.	5 this, and you shall say, "*G* is the Lord
Mt	5.19	them will be called *g* in the kingdom
	12.	6 something *g* than the temple is here.
	12.42	see, something *g* than Solomon is here.
	15.28	"Woman, *g* is your faith! Let it be done
	18.	1 asked, "Who is the *g* in the kingdom
Mk	9.34	argued with one another who was the *g*.
Lk	1.15	he will be *g* in the sight of the Lord. He
	22.24	of them was to be regarded as the *g*.
1 Cor	13.13	these three; and the *g* of these is love.
Rev	2.19	that your last works are *g* than the first.
	18.16	"Alas, alas, the *g* city, clothed in fine

GREATNESS

Deut	3.24 only begun to show your servant your *g*
Ps	145. 3 to be praised; his *g* is unsearchable.
	150. 2 him according to his surpassing *g*!
Ezek	31. 2 hordes: Whom are you like in your *g*?
	38.23 I will display my *g* and my holiness and

GREECE

Dan	8.21 The male goat is the king of *G*, and the
	11. 2 stir up all against the kingdom of *G*.
Zech	9.13 sons, O Zion, against your sons, O *G*,
Acts	20. 2 he came to *G*, where he stayed for three

GREED

Lk	12.15 Be on your guard against all kinds of *g*;
1 Thess	2. 5 words of flattery or with a pretext for *g*;
2 Pet	2. 3 in their *g* they will exploit you with
	2.14 souls. They have hearts trained in *g*.

GREEDY

1 Sam	2.29 "Why then look with *g* eye at my
Prov	1.19 is the end of all who are *g* for gain;
Jer	6.13 of them, everyone is *g* for unjust gain;
	8.10 greatest everyone is *g* for unjust gain;
1 Cor	5.11 or sister who is sexually immoral or *g*,
	6.10 thieves, the *g*, drunkards, revilers,
Eph	5. 5 one who is *g* (that is, an idolater), has

GREEK (GREEKS)

Jn	12.20 to worship at the festival were some *G*.
Acts	14. 1 of both Jews and *G* became believers.
	16. 1 was a believer; but his father was a *G*.
	19.10 of Asia, both Jews and *G* heard the
	20.21 as I testified to both Jews and to *G*
Rom	1.14 I am a debtor both to *G* and to
1 Cor	1.22 demand signs and *G* desire wisdom,

GREET (GREETED GREETING)

1 Sam	6.19 when they *g* the ark of the LORD; and he
Mt	23. 7 to be *g* with respect in the
Mk	12.38 and to be *g* with respect in the
Lk	1.29 pondered what sort of *g* this might be.
	1.41 When Elizabeth heard Mary's *g*, the
	11.43 be *g* with respect in the marketplaces.
Rom	16.16 *G* one another with a holy kiss. All the
1 Cor	16.21 I, Paul, write this *g* with my own hand.
Heb	11.13 from a distance they saw and *g* them.

GRIEF

Prov	14.13 the heart is sad, and the end of joy is *g*.
	17.25 Foolish children are a *g* to their father
2 Cor	7.10 godly *g* produces a repentance that

GRIEVE (GRIEVED GRIEVING)

Gen	6. 6 on the earth, and it *g* him to his heart.
1 Sam	16. 1 "How long will you *g* over Saul? I have
Ps	78.40 the wilderness and *g* him in the desert!
Isa	63.10 But they rebelled and *g* his holy spirit;
Am	6. 6 but are not *g* over the ruin of Joseph!
Mt	14. 9 The king was *g*; yet out of regard for his
Mk	3. 5 he was *g* at their hardness of heart and
	10.22 went away *g*; for he had many
	14.34 "I am deeply *g*, even to death; remain
Eph	4.30 do not *g* the Holy Spirit of God, with
1 Thess	4.13 so that you may not *g* as others do who

GROAN (GROANING GROANS)

Ps	79.11 the *g* of the prisoners come before you;
Prov	29. 2 but when the wicked rule, the people *g*.
Ezek	30.24 of Pharaoh, and he will *g* before him
Joel	1.18 How the animals *g*! The herds of cattle
Acts	7.34 are in Egypt and have heard their *g*,

GROPE

Job	5.14 and *g* at noonday as in the night.
	12.25 They *g* in the dark without light; he
Isa	59.10 We *g* like the blind along a wall,

GROUND

Judg	16.21 shackles; and he *g* at the mill in prison.
Lk	23.22 in him no *g* for the sentence of death;
Acts	7.54 enraged and *g* their teeth at Stephen.

GROUPS

Mk	6.39 all the people to sit down in *g* on the

GROW (GREW)

1 Sam	2.21 the boy Samuel *g* up in the presence of
	3.19 As Samuel *g* up, the LORD was with him
Isa	9. 7 His authority shall *g* continually, and
	53. 2 he *g* up before him like a young plant,
Lk	1.80 The child *g* and became strong in spirit,
	2.40 The child *g* and became strong, filled
Acts	19.20 So the word of the Lord *g* mightily and

GRUMBLED

Deut	1.27 you *g* in your tents and said, "It is
Ps	106. 25 They *g* in their tents, and did not obey

GUARANTEE

2 Cor	5. 5 God, who has given us the Spirit as a *g*.

GUARD (GUARDS)

1 Sam	2. 9 He will *g* the feet of his faithful ones,
Neh	4. 9 to our God, and set a *g* as a protection
Job	7.12 the Dragon, that you set a *g* over me?
Ps	91.11 his angels concerning you to *g* you
	97.10 he *g* the lives of his faithful; he rescues
	140. 4 *G* me, O LORD, from the hands of the
	141. 3 Set a *g* over my mouth, O LORD; keep
Prov	2.11 over you; and understanding will *g* you.
	4. 6 keep you; love her, and she will *g* you.
	13. 3 Those who *g* their mouths preserve their
Eccl	5. 1 *G* your steps when you go to the house
Mt	5.25 to the judge, and the judge to the *g*,
Phil	4. 7 will *g* your hearts and your minds in
1 Tim	6.20 *g* what has been entrusted to you.

GUARDIAN (GUARDIANS)

Gal	4. 2 they remain under *g* and trustees until
1 Cor	4.15 might have ten thousand *g* in Christ,
1 Pet	2.25 to the shepherd and *g* of your souls.

GUEST (GUESTS)

Ps	39.12 For I am your passing *g*, an alien, like
Zeph	1. 7 a sacrifice, he has consecrated his *g*.
Mt	22.10 bad; so wedding hall was filled with *g*.
Lk	22.11 "Where is the *g* room, where I may eat

GUIDANCE

Job	37.12 They turn round and round by his *g*, to
Prov	11.14 Where there is no *g*, a nation falls, but
	24. 6 for by wise *g* you can wage your war,

GUIDE (GUIDED GUIDES)

Deut	32.12 the LORD alone *g* him; no foreign god
Ps	31. 3 for your name's sake lead me and *g*
	48.14 and ever. He will be our *g* forever.
	67. 4 people with equity and *g* the nations
	73.24 You *g* me with your counsel, and
	78.52 sheep, and *g* them in the wilderness
Isa	42.16 they have not known I will *g* them.
	58.11 The LORD will *g* you continually, and
Mt	15.14 if one blind person *g* another, both will
Lk	6.39 "Can a blind person *g* a blind person?
Jn	16.13 truth comes he will *g* you into all truth;
Acts	1.16 Judas, who became a *g* for those who
Rom	2.19 are sure that you are a *g* to the blind,
Gal	5.25 the Spirit, let us also be *g* by the Spirit.

GUILE

Prov	26.26 though hatred is covered with *g*, the

GUILT

Lev	4.22 "When a ruler sins, . . . and incurs *g*,
1 Chr	21. 3 this? Why should he bring *g* on Israel?"
Ps	25.11 O LORD, pardon my *g*, for it is great.

Ezek	16.49 This was the g of your sister Sodom:
Hos	13. 1 in Israel; but he incurred g through Baal
Zech	3. 9 I will remove the g of this land in a

GUILT OFFERING

Lev	7. 1 This is the ritual of the g. It is most

GUILTLESS

2 Sam	3.28 kingdom are forever g before the LORD
2 Cor	7.11 point you have proved yourselves g in

GUILTY

Lev	5. 4 know it , you shall in any of these be g.
Ps	68.21 of those who walk in their g ways.
Isa	5.23 who acquit the g for a bribe, and
	50. 9 who helps me; who will declare me g?
Jer	2. 3 All who ate of it were held g; disaster
	12. 1 Why does the way of the g prosper?
Ezek	22. 4 have become g by the blood that you
Hos	4.15 O Israel, do not let Judah become g.
Lk	23.14 have not found this man g of any of

H

HABAKKUK

Hab	1. 1 The oracle that the prophet H saw. O
	3. 1 A prayer of the prophet H according to

HADES

Mt	16.18 and the gates of H will not prevail
Lk	16.23 In H, where he was being tormented, he
Acts	2.27 For you will not abandon my soul to H,
Rev	6. 8 was Death, and H followed with him;
	20.14 Death and H were thrown into the lake

HAGAR

Gen	16. 1 Egyptian slave-girl whose name was H,
	16.15 H bore Abram a son; and Abram named
	21. 9 Sarah saw the son of H the Egyptian,
	21.14 and a skin of water, and gave it to H,
Gal	4.24 is H, from Mount Sinai, bearing

HAGGAI

Ezra	5. 1 Now the prophets, H and Zechariah son
	6.14 the prophesying of the prophet H
Hag	1. 1 came by the prophet H to Zerubbabel
	2. 1 of the LORD came by the prophet H,

HAIL (HAILSTONES)

Ex	9.18 I will cause the heaviest h to fall that
Josh	10.11 more who died because of the h than

HAIR (HAIRS)

Ps	40.12 they are more than the h of my head,
Prov	23. 7 like a h in the throat, so are they. "Eat
Isa	3.24 and instead of well-set h, baldness;
Mt	10.30 even the h of your head are all counted.
Lk	7.38 her tears and to dry them with her h.
	12. 7 even the h of your head are all counted.
1 Cor	11.15 if a woman has long h, it is her glory?

HALLOW (HALLOWED)

Gen	2. 3 God blessed the seventh day and h it,
Ezek	20.20 and h my sabbaths that they may be a
Mt	6. 9 Our Father in heaven, h be your name.
Lk	11. 2 "Father, h be your name. Your kingdom

HAMATH

Isa	36.19 Where are the gods of H and Arpad?
Am	6. 2 and see; from there go to H the great;

HAMMER

Judg	4.21 and took a h in her hand, and went
1 Kings	6. 7 so that neither h nor axe nor any tool
Jer	23.29 like fire, says the LORD, and like a h
	50.23 the h of the whole earth is cut down

HAND (n)

Gen	9. 2 the sea; into your h they are delivered.
	48.17 saw that his father laid his right h on

Ex	3.19 you go unless compelled by a mighty h.
	4. 2 "What is that in your h?" He said, "A
	15.12 You stretched out your right h, the
	17.11 whenever he lowered his h, Amalek
Lev	4.24 lay his h upon the head of of the goat;
Num	21.34 of him, for I have given him into your h,
Deut	2.15 the LORD's own h was against them, to
	4.34 by war, by a mighty h and an
	5.15 from there with a mighty h and an
	26. 8 brought us out of Egypt with a mighty h
1 Sam	5. 6 The h of the LORD was heavy on the
	12.15 then the h of the LORD will be against
	18.17 "I will not raise a h against him; let the
	23.16 there he strengthened his h through the
2 Sam	3.18 Israel from the h of the Philistines
	24.14 let us fall into the h of the LORD, for his
1 Chr	4.10 and that your h might be with me, and
Ezra	7.28 I took courage, for the h of the LORD my
Job	8.20 person, nor take the h of evildoers.
	12. 9 does not know that the h of the LORD
	19.21 for the h of God has touched me!
	40.14 your own right h can give you victory.
Ps	31.15 My times are in your h; deliver me from
	32. 4 day and night your h was heavy on me;
	74.11 why do you keep your h in your bosom?
	104. 28 when you open your h, they are filled
	106. 10 them from the h of the enemy.
	118. 16 right h of the LORD is exalted; the right
Eccl	9. 1 their deeds are in the h of God; whether
	9.10 Whatever your h finds to do, do with
Isa	5.25 away, and his h is stretched out still.
	8.11 to me while his h was strong upon me,
	9.12 turned away; his h is stretched out still.
	9.17 turned away, his h is stretched out still.
	14.27 His h is stretched out, and who will
	40.12 the waters in the hollow of his h
	59. 1 See, the LORD's h is not too short to
Ezek	3.14 my spirit, the h of the LORD was being
	3.22 h of the LORD was upon me there; and
	13. 9 My h will be against the prophets who
	20.33 a mighty h and an outstretched arm,
	25.16 stretch out my h against the Philistines,
	33.22 h of the LORD had been upon me the
	37. 1 The h of the LORD came upon me, and
Dan	5. 5 fingers of a human h appeared and
Mt	3.12 His winnowing fork is in his h, and he
	5.30 if your right h causes you to sin, cut if
	6. 3 left h know what your right h is doing,
	18. 8 "If your h or your foot causes you to
Mk	3. 5 said to the man, "Stretch out your h." He
	9.43 If your h causes you to stumble, cut it
Lk	6. 6 man there whose right h was withered.
	6.10 He did so, and the h was restored.
Jn	20.25 of the nails and my h in his side, I will
Acts	11.21 The h of the Lord was with them, and a
	13.11 the h of the Lord is against you, and
1 Cor	5. 5 you are to h this man over to Satan for
2 Thess	3.17 Paul, write this greeting with my own h.

HANDS (n)

Num	27.23 he laid his h on him and commissioned
Job	10. 8 Your h fashioned and made me; and
	34.19 poor, for they are all the work of his h?
Ps	24. 4 who have clean h and pure hearts, who
	115. 7 They have h, but do not feel; feet, but
Prov	31.20 and reaches out her h to the needy.
Jer	32.28 this city into the h of the Chaldeans
Mt	15.20 to eat with unwashed h does not defile."
Mk	7. 2 his disciples were eating with defiled h,
Lk	15.19 son; treat me like one of your hired h."
	24.39 Look at my h and my feet; see that it is
Jn	13. 9 feet only but also my h and my head!"
	20.20 he showed them his h and his side.
	20.25 I see the mark of the nails in his h,
Rom	10.21 I have held out my h to a disobedient
2 Cor	5. 1 a house not made with h, eternal in the
1 Jn	1. 1 have looked at and touched with our h,

HANDED

Deut	3.	2 for I have *h* him over to you, along with
Mt	11.27	"All things have been *h* over to me by
	20.18	the Son of Man will be *h* over to the
	26.	2 of Man will be *h* over to be crucified."
	27.	2 led him away, and *h* him over to Pilate
Mk	15.	1 led him away and *h* him over to Pilate.
Lk	18.32	he will be *h* over to the Gentiles; and

HANDSOME

Ps	45.	2 You are the most *h* of men; grace is

HANG (HANGED HANGING HANGS HUNG)

Deut	21.23	for anyone *h* on a tree is under God's
2 Sam	17.23	set his house in order, and *h* himself;
	18.10	told Joab, "I saw Absalom *h* in an oak."
Esth	6.	4 to the king about having Mordecai *h*
	7.	9 And the king said, "*H* him on that."
Job	26.	7 the void, and *h* the earth upon nothing.
Ps	137.	2 On the willows there we *h* up our harps.
Mt	27.	5 departed; and he went and *h* himself.
Acts	10.39	put him to death by *h* him on a tree;

HANNAH

1 Sam	1.	2 two wives; the name of the one was *H*,
	1.13	*H* was praying silently; only her lips
	2.	1 *H* prayed and said, "My heart exults in
	2.21	the LORD took note of *H*; she conceived

HAPPY

Deut	24.	5 at home one year, to be *h* with the wife
	33.29	*H* are you, O Israel! Who is like you, a
1 Kings	10.	8 *H* are your wives! *H* are these your
2 Chr	9.	7 *H* are your people! *H* are these your
Job	5.17	"How *h* is the one whom God reproves;
Ps	1.	1 *H* are those who do not follow the
	32.	1 *H* are those whose transgression is
	34.	8 is good; *h* are those who take refuge
	41.	1 *H* are those who consider the poor; the
	127.	5 *H* is the man who has his quiver full of
	144.	15 *H* are the people whose God is the
	146.	5 *H* are those whose help is the God of
Prov	3.13	*H* are those who find wisdom, and
	8.32	to me: *h* are those who keep my ways.
	28.14	*H* is the one who is never without fear,
	31.28	Her children rise up and call her *h*; her
Mal	3.15	we count the arrogant *h*; evildoers not

HARD (HARDER)

Jer	32.17	arm! Nothing is too *h* for you.
Mt	7.14	road is *h* that leads to life, and there
1 Cor	15.10	I worked *h* than any of them—
2 Pet	3.16	some things in them *h* to understand,

HARDEN (HARDENED HARDENS)

Ex	4.21	but I will *h* his heart, so that he will
	7.	3 I will *h* Pharaoh's heart, and I will
	8.32	But Pharaoh *h* his heart this time also,
Deut	2.30	LORD your God had *h* his spirit and
Josh	11.20	it was the LORD's doing to *h* their hearts
1 Sam	6.	6 Why should you *h* your hearts as the
Ps	95.	8 Do not *h* your hearts, as at Meribah, as
Isa	63.17	stray from your ways and *h* our heart,
Dan	5.20	spirit was *h* so that he acted proudly, he
Mk	6.52	the loaves, but their hearts were *h*.
Jn	12.40	has blinded their eyes and *h* their heart,
Rom	9.18	and he *h* the heart of whomever he
	11.	7 elect obtained it, but the rest were *h*,
2 Cor	3.14	But their minds were *h*. Indeed, to this
Heb	3.	8 do not *h* your hearts as in the rebellion,

HARDENING

Rom	11.25	a *h* has come upon part of Israel, until

HARD-HEARTED

Deut	15.	7 do not be *h* or tight-fisted toward your
Mt	19.	8 because you were so *h* that Moses

HARDNESS

Mk	3.	5 he was grieved at their *h* of heart and
	10.	5 "Because of your *h* of heart he wrote
Eph	4.18	of their ignorance and *h* of heart.

HARDSHIP

Rom	8.35	Will *h*, or distress, or persecution, or

HARM

Gen	44.29	one also from me, and *h* comes to him,
Jer	25.	6 of your hands. Then I will do you no *h*."
	39.12	look after him well and do him no *h*,
Lk	6.	9 to do good or to do *h* on the sabbath,
Acts	16.28	"Do not *h* yourself, for we are all here."

HARMAGEDON

Rev	16.16	at the place that in Hebrew is called *H*.

HARMONY

Rom	15.	5 grant you to live in *h* with one another,
Col	3.14	binds everything together in perfect *h*.

HARP (HARPS)

Ps	108.	2 Awake, O *h* and lyre! I will awake the
	137.	2 On the willows there we hung up our *h*.
1 Cor	14.	7 notes, such as the flute or the *h*.
Rev	5.	8 each holding a *h* and golden bowls full
	14.	2 the sound of harpists playing on their *h*,

HARSH (HARSHLY)

Ruth	1.21	when the LORD dealt *h* with me and the
Mt	25.24	I knew that you were a *h* man, reaping

HARVEST (HARVESTS)

Gen	8.22	as the earth endures, seedtime and *h*,
Lev	23.10	and you reap its *h*, you shall bring the
Prov	25.13	snow in the time of *h* are faithful
Isa	9.	3 rejoice before you as with joy at the *h*,
	16.	9 for the shout over your fruit *h* and your
Jer	5.17	They shall eat up your *h* and your food;
	8.20	"The *h* is past, the summer is ended,
	12.13	They shall be ashamed of their *h*
Joel	3.13	Put in the sickle, for the *h* is ripe. Go
Mt	9.37	"The *h* is plentiful, but the laborers are
	13.30	both of them grow together until the *h*;
Mk	4.29	the sickle, because the *h* has come."
Lk	10.	2 of the *h* to send out laborers into his *h*.
Jn	4.35	'Four months more, then comes the *h*'?
Rom	1.13	that I may reap some *h* among you
2 Cor	9.10	increase the *h* of your righteousness.
Phil	1.11	having produced the *h* of righteousness
Rev	14.15	because the *h* of the earth is fully ripe."

HASTE

Ps	38.22	Make *h* to help me, O Lord, my
	70.	1 deliver me. O LORD, make *h* to help me!
Lk	2.16	went with *h*, and found Mary and

HATE (HATED HATES)

Gen	27.41	Now Esau *h* Jacob because of the
Ps	26.	5 I *h* the company of evildoers, and will
	68.	1 let those who *h* him flee before
	69.	4 are those who *h* me without cause;
	101.	3 I *h* the work of those who fall away; it
	106.	41 so that those who *h* them ruled them.
	119.113	I *h* the doubled-minded, but I love your
Prov	6.16	six things that the LORD *h*, seven that
	19.	7 If the poor are *h* even by their kin, how
Eccl	2.18	I *h* all my toil in which I had toiled
Jer	44.	4 to do this abominable thing that I *h*!"
Am	5.15	*H* evil and love good, and establish
Mal	1.	3 I have loved Jacob but I have *h* Esau; I
Mt	10.22	you will be *h* by all because of my
	24.	9 you will be *h* by all nations because of
Mk	13.13	you will be *h* by all because of my
Lk	6.22	"Blessed are you when people *h* you,
	14.26	comes to me and does not *h* father and
	21.17	You will be *h* by all because of my

Jn	15.18 "If the world *h* you, be aware that it *h*
	15.25 their law, 'They *h* me without a cause.'
	17.14 and the world has *h* them because they
Rom	7.15 what I want, but I do the very thing I *h*.
	9.13 "I have loved Jacob, but I have *h* Esau."
	12. 9 *h* what is evil, hold fast to what is good;
Eph	5.29 no one ever *h* his own body, but he
Heb	1. 9 loved righteousness and *h* wickedness;
1 Jn	4.20 say, "I love God," and *h* their brothers or

HATRED

Num	35.20 if someone pushes another from *h*, or
Ps	25.19 foes, and with what violent *h* they hate
Prov	8.13 fear of the LORD is *h* of evil. Pride and

HAUGHTY

Prov	6.17 *h* eyes, a lying tongue, and hands that
Isa	3.16 Because the daughters of Zion are *h*
	5.15 low, and the eyes of the *h* are humbled.
Jer	13.15 Hear and give ear; do not be *h*, for the
Rom	12.16 do not be *h*, but associate with the

HAWK

Lev	11.16 the sea gull, the *h* of any kind;
Job	39.26 "Is it by your wisdom that the *h* soars,

HEAD

Gen	28.11 of the place, he put it under his *h*
1 Sam	17.51 killed him; then he cut off his *h* with it.
2 Kings	4.19 He complained to his father, "Oh, my *h*,
Song	7. 5 Your *h* crowns you like Carmel, and
Mt	14. 8 "Give me the *h* of John the Baptist here
Mk	6.28 brought his *h* on a platter, and gave it
Jn	13. 9 feet only but also my hands and my *h*!"
1 Cor	11. 3 Christ is the *h* of every man, and the
Eph	1.22 and has made him the *h* over all things
	5.23 the husband is the *h* of the wife just as
Col	1.18 He is the *h* of the body, the church; he

HEAL (HEALED HEALS)

Gen	20.17 prayed to God; and God *h* Abimelech,
Ex	15.26 Egyptians; for I am the LORD who *h* you."
Num	12.13 cried to the LORD, "O God, please *h* her."
Deut	32.39 I kill and I make alive; I wound and I *h*;
2 Chr	7.14 will forgive their sin and *h* their land.
Ps	30. 2 to you for help, and you have *h* me.
	41. 4 me; *h* me, for I have sinned against you."
	103. 3 your iniquity, who *h* all your diseases,
	107. 20 he sent out his word and *h* them, and
	147. 3 He *h* the brokenhearted, and binds up
Isa	30.26 and *h* the wounds inflicted by his blow.
	53. 5 us whole, and by his bruises we are *h*.
	57.19 near, says the LORD; and I will *h* them.
Jer	3.22 children, I will *h* your faithlessness.
	17.14 *H* me, O LORD, and I shall be *h*; save
	30.17 health to you, and your wounds I will *h*,
	33. 6 I will *h* them and reveal to them
	51. 9 We tried to *h* Babylon, but she could
Hos	5.13 is not able to cure you or *h* your wound.
	7. 1 when I would *h* Israel, the corruption of
	11. 3 but they did not know that I *h* them.
	14. 4 I will *h* their disloyalty; I will love them
Mt	13.15 heart and turn— and I would *h* them.'
Mk	6.56 cloak; and all who touched it were *h*.
Lk	6.18 hear him and to be *h* of their diseases;
	8.47 and how she had been immediately *h*.
	9. 2 proclaim the kingdom of God and to *h*.
	22.51 this!" And he touched his ear and *h* him.
Jn	4.47 him to come down and *h* his son,
	5.13 man who had been *h* did not know who
Acts	14. 9 and seeing that he had faith to be *h*,
1 Pet	2.24 by his wounds you have been *h*.

HEALING

Prov	3. 8 It will be *h* for your flesh and a
	29. 1 will suddenly be broken beyond *h*.
Jer	8.15 find no good, for a time of *h*, but found
	14.19 us down so that there is no *h* for us?

Jer	46.11 many medicines; there is no *h* for you.
Ezek	47.12 will be for food, and their leaves for *h*."
Mal	4. 2 shall rise, with *h* in its wings.
1 Cor	12. 9 to another gifts of *h* by the one Spirit,
	12.28 then deeds of power, then gifts of *h*,
Rev	22. 2 of the trees are for the *h* of the nations.

HEALTH (HEALTHY)

Ps	38. 3 is no *h* in my bones because of my sin.
Prov	16.24 to the soul and *h* to the body.
Jer	30.17 For I will restore *h* to you, and your
Lk	11.34 when your eye is *h*, your whole body is
Acts	3.16 Jesus has given him this perfect *h* in
3 Jn	2 well with you and that you may be in *h*,

HEAP

Josh	3.13 cut off; they shall stand in a single *h*."
Job	27.16 Though they *h* up silver like dust, and
Ps	39. 6 they *h* up, and do not know who
Prov	25.22 you will *h* coals of fire on their heads,
Jer	9.11 I will make Jerusalem a *h* of ruins, a

HEAR (HEARD HEARS)

Gen	21.17 God *h* the voice of the boy; and the
Ex	2.24 God *h* their groaning, and God
Deut	4.10 I will let them *h* my words, so that they
	5. 1 *H*, O Israel, the statutes and ordinances
	6. 4 *H*, O Israel: The LORD is our God, the
	31.12 that they may *h* and learn to fear the
2 Sam	5.24 When you *h* the sound of marching in
	22. 7 From his temple he *h* my voice, and my
1 Kings	8.39 then *h* in heaven your dwelling place,
2 Kings	19.16 Incline your ear, O LORD, and *h*; open
2 Chr	6.27 may you *h* in heaven, forgive the sin of
	7.12 "I have *h* your prayer, and have chosen
	33.13 received his entreaty, and *h* his plea,
Neh	8. 9 people wept when they *h* the words of
Job	42. 4 '*H*, and I will speak; I will question
Ps	6. 9 The LORD has *h* my supplication; the
	34.17 the righteous cry for help, the LORD *h*,
	49. 1 *H* this, all peoples; give ear, all
Prov	1. 8 *H*, my child, your father's instruction,
Isa	1. 2 *H*, O heavens, and listen, O earth; for
	33.13 You who are far away, what I have
	40.28 Have you not known? Have you not *h*?
	64. 4 From ages past no one has *h*, no ear
	66. 8 Who has *h* of such a thing? Who has
Jer	18. 2 and there I will let you *h* my words."
	31.18 I *h* Ephraim pleading: "You disciplined
Ezek	3.27 Let those who will *h*, *h*; and let those
	12. 2 see, who have ears to *h*, but do not *h*;
	33.31 and they *h* your words, but they will not
Mic	1. 2 *H*, you peoples, all of you; listen, O
Mt	11. 4 "Go and tell John what you *h* and see:
Mk	4.24 to them, "Pay attention to what you *h*;
Lk	6.18 They had come to *h* him and to be
	7.22 tell John what you have seen and *h*:
Jn	5.24 anyone who *h* my word and believes
	10. 3 the sheep *h* his voice. He calls his own
	12.47 I do not judge anyone who *h* my words
Acts	4.20 about what we have seen and *h*."
	10.44 the Holy Spirit fell on all who *h*
	19.10 of Asia, both Jews and Greeks, *h* the
Rom	10.14 And how are they to *h* without someone
	15.21 and those who have never *h* of him
1 Jn	1. 1 what we have *h*, what we have seen
Rev	1. 3 blessed are those who *h* and who keep

HEARING (n)

Gen	23.10 Abraham in the *h* of the Hittites,
Neh	13. 1 the book of Moses in the *h* of the
1 Cor	12.17 were an eye, where would the *h* be?

HEART

Gen	8.21 the inclination of the human *h* is evil
Ex	28.30 judgment . . . on his *h* before the LORD
	35. 5 let whoever is of a generous *h* bring the
Deut	6. 5 love the LORD your God with all your *h*,

Deut	7.	7 people that the LORD set his *h* on you
	10.12	serve the LORD your God with all your *h*
	10.15	yet the LORD set his *h* in love on your
	17.17	for himself, or else his *h* will turn away;
	28.65	LORD will give you a trembling *h*, failing
	30.	6 God will circumcise your *h* and the *h*
	30.14	mouth and in your *h* for you to observe.
1 Sam	7.	3 Direct your *h* to the LORD, and serve
	10.	9 God gave him another *h*; and all these
	13.14	has sought out a man after his own *h*;
	16.	7 but the LORD looks on the *h*."
	25.37	his *h* died within him; he became like a
2 Sam	17.10	whose *h* is like the *h* of a lion, will
	24.10	David was stricken to the *h* because he
1 Kings	3.	6 in uprightness of *h* toward you; and you
	8.48	if they repent with all their *h* and soul
	11.	9 with Solomon, because his *h* had turned
	15.14	the *h* of Asa was true to the LORD all his
2 Kings	14.10	your *h* has lifted you up. Be content
	22.19	because your *h* was penitent and you
	23.25	turned to the LORD with all his *h*, with
1 Chr	28.	9 him with single mind and willing *h*;
	29.17	I know, my God, that you search the *h*,
2 Chr	16.	9 to strengthen those whose *h* is true
	17.	6 His *h* was courageous in the ways of the
	25.19	your *h* has lifted you up in boastfulness.
	32.25	his *h* was proud. Therefore wrath came
Ezra	6.22	turned the *h* of the king of Assyria to
	7.10	Ezra had set his *h* to study the law of
Neh	2.	2 sick? This can only be sadness of the *h*."
	2.12	had put into my *h* to do for Jerusalem.
Job	11.13	"If you direct your *h* rightly, you will
	23.16	God has made my *h* faint; the Almighty
	31.	9 "If my *h* has been enticed by a woman,
	36.13	"The godless in *h* cherish anger; they do
Ps	19.	8 of the LORD are right, rejoicing the *h*;
	44.21	this? For he knows the secrets of the *h*.
	45.	1 My *h* overflows with a goodly theme; I
	51.10	Create in me a clean *h*, O God, and put
	55.21	than butter, but with a *h* set on war;
	57.	7 My *h* is steadfast, O God, my *h* is
	69.20	Insults have broken my *h*, so that I am
	77.	6 I commune with my *h* in the night; I
	78.18	They tested God in their *h* by
	101.	2 I will walk with integrity of *h* within my
	102.	4 My *h* is stricken and withered like grass;
	104.15	wine to gladden the human *h*, oil to
	108.	1 My *h* is steadfast, O God, my *h* is
	109.22	needy, and my *h* is pierced within me.
	119.11	I treasure your word in my *h*, so that I
	143.	4 within me; my *h* within me is appalled.
Prov	2.10	wisdom will come into your *h*, and
	3.	3 write them on the tablet of your *h*.
	4.23	Keep your *h* with all vigilance, for from
	6.18	a *h* that devises wicked plans, feet that
	18.12	Before destruction one's *h* is haughty,
	20.	9 Who can say, I have made my *h* clean; I
	21.	1 king's *h* is a stream of water in the
	23.26	My child, give me your *h*, and let your
	26.23	vessel are smooth lips with an evil *h*.
	27.19	face, so one human *h* reflects another.
Eccl	5.	2 nor let your *h* be quick to utter a word
	10.	2 The *h* of the wise inclines to the right,
Song	8.	6 Set me as a seal upon your *h*, as a seal
Isa	1.	5 head is sick, and the whole *h* faint.
	38.	3 you in faithfulness with a whole *h*,
	42.25	burned him, but he did not take it to *h*.
	63.17	stray from your ways and harden our *h*,
Jer	3.10	did not return to me with her whole *h*,
	3.15	give you shepherds after my own *h*, who
	4.14	Jerusalem, wash your *h* clean of
	4.19	My *h* is beating wildly; I cannot keep
	17.	9 The *h* is devious above all else; it is
	32.39	I will give them one *h* and one way,
Ezek	11.19	I will give them one *h*, and put a new
	16.30	How sick is your *h*, says the Lord GOD,
	28.	2 Because your *h* is proud and you have

Ezek	33.31	lips, but their *h* is set on their gain.
	36.26	remove from your body the *h* of stone
	44.	7 uncircumcised in *h* and flesh,
Dan	5.22	his son, have not humbled your *h*,
Hos	10.	2 Their *h* is false; now they must bear
Joel	2.12	return to me with all your *h*, with
Am	2.16	who are stout of *h* among the mighty
Mt	5.	8 "Blessed are the pure in *h*, for they will
	5.28	committed adultery with her in his *h*.
	6.21	treasure is, there your *h* will be also.
	9.	2 "Take *h*, son; your sins are forgiven."
	13.15	this people's *h* has grown dull, and their
	14.27	said, "Take *h*, it is I; do not be afraid."
	15.19	out of the *h* come evil intentions,
Mk	6.50	said, "Take *h*, it is I; do not be afraid."
	7.21	it is . . . from the human *h*, that evil
	10.	5 "Because of your hardness of *h* he wrote
	12.30	love the Lord your God with all your *h*,
Lk	2.19	words and pondered them in her *h*.
	2.51	treasured all these things in her *h*.
	6.45	out of the good treasure of the *h*
Jn	1.18	only Son, who is close to the Father's *h*,
	7.38	"Out of the believer's *h* shall flow rivers
Acts	1.24	"Lord, you know everyone's *h*. Show us
	2.26	therefore my *h* was glad, and my tongue
	4.32	who believed were of one *h* and soul,
	7.23	came into his *h* to visit his relatives, the
	7.51	people, uncircumcised in *h* and ears,
	8.21	this, for your *h* is not right before God.
	13.22	son of Jesse, to be a man after my *h*,
	15.	8 God who knows the human *h* testified
	16.14	Lord opened her *h* to listen eagerly to
	21.13	you doing, weeping and breaking my *h*?
	28.27	For this people's *h* has grown dull, and
Rom	8.27	God, who searches the *h*, knows what is
	9.	2 sorrow and unceasing anguish in my *h*.
	10.	9 believe in your *h* that God raised him
1 Cor	2.	9 ear heard, nor the human *h* conceived,
2 Cor	4.	1 in this ministry, we do not lose *h*.
	6.11	to you Corinthians; our *h* is wide open
	7.15	his *h* goes out all the more to you, as
1 Tim	1.	5 is love that comes from a pure *h*,
Heb	4.12	the thoughts and intentions of the *h*.
1 Pet	1.22	love one another deeply from the *h*.

HEARTS

Ex	25.	2 from all those whose *h* prompt them to
Josh	5.	1 they had crossed over, their *h* melted,
	24.23	you, and incline your *h* to the LORD,
2 Sam	15.	6 so Absalom stole the *h* of the people of
1 Kings	18.37	and that you have turned their *h* back."
Ps	14.	1 Fools say in their *h*, "There is no God."
	24.	4 who have clean hands and pure *h*,
	53.	1 Fools say in their *h*, there is no God."
	95.	8 Do not harden your *h*, as at Meribah, as
	112.	8 Their *h* are steady, they will not be
Isa	29.13	their lips, while their *h* are far from me,
	51.	7 who have kept my teaching in your *h*;
Jer	17.	5 whose *h* turn away from the LORD.
	31.33	them and I will write it on their *h*;
Zech	7.12	They made their *h* adamant in order not
Mal	4.	6 He will turn the *h* of parents to their
Mt	15.	8 their lips, but their *h* are far from me;
Mk	2.	8 do you raise such question in your *h*?
	6.52	the loaves, but their *h* were hardened.
	7.	6 their lips, but their *h* are far from me;
	8.17	or understand? Are your *h* hardened?
Lk	1.17	turn the *h* of parents to their children,
	24.32	"Were not our *h* burning within us while
Jn	12.40	blinded their eyes and hardened their *h*,
	14.	1 "Do not let your *h* be troubled. Believe
	14.27	Do not let your *h* be troubled, and do
Rom	2.15	the law requires is written on their *h*,
2 Thess	3.	5 May the Lord direct your *h* to the love
Heb	3.	8 do not harden your *h* as in the
	3.10	'They always go astray in their *h*, and
	4.	7 hear his voice, do not harden your *h*."

Heb	8.10	their minds, and write them on their *h*,
1 Jn	3.20	whenever our *h* condemn us; for God is
Rev	2.23	am the one who searches minds and *h*,

HEAVEN (HEAVENS)

Ex	16. 4	I am going to rain bread from *h* for you;
	20.22	yourselves that I spoke with you from *h*.
Deut	30.12	It is not in *h*, that you should say, "Who
1 Kings	8.27	Even *h* and the highest *h* cannot
2 Chr	6.18	*h* and the highest *h* cannot contain you,
Ps	19. 1	The *h* are telling the glory of God; and
	103. 11	as the *h* are high above the earth, so
	119. 89	forever; your word is firmly fixed in *h*.
	139. 8	I ascend to *h*, you are there; if I make
Isa	14.12	How you are fallen from *h*, O Day Star,
	24. 4	and withers; the *h* languish together
	66. 1	*H* is my throne and the earth is my
Hag	1.10	*h* above you have withheld the dew, and
Mt	5.18	until *h* and earth pass away, not one
	6. 9	"Pray then in this way: Our father in *h*,
Mk	1.10	he saw the *h* torn apart and the Spirit
	13.31	*H* and earth will pass away, but my
	16.19n	Jesus . . . was taken up into *h* and sat
Lk	21.26	for the powers of the *h* will be shaken.
	21.33	*H* and earth will pass away, but my
Acts	9. 3	suddenly a light from *h* flashed
1 Cor	15.49	also bear the image of the man of *h*.
2 Cor	12. 2	ago was caught up to the third *h*—
1 Pet	3.22	Christ, who has gone into *h* and is at
2 Pet	3. 5	by the word of God *h* existed long ago
	3.13	we wait for new *h* and a new earth,
Rev	4. 1	and there in *h* a door stood open!
	19. 1	voice of a great multitude in *h*, saying,
	21. 1	I saw a new *h* and a new earth; for the

HEAVENLY

Jn	3.12	you believe if I tell you about *h* things?
2 Cor	5. 2	to be clothed with our *h* dwelling—
Eph	1. 3	every spiritual blessing in the *h* places,

HEAVY

1 Kings	14. 6	For I am charged with *h* tidings for you.
Ps	32. 4	day and night your hand was *h* on me;
Eccl	6. 1	the sun, and it lies *h* upon humankind:
Mt	11.28	are weary and are carrying *h* burdens,

HEBRON

Gen	13.18	by the oaks of Mamre, which are at *H*;
Judg	1.10	against the Canaanites who lived in *H*
2 Sam	2.11	that David was king in *H* over the house

HEED (HEEDED)

Ex	5. 2	Who is the LORD, that I should *h* him
Deut	4.30	return to the LORD your God and *h* him.
	7.12	If you *h* these ordinances, by diligently
	13. 8	you must not yield to or *h* any such
Judg	6.10	But you have not given *h* to my voice."
1 Sam	12.15	if you will not *h* the voice of the LORD,
2 Chr	11. 4	they *h* the word of the LORD and turned
Ps	31. 7	you have taken *h* of my adversities,
Prov	1.23	Give *h* to my reproof; I will pour out my
Eccl	9.17	words of the wise are more to be *h*
Jer	8. 6	I have given *h* and listened, but they do
	11. 3	Cursed be anyone who does not *h* the
	26. 5	to *h* the words of my servants the

HEEL

Gen	3.15	your head, and you will strike his *h*."
	25.26	out, with his hand gripping Esau's *h*;
Ps	41. 9	my bread, has lifted the *h* against me.

HEIFER

Gen	15. 9	"Bring me a *h* three years old, a female
Num	19. 2	to bring you a red *h* without defect, in
Judg	14.18	"If you had not plowed with my *h*, you

HEIGHT

Rom	8.39	nor *h*, nor depth, nor anything else in

HEIR (HEIRS)

Gen	15. 3	and so a slave . . . is to be my *h*."
Jer	49. 1	Has Israel no sons? Has he no *h*? Why
Mt	21.38	'This is the *h*; come, let us kill him and
Mk	12. 7	'This is the *h*; come, let us kill him, and
Lk	20.14	'This is the *h*; let us kill him so that
Rom	8.17	if children, then *h*, *h* of God and joint *h*
Gal	4. 1	*h*, as long as they are minors, are no
Eph	3. 6	the Gentiles have become fellow *h*,
Heb	11. 7	world and became an *h* to righteousness

HELL

Mt	5.22	fool!' you will be liable to the *h* of fire.
	5.29	your whole body to be thrown into *h*.
	18. 9	eyes and to be thrown into the *h* of fire.
Lk	12. 5	has killed, has authority to cast into *h*.

HELLENISTS

Acts	6. 1	*H* complained against the Hebrews
	9.29	spoke and argued with the *H*; but they

HELMET

Isa	59.17	and a *h* of salvation on his head;
Eph	6.17	Take the *h* of salvation, and the sword
1 Thess	5. 8	love, and for a *h* the hope of salvation.

HELP (n)

2 Sam	22.36	salvation, and your *h* made me great.
Ps	18.35	supported me; your *h* made me great.
	42. 5	God; for I shall again praise him, my *h*
	42.11	God; for I shall again praise him, my *h*
	70. 5	You are my *h* and my deliverer; O LORD,
	121. 2	My *h* comes from the LORD, who made
Isa	30. 7	Egypt's *h* is worthless and empty,
Acts	26.22	To this day I have had *h* from God, and
Phil	4.16	I was in in Thessalonica, you sent me *h*

HELP (HELPED HELPS) (v)

Ex	2.19	"An Egyptian *h* us against the
Deut	28.31	your enemies, without anyone to *h* you.
2 Kings	14.26	bond or free, and no one to *h* Israel.
2 Chr	14.11	*H* us, O LORD our God, for we rely on
	26. 7	God *h* him against the Philistines,
Ps	106. 4	people; *h* me when you deliver them;
	107. 12	labor; they fell down, with none to *h*.
	109. 26	*H* me, O LORD my God! Save me
Isa	49. 8	you, on a day of salvation I have *h* you;
	50. 7	The Lord GOD *h* me; therefore I have
Hos	13. 9	destroy you, O Israel; who can *h* you?
Mt	15.25	knelt before him, saying, "Lord, *h* me."

HELPER

Gen	2.18	I will make him a *h* as his partner."
Ps	10.14	and you have been the *h* of the orphan.
	30.10	be gracious to me! O LORD, be my *h*!"
Heb	13. 6	"The Lord is my *h*, I will not be afraid.

HELPLESS

Jer	6.24	our hands fall *h*; anguish has taken hold

HEM

Ps	139. 5	You *h* me in, behind and before, and lay

HEMORRHAGES

Mk	5.25	been suffering from *h* for twelve years,
Lk	8.43	been suffering from *h* for twelve years;

HERALD

2 Chr	36.22	Persia so that he sent a *h* throughout
Ezra	1. 1	Persia so that he sent a *h* throughout
1 Tim	2. 7	right time. For this I was appointed a *h*

HERE

Isa	40. 9	to the cities of Judah, "*H* is your God!"

HERITAGE

1 Kings	8.53	to be your *h*, just as you promised
Job	31. 2	and my *h* from the Almighty on high?
Ps	2. 8	I will make the nations your *h*, and the

Ps	16. 6 in pleasant places; I have a goodly *h.*
	33.12 people whom he has chosen as his *h.*
	94.14 his people; he will not abandon his *h;*
Jer	12. 7 my house, I have abandoned my *h;*
	17. 4 By your own act you shall lose the *h*
	50.11 though you exult, O plunderers of my *h,*

HERMON

Deut	3. 8 Jordan, from Wadi Arnon to Mount *H*
	4.48 as far as Mount Sirion (that is, *H*),
Josh	11.17 the valley of Lebanon below Mount *H.*
	12. 1 from the Wadi Arnon to Mount *H,* with
Ps	89.12 them; Tabor and *H* joyously praise
	133. 3 It is like the dew of *H,* which falls on
Song	4. 8 Amana, from the peak of Senir and *H,*

HEROD

Mt	2. 1 In the time of King *H,* after Jesus was
	2.13 for *H* is about to search for the child, to
	2.16 When *H* saw that he had been tricked
	2.19 When *H* died, an angel of the Lord
	14. 1 At that time *H* the ruler heard reports
Mk	6.14 King *H* heard of it, for Jesus' name had
	8.15 of the Pharisees and the yeast of *H.*"
Lk	3. 1 and *H* was ruler of Galilee, and his
	13.31 away from here, for *H* wants to kill you."
	23. 7 he sent him off to *H,* who was himself
Acts	4.27 in this city, both *H* and Pontius Pilate,
	12. 1 King *H* laid violent hands upon some
	12.20 Now *H* was angry with the people of
	12.21 day *H* put on his royal robes, took his

HEZEKIAH

2 Kings	16.20 city of David; his son *H* succeeded him.
	19.14 *H* received the letter from the hand of
	20. 1 In those days *H* became sick and was at
2 Chr	30. 1 *H* sent word to all Israel and Judah,
	30.18 But *H* had prayed for them, saying,
	32.30 *H* closed the upper outlet of the waters
Isa	39. 1 envoys with letters and a present to *H,*

HIDE (HID HIDDEN HIDES HIDING)

Gen	3. 8 the man and his wife *h* themselves from
	18.17 "Shall I *h* from Abraham what I am
Ex	2. 2 a fine baby, she *h* him three months.
	2.12 he killed the Egyptian and *h* him in the
	3. 6 Moses *h* his face, for he was afraid to
Josh	2. 4 woman took the two men and *h* them.
1 Sam	3.17 Do not *h* it from me. May God do so to
	10.22 "See, he has *h* himself among the
2 Chr	22.11 — *h* him from Athaliah, so that she did
Ps	10. 1 do you *h* yourself in times of trouble?
	13. 1 forever? How long will you *h* your face
	17. 8 eye; *h* me in the shadow of your wings,
	19.12 their error? Clear me from *h* faults.
	27. 5 he will *h* me in his shelter in the day of
	27. 9 Do not *h* your face from me. Do not
	30. 7 you *h* your face; I was dismayed.
	40.10 I have not *h* your saving help within my
	55. 1 do not *h* yourself from my supplication.
	89.46 O Lᴏʀᴅ? Will you *h* yourself forever?
	104. 29 When you *h* your face, they are
	119.114 You are my *h* place and my shield; I
Prov	27. 5 Better is open rebuke than *h* love.
Isa	1.15 your hands, I will *h* my eyes from you;
	2.10 *h* in the dust from the terror of the
	32. 2 will be like a *h* place from the wind,
	40.27 "My way is *h* from the Lᴏʀᴅ, and my
	45.15 you are a God who *h* himself, O God of
	49. 2 in the shadow of his hand he *h* me;
	64. 5 because you *h* yourself we transgressed.
	65.16 former troubles are forgotten and are *h*
Jer	13. 5 So I went, and *h* it by the Euphrates, as
	36.26 prophet Jeremiah. But the Lᴏʀᴅ *h* them.
Ezek	39.29 I will never again *h* my face from them,
Am	9. 3 they *h* themselves on the top of Carmel,
Mt	5.14 A city built on a hill cannot be *h.*

Mt	25.18 the ground and *h* his master's money.
Mk	4.22 For there is nothing *h,* except to be
Lk	8.17 nothing is *h* that will not be disclosed,
	10.21 have *h* these things from the wise and
Heb	4.13 before him no creature is *h,* but all are

HIGH (HIGHER)

Ezra	9. 6 our iniquities have risen *h* than our
Eccl	10. 6 folly is set in many *h* places, and the
Ezek	17.24 low the *h* tree, I make *h* the low tree;

HIGH PRIEST

Mk	2.26 when Abiathar was *h,* and ate the bread
	14.53 They took Jesus to the *h;* and all the
Jn	18.19 the *h* questioned Jesus about his
Acts	5.17 Then the *h* took action; he and all who
	23. 4 "Do you dare to insult God's *h*?" And
Heb	2.17 be a merciful and faithful *h* in the
	3. 1 Jesus, the apostle and *h* of our
	4.14 have a great *h* who has passed through
	5. 5 did not glorify himself in becoming a *h,*

HIGHWAY (HIGHWAYS)

Ps	84. 5 you, in whose heart are the *h* to Zion;
Isa	11.16 so there shall be a *h* from Assyria for
	19.23 there will be a *h* from Egypt to Assyria,
	35. 8 A *h* shall be there, and it shall be called
	49.11 a road, and my *h* shall be raised up.

HILL (HILLS)

Deut	2. 3 skirting this *h* country long enough.
1 Kings	20.23 "Their gods are gods of the *h,* and so
Ps	24. 3 Who shall ascend the *h* of the Lᴏʀᴅ?

HINDER

| 1 Sam | 14. 6 nothing can *h* the Lᴏʀᴅ from saving by |

HIP

| Gen | 32.25 him on the *h* socket; and Jacob's *h* |

HIRAM

2 Sam	5.11 King *H* of Tyre sent messengers to
1 Kings	5. 1 Now *H* king of Tyre sent his servants to
	7.13 King Solomon invited and received *H*
	7.40 *H* also made the pots, the shovels, and
	9.12 when *H* came from Tyre to see the
1 Chr	14. 1 King *H* of Tyre sent messengers to

HIRED

Deut	23. 4 because they *h* against you Balaam son
2 Chr	24.12 they *h* masons and carpenters to restore
Lk	15.19 son; treat me like one of your *h* hands."

HITTITE (HITTITES)

Gen	15.20 the *H,* the Perizzites, the Rephaim,
	23.10 Ephron the *H* answered Abraham in the
Ex	3. 8 country of the Canaanites, the *H,*
	23.23 brings you to the Amorites, the *H,* the
Deut	7. 1 away many nations before you — the *H,*
1 Kings	9.20 who were left of the Amorites, the *H,*
2 Kings	7. 6 has hired against us the kings of the *H*
Ezra	9. 1 from the Canaanites, the *H,* the

HOLD (HELD HOLDING)

Gen	17. 8 the land of Canaan, for a perpetual *h;*
	48. 4 offspring after you for a perpetual *h.*'
Deut	30.20 God, obeying him, and *h* fast to him;
Josh	22. 5 to *h* fast to him, and to serve him with
	23. 8 but *h* fast to the Lᴏʀᴅ your God, as you
Job	27. 6 I *h* fast my righteousness, and will not
Ps	119.101 I *h* back my feet from every evil way, in
Isa	65. 2 I *h* out my hands all day long to a
Jer	26. 2 I command you; do not *h* back a word.
Ezek	44.28 give them no *h* in Israel; I am their *h.*
Jn	20.17 "Do not *h* on to me, because I have not
Rom	3.28 we *h* that a person is justified by faith
	12. 9 hate what is evil, *h* fast to what is good;

HOLE (HOLES)

Ezek	8.	7 I looked, and there was a *h* in the wall.
Hag	1.	6 wages to put them into a bag with *h*.

HOLINESS

Ex	15.11	Who is like you, majestic in *h*, awesome
Ps	93.	5 very sure; *h* befits your house, O LORD,
Ezek	20.41	I will manifest my *h* among you in the
	36.23	you I display my *h* before their eyes.
	38.16	through you, O Gog, I display my *h*
Lk	1.75	serve him without fear, in *h* and
2 Cor	7.	1 making *h* perfect in the fear of God.
Eph	4.24	of God in true righteousness and *h*.
1 Thess	4.	7 did not call us to impurity but in *h*.
Heb	12.14	and the *h* without which no one will

HOLLOW

Isa	40.12	the waters in the *h* of his hand

HOLY

Ex	3.	5 on which you are standing is *h* ground."
	19.	6 me a priestly kingdom and a *h* nation.
	26.33	for you the *h* place from the most *h*.
	28.36	engraving of a signet, "*H* to the LORD."
	39.30	engraving of a signet, "*H* to the LORD."
Lev	10.	3 who are near me I will show myself *h*,
	10.10	distinguish between the *h* and the
	11.44	therefore, and be *h*, for I am *h*.
	19.	2 You shall be *h*, for I the LORD your God
	20.26	You shall be *h* to me; for I the LORD am
	21.	6 They shall be *h* to their God, and not
	22.	2 that they may not profane my *h* name;
Num	4.20	not go in to look on the *h* things even
	6.	5 they shall be *h*; they shall let the locks
	16.	3 All the congregation are *h*, everyone of
Deut	5.12	Observe the sabbath day and keep it *h*,
	7.	6 For you are a people *h* to the LORD your
	14.	2 For you are a people *h* to the LORD your
	23.14	your camp must be *h*, so that he may
1 Sam	2.	2 "There is no *H* One like the LORD, no
Ezra	8.28	"You are *h* to the LORD, and the vessels
Neh	13.22	the gates, to keep the sabbath day *h*.
Job	5.	1 To which of the *h* ones will you turn?
Ps	16.	3 As for the *h* ones in the land, they are
	22.	3 Yet you are *h*, enthroned on the praises
	30.	4 ones, and give thanks to his *h* name.
	34.	9 O fear the LORD, you his *h* ones, for
	48.	1 in the city of our God. His *h* mountain,
	96.	9 Worship the LORD in *h* splendor; tremble
	99.	3 your great and awesome name. *H* is he!
	134.	2 Lift up your hands to the *h* place, and
Isa	5.16	God shows himself *h* by righteousness.
	6.	3 "*H*, *h*, *h* is the LORD of hosts; the earth
	8.13	of hosts, him you shall regard as *h*;
	35.	8 there, and it shall be called the *H* Way;
	62.	9 gather it shall drink it in my *h* courts.
	62.12	They shall be called, "The *H* People,
Jer	2.	3 Israel was *h* to the LORD, the first fruits
	17.22	but keep the sabbath day *h*, as I
	51.51	aliens have come into the *h* places of
Ezek	42.20	between the *h* and the common.
Dan	7.18	the *h* ones of the Most High shall
	7.27	given to the people of the *h* ones of the
	8.13	Then I heard a *h* one speaking, and
	8.24	powerful and the people of the *h* ones.
	12.	7 the shattering of the power of the *h*
Zech	14.	5 will come, and all the *h* ones with him.
Mt	7.	6 "Do not give what is *h* to dogs; and do
	24.15	sacrilege standing in the *h* place,
Mk	6.20	that he was a righteous and *h* man,
Lk	2.23	first born male shall be designated as *h*
Acts	7.33	the place where you are standing is *h*
Rom	7.12	So the law is *h*, and the commandment
	12.	1 bodies as a living sacrifice, *h* and
1 Cor	7.14	the unbelieving husband is made *h*
	7.34	so that they may be *h* in body and in
Eph	1.	4 of the world to be *h* and blameless

Eph	5.26	in order to make her *h*, by cleansing her
	5.27	that she may be *h* and without blemish.
Heb	7.26	such a high priest, *h*, blameless,
1 Pet	1.15	called you is *h*, be *h* yourselves in all
Jude		14 coming with ten thousand of his *h* ones,
Rev	3.	7 These are the words of the *h* one, the
	4.	8 "*H*, *h*, *h*, is the Lord God the Almighty,
	21.	2 I saw the *h* city, the new Jerusalem,

HOLY ONE

Prov	9.10	and knowledge of the *H* is insight.
Isa	41.14	LORD; your Redeemer is the *H* of Israel.
	43.14	LORD, your Redeemer, the *H* of Israel:
Hab	1.12	not from of old, O LORD my God, my *H*?
Jn	6.69	and know that you are the *H* of God."
Acts	13.35	not let your *H* experience corruption.'

HOLY SPIRIT

Ps	51.11	and do not take your *h* from me.
Mt	1.18	was found to be with child from the *H*.
Mk	1.	8 but he will baptize you with the *H*."
Eph	1.13	with the seal of the promised *H*,
2 Pet	1.21	men and women moved by the *H* spoke

HOME

Ps	68.	6 God gives the desolate a *h* to live in; he
Mk	5.19	"Go *h* to your friends, and tell them
	8.26	he sent him away to his *h*, saying, "Do
Lk	8.39	"Return to your *h*, and declare how
Jn	14.23	to them and make our *h* with them.
	19.27	hour the disciple took her to his own *h*.
1 Cor	11.34	If you are hungry, eat at *h*, so that when
	14.35	know, let them ask their husbands at *h*.
2 Cor	5.	6 while we are at *h* in the body we are
Rev	21.	3 "See, the *h* of God is among mortals.

HOMELAND

Heb	11.14	make it clear that they are seeking a *h*.

HOMETOWN

Mk	6.	1 He left that place and came to his *h*,

HONEST

Lev	19.36	You shall have *h* balances, *h* weights, an
Deut	25.15	You shall have only a full and *h* weight;
Prov	16.11	*H* balances and scales are the LORD's;
Ezek	45.10	You shall have *h* balances, an *h* ephah,
Lk	8.15	hold it fast in an *h* and good heart

HONESTY

Gen	30.33	So my *h* will answer for me later, when

HONEY

Ex	3.	8 land, a land flowing with milk and *h*,
	16.31	taste of it was like wafers made with *h*.
Deut	32.13	he nursed him with *h* from the crags,
1 Sam	14.29	because I tasted a little of this *h*.
Ps	19.10	sweeter also than *h*, and drippings of
	81.16	wheat and with *h* from the rock I would
	119.103	your words to my taste, sweeter than *h*
Prov	24.13	My child, eat *h*, for it is good, and the
Song	4.11	*h* and milk are under your tongue;
Isa	7.15	He shall eat curds and *h* by the time he
Ezek	3.	3 and in my mouth it was as sweet as *h*.
Rev	10.10	sweet as *h* in my mouth, but when I

HONOR (n)

Num	22.17	I will surely do you great *h*, and
2 Sam	6.22	spoken, by them I shall be held in *h*."
2 Chr	1.11	not asked for possessions, wealth, *h*,
Esth	6.	3 "What *h* or distinction has been
Ps	96.	6 *H* and majesty are before him; strength
	104.	1 are very great. You are clothed with *h*
Prov	15.33	in wisdom, and humility goes before *h*.
	29.23	one who is lowly in spirit will obtain *h*.
Dan	2.	6 from me gifts and rewards and great *h*.
Mt	13.57	"Prophets are not without *h* except in
Mk	6.	4 "Prophets are not without *h*, except in
Lk	14.	7 how the guests chose the places of *h*,

Rom	2. 7 doing good seek for glory and *h* and
	12.10 outdo one another in showing *h*.
	13. 7 respect is due, *h* to whom *h* is due.
1 Cor	4.10 You are held in *h*, but we in disrepute.
2 Cor	6. 8 in *h* and dishonor, in ill repute and
1 Tim	6.16 see; to him be *h* and eternal dominion.

HONOR (HONORED HONORS) (v)

Gen	34.19 he was the most *h* of all his family.
Ex	20.12 *H* your father and your mother, so that
Deut	5.16 *H* your father and your mother, as the
1 Sam	2.30 those who *h* me I will *h*, and those who
	15.30 "I have sinned; yet *h* me now before the
1 Chr	4. 9 Jabez was *h* more than his brothers;
Ps	50.23 thanksgiving as their sacrifice *h* me;
Prov	3. 9 *H* the LORD with your substance and
Isa	29.13 and in men will their lips, while their
	43.23 offerings, or *h* me with your sacrifices.
	58.13 if you *h* it, not going your own ways,
Jer	30.19 I will make them *h*, and they shall not
Dan	11.38 He shall *h* the god of fortresses instead
Mal	1. 6 A son *h* his father, and servants their
Mt	15. 4 God said, '*H* your father and your
	15. 8 'This people *h* me with their lips, but
	19.19 *H* your father and mother; also, You
Mk	7.10 said, "*H* your father and your mother';
Lk	14.10 will be *h* in the presence of all who sit
Jn	5.23 all may *h* the Son, just as they *h* the
	8.49 I *h* my father, and you dishonor me.
Eph	6. 2 is right. "*H* your father and mother" —
Phil	2.29 Lord with all joy, and *h* such people,
1 Tim	5. 3 *H* widows who are really widows. If a

HONORABLE

Phil	4. 8 is true, whatever is *h*, whatever is just,

HOPE (n)

Ezra	10. 2 but even now there is *h* for Israel in
Job	5.16 So the poor have *h*, and injustice shuts
	13.15 See, he will kill me; I have no *h*; but I
	14.19 the earth; you destroy the *h* of mortals.
	17.15 where then is my *h*? Who will see my *h*?
	19.10 gone, he has uprooted my *h* like a tree.
	27. 8 what is the *h* of the godless when God
Ps	65. 5 you are the *h* of all the ends of the
	78. 7 so that they should set their *h* in God,
	146. 5 God of Jacob, whose *h* is in the LORD
Prov	10.28 The *h* of the righteous ends in gladness,
	13.12 *H* deferred makes the heart sick, but a
	19.18 your children while there is *h*;
	29.20 There is more *h* for a fool than for
Isa	20. 5 because of Ethiopia their *h* and Egypt
Jer	14.22 We set our *h* on you, for it is you who
	31.17 There is *h* for your future, says the
Ezek	37.11 bones are dried up, and our *h* is lost;
Hos	2.15 make the Valley of Achor a door of *h*.
Acts	28.20 since it is for the sake of the *h* of Israel
Rom	4.18 Hoping against *h*, he believed that he
	12.12 Rejoice in *h*, be patient in suffering,
1 Cor	15.19 for in this life only we have *h* in Christ,
Eph	1.12 who were the first to set our *h* on Christ
	1.18 is the *h* to which he has called you,
Col	1. 5 of the *h* laid up for you in heaven.
	1.23 from the *h* promised by the gospel
	1.27 which is Christ in you, the *h* of glory.
1 Thess	1. 3 love and steadfastness of *h* in our Lord
	2.19 what is our *h* or joy or crown of
Titus	2.13 godly, while we wait for the blessed *h*,
Heb	6.18 encouraged to seize the *h* set before us.
	10.23 us hold fast the confession of our *h*
1 Pet	1. 3 has given us a new birth into a living *h*
1 Jn	3. 3 who have this *h* in him purify

HOPE (HOPED HOPES) (v)

Ps	33.18 him, on those who *h* in his steadfast
	33.22 LORD, be upon us even as we *h* in you.
	42. 5 within me? *H* in God; for I shall again

Ps	43. 5 *H* in God; for I shall again praise him,
	56. 8 steps. As they have *h* to have my life,
	71.14 But I will *h* continually, and will praise
	119. 74 rejoice, because I have *h* in your word.
	119.166 I *h* for your salvation, O LORD, and I
Lam	3.18 and all that I had *h* for from the LORD."
Mt	12.21 And in his name will the Gentiles *h*."
Lk	6.34 to those from whom you *h* to receive,
	24.21 we had *h* that he was the one to
Rom	8.24 is not hope. For who *h* for what is seen?
	15.12 Gentiles; in him the Gentiles shall *h*."
1 Cor	15.19 for in this life only we have *h* in Christ,

HORN (HORNS)

1 Kings	1.50 up and went to grasp the *h* of the altar.
	2.28 the LORD and grasped the *h* of the altar.
Jer	48.25 The *h* of Moab is cut off, and his arm is
Ezek	29.21 I will cause a *h* to sprout up for the
Dan	3. 5 when you hear the sound of the *h*, pipe,
	7. 7 that preceded it, and it had ten *h*.
	8. 3 two *h*. Both *h* were long, but one was
Zech	1.18 I looked up and saw four *h*. I asked the
Rev	17.12 the ten *h* that you saw are ten kings

HORSE (HORSES)

Deut	17.16 he must not acquire many *h* for himself,
Josh	11. 6 you shall hamstring their *h*, and burn
1 Kings	10.28 Solomon's import of *h* was from Egypt
2 Chr	1.16 Solomon's *h* were imported from Egypt
	9.25 Solomon had four thousand stalls for *h*
Job	39.18 aloft, it laughs at the *h* and its rider.
Ps	32. 9 Do not be like a *h* or a mule, without
	33.17 The war *h* is a vain hope for victory,
Prov	21.31 *h* is made ready for the day of battle,
	26. 3 A whip for the *h*, a bridle for the
Am	6.12 Do *h* run on rocks? Does one plow the
Zech	1. 8 the night I saw a man riding on a red *h*!
	6. 2 The first chariot had red *h*, the second
Jas	3. 3 put bits into the mouths of *h* to make

HOSANNAH

Mt	21.15 "*H* to the Son of David!" they became
Mk	11. 9 shouting, "*H*! Blessed is the one who

HOSEA

Hos	1. 1 word of the LORD that came to *H* son of
Rom	9.25 As indeed he says in *H*, "Those who

HOSPITABLE

1 Tim	3. 2 temperate, sensible, respectable, *h*, an
Titus	1. 8 he must be *h*, a lover of goodness,
1 Pet	4. 9 Be *h* to one another without

HOSPITALITY

Rom	12.13 of the saints; extend *h* to strangers.

HOSTILE

Rom	8. 7 that is set on the flesh is *h* to God;
Col	1.21 were once estranged and *h* in mind,

HOSTILITY

Deut	15. 9 view your needy neighbor with *h* and

HOSTS

2 Sam	7.26 'The LORD of *h* is God over Israel'; and
Ps	24.10 is this King of glory? The LORD of *h*,
Isa	1. 9 If the LORD of *h* had not left us a few

HOUR

Mt	20.12 'These last worked only one *h*, and you
	25.13 for you know neither the day nor the *h*.
Mk	13.32 about that day or *h* no one knows,
	14.35 possible, the *h* might pass from him.
	14.41 The *h* has come; the Son of man is
Lk	22.53 But this is your *h*, and the power of
Jn	4.21 me, the *h* is coming when you will
	7.30 him, because his *h* had not yet come.
	12.23 "The *h* has come for the Son of Man to
	12.27 I say — 'Father, save me from this *h*'?

Jn	16.32 The *h* is coming, indeed it has come,		Ps	9.20 the nations know that they are only *h*.	

HOUSE (HOUSES)

Lev	27.14 If a person consecrates a *h* to the LORD,
Deut	8.12 eaten your fill and built fine *h* and live
2 Sam	7.11 to you that the LORD will make you a *h*.
2 Kings	25. 9 burned the *h* of the LORD, the king's *h*,
1 Chr	17. 5 I have not lived in a *h* since the day I
	17.10 to you that the LORD will build you a *h*.
	22. 5 and the *h* that is to be built for the
	28. 2 planned to build a *h* of rest for the ark
2 Chr	5.14 for the glory of the LORD filled the *h* of
	22.12 hidden in the *h* of God, while Athaliah
	24. 4 Joash decided to restore the *h* of
	29.18 "We have cleansed all the *h* of the LORD,
Ezra	3.11 the foundation of the *h* of the LORD
	6.15 this *h* was finished on the third day of
Neh	13.11 said, "Why is the *h* of God forsaken?"
Job	8.14 is gossamer, a spider's *h* their trust.
Ps	42. 4 led them in procession to the *h* of
	52. 8 like a green olive tree in the *h* of God.
	69. 9 zeal for your *h* that has consumed me;
	84.10 be a doorkeeper in the *h* of my God
	92.13 They are planted in the *h* of the LORD;
	122. 1 to me, "Let us go to the *h* of the LORD!"
Prov	25.24 in a *h* shared with a contentious wife.
Eccl	7. 2 better to go to the *h* of mourning than
Isa	2. 3 the LORD, to the *h* of the God of Jacob;
	6. 4 who called, and the *h* filled with smoke.
	22.24 him the whole weight of his ancestral *h*,
	38. 1 Set your *h* in order; for you shall die;
Jer	16. 5 Do not enter the *h* of mourning, or go
	26. 9 'This *h* shall be like Shiloh, and this
	52.13 He burned the *h* of the LORD, the king's
Ezek	10. 4 the *h*; the *h* was filled with the cloud,
Joel	3.18 fountain shall come forth from the *h* of
Hag	1. 4 paneled *h*, while this *h* lies in ruins?
	1. 9 Because my *h* lies in ruins, while all of
Mt	21.13 "My *h* shall be called a *h* of prayer'; but
Mk	5.38 When they came to the *h* of the leader
	6.10 "Whenever you enter a *h*, stay there
	11.17 'My *h* shall be called a *h* of prayer for
Lk	2.49 know that I must be in my Father's *h*?"
	6.48 like a man building a *h*, who dug deeply
	9. 4 Whatever *h* you enter, stay there and
	10. 7 to be paid. Do not go from *h* to *h*.
	11.17 becomes a desert, and *h* falls on *h*.
	13.35 See, your *h* is left to you. And I tell you,
	19.46 'My *h* shall be a *h* of prayer'; but you
Jn	2.16 making my father's *h* a market place!"
Acts	7.48 Most High does not dwell in *h* made
	20.20 teaching you publicly and from *h* to *h*,
1 Cor	16.19 with the church in their *h*, greet you

HOUSEHOLD

Josh	24.15 me and my *h*, we will serve the LORD."
Prov	31.21 for all her *h* are clothed in crimson.
	31.27 She looks well to the ways of her *h*, and
Mt	10.36 foes will be members of one's own *h*.
	13.52 is like the master of a *h* who brings out
Jn	4.53 believed, along with his whole *h*.
Acts	16.31 and you will be saved, you and your *h*."
Phil	4.22 you, especially those of the emperor's *h*.
1 Tim	3. 4 He must manage his own *h* well,
	3.15 one ought to behave in the *h* of God,

HOUSETOP (HOUSETOPS)

Prov	21. 9 live in a corner of the *h* than in a house
Mt	10.27 hear whispered, proclaim from the *h*.
	24.17 the one on the *h* must not go down to
Mk	13.15 the one on the *h* must not go down or
Lk	12. 3 doors will be proclaimed from the *h*.

HUMAN

Job	4.17 Can *h* beings be pure before their
	5. 7 but *h* beings are born to trouble just as
	7.17 What are *h* beings, that you make so

	144. 3 what are *h* beings that you regard them,
Prov	27.19 face, so one *h* heart reflects another.
Jer	10.23 that the way of *h* beings is not in their
Dan	2.34 stone was cut out, not by *h* hands, and
	7.13 I saw one like a *h* being coming with
Rom	3.20 "no *h* being will be justified in his sight"
1 Cor	2.13 in words not taught by *h* wisdom but
	3. 3 behaving according to *h* inclinations?
	3.21 So let no one boast about *h* leaders. For
2 Cor	10. 3 Indeed, we live as *h* beings, but we do
	10. 4 of our warfare are not merely *h*,
Gal	1. 1 Paul an apostle—sent by neither *h*
Heb	2. 6 "What are *h* beings that you are mindful

HUMAN RACE

Prov	8.31 inhabited world and delighting in the *h*.

HUMANITY

Eph	2.15 might create in himself one new *h* in

HUMANKIND

Gen	1.26 God said, "Let us make *h* in our image,

HUMBLE (HUMBLED HUMBLES)

Ex	10. 3 How long will you refuse to *h* yourself
Lev	26.41 if then their uncircumcised heart is *h*
Deut	8. 2 in order to *h* you, testing you to know
1 Kings	21.29 how Ahab has *h* himself before me?
2 Kings	22.19 and you *h* yourself before the LORD,
2 Chr	7.14 are called by my name *h* themselves,
	12. 6 of Israel and the king *h* themselves
	30.11 and Zebulun *h* themselves and came to
	32.26 Hezekiah *h* himself for the pride of his
	34.27 patient and you *h* yourself before God
Ps	55.19 from of old, will hear and *h* them—
	119. 67 Before I was *h* I went astray; but now I
	119. 75 and that in faithfulness you have *h* me.
Isa	5.15 low, and the eyes of the haughty are *h*.
Dan	5.22 And you, Belshazzar his son, have not *h*
	10.12 and to *h* yourself before your God,
Mt	18. 4 Whoever becomes *h* like this child is
	23.12 all those who *h* themselves will be
Lk	18.14 all who *h* themselves will be exalted."
2 Cor	12.21 again, my God may *h* me before you,
Phil	2. 8 he *h* himself and became obedient
Jas	4.10 *H* yourselves before the Lord, and he
1 Pet	5. 6 *H* yourselves therefore under the mighty

HUMBLE (adj)

Num	12. 3 Now the man Moses was very *h*, more
2 Sam	22.28 You deliver a *h* people, but your eyes
Job	22.29 you say it is pride; for he saves the *h*.
Ps	18.27 you deliver a *h* people, but the haughty
	25. 9 He leads the *h* in what is right, and
	149. 4 his people; he adorns the *h* with victory.
Isa	57.15 those who are contrite and *h* in spirit,
Zeph	2. 3 Seek the LORD, all you *h* of the land,
	3.12 the midst of you a people *h* and lowly.
Zech	9. 9 victorious is he, *h* and riding on a
Mt	21. 5 your king is coming to you, *h*, and
1 Pet	3. 8 another, a tender heart, and a *h* mind.

HUMILITY

Prov	15.33 if wisdom, and *h* goes before honor.
	22. 4 reward for *h* and fear of the LORD is
Phil	2. 3 but in *h* regard others as better than

HUNGER

Ps	34.10 young lions suffer want and *h*, but those
Isa	49.10 they shall not *h* or thirst, neither
Jer	38. 9 him in the cistern to die there of *h*,
Lam	2.19 lives of your children, who faint for *h*
Ezek	34.29 they shall no more be consumed with *h*
Mt	5. 6 who *h* and thirst for righteousness,
Acts	27.38 had satisfied their *h*, they lightened
2 Cor	6. 5 labors, sleepless nights, *h*; by purity,
Rev	7.16 They will *h* no more, and thirst no

HUNGRY

1 Sam	2.	5 but those who were *h* are fat with spoil.
Ps	50.12	"If I were *h*, I would not tell you, for the
	107.	9 the thirsty, and the *h* he fills with good
Prov	6.30	satisfy their appetite when they are *h*.
Isa	8.21	the land, greatly distressed and *h*;
Mt	21.18	when he returned to the city, he was *h*.
Mk	2.25	when he and his companions were *h*
	11.12	they came from Bethany, he was *h*.
Lk	1.53	filled the *h* with good things, and sent
	6.21	"Blessed are you who are *h* now, for you
Jn	6.35	whoever comes to me will never be *h*,
Acts	10.10	roof to pray. He became *h* and wanted
1 Cor	4.11	To the present hour we are *h* and
	11.34	If you are *h*, eat at home, so that when
2 Cor	11.27	*h* and thirsty, often without food, cold
Phil	4.12	secret of being well-fed and of going *h*,

HUNT (HUNTED)

Ezek	13.18	lives! Will you *h* down lives among my
Job	10.16	Bold as a lion you *h* me; you repeat
Ps	140.	11 let evil speedily *h* down the violent!
Jer	50.17	Israel is a *h* sheep driven away by lions.

HUNTER

Gen	10.	9 He was a mighty *h* before the Lord;
	25.27	Esau was a skillful *h*, a man of the

HURAM

2 Chr	2.11	Then King *H* of Tyre answered in a

HURRIEDLY

Prov	19.	2 one who moves too *h* misses the way.

HURRY

Gen	19.22	*H*, escape there, for I can do nothing

HURT

1 Chr	4.10	and that you would keep me from *h* and
Eccl	8.	9 authority over another to the other's *h*.
Isa	11.	9 They will not *h* or destroy on all my
Jer	8.21	For the *h* of my poor people I am *h*, I

HUSBAND (HUSBANDS HUSBAND'S)

Gen	3.	6 she also gave some to her *h*, who was
	18.12	I have grown old, and my *h* is old,
Deut	25.	5 Her *h* brother shall go in to her, taking
Esth	1.17	to look with contempt upon their *h*,
Prov	31.23	Her *h* is known in the city gates, taking
Isa	54.	5 For your Maker is your *h*, the Lord of
Jer	31.32	that they broke, though I was their *h*,
Mt	1.16	father of Joseph the *h* of Mary, of whom
Jn	4.16	said to her, "Go, call your *h*, and come
Rom	7.	2 woman is bound by law to her *h*
1 Cor	7.	2 own wife and each woman her own *h*.
	7.14	the unbelieving *h* is made holy through
	7.34	of the world, how to please her *h*.
Eph	5.25	*H*, love your wives, just as Christ loved
	5.33	and a wife should respect her *h*.
Col	3.19	*H*, love your wives, and never treat
1 Tim	3.2	n be above reproach, the *h* of one wife,
1 Pet	3.	7 *H*, in the same way, show consideration

HYMN (HYMNS)

Mt	26.30	When they had sung the *h*, they went
Mk	14.26	When they had sung the *h*, they went
1 Cor	14.26	together, each one has a *h*, a lesson,
Eph	5.19	as you sing psalms and *h* and spiritual
Col	3.16	sing psalms, *h*, and spiritual songs

HYPOCRISY

Lk	12.	1 yeast of the Pharisees, that is, their *h*.

HYPOCRITE (HYPOCRITES)

Mt	6.	2 sound a trumpet before you, as the *h* do
	6.	5 you pray, do not be like the *h*;
	6.16	you fast, do not look dismal, like the *h*,
	7.	5 You *h*, first take the log out of your own
	15.	7 You *h*! Isaiah prophesied rightly about

Mt	23.13	woe to you, scribes and Pharisees, *h*!
	23.23	"Woe to you, scribes and Pharisees, *h*!
Mk	7.	6 Isaiah prophesied rightly about you *h*,
Lk	13.15	"You *h*! does not each of you on the

HYSSOP

Ex	12.22	Take a bunch of *h*, dip it in the blood
Ps	51.	7 Purge me with *h*, and I shall be clean;
Jn	19.29	sponge full of the wine on a branch of *h*

I

IDLE

Mt	20.	3 he saw others standing *i* in the

IDLENESS

2 Thess	3.	6 away from believers who are living in *i*
	3.11	some of you are living in *i*, mere

IDOL (IDOLS)

Ex	20.	4 You shall not make for yourself an *i*,
Lev	26.	1 You shall make for yourselves no *i* and
Deut	5.	8 You shall not make for yourself an *i*,
Judg	17.	3 for my son, to make an *i* of cast metal.
	18.30	Danites set up the *i* for themselves.
1 Sam	19.13	Michal took an *i* and laid it on the bed;
1 Chr	16.26	For all the gods of the peoples are *i*,
2 Chr	15.	8 put away the abominable *i* from all the
Ps	31.	6 those who pay regard to worthless *i*,
	78.58	they moved him to jealousy with their *i*.
	106.	58 they sacrificed to the *i* of Canaan;
Isa	2.	8 Their land is filled with *i*; they bow
	2.18	The *i* shall utterly pass away. Enter the
	19.	3 they will consult the *i* and the spirits of
	40.19	An *i*? —A workman casts it, and a
	44.	9 All who make *i* are nothing, and the
	48.	5 that you would not say, "My *i* did them,
Jer	50.38	land of images, and they go mad over *i*.
Ezek	14.	4 who take their *i* into their hearts and
	20.18	nor defile yourselves with their *i*.
Hos	4.17	Ephraim is joined to *i*— let him alone.
	8.	4 they made *i* for their own destruction.
Mic	1.	7 with fire, and all her *i* I will lay waste;
Acts	15.20	to abstain only from things polluted by *i*
	17.16	to see that the city was full of *i*.
	21.25	from what has been sacrificed to *i*
1 Cor	8.	1 concerning food offered to *i*: we know
	10.19	to *i* is anything, or that an *i* is anything?
1 Thess	1.	9 you turned to God from *i*, to serve a
1 Jn	5.21	Little children, keep yourselves from *i*.

IDOLATER (IDOLATERS)

1 Cor	6.	9 Do not be deceived! Fornicators, *i*,
Eph	5.	5 or one who is greedy (that is, an *i*), has

IGNORANCE (IGNORANT)

Ps	73.22	I was stupid and *i*, I was like a brute
Acts	17.30	has overlooked the times of human *i*,
Eph	4.18	because of their *i* and hardness of heart.

IGNORED

Deut	33.	9 he *i* his kin, and did not acknowledge

ILL

Lk	7.	2 whom he valued highly, and who was *i*
Jn	11.	3 to Jesus, "Lord, he whom you love is *i*."
1 Cor	11.30	this reason many of you are weak and *i*,
Phil	2.26	because you heard that he was *i*.

ILLNESS

Deut	7.15	Lord will turn away from you every *i*;
2 Kings	8.	8 him, whether I shall recover from this *i*."
Ps	41.	3 sickbed; in their *i* you heal all their
Jn	11.	4 "This *i* does not lead to death; rather it

ILL-TREATMENT

Heb	11.25	choosing rather to share *i* with the

IMAGE (IMAGES)

Gen	1.26	"Let us make humankind in our *i*,
Num	33.52	destroy all their molten *i*, and demolish
1 Sam	6. 5	you must make *i* of your tumors and *i*
1 Cor	11. 7	since he is the *i* and reflection of God;
Col	1.15	He is the *i* of the invisible God, the
	3.10	according to the *i* of its creator.

IMAGINE

Eph	3.20	far more than all that we ask or *i*,

IMITATE (IMITATING)

Phil	3.17	join in *i* me, and observe those who live
3 Jn	11	Beloved, do not *i* what is evil but *i* what

IMITATORS

1 Cor	4.16	I appeal to you, then, be *i* of me. For
	11. 1	be saved. Be *i* of me, as I am of Christ.
Eph	5. 1	be *i* of God, as beloved children, and
1 Thess	1. 6	you became *i* of us and of the Lord, for
Heb	6.12	but *i* of those who through faith

IMMANUEL (EMMANUEL)

Isa	7.14	shall bear a son, and shall name him *I*.
	8. 8	will fill the breadth of your land, O *I*.
Mt	1.23	and they shall name him *E*," which

IMMORALITY

1 Cor	5. 1	that there is sexual *i* among you,

IMMORTAL (IMMORTALITY)

Rom	1.23	exchanged the glory of the *i* God for
1 Cor	15.53	and this mortal body must put on *i*.

IMPERISHABLE

1 Cor	15.42	is sown is perishable, what is raised is *i*.
1 Pet	1. 4	into an inheritance that is *i*, undefiled,

IMPLORE

2 Kings	20. 3	"Remember now, O Lord, I *i* you, how I

IMPOSSIBLE

Gen	11. 6	they propose to do will now be *i*
Lk	1.37	"For nothing will be *i* with God."
Heb	10. 4	it is *i* for the blood of bulls and goats to

IMPRISONED

Jer	37.15	Jeremiah, and they beat him and *i* him
Acts	22.19	I *i* and beat those who believed
Rom	11.32	God has *i* all in disobedience, so that

IMPRISONMENT (IMPRISONMENTS)

Acts	20.23	city that *i* and persecutions are waiting
2 Cor	6. 5	hardships, calamities, beatings, *i*, riots,
	11.23	greater labors, far more *i*, with countless
Phil	1.13	to everyone else that my *i* is for Christ;
Heb	11.36	and flogging, and even chains and *i*.

IMPURE (IMPURITY)

Zech	13. 1	to cleanse them from sin and *i*.
Rom	1.24	them up in the lusts of their hearts to *i*,
2 Cor	12.21	have not repented of the *i*, sexual
Eph	4.19	greedy to practice every kind of *i*.
1 Thess	2. 3	does not spring from deceit or *i* motives

IMPUTE (IMPUTES)

1 Sam	22.15	Do not let the king *i* anything to his
Ps	32. 2	those to whom the Lord *i* no iniquity,

INCENSE

Ex	30. 1	shall make an altar on which to offer *i*;
	30.35	make an *i* blended as by the perfumer,
	37.25	He made an altar of *i* of acacia wood,
Num	16.17	of you take his censer, and put *i* on it,
2 Chr	26.16	to make an offering on the altar of *i*.
Ps	141. 2	Let my prayer be counted as *i* before
Ezek	8.11	the fragrant cloud of *i* was ascending.
Mal	1.11	in every place *i* is offered to my name,
Lk	1. 9	the sanctuary of the Lord and offer *i*.

INCITED

1 Chr	21. 1	and *i* David to count the people of
Acts	13.50	But the Jews *i* the devout women of

INCLINATION

Gen	6. 5	every *i* of the thoughts of their hearts
	8.21	for the *i* of the human heart is evil from

INCLINE (INCLINING)

1 Kings	8.58	but *i* our hearts to him, to walk in all
Prov	2. 2	and *i* your heart to understanding;
Dan	9.18	*I* your ear, O my God, and hear. Open

INCOME

Prov	3.14	for her *i* is better than silver, and her

INCREASE (INCREASED INCREASES)

Ps	71.21	You will *i* my honor, and comfort me
	115. 14	May the Lord give you *i*, both you and
Prov	16.21	and pleasant speech *i* persuasiveness.
Eccl	5.11	When goods *i*, they who eat them *i*; and
Isa	26.15	But you have *i* the nation, O Lord, you
Ezek	34.27	the earth shall yield its *i*. They shall be
Lk	2.52	Jesus *i* in wisdom and in years, and in
Jn	3.30	He must *i*, but I must decrease."
Acts	16. 5	in the faith and *i* in numbers daily.
1 Thess	3.12	the Lord make you *i* and abound in love

INCREDIBLE

Acts	26. 8	Why is it thought *i* by any of you that

INDICATE (INDICATES INDICATING)

Jn	21.19	said this to *i* the kind of death by which
Acts	25.27	a prisoner without *i* the charges against
Heb	9. 8	By this the Holy Spirit *i* that the way

INDICTMENT

Job	31.35	that I had the *i* written by my adversary!
Hos	4. 1	Lord has an *i* against the inhabitants
	12. 2	Lord has an *i* against Judah, and will

INDIGNANT

Mk	10.14	when Jesus saw this, he was *i* and said

INDISPENSABLE

1 Cor	12.22	the body that seem to be weaker are *i*,

INDULGE

2 Pet	2.10	who *i* their flesh in depraved lust, and

INFANT (INFANTS)

Hos	11. 4	like those who lift *i* to their cheeks.
Isa	13.16	Their *i* will be dashed to pieces before
Mt	11.25	intelligent and have revealed them to *i*;
Lk	10.21	and revealed them to *i*; yes, for such
	18.15	bringing even *i* to him that he might
1 Cor	3. 1	as people of the flesh, as *i* in Christ.
Heb	5.13	who lives on milk, being still an *i*,

INFERIOR

Job	12. 3	I am not *i* to you. Who does not know
2 Cor	12.11	I am not at all *i* to these super-apostles,

INFIRMITIES

Ps	41. 3	in their illness you heal all their *i*.

INFORMED

Jude	5	to remind you, though you are fully *i*,

INFURIATED

Esth	3. 5	or do obeisance to him, Haman was *i*.

INHABITS (INHABITED)

Isa	57.15	the high and lofty one who *i* eternity,
Jer	17.25	and this city shall be *i* forever.

INHERIT

Lev	20.24	You shall *i* their land, and I will give it
Num	33.54	to your ancestral tribes you shall *i*.
	34.13	This is the land that you shall *i* by lot,

Ps	37.	9 but those who wait for the LORD shall *i*
Zech	2.12	The LORD will *i* Judah as his portion in
Mt	25.34	*i* the kingdom prepared for you from the
Mk	10.17	what must I do to *i* eternal life?"
Lk	10.25	said, "what must I do to *i* eternal life?"
	18.18	what must I do to *i* eternal life?"
Rom	4.13	the promise that he would *i* the world

INHERITANCE

Num	27.	8 you shall pass his *i* on to his daughter.
Deut	18.	1 Levi, shall have no . . . *i* within Israel;
	20.16	God is giving you as an *i*, you must not
Josh	13.14	by fire to the LORD . . . are their *i*,
1 Kings	21.	3 that I should give you my ancestral *i*."
1 Chr	16.18	land of Canaan as your portion for an *i*."
Ps	105.	11 land of Canaan as your portion for an *i*."
Prov	13.22	The good leave an *i* to their children's
Lam	5.	2 Our *i* has been turned over to strangers,
Ezek	47.14	and this land shall fall to you as your *i*.
Acts	20.32	up and to give you the *i* among all who
Gal	3.18	For if the *i* comes from the law, it no
Eph	1.18	of his glorious *i* among the saints,
Col	3.24	you will receive the *i* as your reward;
1 Pet	1.	4 into an *i* which is imperishable,

INIQUITY (INIQUITIES)

Ex	34.	7 forgiving *i* and transgression and sin, yet
	34.	7 visiting the *i* of the parents upon the
2 Sam	7.14	When he commits *i*, I will punish him
Ezra	9.	6 our *i* have risen higher than our heads,
Job	34.32	if I have done *i*, I will do it no more'?
Ps	51.	9 face from my sins, and blot out all my *i*.
	66.18	If I had cherished *i* in my heart, the
	106.	43 and were brought low through their *i*.
Prov	5.22	The *i* of the wicked ensnare them, and
Isa	53.	6 the LORD has laid on him the *i* of us all.
Ezek	36.33	day that I cleanse you from all your *i*,
	39.23	of Israel went into captivity for their *i*,
Titus	2.14	redeem us from all *i* and purify for

INJURED

Ezek	34.16	and I will bind up the *i*, and I will

INJUSTICE

Prov	22.	8 Whoever sows *i* will reap calamity, and
Isa	58.	6 that I choose: to loose the bonds of *i*,
Rom	9.14	Is there *i* on God's part? By no means!

INK

Jer	36.18	and I wrote them with *i* on the scroll."
2 Cor	3.	3 written not with *i* but with the Spirit of
2 Jn	12	rather not use paper and *i*; instead I

INN

Lk	2.	7 there was no place for them in the *i*.
	10.34	brought him to an *i*, and took care of

INNOCENT

Gen	20.	4 said, Lord, will you destroy an *i* people?
Deut	19.13	you shall purge the guilt of *i* blood from
2 Kings	24.	4 filled Jerusalem with *i* blood, and the
Job	4.	7 now, who that was *i* ever perished?
	9.28	for I know you will not hold me *i*.
	17.	8 and the *i* stir themselves up against
	27.17	wear it, and the *i* will divide the silver.
	34.	5 Job has said, 'I am *i*, and God has
Ps	19.13	I shall be blameless, and *i* of great
Isa	3.10	Tell the *i* how fortunate they are, for
Jer	2.35	"I am *i*; surely his anger has turned
	19.	4 filled this place with the blood of the *i*,
Jon	1.14	life. Do not make us guilty of *i* blood;
Mt	10.16	so be wise as serpents and *i* as doves.
	27.24	"I am *i* of this man's blood; see to it
Lk	23.47	God and said, "Certainly this man was *i*!"
1 Tim	1.	9 law is not laid down for the *i* but for

INQUIRE (INQUIRED)

Gen	25.22	do I live?" So she went to *i* of the LORD.

Ex	18.15	the people come to me to *i* of God.
Deut	12.30	do not *i* concerning their gods, saying,
Judg	20.18	to Bethel, where they *i* of God, "Which
1 Sam	14.37	So Saul *i* of God, "Shall I go down after
	23.	2 David *i* of the LORD, "Shall I go and
2 Sam	2.	1 David *i* of the LORD, "Shall I go up into
	5.19	David *i* of the LORD, "Shall I go up
2 Kings	22.13	"Go, *i* of the LORD for me, for the
1 Chr	10.14	David *i* of the LORD, "Shall I go up against
2 Chr	34.21	"Go, *i* of the LORD for me and for those
Jer	8.	2 which they have *i* of and worshiped;
	21.	2 "Please *i* of the LORD on our behalf, for

INSANE

Acts	26.25	Too much learning is driving you *i*!"

INSCRIBED

Job	19.23	down! O that they were *i* in a book!
Dan	5.25	hand was sent and this writing was *i*.
	10.21	tell you what is *i* in the book of truth.

INSCRIPTION

Mk	15.26	The *i* of the charge against him read,
Lk	23.38	There was also an *i* over him, "This is
Jn	19.19	Pilate also had an *i* written and put on

INSIGHT

Dan	1.	4 endowed with knowledge and *i*, and

INSIST

Eph	4.17	I affirm and *i* on in the Lord; you must

INSOLENT

Ps	19.13	Keep back your servant also from the *i*;

INSPIRED

2 Tim	3.16	All scripture is *i* by God and is useful

INSTALLMENT

2 Cor	1.22	us his Spirit in our hearts as a first *i*.

INSTINCTIVELY

Rom	2.14	do *i* what the law requires, these,

INSTRUCT (INSTRUCTED)

2 Chr	26.	5 days of Zechariah, who *i* him in the fear
Ps	32.	8 I will *i* you and teach you the way you
Lk	1.	4 the things of which you have been *i*.
Acts	7.22	Moses was *i* in all the wisdom of the
1 Tim	1.	3 *i* certain people not to teach any
2 Tim	3.	7 who are always being *i* and can never
	3.15	writings that are able to *i* you for

INSTRUCTION

Job	36.10	He opens their ears to *i*, and commands
Prov	8.10	Take my *i* instead of silver, and
Isa	29.24	and those who grumble will accept *i*.
Mic	4.	2 out of Zion shall go forth *i*, and the
Mal	2.	6 True *i* was in his mouth, and no wrong

INSTRUCTORS

Mt	23.10	Nor are you to be called *i*, for you have

INSTRUMENT (INSTRUMENTS)

1 Chr	15.16	as the singers to play on musical *i*,
Am	6.	5 and like David improvise on *i* of music;
Acts	9.15	he is an *i* whom I have chosen to bring

INSULT (INSULTS)

Gen	39.14	has brought among us a Hebrew to *i* us!
Ps	69.	9 the *i* of those who *i* you have fallen on
	69.20	*I* have broken my heart, so that I am in
Prov	17.	5 Those who mock the poor *i* their Maker;
Isa	50.	6 out the beard; I hid not my face from *i*
Hos	12.14	on him and pay him back for his *i*.
Lk	11.45	when you say these things, you *i* us too."
Acts	23.	4 "Do you dare to *i* God's high priest?"
Rom	15.	3 "The *i* of those who *i* you have fallen on
2 Cor	12.10	I am content with weaknesses, *i*,

INTEGRITY

Job 2. 9 "Do you still persist in your *i*? Curse
Titus 2. 7 and in your teaching show *i*, gravity,

INTEND

1 Kings 5. 5 I *i* to build a house for the name of the
2 Cor 8.21 we *i* to do what is right not only in the

INTENTIONS

Mt 15.19 For out of the heart come evil *i*,

INTERCEDE (INTERCEDED INTERCEDES)

Deut 9.20 but I *i* also on behalf of Aaron at the
Jer 27.18 them, then let them *i* with the LORD
Rom 8.26 that very Spirit *i* with sighs too deep for

INTERCESSION

1 Sam 2.25 sins against the LORD, who can make *i*?"
Isa 53.12 many, and made *i* for the transgressors.
Heb 7.25 he always lives to make *i* for them.

INTEREST

Lev 25.36 Do not take *i* in advance or otherwise
Neh 5.10 and grain. Let us stop this taking of *i*.
Ps 15. 5 who do not lend money at *i*, and do not

INTERMARRY

Josh 23.12 left here among you, and *i* with them,

INTERPRET (INTERPRETED)

Lk 12.56 how to *i* the appearance of earth and
24.27 he *i* to them the things about himself in
1 Cor 14.27 three, and each in turn; and let one *i*.

INTERPRETATION

Dan 2. 4 the dream, and we will reveal the *i*."
2.36 dream; now we will tell the king its *i*.
4.18 you, Belteshazzar, declare the *i*, since
5.12 Daniel be called, and he will give the *i*."
2 Pet 1.20 of scripture is a matter of one's own *i*,

INTERPRETER

Gen 42.23 since he spoke with them through an *i*.

INTERVALS

2 Kings 20. 9 advanced ten *i*; shall it retreat ten *i*?"

INTERVENED

Jer 15.11 I have *i* in your life for good, surely I

INVISIBLE

Rom 1.20 divine nature, *i* though they are, have
Col 1.15 He is the image of the *i* God, the
1 Tim 1.17 of the ages, immortal, *i*, the only God,

INVITED

Jn 2. 2 had also been *i* to the wedding.
Rev 19. 9 Blessed are those who are *i* to the

INVOKE

Gen 4.26 people began to *i* the name of the LORD.
12. 8 to the LORD and *i* the name of the LORD.

IRON

Josh 17.16 who live in the plain have chariots of *i*,
2 Kings 6. 6 threw it in there, and made the *i* float.
1 Chr 20. 3 set them to work with saws and *i* picks
Ps 105.18 fetters, his neck was put in a collar of *i*;
Prov 27.17 I sharpens *i*, and one person sharpens
Jer 28.13 broken wooden bars only to forge *i* bars
Dan 2.35 Then the *i*, the clay, the bronze, the

IRON-SMELTER

Deut 4.20 brought you out of the *i*, out of Egypt,

IRONSMITH

Isa 44.12 The *i* fashions it and works over the

ISAAC

His birth foretold, Gen 18.1-15; born, Gen 21.1-7; of-fered to God, Gen 22.1-19; married Rebekah, Gen 24; father of twins, Gen 25.19-26; dwelt in Gerar, Gen 26.1-6; Isaac and Abimelech, Gen 26.7-33; blessed Jacob, Gen 27.1-40; death and burial, Gen 35.29.

Gen 21. 3 Abraham gave the name *I* to his son
Gal 4.28 are children of the promise, like *I*.
Heb 11.20 By faith *I* invoked blessings for the

ISAIAH

Called, Isa 6; father of two sons, Isa 7.3; 8.3; prophe-sied during the reign of Uzziah, Jotham, Ahaz, and Heze-kiah, Isa 1.1; counselled Ahaz, Isa 7; counselled Hezeki-ah, 2 Kings 19—20 (Isa 37—39).

Mt 3. 3 is the one of whom the prophet *I* spoke
15. 7 *I* prophesied rightly about you when he
Lk 4.17 the scroll of the prophet *I* was given to
Acts 8.28 it and heard him reading the prophet *I*.

ISHMAEL

Gen 16.11 shall bear a son; you shall call him *I*,
17.18 God, "O that *I* might live in your sight!"
25.12 These are the descendants of *I*,

ISRAEL

Gen 32.28 shall no longer be called Jacob, but *I*,
Ex 1. 1 of the sons of *I* who came to Egypt
4.22 says the LORD, *I* is my first-born son.
1 Sam 7. 6 And Samuel judged the people of *I* at
1 Kings 4. 1 King Solomon was king over all *I*,
12.19 *I* has been in rebellion against the
17. 1 the LORD the God of *I* lives, before
1 Chr 14. 8 David had been anointed king over all *I*,
2 Chr 30. 1 the passover to the Lord the God of *I*.
Ezra 7. 7 Some of the people of *I*, and some of
Ps 25.22 Redeem *I*, O God, out of all its
103. 7 to Moses, his acts to the people of *I*.
Isa 1. 3 but *I* does not know, my people do not
Mt 2. 6 a ruler who is to shepherd my people *I*.' "
27.42 He is the King of *I*; let him come down
Lk 2.25 looking forward to the consolation of *I*,
Acts 1. 6 when you will restore the kingdom to *I*?"
Rom 11.26 so all *I* will be saved; as it is written,
Eph 2.12 aliens from the commonwealth of *I*,
Heb 8. 8 a new covenant with the house of *I*

ISRAELITES

Ex 14. 8 he pursued the *I*, who were going out
19. 1 after the *I* had gone out of the land of
Josh 4. 8 The *I* did as Joshua commanded. They
Rev 21.12 the names of the twelve tribes of the *I*;

ISSACHAR

Gen 30.18 to my husband"; so she named him *I*.
49.14 *I* is a strong donkey, lying down
Num 26.23 The descendants of *I* by their clans: of
Rev 7. 7 from the tribe of *I* twelve thousand,

IVORY

1 Kings 10.18 king also made a great *i* throne, and
22.39 the *i* house that he built, and all the
Ps 45. 8 From *i* palaces stringed instruments
Am 3.15 the houses of *i* shall perish, and the
6. 4 Alas for those who lie on beds of *i*, and

J

JABBOK

Gen 32.22 children, and crossed the ford of the *J*.
Deut 3.16 up to the *J*, the wadi being boundary of
Josh 12. 2 as far as the river *J*, the boundary of the

JACKALS

Ezek 13. 4 Your prophets have been like *j* among

JACOB (JACOB'S)

Born, Gen 25.19-26; obtained Esau's birthright, Gen 25.27-34; received Isaac's blessing, Gen 27.1-29; fled from Esau, Gen 27.41—28.5; dream at Bethel and his

vow, Gen 28.10-22; served Laban for Rachel and Leah, Gen 29.1-30; dealings with Laban, Gen 30.25-43; departure from Paddan-aram, Gen 31; wrestled at Peniel, Gen 32.24-32; reconciled with Esau, Gen 33.1-16; blessed by God at Bethel, Gen 35.1-15; went down to Egypt, Gen 46—47; blessed Ephraim and Manasseh, Gen 48; blessed his own sons, Gen 49.1-27; death and burial, Gen 49.28—50.14.

Num	24.17 a star shall come out of J, and a scepter
Hos	12.12 J fled to the land of Aram, there Israel
Mt	8.11 Isaac and J in the kingdom of heaven,
Rom	9.13 is written, "I have loved J, but I have
Heb	11.21 By faith J, when dying, blessed each of
Jn	4. 6 J well was there, and Jesus, tired out by

JAIRUS

Mk	5.22 leaders of the synagogue named J came
Lk	8.41 there came a man named J, a leader of

JAMES

Mt	4.21 from there, he saw two other brothers, J
	10. 3 tax collector; J son of Alphaeus, and
Acts	1.13 Matthew, J son of Alphaeus, and Simon
1 Cor	15. 7 Then he appeared to J, then to all the

JAPHETH

Gen	9.27 May God make space for J, and let him

JAR (JARS)

Judg	7.16 and empty j, with torches inside the j,
1 Kings	17.14 "The j of meal will not be emptied, and
Mk	14.13 a man carrying a j of water will meet
Lk	22.10 a man carrying a j of water will meet
Jn	4.28 So the woman left her water j and went
2 Cor	4. 7 we have this treasure in clay j, so that it

JAWBONE

Judg	15.15 Then he found a fresh j of a donkey,

JEALOUS

Gen	37.11 his brothers were j of him, but his
Num	11.29 said to him, "Are you j for my sake?
Deut	4.24 your God is a devouring fire, a j God.
	5. 9 for I the Lord your God am a j God;
	6.15 who is present with you, is a j God;
	32.21 They made me j with what is no god,
Josh	24.19 He is a j God; he will not forgive your
Ps	79. 5 forever? Will your j wrath burn like fire?
	106. 16 They were j of Moses in the camp, and
Ezek	39.25 Israel; and I will be j for my holy name.
Joel	2.18 Then the Lord became j for his land,
Nah	1. 2 A j and avenging God is the Lord, the
Zech	8. 2 I am j for Zion with great jealousy, and
Acts	7. 9 "The patriarchs, j of Joseph, sold him
Rom	11.11 to the Gentiles, so as to make Israel j.

JEALOUSY

Num	5.14 if the spirit of j comes on him, and he
1 Kings	14.22 they provoked him to j with their sins
Prov	6.34 j arouses a husband's fury, and he
Isa	11.13 The j of Ephraim shall depart, the
Ezek	5.13 I, the Lord, have spoken in my j, when I
	8. 3 to the seat of the image of j, which
Mt	27.18 it was out of j that they handed him
Mk	15.10 it was out of j that the chief priests had
1 Cor	3. 3 as long as there is j and quarreling
2 Cor	11. 2 I feel a divine j for you, for I promised

JEHOSHAPHAT

1 Kings	15.24 father David; his son J succeeded him.
	22. 7 But J said, "Is there no other prophet of
2 Chr	20. 1 some of the Meunites, came against J
	20.30 the realm of J was quiet, for his God
	21. 1 J slept with his ancestors and was
Joel	3. 2 and bring them down to the valley of J,

JEPHTHAH

Judg	11. 1 J . . . was a mighty warrior. Gilead was

Judg	11.30 J made a vow to the Lord, and said, "If
	12. 1 said to J, "Why did you cross over to
1 Sam	12.11 Lord sent . . . J, and Samson, and
Heb	11.32 me to tell of Gideon, Barak, Samson, J,

JEREMIAH

Called, Jer 1.1-10; vision of almond rod and boiling pot, Jer 1.11-19; sign of the waist cloth, Jer 13.1-11; sign of the potter's vessel, Jer 18; sign of the earthen flask, Jer 19; put in stocks, Jer 20.1-6; sign of the basket of figs, Jer 24; his life threatened, Jer 26; sign of purchase of field, Jer 32.6-44; prophesied to Rechabites, Jer 35; wrote prophecies, Jer 36; imprisoned, Jer 32.1-5; 37.11—38.28; released, Jer 39.11-14; 40.1-6; taken into Egypt, Jer 43.1-7.

Mt	16.14 but others Elijah, and still others J or

JERICHO

Josh	2. 1 "Go, view the land, especially J." So they
	6. 2 I have handed J over to you, along with
1 Kings	16.34 In his days Hiel of Bethel built J; he
Mk	10.46 and a large crowd were leaving J,
Heb	11.30 By faith the walls of J fell after they

JEROBOAM

1 Kings	11.26 J son of Nebat . . . rebelled against the
	12. 2 When J the son of Nebat heard of it
	12.25 J built Shechem in the hill country of
	13. 1 While J was standing by the altar to
	14. 1 At that time Abijah son of J fell sick.
	14.20 that J reigned was twenty-two years;
	14.30 was war between Rehoboam and J
	15.25 Nadab the son of J began to reign over
	15.34 walking in the way of J and in the sin
2 Kings	14.23 J the son of Joash of Israel began to
	14.28 Now the rest of the acts of J, and all
	14.29 J slept with his ancestors, the kings of
Hos	1. 1 in the days of King J son of Joash of
Am	7.10 the priest of Bethel, sent to King J

JERUSALEM

Judg	19.10 and arrived opposite Jebus (that is, J).
2 Sam	5. 5 at J he reigned over all Israel and Judah
2 Kings	21. 4 Lord had said, "In J I will put my name."
2 Chr	20.28 They came to J, with harps and lyres
	36.19 broke down the wall of J, burned all its
	36.23 charged me to build him a house at J,
Ezra	3. 8 their arrival at the house of God at J,
Ps	51.18 good pleasure; rebuild the walls of J,
	122. 6 Pray for the peace of J! "May they
	137. 5 If I forget you, O J, let my right hand
Isa	31. 5 so the Lord of hosts will protect J;
	40. 9 strength, O J, herald of good tidings,
Mt	23.37 "J, J, the city that kills the prophets
Acts	1. 8 my witnesses in J, in all Judea and
	15. 2 to go up to J to discuss this question
Rom	15.26 with the poor among the saints at J.
Gal	4.26 corresponds to the J above; she is free,
Heb	12.22 to the city of the God, the heavenly J,
Rev	21. 2 saw the holy city, the new J, coming

JESUS

His birth foretold, Lk 1.26-38; born, Mt 1.18-25; Lk 2.1-7; circumcised, Lk 2.21; presented in the temple, Lk 2.22-38; visited by the wise men, Mt 2.1-12; fled to Egypt, Mt 2.13-18; brought to Nazareth, Mt 2.19-23 (Lk 2.39); boyhood visit to Jerusalem, Lk 2.41-50; his brothers and sisters, Mt 13.55-56 (Mk 6.3); baptized, Mt 3.13-17 (Mk 1.9-11; Lk 3.21-22; Jn 1.31-34); tempted by the devil, Mt 4.1-11 (Mk 1.12-13; Lk 4.1-13); called his disciples, Mt 4.18-22 (Mk 1.16-20; Lk 5.1-11); Mt 9.9 (Mk 2.13-14; Lk 5.27-28); Jn 1.35-51; commissioned the twelve, Mt 10.1-4 (Mk 3.13-19; Lk 6.12-16); Sermon on the Mount, Mt 5—7 (Lk 6.17-49); sent out disciples, Mt 9.35—11.1 (Mk 6.7-13; Lk 9.1-6; 10.1-24); foretold his death and resurrection, Mt 16.21-28 (Mk 8.31-38; Lk 9.22-27); Mt 17.22-23 (Mk 9.30-32; Lk 9.43-45); Mt

20.17-28 (Mk 10.32-45; Lk 18.31-34); transfigured, Mt 17.1-8 (Mk 9.2-8; Lk 9.28-36); triumphal entry into Jerusalem, Mt 21.1-11 (Mk 11.1-11; Lk 19.29-44; Jn 12.12-19); instituted the Lord's supper, Mt 26.26-29 (Mk 14.22-25; Lk 22.17-20; 1 Cor 11.23-26); betrayed, arrested, and forsaken, Mt 26.47-57 (Mk 14.43-53; Lk 22.47-54; Jn 18.2-13); crucified, Mt 27.31-56 (Mk 15.20-41; Lk 23.26-49; Jn 19.16-30); appeared after his resurrection, Mt 28.9-20 (Mk 16.9-18n; Lk 24.13-49; Jn 20.11-31); Acts 1.3-8; 1 Cor 15.5-7; ascended to heaven, Lk 24.50-53 (Mk 16.19n); Acts 1.9-11.

JETHRO

Ex	3. 1 keeping the flock of his father-in-law J,
	4. 18 Moses went back to . . . J and said to
	18. 1 J, the priest of Midian . . . heard of all
	18.12 J . . . brought a burnt offering and

JEW (JEWS)

Ezra	4.12 king that the J who came up from you
Neh	1. 2 I asked them about the J that survived,
Esth	2. 5 was a J in the citadel of Susa whose
Dan	3. 8 came forward and denounced the J.
Mt	2. 2 child who has been born king of the J?
	27.11 "Are you the King of the J?" Jesus said,
	27.37 read, "This is Jesus, the King of the J."
Jn	11. 8 the J were just now trying to stone you,
Acts	18. 5 testifying to the J that the Messiah was
	19.10 Asia, both J and Greeks, heard the word
Rom	3. 9 all both J and Greeks, are under the
	9.24 called, not from the J only but also
1 Cor	1.22 For J demand signs and Greeks desire
	9.20 To the J I became a J, in order to win
	10.32 Give no offense to J or to Greeks or to

JEWELS (JEWELRY)

Gen	24.53 the servant brought forth j of silver and
Ex	3.22 neighbor . . . for j of silver and of gold,
Prov	8.11 for wisdom is better than j, and all that

JEWISH

Jn	18.12 officer, and the J police arrested Jesus

JEZREEL

Josh	19.18 Its territory included J, Chesulloth,
1 Kings	21. 1 had a vineyard in J, beside the palace
Hos	1. 4 the house of Jehu for the blood of J,
	2.22 and the oil, and they shall answer J;

JOAB

Murdered Abner, 2 Sam 3.22-30; set Uriah in the forefront, 2 Sam 11.6-22; reconciled David and Absalom, 2 Sam 14.28-33; killed Absalom, 2 Sam 18.9-17; pursued Sheba and slew Amasa, 2 Sam 20.4-22; put to death by Solomon, 1 Kings 2.28-34.

JOB

Job	1. 1 in the land of Uz whose name was J.
	2. 3 "Have you considered my servant J?
	42. 8 go to my servant J, and offer up for
	42.10 the LORD restored the fortunes of J
	42.17 And J died, old and full of days.
Ezek	14.14 even if Noah, Daniel, and J, these
Jas	5.11 You have heard of the endurance of J,

JOEL

Joel	1. 1 The word of the LORD that came to J
Acts	2.16 what was spoken through the prophet J:

JOHN (the Baptist)

Birth foretold, Lk 1.5-25; born, Lk 1.57-66; preached and baptized, Mt 3.1-12 (Mk 1.4-11; Lk 3.1-17; Jn 1.6-8, 19-28); imprisoned, Mt 14.3-4 (Mk 6.17-18; Lk 3.19-20); sent messengers to Jesus, Mt 11.1-6 (Lk 7.18-23); commended by Jesus, Mt 11.7-15 (Lk 7.24-35); beheaded and buried, Mt 14.6-12 (Mk 6.17-29).

JOHN (the Apostle)

Called, Mt 4.21 (Mk 1.19; Lk 5.10); sent out with the twelve, Mt 10.2 (Mk 3.17); desire for revenge rebuked, Lk 9.51-56; selfish request rejected, Mt 20.20-24 (Mk 10.35-41); healed and preached in the temple, Acts 3.1-4.22.

JOIN (JOINED)

2 Kings	23. 3 book. All the people j in the covenant.
Dan	11.34 help, and many shall j them insincerely.
Zech	2.11 Many nations shall j themselves to the
Mt	19. 5 and be j to his wife, and the two shall
	19. 6 what God has j together, let no one
Mk	10. 7 father and mother and be j to his wife,
	10. 9 Therefore what God has j together, let

JONAH

2 Kings	14.25 which he spoke by his servant J son of
Jon	1. 1 Now the word of the LORD came to J
	2. 1 Then J prayed to the LORD his God from
	3. 1 of the LORD came to J a second time,
	4. 1 But this was very displeasing to J, and
Mt	12.40 as J was three days and three nights in
	16. 4 will be given to it except the sign of J."
Lk	11.30 just as J became a sign to the people of
	11.32 see, something greater than J is here!

JONATHAN

Smote the Philistine garrison, 1 Sam 13.2-4; 14.1-15; unknowingly transgressed Saul's oath, 1 Sam 14.24-30; rescued by the people, 1 Sam 14.36-46; made a covenant with David, 1 Sam 18.1-5; friendship with David, 1 Sam 20; killed by the Philistines, 1 Sam 31.2; mourned by David, 2 Sam 1.17-27; covenant with him remembered by David, 2 Sam 9.

JOPPA

2 Chr	2.16 and bring it to you in rafts by sea to J;
Jon	1. 3 He went down to J and found a ship
Acts	9.36 Now in J there was a disciple whose
	10. 5 send men to J for a certain Simon who

JORDAN

Gen	13.10 that the plain of the J was well watered
Deut	1. 1 Moses spoke to all Israel beyond the J
	4.21 he vowed that I should not cross the J
Josh	4. 1 nation had finished crossing over the J,
2 Sam	19.15 king came back to the J; and Judah
2 Kings	5.10 wash in the J seven times, and your
Job	40.23 it is confident though J rushes against
Ps	42. 6 from the land of the J and of Hermon,
Mt	3. 6 were baptized by him in the river J,
	3.13 came from Galilee to John at the J,
	19. 1 to the region of Judea beyond the J.
Jn	3.26 the one who was with you across the J,
	10.40 away again across the J to the place

JOSEPH (Son of Jacob)

Born, Gen 30.22-24; incurred jealousy by his dreams, Gen 37.5-11; sold into Egypt, Gen 37.12-28; refused Potiphar's wife, Gen 39.1-18; imprisoned, Gen 39.19-23; interpreted the prisoners' dreams, Gen 40; interpreted Pharaoh's dreams, Gen 41.1-36; made ruler over Egypt, Gen 41.37-49,53-57; married, had two sons, Gen 41.50-52; met his brothers, Gen 42—43; made himself known to them, Gen 45; saw his father again, Gen 46.28-34; died, Gen 50.22-26; buried in Shechem, Josh 24.32.

Deut	33.13 And of J he said, Blessed by the LORD
Ps	105. 17 He had sent a man ahead of them, J,
Heb	11.22 By faith J, at the end of his life, made

JOSEPH (Husband of Mary, Jesus' mother)

Betrothed to Mary, Mk 1.18 (Lk 1.27); instructed by an angel, Mt 1.19-21; went to Bethlehem, Lk 2.4; fled into Egypt, Mt 2.13-15; returned to Nazareth, Mt 2.19-23.

JOSEPH (of Arimathea)

Mt	27.57 rich man from Arimathea, named J,
Jn	19.38 After these things, J of Arimathea, who

JOSHUA (Son of Nun)

Defeated the Amalekites, Ex 17.8-13; in charge of the place of worship, Ex 33.11; sent with the spies, Num 13.1-16; 14.6-9; chosen to succeed Moses, Num 27.18-23; Deut 3.28; commissioned by Moses, Deut 31.23; 34.9; encouraged by the LORD, Josh 1.1-9; sent spies to Jericho, Josh 2; passed over Jordan, Josh 3; captured Jericho, Josh 6; captured Ai, Josh 7—9; warred against the kings, Josh 10—12; allotted the land, Josh 13.1—22.8; charged the people, Josh 23.1—24.24; made a covenant, Josh 24.25-27; death and burial, Josh 24.29-30.

JOSHUA (Priest, son of Jehozadak)

Hag	1. 1 and to J the son of Jehozadak, the high
	2. 2 and to J the son of Jehozadak, the high
Zech	3. 1 he showed me the high priest J
	6.11 set it on the head of the high priest J

JOSIAH

1 Kings 13.	2 shall be born to the house of David, J
2 Kings 21.24	of the land made his son J king in
	22. 1 J was eight years old when he began to
	23.23 year of King J this passover was kept
2 Chr	35. 1 J kept a passover to the LORD in

JOURNEY

Gen	24.56 LORD has made my j successful; let me

JOY

1 Chr	29.22 before the Lord on that day with great j.
2 Chr	20.27 returned to Jerusalem with j, for the
Neh	8.10 for the j of the LORD is your strength."
Ps	43. 4 to God my exceeding j; and I will praise
	47. 1 shout to God with loud songs of j.
	92. 4 at the works of your hands I sing for j.
	98. 8 clap their hands; let the hills sing for j
Prov	14.10 bitterness, and no stranger shares its j.
Isa	9. 3 before you as with a j at the harvest,
	12. 3 With j you will draw water from the
	35.10 heads; they shall obtain j and gladness,
	51. 3 j and gladness will be found in her,
	55.12 For you shall go out in j, and be lead
	60.15 majestic forever, a j from age to age.
Mt	2.10 stopped, they were overwhelmed with j.
Lk	1.14 You will have j and gladness, and many
	2.10 I am bringing you good news of a great j
Jn	3.29 For this reason my j has been fulfilled.
	15.11 so that my j may be in you, and that
	16.20 have pain, but your pain will turn into j.
	17.13 my j made complete in themselves.
Acts	8. 8 cured. So there was great j in that ci y.
	15. 3 and brought great j to all the believers.
Rom	14.17 and peace and j in the Holy Spirit.
	15.13 fill you with all j and peace in believing,
2 Cor	1.24 we are workers with you for your j,
	7.13 we rejoiced still more at the j of Titus,
Philem	7 I have indeed received much j and
1 Jn	1. 4 writing these things so that our j may

JOYFULLY

Lk	19.37 disciples began to praise God j with a

JUBILEE

Lev	25.10 It shall be a j for you: you shall return,
Num	36. 4 when the j of the Israelites comes, then

JUDAH

Born, Gen 29.35; saved Joseph's life, Gen 37.26-28; Judah and Tamar, Gen 38; pleaded for Benjamin, Gen 44.14-34; blessed by Jacob, Gen 49.8-12.

Tribe of Judah: blessed by Moses, Deut 33.7.

Judg	1.19 the LORD was with J, and he took
1 Sam	18.16 all Israel and J loved David; for it was
2 Sam	5. 5 over all Israel and J thirty-three years.
Ps	78.68 but he chose the tribe of J, Mount Zion,
Isa	5. 3 people of J, judge between me and my
	40. 9 say to the cities of J, "Here is your God!"

Jer	3. 7 not return, and her false sister J saw it.
	39. 1 In the ninth year of Zedekiah king of J,
Lam	1. 3 J has gone into exile with suffering and
Joel	3. 1 when I restore the fortunes of J and

JUDAISM

Acts	13.43 and devout converts to J followed Paul
Gal	1.13 heard, no doubt, of my earlier life in J.

JUDAS (Brother of James)

Mk	6. 3 brother of James and Joses and J and

JUDAS (Iscariot)

Mt	10. 4 and J, the one who betrayed him.
	26.14 was called J, went to the chief priests
	26.25 J, who betrayed him, said, "Surely not I,
	27. 3 When J his betrayer saw that Jesus was
Mk	3.19 and J, who betrayed him.
Lk	22. 3 Then Satan entered into J, who was one
	22.48 "J, is it with a kiss that you are
Jn	6.71 He was speaking of J son of Simon
	12. 4 But J, one of his disciples (the one who
	13. 2 already put it into the heart of J son of
Acts	1.16 concerning J, who became a guide

JUDE

Jude	1 J, a servant of Jesus Christ and brother

JUDEA (JUDEANS)

Jer	32.12 in the presence of all the J who were
Mt	2. 1 Jesus was born in Bethlehem of J, wise
	3. 1 Baptist appeared in the wilderness of J,
Lk	21.21 Then those in J must flee to the
Acts	2.14 "Men of J and all who live in

JUDGE (JUDGES) (n)

Gen	18.25 Shall not the J of all the earth do what
	19. 9 as an alien, and he would play the j!
Ex	2.14 Who made you a ruler and J over us?
	18.13 next day Moses sat as j for the people,
Judg	2.18 Whenever the LORD raised up j for them,
	11.27 let the LORD, who is j, decide today for
Lk	12.58 you may be dragged before the j, and
	18. 2 a j who neither feared God nor had
Acts	7.27 'Who made you a ruler and a j over us?

JUDGE (JUDGED JUDGES) (v)

Gen	31.53 God . . . j between us." So Jacob swore
Num	35.24 congregation shall j between the slayer
Deut	1.16 j rightly between one person and
1 Sam	2.10 The LORD will j the ends of the earth; he
	24.12 May the LORD j between me and you!
1 Chr	16.33 the lord, for he comes to j the earth.
2 Chr	19. 6 for you j not on behalf of human beings
Ps	9. 8 He j the world with righteousness; he j
	58.11 surely there is a God who j on earth."
	72. 2 May he j your people with
	75. 2 time that I appoint I will j with equity.
	96.13 he is coming to j the earth. He will j
Prov	29.14 king j the poor with equity, his throne
Isa	2. 4 He shall j between the nations, and
	11. 4 but with righteousness he shall j the
Jer	11.20 O LORD of hosts, who j righteously, who
Ezek	7. 3 I will j you according to your ways; I
	36.19 with their conduct and their deeds I j
Mt	7. 1 "Do not j, so that you be not j.
Lk	6.37 "Do not j, and you will not be j; do not
	12.57 why do you not j for yourselves what is
Jn	7.24 Do not j by appearances, but j with
	7.51 "Our law does not j people without first
	8.15 You j by human standards, I j no one.
Acts	17.31 will have the world j in righteousness
Rom	2. 1 when you j others; for in passing
	2.16 through Jesus Christ, will j the secret
	3. 6 For then how could God j the world?
	14. 5 while others j all days to be alike.
1 Cor	4. 3 small thing that I should be j by you
	5.12 those who are inside that you are to j?

1 Cor	6.	2 know that the saints will *j* the world?
		3 you not know that we are to *j* angels—
	11.31	But if we *j* ourselves, we would not be *j*.
Jas	2.12	who are to be *j* by the law of liberty.
1 Pet	4.	5 ready to *j* the living and the dead.
Rev	6.10	how long will it be before you *j* and
	19.11	and True, and in righteousness he *j* and
	20.12	the dead were *j* according to their

JUDGMENT (JUDGMENTS)

Gen	15.14	I will bring *j* on the nation that they
Ps	7.	6 O my God; you have appointed a *j*.
	75.	7 but it is God who executes *j*, putting
Eccl	11.	9 these things God will bring you into *j*.
Isa	32.	4 The minds of the rash will have good *j*,
Jer	1.16	I will utter my *j* against them, for all
	25.31	he is entering into *j* with all flesh, and
	48.47	the LORD. Thus far is the *j* on Moab.
Ezek	5.15	I execute *j* on you in anger and fury,
	14.21	my four deadly acts of *j*, sword, famine,
	20.36	I entered into *j* with your ancestors in
Dan	7.22	then *j* was given for the holy ones of
Hos	6.	5 mouth, and my *j* goes forth as the light.
Joel	3.	2 I will enter into *j* with them there, on
Zech	7.	9 Render true *j*, show kindness and mercy
Mt	5.21	'whoever murders shall be liable to *j*.'
Lk	11.32	Nineveh will rise at the *j* with this
Jn	5.22	no one but has given all *j* to the Son,
	12.31	Now is the *j* of this world; now the ruler
	16.	8 about sin and righteousness and *j*:
Rom	5.16	the *j* following one trespass brought
	11.33	How unsearchable are his *j* and how
	14.	3 those who abstain must not pass *j* on
	14.10	For we will all stand before the *j* seat of
1 Cor	11.29	eat and drink *j* against themselves.
2 Cor	5.10	all of us must appear before the *j* seat
Jude		15 to execute *j* on all, and to convict
Rev	18.20	For God has given *j* for you against her."

JUG

1 Kings	17.14	the *j* of oil shall not fail until the day

JUMPING

Acts	3.	8 *J* up, he stood and began to walk, and

JUST

Deut	4.	8 ordinances as *j* as this entire law that I
	32.	4 God, without deceit, *j* and upright is he.
Ezra	9.15	God of Israel, you are *j*, but we have
Neh	9.33	You have been *j* in all that has come
Job	9.	2 so; but how can a man be *j* before God?
Rom	8.	4 so that the *j* requirement of the law
Rev	16.	5 the waters say, "You are *j*, O Holy One,

JUSTICE

Lev	19.15	with *j* shall you judge your neighbor.
Job	34.12	and the Almighty will not pervert *j*.
Ps	82.	3 Give *j* to the weak and the orphan;
Prov	1.	3 in wise dealing, righteousness, *j*,
Eccl	3.16	in the place of *j*, wickedness was there,
Isa	56.	1 Thus says the LORD: Maintain *j*, and do
	59.11	We wait for *j*, but there is none; for
Am	5.24	let *j* roll down like waters, and
Hab	1.	4 law becomes slack and *j* never prevails.
Lk	7.29	acknowledged the *j* of God, because
	18.	3 'Grant me *j* me against my opponent.'
Acts	24.25	And as he discussed *j*, self-control, and
Rom	3.	5 serves to confirm the *j* of God, what

JUSTIFICATION

Rom	4.25	our trespasses and was raised for our *j*.
	5.18	man's act of righteousness leads to *j*
2 Cor	3.	9 does the ministry of *j* abound in glory!
Gal	2.21	if *j* comes through the law, then Christ

JUSTIFY (JUSTIFIED JUSTIFIES)

Ps	51.	4 so that you are *j* in your sentence and
Prov	17.15	One who *j* the wicked and one who

Mt	12.37	by your words you will be *j*, and by your
Lk	10.29	wanting to *j* himself, he asked Jesus,
	18.14	this man went down to his home *j*
Rom	3.20	"no human being will be *j* in his sight"
	3.24	they are now *j* by his grace as a gift,
	3.26	and that he *j* the one who has faith
	4.	2 For if Abraham was *j* by works, he has
1 Cor	6.11	you were *j* in the name of the Lord
Gal	2.16	a person is *j* not by the works of the
	3.24	came, so that we might be *j* by faith.
Titus	3.	7 so that, having been *j* by his grace, we
Jas	2.21	our ancestor Abraham *j* by works when

K

KADESH

Gen	14.	7 and came to Enmishpat (that is, *K*),
Num	20.14	Moses sent messengers from *K* to the
Ps	29.	8 the LORD shakes the wilderness of *K*.

KADESH-BARNEA

Num	32.	8 I sent them from *K* to see the land.
Deut	2.14	length of time we had traveled from *K*
Josh	10.41	Joshua defeated them from *K* to Gaza,

KEEP (KEPT)

Gen	45.	7 and to *k* alive for you many survivors.
Ex	13.	5 you shall *k* this observance in this
Num	6.24	The LORD bless you and *k* you;
	9.	5 They *k* the passover in the first month,
Josh	14.10	the LORD has *k* me alive, as he said,
	22.	5 to *k* his commandments, and to hold
1 Kings	2.43	Why then have you not *k* your oath to
2 Kings	17.13	evil ways and *k* my commandments
	23.21	"*K* the passover to the LORD your God as
2 Chr	13.11	we *k* the charge of the LORD our God,
	30.	1 to *k* the passover to the LORD the God
	34.21	our ancestors did not *k* the word
Ps	25.10	for those who *k* his covenant
	119.	4 your precepts to be *k* diligently.
	119.	55 in the night, O LORD, and *k* your law.
	121.	7 LORD will *k* you from all evil; he will *k*
	132.	12 If your sons *k* my covenant and my
Prov	4.23	*K* your heart with all vigilance, for from
	21.23	and tongue is to *k* out of trouble.
	22.12	eyes of the LORD *k* watch over knowledge,
	28.	7 who *k* the law are wise children, but
	29.18	but happy are those who *k* the law.
Isa	49.	8 I have *k* you and given you as a
	62.	1 For Zion's sake I will not *k* silent, and
Mt	19.17	to enter into life, *k* the commandments."
Rom	2.27	uncircumcised but *k* the law will
2 Tim	4.	7 finished the race, I have *k* the faith.
Jude		1 God the Father and *k* for Jesus Christ:
		6 he has *k* in eternal chains in deepest
		21 *k* yourselves in the love of God; look
		24 who is able to *k* you from falling, and to
Rev	3.10	you have *k* my word of patient

KEEPER

Gen	4.	9 "I do not know; am I my brother's *k*?"
Isa	27.	3 I, the LORD, am its *k*; every moment I

KEY (KEYS)

Isa	22.22	shoulder the *k* of the house of David;
Mt	16.19	I will give you the *k* of the kingdom of
Lk	11.52	have taken away the *k* of knowledge;
Rev	1.18	and I have the *k* of Death and Hades.
	3.	7 the true one, who has the *k* of David,
	20.	1 in his hand the *k* to the bottomless pit

KIDNAPER

Deut	24.	7 the Israelites, then that *k* shall die.

KILL (KILLED KILLS)

Gen	4.	8 up against his brother Abel, and *k* him.
Ex	1.16	if it is a boy, *k* him; but if it is a girl,
	2.12	seeing no one he *k* the Egyptian and

Ex	2.14	Do you mean to *k* me as you *k* the
Num	31.17	*k* every male among the little ones,
1 Kings	21.19	Have you *k*, and also taken possession?"
2 Kings	6.21	"Father, shall I *k* them? Shall I *k* them?"
Job	13.15	See, he will *k* me; I have no hope; but I
Ps	44.22	Because of you we are being *k* all day
Mt	10.28	can *k* the body but cannot *k* the soul;
	21.38	'This is the the heir; come, let us *k* him
	23.37	"Jerusalem, Jerusalem, the city that *k*
Mk	8.31	scribes, and be *k*, and after three days
	10.34	flog him, and *k* him; and after three
Lk	12. 4	do not fear those who *k* the body
	19.47	people kept looking for a way to *k* him;
	20.15	him out of the vineyard and *k* him.
Jn	5.18	were seeking all the more to *k* him,
Acts	2.23	you crucified and *k* by the hands of
	11. 7	saying to me, 'Get up, Peter; *k* and eat.'
Rev	2.13	Antipas . . . was *k* among you, where

KIN

Lev	25.25	If anyone of your *k* falls into difficulty
Deut	23. 7	of the Edomites, for they are your *k*.
Ruth	2.20	a relative of ours, one of our nearest *k*."
	3.	9 over your servant, for you are next-of-*k*."
	4.14	not left you this day without next-of-*k*;
2 Sam	19.12	You are my *k*, you are my bone and my
Prov	18.24	friend sticks closer than one's nearest *k*.
Jer	9. 4	and put no trust in any of your *k*; for all
Neh	5. 8	but now you are selling your own *k* who

KIND (KINDLY)

Josh	2.12	since I have dealt *k* with you, swear to
Prov	11.17	Those who are *k* reward themselves, but
	14.21	happy are those who are *k* to the poor.
	19.17	whoever is *k* to the poor lends to the
Eph	4.32	and be *k* to one another, tenderhearted,
2 Tim	2.24	must not be quarrelsome but *k* to

KINDNESS

Gen	19.19	shown me great *k* in saving my life;
2 Sam	9. 1	I may show *k* for Jonathan's sake?"
Job	6.14	"Those who withhold *k* from a friend
Zech	7. 9	show *k* and mercy to one another;
Rom	2. 4	that God's *k* is meant to lead you
	3.12	there is no one who shows *k*, there is
	11.22	the *k* and severity of God: severity
Titus	3. 4	the goodness and loving *k* of God our

KINDRED

Gen	13. 8	between you and me, . . . for we are *k*.
1 Kings	12.24	shall not go up or fight against your *k*
1 Chr	13. 2	let us send abroad to our *k* who remain
2 Chr	11. 4	shall not go up or fight against your *k*.
Ps	69. 8	I have become a stranger to my *k*, an
Prov	27.10	is a neighbor who is nearby than *k* who

KING

Ex	2.23	After a long time, the *k* of Egypt died.
Deut	17.14	and you say, "I will set a *k* over me, like
Judg	18. 1	In those days there was no *k* in Israel.
	21.25	In those days there was no *k* in Israel;
1 Sam	2.10	he will give strength to his *k*, and exalt
	8. 5	appoint for us, then, a *k* to govern us,
	10.24	all the people shouted, "Long live the *k*!"
	11.15	there they made Saul *k* before the LORD,
	12.12	though the LORD your God was your *k*.
	23.17	you shall be *k* over Israel, and I shall be
2 Sam	19.10	say nothing about bringing the *k* back?"
2 Kings	11.12	they proclaimed him *k*, and anointed
1 Chr	16.31	say among the nations, "The LORD is *k*!"
Job	41.34	is lofty; it is *k* over all that are proud."
Ps	2. 6	"I have set my *k* on Zion, my holy hill."
	5. 2	Listen to the sound of my cry, my *K*
	10.16	The LORD is *k* forever and ever; the
	24. 7	doors! that the *K* of glory may come in.
	44. 4	You are my *K* and my God; you
	47. 8	God is *k* over the nations; God sits on
	72. 1	Give the *k* your justice, O God, and

Ps	93. 1	The LORD is *k*, he is robed in majesty;
	97. 1	The LORD is *k*! Let the earth rejoice; let
	149.	2 the children of Zion rejoice in their *K*.
Eccl	8. 4	the word of the *k* is powerful, and who
	10.16	you, O land, when your *k* is a servant,
Isa	32. 1	See, a *k* will reign in righteousness, and
	43.15	Holy One, the Creator of Israel, your *K*.
Jer	10. 7	Who would not fear you, O *K* of the
	29.16	the *k* who sits on the throne of David,
	30. 9	the LORD their God and David their *k*,
	51.57	sleep and never wake, says the *K*,
Dan	2. 4	The Chaldeans said to the *k* (in
	2.37	You, O *k*, the *k* of kings— to whom the
Hos	3. 5	the LORD their God, and David their *k*;
Mic	2.13	Their *k* will pass on before them, the
Zech	9. 9	Lo, your *k* comes to you; triumphant
Mt	22. 2	to a *k* who gave a wedding banquet
	25.34	the *k* will say to those at his right hand,
Lk	19.38	"Blessed is the *k* who comes in the
	23. 3	asked him, "Are you the *k* of the Jews?"
Jn	1.49	the Son of God! You are the *K* of Israel!"
	6.15	by force to make him *k*, he withdrew
	12.13	the name of the Lord—the *K* of Israel!"
	18.37	"So you are a *k*?" Jesus answered, "You
	19.14	He said to the Jews, "Here is your *K*!"
Acts	7.18	another *k* who had not known Joseph
	17. 7	that there is another *k* named Jesus."
1 Tim	1.17	To the *K* of ages, immortal, invisible,
Rev	9.11	have as *k* over them the angel of the
	19.16	inscribed, "*K* of kings and Lord of lords."

KINGDOM

Ex	19. 6	but you shall be for me a priestly *k* and
1 Sam	13.14	your *k* shall not continue; the LORD has
2 Sam	7.12	your body, and I will establish his *k*.
1 Chr	17.11	own sons, and I will establish his *k*.
	29.11	yours is the *k*, O LORD, and you are
Ps	145. 12	and the glorious splendor of your *k*.
Isa	9. 7	peace for the throne of David and his *k*.
Dan	4. 3	His *k* is an everlasting *k*, and his
	4.17	High is sovereign over the *k* of mortals;
	4.31	The *k* has departed from you! You shall
	11. 4	his *k* shall be broken and divided
Ob	21	Esau; and the *k* shall be the LORD's.
Mt	3. 2	"Repent, for the *k* of heaven has come
	4.17	"Repent, for the *k* of heaven has come
	4.23	proclaiming the good news of the *k* and
	6.33	strive first for the *k* of God and his
	8.11	and Isaac and Jacob in the *k* of heaven,
	10. 7	news, 'The *k* of heaven has come near.'
	18. 3	you will never enter the *k* of heaven.
	19.14	as these that the *k* of heaven belongs."
	21.43	*k* of God will be taken away from you
	24. 7	will rise against nation, and *k* against *k*,
	25.34	inherit the *k* prepared for you from the
	26.29	drink it new with you in my Father's *k*."
Mk	1.15	the *k* of God has come near; repent;
	4.26	"The *k* of God is as if someone would
	9. 1	not taste death until they see that the *k*
	11.10	Blessed is the coming of our ancestor
	12.34	"You are not far from the *k* of God."
	13. 8	will rise against nation, and *k* against *k*;
	14.25	that day when I drink it new in the *k*
Lk	4.43	I must proclaim the good news of the *k*
	8.10	been given to know the secrets of the *k*
	9.11	them, and spoke to them about the *k*
	9.62	the plow and looks back is fit for the *k*
	10. 9	to them, 'The *k* of God has come near
	11.17	"Every *k* divided against itself becomes
	12.31	strive for his *k*, and these things will be
	16.16	good news of the *k* of God is
	17.21	For in fact, the *k* of God is among you.
	18.16	for it to such as these that the *k* of God
	18.29	or children, for the sake of the *k*
	21.10	will rise against nation, and *k* against *k*;
	21.31	place, you know the *k* of God is near.
	22.29	just as my father conferred on me, a *k*,

Jn	3.	5 enter the *k* of God without being born
Acts	1.	6 when you will restore the *k* to Israel?"
	14.22	that we must enter the *k* of God."
	19.	8 argued persuasively about the *k* of God.
	28.23	testifying to the *k* of God and trying to
Rom	14.17	the *k* of God is not food and drink but
1 Cor	4.20	the *k* of God depends not on talk but
	6.10	of these will inherit the *k* of God.
	15.24	end, when he hands over the *k* to God
	15.50	flesh and blood cannot inherit the *k* of
Eph	5.	5 has any inheritance in the *k* of Christ
2 Thess	1.	5 to make you worthy of the *k* of God,
Heb	12.28	are receiving a *k* that cannot be shaken,
2 Pet	1.11	entry into the eternal *k* of our Lord and
Rev	1.	6 made us to be a *k*, priests serving his
	11.15	*k* of the world has become the *k* of our

KINGDOMS

Dan	8.22	four *k* shall arise from his nation, but
Hag	2.22	earth, and to overthrow the throne of *k*;
Mt	4.	8 showed him all the *k* of the world and
Lk	4.	5 him in an instant all the *k* of the world.

KINGS (KING'S)

2 Chr	23.11	he brought out the *k* son, put the crown
Ps	102.	15 LORD, all the *k* of the earth your glory.
Prov	8.15	By me *k* reign, and rulers decree what is
	21.	1 The *k* heart is a stream of water in the
	31.	4 It is not for *k*, O Lemuel, it is not for *k*
Dan	7.17	"As for these four great beasts, four *k*
1 Cor	4.	8 Quite apart from us you have become *k*!
1 Tim	2.	2 for *k* and all who are in high positions,
Rev	16.12	prepare the way for the *k* from the east.

KINGSHIP

1 Sam	10.16	But about the matter of the *k*, of which
Dan	7.27	The *k* and the dominion and the

KINSFOLK

Judg	20.23	again draw near to battle against our *k*
Prov	17.17	times, and *k* are born to share adversity.

KISHON

Judg	5.21	The torrent *K* swept them away, the

KISS (KISSED KISSES KISSING)

Gen	29.11	Then Jacob *k* Rachel, and wept aloud.
	33.	4 him, and fell on his neck and *k* him,
	45.15	he *k* all his brothers and wept upon
	48.10	brought them near him; and he *k* them
Ruth	1.14	Orpah *k* her mother-in-law, but Ruth
1 Sam	20.41	and they *k* each other, and wept with
2 Sam	14.33	the king; and the king *k* Absalom.
Ps	2.12	*k* his feet, or he will be angry, and you
	85.10	meet; righteousness and peace will *k*
Prov	7.13	She seizes him and *k* him, and with
	24.26	who gives an honest answer gives a *k* on
Song	1.	2 Let him *k* me with the *k* of his mouth!
Hos	13.	2 to these," they say. People are *k* calves!
Mt	26.48	"The one I will *k* is the man; arrest him."
Mk	14.44	"The one I will *k* is the man; arrest him
Lk	7.45	You gave me no *k*, but from the time I
	15.20	put his arms around him and *k* him.
	22.47	them. He approached Jesus to *k* him;
Acts	20.37	they embraced Paul and *k* him, grieving
Rom	16.16	Greet one another with a holy *k*. All the
1 Cor	16.20	Greet one another with a holy *k*.
1 Pet	5.14	Greet one another with a *k* of love.

KNEE (KNEES)

1 Kings	19.18	all the *k* that have not bowed to Baal,
Ezra	9.	5 fell on my *k*, spread out my hands to
Isa	45.23	"To me every *k* shall bow, every tongue
Dan	6.10	on his *k* three times a day to pray to his
Lk	5.	8 Peter saw it he fell down at Jesus' *k*,
Rom	14.11	every *k* shall bow to me, and every

KNEEL (KNELT)

Gen	24.11	He made the camels *k* down outside
1 Kings	8.54	the altar of the LORD, where he had *k*
Ps	95.	6 bow down, let us *k* before the LORD, our

KNIFE

Gen	22.	6 he himself carried the fire and the *k*.
	22.10	his hand and took the *k* to kill his son.
Prov	23.	2 put a *k* to your throat if you have a big

KNOCK (KNOCKING)

Mt	7.	7 will find; *k*, and the door will be opened
Lk	11.	9 will find; *k*, and the door will be opened
	13.25	and to *k* at the door, saying, 'Lord,
Acts	12.16	Peter continued *k*; and when they
Rev	3.20	I am standing at the door, *k*; if you hear

KNOW

Ex	1.	8 arose over Egypt, who did not *k* Joseph.
	7.	5 Egyptians shall *k* that I am the LORD,
	18.11	Now I *k* that the LORD is greater than all
	29.46	they shall *k* that I am the LORD their
	31.13	that you may *k* that I, the LORD, sanctify
Lev	23.43	may *k* that I made the people
Judg	2.10	who did not *k* the LORD or the work that
1 Sam	17.47	all this assembly may *k* that the LORD
2 Sam	7.20	to you? For you *k* your servant, O Lord
1 Kings	8.43	may *k* your name and fear you, as do
	8.60	of the earth may *k* that the LORD is God;
	20.13	and you shall *k* that I am the LORD."
1 Chr	28.	9 son Solomon, the God of your father,
Job	8.	9 are but of yesterday, and we *k* nothing,
	19.25	I *k* that my Redeemer lives, and that at
	24.16	themselves up; they do not *k* the light.
	30.23	I *k* that you will bring me to death, and
Ps	25.	4 Make me to *k* your ways, O LORD; teach
	46.10	"Be still, and *k* that I am God! I am
	56.	9 I call. This I *k*, that God is for me.
	73.11	they say, "How can God *k*? Is there
	89.15	are the people who *k* the festal shout,
	100.	3 *K* that the LORD is God. It is he that
	109.	27 *k* that this is your hand; you, O LORD,
	142.	3 When my spirit is faint, you *k* my way.
Prov	28.22	rich and does not *k* that loss is sure to
Eccl	3.14	I *k* that whatever God does endures
	8.	5 and the wise mind will *k* the time and
Isa	1.	3 Israel does not *k*, my people do not
	37.20	may *k* that you alone are the LORD."
	41.20	so that all may see and *k*, all may
	49.26	all flesh shall *k* that I am the LORD
	52.	6 Therefore my people shall *k* my name;
	52.	6 that day they shall *k* that it is I who
	55.	5 You shall call nations that you do not *k*,
Jer	8.	7 but my people do not *k* the ordinance
	12.	3 But you, O LORD, *k* me; you see me and
	24.	7 a heart to *k* that I am the LORD; and
	31.34	or say to each other, "*K* the LORD," for
Ezek	6.14	Then they shall *k* that I am the LORD.
	17.21	wind; and you shall *k* that I, the LORD,
	29.21	Then they shall *k* that I am the LORD.
	32.15	in it, they shall *k* that I am the LORD.
	34.27	and they shall *k* that I am the LORD,
	37.28	nations shall *k* that I the LORD sanctify
	39.	7 nations shall *k* that I am the LORD, the
Hos	6.	3 Let us *k*, let us press on to *k* the LORD;
	11.	3 but they did not *k* that I healed them.
	14.	9 those who are discerning *k* them.
Joel	2.27	You shall *k* that I am in the midst of
Mic	4.12	they do not *k* the thoughts of the LORD;
Mt	6.	3 your left hand *k* what your right hand
	9.	6 that you may *k* that the Son of Man has
	24.50	him and at an hour he does not *k*.
Mk	2.10	that the Son of Man has authority on
	12.24	you *k* neither the scriptures nor the
	13.35	you do not *k* when the master of the
Lk	4.34	us? I *k* who you are, the Holy One
	5.24	that you may *k* that the Son of Man has

Lk	13.27	say, 'I do not *k* where you come from;
	20.21	"Teacher, we *k* that you are right in
Jn	10.14	I *k* my own and my own *k* me,
	13.35	By this everyone will *k* that you are my
	17. 3	life, that they *k* you, the only true God,
	17.23	the world may *k* that you have sent me
Acts	19.15	"Jesus I *k*, and Paul I *k*; but who are
1 Cor	3.16	Do you not *k* that you are God's temple
Gal	4. 9	however, that you have come to *k* God,
Eph	1.18	you may *k* what is the hope to which he
Phil	3.10	I want to *k* Christ and the power of his
2 Tim	1.12	I *k* the one in whom I have put my
Heb	8.11	or say to each other, 'K the Lord,'
1 Jn	4. 6	From this we *k* the spirit of truth and
	5.13	you may *k* that you have eternal life.
1 Jn	5.19	We *k* that we are God's children, and
Rev	2. 2	"I *k* your works, your toil and patient

KNOWS (KNEW KNOWN)

Job	23.10	he *k* the way that I take; when he has
Ps	76. 1	In Judah God is *k*, his name is great in
	103. 14	he *k* how we are made; he remembers
Isa	19.21	will make himself *k* to the Egyptians;
Am	3. 2	You only have I *k* of all the families of
Zech	11.11	watching me, *k* that it was the word
Mt	6. 8	for your Father *k* what you need before
	6.32	heavenly Father *k* that you need all
	12.33	fruit bad; for the tree is *k* by its fruit.
Mk	3.12	ordered them not to make him *k*.
	13.32	about that day or hour no one *k*,
Jn	1.18	Father's heart, who has made him *k*.
	2.25	for he himself *k* what was in everyone.
Acts	7.13	Joseph made himself *k* to his brothers,
	7.18	another king who had not *k* Joseph
	15. 8	God, who *k* the human heart, testified
Rom	1.21	for though they *k* God, they did not
Col	1.25	make the word of God fully *k*, the
2 Pet	2.21	better for them never to have *k* the way
Rev	1. 1	he made it *k* by sending his angel to his

KNOWLEDGE

Gen	2. 9	and the tree of the *k* of good and evil.
Num	24.16	knows the *k* of the Most High, who sees
Ps	139. 6	Such *k* is too wonderful for me; it is so
Prov	1. 4	simple, *k* and prudence to the young—
	9.10	and the *k* of the Holy One is insight.
	14. 6	but *k* is easy for one who understands.
	15. 2	tongue of the wise dispenses *k*, but the
	30. 3	wisdom, nor have I *k* of the holy ones.
Isa	5.13	My people go into exile without *k*; their
	11. 9	earth will be full of the *k* of the LORD
Dan	1.17	To these four young men God gave *k*
Hos	4. 6	My people are destroyed for lack of *k*;
Lk	1.77	give *k* of salvation to his people by the
	11.52	For you have taken away the key of *k*;
1 Cor	5. 1	in him, in speech and *k* of every kind—
	8. 1	K puffs up, but love builds up. Anyone
	8.11	by your *k* those weak believers for
2 Cor	6. 6	by purity, *k*, patience, kindness,
1 Tim	2. 4	saved and to come to the *k* of the truth.

KORAH (KORAH'S)

Num	16. 1	Now *K* the son of Izhar son of Kohath
	16.49	those who died in the affair of *K*.
Jude	11	sake of gain, and perish in *K* rebellion.

L

LABAN

Gen	24.29	brother whose name was *L*; and *L* ran
	27.43	flee at once to my brother *L* in Haran,
	28. 5	to Paddan-aram, to *L* son of Bethuel
	29. 5	"Do you know *L* son of Nahor?" They
	30.25	Jacob said to *L*, "Send me away, that I
	31. 2	Jacob saw that *L* did not regard him as
	31.20	Jacob deceived *L* the Aramean in that
	31.48	*L* said, "This heap is a witness between
	31.55	*L* arose, and kissed his grandchildren

LABOR (LABORS) (n)

Ex	2.11	out to the people and saw their forced *l*.
Ps	48. 6	of them there, pains as of a woman in *l*.
Prov	12.14	things, and manual *l* has its reward.
Isa	21. 3	me, like the pangs of a woman in *l*;
	66. 7	"Before she was in *l* she gave birth;
Jer	6.24	hold of us, pain as of a woman in *l*.
Jn	16.21	When a woman is in *l*, she has pain,
Rom	8.22	whole creation has been groaning in *l*
1 Cor	15.58	that in the Lord your *l* is not in vain.
1 Thess	2. 9	You remember our *l* and toil, brothers
	5. 3	as *l* pains come upon a pregnant
Heb	4.10	rest also cease from their *l* as God did

LABOR (v)

Deut	5.13	Six days you shall *l*, and do all your
Ps	127. 1	the house, those who build it *l* in vain.
Prov	21.25	is fatal, for lazy hands refuse to *l*.
Hab	2.13	that peoples *l* only to feed the flames,

LABORERS

Eccl	5.12	Sweet is the sleep of *l*, whether they eat
Mt	20. 1	in the morning to hire *l* for his vineyard.
Lk	10. 2	harvest is plentiful, but the *l* are few;
Jas	5. 4	wages of the *l* who mowed your fields,

LACERATE

Deut	14. 1	you must not *l* yourselves or shave your

LACK (LACKED LACKING)

Deut	2. 7	has been with you; you have *l* nothing."
Eccl	6. 2	honor, so that they *l* nothing of all that
Mk	10.21	"You *l* one thing; go, sell what you own,
Lk	18.22	"There is still one thing *l*. Sell all that
	22.35	bag, or sandals, did you *l* anything?"

LAKE

Lk	8.33	steep bank into the *l* and were drowned.
Rev	19.20	two were thrown alive into the *l* of fire
	20.10	devil . . . was thrown into the *l* of fire

LAMB (LAMBS)

Gen	22. 7	but where is the *l* for a burnt offering?"
Ex	12. 5	Your *l* shall be without blemish, a
	29.39	One *l* you shall offer in the morning,
2 Sam	12. 3	man had nothing but one little ewe *l*,
Isa	53. 7	like a *l* that is led to the slaughter, and
	65.25	The wolf and the *l* shall feed together,
Jer	11.19	But I was like a gentle *l* led to the
Lk	10. 3	I am sending you out like *l* into the
Jn	1.29	"Here is the *L* of God, who takes away
	21.15	love you." Jesus said to him, "Feed my *l*."
1 Pet	1.19	of Christ, like that of a *l* without defect
Rev	5. 6	a *L* standing as if it had been
	5.12	"Worthy is the *L* that was slaughtered to
	6.16	the throne and from the wrath of the *L*;
	7.10	saying, "Salvation belongs . . . to the *L*!"
	14. 1	there was the *L*, standing on Mount
	17.14	they will make war on the *L*, and the *L*
	19. 7	marriage of the *L* has come, and his
	21. 9	show you the bride, the wife of the *L*."
	21.14	names of the twelve apostles of the *L*.
	21.23	God is its light, and its lamp is the *L*.

LAME

2 Sam	5. 8	attack the *l* and the blind, those whom
Isa	35. 6	then the *l* shall leap like a deer, and
Mt	15.31	maimed whole, the *l* walking, and the
Acts	3. 2	a man *l* from birth was being carried in.

LAMENT (LAMENTED)

1 Sam	7. 2	all the house of Israel *l* after the LORD.
Joel	1. 8	*L* like a virgin dressed in sackcloth for

LAMENTATION

2 Sam	1.17	David intoned this *l* over Saul and his
Jer	6.26	as for an only child, most bitter *l*:
Ezek	27. 2	Now you, mortal, raise a *l* over Tyre,

Am	5.	1 this word that I take up over you in *l*,

LAMP (LAMPS)

Ex	27.20	so that a *l* may be set up to burn
1 Sam	3.	3 *l* of God had not yet gone out, and
2 Sam	22.29	you are my *l*, O LORD, the LORD lightens
1 Kings	11.36	David may always have a *l* before me
	15.	4 God gave him a *l* in Jerusalem, setting
2 Kings	4.10	table, a chair, and a *l*, so that he can
	8.19	since he promised to give a *l* to him
Job	18.	6 their tent, the *l* above them is put out.
	29.	3 when his *l* shone over my head, and by
Ps	18.28	It is you who light my *l*; the LORD, my
	119.105	Your word is a *l* to my feet and a light
Prov	6.23	For the commandment is a *l* and the
	20.20	your *l* will go out in utter darkness.
	20.27	The human spirit is the *l* of the LORD,
	24.20	no future; the *l* of the wicked go out.
	31.18	Her *l* does not go out at night. She puts
Mt	5.15	No one after lighting a *l* puts it under
	6.22	"The eye is the *l* of the body. So, if your
Mk	4.21	"Is a *l* brought in to be put under a
Lk	8.16	"No one after lighting a *l* hides it under
	11.33	"No one after lighting a *l* puts it in a
	11.34	Your eye is the *l* of your body. If your
	12.35	dressed for action and have your *l* lit;
Jn	5.35	He was a burning and shining *l*, and
Rev	21.23	of God is its light, and its *l* is the Lamb.

LAMPSTAND (LAMPSTANDS)

Ex	25.31	You shall make a *l* of pure gold. The
	37.17	He also made the *l* of pure gold. The
Lev	24.	4 He shall set up the lamps on the *l* of
Num	8.	2 lamps shall give light in front of the *l*."
Zech	4.	2 "I see a *l* all of gold, with a bowl on the
Rev	1.12	and on turning I saw seven golden *l*,

LAND (LANDS)

Gen	13.15	all the *l* which you see I will give to you
	35.12	The *l* that I gave to Abraham and Isaac
	47.18	of my lord but our bodies and our *l*.
	50.24	out of this *l* to the *l* that he swore to
Ex	6.	8 I will bring you into the *l* that I swore
Lev	18.25	Thus the *l* became defiled; and I
	25.23	The *l* shall not be sold in perpetuity, for
Num	13.26	and showed them the fruit of the *l*.
	32.	5 let this *l* be given to your servants for a
	32.22	and this *l* shall be your possession
	33.54	You shall apportion the *l* by lot
	35.34	You shall not defile the *l* in which you
Deut	8.	7 God is bringing you into a good *l*, a *l*
	11.10	*l* that you are about to enter to occupy
	11.11	*l* that you are crossing over to occupy is
	29.24	"Why has the LORD done thus to this *l*?
Josh	13.	1 much of the *l* still remains to be
	24.13	I gave you a *l* on which you had not
Neh	9.24	decendants went in and possessed the *l*,
Isa	38.11	not see the LORD in the *l* of the living;
Jer	2.	7 entered you defiled my *l*, and made
	22.29	O *l*, *l*, *l*, hear the word of the LORD!
Ezek	33.24	of these waste places in the *l*
	36.	6 prophesy concerning the *l* of Israel, and
	45.	1 When you allot the *l* as an inheritance,
Hos	9.	3 shall not remain in the *l* of the LORD;
Acts	7.	3 relatives and go to the *l* that I will show
	20.13	intending to go by *l* himself.
2 Cor	10.16	proclaim the good news in *l* beyond

LANDMARK (LANDMARKS)

Job	24.	2 The wicked remove *l*; they seize flocks
Prov	22.28	Do not remove the ancient *l* that your
	23.10	Do not remove an ancient *l* or encroach

LANGUAGE

Gen	11.	1 Now the whole earth had one *l* and the
Neh	13.24	they could not speak the *l* of Judah,
Jer	5.15	a nation whose *l* you do not know,
Ezek	3.	5 of obscure speech and a difficult *l*,

Acts	2.	6 them speaking in the native *l* of each.

LANGUISH (LANGUISHES LANGUISHING)

Ps	6.	2 O LORD, for I am *l*; O LORD, heal me,
	119.	81 My soul *l* for your salvation; I hope in
Isa	19.	8 who spread nets on the water will *l*.

LASHES

2 Cor	11.24	from the Jews the forty *l* minus one.

LAST

Mt	12.45	the *l* state of that person is worse than
	19.30	are first will be *l*, and the *l* will be first."
Mk	10.31	are first will be *l*, and the *l* will be first."
	15.37	gave a loud cry and breathed his *l*.
Lk	13.30	some are *l* who will be first, and some
2 Tim	3.	1 this, that in the *l* days distressing times
Heb	1.	2 but in these *l* days he has spoken to us
Rev	1.17	not be afraid; I am the first and the *l*,

LAUGH (LAUGHED LAUGHS)

Gen	17.17	Abraham fell on his face and *l*, and said
	18.12	So Sarah *l* to herself, saying, "After I
2 Chr	30.10	Zebulun; but they *l* them to scorn, and
Job	5.22	At destruction and famine you shall *l*,
	41.29	as chaff; it *l* at the rattle of javelins.
Ps	2.	4 He who sits in the heavens *l*; the LORD
	37.13	but the LORD *l* at the wicked, for he sees
	52.	6 see, and fear, and will *l* at the evildoer,
	59.	8 But you *l* at them, O LORD; you hold all
Prov	1.26	I also will *l* at your calamity; I will
	31.25	clothing, and she *l* at the time to come.
Mt	9.24	girl is not dead but sleeping." And they *l*
Mk	5.40	And they *l* at him. But he put them all
Lk	6.21	are you who weep now, for you will *l*.
	8.53	they *l* at him, knowing that she was

LAUGHTER

Gen	21.	6 "God has brought *l* for me; everyone
Prov	14.13	Even in *l* the heart is sad, and the end
Eccl	2.	1 said of *l*, "It is mad," and of pleasure,
	7.	3 Sorrow is better than *l*, for by sadness

LAW (LAWS)

Num	5.29	This is the *l* in cases of jealousy, when
	6.13	This is the *l* for the nazirites when the
Deut	1.	5 Moses undertook to expound this *l* as
	17.18	have a copy of this *l* written for him
	31.	9 Then Moses wrote down this *l*, and gave
	31.11	you shall read this *l* before all Israel
	31.26	"Take this book of the *l* and put it
Josh	1.	8 This book of the *l* shall not depart out
	8.34	he read all the words of the *l*, blessings
2 Chr	12.	1 strong, he abandoned the *l* of the LORD,
Neh	9.13	gave them right ordinances and true *l*,
Ps	1.	2 but their delight is in the *l* of the LORD,
	19.	7 The *l* of the LORD is perfect, reviving the
	119.	44 I will keep your *l* continually, forever
Prov	29.	9 If the wise go to *l* with fools, there is
Jer	31.33	I will put my *l* within them, and I will
Dan	6.	5 it in connection with the *l* of his God."
Mt	5.17	think that I have come to abolish the *l*
	11.13	all the prophets and the *l* prophesied
Lk	5.17	Pharisees and teachers of the *l* sitting
	16.17	in the letter of the *l* to become void.
	24.44	everything written about me in the *l*
Acts	15.15	After the reading of the *l* and the
Rom	2.12	all who have sinned under the *l* will be
	4.15	For the *l* brings wrath, but where there
	7.22	I delight in the *l* of God in my
	8.	2 set you free from the *l* of sin and death.
	10.	4 For Christ is the end of the *l* so that
1 Cor	9.21	To those outside the *l* I became as one
Gal	3.10	on the works of the *l* are under a curse;
	3.19	Why then the *l*? It was added because
	3.23	and guarded under the *l* until faith
	4.21	to the *l*, will you not listen to the *l*?
	5.14	the whole *l* is summed up in a single

LAWFUL (cont.)

Gal	6. 2 this way you will fulfill the *l* of Christ.
1 Tim	1. 8 Now we know that the *l* is good, if one
Heb	7.19 (for the *l* made nothing perfect);
Jas	1.25 who looks into the perfect *l*, the *l* of
	2. 9 are convicted by the *l* as transgressors.
	4.11 judges the *l*; but if you judge the *l*, you

LAWFUL

Mt	12. 2 what is not *l* to do on the sabbath."
	12.12 So it is *l* to do good on the sabbath."
	14. 4 him, "It is not *l* for you to have her."
Mk	6.18 telling Herod, "It is not *l* for you to have
1 Cor	6.12 "All things are *l* for me," but not all

LAWLESS

Mk	15.28n says, "And he was counted among the *l*."
Lk	22.37 me, 'And he was counted among the *l*';
2 Thess	2. 3 comes first and the *l* one is revealed,
	2. 8 then the *l* one will be revealed, whom

LAWLESSNESS

2 Thess	2. 7 the mystery of *l* is already at work, but
1 Jn	3. 4 Everyone who commits sin is guilty of *l*;

LAWYER (LAWYERS)

Lk	10.25 a *l* stood up to test Jesus. "Teacher," he
	11.46 he said, "Woe also to you *l*! For you

LAY

Deut	9.18 I *l* prostrate before the LORD as before,
Prov	9. 6 *L* aside immaturity, and live, and walk
	10.14 The wise *l* up knowledge, but the
Mt	8.20 Son of Man has nowhere to *l* his head."
1 Cor	3.11 no one can *l* any foundation other than

LAZARUS

Lk	16.20 at his gate lay a poor man named *L*,
Jn	11. 1 a certain man was ill, *L* of Bethany,
	11.43 cried with a loud voice, "*L*, come out."
	12. 1 the home of *L*, whom he had raised
	12.10 chief priests planned to put *L* to death
	12.17 been with him when he called *L* out

LAZY

Ex	5.17 He said, "You are *l*, *l*; that is why you
Prov	13. 4 appetite of the *l* craves, and gets
	21.25 craving of the *l* person is fatal, for *l*
	22.13 The *l* person says, "There is a lion
	26.15 *l* person buries a hand in the dish, and
	26.16 *l* person is wiser in self-esteem than

LAZYBONES

Prov	6. 6 Go to the ant, you *l*; consider its ways,

LEAD (LEADS LED)

Gen	24.27 the LORD has *l* me on the way to the
	33.14 of his servant, and I will *l* on slowly,
Ex	13.18 So God *l* the people by the roundabout
Josh	24. 3 I him through all the land of Canaan
1 Sam	12. 2 with you. I have *l* you from my youth
Ps	5. 8 *L* me, O LORD, in your righteousness
	23. 2 he *l* me beside still waters; he restores
	25. 5 *L* me in your truth, and teach me, for
	61. 2 *L* me to the rock that is higher than I;
	78.14 In the daytime he *l* them with a cloud,
	107. 7 he *l* them by a straight way, until they
	136. 16 *l* his people through the wilderness,
Isa	11. 6 together, and a little child shall *l* them.
	40.11 bosom, and gently *l* the mother sheep.
	48.17 for your own good, who *l* you in the way
	63.14 Thus you *l* your people, to make for
Jer	2. 6 of Egypt, who *l* us in the wilderness,
Hos	11. 4 I *l* them with cords of human kindness,
Mt	4. 1 Jesus was *l* up by the Spirit into the
Lk	4.29 town and *l* him to the brow of the hill
Acts	8.32 "Like a sheep he was *l* to the slaughter,
Rom	8.14 all who are *l* by the Spirit of God are
1 Cor	7.17 each of you *l* the life that the Lord has
Gal	5.18 if you are *l* by the Spirit, you are not

Eph	4. 1 beg you to *l* a life worthy of the calling
Col	1.10 that you may *l* lives worthy of the Lord,
1 Thess	2.12 pleading that you *l* a life worthy of God,

LEADER

Mt	9.18 I of the synagogue came in and knelt
Lk	8.41 named Jairus, the *l* of the synagogue.
	13.14 the *l* of the synagogue, indignant

LEAF (LEAVES)

Gen	3. 7 they sewed fig *l* together and made
Job	13.25 Will you frighten a windblown *l* and
Ezek	47.12 Their *l* will not wither nor their fruit
Mk	11.13 he found nothing but *l*, for it was not
	13.28 and puts forth its *l*, you know that

LEAGUE

Job	5.23 you shall be in *l* with the stones of the

LEAH

Gen	29.16 the name of the elder was *L*, and the
	29.30 and he loved Rachel more than *L*. He
	30. 9 When *L* saw that she had ceased
	31. 4 called Rachel and *L* into the field where
	35.23 The sons of *L*: Reuben (Jacob's
Ruth	4.11 Rachel and *L*, who together built up the

LEAN

Isa	48. 2 the holy city, and *l* on the God of Israel;

LEAP (LEAPED)

2 Sam	22.30 and by my God I can *l* over a wall.
Lk	1.41 greeting, the child *l* in her womb.

LEARN (LEARNED)

Gen	30.27 I have *l* by divination that the LORD has
Deut	31.12 hear and *l* to fear the LORD your God
Ps	119. 7 when I *l* your righteous ordinances.
	119. 71 that I was humbled, so that I might *l*
Prov	8. 5 O simple ones, *l* prudence; acquire
Isa	1.17 *l* to do good; seek justice, rescue the
	26. 9 inhabitants of the world *l* righteousness.
Jer	10. 2 Do not *l* the way of the nations, or be
Dan	5.21 until he *l* that the Most High God has
Mt	9.13 Go and *l* what this means, 'I desire
	11.29 Take my yoke upon you, and *l* from me;
Phil	4. 9 on doing the things that you have *l*
	4.11 need; for I have *l* to be content with
1 Thess	4. 1 as you *l* from us how you ought to live
Heb	5. 8 was a Son, he *l* obedience through what
Rev	14. 3 No one could *l* that song except the

LEARNING

Prov	1. 5 Let the wise also hear and gain in *l*,
Jn	7.15 "How does this man have such *l*, when
Acts	26.24 Paul! Too much *l* is driving you insane!"

LEAST

Judg	6.15 Manasseh, and I am the *l* in my family."
1 Sam	9.21 a Benjaminite, from the *l* of the tribes
Mt	2. 6 by no means *l* among the rulers of
	5.19 same, will be called *l* in the kingdom
	11.11 the *l* in the kingdom of heaven is
Lk	7.28 John; yet the *l* in the kingdom of God is
	9.48 for the *l* among all of you is the
1 Cor	15. 9 I am the *l* of the apostles, unfit to be
Eph	3. 8 I am the very *l* of all the saints,

LEAVE (LEFT)

Judg	16.20 did not know that the LORD had *l* him.
1 Kings	19.10 I alone am *l*, and they are seeking my
2 Kings	2. 2 and as you yourself live, I will not *l* you."
	4.30 yourself live, I will not *l* without you."
Job	22.17 They said to God; '*L* us alone,' and
Ezek	9. 8 I alone, I fell prostrate on my face, and
Mt	4.22 they *l* the boat and their father, and
	19.27 "Look, we have *l* everything and
Mk	1.18 they *l* their nets and followed him.
	1.20 they *l* their father Zebedee in the boat

Mk 10. 7 man shall *l* his father and mother and
Lk 5.11 to shore, they *l* everything and followed
8.37 the Gerasenes asked Jesus to *l* them;

LEAVEN

Ex 12.15 you shall remove *l* from your houses,
Lev 2.11 bring to the LORD shall be made with *l*,

LEBANON

Deut 1. 7 land of the Canaanites and the *L*, as far
Judg 9.15 bramble and devour the cedars of *L*.'
1 Kings 5. 6 command that cedars from *L* be cut for
10.17 them in the House of the Forest of *L*.
Ezra 3. 7 to bring cedar trees from *L* to the sea,
Ps 29. 5 cedars; the LORD breaks the cedars of *L*.
Song 5.15 His appearance is like *L*, choice as the
Isa 10.34 with an ax, and *L* with its majestic trees
60.13 glory of *L* shall come to you, the
Jer 18.14 Does the snow of *L* leave the crags of

LEFT (n and adj)

Gen 13. 9 the right hand, then I will go to the *l*."
Mt 6. 3 do not let your *l* hand know what your
20.21 at your right hand and one at your *l*,

LEGION (LEGIONS)

Mt 26.53 send me more than twelve *l* of angels?
Mk 5. 9 "My name is *L*; for we are many."

LEGS

Dan 2.33 its *l* of iron, its feet partly of iron and
Jn 19.33 already dead, they did not break his *l*.

LEHI

Judg 15.19 that is at *L*, and water came from it.
2 Sam 23.11 Philistines gathered together at *L*,

LEND (LENDING LENT LENDS)

Ex 22.25 If you *l* money to my people, to the
Deut 28.12 You will *l* to many nations, but you will
1 Sam 1.28 I have *l* him to the LORD; as long as he
Ps 37.26 They are ever giving liberally and *l*, and
Prov 19.17 is kind to the poor *l* to the LORD,
Jer 15.10 I have not *l*, nor have I borrowed, yet all
Lk 6.34 if you *l* to those from whom you hope

LENGTH

Gen 6.15 *l* of the ark three hundred cubits, its
Ezek 40. 5 The *l* of the measuring reed in the
Eph 3.18 saints, what is the breadth and *l* and

LEOPARD (LEOPARDS)

Isa 11. 6 lamb, the *l* shall lie down with the kid,
Jer 13.23 change their skin or the *l* their spots?
Dan 7. 6 as I watched, another appeared, like a *l*.

LEPER (LEPERS)

Mt 8. 2 a *l* who came to him and knelt before
11. 5 the lame walk, the *l* are cleansed, the
26. 6 at Bethany in the house of Simon the *l*,
Mk 1.40 A *l* came to him begging him, and
14. 3 in the house of Simon the *l*, as he sat
Lk 4.27 many *l* in Israel in the time of the
7.22 lame walk, *l* are cleansed, the deaf hear,
17.12 ten *l* approached him. Keeping their

LEPROSY

2 Kings 5. 1 a mighty warrior, suffered from *l*.
5.27 the *l* of Naaman shall cling to you, and
Lk 5.12 there was a man covered with *l*. When

LEPROUS

Ex 4. 6 when he took it out, his hand was *l*, as
Lev 13. 2 and it turns into a *l* disease on the skin
14. 2 This shall be the ritual for the *l* person
14.34 and I put a *l* disease in a house in the
Num 5. 2 put out of the camp everyone who is *l*,
12.10 Miriam was *l*, as white as snow. And
2 Kings 7. 3 there were four *l* men outside the city

2 Kings 15. 5 LORD struck the king, so that he was *l*
2 Chr 26.19 angry with the priests a *l* disease broke

LETTER (LETTERS)

2 Sam 11.14 David wrote a *l* to Joab, and sent it by
1 Kings 21. 8 she wrote *l* in Ahab's name and sealed
2 Kings 5. 6 He brought the *l* to the king of Israel,
2 Chr 21.12 A *l* came to him from the prophet
30. 1 wrote *l* also to Ephraim and Manasseh,
Ezra 5. 5 and then answer was returned by *l*
Neh 6. 5 sent his servant to me with an open *l*
Isa 37.14 Hezekiah received the *l* from the hand
Jer 29. 1 of the *l* that the prophet Jeremiah
Acts 9. 2 for *l* to the synagogues at Damascus,
15.23 with the following *l*: "The brothers, both
15.30 together, they delivered the *l*.
22. 5 received *l* to the brothers in Damascus,
23.25 the governor." He wrote a *l* to this effect:
23.33 and delivered the *l* to the governor,
2 Cor 3. 1 need, as some do, *l* of recommendation
3. 2 You yourselves are our *l*, written on our
3. 6 of spirit; for the *l* kills, but the Spirit
10. 9 I am trying to frighten you with my *l*.
Gal 6.11 See what large *l* I make when I am
Col 4.16 when this *l* has been read among you,
2 Thess 2. 2 either by spirit or by word or by *l*,
3.14 who do not obey what we say in this *l*;
3.17 This is the mark in every *l* of mine; it
2 Pet 3.16 speaking of this as he does in all his *l*.

LEVI

Gen 29.34 three sons"; therefore he was named *L*.
Ex 2. 1 Now a man from the house of *L* went
Num 1.49 Only the tribe of *L* you shall not enroll,
Deut 10. 8 the LORD set apart the tribe of *L* to carry

LEVIATHAN

Job 41. 1 "Can you draw out *L* with a fishhook, or
Isa 27. 1 strong sword will punish *L* the fleeing

LEVITES

Josh 14. 4 no portion was given to the *L* in the
2 Chr 31. 2 to his service, the priests and the *L*,
34. 9 which the *L*, the keepers of the
35. 3 He said to the *L* who taught all Israel

LIAR (LIARS)

Ps 116.11 in my consternation, "Everyone is a *l*."
Jn 8.55 not know him, I would be a *l* like you.
Rom 3. 4 Although everyone is a *l*, let God be
1 Jn 5.10 made him a *l* by not believing in the
Rev 21. 8 and all *l*, their place will be in the lake

LIBERTY

Lev 25.10 shall proclaim *l* throughout the land
Ps 119. 45 I shall walk at *l*, for I have sought your
Jer 34. 8 to make a proclamation of *l* to them,
Ezek 46.17 his to the year of *l*; then it shall revert
1 Cor 8. 9 take care that this *l* of yours does not
10.29 why should my *l* be subject to the

LIE (LIES)

Num 23.19 is not a human being, that he should *l*,
Ps 4. 8 I will both *l* down and sleep in peace;
119. 69 The arrogant smear me with *l*, but with
Prov 14. 5 A faithful witness does not *l*, but a false
Isa 28.15 we have made *l* our refuge, and in
59. 3 your lips have spoken *l*, your tongue
Jer 27.10 For they are prophesying a *l* to you,
Jn 8.44 When he *l*, he speaks according to his
Acts 5. 3 has Satan filled your heart to *l*
Rom 1.25 exchanged the truth about God for a *l*
Col 3. 9 Do not *l* to one another, seeing that you
Rev 14. 5 in their mouth no *l* was found; they are

LIFE

Gen 1.30 everything that has the breath of *l*, *l*
2. 9 tree of *l* also in the midst of the garden,

Lev	17.11 For the *l* of the flesh is in the blood;
Deut	30.15 I have set before you today *l* and
	30.20 for that means *l* to you and length of
1 Sam	2. 6 The LORD kills and brings to *l*; he brings
	25.29 to seek your *l*, the *l* of my lord shall be
2 Sam	15.21 whether for death or for *l*, there also
1 Kings	20.42 your *l* shall be for his *l*, and your people
2 Kings	13.21 the bones of Elisha, he came to *l*;
Job	7. 7 "Remember that my *l* is a breath; my
	33. 4 the breath of the Almighty gives me *l*.
	33.30 Pit, so that they may see the light of *l*.
Ps	16.11 You show me the path of *l*. In your
	34.12 Which of you desires *l*, and covets many
	36. 9 For with you is the fountain of *l*; in
	63. 3 your steadfast love is better than *l*,
	94.21 together against the *l* of the righteous,
Prov	3.22 and they will be *l* for your soul
	4.22 they are *l* to those who find them, and
	8.35 For whoever finds me finds *l* and
	12.28 In the path of righteousness there is *l*,
	14.27 The fear of the LORD is a fountain of *l*,
Eccl	2.17 I hated *l*, because what is done under
	9. 9 Enjoy *l* with the wife whom you love,
Isa	4. 3 has been recorded for *l* in Jerusalem,
	38.17 held back my *l* from the pit of
Jer	8. 3 Death shall be preferred to *l* by all the
	21. 8 I am setting before you the way of *l* and
Ezek	3.21 warning; and you will have saved your *l*.
Jon	4. 3 now, O LORD, please take my *l* from me,
Mt	7.14 and the road is hard that leads to *l*,
	10.39 those who lose their *l* for my sake will
	16.26 gain the whole world and forfeit their *l*?
	25.46 but the righteous into eternal *l*."
Mk	8.35 those who want to save their *l* will lose
	8.36 gain the whole world and forfeit their *l*?
	10.30 and in the age to come eternal *l*.
Lk	9.24 who want to save their *l* will lose it, and
	12.22 do not worry about your *l*, what you will
	18.18 what must I do to inherit eternal *l*?"
Jn	1. 4 In him was *l*, and the *l* was the light of
	3.36 believes in the Son has eternal *l*;
	4.14 spring of water gushing up to eternal *l*."
	5.24 believes him who sent me has eternal *l*,
	6.68 we go? You have the words of eternal *l*.
	10.10 I came that they may have *l*, and have
	10.15 Father. I lay down my *l* for the sheep.
	10.28 I give them eternal *l*, and they will
	11.25 "I am the resurrection and the *l*. Those
	14. 6 "I am the way and the truth, and the *l*;
	17. 3 this is eternal *l*, that they know you, the
	20.31 that through believing you may have *l*
Acts	5.20 people the whole message about this *l*."
	17.25 he himself gives to all mortals *l* and
Rom	6.13 who have been brought from death to *l*,
	6.23 but the free gift of God is eternal *l*
	8.10 the Spirit is *l* because of righteousness.
	8.38 neither death, nor *l*, nor angels, nor
2 Cor	2.16 to the other a fragrance from *l* to *l*.
	3. 6 for the letter kills, but the Spirit gives *l*.
	4.10 that the *l* of Jesus may be made visible
	4.12 So death is at work in us, but *l* in you.
Gal	1.13 no doubt, of my earlier *l* in Judaism.
	2.20 the *l* I now live in the flesh I live by
Eph	2.10 prepared beforehand to be our way of *l*.
Col	3. 3 and your *l* is hidden with Christ in God.
1 Tim	2. 2 lead a quiet and peaceable *l* in all
Heb	7.16 the power of an indestructible *l*.
Jas	4.14 What is your *l*? for you are a mist that
1 Pet	3.10 "Those who desire *l* and desire to see
1 Jn	3.14 we have passed from death to *l* because
	3.16 by this, that he laid down his *l* for us
Rev	2. 7 give permission to eat from the tree of *l*
	3. 5 not blot your name out of the book of *l*;
	11.11 breath of *l* from God entered them, and
	12.11 they did not cling to *l* even in the face
	13. 8 in the book of *l* of the Lamb that was
	20. 4 They came to *l*, and reigned with Christ

Rev	21. 6 a gift from the spring of the water of *l*.
	21.27 are written in the Lamb's book of *l*.
	22.17 who wishes take the water of *l* as a gift.

LIFT (LIFTED LIFTING)

Ps	24. 7 *L* up your heads, O gates! and be *l* up,
	25. 1 To you, O LORD, I *l* up my soul. O my
	75. 6 not from the wilderness comes *l* up; but
	86. 4 for to you, O LORD, I *l* up my soul.
	121. 1 I *l* up my eyes to the hills — from where
	131. 1 O LORD, my heart is not *l* up, my eyes
	134. 2 *L* up your hands to the holy place, and
Lk	1.52 from their thrones, and *l* up the lowly;
Jn	3.14 so must the Son of man be *l* up, that
	8.28 "When you have *l* up the Son of Man,
	12.32 And I, when I am *l* up from the earth,

LIGHT (LIGHTS)

Gen	1. 3 said, "Let there be *l*"; and there was *l*.
	1.15 let there be *l* in the dome of the sky to
Ex	10.23 but all the Israelites had *l* where they
Lev	24. 2 the lamp, that a *l* may be kept burning
2 Sam	23. 4 is like the *l* of morning, like the sun
Job	24.16 themselves up; they do not know the *l*.
Ps	27. 1 The LORD is my *l* and my salvation;
	37. 6 make your vindication shine like the *l*,
	43. 3 O send out your *l* and your truth; let
	49.19 who will never more see the *l*.
	97.11 *L* dawns for the righteous, and joy for
	119.105 is a lamp to my feet and a *l* to my path.
	119.130 The unfolding of your words gives *l*; it
	139. 12 as the day, for darkness is as *l* to you.
Prov	4.18 of the righteous is like the *l* of dawn,
	13. 9 The *l* of the righteous rejoices, but the
Eccl	11. 7 *L* is sweet, and it is pleasant for the
Isa	2. 5 come, let us walk in the *l* of the LORD!
	5.20 put darkness for *l* and *l* for darkness,
	42. 6 to the people, a *l* to the nations,
	45. 7 I form *l* and create darkness, I make
	49. 6 I will give you as a *l* to the nations, that
	58. 8 Then your *l* shall break forth like the
	60. 1 Arise, shine; for your *l* has come, and
	60. 3 Nations shall come to your *l*, and kings
Mic	7. 8 in darkness, the LORD will be a *l* to me.
Mt	4.16 who sat in darkness have seen a great *l*,
	5.16 let your *l* shine before others, so that
Lk	1.79 *l* to those who sit in darkness and in
	2.32 a *l* for revelation to the Gentiles and for
	12. 3 said in the dark will be heard in the *l*,
Jn	1. 5 The *l* shines in the darkness, and the
	3.19 that the *l* has come into the world,
	8.12 "I am the *l* of the world. Whoever
	9. 5 in the world, I am the *l* of the world,"
	12.35 believe in the *l*, so that you may
Acts	9. 3 suddenly a *l* from heaven flashed
	13.47 have set you to be a *l* for the Gentiles,
	22. 6 a great *l* from heaven suddenly shone
	26.13 your Excellency, I saw a *l* from heaven,
	26.18 that they may turn from darkness to *l*
Rom	13.12 of darkness and put on the armor of *l*;
1 Cor	4. 5 comes, who will bring to *l* the things
2 Cor	4. 4 to keep them from seeing the *l* of the
	4. 6 "Let *l* shine out of darkness," who has
	6.14 is there between *l* and darkness?
Eph	5. 8 darkness, but now in the Lord you are *l*.
	5.14 for everything that becomes visible is *l*.
Jas	1.17 coming down from the father of *l*, with
1 Pet	2. 9 out of darkness into his marvelous *l*.
1 Jn	1. 5 that God is *l* and in him there is no
	1. 7 but if we walk in the *l*, as he himself is
	2. 8 away and the true *l* is already shining.
Rev	22. 5 they need no *l* of lamp or sun, for the

LIGHTNING (LIGHTNINGS)

Ps	18.14 and scattered them; he flashed forth *l*,
Mt	24.27 as the *l* comes from the east and flashes
Lk	17.24 as the *l* flashes and lights up the sky

Rev	8.	5 of thunder, rumblings, flashes of *l*, and

LIKENESS

Gen	5.	1 he made them in the *l* of God.
Isa	40.	18 liken God, or what *l* compare with him?
Rom	8.	3 his own Son in the *l* of sinful flesh,
Phil	2.	7 form of a slave, being born in human *l*.

LILY (LILIES)

Song	2.	2 As a *l* among brambles, so is my love
Mt	6.	28 Consider the *l* of the field, how they
Lk	12.	27 Consider the *l*, how they grow; they

LINEN

Mk	15.	46 the body, wrapped it in the *l* cloth,
Rev	19.	8 with fine *l*, bright and pure" —for the

LION (LIONS LION'S)

1 Sam	17.	34 whenever a *l* or a bear came, and took a
2 Sam	23.	20 went down and killed a *l* in a pit on a
1 Kings	13.	24 he went away, a *l* met him on the road
1 Chr	11.	22 killed a *l* in a pit on a day when snow
Ps	7.	2 or like a *l* they will tear me apart; they
	22.	21 dog! Save me from the mouth of the *l*!
	104.	21 The young *l* roar for their prey, seeking
Prov	26.	13 The lazy person says, "There is a *l* in
Jer	12.	8 has become to me like a *l* in the forest;
Dan	6.	16 brought and thrown into the den of *l*.
	7.	4 first was like a *l* and had eagle's wings.
Hos	5.	14 I will be like a *l* to Ephraim, and like a
Am	5.	19 not light; as if someone fled from a *l*,
2 Tim	4.	17 it. So I was rescued from the *l* mouth.
Heb	11.	33 shut the mouths of *l*, quenched the
1 Pet	5.	8 Like a roaring *l* your adversary the devil
Rev	5.	5 the *L* of the tribe of Judah, the Root of

LIPS

Ps	12.	4 will prevail; our *l* are our own—who is
	34.	13 evil, and your *l* from speaking deceit.
Prov	12.	19 Truthful *l* endure forever, but a lying
	16.	13 Righteous *l* are the delight of a king,
	20.	15 but the *l* informed by knowledge are a
Song	4.	3 Your *l* are like a crimson thread, and
Isa	29.	13 honor me with their *l*, while their hearts
Mt	15.	8 This people honors me with their *l*, but
Mk	7.	6 'This people honors me with their *l*, but
Rom	3.	13 "The venom of vipers is under their *l*."
	10.	8 "The word is near you, on your *l* and in

LISTED

Judg	8.	14 questioned him; and he *l* for him the

LISTEN (LISTENED LISTENING LISTENS)

Ex	23.	21 Be attentive to him and *l* to his voice;
Josh	5.	6 not having *l* to the voice of the Lord. To
Judg	13.	9 God *l* to Manoah, and the angel of God
1 Sam	8.	19 the people refused to *l* to the voice of
2 Kings	21.	9 But they did not *l*, Manasseh misled
Job	36.	11 If they *l*, and serve him, they complete
Prov	12.	15 way is right, but the wise *l* to advice.
	23.	22 *L* to your father who begot you, and do
Eccl	5.	1 to draw near to *l* is better than the
Isa	6.	9 'Keep *l*, but do not comprehend; keep
	51.	1 *L* to me, you that pursue righteousness,
Jer	12.	17 But if any nation will not *l*, then I will
	17.	24 But if you *l* to me, says the Lord, and
	18.	10 not *l* to my voice, then I will change my
	26.	3 It may be that they will *l*, all of them,
Dan	9.	19 forgive; O Lord, *l* and act and do not
Mal	3.	16 The Lord took note and *l*, and a book of
Mk	9.	7 "This is my Son, the Beloved; *l* to him!"
Lk	9.	35 "This is my Son, my Chosen; *l* to him!"
	10.	16 "Whoever *l* to you *l* to me, and whoever
	10.	16 them also, and they will *l* to my voice.
Jn		
Acts	28.	26 You will indeed *l*, but never understand,
Jas	1.	19 let everyone be quick to *l*, slow to

LITTLE

Ps	37.	16 Better is a *l* that the righteous one has
Prov	13.	11 but those who gather *l* by *l* will increase
Isa	28.	10 line, line upon line, here a *l*, there a *l*."
Mic	5.	2 who are one of the *l* clans of Judah,
Mt	6.	30 much more clothe you—you of *l* faith?
	8.	26 "Why are you afraid, you of *l* faith?"
	10.	42 cold water to one of these *l* ones in the
	14.	31 him, "You of *l* faith, why did you doubt?"
	16.	8 "You of *l* faith, why are you talking
	18.	6 stumbling block before one of these *l*
Lk	7.	47 the one to whom *l* is forgiven, loves *l*."
	17.	2 to cause one of these *l* ones to stumble.
2 Cor	8.	15 the one who had *l* did not have too *l*."

LIVE (v)

Gen	13.	6 so great that they could not *l* together,
Ex	1.	17 them, but they let the boys *l*.
	9.	16 this is why I have let you *l*: to show you
	33.	20 face; for no one shall not see me and *l*."
Lev	18.	5 by doing so one shall *l*: I am the Lord.
Num	21.	9 look at the serpent of bronze and *l*.
Deut	4.	1 that you may *l* to enter and occupy the
	5.	24 to someone and the person may still *l*.
	5.	33 that you may *l*, and that it may go well
	8.	1 that you may *l* and increase, and go in
	8.	3 one does not *l* by bread alone, but by
	16.	20 that you may *l* and occupy the land that
	30.	20 that you may *l* in the land that the Lord
Josh	15.	63 the Jebusites *l* with the people of Judah
1 Sam	10.	24 all the people shouted, "Long *l* the king!"
1 Kings	1.	34 and say, 'Long *l* King Solomon!'
Job	14.	14 If mortals die, will they *l* again? All the
Ps	27.	4 to *l* in the house of the Lord all the
	84.	4 Happy are those who *l* in your house,
	91.	1 You who *l* in the shelter of the Most
	107.	36 there he lets the hungry *l*, and they
	119.	17 so that I may *l* and observe your word.
	119.	144 give me understanding that I may *l*.
	133.	1 it is when kindred *l* together in unity!
	146.	2 I will praise the Lord as long as I *l*; I
Prov	4.	4 words; keep my commandments, and *l*;
	9.	6 Lay aside immaturity, and *l*, and walk
	21.	9 It is better to *l* in a corner of the
Isa	26.	19 Your dead shall *l*, their corpses shall
	33.	14 among us can *l* with the devouring fire?
	55.	3 come to me; listen, so that you may *l*;
Jer	27.	12 and serve him and his people, and *l*.
Ezek	16.	6 you lay in your blood, I said to you, "*L*,
	18.	9 a one is righteous, he shall surely *l*,
	18.	22 that they have done they shall *l*.
	20.	11 by whose observance everyone shall *l*.
	33.	19 is lawful and right, they shall *l* by it.
	37.	3 said to me, "Mortal, can these bones *l*?"
Hos	6.	2 raise us up, that we may *l* before him.
	12.	9 I will make you *l* in tents again, as in
	14.	7 They shall again *l* beneath my shadow,
Am	5.	14 Seek good and not evil, that you may *l*;
Mt	4.	4 "One does not *l* by bread alone, but by
	9.	18 lay your hand on her, and she will *l*."
Mk	7.	5 disciples not *l* according to the tradition
	12.	44 everything she had, all she had to *l* on."
Lk	4.	4 'One does not *l* by bread alone.'
	10.	28 the right answer; do this, and you will *l*."
Jn	6.	58 But the one who eats this bread will *l*
	14.	19 will see me; because I *l*, you also will *l*.
Acts	17.	28 For 'In him we *l* and move and have
Rom	8.	13 if you *l* according to the flesh, you will
	10.	5 who does these things will *l* by them."
	13.	13 let us *l* honorably as in the day, not in
	14.	7 We do not *l* to ourselves, and we do not
Gal	3.	11 one who is righteous will *l* by faith."
	5.	16 *L* by the Spirit, I say, and do not gratify
	5.	25 If we *l* by the Spirit, let us also be
Eph	4.	17 no longer *l* as the Gentiles *l*, in the
	5.	2 *l* in love, as Christ loved us and gave
	5.	8 you are light. *L* as children of light—

Col	2. 6 continue to *l* your lives in him, rooted
2 Tim	2.11 died with him, we will also *l* with him;
Titus	2.12 to *l* lives that are self-controlled,

LIVES (LIVED LIVING) (v)

Gen	14.12 took Lot . . . who *l* in Sodom, and his
	19.30 in Zoar; so he *l* in a cave with his two
2 Sam	7. 2 I am *l* in a house of cedar, but the ark
Job	19.25 I know that my Redeemer *l*, and at the
Lk	1. 6 righteous before God, *l* blamelessly
Jn	1.14 Word became flesh and *l* among us, and
Acts	9.31 L in the fear of the Lord and in the
Eph	2. 2 trespasses and sins in which you once *l*,
Phil	1.21 For to me, *l* is Christ and dying is
1 Pet	4. 3 Gentiles like to do, *l* in licentiousness,
1 Jn	4.12 if we love one another, God *l* in us, and

LIVES (n)

Prov	11.30 a tree of life, but violence takes *l* away.
Jer	51. 6 of Babylon, save your *l*, each of you!
Ezek	13.18 you hunt down *l* among my people, and
Acts	15.26 who have risked their *l* for the sake of
Heb	13. 5 Keep your *l* free from love of money,
2 Pet	3.11 in leading *l* of holiness and godliness,

LIVING (n and adj)

Gen	2. 7 of life; and the man became a *l* being.
Num	16.48 He stood between the dead and the *l*;
Josh	3.10 among you is the *l* God who without
1 Sam	17.36 he has defied the armies of the *l* God."
2 Kings	19. 4 of Assyria has sent to mock the *l* God,
Ps	42. 2 My soul thirsts for God, for the *l* God.
	66. 9 who has kept us among the *l*, and has
	69.28 be blotted out of the book of the *l*;
Eccl	4. 2 already died, more fortunate than the *l*
	9. 5 the *l* know that they will die, but the
Isa	8.19 their gods, the dead on behalf of the *l*,
	38.19 The *l*, the *l*, they thank you, as I do this
Jer	10.10 is the *l* God and the everlasting King.
Zech	14. 8 that day *l* waters shall flow out of
Mt	22.32 He is God not of the dead, but of the *l*."
Mk	12.27 He is God not of the dead, but of the *l*;
Lk	15.13 squandered his property in dissolute *l*.
	24. 5 do you look for the *l* among the dead?
Jn	4.10 and he would have given you *l* water."
	6.51 I am the *l* bread that came down from
	6.57 the *l* Father sent me, and I live because
1 Cor	15.45 "The first man, Adam, became a *l* being";
1 Thess	1. 9 from idols, to serve a *l* and true God,
1 Tim	4.10 we have our hope set on the *l* God, who
Heb	3.12 heart that turns away from the *l* God.
Rev	1.18 and the *l* one. I was dead, and see, I am

LIZARD

Lev	11.29 . . . the great *l* according to its kind,
Prov	30.28 the *l* can be grasped in the hand, yet it

LOAN (LOANS)

Deut	23.19 shall not charge interest on *l* to another
	24.10 When you make your neighbor a *l* of

LOATHE (LOATHED)

Job	10. 1 "I *l* my life; I will give free utterance to
Ps	95.10 For forty years I *l* that generation and
	139. 21 I not *l* those who rise up against you?
Ezek	36.31 you shall *l* yourselves for your iniquities

LOAVES

Mt	14.17 nothing here but five *l* and two fish."
	15.34 "How many *l* have you?" They said,
Mk	6.38 "How many *l* have you? Go and see."
	8. 5 asked them, "How many *l* do you have?"
Lk	9.13 "We have no more than five *l* and two
	11. 5 'Friend, lend me three *l* of bread; for a
Jn	6. 9 here who has five barley *l* and two fish.
	6.26 but because you ate your fill of the *l*.

LOCK

Mt	23.13 For you *l* people out of the kingdom of

LOCUST (LOCUSTS)

Ex	10. 4 tomorrow I will bring *l* into your
Lev	11.22 of them you may eat: the *l* according to
Judg	6. 5 even bring their tents, as thick as *l*;
Ps	105. 34 He spoke, and the *l* came, and young *l*
Prov	30.27 the *l* have no king, yet all of them
Joel	1. 4 What the cutting *l* left, the swarming *l*
Am	7. 1 he was forming *l* at the time the latter
Mt	3. 4 and his food was *l* and wild honey.
Mk	1. 6 his waist, and he ate *l* and wild honey.
Rev	9. 3 from the smoke came *l* on the earth,

LODGE (LODGED)

Ruth	1.16 you go, I will go; Where you *l*, I will *l*,
1 Sam	7. 2 day that the ark was *l* at Kiriath-jearim,

LOFTY

Job	22.12 See the highest stars, how *l* they are!
Isa	57.15 high and *l* one who inhabits eternity,
1 Cor	2. 1 the mystery of God to you in *l* words or

LONELY

Ps	25.16 gracious to me, for I am *l* and afflicted.

LONG (LONGED LONGING LONGS)

Job	3.21 to the bitter in soul, who *l* for death,
Ps	42. 1 As a deer *l* for flowing streams, so my
	84. 2 My soul *l*, indeed it faints for the courts
	119. 20 is consumed with *l* for your ordinances
	119. 40 I have *l* for your precepts; in your
Mt	13.17 righteous people *l* to see what you see,
Lk	17.22 days are coming when you will *l* to see
Rom	8.19 creation waits with eager *l* for the
Rev	18.14 "The fruit for which your soul *l* has

LOOK (LOOKED LOOKING LOOKS)

Gen	13.14 eyes now, and *l* from the place where
	15. 5 "L toward heaven, and count the stars,
	19.17 "Flee for your life; do not *l* back or stop
	19.26 But Lot's wife . . . *l* back, and she
	22.13 Abraham *l* up and saw a ram, caught in
Num	21. 9 person would *l* at the serpent of bronze
Deut	26.15 L down from your holy habitation, from
1 Sam	16. 7 "Do not *l* on his appearance or on the
2 Sam	22.42 They *l*, but there was no one to save
Job	36.25 All people have *l* on it; everyone
Ps	8. 3 When I *l* at your heavens, the work of
	33.13 The Lord *l* down from heaven, he sees
	84. 9 O God; *l* on the face of your anointed.
	102. 19 from heaven the Lord *l* at the earth,
	104. 27 These all *l* to you, to give them their
	119.153 L on my misery and rescue me, for I do
Isa	22.11 But you did not *l* to him who did it, or
	33.20 L on Zion, the city of our appointed
	42.18 and you that are blind, *l* up and see!
	51. 1 L to the rock from which you were
	51. 6 the heavens, and *l* at the earth beneath;
	63. 5 I *l*, but there was no helper; I stared,
Mic	7. 7 But as for me, I will *l* to the Lord, I will
Hab	1.13 evil, and you cannot *l* on wrongdoing;
Hag	1. 9 You have *l* for much, and, lo, it came to
Mt	5.28 who *l* at a woman with lust had already
	6.16 whenever you fast, do not *l* dismal, like
	13.14 you will indeed *l*, but never perceive.
	23.28 on the outside *l* righteous to others,
Mk	4.12 'they may indeed *l*, but not perceive,
Lk	1.48 for he has *l* with favor on the lowliness
	2.25 *l* forward to consolation of Israel,
	9.38 "Teacher, I beg you to *l* at my son; he is
	13. 7 I have come *l* for fruit on this fig tree,
	24. 5 "Why do you *l* for the living among the
Jn	6.26 you are *l* for me, not because you saw
	18. 4 and asked them, "Whom are you *l* for?"
	20.15 are you weeping? Whom are you *l* for?"
Acts	1.11 why do you stand *l* up toward heaven?

Acts 28.26 you will indeed *l* but never perceive.
2 Cor 10. 7 *L* at what is before your eyes. If you are
Heb 11.10 he *l* forward to the city that has
 12. 2 *l* to Jesus the pioneer and perfector of
Jas 1.25 those who *l* into the perfect law, the

LOOSE (LOOSED LOOSES)

Job 12.21 on princes, and *l* the belt of the strong.
Ps 78.49 He let *l* on them his fierce anger, wrath,
 116. 16 You have *l* my bonds. I will offer to you
Prov 5. 3 For the lips of a *l* woman drip honey,
Isa 58. 6 I choose: to *l* the bonds of injustice,
Mt 16.19 whatever you *l* on earth will be *l* in
 18.18 whatever you *l* on earth will be *l* in

LORD

Gen 2. 4 day that the *L* God made the earth and
 6. 8 Noah found favor in the sight of the *L*.
 12. 1 Now the *L* said to Abram, "Go from
Ex 6. 3 by my name 'The *L*' I did not make
 12.51 very day the *L* brought the Israelites
 15. 1 the Israelites sang this song to the *L*:
Deut 34.10 Moses, whom the *L* knew face to face.
1 Kings 1.31 said, "May my *l* King David live forever!"
Ps 1. 2 but their delight is in the law of the *L*,
 83.18 that you alone, whose name is the *L*,
 84. 1 is your dwelling place, O *L* of hosts!
Isa 53. 6 and the *L* has laid on him the iniquity
Mt 12. 8 For the Son of Man is *l* of the sabbath."
Mk 1. 3 Prepare the way of the *L*, make his
Jn 14. 5 "*L*, we do not know where you are
 20.28 answered him, "My *L* and my God!"
Acts 2.36 God has made him both *L* and Messiah,
1 Cor 12. 3 no one can say "Jesus is *L*" except by
Phil 2.11 should confess that Jesus Christ is *L*,
Heb 1.10 beginning, *L*, you founded the earth,
Rev 19. 6 "Hallelujah! for the *L* our God the

LORD JESUS

Acts 15.11 be saved through the grace of the *L*,
 16.31 "Believe on the *L*, and you will be

LORD JESUS CHRIST

Acts 11.17 he gave us when we believed in the *L*,
Rom 5. 1 we have peace with God through our *L*.
1 Cor 15.57 who gives us the victory through our *L*.
2 Cor 8. 9 you know the generous act of our *L*,
2 Pet 1.16 to you the power and coming of our *L*,

LORD OF HOSTS

Ps 46. 7 The *L* is with us; the God of Jacob is
Isa 8.13 the *L*, him you shall regard as holy; let

LORDS

1 Cor 8. 5 fact there are many gods and many *l*—

LOSE (LOSES LOST)

Ps 119.176 I have gone astray like a *l* sheep; seek
Eccl 5.14 riches were *l* in a bad venture; though
Isa 6. 5 "Woe is me! I am *l*, for I am a man of
Ezek 37.11 bones are dried up, and our hope is *l*;
Mt 10. 6 go rather to the *l* sheep of the house of
 10.39 Those who find their life will *l* it, and
 15.24 was sent only to the *l* sheep of the
 16.25 who want to save their life will *l* it,
 18.14 that one of these little ones should be *l*.
Mk 8.35 it, and those who *l* their life for my sake
Lk 9.24 those who *l* their life for my sake will
 15. 8 if she *l* one of them, does not light a
 15.24 is alive again; he was *l*, and is found!'
 17.33 it, but those who *l* their life will keep it.
Jn 6.39 should *l* nothing of all that he has given
 18. 9 "I did not *l* a single one of those whom

LOST (n)

Ezek 34.16 I will seek the *l*, and I will bring back
Mt 18.11n For the Son of Man came to save the *l*.
Lk 19.10 Man came to seek out and to save the *l*."

LOT

Accompanied Abram to Canaan, Gen 11.31–12.5; separated from Abram to live at Sodom, Gen 13; rescued by Abram, Gen 14.1-16; sheltered angels, Gen 19.1-11; fled to Zoar, Gen 19.15-23; Lot and his daughters, Gen 19.30-38.

Gen 12. 4 and *L* went with him. Abram was
 14.16 brought back his nephew *L* with his
 19. 1 *L* was sitting in the gateway of Sodom.
Lk 17.28 just as it was in the days of *L*: they
2 Pet 2. 7 if he rescued *L*, a righteous man greatly

LOT (LOTS)

Lev 16. 8 Aaron shall cast *l* on the two goats, one
1 Sam 14.42 Then Saul said, "Cast the *l* between me
Ps 22.18 and for my clothing they cast *l*.
Prov 1.14 Throw in your *l* among us; we will all
 16.33 The *l* is cast into the lap, but the
Eccl 3.22 enjoy their work, for that is their *l*;
Ob 11 his gates and cast *l* for Jerusalem,
Jon 1. 7 they cast lots, and the *l* fell on Jonah.
Mt 27.35 clothes among themselves by casting *l*;
Lk 1. 9 he was chosen by *l*, according to the
Jn 19.24 "Let us not tear it, but cast *l* for it to
Acts 1.26 and the *l* fell on Matthias; and he was

LOVE (n)

1 Sam 20.14 show me the faithful *l* of the LORD;
2 Sam 7.15 I will not take my steadfast *l* from him,
Prov 7.18 let us take our fill of *l* until morning;
 10.12 stirs up strife, but *l* covers all offenses.
 15.17 is a dinner of vegetables where *l* is
 27. 5 Better is open rebuke than hidden *l*.
Song 1. 2 For your *l* is better than wine, your
 1.15 you are beautiful, my *l*; ah, you are
 4. 1 How beautiful you are, my *l*, how very
 4.10 How much better is your *l* than wine,
 5. 1 Eat, friends, drink, and be drunk with *l*.
 8. 6 for *l* is strong as death, passion fierce as
 8. 7 Many waters cannot quench *l*, neither
Isa 63. 9 in his *l* and in his pity he redeemed
Ezek 33.32 To them you are like a singer of *l* songs,
Hos 6. 4 Your *l* is like a morning cloud, like the
 11. 4 of human kindness, with bands of *l*.
Mt 24.12 the *l* of many will grow cold.
Lk 11.42 and neglect justice and the *l* of God;
Jn 15.13 No one has greater *l* than this, to lay
 17.26 so that the *l* with which you have loved
Rom 5. 5 God's *l* has been poured into our hearts
 5. 8 But God proves his *l* for us in that while
 8.39 be able to separate us from the *l* of God
 12. 9 Let *l* be genuine; hate what is evil, hold
1 Cor 8. 1 Knowledge puffs up, but *l* builds up.
 13. 1 but do not have *l*, I am a noisy gong or
 13.13 three; and the greatest of these is *l*.
2 Cor 5.14 the *l* of Christ urges us on, because we
 6. 6 kindness, holiness of spirit, genuine *l*,
 8. 8 I am testing the genuineness of your *l*
 8.24 show them the proof of your *l* and of
 13.13 Christ, the *l* of God, and the
Gal 5. 6 that counts is faith working through *l*.
 5.13 through *l* become slaves to one another.
Eph 1.15 your *l* toward all the saints, and for this
 3.19 *l* of Christ that surpasses knowledge,
 4.15 speaking the truth in *l*, we must grow
 5. 2 live in *l*, as Christ loved us and gave
Phil 1. 9 is my prayer, that your *l* may overflow
 1.16 These proclaim Christ out of *l*, knowing
Col 1. 4 Jesus and of the *l* that you have for all
 3.14 Above all, clothe yourselves with *l*,
1 Thess 1. 3 your work of faith and labor of *l* and
 4. 9 concerning *l* of the brothers and sisters,
2 Tim 4.10 Demas, in *l* with this present world, has
Heb 13. 1 Let mutual *l* continue. Do not neglect
1 Pet 4. 8 another, for *l* covers a multitude of sins.
1 Jn 3. 1 See what *l* the Father has given us, that
 3.16 We know *l* by this, that he laid down

Jude	12	These are blemishes on your *l*-feasts,
Rev	2. 4	that you have abandoned the *l* you had

LOVE (v)

Ex	20. 6	generation of those who *l* me and keep
	21. 5	"I *l* my master, my wife, and my
Lev	19.18	you shall *l* your neighbor as yourself: I
Deut	5.10	generation of those who *l* me
	6. 5	You shall *l* the Lord your God with all
	7.13	he will *l* you, bless you, and multiply
	10.12	to *l* him, to serve the Lord your God
	10.19	You shall also *l* the stranger, for you
	13. 3	to know whether you indeed *l* the Lord
	30. 6	so that you will *l* the Lord your God
Josh	23.11	very careful . . . to *l* the Lord your God.
2 Chr	19. 2	wicked and *l* those who hate the Lord?
Neh	1. 5	*l* with those who *l* him and keep his
Ps	18. 1	I *l* you, O Lord, my strength. The Lord
	31.23	*L* the Lord, all you his saints. The Lord
	45. 7	you *l* righteousness and hate
	60. 5	that those whom you *l* may be rescued.
	70. 4	Let those who *l* your salvation say
	91.14	Those who *l* me, I will deliver; I will
	116. 1	I *l* the Lord, because he has heard my
	119. 97	Oh, how I *l* your law! It is my
Prov	4. 6	keep you; *l* her, and she will guard you.
	8.17	I *l* those who *l* me, and those who seek
	20.13	Do not *l* sleep, or else you will come to
	22.11	who *l* a pure heart and are gracious
Eccl	3. 8	time to *l*, and a time to hate; a time for
	9. 9	life with the wife whom you *l*, all the
Isa	61. 8	For I the Lord *l* justice, I hate robbery
Hos	3. 1	*l* a woman who has a lover and is an
	9.15	I will *l* them no more; all their officials
	14. 4	I will *l* them freely, for my anger has
Am	5.15	Hate evil and *l* good, and establish
Mic	3. 2	you who hate the good and *l* the evil,
	6. 8	do justice, to *l* kindness, and to walk
Mt	5.43	'You shall *l* your neighbor and hate
	19.19	You shall *l* your neighbor as yourself."
	22.37	"You shall *l* the Lord your God with all
	23. 6	They *l* to have the place of honor at
Mk	12.30	you shall *l* the Lord your God with all
Lk	6.27	*L* your enemies, do good to those who
	6.32	"If you *l* those who *l* you, what credit is
	10.27	"You shall *l* the Lord your God with all
	16.13	will either hate the one and *l* the other,
Jn	8.42	God were your Father, you would *l* me,
	11. 3	to Jesus, "Lord, he whom you *l* is ill."
	12.25	Those who *l* their life will lose it, and
	13.34	commandment, that you *l* one another.
	14.15	"If you *l* me, you will keep my
	14.21	and keep them are those who *l* me;
	15.12	that you *l* one another as I have *l* you.
	21.15	"Yes, Lord; you know that I *l* you." Jesus
Rom	8.28	together for good for those who *l* God,
	13. 8	one anything, except to *l* one another;
1 Cor	2. 9	God has prepared for those who *l* him"
2 Cor	12.15	If I *l* you more, am I to be *l* less? Let it
Eph	5.25	Husbands, *l* your wives, just as Christ
Col	3.19	Husbands, *l* your wives, and never treat
Titus	2. 4	the young women to *l* their husbands,
Jas	2. 5	he has promised to those who *l* him?
1 Pet	1. 8	you have not seen him, you *l* him;
	2.17	everyone. *L* the family of believers.
1 Jn	2.15	Do not *l* the world or the things in the
	3.11	that we should *l* one another.
	4. 7	let us *l* one another, because *l* is from
	4.19	We *l*, because he first loved us.
	5. 2	we *l* God and obey his commandments.
Rev	3.19	I reprove and discipline those whom I *l*.

LOVES (LOVED)

Gen	24.67	she became his wife; and he *l* her. So
	25.28	Isaac *l* Esau . . . , but Rebekah *l* Jacob.
	37. 3	Now Israel *l* Joseph more than any
	44.20	mother's children, and his father *l* him.'

Deut	4.37	because he *l* your ancestors, he chose
	15.16	because he *l* you and your household,
	23. 5	you, because the Lord your God *l* you.)
1 Sam	1. 5	gave a double portion, because he *l* her,
	16.21	Saul *l* him greatly, and he became his
	18. 1	and Jonathan *l* him as his own soul.
	18.16	all Israel and Judah *l* David; for it was
	18.28	and that Saul's daughter Michal *l* him,
	20.17	him, for he *l* him as he *l* his own life.
1 Kings	3. 3	Solomon *l* the Lord, walking in the
	10. 9	Because the Lord *l* Israel forever, he has
	11. 1	Solomon *l* many foreign women along
2 Chr	2.11	"Because the Lord *l* his people he has
Ps	78.68	tribe of Judah, Mount Zion, which he *l*.
	97.10	The Lord *l* those who hate evil; he
Prov	3.12	for the Lord reproves the one he *l*, as a
	12. 1	Whoever *l* discipline *l* knowledge, but
	15. 9	he *l* the one who pursues righteousness.
	17.17	A friend *l* at all times, and kinsfolk are
	17.19	One who *l* transgression *l* strife; one
	21.17	Whoever *l* pleasure will suffer want;
Song	3. 1	at night I sought him whom my soul *l*;
Isa	48.14	Lord *l* him; he shall perform his
Jer	31. 3	I have *l* you with an everlasting love;
Hos	11. 1	When Israel was a child, I *l* him, and
Mal	1. 2	I have *l* you, says the Lord. But you say,
Mt	10.37	Whoever *l* father or mother more than
Mk	10.21	Jesus, looking at him, *l* him and said,
Lk	7. 5	he *l* our people, and it is he who built
	7.47	forgiven, hence she has shown great *l*.
Jn	3.16	"For God so *l* the world that he gave his
	5.20	The Father *l* the Son and shows him all
	10.17	For this reason the Father *l* me,
	11.36	So the Jews said, "See how he *l* him!"
	12.43	for they *l* human glory more than the
	13. 1	were in the world, he *l* them to the end.
	15. 9	As the Father has *l* me, so I have *l* you;
	16.27	for the Father himself *l* you, because
	17.23	that you have sent me and have *l* them
	19.26	and the disciple whom he *l* standing
Rom	9.13	"I have *l* Jacob, but I have hated Esau."
1 Cor	8. 3	but anyone who *l* God is known by him.
2 Cor	9. 7	compulsion, for God *l* a cheerful giver.
Gal	2.20	in the Son of God, who *l* me and gave
Eph	2. 4	out of the great love with which he *l* us
Heb	1. 9	You have *l* righteousness and hated
1 Jn	2.10	whoever *l* a brother or sister lives in the
Rev	1. 5	To him who *l* us and freed us from our

LOVELY

Ps	84. 1	How *l* is your dwelling place, O Lord of

LOVER (LOVERS)

Eccl	5.10	the *l* of money will not be satisfied with
Jer	4.30	Your *l* despise you; they seek your life.
	22.22	and your *l* shall go into captivity;
	30.14	All your *l* have forgotten you; they care
Ezek	16.33	but you gave your gifts to all your *l*,
	23.22	I will rouse against you your *l* from
Hos	8. 9	alone; Ephraim has bargained for *l*.
2 Tim	3. 2	people will be *l* of themselves, *l* of

LOVE-SONG

Isa	5. 1	beloved my *l* concerning his vineyard:

LOW (LOWEST)

Isa	2.11	eyes of people will be brought *l*,
	10.33	down, and the lofty will be brought *l*.
	26. 5	city he lays *l*. He lays it *l* to the ground,
Lk	14. 9	you would start to take the *l* place.

LOWLY

Prov	16.19	It is better to be of a *l* spirit among the
	29.23	one who is *l* in spirit will obtain honor.
Zeph	3.12	the midst of you a people humble and *l*.

LOYAL (LOYALLY)

Deut	18.13	You must remain completely *l* to the

LOYALTY

2 Sam	22.26 "With the *l* you show yourself *l*; with the
1 Chr	19. 2 "I will deal *l* with Hanun son of Nahash,
Ps	18.25 With the *l* you show yourself *l*; with the

LOYALTY

Ruth	3.10 this last instance of your *l* is better than
2 Sam	2. 5 because you showed this *l* to Saul your
Prov	19.22 What is desirable in a person is *l*, and it

LUKE

Col	4.14 *L*, the beloved physician, and Demas
2 Tim	4.11 Only *L* is with me. Get Mark and bring
Philem	24 Demas, and *L*, my fellow workers.

LUKEWARM

Rev	3.16 because you are *l*, and neither cold nor

LUMP

Isa	38.21 had said, "Let them take a *l* of figs,

LURE

Mk	4.19 cares of the world, and the *l* of wealth,

LUST

Mt	5.28 everyone who looks at a woman with *l*

LYING

Ps	31.18 Let the *l* lips be stilled that speak
	109. 2 me, speaking against me with *l* tongues.
Prov	6.17 haughty eyes, a *l* tongue, and hands

LYRE

Gen	4.21 ancestor of all those who play the *l* and
Ps	33. 2 Praise the LORD with the *l*, make the

LYSTRA

Acts	14. 6 of it and fled to *L* and Derbe, cities
	14.21 they returned to *L*, then on to Iconium
	16. 1 Paul went on also to Derbe and to *L*,
2 Tim	3.11 and *L*. What persecutions I endured!

M

MACEDONIA

Acts	16. 9 stood a man of *M* pleading with him
	18. 5 Silas and Timothy arrived from *M*, Paul
	19.22 his helpers, Timothy and Erastus, to *M*,
Rom	15.26 *M* and Achaia have been pleased to
2 Cor	9. 2 boasting about you to the people of *M*,
Phil	4.15 when I left *M*, no church shared with
1 Thess	1. 8 sounded forth from you not only in *M*

MAD

Deut	28.34 driven *m* by the sight that your eyes
1 Sam	21.13 he pretended to be *m* in their presence.

MADE

Eph	2.10 For we are what he has *m* us, created in

MADNESS

Eccl	2.12 to consider wisdom and *m* and folly;

MAGGOT (MAGGOTS)

Job	25. 6 less mortal, who is a *m*, and a
Hos	5.12 Therefore I am like *m* to Ephraim, and

MAGNIFICENT

1 Chr	22. 5 for the LORD must be exceedingly *m*,

MAGNIFY (MAGNIFIED MAGNIFIES)

2 Sam	7.26 your name will be *m* forever in the
1 Chr	17.24 name will be established and *m* forever
Ps	34. 3 O me the LORD with me, and let us exalt
Isa	10.15 or the saw *m* itself against the one who
	42.21 *m* his teaching and make it glorious.
Lk	1.47 "My soul *m* the Lord, and my spirit

MAGOG

Ezek	38. 2 your face toward Gog, of the land of *M*,
Rev	20. 8 Gog and *M*, in order to gather them for

MAID

Prov	30.23 and a *m* when she succeeds her

MAIDEN (MAIDENS)

Song	1. 3 poured out; therefore the *m* love you.
Am	5. 2 Fallen, no more to rise, is *m* Israel;

MAINTAIN

Job	16.21 he would *m* the right of a mortal with

MAINTENANCE

1 Chr	26.27 dedicated gifts for the *m* of the house of

MAJESTIC

Ps	8. 1 Sovereign, how *m* is your name in all
	8. 9 Sovereign, how *m* is your name in all

MAJESTY

Job	13.11 Will not his *m* terrify you, and the dread
	40.10 "Deck yourself with *m* and dignity;
Isa	33.21 there the LORD in *m* will be for us a
Lam	1. 6 daughter Zion has departed all her *m*.
Dan	4.30 mighty power and for my glorious *m*?"
	4.36 and my *m* and splendor were restored to
Mic	5. 4 LORD, in the *m* of the name of the LORD
Acts	19.27 she will be deprived of her *m* that

MAKER

Gen	14.19 God Most High, *m* of heaven and earth;
Job	35.10 no one says, 'Where is God my *M*, who
Ps	95. 6 let us kneel before the LORD, our *M*!
Isa	17. 7 On that day people will regard their *M*,
	45. 9 "Woe to you who strive with your *M*,
	54. 5 For your *M* is your husband, the LORD of

MALACHI

Mal	1. 1 The word of the LORD to Israel by *M*.

MALE

Gen	1.27 them; *m* and female he created them.
	17.10 Every *m* among you shall be
Gal	3.28 there is no longer *m* nor female; for all

MALTA

Acts	28. 1 learned that the island was called *M*.

MAN (MEN)

Gen	2. 7 God formed *m* from the dust of the
	2.19 the *m* called every living creature,
	3. 8 the *m* and his wife hid themselves from
1 Sam	4. 9 Take courage, and be *m*, O Philistines,
2 Sam	12. 7 Nathan said to David, "You are the *m*!
Rom	5.12 sin came into the world through one *m*,
1 Cor	11. 8 *m* was not made from woman, but

MAN OF GOD

Judg	13. 6 told her husband, "A *m* came to me,
1 Sam	2.27 A *m* came to Eli and said to him, "Thus
	9. 6 "There is a *m* in this town; he is a man
1 Kings	13. 1 a *m* came out of Judah by the word of
	13.26 "It is the *m* who disobeyed the word of
	17.24 now I know that you are a *m*, and that
	20.28 A *m* approached and said to the king of
2 Kings	1.10 "If I am a *m*, let fire come down from
	7.17 in the gate, just as the *m* had said
2 Chr	25. 7 a *m* came to him and said, "O king, do

MANAGEMENT

Lk	16. 2 Give me an accounting of your *m*,

MANAGER

Mt	20. 8 the owner of the vineyard said to his *m*,
Lk	12.42 is the faithful and prudent *m* whom his
	16. 1 a rich man who had a *m*, and charges

MANASSEH

Gen	41.51 Joseph named the firstborn *M*, "For," he
	48. 1 with him his two sons, *M* and Ephraim,
Num	1.34 The descendants of *M*, their lineage, in

Deut	3.13	I give to the half-tribe of *M* the rest of
Judg	6.15	my clan is the weakest in *M*, and I am
2 Kings	21. 1	*M* was twelve years old when he began
	21.16	*M* shed very much innocent blood, until
	21.18	*M* slept with his ancestors, and was
	23.12	the altars that *M* had made in the two
2 Chr	33. 1	*M* was twelve years old when he began
	33.13	Then *M* knew that the LORD indeed
	33.23	humble himself before the LORD, as *M*

MANDRAKES

Gen	30.14	Reuben went and found *m* in the field,
Song	7.13	The *m* give forth fragrance, and over our

MANGER

Lk	2. 7	and laid him in a *m*, because there was

MANIFESTED

Ps	90.16	Let your work be *m* to your servants,

MANIFESTATION

1 Cor	12. 7	To each is given the *m* of the Spirit for
1 Tim	6.14	spot or blame until the *m* of our Lord

MANNA

Ex	16.31	Israel called it *m*; it was like coriander
	16.35	Israelites ate *m* forty years, until they
Num	11. 6	there is nothing at all but this *m* to
Josh	5.12	The *m* ceased on the day they ate the
Ps	78.24	he rained down on them *m* to eat, and
Jn	6.31	Our ancestors ate *m* in the wilderness;
Rev	2.17	I will give some of the hidden *m*,

MANTLE

2 Kings	2.13	He picked up the *m* of Elijah that had

MARK

Cousin of Barnabas, Col 4.10; lived in Jerusalem, Acts 12.12; accompanied Barnabas and Paul to Antioch, Acts 12.25; began missionary work, Acts 13.5; deserted the group at Perga, Acts 13.13; subject of contention, Acts 15.37-38; went with Barnabas to Cyprus, Acts 15.39; ministered to Paul in Rome, Col 4.10; Philem 24; companion of Peter, 1 Pet 5.13.

MARK (MARKED MARKS)

Gen	4.15	LORD put a *m* on Cain, so that no one
Ps	37.37	*M* the blameless, and behold the
	50.22	"*M* this, then, you who forget God, or I
	130. 3	If you, O LORD, should *m* iniquities,
Ezek	9. 4	put a *m* upon the foreheads of those
Hab	1.12	O LORD, you have *m* them for judgment;
Gal	6.17	the *m* of Jesus branded on my body.
Rev	13.16	and slave, to be *m* on the right hand or
	14. 9	and receive a *m* on their foreheads or
	19.20	received the *m* of the beast and those

MARKET (MARKETS)

Ezek	27.15	coastlands were your own special *m*,
1 Cor	10.25	Eat whatever is sold in the meat *m*

MARKETPLACE (MARKETPLACES)

Lk	7.32	like children sitting in the *m* and calling
	20.46	love to be greeted in the *m*, and to have
Acts	17.17	and also in the *m* every day with those

MARRIAGE (MARRIAGES)

Gen	34. 9	Make *m* with us; give your daughters to
Deut	24. 1	Suppose a man enters into *m* with a
2 Cor	11. 2	I promised you in *m* to one husband, to
1 Tim	4. 3	They forbid *m* and demand abstinence
Heb	13. 4	Let *m* be held in honor by all, and let

MARRY (MARRIED MARRIES)

Num	12. 1	of the Cushite woman whom he had *m*,
Mal	2.11	*m* the daughter of a foreign god. May
Mt	5.32	and whoever *m* a divorced woman
	19. 9	and *m* another commits adultery."
Mk	10.11	divorces his wife and *m* another

Mk	12.25	they rise from the dead, they neither *m*
Lk	16.18	who divorces his wife and *m* another
	20.35	from the dead neither *m* nor are given
1 Cor	7.10	To the *m* I give this command, — not I
	7.33	the *m* man is anxious about the affairs

MARTHA

Lk	10.38	*M* welcomed him into her house.
Jn	11. 1	the village of Mary and her sister *M*.
	11.24	*M* said to him, "I know that he will rise
	12. 2	they gave a dinner for him. *M* served,

MARVELOUS

Job	5. 9	unsearchable, *m* things without number.
	9.10	and *m* things without number.
Ps	118. 23	This is the LORD's doing; it is *m* in our

MARY (Mother of Jesus)

Betrothed to Joseph, Mt 1.18 (Lk 1.27); Jesus' birth foretold to her, Lk 1.26-38; visited Elizabeth, Lk 1.39-45; The Song of Mary, Lk 1.46-55; went to Bethlehem, Lk 2.4-5; birth of Jesus, Mt 1.25 (Lk 2.7); found Jesus in the temple, Lk 2.41-51; attended the marriage at Cana, Jn 2.1-5; concerned over Jesus' ministry, Mk 3.31-35; at the cross, Jn 19.25-27; in the upper room, Acts 1.14.

MARY (Magdalene)

Healed of demons, Lk 8.2; stood by the cross, Mt 27.56 (Mk 15.40; Jn 19.25); watched Jesus' burial, Mt 27.61 (Mk 15.47); came early to the tomb, Mt 28.1 (Mk 16.1; Lk 24.1-10; Jn 20.1); saw the risen Lord, Mt 28.9 (Mk 16.9n; Jn 20.11-18).

MARY (of Bethany)

Listened to the Lord's teaching, Lk 10.38-42; present at the raising of Lazarus, Jn 11.1-45; anointed Jesus, Jn 12.1-8.

MASTER (MASTERS)

Gen	39. 3	His *m* saw that the LORD was with him,
Ex	21. 5	"I love my *m*, my wife, and my children;
Prov	27.18	who takes care of a *m* will be honored.
Jer	3.14	I am your *m*; I will take you, one from a
Dan	1. 3	commanded his palace *m* Ashpenaz
Mt	6.24	"No one can serve two *m*; for a slave
Eph	6. 9	both of you have the same *M* in heaven,
1 Tim	6. 2	Those who have believing *m* must not
1 Pet	2.18	Slaves, accept the authority of your *m*

MATTHEW

Mt	9. 9	he saw a man called *M* sitting at the
	10. 3	Thomas and *M* the tax collector; James
Mk	3.18	and *M*, and Thomas, and James son of
Lk	6.15	and *M*, and Thomas, and James son of
Acts	1.13	and Thomas, Bartholomew and *M*,

MATURE (MATURITY)

1 Cor	2. 6	Yet among the *m* we do speak wisdom,
Eph	4.13	to *m*, to the measure of the full stature

MEASURE (MEASURED MEASURING)

Ps	39. 4	my end, and what is the *m* of my days;
Isa	40.12	Who has *m* the waters in the hollow of
Jer	31.37	If the heavens above can be *m*, and the
Zech	2. 1	looked up and saw a man with a *m* line
Mk	4.24	the *m* you give will be the *m* you get,
Lk	6.38	for the *m* you give will be the *m* you get
Rev	11. 1	"Come and *m* the temple of God and
	21.15	had a *m* rod of gold to *m* the city and

MEDE (MEDES)

2 Kings	17. 6	of Gozan, and in the cities of the *M*.
Esth	1.19	the laws of the Persians and the *M*
Jer	51.11	up the spirit of the kings of the *M*,
Dan	5.28	and given to the *M* and Persians."
	6. 8	according to the law of the *M* and the
	9. 1	by birth a *M*, who became king over the

MEDIA

Ezra	6.	2 province of M, that a scroll was found
Esth	1.	3 The army of Persia and M and the
	10.	2 written in the annals of the kings of M
Dan	8.	20 the two horns, these are the kings of M

MEDIATOR

Job	33.	23 be for one of them an angel, a m,
Gal	3.	20 Now a m involves more than one party;
1 Tim	2:	5 one m between God and humankind,
Heb	9.	15 reason he is the m of a new covenant,
	12.	24 to Jesus, the m of a new covenant, and

MEDITATE

Josh	1.	8 you shall m on it day and night, so that
Ps	1.	2 and on his law they m day and night.
	63.	6 I think of you on my bed, and m on you
	77.	12 I will m on all your work, and muse on
	119.	15 I will m on your precepts, and fix my
	119.	78 as for me, I will m on your precepts.
	143.	5 deeds, I m on the works of your hands.

MEDITATION

Job	15.	4 of God, and hindering m before God.
Ps	19.	14 and the m of my heart be acceptable
	49.	3 speak wisdom; the m of my heart shall
	104.	34 May my m be pleasing to him, for I
	119.	97 I love your law! It is my m all day long.

MEEK

Ps	10.	17 you will hear the desire of the m; you
	37.	11 But the m shall inherit the land, and
Isa	29.	19 The m shall obtain fresh joy in the
Mt	5.	5 "Blessed are the m, for they will inherit

MEEKNESS

2 Cor	10.	1 by the m and gentleness of Christ—
Jas	1.	21 welcome with m the implanted word

MEET

Ex	25.	22 There I will m with you, and from above
Am	4.	12 to you, prepare to m your God, O Israel!
Mt	8.	34 the whole town came out to m Jesus;
1 Thess	4.	17 with them to m the Lord in the air;
Heb	10.	25 not neglecting to m together, as is the

MEETING

Ps	74.	8 they burned all the m places of God in

MEGIDDO

Josh	12.	21 of Taanach, one; the king of M, one;
	17.	11 the inhabitants of M and its villages
1 Kings	4.	12 in Taanach, M, and all Bethshean,
2 Kings	9.	27 Then he fled to M, and died there.
	23.	29 when Pharaoh Neco met him at M, he
Zech	12.	11 for Hadad-rimmon in the plain of M.

MELCHIZEDEK

Gen	14.	18 King M of Salem brought out bread and
Ps	110.	4 forever according to the order of M."
Heb	5.	6 forever, according to the order of M."
	6.	20 forever according to the order of M.
	7.	1 This "King M of Salem, priest of the
	7.	10 loins of his ancestor when M met him.
	7.	15 another priest arises, resembling M,

MELT (MELTED MELTS)

Ex	15.	15 all the inhabitants of Canaan m away.
Josh	2.	11 As soon as we heard it, our hearts m,
	5.	1 they had crossed over, their hearts m,
	7.	5 The hearts of the people m and turned
Ps	22.	14 my heart is like wax; it is m within my
	97.	5 The mountains m like wax before the
Ezek	22.	22 m in a smelter, so you shall be m in it;

MEMBER (MEMBERS)

Mt	18.	15 "If another m of the church sins against
	18.	21 if another m of the church sins against

Rom	6.	13 No longer present your m to sin as
	12.	4 as in one body we have many m, and
1 Cor	6.	15 know that your bodies are m of Christ?
Eph	5.	30 church, because we are m of his body.

MEMORIAL

Josh	4.	7 shall be to the Israelites a m forever."
Acts	10.	4 prayers and alms have ascended as a m

MEMORY

Deut	32.	26 out the m of them from humankind;
Job	18.	17 Their m perishes from the earth, and
Ps	109.	15 may his m be cut off from the earth.
Prov	10.	7 The m of the righteous is a blessing,
Eccl	9.	5 reward, and even the m of them is lost.

MENE

Dan	5.	25 that was inscribed: M, M, TEKEL, and

MEPHIBOSHETH

Crippled by a fall, 2 Sam 4.4; dined continually at the royal table, 2 Sam 9; reported to David as a deserter, 2 Sam 16.1-4; cleared himself before David, 2 Sam 19.24-30.

MERCHANT (MERCHANTS)

Nah	3.	16 You increased your m more than the
Mt	13.	45 is like a m in search of fine pearls;
Rev	18.	3 the m of the earth have grown rich from

MERCIFUL

Gen	19.	16 LORD being m to him, and they brought
1 Kings	20.	31 kings of the house of Israel are m kings;
Ps	86.	15 you, O Lord, are a God m and gracious,
Jon	4.	2 that you are a gracious God and m,
Mt	5.	7 "Blessed are the m, for they will receive
Lk	6.	36 Be m, just as your Father is m.
Heb	8.	12 I will be m toward their iniquities, and I

MERCY (MERCIES)

Gen	43.	14 may God Almighty grant you m before
Ex	33.	19 will show m on whom I will show m.
Deut	7.	2 with them and show them no m.
1 Chr	21.	13 of the LORD, for his m is very great;
Neh	1.	11 today, and grant him m in the sight of
Ps	51.	1 Have m on me, O God, according to
	103.	4 crowns you with steadfast love and m,
Jer	31.	20 for him; I will surely have m on him,
	42.	12 I will grant you m, and he will have m
Lam	3.	22 ceases, his m never come to an end;
Dan	2.	18 told them to seek m from the God of
Hab	3.	2 known; in wrath may you remember m.
Mt	9.	13 means, 'I desire m and not sacrifice.'
	12.	7 means, 'I desire m and not sacrifice,'
	15.	22 "Have m on me, Lord, Son of David; my
	20.	30 they shouted, "Lord, have m on us, Son
	23.	23 of the law, justice and m and faith.
Mk	5.	19 for you, and what m he has shown you."
Lk	1.	50 His m is on those who fear him from
	1.	72 he has shown m promised to our
	10.	37 He said, "The one who showed him m."
	16.	24 'Father Abraham, have m on me, and
	18.	38 "Jesus, Son of David, have m on me!
Rom	9.	15 "I will have m on whom I have m, and I
	9.	18 he has m upon whomever he chooses,
	9.	23 riches of his glory for the objects of m,
	11.	30 but now have received m because of
2 Cor	4.	1 by God's m that we are engaged in this
Phil	2.	27 But God had m on him, and not only on

MERCY SEAT

Ex	25.	22 meet with you, and from above the m,
Lev	16.	2 inside the curtain before the m that is

MEROM

Josh	11.	5 at the waters of M, to fight with Israel.
	11.	7 by the waters of M, and fell upon them.

MESSAGE

Judg	3.20	and said, "I have a *m* from God for you."
Hag	1.13	spoke to the people with the LORD's *m*,
Mk	16.20n	confirmed the *m* by the signs that
Acts	5.20	and tell the people the whole *m* about
	15. 7	Gentiles would hear the *m* of the good
	17.11	they welcomed the *m* very eagerly and
	20.32	you to God and to the *m* of his grace,
2 Tim	4. 2	I solemnly urge you: proclaim the *m*; be
2 Pet	1.19	we have the prophetic *m* more fully
1 Jn	1. 5	This is the *m* we have heard from him

MESSENGER (MESSENGERS)

Gen	32. 3	Jacob sent *m* before him to his brother
2 Chr	36.15	sent persistently to them by his *m*,
Prov	25.13	harvest are faithful *m* to those who send
Jer	49.14	a *m* has been sent among the nations:
Ezek	30. 9	On that day, *m* shall go out from me in
Mal	2. 7	his mouth, for he is the *m* of the LORD
	3. 1	I am sending my *m* to prepare the way
Mt	11.10	I am sending my *m* ahead of you, who
Mk	1. 2	I am sending my *m* ahead of you, who
Lk	7.27	"See, I am sending my *m* ahead of you,
	9.52	And he sent *m* ahead of him. On their
2 Cor	12. 7	was given me in the flesh, a *m* of Satan

MESSIAH

Mt	1.16	Jesus was born, who is called the *M*.
	16.16	Peter answered, "You are the *M*, the
Jn	1.41	and said to him, "We have found the *M*"
	4.25	said to him, "I know that *M* is coming"

METHUSELAH

Gen	5.27	Thus all the days of *M* were nine

MICAH

Jer	26.18	"*M* of Moresheth, who prophesied
Mic	1. 1	word of the LORD that came to *M* of

MICHAL

Married to David, 1 Sam 18.20-30; helped David escape, 1 Sam 19.12-17; restored to David, 2 Sam 3.13-16; rebuked for despising David, 2 Sam 6.12-23.

1 Sam	14.49	and the name of the younger, *M*.
2 Sam	3.13	unless you bring Saul's daughter *M*
1 Chr	15.29	*M* daughter of Saul looked out of the

MICHMASH

1 Sam	13. 2	two thousand were with Saul in *M* and
	14. 5	crag rose on the north in front of *M*,
Isa	10.28	Migron, at *M* he stores his baggage;

MIDIAN

Gen	25. 2	She bore him . . . *M*, Ishbak, and Shuah.
Ex	2.15	Moses . . . settled in the land of *M*, and
	4.19	The LORD said to Moses in *M*, "Go back
	18. 1	Jethro, the priest of *M* . . . heard of all
Num	22. 4	Moab said to the elders of *M*, "This
Judg	6. 1	them into the hand of *M* seven years.
	7. 8	The camp of *M* was below him in the
1 Kings	11.18	They set out from *M* and came to
Ps	83. 9	Do to them as you did to *M*, as to
Isa	9. 4	you have broken as on the day of *M*.
	10.26	against them, as when he struck *M* at

MIDIANITE

Gen	37.28	When some *M* traders passed by, they

MIDNIGHT

Judg	16. 3	But Samson lay only until *m*. Then at *m*
Ps	119. 62	At *m* I rise to praise you, because of
Acts	16.25	About *m* Paul and Silas were praying
	20. 7	day, he continued speaking until *m*.

MIDWIVES

Ex	1.15	king of Egypt said to the Hebrew *m*,

MIGHT

Judg	6.14	"Go in this *m* of yours and deliver Israel
1 Sam	2. 9	darkness; for not by *m* does one prevail.
Job	39.19	"Do you give the horse its *m*? Do you
Ps	59.16	But I will sing of your *m*; I will sing
	118. 14	The LORD is my strength and my *m*; he
Isa	12. 2	the LORD GOD is my strength and my *m*;
Eccl	9.10	your hand finds to do, do with your *m*;
Hab	1.11	become guilty; their own *m* is their god!
Zech	4. 6	Not by *m*, nor by power, but by my

MIGHTY (MIGHTIER)

2 Sam	1.25	How the *m* have fallen in the midst of
Job	21. 7	reach old age, and grow *m* in power?
	36. 5	"Surely God is *m* and does not despise
Ps	71.16	I will come praising the *m* deeds of the
Prov	24. 5	Wise warriors are *m* than strong ones,
Isa	1.24	LORD of hosts, the *M* One of Israel: Ah,
	9. 6	Wonderful Counselor, *M* God,
	63. 1	is I, announcing vindication, *m* to save."

MILE

Mt	5.41	you to go one *m*, go also the second *m*.

MILITARY

1 Cor	9. 7	pays the expenses for doing *m* service?

MILK

Gen	18. 8	Then he took curds and *m* and the calf
Ex	3. 8	land, a land flowing with *m* and honey,
Judg	4.19	she opened a skin of *m* and gave him a
Job	10.10	Did you not pour me out like *m* and
1 Cor	3. 2	I fed you with *m*, not solid food, for you
	9. 7	a flock and does not get any of its *m*?
Heb	5.12	You need *m*, not solid food; for

MILLSTONE

Judg	9.53	But a certain woman threw an upper *m*
Mt	18. 6	great *m* were fastened around your neck
Mk	9.42	better for you if a great *m* were hung
Lk	17. 2	better for you if a *m* were hung around

MIND (MINDS)

Gen	37.11	but his father kept the matter in *m*.
Deut	29. 4	has not given you a *m* to understand,
2 Sam	7. 3	do all that you have in *m*; for the LORD
1 Kings	3. 9	there an understanding *m* to govern
2 Kings	6.11	*m* of the king of Aram was greatly
1 Chr	17. 2	"Do all that you have in *m*, for God is
2 Chr	6. 7	David had it in *m* to build a house for
Neh	4. 6	height; for the people had a *m* to work.
Ps	77.11	I will call to *m* the deeds of the LORD; I
Prov	14.30	A tranquil *m* gives life to the flesh, but
	16. 9	The human *m* plans his way, but the
	17.20	The crooked of *m* do not prosper, and
Isa	6.10	Make the *m* of this people dull, and
	26. 3	Those of steadfast *m* you keep in peace
	44.20	deluded *m* has led him astray, and
Jer	23.16	They speak visions of their own *m*, not
Dan	4.16	his *m* be changed from that of a human,
Mk	5.15	sitting there, clothed and in his right *m*,
Rom	8. 7	the *m* that is set on the flesh is hostile
	11.34	"For who has known the *m* of the Lord?
1 Cor	2.16	him?" But we have the *m* of Christ.
	14.15	spirit, but I will pray with the *m* also.
	14.19	rather speak five words with my *m*,
2 Cor	3.15	Moses is read, a veil lies over their *m*;
	9. 7	must give as you have made up your *m*,
Phil	2. 5	Let the same *m* be in you that was in
	4. 2	I urge Syntyche to be of the same *m*
Col	3. 2	Set your *m* on things that are above, not

MINDFUL

Ps	25. 6	Be *m* of your mercy, O LORD, and of
	115. 12	The LORD has been *m* of us; he will
Zeph	2. 7	their God will be *m* of them and restore

MINISTER (MINISTERED MINISTERING MINISTERS)

Deut	18.	7 he may *m* in the name of the LORD his
1 Sam	2.11	while the boy remained to *m* to the
	3.	1 Samuel was *m* to the LORD under Eli.
1 Chr	6.32	They *m* with song before the tabernacle
Ps	104.	4 your messengers, fire and flame your *m*.
Isa	56.	6 themselves to the LORD, to *m* to him,
	60.10	walls, and their kings shall *m* to you;
Ezek	44.11	They shall be *m* in my sanctuary, having
Rom	15.16	me by God to be a *m* of Christ Jesus
2 Cor	11.23	Are they *m* of Christ? I am talking like a
Col	4.	7 he is a beloved brother, a faithful *m*,

MINISTRY

Rom	11.13	apostle to the Gentiles, I glorify my *m*.
	12.	7 in proportion to faith; *m*, in ministering;
	15.25	going to Jerusalem in a *m* to the saints;
Eph	4.12	equip the saints for the work of *m*, for

MIRACLES

1 Chr	16.12	wonderful works he has done, his *m*,
1 Cor	12.10	to another the working of *m*, to another
Gal	3.	5 with the Spirit and work *m* among you

MIRIAM

Song of Miriam, Ex 15.20-21; became leprous for criticizing Moses, Num 12.1-10; her leprosy healed, Num 12.11-16; died in Kadesh, Num 20.1.

MIRROR (MIRRORS)

Ex	38.	8 from the *m* of the women who served at
Job	37.18	out the skies, hard as a molten *m*?
1 Cor	13.12	now we see in a *m*, dimly, but then we
Jas	1.23	those who look at themselves in a *m*.

MISCHIEF

Judg	15.	3 when I do *m* to the Philistines, I will be
Ps	7.14	evil, and are pregnant with *m*, and bring
	36.	4 They plot *m* while on their beds; they
1 Pet	4.15	thief, a criminal, or even as a *m* maker.

MISERABLE

Job	16.	2 such things; *m* comforters are you all.

MISERY

Ex	3.	7 "I have observed the *m* of my people
Num	11.15	sight—and do not let me see my *m*."

MISFORTUNE

Prov	13.21	*M* pursues sinners, but prosperity

MISLEAD

2 Kings	4.28	for a son? Did I not say, Do not *m* me?"

MISS (MISSED)

Judg	20.16	could sling a stone at a hair and not *m*.
1 Sam	20.18	you will be *m*, because your place will
Job	5.24	shall inspect your fold and *m* nothing.
Prov	8.36	but those who *m* me injure themselves;

MIST

Jas	4.14	you are a *m* that appears for a little

MISTAKE

Jer	42.20	you today that you have made a fatal *m*.

MIZPAH

Gen	31.49	and the pillar *M*, for he said, "The LORD
Judg	11.11	all his words before the LORD at *M*.
1 Sam	7.	5 "Gather all Israel at *M*, and I will pray
	10.17	summoned the people to the LORD at *M*
Jer	41.10	the rest of the people who were in *M*,

MOCK (MOCKED MOCKING MOCKS)

Gen	27.12	I shall seem to be *m* him, and bring a
Judg	16.10	you have *m* me, and told me lies; please
1 Kings	18.27	At noon Elijah *m* them, saying, "Cry
2 Kings	19.	4 of Assyria has sent to *m* the living God,

2 Kings	19.22	"Whom have you *m* and reviled? Against
2 Chr	36.16	kept *m* the messengers of God, despising
Job	21.	3 speak; then after I have spoken, *m* on.
Ps	22.	7 All who see me *m* at me, they make
Prov	17.	5 who *m* the poor insult their Maker;
Isa	37.	4 of Assyria has sent to *m* the living God,
Jer	20.	7 all day long; everyone *m* me.
Ezek	22.	5 those who are far from you will *m* you,
Mt	27.29	before him and *m* him, saying, "Hail,
Mk	10.34	will *m* him, and spit upon him,
	15.31	along with the scribes, were also *m* him
Lk	18.32	Gentiles; and he will be *m* and insulted
	23.36	The soldiers also *m* him, coming up and

MOCKERY

Ezek	5.15	You shall be a *m* and a taunt, a warning
Joel	2.19	more make you a *m* among the nations.

MOLECH

Lev	18.21	of your offspring to sacrifice them to *M*,
2 Kings	23.10	pass through fire as an offering to *M*.

MONEY

Num	3.49	Moses took the redemption *m* from
Deut	14.25	you may turn it into *m*. With the *m*
2 Kings	12.11	would give the *m* that was weighed
Eccl	5.10	The lover of *m* will not be satisfied with
	7.12	of wisdom is like the protection of *m*;
	10.19	gladdens life, and *m* meets every need.
Mt	27.	6 the treasury, since they are blood *m*."
	28.12	a plan to give a large sum of *m* to the
Lk	16.14	Pharisees, who were also lovers of *m*,
Acts	4.37	then brought the *m*, and laid it at the
	8.18	he offered them *m*, saying, "Give me
1 Tim	6.10	love of *m* is a root of all kinds of evils,
Heb	13.	5 Keep your lives free from love of *m*, and

MONEY CHANGERS

Mt	21.12	overturned the tables of the *m* and the
Mk	11.15	overturned the tables of the *m* and the
Jn	2.14	doves, and the *m* seated at their tables.

MOON

Song	6.10	fair as the *m*, bright as the sun, terrible
Isa	13.10	rising, and the *m* will not shed its light.
	30.26	light of the *m* will be like the light of
Jer	31.35	and the fixed order of the *m* and the
Ezek	32.	7 cloud, and the *m* shall not give its light.
Mt	24.29	and the *m* will not give its light,
Acts	2.20	turned to darkness and the *m* to blood,
1 Cor	15.41	another glory of the *m*, and another

MORALS

1 Cor	15.33	deceived: "Bad company ruins good *m*."

MORDECAI

Counseled Esther, Esth 2.5-20; informed Esther of a conspiracy, Esth 2.21-23; refused to reverence Haman, Esth 3.2-6; arrayed in royal apparel, Esth 6.1-11; promoted next to the king, Esth 8.1-2; 10.3; reversed Haman's decree, Esth 8.3 – 9.4; decreed feast of Purim, Esth 9.20-31.

MORIAH

Gen	22.	2 go to land of *M*, and offer him there as
2 Chr	3.	1 of the LORD in Jerusalem on Mount *M*,

MORNING

Ps	5.	3 O LORD, in the *m* you hear my voice; in
	30.	5 for the night, but joy comes with the *m*.
Isa	21.12	The sentinel says: "*M* comes, and also
Mk	1.35	In the *m*, while it was still very dark, he
Rev	2.28	who conquers I will also give the *m* star.
	22.16	descendant of David, the bright *m* star."

MORSEL

Prov	17.	1 Better is a dry *m* with quiet than a

MORTAL (MORTALS)

Job	4.17 'Can *m* be righteous before God? Can
	14.10 But *m* die, and are laid low; humans
	15.14 What are *m*, that they can be clean? Or
Ps	8. 4 of them, *m* that you care for him?
Ezek	2. 1 O *m*, stand up on your feet, and I will
	3.17 *M*, I have made you a sentinel for the
	20. 3 *M* speak to the elders of Israel, and say
	30.21 *M* I have broken the arm of Pharaoh
Job	9.32 he is not a *m*, as I am, that I might
	14. 1 "A *m*, born of a woman, few of days and
Am	4.13 reveals his thoughts to *m*, makes the
Acts	14.15 We are *m* just like you, and we bring
Rom	6.12 sin exercise dominion in your *m* bodies,
1 Cor	15.53 this *m* body must put on immortality.
1 Jn	5.16 There is sin that is *m*; I do not say that

MOSES (MOSES')

Born, Ex 2.1-2; adopted by Pharaoh's daughter, Ex 2.5-10; trained at the Egyptian court, Acts 7.22; killed an Egyptian, Ex 2.11-12; Fled to Midian, Ex 2.15-20; married Zipporah, Ex 2.21-22; called by God, Ex 3.1–4.17; returned to Egypt, Ex 4.18-31; interceded with Pharaoh, Ex 5—11; led the Israelites across the Red Sea, Ex 14; sang for triumph, Ex 15.1-18; appointed rulers, Ex 18.13-26; met God on Mount Sinai, Ex 19.3-13; 24—31; enraged by Israel's idolatry, Ex 32; talked with the LORD, Ex 33—34; built the tabernacle, Ex 35—40; numbered the people, Num 1; vindicated before Aaron and Miriam, Num 12; sent twelve spies to Canaan, Num 13.1-20; consecrated Joshua as his successor, Num 27.18-23; Deut 31.23; recounted Israel's history, Deut 1—3; exhorted Israel to obedience, Deut 4.1-40; song of Moses, Deut 32.1-43; viewed Canaan, Deut 3.23-27; 32.48-52; 34.1-4; blessed the tribes, Deut 33; death and burial in Moab, Deut 34.5-7. (See also Acts 7.20-44.)

Josh	1. 5 As I was with *M*, so I will be with you; I
Ps	77.20 a flock by the hand of *M* and Aaron.
	103. 7 He made his ways known to *M*, his acts
	106. 23 he would destroy them—had not *M*,
Isa	63.12 arm to march at the right hand of *M*,
Jer	15. 1 Though *M* and Samuel stood before me,
Mt	17. 3 there appeared to them *M* and Elijah,
	19. 8 *M* allowed you to divorce your wives,
Mk	7.10 For *M* said, 'Honor your father and
Lk	16.29 Abraham replied, 'They have *M* and the
	24.27 beginning with *M* and all the prophets,
Jn	1.17 The law indeed was given through *M*;
	3.14 just as *M* lifted up the serpent in the
	5.46 If you believed *M*, you would believe
Acts	3.22 *M* said, 'The Lord your God will raise
Rom	5.14 exercised dominion from Adam to *M*,
1 Cor	10. 2 all were baptized into *M* in the cloud
2 Cor	3. 7 Israel could not gaze at *M* face because
	3.15 whenever *M* is read, a veil lies over
2 Tim	3. 8 As Jannes and Jambres opposed *M*, so
Heb	3. 2 just as *M* also "was faithful in all God's
	11.23 By faith *M* was hidden by his parents
Jude	9 devil and disputed about the body of *M*,
Rev	15. 3 they sing the song of *M*, the servant of

MOTH

Ps	39.11 for sin, consuming like a *m* what is dear
Mt	6.19 on earth, where *m* and rust consume

MOTHER (MOTHERS MOTHER'S)

Gen	3.20 because she was the *m* of all living.
Ex	2. 8 the girl went and called the child's *m*.
Judg	5. 7 arose, Deborah, arose as a *m* in Israel.
1 Sam	2.19 His *m* used to make for him a little
1 Kings	3.27 living boy; do not kill him. She is his *m*."
2 Chr	15.16 Asa even removed his *m* Maacah from
Ps	113. 9 a home, making her the joyous *m*
Prov	4. 3 my father, tender, and my favorite,
Isa	66.13 As a *m* comforts her child, so I will
Mt	12.48 Jesus replied, "Who is my *m*, and who
	12.50 heaven is my brother and sister and *m*."

Mt	19. 5 man shall leave his father and *m* and be
Mk	3.33 replied, "Who are my *m* and brothers?"
	7.10 said, 'Honor your father and your *m*';
Jn	19.27 he said to the disciple, "Here is your *m*."
Gal	4.26 above; she is free, and she is our *m*.
1 Tim	5. 2 to older women as *m*, to younger
2 Tim	1. 5 Lois and your *m* Eunice and now, I am

MOTHER-IN-LAW

Ruth	3. 1 Naomi her *m* said to her, "My daughter,
Mk	1.30 Simon's *m* was in bed with a fever, and

MOUNT OF OLIVES

Zech	14. 4 that day his feet shall stand on the *M*,
Mt	21. 1 Bethphage, at the *M*, Jesus sent
	24. 3 When he was sitting on the *M*, the
	26.30 sung the hymn, they went out to the *M*.
Lk	21.37 and spend the night on the *M*, as it was
Jn	8. 1 went home, while Jesus went to the *M*.

MOUNTAIN (MOUNTAINS)

Deut	1. 6 "You have stayed long enough at this *m*.
Ps	36. 6 Your righteousness is like the mighty *m*
	46. 2 should change, though the *m* shake
	68.15 O mighty *m*, *m* of Bashan; O
Isa	2. 2 days to come the *m* of the LORD's house
	11. 9 not hurt or destroy in all my holy *m*;
	25. 6 On this *m* the LORD of hosts will make
	30.29 of the flute to go to the *m* of the LORD,
	45. 2 I will go before you and level the *m*, I
Ezek	6. 3 You *m* of Israel, hear the word of the
	20.40 on my holy *m*, the *m* height of Israel,
Dan	2.35 that struck the statue became a great *m*
Ob	16 For as you have drunk on my holy *m*,
Mic	1. 4 Then the *m* will melt under him and
	4. 1 be established as the highest of the *m*,
	6. 2 Hear, you *m*, the controversy of the
Nah	1.15 On the *m* the feet of one who brings
Zech	8. 3 LORD of hosts shall be called the holy *m*.
Mt	4. 8 devil took him to a very high *m* and
	5. 1 he went up on the *m*; and after he sat
	17. 1 brother John and led them up a high *m*,
Mk	6.46 to them, he went up on the *m* to pray.
	11.23 if you say to this *m*, 'Be taken up and
	13.14 then those in Judea must flee to the *m*;
Lk	9.28 James and went up on the *m* to pray.
Jn	6.15 him king, he withdrew again to the *m*
1 Cor	13. 2 if I have all faith, so as to remove *m*,

MOURN (MOURNED MOURNING)

Gen	37.34 his loins, and *m* for his son many days.
2 Sam	1.12 They *m* and wept, and fasted until
	13.37 David *m* for his son day after day.
Dan	10. 2 time I, Daniel, had been *m* for three
Am	5.16 They shall call the farmers to *m*, and
	8.10 I will turn your feasts into *m*, and all
Mt	5. 4 "Blessed are those who *m*, for they will
1 Cor	7.30 those who *m* as though they were not
Rev	21. 4 Death will be no more; *m* and crying

MOURNFULLY

Ps	43. 2 Why must I walk about *m* because of

MOUTH (MOUTHS)

Deut	8. 3 that comes from the *m* of the LORD.
2 Kings	4.34 the child, putting his *m* upon his *m*,
Job	40. 4 I answer you? I lay my hand on my *m*.
Ps	34. 1 his praise shall continually be in my *m*.
	71. 8 My *m* is filled with your praise, and
	109. 2 and deceitful *m* are opened against me,
	135. 16 They have *m*, but they do not speak;
	141. 3 Set a guard over my *m*, O LORD, keep
Prov	30.32 devising seraph, put your hand on your *m*.
Isa	6. 7 The seraph touched my *m* with it and
Mal	2. 6 True instruction was in his *m*, and no
Rom	3.14 "Their *m* are full of cursing and
	3.19 that every *m* may be silenced, and the

MOVE (MOVED MOVING)

Deut	19.14	You must not *m* your neighbor's
2 Sam	7. 6	I have been *m* about in a tent and a
1 Chr	17. 6	I have *m* about among all Israel,
Ps	16. 8	he is at my right hand, I shall not be *m.*
	21. 7	of the Most High he shall not be *m.*
	46. 5	the midst of the city; it shall not be *m;*
	121. 3	He will not let your foot be *m,* he who
Acts	17.28	For 'In him we live and *m* and have our
2 Pet	1.21	men and women *m* by the Holy Spirit

MUD

Jn	9. 6	made *m* with the saliva and spread the

MULTIPLY (MULTIPLIED)

Gen	1.22	the seas, and let birds *m* on the earth."
	9. 1	"Be fruitful and *m,* and fill the earth.
	35.11	be fruitful and *m,* a nation and a
Deut	7.13	he will love you, bless you, and *m* you;
Isa	9. 3	You have *m* the nation, you have

MULTITUDE (MULTITUDES)

Gen	2. 1	the earth were finished, and all their *m.*
Ps	42. 4	of thanksgiving, a *m* keeping festival.
Joel	3.14	*M, m,* in the valley of decision! For the
1 Pet	4. 8	one another, for love covers a *m* of sins.
Rev	7. 9	was a great *m* that no one could count,

MURDER (MURDERS)

Ex	20.13	You shall not *m.*
Deut	5.17	You shall not *m.*
Mt	5.21	and 'whoever *m* shall be liable to
	15.19	of the heart come evil intentions, *m,*
	19.18	Jesus said, "You shall not *m;* You shall
Mk	15. 7	with the rebels who had committed *m*
Lk	23.19	who had been put in prison . . . for *m.*)

MURDERER

Jn	8.44	He was a *m* from the beginning and
Acts	3.14	and asked to have a *m* given to you,

MURMURED (MURMURING)

Josh	9.18	the congregation *m* against the leaders.
Phil	2.14	Do all things without *m* or arguing, so

MUSTARD

Mt	13.31	is like a *m* seed that someone took and
	17.20	if you have faith the size of a *m* seed,
Mk	4.31	It is like a *m* seed, which, when sown
Lk	13.19	It is like a *m* seed that someone took
	17. 6	"If you had faith the size of a *m* seed,

MUTE

Ps	38.13	not hear; like the *m,* who cannot speak.
Mt	9.32	a demoniac who was *m* was brought to
	12.22	who had been *m* could speak and see.
	15.30	lame, the maimed, the blind, the *m,*
Mk	7.37	the deaf to hear and the *m* to speak."
Lk	1.20	you will be *m,* unable to speak, until
	11.14	the one who had been *m* spoke, and the

MUZZLE

Ps	39. 1	I will keep a *m* on my mouth, as long as

MYRRH

Ps	45. 8	your robes are all fragrant with *m* and
Mt	2.11	him gifts of gold, frankincense, and *m.*
Mk	15.23	they offered him wine mixed with *m;*

MYRTLE

Isa	55.13	of the brier shall come up the *m;*
Zech	1. 8	He was standing among the *m* trees in

MYSTERY (MYSTERIES)

Dan	2.18	the God of heaven concerning this *m,*
Rom	11.25	I want you to understand this *m*: a
	16.25	according to the revelation of the *m*
1 Cor	4. 1	of Christ and stewards of God's *m.*
	13. 2	prophetic powers, and understand all *m*

1 Cor	15.51	Listen, I will tell you a *m*! We will not
Eph	1. 9	has made known to us the *m* of his will,
	3. 4	my understanding the *m* of Christ.
	5.32	This is a great *m,* and I am applying it
	6.19	with boldness the *m* of the gospel,
Col	1.26	the *m* that has been hidden throughout
	2. 2	and have the knowledge of God's *m,*
2 Thess	2. 7	the *m* of lawlessness is already at work,
1 Tim	3. 9	must hold fast to the *m* of the faith
	3.16	doubt, the *m* of our religion is great:
Rev	10. 7	the *m* of God will be fulfilled, as he
	17. 5	was written a name, a *m*: "Babylon the

MYTHS

1 Tim	1. 4	not to occupy themselves with *m* and
Titus	1.14	not paying attention to Jewish *m* or to
2 Pet	1.16	we did not follow cleverly devised *m*

N

NAAMAN

2 Kings	5. 1	*N,* commander of the army of the king
Lk	4.27	them was cleansed except *N* the Syrian."

NAHUM

Nah	1. 1	Nineveh. The book of the vision of *N* of

NAILING

Col	2.14	He set this aside, *n* it to the cross. He

NAILS

Eccl	12.11	like *n* firmly fixed are the collected
Jn	20.25	"Unless I see the mark of the *n* in his

NAKED

Job	1.21	"*N* I came from my mother's womb, and
	24.10	They go about *n,* without clothing;
Eccl	5.15	so they shall go again, *n* as they came;
Isa	20. 3	Isaiah has walked *n* and barefoot
	58. 7	when you see the *n,* to cover them, and
Ezek	16.39	objects and leave you *n* and bare
Mk	14.52	but he left the linen cloth and ran off *n.*

NAKEDNESS

Lev	18. 7	shall not uncover the *n* of your father,
Isa	47. 3	Your *n* shall be uncovered, and your

NAME

Gen	12. 8	the LORD and invoked the *n* of the LORD.
	32.29	"Please tell me your *n.*" But he said,
Ex	3.13	ask me, 'What is his *n?*' what shall I
	6. 3	by my *n* 'the LORD' I did not make
	9.16	and to make my *n* resound through all
	15. 3	The LORD is a warrior; the LORD is his *n.*
	20. 7	make wrongful use of the *n* of the LORD
	34. 5	there, and proclaimed the *n,* "The LORD."
Lev	24.11	son blasphemed the *N* in a curse.
Deut	5.11	shall not make wrongful use of the *n* of
	28.10	that you are called by the *n* of the LORD,
	28.58	fearing this glorious and awesome *n,*
	32. 3	I will proclaim the *n* of the LORD.
Josh	7. 9	Then what will you do for your great *n?*"
Judg	13.17	"What is your *n,* so that we may honor
2 Sam	7.26	take the city, and it be called by my *n.*"
1 Kings	9. 3	have built, and put my *n* there forever;
1 Chr	16. 2	he blessed the people in the *n* of the
	17. 8	I will make for you a *n,* like the *n* of the
	29.13	to you and praise your glorious *n.*
Ps	8. 9	our Sovereign, how majestic is your *n* in
	9.10	those who know your *n* put their trust
	72.17	May his *n* endure forever, his fame
	102. 12	your *n* endures to all generations.
	118. 26	one who comes in the *n* of the LORD.
	138. 2	you have exalted your *n* and your word
Prov	18.10	The *n* of the LORD is a strong tower; the
	22. 1	A good *n* is to be chosen rather than
Eccl	7. 1	A good *n* is better than precious
Isa	30.27	*n* of the LORD comes from far away,

Isa	40.26 numbers them, calling them all by *n*;
	44. 5 "The LORD's," and adopt the *n* of Israel.
	52. 5 all day long my *n* is despised.
	56. 5 I will give them an everlasting *n* better
	62. 2 you shall be called by a new *n* that the
Jer	7.11 this house, which is called by my *n*,
	10. 6 are great, and your *n* is great in might.
	14.14 prophets are prophesying lies in my *n*;
Ezek	36.21 But I had concern for my holy *n*, which
	39.25 and I will be jealous for my holy *n*.
Hos	12. 5 the God of hosts, the LORD is his *n*!
Joel	2.32 Then everyone who calls upon the *n* of
Am	6.10 We must not mention the *n* of the LORD."
	9.12 all the nations who are called by my *n*,
Mt	7.22 Lord, did we not prophesy in your *n*,
	28.19 baptizing them in the *n* of the Father
Mk	9.38 someone casting out demons in your *n*,
	13. 6 Many will come in my *n* and say, 'I am
Lk	1.31 bear a son, and you will *n* him Jesus.
	9.49 saw some casting out demons in your *n*,
	11. 2 pray, say: "Father, hallowed be your *n*.
Jn	5.43 I have come in my father's *n*, and you
	12.28 Father, glorify your *n*." Then a voice
	16.23 you ask anything of the Father in my *n*,
Acts	3.16 by faith in his *n*, his *n* itself has made
	4.10 in good health by the *n* of Jesus Christ
	4.12 there is no other *n* under heaven given
	4.30 performed through the *n* of your holy
	8.12 and the *n* of Jesus Christ, they were
	9.15 chosen to bring my *n* before Gentiles
	19.17 and the *n* of the Lord Jesus was
	21.13 die in Jerusalem for the *n* of the Lord
Rom	2.24 "The *n* of God is blasphemed among the
	9.17 you, so that my *n* may be proclaimed in
Phil	2. 9 gave him the *n* that is above every *n*,
Col	3.17 do everything in the *n* of the Lord
2 Tim	2.19 everyone who calls on the *n* of the Lord
Heb	1. 4 the *n* he has inherited is more excellent
Jas	2. 7 blaspheme the excellent *n* that was
1 Pet	4.14 If you are reviled for the *n* of Christ,
Rev	2.17 on the white stone is written a new *n*
	15. 4 who will not fear and glorify your *n*?

NAMED (NAMES)

Gen	2.20 The man gave *n* to all cattle, and to the
Ex	28. 9 engrave on them the *n* of the sons of
Mt	1.25 had borne a son; and he *n* him Jesus.
	10. 2 the *n* of the twelve apostles: first,
Lk	10.20 you, but rejoice that your *n* are written
Phil	4. 3 whose *n* are in the book of life.

NAPHTALI

Gen	30. 8 have prevailed"; so she named him *N*.
	49.21 *N* is a doe let loose that bears lovely
Deut	33.23 of *N* he said: O *N*, sated with favor, full
Judg	1.33 *N* did not drive out the inhabitants of
Ps	68.27 princes of Zebulun, the princes of *N*.
Isa	9. 1 the land of Zebulun and the land of *N*,
Mt	4.13 land of *N*, on the road by the sea,

NAPHTALITES

Num	26.50 These are the *N* by their clans: the

NARROW

Mt	7.13 "Enter through the *n* gate; for the gate
Lk	13.24 "Strive to enter through the *n* door; for

NATHAN

Counseled David about the people, 2 Sam 7.2-17 (1 Chr 17.1-15); rebuked David, 2 Sam 12.1-23; anointed Solomon as king, 1 Kings 1.8-45.

NATHANAEL

Jn	1.45 Philip found *N*, and said to him, "We

NATION

Gen	12. 2 I will make of you a great *n*, and I will
	18.18 shall become a great and mighty *n*,

Gen	46. 3 Egypt, for I will make of you a great *n*
Deut	4. 7 what other great *n* has a god so near to
	4.34 to take a *n* for himself from the midst
	26. 5 and there he became a *n*, mighty and
	28.49 LORD will bring a *n* from far away, from
2 Sam	7.23 Is there another *n* on earth whose God
Ps	106. 5 I may rejoice in the gladness of your *n*,
Prov	14.34 Righteousness exalts a *n*, but sin is a
Isa	2. 4 *n* shall not lift up sword against *n*,
	9. 3 You have multiplied the *n*, you have
Jer	7.28 This is the *n* that did not obey the voice
	31.36 Israel would cease to be a *n* before me
Ezek	37.22 I will make them one *n* in the land, on
Mt	21.43 given to a *n* that produces the fruits of
Acts	10.35 in every *n* anyone who fears him and

NATIONS

Gen	10. 5 language, by their families, in their *n*.
	17. 5 you the ancestor of a multitude of *n*.
	22.18 all the *n* of the earth gain blessing for
	26. 4 all the *n* of the earth shall gain blessing
Lev	25.44 from the *n* around you that you may
1 Sam	8. 5 then, a king to govern us, like other *n*."
1 Chr	16.24 Declare his glory among the *n*, his
	16.35 gather and rescue us from among the *n*,
Ps	18.43 You made me the head of the *n*;
	33.10 brings the counsel of the *n* to nothing;
	67. 4 Let the *n* be glad and sing for joy, for
	79. 6 Pour out your anger on the *n* that do
	96. 3 Declare his glory among the *n*, his
	110. 6 He will execute judgment among the *n*,
	126. 2 then it was said among the *n*, "The LORD
Isa	2. 2 the hills; all the *n* shall stream to it.
	40.15 the *n* are like a drop from a bucket, and
	49. 6 I will give you as a light to the *n*, that
	60. 3 *N* shall come to your light, and kings to
	66.18 I am coming to gather all *n* and
	66.19 shall declare my glory among the *n*.
Jer	4. 2 then *n* shall be blessed by him, and by
	27. 7 All the *n* shall serve him and his son
Ezek	7.24 the worst of the *n* to take possession
	11.16 removed them far away among the *n*,
	36.23 the *n* shall know that I am the LORD,
	39.21 I will display my glory among the *n*; and
Joel	2.17 a mockery, a byword among the *n*.
	3. 2 I will gather all the *n* and bring them
	3.12 Let the *n* rouse themselves, and come
Mic	5.15 vengeance on the *n* that did not obey.
Hab	1. 5 Look at the *n*, and see! Be astonished!
Zech	14. 2 I will gather all the *n* against Jerusalem
Mal	1.11 setting my name is great among the *n*,
	3.12 all *n* will count you happy, for you will
Mt	24. 9 be hated by all *n* because of my name.
Mk	11.17 called a house of prayer for all the *n*'?
Lk	24.47 is to be proclaimed in his name to all *n*,
Rev	11.18 The *n* raged, but your wrath has come,
	18.23 and all *n* were deceived by your sorcery.
	21.24 The *n* will walk by its light, and the

NATURE

Rom	11.24 from what is by *n* a wild olive tree and

NAZARETH

Mt	2.23 made his home in a town called *N*,
	4.13 He left *N* and made his home in
	21.11 is the prophet Jesus from *N* in Galilee."
	26.71 "This man was with Jesus of *N*."
Mk	16. 6 you are looking for Jesus of *N*, who was
Jn	1.45 wrote, Jesus son of Joseph from *N*."
Acts	2.22 Jesus of *N*, a man attested to you by
	10.38 how God anointed Jesus of *N* with the
	22. 8 said to me, 'I am Jesus of *N* whom you

NAZIRITE

Num	6. 2 the vow of a *n*, to separate themselves
Judg	13. 5 the boy shall be a *n* to God from birth.

NEBO

Deut 34. 1 Moses went up . . . to Mount *N*, to the

NEBUCHADNEZZAR (NEBUCHADREZZAR)

Won the battle of Carchemish, 2 Kings 24.1-7; Jer 46.2; conquered Judah, 2 Kings 24.10—25.10 (2 Chr 36.6-19; Jer 39.1-8; 52.1-14); deported the people, 2 Kings 24.14-16; 25.11-21 (2 Chr 36.20-21; Jer 39.9-10; 52.15-30); favored Jeremiah, Jer 39.11-14; his dreams revealed, Dan 2.1-13; 4.4-18; set up the golden image, Dan 3.1-7; punished for boasting, Dan 4.31-33; his reason returned, Dan 4.34-37.

NECK (NECKS)

Josh 10.24 Come near, put your feet on the *n* of
Song 4. 4 Your *n* is like the tower of David, built
Jer 30. 8 I will break the yoke from off his *n*, and
Rom 16. 4 and who risked their *n* for my life, to

NEED (NEEDS)

Deut 15. 7 If there is among you anyone in *n*, a
 15.11 there will never cease to be some in *n*
Dan 3.16 we have no *n* to present a defense to
Mt 7.12 knows that you *n* all these things.
 21. 3 to you, just say this, 'The Lord *n* them.'
Mk 11. 3 just say this, 'The Lord *n* it and will
Lk 10.42 there is *n* of only one thing . Mary has
 11. 8 will get up and give him whatever he *n*.
 19.31 it?' just say this, 'The Lord *n* it.' "
Acts 4.35 it was distributed to each as any had *n*.
Rom 12.13 Contribute to the *n* of the saints;
Phil 4.11 Not that I am referring to being in *n*;

NEEDLE

Lk 18.25 camel to go through the eye of a *n* than

NEEDY

Ps 37.14 bows to bring down the poor and *n*
 40.17 I am poor and *n*; but the LORD takes
 107. 41 but he raises up the *n* out of distress,
Prov 14.31 those who are kind to the *n* honor him.
 31.20 and reaches out her hands to the *n*.
Isa 14.30 will graze, and the *n* lie down in safety;
Am 2. 6 silver, and the *n* for a pair of sandals—
Acts 4.34 There was not a *n* person among them,

NEGLECT (NEGLECTED NEGLECTING)

Neh 10.39 We will not *n* the house of our God.
Mt 23.23 have *n* the weightier matters of the law:
Lk 11.42 to have practiced, without *n* the others.
Heb 2. 3 we escape if we *n* so great a salvation?

NEHEMIAH

Neh 1. 1 The words of *N* the son of Hacaliah. In
 3.16 After him *N* son of Azbuk, ruler of half
 12.26 in the days of the governor *N* and of the

NEIGHBOR (NEIGHBORS NEIGHBOR'S)

Lev 19.18 you shall love your *n* as yourself: I am
Josh 9.16 they heard that they were their *n* and
Ps 15. 3 nor take up a reproach against their *n*;
 28. 3 who speak peace with their *n*, while
 31.11 of all my adversaries, a horror to my *n*,
 38.11 my affliction, and my *n* stand afar off.
 101. 5 One who secretly slanders his *n* I will
Prov 3.29 Do not plan harm against your *n* who
 6. 1 if you have given your pledge to your *n*,
 6.29 So is he who sleeps with his *n* wife; no
 11. 9 the godless would destroy their *n*,
 14.21 Those who despise their *n* are sinners,
 25.17 your foot be seldom in your *n* house,
 27.10 Better is a *n* who is nearby than kindred
Jer 9. 8 They all speak friendly words to their *n*,
 34.17 me by granting a release to your *n*
Hab 2.15 who make your *n* drink, pouring out
Mt 5.43 shall love your *n* and hate your enemy.'
 22.39 it: 'You shall love your *n* as yourself.'
Mk 12.31 this, 'You shall love your *n* as yourself.'

Lk 6.41 do you see the speck in your *n* eye,
 10.29 he asked Jesus, "And who is my *n*?"
Rom 13. 9 in this word, "Love your *n* as yourself."
Gal 5.14 "You shall love your *n* as yourself."
Jas 2. 8 "You shall love your *n* as yourself."

NEPHILIM

Gen 6. 4 The *N* were on the earth in those
Num 13.33 There we saw the *N* (the Anakites come

NET (NETS)

Ps 10. 9 the poor and drag them off in their *n*.
 31. 4 take me out of the *n* that is hidden for
Prov 1.17 For in vain is the *n* baited while the
Isa 19. 8 and who spread *n* on the water will
Ezek 17.20 I will spread my *n* over him, and he
Mt 13.47 kingdom of heaven is like a *n* that was
Mk 1.16 and his brother Andrew casting a *n* into
 1.19 who were in their boat mending the *n*.

NEW

Num 16.30 if the LORD creates something *n*, and the
Ps 40. 3 He put a *n* song in my mouth, a song of
 96. 1 O sing to the LORD a *n* song; sing to the
 149. 1 Sing to the LORD a *n* song, his praise in
Eccl 1.10 "See, this is *n*"? It has already been, in
Isa 42. 9 to pass and *n* things I now declare;
 43.19 I am about to do a *n* thing; now it
 48. 6 time forward I make you hear *n* things,
 62. 2 you shall be called by a *n* name that
 66.22 the *n* heavens and the *n* earth, which I
Jer 31.31 when I will make a *n* covenant with the
Lam 3.23 they are *n* every morning; great is your
Ezek 36.26 A *n* heart I will give you, and a *n* spirit
Mk 14.24n "This is my blood of the *n* covenant,
Lk 5.36 tears a piece from a *n* garment and
Jn 13.34 I give you a *n* commandment, that you
Acts 17.21 but telling or hearing something *n*.
Rom 7. 6 code but in the *n* life of the Spirit.
1 Cor 11.25 "This cup is the *n* covenant in my
2 Cor 3. 6 to be ministers of a *n* covenant,
 5.17 is in Christ, there is a *n* creation:
Rev 5. 9 They sing a *n* song: "You are worthy to
 21. 1 I saw a *n* heaven and a *n* earth; for the
 21. 5 throne said, "See, I make all things *n*."

NEWNESS

Rom 6. 4 so we too might walk in *n* of life.

NICODEMUS

Jn 3. 1 there was a Pharisee named *N*, a leader
 7.50 *N*, who had gone to Jesus before, and
 19.39 *N*, who had at first come to Jesus by

NIGHT

Gen 1. 5 light Day, and the darkness he called *N*.
2 Chr 1. 7 That *n* God appeared to Solomon, and
Ps 19. 2 speech, and *n* to *n* declares knowledge.
 42. 8 at *n* his song is with me, a prayer to the
 104. 20 You make darkness, and it is *n*, when
Prov 7. 9 evening, at the time of *n* and darkness.
Lk 5. 5 have worked all *n* long but have caught
 12.20 This very *n* your life is being demanded
Jn 3. 2 He came to Jesus by *n* and said to him,
 9. 4 me while it is day; *n* is coming when
 11.10 But those who walk at *n* stumble
 13.30 he immediately went out; and it was *n*.
Rev 21.25 by day—and there will be no *n* there.

NILE

Ex 7.18 be unable to drink water from the *N*.' "
Ezek 29. 3 saying, "My *N* is my own; I made it for

NIMROD

Gen 10. 8 Cush became the father of *N*; he was

NINE

Acts 2.15 for it is only *n* o'clock in the morning.

NINEVEH

Gen	10.11 land he went into Assyria, and built *N*,
Jon	1. 2 "Go at once to *N*, that great city, and
	4.11 And should I not be concerned about *N*,
Nah	2. 8 *N* is like a pool whose waters run away.
Mt	12.41 the people of *N* will rise up at the
Lk	11.30 became a sign to the people of *N*,
	11.32 The people of *N* will rise up at the

NOAH

Born, Gen 5.29; walked with God, Gen 6.9; built the ark, Gen 6.11-22; preserved through the flood, Gen 7.1—8.19; built an altar, Gen 8.20-22; covenant with God, Gen 9.8-17; his drunkenness, Gen 9.20-21; prophesied concerning his sons, Gen 9.22-27; died, Gen 9.28-29.

NOBLE

Prov	8. 6 Hear, for I will speak *n* things, and from
1 Cor	1.26 powerful, not many were of *n* birth.

NOISE

Ps	66. 1 Make a joyful *n* to God, all the earth;
	100. 1 Make a joyful *n* to the LORD, all the
Jer	10.22 Hear, a *n*! Listen, it is coming—a great

NOON

Acts	10. 9 About *n* the next day, as they were on

NORTH

Isa	41.25 I stirred up one from the *n*, and he has
	43. 6 I will say to the *n*, "Give them up," and

NOTHING

Job	1. 9 the LORD, "Does Job fear God for *n*?
Ezek	12.22 prolonged and every vision comes to *n*"?
Hag	2. 3 to you now? Is it not in your sight as *n*?
1 Cor	13. 3 boast, but do have not love, I gain *n*.

NOTICE

Ex	13.19 "God will surely take *n* of you, and then

NUMBER (NUMBERED)

1 Chr	21. 2 "Go, *n* Israel, from Beer-sheba to Dan,
Job	14.16 then you would not *n* my steps, you
Isa	53.12 death, and was *n* with the transgressors;
Acts	2.47 day by day the Lord added to their *n*
Rev	13.18 of the beast, for it is the *n* of a person.

O

OAK (OAKS)

Isa	1.30 shall be like an *o*, whose leaf withers,
	6.13 or an *o* whose stump remains standing
	61. 3 They will be called of *o* of righteousness,

OATH

Gen	24. 8 then you will be free from this *o* of
	24.41 her to you, you will be free from my *o*.'
Num	5.19 the priest shall make her take an *o*,
Ps	15. 4 who stand by their *o* even to their hurt;
Neh	10.29 a curse and an *o* to walk in God's law,
Zech	8.17 love no false *o*; for all these are things
Lk	1.73 *o* which he swore to our ancestor
Acts	23.21 by an *o* neither to eat nor drink until
Heb	7.20 this one became a priest with an *o*,

OBADIAH

Ob	1 The vision of *O*. Thus says the Lord GOD

OBEDIENCE

Gen	49.10 to him; and the *o* of the peoples is his.
Rom	1. 5 apostleship to bring about *o* of faith
	16.19 while your *o* is known to all, so that I

OBEDIENT

Isa	1.19 If you are willing and *o*, you shall eat
Lk	2.51 and was *o* to them. His mother
Acts	6. 7 of the priests became *o* to the faith.
Phil	2. 8 and became *o* to the point of death—

1 Pet	1. 2 sanctified by the Spirit to be *o* to Jesus

OBEY (OBEYED OBEYING)

Gen	22.18 because you have *o* my voice."
	26. 5 because Abraham *o* my voice and kept
	27.13 my son; only *o* my word, and go, get
	27.43 my son, *o* my voice; flee at once to my
Ex	19. 5 if you will *o* my voice and keep my
Deut	12.28 Be careful to *o* all these words that I
	13. 4 his voice you shall *o*, him shall you
	21.20 "This son of ours . . . will not *o* us. He
	28.13 if you *o* the commandments of the LORD
	28.45 because you did not *o* the LORD your
	30. 2 you and your children *o* him with all
	30. 8 Then you shall again *o* the LORD,
	34. 9 the Israelites *o* him, doing as the LORD
Josh	1.17 Moses in all things, so we will *o* you.
1 Sam	15.19 Why then did you not *o* the voice of the
	15.22 Surely, to *o* is better than sacrifice, and
2 Kings	18.12 because they did not *o* the voice of the
Neh	9.17 they refused to *o*, and were not mindful
Jer	3.13 green tree, and have not *o* my voice,
	7.23 I gave them, "*O* my voice, and I
	7.28 is the nation that did not *o* the voice
	26.13 your doings, and *o* the voice of the LORD
	32.23 But they did not *o* your voice or follow
	35. 8 We have *o* the charge of our ancestor
	38.20 Just *o* the voice of the LORD in what I
	42. 6 or good, we will *o* the voice of the LORD
	43. 4 and all the people did not *o* the voice
Dan	7.27 and all dominions shall serve and *o*
Hag	1.12 all the remnant of the people, *o* the
Zech	6.15 This will happen if you diligently *o* the
Mt	8.27 that even the winds and the sea *o* him?"
	28.20 teaching them to *o* everything that I
Mk	1.27 the unclean spirits, and they *o* him."
	4.41 this, that even wind and the sea *o* him?"
Lk	8.25 winds and the waters, and they *o* him?"
Acts	5.29 "We must *o* God rather than human
Rom	2. 8 and who *o* not the truth but
2 Cor	10. 5 take every thought captive to *o* Christ.
Gal	5. 7 who prevented you from *o* the truth?
2 Thess	3.14 note of those who do not *o* what we say
Heb	5. 9 of eternal salvation for all who *o* him,
	11. 8 By faith Abraham *o* when he was called
	13.17 *O* your leaders and submit to them, for
1 Pet	3. 6 Thus Sarah *o* Abraham and called him
	4.17 end for those who do not *o* the gospel

OBJECT

Rom	9.21 of the same lump one *o* for special use

OBLIGED

Gal	5. 3 that he is *o* to obey the entire law.

OBSERVE (OBSERVES OBSERVING)

Ex	12.17 You shall *o* the festival of unleavened
	31.16 shall keep the sabbath, *o* the sabbath
Deut	4. 6 You must *o* them diligently, for this will
	17.19 diligently *o* all the words of this law,
Ps	33.15 hearts of them all, and *o* all their deeds.
	105. 45 might keep his statutes and *o* his laws.
	106. 3 Happy are those who *o* justice, who do
	119. 34 your law and *o* it with my whole heart.
Eccl	11. 4 Whoever *o* the wind will not sow; and
Gal	4.10 You are *o* special days, and months, and

OCCUPATION

Gen	46.33 calls you, and says, 'What is your *o*?'
Jon	1. 8 What is your *o*? Where do you come

OCCUPY

Deut	3.18 God has given you this land to *o*, all
	6.18 that you may go in and *o* the good land

OFFEND (OFFENDED)

Gen	40. 1 and his baker *o* their lord the king of
Prov	18.19 An ally *o* is stronger than a city; such

Jn 6.61 it, said to them, "Does this *o* you?

OFFENSE

Mt 11. 6 is anyone who takes no *o* at me."
 15.12 the Pharisees took *o* when they heard
Mk 6. 3 here with us?" And they took *o* at him.
Lk 7.23 is anyone who takes no *o* at me."
Acts 25. 8 in no way committed an *o* against the
1 Cor 10.32 Give no *o* to Jews or to Greeks or to the
Gal 5.11 the *o* of the cross has been removed.

OFFER (OFFERED)

Gen 22. 2 and *o* him there as a burnt offering
 46. 1 he *o* sacrifices to the God of his father
Ex 34.25 You shall not *o* the blood of my
Lev 10. 1 and they *o* unholy fire before the LORD,
 22.20 shall not *o* anything that has a blemish,
Judg 5. 9 Israel who *o* themselves willingly among
2 Sam 24.22 *o* up what seems good to him; here are
1 Chr 29. 9 mind they had *o* freely to the LORD;
2 Chr 8.12 Solomon *o* up burnt offerings to the
Ezra 7.15 counselors have freely *o* to the God of
Neh 11. 2 who willingly *o* to live in Jerusalem.
Ps 4. 5 O right sacrifices, and put your trust in
 27. 6 I will *o* in his tent sacrifices with shouts
 50.14 *O* to God a sacrifice of thanksgiving,
Jon 1.16 they *o* a sacrifice to the LORD and made
Mt 5.24 or sister, and then come and *o* your gift.
Acts 7.42 'Did you *o* to me slain victims and
1 Cor 8. 4 as to the eating of food *o* to idols, we
Heb 11. 4 By faith Abel *o* to God a more
 11.17 when put to the test, *o* up Isaac.
 12.28 we *o* to God an acceptable worship

OFFERING (OFFERINGS)

Ex 35. 5 Take from among you an *o* to the LORD;
1 Chr 16.29 due his name; bring an *o*, and come
Ps 20. 3 May he remember all your *o*, and regard
Isa 66.20 kindred from all the nations as an *o*
Jer 11.12 out to the gods to whom they make *o*,
Ezek 44.30 every *o* of all kinds shall belong to the
Mal 3. 4 the *o* of Judah and Jerusalem will be
Rom 15.16 so that the *o* of the Gentiles may be

OFFICER

Jer 20. 1 was chief *o* in the house of the LORD,

OFFICIAL (OFFICIALS)

Jer 26.10 When the *o* of Judah heard these
Mic 7. 3 the *o* and the judge ask for a bribe, and
Acts 18.17 Sosthenes, the *o* of the synagogue,

OFFSPRING

Gen 3.15 the woman, between your *o* and hers;
 12. 7 said, "To your *o* I will give this land."
 17. 8 I will give you, and your *o* after you, the
 21.12 is through Isaac that *o* shall be named
 26. 4 and will give to your *o* all these lands;
Job 5.25 be many, your *o* like the grass of the
Mal 2.15 what does the one God desire? Godly *o*.
Acts 17.28 poets have said, 'For we too are his *o*.'

OIL

Ex 30.25 make of these a sacred anointing *o*
2 Kings 4. 2 nothing in the house, except a jar of *o*."
Ps 23. 5 you anoint my head with *o*; my cup
 45. 7 has anointed you with the *o* of gladness
Isa 1. 6 drained or bound up or softened with *o*.
Mt 25. 4 but the wise took flasks of *o* with their
Mk 6.13 anointed with *o* many who were sick

OINTMENT (OINTMENTS)

Eccl 10. 1 Dead flies make the perfumer's *o* give
Mt 26. 7 alabaster jar of very costly *o*, and she
Mk 14. 3 with an an alabaster jar of very costly *o*
Lk 23.56 returned, and prepared spices and *o*.

OLD (OLDER)

Josh 23. 2 said to them, "I am now *o* and well

2 Chr 10. 8 rejected the advice that the *o* men gave
Mt 9.16 piece of unshrunk cloth on an *o* cloak,
Mk 2.21 piece of unshrunk cloth on an *o* cloak;
Lk 3.23 Jesus was about thirty years *o* when he
2 Cor 3.14 they hear the reading of the *o* covenant,

OLIVE

Gen 8.11 in its beak was a freshly plucked *o* leaf;
Deut 24.20 When you beat your *o* trees, do not
Ps 128. 3 your children will be like *o* shoots
Hos 14. 6 his beauty shall be like the *o* tree, and
Zech 4. 3 And by it there are two *o* trees, one on
Rom 11.17 you, a wild *o* shoot, were grafted in
Rev 11. 4 These are the two *o* trees and the two

OLIVET

Acts 1.12 to Jerusalem from the mount called *O*,

ONE

Gen 2.24 to his wife, and they become *o* flesh.
Mk 10. 8 the two shall become *o* flesh.' So they
Acts 17.26 ancestor he made all nations to
1 Cor 8. 6 and *o* Lord, Jesus Christ, through whom
Eph 5.31 wife, and the two will become *o* flesh."

ONESIMUS

Col 4. 9 he is coming with *O*, the faithful and
Philem 10 I am appealing to you for my child, *O*,

OPEN (OPENED OPENS)

Gen 3. 5 your eyes will be *o*, and you will be like
 3. 7 the eyes of both were *o*, and they knew
Num 22.28 the LORD *o* the mouth of the donkey,
Judg 11.35 I have *o* my mouth to the LORD, and I
2 Kings 6.17 LORD *o* the eyes of the servant, and he
Job 33.16 then he *o* their ears, and terrifies them
Ps 51.15 Lord, *o* my lips, and my mouth will
 104. 28 when you *o* your hand, they are filled
 119. 18 *O* my eyes, so that I may behold
Prov 20.13 *o* your eyes, and you will have plenty of
 31.26 She *o* her mouth with wisdom, and the
Song 5. 2 "*O* to me, my sister, my love, my dove,
 5. 6 I *o* to my beloved but my beloved had
Isa 22.22 he shall *o*, and no one shall shut; he
 26. 2 *O* the gates, so that the righteous
 50. 5 The Lord GOD has *o* my ear, and I was
 60.11 Your gates shall always be *o*; day and
Ezek 3. 2 So I *o* my mouth, and he gave me the
Dan 9.18 *O* your eyes and look at our desolation
Mt 3.16 the heavens were *o* to him and he saw
 9.30 And their eyes were *o*. Then Jesus
 13.35 "I will *o* my mouth to speak in parables;
 27.52 The tombs also were *o*, and many
Lk 24.31 their eyes were *o* and they recognized
 24.45 he *o* their minds to understand the
Jn 9.14 Jesus made the mud and *o* his eyes.
Acts 14.27 and how he had *o* a door of faith for
 16.14 The Lord *o* her heart to listen eagerly to
 26.18 I am sending you to *o* their eyes so that
1 Cor 16. 9 door for effective work has *o* to me,
2 Cor 2.12 Christ, a door was *o* for me in the Lord;
Rev 3. 8 I have set before you an *o* door, which
 6. 1 saw the Lamb *o* one of the seven seals,

OPENLY

Mk 1.45 Jesus could no longer go into a town *o*,
Jn 7.13 Yet no one would speak *o* about him for

OPPORTUNITY

Acts 24.25 when I have an *o*, I will send for you.
Phil 4.10 were concerned for me, but had no *o* to

OPPOSE (OPPOSED OPPOSES)

Gal 2.11 Cephas came to Antioch, I *o* him to
2 Thess 2. 4 He *o* and exalts himself above every
2 Tim 3. 8 and counterfeit faith, also *o* the truth.
1 Pet 5. 5 "God *o* the proud, but gives grace to the

OPPRESS (OPPRESSED OPPRESSES OPPRESSING)

Gen	15.13	they shall be *o* for four hundred years;
Ex	23. 9	You shall not *o* a resident alien; you
Ps	42. 9	mournfully because the enemy *o* me?
Prov	14.31	who *o* the poor insult their Maker,
	22.16	*O* the poor in order to enrich oneself,
	28. 3	A ruler who *o* the poor is a beating rain
Jer	7. 6	if you do not *o* the alien, the orphan,
Ezek	18.12	*o* the poor and needy, commits robbery,
Hos	12. 7	hands are false balances, he loves to *o*.
Am	4. 1	who *o* the poor, who crush the needy,
Mic	2. 2	they *o* the householder and house,
Zech	7.10	do not *o* the widow, the orphan, the
Mal	3. 5	against those who *o* the hired workers

OPPRESSED (n)

Ps	69.32	Let the *o* see it and be glad; you who
	76. 9	to save all the *o* of the earth.
Isa	1.17	seek justice, rescue the *o*, defend the
	51.14	The *o* shall speedily be released; they
	61. 1	sent me to bring good news to the *o*,
Dan	4.27	and your iniquities with mercy to the *o*,

OPPRESSION (OPPRESSIONS)

Ps	55.11	*o* and fraud do not depart from its
Eccl	4. 1	I saw all the *o* that are practiced under
	7. 7	*o* makes the wise foolish, and a bribe
Isa	30.12	reject this word, and put your trust in *o*
Jer	22.17	blood, and for practicing *o* and violence.

OPPRESSOR

Ps	72. 4	to the needy, and crush the *o*.
Isa	14. 4	How the *o* has ceased! How his
	51.13	But where is the fury of the *o*?
Zech	8	no *o* shall again overrun them, for now I

ORACLE (ORACLES)

Isa	13. 1	The *o* concerning Babylon that Isaiah
	17. 1	An *o* concerning Damascus. See,
	19. 1	An *o* concerning Egypt. See, the LORD is
	21. 1	*o* concerning the wilderness of the sea.
	21.13	The *o* concerning the desert plain. In
	23. 1	The *o* concerning Tyre. Wail, O ships of
Nah	1. 1	An *o* concerning Nineveh. The book of
Hab	1. 1	The *o* that the prophet Habakkuk saw.
Zech	9. 1	An *O*. The word of the LORD is against
	12. 1	An *O*. The word of the LORD concerning
Mal	1. 1	An *o*. The word of the LORD to Israel by
Rom	3. 2	the Jews were entrusted with the *o*
Heb	5.12	the basic elements of the *o* of God.

ORDAIN (ORDAINED)

Ex	28.41	shall anoint them and *o* them and
	32.29	Today you have *o* yourselves for the
2 Sam	17.14	the LORD had *o* to defeat the good
Isa	26.12	O LORD, you will *o* peace for us, for
Lam	3.37	and have it done, if the Lord has *o* it?
Acts	10.42	that he is the one *o* by God as judge
Gal	3.19	it was *o* through angels by a mediator.

ORDEAL

2 Cor	8. 2	during a severe *o* of affliction, their
Rev	7.14	they who have come out of the great *o*;

ORDER (ORDERED ORDERS)

Lev	25.21	I will *o* my blessing for you in the sixth
Ps	110. 4	according to the *o* of Melchizedek."
Mt	12.44	it finds it empty, swept, and put in *o*.
	17.	Jesus *o* them, "Tell no one about the
Mk	5.43	strictly *o* them that no one should know
	9. 9	he *o* them to tell no one about what
Lk	8.56	but he *o* them to tell no one what had
Acts	5.28	"We gave you strict *o* not to teach in his
1 Cor	14.40	should be done decently and in *o*.

ORDINANCES

Deut	4. 8	nation has . . . *o* as just as this entire

Job	38.33	Do you know the *o* of the heavens? Can

ORGANIZED

1 Chr	24. 3	David *o* them according to the
2 Chr	23.18	the levitical priests whom David had *o*

ORNAMENT

Titus	2.10	they may be an *o* to the doctrine of God

ORPHAN (ORPHANS)

Deut	10.18	who executes justice for the *o* and
	14.29	the resident aliens, the *o*, and the
Job	6.27	You would even cast lots over the *o*,
	22. 9	and the arms of the *o* you have crushed.
	24. 9	There are those who snatch the *o* child
	29.12	cried, and the *o* who had no helper.
Ps	10.14	you; you have been the helper of the *o*.
Jer	49.11	Leave your *o*, I will keep them alive;

OUT

1 Cor	10.13	he will also provide the way *o* so that

OUTWITTED

2 Cor	2.11	this so that we may not be *o* by Satan;

OVEN

Lk	12.28	and tomorrow is thrown into the *o*,

OVERCOME

Rom	12.21	not be *o* by evil, but *o* evil with good.

OVERFLOW (OVERFLOWED OVERFLOWING OVERFLOWS)

Ps	73. 7	with fatness; their hearts *o* with follies.
Mal	3.10	and pour down for you an *o* blessing.
2 Cor	9.12	saints but also *o* in many thanksgivings
1 Tim	1.14	grace of our Lord *o* for me with the

OVERLOOK (OVERLOOKED)

Acts	17.30	has *o* the times of human ignorance,
Heb	6.10	is not unjust; he will not *o* your work

OVERPOWERS

Lk	11.22	he attacks him and *o* him, he takes

OVERSEERS

Acts	20.28	which the Holy Spirit has made you *o*,

OVERTHROW

Jer	1.10	to destroy and to *o*, to build and to
Hag	2.22	earth, and to *o* the throne of kingdoms;
Rom	3.31	Do we then *o* law by this faith? By no

OVERWHELM (OVERWHELMED OVERWHELMS)

Ps	55. 5	come upon me, and horror *o* me.
	88. 7	me, and you *o* me with all your waves.
2 Cor	2. 7	he may not be *o* by excessive sorrow.

OWE (OWED)

Mt	18.24	one who *o* him ten thousand talents
Rom	13. 8	*O* no one anything, except to love one

OWN

Ex	15.17	on the mountain of your *o* possession,
Phil	3.12	Christ Jesus has made me his *o*.

OWNER

Isa	1. 3	The ox knows its *o*, and the donkey its
2 Tim	2.21	and useful to the *o* of the house,

OX

Ex	21.28	"When an *o* gores a man or a woman to
Num	22. 4	around us, as the *o* licks up the grass of
Deut	25. 4	You shall not muzzle an *o* while it is
Prov	7.22	her, and goes like an *o* to the slaughter,
Isa	1. 3	The *o* knows its owner, and the donkey
Lk	14. 5	*o* that has fallen into a well, will you
1 Cor	9. 9	"You shall not muzzle an *o* while it is
1 Tim	5.18	you shall not muzzle an *o* when it is

P

PAIN

Job	14.22 They feel only the *p* of their own
Eccl	2.23 all their days are full of *p*, and their
	11.10 put away *p* from your body; for youth
Jer	30.15 Your *p* is incurable. Because your guilt
Jn	16.20 have *p*, but your *p* will turn into joy.
2 Cor	2. 2 if I cause you *p*, who is there to make
Gal	4.19 for whom I am again in the *p* of

PAINTED

2 Kings	9.30 Jezebel . . . *p* her eyes, and adorned her
Ezek	23.40 them you bathed yourself, *p* your eyes,

PALACE (PALACES)

Ps	45. 8 From ivory *p* stringed instruments make
	45.15 along as they enter the *p* of the king.

PALM

Ps	92.12 The righteous flourish like the *p* tree,
Song	7. 8 I say I will climb the *p* tree and lay
Jn	12.13 they took branches of *p* trees and went

PANGS

Gen	3.16 greatly increase your *p* in childbearing;
Jer	13.21 Will not *p* take hold of you, like those
Hos	13.13 *p* of childbirth come for him, but he is

PANIC

Isa	28.16 foundation: "One who trusts will not *p*."

PARABLE (PARABLES)

Ps	78. 2 I will open my mouth in a *p*; I will utter
Mt	13. 3 he told them many things in *p*, saying,
Mk	4.30 of God, or what *p* will we use for it?
	4.34 he did not speak to them except in *p*,
Lk	8.11 *p* is this: The seed is the word of God.

PARADISE

Lk	23.43 tell you, today you will be with me in *P*."
2 Cor	12. 3 was caught up into *P* and heard things

PARALYTIC (PARALYTICS)

Mt	4.24 epileptics, and *p*, and he cured them.
	9. 2 Jesus saw their faith, he said to the *p*,

PARALYZED

Mt	8. 6 "Lord, my servant is lying at home *p*, in
Mk	2. 3 people came, bringing to him a *p* man,
Lk	5.18 carrying a *p* man on a bed. They were
Acts	9.33 bedridden for eight years, for he was *p*.

PARDON (PARDONING)

Ex	34. 9 *p* our iniquity and our sin, and take us
Deut	29.20 LORD will be unwilling to *p* them, for
1 Sam	15.25 *p* my sin, and return with me, so that I
2 Kings	5.18 may the LORD *p* your servant on one
	24. 4 and the LORD was not willing to *p*.
2 Chr	30.18 for them saying, "The good LORD *p* all
Job	7.21 Why do you not *p* my transgression and
Ps	25.11 sake, O LORD, *p* my guilt, for it is great.
Isa	55. 7 to our God, for he will abundantly *p*.
Jer	5. 1 truth — so that I may *p* Jerusalem.
	5. 7 How can I *p* you? Your children have
	50.20 be found; for I will *p* the remnant that I
Mic	7.18 Who is a God like you, *p* iniquity and

PARENT (PARENTS)

Deut	24.16 shall children be put to death for the *p*;
2 Kings	14. 6 *p* shall not be put to death for the
Prov	17.21 gets trouble; the *p* of a fool has no joy.
Ezek	18.20 nor a *p* suffer for the iniquity of a child;
Mal	4. 6 turn the hearts of *p* to their children
Mt	10.21 children will rise against *p* and have
Lk	1.17 go before him, to turn the hearts of *p* to
	2.41 every year his *p* went to Jerusalem for
Jn	9. 2 who sinned, this man or his *p*, that he
	9.18 they called the *p* of the man who had

2 Cor	12.14 up for their *p*, but *p* for their children.
Eph	6. 1 Children, obey your *p* in the Lord, for
2 Tim	3. 2 disobedient to their *p*, ungrateful,

PARTAKE

Ezra	2.63 were not to *p* of the most holy food,
Neh	7.65 not to *p* of the most holy food, until a
1 Cor	10.17 one body, for we all *p* of the one bread.

PARTED

2 Kings	2. 8 the water was *p* to the one side and to

PARTIAL

Lev	19.15 you shall not be *p* to the poor or defer
Deut	1.17 You must not be *p* in judging; hear out
	10.17 the great God . . . is not *p* and takes no
Prov	18. 5 It is not right be *p* to the guilty, or to

PARTIALITY

Deut	16.19 distort justice; you must not show *p*;
2 Chr	19. 7 with the LORD our God, or *p*, or taking
Prov	24.23 *P* in judging is not good. Whoever says
	28.21 To show *p* is not good — yet for a piece
Acts	10.34 I truly understand that God shows no *p*,
Rom	2.11 also the Greek. For God shows no *p*.
Gal	2. 6 God shows no *p*) — those leaders
Eph	6. 9 in heaven, and with him there is no *p*.
1 Tim	5.21 doing nothing on the basis of *p*.
Jas	2. 9 if you show *p*, you commit sin and are

PARTNER (PARTNERS)

Prov	29.24 To be a *p* of a thief is to hate one's
Lk	5. 7 signaled their *p* in the other boat to
1 Cor	10.20 I do not want you to be *p* with demons.
Philem	17 if you consider me your *p*, welcome him

PARTNERSHIP

2 Cor	6.14 what *p* is there between righteousness

PARTRIDGE

1 Sam	26.20 like one who hunts a *p* in the
Jer	17.11 Like the *p* hatching what it did not lay,

PASCHAL

1 Cor	5. 7 For our *p* lamb, Christ, has been

PASS (PASSED)

Ex	12.23 LORD will *p* over that door and will not
Josh	3. 4 go, for you have not *p* this way before.
Ps	31.12 I have *p* out of mind like one who is
Prov	9.15 calling to those who *p* by, who are
Eccl	6.12 vain life, which they *p* like a shadow?
Isa	14.24 as I have planned, so shall it come to *p*:
	43. 2 When you *p* through the waters, I will
Lam	1.12 all you who *p* by? Look and see if there
Mt	24.35 will *p* away, but my words will not *p*
Mk	1.16 As Jesus *p* along the Sea of Galilee, he
	13.31 Heaven and earth will *p* away, but my
Lk	10.31 he saw him, he *p* by on the other side.
1 Jn	3.14 know that we have *p* from death to life

PASSION (PASSIONS)

Prov	14.30 to the flesh, but *p* makes the bones rot.
Song	8. 6 is strong as death, *p* fierce as the grave.
Rom	1.27 were consumed with *p* for one another.
1 Cor	7.36 if his *p* are strong, and so it has to be
Eph	2. 3 lived among them in the *p* of our flesh,

PASSOVER

Ex	12.11 eat it hurriedly. It is the *p* of the LORD.
Lev	23. 5 twilight, there shall be a *p* offering to
Num	9. 5 They kept the *p* in the first month, on
	28.16 there shall be a *p* offering to the LORD.
Deut	16. 1 by keeping the *p* for the LORD your God,
Josh	5.11 On the day after the *p*, on that very day,
2 Kings	23.21 "Keep the *p* to the LORD your God as
2 Chr	30. 1 Jerusalem to keep the *p* to the LORD the
	35.17 of Israel who were present kept the *p* at
Ezra	6.19 month the returned exiles kept the *p*.

Mt	26. 2 after two days the *P* is coming, and the
Mk	14. 1 It was two days before the *P* and the
	14.14 I may eat the *P* with my disciples?'
Lk	22. 7 Bread, on which the *P* lamb had
Jn	13. 1 before the festival of the *P*, Jesus knew
	18.39 that I release someone for you at the *P*.
Heb	11.28 By faith he kept the *P* and the

PASTORS

Eph	4.11 some evangelists, some *p* and teachers.

PASTURE (PASTURES)

Ps	23. 2 He makes me lie down in green *p*; he
Jer	50.19 I will restore Israel to its *p*, and it shall

PATH (PATHS)

Job	8.13 the *p* of all who forget God; the hope of
Ps	8. 8 whatever passes along the *p* of the seas.
	17. 5 My steps have held fast to your *p*, my
	119. 35 me in the *p* of your commandments,
	119.105 a lamp to my feet and a light to my *p*.
Prov	4.18 But the *p* of the righteous is like the
	15.24 For the wise the *p* of life leads upward,
Isa	40.14 and who taught him the *p* of justice?
	42.16 by *p* they have not known I will guide
	45.13 and I will make all his *p* straight;
Jer	31. 9 walk by brooks of water, in a straight *p*
Mt	13. 4 some seeds fell on the *p*, and the birds
Mk	4. 4 some seed fell on the *p*, and the birds

PATHWAYS

Hab	3. 6 his ancient *p* the everlasting hills sank

PATIENCE

Mic	2. 7 Is the LORD's *p* exhausted? Are these his
Mt	18.29 with him, "Have *p* with me, and I will
Rom	8.25 we do not see, we wait for it with *p*.
	9.22 has endured with much *p* the objects of
Col	3.12 kindness, humility, meekness, and *p*.
Jas	5.10 As an example of suffering and *p*,
2 Pet	3.15 regard the *p* of our Lord as salvation. So

PATIENT

Lk	8.15 heart, and bear fruit with *p* endurance.
Rom	12.12 Rejoice in hope, be *p* in suffering,
1 Cor	4 Love is *p*; love is kind; love is not
Jas	5. 8 be *p*. Strengthen your hearts, for the
Rev	2. 2 works, your toil and your *p* endurance.
	2.19 love, faith, service, and *p* endurance.

PATMOS

Rev	1. 9 was on the island called *P* because of

PAUL

Born in Tarsus, Acts 22.3; educated under Gamaliel, Acts 22.3; consented to Stephen's death, Acts 7.58; 8.1 (22.20); persecuted the church, Acts 8.3; 9.1-2 (22.4-5; 26.10-11; 1 Cor 15.9; Gal 1.13; Phil. 3.6); went into Arabia, Gal 1.17; preached in Damascus, Gal 1.17; went up to Jerusalem, Acts 9.26-28; Gal 1.18-19; name changed to Paul, Acts 13.9; missionary work, Acts 13 — 14; 15.36 — 18.22; 18.23 — 21.17; attended the Council of Jerusalem, Acts 15.1-29; Gal. 2.1-10; arrested in Jerusalem, Acts 21.27-40; imprisoned in Caesarea, Acts 23.23-35; defended himself before Felix, Acts 24; appealed to Caesar, Acts 25.10-12; defended himself before Agrippa, Acts 26; journeyed to Rome, Acts 27.1 — 28.16; preached during imprisonment, Acts 28.17-31.

1 Cor	1.13 been divided? Was *P* crucified for you?
	3. 4 For when one says, "I belong to *P*," and
2 Pet	3.15 our beloved brother *P* wrote to you

PAWN

Ex	22.26 If you take your neighbor's cloak in *p*,

PAY (PAID PAYING PAYS)

Gen	50.15 bears a grudge against us and *p* us back
Num	20.19 and our livestock, then we will *p* for it.

Ps	66.13 I will *p* you my vows, those that my lips
	116. 18 I will *p* my vows to the LORD in the
	137. 8 Happy shall they be who *p* you back
Isa	40. 2 served her term, that her penalty is *p*,
Joel	3. 4 Are you *p* me back for something? If
Rom	13. 7 *P* all what is due them — taxes to whom
2 Tim	4.14 great harm; the Lord will *p* him back

PAYMENT

Lev	25.52 they shall make *p* for their redemption.
Ezek	16.34 *p*, while no *p* was given to you; you
Mt	10. 8 You received without *p*, give without *p*.

PEACE

Lev	26. 6 I will grant *p* in the land, and you shall
Num	6.26 countenance upon you, and give you *p*.
Deut	20.10 to fight against it, offer it terms of *p*.
Judg	6.23 "*P* be to you; do not fear, you shall not
1 Sam	10.27 him no present. But he held his *p*.
1 Kings	2.33 there shall be *p* from the LORD
2 Kings	20.19 "Why not, if there will be *p* and security
1 Chr	12.18 son of Jesse! *P*, *p* to you, and *p* to the
	19.19 by Israel, they made *p* with David,
	22. 9 he shall be a man of *p*. I will give him *p*
2 Chr	14. 6 in those years, for the LORD gave him *p*.
Job	5. 23 the wild animals shall be at *p* with you.
Ps	35.20 For they do not speak *p*, but they
	85.10 will meet; righteousness and *p* will kiss
	119.165 Great *p* have those who love your law;
	120. 7 I am for *p*; but when I speak, they are
	122. 6 Pray for the *p* of Jerusalem: "May they
Prov	3.17 lay hold of her; and all her paths are *p*.
Song	8.10 I was in his eyes as one who brings *p*.
Isa	9. 7 there shall be endless *p* for the throne
	26. 3 you keep in *p* — in *p* because they trust
	26.12 O LORD, you will ordain *p* for us, for
	27. 5 let it make *p* with me, let it make *p*
	32. 1 The effect of righteousness will be *p*,
	36.16 king of Assyria: 'Make your *p* with me
	39. 8 will be *p* and security in my days."
	48.22 "There is no *p*," says the LORD, "for the
	52. 7 feet of the messenger who announces *p*,
	54.10 my covenant of *p* shall not be removed,
	55.12 go out in joy, and be led back in *p*;
	57.19 *P*, *p*, to the far and the near, says the
	60.17 I will anoint *P* as your overseer and
Jer	6.14 saying, "*P*, *p*," when there is no *p*.
	8.11 saying, "*P*, *p*," when there is no *p*.
	14.19 We look for *p*, but find no good; for a
Ezek	7.25 will seek *p*, but there shall be none.
	13.10 people, saying, "*P*," when there is no *p*;
	13.16 saw visions of *p* for it, when there was
	34.25 I will make with them a covenant of *p*
	37.26 I will make a covenant of *p* with them;
Mic	3. 5 who lead my people astray, who cry "*P*"
Nah	1.15 brings good tidings, who proclaims *p*!
Zech	9.10 and he shall command *p* to the nations;
Mt	10.34 I have not come to bring *p*, but a sword.
Mk	4.39 said to the sea, "*P*! Be still!" Then the
	9.50 and be at *p* with one another."
Lk	1.79 to guide our feet into the way of *p*."
	2.14 and on earth *p* among those whom he
	7.50 "Your faith has saved you; go in *p*."
	8.48 your faith has made you well; go in *p*."
	10. 5 you enter, first say, '*P* to this house!'
	12.51 I have come to give *p* on earth? No,
	24.36 them and said to them, "*P* be with you!"
Jn	14.27 *P* I leave with you; my *p* I give to you. I
	16.33 to you so that in me you may have *p*.
	20.19 among them and said, "*P* be with you."
	20.21 said to them again, "*P* be with you.
Acts	10.36 Israel, preaching through Jesus Christ
Rom	5. 1 faith, we have *p* with God through our
	14.19 us then pursue what makes for *p* and
	16.20 The God of *p* will shortly crush Satan
2 Cor	1. 2 Grace to you and *p* from God our

Eph	2.14 for he is our *p*; in his flesh he has made
	2.15 in place of the two, thus making *p*
	2.17 proclaimed *p* to you who were far off
Phil	4. 7 the *p* of God, which surpasses all
	4. 9 me, and the God of *p* will be with you.
Col	1.20 *p* through the blood of his cross.
	3.15 let the *p* of Christ rule in your hearts,
Heb	13.20 may the God of *p*, who brought back
1 Pet	3.11 do good; let them seek *p* and pursue it.
Rev	6. 4 rider was permitted to take *p* from the

PEACEABLY

Gen	37. 4 him, and could not speak *p* to him.
1 Kings	2.13 asked, "Do you come *p*?" He said, "*P*."
Rom	12.18 far as it depends on you, live *p* with all.

PEACEMAKERS

Mt	5. 9 "Blessed are the *p*, for they will be

PEARLS

Mt	7. 6 and do not throw your *p* before swine,
	13.45 is like a merchant in search of fine *p*,

PEN

Job	19.24 O that with an iron *p* and with lead
Ps	45. 1 to the king; my tongue is like the *p* of a
Jer	8. 8 the false *p* of the scribes has made it
	17. 1 sin of Judah is written with an iron *p*;
3 Jn	13 but I would rather not write with *p* and

PENNY

Mt	10.29 Are now two sparrows sold for a *p*? Yet
Mk	12.42 copper coins, which are worth a *p*.

PENTECOST

Acts	2. 1 When the day of *P* had come, they were
1 Cor	16. 8 But I will stay in Ephesus until *P*,

PEOPLE

Ex	2.11 he went out to his *p* and saw their
	6. 7 I will take you as my *p*, and I will be
	7.16 "Let my *p* go, so that they may worship
	15.16 until your *p*, O LORD, passed by, . . . the
	32.11 your wrath burn hot against your *p*,
	33.13 Consider too that this nation is your *p*."
Lev	26.12 be your God, and you shall be my *p*.
Num	14.14 you, O LORD, are in the midst of this *p*;
Deut	9.27 attention to the stubbornness of this *p*,
	14. 2 you are a *p* holy to the LORD your God;
	26.18 to be a treasured *p*, as he promised you,
	29.13 he may establish you today as his *p*,
	32. 9 LORD's own portion was his *p*, Jacob his
Judg	2. 7 The *p* worshiped the LORD all the days
Ruth	1. 6 LORD had considered his *p* and given
	1.16 your *p* shall be my *p*, and your God, my
1 Sam	27.12 himself utterly abhorrent to his *p* Israel;
2 Sam	3.18 my servant David I will save my *p* Israel
	7.24 established your *p* Israel to be your *p*
1 Kings	8.16 Since the day that I brought my *p* Israel
	22. 4 my *p* are your *p*, my horses are your
2 Kings	3. 7 I am with you, my *p* are your *p*, my
	11.17 and *p*, that they should be the LORD's *p*;
1 Chr	17. 9 I will appoint a place for my *p* Israel,
	17.21 your *p* whom you redeemed from Egypt?
	17.22 made your *p* Israel to be your *p* forever;
2 Chr	7.14 if my *p* who are called by my name
	36.15 because he had compassion on his *p*
Ps	78.52 Then he led out his *p* like sheep, he
	100. 3 we are his; we are his *p*, and the sheep
	106. 40 of the LORD was kindled against his *p*,
	110. 3 Your *p* will offer themselves willingly on
	125. 2 Jerusalem, so the LORD surrounds his *p*,
	144. 15 blessings fall; happy the *p* whose God is
	148. 14 He has raised up a horn for his *p*,
	149. 4 For the LORD takes pleasure in his *p*; he
Isa	2. 6 you have forsaken the ways of your *p*,
	3.12 My *p*—children are their oppressors,
	5.13 my *p* go into exile without knowledge;

Isa	9. 2 The *p* who walked in darkness have
	40. 5 revealed, and all *p* shall see it together,
	40. 6 "What shall I cry?" All *p* are grass, and
	47. 6 I was angry with my *p*, I profaned my
	58. 1 Announce to my *p* their rebellion, to
	63. 8 "Surely they are my *p*, children who will
	65.19 in Jerusalem, and delight in my *p*;
Jer	2.13 my *p* have committed two evils: they
	7.23 be your God, and you shall be my *p*;
	13.11 might be for me a *p*, a name, a praise,
	18.15 But my *p* have forgotten me, they burn
	24. 7 they shall be my *p* and I will be their
	30.22 And you shall be my *p*, and I will be
	32.38 They shall be my *p*, and I will be their
Ezek	11.20 Then they shall be my *p*, and I will be
	14.11 Then they shall be my *p*, and I will be
	36.28 and you shall be my *p*, and I will be
Hos	1.10 it was said to them, "You are not my *p*,"
	2.23 I will say to Lo-ammi, "You are my *p*";
Joel	2.18 for his land, and had pity on his *p*.
Am	9. 7 like the Ethiopians to me, O *p* of Israel?
Mic	6. 2 LORD has a controversy with his *p*, and
Acts	18.10 are many in this city who are my *p*."
Rom	9.25 who were not my *p* I will call 'my *p*,'
1 Pet	2.10 were not a *p*, but now you are God's *p*;

PEOPLES

1 Kings	8.60 all the *p* of the earth may know that the
Ps	67. 5 Let the *p* praise you, O God; let all the
Mic	4. 1 *P* shall stream to it, and many nations

PERCEIVE (PERCEIVED PERCEIVES)

Judg	6.22 Gideon *p* that it was the angel of the
Ps	73.17 sanctuary of God; then I *p* their end.
	138. 6 but the haughty he *p* from far away.
Isa	64. 4 no ear has *p*, no eye has seen any God
Mt	13.14 and you will indeed look, but never *p*.
Mk	4.12 'they may indeed look, but not *p*, and
	8.17 no bread? Do you still not *p* or

PERFECT

2 Sam	22.31 This God—his way is *p*; the promise of
Job	36. 4 not false; one who is *p* in knowledge is
Ps	18.30 This God—his way is *p*; the promise of
Song	6. 9 My dove, my *p* one, is only one, the
Mt	5.48 Be *p*, therefore, as your heavenly Father
	19.21 "If you wish to be *p*, go, sell your
Heb	2.10 the pioneer of their salvation *p* through
	5. 9 having been made *p*, he became the
	7.28 a Son who has been made *p* forever.
	9. 9 are offered that cannot *p* the conscience
Jas	1.17 every *p* gift is from above, coming down

PERFECTION

Ps	50. 2 Out of Zion, the *p* of beauty, God
	119. 96 I have seen a limit to all *p*, but your
Heb	6. 1 let us go on toward *p*, leaving behind
	7.11 Now if *p* had been attainable through
1 Jn	2. 5 person the love of God has reached *p*.

PERFORM (PERFORMED)

2 Kings	23. 3 to *p* the words of this covenant that
Ps	76.11 vows to the LORD your God, and *p* them;
Isa	41. 4 Who has *p* and done this, calling the

PERIL

Lam	5. 9 We get our bread at the *p* of our lives,

PERISH (PERISHED PERISHES PERISHING)

Lev	26.38 You shall *p* among the nations, and the
Num	24.20 was Amalek, but its end is to *p* forever."
Deut	4.26 you will soon utterly *p* from the land
	8.19 warn you today that you shall surely *p*.
Josh	23.16 and you shall *p* quickly from the good
Judg	5.31 "So *p* all your enemies, O LORD! But
Esth	4.16 it is against the law; and if I *p*, I *p*."
Job	20. 7 they will *p* forever like their own dung;
Ps	9. 3 back, they stumbled and *p* before you.

Ps	37.20	But the wicked *p*, the enemies of the
	73.27	those who are far from you will *p*; you
	102.26	They will *p*, but you endure; they will
Prov	11.7	When the wicked die, their hope *p*, and
	28.28	but when they *p*, the righteous increase.
Jer	8.14	our God has doomed us to *p*, and he
Jon	3.9	his fierce anger, so that we do not *p*."
Mt	26.52	who take the sword will *p* by the sword.
Lk	13.3	but unless you repent, you will all *p* as
2 Cor	4.3	is veiled, it is veiled to those who are *p*.
Heb	1.11	they will *p*, but you remain; they will all

PERISHABLE

1 Cor	9.25	they do it to receive a *p* wreath, but we
	15.42	What is sown is *p*, what is raised is
1 Pet	1.18	not with *p* things like silver or gold, but

PERMITS (PERMITTED)

Jn	18.31	"We are not *p* to put anyone to death."
1 Cor	16.7	some time with you, if the Lord *p*.
Heb	6.3	we will do this, if God *p*. For it is

PERPLEXED

Lk	9.7	Herod . . . was *p*, because it was said by
	24.4	While they were *p* about this, suddenly
2 Cor	4.8	crushed; *p*, but not driven to despair;

PERSECUTE (PERSECUTED PERSECUTING)

Mt	5.10	are those who are *p* for righteousness'
	5.11	when people revile you and *p* you and
	10.23	When they *p* you in one town, flee to
Lk	11.49	some of whom they will kill and *p*,'
	21.12	they will arrest and *p* you; they will
Jn	5.16	Therefore the Jews started *p* Jesus,
	15.20	If they *p* me, they will *p* you; if they
Acts	7.52	the prophets did your ancestors not *p*?
	9.4	to him, "Saul, Saul, why do you *p* me?"
	22.4	I *p* this Way up to the point of death,
	22.7	to me, 'Saul, Saul, why are you *p* me?'
Rom	12.14	Bless those who *p* you; bless and do not
1 Cor	4.12	reviled, we bless; when *p*, we endure;
	15.9	apostle, because I *p* the church of God.
2 Cor	4.9	driven to despair; *p*, but not forsaken;
Gal	1.13	I was violently *p* the church of God and
	4.29	*p* the child born according to the Spirit,
	6.12	may not be *p* for the cross of Christ.
2 Tim	3.12	a godly life in Christ Jesus will be *p*.

PERSECUTION (PERSECUTIONS)

Mt	13.21	when trouble or *p* arises on account of
Mk	10.30	and fields with *p* —and in the age to
Jn	16.33	In the world you face *p*. But take
Acts	8.1	day a severe *p* arose against the church
	11.19	who were scattered because of the *p*
	14.22	"It is through many *p* that we must
1 Thess	3.4	beforehand that we were to suffer *p*;
2 Thess	1.4	faith during all your *p* and the
2 Tim	3.1	and Lystra. What *p* I endured! Yet the
Rev	1.9	share with you in Jesus the *p* and the

PERSECUTORS

Jer	17.18	Let my *p* be shamed, but do not let me

PERSEVERE (PERSEVERED)

Dan	12.12	Happy are those who *p* and attain the
Heb	11.27	he *p* as though he saw him who is

PERSIA

Ezra	1.1	In the first year of King Cyrus of *P*, in
	4.7	wrote to King Artaxerxes of *P*;
	4.24	year of the reign of King Darius of *P*.
Esth	1.3	The army of *P* and Media and the
Dan	10.13	with the prince of the kingdom of *P*,

PERSON

Deut	1.16	judge rightly between one *p* and
	4.42	who unintentionally kills another *p*,
	19.4	has killed another *p* unintentionally
Prov	27.17	and one *p* sharpens the wits of another.

Ezek	18.4	it is only the *p* who sins that shall die.

PERSUADE (PERSUADED PERSUADING)

Acts	17.4	Some of them were *p*, and joined Paul
	18.13	man is *p* people to worship God in ways
	19.26	Paul has *p* and drawn away a
2 Cor	5.11	the fear of the Lord, we try to *p* others;

PERVERSE (PERVERSELY)

Ex	32.7	at once! Your people, . . . have acted *p*;
Ps	14.3	all gone astray, they are all alike *p*;

PERVERSITY

Ezek	9.9	and the city full of *p*; for they say, 'The

PERVERT (PERVERTED PERVERTING)

Job	8.3	Or does the Almighty *p* the right?
	34.12	and the Almighty will not *p* justice.
Jer	3.21	children, because they have *p* their way,
	23.36	so you *p* the words of the living God,
Mic	3.9	who abhor justice and *p* all equity,
Lk	23.2	"We found this man *p* our nation,

PESTERED

Judg	16.16	day, and *p* him, he was tired to death.

PESTILENCE

Ex	9.3	will strike with a deadly *p* your livestock
Deut	28.21	The LORD will make the *p* cling to you
2 Sam	24.13	there be three days' *p* in your land?
Ps	91.6	files by, or the *p* that stalks in darkness,
Jer	29.17	let loose on them sword, famine, and *p*,

PETER (CEPHAS SIMON SIMEON)

Called to be a fisher of men, Mt 4.18-20 (Mk 1.16-18; Lk 5.1-11); also named Cephas, which means "rock," Jn 1.42n; sent out with the twelve, Mt 10.2 (Mk 3.16); walked on the sea, Mt 14.28-33; confessed Jesus as the Christ, Mt 16.13-20 (Mk 8.27-30; Lk 9.18-22); interceded for by the Lord, Lk 22.31-32; cut off the servant's ear, Jn 18.10-11; denied Jesus three times, Mt 26.69-75 (Mk 14.66-72; Lk 22.54-62; Jn 18.15-18,25-27); "Feed my sheep," Jn 21.15-19; addressed the disciples, Acts 1.15-26; preached on Pentecost, Acts 2.14-42; healed the lame man, Acts 3.1-10; witnessed in Solomon's portico, Acts 3.11-26; preached to the Council, Acts 4.1-12; imprisoned and released, Acts 5.17-42; denounced Simon Magus, Acts 8.14-24; visited Cornelius after the vision, Acts 10; reported to the Jerusalem Church, Acts 11.1-18; imprisoned and delivered, Acts 12.1-19; at the Council of Jerusalem, Acts 15.6-12; visited by Paul, Gal 1.18; blamed by Paul, Gal 2.11-14; Peter's wife's mother, Mt 8.14 (Mk 1.30; Lk 4.38); his wife, 1 Cor 9.5.

PETITIONS

Ps	20.5	banners. May the LORD fulfill all your *p*.

PHARISEE (PHARISEES)

Mt	3.7	when he saw many *P* and Sadducees
	5.20	exceeds that of the scribes and *P*,
	9.11	When the *P* saw this, they said to his
	12.2	When the *P* saw it, they said to him,
	12.14	the *P* went out and conspired against
	16.6	and beware of the yeast of the *P* and
	19.3	Some *P* came to him, and to test him
	22.15	the *P* went and plotted to entrap him in
	23.2	scribes and the *P* sit on Moses' seat;
	27.62	priests and the *P* gathered before Pilate
Jn	3.1	Now there was a *P* named Nicodemus,
	8.3	The scribes and the *P* brought a woman
Acts	15.5	the *P* stood up and said, "It is necessary
	23.6	were Sadducees and the others were *P*,

PHILEMON

Philem	1	To *P* our dear friend and co-worker, to

PHILIP

Mt	10.3	*P* and Bartholomew; Thomas and
Jn	1.43	He found *P* and said to him, "Follow

PHILIPPI

Jn	6. 5 Jesus said to *P*, "Where are we to buy
	12.21 some Greeks. They came to *P*, who was
	14. 8 *P* said to him, "Lord, show us the
Acts	1.13 and Andrew, *P* and Thomas,
	8. 5 *P* went down to a city of Samaria, and
	8.40 But *P* found himself at Azotus, and as
	21. 8 we went into the house of *P* the

PHILIPPI

Acts	16.12 and from there to *P*, which is a leading
	20. 6 we sailed from *P* after the days of
Phil	1. 1 the saints in Christ Jesus who are in *P*,
1 Thess	2. 2 and been shamefully mistreated at *P*,

PHILISTIA

Ex	15.14 pangs seized the inhabitants of *P*.
Joel	3. 4 and Sidon, and all the regions of *P*?
Zech	9. 6 I will make an end of the pride of *P*.

PHILISTINES

Gen	26. 1 to Gerar, to King Abimelech of the *P*.
Judg	16.21 the *P* seized him and gouged out his
1 Sam	4. 1 In those days the *P* mustered for war
	5. 1 When the *P* captured the ark of God,
	7. 3 deliver you out of the hand of the *P*."
	31. 1 Now the *P* fought against Israel; and
2 Sam	8. 1 David attacked the *P* and subdued
Isa	2. 6 the east and of soothsayers like the *P*,
	14.29 Do not rejoice, all you *P*, that the rod
Am	9. 7 the *P* from Caphtor and the Arameans

PHILOSOPHERS

Acts	17.18 Epicurean and Stoic *p* debated with

PHILOSOPHY

Col	2. 8 you captive through *p* and empty deceit,

PHYSICAL

1 Cor	15.44 If there is a *p* body, there is also a
Gal	4.13 was because of a *p* infirmity that I first

PHYSICIAN (PHYSICIANS)

Gen	50. 2 his father. So the *p* embalmed Israel.
Job	13. 4 with lies; all of you are worthless *p*.
Jer	8.22 no balm in Gilead? Is there no *p* there?
Mt	9.12 who are well have no need of a *p*,
Mk	2.17 who are well have no need of a *p*,
	5.26 She had endured much under many *p*,
Lk	5.31 who are well have no need of a *p*,
	8.43 she had spent all she had on *p*, no one
Col	4.14 Luke, the beloved *p*, and Demas greet

PIECES

Mk	6.43 took up twelve baskets full of broken *p*
	8.19 how many baskets full of broken *p* did
Lk	9.17 gathered up, twelve baskets of broken *p*.

PIERCE (PIERCED)

Zech	12.10 they look on the one whom they have *p*,
Lk	2.35 —and a sword will *p* your own soul
Jn	19.34 Instead, one of the soldiers *p* his side
Rev	1. 7 shall see him, even those who *p* him;

PIETY

Mt	6. 1 "Beware of practicing your *p* before
Acts	3.12 as though by our own power or *p* we

PIG (PIGS PIG'S)

Lev	11. 7 The *p*, for even though it has divided
Prov	11.22 a gold ring in a *p* snout is a beautiful
Lk	15.15 who sent him to his fields to feed the *p*.

PIGEON (PIGEONS)

Gen	15. 9 me . . . a turtledove, and a young *p*."
Lev	1.14 shall choose your offering from . . . *p*.

PILATE

Governor of Judea, Lk 3.1; killed some Galileans, Lk 13.1; sentenced Jesus to be crucified, Mt 27.1-25 (Mk 15.1-15; Lk 23.1-26; Jn 18.28 — 19.22); Jesus suffered under Pontius Pilate, Acts 3.13; 13.28; 1 Tim 6.13.

PILLAR (PILLARS)

Gen	19.26 back, and she became a *p* of salt.
	28.18 set it up for a *p* and poured oil on the
Ex	13.21 in front of them in a *p* of cloud by day,
Judg	16.26 "Let me feel the *p* on which the house
2 Sam	18.18 set up for himself the *p* that is in the
2 Kings	10.26 They brought out the *p* that was in the
Neh	9.12 and by night with a *p* of fire, to give
Gal	2. 9 who were acknowledged *p*, recognized

PIONEER

Heb	2.10 should make the *p* of their salvation
	12. 2 looking to Jesus the *p* and perfecter of

PIT

Ps	16.10 Sheol, or let your faithful one see the *P*.
Ezek	28. 8 They shall thrust you down to the *P*,
Jon	2. 6 yet you brought up my life from the *P*,

PITY (PITIED)

Ex	2. 6 He was crying, and she took *p* on him;
Deut	7.16 showing them no *p*; you shall not serve
Job	19.21 have *p* on me, O you my friends, for the
	27.22 It hurls at them without *p*; they flee
Ps	72.13 He has *p* on the weak and needy, and
Isa	49.10 he who has *p* on them will lead them,
Ezek	7. 4 will not spare you, I will have no *p*. I
	8.18 eye will not spare, nor will I have *p*; and
	16. 5 No eye *p* you, to do any of these things
Hos	1. 7 I will have *p* on the house of Judah,
Joel	2.18 for his land, and had *p* on his people.
Zech	11. 6 For I will no longer have *p* on the
Mt	18.27 out of *p* for him, the lord of that slave
Mk	1.41 Moved with *p*, Jesus stretched out his
	9.22 do anything, have *p* on us and help us."
Lk	10.33 he saw him, he was moved with *p*.
1 Cor	15.19 we are of all people most to be *p*.

PLACE (PLACES)

Gen	8. 9 the dove found no *p* to set its foot, and
Mt	24.34 until all these things have taken *p*.
Lk	2. 7 there was no *p* for them in the inn.
Jn	14. 2 my Father's house are many dwelling *p*.

PLAGUE (PLAGUES)

Gen	12.17 his house with great *p* because of Sarai,
Ex	11. 1 "I will bring one more *p* upon Pharaoh
Num	11.33 struck the people with a very great *p*.
	14.37 the land died by a *p* before the LORD.
	16.47 where the *p* had already begun among
	25. 9 those that died by the *p* were
1 Chr	21.22 —so that the *p* may be averted from
Ps	106. 30 and interceded, and the *p* was stopped.
Zech	14.12 This shall be the *p* with which the LORD

PLAN (PLANNED PLANS)

1 Chr	28. 2 I had *p* to build a house of rest for the
Ezra	4. 5 they bribed officials to frustrate their *p*,
Job	17.11 past, my *p* are broken off, the desires of
	21.16 *p* of the wicked are repugnant to me.
Ps	83. 3 They lay crafty *p* against your people;
Prov	15.26 Evil *p* are an abomination to the LORD,
	19.21 human mind may devise many *p*, but it
	20.18 *P* are established by taking advice; wage
Isa	5.19 let the *p* of the Holy One of Israel
	14.26 This is the *p* that is *p* concerning the
	19.17 fear because of the *p* that the LORD of
	30. 1 LORD, who carry out a *p*, but not mine;
Jer	18.11 you and devising a *p* against you.
	29.11 For surely I know the *p* I have for you,
Acts	2.23 according to the definite *p* and
	5.38 if this *p* or this undertaking is of human
Eph	1.10 a *p* for the fullness of time, to gather up
	3. 9 what is the *p* of the mystery hidden for

PLANT (PLANTED PLANTS)

Gen	1.11	"Let the earth put forth vegetation, *p*
	2. 5	when no *p* of the field was yet in the
Ex	15.17	You brought them in and *p* them on the
1 Chr	17. 9	for my people Israel, and will *p* them,
Job	12. 8	ask the *p* of the earth, and they will
Ps	44. 2	drove out the nations, but them you *p*;
	80.15	this vine, stock that your right hand *p*.
Jer	2.21	Yet I *p* you as a choice vine, from the
	32.41	I will *p* them in this land in
Am	9.15	I will *p* them upon their land, and they
Mt	15.13	Father has not *p* will be uprooted.
1 Cor	3. 6	I *p*, Apollos watered, but God gave the
	9. 7	Who *p* a vineyard and does not eat any

PLATFORM

Neh	8. 4	The scribe Ezra stood on a wooden *p*
Acts	12.21	took his seat on the *p*, and delivered a

PLATTER

Mk	6.25	the head of John the Baptist on a *p*."

PLAY (PLAYING)

Gen	21. 9	borne to Abraham, *p* with her son Isaac.
Isa	11. 8	child shall *p* over the hole of the asp,

PLEA

Jer	42. 2	"Be good enough to listen to our *p*, and

PLEAD (PLEADS)

Ps	5. 3	my voice; in the morning I *p* my case to
	119.154	*P* my cause and redeem me; give me
Prov	22.23	the LORD *p* their cause and despoils the
Isa	51.22	God who *p* the cause of his people:
Hos	2. 2	*P* with your mother, *p* — for she is not
Lk	15.28	came out and began to *p* with him,

PLEADINGS

Ps	28. 6	for he has heard the sound of my *p*.

PLEASANT

Gen	2. 9	God made to grow every tree that is *p*
Ps	16. 6	lines have fallen for me in *p* places;
	106.24	Then they despised the *p* land, having
	133. 1	good and *p* it is when kindred live
Prov	2.10	and knowledge will be *p* to your soul;
	9.17	is sweet, and bread eaten in secret is *p*."

PLEASANTNESS

Prov	3.17	Her ways are ways of *p*, and all her

PLEASE (PLEASED PLEASES)

Num	14. 8	If the LORD is *p* with us, he will bring us
Judg	14. 3	"Get her for me, because she *p* me."
1 Sam	12.22	it has *p* the LORD to make you a people
	18.26	David was well *p* to be the king's
2 Sam	3.36	just as everything the king did *p* all the
	7.29	may it *p* you to bless the house of your
	17. 4	The advice *p* Absalom and all the elders
1 Kings	3.10	It *p* the Lord that Solomon had asked
1 Chr	17.27	may it *p* you to bless the house of your
Neh	2. 6	So it *p* the king to send me, and I set
Esth	2. 4	let the girl who *p* the king be queen
Job	6. 9	that it would *p* God to crush me, that
Ps	135. 6	Whatever the LORD *p* he does, in heaven
Prov	16. 7	When the ways of people *p* the LORD, he
Eccl	7.26	one who *p* God escapes her, but the
	8. 3	unpleasant, for he does whatever he *p*.
Isa	42.21	The LORD was *p*, for the sake of his
Jon	1.14	"*P*, O LORD, we pray, do not let us
Mic	6. 7	the LORD be *p* with thousands of rams,
Mal	1. 8	he be *p* with you or show you favor?
Mt	3.17	my Beloved, with whom I am well *p*."
	17. 5	my Beloved, with whom I am well *p*;"
Mk	1.11	Son, the Beloved; with you I am well *p*."
Lk	3.22	Son, the Beloved; with you I am well *p*."
Rom	8. 8	who are in the flesh cannot *p* God.
	15. 1	of the weak, and not to *p* ourselves.

1 Cor	7.32	affairs of the Lord, how to *p* the Lord;
	10. 5	God was not *p* with most of them, and
	10.33	just as I try to *p* everyone in everything
2 Cor	5. 9	or away, we make it our aim to *p* him.
Gal	1.10	Or am I trying to *p* people? If I were
	1.15	his grace, was *p* to reveal his Son
Col	1.19	all the fullness of God was *p* to dwell,
1 Thess	2. 4	speak, not to *p* mortals, but to *p* God
2 Tim	2. 4	aim is to *p* the enlisting officer.
Heb	11. 5	he was taken away that "he had *p* God."
1 Jn	3.22	his commandments and do what *p* him.

PLEASING

Eccl	12.10	The Teacher sought to find *p* words,
Jn	8.29	alone, for I always do what is *p* to him."
Eph	5.10	Try to find out what is *p* to the Lord.
Phil	4. 8	is just, whatever is pure, whatever is *p*,
	4.18	offering, a sacrifice acceptable and *p*
Col	1.10	lead lives worthy of the Lord, fully *p*
Heb	13.16	have, for such sacrifices are *p* to God.

PLEASURE (PLEASURES)

Job	22. 3	Is it any *p* to the Almighty if you are
Ps	16.11	fullness of joy; in your right hand are *p*
	147.11	but the LORD takes *p* in those who fear
	149. 4	the LORD takes *p* in his people; he
Prov	21.17	Whoever loves *p* will suffer want;
Eccl	2. 1	"Come now, I will make a test of *p*;
	2.10	I kept my heart from no *p*, for my heart
	5. 4	for he has no *p* in fools. Fulfill what
Ezek	18.23	Have I any *p* in the death of the
	33.11	I have no *p* in the death of the wicked,
Hag	1. 8	the house, that I may take *p* in it and
Mal	1.10	on my altar in vain! I have no *p* in you,
Lk	8.14	choked by the cares and riches and *p* of
	12.32	it is your Father's good *p* to give you
Phil	2.13	both to will and to work for his good *p*.
2 Thess	2.12	but took *p* in unrighteousness will be
Heb	10. 6	and sin offerings you have no *p*.
	11.25	of God than to enjoy the fleeting *p*
Jas	5. 5	lived on the earth in luxury and in *p*;

PLEDGE

Lev	6. 2	neighbor in a matter of a deposit or a *p*,
Deut	24. 6	take a mill or an upper millstone for a *p*,
	24.12	sleep in the garment given you as the *p*;
2 Chr	34.32	and in Benjamin *p* themselves
Prov	20.16	seize the *p* given as surety for
	27.13	seize the *p* given as surety for
Ezek	33.15	If the wicked restores the *p*, give back
Am	2. 8	every altar on garments taken in *p*;
Eph	1.14	Spirit; this is the *p* of our inheritance

PLENTY

Gen	41.29	There will come seven years of great *p*
Prov	12.11	Those who till their land will have *p* of
Phil	4.12	of having *p* and of being in need.

PLOT (PLOTTED)

Neh	4.15	enemies heard that their *p* was known
Isa	7. 5	son of Remaliah, has *p* evil against you
Nah	1. 9	Why do you *p* against the LORD? He will
Mt	22.15	Pharisees went and *p* to entrap him in

PLOW (PLOWED)

Deut	22.10	shall not *p* with an ox and a donkey
Job	4. 8	those who *p* iniquity and sow trouble
Ps	129. 3	The plowers *p* upon my back; they
Prov	20. 4	The lazy person does not *p* in season;
Isa	28.24	those who *p* for sowing *p* continually?
Jer	26.18	Zion shall be *p* as a field; Jerusalem
Hos	10.13	You have *p* wickedness, you have
Mic	3.12	of you Zion shall be *p* as a field;
Lk	9.62	puts a hand to the *p* and looks back
1 Cor	9.10	whoever plows should *p* in hope and

PLOWSHARES

Joel	3.10	Beat your *p* into swords, and your

Mic 4. 3 they shall beat their swords into *p*, and

PLUCK

Jer 12.14 and I will *p* up the house of Judah from

PLUMB LINE

Am 7. 7 beside a wall built with a *p*, with a *p* in

PLUNDER (PLUNDERED PLUNDERING)

Gen 34.27 *p* the city, because their sister had been
Ex 3.22 and so you shall *p* the Egyptians."
12.36 asked. And so they *p* the Egyptians.
Num 31.53 (The troops had all taken *p* for
2 Kings 7.16 out, and *p* the camp of the Arameans.
Isa 17.14 us, and the lot of those who *p* us.
Hab 2. 8 Because you have *p* many nations, all
Mt 12.29 strong man's house and *p* his property,
Heb 10.34 accepted the *p* of your possessions,

POLICE

Jn 7.46 The *p* answered, "Never has anyone

POMP

Ps 49.12 Mortals cannot abide in their *p*; they
Isa 14.11 Your *p* is brought down to Sheol, and

PONDER (PONDERED)

Ps 4. 4 not sin; *p* it on your beds, and be silent.
48. 9 We *p* your steadfast love, O God, in the
Lk 2.19 treasured all these words and *p* them

POOL (POOLS)

Isa 42.15 the rivers into islands, and dry up the *p*.
Jn 5. 2 by the Sheep Gate there is a *p*,
9. 7 him, "Go, wash in the *p* of Siloam"

POOR

Ex 23.11 so that the *p* of your people may eat;
30.15 the *p* shall not give less, than the half
Lev 19.10 you shall leave them for the *p* and the
23.22 you shall leave them for the *p* and for
1 Sam 2. 8 He raises up the *p* from the dust; he
2 Sam 12. 3 the *p* man had nothing but one little
Job 5.16 So the *p* have hope, and injustice shuts
20.19 have crushed and abandoned the *p*,
24. 4 off the road; the *p* of the earth all hide
29.12 because I delivered the *p* who cried,
31.16 If I have withheld anything that the *p*
Ps 9.18 forgotten, nor the hope of the *p* perish
10. 2 arrogance the wicked persecute the *p*—
22.26 The *p* shall eat and be satisfied; those
34. 6 This *p* soul cried, and was heard by the
40.17 As for me, I am *p* and needy, but the
41. 1 Happy are those who consider the *p*;
72. 4 May he defend the cause of the *p* of the
86. 1 and answer me, for I am *p* and needy.
109. 22 For I am *p* and needy, and my heart is
113. 7 He raises the *p* from the dust, and lifts
Prov 10.15 the poverty of the *p* is their ruin.
19. 1 Better the *p* walking in integrity than
19. 7 If the *p* are hated even by their kin,
22. 2 The rich and the *p* have this in
29.14 If a king judges the *p* with equity, his
Isa 3.14 the spoil of the *p* is in your houses.
11. 4 with righteousness he shall judge the *p*,
25. 4 you have been a refuge to the *p*, a
Am 4. 1 who oppress the *p*, who crush the
5.11 because you trample upon the *p* and
8. 6 buying the *p* for silver and the needy for
Mt 5. 3 "Blessed are the *p* in spirit, for theirs is
11. 5 the good news brought to them.
19.21 and give the money to the *p*,
26.11 you always have the *p* with you, but you
Mk 10.21 sell what you own, and give to the *p*,
14. 5 denarii, and the money given to the *p*."
Lk 4.18 me to bring good news to the *p*.
6.20 "Blessed are you who are *p*, for yours is
14.13 when you give a banquet, invite the *p*,

Lk 16.20 at his gate lay a *p* man named Lazarus,
18.22 distribute the money to the *p*, and you
19. 8 possessions, Lord, I will give to the *p*;
Jn 12. 5 denarii and the money given to the *p*?"
2 Cor 6.10 rejoicing; as *p*, yet making many rich;
8. 9 was rich, yet for your sake he became *p*,
9. 9 "He scatters abroad, he gives to the *p*;
Gal 2.10 one thing, that we remember the *p*,
Jas 2. 5 God chosen the *p* in the world to be
Rev 3.17 you are wretched, pitiable, *p*, blind, and

POOREST

2 Kings 25.12 guard left some of the *p* people of the

PORTENT (PORTENTS)

Ps 71. 7 I have been as a *p* to many, but you are
Joel 2.30 I will show *p* in the heavens and on the
Acts 2.19 I will show *p* in the heaven above and
Rev 12. 1 A great *p* appeared in heaven: a woman
15. 1 I saw another *p* in heaven, great and

PORTION (PORTIONS)

Deut 32. 9 LORD's own *p* is his people, Jacob his
1 Sam 1. 5 to Hannah he gave a double *p*, because
2 Sam 20. 1 "We have no *p* in David, no share in the
Neh 8.10 send *p* of them to those for whom
Job 20.29 This is the *p* of the wicked from God,
Ps 16. 5 The LORD is my chosen *p* and my cup;
119. 57 The LORD is my *p*; I promise to keep
142. 5 "You are my refuge, my *p* in the land of
Jer 10.16 like these is the LORD, the *p* of Jacob,
Lam 3.24 LORD is my *p*," says my soul, "therefore I

POSSESS (POSSESSING)

Num 14.24 he went, and his descendants shall *p* it.
36. 8 continue to *p* their ancestral inheritance
Deut 33.23 of the LORD, *p* the west and the south.
Judg 11.24 Should you not *p* what your god
18. 9 slow to go, but enter in and *p* the land.
Neh 9.15 you told them to go in to *p* the land
Ps 25.13 and their children shall *p* the land.
Isa 14. 2 Israel will *p* the nations as male and
34.17 they shall *p* it forever, from generation
54. 3 your descendants will *p* the nations and
60.21 righteous; they shall *p* the land forever.
Ezek 33.26 wife; shall you then *p* the land?
36.12 people Israel— and they shall *p* you,
Dan 7.18 kingdom and *p* the kingdom forever—
Zech 8.12 remnant of this people to *p* all these
2 Cor 6.10 as having nothing, yet *p* everything.

POSSESSION (POSSESSIONS)

Ex 19. 5 you shall be my treasured *p* out of all
Lev 25.34 be sold; for that is their *p* for all time.
Num 32.22 this land shall be your *p* before the
Deut 1. 8 go in and take *p* of the land that I
1.39 I will give it, and they shall take *p* of it.
4.20 to become a people of his very own *p*,
14. 2 earth to be his people, his treasured *p*.
15. 4 your God is giving you as a *p* to occupy
21.16 the day when he wills his *p* to his sons,
Josh 1.11 to go in to take *p* of the land that the
18. 3 slack about going in and taking *p* of the
2 Chr 20.11 us by coming to drive us out of your *p*
Ps 78.55 he apportioned them for a *p* and settled
135. 4 Jacob for himself, Israel as his own *p*.
Eccl 2. 7 I had also great *p* of herds and flocks,
Jer 32.23 and they entered and took *p* of it.
Ob 17 house of Jacob shall take *p* of those
Mal 3.17 my special *p* on the day when I act, and
Mt 19.22 went away grieving; for he had many *p*.
24.47 will put that one in charge of all his *p*.
Lk 12.15 does not consist in the abundance of *p*."

POSSIBLE

Mt 19.26 impossible, but for God all things are *p*."
Mk 10.27 not for God; for God all things are *p*."

Mk	14.35 prayed that, if it were *p*, the hour might
Lk	18.27 is impossible for mortals is *p* for God."

POSTERITY

Ps	22.30 *P* shall serve him; future generations
	109. 13 May his *p* be cut off; may his name be

POT (POTS)

2 Kings	4.40 "O man of God, there is death in the *p*!"
Jer	1.13 "I see a boiling *p*, tilted away from the
Rev	2.27 iron rod, as when clay *p* are shattered

POTTER (POTTER'S)

Ps	2. 9 and dash them in pieces like a *p* vessel."
Isa	30.14 is like that of a *p* vessel that is smashed
	41.25 rulers as mortar, as the *p* treads clay.
	45. 9 your Maker, earthen vessels with the *p*!
Jer	18. 2 "Come, go down to the *p* house, and
	18. 6 like the clay in the *p* hand, so are you
	19. 1 the LORD: Go and buy a *p* earthenware
Lam	4. 2 as earthen pots, the work of a *p* hands!
Mt	27. 7 they used them to buy the *p* field as a
Rom	9.21 Has the *p* no right over the clay, to

POUR (POURED POURING)

1 Sam	1.15 I have been *p* out my soul before the
	7. 6 drew water and *p* it out before the LORD,
2 Sam	23.16 not drink of it; he *p* it out to the LORD,
1 Chr	11.18 not drink of it; he *p* it out to the LORD,
Ps	42. 4 things I remember, as I *p* out my soul:
Isa	32.15 until a spirit from on high is *p* out on
	44. 3 *p* water on the thirsty land, and streams
Jer	6.11 *P* it out on the children in the street,
	7.20 My anger and my wrath will be *p* out on
	10.25 *P* out your wrath on the nations that do
Ezek	7. 8 now I will *p* out my wrath upon you;
Hos	5.10 them I will *p* out my wrath like water.
Joel	2.28 I will *p* out my spirit on all flesh;
Zech	12.10 I will *p* out a spirit of compassion and
Mt	26. 7 ointment, and she *p* it on his head.
Mk	14. 3 the jar and *p* the ointment on his head.
Acts	2.17 I will *p* out my Spirit upon all flesh,
Rom	5. 5 God's love has been *p* into our hearts

POVERTY

Prov	6.11 and *p* will come upon you like a robber,
	13.18 *P* and disgrace are for the one who
	24.34 and *p* will come upon you like a robber,
	28.19 worthless pursuits will have plenty of *p*.
Mk	12.44 but she out of her *p* has put in
2 Cor	8. 2 joy and their extreme *p* have overflowed
Rev	2. 9 I know your affliction and your *p*, even

POWER

Lev	26.37 you shall have no *p* to stand against
Num	11.23 "Is the LORD's *p* limited? Now you shall
1 Chr	29.11 Yours, O LORD, are the greatness, the *p*,
2 Chr	25. 8 for God has *p* to help or to overthrow."
Job	23. 6 with me in the greatness of his *p*?
	26.14 But the thunder of his *p* who can
Ps	21.13 strength! We will sing and praise your *p*.
	49.15 ransom my soul from the *p* of Sheol,
	66. 3 of your great *p*, your enemies cringe
	67. 2 earth, your saving *p* among all nations.
	68.34 Ascribe *p* to God, whose majesty is over
	145. 11 of your kingdom, and tell of your *p*,
Prov	3.27 it is due, when it is in your *p* to do
Eccl	8. 8 No one has *p* over the wind to restrain
Isa	40.26 great in strength, mighty in *p*, not one
	40.29 He gives *p* to the faint, and strengthens
Jer	16.21 time I am going to teach them my *p*
	32.17 heavens and the earth by your great *p*
Dan	8.24 He shall grow strong in *p*, shall cause
Mic	3. 8 as for me, I am filled with *p*, with the
Zech	4. 6 by might, nor by *p*, but by my spirit,
Mt	6.13n and the *p* and the glory are yours
	22.29 neither the scriptures nor the *p* of God.
Mk	5.30 aware that *p* had gone forth from him,

Mk	9. 1 the kingdom of God has come with *p*."
	9.39 for no one who does a deed of *p* in my
	12.24 neither the scriptures nor the *p* of God?
	14.62 of Man seated at the right hand of *P*,'
Lk	1.35 and the *p* of the Most High will
	5.17 and the *p* of the Lord was with him to
	6.19 touch him, for *p* came out of him and
	8.46 I noticed that *p* had gone out from me."
	19.12 country to get royal *p* for himself
	21.27 coming in a cloud' with *p* and great
	22.53 this is your hour, and the *p* of darkness!"
	22.69 at the right hand of the *p* of God."
	24.49 have been clothed with *p* from on high
Jn	10.18 I have *p* to lay it down, and I have *p* to
	19.10 that I have *p* to release you, and *p* to
Acts	1. 8 you will receive *p* when the Holy Spirit
	2.11 them speaking about God's deeds of *p*."
	3.12 as though by our own *p* or piety we
	4.33 with great *p* the apostles gave their
	6. 8 Stephen, full of grace and *p*, did great
	8.10 "This man is the *p* of God that is called
	26.18 from the *p* of Satan to God, so they
Rom	1.16 the gospel; it is the *p* of God for
	15.13 you may abound in hope by the *p* of the
	15.19 wonders, by the *p* of the Spirit of God.
1 Cor	1.18 who are being saved it is the *p* of God.
	2. 4 with a demonstration of Spirit and of *p*,
	2. 5 on human wisdom but on the *p* of God.
	5. 4 is present with the *p* of our Lord Jesus,
	15.24 every ruler and every authority and *p*.
	15.43 It is sown in weakness, it is raised in *p*.
2 Cor	6. 7 truthful speech, and the *p* of God; with
	12. 9 so that the *p* of Christ may dwell in me.
	12. 9 you, for *p* is made perfect in weakness."
	13. 4 in weakness, but lives by the *p* of God.
Eph	1.19 greatness of his *p* in us who believe,
	3.20 to him who by the *p* at work within us
Phil	3.10 Christ and the *p* of his resurrection
1 Thess	1. 5 not in word only, but also in *p* and in
Heb	2.14 destroy the one who has the *p* of death,
1 Pet	1. 5 are being protected by the *p* of God
2 Pet	1. 3 His divine *p* has given us everything
Rev	11.17 for you have taken your great *p* and
	17.13 These are united in yielding their *p* and

POWERFUL

Lk	3.16 one who is more *p* than I is coming; I

PRAISE (PRAISES) (n)

Deut	10.21 He is your *p*; he is your God, who has
1 Chr	16. 7 David first appointed the singing of *p* to
Ps	47. 6 Sing *p* to God, sing *p*; sing *p* to our
	48.10 God, like your *p*, reaches to the ends of
	61. 8 So I will always sing *p* to your name, as
	65. 1 *P* is due to you, O God, in Zion; and to
	71. 8 My mouth is filled with your *p*, and
	119.108 Accept my offerings of *p*, O LORD, and
Rom	14.11 to me, and every tongue shall give *p*
Jas	5.13 cheerful? They should sing songs of *p*.

PRAISE (PRAISED PRAISING) (v)

1 Chr	16.25 great is the LORD, and greatly to be *p*;
	29.13 we give thanks to you and *p* your
Ps	33. 2 *P* the LORD with the lyre; make melody
	71.22 I will also *p* you with the harp for your
	76.10 Human wrath serves only to *p* you,
	113. 1 *P* the LORD! *P*, O servants of the LORD; *p*
	119. 62 At midnight I rise to *p* you, because of
	147. 12 *P* the LORD, O Jerusalem! *P* your God, O
	148. 2 *P* him, all his angels; *p* him, all his
	150. 6 Let everything that breathes *p* the LORD!
Prov	27. 2 Let another *p* you, and not your own
Isa	38.18 cannot thank you, death cannot *p* you;
Dan	4.34 I blessed the Most High, and *p* and
Lk	1.64 freed, and he began to speak, *p* God.
	2.28 took him in his arms and *p* God,
Acts	11.18 they were silenced. And they *p* God,

Acts	19.17 and the name of the Lord Jesus was *p*.
Rom	15.11 "*P* the Lord, all you Gentiles, and let all

PRAY

Ex	8. 8 "*P* to the LORD to take away the frogs
1 Sam	12.19 "*P* to the LORD your God for your
	12.23 the LORD by ceasing to *p* for you;
2 Sam	7.27 servant has found courage to *p* this
	15.31 David said, "O LORD, I *p* you, turn the
	24.17 Let your hand, I *p*, be against me and
1 Kings	8.33 confess your name, *p* and plead with
1 Chr	17.25 has found it possible to *p* before you.
Job	42. 8 Job shall *p* for you, for I will accept his
Ps	122. 6 *P* for the peace of Jerusalem: "May they
Isa	16.12 his sanctuary to *p*, he will not prevail.
Jer	7.16 As for you, do not *p* for this people, do
	11.14 As for you, do not *p* for this people, or
	29.12 come and *p* to me, and I will hear you.
	37. 3 Jeremiah saying, "*P* for us to the LORD
Dan	6.10 three times a day to *p* to his God and
Mt	5.44 and *p* for those who persecute you,
	6. 5 they love to stand and *p* in the
	6. 9 "*P* then in this way: Our Father in
	14.23 up into the mountains by himself to *p*.
	19.13 he might lay his hands on them and *p*.
	24.20 *P* that your flight may not be in winter
	26.36 "Sit here while I go over there and *p*."
	26.41 Stay awake and *p* that you may not
Mk	6.46 he went up on the mountain to *p*.
	13.18 *P* that it may not be in winter.
	13.33n Beware, keep alert and *p*; for you do
	14.32 said to his disciples, "Sit here while I *p*."
	14.38 Keep aware and *p* that you may not
Lk	5.16 withdraw to deserted places and *p*.
	5.33 the Pharisees, frequently fast and *p*, but
	6.12 he went out to the mountain to *p*; and
	6.28 curse you, *p* for those who abuse you.
	9.28 and went up on the mountain to *p*.
	11. 1 "Lord, teach us to *p*, as John taught his
	18. 1 them a parable about their need to *p*
Acts	8.24 Simon answered, "*P* for me to the Lord,
Rom	8.26 we do not know how to *p* as we ought,
1 Cor	11.13 to *p* to God with her head unveiled?
	14.15 spirit, but I will *p* with the mind also;
2 Cor	13. 7 *p* to God that you may not do anything
Eph	6.18 *P* in the Spirit at all times in every
1 Thess	3.10 Night and day we *p* most earnestly that
	5.17 Rejoice always, *p* without ceasing, give
2 Thess	1.11 To this end we always *p* for you, asking
1 Tim	2. 8 that in every place the men should *p*,
Heb	13.18 *P* for us; we are sure that we have a
Jas	5.13 among you suffering? They should *p*.
Jude	20 most holy faith; *p* in the Holy Spirit;

PRAYS (PRAYED PRAYING)

Gen	20.17 Then Abraham *p* to God; and God
Num	11. 2 Moses *p* to the LORD, and the fire
Deut	9.26 I *p* to the LORD and said, "Lord GOD, do
1 Sam	1.10 was deeply distressed and *p* to the LORD,
	1.27 For this child I *p*; and the LORD granted
	8. 6 to govern us." And Samuel *p* to the LORD,
2 Kings	4.33 on the two of them, and *p* to the LORD.
	6.17 Elisha *p*: "O LORD, please open his eyes
	19.15 Hezekiah *p* before the LORD, and said,
	20. 2 turned his face to the wall and *p* to the
2 Chr	32.20 the prophet Isaiah son of Amoz *p*
	33.13 He *p* to him, and God received his
Neh	1. 4 for days, fasting and *p* before the God
	4. 9 we *p* to our God, and set a guard as a
Job	42.10 the fortunes of Job, when he had *p* for
	33.26 Then he *p* to God, and is accepted by
Ps	35.13 I *p* with head bowed on my bosom,
Isa	37.15 And Hezekiah *p* to the LORD, saying: "O
	38. 2 turned his face to the wall, and *p*
	45.20 and keep *p* to a god that cannot save.
Dan	6. 7 whoever *p* to anyone, divine or human,
Jon	2. 1 Then Jonah *p* to the LORD his God from

Mt	26.44 he went away and *p* for the third time,
Mk	1.35 out to a deserted place, and there he *p*.
Lk	1.10 assembly of people was *p* outside.
	3.21 been baptized and was *p*, the heaven
	9.18 when Jesus was *p* alone, with only the
	18.11 standing by himself, was *p* thus,
	22.41 knelt down, and *p*, "Father, if you are
Acts	1.24 they *p* and said, "Lord, you know
	4.31 When they had *p*, the place in which
	8.15 The two went down and *p* for them that
	9.11 named Saul. At this moment he is *p*,
	9.40 outside, and then he knelt down and *p*.
	10.30 I was *p* in my house when suddenly a
	12. 5 kept in prison; the church *p* fervently
	12.12 where many had gathered and were *p*.
	13. 3 after fasting and *p* they laid their hands
	16.25 Paul and Silas were *p* and singing
	21. 5 we knelt down on the beach and *p*
	28. 8 Paul visited him and cured him by *p*
Col	1. 9 we have not ceased *p* for you and

PRAYER

Gen	25.21 LORD granted his *p*, and his wife
2 Chr	6.19 Regard your servant's *p* and his plea, O
	30.27 heard; their *p* came to his holy dwelling
Ps	6. 9 my supplication; the LORD accepts my *p*.
	17. 1 my cry; give ear to my *p* from lips free
	32. 6 let all who are faithful offer *p* to you; at
	42. 8 night his song is with me, a *p* to the
	65. 2 O you who answer *p*! To you all flesh
	72.15 May *p* be made for him continually and
	102. 17 He will regard the *p* of the destitute,
	109. 4 they accuse me, even as I make *p* for
	141. 2 Let my *p* be counted as incense before
Prov	15. 8 but the *p* of the upright is his delight.
	15.29 but he hears the *p* of the righteous.
Isa	26.16 they sought you, they poured out a *p*
	37. 4 therefore lift up your *p* for the remnant
	56. 7 be called a house of *p* for all peoples.
Lam	3. 8 call and cry for help, he shuts out my *p*;
	3.44 a cloud so that no *p* can pass through.
Dan	9. 3 to the Lord God, to seek an answer by *p*
Mt	17.21n kind does not come out except by *p*
	21.13 My house shall be called a house of *p*';
	21.22 Whatever you ask for in *p* with faith,
Mk	9.29 kind can come out only through *p*."
	11.17 'My house shall be called a house of *p*
	11.24 whatever you ask for in *p*, believe that
Lk	1.13 Zechariah, for your *p* has been heard.
	19.46 'My house shall be a house of *p*'; but
Acts	1.14 constantly devoting themselves to *p*,
	3. 1 temple at the hour of *p*, three o'clock in
	6. 4 for our part, will devote ourselves to *p*
	14.23 with *p* and fasting, they entrusted them
	16.13 we supposed there was a place of *p*;
Rom	12.12 be patient in suffering, persevere in *p*.
	15.30 Spirit, to join me in earnest *p* to God
1 Cor	7. 5 for a set time, to devote yourselves to *p*,
Phil	4. 6 in everything by *p* and supplication with
Col	4. 2 Devote yourselves to *p*, keeping alert in
Jas	5.16 The *p* of the righteous is powerful and

PRAYERS

Mt	23.14n sake of appearance you make long *p*;
Mk	12.40 for the sake of appearance say long *p*.
Lk	20.47 for the sake of appearance say long *p*.
Acts	2.42 to the breaking of bread and the *p*.
	10. 4 "Your *p* and your alms have ascended as
Rom	1. 9 ceasing I remember you always in my *p*,
2 Cor	1.11 You also join in helping us by your *p*,
Phil	1. 4 joy in every one of my *p* for all of you,
Col	4.12 always wrestling in his *p* on your behalf,
1 Tim	2. 1 I urge that supplications, *p*,
	5. 5 in supplications and *p* night and day;
2 Tim	1. 3 I remember you constantly in my *p*
Heb	5. 7 Jesus offered up *p* and supplications,
1 Pet	3. 7 life—so that nothing may hinder your *p*.

1 Pet	4. 7 yourselves for the sake of your *p*.
Rev	5. 8 incense, which are the *p* of the saints.

PREACH (PREACHING)

Mic	2. 6 "Do not *p*"—thus they *p*—"one should
Rom	2.21 While you *p* against stealing, do you
1 Tim	5.17 those who labor in *p* and teaching;

PREACHER

Mic	2.11 a one would be the *p* for this people!

PRECEPT (PRECEPTS)

Ps	19. 8 the *p* of the LORD are right, rejoicing the
	111. 7 and just; all his *p* are trustworthy.
	119. 63 who fear you, of those who keep your *p*.
	119. 93 I will never forget your *p*, for by them
Prov	4. 2 for I give you good *p*; do not forsake my
Isa	28.10 For it is *p* upon *p*, *p* upon *p*, line upon

PRECIOUS

Job	28.10 rocks and their eyes see every *p* thing.
Ps	36. 7 How *p* is your steadfast love, O God! All
	72.14 life; and *p* is their blood in his sight.
	116. 15 *P* in the sight of the LORD is the death
	133. 2 like the *p* oil on the head, running
Prov	3.15 She is more *p* than jewels, and nothing
	20.15 informed by knowledge are a *p* jewel.
	31.10 can find? She is far more *p* than jewels.
Isa	43. 4 you are *p* in my sight, and honored, and
1 Pet	1. 7 of your faith—being more *p* than gold
	2. 6 a stone, a cornerstone chosen and *p*;
2 Pet	1. 1 who have received a faith as *p* as ours

PREDESTINED

Acts	4.28 hand and your plan had *p* to take place
Rom	8.30 those whom he *p* he also called; and

PREDICTED

2 Kings	23.17 and *p* these things that you have done
Rom	9.29 And as Isaiah *p*, "If the Lord of hosts

PREDICTION

Isa	44.26 and fulfills the *p* of his messengers;

PREGNANT

Ex	21.22 injure a *p* woman so that there is a
Mt	24.19 Woe to those who are *p* and to those
Rev	12. 2 she was *p* and was crying out in

PREPARATION (PREPARATIONS)

2 Chr	35. 4 Make *p* by your ancestral houses by
Mt	26.17 "Where do you want us to make *p* for
Mk	14.12 and make *p* for you to eat the Passover?"
	15.42 since it was the day of *P*, that is, the
Lk	23.54 It was the day of *P*, and the sabbath

PREPARE (PREPARED PREPARES)

Neh	8.10 to those for whom nothing is *p*, for this
Ps	132. 17 David; I have *p* a lamp for my anointed
	147. 8 with clouds, *p* rain for the earth,
Isa	30.33 For his burning place has long been *p*;
	40. 3 "In the wilderness *p* the way of the
	62.10 the gates, *p* the way for the people;
Am	4.12 to you, *p* to meet your God, O Israel!"
Zeph	1. 7 the LORD has *p* a sacrifice, he has
Mt	20.23 for whom it has been *p* by my Father."
Mk	1. 3 '*P* the way of the Lord, make his paths
	10.40 it is for those for whom it has been *p*."
Lk	1.17 to make ready a people *p* for the Lord."
	1.76 will go before the Lord to *p* his ways,
	2.31 which you have *p* in the presence of all
	3. 4 '*P* the way of the Lord, make his paths
	7.27 of you, who will *p* your way before you."
	12.47 but did not *p* himself or do what was
Jn	14. 3 And if I go and *p* a place for you, I will
Rom	9.23 which he has *p* beforehand for glory—
1 Cor	2. 9 what God has *p* for those who love
Philem	22 —*p* a guest room for me, for I am
Heb	10. 5 desired, but a body you have *p* for me;

PRESENCE

Gen	4.16 Cain went away from the *p* of the LORD,
Ex	33.15 "If your *p* will not go, do not carry us
Ps	16.11 in your *p* there is fullness of joy; in your
	114. 7 Tremble, O earth at the *p* of the LORD,
Jon	1.10 he was fleeing from the *p* of the LORD,
Lk	1.19 I am Gabriel. I stand in the *p* of God,
Acts	10.33 all of us are here in the *p* of God to
Heb	9.24 now to appear in the *p* of God on our
Jude	24 you stand without blemish before the *p*

PRESENT (PRESENTED)

Gen	32.13 him he took a *p* for his brother Esau,
	47. 2 took five men and *p* them to Pharaoh.
Num	7.12 The one who *p* his offering the first day
Josh	15.19 "Give me a *p*; since you have set me in
2 Kings	16. 8 and sent a *p* to the king of Assyria.
Jer	40. 5 gave him an allowance of food and a *p*,
Lk	2.22 up to Jerusalem to *p* him to the Lord
Rom	6.19 now *p* your members as slaves to
	12. 1 of God, to *p* your bodies as a living
2 Cor	11. 2 husband, to *p* you as a chaste virgin to
Eph	5.27 so as to *p* the church to himself in
Col	1.22 to *p* you holy and blameless and
	1.28 we may *p* everyone mature in Christ.

PRESERVE (PRESERVED PRESERVES PRESERVING)

Gen	45. 5 for God sent me before you to *p* life.
1 Sam	30.23 he has *p* us and handed over to us the
Ps	25.21 May integrity and uprightness *p* me, for
	32. 7 you *p* me from trouble; you surround
	64. 1 *p* my life from the dread enemy,
	119.149 voice; O LORD, in your justice *p* my life.
	138. 7 you *p* me against the wrath of my
Prov	2. 8 and *p* the way of his faithful ones.
	16.17 those who guard their way *p* their lives.
	20.28 Loyalty and faithfulness *p* the king, and

PRESS (PRESSED)

Ruth	1.16 "Do not *p* me to leave you or to turn
Hos	6. 3 us know, let us *p* on to know the LORD;
Phil	1.23 I am hard *p* between the two: my desire
	3.14 I *p* on toward the goal for the prize of

PRESSURE

2 Cor	8.13 be relief for others and *p* on you,

PREVAILED

Gen	32.28 with God and with humans, and have *p*."
Ex	17.11 Moses held up his hand, Israel *p*;
Hos	12. 4 strove with the angel and *p*, he wept

PREVENT (PREVENTED)

Mt	3.14 John would have *p* him, saying, "I need
Acts	8.37 What is to *p* me from being baptized?"

PRICE

Gen	23.13 I will give the *p* of the field; accept it
Isa	55. 1 and milk without money and without *p*.
1 Cor	6.20 For you were bought with a *p*; therefore
	7.23 You were bought with a *p*; do not

PRIDE

Job	33.17 their deeds, and keep them from *p*,
Ps	20. 7 our *p* is in the name of the LORD our
Prov	8.13 *P* and arrogance and the way of evil and
	11. 2 When *p* comes, then comes disgrace;
	16.18 *P* goes before destruction, and a
Isa	9. 9 but in *p* and arrogance of heart they
Jer	48.29 We have heard of the *p* of Moab—he is
Ezek	7.10 The rod has blossomed, *p* has budded.
Hos	5. 5 Israel's *p* testifies against him; Ephraim
Zeph	2.10 shall be their lot in return for their *p*,
Mk	7.22 licentiousness, envy, slander, *p*, folly.

PRIEST (PRIESTS)

Gen	14.18 King Melchizedek . . . was *p* of God

Gen	47.26 The land of the *p* alone did not become
Ex	19.22 Even the *p* who approach the LORD must
1 Sam	2.35 I will raise up for myself a faithful *p*,
	22.17 "Turn and kill the *p* of the LORD,
2 Kings	23. 5 He deposed the idolatrous *p* whom the
2 Chr	11.15 appointed his own *p* for the high places,
	13. 9 you not driven out the *p* of the LORD,
Ps	110. 4 "You are a *p* forever according to the
Isa	24. 2 be, as with the people, so with the *p*;
	61. 6 you shall be called *p* of the LORD, you
Lam	4.13 and the iniquities of her *p*, who shed
Ezek	44.15 levitical *p*, the descendants of Zadok,
Joel	1.13 Put on sackcloth and lament, you *p*,
Zech	6.13 There shall be a *p* by his throne, with
Mal	1. 6 to you, O *p*, who despise my name.
Lk	1. 8 when he was serving as *p* before God
	5.14 he said, "and show yourself to the *p*,
	6. 4 which it is not lawful for any but the *p*
Acts	6. 7 a great many of the *p* became obedient
Heb	10.21 have a great *p* over the house of God,
Rev	1. 6 us to be a kingdom, *p* serving his God
	5.10 made them to be a kingdom and *p*

PRIESTHOOD

Num	16.10 with you; yet you seek the *p* as well!
	18. 7 I give your *p* as a gift; any outsider who
Heb	7.11 attainable through the levitical *p* —
	7.24 he holds his *p* permanently, because he
1 Pet	2. 5 a holy *p*, to offer spiritual sacrifices

PRIESTLY

| Ex | 19. 6 you shall be for me a *p* kingdom and a |

PRINCE (PRINCES)

Deut	33.16 the brow of the *p* among his brothers.
1 Sam	25.30 and has appointed you *p* over Israel,
2 Sam	7. 8 the sheep to be *p* over my people
Isa	1.23 Your *p* are rebels and companions of
	9. 6 God, Everlasting Father, *P* of Peace.
Ezek	28. 2 say to the *p* of Tyre, Thus says the Lord
Dan	8.25 even rise up against the *P* of princes.

PRISON

Gen	39.20 took him and put him into the *p*,
	42.16 while the rest of you remain in *p*, in
2 Kings	25.27 King Jehoiachin of Judah from *p*;
Ps	142. 7 Bring me out of *p*, so that I may give
Eccl	4.14 One can indeed come out of *p* to reign,
Jer	52.11 put him in *p* until the day of his death.
Mt	5.25 to the guard, and you be thrown in *p*.
	14. 3 John, bound him, and put him in *p*
	18.30 threw him into *p* until he would pay the
	25.36 of me, I was in *p* and you visited me.'
Mk	6.17 John, bound him, and put him in *p*
Lk	3.20 to them all by shutting up John in *p*.
Acts	12. 5 While Peter was kept in *p*, the church
	16.23 they threw them into *p* and ordered the
	16.40 After leaving the *p*, they went to Lydia's
	26.10 only locked up many of the saints in *p*,
Heb	10.34 compassion for those who were in *p*,
1 Pet	3.19 made a proclamation to the spirits in *p*,
Rev	2.10 is about to throw some of you into *p*

PRISONER (PRISONERS)

Ps	79.11 Let the groans of the *p* come before
	102. 20 to hear the groans of the *p*, to set free
	107. 10 and in gloom, *p* in misery and in irons,
	146. 7 to the hungry. The LORD sets the *p* free;
Isa	42. 7 to bring out the *p* from the dungeon,
Zech	9.12 Return to your stronghold, O *p* of hope;
Mt	27.16 they had a notorious *p*, called Jesus
Mk	15. 6 festival he used to release a *p* for them,
Acts	27.42 The soldiers plan was to kill the *p*, so
Eph	3. 1 that I, Paul, am a *p* for Christ Jesus
	4. 1 I therefore, the *p* for the Lord, beg you
Philem	1 Paul, a *p* of Christ Jesus, and Timothy

PROCEED

| Deut | 2.24 "*P* on your journey and cross the Wadi |
| Josh | 1. 2 Now *p* to cross the Jordan, you and all |

PROCLAIM (PROCLAIMED PROCLAIMING)

Lev	25.10 you shall *p* liberty throughout the land
Deut	32. 3 I will *p* the name of the LORD; ascribe
2 Sam	1.20 it not in Gath, *p* it not in the streets
Ps	22.31 and *p* his deliverance to a people yet
Prov	20. 6 Many *p* themselves loyal, but who can
Isa	62.11 The LORD has *p* to the end of the earth:
Jer	3.12 Go, and *p* these words toward the north
	7. 2 the LORD's house, and *p* there this word,
	31. 7 *p*, give praise, and say, "Save, O LORD,
Joel	3. 9 *P* this among the nations: Prepare war,
Jon	3. 2 go to Nineveh, that great city, and *p* to
Mt	3. 1 appeared in the wilderness of Judea, *p*,
	9.35 *p* the good news of the kingdom, and
	10.27 hear whispered, *p* from the housetops.
	26.13 wherever this good news is *p* in the
Mk	1. 7 He *p*, "The one who is more powerful
	1.45 he went out and began to *p* it freely,
	3.14 to be sent out to *p* the message.
	5.20 away and began to *p* in the Decapolis
	6.12 went out and *p* that all should repent
	13.10 the good news must first be *p* to all
	16.15n *p* the good news to the whole creation.
Lk	3. 3 around the Jordan, *p* a baptism of
	4.43 "I must *p* the good news of the kingdom
	8.39 he went away, *p* throughout the city
	9. 2 he sent them out to *p* the kingdom of
	24.47 forgiveness of sins is to be *p* in his
Acts	4. 2 *p* that in Jesus there is the resurrection
	8. 4 went from place to place, *p* the word.
	8.35 scripture, he *p* to him the good news
	9.20 immediately he began to *p* Jesus in the
	13. 5 at Salamis, they *p* the word of God in
	16.10 God had called us to *p* the good news
	17.23 you worship as unknown, this I *p*
	18. 5 Paul was occupied with *p* the word,
	28.31 *p* the kingdom of God and teaching
Rom	10.14 they to hear without someone to *p* him?
	10.15 are they to *p* him unless they are sent?
	15.20 it my ambition to *p* the good news,
1 Cor	1.17 send me to baptize but to *p* the gospel,
	2. 1 not come *p* the mystery of God to you
	9.14 those who *p* the gospel should get their
	11.26 drink the cup, you *p* the Lord's death
2 Cor	4. 5 we do not *p* ourselves; we *p* Jesus
Gal	1.23 formerly was persecuting us is now *p*
Phil	1.15 Some *p* Christ from envy and rivalry,
	1.17 others *p* Christ out of selfish ambition,
1 Thess	2. 9 any of you while we *p* to you the gospel
2 Tim	4. 2 I urge you: *p* the message; be persistent

PROCLAMATION

Jon	3. 7 he had a *p* made in Nineveh: "By the
1 Cor	2. 4 and my *p* were not with plausible words
1 Pet	3.19 and made a *p* to the spirits in prison,

PRODUCE

| Mt | 21.34 slaves to the tenants to collect his *p*. |

PROFANE (PROFANED PROFANES)

Ex	31.14 everyone who *p* it shall be put to death;
Lev	18.21 and so *p* the name of your God:
	19.29 Do not *p* your daughter by making her a
Ezek	22.26 sabbaths, so that I am *p* among them.
	28.18 of your trade, you *p* your sanctuaries;
	39. 7 I will not let my holy name be *p* any
Dan	11.31 occupy and *p* the temple and fortress.
Acts	10.15 has made clean, you must not call *p*."

PROFIT (PROFITS)

Job	34. 9 said, 'It *p* one nothing to take delight
Ps	30. 9 "What *p* is there in my death, if I go
Prov	14.23 In all toil there is *p*, but mere talk leads

Isa	30.	5 through a people that cannot *p* them,
Mt	16.26	what will it *p* them if they gain the
Mk	8.36	what will it *p* them to gain the whole

PROLIFIC

Ex	1.	7 But the Israelites were fruitful and *p*;

PROMINENT

1 Chr	5.	2 though Judah became *p* among his

PROMISE (PROMISES) (n)

2 Chr	1.	9 God, let your *p* to my father David now
Ps	77.	8 Are his *p* at an end for all time?
	106.	24 pleasant land, having no faith in his *p*.
	119.	82 My eyes fail with watching for your *p*; I
Acts	1.	4 wait there for the *p* of the Father. "This,"
	2.39	*p* is for you, for your children, and for
	7.17	drew near for the fulfillment of the *p*
	13.34	will give you the holy *p* given to David.'
	26.	6 on trial on account of my hope in the *p*
Rom	4.13	the *p* that he would inherit the world
	4.16	that the *p* may rest on grace and be
	9.	8 but the children of the *p* are counted as
	15.	8 confirm the *p* given to the patriarchs,
2 Cor	1.20	him every one of the *p* of God is a "Yes."
	7.	1 Since we have these *p*, beloved, let us
Gal	3.16	the *p* were made to Abraham and to his
	3.21	the law then opposed to the *p* of God?
	4.23	free woman, was born through the *p*.
	4.28	friends, are children of the *p*, like Isaac.
Eph	3.	6 and sharers in the *p* in Christ Jesus
Heb	4.	1 while the *p* of entering his rest is still
	6.12	faith and patience inherit the *p*.
	8.	6 has been enacted through better *p*.
2 Pet	1.	4 his precious and very great *p*, so that
	3.	4 "Where is the *p* of his coming? For ever
	3.	9 Lord is not slow about his *p*, as some

PROMISE (PROMISED) (v)

Deut	1.11	more and bless you, as he has *p* you!
	12.20	enlarges your territory, as he has *p* you,
	19.	8 will give you all the land that he *p* your
Josh	23.	5 their land, as the LORD your God *p* you.
2 Sam	7.28	you have *p* this good thing to your
1 Kings	5.12	gave Solomon wisdom, as he *p* him.
	8.56	people Israel according to all that he *p*;
2 Chr	6.10	on the throne of Israel, as the LORD *p*,
Jer	32.42	them all the good fortune that I now *p*
Lk	24.49	I am sending you what my Father *p*; so
Acts	7.	5 but *p* to give it to him as his possession
	13.32	news that what God *p* to our ancestors
Rom	1.	2 which he *p* beforehand through his
	4.21	that God was able to do what he *p*.
Titus	1.	2 life that God, who never lies, *p* before
Heb	9.15	may receive the *p* eternal inheritance,
	10.36	of God, you may receive what was *p*.
	11.39	did not receive what was *p*, since God
Jas	1.12	the Lord has *p* to those who love him.
2 Pet	2.19	They *p* them freedom, but they

PRONOUNCED

Jer	44.26	my name shall no more be *p* on the lips

PROOF (PROOFS)

Ps	95.	9 tested me, and put me to the *p*,
Acts	1.	3 alive to them by many convincing *p*,
2 Cor	8.24	show them the *p* of your love and of our
	13.	3 desire *p* that Christ is speaking in me.

PROPHECY

Prov	29.18	Where there is no *p*, the people cast off
Lk	1.67	with the Holy Spirit and spoke this *p*:
Rom	12.	6 given to us: *p*, in proportion to faith;
1 Cor	12.10	the working of miracles, to another *p*,
Rev	22.	7 keeps the words of the *p* of this book.

PROPHESY (PROPHESIED PROPHESIES PROPHESYING)

Num	11.25	the spirit rested upon them, they *p*.
1 Chr	25.	1 who should *p* with lyres, harps, and
2 Chr	18.	7 him, for he never *p* anything favorable
Isa	30.10	speak to us smooth things, *p* illusions,
Jer	5.31	the prophets *p* falsely, and the priests
	11.21	"You shall not *p* in the name of the
	14.14	The prophets are *p* lies in my name; I
	19.14	where the LORD had sent him to *p*,
	23.13	they *p* by Baal and led my people Israel
	23.21	ran; I did not speak to them, yet they *p*.
	23.32	I am against those who *p* lying dreams,
	25.30	"You, therefore, shall *p* against them all
	26.18	"Micah of Moresheth, who *p* during the
	29.	9 for it is a lie that they are *p* to you in
	32.	3 "Why do you *p* and say, Thus says the
Ezek	4.	7 your arm bared you shall *p* against it.
	11.	4 Therefore *p* against them, *p*, O mortal."
	13.	2 *p* against the prophets of Israel, who are
	21.	2 sanctuaries; *p* against the land of Israel
	36.	1 *p* to the mountains of Israel, and say: O
	37.	4 "*P* to these bones, and say to them: O
	38.14	mortal, *p*, and say to Gog, Thus says the
Am	2.12	the prophets, saying, "You shall not *p*."
	7.12	of Judah, earn your bread there, and *p*
Mt	7.22	'Lord, Lord, did we not *p* in your name,
	26.68	saying, "*P* to us, you Messiah! Who is it
Mk	14.65	and to strike him, saying to him, "*P*!"
Lk	22.64	him, "*P*! Who is it that struck you?"
Acts	2.17	sons and your daughters shall *p*, and
	19.	6 them, and they spoke in tongues and *p*.
1 Cor	13.	9 only in part, and we *p* only in part;
	14.	5 speak in tongues, but even more to *p*.
Jude	14	*p*, saying, "See, the Lord is coming with
Rev	10.11	"You must *p* again about many peoples

PROPHET

Gen	20.	7 return the man's wife; for he is a *p*, and
Ex	7.	1 and your brother shall be your *p*.
Deut	18.15	God will raise up for you a *p* like me
	34.10	has there arisen a *p* in Israel like Moses
Judg	6.	8 the LORD sent a *p* to the Israelites; and
1 Sam	3.20	knew that Samuel was a trustworthy *p*.
1 Kings	13.11	Now there lived an old *p* in Bethel. One
	22.	7 "Is there no other *p* of the LORD here of
2 Kings	5.	8 he may learn that there is a *p* in Israel."
2 Chr	18.	6 Is there no other *p* of the LORD here of
	28.	9 a *p* of the LORD was there, whose name
	36.12	humble himself before the *p* Jeremiah
Ps	74.	9 there is no longer any *p*, and there is no
Jer	8.10	unjust gain; from *p* to priest everyone
Ezek	2.	5 they shall know that there has been a *p*
	14.	9 I, the LORD, have deceived that *p*, and I
	33.33	know that a *p* has been among them.
Hos	9.	7 "The *p* is a fool, the man of the spirit is
	12.13	By a *p* the LORD brought Israel up from
Am	7.14	Amos answered Amaziah, "I am no *p*,
Mt	10.41	welcomes a *p* in the name of a *p* will
	21.	4 what had been spoken through the *p*,
	21.11	"This is the *p* Jesus from Nazareth in
Mk	11.32	for all regarded John as truly a *p*.
Lk	4.24	no *p* is accepted in the prophet's
	7.16	saying, "A great *p* has arisen among us:"
	20.	6 they are convinced that John was a *p*.
Jn	1.21	"Are you the *p*?" He answered, "No."
	4.19	said to him, Sir, I see that you are a *p*.
	7.40	in the crowd said, "This is really the *p*."
Acts	7.37	God will raise up a *p* for you from your
Titus	1.12	of them, their very own *p*, who said,
Rev	19.20	with it the false *p* who had performed

PROPHETESS

Judg	4.	4 Deborah, a *p*, the wife of Lappidoth,
Isa	8.	3 And I went to the *p*, and she conceived

PROPHETIC

1 Cor	13. 2 And if I have *p* powers, and understand
2 Pet	1.19 the *p* message more fully confirmed.

PROPHETS

Num	11.29 Would that all the LORD's people were *p*,
	12. 6 When there were *p* among you, I the
Deut	13. 1 If *p* or those who divine by dreams
1 Sam	10. 5 you will meet a band of *p* coming down
	10.11 son of Kish? Is Saul also among the *p*?"
	19.24 it is said, "Is Saul also among the *p*?"
2 Kings	2. 2 that he spoke by his servants the *p*.
2 Chr	20.20 you will be established; believe his *p*."
Neh	9.30 them by your Spirit through your *p*;
Isa	9.15 head, and *p* who teach lies are the tail;
Jer	4. 9 shall be appalled and the *p* astounded.
	5.13 The *p* are nothing but wind, for the
	7.25 persistently sent all my servants the *p*
	27. 9 therefore, must not listen to your *p*,
	44. 4 sent to you all my servants the *p*,
Lam	2.14 *p* have seen for you false and deceptive
	4.13 It was for the sins of her *p* and the
Zeph	3. 4 Its *p* are reckless, faithless persons; its
Mt	13.57 "*P* are not without honor except in their
	23.37 the city that kills the *p* and stones
	24.24 false messiahs and false *p* will appear
Mk	6. 4 "*P* are not without honor, except in
	8.28 Elijah; and still others, one of the *p*."
Lk	6.26 what their ancestors did to the false *p*.
	9.19 that one of the ancient *p* has arisen."
	10.24 many *p* and kings desired to see what
	13.34 Jerusalem, the city that kills the *p* and
	24.44 Moses, the *p*, and the psalms must be
Acts	13.15 After the reading of the law and the *p*,
Rom	11. 3 "Lord, they have killed your *p*, they
1 Cor	12.28 the church first apostles, second *p*,
	14.32 And the spirits of *p* are subject to the *p*,
Eph	4.11 that some would be apostles, some *p*,
1 Pet	1.10 the *p* who prophesied of the grace
2 Pet	2. 1 false *p* also arose among the people,
Rev	10. 7 as he announced to his servants the *p*."

PROSPER (PROSPERED PROSPERS)

Gen	39.23 whatever he did, the LORD made it *p*.
1 Kings	2. 3 that you may *p* in all that you do and
2 Kings	18. 7 was with him; wherever he went, he *p*.
2 Chr	26. 5 he sought the LORD, God made him *p*.
	31.21 God, he did with all his heart, and he *p*.
Ezra	5. 8 done diligently and *p* in their hands.
Ps	1. 3 not wither. In all that they do, they *p*.
	37. 7 do not fret over those who *p* in their
	90.17 our hands— O *p* the work of our hands!
	122. 6 of Jerusalem: "May they *p* who love you!
Prov	17. 8 who give it; wherever they turn they *p*.
	28.13 one who conceals transgressions will *p*,
Isa	48.15 brought him, and he will *p* in his way.
	53.10 him the will of the LORD shall *p*.
	54.17 that is fashioned against you shall *p*,
Jer	2.37 trust, and you will not *p* through them.
	12. 1 Why does the way of the guilty *p*? Why
Dan	6.28 Daniel *p* during the reign of Darius and

PROSPERITY

Job	21.23 One dies in full *p*, being wholly at ease
Ps	25.13 They will abide in *p*, and their children
	30. 6 As for me, I said in my *p*, "I shall never
	37.11 and delight themselves in abundant *p*.
Eccl	7.14 In the day of *p* be joyful, and in the day
Isa	48.18 your *p* would have been like a river,
	66.12 LORD: I will extend *p* to her like a river,
Hag	2. 9 of hosts; and in this place I will give *p*,

PROSPEROUS

Josh	1. 8 Only then shall you make your way *p*,

PROSTITUTE

Gen	38.15 he thought her to be a *p*, for she had

Josh	6.17 Only Rahab the *p* and all who are with
Judg	16. 1 went to Gaza, where he saw a *p* and
Prov	7.10 comes toward him, decked out like a *p*,
	23.27 "For a *p* is a deep pit; an adulteress is a
Heb	11.31 By faith Rahab the *p* did not perish
Jas	2.25 Rahab the *p* also justified by works

PROSTRATED

1 Chr	29.20 bowed their heads and *p* themselves

PROTECT (PROTECTED PROTECTS)

Josh	24.17 He *p* us along all the way that we went,
Ps	16. 1 *P* me, O God, for in you I take refuge.
	20. 1 The name of the God of Jacob *p* you!
	41. 2 The LORD *p* them and keeps them alive;
	59. 1 my God, *p* me from those who rise up
	116. 6 The LORD *p* the simple; when I was
Isa	31. 5 he will *p* and deliver it, he will spare
Zech	9.15 LORD of hosts will *p* them, and they
Jn	17.11 Father, *p* them in your name that you
1 Pet	1. 5 who are being *p* by the power of God

PROUD

2 Chr	26.16 when he had become strong he grew *p*,
Job	40.11 look on all who are *p*, and abase them.
	41.34 is lofty; it is king over all that are *p*."
Ps	123. 4 who are at ease, the contempt of the *p*.
Prov	21. 4 Haughty eyes and a *p* heart— the lamp
Ob	3 Your *p* heart has deceived you, you that
Lk	1.51 he has scattered the *p* in the thoughts
Jas	4. 6 "God opposes the *p*, but gives grace to

PROVE (PROVING)

Ps	26. 2 *P* me, O LORD, and try me; test my heart
Jn	16. 8 he will *p* the world wrong about sin and
Acts	9.22 by *p* that Jesus was the Messiah.
	17. 3 and *p* that it was necessary for the
	24.13 Neither can they *p* to you the charge
	25. 7 against him, which they could not *p*.

PROVERB (PROVERBS)

Deut	28.37 shall become an object of horror, a *p*,
1 Sam	10.12 Therefore it became a *p*, "Is Saul also
1 Kings	4.32 He composed three thousand *p*, and his
	9. 7 Israel will become a *p* and a taunt
Ps	49. 4 I will incline my ear to a *p*; I will solve
Prov	1. 6 skill, to understand a *p* and a figure,
	26. 9 drunkard is a *p* in the mouth of a fool.
Ezek	12.22 Mortal, what is this *p* of yours about
	16.44 use this *p* about you, "Like mother, like
Lk	4.23 quote me this *p*, 'Doctor, cure yourself!'

PROVIDE (PROVIDED PROVIDES)

Gen	22. 8 "God himself will *p* the lamb for a burnt
	45.11 I will *p* for you there —since there are
	47.12 And Joseph *p* his father, his brothers,
1 Chr	22.14 I have *p* for the house of the LORD one
	29. 2 I have *p* for the house of my God, so far
Job	38.41 Who *p* for the raven its prey, when its
Prov	31.15 still night and *p* food for her household
Jon	1.17 But the LORD *p* a large fish to swallow
Mt	27.55 Jesus from Galilee and had *p* for him.

PROVISION (PROVISIONS)

Gen	45.23 with grain, bread, and *p* for his father
Josh	9. 4 they went and prepared *p*, and took
1 Kings	4.22 Solomon's *p* for one day was thirty cors
Rom	13.14 and make no *p* for the flesh, to gratify

PROVOKE (PROVOKED PROVOKING)

Deut	9.22 you have *p* the LORD to wrath.
	32.21 what is no god, *p* me with their idols.
Judg	2.12 to them, and they *p* the LORD to anger.
1 Sam	1. 6 Her rival used to *p* her severely, to
1 Kings	14.22 they *p* him to jealousy with their sins
	22.53 he *p* the LORD, the God of Israel, to
2 Kings	14.10 why should you *p* trouble so that you
	17.17 in the sight of the Lord, *p* him to anger.

PRUDENCE

2 Chr	25.19	at home; why should you *p* trouble so
	28.25	offerings to other gods, *p* to anger the
Ps	78.41	and again, and *p* the Holy One of Israel.
	78.58	they *p* him to anger with their high
Isa	65. 3	people who *p* me to my face
Jer	7.19	Is it I whom they *p*? says the LORD.
	44. 8	Why do you *p* me to anger with the
1 Cor	10.22	Or are we *p* the Lord to jealousy? Are
Eph	6. 4	fathers, do not *p* your children to anger,
Heb	10.24	consider how to *p* one another to love

PRUDENCE

Prov	5. 2	so that you may hold on to *p*, and your

PRUDENT

Prov	19.14	parents, but a *p* wife is from the LORD.
Am	5.13	Therefore the *p* will keep silent in such

PSALMS

Lk	24.44	prophets, and the *p* must be fulfilled."
Eph	5.19	as you sing *p* and hymns and spiritual
Col	3.16	in your hearts sing *p*, hymns, and

PUFFED (PUFFS)

1 Cor	4. 6	so that none of you will be *p* up in
	8. 1	Knowledge *p* up, but love builds up.

PULLED

Jer	38.13	the ropes and *p* him out of the cistern.

PUNISH (PUNISHED)

Ex	32.34	punishment, I will *p* them for their sin."
Lev	26.18	I will continue to *p* you sevenfold
	26.28	I in turn will *p* you myself sevenfold for
Ps	89.32	then I will *p* their transgression with the
Isa	10.12	he will *p* the arrogant boasting of the
	13.11	*p* the world for its evil, and the wicked
	24.21	day the LORD will *p* the host of heaven
Jer	5. 9	Shall I not *p* them for these things?
	9. 9	Shall I not *p* them for these things?
	21.14	I will *p* you according to the fruit of
	51.47	when I will *p* the images of Babylon;
Hos	2.13	I will *p* her for the festival days of the
	8.13	their iniquity, and *p* their sins;
	9. 9	their iniquity, he will *p* their sins.
	10.10	against the wayward people to *p* them;
	12. 2	and will *p* Jacob according to his ways,
Am	3.14	On the day I *p* Israel for its
2 Cor	6. 9	are alive; as *p*, and yet not killed;

PUNISHMENT

Gen	4.13	LORD, "My *p* is greater than I can bear.
Isa	10. 3	What will you do on the day of *p*, in the
	53. 5	upon him was the *p* that made us
Lam	4. 6	hs been greater than the *p* of Sodom,
Ezek	4. 5	and so you shall bear the *p* of the
	14.10	they shall bear their *p* — the *p* of the
Hos	9. 7	The days of *p* have come, the days of
Hab	1.12	O Rock, have established them for *p*.
2 Cor	2. 6	*p* by the majority is enough for such a
2 Thess	1. 9	will suffer the *p* of eternal destruction,

PURCHASE (PURCHASED)

Gen	25.10	the field that Abraham *p* from the
Jer	32.12	and I gave the deed of *p* to Baruch son

PURE (PURER)

2 Sam	22.27	With the *p* you show yourself *p*, and
Job	4.17	human beings be *p* before their Maker?
	8. 6	if you are *p* and upright, surely then he
	11. 4	you say, "My conduct is *p*, and I am
Ps	12. 6	of the LORD are promises that are *p*,
	18.26	with the *p* you show yourself *p*; and
	19. 9	the fear of the LORD is *p*, enduring
	24. 4	who have clean hands and *p* hearts,
	73. 1	the upright, to those who are *p* in heart.
	119. 9	can young people keep their way *p*?
Prov	15.26	to the LORD, but gracious words are *p*.
	16. 2	one's ways may be *p* in one's own eyes,

Prov	30.12	are those who are *p* in their own eyes
Hab	1.13	Your eyes are too *p* to behold evil, and
Mt	5. 8	"Blessed are the *p* in heart, for they will
2 Cor	11. 3	led astray from a sincere and *p* devotion
1 Tim	5.22	in the sins of others; keep yourself *p*.
Titus	1.15	To the *p* all things are *p*, but to the

PURGE (PURGED)

2 Chr	34. 5	their altars, and *p* Judah and Jerusalem.
Ps	51. 7	*P* me with hyssop, and I shall be clean;
Ezek	20.38	I will *p* out the rebels among you, and

PURIFICATION

Lk	2.22	when the time came for their *p*
Jn	3.25	a discussion about *p* arose between
Heb	1. 3	When he had made *p* for sins, he sat

PURIFY (PURIFIED)

Num	19.13	who has died, and do not *p* themselves,
	31.20	You shall *p* every garment, every article
Neh	12.30	and the Levites *p* themselves; and they
Isa	52.11	out from the midst of it, *p* yourselves,
Dan	12.10	Many shall be *p*, cleansed, and refined,
Mal	3. 3	he will *p* the descendants of Levi and
Acts	21.26	having *p* himself, he entered the temple
Heb	9.14	*p* our conscience from dead works to
	9.22	law almost everything is *p* with blood,
1 Pet	1.22	you have *p* your souls by your
1 Jn	3. 3	have this hope in him *p* themselves,

PURITY

1 Pet	3. 2	see the *p* and reverence of your lives.

PURPOSE (PURPOSES)

Prov	20. 5	The *p* in the human mind are like deep
Isa	46.10	"My *p* shall stand, and I will fulfill my
Jer	51.29	for the LORD's *p* against Babylon stand,
Lk	7.30	and the lawyers rejected God's *p* for
Acts	20.27	declaring to you the whole *p* of God.
Eph	1.11	*p* of him who accomplishes all things
	3.11	was in accordance with the eternal *p*
2 Tim	1. 9	to our works but according to his own *p*
Heb	6.17	the unchangeable character of his *p*,
Rev	17.17	put into their hearts to carry out his *p*

PURSUE (PURSUED PURSUES)

Ex	14. 8	Pharoah . . . *p* the Israelites, who were
Job	19.22	Why do you, like God, *p* me, never
Ps	83.15	so *p* them with your tempest and terrify
	109. 16	kindness, but *p* the poor and needy
Prov	21.21	Whoever *p* righteousness and kindness
Jer	29.18	I will *p* them with the sword, with
Lam	3.66	*P* them in anger and destroy them from
Am	1.11	he *p* his brother with the sword,
Acts	26.11	at them, I *p* them even to foreign cities.
Rom	14.19	Let us then *p* what makes for peace and
1 Tim	6.11	*p* righteousness, godliness, faith, love,
Heb	12.14	*P* peace with everyone, and the holiness

PUT

Rom	13.14	Instead, *p* on the Lord Jesus Christ, and
2 Cor	11.20	you *p* up with it when someone makes
Eph	4.22	to *p* away your former way of life,

Q

QUARREL (QUARRELED QUARRELING QUARRELS)

Ex	17. 3	The people *q* with Moses, and said,
Prov	17.14	out water; so stop before the *q* breaks
	19.13	and a wife's *q* is a continual dripping of
1 Cor	1.11	people that there are *q* among you,
	3. 3	as there is jealousy and *q* among you,
2 Cor	12.20	I fear that there may perhaps be *q*,

QUEEN

Esth	2.17	head and made her *q* instead of Vashti.
Ps	45. 9	honor; at your right hand stands the *q*
Mt	12.42	The *q* of the South will rise up at the

QUENCH

Lk 11.31 The *q* of the South will rise at the

QUENCH (QUENCHED)

Song 8. 7 Many waters cannot *q* love, neither can
Isa 1.31 burn together, with no one to *q* them.
 42. 3 and a dimly burning wick he will not *q*;
Mt 12.20 a bruised reed or *q* a smoldering wick
Mk 9.48 worm never dies, and the fire is never *q*.
1 Thess 5.19 Do not *q* the Spirit. Do not despise the

QUESTION (QUESTIONING QUESTIONS)

1 Kings 10. 1 she came to test him with hard *q*.
2 Chr 9. 1 to Jerusalem to test him with hard *q*,
Isa 45.11 Will you *q* me about my children,
Mk 2. 8 do you raise such *q* in your hearts?
Lk 3.15 were *q* in their hearts concerning John

QUICK-TEMPERED

Prov 14.17 One who is *q* acts foolishly, and the

QUIET (QUIETLY)

Job 34.29 When he is *q*, who can condemn? When
Eccl 4. 6 Better is a handful with *q* than two
Mt 1.19 disgrace, planned to dismiss her *q*.
1 Thess 4.11 to aspire to live *q*, to mind your own

QUIETNESS

Isa 32.17 the result of righteousness, *q* and trust

QUIVER

Ps 127. 5 Happy is the man who has his *q* full of

R

RACE

Eccl 9.11 under the sun the *r* is not to the swift,
1 Cor 9.24 in a *r* the runners all compete, but only
Heb 12. 1 let us run with perseverance the *r* that

RACHEL

Gen 29. 6 and here is his daughter *R*, coming with
 29.16 and the name of the younger was *R*.
 29.18 Jacob loved *R*; so he said, "I will serve
 29.30 to *R* also, and he loved *R* more than
 30.22 Then God remembered *R*, and God
 31.34 *R* had taken the household gods and
 35.19 So *R* died, and she was buried on the
Ruth 4.11 like *R* and Leah, who together built up
Mt 2.18 *R* weeping for her children; she refused

RADIANT

Ps 34. 5 Look to him, and be *r*; so your faces
Isa 60. 5 Then you shall see and be *r*; your heart
Jer 31.12 and they shall be *r* over the goodness of

RAFTS

1 Kings 5. 9 I will make it into *r* to go by sea to the
2 Chr 2.16 bring it to you as *r* by sea to Joppa; you

RAGES (RAGED RAGING)

Prov 19. 3 to ruin, yet the heart *r* against the Lord.
Isa 37.28 and coming in, and your *r* against me.
Rev 11.18 The nations *r*, but your wrath has come,

RAIL

Num 16.11 What is Aaron that you *r* against him?"

RAIN (RAINS)

Gen 2. 5 God had not caused it to *r* upon the
 7. 4 For in seven days I will send *r* on the
Lev 26. 4 I will give you your *r* in their season,
Deut 11.14 then he will give the *r* for your land in
 28.12 to give the *r* of your land in its season
1 Kings 8.35 there is no *r* because they have sinned
 17. 1 shall be neither dew nor *r* these years,
 18.41 for there is a sound of the rushing *r*."
Job 5.10 He gives *r* on the earth and sends
 38.28 "Has the *r* a father, or who has begotten
Ps 68. 9 *R* in abundance, O God, you showered
Isa 44.14 plants a cedar, and the *r* nourishes it.

Isa 45. 8 and let the skies *r* down righteousness;
 55.10 as the *r* and the snow come down from
Jer 5.24 our God, who gives the *r* in its season,
Joel 2.23 abundant *r*, the early and the latter *r*, as
Am 4. 7 I also withheld the *r* from you when
Zech 10. 1 Ask *r* from the Lord in the season of
 14.17 of hosts, there will be no *r* upon them.
Mt 5.45 sends *r* on the righteous and on the
 7.25 The *r* fell, the floods came, and the
Acts 14.17 giving you *r* from heaven and fruitful
Rev 11. 6 that no *r* may fall during the days of

RAINBOW

Rev 4. 3 around the throne is a *r* that looks like

RAISE (RAISED RAISES)

Ps 41.10 to me, and *r* me up, that I may repay
 148. 14 He has *r* up a horn for his people,
Mt 14. 2 Baptist; he has been *r* from the dead,
 16.21 and be killed, and on the third day be *r*.
 17. 9 Son of Man has been *r* from the dead.
 20.19 and on the third day he will be *r*."
 26.32 after I am *r* up, I will go ahead of you
 27.64 people, 'He has been *r* from the dead,
 28. 6 He is not here; for he has been *r*, as he
Mk 6.14 "John the baptizer has been *r* from the
 14.28 after I am *r* up, I will go before you to
 16. 6 He has been *r*; he is not here. Look,
Lk 9. 7 that John had been *r* from the dead
 21.28 take place, stand up and *r* your heads,
Jn 5.21 just as the father *r* the dead and gives
 6.39 given me, but *r* it up at the last day.
Acts 3.15 Author of life, whom God *r* from the
 10.40 God *r* him on the third day and allowed
 13.30 But God *r* him from the dead;
 26. 8 by any of you that God *r* the dead?
Rom 9.17 to Pharaoh, "I have *r* you up for the very
1 Cor 6.14 And God *r* the Lord and will also *r* us
 15. 4 that he was *r* on the third day in
 15.13 of the dead, then Christ has not been *r*;
2 Cor 4.14 the one who *r* the Lord Jesus will *r* us
Eph 1.20 when he *r* him from the dead and
 2. 6 *r* us up with him and seated us with
Col 3. 1 if you have been *r* with Christ, seek the
2 Tim 2. 8 Remember Jesus Christ, *r* from the
Jas 5.15 the sick, and the Lord will *r* them up;
1 Pet 1.21 to trust in God, who *r* him from the

RAM

Gen 15. 9 Bring me . . . a *r* three years old, a
 22.13 and saw a *r*, caught in a thicket by its

RAMAH

1 Sam 1.19 they went back to their house at *R*.
 2.11 Then Elkanah went home to *R*, while
 8. 4 together and came to Samuel at *R*,
 19.18 and escaped; he came to Samuel at *R*,
 28. 3 mourned for him and buried him in *R*,
2 Chr 16. 1 against Judah, and built *R*, to prevent
Isa 10.29 *R* trembles, Gibeah of Saul has fled. Cry
Jer 31.15 A voice is heard in *R*, lamentation and
Mt 2.18 "A voice was heard in *R*, wailing and

RAMOTH-GILEAD

1 Kings 22. 6 "Shall I go to battle against *R*, or shall I
2 Kings 9. 1 flask of oil in your hand, and go to *R*.

RAMPART

Hab 2. 1 watchpost, and station myself on the *r*,

RANK

Gen 49. 3 of my vigor, excelling in *r* and excelling

RANSOM (RANSOMED)

Ex 30.12 all of them shall give a *r* for their lives
1 Sam 14.45 So the people *r* Jonathan, and he did
Job 6.23 hand'? Or, '*R* me from the hand
 33.24 down into the Pit; I have found a *r*;

Job	36.18	not let the greatness of the r turn you
Ps	49. 7	Truly, no r avails for one's life, there is
	49. 8	For the r of life is costly, and can never
Prov	21.18	The wicked is a r for the righteous, and
Isa	43. 3	I give Egypt as your r, Ethiopia and
Hos	13.14	Shall I r them from the power of Sheol?
Mt	20.28	serve, and to give his life a r for many."
Mk	10.45	serve, and to give his life a r for many."
1 Tim	2. 6	human, who gave himself as a r for all
1 Pet	1.18	You know that you were r from the
Rev	5. 9	by your blood you r for God saints from

RARE

1 Sam	3. 1	word of the LORD was r in those days;
Isa	13.12	I will make mortals more r than fine

RASH

Job	6. 3	sea; therefore my words have been r.
Eccl	5. 2	Never be r with your mouth, nor let

RAVAGED (RAVAGING)

Nah	2. 2	though ravagers have r them and ruined
Acts	8. 3	But Saul was r the church by entering

RAVEN (RAVENS)

Gen	8. 7	and sent out the r; and it went to and
1 Kings	17. 4	commanded the r to feed you there."
Job	38.41	Who provides for the r its prey, when its
Lk	12.24	Consider the r: they neither sow nor

RAVENOUS

Prov	27. 7	but to a r appetite even the bitter

RAVISH (RAVISHED)

Judg	19.24	R them and do whatever you want to
Song	4. 9	you have r my heart with a glance of

RAZOR

Num	6. 5	vow no r shall come upon the head;
Ps	52. 2	Your tongue is like a sharp r, you
Isa	7.20	the Lord will shave with a r hired
Ezek	5. 1	sword; use it as a barber's r and run it

READ (READING READS)

Deut	17.19	he shall r in it all the days of his life,
	31.11	you shall r this law before all Israel in
2 Kings	23. 2	he r in their hearing all the words of
Neh	8. 3	he r from it facing the square before the
	13. 1	they r from the book of Moses in the
Isa	29.11	"R this," they say, "I cannot, for it is
	34.16	r from the book of the LORD: Not one of
Jer	36. 6	house you shall r the words of the LORD
	36.21	and Jehudi r it to the king and all the
Dan	5. 7	"Whoever can r this writing and tell me
	5.17	I will r the writing to the king and let
Hab	2. 2	on tablets, so that a runner may r it.
Mt	21.42	"Have you never r in the scriptures:
Mk	12.10	Have you not r this scripture: 'The
	12.26	have you not r in the book of Moses, in
Lk	6. 3	"Have you not r what David did when
Acts	8.28	his chariot, he was r the prophet Isaiah.
2 Cor	3. 2	on our hearts, to be known and r by all;
Rev	1. 3	Blessed is the one who r aloud the

READY

Song	2. 7	not stir up or awaken love until it is r.
	3. 5	not stir up or awaken love until it is r.
	8. 4	not stir up or awaken love until it is r.
Mt	22. 4	and everything is r; come to my
	22. 8	The wedding is r, but those invited
	24.44	you also must be r, for the Son of Man
	25.10	those who were r went with him into
1 Cor	14. 8	sound, who will get r for battle?
2 Cor	9. 2	saying that Achaia has been r since last

REALIZED

Mk	15.10	he r that it was out of jealousy that the
Lk	20.19	and chief priests r that he had told this

REALM

Dan	11. 5	shall rule a r greater than his own r.

REAP (REAPS)

Lev	19. 9	r . . ., you shall not r to the very edges
	23.22	r . . ., you shall not r to the very edges
Job	4. 8	iniquity and sow trouble r the same.
Ps	126. 5	who sow in tears r with shouts of joy.
Prov	22. 8	Whoever sows injustice will r calamity,
Eccl	11. 4	whoever regards the clouds will not r.
Mic	6.15	You shall sow, but not r; you shall tread
Mt	6.26	they neither sow nor r nor gather into
Jn	4.37	holds true, 'One sows and another.'
1 Cor	9.11	too much if we r your material benefits?
Gal	6. 7	mocked, for you r whatever you sow.
Rev	14.15	r, for the hour to r has come, because

REBEKAH (REBECCA)

Gen	22.23	Bethuel became the father of R. These
	24.15	he had finished speaking, there was R,
	24.59	So they sent away their sister R and her
	24.67	He took R, and she became his wife,
	25.28	was fond of game; but R loved Jacob.
	27. 5	R was listening when Isaac spoke to his
	49.31	there Isaac and his wife R were buried;
Rom	9.10	to R when she had conceived children

REBEL (REBELS) (n)

Num	20.10	"Listen, you r, shall we bring water for
Isa	1.23	Your princes are r and companions of
	1.28	r and sinners shall be destroyed
	48. 8	and that from birth you were called a r.

REBEL (REBELLED REBELLING REBELS)

Num	14. 9	do not r against the LORD; and do not
	16.41	of the Israelites r against Moses
	20.24	because you r against my command at
	27.14	because you r against my word in the
Deut	1.26	You r against the command of the LORD
	1.43	You r against the command of the LORD
2 Kings	3. 5	of Moab r against the king of Israel.
Neh	2.19	are doing? Are you r against the king?"
Job	24.13	There are those who r against the light,
Ps	5.10	them out, for they have r against you.
	78.17	against him, r against the Most High
	78.40	How often they r against him in the
	107. 11	for they had r against the words of God,
Prov	28. 2	When a land r it has many rulers; but
Isa	1. 2	them up, but they have r against me.
	1.20	but if you refuse and r, you shall be
	36. 5	now rely, that you have r against me?
	63.10	they r and grieved his holy spirit;
Jer	4.17	of a field, because she has r against me,
Ezek	2. 3	nation of rebels, who have r against me;
	20.13	Israel r against me in the wilderness;
Hos	13.16	because she has r against her God;

REBELLION

Josh	22.16	yourselves an altar today in r against
1 Sam	15.23	r is no less a sin than divination, and
1 Kings	12.19	Israel has been in r against the house of
2 Chr	10.19	So Israel has been in r against the
Job	34.37	For he adds r to his sin; he claps his
Jer	29.32	for he has spoken r against the LORD.

REBELLIOUS

Deut	21.18	and r son who will not obey his father
Ezra	4.15	this is a r city, hurtful to kings and
Isa	30. 1	Oh, r children, says the LORD, who carry
Ezek	17.12	Say now to the r house: Do you not

REBUILD (REBUILT)

Ezra	1. 3	in Judah, and r the house of the LORD,
Neh	4. 6	So we r the wall, and all the wall was
Job	12.14	If he tears down, no one can r; if he
Ps	51.18	r the walls of Jerusalem, then you will

REBUKE (n)

Job	26.11 tremble, and are astounded at his r.
Ps	76. 6 At your r, O God of Jacob, both rider
	104. 7 At your r they flee; at the sound of your
Prov	17.10 A r strikes deeper into a discerning
	27. 5 Better is open r than hidden love. Well

REBUKE (REBUKED) (v)

Gen	31.42 and the labor of my hands, and r you
	37.10 to his brothers, his father r him, and
1 Chr	16.21 them; he r kings on their account,
Job	13.10 He will surely r you if in secret you
Ps	6. 1 O Lord, do not r me in your anger, or
	38. 1 O Lord, do not r me in your anger, or
	50. 8 Not for your sacrifices do I r you; your
	105. 14 them; he r kings on their account,
	106. 9 He r the Red Sea, and it became dry; he
	119. 21 You r the insolent, accursed ones, who
Prov	24.25 who r the wicked will have delight,
Jer	29.27 why have you not r Jeremiah of
Zech	3. 2 "The Lord r you, O Satan! The Lord
Mt	16.22 took him aside and began to r him,
	17.18 Jesus r the demon, and it came out of
Mk	8.32 took him aside and began to r him.
	9.25 he r the unclean spirit, saying to it,
Lk	4.35 Jesus r him, saying "Be silent, and
	9.42 Jesus r the unclean spirit, healed the
	9.55 But he turned and r them. Then they
Jude	9 against him, but said, "The Lord r you!"

RECEIVE (RECEIVED RECEIVES)

Job	2.10 at the hand of God, and not r the bad?"
	22.22 R instruction from his mouth, and lay
	27.13 and the heritage that oppressors r from
	35. 7 to him; and what does he r from your
Ps	24. 5 They will r blessing from the Lord, and
	49.15 the power of Sheol, for he will r me.
	73.24 and afterward you will r me with honor.
Mt	7. 8 For everyone who asks r, and everyone
	20.10 came, they thought they would r more;
	21.22 ask for in prayer with faith, you will r."
Mk	4.16 the word, they immediately r it with joy;
	10.15 does not r the kingdom as a little child
	10.30 who will not r a hundredfold now in
Lk	6.34 sinners lend to sinners, to r as much
	9.53 they did not r him, because his face
	11.10 For everyone who asks r, and everyone
	18.42 to him, "R your sight; your faith has
Jn	1.12 But to all who r him, who believed in
	3.27 "No one can r anything except what has
	13.20 and whoever r me r him who sent me."
	20.22 "R the Holy Spirit. If you forgive the
Acts	19. 2 "Did you r the Holy Spirit when you
1 Cor	2.14 who are unspiritual do not r the gifts of
	11.23 I r from the Lord what I also handed on
	15. 3 what I in turn had r: that Christ died
Gal	3. 2 Did you r the Spirit by doing the works
	3.14 that we might r the promise of the
	4. 5 so that we might r adoption as children.
	6. 1 who have r the Spirit should restore
Col	2. 6 therefore have r Christ Jesus the Lord,
1 Thess	1. 6 of persecution you r the word with joy
2 Jn	8 worked for, but may r a full reward.

RECEPTIVE

Acts	17.11 These Jews were more r than those in

RECITE

Deut	6. 7 R them to your children and talk about

RECKONS (RECKONED RECKONING)

Gen	15. 6 the Lord; and the Lord r it to him as
	42.22 So now there comes a r for his blood."
Ps	106. 31 that has been r to him as righteousness
Prov	18.24 When he began the r, one who owed
Rom	4. 3 "Abraham believed God, and it was r to
	4. 6 to whom God r righteousness apart

Rom	4. 9 "Faith was r to Abraham as
	4.22 his faith was "r to him as righteousness."
	5.13 but sin is not r when there is no law.

RECOGNIZED

Gen	42. 8 Although Joseph had r his brothers,

RECOMPENSED

2 Sam	22.25 the Lord has r me according to my
Ps	18.24 Therefore the Lord has r me according

RECONCILE (RECONCILED)

Mt	5.24 first be r to your brother or sister, and
Rom	5.10 enemies, we were r to God through the
1 Cor	7.11 unmarried or else be r to her husband),
2 Cor	5.18 is from God, who r us to himself
Eph	2.16 might r both groups to God in one body
Col	1.20 was pleased to r to himself all things,

RECONCILIATION

Rom	5.11 through whom we have now received r.
	11.15 if their rejection is the r of the world,

RECOUNT

Ps	118. 17 not die, but I shall live, and r the deeds
Isa	63. 7 I will r the gracious deeds of the Lord,

RECOVER

2 Kings	8. 8 him, whether I shall r from this illness."
Isa	11.11 yet a second time to r the remnant

RED SEA

Ex	10.19 the locusts and drove them into the R;
	15. 4 his picked officers were sunk in the R.
	15.22 ordered Israel to set out from the R,
Josh	4.23 God did to the R, which he dried up for
Ps	106. 9 He rebuked the R, and it became dry;
Acts	7.36 wonders and signs in Egypt, at the R,
Heb	11.29 faith the people passed through the R

REDEEM (REDEEMED REDEEMS)

Gen	48.16 the angel who has r me from all harm,
Ex	6. 6 I will r you with an outstretched arm
	15.13 love you led the people whom you r;
	21. 8 then he shall let her be r; he shall have
	34.20 if a donkey you shall r with a lamb,
Num	18.15 first-born of human beings you shall r,
Deut	7. 8 and r you from the house of slavery,
	9.26 whom you r in your greatness, whom
Ruth	4. 4 If you will r it, r it; but if you will not,
2 Sam	4. 9 As the Lord lives, who has r my life out
	7.23 whose God went to r it as a people,
1 Chr	17.21 whom God went to r to be his people,
Neh	1.10 your people, whom you r by your great
Job	5.20 In famine he will r you from death, and
	33.28 He has r my soul from going down to
Ps	25.22 R Israel, O God, out of all its troubles.
	26.11 integrity; r me, and be gracious to me.
	31. 5 my spirit; you have r me, O Lord,
	34.22 The Lord r the life of his servants; none
	44.26 Rise up, come to our help. R us for the
	69.18 Draw near to me, r me, set me free
	77.15 With your strong arm you r your people,
	103. 4 diseases, who r your life from the Pit,
	130. 7 love, and with him is great power to r.
Isa	1.27 Zion shall be r by justice, and those in
	43. 1 O Israel: Do not fear, for I have r you;
	48.20 say, "The Lord has r his servant Jacob!"
	52. 3 and you shall be r without money.
Jer	15.21 the wicked, and r you from the grasp of
Hos	7.13 I would r them, but they speak lies
Mic	6. 4 and r you from the house of slavery;
Zech	10. 8 and gather them in, for I have r them,
Lk	1.68 favorably to his people and r them
	24.21 hoped that he was the one to r Israel.
Gal	3.13 Christ r us from the curse of the law by
	4. 5 to r those who were under the law,
Titus	2.14 us that he might r us from all iniquity

REDEEMED (n)

Ps 107. 2 Let the *r* of the LORD say so, those he *r*
Isa 35. 9 found there, but the *r* shall walk there.
 51.10 of the sea a way for the *r* to cross over?
 62.12 "The Holy People, The *R* of the LORD";

REDEEMER

Job 19.25 For I know that my *R* lives, and that at
Ps 19.14 to you, O LORD, my rock and my *r*.
 78.35 their rock, the Most High God their *r*.
Prov 23.11 for their *R* is strong; he will plead their
Isa 41.14 says the LORD; your *R* is the Holy One
 44. 6 King of Israel, and his *R*, the LORD of
 47. 4 Our *R*—the LORD of hosts is his
 54. 8 on you, says the LORD, your *R*.
 59.20 he will come to Zion as *R*, to those in
Jer 50.34 Their *R* is strong; the LORD of hosts is

REDEMPTION

Ex 21.30 is imposed for the *r* of the victim's life.
Lev 25.24 you shall provide for the *r* of the land.
 25.29 sale; the right of *r* shall be for one year.
 25.52 they shall make payment for their *r*.
Num 3.49 So Moses took the *r* money from those
Ruth 4. 6 Take my right of *r* yourself, for I cannot
Ps 111. 9 He sent *r* to his people; he has
Jer 32. 7 Anathoth, for the right of *r* by purchase
Lk 2.38 were looking for the *r* of Jerusalem.
 21.28 heads, because your *r* is drawing near."
Rom 3.24 through the *r* which is in Christ Jesus,
1 Cor 1.30 and sanctification and *r*, in order that,
Eph 1. 7 we have *r* through his blood, the
 4.30 marked with a seal for the day of *r*.
Heb 9.12 his own blood, thus obtaining eternal *r*.

REED

2 Kings 18.21 Egypt, that broken *r* of a staff, which
Isa 42. 3 bruised *r* he will not break, and a dimly
Ezek 40. 3 a measuring *r* in his hand; and he was
Mt 11. 7 to look at? A *r* shaken by the wind?
 12.20 He will not break a bruised *r* or quench
Lk 7.24 to look at? A *r* shaken by the wind?

REFINE (REFINED REFINES)

Isa 48.10 See, I have *r* you, but not like silver; I
Jer 9. 7 I will now *r* and test them, for what else
Zech 13. 9 into the fire, *r* them as one *r* silver,
Rev 3.18 buy from me gold *r* by fire so that you

REFLECTS (REFLECTION)

Prov 27.19 the face, so one human heart *r* another.
Heb 1. 3 He is the *r* of God's glory and the exact

REFRESH (REFRESHED)

Gen 18. 5 a little bread, that you may *r* yourselves,
Ex 23.12 slave and the resident alien may be *r*.
Prov 25.13 them; they *r* the spirit of their masters.
Song 2. 5 *r* me with apples; for I am faint with
Rom 15.32 you with joy and be *r* in your company.
1 Cor 16.18 for they *r* my spirit as well as yours. So
2 Tim 1.16 of Onesiphorus, because he often *r* me
Philem 7 of the saints have been *r* through you.
2 Pet 1.13 as I am in this body, to *r* your memory,

REFUGE

Num 35. 6 shall include six cities of *r*, where you
 35.11 select cities to be cities of *r* for you,
Deut 32.37 gods, the rock in which they took *r*,
Josh 20. 2 'Appoint the cities of *r*, of which I
Ruth 2.12 under whose wings you have come for *r*!"
Ps 2.12 kindled. Happy are all who take *r*
 7. 1 O LORD my God, in you I take *r*; save
 14. 6 of the poor, but the LORD is their *r*.
 16. 1 Protect me. O God, for in you I take *r*. I
 31. 1 In you, O LORD, I seek *r*; do not let me
 46. 1 God is our *r* and strength, a very
 57. 1 the shadow of your wings I will take *r*,
 61. 3 for you are my *r*, a strong tower against

Ps 61. 4 tent forever, find *r* under the shelter of
 71. 1 In you, O LORD, I take *r*; never let me be
 71. 7 to many, but you are my strong *r*.
 73.28 made the Lord GOD my *r*, to tell of all
 91. 2 say to the LORD, "My *r* and my fortress;
 118. 8 better to take *r* in the LORD than to put
 142. 4 notice of me; no *r* remains to me; no
Prov 14.32 the righteous find a *r* in their integrity.
 30. 5 true; he is a shield to those who take *r*
Isa 4. 6 and a *r* and a shelter from the storm
 25. 4 you have been a *r* to the poor, a *r* to
 28.15 we have made lies our *r*, and in
 33.16 their *r* will be the fortresses of rocks;
 57.13 whoever takes *r* in me shall possess the
Jer 16.19 stronghold, my *r* in the day of trouble,
 17.17 me; you are my *r* in the day of disaster;
Joel 3.16 the LORD is a *r* for his people, a
Nah 1. 7 he protects those who take *r* in him,
Zeph 3.12 They shall seek *r* in the name of the

REFUSE (REFUSED)

Gen 39. 8 But he *r* and said to his master's wife,
Num 20.21 Thus Edom *r* to give Israel passage
1 Sam 8.19 the people *r* to listen to the voice of
Neh 9.17 they *r* to obey, and were not mindful of
Esth 1.12 But Queen Vashti *r* to come at the
Ps 78.10 but *r* to walk according to his law.
Prov 1.24 Because I have called and you *r*, have
Isa 7.15 the time he knows how to *r* the evil and
Jer 5. 3 them, but they *r* to take correction.
 9. 6 upon deceit! They *r* to know me, says
 13.10 evil people, who *r* to hear my words,
Hos 11. 5 because they have *r* to return to me.
Zech 7.11 But they *r* to listen, and turned a
2 Thess 2.10 because they *r* to love the truth and so
Heb 11.24 grown up, *r* to be called the son of
 12.25 you do not *r* the one who is speaking;

REFUTE (REFUTED)

Acts 18.28 he powerfully *r* the Jews in public,
Titus 1. 9 and to *r* those who contradict it.

REGARD (REGARDED REGARDS)

Gen 4. 4 the LORD had *r* for Abel and his offering,
1 Kings 8.28 *R* your servant's prayer and his plea, O
Job 34.19 nor *r* the rich more than the poor, for
 37.24 he does not *r* any who are wise in their
Ps 80.14 heaven, and see; have *r* for this vine,
 106. 44 he *r* their distress, when he heard their
Isa 17. 7 people will *r* their Maker, and their eyes
Jer 24. 5 I will *r* as good the exiles from Judah,
Mk 12.14 you do not *r* people with partiality, but
Phil 3. 8 I *r* everything as loss because of the

REGISTER (REGISTERED)

Num 3.10 you shall make a *r* of Aaron and his
Lk 2. 1 Augustus that all the world should be *r*.

REGRET

1 Sam 15.11 "I *r* that I have made Saul king, for he

REGULAR

Dan 8.11 took the *r* burnt offering away from him

REGULATIONS

Num 9. 3 according to its statutes and all its *r*

REHOBOAM

1 Kings 11.43 David; and his son *R* succeeded him.
 12. 1 *R* went to Shechem, for all Israel had
 14.21 *R* was forty-one years old when he
 15. 6 war between *R* and Jeroboam continued
Mt 1. 7 Solomon the father of *R*, and *R* the

REIGN (REIGNED REIGNS)

Gen 37. 8 "Are you indeed to *r* over us? Are you
Ex 15.18 The LORD will *r* forever and ever."
1 Sam 11.12 is it that said, 'Shall Saul *r* over us?'
1 Kings 2.11 time that David *r* over Israel was forty

Job 34.30 so that the godless should not r, or
Ps 146. 10 The LORD will r forever, your God, O
Prov 8.15 By me kings r, and rulers decree what is
Eccl 4.14 One can indeed come out of prison to r,
Isa 24.23 for the LORD of hosts will r on Mount
 32. 1 king will r in righteousness, and princes
Jer 23. 5 and he shall r as king and deal wisely,
Lam 5.19 But you, O LORD, r forever; your throne
Mic 4. 7 the LORD will r over them in Mount Zion
Lk 1.33 He will r over the house of Jacob
1 Cor 15.25 he must r until he has put all his
Rev 11.15 Messiah, and he will r forever and ever."
 19. 6 For the Lord our God the Almighty r.
 20. 4 life and r with Christ a thousand years.

REJECT (REJECTED REJECTING REJECTS)

Num 11.20 you have r the LORD who is among you,
1 Sam 8. 7 not r you, but they have r me from
 10.19 today you have r your God, who saves
Ps 36. 4 way that is not good; they do not r evil.
 118. 22 The stone that the builders r has
Prov 10.17 life, but one who r a rebuke goes astray.
Isa 30.12 Because you r this word, and put your
Jer 2.37 the LORD has r those in whom you trust,
 6.19 and as for my teaching, they have r it.
 6.30 They are called "r silver," for the LORD
 7.29 the LORD has r and forsaken the
Lam 5.22 unless you have utterly r us, and are
Ezek 5. 6 her, r my ordinances and not following
Hos 4. 6 knowledge, I r you from being a priest
Am 2. 4 because they have r the law
Mt 21.42 stone that the builders r has become
Mk 7. 9 have a fine way of r the commandment
 12.10 stone that the builders r has become
Lk 9.22 be r by the elders, chief priests, and
 10.16 r you r me, whoever r me r the one who
 17.25 suffering and be r by this generation.
 20.17 stone that the builders r has become
Jn 12.48 The one who r me and does not receive
Rom 11. 1 I ask then, has God r his people? By no

REJOICE

Lev 23.40 you shall r before the LORD your God for
Deut 16.11 R before the LORD your God —you and
1 Chr 16.10 the hearts of those who seek the LORD r.
Ps 5.11 But let all who take refuge in you r; let
 33. 1 R in the LORD, O you righteous. Praise
 35. 9 Then my soul shall r in the LORD,
 58.10 The righteous will r when they see
 85. 6 again, so that your people may r in you?
 118. 24 has made; let us r and be glad in it.
 149. 2 let the children of Zion r in their King!
Prov 5.18 blessed, and r in the wife of your youth,
 29. 2 righteous are in authority, the people r;
Isa 1.10 I will greatly r in the LORD, my whole
 35. 1 be glad, the desert shall r and blossom;
 41.16 Then you shall r in the LORD; in the
 62. 5 the bride, so shall your God r over you.
 66.10 R with Jerusalem, and be glad for her,
Jer 31.13 shall the young women r in the dance,
Lam 2.17 he has made the enemy r over you, and
Ezek 7.12 let not the buyer r, nor the seller
Joel 2.23 of Zion, be glad and r in the LORD
Hab 3.18 yet I will r in the LORD; I will exult in
Zech 9. 9 R greatly, O daughter Zion! Shout
Mt 5.12 R and be glad, for your reward is great
Lk 6.23 R in that day and leap for joy, for surely
 10.20 do not r at this, that the spirits submit
Jn 14.28 If you loved me, you would r that I am
Rom 12.15 R with those who r, weep with those
 15.10 he says, "R, O Gentiles, with his people";
1 Cor 7.30 those who r as though they were not
 13. 6 it does not r in wrongdoing, but rejoices
Phil 1.18 of false motives or true; and in that I r.
 3. 1 my brothers and sisters, r in the Lord.
 4. 4 R in the Lord always; again I will say,
1 Thess 5.16 R always, pray without ceasing, give

1 Pet 1. 8 see him now, you believe in him and r
 4.13 But r insofar as you are sharing Christ's

REJOICES (REJOICED REJOICING)

Num 10.10 Also on your days of r, at your
1 Sam 6.13 the ark, they went with r to meet it.
1 Chr 29. 9 Then the people r because these had
Esth 8.15 while the city of Susa shouted and r.
Ps 19. 8 of the LORD are right, r the heart;
Prov 11.10 goes well with the righteous, the city r;
 15.30 The light of the eyes r the heart, and
Mt 18.13 he r over it more than over the
Lk 1.47 Lord, and my spirit r in God my Savior,
 13.17 crowd was r at all the wonderful things
 15. 5 it, he lays it on his shoulders and r.
Jn 8.56 Abraham r that he would see my day;
Acts 16.34 he and his entire household r that he

REKINDLE

2 Tim 1. 6 remind you to r the gift of God that is

RELAX

Lk 12.19 goods laid up for many years; r, eat,

RELEASE (RELEASED)

Job 14.14 I would wait, until my r should come.
Mk 15. 6 he used to r a prisoner for them,
 15.15 Pilate . . . r Barabbas for them; and after
Lk 23.16 therefore have him flogged and r him."
Jn 18.39 have a custom that I r someone for you
Rev 20. 7 Satan will be r from his prison and will

RELENT (RELENTED)

2 Sam 24.16 LORD r concerning the evil, and said to
1 Chr 21.15 the LORD took note and r concerning the
Am 7. 3 The LORD r concerning this; "It shall not
Jon 3. 9 God may r and change his mind;

RELIEF

Gen 5.29 this one shall bring us r from our work
Job 32.20 I must speak, so that I may find r; I
Acts 11.29 each would send r to the believers

RELIGION

Acts 26. 5 belonged to the strictest sect of our r
1 Tim 3.16 any doubt, the mystery of our r is great:
Jas 1.27 R that is pure and undefiled before

RELIGIOUS

Acts 17.22 I see how how extremely r you are
Jas 1.26 If any think they are r, and do not

RELY (RELYING)

2 Kings 18.21 you are r now on Egypt, that broken
 18.30 let Hezekiah make you to r on the LORD
2 Chr 14.11 God, for we r on you, and in your name
 16. 7 and did not r on the LORD your God,
Isa 59. 4 they r on empty pleas, they speak lies,
2 Cor 1. 9 so that we would r not on ourselves but

REMAIN (REMAINED REMAINS)

Gen 49.24 Yet his bow r taut, and his arms were
Josh 13. 1 much of the land still r to be possessed.
1 Sam 1.22 of the LORD, and r there forever;
 5. 7 of the God of Israel must not r with us;
Ps 101. 7 No one who practices deceit shall r in
Eccl 1. 4 comes, but the earth r forever.
Jer 42.10 If you will only r in this land, then I
Hos 3. 4 Israelites shall r many days without king
Mk 14.34 deeply grieved, even to death; r here,
Lk 10. 7 R in the same house, eating and
Jn 21.22 If it is my will that he r until I come,
1 Cor 7.24 brothers and sisters, there r with God.
1 Jn 2.19 to us, they would have r with us.

REMEMBER

Gen 9.15 I will r my covenant that is between me
 41. 9 said to Pharaoh, "I r my faults today.
Ex 13. 3 "R this day on which you came out of

Ex	32.13 *R* Abraham, Isaac, and Israel, your
Lev	26.42 *r* my covenant with Jacob; I will *r* also
Num	11. 5 We *r* the fish we used to eat in Egypt
	15.39 when you see it, you will *r* all the
Deut	7.18 Just *r* what the LORD your God did to
	9. 7 *R* . . . how you provoked the LORD your
	15.15 *R* that you were a slave in the land of
	16.12 *R* that you were a slave in Egypt, and
	24.18 *R* that you were a slave in Egypt and
	32. 7 *R* the days of old, consider the years
Judg	8.34 Israelites did not *r* the LORD their God,
	16.28 "Lord GOD, *r* me and strengthen me only
1 Sam	1.11 on the misery of your servant, and *r* me,
2 Kings	20. 3 "*R* now, O LORD, I implore you, how I
1 Chr	16.12 *R* the wonderful works he has done, his
2 Chr	6.42 *R* your steadfast love for your servant
	24.22 Joash did not *r* the kindness that
Neh	1. 8 *R* the word that you commanded your
	4.14 *R* the LORD, who is great and awesome,
	5.19 *R* for my good, O my God, all that I
	6.14 *R* Tobiah and Sanballat, O my God,
	13.14 *R* me, O my God, concerning this, and
Ps	42. 6 cast down within me; therefore I *r* you
	74. 2 *R* your congregation, which you
	79. 8 Do not *r* against us the iniquities of our
	89.47 *R* how short my time is— for whatever
	105. 5 *R* the wonderful works he has done, his
	137. 7 *R*, O LORD, against the Edomites the day
Prov	31. 7 poverty, and *r* their misery no more.
Eccl	11. 8 *r* that the days of darkness will be
	12. 1 *R* your creator in the days of your
Isa	38. 3 "*R* now, O LORD, I implore you, how I
	43.18 Do not *r* the former things, or consider
	43.25 my own sake, and I will not *r* your sins.
	46. 8 *R* this and consider, recall it to mind,
Jer	2. 2 I *r* the devotion of your youth, your love
	18.20 *R* how I stood before you to speak good
Ezek	16.22 you did not *r* the days of your youth,
	20.43 There you shall *r* your ways and all the
	36.31 Then you will *r* your evil ways, and your
Hos	7. 2 consider that I *r* all their wickedness.
Am	1. 9 and did not *r* the covenant of kinship.
Mic	6. 5 O my people, *r* now what King Balak of
Hab	3. 2 it known; in wrath may you *r* mercy.
Zech	10. 9 yet in far countries they shall *r* me,
Mal	4. 4 *R* the teaching of my servant Moses, the
Mt	5.23 if you *r* that your brother or sister has
Lk	16.25 Abraham said, "Child, *r* that during your
	17.32 field must not turn back. *R* Lot's wife.
	23.42 "Jesus, *r* me when you come into your
Jn	15.20 *R* the word that I said to you, 'Servants
Gal	2.10 only one thing, that we *r* the poor,
Eph	2.11 So then, *r* that at one time you Gentiles
2 Tim	2. 8 *R* Jesus Christ, raised from the dead, a
Heb	8.12 and I will *r* their sins no more."
	13. 3 *R* those who are in prison, as though
Jude	17 beloved, must *r* the predictions of the
Rev	3. 3 *R* then what you received and heard;

REMEMBERS (REMEMBERED REMEMBERING)

Gen	8. 1 God *r* Noah and all the wild animals
	19.29 God *r* Abraham, and sent Lot out of the
	30.22 Then God *r* Rachel, and God heeded
	42. 9 Joseph also *r* the dreams that he had
Ex	2.24 God *r* his covenant with Abraham,
	6. 5 as slaves, and I have *r* my covenant.
	20.24 place where I cause my name to be *r*
Num	10. 9 so that you may be *r* before the LORD
Esth	9.28 These days should be *r* and kept
Ps	78.35 They *r* that God was their rock, the
	98. 3 He has *r* his steadfast love and
	112. 6 never be moved; they will be *r* forever.
	136. 23 It is he who *r* us in our low estate, for
Eccl	1.11 The people of long ago are not *r*, nor
Isa	65.17 former things shall not be *r* or come to
Lam	1. 7 Jerusalem *r*, in the day of her affliction
Ezek	23.19 increased her whorings, *r* the days of

Jon	2. 7 I *r* the LORD; and my prayer came to
Mt	26.75 Peter *r* what Jesus had said: "Before the
Lk	24. 8 Then they *r* his words, and returning
Rev	18. 5 as heaven, and God has *r* her iniquities.

REMEMBRANCE

Ex	28.12 Aaron shall bear their names . . . for *r*.
	39. 7 the ephod, to be stones of *r* for the sons
1 Kings	17.18 have come to me to bring my sin to *r*,
Ps	6. 5 For in death there is no *r* of you; in
Mal	3.16 a book of *r* was written before him of
Mt	26.13 she has done will be told in *r* of her."
Lk	22.19 is given for you. Do this in *r* of me."
1 Cor	11.24 body that is for you. Do this in *r* of me."

REMIND

Isa	62. 6 You who *r* the LORD, take no rest, and

REMINDER

Ex	13. 9 your hand and as a *r* on your forehead,
	17.14 "Write this as a *r* in a book and recite it
	30.16 it will be a *r* to the Israelites of the
Num	10.10 they shall serve as a *r* on your behalf

REMISSION

Deut	15. 1 year you shall grant a *r* of debts.
	31.10 seventh year, in the scheduled year of *r*,

REMNANT

2 Kings	19.30 The surviving *r* of the house of Judah
	21.14 I will cast off the *r* of my heritage, and
2 Chr	30. 6 he may turn again to the *r* of you who
Ezra	9. 8 our God, who has left us a *r*, and given
Isa	10.20 On that day the *r* of Israel and the
	37. 4 lift up your prayer for the *r* that is left."
	37.31 surviving *r* of the house of Judah shall
	46. 3 of Jacob, all the *r* of the house of Israel,
Jer	23. 3 I myself will gather the *r* of my flock
	31. 7 O LORD, your people, the *r* of Israel."
	40.11 king of Babylon had left a *r* in Judah
Am	5.15 will be gracious to the *r* of Joseph.
	9.12 that they may possess the *r* of Edom
Mic	4. 7 The lame I will make the *r*, and those
	5. 8 among the nations the *r* of Jacob,
	7.18 of the *r* of your possession?
Zeph	3.13 the *r* of Israel; they shall do no wrong
Zech	8. 6 though it seems impossible to the *r*
	8.12 cause the *r* of this people to possess
Rom	9.27 the sea, only a *r* of them will be saved;
	11. 5 time there is a *r*, chosen by grace.

REMOVE (REMOVED REMOVES)

2 Kings	23.27 LORD said, "I will *r* Judah also out of my
Ps	103. 12 the west, so far he *r* our transgressions
Prov	22.28 Do not *r* the ancient landmark that your
Isa	54.10 may depart and the hills be *r*, but
Zech	3. 9 I will *r* the guilt of this land in a single

RENDER (RENDERED)

Ps	28. 4 of their hands; *r* them their due reward.
Isa	59.18 to the coastlands he will *r* requital.
Rev	18. 6 *R* to her as she herself has *r*, and repay

RENEW (RENEWED)

1 Sam	11.14 go to Gilgal, and there *r* the kingship."
Ps	103. 5 so that your youth is *r* like the eagle's.
Isa	40.31 wait for the LORD shall *r* their strength,
Lam	5.21 may be restored; *r* our days as of old—
Zeph	3.17 with gladness, he will *r* you in his love;
Col	3.10 which is being *r* in knowledge according

RENEWAL

Mt	19.28 at the *r* of all things, when the Son of

RENOUNCE

Ps	10. 3 greedy for gain curse and *r* the LORD.

RENOWN (RENOWNED)

Gen	6. 4 heroes that were of old, warriors of *r*.

Ps 135. 13 forever, your r, O Lord, throughout all
Isa 62. 7 and makes it r throughout the earth.

REPAIR (REPAIRED REPAIRING REPAIRS)

1 Kings 18.30 First he r the altar of the Lord that had
2 Kings 12. 5 let them r the house wherever any need
12.14 given to the workers who were r the
22. 5 at the house of the Lord, r the house,
Neh 3. 4 made r. Next to them Meshullam
Prov 6.15 in a moment, damage beyond r.

REPAY

Ezek 23.49 They shall r you for your lewdness, and
Job 34.11 according to their deeds he will r them,
Ps 35.12 They r me evil for good; my soul is
62.12 Lord. For you r to all according to their
103. 10 to our sins, nor r us according to our
Jer 16.18 And I will doubly r their iniquity and
25.14 I will r them according to their deeds
50.29 R her according to her deeds; just as
Hos 4. 9 their ways, and r them for their deeds.
Joel 2.25 I will r you for the years that the
Rom 2. 6 he will r according to each one's deeds:

REPENT (REPENTED REPENTS)

1 Kings 8.47 have been taken captive, and r, and
2 Chr 6.38 if they r with all their heart and soul in
Job 42. 6 therefore I despise myself, and r in dust
Isa 1.27 those in her who r, by righteousness.
Jer 8. 6 no one r of wickedness, saying, "What
Ezek 14. 6 Thus says the Lord God: R and turn
18.30 R and turn away from all your
Mt 3. 2 "R, for the kingdom of heaven has come
4.17 proclaim, "R, for the kingdom of heaven
11.20 had been done, because they did not r.
12.41 they r at the preaching of Jonah, and
27. 3 he r and brought back the thirty pieces
Mk 6.12 out and proclaimed that all should r.
Lk 10.13 and Sidon, they would have r long ago,
11.32 they r at the preaching of Jonah,
13. 3 but unless you r you will all perish as
16.30 to them from the dead, they will r.'
Acts 2.38 Peter said to them, "R, and be baptized
3.19 R therefore, and turn to God so that
17.30 commands all people everywhere to r,
2 Tim 2.25 grant that they will r and come to know
Heb 12.17 for he found no chance to r, even
Rev 2. 5 r, and do the works you did at first. If
2.16 R then. If not, I will come to you soon
2.21 I gave her time to r, but she refuses to r
9.20 The rest of humankind . . . did not r of
16. 9 and they did not r and give him glory.

REPENTANCE

Mt 3. 8 Bear fruit worthy of r.
Mk 1. 4 proclaiming a baptism of r for the
Lk 3. 3 proclaiming a baptism of r for the
3. 8 Bear fruits worthy of r. Do not begin to
5.32 call not the righteous but sinners to r."
15. 7 righteous persons who need no r.
24.47 that r and forgiveness of sins is to be
Acts 5.31 he might give r to Israel and forgiveness
11.18 given even to the Gentiles the r that
20.21 to both Jews and Greeks about r
26.20 to God and do deeds consistent with r.
Rom 2. 4 kindness is meant to lead you to r?

REPORT (REPORTS)

Dan 11.44 r from the east and the north shall
Mt 14. 1 At that time Herod the ruler heard r
Acts 25. 2 of the Jews gave him a r against Paul.

REPROACH (REPROACHES)

Gen 30.23 and said, "God has taken away my r";
Ruth 2.15 the standing sheaves, and do not r her.
Prov 27.11 so that I may answer whoever r me.
Jer 20. 8 become for me a r and derision all day
1 Tim 3. 2 a bishop must be above r, married only

REPROOF

Prov 1.23 Give heed to my r; I will pour out my
5.12 discipline, and my heart despised r!
13.18 but one who heeds r is honored.
29.15 The rod and r give wisdom, but a

REPROVE (REPROVED)

Prov 19.25 r the intelligent, and they will gain
29. 1 who is often r, yet remains stubborn,
1 Cor 14.24 outsider who enters is r by all and

REPUTE

1 Sam 18.23 that I am a poor man and of no r?"

REQUEST

Esth 5. 3 is it Queen Esther? What is your r?
7. 3 the lives of my people—that is my r.
Job 6. 8 "O that I might have my r, and that God
Ps 21. 2 and have not withheld the r of his lips.
Dan 2.49 Daniel made r of the king, and he

REQUIRE (REQUIRED)

Deut 10.12 God r of you? Only to fear the Lord
Ezra 7.20 whatever else is r for the house of your
Ezek 3.18 but their blood I will r at your hand.
33. 6 but their blood I will r at the sentinel's
Mic 6. 8 what does the Lord of you but to do

RESCUE (RESCUED RESCUES RESCUING)

Num 35.25 the congregation shall r the slayer from
1 Sam 30.18 had taken; and David r his two wives.
1 Chr 16.35 gather and r us from among the
Ps 35.17 you look on? R me from their ravages,
37.40 The Lord helps them and r them; he r
69.14 help r me from sinking in the mire;
71. 2 your righteousness deliver me and r me;
71.23 to you; my soul also, which you have r.
136. 24 and r us from our foes, for his steadfast
Prov 24.11 if you hold back from r those taken
Isa 1.17 seek justice, r the oppressed, defend the
Jer 30. 7 for Jacob; yet he shall be r from it.
Ezek 34.10 I will r my sheep from their mouths, so
Dan 8. 4 it, and no one could r from its power;
Acts 7.25 that God through him was r them,
12.11 the Lord has sent his angel and r me
Rom 7.24 Who will r me from this body of death?
2 Cor 1.10 He who r us from so deadly a peril will
Col 1.13 He has r us from the power of darkness
2 Tim 4.18 The Lord will r me from every evil
2 Pet 2. 7 and if he r Lot, a righteous man greatly

RESERVED

2 Pet 3. 7 heavens and earth have been r for fire,

RESIDE (RESIDES RESIDING)

Lev 19.33 When an alien r with you in your land,
Num 9.14 Any alien r among you who wishes to
2 Chr 6.18 "But will God indeed r with mortals on
Job 11.14 and do not let wickedness r in your

RESIST (RESISTED)

Job 9. 4 —who has r him, and succeeded?—
Jas 4. 7 R the devil, and he will flee from you.
1 Pet 5. 9 R him, steadfast in your faith, for you

RESOLVED

Dan 1. 8 Daniel r that he would not defile

RESOURCES

Ezra 2.69 According to their r they gave to the

RESPECT

Dan 11.37 He shall pay no r to the gods of his
Mt 21.37 to them, saying, 'They will r my son.'
Mk 12. 6 to them, saying, 'They will r my son.'
Lk 20.13 beloved son; perhaps they will r him.'
Eph 5.33 and a wife should r her husband.

RESPONSIBLE

Acts 20.26 this day that I am not *r* for the blood of

REST (n)

Lev 16.31 a sabbath of complete *r* to you, and you
25. 4 there shall be a sabbath of complete *r*
Deut 3.20 When the LORD gives *r* to your kindred,
12.10 when he gives you *r* from your enemies
25.19 God has given you *r* from all your
Josh 1.15 until the LORD gives *r* to your kindred as
11.23 And the land had *r* from war.
23. 1 LORD had given *r* to Israel from all their
Judg 3.11 the land had *r* forty years. Then Othniel
5.31 in its might." And land had *r* forty years.
2 Sam 7. 1 LORD had given him *r* from all his
2 Kings 25.11 Babylon— all the *r* of the population.
1 Chr 28. 2 I had planned to build a house of *r* for
Neh 9.28 after they had *r*, they again did evil
Job 3.17 troubling, and there the weary are at *r*.
11.18 be protected and take your *r* in safety.
Ps 95.11 I swore, "They shall not enter my *r*."
116. 7 Return, O my soul, to your *r*, for the
Isa 30.15 In returning and *r* you shall be saved;
Mic 5. 3 then the *r* of his kindred shall return to
Mt 11.28 heavy burdens, and I will give you *r*.
Mk 14.41 you still sleeping and taking your *r*?
2 Cor 7. 5 Macedonia, our bodies had no *r*, but we
Heb 3.11 I swore, 'They will not enter my *r*.' "
4. 9 a sabbath *r* still remains for the people
Rev 11.13 the *r* were terrified and gave glory to

REST (RESTED RESTS)

Gen 2. 2 he *r* on the seventh day from all the
18. 4 feet, and *r* yourselves under the tree,
Ex 23.12 work, but on seventh day you shall *r*;
Lev 26.34 the land shall *r*, and enjoy its sabbath
Deut 33.12 the beloved *r* between his shoulders.
Ruth 3.18 the man will not *r*, but will settle the
2 Kings 2.15 "The spirit of Elijah *r* on Elisha."
Eccl 2.23 even at night their minds do not *r*.
Isa 11. 2 spirit of the LORD shall *r* on him, the
Dan 12.13 you, go your way, and *r*; you shall rise
Heb 4. 4 "And God *r* on the seventh day from all
Rev 14.13 "they will *r* from their labors, for their

RESTING PLACE

Isa 66. 1 build for me, and what is my *r*?
Lk 11.24 waterless regions looking for a *r*,

RESTORE (RESTORED RESTORES)

2 Kings 8. 1 the woman whose son he had *r* to life,
2 Chr 24. 4 afterward Joash decided to *r* the house
33.16 He also *r* the altar of the LORD and
Ps 23. 3 he *r* my soul. He leads me in right
80.19 *R* us, O LORD God of hosts; let your face
85. 4 *R* us again, O God of our salvation, and
Isa 1.26 I will *r* your judges as at the first, and
Jer 8.22 health of my poor people not been *r*?
33.26 For I will *r* their fortunes, and will have
Lam 5.21 *R* us to yourself, O LORD, that we may
Dan 8.14 then the sanctuary shall be *r* to its
9.25 went out to *r* and rebuild Jerusalem
Mt 12.13 He stretched it out, and it was *r*, as
17.11 is indeed coming and will *r* all things;
Lk 6.10 hand." He did so, and his hand was *r*.
Acts 1. 6 the time when you will *r* the kingdom
Gal 6. 1 the Spirit should *r* such a one in a spirit
Heb 6. 4 it is impossible to *r* again to repentance

RESTRAIN (RESTRAINED RESTRAINING)

Ex 36. 6 So people were *r* from bringing;
1 Sam 3.13 God, and he did not *r* them.
Job 7.11 I will not *r* my mouth; I will speak in
Isa 64.12 all this, will you *r* yourself, O LORD?
2 Thess 2. 6 you know what is now *r* him, so that he

RESTRAINT

Prov 14.16 from evil, but the fool throws off *r* and

Prov 29.18 is no prophecy, the people cast off *r*,
1 Cor 7.35 own benefit, not to put any *r* upon you,

RESURRECTION

Mt 22.23 came to him, saying there is no *r*;
Mk 12.18 Sadducees, who say that there is no *r*,
Lk 14.14 will be repaid at the *r* of the righteous."
20.27 those who say that there is no *r*,
Jn 5.29 who have done good, to the *r* of life,
11.25 said to her, "I am the *r* and the life.
Acts 1.22 must become a witness with us to his *r*."
2.31 David spoke of the *r* of the Messiah,
17.18 the good news about Jesus and the *r*.)
23. 6 the hope of the *r* of the dead."
24.15 that there will be a *r* of both the
Rom 6. 5 be united with him in a *r* like his.
1 Cor 15.12 of you say there is no *r* of the dead?
2 Tim 2.18 truth by claiming that the *r* has already
Heb 11.35 Women received their dead by *r*. Others
1 Pet 1. 3 a living hope through the *r* of Jesus
Rev 20. 5 years were ended.) This is the first *r*.

RETAIN

Num 36. 7 Israelites shall *r* the inheritance of their

RETRIBUTION

Jer 15.15 visit me, and bring down *r* for me on

RETURN (RETURNED RETURNING RETURNS)

Gen 16. 9 said to her, "*R* to your mistress, and
20. 7 Now then, *r* the man's wife; for he is a
31. 3 Jacob, "*R* to the land of your ancestors
32. 9 '*R* to your country and to your kindred,
44. 4 "Why have you *r* evil for good? Why
50.14 Joseph *r* to Egypt with his brothers and
Num 10.36 "*R*, O LORD of the ten thousand
Deut 4.30 you will *r* to the LORD your God and
22. 2 the owner claims it; then you shall *r* it.
30. 2 and *r* to the LORD your God, and you
Josh 22. 9 half-tribe of Manasseh *r* home, parting
1 Sam 7. 3 "If you are *r* to the LORD with all your
Job 10.21 before I go, never to *r*, to the land of
22.23 If you *r* to the Almighty, you will be
Ps 51.13 your ways, and sinners will *r* to you.
116. 7 *R*, O my soul, to your rest; for the LORD
116. 12 What shall I *r* to the LORD for all his
Eccl 12. 7 and the breath *r* to God who gave it.
Song 6.13 *R, r*, O Shulammite! *R, r*, that we may
Isa 35.10 ransomed of the LORD shall *r*, and come
44.22 like mist; *r* to me, for I have redeemed
51.11 ransomed of the LORD shall *r*, and come
55.11 it shall not *r* to me empty, but it shall
Jer 3. 1 many lovers; and would you *r* to me?
3.12 *R*, faithless Israel, says the LORD. I will
4. 1 If you *r*, O Israel, says the LORD, if you *r*
24. 7 shall *r* to me with their whole heart.
30.10 Jacob shall *r* and have quiet and ease,
Hos 2. 7 "I will go and *r* to my first husband, for
6. 1 "Come, let us *r* to the LORD; for it is he
14. 1 *R*, O Israel, to the LORD your God, for
Am 4. 8 not satisfied; yet you did not *r* to me,
Zech 1. 3 *R* to me, says the LORD of hosts, and I
Mal 3. 7 *R* to me, and I will *r* to you, says the
Lk 8.39 "*R* to your home, and declare how much
11.24 it says, 'I will *r* to my house from which
17.18 Was none of them found to *r* and give
Acts 15.16 'After this I will *r*, and I will rebuild the

REUBEN

Born, Gen 29.32; found mandrakes for Leah, Gen 30.14; rescued Joseph, Gen 37.21-22; blessed by Jacob, Gen 49.3-4.

Tribe of Reuben: blessed by Moses, Deut 33.6.

REVEAL (REVEALED REVEALING REVEALS)

Deut 29.29 but the *r* things belong to us and to our
1 Sam 3. 7 of the LORD had not yet been *r* to him.
3.21 LORD *r* himself to Samuel at Shiloh by

1 Sam	9.15	Saul came, the LORD had r to Samuel:
Ps	98.	2 he has r his vindication in the sight of
Prov	20.19	A gossip r secrets; therefore do not
Isa	22.14	LORD of hosts has r himself in my ears:
	53.	1 whom has the arm of the LORD been r?
	56.	1 will come, and my deliverance be r.
Dan	2.19	the mystery was r to Daniel in a vision
	2.28	God in heaven who r mysteries, and he
Am	3.	7 God does nothing, without r his secret
Mt	11.25	intelligent and have r them to infants;
	11.27	to whom the Son chooses to r him.
	16.17	flesh and blood has not r this to you,
Lk	2.26	It had been r to him by the Holy Spirit
	2.35	the inner thoughts of many will be r."
	10.21	intelligent and have r them to infants;
	10.22	to whom the Son chooses to r him."
	17.30	on the day that the Son of man is r.
Jn	1.31	this reason, that he might be r to Israel."
	12.38	whom has the arm of the Lord been r?"
Rom	1.17	righteousness of God is r through faith
	8.19	longing for the r of the children of God;
1 Cor	1.	7 gift as you wait for the r of our Lord
	2.10	God has r to us through the Spirit;
	3.13	because it will be r with fire, and the
Gal	1.16	grace, was pleased to r his Son to me,
Col	3.	4 is r, then you also will be r with him
2 Thess	1.	7 when the Lord Jesus is r from heaven
1 Pet	1.12	It was r to them that they were serving
	1.13	Jesus Christ will bring you when he is r.
	4.13	and shout for joy when his glory is r.
1 Jn	1.	2 this life was r, and we have seen it and
	3.	2 what we shall be has not yet been r.
	4.	9 God's love was r among us in this way:

REVEL

Ex	32.	6 down to eat and drink, and rose up to r.

REVELATION

Rom	16.25	you according to the r of the mystery
Gal	1.12	I received it through a r of Jesus Christ.
	2.	2 I went up in response to a r. Then I laid
Eph	3.	3 was made known to me by r, as I wrote

REVENGE

Judg	15.	7 not stop until I have taken r on you."
	16.28	with this one act of r I may pay back
Esth	8.13	were to be ready on that day to take r
Prov	6.34	he shows no restraint when he takes r.
Jer	20.10	against him, and take our r on him."

REVENUE

Ezra	4.13	or toll, and the royal r will be reduced.
Isa	23.	3 waters; your r was the grain of Shihor,
Rom	13.	7 taxes are due, r to whom r is due,

REVERE (REVERED)

Josh	24.14	"Now therefore r the LORD, and serve
1 Chr	16.25	to be praised; he is r above all gods.
Mal	3.16	those who r the LORD spoke with one

REVERENCE

Lev	19.30	keep my sabbaths and r my sanctuary: I
	26.	2 keep my sabbaths and r my sanctuary: I
1 Pet	3.	2 they see the purity and r of your lives.
	3.15	in you; yet do it with gentleness and r.

REVERENT

Titus	2.	3 the older women to be r in behavior,

REVILE (REVILED)

Ex	22.28	"You shall not r God, or curse a leader
2 Kings	19.22	Whom have you mocked and r? Against
Ps	74.10	to scoff? Is the enemy to r your name
Isa	65.	7 the mountains and r me upon the hills,
Mt	5.11	"Blessed are you when people r you and
1 Cor	4.12	When r, we bless; when persecuted, we
1 Pet	4.14	If you are r for the name of Christ, you

REVIVE (REVIVED REVIVING)

Gen	45.27	him, the spirit of their father Jacob r.
Judg	15.19	he drank, his spirit returned, and he r.
1 Kings	17.22	child came into him again, and he r.
Neh	4.	2 Will they r the stones out of the heaps
Ps	19.	7 law of the LORD is perfect, r the soul;
	85.	6 Will you not r us again, so that your
	119.	25 the dust; r me according to your word.
Isa	57.15	in spirit, to r the spirit of the humble,
Lam	1.11	treasures for food to r their strength.
Hos	6.	2 After two days he will r us; on the third
Hab	3.	2 In our own time r it; in our own time
Phil	4.10	at last you have r your concern for me;

REWARD

Gen	15.	1 your shield; your r shall be very great."
1 Sam	24.19	So may the LORD r you with good for
Ps	19.11	in keeping them there is great r.
	58.11	"Surely there is a r for the righteous;
	109.	5 So they r me evil for good, and hatred
Isa	40.10	his r is with him, and his recompense
Mt	5.12	be glad, for your r is great in heaven,
	5.46	who love you, what r do you have?
	6.	6 Father who sees in secret will r you.
	10.41	of a prophet will receive a prophet's r;
Mk	9.41	of Christ will by no means lose the r.
Lk	6.35	nothing in return." Your r will be great,
1 Cor	9.18	What then is my r? Just this: that in my

RIBS

Gen	2.21	then he took one of his r and closed up

RICH (RICHER)

Gen	13.	2 Now Abram was very r in livestock, in
	14.23	might not say, 'I have made Abram r.'
Ex	30.15	The r shall not give more, and the poor
2 Sam	12.	2 The r man had very many flocks and
Job	15.29	they will not be r, and their wealth will
Prov	10.22	The blessing of the LORD makes r, and
	11.24	Some give freely, yet grow all the r;
	14.20	neighbors, but the r have many friends.
	22.	2 The r and the poor have this in
	23.	4 Do not wear yourself out to get r; be
Mt	19.23	be hard for a r person to enter the
	27.57	there came a r man from Arimathea,
Mk	10.25	who is r to enter the kingdom of God.
Lk	1.53	good things, and sent the r away empty.
	6.24	"But woe to you who are r, for you have
	12.16	land of a r man produced abundantly.
	16.	1 "There was a r man who had a manager,
	16.19	"There was a r man, who was dressed in
	18.23	this, he became sad, for he was very r.
1 Cor	4.	8 you want! Already you have become r!
1 Tim	6.	9 who want to be r fall into temptation
	6.17	who are in the present age r, command
Jas	1.10	the r will disappear like a flower in the
	5.	1 you r people, weep and wail for the
Rev	2.	9 your poverty, even though you are r.
	3.17	For you say, 'I am r, I have prospered,
	18.	3 merchants of the earth have grown r

RICHES

1 Kings	10.23	excelled all the kings of the earth in r
Job	20.15	They swallow down r and vomit them
Ps	119.	14 way of your decrees as much as in all r.
Prov	11.	4 R do not profit in the day of wrath, but
	11.16	destitute, but the aggressive gain r.
	11.28	Those who trust in their r will wither,
	27.24	for r do not last forever; nor a crown for
Jer	48.36	for the r they gained have perished.
Rom	2.	4 the r of his kindness and forbearance
	11.12	if their stumbling means r for the world,
	11.33	O the depth of the r and wisdom and
Eph	3.	8 the news of the boundless r of Christ,
	3.16	according to the r of his glory, he may
Phil	4.19	need of yours according to his r in glory

RIDDLE

Judg	14.12 "Let me now put a r to you. If you can
	14.19 to those who had explained the r.

RIDICULE (RIDICULED)

Lk	14.29 to finish, all who see it begin to r him,
	16.14 money, heard all this, and they r him.

RIGHT

Gen	13. 9 then I will go to the r; or if you take the
	38.26 "She is more in the r than I, since I did
Deut	6.25 has commanded us, we will be in the r."
Judg	17. 6 people did what was r in their own eyes.
	21.25 people did what was r in their own eyes.
2 Chr	24. 2 Joash did what was r in the sight of the
Job	33.12 in this you are not r. I will answer you:
	35. 2 be just? You say, 'I am r before God.'
	36. 6 alive, but gives the afflicted their r.
	42. 7 not spoken of me what is r, as my
Ps	17. 2 come; let your eyes see the r.
	58. 1 you indeed decree what is r, you gods?
Isa	43.26 your case, so that you may be proved r.
Lam	1.18 The LORD is in the r, for I have rebelled
Hab	2. 4 Look at the proud! Their spirit is not r
Mt	20.21 one at your r hand and one at your left,
Mk	16.19n and sat down at the r hand of God.
Acts	2.33 exalted at the r hand of God, and
	7.55 of God and Jesus standing at the r hand
	10.35 him and does what is r is acceptable
2 Cor	5.13 for God; if we are in our r mind, it is for
	8.21 we intend to do what is r not only in
Eph	1.20 the dead and seated him at his r hand
Jas	4.17 who knows the r thing to do and fails to
1 Jn	2.29 everyone who does r is born of him.

RIGHTS

Prov	29. 7 The righteous know the r of the poor;
	31. 9 righteously, defend the r of the poor
Jer	5.28 they do not defend the r of the needy.
1 Cor	9.18 to make full use of my r in the gospel.

RIGHTEOUS

Gen	6. 9 Noah was a r man, blameless in his
	18.24 Suppose there are fifty r within the city;
1 Sam	24.17 "You are more r than I; for you have
1 Kings	8.32 vindicating the r by rewarding them
Job	4.17 'Can mortals be r before God? Can
	17. 9 Yet the r hold to their way, and they
	25. 4 then can a mortal be r before God?
	32. 1 Job, because he was r in his own eyes.
Ps	1. 6 the LORD watches over the way of the r,
	7.11 God is a r judge, and a God who has
	11. 3 are destroyed, what can the r do?"
	14. 5 for God is with the comapny of the r.
	37.29 The r shall inherit the land, and live in
	64.10 Let the r rejoice in the LORD, and take
	68. 3 But let the r be joyful; let them exult
	71.15 My mouth will tell of your r acts, of
	92.12 The r flourish like the palm tree, and
	97.11 Light dawns for the r, and joy for the
	119.137 You are r, O LORD, and your judgments
	141. 5 Let the r strike me; let the faithful
	143. 2 for no one living is r before you.
Prov	4.18 But the path of the r is like the light of
	10. 7 The memory of the r is a blessing, but
	10.16 The wage of the r leads to life, the gain
	10.28 The hope of the r ends in gladness, but
	12.13 their lips, but the r escape from trouble.
	12.26 The r gives good advice to friends, but
	15. 6 In the house of the r there is much
	18.10 tower; the r run into it and are safe.
	20. 7 The r walk in integrity — happy are the
	21.15 justice is done, it is a joy to the r,
	25.26 the r who give way before the wicked.
	28. 1 pursues, but the r are as bold as a lion.
	28.28 but when they perish, the r increase.
Eccl	3.17 God will judge the r and the wicked, for
Eccl	7.20 there is no one on the earth so r as to
	8.14 that there are r people who are treated
	9. 2 the same fate comes to all, to the r and
Isa	26. 2 Open the gates, so that the r nation
	53.11 r one, my servant, shall make many r,
	57. 1 The r perish, and no one takes it to
	64. 6 all our r deeds are like a filthy cloth.
Jer	33.15 time I will cause a r Branch to spring
Ezek	3.21 you warn the r not to sin, they shall
	18. 5 If a man is r and does what is lawful
	18.24 But when the r turn away from their
	18.26 When the r turn away from their
Hab	2. 4 in them, but the r live by their faith.
Mt	1.19 Her husband Joseph, being a r man and
	5.45 and sends rain on the r and the
Mk	6.20 knowing that he was a r and holy man,
Lk	1. 6 Both of them were r before God, living
	2.25 Simeon; this man was r and devout,
	18. 9 r and regarded others with contempt:
Rom	1.17 "The one who is r will live by faith."
	3.10 "There is no one who is r, not even one;
	3.26 that he himself is r and that he justifies
	5. 7 rarely will anyone die for a r person
	5.19 obedience the many will be made r.
Gal	3.11 for "The one who is r will live by faith."
Heb	10.38 delay; but my r one will live by faith.
Jas	5. 6 condemned and murdered the r one,
1 Pet	3.18 once for all, the r for the unrighteous,
	4.18 If it is hard for the r to be saved, what
2 Pet	2. 7 if he rescued Lot, a r man greatly
	2. 8 (for that r man, living among them day
Rev	19. 8 fine linen is the r deeds of the saints.

RIGHTEOUSNESS

Gen	15. 6 and the LORD reckoned it to him as r.
	18.19 way of the LORD by doing r and justice;
Deut	9. 4 "It is because of my r that the LORD has
1 Sam	26.23 The LORD rewards everyone for his r and
Job	27. 6 I hold fast my r, and will not let it go;
	29.14 I put on r, and it clothed me; my justice
	36. 3 far away and ascribe r to my Maker.
	37.23 and abundant r he will not violate.
Ps	33. 5 He loves r and justice; the earth is full
	36. 6 Your r is like the mighty mountains,
	45. 7 equity; you love r and hate wickedness.
	50. 6 The heavens declare his r, for God
	71.19 Your power and your r, O God, reach
	89.14 R and justice are the foundation of your
	89.16 name all day long, and extol your r.
	96.13 He will judge the world with r, and the
	106. 31 And that has been reckoned to him as r
	112. 3 houses, and their r endures forever.
	119.142 Your r is an everlasting r, and your law
Prov	2. 9 Then you will understand r and justice
	10. 2 do not profit, but r delivers from death.
	11.19 Whoever is steadfast in r will live, but
	12.28 In the path of r is life, in walking its
	14.34 R exalts a nation, but sin is a reproach
	16.12 evil, for the throne is established by r.
	21.21 Whoever pursues r and kindness will
Eccl	7.15 righteous people who perish in their r,
Isa	5. 7 but saw bloodshed; r, but heard a cry!
	11. 4 hear; but with r he shall judge the poor,
	32.16 and r abide in the fruitful field.
	33. 5 high; he filled Zion with justice and r;
	45.24 shall be said of me, are r and strength;
	54.14 In r you shall be established; you shall
	57.12 I will concede your r and your works,
	58. 2 as if they were a nation that practiced r
	59.17 put on r like a breastplate, and a
	61. 3 spirit. They will be called oaks of r,
	61.10 he has covered me with the robe of r,
Jer	22. 3 Act with justice and r, and deliver from
	23. 6 he will be called: "The LORD is our r."
Ezek	14.14 save only their own lives by their r,
	18.22 for the r that they have done they shall
	33.12 r of the righteous shall not save them

Dan	4.27 atone for your sins with *r*, and your
	9. 7 "*R* is on your side, O Lord, but open to
	9.18 before you on the ground of our *r*, but
Hos	10.12 Sow for yourselves *r*; reap steadfast love;
Am	5.24 and *r* like an everflowing stream.
Mt	3.15 proper for us in this way to fulfill all *r*."
	5.20 unless your *r* exceeds that of the scribes
	21.32 John came to you in the way of *r* and
Lk	1.75 fear, in holiness and *r* before him
Jn	16. 8 wrong about sin and *r* and judgment:
Acts	17.31 he will have the world judged in *r* by a
Rom	1.17 in it the *r* of God is revealed through
	3.21 law, the *r* of God has been disclosed,
	4. 3 God, and it was reckoned to him as *r*."
	4. 6 whom God reckons *r* apart from works:
	5.18 one man's act of *r* leads to justification
	6.19 present your members as slaves to *r* for
	9.30 Gentiles who did not strive for *r*, have
	10. 3 being ignorant of the *r* that comes from
1 Cor	1.30 for us wisdom from God, and *r* and
2 Cor	5.21 so that we might become the *r* of God.
Gal	3. 6 God, and it was reckoned to him as *r*."
	3.21 *r* would indeed come through the law.
Eph	4.24 likeness of God in true *r* and holiness.
Phil	3. 9 Christ, the *r* from God based on faith.
1 Tim	6.11 all this; pursue *r*, godliness, faith, love,
2 Tim	3.16 for correction, and for training in *r*,
Heb	11. 7 an heir to the *r* that is in accordance
Jas	1.20 your anger does not produce God's *r*.
	3.18 harvest of *r* is sown in peace for those

RING (RINGS)

Gen	35. 4 had, and the *r* that were in their ears;
Ex	32. 2 "Take off the gold *r* that are on the ears
Esth	3.10 the king took his signet *r* from his hand
Lk	15.22 put a *r* on his finger and sandals on his

RIOT

Mt	26. 5 the festival, or there may be a *r* among
Mk	14. 2 the festival, or there may be a *r* among

RISE (RISEN RISING)

Gen	13.17 R up, walk through the length and the
Ps	9.19 R up, O Lord! Let not mortals prevail;
	17.13 R up, O Lord, confront them, overthrow
	44.26 R up, come to our help. Redeem us for
	68. 1 Let God r up, let his enemies be
	113. 3 From the *r* of the sun to its setting the
Prov	24.16 though they fall seven times, they will *r*
Isa	30.18 therefore he will *r* up to show mercy
	52. 2 the dust, *r* up, O captive Jerusalem;
	58.10 your light *r* in the darkness and your
Mk	8.31 be killed, and after three days *r* again.
	9. 9 the Son of Man had *r* from the dead.
	9.31 days after being killed, he will *r* again."
Lk	2.34 for the falling and *r* of many in Israel,
	7.14 he said, "Young man, I say to you, *r*."
	24. 5 the dead? He is not here, but has *r*
	24. 7 crucified, and on the third day *r* again."
	24.34 "The Lord has *r* indeed, and he has
Jn	11.23 said to her, "Your brother will *r* again."
Acts	26.23 by being the first to *r* from the dead, he
Eph	5.14 "Sleeper, awake! R from the dead, and
1 Thess	4.16 and the dead in Christ will *r* first.

RITUAL

Lev	6. 9 This is the *r* of the burnt offering.
	6.14 This is the *r* of the grain offering: The
	6.25 This is the *r* of the sin offering. The sin
	7. 1 This is the *r* of the guilt offering. It is
	7.11 This is *r* of the sacrifice of the offering

RIVER (RIVERS)

Gen	2.10 A *r* flows out of Eden to water the
Ps	46. 4 There is a *r* whose streams make glad
	107. 33 He turns *r* into a desert, springs of
	137. 1 By the *r* of Babylon—there we sat
Isa	7.20 with a razor hired beyond the *R*—

Isa	33.21 for us a place of broad *r* and streams,
	41.18 open *r* on the bare heights, and
	48.18 prosperity would have been like a *r*,
	66.12 I will extend prosperity to her like a *r*,
Lam	3.48 My eyes flow with *r* of tears because of
Rev	22. 1 showed me the *r* of the water of life,

ROAD (ROADS ROADSIDE)

Mt	2.12 left for their own country by another *r*.
Mk	10.46 a blind beggar, was sitting by the *r*.
Lk	14.23 'Go out into the *r* and lanes, and

ROAR (ROARS)

1 Chr	16.32 Let the sea *r*, and all that fills it; let the
Ps	96.11 and let the earth rejoice; let the sea *r*,
Hos	11.10 go after the Lord, who *r* like a lion;
Am	1. 2 The Lord *r* from Zion, and utters his
	3. 4 Does a lion *r* in the forest, when it has

ROB (ROBBED ROBBING ROBS)

Prov	22.22 Do not *r* the poor because they are
	28.24 Anyone who *r* father or mother and
Mal	3. 8 Will anyone *r* God? Yet you are *r* me!
2 Cor	11. 8 I *r* other churches by accepting support

ROBBERS

Jer	7.11 called by my name, become a den of *r*
Mk	11.17 But you have made it a den of *r*."
Lk	10.30 fell into the hands of *r*, who stripped
Acts	19.37 men here who are neither temple *r* nor

ROBE (ROBES)

Gen	37. 3 he had made him a long *r* with sleeves.
	37.23 they stripped him of his *r*, the long *r*
	37.31 a goat, and dipped the *r* in the blood.
Ex	39.22 He also made the *r* of the ephod all of
1 Sam	15.27 Saul caught hold of the hem of his *r*,
Ps	45. 8 your *r* are all fragrant with myrrh and
	45.13 in her chamber with gold-woven *r*;
Isa	22.21 will clothe him with your *r* and bind
	61.10 covered me with the *r* of righteousness,
Mt	22.11 there who was not wearing a wedding *r*,
Lk	15.22 'Quickly, bring out a *r*—the best
Jn	13. 4 took off his outer *r*, and tied a towel
	19. 5 the crown of thorns and the purple *r*.
Rev	6.11 They were each given a white *r* and told

ROCK

Ex	17. 6 Strike the *r*, and water will come out of
Num	20. 8 command the *r* before their eyes to
	20.11 up his hand and struck the *r* twice
Deut	32. 4 The *R*, his work is perfect, and all his
	32.31 their *r* is not as our *R*; our enemies are
1 Sam	2. 2 besides you; there is no *R* like our God.
2 Sam	22. 2 "The Lord is my *r*, my fortress, and my
Ps	18. 2 The Lord is my *r*, and my fortress, and
	18.31 And who is a *r* besides our God?—
	27. 5 of his tent; he will set me high on a *r*.
	28. 1 Lord, I call; my *r*, do not refuse to hear
	40. 2 and set my feet upon a *r*, making my
	61. 2 Lead me to the *r* that is higher than I;
	62. 6 He alone is my *r* and my salvation, my
	71. 3 Be to me a *r* of refuge, a strong fortress,
	78.16 He made streams come out of the *r*,
	89.26 my God, and the *R* of my salvation!'
	92.15 that the Lord is upright; he is my *r*,
	105. 41 He opened the *r*, and water gushed out;
	114. 8 who turns the *r* into a pool of water,
Isa	17.10 not remembered the *R* of your refuge;
	32. 2 the shade of a great *r* in a weary land.
	51. 1 to the *r* from which you were hewn,
Jer	23.29 and like a hammer that breaks a *r* in
Mt	7.24 a wise man who built his house on *r*.
	16.18 and on this *r* I will build my church,
Lk	6.48 deeply and laid the foundation on *r*;
1 Cor	10. 4 they drank from the spiritual *r* that

ROD

Ps	2. 9 You shall break them with a r of iron,
Prov	13.24 who spare the r hate their children,
	22.15 boy, but the r of discipline drives it far
	23.14 If you beat them with the r, you will
	26. 3 donkey, and a r for the back of fools.
Isa	10. 5 Assyria, the r of my anger— the club in
1 Cor	4.21 Am I to come to you with a r, or with

ROLL

Mk	16. 3 "Who will r away the stone for us from
Heb	1.12 like a cloak you will r them up, and like

ROMAN (ROMANS)

Jn	11.48 and the R will come and destroy both
Acts	16.21 that are not lawful for us as R to adopt
	22.25 for you to flog a R citizen who is
	25.16 not the custom of the R to hand over

ROME

Acts	2.10 Cyrene, and visitors from R, both Jews
	18. 2 had ordered all Jews to leave R.
	23.11 so you must bear witness also at R."
	28.16 When we came into R, Paul was
Rom	1. 7 To all God's beloved in R, who are in
	1.15 the gospel to you also who are in R.
2 Tim	1.17 he arrived in R, he eagerly searched

ROOF

Gen	6.16 Make a r for the ark, and finish it to a
Mk	2. 4 they removed the r above him; and after
Acts	10. 9 Peter went up on the r to pray. He

ROOM

Ps	4. 1 You gave me r when I was in distress.
Mt	6. 6 whenever you pray, go into your r and
Lk	14.22 has been done, and still there is r.'
	22.12 He will show you a large r upstairs,
Acts	1.13 they went up to the r upstairs where
Philem	22 —prepare a guest r for me, for I am

ROOT (ROOTED)

1 Kings	14.15 he will r up Israel out of this good land
Prov	2.22 land, and the treacherous will be r out
	12. 3 but the r of the righteous will never be
Isa	11.10 On that day the r of Jesse shall stand
	37.31 Judah shall again take r downward, and
	40.24 scarcely has their stem taken r in the
Mt	3.10 ax is lying at the r of the trees; every
Rom	15.12 Isaiah says, "The r of Jesse shall come,
Eph	3.17 as you are being r and grounded in love.
Col	2. 7 r and built up in him and established in
1 Tim	6.10 For the love of money is the r of all
Rev	22.16 I am the r and the descendant of David,

ROPE (ROPES)

Josh	2.15 she let them down by a r through a
Jer	38.13 they drew Jeremiah up by the r and

ROSE

Song	2. 1 I am a r of Sharon, a lily of the valleys.

ROUSE

Joel	3.12 Let the nations r themselves, and come

ROYAL

Esth	4.14 perhaps you have come to r dignity for

RUDE

1 Cor	13. 5 not envious or boastful or arrogant or r.

RUIN (RUINS)

Deut	13.16 It shall remain a perpetual r, never to
Ps	35. 8 Let r come upon them unawares. And
	89.40 walls; you have laid his strongholds in r.
Prov	19. 3 One's own folly leads to r, yet the heart
Isa	25. 2 the city a heap, the fortified city a r;
Jer	25.11 This whole land shall become a r and a
	46.19 Memphis shall become a waste, a r,

Ezek	21.27 A r, a r, a r—I will make it! (Such has
Am	6. 6 but are not grieved over the r of Joseph!

RULE (n)

1 Cor	7.17 you. This is my r in all the churches.
Gal	6.16 As for those who will follow this r—
Eph	1.21 far above all r and authority and power

RULE (RULED RULES) (v)

Gen	1.16 day and the lesser light to r the night
	3.16 your husband, and he shall r over you."
Deut	15. 6 you will r over many nations, but they
Judg	8.23 not r over you; the LORD will r over you."
2 Chr	1.10 people, for who can r this great people
	9.26 He r over all the kings from the
Ps	22.28 to the LORD, and he r over the nations.
	89. 9 You r the raging of the sea; when its
	106. 41 that those who hated them r over them.
	110. 2 scepter. R in the midst of your foes.
Prov	19.10 in luxury, much less for a slave to r
Isa	3. 4 princes, and babes shall r over them.
	26.13 lords besides you have r over us, but we
	40.10 with might, and his arm r for him;
Ezek	34. 4 force and harshness you have r them.
Dan	11. 3 arise, who shall r with great dominion
Mic	5. 2 forth for me one who is to r in Israel,
Lk	19.14 saying, 'We do not want this man to r
Rev	2.27 to r them with an iron rod, as when
	12. 5 male child, who is to r all the nations
	19.15 he will r them with a rod of iron; he

RULER (RULERS)

Gen	45. 8 house and r over all the land of Egypt.
	45.26 Joseph is still alive! He is even r over
Lev	4.22 When a r sins, doing unintentionally
Ps	2.10 be wise; be warned, O r of the earth.
Prov	6. 7 Without having any chief or officer or r,
	23. 1 When you sit down to eat with a r,
	29.12 If a r listens to falsehood, all his
Isa	33.22 The LORD is our judge, the LORD is our r,
	40.23 makes the r of the earth as nothing.
Jer	2. 8 know me; the r transgressed against me;
Jn	12.31 the r of this world will be driven out.
	16.11 r of this world has been condemned.
Acts	4. 8 Spirit said to them, "R of the people
	7.10 appointed him r over Egypt and over all
Rom	13. 3 For r are not a terror to good conduct,
1 Cor	2. 8 None of the r of this age understood
	15.24 after he has destroyed every r and every
Rev	1. 5 dead, and the r of kings of the earth.

RUMOR (RUMORS)

2 Kings	19. 7 he shall hear a r and return to his own
Isa	37. 7 so that he shall hear a r, and return to
Mt	24. 6 you will hear of wars and r of wars; see

RUN (RAN RUNNING RUNS)

Gen	16. 6 with her, and she r away from her.
Neh	6.11 "Should a man like me r away? Would a
Ps	119. 32 I r the way of your commandments, for
	147. 15 to the earth; his word r swiftly.
Jer	5. 1 R to and fro through the streets of
Dan	12. 4 Many shall be r back and forth, and evil
Mt	28. 8 and great joy, and r to tell his disciples.
Jn	20. 2 So she r and went to Simon Peter and
Gal	2. 2 that I was not r, or had not r, in vain.
	5. 7 You were r well; who prevented you
Heb	12. 1 let us r with perseverance the race that

RUNNER (RUNNERS)

Job	9.25 "My days are swifter than a r; they flee
Hab	2. 2 in plain tablets, so that a r may read it.
1 Cor	9.24 in a race the r all compete, but only

RUTH

Ruth	1. 4 Orpah, and the name of the other R.
	2. 2 R the Moabite said to Naomi, "Let me
	3. 9 "I am R, your servant; spread your cloak

Ruth 4.13 Boaz took *R* and she became his wife.
Mt 1. 5 Boaz the father of Obed by *R*, and Obed

S

SABBATH (SABBATHS)

Ex 16.26 day, which is a *s*, there will be none."
 20. 8 Remember the *s* day, and keep it holy.
 31.16 shall keep the *s*, observing the *s*
Lev 16.31 a *s* of complete rest to you, and you
 19.30 You shall keep my *s* and reverence my
 25. 4 there shall be a *s* of complete rest for
 26. 2 You shall keep my *s* and reverence my
Num 15.32 a man gathering sticks on the *s* day.
Deut 5.12 Observe the *s* day and keep it holy, as
Neh 13.17 that you are doing, profaning the *s* day?
Isa 56. 2 who keeps the *s*, not profaning it, and
 58.13 If you refrain from trampling the *s*, from
 66.23 from *s* to *s*, all flesh shall come to
Jer 17.21 do not bear a burden on the *s* day or
Ezek 20.12 I gave them my *s*, as a sign between me
 44.24 festivals, and they shall keep my *s* holy.
Mt 12. 1 went through the grainfields on the *s*;
 24.20 flight may not be in winter or on a *s*.
 28. 1 After the *s*, as the first day of the week
Mk 2.23 One *s* he was going through the
 3. 2 to see if he would cure him on the *s*,
 16. 1 When the *s* was over, Mary Magdalene,
Lk 4.16 he went to the synagogue on the *s* day,
 6. 1 One *s* while Jesus was going through
 13.14 because Jesus had cured on the *s*,
 14. 1 to eat a meal on the *s*, they were
Jn 5.10 "It is the *s*; it is not lawful for you to
 7.23 If a man receives circumcision on the *s*
 9.14 was a *s* day when Jesus made the mud
Acts 16.13 On the *s* day we went outside the gate

SACKCLOTH

1 Kings 20.32 So they tied *s* around their waists, put
 21.27 he fasted, lay in the *s*, and went about
2 Kings 19. 1 tore his clothes, covered himself with *s*,
Esth 4. 1 tore his clothes and put on *s* and ashes,
Ps 35.13 for me, when they were sick, I wore *s*;
 69.11 When I made *s* my clothing, I became a
Isa 20. 2 loose the *s* from your loins and take the
 37. 1 tore his clothes, covered himself with *s*,
Jon 3. 5 and everyone, great and small, put on *s*.
Lk 10.13 long ago, sitting in *s* and ashes.

SACRED

Ezek 44. 8 have not kept charge of my *s* offerings;
2 Tim 3.15 you have known the *s* writings

SACRIFICE (SACRIFICES) (n)

1 Sam 15.22 to obey is better than *s*, and to heed
1 Chr 29.21 the next day they offered *s* and burnt
Ps 40. 6 S and offering you do not desire, but
 51.16 For you have no delight in *s*; if I were
Prov 15. 8 *s* of the wicked is an abomination to
 21. 3 is more acceptable to the Lord than *s*.
 21.27 The *s* of the wicked is an abomination;
Eccl 5. 1 is better than the *s* offered by fools;
Isa 1.11 What to me is the multitude of your *s*?
Jer 6.20 not acceptable, nor are your *s* pleasing
Dan 9.27 he shall make *s* and offering cease;
Hos 6. 6 For I desire steadfast love and not *s*,
 8.13 Though they offer choice *s*, though they
Am 4. 4 bring your *s* every morning, your tithes
Mal 1. 8 When you offer blind animals in *s*, is it
Mt 9.13 what this means, 'I desire mercy, not *s*.'
 12. 7 this means, 'I desire mercy, and not *s*,'
Mk 12.33 than all whole burnt offerings and *s*."
Lk 2.24 they offered a *s* according to what is
Rom 12. 1 present your bodies as a living *s*, holy
 3.25 Christ, whom God put forward as a *s*
Eph 5. 2 for us, a fragrant offering and *s* to God.
Phil 4.18 offering, a *s* acceptable and pleasing
Heb 2.17 to make a *s* of atonement for the sins of

Heb 9.26 age to remove sin by the *s* of himself.
 10.12 offered for all time a single *s* for sins,
1 Jn 2. 2 he is the atoning *s* for our sins, and not
 4.10 his Son to be the atoning *s* for our sins.

SACRIFICE (SACRIFICED) (v)

Ex 3.18 wilderness, so that we may *s* to the
Deut 15.21 you shall not *s* it to the Lord your God;
1 Kings 13. 2 he shall *s* on you the priests of the high
Ps 54. 6 With a freewill offering I will *s* to you; I
Eccl 9. 2 to those who *s* and those who do not *s*.
Jon 2. 9 the voice of thanksgiving will *s* to you;
1 Cor 5. 7 our paschal lamb, Christ, has been *s*.
 10.20 that what pagans *s* they *s* to demons

SACRILEGE

Mt 24.15 "So when you see the desolating *s*
Mk 13.14 when you see the desolating *s* set up

SADDUCEES

Mt 3. 7 Pharisees and *S* coming for baptism,
 16. 1 The Pharisees and *S* came, and to test
 16. 6 of the yeast of the Pharisees and *S*."
 22.23 The same day some *S* came to him,
Acts 4. 1 and the *S* came to them, much annoyed
 5.17 sect of the *S*), being filled with jealousy,
 23. 6 Paul noticed that some were *S* and

SAFE (SAFELY)

Ps 18.32 me with strength, and made my way *s*.
 119.117 Hold me up, that I may be *s* and have
Acts 23.24 Paul to ride, and take him *s* to Felix

SAFETY

Ps 4. 8 alone, O Lord, make me lie down in *s*.
 12. 5 "I will place them in the *s* for which
Isa 14.30 will graze, and the needy lie down in *s*;

SAGES

Isa 19.12 Where now are your *s*? Let them tell

SAIL (SAILED)

Acts 13. 4 and from there they *s* to Cyprus.
 18.18 and *s* for Syria, accompanied by Priscilla
 27. 1 was decided that we were to *s* for Italy,

SAINTS (SAINTS')

Mt 27.52 bodies of the *s* who had fallen asleep
Acts 9.13 how much evil he has done to your *s* in
 26.10 I not only locked up many of the *s* in
Rom 12.13 Contribute to the needs of the *s*; extend
 15.25 to Jerusalem in a ministry to the *s*;
1 Cor 1. 2 called to be *s*, together with all those
 6. 2 know that the *s* will judge the world?
2 Cor 9. 1 to you about the ministry for the *s*,
Eph 5. 3 among you, as is proper among *s*.
Col 1.26 but has now been revealed to his *s*.
1 Tim 5.10 shown hospitality, washed the *s* feet,
Philem 7 the hearts of the *s* have been refreshed
Rev 8. 3 with the prayers of all the *s* on the
 13. 7 it was allowed to make war on the *s*
 14.12 is a call for the endurance of the *s*,
 16. 6 they shed the blood of *s* and prophets,
 20. 9 surrounded the camp of the *s* and the

SALT (SALTED)

Gen 19.26 back, and she became a pillar of *s*.
Mt 5.13 "You are the *s* of the earth; but if the
Mk 9.49 For everyone will be *s* with fire.
Lk 14.34 "S is good; but if *s* has lost its taste,

SALVATION

Gen 49.18 I wait for your *s*, O Lord.
Ex 15. 2 and he has become my *s*; this is my
2 Sam 22. 3 my shield and the horn of my *s*, my
1 Chr 16.23 Tell of his *s* from day to day. Declare
Ps 13. 5 love; my heart shall rejoice in your *s*.
 27. 1 The Lord is my light and my *s*; whom
 35. 3 pursuers; say to my soul, "I am your *s*!"

Ps	37.39 The s of the righteous is from the LORD;
	50.23 the right way I will show the s of God."
	51.12 Restore to me the joy of your s, and
	62. 1 waits in silence; from him comes my s.
	70. 4 Let those who love your s say evermore,
	91.16 will satisfy them, and show them my s.
	116. 13 I will lift up the cup of s and call on
	118. 14 and my might; he has become my s.
	119.123 My eyes fail from watching for your s,
Isa	12. 2 God is my s; I will trust, and will not be
	33. 2 morning, our s in the time of trouble.
	45. 8 the earth open, that s may spring up,
	45.17 is saved by the LORD with everlasting s;
	51. 6 but my s will be forever, and my
	52. 7 who announces s, who says to Zion,
	56. 1 for soon my s will come, and my
	60.18 you shall call your walls S, and your
Jer	3.23 in the LORD our God is the s of Israel.
Lam	3.26 that one should wait quietly for the s of
Mic	7. 7 LORD, I will wait for the God of my s;
Hab	3.18 LORD; I will exult in the God of my s.
Lk	1.77 give knowledge of s to his people by the
	2.30 for my eyes have seen your s,
	3. 6 and all flesh shall see the s of God."
	19. 9 "Today s has come to this house,
Jn	4.22 what we know, for s is from the Jews.
Acts	4.12 There is s in no one else, for there is no
	13.47 may bring s to the ends of the earth.' "
	28.28 this s of God has been sent to the
Rom	1.16 the gospel; it is the power of God for s
	13.11 For s is nearer to us now than when we
2 Cor	6. 2 time; see, now is the day of s.
Eph	1.13 the word of truth, the gospel of your s,
Phil	1.28 of their destruction, but of your s.
	2.12 work out your own s with fear and
1 Thess	5. 9 for obtaining s through our Lord Jesus
Heb	1.14 the sake of those who are to inherit s?
1 Pet	1. 9 of your faith, the s of your souls.
2 Pet	3.15 regard the patience of our Lord as s. So
Jude	3 write to you about the s we share, I find
Rev	7.10 "S belongs to our God who is seated on
	12.10 "Now have come the s and the power
	19. 1 "Hallelujah! S and glory and power to

SAMARIA

1 Kings	16.24 He bought the hill of S from Shemer for
	16.29 Ahab . . . reigned over Israel in S
2 Kings	17. 6 king of Assyria captured S; he carried
Isa	7. 9 The head of Ephraim is S, and the head
Ezek	16.46 Your elder sister is S, who lived with
Hos	8. 5 Your calf is rejected, O S. My anger
Mic	1. 6 Therefore I will make S a heap in the
Lk	17.11 the region between S and Galilee.
Jn	4. 4 But he had to go through S. So he came
Acts	1. 8 in Jerusalem, in all Judea and S,
	8. 5 Philip went down to the city of S, and

SAMARITAN (SAMARITANS)

Mt	10. 5 and enter no town of the S, but go
Jn	4. 7 A S woman came to draw water , and
Acts	8.25 good news to many villages of the S.

SAME

Eccl	9. 2 is vanity, since the s fate comes to all,

SAMSON

Judg	13.24 woman bore a son, and named him S.
	14. 1 Once S went to Timnah, and at
	15. 1 S went to visit his wife, bringing along a
	16. 1 Once S went to Gaza, where he saw a
	16.30 Then S said, "Let me die with the
Heb	11.32 fail me to tell of Gideon, Barak, S

SAMUEL

Born, 1 Sam 1.19-20; dedicated to God, 1 Sam 1.21-28; ministered before God, 1 Sam 2.11,18-21; called, 1 Sam 3.1-18; judged Israel, 1 Sam 7.3-17; warned Israel for requesting a king, 1 Sam 8.10-18; anointed Saul king, 1

	Sam 10.1-8; reasoned with Israel, 1 Sam 12; reproved Saul, 1 Sam 13.8-15; 15.10-23; hewed Agag in pieces, 1 Sam 15.33; anointed David, 1 Sam 16.1-13; died, 1 Sam 25.1; 28.3.
Jer	15. 1 Though Moses and S stood before me,
Acts	3.24 from S and those after him, also
	13.20 judges until the time of the prophet S.

SANCTIFICATION

1 Cor	1.30 righteousness and s and redemption, in
1 Thess	4. 3 this is the will of God, your s: that you

SANCTIFY (SANCTIFIED SANCTIFIES)

Ex	29.43 there, and it will be s by my glory;
Lev	22.32 my holy name, that I may be s among
Josh	3. 5 "S yourselves; for tomorrow the LORD
	7.13 Proceed to s the people, and say, 'S
1 Chr	15.14 the priests and the Levites s themselves
2 Chr	29. 5 to me, Levites! S yourselves, and s
Isa	29.23 in his midst, they will s my name;
Ezek	20.12 they might know that I the LORD s them.
Joel	1.14 S a fast, call a solemn assembly. Gather
Jn	17.17 to the world. S them in the truth; your
Acts	26.18 and a place among those who are s by
1 Cor	1. 2 to those who are s in Christ Jesus,
	6.11 you were washed, you were s, you were
1 Thess	5.23 May the God of peace himself s you
Heb	2.11 the one who s and those who are s
	9.13 of the ashes of a heifer, s those
	10.10 have been s through the offering of the
	10.14 perfected for all time those who are s.
	13.12 order to s the people by his own blood.

SANCTUARY

Ex	25. 8 have them make me a s, so that I may
	36. 1 in the construction of the s shall work
Lev	12. 4 any holy thing, or come into the s,
	21.12 outside the s and thus profane the s of
1 Chr	22.19 Go and build the s of the LORD God so
	28.10 chosen you to build a house as the s;
2 Chr	26.18 Go out of the s; for you have done
Ps	20. 2 May he send you help from the s, and
	63. 2 So I have looked upon you in the s,
	73.17 task, until I went into the s of God;
	74. 7 They set your s on fire; they desecrated
	114. 2 Judah became God's s, Israel his
Isa	8.14 He will become a s, a stone one strikes
	16.12 when he comes to his s to pray, he will
Jer	17.12 from the beginning, the shrine of our s!
Lam	1.10 has even seen the nations invade her s,
	2. 7 has scorned his altar, disowned his s;
Ezek	5.11 because you have defiled my s with all
	11.16 yet I have been a s to them for a little
	23.38 they have defiled my s on the same day
	24.21 I will profane my s, the pride of your
	48. 8 the west, with the s in the middle of it.
Dan	8.14 then the s shall be restored to its
	9.17 your face shine upon your desolate s.
Am	7.13 prophesy at Bethel, for it is the king's s;
Mal	2.11 Judah has profaned the s of the LORD,
Heb	9. 1 regulations for worship and an earthly s.
	9. 8 way into the s has not yet been
	10.19 confidence to enter the s by the blood

SAND

Gen	22.17 as . . . s that is on the seashore."
	32.12 make your offspring as the s of the sea,"
Prov	27. 3 is heavy, and s is weighty, but a fool's
Isa	10.22 people Israel were like the s of the sea,
Hos	1.10 the people of Israel shall be like the s
Mt	7.26 man who built his house upon the s;
Rom	9.27 children of Israel were like the s of the
Heb	11.12 and as the innumerable grains of s by

SANDAL (SANDALS)

Ex	3. 5 Remove the s from your feet, for the
Deut	25. 9 pull his s off his foot, spit in his face,

Josh	5.15	"Remove the s from your feet, for the
Ruth	4. 7	took off his s and gave it to the other;
Mk	1. 7	down and untie the thong of his s.
	6. 9	but to wear s and not to put on two
Lk	3.16	not worthy to untie the thong of his s.
	15.22	a ring on his finger and s on his feet.
Acts	7.33	'Take off the s from your feet, for the
	13.25	not worthy to untie the thong of the s

SARAH (SARAH'S SARAI)

Wife of Abraham, Gen 11.29; barren, Gen 11.30; Sarai and Hagar, Gen 16.1-6; represented as Abraham's sister, Gen 12.10-20; 20.1-18; name changed to Sarah, Gen 17.15; laughed at the LORD's promise, Gen 18.9-15; bore Isaac, Gen 21.1-8; jealous of Ishmael, Gen 21.9-13; died at Hebron, Gen 23.2; buried in Machpelah, Gen 23.19.

Gen	11.30	Now S was barren; she had no child.
	16. 1	S, Abram's wife, bore him no children.
	18. 9	"Where is your wife S?" And he said,
	21. 1	LORD dealt with S as he had said, and
Rom	4.19	considered the barrenness of S womb.
Heb	11.11	too old —and S herself was barren—
1 Pet	3. 6	Thus S obeyed Abraham, and called

SATAN

1 Chr	21. 1	S stood up against Israel, and incited
Job	1. 6	the LORD, and S also came among them.
	2. 1	and S also came among them to present
Zech	3. 1	S standing at his right hand to accuse
Mt	4.10	Jesus said to him, "Away with you, S!"
	12.26	If S casts out S, he is divided against
	16.23	and said to Peter, "Get behind me, S!"
Lk	10.18	to them, "I watched S fall from heaven
Acts	5. 3	asked, "Why has S filled your heart
2 Cor	2.11	so we may not be outwitted by S; for we
	11.14	Even S disguises himself as an angel of
Rev	2. 9	and are not, but are a synagogue of S.
	12. 9	serpent, who is called the Devil and S,
	20. 2	ancient serpent, who is the Devil and S,

SATISFACTION

Isa	53.11	he shall find s through his knowledge.

SATISFY (SATISFIED SATISFIES)

Josh	22.30	and the Manassites spoke, they were s.
Ps	22.26	The poor shall eat and be s; those who
	65. 4	be s with the goodness of your house,
	90.14	S us in the morning with your steadfast
	104. 13	the earth is s with the fruit of your
	107. 9	For he s the thirsty, and the hungry he
	132. 15	provisions; I will s its poor with bread.
Prov	27.20	never s, and human eyes are never s.
	30.15	give," they cry. Three things are never s;
Eccl	1. 8	the eye is not s with seeing, or the ear
	5.10	of money will not be s with money;
Isa	55. 2	your labor for that which does not s?
	58.11	and s your needs in parched places,
Jer	31.14	my people shall be s with my bounty,
	31.25	I will s the weary, and all who are faint
Ezek	7.19	They shall not s their hunger or fill
Mic	6.14	You shall eat, but not be s, and there
Mt	28.14	we will s him and keep you out of
Lk	3.14	accusations, and be s with your wages."
Jn	14. 8	show us the Father, and we will be s."
Acts	27.38	they had s their hunger, they lightened
Phil	4.19	my God will fully s every need of yours

SAUL (King of Israel)

Son of Kish, 1 Sam 9.1-2; met Samuel, 1 Sam 9.5-24; anointed by Samuel, 1 Sam 10.1-8; prophesied with the prophets, 1 Sam 10.9-13; chosen king at Mizpah, 1 Sam 10.20-24; defeated the Ammonites, 1 Sam 11.5-11; made king in Gilgal, 1 Sam 11.12-15; reproved for his burnt offering, 1 Sam 13.8-15; built an altar, 1 Sam 14.35; rejected as king, 1 Sam 15.11-30; refreshed by David's harp playing, 1 Sam 16.14-23; became jealous of David, 1 Sam 18.6-30; sought to kill David, 1 Sam 19.1-17;

killed the priests of Nob, 1 Sam 22.11-19; spared by David, 1 Sam 24.1-7; 26.1-12; consulted the woman of Endor, 1 Sam 28.3-25; died and buried, 1 Sam 31.

Acts	13.21	asked for a king; and God gave them S

SAUL (Paul)

Acts	13. 9	But S, also known as Paul, filled with

SAVE

Deut	23.14	to s you and to hand over your enemies.
1 Sam	4. 3	may come among us and s us from the
	17.47	the LORD does not s by sword and spear;
2 Kings	19.19	So now, O LORD our God, s us, I pray
	19.34	I will defend this city to s it, for my
1 Chr	16.35	Say also: "S us, O God of our salvation,
2 Chr	20. 9	in our distress, and you will hear and s.'
Ps	28. 9	O s your people, and bless your
	69.35	God will s Zion and rebuild the cities of
	76. 9	judgment, to s all the oppressed
	86. 2	to you; s your servant who trusts
	116. 4	of the LORD: "O LORD, I pray, s my life!"
Prov	2.12	It will s you from the way of evil, from
	6. 5	s yourself like a gazelle from the hunter,
	23.14	them with a rod, you will s their lives
Isa	25. 9	waited for him, so that he might s us.
	36.18	you by saying, The LORD will s us.
	37.20	God, s us from his hand, so that all the
	44.17	it and says, "S me, for you are my god!"
	47.15	own paths; there is no one to s you.
	63. 1	I, announcing vindication, mighty to s."
Jer	15.20	for I am with you to s you and deliver
	17.14	be healed; s me, and I shall be saved;
	30.10	I am going to s you from far away, and
	39.17	I will s you on that day, says the LORD,
	46.27	I am going to s you from far away, and
	51. 6	of Babylon, s your lives, each of you!
Ezek	3.18	their wicked way in order to s their life,
	7.19	Their silver and gold cannot s them on
	34.22	I will s my flock, and they will no
Hos	13.10	now is your king, that he may s you?
	14. 3	Assyria shall not s us; we will not ride
Am	2.14	strength, nor shall the mighty s their
Hab	3.13	You came forth to s your people, to s
Zeph	3.19	And I will s the lame and gather the
Mt	1.21	name him Jesus, for he will s his people
	8.25	saying, "Lord, s us! We are perishing!"
	14.30	to sink, he cried out, "Lord, s me!"
	16.25	who want to s their life will lose it,
	18.11n	For the Son of man came to s the lost
	27.40	and build it in three days, s yourself!
Mk	8.35	those who want to s their life will lose
	15.30	s yourself, and come down from the
Lk	9.24	those who want to s their life will lose
	9.56n	lives of human beings but to s them."
1 Cor	7.16	you might s your husband. Husband, for
	9.22	that I might by all means s some.
1 Tim	1.15	came into the world to s sinners—
	4.16	will s both yourself and your hearers.
Heb	7.25	all time to s those who approach God
	9.28	but to s those who are eagerly waiting
Jas	5.20	will s the sinner's soul from death
Jude	23	s others by snatching them out of the

SAVES (SAVED SAVING)

Ex	14.30	Thus the LORD s Israel that day from
Num	10. 9	your God and be s from your enemies.
Deut	33.29	Who is like you, a people s by the LORD,
1 Sam	14. 6	nothing can hinder the LORD from s by
2 Sam	22. 4	praised, and I am s from my enemies.
1 Kings	1.29	"As the LORD lives, who has s my life
2 Chr	32.22	So the LORD s Hezekiah and the
Job	5.15	But he s the needy from the sword of
Ps	18. 3	so I shall be s from my enemies.
	34. 6	and was heard by the LORD, and was s
	80. 3	let your face shine, that we may be s.
	106. 8	Yet he s them for his name's sake, so
	107. 19	and he s them from their distress;

Isa	30.15 In returning and rest you shall be *s*;
Jer	8.20 the summer is ended, and we are not *s*."
	23. 6 In his days Judah will be *s* and Israel
	33.16 In those days Judah will be *s* and
Ezek	3.19 iniquity; but you will have *s* your life.
Ob	21 have been *s* shall go up to Mount Zion
Mic	6. 5 you may know the *s* acts of the LORD."
Mt	19.25 and said, "Then who can be *s*?"
	24.13 one who endures to the end will be *s*.
Mk	10.26 to one another, "Then who can be *s*?"
Lk	7.50 to the woman, "Your faith has *s* you; go
	13.23 asked him, "Lord, will only a few be *s*?"
	18.26 who heard it said, "Then who can be *s*?"
	23.35 "He *s* others; let him save himself if he
Jn	5.34 I say these things so that you may be *s*.
Acts	2.21 on the name of the Lord shall be *s*.'
	11.14 and your entire household will be *s*.'
	15. 1 the custom of Moses, you cannot be *s*."
	15.11 that we will be *s* through the grace of
	16.30 and said, "Sirs, what must I do to be *s*?"
	27.31 men stay in the ship, you cannot be *s*."
Rom	5. 9 we be *s* through him from the wrath
	8.24 For in hope we were *s*. Now hope that
	10. 1 to God for them is that they may be *s*.
	10. 9 raised him from the dead, you will be *s*.
	11.26 And so all Israel will be *s*; as it is
1 Cor	1.18 but to us who are being *s* it is the
	3.15 the builder will be *s*, but only as
	5. 5 so that his spirit may be *s* in the day of
	10.33 but that of many, so that they may be *s*.
	15. 2 through which you also are being *s*, if
1 Thess	2.16 to the Gentiles so that they may be *s*.
2 Tim	1. 9 of God, who *s* us and called us with a
Titus	3. 5 he *s* us, not because of any works of
1 Pet	3.20 is, eight persons, were *s* through water.
	4.18 If it is hard for the righteous to be *s*,
Jude	5 once for all *s* a people out of the land

SAVIOR

2 Kings	13. 5 the LORD gave Israel a *s*, so that they
Ps	106. 21 They forgot God, their *S*, who had done
Isa	19.20 he will send them a *s*, and will defend
	43. 3 God, the Holy One of Israel, your *S*.
	43.11 the LORD, and besides me there is no *s*.
	45.21 a righteous God and *S*; there is no one
	60.16 shall know that I, the LORD, am your *S*
Jer	14. 8 O hope of Israel, its *s* in time of
Hos	13. 4 but me, and besides me there is no *s*.
Lk	1.47 and my spirit rejoices in God my *S*,
	1.69 He has raised up a mighty *s* for us in
	2.11 is born this day in the city of David a *S*,
Acts	13.23 God has brought to Israel a *S*, Jesus, as
1 Tim	2. 3 acceptable in the sight of God our *S*,
	4.10 living God, who is the *S* of all people,
1 Jn	4.14 has sent his Son as the *S* of the world.
Jude	25 only God, our *S*, through Jesus Christ

SAY (SAYING)

Lk	5. 5 nothing. Yet if you *s* so, I will let down
1 Tim	1.15 The *s* is sure and worthy of full
	4. 9 The *s* is sure and worthy of full

SCALES

Prov	16.11 Honest balances and *s* are the LORD's;
	20.23 to the LORD, and false *s* are not good.
Dan	5.27 you have been weighed on the *s*
Mic	6.11 Can I tolerate wicked *s* and a bag of
Rev	6. 5 Its rider held a pair of *s* in his hand,

SCARLET

Isa	1.18 though your sins are like *s*, they shall
Mt	27.28 stripped him and put a *s* robe on him,

SCATTER (SCATTERED SCATTERS)

Gen	49. 7 them in Jacob, and *s* them in Israel.
Lev	26.33 I will *s* you among the nations, and I
Deut	4.27 The LORD will *s* you among the peoples;
	28.64 The LORD will *s* you among all peoples,

Jer	9.16 I will *s* them among the nations that
	10.21 not prospered, and all their flock is *s*.
	13.24 I will *s* you like chaff driven by the
	18.17 east, I will *s* them before the enemy.
Ezek	11.16 though I *s* them among the countries,
	20.23 in the wilderness that I would *s* them
Zech	1.21 "These are the horns that *s* Judah, so
	7.14 I *s* them with a whirlwind all the
	10. 9 Though I *s* them among the nations, yet
Jn	10.12 wolf snatches them and *s* them.
	16.32 indeed it has come, when you will be *s*,
Acts	8. 4 those who were *s* went from place to

SCEPTER

Gen	49.10 The *s* shall not depart from Judah, nor
Num	21.18 people dug, with the *s*, with the staff.
	24.17 a *s* shall rise out of Israel; it shall crush
Ps	45. 6 and ever. Your royal *s* is a *s* of equity;
	60. 7 Ephraim is my helmet; Judah is my *s*.

SCHEMES

Job	10. 3 hands and favor the *s* of the wicked?

SCOFFED

Deut	32.15 him, and *s* at the Rock of his salvation.
Acts	17.32 resurrection of the dead, some *s*; but

SCOFFER (SCOFFERS)

Ps	1. 1 sinners tread, or sit in the seat of *s*;
Prov	1.22 How long will *s* delight in their
	13. 1 but a *s* does not listen to rebuke.
	14. 6 A *s* seeks wisdom in vain, but
	15.12 *S* do not like to be rebuked; they will
	19.25 Strike a *s*, and the simple will learn
Isa	29.20 be no more, and the *s* shall cease to be;
Acts	13.41 'Look, you *s*! Be amazed and perish, for

SCOLDED

Mk	14. 5 given to the poor." And they *s* her.

SCORCH (SCORCHED)

Mt	13. 6 But when the sun rose, they were *s*; and
Rev	16. 8 and it was allowed to *s* them with fire;

SCORN (SCORNED)

2 Sam	12.14 this deed you have utterly *s* the LORD,
2 Chr	30.10 they laughed them to *s*, and mocked
Ps	31.11 I am the *s* of all my adversaries, a
	89.41 he has become the *s* of his neighbors.
Ezek	23.32 wide; you shall be *s* and derided, it
Jer	6.10 of the LORD is to them an object of *s*;
Mic	6.16 so you shall bear the *s* of my people.
Gal	4.14 you did not *s* or despise me, but

SCOURGE

Job	5.21 be hidden from the *s* of the tongue,

SCRIBE (SCRIBES)

Ezra	7.12 Ezra, the *s* of the law of the God of
Mt	8.19 A *s* then approached and said, "Teacher,
	13.52 every *s* who has been trained for the
	23. 2 "The *s* and the Pharisees sit on Moses'
Mk	3.22 *s* who came down from Jerusalem said,
	9.14 them, and some *s* arguing with them.
	12.38 "Beware of the *s*, who like to walk
1 Cor	1.20 is the one who is wise? Where is the *s*?

SCRIPTURE (SCRIPTURES)

Mt	21.42 "Have you never read in the *s*: 'The
	22.29 you know neither the *s* nor the power of
	26.54 But how then would the *s* be fulfilled,
Mk	12.10 Have you not read this *s*: 'The stone
	12.24 you know neither the *s* nor the power of
	14.49 not arrest me. But let the *s* be fulfilled."
	15.28n that *s* was fulfilled which says, "And he
Lk	4.21 "Today this *s* has been fulfilled in your
	24.32 road, while he was opening the *s* to us?"
	24.45 opened their minds to understand the *s*,
Jn	2.22 they believed the *s* and the word that

Jn	5.39 You search the s because you think that
	10.35 —and the s cannot be annulled—
	13.18 to fulfill the s, 'The one who ate my
	17.12 be lost, so that the s might be fulfilled.
	19.24 This was to fulfill what the s says,
	19.28 (in order to fulfill the s), "I am thirsty."
	19.37 of s says, "They will look on the one
Acts	8.35 starting with this s, he proclaimed to
	17. 2 argued with them from the s, explaining
	17.11 examined the s every day to see
	18.24 an eloquent man, well-versed in the s
Rom	9.17 For the s says to Pharaoh, "I have raised
	15. 4 of the s we might have hope.
1 Cor	15. 3 for our sins in accordance with the s,
Gal	3. 8 the s, foreseeing that God would justify
	3.22 the s has imprisoned all things under
	4.30 does the s say? "Drive out the slave
Jas	2. 8 fulfill the royal law according to the s,
	2.23 Thus the s was fulfilled that says,
	4. 5 that it is for nothing that the s says,
2 Pet	1.20 no prophecy of s is a matter of one's
	3.16 own destruction, as they do the other s.

SCROLL

Ps	40. 7 I am; in the s of the book it is written
Isa	34. 4 rot away, and the skies roll up like a s.
Jer	36. 2 Take a s and write on it all the words
	36.18 me, and I wrote them with ink on the s."
	36.23 the entire s was consumed in the fire
	36.32 Then Jeremiah took another s and gave
	51.60 Jeremiah wrote in a s all the disasters
Ezek	2. 9 out to me, and a written s was in it;
Zech	5. 1 Again I looked up and saw a flying s.
Lk	4.17 read and the s of the prophet Isaiah was
Heb	9.19 sprinkled both the s itself and all the
	10. 7 (in the s of the book it is written of
Rev	5. 1 s written on the inside and on the back,
	6.14 The sky vanished like a s rolling itself
	10. 2 He had a little s open in his hand.
	10. 9 told him to give me the little s; and he

SEA (SEAS)

Gen	1.10 that were gathered together he called S.
Ex	14.21 The Lord drove the s back by a strong
2 Chr	2.16 bring it to you as rafts by s to Joppa;
Neh	9.11 you divided the s before them, so that
Eccl	1. 7 run to the s, but the s is not full;
Mt	8.24 A windstorm arose on the s, so great
Mk	6.48 early in the morning, walking on the s.
Jn	6.19 they saw Jesus walking on the s and
1 Cor	10. 2 into Moses in the cloud and in the s,
Rev	15. 2 standing beside the s of glass with
	21. 1 passed away, and the s was no more.

SEA OF GALILEE

Mt	4.18 As he walked by the S, he saw two
	15.29 he passed along the S, and he went up
Jn	6. 1 Jesus went to the other side of the S,

SEAL (SEALS) (n)

Jn	6.27 him that God the Father has set his s."
Rom	4.11 the sign of circumcision as a s of the
1 Cor	9. 2 you; for you are the s of my apostleship
2 Cor	1.22 by putting his s on us and giving us his
Eph	1.13 with the s of the promised Holy Spirit;
	4.30 you were marked with a s for the day of
Rev	6. 1 Lamb opened one of the seven s, and I
	7. 3 marked the servants of our God with a s
	8. 1 the Lamb opened the seventh s, there
	9. 4 who have not the s of God on their

SEAL (SEALED SEALING)

Esth	8. 8 the king, and s it with the king's ring;
Job	14.17 my transgression would be s up in a
Isa	29.11 for you like the words of a s document.
Dan	9.24 to s both vision and prophet, and to
	12. 4 the words and the secret and the book s
	12. 9 the words are to remain secret and s

Mt	27.66 made the tomb secure by s the stone.
Rev	5. 1 and on the back, s with seven seals;
	10. 4 "S up what the seven thunders have
	22.10 "Do not s up the words of the prophecy

SEARCH (SEARCHED SEARCHES SEARCHING)

Job	5.27 See, we have s this out; it is true. Hear,
Ps	139. 1 O Lord, you have s me and known me.
	139. 23 S me, O God, and know my heart; test
Jer	17.10 the Lord test the mind and s the heart,
	29.13 When you s for me, you will find me; if
Am	9. 3 from there I will s out and take them;
Zeph	1.12 that time I will s Jerusalem with lamps,
Mt	2. 8 "Go and s diligently for the child, and
	7. 7 s, and you will find; knock, and the
	18.12 and go in s of the one that went astray?
Mk	1.37 they said to him, "Everyone is s for you.
Jn	5.39 "You s the scriptures because you think
	7.34 You will s for me, but you will not find
	7.52 S and you will see that no prophet is to
	8.21 and you will s for me, but you will not
Acts	17.27 so that they would s for God, and
Rom	8.27 God, who s the heart, knows what is in
1 Cor	2.10 for the Spirit s everything, even the
Rev	2.23 I am the one who s minds and hearts,

SEASON (SEASONS)

Gen	1.14 and let them be for signs and for s and
Eccl	3. 1 For everything there is a s, and a time
Mk	9.50 has lost its saltness, how can you s it?"

SEAT (SEATED)

2 Kings	25.28 gave him a s above the seats of the
Job	29. 7 of the city, I took my s in the public
Mk	14.62 see the Son of Man s at the right hand
Lk	11.43 for you love the s of honor in the

SECRET (SECRETS)

Deut	29.29 The s things belong to the Lord our
2 Sam	15.10 Absalom sent s messengers throughout
Ps	44.21 this? For he knows the s of the heart.
	90. 8 our s sins in the light of your
Prov	11.13 A gossip goes about telling s, but one
Eccl	12.14 deed into judgment, including every s
Isa	45.19 I did not speak in s, in a land of
	48.16 I have not spoken in s, from the time it
Jer	23.24 Who can hide in s places so that I
Am	3. 7 without revealing his s to his servants
Mt	6. 4 so that your alms may be done in s; and
	13.11 given to know the s of the kingdom
Mk	4.11 has been given the s of the kingdom
	4.22 is anything s, except to come to light.
Rom	2.16 Christ, will judge the s thoughts of all.
1 Cor	2. 7 we speak God's wisdom, s and hidden,
	14.25 After the s of the unbeliever's heart are

SECRETLY

Gen	31.27 Why did you flee s and deceive me and
2 Kings	17. 9 Israel did s things that were not right
Jer	37.17 The king questioned him s in his house,
Mt	2. 7 Then Herod s called for the wise men

SECT

Acts	24. 5 a ringleader of the s of the Nazarenes.
	28.22 with regard to this s we know that

SECURE (SECURELY)

Judg	18. 7 people who were there living s, after the
Ps	112. 7 their hearts are firm, s in the Lord.
Lk	17.33 who try to make their life s will lose it,

SECURITY

Job	24.23 He gives them s, and they are
Isa	38.14 O Lord, I am oppressed; be my s!

SEE (SEEING SEEN SEES)

Gen	16.13 God and remained alive after s him?"
	45.28 alive. I must go and s him before I die."
Deut	34. 4 I have let you s it with your eyes, but

1 Sam	9. 16 I have *s* the suffering of my people,	
	16. 7 for the Lord does not *s* as mortals *s*;	
Job	19. 26 then in my flesh I shall *s* God,	
Prov	27. 12 The clever *s* danger and hide; but the	
	28. 11 poor person *s* through the pose.	
Eccl	11. 7 it is pleasant for the eyes to *s* the sun.	
Isa	5. 12 of the Lord, or *s* the work of his hands!	
	29. 15 who say, "Who *s* us? Who knows us?"	
	44. 18 eyes are shut, so that they cannot *s*,	
	52. 10 ends of the earth shall *s* the salvation	
	53. 10 he shall *s* his offspring, and shall	
Mal	3. 18 you shall *s* the difference between the	
Mt	4. 16 who sat in darkness have *s* a great light,	
	5. 8 the pure in heart, for they will *s* God.	
	6. 1 before others in order to be *s* by them;	
	11. 4 "Go and tell John what you hear and *s*:	
	28. 6 Come, *s* the place where he lay.	
Lk	3. 6 all flesh shall *s* the salvation of God.' "	
	7. 22 "Go and tell John what you have *s* and	
Jn	3. 21 may be clearly *s* that their deeds have	
	4. 35 around you, *s* how the fields are ripe	
	8. 51 keeps my word, will never *s* death."	
	9. 25 know, that though I was blind, now I *s*."	
	9. 39 so that those who do not *s* may *s*,	
	12. 21 said to him, "Sir, we wish to *s* Jesus."	
	16. 16 again a little while, and you will *s* me."	
	17. 24 be with me where I am, to *s* my glory,	
	20. 25 "Unless I *s* the mark of the nails in his	
Acts	4. 20 from speaking about what we have *s*	
	9. 27 on the road he had *s* the Lord, who had	
1 Cor	13. 12 now we *s* in a mirror, dimly, but then	
2 Cor	3. 18 all of us, with unveiled face, *s* the glory	
	4. 4 keep them from *s* the light of the gospel	
Heb	2. 9 but we do *s* Jesus, who for a little while	
1 Jn	1. 1 I have heard, what we have *s* with our	
	3. 2 be like him, for we will *s* him as he is	
Rev	1. 7 every eye will *s* him, even those who	

SEED

Gen	1. 29 I have given you every plant yielding *s*	
Ps	126. 6 out weeping, bearing the *s* for sowing,	
Eccl	11. 6 In the morning sow your *s*, and at	
Mt	13. 24 someone who sowed good *s* in his field;	
	13. 38 the good *s* are the children of the	
Mk	4. 26 of God is as if someone would scatter *s*	
1 Jn	3. 9 sin, because God's *s* abides in them;	

SEEK (SEEKS SOUGHT)

Num	10. 33 day's journey, to *s* out a resting place	
Deut	4. 29 From there you will *s* the Lord your	
1 Sam	22. 23 the one who *s* my life *s* your life; you	
1 Chr	16. 11 *S* the Lord and his strength, *s* his	
	28. 9 If you *s* him, he will be found by you;	
2 Chr	7. 14 pray, *s* my face, and turn from their	
	14. 4 and commanded Judah to *s* the Lord,	
	16. 12 yet even in his disease he did not *s* the	
	19. 3 land, and have set your heart to *s* God."	
	31. 21 to *s* his God, he did with all his heart;	
Ps	9. 10 have not forsaken those who *s* you.	
	14. 2 are any who are wise; who *s* after God.	
	24. 6 who *s* the face of the God of Jacob.	
	27. 8 my heart says, "*s* his face!" Your face,	
	40. 16 But may all who *s* you rejoice and be	
	53. 2 are any who are wise, who *s* God.	
	54. 3 risen against me, the ruthless *s* my life	
	63. 1 you are my God, I *s* you, my soul thirsts	
	69. 32 glad; who *s* God, let your hearts revive.	
	105. 3 hearts of those who *s* the Lord rejoice.	
	119. 2 who *s* him with their whole heart, who	
	122. 9 of the Lord our God, I will *s* your good.	
Prov	1. 28 they will *s* me diligently, but will not	
Eccl	1. 13 mind to *s* and to search out by wisdom	
	3. 15 is; and God *s* out what has gone by.	
	12. 10 The Teacher *s* to find pleasing words,	
Song	3. 1 at night I *s* him whom my soul loves;	
Isa	9. 13 who struck them, or *s* the Lord of hosts.	
	26. 9 night, my spirit within me earnestly *s*	

Isa	34. 16 *S* and read from the book of the Lord:	
	45. 19 the offspring of Jacob, "*S* me in chaos."	
	55. 6 *S* the Lord while he may be found, call	
Jer	45. 5 you, do you *s* great things for yourself?	
Lam	3. 25 wait for him, to the soul that *s* him.	
Ezek	7. 25 will *s* peace, but there shall be none.	
	22. 30 I *s* for anyone among them who would	
	34. 12 so will I *s* out my sheep. I will rescue	
Dan	9. 3 the Lord God, to *s* an answer by prayer	
Hos	3. 5 Israelites shall return and *s* the Lord	
	5. 15 acknowledge their guilt and *s* my face.	
Am	5. 4 Israel: *S* me and live; but do not *s*	
	5. 14 *S* good, and not evil, that you may live;	
Zeph	2. 3 *S* the Lord, all you humble of the land,	
Zech	8. 22 nations shall come to *s* the Lord of	
Lk	11. 9 *s*, and you will find; knock, and the	
	19. 10 Son of Man came to *s* and to save the	
Jn	4. 23 truth, for the Father *s* such as these	
	5. 30 I *s* to do not my own will, but the will	
	8. 50 Yet I do not *s* my own glory; there is	
Acts	15. 17 that all other peoples may *s* the Lord—	
Rom	3. 11 there is no one who *s* God. All have	
	11. 3 I alone am left, and they *s* my life."	
Col	3. 1 *s* the things that are above, where	

SEER (SEERS)

1 Sam	9. 9 a prophet was formerly called a *s*.)	
Isa	30. 10 say to the *s*, "Do not see"; and to the	
Mic	3. 7 the *s* shall be disgraced, and the	

SELF-CONDEMNED

Gal	2. 11 him to his face, because he stood *s*.	

SELF-CONTROL

Prov	25. 28 without walls, is one who lacks *s*.	
Acts	24. 25 he discussed justice, *s*, and the coming	
1 Cor	7. 5 if they are not practicing *s*, they should	
	9. 25 Athletes exercise *s* in all things; they do	

SELFISH (SELFISHNESS)

2 Cor	12. 20 anger, *s*, slander, gossip, conceit, and	
Phil	2. 3 Do nothing from *s* ambition or conceit,	

SELL (SELLS SOLD)

Gen	25. 31 Jacob said, "First *s* me your birthright."	
	31. 15 For he has *s* us, and he has been using	
	37. 28 and *s* him to the Ishmaelites for twenty	
	41. 56 the storehouses, and *s* to the Egyptians,	
	45. 4 brother, Joseph, whom you *s* into Egypt.	
Lev	25. 23 The land shall not be *s* in perpetuity,	
	27. 28 may be *s* or redeemed; every devoted	
Judg	2. 14 he *s* them into the power of their	
1 Kings	21. 25 Ahab, who *s* himself to do what was evil	
2 Kings	17. 17 they *s* themselves to do evil in the sight	
Esth	7. 4 we have been *s*, I and my people, to be	
Ps	44. 12 You have *s* your people for a trifle,	
	105. 17 of them, Joseph, who was *s* as a slave.	
Am	2. 6 because they *s* the righteous for silver,	
Mt	13. 44 in his joy he goes and *s* all that he has	
Lk	12. 33 *S* your possessions, and give alms. Make	
Acts	4. 34 many as owned lands or houses *s* them	
	7. 9 patriarchs, jealous of Joseph, *s* him	
Rom	7. 14 but I am of the flesh, *s* into slavery	

SEND (SENDING SENDS SENT)

Gen	45. 5 for God *s* me before you to preserve life.	
Ex	3. 10 Come now, I will *s* you to Pharaoh to	
Ps	43. 3 O *s* out your light and your truth; let	
	57. 3 He will *s* from heaven and save me; my	
	147. 15 He *s* out his command to the earth; his	
Eccl	11. 1 *S* out your bread upon the waters, for	
Isa	6. 8 go for us?" And I said, "Here am I; *s* me!"	
Jer	26. 12 "It is the Lord who *s* me to prophesy	
Mal	3. 1 I am *s* my messenger to prepare the way	
Mt	9. 38 to *s* out laborers into his harvest."	
	10. 5 These twelve Jesus *s* out, with the	
	10. 40 me welcomes the one who *s* me.	
	11. 2 he *s* word by his disciples and said to	

Mt	13.41	The Son of Man will *s* his angels, and
Mk	1. 2	"See, I am *s* my messenger ahead of
	5.12	spirits begged him, "*S* us to the swine;
	11. 1	of Olives, he *s* two of his disciples,
Lk	19.29	of Olives, he *s* two of the disciples,
Jn	6.57	the living Father *s* me, and I live
	17. 8	and they have believed that you *s* me.
	17.18	As you have *s* me into the world, so I
	20.21	the Father has *s* me, even so I *s* you."
1 Cor	1.17	Christ did not *s* me to baptize but to
2 Cor	2.17	as persons *s* from God and standing in
Gal	4. 4	of time had come, God *s* his Son,
	4. 6	God has *s* the Spirit of his Son into our
1 Jn	4. 9	God *s* his only Son into the world so

SENNACHERIB

2 Kings	18.13	*S* king of Assyria came up against all
	19.16	hear the words of *S*, which he has sent
	19.36	*S* of Assyria left, went home, and lived
2 Chr	32. 1	King *S* of Assyria came and invaded
Isa	37.17	hear all the words of *S*, which he has
	37.37	Then *S* king of Assyria left, went home,

SENSE

1 Sam	25.33	Blessed be your good *s*, and blessed be

SENTINEL (SENTINELS)

2 Sam	18.25	The *s* shouted and told the king. The
Isa	21.11	"*S*, what of the night? *S*, what of the
	62. 6	your walls, O Jerusalem, I have set *s*;
Jer	6.17	I raised up *s* for you: "Give heed to the
	31. 6	For there shall be a day when *s* will call
Ezek	3.17	I have made you a *s* for the house of
	33. 6	But if the *s* sees the sword coming and
Hos	9. 8	prophet is a *s* for my God over Ephraim,

SEPARATE (SEPARATED SEPARATES)

Gen	1. 4	and God *s* the light from the darkness.
	1.14	of the sky to *s* the day from the night;
	13.11	eastward; thus they *s* from each other.
Ex	26.33	the veil shall *s* for you the holy place
Lev	15.31	of Israel *s* from their uncleanness,
	20.24	God. I have *s* you from the peoples.
1 Kings	8.53	for you have *s* them from among all the
Ezra	9. 1	Levites have not *s* themselves from the
	10.11	do his will; *s* yourselves from the
Neh	13. 3	they *s* from Israel all those of foreign
Mt	19. 6	God has joined together, let no one *s*."
	25.32	he will *s* the people one from another
Rom	8.35	Who will *s* us from the love of Christ?
	8.39	will be able to *s* us from the love of God
1 Cor	7.15	if the unbelieving partner *s*, let it be so;
2 Cor	6.17	them, be *s* from them, says the Lord,
Gal	2.12	*s* for fear of the circumcision faction.

SEPARATION

Ezek	42.20	to make a *s* between the holy and the

SERAPHS

Isa	6. 2	*S* were in attendance above him; each

SERPENT (SERPENTS)

Gen	3. 1	Now the *s* was more crafty than any
Num	21. 6	Lord sent poisonous *s* among the
	21. 8	"Make a poisonous *s*, and set it on a
2 Kings	18. 4	broke in pieces the bronze *s* that Moses
Prov	23.32	the last it bites like a *s*, and stings like
Isa	27. 1	will punish Leviathan the fleeing *s*,
Jn	3.14	Just as Moses lifted up the *s* in the
2 Cor	11. 3	*s* deceived Eve by its cunning, your
Rev	20. 2	the dragon, that ancient *s*, who is the

SERVANT (SERVANTS)

Lev	25.42	For they are my *s*, whom I brought out
	25.55	Israel are *s*; they are my *s* whom I
Num	12. 7	Not so with my *s* Moses; he is entrusted
1 Sam	25.24	please let your *s* speak in your ears, and
2 Sam	14. 6	Your *s* had two sons, and they fought

1 Kings	12. 7	"If you will be a *s* to this people today
2 Kings	24. 2	that he spoke by his *s* the prophets.
Job	2. 3	"Have you considered my *s* Job? There
	42. 8	my *s* Job shall pray for you, for I will
Ps	19.13	Keep back your *s* also from the
	78.70	He chose his *s* David, and took him
	86.16	to me; give your strength to your *s*,
	109. 28	be put to shame; may your *s* be glad.
	143. 12	all my adversaries, for I am your *s*.
Prov	30.10	Do not slander a *s* to a master, or the
Isa	41. 8	But you, Israel, my *s*, Jacob, whom I
	42. 1	Here is my *s*, whom I uphold, my
	42.19	Who is blind but my *s*, or deaf like my
	43.10	Lord, and my *s* whom I have chosen,
	44. 1	But now hear, O Jacob my *s*, Israel
	52.13	my *s* shall prosper; he shall be exalted
	66.14	that the hand of the Lord is with his *s*,
Jer	7.25	persistently sent all my *s* the prophets
	25. 4	sent you all his *s* the prophets,
	25. 9	Babylon, my *s*, and I will bring them
	30.10	have no fear, my *s* Jacob, says the Lord,
Ezek	34.23	one shepherd, my *s* David, and he shall
Dan	6.20	Daniel, *s* of the living God, has your
Zech	3. 8	I am going to bring my *s* the Branch.
Mt	23.11	The greatest among you will be your *s*.
Mk	9.35	be first must be last of all and *s* of all."
	10.43	great among you must be yours,
Lk	1.38	said, "Here am I, the *s* of the Lord;
	1.54	He has helped his *s* Israel, in
	2.29	now you are dismissing your *s* in peace,
Jn	13.16	*s* are not greater than their master, nor
	15.15	I do not call you *s* any longer, because
Acts	3.26	When God raised up his *s*, he sent him
	4.25	through our ancestor David, your *s*:
	4.27	gathered against your holy *s* Jesus,
Rom	1. 1	Paul, a *s* of Jesus Christ, called to be an
	13. 4	approval, for it is God's *s* for your good.
Col	1.23	I, Paul, became a *s* of this gospel.
2 Tim	2.24	the Lord's *s* must not be quarrelsome
Heb	3. 5	house as a *s*, to testify to the things
Rev	7. 3	marked the *s* of our God with a seal on
	22. 3	will be in it, and his *s* will worship him;

SERVANT-GIRL

Mt	26.71	another *s* saw him, and she said to the

SERVE (SERVED SERVES SERVING)

Gen	25.23	the other, the elder shall *s* the younger."
Ex	14.12	us alone and let us *s* the Egyptians'?
	28. 1	to *s* me as priests — Aaron and Aaron's
Deut	6.13	him you shall *s*, and by his name alone
	20.11	people in it shall *s* you at forced labor.
	28.36	where you shall *s* other gods, of wood
Josh	22. 5	to *s* him with all your heart and with all
	24. 2	beyond the Euphrates and *s* other gods.
	24.15	and my household, we will *s* the Lord."
1 Sam	7. 4	the Astartes, and they *s* the Lord only.
2 Sam	22.44	people whom I had not known *s* me.
1 Kings	12. 4	that he placed on us, and we will *s* you."
2 Kings	17.12	they *s* idols, of which the Lord had said
	25.24	live in the land, *s* the king of Babylon,
1 Chr	28. 9	and *s* him with single mind and willing
Job	21.15	is the Almighty, that we should *s* him?
Ps	2.11	*S* the Lord with fear, with trembling
	106. 36	They *s* their idols, which became a
Isa	60.12	that will not *s* you shall perish;
Jer	25.11	nations shall *s* the king of Babylon
	27. 7	All the nations shall *s* him and his son
	30. 9	But they shall *s* the Lord their God and
Dan	3.18	we will not *s* your gods and we will not
	7.10	A thousand thousands *s* him, and ten
Mal	3.14	You have said, "It is vain to *s* God.
Mt	8.15	her and she got up and began to *s* him.
	20.28	of man came not to be served but to *s*,
Mk	1.31	fever left her; and she began to *s* them.
Lk	4.39	Immediately she got up and began to *s*
	16.13	No slave can *s* two masters; for a slave

Lk	22.26 youngest, and the leader like one who *s*.
Jn	12.26 Whoever *s* me must follow me, and
Acts	6. 4 ourselves to prayer and to *s* the word."
	26.16 purpose, to appoint you to *s* and testify
Rom	16.18 such people do not *s* our Lord Christ,
Phil	2.22 a father he has *s* with me in the work of
Heb	1.14 in the divine service, sent to *s* for the
	6.10 you showed for his sake in *s* the saints,

SERVICE

Ex	1.14 made their lives bitter with hard *s* in
Num	3. 7 of meeting, doing *s* at the tabernacle;
Job	7. 1 "Do not human beings have a hard *s* on
1 Cor	9.13 who are employed in the temple *s* get
	16.15 themselves to the *s* of the saints;

SETH

Gen	4.25 she bore a son and named him *S*, for
	5. 3 to his image, and named him *S*.
Lk	3.38 son of Enos, son of *S*, the son of Adam,

SETTLED

Gen	13.12 Abram *s* in the land of Canaan, while

SEVEN

Josh	6. 4 march around the city *s* times, the
Ps	119.164 *S* times a day I praise you for your
Mt	16.10 Or the *s* loaves for the four thousand,
	18.21 should I forgive? As many as *s* times?"
	22.25 Now there were *s* brothers among us;
Lk	20.29 Now there were *s* brothers; the first
Rev	3. 1 has the *s* spirits of God and the *s* stars:

SEVENFOLD

Gen	4.24 If Cain is avenged *s*, truly Lamech
Lev	26.18 continue to punish you *s* for your sins,
Prov	6.31 if they are caught, they will pay *s*; they

SEVENTH

Gen	2. 2 on the *s* day God finished his work that
Ex	20.10 the *s* day is a sabbath to the LORD your
Heb	4. 4 "And God rested on the *s* day from all

SEVENTY

Jer	25.11 shall serve the king of Babylon *s* years.
	29.10 when Babylon's *s* years are completed
Dan	9. 2 of Jerusalem, namely, *s* years.
	9.24 "*S* weeks are decreed for your people
Lk	10. 1 the Lord appointed *s* others and sent

SEVERE

Gen	12.10 an alien, for famine was *s* in the land.
2 Cor	13.10 I may not have to be *s* in using the

SEX

1 Pet	3. 7 honor to the woman as the weaker *s*,

SHADOW

2 Kings	20.10 rather let the *s* retreat ten intervals."
1 Chr	29.15 our days on earth are like a *s*, and there
Job	14. 2 a flower and withers, flees like a *s* and
Ps	102. 11 My days are like an evening *s*; I wither
Eccl	6.12 their vain life, which they pass like a *s*?
Song	2. 3 With great delight I sat in his *s*, and his
Acts	5.15 that Peter's *s* might fall on some of
Col	2.17 These are only a *s* of what is to come,
Heb	10. 1 Since the law has only a *s* of the good

SHADRACH

Dan	1. 7 Hananiah he called *S*, Mishael he called
	2.49 and he appointed *S*, Meshach, and
	3.12 the affairs of the province of Babylon: *S*,
	3.23 *S*, Meshach, and Abednego, fell down,
	3.30 Then the king promoted *S*, Meshach,

SHAKE (SHAKEN SHAKES SHOOK)

Judg	16.20 out as at other times and *s* myself free."
Ps	29. 8 The voice of the LORD *s* in the
Am	9. 9 and *s* the house of Israel among all the

Hab	3. 6 He stopped and *s* the earth; he looked
Hag	2. 6 I will *s* the heavens and the earth and
Mt	10.14 *s* off the dust from your feet as you
Acts	2.25 at my right hand so that I will not be *s*;
	4.31 they were gathered together was *s*;
Heb	12.26 I will *s* not only the earth but also the

SHAME

2 Sam	19. 5 covered with *s* the faces of all your
2 Chr	32.21 So he returned in *s* to his own land.
Ps	4. 2 you people, shall my honor suffer *s*?
	22. 5 you they trusted, and were not put to *s*.
	31. 1 refuge; do not let me ever be put to *s*;
	31.17 Do not let me ever be put to *s*, O LORD,
	53. 5 will be put to *s*, for God has rejected
	109. 29 may they be wrapped in their own *s* as
	119. 6 Then I shall not be put to *s*, having my
Prov	25. 8 end, when your neighbor puts you to *s*?
Isa	23. 9 glory, to *s* all the honored of the earth,
	30. 3 of Pharaoh shall become your *s*,
	45.17 you shall not be put to *s* or confounded
	49.23 who wait for me shall not be put to *s*.
	54. 4 for you will forget the *s* of your youth,
	61. 7 Because their *s* was double, and
Jer	50. 2 Babylon is taken, Bel is put to *s*,
Ezek	7.18 *S* shall be on all faces, baldness on all
Hos	4. 7 me; they changed their glory into *s*.
	10. 6 Ephraim shall be put to *s*, and Israel
Joel	2.26 my people shall never again be put to *s*.
Lk	13.17 all his opponents were put to *s*; and the
1 Cor	6. 5 I say this to your *s*. Can it be that there
	15.34 knowledge of God. I say this to your *s*.
1 Jn	2.28 not be put to *s* before him at the time

SHAMEFUL

2 Cor	4. 2 We have renounced the *s* things that

SHARE (SHARED SHARING)

1 Kings	12.16 "What *s* have we in David? We have no
Jn	4. 9 (Jews do not *s* things in common with
Rom	15.26 to *s* their resources with the poor
	15.27 Gentiles have come to *s* in their
1 Cor	9.13 who serve at the altar *s* in what is
	10.16 is it not a *s* in the body of Christ?
2 Cor	1. 7 as you *s* in our sufferings, so also you
	9.13 by the generosity of your *s* with them
Gal	6. 6 who are taught the word must *s* in all
Phil	1. 5 because of your *s* in the gospel from the
	2. 1 from love, any *s* in the Spirit,
	3.10 and the *s* of his sufferings by becoming
	4.15 Macedonia, no church *s* with me in the
Col	1.12 you to *s* in the inheritance of the saints
Heb	2.14 the children *s* flesh and blood, he
	13.16 to do good and to *s* what you have,
1 Pet	4.13 insofar as you are *s* Christ's sufferings,

SHARP

Ps	45. 5 Your arrows are *s* in the heart of the
	140. 3 They make their tongue *s* as a snake's,

SHATTER (SHATTERED SHATTERING)

Ps	68.21 God will *s* the heads of his enemies, the
Dan	12. 7 when the *s* of the power of the holy
Ob	9 Your warriors shall be *s*, O Teman, so
Mal	1. 4 says, "We are *s* but we will rebuild

SHAVE (SHAVED SHAVING)

2 Sam	10. 4 David's envoys, *s* off half the beard
Isa	7.20 Lord will *s* with a razor hired beyond
Ezek	44.20 They shall not *s* their heads or let their
Acts	21.24 them, and pay for the *s* of their heads.

SHEAVES

Ps	126. 6 with shouts of joy, carrying their *s*.

SHEBA

1 Kings	10. 1 When the queen of *S* heard of the fame
Ps	72.10 may the kings of *S* and Seba bring gifts.

Jer 6.20 me is frankincense that comes from S,

SHECHEM
Gen 37.12 to pasture their father's flock near S.
Judg 9.41 kinsfolk, so they could not live on at S.
Acts 7.16 their bodies were brought back to S and

SHED
Deut 21. 7 "Our hands did not s this blood, nor
2 Kings 21.16 Manasseh s very much innocent blood,

SHEEP
Num 27.17 may not be like s without a shepherd."
1 Sam 16.19 me your son David who is with the s."
2 Sam 7. 8 from following the s to be prince over
 24.17 but these s, what have they done? Let
1 Kings 22.17 like s that have no shepherd;
1 Chr 21.17 But these s, what have they done? Let
2 Chr 18.16 mountains, like s without a shepherd;
Ps 44.11 You have made us like s for slaughter,
 44.22 and accounted as s for the slaughter.
 49.14 Like s they are appointed for Sheol;
 74. 1 does your anger smoke against the s
 78.52 Then he led out his people like s, and
 95. 7 of his pasture, and the s of his hand.
 100. 3 are his people, and the s of his pasture.
 119.176 I have gone astray like a lost s; seek out
Isa 53. 6 we like s have gone astray; we have all
Jer 12. 3 Pull them out like s for the slaughter,
 23. 1 destroy and scatter the s of my pasture!
 50. 6 My people have been lost s; their
Ezek 34.31 You are my s, the s of my pasture and I
Mt 9.36 and helpless, like s without a shepherd.
 10. 6 to the lost s of the house of Israel.
 12.11 has only one s and it falls into a pit on
 25.32 as a shepherd separates the s from the
 26.31 and the s of the flock will be scattered.'
Mk 14.27 shepherd, and the s will be scattered.'
Lk 15. 4 having a hundred s, and losing one of
Jn 10.15 Father. And I lay down my life for the s.
 10.27 My s hear my voice. I know them and
 21.16 love you." Jesus said to him, "Tend my s."
Acts 8.32 "Like a s he was led to the slaughter,
Rom 8.36 are accounted as s to be slaughtered."
1 Pet 2.25 you were going astray like s, but now

SHEEPFOLD (SHEEPFOLDS)
Ps 78.70 servant David, and took him from the s;
Jn 10. 1 who does not enter the s by the gate

SHEET
Acts 10.11 something like a large s coming down,

SHEKEL
Ex 30.13 half a s according to the s of the

SHELTER
Ps 27. 5 For he will hide me in his s in the day
 31.20 In the s of your presence you hide them
 91. 1 You who live in the s of the Most High,
Isa 25. 4 a s from the rainstorm and a shade

SHEM
Gen 9.26 "Blessed by the Lord my God be S; and

SHEOL
Job 26. 6 S is naked before God, and Abaddon
Ps 9.17 The wicked shall depart to S, all the
 16.10 For you do not give me up to S, or let
 139. 8 if I make my bed in S, you are there. If
Prov 5. 5 to death; her steps follow the path to S.
 7.27 Her house is the way to S, going down
 15.11 S and Abaddon lie open before the
Isa 5.14 S has enlarged its appetite and opened
 14. 9 S beneath is stirred up to meet you
 28.15 and with S we have an agreement;
 57. 9 far away, and sent down even to S.
Ezek 32.21 out of the midst of S: "They have come
Hos 13.14 O S, where is your destruction?

SHEPHERD (SHEPHERDS)
Gen 46.32 The men are s, for they have been
Num 14.33 your children shall be s in the
 27.17 Lord may not be like sheep without a s."
2 Sam 5. 2 you who shall be s of my people Israel,
Ps 23. 1 The Lord is my s, I shall not want. He
 80. 1 Give ear, O S of Israel, you who lead
Isa 40.11 feed his flock like a s; he will gather
 44.28 says of Cyrus, "He is my s, and he shall
 56.11 s also have no understanding; they have
 63.11 them up out of the sea with the s
Jer 10.21 For the s are stupid, and do not inquire
 23. 1 Woe to the s who destroy and scatter
 23. 4 I will raise up s over them who will s
 25.34 Wail, you s, and cry out; roll in ashes,
 51.23 with you I smash s and their flocks;
Ezek 34. 2 prophesy against the s of Israel:
 34. 7 you s, hear the word of the Lord:
 34.23 I will set up over them one s, my
Am 1. 1 Amos, who was among the s of Tekoa,
Mic 7.14 S your people with your staff, the flock
Nah 3.18 Your s are asleep, O king of Assyria;
Zech 10. 2 like sheep; they suffer for lack of a s.
 11. 7 I became the s of the flock doomed to
 11.16 a s who does not care for the perishing,
 13. 7 "Awake, O sword, against my s, against
Mt 2. 6 a ruler who is to s my people Israel.' "
 9.36 and helpless, like sheep without a s.
 26.31 "I will strike the s, and the sheep of the
Mk 6.34 they were like sheep without a s;
 14.27 'I will strike the s, and the sheep will
Lk 2. 8 there were s living in the fields, keeping
 2.20 The s returned, glorifying and praising
Jn 10. 2 The one who enters by the gate is the s
 10.11 "I am the good s. The good s lays down
Acts 20.28 you overseers, to s the church of God
Heb 13.20 Jesus, the great s of the sheep, by the
1 Pet 5. 4 when the chief s appears, you will win
Rev 7.17 will be their s, and he will guide them

SHIBBOLETH
Judg 12. 6 "Then say S," and he said, "Sibboleth,"

SHIELD
2 Sam 22. 3 my s and the horn of my salvation, my
Ps 3. 3 But you, O Lord, are a s around me, my
 5.12 you cover them with favor as with a s.
 7.10 God is my s, who saves the upright in
 18. 2 my rock in whom I take refuge, my s,
 18.30 true; he is a s for all who take refuge
 18.35 have given me the s of your salvation,
 28. 7 The Lord is my strength and my s; in
 35. 2 Take hold of s and buckler, and rise up
 84.11 the Lord God is a sun and s; he bestows
 89.18 For our s belongs to the Lord, our king
 91. 4 his faithfulness is a s and buckler. You
 115. 9 in the Lord! He is their help and their s.
Prov 2. 7 the upright; he is a s to those who walk
Zech 12. 8 Lord will s the inhabitants of Jerusalem
Eph 6.16 take the s of faith, with which you will

SHILOH
Josh 18. 8 lots for you here before the Lord in S."
1 Sam 1. 3 to sacrifice to the Lord of hosts at S,
 14. 3 the priest of the Lord in S, carrying an
Ps 78.60 He abandoned his dwelling at S, the
Jer 26. 6 I will make this house like S, and I will

SHINE (SHINED)
Num 6.25 the Lord make his face to shine upon you,
Job 22.28 for you, and light will s on your ways.
Eccl 8. 1 Wisdom makes one's face s, and the
Isa 9. 2 of deep darkness— on them light has s.
Dan 12. 3 Those who are wise shall s like the
Zech 9.16 of a crown they shall s on his land.
Mt 5.16 same way, let your light s before others,
 13.43 Then the righteous will s like the sun in

Eph 5.14 from the dead, and Christ will *s* on you."
Phil 2.15 in which you *s* like stars in the world.

SHIP (SHIPS)

1 Kings 22.48 Jehoshaphat made *s* of the Tarshish
Ps 104. 26 There go the *s*, and Leviathan that you
 107. 23 Some went down to the sea in *s*, doing
Prov 30.19 way of a *s* on the high seas, and the
Ezek 30. 9 messengers shall go out from me in *s* to

SHIPWRECK (SHIPWRECKED)

2 Cor 11.25 Three times I was *s*; for a night and a
1 Tim 1.19 persons have suffered *s* in the faith;

SHIRT

Lk 6.29 your coat do not withhold even your *s*

SHORT (SHORTENED)

Isa 50. 2 Is my hand *s*, that it cannot redeem?
Mt 24.22 And if those days had not been cut *s*,
Mk 13.20 if the Lord had not cut *s* those days, no

SHOUT (SHOUTED SHOUTS)

Josh 6.16 "*S*; for the Lord has given you the city.
Isa 12. 6 *S* aloud and sing for joy, O royal Zion,
 42.13 he cries out, he *s* aloud, he shows
Mt 20.30 passing by, they *s*, "Lord, have mercy
Lk 19.40 were silent, the stones would *s* out."

SHOW (SHOWED SHOWN SHOWS)

Ex 33.18 Moses said, "*S* me your glory, I pray."
Deut 34. 1 the Lord *s* him the whole land: Gilead
Mic 6. 8 He has *s* you, O mortal, what is good;
 7.15 land of Egypt, *s* us marvelous things.
Mt 8. 4 but go, *s* yourself to the priest, and
Lk 1.72 he has *s* the mercy promised to our
 24.40 said this, he *s* them his hands and his
Jn 14. 8 "Lord, *s* us the Father, and we will be
Acts 10.28 but God has *s* me that I should not call
Rom 3.25 He did this to *s* his righteousness,
 5. 8 But God *s* his love for us in that while
Gal 2. 6 God *s* no partiality)—those leaders

SHOWERS

Jer 3. 3 Therefore the *s* have been withheld, and
Ezek 34.26 their season; they shall be *s* of blessing.
Hos 6. 3 he will come to us like the *s*, like the
Mic 5. 7 dew from the Lord, like *s* on the grass,

SHRIVELED

Ps 22.16 My hands and feet have *s*; I can count

SHUN

1 Cor 6.18 *S* fornication! Every sin that a person
1 Tim 6.11 for you, man of God, *s* all this; pursue

SHUT

Gen 7.16 him; and the Lord *s* him in.
Isa 22.22 open, and no one shall *s*; he shall *s*,

SICK

2 Kings 20. 1 Hezekiah became *s* and was at the
Ps 107. 17 Some were *s* through their sinful ways,
Prov 13.12 Hope deferred makes the heart *s*, but
Isa 1. 5 The whole head is *s*, and the whole
Jer 8.18 is gone, grief is upon me, my heart is *s*.
Mt 9.12 of a physician, but those who are *s*.
Lk 4.40 all those who had any who were *s* with
 5.31 of a physician, but those who are *s*;
Acts 5.15 they even carried out the *s* into the
Jas 5.14 Are any among you *s*? They should call

SICKLE

Deut 23.25 you shall not put a *s* to your neighbor's
Joel 3.13 Put in the *s*, for the harvest is ripe. Go
Rev 14.15 "Use your *s* and reap, for the hour to

SICKNESS

Eccl 5.17 in much vexation and *s* and resentment.

Isa 10.16 wasting *s* among his stout warriors,
Hos 5.13 When Ephraim saw his *s*, and Judah his

SIDE

Ps 124. 1 not been the Lord who was on our *s*,
Jn 19.34 one of the soldiers pierced his *s*

SIDON

Gen 10.15 Canaan became the father of *S* his
Mt 11.21 in you had been done in Tyre and *S*,
 15.21 went away to the district of Tyre and *S*.
Mk 3. 8 and the region around Tyre and *S*.
Lk 4.26 except to a widow at Zarephath in *S*,
Acts 27. 3 The next day we put in at *S*; and Julius

SIDONIANS

Deut 3. 9 (the *S* call Hermon Sirion, while the
Judg 18. 7 they were far from the *S* and had no
1 Kings 5. 6 knows how to cut timber like the *S*."
2 Kings 23.13 for Astarte the abomination of the *S*,

SIGH (SIGHING)

Ps 31.10 spent with sorrow, and my years with *s*;
 90. 9 our years come to an end like a *s*.

SIGHT

Gen 6. 8 Noah found favor in the *s* of the Lord.
Deut 34. 7 his *s* was unimpaired and his vigor had
1 Kings 15.11 did what was right in the *s* of the Lord,
Eccl 6. 9 Better is the *s* of the eyes than the
Isa 65.16 are forgotten and are hidden from my *s*.
2 Cor 8.21 not only in the Lord's *s* but also in the

SIGN

Gen 9.12 "This is the *s* of the covenant that I
Ex 4. 8 first *s*, they may believe the second *s*.
 31.13 for this is a *s* between me and you
Num 16.38 Thus they shall be a *s* to the Israelites.
Josh 4. 6 this may be a *s* among you. When your
Judg 6.17 then show me a *s* that it is you who
1 Sam 2.34 shall be *s* to you— both of them
1 Kings 13. 3 He gave a *s* the same day, saying, "This
Isa 7.11 Ask a *s* of the Lord your God; let it be
 7.14 the Lord himself will give you a *s*.
 37.30 this shall be the *s* for you: This year eat
 38. 7 "This is the *s* to you from the Lord, that
 55.13 everlasting *s* that shall not be cut off.
Jer 44.29 This shall be the *s* to you, says the
Ezek 4. 3 it. This is a *s* for the house of Israel.
 12. 6 the land; for I have made you a *s* for
 14. 8 make them a *s* and a byword and cut
 24.24 Ezekiel shall be a *s* to you; you shall do
Mt 12.39 but no *s* will be given to it except the *s*
 16. 1 asked him to show them a *s* from
 24. 3 what will be the *s* of your coming and
 26.48 Now the betrayer had given them a *s*,
Mk 8.11 asking him for a *s* from heaven, to test
 13. 4 what will be the *s* that all these things
 14.44 betrayer had given them a *s*, saying,
Lk 2.12 This will be a *s* for you: you will find a
 2.34 and to be a *s* that will be opposed
 11.16 demanding from him a *s* from heaven.
 11.29 it asks for a *s*, but no *s* will be given to
 21. 7 what will be the *s* that this is about to
 23. 8 was hoping to see him perform some *s*.
Jn 2.18 "What *s* can you show us for doing this?"
 10.41 "John performed no *s*, but everything
Acts 4.16 a notable *s* has been done through
Rom 4.11 He received the *s* of circumcision as a
1 Cor 14.22 Tongues, then, are not a *s* for believers

SIGNS

Gen 1.14 and let them be for *s* and for seasons
Isa 8.18 whom the Lord has given me are *s*
Jer 10. 2 or be dismayed at the *s* of the heavens;
Dan 4. 3 How great are his *s*, how mighty his
Mt 16. 3 you cannot interpret the *s* of the times.
Mk 13.22 false prophets will appear and produce *s*

Mk	16.17 these s will accompany those who
Jn	2.11 Jesus did this, the first of his s, in Cana
	2.23 they saw the s that he was doing.
	4.48 "Unless you see s and wonders you will
	6. 2 following him, because they saw the s
	20.30 Now Jesus did many other s in the
Acts	5.12 Now many s and wonders were done
	15.12 of all the s and wonders God had done
1 Cor	1.22 Jews demand s and Greeks desire
Rev	13.13 It performs great s, even making fire
	13.14 by the s that it is allowed to perform on
	16.14 demonic spirits, performing s, who go

SIGNAL

Isa	5.26 He will raise a s for a nation far away,
	11.10 the root of Jesse shall stand as a s to
	13. 2 On a bare hill raise a s, cry aloud to
	18. 3 when a s is raised on the mountains,
Zech	10. 8 I will s for them and gather them in, for

SIGNET

| Jer | 22.24 Judah were the s ring on my right hand, |
| Dan | 6.17 king sealed it with his own s and with |

SILAS (SILVANUS)

Acts	15.22 sent Judas called Barsabbas, and S,
	15.40 But Paul chose S and set out, the
	16.19 they seized Paul and S and dragged
	17. 4 were persuaded and joined Paul and S,
	18. 5 When S and Timothy arrived from
2 Cor	1.19 we proclaimed among you, S and
1 Thess	1. 1 Paul, S and Timothy, To the church of
1 Pet	5.12 Through S, whom I consider a faithful

SILENCE (SILENCED)

| 1 Kings 19.12 and after the fire the sound of sheer s. |
Esth	4.14 if you keep s at such a time as this,
Ps	32. 3 While I kept s, my body wasted away
	83. 1 O God, do not keep s; do not hold your
Hab	2.20 let all the earth keep s before him.
Rom	3.19 that every mouth may be s, and the
1 Tim	2.11 Let a woman learn in s with full
Rev	8. 1 seal, there was s in heaven for about

SILENT

| 2 Kings 18.36 the people were s and answered him |
Ps	4. 4 sin; ponder it on your beds, and be s.
	39. 2 I was s and still; I held my peace to no
Prov	17.28 fools who keep s are considered wise;
Zeph	1. 7 Be s before the Lord GOD! For the day
Zech	2.13 Be s, all people, before the LORD; for he
Mt	26.63 But Jesus was s. Then the high priest
Mk	1.25 saying, "Be s, and come out of him!"
1 Cor	14.28 is no one to interpret, let them be s
	14.34 women should be s in the churches.

SILLY

| 2 Tim | 3. 6 and captivate s women, overwhelmed by |

SILOAM

| Lk | 13. 4 were killed when the tower of S fell |
| Jn | 9. 7 to him, "Go, wash in the pool of S" |

SILVER

Ps	12. 6 are promises that are pure, s refined
Prov	8.19 fine gold, and my yield than choice s.
Isa	1.22 Your s has become dross, your wine is
Jer	6.30 They are called "rejected s," for the LORD
Hag	2. 8 The s is mine, and the gold is mine,
Mt	26.15 you?" They paid him thirty pieces of s.
	27. 3 and brought back the thirty pieces of s
Lk	15. 8 having ten s coins, if she loses one
Acts	3. 6 Peter said, "I have no s or gold, but

SILVERSMITH

| Judg | 17. 4 gave it to a s, who made it into an idol |
| Acts | 19.24 Demetrius, a s, who made silver shrines |

SIMEON (Son of Jacob)

Born, Gen 29.33; with Levi, took revenge on Shechem, Gen 34; detained as a hostage, Gen 42.24; his future predicted, Gen 49.5-7.

SIMEON (the Prophet)

| Lk | 2.25 Jerusalem whose name was S; this man |
| | 2.34 Then S blessed them and said to his |

SIMON

Mt	10. 4 S the Cananaean, and Judas Iscariot,
Mk	3.18 Thaddaeus, and S the Cananaean, and
Acts	1.13 Alphaeus, and S the Zealot, and Judas

SIMPLE

Ps	19. 7 of the LORD are pure, making wise the s;
	116. 6 The LORD protects the s; when I was
	119.130 light; it imparts understanding to the s.
Prov	1.22 "How long, O s ones, will you love
	9. 4 "You that are s, turn in here!" To those

SIN (n)

Gen	4. 7 do not do well, s is lurking at the door;
	31.36 What is my s, that you have hotly
Lev	24.15 who curses God shall bear the s.
Num	12.11 do not punish us for a s that we have so
	32.23 and be sure your s will find you out.
1 Sam	2.17 the s of the young men was very great
1 Kings	8.36 forgive the s of your servants, your
	17.18 to me to bring my s to remembrance,
2 Kings	21.16 besides the s that he caused Judah to s
2 Chr	6.25 forgive the s of your people, and bring
Job	10. 6 out my iniquity and search for my s,
	13.23 me know my transgression and my s.
Ps	32. 5 Then I acknowledged my s to you, and I
	38.18 confess my iniquity; I am sorry for my s.
Prov	5.22 they are caught in the toils of their s.
	20. 9 my heart clean; I am pure from my s"?
	24. 9 The devising of folly is s, and the
Eccl	5. 6 Do not let your mouth lead you into s,
Isa	5.18 who drag s as with cart ropes,
	30. 1 but against my will, adding s to s;
Jer	17. 1 The s of Judah is written with an iron
Mic	6. 7 fruit of my body for the s of my soul?"
Mt	12.31 forgiven for every s and blasphemy, but
	13.41 out of his kingdom all causes of s
Jn	1.29 God who takes away the s of the world!
	8. 7 anyone among you who is without s
	8.21 for me, but you will die in your s.
	8.46 Which of you convicts me of s? If I tell
	15.22 but now they have no excuse for their s.
	16. 8 he will prove the world wrong about s
Acts	7.60 "Lord, do not hold this s against them."
Rom	3. 9 and Greeks, are under the power of s,
	5.12 just as s came into the world through
	6.14 For s will have no dominion over you,
	6.23 For the wages of s is death, but the free
	7. 7 for the law, I would not have known s.
	7.13 It was s, working death in me through
	14.23 does not proceed from faith is s.
2 Cor	5.21 he made him to be s who knew no s, so
Gal	3.22 all things under the power of s,
1 Tim	5.20 As for those who persist in s, rebuke
Heb	3.13 be hardened by the deceitfulness of s.
	4.15 been tested as we are, yet without s.
	12. 4 In your struggle against s you have not
1 Pet	2.22 "He committed no s; and no deceit was
1 Jn	1. 8 If we say we have no s, we deceive
	3. 5 away sins, and in him there is no s.
	5.16 what is not a mortal s, you will ask, and

SINS (n)

| Lev | 26.21 to plague you sevenfold for your s. |
| 2 Kings 13. 6 did not depart from the s of the house |
2 Chr	25. 4 all shall be put to death for their own s."
	28.10 What have you except s against the
Ps	25. 7 Do not remember the s of my youth or

Ps	79.	9 deliver us, and forgive our *s*, for your
	103.	10 not deal with us according to our *s*,
Isa	38.	17 have cast all my *s* behind your back.
	43.	24 burdened me with your *s*; you have
	58.	1 rebellion, to the house of Jacob their *s*.
Lam	4.	13 It was for the *s* of her prophets and the
Dan	4.	27 atone for your *s* with righteousness, and
Am	5.	12 and how great are your *s* — you who
Mt	1.	21 for he will save his people from their *s*.
Mk	2.	5 the paralytic, "Son, your *s* are forgiven."
	3.	28 people will be forgiven for their *s* and
Lk	5.	20 said, "Friend, your *s* are forgiven you."
Jn	20.	23 If you forgive the *s* of any, they are
Acts	22.	16 be baptized, have your *s* washed away,
1 Cor	15.	17 faith is futile and you are still in your *s*.
Gal	1.	4 who gave himself for our *s* to set us free
Eph	2.	1 were dead through the trespasses and *s*
Heb	9.	7 that he offers for himself and for the *s*
	10.	17 their *s* and their lawless deeds
1 Pet	2.	24 He himself bore our *s* in his body on
	3.	18 Christ also suffered for *s* once for all,

SIN (SINS SINNING) (v)

Gen	39.	9 great wickedness, and *s* against God?"
Lev	4.	2 When anyone *s* unintentionally in any
Deut	20.	18 you thus *s* against the LORD your God.
1 Sam	2.	25 but if someone *s* against the LORD, who
	12.	23 me that I should *s* against the LORD
	14.	33 the troops are *s* against the LORD by
	19.	4 "The king should not *s* against his
1 Kings	8.	46 there is no one who does not *s* —
2 Chr	6.	36 "If they *s* against you — for there is no
Job	7.	20 If I *s*, what do I do to you, you watcher
	10.	14 If I *s*, you watch me, and do not acquit
Ps	119.	11 heart, so that I might not *s* against you.
Eccl	7.	20 righteous as to do good without ever *s*.
Mt	5.	29 If your right eye causes you to *s*, tear it
	18.	15 another member of the church *s* against
Lk	17.	3 If another disciple *s*, you must rebuke
Jn	5.	14 been made well! Do not *s* any more,
1 Cor	6.	18 but the fornicator *s* against the body
	8.	12 when it is weak, you *s* against Christ.
Heb	10.	26 if we willfully persist in *s* after having
1 Jn	2.	1 things to you so that you may not *s*.
	3.	6 no one who *s* has either seen him or
	3.	9 who have been born of God do not *s*,

SINNED

Ex	9.	27 said to them, "This time I have *s*;
	32.	30 "You have *s* a great sin. But now I will
Num	14.	40 that God has promised, for we have *s*."
	22.	34 "I have *s*, for I did not know that you
Deut	1.	41 "We have *s* against the LORD! We are
	9.	16 that you had indeed *s* against the LORD
Josh	7.	11 Israel has *s*; they have transgressed my
Judg	10.	10 "We have *s* against you, because we
1 Sam	7.	6 and said, "We have *s* against the LORD."
	15.	24 Saul said to Samuel, "I have *s*; for I
	24.	11 I have not *s* against you, though you are
2 Sam	12.	13 to Nathan, "I have *s* against the LORD."
	24.	10 "I have *s* greatly in what I have done.
1 Kings	14.	16 which he *s* and which he caused Israel
2 Kings	17.	7 people of Israel had *s* against the LORD
1 Chr	21.	8 David said to God, "I have *s* greatly in
Neh	1.	6 of Israel, which we have *s* against you.
Job	33.	27 'I *s*, and perverted what was right, and
	35.	6 If you have *s*, what do you accomplish
Ps	78.	32 In spite of all this they still *s*; they did
Isa	42.	24 not the LORD, against whom we have *s*,
Jer	8.	14 because we have *s* against the LORD.
	14.	7 are many, and we have *s* against you.
Lam	1.	8 Jerusalem *s* grievously, so she has
	5.	7 Our ancestors *s*; they are no more, and
Dan	9.	5 we have *s* and done wrong, acted
Hos	10.	9 the days of Gibeah you have *s*, O Israel;
Mic	7.	9 the LORD, because I have *s* against him,
Mt	27.	4 "I have *s* in betraying innocent blood."

Lk	15.	18 "Father, I have *s* against heaven and
Jn	9.	2 who *s*, this man or his parents, that he
Rom	2.	12 All who have *s* apart from the law will
	3.	23 all have *s* and fall short of the glory of

SIN OFFERING

Ex	29.	14 with fire outside the camp; it is a *s*.
Lev	4.	3 herd without blemish as a *s* to the LORD.
	5.	6 from the flock, a sheep or a goat, as a *s*;
	6.	25 the ritual of the *s*. The *s* shall be

SINAI

Ex	19.	1 day, they came into the wilderness of *S*.
	19.	20 the LORD descended upon Mount *S*,
	34.	29 Moses came down from Mount *S*. As he
Deut	33.	2 The LORD came from *S*, and dawned
Ps	68.	8 at the presence of God, the God of *S*,
Gal	4.	24 is Hagar, from Mount *S*, bearing

SINFUL

Isa	1.	4 Ah, *s* nation, people laden with iniquity,
Lk	5.	8 away from me, Lord, for I am a *s* man!"
1 Tim	1.	9 for the godless and the *s*, for the unholy

SING

Num	21.	17 this song: "Spring up, O well! — *S* to it!
1 Chr	16.	9 *S* to him, *s* praises to him, tell of all his
2 Chr	20.	21 appointed those who were to *s* to the
Job	29.	13 and I caused the widow's heart to *s* for
Ps	59.	16 But I will *s* of your might; I will *s* aloud
	75.	9 I will *s* praises to the God of Jacob.
	81.	1 *S* aloud to God our strength; shout for
	89.	1 I will *s* of your steadfast love, O LORD,
	95.	1 O come, let us *s* to the LORD; let us
	96.	2 *S* to the LORD, bless his name; tell of his
	108.	1 is steadfast; I will *s* and make melody.
Prov	29.	6 a snare, but the righteous *s* and rejoice.
Isa	12.	5 *S* praises to the LORD, for he has done
	26.	19 in the dust, awake and *s* for joy!
	35.	6 the tongue of the speechless *s* for joy.
	38.	20 and we will *s* to stringed instruments
	42.	10 *S* to the LORD a new song, his praise
	44.	23 *S*, O heavens, for the LORD has done it;
	52.	8 together they *s* for joy; for in plain sight
	54.	1 *S*, O barren one who did not bear; burst
	65.	14 servants shall *s* for gladness of heart,
Jer	20.	13 *S* to the LORD; praise the LORD! For he
Zech	2.	10 *S* and rejoice, O daughter Zion! For lo, I
Rom	15.	9 you among the Gentiles, and *s* praises
1 Cor	14.	15 but I will *s* praise with the mind also.
Rev	14.	3 they *s* a new song before the throne and

SINGING

Song	2.	12 the time of *s* has come, and the voice
Isa	14.	7 rest and quiet; they break forth into *s*.
Zeph	3.	17 he will exult over you with loud *s* as on
Acts	16.	25 Silas were praying and *s* hymns to God,

SINNER (SINNERS)

Ps	25.	8 therefore he instructs *s* in the way.
	104.	35 Let *s* be consumed from the earth, and
Prov	13.	21 Misfortune pursues *s*, but prosperity
Eccl	2.	26 but to the *s* he gives the work of
Isa	13.	9 desolation, and to destroy its *s* from it.
Mt	9.	10 many tax collectors and *s* came and
	9.	13 come to call not the righteous but *s*."
Mk	2.	15 tax collectors and *s* were also sitting
	2.	17 come to call not the righteous but *s*."
	14.	41 of Man is betrayed into the hands of *s*.
Lk	6.	32 For even *s* love those who love them.
	6.	34 Even *s* lend to *s*, to receive as much
	7.	37 a woman in the city, who was a *s*,
	13.	2 were worse *s* than all other Galileans?
	15.	2 "This fellow welcomes *s* and eats
	15.	7 more joy in heaven over one *s* who
	19.	7 gone to be the guest of one who is a *s*."
Jn	9.	16 "How can a man who is a *s* perform
	9.	24 to God! We know that this man is a *s*."

Rom	3.	7 why am I still being condemned as a s?
	5.19	disobedience the many were made s,
Gal	2.17	we ourselves have been found to be s, is
Jas	5.20	whoever brings back a s from wandering

SISTER (SISTERS)

Gen	12.13	Say you are my s, so that it may go well
	20. 2	said of his wife Sarah, "She is my s."
	26. 7	about his wife, he said, "She is my s";
Ex	2. 4	His s stood at a distance, to see what
Prov	7. 4	Say to wisdom, "You are my s," and call
Song	4. 9	have ravished my heart, my s, my bride,
	8. 8	We have a little s, she has no breasts.
Ezek	16.48	your s Sodom and her daughters has
Mk	3.35	God is my brother, and s, and mother."
Acts	23.16	the son of Paul's s heard about the
1 Cor	9. 5n	right to be accompanied by a s as wife,
1 Thess	4. 6	no one wrong or exploit a brother or s
1 Tim	5. 2	mothers, to younger women as s—
2 Jn	13	children of your elect s send their

SIT (SAT SITTING)

Judg	21. 2	and s there till evening before God, and
Ps	110. 1	"S at my right hand, until I make your
Isa	6. 1	I saw the Lord s on a throne, high and
Jer	15.17	I did not s in the company of
Ezek	3.15	river Chebar. And I s among them,
Mic	4. 4	they shall all s under their own vines
Mk	10.37	"Grant us to s, one at your right hand
	12.36	said to my Lord, "S at my right hand,
	16.19	heaven and s down at the right hand
Lk	7.32	are like children s in the marketplace
	20.42	said to my Lord, "S at my right hand,
Acts	2.34	said to my Lord, "S at my right hand,
Heb	1. 3	he s down at the right hand of the
	10.12	"he s down at the right hand of God,"

SIXTH

Lk	1.26	In the s month the angel Gabriel was

SKETCH

Heb	8. 5	is a s and shadow of the heavenly one;

SKILL (SKILLFUL)

1 Sam	16.16	someone who is s in playing the lyre;
1 Kings	7.14	was full of s, intelligence, and
Ps	78.72	them, and guided them with a s hand.
Prov	22.29	you see those who are s in their work?

SKIN (SKINS)

Gen	3.21	God made garments of s for the man
	21.14	took bread and a s of water, and gave it
Job	2. 4	"S for s! All that people have they will
	7. 5	and dirt; my s hardens, then breaks out
	19.20	I have escaped by the s of my teeth.
Jer	13.23	Can Ethiopians change their s or the
Mk	2.22	otherwise, the wine will burst the s,

SKULL

Mt	27.33	Golgotha (which means Place of a S),
Mk	15.22	(which means the place of a s).
Lk	23.33	is called The S, they crucified Jesus
Jn	19.17	out to what is called the Place of the S,

SKY (SKIES)

Gen	1. 8	God called the dome S. And there was
2 Kings	7. 2	Lord were to make windows in the s,
Ps	85.11	will look down from the s.
Isa	34. 4	rot away, and the s roll up like a scroll.
Lk	12.56	interpret the appearance of earth and s;
Rev	6.14	The s vanished like a scroll rolling itself

SLANDER (SLANDERED SLANDERS)

Ps	15. 3	who do not s with their tongue, and do
	50.20	your kin; you s your own mother's child.
	101. 5	who secretly s a neighbor I will destroy.
Prov	30.10	Do not s a servant to his master, or the
1 Cor	4.13	we endure; when s, we speak kindly.
2 Pet	2.10	they are not afraid to s the glorious

SLANDERER (SLANDERERS)

Lev	19.16	You shall not go around as a s among
Rom	1.30	they are gossips, s, God-haters, insolent,

SLAP

2 Cor	11.20	or puts on airs, or gives you a s in the

SLAUGHTER (SLAUGHTERED)

Ps	44.22	long, and accounted as sheep for the s.
Jer	11.19	I was like a gentle lamb led to the s.
Rom	8.36	we are accounted as sheep to be s."
Rev	6. 9	those who had been s for the word of
	13. 8	in book of life of the Lamb that was s.

SLAVE (SLAVES)

Gen	9.25	"Cursed be Canaan; lowest of s shall he
	21.10	Cast out this s woman with her son; for
Deut	5.15	Remember you were a s in the land of
	6.21	"We were Pharaoh's s in Egypt, but the
	21.14	You must not treat her as a s, since you
Josh	9.23	some of you shall always be s, hewers
Prov	19.10	luxury, much less for a s to rule over
Eccl	10. 7	I have seen s on horseback, and princes
Jer	2.14	Is Israel a s? Is he a homeborn servant?
	34.11	and took back the male and female s
Lam	5. 8	S rule over us; there is no one to deliver
Mt	20.27	to be first among you must be your s;
	21.34	he sent his s to the tenants to collect
	25.14	summoned his s and entrusted his
	25.23	'Well done, good and trustworthy s;
Mk	10.44	wishes be first among you must be s
	12. 2	he sent a s to the tenants, to collect
	14.47	struck the s of the high priest, cutting
Lk	17. 9	Do you thank the s for doing what was
	19.17	"Well done, good s! Because you have
	20.10	he sent a s to the tenants in order that
	22.50	of them struck the s of the high priest
Jn	8.34	everyone who commits sin is a s to sin.
Rom	6.16	yourselves to anyone as obedient s,
	7. 6	we are s not under the old written code
1 Cor	7.21	Were you a s when called? Do not be
2 Cor	4. 5	Christ as Lord and ourselves as your s
Gal	3.28	there is no longer s or free, there is no
	4. 1	as they are minors, are no better than s,
Eph	6. 5	S, obey your earthly masters with fear
Col	3.22	S, obey your earthly masters in
Titus	2. 9	Tell s to be submissive to their masters
Philem	16	no longer as a s but more than a s, a
1 Pet	2.18	S, accept the authority of your masters
2 Pet	2.19	but they themselves are s of corruption;

SLAVE-GIRL

Gen	16. 2	from bearing children; go in to my s;

SLAVERY

Ex	20. 2	the land of Egypt, out of the house of s.
Deut	5. 6	the land of Egypt, out of the house of s.
Rom	8.15	you did not receive a spirit of s to fall
Gal	5. 1	and do not submit again to a yoke of s.
Heb	2.15	lives were held in s by the fear of death.

SLEEP (n)

Gen	2.21	God caused a deep s to fall upon the
1 Sam	26.12	a deep s from the Lord had fallen upon
Ps	127. 2	toil; for he gives s to his beloved.
	132. 4	I will not give s to my eyes or slumber
Prov	3.24	you lie down, your s will be sweet.
	6. 4	Give your eyes no s and your eyelids no
	24.33	little s, a little slumber, a little folding
Eccl	5.12	Sweet is the s of laborers, whether they
Isa	29.10	poured out upon you a spirit of deep s,
Jer	51.39	become merry and then s a perpetual s

SLEEP (SLEEPING SLEPT)

Ps	3. 5	I lie down and s; I wake again, for the
	13. 3	to my eyes, or I will s the s of death,
	121. 4	keeps Israel will neither slumber nor s.
Song	5. 2	I s, but my heart was awake. Listen! my

SLIP

Dan	12. 2 of those who s in the dust of the earth
Mt	9.24 "Go away, for the girl is not dead but s."
	26.40 came to the disciples and found them s;
Mk	5.39 and weep? The child is not dead but s."
	14.37 He came and found them s; and he said
	14.40 once more he came and found them s,
Lk	22.45 and found them s because of grief

SLIP (SLIPPED SLIPS)

Deut	32.35 for the time when their foot shall s;
Ps	17. 5 fast to your paths, my feet have not s.
	18.36 steps under me, and my feet did not s.
	37.31 is in their hearts; their steps do not s.
	38.16 who boast against me when my foot s."

SLIPPERY

Ps	35. 6 Let their way be dark and s, with the
	73.18 you set them in s places; you make

SLOW

Prov	16.32 who is s to anger is better than the
	19.11 Those with good sense are s to anger,

SLUMBER (SLUMBERS)

Ps	121. 3 be moved; he who keeps you will not s.
Prov	6.10 A little sleep, a little s, a little folding
Isa	5.27 weary, none stumbles, none s or sleeps,

SMALL (SMALLEST)

Job	40. 4 I am of s account; what shall I answer
Mt	13.32 it is the s of all seeds, but when it has

SMASHES

Dan	2.40 just as iron crushes and s everything, it

SMELLED

Gen	27.27 he s the smell of his garments, and he

SMELT

Isa	1.25 I will s away your dross as with lye and

SMITH

1 Sam	13.19 there was no s to be found throughout
Isa	54.16 I who have created the s who blows the

SMITTEN

Ps	102. 4 My heart is s and withered like grass; I

SMOKE

Gen	19.28 s of the land going up like the s of a
Ps	68. 2 As s is driven away, so drive them away;
Prov	10.26 and s to the eyes, so are the lazy to
Rev	15. 8 the temple filled with s from the glory

SMOOTH

Prov	2.16 from the adulteress with her s words,
Isa	30.10 speak to us s things, prophesy illusions,
Lk	3. 5 straight, and the rough ways made s;

SNAKE (SNAKES)

Ex	4. 3 on the ground, and it became a s;
	7.10 down his staff . . . , and it became a s.
Jer	8.17 I am letting s loose among you, adders
Mt	23.33 You s, you brood of vipers! How can you
Mk	16.18n they will pick up s in their hands, and if
Lk	10.19 authority to tread on s and scorpions,

SNARE (SNARES)

Ex	23.33 their gods, it will surely be a s to you.
Deut	7.16 their gods, for that would be a s to you.
Judg	2. 3 you, and their gods shall be a s to you."
	8.27 and it became a s to Gideon and to his
1 Sam	18.21 her to him that she may be a s for him,
Job	22.10 Therefore a s is around you, and sudden
Ps	38.12 Those who seek my life lay their s;
	64. 5 they talk of laying s secretly, thinking,
	69.22 their table be a trap for them, a s for
Prov	18. 7 are their ruin, and their lips are a s to
	22.25 their ways and entangle yourself in a s.
	29.25 The fear of others lays a s, but one who

Jer	18.22 pit to catch me, and laid s for my feet.
	50.24 You set a s for yourself and you were
Ezek	12.13 him and he shall be caught in my s;
Lk	21.35 day catch you unexpectedly, like a s.
1 Tim	3. 7 fall into disgrace and the s of the devil.

SNATCH (SNATCHING)

Job	24. 9 There are those who s the orphan child
Jn	10.28 never perish. No one will s them out
Jude	23 save others, by s them out of the fire;

SNOW (SNOWS)

2 Sam	23.20 lion in a pit on a day when s had fallen.
Job	38.22 you entered the storehouses of the s,
Ps	51. 7 wash me, and I shall be whiter than s.
	147. 16 He gives s like wool; he scatters frost
Prov	25.13 Like the cold of s in the time of harvest
	26. 1 Like s in summer or rain in harvest, so
	31.21 not afraid for her household when it s,
Isa	1.18 sins are like scarlet, they shall be like s;
Jer	18.14 Does the s of Lebanon leave the crags
Lam	4. 7 Her princes were purer than s, whiter
Mt	28. 3 lightning, and his clothing white as s.

SOAP

Job	9.30 If I wash myself with s and cleanse my

SOBER

1 Thess	5. 6 do, but let us keep awake and be s;

SODOM

Gen	10.19 as far as Gaza, in the direction of S,
	13.13 Now the people of S were wicked, great
	14.12 they took Lot . . . who lived in S, and
	19.24 LORD rained on S . . . sulfur and fire
Jer	50.40 as when God overthrew S and
Mt	10.15 it will more tolerable for the land of S
	11.23 power done in you had been done in S,
Lk	17.29 on the day that Lot left S, it rained fire
Rev	11. 8 great city that is prophetically called S

SOFT

Prov	15. 1 A s answer turns away wrath, but a
Mt	11. 8 out to see? Someone dressed in s robes?

SOIL (SOILED)

Gen	9.20 Noah, a man of the s, was the first to
Rev	3. 4 who have not s their clothes; they will

SOLDIERS

Mt	28.12 to give a large sum of money to the s,
Lk	3.14 S also asked him, "And we, what should
	7. 8 set under authority, with s under me:
Jn	19.23 When the s had crucified Jesus, they

SOLE

Josh	1. 3 Every place that the s of your foot will

SOLID

1 Cor	3. 2 I fed you with milk, not s food, for you
Heb	5.12 of God. You need milk, not s food;

SOLOMON (SOLOMON'S)

Born, 2 Sam 12.24; anointed king, 1 Kings 1.32-40; established his kingdom, 1 Kings 2.12-46; married Pharaoh's daughter, 1 Kings 3.1; asked for wisdom, 1 Kings 3.5-15; judged wisely, 1 Kings 3.16-28; conferred with Hiram, 1 Kings 5; 7.13-14; built the temple, 1 Kings 6; 7.15-51; built his own house, 1 Kings 7.1-12; dedicated the temple, 1 Kings 8; the LORD's covenant with Solomon, 1 Kings 9.1-9; visited by the queen of Sheba, 1 Kings 10.1-13; turned from the LORD, 1 Kings 11.1-40; died, 1 Kings 11.41-43. (See also 2 Chr 1—9.)

Prov	1. 1 proverbs of S, son of David, king of
Song	1. 1 The Song of Songs, which is S.
Mt	6.29 even S in all his glory was not clothed
Lk	11.31 the earth to listen to the wisdom of S,
	11.31 see, something greater than S is here.
Jn	10.23 in the temple, in the portico of S.

Acts 3.11 in the portico called *S* Portico, utterly

SON

Gen	18.10 and your wife Sarah shall have a *s*."
	22. 2 "Take your *s*, your only *s* Isaac, whom
Deut	21.18 stubborn and rebellious *s* who will not
2 Sam	7.14 to him, and he shall be a *s* to me.
	18.33 "O my *s* Absalom, my *s*, my *s* Absalom!
2 Kings	4.14 "Well, she has no *s*, and her husband is
	4.16 in due time, you shall embrace a *s*."
	8. 1 woman whose *s* he had restored to life,
1 Chr	17.13 to him, and he shall be a *s* to me.
Ps	2. 7 He said to me, "You are my *s*; today I
Prov	3.12 the one he loves, as a father the *s*
Isa	7.14 shall bear a *s*, and shall name him
	9. 6 has been born for us, a *s* given to us;
Jer	31.20 Is Ephraim my dear *s*? Is he the child I
Am	7.14 "I am no prophet, nor a prophet's *s*; but
Mic	7. 6 *s* treats the father with contempt, and
Mt	9.27 loudly, "Have mercy on us, *S* of David."
	12.23 and said, "Can this be the *S* of David?"
	13.55 Is not this the carpenter's *s*? Is not his
	21.37 them saying, 'They will respect my *s*.'
	22. 2 who gave a wedding banquet for his *s*,
	22.42 he?" They said to him, "The *s* of David."
Mk	1.11 "You are my *S*, the Beloved; with you I
	9. 7 "This is my *S*, the Beloved; listen to
	9.17 "Teacher, I brought you my *s*; he has a
	12. 6 He had still one other, a beloved *s*;
	14.61 the Messiah, the *S* of the Blessed One?"
Lk	1.31 and bear a *s*, and you will name him
	1.57 to give birth, and she bore a *s*.
	7.12 mother's only *s*, and she was a widow;
	9.38 "Teacher, I beg you to look at my *s*, he
	12.53 be divided, father against *s* and *s*
	15.21 no longer worthy to be called your *s*.'
	19. 9 because he too is a *s* of Abraham.
	20.13 I will send my beloved *s*; perhaps they
	20.44 calls him Lord; so how can he be his *s*?"
Jn	1.14 glory as of a father's only *s*, full of grace
	3.16 loved the world that he gave his only *S*,
	4.47 him to come down and heal his *s*,
	8.36 So if the *S* makes you free, you will be
	9.20 is our *s*, and that he was born blind;
	10.36 because I said, 'I am God's *S*'?
	17.12 n was lost except the *s* of destruction
	19.26 to his mother, "Woman, here is your *s*."
Acts	3.10 "You *s* of the devil, you enemy of all
	13.33 'You are my *S*; today I have begotten
Gal	1.16 was pleased to reveal his *S* to me,
	4. 4 of time had come, God sent his *S*,
Col	1.13 us into the kingdom of his beloved *S*,
Heb	1. 2 last days he has spoken to us by a *S*,
	3. 6 was faithful over God's house as a *s*.
	5. 5 said to him, "You are my *S*, today I have
	11.17 was ready to offer up his only *s*,
1 Jn	1. 3 the Father and with his *S* Jesus Christ.
	2.23 No one who denies the *S* has the
	4. 9 God sent his only *S* into the world so
	4.14 Father has sent his *S* as the Savior of
	5.12 Whoever has the *S* has life; whoever

SONS

Gen	6. 2 the *s* of God saw that they were fair;
Ps	127. 3 *S* are indeed a heritage from the LORD,
	132. 12 If your *s* keep my covenant and my
	144. 12 May our *s* in their youth be like plants
Jer	16. 2 not take a wife, nor shall you have *s* or
Mt	21.28 A man had two *s*; he went to the first

SON OF GOD

Mt	4. 3 "If you are the *S*, command these
	8.29 "What have you to do with us, *S*?
	14.33 him, saying, "Truly you are the *S*."
	26.63 tell us if you are the Messiah, the *S*."
	27.40 yourself! If you are the *S*, come down
Lk	1.35 will be holy; he will be called the *S*.

Jn	1.34 and have testified that this is the *S*."
	3.18 not believed in the name of the only *S*.
	19. 7 die because he has claimed to be the *S*."
Acts	9.20 in the synagogues, saying, "He is the *S*."
Rom	1. 4 and was declared to be *S* with power
Eph	4.13 the faith and of the knowledge of the *S*,
Heb	4.14 through the heavens, Jesus, the *S*,
	6. 6 own they are crucifying again the *S*
	10.29 by those who have spurned the *S*,
1 Jn	4.15 those who confess that Jesus is the *S*,
Rev	2.18 These are the words of the *S*, who has

SON OF MAN

Mt	8.20 but the *S* has nowhere to lay his head."
	9. 6 know that the *S* has authority on earth
	10.23 the towns of Israel, before the *S* comes.
	12. 8 For the *S* is lord of the sabbath."
	12.32 whoever speaks a word against the *S*
	13.37 one who sows the good seed is the *S*;
	16.27 *S* is to come with his angels in the glory
	17.22 "The *S* is going to be betrayed into
	24.27 west, so will be the coming of the *S*.
	24.30 Then the sign of the *S* will appear in
	25.31 "When the *S* comes in his glory, and all
	26. 2 and the *S* will be handed over to be
	26.24 The *S* goes as it is written of him, but
	26.64 from now on you will see the *S* seated
Mk	2.10 the *S* has authority on earth to forgive
	9.31 "The *S* is to be betrayed into human
	14.21 For the *S* goes as it is written of him,
	14.62 'you will see the *S* seated at the right
Lk	6. 5 to them, "The *S* is lord of the sabbath."
	9.22 "The *S* must undergo great suffering,
	9.44 your ears: The *S* is going to be betrayed
	22.69 the *S* will be seated at the right hand of
Jn	3.13 one who descended from heaven, the *S*.
	3.14 wilderness, so must the *S* be lifted up,
Acts	7.56 "I see the heavens opened, and the *S*
Rev	1.13 I saw one like the *S*, clothed with a
	14.14 seated on the cloud was one like the *S*,

SONG (SONGS)

Ex	15. 1 the Israelites sang this *s* to the LORD:
Deut	31.19 therefore write this *s*, and teach it to
Job	30. 9 "And now they mock me in *s*; I am a
Ps	28. 7 exults, and with my *s* I give thanks
	33. 3 Sing to him a new *s*; play skillfully on
	40. 3 He put a new *s* in my mouth, as a
	69.12 and the drunkards make *s* about me.
	81. 2 Raise a *s*, sound the tambourine, the
	95. 2 a joyful noise to him with *s* of praise!
	119. 54 Your statutes have been my *s* wherever I
	137. 3 For there our captors asked us for *s*,
	144. 9 I will sing a new *s* to you, O God; upon
	149. 1 Sing to the LORD a new *s*, his praise in
Prov	25.20 is one who sings *s* to a heavy heart.
Isa	26. 1 On that day this *s* will be sung in the
	30.29 have a *s* as in the night when a holy
Ezek	33.32 To them you are like a singer of love *s*,
Mic	2. 4 they shall take up a taunt *s* against you,
Rev	5. 9 They sing a new *s*: "You are worthy to
	15. 3 they sing the *s* of Moses, the servant of

SORCERER

Ex	22.18 You shall not permit a female *s* to live.

SORROW (SORROWS)

Ps	13. 2 my soul, and have *s* in my heart all day
	16. 4 choose another god multiply their *s*;
	31.10 For my life is spent with *s*, and my
	119. 28 My soul melts away for *s*; strengthen
Eccl	1.18 who increase knowledge increase *s*.
	7. 3 *S* is better than laughter, for by sadness
Isa	35.10 gladness, and *s* and sighing shall flee
	51.11 gladness, and *s* and sighing shall flee
Jer	20.18 forth from the womb to see toil and *s*,
	45. 3 me! The LORD has added *s* to my pain;

Lam	1.12	Look and see if there is any s like my s,
Ezek	23.33	shall be filled with drunkenness and s.
Jn	16.	6 things to you, s has filled your hearts.
Rom	9.	2 I have great s and unceasing anguish in
2 Cor	2.	7 may not be overwhelmed by excessive s.

SORROWFUL

2 Cor	6.10	as s, yet always rejoicing; as poor, yet

SORRY

Gen	6.	6 LORD was s that he had made
1 Sam	15.35	the LORD was s that he had made Saul
Ps	38.18	I confess my iniquity; I am s for my sin.

SOSTHENES

Acts	18.17	seized S, the official of the synagogue,
1 Cor	1.	1 by the will of God, and our brother S,

SOUL (SOULS)

Deut	6.	5 all your heart, and with all your s,
1 Sam	18.	1 the s of Jonathan was bound to the s of
2 Chr	6.38	repent with all their heart and s in the
Job	7.11	will complain in the bitterness of my s.
	30.16	now my s is poured out within me;
Ps	23.	3 me beside still waters; he restores my s.
	42.11	Why are you cast down, O my s, and
	56.13	For you have delivered my s from death,
	103.	1 Bless the LORD, O my s; and all that is
Prov	21.10	The s of the wicked desire evil; their
	27.	9 heart glad, but the s is torn by trouble.
Song	1.	7 Tell me, you whom my s loves, where
Isa		1.14 and your appointed festivals my s hates;
Jer	13.17	my s will weep in secret for your pride;
Mic	6.	7 the fruit of my body for the sin of my s?"
Mt	10.28	who kill the body but cannot kill the s;
	22.37	with all your heart, and with all your s,
Mk	12.30	with all your heart, and with all your s,
Lk	1.47	Mary said, "My s magnifies the Lord,
	12.19	say to my s, "S, you have ample goods
	21.19	By your endurance you will gain your s.
Acts	2.27	For you will not abandon my s to
1 Pet	1.22	have purified your s by your obedience
3 Jn	2	health, just as it is well with your s.
Rev	18.14	fruit for which your s longed has gone
	20.	4 I saw the s of those who had been

SOUND

Gen	3.	8 They heard the s of the LORD God
Ezek	1.24	the s of their wings like the s of mighty
Zeph	1.14	the s of the day of the LORD is bitter,
2 Tim	1.13	Hold to the standard of s teaching that
Titus	2.	2 prudent, and s in faith, in love, and in
	2.	8 s speech that cannot be censured; then

SOUNDNESS

Ps	38.	3 There is no s in my flesh because of
Isa	1.	6 there is no s in it, but bruises and sores

SOVEREIGN (SOVEREIGNTY)

1 Kings	4.21	Solomon was s over all the kingdoms
Dan	4.17	the Most High is s over the kingdom
	4.25	High has s over the kingdom of mortals,
	4.32	the Most High has s over the kingdom
	4.34	For his s is an everlasting s, and his

SOW (SOWED SOWN SOWS)

Gen	26.12	Isaac s in that land, and in the same
	47.23	here is seed for you; s the land.
Ps	107.	37 they s fields, and plant vineyards, and
	126.	5 those who s in tears reap with shouts
Prov	6.19	and one who s discord in a family.
	22.	8 Whoever s injustice will reap calamity,
Eccl	11.	4 Whoever observes the wind will not s;
Isa	32.20	will you be who s beside every stream,
Jer	4.	3 fallow ground, and s not among thorns.
	12.13	have s wheat and have reaped thorns,
	31.27	when I will s the house of Israel and
Hos	8.	7 For they s the wind, and they shall reap

Hos	10.12	S for yourselves righteousness; reap
Mic	6.15	You shall s, but not reap; you shall
Mt	6.26	birds of the air; they neither s nor reap
	13.27	'Master, did you not s good seed in
	25.26	did you, that I reap where I did not s,
Mk	4.	3 "Listen! A sower went out to s.
Lk	12.24	the ravens: they neither s nor reap,
Jn	4.37	holds true, 'One s and another reaps.'
1 Cor	9.11	If we have s spiritual good among you,
	15.36	What you s does not come to life unless
2 Cor	9.	6 one who s sparingly will also reap
Gal	6.	7 mocked, for you reap whatever you s.

SOWER

Mt	13.	3 saying: "Listen! A s went out to sow.
	13.18	"Hear then the parable of the s.
Mk	4.14	The s sows the word.
Lk	8.	5 "As went out to sow his seed; and as

SPAIN

Rom	15.24	come to you when I go to S. For I do
	15.28	I will set out by way of you to S; and I

SPAN

Mt	6.27	add a single hour to your s of life?
Lk	12.25	add a single hour to your s of life?

SPARE (SPARED SPARES)

Josh	6.25	Rahab . . . Joshua s. Her family has
1 Sam	15.	9 Saul and the people s Agag, and the
	24.10	some urged me kill you, but I s you.
2 Sam	21.	7 the king s Mephibosheth, the son of
Job	2.	6 well, he is in your power; only s his life."
	21.30	that the wicked are s in the day of
Ps	119.	88 In your steadfast love s my life, so that
Prov	13.24	who s the rod hate their children, but
	17.27	One who s words is knowledgeable, one

SPARROW (SPARROWS)

Ps	84.	3 Even the s finds a home, and the
Mt	10.29	Are not two s sold for a penny?
Lk	12.	6 Are not five s sold for two pennies? Yet

SPEAK (SPEAKING SPEAKS SPOKE SPOKEN)

Ex	20.	1 Then God s all these words:
	20.19	but do not let God s to us, or we will
	33.	9 tent, and the LORD would s with Moses.
Num	7.89	into tent of meeting to s with the LORD,
	11.25	came down in the cloud and s to him,
	12.	8 With him I s face to face —clearly, not
Deut	5.	4 The LORD s with you face to face at the
	5.24	Today we have seen that God may s to
1 Sam	3.	9 "S, LORD, for your servant is listening.' "
1 Kings	22.14	the LORD says to me, that I will s."
2 Chr	18.13	lives, whatever God says, that I will s."
Job	33.14	For God s in one way, and in two,
Ps	50.	1 LORD, s and summons the earth from
	85.	8 will s, for he will s peace to his people,
	87.	3 Glorious things are s of you, O city of
	139.	20 those who s of you maliciously, and lift
Eccl	3.	7 a time to keep silence, and a time to s;
Isa	40.	2 S tenderly to Jerusalem, and cry to her
Jer	1.	6 I do not know how to s, for I am only a
Hos	2.14	the wilderness, and s tenderly to her
Mt	17.25	Jesus s of it first, asking, "What do you
Mk	2.	2 door, and he was s the word to them.
Lk	4.32	teaching, because he s with authority.
	4.41	them and would not allow them to s,
	12.10	everyone who s a word against the Son
Jn	7.46	answered, "Never has anyone s like this!"
Acts	2.	4 and began to s in other languages,
	5.40	them not to s in the name of Jesus,
1 Tim	5.	1 Do not s harshly to an older man, but s
Heb	11.	4 he died, but through his faith he still s.
Jas	4.11	Whoever s evil against another or judges

SPEAR (SPEARS)

1 Sam	26.	8 to the ground with one stroke of the s;

Isa 2. 4 and their *s* into pruning hooks;
Jn 19.34 of the soldiers pierced his side with a *s*,

SPECIAL

2 Tim 2.20 clay, some for *s* use, some for ordinary.

SPECK

Mt 7. 3 do you see the *s* in your neighbor's eye,
Lk 6.41 do you see the *s* in your neighbor's eye,

SPECTACLE

Nah 3. 6 you with contempt, and make you a *s*.

SPEECH

Ex 4.10 but I am slow of *s* and of tongue."
Ps 19. 2 Day to day pours forth *s*, and night to
Prov 17. 7 Fine *s* is not becoming to a fool; still
29.20 Do you see someone who is hasty in *s*?
Ezek 3. 5 not sent to a people of obscure *s* and
Zeph 3. 9 change the *s* of the peoples to a pure *s*,
1 Cor 1. 5 enriched in him, in *s* and knowledge of
2 Cor 10.10 is weak, and his *s* is contemptible"
Col 4. 6 Let your *s* always be gracious, seasoned

SPEECHLESS

Ezek 3.26 shall be *s* and unable to reprove them;
Dan 10.15 my face toward the ground and was *s*.
Mt 22.12 without a wedding robe?' And he was *s*.
Acts 9. 7 who were traveling with him stood *s*,

SPELLBOUND

Mk 11.18 the whole crowd was *s* at his teaching.

SPEND (SPENT)

Gen 19. 2 *s* the night, and wash your feet; then
47.18 from my lord that our money is all *s*;
Ps 38. 8 I am utterly *s* and crushed; I groan

SPEWED

Jon 2.10 spoke to the fish, and it *s* Jonah out

SPICE (SPICES)

Song 4.10 the fragrance of your oils than any *s*!
Jn 19.40 wrapped it with the *s* in linen cloths

SPIES

Josh 2. 1 sent two men ecretly from Shittim as *s*,
6.23 men who had been *s* went in and
Judg 1.24 When the *s* saw a man coming out of

SPIRIT

Gen 6. 3 "My *s* shall not abide in mortals forever,
Ex 31. 3 I have filled him with divine *s*, with
Num 11.17 will take some of the *s* which is on you
11.29 the LORD would put his *s* upon them!"
27.18 son of Nun, a man in whom is the *s*,
Judg 9.23 God sent an evil *s* between Abimelech
1 Sam 19. 9 an evil *s* from the LORD came upon Saul,
28. 8 "Consult a *s* for me, and bring up for
1 Kings 22.21 until a *s* came forward and stood before
2 Kings 2.15 "The *s* of Elijah rests on Elisha."
5.26 " Did I not go with you in *s* when
Neh 9.20 You gave your good *s* to instruct them,
Job 15.13 so that you turn your *s* against God,
32. 8 But truly it is the *s* in a mortal, the
Ps 34.18 and saves the crushed in *s*.
77. 3 and I moan; I meditate, and my *s* faints.
78. 8 whose *s* was not faithful to God.
104. 30 you send forth your *s*, they are created;
106. 33 for they made his *s* bitter, and he spoke
139. 7 Where can I go from your *s*? Or where
142. 3 When my *s* is faint, you know my way.
143. 10 Let your good *s* lead me on a level
Prov 16. 2 own eyes, but the LORD weighs the *s*.
17.22 but a downcast *s* dries up the bones.
18.14 human *s* will endure sickness; but a
20.27 The human *s* is the lamp of the LORD,
Eccl 3.21 Who knows whether the human *s* goes
Isa 4. 4 its midst by a *s* of judgment and by a *s*

Isa 32.15 until a *s* from on high is poured out on
42. 1 I have put my *s* upon him; he will bring
44. 3 I will pour my *s* upon your descendants,
Ezek 1.12 wherever the *s* would go, they went,
1.20 the *s* of the living creatures was in the
8. 3 *s* lifted me up between earth and
10.17 for the *s* of the living creatures was
36.27 I will put my *s* within you, and make
37.14 I will put my *s* within you, and you
Dan 4. 8 is endowed with a *s* of the holy gods—
5.11 is endowed with a *s* of the holy gods.
Joel 2.28 I will pour out my *s* on all flesh;
Hab 2. 4 Look at the proud! Their *s* is not right
Hag 2. 5 My *s* abides among you; do not fear.
Zech 4. 6 by might, nor by power, but by my *s*,
12. 1 earth and formed the human *s* within:
Mt 4. 1 Jesus was led up by the *S* into the
5. 3 "Blessed are the poor in *s*, for theirs is
10.20 but the *S* of your Father speaking
12.18 I will put my *S* upon him, and he will
26.41 the *s* indeed is willing, but the flesh is
Mk 1.23 synagogue a man with an unclean *s*;
14.38 the *s* indeed is willing, but the flesh is
Lk 1.47 and my *s* rejoices in God my Savior,
4. 1 was led by the *S* into the wilderness,
Jn 3. 6 is flesh, and what is born of the *S* is *s*.
3.34 for he gives the *S* without measure.
6.63 It is the *s* that gives life; the flesh is
Acts 2.17 I will pour out my *S* upon all flesh, and
20.22 And now, as a captive to the *S*, I am on
Rom 1. 4 power according to the *s* of holiness
8. 2 the law of the *S* of life in Christ Jesus
8. 4 to the flesh but according to the *S*.
8. 5 those who live according to the *S* set
8. 6 is death, but to set the mind on *S* is life
1 Cor 2.10 God has revealed to us through the *S*;
3.16 temple and that God's *S* dwells in you?
12.13 For in the one *S* we were all baptized
2 Cor 1.22 giving us his *S* in our hearts as a first
Gal 4. 6 God has sent the *S* of his Son into our
6. 8 if you sow to the *S* you will reap eternal
Eph 5.18 is debauchery; but be filled with the *S*,
1 Thess 5.19 Do not quench the *S*. Do not despise
2 Tim 1. 7 rather a *s* of power and of love and of
Heb 9.14 through the eternal *S* offered himself
Jas 2.26 just as the body without the *s* is dead,
4. 5 "God yearns jealously for the *s* that he
1 Jn 3.24 in us, by the *S* which he has given us.
5. 8 the *S*, and the water, and the blood,
Rev 2. 7 listen to what the *S* is saying to the
22.17 The *S* and the Bride say, "Come." And

SPIRITS

Lk 4.36 he commands the unclean *s*, and out
Heb 1.14 not all angels *s* in the divine service,
Rev 3. 1 of him who has the seven *s* of God
4. 5 torches, which are the seven *s* of God;

SPIRIT OF GOD

Gen 1.2n while the *s* swept over the face of the
41.38 else like this— one in whom is the *s*?"
Num 24. 2 by tribe. Then the *S* came upon him,
1 Sam 11. 6 the *s* came upon Saul in power when he
19.20 the *s* came upon the messengers of
2 Chr 15. 1 The *S* came upon Azariah son of Oded.
24.20 the *S* took possession of Zachariah son
Job 27. 3 is in me and the *s* is in my nostrils,
33. 4 The *s* has made me, and the breath of
Rom 8.14 all who are led by the *S* are children
15.19 and wonders, by the power of the *S*
Phil 3. 3 circumcision, who worship in the *S* and
1 Jn 4. 2 By this you know the *S*: every spirit that

SPIRIT OF THE LORD

Judg 3.10 the *s* came upon him, and he judged
6.34 the *s* took possession of Gideon; and he
11.29 the *s* came upon Jephthah, and he

Judg	13.25 The *s* began to stir him at
	15.14 the *s* rushed on him, and the ropes that
1 Sam	16.13 the *s* came mightily upon David from
1 Kings	18.12 the *s* will carry you I know not where;
	22.24 "Which way did the *s* pass from me to
2 Chr	20.14 the *S* came upon Jahaziel son of
Isa	11. 2 The *S* shall rest on him, the spirit of
	40.13 Who has directed the *s*, or as his
Ezek	11. 5 Then the *S* fell upon me, and he said to
Lk	4.18 "The *S* is upon me, because he has
Acts	5. 9 agreed together to put the *S* to the test?
2 Cor	3.17 Lord is the Spirit, and where the *S* is,

SPIRITUAL

Rom	2.29 of the heart — it is *s* and not literal.
	7.14 we know that the law is *s*; but I am of
1 Cor	2.13 by the Spirit, interpreting *s* things
	3. 1 I could not speak to you as *s* people,
	10. 3 in the sea, and all ate the same *s* food,
	12. 1 Now concerning *s* gifts, brothers and
	15.44 a physical body, it is raised a *s* body.

SPIT (SPAT)

Deut	25. 9 *s* in his face, and declare, "This is what
Mt	26.67 Then they *s* in his face and struck him;
Mk	7.33 ears and he *s* and touched his tongue.
	14.65 Some began to *s* on him, to blindfold
	15.19 his head with a reed, *s* upon him,
Rev	3.16 cold not hot, I am about to *s* you out

SPLENDOR

Ps	29. 2 of his name; worship the LORD in holy *s*.
	96. 9 Worship the LORD in holy *s*; tremble
Ezek	16.14 for it was perfect because of my *s*
Hag	2. 9 The latter *s* of this house shall be

SPOIL (SPOILS)

Judg	5.19 of Megiddo, they got no *s* of silver.
Ps	44.10 our foe, and our enemies have gotten *s*.
	119.162 at your word like one who finds great *s*.

SPOT

Tim	6.14 the commandmant without *s* or blame

SPREAD (SPREADING)

2 Sam	5.18 Philistines had come and *s* out in the
2 Kings	19.14 of the LORD and *s* it before the LORD.
Ps	88. 9 you, O LORD; I *s* out my hands to you.
Prov	29. 5 flatters a neighbor is *s* a net for the
Ezek	16. 8 I *s* the edge of my cloak over you, and
Mt	21. 8 large crowd *s* their cloaks on the road.
Mk	11. 8 Many people *s* their cloaks on the road,
Lk	19.36 people kept *s* their cloaks on the road.
Phil	1.12 me has actually helped to *s* the gospel,

SPRING (SPRINGS)

Josh	15.19 gave her the upper *s* and the lower *s*.
Ps	104. 10 You make *s* gush forth in the valleys;
Hos	13.15 shall dry up, his *s* shall be parched.
Jas	3.11 Does a *s* pour forth from the same
2 Pet	2.17 These are waterless *s* and mists driven
Rev	21. 6 as a gift from the *s* of the water of life.

SPROUT

Num	17. 5 staff of the man whom I choose shall *s*;
Ps	92. 7 though the wicked *s* like grass and all

SPURN (SPURNED)

Lev	26.15 if you *s* my statutes, and abhor my
Heb	10.29 by those who have *s* the Son of God,

SPY (SPIED SPYING)

Gen	42.30 us, and charged us with *s* on the land.
Num	13. 2 "Send men to *s* out the land of Canaan,
	13.17 sent them to *s* out the land of Canaan,
	13.21 So they went and *s* out the land from
1 Chr	19. 3 search and to overthrow and to *s* out
Gal	2. 4 who slipped in to *s* on the freedom we

SQUANDER (SQUANDERED)

Prov	29. 3 company with prostitutes is to *s* one's
Lk	15.13 and there he *s* his property in dissolute

STABILITY

Prov	29. 4 By justice a king gives *s* to the land, but
Isa	33. 6 he will be the *s* of your times,

STAFF

Ex	4. 2 is that in your hand?" He said, "A *s*."
	4.20 and Moses carried the *s* of God in his
Num	17. 3 and write Aaron's name on the *s* of
Judg	5.14 those who bear the marshal's *s*;
2 Kings	4.29 and lay my *s* upon the face of the child."
Mk	6. 8 nothing for their journey except a *s*;

STAGGER (STAGGERED)

Job	12.25 light; he makes them *s* like a drunkard.
Ps	107. 27 they reeled and *s* like drunkards, and

STALLS

2 Chr	9.25 Solomon had four thousand *s* for horses

STALK

Mk	4.28 of itself, first the *s*, then the head,

STAMMERING

Isa	28.11 *s* lip and with alien tongue he will
	33.19 *s* in a language that you cannot

STAND (STANDING STANDS STOOD)

Gen	18.22 Abraham remained *s* before the LORD.
Num	16.48 He *s* between the dead and the living;
Deut	7.24 no one will be able to *s* against you,
	10. 8 to *s* before the LORD to minister to him,
	29.10 You *s* assembled today, all of you,
Josh	10.13 And the sun *s* still, and the moon
Neh	8. 5 when he opened it, all the people *s*.
Ps	5. 5 The boastful will not *s* before your eyes;
	130. 3 mark iniquities, Lord, who could *s*?
	135. 2 you that *s* in the house of the LORD, in
Jer	6.16 *S* at the crossroads, and look, and ask
Ezek	2. 1 O mortal, *s* up on your feet, and I will
Mt	9. 6 to the paralytic— "*S* up, take your bed
Mk	2.11 *s* up, take your mat and go to your
Lk	5.24 to you, *s* up and take up your bed and
	21.36 place, and to *s* before the Son of man."
Jn	5. 8 to him, "*S* up, take your mat and walk."
Acts	7.56 and the Son of Man *s* at the right hand
1 Cor	6. 4 appoint as judges those who have no *s*
	10.12 if you think you are *s*, watch out that
	16.13 Keep alert, *s* firm in your faith, be
Gal	5. 1 Christ has set us free. *S* firm, therefore,
Phil	4. 1 crown, *s* firm in the Lord in this way,
1 Thess	3. 8 if you continue to *s* firm in the Lord.
2 Tim	2.19 But God's firm foundation *s*, bearing
1 Pet	5.12 is the true grace of God. *S* fast in it.
Jude	24 to make you *s* without blemish in the

STANDARD

Num	10.14 The *s* of the camp of Judah set out
Isa	31. 9 and his officers desert the *s* in panic,"
Jer	4. 6 Raise a *s* toward Zion, flee for safety, do

STAR (STARS)

Gen	1.16 light to rule the night — and the *s*.
	15. 5 "Look toward heaven and count the *s*, if
	22.17 your offspring as numerous as the *s*
Num	24.17 as shall come out of Jacob, and a
Deut	1.10 you are as numerous as the *s* of heaven.
	10.22 has made you as numerous as the *s*
	28.62 once you were as numerous as the *s*
Judg	5.20 The *s* fought from heaven, from their
1 Chr	27.23 to make Israel as numerous as the *s* of
Neh	4.21 break of dawn until the *s* came out.
Job	38. 7 when the morning *s* sang together, and
Ps	147. 4 He determines the number of the *s*; he
Isa	14.12 you are fallen from heaven, O Day *S*,

Dan	8.10 some of the s, and trampled on them.
	12. 3 many to righteousness, like the s forever
Mt	2. 2 For we observed his s at its rising, and
Heb	11.12 were born, "as many as the s of heaven
2 Pet	1.19 and the morning s rises in your hearts.
Rev	1.16 In his right hand he held seven s, and
	8.10 a great s fell from heaven, blazing like a
	22.16 of David, the bright morning s."

STARED

Isa	63. 5 I s, but there was no one to sustain me;

STATE

Mt	12.45 the last s of that person is worse than
Lk	11.26 and the last s of that person is worse

STATUE

Dan	2.31 O king, and lo! there was a great s.
Acts	19.35 the great Artemis and of the s that fell

STATUTE (STATUTES)

Lev	18. 5 You shall keep my s and my ordinances;
Num	35.29 These things shall be a s and ordinance
Ps	119. 48 which I love, I will meditate on your s.
Ezek	5. 6 against my ordinances and my s,

STAY (STAYED STAYING)

Ex	2.21 Moses agreed to s with the man, and He
	16.29 each of you s where you are; do not
Jer	42.15 hungry for bread, and there we will s,'
Mt	10.11 it is worthy and s there until you leave.
Lk	19. 5 down; for I must s at your house today."
Jn	1.38 Teacher), where are you s?" He said to
Acts	1. 4 While s with them, he ordered them not
Heb	11. 9 By faith he s for a time in the land he

STEADFAST

Ps	57. 7 My heart is s, O God, my heart is s. I
1 Cor	15.58 be s, immovable, always excelling

STEADFAST LOVE

Gen	24.12 and show s to my master Abraham.
	32.10 I am not worthy of the least of all the s
	39.21 was with Joseph and showed him s;
Ex	34. 7 keeping s for the thousandth generation,
1 Chr	16.34 for he is good; for his s endures forever.
2 Chr	7. 3 he is good, for his s endures forever."
Ezra	7.28 who extended to me s before the king
Ps	17. 7 Wondrously show your s, O savior of
	25. 6 of your mercy, O Lord, and of your s,
	25. 7 according to your s remember me, for
	26. 3 For your s is before my eyes, I walk in
	36. 7 How precious is your s, O God! All
	40.10 I have not concealed your s and your
	63. 3 your s is better than life, my lips will
	69.16 Answer me, O Lord, for your s is good;
	77. 8 Has his s ceased forever? Are his
	85.10 S and faithfulness will meet;
	89. 2 that your s is established forever;
	92. 2 declare your s in the morning, and your
	100. 5 the Lord is good; his s endures forever,
	103. 17 But the s of the Lord is from everlasting
	107. 8 Let them thank the Lord for his s, for
	107. 43 things, and consider the s of the Lord.
	118. 1 for he is good; his s endures forever.
	119. 88 In your s spare my life, so that I may
	136. 1 for he is good, for his s endures forever.
Isa	63. 7 according to the abundance of his s.
Jer	16. 5 people, says the Lord, my s and mercy.
Lam	3.22 The s of the Lord never ceases, his
Hos	6. 6 I desire s and not sacrifice, the

STEADFASTNESS

Rom	15. 4 written for our instruction, so that by s
2 Thess	3. 5 the love of God and to the s of Christ.

STEAL (STEALING STEALS STOLE)

Gen	31.30 father's house, why did you s my gods?"
Ex	20.15 You shall not s.

Ex	22. 1 When someone s an ox or a sheep, and
Deut	5.19 Neither shall you s.
2 Sam	15. 6 Absalom s the hearts of the people of
Prov	6.30 who s only to satisfy their appetite
Jer	7. 9 Will you s, murder, commit adultery,
Mt	6.20 where thieves do not break in and s.
	19.18 You shall not s; You shall not bear false
Eph	4.28 Thieves must give up s; rather let them

STEEP

Mt	8.32 the whole herd rushed down the s bank

STEP (STEPS)

1 Sam	20. 3 there is but a s between me and death."
Job	14.16 then you would not number my s, you
	18. 7 Their strong s are shortened, and their
	31. 4 not see my ways, and number all my s?
Ps	18.36 You gave me a wide place for my s
	37.23 Our s are made firm by the Lord, when
	44.18 turned back, nor have our s departed
	73. 2 stumbled; my s had nearly slipped.
	119.133 Keep my s steady according to your
Prov	16. 9 the way but the Lord directs the s.
	20.24 All our s are ordered by the Lord; how
Isa	38. 8 sun on the dial of Ahaz turn back ten s."
Jer	10.23 as they walk cannot direct their s.
Lam	4.18 They dogged our s so that we could not
2 Cor	12.18 spirit? Did we not take the same s?

STEPHEN

Acts	6. 5 they chose S, a man full of faith and
	6. 9 and Asia, stood up and argued with S.
	7.59 While they were stoning S, he prayed,
	8. 2 Devout men buried S, and made loud
	11.19 persecution that took place over S
	22.20 the blood of your witness S was shed,

STEWARDS

1 Cor	4. 1 of Christ and s of God's mysteries.

STICK (STICKS)

Num	15.32 a man gathering s on the sabbath day.
Prov	18.24 but a true friend s closer than one's
Ezek	37.16 take a s and write on it, "For Judah,

STIFF-NECKED

Ex	33. 3 you on the way, for you are a s people."
2 Chr	30. 8 Do not now be s as your ancestors were,
Acts	7.51 "You s people, uncircumcised in heart

STILL

Josh	10.13 And the sun stood s, and the moon
Ps	37. 7 Be s before the Lord, and wait patiently
	39. 2 I was silent and s; I held my peace to
	46.10 "Be s, and know that I am God! I am
	107. 29 he made the storm be s, and the waves

STING

1 Cor	15.55 your victory? Where, O death, is your s?"

STINGERS

Rev	9.10 tails like scorpions, with s, and in their

STIRS (STIRRED)

Ex	35.21 they came, everyone whose heart was s,
2 Chr	36.22 Lord s up the spirit of King Cyrus of
Prov	28.25 The greedy person s up strife, but
Hag	1.14 the Lord s up the spirit of Zerubbabel
Lk	23. 5 "He s up the people by teaching
Jn	5.4n into the pool, and s up the water;
	5. 7 into the pool when the water is s up;
Acts	6.12 They s up the people as well as the
2 Cor	9. 2 and your zeal has s up most of them.

STOCKS

Job	13.27 You put my feet in the s, and watch all
Jer	20. 2 prophet Jeremiah, and put him in the s
Acts	16.24 cell and fastened their feet in the s.

STOLEN

2 Sam 19.41 have the people of Judah s you away,

STOMACH

Mt	15.17	goes into the mouth enters the s,
Mk	7.19	since it enters, not the heart but the s,
1 Cor	6.13	is meant for the s and the s for food,"
1 Tim	5.23	take a little wine for the sake of your s

STONE (STONES) (n)

Ex	28.11	you shall engrave the two s with the
Deut	5.22	He wrote them on two s tablets, and
	10. 1	"Carve out two s tablets like the former
Josh	4. 6	time to come, 'What do those s mean
	24.26	he took a large s, and set it up there
1 Sam	6.18	The great s, beside which they set down
	7.12	Samuel took a s and set it up between
	17.40	and chose five smooth s from the wadi,
	25.37	died within him; he became like a s.
Ps	118.22	The s that the builders rejected has
Prov	27. 3	As is heavy, and sand is weighty, but a
Isa	28.16	laying in Zion a foundation s, a tested s,
Jer	2.27	father," and to a s, "You gave me birth."
Ezek	11.19	I will remove the heart of s from their
Dan	2.35	the s that struck the statue became a
Hab	2.11	The very s will cry out from the wall,
Mt	7. 9	child asks for bread, will give him a s?
	21.42	'The s which the builders rejected has
	21.44	who falls on this s will be broken to
	24. 2	I tell you, not one s will be left here
	27.66	made the tomb secure by sealing the s.
Mk	12.10	the s which the builders rejected has
	13. 2	Not one s will be left here upon
	16. 4	looked up, they saw that the s, which
Lk	3. 8	is able from these s to raise up children
	4. 3	God, command this s to become a loaf
	11.11	n bread, will give a s; or if your child asks
	19.40	were silent, the s would shout out."
	20.17	'The s which the builders rejected has
	21. 6	will come when not one s will be left
	24. 2	They found the s rolled away from the
Jn	8.59	they picked up s to throw at him, but
	11.39	Jesus said, "Take away the s." Martha,
	20. 1	and saw that the s had been removed
Acts	4.11	Jesus is 'the s that was rejected by you,
2 Cor	3. 3	not on tablets of s but on tablets of
1 Pet	2. 6	"See, I am laying in Zion a s, a

STONE (STONED STONES STONING)

Lev	24.14	and let the whole congregation s him.
Num	14.10	congregation threatened to s them.
	15.36	outside the camp and s him to death,
Deut	13.10	S them to death for trying to turn you
	21.21	men of the town shall s him to death,
Josh	7.25	And all Israel s him to death; they
1 Sam	30. 6	danger; for the people spoke of s him,
Mt	23.37	city that kills the prophets and s those
Jn	8. 5	Moses commanded us to s such women.
	10.31	Jews took up stones again to s him.
2 Cor	11.25	beaten with rods; once I received a s.
Acts	7.58	him out of the city and began to s him;

STOP (STOPPED)

Num	11.28	men, said, "My lord Moses, s them!"
Job	9.12	He snatches away; who can s him? Who
Ps	63.11	exult, for the mouths of liars will be s.

STORE (STORED STORING)

Gen	41.49	So Joseph s up grain in such
Mt	6.19	"Do not s up for yourselves treasures on
1 Tim	6.19	thus s up for themselves the treasure of

STOREHOUSE (STOREHOUSES)

Gen	41.56	Joseph opened all the s, and sold to the
Job	38.22	"Have you entered the s of the snow, or
Ps	33. 7	sea in a bottle; he put the deeps in s.
Isa	39. 2	armory, all that was found in his s.
Jer	10.13	and he brings out the wind from his s.

Mal	3.10	Bring the full tithe into the s, so that

STORK

Lev	11.19	the s, the heron of any kind, the
Jer	8. 7	Even the s in the heavens knows its

STORM

Ps	107.29	he made the s be still, and the waves of
Jer	23.19	Look, the s of the LORD! Wrath has gone
Jon	1.12	me that this great s has come upon you."

STRAIGHT

Prov	3. 6	him, and he will make s your paths.
	11. 5	of the blameless keeps their ways s,
Eccl	7.13	can make s what he has made crooked?
Isa	45.13	and I will make all his paths s;
Acts	9.11	"Get up and go to the street called S,

STRAIGHTFORWARD

Eccl 7.29 God made human beings s, but they

STRAIN (STRAINING)

Mt	23.24	guides, you s out a gnat but swallow
Phil	3.13	and s forward to what lies ahead,

STRANGE

Ps 44.20 or spread out our hands to a s god,

STRANGER (STRANGERS)

Gen	23. 4	"I am a s and an alien residing among
Deut	10.18	who loves the s, providing them food
	10.19	shall also love the s, for you were s
Job	31.32	the s has not lodged in the street; I
Ps	69. 8	I have become a s to my kindred, an
	146. 9	The LORD watches over the s, he
Jer	14. 8	why should you be like a s in the land,
Lam	5. 2	inheritance has been turned over to s,
Joel	3.17	be holy, and s shall never again pass
Mt	25.35	I was a s and you welcomed me,
Eph	2.12	s to the covenants of promise, having

STRAW

Ex	5. 7	You shall no longer give the people s to
Job	21.18	How often are they like s before the
Jer	23.28	What has s in common with wheat?
1 Cor	3.12	silver, precious stones, wood, hay, s —

STREAM (STREAMS)

Gen	2. 6	but a s would rise from the earth, and
Ps	1. 3	They are like a s trees planted by s of
	42. 1	As a deer longs for flowing s, so my
	119.136	My eyes shed s of tears because your
Isa	2. 2	the hills; all the nations shall s to it.
	32. 2	tempest, like s of water in a dry place,
	35. 6	in the wilderness, and s in the desert;

STREET (STREETS)

Ps	18.42	I cast them out like the mire of the s.
Acts	9.11	"Get up and go to the s called Straight,

STRENGTH

Ex	15. 2	The LORD is my s and my might, and he
Num	11. 6	but now our s is dried up, and there is
Deut	33.25	bronze; and as your days, so is your s.
Judg	16. 6	tell me what makes your s so great, and
2 Sam	22.40	you girded me with s for the battle; you
Job	6.11	What is my s, that I should wait? And
	9.19	If it is a contest of s, he is the strong
	18.12	Their s is consumed by hunger, and
	35.10	'Where is God my Maker, who gives s
Ps	18.32	the God who girded me with s, and
	21. 1	In your s the king rejoices, O LORD, and
	29. 1	beings, ascribe to the LORD glory and s.
	29.11	May the LORD give s to his people! May
	68.28	your might, O God; show yours, O God,
	73.26	but God is the s of my heart and my
	81. 1	Sing aloud to God our s; shout for joy
	84. 5	Happy are those whose s is in you, in
	96. 6	him; s and beauty are in his sanctuary.

Ps 102. 23 He has broken my *s* in midcourse; he
105. 4 Seek the Lord and his *s*; seek his
118. 14 The Lord is my *s* and my might; he has
Eccl 7. 19 Wisdom gives *s* to the wise more than
10. 17 time — for *s*, and not for drunkenness!
Isa 10. 13 "By the *s* of my hand I have done it,
30. 15 quietness and in trust shall be your *s*.
40. 9 good tidings; lift up your voice with *s*,
49. 5 Lord, and my God has become my *s* —
51. 9 awake, put on *s*, O arm of the Lord!
52. 1 Awake, awake, put on your *s*, O Zion!
Jer 16. 19 Lord, my *s* and my stronghold, my
Hab 3. 19 God, the Lord, is my *s*; he makes my
Lk 1. 51 He has shown *s* with his arm; he has
21. 36 praying that you may have *s* to escape
1 Cor 10. 13 will not let you be tested beyond your *s*,
Eph 6. 10 in the Lord and in the *s* of his power.
Col 1. 11 May you be made strong with all the *s*
1 Pet 4. 11 do so with the *s* that God supplies,

STRENGTHEN (STRENGTHENED STRENGTHENING STRENGTHENS)

1 Sam 23. 16 there he *s* his hand through the Lord.
30. 6 David *s* himself in the Lord his God.
Job 4. 3 many; you have *s* the weak hands.
Ps 89. 21 with him; my arm also shall *s* him.
Isa 35. 3 *S* the weak hands, and make firm the
41. 10 I will *s* you, I will help you, I will
54. 2 lengthen your cords and *s* your stakes.
Ezek 34. 16 and I will *s* the weak, but the fat and
Dan 10. 18 in human form touched me and *s* me.
Zech 10. 6 I will *s* the house of Judah, and I will
Acts 15. 41 Syria and Cilicia, *s* the churches.
18. 23 Galatia and Phrygia, *s* all the disciples.
Rom 16. 25 to God who is able to *s* you according
1 Cor 1. 8 He will also *s* you to the end, so that
Eph 3. 16 he may grant that you may be *s* in your
Phil 4. 13 do all things through him who *s* me.
1 Thess 3. 2 to *s* and encourage you for the sake of
3. 13 may he so *s* your hearts in holiness that
1 Pet 5. 10 Christ, will himself restore, support, *s*
Rev 3. 2 Wake up, and *s* what remains and is on

STRETCH (STRETCHED STRETCHES)

1 Kings 17. 21 he *s* himself upon the child three times,
Job 9. 8 who alone *s* out the heavens and
Ps 68. 31 let Ethiopia hasten to *s* out its hands to
104. 2 You *s* out the heavens like a tent, you
Lam 1. 17 Zion *s* out her hands, but there is no
Mt 12. 13 he said to the man, "*S* out your hand."

STRICKEN

1 Sam 24. 5 David was *s* to the heart because he
2 Sam 24. 10 David was *s* to the heart because he

STRIFE

Gen 13. 7 *s* between the herders of Abram's
Ps 55. 9 for I see violence and *s* in the city.
Prov 13. 10 By insolence the heedless make *s*, but
17. 1 than a house full of feasting with *s*.
17. 14 The beginning of *s* is like letting out
18. 6 A fool's lips bring *s*, and a fool's mouth
28. 25 The greedy person stirs up *s*, but
29. 22 One given to anger stirs up *s*, and the
30. 33 blood, so pressing anger produces *s*.

STRIKE (STRUCK)

Gen 3. 15 He will *s* your head, and you will *s* his
Ex 12. 12 I will *s* down every firstborn in the land
12. 29 the Lord *s* down all the firstborn in the
Num 20. 11 lifted up his hand and *s* the rock twice
2 Sam 12. 9 You have *s* down Uriah the Hittite with
12. 15 The Lord *s* the child that Uriah's wife
Ps 121. 6 The sun shall not *s* you by day, nor the
141. 5 Let the righteous *s* me; let the faithful
Isa 27. 7 Has he *s* them down as he *s* down those
53. 4 accounted him stricken, *s* down by God,
Jer 5. 3 You have *s* them, but they felt no

Hag 2. 17 I *s* you and all the products of your toil
Mk 14. 27 'I will *s* the shepherd, and the sheep

STRIP (STRIPPED)

Lev 19. 10 You shall not *s* your vineyard bare, or
Num 20. 28 Moses *s* Aaran of his vestments, and
Job 19. 9 He has *s* my glory from me, and taken

STRIVE (STRIVEN STRIVING)

Gen 32. 28 but Israel, for you have *s* with God
Isa 41. 11 those who *s* against you shall be as
Mt 6. 33 But *s* first for the kingdom of God and
Lk 12. 31 Instead, *s* for his kingdom, and these
13. 24 "*S* to enter through the narrow door; for
1 Cor 12. 31 But *s* for greater gifts. And I will show
14. 12 for spiritual gifts, *s* to excel in them
Phil 1. 27 *s* side by side with one mind for the
2 Pet 3. 14 *s* to be found by him at peace, without

STRONG (STRONGER)

Judg 14. 14 eat. Out of the *s* came something sweet."
2 Sam 3. 1 David grew *s* and *s*, while the house of
1 Chr 19. 13 Be *s*, and let us be courageous for our
28. 20 "Be *s* and of good courage, and act. Do
2 Chr 26. 16 when he had become *s* he grew proud,
Ps 27. 14 Wait for the Lord; be *s*, and let your
140. 7 Lord, my *s* deliverer, you have covered
Eccl 6. 10 able to dispute with those who are *s*.
9. 11 nor the battle to the *s*, nor bread to the
Mt 12. 29 how can one enter as a man's house and
Lk 11. 21 When a *s* man, fully armed, guards his
Rom 15. 1 *s* ought to put up with the failings of
1 Cor 1. 25 weakness is *s* than human strength.
1. 27 is weak in the world to shame the *s*;
Eph 6. 10 Finally, be *s* in the Lord and in the
2 Tim 2. 1 my child, be *s* in the grace that is in
1 Jn 2. 14 young people, because you are *s* and

STRONGHOLD

Ps 9. 9 The Lord is a *s* for the oppressed, a *s* in
18. 2 and the horn of my salvation, my *s*.
27. 1 The Lord is the *s* of my life; of whom
94. 22 But the Lord has become my *s*, and my
Joel 3. 16 his people, a *s* for the people of Israel.
Nah 1. 7 Lord is good, a *s* in a day of trouble;

STRUGGLE (STRUGGLING)

Prov 28. 4 but those who keep the law *s* against
Eph 6. 12 our *s* is not against enemies of blood
Col 2. 1 you to know how much I am *s* for you,

STUBBLE

Ex 5. 12 the land of Egypt, to gather *s* for straw.
Isa 47. 14 they are like *s*, the fire consumes them;
Mal 4. 1 arrogant and all evildoers will be *s*;

STUBBORN

Deut 9. 6 righteousness, for you are a *s* people.
29. 19 safe even though we go our own *s* ways"
Judg 2. 19 any of their practices or their *s* ways.
2 Kings 17. 14 not listen, but were *s*, as their ancestors
Ps 81. 12 So I gave them over to their *s* hearts, to
Ezek 3. 7 have a hard forehead and a *s* heart.

STUBBORNNESS

1 Sam 15. 23 and *s* is like iniquity and idolatry.
Mk 16. 14n them for their lack of faith and *s*,

STUDENTS

Mt 23. 8 you have one teacher, and you are all *s*.

STUDY

Ps 101. 2 I will *s* the way that is blameless. When
Eccl 12. 12 and much *s* is a weariness of the flesh.

STUMBLE (STUMBLED STUMBLING)

Prov 3. 23 way securely, and your foot will not *s*.
4. 19 they do not know what they *s* over.
Isa 3. 8 Jerusalem has *s*, and Judah has fallen,

STUMBLING BLOCK

Jer	13.16 and before your feet s on the mountains
	20.11 my persecutors will s, and they will not
	50.32 The arrogant one shall s and fall, with
Mt	18. 8 or your foot causes you to s, cut it off
Mk	9.43 If your hand causes you to s, cut it off;
Lk	17. 1 "Occasions for s are bound to come, but
	17. 2 to cause one of these little ones to s.
Jn	11. 9 who walk during the day do not s,
Rom	9.32 on works. They have s over the s stone,
	11.11 have they s so as to fall? By no means!
	14.21 that makes your brother or sister s.

STUMBLING BLOCK (STUMBLING BLOCKS)

Jer	6.21 I am laying before this people s against
Mt	16.23 "Get behind me, Satan! You are a s to
Rom	14.13 resolve instead never to put a s or
1 Cor	1.23 proclaim Christ crucified, a s to Jews
	8. 9 not somehow become a s to the weak.
Rev	2.14 who taught Balak to put a s before the

STUNNED

Ezek	3.15 sat there among them, s, for seven days.

SUBDUE (SUBDUED)

Gen	1.28 and multiply, and fill the earth and s it;
Ps	47. 3 He s peoples under us, and nations
	81.14 Then I would quickly s their enemies,
Mk	5. 4 and no one had the strength to s him.

SUBJECT (SUBJECTED)

2 Sam	10.19 with Israel, and became s to them.
1 Chr	19.19 peace with David, and became s to him.
Rom	13. 1 person be s to the governing authorities;
1 Cor	14.32 spirits of prophets are s to prophets, for
	15.28 Son himself will also be s to the one
Eph	5.22 Wives, be s to your husbands as you are
Col	3.18 Wives, be s to your husbands, as is
Titus	3. 1 Remind them to be s to rulers and

SUBMISSION

Heb	5. 7 he was heard because of his reverent s.

SUBMISSIVE

Titus	2. 9 Tell slaves to be s to their masters and

SUBMIT

Lk	10.17 in your name, even the demons s to us!"

SUBORDINATE

1 Cor	14.34 not permitted to speak, but should be s,

SUBSTANCE

Prov	3. 9 Honor the LORD with your s and with

SUCCEED (SUCCEEDED)

1 Sam	26.25 will do many things and will s in them."
1 Chr	22.11 you may s in building the house of the
Job	9. 4 has resisted him, and s?—
Isa	55.11 purpose, s in the thing for which I sent
Jer	22.30 man as childless, a man who shall not s
	32. 5 against the Chaldeans, you shall not s?"
Ezek	17.15 Will he s? Can one escape who does

SUCCESS (SUCCESSFUL)

Gen	24.21 or not the LORD had made his journey s.
	24.40 angel with you and make your way s.
	39. 2 with Joseph, and he became a s man;
Josh	1. 8 prosperous, and then you shall be s.
1 Sam	18.30 David had more s than all the servants

SUFFER (SUFFERED SUFFERING SUFFERS)

Ps	9.13 See what I s from those who hate me,
Prov	27.12 hide; but the simple go on, and s for it.
Mt	17.12 So also the Son of man is about to s at
	17.15 for he is an epileptic and he s terribly;
	27.19 I have s a great deal because of a dream
Lk	24.26 necessary that the Messiah should s
	24.46 it is written, that the Messiah is to s
Acts	3.18 the prophets, that his Messiah should s.

Acts	5.41 were considered worthy to s dishonor
	26.23 that the Messiah must s, and that, by
Rom	8.17 we s with him so that we may also be
1 Cor	12.26 If one member s, all s together
Phil	1.29 in Christ, but of s for him as well—
1 Thess	2. 2 but though we had already s and been
Heb	2.18 he himself was tested by what he s, he
1 Pet	2.21 called, because Christ also s for you,
	2.23 when he s, he did not threaten; but he
	3.18 Christ also s for sins once for all, the
	4. 1 Christ s in the flesh, arm yourselves
	4.15 let none of you s as a murderer, a thief,

SUFFERING (SUFFERINGS)

Ex	3. 7 taskmasters. Indeed, I know their s,
Isa	53. 3 a man of s and acquainted with
Mt	24.21 For at that time there will be great s,
	24.29 "Immediately after the s of those days
Mk	8.31 the Son of Man must undergo great s,
	13.19 there will be s, such as has not been
	13.24 after that s, the sun will darkened, and
Lk	9.22 "The Son of Man must undergo great s,
	17.25 first he must endure much s and be
Rom	5. 3 knowing that s produces endurance, and
	12.12 Rejoice in hope, be patient in s,
Eph	3.13 may not lose heart over my s for you;
Col	1.24 am now rejoicing in my s for your sake,
2 Tim	2. 3 Share in s like a good soldier of Christ

SUFFICIENT

2 Cor	12. 9 "My grace is s for you, for power is

SULFUR

Gen	19.24 the LORD rained on Sodom . . . s and fire
Lk	17.29 Lot left Sodom, it rained fire and s from
Rev	14.10 tormented with fire and s in the
	19.20 into the lake of fire that burns with s.

SUITABLE

Eccl	3.11 He has made everything s for its time;

SUMMED

Gal	5.14 For the whole law is s up in a single

SUMMER

Gen	8.22 s and winter, day and night, shall not
Prov	26. 1 Like snow in s or rain in harvest, so
Jer	8.20 "The harvest is past, the s is ended, and

SUMMONED

Ex	19.20 the LORD s Moses to the top of the
Isa	41.25 the rising of the sun he was s by name.
Mt	10. 1 Jesus s his twelve disciples and gave

SUN

Josh	10.12 "S, stand still at Gibeon, and Moon, in
Ps	19. 4 the heavens he has set a tent for the s,
	84.11 the LORD God is a s and shield; he
	113. 3 From the rising of the s to its setting
Eccl	1. 9 done; there is nothing new under the s.
Isa	13.10 s will be dark at its rising, and the
Jer	31.35 says the LORD, who gives the s for light
Ezek	32. 7 cover the s with a cloud, and the moon
Joel	2.31 s shall be turned to darkness, and the
Am	8. 9 I will make the s go down at noon, and
Hab	3.11 the s stood still in its exalted place, at
Mal	4. 2 name the s of righteousness shall rise,
Mt	5.45 he makes his s to rise on the evil and
	24.29 the s will be darkened, and the moon
Acts	2.20 The s shall be turned into darkness and
1 Cor	15.41 There is one glory of the s, another
Eph	4.26 do not sin; do not let the s go down on

SUPPER

Lk	22.20 he did the same with the cup after s,
Jn	13. 2 betray him. And during s Jesus,
1 Cor	11.20 it is not really to eat the Lord's s s.

SUPPLANT

Hos 12. 3 In the womb he tried to *s* his brother,

SUPPLICATION

2 Sam 24.25 LORD answered his *s* for the land, and
Job 8. 5 If you will seek God and make *s* to the
Ps 28. 2 Hear the voice of my *s*, as I cry to you
Isa 45.14 They will make *s* to you, saying, "God is

SUPPORT

Gen 13. 6 the land could not *s* both of them living
Ezek 30. 6 Those who *s* Egypt shall fall, and it
Mt 15. 5 'Whatever *s* you might have had from
Acts 20.35 by such work we must *s* the weak,
2 Cor 11. 8 churches by accepting *s* from them
3 Jn 8 Therefore we ought to *s* such people, so

SUPPORTERS

Job 31.21 because I saw I had *s* at the gate;

SURE

1 Jn 2. 3 by this we may be *s* that we know him,

SURROUND (SURROUNDED)

Gen 19. 4 and old, all the people . . . *s* the house;
Ps 118. 11 They *s* me, *s* me on every side; in the
Lk 8.45 "Master, the crowds *s* you and press in
Heb 12. 1 since we are *s* by so great a crowd of

SURVIVORS

Neh 1. 3 "The *s* there in the province who
Joel 2.32 among the *s* shall be those whom the
Mic 2.12 I will gather the *s* of Israel; I will set

SUSA

Neh 1. 1 year, while I was in *S* the capital,
Esth 1. 2 sat his royal throne in the citadel of *S*,
2. 5 was a Jew in the citadel of *S* whose
8.15 the city of *S* shouted and rejoiced.
9.18 the Jews who were in *S* gathered on the

SUSPENSE

Jn 10.24 "How long will you keep us in *s*? If you

SUSTAIN (SUSTAINED)

Neh 9.21 years you *s* them in the wilderness
Ps 55.22 burden on the LORD, and he will *s* you;

SWALLOW (n)

Isa 38.14 Like a *s* or a crane I clamor, I moan
Jer 8. 7 the turtledove, *s*, and crane observe the

SWALLOW (SWALLOWED SWALLOWS)

Num 16.30 ground opens its mouth and *s* them up,
Ps 35.25 Do not let them say, "We have *s* you up."
Isa 25. 7 all nations; he will *s* up death forever.
Jon 1.17 provided a large fish to *s* up Jonah;
1 Cor 15.54 "Death has been *s* up in victory."
2 Cor 5. 4 so that what is mortal may be *s* up

SWARM (SWARMS)

Gen 1.20 "Let the waters bring forth *s* of living
Ex 8.21 I will send *s* of flies on you, your
Lev 11.41 All creatures that *s* upon the earth are

SWEAR (SWEARS SWORE SWORN)

Gen 24. 3 I will make you *s* by the LORD, the God
Lev 19.12 You shall not *s* falsely by my name,
Deut 6.10 the land that he *s* to your ancestors,
Ps 110. 4 LORD has *s* and will not change his
Isa 48. 1 who *s* by the name of the LORD, and
62. 8 LORD has *s* by his right hand and by his
Jer 4. 2 if you *s*, "As the LORD lives!" in truth, in
22. 5 words, I *s* by myself, says the LORD,
44.26 Lo, I *s* by my great name, says the LORD,
Am 4. 2 GOD has *s* by his holiness: The time is
Zech 5. 3 everyone who *s* falsely shall be cut off
Mt 5.34 Do not *s* at all, either by heaven, for it
23.16 whoever *s* by the gold of the sanctuary,

Jas 5.12 do not *s*, either by heaven or by earth

SWEAT

Gen 3.19 "By the *s* of your face you shall eat
Lk 22.44 his *s* became like great drops of blood

SWEET

Judg 14.14 Out of the strong came something *s*."
Ps 119.103 How *s* are your words to my taste,

SWEPT

Gen 1. 2 a mighty wind *s* over the face of the
Isa 44.22 *s* away your transgressions like a cloud,
Mt 12.44 it finds it empty, *s*, and put in order.

SWIFT

Eccl 9.11 the race is not to the *s*, nor the battle

SWINE

Mt 8.31 cast us out, send us into the herd of *s*."
Mk 5.12 "Send us to the *s*, let us enter them."
Lk 8.32 herd of *s* was feeding; and the demons

SWORD (SWORDS)

Gen 3.24 a *s* flaming and turning to guard the
Judg 7.14 "This is no other than the *s* of Gideon
7.20 cried, "A *s* for the LORD and for Gideon!"
1 Kings 3.24 king said, "Bring me a *s*," and they
Isa 2. 4 beat their *s* into plowshares, and their
49. 2 made my mouth like a sharp *s*, in the
Jer 9.16 I will send the *s* after them, until I have
25.38 become waste because of the cruel *s*,
Ezek 21. 9 Say: A *s*, a *s* is sharpened, it is also
Joel 3.10 Beat your plowshares into *s*, and your
Mic 4. 3 they shall beat their *s* into plowshares,
Zech 13. 7 "Awake, O *s*, against my shepherd,
Mt 10.34 I have not come to bring peace, but a *s*.
26.51 on his *s*, drew it, and struck the slave of
Mk 14.47 drew his *s*, and struck the slave of the
Lk 2.35 a *s* will pierce your own soul
Eph 6.17 the *s* of the Spirit, which is the word of
Heb 4.12 sharper than any two-edged *s*, piercing
Rev 1.16 his mouth came a sharp two-edged *s*,
19.15 from his mouth comes a sharp *s* with

SYCAMORE

Am 7.14 a herdsman, and a dresser of *s* trees,
Lk 19. 4 So he ran ahead and climbed a *s* tree to

SYCHAR

Jn 4. 5 he came to a Samaritan city called *S*,

SYMPATHY

Job 42.11 they showed *s* and comforted him for
1 Pet 3. 8 all of you, have unity of spirit, *s*, love

SYNAGOGUE

Mk 5.38 to the house of the leader of the *s*,
6. 2 the sabbath he began to teach in the *s*,
Lk 7. 5 and it is he who built our *s* for us."
8.41 a man named Jairus, a leader of the *s*.
Acts 18. 4 Every sabbath he would argue in the *s*
19. 8 He entered the *s* and for three months

SYRIA

Mt 4.24 So his fame spread throughout all *S*,
Lk 2. 2 while Quirinius was governor of *S*.
Acts 15.41 He went through *S* and Cilicia,

T

TABERNACLE

Ex 25. 9 pattern of the *t* and of all its furniture,
26.30 you shall erect the *t* according to the
40. 2 you shall set up the *t* of the tent of

TABLE (TABLES)

Ex 25.23 You shall make a *t* of acacia wood, two
37.10 He also made the *t* of acacia wood, two
2 Kings 4.10 put there for him a bed, a *t*, a chair,

Ps	23. 5 You prepare a *t* before me in the
	69.22 Let their *t* be a trap for them, a snare
	78.19 "Can God spread a *t* in the wilderness?
Mal	1.12 you say that the LORD's *t* is polluted,
Acts	6. 2 the word of God in order to wait on *t*.
1 Cor	10.21 partake of the *t* of the Lord and the *t* of

TABLET (TABLETS)

Ex	31.18 the two *t* of the covenant, *t* of stone,
	34. 1 "Cut two *t* of stone like the first; and I
Deut	9.10 LORD gave me the two stone *t* written
Isa	8. 1 Take a large *t* and write on it in
Lk	1.63 He asked for a writing *t*, and wrote,
2 Cor	3. 3 on *t* of stone but on *t* of human hearts.

TAKE (TAKEN TAKES)

Ex	25. 2 the Israelites to *t* for me an offering;
Prov	8.10 *T* my instruction instead of silver, and
	11.30 a tree of life, but violence *t* lives away.
Lam	3.58 You have *t* up my cause, O Lord, you
Mt	26.26 and said, "*T*, eat; this is my body."
Mk	14.22 it to them, and said "*T*; this is my body."
Jn	14. 3 I will come again and will *t* you to
Heb	11. 5 was not found, because God had *t* him."
Rev	22.19 if anyone *t* away from the words of the

TALE

Lk	24.11 these words seemed to them an idle *t*,

TALENTS

Mt	18.24 one who owed him ten thousand *t* was
	25.15 to one he gave five *t*, to another two, to

TALK (TALKED TALKING)

Job	11. 2 and should one full of *t* be vindicated?
	15. 3 Should they argue in unprofitable *t*, or
Ps	71.24 my tongue will *t* of your righteous help,
Prov	4.24 speech, and put devious *t* far from you.
Zech	1.14 the angel who *t* with me said to me,
Mt	16. 8 little faith, why are you *t* about having
Lk	24.15 While they were *t* and discussing, Jesus

TAME

Jas	3. 8 no one being can *t* the tongue — a

TARSHISH

Gen	10. 4 The descendants of Javan: . . . *T*,
2 Chr	9.21 the king's ships went to *T* with the
	20.36 joined him in building ships to go to *T*;
Ps	48. 7 an east wind shatters the ships of *T*.
	72.10 the kings of *T* and of the isles render
Isa	23.14 Wail, O ships of *T*, for your fortress is
Jon	1. 3 Jonah set out to flee to *T* from the

TARSUS

Acts	9.11 Judas look for a man of *T* named Saul.
	11.25 Barnabas went to *T* to look for Saul,
	21.39 replied, "I am a Jew, from *T* in Cilicia,

TASKMASTERS

Ex	1.11 they set *t* over them to oppress them
	5. 6 Pharaoh commanded the *t* of the

TASTE (TASTED)

Ps	34. 8 O *t* and see that the LORD is good;
Mt	5.13 but if salt has lost its *t*, how can its
	16.28 who will not *t* death before they see the
Mk	9. 1 who will not *t* death until they see that
Lk	9.27 who will not *t* death before they see the
Acts	23.14 by an oath to *t* no food until we have
Col	2.21 not handle, Do not *t*, Do not touch"?
Heb	2. 9 of God he might *t* death for everyone.
	6. 4 and have *t* the heavenly gift,
1 Pet	2. 3 indeed you have *t* that the Lord is good.

TAUNT

Ps	42.10 my adversaries *t* me, while they say to
	44.13 You have made us the *t* of our
	102. 8 All day long my enemies *t* me; those

Isa	14. 4 up this *t* against the king of Babylon:
Hab	2. 6 Shall not everyone *t* such people and,

TAUNT-SONGS

Lam	3.63 I am the object of their *t*.

TAX (TAXES)

Mt	9. 9 called Matthew sitting at the *t* booth,
	17.24 your teacher not pay the temple *t*?"
	22.17 Is it lawful to pay *t* to the emperor,
Mk	2.14 son of Alphaeus sitting at the *t* booth,
	12.14 Is it lawful to pay *t* to the emperor, or
Lk	5.27 named Levi, sitting at the *t* booth;
	20.22 Is it lawful for us to pay *t* to the
Rom	13. 6 also pay *t*, for the authorities are God's

TAX COLLECTOR (TAX COLLECTORS)

Mt	21.31 *t* and the prostitutes go into the
Mk	2.15 many *t* and sinners were also sitting
Lk	3.12 Even *t* came to be baptized, and they
	5.30 "Why do you eat and drink with *t* and
	7.29 including the *t* acknowleged the justice
	7.34 and drunkard, a friend of *t* and sinners!'
	18.10 pray, one a Pharisee and the other a *t*.
	19. 2 Zacchaeus; he was a chief *t* and was

TEACH

Ex	4.12 I will . . . *t* you what you shall speak."
	18.20 and *t* them the statutes and instructions
Lev	10.11 you are to *t* the people of Israel all the
Deut	4. 5 I now *t* you statutes and ordinances for
	4.10 the earth, and may *t* their children so";
	5.31 that you shall *t* them, so that they may
	11.19 *T* them to your children, talking about
	20.18 that they may not *t* you to do all the
	31.19 write this song, and *t* it to the Israelites;
	33.10 They *t* Jacob your ordinances, and
Judg	13. 8 again to us, and *t* us what we are to do
Ezra	7.10 and to *t* the statutes and ordinances in
Job	12. 7 ask the animals, and they will *t* you; the
	21.22 Will any *t* God knowledge, seeing that
Ps	25. 4 your ways. O LORD; *t* me your paths.
	25.12 He will *t* them the way that they should
	27.11 *T* me your way, O LORD; and lead me on
	34.11 to me; I will *t* you the fear of the LORD.
	86.11 *T* me your way, O LORD, that I may walk
	90.12 So *t* us to count our days that we may
	119. 12 are you, O LORD; *t* me your statutes.
	119. 33 *T* me, O LORD, the way of your statutes,
	143. 10 *T* me to do your will, for you are my
Prov	9. 9 *t* the righteous and they will gain in
Isa	2. 3 that he may *t* us his ways and that we
	28. 9 "Whom will he *t* knowledge, and to
Jer	31.34 No longer shall they *t* one another, or
Ezek	44.23 *t* my people the difference between the
Mic	3.11 for a bribe, its priests *t* for a price,
	4. 2 that he may *t* us his ways and that we
Mt	13.54 began to *t* the people in their
Mk	4. 2 He began to *t* them many things in
	6. 2 On the sabbath he began to *t* in the
	8.31 began to *t* them that the Son of Man
Lk	4.15 He began to *t* in their synagogues and
	11. 1 "Lord, *t* us to pray, as John taught his
	12.12 for the Holy Spirit will *t* you at that very
Jn	14.26 send in my name, will *t* you everything,
Acts	4.18 ordered them not to speak or *t* at all in
	5.42 they did not cease to *t* and proclaim
Rom	2.21 that *t* others, will you not *t* yourself?
Col	3.16 you richly; *t* and admonish one another
1 Tim	2.12 I permit no woman to *t* or to have
Heb	8.11 they shall not *t* one another or say to

TEACHES (TEACHING TAUGHT)

Deut	4. 1 ordinances which I am *t* you to observe,
2 Chr	15. 3 the true God, and without a *t* priest,
	17. 9 They *t* in Judah, having the book of the
Ps	94.10 He who *t* knowledge to humankind,
Prov	4.11 I have *t* you the way of wisdom; I have

Isa	50.	4 my ear to listen as those who are *t*.
Jer	32.	33 though I have *t* them persistently, they
Dan	1.	4 were to be *t* the literature and language
Mt	4.	23 Galilee, *t* in their synagogues
	7.	29 for he *t* them as one having authority,
Mk	1.	22 for he *t* them as one having authority,
	9.	31 he was *t* his disciples, saying to them,
	14.	49 after day I was with you in the temple *t*,
Lk	4.	31 Galilee, and was *t* them on the sabbath.
Jn	6.	45 'And they shall all be *t* by God.'
Acts	1.	1 wrote about all that Jesus did and *t*
	5.	25 prison are standing in the temple and *t*
	15.	35 and there, with many others, they *t*
	18.	25 and *t* accurately the things concerning
	21.	28 This is the man who is *t* everyone
Gal	6.	6 Those who are *t* the word must share in
Eph	4.	21 heard about him and were *t* in him,
1 Tim	6.	3 Whoever *t* otherwise and does not agree
1 Jn	2.	27 as his anointing *t* you about all things,

TEACHER (TEACHERS)

Job	36.	22 in his power; who is a *t* like him?
Ps	119.	99 have more understanding than all my *t*,
Eccl	1.	1 The words of the *T*, the son of David,
Isa	30.	20 your *T* will not hide himself any more,
Mt	10.	24 "A disciple is not above his *t*, nor a
	17.	24 "Does your *t* not pay the temple tax?"
	23.	8 to be called rabbi, for you have one *t*,
	26.	18 "The *T* says, My time is near; I will
Mk	5.	35 is dead. Why trouble the *t* any further?"
Lk	5.	17 Pharisees and *t* of the law were sitting
	6.	40 A disciple is not above the *t*, but
Jn	11.	28 privately, "The *T* is here and is calling
	20.	16 in Hebrew, "Rabboni!" (which means *T*).
Eph	4.	11 some pastors and *t*, to equip the saints
1 Tim	1.	7 talk, desiring to be *t* of the law,

TEACHING (TEACHINGS)

Deut	32.	2 May my *t* drop like the rain, my speech
Prov	1.	8 and do not reject your mother's *t*;
	13.	14 The *t* of the wise is a fountain of life,
Isa	51.	7 people who have my *t* in your hearts;
Jer	6.	19 and as for my *t*, they have rejected it.
Mt	16.	12 of bread, but of the *t* of the Pharisees
Lk	4.	32 They were astonished at his *t*, because
Jn	7.	16 answered them, "My *t* is not mine, but
	18.	19 about his disciples and about his *t*.
Acts	2.	42 devoted themselves to the apostles' *t*
	5.	28 you have filled Jerusalem with your *t*
	17.	19 "May we know what this new *t* is that
Rom	6.	17 form of *t* to which you were entrusted,
1 Tim	4.	13 reading of scripture, to exhorting, to *t*.
	5.	17 those who labor in preaching and *t*;
	6.	3 *t* that is in accordance with godliness,
2 Tim	3.	10 you have observed my *t*, my conduct,
	3.	16 and is useful for *t*, for reproof, for
2 Jn		9 who does not abide in the *t* of Christ,

TEAR (TEARS) (n)

Ps	42.	3 My *t* have been my food day and night,
	56.	8 put my *t* in your bottle. Are they not in
Isa	25.	8 GOD will wipe away the *t* from all faces,
	38.	5 heard your prayer, I have seen your *t*;
2 Cor	2.	4 and with many *t*, not to cause you pain,
Rev	7.	17 God will wipe away every *t* from their
	21.	4 he will wipe away every *t* from their

TEAR (TORN) (v)

1 Sam	15.	28 "The LORD has *t* the kingdom of Israel
Mt	5.	29 your right eye causes you to sin, *t* it out
Mk	15.	38 curtain of the temple was *t* in two, from
Gal	4.	15 you would have *t* out your eyes and

TEKOA

2 Sam	14.	2 Joab sent to *T*, and brought from there
2 Chr	20.	20 and went out into the wilderness of *T*;
Jer	6.	1 Blow the trumpet in *T*, and raise a
Am	1.	1 who was among the shepherds of *T*,

TELL (TOLD)

2 Sam	1.	20 *T* it not in Gath, proclaim it not in the
Neh	9.	23 into the land that you had *t* their
Ps	40.	9 I have *t* the glad news of deliverance in
	105.	2 to him; *t* of all his wonderful works.
Isa	41.	22 bring them, and *t* us what is to happen.
Jer	33.	3 will *t* you great and hidden things that
	38.	15 Jeremiah said to Zedekiah, "If I *t* you,
Mt	28.	7 go quickly and *t* his disciples, 'He has
Mk	5.	14 The swineherds ran off and *t* it in the
	16.	7 go, *t* his disciples and Peter that he is
2 Cor	12.	4 and heard things that are not to be *t*,

TEMPEST

Prov	10.	25 When the *t* passes, the wicked are no

TEMPESTUOUS

Jon	1.	11 the sea was growing more and more *t*.

TEMPLE

Ps	11.	4 The LORD is in his holy *t*; the LORD's
	29.	9 forest bare; and in his *t* all say, "Glory!"
	48.	9 love, O God, in the midst of your *t*.
	65.	4 the goodness of your house, your holy *t*.
	79.	1 they have defiled your holy *t*;
Isa	44.	28 of the *t*, "Your foundation shall be laid."
Jer	7.	4 in these deceptive words: "This is the *t*
Ezek	43.	5 and the glory of the LORD filled the *t*.
	43.	11 make known to them the plan of the *t*,
Dan	11.	31 by him shall occupy and profane the *t*
Hab	2.	20 the LORD is in his holy *t*; let all the
Zech	6.	12 and he shall build the *t* of the LORD.
Mt	4.	5 placed him on the pinnacle of the *t*,
	21.	12 all who were selling and buying in the *t*,
	24.	1 point out to him the buildings of the *t*.
	26.	61 I am able to destroy the *t* of God, and
	27.	40 "You who would destroy the *t* and build
Mk	11.	15 he entered the *t* and began to drive out
	11.	16 anyone to carry anything through the *t*.
	14.	58 heard him say, "I will destroy this *t* that
	15.	29 You who would destroy the *t* and build
Lk	2.	46 they found him in the *t*, sitting among
	4.	9 placed him on the pinnacle of the *t*,
	18.	10 "Two men went up to the *t* to pray, one
	19.	45 he entered the *t* and began to drive out
Jn	2.	14 In the *t* he found people selling cattle,
	2.	19 "Destroy this *t*, and in three days I will
Acts	24.	6 He even tried to profane the *t*, and so
1 Cor	3.	16 not know that you are God's *t* and that
	6.	19 your body is a *t* of the Holy Spirit
2 Cor	6.	16 For we are the *t* of the living God; as
Eph	2.	21 and grows into a holy *t* in the Lord;
Rev	11.	1 "Come and measure the *t* of God and
	11.	19 God's *t* in heaven was opened, and the
	15.	8 the *t* was filled with smoke from the
	21.	22 I saw no *t* in the city, for its *t* is the

TEMPORARY

2 Cor	4.	18 for what can be seen is *t*, but what

TEMPT (TEMPTED)

Mk	1.	13 in the wilderness forty days, *t* by Satan;
Lk	4.	2 for forty days he was *t* by the devil.
1 Cor	7.	5 so that Satan may not *t* you because of
Jas	1.	13 No one, when *t*, should say, "I am being

TEMPTER

Mt	4.	3 The *t* came and said to him, "If you are
1 Thess	3.	5 that somehow the *t* had tempted you

TEN

Gen	18.	32 Suppose *t* are found there." He
Deut	4.	13 observe, that is, the *t* commandments;
Lk	17.	12 a village, *t* lepers approached him.

TENANTS

Mt	21.	33 Then he leased it to *t* and went to
Mk	12.	1 watchtower, then he leased it to *t*

Lk 20.16 come and destroy those *t* and give the

TEND (TENDED)

Ps 78.72 With upright heart he *t* them, and
1 Pet 5. 2 elders among you to *t* the flock of God

TENT (TENTS)

Gen 4.20 the ancestor of those who live in *t* and
12. 8 on the east of Bethel, and pitched his *t*,
13. 3 to the place where his *t* had been at the
Ex 29.44 I will consecrate the *t* of meeting and
33. 7 the camp; he called it the *t* of meeting.
Lev 1. 1 and spoke to him from the *t* of meeting,
Josh 18. 1 at Shiloh, and set up the *t* of meeting
2 Sam 7. 2 of cedar, but the ark of God stays in a *t*."
1 Chr 17. 1 of the covenant of the LORD is under a *t*."
Job 29. 4 the friendship of God was upon my *t*;
Ps 15. 1 O LORD, who may abide in your *t*? Who
19. 4 the heavens he has set a *t* for the sun,
Prov 14.11 but the *t* of the upright flourishes.
Isa 33.20 a quiet habitation, an immovable *t*,
40.22 like a curtain, and spreads them like a *t*
Jer 10.20 My *t* is destroyed, and all my cords are
Acts 7.44 ancestors had the *t* of testimony in the
2 Cor 5. 1 that if the earthly *t* we live in is
Heb 8. 5 when he was about to erect the *t*,
Rev 15. 5 temple of the *t* of witness in heaven

TENTH

Gen 14.20 And Abram gave him a *t* of everything.
28.22 that you give me I will surely give one *t*
Lev 27.32 All tithes of herd and flock, every *t* one
Isa 6.13 Even if a *t* remain in it, it will be
Heb 7. 2 to him Abraham apportioned "one-*t* of

TENT-MAKERS

Acts 18. 3 worked together— by trade they were *t*.

TERM

Isa 40. 2 cry to her that she has served her *t*, that

TERRIFY (TERRIFIED)

Job 15.24 distress and anguish *t* them; they
23.16 my heart faint; the Almighty has *t* me;
Ps 2. 5 in his wrath, and *t* them in his fury,
Mt 14.26 him walking on the sea, they were *t*,
27.54 they were *t* and said, "Truly this man
Lk 9.34 they were *t* as they entered the cloud.

TERROR

Lev 26.16 will do this to you: I will bring *t* on you;
Ps 91. 5 You will not fear the *t* of the night, or
Isa 2.19 of the ground, from the *t* of the LORD,
17.14 At evening time, lo, *t*! Before morning,
Jer 8.15 for a time of healing, but there is *t*
20. 4 I am making you a *t* to yourself and to
48.44 Everyone who flees from the *t* shall fall
Mk 16. 8 for *t* and amazement had seized them;

TEST (n)

Ex 15.25 and there he put them to the *t*.
Deut 6.16 not put the LORD . . . to the *t*, as you
Ps 106. 14 and put God to the *t* in the desert;
Isa 7.12 ask, and I will not put the LORD to the *t*.
Mal 3.10 and thus put me to the *t*, says the LORD
3.15 when they put God to the *t* they escape."
Mt 4. 7 not put the Lord your God to the *t*.' "
22.18 "Why are you putting me to the *t*, you
Mk 12.15 "Why put me to the *t*? Bring me a
Lk 4.12 not put the Lord your God to the *t*.' "
Acts 5. 9 to put the Spirit of the Lord to the *t*?
15.10 why are you putting God to the *t* by
1 Cor 10. 9 We must not put Christ to the *t*, as

TEST (TESTED TESTING TESTS)

Gen 22. 1 God *t* Abraham. He said to him,
42.15 Here is how you shall be *t*: as Pharaoh
Ex 17. 7 the Israelites quarreled and *t* the LORD,
Num 14.22 and yet you have *t* me these ten times

Deut 8. 2 to humble you, *t* you to know what was
13. 3 God is *t* you, to know whether you
Judg 2.22 In order to *t* Israel, whether or not they
1 Kings 10. 1 she came to *t* him with hard questions.
Job 12.11 Does not the ear *t* words as the palate
Ps 7. 9 you who *t* the minds and hearts, O
11. 5 The LORD *t* the righteous and the
66.10 for you, O God, have *t* us; you have
78.18 They *t* God in their heart by demanding
78.56 they *t* the Most High God, and rebelled
81. 7 I *t* you at the waters of Meribah.
95. 9 when your ancestors *t* me, and put me
105. 19 pass, the word of the LORD kept *t* him.
139. 23 my heart; *t* me and know my thoughts.
Prov 17. 3 is for gold, but the LORD *t* hearts.
Jer 12. 3 O LORD, know me; You see me and *t* me
17.10 "I the LORD *t* the mind and search the
20.12 O LORD of hosts, you *t* the righteous,
Lam 3.40 Let us *t* and examine our ways, and
Dan 1.12 "Please *t* your servants for ten days; Let
Mt 19. 3 and to *t* him they asked, "Is it lawful for
Mk 8.11 him for a sign from heaven, to *t* him.
Lk 11.16 Others, to *t* him, kept demanding from
Jn 6. 6 He said this to *t* him, for he himself
8. 6 They said this to *t* him, so that they
2 Cor 13. 5 you are living in the faith. *T* yourselves.
Gal 6. 4 All must *t* their own work, then that
1 Thess 5.21 but *t* everything; hold fast to what is
Heb 2.18 is able to help those who are being *t*.
4.15 has been *t* as we are, yet without sin.
1 Jn 4. 1 but *t* the spirits to see whether they are

TESTIFY (TESTIFIED TESTIFIES)

Deut 19.18 witness, having *t* falsely against another,
1 Sam 12. 3 Here I am; *t* against me before the LORD
Job 15. 6 and not I; your own lips *t* against you.
Ps 50. 7 O Israel, I will *t* against you. I am God,
Isa 59.12 you are many, and our sins *t* against us.
Jer 14. 7 Although our iniquities *t* against us, act,
Hos 5. 5 Israel's pride *t* against him; Ephraim
7.10 Israel's pride *t* against him; yet they do
Mt 23.31 Thus you *t* against yourselves that you
Lk 21.13 This will give you an opportunity to *t*.
Jn 1. 7 He came as a witness to *t* to the light,
1.34 and have *t* that this is the Son of God."
3.11 we know and *t* to what we have seen;
3.26 to whom you *t*, here he is baptizing,
5.32 He *t* to what he has seen and heard, yet
5.31 If I *t* about myself, my testimony is not
5.37 And the Father who sent me has *t* on
5.39 life; and it is they that *t* on my behalf.
7. 7 hates me because I *t* against it that its
15.26 from the Father, he will *t* on my behalf.
15.27 "You also are to *t* because you have
18.23 I have spoken wrongly, *t* to the wrong.
21.24 is the disciple who is *t* to these things
Acts 8.25 after Peter and John had *t* and spoken
14. 3 who *t* to the word of his grace by
20.21 as I *t* both to Jews and to Greeks about
26.16 to appoint you to serve and *t* to the
1 Pet 1.11 when it *t* in advance to the sufferings
1 Jn 4.14 we have seen and do *t* that the Father
3 Jn 3 and *t* to your faithfulness to the truth,
12 We also *t* for him, and you know that
Rev 1. 2 who *t* to the word of God and to the
22.20 The one who *t* to these things says,

TESTIMONY

Isa 8.16 Bind up the *t*, seal the teaching among
Mt 8. 4 that Moses commanded, as a *t* to them."
24.14 the world, as a *t* to all nations;
26.59 were looking for false *t* against Jesus
Mk 1.44 what Moses commanded, for a *t*
6.11 dust that is on your feet as a *t* against
13. 9 kings because of me, as a *t* to them.
14.55 council were looking for *t* against Jesus
Lk 5.14 for your cleansing, for a *t* to them."

Lk	9.	5 town shake the dust off your feet as a *t*
	22.71	"What further *t* do we need? We have
Jn	4.39	in him because of the woman's *t*,
	8.13	on your own behalf; your *t* is not valid."
	8.17	that the *t* of two witnesses is valid.
1 Cor	1.	6 as the *t* of Christ has been strengthened
2 Cor	1.12	is our boast, the *t* of our conscience:
1 Jn	5.	9 If we receive human *t*, the *t* of God is
Rev	6.	9 for the word of God and for the *t* they
	12.17	of God and hold the *t* of Jesus.
	19.10	For the *t* of Jesus is the spirit of
	22.16	to you with this *t* for the churches.

TESTING (n)

Lk	8.13	for a while and in a time of *t* fall away.
1 Cor	10.13	No *t* has overtaken you that is not
Jas	1.	3 know that the *t* of your faith produces

THADDAEUS

Mt	10.	3 James son of Alphaeus, and *T*;
Mk	3.18	*T*, and Simon the Cananaean, and Judas

THANK (THANKED)

Ps	107.	21 Let them *t* the LORD for his steadfast
Isa	38.18	For Sheol cannot *t* you, death cannot
Mt	11.25	Jesus said, "I *t* you, Father, Lord of
Lk	10.21	"I *t* you, Father, Lord of heaven and
	17.	9 Do you *t* the slave for doing what was
	17.16	himself at Jesus' feet and *t* him.
Jn	11.41	"Father, I *t* you for having heard me.
Acts	28.15	On seeing them, Paul *t* God and took
Rom	1.	8 First, I *t* my God through Jesus Christ
Phil	1.	3 I *t* God every time I remember you,
1 Thess	3.	9 How can we *t* God enough for you in

THANK OFFERING (THANK OFFERINGS)

Lev	7.12	you shall offer with the *t* unleavened
2 Chr	29.31	bring sacrifices and *t* to the house of
Ps	56.12	perform, O God; I will render *t* to you.
Jer	17.26	and bringing *t* to the house of the LORD.
Am	4.	5 bring a *t* of leavened bread, and

THANKS

2 Chr	7.	3 and worshiped and gave *t* to the LORD,
Neh	12.40	of those who gave *t* stood in the house
Ps	7.17	I will give to the LORD the *t* due to his
	30.12	my God, I will give *t* to you forever.
	75.	1 We give *t* to you, O God; we give *t*; your
	92.	1 It is good to give *t* to the LORD, to sing
	100.	4 praise. Give *t* to him, bless his name.
	107.	1 O give *t* to the LORD, for he is good; for
	138.	1 I give you *t*, O LORD, with my whole
Isa	12.	1 will say in that day: I will give *t* to you,
Dan	2.23	I give *t* and praise, for you have given
Mt	15.36	after giving *t* he broke them and gave
Acts	27.35	he took bread; and giving *t* to God in
Rom	1.21	not honor him as God or give *t* to him,
	6.17	But *t* be to God that you, having once
	7.25	of death? *T* be to God through Jesus
	14.	6 in honor of the Lord and give *t* to God.
1 Cor	14.17	you may give *t* well enough, but the
	15.57	But *t* be to God, who gives us the
2 Cor	2.14	But *t* be to God, who in Christ always
	8.16	But *t* be to God who put in the heart of
Eph	1.16	I do not cease to give *t* for you as I
	5.20	your hearts, giving *t* to God the Father
Col	3.17	Lord Jesus, giving *t* to God the Father
1 Thess	2.13	We also constantly give *t* to God for
	5.18	ceasing, give *t* in all circumstances;
2 Thess	1.	3 We must always give *t* to God for you,

THANKSGIVING

Lev	22.29	When you sacrifice a *t* offering to the
Ps	26.	7 singing aloud a song of *t*, and telling all
	50.14	Offer to God a sacrifice of *t*, and pay
	50.23	Those who bring *t* as their sacrifice
	69.30	with a song; I will magnify him with *t*.
	116.	17 I will offer to you a *t* sacrifice and call

Isa	51.	3 be found in her, *t* and the voice of song.
Jer	30.19	Out of them shall come *t*, and the
1 Tim	4.	4 rejected, provided it is received with *t*;
Rev	7.12	glory and wisdom and *t* and honor and

THESSALONICA

Acts	17.	1 they came to *T*, where there was a
	17.11	were more receptive than those in *T*,
	27.	2 by Aristarchus, a Macedonian from *T*.
Phil	4.16	even when I was in *T*, you sent me help
2 Tim	4.10	world, has deserted me and gone to *T*;

THICKET

Gen	22.13	looked up and saw a ram, caught in a *t*

THIEF (THIEVES)

Ps	50.18	You make friends with a *t* when you see
Prov	6.30	*T* are not despised who steal only to
	29.24	partner of a *t* is to hate one's own life;
Jer	2.26	As a *t* is shamed when caught, so the
Mt	6.19	and where *t* break in and steal;
	24.43	what part of the night the *t* was coming,
Lk	12.39	known at what hour the *t* was coming,
Jn	12.	6 but because he was a *t*; he kept the
2 Pet	3.10	the day of the Lord will come like a *t*,
Rev	3.	3 I will come like a *t*, and you will not

THIGH

Gen	24.	2 that he had, "Put your hand under my *t*,

THINK (THINKING)

Ps	63.	6 when I *t* of you on my bed, and
Prov	12.15	Fools *t* their own way is right, but the
Mt	5.17	"Do not *t* that I have come to abolish
	22.42	"What do you *t* of the Messiah? Whose
Lk	6.	8 he knew what they were *t*, he said
	11.17	But he knew what they were *t* and said
Rom	12.	3 ought to *t*, but *t* with sober judgement,
2 Cor	12.	6 that no one may *t* better of me than
Gal	6.	3 who are nothing *t* they are something,
2 Tim	2.	7 *T* over what I say, for the Lord will give

THIRD

Mt	17.23	him, and on the *t* day he will be raised."
	26.44	he went away and prayed for the *t* time,

THIRST (THIRSTS)

Ps	42.	2 my soul *t* for God, for the living God.
	63.	1 my soul *t* for you, my flesh faints for
	69.21	food, and for my *t* they gave me vinegar
	143.	6 hands to you; my soul *t* for you like a
Isa	48.21	They did not *t* when he led them
	41.17	and their tongue is parched with *t*,
	55.	1 Ho, every one who *t*, come to the
Am	8.13	and the young men shall faint for *t*.
Mt	5.	6 who hunger and *t* for righteousness,
Rev	7.16	will hunger no more, and *t* no more;

THIRSTY

Prov	25.25	Like cold water to a *t* soul, so is good
Isa	29.	8 a *t* person dreams of drinking and
	32.	6 and to deprive the *t* of drink.
	35.	7 pool, and the *t* ground springs of water;
	65.13	servants shall drink, but you shall be *t*;
Mt	25.35	I was *t* and you gave me something to
Jn	7.37	"Let anyone who is *t* come to me, and
	19.28	order to fulfill the scripture), "I am *t*."
Rom	12.20	them; if they are *t*, give them something
2 Cor	11.27	hungry and *t*, often without food, cold
Rev	22.17	"Come." And let everyone who is *t* come.

THIRTY

Zech	11.12	out as my wages *t* shekels of silver.
Mt	26.15	They paid him *t* pieces of silver.
	27.	3 and brought back the *t* pieces of silver

THOMAS

Mt	10.	3 Bartholomew; *T* and Matthew the tax
Mk	3.18	Matthew, and *T*, and James son of

Jn	11.16	T, who was called the Twin, said to his
	14. 5	T said to him, "Lord, we do not know
	20.27	he said to T, "Put your finger here and
	21. 2	were Simon Peter, T called the Twin,

THONG

Mk	1. 7	down and untie the t of his sandals.

THORN (THORNS)

Gen	3.18	t and thistles it shall bring forth for
Num	33.55	barbs in your eyes and t in your sides;
Isa	5. 6	it shall be overgrown with briers and t;
Mt	13. 7	Other seeds fell upon t, and the t grew
	27.29	twisting some t into a crown, they put it
Mk	4. 7	Other seed fell among t and the t grew
	15.17	twisting some t into a crown, they put it
Lk	6.44	Figs are not gathered from t, nor are
	8. 7	Some fell among t; and the t grew with
Jn	19. 5	Jesus came out, wearing the crown of t
2 Cor	12. 7	elated, a t was given me in the flesh,
Heb	6. 8	if it produces t and thistles, it is

THOUGHT (THOUGHTS)

Job	21.27	"Oh, I know your t, and your schemes
Ps	10. 4	it out"; all their t are, "There is no God."
	40. 5	wondrous deeds and your t toward us;
	40.17	and needy, but the LORD takes t for me.
	56. 5	cause; all their t are against me for evil.
	92. 5	works, O LORD! Your t are very deep!
	94.11	The LORD knows our t, that they are
	139. 17	How weighty to me are your t, O God!
Prov	1.23	I will pour out my t to you; I will make
	12. 5	The t of the righteous are just; the
Isa	55. 8	For my t are not your t, nor are your
	59. 7	innocent blood; their t are t of iniquity,
	66.18	For I know their works and their t, and
Dan	2.30	you may understand the t of your mind.
Am	4.13	reveals his t to mortals, makes the
Mic	4.12	But they do not know the t of the LORD;
Mt	9. 4	But Jesus, perceiving their t, said, "Why
1 Cor	3.20	Lord knows the t of the wise, that they
2 Cor	10. 5	and we take every t captive to obey
Heb	4.12	it is able to judge the t and intentions

THOUSAND (THOUSANDS)

1 Sam	18. 7	has killed his t, and David his ten t."
Ps	50.10	forest is mine, the cattle on a t hills.
	68.17	t upon t, the LORD came from Sinai into
	84.10	a day in your courts is better than a t
Eccl	7.28	One man among a t I found, but a
Song	5.10	and ruddy, distinguished among ten t.
2 Pet	3. 8	one day is like a t years, and a t years
Rev	20. 2	and Satan, and bound him for a t years,

THREATS

Prov	13. 8	for a person's life, but the poor get no t.
Lk	3.14	"Do not extort money from anyone by t

THREE

Dan	6.13	he is saying his prayers t times a day."
Mt	17. 4	I will make t dwellings here, one for
1 Jn	5. 8	water and the blood, and these t agree.

THRESH (THRESHED THRESHES THRESHING)

Ruth	3. 2	winnowing barley tonight at the t floor.
Isa	41.15	you shall t the mountains and crush
Jer	51.33	Babylon is like a t floor at the time
Hos	10.11	was a trained heifer that loved to t,
Am	1. 3	because they have t Gilead with t
1 Cor	9.10	whoever t should t in hope of a share in

THROAT (THROATS)

Prov	23. 7	like a hair in the t, so are they. "Eat
Hab	2. 5	They open their t as wide as Sheol; like
Mt	18.28	seizing him by the t, he said, 'Pay what
Rom	3.13	"Their t are opened graves; they use

THRONE (THRONES)

1 Kings	1.13	me as king, and he shall sit upon my t?

1 Kings	1.37	make his t greater than the t of my lord
	9. 5	I will establish your royal t over Israel
	10.18	The king also made a great ivory t, and
1 Chr	17.12	for me, and I will establish his t forever.
Ps	9. 4	just cause; you have sat on the t giving
	45. 6	Your t, O God, endures forever and ever.
	93. 2	your t is established from of old; you
	103. 19	LORD has established his t in the
	132. 11	sons of your body I will set on your t."
Prov	16.12	to do evil, for the t is established by
	25. 5	king, and his t will be established in
Isa	6. 1	died, I saw the Lord sitting on a t,
	16. 5	a t shall be established in steadfast love
	66. 1	Heaven is my t and the earth is my
Jer	3.17	time Jerusalem shall be called the t
	17.12	O glorious t, exalted from the
	43.10	and he will set his t above these stones
Lam	5.19	your t endures to all generations.
Dan	7. 9	As I watched, t were set in place, and
Mt	19.28	followed me will also sit on twelve t,
Lk	1.32	give to him the t of his ancestor David.
Acts	7.49	'Heaven is my t, and the earth is my
Heb	1. 8	"Your t, O God, is forever and ever, and
	4.16	Let us therefore approach the t of grace
	8. 1	at the right hand of the t of the Majesty
Rev	4. 2	there in heaven stood a t, with one
	4. 4	twenty-four t, and seated on the t are
	20. 4	Then I saw t, and those seated on them
	20.11	I saw a great white t and one who sat
	22. 1	as crystal, flowing from the t of God

THRONG

Ps	109. 30	I will praise him in the midst of the t.

THROW (THREW THROWN)

Isa	22.18	and t you like a ball into a wide land;
Mt	4. 6	are the Son of God, t yourself down;
	8.12	heirs of the kingdom will be t into the
	13.42	and they will t them into the furnace of
Lk	20.15	they t him out of the vineyard and

THUMMIN

Ex	28.30	shall put the Urim and the T, and they
Lev	8. 8	breastplate he put the Urim and the T.

THUNDER (THUNDERS THUNDERED)

1 Sam	12.17	the LORD, that he may send t and rain;
2 Sam	22.14	The LORD t from heaven, the Most High
Ps	18.13	LORD also t in the heavens, and the
	29. 3	over the waters; the God of glory t, the
Mk	3.17	the name Boanerges, that is, sons of t);

TIDINGS

1 Kings	14. 6	For I am charged with heavy t for you.
Ps	68.11	is the company of those who bore the t:
Isa	40. 9	O Zion, herald of good t; lift up your
	41.27	I give to Jerusalem a herald of good t.

TIGLATH-PILESER (PUL)

Received tribute from Menahem, 2 Kings 15.19-20; carried him captive to Assyria, 2 Kings 15.29; paid homage by Ahaz, 2 Kings 16.7-10 (2 Chr 28.20-21); deported some of the tribes of Israel, 1 Chr 5.26.

TIGRIS

Gen	2.14	name of the third river is T, which flows
Dan	10. 4	bank of the great river (that is, the T),

TILL (TILLER)

Gen	2. 5	and there was no one to t the ground;
	3.23	God sent him . . . to t the ground from
Zech	13. 5	"I am no prophet, I am a t of the soil;

TIME (TIMES)

Gen	21. 2	age, at the t of which God had spoken
Ex	12.40	The t that the Israelites had lived in
2 Kings	5.26	Is this a t to accept money and to
Esth	4.14	to royal dignity for such a t as this."
Ps	31.15	My t are in your hand; deliver me from

Ps	34. 1 I will bless the LORD at all *t*; his praise
	89.47 Remember how short my *t* is — for what
	119.126 It is *t* for the LORD to act, for your law
Eccl	3. 1 is a season, and a *t* for every matter
	8. 6 For every matter has its *t* and way,
	9.11 but *t* and chance happen to them all.
Ezek	12.27 years ahead; he prophesies for distant *t*."
	30. 3 will be a day of clouds, a *t* of doom for
Hab	2. 3 is still a vision for the appointed *t*;
Hag	1: 2 These people say the *t* has not yet
Mt	8.29 come here to torment us before the *t*?"
	26.18 'The Teacher says, My *t* is near; I will
Jn	7. 6 "My *t* has not yet come, but your *t* is
1 Cor	7.29 appointed *t* has grown short; from now
Eph	5.16 making the most of the *t*, because the
Col	4. 5 outsiders, making the most of the *t*.
Rev	1. 3 what is written in it; for the *t* is near.
	12.14 she is nourished for a *t*, and *t*, and half a

TIMOTHY

Paul's son in the Lord, 1 Cor 4.17; 1 Tim 1.2,18; 2 Tim 1.2; son of a Greek father and a Jewish mother, Acts 16.1; brought up in a devout home, 2 Tim 1.5; 3.14-15; lived in Lystra (or Derbe), Acts 16.1; circumcised, Acts 16.3; accompanied Paul in his second missionary journey, Acts 16.1-4; 17.14-15; 18.5; 1 Thess 3.2-6; ordained, 1 Tim 4.14; 2 Tim 1.6; sent to the church in Corinth, 1 Cor 4.17; 16.10; accompanied Paul in the third missionary journey, Acts 20.4; in charge of the church in Ephesus, 1 Tim 1.3; 4.12; urged by Paul to visit him in prison, 2 Tim 4.9,13; imprisoned and released, Heb 13.23.

1 Cor	4.17 For this reason I sent you *T*, who is my
	16.10 If *T* comes, see that he has nothing to

TITHE (TITHES)

Lev	27.31 If persons wish to redeem any of their *t*,
Num	18.21 To the Levites I have given every *t* in
	18.24 Levites as their portion of the *t* of the
Deut	14.22 Set apart a *t* of all the yield of your
	26.12 finished paying all the *t* of your produce
Neh	10.37 to bring to the Levites the *t* from our
Mal	3. 8 "How are we robbing you?" In your *t* and
Mt	23.23 hypocrites! For you *t* mint, dill, and
Lk	11.42 woe to you Pharisees! for you *t* mint
Heb	7. 9 who receives *t*, paid *t* through Abraham,

TITLE

Mt	22.20 "Whose head is this, and whose *t*?"
Mk	12.16 "Whose head is this, and whose *t*?"

TITUS

2 Cor	2.13 I did not find my brother *T* there.
	7. 6 consoled us by the arrival of *T*,
	8. 6 so that we might urge *T* that, as he had
	8.23 As for *T*, he is my partner and
	12.18 *T* did not take advantage of you, did
Gal	2. 1 with Barnabas, taking *T* along
2 Tim	4.10 has gone to Galatia, *T* to Dalmatia.
Titus	1. 4 To *T*, my loyal child in the faith we

TODAY (TODAY'S)

Ps	95. 7 of his hand. O that *t* you would listen
Mt	6.34 of its own. *T* trouble is enough for *t*.
Lk	23.43 I tell you, *t* you will be with me in
Heb	3.15 "*T*, if you hear his voice, do not harden

TOGETHER

Gen	22. 8 son." So the two of them walked on *t*.
Acts	2. 1 had come, they were all *t* in one place.
	2.46 they spent much time *t* in the temple,
Col	1.17 all things, and in him all things hold *t*.

TOIL

Prov	14.23 In all *t* there is profit, but mere talk
Eccl	1. 3 What do people gain from all the *t* at
	3.13 drink and take pleasure in all their *t*.
	4. 4 I saw that all *t* and all skill in work
	4. 6 with quiet than two handfuls with *t*,

Eccl	4. 8 yet there is no end to all their *t*, and
	5.19 and find enjoyment in their *t* — this is
	6. 7 All human *t* is for the mouth, yet the
	10.15 The *t* of fools wears them out, for they
Lk	12.27 how they grow: they neither *t* nor spin;
2 Cor	11.27 in *t* and hardship, through many a
Col	1.29 For this I *t* and struggle with all the
Rev	2. 2 "I know your works, your *t* and your

TOLL

Ezra	4.13 they will not pay tribute, custom, or *t*,
	7.24 custom, or *t* on any of the priests,
Mt	17.25 from whom do kings of the earth take *t*

TOMB (TOMBS)

Mt	23.27 For you are like whitewashed *t*, which
	27.60 rolled a great stone to the door of the *t*
Mk	6.29 and took his body, and laid it in a *t*.
	15.46 laid it in a *t* that had been hewn out of
Lk	8.27 he did not live in a house but in the *t*.
	11.47 you build the *t* of the prophets whom
	24. 1 they came to the *t*, taking the spices
Jn	11.31 she was going to the *t* to weep there.
	19.41 and in the garden there was a new *t* in
	20. 6 went into the *t*. He saw the linen

TOMORROW

Prov	27. 1 Do not boast about *t*, for you do not
Isa	22.13 "Let us eat and drink, for *t* we die."
Mt	6.30 is alive today and *t* is thrown into the
1 Cor	15.32 "Let us eat and drink, for *t* we die."
Jas	4.14 you do not even know what *t* will bring.

TONGUE (TONGUES)

Job	5.21 hidden from the scourge of the *t*, and
Ps	5. 9 are open graves; they flatter with their *t*.
	31.20 under your shelter from contentious *t*.
	34.13 Keep your *t* from evil, and your lips
	35.28 Then my *t* shall tell of your
	39. 1 my ways that I may not sin with my *t*;
	45. 1 my *t* is like the pen of a ready scribe.
	52. 2 Your *t* is like a sharp razor, you worker
	64. 3 who whet their *t* like swords, who aim
Prov	10.20 The *t* of the righteous is choice silver;
	10.31 but the perverse *t* will be cut off.
	12.18 but the *t* of the wise brings healing.
	18.21 Death and life are in the power of the *t*,
	25.15 and a soft *t* can break bones.
Isa	45.23 knee shall bow, every *t* shall swear."
	54.17 you shall confute every *t* that rises
Jer	9. 5 they have taught their *t* to speak lies;
	9. 8 Their *t* is a deadly arrow; it speaks
Mk	7.35 opened, his *t* was released, and he
	16.17n out demons; they will speak in new *t*;
Acts	2. 3 Divided *t*, as of fire, appeared among
	19. 6 they spoke with *t* and prophesied —
Rom	3.13 graves; they use their *t* to deceive."
1 Cor	12.10 to another various kinds of *t*, to another
	13. 1 If I speak in *t* of mortals and of angels,
	14. 2 those who speak in a *t* do not speak to
	14.21 written, "By people of strange *t* and by
	14.22 *T*, then, are a sign not for believers but
Jas	1.26 and do not bridle their *t* but deceive
	3. 5 the *t* is a small member, yet it boasts of

TOOTH (TEETH)

Ex	21.24 eye for eye, *t* for *t*, hand for hand, foot
Deut	19.21 eye for eye, *t* for *t*, hand for hand, foot
Job	19.20 and I have escaped by the skin of my *t*.
Prov	25.19 Like a bad *t* or a lame foot is trust in a
Song	4. 2 Your *t* are like a flock of shorn ewes
Ezek	18. 2 and the children's *t* are set on edge"?

TORCH (TORCHES)

Gen	15.17 flaming *t* passed between these pieces.
Judg	7.16 and empty jars, with *t* inside the jars,
Rev	4. 5 of the throne burn seven flaming *t*,

TORMENT (TORMENTED TORMENTS)

Job 19. 2 "How long will you *t* me, and break me
Ps 32.10 Many are the *t* of the wicked, but
Isa 50.11 from my hand: you shall lie down in *t.*
Mt 8.29 Have you come here to *t* us before the
15.22 of David; my daughter is *t* by a demon."
Mk 5. 7 God? I adjure you by God, do not *t* me."
Lk 8.28 High God? I beg you, do not *t* me"—
16.23 in Hades, where he was being *t*, he
Rev 20.10 they will be *t* day and night forever and

TOSSED (TOSSING)

Ex 14.27 the LORD *t* the Egyptians into the sea.
Job 7. 4 is long and I am full of *t* till the dawn.
Isa 57.20 wicked are like the *t* sea that cannot

TOUCH (TOUCHED TOUCHES)

Gen 3. 3 of the garden, nor shall you *t* it, or you
1 Sam 10.26 went warriors whose hearts God had *t.*
Job 4. 5 it *t* you, and you are dismayed.
5.19 troubles; in seven no harm shall *t* you.
Ps 105. 15 saying, "Do not *t* my anointed ones; do
Jer 1. 9 LORD put out his hand and *t* my mouth;
Zech 2. 8 one who *t* you *t* the apple of my eye.
Mt 8. 3 He stretched out his hand and *t* him,
8.15 he *t* her hand, and the fever left her,
9.21 "If I only *t* his cloak, I will be made
9.29 Then he *t* their eyes and said,
14.36 might *t* even the fringe of his cloak;
20.34 with compassion, Jesus *t* their eyes.
Mk 5.28 "If I but *t* his clothes, I will be made
6.56 they might *t* even the fringe of his
Lk 8.45 "Someone *t* me; for I noticed that power
1 Cor 7. 1 "It is well for a man not to *t* a woman."
2 Cor 6.17 and *t* nothing unclean; then I will
1 Jn 5.18 them, and the evil one does not *t* them.

TOWEL

Jn 13. 4 outer robe, and tied a *t* around himself.

TOWER

Gen 11. 4 let us build ourselves a city, and a *t*
Lk 13. 4 were killed when the *t* of Siloam fell
14.28 intending to build a *t*, does not first sit

TRADE (TRADED)

Ezek 27.17 Judah and the land of Israel *t* with you;
Mt 25.16 went off at once and *t* with them;
Acts 19.25 together, with the workers of same *t,*

TRADITION (TRADITIONS)

Mt 15. 2 your disciples break the *t* of the elders?
Mk 7. 5 disciples not live according to the *t* of
7. 8 of God and hold to human *t.*
2 Thess 2.15 stand firm and hold to the *t* that you

TRAIN (TRAINED TRAINING TRAINS)

Gen 14.14 taken captive, he led forth his *t* men,
Ps 144. 1 rock, who *t* my hands for war, and my
Prov 22. 6 *T* children in the right way, and when
1 Tim 1. 4 than the divine *t* that is known by faith.
4. 8 physical *t* is of some value, godliness is
Titus 2.12 *t* us to renounce impiety and worldly

TRAITOR

Lk 6.16 and Judas Iscariot, who became a *t.*

TRAMPLE (TRAMPLED)

Job 9. 8 the heavens and *t* the waves of the Sea;
Ps 56. 1 to me, O God, for people *t* on me;
Hab 3.15 You *t* the sea with your horses,

TRANCE

Dan 10. 9 of his words, I fell into a *t*, face to the

TRANSFER (TRANSFERRED)

2 Sam 3.10 to *t* the kingdom from the house of
Col 1.13 and *t* us into the kingdom of his

TRANSFIGURED

Mt 17. 2 he was *t* before them, and his face
Mk 9. 2 themselves. And he was *t* before them,

TRANSFORM (TRANSFORMED)

Rom 12. 2 be *t* by the renewing of your minds, so
2 Cor 3.18 are being *t* into the same image from
Phil 3.21 He will *t* the body of our humiliation

TRANSGRESS (TRANSGRESSED)

Deut 26.13 I have neither *t* nor forgotten any of
Josh 23.16 If you *t* the covenant of the LORD your
Judg 2.20 people have *t* my covenant that I
2 Kings 18.12 but *t* his covenant —all that Moses the
1 Chr 5.25 But they *t* against the God of their
Ps 17. 3 in me; my mouth does not *t.*
Jer 34.18 those who *t* my covenant and did not
Lam 3.42 We have *t* and rebelled, and you have
Hos 6. 7 at Adam they *t* the covenant; there they
Am 4. 4 Come to Bethel—and *t*; to Gilgal—and

TRANSGRESSION (TRANSGRESSIONS)

Lev 16.16 and because of their *t*, all their sins;
Job 31.33 if I have concealed my *t* as others do,
Ps 32. 1 Happy are those whose *t* is forgiven,
39. 8 Deliver me from all my *t*. Do not make
51. 3 For I know my *t*, and my sin is ever
89.32 I will punish their *t* with the rod and
Prov 10.19 When words are many, *t* is not lacking,
28.13 No one who conceals *t* will prosper, but
Isa 57. 4 Are you not children of *t*, the offspring
59.12 our *t* before you are many, and our sins
6 because their *t* are many, their
Ezek 18.22 None of the *t* that they have committed
39.24 to their uncleanness and their *t,*
Am 1. 3 For three *t* of Damascus, and for four, I
3.14 On the day I punish Israel for its *t*, I
Mic 1. 5 All this is for the *t* of Jacob and for the
Rom 5.14 whose sins were not like the *t* of Adam,
Gal 6. 1 if anyone is detected in a *t*, you who

TRANSGRESSOR

Gal 2.18 down, then I demonstrate that I am a *t.*

TRAVEL (TRAVELED TRAVELS)

Deut 23.14 God *t* along with your camp, to save
Ezek 27.25 The ships of Tarshish *t* for you in your
2 Cor 8.19 appointed by the churches to *t* with us

TRAVELER

Job 31.32 I have opened my doors to the *t*—

TREACHEROUS

Job 6.15 My companions are *t* like a torrent-bed,
Prov 11. 3 but the crookedness of the *t* destroys
Isa 24.16 the *t* deal treacherously, the *t* deal very
2 Tim 3. 4 haters of good, *t*, reckless, swollen with

TREACHERY

Lev 26.40 in that they committed *t* against me,
Josh 22.16 'What is this *t* that you have committed
Jer 5.27 full of birds, their houses are full of *t;*

TREAD (TREADING)

Ps 44. 5 our foes; through your name we *t* down
91.13 You will *t* on the lion and the adder,
Mic 7.19 us; he will *t* our iniquities under foot.
Hab 3.19 deer, and makes me *t* upon the heights.
Mal 4. 3 you shall *t* down the wicked, for they
1 Cor 9. 9 muzzle an ox while it is *t* out the grain."

TREASON

2 Kings 9.23 about and fled, saying to Ahaziah, "*T,*
11.14 tore her clothes and cried, "*T! T!*"
2 Chr 23.13 tore her clothes, and cried, "*T! T!*"

TREASURE (TREASURED TREASURES)

Gen 43.23 must have put *t* in your sacks for you;
1 Kings 14.26 he took away the *t* of the house of the

2 Kings 20.13 he showed them all his *t* house, the
Job 23.12 his lips; I have *t* in my bosom the words
Prov 2. 1 my words and *t* up my commandments
2. 4 and search for it as for hidden *t* —
15. 6 house of the righteous there is much *t*,
15.16 fear of the LORD than great *t* and trouble
21.20 Precious *t* remains in the house of the
Eccl 2. 8 for myself silver and gold and the *t*
Isa 33. 6 the fear of the LORD is Zion's *t*.
45. 3 give you the *t* of darkness and riches
Jer 15.13 your *t* I will give as plunder, without
20. 5 *t* of the kings of Judah into the hand of
Mic 6.10 Can I forget the *t* of wickedness in the
Hag 2. 7 so that the *t* of all nations shall come,
Mt 6.19 "Do not store up for yourselves *t* on
12.35 brings good things out of a good *t*,
13.44 of heaven is like *t* hidden in a field,
13.52 brings out of his *t* what is new and
Lk 6.45 person out of the good *t* of his heart
12.21 those who store up *t* for themselves
12.34 For where your *t* is, there your heart
2 Cor 4. 7 we have this *t* in clay jars, so that it
Col 2. 3 in whom are hidden all the *t* of wisdom

TREASURE CHESTS

Mt 2.11 opening their *t* they offered him gifts

TREASURY

Josh 6.19 they shall go into the *t* of the LORD."
Zech 11.13 "Throw it into the *t*" — this lordly price
Mk 12.41 the crowd putting money into the *t*.
Jn 8.20 he was teaching in the *t* of the temple,

TREATED

Jer 6.14 *t* the wound of my people carelessly,

TREATY

Josh 9. 6 a far country; so now make a *t* with us."
Isa 33. 8 The *t* is broken, its oaths are despised,

TREE (TREES)

Gen 2. 9 *t* of life also in the midst of the garden,
Deut 16.21 shall not plant any *t* as a sacred pole
20.19 you must not not destroy its *t* by
21.23 anyone hung on a *t* is under God's
1 Kings 19. 4 and sat down under a solitary broom *t*.
Job 14. 7 hope for a *t*, if it be cut down, that it
Ps 52. 8 I am like a green olive *t* in the house of
104. 16 The *t* of the LORD are watered
Prov 15. 4 A gentle tongue is a *t* of life, but
Jer 17. 8 like a *t* planted by water, sending out
Ezek 31. 8 no *t* in the garden of God was like it in
47. 7 I saw upon the bank a great many *t* on
Dan 4.10 there was a *t* at the center of the earth,
Mic 4. 4 own vines and under their own fig *t*,
Mt 7.17 same way, every good *t* bears good fruit,
12.33 for the *t* is known by its fruit;
Lk 6.43 "No good *t* bears bad fruit, nor again
19. 4 ahead and climbed a sycamore *t* to see
Acts 13.29 they took him down from the *t* and laid
Gal 3.13 "Cursed is everyone who hangs on a *t*" —
Rev 2. 7 to eat from the *t* of life that is in the
22. 2 the *t* of life with its twelve kinds of
22.14 they will have the right to the *t* of life

TREMBLE (TREMBLING)

Ps 99. 1 LORD is king; let the peoples *t*! He sits
Isa 13.13 I will make the heavens *t*, and the earth
14.16 "Is this the man who made the earth *t*,
24.18 and the foundations of the earth *t*.
32.11 *T*, you women who are at ease, shudder,
64. 2 the nations might *t* at your presence!
66. 5 of the LORD, you who *t* at his word:
Am 8. 8 Shall not the land *t* on this account,
Mk 5.33 happened to her, came in fear and *t*

TRESPASS (TRESPASSES)

1 Sam 25.28 Please forgive the *t* of your servant; for

Mt 6.14 For if you forgive others their *t*, your
Mk 11.26 in heaven may also forgive your *t*."
Rom 4.25 handed over to death for our *t* and was
2 Cor 5.19 not counting their *t* against them,
Col 2.13 when he forgave us all our *t*, erasing the

TRIAL (TRIALS)

Judg 6.39 let me, please, make *t* just once more;
Mt 6.13 And do not bring us to the time of *t*,
26.41 you may not come into the time of *t*;
Mk 14.38 you may not come into the time of *t*;
Lk 11. 4 And do not bring us to the time of *t*."
22.28 who have stood by me in my *t*; and I
Acts 20.19 with tears, enduring the *t* that came
2 Pet 2. 9 knows how to rescue the godly from *t*,
Rev 3.10 I will keep you from the hour of *t* that

TRIBE (TRIBES)

Judg 21. 6 and said, "One *t* is cut off from Israel
Ps 122. 4 To it the *t* go up, the *t* of the LORD, as
Jer 51.19 and Israel is the *t* of his inheritance;
Rev 7. 4 sealed out of every *t* of the people of

TRIBULATION

Lam 3. 5 and enveloped me with bitterness and *t*;

TRIBUTE

Num 31.37 the LORD's *t* of sheep and goats was six
Judg 3.15 Israelites sent *t* by him to King Eglon of

TRICKED

Gen 3.13 said, "The serpent *t* me, and I ate."

TRICKERY

Eph 4.14 wind of doctrine, by people's *t*, by their

TRIUMPH (TRIUMPHED TRIUMPHING TRIUMPHS)

Ex 15.21 to the LORD, for he has *t* gloriously;
Judg 5.11 repeat the *t* of the LORD, the *t* of his
Ps 18.50 Great *t* he gives to his king, and shows
41.11 because my enemy has not *t* over me.
Prov 28.12 When the righteous *t*, there is great
Isa 45.25 LORD all the offspring of Israel shall *t*
Col 2.15 example of them, *t* over them in him.

TRIUMPHAL

2 Cor 2.14 in Christ always leads us in *t* procession

TROAS

Acts 16. 8 passing by Mysia, they went down to *T*.
20. 5 ahead and were waiting for us in *T*;
2 Cor 2.12 When I came to *T* to proclaim the good
2 Tim 4.13 the cloak that I left with Carpus at *T*,

TROUBLE (TROUBLES) (n)

Josh 7.25 said, "Why did you bring *t* on us?
Judg 11. 7 you come to me now when you are in *t*?"
1 Kings 20. 7 See how this man is seeking *t*; for he
Job 3.26 am I quiet; I have no rest; but *t* comes."
5. 7 human beings are born to *t* just as
5.19 He will deliver you from six *t*; in seven
14. 1 of woman, few of days, and full of *t*,
Ps 27. 5 hide me in his shelter in the day of *t*;
34. 6 the LORD, and was saved from every *t*.
37.39 LORD; he is their refuge in the time of *t*.
46. 1 and strength, a very present help in *t*.
50.15 Call on me in the day of *t*; I will deliver
66.14 my mouth promised when I was in *t*.
73. 5 They are not in *t* as others are; they are
90.10 even then their span is only toil and *t*;
Prov 15.16 of the LORD than great treasure and *t*
27. 9 the heart glad, but the soul is torn by *t*.
Nah 1. 7 LORD is good, a stronghold in a day of *t*;
Mt 13.21 while and when *t* or persecution arises
Gal 6.17 From now on, let no one make *t* for me;

TROUBLE (TROUBLED) (v)

Num 33.55 they shall *t* you in the land where you

Ezek	32.	9 I will *t* the hearts of many peoples, as I
Dan	7.15	me, Daniel, my spirit was *t* within me,
Mt	26.10	"Why do you *t* the woman? She has
Mk	14.	6 why do you *t* her? She has performed a
Lk	8.49	daughter is dead; do not *t* the teacher
Jn	12.27	"Now is my soul *t*. And what should I
	13.21	After saying this Jesus was *t* in spirit,
	14.	1 "Do not let your hearts be *t*. Believe in

TRUE

1 Kings	11.	4 his heart was not *t* to the LORD his God,
2 Chr	15.17	Nevertheless the heart of Asa was *t* all
	16.	9 those whose heart is *t* to him.
Jn	15.	1 "I am the *t* vine, and my Father is the
Rom	3.	4 everyone is a liar, let God be *t*,
Phil	1.18	way, whether out of false motives or *t*;
	4.	8 Finally, beloved, whatever is *t*, whatever
Titus	1.13	That testimony is *t*. For this reason

TRUMPET (TRUMPETS)

Ex	19.16	and a blast of a *t* so loud that all the
Lev	23.24	commemmorated with *t* blasts.
Num	10.	2 "Make two silver *t*; you shall make them
Judg	7.16	put *t* into the hands of all of them, and
2 Kings	9.13	they blew the *t*, and proclaimed, "Jehu
Ps	98.	6 With *t* and the sound of the horn make
Isa	27.13	on that day a great *t* will be blown, and
Ezek	33.	5 They heard the sound of the *t* and did
Joel	2.	1 Blow the *t* in Zion; sound the alarm on
Am	3.	6 Is a *t* blown in a city, and the people
Zech	9.14	Lord GOD will sound the *t* and march
Mt	6.	2 you give alms, do not sound a *t*
1 Cor	15.52	*t* will sound, and the dead will be raised
1 Thess	4.16	with the sound of God's *t*, will descend

TRUST (n)

Deut	1.32	spite of this, you have no *t* in the LORD
Job	8.14	is gossamer, a spider's house their *t*.
	31.24	"If I have made gold my *t*, or called fine
Ps	40.	4 are those who make the LORD their *t*,
	146.	3 Do not put your *t* in princes, in mortals,
Prov	20.	6 loyal, but who can find one worthy of *t*?
	22.19	So that your *t* may be in the LORD, I
	25.19	tooth or a lame foot is *t* in a faithless
Isa	32.17	righteousness, quietness and *t* forever.
Mic	7.	5 Put no *t* in a friend, have no confidence
Heb	2.13	And again, "I will put my *t* in him." And

TRUST (TRUSTED TRUSTING TRUSTS)

Num	20.12	"Because you did not *t* in me, to show
Deut	9.23	LORD your God, neither *t* nor obeying
	28.52	and fortified walls, in which you *t*,
2 Kings	18.	5 He *t* in the LORD the God of Israel; so
Job	18.14	from the tent in which they *t*, and are
Ps	13.	5 But I *t* in your steadfast love; my heart
	21.	7 For the king *t* in the LORD, and through
	25.	2 O my God, in you I *t*; do not let me be
	31.14	But I *t* in you, O LORD; I say, "You are
	33.21	in him, because we *t* in his holy name.
	37.	3 *T* in the LORD, and do good; so you will
	49.	6 those who *t* in their wealth and boast of
	52.	7 but *t* in abundant riches, and sought
	55.23	out half their days. But I will *t* in you.
	62.	8 *T* in him at all times, O people; pour
	84.12	hosts, happy is everyone who *t* in you.
	91.	2 and my fortress; my God, in whom I *t*."
	115.	8 are like them; so are all who *t* in them.
	125.	1 Those who *t* in the LORD are like Mount
Prov	3.	5 *T* in the LORD with all your heart, and
	11.28	Those who *t* in their riches will wither,
	16.20	will prosper, and happy are those who *t*
	28.25	whoever *t* in the LORD will be enriched.
Isa	26.	4 *T* in the Lord forever, for in the LORD
	28.16	foundation: "One who *t* will not panic."
	31.	1 who rely on horses, who *t* in chariots
	42.17	put to shame — who *t* in carved images,
	50.10	no light, yet *t* in the name of the LORD

Jer	7.	4 not *t* in these deceptive words: "This is
	13.25	you have forgotten me and *t* in lies.
	17.	5 "Cursed are those who *t* in mere
	17.	7 Blessed are those who *t* in the LORD,
	29.31	send him, and has led you to *t* in a lie,
	48.	7 because you *t* in your strongholds and
Dan	6.23	on him, because he had *t* in his God.
Hos	10.13	Because you have *t* in your power and
Mk	10.24n	for those who *t* in riches to enter the
Rom	4.	5 works *t* him who justifies the ungodly,
1 Pet	1.21	him you have come to *t* in God,

TRUSTWORTHY

Ps	111.	7 faithful and just; all his precepts are *t*.
Mt	25.21	"Well done, good and *t* slave; you have
Lk	19.17	you have been *t* in a very small thing,
1 Cor	4.	2 of stewards that they should be found *t*.
Rev	21.	5 this, for these words are *t* and true."

TRUTH

Ps	15.	2 is right and speak *t* from their heart;
Prov	12.17	Whoever speaks the *t* gives honest
	23.23	Buy *t*, and do not sell it; buy wisdom,
Isa	45.19	I the LORD speak the *t*, I declare what is
	48.	1 the God of Israel, but not in *t* or right.
Dan	4.37	for all his works are *t*, and his ways are
	8.12	it cast *t* to the ground, and kept
Lk	1.	4 so that you may know the *t* concerning
Jn	8.32	and you will know the *t*, and the *t* will
	14.	6 "I am the way, and the *t*, and the life.
	18.38	my voice." Pilate asked him, "What is *t*?"
Rom	1.25	they exchanged the *t* about God for a
1 Cor	5.	8 the unleavened bread of sincerity and *t*.
	13.	6 in wrongdoing, but rejoices in the *t*.
2 Cor	13.	8 against the *t*, but only for the *t*.
Eph	4.21	and were taught in him, as *t* is in Jesus.
1 Jn	2.	4 in such a person the *t* does not exist;

TRUTHFUL

Prov	12.19	*T* lips endure forever, but a lying tongue
	14.25	A *t* witness saves lives, but one who

TRY (TRIED)

Job	23.10	when he has *t* me, I shall come out like
	34.36	Would that Job were *t* to the limit,
Ps	17.	3 If you *t* my heart, if you visit me by
	26.	2 Prove me, O LORD, and *t* me; test my
	119.140	Your promise is well *t*, and your servant

TUMULT

Isa	22.	5 a day of *t* and trampling and confusion
Hos	10.14	therefore the *t* of war shall rise against

TUNIC (TUNICS)

Mk	6.	9 wear sandals and not to put on two *t*.
Lk	9.	3 bread, nor money — not even an extra *t*.

TURMOIL

Job	30.27	My inward parts are in *t*, and are never
Ps	39.	6 Surely for nothing they are in *t*; they

TURN (TURNED TURNING TURNS)

Deut	23.	5 your God *t* the curse into a blessing for
2 Kings	17.13	"*T* from your evil ways and keep my
	23.25	no king like him, who *t* to the LORD
Ezra	6.22	had *t* the heart of the king of Assyria to
Ps	6.	4 *T*, O LORD, save my life; deliver me for
	40.	4 who do not *t* to the proud, to those who
	90.	3 to dust, and say, "*T* back, you mortals."
	119.	36 *T* my heart to your decrees, and not to
	119.	51 me, but I do not *t* away from your law.
Prov	4.27	or to the left; *t* your foot away from evil.
Eccl	7.25	I *t* my mind to know and to search out
Isa	2.22	*T* away from mortals, who have only
	6.10	with their minds, and *t* and be healed."
	45.22	*T* to me and be saved, all the ends of
	53.	6 astray; we have all *t* to our own way,
Jer	5.23	heart; they have *t* aside and gone away.

TURTLEDOVE (continued)

Jer	15.	7 people; they did not *t* from their ways.
	15.19	If you *t* back, I will take you back, and
	18.	8 *t* from its evil, I will change my mind
	25.	5 "*T* now, everyone of you, from your evil
	31.13	I will *t* their mourning into joy, I will
	35.15	'*T* now everyone of you from your evil
Ezek	14.	6 Repent and *t* away from your idols; and
	33.11	*t* back from your evil ways; for why will
Mt	5.39	you on the right cheek, *t* the other also;
	13.15	understand with their heart and *t*
Mk	4.12	understand; so they may not *t* again and
Lk	1.16	He will *t* many of the people of Israel to
	22.32	once you have *t* back, strengthen your
Acts	14.15	should *t* from these worthless things
	17.	6 who have been *t* the world upside down
	28.27	understand with their heart and *t*
1 Thess	1.	9 how you *t* to God from idols, to serve a

TURTLEDOVE (TURTLEDOVES)

Gen	15.	9 "Bring me . . . a *t*, and a young pigeon."
Lev	1.14	you shall choose your offering from *t* or
Song	2.12	and the voice of the *t* is heard in our
Lk	2.24	law of the Lord, "a pair of *t*, or two

TWELVE

1 Kings	11.30	he was wearing and tore it into *t* pieces.
Mt	10.	2 These are the names of the *t* apostles:
Mk	3.14	And he appointed *t*, whom he also
	6.	7 He called the *t*, and began to send
	14.17	it was evening, he came with the *t*.
Lk	2.42	And when he was *t* years old, they went
	6.13	called his disciples and chose *t* of them
	8.42	he had an only daughter, about *t* years
Jn	6.67	So Jesus asked the *t*, "Do you also wish

TWINKLING

1 Cor	15.52	in the *t* of an eye, at the last trumpet.

TWINS

Gen	25.24	was at hand, there were *t* in her womb.
	38.27	came, there were *t* in her womb.

TWO

Gen	6.19	shall bring *t* of every kind into the ark,
Eccl	4.	9 *T* are better than one, because they
Isa	6.	2 with *t* they covered their faces, and with
Mt	6.24	"No one can serve *t* masters; for a slave
	18.20	where *t* or three are gathered in my
	21.28	A man had *t* sons; he went to the first
	24.40	Then *t* will be in the field; one will be
	27.21	"Which of the *t* do you want me to
Lk	24.13	on that same day *t* of them were going
1 Cor	6.16	For it is said, "The *t* shall be one flesh."

TYPE

Rom	5.14	who is a *t* of the one who was to come.

TYRANTS

Mt	20.25	and their great ones are *t* over them.

TYRE (TYRIAN)

Josh	19.29	reaching to the fortified city of *T*;
1 Kings	5.	1 King Hiram of *T* sent his servants to
	9.11	Hiram of *T* having supplied Solomon
2 Chr	2.14	of the Danite women, his father a *T*.
Ps	45.12	people of *T* will seek your favor with
Isa	23.	1 The oracle concerning *T*. Wail, O ships
Mk	3.	8 and the region around *T* and Sidon.
Lk	10.13	in you had been done in *T* and Sidon,
Acts	21.	3 left, we sailed to Syria and landed at *T*,

U

UNAWARE

1 Cor	10.	1 I do not want you to be *u*, brothers and
2 Cor	1.	8 We do not want you to be *u*, brothers

UNBELIEF

Mt	13.58	of power there, because of their *u*.

Mk	6.	6 And he was amazed at their *u*. Then he
	9.24	child cried out, "I believe; help my *u*!"
Rom	11.20	were broken off because of their *u*,

UNBELIEVERS

1 Cor	6.	6 court against a believer—and before *u*
	14.23	in tongues, and outsiders or *u* enter,
2 Cor	6.14	Do not be mismatched with *u*. For what

UNBELIEVING

1 Cor	7.14	the *u* husband is made holy through his
Titus	1.15	to the corrupt and *u* nothing is pure.

UNCHASTITY

Mt	5.32	his wife, except on the ground of *u*,

UNCIRCUMCISED

Ex	12.48	land. But no *u* person shall eat of it;
Judg	14.	3 and take a wife from the *u* Philistines?"
Rom	3.30	faith and the *u* through that same faith.
1 Cor	7.18	Was anyone at the time of his call *u*?

UNCLEAN

Lev	13.	3 he shall pronounce him ceremonially *u*.
	13.45	cover his upper lip and cry out, "*U*, *u*."
Num	19.11	any human being shall be *u* seven days.
Isa	6.	5 me! I am lost, for I am a man of *u* lips,
	52.	1 and the *u* shall enter you no more.
	64.	6 all become like one who is *u*, and all
Hag	2.14	hands; and what they offer there is *u*.
Mt	12.43	"When the *u* spirit has gone of a person,
Mk	5.	2 of the tombs with an *u* spirit met him.
	7.25	whose little daughter had an *u* spirit
Lk	4.33	man who had the spirit of an *u* demon,
	9.42	Jesus rebuked the *u* spirit, healed the
	11.24	"When the *u* spirit has gone out of a
Acts	10.14	eaten anything that is profane or *u*."
	10.28	I should not call anyone profane or *u*.
1 Cor	7.14	Otherwise, your children would be *u*,

UNCLEANNESS

Lev	5.	3 when you touch human *u*—any *u* by
Ezra	9.11	have filled it end to end with their *u*.

UNCONDEMNED

Acts	16.37	"They have beaten us in public, *u*, men
	22.25	you to flog a Roman citizen who is *u*?"

UNCOVERED

Mt	10.26	nothing is covered that will not be *u*,
Lk	12.	2 is covered up that will not be *u*,

UNDEFILED

Heb	7.26	blameless, *u*, separated from sinners,

UNDERGOING

1 Pet	5.	9 world are *u* the same kinds of suffering.

UNDERSTAND (UNDERSTOOD)

Gen	11.	7 they will not *u* one another's speech."
2 Kings	18.26	Aramaic language, for we *u* it; do not
Neh	8.	8 sense, so that the people *u* the reading.
Job	26.14	the thunder of his power who can *u*?"
	42.	3 I have uttered what I did not *u*,
Ps	119.100	I *u* more than the aged, for I keep your
Prov	28.	5 The evil do not *u* justice, but those who
Isa	36.11	to your servants in Aramaic, for we *u* it;
Jer	9.12	Who is wise enough to *u* this? To whom
	23.20	his mind. In the latter days you will *u*
Dan	8.17	"*U*, O mortal, that the vision is for the
Mt	13.14	'You will indeed listen, but never *u*,
	13.51	"Have you *u* all this?" They answered,
Mk	6.52	they did not *u* about the loaves, but
	7.18	"Then do you also fail to *u*? Do you not
Jn	20.	9 as yet they did not *u* the scripture, that
Acts	8.30	asked, "Do you *u* what you are reading?"
	10.34	"I truly *u* that God shows no partiality,
	28.27	and *u* with their heart and turn—and I
Rom	1.20	they are, have been *u* and seen through

Rom 11.25 I want you to u this mystery: a
2 Cor 1.14 as you have already u us in part—

UNDERSTANDING (n)

Deut 32.28 void of sense; there is no u in them.
Job 17. 4 Since you have closed their minds to u,
Ps 136. 5 who by u made the heavens, for his
 147. 5 in power; his u is beyond measure.
Prov 2.11 watch over you; and u will guard you.
 15.32 but those who heed admonition gain u.
 18. 2 A fool takes no pleasure in u, but only
Isa 29.16 of the one who formed it, "He has no u?"
 40.14 and showed him the way of u?
Jer 10.12 and by his u stretched out the heavens.
Hos 4.14 thus a people without u comes to ruin.
Mt 15.16 he said, "Are you also still without u?
Mk 12.33 with all the heart and with all the u,
Lk 2.47 him were amazed at his u and answers.

UNDO

Eccl 10. 4 post, for calmness will u great offenses.

UNDYING

Eph 6.24 with all who have an u love for our Lord

UNFAIR

Ezek 18.25 "The way of the Lord is u." Hear now, O

UNFAITHFUL (UNFAITHFULNESS)

1 Chr 10.13 So Saul died for his u; he was u to the
Lk 12.46 him in pieces, and put him with the u.

UNGODLY

Job 16.11 God gives me up to the u, and casts me
 18.21 such are the dwellings of the u, such is
Ps 43. 1 God, and defend my cause against an u
Rom 5. 6 at the right time Christ died for the u.

UNINTENTIONALLY

Lev 4. 2 When anyone sins u in any of the
Num 15.24 then if it was done u without the
Deut 19. 4 who has killed another person u

UNITED

Judg 20.11 gathered against the city, u as one.
1 Cor 6.17 anyone u to the Lord becomes one
Heb 4. 2 because they were not u by faith with

UNITY

Ps 133. 1 it is when kindred live together in u!
Eph 4. 3 effort to maintain the u of the Spirit
 4.13 until all of us come to the u of the faith

UNJUST (UNJUSTLY)

Lev 19.15 You shall not render an u judgment;
Ps 71. 4 of the wicked, from the grasp of the u
 82. 2 "How long will you judge u and show
Prov 28.16 but one who hates u gain will enjoy a
 29.27 The u are an abomination to the
Zeph 3. 5 without fail; but the u knows no shame.

UNKNOWN

Acts 17.23 with this inscription, 'To an u god.'
2 Cor 6. 9 as u, and yet are well known; as dying,

UNLEAVENED

Lev 23. 6 the festival of u bread to the Lord;
Deut 16. 8 days you shall continue to eat u bread,
2 Chr 30.21 at Jerusalem kept the feast of u bread

UNMARRIED

1 Cor 7. 8 To the u and the widows I say it is well

UNPRODUCTIVE

1 Cor 14.14 my spirit prays but my mind is u.
Titus 3.14 needs, so that they may not be u.

UNRIGHTEOUS (UNRIGHTEOUSNESS)

Jer 22.13 Woe to him who builds his house by u,
Mt 5.45 rain on the righteous and on the u.

UNROLLED

Lk 4.17 He u the scroll and found the place

UNSEARCHABLE

Job 5. 9 He does great things and u, marvelous
Ps 145. 3 greatly to be praised; his greatness is u.
Prov 25. 3 for depth, so the mind of kings is u.
Rom 11.33 How u are his judgments and how

UNSKILLED

Heb 5.13 infant, is u in the word of righteousness,

UNSTAINED

Jas 1.27 and to keep oneself u by the world.

UNTIE

Mk 1. 7 not worthy to stoop down and u the
Lk 19.30 been ridden. U it and bring it here.

UNTRAINED

2 Cor 11. 6 I may be u in speech, but not in

UNVEILED

1 Cor 11. 5 prays or prophesies with her head u
2 Cor 3.18 all of us, with u faces, seeing the glory

UNWORTHY

1 Cor 11.27 or drinks the cup of the Lord in an u

UPBUILDING

1 Cor 14. 3 speak to other people for their u

UPHOLD (UPHOLDS)

Ps 37.17 be broken, but the Lord u the righteous.
 63. 8 clings to you; your right hand u me.
Jer 30.13 There is no one to u your cause, no

UPRIGHT (UPRIGHTLY)

Num 23.10 Let me die the death of the u, and let
Job 4. 7 perished? Or where were the u cut off?
Ps 7.10 is my shield, who saves the u in heart.
 11. 7 deeds; the u shall behold his face.
 32.11 and shout for joy, all you u in heart.
 107. 42 The u see it and are glad; and all
Prov 2.21 For the u will abide in the land, and
 3.32 Lord, but the u are in his confidence.
 14. 2 Those who walk u fear the Lord, but

UPROAR

Ps 46. 6 The nations are in an u, the kingdoms
Acts 21.31 cohort that all Jerusalem was in an u.

UPROOT (UPROOTED)

Mt 13.29 the weeds you would u the wheat
 15.13 Father has not planted will be u.

UPSTAIRS

Lk 22.12 He will show you a large room u,
Acts 1.13 they went to the room u, where they

UR

Gen 11.28 Terah in the land of his birth, in U
 11.31 they went out together from U of the
 15. 7 I am the Lord who brought you from U
Neh 9. 7 chose Abram and brought him out of U

URGE (URGED URGES)

2 Kings 4. 8 lived, who u him to have a meal.
 5.23 "Please accept two talents." He u him
Lk 24.29 they u him strongly, saying, "Stay with
Acts 27.22 I u you now to keep up your courage,
2 Cor u the love of Christ u us on, because we
 6. 1 we u you also not to accept the grace of
 9. 5 it necessary to u the brothers to go on

URIM

Ex 28.30 shall put the U and the Thummin, and
Lev 8. 8 in the breastpiece he put the U and the
1 Sam 28. 6 answer him, not by dreams, or by U,

USE
Hab 2.18 What *u* is an idol once its maker has

USEFUL
2 Tim 4.11 with you, for he is *u* in my ministry.
Philem 11 you, but now he is indeed *u* both to you

UTENSILS
2 Tim 2.20 there are *u* not only of gold and silver

UZ
Gen 10.23 The descendants of Aram: *U*, Hul,
Job 1. 1 in the land of *U* whose name was Job.
Lam 4.21 Edom, you that live in the land of *U*;

UZZIAH
2 Chr 26. 1 people of Judah took *U*, who was
26.11 Moreover *U* had an army of soldiers, fit
26.18 "It is not for you, *U*, to make offering to
26.21 King *U* was leprous to the day of his
27. 2 LORD just as his father *U* had done—
Isa 1. 1 Judah and Jerusalem in the days of *U*,
6. 1 In the year that King *U* died, I saw the
Mt 1. 8 and Joram the father of *U*, and *U* the

V

VAIN
Ps 127. 1 the house, those who build it labor in *v*.
Prov 31.30 Charm is deceitful, and beauty is *v*, but
1 Cor 15.14 then our proclamation has been in *v*

VALLEY (VALLEYS)
1 Kings 20.28 of the hills but he is not a god of the *v*,'
Ps 23. 4 through the darkest *v*, I fear no evil;
Isa 22. 1 The oracle concerning the *v* of vision.
40. 4 Every *v* shall be lifted up, and every
Jer 19. 6 son of Hinnom, but the *v* of Slaughter.
Ezek 37. 1 the middle of a *v*; it was full of bones.
Joel 3.14 multitudes, in the *v* of decision!
Lk 3. 5 Every *v* shall be filled, and every

VALUE
Mt 13.46 on finding one pearl of great *v*,
Lk 12. 7 you are of more *v* than many sparrows.
1 Tim 4. 8 while physical training is of some *v*,

VANISH (VANISHED)
Judg 6.21 the angel of the LORD *v* from his sight.
Ps 78.33 So he made their days *v* like a breath,
Ezek 26.17 How you have *v* from the seas, O city
Lk 24.31 him; and he *v* from their sight.
Rev 6.14 The sky *v* like a scroll rolling itself up,

VANITY
Eccl 1. 2 *V* of vanities, says the Teacher, *v* of
2.21 toil for it. This also is *v* and a great evil.
12. 8 *V* of vanities, says the Teacher; all is *v*.

VARIETIES
1 Cor 12. 4 there are *v* of gifts, but the same Spirit;
12. 5 there are *v* of activities, but it is the

VEIL (VEILED)
Gen 24.65 So she took her *v* and covered herself.
Ex 26.33 the *v* shall separate for you the holy
34.33 with them, he put a *v* on his face;
36.35 He made the *v* of blue, purple, and
2 Cor 3.14 of the old covenant, that same *v* is still
4. 3 even if our gospel is *v*, it is *v* to those

VENGEANCE
Gen 4.15 kills Cain will suffer a sevenfold *v*."
Lev 19.18 You shall not take *v* or bear any grudge
Deut 32.35 *V* is mine, and recompense, for the time
Ps 58.10 righteous will rejoice when they see *v*
94. 1 you God of *v*, you God of *v*, shine forth!
Isa 63. 4 day of *v* was in my heart, and the year
Jer 50.15 this is the *v* of the LORD: take *v* on her,

VERSED
Esth 1.13 all who were *v* in law and custom,
Acts 18.24 eloquent man, well-*v* in the scriptures.

VESSEL (VESSELS)
2 Kings 4. 3 borrow *v* . . . , empty *v* and not just a few.
Ps 31.12 is dead; I have become like a broken *v*.
Prov 26.23 Like the glaze covering an earthen *v* are
Isa 52.11 you who carry the *v* of the LORD.
Jer 18. 4 the *v* he was making of clay was spoiled
19.11 and this city, as one breaks a potter's *v*,
22.28 despised broken pot, a *v* no one wants?
Hos 8. 8 are among the nations as a useless *v*.

VESTMENTS
Ex 28. 2 You shall make sacred *v* for the glorious

VICTOR
Isa 41. 2 Who has roused a *v* from the east,

VICTORIOUS
Isa 41.10 I will uphold you with my *v* right hand.
Zech 9. 9 and *v* is he, humble and riding

VICTORY
Deut 20. 4 who goes with you . . . to give you the *v*."
1 Sam 2. 1 my enemies, because I rejoice in my *v*.
14.23 So the LORD gave Israel *v* that day. The
14.45 die, who has accomplished this great *v*
2 Sam 8. 6 The LORD gave *v* to David wherever he
19. 2 *v* that day was turned into mourning for
2 Kings 13.17 arrow of *v*, the arrow of *v* over Aram!
1 Chr 18. 6 The LORD gave *v* to David wherever he
2 Chr 20.17 your position, stand still, and see the *v*
Job 40.14 your own right hand can give you *v*.
Ps 20. 5 May we shout for joy over your *v*, and
44. 3 nor did their own arm give them *v*;
144. 10 the one who gives *v* to kings, who
Prov 21.31 of battle, but the *v* belongs to the LORD.
Isa 63. 5 so my own arm brought me *v*, and my
Zeph 3.17 is in your midst, a warrior who gives *v*;
Zech 12. 7 LORD will give *v* to the tents of Judah
Mt 12.20 wick until he brings justice to *v*.
1 Cor 15.54 "Death has been swallowed up in *v*."
1 Jn 5. 4 this is the *v* that conquers the world,

VIGILANCE
Prov 4.23 Keep your heart with all *v*; for from it

VILE
2 Sam 13.12 done in Israel; do not do anything so *v*!

VINDICATE (VINDICATES VINDICATING)
Deut 32.36 Indeed the LORD will *v* his people, have
1 Kings 8.32 *v* the righteous by rewarding them
2 Chr 6.23 *v* those who are in the right by
Ps 43. 1 *V* me, O God, and defend my cause
135. 14 For the LORD will *v* his people, and have
Isa 50. 8 he who *v* me is near. Who will contend

VINDICATION
Ps 24. 5 and *v* from the God of their salvation.
98. 2 he has revealed his *v* in the sight of the
103. 6 The LORD works *v* and justice for all
Mic 7. 9 me out to the light; I shall see his *v*.

VINE (VINES)
1 Kings 4.25 all of them under their *v* and fig trees.
Ps 80. 8 You brought a *v* out of Egypt; you drove
80.14 heaven, and see; have regard for this *v*,
Isa 5. 2 of stones, and planted it with choice *v*;
Ezek 19.10 Your mother was like a *v* in a vineyard
Hos 10. 1 Israel is a luxuriant *v* that yields its
Joel 1. 7 It has laid waste my *v*, and splintered
Mic 4. 4 they shall all sit under their own *v* and

Mt	26.29	never again drink of this fruit of the *v*
Mk	14.25	never again drink of the fruit of the *v*
Jn	15. 1	"I am the true *v*, and my Father is the

VINEGAR

Ps	69.21	food, and for my thirst they gave me *v*
Prov	10.26	Like *v* to the teeth, and smoke to the

VINEYARD (VINEYARDS)

Gen	9.20	of the soil, was the first to plant a *v*.
Deut	20. 6	Has anyone planted a *v* but not yet
	22. 9	shall not sow your *v* with a second kind
1 Kings	21. 1	Naboth . . . had a *v* in Jezreel, beside
Song	1. 6	but my own *v* I have not kept!
	2.15	ruin the *v* — for our *v* are in blossom."
Isa	5. 1	beloved my love-song concerning his *v*:
	27. 2	On that day: A pleasant *v*, sing about it!
Mt	20. 1	in the morning to hire laborers for his *v*.
	21.28	'Son, go and work in the *v* today.'
	21.33	landowner who planted a *v*, put a fence
Mk	12. 1	them in parables. "A man planted a *v*,
Lk	20. 9	"A man planted a *v*, and leased it to

VINTAGE

Isa	32.10	for the *v* will fail, the fruit harvest will
Jer	48.32	fruits of your *v* the destroyer has
Rev	14.19	gathered the *v* of the earth, and he

VIOLATE (VIOLATED)

Job	37.23	abundant righteousness he will not *v*.
Heb	10.28	Anyone who has *v* the law of Moses

VIOLENCE

Job	16.17	though there is no *v* in my hands, and
	19. 7	Even when I cry out, '*V*!' I am not
Ps	7.16	on their own heads their *v* descends.
	73. 6	necklace; *v* covers them like a garment.
Jer	22. 3	do no wrong or *v* to the alien, the
Hab	1. 3	Destruction and *v* are before me; strife
Mal	2.16	and covering one's garment with *v*,
Mt	11.12	the kingdom of heaven has suffered *v*,

VOILENT

2 Sam	22.49	you delivered me from the *v*.
Acts	27.14	soon a *v* wind, called the northeaster,

VIPER (VIPERS)

Job	20.16	of asps; the tongue of a *v* will kill them.
Mt	3. 7	brood of *v*! Who warned you to flee
	12.34	brood of *v*! How can you speak good
Acts	28. 3	when a *v*, driven out by the heat,

VIRGIN (VIRGINS)

Gen	24.16	The girl was very fair to look upon, a *v*,
Lev	21.14	He shall marry a *v* of his own kin,
Judg	21.12	four hundred young *v* who had never
1 Kings	1. 2	"Let a young *v* be sought for my lord
Ps	45.14	her the *v*, her companions, follow.
Jer	14.17	the *v* daughter—my people —is struck
Lam	2.13	I may comfort you, O *v* daughter Zion?
Joel	1. 8	Lament like a *v* dressed in sackcloth for
Mt	1.23	the *v* shall conceive and bear a son,
Lk	1.27	to a *v* engaged to a man whose name
1 Cor	7.28	sin, and if a *v* marries, she does not sin.
2 Cor	11. 2	to present you as a chaste *v* to Christ.
Rev	14. 4	with women, for they are *v*; these follow

VIRGINITY

Deut	22.14	her, I did not find evidence of her *v*."
	22.15	the evidence of the young woman's *v*
Judg	11.38	her companions, and bewailed her *v*

VISION (VISIONS)

Gen	15. 1	word of the LORD came to Abram in a *v*,
Num	12. 6	LORD make myself known to them in *v*,
1 Sam	3. 1	in those days; *v* were not widespread.
Job	4.13	Amid thoughts from *v* of the night,
	7.14	me with dreams and terrify me with *v*,
Isa	1. 1	The *v* of Isaiah the son of Amoz, which

Isa	22. 1	The oracle concerning the valley of *v*.
	29.11	The *v* of all this has become for you
Jer	14.14	prophesying to you a lying *v*, worthless
	23.16	They speak *v* of their own minds, not
Lam	2. 9	no more, and her prophets obtain no *v*
Ezek	1. 1	were opened, and I saw *v* of God.
	7.26	shall keep seeking a *v* from the prophet;
	11.24	lifted me up and brought me in a *v*
	12.22	and every *v* comes to nothing"?
	13. 7	Have you not seen a false *v*, and uttered
	40. 2	brought me, in *v* of God, to the land of
Dan	1.17	Daniel also had insight into all *v* and
	7. 2	I, Daniel, saw in my *v* by night the four
	10. 7	I, Daniel, alone saw the *v*; the people
Hos	12.10	it was I who multiplied *v*, and through
Ob	1	The *v* of Obadiah. Thus says the Lord
Hab	2. 2	Write the *v*; make it plain on tablets, so
Zech	13. 4	will be ashamed, every one, of their *v*
Lk	24.23	that had indeed seen a *v* of angels who
Acts	2.17	your young men shall see *v*, and your
	11. 5	praying, and in a trance I saw a *v*.
	16. 9	During the night Paul had a *v*; there
	18. 9	One night the Lord said to Paul in a *v*,
	26.19	I was not disobedient to the heavenly *v*,
2 Cor	12. 1	but I will go on to *v* and revelations of

VISIT

Job	7.18	on them, *v* them every morning, test
Ps	65. 9	You *v* the earth and water it, you greatly
Jer	29.10	years are completed will I *v* you,

VOICE (VOICES)

Gen	27.22	"The *v* is Jacob's *v*, but the hands are
Num	7.89	he would hear the *v* speaking to him
Deut	4.12	but saw no form; there was only a *v*.
	4.33	ever heard the *v* of a god speaking out
	8.20	you would not obey the *v* of the LORD
1 Sam	1.13	lips moved, but her *v* was not heard;
1 Kings	19.13	Then there came a *v* to him that said,
Ps	29. 3	The *v* of the LORD is over the waters;
	68.33	listen, sends out his *v*, his mighty *v*.
	81. 5	I hear a *v* I had not known: "I relieved
	95. 7	O that you would listen to his *v*! Do not
Song	2. 8	The *v* of my beloved! Look, he comes,
Isa	6. 8	I heard the *v* of the Lord saying, "Whom
	30.30	will cause his majestic *v* to be heard
	40. 6	A *v* says, "Cry out!" And I said, "What
	66. 6	A *v* from the temple! The *v* of the LORD,
Jer	7.34	mirth and gladness, the *v* of the bride
	16. 9	the *v* of mirth and the *v* of gladness,
	42. 6	with us when we obey the *v* of the LORD
Joel	2.11	The LORD utters his *v* at the head of his
Mic	6. 9	*v* of the LORD cries to the city (it is
Mt	3. 3	"The *v* of one crying out in the
	3.17	And a *v* from heaven said, "This is my
	17. 5	and from the cloud a *v* said, "This is my
Mk	1.11	And a *v* came from heaven, "You are my
	9. 7	from the cloud there came a *v*, "This is
Lk	3. 4	Isaiah, "The *v* of one crying out in the
	9.35	came a *v* that said, "This is my Son,
Jn	1.23	"I am the *v* of one crying out in the
	5.25	the dead will hear the *v* of the Son
	5.37	You have never heard his *v* or seen his
	10.16	them also, and they will listen to my *v*.
Acts	4.24	they raised their *v* together to God and
	7.31	to look, there came the *v* of the Lord:
	12.22	"The *v* of a god, and not of a mortal!"
	26.14	I heard a *v* saying to me in the Hebrew
Rom	10.18	"Their *v* has gone out to all the earth
2 Pet	1.18	heard this *v* come from heaven,
Rev	14. 2	I heard a *v* from heaven like the sound

VOID

Gen	1. 2	the earth was a formless *v* and darkness
Jer	4.23	on the earth, and lo, it was waste and *v*;
	19. 7	I will make *v* the plans of Judah and

VOMIT (VOMITED)

Lev	18.25 and the land *v* out its inhabitants.
Job	20.15 swallow down riches and *v* them up
Prov	25.16 or else, having too much, you will *v* it.
	26.11 Like a dog that returns to its *v* is a fool
2 Pet	2.22 "The dog turns back to its own *v*," and,

VOW (VOWS)

Gen	28.20 Then Jacob made a *v*, saying, "If God
	31.13 anointed a pillar and made a *v* to me.
Lev	22.18 whether in payment of a *v* or as a
	27. 2 When a person makes an explicit *v* to
Num	6. 2 make a special *v*, the *v* of a nazirite, to
	21. 2 Then Israel made a *v* to the Lord and
	30. 2 When a man makes a *v* to the Lord, or
Deut	23.21 If you make a *v* to the Lord your God,
Judg	11.30 Jephthah made a *v* to the Lord, and
1 Sam	1.11 She made this *v* : "O Lord of hosts, if
Ps	22.25 my *v* I will pay before those
	56.12 My *v* to you I must perform, O God; I
	65. 1 to you shall *v* be performed, O you who
	116. 18 I will pay my *v* to the Lord in the
Eccl	5. 4 no pleasure in fools. Fulfill what you *v*.
Acts	18.18 had his hair cut, for he was under a *v*.

VOYAGE

Acts	27.10 I can see that the *v* will be with danger

VULTURES

Lk	17.37 "Where the corpse is, there the *v* will

W

WAGES

Gen	30.28 name your *w*, and I will give it."
	31. 7 me and changed my *w* ten times,
Ex	2. 9 it for me, and I will give you your *w*."
Jer	22.13 and does not give them their *w*;
Hag	1. 6 earn *w* earn *w* to put them into a bag
Lk	3.14 and be satisfied with your *w*."
Rom	6.23 the *w* of sin is death, but the free gift of
1 Cor	3. 8 will receive *w* according to the labor

WAILING

Lk	8.52 they were all weeping and *w* for her;

WAIT (WAITED WAITING WAITS)

Ps	25. 3 those who *w* for you be put to shame;
	25. 5 of my salvation; for you I *w* all day long.
	27.14 *W* for the Lord; be strong, and let your
	37. 7 Be still before the Lord, and *w* patiently
	37.34 *W* for the Lord, and keep to his way,
	40. 1 I *w* patiently for the Lord; he inclined
	62. 1 for God alone my soul *w* in silence;
	69. 3 My eyes grow dim with *w* for my God.
	130. 5 I *w* for the Lord, my soul *w*, and in his
Prov	20.22 repay evil"; *w* for the Lord, and he will
Isa	8.17 I will *w* for the Lord, who is hiding his
	26. 8 O Lord, we *w* for you; your name and
	30.18 the Lord *w* to be gracious to you,
	40.31 those who *w* for the Lord shall renew
	42. 4 and the coastlands *w* for his teaching,
	49.23 those who *w* for me shall not be put to
	59.11 We *w* for justice, but there is none; for
	60. 9 the coastlands shall *w* for me, the ships
	64. 4 besides you, who works for those who *w*
Lam	3.26 It is good that one should *w* quietly for
Hos	12. 6 justice, and *w* continually for your God.
Mic	7. 7 I will *w* for the God of my salvation; my
Zeph	3. 8 Therefore *w* for me, says the Lord, for
Mk	15.43 who was also himself *w* expectantly for
Lk	8.40 him, for they were all *w* for him.
	12.36 be like those who are *w* for their master
Rom	8.23 groan inwardly while we *w* for adoption,
1 Cor	1. 7 spiritual gift as you *w* for the revealing
	11.33 together to eat, *w* for one another.
Gal	5. 5 by faith, we *w* eagerly for the hope of
1 Thess	1.10 to *w* for his Son from heaven, whom he

Titus	2.13 while we *w* for the blessed hope, and
2 Pet	3.12 *w* for and hastening the day of God,

WAKE

Rom	13.11 the moment for you to *w* from sleep.

WAKENS

Isa	50. 4 Morning by morning he *w* — *w* my ear

WALK

Gen	13.17 Rise up, *w* through the length and
	17. 1 "I am God Almighty; *w* before me, and
	24.40 Lord, before whom I *w*, will send his
Lev	26.12 And I will *w* among you, and will be
Deut	10.12 to *w* in all his ways, to love him, to
Josh	22. 5 to *w* in all his ways, to keep his
1 Kings	3.14 If you will *w* in my ways, keeping my
	9. 4 if you will *w* before me, as David your
2 Kings	21.22 and did not *w* in the way of the Lord.
2 Chr	6.14 with your servants who *w* before you
	7.17 for you, if you *w* before me, your father
Neh	5. 9 Should you not *w* in the fear of our
	10.29 a curse and an oath to *w* in God's law,
Ps	48.12 *W* about Zion, go all around it, count
	56.13 so that I may *w* before God in the light
	78.10 but refused to *w* according to his law.
	81.13 to me, that Israel would *w* in my ways!
	82. 5 they *w* around in darkness; all the
	89.15 who *w*, O Lord, in the light of your
	101. 2 I will *w* with integrity of heart within
	116. 9 I *w* before the Lord in the land of the
	119. 1 who *w* in the law of the Lord.
	138. 7 Though I *w* in the midst of trouble, you
Prov	1.15 my child, do not *w* in their way, keep
	2.20 Therefore *w* in the way of the good,
	8.20 I *w* in the way of righteousness, along
	28. 6 Better to be poor and *w* in integrity
Eccl	2.14 in their head, but fools *w* in darkness.
Isa	2. 3 ways and that we may *w* in his paths."
	8.11 warned me not to *w* in the way of this
	30.21 you, saying, "This is the way, *w* in it."
	33.15 Those who *w* righteously and speak
	40.31 be weary, they shall *w* and not faint.
	42. 5 upon it and spirit to those who *w* in it:
	42.24 in whose ways they would not *w*, and
	57. 2 those who *w* uprightly will rest on their
	65. 2 rebellious people, who *w* in a way that
Jer	6.16 where the good way lies; and *w* in it,
	10.23 that mortals as they *w* cannot direct
	31. 9 I will let them *w* by brooks of water, in
Am	3. 3 Do two *w* together unless they have
Mic	4. 5 peoples *w*, each in the name of its god,
	6. 8 and to *w* humbly with your God?
Zech	3. 7 If you will *w* in my ways and keep my
	10.12 the Lord, and they shall *w* in his name,
Mt	9. 5 forgiven,' or to say, 'Stand up and *w*'?
Jn	5. 8 "Stand up, take your mat and *w*." At
	11. 9 Those who *w* during the day do not
	12.35 *W* while you have the light, so that
Acts	3. 6 Christ of Nazareth, stand up and *w*."
Rom	6. 4 so we too might *w* in newness of life.
	8. 4 who *w* not according to the flesh but
2 Cor	6.16 "I will live in them and *w* among them,
1 Jn	2. 6 in him," ought to *w* just as he walked.
Rev	3. 4 they shall *w* with me, dressed in white,

WALKS (WALKED WALKING)

Gen	3. 8 sound of the Lord God *w* in the garden
	5.22 Enoch with God after the birth of
	6. 9 in his generation; Noah *w* with God.
Deut	30.16 *w* in his ways, and observing his
1 Kings	3. 3 David, because he *w* before you in
	16.26 he *w* in all the way of Jeroboam son of
2 Kings	13. 6 he caused Israel to sin, but *w* in them;
	16. 3 he *w* in the way of the kings of Israel.
	17. 8 *w* in the customs of the nations whom
	17.19 but *w* in the customs that Israel had

Ps	69. 1 for the *w* have come up to my neck.
Prov	11.25 and one who gives *w* will get *w*.
	25.25 Like cold *w* to a thirsty soul, so is good
Song	8. 7 Many *w* cannot quench love, neither
Isa	12. 3 will draw *w* from the wells of salvation.
	33.16 food will be supplied, their *w* assured.
	43. 2 When you pass through the *w*, I will be
	44. 3 For I will pour *w* on the thirsty land,
	58.11 a spring of *w*, whose *w* never fail.
Jer	9. 1 O that my head were a spring of *w*, and
	14. 3 they find no *w*, they return with their
	17. 8 They shall be like a tree planted by *w*,
	17.13 the fountain of living *w*, the LORD.
Ezek	36.25 I will sprinkle clean *w* upon you, and
	47. 1 *w* was flowing from below the threshold
Am	5.24 let justice roll down like *w*, and
Hab	2.14 of the LORD, as the *w* cover the sea.
Zech	14. 8 On that day living *w* shall flow out from
Mt	3.11 I baptize you with *w* for repentance,
	10.42 cup of cold *w* to one of these little ones
	27.24 took some *w* and washed his hands
Mk	9.41 *w* to drink because you bear the name
Lk	3.16 "I baptize you with *w*; but one who is
	16.24 the tip of his finger in *w* and cool my
Jn	1.26 "I baptize with *w*. Among you stands
	2. 7 said to them, "Fill the jars with *w*."
	3. 5 God without being born of *w* and Spirit.
	4.14 those who drink of the *w* that I will give
	5.3n waiting for the stirring of the *w*; for an
	7.38 heart shall flow rivers of living *w*.' "
Acts	8.36 eunuch said, "Look, here is *w*! What is
	10.47 "Can anyone withhold the *w* for
1 Jn	5. 6 Christ, not with the *w* only but with the
Rev	22.17 anyone who wishes take the *w* of life

WATER (WATERED) (v)

Gen	2. 6 and *w* whole face of the ground—
	13.10 that the plain of the Jordan was well *w*
	29.10 Jacob . . . *w* the flock of his mother's
Isa	27. 3 am its keeper; every moment I *w* it.
1 Cor	3. 6 I planted, Apollos *w*, but God gave the

WATERCOURSES

Joel	1.20 cry to you because the *w* are dried up,

WAVE (WAVES)

Ps	42. 7 cataracts; all your *w* and your billows
	88. 7 and you overwhelm me with all your *w*.
Jon	2. 3 all your *w* and your billows passed over
Mt	14.24 the boat, battered by the *w*, was far
Mk	4.37 and the *w* beat into the boat, so that
Jas	1. 6 the one who doubts is like a *w* of the

WAVERING

Ps	26. 1 I have trusted in the LORD without *w*.
Heb	10.23 the confession of our hope without *w*,

WAY

Gen	3.24 to guard the *w* to the tree of life.
Num	21. 4 the people became impatient on the *w*.
Judg	2.22 take care to walk in the *w* of the LORD
1 Sam	9. 8 it to the man of God, to tell us our *w*."
2 Sam	22.31 This God—his *w* is perfect; the
1 Kings	16.26 walked in all the *w* of Jeroboam son of
Job	16.22 I shall go the *w* from which I shall not
	19. 8 He has walled up my *w* so I cannot
	23.10 he knows the *w* that I take; when he
	28.13 Mortals do not know the *w* to it, and it
	28.23 "God understands the *w* to it, and he
	38.19 "Where is the *w* to the dwelling of light,
Ps	1. 6 watches over the *w* of the righteous, but
	5. 8 make your *w* straight before me.
	18.30 This God—his *w* is perfect; the
	25. 9 is right, and teaches the humble his *w*.
	37. 5 Commit your *w* to the LORD; trust in
	37.23 by the LORD, when he delights in our *w*;
	37.34 Wait for the LORD, and keep to his *w*,
	67. 2 that your *w* may be known upon the

Ps	77.13 Your *w*, O God, is holy. What god is so
	101. 6 walks in the *w* that is blameless
	119. 9 can young people keep their *w* pure?
	139. 24 in me, and lead me in the *w* everlasting.
Prov	2. 8 and preserving the *w* of his faithful
	7.27 Her house is the *w* to Sheol, going
	8.20 I walk in the *w* of righteousness, along
	10.29 The *w* of the LORD is a stronghold for
	13.15 but the *w* of the faithless is their ruin.
	14.12 There is a *w* which seems right to a
	15. 9 The *w* of the wicked is an abomination
	15.19 The *w* of the lazy is overgrown with
	16.25 there is a *w* which seems to be right,
	22. 6 Train children in the right *w*, and when
Isa	30.21 you, saying, "This is the *w*, walk in it."
	40. 3 wilderness prepare the *w* of the LORD,
	40.27 "My *w* is hidden from the LORD, and my
	43.16 who makes a *w* in the sea, a path in the
	53. 6 astray; we have all turned to our own *w*,
	57.14 said, "Build up, build up, prepare the *w*,
	59. 8 The *w* of peace they do not know, and
Jer	5. 4 for they do not know the *w* of the LORD,
	10.23 that the *w* of human beings is not in
	21. 8 I am setting before you the *w* of life
	23.12 their *w* shall be to them like slippery
Ezek	18.25 you say, "The *w* of the Lord is unfair."
	33.17 say, "The *w* of the Lord is not just,"
Nah	1. 3 His *w* is in whirlwind and storm, and
Mt	3. 3 'Prepare the *w* of the Lord, make his
	11.10 who will prepare your *w* before you.'
	22.16 teach the *w* of God in accordance with
Mk	1. 2 before you, who will prepare your *w*;
	12.14 but teach the *w* of God in accordance
Lk	3. 4 'Prepare the *w* of the Lord, make his
	7.27 who will prepare your *w* before you.'
Jn	14. 6 "I am the *w*, and the truth, and the life.
Acts	9. 2 if he found any who belonged to the *W*,
	16.17 who proclaim to you a *w* of salvation."
	18.26 and explained the *W* of God to him
	19.23 broke out concerning the *W*.
	22. 4 I persecuted this *W* up to the point of
	24.14 the *W*, which they call a sect, I worship
Rom	3.17 the *w* of peace they have not known."
Heb	9. 8 the *w* into the sanctuary has not yet
	10.20 by the new and living *w* that he opened
2 Pet	2.21 known the *w* of righteousness than,
Rev	16.12 to prepare the *w* for the kings from the

WAYFARER

Judg	19.17 the old man looked up and saw the *w*
Jer	14. 8 in the land, like a *w* turning aside for

WAYS

2 Sam	22.22 For I have kept the *w* of the LORD, and
1 Kings	2. 3 your God, walking in his *w* and keeping
	3.14 If you will walk in my *w*, keeping my
Job	21.14 We do not desire to know your *w*.
	24.23 supported; his eyes are upon their *w*.
	31. 4 Does not he see my *w*, and number all
Ps	18.21 For I have kept the *w* of the LORD, and
	95.10 go astray, and they do not regard my *w*."
	103. 7 He made known his *w* to Moses, his
Prov	5.21 For human are under the eyes of the
	16. 2 All one's *w* may be pure in one's own
	20.24 then can we understand our own *w*?
	31.27 looks well to the *w* of her household,
Isa	2. 3 that he may teach us his *w* and that we
	55. 9 so are my *w* higher than your *w* and my
Jer	4.18 Your *w* and your doings have brought
	16.17 my eyes are on all their *w*; they are not
	17.10 to give to all according to their *w*,
Ezek	7. 3 judge you according to your *w*; I will
	33.11 the wicked turn from their *w* and live;
Dan	4.37 works are truth, and his *w* are justice;
Mic	4. 2 that he may teach us his *w* and that we
Rom	11.33 judgments and how inscrutable his *w*!
Rev	15. 3 Just and true are your *w*, King of the

WEAK

Ezek	34.	4 You have not strengthened the *w*, you
Acts	20.35	we must support the *w*, remembering
Rom	5.	6 While we were still *w*, at the right time
	14.	1 Welcome those who are *w* in faith, but
	15.	1 to put up with the failings of the *w*,
1 Cor	1.27	God chose what is *w* in the world to
	4.10	in Christ. We are *w*, but you are strong.
	8.	7 their conscience, being *w*, is defiled.
	9.22	To the *w* I became *w*, so that I might
2 Cor	11.29	Who is *w*, and I am not *w*? Who is
	12.10	for whenever I am *w*, then I am strong.
1 Thess	5.14	hearted, help the *w*, be patient with all

WEAKNESS (WEAKNESSES)

1 Cor	1.25	and God's *w* is stronger than human
	2.	3 I came to you in *w* and in fear and in
2 Cor	13.	4 he was crucified in *w*, but lives by the
Heb	4.15	is unable to sympathize with our *w*,

WEALTH

Deut	8.17	of my own hand have gotten me this *w*."
Job	31.25	if I have rejoiced because my *w* was
Ps	49.	6 those who trust in their *w* and boast of
	112.	3 *W* and riches are in their houses, and
Prov	12.27	but the diligent obtain precious *w*.
	13.	7 pretend to be poor, yet have great *w*.
	13.11	*W* hastily gotten will dwindle, but those
	13.22	sinner's *w* is laid up for the righteous.
Eccl	5.19	Likewise all to whom God gives *w* and
Song	8.	7 If one offered for love all the *w* of his
Isa	61.	6 you shall enjoy the *w* of the nations,
Jer	17.11	lay, so are all who amass *w* unjustly;
Ezek	28.	5 your heart has become proud in your *w*.
Hab	2.	5 Moreover, *w* is treacherous; the arrogant
Mt	6.24	the other. You cannot serve God and *w*.
	13.22	the lure of *w* choke the word, and it
Mk	4.19	cares of the world, and the lure of *w*,
	10.23	it will be for those who have *w* to enter
Lk	16.	9 for yourselves by means of dishonest *w*
2 Cor	8.	2 have overflowed in a *w* of generosity on
Heb	11.26	suffered for the Christ to be greater *w*
Rev	18.17	one hour all this *w* has been laid waste."

WEAPON (WEAPONS)

Eccl	9.18	Wisdom is better than *w* of war, but
Jer	51.20	You are my war club, my *w* of battle:
2 Cor	6.	7 with the *w* of righteousness for the right
	10.	4 for the *w* of our warfare are not merely

WEAR (WEARS)

Deut	22.	5 A woman shall not *w* a man's apparel,
Prov	23.	4 Do not *w* yourself out to get rich; be
Eccl	10.15	The toil of fools *w* them out, for they
Lk	18.	5 so that she may not *w* me out by

WEARINESS

Eccl	12.12	end, and much study is a *w* of the flesh.

WEARISOME

Eccl	1.	8 All things are *w*; more than one can

WEARY (WEARIED)

2 Sam	21.15	the Philistines, and David grew *w*.
Job	3.17	troubling, and there the *w* are at rest.
Isa	1.14	burden to me, I am *w* of bearing them.
	5.27	None of them is *w*, none stumbles,
	7.13	to *w* mortals, that you *w* my God also?
	43.22	but you have been *w* of me, O Israel!
	43.24	you have *w* me with your iniquities.
	47.13	are *w* with your many consultations;
	57.10	You grew *w* from your many wanderings;
Jer	15.	6 destroyed you – I am *w* of relenting.
	31.25	I will satisfy the *w*, and all who are
Mic	6.	3 In what have I *w* you? Answer me! For I
Mal	2.17	You have *w* the LORD with your words.
Gal	6.	9 let us not grow *w* in doing what is right,
2 Thess	3.13	do not be *w* in doing what is right.

WEATHER

Mt	16.	2 you say, 'It will be fair *w*, for the sky is

WEAVER (WEAVER'S)

Job	7.	6 My days are swifter than a *w* shuttle,
Isa	38.12	like a *w* I have rolled up my life; he

WEDDING

Mt	22.	2 to a king who gave a *w* banquet
	22.	8 'The *w* is ready, but those invited were
	25.10	went with him into the *w* banquet;
Lk	12.36	to return home from the *w* banquet,

WEEDS

Mt	13.25	his enemy came and sowed *w* among

WEEKS

Deut	16.10	you shall keep the festival of *w* for the
Dan	9.24	"Seventy *w* are decreed for your people

WEEP (WEEPING WEEPS WEPT)

Gen	27.38	father!" And Esau lifted his voice and *w*.
	42.24	He turned away from them and *w*; then
	43.30	went into a private room and *w* there.
	45.	2 he *w* so loudly that the Egyptians heard
	46.29	fell on his neck, and *w* on his neck a
Judg	20.23	went up and *w* before the LORD
1 Sam	30.	4 until they had no more strength to *w*.
2 Sam	18.33	up to the chamber over the gate, and *w*;
Ezra	3.12	*w* with a loud voice when they saw this
Neh	1.	4 I heard these words I sat down and *w*,
	8.	9 all the people *w* when they heard the
Job	16.16	My face is red with *w*, and deep
Ps	6.	6 tears; I drench my couch with my *w*.
	6.	8 the LORD has heard the sound of my *w*.
	30.	5 *W* may linger for the night, but joy
	137.	1 and we *w* when we remembered Zion.
Eccl	3.	4 a time to *w*, and a time to laugh; a time
Isa	15.	2 to the temple, to the high places to *w*;
Jer	13.17	not listen, my soul will *w* in secret for
	22.10	Do not *w* for him who is dead, nor
	31.15	bitter *w*. Rachel is *w* for her children;
Lam	1.16	For these things I *w*; my eyes flow with
	2.11	My eyes are spent with *w*; my stomach
Ezek	8.14	were sitting there *w* for Tammuz.
	27.31	they *w* over you in bitterness of soul,
Joel	2.17	the priests, the ministers of the LORD, *w*.
Mic	1.10	Tell it not in Gath, *w* not at all; in
Zech	12.10	*w* bitterly over him, as one *w* over a
Mt	2.18	Rachel *w* for her children;
	8.12	there will be *w* and gnashing of teeth
	24.51	there will be *w* and gnashing of teeth.
	26.75	And he went out and *w* bitterly.
Mk	14.72	three times." And he broke down and *w*.
Lk	6.21	"Blessed are you who *w* now, for you
	8.52	"Do not *w*; for she is not dead but
	19.41	near and saw the city, he *w* over it,
	22.62	times." And he went out and *w* bitterly.
	23.28	do not *w* for me, but *w* for yourselves
Jn	11.31	she was going to the tomb to *w* there.
	11.35	Jesus began to *w*.
	20.11	But Mary stood *w* outside the tomb. As
	20.15	"Woman, why are you *w*? Whom are you
Acts	21.13	"What are you doing, *w* and breaking
Rom	12.15	those who rejoice, *w* with those who *w*.
Rev	5.	4 I began to *w* bitterly because no one
	18.	9 will *w* and wail over her when they see

WEIGH (WEIGHED WEIGHS)

1 Sam	2.	3 of knowledge, and by him actions are *w*.
Job	6.	2 "O that my vexation were *w*, and all my
	31.	6 let me be *w* in a just balance, and let
Prov	16.	2 own eyes, but the LORD *w* the spirit.
	21.	2 of the doer, but the LORD *w* the heart.
	24.12	not he who *w* the heart perceive it?
Isa	40.12	and *w* the mountains in scales and the
Jer	32.10	and and *w* the money on scales.
Dan	5.27	TEKEL, you have been *w* on the scales

Zech	11.12 So they *w* out as my wages thirty
1 Cor	14.29 and let the others *w* what is said.

WEIGHTS

Deut	25.13 not have in your bag two kinds of *w*,
Prov	20.10 Diverse *w* and diverse measures are

WEIGHTY

Ps	139. 17 How *w* to me are your thoughts, O God!

WELCOME (WELCOMED WELCOMES)

Mt	10.40 "Whoever *w* you *w* me, and whoever *w*
	18. 5 Whoever *w* one such child in my name
Mk	6.11 If any place will not *w* you and they
	9.37 "Whoever *w* one such child in my name
Lk	8.40 when Jesus returned, the crowd *w* him
	9. 5 Wherever they do not *w* you, as you are
	9.11 he *w* them, and spoke to them about
	9.48 *w* this child in my name *w* me,
	10.10 enter a town and they do not *w* you,
	19. 6 hurried down, and was happy to *w* him.
Acts	2.41 who *w* his message were baptized, and
	28.30 expense, and *w* all who came to him,
Rom	15. 7 *W* one another, therefore, just as Christ
	16. 2 so that you may *w* her in the Lord as is
Gal	4.14 me, but *w* me as an angel of God,

WELFARE

Gen	43.27 He inquired about their *w*, and said, "Is
Neh	2.10 had come to seek the *w* of the people
Ps	35.27 who delights in the *w* of his servant."
Prov	3. 2 life and abundant *w* will they give you.
Jer	29. 7 behalf, for in its *w* you will find your *w*.
	38. 4 is not seeking the *w* of his people, but

WELL (WELLS) (n)

Gen	21.19 her eyes and she saw a *w* of water.
	21.25 to Abimelech about a *w* of water
	24.11 down outside the city by the *w* of water;
	26.22 moved from there and dug another *w*,
Num	21.17 Israel sang this song: "Spring up, O *w*!
2 Sam	23.15 drew water from the *w* of Bethlehem
Song	4.15 a *w* of living water, and flowing streams
Isa	12. 3 will draw water from the *w* of salvation.
Jer	6. 7 As a *w* keeps its water fresh, so she
Lk	14. 5 child or an ox that has fallen into a *w*,
Jn	4. 6 Jacob's *w* was there, and Jesus, tired

WELL (adv)

2 Sam	18.29 "Is it *w* with the young man Absalom?"
Prov	27. 6 *W* meant are the wounds a friend
Mt	9.22 daughter; your faith has made you *w*."
Mk	5.23 so that she may be made *w*, and live."

WELL-BEING

Lev	3. 1 If the offering is a sacrifice of *w*, if you
	7.11 of the sacrifice of the offering of *w*

WEST

Ps	103. 12 as far as the east is from the *w*, so far
Mt	8.11 many will come from east and *w* and
Lk	13.29 people will come from east and *w*, from

WHEAT

Judg	6.11 Gideon was beating out *w* in the wine
Jer	23.28 What has straw in common with *w*?
Mt	13.25 came and sowed weeds among the *w*,
	13.29 you uproot the *w* along with them.
Lk	3.17 and to gather the *w* into his granary;
Jn	12.24 unless a grain of *w* falls into the earth

WHEEL

Jer	18. 3 and there he was working at his *w*.
Ezek	1.16 being something like a *w* within a *w*.
	10.10 alike, something like a *w* within a *w*.

WHIP

Prov	26. 3 A *w* for the horse, a bridle for the
Isa	10.26 of hosts will wield a *w* against them,

Jn	2.15 Making a *w* of cords, he drove all of

WHIRLWIND

2 Kings	2.11 and Elijah ascended in a *w* into heaven.
Isa	5.28 like flint, and their wheels like the *w*.
Hos	8. 7 the wind, and they shall reap the *w*.

WHISPER

Ps	41. 7 All who hate me *w* together about me;
Isa	29. 4 and your speech shall *w* out of the dust.

WHISPERER

Prov	16.28 strife, and a *w* separates close friends.
	18. 8 The words of a *w* are like delicious
	26.22 The words of a *w* are like delicious

WHITE

Eccl	9. 8 Let your garments be always *w*; do not
Mk	9. 3 and his clothes became dazzling *w*,
Acts	1.10 heaven, suddenly two men in *w* robes
Rev	1.14 head and his hair were *w* as *w* wool,

WHITEWASH (WHITEWASHED)

Job	13. 4 As for you, you *w* with lies; all of you
Mt	23.27 hypocrites! For you are like *w* tombs,
Acts	23. 3 "God will strike you, you *w* wall! Are

WHOLESOME

2 Kings	2.21 the LORD, I have made this water *w*;
Prov	15.31 The ear that heeds *w* admonition will

WHORE (WHORES)

Jer	3. 1 You have played the *w* with many
Ezek	16.28 You played the *w* with the Assyrians,
	23. 5 Oholah played the *w* while she was
Hos	2. 5 their mother has played the *w*; she who
Rev	17. 5 "Babylon the great, mother of *w* and of

WICK

Isa	42. 3 a dimly burning *w* he will not quench;
Mt	12.20 or quench a smoldering *w*, until he

WICKED

Gen	13.13 the people of Sodom were *w*, great
2 Chr	19. 2 "Should you help the *w* and love those
Job	9.24 earth is given into the hand of the *w*;
	11.20 the eyes of the *w* will fail; all the way of
	15.20 The *w* man writhes in pain all their
	21.30 that the *w* are spared in the day of
	27.13 "This is the portion of the *w* with God,
Ps	10.15 Break the arm of the *w* and evildoers;
	37.10 little while, and the *w* will be no more;
	37.35 I have seen the *w* oppressing, and
	94. 3 shall the *w*, how long shall the *w* exult?
	112. 10 The *w* see it and are angry; they gnash
	119. 53 indignation seizes me because of the *w*,
	139. 19 O that you would kill the *w*, O God,
	141. 5 Never let the oil of the *w* anoint my
Prov	2.22 but the *w* will be cut off from the land,
	10. 6 the mouth of the *w* conceals violence.
	10.30 but the *w* will not remain in the land.
	13. 6 is upright, but sin overthrows the *w*.
	16. 4 even the *w* for the day of trouble.
	28. 1 The *w* flee when no one pursues, but
Isa	26.10 If favor is shown to the *w*, they do not
	53. 9 They made his grave with the *w* and his
Ezek	18.27 when the *w* turn away from the
	33.15 if the *w* restore the pledge, give back
Dan	12.10 the *w* shall continue to act wickedly.
Mt	18.32 'You *w* slave! I forgave you all that debt
	25.26 'You *w* and lazy slave! You knew, did
Acts	3.26 turning each of you from your *w* ways."
1 Cor	5.13 outside. "Drive out the *w* person from

WICKEDLY

Judg	19.23 "No, my brothers, do not act so *w*.
1 Chr	21.17 is I who have sinned and done very *w*.
Neh	9.33 dealt faithfully and we have acted *w*;

WICKEDNESS

Gen	6. 5 LORD saw that the *w* of humankind was
1 Sam	24.13 says, Out of the wicked comes forth *w*';
Job	20.12 "Though *w* is sweet in their mouth,
Prov	8. 7 truth; *w* is an abomination to my lips.
Isa	9.18 For *w* burned like a fire, consuming
Jer	6. 7 so she keeps fresh her *w*; violence and
Ezek	16.57 before your *w* was uncovered? Now you
Rom	1.18 who by their *w* suppress the truth.
	1.29 They were filled with every kind of *w*,

WIDOW (WIDOWS WIDOW'S WIDOWS')

Deut	14.29 the orphans, and the *w* in your towns,
	24.17 you shall not take a *w* garment in
Job	22. 9 You have sent *w* away empty-handed,
	29.13 upon me, I caused the *w* heart to sing
Ps	109. 9 children be orphans, and his wife a *w*.
Prov	15.25 proud, but maintains the *w* boundaries.
Isa	1.17 defend the orphan, plead for the *w*.
	10. 2 of their right, that *w* may be their spoil,
Jer	49.11 them alive; and let your *w* trust in me.
Lam	1. 1 How like a *w* has she become, she that
Mt	23.14n For you devour *w* houses and for the
Mk	12.40 They devour *w* houses and for the sake
	12.42 A poor *w* came and put in two small
Lk	4.25 there were many *w* in Israel in the time
	7.12 his mother's only son, and she was a *w*;
	21. 2 he also saw a poor *w* put in two small
Acts	6. 1 their *w* were being neglected in the
1 Tim	5. 3 Honor *w* who are really *w*. If a *w* has

WIFE (WIFE'S WIVES)

Gen	12.12 'This is his *w*'; then they will kill me,
Num	5.12 If any man's *w* goes astray and is
Ruth	4.13 Boaz took Ruth and she became his *w*.
1 Sam	25.39 David wooed Abigail, to make her his *w*.
Job	31.10 then let my *w* grind for another, and let
Ps	128. 3 Your *w* will be like a fruitful vine within
Prov	5.18 blessed, rejoice in the *w* of your youth,
	6.24 to preserve you from the *w* of another,
	6.29 is he who sleeps with his neighbor's *w*;
	18.22 He who finds a *w* finds a good thing,
	19.13 and a *w* quarreling is a continual
	19.14 but a prudent *w* is from the LORD.
	31.10 A capable *w* who can find? She is far
Eccl	9. 9 Enjoy life with the *w* whom you love,
Jer	3. 1 If a man divorces his *w* and she goes
	3.20 as a faithless *w* leaves her husband, so
Ezek	24.18 morning , and at evening my *w* died.
Hos	1. 2 "Go, take for yourself a *w* of whoredom
	2.19 I will take you as my *w* forever; I will
	12.12 Israel served for a *w*, and for a *w* he
Mal	2.14 companion and your *w* by covenant.
Mt	1.24 he took her as his *w*, but had no
	5.31 "Whoever divorces his *w*, let him give
	19. 5 and be joined to his *w*, and the two
	27.19 judgment seat, his *w* sent word to him,
Mk	10. 2 "Is it lawful for a man to divorce his *w*?"
	12.19 brother dies, leaving a *w* but no child,
Lk	17.32 must not turn back. Remember Lot's *w*.
Acts	5. 7 his *w* came in, not knowing what had
1 Cor	7. 4 the *w* does not have authority over her
	7.27 Are you free from a *w*? Do not seek a *w*.
	7.39 A *w* is bound as long as her husband
	9. 5 to be accompanied by a believing *w*,
Eph	5.22 W, be subject to your husbands as you
	5.31 be joined to his *w*, and the two will
Col	3.18 W, be subject to your husbands, as is
1 Thess	4.4n you know how to take a *w* for himself
1 Pet	3. 1 W, in the same way, accept the

WILD

Ex	32.25 the people were running *w* (for Aaron

WILDERNESS

Num	26.65 "They shall die in the *w*." Not one of
Deut	8.15 you through the great and terrible *w*,

1 Sam	23.14 remained in the strongholds in the *w*,
Song	3. 6 What is that coming up from the *w*, like
Isa	35. 1 *w* and the dry land shall be glad, the
	41.18 I will make the *w* a pool of water, and
	64.10 Your holy cities have become a *w*, Zion
Ezek	20.10 of Egypt and brought them into the *w*.
Mk	1.13 He was in the *w* forty days, tempted by
Lk	4. 1 the Spirit in the *w*, where for forty days
	7.24 did you go out into the *w* to look at?

WILL (WILLS)

Ezra	7.18 may do, according to the *w* of your God.
Ps	40. 1 delight to do your *w*, O my God; your
Isa	53.10 it was the *w* of the LORD to crush him
Mt	6.10 Your *w* be done, On earth as it is in
	12.50 whoever does the *w* of my Father in
	18.14 it is not the *w* of your Father in heaven
	26.42 pass unless I drink it, your *w* be done."
Mk	3.35 Whoever does the *w* of God is my
Jn	4.34 "My food is to do the *w* of him who
	5.30 own *w*, but the *w* of him who sent me.
	6.38 own *w*, but the *w* of him who sent me.
	7.17 who resolves to do the *w* of God
Acts	21.14 except to say, "The Lord's *w* be done."
Rom	1.10 by God's *w* I may somehow at last
	2.18 know his *w* and determine what is best
	9.16 it depends not on human *w* or exertion,
	12. 2 you may discern what is the *w* of God
1 Cor	9.17 if I do this of my own *w*, I have a
2 Cor	8. 5 to the Lord and, by the *w* of God, to us,
Gal	1. 4 evil age, according to the *w* of our God
Eph	5.17 understand what the *w* of the Lord is.
Phil	2.13 you both to *w* and to work for his good
Col	4.12 fully assured in everything that God *w*.
1 Thess	4. 3 this is the *w* of God, your sanctification:
Heb	10. 7 'See, God, I have come to do your *w*, O
1 Pet	2.15 is God's *w* that by doing right you
	3.17 good, if suffering should be God's *w*,
	4. 2 by human desires but by the *w* of God.
1 Jn	2.17 those who do the *w* of God live forever.
Rev	4.11 and by your *w* they existed and were

WILLING (WILLINGLY)

1 Chr	29. 5 Who then will offer *w*, consecrating
Ps	110. 3 Your people will offer themselves *w* on
Lk	22.42 "Father, if you are *w*, remove this cup

WILLOWS

Lev	23.40 of leafy trees and *w* of the brook;
Ps	137. 2 On the *w* there we hung up our harps.

WIN

1 Cor	9.19 to all, so that I might *w* more of them.

WIND

Gen	1.2n while a mighty *w* swept over the face of
1 Kings	19.11 a great, *w*, so strong that it was splitting
Job	26.13 By his *w* the heavens were made fair;
Ps	55. 8 myself from the raging *w* and tempest."
Eccl	8. 8 No one has power over the *w*, to
Ezek	1. 4 a stormy *w* came out of the north; a
Hos	8. 7 For they sow the *w*, and they shall reap
	12. 1 Ephraim herds the *w*, and pursues the
	13.15 east *w* shall come, a blast from the
Lk	8.24 And he woke up and rebuked the *w* and
Jn	3. 8 The *w* blows where it chooses, and you
Acts	2. 2 a sound like the rush of a violent *w*,

WINDOW (WINDOWS)

Gen	7.11 and *w* of the heavens were opened.
2 Kings	7. 2 if the LORD were to make *w* in the sky,
Dan	6.10 which had *w* in its upper room open
2 Cor	11.33 was let down in a basket through a *w* in

WINDSTORM

Mt	8.24 A *w* arose on the sea, so great that the
Mk	4.37 A great *w* arose, and the waves beat

WINE

Gen	9.24 Noah awoke from his *w* and knew what
	19.35 they made their father drink *w* that
Lev	10. 8 Drink no *w* nor strong drink, neither
Num	6. 3 they shall separate themselves from *w*
Judg	13. 4 Now be careful not to drink *w* or strong
2 Sam	13.28 when Amnon's heart is merry with *w*,
Esth	1.10 day, when the king was merry with *w*,
Prov	20. 1 *W* is a mocker, strong drink a brawler,
	23.30 Those who linger late over *w*, those who
Eccl	2. 3 mind how to cheer my body with *w*—
Song	1. 2 For your love is better than *w*, your
Isa	5.11 in the evening to be inflamed by *w*,
	5.22 you who are heroes in drinking *w* and
	24.11 is an outcry in the streets for lack of *w*;
	56.12 "Come," they say, "let us get *w*; let us fill
Jer	35. 6 they answered, "We will drink no *w*, for
Ezek	44.21 No priest shall drink *w*, when he enters
Dan	5. 4 drank *w* and praised the gods of gold
Hos	4.11 *W* and new *w* take away the
Am	6. 6 who drink *w* in bowls, and anoint
Mt	27.34 they offered him *w* to drink, mixed with
Mk	2.22 no one puts new *w* into old wineskins;
	15.23 they offered him *w* mixed with myrrh;
Lk	5.37 And no one puts new *w* into old
Jn	2. 9 tasted the water that had become *w*,
Acts	2.13 and said, "They are filled with new *w*."
Eph	5.18 Do not get drunk with *w*, for that is
1 Tim	5.23 but take a little *w* for the sake of your

WINE PRESS

Judg	6.11 beating out wheat in the *w*, to hide it
Isa	63. 3 "I have trodden the *w* alone, and from
Rev	14.19 he threw it into the great *w* of the

WINESKINS

Mt	9.17 Neither is new wine put into old *w*;
Lk	5.37 And no one puts new wine into old *w*;

WINGS

Ex	19. 4 how I bore you on eagles' *w* and
Ruth	2.12 the God of Israel, under those *w* you
Ps	17. 8 hide me in the shadow of your *w*, from
	18.10 he came swiftly upon the *w* of the wind.
	36. 7 take refuge in the shadow of your *w*.
	55. 6 And I say, "O that I had *w* like a dove! I
	61. 4 find refuge under the shelter of your *w*.
Prov	23. 5 it takes *w* to itself, flying like an eagle
Isa	6. 2 attendance above him; each had six *w*:

WINKING (WINKS)

Prov	6.13 with crooked speech, *w* the eyes,
	10.10 Whoever *w* the eye causes trouble, but

WINNOW

Isa	41.16 You shall *w* them and the wind shall
Jer	51. 2 to Babylon, and they shall *w* her.

WINTER

Gen	8.22 night, summer and *w* shall not cease."
Song	2.11 away; for *w* is past, the rain is over
Acts	27.12 was not suitable for spending the *w*,
1 Cor	16. 6 with you or even spend the *w*, so that
2 Tim	4.21 Do your best to come before *w*. Eubulus
Titus	3.12 for I have decided to spend the *w* there.

WIPED

Acts	3.19 to God so that your sins may be *w* out,

WISDOM

Deut	4. 6 this will show your *w* and discernment
2 Sam	14.20 my lord has *w* like the *w* of the angel of
1 Kings	4.29 God gave Solomon very great *w*
	10. 4 of Sheba observed all the *w* of Solomon,
	10.23 kings of the earth in riches and in *w*.
2 Chr	1.10 Give me now *w* and knowledge to go
	9. 6 of your *w* had been told to me;
Job	12. 2 are the people, and *w* will die with you.

Job	28.12 "But where shall *w* be found? And
	38.36 Who has put *w* in the inward parts, or
Ps	37.30 The mouths of the righteous utter *w*,
	49. 3 My mouth shall speak *w*; the
	111. 10 fear of the LORD is the beginning of *w*;
Prov	1. 2 For learning about *w* and instruction,
	1.20 *W* cries out in the street; in the squares
	2.10 *w* will come into your heart, and
	8.11 *w* is better than jewels, and all that you
	16.16 How much better to get *w* than gold! To
	19. 8 To get *w* is to love oneself; to keep
	21.30 No *w*, no understanding, no counsel,
	24. 3 By *w* a house is built, and by
	31.26 She opens her mouth with *w*, and the
Eccl	1.13 mind to seek and to search out by *w* all
	7.12 For the protection of *w* is like the
	9.16 yet the poor man's *w* is despised,
Isa	11. 2 him, the spirit of *w* and understanding,
Jer	49. 7 Is there no longer *w* in Teman? Has
	51.15 who established the world by his *w*,
Dan	1.20 In every matter of *w* and understanding
	5.11 and *w* like the *w* of the gods.
	9.22 I have now come out to give you *w* and
Mt	11.19 Yet *w* is vindicated by her deeds."
	12.42 the earth to listen to the *w* of Solomon,
	13.54 "Where did this man get this *w* and
Lk	2.52 And Jesus increased in *w* and in years,
	7.35 Nevertheless, *w* is vindicated by all her
	11.31 the earth to listen to the *w* of Solomon,
	21.15 I will give you words and a *w* that none
Acts	7.22 Moses was instructed in all the *w* of the
Rom	11.33 the riches and *w* and knowledge of God!
1 Cor	1.17 the gospel, and not with eloquent *w*,
	1.24 is the power of God and the *w* of God.
	1.30 Jesus, who became for us *w* from God,
	2. 6 among the mature we do speak *w*,
	3.19 the *w* of this world is foolishness with
	12. 8 through the Spirit the utterance of *w*,
Eph	1.17 may give you a spirit of *w* and
	3.10 that through the church the *w* of God
Jas	1. 5 If any of you is lacking in *w*, ask God,
	3.17 the *w* from above is first pure, then
2 Pet	3.15 to you according to the *w* given him,

WISE

Deut	32.29 If they were *w*, they would understand
1 Kings	3.12 I give you a *w* and discerning mind; no
Job	5.13 He takes the *w* in their own craftiness;
Ps	49.10 When he looks at the *w*, they die; fool
Prov	10. 8 *w* of heart will heed commandments
	13. 1 A *w* child loves discipline, but a scoffer
	14. 1 The *w* woman builds her house, but the
	16.14 death, and whoever is *w* will appease it.
	22.17 The words of the *w*: Incline your ear
Isa	5.21 who are *w* in their own eyes, and
Jer	8. 8 How can you say, "We are *w*, and the
Dan	2.12 all the *w* men of Babylon be destroyed.
	12. 3 Those who are *w* shall shine like the
Hos	14. 9 Those who are *w* understand these
Mt	2. 1 *w* men from the East came to
	7.24 will be like a *w* man who built his
	10.16 be *w* as serpents and innocent as doves.
	11.25 have hidden these things from the *w*
	24.45 "Who then is the faithful and *w* slave
1 Cor	1.20 Where is the one who is *w*? Where is
2 Cor	11.19 put up with fools, being *w* yourselves!
Eph	5.15 you live, not as unwise people but as *w*,
Jas	3.13 Who is *w* and understanding among

WISER

Ps	119. 98 Your commandment makes me *w* than
Ezek	28. 3 You are indeed *w* than Daniel; no secret

WISHES

Esth	6. 6 for the man whom the king *w* to honor?"
	6.11 for the man whom the king *w* to honor."
Jas	4.15 you ought to say, "If the Lord *w*,

WITHER (WITHERED WITHERS)

Ps	37. 2 the grass, and *w* like the green herb.
Isa	40. 7 The grass *w*, the flower fades, when the
Ezek	47.12 Their leaves will not *w* nor their fruit
Mt	12.10 a man was there with a *w* hand, and
	21.19 And the fig tree *w* at once.
Mk	3. 1 a man was there who had a *w* hand.
	4. 6 and since it had no root, it *w* away.
	11.21 The fig tree that you cursed has *w*."
Lk	6. 6 a man there whose right hand was *w*.

WITHHOLD (WITHHELD)

Gen	22.12 you have not *w* your son, your only son,
Deut	24.14 You shall not *w* the wages of poor and
Job	31.16 "If I have *w* anything that the poor
Ps	21. 2 and have not *w* the request of his lips.
	84.11 No good thing does the LORD *w* from
Prov	3.27 Do not *w* good from those to whom it is
Am	4. 7 I also *w* the rain from you when there
Lk	6.29 your coat do not *w* even your shirt.
Rom	8.32 He who did not *w* his own Son, but

WITNESS (WITNESSES) (n)

Gen	21.30 that you may be a *w* for me that I dug
	31.50 that God is *w* between you and me."
Ex	20.16 You shall not bear false *w* against your
Num	35.30 to death on the testimony of a single *w*.
Deut	5.20 Neither shall you bear false *w* against
	17. 6 On the evidence of two or three *w* the
	19.15 on the evidence of two or three *w* shall
	31.19 that this song may be a *w* for me
Josh	22.27 to be a *w* between us and you, and
	24.22 to serve him. And they said, "We are *w*."
Judg	11.10 LORD will be *w* between us; we will
Ruth	4.11 "We are *w*. May the LORD make the
Job	16.19 Even now, in fact, my *w* is in heaven,
Prov	14. 5 A faithful *w* does not lie, but a false *w*
	14.25 A truthful *w* saves lives, but one who
	19. 5 A false *w* will not go unpunished, and
	24.28 Do not be a *w* against your neighbor
	25.18 who bears false *w* against a neighbor.
Isa	43.10 You are my *w*, says the LORD, and my
	44. 8 of old and declared it? You are my *w*!
	55. 4 See, I made him a *w* to the peoples, a
Jer	29.23 I am the one who knows and bears *w*,
	32.10 I signed the deed, sealed it, got *w*, and
	42. 5 be a true and faithful *w* against us if we
Mic	1. 2 let the Lord GOD be a *w* against you,
Mal	2.14 the LORD was *w* between you and the
	3. 5 be swift to bear *w* against the sorcerers,
Mt	18.16 by the evidence of two or three *w*.
Mk	14.63 and said, "Why do we still need *w*?
Lk	24.48 Jerusalem. You are *w* of these things.
Acts	1. 8 you will be my *w* in Jerusalem, in all
	2.32 raised up, and of that all of us are *w*.
	5.32 we are *w* to these things, and so is the
	10.39 We are *w* to all that he did both in
	14.17 yet he has not left himself without a *w*
	22.15 you will be his *w* to all the world of
	22.20 blood of your *w* Stephen was shed, I
	23.11 you must bear *w* also in Rome."
Rom	1. 9 is my *w* that without ceasing I
	8.16 Spirit bearing *w* with our spirit that we
2 Cor	13. 1 by the evidence of two or three *w*."
1 Thess	2.10 You are *w*, and God also, how pure,
Heb	12. 1 are surrounded by so great a cloud of *w*,
Rev	1. 5 Jesus Christ, the faithful *w*, the firstborn
	3.14 the Amen, the faithful and true *w*, the
	11. 3 I will grant my two *w* authority to
	17. 6 saints and the blood of the *w* to Jesus.

WITNESS (v)

Deut	4.26 I call heaven and earth to *w* against you
	30.19 I call heaven and earth to *w* against you

WOE

Job	10.15 If I am wicked, *w* to me! If I am

Isa	6. 5 "*W* is me! I am lost, for I am a man of
	45. 7 I make weal and create *w*; I the LORD do
Mk	14.21 *w* to that one by whom the Son of Man
1 Cor	9.16 *w* to me if I do not proclaim the gospel!
Rev	8.13 midheaven, "*W*, *w*, *w* to the inhabitants

WOLF (WOLVES)

Isa	11. 6 The *w* shall live with the lamb, the
	65.25 The *w* and the lamb shall feed together,
Acts	20.29 after I have gone, savage *w* will come in

WOMAN (WOMEN)

Gen	2.23 this one shall be called *W*, for out of
	3.12 "The *w* whom you gave to be with me,
1 Kings	11. 1 Solomon loved many foreign *w* along
Prov	9.13 The foolish *w* is loud; she is ignorant
	31.30 but a *w* who fears the LORD is to be
Eccl	7.26 bitter than death the *w* who is a trap,
Isa	4. 1 Seven *w* shall take hold of one man in
	7.14 Look, the young *w* is with child and
	32. 9 Rise up, you *w* who are at ease, hear
	62. 5 For as a young man marries a young *w*,
Mt	9.20 a *w* who had been suffering from
Mk	15.40 were also *w* looking on from a distance;
Lk	7.37 And a *w* in the city, who was a sinner,
	13.11 there appeared a *w* with a spirit that
	17.35 will be two *w* grinding meal together;
	23.49 including the *w* who had followed him
Jn	2. 4 "*W*, what concern is that to you and to
	8. 3 a *w* who had been caught in adultery;
	16.21 When a *w* is in labor, she has pain,
Rom	1.27 giving up natural intercourse with *w*
1 Cor	7. 1 "It is well for a man not to touch a *w*."
	11. 9 created for the sake of *w*, but *w* for the
	14.34 *w* should be silent in the churches.
Gal	4. 4 God sent his Son, born of a *w*, born
1 Tim	2. 9 the *w* should dress themselves modestly
Heb	11.35 *W* received their dead by resurrection.
Rev	12. 1 a *w* clothed with the sun, with the
	12. 6 the *w* fled into the wilderness, where
	17. 3 a *w* sitting on a scarlet beast that was

WOMB

Eccl	11. 5 comes to the bones in the mother's *w*,
Lk	11.27 "Blessed is the *w* that bore you and the
Jn	3. 4 enter a second time into the mother's *w*

WONDER (WONDERS)

Ex	3.20 So I will . . . strike Egypt with all my *w*
	7. 9 Pharaoh says to you, 'Perform a *w*,'
	15.11 awesome in splendor, doing *w*?
Ps	88.10 Do you work *w* for the dead? Do the
	136. 4 who alone does great *w*, for his
Acts	3.12 You Israelites, why do you *w* at this, or

WONDERFUL

Gen	18.14 Is anything too *w* for the LORD? At the
Judg	13.18 "Why do you ask my name? It is too *w*."
2 Sam	1.26 your love to me was *w*, passing the love
Job	42. 3 what I did not understand, things too *w*
Ps	119.129 Your decrees are *w*; therefore my soul
	139. 6 Such knowledge is too *w* for me; it is so
	139. 14 wonderfully made. *W* are your works;
Prov	30.18 Three things are too *w* for me; four I do
Isa	9. 6 he is named *W* Counselor, Mighty God,
	25. 1 for you have done *w* things, plans

WONDROUS

Ps	26. 7 and telling all your *w* deeds.
	72.18 God of Israel, who alone does *w* things.
	119. 18 I may behold *w* things out of your law.

WOOD

Ex	15.25 the LORD showed him a piece of *w*; he
Prov	25.20 Like a moth in clothing or a worm in *w*,

WOOL

Deut	22.11 not wear clothes made of *w* and linen

Prov	31.13 She seeks *w* and flax, and works with
Isa	1.18 like crimson, they shall become like *w*.

WORD

Num	11.23 shall see whether my *w* will come true
Deut	8. 3 but by every *w* that comes from the
	30.14 No, the *w* is very near to you; it is in
Job	4. 2 "If one ventures a *w* with you, will you
	29.22 again, and my *w* dropped upon them
Ps	56.10 In God, whose *w* I praise, in the Lord,
	107. 20 he sent out his *w* and healed them, and
	119. 9 By guarding it according to your *w*.
	119. 11 I treasure your *w* in my heart, so that I
	119. 89 forever; your *w* is firmly fixed in heaven.
	147. 15 to the earth; his *w* runs swiftly.
Prov	12.25 human heart, but a good *w* cheers it up.
	15.23 and a *w* in season, how good it is!
	25.11 A *w* fitly spoken is like apples of gold in
Isa	40. 8 fades; but the *w* of our God will stand
	45.23 righteousness *w* that shall not return:
	55.11 so shall my *w* be that goes out from my
Jer	23.28 let the one who has my *w* speak my *w*
Mt	4. 4 by bread alone, but by every *w* that
	8. 8 only speak the *w*, and my servant will
	12.36 give account for every careless *w* you
Mk	2. 2 and he was speaking the *w* to them.
	4.14 The sower sows the *w*.
Lk	1. 2 eyewitnesses and servants of the *w*,
	2.29 servant in peace, according to your *w*;
	7. 7 only speak the *w*, and let my servant
Jn	1. 1 *W* was with God, and the *W* was God.
	5.24 who hears my *w* and believes him who
	5.38 do not have his *w* abiding in you,
	8.31 "If you continue in my *w*, you are truly
	8.37 there is no place in you for my *w*.
	15. 3 have already been cleansed by the *w*
	17. 6 them to me, and they have kept your *w*.
	17.17 them in the truth; your *w* is truth.
Acts	10.44 Spirit fell upon all who heard the *w*.
Rom	10. 8 "The *w* is near you, on your lips and in
	10.17 and what is heard comes through the *w*
	15.18 from the Gentiles, by *w* and deed,
2 Cor	2.17 we are not peddlers of God's *w* like so
Gal	6. 6 Those who are taught the *w* must share
Eph	5.26 her with the washing of water by the *w*,
Phil	1.14 to speak the *w* with greater boldness
	2.16 It is by your holding fast the *w* of life
Col	3.16 Let the *w* of Christ dwell in you richly,
1 Thess	1. 6 persecution you received the *w* with joy
1 Tim	4. 5 is sanctified by God's *w* and by prayer.
2 Tim	2.15 rightly explaining the *w* of truth.
Titus	1. 9 He must have a firm grasp of the *w* that
Heb	7.28 but the *w* of the oath, which came later
Jas	1.21 with meekness the implanted *w*
1 Pet	3. 1 they may be won over without a *w* by
1 Jn	1. 1 our hands, concerning the *w* of life—
	1.10 make him a liar, and his *w* is not in us.
	2. 5 whoever obeys his *w*, truly in this
Rev	3. 8 and yet you have kept my *w* and have

WORD OF GOD

1 Sam	9.27 that I may make known to you the *w*."
1 Kings	12.22 But the *w* came to Shemaiah the man
Prov	30. 5 Every *w* proves true; he is a shield to
Mt	15. 6 tradition, you make void the *w*.
Mk	7.13 making void the *w* through your
Lk	3. 2 the *w* came to John son of Zechariah in
	5. 1 was pressing in on him to hear the *w*,
	8.11 the parable is this: The seed is the *w*.
	8.21 are those who hear the *w* and do it."
	11.28 are those who hear the *w* and keep it!"
Acts	6. 2 not right that we should neglect the *w*
	6. 7 The *w* continued to spread; the number
	8.14 heard that Samaria had accepted the *w*,
	11. 1 the Gentiles had also accepted the *w*.
	12.24 the *w* continued to advance and gain
	13.46 "It was necessary that the *w* should be

Rom	9. 6 It is not as though the *w* had failed.
Eph	6.17 the sword of the Spirit, which is the *w*.
1 Thess	2.13 when you received the *w* that you heard
2 Tim	2. 9 a criminal. But the *w* is not chained.
Titus	2. 5 so that the *w* may not be discredited.
Heb	4.12 the *w* is living and active, sharper
	6. 5 tasted the goodness of the *w* and the
1 Pet	1.23 seed, through the living and enduring *w*.
2 Pet	3. 5 by the *w* heavens existed long ago and
1 Jn	2.14 you are strong and the *w* abides in you,
Rev	1. 2 who testified to the *w* and to the
	6. 9 slaughtered for the *w* and for the
	19.13 in blood, and his name is called The *W*.
	20. 4 their testimony to Jesus and for the *w*.

WORD(S) OF THE LORD

Gen	15. 1 things the *w* came to Abram in a vision,
Ex	9.20 officials of Pharaoh who feared the *w*
Num	24.13 I would not be able to go beyond the *w*,
Deut	5. 5 to declare to you the *w*, for you
1 Sam	3. 1 The *w* was rare in those days; visions
	15. 1 Israel; now therefore listen to the *w*."
2 Sam	7. 4 that same night the *w* came to Nathan:
1 Kings	14.18 according to the *w*, which he spoke by
2 Kings	9.36 "This is the *w*, which he spoke by his
	20.19 to Isaiah, "The *w* that you have spoken
	23.16 defiled it, according to the *w* that the
1 Chr	17. 3 that same night the *w* came to Nathan,
Ps	33. 4 For the *w* is upright; and all his work is
	33. 6 By the *w* the heavens were made, and
	105. 19 came to pass, the *w* kept testing him.
Isa	2. 3 instruction, and the *w* from Jerusalem.
	38. 4 Then the *w* came to Isaiah: "Go and say
	39. 8 "The *w* that you have spoken is good."
	66. 5 Hear the *w*, you who tremble at his
Jer	1. 2 the *w* came in the days of King Josiah
	6.10 The *w* is to them an object of scorn;
	8. 9 they have rejected the *w*, what wisdom
	20. 8 the *w* has become for me a reproach
	36. 6 you shall read the *w* from the scroll
Hos	1. 1 The *w* that came to Hosea son of Beeri,
Joel	1. 1 The *w* that came to Joel son of Pethuel;
Am	8.11 a thirst for water, but of hearing the *w*.
Jon	1. 1 Now the *w* came to Jonah the son of
Zeph	1. 1 The *w* that came to Zephaniah son of
Acts	16.32 They spoke the *w* to him and to all who
	19.20 So the *w* grew mightily and prevailed.
2 Thess	3. 1 so that the *w* may spread rapidly and be

WORDS

Gen	11. 1 had one language and the same *w*.
Deut	4.10 I will let them hear my *w*, so that they
	11.18 shall put these *w* of mine in your heart
	18.18 I will put my *w* in the mouth of the
2 Kings	6.12 the king of Israel the *w* that you speak
Job	6.10 for I have not denied the *w* of the Holy
	6.26 Do you think that you can reprove *w*, as
	15. 3 in *w* with which they can do no good?
	18. 2 "How long will you hunt for *w*?
	22.22 mouth, and lay up his *w* in your heart.
	23.12 I have treasured in my bosom the *w* of
Ps	19. 3 There is no speech, nor are there *w*;
	19.14 Let the *w* of my mouth and the
Prov	30. 1 The *w* of Agur son of Jakeh. An oracle.
Eccl	5. 2 upon earth; therefore let your *w* be few.
	10.12 *W* spoken by the wise bring favor,
Jer	15.16 Your *w* were found, and I ate them, and
	18.18 him, and let us not heed any of his *w*."
	44.28 shall know whose *w* will stand, mine or
Mt	24.35 pass away, but my *w* will not pass away.
Mk	13.31 pass away, but my *w* will not pass away.
Lk	21.33 pass away, but my *w* will not pass away.
Jn	6.68 we go? You have the *w* of eternal life.
	14.10 The *w* that I say to you I do not speak
1 Cor	14.19 rather speak five *w* with my mind,

WORK (WORKS) (n)

Gen	2.	2 on the seventh day from all the *w*
Ex	23.12	Six days you shall do your *w*, but on
1 Chr	16.	9 to him, tell of all his wonderful *w*.
Neh	3.	5 their shoulders to the *w* of their Lord
Job	10.	3 to despise the *w* of your hands and
	37.14	Job; stop and consider the wondrous *w*
Ps	28.	5 of the LORD, or the *w* of his hands,
	102.	25 the heavens are the *w* of your hands.
	104.	23 People go out to their *w* and to their
	104.	24 O LORD, how manifold are your *w*! In
	145.	10 All your *w* shall give thanks to you, O
Prov	16.	3 Commit your *w* to the LORD, and your
	31.31	and let her *w* praise her in the city
Eccl	8.17	I saw all the *w* of God, that no one can
Isa	66.18	I know their *w* and their thoughts, and I
Hab	1.	5 For a *w* is being done in your days that
	3.	2 and I stand in awe, O LORD, of your *w*.
Jn	5.36	*w* that the Father has given me to
	9.	3 blind so that God's *w* might be revealed
	10.25	The *w* that I do in my Father's name
	17.	4 earth by finishing the *w* that you gave
Acts	9.36	She was devoted to good *w* and acts of
Rom	4.	5 to one who without *w* trusts him who
	9.12	not by *w* but by his call) she was told,
	11.	6 grace, it is no longer on the basis of *w*,
1 Cor	3.13	the *w* of each builder will become
	9.	1 Are not you my *w* in the Lord? If I am
Gal	3.	2 the Spirit by doing the *w* of the law or
	5.19	Now the *w* of the flesh are obvious:
Eph	2.	9 — not the result of *w*, so that no one
Phil	2.30	came close to death for the *w* of Christ,
1 Thess	5.13	very highly in love because of their *w*.
2 Thess	2.17	and strengthen them in every good *w*
1 Tim	6.18	to be rich in good *w*, generous, and
2 Tim	3.17	proficient, equipped for every good *w*.
Titus	3.	5 he saved us, not because of any *w* of
Heb	1.10	the heavens are the *w* of your hands;
Jas	2.17	So faith by itself, if it has no *w*, is dead.
	2.21	our ancestor Abraham justified by *w*,
Rev	20.12	dead were judged according to their *w*,

WORK (WORKED WORKING WORKS)

Neh	4.	6 height; for the people had a mind to *w*.
Prov	31.13	and flax, and *w* with willing hands.
Jer	18.	3 house, and there he was *w* at his wheel.
Hag	2.	4 *w*, for I am with you, says the LORD of
Mt	20.12	'These last *w* only one hour, and you
Mk	16.20	while the Lord *w* with them and
Lk	5.	5 "Master, we *w* all night but we have
Jn	5.17	"My Father is still *w*, and I also am *w*."
	6.27	Do not *w* for the food which perishes,
	9.	4 We must *w* the works of him who sent
Rom	8.28	all things *w* together for good for those
1 Cor	3.	9 we are God's servants, *w* together; you
2 Cor	6.	1 As we *w* together with him, we urge you
Gal	2.	8 (for he who *w* through Peter making
Phil	2.12	*w* out your own salvation with fear and
2 Thess	3.10	Anyone unwilling to *w*, should not eat.

WORKER (WORKERS)

Prov	16.26	The appetite of *w* works for them; their
2 Tim	2.15	a *w* who has no need to be ashamed,

WORLD (WORLDS)

Ps	19.	4 and their words to the end of the *w*.
Mt	13.38	the field is the *w*, and the good seed
Mk	16.15n	"Go into all the *w* and proclaim the
Lk	9.25	if they gain the whole *w*, but lose or
Jn	8.23	you are of this *w*, I am not of this *w*.
	9.39	"I came into this *w* for judgment so
	12.19	Look, the *w* has gone after him!"
	16.33	In the *w* you face persecution. But take
	17.14	the *w*, just as I do not belong to the *w*.
	17.21	us, so that the *w* may believe that you
Acts	17.	6 have been turning the *w* upside down
Rom	5.12	as sin came into the *w* through one

1 Cor	4.	9 become a spectacle to the *w*, to angels
Heb	11.	3 the *w* were prepared by the word of
	11.38	of whom the *w* was not worthy. They
1 Jn	2.15	Do not love the *w* or the things in the
	3.13	and sisters, that the *w* hates you.
	4.	5 They are from the *w*, therefore what

WORM (WORMS)

Ps	22.	6 But I am a *w*, and not human; scorned
Isa	41.14	Do not fear, you *w* Jacob, you insect
Mk	9.48	where their *w* never dies, and the fire is
Acts	12.23	down, and he was eaten by *w* and died.

WORRY (WORRIED WORRIES)

Mt	6.25	do not *w* about your life, what you will
	10.19	do not *w* about how you are to speak or
Lk	10.41	Martha, you are *w* and distracted
	12.11	do not *w* about how you are to defend
	21.34	and drunkenness and *w* of this life,
Phil	4.	6 Do not *w* about anything, but in

WORSE

Ps	39.	2 my distress grew *w*, my heart became
Mt	12.45	state of the person is *w* than the first.
2 Tim	3.13	will go from bad to *w*, deceiving

WORSHIP

Gen	22.	5 we will *w*, and then we will come back
Ex	3.12	you shall *w* God upon this mountain."
	20.	5 shall not bow down to them or *w* them;
	24.	1 the elders of Israel, and *w* at a distance.
	34.14	(for you shall *w* no other god, because
1 Sam	1.	3 go up year by year from his town to *w*
1 Chr	16.29	*W* the LORD in holy splendor; tremble
Ps	22.27	of the nations shall *w* before him.
	29.	2 his name; *w* the LORD in holy splendor
	95.	6 O come, let us *w* and bow down, let us
	96.	9 *W* the LORD in holy splendor; tremble
	132.	7 dwelling place; let us *w* at his footstool."
Isa	2.20	which they made for themselves to *w*,
	27.13	will come and *w* the LORD on the holy
	36.	7 'You shall *w* before this altar'?
Jer	7.	2 Judah, you that enter these gates to *w*
Dan	3.28	serve and *w* any god except their own
Zech	14.16	go up year after year to *w* the King,
Mt	4.	9 you, if you will fall down and *w* me."
	4.10	'*W* the Lord your God, and serve only
Lk	4.	7 If you, then, will *w* me, it will all be
Jn	4.21	when you will *w* the Father neither on
	4.24	who *w* him must *w* in spirit and truth."
	12.20	among those who went up to *w* at the
	16.	2 by doing so they are offering *w* to God.
Acts	7.42	them over to *w* the host of heaven,
	18.13	man is persuading people to *w* God
	19.27	brought all Asia and the world to *w* her."
1 Cor	14.25	before God and *w* him, declaring, "God
Phil	3.	3 circumcision, who *w* in the Spirit of
Heb	1.	6 he says, "Let all God's angels *w* him."
Rev	7.15	throne of God, and *w* him day and night
	13.	8 all the inhabitants of the earth will *w* it,
	14.	7 *w* him who made heaven and earth, the
	19.10	I fell down at his feet to *w* him, but he
	22.	8 I fell down to *w* at the feet of the angel

WORSHIPED (WORSHIPING WORSHIPS)

Gen	24.26	man bowed his head and *w* the LORD
Ex	4.31	their misery, they bowed down and *w*.
	12.27	And the people bowed down and *w*.
Deut	17.	3 going to serve other gods and *w* them
Judg	2.	7 The people *w* the LORD all the days of
	3.	6 to their sons, and they *w* their gods.
	10.13	have abandoned me and *w* other gods;
1 Sam	1.19	in the morning and *w* before the LORD;
2 Sam	12.20	went into the house of the LORD, and *w*;
	15.32	came to the summit, where God was *w*,
2 Kings	17.33	So they *w* the LORD but also served their
2 Chr	20.18	Jerusalem fell down before the LORD, *w*
Job	1.20	his head, and fell on the ground and *w*.

Ps	66. 4 All the earth *w* you; they sing praises to
Isa	44.15 Then he makes a god and *w* it, makes it
Mt	14.33 And those in the boat *w* him, saying,
	28. 9 him, took hold of his feet, and *w* him.
Lk	2.37 temple, but *w* with fasting and prayer
	24.52 And they *w* him, and returned to
Jn	9.31 he does listen to one who *w* him and
	9.38 He said, "Lord, I believe." And he *w* him.
Acts	10.25 met him, and falling at his feet, *w* him.
Rev	5.14 "Amen!" And the elders fell down and *w*.
	13. 4 They *w* the dragon, for he had given

WORSHIPERS

2 Kings	10.21 all the *w* of Baal came, so that there

WORTH

2 Sam	18. 3 you are not ten thousand of us; therefore
Rom	8.18 time are not *w* comparing with the glory
Phil	2.22 But Timothy's *w* you know, how like a

WORTHLESS

Ps	60.11 against the foe, for human help is *w*.
Lk	17.10 ordered to do, say, 'We are *w* slaves;
Acts	14.15 turn from these *w* things to the living

WORTHY

Gen	32.10 I am not *w* of the least of all the
Ruth	3.11 people know that you are a *w* woman.
Prov	20. 6 loyal, but who can find one *w* of trust?
Mt	3.11 me; I am not *w* to carry his sandals.
	8. 8 "Lord, I am not *w* to have you come
	10.37 father or mother more than me is not *w*
Mk	1. 7 I am not *w* to stoop down and untie the
Lk	7. 4 "He is *w* of having you do this for him,
	7. 6 I am not *w* to have you come under my
	15.21 you; I am no longer *w* to be called
Jn	1.27 I am not *w* to untie the thong of his
Acts	5.41 were considered *w* to suffer dishonor
	13.25 I am not *w* to untie the thong of the
2 Thess	1.11 our God may make you *w* of his call
Heb	3. 3 Jesus is *w* of more glory than Moses,
	11.38 of whom the world was not *w*. They
Rev	3. 4 me, dressed in white, for they are *w*.
	4.11 "You are *w*, our Lord and God, to
	5. 2 "Who is *w* to open the scroll and break
	5. 9 "You are *w* to take the scroll and to

WOUND (WOUNDED WOUNDS)

Deut	32.39 I kill and I make alive; I *w* and I heal;
1 Kings	22.34 carry me out of the battle, for I am *w*."
2 Chr	18.33 carry me out of the battle, for I am *w*."
Ps	38. 5 My *w* grow foul and fester because of
Prov	23.29 Who has *w* without cause? Who had
	27. 6 Well meant are the *w* a friend inflicts,
Isa	1. 6 but bruises and sores and bleeding *w*;
	53. 5 But he was *w* for our transgressions,
Jer	10.19 me because of my hurt! My *w* is severe.
	15.18 is my pain unceasing, my *w* incurable,
	30.12 hurt is incurable, your *w* is grievous.
Mic	1. 9 For her *w* is incurable. It has come to
Nah	3.19 assuaging your hurt, your *w* is mortal.
Zech	13. 6 "What are these *w* on your chest?" the
Lk	10.34 bandaged his *w*, having poured oil
	20.12 this one they also *w* and threw out.
1 Cor	8.12 *w* their conscience when it is weak, you
Rev	13. 3 but its mortal *w* had been healed. In

WRAPPED

Lam	3.44 you have *w* yourself with a cloud so
Mk	15.46 down the body, *w* it in the linen cloth,
Lk	2. 7 son and *w* him in bands of cloth,

WRATH

2 Kings	22.13 great is the *w* of the LORD that is
Ezra	10.14 until the fierce *w* of our God on this
Job	16. 9 He has torn me in his *w*, and hated me;
Ps	76.10 Human *w* serves only to praise you,
Hos	5.10 them I will pour out my *w* like water.

Hab	3. 2 known; in *w* may you remember mercy.
	3. 8 Was your *w* against the rivers, O LORD?
Zeph	2. 2 upon you the day of the LORD's *w*.
Mt	3. 7 warned you to flee from the *w* to come?
Jn	3.36 not see life, but must endure God's *w*.
Rom	2. 5 up *w* for yourself on the day of *w*,
	3. 5 That God is unjust to inflict *w* on us?
	4.15 for the law brings *w*; but where there is
Col	3. 6 the *w* of God is coming on those who
1 Thess	1.10 —Jesus, who rescues us from the *w*
Rev	6.16 the throne and from the *w* of the Lamb;
	14.19 the great wine press of the *w* of God.

WREATH (WREATHS)

1 Kings	7.17 of checker work with *w* of chain work
1 Cor	9.25 they do it to receive a perishable *w*, but

WRESTLED (WRESTLING)

Gen	30. 8 I have *w* with my sister, and have
	32.24 and a man *w* with him until daybreak.
Col	4.12 always *w* in his prayers on your behalf,

WRETCHED

Rom	7.24 *W* man that I am! Who will rescue me

WRITE (WRITTEN WROTE)

Ex	17.14 *W* this as a reminder in a book and
	24. 4 Moses *w* all the words of the LORD. He
	31.18 of stone, *w* with the finger of God.
	34. 1 I will *w* on the tablets the words that
Deut	6. 9 *w* them on the doorposts of your house
	11.20 *W* them on the doorposts of your house
	17.18 a copy of this law *w* for him in the
	27. 3 You shall *w* on them all the words of
	31. 9 Moses *w* down this law, and gave it to
2 Chr	23.18 as it is *w* in the law of Moses, with
Neh	10.34 the LORD our God, as it is *w* in the law.
Ps	40. 7 I am; in the scroll of the book it is *w*
Prov	7. 3 *w* them on the tablet of your heart. Say
	22.20 Have I not *w* for you thirty sayings of
Eccl	12.10 words, and he *w* words of truth plainly.
Jer	17. 1 The sin of Judah is *w* with an iron pen;
	30. 2 *W* in a book all the words that I have
	36. 2 Take a scroll and *w* on it all the words
	36.18 and I *w* them with ink on the scroll."
Dan	12. 1 everyone who is found *w* in the book.
Hos	8.12 Though I *w* for him the multitude of my
Hab	2. 2 *W* the vision; make it plain on tablets,
Mk	9.12 How then is it *w* about the Son of Man,
Lk	10.20 that your names are *w* in heaven."
Jn	8. 6 Jesus bent down and *w* with his finger
	19.22 answered, "What I have *w* I have *w*."
	20.30 signs which are not *w* in this book.
Acts	13.33 by raising Jesus; as also it is *w* in the
Rom	15. 4 whatever was *w* in former days was *w*
Heb	8.10 minds, and *w* them on their hearts,
	10.16 and I will *w* them on their minds,"
2 Pet	3.15 our beloved brother Paul *w* to you
1 Jn	5.13 I *w* these things to you who believe in
Rev	1.19 Now *w* what you have seen, what is,
	3.12 I will *w* on you the name of my God,

WRITING (WRITINGS)

Ex	32.16 the *w* was the *w* of God, engraved upon
Ezek	9. 2 a man clothed in linen, with a *w* case
Lk	1.63 He asked for a *w* tablet and wrote, "His
2 Tim	3.15 you have known the sacred *w* which are

WRONG (WRONGED WRONGS)

Ex	2.13 he said to the one who was in the *w*,
Num	5. 7 shall make full restitution for his *w*,
1 Sam	26.21 Saul said, "I have done *w*; come back,
2 Kings	18.14 "I have done *w*; withdraw from me;
Job	6.24 me understand how I have gone *w*.
	32. 3 they had declared Job to be in the *w*.
Ps	7. 3 done this, if there is *w* in my hands,
	58. 2 No, in your hearts you devise *w*; your
Prov	30.20 her mouth, and says, "I have done no *w*."

Jer	37.18 also said to King Zedekiah, "What *w*
Mk	12.24 "Is not this the reason you are *w*, that
Lk	23.41 but this man has done nothing *w*."
Acts	25.10 I have done no *w* to the Jews, as you
1 Cor	6. 7 a defeat for you. Why not rather be *w*?
2 Cor	7. 2 we have *w* no one, we have corrupted
	12.13 did not burden you? Forgive me this *w*!
Philem	18 If he has *w* you in any way, or owes you

Y

YEAR (YEARS)

Lev	16.34 atonement . . . once in the *y* for all their
Ps	102. 27 are the same, and your *y* have no end.
Prov	10.27 but the *y* of the wicked will be short.
Isa	61. 2 to proclaim the *y* of the Lord's favor,
	63. 4 and the *y* for my redeeming had come.
Ezek	46.17 his to the *y* of liberty; then it shall
Lk	2.52 Jesus increased in wisdom and in *y*,
Rev	20. 6 they will reign with him a thousand *y*.

YEARNING

2 Sam	13.39 of the king went out, *y* for Absalom;

YEAST

Mt	13.33 "The kingdom of heaven is like *y* that a
	16. 6 and beware of the *y* of the Pharisees
Mk	8.15 beware of the *y* of the Pharisees and the
Lk	12. 1 "Beware of the *y* of the Pharisees, that
	13.21 It is like *y* that a woman took and
1 Cor	5. 6 that a little *y* leavens the whole batch
Gal	5. 9 you. A little *y* leavens the whole batch

YES

Mt	5.37 let your word be 'Y, Y' or 'No, No';
2 Cor	1.17 ready to say "Y, y" and "No, no" at the
	1.20 every one of God's promises is a "Y."

YESTERDAY

Job	8. 9 for we are but of *y*, and we know
Heb	13. 8 is the same *y* and today and forever.

YIELD

2 Chr	30. 8 but *y* yourselves to the Lord and come

YOKE

Lev	26.13 I have broken the bars of your *y* and
1 Kings	12. 4 "Your father made our *y* heavy. Now
2 Chr	10. 4 "Your father made our *y* heavy.
Isa	9. 4 For the *y* of their burden, and the bar
	10.27 and his *y* will be destroyed from your
	14.25 his *y* shall be removed from them, and
	58. 6 to undo the thongs of the *y*, to let the
Jer	28. 2 broken the *y* of the king of Babylon.
Lam	1.14 My transgressions were bound into a *y*;
Nah	1.13 I will break his *y* from you and snap the
Mt	11.29 Take my *y* upon you, and learn from
Acts	15.10 placing on the neck of the disciples a *y*

YOUNG (YOUNGER)

Gen	25.23 the other, the elder shall serve the *y*."
1 Chr	29. 1 God has chosen, is *y* and inexperienced,
Job	30. 1 they make sport of me, those who are *y*
	39.16 It deals cruelly with its *y*, as if they
Prov	1. 4 knowledge and prudence to the *y*—
Eccl	11. 9 Rejoice, *y* man, while you are *y*, and let
Dan	1. 4 *y* men without physical defect and
Mt	19.20 The *y* man said to him, "I have kept all
Mk	14.51 *y* man following him, wearing
	16. 5 entered the tomb, they saw a *y* man,
Lk	15.12 The *y* of them said to his father,
Jn	21.18 when you were *y*, you used to fasten
Acts	23.17 "Take this *y* man to the tribune, for he
Rom	9.12 was told, "The elder shall serve the *y*."
Titus	2. 6 urge the *y* men to be self-controlled.
1 Jn	2.13 I am writing to you, *y* people, because

YOUTH

Gen	8.21 of the human heart is evil from *y*;

Ps	25. 7 Do not remember the sins of my *y*, or
	103. 5 that your *y* is renewed like the eagle's.
	110. 3 the morning, like dew, your *y* will come
Eccl	12. 1 your creator in days of your *y*,
Isa	65.20 a hundred years will be considered a *y*,
Jer	22.21 This has been your way from your *y*, for
Mal	2.14 you and the wife of your *y*, to whom
Mk	10.20 I have kept all these from my *y*."
Lk	18.21 "I have kept all these since my *y*."
Acts	26. 4 Jews know my way of life from my *y*,
1 Tim	4.12 Let no one despise your *y*, but set the

Z

ZACCHAEUS

Lk	19. 2 named *Z*; he was a chief tax collector
	19. 5 "*Z*, hurry and come down; for I must
	19. 8 *Z* stood there and said to the Lord,

ZAPHON

Job	26. 7 He stretches out *Z* over the void, and

ZEAL

2 Kings	10.16 with me, and see my *z* for the Lord."
	19.31 survivors. The *z* of the Lord will do this.
Ps	69. 9 It is *z* for your house that has consumed
	119.139 My *z* consumes me because my foes
Isa	9. 7 The *z* of the Lord of hosts will do this.
	26.11 Let them see your *z* for your people,
	37.32 The *z* of the Lord of hosts will do this.
	63.15 Where are your *z* and your might? The
Jn	2.17 written, "*Z* for your house will consume
Rom	10. 2 they have a *z* for God, but it is not
2 Cor	7. 7 your *z* for me, so that I rejoiced
	7.12 your *z* for us might be made known to
	9. 2 last year; and your *z* has stirred up most
Phil	3. 6 as to *z*, a persecutor of the church;

ZEALOUS

Num	25.13 he was *z* for his God, and made
Acts	21.20 the Jews, and they are all *z* for the law.
	22. 3 being *z* for God, just as all of you are
Gal	1.14 *z* for the traditions of my ancestors.

ZEBULUN

Gen	30.20 him six sons"; so she named him *Z*.
	49.13 *Z* shall settle at the shore of the sea; he
Num	26.26 The descendants of *Z* by their clans: of
Deut	33.18 of *Z* he said, "Rejoice, *Z*, in your going
Ps	68.27 in a body, the princes of *Z*, the princes
Isa	9. 1 he brought into contempt the land of *Z*
Mt	4.13 sea, in the territory of *Z* and Naphtali,
Rev	7. 8 from the tribe of *Z* twelve thousand,

ZECHARIAH

Ezra	5. 1 Now the prophets, Haggai and *Z* son of
	6.14 of the prophet Haggai and *Z* son of
Zech	1. 1 word of the Lord came to the prophet *Z*
	7. 1 the word of the Lord came to *Z* on the

ZEPHANIAH

Zeph	1. 1 The word of the Lord that came to *Z*

ZERUBBABEL

Ezra	2. 2 They came with *Z*, Jeshua, Nehemiah,
	4. 2 they approached *Z* and the heads of the
	5. 2 Then *Z* the son of Shealtiel and Jeshua
Neh	7. 7 They came with *Z*, Jeshua, Nehemiah,
Hag	1. 1 Lord came by the prophet Haggai to *Z*
	2. 2 Speak now to *Z* son of Shealtiel,
Zech	4. 6 "This is the word of the Lord to *Z*: Not

ZION

Ps	2. 6 "I have set my king on *Z*, my holy hill."
	48. 2 Mount *Z*, in the far north, the city of
	50. 2 Out of *Z*, the perfection of beauty, God
Isa	1. 8 And daughter *Z* is left like a booth in a
	2. 3 For out of *Z* shall go forth instruction,
Heb	12.22 you have come to Mount *Z* and to the

MAP INDEX

Index to Color Maps

The following index will enable you to locate places on the color maps quickly and easily. There are six maps in all: Map 1–World of the Patriarchs; Map 2–Palestine and Syria; Map 3–Kingdom of David and Solomon; Map 4–Jesus' Ministry; Map 5–Paul's Missionary Journeys; Map 6–Jerusalem in Jesus' Time. The first number of each index entry refers to the number of the map; the second one to the location of the place on that map.

WORLD OF THE PATRIARCHS

→ Abraham's journeys

Possible location of Biblical "Ur of the Chaldeans," where Abraham's migration began

Possible location of Sodom and Gomorrah

CAUCASUS MTS.

Mt. Ararat
Araxes R.
Lake Urmia
Caspian Sea

Nineveh
Asshur
Nuzi

BABYLONIANS

Tigris
Euphrates R.

Babylon
Nippur
Erech (Uruk)
Ur

Persian Gulf

ARABIA

Haran
PADDAN ARAM
Tadmor
Mari

Carchemish
Aleppo
Ugarit Ebla
HITTITES
Hattusha
TAURUS MTS.

Damascus
Hazor
Shechem
Ai
Hebron
Zoar?
Kadesh Barnea

Byblos
Megiddo
Dothan
Bethel
Beersheba
Gerar
Succoth
On (Heliopolis)
Zoan (Tanis)
Noph (Memphis)

EGYPTIANS
SINAI
Nile R.
Red Sea

The Great Sea

Kittim (Cyprus)
Knossos
Caphtor (Crete)
Aegean Sea
Troy
Mycenae

Black Sea

| 0 | 100 | 200 | 300 mi. |
| 0 | 100 | 200 | 300 | 400 km. |

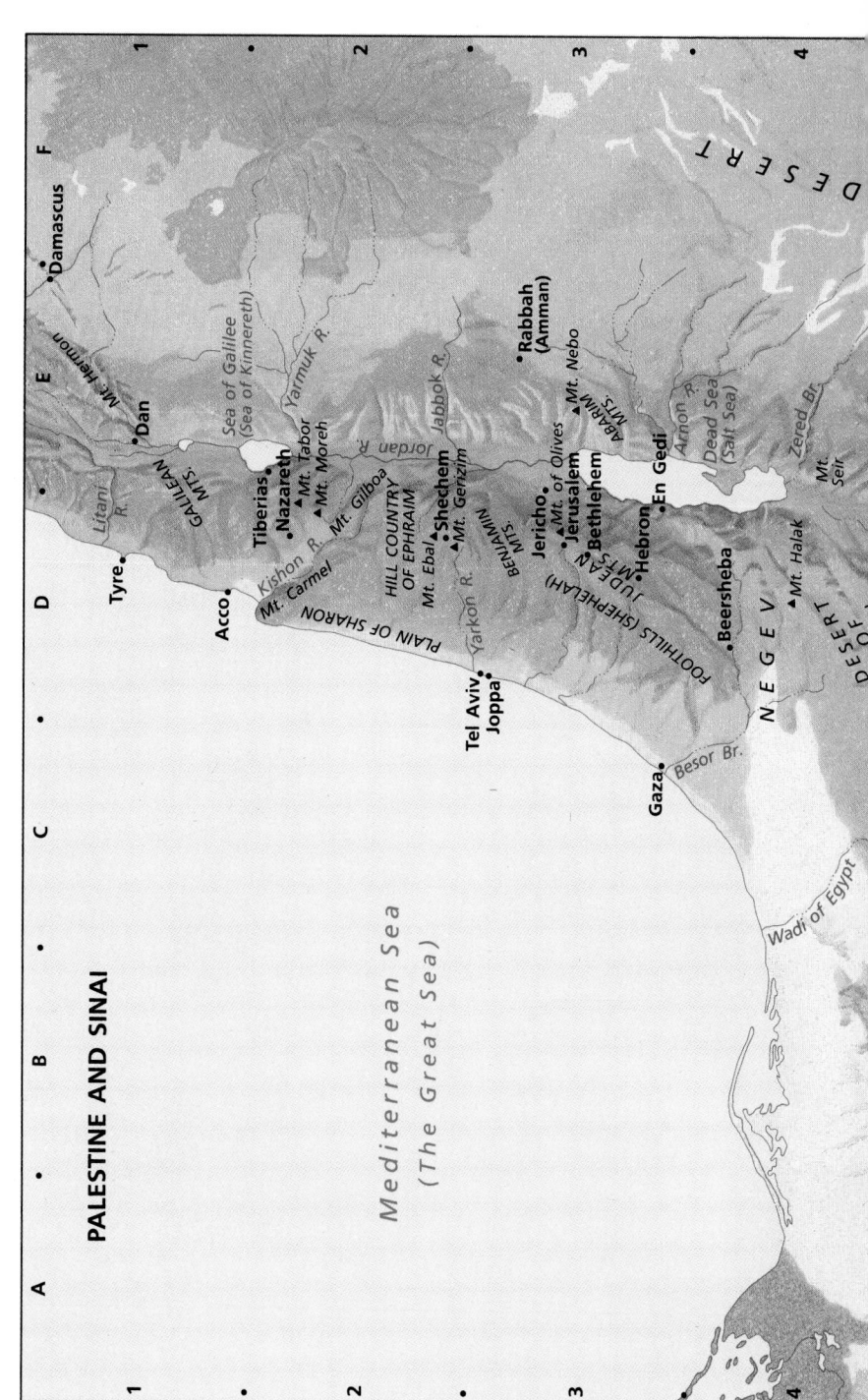

PALESTINE AND SINAI

Mediterranean Sea
(The Great Sea)

Damascus

Mt. Hermon

Dan

Tyre

GALILEAN MTS.

Litani R.

Sea of Galilee
(Sea of Kinnereth)

Yarmuk R.

Tiberias

Nazareth
Mt. Tabor
Mt. Moreh

Jordan R.

Jabbok R.

Mt. Gilboa

Kishon R.

Mt. Carmel

Acco

PLAIN OF SHARON

HILL COUNTRY
OF EPHRAIM

Shechem
Mt. Ebal
Mt. Gerizim

Rabbah
(Amman)

Mt. Nebo

ABARIM
MTS.

Tel Aviv
Joppa

Yarkon R.

BENJAMIN
MTS.

Jericho
Mt. of Olives
Jerusalem
Bethlehem

En Gedi

Arnon R.

Dead Sea
(Salt Sea)

Zered Br.

Gaza

Besor Br.

FOOTHILLS (SHEPHELAH)

JUDEAN
MTS.

Hebron

Beersheba

NEGEV

Mt. Halak

Mt. Seir

DESERT OF

DESERT

Wadi of Egypt